THE

Oxford
American
Desk
Dictionary

THE

Oxford
American
Desk
Dictionary

Edited by

Frank Abate

New York   Oxford
Oxford University Press
1998

Oxford University Press

Oxford   New York
Athens   Auckland   Bangkok   Bogota   Bombay
Buenos Aires   Calcutta   Cape Town   Dar es Salaam
Delhi   Florence   Hong Kong   Istanbul   Karachi
Kuala Lumpur   Madras   Madrid   Melbourne
Mexico City   Nairobi   Paris   Singapore
Taipei   Tokyo   Toronto   Warsaw

and associated companies in
Berlin   Ibadan

This is a revised edition of the Oxford Essential Dictionary,
prepared by Oxford University Press for publication in 1998
by The Berkley Publishing Group.

Published by Oxford University Press, Inc.,
198 Madison Avenue, New York, New York 10016
Oxford is a registered trademark of Oxford University Press.

Library of Congress Cataloging-in-Publication Data
The Oxford American desk dictionary.
p.   cm.
Rev. ed. of Oxford essential dictionary: American edition
ISBN 0–19–512673–4 (alk. paper)
1. English language—Dictionaries. I. Abate, Frank, 1951–   .
II. Oxford essential dictionary.
PE1628.08615   1998
423—dc21   98-17237
CIP

3   5   7   9   8   6   4   2
Printed in the United States of America
on acid free paper

Contents

Preface

The *Oxford American Desk Dictionary* is intended as a quick-reference, compact dictionary for the home, school, or office. The dictionary covers the essential vocabulary of American English, with features that include syllabification, pronunciation, derivatives and inflected forms, and clear, concise definitions. The text is accompanied by hundreds of illustrations and usage notes, as well as unique word origin information presented in text boxes for quick look-up.

Special Reference Sections at the back of the book provide up-to-the-minute information on such useful topics as Weights and Measures, Chemical Elements, Presidents of the United States, and Countries of the World.

This handy desk dictionary is an excellent yet economical choice for students, writers, business people, and all those who want to use American English accurately and appropriately. Among the most full-featured dictionaries of its size, the *Oxford American Desk Dictionary*, with its attention to quality, thoroughness, and currency, continues the tradition of Oxford—the world's most trusted name in dictionaries.

Project Staff

Editor-in-Chief: Frank R. Abate

Managing Editor: Elizabeth J. Jewell

Editors: Deborah Argosy
Patricia Baldwin
Archie Hobson
Christine A. Lindberg
Andrea R. Nagy
Laurie H. Ongley

Special Editorial Assistance: Jeffrey Triggs

Proofreaders: Linda Costa
Julie Marsh

Data Entry: Kim Roberts

Illustrator: Mike Malkovas

How to Use the Oxford American Desk Dictionary

The "entry map" below explains the different parts of a typical entry in this dictionary.

Boldface main entry — Sense numbers and letters in **boldface** — New part of speech signaled by • — Pronunciation set off with slashes / / — Parts of speech in *italic* — Inflected forms in **boldface** — Idioms and phrases signaled by □ — Derivatives signaled by □□

Main entries and other boldface forms

Main entries appear in boldface type, as do inflected forms, idioms and phrases, and derivatives. Main entries, inflected forms, and derivatives of two or more syllables show syllabification with centered dots. On a derivative, an accent mark follows the stressed syllable(s).

Cross references

Cross references to main entries appear in small capitals. For example, in the entry **adrenaline**, a cross reference is given in small capitals to the entry **epinephrine**:

a·dren·a·line /ədrénəlin/ = EPINEPHRINE.

Cross references to derivatives and compounds are given in italic type. For example, in the entry **division**, a cross reference is given to *long division* (see LONG¹); the italic type indicates that the compound (*long division*) can be found under its main entry (LONG¹):

di·vi·sion /divízhən/ *n.* **1** dividing; being divided. **2** *Math.* dividing one number by another (see also *long division* (see LONG¹)). **3** disagreement or discord (*division of opinion*). **4 a** one of two or more parts into which a thing is divided. **b** point at which a thing is divided. **5** unit of administration or organization. □ **division sign** sign (÷) indicating that one quantity is to be divided by another. □□ **di·vi′sion·al** *adj.*

List words

Words beginning with common prefixes (*in-*, *non-*, *over-*, *re-*, *self-*, *sub-*, and *un-*) are given in lists where the sense of the word (e.g., *inexpensive*) is clear from an understanding of the meaning of the prefix (*in-* = 'not,' 'without') and the root of the word (*expensive* = 'costing or charging much').

Word histories

Brief word histories are provided for hundreds of entries from **ache** to **war**. These special boxed features highlight some of the most useful and surprising accounts of how the English language has evolved over the centuries. For example, at the entry **pay**, the word history reveals the connection between 'money' and 'peace':

> **pay** Middle English (in the sense 'pacify'):
> from Old French *paie* (noun), *payer* (verb),
> from Latin *pacare* 'appease,' from *pax, pac-*
> 'peace.' The notion of 'payment' arose from
> the sense of 'pacifying' a creditor.

Usage notes

Usage notes, found throughout the text, offer guidance on troublesome words, formal and informal style, sensitive terms, spelling, pronunciation, and other key points not covered by traditional dictionary definitions. For example, the entry **classic** features a discussion of the differences between 'classic' and 'classical':

> ¶ Traditionally, **classic** means 'typical; excellent as an example; timeless' and **classical** means 'of (esp. Greek or Roman) antiquity.' Thus: *John Ford directed many classic Westerns. The museum was built in the classical style.* Great art is considered **classic**, not **classical,** unless it is created in the forms of antiquity. *Classical music* is formal and sophisticated music adhering to certain stylistic principles, esp. those of the late 18th century, but a *classic folk song* is one that well expresses its culture. A *classical education* exposes a student to *classical* literature, disciplines, and languages (especially Latin and Greek), but the study of Greek and Latin languages and their literature is also referred to as *classics*, as in *he majored in classics at college.*

Abbreviations Used in This Book

abbr.	abbreviation
absol.	absolute, absolutely
adj.	adjective
adv.	adverb
Aeron.	Aeronautics
Amer.	America, American
Anat.	Anatomy
Anthropol.	Anthropology
Antiq.	Antiquity
Archaeol.	Archaeology
Archit.	Architecture
assim.	assimilated
Astrol.	Astrology
Astron.	Astronomy
Astronaut.	Astronautics
attrib.	attributive, attributively
attrib.adj.	attributive adjective
Austral.	Australia, Australian
aux.	auxiliary
Bibl.	Biblical
Biochem.	Biochemistry
Biol.	Biology
Bot.	Botany
Brit.	British
c.	century, circa
cf.	compare
Ch.	Church
Chem.	Chemistry
Cinematog.	Cinematography
class.	classical
coarse sl.	coarse slang
collect.	collective, collectively
colloq.	colloquial, colloquially
comb.	combination, combining
compar.	comparative
compl.	complement
conj.	conjunction
contr.	contraction
corresp.	corresponding
Criminol.	Criminology
def.	definite
demons.adj.	demonstrative adjective

Abbreviations Used in This Book xii

demons.pron.	demonstrative pronoun
deriv.	derivative
derog.	derogatory
dial.	dialect
dimin.	diminutive
disp.	disputed (use or pronunciation)
Eccl.	Ecclesiastical
Ecol.	Ecology
Econ.	Economics
e.g.	for example
Electr.	Electricity
ellipt.	elliptical, elliptically
emphat.	emphatic, emphatically
Engin.	Engineering
Engl.	England, English
Entomol.	Entomology
erron.	erroneous, erroneously
esp.	especially
etc.	et cetera ("and so on")
euphem.	euphemism
exc.	except
exclam.	exclamation
fam.	familiar
fem.	feminine
fig.	figurative, figuratively
fl.	flourished
foll.	followed, following
form.	formation
Geog.	Geography
Geol.	Geology
Geom.	Geometry
Gram.	Grammar
Gk.	Greek
Hist.	History
hist.	with historical reference
Horol.	Horology
i.e.	that is to say
imit.	imitative
imper.	imperative
incl.	including, inclusive
Ind.	India, Indian
infin.	infinitive
int.	interjection
interrog.	interrogative, interrogatively
interrog.adj.	interrogative adjective
intr.	intransitive

iron.	ironic, ironically
irreg.	irregular, irregularly
joc.	jocular, jocularly
lang.	language
lit.	literal, literally
masc.	masculine
Math.	Mathematics
Mech.	Mechanics
Med.	Medicine
Meteorol.	Meteorology
Mil.	Military
Mineral.	Mineralogy
mod.	modern
Mus.	Music
Mythol.	Mythology
n.	noun
N.Amer.	North America, North American
Naut.	Nautical
neg.	negative, negatively
neut.	neuter
n.pl.	noun plural
num.	numeral
obj.	object, objective
obs.	obsolete
occas.	occasional, occasionally
offens.	offensive
opp.	(as) opposed (to), opposite (of)
orig.	origin, original, originally
part.	participle
past part.	past participle
perf.	perfect (tense)
perh.	perhaps
pers.	person, personal
Pharm.	Pharmacy, Pharmacology
Philol.	Philology
Philos.	Philosophy
Phonet.	Phonetics
Photog.	Photography
phr.	phrase
Physiol.	Physiology
pl.	plural
poet.	poetical
Polit.	Politics
pop.	popular, not technical
poss.	possessive
prec.	preceded, preceding

predic.	predicate, predicative, predicatively
prep.	preposition
pres.part.	present participle
prob.	probable, probably
pron.	pronoun
pronunc.	pronunciation
propr.	proprietary term, trademark
Psychol.	Psychology
RC Ch.	Roman Catholic Church
ref.	reference
refl.	reflexive, reflexively
rel.	related, relative
rel.adj.	relative adjective
Relig.	Religion
rel.pron.	relative pronoun
repr.	representing
Rhet.	Rhetoric
rhet.	rhetorical, rhetorically
Rom.	Roman
Sc.	Scottish
Sci.	Science
sing.	singular
sl.	slang
Sociol.	Sociology
spec.	special, specially
Stock Exch.	Stock Exchange
subj.	subject, subjunctive
superl.	superlative
syll.	syllable
symb.	symbol
syn.	synonym
Telev.	Television
Theatr.	Theater, Theatrical
Theol.	Theology
tr.	transitive
transl.	translation
ult.	ultimate, ultimately
US	American, in American use, in the United States
usu.	usual, usually
v.	verb
var.	variant(s)
v.aux.	auxiliary verb
v.intr.	intransitive verb
v.refl.	reflexive verb
v.tr.	transitive verb
Zool.	Zoology

Abbreviations Used in This Book

Note on proprietary status
This book includes some words that are, or are asserted to be, proprietary names or trademarks. Their inclusion does not imply that they have acquired for legal purposes a nonproprietary or general significance. In cases where the editor has some evidence that a word is used as a proprietary name or trademark, this is indicated by the designation *propr.,* but no judgment concerning the legal status of such words is made or implied thereby.

Key to the Pronunciations

This book uses a simple respelling system to show how entries are pronounced, using the following symbols:

a, á	*as in*	**pat** /pat/, **fasten** /fásən/
aa, áa	*as in*	**father** /faáthər/, **barnyard** /baárnyaard/
air, áir	*as in*	**fair** /fair/, **share** /shair/, **heir** /air/
aw, áw	*as in*	**law** /law/, **caught** /kawt/, **thought** /thawt/
ay, áy	*as in*	**day** /day/, **raid** /rayd/, **made** /mayd/, **prey** /pray/
ch	*as in*	**church** /chərch/, **picture** /píkchər/
e, é	*as in*	**men** /men/, **said** /sed/
ee, ée	*as in*	**feet** /feet/, **receive** /riséev/
ə	*as in*	**along** /əlóng/, **soda** /sódə/, **civil** /sívəl/
ər, ə́r	*as in*	**parade** /pəráyd/, **bitter** /bítər/, **person** /pə́rsən/
g	*as in*	**get** /get/, **exhaust** /igzáwst/, **egg** /eg/
i, í	*as in*	**pin** /pin/, **guild** /gild/, **women** /wímin/
ī, í̄	*as in*	**time** /tīm/, **fight** /fīt/, **guide** /gīd/
īr, í̄r	*as in*	**fire** /fīr/, **desire** /dizí̄r/
j	*as in*	**judge** /juj/, **carriage** /kárij/
<u>kh</u>	*as in*	**loch** /lo<u>kh</u>/, **Bach** /baa<u>kh</u>/
ɴ	*as in*	**en route** /oɴ root/ (preceding vowel is nasalized)
ng	*as in*	**sing** /sing/, **anger** /ánggər/
o, ó	*as in*	**rob** /rob/, **pocket** /pókit/
ō, ố	*as in*	**go** /gō/, **promote** /prəmốt/
ö, ő	*as in*	**hors d'oeuvre** /awrdốrvrə; –dörv/
o͞o, o͝o	*as in*	**wood** /wo͝od, **football** /fo͝otbawl/
o͞o, o͞ó	*as in*	**food** /fo͞od/, **music** /myo͞ósik/
ow, ów	*as in*	**mouse** /mows/, **coward** /kówərd/
oy, óy	*as in*	**boy** /boy/, **noisy** /nóyzee/
r	*as in*	**run** /run/, **fur** /fər/, **spirit** /spírit/

Key to the Pronunciations

sh	*as in*	**shut** /shut/, **social** /sṓshəl/, **action** /ákshən/
th	*as in*	**thin** /thin/, **truth** /trōoth/
<u>th</u>	*as in*	**then** /<u>th</u>en/, **mother** /mú<u>th</u>ər/
u, ú	*as in*	**cut** /kut/, **blood** /blud/, **enough** /inúf/
y	*as in*	**yet** /yet/, **accuse** /əkyōoz/
<u>zh</u>	*as in*	**measure** /mé<u>zh</u>ər/, **vision** /ví<u>zh</u>ən/

Variants

More than one acceptable pronunciation may be given, with commas between the variants; for example:

news /nōoz, nyōoz/

If the pronunciations of a word differ only in part, then the syllable or syllables affected are shown as follows:

bedroom /bédrōom, –rŏŏm/, **forest** /fáwrist, fór–/

The same principle applies to derivative forms that are given within the main entry; for example:

complete /kəmpleét/, **completion** /–pleéshən/

Stress

The mark that appears over the vowel symbol in words of more than one syllable indicates the part of the word that carries the stress. Where a word has two or more stress markers then the main stress may vary according to the context in which a word is used; for example:

afternoon /áftərnōon/

In the phrase "afternoon tea" the main stress falls on the first syllable /áftər–/, but in the phrase "all afternoon" the main stress falls on the last syllable /–nōon/.

Aa

A¹ /ay/ n. (also **a**) (pl. **As** or **A's; a's**) **1** first letter of the alphabet. **2** Mus. sixth note of the diatonic scale of C major. **3** first hypothetical person or example. **4** highest class or category (of academic grades, etc.). **5** human blood type.

A² /ay/ abbr. (also **A.**) **1** ampere(s). **2** answer. **3** Associate of. **4** atomic (energy, etc.).

a¹ /ə, ay/ adj. (also **an** before a vowel) **1** one; some; any. **2** one like (a Judas). **3** one single (not a thing in sight). **4** the same. **5** in, to, or for each (twice a year).

a² /ə/ prep. (usu. as prefix) **1** to; toward (ashore). **2** in the process of; in a specified state (a-wandering; abuzz). **3** on (afire).

Å abbr. ångström(s).

a- /ay, ə/ prefix not; without (amoral).

AA abbr. **1** Alcoholics Anonymous. **2** Mil. antiaircraft.

aard·vark /aárdvaark/ n. anteating nocturnal mammal of southern Africa.

AB /áybeé/ n. human blood type.

ab- /əb, ab/ prefix off; away; from (abduct; abnormal; abuse).

a·back /əbák/ adv. archaic backward; behind. □ **take aback** surprise; disconcert (your request took me aback).

ab·a·cus /ábəkəs, əbákəs/ n. (pl. **ab·a·cus·es**) oblong frame with wires along which beads are slid, used for calculating.

ABACUS

a·baft /əbáft/ Naut. • adv. in the stern half of a ship. • prep. nearer the stern than; aft of.

ab·a·lo·ne /ábəlónee/ n. salt-water mollusk with a shallow ear-shaped shell.

a·ban·don /əbándən/ • v.tr. **1** give up completely or before completion. **2** forsake, desert, or leave. • n. lack of inhibition or restraint. □□ **a·ban'do·ner** n. **a·ban'don·ment** n.

a·ban·doned /əbándənd/ adj. **1** deserted; forsaken. **2** unrestrained; profligate.

a·base /əbáys/ v.tr. humiliate or degrade. □□ **a·base'ment** n.

a·bash /əbásh/ v.tr. (usu. as **abashed** adj.) embarrass; disconcert. □□ **a·bash'ment** n.

a·bate /əbáyt/ v. make or become less strong, severe, intense, etc. □□ **a·bate'ment** n.

ab·at·toir /ábətwaar/ n. slaughterhouse.

ab·bess /ábis/ n. head of a community of nuns.

ab·bey /ábee/ n. (pl. **–beys**) **1** building(s) occupied by a community of monks or nuns. **2** the community itself.

ab·bot /ábət/ n. head of a community of monks.

abbr. abbr. (also **abbrev.**) abbreviation.

ab·bre·vi·ate /əbreévee-ayt/ v.tr. shorten, esp. represent (a word, etc.) by a part of it. □□ **ab·bre·vi·a·tion** /–áyshən/ n.

ABC /áybeeseé/ n. **1** the alphabet. **2** (usu. pl.) rudiments of any subject.

ab·di·cate /ábdikayt/ v.tr. **1** give up or renounce (esp. a throne). **2** renounce (a responsibility, duty, etc.). □□ **ab·di·ca'tion** /–káyshən/ n. **ab'di·ca·tor** n.

ab·do·men /ábdəmən, abdó–/ n. **1** part of the body containing digestive and reproductive organs. **2** Zool. hind part of an insect, crustacean, etc. □□ **ab·dom·i·nal** /abdóminəl/ adj. **ab·dom'i·nal·ly** /abdóminəlee/ adv.

ab·duct /əbdúkt/ v.tr. carry off or kidnap (a person) illegally. □□ **ab·duc'tion** /–dúkshən/ n. **ab·duc'tor** n.

a·beam /əbeém/ adv. at right angles to a ship's or aircraft's length.

ab·er·ra·tion /ábəráyshən/ n. **1** departure from what is normal or regarded as right. **2** moral or mental lapse. □□ **ab·er'rant** adj. **ab·er·ra'tion·al** adj.

a·bet /əbét/ v.tr. (**a·bet·ted, a·bet·ting**) (usu. in **aid and a·bet**) encourage or assist (an offender or offense). □□ **a·bet'ment** n.

a·bey·ance /əbáyəns/ n. (usu. prec. by in, into) state of temporary disuse or suspension. □□ **a·bey·ant** /–ənt/ adj.

abhor /əbháwr/ v.tr. (**ab·horred, ab·hor·ring**) detest; regard with disgust and hatred. □□ **ab·hor'rence** n. **ab·hor'rer** n.

ab·hor·rent /əbháwrənt, –hór–/ adj. disgusting; repugnant; hateful; detestable.

a·bide /əbíd/ v. (past **a·bode** /əbód/ or **a·bid·ed**) **1** tr. tolerate; endure. **2** intr. **a** act in accordance with **b** remain faithful to (a promise). □□ **a·bid'ance** n.

a·bid·ing /əbíding/ adj. enduring; permanent (an abiding sense of loss). □□ **a·bid'ing·ly** adv.

a·bil·i·ty /əbíleteé/ n. (pl. **–ties**) **1** capacity or power. **2** cleverness; talent; mental power.

-ability /əbíleteé/ suffix forming nouns of quality from, or corresponding to, adjectives in –able (capability; vulnerability).

ab·ject /ábjekt, abjékt/ adj. **1** miserable; wretched. **2** degraded; self-abasing; humble. **3** despicable. □□ **ab·jec'tion** n. **ab·ject'ly** adv. **ab·ject'ness** n.

ab·jure /əbjoôr/ v.tr. renounce under oath. □□ **ab·ju·ra'tion** /–ráyshən/ n.

ab·la·tive /áblətiv/ Gram. • n. case (esp. in

Latin) of nouns and pronouns indicating an agent, instrument, or location. ● *adj.* of or in the ablative.

a·blaze /əbláyz/ *adj. & adv.* **1** on fire. **2** glittering; glowing; radiant. **3** greatly excited.

a·ble /áybəl/ *adj.* (**a·bler, a·blest**) **1** (often foll. by *to*) having the capacity or power (*able to come*). **2** having great ability; clever. □ **able-bodied** fit; healthy.

-able /əbəl/ *suffix* forming adjectives meaning: **1** that may or must be (*eatable*). **2** that can be made the subject of (*dutiable; objectionable*). **3** relevant to or in accordance with (*fashionable*).

ab·lu·tion /əblóoshən/ *n.* (usu. in *pl.*) **1** ceremonial washing of hands, sacred vessels, etc. **2** *colloq.* ordinary washing of the body. □□ **ab·lu′tion·ar·y** *adj.*

-ably /əblee/ *suffix* forming adverbs corresponding to adjectives in *-able.*

ABM *abbr.* antiballistic missile.

ab·ne·gate /ábnigayt/ *v.tr.* **1** give up or deny oneself (a pleasure, etc.). **2** renounce or reject (a right or belief). □□ **ab·ne·ga·tion** /-gáyshən/ *n.* **ab′ne·ga·tor** *n.*

ab·nor·mal /abnáwrməl/ *adj.* deviating from the norm; exceptional. □□ **ab·nor·mal′i·ty** *n.* **ab·nor′mal·ly** *adv.*

a·board /əbáwrd/ *adv. & prep.* **1** on or into (a ship, aircraft, etc.). **2** alongside.

a·bode[1] /əbód/ *n.* dwelling; one's home.

a·bode[2] *past of* ABIDE.

a·bol·ish /əbólish/ *v.tr.* put an end to (esp. a custom or institution). □□ **a·bol′ish·a·ble** *adj.* **a·bol′ish·er** *n.* **a·bol′ish·ment** *n.*

ab·o·li·tion /ábəlíshən/ *n.* **1** abolishing or being abolished. **2** the ending of a practice or institution, esp. (in US hist.) slavery. □□ **ab·o·li′tion·ist** *n.*

A-bomb /áybom/ *n.* = atom bomb.

a·bom·i·na·ble /əbóminəbəl/ *adj.* **1** detestable; loathsome; morally reprehensible. **2** *colloq.* very unpleasant. □□ **a·bom′i·na·bly** *adv.*

a·bom·i·nate /əbóminayt/ *v.tr.* detest; loathe. □□ **a·bom·i·na·tion** /-náyshən/ *n.* **a·bom′i·na·tor** *n.*

ab·o·rig·i·nal /ábəríjinəl/ *adj.* **1** inhabiting or existing in a land from the earliest times or from before the arrival of colonists. **2** (usu. **Aboriginal**) of the Australian Aborigines.

ab·o·rig·i·ne /ábəríjinee/ *n.* (usu. in *pl.*) **1** aboriginal inhabitant. **2** (usu. **Aborigine**) aboriginal inhabitant of Australia. **3** aboriginal plant or animal.

a·bort /əbáwrt/ ● *v.* **1** *intr.* miscarry. **2** *tr.* effect abortion. **3** *a tr.* cause to end fruitlessly or prematurely. **b** *intr.* end unsuccessfully or prematurely. ● *n.* **1** prematurely terminated space flight or other undertaking. **2** termination of such an undertaking.

a·bor·tion /əbáwrshən/ *n.* expulsion of a fetus (naturally or esp. by medical induction) from the womb before it is able to survive independently. □□ **a·bor′tion·ist** *n.*

a·bor·tive /əbáwrtiv/ *adj.* fruitless; unsuccessful; unfinished. □□ **a·bor′tive·ly** *adv.*

ABO system /áybee-ó/ *n.* system of four types (A, AB, B, and O) by which human blood may be classified.

a·bound /əbównd/ *v.intr.* **1** be plentiful. **2** (foll. by *in, with*) be rich; teem or be infested.

a·bout /əbówt/ ● *prep.* **1 a** on the subject of. **b** relating to. **c** in relation to (*symmetry about a plane*). **d** so as to affect (*can do nothing about it*). **2** at a time near to. **3** in; around. ● *adv.* **1 a** approximately. **b** *colloq.* used to indicate understatement (*just about had enough*). **2** at points nearby (*a lot of flu about*). **3** in every direction.

a·bout-face /əbówtfáys/ ● *n.* **1** turn made to face the opposite direction. **2** change of opinion or policy, etc. ● *v.intr.* make an about-face. ● *int. Mil.* a command to make an about-face.

a·bove /əbúv/ ● *prep.* **1** over; on the top of; higher than. **2** more than (*above average*). **3** higher in rank, importance, etc., than. ● *adv.* **1** at or to a higher point; overhead. **2** upstairs. **3** (of a text reference) further back on a page or in a book (*as noted above*). ● *adj.* preceding. ● *n.* (prec. by *the*) what is mentioned above. □ **above all** more than anything else.

a·bove·board /əbúvbawrd/ *adj. & adv.* without concealment; fair or fairly; open or openly.

ab·ra·ca·da·bra /ábrəkədábrə/ *int.* word used in performing a magic trick.

a·brade /əbráyd/ *v.tr.* scrape or wear away (skin, rock, etc.) by rubbing. □□ **a·brad′er** *n.*

a·bra·sion /əbráyzhən/ *n.* **1** result of abrading. **2** damaged area resulting from this.

a·bra·sive /əbráysiv/ ● *adj.* **1 a** tending to rub or abrade. **b** capable of polishing by rubbing or grinding. **2** harsh or hurtful in manner. ● *n.* abrasive substance.

a·breast /əbrést/ *adv.* **1** side by side and facing the same way. **2 a** up to date. **b** well-informed.

a·bridge /əbríj/ *v.tr.* **1** shorten (a book, movie, etc.). **2** curtail. □□ **a·bridg′a·ble** or **a·bridge′a·ble** *adj.* **a·bridg′er** *n.* **a·bridg′ment** or **a·bridge′ment** *n.*

a·broad /əbráwd/ *adv.* **1** in or to a foreign country or countries. **2** over a wide area. **3** in circulation.

ab·ro·gate /ábrəgayt/ *v.tr.* repeal, annul, or abolish (a law or custom). □□ **ab·ro·ga·tion** /-gáyshən/ *n.* **ab′ro·ga·tor** *n.*

a·brupt /əbrúpt/ *adj.* **1** sudden; hasty. **2** (of speech, manner, etc.) curt. **3** steep. □□ **ab·rupt′ly** *adv.* **ab·rupt′ness** *n.*

ABS *abbr.* antilock brake (or braking) system.

ab·scess /ábses/ *n.* swelling containing pus. □□ **ab′scessed** *adj.*

ab·scis·sa /əbsísə/ *n.* (*pl.* **ab·scis·sae** /-ee/ or **ab·scis·sas**) *Math.* (in a system of coordinates) shortest distance from a point to the vertical or *y*-axis (cf. ORDINATE).

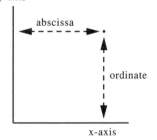

ABSCISSA

ab·scond /əbskónd/ v.intr. depart hurriedly and furtively, esp. unlawfully or to avoid arrest. □□ **ab·scond′er** n.

ab·sence /ábsəns/ n. **1** state of being away. **2** time of this. **3** lack.

ab·sent ● adj. /ábsənt/ **1** not present. **2** not existing. **3** inattentive. ● v.refl. /ábsént/ **1** stay away. **2** withdraw. □□ **ab′sent·ly** adv. (in sense 3 of adj.).

ab·sen·tee /ábsəntee/ n. person not present. □ **absentee landlord** a landlord who rents out a property while living elsewhere.

ab·sen·tee·ism /ábsənteéeizəm/ n. habitual absence from work, school, etc.

ab·sent·mind·ed /ábsəntmíndid/ adj. forgetful or inattentive. □□ **ab′sent·mind·ed·ly** adv. **ab′sent·mind′ed·ness** n.

ab·sinthe /ábsinth/ n. (also **ab′sinth**) aniseed-flavored potent liqueur based on wormwood.

ab·so·lute /ábsəlŏŏt/ adj. **1** complete; utter. **2** unconditional. **3** despotic. **4** (of a standard or other concept) not relative or comparative. **5** (of a legal decree, etc.) final. □ **absolute majority 1** majority over all others combined. **2** more than half. **absolute pitch** Mus. ability to recognize or sound any given note. **absolute zero** theoretical lowest possible temperature, calculated as −273.15° C (or 0° K). □□ **ab·so·lute′ness** n.

ab·so·lute·ly /ábsəlŏŏtlee/ adv. **1** completely; utterly. **2** in an absolute sense. **3** colloq. in actual fact; positively. **4** colloq. (used in reply) quite so; yes.

ab·so·lu·tion /ábsəlŏŏshən/ n. formal release or forgiveness from guilt, sin, obligation, or punishment.

ab·so·lut·ism /ábsəlŏŏtizəm/ n. acceptance of or belief in absolute principles in politics, theology, etc. □□ **ab′so·lut·ist** n. & adj.

ab·solve /əbzólv, –sólv/ v.tr. **1 a** free from blame or obligation, etc. **b** acquit; pronounce not guilty. **2** pardon or give absolution for (a sin, etc.). □□ **ab·solv′er** n.

ab·sorb /əbsáwrb, –záwrb/ v.tr. **1** incorporate as part of itself or oneself. **2** take in; suck up. **3** reduce the effect or intensity of. **4** consume. **5** engross the attention of. □□ **ab·sorb′a·ble** adj. **ab·sorb·a·bil′i·ty** n. **ab·sorb′er** n.

ab·sorbed /əbsáwrbd, –záwrbd/ adj. intensely engaged or interested. □□ **ab·sorb·ed·ly** /–bidlee/ adv.

ab·sor·bent /əbsáwrbənt, –záwr–/ ● adj. tending to absorb. ● n. absorbent substance. □□ **ab·sor·ben·cy** /–bənsee/ n.

ab·sorb·ing /əbsáwrbing, –záwr–/ adj. engrossing; intensely interesting. □□ **ab·sorb′ing·ly** adv.

ab·sorp·tion /əbsáwrpshən, –záwrp–/ n. **1** absorbing or being absorbed. **2** mental engrossment. □□ **ab·sorp′tive** adj.

ab·stain /əbstáyn/ v.intr. **1** refrain from. **2** formally decline to use one's vote. □□ **ab·stain′er** n. **ab·sten·tion** /əbsténshən/ n.

ab·ste·mi·ous /əbsteémeeəs/ adj. moderate, esp. in eating and drinking. □□ **ab·ste′mi·ous·ly** adv. **ab·ste′mi·ous·ness** n.

ab·sti·nence /ábstinəns/ n. abstaining, esp. from food, alcohol, or sexual relations. □□ **ab′sti·nent** adj.

ab·stract ● adj. /ábstrakt/ **1 a** of or existing in thought or theory rather than matter or prac-

tice; not concrete. **b** (of a word, esp. a noun) denoting a quality, condition, etc., not a concrete object. **2** (of art) achieving its effect by shapes and colors rather than by realism. ● v.tr. /əbstrákt/ **1** extract; remove. **2** summarize. ● n. /ábstrakt/ **1** summary. **2** abstract work of art. □□ **ab·stract′ly** adv. **ab·stract′or** n. (in sense 2 of v.).

ab·strac·tion /əbstrákshən/ n. **1** removal or taking away. **2** abstract or visionary idea. **3 a** abstract qualities (esp. in art). **b** abstract work of art. **4** absentmindedness.

ab·struse /əbstrŏŏs/ adj. hard to understand; obscure; profound. □□ **ab·struse′ly** adv. **ab·struse′ness** n.

ab·surd /əbsárd/ adj. wildly illogical or inappropriate. □□ **ab·surd′i·ty** n. **ab·surd′ly** adv.

a·bun·dance /əbúndəns/ n. very great quantity; more than enough. □□ **a·bun′dant** adj. **a·bun′dant·ly** adv.

a·buse ● v.tr. /əbyŏŏz/ **1 a** use improperly; misuse. **b** take (a drug) for a purpose other than a therapeutic one; be addicted to (a substance). **2** insult verbally. **3** maltreat; assault (esp. sexually). ● n. /əbyŏŏs/ **1** improper use. **2** insulting language. **3** unjust or corrupt practice. **4** maltreatment. □□ **a·bused** /əbyŏŏzd/ adj. **a·bus·er** /əbyŏŏzər/ n. **a·bu·sive** /əbyŏŏsiv/ adj. **a·bu′sive·ly** adv. **a·bu′sive·ness** n.

a·but /əbút/ v. (**a·but·ted**, **a·but·ting**) **1** intr. (of land, etc.) adjoin (another). **2** tr. border on.

a·but·ment /əbútmənt/ n. **1** lateral supporting structure of a bridge, arch, etc. **2** point of junction between such a support and the thing supported.

a·bys·mal /əbízməl/ adj. **1** colloq. extremely bad. **2** profound; utter. □□ **a·bys′mal·ly** adv.

a·byss /əbís/ n. **1** deep chasm. **2** immeasurable depth. **3** primal chaos; hell.

AC abbr. **1** (also **ac**) alternating current. **2** air conditioning.

Ac symb. Chem. actinium.

ac- /ək/ prefix assim. form of AD- before c, k, q.

-ac /ak/ suffix forming adjectives often (or only) used as nouns (cardiac; maniac).

a·ca·cia /əkáyshə/ n. tree with yellow or white flowers, esp. one yielding gum arabic.

ac·a·de·mi·a /ákədeémeeə/ n. (also **ac·a·deme** /ákədeem/) academic world; scholastic life. □□ **ac·a·de·mi·cian** /ákədəmíshən/ n.

ac·a·dem·ic /ákədémik/ ● adj. **1 a** scholarly; of learning. **b** of or relating to a scholarly institution (academic dress). **2** theoretical; not of practical relevance. ● n. teacher or scholar in a university, etc. □□ **ac·a·dem′i·cal·ly** adv.

a·cad·e·my /əkádəmee/ n. (pl. **-mies**) **1 a** place of specialized training. **b** hist. place of study. **2** (usu. **Academy**) society or institution of distinguished scholars, artists, scientists, etc.

a·can·thus /əkánthəs/ n. herbaceous plant with spiny leaves.

a cap·pel·la /áa kəpélə/ adj. & adv. Mus. (of choral singing) unaccompanied.

ac·cede /akseéd/ v.intr. **1** assent or agree. **2** take office.

ac·cel·er·ate /aksélərayt/ v. **1** intr. **a** move or begin to move more quickly; increase speed. **b** happen or reach completion more quickly. **2**

tr. **a** cause to increase speed. **b** cause to happen more quickly. □□ **ac·cel·er·a·tion** /–ráyshən/ *n.*

ac·cel·er·a·tor /əkséləraytər/ *n.* **1** device for increasing speed, esp. the pedal that controls the speed of a vehicle's engine. **2** *Physics* apparatus for imparting high speeds to charged particles.

ac·cent • *n.* /áksent/ **1** particular mode of pronunciation, esp. local or national. **2** prominence given to a syllable by stress or pitch. **3** mark on a letter or word to indicate pitch, stress, or vowel quality. **4** distinctive feature or emphasis. • *v.tr.* (also /aksént/) **1** emphasize (a word or syllable). **2** write or print accents on (words, etc.). **3** accentuate. □□ **ac·cen·tu·al** /aksénchōoəl/ *adj.*

ac·cen·tu·ate /aksénchōoayt/ *v.tr.* emphasize; make prominent. □□ **ac·cen·tu·a·tion** /–áyshən/ *n.*

ac·cept /aksépt/ *v.tr.* **1** willingly receive. **2** answer affirmatively. **3** regard favorably; treat as welcome. **4 a** believe. **b** be prepared to subscribe to (a belief, philosophy, etc.).

¶ **Accept,** which means 'to take that which is offered,' may be confused with the verb **except,** which means 'to exclude.' Thus: *I accept the terms of your offer, but I wish to except the clause calling for repayment of the deposit.*

ac·cept·a·ble /akséptəbəl/ *adj.* **1 a** worth accepting. **b** welcome. **2** adequate. **3** tolerable. □□ **ac·cept·a·bil·i·ty** /–bílitee/ *n.* **ac·cept'a·ble·ness** *n.* **ac·cept'a·bly** *adv.*

ac·cept·ance /akséptəns/ *n.* **1** willingness to receive. **2** affirmative answer to an invitation.

ac·cess /ákses/ • *n.* **1** way of approach or entry. **2 a** right or opportunity to reach or use or visit; admittance. **b** accessibility. • *v.tr. Computing* gain access to (data, a file, etc.).

ac·ces·si·ble /aksésibəl/ *adj.* **1** readily reached, entered, or used. **2** readily available. **3** easy to understand. □□ **ac·ces·si·bil·i·ty** /–bílitee/ *n.* **ac·ces'si·bly** *adv.*

ac·ces·sion /akséshən/ • *n.* **1** taking office (esp. the throne). **2** thing added (e.g., book to a library); increase. • *v.tr.* record the addition of (a new item) to a library, etc.

ac·ces·so·ry /aksésəree/ • *n.* (*pl.* **–ries**) **1** additional or extra thing. **2** (usu. in *pl.*) **a** small attachment or fitting. **b** small item of (esp. a woman's) dress (e.g., shoes, gloves, etc.). **3** person who helps in or knows the details of an (esp. illegal) act. • *adj.* additional; contributing or aiding in a minor way; dispensable. □□ **ac·ces·so·ri·al** /áksesáwreeəl/ *adj.*

ac·ci·dent /áksidənt/ *n.* **1** event that is without apparent cause or that is unexpected. **2** unfortunate event, esp. one causing physical harm or damage. **3** occurrence of things by chance. □ **accident-prone** (of a person) subject to frequent accidents.

ac·ci·den·tal /áksidént'l/ • *adj.* happening by chance or unexpectedly. • *n.* **1** *Mus.* sign indicating a momentary departure from the key signature. **2** something not essential. □□ **ac·ci·den'tal·ly** *adv.*

ac·claim /əkláym/ • *v.tr.* welcome or applaud enthusiastically; praise publicly. • *n.* applause; welcome; public praise. □□ **ac·claim'er** *n.*

ac·cla·ma·tion /ákləmáyshən/ *n.* **1** loud and eager assent. **2** act or process of acclaiming.

ac·cli·mate /áklimayt, əklímit/ *v.tr.* acclimatize.

ac·cli·ma·tize /əklímətīz/ *v.* **1** *tr.* accustom to a

new climate or conditions. **2** *intr.* become acclimatized. □□ **ac·cli·ma·tiz·a'tion** *n.*

ac·co·lade /ákəláyd/ *n.* awarding of praise; acknowledgment of merit.

ac·com·mo·date /əkómədayt/ *v.tr.* **1** provide lodging or room for. **2** adapt; harmonize; reconcile. **3** do a favor for.

ac·com·mo·dat·ing /əkómədayting/ *adj.* obliging; compliant. □□ **ac·com'mo·dat·ing·ly** *adv.*

ac·com·mo·da·tion /əkómədáyshən/ *n.* **1** (in *pl.*) **a** lodgings; place to live. **b** room and board. **2 a** adjustment or adaptation. **b** settlement or compromise. **3** act or process of accommodating or being accommodated. **4** (in *pl.*) seat or other facilities for a passenger of a public vehicle.

ac·com·pa·ni·ment /əkúmpənimənt/ *n.* **1** *Mus.* instrumental or orchestral support for a solo instrument, voice, or group. **2** accompanying thing. □□ **ac·com'pa·nist** *n.*

ac·com·pa·ny /əkúmpənee/ *v.tr.* (**–nies, –nied**) **1** go with; escort. **2 a** supplement. **b** have as a result (*pills accompanied by side effects*). **3** *Mus.* support or partner with accompaniment.

ac·com·plice /əkómplis, əkúm–/ *n.* partner in a crime.

---

accomplice mid-16th cent.: alteration (probably by association with ACCOMPANY) of Middle English *complice* 'an associate,' via Old French from late Latin *complex, complic-* 'allied,' from *com-* 'together' + the root of *plicare* 'to fold.'

---

ac·com·plish /əkómplish/ *v.tr.* perform; complete; succeed in doing. □□ **ac·com'plish·a·ble** *adj.*

ac·com·plished /əkómplisht/ *adj.* clever; skilled.

ac·com·plish·ment /əkómplishmənt/ *n.* **1** completion (of a task, etc.). **2** acquired (esp. social) skill. **3** thing achieved.

ac·cord /əkáwrd/ • *v.* **1** *intr.* be in harmony; be consistent. **2** *tr.* grant (permission, a request, etc.). • *n.* **1** agreement; consent. **2** harmony. **3** formal treaty or agreement. □ **of one's own accord** voluntarily.

ac·cord·ance /əkáwrd'ns/ *n.* harmony; agreement.

ac·cord·ing /əkáwrding/ *adv.* **1** (foll. by *to*) as stated by (*according to my sister*). **2** in proportion to.

ac·cord·ing·ly /əkáwrdinglee/ *adv.* **1** as suggested or required by the (stated) circumstances. **2** consequently.

ac·cor·di·on /əkáwrdeeən/ *n.* musical reed instrument with bellows, keys, and buttons. □□ **ac·cor'di·on·ist** *n.*

ACCORDION

ac·cost /əkáwst, əkóst/ *v.tr.* **1** approach and address (a person), esp. boldly. **2** (of a prostitute) solicit.

ac·count /əkównt/ • *n.* **1** narration or description. **2** arrangement at a bank, etc., for commercial or financial transactions, esp. for depositing and withdrawing money. **3** (often in *pl.*) record or statement of financial transactions. • *v.tr.* (foll. by *to be* or compl.) consider; regard as (*account it a misfortune*). ¶ Use with *as* (*we accounted him as wise*) is considered incorrect. □ **account for 1** serve as or provide an explanation for. **2 a** give a reckoning of (money, etc., entrusted). **b** answer for (one's conduct). **on no account** under no circumstances. **take account of** (or **take into account**) consider along with other factors (*took their age into account*).

ac·count·a·ble /əkówntəbəl/ *adj.* **1** responsible; required to account for (one's conduct). **2** understandable. □□ **ac·count·a·bil·i·ty** /–bilitee/ *n.* **ac·count′a·ble·ness** *n.* **ac·count′a·bly** *adv.*

ac·count·ant /əkównt′nt/ *n.* professional keeper or inspector of accounts. □□ **ac·count′an·cy** *n.*

ac·count·ing /əkównting/ *n.* **1** process or practice of keeping and verifying accounts. **2** in sense of ACCOUNT *v.*

ac·cou·ter·ment /əkóóŏtərmənt, –trəmənt/ *n.* (also **ac·cou′tre·ment**) (usu. in *pl.*) **1** equipment. **2** *Mil.* soldier's equipment.

ac·cred·it /əkrédit/ *v.tr.* **1** attribute. **2** send (an ambassador, etc.) with credentials. **3** make credible (an adviser, a statement, etc.). **4** certify (esp. an educational institution) as maintaining professional standards. □□ **ac·cred·i·ta′tion** *n.* **ac·cred′it·ed** *adj.*

ac·cre·tion /əkréeshən/ *n.* **1** growth by organic enlargement. **2 a** growing of separate things into one. **b** product of such growing. **3 a** extraneous matter added to anything. **b** the adhesion of this. □□ **ac·cre′tive** *adj.*

ac·crue /əkróŏ/ *v.intr.* (**ac·crued**, **ac·cru·ing**) come as a natural increase or advantage, esp. financial. □□ **ac·cru′al** *n.* **ac·crued′** *adj.* **ac·crue′ment** *n.*

acct. *abbr.* **1** account. **2** accountant.

ac·cu·mu·late /əkyóómyəlayt/ *v.tr.* **1** acquire an increasing number or quantity of. **2** produce or acquire (a resulting whole) in this way. □□ **ac·cu·mu·la·tion** /–láyshən/ *n.* **ac·cu·mu·la·tive** /–laytiv, –lətiv/ *adj.* **ac·cu′mu·la·tor** *n.*

ac·cu·ra·cy /ákyərəsee/ *n.* exactness or careful precision.

ac·cu·rate /ákyərət/ *adj.* **1** careful; precise; lacking errors. **2** conforming exactly with a qualitative standard, physical or quantitative target, etc. □□ **ac′cu·rate·ly** *adv.* **ac′cu·rate·ness** *n.*

ac·curs·ed /əkɔ́rsid, əkɔ́rst/ *adj.* **1** under a curse. **2** *colloq.* detestable; annoying.

ac·cu·sa·tion /ákyəzáyshən/ *n.* **1** accusing or being accused. **2** statement charging a person with an offense or crime. □□ **ac·cu·sa·to·ry** /əkyóŏzətawree/

ac·cu·sa·tive /əkyóŏzətiv/ *Gram.* • *n.* case of nouns, pronouns, and adjectives expressing the object of an action. • *adj.* of or in this case. □□ **ac·cu·sa·ti·val** /–tíŏvəl/ *adj.* **ac·cu′sa·tive·ly** *adv.*

ac·cuse /əkyóŏz/ *v.tr.* **1** (foll. by *of*) charge with a fault or crime; indict. **2** blame. □□ **ac·cus′er** *n.* **ac·cus′ing·ly** *adv.*

ac·cus·tom /əkústəm/ *v.tr.* (foll. by *to*) make (a person or thing) used to (*the army accustomed him to discipline*).

ac·cus·tomed /əkústəmd/ *adj.* **1** (usu. foll. by *to*) used to. **2** customary; usual.

ace /ays/ • *n.* **1** playing card with a single spot and generally having the highest value. **2 a** person who excels in some activity. **b** *Mil.* pilot who has shot down many enemy aircraft. **3** *Tennis* **a** unreturnable serve. **b** point scored in this way. **4** *Golf* hole in one. • *adj. sl.* excellent. □ **within an ace of** on the verge of.

-aceous /áyshəs/ *suffix* forming adjectives, esp. from nouns in *-acea*, *-aceae* (*herbaceous; rosaceous*).

a·cer·bic /əsérbik/ *adj.* **1** astringently sour; harsh-tasting. **2** bitter in speech, manner, or temper. □□ **a·cer′bi·cal·ly** *adv.* **a·cer′bi·ty** *n.* (*pl.* **-ties**).

a·cet·a·min·o·phen /əseetəmínəfən/ *n.* common drug used medically to reduce fever and pain.

ac·e·tate /ásitayt/ *n.* **1** salt or ester of acetic acid. **2** fabric made from this.

a·ce·tic /əseétik/ *adj.* of or like vinegar. □ **acetic acid** clear liquid acid that gives vinegar its characteristic taste.

ac·e·tone /ásitōn/ *n.* colorless, volatile liquid that dissolves organic compounds, esp. paints, varnishes, etc.

a·cet·y·lene /əsétileen/ *n.* colorless hydrocarbon gas, burning with a bright flame, used esp. in welding.

ache /ayk/ • *n.* **1** continuous dull pain. **2** mental distress. • *v.intr.* **1** suffer an ache. **2** desire greatly. □□ **ach′ing·ly** *adv.* **ach′y** *adj.* (**ach·i·er, ach·i·est**).

---

ache Old English *æce* (noun), *acan* (verb). In Middle and early modern English the noun was spelled *atche* and pronounced so as to rhyme with 'batch,' the verb was spelled and pronounced as it is today. The noun began to be pronounced like the verb around 1700. The modern spelling is largely due to lexicographer Samuel Johnson, who mistakenly assumed its derivation to be from Greek *akhos* 'pain.'

---

a·chieve /əcheev/ *v.tr.* **1 a** attain by effort. **b** acquire; gain; earn. **2** accomplish. **3** *absol.* be successful. □□ **a·chiev′a·ble** *adj.* **a·chiev′er** *n.*

a·chieve·ment /əcheevmənt/ *n.* **1** something achieved. **2** act of achieving.

A·chil·les heel /əkíleez/ *n.* person's weak or vulnerable point.

A·chil·les ten·don /əkíleez/ *n.* tendon connecting the heel with the calf muscles.

ach·ro·mat·ic /ákrōmátik/ *adj. Optics* transmitting light without separating it into constituent colors. □□ **ach·ro·ma′tic·al·ly** *adv.* **a·chro·ma·tic·i·ty** /əkrōmətísitee/ *n.* **a·chro·ma·tism** /əkrómətizəm/ *n.*

ac·id /ásid/ • *n.* **1** *Chem.* **a** any of a class of substances that liberate hydrogen ions in water, are usu. sour and corrosive, and have a pH of less than 7. **b** any compound or atom donating protons. **2** any sour substance. **3** *sl.* the drug LSD. • *adj.* **1** sour. **2** biting; sharp. **3** *Chem.* having the properties of an acid. □ **acid rain** overly acidic rainwater, as from pollution. **acid test** severe or conclusive test. □□ **a·cid·ic** /əsídik/ *adj.* **a·cid·i·fy** /əsídifī/ *v.* **a·cid′i·ty** *n.* **ac′id·ly** *adv.* **ac′id·ness** *n.*

a·cid·u·lous /əsídyooləs/ *adj.* somewhat acid.

-acity /ásitee/ *suffix* forming nouns of quality or state corresponding to adjectives in *-acious.*

ac·knowl·edge /əknólij/ *v.tr.* **1** recognize; accept as truth. **2** confirm the receipt of (*acknowledged her letter*). **3 a** show that one has noticed. **b** express appreciation for. **4** recognize the validity of. □□ **ac·knowl′edge·a·ble** *adj.* **ac·knowl′edg·ment** or **ac·knowl′edge·ment** *n.*

ACLU *abbr.* American Civil Liberties Union.

ac·me /ákmee/ *n.* highest point.

ac·ne /áknee/ *n.* skin condition characterized by pimples. □□ **ac′ned** *adj.*

ac·o·lyte /ákəlīt/ *n.* **1** person assisting a priest; altar boy or girl. **2** assistant; beginner.

ac·o·nite /ákənīt/ *n.* **1** any of various poisonous plants, esp. monkshood or wolfsbane. **2** drug obtained from this. □□ **ac·o·nit·ic** /–nítik/ *adj.*

a·corn /áykorn/ *n.* fruit of the oak, with a smooth nut in a rough cuplike base.

a·cous·tic /əko͞ostik/ • *adj.* **1** relating to sound or the sense of hearing. **2** (of a musical instrument) not having electrical amplification. **3** (of building materials) used for soundproofing. • *n.* **1** (usu. in *pl.*) properties or qualities (esp. of a room, etc.) in transmitting sound. **2** (in *pl.*; usu. treated as *sing.*) science of sound. □□ **a·cous′ ti·cal** *adj.* **a·cous′ti·cal·ly** *adv.* **ac·ous·ti·cian** /ákoostíshən/ *n.*

ac·quaint /əkwáynt/ *v.tr.* (usu. foll. by *with*) make aware of or familiar with.

ac·quaint·ance /əkwáyntəns/ *n.* **1** slight knowledge (of a person or thing). **2** being acquainted. **3** person one knows slightly. □□ **ac·quaint′ ance·ship** *n.*

ac·qui·esce /ákwee-és/ *v.intr.* **1** agree, esp. tacitly. **2** raise no objection. **3** accept (an arrangement, etc.). □□ **ac·qui·es′cence** *n.* **ac·′qui·es′ cent** *adj.*

ac·quire /əkwír/ *v.tr.* **1** gain by and for oneself. **2** come into possession of. □ **acquired immune deficiency syndrome** *Med.* see AIDS. □□ **ac·quir′ a·ble** *adj.* **ac·quire′ment** *n.*

ac·qui·si·tion /ákwizíshən/ *n.* **1** something acquired. **2** act of acquiring.

ac·quis·i·tive /əkwízitiv/ *adj.* eager to acquire things. □□ **ac·quis′i·tive·ly** *adv.* **ac·quis′i·tive· ness** *n.*

ac·quit /əkwít/ *v.* (**ac·quit·ted, ac·quit·ting**) **1** *tr.* declare not guilty. **2** *refl.* **a** conduct oneself or perform in a specified way. **b** discharge (a duty or responsibility). □□ **ac·quit′tal** /əkwít′l/ *n.*

a·cre /áykər/ *n.* measure of land, 4,840 sq. yds. □□ **a′cred** *adj.* (also in *comb.*).

---

acre Old English *æcer* (denoting the amount of land a yoke of oxen could plow in a day), of Germanic origin; related to Dutch *akker* and German *Acker* 'field,' from an Indo-European root shared by Sanskrit *ajra* 'field,' Latin *ager,* and Greek *agros.*

---

a·cre·age /áykərij, áykrij/ *n.* unspecified number of acres.

ac·rid /ákrid/ *adj.* (**ac·rid·er, ac·rid·est**) bitterly pungent. □□ **a·crid′i·ty** *n.* **ac′rid·ly** *adv.*

ac·ri·mo·ni·ous /ákrimóneeəs/ *adj.* bitter in manner or temper. □□ **ac·ri·mo′ni·ous·ly** *adv.* **ac·ri·mo·ny** /ákrimōnee/ *n.*

ac·ro·bat /ákrəbat/ *n.* performer of gymnastic feats. □□ **ac·ro·bat′ic** *adj.* **ac·ro·bat′i·cal·ly** *adv.*

ac·ro·bat·ics /ákrəbátiks/ *n.pl.* **1** acrobatic feats. **2** (as *sing.*) art of performing these. **3** skill requiring ingenuity (*mental acrobatics*).

ac·ro·nym /ákrənim/ *n.* usu. pronounceable word formed from the initial letters of other words (e.g., *laser, NATO*).

ac·ro·pho·bi·a /ákrəfóbeeə/ *n. Psychol.* abnormal dread of heights. □□ **ac·ro·pho·bic** /–fó bik/ *adj.*

a·crop·o·lis /əkrópəlis/ *n.* **1** elevated, fortified part of esp. an ancient Greek city. **2** (**Acropolis**) ancient citadel at Athens.

a·cross /əkráws, əkrós/ • *prep.* **1** to or on the other side of. **2** from one side to another side of. **3** at or forming an angle (esp. a right angle) with. • *adv.* **1** to or on the other side. **2** from one side to another. □ **across the board** generally; applying to all.

¶ Avoid pronouncing **across** with a *t*-sound at the end of the word; many regard this as uneducated pronunciation.

a·cros·tic /əkráwstik, əkrós–/ *n.* poem, puzzle, etc., in which certain letters in each line form a word or words.

a·cryl·ic /əkrilik/ • *adj.* **1** of synthetic material made from acrylic acid. **2** *Chem.* of or derived from acrylic acid. • *n.* acrylic fiber.

act /akt/ • *n.* **1** something done; deed. **2** process of doing. **3 a** piece of entertainment. **b** performer(s) of this. **4** pretense. **5** main division of a play or opera. **6** statute law. • *v.intr.* **1** behave. **2** perform actions or functions; take action. **3** (also foll. by *on*) exert energy or influence. **4 a** perform a part in a play, movie, etc. **b** pretend. □ **act up** *colloq.* misbehave; give trouble. **get one's act together** *sl.* become properly organized.

act·ing /ákting/ • *n.* art or occupation of an actor. • *attrib.adj.* serving temporarily.

ac·tin·i·um /aktíneeəm/ *n. Chem.* radioactive metallic element. ¶ Symb.: **Ac.**

ac·tion /ákshən/ • *n.* **1** process of doing or acting. **2** forcefulness or energy. **3** exertion of energy or influence. **4** deed or act. **5 a** series of events in a story, play, etc. **b** *sl.* exciting activity. **6 a** armed conflict; fighting (*killed in action*). **b** minor military engagement. **7 a** way in which a machine, instrument, etc., works. **b** mechanism of an instrument, etc. **8** lawsuit. • *v.tr.* bring a legal action against.

ac·tion·a·ble /ákshənəbəl/ *adj.* giving cause for legal action. □□ **ac′tion·a·bly** *adv.*

ac·ti·vate /áktivayt/ *v.tr.* **1** make active. **2** *Chem.* cause reaction in. **3** *Physics* make radioactive. □□ **ac·ti·va·tion** /–váyshən/ *n.* **ac′ti·va·tor** *n.*

ac·tive /áktiv/ • *adj.* **1 a** marked by action; energetic. **b** able to move about or accomplish practical tasks. **2** working; operative (*active volcano*). **3** originating action (*active support*). **4** *Gram.* designating the voice that attributes the action of a verb to the person or thing from which it logically proceeds (e.g., of the verb in *guns kill*). • *n. Gram.* active form or voice of a verb. □□ **ac′tive·ly** *adv.* **ac′tive·ness** *n.*

ac·tiv·ism /áktivizəm/ *n.* policy of vigorous action in a cause, esp. in politics. □□ **ac′tiv·ist** *n.*

ac·tiv·i·ty /aktívitee/ *n.* (*pl.* **–ties**) **1 a** condition of being active or moving about. **b** exertion of energy; vigorous action. **2** (often in *pl.*) particular occupation or pursuit.

ac·tor /áktər/ *n.* performer in a play, movie, etc.

ac·tress /áktris/ *n.* female actor.

ac·tu·al /ákchŏŏəl/ *adj.* (usu. *attrib.*) **1** existing in fact; real. **2** current. □□ **ac′tu·al·ize** *v.* **ac·tu·al·i·za′tion** *n.*

ac·tu·al·i·ty /ákchŏŏ-álitee/ *n.* (*pl.* **–ties**) **1** reality. **2** (in *pl.*) existing conditions.

ac·tu·al·ly /ákchŏŏəlee/ *adv.* **1** as a fact; really. **2** in truth; strange as it may seem. **3** at present.

ac·tu·ar·y /ákchŏŏeree/ *n.* (*pl.* **–ies**) statistician, esp. one who calculates insurance risks and premiums. □□ **ac·tu·ar·i·al** /–chŏŏáireeəl/ *adj.* **ac·tu·ar′i·al·ly** *adv.*

ac·tu·ate /ákchŏŏ-ayt/ *v.tr.* **1** cause the operation of (an electrical device, etc.). **2** cause to act. □□ **ac·tu·a·tion** /–áyshən/ *n.* **ac′tu·a·tor** *n.*

a·cu·i·ty /əkyŏóitee/ *n.* sharpness; acuteness.

a·cu·men /ákyəmən, əkyŏó–/ *n.* keen insight or discernment.

ac·u·pres·sure /ákyəpreshər/ *n.* method of treating various conditions by applying pressure with the fingers to specific points on the body.

ac·u·punc·ture /ákyəpungkchər/ *n.* method (orig. Chinese) of treating various conditions by pricking the skin with needles. □□ **ac·u·punc′tur·ist** *n.*

a·cute /əkyŏót/ ● *adj.* (**a·cut·er**, **a·cut·est**) **1 a** (of senses, etc.) keen; penetrating. **b** (of pain) intense; severe. **2** (of a disease) coming sharply to a crisis; not chronic. **3 a** (of an angle) less than 90°. **b** sharp; pointed. ● *n.* = *acute accent.* □ **acute accent** mark (′) placed over letters in some languages to show vowel length, pronunciation (e.g., *maté*), etc. □□ **a·cute′ly** *adv.* **a·cute′ness** *n.*

-acy /əsee/ *suffix* forming nouns of state or quality (*accuracy; piracy; supremacy*), or an instance of it (*conspiracy; fallacy*).

A.D. *abbr.* (of a date) of the Christian era (Latin *Anno Domini*, 'in the year of the Lord').

ad /ad/ *n. colloq.* advertisement.

ad- /əd, ad/ *prefix* (also **a-** before *sc, sp, st,* **ac-** before *c, k, q,* **af-** before *f,* **ag-** before *g,* **al-** before *l,* **an-** before *n,* **ap-** before *p,* **ar-** before *r,* **as-** before *s,* **at-** before *t*) with the sense of motion or direction; reduction or change into; addition, adherence, increase, or intensification.

ad·age /ádij/ *n.* traditional maxim; proverb.

a·da·gio /ədáazheeō/ *Mus.* ● *adv. & adj.* in slow time. ● *n.* (*pl.* **–gios**) adagio movement or passage.

Ad·am /ádəm/ *n.* Biblical first man. □ **Adam's apple** projection of cartilage of the larynx, esp. as prominent in men.

ad·a·mant /ádəmənt/ *adj.* stubbornly resolute; resistant to persuasion. □□ **ad′a·mant·ly** *adv.*

a·dapt /ədápt/ *v.* **1** *tr.* (foll. by *to*) fit; adjust (one thing to another). **2** *intr. & refl.* (usu. foll. by *to*) become adjusted to new conditions. □□ **a·dapt′a·ble** *adj.* **ad·ap·ta′tion** *n.* **a·dapt′er** or **a·dap′tor** *n.* **a·dap′tive** *adj.* **a·dap′tive·ly** *adv.*
¶ Avoid confusing **adapt** with **adopt**. Trouble sometimes arises because in *adapting* to new conditions an animal or plant can be said to *adopt* something—e.g., a new color or behavior pattern.

add /ad/ *v.tr.* **1** join (one thing to another) as an increase or supplement. **2** put together (numbers) to find their total value. **3** say further. □ **add up 1** find the total of. **2** (foll. by *to*) amount to (*adds up to a disaster*). **3** *colloq.* make sense. □□ **add′ed** *adj.*

ad·den·dum /ədéndəm/ *n.* (*pl.* **ad·den·da** /–də/) **1** thing to be added, esp. (in *pl.*) as additional matter at the end of a book. **2** appendix; addition.

ad·der /ádər/ *n.* any of various small venomous snakes, esp. the common viper.

ad·dict ● *v.tr. & refl.* /ədíkt/ (usu. foll. by *to*) devote or apply habitually or compulsively; make addicted. ● *n.* /ádikt/ **1** person addicted to a habit, esp. to a drug. **2** *colloq.* devotee. □□ **ad·dic·tion** /–díkshən/ *n.* **ad·dic′tive** *adj.*

ad·di·tion /ədíshən/ *n.* **1** adding or being added. **2** person or thing added. □ **in addition** moreover; furthermore. **in addition to** as well as; as something added to.

ad·di·tion·al /ədíshənəl/ *adj.* added; extra; supplementary. □□ **ad·di′tion·al·ly** *adv.*

ad·di·tive /áditiv/ ● *n.* substance added to another so as to give it specific qualities. ● *adj.* characterized by addition (*additive process*).

ad·dle /ád′l/ ● *v.* **1** *tr.* muddle; confuse. **2** *intr.* (of an egg) become rotten. ● *adj.* **1** muddled; unsound (*addlebrained*). **2** empty; vain.

ad·dress /ədrés/ ● *n.* **1** (also /ádres/) **a** place where a person lives or an organization is situated. **b** particulars of this, esp. for postal purposes. **c** *Computing* location of an item of stored information. **2** discourse delivered to an audience. ● *v.tr.* **1** write postal directions on (an envelope, package, etc.). **2** speak or write to, esp. formally (*addressed the audience*). **3** direct one's attention to. □□ **ad·dress′er** *n.*

ad·dress·ee /ádresee/ *n.* person to whom something (esp. a letter) is addressed.

ad·duce /ədŏós, ədyŏós/ *v.tr.* cite as an instance or as proof or evidence. □□ **ad·duc′i·ble** *adj.*

ad·duc·tor /ədúktər/ *n.* muscle that moves one part of the body toward another or toward the midline of the body.

-ade[1] /ayd/ *suffix* forming nouns: **1** an action done (*blockade; tirade*). **2** the body concerned in an action or process (*cavalcade*). **3** the product or result of a material or action (*arcade; lemonade; masquerade*).

-ade[2] /ayd/ *suffix* forming nouns: (*decade*).

-ade[3] /ayd/ *suffix* forming nouns: **1** = -ADE[1] (*brocade*). **2** a person concerned (*renegade*).

ad·e·noids /ád′noydz/ *n.pl. Med.* mass of lymphatic tissue between the back of the nose and the throat. □□ **ad·e·noi·dal** /–nóyd′l/ *adj.*

a·dept ● *adj.* /ədépt/ thoroughly proficient. ● *n.* /ádept/ skilled performer; expert. □□ **a·dept′ly** *adv.* **a·dept′ness** *n.*

ad·e·quate /ádikwət/ *adj.* sufficient; satisfactory. □□ **ad′e·qua·cy** *n.* **ad′e·quate·ly** *adv.*

ad·here /ədheér/ *v.intr.* **1** (of a substance) stick fast to a surface, etc. **2** (foll. by *to*) behave according to. **3** (foll. by *to*) give support or allegiance.

ad·her·ent /ədheérənt, –hér–/ ● *n.* **1** supporter. **2** devotee. ● *adj.* **1** faithfully observing a rule, etc. **2** (of a substance) sticking fast. □□ **ad·her′ence** /–rəns/ *n.*

ad·he·sion /ədhéezhən/ n. 1 adhering. 2 Med. unnatural union of body tissues.

ad·he·sive /ədhéesiv, –ziv/ • adj. sticky; causing adhesion. • n. adhesive substance. □□ **ad·he′sive·ly** adv. **ad·he′sive·ness** n.

ad hoc /ád hók/ adv. & adj. for one particular (usu. exclusive) purpose (an ad hoc appointment).

a·dieu /ədyōo, ədōo/ • int. good-bye. • n. (pl. **a·dieus** or **a·dieux** /ədyōoz, ədōoz/) a good-bye.

ad in·fi·ni·tum /ad ínfinítəm/ adv. without limit; for ever.

ad·i·os /áadee-ós, ádee–/ int. good-bye.

ad·i·pose /ádipōs/ adj. fat; fatty. □□ **ad·i·pos·i·ty** /–pósitee/ n.

ad·ja·cent /əjáysənt/ adj. (often foll. by to) lying near or adjoining. □□ **ad·ja·cen·cy** /–sənsee/ n.

ad·jec·tive /ájiktiv/ n. word used to modify or describe a noun or pronoun. □□ **ad·jec·ti·val** /ájiktívəl/ adj. **ad·jec·ti′val·ly** adv.

ad·join /əjóyn/ v.tr. (often as **adjoining** adj.) be next to and joined with.

ad·journ /əjárn/ v. 1 tr. a put off; postpone. b break off (a meeting, etc.) temporarily. 2 intr. of persons at a meeting: a break off proceedings and disperse. b (foll. by to) transfer the meeting to another place. □□ **ad·journ′ment** n.

ad·judge /əjúj/ v.tr. 1 adjudicate (a matter). 2 pronounce or award judicially.

ad·ju·di·cate /əjōodikayt/ v. 1 intr. act as judge in a competition, court, etc. 2 tr. a decide judicially regarding (a claim, etc.). b (foll. by to be + compl.) pronounce (was adjudicated to be bankrupt). □□ **ad·ju·di·ca·tion** /–dikáyshən/ n. **ad·ju′di·ca·tive** adj. **ad·ju′di·ca·tor** n.

ad·junct /ájungkt/ n. 1 (foll. by to, of) subordinate or incidental thing. 2 subordinate person, esp. one with temporary appointment only. □□ **ad·junc·tive** /əjúngktiv/ adj. **ad·junc′tive·ly** adv.

ad·jure /əjōor/ v.tr. (usu. foll. by to + infin.) charge or request (a person) solemnly or earnestly, esp. under oath. □□ **ad·ju·ra′tion** n. **ad·jur′a·to·ry** adj.

ad·just /əjúst/ v. 1 tr. a put in the correct order or position. b regulate. 2 tr. make suitable. 3 tr. assess (loss or damages). 4 intr. (usu. foll. by to) adapt oneself. □□ **ad·just′a·ble** adj. **ad·just·a·bil′i·ty** n. **ad·just′er** n. **ad·just′ment** n.

ad·ju·tant /ájət′nt/ n. 1 Mil. officer who assists superior officers. 2 assistant. □□ **ad·ju·tan·cy** /–t′nsee/ n.

ad lib /ád líb/ • v.intr. (**ad libbed, ad lib·bing**) improvise. • adj. improvised. • adv. as one pleases. • n. something spoken or played extempore.

ad loc abbr. to or at that place.

ad·man /ádman/ n. (pl. **ad·men**) colloq. person who produces advertisements commercially.

ad·min·is·ter /ədmínistər/ v. 1 tr. manage. 2 tr. a be responsible for the implementation of (the law, justice, punishment, etc.). b Eccl. perform the rites of (a sacrament). 3 tr. a provide; apply (a remedy). b give; deliver (a rebuke). 4 intr. act as administrator. □□ **ad·min′is·tra·ble** adj.

ad·min·is·trate /ədmínistrayt/ v. administer (esp. business affairs); act as an administrator.

□□ **ad·min′is·tra·tive** adj. **ad·min′is·tra·tive·ly** adv.

ad·min·is·tra·tion /ədmínistráyshən/ n. 1 management; government. 2 the government in power. 3 president's period of office. 4 (foll. by of) a administering of justice, an oath, etc. b application of remedies.

ad·min·is·tra·tor /ədmínistraytər/ n. 1 manager. 2 Law person appointed to manage the estate of one who has died intestate.

ad·mi·ra·ble /ádmərəbəl/ adj. 1 deserving admiration. 2 excellent. □□ **ad′mi·ra·bly** adv.

ad·mi·ral /ádmərəl/ n. 1 commander in chief of a fleet. 2 naval officer of high rank. □□ **ad′mi·ral·ship** n.

Ad·mi·ral·ty /ádmərəltee/ n. (pl. **–ties**) (hist. except in titles) (in the UK) department administering the Royal Navy.

---

admiral Middle English (denoting an emir or Saracen commander): from Old French amiral, admirail, via medieval Latin from Arabic 'amīr 'commander' (from 'amara 'to command'). The ending -al was from Arabic -al- in the sense 'of the' used in forming titles (e.g. 'amīr-al-'umarā 'ruler of rulers'), later assimilated to the familiar Latinate suffix -AL.

---

ad·mi·ra·tion /ádmiráyshən/ n. 1 pleased contemplation. 2 respect; warm approval. 3 object of this.

ad·mire /ədmír/ v.tr. 1 regard with approval, respect, or satisfaction. 2 express one's admiration of. □□ **ad·mir′er** n. **ad·mir′ing** adj. **ad·mir′ing·ly** adv.

ad·mis·si·ble /ədmísibəl/ adj. 1 (of an idea or plan) worth accepting or considering. 2 Law allowable as evidence. □□ **ad·mis·si·bil·i·ty** /–bílitee/ n.

ad·mis·sion /ədmíshən/ n. 1 acknowledgment. 2 a process or right of entering. b charge for this.

¶ **Admission** traditionally referred to the price paid for entry or the right to enter: Admission was $5. **Admittance** more often referred to physical entry: We were denied admittance by a large man with a forbidding scowl. In the sense of 'permission or right to enter,' these words have become almost interchangeable, although **admittance** is more formal and technical.

ad·mit /ədmít/ v. (**ad·mit·ted, ad·mit·ting**) 1 tr. acknowledge; recognize as true. 2 intr. a (foll. by to) confess. b (foll. by of) allow for something to exist, have influence, etc. 3 tr. allow (a person) entrance or access. 4 tr. (of an enclosed space) accommodate. □□ **ad·mit′ta·ble** adj. **ad·mit′tance** n.

ad·mit·ted·ly /ədmítidlee/ adv. as an acknowledged fact.

ad·mix·ture /admíkschər/ n. 1 thing added, esp. a minor ingredient. 2 act of adding this.

ad·mon·ish /ədmónish/ v.tr. 1 reprove. 2 urge. 3 give earnest advice to. 4 warn. □□ **ad·mon′ish·ment** n. **ad·mo·ni·tion** /ádmənishən/ n. **ad·mon′i·to·ry** adj.

ad nau·se·am /ad náwzeeəm/ adv. to an excessive or disgusting degree.

a·do /ədōo/ n. (pl. **a·dos**) fuss; busy activity; trouble; difficulty. □ **without further** (or **more**) **ado** immediately.

a·do·be /ədóbee/ n. 1 sun-dried brick of clay and

straw. **2** clay used for making this. **3** structure of such bricks.

ad·o·les·cent /ádəlésənt/ • *adj.* between childhood and adulthood. • *n.* adolescent person. □□ **ad·o·les′cence** /–səns/ *n.*

A·don·is /ədónis, ədŏ–/ *n.* handsome young man.

a·dopt /ədópt/ *v.tr.* **1** legally take another's child as one's own. **2** choose to follow (a course of action, etc.). **3** take over (a name, idea, etc.). □□ **a·dop′tion** /–dópshən/ *n.* **a·dop′tive** *adj.* ¶ See note at ADAPT.

a·dor·a·ble /ədáwrəbəl/ *adj.* **1** deserving adoration. **2** *colloq.* delightful; charming. □□ **a·dor′a·bly** *adv.*

a·dore /ədáwr/ *v.tr.* **1** regard with honor and deep affection. **2** worship as divine. **3** *colloq.* like very much. □□ **ad·o·ra·tion** /ádəráyshən/ *n.* **a·dor′er** *n.* **a·dor′ing** *adj.* **a·dor′ing·ly** *adv.*

a·dorn /ədáwrn/ *v.tr.* add beauty to; decorate. □□ **a·dorn′ment** *n.*

ADP *abbr.* **1** adenosine diphosphate, a nucleic acid essential to living cells. **2** automatic data processing.

a·dre·nal /ədreénəl/ • *adj.* **1** at or near the kidneys. **2** of the adrenal glands. • *n.* (in full **adre′nal gland**) either of two ductless glands above the kidneys, secreting adrenaline.

a·dren·a·line /ədrénəlin/ = EPINEPHRINE.

a·drift /ədríft/ *adv. & predic. adj.* **1** drifting. **2** powerless; aimless.

a·droit /ədróyt/ *adj.* dexterous; skillful. □□ **a·droit′ly** *adv.* **a·droit′ness** *n.*

ad·sorb /adsáwrb, –záwrb/ *v.tr.* (usu. of a solid) hold (molecules of a gas or liquid, etc.) to its surface, as a thin film. □□ **ad·sorb′a·ble** *adj.* **ad·sorb′ent** *adj. & n.* **ad·sorp·tion** /–sáwrp–, –záwrp–/ *n.* (also **ad·sorb′tion**).

ad·u·late /ájəlayt/ *v.tr.* flatter obsequiously. □□ **ad·u·la·tion** /–láyshən/ *n.* **ad′u·la·tor** *n.* **ad·u·la·to·ry** /–lətáwree/ *adj.*

a·dult /ədúlt, ádúlt/ • *adj.* **1** mature; grown-up. **2** a of or for adults. **b** *euphem.* sexually explicit; indecent (*adult films*). • *n.* adult person. □□ **a·dult′hood** *n.* **a·dult′ly** *adv.*

a·dul·ter·ate • *v.intr.* /ədúltərayt/ debase (esp. foods) by adding other or inferior substances. • *adj.* /ədúltərət/ spurious; debased; counterfeit. □□ **a·dul·ter·ant** /ədúltərənt/ *adj. & n.* **a·dul·ter·a·tion** /–ráyshən/ *n.* **a·dul′ter·a·tor** *n.*

a·dul·ter·y /ədúltəree/ *n.* voluntary sexual intercourse between a married person and a person (married or not) other than his or her spouse. □□ **a·dul·ter·er** *n.* **a·dul′ter·ous** *adj.* **a·dul′ter·ous·ly** *adv.*

ad·um·brate /ádumbrayt/ *v.tr.* **1** indicate faintly. **2** represent in outline. **3** foreshadow. **4** overshadow. □□ **ad·um·bra·tion** /–bráyshən/ *n.* **ad·um′bra·tive** /ədúmbrətiv/ *adj.*

ad·vance /ədváns/ • *v.* **1** *tr.* & *intr.* move or put forward. **2** *intr.* make progress. **3** *tr.* **a** pay (money) before it is due. **b** lend (money). **4** *tr.* promote (a person, cause, or plan). **5** *tr.* put forward (a suggestion, etc.). **6** *tr.* (as **advanced** *adj.*) **a** far on in progress. **b** ahead of the times. • *n.* **1** progress. **2** prepayment. **3** loan. **4** (esp. *pl.*) amorous approach. **5** rise in price. • *adj.* beforehand (*advance warning*). □ **in advance** ahead in place or time. □□ **ad·vance′ment** *n.* **ad·vanc′er** *n.*

ad·van·tage /ədvántij/ • *n.* **1** beneficial feature. **2** benefit; profit. **3** superiority. **4** (in tennis) the next point won after deuce. • *v.tr.* **1** be beneficial or favorable to. **2** further; promote. □ **take advantage of 1** make good use of. **2** exploit, esp. unfairly. **3** *euphem.* seduce. □□ **ad·van·ta·geous** /ádvəntáyjəs/ *adj.* **ad·van·ta′geous·ly** *adv.*

Ad·vent /ádvent/ *n.* **1** season before Christmas. **2** coming of Christ. **3** (**advent**) important arrival.

adven·ti·tious /ádventíshəs/ *adj.* accidental; casual. □□ **ad·ven·ti′tious·ly** *adv.*

ad·ven·ture /ədvénchər/ • *n.* **1** unusual and exciting experience. **2** daring enterprise. • *v.intr.* **1** (often foll. by *into, upon*) dare to go or come. **2** dare to undertake. **3** incur risk. □□ **ad·ven′ture·some** *adj.* **ad·ven′tur·ous** *adj.*

ad·ven·tur·er /ədvénchərər/ *n.* (*fem.* **ad·ven·tur·ess** /–chəris/) **1** person who seeks adventure. **2** financial speculator.

ad·verb /ádvərb/ *n.* word or phrase that modifies or qualifies an adjective, verb, or other adverb (e.g., *gently, quite, then, there*). □□ **ad·ver·bi·al** /ədvárbeeəl/ *adj.*

ad·ver·sar·y /ádvərseree/ • *n.* (*pl.* **–ies**) **1** enemy. **2** opponent. • *adj.* opposed; antagonistic. □□ **ad·ver·sar·i·al** /ádvərsáireeəl/ *adj.*

ad·verse /advárs, ád–/ *adj.* **1** contrary; hostile. **2** harmful; injurious. □□ **ad·verse′ly** *adv.* ¶ **Adverse** means 'hostile, unfavorable, opposed,' and is usually applied to situations, conditions, or events, not people, e.g., *The dry weather has had an adverse effect on the garden.* **Averse** is related in origin and also has the sense of 'opposed,' but is usually employed to describe a person's attitude, e.g., *I would not be averse to making the repairs myself.*

ad·ver·si·ty /ədvársitee/ *n.* (*pl.* **–ties**) **1** adverse fortune. **2** misfortune.

ad·vert /ədvárt/ *v.intr.* (foll. by *to*) *literary* refer in speaking or writing.

ad·ver·tise /ádvərtīz/ *v.* **1** *tr.* promote (goods or services) publicly to increase sales. **2** *tr.* make generally known. **3** *intr.* (foll. by *for*) place an advertisement. **4** *tr.* (usu. foll. by *that* + clause) notify. □□ **ad·ver′tis·er** *n.*

ad·ver·tise·ment /ádvərtízmənt, ədvártis–, –tiz–/ *n.* public notice or announcement.

ad·vice /ədvís/ *n.* **1** recommendation about future action or behavior. **2** information given; news.

ad·vis·a·ble /ədvízəbəl/ *adj.* **1** to be recommended. **2** expedient. □□ **ad·vis·a·bil′i·ty** *n.* **ad·vis′a·bly** *adv.*

ad·vise /ədvíz/ *v.tr.* **1** (also *absol.*) give advice to. **2** recommend. **3** inform. □□ **ad·vis′er** or **ad·vi′sor** *n.*

ad·vi·so·ry /ədvízəree/ • *adj.* giving advice. • *n.* (*pl.* **–ries**) information, esp. warning about bad weather, etc.

ad·vo·cate • *n.* /ádvəkət/ **1** person who supports or speaks in favor. **2** person who pleads for another. **3** professional pleader in a court of justice. • *v.tr.* /ádvəkayt/ **1** recommend by argument (a cause, etc.). **2** plead for; defend. □□ **ad′vo·ca·cy** *n.* **ad·vo·cate′ship** *n.* **ad·voc·a·to·ry** /ádvəkə-táwree, ádvəkə–, ədvákətəree/ *adj.*

adze /adz/ (also **adz**) *n.* axelike tool for cutting away the surface of wood.

ae·gis /eéjis/ *n.* protection; impregnable defense.

ae·on var. of EON.

aer·ate /áirayt/ v.tr. **1** charge a liquid with carbon dioxide. **2** expose to air. □□ **aer·a·tion** /-ráyshən/ n. **aer'a·tor** n.

ae·ri·al /áireeəl/ • n. radio or TV antenna. • adj. **1** by, in, or from the air. **2** existing, moving, or happening in the air. **3** thin as air; ethereal. □□ **aer'i·al·ly** adv.

aer·i·al·ist /áireeəlist/ n. high-wire or trapeze artist.

aer·ie /áiree, áree/ n. (also **ey'rie**) **1** lofty nest of a bird of prey. **2** house, etc., perched high up.

aer·o·bat·ics /áirəbátiks/ n.pl. feats of expert and usu. spectacular flying of aircraft.

aer·o·bic /airóbik/ adj. **1** existing or active only in the presence of oxygen. **2** of or relating to aerobics.

aer·o·bics /airóbiks/ n.pl. vigorous exercises designed to increase the body's heart rate and oxygen intake.

aer·o·dy·nam·ics /áirōdīnámiks/ n.pl. (usu. treated as sing.) study of solid bodies moving through air. □□ **aer·o·dy·nam'ic** adj. **aer·o·dy·nam'i·cal·ly** adv. **aer·o·dy·nam·i·cist** /-misist/ n.

aer·o·nau·tics /áirənáwtiks/ n.pl. (usu. treated as sing.) science or practice of motion in the air. □□ **aer·o·nau'tic** adj. **aer·o·nau'ti·cal** adj.

aer·o·sol /áirəsawl, -sol/ n. **1** pressurized container for releasing a substance as a fine spray. **2** system of colloidal particles dispersed in a gas (e.g., fog or smoke).

aer·o·space /áirōspays/ n. **1** earth's atmosphere and outer space. **2** technology of aviation in this region.

aes·thete /és-theet/ n. (also **es'thete**) person who has or professes a special appreciation of beauty.

aes·thet·ic /es-thétik/ (also **es·thet'ic**) • adj. **1** concerned with beauty or the appreciation of beauty. **2** sensitive to beauty. • n. **1** (in pl.) philosophy of the beautiful, esp. in art. **2** set of principles of good taste and the appreciation of beauty. □□ **aes·thet'i·cal·ly** adv. **aes·thet·i·cism** /-tisizəm/ n.

---

aesthetic late 18th cent. (in the sense 'relating to perception by the senses'): from Greek aisthētikos, from aisthēta 'perceptible things,' from aisthesthai 'perceive.' The sense 'concerned with beauty' was coined in German in the mid-18th cent. and adopted into English in the early 19th cent., but its use was controversial until much later in the century.

---

a·far /əfáar/ adv. at or to a distance.

AFB abbr. Air Force Base.

af·fa·ble /áfəbəl/ adj. **1** friendly. **2** kind and courteous. □□ **af·fa·bil'i·ty** n. **af'fa·bly** adv.

af·fair /əfáir/ n. **1** concern, business, or matter to be attended to. **2 a** celebrated or notorious happening. **b** colloq. noteworthy thing or event. **3** amorous relationship. **4** (in pl.) **a** ordinary pursuits of life. **b** business dealings. **c** public matters (current affairs).

af·fect[1] /əfékt/ v.tr. **1 a** produce an effect on. **b** (of a disease, etc.) attack (his liver is affected). **2** touch the feelings of. □□ **af·fect'ing** adj. **af·fect'ing·ly** adv.

¶ Both **affect** and **effect** are both verbs and nouns, but only **effect** is common as a noun, usually meaning 'a result, consequence, impression, etc.,' e.g., My father's warnings had no effect on my adventurousness. As verbs they are used differently. **Affect** means 'to produce an effect upon,' e.g., Smoking during pregnancy can affect the baby's development. **Effect** means 'to bring about,' e.g., The negotiators effected an agreement despite many difficulties.

af·fect[2] /əfékt/ v.tr. **1** pretend. **2** pose as.

af·fect[3] /áfekt/ n. Psychol. feeling or emotion.

af·fec·ta·tion /áfektáyshən/ n. **1** assumed or contrived manner of behavior. **2** pretense.

af·fect·ed /əféktid/ adj. **1** in senses of AFFECT[1], AFFECT[2]. **2** artificial; pretended. **3** disposed, inclined. □□ **af·fect'ed·ly** adv. **af·fect'ed·ness** n.

af·fec·tion /əfékshən/ n. **1** goodwill; fond feeling. **2** disease; diseased condition.

af·fec·tion·ate /əfékshənət/ adj. loving; tender; showing love or tenderness. □□ **af·fec'tion·ate·ly** adv.

af·fi·da·vit /áfidáyvit/ n. written statement confirmed under oath, for use as evidence in court.

af·fil·i·ate • v. /əfileeayt/ **1** tr. attach or connect (a person or society) with a larger organization. **2** tr. (of an institution) adopt (persons as members, societies as branches, etc.). **3** intr. associate oneself with a society. • n. /əfileeət/ affiliated person or organization. □□ **af·fil·i·a·tion** /-áyshən/ n.

af·fin·i·ty /əfinitee/ n. (pl. **-ties**) **1** liking for or attraction to a person or thing. **2** relationship, esp. by marriage. **3** similarity of character suggesting a relationship.

af·firm /əfərm/ v. **1** tr. assert strongly; state as a fact. **2** intr. a Law make an affirmation. **b** make a formal declaration. □□ **af·fir·ma'tion** n. **af·firm'a·to·ry** adj. **af·firm'er** n.

af·fir·ma·tive /əfərmətiv/ • adj. **1** affirming; asserting that a thing is so. **2** (of a vote) expressing approval. • n. **1** affirmative statement, reply, or word. **2** (prec. by the) positive or affirming position. • **affirmative action** action favoring minorities, etc., who have been discriminated against. □□ **af·firm'a·tive·ly** adv.

af·fix • v.tr. /əfiks/ **1** attach; fasten. **2** add in writing. **3** impress (a seal or stamp). • n. /áfiks/ **1** addition. **2** Gram. prefix or suffix.

af·flict /əflikt/ v.tr. inflict bodily or mental suffering on. □□ **af·flic·tion** /əflikshən/ n. **af·flic'tive** adj.

af·flu·ent /áflooənt/ adj. **1** wealthy; rich. **2** abundant. □□ **af'flu·ence** n. **af'flu·ent·ly** adv.

af·ford /əfáwrd/ v.tr. **1 a** have enough money, means, time, etc., for; be able to spare (can afford $50). **b** be in a position to do something. **2** yield a supply of. **3** provide. □□ **af·ford'a·ble** adj. **af·ford·a·bil'i·ty** n.

af·for·est /əfáwrist, əfór-/ v.tr. plant with trees. □□ **af·for·es·ta'tion** n.

af·fray /əfráy/ n. loud public brawl.

af·front /əfrúnt/ n. open insult. • v.tr. **1** insult openly. **2** offend the modesty or self respect of.

Af·ghan /áfgan/ • n. **1 a** native or inhabitant of Afghanistan. **b** person of Afghan descent. **2** official language of Afghanistan (also called PASHTO). **3** (**afghan**) knitted or crocheted shawl or throw. • adj. of or relating to Afghanistan or its people or language. □ **Afghan hound** tall hunting dog with long silky hair.

a·fi·cio·na·do /əfisheeənaʹádō, əfisee–/ n. (pl. –dos) devotee of a sport or pastime (orig. of bullfighting).

a·field /əfeʹeld/ adv. 1 away from home. 2 to or on a field. 3 astray.

a·flame /əfláym/ adv. & adj. in flames.

a·float /əflṓt/ adv. & adj. 1 floating in water or on air. 2 at sea; on board ship.

a·foot /əfŏŏt/ adv. & adj. 1 in operation; progressing. 2 astir; on the move.

afore– /əfáwr/ comb. form before; previously (aforesaid).

a·fore·thought /əfáwrthawt/ adj. premeditated.

a·foul /əfówl/ adv. foul. □ **run afoul of** come into conflict with.

a·fraid /əfráyd/ adj. alarmed; frightened. □ **be afraid** colloq. politely regret (I'm afraid there's none left).

a·fresh /əfrésh/ adv. anew; with a fresh beginning.

Af·ri·can /áfrikən/ • n. 1 native of Africa (esp. a black person). 2 person of African descent. • adj. of or relating to Africa. □ **African-American** n. American citizen of black African origin or descent. • adj. of or relating to American blacks or their culture. **African violet** houseplant with heart-shaped velvety leaves and blue, purple, or pink flowers.

Af·ri·kaans /áfrikaʹaans/ n. language derived from Dutch, spoken in S. Africa.

Af·ri·ka·ner /áfrikaʹanər/ n. Afrikaans-speaking white person in S. Africa.

Af·ro /áfrō/ • adj. (of hair) tightly curled and bushy, as naturally worn originally by blacks. • n. (pl. –ros) Afro hairstyle.

Afro– /áfrō/ comb. form African (Afro-Asian).

Af·ro-A·mer·i·can /áfrōəmérikən/ adj. & n. = African-American.

Af·ro-Car·ib·be·an /áfrōkáribeʹən, –kəribeeən/ • n. person of African descent in or from the Caribbean. • adj. of or relating to the Afro-Caribbeans or their culture.

aft /aft/ adv. Naut. & Aeron. at or toward the stern or tail.

af·ter /áftər/ • prep. 1 a following in time; later than (after six months). b specifying time (quarter after eight). 2 in view of (after your behavior tonight what do you expect?). 3 in spite of (after all my efforts I'm no better off). 4 behind (shut the door after you). 5 in pursuit or quest of. 6 about; concerning. 7 in allusion to (named after his uncle). 8 in imitation of. 9 next in importance to. 10 according to (after a fashion). • conj. later than. • adv. 1 later in time (soon after). 2 behind. • adj. 1 later; following. 2 Naut. nearer the stern.

af·ter·birth /áftərbərth/ n. Med. placenta and fetal membranes discharged from the womb after childbirth.

af·ter·burn·er /áftərbərnər/ n. auxiliary burner in a jet engine to increase thrust.

af·ter·care /áftərkair, –ker/ n. care of a patient after a stay in the hospital or of a person on release from prison.

af·ter·ef·fect /áftərəfékt/ n. delayed effect following an accident, trauma, etc.

af·ter·life /áftərlīf/ n. 1 life after death. 2 life at a later time.

af·ter·math /áftərmath/ n. consequences; after-effects.

af·ter·noon /áftərnṓn/ n. time from noon to evening.

af·ter·thought /áftərthawt/ n. thing thought of or added later.

af·ter·ward /áftərwȯrd/ adv. (also **af'ter·wards**) later; subsequently.

Ag symb. Chem. silver.

a·gain /əgén/ adv. 1 another time; once more. 2 as previously (back again). 3 in addition. 4 further; besides. 5 on the other hand. □ **again and again** repeatedly.

a·gainst /əgénst/ prep. 1 in opposition to (arson is against the law). 2 into collision or in contact with. 3 to the disadvantage of. 4 in contrast to. 5 in anticipation of.

a·gape /əgáyp/ adv. & adj. gaping, open-mouthed.

a·gar /áygaar/ n. (also **a'gar-a'gar**) gelatinous substance from seaweed, used in food, microbiological media, etc.

ag·ate /ágət/ n. 1 any of several varieties of hard usu. streaked chalcedony. 2 colored toy marble resembling this.

a·ga·ve /əgaʹavee, əgáy–/ n. plant with rosettes of narrow spiny leaves and tall inflorescences, e.g., the aloe.

age /ayj/ • n. 1 a length of time that a person or thing has existed. b particular point in or part of one's life (old age). 2 a colloq. long time (often in pl.) a long time. b distinct historical or geological period. 3 old age. • v.intr. (pres. part. **ag·ing, age·ing**) 1 show signs of advancing age. 2 grow old. 3 mature. □ **of age** adult.

-age /ij/ suffix forming nouns denoting: 1 action (breakage). 2 condition (bondage). 3 aggregate or number of (acreage). 4 cost (postage). 5 product of an action (wreckage). 6 place; abode (anchorage; orphanage).

a·ged adj. 1 /ayjd/ a of the age of (aged ten). b allowed to reach maturity or ripeness in storage (aged cheese). 2 /áyjid/ old.

age·ism /áyjizəm/ n. (also **ag'ism**) prejudice or discrimination on the grounds of age. □□ **age'ist** adj. & n.

age·less /áyjlis/ adj. 1 never growing or appearing old or outmoded. 2 eternal; timeless.

a·gen·cy /áyjənsee/ n. (pl. –cies) 1 business or establishment of an agent. 2 a action. b intervention. 3 governmental department.

a·gen·da /əjéndə/ n. 1 (pl. **agen·das**) list of items of business to be considered at a meeting. 2 things to be done. 3 underlying motivation.

a·gent /áyjənt/ n. 1 a person who acts for another in business, etc. b a spy. 2 a person or thing that exerts power or produces an effect. b cause of a natural force or effect on matter (oxidizing agent). □□ **a·gen·tial** /əjénshəl/ adj.

a·gent pro·voc·a·teur /aʹazhoɴ prəvókətȯr/ n. (pl. **a·gents pro·voc·a·teurs** pronunc. same) person employed to detect suspected offenders by tempting them to overt self-incriminating action.

ag·glom·er·ate • v. /əglómərayt/ 1 collect into a mass. 2 accumulate in a disorderly way. • n. /əglómərət/ 1 mass or collection of things. 2

Geol. mass of large volcanic fragments bonded under heat (cf. CONGLOMERATE). • *adj.* /əglómərət/ collected into a mass.

ag·glu·ti·nate /əglóō't'nayt/ *v.tr.* unite as with glue. □□ **ag·glu·ti·na·tion** /–náyshən/ *n.* **ag·glu·ti·na·tive** /əglóō't'nǝtiv, –aytiv/ *adj.*

ag·gran·dize /əgrándīz/ *v.tr.* 1 increase the power, rank, or wealth of (a person or nation). 2 cause to appear greater than is the case. □□ **ag·gran·dize·ment** /–dizmənt/ *n.* **ag·gran'diz·er** *n.*

ag·gra·vate /ágrəvayt/ *v.tr.* 1 increase the seriousness of (an illness, offense, etc.). 2 *disp.* annoy; exasperate (a person). □□ **ag·gra·va·tion** /–váyshən/ *n.*
¶ This word is used informally to mean 'to annoy or exasperate,' rather than 'to make worse or more serious.' An example of more correct usage is *Heavy lifting aggravated the strain on my back.*

ag·gre·gate • *n.* /ágrigət/ 1 total amount assembled. 2 crushed stone, gravel, etc., used in making concrete. 3 *Geol.* mass of minerals formed into solid rock. • *adj.* /ágrigət/ 1 (of disparate elements) collected into one mass. 2 constituted by the collection of many units into one body. • *v.* /ágrigayt/ 1 *tr.* & *intr.* combine into one mass. 2 *tr. colloq.* amount to. □□ **ag·gre·ga·tion** /–gáyshən/ *n.* **ag·gre·ga'tive** *adj.*

ag·gres·sion /əgréshən/ *n.* 1 unprovoked attack. 2 self-assertiveness; forcefulness. 3 *Psychol.* hostile or destructive behavior. □□ **ag·gres·sor** /əgrésər/ *n.*

ag·gres·sive /əgrésiv/ *adj.* 1 of a person: **a** given to aggression; hostile. **b** forceful; self-assertive. 2 (of an act) offensive; hostile. 3 of aggression. □□ **ag·gres'sive·ly** *adv.* **ag·gres'sive·ness** *n.*

ag·grieved /əgrée'vd/ *adj.* having a grievance. □□ **ag·griev'ed·ly** *adv.*

a·ghast /əgást/ *adj.* filled with dismay or consternation.

---

aghast late Middle English: past participle of the obsolete verb *agast, gast* 'frighten,' from Old English *gǣsten.* The spelling with *gh* (originally Scots) became general by about 1700, probably influenced by GHOST; compare with GHASTLY.

---

ag·ile /ájəl, ájīl/ *adj.* quick-moving; nimble; active. □□ **ag'ile·ly** *adv.* **a·gil·i·ty** /əjílitee/ *n.*

ag·i·tate /ájitayt/ *v.* 1 *tr.* (often as **agitated** *adj.*) disturb or excite (a person or feelings). 2 *intr.* stir up concern, esp. publicly (*agitated for tax reform*). 3 *tr.* shake or move, esp. briskly. □□ **ag'i·tat·ed·ly** *adv.* **ag·i·ta·tion** /–táyshən/ *n.* **ag'i·ta·tive** *adj.* **ag'i·ta·tor** *n.*

a·glow /əglṓ/ • *adv.* glowingly. • *adj.* glowing.

ag·nos·tic /agnóstik/ • *n.* person who believes that the existence or nature of God cannot be proven. • *adj.* of agnosticism. □□ **ag·nos'ti·cism** *n.*

a·go /əgṓ/ *adv.* earlier; before the present.

a·gog /əgóg/ • *adv.* eagerly; expectantly. • *adj.* eager; expectant.

ag·o·nize /ágənīz/ *v.* 1 *intr.* suffer agony. 2 *tr.* (often as **agonizing** *adj.*) cause agony to. □□ **ag'o·niz·ing·ly** *adv.*

ag·o·ny /ágənee/ *n.* (*pl.* **–nies**) 1 extreme mental or physical suffering. 2 severe struggle.

ag·o·ra·pho·bi·a /ágərəfóbeeə/ *n. Psychol.* abnormal fear of open spaces or public places. □□ **ag·o·ra·pho'bic** *adj. & n.*

a·grar·i·an /əgráireeən/ *adj.* 1 of the land or its cultivation. 2 relating to the ownership of land.

a·gree /əgrée'/ *v.* (**a·grees, a·greed, a·gree·ing**) 1 hold a similar opinion. 2 consent. 3 **a** become or be in harmony. **b** be good for; suit. **c** *Gram.* have the same number, gender, case, or person as.
¶ Note the distinction between *agreeing to* something like a plan, scheme, or project; and *agreeing with* somebody: *I agree to the repayment schedule suggested. Danielle agrees with Eric that we should all go hiking on Saturday. Humid weather does not agree with me. Agree with* is also used regarding two things that go together: *That story does not agree with the facts. The verb must agree with the noun in person and number.*

a·gree·a·ble /əgrée'əbəl/ *adj.* 1 pleasing. 2 willing to agree. □□ **a·gree·a·bil·i·ty** /–bílitee/ *n.* **a·gree'a·ble·ness** *n.* **a·gree'a·bly** *adv.*

a·gree·ment /əgrée'mənt/ *n.* 1 act of agreeing. 2 mutual understanding. 3 arrangement or contract.

ag·ri·busi·ness /ágribiznis/ *n.* large-scale farming and related commerce, as food processing, etc.

ag·ri·cul·ture /ágrikulchər/ *n.* cultivating the soil and rearing animals. □□ **ag·ri·cul·tur·al** /–kúlchərəl/ *adj.* **ag·ri·cul'tur·al·ist** *n.* **ag·ri·cul'tur·al·ly** *adv.* **ag·ri·cul'tur·ist** *n.*

a·gron·o·my /əgrónəmee/ *n.* science of soil management and crop production. □□ **ag·ro·nom·ic** /ágrənómik/ *adj.* **a·gron·o·mist** /–grón–/ *n.*

a·ground /əgrównd/ *adj. & adv.* (of a ship) on or on to the bottom of shallow water (*run aground*).

a·gue /áygyṓo/ *n.* 1 *hist.* malarial fever. 2 shivering fit. □□ **a'gued** *adj.* **a'gu·ish** *adj.*

ah /aa/ *int.* expressing surprise, pleasure, realization, etc.

a·ha /aahá'a, əha'a/ *int.* expressing surprise, triumph, mockery, irony, etc.

a·head /əhéd/ *adv.* 1 further forward in space or time. 2 in the lead.

a·hem /əhém/ *int.* used to attract attention, gain time, or express disapproval.

-aholic /əhólik/ *suffix* (also **-oholic**) denoting one addicted to or compulsively in need of what is specified in the initial element (*workaholic, chocoholic*).

a·hoy /əhóy/ *int. Naut.* call used in hailing.

AI *abbr.* 1 artificial intelligence. 2 artificial insemination.

aid /ayd/ • *n.* 1 help. 2 financial or material help. 3 person or thing that helps. • *v.tr.* 1 help. 2 promote or encourage.

aide /ayd/ *n.* 1 aide-de-camp. 2 assistant.

aide-de-camp /áyd-dəkámp/ *n.* (*pl.* **aides-de-camp** *pronunc.* same) officer acting as a confidential assistant to a senior officer.

AIDS /aydz/ *n.* acquired immune deficiency syndrome, a viral disorder marked by severe loss of resistance to infection. □ **AIDS-related complex** symptoms of a person affected with the AIDS virus who has not developed the disease.

ail /ayl/ *v.* 1 *tr.* trouble or afflict (*what ails him?*). 2 *intr.* (usu. **be ailing**) be ill.

ai·le·ron /áyləron/ *n.* hinged surface in the

trailing edge of an airplane wing, used to control lateral balance, etc.

AILERON

ail·ment /áylmənt/ *n.* minor or chronic illness.

aim /aym/ • *v.* **1** *intr.* (foll. by *at, to*) intend or try. **2** *tr.* direct or point (a weapon, remark, etc.). **3** *intr.* take aim. **4** *intr.* (foll. by *at, for*) seek to attain or achieve. • *n.* **1** purpose or object. **2** directing of a weapon, etc., at an object. □ **take aim** direct a weapon, etc., at an object.

aim·less /áymlis/ *adj.* without aim or purpose. □□ **aim′less·ly** *adv.* **aim′less·ness** *n.*

ain't /aynt/ *contr. colloq.* **1** am not; are not; is not. **2** has not; have not.
¶ Although this form has been used for hundreds of years, it is generally thought incorrect, and should be avoided in formal contexts.

air /air/ • *n.* **1** gaseous mixture, mainly of oxygen and nitrogen, surrounding the earth. **2** earth's atmosphere. **3 a** distinctive impression. **b** one's manner or bearing, esp. a confident one. **c** (esp. in *pl.*) pretentiousness. **4** *Mus.* tune. • *v.tr.* **1** expose (a room, etc.) to the open air; ventilate. **2** express publicly. **3** broadcast. □ **air bag** safety device that fills with nitrogen on impact to protect the occupants of a vehicle in a collision. **air base** base for the operation of military aircraft. **air-conditioned** (of a room, building, etc.) equipped with air-conditioning. **air conditioner** air-conditioning apparatus. **air-conditioning** system for regulating the humidity, ventilation, and temperature in a building. **air force** branch of the armed forces concerned with fighting or defense in the air. **air raid** attack by aircraft. **in the air** prevalent. **up in the air** uncertain. □□ **air′less** *adj.* **air′less·ness** *n.*

air·borne /áirbawrn/ *adj.* **1** transported by air. **2** (of aircraft) in the air after taking off.

air·craft /áirkraft/ *n.* (*pl.* same) machine capable of flight, esp. an airplane or helicopter. □ **aircraft carrier** warship that carries and serves as a base for airplanes.

Aire·dale /áirdayl/ *n.* **1** large terrier of a rough-coated breed. **2** this breed.

air·field /áirfeeld/ *n.* area with runways for aircraft.

air·head /áirhed/ *n. sl.* silly or stupid person.

air·lift /áirlift/ • *n.* emergency transport of supplies by air. • *v.tr.* transport in this way.

air·line /áirlīn/ *n.* organization providing a regular public service of air transport on one or more routes.

air·lin·er /áirlīnər/ *n.* passenger aircraft, esp. a large one.

air·lock /áirlok/ *n.* **1** stoppage of the flow in a

pump or pipe, caused by an air bubble. **2** airtight compartment between areas of different pressures.

air·mail /áirmayl/ • *n.* **1** system of transporting mail by air. **2** mail carried by air. • *v.tr.* send by airmail.

air·man /áirmən/ *n.* (*pl.* **–men**) **1** pilot or member of the crew of an aircraft. **2** member of the USAF below commissioned rank.

air·plane /áirplayn/ *n.* powered heavier-than-air flying vehicle with fixed wings.

air·port /áirpawrt/ *n.* complex of runways and buildings for the takeoff, landing, and maintenance of civil aircraft, with facilities for passengers.

air·ship /áirship/ *n.* power-driven aircraft lighter than air.

air·sick /áirsik/ *adj.* nauseated from air travel. □□ **air′sick·ness** *n.*

air·space /áirspays/ *n.* air above a country and subject to its jurisdiction.

air·speed /áirspeed/ *n.* speed of an aircraft relative to the air.

air·strip /áirstrip/ *n.* strip of ground suitable for the takeoff and landing of aircraft but usu. without other facilities.

air·tight /áirtīt/ *adj.* **1** not allowing air to pass through. **2** having no visible or apparent weaknesses (*an airtight alibi*).

air·waves /áirwayvz/ *n.pl. colloq.* radio waves used in broadcasting.

air·way /áirway/ *n.* **1 a** recognized route followed by aircraft. **b** (often in *pl.*) = AIRLINE. **2** *Med.* (often in *pl.*) breathing passage(s).

air·wom·an /áirwŏŏmən/ *n.* (*pl.* **–wom·en**) **1** woman pilot or member of the crew of an aircraft. **2** woman member of the USAF below commissioned rank.

air·wor·thy /áirwərthee/ *adj.* (of an aircraft) fit to fly.

air·y /áiree/ *adj.* (**air·i·er, air·i·est**) **1** well ventilated; breezy. **2** flippant; superficial. **3 a** light as air. **b** graceful; delicate. **4** insubstantial; ethereal. □□ **air′i·ly** *adv.* **air′i·ness** *n.*

aisle /īl/ *n.* **1** passage between rows of pews, seats, etc. **2** passageway in a supermarket, department store, etc. □□ **aisled** *adj.*

aitch /aych/ *n.* name of the letter H.

a·jar /əjáar/ *adv. & adj.* (of a door) slightly open.

AK *abbr.* Alaska (in official postal use).

a.k.a. *abbr.* also known as.

a·kim·bo /əkímbō/ *adj. & adv.* (of the arms) with hands on the hips and elbows turned outwards.

a·kin /əkín/ *adj.* **1** related by blood. **2** (often foll. by *to*) of similar or kindred character.

AL *abbr.* Alabama (in official postal use).

Al *symb. Chem.* aluminum.

-al /əl/ *suffix* **1** forming adjectives meaning 're-lating to; of the kind of': **a** from Latin or Greek words (*central; tropical*) (cf. -IAL, -ICAL). **b** from English nouns (*tidal*). **2** forming nouns, esp. of verbal action (*arrival; trial*).

Ala. *abbr.* Alabama.

à la /áa laa/ *prep.* after the manner of (*à la russe*).

al·a·bas·ter /áləbastər/ • *n.* translucent usu.

white form of gypsum, often carved. ● *adj.* **1** of alabaster. **2** white or smooth. □□ **al·a·bas·trine** /–bástrin/ *adj.*

à la carte /aʼa laa kaʼart/ *adv. & adj.* ordered as separately priced item(s) from a menu, not as part of a set meal.

a·lac·ri·ty /əlákritee/ *n.* briskness or cheerful readiness.

à la mode /aʼa laa mód/ *adv. & adj.* **1** in fashion; fashionable. **2** served with ice cream, esp. pie or cake.

a·larm /əlaʼarm/ ● *n.* **1** warning of danger, etc. **2 a** warning sound or device. **b** = *alarm clock.* **3** apprehension. ● *v.tr.* **1** frighten or disturb. **2** warn. □ **alarm clock** clock that rings at a set time. □□ **a·larm′ing** *adj.* **a·larm′ing·ly** *adv.*

a·larm·ist /əláʼarmist/ ● *n.* person spreading needless alarm. ● *adj.* creating needless alarm. □□ **a·larm′ism** *n.*

Alas. *abbr.* Alaska.

a·las /əlás/ *int.* expression of grief, pity, or concern.

alb /alb/ *n.* long white vestment worn by Christian priests.

al·ba·core /álbəkawr/ *n.* **1** long-finned tuna. **2** any of various other related fish.

Al·ba·ni·an /albáyneeən, awl–/ ● *n.* **1 a** native or inhabitant of Albania in SE Europe. **b** person of Albanian descent. **2** language of Albania. ● *adj.* of or relating to Albania or its people or language.

al·ba·tross /álbətraws, –tros/ *n.* **1** long-winged, web-footed, stout-bodied sea bird. **2** encumbrance.

---

albatross late 17th cent.: alteration (influenced by Latin *albus* 'white') of 16th-cent. *alcatras,* applied to various seabirds including the frigate bird and pelican, from Spanish and Portuguese *alcatraz,* from Arabic *al-ġaṭṭās* 'the diver.'

---

al·be·it /áwlbéeit/ *conj. formal* though.

al·bi·no /albínō/ *n.* (*pl.* **–nos**) **1** person or animal lacking pigment in the skin and hair (which are white), and the eyes (usu. pink). **2** plant lacking normal coloring. □□ **al·bi·nism** /álbinizəm/ *n.* **al·bi·not·ic** /álbinótik/ *adj.*

al·bum /álbəm/ *n.* **1** blank book for photographs, stamps, etc. **2 a** long-playing phonograph, audio cassette, or compact disc recording. **b** set of these.

al·bu·men /albyoo̅omin/ *n.* **1** egg white. **2** *Bot.* substance found between the skin and embryo of many seeds, usu. the edible part.

al·bu·min /albyoo̅omin/ *n.* water-soluble proteins found in egg white, milk, blood, etc. □□ **al·bu′min·ous** *adj.*

al·che·my /álkəmee/ *n.* (*pl.* **–mies**) medieval chemistry, esp. seeking to turn base metals into gold. □□ **al·chem·ic** /alkémik/ *adj.* **al·chem′i·cal** *adj.* **al′che·mist** *n.* **al′che·mize** *v.tr.*

al·co·hol /álkəhawl, –hol/ *n.* **1** colorless volatile flammable liquid forming the intoxicating element in wine, beer, liquor, etc., and also used as a solvent, as fuel, etc. **2** any liquor containing this. **3** *Chem.* any of a large class of organic compounds that contain one or more hydroxyl groups attached to carbon atoms.

alcohol mid-16th cent.: French (earlier form of *alcool*), or from medieval Latin, from Arabic *al-kuḥl* 'the kohl.' In early use the term denoted powders, specifically kohl, and especially those obtained by sublimation; later 'a distilled or rectified spirit' (mid-17th cent).

al·co·hol·ic /álkəháwlik, –hól–/ ● *adj.* of, relating to, containing, or caused by alcohol. ● *n.* person suffering from alcoholism.

al·co·hol·ism /álkəhawlízəm, –ho–/ *n.* addiction to the consumption of alcoholic liquor; condition resulting from this.

al·cove /álkōv/ *n.* recess, esp. in the wall of a room.

al den·te /aal déntay, al déntee/ *adj.* (of pasta, etc.) cooked so as to be still firm when bitten.

al·der /áwldər/ *n.* tree related to the birch.

al·der·man /áwldərmən/ *n.* (*pl.* **–men**; *fem.* **al·der·wom·an**, *pl.* **-wom·en**) elected municipal official serving on the governing council of a city. □□ **al·der·man·ic** /–mánik/ *adj.* **al′der·man·ship** *n.*

ale /ayl/ *n.* beverage like beer, but stronger.

a·le·a·to·ry /áyleeətawree/ *adj.* depending on chance.

a·lem·bic /əlémbik/ *n.* **1** *hist.* apparatus used in distilling. **2** means of refining or extracting.

a·lert /əlórt/ ● *adj.* **1** watchful or vigilant. **2** quick (esp. of mental faculties); attentive. ● *n.* **1** alarm. **2** state or period of special vigilance. ● *v.tr.* warn. □ **on the alert** vigilant. □□ **a·lert′ly** *adv.* **a·lert′ness** *n.*

Al·eut /əlóot/ *n.* **1 a** N. American people native to the Aleutian Islands and western Alaska. **b** member of this people. **2** language of this people. □□ **A·leu·tian** /–shən/ *adj.*

al·fal·fa /alfálfə/ *n.* cloverlike plant used for fodder.

al·fres·co /alfréskō/ *adv. & adj.* in the open air; out doors.

al·ga /álgə/ *n.* (*pl.* **al·gae** /áljee/ also **al·gas**) (usu. in *pl.*) nonflowering stemless water plant, esp. seaweed and phytoplankton. □□ **al′gal** *adj.* **al′goid** *adj.*

al·ge·bra /áljibrə/ *n.* branch of mathematics that uses letters, etc., to represent numbers and quantities. □□ **al·ge·bra·ic** /áljibráyik/ *adj.* **al·ge·bra′i·cal** *adj.* **al·ge·bra′i·cal·ly** *adv.*

---

algebra late Middle English: from Italian, Spanish, and medieval Latin, from Arabic *al-jabr* 'the reunion of broken parts,' 'bonesetting,' from *jabara* 'reunite, restore.' The original sense, 'the surgical treatment of fractures,' probably came via Spanish, in which it survives; the mathematical sense comes from the title of a book, '*ilm al-jabr wa'l-muķābala* 'The Science of Restoring What Is Missing and Equating Like with Like,' by the mathematician al-Ḵwārizmī.

Al·gon·qui·an /algóngkweeən/ *n.* any of the languages or dialects used by the Algonquin peoples, native to eastern N. America.

al·go·rithm /álgərithəm/ *n.* *Math.* process or set of rules used for calculation or problem-solving, esp. with a computer. □□ **al·go·rith′mic** /álgərithmik/ *adj.*

a·li·as /áyleeəs/ • *adv.* also named or known as. • *n.* false or assumed name.

al·i·bi /álibī/ (*pl.* **al·i·bis**) • *n.* **1** claim or proof that when an alleged act took place one was elsewhere. **2** excuse. • *v.* (**al·i·bis, al·i·bied, al·i·bi·ing**) *colloq.* **1** *tr.* provide an alibi or offer an excuse for (a person). **2** *intr.* provide an alibi. ¶ The chief meaning of this Latin word is 'evidence that when something took place one was elsewhere,' e.g., *He has no alibi for the evening in question.* It is also used informally, however, to mean 'an excuse, pretext, or justification'; many consider this incorrect.

al·ien /áyleeən/ • *adj.* **1 a** unfamiliar; unacceptable or repugnant. **b** different or separated. **2** foreign. **3** of or relating to beings supposedly from other worlds. • *n.* **1** foreigner, esp. one who is not a citizen of the country where he or she is living. **2** being supposedly from another world. □□ **al′ien·ness** *n.*

al·ien·ate /áyleeənayt/ *v.tr.* **1 a** cause (a person) to become unfriendly or hostile. **b** (often foll. by *from*) cause (a person) to feel isolated or estranged from (friends, society, etc.). **2** transfer ownership of. □□ **al·ien·a′tion** /-áyshən/ *n.* **al′ien·a·tor** *n.*

a·light¹ /əlít/ *v.intr.* **1 a** descend from a vehicle. **b** dismount from a horse. **2** settle; come to earth from the air.

a·light² /əlít/ *adj.* **1** on fire. **2** lit up; excited.

a·lign /əlín/ *v.tr.* (also **a·line′**) **1** put or bring into line. **2** bring (oneself, etc.) into agreement or alliance with (a cause, party, etc.). □□ **a·lign′ment** *n.*

a·like /əlík/ • *adj.* similar; like. • *adv.* in a similar way.

al·i·men·ta·ry /áliméntəree/ *adj.* of or providing nourishment or sustenance. □ **alimentary canal** *Anat.* passage along which food is passed during digestion. □□ **al·i·men·ta′tion** *n.*

al·i·mo·ny /álimōnee/ *n.* money payable to a spouse after divorce or legal separation.

a·live /əlív/ *adj.* **1** living; not dead. **2 a** (of a thing) existing; continuing (*kept his interest alive*). **b** under discussion (*topic is very much alive*). **3** lively; active. **4** (foll. by *to*) aware of; alert. **5** (foll. by *with*) swarming or teeming with. □□ **a·live′ness** *n.*

al·ka·li /álkəlī/ *n.* (*pl.* **al·ka·lis**) **1** any of a class of substances that liberate hydroxide ions in water, usu. form caustic or corrosive solutions, and have a pH of more than 7. **2** *Chem.* any substance that reacts with or neutralizes acids. □□ **al′ka·line** /-līn/ *adj.* **al·ka·lin′i·ty** /-línitee/ *n.*

al·ka·loid /álkəloyd/ *n.* nitrogenous organic compounds of plant origin, e.g., morphine, quinine.

al·kyd /álkid/ *n.* synthetic resin derived from various alcohols and acids.

all /awl/ • *adj.* **1 a** whole amount, quantity, or extent of. **b** (with *pl.*) entire number of (*all the others left*). **2** any whatever (*beyond all doubt*). **3** greatest possible (*with all speed*). • *n.* **1 a** all concerned (*all were present*). **b** everything. **2** (foll. by *of*) **a** the whole of. **b** every one of. **3** (in games) each (*score was two all*). • *adv.* **1** entirely; quite (*dressed all in black*). **b** as an intensifier (*a book all about ships*). **2** to that extent (*if they go, all the better*). □ **all-America(n)** *1* representing the whole of (or only) America or the US. **2** truly American (*all-American boy*). **3** *Sports* recognized as one of the best in a particular sport. **all-**

around (of a person) versatile. **all but** very nearly (*it was all but impossible*). **all in all** everything considered. **all right** (*predic.*) **1** satisfactory; in good condition. **2** satisfactorily; as desired. **at all** in any way; to any extent. ¶ Although found widely, **alright** remains nonstandard, even where standard spelling leads to awkwardness, e.g., *I wanted to make sure it was all all right.*

Al·lah /álə, aálaa/ *n.* name of God in Islam.

al·lay /əláy/ *v.tr.* **1** diminish (fear, suspicion, etc.). **2** relieve or alleviate (pain, hunger, etc.).

al·le·ga·tion /áligáyshən/ *n.* **1** assertion, esp. unproved. **2** alleging.

al·lege /əléj/ *v.tr.* **1** declare, esp. without proof. **2** advance as an argument or excuse. □□ **al·leged** *adj.* **al·leg′ed·ly** *adv.*

al·le·giance /əléejəns/ *n.* **1** loyalty (to a person or cause, etc.). **2** the duty of a subject to his or her government.

al·le·go·ry /áligawree/ *n.* (*pl.* **–ries**) story, etc., whose characters are represented symbolically. □□ **al′le·go·rist** *n.*

al·le·gret·to /áligrétō/ *Mus.* • *adv.* & *adj.* in a fairly brisk tempo. • *n.* (*pl.* **–tos**) such a passage or movement.

al·le·gro /əléggrō, əláy-/ *Mus.* • *adv.* & *adj.* in a brisk tempo. • *n.* (*pl.* **–gros**) such a passage or movement.

al·le·lu·ia /álilóoyə/ (also **al·le·lu′ya, hal·le·lu·jah** /hál-/) • *int.* God be praised. • *n.* praise to God.

Al·len wrench /álən/ *n.* hexagonal wrench designed to fit into and turn a screw with a hexagonal head.

al·ler·gen /álərjen/ *n.* any substance that causes an allergic reaction. □□ **al·ler·gen′ic** /-jénik/ *adj.*

al·ler·gic /əlórjik/ *adj.* **1** (foll. by *to*) **a** having an allergy to. **b** *colloq.* having a strong dislike for. **2** caused by an allergy.

al·ler·gy /álərjee/ *n.* (*pl.* **–gies**) **1** *Med.* adverse reaction to certain substances, as particular foods, pollen, fur, or dust. **2** *colloq.* dislike. □□ **al′ler·gist** *n.*

al·le·vi·ate /əléeveeayt/ *v.tr.* lessen or make less severe (pain, suffering, etc.). □□ **al·le·vi·a·tion** /-áyshən/ *n.* **al·le′vi·a·tive** *adj.* **al·le′vi·a·tor** *n.* **al·le′vi·a·to·ry** /-veeatáwree/ *adj.*

al·ley /álee/ *n.* (*pl.* **–leys**) **1** (also **al·ley·way**) narrow streetlike passageway, esp. between or behind buildings. **2** place for bowling, etc.

al·li·ance /əlíəns/ *n.* **1** union or agreement to cooperate, esp. of nations by treaty or families by marriage. **2** the parties involved.

al·lied /əlíd, álīd/ *adj.* **1 a** associated in an alliance. **b** (**Allied**) of or relating to the US and its allies in World War I and World War II. **2** connected or related.

al·li·ga·tor /áligaytor/ *n.* large reptile of the crocodile family native to the Americas and China, with a head broader and shorter than that of the crocodile. □ **alligator pear** avocado.

al·lit·er·a·tion /əlítəráyshən/ *n.* occurrence of the same letter or sound at the beginning of adjacent or closely connected words (e.g., *calm, cool, and collected*). □□ **al·lit·er·ate** /əlítərayt/ *v.* **al·lit′er·a·tive** /əlítəraytiv, –rətiv/ *adj.*

al·lo·cate /áləkayt/ *v.tr.* assign, apportion, or

devote to (a purpose, person, or place). □□ **al·lo·ca·ble** /–kəbəl/ adj. **al·lo·ca·tion** /–káyshən/ n. **al·lo·ca·tor** /–/ n.

al·lot /əlót/ v. tr. (**al·lot·ted, al·lot·ting**) apportion or distribute to (a person) as a share or task. □□ **al·lot′ment** n.

al·low /əlów/ v. **1** tr. permit (a thing to happen, etc.). **2** tr. permit (a person) to have (a limited quantity or sum) (we were allowed $500 a year). **3** tr. provide or set aside for a purpose. **4** tr. **a** admit; concede. **b** assert. **5** refl. indulge oneself in (conduct). **6** intr. take into consideration or account. □□ **al·low′a·ble** adj. **al·low′a·bly** adv.

al·low·ance /əlówəns/ • n. **1** amount or sum allowed. **2** deduction or discount. **3** tolerance of. • v. tr. make an allowance to (a person). □ **make allowances 1** take into consideration (mitigating circumstances). **2** look with tolerance upon.

al·loy /áloy, əlóy/ • n. **1** mixture of two or more metals. **2** inferior metal mixed esp. with gold or silver. • v. tr. **1** mix (metals). **2** debase (a pure substance) by admixture. **3** moderate.

all·spice /áwlspīs/ n. **1** aromatic spice obtained from the ground berry of the pimento tree. **2** berry of this.

al·lude /əlŏŏd/ v. intr. **1** refer, esp. indirectly, covertly, or briefly to. **2** mention.

al·lure /əlŏŏr/ • v. tr. attract, charm, or fascinate. • n. attractiveness; personal charm; fascination. □□ **al·lure′ment** n. **al·lur′ing** adj. **al·lur′ing·ly** adv.

al·lu·sion /əlŏŏzhən/ n. reference, esp. a covert, passing, or indirect one. □□ **al·lu·sive** /əlŏŏsiv/ adj.

al·lu·vi·um /əlŏŏveeəm/ n. (pl. **al·lu·vi·ums** or **al·lu·vi·a** /–ə/) deposit of usu. fine fertile soil left behind by a flood. □□ **al·lu′vi·al** adj.

al·ly /álī/ • n. (pl. **–lies**) **1** government formally cooperating or united with another, esp. by a treaty. **2** person or organization that cooperates with or helps another. • v. tr. also /əlí/ (**–lies, –lied**) combine or unite in alliance.

-ally /əlee/ suffix forming adverbs from adjectives in -al (cf. -AL, -LY², -ICALLY).

al·ma ma·ter /a̐almə máatər, álmə máytər/ n. (also **Al·ma Ma·ter**) **1** university, school, or college one attends or attended. **2** official school anthem or song.

al·ma·nac /áwlmənak, ál–/ n. calendar, usu. with astronomical data and other reference information.

al·might·y /áwlmītee/ • adj. **1** having complete power; omnipotent. **2** (**the Al·might·y**) God. **3** sl. very great (an almighty crash). • adv. sl. extremely; very much.

al·mond /áamənd, ám–/ n. **1** nutlike seed (kernel) of a fruit related to the peach and plum. **2** tree itself.

al·most /áwlmōst/ adv. all but; very nearly.

alms /aamz/ n. pl. hist. charitable donation of money or food to the poor.

alms·house /áamz-hows/ n. esp. Brit. hist. a house founded by charity for the poor.

al·oe /álō/ n. plant of the lily family, usu. having toothed fleshy leaves.

a·loft /əláwft, əlóft/ predic. adj. & adv. **1** high up; overhead. **2** upwards.

a·lo·ha /əlóhaa, aa–/ int. Hawaiian salutation at meeting or parting.

a·lone /əlón/ predic. adj. & adv. **1** without others. **2** lonely. **3** only; exclusively. □□ **a·lone′ness** n.

a·long /əláwng, əlóng/ • prep. **1** from one end to the other end of. **2** on, beside, or through any part of the length of. • adv. **1** onward. **2** arriving. **3** with oneself or others.

a·long·side /əláwngsíd, əlóng–/ • adv. at or to the side. • prep. close to the side of.

a·loof /əlŏŏf/ • adj. distant; unsympathetic. • adv. away; apart. □□ **a·loof′ness** n.

a·loud /əlówd/ adv. audibly; not silently or in a whisper.

alp /alp/ n. **1** high mountain. **2** (**the Alps**) high range of mountains in Switzerland and adjoining countries.

al·pac·a /alpákə/ n. **1** S. American mammal related to the llama, with long shaggy hair. **2** wool from the animal. **3** fabric made from the wool.

al·pha /álfə/ n. **1** first letter of the Greek alphabet (A, α). **2** beginning. □ **alpha and omega** beginning and end. **alpha particle** helium nucleus emitted by a radioactive substance.

al·pha·bet /álfəbet/ n. set of letters used in writing a language. □□ **al·pha·bet′i·cal** adj. **al·pha·bet′i·cal·ly** adv.

al·pha·bet·ize /álfəbətīz/ v. tr. arrange (words, names, etc.) in alphabetical order. □□ **al·pha·bet·i·za·tion** /–izáyshən/ n.

al·pha·nu·mer·ic /álfənōōmérik, –nyōō–/ adj. (also **al·pha·nu·mer′i·cal**) containing both alphabetical and numerical symbols.

al·pine /álpīn/ adj. **1** of, relating to, or found in high mountains. **2** (**Alpine**) of or relating to the Alps.

al·read·y /áwlrédee/ adv. **1** before the time in question. **2** as early or as soon as this.

al·right /áwlrít/ adj., adv., & int. disp. = all right. ¶ See note at all right.

ALS abbr. AMYOTROPHIC LATERAL SCLEROSIS.

al·so /áwlsō/ adv. in addition; likewise; besides. □ **also-ran 1** one who does not win a competition. **2** undistinguished person.

alt. abbr. **1** alternate **2** altimeter. **3** altitude.

al·tar /áwltər/ n. **1** table or flat block for sacrifice or offering to a deity. **2** raised surface or table used in a Christian service.

al·tar·piece /áwltərpees/ n. piece of art, esp. a painting, set above or behind an altar.

al·ter /áwltər/ v. **1** tr. & intr. make or become different; change. **2** tr. castrate or spay. □□ **al′ter·a·ble** adj. **al·ter·a′tion** n.

al·ter·cate /áwltərkayt/ v. intr. dispute hotly; wrangle. □□ **al·ter·ca·tion** /–káyshən/ n.

al·ter e·go /áwltər ée̐gō, ég̐ō/ n. **1** intimate and trusted friend. **2** person's secondary or alternative personality.

al·ter·nate • v. intr. /áwltərnayt, ál–/ **1** (of two things) succeed each other in turn. **2** change repeatedly (between two conditions). • adj. /áwltərnət, ál–/ **1** every other. **2** (of things of two kinds) each following and succeeded by one of the other kind. • n. /áwltərnət, ál–/ alternative; deputy or substitute. □ **alternating current** electric current that reverses its direction at regular intervals. □□ **al′ter·nate·ly** adv. **al·ter·na·tion** /–náyshən, ál–/ n.

¶ In both American and British English **alternate** means 'every other,' e.g., There will be a dance on *alternate Saturdays,* and **alternative** means 'available as another choice,' e.g., *an alternative route.* In American usage, however, **alternate** can also be used to mean 'available as another choice,' e.g., *An alternate plan called for construction to begin immediately rather than waiting for spring.*

al·ter·na·tive /awltə́rnətiv, al–/ • *adj.* **1** available or usable instead of another. **2** (of two things) mutually exclusive. **3** unconventional. • *n.* **1** any of two or more possibilities. **2** choice. □□ **al·ter′na·tive·ly** *adv.* ¶ See note at ALTERNATE.

al·ter·na·tor /áwltərnaytər, ál–/ *n.* generator that produces an alternating current.

al·though /awltͪó/ *conj.* = THOUGH *conj.* 1–3.

al·tim·e·ter /altímitər, áltimeetər/ *n.* instrument for showing height above sea or ground level.

al·ti·tude /áltitōod, –tyōod/ *n.* height of an object in relation to a given point, esp. sea level or the horizon.

al·to /áltō/ *n.* (*pl.* **–tos**) **1** = CONTRALTO. **2** = COUNTERTENOR. **3** instrument pitched next below a soprano of its type.

al·to·geth·er /áwltəgéthər/ *adv.* **1** totally; completely. **2** on the whole. **3** in total. □ **in the altogether** *colloq.* naked. ¶ **Altogether** and **all together** are used in different contexts. **Altogether** means 'in total,' e.g., *The hotel has twenty rooms altogether. Altogether, I spent five years on the island.* **All together** means 'all at once' or 'all in one place or in one group,' e.g., *The packages arrived all together. We managed to get three bedrooms all together* (i.e., near each other).

al·tru·ism /áltrōoizm/ *n.* unselfishness as a principle of action. □□ **al·tru·ist** /–trooist/ *n.* **al·tru·is′tic** /–ístik/ *adj.* **al·tru·is′ti·cal·ly** *adv.*

al·um /áləm/ *n.* sulfate of aluminum and potassium.

a·lu·mi·na /əlōominə/ *n.* aluminum oxide occurring naturally as corundum and emery.

a·lu·mi·num /əlōominəm/ *n.* silvery light and malleable metallic element. ¶ Symb.: **Al.**

a·lum·nus /əlúmnəs/ *n.* (*pl.* **a·lum·ni** /–nī/; *fem.* **a·lum·na,** *pl.* **a·lum·nae** /–nee, nī/) former pupil or student of a particular school, college, or university.

al·ways /áwlwayz/ *adv.* **1** at all times; on all occasions. **2** whatever the circumstances. **3** repeatedly; often.

Alz·hei·mer's dis·ease /áalts-hī́mərz, álts–, áwlts–, áwlz–/ *n.* brain disorder causing premature senility.

AM *abbr.* **1** amplitude modulation. **2** Master of Arts.

Am *symb.* *Chem.* americium.

am *1st person sing. present* of BE.

a.m. *abbr.* (also **A.M.** or **AM**) between midnight and noon.

a·mal·gam /əmálgəm/ *n.* **1** mixture or blend. **2** alloy of mercury with one or more other metals.

a·mal·ga·mate /əmálgəmayt/ *v.* combine or unite. □□ **a·mal·ga·ma·tion** /–máyshən/ *n.*

a·man·u·en·sis /əmányōo-énsis/ *n.* (*pl.* **a·man·u·en′ses** /–seez/) person who writes from dictation or copies manuscripts.

am·a·ranth /áməranth/ *n.* **1** plant with small green, red, or purple tinted flowers. **2** imaginary flower that never fades. □□ **am·a·ran′thine** /–əránthin, –thīn/ *adj.*

am·a·ryl·lis /ámərílis/ *n.* bulbous lilylike plant with white, pink, or red flowers.

a·mass /əmás/ *v.tr.* **1** gather or heap together. **2** accumulate (esp. riches). □□ **a·mass′er** *n.* **a·mass′ment** *n.*

am·a·teur /áməchōor, –chər, –tər, –tər/ • *n.* **1** person who engages in a pursuit as a pastime rather than a profession. **2** *derog.* person who does something unskillfully. • *adj.* for or done by amateurs; amateurish; unskillful. □□ **am′a·teur·ish** *adj.* **am·a·teur′ish·ly** *adv.*

am·a·to·ry /ámətawree/ *adj.* sexual love or desire.

a·maze /əmáyz/ *v.tr.* surprise greatly; overwhelm with wonder. □□ **a·maze′ment** *n.* **a·maz·ing** *adj.* **a·maz′ing·ly** *adv.*

Am·a·zon /áməzon, –zən/ *n.* **1** female warrior of a mythical race. **2** (**amazon**) tall, strong, or athletic woman. □□ **Am·a·zo·ni·an** /–zṓneeən/ *adj.*

am·bas·sa·dor /ambásədər, –dawr/ *n.* **1** accredited diplomat sent by a nation as its representative in a foreign country. **2** representative or promoter. □□ **am·bas·sa·do·ri·al** /–dáwreeəl/ *adj.* **am·bas′sa·dor·ship** *n.*

am·ber /ámbər/ *n.* **1** yellowish translucent fossilized resin deriving from extinct (esp. coniferous) trees and used in jewelry. **2** color of this.

am·ber·gris /ámbərgris, –grees/ *n.* waxlike secretion of the sperm whale, used in perfumes.

am·bi·dex·trous /ámbidékstrəs/ *adj.* **1** able to use either hand equally well. **2** versatile; skillful. □□ **am·bi·dex·ter·i·ty** /–stéritee/ *n.* **am·bi·dex′trous·ly** *adv.* **am·bi·dex′trous·ness** *n.*

am·bi·ence /ámbeeəns, aaNbeeáaNs/ *n.* (also **am′bi·ance**) surroundings or atmosphere of a place.

am·bi·ent /ámbeeənt/ *adj.* surrounding.

am·big·u·ous /ambígyōoəs/ *adj.* **1** having an obscure or double meaning. **2** difficult to classify. □□ **am·bi·gu·i·ty** /ámbigyōóitee/ *n.* **am·big′u·ous·ly** *adv.*

am·bi·tion /ambíshən/ *n.* **1** determination to succeed. **2** object of this.

am·bi·tious /ambíshəs/ *adj.* **1 a** full of ambition. **b** showing ambition. **2** strongly determined. □□ **am·bi′tious·ly** *adv.*

am·biv·a·lence /ambívələns/ *n.* (also **am·biv′a·len·cy**) simultaneous conflicting feelings. □□ **am·biv′a·lent** *adj.* **am·biv′a·lent·ly** *adv.*

am·ble /ámbəl/ • *v.intr.* move at an easy pace. • *n.* such a pace.

am·bro·sia /ambrṓzhə/ *n.* **1** (in Greek and Roman mythology) food of the gods. **2** anything very pleasing to taste or smell. □□ **am·bro′sial** *adj.* **am·bro′sian** *adj.*

am·bu·lance /ámbyələns/ *n.* vehicle equipped for conveying the sick or injured to and from a hospital.

am·bu·la·to·ry /ámbyələtawree/ *adj.* **1** (of a patient) able to walk about. **2** of or for walking.

am·bus·cade /ámbəskáyd/ *n.* & *v.* = AMBUSH.

am·bush /ámbōosh/ *n.* **1** surprise attack from a concealed position. **2 a** concealment of troops, etc., to make such an attack. **b** place where they are concealed. • *v. tr.* **1** attack by ambush. **2** lie in wait for.

a·me·ba var. of AMOEBA.

a·me·lio·rate /əmeélyərayt/ *v.* make or become better; improve. □□ **a·mel·io·ra·tion** /–ráyshən/ *n.* **am·el′io·ra·tive** *adj.* **a·mel′io·ra·tor** *n.*

a·men /a′ámén, áy–/ *int.* word uttered at the end of a prayer, etc., meaning 'so be it.'

a·me·na·ble /əmeénəbəl, əmén–/ *adj.* **1** responsive. **2** (of a person) responsible to law. □□ **a·me·na·bil′i·ty** *n.* **a·me′na·bly** *adv.*

a·mend /əménd/ *v. tr.* **1** make minor improvements in (a text, etc.). **2** correct an error in (a document). **3** improve. **4** modify formally, as a legal document. □□ **a·mend′a·ble** *adj.* **a·mend′er** *n.*

a·mend·ment /əméndmənt/ *n.* **1** minor change in a document (esp. a legal or statutory one). **2** article added to the US Constitution.

a·mends /əméndz/ *n.* □ **make amends** compensate or make up (for).

a·men·i·ty /əménitee, əmee′–/ *n.* (*pl.* **–ties**) **1** (usu. in *pl.*) pleasant or useful feature. **2** pleasantness (of a place, etc.).

Am·er·a·sian /aməráyzhən/ *n.* person of American and Asian descent.

a·merce /əmɔ́rs/ *v. tr.* **1** *Law* punish by fine. **2** punish arbitrarily. □□ **a·merce′ment** *n.*

A·mer·i·can /əmérikən/ • *adj.* **1** of, relating to, or characteristic of the United States or its inhabitants. **2** (usu. in *comb.*) of or relating to the continents of America (*Latin-American*). • *n.* **1** native or citizen of the United States. **2** native or inhabitant of the continents of America. **3** (also **Amer′ican Eng′lish**) the English language as it is used in the United States. □ **American Indian** member of the aboriginal peoples of America or their descendants. □□ **A·mer·i·can·i·za′tion** *n.* **A·mer′i·can·ize** *v.*

A·mer·i·ca·na /əmérikánə, –ka′anə, –káynə/ *n.pl.* things connected with America, esp. with the United States.

A·mer·i·can·ism /əmérikənizəm/ *n.* **1 a** word, sense, or phrase peculiar to or originating from the United States. **b** thing or feature characteristic of the United States. **2** attachment to or sympathy for the United States.

am·er·i·ci·um /ámərísheeəm/ *n. Chem.* artificial radioactive metallic element. ¶ Symb.: **Am.**

Am·er·in·di·an /áməríndeeən/ *adj. & n.* (also **Am·er·ind** /ámərind/) = *American Indian.* □□ **Am·er·in′dic** /–ríndik/ *adj.*

am·e·thyst /ámithist/ *n.* semiprecious stone of a violet or purple variety of quartz. □□ **am·e·thys·tine** /–thísteen/ *adj.*

a·mi·a·ble /áymeeəbəl/ *adj.* friendly and pleasant, likable. □□ **a·mi·a·bil′i·ty** *n.* **a′mi·a·ble·ness** *n.* **a′mi·a·bly** *adv.*

---

amiable late Middle English (originally in the senses 'kind,' and 'lovely, lovable'): via Old French from late Latin *amicabilis* 'amicable.' The current sense, influenced by modern French *aimable* 'trying to please,' dates from the mid-18th cent.

---

am·i·ca·ble /ámikəbəl/ *adj.* showing or done in a friendly spirit. □□ **am·i·ca·bil′i·ty** *n.* **am′i·ca·bly** *adv.*

a·mid /əmíd/ *prep.* (also **a·midst** /əmídst/) **1** in the middle of. **2** in the course of.

am·ide /áymīd, ám–/ *n. Chem.* compound formed from ammonia.

a·mid·ships /əmídships/ *adv.* (also **a·mid′ship**) in or into the middle of a ship.

a·mi·go /əmeégō/ *n.* (*pl.* **–gos**) friend or comrade.

a·mine /əmeén, ámeen/ *n. Chem.* compound formed from ammonia.

a·mi·no ac·id /əmeénō/ *n. Biochem.* any of a group of nitrogenous organic acids forming the basic constituents of proteins.

a·miss /əmís/ • *adj.* wrong; out of order. • *adv.* wrong; wrongly; inappropriately.

am·i·ty /ámitee/ *n.* friendship; friendly relations.

am·me·ter /ám-meetər/ *n.* instrument for measuring electric current in amperes.

am·mo /ámō/ *n. colloq.* ammunition.

am·mo·nia /əmṓnyə/ *n.* **1** pungent, strongly alkaline gas. ¶ Chem. formula: NH_3. **2** solution of ammonia gas in water.

am·mu·ni·tion /ámyəníshən/ *n.* **1** supply of bullets, shells, grenades, etc. **2** points usable to advantage in an argument.

am·ne·sia /amneézhə/ *n.* partial or total loss of memory. □□ **am·ne′si·ac** /–zeeak, –zheeak/ *n.* **am·ne′sic** *adj. & n.*

am·nes·ty /ámnistee/ • *n.* (*pl.* **–ties**) general pardon, esp. for political offenses. • *v. tr.* (**–ties, –tied**) grant an amnesty to.

am·ni·o·cen·te·sis /ámneeōsente′esis/ *n.* (*pl.* **am·ni·o·cen·te·ses** /–seez/) *Med.* sampling of amniotic fluid to determine health of a fetus.

am·ni·on /ámneeon/ *n.* (*pl.* **am·ni·a**) *Zool. & Physiol.* innermost membrane that encloses an embryo. □□ **am·ni·ot·ic** /ámneeótik/ *adj.*

a·moe·ba /əmeébə/ *n.* (also **a·me′ba**) (*pl.* **a·moe·bas** or **a·moe·bae** /–bee/) any usu. aquatic protozoan capable of changing shape. □□ **a·moe·bic** *adj.* **a·moe′boid** *adj.*

a·mok /əmúk, əmók/ *adv.* (also **a·muck** /əmúk/) □ **run amok** run about wildly in an uncontrollable violent rage.

a·mong /əmúng/ *prep.* (also **a·mongst** /əmúngst/) **1** surrounded by; in the company of. **2** included in. **3** in the class or category of (*is among the richest men alive*). **4 a** shared by (*had $5 among us*). **b** from the joint resources of. **5** with one another. **6** as distinguished from (*she is one among many*).
¶ See note at BETWEEN.

a·mor·al /áymáwrəl, –mór–/ *adj.* **1** not concerned with or outside the scope of morality (cf. IMMORAL). **2** having no moral principles. □□ **a·mor′al·ism** *n.* **a·mo·ral·i·ty** /–rálitee/ *n.*
¶ See note at IMMORAL.

am·o·rous /ámərəs/ *adj.* **1** showing, feeling, or inclined to sexual love. **2** of or relating to sexual love. □□ **am′o·rous·ly** *adv.* **am′o·rous·ness** *n.*

a·mor·phous /əmáwrfəs/ *adj.* **1** shapeless. **2** ill-organized; unclassifiable. **3** *Mineral. & Chem.* noncrystalline. □□ **a·mor′phous·ly** *adv.* **a·mor′phous·ness** *n.*

am·or·tize /ámərtīz, əmáwr–/ *v. tr. Commerce* gradually extinguish (a debt) by regular payments.

a·mount /əmównt/ • *n.* **1** quantity, esp. the total in number, size, value, extent, etc. **2** full effect.

• v.intr. (foll. by *to*) **1** be equivalent to in number, significance, etc. **2** (of a person) develop into; become.

a·mour /əmŏŏr/ *n.* love affair, esp. a secret one.

a·mour pro·pre /a'amŏŏrr práwprə/ *n.* self-respect.

amp /amp/ *n.* **1** ampere. **2** amperage. **3** amplifier.

amp·er·age /ámpərij/ *n. Electr.* strength of an electric current in amperes.

am·pere /ámpeer/ *n. Electr.* base unit of electric current. ¶ Symb.: **A**.

am·per·sand /ámpərsand/ *n.* character representing the word *and*: & .

am·phet·a·mine /amfétəmeen, –min/ *n.* synthetic drug used esp. as a stimulant.

am·phib·i·an /amfíbeeən/ • *adj.* **1** of a class of vertebrates living both on land and in water. **2** (of a vehicle) able to operate on land and water. • *n.* **1** *Zool.* class of vertebrates including frogs, toads, newts, and salamanders. **2** (in general use) creature living both on land and in water. **3** amphibian vehicle. □□ **am·phib'i·ous** *adj.* **am·phib'i·ous·ly** *adv.*

---

amphibian mid-17th cent. (in the sense 'having two modes of existence or of doubtful nature'): from modern Latin *amphibium* 'an amphibian,' from Greek *amphibion* (noun use of *amphibios* 'living both in water and on land,' from *amphi* 'both' + *bios* 'life').

---

am·phi·the·a·ter /ámfitheeətər/ *n.* round, usu. unroofed building with tiers of seats surrounding a central space.

am·pho·ra /ámfərə/ *n.* (*pl.* **am·pho·rae** /–ree/ or **am·pho·ras**) Greek or Roman vessel with two handles and a narrow neck.

am·ple /ámpəl/ *adj.* (**am·pler, am·plest**) **1 a** plentiful; abundant; extensive. **b** *euphem.* (esp. of a person) large; stout. **2** enough or more than enough. □□ **am'ple·ness** *n.* **am'ply** *adv.*

am·pli·fi·er /ámplifiər/ *n.* electronic device for increasing the strength of electrical signals, esp. for conversion into sound.

am·pli·fy /ámplifī/ *v.* (**–fies, –fied**) **1** *tr.* increase the strength of (sound, electrical signals, etc.). **2** *tr.* enlarge upon or add detail to (a story, etc.). **3** *intr.* expand what is said or written. □□ **am·pli·fi·ca'tion** *n.*

am·pli·tude /ámplitŏŏd, –tyŏŏd/ *n.* **1 a** *Physics* maximum extent of a vibration or oscillation from the position of equilibrium. **b** *Electr.* maximum departure of the value of an alternating current or wave from the average value. **2 a** spaciousness; breadth; wide range. **b** abundance. □ **amplitude modulation** *Electr.* **1** modulation of a wave by variation of its amplitude. **2** system using such modulation.

am·poule /ámpŏŏl, –pōōl/ *n.* (also **am'pule** or **am'pul**) sealed capsule holding a solution for injection.

am·pu·tate /ámpyətayt/ *v.tr.* cut off by surgical operation (a limb, etc.). □□ **am·pu·ta'tion** /–táyshən/ *n.* **am'pu·ta·tor** *n.*

am·pu·tee /ámpyətée/ *n.* person who has lost a limb, etc., by amputation.

Am·trak /ámtrak/ *n. propr.* US passenger railroad system.

a·muck var. of AMOK.

am·u·let /ámyəlit/ *n.* charm worn against evil.

---

a·muse /əmyŏŏz/ *v.* **1** *tr.* cause to laugh or smile. **2** *tr. & refl.* interest or occupy; keep entertained. □□ **a·mus'ing** *adj.* **a·mus'ing·ly** *adv.*

a·muse·ment /əmyŏŏzmənt/ *n.* **1** something that amuses. **2 a** state of being amused. **b** act of amusing. □ **amusement park** park with rides such as a roller coaster, etc., and other entertainment.

a·my·o·troph·ic lat·er·al scle·ro·sis /aymīə-trófik, –tró–/ *n.* incurable degenerative disease of the nervous system leading to paralysis. Also called **Lou Gehrig's disease**. ¶ Abbr.: **ALS**.

an /an, ən/ *adj.* form of the indefinite article (see A).

an- /ən, an/ *prefix* **1** not; without (*anarchy*) (cf. A-). **2** assim. form of AD- before *n*.

-an /ən/ *suffix* (also **–ean, –ian**) forming adjectives and nouns, esp. from names of places, systems, classes or orders, and founders (*Mexican; Anglican; crustacean; Lutheran*).

an·a·bol·ic /ánəbólik/ *adj. Biochem.* of or relating to anabolism. □ **anabolic steroid** synthetic steroid hormones used to increase muscle size.

a·nab·o·lism /ənábəlizəm/ *n. Biochem.* synthesis of complex molecules in living organisms from simpler ones.

a·nach·ro·nism /ənákrənizəm/ *n.* **1 a** attribution of a custom, event, etc., to the wrong period. **b** thing attributed in this way. **2** out-of-date person or thing. □□ **a·nach·ro·nis·tic** /–nístik/ *adj.* **a·nach·ro·nis'ti·cal·ly** *adv.*

an·a·con·da /ánəkóndə/ *n.* large nonpoisonous snake that kills its prey by constriction.

an·aer·obe /ánərōb, anáirōb/ *n.* organism able to live without air or water. □□ **an·aer·o'bic** *adj.*

an·a·gram /ánəgram/ *n.* word or phrase formed by transposing the letters of another word or phrase. □□ **an·a·gram·mat·ic** /–mátik/ *adj.* **an·a·gram·mat'i·cal** *adj.* **an·a·gram·ma·tize** /–grámətīz/ *v.tr.*

a·nal /áynəl/ *adj.* **1** of or near the anus. **2** = *anal retentive.* □ **anal retentive** (of a person) excessively orderly and fussy. □□ **a'nal·ly** *adv.*

an·al·ge·si·a /ánəlje'ezeeə, –seeə/ *n.* absence or relief of pain.

an·al·ge·sic /ánəlje'ezik, –sik/ • *adj.* relieving pain. • *n.* analgesic drug.

an·a·log /ánəlog/ *n.* **1** analogous thing. **2** (*attrib.*) (of a computer or electronic process) using physical variables, e.g., voltage, weight, etc., to represent numbers (cf. DIGITAL).

a·nal·o·gize /ənáləjīz/ *v.* **1** *tr.* represent or explain by analogy. **2** *intr.* use analogy.

a·nal·o·gous /ənáləgəs/ *adj.* (usu. foll. by *to*) partially similar or parallel; showing analogy. □□ **a·nal'o·gous·ly** *adv.*

a·nal·o·gy /ənálojee/ *n.* (*pl.* **–gies**) **1** correspondence or partial similarity. **2** *Logic* arguing from parallel cases. **3** = ANALOG 1. □□ **an·a·log·i·cal** /ánəlójikəl/ *adj.* **an·a·log'i·cal·ly** *adv.*

a·nal·y·sis /ənálisis/ *n.* (*pl.* **a·nal·y·ses** /–seez/) **1 a** detailed examination of elements or structure. **b** statement of the result of this. **2** *Chem.* determination of the constituent parts of a mixture or compound. **3** psychoanalysis. □□ **an·a·lyt·ic** /ánəlítik/ *adj.* **an·a·lyt'i·cal** *adj.* **an·a·lyt'i·cal·ly** *adv.*

an·a·lyst /ánəlist/ *n.* **1** person skilled in analysis. **2** psychoanalyst.

an·a·lyze /ánəlīz/ *v.tr.* **1** examine in detail. **2 a** *Chem.* ascertain the constituents of. **b** break (something) down into its constituent parts. **3** psychoanalyze. □□ **an'a·lyz·a·ble** *adj.* **an'a·lyz·er** *n.*

an·a·pest /ánəpest/ *n. Prosody* metrical foot consisting of two short or unstressed syllables followed by one long or stressed syllable. □□ **an·a·pes'tic** *adj.*

an·a·phy·lax·is /ánəfiláksis/ *n.* (*pl.* **an·a·phy·lax·es** /–seez/) *Med.* hypersensitivity of tissues to a dose of antigen, as a reaction against a previous dose. □□ **an·a·phy·lac·tic** /–láktik/ *adj.*

an·ar·chism /ánərkizəm/ *n.* doctrine that all government and laws should be abolished. □□ **an'ar·chist** *n.* **an·ar·chis'tic** *adj.*

an·ar·chy /ánərkee/ *n.* **1** disorder, esp. political or social. **2** lack of government in a society. □□ **an·ar'chic** *adj.* **an·ar'chi·cal** *adj.* **an·ar'chi·cal·ly** *adv.*

A·na·sa·zi /onəsáazee/ *n.* **1 a** prehistoric N. American people native to the southwestern US. **b** member of this people. **2** language of this people.

anat. *abbr.* **1** anatomical. **2** anatomy.

a·nath·e·ma /ənáthəmə/ *n.* (*pl.* **a·nath·e·mas**) **1** detested thing or person. **2** ecclesiastical rejection of a person or doctrine.

a·nath·e·ma·tize /ənáthəmətīz/ *v.* curse.

a·nat·o·mize /ənátəmīz/ *v.tr.* **1** examine in detail. **2** dissect.

a·nat·o·my /ənátəmee/ *n.* (*pl.* **–mies**) **1** science of the bodily structure of animals and plants. **2** this structure. **3** *colloq.* human body. **4** analysis. □□ **an·a·tom·i·cal** /ánətómikəl/ *adj.* **a·nat·o·mist** /ənátəmist/ *n.*

ANC *abbr.* African National Congress.

-ance /əns/ *suffix* forming nouns expressing: **1** quality or state or an instance of (*appearance; resemblance*). **2** action (*assistance*).

an·ces·tor /ánsestər/ *n.* (*fem.* **an·ces·tress** /–stris/) **1** any (esp. remote) person from whom one is descended. **2** early type of animal or plant from which others have evolved. **3** prototype or forerunner. □□ **an·ces·tral** /ánséstrəl/ *adj.*

an·ces·try /ánsestree/ *n.* (*pl.* **–tries**) **1** family descent. **2** one's ancestors collectively.

an·chor /ángkər/ ● *n.* **1** heavy metal weight used to moor a ship or a balloon. **2** thing affording stability. **3** source of confidence. **4** (in full **anchor·man, an'chor·per·son, an'chor·wom·an**) a person who plays a vital part, as the last member of a relay team, etc. **b** news broadcaster who introduces segments and reads news. ● *v.* **1** *tr.* secure by means of an anchor. **2** *tr.* fix firmly. **3** *intr.* cast anchor. **4** *intr.* be moored by means of an anchor.

an·chor·age /ángkərij/ *n.* **1** place where a ship may be anchored. **2** anchoring or lying at anchor.

an·cho·rite /ángkərīt/ *n.* hermit; religious recluse.

an·cho·vy /ánchóvee/ *n.* (*pl.* **–vies**) small strong-flavored fish of the herring family.

an·cient /áynshənt/ ● *adj.* **1** of long ago. **2** having lived or existed long. ● *n.* very old person. □□ **an'cient·ness** *n.*

an·cil·lar·y /ánsəleree/ ● *adj.* **1** providing essential support to a central service or industry, esp. the medical service. **2** subordinate; subservient. ● *n.* (*pl.* **–ies**) **1** ancillary worker. **2** accessory.

-ancy /ənsee/ *suffix* forming nouns denoting a quality (*constancy*) or state (*infancy*) (cf. –ANCE).

and /and, ənd/ *conj.* **1** connecting words, clauses, or sentences to be taken jointly (*buy and sell*). **2** implying: **a** progression (*better and better*). **b** causation (*do that and I'll hit you*). **c** great duration (*he cried and cried*). **d** great number (*miles and miles*). **e** addition (*two and two*). **3** *colloq.* to (*try and open it*). □ **and/or** either or both of two stated possibilities.

an·dan·te /aandáantay, andántee/ *Mus.* ● *adv. & adj.* in a moderately slow tempo. ● *n.* andante passage or movement.

and·i·ron /ándīrn/ *n.* one of a pair of supports for logs in a fireplace.

an·dro·gen /ándrəjən/ *n.* male sex hormone or other substance that reinforces certain male sex characteristics. □□ **an·dro·gen·ic** /–jénik/ *adj.*

an·drog·y·nous /andrójinəs/ *adj.* **1** hermaphroditic. **2** exhibiting the appearance or attributes of both sexes. **3** *Bot.* with stamens and pistils in the same flower. □□ **an·drog'y·ny** /andrójinee/ *n.*

an·droid /ándroyd/ *n.* robot with a human appearance.

-ane¹ /ayn/ *suffix* var. of –AN; usu. with distinction of sense (*germane; humane; urbane*) but sometimes with no corresponding form in -an (*mundane*).

-ane² /ayn/ *suffix Chem.* forming names of saturated hydrocarbons (*methane; propane*).

an·ec·dote /ánikdōt/ *n.* short account of an entertaining or interesting incident. □□ **an·ec·do·tal** /–dót'l/ *adj.* **an·ec·do'tal·ist** *n.* **an·ec·dot·ic** /–dótik/ *adj.* **an·ec·dot·ist** /–dót–/ *n.*

anchor with arm and flukes   mushroom anchor

ANCHOR, 1

a·ne·mi·a /əne'emeeə/ *n.* deficiency of red cells or their hemoglobin.

a·ne·mic /əne'emik/ *adj.* **1** relating to or suffering from anemia. **2** pale; lacking in vitality.

an·e·mom·e·ter /ánimómitər/ *n.* instrument for measuring the force of the wind.

a·nem·o·ne /ənémənee/ *n.* plant akin to the buttercup, with flowers of various vivid colors.

-aneous /áyneeəs/ *suffix* forming adjectives (*cutaneous; miscellaneous*).

an·er·oid /ánəroyd/ ● *adj.* (of a barometer) that measures air pressure by its action on the elastic lid of a box containing a vacuum. ● *n.* aneroid barometer.

an·es·the·sia /ánis-theézhə/ n. absence of sensation, esp. artificially induced before surgery. □□ **an·es·the·si·ol·o·gy** /–zeeóləjee/ n.

an·es·thet·ic /ánis-thétik/ • n. substance that produces insensibility to pain, etc. • adj. producing partial or complete insensibility to pain, etc. □□ **an·es·the·tize** /ənés-thətīz/ v.

an·es·the·tist /ənés-thətist/ n. specialist in the administration of anesthetics.

an·eu·rysm /ányərizəm/ n. (also **an'eu·rism**) excessive localized enlargement of an artery. □□ **an·eu·rys'mal** /–rízməl/ adj. (also **an·eu·ris'mal**).

a·new /ənoó, ənyoó/ adv. 1 again. 2 in a different way.

an·gel /áynjəl/ n. 1 a attendant or messenger of God. b conventional representation of this in human form with wings. 2 a very virtuous person. b obliging person (be an angel and answer the door). 3 sl. financial backer of an enterprise, esp. in the theater. □□ **an·gel·ic** /–jél–/ adj. **an·gel'i·cal** adj. **an·gel'i·cal·ly** adv.

an·ger /ánggər/ • n. extreme or passionate displeasure. • v.tr. make angry; enrage.

an·gin·a /anjínə, ánjənə/ n. 1 attack of intense constricting pain often causing suffocation. 2 (in full **an·gi·na pec·tor·is** /péktəris/) pain in the chest brought on by exertion, owing to an inadequate blood supply to the heart.

an·gi·o·sperm /ánjeeəspərm/ n. plant propagating by seeds in ovules (opp. GYMNOSPERM). □□ **an·gi·o·sper'mous** adj.

an·gle[1] /ánggəl/ • n. 1 a space between two meeting lines or surfaces. b inclination of two lines or surfaces to each other. 2 corner. 3 a point of view. b approach, technique, etc. • v. 1 tr. & intr. move or place obliquely. 2 tr. present (information) in a biased way. □□ **an·gled** adj.

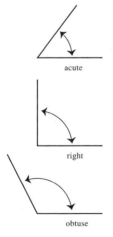

acute

right

obtuse

ANGLES

an·gle[2] /ánggəl/ v.intr. 1 fish with hook and line. 2 (foll. by for) seek an objective by devious means (angled for a pay raise).

An·gli·can /ángglikən/ • adj. of or relating to

the Church of England or any church in communion with it. • n. member of an Anglican Church. □□ **An'gli·can·ism** n.

An·gli·cism /ánggliszəm/ n. peculiarly English word or custom.

An·gli·cize /ánggliszīz/ v.tr. make English in form or character.

An·glo /ánggló/ n. (pl. **–glos**) 1 person of British or northern European origin. 2 non-Hispanic white person.

Anglo- /ánggló/ comb. form 1 Anglican (Anglo-Catholic). 2 of English origin (an Anglo-American). 3 English or British and (Anglo-American agreement).

Anglo-French /ángglófrénch/ • adj. English (or British) and French. • n. French language as developed in England after the Norman Conquest.

An·glo·phile /ánggləfīl/ • n. person who greatly admires England or the English. • adj. being or characteristic of an Anglophile.

An·glo-Sa·xon /ángglósáksən/ • adj. 1 of the English Saxons (as distinct from the Old Saxons of the European continent, and from the Angles) before the Norman Conquest. 2 of English descent. • n. 1 Anglo-Saxon person. 2 Old English. 3 colloq. plain (esp. crude) English.

an·go·ra /anggáwrə/ n. 1 fabric or wool made from the hair of the angora goat or rabbit. 2 long-haired variety of cat, goat, or rabbit.

an·gry /ánggree/ adj. (**an·gri·er**, **an·gri·est**) 1 feeling or showing anger. 2 (of a wound, sore, etc.) inflamed; painful. 3 stormy (an angry sky). □□ **an'gri·ly** adv.

angst /aangkst/ n. 1 anxiety. 2 feeling of guilt or remorse.

ang·strom /ángstrəm/ n. (also **ång·ström** /áwngström/) unit of length equal to 10^{-10} meter. ¶ Symb.: **Å**.

an·guish /ánggwish/ • n. severe mental suffering. • v.tr. (often as **anguished** adj.) cause to suffer physical or mental pain.

an·gu·lar /ánggyələr/ adj. 1 a having angles or sharp corners. b (of a person) having sharp features. 2 forming an angle. 3 measured by angle. □□ **an·gu·lar·i·ty** /–láritee/ n. **an'gu·lar·ly** adv.

an·i·line /ánillin, –līn/ n. colorless oily liquid used in the manufacture of dyes, drugs, and plastics.

an·i·mad·vert /ánimadvərt/ v.intr. criticize; censure. □□ **an·i·mad·ver·sion** /–vərzhən/ n.

an·i·mal /ániməl/ • n. 1 living organism that feeds on organic matter, usu. one with specialized sense organs and a nervous system, and able to respond rapidly to stimuli. 2 such an organism other than human beings. 3 brutish or uncivilized person. • adj. characteristic of animals.

an·i·mal·ism /ániməlizəm/ n. 1 nature and activity of animals. 2 belief that humans are mere animals. 3 sensuality.

an·i·mate • adj. /ánimət/ 1 having life. 2 lively. • v.tr. /ánimayt/ 1 enliven. 2 give life to. 3 inspire. 4 encourage.

an·i·mat·ed /ánimaytid/ adj. 1 lively; vigorous. 2 having life. 3 (of a movie, etc.) using techniques of animation. □□ **an'i·mat·ed·ly** adv. **an'i·ma·tor** n. (in sense 3).

an·i·ma·tion /ánimáyshən/ *n.* **1** vivacity; ardor. **2** state of being alive. **3** *Cinematog.* technique of filming successive drawings, positions of puppets, etc., to create an illusion of movement.

an·i·mism /ánimizəm/ *n.* attribution of a living soul to plants, inanimate objects, and natural phenomena. □□ **an′i·mist** *n.* **an·i·mis′tic** /–místik/ *adj.*

an·i·mos·i·ty /ánimósitee/ *n.* (*pl.* **–ties**) spirit or feeling of strong hostility.

an·i·mus /ánimɵs/ *n.* **1** animosity. **2** ill feeling.

an·i·on /ánīɵn/ *n.* negatively charged ion (opp. CATION). □□ **an·i·on·ic** /ánīónik/ *adj.*

an·ise /ánis/ *n.* umbelliferous plant having aromatic seeds, used to flavor liqueurs and candy.

ankh /angk/ *n.* cross with a loop at the top.

ANKH

an·kle /ángkəl/ *n.* **1** joint connecting the foot with the leg. **2** this part of the leg.

ank·let /ángklit/ *n.* **1** ornament worn around the ankle. **2** short sock.

an·ky·lo·sis /ángkilósis/ *n.* **1** abnormal stiffening of a joint by fusion of the bones. **2** such fusion. □□ **an·ky·lot·ic** /–lótik/ *adj.*

an·nals /ánəlz/ *n.pl.* **1** narrative of events year by year. **2** historical records. □□ **an′nal·ist** *n.* **an·nal·is′tic** *adj.* **an·nal·is′ti·cal·ly** *adv.*

an·neal /əneél/ *v.tr.* **1** heat (metal or glass) and cool slowly, esp. to toughen it. **2** toughen. □□ **an·neal′er** *n.*

an·ne·lid /án′lid/ *n.* segmented worm, e.g., earthworms, etc.

an·nex /anéks, áneks/ • *v.tr.* **1** add as a subordinate part. **2** incorporate (territory of another) into one's own. • *n.* **1** separate or added building, esp. for extra accommodation. **2** addition to a document. □□ **an·nex·a′tion** *n.*

an·ni·hi·late /ənfələyt/ *v.tr.* **1** completely destroy. **2** defeat utterly; make powerless. □□ **an·ni·hi·la·tion** /–láyshən/ *n.* **an·ni·hi·la·tor** *n.*

an·ni·ver·sa·ry /ániv⒜rsəree/ *n.* (*pl.* **–ries**) **1** date on which an event took place in a previous year. **2** celebration of this.

an·no·tate /ánōtayt/ *v.tr.* add explanatory notes to (a book, document, etc.). □□ **an·no·ta·tion** /–táyshən/ *n.* **an′no·ta·tive** *adj.* **an′no·ta·tor** *n.*

an·nounce /ənówns/ *v.* **1** *tr.* make publicly known. **2** *tr.* make known the arrival or imminence of (a guest, etc.). **3** *intr.* declare one's candidacy for office. **4** *tr.* be a sign of. □□ **an·nounce′ment** *n.*

an·nounc·er /ənównsər/ *n.* person who announces, esp. in broadcasting.

an·noy /ənóy/ *v.tr.* **1** cause slight anger or mental distress to. **2** (in *passive*) be somewhat angry. **3** molest; harass repeatedly. □□ **an·noy′ance** *n.* **an·noy′er** *n.* **an·noy′ing** *adj.*

an·nu·al /ányōōəl/ • *adj.* **1** reckoned by the year. **2** occurring every year. **3** living or lasting for one year. • *n.* **1** book, etc., published once a year; yearbook. **2** plant that lives only for a year or less. □□ **an′nu·al·ly** *adv.*

an·nu·i·ty /ənōóitee, ənyōó–/ *n.* (*pl.* **–ties**) **1** yearly grant or allowance. **2** investment yielding a fixed annual sum. **3** sum paid.

an·nul /ənúl/ *v.tr.* (**an·nulled, an·nul·ling**) **1** declare (a marriage, etc.) invalid. **2** cancel; abolish. □□ **an·nul′ment** *n.*

an·nu·lar /ányələr/ *adj.* ring-shaped; forming a ring. □ **annular eclipse** eclipse of the sun in which the moon leaves a ring of sunlight visible around it. □□ **an′nu·lar·ly** *adv.*

an·nun·ci·a·tion /ənúnseeáyshən/ *n.* **1** (**Annunciation**) **a** announcing of the Incarnation, made by the angel Gabriel to Mary, related in Luke 1:26-38. **b** festival commemorating this. **2 a** act or process of announcing. **b** announcement.

an·ode /ánōd/ *n. Electr.* positive electrode in an electrolytic cell. □□ **an·od·ic** /ənódik/ *adj.*

an·o·dize /ánədīz/ *v.tr.* coat (a metal, esp. aluminum) with a protective oxide layer by electrolysis. □□ **an′o·diz·er** *n.*

an·o·dyne /ánədīn/ • *adj.* **1** able to relieve pain. **2** mentally soothing. • *n.* anodyne drug or medicine.

a·noint /ənóynt/ *v.tr.* **1** apply oil or ointment to, esp. as a religious ceremony (e.g., at baptism, etc.). **2** smear; rub. □□ **a·noint′er** *n.*

a·nom·a·lous /ənómələs/ *adj.* irregular; deviant; abnormal. □□ **a·nom′a·lous·ly** *adv.* **a·no′m·alous·ness** *n.*

a·nom·a·ly /ənómələe/ *n.* (*pl.* **–lies**) **1** anomalous thing; irregularity. **2** irregularity of motion, behavior, etc.

a·non /ənón/ *adv. archaic* or *literary* soon; shortly.

anon. /ənón/ *abbr.* anonymous; anonymous author.

a·non·y·mous /ənóniməs/ *adj.* **1** of unknown name. **2** of undeclared authorship. **3** without character; featureless. □□ **a·no·nym·i·ty** /ánənímitee/ *n.* **a·non′y·mous·ly** *adv.*

a·noph·e·les /ənófileez/ *n.* any of various mosquitoes that transmit malaria to humans.

an·o·rak /ánərak/ *n.* warm jacket, usu. with a hood; parka.

an·o·rex·i·a /ánərékseeə/ *n.* **1** lack of appetite for food. **2** (in full **an·o·rex′ia ner·vo·sa** /nərvōsə/) psychological illness, esp. in young women, characterized by an obsessive desire to lose weight by refusing to eat. □□ **an·o·rex′ic** *adj.*

an·oth·er /ənúthər/ • *adj.* **1** additional (*have another piece of cake*). **2** person like (*another Lincoln*). **3** a different (*quite another matter*). **4** some or any other (*will not do another person's work*). • *pron.* **1** additional one. **2** different one. **3** some or any other one (*I know another*).

an·swer /ánsər/ • *n.* **1** something said or done in reaction to a question, statement, or circumstance. **2** solution to a problem. • *v.* **1** *tr.* & *intr.* make an answer to (*answer me*). **2** *tr.* respond to the summons or signal of (*answer the door*). **3** *tr.* be satisfactory for (a purpose or need). **4** *intr.* **a** (foll. by *for, to*) be responsible. **b** vouch (for a person, etc.). **5** *intr.* correspond, esp. to a description. □ **answer back** answer impudently. **answering machine** device that supplies a recorded answer to a telephone call and usu. records incoming messages. **answering service** business that receives and answers telephone calls for its clients. □□ **an'swer•a•ble** *adj.*

ant /ant/ *n.* small insect living in complex social colonies, usu. wingless, and proverbial for industry.

-ant /ənt/ *suffix* **1** forming adjectives denoting attribution of an action (*repentant*) or state (*arrogant*). **2** forming nouns denoting an agent (*assistant*).

ant•ac•id /antásid/ *n.* substance that prevents or corrects acidity.

an•tag•o•nism /antágənizəm/ *n.* active opposition or hostility.

an•tag•o•nist /antágənist/ *n.* opponent or adversary. □□ **an•tag•o•nis'tic** *adj.* **an•tag•o•nis'ti•cal•ly** *adv.*

an•tag•o•nize /antágənīz/ *v.tr.* evoke hostility or opposition or enmity in. □□ **an•tag•o•ni•za'tion** *n.*

Ant•arc•tic /antaárktik/ • *adj.* of the south polar regions. • *n.* this region. □ **Antarctic Circle** parallel of latitude 66° 32' S., delimiting this region.

an•te /ántee/ • *n.* **1** stake put up by a player in poker, etc., before receiving cards. **2** amount to be paid in advance. • *v.tr.* (**an•tes, an•ted**) **1** put up as an ante. **2 a** bet; stake. **b** (foll. by *up*) pay.

ante- /ántee/ *prefix* forming nouns and adjectives meaning 'before; preceding' (*anteroom*).

ant•eat•er /ánteetər/ *n.* any of various mammals feeding on ants and termites.

an•te•bel•lum /ánteebéləm/ *adj.* before the US Civil War.

an•te•ced•ent /ántiseé'nt/ • *n.* **1** preceding thing or circumstance. **2** *Gram.* word, phrase, etc., to which another word (esp. a relative pronoun) refers. **3** (in *pl.*) past history, esp. of a person. • *adj.* previous. □□ **an•te•ce'dence** *n.* **an•te•ced'ent•ly** *adv.*

an•te•cham•ber /ánteechaymbər/ *n.* = ANTEROOM.

an•te•date /ántidáyt/ • *v.tr.* **1** precede in time. **2** assign an earlier date to. • *n.* date earlier than the actual one.

an•te•di•lu•vi•an /ánteedilóoveeən/ *adj.* **1** of the time before the Biblical flood. **2** *colloq.* very old or out of date.

an•te•lope /ántilōp/ *n.* (*pl.* same or **an•te•lopes**) **1** swift-moving deerlike ruminant, e.g., gazelle and impala. **2** leather made from the skin of any of these.

an•ten•na /anténə/ *n.* (*pl.* **an•ten•nae** /–ee/) **1** *Zool.* one of a pair of feelers on the heads of insects, crustaceans, etc. **2** (*pl.* **an•ten•nas**) metal rod, wire, or other structure by which broadcast signals are transmitted or received.

an•te•ri•or /anteéreeər/ *adj.* **1** nearer the front. **2** earlier; prior. □□ **an•te•ri•or•i•ty** /–reeáwritee/ *n.* **an•te'ri•or•ly** *adv.*

an•te•room /ánteeróom, –róom/ *n.* small room leading to a main one.

an•them /ánthəm/ *n.* **1** elaborate choral composition usu. based on a passage of scripture. **2** solemn hymn of praise, etc., esp. = *national anthem.*

an•ther /ánthər/ *n. Bot.* apical portion of a stamen containing pollen. □□ **an'the•ral** *adj.*

ant•hill /ánt-hil/ *n.* moundlike nest built by ants or termites.

an•thol•o•gy /anthóləjee/ *n.* (*pl.* **–gies**) published collection of passages from literature, songs, reproductions of paintings, etc. □□ **an•thol'o•gist** *n.* **an•thol'o•gize** *v.*

---

anthology mid-17th cent.: via French or medieval Latin from Greek *anthologia*, from *anthos* 'flower' + *-logia* 'collection' (from *legein* 'gather'). In Greek, the word originally denoted a collection of the "flowers"of verse, i.e. small choice poems or epigrams, by various authors.

---

an•thra•cite /ánthrəsīt/ *n.* coal of a hard variety burning with little flame and smoke. □□ **an•thra•cit•ic** /–sítik/ *adj.*

an•thrax /ánthraks/ *n.* disease of sheep and cattle transmissible to humans.

an•thro•po•cen•tric /ánthrəpōséntrik/ *adj.* regarding humankind as the center of existence. □□ **an•thro•po•cen'tri•cal•ly** *adv.* **an•thro•po•cen'trism** *n.*

an•thro•poid /ánthrəpoyd/ • *adj.* **1** human in form. **2** *colloq.* (of a person) apelike. • *n.* anthropoid ape.

an•thro•pol•o•gy /ánthrəpóləjee/ *n.* study of humankind, esp. its societies and customs. □□ **an•thro•pol•og•i•cal** /–pəlójikəl/ *adj.* **an•thro•pol'o•gist** *n.*

an•thro•po•mor•phism /ánthrəpəmáwrfizəm/ *n.* attribution of human characteristics to a god, animal, or thing. □□ **an•thro•po•mor'phic** *adj.* **an•thro•po•mor'phi•cal•ly** *adv.* **an•thro•po•mor'phize** *v.tr.*

an•thro•po•mor•phous /ánthrəpəmáwrfəs/ *adj.* human in form.

an•ti /ántee, –tī/ • *prep.* opposed to (*is anti everything*). • *n.* (*pl.* **an•tis**) person opposed to a particular policy, etc.

anti- /ántee/ *prefix* (also **ant-** before a vowel or *h*) forming nouns and adjectives meaning: **1** opposed to; against (*antivivisectionism*). **2** preventing (*antiscorbutic*). **3** opposite of (*anticlimax*). **4** rival (*antipope*). **5** unlike the conventional form (*antihero*).

an•ti•air•craft /ánteeáirkraft, ántī–/ *adj.* (of a gun, missile, etc.) used to attack enemy aircraft.

an•ti•bi•ot•ic /ántibīótik, ántī–/ *Pharm.* • *n.* substance (e.g., penicillin) that can inhibit or destroy susceptible microorganisms. • *adj.* functioning as an antibiotic.

an•ti•bod•y /ántibodee, ántī–/ *n.* (*pl.* **–ies**) blood protein produced in response to and then counteracting antigens.

an•tic /ántik/ *n.* (usu. in *pl.*) absurd or foolish behavior or action; prank.

An•ti•christ /ánteekrīst, ántī–/ *n.* archenemy of Christ.

an•tic•i•pate /antísipayt/ *v.tr.* **1** deal with or use before the proper time. **2** expect; foresee. **3** forestall (a person or thing). **4** look forward to. □□ **an•tic•i•pa'tion** /–páyshən/ *n.* **an•tic'i•pat•or** *n.* **an•tic•i•pa•to•ry** /–pətawree/ *adj.*

¶ **Anticipate** in the sense 'expect, foresee' is well-established in informal use (e.g., *He anticipated* *a restless night*), but is regarded as incorrect by some people. The formal sense, 'deal with or use before the proper time,' is illustrated by the sentence *The doctor anticipated the possibility of a relapse by prescribing new medications.*

an·ti·cli·max /ánteeklímaks, ántī–/ *n.* disappointingly trivial conclusion to something significant. □□ **an·ti·cli·mac·tic** /–máktik/ *adj.* **an·ti·cli·mac′ti·cal·ly** *adv.*

an·ti·de·pres·sant /ánteediprésənt, ántī–/ ● *n.* drug that alleviates depression. ● *adj.* alleviating depression.

an·ti·dote /ántidōt/ *n.* **1** medicine, etc., used to counteract poison. **2** anything that counteracts something unpleasant. □□ **an·ti·dot′al** *adj.*

an·ti·freeze /ántifreez, ántee–/ *n.* substance added to water to lower its freezing point, esp. in the radiator of a motor vehicle.

an·ti·gen /ántijən/ *n.* foreign substance (e.g., toxin) that causes the body to produce antibodies. □□ **an·ti·gen·ic** /–jénik/ *adj.*

an·ti·he·ro /ánteeheerō, ántī–/ *n.* (*pl.* **–roes**) (in a story) central character lacking conventional heroic attributes.

an·ti·his·ta·mine /ánteehístəmin, –meen, ántī–/ *n.* substance used esp. in the treatment of allergies.

an·ti·lock /ánteelók, ántī–/ *adj.* (of brakes) designed so as to prevent locking and skidding when applied suddenly.

an·ti·log·a·rithm /ánteelάwgərithəm, –lóg–, ántī–/ *n.* number to which a logarithm belongs.

an·ti·mat·ter /ánteemátər, ántī–/ *n. Physics* matter composed solely of antiparticles.

an·ti·mo·ny /ántimónee/ *n. Chem.* brittle silvery metallic element used esp. in alloys. ¶ Symb.: **Sb**.

an·ti·par·ti·cle /ánteepaartikəl, ántī–/ *n. Physics* elementary particle having the same mass as a given particle but opposite electric or magnetic properties.

an·ti·pas·to /ánteepa′astō/ *n.* (*pl.* **–tos** or **an·ti·pas·ti** /–tee/) assorted appetizers, esp. of marinated vegetables.

an·tip·a·thy /antípəthee/ *n.* (*pl.* **–thies**) strong or deep-seated aversion or dislike.

an·ti·per·spi·rant /ánteepə́rspirənt, ántī–/ *n.* substance applied to the skin to prevent or reduce perspiration.

an·ti·phon /ántifon/ *n.* **1** hymn sung or recited alternately by two groups. **2** phrase from this. □□ **an·tiph·o·nal** /antífənəl/ *adj. & n.* **an·tiph′o·nal·ly** *adv.*

an·tip·o·des /antípədeez/ *n.pl.* (also **Antipodes**) places diametrically opposite to one another, esp. Australasia in relation to N. America or Europe. □□ **an·tip′o·dal** *adj.* **an·tip·o·de·an** /–de′e-ən/ *adj. & n.*

an·ti·quar·i·an /ántikwáireeən/ ● *adj.* of or dealing in antiques or rare books. ● *n.* antiquary. □□ **an·ti·quar′i·an·ism** *n.*

an·ti·quar·y /ántikweree/ *n.* (*pl.* **–ies**) student or collector of antiques or antiquities.

an·ti·quat·ed /ántikwaytid/ *adj.* old-fashioned; out of date.

an·tique /anteék/ ● *n.* old object, item of furniture, etc., esp. one valued for its beauty or

quality. ● *adj.* **1** of or existing from an early date. **2** old-fashioned. ● *v.tr.* (**an·tiques, an·tiqued, an·ti·quing**) give an antique appearance to (furniture, etc.) by artificial means.

an·tiq·ui·ty /antíkwitee/ *n.* (*pl.* **–ties**) **1** ancient times, esp. before the Middle Ages. **2** great age. **3** (usu. in *pl.*) relics from ancient times, esp. buildings and works of art.

an·ti-Sem·ite /ánteesémīt, ántī–/ *n.* person prejudiced against Jews. □□ **an·ti-Se·mit·ic** /–simítik/ *adj.* **an·ti-Sem·i·tism** /–sémitizəm/ *n.*

an·ti·sep·tic /ántiséptik/ ● *adj.* **1** counteracting sepsis, esp. by preventing the growth of disease-causing microorganisms. **2** sterile or free from contamination. **3** lacking character. ● *n.* antiseptic agent. □□ **an·ti·sep′ti·cal·ly** *adv.*

an·ti·se·rum /ántisee′erəm/ *n.* (*pl.* **an·ti·se·ra** /–rə/) blood serum with a high antibody count.

an·ti·so·cial /ánteesóshəl, ántī–/ *adj.* **1** harmful to the existing social order. **2** not sociable.

an·tith·e·sis /antíthisis/ *n.* (*pl.* **an·tith·e·ses** /–seez/) **1** direct opposite. **2** contrast or opposition between two things. □□ **an·ti·thet·i·cal** /–thót–/ *adj.* **an·ti·thet′i·cal·ly** *adv.*

an·ti·tox·in /ánteetóksin/ *n.* antibody that counteracts a toxin. □□ **an·ti·tox′ic** *adj.*

an·ti·trust /ánteetrúst, ántī–/ *adj.* (of a law, etc.) opposed to or controlling trusts or other monopolies.

an·ti·vi·ral /ánteevírəl, ántī–/ *adj.* effective against viruses.

ant·ler /ántlər/ *n.* each of the branched horns of a stag or other (usu. male) deer. □□ **ant′lered** *adj.*

an·to·nym /ántonim/ *n.* word opposite in meaning to another (opp. SYNONYM). □□ **an·ton·y·mous** /antóniməs/ *adj.*

a·nus /áynəs/ *n. Anat.* excretory opening at the end of the alimentary canal.

an·vil /ánvil/ *n.* block (usu. of iron) on which metals are shaped.

ANVIL

anx·i·e·ty /angzíətee/ *n.* (*pl.* **–ties**) **1** being anxious. **2** worry or concern. **3** anxious desire.

anx·ious /ángkshəs/ *adj.* **1** mentally troubled. **2** causing or marked by anxiety. **3** earnestly or uneasily wanting or trying. □□ **anx′ious·ly** *adv.* **anx′ious·ness** *n.*

an·y /énee/ ● *adj.* **1** (with *interrog., neg.,* or conditional expressed or implied) **a** one, no matter which, of several. **b** some, no matter how much or many or of what sort. **2** whichever (*any fool knows that*). **3** appreciable or significant. ● *pron.* **1** any one. **2** any number or amount. ● *adv.* (usu. with *neg.* or *interrog.*) at all; in some degree.

an·y·bod·y /éneebudee, –bodee/ *n. & pron.* **1** person of any kind. **2** person of importance.

an·y·how /éneehow/ *adv.* **1** anyway. **2** in a disorderly manner or state (*does his work anyhow*).

an·y·one /éneewun/ *pron.* anybody.
¶ **Anyone** is written as two words only to emphasize singularity, e.g., *Any one of us could do the job*. Otherwise it is written as one word (e.g., *Anyone who wants to come is welcome*).

an·y·thing /éneething/ *pron.* **1** a thing, no matter which. **2** thing of any kind. □ **anything but** not at all.

an·y·way /éneeway/ *adv.* (also *dial.* **an·y·ways** /éneewayz/) **1** in any way or manner. **2** at any rate. **3** in any case. **4** to resume (*anyway, as I was saying*).

an·y·where /éneehwair, –wair/ • *adv.* in or to any place. • *pron.* any place (*anywhere will do*).

A-OK *abbr. colloq.* excellent; in good order.

a·or·ta /ayáwrtə/ *n.* (*pl.* **a·or·tas**) main artery through which oxygenated blood is supplied to the body from the heart. □□ **a·or´tic** *adj.*

a·pace /əpáys/ *adv. literary* swiftly; quickly.

A·pach·e /əpáchee/ *n.* member of a N. American Indian tribe of the southwestern US.

a·part /əpaárt/ *adv.* **1** separately; not together. **2** into pieces. **3** to or on one side. **4** to or at a distance. □ **apart from 1** excepting; not considering. **2** in addition to (*apart from roses we grow irises*).

a·part·heid /əpaárt-hayt, –hīt/ *n.* (in S. Africa) racial segregation or discrimination.

a·part·ment /əpaártmənt/ *n.* room or suite of rooms, usu. on one floor, used as a residence. □ **apartment building** (or **house**) building containing a number of separate apartments.

ap·a·thy /ápəthee/ *n.* lack of interest or feeling; indifference. □□ **ap·a·thet·ic** /ápəthétik/ *adj.* **ap·a·thet´i·cal·ly** *adv.*

ap·a·to·sau·rus /əpátəsáwrəs/ *n.* = BRONTO- SAURUS.

ape /ayp/ • *n.* **1** monkeylike primate characterized by the absence of a tail, e.g., the gorilla, chimpanzee, etc. **2** (in general use) any monkey. **3 a** imitator. **b** apelike person. • *v.tr.* imitate; mimic.

a·pe·ri·tif /əperite´ef/ *n.* alcoholic drink taken before a meal to stimulate the appetite.

ap·er·ture /ápərchər/ *n.* opening; gap.

a·pex /áypeks/ *n.* (*pl.* **a·pex·es** or **a·pi·ces** /áypiseez/) **1** highest point. **2** climax. **3** tip or pointed end.

a·pha·si·a /əfáyzhə/ *n. Med.* loss of ability to understand or express speech. □□ **a·pha·sic** /–zik/ *adj. & n.*

aph·e·li·on /əfe´eleeən, ap-he´eleeən/ *n.* (*pl.* **a·phe·li·a** /–leeə/) point in an orbit farthest from the sun (opp. PERIHELION). ¶ *Symb.*: **Q**.

a·phid /áyfid, áfid/ *n.* small insect that feeds by sucking sap from leaves, stems, or roots of plants.

aph·o·rism /áfərizəm/ *n.* short pithy maxim. □□ **aph·o·ris´tic** *adj.* **aph·o·ris´ti·cal·ly** *adv.* **aph´o·rize** *v.intr.*

aph·ro·di·si·ac /áfrəde´ezeeak, –díz–/ • *adj.* that arouses sexual desire. • *n.* aphrodisiac drug.

a·pi·ar·y /áypee-eree/ *n.* (*pl.* **–ies**) place where bees are kept. □□ **a´pi·a·rist** *n.*

ap·i·cal /áypikəl, áp–/ *adj.* of, at, or forming an apex. □□ **a´pi·cal·ly** *adv.*

a·piece /əpe´es/ *adv.* for each one; severally; individually.

a·plomb /əplóm, əplúm/ *n.* assurance; self-confidence.

APO *abbr.* Army post office.

a·poc·a·lypse /əpókəlips/ *n.* **1** (**the Apocalypse**) Revelation, the last book of the New Testament. **2** grand or violent event resembling those described in the Apocalypse. □□ **a·poc·a·lyp·tic** /–líptik/ *adj.* **a·poc·a·lyp´ti·cal·ly** *adv.*

A·poc·ry·pha /əpókrifə/ *n.pl.* **1** books included in the Septuagint and Vulgate versions of the Old Testament but not in the Hebrew Bible. **2** (**apocrypha**) writings or reports not considered genuine.

a·poc·ry·phal /əpókrifəl/ *adj.* of doubtful authenticity.

ap·o·gee /ápəjee/ *n.* **1** point in an orbit farthest from the earth (opp. PERIGEE). **2** point in a celestial body's orbit where it is farthest from the body being orbited. □□ **ap·o·ge´an** *adj.*

a·po·lit·i·cal /áypəlítikəl/ *adj.* not interested in or concerned with politics.

a·pol·o·get·ic /əpóləjétik/ • *adj.* **1** regretfully acknowledging or excusing an offense or failure. **2** diffident. • *n.* (usu. in *pl.*) reasoned defense, esp. of Christianity. □□ **a·pol·o·get´i·cal·ly** *adv.*

a·pol·o·gist /əpóləjist/ *n.* person who defends something by argument.

a·pol·o·gize /əpóləjīz/ *v.intr.* make an apology for an offense or failure; express regret.

a·pol·o·gy /əpóləjee/ *n.* (*pl.* **–gies**) **1** regretful acknowledgment of an offense or failure. **2** assurance that no offense was intended. **3** explanation or defense. **4** (foll. by *for*) poor or scanty specimen of (*this apology for a letter*).

ap·o·plex·y /ápəpleksee/ *n.* sudden loss of consciousness, voluntary movement, and sensation caused by blockage or rupture of a brain artery; stroke.

a·pos·ta·sy /əpóstəsee/ *n.* (*pl.* **–sies**) **1** renunciation of a belief or faith, esp. religious. **2** abandonment of principles or of a party. **3** instance of apostasy.

a·pos·tate /əpóstayt/ • *n.* person who renounces a former belief, adherence, etc. • *adj.* engaged in apostasy. □□ **ap·o·stat·i·cal** /ápəstátikəl/ *adj.* **a·pos·ta·tize** /–tətīz/ *v.*

a pos·te·ri·o·ri /áy póste´eree-áwree, –áwrī/ • *adj.* (of reasoning) inductive; empirical; proceeding from effects to causes. • *adv.* inductively (opp. A PRIORI).

a·pos·tle /əpósəl/ *n.* **1** (**Apostle**) **a** any of the twelve men first sent out by Christ to preach the gospel. **b** first successful Christian missionary in a country or to a people. **2** leader or outstanding figure, esp. of a reform movement. □□ **a·pos´tle·ship** *n.*

ap·os·tol·ic /ápəstólik/ *adj.* **1** of or relating to the Apostles. **2** of the pope regarded as the successor of St. Peter.

a·pos·tro·phe /əpóstrəfee/ *n.* punctuation mark used to indicate: **1** omission of letters or numbers (e.g., *can't*; *Class of '92*). **2** possessive case (e.g., *Harry's book*).

a·poth·e·car·y /əpóthəkeree/ *n.* (*pl.* **–ies**) *archaic* pharmacist.

ap·o·thegm /ápəthem/ = APHORISM. □□ **ap·o· theg·mat·ic** /–thegmátik/ *adj.*

a·po·the·o·sis /əpóthee-ósis/ *n.* (*pl.* **a·poth·e·o·ses** /–seez/) **1** elevation to divine status; deification. **2** glorification of a thing; sublime example.

ap·pall /əpáwl/ *v.tr.* (also **ap·pal**) (**ap·palled, ap·pal·ling**) **1** greatly dismay or horrify. **2** (as **ap·palling** *adj.*) *colloq.* shocking; unpleasant; bad. □□ **ap·pal′ling·ly** *adv.*

ap·pa·rat·us /ápərátəs, –ráytəs/ *n.* **1** equipment for a particular function, esp. scientific or technical. **2** political or other complex organization.

ap·par·el /əpárəl/ ● *n.* clothing; dress. ● *v.tr.* (**ap·par·eled, ap·par·el·ing; ap·par·elled, ap·par·el·ling**) clothe.

ap·par·ent /əpárənt/ *adj.* **1** readily visible or perceivable. **2** seeming. □□ **ap·par′ent·ly** *adv.*

ap·pa·ri·tion /ápəríshən/ *n.* sudden or dramatic appearance, esp. of a ghost or phantom; visible ghost.

ap·peal /əpeél/ ● *v.intr.* **1** make an earnest or formal request; plead. **2** be attractive or of interest; be pleasing. **3** (foll. by *to*) resort to for support. **4** *Law* apply (to a higher court) for a reconsideration of a decision. ● *n.* **1** act or instance of appealing. **2** formal or urgent request for public support, esp. financial. **3** *Law* referral of a case to a higher court. **4** attractiveness. □□ **ap·peal′er** *n.*

ap·peal·ing /əpeéling/ *adj.* attractive; likable. □□ **ap·peal′ing·ly** *adv.*

ap·pear /əpeér/ *v.intr.* **1** become or be visible. **2** be evident (*a new problem appeared*). **3** seem. **4** present oneself publicly or formally. **5** be published.

ap·pear·ance /əpeérəns/ *n.* **1** act or instance of appearing. **2** outward form as perceived (*gives the appearance of trying hard*). **3** semblance. □ **keep up appearances** maintain an impression or pretense. **make** (or **put in**) **an appearance** be present, esp. briefly.

ap·pease /əpeéz/ *v.tr.* **1** make calm or quiet, esp. conciliate (a potential aggressor) by making concessions. **2** satisfy (an appetite, scruples). □□ **ap·pease′ment** *n.* **ap·peas′er** *n.*

ap·pel·lant /əpélənt/ *n. Law* person who appeals to a higher court.

ap·pel·late /əpélət/ *adj. Law* (esp. of a court) concerned with or dealing with appeals.

ap·pel·la·tion /ápəláyshən/ *n. formal* name or title; nomenclature.

ap·pend /əpénd/ *v.tr.* (usu. foll. by *to*) attach, affix, add, esp. to a written document, etc.

ap·pend·age /əpéndij/ *n.* something attached; addition.

ap·pen·dec·to·my /ápəndéktəmee/ *n.* (*pl.* –mies) surgical removal of the appendix.

ap·pen·di·ci·tis /əpéndisítis/ *n.* inflammation of the appendix.

ap·pen·dix /əpéndiks/ *n.* (*pl.* **ap·pen·di·ces** /–diseez/; **ap·pen·dix·es**) **1** (in full **verm·i·form ap·pen·dix**) *Anat.* small outgrowth of tissue attached to the large intestine. **2** subsidiary matter at the end of a book or document.

ap·per·tain /ápərtáyn/ *v.intr.* (foll. by *to*) **1** relate. **2** belong as a possession or right. **3** be appropriate.

ap·pe·tite /ápitīt/ *n.* **1** natural desire to satisfy bodily needs, esp. for food or sexual activity. **2** inclination or desire. □□ **ap·pe·ti′tive** *adj.*

ap·pe·tiz·er /ápitīzər/ *n.* small amount, esp. of food served before a meal, to stimulate an appetite.

ap·pe·tiz·ing /ápitīzing/ *adj.* stimulating an appetite, esp. for food. □□ **ap′pe·tiz·ing·ly** *adv.*

ap·plaud /əpláwd/ *v.* express approval or praise, esp. by clapping.

ap·plause /əpláwz/ *n.* **1** approbation, esp. from an audience, etc., by clapping. **2** emphatic approval.

ap·ple /ápəl/ *n.* **1** rounded firm edible fruit with a crisp flesh. **2** tree bearing this. □ **apple-pie order** extreme neatness.

ap·ple·jack /ápəljak/ *n.* brandy distilled from fermented apple cider.

ap·pli·ance /əplīəns/ *n.* device for a specific task, esp. a household device for washing, drying, cooking, etc.

ap·pli·ca·ble /áplikəbəl, əplíkə–/ *adj.* **1** that may be applied. **2** having reference; appropriate. □□ **ap·pli·ca·bil′i·ty** *n.* **ap′pli·ca·bly** *adv.*

ap·pli·cant /áplikənt/ *n.* person who applies for something, esp. a job.

ap·pli·ca·tion /áplikáyshən/ *n.* **1** act or instance of applying. **2** formal request, usu. in writing. **3 a** relevance. **b** use. **4** diligence.

ap·pli·ca·tor /áplikaytər/ *n.* device for applying a substance to a surface.

ap·plied /əplíd/ *adj.* (of a subject of study) put to practical use as opposed to being theoretical (cf. PURE *adj.* 5).

ap·pli·qué /áplikáy/ ● *n.* attachment of cut-out fabric patterns to the surface of another fabric to form pictures or patterns. ● *adj.* executed in appliqué. ● *v.tr.* (**ap·pli·qués, ap·pli·quéd, ap·pli·qué·ing**) decorate with appliqué.

ap·ply /əplí/ *v.* (**–plies, –plied**) **1** *intr.* formally request. **2** *intr.* have relevance. **3** *tr.* **a** make use of; employ. **b** operate (*apply the hand brake*). **4** *tr.* put or spread on. **5** *refl.* devote oneself. □□ **ap·pli′er** *n.*

ap·point /əpóynt/ *v.tr.* **1** assign a job or office to (*appoint him governor*). **2** fix (a time, place, etc.). **3** (as **appointed** *adj.*) equipped; furnished. □□ **ap·point·ee** /–teé/ *n.* **ap·point′er** *n.* **ap·poin′tive** *adj.*

ap·point·ment /əpóyntmənt/ *n.* **1** arrangement to meet at a specific time and place. **2 a** job or office, esp. one available for applicants. **b** person appointed. **c** act or instance of appointing. **3** (usu. in *pl.*) **a** furniture; fittings. **b** equipment.

ap·por·tion /əpáwrshən/ *v.tr.* share out; assign as a share. □□ **ap·por′tion·a·ble** *adj.* **ap·por′tion·ment** *n.*

ap·po·site /ápəzit/ *adj.* **1** apt; well chosen. **2** well expressed. □□ **ap·pos′ite·ly** *adv.* **ap′po·site·ness** *n.*

ap·po·si·tion /ápəzíshən/ *n. Gram.* placing of a word next to another to qualify or explain the first (e.g., *William the Conqueror, my friend Sue*). □□ **ap·po·si′tion·al** *adj.*

ap·praise /əpráyz/ *v.tr.* **1** estimate the value or quality of. **2** (esp. officially) set a price on. □□ **ap·prais′a·ble** *adj.* **ap·prais′al** *n.* **ap·prais′er** *n.*

¶ **Appraise**, meaning 'evaluate,' should not be confused with *apprise*, which means 'inform': *The painting was appraised at $3 million. They gasped when apprised of this valuation.*

ap·pre·cia·ble /əpreéshəbəl/ *adj.* significant; considerable. □□ **ap·pre′cia·bly** *adv.*

ap·pre·ci·ate /əpre'eesheeáyt/ *v.* **1** *tr.* **a** esteem highly; value. **b** be grateful for. **2** *tr.* understand; recognize. **3 a** *intr.* (of property, etc.) rise in value. **b** *tr.* raise in value. □□ **ap·pre·cia·tive** /‑shətiv, ‑shee‑áytiv/ *adj.* **ap·pre′cia·tive·ly** *adv.* **ap·pre′cia·tive·ness** *n.* **ap·pre′ci·a·tor** *n.* **ap·pre·ci·a·to·ry** /‑sheeətáwree/ *adj.*

ap·pre·ci·a·tion /əpre'eeshee‑áyshən/ *n.* **1** favorable or grateful recognition. **2** sensitive understanding or judgment. **3** increase in value.

ap·pre·hend /áprihénd/ *v.tr.* **1** seize; arrest. **2** understand; perceive. **3** anticipate with uneasiness or fear.

ap·pre·hen·sion /áprihénshən/ *n.* **1** uneasiness; dread. **2** understanding; perception. **3** arrest; capture.

ap·pre·hen·sive /áprihénsiv/ *adj.* uneasily fearful; dreading. □□ **ap·pre·hen′sive·ly** *adv.* **ap·pre·hen′sive·ness** *n.*

ap·pren·tice /əpréntis/ ● *n.* **1** person learning a trade by being employed in it usu. at low wages. **2** novice. ● *v.tr.* engage or bind as an apprentice. □□ **ap·pren′tice·ship** *n.*

ap·prise /əpríz/ *v.tr.* inform. □ **be apprised of** be aware of.
¶ See note at APPRAISE.

ap·proach /əpróch/ ● *v.* **1** *tr.* come near or nearer to (a place or time). **2** *intr.* come near or nearer in space or time (*the hour approaches*). **3** *tr.* make a tentative proposal or suggestion to. **4** *tr.* **a** be similar to. **b** approximate to. **5** *tr.* set about. ● *n.* **1** act or means of approaching. **2** approximation. **3** way of dealing with a person or thing.

ap·proach·a·ble /əpróchəbəl/ *adj.* **1** friendly; easy to talk to. **2** able to be approached. □□ **ap·proach·a·bil′i·ty** *n.*

ap·pro·ba·tion /áprəbáyshən/ *n.* approval; consent. □□ **ap·pro·ba′tive** *adj.* **ap·pro·ba·to·ry** /əprób́ətawree/ *adj.*

ap·pro·pri·ate ● *adj.* /əprópreeət/ suitable or proper. ● *v.tr.* /əprópreeayt/ **1** take possession of, esp. without authority. **2** devote (money, etc.) to special purposes. □□ **ap·pro′pri·ate·ly** *adv.* **ap·pro′pri·ate·ness** *n.* **ap·pro·pri·a·tion** /‑áyshən/ *n.* **ap·pro′pri·a·tor** *n.*

ap·prov·al /əproovəl/ *n.* **1** approving. **2** consent; favorable opinion. □ **on approval** (of goods supplied) to be returned if not satisfactory.

ap·prove /əproov/ *v.* **1** *tr.* confirm; sanction. **2** *intr.* give or have a favorable opinion. **3** *tr.* commend. □□ **ap·prov′er** *n.* **ap·prov′ing·ly** *adv.*

approx. *abbr.* **1** approximate. **2** approximately.

ap·prox·i·mate ● *adj.* /əpróksimət/ fairly correct; near to the actual. ● *v.* /əpróksimayt/ bring or come near (esp. in quality, number, etc.). □□ **ap·prox′i·mate·ly** /‑mətlee/ *adv.* **ap·prox·i·ma·tion** /‑máyshən/ *n.*

ap·pur·te·nance /əpə́rt'nəns/ *n.* (usu. *pl.*) belonging; appendage; accessory.

APR *abbr.* annual or annualized percentage rate.

Apr. *abbr.* April.

a·pri·cot /áprikot, áypri‑/ ● *n.* **1 a** small, juicy, soft fruit, of an orange-yellow color. **b** tree bearing it. **2** its color. ● *adj.* orange-yellow.

A·pril /áypril/ *n.* fourth month of the year. □ **April Fool's** (or **Fools′**) **Day** April 1.

a pri·o·ri /a'a pree‑áwree, áy prī‑áwrī/ ● *adj.* **1** (of reasoning) deductive; proceeding from causes to effects (opp. A POSTERIORI). **2** (of concepts,

etc.) logically independent of experience (opp. EMPIRICAL). **3** not submitted to critical investigation. ● *adv.* **1** deductively. **2** as far as one knows. □□ **a·pri·o·rism** /aypri'ərizəm/ *n.*

a·pron /áyprən/ *n.* **1** garment covering and protecting the front of a person's clothes. **2** *Theatr.* part of a stage in front of the curtain. **3** paved area of an airfield for maneuvering or loading aircraft. □□ **a′proned** *adj.* **a′pron·ful** *n.* (*pl.* **‑fuls**)

ap·ro·pos /áprəpó/ ● *adj.* to the point; appropriate. ● *adv.* appropriately. ● *prep.* in respect to.

apse /aps/ *n.* large semicircular or polygonal recess, arched or with a domed roof, at the eastern end of a church.

apt /apt/ *adj.* **1** appropriate; suitable. **2** having a tendency. **3** clever; quick to learn. □□ **apt′ly** *adv.* **apt′ness** *n.*

apt. *abbr.* **1** apartment. **2** aptitude.

ap·ti·tude /áptitōod, ‑tyōod/ *n.* **1** natural talent. **2** ability or suitability.

aq·ua /ákwə, a'akwə/ *n.* the color aquamarine.

aq·ua·ma·rine /ákwəməre'en, a'akwə‑/ *n.* **1** light bluish green beryl. **2** its color.

aq·ua·naut /ákwənawt, a'akwə‑/ *n.* underwater swimmer or explorer.

aq·ua·plane /ákwəplayn, a'akwə‑/ ● *n.* board for riding on the water, pulled by a speedboat. ● *v.intr.* ride on this.

a·quar·i·um /əkwáireeəm/ *n.* (*pl.* **a·quar·i·ums** or **a·quar·i·a** /‑reeə/) **1** tank of water with transparent sides for keeping live aquatic plants and animals. **2** building where aquatic plants and animals are kept for study and exhibition.

A·quar·i·us /əkwáireeəs/ *n.* **1** constellation and eleventh sign of the zodiac (the Water Carrier). **2** person born under this sign. □□ **A·quar′i·an** *adj.* & *n.*

a·quat·ic /əkwátik, əkwótik/ ● *adj.* **1** growing or living in water. **2** (of a sport) played in or on water. ● *n.* **1** aquatic plant or animal. **2** (in *pl.*) aquatic sports.

aq·ua vi·tae /a'akwə vitee, ve'e‑/ *n.* strong alcoholic liquor.

aq·ue·duct /ákwidukt/ *n.* artificial channel for conveying water, esp. in the form of a bridge supported by tall columns across a valley.

a·que·ous /áykweeəs, ák‑/ *adj.* of, containing, or like water.

aq·ui·fer /ákwifər/ *n.* Geol. layer of rock or soil able to hold or transmit much water.

aq·ui·line /ákwilīn/ *adj.* **1** of or like an eagle. **2** (of a nose) curved like an eagle's beak.

AR *abbr.* Arkansas (in official postal use).

Ar *symb. Chem.* argon.

-ar¹ /ər/ *suffix* **1** forming adjectives (*angular; linear; nuclear; titular*). **2** forming nouns (*scholar*).

-ar² /ər/ *suffix* forming nouns (*pillar*).

-ar³ /ər/ *suffix* forming nouns (*bursar; exemplar; mortar; vicar*).

-ar⁴ /ər/ *suffix* assim. form of ‑ER¹, ‑OR¹ (*liar; beggar*).

Ar·ab /árəb/ ● *n.* member of a Semitic people inhabiting Saudi Arabia and the Middle East generally. ● *adj.* of Arabia or the Arabs (esp. with ethnic reference).

ar·a·besque /árəbésk/ *n.* 1 *Ballet* posture with one leg extended horizontally backward, torso extended forward, and arms outstretched. 2 design of intertwined leaves, scrolls, etc.

A·ra·bi·an /əráybeeən/ • *adj.* of or relating to Arabia (esp. with geographical reference). • *n.* 1 native of Arabia. 2 (in full **Ara′bian horse′**) horse of a breed orig. native to Arabia.

Ar·a·bic /árəbik/ • *n.* Semitic language of the Arabs. • *adj.* of or relating to Arabia (esp. with reference to language or literature). □ **Arabic numeral** any of the numerals 0, 1, 2, 3, 4, 5, 6, 7, 8, and 9 (cf. *Roman numeral*).

ar·a·ble /árəbəl/ *adj.* (of land) suitable for crop production.

a·rach·nid /əráknid/ • *n.* any arthropod of a class comprising scorpions, spiders, etc. • *adj.* of or pertaining to the arachnids. □□ **a·rach′ni·dan** *adj.* & *n.*

Ar·a·ma·ic /árəmáyik/ • *n.* branch of the Semitic languages, esp. the language of Syria, used as a lingua franca in the Near East. • *adj.* of or in Aramaic.

A·rap·a·ho /ərápəhō/ *n.* 1 a N. American people native to the central plains of Canada and the US. b member of this people. 2 the language of this people.

ar·bi·ter /aárbitər/ *n.* arbitrator; judge.

ar·bi·trar·y /aárbitreeree/ *adj.* 1 random; capricious. 2 despotic. □□ **ar·bi·trar′i·ly** *adv.* **ar·bi·trar′i·ness** *n.*

ar·bi·trate /aárbitrayt/ *v.* decide by or as an arbitrator. □□ **ar·bi·tra·tion** /-tráyshən/ *n.*

ar·bi·trat·or /aárbitraytər/ *n.* person appointed to settle a dispute; arbiter.

ar·bor /aárbər/ *n.* shady garden alcove enclosed by trees or climbing plants; bower. □□ **ar·bored** *adj.*

ar·bo·re·al /aarbáwreeəl/ *adj.* of or living in trees.

ar·bo·re·tum /aárbəre′etəm/ *n.* (*pl.* **ar·bo·re·tums** or **ar·bo·re·ta** /-tə/) botanical garden devoted to trees, shrubs, etc.

ar·bor vi·tae /aárbər vī́tee/ *n.* any of various evergreen conifers, usu. of pyramidal shape with flattened shoots bearing scalelike leaves.

ar·bu·tus /aarbyṓotəs/ *n.* evergreen tree or shrub having white or pink clusters of flowers and strawberrylike berries. □ **trailing arbutus** mayflower, a creeping plant of the heath family with pink or white flowers.

arc /aark/ • *n.* 1 part of the circumference of a circle or any other curve. 2 *Electr.* luminous discharge between two electrodes. • *v.intr.* (**arced** /aarkt/, **arc·ing** /aárking/) form an arc or move in a curve.

ar·cade /aarkáyd/ *n.* 1 passage with an arched roof. 2 covered walk, esp. lined with shops. 3 *Archit.* series of arches supporting or set along a wall. 4 entertainment establishment with coin-operated games, etc. □□ **ar·cad′ed** *adj.*

ar·cane /aarkáyn/ *adj.* mysterious; secret. □□ **ar·cane′ly** *adv.*

arch¹ /aarch/ • *n.* 1 a curved structure as an opening or a support for a bridge, roof, floor, etc. b arch used in building as an ornament. 2 any arch-shaped curve. • *v.tr.* 1 form an arch. 2 span like an arch.

arch² /aarch/ *adj.* self-consciously or affectedly playful or teasing. □□ **arch′ly** *adv.* **arch′ness** *n.*

arch- /aarch/ *comb. form* chief; principal (*archbishop*; *archenemy*).

ar·chae·ol·o·gy /aárkee-óləjee/ *n.* (also **ar·che·ol′o·gy**) study of ancient cultures, esp. through the excavation and analysis of physical remains. □□ **ar·chae·o·log·ic** /-keeəlójik/ *adj.* **ar·chae·o·log′i·cal** *adj.* **ar·chae·ol′o·gist** *n.*

ar·cha·ic /aarkáyik/ *adj.* 1 a antiquated. b (of a word, etc.) no longer in ordinary use. 2 primitive. 3 of an early period of culture. □□ **ar·cha′i·cal·ly** *adv.*

ar·cha·ism /aárkeeizəm, -kay-/ *n.* 1 retention or imitation of the old or obsolete, esp. in language or art. 2 archaic word or expression. □□ **ar′cha·ist** *n.* **ar·cha·is′tic** *adj.*

arch·an·gel /aárkaynjəl/ *n.* angel of the highest rank.

arch·bish·op /aárchbíshəp/ *n.* bishop of highest rank. □□ **arch·bish′op·ric** *n.*

arch·dea·con /aárchdee′ekən/ *n.* cleric in various churches ranking below a bishop. □□ **arch·dea′con·ry** *n.* (*pl.* **-ries**) **arch·dea′con·ship** *n.*

arch·di·o·cese /aárchdī́əsis, -sees, -seez/ *n.* diocese of an archbishop. □□ **arch·di·oc·e·san** /aárchdīósisən/ *adj.*

arch·duke /aárchdṓok, -dyṓok/ *n.* (*fem.* **arch·duch·ess** /-dúchis/) *hist.* chief duke (esp. as the title of a son of the Emperor of Austria). □□ **arch·du′cal** *adj.* **arch·duch·y** /-dúchee/ *n.* (*pl.* **-ies**)

arch·en·e·my /aárchénəmee/ *n.* (*pl.* **-mies**) 1 chief enemy. 2 the Devil.

ar·che·ol·o·gy var. of ARCHAEOLOGY.

arch·er /aárchər/ *n.* 1 person who shoots with a bow and arrows. 2 (**the Archer**) the zodiacal sign or constellation Sagittarius.

ar·cher·y /aárchəree/ *n.* shooting with a bow and arrows, esp. as a sport.

ar·che·type /aárkitīp/ *n.* 1 original model; prototype. 2 typical specimen. □□ **ar′che·typ·al** *adj.* **ar·che·typ·i·cal** /-típikəl/ *adj.*

ar·chi·pel·a·go /aárkipéləgō/ *n.* (*pl.* **-gos** or **-goes**) 1 group of islands. 2 sea with many islands.

ar·chi·tect /aárkitekt/ *n.* 1 designer of buildings, ships, etc., supervising their construction. 2 person who brings about a specified thing (*the architect of the tax reform bill*).

ar·chi·tec·ton·ic /aárkitektónik/ • *adj.* 1 of or relating to architecture or architects. 2 of or relating to the systematization of knowledge. • *n.* (in *pl.*; usu. treated as *sing.*) 1 scientific study of architecture. 2 study of the systematization of knowledge.

ar·chi·tec·ture /aárkitekchər/ *n.* 1 design and construction of buildings. 2 style of a building. 3 buildings collectively. □□ **ar·chi·tec′tur·al** *adj.* **ar·chi·tec′tur·al·ly** *adv.*

ar·chi·trave /aárkitrayv/ *n.* 1 (in classical architecture) main beam resting across the tops of columns. 2 molded frame around a doorway or window. 3 molding around the exterior of an arch.

ar·chive /aárkīv/ • *n.* (usu. in *pl.*) 1 collection of esp. public or corporate documents or records. 2 place where these are kept. • *v.tr.* 1 place or store in an archive. 2 *Computing* transfer (data) to a less frequently used file or less easily accessible medium, e.g., from disk to tape. □□ **ar·chi′val** *adj.* **ar·chi·vist** /aárkivist, aárkī-/ *n.*

arch•way /a'archway/ *n.* **1** vaulted passage. **2** arched entrance.

Arc•tic /a'arktik, a'artik/ • *adj.* **1** of the north polar regions. **2** (**arctic**) *colloq.* very cold. • *n.* Arctic regions. □ **Arctic Circle** parallel of latitude 66° 30′ N, forming an imaginary line around this region.

-ard /ərd/ *suffix* **1** forming nouns in depreciatory senses (*drunkard; sluggard*). **2** forming nouns in other senses (*Spaniard; wizard*).

ar•dent /a'ard'nt/ *adj.* **1** eager; zealous; fervent; passionate. **2** burning. □□ **ar•den•cy** /-d'nsee/ *n.* **ar'dent•ly** *adv.*

ar•dor /a'ardər/ *n.* zeal; burning enthusiasm; passion.

ar•du•ous /a'arjठ̄ठ̄əs/ *adj.* **1** hard to achieve or overcome; difficult; laborious. **2** strenuous. □□ **ar'du•ous•ly** *adv.* **ar'du•ous•ness** *n.*

are *2nd sing. present & 1st, 2nd, 3rd pl. present* of BE.

a•re•a /áireeə/ *n.* **1** extent or measure of a surface (*3 acres in area*). **2** region. **3** space for a specific purpose. **4** scope or range. □ **area code** three-digit number that identifies telephone service region. □□ **ar'e•al** *adj.*

a•re•na /əréenə/ *n.* **1** central part of an amphitheater, etc. **2** scene of conflict; sphere of action or discussion.

aren't /aarnt, a'arənt/ *contr.* **1** are not. **2** (in *interrog.*) am not (*aren't I coming too?*).

Ar•gen•tine /a'arjənteen, -tīn/ (also **Ar•gen•tin•e•an** /-tíneeən/) • *adj.* of or relating to Argentina in S. America. • *n.* **1** native or citizen of Argentina. **2** person of Argentine descent.

ar•gon /a'argon/ *n. Chem.* inert gaseous element. ¶ Symb.: **Ar.**

ar•go•sy /a'argəsee/ *n.* (*pl.* **-sies**) *poet.* large merchant ship.

ar•got /a'argō, -gət/ *n.* jargon of a group or class.

ar•gue /a'argōō/ *v.* (**ar•gues, ar•gued, ar•gu•ing**) **1** *intr.* exchange views or opinions heatedly or contentiously. **2** *tr.* & *intr.* indicate; maintain by reasoning. **3** *tr.* persuade. □□ **ar'gu•a•ble** *adj.* **ar'gu•a•bly** *adv.* **ar'gu•er** *n.*

ar•gu•ment /a'argyəmənt/ *n.* **1** exchange of views, esp. a contentious or prolonged one. **2** reason advanced; reasoning process.

ar•gu•men•ta•tion /a'argyəmentáyshən/ *n.* **1** methodical reasoning. **2** debate or argument.

ar•gu•men•ta•tive /a'argyəméntətiv/ *adj.* fond of arguing. □□ **ar•gu•men'ta•tive•ly** *adv.* **ar•gu•men'ta•tive•ness** *n.*

a•ri•a /a'areeə/ *n. Mus.* solo in an opera, etc.

-arian /áireeən/ *suffix* forming adjectives and nouns meaning '(one) concerned with or believing in' (*agrarian; antiquarian; humanitarian; vegetarian*).

ar•id /árid/ *adj.* **1 a** dry; parched. **b** barren. **2** uninteresting. □□ **a•rid•i•ty** /əríditee/ *n.* **ar'id•ly** *adv.* **ar'id•ness** *n.*

A•ries /áireez/ *n.* **1** constellation and the first sign of the zodiac (the Ram). **2** person born under this sign. □□ **Ar•i•an** /-reeən/ *adj. & n.*

a•right /ərít/ *adv.* rightly.

a•rise /əríz/ *v.intr.* (*past* **a•rose** /ərōz/; *past part.* **a•risen** /ərízən/) **1** originate. **2** result. **3** emerge. **4** rise.

ar•is•to•cra•cy /áristókrəsee/ *n.* (*pl.* **-cies**) **1 a** highest class in society; the nobility. **b** the nobility as a ruling class. **2 a** government by a privileged group. **b** nation so governed.

a•ris•to•crat /ərístəkrat, áris-/ *n.* member of the aristocracy. □□ **a•ris•to•crat'ic** *adj.* **a•ris•to•crat'i•cal•ly** *adv.*

ar•ith•me•tic • *n.* /əríthmətik/ **1** science of numbers. **2** use of numbers; computation. • *adj.* /árithmétik/ (also **ar•ith•met'i•cal** /-métikəl/) of arithmetic. □□ **a•rith•me•ti•cian** /əríthmətishən/ *n.*

Ariz. *abbr.* Arizona.

Ark. *abbr.* Arkansas.

ark /aark/ *n.* **1** (usu. **Noah's Ark**) ship used by Noah to save his family and the animals from the biblical flood. **2** *archaic* chest; box.

arm[1] /aarm/ *n.* **1** each of the upper limbs of the human body from shoulder to hand. **2** forelimb or tentacle of an animal. **3 a** sleeve of a garment. **b** arm support of a chair. **c** thing resembling an arm in branching from a main stem (*an arm of the sea*). □ **at arm's length** at a distance. **with open arms** cordially. □□ **arm•ful** *n.* (*pl.* **-fuls**) **arm•less** *adj.*

arm[2] /aarm/ • *n.* **1** (usu. *pl.*) **a** weapon. **b** = FIREARM. **2** (*pl.*) military profession. **3** branch of the military. • *v.tr.* & *refl.* **1** supply with weapons. **2** make (a bomb, etc.) able to explode. □ **take up arms** begin fighting.

ar•ma•da /aarma'adə/ *n.* fleet of warships, esp. that sent by Spain against England in 1588.

ar•ma•dil•lo /a'armədílō/ *n.* (*pl.* **-los**) tropical American mammal with a body covered in bony plates.

ARMADILLO

Ar•ma•ged•don /a'armagéd'n/ *n.* **1** (in the New Testament) last battle between good and evil before the Day of Judgment. **2** any huge bloody battle or struggle.

ar•ma•ment /a'arməmənt/ *n.* **1** (often *pl.*) military weapons and equipment. **2** equipping for war. **3** force equipped for war.

ar•ma•ture /a'arməchठ̄ठ̄r/ *n.* **1 a** rotating part of a generator or electric motor. **b** any moving part of an electrical machine in which a voltage is induced by a magnetic field. **2** iron bar placed in contact with the poles of a horseshoe magnet to preserve its power. **3** metal framework on which a clay, etc., sculpture is molded.

arm•chair *n.* /a'armchair/ **1** chair with arm supports. **2** (*attrib.*) theoretical rather than active (*armchair critic*).

Ar•me•ni•an /aarméeneeən/ • *n.* **1 a** native of Armenia. **b** person of Armenian descent. **2** language of Armenia. • *adj.* of or relating to Armenia, its language, or the Christian Church established there *c.*300.

arm•hole /a'armhōl/ *n.* each of two holes for arms in a garment.

ar•mi•stice /a'armistis/ *n.* truce, esp. permanent. □ **Armistice Day** former name of Veteran's Day.

arm•let /a'armlit/ *n.* band worn around the arm.

ar·moire /aarmwaʹar/ *n.* tall, upright cupboard or closet.

ar·mor /aʹarmər/ • *n.* 1 defensive covering, usu. of metal. 2 armored vehicles collectively. • *v.tr.* (usu. as **armored** *adj.*) provide with armor and often with guns.

ar·mor·y /aʹarməree/ *n.* (*pl.* **–ies**) 1 arsenal. 2 arms factory.

arm·pit /aʹarmpit/ *n.* hollow under the arm at the shoulder.

arm·rest /aʹarmrest/ *n.* = ARM¹ 3b.

ar·my /aʹarmee/ *n.* (*pl.* **–mies**) 1 organized armed land force. 2 very large number.

a·ro·ma /ərṓmə/ *n.* fragrance; distinctive and esp. pleasing smell.

ar·o·ma·tic /árəmátik/ • *adj.* fragrant; pleasantly pungent. • *n.* aromatic substance. □□ **ar·o·mat'ic·al·ly** *adv.*

a·rose *past* of ARISE.

a·round /ərównd/ • *adv.* 1 on every side; on all sides. 2 in various places; here and there (*shop around*). 3 *colloq.* **a** in existence; available. **b** near at hand. 4 approximately. 5 in circumference. • *prep.* 1 on or along the circuit of. 2 on every side of. 3 here and there; in or near. 4 about; at a time near to.

a·rouse /ərówz/ *v.tr.* 1 induce (esp. a feeling, etc.). 2 awake from sleep. 3 stir into activity. 4 stimulate sexually. □□ **a·rous'a·ble** *adj.* **a·rous'al** *n.* **a·rous'er** *n.*

ar·peg·gio /aarpéjeeṓ/ *n.* (*pl.* **–gios**) *Mus.* notes of a chord played in succession.

ar·raign /əráyn/ *v.tr.* indict; formally accuse. □□ **ar·raign'ment** *n.*

ar·range /əráynj/ *v.* 1 *tr.* put into order; classify. 2 *tr.* plan or provide for. 3 *tr.* agree about. 4 *intr.* make plans. 5 *tr. Mus.* adapt (a composition) for performance with instruments or voices. □□ **ar·range'a·ble** *adj.* **ar·rang'er** *n.* (esp. in sense 5).

ar·range·ment /əráynjmənt/ *n.* 1 arranging or being arranged. 2 manner in which a thing is arranged. 3 something arranged. 4 (*pl.*) plans; preparations. 5 *Mus.* composition arranged for performance by different instruments or voices.

ar·rant /árənt/ *attrib.adj.* downright; utter. □□ **ar'rant·ly** *adv.*

ar·ras /árəs/ *n. hist.* rich tapestry or hanging.

ar·ray /əráy/ • *n.* 1 imposing or well-ordered series or display. 2 ordered arrangement, esp. of troops. • *v.tr.* 1 deck; adorn. 2 set in order; marshal (forces).

ar·rears /əreʹerz/ *n.pl.* amount (esp. of work or debt) still outstanding or uncompleted. □□ **ar·rear'age** *n.*

ar·rest /ərést/ • *v.tr.* 1 lawfully seize (a person, ship, etc.). 2 stop or check (esp. a process or moving thing). 3 attract (a person's attention). • *n.* 1 arresting or being arrested. 2 stoppage. □ **under arrest** in custody. □□ **ar·rest'ing** *adj.* **ar·rest'ing·ly** *adv.*

ar·riv·al /əríʹvəl/ *n.* 1 **a** arriving. **b** appearance on the scene. 2 person or thing that has arrived.

ar·rive /ərív/ *v.intr.* (often foll. by *at, in*) 1 reach a destination. 2 (foll. by *at*) reach (a conclusion, etc.). 3 *colloq.* become successful. 4 (of a thing) be brought. 5 come.

ar·ri·viste /áreeveʹest/ *n.* 1 ambitious or ruthless person. 2 person who is newly arrived in social status, wealth, etc.

ar·ro·gant /árəgənt/ *adj.* aggressively assertive or presumptuous. □□ **ar'ro·gance** *n.* **ar'ro·gant·ly** *adv.*

ar·ro·gate /árəgayt/ *v.tr.* claim (power, responsibility, etc.) without justification. □□ **ar·ro·ga·tion** /–gáyshən/ *n.*

ar·row /árṓ/ *n.* 1 sharp pointed wooden or metal missile shot from a bow. 2 representation of an arrow indicating a direction.

ar·row·head /árṓhed/ *n.* pointed end of an arrow.

ar·row·root /árṓrŏŏt, –rŏŏt/ *n.* 1 type of nutritious starch. 2 plant yielding this.

ar·se·nal /aʹarsənəl/ *n.* 1 store of weapons. 2 government establishment for the storage and manufacture of weapons and ammunition. 3 resources regarded collectively.

ar·se·nic • *n.* /aʹarsənik/ 1 nonscientific name for arsenic trioxide, a poisonous white powder used in weed killers, rat poison, etc. 2 *Chem.* brittle semimetallic element. ¶ Symb.: **As**. • *adj.* /aarsénik/ of or containing arsenic. □□ **ar·sen'i·cal** *adj. & n.*

ar·son /aʹarsən/ *n.* act of maliciously setting fire to property. □□ **ar'son·ist** *n.*

art¹ /aart/ *n.* 1 **a** human creative skill or its application. **b** work exhibiting this. 2 **a** (*pl.*; prec. by *the*) various branches of creative activity concerned with the production of imaginative designs, sounds, or ideas, e.g., painting, music, writing, etc. **b** any one of these branches. 3 creative activity, esp. painting and drawing, resulting in visual representation. 4 human skill as opposed to nature. 5 skill, aptitude, or knack. 6 (*pl.*; usu. prec. by *the*) = *liberal arts.*

art² /aart/ *archaic* or *dial. 2nd sing. present* of BE.

ar·te·ri·al /aarteʹereeəl/ *adj.* 1 of or relating to an artery. 2 (esp. of a road) main, important.

ar·te·ri·o·scle·ro·sis /aarteʹereeōsklərṓsis/ *n.* loss of elasticity and thickening of the walls of the arteries, esp. in old age; hardening of the arteries. □□ **ar·te·ri·o·scle·rot·ic** /–rótik/ *adj.*

ar·te·ry /aʹartəree/ *n.* (*pl.* **–ries**) 1 any of the blood vessels carrying oxygen-enriched blood from the heart (cf. VEIN). 2 main road or railroad line.

ar·te·sian well /aarteʹezhən/ *n.* well in which natural pressure produces a constant supply of water.

art·ful /aʹartfŏŏl/ *adj.* 1 crafty; deceitful. 2 skillful; clever. □□ **art'ful·ly** *adv.* **art'ful·ness** *n.*

ar·thri·tis /aarthrítis/ *n.* inflammation of a joint or joints. □□ **ar·thrit·ic** /–thrítik/ *adj. & n.*

ar·thro·pod /aʹarthrəpod/ *n. Zool.* invertebrate with a segmented body, jointed limbs, and an external skeleton, e.g., spider, crustacean, etc.

ar·ti·choke /aʹartichōk/ *n.* 1 plant allied to the thistle. 2 flower head of the artichoke, the bracts of which have edible bases.

ar·ti·cle /aʹartikəl/ • *n.* 1 (often in *pl.*) item or commodity. 2 nonfictional journalistic essay. 3 separate clause or portion of any document. 4 *Gram.* word (e.g., *a, an, the*) preceding a noun and signifying a specific instance (*the*) or any of several instances (*a, an*). • *v.tr.* bind by articles of apprenticeship.

ar·tic·u·lar /aartíkyələr/ *adj.* of or relating to the joints.

ar·ti·cu·late • *adj.* /aartíkyələt/ **1** able to speak fluently and coherently. **2** (of sound or speech) having clearly distinguishable parts. **3** having joints. • *v.* /aartíkyəlayt/ **1** pronounce clearly and distinctly. **2** express (an idea, etc.) coherently (*was quite unable to articulate*). **3** connect by joints. □□ **ar·tic′u·late·ly** *adv.* **ar·tic′u·late·ness** *n.* **ar·tic·u·la·tion** /-láyshən/ *n.*

ar·ti·fact /áartifakt/ *n.* man-made object.

ar·ti·fice /áartifis/ *n.* **1** clever device; contrivance. **2** cunning. **3** skill; dexterity.

ar·ti·fi·cer /aartífisər/ *n.* **1** inventor. **2** craftsman.

ar·ti·fi·cial /áartifíshəl/ *adj.* **1** produced by human art or effort; not natural. **2** imitation; fake. **3** affected; insincere. □ **artificial insemination** injection of semen into the uterus other than by sexual intercourse. **artificial intelligence** application of computers to areas normally regarded as requiring human intelligence. **artificial respiration** restoration or initiation of breathing by manual or mechanical methods. □□ **ar·ti·fi·ci·al·i·ty** /-sheeálitee/ *n.* **ar·ti·fi′cial·ly** *adv.*

ar·til·ler·y /aartíləree/ *n.* (*pl.* **–ies**) **1** large-caliber guns used in warfare on land. **2** branch of the armed forces that uses these. □□ **ar·til′ler·y·man** *n.*

ar·ti·san /áartizən, –sən/ *n.* skilled manual worker or craftsman.

art·ist /áartist/ *n.* **1** painter. **2** person who practices any of the arts. **3** professional performer, esp. a singer or dancer. **4** habitual or skillful practitioner of a specified activity. □□ **art′ist·ry** *n.*

ar·tis·tic /aartístik/ *adj.* **1** having natural skill in art. **2** made or done with art. **3** of art or artists. □□ **ar·tis′ti·cal·ly** *adv.*

art·less /áartlis/ *adj.* **1** guileless; ingenuous. **2** not resulting from or displaying art. **3** clumsy. □□ **art′less·ly** *adv.* **art′less·ness** *n.*

art·work /áartwərk/ *n.* **1** artistic work, esp. in the visual arts. **2** illustrations in a printed work.

art·y /áartee/ *adj.* (**art·i·er**, **art·i·est**) *colloq.* pretentiously or affectedly artistic. □□ **art′i·ness** *n.*

a·rum /áirəm/ *n.* usu. stemless plant with arrow-shaped leaves.

-ary[1] /eree/ *suffix* **1** forming adjectives (*budgetary; contrary; primary*). **2** forming nouns (*dictionary; fritillary; granary*).

-ary[2] /eree/ *suffix* **1** forming adjectives (*military*).

Ar·y·an /áireeən/ • *n.* **1** member of the peoples speaking any of the Indo-European languages. **2** parent language of this family. **3** *improperly* (in Nazi ideology) a Caucasian not of Jewish descent. • *adj.* of or relating to Aryan or the Aryans.

As *symb. Chem.* arsenic.

as /az, *unstressed* əz/ • *adv. & conj.* (*adv.* as antecedent in main sentence; *conj.* in relative clause expressed or implied) . . . to the extent to which . . . is or does, etc. (*I am as tall as he; it is not as easy as you think*). • *conj.* (with relative clause expressed or implied) **1** (with antecedent *so*) expressing result or purpose (*came early so as to meet us*). **2** although (*good as it is* = although it is good). **3** (without antecedent adverb) **a** in the manner in which (*do as you like*). **b** in the capacity or form of (*Olivier as Hamlet*). **c** during or at the time that (*fell just as I reached the door*). **d** since (*as you are here, we can talk*). **e** for instance (*composers, as Monteverdi*). • *pron.* (with verb of relative clause expressed or implied) **1** that; who; which (*I had the same trouble*

as you). **2** (with sentence as antecedent) a fact that (*he lost, as you know*). □ **as for** with regard to. **as if** (or **though**) as would be the case if (*acts as if she were in charge*). **as it is** (or **as is**) in the existing circumstances or state. **as it were** in a way; to a certain extent. **as well** see WELL[1]. ¶ See note at LIKE.

a.s.a.p. *abbr.* (also **ASAP**) as soon as possible.

as·bes·tos /asbéstəs, az–/ *n.* fibrous silicate mineral, esp. used as a heat-resistant or insulating material.

as·cend /əsénd/ *v.* **1** *intr.* move upwards; rise. **2** *intr.* **a** slope upwards. **b** lie along an ascending slope. **3** *tr.* climb; go up. □ **ascend the throne** become king or queen.

as·cen·dan·cy /əséndənsee/ *n.* (also **as·cen′den·cy**) superior or dominant condition or position.

as·cen·dant /əséndənt/ *adj.* **1** rising. **2** ASTRON. RISING TOWARD THE ZENITH. **3** predominant. □ **in the ascendant** rising; gaining power or authority.

as·cen·sion /əsénshən/ *n.* **1** ascent. **2** (ASCENSION) ascent of CHRIST INTO HEAVEN. □□ **as·cen′sion·al** *adj.*

as·cent /əsént/ *n.* **1** ascending; rising; progressing. **2** upward slope.

as·cer·tain /ásərtáyn/ *v.tr.* find out as a definite fact. □□ **as·cer·tain′a·ble** *adj.* **as·cer·tain′ment** *n.*

as·cet·ic /əsétik/ • *n.* person who practices severe self-discipline and abstains from all forms of pleasure, esp. for religious or spiritual reasons. • *adj.* relating to or characteristic of ascetics or asceticism; abstaining from pleasure. □□ **as·cet′i·cal·ly** *adv.* **as·cet·i·cism** /–tisizəm/ *n.*

ASCII /áskee/ *abbr. Computing* American Standard Code for Information Interchange.

a·scor·bic ac·id /əskáwrbik/ *n.* vitamin C.

as·cot /áskot, –kət/ *n.* scarflike item of neckwear with broad ends worn looped to lie flat one over the other against the chest.

as·cribe /əskríb/ *v.tr.* (usu. foll. by *to*) **1** attribute or impute. **2** regard as belonging. □□ **a·scrib′a·ble** *adj.* **as·crip·tion** /–kríp–/ *n.*

a·sep·sis /aysépsis/ *n.* **1** absence of harmful microorganisms. **2** method of achieving asepsis in surgery. □□ **a·sep′tic** *adj.*

a·sex·u·al /aysékshōōəl/ *adj.* BIOL. **1** without sex or sexual organs. **2** (of reproduction) not involving the fusion of gametes. □□ **a·sex·u·al·i·ty** /–shōōálitee/ *n.* **a·sex′u·al·ly** *adv.*

ash[1] /ash/ *n.* **1** (often in *pl.*) powdery residue left after burning. **2** (*pl.*) remains of the human body after cremation. **3** grayish color. □ ASH WEDNESDAY first day of LENT.

ash[2] /ash/ *n.* **1** tree with silvery-gray bark. **2** its hard, pale wood.

a·shamed /əsháymd/ *adj.* **1** embarrassed by shame. **2** hesitant; reluctant (but usu. not actually refusing or declining) (*ashamed to admit* I WAS WRONG). □□ **a·sham·ed·ly** /–midlee/ *adv.*

ash·en /áshən/ *adj.* like ashes; esp. gray or pale.

ash·lar /áshlər/ *n.* **1** large square-cut stone used in building. **2** masonry made of ashlars. **3** such masonry used as a facing for walls.

a·shore /əsháwr/ adv. toward or on the shore or land.

ash·ram /aáshrəm/ n. Ind. place of religious retreat for Hindus; a hermitage.

ash·tray /áshtray/ n. small receptacle for cigarette ashes, butts, etc.

ash·y /áshee/ adj. (**ash·i·er, ash·i·est**) 1 = ASHEN. 2 covered with ashes.

A·sian /áyzhən, –shən/ • n. 1 native of Asia. 2 person of Asian descent. • adj. of or relating to Asia or its people, customs, or languages.

A·si·at·ic /áyzheeátik, –shee–, –zee–/ • n. offens. an Asian. • adj. Asian.

a·side /əsíd/ • adv. 1 to or on one side; away. 2 out of consideration (placed after noun: joking aside). • n. 1 words spoken in a play for the audience to hear, but supposed not to be heard by the other characters. 2 incidental remark.

as·i·nine /ásinīn/ adj. like an ass, esp. stubborn or stupid. □□ **as·i·nin·i·ty** /–nínitee/ n.

ask /ask/ v. 1 tr. call for an answer to or about. 2 tr. seek to obtain from another person. 3 tr. invite; request the company of. 4 intr. **a** seek to obtain, meet, or be directed to (ask for a donation; asking for you). **b** bring upon oneself (they were asking for trouble). □ **ask after** inquire about (esp. a person). □□ **ask'er** n.

a·skance /əskáns/ adv. (also **a·skant** /–skánt/) sideways or squinting. □ **look askance at** regard with suspicion.

a·skew /əskyoõ/ • adv. obliquely; awry. • adj. oblique; awry.

a·slant /əslánt/ • adv. obliquely or at a slant. • prep. obliquely across (lay aslant the path).

a·sleep /əsleep/ adj. & adv. 1 **a** in or into a state of sleep. **b** inactive; inattentive. 2 (of a limb, etc.) numb. 3 euphem. dead.

asp /asp/ n. small venomous snake of North Africa and southern Europe.

as·par·a·gus /əspárəgəs/ n. 1 plant of the lily family. 2 edible young shoots of this.

as·pect /áspekt/ n. 1 **a** particular component or feature of a matter (one aspect of the problem). **b** particular way in which a matter may be considered. 2 appearance.

as·pen /áspən/ n. poplar tree with especially tremulous leaves.

as·per·i·ty /əspéritee/ n. (pl. **–ties**) 1 harshness or sharpness of temper or tone. 2 roughness. 3 rough excrescence.

as·per·sion /əspérzhən/ n. slander; false insinuation.

as·phalt /ásfalt/ • n. 1 dark bituminous pitch occurring naturally or made from petroleum. 2 mixture of this with sand, gravel, etc., for surfacing roads, etc. • v.tr. surface with asphalt. □□ **as'phalt·er** n. **as·phal'tic** /–fáltik/ adj.

as·pho·del /ásfədel/ n. plant of the lily family.

as·phyx·i·ate /asfikseeayt/ v.tr. suffocate. □□ **as·phyx·i·a·tion** /–áyshən/ n. **as·phyx'i·a·tor** n.

as·pic /áspik/ n. savory meat jelly used as a garnish or to contain meat, eggs, etc.

as·pi·rant /áspirənt, əspírənt/ • adj. aspiring. • n. person who aspires.

as·pi·rate /áspirət/ • adj. pronounced with an exhalation of breath with the sound of h. • n. 1 consonant pronounced in this way. 2 sound of h. • v. also /áspirayt/ **1 a** tr. pronounce with a breath. **b** intr. make the sound of h. 2 tr. draw (fluid) by suction from a vessel or cavity. 3 tr. draw (air, fluid, etc.) into the lungs, as by breathing.

as·pi·ra·tion /áspiráyshən/ n. 1 strong desire; ambition. 2 drawing breath. 3 aspirating.

as·pi·ra·tor /áspiraytər/ n. apparatus for aspirating fluid.

as·pire /əspír/ v.intr. have ambition or strong desire.

as·pi·rin /ásprin/ n. (pl. same or **as·pi·rins**) 1 white powder, acetylsalicylic acid, used to relieve pain and reduce fever. 2 tablet of this.

ass /as/ n. 1 **a** four-legged long-eared mammal related to the horse. **b** donkey. 2 stupid person.

as·sail /əsáyl/ v.tr. attack physically or verbally. □□ **as·sail'a·ble** adj. **as·sail'ant** n.

as·sas·sin /əsásin/ n. killer, esp. of a political or religious leader.

as·sas·si·nate /əsásinayt/ v.tr. kill for political or religious motives. □□ **as·sas·si·na'tion** /–náyshən/ n. **as·sas'si·na·tor** n.

as·sault /əsáwlt/ • n. 1 violent physical or verbal attack. 2 **a** Law act that threatens physical harm. **b** euphem. rape. • v.tr. 1 make an assault on. 2 euphem. rape. □□ **as·sault'er** n.

as·say /əsáy, ásay/ • n. testing of a metal or ore to determine its ingredients and quality. • v. make an assay of (a metal or ore). □□ **as·say'er** n.

as·sem·blage /əsémblij/ n. 1 bringing or coming together. 2 assembled group. 3 work of art made by grouping found or unrelated objects.

as·sem·ble /əsémbəl/ v. 1 tr. & intr. gather together; collect. 2 tr. arrange in order. 3 tr. esp. Mech. fit together the parts of. □□ **as·sem'bler** n.

as·sem·bly /əsémblee/ n. (pl. **–blies**) 1 assembling. 2 **a** group of persons gathered together, esp. as a deliberative body. **b** gathering of the entire membership of a school. 3 assembling of a machine or structure or its parts.

as·sent /əsént/ • v.intr. (usu. foll. by to) 1 express agreement. 2 consent. • n. 1 mental or inward acceptance or agreement. 2 consent or sanction, esp. official. □□ **as·sen'tor** n. (also **as·sent'er**).

as·sert /əsért/ v. 1 tr. declare; state clearly. 2 refl. insist on one's rights. 3 tr. vindicate a claim to. □□ **as·ser'tor** n.

as·ser·tion /əsérshən/ n. 1 declaration; forthright statement. 2 act or instance of asserting.

as·ser·tive /əsértiv/ adj. tending to assert oneself; forthright. □□ **as·ser'tive·ly** adv. **as·ser'tive·ness** n.

as·sess /əsés/ v.tr. 1 estimate the size or quality of. 2 estimate the value of (a property) for taxation. □□ **as·sess'a·ble** adj. **as·sess'ment** n. **as·ses'sor** n.

as·set /áset/ n. 1 **a** useful or valuable quality. **b** person or thing possessing such a quality. 2 property and possessions.

as·sev·er·ate /əsévərayt/ v.tr. declare solemnly. □□ **as·sev·er·a'tion** /–ráyshən/ n. **as·sev·er·a·tive** /–rətiv/ adj.

as·sid·u·ous /əsíjooəs/ adj. 1 persevering; hardworking. 2 attending closely. □□ **as·sid'u·ous·ly** adv. **as·sid'u·ous·ness** n.

as·sign /əsín/ • *v.tr.* **1 a** allot as a share or responsibility. **b** appoint to a position, task, etc. **2** fix (a time, place, etc.) for a specific purpose. **3** ascribe or refer to. • *n.* person to whom property or rights are legally transferred. □□ **as·sign′a·ble** *adj.* **as·sign′er** *n.*

as·sig·na·tion /ásignáyshən/ *n.* appointment to meet, esp. in secret.

as·sign·ee /ásínée/ *n.* *Law* person assigned a property, duty, etc.

as·sign·ment /əsínmənt/ *n.* **1** task or mission. **2** assigning or being assigned.

as·sim·i·late /əsímilayt/ *v.* **1** *tr.* **a** absorb and digest (food, etc.) into the body. **b** absorb (information, etc.) into the mind. **2** *tr.* make like; cause to resemble. **3** *intr.* be absorbed into the body, mind, or a larger group. □□ **as·sim·i·la·tion** /–láyshən/ *n.* **as·sim′i·la·tive** *adj.* **as·sim′i·la·tor** *n.*

as·sist /əsíst/ • *v.tr.* help. • *n.* act of helping. □□ **as·sis′tance** *n.* **as·sist′er** *n.*

as·sis·tant /əsístənt/ *n.* **1** helper. **2** person who assists, esp. as a subordinate.

assn. *abbr.* association.

Assoc. *abbr.* (as part of a title) Association.

as·so·ci·ate • *v.* /əsósheeayt, –see–/ **1** *tr.* connect in the mind. **2** *tr.* join or combine. **3** *refl.* declare oneself in agreement (*want to associate ourselves with the plan*). **4** *intr.* combine for a common purpose. **5** *intr.* meet frequently or have dealings. • *n.* /əsósheeət, –see–/ **1** business partner or colleague. **2** friend or companion. **3** subordinate member of a body, institute, etc. • *adj.* /əsóshiət, əsósee–/ **1** joined or allied. **2** of less than full status. □□ **as·so′ci·ate·ship** *n.* **as·so·ci·a·tive** /əsósheeətiv, –see–/ *adj.*

as·so·ci·a·tion /əsósseeáyshən/ *n.* **1** group organized for a joint purpose; society. **2** associating. **3** fellowship. **4** mental connection between ideas.

as·so·nance /ásənəns/ *n.* resemblance of sound (often of vowels) between two syllables in nearby words, e.g., *saw, caught; cold, culled.* □□ **as′so·nant** *adj.* **as·so·nate** /–nayt/ *v.intr.*

as·sort /əsáwrt/ *v.* **1** *tr.* classify or arrange in groups. **2** *intr.* suit; harmonize with.

as·sort·ed /əsáwrtid/ *adj.* **1** of various kinds put together. **2** sorted into groups. **3** matched.

as·sort·ment /əsáwrtmənt/ *n.* diverse group or mixture.

Asst. *abbr.* Assistant.

as·suage /əswáyj/ *v.tr.* **1** calm or soothe. **2** appease (an appetite). □□ **as·suage′ment** *n.* **as·suag′er** *n.*

as·sume /əsóóm/ *v.tr.* **1** take or accept as being true. **2** simulate or pretend (ignorance, etc.). **3** undertake (an office or duty). **4** take or put on (an aspect, attribute, etc.). □□ **as·sum′a·ble** *adj.* **as·sum′ed·ly** *adv.*

as·sumed /əsóómd/ *adj.* **1** false; adopted. **2** supposed; accepted.

as·sum·ing /əsóóming/ *adj.* arrogant; presumptuous.

as·sump·tion /əsúmpshən/ *n.* **1** assuming. **2** accepting without proof. **3** arrogance. **4** (**Assumption**) reception of the Virgin Mary bodily into heaven.

as·sur·ance /əshóórəns/ *n.* **1** positive declaration. **2** solemn promise or guarantee. **3** certainty. **4 a** self-confidence. **b** impudence.

as·sure /əshóór/ *v.tr.* **1 a** convince. **b** confirm confidently. **2 a** make certain of. **b** make safe (against overthrow, etc.). **3** (as **assured** *adj.*) **a** guaranteed. **b** self-confident. □□ **as·sur′a·ble** *adj.* **as·sur′er** *n.* ¶ See note at INSURE.

as·ta·tine /ástəteen, –tin/ *n.* *Chem.* radioactive element. ¶ Symb.: **At.**

as·ter /ástər/ *n.* plant with bright daisylike flowers.

as·ter·isk /ástərisk/ • *n.* symbol (*) used in printing and writing to mark words, etc., for reference, to stand for omitted matter, etc. • *v.tr.* mark with an asterisk. ¶ Avoid pronouncing this word "as-tuhr-riks," many regard this as uneducated.

a·stern /əstə́rn/ *adv.* *Naut.* & *Aeron.* **1** aft; away to the rear. **2** backward.

as·ter·oid /ástəroyd/ *n.* any of the small celestial bodies revolving around the sun, mainly between the orbits of Mars and Jupiter. □□ **as·ter·oi′dal** /ástəróyd′l/ *adj.*

asth·ma /ázmə, ás–/ *n.* usu. allergic respiratory disorder, often with paroxysms of difficult breathing. □□ **asth·mat·ic** /azmátik, as–/ *adj.* & *n.*

a·stig·ma·tism /əstígmətizəm/ *n.* defect in the eye or lens resulting in distorted images. □□ **as·tig·mat·ic** /ástigmátik/ *adj.*

a·stir /əstə́r/ *predic.adj.* & *adv.* **1** in motion. **2** out of bed.

as·ton·ish /əstónish/ *v.tr.* amaze; surprise greatly. □□ **as·ton′ish·ing** *adj.* **ast·on′ish·ing·ly** *adv.* **as·ton′ish·ment** *n.*

as·tound /əstównd/ *v.tr.* shock with alarm or surprise; amaze. □□ **as·tound′ing** *adj.* **as·tound′ing·ly** *adv.*

a·strad·dle /əstrád′l/ *adv.* & *predic.adj.* in a straddling position.

as·tra·khan /ástrəkán/ *n.* dark curly fleece of young lambs from Astrakhan.

as·tral /ástrəl/ *adj.* **1** of the stars. **2** starry.

a·stray /əstráy/ *adv.* & *predic. adj.* **1** in or into error or sin (esp. lead astray). **2** out of the right way.

a·stride /əstríd/ • *adv.* **1** with a leg on each side. **2** with legs apart. • *prep.* with a leg on each side of; extending across.

as·trin·gent /əstrínjənt/ • *adj.* **1** causing the contraction of body tissues. **2** checking bleeding. **3** severe; austere. • *n.* astringent substance or drug. □□ **as·trin·gen·cy** /–jənsee/ *n.* **as·trin′gent·ly** *adv.*

astro- /ástrō/ *comb. form* **1** relating to the stars or celestial bodies. **2** relating to outer space.

as·tro·labe /ástrəlayb/ *n.* instrument formerly used to measure the altitudes of celestial bodies.

as·trol·o·gy /əstróləjee/ *n.* study of the movements and relative positions of celestial bodies interpreted as an influence on human affairs. □□ **as·trol′o·ger** *n.* **as·tro·log·i·cal** /ástrəlójikəl/ *adj.* **as·trol′o·gist** *n.*

as·tro·naut /ástrənawt/ *n.* person trained to travel in a spacecraft. □□ **as·tro·nau′ti·cal** *adj.* **as·tro·nau′tics** *n.*

as·tro·nom·i·cal /ástrənómikəl/ *adj.* (also **as·tro·nom′ic**) **1** of astronomy. **2** extremely large. □ **astronomical unit** unit of measurement equal to the mean distance from the center of the earth to the center of the sun, 1.496 x 10^{11} meters or 92.9 million miles. □□ **as·tro·nom′i·cal·ly** *adv.*

as·tron·o·my /əstrónəmee/ *n.* scientific study of celestial bodies. □□ **as·tron′o·mer** *n.*

as·tro·phys·ics /ástrōfíziks/ *n.* branch of astronomy concerned with the physics and chemistry of celestial bodies. □□ **as·tro·phys′i·cal** *adj.* **as·tro·phys′i·cist** /–zisist/ *n.*

as·tute /əstōot, əstyōot/ *adj.* **1** shrewd; sagacious. **2** crafty. □□ **as·tute′ly** *adv.* **as·tute′ness** *n.*

a·sun·der /əsúndər/ *adv. literary* apart.

a·sy·lum /əsíləm/ *n.* **1** sanctuary; protection, esp. for those pursued by the law. **2** *hist.* institution for the mentally ill or destitute.

a·sym·me·try /aysímitree/ *n.* lack of symmetry. □□ **a·sym·met·ric** /–métrik/ *adj.* **a·sym·met′ri·cal** *adj.* **a·sym·met′ri·cal·ly** *adv.*

At *symb. Chem.* astatine.

at /at, *unstressed* ət/ *prep.* **1** expressing position (*at the corner*). **2** expressing a time (*at dawn*). **3** expressing a point in a scale (*at his best*). **4** expressing engagement in a state or activity (*at war*). **5** expressing a value or rate (*sell at $10 each*). **6 a** with or with reference to (*at a disadvantage; annoyed at losing*). **b** by means of (*starts at a touch*). **7** expressing: **a** motion toward (*arrived at the station*). **b** aim toward or pursuit of (*aim at the target; work at a solution*).

at·a·vism /átəvizəm/ *n.* **1** resemblance to remote ancestors rather than to parents in plants or animals. **2** reversion to an earlier type. □□ **at·a·vis′tic** *adj.* **at·a·vis′ti·cal·ly** *adv.*

at·ax·i·a /ətákseeə/ *n.* (also **a·tax·y** /–see/) *Med.* loss of full control of bodily movements. □□ **a·tax′ic** *adj.*

ate *past of* EAT.

-ate¹ /ət, ayt/ *suffix* **1** forming nouns denoting status or office (*doctorate; episcopate*). **2** forming nouns denoting state or function (*curate; mandate*).

-ate² /ayt/ *suffix* forming verbs (*associate; duplicate; hyphenate*).

a·te·lier /átəlyáy/ *n.* workshop or artist's studio.

a·the·ism /áytheeizəm/ *n.* belief that God does not exist. □□ **a′the·ist** *n.* **a·the·is′tic** *adj.* **a·the·is′ti·cal** *adj.*

ath·er·o·scle·ro·sis /áthərōsklərósis/ *n.* degeneration of the arteries because of a buildup of fatty deposits. □□ **ath·er·o·scle·rot·ic** /–rótik/ *adj.*

ath·lete /áthleet/ *n.* skilled performer in sports and physical activities. □ **athlete's foot** fungal foot condition.

ath·let·ic /athlétik/ *adj.* **1** of athletes or athletics. **2** muscular or physically powerful. □□ **ath·let′i·cal·ly** *adv.* **ath·let·i·cism** /–tisizəm/ *n.*

ath·let·ics /athlétiks/ *n.pl.* (usu. treated as *sing.*) **1** physical exercises, games, sports, etc. **2** practice of these.

-atic /átik/ *suffix* forming adjectives and nouns (*aquatic; fanatic; idiomatic*).

-ation /áyshən/ *suffix* **1** forming nouns denoting an action or an instance of it (*alteration*). **2** forming nouns denoting a result or product of action (*plantation; starvation*) (see also –FICATION).

-ative /ətiv, aytiv/ *suffix* forming adjectives denoting a characteristic or propensity (*authoritative; imitative; talkative*).

At·lan·tic /ətlántik/ • *n.* ocean separating the Americas from Europe and Africa. • *adj.* of or adjoining the Atlantic.

at·las /átləs/ *n.* book of maps or charts.

ATM *abbr.* automatic teller machine.

at·mo·sphere /átməsfeer/ *n.* **1 a** gases surrounding the earth, any other planet, or any substance. **b** air in any particular place. **2 a** pervading tone or mood of a place or situation. **b** feelings or emotions evoked by a work of art, a piece of music, etc. **3** *Physics* unit of pressure equal to mean atmospheric pressure at sea level, 101,325 pascals or 14.7 pounds per square inch. ¶ Abbr.: **atm.** □□ **at·mos·pher·ic** /–férik, –feér–/ *adj.* **at·mos·pher′i·cal** *adj.* **at·mos·pher′i·cal·ly** *adv.*

a·tom·ic /ətómik/ *adj.* **1** concerned with or using atomic energy or atomic bombs. **2** of atoms. □ **atomic bomb** = *atom bomb.* **atomic energy** nuclear energy. **atomic number** number of protons in the nucleus of an atom. **atomic weight** ratio of the average mass of one atom of an element to one twelfth of the mass of an atom of carbon-12. □□ **a·tom′i·cal·ly** *adv.*

at·om·ize /átəmíz/ *v.tr.* reduce to atoms or fine particles. □□ **at·om·i·za′tion** *n.*

at·om·iz·er /átəmīzər/ *n.* instrument for emitting liquids as a fine spray.

a·ton·al /áytón′l/ *adj. Mus.* not written in any key or mode. □□ **a·to·nal·i·ty** /–nálitee/ *n.*

a·tone /ətón/ *v.intr.* make amends.

a·tone·ment /ətónmənt/ *n.* **1** expiation; reparation for a wrong.

-ator /áytər/ *suffix* forming agent nouns, usu. from Latin words (sometimes via French) (*agitator; creator; escalator*). See also –OR¹.

-atory /ətáwree/ *suffix* forming adjectives meaning 'relating to or involving (a verbal action)' (*amatory; explanatory; predatory*). See also –ORY².

a·tri·um /áytreeəm/ *n.* (*pl.* **a·tri·ums** or **a·tri·a** /–treeə/) **1 a** central court of an ancient Roman house. **b** usu. skylit central court rising through several stories. **c** (in a modern house) central hall or courtyard with rooms opening off it. **2** *Anat.* one of the two upper cavities of the heart. □□ **a′tri·al** *adj.*

a·tro·cious /ətróshəs/ *adj.* **1** very bad or unpleasant. **2** extremely savage or wicked. □□ **a·tro′cious·ly** *adv.*

a·troc·i·ty /ətrósitee/ *n.* (*pl.* **–ties**) **1** extremely evil or cruel act. **2** extreme wickedness.

at·ro·phy /átrəfee/ • *v.* (**–phies, –phied**) **1** *intr.* waste away through lack of use; become emaciated. **2** *tr.* cause to atrophy. • *n.* process of atrophying; emaciation.

at·ro·pine /átrəpeen, –pin/ *n.* poisonous alkaloid in deadly nightshade.

at·tach /ətách/ *v.* **1** *tr.* fasten; affix; join. **2** *tr.* (in *passive*; foll. by *to*) be very fond of or devoted to. **3** *tr.* attribute; assign. **4** *a tr.* include. **b** *intr.* (foll. by *to*) be an attribute or characteristic. **5** *refl.* (usu. foll. by *to*) (of a thing) adhere; (of a person) join. **6** *tr. Law* seize by legal authority. □□ **at·tach′a·ble** *adj.* **at·tach′er** *n.*

at·ta·ché /atasháy/ *n.* person appointed to an ambassador's staff, usu. with a special sphere of activity. □ **attaché case** small flat rectangular case for carrying documents, etc.

at·tach·ment /ətáchmənt/ n. **1** thing attached, esp. for a special function. **2** affection; devotion. **3** means of attaching. **4** attaching or being attached. **5** legal seizure.

at·tack /əták/ • v.tr. **1** act against with (esp. armed) force. **2** seek to hurt or defeat. **3** criticize adversely. **4** act harmfully upon. **5** vigorously apply oneself to. • n. **1** act of attacking. **2** a offensive operation. **b** severe criticism. **3** sudden occurrence of an illness. □□ **at·tack′er** n.

at·tain /ətáyn/ v. **1** tr. reach (a goal, etc.). **2** tr. gain; accomplish. **3** intr. arrive at. □□ **at·tain′a·ble** adj. **at·tain·a·bil′i·ty** n. **at·tain′ment** n.

at·tar /átaar/ n. (also **ot·to** /ótō/) fragrant essential oil, esp. from rose petals.

at·tempt /ətémpt/ • v.tr. seek to achieve, complete, or master. • n. attempting; endeavor. □□ **at·tempt′a·ble** adj.

at·tend /əténd/ v. **1** tr. **a** be present at. **b** go regularly to. **2** intr. **a** be present. **b** wait on. **3** tr. escort. **4** intr. **a** turn or apply one's mind. **b** deal with. □□ **at·tend′er** n.

at·tend·ance /əténdəns/ n. **1** attending or being present. **2** number present.

at·tend·ant /əténdənt/ • n. person employed to wait on others or provide a service. • adj. **1** accompanying. **2** waiting on; serving.

at·tend·ee /áténdée/ n. person who attends.

at·ten·tion /əténshən/ n. **1** act or faculty of applying one's mind. **2 a** consideration. **b** care. **3** (in pl.) **a** ceremonious politeness. **b** wooing; courting. **4** Mil. erect stance.

at·ten·tive /əténtiv/ adj. **1** concentrating; paying attention. **2** assiduously polite. □□ **at·ten′tive·ly** adv. **at·ten′tive·ness** n.

at·ten·u·ate • v.tr. /ətényōoayt/ **1** make thin. **2** reduce in force, value, etc. • adj. /ətényōoət/ **1** slender. **2** tapering gradually. □□ **at·ten′u·at·ed** adj. **at·ten·u·a′tion** /-áyshən/ n. **at·ten′u·a·tor** n.

at·test /ətést/ v. **1** tr. certify the validity of. **2** intr. (foll. by to) bear witness to. □□ **at·test′a·ble** adj. **at·tes·ta′tion** n. **at·tes′tor** n.

At·tic /átik/ • adj. of ancient Athens or Attica, or the form of Greek spoken there. • n. form of Greek used by the ancient Athenians.

at·tic /átik/ n. uppermost story in a house, usu. under the roof.

at·tire /ətír/ formal • v.tr. dress. • n. clothes.

at·ti·tude /átitōod, -tyōod/ n. **1 a** opinion or way of thinking. **b** behavior reflecting this. **2 a** bodily posture. **b** pose. **3** position of an aircraft, spacecraft, etc., in relation to specified directions. □□ **at·ti·tu′di·nal** /-tōod′nəl, -tyōod-/ adj.

at·ti·tu·di·nize /átitōod′nīz, -tyōod-/ v.intr. adopt affected attitudes.

at·tor·ney /ətɔ́rnee/ n. (pl. **-neys**) **1** person, esp. a lawyer, appointed to act for another in business or legal matters. **2** lawyer. □□ **attorney general** chief legal officer in the US and some other countries.

at·tract /ətrákt/ v.tr. **1** draw or bring to oneself or itself. **2** be attractive to; fascinate. □□ **at·tract′a·ble** adj. **at·trac′tor** n.

at·trac·tion /ətrákshən/ n. **1 a** attracting or being attracted. **b** person or thing that attracts. **2** Physics the force by which bodies attract or approach each other (opp. REPULSION).

at·trac·tive /ətráktiv/ adj. **1** attracting. **2** aesthetically pleasing. □□ **at·trac′tive·ly** adv. **at·trac′tive·ness** n.

at·tri·bute • v.tr. /ətríbyōot/ **1** regard as belonging or appropriate. **2** ascribe to a cause. • n. /átribyōot/ **1** characteristic quality ascribed to a person or thing. **2** material object recognized as appropriate to a person, office, or status. □□ **at·trib′ut·a·ble** adj. **at·tri·bu′tion** n.

at·trib·u·tive /ətríbyətiv/ adj. Gram. (of an adjective or noun) preceding the word described, as old in the old dog (opp. PREDICATIVE). □□ **at·trib′u·tive·ly** adv.

at·tri·tion /ətríshən/ n. **1 a** gradual wearing out, esp. by friction. **b** abrasion. **2** gradual reduction, as by retirement, etc., in a work force. □□ **at·tri′tion·al** adj.

at·tune /ətōon, ətyōon/ v.tr. **1** adjust to a situation. **2** bring (an orchestra, instrument, etc.) into musical accord.

atty. abbr. attorney.

ATV abbr. all-terrain vehicle.

a·typ·i·cal /áytípikəl/ adj. not typical. □□ **a·typ′i·cal·ly** adv.

Au symb. Chem. gold.

au·burn /áwbərn/ adj. reddish brown (usu. of a person's hair).

---

auburn late Middle English: from Old French *auborne, alborne*, from Latin *alburnus* 'whitish,' from *albus* 'white.' The original sense was 'yellowish white,' but the word became associated with brown because in the 16th and 17th centuries it was often written *abrune* or *abroun*.

---

auc·tion /áwkshən/ • n. sale in which articles are sold to the highest bidder. • v.tr. sell at auction.

auc·tion·eer /áwkshəneér/ n. person who conducts auctions professionally. □□ **auc·tion·eer′ing** n.

au·da·cious /awdáyshəs/ adj. **1** daring; bold. **2** impudent. □□ **au·da′cious·ly** adv. **au·da′cious·ness** n. **au·dac·i·ty** /awdásitee/ n.

au·di·ble /áwdibəl/ adj. capable of being heard. □□ **au·di·bil′i·ty** n. **au′di·ble·ness** n. **au′di·bly** adv.

au·di·ence /áwdeeəns/ n. **1 a** assembled listeners or spectators at an event, esp. a stage performance, concert, etc. **b** people addressed by a movie, book, play, etc. **2** formal interview with a person in authority.

au·di·o /áwdeeō/ n. sound or its reproduction. □ **audio frequency** frequency perceivable by the human ear.

au·di·o·phile /áwdeeōfīl/ n. high-fidelity sound enthusiast.

au·di·o·vi·su·al /áwdeeōvízhyōoəl/ adj. (esp. of teaching methods) using both sight and sound.

au·dit /áwdit/ • n. official examination of accounts. • v.tr. **1** conduct an audit of. **2** attend (a college-level class) for no credit.

au·di·tion /awdíshən/ • n. test for a performer's ability or suitability. • v. assess or be assessed at an audition.

au·di·tor /áwditər/ n. **1** person who audits accounts. **2** person who audits a class.

au·di·to·ri·um /áwditáwreeəm/ n. (pl. **au·di·to·ri·ums** or **au·di·to·ri·a** /-reeə/) **1** large room or building for meetings, etc. **2** part of a theater, etc., in which the audience sits.

au·di·to·ry /áwditawree/ *adj.* concerned with hearing.

au fait /ō fáy/ *adj.* conversant.

Aug. *abbr.* August.

au·ger /áwgər/ *n.* tool resembling a large corkscrew, for boring holes in wood, the ground, etc.

aught[1] /awt/ *n.* (also **ought**) *archaic* anything.

aught[2] /awt/ *n.* (also **ought**) *colloq.* zero.

aug·ment /awgmént/ *v.* **1** make or become greater; increase. **2** add to; supplement. □□ **aug·men·ta′tion** *n.* **aug·men′ta·tive** *adj.* **aug′ment′er** *n.*

au gra·tin /ō gratáN/ *adj. Cookery* cooked with a crisp brown crust, usu. of bread crumbs or melted cheese.

au·gur /áwgər/ • *v.intr.* **1** (of an event, circumstance, etc.) suggest a specified outcome (usu. *augur well* or *ill*). **2** portend; bode. • *n.* ancient Roman religious soothsayer.

au·gu·ry /áwgyəree/ *n.* (*pl.* **–ries**) **1** omen; portent. **2** interpretation of omens; prophecy. □□ **au′gu·ral** *adj.*

Au·gust /áwgəst/ *n.* eighth month of the year.

au·gust /awgúst/ *adj.* inspiring reverence and admiration; venerable; impressive. □□ **au·gust′ly** *adv.* **au·gust′ness** *n.*

Au·gus·tan /awgústən/ *adj.* of the reign of the Roman emperor Augustus, esp. as an outstanding period of Latin literature.

auk /awk/ *n.* black and white diving bird, e.g., the puffin and razorbill.

auld lang syne /áwld lang zīn, sín/ *n.* times long past.

aunt /ant, aant/ *n.* **1** sister of one's father or mother. **2** uncle's wife. **3** *colloq.* unrelated woman friend of a child or children.

au pair /ō páir/ *n.* young foreign person who helps with child care, housework, etc., in exchange for room and board.

au·ra /áwrə/ *n.* (*pl.* **au·rae** /–ree/ or **au·ras**) **1** distinctive atmosphere. **2** subtle emanation or aroma.

au·ral /áwrəl/ *adj.* of the ear; or hearing. □□ **au′ral·ly** *adv.*

au·re·ole /áwreeōl/ *n.* (also **au·re·o·la** /awréeə-lə/) **1** halo, esp. around the head in a religious painting. **2** corona around the sun or moon.

au re·voir /ō rəvwaár/ *int. & n.* good-bye (until we meet again).

au·ri·cle /áwrikəl/ *n. Anat.* **1 a** small muscular pouch on the surface of each atrium of the heart. **b** the atrium itself. **2** external ear of animals. Also called **pinna.**

au·ro·ra /awráwrə/ *n.* (*pl.* **au·ro·ras** or **au·ro·rae** /–ree/) luminous phenomenon, usu. of streamers of light in the night sky above the northern or southern magnetic pole. □ **aurora australis** /awstráylis/ southern occurrence of aurora. **aurora borealis** /báwree-ális/ northern occurrence of aurora.

aus·cul·ta·tion /áwskəltáyshən/ *n.* listening, esp. to sounds from the heart, lungs, etc., as a part of medical diagnosis.

aus·pice /áwspis/ *n.* **1** (in *pl.*) patronage. **2** forecast.

aus·pi·cious /awspíshəs/ *adj.* of good omen; favorable. □□ **aus·pi′cious·ly** *adv.* **aus·pi′cious·ness** *n.*

Aus·sie /áwsee, –zee/ (also **Os·sie, Oz·zie**) *colloq.* • *n.* **1** an Australian. **2** Australia. • *adj.* Australian.

aus·tere /awsteér/ *adj.* (**aus·ter·er, aus·ter·est**) **1** severely simple. **2** morally strict. **3** harsh; stern. □□ **aus·tere′ly** *adv.*

aus·ter·i·ty /awstéritee/ *n.* (*pl.* **–ties**) **1** sternness; moral severity. **2** severe simplicity, e.g., of economies. **3** (esp. in *pl.*) austere practice (*the austerities of a monk's life*).

Aus·tral·i·an /awstráylyən/ • *n.* **1** native or inhabitant of Australia. **2** person of Australian descent. **3** any of the aboriginal languages of Australia. • *adj.* of or relating to Australia. □□ **Aus·tral′ian·ism** *n.*

auth. *abbr.* **1** authentic. **2** author. **3** authority. **4** authorized.

au·then·tic /awthéntik/ *adj.* **1** of undisputed origin; genuine. **2** reliable or trustworthy. □□ **au·then′ti·cal·ly** *adv.* **au·then·tic·i·ty** /–tísitee/ *n.*

au·then·ti·cate /awthéntikayt/ *v.tr.* **1** establish the truth or genuineness of. **2** validate. □□ **au·then·ti·ca·tion** /–káyshən/ *n.* **au·then′ti·ca·tor** *n.*

au·thor /áwthər/ • *n.* (*fem.* **au·thor·ess** /áwthris, áwthrés/) **1** writer, esp. of books. **2** originator of an event, condition, etc. • *v.tr.* be the author of (a book, the universe, a child, etc.). □□ **au·tho·ri·al** /awtháwriəl/ *adj.* **au′thor·ship** *n.*

---

author Middle English (in the sense 'a person who invents or causes something'): from Old French *autor*, from Latin *auctor*, from *augere* 'increase, originate, promote.' The spelling with *th* arose in the 15th cent., and perhaps became established under the influence of *authentic*.

---

au·thor·i·tar·i·an /ətháwritáireeən, əthór–/ • *adj.* **1** favoring or enforcing strict obedience to authority. **2** tyrannical or domineering. • *n.* person favoring absolute obedience to a constituted authority. □□ **au·thor·i·tar′i·an·ism** *n.*

au·thor·i·ta·tive /ətháwritáytiv, əthór–/ *adj.* **1** recognized as true or dependable. **2** (of a person, behavior, etc.) commanding or self-confident. **3** official. □□ **au·thor′i·ta·tive·ly** *adv.* **au·thor′i·ta·tive·ness** *n.*

au·thor·i·ty /ətháwritee, əthór–/ *n.* (*pl.* **–ties**) **1 a** power or right to enforce obedience. **b** delegated power. **2** (esp. *pl.*) person or body having authority. **3 a** influence based on recognized knowledge or expertise. **b** such an influence expressed in a book, etc. **c** expert.

au·thor·ize /áwthəriz/ *v.tr.* **1** sanction. **2 a** give authority. **b** commission (a person or body) (*authorized to trade*). □□ **au·thor·i·za′tion** *n.*

au·tism /áwtizəm/ *n. Psychol.* mental condition, usu. present from childhood, characterized by complete self-absorption and social withdrawal. □□ **au·tis·tic** /awtístik/ *adj.*

au·to /áwtō/ *n.* (*pl.* **–tos**) *colloq.* automobile.

auto- /áwtō/ *comb. form* (usu. **aut-** before a vowel) **1** self (*autism*). **2** one's own (*autobiography*). **3** by oneself or spontaneous (*autosuggestion*). **4** by itself or automatic (*automobile*).

au·to·bi·og·ra·phy /áwtōbīógrəfee/ *n.* (*pl.* **–phies**) **1** written account of one's own life. **2** this as a literary form. □□ **au·to·bi·og′ra·pher** *n.* **au·to·bi·o·graph·ic** /–bíəgráfik/ *adj.* **au·to·bi·o·graph′i·cal** *adj.*

au·to·clave /áwtōklayv/ *n.* sterilizer using steam.

au·toc·ra·cy /awtókrəsee/ n. (pl. –cies) 1 absolute government by one person; tyranny. 2 dictatorship. □□ **au·to·crat** /áwtəkrat/ n. **au·to·crat´ic** adj. **au·to·crat´i·cal·ly** adv.

au·to·da·fé /áwtōdaafáy/ n. (pl. **au·tos-da-fé** /áwtōz–/) 1 judgment of heretics by the Spanish Inquisition. 2 public burning of a heretic.

au·to·di·dact /áwtōdídakt, –dákt/ n. self-taught person. □□ **au·to·di·dac´tic** adj.

au·to·graph /áwtəgraf/ • n. 1 signature, esp. that of a celebrity. 2 manuscript in an author's own handwriting. • v.tr. sign (a photograph, autograph album, etc.).

au·to·im·mune /áwtōimyóon/ adj. Med. (of a disease) caused by antibodies produced against substances naturally present in the body. □□ **au·to·im·mu´ni·ty** n.

au·to·mate /áwtəmayt/ v.tr. convert to or operate by automation. □ **automated teller machine** electronic machine that allows customers to deposit or withdraw funds, etc. ¶ Abbr.: **ATM.**

au·to·mat·ic /áwtəmátik/ • adj. 1 (of a machine, etc.) working by itself, without any direct human intervention. 2 a done spontaneously. b necessary and inevitable. 3 Psychol. performed unconsciously or subconsciously. 4 (of a firearm) able to be loaded and fired continuously. 5 (of a motor vehicle or its transmission) using gears that change automatically. • n. 1 automatic device, esp. a gun or transmission. 2 colloq. vehicle with automatic transmission. □ **automatic pilot** device for keeping an aircraft on a set course. □□ **au·to·mat´i·cal·ly** adv. **au·to·ma·tic·i·ty** /áwtəmətísitee/ n.

au·to·ma·tion /áwtəmáyshən/ n. use of automatic manufacturing equipment.

au·tom·a·tism /awtómətizəm/ n. involuntary, unthinking action.

au·tom·a·ton /awtómətən, –ton/ n. (pl. **au·tom·a·ta** /–tə/ or **au·tom·a·tons**) 1 mechanism with concealed motive power. 2 person who behaves like a robot.

au·to·mo·bile /áwtəməbeel/ n. motor vehicle for road use with an enclosed passenger compartment; car.

au·to·mo·tive /áwtəmótiv/ adj. concerned with motor vehicles.

au·to·nom·ic /áwtənómik/ adj. esp. Physiol. functioning involuntarily. □ **autonomic nervous system** nervous system controlling involuntary bodily functions, e.g., heartbeat.

au·ton·o·mous /awtónəməs/ adj. 1 having self-government. 2 acting independently or having the freedom to do so. □□ **au·ton´o·mous·ly** adv.

au·ton·o·my /awtónəmee/ n. (pl. –mies) 1 self-government. 2 personal freedom. □□ **au·ton´o·mist** n.

au·to·pi·lot /áwtōpīlət/ n. = automatic pilot.

au·top·sy /áwtopsee/ n. (pl. –sies) postmortem examination to determine cause of death, etc.

au·tumn /áwtəm/ n. 1 season between summer and winter. Also called **fall.** 2 time of maturity or incipient decay. □□ **au·tum·nal** /awtúmnəl/ adj. (see also EQUINOX).

aux·il·ia·ry /awgzílyəree/ • adj. 1 (of a person or thing) that gives help. 2 (of services or equipment) subsidiary; additional. • n. (pl. –ries) 1 auxiliary person or thing. 2 Gram.= auxiliary verb. □ **auxiliary verb** Gram. one used in forming

37 autocracy ~ avian

tenses or moods of other verbs, e.g., have in I have seen.

AV abbr. audiovisual (teaching aids, etc.).

a·vail /əváyl/ • v. 1 tr. help; benefit. 2 refl. (foll. by of) profit by; take advantage of. 3 intr. a provide help. b be of use, value, or profit. • n. use; profit (to no avail).

a·vail·a·ble /əváyləbəl/ adj. 1 capable of being used; at one's disposal. 2 within one's reach. 3 (of a person) a free. b able to be contacted. □□ **a·vail·a·bil´i·ty** n. **a·vail´a·bly** adv.

av·a·lanche /ávəlanch/ n. 1 mass of snow and ice tumbling rapidly down a mountain. 2 sudden appearance or arrival of anything in large quantities.

a·vant-garde /avón-gaárd/ • n. pioneers or innovators, esp. in art and literature. • adj. (of ideas, etc.) new; progressive. □□ **a·vant´-gard´ism** n. **a·vant´-gard´ist** n.

av·a·rice /ávəris/ n. extreme greed for money or gain; cupidity. □□ **av·a·ri·cious** /–ríshəs/ adj. **av·a·ri´cious·ly** adv. **av·a·ri´cious·ness** n.

a·vast /əvást/ int. Naut. stop; cease.

av·a·tar /ávətaar/ n. (in Hindu mythology) descent of a deity, etc., to earth in bodily form.

Ave. abbr. Avenue.

a·venge /əvénj/ v.tr. 1 inflict retribution on behalf of. 2 take vengeance for (an injury). □□ **a·veng´er** n.

av·e·nue /ávənōo, –nyōō/ n. 1 broad, often treelined road or street. 2 approach.

a·ver /əvór/ v.tr. (**a·verred, a·ver·ring**) formal assert; affirm; declare.

av·er·age /ávərij, ávrij/ • n. 1 a usual amount, extent, or rate. b ordinary standard. 2 amount obtained by dividing the total of given amounts by the number of amounts in the set. • adj. 1 a usual; typical. b mediocre. 2 estimated by average. • v.tr. 1 amount on average to (sales averaged $1000 a day). 2 do on average. 3 estimate average of. □ **average out** result in an average of. **on** (or **on an**) **average** as an average rate or estimate.
¶ See note at MEAN.

---

average late 15th cent.: from French avarie 'damage to ship or cargo,' earlier 'customs duty,' from Italian avaria, from Arabic 'awār 'damage to goods'; the suffix -age on the pattern of damage. Originally denoting a charge or customs duty payable by the owner of goods to be shipped, the term later denoted the financial liability from goods lost or damaged at sea, and specifically the equitable apportionment of this between the owners of the vessel and the cargo (late 16th cent.); this gave rise to the general sense of the equalizing out of gains and losses by calculating the mean (mid-18th cent.).

---

a·verse /əvórs/ predic.adj. opposed; disinclined.
¶ See note at ADVERSE.

a·ver·sion /əvórzhən, –shən/ n. 1 dislike or unwillingness. 2 object of dislike.

a·vert /əvórt/ v.tr. 1 turn away (one's eyes or thoughts). 2 prevent or ward off (an undesirable occurrence).

avg. abbr. average.

a·vi·an /áyveeən/ adj. of or relating to birds.

a·vi·ar·y /áyvee–eree/ *n.* (*pl.* **–ies**) large enclosure or building for keeping birds.

a·vi·a·tion /áyveeáyshən/ *n.* **1** skill or practice of operating aircraft. **2** aircraft manufacture.

a·vi·a·tor /áyveeaytər/ *n.* (*fem.* **a·vi·a·trix** /áyveeáytriks/) person who pilots an aircraft.

av·id /ávid/ *adj.* eager; greedy. □□ **a·vid·i·ty** /əvíditee/ *n.* **a·vid·ly** *adv.*

a·vi·on·ics /áyveeóniks/ *n.pl.* (treated as *sing.*) electronics as applied to aviation.

av·o·ca·do /ávəkaádō, aávə–/ *n.* (*pl.* **–dos**) **1** pear-shaped fruit with rough leathery skin, smooth flesh, and a large stone. **2** tropical tree bearing this fruit. Also called **alligator pear.**

av·o·ca·tion /ávōkáyshən/ *n.* hobby.

a·void /əvóyd/ *v.tr.* **1** refrain or keep away from. **2** escape; evade. **3** *Law* **a** nullify. **b** quash. □□ **a·void'a·ble** *adj.* **a·void'a·bly** *adv.* **a·void'ance** *n.* **a·void'er** *n.*

av·oir·du·pois /ávərdəpóyz/ *n.* (in full **av'oir·du·pois' weight'**) system of weights based on a pound of 16 ounces or 7,000 grains.

a·vow /əvów/ *v.tr.* admit; confess. □□ **a·vow'al** *n.* **a·vow'ed·ly** *adv.*

a·vun·cu·lar /əvúngkyələr/ *adj.* like or of an uncle; kind and friendly, esp. toward a younger person.

a·wait /əwáyt/ *v.tr.* **1** wait for. **2** be in store for.

a·wake /əwáyk/ ● *v.* (*past* **a·woke** /əwṓk/; *past part.* **a·wok·en** /əwṓkən/) **1** *intr.* **a** cease to sleep. **b** become active. **2** *intr.* (foll. by *to*) become aware of. **3** *tr.* rouse, esp. from sleep. ● *predic.adj.* **1** a not asleep. **b** vigilant. **2** (foll. by *to*) aware of.

a·wak·en /əwáykən/ *v.* = AWAKE *v.*

a·ward /əwáwrd/ ● *v.tr.* **1** give or order to be given as a payment or prize. **2** grant; assign. ● *n.* **1 a** payment, compensation, or prize awarded. **b** the act or process of awarding. **2** judicial decision. □□ **a·ward'er** *n.*

a·ware /əwáir/ *predic.adj.* **1** conscious; having knowledge. **2** well-informed. □□ **a·ware'ness** *n.*

a·wash /əwósh, əwáwsh/ *predic.adj.* **1** level with the surface of water, so that it just washes over. **2** overflowing, abounding.

a·way /əwáy/ ● *adv.* **1** to or at a distance from. **2** toward or into nonexistence. **3** constantly; persistently. **4** without delay. ● *adj.* **1** *Sports* played at an opponent's field, etc. **2** absent or distant. **3** *Baseball* out. ● *n. Sports* away game or win. □ **away with** (as *imper.*) take away.

awe /aw/ ● *n.* reverential fear or wonder. ● *v.tr.* inspire with awe. □ **awe-inspiring** causing awe; magnificent.

a·weigh /əwáy/ *predic.adj. Naut.* (of an anchor) clear of the sea or river bed; hanging.

awe·some /áwsəm/ *adj.* **1** inspiring awe. **2** *colloq.* excellent; superb. □□ **awe'some·ly** *adv.* **awe'some·ness** *n.*

aw·ful /áwfool/ *adj.* **1** *colloq.* **a** unpleasant or horrible. **b** poor in quality. **c** excessive. **2** *poet.* inspiring awe. □□ **aw'ful·ness** *n.*

aw·ful·ly /áwfəlee, –flee/ *adv.* **1** *colloq.* unpleasantly, badly. **2** *colloq.* very.

a·while /əhwíl, əwíl/ *adv.* for a short time.

awk·ward /áwkwərd/ *adj.* **1** difficult to use. **2** clumsy or bungling. **3 a** embarrassed. **b** embarrassing. □□ **awk'ward·ly** *adv.* **awk'ward·ness** *n.*

awl /awl/ *n.* small pointed tool used for piercing holes.

AWL

awn /awn/ *n.* stiff bristle growing from the grain sheath of grasses, or terminating a leaf, etc.

awn·ing /áwning/ *n.* sheet of canvas or similar material stretched on a frame and used as a shelter from the sun or rain.

a·woke *past* of AWAKE.

a·wok·en *past part.* of AWAKE.

AWOL /áywawl/ *abbr.* absent without leave.

a·wry /ərí/ ● *adv.* **1** crookedly or askew. **2** improperly or amiss. ● *predic. adj.* crooked; unsound.

ax /aks/ (also **axe**) ● *n.* **1** chopping tool, usu. of iron with a steel edge at a right angle to a wooden handle. **2** drastic cutting or elimination of expenditure, staff, etc. ● *v.tr.* (**ax·ing**) **1** use an ax. **2** cut (esp. costs or services) drastically. **3** remove or dismiss. □ **an ax to grind** private or selfish purpose to serve.

AX

ax·i·al /ákseeəl/ *adj.* of, forming, or placed around an axis. □□ **ax'i·al·ly** *adv.*

ax·i·om /ákseeəm/ *n.* **1** established or widely accepted principle. **2** esp. *Geom.* self-evident truth. □□ **ax·i·o·mat'ic** *adj.* **ax·i·o·mat'i·cal·ly** *adv.*

ax·is /áksis/ *n.* (*pl.* **ax·es** /–seez/) **1 a** imaginary line about which a body rotates. **b** line that divides a regular figure symmetrically. **2** *Math.* fixed reference line for the measurement of coordinates, etc. **3** (**the Ax·is**) alliance of Germany and Italy during World War II, later also Japan.

ax·le /áksəl/ *n.* spindle on which a wheel is fixed.

ax·o·lotl /áksəlot'l/ *n.* aquatic newtlike salamander from Mexico.

ax·on /ákson/ *n. Anat. & Zool.* long threadlike part of a nerve cell, conducting impulses from the cell body.

a·ya·tol·lah /fətólə/ *n.* Shiite religious leader in Iran.

aye /ī/ (also **ay**) ● *adv. archaic* or *dial.* yes. ●

n. affirmative answer or assent, esp. in voting.

AZ *abbr.* Arizona (in official postal use).

a·za·lea /əzáylyə/ *n.* kind of rhododendron.

az·i·muth /áziməth/ *n.* angular distance from a north or south point of the horizon to the intersection with the horizon of a vertical circle passing through a given celestial body. □□ **az·i·muth·al** /–múthəl/ *adj.*

AZT *n.* drug used against the AIDS virus.

Az·tec /áztek/ • *n.* **1** member of the native people dominant in Mexico before the Spanish conquest of the 16th century. **2** language of the Aztecs. • *adj.* of the Aztecs or their language (see also NAHUATL).

az·ure /ázhər/ • *n.* **1** deep sky-blue color. **2** *poet.* clear sky. • *adj.* of the color azure.

Bb

B¹ /bee/ *n.* (also **b**) (*pl.* **Bs** or **B's**; **b's**) **1** second letter of the alphabet. **2** second class or category (of sizes, academic marks, etc.). **3** *Algebra* (usu. **b**) second known quantity. **4** human blood type. □ **B movie** low-budget movie.

B² *symb.* **1** *Chem.* boron. **2** *Physics* magnetic flux density.

B³ *abbr.* (also **B.**) **1** bachelor. **2** bishop. **3** black (pencil lead). **4** *Baseball* base; baseman.

b *abbr.* (also **b.**) *Physics* barn.

b. *abbr.* **1** born. **2** billion.

BA *abbr.* **1** Bachelor of Arts. **2** *Baseball* batting average.

Ba *symb. Chem.* barium.

baa /baa/ • *v.intr.* (**baas, baaed** or **baa'd**) (esp. of a sheep) bleat. • *n.* (*pl.* **baas**) cry of a sheep or lamb.

bab·ble /bábəl/ • *v.* **1** *intr.* **a** talk inarticulately or incoherently. **b** chatter excessively or irrelevantly. **c** (of a stream, etc.) murmur. **2** *tr.* repeat foolishly; divulge through chatter. • *n.* **1 a** incoherent speech. **b** foolish talk. **2** murmur of voices, water, etc. □□ **bab'bler** *n.*

babe /bayb/ *n.* **1** esp. *literary* baby. **2** innocent or helpless person. **3** sometimes *derog. sl.* young woman.

ba·bel /báybəl, báb-/ *n.* **1** confused noise, esp. of voices. **2** noisy assembly. **3** scene of confusion.

ba·boon /babōn/ *n.* **1** monkey having a long doglike snout, large teeth, and a short tail. **2** ugly or uncouth person.

ba·by /báybee/ • *n.* (*pl.* **-bies**) **1** very young child or infant. **2** childish person (*is a baby about injections*). **3** youngest member of a family, team, etc. **4** young or newly born animal. **5** *sl.* young woman; sweetheart (often as a form of address). **6** *sl.* person or thing regarded with affection or familiarity. • *v.tr.* (**-bies, -bied**) **1** treat like a baby. **2** pamper. □ **baby boom** *colloq.* temporary marked increase in the birthrate. **baby boomer** person born during a baby boom, esp. that following World War II. **baby carriage** four-wheeled carriage for pushing a baby. **baby grand** smallest grand piano. **baby-sit** look after a child while the parents are out. **baby-sitter** person who baby-sits. **baby talk** childish talk used by or to young children. **throw out the baby with the bath water** reject the essential with the inessential. □□ **ba'by·hood** *n.* **ba'by·ish** *adj.*

bac·ca·lau·re·ate /bákəláwreeət/ *n.* **1** college or university bachelor's degree. **2** examination intended to qualify successful candidates for higher education.

bac·cha·nal /bákənál, bákənəl/ • *n.* **1** (also **bac·cha·na·li·a** /bákənáylyə/) wild and drunken revelry. **2** reveler. **3** priest, worshiper, or follower of Bacchus. • *adj.* **1** of or like Bacchus, the Greek or Roman god of wine, or his rites. **2** riotous.

bach·e·lor /báchələr, báchlər/ *n.* **1** unmarried man. **2** man or woman who has taken the degree of Bachelor of Arts or Science, etc. □□ **bach' e·lor·hood** *n.*

ba·cil·lus /bəsíləs/ *n.* (*pl.* **ba·cil·li** /-lī/) **1** any rod-shaped bacterium. **2** (usu. in *pl.*) any pathogenic bacterium.

back /bak/ • *n.* **1 a** rear surface of the human body from shoulders to hips. **b** upper surface of an animal's body. **c** spine. **2 a** any backlike surface, e.g., of the head, a chair, etc. **b** part of a garment that covers the back. **3 a** less active or visible or important part (*write it on the back*). **b** distant part. **4** player or position in some games. • *adv.* **1** to the rear. **2 a** in or into an earlier or normal position or condition (*went back home*). **b** in return (*pay back*). **3** in or into the past (*back in June*). **4** at a distance (*stand back from the road*). **5** in check (*hold him back*). **6** (foll. by *of*) behind. • *v.* **1** *tr.* **a** help with moral or financial support. **b** bet on. **2** *tr. & intr.* move, or cause (a vehicle, etc.) to move, backward. **3** *tr.* **a** put or serve as a back or support to. **b** *Mus.* accompany. **4** *tr.* lie at the back of (*a beach backed by steep cliffs*). • *adj.* **1** situated behind, esp. as remote or subsidiary (*back entrance*). **2** past; not current (*back pay*). **3** reversed (*back flow*). □ **back and forth** to and fro. **back down** withdraw one's claim; concede defeat in an argument. **back off 1** draw back; retreat. **2** abandon one's intention, stand, etc. **back out** withdraw from a commitment. **back talk** *colloq.* rude or impudent response. **back up 1** give (esp. moral) support to. **2** *Computing* copy (a file, disk, etc.). **3** (of running water, etc.) accumulate behind an obstruction. **4** move (a vehicle) backward. **get** (or **put**) **a person's back up** annoy or anger a person. **get off a person's back** stop troubling a person. **go back on** fail to honor (a promise or commitment). **turn one's back on 1** abandon. **2** disregard; ignore. □□ **back'er** *n.* (in sense 1 of *v.*). **back'less** *adj.*

back·ache /bákayk/ *n.* (usu. prolonged) pain in one's back.

back·bite /bákbīt/ *v.tr.* speak badly of. □□ **back'bit·er** *n.*

back·bone /bákbōn/ *n.* **1** spine. **2** main support. **3** firmness of character.

back·break·ing /bákbrayking/ *adj.* extremely hard.

back·date /bákdáyt/ *v.tr.* put an earlier date on (an agreement, etc.) than the actual one.

back·door /bákdáwr/ *adj.* (of an activity) clandestine; underhand (*backdoor deal*).

back·drop /bákdrop/ *n. Theatr.* painted cloth at the back of the stage as a main part of the scenery.

back·fire /bákfīr/ • *v.intr.* **1** undergo a mistimed explosion in the cylinder or exhaust of an internal combustion engine. **2** (of a plan, etc.) fail adversely. • *n.* instance of backfiring.

back·gam·mon /bákgámən/ *n.* board game for two with pieces moved according to throws of the dice.

back·ground /bákgrownd/ *n.* **1** part of a scene

or picture farthest from the observer. **2** inconspicuous or obscure position (esp. as *in the background*). **3** person's education, knowledge, or social circumstances. **4** explanatory or contributory information or circumstances.

back·hand /bák-hand/ *n. Tennis*, etc. **1** stroke played with the back of the hand turned toward the opponent. **2** (*attrib.*) of or made with a backhand (*backhand volley*).

back·hand·ed /bák-hándid/ *adj.* **1** (of a blow, etc.) delivered with the back of the hand. **2** indirect. **3** = BACKHAND *attrib.*

back·ing /báking/ *n.* **1 a** support. **b** body of supporters. **c** material used to form a back or support. **2** musical accompaniment, esp. to a singer; backup.

back·lash /báklash/ *n.* **1** excessive or marked adverse reaction. **2** sudden recoil in a mechanism.

back·log /báklawg, -log/ *n.* **1** accumulation of uncompleted work, etc. **2** reserve; reserves (*backlog of goodwill*).

back·pack /bákpak/ • *n.* bag with shoulder straps for carrying on the back. • *v.intr.* travel or hike with this. □□ **back′pack·er** *n.*

back·ped·al /bákped'l/ *v.* (**-ped·aled, -ped·al·ing**) **1** pedal backward. **2** reverse one's previous action or opinion.

back·rest /bákrest/ *n.* support for the back.

back·seat /bákseet/ *n.* **1** seat in the rear. **2** inferior position or status. □ **backseat driver** person eager to advise without taking or having responsibility.

back·side /báksīd/ *n. colloq.* buttocks.

back·slash /bákslash/ *n.* backward-sloping diagonal line.

back·slide /bákslīd/ *v.intr.* (*past* **-slid** /-slid/; *past part.* **-slid** or **-slid·den** /-slid′n/) relapse into bad ways or error. □□ **back′slid·er** *n.*

back·space /bákspays/ *v.intr.* move a computer cursor, etc., back one or more spaces.

back·spin /bákspin/ *n.* backward spin imparted to a ball.

back·stage /bákstáyj/ • *adv. Theatr.* out of view of the audience. • *adj.* concealed.

back·stairs /bákstairz/ *adj.* (also **back′stair**) underhand; clandestine.

back·stop /bákstaap/ *n. Baseball* fence or screen positioned behind home plate.

back·stroke /bákstrōk/ *n.* swimming stroke performed on the back.

back·track /báktrak/ *v.intr.* **1** retrace one's steps. **2** reverse one's previous action or opinion.

back·up /bákup/ *n.* **1** moral or technical support. **2** reserve. **3** *Computing* security copies of data.

back·ward /bákwərd/ • *adv.* (also **back′wards**) **1** away from one's front. **2 a** with the back foremost. **b** in reverse of the usual way. **3 a** into a worse state. **b** into the past. **c** back toward the starting point. • *adj.* **1** directed to the rear or starting point. **2** reversed. **3 a** mentally retarded or slow. **b** slow to progress. **4** reluctant; shy. □ **bend** (or **fall** or **lean**) **over backward** *colloq.* make every effort, esp. to be fair or helpful. □□ **back′ward·ness** *n.*

back·wash /bákwosh, -wawsh/ *n.* **1** receding waves created by the motion of a ship, etc. **2** repercussions.

back·wa·ter /bákwawtər, -wotər/ *n.* **1** place remote from the center of activity. **2** stagnant water.

back·woods /bákwŏŏdz/ *n.pl.* **1** remote uncleared forest land. **2** any remote or sparsely inhabited region. □□ **back′woods·man** *n.* (*pl.* **-men**)

back·yard /bakya'ard/ *n.* yard at the back of a house, etc. □ **in one's own backyard** *colloq.* near at hand.

ba·con /báykən/ *n.* cured meat from the back or sides of a pig.

bac·te·ri·a *pl.* of BACTERIUM.

bac·te·ri·cide /bakte'erisīd/ *n.* substance capable of destroying bacteria. □□ **bac·te·ri·ci′dal** *adj.*

bac·te·ri·ol·o·gy /bákteereeóləjee/ *n.* the study of bacteria. □□ **bac·te·ri·o·log′i·cal** /-reeəlójikəl/ *adj.* **bac·te·ri·o·log′i·cal·ly** *adv.* **bac·te·ri·ol·o·gist** /-óləjist/ *n.*

bac·te·ri·um /bakte'ereeəm/ *n.* (*pl.* **bac·te·ri·a** /-reeə/) unicellular microorganism lacking an organized nucleus, esp. that can cause disease. □□ **bac·te′ri·al** *adj.*

bad /bad/ • *adj.* (**worse** /wərs/; **worst** /wərst/) **1** inferior; inadequate; defective. **2 a** unpleasant; unwelcome. **b** unsatisfactory; unfortunate. **3** harmful. **4 a** (of food) decayed; putrid. **b** polluted. **5** ill; injured. **6** *colloq.* regretful; guilty. **7** serious; severe. **8** morally unacceptable. **b** disobedient. **9** not valid. **10** (**bad·der, bad·dest**) *sl.* good; excellent. • *n.* **1** ill fortune. **2** ruin. • *adv. colloq.* badly. □ **bad blood** ill feeling. **bad debt** debt that is not recoverable. **bad faith** see FAITH. **bad-mouth** *v.tr.* subject to malicious gossip or criticism. **bad news** *colloq.* unpleasant or troublesome person or thing. **not** (or **not so**) **bad** *colloq.* fairly good. **too bad** *colloq.* regrettable. □□ **bad′ness** *n.*

¶ Confusion in the use of **bad** and **good** vs. **badly** and **well** usually has to do with verbs called copulas, such as **feel** or **seem**: Thus, standard usage calls for *I feel bad* and *I feel well*, but *I feel badly*, to a precise speaker or writer, means 'I do not have a good sense of touch.' See note at GOOD.

bade see BID.

badge /baj/ *n.* **1** distinctive emblem worn as a mark of office, membership, achievement, etc. **2** thing that reveals a condition or quality.

bad·ger /bájər/ • *n.* omnivorous gray-coated nocturnal mammal with a black and white striped head. • *v.tr.* pester; harass; tease.

bad·i·nage /bád′naázh/ *n.* humorous or playful ridicule.

bad·lands /bádlandz/ *n.* extensive barren eroded tracts in arid areas.

bad·ly /bádlee/ *adv.* (**worse** /wərs/; **worst** /wərst/) **1** in a bad manner. **2** *colloq.* very much (*wants it badly*). **3** severely.

bad·min·ton /bádmint′n/ *n.* game with rackets in which a shuttlecock is volleyed back and forth across a net.

bad-tem·pered /bádtémpərd/ *adj.* having a bad temper.

baf·fle /báfəl/ • *v.tr.* **1** confuse. **2** frustrate; hinder. • *n.* device that checks the flow of fluid, gas, sound, etc. □□ **baf′fle·ment** *n.* **baf′fling** *adj.* **baf′fling·ly** *adv.*

bag /bag/ • *n.* **1** receptacle of flexible material with an opening at the top. **2 a** piece of luggage. **b** handbag. **3** (in *pl.*) *colloq.* large amount. **4** amount of game shot or allowed. **5** (usu. in *pl.*) baggy skin under the eyes. **6** *sl.* particular interest. • *v.* (**bagged, bag·ging**) **1** *tr.* put in a bag. **2** *colloq.* *tr.* **a** secure. **b** *colloq.* steal. **c** shoot (game). **3 a** *intr.* hang loosely; bulge. **b** *tr.* cause to do this. **bag lady** homeless woman who carries her possessions in shopping bags. **in the bag** *colloq.* achieved; secured. □□ **bag′ful** *n.* (*pl.* **-fuls**).

bag·a·telle /bágətél/ *n.* mere trifle.

ba·gel /báygəl/ *n.* hard bread roll in the shape of a ring.

bag·gage /bágij/ *n.* luggage.

bag·gy /bágee/ *adj.* (**bag·gi·er, bag·gi·est**) **1** hanging in loose folds. **2** puffed out. □□ **bag′gi·ly** *adv.* **bag′gi·ness** *n.*

bag·pipe /bágpīp/ *n.* (usu. in *pl.*) musical instrument consisting of a windbag connected to reeded pipes. □□ **bag′pip·er** *n.*

BAGPIPES

ba·guette /bagét/ *n.* long narrow French loaf.

bah /baa/ *int.* expression of contempt or disbelief.

bail[1] /bayl/ • *n.* **1** money, etc., required as security for the temporary release of a person in custody pending trial. **2** person(s) giving such security. • *v. tr.* **1** release or secure the release of (a prisoner) on payment of bail. **2** release from a difficulty; rescue. □ **forfeit** (*colloq.* **jump**) **bail** fail to appear for trial after being released on bail. □□ **bail′a·ble** *adj.*

bail[2] /bayl/ *n.* **1** bar on a typewriter holding the paper against the platen. **2** arched usu. wire handle, as of a pail.

bail[3] /bayl/ *v. tr.* scoop water out of (a boat, etc.). □ **bail out 1** parachute from an aircraft. **2** leave or desert a problematic situation. □□ **bail′er** *n.*

bai·liff /báylif/ *n.* official in a court of law who keeps order, looks after prisoners, etc.

bai·li·wick /báyliwik/ *n.* **1** *Law* district or jurisdiction of a bailiff. **2** *joc.* person's sphere of operations or particular area of interest.

bail·out /báylowt/ *n.* a rescue from a dire situation (*a financial bailout for an ailing company*).

bait /bayt/ • *n.* **1** food used to entice a prey, esp. a fish or an animal. **2** allurement. • *v.* **1** *tr.* **a** harass or annoy (a person). **b** torment (a chained animal). **2** *tr.* put bait on (a hook, trap, etc.).

baize /bayz/ *n.* coarse, usu. green woolen material resembling felt used as a covering or lining, esp. on the tops of billiard and card tables.

bake /bayk/ • *v.* **1** *tr.* cook or process (food,

etc.) by dry heat in an oven or on a hot surface, without direct exposure to a flame. **2** *intr.* undergo the process of being baked. • *n.* act or an instance of baking. □ **baked Alaska** sponge cake and ice cream with a meringue covering browned in an oven. **baking powder** mixture of sodium bicarbonate, cream of tartar, etc., used as a leavening agent. **baking soda** sodium bicarbonate. □□ **bak′er** *n.*

bak·er·y /báykəree/ *n.* (*pl.* **-ies**) place where bread and cakes are made or sold.

bak·la·va /baaklavaá/ *n.* rich dessert of flaky pastry, honey, and nuts.

bak·sheesh /bákshéesh/ *n.* gratuity.

bal·a·cla·va /báləklaávə/ *n.* tight covering for the whole head and neck except for the eyes, nostrils, and mouth.

bal·a·lai·ka /báləlíkə/ *n.* guitarlike stringed instrument with a triangular body.

BALALAIKA

bal·ance /báləns/ • *n.* **1** apparatus for weighing, esp. one with a central pivot, beam, and two scales. **2 a** counteracting weight or force. **b** (in full **bal′ance wheel**) regulating device in a clock, etc. **3 a** even distribution of weight or amount. **b** stability of body or mind. **4** decisive weight or amount. **5 a** agreement between or the difference between credits and debits in an account. **b** amount outstanding. **6 a** *Art* harmony and proportion. **b** *Mus.* relative volume of sources of sound. **7** (**the Balance**) zodiacal sign or constellation Libra. • *v.* **1** *tr.* offset or compare (one thing) with another. **2** *tr.* counteract, equal, or neutralize the weight or importance of. **3 a** *tr.* bring into or keep in equilibrium. **b** *intr.* be in equilibrium (*balanced on one leg*). **4** *tr.* make well-proportioned and harmonious. **5 a** *tr.* compare and esp. equalize debits and credits of (an account). **b** *intr.* (of an account) have credits and debits equal. □ **balance of payments** difference in value between payments into and out of a country. **balance of power** situation in which the chief nations of the world have roughly equal power. **balance of trade** difference in value between imports and exports. **balance sheet** statement giving the balance of an account. □□ **bal′anc·er** *n.*

bal·co·ny /bálkənee/ *n.* (*pl.* **-nies**) **1 a** usu. balustraded platform on the outside of a building, with access from an upper floor window or door. **b** such a balustraded platform inside a building; gallery. **2** upper tier of seats in a theater, etc. □□ **bal′co·nied** *adj.*

bald /bawld/ *adj.* **1** with the scalp wholly or partly lacking hair. **2** lacking the usual hair, feathers, leaves, etc. **3** *colloq.* with the surface worn away (*a bald tire*). **4** blunt; unelaborated (*a bald statement*). **5** marked with white, esp. on the face (*a bald horse*). □ **bald eagle** white-headed eagle used as the emblem of the United States. □□ **bald′ing** *adj.* (in senses 1–3). **bald′ish** *adj.* **bald′ly** *adv.* (in sense 4). **bald′ness** *n.*

bal·der·dash /báwldərdash/ *n.* nonsense.

bale /bayl/ • *n.* tightly bound bundle of merchandise or hay. • *v.tr.* make up into bales.

ba·leen /bəleén/ *n.* whalebone.

bale·ful /báylfŏŏl/ *adj.* **1** (esp. of a manner, look, etc.) gloomy; menacing. **2** harmful; malignant; destructive. □□ **bale′ful·ly** *adv.* **bale′ful·ness** *n.*

balk /bawk/ • *v.intr.* **1** refuse to go on. **2** (often foll. by *at*) hesitate. • *n.* **1** hindrance; stumbling block. **2** heavy timber. **3** *Baseball* illegal action made by a pitcher. □□ **balk′er** *n.*

ball[1] /bawl/ • *n.* **1 a** sphere, esp. for use in a game. **b** game played with such a sphere. **2 a** ball-shaped object; material forming the shape of a ball (*ball of snow*). **b** rounded part of the body (*ball of the foot*). **3** solid nonexplosive missile for a cannon, etc. **4** *Baseball* pitched ball that is not swung at by the batter and that does not pass through the strike zone. • *v.* form into a ball. □ **ball-and-socket joint** *Anat.* joint in which a rounded end pivots in a concave socket. **ball bearing 1** bearing in which friction is relieved by a ring of metal balls. **2** one of these balls. **ball cock** floating ball on a hinged arm that controls the water level in a cistern, etc. **ball game 1** game played with a ball, esp. a game of baseball. **2** *colloq.* affair or concern (*a whole new ball game*). **on the ball** *colloq.* alert. **play ball 1** start or continue a ball game. **2** *colloq.* cooperate. **start** (or **get**) **the ball rolling** set an activity in motion; make a start.

ball[2] /bawl/ *n.* **1** formal social gathering for dancing. **2** *sl.* enjoyable time (esp. *have a ball*).

bal·lad /báləd/ *n.* **1** poem or song narrating a popular story. **2** slow sentimental song. □□ **bal·lad·eer′** *n.* **bal′lad·ry** *n.*

---

ballad late 15th century (denoting a light, simple song): from Old French *balade*, from Provençal *balada* 'dance, song to dance to,' from *balar* 'to dance,' from late Latin *ballare*, from Greek *ballizein* 'to dance.' The sense 'narrative poem' dates from the mid-18th century.

---

bal·last /báləst/ • *n.* **1** any heavy material placed in a ship's hold, etc., for stability. **2** coarse stone, etc., used to form the bed of a railroad track or road. • *v.tr.* provide with ballast.

ball·boy /báwlboy/ *n.* (*fem.* **ball·girl** /-gərl/) boy or girl who retrieves balls that go out of play during a game.

bal·le·ri·na /báləreénə/ *n.* female ballet dancer.

bal·let /baláy, bálay/ *n.* **1** dramatic or representational style of dancing to music. **2** particular piece or performance of ballet. □□ **bal·let·ic** /balétik/ *adj.*

bal·lis·tic /bəlístik/ *adj.* **1** of or relating to projectiles. **2** moving under the force of gravity only. □ **ballistic missile** missile that is initially powered and guided but falls under gravity on its target. □□ **bal·lis′ti·cal·ly** *adv.*

bal·lis·tics /bəlístiks/ *n.pl.* (usu. treated as *sing.*) science of projectiles and firearms.

bal·loon /bəlŏŏn/ • *n.* **1** small inflatable rubber pouch with a neck, used as a toy or decoration. **2** large bag inflatable with hot air or gas to make it rise in the air, often carrying a basket for passengers. **3** balloon shape enclosing dialogue in a comic strip or cartoon. • *v.* **1** *intr.* & *tr.* swell out or cause to swell out like a balloon. **2** *intr.* travel by balloon. □□ **bal·loon′ist** *n.*

bal·lot /bálət/ • *n.* **1** process of recorded voting, usu. secret. **2** total of votes recorded in a ballot. **3** paper or ticket, etc., used in voting. • *v.* (**bal·lot·ed, bal·lot·ing**) **1** *intr.* give a vote. **2** *tr.* take a ballot of (*the union balloted its members*). □ **ballot box** sealed box into which voters put completed ballot papers.

ball·park /báwlpaark/ *n.* **1** baseball field. **2** (*attrib.*) *colloq.* approximate. □ **in the** (**right**) **ballpark** *colloq.* approximately correct.

ball·point /báwlpoynt/ *n.* (in full **ball′point·pen′**) pen with a tiny ball as its writing point.

ball·room /báwlrŏŏm, -rŏŏm/ *n.* large room for dancing.

bal·ly·hoo /báleehŏŏ/ *n.* **1** loud noise or fuss; confused state or commotion. **2** extravagant or sensational publicity.

balm /baam/ *n.* aromatic soothing ointment or oil.

balm·y /ba'amee/ *adj.* (**balm·i·er, balm·i·est**) **1** mild; soothing. **2** fragrant. □□ **balm′i·ly** *adv.* **balm′i·ness** *n.*

ba·lo·ney /bəlónee/ *n.* (*pl.* **-neys**) *sl.* **1** nonsense. **2** = BOLOGNA.

bal·sa /báwlsə/ *n.* **1** (in full **bal′sa wood**) tough lightweight wood used for making models, etc. **2** tropical American tree from which it comes.

bal·sam /báwlsəm/ *n.* **1** resin exuded from various trees and shrubs. **2** ointment, esp. containing oil or turpentine. **3** any of various trees or shrubs that yield balsam. □□ **bal·sam·ic** /-sámik/ *adj.*

bal·us·ter /báləstər/ *n.* short post or pillar supporting a rail.

---

baluster early 17th century: from French *balustre*, from Italian *balaustro*, from *balaust(r)a* 'wild pomegranate flower' (via Latin from Greek *balaustion*), so named because part of the pillar resembles the curving calyx tube of the flower.

---

bal·us·trade /báləstráyd/ *n.* railing supported by balusters.

BALUSTRADE

bam·boo /bambóo/ *n.* **1** tropical giant woody grass with hollow jointed stem. **2** its stem used for canes, furniture, etc.

bam·boo·zle /bambóozəl/ *v.tr. colloq.* cheat; hoax; mystify. □□ **bam·boo′zle·ment** *n.* **bam·boo′zler** *n.*

ban /ban/ • *v.tr.* (**banned, ban·ning**) forbid; prohibit, esp. formally. • *n.* formal or authoritative prohibition.

ba·nal /bənál, báynəl, bənáal/ *adj.* trite; feeble; commonplace. □□ **ba·nal·i·ty** /-nálitee/ *n.* (*pl.* **-ties**). **ba′nal·ly** *adv.*

ba·nan·a /bənánə/ *n.* **1** long curved fruit with soft pulpy flesh and yellow skin. **2** treelike plant bearing this. □ **banana republic** *derog.* small nation, esp. in Central America, dependent on one export crop. **go bananas** *sl.* go crazy.

band¹ /band/ • *n.* **1** flat, thin strip or loop of material (e.g., paper, metal, or cloth) put around something esp. to hold or decorate it. **2 a** strip of material forming part of a garment. **b** stripe. **3** a range of frequencies or wavelengths in a spectrum (esp. of radio frequencies). **b** range of values within a series. • *v.tr.* **1** put a band on. □ **band saw** mechanical saw with a blade formed by an endless toothed band.

band² /band/ • *n.* organized group, esp. of nonclassical musicians. • *v.tr* unite (esp. as *band together*).

band·age /bándij/ • *n.* strip of material for binding up a wound, etc. • *v.tr.* bind with a bandage.

Band-Aid /bándayd/ *n.* **1** *propr.* adhesive strip with a gauze pad for covering minor wounds. **2** (**band-aid**) stopgap solution to a problem.

ban·dan·na /bandánə/ *n.* (also **ban·dan′a**) a large patterned handkerchief.

b. & b. *abbr.* (also **B & B**) bed and breakfast.

band·box /bándboks/ *n.* cardboard box to hold hats, collars, etc.

ban·deau /bandó/ *n.* (*pl.* **ban·deaux** /-dōz/) narrow ribbon.

ban·dit /bándit/ *n.* robber; outlaw. □□ **ban′dit·ry** *n.*

ban·do·lier /bándəléeʹr/ *n.* (also **ban·do·leer′**) shoulder belt with loops or pockets for cartridges.

bandolier

BANDOLIER

bands·man /bándzmən/ *n.* (*pl.* **-men**) player in a band.

band·stand /bándstand/ *n.* covered outdoor platform for a band to play on, usu. in a park.

band·wag·on /bándwagən/ *n.* wagon used for carrying a band in a parade, etc. □ **climb** (or **jump**) **on the bandwagon** join a popular or successful cause, etc.

ban·dy¹ /bándee/ *adj.* (**ban·di·er, ban·di·est**) **1** (of the legs) curved so as to be wide apart at the knees. **2** (also **ban′dy-leg·ged** /-légəd, -legd/) (of a person) having bandy legs.

ban·dy² /bándee/ *v.tr.* (**-dies, -died**) **1** pass (a story, rumor, etc.) back and forth. **2** discuss disparagingly. **3** exchange (blows, insults, etc.).

bane /bayn/ *n.* **1** cause of ruin or trouble. **2** ruin; woe. □□ **bane′ful** *adj.* **bane′ful·ly** *adv.*

bang /bang/ • *n.* **1** loud short sound. **2** sharp blow. **3** (esp. in *pl.*) fringe of hair cut straight across the forehead. • *v.* **1** strike or shut noisily. **2** make or cause to make a bang. • *adv.* with a bang.

ban·gle /bánggəl/ *n.* rigid bracelet or anklet.

ban·ish /bánish/ *v.tr.* **1** condemn to exile. **2** dismiss from one's presence or mind. □□ **ban′ish·ment** *n.*

ban·is·ter /bánistər/ *n.* (also **ban′nis·ter**) uprights and handrail at the side of a staircase.

ban·jo /bánjō/ *n.* (*pl.* **-jos** or **-joes**) guitarlike stringed instrument with a circular body. □□ **ban′jo·ist** *n.*

bank¹ /bangk/ • *n.* **1** area of sloping land alongside a river. **2** raised shelf of ground; slope. **3** mass of cloud, fog, snow, etc. • *v.* **1** *tr. & intr.* heap or rise into banks. **2** *tr.* heap up (a fire) tightly so that it burns slowly. **3 a** *intr.* (of a vehicle or aircraft or its occupant) travel with one side higher than the other in rounding a curve. **b** *tr.* cause to do this.

bank² /bangk/ • *n.* **1 a** establishment for depositing, withdrawing, and borrowing money. **b** building in which this business takes place. **2** kitty in some gambling games. **3** storage place. • *v.tr.* deposit (money or valuables) in a bank. □ **bank on** rely on. □□ **bank′a·ble** *adj.*

bank³ /bangk/ *n.* row of similar objects, e.g., lights, switches, oars.

bank·book /bángkbŏŏk/ *n.* = PASSBOOK.

bank·card /bángk-kard/ *n.* bank-issued credit card or automatic teller machine card.

bank·er /bángkər/ *n.* **1** person who manages or owns a bank. **2** keeper of the bank in some gambling games.

bank·ing /bángking/ *n.* business transactions of a bank.

bank·note /bángknōt/ *n.* banker's promissory note, payable on demand.

bank·rupt /bángkrupt/ • *adj.* **1** insolvent; declared in law unable to pay debts. **2** exhausted or drained (of some quality, etc.); deficient; lacking. • *n.* insolvent person. • *v.tr.* make bankrupt. □□ **bank·rupt·cy** /-ruptsee/ *n.* (*pl.* **-cies**).

ban·ner /bánər/ *n.* **1** large sign bearing a slogan or design used esp. in a demonstration or procession. **2** flag. □□ **ban′nered** *adj.*

ban′nis·ter var. of BANISTER.

banns /banz/ *n.pl.* notice in a parish church announcing an intended marriage.

ban·quet /bángkwit/ • *n.* elaborate usu. extensive feast. • *v.* **1** *intr.* hold a banquet; feast. **2** *tr.* entertain with a banquet. □□ **ban′quet·er** *n.*

ban·quette /bangkét/ *n.* upholstered bench along a wall, esp. in a restaurant or bar.

ban·shee /bánshee, -shée/ *n.* female spirit whose wailing warns of a death in a house.

ban·tam /bántəm/ *n.* **1** any of several small breeds of domestic fowl. **2** small but aggressive person.

ban·tam·weight /bántəmwayt/ *n.* **1** weight in certain sports between flyweight and featherweight. **2** athlete of this weight.

ban·ter /bántər/ • *n.* good-humored teasing. • *v.* **1** *tr.* ridicule in a good-humored way. **2** *intr.* talk humorously or teasingly. □□ **ban′ter·er** *n.*

Ban·tu /bántoo/ • *n.* (*pl.* same or **Ban·tus**) **1** often *offens.* large group of Negroid peoples of central and southern Africa. **2** group of languages spoken by them. • *adj.* of these peoples or languages.

ban·yan /bányən/ *n.* Indian fig tree with self-rooting branches.

---

banyan late 16th century: from Portuguese, from Gujarati *vāṇiyo* 'man of the trading caste,' from Sanskrit. Originally denoting a Hindu trader or merchant, the term was applied by Europeans in the mid-17th century to a particular tree under which such traders had built a pagoda.

---

ba·o·bab /báyōbab, ba´a-/ *n.* African tree with a massive trunk and large edible fruit.

bap·tism /báptizəm/ *n.* **1** religious rite symbolizing admission to the Christian Church, with water and usu. name giving. **2** any initiation. □□ **bap·tis·mal** /-tízməl/ *adj.*

Bap·tist /báptist/ *n.* Christian advocating baptism by total immersion.

bap·tis·ter·y /báptistree/ *n.* (also **bap′tis·try**) (*pl.* **-tries**) **1** part of a church used for baptism. **2** (in a Baptist chapel) sunken receptacle used for total immersion.

bap·tize /baptíz/ *v.tr.* **1** administer baptism to. **2** give a name or nickname to.

bar[1] /baar/ • *n.* **1** long piece of rigid material used to confine or obstruct. **2** something resembling this in being straight, rigid, narrow, etc. **3** barrier or restriction. **4 a** counter in a restaurant, etc., for serving alcohol or refreshments. **b** room in which alcohol is served and customers may sit and drink. **c** establishment selling alcoholic drinks to be consumed on the premises. **d** small store or stall serving refreshments. **5** enclosure in which a defendant stands in a court of law. **6** *Mus.* any of the sections of usu. equal time value into which a musical composition is divided by vertical lines. **7** (**the Bar**) *Law* **a** lawyers collectively. **b** the profession of lawyers. • *v.tr.* (**barred, bar·ring**) **1 a** fasten (a door, window, etc.) with a bar or bars. **b** (usu. foll. by *in, out*) shut or keep in or out. **2** obstruct; prevent. • *prep.* except (*all were there bar a few*). □ **bar code** machine-readable striped code on packaging. **behind bars** in prison.

bar[2] /baar/ *n.* esp. Meteorol. unit of pressure, 10^5 newtons per square meter, approx. one atmosphere.

barb /baarb/ • *n.* **1** secondary, backward facing

---

projection from an arrow, fishhook, etc. **2** hurtful remark. • *v.tr.* **1** provide (an arrow, fishhook, etc.) with a barb or barbs. **2** (as **barbed** *adj.*) (of a remark, etc.) deliberately hurtful.

bar·bar·i·an /baarbáireeən/ • *n.* **1** uncultured or brutish person. **2** member of a primitive community or tribe. • *adj.* **1** rough and uncultured. **2** uncivilized.

bar·bar·ic /baarbárik/ *adj.* **1** brutal; cruel. **2** rough and uncultured. **3** primitive. □□ **bar·bar′i·cal·ly** *adv.*

bar·ba·rism /ba´arbərizəm/ *n.* **1** absence of culture and civilized standards; rudeness. **2** nonstandard word or expression.

bar·bar·i·ty /baarbáritee/ *n.* (*pl.* **-ties**) **1** savage cruelty. **2** example of this.

bar·ba·rous /ba´arbərəs/ *adj.* = BARBARIC. □□ **bar′ba·rous·ly** *adv.* **bar′ba·rous·ness** *n.*

bar·be·cue /ba´arbikyoo/ • *n.* **1 a** meal cooked over an open fire, often out of doors. **b** party at which such a meal is cooked and eaten. **c** marinated or seasoned meat prepared for cooking this way. **2 a** grill used for this. **b** fireplace containing such a grill. • *v.tr.* (**bar·be·cues, bar·be·cued, bar·be·cuing**) cook on a barbecue.

---

barbecue mid-17th century: from Spanish *barbacoa*, perhaps from Arawak *barbacoa* 'wooden frame on posts.' The original sense was 'wooden framework for sleeping on, or for storing meat or fish to be dried.'

---

bar·bel /baárbəl/ *n.* fleshy filament growing from the mouth of some fishes.

bar·bell /baárbel/ *n.* iron bar with removable weights at each end, used for weightlifting.

bar·ber /baárbər/ • *n.* person who cuts men's hair as an occupation. • *v.tr.* cut the hair of; shave or trim the beard of. □□ **bar′ber·shop** *n.*

bar·ber·ry /baárberee/ *n.* (*pl.* **-ries**) **1** shrub with yellow flowers and red berries. **2** its berry.

bar·bi·tu·rate /baarbítchərət, -rayt/ *n.* sedative or sleep-inducing drug derived from an organic, white crystalline acid.

bar·ca·role /baárkərōl/ *n.* (also **bar′ca·rolle**) **1** song sung by Venetian gondoliers. **2** music in imitation of this.

bard /baard/ *n.* **1** poet. **2** *hist.* Celtic minstrel. □□ **bard′ic** *adj.*

bare /bair/ • *adj.* **1** unclothed or uncovered. **2** leafless; unfurnished; empty. **3** unadorned. **4** scanty; mere. • *v.tr.* uncover; reveal. □□ **bare′ness** *n.*

bare·back /báirbak/ *adj.* & *adv.* without a saddle.

bare·faced /báirfayst/ *adj.* undisguised; impudent (*barefaced lie*).

bare·foot /báirfoot/ *adj.* & *adv.* (also **bare·foot·ed** /-footid/) with nothing on the feet.

bare·head·ed /báirhédid/ *adj.* & *adv.* without a covering for the head.

bare·ly /báirlee/ *adv.* **1** only just; scarcely. **2** scantily.

bar·gain /baárgin/ • *n.* **1 a** agreement on the terms of a transaction or sale. **b** this from the buyer's viewpoint. **2** something acquired or offered cheaply. • *v.intr.* discuss the terms of a transaction. □ **bargain for** (or *colloq.* **on**) (usu. with *neg.* actual or implied) be prepared for; expect. **in** (also **into**) **the bargain** moreover; in addition to what was expected. □□ **bar'gain•er** *n.*

barge /baarj/ • *n.* **1** long flat-bottomed cargo boat on canals, rivers, etc. **2** long ornamental pleasure boat. • *v. intr.* **1** intrude or interrupt rudely or awkwardly. **2** collide with.

bar•i•tone /báritōn/ • *n.* **1 a** second-lowest adult male singing voice. **b** singer with this voice. **2** instrument pitched second-lowest in its family.

bar•i•um /báireeəm, bár-/ *n. Chem.* white, reactive, soft metallic element of the alkaline earth group. ¶ Symb.: **Ba.**

bark[1] /baark/ • *n.* **1** sharp explosive cry of a dog, fox, etc. **2** sound resembling this. • *v.* **1** *intr.* (of a dog, fox, etc.) give a bark. **2** *tr.* & *intr.* speak or utter sharply or brusquely. □ **bark up the wrong tree** make an effort in the wrong direction.

bark[2] /baark/ • *n.* **1** tough protective outer sheath of tree trunks, branches, etc. • *v. tr.* graze or scrape (one's shin, etc.).

bar•keep•er /báarkeepər/ *n.* (also **bar'keep**) person who owns or serves drinks in a bar.

bark•er /báarkər/ *n.* person at an auction, sideshow, etc., who calls out to passersby as advertising.

bar•ley /báarlee/ *n.* cereal widely used as food and in malt liquors and spirits.

bar•maid /báarmayd/ *n.* female bartender.

bar•man /báarmən/ *n.* (*pl.* **-men**) male bartender.

bar mitz•vah /baar mítsvə/ *n.* **1** religious initiation ceremony of a Jewish boy who has reached the age of 13. **2** boy undergoing this ceremony.

barn /baarn/ *n.* large farm building for storing grain, housing livestock, etc.

bar•na•cle /báarnəkəl/ *n.* **1** any of various species of small marine crustaceans that cling to rocks, ships' hulls, etc. **2** tenacious attendant or follower. □□ **bar'na•cled** *adj.*

barn•storm /báarnstawrm/ *v. intr.* **1** tour rural districts as an entertainer or political campaigner. **2** *Aeron.* give informal flying exhibitions; do stunt flying. □□ **barn'storm•er** *n.*

barn•yard /báarnyaard/ *n.* area around a barn.

ba•rom•e•ter /bərómitər/ *n.* **1** instrument measuring atmospheric pressure, esp. in forecasting the weather. **2** anything that reflects change. □□ **bar•o•met•ric** /báarométrik/ *adj.* **bar•o•met'ri•cal** *adj.* **ba•rom'e•try** *n.*

bar•on /báron/ *n.* **1** member of the lowest order of the British nobility. **2** important businessman or other powerful or influential person (*newspaper baron*).

bar•on•ess /báronis/ *n.* **1** woman holding the rank of baron. **2** wife or widow of a baron.

bar•on•et /báronit, -nét/ *n.* member of the lowest hereditary British order.

bar•o•ny /báronee/ *n.* (*pl.* **-nies**) domain or rank of a baron.

ba•roque /bərók/ • *adj.* **1** highly ornate and extravagant in style, esp. of European art, architecture, and music of the 17th and 18th c. **2** of or relating to this period. • *n.* baroque style or art.

bar•rack /báarək/ • *n.* (usu. in *pl.*, often treated as *sing.*) **1** housing for soldiers. **2** large bleak building. • *v. tr.* place (soldiers, etc.) in barracks.

bar•ra•cu•da /báarəkŏŏdə/ *n.* (*pl.* same or **-das**) large voracious tropical marine fish.

bar•rage /bəráazh/ *n.* **1** concentrated artillery bombardment. **2** rapid succession of questions or criticisms.

barre /baar/ *n.* horizontal bar at waist level used in dance exercises.

bar•rel /báral/ • *n.* **1** cylindrical container usu. bulging out in the middle. **2** its contents. **3** measure of capacity, usu. varying from 30 to 40 gallons. **4** cylindrical tube forming part of an object such as a gun or pen. • *v.* (**bar•reled,** **bar•rel•ing; bar•relled, bar•rel•ling**) **1** *tr.* put into a barrel or barrels. **2** *intr. sl.* drive or move fast. □ **barrel organ** mechanical musical instrument in which a rotating pin-studded cylinder acts on a series of pipe valves, strings, or metal tongues.

bar•ren /báron/ *adj.* **1 a** unable to bear young. **b** unable to produce fruit or vegetation. **2** unprofitable. **3** dull. □□ **bar'ren•ly** *adv.* **bar'ren•ness** *n.*

bar•rette /bərét/ *n.* hair clip.

bar•ri•cade /bárikáyd/ • *n.* barrier, esp. improvised. • *v. tr.* block or defend with a barricade.

bar•ri•er /báreeər/ *n.* **1** fence, etc., that bars advance or access. **2** obstacle (*language barrier*).

bar•ring /báaring/ *prep.* except; not including.

bar•ri•o /báareeō, bár-/ *n.* (*pl.* **-os**) Spanish-speaking quarter or neighborhood of a town or city.

bar•room /báarōōm, -rŏŏm/ *n.* establishment specializing in serving alcoholic drinks.

bar•row[1] /báarō/ *n.* **1** two-wheeled handcart. **2** = WHEELBARROW.

bar•row[2] /báarō/ *n. Archaeol.* ancient grave mound.

bar•tend•er /báartendər/ *n.* person serving behind the bar of a tavern, bar, etc.

bar•ter /báartər/ • *v.* **1** *tr.* exchange (goods or services) without using money. **2** *intr.* make such an exchange. • *n.* trade by exchange of goods. □□ **bar'ter•er** *n.*

bar•y•on /báreeon/ *n. Physics* heavy elementary particle (i.e., a nucleon or hyperon). □□ **bar•y•on'ic** *adj.*

ba•sal /báysəl, -zəl/ *adj.* of, at, or forming a base. □ **ba'sal me•tab'o•lism** amount of energy consumed by an organism at complete rest.

ba•salt /bəsáwlt, báysawlt/ *n.* dark volcanic rock. □□ **ba•sal'tic** /-sáwltik/ *adj.*

base[1] /bays/ • *n.* **1 a** part supporting from beneath or serving as a foundation. **b** notional structure or entity (*power base*). **2** principle or starting point. **3** headquarters. **4** main or important ingredient. **5** *Chem.* substance capable of combining with an acid to form a salt. **6** *Math.* number in terms of which other numbers or logarithms are expressed. **7** *Baseball,* etc., one of the four stations that must be reached in turn to score a run. • *v. tr.* **1** found or establish. **2** station (*troops were based in Malta*).

base[2] /bays/ *adj.* **1** cowardly; despicable. **2** menial. **3** not pure; alloyed. **4** (of a metal) low in value. □□ **base'ly** *adv.* **base'ness** *n.*

base•ball /báysbawl/ *n.* **1** game played with a bat and ball, and a circuit of four bases that must be completed to score. **2** ball used in this game.

base•board /báysbawrd/ *n.* narrow board, etc., along the bottom of the wall of a room.

base·less /báyslis/ *adj.* unfounded; groundless. □□ **base′less·ly** *adv.* **base′less·ness** *n.*

base·line /báyslīn/ *n.* **1** line used as a base or starting point. **2** (in tennis, basketball, etc.) line marking each end of a court. **3** *Baseball* either of the lines leading from home plate and determining the boundaries of fair territory.

base·ment /báysmənt/ *n.* lowest floor of a building, usu. at least partly below ground level.

bash /bash/ • *v.tr.* strike bluntly or heavily. • *n.* **1** heavy blow. **2** *sl.* party. □□ **bash′er** *n.*

bash·ful /báshfŏŏl/ *adj.* **1** shy; diffident; self-conscious. **2** sheepish. □□ **bash′ful·ly** *adv.* **bash′ful·ness** *n.*

BASIC /báysik/ *n.* computer programming language using familiar English words and designed for beginners.

bas·ic /báysik/ • *adj.* **1** serving as a base. **2** fundamental. • *n.* (usu. in *pl.*) fundamental facts or principles. □□ **ba′si·cai·ly** *adv.*

ba·sil /bázəl, báyzəl/ *n.* aromatic herb used as a flavoring.

ba·sil·i·ca /bəsílikə/ *n.* **1** ancient Roman public hall used as a court of law, etc. **2** similar building used as a Christian church.

ba·sin /báysən/ *n.* **1** shallow, open container for holding water; sink. **2** hollow depression. **3** any sheltered mooring area. **4** area drained by rivers and tributaries. □□ **ba′sin·ful** *n.* (*pl.* **-fuls**).

ba·sis /báysis/ *n.* (*pl.* **ba·ses** /-seez/) **1** foundation or support. **2** main or determining principle or ingredient. **3** starting point for a discussion, etc.

bask /bask/ *v.intr.* **1** relax in warmth and light. **2** (foll. by *in*) derive great pleasure (from).

bas·ket /báskit/ *n.* **1** container made of interwoven cane, etc. **2** amount held by this. **3** goal in basketball, or a goal scored. □ **basket case** person who cannot function because of tension, etc. □□ **bas′ket·ful** *n.* (*pl.* **-fuls**).

bas·ket·ball /báskitbawl/ *n.* **1** game between two teams in which points are scored by making the ball drop through hooped nets fixed at each end of the court. **2** ball used in this game.

bas·ket·ry /báskitree/ *n.* **1** art of making baskets. **2** baskets collectively.

bas·ket·work /báskitwərk/ *n.* = BASKETRY.

bas mitz·vah /bas mítsvə/ *n.* (also **bat mitz′vah**) **1** initiation ceremony for a Jewish girl who has reached the age of 12 or 13. **2** girl undergoing this ceremony.

Basque /bask/ • *n.* **1** member of a people of the Western Pyrenees. **2** their language. • *adj.* the Basques or their language.

bas-re·lief /ba′a-rileéf, bás-/ *n.* sculpture or carving in which the figures project slightly from the background.

bass[1] /bays/ • *n.* **1 a** lowest adult male singing voice. **b** singer with this voice. **2** instrument pitched lowest in its family. **3** *colloq.* bass guitar or double bass. **4** low-frequency output of a radio, CD player, etc. • *adj.* **1** lowest in musical pitch. **2** deep sounding. □□ **bass′ist** *n.* (in sense 3).

bass[2] /bas/ *n.* (*pl.* same or **bass·es**) any of various edible fishes including the common perch.

bas·set /básit/ *n.* (in full **bas′set hound**) sturdy hunting dog with a long body, short legs, and big ears.

bas·si·net /básinét/ *n.* baby's wicker cradle, usu. hooded.

bas·so /básō, ba′a-/ *n.* (*pl.* **-sos** or **bas·si** /-see/) singer with a bass voice.

bas·soon /bəsŏ̄on/ *n.* bass instrument of the oboe family.

BASSOON

bast /bast/ *n.* fiber from the inner bark of a tree used for ropes, etc.

bas·tard /bástərd/ usu. *offens.* • *n.* **1** person born of parents not married to each other. **2** *sl.* unpleasant or despicable person. **3** *sl.* difficult or awkward thing, undertaking, etc. • *adj.* **1** illegitimate by birth. **2** (of things) unauthorized; counterfeit; hybrid. □□ **bas′tard·y** *n.* (in sense 1 of *n.*).

¶ In the past the word **bastard** was the standard term in both legal and non-legal use for 'an illegitimate child.' Today, however, it has little importance as a legal term and is retained in this older sense only as a term of abuse.

---

bastard Middle English: via Old French from medieval Latin *bastardus*, probably from *bastum* 'packsaddle'; compare with Old French *fils de bast*, literally 'packsaddle son' (i.e., the son of a mule driver who uses a packsaddle for a pillow and is gone by morning).

---

bas·tard·ize /bástərdīz/ *v.tr.* **1** declare (a person) illegitimate. **2** corrupt; debase. □□ **bas·tard·i·za′tion** *n.*

baste[1] /bayst/ *v.tr.* moisten (meat) with gravy or melted fat during cooking.

baste[2] /bayst/ *v.tr.* stitch loosely together in preparation for sewing; tack.

bas·tion /báschən, -teeən/ *n.* **1** projecting part of a fortification. **2** thing regarded as protecting (*bastion of freedom*).

bat[1] /bat/ • *n.* **1** implement with a handle, used for hitting balls in games. **2** player's turn with this. • *v.* (**bat·ted, bat·ting**) **1** *tr.* hit with or as with a bat. **2** *intr.* take a turn at batting.

bat[2] /bat/ *n.* mouselike nocturnal flying mammal.

bat[3] /bat/ *v.tr.* (**bat·ted, bat·ting**) blink.

batch /bach/ • *n.* **1** group of things or persons

dealt with together. **2** loaves, panfuls, etc., produced at one baking. **3** *Computing* group of records processed as a single unit. • *v.tr.* arrange or deal with in batches.

bat·ed /báytid/ *adj.* □ **with bated breath** very anxiously.

bath /bath/ *n.* (*pl.* **baths** /bathz, baths/) **1** = BATH-TUB. **2** act of washing the body in a tub. **3** liquid in which something is immersed, treated, etc.

bathe /bayth/ *v.* **1** *intr.* immerse oneself in water, esp. to wash. **2** *tr.* soak. **3** *tr.* (of sunlight, etc.) envelop. □ **bathing suit** garment worn for swimming.

bath·house /báth-hows/ *n.* **1** building with baths for public use. **2** building with changing rooms, as at the beach.

ba·th·os /báythaws, -thos/ *n.* lapse in mood from the sublime to the absurd or trivial; anticlimax. □□ **ba·thet·ic** /bəthétik/ *adj.*

bath·robe /báthrōb/ *n.* loose robe, often of toweling, worn before and after taking a bath.

bath·room /báthrōom, -rŏom/ *n.* room with a toilet and sink and often a bathtub or shower.

bath·tub /báthtəb/ *n.* container for liquid, usu. water, used for bathing the body.

bath·y·scaphe /báthiskaf/ *n.* manned vessel controlled by ballast for deep-sea diving.

bath·y·sphere /báthisfeer/ *n.* spherical vessel connected to a surface vessel by cables, used for deep-sea observation.

ba·tik /bətéek, bátik/ *n.* method of producing colored designs on textiles by applying wax to the parts to be left uncolored; piece of cloth treated in this way.

bat mitz·vah /bat mítsvə/ *var.* of BAS MITZVAH.

ba·ton /bətón, bə-, bát'n/ *n.* **1** thin stick used by a conductor to direct an orchestra. **2** *Sports* short stick carried and passed on in a relay race. **3** stick carried by a drum major. **4** staff of office.

bat·tal·ion /bətályən/ *n.* army unit, part of a division.

bat·ten[1] /bát'n/ • *n.* **1** narrow flat strip of wood used as a stiffener, etc. **2** strip of wood used for clamping the boards of a door, etc. **3** *Naut.* strip for securing tarpaulin over a ship's hatchway. • *v.tr.* strengthen or fasten with battens. □ **batten down the hatches 1** *Naut.* secure a ship's tarpaulins. **2** prepare for a difficulty or crisis.

bat·ten[2] /bát'n/ *v.intr.* (foll. by *on*) thrive or prosper at another's expense.

bat·ter[1] /bátər/ *v.* **1 a** *tr.* strike repeatedly with hard blows. **b** *intr.* pound heavily and insistently (*batter at the door*). **2** *tr.* handle roughly, esp. over a long period. □□ **bat'ter·er** *n.* **bat'ter·ing** *n.*

bat·ter[2] /bátər/ *n.* mixture of flour, egg, and liquid used in cooking, esp. for cakes, etc.

bat·ter[3] /bátər/ *n.* *Sports* player batting, esp. in baseball.

bat·ter·y /bátəree/ *n.* (*pl.* **-ies**) **1** cell or cells carrying an electric charge, as a source of current. **2** set of similar units of equipment, esp. connected. **3** series of tests. **4** fortified emplacement for heavy guns. **5** *Law* unlawful personal violence on another (see ASSAULT).

bat·tle /bát'l/ • *n.* **1** prolonged fight between armed forces. **2** contest; difficult struggle. • *v.*

1 *intr.* struggle; fight. **2** *tr.* engage in battle with. □ **battle-ax 1** large ax used in ancient warfare. **2** *colloq.* formidable older woman. **battle cruiser** warship faster and more lightly armored than a battleship. **battle cry** cry or slogan used in a battle. **battle fatigue** = *combat fatigue*. **battle royal 1** battle of many combatants; free fight. **2** heated argument. □□ **bat'tler** *n.*

bat·tle·field /bát'lfeeld/ *n.* (also **bat·tle·ground** /-grownd/) piece of ground on which a battle is or was fought.

bat·tle·ment /bát'lmənt/ *n.* (usu. in *pl.*) recessed parapet along the top of a fortification.

BATTLEMENT

bat·tle·ship /bát'lship/ *n.* heaviest armored warship.

bat·ty /bátee/ *adj.* (**bat·ti·er, bat·ti·est**) *sl.* crazy.

bau·ble /báwbəl/ *n.* showy trinket or toy of little value.

baud /bawd/ *n.* (*pl.* same or **bauds**) *Computing*, etc., unit to express the speed of electronic code signals, corresponding to one information unit or one bit per second.

baux·ite /báwksīt/ *n.* claylike ore, the source of aluminum.

bawd /bawd/ *n.* woman who runs a brothel.

bawd·y /báwdee/ • *adj.* (**bawd·i·er, bawd·i·est**) (esp. humorously) indecent; raunchy. • *n.* bawdy talk or writing. □ **bawdy house** brothel. □□ **bawd'i·ly** *adv.* **bawd'i·ness** *n.*

bawl /bawl/ *v.* **1** speak or call out noisily. **2** *intr.* weep loudly. □ **bawl out** *colloq.* reprimand angrily. □□ **bawl'er** *n.*

bay[1] /bay/ *n.* broad inlet of the sea where the land curves inward.

bay[2] /bay/ *n.* **1** laurel having deep green leaves and purple berries. **2** (in *pl.*) bay wreath for a victor or poet. □ **bay leaf** aromatic (usu. dried) leaf of the bay tree, used in cooking.

bay[3] /bay/ *n.* **1** space created by a window line projecting outward from a wall. **2** recess; alcove. **3** compartment (*bomb bay*). **4** area specially allocated (*loading bay*).

bay[4] /bay/ • *adj.* (esp. of a horse) dark reddish brown. • *n.* bay horse with a black mane and tail.

bay[5] /bay/ • *v.* **1** *intr.* bark or howl loudly and plaintively. **2** *tr.* bay at. • *n.* sound of baying, esp. in chorus from hounds in close pursuit. □ **at bay** cornered; unable to escape. **hold** (or **keep**) **at bay** hold off (a pursuer).

bay·ber·ry /báyberee/ *n.* (*pl.* **-ries**) N. American plants bearing waxy berries.

bay·o·net /báyənét/ • *n.* **1** stabbing blade attachable to the muzzle of a rifle. **2** electrical or other fitting engaged by being pushed into a socket and twisted. • *v.tr.* stab with a bayonet.

bay·ou /bī-ōō/ *n.* marshy offshoot of a river, etc.

ba·zaar /bəzáar/ *n.* **1** market in an Eastern or Middle Eastern country. **2** fund-raising sale, esp. for charity.

ba·zoo·ka /bəzóbkə/ *n.* **1** anti-tank rocket launcher. **2** crude trombone-like musical instrument.

BB *abbr.* pellet about .18 inch in diameter, for use in a BB gun or air gun.

bbl. *abbr.* barrels (esp. of oil).

BC *abbr.* **1** (of a date) before Christ. **2** British Columbia.

bdrm. *abbr.* bedroom.

Be *symb. Chem.* beryllium.

be /bee/ (*sing. present* **am** /am, əm/, **is** /iz/; *pl. present* **are**; *1st and 3rd sing. past* **was** /wuz, woz, wəz/; *2nd sing. past and pl. past* **were** /wər/; *present subj.* **be**; *past subj.* **were**; *pres. part.* **be·ing**; *past part.* **been** /bin/) • *v.intr.* **1** exist; live (*I think, therefore I am*). **2 a** occur; take place. **b** occupy a position. **3** remain; continue. **4** linking subject and predicate, expressing: **a** identity (*she is the person*). **b** condition (*he is ill*). **c** state or quality (*he is kind*). **d** opinion (*I am against hanging*). **e** total (*two and two are four*). **f** cost or significance (*it is nothing to me*). • *v.aux.* **1** with a past participle to form the passive mood (*it was done*). **2** with a present participle to form continuous tenses (*we are coming*). **3** with an infinitive to express duty or commitment, intention, possibility, destiny, or hypothesis (*we are to wait here*).

be- /bee/ *prefix* forming verbs: **1** (from transitive verbs) **a** all over; all around (*beset*). **b** thoroughly; excessively (*begrudge*; *belabor*). **2** (from intransitive verbs) expressing transitive action (*bemoan*). **3** (from adjectives and nouns) expressing transitive action (*befoul*). **4** (from nouns) **a** affect with (*befog*). **b** treat as (*befriend*). **c** (forming adjectives, ending in -ed) having (*bejeweled*).

beach /beech/ • *n.* pebbly or sandy shore. • *v.tr.* run or haul up (a boat, etc.) onto a beach.

beach·comb·er /béechkōmər/ *n.* vagrant who lives by searching beaches for articles of value.

beach·head /béech-hed/ *n. Mil.* fortified position established on a beach by landing forces.

bea·con /béekən/ *n.* **1** visible warning or guiding device (e.g., lighthouse, navigation buoy, etc.). **2** radio transmitter whose signal helps fix the position of a ship or aircraft.

bead /beed/ • *n.* **1 a** small usu. rounded and perforated piece of glass, stone, etc., for threading with others or sewing on to fabric, etc. **b** (in *pl.*) string of beads; rosary. **2** drop of liquid. **3** small knob in the foresight of a gun. **4** inner edge of a pneumatic tire that grips the rim of the wheel. • *v. tr.* decorate with beads. □ **draw a bead on** take aim at. □□ **bead′ed** *adj.*

bead·ing /béeding/ *n.* **1** decoration of or resembling beads. **2** *Archit.* molding like a series of beads. **3** bead of a tire.

bead·y /béedee/ *adj.* (**bead·i·er, bead·i·est**) **1** (of the eyes) small, round, and bright. **2** covered with beads or drops. □ **beady-eyed** with beady eyes. □□ **bead′i·ly** *adv.* **bead′i·ness** *n.*

bea·gle /béegəl/ *n.* small short-haired hound.

beak /beek/ *n.* **1** bird's horny projecting jaws;

bill. **2** similar jaw of a turtle, etc. □□ **beaked** *adj.* **beak′y** *adj.*

beak·er /béekər/ *n.* **1** tall drinking vessel. **2** lipped cylindrical vessel for scientific experiments.

beam /beem/ • *n.* **1** long sturdy piece of timber or metal spanning an opening or room, usu. to support the structure above. **2** ray or shaft of light. **3** series of radio or radar signals as a guide to a ship or aircraft. **4** crossbar of a balance. **5** ship's breadth at its widest point. • *v.* **1** *tr.* emit or direct (light, radio waves, etc.). **2** *intr.* **a** shine. **b** look or smile radiantly. • *adj.* (*or* **off the**) beam *colloq.* mistaken. **on the beam** *colloq.* on the right track.

bean /been/ • *n.* **1 a** plant with edible seeds in long pods. **b** one of these seeds. **2** similar seed of coffee, etc. **3** *sl.* source of common sense. • *v.tr. sl.* hit on the head. □ **bean counter** *colloq.* accountant.

bean·bag /béenbag/ *n.* **1** small bag filled with dried beans and used esp. in children's games. **2** (in full **bean′bag chair**) large cushion filled usu. with polystyrene beads and used as a seat.

bean·pole /béenpōl/ *n.* **1** stick for supporting bean plants. **2** *colloq.* tall thin person.

bear¹ /bair/ *v.* (*past* **bore** /bor/; *past part.* **borne, born** /bawrn/) **1** *tr.* carry, bring, or take. **2** *tr.* show; have as an attribute or characteristic (*bear marks of violence*). **3** *tr.* **a** produce; yield (fruit, etc.). **b** give birth to. **4** *tr.* **a** sustain (a weight, responsibility, cost, etc.). **b** endure (an ordeal, difficulty, etc.). **5** *tr.* **a** tolerate. **b** admit of. **6** *intr.* veer in a given direction (*bear left*). □ **bear down** exert downward pressure. **bear down on** approach rapidly or purposefully. **bear on** (*or* **upon**) be relevant to. **bear out** support or confirm (an account or the person giving it). **bear with** tolerate. **bear witness** testify. □□ **bear′a·ble** *adj.* **bear′a·bly** *adv.* **bear′er** *n.*

bear² /bair/ • *n.* **1** large heavy mammal having thick fur and walking on its soles. **2** rough or uncouth person. **3** *Stock Exch.* person who sells shares hoping to buy them back later at a lower price. □□ **bear·ish** *adj.*

beard /beerd/ • *n.* **1** facial hair growing on the chin, etc. **2** similar tuft on an animal. • *v.tr.* oppose openly; defy. □□ **beard′ed** *adj.* **beard′less** *adj.*

bear·ing /báiring/ *n.* **1** person's bodily attitude or outward behavior. **2** relevance (*has no bearing on the subject*). **3** part of a machine that supports a rotating or other moving part. **4** direction or position relative to a fixed point. **5** (in *pl.*) sense of one's orientation (*get my bearings*).

Bé·ar·naise sauce /báirnáyz/ *n.* rich, savory sauce thickened with egg yolks.

bear·skin /báirskin/ *n.* **1** skin of a bear. **2** wrap, etc., made of this.

beast /beest/ *n.* **1** animal, esp. a wild quadruped. **2** brutal, objectionable person.

beast·ly /béestlee/ *adj.* (**beast·li·er, beast·li·est**) **1** *colloq.* objectionable; unpleasant. **2** like a beast; brutal. □□ **beast′li·ness** *n.*

beat /beet/ • *v.* (*past* **beat**; *past part.* **beat·en** /béet′n/) **1 a** strike persistently or repeatedly, esp. to harm or punish. **b** strike (a thing) repeatedly, e.g., to remove dust from (a carpet, etc.), or to sound (a drum, etc.). **2** *tr.* **a** overcome;

surpass. **b** complete an activity before (another person, etc.). **c** be too hard for; perplex. **3** *tr.* stir (eggs, etc.) vigorously. **4** *tr.* shape (metal, etc.) by blows. **5** *intr.* (of the heart, etc.) pulsate rhythmically. **6** *tr.* **a** indicate (a tempo or rhythm) by tapping, etc. **b** sound (a signal, etc.) by striking a drum. **7** move or cause (wings) to move up and down. **8** *tr.* make (a path, etc.) by trampling. • *n.* **1 a** main stress accent in music or verse. **b** indication of rhythm by a conductor. **2** stroke, blow, or measured sequence of strokes. **3** route or area allocated to a police officer, etc. • *adj. sl.* exhausted; tired out. □ **beat generation** members of a movement of young people, esp. in the 1950s, who rejected conventional society in their dress, habits, and beliefs. **beat it** *sl.* go away. **beat off** drive back (an attack, etc.). **beat up** give a beating to, esp. with punches and kicks. **beat-up** *adj. colloq.* dilapidated; in a state of disrepair. □□ **beat′a•ble** *adj.*

beat•en /beét'n/ *adj.* **1** outwitted; defeated. **2** exhausted; dejected. **3** (of metal) shaped by a hammer. **4** (of a path, etc.) much used.

beat•er /beétər/ *n.* implement used for beating (esp. a carpet or eggs).

be•a•tif•ic /beéətifik/ *adj.* **1** *colloq.* blissful (*beatific smile*). **2 a** of or relating to blessedness. **b** making blessed. □□ **be•a•tif′i•cal•ly** *adv.*

be•at•i•fy /beeátifī/ *v.tr.* (**-fies, -fied**) **1** *RC Ch.* declare a dead person "blessed," often a step toward canonization. **2** make happy. □□ **be•at•i•fi•ca′tion** *n.*

beat•ing /beéting/ *n.* **1** physical punishment or assault. **2** defeat. □ **take a beating** suffer a defeat or setback.

be•at•i•tude /beeátitŏod, -tyŏod/ *n.* **1** blessedness. **2** (in *pl.*) declarations of blessedness in Matt. 5:3-11.

beat•nik /beétnik/ *n.* member of the beat generation (see BEAT).

beau /bō/ *n.* (*pl.* **beaux** or **beaus** /bōz/) boyfriend.

Beau•fort scale /bófərt/ *n.* scale of wind speed ranging from 0 (calm) to 12 (hurricane).

beau•te•ous /byŏoteeəs/ *adj. poet.* beautiful.

beau•ti•cian /byŏotíshən/ *n.* specialist in beauty treatment.

beau•ti•ful /byŏotifŏol/ *adj.* **1** delighting the aesthetic senses. **2** pleasant; enjoyable (*had a beautiful time*). **3** excellent (*beautiful specimen*). □□ **beau′ti•ful•ly** *adv.*

beau•ti•fy /byŏotifī/ *v.tr.* (**-fies, -fied**) make beautiful; adorn. □□ **beau•ti•fi•ca•tion** *n.* **beau′ti•fi•er** *n.*

beau•ty /byŏotee/ *n.* (*pl.* **-ties**) **1** combination of shape, color, etc., that pleases the senses. **2** *colloq.* **a** excellent specimen. **b** attractive feature; advantage. □ **beauty parlor** (or **salon** or **shop**) establishment for manicure, hairdressing, makeup, etc.

bea•ver /beévər/ • *n.* (*pl.* same or **bea•vers**) **1 a** amphibious broad-tailed rodent native to N. America, Europe, and Asia able to cut down trees and build dams. **b** its fur. **c** hat of this. • *v.intr. colloq.* work hard. □ **eager beaver** *colloq.* over-zealous person.

be•bop /beébop/ *n.* type of jazz characterized by complex harmony and rhythms. □□ **be′bop•per** *n.*

be•calm /bikaám/ *v.tr.* deprive (a ship) of wind.

be•came *past* of BECOME.

be•cause /bikáwz, -kúz/ *conj.* for the reason that; since. □ **because of** on account of; by reason of.

bé•cha•mel /béshəmel/ *n.* kind of thick white sauce.

beck /bek/ □ **at a person's beck and call** having constantly to obey a person's orders.

beck•on /békən/ *v.* **1** *tr.* summon by gesture. **2** *intr.* make a signal to attract a person's attention.

be•come /bikúm/ *v.* (*past* **be•came** /bikáym/; *past part.* **be•come**) **1** *intr.* begin to be; come to be; turn into (*tadpoles become frogs*). **2** *tr.* **a** look well on; suit. **b** befit (*it ill becomes you to complain*). **3** *intr.* (as **becoming** *adj.*) **a** flattering the appearance. **b** suitable; decorous. □ **become of** happen to (*what will become of me?*). □□ **be•com′ing•ly** *adv.*

bed /bed/ • *n.* **1** piece of furniture or padding, etc. for sleeping on. **2** garden plot, esp. for flowers. **3 a** bottom of the sea or a river. **b** foundations of a road or railroad. **4** stratum; layer. • *v.* (**bed•ded, bed•ding**) **1** *tr.* & *intr.* put or go to bed. **2** *tr.* plant in a garden bed. **3 a** *tr.* arrange as a layer. **b** *intr.* be or form a layer. □ **bed and board** lodging and food. **bed and breakfast 1** one night's lodging and breakfast in a hotel, etc. **2** establishment that provides this. **get out of bed on the wrong side** be bad-tempered all day long. **make one's bed and lie in it** accept the consequences of one's acts.

be•daz•zle /bidázəl/ *v.tr.* **1** dazzle. **2** confuse (a person). □□ **be•daz′zle•ment** *n.*

bed•bug /bédbug/ *n.* biting parasites infesting beds, etc.

bed•clothes /bédklōthz, -klōz/ *n.pl.* coverings for a bed, such as sheets, blankets, etc.

bed•ding /béding/ *n.* **1** mattress and bedclothes. **2** geological strata.

be•deck /bidék/ *v.tr.* adorn.

be•dev•il /bidévəl/ *v.tr.* (**-iled, -il•ing**) **1** plague; afflict. **2** confound; confuse. **3** bewitch. **4** torment or abuse. □□ **be•dev′il•ment** *n.*

bed•fel•low /bédfelō/ *n.* **1** person who shares a bed. **2** associate.

bed•lam /bédləm/ *n.* scene of uproar and confusion.

Bed•ou•in /bédŏoin/ (also **Bed′u•in**) (*pl.* same) *n.* **1** nomadic Arab of the desert. **2** wanderer; nomad.

bed•pan /bédpan/ *n.* toilet for a bedridden patient.

be•drag•gle /bidrágəl/ *v.tr.* **1** (often as **bedraggled** *adj.*) wet (a dress, etc.) by trailing it, or so that it hangs limp. **2** (as **bedraggled** *adj.*) untidy; disheveled.

bed•rid•den /bédrid'n/ *adj.* confined to bed by infirmity.

bed•rock /bédrok/ *n.* **1** solid underlying rock. **2** underlying principles or facts.

bed•room /bédrŏom, -rŏom/ *n.* room for sleeping in.

bed•side /bédsīd/ *n.* space beside esp. a patient's bed. □ **bedside manner** (of a doctor) way with a patient.

bed•sore /bédsawr/ *n.* sore developed by lying in bed.

bed•spread /bédspred/ *n.* decorative cover for a bed.

bed•stead /bédsted/ *n.* framework of a bed.

bed•wet•ting /bédweting/ *n.* involuntary urination during the night.

bee /bee/ *n.* **1** any four-winged social insect that collects nectar and pollen and produces wax and honey. **2** meeting for communal work or amusement. □ **bee in one's bonnet** obsession.

beech /beech/ *n.* **1** large tree with smooth gray bark and glossy leaves. **2** its wood.

beef /beef/ • *n.* **1** flesh of the ox, bull, or cow for eating. **2** *colloq.* well-developed male muscle. **3** (*pl.* **beeves** /beevz/ or **beefs**) cow, bull, or ox fattened for beef. **4** (*pl.* **beefs**) *sl.* complaint. • *v.intr. sl.* complain. □ **beef up** *sl.* strengthen; reinforce.

beef·cake /beéfkayk/ *n. sl.* well-developed male muscles, esp. when photographed and displayed for admiration.

beef·steak /beéfstáyk/ *n.* thick slice of beef, usu. for grilling or frying.

beef·y /beéfee/ *adj.* (**beef·i·er, beef·i·est**) **1** like beef. **2** solid; muscular. □□ **beef'i·ly** *adv.* **beef'i·ness** *n.*

bee·hive /beéhīv/ *n.* **1** artificial habitation for bees. **2** busy place.

bee·keep·er /beékeepər/ *n.* keeper of bees. □□ **bee'keep·ing** *n.*

bee·line /beélīn/ *n.* straight line between two places.

Be·el·ze·bub /bee-élzibub/ *n.* the Devil.

been *past part.* of BE.

beep /beep/ • *n.* **1** sound of an automobile horn. **2** any similar high-pitched noise. • *v.intr.* emit a beep.

beep·er /beépər/ *n.* portable electronic device that receives signals and emits a beep to page the person carrying it.

beer /beer/ *n.* **1** alcoholic drink made from yeast-fermented malt, etc., flavored with hops. **2** fermented nonalcoholic drinks, e.g., ginger beer, root beer.

beet /beet/ *n.* plant with an edible root (see *sugar beet*).

bee·tle[1] /beét'l/ *n.* insect with modified front wings forming hard protective cases closing over the back wings.

bee·tle[2] /beét'l/ *n.* tool with a heavy head and handle, used for ramming, crushing, driving wedges, etc.

bee·tle[3] /beét'l/ • *adj.* (esp. of the eyebrows) projecting; shaggy; scowling. • *v.intr.* (usu. as **beetling** *adj.*) (of brows, cliffs, etc.) projecting; overhanging threateningly. □ **beetle-browed** with shaggy or projecting eyebrows.

beeves *pl.* of BEEF.

be·fall /bifáwl/ *v.* (*past* **be·fell** /bifél/; *past part.* **be·fall·en** /bifáwlən/) *poet.* **1** *intr.* happen (*so it befell*). **2** *tr.* happen to.

be·fit /bifít/ *v.tr.* (**be·fit·ted, be·fit·ting**) be appropriate for; suit. □□ **be·fit'ting** *adj.* **be·fit'ting·ly** *adv.*

be·fog /bifawg, -fóg/ *v.tr.* (**be·fogged, be·fog·ging**) **1** confuse; obscure. **2** envelop in fog.

be·fore /bifáwr/ • *conj.* **1** earlier than the time when. **2** rather than that. • *prep.* **1** in front of; ahead of. **2** earlier than; preceding. **3** rather than. **4 a** in the presence of. **b** for the attention of. • *adv.* **1 a** earlier than the time in question; already. **b** in the past (*happened long before*). **2** ahead.

be·fore·hand /bifáwrhand/ *adv.* in advance; in readiness.

be·fud·dle /bifúd'l/ *v.tr.* **1** make drunk. **2** confuse. □□ **be·fud'dle·ment** *n.*

beg /beg/ *v.* (**begged, beg·ging**) **1 a** *tr. & intr.* ask for (esp. food, money, etc.). **b** *intr.* live by begging. **2** *tr.* ask earnestly or humbly. **3** *tr.* ask formally for. **4** *intr.* (of a dog, etc.) sit up with the front paws raised expectantly. **5** *tr.* take or ask leave (to do something). □ **beg off 1** decline to take part in or attend. **2** get (a person) excused from a penalty, etc.

be·get /bigét/ *v.tr.* (**be·get·ting**; *past* **be·got** /bigót/; *archaic* **be·gat** /bigát/; *past part.* **be·got·ten** /bigót'n/) *literary* **1** father; procreate. **2** cause. □□ **be·get'ter** *n.*

beg·gar /bégər/ • *n.* **1** person who lives by begging. **2** poor person. • *v.tr.* **1** reduce to poverty. **2** cause one's ability for (description, etc.) to be inadequate. □□ **beg·gar·ly** *adj.* **beg·gar·y** *n.*

be·gin /bigín/ *v.* (**be·gin·ning**; *past* **be·gan** /bigán/; *past part.* **be·gun** /bigún/) **1** *tr.* perform the first part of; start. **2** *intr.* come into being. **3** *tr.* start at a certain time. **4** *intr.* be begun.

be·gin·ner /bigínər/ *n.* person just beginning to learn.

be·gin·ning /bigíning/ *n.* **1** time or place at which anything begins. **2** source or origin. **3** first part.

be·gone /bigáwn, -gón/ *int. poet.* go away at once!

be·go·nia /bigónyə/ *n.* plant with brightly colored sepals and no petals, and often having brilliant glossy foliage.

be·got *past* of BEGET.

be·got·ten *past part.* of BEGET.

be·grudge /bigrúj/ *v.tr.* **1** resent; be dissatisfied at. **2** envy (a person) the possession of. □□ **be·grudg'ing·ly** *adv.*

be·guile /bigíl/ *v.tr.* **1** charm; amuse. **2** divert attention pleasantly from (work, etc.). **3** delude; cheat. □□ **be·guile'ment** *n.* **be·guil'er** *n.* **be·guil'ing** *adj.* **be·guil'ing·ly** *adv.*

be·guine /bigéen/ *n.* popular dance of W. Indian origin.

be·gun *past part.* of BEGIN.

be·half /biháf/ *n.* □ **on** (also **in**) **behalf of** (or **on a person's behalf**) **1** in the interests of (a person, principle, etc.). **2** as representative of (*acting on behalf of my client*).

be·have /biháyv/ *v.tr.* **1** act or react (in a specified way). **2** (esp. to or of a child) conduct oneself properly. **3** (of a machine, etc.) work well (or in a specified way).

be·hav·ior /biháyvyər/ *n.* **1 a** way one conducts oneself; manners. **b** treatment of others. **2** way in which a ship, machine, etc., acts or works. **3** *Psychol.* response (of a person, animal, etc.) to a stimulus. □□ **be·hav'ior·al** *adj.*

be·head /bihéd/ *v.tr.* cut off the head.

be·held *past* and *past part.* of BEHOLD.

be·he·moth /bihéeməth, beéə-/ *n.* huge creature or thing.

be·hest /bihést/ *n. literary* command; entreaty.

be·hind /bihínd/ • *prep.* **1 a** in, toward, or to the rear of. **b** on the farther side of. **c** hidden by. **2 a** in the past in relation to. **b** late in relation to. **3** inferior to; weaker than. **4 a** in support of. **b** responsible for. • *adv.* **1 a** in or to the rear; farther back. **b** on the farther side (*a high wall with a field behind*). **2** remaining. **3 a** in arrears. **b** late in accomplishing a task, etc. **4** in a weak position;

backward (*behind in Latin*). • *n. colloq.* buttocks. □ **behind the times** old-fashioned; antiquated.

be·hold /bihóld/ *v.tr.* (*past & past part.* **be·held** /bihéld/) *literary* (esp. in *imper.*) see; observe. □□ **be·hold'er** *n.*

be·hold·en /bihóldən/ *adj.* under obligation.

be·hoove /bihóōv/ *v.tr.* **1** be incumbent on. **2** befit.

beige /bayzh/ • *n.* pale sandy color. • *adj.* of this color.

be·ing /bééing/ *n.* **1** existence. **2** nature or essence. **3** human being. **4** anything that exists or is imagined.

be·la·bor /biláybər/ *v.tr.* **1** thrash; beat. **2** argue or elaborate (a subject) in excessive detail.

be·lat·ed /biláytid/ *adj.* late or too late. □□ **be·lat'ed·ly** *adv.* **be·lat'ed·ness** *n.*

be·lay /biláy/ • *v.* **1** *tr.* fix (a running rope) around a cleat, etc., to secure it. **2** *tr. & intr.* (usu. in *imper.*) *Naut. sl.* stop; enough!

bel can·to /bel kántō, ka'an-/ *n.* lyrical style of operatic singing using a full rich broad tone and smooth phrasing.

belch /belch/ • *v.* **1** *intr.* emit wind noisily from the stomach through the mouth. **2** *tr.* (of a chimney, gun, etc.) send (smoke, etc.) out or up. • *n.* act of belching.

be·lea·guer /biléégər/ *v.tr.* **1** besiege. **2** vex; harass.

bel·fry /bélfree/ *n.* (*pl.* **-fries**) **1** bell tower. **2** space for bells in a church tower. □ **have bats in the belfry** be eccentric or crazy.

be·lie /bilí/ *v.tr.* (**be·lied**, **be·ly·ing**) **1** give a false notion of. **2** fail to fulfill or justify.

be·lief /bileéf/ *n.* **1 a** religious conviction. **b** firm opinion. **c** acceptance. **2** trust or confidence.

be·lieve /bileév/ *v.* **1** *tr.* accept as true or as conveying the truth. **2** *tr.* think; suppose. **3** *intr.* (foll. by *in*) **a** have faith in the existence of. **b** have confidence in. **c** have trust in the advisability of. **4** *intr.* have (esp. religious) faith. □ **make believe** pretend. □□ **be·liev'a·ble** *adj.* **be·liev·a·bil'i·ty** *n.* **be·liev'er** *n.*

be·lit·tle /bilít'l/ *v.tr.* **1** disparage. **2** make small; dwarf. □□ **be·lit'tle·ment** *n.* **be·lit'tler** *n.* **be·lit'tling·ly** *adv.*

bell /bel/ • *n.* **1** hollow usu. metal object in the shape of a cup usu. widening at the lip, made to sound a clear musical note when struck. **2** sound or stroke of a bell, esp. as a signal. **3** anything that sounds like or functions as a bell. • *v.tr.* provide with a bell or bells. □ **bell-bottom** marked flare below the knee (of a pants leg). **bell jar** bell-shaped glass cover or container. **bells and whistles** *colloq.* attractive but unnecessary additional features. **saved by the bell 1** *Boxing* spared a knockout by the bell signaling the end of a round. **2** spared an unwanted task, etc., by another claim on one's attention.

bel·la·don·na /bélədónə/ *n.* **1** *Bot.* poisonous plant with purple flowers and purple-black berries. Also called **deadly nightshade**. **2** *Med.* drug from this.

bell·boy /bélboy/ *n.* = BELLHOP.

belle /bel/ *n.* beautiful woman.

bel·les let·tres /bel-létrə/ *n.pl.* (also treated as *sing.*) writings or studies of a literary nature, esp. essays and criticisms. □□ **bel·le·trism** /bel-létrizəm/ *n.* **bel·let·rist** /bel-létrist/ *n.* **bel·let·ris·tic** /bél-letrístik/ *adj.*

bell·hop /bélhop/ *n.* person who carries luggage, runs errands, etc., in a hotel or club.

bel·li·cose /bélikōs/ *adj.* eager to fight; warlike. □□ **bel·li·cos·i·ty** /-kósitee/ *n.*

bel·lig·er·ent /bilíjərənt/ • *adj.* **1** engaged in war or conflict. **2** given to constant fighting; pugnacious. • *n.* nation or person engaged in war or conflict. □□ **bel·lig'er·ence** *n.* **bel·lig'er·ent·ly** *adv.*

bel·low /bélō/ • *v.* **1** *intr.* emit a deep loud roar. **2** *tr.* utter loudly. • *n.* bellowing sound.

bel·lows /bélōz/ *n.pl.* (also treated as *sing.*) **1** device that emits a stream of air when squeezed, esp. (in full **pair of bel·lows**) kind with two handles used for blowing air onto a fire. **2** expandable component, e.g., of a camera.

BELLOWS

bel·ly /bélee/ • *n.* (*pl.* **-lies**) **1** part of the human body below the chest, containing the stomach and bowels. **2** stomach. **3** front of the body from the waist to the groin. **4** underside of a four-legged animal. **5** cavity or bulging part. • *v.* (**-lies**, **-lied**) swell or cause to swell; bulge. □ **belly button** *colloq.* navel. **belly dance** Middle Eastern dance performed by a woman, involving voluptuous movements. **belly laugh** loud unrestrained laugh.

bel·ly·ache /béleeayk/ • *n. colloq.* stomach pain. • *v.intr. sl.* complain noisily or persistently. □□ **bel'ly·ach·er** *n.*

bel·ly·flop /béleeflop/ *colloq. n.* dive with the belly landing flat on the water.

bel·ly·ful /béleefŏol/ *n.* (*pl.* **-fuls**) **1** enough to eat. **2** *colloq.* more than enough of anything (esp. unwelcome).

be·long /bil+áwng, -lóng/ *v.intr.* **1** (foll. by *to*) **a** be the property of. **b** be rightly assigned to. **c** be a member of. **2** fit socially.

be·long·ing /bilÁwnging, -lóng-/ *n.* **1** (in *pl.*) movable possessions or luggage. **2** membership; relationship.

be·lov·ed /bilúvid, -lúvd/ • *adj.* much loved. • *n.* much loved person.

be·low /bilō/ • *prep.* **1 a** lower in position than. **b** south of. **2** beneath the surface of. **3** unworthy of. • *adv.* **1** at or to a lower point or level. **2 a** downstairs. **b** downstream. **3** (of a text reference) further forward on a page or in a book (*as noted below*).

belt /belt/ • *n.* **1** strip of leather, etc., esp. worn around the waist. **2 a** circular band of material used as a driving medium in machinery. **b** conveyor belt. **3** distinct region or extent. **4** *sl.* heavy blow. • *v.* **1** *tr.* put a belt around. **2** *tr.* fasten with a belt. **3** *tr. sl.* hit hard. □ **below the belt** unfair or unfairly. **belt out** *sl.* sing loudly. **tighten one's belt** live more frugally. **under one's belt** securely acquired. □□ **belt′er** *n.* (esp. in sense of *belt out*).

belt·way /béltway/ *n.* highway skirting a metropolitan region.

be·muse /bimyōbz/ *v.tr.* stupefy or bewilder (a person). □□ **be·mus·ed·ly** /-zidlee/ *adv.* **be·muse′ment** *n.*

bench /bench/ • *n.* **1** long seat of wood, stone, etc. **2** strong worktable. **3** (prec. by *the*) **a** office of judge or magistrate. **b** judge's seat in a court of law. **c** court of law. **d** judges and magistrates collectively. **4** *Sports* **a** seating to the side of a field for coaches and players not taking part. **b** those players not taking part in a game. • *v.tr.* **1** *Sports* **a** keep (a player) on the bench. **b** withdraw (a player) from a game.

bench·mark /bénchmaark/ *n.* **1** surveyor's mark used as a reference point. **2** standard or point of reference.

bend[1] /bend/ • *v.* (*past* **bent**; *past part.* **bent** exc. in *bended knee*) **1 a** *tr.* force or adapt (something straight) into a curve or angle. **b** *intr.* (of an object) be so altered. **2** *intr.* move or stretch in a curved course. **3** *intr.* & *tr.* (often foll. by *down, over,* etc.) incline or cause to incline from the vertical. **4** *tr.* interpret or modify (a rule) to suit oneself. **5** *tr.* & *refl.* (foll. by *to, on*) direct or devote (oneself or one's attention, energies, etc.). **6** *tr.* turn (one's steps or eyes) in a new direction. **7 a** *intr.* stoop or submit. **b** *tr.* force to submit. • *n.* **1** curve. **2** departure from a straight course. **3** bent part. **4** (in *pl.*; prec. by *the*) *colloq.* decompression sickness. □□ **bend′a·ble** *adj.*

bend[2] /bend/ *n. Naut.* any of various rope knots.

bend·er /béndər/ *n. sl.* wild drinking spree.

be·neath /bineéth/ • *prep.* **1** not worthy of. **2** below; under. • *adv.* below; underneath.

ben·e·dic·tion /bénidíkshən/ *n.* **1** blessing, esp. as part of a religious service. **2** state of being blessed.

ben·e·fac·tion /bénifákshən/ *n.* **1** donation or gift. **2** giving or doing good.

ben·e·fac·tor /bénifaktər/ *n.* (*fem.* **ben·e·fac·tress** /-tris/) person who gives support (esp. financial) to a person or cause.

ben·e·fice /bénifis/ *n.* income from a church office.

ben·ef·i·cent /binéfisənt/ *adj.* doing good; generous; actively kind. □□ **be·nef′i·cence** *n.* **be·nef′i·cent·ly** *adv.*

ben·e·fi·cial /bénifishəl/ *adj.* advantageous; having benefits. □□ **ben·e·fi′cial·ly** *adv.*

ben·e·fi·ci·ar·y /bénifishee-e-ree, -fishəree/ *n.* (*pl.* **-ies**) person who benefits, esp. from a will.

ben·e·fit /bénifit/ • *n.* **1** favorable or helpful factor or circumstance. **2** (often in *pl.*) insurance, social security, welfare, etc., payment. **3** public performance or game in aid of a charitable cause. • *v.* (**ben·e·fit·ed, ben·e·fit·ing; ben·e·fit·ted, ben·e·fit·ing**) **1** *tr.* do good to; bring advantage to. **2** *intr.* receive an advantage. □ **the benefit of the doubt** concession that a person is innocent, etc., although doubt exists.

be·nev·o·lent /binévələnt/ *adj.* **1** wishing to do good; actively friendly and helpful. **2** charitable. □□ **be·nev′o·lence** *n.* **be·nev′o·lent·ly** *adv.*

be·night·ed /binítid/ *adj.* intellectually or morally ignorant. □□ **be·night′ed·ness** *n.*

be·nign /binín/ *adj.* **1** gentle; mild; kind **2** fortunate; salutary. **3** *Med.* (of a tumor, etc.) not malignant. □□ **be·nign′ly** *adv.*

be·nig·nant /binígnənt/ *adj.* **1** kindly, esp. to inferiors. **2** salutary; beneficial. □□ **be·nig·nan·cy** /-nənsee/ *n.* **be·nig′nant·ly** *adv.*

be·nig·ni·ty /binígnitee/ *n.* (*pl.* **-ties**) kindliness.

bent[1] /bent/ *past* and *past part.* of BEND[1] *v.* • *adj.* **1** curved; having an angle. **2** (foll. by *on*) determined to do or have. • *n.* **1** inclination or bias. **2** talent for something specified (*bent for mimicry*).

bent[2] /bent/ *n.* **1** any of various grasslike reeds, rushes, or sedges. **2** stiff stalk of a grass usu. with a flexible base.

bent·wood /béntwŏŏd/ *n.* wood that is artificially shaped for use in making furniture.

be·numb /binúm/ *v.tr.* **1** make numb; deaden. **2** paralyze (the mind or feelings).

ben·zene /bénzeen/ *n.* colorless carcinogenic volatile liquid found in coal tar, petroleum, etc., and used as a solvent and in the manufacture of plastics, etc.

be·queath /bikweéth, -kweéth/ *v.tr.* **1** leave (a personal estate) to a person by a will. **2** hand down to posterity. □□ **be·queath′al** *n.* **be·queath′er** *n.*

be·quest /bikwést/ *n.* **1** bequeathing. **2** thing bequeathed.

be·rate /biráyt/ *v.tr.* scold; rebuke.

Ber·ber /bárbər/ • *n.* **1** member of the indigenous mainly Muslim peoples of N. Africa. **2** language of these peoples. • *adj.* of the Berbers or their language.

be·reave /bireév/ *v.tr.* (esp. as **bereaved** *adj.*) deprive of a relation, friend, etc., esp. by death. □□ **be·reave′ment** *n.*

be·reft /biréft/ *adj.* deprived (esp. of a nonmaterial asset).

be·ret /bəráy/ *n.* round, flattish, visorless cap of felt or cloth.

berg /bərg/ *n.* = ICEBERG.

beri·beri /béreebéree/ *n.* nerve disease caused by a deficiency of vitamin B_1.

ber·ke·li·um /bərkeéleeəm, bə́rkleeəm/ *n. Chem.* transuranic radioactive metallic element. ¶ Symb.: **Bk.**

ber·ry /béree/ *n.* (*pl.* **-ries**) **1** any small roundish juicy fruit without a stone. **2** *Bot.* fruit with its seeds enclosed in a pulp (e.g., banana, tomato). □□ **ber′ried** *adj.* in *comb.*).

ber·serk /bərsórk, -zórk/ *adj.* (esp. in **go berserk**) **wild; frenzied; in a violent rage.**

berth /bərth/ • *n.* **1** fixed bunk on a ship, train, etc. **2** ship's place at a wharf. • *v.* **1** *tr.* moor (a ship) in its berth. **2** *tr.* provide a sleeping place for. □ **give a wide berth to** stay away from.

ber·yl /béril/ *n.* transparent precious stone, esp. emerald and aquamarine.

be·ryl·li·um /bərileeəm/ *n. Chem.* hard white metallic element. ¶ Symb.: **Be.**

be·seech /biseéch/ *v.tr.* (*past* and *past part.* **besought** /-sáwt/ or **beseeched**) ask earnestly. □□ **be·seech′ing** *adj.*

be·set /bisét/ *v.tr.* (**be·set·ting;** *past* and *past part.* **be·set**) **1** attack or harass persistently. **2** surround or hem in. □□ **be·set′ment** *n.*

be·side /bisíd/ *prep.* **1** at the side of; near. **2**

compared with. **3** irrelevant to. □ **beside oneself** overcome with worry, anger, etc.

be·sides /bisídz/ • *prep.* in addition to; apart from. • *adv.* also; as well; moreover.

be·siege /biseéj/ *v.tr.* **1** lay siege to. **2** crowd around oppressively. **3** harass with requests. □□ **be·sieg′er** *n.*

be·smirch /bismərch/ *v.tr.* **1** soil. **2** dishonor.

be·sot·ted /bisótid/ *adj.* **1** intoxicated; stupefied. **2** infatuated.

be·sought *past* and *past part.* of BESEECH.

be·spat·ter /bispátər/ *v.tr.* **1** spatter (an object) all over. **2** overwhelm with abuse, slander, etc.

be·speak /bispeék/ *v.tr.* (*past* **be·spoke** /-spók/; *past part.* **be·spo·ken** /-spókən/ or as *adj.* **be·spoke**) **1** engage in advance. **2** suggest; be evidence of.

best /best/ • *adj.* (*superl.* of GOOD) of the most excellent or desirable kind. • *adv.* (*superl.* of WELL[1]). **1** in the best manner. **2** to the greatest degree. **3** most usefully. • *n.* **1** that which is best. **2** chief merit or advantage. **3** (foll. by *of*) winning majority of (games, etc., played). **4** = *Sunday best.* • *v.tr. colloq.* defeat, outwit, outbid, etc. □ **at best** on the most optimistic view. **get the best of** defeat; outwit. **had best** would find it wisest to. **make the best of** derive what limited advantage one can from (something unsatisfactory or unwelcome).

bes·tial /béschəl, bées-/ *adj.* **1** brutish; cruel; savage. **2** of or like a beast. □□ **bes′tial·ize** *v.tr.* **bes′tial·ly** *adv.*

bes·ti·al·i·ty /béscheeálitee, bées-/ *n.* (*pl.* **-ties**) **1** bestial behavior. **2** sexual intercourse between a person and an animal.

bes·ti·ar·y /béschee-eree, bées-/ *n.* (*pl.* **-ies**) moralizing medieval treatise on real and imaginary beasts.

be·stir /bistər/ *v.refl.* (**be·stirred, be·stir·ring**) exert or rouse (oneself).

be·stow /bistó/ *v.tr.* confer (a gift, right, etc.). □□ **be·stow′al** *n.*

be·strew /bistró/ *v.tr.* (*past part.* **be·strewed** or **be·strewn** /-stróɒn/) **1** (foll. by *with*) cover or partly cover (a surface). **2** scatter (things) about. **3** lie scattered over.

bet /bet/ • *v.* (**bet·ting**; *past* and *past part.* **bet** or **bet·ted**) **1** *intr.* risk money, etc., on the outcome of an event (esp. a race, game, etc.). **2** *tr.* risk (an amount) on such an outcome. **3** *tr. colloq.* feel sure. • *n.* **1** act of betting. **2** money, etc., staked. **3** *colloq.* choice or course of action. □ **you bet** *colloq.* you may be sure. □□ **bet·tor** or **bet·ter** *n.*

bet. *abbr.* between.

be·ta /báytə, beé-/ *n.* second letter of the Greek alphabet (B, β). □ **beta-blocker** *Pharm.* drug that prevents the stimulation of increased cardiac action, used to treat angina and reduce high blood pressure. **beta particle** (or **ray**) fast-moving electron emitted by radioactive decay.

be·ta·tron /báytətron, beé-/ *n. Physics* apparatus for accelerating electrons in a circular path by magnetic induction.

be·tel /beét'l/ *n.* leaf chewed in parts of Asia with the betel nut. □ **betel nut** astringent seed of a tropical palm.

bête noire /bet nwaár/ *n.* (*pl.* **bêtes noires** *pronunc.* same) person or thing one particularly dislikes or fears.

be·think /bithíngk/ *v.refl.* (*past* and *past part.*

be·thought /-tháwt/) (foll. by *of, how,* or *that* + clause) *formal* **1** reflect; stop to think. **2** be reminded by reflection.

be·tray /bitráy/ *v.tr.* **1** be disloyal or treacherous to (another person, etc.). **2** reveal involuntarily or treacherously; be evidence of. □□ **be·tray′al** *n.* **be·tray′er** *n.*

be·troth /bitróth, -tráwth/ *v.tr.* (usu. as **betrothed** *adj.*) bind with a promise to marry. □□ **be·troth′al** *n.*

bet·ter /bétər/ • *adj.* (*compar.* of GOOD). **1** of a more excellent or desirable kind. **2** partly or fully recovered from illness. • *adv.* (*compar.* of WELL[1]). **1** in a better manner. **2** to a greater degree. **3** more usefully or advantageously. • *n.* **1** that which is better. **2** (usu. in *pl.*; prec. by *my,* etc.) one's superiors. • *v.tr.* **1** surpass. **2** improve. □ **better off** in a better (esp. financial) position. **get the better of** defeat; outwit. **had better** would find it wiser to.

bet·ter·ment /bétərmənt/ *n.* improvement.

be·tween /bitweén/ • *prep.* **1 a** at or to a point in the area or interval bounded by two points in space, time, etc. (*broke down between Boston and Providence*). **b** along the extent of such an area. **2** separating. **3 a** shared by. **b** by joint action. **4** to and from. **5** taking one and rejecting the other of. • *adv.* (also **in be·tween**) at a point or in the area bounded by two or more other points in space, time, sequence, etc. (*not fat or thin but in between*). □ **between ourselves** (or **you and me**) in confidence. ¶ **1. Between** is used in speaking of only two things, people, etc.: *We must choose between two equally unattractive alternatives.* **Among** is used when more than two are involved: *Agreement on landscaping was reached among all the neighbors.* But where there are more than two parties involved, **between** may be proper to emphasize the relationship of pairs within the group or the sense 'shared by': *There is close friendship between the members of the club; relations between the United States, Canada, and Mexico.* **2.** *Between you and I, between you and he,* etc., are incorrect; **between** should be followed only by the objective case: *me, her, him, them.*

be·twixt /bitwíkst/ *prep. & adv.* between. □ **betwixt and between** *colloq.* neither one thing nor the other.

BEVEL GEAR

bev·el /bévəl/ • *n.* **1** slope from the horizontal or vertical; sloping surface or edge. **2** (in full **bevel square**) tool for marking angles. • *v.* (**bev·eled, bev·el·ing; bev·elled, bev·el·ling**) **1** *tr.* reduce (a square edge) to a sloping edge. **2** *intr.* slope at an angle. □ **bevel gear** gear working another gear at an angle.

bev·er·age /bévərij, bévrij/ *n.* drink.

bev·y /bévee/ n. (pl. **-ies**) **1** flock of quails or larks. **2** company or group (orig. of women).

be·wail /biwáyl/ v.tr. **1** lament. **2** wail over. □□ **be·wail′er** n.

be·ware /biwáir/ v. (only in imper. or infin.) **1** intr. take heed. **2** tr. be cautious of.

be·wil·der /biwíldər/ v.tr. utterly perplex or confuse. □□ **be·wil′dered·ly** adv. **be·wil′der·ing** adj. **be·wil′der·ing·ly** adv. **be·wil′der·ment** n.

be·witch /biwích/ v.tr. **1** enchant; greatly delight. **2** cast a spell on. □□ **be·witch′ing** adj. **be·witch′ing·ly** adv.

be·yond /biyónd/ • prep. **1** at or to the farther side of. **2** outside the scope or understanding of. **3** more than. • adv. **1** at or to the farther side. **2** farther on. • n. (prec. by the) the unknown after death.

bez·el /bézəl/ n. **1** sloped edge of a chisel. **2** oblique faces of a cut gem. **3** groove holding a watch crystal or gem.

Bh symb. Chem. bohrium.

Bi symb. Chem. bismuth.

bi- /bī/ comb. form (often **bin-** before a vowel) forming nouns and adjectives meaning: **1** having two; thing having two (bilateral). **2 a** occurring twice in every one or once in every two (biweekly). **b** lasting for two (biennial).

bi·an·nu·al /bī-ányōōəl/ adj. occurring, appearing, etc., twice a year (cf. BIENNIAL). □□ **bi·an′nu·al·ly** adv.

¶ see note at BIENNIAL.

bi·as /bíəs/ • n. **1** predisposition or prejudice. **2** edge cut obliquely across the weave of a fabric. • v.tr. (**bi·ased**, **bi·as·ing**) (esp. as **biased** adj.) influence (usu. unfairly); prejudice. □ **on the bias** obliquely; diagonally.

bi·ath·lon /bī-áthlon, -lən/ n. Sports athletic contest in skiing and shooting. □□ **bi·ath′lete** n.

bib /bib/ n. **1** piece of cloth fastened around a child's neck while eating. **2** top front part of an apron, overalls, etc.

bibl. abbr. (also **Bibl.**) biblical.

Bi·ble /bíbəl/ n. **1 a** Christian scriptures consisting of the Old and New Testaments. **b** Jewish scriptures. **2** (**bible**) colloq. any authoritative book (the woodworker's bible). □ **Bible belt** area of the southern and central US where fundamentalist Protestant beliefs prevail. □□ **bib·li·cal** /bíblikəl/ adj. **bib′li·cal·ly** adv.

bibliog. abbr. bibliography.

bib·li·og·ra·phy /bíbleeógrəfee/ n. (pl. **-phies**) **1 a** list of books referred to in a scholarly work, usu. as an appendix. **b** list of books by a specific author or publisher, or on a specific subject, etc. **2** history or description of books, including authors, editions, etc. □□ **bib·li·og′ra·pher** n. **bib·li·o·graph·ic** /-leeəgráfik/ adj. **bib·li·o·graph′i·cal** adj. **bib·li·o·graph′i·cal·ly** adv.

bib·li·o·phile /bíbleeōfīl/ n. collector or lover of books. □□ **bib·li·o·phil·ic** /-fílik/ adj. **bib·li·oph′i·ly** /-leeófilee/ n.

bib·u·lous /bíbyələs/ adj. given to drinking alcoholic beverages. □□ **bib′u·lous·ly** adv. **bib′u·lous·ness** n.

bi·cam·er·al /bīkámərəl/ adj. (of a legislative body) having two chambers. □□ **bi·cam′er·al·ism** n.

bi·carb /bikaárb/ n. colloq. = BICARBONATE.

bi·car·bon·ate /bīkaárbənit/ n. (in full **bi·car′bo·nate of so′da**) sodium bicarbonate used as an antacid or in baking powder.

bi·cen·ten·ni·al /bísenténeeəl/ • n. two-hundredth anniversary. • adj. lasting two hundred years or occurring every two hundred years.

bi·ceps /bíseps/ n. muscle having two heads or attachments, esp. the one that bends the elbow.

bick·er /bíkər/ v.intr. quarrel pettily; wrangle.

bi·con·cave /bīkónkayv, bíkonkáyv/ adj. (esp. of a lens) concave on both sides.

bi·con·vex /bīkónveks, bíkonvéks/ adj. (esp. of a lens) convex on both sides.

bi·cus·pid /bīkúspid/ • adj. having two cusps. • n. the premolar in humans. □□ **bi·cus′pi·date** adj.

bi·cy·cle /bísikəl, -sīkəl/ • n. two-wheeled vehicle propelled by pedals and steered with handlebars attached to the front wheel. • v.intr. ride a bicycle.

bid /bid/ • v. (**bid·ding**; past **bid**, **bade** /bayd, bad/; past part. **bid**) **1** tr. & intr. (past and past part. **bid**) (often foll. by for, against) **a** (esp. at an auction) offer (a certain price) (bid $20). **b** offer to do work, etc., for a stated price. **2** tr. command; invite. **3** tr. archaic or literary utter (greeting or farewell) to. **4** tr. & intr. (past and past part. **bid**) Cards state before play how many tricks one intends to make. • n. **1 a** offer (of a price). **b** offer (to do work, etc.) at a stated price. **2** attempt; effort. □□ **bid′da·ble** adj. **bid·da·bil′i·ty** n. **bid′der** n.

bid·ding /bíding/ n. **1** bids at an auction or card game. **2** command; request; invitation.

bid·dy /bídee/ n. (pl. **-dies**) sl. derog. woman (esp. old biddy).

bide /bīd/ □ **bide one's time** await one's best opportunity.

bi·det /beedáy/ n. low, oval, basinlike bathroom fixture used esp. for washing the genital area.

bi·en·ni·al /bī-éneeəl/ • adj. **1** lasting two years. **2** recurring every two years (cf. BIANNUAL). • n. **1** Bot. plant that takes two years to grow from seed to fruition and die. **2** event celebrated or taking place every two years. □□ **bi·en′ni·al·ly** adv.

¶ **Biennial** means 'lasting or occurring every two years': Congressional elections are a biennial phenomenon. A biennial plant is one that lives a two-year cycle, flowering and producing seed in the second year. **Biannual** means 'twice a year': The solstice is a biannual event.

bier /beer/ n. movable frame for a coffin.

bi·fo·cal /bīfókəl/ • adj. having two focuses, esp. of a lens with a part for distant vision and a part for near vision. • n. (in pl.) bifocal eyeglasses.

bi·fur·cate /bífərkayt/ • v. divide into two branches; fork. • adj. forked; branched. □□ **bi·fur·ca·tion** /-káyshən/ n.

big /big/ • adj. (**big·ger**, **big·gest**) **1 a** of considerable size, amount, intensity, etc. **b** of a large or the largest size. **2** important; significant; outstanding. **3 a** grown up. **b** elder. **4** colloq. **a** boastful. **b** often iron. generous. **c** ambitious. **d** popular. **5** advanced in pregnancy. • adv. colloq. in a big manner, esp.: **1** effectively (went over big). **2** boastfully. **3** ambitiously. □ **Big Apple** sl. New York City. **big bang theory** theory that the universe began with the explosion of dense matter. **Big Dipper** constellation of seven bright stars in Ursa Major in the shape of a dipper. **big top** main tent in a circus. □□ **big′gish** adj. **big′ness** n.

big·a·my /bígəmee/ n. (pl. **-mies**) crime of marrying when one is lawfully married to another person. □□ **big′a·mist** n. **big′a·mous** adj.

big·heart·ed /bíghártid/ adj. generous.

big·horn /bíghawrn/ n. American wild sheep, esp. native to the Rocky Mountains.

bight /bīt/ n. **1** curve or recess in a coastline, river, etc. **2** loop of rope.

big·mouth /bígmowth/ n. colloq. boastful or talkative person.

big·ot /bígət/ n. obstinate and intolerant believer in a religion, etc. □□ **big′ot·ed** adj. **big′ot·ry** n.

big·wig /bígwig/ n. colloq. important person.

bike /bīk/ • n. colloq. bicycle or motorcycle. • v.intr. ride a bicycle or motorcycle. □□ **bik′er** n.

bi·ki·ni /bikéenee/ n. brief two-piece swimsuit for women.

---

bikini 1940s: named after Bikini atoll in the Pacific, (where an atom bomb was tested in 1946) because of the supposed "explosive" effect created by the garment.

---

bi·lat·er·al /bīlátərəl/ adj. **1** of, on, or with two sides. **2** affecting or between two parties, countries, etc. (bilateral negotiations). □ **bilateral symmetry** symmetry about a plane. □□ **bi·lat′er·al·ly** adv.

bile /bīl/ n. **1** bitter fluid that aids digestion and is secreted by the liver. **2** bad temper; peevish anger.

bilge /bilj/ n. **1 a** almost flat part of a ship's bottom, inside or out. **b** (in full **bilge wa·ter**) filthy water that collects there. **2** sl. nonsense; worthless ideas.

bi·lin·gual /bīlínggwəl/ • adj. **1** able to speak two languages. **2** spoken or written in two languages. • n. bilingual person. □□ **bi·lin′gual·ism** n.

bil·ious /bílyəs/ adj. **1** affected by a disorder of the bile. **2** bad-tempered. □□ **bil′ious·ly** adv. **bil′ious·ness** n.

bilk /bilk/ v.tr. sl. **1** cheat. **2** give the slip to. **3** avoid paying (a creditor or debt). □□ **bilk′er** n.

bill¹ /bil/ • n. **1 a** statement of charges for goods or services rendered. **b** amount owed (ran up a bill of $300). **2** draft of a proposed law. **3 a** poster; placard. **b** = HANDBILL. **4** a printed list, esp. a theater program. **b** the entertainment itself (top of the bill). **5** piece of paper money. • v.tr. **1** put in the program; announce. **2** send a note of charges to. □ **bill of exchange** Econ. written order to pay a sum of money on a given date to the drawer or to a named payee. **bill of fare** menu. **bill of goods** shipment of merchandise, often for resale. **2** colloq. item that is misrepresented, fraudulent, etc. **bill of lading** Naut. detailed list of cargo. **Bill of Rights** original ten amendments to the U.S. Constitution, affirming civil rights. **bill of sale** Econ. certificate of transfer of personal property. □□ **bill′a·ble** adj.

bill² /bil/ • n. bird's beak. • v.intr. (of doves, etc.) stroke a bill with a bill. □□ **billed** adj. (usu. in comb.).

bill·board /bílbawrd/ n. large outdoor advertising sign.

bil·let /bílit/ • n. **1** place where troops, etc.,

are lodged. **2** colloq. job. • v.tr. (usu. foll. by on, in, at) quarter (soldiers, etc.). □□ **bil′let·er** n.

bil·let-doux /bílaydōō/ n. (pl. **bil·lets-doux** /-dōōz/) often joc. love letter.

bill·fold /bílfōld/ n. wallet for keeping paper money.

bil·liards /bílyərdz/ n. any of several games played on an oblong cloth-covered table, esp. one with three balls struck with cues into pockets around the edge of the table.

bil·lion /bílyən/ n. (pl. same or (in sense 2) **billions**) (in sing. prec. by a or one) **1** a thousand million (1,000,000,000 or 10⁹). **2** colloq. very large number (billions of years). □□ **bil′lionth** adj. & n.

bil·lion·aire /bílyənáir/ n. person possessing over a billion dollars, pounds, etc.

bil·low /bílō/ n. **1** wave. **2** any large soft mass. □□ **bil′low·y** adj.

bil·ly /bílee/ n. (pl. **-lies**) (in full **bil′ly club**) bludgeon.

bil·ly goat /bíligōt/ n. male goat.

bim·bo /bímbō/ n. (pl. **-bos** or **-boes**) sl. usu. derog. **1** foolish person. **2 a** physically attractive but simple-minded woman. **b** disreputable woman.

bi·me·tal·lic /bímitálik/ adj. made of two metals.

bi·month·ly /bímúnthlee/ • adj. occurring twice a month or every two months. • adv. twice a month or every two months. • n. (pl. **-lies**) periodical produced bimonthly.

bin /bin/ n. large receptacle for storage or garbage.

bi·na·ry /bíneree/ • adj. **1 a** dual. **b** of or involving pairs. **2** of the arithmetical system using 2 as a base. • n. (pl. **-ries**) **1** something having two parts. **2** binary number. □ **binary code** Computing coding system using the binary digits 0 and 1 to represent a letter, digit, or other character. **binary star** system of two stars orbiting each other.

bind /bīnd/ • v. (past and past part. **bound** /bownd/) **1** tr. tie or fasten tightly. **2** tr. **a** restrain. **b** (as **-bound** adj.) constricted; obstructed (snowbound). **3** tr. cause to cohere. **4** tr. fasten or hold together as a single mass. **5** tr. compel; impose. **6** tr. **a** edge (fabric, etc.) with braid, etc. **b** fasten (the pages of a book) in a cover. **7** tr. ratify (a bargain, agreement, etc.). **8** tr. (in passive) be required by an obligation or duty (am bound to answer). **9** tr. (often foll. by up) bandage. • n. colloq. **1** nuisance; restriction. **2** tight or difficult situation.

bind·er /bíndər/ n. **1** cover for sheets of paper, etc. **2** substance that acts cohesively. **3** reaping machine that binds grain into sheaves. **4** bookbinder.

bind·er·y /bíndəree/ n. (pl. **-ies**) bookbinder's workshop.

bind·ing /bínding/ • n. something that binds, esp. the covers, glue, etc., of a book. • adj. obligatory.

binge /binj/ sl. • n. spree; period of uncontrolled eating, drinking, etc. • v.intr. indulge in a binge.

bin·go /bínggō/ n. game in which each player has a card of squares with numbers that are marked off as they are randomly drawn and called.

bin·na·cle /bínəkəl/ *n.* housing for a ship's compass.

BINNACLE

bin·oc·u·lar /bínókyələr/ *adj.* adapted for or using both eyes.

bin·oc·u·lars /binókyələrz/ *n.pl.* optical instrument with a lens for each eye, for viewing distant objects.

bi·no·mi·al /bīnṓmeeəl/ ● *n.* algebraic expression of the sum or the difference of two terms. ● *adj.* consisting of two terms. □□ **bi·no′mi·al·ly** *adv.*

bi·o /bī-ō/ ● *n.* **1** biology. **2** (*pl.* **bi·os**) biography. ● *adj.* biological.

bio- /bī-ō/ *comb. form* **1** life (*biography*). **2** biological (*biomathematics*). **3** of living beings (*biophysics*).

bi·o·chem·is·try /bī-ōkémistree/ *n.* study of the chemical and physicochemical processes of living organisms. □□ **bi·o·chem′i·cal** *adj.* **bi·o·chem′ist** *n.*

bi·o·de·grad·a·ble /bī-ōdigráydəbəl/ *adj.* capable of being decomposed by bacteria or other living organisms. □□ **bi·o·de·grad·a·bil′i·ty** *n.* **bi·o·deg·ra·da·tion** /bī-ōdégrədáyshən/ *n.*

bi·o·di·ver·si·ty /bī-ōdivə́rsitee/ *n.* variety of plant and animal life in a particular habitat.

bi·o·feed·back /bī-ōfeédbak/ *n.* technique of using the feedback of a normally automatic bodily response to a stimulus in order to acquire voluntary control of that response.

biog. *abbr.* **1** biographer. **2** biographical. **3** biography.

bi·o·gen·e·sis /bī-ōjénisis/ *n.* **1** synthesis of substances by living organisms. **2** hypothesis that a living organism arises only from another similar living organism. □□ **bi·o·ge·net·ic** /-jinétik/ *adj.*

bi·og·ra·phy /bī-ógrəfee/ *n.* (*pl.* **-phies**) **1** written account of a person's life, usu. by another. **2** such writing as a branch of literature. □□ **bi·og′ra·pher** *n.* **bi·o·graph·ic** /bī·əgráfik/ *adj.* **bi·o·graph′i·cal** *adj.*

biol. *abbr.* **1** biologic. **2** biological. **3** biologist. **4** biology.

bi·o·log·i·cal /bī·əlójikəl/ *adj.* **1** of or relating to biology or living organisms. **2** related genetically, not by marriage, adoption, etc. □ **biological clock** innate mechanism controlling the rhythmic physiological activities of an organism. **biological warfare** warfare involving the use

of toxins or microorganisms. □□ **bi·o·log′i·cal·ly** *adv.*

bi·ol·o·gy /bī-óləjee/ *n.* the study of living organisms. □□ **bi·ol′o·gist** *n.*

bi·o·mass /bī-ōmas/ *n.* total quantity or weight of organisms in a given area or volume.

bi·on·ic /bī-ónik/ *adj.* having electronically or mechanically operated body parts. □□ **bi·on′i·cal·ly** *adv.*

bi·on·ics /bī-óniks/ *n.pl.* (treated as *sing.*) the study of mechanical systems that function like living organisms.

bi·o·phys·ics /bī-ōfíziks/ *n.pl.* (treated as *sing.*) science of the application of the laws of physics to biological phenomena. □□ **bi·o·phys′i·cal** *adj.* **bi·o·phys′i·cist** *n.*

bi·op·sy /bī́opsee/ *n.* (*pl.* **-sies**) examination of tissue removed for diagnosis.

bi·o·rhythm /bī-ṓrithəm/ *n.* any recurring biological cycle thought to affect a person's emotional, intellectual, and physical activity. □□ **bi·o·rhyth·mic** /-ərithmik/ *adj.* **bi·o·rhyth′mi·cal·ly** *adv.*

bi·o·sphere /bī-ōsfeer/ *n.* regions of the earth's crust and atmosphere occupied by living organisms.

bi·o·syn·the·sis /bī-ōsínthisis/ *n.* production of organic molecules by living organisms. □□ **bi·o·syn·thet·ic** /-thétik/ *adj.*

bi·o·tech·nol·o·gy /bī-ōteknóləjee/ *n.* exploitation of biological processes in industry, medicine, etc.

bi·o·tin /bī́ətin/ *n.* vitamin of the B complex.

bi·par·ti·san /bīpáartizən, -sən/ *adj.* of or involving two (esp. political) parties. □□ **bi·par′ti·san·ship** *n.*

bi·par·tite /bīpáartīt/ *adj.* **1** consisting of two parts. **2** shared by or involving two parties.

bi·ped /bī́ped/ ● *n.* two-footed animal. ● *adj.* two-footed. □□ **bi·ped′al** *adj.*

bi·plane /bī́playn/ *n.* type of airplane having two sets of wings, one above the other.

birch /bərch/ ● *n.* **1** hardwood tree with thin peeling bark. **2** its wood. **3** (in full **birch rod**) bundle of birch twigs used for flogging. ● *v.tr.* beat with a birch (in sense 3).

bird /bərd/ *n.* egg-laying feathered vertebrate with a beak, two wings, and two feet, and usu. able to fly. □ **bird in the hand** something secured or certain. **the birds and the bees** *euphem.* sexual activity and reproduction. **bird's-eye view** general view from above. **birds of a feather** people of like character. **for** (or **strictly for**) **the birds** *colloq.* trivial; uninteresting.

bird·bath /bə́rdbath/ *n.* basin in a garden, etc., with water for birds to bathe in.

bird·brain /bə́rdbrayn/ *n.* *colloq.* stupid or flighty person. □□ **bird′brained** *adj.*

bird·ie /bə́rdee/ *Golf* ● *n.* score of one stroke less than par at any hole. ● *v.tr.* (**-ies, -ied, -ie·ing**) play (a hole) in one stroke less than par.

bi·ret·ta /birétə/ *n.* square, usu. black cap worn by (esp. Roman Catholic) clergymen.

birth /bərth/ ● *n.* **1** emergence of an infant or other young from the body of its mother. **2** *rhet.* beginning (*birth of socialism*). **3** origin; descent; ancestry (*of noble birth*). ● *v.tr. colloq.* give birth to. □ **birth control** contraception.

birth·day /bə́rthday/ *n.* **1** day on which one was born. **2** anniversary of this. □ **in one's birthday suit** *joc.* naked.

birth·mark /bə́rthmaark/ *n.* brown or red mark on one's body at or from birth.

birth·place /bə́rthplays/ *n.* place where one was born.

birth·right /bə́rthrīt/ *n.* right of possession or privilege one has from birth.

birth·stone /bə́rthstōn/ *n.* gemstone popularly associated with the month of one's birth.

bis·cuit /bískit/ *n.* small leavened bread or cake.

biscuit Middle English: from Old French *bescuit*, based on Latin *bis* 'twice' + *coctus*, past participle of *coquere* 'to cook' (so named because originally biscuits were cooked in a twofold process: first baked and then dried out in a slow oven so that they would keep).

bi·sect /bísékt/ *v.tr.* divide into two (equal) parts. □□ **bi·sec·tion** /-sékshən/ *n.* **bi·sec′tor** *n.*

bi·sex·u·al /bíséksho͞oəl/ • *adj.* **1** sexually attracted to persons of both sexes. **2** *Biol.* having characteristics of both sexes. **3** of or concerning both sexes. • *n.* bisexual person. □□ **bi·sex·u·al·i·ty** /-sékshoo-álitee, -séksyoo-álitee/ *n.*

bish·op /bíshəp/ *n.* **1** senior member of the Christian clergy usu. in charge of a diocese. **2** chess piece that is moved diagonally.

bish·op·ric /bíshəprik/ *n.* office or diocese of a bishop.

bis·muth /bízməth/ *n. Chem.* metallic element used in alloys. ¶ Symb.: **Bi.**

bi·son /bísən/ *n.* (*pl.* same) humpbacked shaggy-haired oxen of N. America or Europe.

bisque /bisk/ *n.* rich shellfish soup, made esp. from lobster.

bis·tro /béestrō, bís-/ *n.* (*pl.* **-tros**) small restaurant.

bit¹ /bit/ *n.* **1** small piece or quantity. **2** (*prec.* by *a*) **a** fair amount. **b** *colloq.* somewhat (*am a bit tired*). **3** short time or distance. □ **bit by bit** gradually. **do one's bit** *colloq.* make a useful contribution. **two bits** 25 cents.

bit² /bit/ *n.* **1** metal mouthpiece on a bridle. **2** (usu. metal) tool or piece for boring or drilling. **3** cutting or gripping part of a plane, pliers, etc.

bit³ /bit/ *n. Computing* unit of information; 0 or 1 in binary notation.

bitch /bich/ • *n.* **1** female dog or other canine animal. **2** *sl. offens.* spiteful woman. **3** *sl.* very unpleasant or difficult thing. • *v. colloq.* **1** *intr.* (often foll. by *about*) speak scathingly. **2** complain.

bitch·y /bíchee/ *adj.* (**bitch·i·er, bitch·i·est**) *sl.* spiteful; bad-tempered. □□ **bitch′i·ly** *adv.* **bitch′i·ness** *n.*

bite /bīt/ • *v.* (*past* **bit** /bit/; *past part.* **bit·ten** /bit′n/) **1** *tr.* cut or puncture using the teeth. **2** *tr.* (often foll. by *off*, etc.) detach with the teeth. **3** *tr.* (of an insect, etc.) sting. **4** *intr.* (of a wheel, screw, etc.) grip; penetrate. **5** *intr.* accept bait or an inducement. **6** *tr.* (as **bitten** *adj.*) cause smarting pain. • *n.* **1** act of biting. **2** wound made by biting. **3 a** mouthful of food. **b** snack. **4** taking of bait by a fish. **5** pungency (esp. of flavor). **6** incisiveness; sharpness. □ **bite the bullet** *sl.* behave bravely or stoically. **bite the dust**

sl. **1** die. **2** fail; break down. **bite a person's head off** *colloq.* respond angrily. **bite one's lip** see LIP. □□ **bit′er** *n.*

bit·ing /bíting/ *adj.* **1** stinging; intensely cold. **2** sharp; effective. □□ **bit′ing·ly** *adv.*

bit·ter /bítər/ • *adj.* **1** having a sharp pungent taste; not sweet. **2** caused by, feeling, or showing mental pain or resentment. **3 a** harsh; virulent. **b** piercingly cold. • *n.* (in *pl.*) liquor with a bitter flavor used as an additive in cocktails. □□ **bit′ter·ly** *adv.* **bit′ter·ness** *n.*

bit·tern /bítərn/ *n.* wading bird of the heron family.

bit·ter·sweet /bítərswēt/ • *adj.* sweet with a bitter aftertaste. • *n.* **1** such sweetness. **2** scarlet-berried climbing nightshade of N. America.

bi·tu·men /bīto͞omin, -tyo͞o-, bi-/ *n.* any of various oily tarlike mixtures of hydrocarbons derived from petroleum.

bi·tu·mi·nous /bīto͞ominəs, -tyo͞o-, bi-/ *adj.* of, relating to, or containing bitumen. □ **bituminous coal** soft coal burning with a smoky flame.

bi·valve /bívalv/ *n.* any of a group of aquatic mollusks with two hinged shells, e.g., oysters.

biv·ou·ac /bívo͞o-ak, bívwak/ • *n.* temporary open encampment without tents. • *v.intr.* (**biv·ou·acked, biv·ou·ack·ing**) camp in a bivouac.

biz /biz/ *n. colloq.* business.

bi·zarre /bizaár/ *adj.* strange; eccentric; grotesque. □□ **bi·zarre′ly** *adv.* **bi·zarre′ness** *n.*

Bk *symb. Chem.* berkelium.

bk. *abbr.* book.

blab /blab/ • *v.* (**blabbed, blab·bing**) **1** talk foolishly or indiscreetly. **2** reveal secrets. • *n.* person who blabs.

black /blak/ • *adj.* **1** having no color from the absorption of all or nearly all incident light (like coal or soot). **2** completely dark. **3 a** of the human group having dark-colored skin, esp. of African descent. **b** of or relating to black people. **4** (of the sky, etc.) dusky; heavily overcast. **5** angry; threatening. **6** wicked; sinister; deadly. **7** gloomy; depressed; sullen (*a black mood*). **8** with sinister or macabre, as well as comic, import (*black comedy*). **9** (of coffee or tea) without milk. • *n.* **1** black color or pigment. **2** black clothes (*wears nothing but black*). **3** credit side of an account (*in the black*). **4** member of a dark-skinned race, esp. one of African descent. • *v.tr.* make black (*blacked his eyebrows*). □ **black and blue** discolored by bruises. **black belt 1** black belt worn by an expert in judo, etc. **2** person qualified to wear this. **black box** flight recorder in an aircraft. **black eye** bruised skin around the eye resulting from a blow. **black-eyed Susan** daisylike flower with yellow petals and a dark center. **black hole** region of space possessing a strong gravitational field from which matter and radiation cannot escape. **black ice** thin, hard transparent ice, esp. on a road surface. **black light** *Physics* invisible ultraviolet or infrared radiations of the electromagnetic spectrum. **black magic** magic involving supposed invocation of evil spirits. **black mark** mark of discredit. **black market** illicit traffic in officially controlled or scarce commodities. **black marketeer** person who engages in a black market. **Black Mass** ceremony in worship of Satan. **Black Power** movement, esp. in the 1960s in support of black rights and political power. **black sheep** *colloq.* unsatisfactory or disreputable member of a family, group, etc. **black tie 1** black bow tie worn with a dinner jacket. **2** *colloq.* man's formal evening dress. **black widow** venomous spider, of which the female has an hourglass-shaped red mark on her abdomen. □□ **black′ish** *adj.* **black′ly** *adv.* **black′ness** *n.*

¶ **Black,** designating Americans of African heritage, became the most widely used and accepted term in the 1960s and 1970s, replacing **Negro.** It is not usually capitalized: *black Americans.* Through the 1980s, the more formal **African American** replaced **black** in much usage, but both are now generally acceptable. **Afro-American,** an earlier alternative to **black,** is heard mostly in anthropological and cultural contexts. 'Colored people', common earlier in the twentieth century, is now usually regarded as derogatory, although the phrase survives in the full name of the NAACP. An inversion, 'people of color' has gained some favor, but is also used for all nonwhite ethnic groups: *a gathering spot for African-Americans and other people of color interested in reading about their cultures.*

black·ball /blákbawl/ *v.tr.* **1** reject (a candidate) in a ballot (orig. by voting with a black ball). **2** exclude; ostracize.

black·ber·ry /blákberee/ *n.* (*pl.* **-ries**) **1** thorny rosaceous shrub. Also called **bramble. 2** black fleshy edible fruit of this plant.

black·bird /blákbərd/ *n.* **1** common thrush of which the male is black with an orange beak. **2** any of various birds, esp. a grackle, with black plumage.

black·board /blákbawrd/ *n.* board with a smooth, usu. dark surface for writing on with chalk.

black·en /blákən/ *v.* **1** *tr.* & *intr.* make or become black or dark. **2** *tr.* speak evil of; defame.

black·guard /blágaard, -ərd/ *n.* villain; scoundrel. □□ **black′guard·ly** *adj.*

black·head /blák-hed/ *n.* black-topped pimple on the skin.

black·jack /blákjak/ *n.* **1** card game in which players try to acquire cards with a face value totaling 21 and no more. **2** flexible leaded bludgeon.

black·list /bláklist/ • *n.* list of people in disfavor, etc. • *v.tr.* put on a blacklist.

black·mail /blákmayl/ • *n.* **1** extortion of payment in return for not disclosing a secret, etc. **2** any payment extorted in this way. • *v.tr.* extort money, etc., by blackmail. □□ **black′mail·er** *n.*

black·out /blákowt/ *n.* **1** temporary loss of consciousness or memory. **2** temporary loss of power, etc. **3** compulsory darkness as a precaution against air raids. **4** suppression of news. **5** sudden darkening of a theater stage.

black·smith /bláksmith/ *n.* smith who works in iron.

black·thorn /blákthawrn/ *n.* thorny rosaceous shrub bearing white flowers and small blue-black fruits.

black·top /bláktop/ *n.* type of surfacing material for roads, playgrounds, etc.

blad·der /bládər/ *n.* **1 a** membranous sac in some animals, esp. that which stores urine. **b** this or a similar object prepared for various uses. **2** inflated vesicle in various plants.

blade /blayd/ *n.* **1 a** cutting edge of a knife, etc. **b** flat piece of metal with a sharp edge or edges

used in a razor. **2** flattened part of an oar, propeller, etc. **3 a** flat, narrow leaf of grass and cereals. **b** *Bot.* broad thin part of a leaf. **4** *poet.* sword. □□ **blad·ed** *adj.* (also in *comb.*).

blame /blaym/ • *v.tr.* **1** assign fault or responsibility to. **2** (foll. by *on*) assign the responsibility for (an error or wrong) to a person, etc. • *n.* **1** responsibility for a bad result. **2** blaming or attributing responsibility. □ **be to blame** (often foll. by *for*) be responsible; deserve censure. □□ **blam′a·ble** or **blame′a·ble** *adj.* **blame′ful** *adj.*

blame·less /bláymlis/ *adj.* innocent; free from blame. □□ **blame′less·ly** *adv.* **blame′less·ness** *n.*

blanch /blanch/ *v.* **1** *tr.* make or become white or pale. **2** *tr. Cookery* prepare by briefly immersing in boiling water.

bland /bland/ *adj.* **1 a** mild; not irritating. **b** tasteless; insipid. **2** gentle in manner; smooth. □□ **bland′ly** *adv.* **bland′ness** *n.*

blan·dish /blándish/ *v.tr.* flatter; coax; cajole. □□ **blan′dish·ment** *n.*

blank /blangk/ • *adj.* **1 a** (of paper) not written or printed on. **b** (of a document) with spaces left for a signature or details. **2 a** empty. **b** undecorated. **3 a** puzzled; nonplussed. **b** having (temporarily) no knowledge. • *n.* **1 a** unfilled space in a document. **b** document having blank spaces to be filled. **2** (in full **blank cartridge**) cartridge containing gunpowder but no bullet. • *v.tr.* (usu. foll. by *off, out*) screen; obscure. □ **blank check 1** check with the amount left for the payee to fill in. **2** *colloq.* freedom of action. **blank verse** unrhymed verse, esp. iambic pentameters. □□ **blank′ly** *adv.* **blank′ness** *n.*

blan·ket /blángkit/ • *n.* **1** large piece of woolen or other material used for warmth, esp. as a bed covering. **2** (usu. foll. by *of*) thick covering mass or layer. • *adj.* covering all cases or classes; inclusive. • *v.tr.* **1** cover. **2** stifle; keep quiet.

blare /blair/ • *v.tr. & intr.* sound or utter loudly. **2** *intr.* make the sound of a trumpet. • *n.* loud sound.

blar·ney /bláarnee/ • *n.* cajoling talk; flattery. • *v.* (**-neys, -neyed**) *tr.* flatter; cajole.

bla·sé /blaazáy/ *adj.* bored; indifferent.

blas·pheme /blasfeém, blásfeem/ *v.* **1** *intr.* talk profanely, making use of religious names, etc. **2** *tr.* talk profanely about; revile. □□ **blas·phem′er** *n.*

blas·phe·my /blásfəmee/ *n.* (*pl.* **-mies**) **1** profane talk. **2** instance of this. □□ **blas′phe·mous** *adj.* **blas′phe·mous·ly** *adv.*

blast /blast/ • *n.* **1** strong gust of wind, heat, etc. **2 a** explosion. **b** destructive wave of air from this. **3** loud note of a wind instrument, car horn, etc. **4** *colloq.* severe reprimand. • *v.* **1** *tr.* blow up with explosives. **2** *tr.* wither; shrivel. **3** *intr. & tr.* make or cause to make a loud noise. **4** *colloq.* reprimand severely. □ **at full blast** *colloq.* working at maximum speed, etc. **blast off** (of a rocket, etc.) take off from a launching site.

bla·tant /bláyt'nt/ *adj.* **1** flagrant; unashamed. **2** offensively obtrusive. □□ **bla·tan·cy** /-t'nsee/ *n.* **bla′tant·ly** *adv.*

blaze¹ /blayz/ • *n.* **1** bright flame or fire. **2** bright glaring light. **3** violent outburst (of passion, etc.). • *v.intr.* **1** burn with a bright flame. **2** be brilliantly lit. **3** be consumed with anger, excitement, etc. □ **blaze away** (often foll. by *at*) shoot continuously. □□ **blaz'ing** *adj.* **blaz' ing•ly** *adv.*

blaze² /blayz/ • *n.* **1** white mark on an animal's face. **2** mark cut on a tree, esp. to mark a route. • *v.tr.* mark (a tree or path) with blazes.

blaz•er /bláyzər/ *n.* solid-color jacket not worn with matching trousers.

bla•zon /bláyzən/ • *v.tr.* proclaim. • *n. Heraldry* coat of arms.

bldg. *abbr.* building.

bleach /bleech/ • *v.* whiten by sunlight or chemical process. • *n.* bleaching substance.

bleach•er /bléechər/ *n.* (usu. in *pl.*) usu. uncovered, inexpensive bench seat at a sports field or arena.

bleak /bleek/ *adj.* **1** exposed; windswept. **2** dreary. □□ **bleak'ly** *adv.* **bleak'ness** *n.*

blear•y /bléeree/ *adj.* (**blear•i•er**, **blear•i•est**) **1** (of the eyes or mind) dim; blurred. **2** indistinct. □ **bleary-eyed** having dim sight or wits. □□ **blear'i•ly** *adv.* **blear'i•ness** *n.*

bleat /bleet/ • *v.* **1** *intr.* (of a sheep, goat, or calf) make a wavering cry. **2** *intr.* & *tr.* (often foll. by *out*) speak feebly, foolishly, or plaintively. • *n.* **1** sound made by a sheep, goat, etc. **2** weak cry. □□ **bleat'er** *n.* **bleat'ing•ly** *adv.*

bleed /bleed/ • *v.* (*past* and *past part.* **bled** /bled/) **1** *intr.* emit blood. **2** *tr.* draw blood from surgically. **3** *tr.* extort money from. **4** *tr.* allow (fluid or gas) to escape from a closed system through a valve, etc.

bleed•er /bléedər/ *n. colloq.* hemophiliac.

bleep /bleep/ • *n.* intermittent high-pitched sound made electronically. • *v.* **1** *intr.* & *tr.* make such a sound, esp. as a signal. **2** *tr.* obliterate obscenities with a bleep, as on a broadcast.

blem•ish /blémish/ • *n.* defect; stain; flaw. • *v.tr.* spoil; stain.

blench /blench/ *v.intr.* flinch; quail.

blend /blend/ • *v.* **1** *tr.* **a** mix together. **b** produce by this method. **2** *intr.* harmonize; become one. **3** *intr.* (esp. of colors): **a** merge imperceptibly. **b** go well together; harmonize. • *n.* mixture.

blend•er /bléndər/ *n.* kitchen appliance for liquefying, chopping, or puréeing food.

bless /bles/ *v.tr.* (*past* and *past part.* **bless•ed**, *poet.* **blest** /blest/) **1** (of a priest, etc.) pronounce words, esp. in a religious rite, asking for divine favor. **2 a** consecrate (esp. bread and wine). **b** sanctify by the sign of the cross. **3** glorify (God). **4** thank. **5** (usu. in *passive*; often foll. by *with*) make happy or successful. □ (**God**) **bless you!** exclamation of endearment, gratitude, etc., or to a person who has just sneezed.

---

bless Old English *blēdsian*, *blētsian*, based on *blōd* 'blood' (i.e., originally perhaps 'mark or consecrate with blood'). The meaning was influenced by its being used to translate Latin *benedicere* 'to praise, worship,' and later by association with **bliss**.

---

bless•ed /blésid, blest/ *adj.* (also *poet.* **blest**) **1** consecrated. **2** /blest/ (usu. foll. by *with*) often *iron.* fortunate (in the possession of). **3** *euphem.* cursed. **4** *RC Ch.* beatified. □□ **bless'ed•ly** *adv.* **bless'ed•ness** *n.*

bless•ing /blésing/ *n.* **1** invoking (esp. divine)

favor. **2** grace said before or after a meal. **3** gift of God, nature, etc.

blew *past* of BLOW¹.

blight /blīt/ • *n.* **1** plant disease caused by mildew, insects, etc. **2** such an insect. **3** harmful or destructive force. **4** unsightly or neglected urban area. • *v.tr.* **1** affect with blight. **2** harm; destroy. **3** spoil.

blimp /blimp/ *n.* small nonrigid airship.

blind /blīnd/ • *adj.* **1** lacking the power of sight. **2 a** without discernment. **b** (often foll. by *to*) unwilling or unable to appreciate (a circumstance, etc.). **3** not governed by purpose or reason. **4 a** concealed. **b** closed at one end. **5** *Aeron.* (of flying) using instruments only. • *v.tr.* **1** deprive of sight. **2** (often foll. by *to*) rob of judgment. • *n.* **1** shade for a window. **2** pretext. **3** obstruction to sight or light. **4** camouflaged shelter used for observing wildlife or hunting animals. □ **blind date 1** social engagement between two people who have not previously met. **2** either of such people. **blind spot 1** *Anat.* point on the retina insensitive to light. **2** area in which a person lacks understanding or impartiality. **turn a** (or **one's**) **blind eye to** pretend not to notice. □□ **blind'ly** *adv.* **blind'ness** *n.*

blind•er /blíndər/ *n. colloq.* (in *pl.*) either of a pair of flaps attached to a horse's bridle to prevent it from seeing sideways.

blind•fold /blíndfōld/ • *v.tr.* **1** cover the eyes with a cloth, etc. **2** deprive of understanding; hoodwink. • *n.* cloth used to blindfold. • *adj.* & *adv.* with eyes bandaged.

blind•side /blíndsīd/ *v.tr.* strike or attack unexpectedly.

blink /blingk/ • *v.* **1** *intr.* shut and open the eyes quickly. **2** *intr.* look with eyes opening and shutting. **3** *tr.* (often foll. by *back*) prevent (tears) by blinking. **4** *tr.* & (foll. by *at*) *intr.* ignore; condone. • *n.* **1** act of blinking. **2** momentary gleam or glimpse. □ **on the blink** *sl.* out of order.

blink•er /blíngkər/ • *n.* **1** device that blinks, esp. a vehicle's turn indicator. **2** = BLINDER. • *v.tr.* obscure with blinders.

blip /blip/ • *n.* **1** small image of an object on a radar screen. **2** minor deviation or error. • *v.* (**blipped, blip•ping**) *intr.* make a blip.

bliss /blis/ *n.* **1** perfect joy; gladness. **2** being in heaven. □□ **bliss'ful** *adj.* **bliss'ful•ly** *adv.* **bliss' ful•ness** *n.*

blis•ter /blístər/ • *n.* **1** small bubble on the skin filled with fluid and caused by friction, etc. **2** similar swelling on any surface. • *v.* **1** *tr.* raise a blister on. **2** *intr.* come up in blisters. **3** *tr.* attack sharply. **4** (as **blistering** *adj.*) causing blisters. □□ **blis'ter•y** *adj.*

blithe /blīth/ *adj.* **1** *poet.* joyous. **2** careless; casual. □□ **blithe'ly** *adv.* **blithe'ness** *n.* **blithe'some** /blíthsəm/ *adj.*

blitz /blits/ *colloq.* • *n.* **1** intensive or sudden (esp. aerial) attack. **2** (**the Blitz**) German air raids on London in 1940 during World War II. • *v.tr.* attack, damage, or destroy by a blitz.

bliz•zard /blízərd/ *n.* severe snowstorm with high winds.

bloat /blōt/ *v.* **1** *tr.* & *intr.* inflate; swell. **2** *tr.* (as **bloated** *adj.*) **a** swollen; puffed. **b** puffed up with pride or excessive wealth (*bloated plutocrat*).

blob /blob/ *n.* **1** small drop of matter. **2** drop; spot.

bloc /blok/ *n.* combination of parties, governments, etc., sharing a common purpose. □ **bloc vote** vote proportional in power to the number of people a delegate represents.

block /blok/ • *n.* **1** solid piece of hard material, esp. of stone or wood. **2** this as a base for chopping, etc. **3** compact mass of buildings bounded by (usu. four) streets. **4** obstruction. **5** pulley or system of pulleys mounted in a case. **6** (in *pl.*) any of a set of solid cubes, etc., used as a child's toy. **7** *Printing* piece of wood or metal engraved for printing. • *v.tr.* obstruct. □ **block and tackle** system of pulleys and ropes, esp. for lifting. □□ **block′er** *n.*

BLOCK AND TACKLE

block·ade /blokáyd/ • *n.* blocking of a place, esp. a port, by an enemy to prevent entry and exit. • *v.tr.* subject to a blockade.

block·bust·er /blókbustər/ *n. sl.* **1** thing of great power, esp. an extremely popular movie or book. **2** highly destructive bomb.

block·head /blókhed/ *n.* stupid person. □□ **block′head·ed** *adj.*

block·house /blókhows/ *n.* **1** reinforced concrete shelter. **2** *hist.* small timber fort.

blond /blond/ • *adj.* (also *fem.* **blonde**) **1** (of hair) light-colored; fair. **2** (of the complexion, esp. as an indication of race) light-colored. • *n.* person with fair hair and skin. □□ **blond′ish** *adj.* **blond′ness** *n.*

blood /blud/ • *n.* **1** usu. red fluid circulating in the arteries and veins of vertebrates. **2** corresponding fluid in invertebrates. **3** bloodshed. **4** passion; temperament. **5** race; descent; parentage. **6** relationship; relations. • *v.tr.* **1** give (a hound) a first taste of blood. **2** initiate (a person) by experience. □ **blood bank** store of blood or plasma for transfusion. **blood bath** massacre. **blood count** number of corpuscles in a specific amount of blood. **blood group** any of the types of human blood. **blood relation** (or **relative**) relative by birth. **blood vessel** vein, artery, or capillary carrying blood.

blood·cur·dling /blúdkərdling/ *adj.* horrifying.

blood·hound /blúdhownd/ *n.* **1** large hound used in tracking, having a keen sense of smell. **2** this breed.

blood·less /blúdlis/ *adj.* **1** without blood. **2** unemotional; cold. **3** pale. **4** without bloodshed.

5 feeble; lifeless. □□ **blood′less·ly** *adv.* **blood′less·ness** *n.*

blood·mo·bile /blúdmōbeel/ *n.* van, truck, or bus equipped and staffed to take blood from donors.

blood·shed /blúdshed/ *n.* **1** spilling of blood. **2** slaughter.

blood·shot /blúdshot/ *adj.* (of an eyeball) inflamed.

blood·stain /blúdstayn/ *n.* discoloration caused by blood. □□ **blood′stained** *adj.*

blood·stream /blúdstreem/ *n.* blood in circulation.

blood·suck·er /blúdsukər/ *n.* **1** animal or insect that sucks blood, esp. a leech. **2** extortionist. **3** person who lives off others. □□ **blood′suck·ing** *adj.*

blood·thirst·y /blúdthərstee/ *adj.* (**blood·thirst·i·er**, **blood·thirst·i·est**) eager for bloodshed. □□ **blood′thirst·i·ly** *adv.* **blood′thirst·i·ness** *n.*

blood·y /blúdee/ • *adj.* (**blood·i·er**, **blood·i·est**) **1 a** of or like blood. **b** running or smeared with blood. **2 a** involving bloodshed. **b** sanguinary; cruel. **3** red. *v.tr.* (**-ies**, **-ied**) stain with blood. □ **Bloody Mary** mixed drink of vodka and tomato juice. □□ **blood′i·ly** *adv.* **blood′i·ness** *n.*

bloom /bloom/ • *n.* **1 a** flower, esp. cultivated. **b** state of flowering. **2** one's prime. **3 a** (of the complexion) glow. **b** delicate powder on fruits, leaves, etc. • *v.* **1** *intr.* bear flowers; be in flower. **2** *intr.* **a** come into, or remain in, full beauty. **b** flourish.

bloom·ers /bloomərz/ *n.pl.* women's loose, almost knee-length underpants or knee-length trousers.

bloom·ing /blooming/ *adj.* flourishing; healthy.

blos·som /blósəm/ • *n.* **1** flower or mass of flowers, esp. of a fruit tree. **2** promising stage. • *v.intr.* **1** open into flower. **2** mature; thrive. □□ **blos′som·y** *adj.*

blot /blot/ • *n.* **1** spot or stain esp. of ink, etc. **2** disgraceful act or quality. **3** any blemish. • *v.* (**blot·ted**, **blot·ting**) **1 a** *tr.* spot or stain, esp. with ink. **b** *intr.* (of a pen, ink, etc.) make blots. **2** *tr.* **a** use blotting paper to absorb excess liquid, esp. ink. **b** (of blotting paper, etc.) soak up (esp. ink). □ **blot out 1** obliterate (writing). **2** obscure (a view, sound, etc.). **blotting paper** absorbent paper for drying excess ink.

blotch /bloch/ • *n.* **1** discolored or inflamed patch on the skin. **2** irregular patch of color. • *v.tr.* cover with blotches. □□ **blotch′y** *adj.* (**blotch·i·er**, **blotch·i·est**)

blot·ter /blótər/ *n.* **1** sheet of blotting paper. **2** logbook, esp. a police charge sheet.

blouse /blows, blowz/ • *n.* **1** woman's loose upper garment, usu. buttoned and collared. **2** upper part of a military uniform. • *v.tr.* make (a shirt, etc.) full like a blouse.

blow[1] /blō/ • *v.* (*past* **blew** /bloo/; *past part.* **blown** /blōn/) **1 a** *intr.* (of the wind or air) move rapidly. **b** *intr.* be driven by an air current. **c** *tr.* drive with an air current. **2 a** *tr.* send out (esp. air) by breathing. **b** *intr.* send a directed air current from the mouth. **3** *tr. & intr.* sound or be sounded by blowing. **4** *tr.* clear (the nose) by blowing. **5 a** *intr.* puff; pant. **b** *tr.* (esp. in *passive*) exhaust of breath. **6** *sl.* **a** *tr.* depart suddenly from (*blew town yesterday*). **b** *intr.* depart suddenly. **7** *tr.* shatter by an explosion. **8** *tr.* make or shape (glass or a bubble) by blowing. **9** *tr.* & *intr.* melt or cause to melt from overloading (*the fuse has blown*). **10** *tr.* break into (a safe, etc.) with explosives. **11** *tr. sl.* **a** squander; spend recklessly (*blew $20 on a meal*). **b** spoil; bungle (an opportunity, etc.). **c** reveal (a secret, etc.). • *n.* **1** act of blowing (e.g., one's nose, a wind instrument). **2 a** gust of wind or air. **b** exposure to fresh air. □ **blow-dry** arrange (the hair) while drying it with a hand-held dryer. **blow hot and cold** *colloq.* vacillate. **blow in** *colloq.* arrive unexpectedly. **blow a person's mind** *sl.* **1** cause to have drug-induced hallucinations, etc. **2** amaze. **blow out 1** extinguish by blowing. **2** (of a tire) burst. **blow over** (of trouble, etc.) fade away. **blow one's top** (or **stack**) *colloq.* explode in rage. **blow up 1 a** shatter or destroy by an explosion. **b** explode; erupt. **2** *colloq.* rebuke strongly. **3** inflate (a tire, etc.). **4** *colloq.* **a** enlarge (a photograph). **b** exaggerate. **5** *colloq.* lose one's temper. **blow-up** *n.* **1** *colloq.* enlargement (of a photograph, etc.). **2** explosion.

blow[2] /blō/ • *n.* **1** hard stroke with a hand or weapon. **2** sudden shock or misfortune. □ **blow-by-blow** (of a description, etc.) giving all the details in sequence.

blow·fly /blṓflī/ *n.* (*pl.* **-flies**) fly that lays eggs on meat or flesh.

blow·gun /blṓgun/ *n.* tube for propelling arrows or darts by blowing.

blow·hole /blṓhōl/ *n.* **1** nostril of a whale or other cetacean, on the top of its head. **2** vent for air, smoke, etc.

blown *past part.* of BLOW[1].

blow·out /blṓ-owt/ *n. colloq.* **1** burst tire. **2** melted fuse. **3** large party. **4** victory by a wide margin.

blow·pipe /blṓpīp/ *n.* **1** = BLOWGUN. **2** tube used to intensify the heat of a flame by blowing air or other gas through it.

blow·torch /blṓtawrch/ *n.* portable device with a very hot flame used for burning off paint, soldering, etc.

blow·zy /blṓwzee/ *adj.* (**blow·zi·er**, **blow·zi·est**) slovenly. □□ **blow′zi·ly** *adv.* **blow′zi·ness** *n.*

BLT *abbr.* bacon, lettuce, and tomato sandwich.

blub·ber /blúbər/ • *n.* **1 a** whale fat. **b** thick or excessive fat. **2** spell of weeping. • *v.* **1** *intr.* sob loudly. **2** *tr.* sob out (words). □□ **blub′ber·er** *n.* **blub′ber·ing·ly** *adv.* **blub′ber·y** *adj.*

blud·geon /blújən/ • *n.* heavy club. • *v.tr.* **1** beat with a bludgeon. **2** coerce.

blue /blōō/ • *adj.* **1** having the color of a clear sky. **2** sad; depressed. **3** pornographic. • *n.* **1** blue color or pigment. **2** blue clothes or material (*looks good in blue*). □ **blue baby** baby with a blue complexion due to a congenital heart defect. **blue blood** aristocrat. **blue cheese** cheese with veins of blue mold. **blue-chip 1** (of stock) sound and usu. paying a dividend. **2** high quality. **blue-collar** manual; industrial. **blue jay** common crested bird with a blue back and head. **blue jeans** pants made of blue denim. **blue-pencil** (**-pen·ciled**, **-pen·cil·ing**) edit (a manuscript, movie, etc.).

blue·bell /blōōbel/ *n.* any of various woodland plants with bell-shaped blue flowers.

blue·ber·ry /blōōberee/ *n.* (*pl.* **-ries**) small, blue-black edible fruit of various plants.

blue·bird /blōōbərd/ *n.* any of various blue songbirds.

blue·bot·tle /blōōbot′l/ *n.* large buzzing blowfly with a metallic blue body.

blue·grass /blōōgras/ *n.* **1** any of several bluish green grasses, esp. Kentucky bluegrass. **2** variety of country music.

blue·print /blōōprint/ • *n.* **1** photographic print of plans in white on a blue background. **2** detailed plan. • *v.tr.* work out (a program, plan, etc.).

blues /blōōz/ *n.pl.* **1** (prec. by *the*) bout of depression. **2** (prec. by *the*; often treated as *sing.*) melancholic music of African-American folk origin. □□ **blues′y** *adj.* (in sense 2).

bluff[1] /bluf/ • *v.* **1** *intr.* feign strength, confidence, etc. **2** *tr.* mislead by bluffing. • *n.* act of bluffing. □ **call a person's bluff** challenge a person to prove a claim. □□ **bluff′er** *n.*

bluff[2] /bluf/ • *adj.* **1** (of a cliff, or a ship's bows) having a steep broad front. **2** (of a person or manner) blunt; frank. • *n.* steep cliff or headland. □□ **bluff′ly** *adv.* (in sense 2 of *adj.*). **bluff′ness** *n.* (in sense 2 of *adj.*).

blun·der /blúndər/ • *n.* serious or foolish mistake. • *v.* **1** *intr.* make a blunder; act clumsily or ineptly. **2** *tr.* deal incompetently with. **3** *intr.* stumble. □□ **blun′der·er** *n.* **blun′der·ing·ly** *adv.*

blun·der·buss /blúndərbus/ *n. hist.* short, large-bored gun.

blunt /blunt/ • *adj.* **1** (of a knife, pencil, etc.) not sharp or pointed. **2** (of a person or manner) direct; outspoken. • *v.tr.* make less sharp. □□ **blunt′ly** *adv.* (in sense 2 of *adj.*). **blunt′ness** *n.*

blur /blər/ • *v.* (**blurred, blur·ring**) **1** *tr.* & *intr.* make or become unclear or less distinct. **2** *tr.* smear. • *n.* something that appears or sounds indistinct or unclear. □□ **blur′ry** *adj.* (**blur·ri·er, blur·ri·est**).

blurb /blərb/ *n.* promotional description of a book.

blurt /blərt/ *v.tr.* (usu. foll. by *out*) utter abruptly, thoughtlessly, or tactlessly.

blush /blush/ • *v.intr.* **1 a** become pink in the face from embarrassment. **b** (of the face) redden thus. **2** feel embarrassed or ashamed. **3** become red or pink. • *n.* **1** act of blushing. **2** pink tinge. □ **at first blush** on the first glimpse.

blush·er /blúshər/ *n.* rouge.

blus·ter /blústər/ • *v.intr.* **1** behave pompously and boisterously. **2** (of the wind, etc.) blow fiercely. • *n.* **1** noisily self-assertive talk. **2** empty threats. □□ **blus′ter·er** *n.* **blus′ter·y** *adj.*

blvd. *abbr.* boulevard.

BM *abbr.* **1** Bachelor of Medicine. **2** Bachelor of Music. **3** British Museum. **4** basal metabolism. **5** bowel movement.

BO *abbr. colloq.* body odor.

bo·a /bṓə/ *n.* **1** large snake that kills its prey by crushing and suffocating. **2** long scarf of feathers or fur.

boar /bawr/ *n.* **1** tusked wild pig. **2** uncastrated male pig.

board /bawrd/ • *n.* **1** long, flat, thin piece of sawn lumber. **2** provision of regular meals for payment. **3** directors of a company; committee or group of councilors, etc. **4** (in *pl.*) stage of a theater. **5** *Naut.* side of a ship. • *v.* **1** *tr.* go on board (a ship, train, etc.). **2** *intr.* **a** receive regular meals for payment. **b** *tr.* provide with regular meals. **3** *tr.* cover with boards. □ **go by the board** be neglected or discarded. **on board** on or onto a ship, aircraft, etc. □□ **board'er** *n.*

board·ing·house /báwrdinghows/ *n.* establishment providing board and lodging.

board·walk /báwrdwawk/ *n.* promenade, esp. of wood, along a beach.

boast /bōst/ • *v.* **1** *intr.* talk about oneself with indulgent pride. **2** *tr.* own or have with pride. • *n.* **1** act of boasting. **2** thing one is proud of. □□ **boast'er** *n.* **boast'ful** *adj.* **boast'ful·ly** *adv.* **boast'ful·ness** *n.* **boast'ing·ly** *adv.*

boat /bōt/ • *n.* **1** small vessel propelled on water by an engine, oars, or sails. **2** (in general use) any ship. **3** elongated boat-shaped container used for sauce, gravy, etc. • *v.intr.* go in a boat, esp. for pleasure. □ **boat people** refugees who have left a country by sea. **in the same boat** sharing the same problems. □□ **boat'ful** *n.* (*pl.* **-fuls**).

boat·er /bótər/ *n.* **1** person who boats. **2** flat-topped straw hat with a stiff brim.

boat·house /bót-hows/ *n.* waterside shelter for housing boats.

boat·ing /bóting/ *n.* rowing or sailing as recreation.

boat·swain /bós'n/ *n.* (also **bo'sun, bo'sun, bo's'n**) ship's officer in charge of equipment and the crew. □ **boatswain's chair** seat suspended from ropes for work on the side of a ship or building.

bob /bob/ • *v.intr.* (**bobbed, bob·bing**) **1** move quickly up and down. **2** emerge suddenly; become active or conspicuous again after a defeat, etc. • *n.* jerking or bouncing movement, esp. upward.

bob·bin /bóbin/ *n.* cylinder for thread.

bob·ble /bóbəl/ *n.* fumble, esp. of a baseball or football.

bob·by pin /bóbeepin/ *n.* flat, closed hairpin.

bob·by socks *n.pl.* (also **bob'by sox**) short socks reaching just above the ankle.

bob·cat /bóbkat/ *n.* small N. American lynx with a spotted reddish-brown coat and a short tail.

bob·sled /bóbsled/ • *n.* mechanically steered and braked sled used for racing down a steep ice-covered run. • *v.intr.* race in a bobsled.

bob·white /bóbhwít, bóbwít/ *n.* American quail.

bode /bōd/ *v. tr.* portend; foreshow. □ **bode well** (or **ill**) be a good (or bad) sign. □□ **bod'ing** *n.*

bod·ice /bódis/ *n.* part of a woman's dress above the waist.

bod·i·ly /bód'lee/ • *adj.* of the body. • *adv.* **1** as a whole (*threw them bodily*). **2** in the body; as a person.

bod·kin /bódkin/ *n.* **1** blunt thick needle for drawing tape, etc., through a hem. **2** small pointed instrument for piercing cloth, etc.

bod·y /bódee/ *n.* (*pl.* **-ies**) **1** physical structure, including the bones, flesh, and organs, of a person or animal. **2** = TRUNK 2. **3** a main or central part. **b** bulk or majority. **4 a** group regarded collectively. **b** collection. **5** quantity. **6** piece of matter. **7** full or substantial quality of flavor, tone, etc. □ **body language** communicating through gestures and poses. **body politic** nation or government as a corporate body. **body shop** workshop where bodies of vehicles are repaired. **body stocking** tight-fitting garment covering the torso.

bod·y·build·ing /bódeebílding/ *n.* strengthening and enlarging the muscles by exercise.

bod·y·guard /bódeegaard/ *n.* person or group of persons escorting and protecting another person (esp. a dignitary).

bod·y·suit /bódeesōot/ *n.* close-fitting, one-piece stretch garment, used mainly for sport.

Boer /bōr, bawr/ • *n.* South African of Dutch descent. • *adj.* of or relating to the Boers.

bog /bog, bawg/ • *n.* wet, spongy ground. • *v.tr.* (**bogged, bog·ging**) (foll. by *down*) impede. □□ **bog'gy** *adj.* (**bog·gi·er, bog·gi·est**). **bog'gi·ness** *n.*

bo·gey[1] /bógee/ *Golf* • *n.* (*pl.* **-geys**) score of one stroke more than par at any hole. • *v.tr.* (**-geys, -geyed**) play (a hole) in one stroke more than par.

bo·gey[2] /bógee/ *n.* (also **bo·gy**) (*pl.* **-geys** or **-gies**) evil or mischievous spirit; devil.

bo·gey·man /bŏŏgeeman, bógee-, bŏŏgee-/ *n.* (also **bo'gy·man, boog'ey·man, boog'ie·man**) (*pl.* **-men**) person (real or imaginary) causing fear or difficulty.

bog·gle /bógəl/ *v.intr.* *colloq.* **1** be startled or baffled (esp. *the mind boggles*). **2** (usu. foll. by *about, at*) hesitate; demur.

bo·gus /bógəs/ *adj.* sham; fictitious; spurious. □□ **bo'gus·ly** *adv.* **bo'gus·ness** *n.*

Bo·he·mi·an /bōhéemeeən/ • *n.* **1** native of Bohemia; Czech. **2** (also **bohemian**) socially unconventional person, esp. an artist or writer. • *adj.* **1** of Bohemia or its people. **2** socially unconventional. □□ **bo·he'mi·an·ism** *n.* (sense 2).

bohr·i·um /báwreeəm/ *n.* artificially produced radioactive element. ¶ Symb.: **Bh**.

boil[1] /boyl/ • *v.* **1** *intr.* **a** (of a liquid) start to bubble up and turn into vapor; reach a temperature at which this happens. **b** (of a vessel) contain boiling liquid. **2 a** *tr.* cause to boil. **b** *tr.* cook by boiling. **c** *intr.* (of food) be cooked by boiling. **3** *intr.* be very angry. • *n.* act or process of boiling. □ **boil down 1** reduce volume by boiling. **2** reduce to essentials. **3** (foll. by *to*) amount to. **boil over** lose one's temper.

boil[2] /boyl/ *n.* inflamed pus-filled swelling caused by infection of a hair follicle, etc.

boil·er /bóylər/ *n.* **1** apparatus for heating a hot water supply. **2** tank for turning water to steam.

boil·ing point /bóyling poynt/ *n.* **1** temperature at which a liquid starts to boil. **2** high excitement.

bois·ter·ous /bóystərəs/ *adj.* **1** (of a person) rough; noisily exuberant. **2** (of the sea, etc.) stormy. □□ **bois'ter·ous·ly** *adv.* **bois'ter·ous·ness** *n.*

bold /bōld/ *adj.* **1** confidently assertive; adventurous; courageous. **2** impudent. **3** vivid. □□ **bold'ly** *adv.* **bold'ness** *n.*

bole /bōl/ *n.* stem or trunk of a tree.

bo·le·ro /bōláirō, bə-/ *n.* (*pl.* **-ros**) **1 a** Spanish dance in simple triple time. **b** music for it. **2** woman's short open jacket.

boll /bōl/ *n.* rounded seedpod of flax or cotton.

bo·lo·gna /bəlónee, -nyə/ *n.* large meat sausage sold ready for eating.

Bol·she·vik /bólshəvik, ból-/ • *n.* **1** *hist.* member of the radical faction of the Russian Social

Democratic party, which became the Communist party in 1918. **2** Russian communist. **3** any revolutionary socialist. ● *adj.* **1** of the Bolsheviks. **2** communist. □□ **Bol'she·vism** *n.* **Bol'she·vist** *n.*

bol·ster /bṓlstər/ ● *n.* long, thick pillow. ● *v.tr.* (usu. foll. by *up*) encourage; reinforce. □□ **bol' ster·er** *n.*

bolt /bōlt/ ● *n.* **1** sliding bar and socket used to fasten a door, etc. **2** threaded pin, usu. metal, used with a nut to hold things together. **3** discharge of lightning. **4** act of bolting (cf. sense 3 of *v.*). **5** *hist.* arrow for shooting from a crossbow. **6** roll of fabric, wallpaper, etc. ● *v.* **1** *tr.* fasten with a bolt. **2** *tr.* fasten together with bolts. **3** *intr.* **a** dash suddenly away. **b** (of a horse) suddenly gallop out of control. **4** *tr.* gulp down (food) unchewed. ● *adv.* rigidly; stiffly (esp. as *bolt upright*). □ **bolt from the blue** complete surprise. □□ **bolt'er** *n.* (in sense 3 of *v.*).

TOGGLE BOLT   CARRIAGE BOLT

HEX-HEAD BOLT

BOLT, 2

bomb /bom/ ● *n.* **1** container with explosive, incendiary material, etc., designed to explode and cause damage. **2** small pressurized container that sprays liquid, foam, or gas. **3** *colloq.* failure (esp. a theatrical one). ● *v.* **1** *tr.* attack with bombs. **2** *intr.* throw or drop bombs. **3** *intr. sl.* fail badly.

bom·bard /bombård/ *v.tr.* **1** attack with heavy guns or bombs. **2** subject to persistent questioning. **3** *Physics* direct a stream of high-speed particles at (a substance). □□ **bom·bard' ment** *n.*

bom·bar·dier /bómbərdéer/ *n.* member of a bomber crew responsible for aiming and releasing bombs.

bom·bast /bómbast/ *n.* pompous, pretentious, or extravagant language. □□ **bom·bas'tic** *adj.* **bom·bas'ti·cal·ly** *adv.*

bomb·er /bómər/ *n.* **1** aircraft equipped to drop bombs. **2** person using bombs.

bomb·shell /bómshel/ *n.* **1** overwhelming surprise. **2** artillery bomb. **3** *sl.* very attractive woman.

bo·na fi·de /bónə fīd, fīdee, bónə/ ● *adj.* genuine; sincere. ● *adv.* genuinely; sincerely.

bo·nan·za /bənánzə/ *n.* **1** source of wealth. **2** rich lode. **3** prosperity.

bon·bon /bónbon/ *n.* piece of candy.

bond /bond/ ● *n.* **1 a** thing that fastens down or together. **b** (usu. in *pl.*) thing restraining bodily freedom. **2** (often in *pl.*) **a** uniting force. **b** restraint; responsibility. **3** binding agreement. **4** *Commerce* certificate issued by a government or a company promising to repay borrowed money at a fixed rate of interest. **5** (also **bail bond**) money deposited to guarantee appearance in court. ● *v.* **1** *intr.* adhere; hold together. **2** *tr.* connect with a bond. **3** *tr.* place (goods) in bond. □ **bond paper** high-quality writing paper.

bond·age /bóndij/ *n.* **1** slavery. **2** subjection to constraint, influence, etc.

bonds·man /bóndzmən/ *n.* (*pl.* **-men**) **1** slave. **2** person who provides bond (sense 5).

bone /bōn/ ● *n.* **1** any piece of hard tissue making up the skeleton in vertebrates. **2** (in *pl.*) **a** skeleton, esp. as remains after death. **b** the body, esp. as a seat of intuitive feeling (*felt it in my bones*). **3 a** material of which bones consist. **b** similar substance such as ivory, dentine, or whalebone. ● *v. tr.* take out bones from (meat or fish). □ **bone china** fine china made of clay mixed with bone ash. **bone-dry** quite dry. **bone of contention** source of dispute. **bone up** (often foll. by *on*) *colloq.* study (a subject) intensively. □□ **bone'less** *adj.*

bone·meal /bónmeel/ *n.* crushed or ground bones used esp. as a fertilizer.

bon·fire /bónfīr/ *n.* large open-air fire.

bon·go /bónggō/ *n.* (*pl.* **-gos** or **-goes**) either of a pair of small connected drums usu. held between the knees and played with the fingers.

bo·ni·to /bənéetō/ *n.* (*pl.* same or **-tos**) any of several fish similar to the tuna and striped like mackerel.

bonk /bongk/ ● *v.* **1** *tr.* hit resoundingly. **2** *intr.* bang; bump. ● *n.* instance of bonking (*a bonk on the head*). □□ **bonk·er** *n.*

bon·kers /bóngkərz/ *adj. sl.* crazy.

bon mot /bawn mó/ *n.* (*pl.* **bons mots** *pronunc.* same or /-mōz/) witty saying.

bon·net /bónit/ *n.* woman's or child's hat tied under the chin.

bon·sai /bónsī, -zī/ *n.* (*pl.* same) **1** art of cultivating ornamental, artificially dwarfed trees and shrubs. **2** such a tree or shrub.

bo·nus /bónəs/ *n.* **1** extra benefit. **2** usu. seasonal gratuity to employees beyond their normal pay.

bon voyage /báwn vwaaya'azh/ expression of good wishes to a departing traveler.

bon·y /bónee/ *adj.* (**bon·i·er, bon·i·est**) **1** thin with prominent bones. **2** having many bones. **3** of or like bone. □□ **bon'i·ness** *n.*

boo /boo/ ● *int.* **1** expression of disapproval or contempt. **2** sound intended to surprise. ● *n.* utterance of *boo*, esp. made to a performer, etc. ● *v.* (**boos, booed**) **1** *intr.* utter boos. **2** *tr.* jeer at by booing.

boob /boob/ *sl. n.* simpleton. □ **boob tube** *sl.* television set.

boo·boo /booboo/ *n. sl.* **1** mistake. **2** (esp. by or to a child) minor injury.

boo·by /boobee/ *n.* (*pl.* **-bies**) **1** stupid or childish person. **2** gannet with a bright bill and bright feet. □ **booby prize** prize given to the least successful competitor in any contest. **booby trap** *Mil.* apparently harmless explosive device intended to kill or injure anyone touching it. **booby-trap** *v.tr.* place a booby trap or traps in or on.

boo·dle /bood'l/ *n. sl.* money, esp. gained or used dishonestly.

boog·ey·man var. of BOGEYMAN.

boo·gie /boogee/ • *v.intr.* (**-gies, -gied, -gy·ing**) *sl.* **1** dance enthusiastically to pop music. **2** leave, esp. quickly. • *n.* **1** = BOOGIE-WOOGIE. **2** *sl.* dance to jazz music.

boog·ie·man var. of BOGEYMAN.

boog·ie-woog·ie /boogeewoogee, boogeewoogee/ *n.* style of playing blues or jazz, esp. on the piano.

book /book/ • *n.* **1 a** written or printed work consisting of pages glued or sewn together along one side and bound in covers. **b** literary composition intended for publication (*working on her book*). **2** bound set of tickets, stamps, matches, etc. **3** (in *pl.*) set of records or accounts. **4** main division of a literary work, or of the Bible. **5** libretto, script of a play, etc. **6** telephone directory. **7** record of bets. • *v.* **1** *tr.* **a** reserve (a seat, etc.) in advance. **b** engage (a guest, musical act, etc.) for some occasion. **2** *tr.* record the personal details of (esp. a criminal offender). □ **go by the book** proceed according to the rules. **the Good Book** the Bible. **make book** take bets and pay out winnings on a race, etc. **throw the book at** *colloq.* charge or punish to the utmost.

book·bind·er /bookbīndər/ *n.* person who binds books professionally. □□ **book'bind·ing** *n.*

book·case /book-kays/ *n.* set of shelves for books in the form of a cabinet.

book·end /bookend/ *n.* usu. ornamental prop used to keep a row of books upright.

book·ie /bookee/ *n. colloq.* = BOOKMAKER.

book·ing /booking/ *n.* reservation or engagement (see BOOK *v.* 1).

book·ish /bookish/ *adj.* **1** studious; fond of reading. **2** acquiring knowledge mainly from books. □□ **book'ish·ly** *adv.* **book'ish·ness** *n.*

book·keep·er /book-keepər/ *n.* person who keeps accounts for a business, etc. □□ **book'keep·ing** *n.*

book·let /booklit/ *n.* small book, usu. with paper covers.

book·mak·er /bookmaykər/ *n.* professional taker of bets. □□ **book'mak·ing** *n.*

book·mark /bookmaark/ *n.* strip of leather, cardboard, etc., used to mark one's place in a book.

book·mo·bile /bookmōbeel/ *n.* mobile library.

book·plate /bookplayt/ *n.* decorative personalized label stuck in the front of a book.

book·sell·er /bookselər/ *n.* dealer in books.

book·store /bookstawr/ *n.* store where books are sold.

boom¹ /boom/ • *n.* deep resonant sound. • *v.intr.* make or speak with a boom. □ **boom box** *sl.* stereo with powerful speakers.

boom² /boom/ • *n.* period of economic prosperity or activity. • *v.intr.* be suddenly prosperous.

boom³ /boom/ *n.* **1** *Naut.* pivoted spar to which a sail is attached. **2** long pole over a movie or television stage set, carrying microphones and other equipment. **3** floating barrier across the mouth of a harbor or river, or enclosing an oil spill.

boo·mer·ang /boomərang/ • *n.* **1** curved flat

missile able to return to the thrower. **2** plan that recoils on its originator. • *v.intr.* (of a plan, etc.) backfire.

BOOMERANG, 1

boon¹ /boon/ *n.* **1** advantage; blessing. **2 a** thing asked for. **b** gift.

boon² /boon/ *adj.* intimate; favorite (esp. as *boon companions*).

boon·docks /boondoks/ (also **boon·ies**) *n. sl.* rough, remote, or isolated country.

boon·dog·gle /boondogəl, -daw-/ • *n.* **1** trivial work done to appear busy. **2** questionable public project that typically involves political patronage and graft. • *v.intr.* participate in a boondoggle.

boor /boor/ *n.* rude, unmannerly person. □□ **boor'ish** *adj.* **boor'ish·ly** *adv.* **boor'ish·ness** *n.*

boost /boost/ *colloq.* • *v.tr.* **1 a** promote by praise or advertising; push; increase. **b** push from below. **2** increase or amplify (voltage, a radio signal, etc.). • *n.* act or result of boosting.

boost·er /boostər/ *n.* **1** device for increasing power or voltage. **2** auxiliary engine or rocket for initial acceleration. **3** (also **boost·er shot**) *Med.* dose of an immunizing agent to reinforce an earlier one. **4** *colloq.* person who boosts by helping or encouraging.

boot¹ /boot/ • *n.* outer foot covering reaching above the ankle. • *v.tr.* **1** kick. **2** (often foll. by *out*) dismiss (a person) forcefully. **3** put (a computer) in a state of readiness. □ **you bet your boots** *sl.* it is quite certain. □□ **boot'ed** *adj.*

boot² /boot/ *n.* □ **to boot** as well; to the good; in addition.

booth /booth/ *n.* (*pl.* **booths** /boothz, booths/) **1** small temporary structure used esp. for sale or display of goods at a market, etc. **2** enclosure for telephoning, voting, etc. **3** set of a table and benches in a restaurant or bar.

boot·leg /bootleg/ • *adj.* (esp. of liquor) smuggled; illicitly sold. • *v.tr.* (**-legged, -leg·ging**) make, distribute, or smuggle (illicit goods). □□ **boot'leg·ger** *n.*

boot·less /bootlis/ *adj.* unavailing; useless.

boot·strap /bootstrap/ *n.* loop at the back of a boot used to pull it on. □ **pull oneself up by one's bootstraps** better oneself by one's own efforts.

boo·ty /bootee/ n. **1** plunder gained esp. in war or by piracy. **2** colloq. something gained or won.

booze /booz/ colloq. • n. alcohol, esp. hard liquor. • v.intr. drink alcohol esp. excessively or habitually. □□ **booz'er** n.

bop¹ /bop/ • n. colloq. = BEBOP. • v.intr. sl. proceed; go (let's bop on over to the library). □□ **bop'per** n.

bop² /bop/ colloq. • v.tr. (**bopped, bop·ping**) hit; punch lightly. • n. light blow or hit.

bor. abbr. borough.

bo·rax /báwraks/ n. mineral salt, sodium borate, used in making glass and china, and as an antiseptic.

bor·der /báwrdər/ • n. **1** edge or boundary, or the part near it. **2** a line separating two countries. **b** district on each side of this. **3** edging around anything. • v. **1** tr. be on or along a border. **2** tr. provide with a border. **3** intr. (usu. foll. by on, upon) **a** adjoin; come close to being. **b** approximate; resemble.

bor·der·land /báwrdərland/ n. **1** district near a border. **2** area for debate.

bor·der·line /báwrdərlīn/ • n. **1** line dividing two conditions. **2** line marking a boundary. • adj. **1** on the borderline. **2** barely acceptable.

bore¹ /bawr/ • v.tr. **1** make a hole, esp. with a revolving tool. **2** hollow out (a tube, etc.). • n. **1** hollow of a firearm barrel or of a cylinder in an internal combustion engine. **2** diameter of this; caliber.

bore² /bawr/ • n. tiresome or dull person or thing. • v.tr. weary by tedious talk or dullness. □□ **bor'ing** adj.

bore³ /bawr/ n. high tidal wave rushing up a narrow estuary.

bore⁴ past of BEAR¹.

bore·dom /báwrdəm/ n. state of being bored; ennui.

bor·ic /báwrik/ □ **boric acid** acid derived from borax, used as a mild antiseptic.

born /bawrn/ adj. **1** existing as a result of birth. **2 a** of natural ability or quality. **b** destiny. **3** (in comb.) of a certain status by birth (French-born; well-born). □ **born-again** (attrib.) converted (esp. to fundamentalist Christianity).

¶ **Born** refers to birth (e.g., born in Detroit in 1947). **Borne**, meaning 'carried,' is used in the expression borne by followed by the name of the mother (e.g., the baby borne by Sarah), as well as in other senses (e.g., a litter borne by slaves).

borne /bawrn/ **1** past part. of BEAR¹. **2** (in comb.) carried by.

bo·ron /báwron/ n. Chem. nonmetallic crystalline element. ¶ Symb.: **B**.

bor·ough /bórō, búrō/ n. **1** (in some states) incorporated municipality. **2** each of five political divisions of New York City. **3** (in Alaska) a county equivalent.

bor·row /bórō, báwrō/ v. **1 a** tr. acquire temporarily with the promise or intention of returning. **b** intr. obtain money in this way. **2** tr. use (an idea, etc.) originated by another; plagiarize. □□ **bor'row·er** n. **bor'row·ing** n.

borscht /bawrsht/ n. (also **borsch** /bawrsh, bawrshch/) Russian soup made primarily with beets.

bor·zoi /báwrzoy/ n. **1** large Russian wolfhound of a breed with a narrow head and silky, usu. white, coat. **2** this breed.

bosh /bosh/ n. & int. sl. nonsense; foolish talk.

bo's·n var. of BOATSWAIN.

bo·som /boozəm/ • n. **1 a** person's breast. **b** colloq. each of a woman's breasts. **c** enclosure formed by the breast and arms. **2** emotional center. • adj. (esp. in **bos·om friend**) close; intimate. □□ **bos'om·y** adj.

boss¹ /baws, bos/ n. **1** employer; manager; overseer. **2** one who controls a political organization. • v.tr. **1** treat domineeringly. **2** be the master or manager of.

boss² /baws, bos/ n. round knob, stud, or other protuberance, esp. in the center of a shield or in ornamental work.

bos·sa no·va /bósə nóvə, báwsə/ n. **1** Brazilian dance like the samba. **2** music for this.

boss·y /báwsee, bós-/ adj. (**boss·i·er, boss·i·est**) colloq. domineering; tending to boss. □□ **boss' i·ly** adv. **boss'i·ness** n.

bo·sun (also **bo'sun**) var. of BOATSWAIN.

bot. abbr. **1** bottle. **2** botanic; botanical; botany.

bot·a·ny /bót'nee/ n. the study of plants. □□ **bo·tan·ic** /bətánik/ adj. **bo·tan'i·cal** adj. **bo·tan'i·cal·ly** adv. **bot·a·nist** /bót'nist/ n.

botch /boch/ • v.tr. **1** bungle; do badly. **2** repair clumsily. • n. bungled or spoiled work. □□ **botch'er** n.

both /bōth/ • adj. & pron. the two; not only one (both boys; both the boys; the boys are both here). • adv. with equal truth in two cases (both angry and sad).

¶ Avoid using **both** when you mean **each**: Q: Would you like vanilla or chocolate? A: May I have a little of each? (not "of both"); Each child (not "Both children" would take the toy.

both·er /bóthər/ • v. **1** tr. **a** give trouble to; worry; disturb. **b** refl. be anxious or concerned. **2** intr. **a** worry oneself. **b** (foll. by with) be concerned. • n. **1** person or thing that bothers; nuisance. **2** trouble; worry; fuss. □□ **both'er·some** adj.

bot·tle /bót'l/ • n. **1** container, usu. of glass or plastic, for storing liquid. **2** amount filling it. • v.tr. **1** put into bottles or jars. **2** (foll. by up) **a** conceal or restrain (esp. a feeling). **b** keep (an enemy force, etc.) contained or entrapped. □ **hit the bottle** sl. drink heavily. □□ **bot'tle·ful** n. (pl. **-fuls**). **bot·tler** /bótlər/ n.

bot·tle·neck /bót'lnek/ n. **1** point at which the flow of traffic, production, etc., is constricted. **2** any impedance to progress.

bot·tom /bótəm/ • n. **1 a** lowest point or part. **b** base. **c** undermost part. **2** colloq. **a** buttocks. **b** seat of a chair, etc. **3** ground under the water of a lake, etc. **4** basis; origin. • adj. **1** lowest. **2** last. □ **at bottom** basically; essentially. **bottom line** colloq. underlying truth; ultimate, esp. financial, criterion. □□ **bot'tom·most** adj.

bot·tom·less /bótəmlis/ adj. **1** without a bottom. **2** (of a supply, etc.) inexhaustible.

bot·u·lism /bóchəlizəm/ n. poisoning caused by a bacillus growing in spoiled food.

bou·doir /boodwaar/ n. woman's private room or bedroom.

bouf·fant /boofáant/ adj. (of a dress, hair, etc.) puffed out.

bou·gain·vil·le·a /bóōgənvílyə, -véeə/ *n.* tropical plant with large colored bracts.

bough /bow/ *n.* branch of a tree, esp. a main one.

bought *past* and *past part.* of BUY.

bouil·la·baisse /bóōyəbés, bóōlyəbáys/ *n. Cookery* rich, spicy fish stew.

bouil·lon /bóōlyən, -yon, bōōyóN/ *n.* clear soup; broth.

boul·der /bóldər/ *n.* large rock.

bou·le·vard /bóōləvaard/ *n.* 1 broad, tree-lined avenue. 2 broad main road.

bounce /bowns/ • *v.* 1 a *intr.* (of a ball, etc.) rebound. b *tr.* cause to rebound. 2 *intr. sl.* (of a check) be returned by a bank when there are insufficient funds to meet it. 3 *intr.* jump, spring, or rush noisily, enthusiastically, etc. • *n.* 1 a rebound. b power of rebounding. 2 *colloq.* a liveliness. b resilience. 3 *sl.* (often prec. by *the*) dismissal or ejection. □□ **bounc'i·ness** *n.* **bounc'y** *adj.* (**bounc·i·er, bounc·i·est**).

bounc·er /bównsər/ *n. sl.* person employed to eject troublemakers from a bar, club, etc.

bounc·ing /bównsing/ *adj.* (esp. of a baby) big and healthy.

bound[1] /bownd/ • *v.intr.* 1 a spring; leap. b walk or run with leaping strides. 2 (of a ball, etc.) bounce. • *n.* 1 springy leap. 2 bounce.

bound[2] /bownd/ • *n.* (usu. in *pl.*) 1 limitation; restriction. 2 border; boundary. • *v.tr.* 1 (esp. in *passive*; foll. by *by*) set bounds to; limit. 2 be the boundary of. □ **out of bounds** 1 outside a permitted area. 2 beyond what is acceptable.

bound[3] /bownd/ *adj.* 1 on one's way. 2 (in *comb.*) moving in a specified direction (*northbound*).

bound[4] /bownd/ *past* and *past part.* of BIND. □ **bound to** certain to (*he's bound to come*).

bound·a·ry /bówndəree, -dree/ *n.* (*pl.* **-ries**) real or notional line marking the limits of an area, territory, etc.

bound·en /bówndən/ *adj. archaic* □ **bounden duty** solemn responsibility.

bound·less /bówndlis/ *adj.* unlimited; immense (*boundless enthusiasm*). □□ **bound'less·ly** *adv.* **bound'less·ness** *n.*

boun·te·ous /bównteeəs/ *adj. poet.* generous; liberal. □□ **boun'te·ous·ly** *adv.* **boun'te·ous·ness** *n.*

boun·ti·ful /bówntifŏol/ *adj.* 1 = BOUNTEOUS. 2 ample. □□ **boun'ti·ful·ly** *adv.*

boun·ty /bówntee/ *n.* (*pl.* **-ties**) 1 generosity. 2 reward; premium.

bou·quet /bōōkáy, bō-/ *n.* 1 bunch of flowers. 2 scent of wine, etc. 3 compliment.

bour·bon /bárbən/ *n.* whiskey distilled from corn mash.

bour·geois /bŏŏrzhwaá/ *often derog.* • *adj.* 1 a conventional. b humdrum. c selfishly materialistic. 2 capitalistic; noncommunist. • *n.* bourgeois person.

bour·geoi·sie /bŏŏrzhwaazée/ *n.* 1 capitalist class. 2 middle class.

bout /bowt/ *n.* 1 limited period. 2 a wrestling or boxing match. b trial of strength.

bou·tique /bŏōtéek/ *n.* small shop, esp. one selling fashionable goods.

bou·ton·niere /bŏōtənéer, -tənyáir/ *n.* (also **bou·ton·nière'**) flower worn in a buttonhole.

bo·vine /bóvīn, -veen/ *adj.* 1 of or relating to cattle. 2 stupid; dull. □□ **bo'vine·ly** *adv.*

bow[1] /bō/ • *n.* 1 a slipknot with a double loop. b ribbon, shoelace, etc., tied with this. 2 device for shooting arrows with a taut string joining the ends of a curved piece of wood, etc. 3 rod with horsehair stretched along its length, used for playing the violin, cello, etc. 4 shallow curve or bend. • *v.tr.* use a bow on (a violin, etc.). □ **bow tie** necktie in the form of a bow (sense 1).

bow[2] /bow/ • *v.* 1 *intr.* incline the head or trunk, esp. in greeting or acknowledgment. 2 *intr.* submit. 3 *tr.* cause to incline or submit. • *n.* act of bowing. □ **take a bow** acknowledge applause.

bow[3] /bow/ *n. Naut.* forward end of a boat or ship.

bowd·ler·ize /bówdlərīz/ *v.tr.* delete offensive words from (a book, etc.). □□ **bowd'ler·ism** *n.* **bowd·ler·i·za'tion** *n.*

bow·el /bówəl/ *n.* 1 intestine. 2 (in *pl.*) depths; innermost parts. □ **bowel movement** defecation.

bow·er /bówər/ *n.* secluded place enclosed by foliage; arbor. □□ **bow'er·y** *adj.*

bowl[1] /bōl/ *n.* 1 a usu. round deep basin for food or liquid. b contents of a bowl. 2 a any deep-sided container shaped like a bowl. b bowl-shaped part of a tobacco pipe, spoon, balance, etc. □□ **bowl'ful** *n.* (*pl.* **-fuls**).

bowl[2] /bōl/ • *n.* wooden or hard rubber ball used in the game of bowls. • *v.* 1 a *tr.* roll (a hoop, etc.) along the ground. b *intr.* play bowling or skittles. 2 *intr.* (foll. by *along*) go along rapidly. □ **bowl over** 1 knock down. 2 *colloq.* a impress greatly. b overwhelm.

bow·legs /bólegz/ *n.* legs that curve outward at the knee. □□ **bow·leg·ged** /bólegid/ *adj.*

bowl·er[1] /bólər/ *n.* player at bowls or bowling.

bowl·er[2] /bólər/ *n.* (in full **bowl'er hat**) man's hard felt hat.

bowl·ing /bóling/ *n.* games of tenpins, skittles, or bowls as a sport or recreation. □ **bowling alley** 1 long lane used for tenpin bowling. 2 building containing these. **bowling green** lawn used for playing bowls.

bow·man /bómən/ *n.* (*pl.* **-men**) archer.

bow·sprit /bówsprit/ *n. Naut.* spar running out from a ship's bow to which the forestays are fastened.

bow·string /bóstring/ *n.* string of an archer's bow.

box[1] /boks/ • *n.* 1 container, usu. flat sided and firm. 2 amount that will fill a box. 3 separate seating area in a theater, etc. 4 facility at a post office, etc., for receiving mail or messages. 5 enclosed area for a jury or witnesses in a courtroom. 6 space or area of print on a page, enclosed by a border. • *v.tr.* 1 put in or provide with a box. 2 confine. □ **box office 1** ticket office at a theater, etc. 2 the commercial aspect of a performance. □□ **box'ful** *n.* (*pl.* **-fuls**). **box'like** *adj.*

box[2] /boks/ • *v.* 1 a *tr.* fight (an opponent) at boxing. b *intr.* practice boxing. 2 slap (esp. a person's ears). • *n.* slap with the hand, esp. on the ears.

box[3] /boks/ *n.* 1 small evergreen tree with glossy dark green leaves. 2 its wood.

box·car /bókskaar/ *n.* enclosed railroad freight car.

box·er /bóksər/ *n.* 1 person who boxes, esp. for

sport. **2** medium-sized dog with a smooth brown coat and puglike face. □ **boxer shorts** (also **box·ers**) underpants similar to shorts worn in boxing, with an elastic waist.

box·ing /bóksing/ *n.* fighting with the fists, esp. as a sport.

boy /boy/ • *n.* **1** male child or youth. **2** young man. **3** (**the boys**) *colloq.* group of men mixing socially. • *int.* expressing pleasure, surprise, etc. □ **boy scout** (also **Boy Scout**) member of an organization of boys, esp. the Boy Scouts of America, that promotes character, outdoor activities, community service, etc. □□ **boy′hood** *n.* **boy′ish** *adj.* **boy′ish·ly** *adv.* **boy′ish·ness** *n.*

boy·cott /bóykot/ • *v.tr.* refuse social or commercial relations with (a person, country, etc.). • *n.* such a refusal.

boy·friend /bóyfrend/ *n.* person's regular male companion or lover.

bps *abbr.* (also **BPS**) *Computing* bits per second.

Br *symb. Chem.* bromine.

bra /braa/ *n. colloq.* = BRASSIERE.

brace /brays/ • *n.* **1 a** device that clamps or fastens tightly. **b** strengthening piece of metal, wood, etc., in building. **2** (in *pl.*) wire device for straightening the teeth. **3** (*pl.* same) pair (esp. of game). **4** connecting mark { or } in printing. • *v.tr.* **1** give strength to. **2** make steady by supporting. **3** (esp. as **bracing** *adj.*) invigorate; refresh. **4** (often *refl.*) prepare for a difficulty, shock, etc. □ **brace and bit** revolving tool with a D-shaped central handle for boring. □□ **brac′ing·ly** *adv.* **brac′ing·ness** *n.*

BRACE AND BIT

brace·let /bráyslit/ *n.* **1** ornamental band or chain worn on the wrist or arm. **2** *sl.* handcuff.

brack·en /brákən/ *n.* **1** large coarse fern. **2** mass of such ferns.

brack·et /brákit/ • *n.* **1** support projecting from a vertical surface. **2 a** each of a pair of marks [ ] (**square brack·ets**) or < > (**an·gle brack·ets**) used to enclose words or figures. **b** = PARENTHESIS 1b. **c** = BRACE 4. **3** group or classification. • *v.tr.* **1 a** combine within brackets. **b** imply a connection or equality between. **2** enclose in brackets.

brack·ish /brákish/ *adj.* (of water, etc.) slightly salty. □□ **brack′ish·ness** *n.*

bract /brakt/ *n.* often brightly colored leaflike part of a plant growing below a flower. □□ **brac′te·al** *adj.* **brac·te·ate** /-tee-it, -ayt/ *adj.*

bract

BRACT

brad /brad/ *n.* thin flat nail with a small head.

brag /brag/ • *v.* (**bragged, brag·ging**) **1** *intr.* talk boastfully. **2** *tr.* boast about. • *n.* boastful statement or talk. □□ **brag′ger** *n.* **brag′ging·ly** *adv.*

brag·gart /brágort/ • *n.* person given to bragging. • *adj.* boastful.

Brah·ma /bráʼamə/ *n.* supreme Hindu divinity.

Brah·man /bráʼamən/ *n.* (also **brah′man**) (*pl.* **-mans**) **1** member of the highest or priestly Hindu caste. **2** = BRAHMA. □□ **Brah·man·ic** /-mánik/ *adj.* **Brah·man′i·cal** *adj.* **Brah′man·ism** *n.*

Brah·min /bráʼamin/ *n.* **1** = BRAHMAN. **2** (esp. in New England) socially or culturally superior person.

braid /brayd/ • *n.* **1** woven band as edging or trimming. **2** length of hair, straw, etc., in three or more interlaced strands. • *v.tr.* intertwine. □□ **braid′er** *n.* **braid′ing** *n.*

Braille /brayl/ • *n.* system of writing and printing for the blind with patterns of raised dots.

brain /brayn/ • *n.* **1** organ of soft nervous tissue contained in the skull of vertebrates, the center of sensation and of nervous and intellectual activity. **2** (in *pl.*) the substance of the brain, esp. as food. **3 a** person's intellectual capacity. **b** (often in *pl.*) intelligence. **4** *colloq.* intelligent person. • *v.tr. colloq.* strike very hard on the head. □ **brain drain** *colloq.* loss of skilled personnel by emigration. **brain wave 1** (usu. in *pl.*) electrical impulse in the brain. **2** *colloq.* sudden bright idea.

brain·child /bráynchīld/ *n.* (*pl.* **-chil·dren**) *colloq.* clever idea or invention.

brain·less /bráynlis/ *adj.* stupid; foolish.

brain·storm /bráynstawrm/ • *n.* spontaneous ingenious idea or invention. • *v.* **1** *intr.* discuss ideas spontaneously and openly. **2** *tr.* discuss (an issue) in this way. □□ **brain·storm·ing** *n.*

brain·wash /bráynwosh, -wawsh/ *v.tr.* subject (a person) to a process by which ideas are implanted in the mind. □□ **brain·wash·ing** *n.*

brain·y /bráynee/ *adj.* (**brain·i·er, brain·i·est**) intellectually clever or active. □□ **brain′i·ly** *adv.* **brain′i·ness** *n.*

braise /brayz/ *v.tr.* sauté lightly and then stew slowly with a little liquid in a closed container.

brake /brayk/ • *n.* (often *pl.*) device for stopping or slowing a wheel, vehicle, etc. • *v.* **1** *intr.* apply a brake. **2** *tr.* retard or stop with a brake. □□ **brake′less** *adj.*

brake·man /bráykmən/ *n.* (*pl.* **-men**) railroad worker responsible for maintenance on a journey.

bram·ble /brámbəl/ *n.* any of various thorny shrubs bearing fleshy red or black berries. □□ **bram′bly** *adj.*

bran /bran/ *n.* grain husks separated from the flour.

branch /branch/ • *n.* **1** limb of a tree. **2** lateral extension or subdivision, esp. of a river or railroad. **3** conceptual extension or subdivision, as of a family, knowledge, etc. **4** local office, etc., of a large business. • *v.intr.* (often foll. by *off*) **1** diverge. **2** divide into branches. □ **branch out** extend one's field of interest. □□ **branched** *adj.* **branch′let** *n.* **branch′like** *adj.*

brand /brand/ • *n.* **1 a** particular make of goods. **b** identifying trademark, label, etc. **2** characteristic kind. **3** identifying mark burned on livestock, etc. **4** iron used for this. **5** piece of burning, smoldering, or charred wood. **6** stigma; mark of disgrace. • *v.tr.* **1** mark with a hot iron. **2** stigmatize (*was branded for life*). **3** impress unforgettably on one's mind. □ **brand-new** completely new. □□ **brand′er** *n.*

bran·dish /brándish/ *v.tr.* wave or flourish as a threat or in display. □□ **bran′dish·er** *n.*

bran·dy /brándee/ *n.* (*pl.* **-dies**) strong alcoholic spirit distilled from wine or fermented fruit juice.

brash /brash/ *adj.* **1** vulgarly self-assertive. **2** hasty; rash. **3** impudent. □□ **brash′ly** *adv.* **brash′ness** *n.*

brass /bras/ • *n.* **1** yellow alloy of copper and zinc. **2** brass objects collectively. **3** *Mus.* brass wind instruments. **4** (in full **top brass**) *colloq.* persons of high (esp. military) rank. **5** *colloq.* effrontery. • *adj.* made of brass. □ **brass tacks** *sl.* actual details.

bras·siere /brəzéer/ *n.* undergarment worn by women to support the breasts.

brass·y /brásee/ *adj.* (**brass·i·er**, **brass·i·est**) **1** impudent. **2** pretentious; showy. **3** loud and blaring. **4** of or like brass. □□ **brass′i·ly** *adv.* **brass′i·ness** *n.*

brat /brat/ *n.* usu. *derog.* child, esp. a badly-behaved one. □□ **brat·ty** *adj.*

bra·va·do /brəváadō/ *n.* show of boldness.

brave /brayv/ • *adj.* **1** able or ready to face and endure danger or pain. **2** splendid; spectacular. • *n.* Native American warrior. • *v.tr.* defy; encounter bravely. □□ **brave′ly** *adv.* **brave′ness** *n.* **brav′er·y** *n.*

bra·vo /bráávō/ • *int.* expressing approval. • *n.* (*pl.* **-vos**) cry of bravo.

bra·vu·ra /brəvŏŏrə, -vyŏŏrə/ *n.* **1** brilliant action or display. **2** passage of (esp. vocal) music requiring exceptional ability.

brawl /brawl/ • *n.* noisy quarrel or fight. • *v.intr.* quarrel noisily or roughly. □□ **brawl′er** *n.*

brawn /brawn/ *n.* **1** muscular strength. **2** muscle; lean flesh. □□ **brawn·y** *adj.* (**brawn·i·er**, **brawn·i·est**). **brawn′i·ness** *n.*

bray /bray/ • *n.* cry of a donkey. • *v.intr.* make such a sound.

braze /brayz/ *v.tr.* solder with an alloy of brass and zinc.

bra·zen /bráyzən/ • *adj.* **1** (also **bra′zen-faced**) shameless; insolent. **2** made of brass. **3** of or like brass. • *v.tr.* (foll. by *out*) face or undergo defiantly. □□ **bra′zen·ly** *adv.* **bra′zen·ness** *n.*

bra·zier /bráyzhər/ *n.* metal pan or stand for holding lighted coals.

Bra·zil /brəzíl/ *n.* (in full **Bra·zil nut**) large three-sided nut with an edible kernel from a S. American tree.

breach /breech/ • *n.* **1** breaking of or failure to observe a law, contract, etc. **2 a** breaking of relations. **b** quarrel. **3** gap; opening. • *v.tr.* **1** break through; make a gap in. **2** break (a law, contract, etc.).

bread /bred/ • *n.* **1** baked dough of flour and liquid usu. leavened with yeast. **2 a** necessary food. **b** (also **dai·ly bread**) one's livelihood. **3** *sl.* money. • *v.tr.* coat with breadcrumbs for cooking. □ **bread basket 1** *sl.* the stomach. **2** farming area producing staple crops.

breadth /bredth/ *n.* **1** distance or measurement from side to side of a thing. **2** extent; distance; room. □□ **breadth′ways** *adv.* **breadth′wise** *adv.*

bread·win·ner /brédwinər/ *n.* person who earns the money to support a family.

break /brayk/ • *v.* (*past* **broke** /brōk/; *past part.* **bro·ken** /brōkən/) **1** *tr.* & *intr.* **a** separate into pieces, as from a blow; shatter. **b** make or become inoperative. **2 a** *tr.* cause or effect an interruption in. **b** *intr.* have an interval between periods of work. **3** *tr.* fail to keep (a law, promise, etc.). **4 a** *tr.* & *intr.* make or become subdued or weakened; yield or cause to yield. **b** *tr.* weaken the effect of (a fall, etc.). **c** *tr.* tame or discipline (an animal); accustom (a horse) to saddle and bridle, etc. **d** *tr.* defeat; destroy. **e** *tr.* defeat the object of (a strike, e.g., by hiring other personnel). **5** *tr.* surpass (a record, etc.). **6** *intr.* (foll. by *with*) quarrel or cease association with (another person, etc.). **7** *tr.* **a** be no longer subject to (a habit). **b** free (a person) of a habit. **8** *tr.* & *intr.* reveal or be revealed. **9** *intr.* **a** (of the weather) change suddenly. **b** (of waves) curl over and foam. **c** (of the day) dawn. **d** (of clouds) move apart. **e** (of a storm) begin violently. **10** *tr. Electr.* disconnect (a circuit). **11** *intr.* **a** (of the voice) change with emotion. **b** (of a boy's voice) change at puberty. **12** *tr.* **a** divide (a set, etc.) into parts. **b** change (a bill, etc.) for coins or smaller denominations. **13** *tr.* ruin financially (see also **BROKE** *adj.*). **14** *tr.* penetrate (e.g., a safe) by force. **15** *tr.* decipher (a code). **16** *tr.* make (a path, etc.) by separating obstacles. **17** *intr.* burst forth. **18 a** *intr.* escape from constraint by a sudden effort. **b** *tr.* escape or emerge from (prison, cover, etc.). • *n.* **1 a** act or instance of breaking. **b** gap; split. **2** interval; interruption; pause. **3** sudden dash (esp. to escape). **4** *colloq.* piece of good luck. □ **bad break** *colloq.* **1** piece of bad luck. **2** mistake or blunder. **break down 1 a** fail; cease to function. **b** (of human relationships, etc.) collapse. **c** be overcome by emotion. **2 a** demolish. **b** suppress (resistance). **c** force (a person) to yield under pressure. **3** analyze into components (see also BREAKDOWN). **break even** make neither profit nor loss. **break in 1** enter by force. **2** interrupt. **3 a** accustom to a habit, etc. **b** wear, etc., until comfortable. **c** = BREAK 4c. **break-in** *n.* illegal forced entry into premises, esp. with criminal intent.

break into 1 enter forcibly. **2 a** burst forth with. **b** suddenly change one's pace for (a faster one). **3** interrupt. **break off 1** detach by breaking. **2** bring to an end. **break out 1** escape by force, esp. from prison. **2** begin suddenly; burst forth. **3** become covered in (a rash, etc.). **break up 1** disperse; disband. **2** terminate a relationship. **3** convulse or be convulsed (see also BREAKUP). □□ **break′a·ble** adj.

break·age /bráykij/ n. **1 a** broken thing. **b** damage or loss caused by breaking. **2** act or instance of breaking.

break·down /bráykdown/ n. **1 a** mechanical failure. **b** loss of (esp. mental) health. **2** collapse. **3** detailed analysis.

break·er /bráykər/ n. heavy breaking wave.

break·fast /brékfəst/ • n. first meal of the day. • v.intr. have breakfast. □□ **break′fas·ter** n.

break·neck /bráyknek/ adj. (of speed) dangerously fast.

break·through /bráykthrōo/ n. **1** major advance or discovery. **2** act of breaking through an obstacle, etc.

break·up /bráykup/ n. **1** disintegration; collapse. **2** dispersal.

break·wa·ter /bráykwawtər, -wotər/ n. barrier built out into the sea to break the force of waves.

breast /brest/ • n. **1 a** either of two milk-secreting organs on a woman's chest. **b** corresponding part of a man's body. **2 a** chest. **b** corresponding part of an animal. **3** part of a garment that covers the breast. • v.tr. **1** face; meet in full opposition. **2** contend with. □□ **breast′ed** adj. (also in comb.). **breast′less** n.

breast·bone /bréstbōn/ n. thin, flat vertical bone and cartilage in the chest connecting the ribs.

breast·stroke /bréststrōk/ n. stroke made while swimming face down by extending arms forward and sweeping them back in unison.

breath /breth/ n. **1 a** air taken into or expelled from the lungs. **b** respiration. **2 a** breeze. **b** whiff of perfume, etc. **3** whisper. **4** spirit; vitality. □ **below** (or **under**) **one's breath** in a whisper. **catch one's breath 1** cease breathing momentarily in surprise, suspense, etc. **2** rest to restore normal breathing. **hold one's breath 1** cease breathing temporarily. **2** colloq. wait in eager anticipation. **take a person's breath away** awe; delight.

breathe /breeth/ v. **1** intr. take air into and expel it from the lungs. **2** intr. be or seem alive. **3** tr. **a** utter. **b** express; display.

breath·er /bréethər/ n. colloq. brief pause for rest.

breath·ing /bréething/ n. process of taking air into and expelling it from the lungs.

breath·less /bréthlis/ adj. **1** panting; out of breath. **2** (as if) holding the breath because of excitement, etc. **3** windless; still. □□ **breath′less·ly** adv. **breath′less·ness** n.

breath·tak·ing /bréthtayking/ adj. astounding; awe-inspiring. □□ **breath′tak·ing·ly** adv.

breath·y /bréthee/ adj. (**breath·i·er, breath·i·est**) (of a voice, etc.) containing the sound of breathing. □□ **breath′i·ly** adv. **breath′i·ness** n.

bred /bred/ past and past part. of BREED.

breech /breech/ n. back part of a rifle or gun barrel. □ **breech birth** (or **delivery**) delivery of a baby with the buttocks and feet foremost.

breech·es /bríchiz/ n.pl. (also **pair of breeches** sing.) short trousers, esp. fastened below the knee, now used esp. for riding. □ **breeches buoy** lifebuoy suspended from a rope with canvas breeches for the user's legs.

breed /breed/ • v. (past and past part. **bred** /bred/) **1** tr. & intr. generate (offspring); reproduce. **2** tr. & intr. propagate or cause to propagate. **3** tr. **a** produce; result in. **b** spread (discontent bred by rumor). **4** intr. arise; spread. **5** tr. bring up; train. • n. **1** stock of genetically similar animals or plants. **2** race; lineage. **3** sort; kind. □ **breeder reactor** nuclear reactor creating surplus fissile material. □□ **breed′er** n.

breed·ing /bréeding/ n. **1** developing or propagating (animals, plants, etc.). **2** generation; childbearing. **3** good manners (has no breeding).

breeze /breez/ • n. **1** gentle wind. **2** colloq. easy task. • v.intr. (foll. by in, out, along, etc.) colloq. come or go casually.

breez·y /bréezee/ adj. (**breez·i·er, breez·i·est**) **1** pleasantly windy. **2** colloq. lively; jovial. **3** colloq. careless. □□ **breez′i·ly** adv. **breez′i·ness** n.

breth·ren see BROTHER 3.

breve /brev, breev/ n. **1** Mus. note having the time value of two whole notes. **2** written or printed mark (˘) indicating a short or unstressed vowel.

bre·vi·ar·y /bréevee-eree, brév-/ n. (pl. **-ies**) RC Ch. book containing the service for each day.

brev·i·ty /brévitee/ n. **1** conciseness. **2** shortness (of time, etc.).

brew /brōo/ • v. **1** tr. **a** make (beer, etc.) by infusion, boiling, and fermentation. **b** make (tea, etc.) by infusion. **2** intr. undergo these processes. **3** intr. gather force; threaten. **4** tr. bring about; concoct. • n. **1 a** amount brewed. **b** serving (of beer, etc.). □□ **brew′er** n.

brew·er·y /brōoəree, brōoree/ n. (pl. **-ies**) place where beer, etc., is brewed commercially.

bri·ar[1] var. of BRIER[1].

bri·ar[2] var. of BRIER[2].

bribe /brīb/ • v.tr. persuade to act improperly by a gift of money, etc. • n. money or services offered in bribing. □□ **brib′a·ble** adj. **brib′er** n. **brib′er·y** n.

bric-à-brac /bríkəbrak/ n. (also **bric′-a-brac, bric′a·brac**) miscellaneous, cheap ornaments.

brick /brik/ • n. **1 a** block of fired or sun-dried clay, used in building. **b** similar block of concrete, etc. **2** brick-shaped solid object. • v.tr. close, pave, or block with bricks. • adj. built of brick.

brick·bat /bríkbat/ n. **1** piece of brick, esp. when used as a missile. **2** uncomplimentary remark.

brick·lay·er /bríklayər/ n. worker who builds with bricks. □□ **brick′lay·ing** n.

brid·al /bríd'l/ adj. of a bride or wedding.

bride /brīd/ n. woman on her wedding day and for some time before and after it.

bride·groom /brídgrōom, -grŏom/ n. man on his wedding day and for some time before and after it.

brides·maid /brídzmayd/ n. girl or woman attending a bride on her wedding day.

bridge[1] /brij/ • n. **1 a** structure providing a way across a river, ravine, road, etc. **b** thing joining or connecting. **2** operational superstructure on a ship. **3** upper bony part of the nose. **4** Mus. upright piece of wood on a violin, etc., over which

the strings are stretched. **5** = BRIDGEWORK. •
v. tr. **1 a** be a bridge over. **b** make a bridge over.
2 span as if with a bridge. □□ **bridge′a•ble** *adj.*

bridge² /brij/ *n.* card game derived from whist.

bridge•head /brijhed/ *n. Mil.* fortified position
held on the enemy's side of a river or other
obstacle.

bridge•work /brijwərk/ *n. Dentistry* dental structure used to cover a gap.

bri•dle /brīd′l/ • *n.* **1** headgear to control a
horse, including reins and bit. **2** restraining
thing. • *v.* **1** *tr.* put a bridle on. **2** *tr.* bring under
control; curb. **3** *intr.* (often foll. by *at* or *up at*)
express offense, etc., esp. by throwing up the
head. □ **bridle path** rough path or road suitable
for horseback riding.

BRIDLE, 1

brief /breef/ • *adj.* **1** of short duration. **2** concise. **3** abrupt; brusque. **4** scanty. • *n.* **1** (in *pl.*)
brief underpants. **2** *Law* summary of a case. •
v. tr. instruct in preparation for a task; inform
in advance. □□ **brief′ly** *adv.* **brief′ness** *n.*

brief•case /breefkays/ *n.* flat, rectangular document case.

bri•er¹ /brīər/ *n.* (also **bri′ar**) any prickly bush,
esp. of a wild rose. □□ **bri′er•y** *adj.*

bri•er² /brīər/ *n.* (also **bri′ar**) **1** white heath native to S. Europe. **2** tobacco pipe made from
its root.

brig /brig/ *n.* **1** two-masted square-rigged ship.
2 prison, esp. in the navy.

bri•gade /brigáyd/ *n.* **1** *Mil.* subdivision of an
army consisting usu. of three battalions and
forming part of a division. **2** organized or uni-
formed band of workers (*fire brigade*).

brig•a•dier /brigədeér/ *n. Mil.* (in full **brig′a•
dier gen′er•al**) officer ranking between colonel
and major general.

brig•and /brigənd/ *n.* member of a robber band.
□□ **brig′and•age** *n.*

brig•an•tine /brigənteen/ *n.* type of two-masted
ship.

bright /brīt/ *adj.* **1** emitting or reflecting much
light; shining. **2** intense; vivid. **3** talented. **4 a**
(of a person) cheerful; vivacious. **b** (of prospects, etc.) promising; hopeful. □□ **bright′ish**
adj. **bright′ly** *adv.* **bright′ness** *n.*

bright•en /brīt′n/ *v.* **1** make or become brighter.
2 make or become more cheerful or hopeful.

bril•liant /brilyənt/ • *adj.* **1** very bright; sparkling. **2** outstandingly talented. **3** showy. • *n.*

diamond of the finest cut with many facets.
□□ **bril′liance** *n.* **bril′liant•ly** *adv.*

bril•lian•tine /brilyənteen/ *n.* dressing for making the hair glossy.

brim /brim/ • *n.* **1** edge or lip of a vessel. **2**
projecting edge of a hat. • *v.* (**brimmed, brim•
ming**) fill or be full to the brim. □□ **brim′less**
adj. **brimmed** *adj.* (usu. in *comb.*).

brim•stone /brimstōn/ *n.* sulfur.

brin•dled /brind′ld/ *adj.* (also **brin′dle**) brownish or tawny with streaks of other color(s) (esp.
of domestic animals).

brine /brīn/ *n.* **1** water saturated or strongly impregnated with salt. **2** sea water. □□ **brin′y** *adj.*
(**brin•i•er, brin•i•est**). **brin′i•ness** *n.*

bring /bring/ *v. tr.* (*past* and *past part.* **brought**
/brawt/) **1 a** come carrying or leading. **b** come
with. **2** cause to come or be present. **3** cause or
result in (*war brings misery*). **4** be sold for; produce as income. □ **bring about** cause to happen.
bring forth give birth to. **bring off** achieve successfully. **bring out 1** emphasize; make evident.
2 publish. **bring up 1** rear (a child). **2** vomit. **3**
call attention to. □□ **bring′er** *n.*

brink /bringk/ *n.* **1** extreme edge. **2** furthest point
before something dangerous or exciting is
discovered. □ **on the brink of** about to experience
or suffer.

brink•man•ship /bringkmənship/ *n.* pursuing a
dangerous course to the brink of catastrophe.

bri•quette /brikét/ *n.* (also **bri•quet′**) block of
compressed coal dust or charcoal used as fuel.

brisk /brisk/ • *adj.* **1** quick; lively. **2** enlivening.
3 curt; peremptory. • *v.* make or grow brisk.
□□ **brisk′ly** *adv.* **brisk′ness** *n.*

bris•ket /briskit/ *n.* animal's breast, esp. as a cut
of meat.

bris•tle /brisəl/ • *n.* **1** short stiff hair, esp. one
of those on an animal's back. **2** this, or an artificial substitute, used in brushes. • *v.* **1 a** *intr.*
(of the hair) stand upright. **b** *tr.* make (the hair)
do this. **2** *intr.* show irritation. **3** *intr.* be covered
or abundant (in).

Brit /brit/ *n. colloq.* British person.

Brit. *abbr.* **1** British. **2** Britain.

Bri•tan•nia /britányə/ *n.* personification of Britain, esp. as a helmeted woman with shield and
trident.

Brit•i•cism /britisizəm/ *n.* (also **Brit•ish•ism**
/-tishizəm/) term used or originating in Britain.

Brit•ish /british/ • *adj.* **1** of Great Britain or
the United Kingdom, or to its people or language. **2** of the British Commonwealth. • *n.* **1**
(prec. by *the*; treated as *pl.*) the British people.
2 = *British English.* □ **British English** English as
used in Great Britain. **British thermal unit** see
THERMAL. □□ **Brit′ish•ness** *n.*

Brit•on /britən/ *n.* **1** one of the people of S.
Britain before the Roman conquest. **2** native or
inhabitant of Great Britain.

brit•tle /brit′l/ • *adj.* **1** hard and fragile; apt to
break. **2** frail; weak; unstable. • *n.* brittle confection made from nuts and hardened melted
sugar. □□ **brit′tle•ly** *adv.* **brit′tle•ness** *n.*

broach /brōch/ • *v. tr.* **1** raise for discussion. **2**
pierce (a cask) to draw liquor, etc. • *n.* bit for
boring.

broad /brawd/ • *adj.* **1** large in extent from one side to the other; wide. **2** spacious or extensive (*broad plain*). **3** full and clear (*broad daylight*). **4** explicit. **5** not taking account of detail. • *n.* **1** broad part of something. **2** *sl.* woman. □ **broad-minded** tolerant; liberal. **broad spectrum** (of a drug) effective against many microorganisms. □□ **broad′ly** *adv.* **broad′-mind·ed·ly** *adv.* **broad′-mind′ed·ness** *n.* **broad′ness** *n.* **broad′ways** *adv.* **broad′wise** *adv.*

broad·cast /bráwdkast/ • *v.* (*past* **broad·cast** or **broad·cast·ed**; *past part.* **broad·cast**) **1** *tr.* a transmit by radio or television. **b** disseminate widely. **2** *intr.* undertake or take part in a radio or television transmission. **3** *tr.* scatter (seed, etc.) widely. • *n.* radio or television program or transmission. • *adj.* **1** transmitted by radio or television. **2** a scattered widely. **b** widely disseminated. • *adv.* over a large area. □□ **broad′cast·er** *n.* **broad′cast·ing** *n.*

broad·cloth /bráwdklawth, -kloth/ *n.* fine cloth of wool, cotton, or silk.

broad·en /bráwdən/ *v.* make or become broader.

broad·loom /bráwdloom/ *adj.* (esp. of carpet) woven in broad widths.

broad·side /bráwdsīd/ *n.* **1** firing of all guns from one side of a ship. **2** vigorous verbal onslaught. **3** side of a ship above the water.

broad·sword /bráwdsawrd/ *n.* sword with a broad blade, for cutting rather than thrusting.

Broad·way /bráwdway/ *n.* principal thoroughfare in New York City, noted as the center of U.S. commercial theater production.

bro·cade /brōkáyd/ • *n.* rich fabric woven with a raised pattern. • *v.tr.* weave with this design.

broc·co·li /brókəlee/ *n.* green vegetable with edible flower heads.

bro·chure /brōshoor/ *n.* pamphlet or leaflet.

brogue¹ /brōg/ *n.* **1** strong outdoor shoe with ornamental perforated bands. **2** rough shoe of untanned leather.

brogue² /brōg/ *n.* marked dialect or accent, esp. Irish.

broil /broyl/ *v.* **1** *tr.* cook (meat) on a rack or a grill. **2** *tr.* & *intr.* make or become very hot.

broil·er /bróylər/ *n.* **1** young chicken for broiling. **2** device or oven setting on a stove for radiating heat downward. **3** *colloq.* a very hot day.

broke /brōk/ *past* of BREAK. • *predic.adj. colloq.* having no money; financially ruined. □ **go for broke** *sl.* risk everything in a strenuous effort.

bro·ken /brókən/ *past part.* of BREAK. • *adj.* **1** that has been broken. **2** reduced to despair. **3** (of language) badly spoken, as by a foreigner. **4** interrupted. **5** uneven (*broken ground*). **6** tamed. □ **broken-down 1** worn out by age, use, etc. **2** out of order. **broken home** family in which the parents are divorced or separated. □□ **bro′ken·ly** *adv.* **bro′ken·ness** *n.*

bro·ken·heart·ed /brókənháartid/ *adj.* overwhelmed with sorrow or grief. □□ **bro′ken·heart·ed·ness** *n.*

brok·er /brókər/ *n.* **1** agent who buys and sells for others; intermediary. **2** member of the stock exchange dealing in stocks and bonds. □□ **bro′ker·age** *n.* **bro′ker·ing** *n.*

bro·mide /brómīd/ *n.* **1** *Chem.* any binary compound of bromine. **2** *Pharm.* preparation of usu.

potassium bromide, used as a sedative. **3** trite remark.

bro·mine /brómeen/ *n.* *Chem.* poisonous liquid element with a choking irritating smell. ¶ *Symb.*: **Br**.

bron·chi·al /bróngkeeəl/ *adj.* of or relating to the bronchi or bronchioles.

bron·chi·tis /brongkítis/ *n.* inflammation of the mucous membrane in the bronchial tubes. □□ **bron·chit·ic** /-kítik/ *adj.* & *n.*

bron·chus /bróngkəs/ *n.* (*pl.* **bron·chi** /-kī/) either of the two main divisions of the windpipe.

bron·co /bróngkō/ *n.* (*pl.* **-cos**) wild or half-tamed horse of western N. America.

bron·to·sau·rus /bróntəsáwrəs/ *n.* (also **bron·to·saur** /bróntəsawr/) large plant-eating dinosaur with a long whiplike tail and trunk-like legs. Now more correctly **apatosaurus**.

bronze /bronz/ • *n.* **1** alloy of copper and tin. **2** its brownish color. **3** thing of bronze, esp. a sculpture. • *adj.* made of or colored like bronze. • *v.* **1** *tr.* give a bronzelike surface to. **2** *tr.* & *intr.* make or become brown; tan. □□ **bronz′y** *adj.*

brooch /brōch, brooch/ *n.* ornamental pin.

brood /brood/ • *n.* **1** young of an animal (esp. a bird) produced at one time. **2** *colloq.* children in a family. • *v.* **1** *intr.* (often foll. by *on, over*, etc.) worry or ponder (esp. resentfully). **2** *tr.* sit as a hen on eggs to hatch them. **3** *intr.* (usu. foll. by *over*) (of silence, a storm, etc.) hang or hover closely. □□ **brood′ing·ly** *adv.*

brook¹ /brook/ *n.* small stream. □□ **brook·let** /-lət/ *n.*

brook² /brook/ *v.tr.* (usu. with *neg.*) *formal* tolerate; allow.

broom /broom, broom/ *n.* **1** long-handled brush for sweeping. **2** any of various shrubs bearing bright yellow flowers.

broom·stick /broomstik, broom-/ *n.* handle of a broom.

Bros. *abbr.* Brothers (esp. in the name of a business).

broth /brawth, broth/ *n.* *Cookery* thin soup of meat or fish stock.

broth·el /bróthəl/ *n.* house for prostitutes.

broth·er /brúthər/ *n.* **1** male sibling. **2** close male friend or associate. **3** (*pl.* also **breth·ren** /bréthrin/) **a** member of a male religious order; a monk. **b** fellow member of a congregation, religion, or (formerly) guild, etc. □ **brother-in-law** (*pl.* **broth·ers-in-law**) **1** brother of one's wife or husband. **2** husband of one's sister or sister-in-law. □□ **broth′er·less** *adj.* **broth′er·ly** *adj.* & *adv.* **broth′er·li·ness** *n.*

broth·er·hood /brúthərhood/ *n.* **1 a** relationship between brothers. **b** brotherly friendliness. **2** association of people linked by a common interest. **b** its members collectively. **3** labor union.

brought *past* and *past part.* of BRING.

brou·ha·ha /broohaahaa/ *n.* commotion; sensation.

brow /brow/ *n.* **1** forehead. **2** (usu. in *pl.*) eyebrow. **3** summit of a hill or pass. **4** edge of a cliff, etc. □□ **browed** *adj.*

brow·beat /brówbeet/ *v.tr.* (*past* **-beat**; *past part.* **-beat·en**) intimidate with stern looks and words. □□ **brow′beat·er** *n.*

brown /brown/ • *adj.* **1** having the color as of dark wood or rich soil. **2** dark-skinned or sun-tanned. **3** (of bread) made from a dark flour such as whole wheat. • *n.* **1** brown color or pigment. **2** brown clothes or material. • *v.* make or become brown by cooking, sunburn, etc. □ **brown-bag** take one's lunch to work, etc., in a brown paper bag. **brown rice** unpolished rice. □□ **brown'ish** *adj.* **brown'ness** *n.* **brown'y** *adj.*

brown-ie /brównee/ *n.* **1** (**Brownie**) junior Girl Scout. **2** *Cookery* small square of rich, usu. chocolate, cake with nuts. **3** benevolent elf. □ **Brownie point** *colloq.* notional credit for something done to please.

brown-out /brównowt/ *n.* period during which electrical voltage is reduced to avoid a blackout.

brown-stone /brównstōn/ *n.* **1** kind of reddish brown sandstone used for building. **2** building faced with this.

browse /browz/ • *v.* **1** *intr.* & *tr.* read or survey desultorily. **2** *intr.* feed (on leaves, twigs, etc.). • *n.* **1** twigs, young shoots, etc., as fodder. **2** act of browsing. □□ **brows'er** *n.*

bruise /brooz/ • *n.* **1** injury appearing as a discoloration of the skin. **2** similar damage on a fruit, etc. • *v.* **1** *tr.* **a** inflict a bruise on. **b** hurt mentally. **2** *intr.* be susceptible to bruising.

bruis-er /broozər/ *n. colloq.* large tough-looking person.

bruit /broot/ *v.tr.* (often foll. by *about*) spread (a report or rumor).

brunch /brunch/ • *n.* late-morning meal eaten as the first meal of the day. • *v.intr.* eat brunch.

bru-nette /broonét/ (also *masc.* **bru-net'**) • *n.* person with dark hair. • *adj.* having dark hair.

brunt /brunt/ *n.* chief impact of an attack, task, etc. (esp. *bear the brunt of*).

brush /brush/ • *n.* **1** implement with bristles, hair, wire, etc., set into a handle, for arranging the hair, cleaning, painting, etc. **2** application of a brush; brushing. **3** a short, esp. unpleasant encounter. **b** skirmish. **4** bushy tail of a fox. **5** *Electr.* piece of carbon or metal serving as an electrical contact, esp. with a moving part. **6** undergrowth. • *v.* **1** *tr.* **a** sweep, scrub, or put in order with a brush. **b** treat (a surface) with a brush so as to change its nature or appearance. **2** *tr.* remove or apply with a brush. **3** *tr.* & *intr.* graze in passing. **4** *intr.* perform a brushing action or motion. □ **brush aside** dismiss curtly. **brush-off** *n.* abrupt dismissal. **brush up** (often foll. by *on*) revive one's former knowledge of (a subject). □□ **brush'like** *adj.* **brush'y** *adj.*

brush-wood /brúshwŏŏd/ *n.* **1** cut or broken twigs, etc. **2** undergrowth; a thicket.

brush-work /brúshwərk/ *n.* **1** manipulation of the brush in painting. **2** painter's style in this.

brusque /brusk/ *adj.* abrupt or offhand. □□ **brusque'ly** *adv.* **brusque'ness** *n.*

Brus-sels sprout /brúsəlz/ *n.* **1** vegetable with small, compact cabbage-like buds. **2** any of these buds.

bru-tal /broot'l/ *adj.* **1** savagely or viciously cruel. **2** harsh; merciless. □□ **bru-tal-i-ty** /-tálitee/ *n.* (*pl.* **-ties**). **bru'tal-ly** *adv.*

bru-tal-ize /broot'līz/ *v.tr.* **1** make brutal. **2** treat brutally. □□ **bru-tal-i-za'tion** *n.*

brute /broot/ • *n.* **1** brutal or violent person or animal. **2** animal as opposed to a human being. • *adj.* **1** not possessing the capacity to reason. **2 a** cruel. **b** stupid. **3** unthinking; merely physical. □□ **brut'ish** *adj.* **brut'ish-ly** *adv.* **brut'ish-ness** *n.*

BS *abbr.* **1** Bachelor of Science. **2** Bachelor of Surgery. **3** Blessed Sacrament.

B.Sc. *abbr.* Bachelor of Science.

BTU *abbr.* (also **B.t.u.**) British thermal unit(s).

bub-ble /búbəl/ • *n.* **1 a** thin sphere of liquid enclosing air, etc. **b** air-filled cavity in a liquid or a solidified liquid such as glass or amber. **c** (in *pl.*) froth; foam. **2** sound or appearance of boiling. **3** semicylindrical or domed structure. **4** visionary or unrealistic project. • *v.intr.* **1** rise in or send up bubbles. **2** make the sound of boiling. □ **bubble gum** chewing gum that can be blown into bubbles. **bubble memory** *Computing* type of memory that stores data as a pattern of magnetized regions in a thin layer of magnetic material. **bubble wrap** clear plastic wrap with air bubbles in it.

bub-bly /búblee/ • *adj.* (**bub-bli-er, bub-bli-est**) **1** having bubbles. **2** exuberant. • *n. colloq.* champagne.

bu-bo /byŏŏbō, bŏŏ-/ *n.* (*pl.* **-boes**) swollen inflamed lymph node, esp. in the armpit or groin.

bu-bon-ic plague /byŏŏbónik, bŏŏ-/ *n.* contagious bacterial disease characterized by fever, delirium, and buboes.

buc-ca-neer /búkənéer/ • *n.* **1** pirate. **2** unscrupulous adventurer. • *v.intr.* be a buccaneer. □□ **buc-ca-neer'ing** *n.* & *adj.* **buc-ca-neer'ish** *adj.*

buck[1] /buk/ • *n.* male deer, hare, rabbit, etc. • *v.* **1** *intr.* (of a horse) jump upward with back arched and feet drawn together. **2** *tr.* **a** throw (a rider) in this way. **b** oppose; resist. **3** *tr.* & *intr.* (usu. foll. by *up*) *colloq.* make or become more cheerful. □□ **buck'er** *n.*

buck[2] /buk/ *n. sl.* dollar. □ **a fast buck** easy money.

buck[3] /buk/ *n. sl.* article placed as a reminder before a player whose turn it is to deal at poker. □ **pass the buck** *colloq.* shift responsibility (to another).

buck-board /búkbawrd/ *n.* horse-drawn vehicle with the body formed by a plank fixed to the axles.

buck-et /búkit/ • *n.* **1 a** roughly cylindrical open container with a handle, for carrying, catching, or holding water, etc. **b** amount contained in this. **2** (in *pl.*) large quantities, esp. rain or tears. **3** compartment on the outer edge of a waterwheel. **4** scoop of a dredger or a grain elevator. • *v. intr.* (esp. of rain) pour heavily. □ **bucket seat** seat with a rounded back to fit one person, esp. in a car. □□ **buck'et-ful** *n.* (*pl.* **-fuls**).

buck-le /búkəl/ • *n.* **1** clasp with a hinged pin, used for securing a belt, strap, etc. **2** similarly shaped ornament, esp. on a shoe. • *v.* **1** *tr.* (often foll. by *up, on,* etc.) fasten with a buckle. **2** *tr.* & *intr.* give way or cause to give way under longitudinal pressure; crumple. □ **buckle down** make a determined effort.

buck-ram /búkrəm/ *n.* coarse linen or other cloth stiffened with gum or paste.

buck-saw /búksaw/ *n.* two-handed saw set in an H-shaped frame and used for sawing wood.

buck-shot /búkshot/ *n.* large-sized lead shot.

buck-skin /búkskin/ *n.* **1** leather made from a buck's skin. **2** thick, smooth cotton or wool cloth.

buck·tooth /búktŏŏth/ n. upper tooth that projects.

buck·wheat /búkhweet, -weet/ n. any cereal plant with seeds used for fodder and flour.

bu·col·ic /byŏŏkólik/ • adj. of or concerning shepherds, etc.; rural. • n. 1 (usu. in pl.) pastoral poem or poetry. 2 peasant. □□ **bu·col'i·cal·ly** adv.

bud /bud/ • n. 1 a shoot from which a stem, leaf, or flower develops. b flower or leaf not fully open. 2 anything still undeveloped. • v.intr. (**bud·ded, bud·ding**) 1 Bot. & Zool. form a bud. 2 begin to grow or develop.

Bud·dha /bŏŏdə, bŏŏdə/ n. title given to successive teachers of Buddhism, esp. to its founder, Gautama.

Bud·dhism /bŏŏdizəm, bŏŏd-/ n. widespread Asian religion or philosophy, founded by Gautama Buddha in India in the 5th c. BC. □□ **Bud'dhist** n. & adj.

bud·dy /búdee/ colloq. • n. (pl. **-dies**) close friend or companion. • v.intr. (**-dies, -died**) become friendly.

budge /buj/ v. (usu. with neg.) 1 intr. a make the slightest movement. b change one's opinion. 2 tr. cause or compel to budge.

bud·ger·i·gar /bújəreegaar/ n. small parrot kept as a pet.

bud·get /bújit/ • n. 1 amount of money needed or available. 2 estimate or plan of revenue and expenditure. • v. allow or arrange for in a budget. □□ **budg'et·ar·y** adj.

buff /buf/ • adj. of a yellowish beige color. • n. 1 this color. 2 colloq. enthusiast. 3 colloq. human skin unclothed. 4 velvety dull yellow ox leather. • v.tr. 1 polish (metal, etc.). 2 make (leather) velvety. □ **in the buff** colloq. naked.

buf·fa·lo /búfəlō/ • n. (pl. same or **-loes**) 1 N. American bison. 2 wild ox of Africa or Asia. • v.tr. (**-loes, -loed**) sl. outwit.

buf·fer /búfər/ • n. 1 a device that deadens an impact, etc. b such a device on the front and rear of a railroad vehicle or at the end of a track. 2 Biochem. substance that maintains the hydrogen ion concentration of a solution when an acid or alkali is added. 3 Computing temporary memory area for data. • v.tr. 1 act as a buffer to. 2 Biochem. treat with a buffer. □ **buffer state** small nation situated between two larger ones regarded as reducing friction. **buffer zone** any area separating those in conflict.

buf·fet[1] /bŏŏfáy, bə-/ n. 1 meal consisting of several dishes set out on a table from which guests serve themselves. 2 restaurant or counter where light meals or snacks may be bought. 3 sideboard. □ **buffet car** railroad car serving refreshments.

buf·fet[2] /búfit/ • v. tr. strike repeatedly. • n. 1 blow, esp. of the hand or fist. 2 shock.

buf·foon /bəfŏŏn/ n. 1 jester; mocker. 2 stupid person. □□ **buf·foon'er·y** n. **buf·foon'ish** adj.

bug /bug/ • n. 1 a any of various insects with mouthparts modified for piercing and sucking. b colloq. any insect. 2 sl. virus; infection. 3 concealed microphone. 4 error in a computer program or system, etc. 5 sl. a obsession, enthusiasm, etc. b enthusiast. • v. (**bugged, bug·ging**) 1 tr. conceal a microphone in. 2 tr. sl.

annoy. 3 intr. sl. leave quickly. □ **bug-eyed** with bulging eyes.

bug·bear /búgbair/ n. 1 cause of annoyance; bête noire. 2 object of baseless fear.

bug·gy /búgee/ n. (pl. **-gies**) 1 small light, horse-drawn vehicle. 2 small, sturdy, esp. open, motor vehicle (beach buggy). 3 baby carriage.

bu·gle /byŏŏgəl/ • n. (also **bu'gle horn**) brass military instrument like a small trumpet. • v. 1 intr. sound a bugle. 2 tr. sound (a note, a call, etc.) on a bugle. □□ **bu'gler** /byŏŏglər/ n. **bu'glet** /byŏŏglit/ n.

build /bild/ • v.tr. (past and past. part. **built** /bilt/) 1 a construct. b commission, finance, and oversee the building of. 2 a establish, develop, make, or accumulate. b (often foll. by on) base (hopes, theories, etc.). 3 (as **built** adj.) having a specified build. • n. 1 physical proportions. 2 style of construction. □ **build in** incorporate. **build on** add (an extension, etc.). **build up 1** increase in size or strength. 2 praise; boost. 3 gradually become established. **built-in** integral. **built-up 1** (of a locality) densely developed. 2 increased in height, etc., by the addition of parts. □□ **build'er** n.

build·ing /bílding/ n. 1 permanent fixed structure. 2 constructing of such structures.

build-up /bíldəp/ n. 1 favorable advance publicity. 2 gradual approach to a climax.

built past and past part. of BUILD.

bulb /bulb/ n. 1 a underground fleshy-leaved storage organ of some plants (e.g., lily, onion) sending roots downward and leaves upward. b plant grown from this. 2 = LIGHTBULB. 3 any object or part shaped like a bulb.

bul·bous /búlbəs/ adj. shaped like a bulb; fat or bulging.

bulge /bulj/ • n. 1 irregular swelling; lump. 2 colloq. temporary increase in quantity or number. • v. 1 intr. swell. 2 intr. be full or replete. 3 tr. swell (a bag, etc.). □□ **bulg'ing·ly** adv. **bulg'y** adj.

bu·li·ma·rex·i·a /bŏŏlímərékseeə, -lĕemə-, byŏŏ-/ n. = BULIMIA 2. □□ **bu·lim·a·rex'ic** adj. & n.

bu·lim·i·a /bŏŏléemeeə, -li-, byŏŏ-/ n. Med. 1 insatiable overeating. 2 (in full **bu·lim'i·a ner·vo'sa**) emotional disorder in which bouts of overeating are followed by self-induced vomiting, etc. □□ **bu·lim'ic** adj. & n.

bulk /bulk/ • n. 1 a magnitude (esp. large). b large mass. c large quantity. 2 large shape, body, or person. 3 (treated as pl.) the greater part or number. 4 roughage. • v. 1 intr. seem in respect to size or importance; loom. 2 tr. make (a book, etc.) seem thicker (bulked it with irrelevant stories). □ **in bulk** in large quantities.

bulk·head /búlk-hed/ n. 1 upright partition separating compartments in a ship, aircraft, etc. 2 embankment, esp. along a waterfront.

bulk·y /búlkee/ adj. (**bulk·i·er, bulk·i·est**) awkwardly large; unwieldy. □□ **bulk'i·ly** adv. **bulk'i·ness** n.

bull[1] /bŏŏl/ • n. 1 a uncastrated male bovine animal. b male of the whale, elephant, etc. 2 (**the Bull**) zodiacal sign or constellation Taurus. 3 Stock Exch. person who buys shares hoping to sell them at a higher price (cf. BEAR[2]). • adj. like that of a bull. • v. 1 tr. & intr. act or treat violently. 2 Stock Exch. a intr. speculate for a rise in stock prices. b tr. raise price of (stocks, etc.). □ **bull pen** (also **bull'pen**) 1 Baseball a area where relief pitchers warm up. **b** relief pitchers on a team. **2** large temporary holding cell for prisoners. **bull's-eye** center of a target; direct hit. **take the bull by the horns** face danger or challenge boldly. □□ **bull′ish** adj.

bull² /bŏŏl/ n. a papal edict.

bull·dog /bŏŏldawg, -dog/ n. **1 a** dog of a sturdy powerful breed with a large head and smooth hair. **b** this breed. **2** tenacious and courageous person.

bull·doze /bŏŏldōz/ v.tr. **1** clear with a bulldozer. **2** colloq. **a** intimidate. **b** make (one's way) forcibly.

bull·doz·er /bŏŏldōzər/ n. powerful tractor with a broad curved vertical blade at the front for clearing ground.

bul·let /bŏŏlit/ n. small missile fired from a rifle, revolver, etc.

bul·le·tin /bŏŏlitin/ n. **1** short official statement of news. **2** regular periodical issued by an organization. □ **bulletin board 1** board for posting notices, information, etc. **2** Computing public computer file serving the function of a bulletin board.

---

bulletin mid-17th century (denoting an official warrant in some European countries) from French, from Italian bullettino, diminutive of bulletta 'passport,' diminutive of bulla 'official seal on a document.'

---

bul·let·proof /bŏŏlitprŏŏf/ ● adj. (of a material) designed to protect from bullets. ● v.tr. make bulletproof.

bull·fight /bŏŏlfit/ n. sport of baiting and (usu.) killing bulls. □□ **bull′fight·er** n. **bull′fight·ing** n.

bull·frog /bŏŏlfrawg, -frog/ n. large frog native to eastern N. America, with a deep croak.

bull·head·ed /bŏŏlhédid/ adj. obstinate; impetuous; blundering. □□ **bull′head·ed·ly** adv. **bull′head·ed·ness** n.

bull·horn /bŏŏlhawrn/ n. portable voice amplifier.

bul·lion /bŏŏlyən/ n. gold or silver in bulk before coining, or valued by weight.

bull·ish /bŏŏlish/ adj. **1** like a bull, esp. in size or temper. **2 a** associated with rising stock prices. **b** optimistic.

bul·lock /bŏŏlək/ n. castrated bull; steer.

bull·ring /bŏŏlring/ n. arena for bullfights.

bul·ly /bŏŏlee/ ● n. (pl. **-lies**) person intimidating others. ● v.tr. (**-lies, -lied**) **1** persecute. **2** pressure (a person) to do something (bullied him into agreeing).

bul·rush /bŏŏlrush/ n. **1** rushlike water plant. **2** Bibl. papyrus.

bul·wark /bŏŏlwərk/ ● n. **1** defensive wall, esp. of earth; a rampart. **2** person, principle, etc., that acts as a defense. **3** (usu. in pl.) ship's side above deck. ● v.tr. serve as a bulwark to; protect.

bum /bum/ sl. ● n. **1** habitual loafer or tramp; lazy dissolute person. ● v. (**bummed, bum·ming**) **1** intr. loaf or wander around. **2** tr. cadge. ● attrib.adj. **1** of poor quality. **2** false; fabricated. **3** not entirely functional (bum ankle).

bum·ble /búmbəl/ v.intr. **1** speak in a rambling way. **2** (often as **bumbling** adj.) blunder. □□ **bum′bler** n.

bum·ble·bee /búmbəlbee/ n. any large loud humming bee.

bump /bump/ ● n. **1** dull-sounding blow or collision. **2** swelling or dent so caused. **3** uneven patch on a road, etc. ● v. **1 a** tr. hit or come against with a bump. **b** intr. (of two objects) collide. **2** intr. hit with a bump; collide with. **3** tr. hurt or damage by striking. **4** intr. (usu. foll. by along) move with much jolting. ● adv. with a bump. □ **bump into** colloq. meet by chance. **bump off** sl. murder. □□ **bump′i·ly** adv. **bump′i·ness** n. **bump′y** adj. (**bump·i·er, bump·i·est**).

bump·er /búmpər/ n. **1** horizontal bar across the front or back of a vehicle, at the end of a track, etc., to reduce damage in a collision. **2** unusually large or fine (a bumper crop).

bump·kin /búmpkin/ n. rustic or socially inept person.

bump·tious /búmpshəs/ adj. offensively self-assertive or conceited. □□ **bump′tious·ly** adv. **bump′tious·ness** n.

bun /bun/ n. **1** small bread, roll, or cake. **2** hair worn in the shape of a bun.

bunch /bunch/ ● n. **1** things growing or fastened together (bunch of grapes). **2** collection. **3** colloq. group; gang. ● v. **1** tr. gather into close folds. **2** intr. form into a group or crowd. □□ **bunch′y** adj.

bun·co /búngkō/ (also **bun′ko**) sl. n. (pl. **-cos**) swindle, esp. by card sharping or a confidence trick.

bun·dle /búndəl/ ● n. **1** things tied or fastened together. **2** set of nerve fibers, etc. **3** sl. large amount of money. ● v.tr. **1** tie or make into a bundle. **2** (usu. foll. by into) throw or push, esp. quickly or confusedly. **3** send away hurriedly.

bung /bung/ ● n. stopper for a cask. ● v.tr. stop with a bung.

bun·ga·low /búnggəlō/ n. one-storied house.

bun·gee /búnjee/ n. (in full **bun′gee cord**) elasticized cord used for securing baggage, etc. □ **bungee jumping** sport of jumping from a height while secured by a bungee from the ankles or a harness.

bun·gle /búnggəl/ ● v. **1** tr. mismanage or fail at (a task). **2** intr. work badly or clumsily. ● n. bungled attempt or work. □□ **bun′gler** n.

bun·ion /búnyən/ n. swelling on the foot, esp. at the base of the big toe.

bunk¹ /bungk/ ● n. shelflike bed against a wall, e.g., in a ship. ● v.intr. sleep in a bunk. □ **bunk bed** each of two or more beds one above the other, forming a unit.

bunk² /bungk/ n. sl. nonsense; humbug.

bunk·er /búngkər/ ● n. **1** large container or compartment for storing fuel. **2** reinforced underground shelter. **3** sand-filled hollow as an obstacle in a golf course. ● v.tr. fill the fuel bunkers of (a ship, etc.).

bun·kum /búngkəm/ n. nonsense; humbug.

bun·ny /búnee/ n. (pl. **-nies**) child's word for a rabbit.

Bun·sen burn·er /búnsən/ n. small adjustable gas burner used in scientific work as a source of intense heat.

bunt /bunt/ ● v. **1** tr. & intr. push with the head or horns; butt. **2** tr. Baseball tap or push (a ball) with the bat without swinging. ● n. act of bunting.

bun·ting¹ /búnting/ n. any of numerous seed-eating birds related to the finches and sparrows.

bunt·ing[2] /búnting/ n. 1 flags and other decorations. 2 loosely woven fabric used for these.

buoy /bōo-ee, boy/ • n. 1 anchored float as a navigation mark, etc. 2 lifebuoy. • v.tr. 1 (usu. foll. by *up*) a keep afloat. b uplift; encourage. 2 mark with a buoy.

buoy·ant /bóyənt/ adj. 1 a able or apt to keep afloat. b (of a liquid or gas) able to keep something afloat. 2 lighthearted; resilient. □□ **buoy·an·cy** /bóyənsee/ n. **buoy′ant·ly** adv.

bur /bər/ n. var. of BURR.

bur. abbr. bureau.

bur·den /bárdən/ • n. 1 load, esp. a heavy one. 2 oppressive duty, expense, emotion, etc. 3 ship's carrying capacity; tonnage. • v.tr. load with a burden; oppress. □□ **bur′den·some** adj. **bur′den·some·ness** n.

bur·dock /bárdok/ n. plant with prickly flowers and leaves.

bu·reau /byŏŏrō/ n. (pl. **bu·reaus** or **bu·reaux** /-rōz/) 1 chest of drawers. 2 a office or department for specific business. b government department.

bu·reau·cra·cy /byŏŏrókrəsee/ n. (pl. **-cies**) 1 a government by central administration. b nation so governed. 2 officials of such a government, esp. regarded as oppressive and inflexible. 3 conduct typical of these. □□ **bu·reau·crat** /byŏŏrəkrat/ n. **bu·reau·crat′ic** adj. **bu·reau·crat′i·cal·ly** adv.

bur·geon /bárjən/ literary • v.intr. grow rapidly; flourish. • n. bud; sprout.

burg·er /bárgər/ n. colloq. hamburger.

bur·gher /bárgər/ n. citizen of a town.

bur·glar /bárglər/ n. person who commits burglary.

bur·glar·ize /bárglərīz/ v. 1 tr. commit burglary against (a building or person). 2 intr. commit burglary.

bur·gla·ry /bárgləree/ n. (pl. **-ries**) 1 entry into a building illegally with intent to commit a felony. 2 instance of this.

¶ Traditionally (under common law), **burglary** was the crime of breaking into a dwelling with the intent of committing a felony. It was essentially a crime against the security of one's home. Today, common usage and statutes have made burglary the crime of breaking into any building at any time with intent to steal or commit a felony; it is now essentially a crime against property.

bur·gle /bárgəl/ v. = BURGLARIZE.

bur·gun·dy /bárgəndee/ n. (pl. **-dies**) 1 a wine of Burgundy in E. France. b similar wine from another place. 2 dark red color of Burgundy wine.

bur·i·al /béreeəl/ n. 1 burying of a dead body. 2 Archaeol. grave or its remains.

bur·lesque /bərlésk/ • n. 1 a comic imitation; parody. b performance or work of this kind. 2 variety show, often including striptease. • adj. of or in the nature of burlesque. • v.tr. (**bur·lesques, bur·lesqued, bur·lesqu·ing**) parody. □□ **bur·lesqu′er** n.

bur·ly /bárlee/ adj. (**bur·li·er, bur·li·est**) of stout sturdy build; big and strong. □□ **bur′li·ness** n.

burn /bərn/ • v. (past and past part. **burned** or **burnt**) 1 tr. & intr. be or cause to be consumed or destroyed by fire. 2 intr. blaze or glow with fire. 3 tr. & intr. be or cause to be injured or damaged by fire, heat, or radiation. 4 tr. & intr. use or be used as fuel. 5 tr. & intr. char in cooking. 6 tr. produce (a hole, a mark, etc.) by fire or heat. 7 tr. & intr. put or be put to death by fire or electrocution. 8 tr. cauterize; brand. 9 tr. & intr. make, be, or feel hot, esp. painfully. 10 a tr. & intr. make or be passionate; feel or cause to feel great emotion. b intr. (usu. foll. by *to* + infin.) desire passionately; long. • n. mark or injury caused by burning. □ **burn down** destroy or be destroyed by fire. **burn out** 1 be reduced to nothing by burning. 2 fail or cause to fail by burning. 3 (usu. refl.) suffer exhaustion. **burn up** 1 get rid of by fire. 2 sl. be or make furious.

burn·er /bárnər/ n. part of a gas stove, lamp, etc., that emits and shapes the flame.

burn·ing /bárning/ adj. 1 ardent; intense. 2 hotly discussed; exciting. 3 flagrant (*burning shame*). 4 that burns; on fire; very hot. □□ **burn′ing·ly** adv.

bur·nish /bárnish/ v.tr. polish by rubbing. □□ **bur′nish·er** n.

bur·noose /bərnōōs/ n. Arab or Moorish hooded cloak.

burn·out /bárnowt/ n. 1 physical or emotional exhaustion. 2 extinguishing of a rocket motor when fuel is exhausted.

burnt see BURN.

burp /bərp/ colloq. • v. 1 intr. belch. 2 tr. make (a baby) belch. • n. belch.

burr /bər/ • n. 1 a whirring sound. b rough sounding of the letter *r*. 2 a rough edge on cut metal or paper. b surgeon's or dentist's small drill. 3 a prickly clinging seedcase or flowerhead. b any plant producing these. • v. 1 tr. pronounce with a burr. 2 intr. speak indistinctly. 3 intr. make a whirring sound.

bur·ri·to /bəreétō/ n. (pl. **-tos**) tortilla rolled around a usu. meat or bean filling.

bur·ro /bárō, bŏŏrō, búrō/ n. (pl. **-ros**) small donkey.

bur·row /bárō, búrō/ • n. hole or tunnel dug by a small animal as a dwelling. • v. 1 intr. make a burrow. 2 tr. make (a hole, etc.) by digging. 3 intr. hide oneself. 4 intr. (foll. by *into*) investigate; search. □□ **bur′row·er** n.

bur·sa /bársə/ n. (pl. **bur·sae** /-see/ or **bur·sas**) Anat. fluid-filled sac or cavity that eases friction. □□ **bur′sal** adj.

bur·sar /bársər/ n. treasurer, esp. of a college.

bur·si·tis /bərsítis/ n. inflammation of a bursa.

burst /bərst/ • v. (past and past part. **burst**) 1 a intr. break suddenly apart from within. b tr. cause to do this. 2 a tr. open forcibly. b intr. come open or be opened forcibly. 3 a intr. make one's way suddenly, dramatically, or by force. b tr. break away from or through. 4 tr. & intr. fill or be full to overflowing. 5 intr. appear or come suddenly (*burst into flame*). 6 intr. suddenly begin to shed or utter (*burst into tears* or laughter or song). 7 intr. be as if about to burst because of effort, excitement, etc. • n. 1 act of bursting; split. 2 sudden issuing forth. 3 sudden outbreak. 4 sudden effort; spurt. 5 explosion.

bur·y /béree/ v.tr. (**-ies, -ied**) 1 place (a dead body) in the earth, a tomb, or the sea. 2 lose by death. 3 a put under ground (*bury alive*). b hide (treasure, a bone, etc.) in the earth. c cover up; submerge. 4 involve deeply.

bus /bus/ • *n.* (*pl.* **bus·es** or **bus·ses**) **1** large passenger vehicle, usu. on a fixed route. **2** *Computing* defined set of conductors carrying data and control signals within a computer. • *v.* (**bus·es, bused, bus·ing; bus·ses, bussed, bus·sing**) **1** *intr.* go by bus. **2** *tr.* transport by bus.

bus. *abbr.* business.

bus·boy /búsboy/ *n.* assistant to a restaurant waiter who fills water glasses, removes dirty dishes, etc.

bus·by /búzbee/ *n.* (*pl.* **-bies**) tall fur hat worn by some military units.

BUSBY

bush /boosh/ *n.* **1** shrub or clump of shrubs. **2** thing resembling this, esp. a clump of hair or fur. □□ **bush′i·ly** *adv.* **bush′i·ness** *n.* **bush′y** *adj.* (**bush·i·er, bush·i·est**).

bushed /boosht/ *adj. colloq.* tired out.

bush·el /booshal/ *n.* measure of capacity equivalent to 64 pints. □□ **bush′el·ful** *n.* (*pl.* **-fuls**).

bush·ing /booshing/ *n.* metal lining for a hole enclosing a revolving shaft, etc.

bush·man /booshman/ *n.* (*pl.* **-men**) **1** person who lives or travels in the Australian bush. **2** (**Bushman**) member or language of an aboriginal people in S. Africa.

bush·mas·ter /booshmastar/ *n.* venomous viper of Central and S. America.

bush·whack /boosh-hwak, -wak/ *v.* **1** *intr.* **a** clear woods and bush country. **b** live or travel in bush country. **2** *tr.* ambush.

busi·ness /bíznis/ *n.* **1** one's regular occupation, profession, or trade. **2** one's own concern. **3 a** task or duty. **b** reason for coming. **4** *derog.* affair; matter. **5** commercial firm. □ **business card** card printed with one's name and professional details. **the business end** *colloq.* functional part of a tool or device. **business reply mail** system of sending business mail in envelopes prepaid by the addressee. **business suit 1** man's suit consisting of a jacket, trousers, and sometimes a vest. **2** woman's suit, consisting of a jacket and usu. a skirt. **has no business to** has no right to. **in business 1** trading or dealing. **2** able to begin operations. **in the business of 1** engaged in. **2** intending to (*we are not in the business of surrendering*). **mind one's own business** not meddle.

busi·ness·like /bíznislīk/ *adj.* efficient; systematic; practical.

busi·ness·man /bíznismən/ *n.* (*pl.* **-men**; *fem.* **busi·ness·wom·an,** *pl.* **-wom·en**) person engaged in commerce.

bus·man /búsmən/ *n.* (*pl.* **-men**) driver of a bus. □ **busman's holiday** leisure time spent in an activity similar to one's regular work.

buss /bus/ *colloq.* • *n.* kiss. • *v.tr.* kiss.

bust¹ /bust/ *n.* **1** human chest, esp. that of a woman; bosom. **2** sculpture of a person's head, shoulders, and chest.

bust² /bust/ *colloq.* • *v.* (*past* and *past part.* **bust·ed** or **bust**) **1** *tr.* & *intr.* burst; break. **2** *tr.* reduce (a soldier, etc.) to a lower rank. **3** *tr.* **a** raid; search. **b** arrest. • *n.* **1** sudden failure. **2 a** police raid. **b** arrest. • *adj.* (also **bust·ed**) **1** broken; burst. **2** bankrupt. **3** arrested. □ **bust up** (of esp. a married couple) separate.

bust·er /bústər/ *n. sl.* buddy; fellow (used esp. as a disrespectful form of address).

bus·tle /búsəl/ • *v.* **1** *intr.* **a** work, etc., showily and energetically. **b** hasten. **2** *tr.* make (a person) hurry or work hard. **3** *intr.* (as **bustling** *adj.*) *colloq.* full of activity. • *n.* excited activity; fuss. □□ **bus′tler** *n.*

bus·y /bízee/ • *adj.* (**bus·i·er, bus·i·est**) **1** occupied or engaged. **2** full of activity; fussy. **3** (of a telephone line) in use. • *v.tr.* (**-ies, -ied**) (often *refl.*) keep busy; occupy. □ **busy signal** intermittent buzzing sound indicating that a telephone line is in use. □□ **bus′i·ly** /bízilee/ *adv.* **bus′y·ness** /bízeenis/ *n.* (cf. BUSINESS).

bus·y·bod·y /bízeebodee, -budee/ *n.* (*pl.* **-ies**) **1** meddlesome person. **2** mischief maker.

but /but, bət/ • *conj.* **1 a** nevertheless; however. **b** on the other hand; on the contrary. **2** except; other than; otherwise than (*what could we do but run?*). **3** without the result that (*it never rains but it pours*). • *prep.* except; apart from; other than (*everyone went but me*). • *adv.* **1** only; no more than; only just (*we can but try; did it but once*). **2** introducing emphatic repetition; definitely (*wanted to see nobody, but nobody*). • *rel.pron.* who not; that not (*there is not a man but feels pity*). • *n.* objection (*ifs and buts*). • *v.tr.* (in phr. **but me no buts**) do not raise objections. □ **but for** without the help or hindrance, etc., of (*but for you I'd be rich by now*).

bu·tane /byootayn/ *n. Chem.* gaseous hydrocarbon used as fuel.

butch /booch/ *sl.* • *adj.* masculine; tough-looking. • *n.* **1** mannish woman. **2** mannish lesbian.

butch·er /boochər/ • *n.* **1 a** person who deals in meat. **b** person who slaughters animals for food. **2** person who kills indiscriminately or brutally. • *v.tr.* **1** slaughter or cut up (an animal) for food. **2** kill (people) wantonly or cruelly. **3** ruin through incompetence.

butch·er·y /boochəree/ *n.* (*pl.* **-ies**) **1** needless or cruel slaughter (of people). **2** butcher's trade.

but·ler /bútlər/ *n.* principal manservant of a household.

butt¹ /but/ • *v.* **1** *tr.* & *intr.* push with the head or horns. **2** *intr.* meet end to end with; abut. • *n.* **1** a push with the head. **2** joining of two edges. □ **butt in** interrupt; meddle.

butt² /but/ *n.* **1** object (of ridicule, etc.). **2 a** mound behind a target. **b** (in *pl.*) shooting range.

butt³ /but/ *n.* **1** (also **butt end**) thicker end, esp. of a tool or a weapon. **2** stub of a cigar or a cigarette. **3** *sl.* buttocks.

butt⁴ /but/ *n.* cask, esp. as a measure of wine or ale.

but·ter /bútər/ • *n.* **1 a** solidified churned cream used as a spread and in cooking. **b** substance of a similar consistency. • *v.tr.* spread, cook, or serve with butter. □ **butter bean 1** dried lima bean. **2** wax bean. **butter cream** (or **icing**) mixture of butter, confectioner's sugar, etc., used as a filling or topping for a cake. **butter up** *colloq.* flatter excessively.

but·ter·fat /bútərfat/ *n.* essential fats of pure butter.

but·ter·fin·gers /bútərfingərz/ *n. colloq.* clumsy person.

but·ter·fly /bútərflī/ *n.* (*pl.* **-flies**) **1** insect with four usu. brightly colored wings erect when at rest. **2** (in *pl.*) *colloq.* nervous sensation felt in the stomach. □ **butterfly stroke** stroke in swimming, with both arms raised out of the water and lifted forward together.

but·ter·milk /bútərmilk/ *n.* slightly acid liquid left after churning butter.

but·ter·scotch /bútərskoch/ *n.* **1** brittle candy made from butter, brown sugar, etc. **2** this flavor in desserts, etc.

but·ter·y¹ /bútəree/ *n.* (*pl.* **-ies**) pantry.

but·ter·y² /bútəree/ *adj.* like, containing, or spread with butter. □□ **but′ter·i·ness** *n.*

but·tock /bútək/ *n.* (usu. in *pl.*) **1** each of two fleshy protuberances on the lower rear part of the human trunk. **2** the corresponding part of an animal.

but·ton /bút'n/ • *n.* **1** small disk or knob sewn to a garment as a fastener or as an ornament. **2** knob on electronic equipment that is pressed to operate it. • *v.* **1** *tr.* & *intr.* = button up 1. **2** *tr.* supply with buttons. □ **button up 1** fasten with buttons. **2** *colloq.* complete (a task, etc.) satisfactorily. **3** *colloq.* become silent. □□ **but′toned** *adj.* **but′ton·less** *adj.*

but·ton·hole /bút'nhōl/ • *n.* **1** slit in a garment for a button. **2** flower worn in a lapel buttonhole; boutonniere. • *v.tr. colloq.* accost and detain (a reluctant listener).

but·tress /bútris/ • *n.* **1** projecting support of stone or brick, etc., built against a wall. **2** source of help or encouragement. • *v.tr.* **1** support with a buttress. **2** support by argument, etc.

bu·xom /búksəm/ *adj.* (esp. of a woman) plump and healthy-looking; large bosomed. □□ **bux′om·ly** *adv.* **bux′om·ness** *n.*

buy /bī/ • *v.* (**buys**, **buy·ing**; *past* and *past part.* **bought** /bawt/) **1** *tr.* **a** obtain in exchange for money. **b** (usu. in *neg.*) serve to obtain (*money can't buy happiness*). **2** *tr.* bribe. **3** *tr.* get by sacrifice, great effort, etc. **4** *tr. sl.* accept; believe in; approve of. **5** *absol.* be a buyer for a store, etc. • *n. colloq.* purchase. □ **buy off** get rid of by payment. **buy out** pay (a person) to give up an ownership, interest, etc. **buy up** buy as much as possible of.

buy·er /bīər/ *n.* **1** person employed to purchase stock for a large store, etc. **2** customer. □ **buyer's** (or **buyers'**) **market** trading conditions favorable to buyers.

buy·out /bīowt/ *n.* purchase of a controlling share in a company, etc.

buzz /buz/ • *n.* **1** hum of a bee, etc. **2** sound of a buzzer. **3 a** murmur, as of conversation. **b** hurried activity. **c** *colloq.* rumor. **4** *sl.* telephone call. **5** *sl.* thrill; euphoric sensation. • *v.* **1** *intr.* make a humming sound. **2 a** *tr.* & *intr.* signal or signal to with a buzzer. **b** *tr. sl.* telephone. **3** *intr.* **a** (often foll. by *about*) move busily. **b** (of a place) have an air of excitement or purposeful activity. **4** *tr. Aeron. colloq.* fly fast and very close to (another aircraft, the ground, etc.). □ **buzz off** *sl.* go or hurry away. **buzz saw** circular saw.

buz·zard /búzərd/ *n.* turkey vulture.

buzz·er /búzər/ *n.* **1** electrical device that makes a buzzing noise. **2** whistle or siren.

buzz·word /búzwərd/ *n. sl.* **1** fashionable technical or computer jargon. **2** catchword; slogan.

BVM *abbr.* Blessed Virgin Mary.

by /bī/ • *prep.* **1** near; beside. **2** through the agency or means of. **3** not later than. **4 a** past; beyond. **b** passing through; via. **5** in the circumstances of (*by day*). **6** to the extent of. **7** according to. **8** with the succession of. **9** concerning; in respect of. **10** placed between specified lengths in two directions (*three feet by two*). **11** inclining to (*north by northwest*). • *adv.* **1** near. **2** aside; in reserve (*put $5 by*). **3** past (*marched by*). • *n.* = BYE². □ **by and by** before long; eventually. **by and large** on the whole. **by the by** (or **bye**) incidentally.

by- /bī/ *prefix* (also **bye-**) subordinate; incidental (*byroad*).

bye¹ /bī/ *n.* status of an unpaired competitor in a sport, who proceeds to the next round as if having won.

bye² /bī/ *int. colloq.* = GOOD-BYE.

by·gone /bígawn, -gon/ • *adj.* past; antiquated. • *n.* (in *pl.*) past offenses (*let bygones be bygones*).

by·law /bīlaw/ *n.* (also **bye′law**) regulation made by a society or corporation.

by·line /bīlīn/ *n.* **1** line in a newspaper, etc., naming the writer of an article. **2** secondary line of work.

by·pass /bípas/ • *n.* **1** road passing around a town or its center. **2 a** secondary channel or pipe, etc., used in emergencies. **b** alternative passage for the circulation of blood to the heart. • *v.tr.* avoid; go around.

by·play /bíplay/ *n.* secondary action, esp. in a play.

by·prod·uct /bíprodəkt/ *n.* **1** incidental product of the manufacture of something else. **2** secondary result.

by·road /bírōd/ *n.* minor road.

by·stand·er /bístandər/ *n.* person who stands by but does not take part; mere spectator.

byte /bīt/ *n. Computing* group of eight binary digits, often used to represent one character.

by·way /bíway/ *n.* small seldom-traveled road.

by·word /bíwərd/ *n.* **1** person or thing as a notable example. **2** familiar saying; proverb.

Byz·an·tine /bízənteen, -tīn, bizántin/ • *adj.* **1** of Byzantium or the E. Roman Empire. **2** (of a political situation, etc.): **a** extremely complicated. **b** inflexible. **c** underhand. **3** *Archit.* & *Painting* of Byzantium's highly decorated style. • *n.* citizen of Byzantium or the E. Roman Empire. □□ **By′zan·tin·ism** *n.* **Byz′an·tin·ist** *n.*

Cc

C¹ /see/ *n.* (also **c**) (*pl.* **Cs** or **C's**; **c's**) **1** third letter of the alphabet. **2** *Mus.* first note of the diatonic scale of C major. **3** third hypothetical person or example. **4** third highest class or category. **5** (as a Roman numeral) 100. **6** (also ©) copyright.

C² *symb. Chem.* carbon.

C³ *abbr.* (also **C.**) Celsius; centigrade.

c. *abbr.* **1** century; centuries. **2** chapter. **3** cent(s). **4** cubic. **5** *Baseball* catcher. **6** circa; about.

CA *abbr.* California (in official postal use).

Ca *symb. Chem.* calcium.

cab /kab/ *n.* **1** taxi. **2** driver's compartment in a truck, train, crane, etc.

ca·bal /kəbál/ *n.* **1** secret intrigue. **2** political clique.

cab·a·ret /kabəráy/ *n.* **1** entertainment in a nightclub or restaurant. **2** such a nightclub, etc.

cab·bage /kábij/ *n.* vegetable with thick green or purple leaves forming a round heart or head.

cab·by /kábee/ *n.* (also **cab'bie**) (*pl.* **-bies**) *colloq.* cab driver.

cab·in /kábin/ *n.* **1** small shelter or house, esp. of wood. **2** room or compartment in an aircraft or ship. □ **cabin fever** state of restlessness and irritability from having been confined for an extended period.

cab·i·net /kábinit/ *n.* **1 a** cupboard or case for storing or displaying articles. **b** piece of furniture housing a radio or television, etc. **2** (**Cabinet**) committee of senior government advisers.

cab·i·net·mak·er /kábinitmáykər/ *n.* skilled furniture maker.

cab·i·net·ry /kábinitree/ *n.* finished woodwork, esp. of professional quality.

ca·ble /káybəl/ • *n.* **1** thick rope of wire or hemp. **2** encased group of insulated wires for transmitting electricity or electrical signals. **3** cablegram. • *v.tr.* **1** transmit (a message) by cablegram. **2** inform (a person) by cablegram. □ **cable-ready** (of a TV, VCR, etc.) designed for direct connection to a coaxial cable TV system. **cable television** broadcasting system with signals transmitted by cable to subscribers' sets.

ca·ble·gram /káybəlgram/ *n.* telegraph message sent by undersea cable, etc.

ca·boo·dle /kəbo͞od'l/ *n.* □ **the whole (kit and) caboodle** *sl.* the whole lot (of persons or things).

ca·boose /kəbo͞os/ *n.* crew car at the rear of a freight train.

ca·ca·o /kəka'a-ō, -káyō/ *n.* (*pl.* **-os**) **1** seed pod from which cocoa and chocolate are made. **2** small, widely cultivated evergreen tree bearing these.

cache /kash/ • *n.* **1** hiding place for treasure, provisions, ammunition, etc. **2** what is hidden in a cache. • *v.tr.* put in a cache.

ca·chet /kasháy/ *n.* **1** distinguishing mark or seal. **2** prestige.

cack·le /kákəl/ • *n.* **1** clucking sound as of a hen or a goose. **2** loud, silly laugh. **3** noisy, inconsequential talk. • *v.* **1** *intr.* emit a cackle. **2** *intr.* talk noisily and inconsequentially. **3** *tr.* utter or express with a cackle.

cac·o·de·mon /kákəde'emən/ *n.* (also **cac·o·dae'mon**) **1** evil spirit. **2** malignant person.

ca·coph·o·ny /kəkófənee/ *n.* (*pl.* **-nies**) **1** harsh discordant mixture of sound. **2** dissonance; discord. □□ **ca·coph'o·nous** *adj.*

cac·tus /káktəs/ *n.* (*pl.* **cac·ti** /-tī/ or **cac·tus·es**) succulent plant with a thick fleshy stem and usu. spines but no leaves.

CAD /kad/ *abbr.* computer-aided design.

cad /kad/ *n.* man who behaves dishonorably. □□ **cad'dish** *adj.* **cad'dish·ly** *adv.* **cad'dish·ness** *n.*

ca·dav·er /kədávər/ *n.* esp. *Med.* corpse.

ca·dav·er·ous /kədávərəs/ *adj.* **1** corpselike. **2** deathly pale.

cad·die /kádee/ (also **cad'dy**) • *n.* (*pl.* **-dies**) person who assists a golfer during a match, by carrying clubs, etc. • *v.intr.* (**cad·dies, cad·died, cad·dy·ing**) act as caddie.

---

caddie mid-17th century (originally Scots): from French *cadet*. The original term denoted a gentleman who joined the army without a commission, intending to learn the profession and follow a military career, later coming to mean 'odd-job man.' The current sense dates from the late 18th century.

---

cad·dy /kádee/ *n.* (*pl.* **-dies**) small container, esp. a box for holding tea.

ca·dence /káyd'ns/ *n.* **1** fall in pitch of the voice, esp. at the end of a phrase or sentence. **2** intonation; tonal inflection. **3** *Mus.* close of a musical phrase. **4** rhythm; measure or beat of sound or movement. □□ **ca'denced** *adj.*

ca·den·za /kədénzə/ *n.* *Mus.* virtuosic solo passage, somtimes improvised.

ca·det /kədét/ *n.* young trainee, as in the armed services or police force.

cadge /kaj/ *v.* **1** *tr.* get or seek by begging. **2** *intr.* beg. □□ **cadg'er** *n.*

cad·mi·um /kádmeeəm/ *n.* soft, bluish-white metallic element. ¶ Symb.: **Cd**. □ **cadmium yellow** an intense yellow pigment.

cad·re /kádree, ka'adray/ *n.* basic unit, esp. of servicemen.

ca·du·ce·us /kədo͞oseeəs, -shəs, -dyo͞o/ *n.* (*pl.* **ca·du·ce·i** /-see-ī/) winged staff of Mercury; symbol of the medical profession.

CADUCEUS

Cae·sar /se'ezər/ *n.* **1** title of the Roman emperors, esp. from Augustus to Hadrian. **2** autocrat.

Cae·sar·e·an (also **Cae·sar′i·an**) var. of CE-SAREAN.

cae·su·ra /sizhŏŏrə, -zŏŏrə/ *n.* (*pl.* **cae·su·ras** or **cae·su·rae** /-zhŏŏree, -zŏŏree/) *Prosody* pause near the middle of a line. □□ **cae·su′ral** *adj.*

ca·fé /kafáy/ *n.* (also **ca·fe**/) **1** small coffeehouse; simple restaurant. **2** bar. □ **café au lait** /ō láy/ **1** coffee with milk. **2** color of this. **café noir** /nwaar/ black coffee.

caf·e·te·ri·a /káfite'ereeə/ *n.* restaurant in which customers collect their meals on trays at a counter.

caf·feine /káfeen, kafe'en/ *n.* alkaloid drug with stimulant action found in tea leaves and coffee beans.

caf·tan /káftan/ *n.* (also **kaf′tan**) **1** long tunic worn in the Near East. **2 a** long, loose dress. **b** loose shirt or top.

cage /kayj/ • *n.* **1** structure of bars or wires, esp. for confining animals or birds. **2** any similar open framework, as in a freight elevator, etc. • *v.tr.* place or keep in a cage.

ca·gey /káyjee/ *adj.* (also **cag′y**) (**cag·i·er**, **cag·i·est**) *colloq.* cautious and uncommunicative; wary. □□ **cag′i·ly** *adv.* **cag′i·ness** *n.*

ca·hoots /kəhŏŏts/ *n.pl.* □ **in cahoots** *sl.* in collusion.

CAI *abbr.* computer-assisted (or -aided) instruction.

Cain /kayn/ *n.* □ **raise Cain** *colloq.* make a disturbance.

cairn /kairn/ *n.* mound of rough stones as a monument or landmark.

cais·son /káyson, -sən/ *n.* watertight chamber in which underwater construction work can be done.

ca·jole /kəjṓl/ *v.tr.* persuade by flattery, deceit, etc. □□ **ca·jole′ment** *n.* **ca·jol′er** *n.* **ca·jol′er·y** *n.*

cake /kayk/ • *n.* **1** baked mixture of flour, butter, eggs, sugar, etc., often iced. **2** other food in a flat round shape. **3** flattish compact mass. • *v.* **1** *tr.* & *intr.* form into a compact mass. **2** *tr.* cover (with a hard or sticky mass). □ **piece of cake** *colloq.* something easily achieved.

Cal *abbr.* large calorie(s).

cal *abbr.* small calorie(s).

cal·a·bash /kálǝbash/ *n.* **1 a** gourd-bearing evergreen tree native to tropical America. **b** gourd from this tree. **2** shell of this or a similar gourd used as a vessel for water, etc.

cal·a·boose /kálǝbŏŏs/ *n. sl.* prison.

cal·a·mine /kálǝmīn/ *n.* pink powder consisting of zinc carbonate and ferric oxide, used in lotion or ointment.

ca·lam·i·ty /kəlámitee/ *n.* (*pl.* **-ties**) **1** disaster; great misfortune. **2** adversity. **b** deep distress. □□ **ca·lam′i·tous** *adj.* **ca·lam′i·tous·ly** *adv.*

cal·cif·er·ous /kalsífərəs/ *adj.* yielding calcium salts, esp. calcium carbonate.

cal·ci·fy /kálsifī/ *v.* (**-fies, -fied**) **1** harden or become hardened by deposition of calcium salts; petrify. **2** convert or be converted to calcium carbonate. □□ **cal·cif·ic** /-sífik/ *adj.* **cal·ci·fi·ca′tion** *n.*

cal·cine /kálsīn, -sin/ *v.* **1** *tr.* **a** reduce, oxidize, or desiccate by strong heat. **b** burn to ashes. **2** *tr.* consume or purify as if by fire. **3** *intr.* undergo any of these. □□ **cal·ci·na′tion** /-sináyshən/ *n.*

cal·cite /kálsīt/ *n.* natural crystalline calcium carbonate.

cal·ci·um /kálseeəm/ *n.* soft, gray metallic element of the alkaline earth group occurring naturally in limestone, marble, chalk, etc. ¶ Symb.: **Ca.** □ **calcium carbonate** white, insoluble solid occurring naturally as chalk, limestone, marble, and calcite.

cal·cu·late /kálkyəlayt/ *v.tr.* **1** ascertain or determine beforehand, esp. by arithmetic. **2** plan deliberately. □□ **cal·cu·la·ble** /-ləbəl/ *adj.* **cal·cu·la·tive** /-lətiv/ *adj.*

cal·cu·lat·ed /kálkyǝlaytid/ *adj.* **1** (of an action) done with awareness of the likely consequences. **2** (foll. by *to* + infin.) designed or suitable; intended. □□ **cal′cu·lat·ed·ly** *adv.*

cal·cu·lat·ing /kálkyǝlayting/ *adj.* shrewd; scheming.

cal·cu·la·tion /kálkyǝláyshən/ *n.* **1** act or process of calculating. **2** result from calculating. **3** reckoning or forecast.

cal·cu·la·tor /kálkyǝlaytǝr/ *n.* device (esp. a small electronic one) used for making mathematical calculations.

cal·cu·lus /kálkyǝlǝs/ *n.* (*pl.* **cal·cu·li** /-lī/ or **cal·cu·lus·es**) **1** *Math.* particular method of calculation or reasoning (*calculus of probabilities*). **2** *Med.* stone or concretion of minerals formed within the body.

cal·dron var. of CAULDRON.

cal·en·dar /kálindǝr/ *n.* **1** system by which the beginning, length, and subdivisions of the year are fixed. **2** chart or series of pages showing the days, weeks, and months of a particular year. **3** timetable of appointments, special events, etc.

cal·en·der /kálǝndǝr/ • *n.* machine in which cloth, paper, etc., is rolled to glaze or smooth it. • *v.tr.* press in a calender.

calf[1] /kaf/ *n.* (*pl.* **calves** /kavz/) **1** young bovine animal. **2** young of other animals, e.g., elephant, deer, and whale. □□ **calf′hood** *n.* **calf′ish** *adj.* **calf′like** *adj.*

calf[2] /kaf/ *n.* (*pl.* **calves** /kavz/) fleshy hind part of the human leg below the knee.

calf·skin /káfskin/ *n.* calf leather.

cal·i·ber /kálibǝr/ *n.* **1 a** internal diameter of a gun or tube. **b** diameter of a bullet or shell. **2** strength or quality of character; ability; importance. □□ **cal′i·bered** *adj.* (also in *comb.*).

cal·i·brate /kálibrayt/ *v.tr.* **1** mark (a gauge) with a scale of readings. **2** correlate the readings of (an instrument) with a standard. □□ **cal·i·bra·tion** /-bráyshən/ *n.* **cal′i·bra·tor** *n.*

cal·i·co /kálikō/ • *n.* (*pl.* **-coes** or **-cos**) printed cotton fabric. • *adj.* **1** made of calico. **2** multicolored; piebald.

Calif. *abbr.* California.

cal·i·for·ni·um /kálifáwrneeəm/ *n. Chem.* transuranic radioactive metallic element produced artificially. ¶ Symb.: **Cf.**

cal·i·per /kálipǝr/ *n.* (in *pl.*) compasses for measuring diameters or internal dimensions.

ca·liph /káylif, kál-/ *n.* esp. *hist.* chief Muslim civil and religious ruler. □□ **ca′liph·ate** *n.*

cal·is·then·ics /kálisthéniks/ *n.pl.* fitness exercises. □□ **cal·is·then′ic** *adj.*

calk var. of CAULK.

call /kawl/ • *v.* **1** *intr.* **a** cry; shout; speak loudly. **b** (of a bird or animal) emit its characteristic note or cry. **2** *tr.* communicate with by telephone or radio. **3** *tr.* summon. **4** *intr.* pay a brief visit (*called at the house*). **5** *tr.* announce or order to take place. **6** *tr.* name; describe as. **7** *intr.* guess the outcome of tossing a coin, etc. **8** *intr.* (foll. by *for*) order; demand (*called for silence*). **9** *intr.* (foll. by *on, upon*) appeal to; request (*called on us to be quiet*). • *n.* **1** shout or cry. **2 a** characteristic cry of a bird or animal. **b** imitation of this. **c** instrument for imitating it. **3** brief visit (*paid them a call*). **4** act of telephoning. **5** invitation; appeal. **6** duty, need, or occasion (*no call to be rude*). **7** signal on a bugle, etc. **8** *Stock Exch.* option of buying stock at a fixed price at a given date. □ **call girl** female prostitute who accepts appointments by telephone. **calling card** **1** card with a person's name, etc., sent or left in lieu of a formal visit. **2** identifying mark, etc., left behind (by someone). **3** card used to pay for a telephone call. **call off 1** cancel (an arrangement, etc.). **2** order (an attacker or pursuer) to desist. **call of nature** a need to urinate or defecate. **call out 1** summon (troops, etc.) to action. **2** order (workers) to strike. **call the shots** (or **tune**) be in control; take the initiative. **call to order 1** request to be orderly. **2** declare (a meeting) open. **call up 1** reach by telephone. **2** imagine; recollect. **3** summon, esp. to military duty. **on call** (of a doctor, etc.) available if required.

call·er /káwlər/ *n.* person who calls, esp. one who pays a visit or makes a telephone call.

cal·lig·ra·phy /kəlígrəfee/ *n.* art of fine handwriting. □□ **cal·lig′ra·pher** *n.* **cal·li·graph·ic** /káligráfik/ *adj.* **cal·lig′ra·phist** *n.*

---

calligraphy mid-19th century (as a noun): from Greek *kalligraphia*, from *kalligraphos* 'person who writes beautifully,' from *kallos* 'beauty' + *graphein* 'write.' The verb dates from the late 19th century.

---

call·ing /káwling/ *n.* profession or occupation.

cal·li·o·pe /kəlíəpee/ *n.* keyboard instrument resembling an organ, with a set of steam whistles producing musical notes.

cal·los·i·ty /kəlósitee/ *n.* (*pl.* **-ties**) hard, thick area of skin.

cal·lous /káləs/ *adj.* **1** unfeeling; insensitive. **2** (of skin) hardened. □□ **cal′lous·ly** *adv.* (in sense 1). **cal′lous·ness** *n.*

cal·low /kálō/ *adj.* inexperienced; immature.

cal·lus /káləs/ *n.* hard thick area of skin or tissue.

calm /kaam/ • *adj.* **1** tranquil; quiet; windless. **2** settled; not agitated. • *n.* **1** state of being calm; stillness; serenity. **2** period without wind or storm. • *v.* make or become calm. □□ **calm′ly** *adv.* **calm′ness** *n.*

ca·lo·ric /kəláwrik, -lór-/ *adj.* of heat or calories.

cal·o·rie /káləree/ *n.* unit of quantity of heat: **1** (in full **small calorie**) amount needed to raise the temperature of 1 gram of water through 1°C. ¶ Abbr.: **cal.** **2** (in full **large calorie**) amount needed to raise the temperature of 1 kilogram of water through 1°C, often used to measure the energy value of foods. ¶ Abbr.: **Cal.**

cal·o·rif·ic /kálərífik/ *adj.* producing heat.

cal·u·met /kályəmét/ *n.* Native American ceremonial peace pipe.

ca·lum·ni·ate /kəlúmneeayt/ *v.tr.* slander. □□ **ca·lum·ni·a·tion** /-neeáyshən/ *n.* **ca·lum′ni·a·tor** *n.*

cal·um·ny /káləmnee/ *n.* (*pl.* **-nies**) slander. □□ **ca·lum·ni·ous** /-lúmneeəs/ *adj.*

cal·va·dos /kálvədōs/ *n.* (also **Cal·va·dos**) apple brandy.

calve /kav/ *v.intr.* give birth to a calf.

calves *pl.* of CALF[1], CALF[2].

Cal·vin·ism /kálvinizəm/ *n.* theology of J. Calvin (d. 1564) or his followers, in which predestination and justification by faith are important elements. □□ **Cal′vin·ist** *n.* **Cal·vin·is′tic** *adj.*

ca·lyp·so /kəlípsō/ *n.* (*pl.* **-sos**) W. Indian musical style with syncopated rhythm.

ca·lyx /káyliks, kál-/ *n.* (*pl.* **ca·lyx·es** or **ca·ly·ces** /-liseez/) **1** *Bot.* sepals collectively, forming the protective layer of a flower in bud. **2** *Biol.* any cuplike cavity or structure.

cam /kam/ *n.* projection on a rotating part in machinery, shaped to impart a particular motion.

ca·ma·ra·de·rie /ka'amərə'ádəree/ *n.* mutual trust and sociability among friends.

cam·ber /kámbər/ • *n.* slightly convex or arched shape of the surface of a ship's deck, aircraft wing, etc. • *v.* **1** *intr.* (of a surface) have a camber. **2** *tr.* build with a camber.

Cam·bo·di·an /kambódeeən/ • *n.* **1 a** native or national of Cambodia (Kampuchea) in SE Asia. **b** person of Cambodian descent. **2** language of Cambodia. • *adj.* of or relating to Cambodia or its people or language.

Cam·bri·an /kámbreeən/ • *adj.* **1** Welsh. **2** *Geol.* of the first period in the Paleozoic era. • *n.* this period.

cam·bric /kámbrik/ *n.* a fine white linen or cotton fabric.

cam·cor·der /kámkawrdər/ *n.* combined video camera and sound recorder.

came *past* of COME.

cam·el /káməl/ *n.* large, cud-chewing mammal having slender legs and one hump (**Arabian camel**) or two humps (**Bactrian camel**).

ca·mel·li·a /kəmeélyə/ *n.* evergreen shrub native to E. Asia, with shiny leaves and showy flowers.

Cam·em·bert /káməmbair/ *n.* a soft, creamy cheese, usu. with a strong flavor.

cam·e·o /kámeeō/ *n.* (*pl.* **-os**) **1** relief carving with a background of a different color. **2** small character part in a play or film played by a distinguished actor.

cam·er·a /kámrə, kámərə/ *n.* **1** apparatus for taking still or motion pictures. **2** *Telev.* equipment that converts images into electrical impulses for transmission or storage. □ **in camera** *Law* in a judge's private room.

cam·i·sole /kámisōl/ *n.* an upper-body undergarment.

cam·o·mile var. of CHAMOMILE.

cam·ou·flage /káməflaazh/ • *n.* **1** disguising of soldiers, vehicles, aircraft, etc., so that they blend with their surroundings. **2** such a disguise. **3** misleading or evasive precaution or expedient. • *v.tr.* hide by camouflage.

---

camouflage World War I: from French, from *camoufler* 'to disguise' (originally thieves' slang), from Italian *camuffare* 'disguise, deceive,' perhaps by association with French *camouflet* 'whiff of smoke in the face.'

camp[1] /kamp/ • *n.* **1** place where troops are lodged or trained. **2** temporary accommodations, as huts or tents. **3** adherents of a particular party or doctrine regarded collectively. • *v. intr.* set up or spend time in a camp. □□ **camp′ing** *n.*

camp[2] /kamp/ *colloq.* • *adj.* done in an exaggerated way for effect. • *v.* behave or do in a camp way. □□ **camp′y** *adj.* (**camp·i·er, camp·i·est**). **camp′i·ly** *adv.* **camp′i·ness** *n.*

cam·paign /kampáyn/ • *n.* **1** organized course of action. **2** series of military operations. • *v. intr.* conduct or take part in a campaign. □□ **cam·paign′er** *n.*

campaign early 17th century (denoting a tract of open country): from French *campagne* 'open country,' via Italian from late Latin *campania,* from *campus* 'level ground.' The change in sense arose from the army's practice of 'taking the field' (i.e., moving from fortress or town, etc., to open country) at the onset of summer.

cam·pa·ni·le /kámpəneélee, -neéel/ *n.* bell tower (usu. freestanding), esp. in Italy.

camp·er /kámpər/ *n.* **1** person who camps. **2** large motor vehicle with beds, etc.

cam·phor /kámfər/ *n.* white, crystalline volatile substance with aromatic smell used to make celluloid and in medicine.

camp·site /kámpsīt/ *n.* place suitable for camping.

cam·pus /kámpəs/ *n.* (*pl.* **cam·pus·es**) grounds of a university or other institution.

cam·shaft /kámshaft/ *n.* shaft with one or more cams.

can[1] /kan, kən/ *v. aux.* (*past* **could** /kŏŏd/) **1 a** be able to; know how to (*I can run fast; can you speak German?*). **b** be potentially capable of (*you can do it if you try*). **2** be permitted to (*can we go to the party?*).
¶ **Can** is properly used to mean 'be able to': *I can solve any problem on this list.* **May** means 'be permitted to or have approval to': *May I leave now? You may take anything you like.*

can[2] /kan/ • *n.* **1** metal vessel for liquid. **2** metal container in which food or drink is sealed. **3** (prec. by *the*) *sl.* **a** prison. **b** toilet. • *v. tr.* (**canned, can·ning**) put or preserve in a can. □ **can of worms** *colloq.* complicated problem. **in the can** *colloq.* completed; ready. □□ **can′ner** *n.*

Can·a·da goose /kánədə/ *n.* wild goose of N. America, with a brownish-gray body and white cheeks and breast.

ca·nal /kənál/ *n.* **1** artificial waterway for inland navigation or irrigation. **2** tubular duct in a plant or animal.

ca·na·pé /kánəpay, -pee/ *n.* small piece of bread or pastry with a savory food on top, often served as an hors d'oeuvre.

ca·nard /kənáard/ *n.* unfounded rumor or story.

ca·nar·y /kənáiree/ *n.* (*pl.* **-ies**) songbird native to the Canary Islands, with mainly yellow plumage.

ca·nas·ta /kənástə/ *n.* **1** card game using two decks and resembling rummy. **2** set of seven cards in this game.

can·can /kánkan/ *n.* lively stage dance with high kicking.

can·cel /kánsəl/ *v.* (**can·celed, can·cel·ing; can·celled, can·cel·ling**) **1** *tr.* withdraw, revoke, or discontinue (an arrangement). **2** *tr.* obliterate; delete; invalidate. **3** *intr. & tr.* neutralize; counterbalance. **4** *tr. Math.* strike out (an equal factor) on each side of an equation, etc. □□ **can·cel·la′tion** *n.*

can·cer /kánsər/ *n.* **1** malignant growth or tumor of body cells. **2** evil influence or corruption spreading uncontrollably. **3** (**Cancer**) a constellation and fourth sign of the zodiac (the Crab). **b** person born under this sign. □□ **Can·cer·i·an** /-séreeən/ *n. & adj.* (in sense 3). **can′cer·ous** *adj.*

cancer Old English, from Latin, 'crab or creeping ulcer,' translating Greek *karkinos,* which is said to have been applied to such tumors because the swollen veins around them resembled the limbs of a crab. *Canker* was the usual form until the 17th century.

can·de·la·brum /kánd'láábrəm/ *n.* (also **can·de·la·bra** /-brə/) (*pl.* **can·de·la·bra, can·de·la·brums, can·de·la·bras**) large branched candlestick or lamp holder.

can·did /kándid/ *adj.* **1** frank. **2** (of a photograph) taken informally. □□ **can′did·ly** *adv.* **can′did·ness** *n.*

can·di·date /kándidət, -dayt/ *n.* nominee, office seeker, or entrant. □□ **can·di·da·cy** /-dəsee/ *n.*

can·dle /kánd'l/ *n.* cylinder or block of wax or tallow with a central wick, for giving light when burning. □ **cannot hold a candle to** cannot be compared with; is much inferior to. □□ **can′dler** *n.*

can·dle·light /kánd'l-līt/ *n.* light provided by candles. □□ **can′dle·lit** *adj.*

can·dle·pow·er /kánd'lpowr/ *n.* unit of luminous intensity.

can·dle·stick /kánd'lstik/ *n.* holder for one or more candles.

can·dor /kándər/ *n.* candid behavior or action.

can·dy /kándee/ • *n.* (*pl.* **-dies**) sweet confection, usu. containing sugar, chocolate, etc. • *v. tr.* (**-dies, -died**) (usu. as **candied** *adj.*) preserve by coating and impregnating with a sugar syrup (*candied fruit*). □ **candy stripe** pattern consisting of alternate stripes of white and a color (usu. pink). **candy striper** hospital volunteer, esp. a teenager.

cane /kayn/ • *n.* **1 a** hollow jointed stem of giant reeds or grasses. **b** solid stem of slender palms. **2** = *sugar cane.* **3** material of cane used for wickerwork, etc. **4** cane used as a walking stick or an instrument of punishment. • *v. tr.* **1** beat with a cane. **2** weave cane into (a chair, etc.). □ **cane sugar** sugar obtained from sugar cane. □□ **can′er** *n.* (in sense 2 of *v.*). **can′ing** *n.*

ca·nine /káynīn/ • *adj.* of a dog or dogs. • *n.* **1** dog. **2** (in full **canine tooth**) pointed tooth between incisors and premolars.

can·is·ter /kánistər/ *n.* **1** rigid container for storage. **2** cylinder of shot, tear gas, etc.

can·ker /kángkər/ • *n.* **1** destructive fungus disease of trees and plants. **2** *Zool.* ulcerous ear disease of animals, esp. cats and dogs. **3** corrupting influence. • *v.tr.* **1** consume with canker. **2** corrupt. □□ **can′ker•ous** *adj.*

can•na•bis /kánəbis/ *n.* **1** hemp plant. **2** parts of this used as an intoxicant or hallucinogen.

canned /kand/ *adj.* **1** prerecorded. **2** supplied in a can.

can•nel•lo•ni /kánəlónee/ *n.pl.* tubes or rolls of pasta stuffed with meat or a vegetable mixture.

can•ner•y /kánəree/ *n.* (*pl.* **-ies**) canning factory.

can•ni•bal /kánibəl/ *n.* **1** person who eats human flesh. **2** animal that feeds on flesh of its own species. □□ **can′ni•bal•ism** *n.* **can•ni•bal•is′tic** *adj.*

can•ni•bal•ize /kánibəlīz/ *v.tr.* use (a machine, etc.) as a source of spare parts for others. □□ **can•ni•bal•i•za′tion** *n.*

can•non /kánən/ *n. hist.* (*pl.* same) heavy gun installed on a carriage or mounting.

can•non•ade /kánənáyd/ • *n.* period of continuous heavy gunfire. • *v.tr.* bombard with a cannonade.

can•non•ball /kánənbawl/ *n.* large, usu. metal ball fired by a cannon.

can•not /kánot, kanót/ *v.aux.* can not.

can•ny /kánee/ *adj.* (**can•ni•er**, **can•ni•est**) shrewd; worldly-wise. □□ **can′ni•ly** *adv.* **can′ni•ness** *n.*

ca•noe /kənoo/ • *n.* narrow boat with pointed ends usu. propelled by paddling. • *v.intr.* (**ca•noes**, **ca•noed**, **ca•noe•ing**) travel in a canoe. □□ **ca•noe′ist** *n.*

can•o•la oil′ /kənólə/ *n.* type of cooking oil derived from the seed of a variety of the rape plant.

can•on /kánən/ *n.* **1 a** general law, rule, principle, or criterion. **b** church decree or law. **2** (*fem.* **can•on•ess**) member of a cathedral chapter. **3** collection or list of books, etc., accepted as genuine. **4** *Mus.* piece with different parts taking up the same theme successively. □ **canon law** ecclesiastical law.

ca•non•i•cal /kənónikəl/ *adj.* (also **ca•non•ic** /kənónik/) **1 a** according to or ordered by canon law. **b** included in the canon of Scripture. **2** authoritative; standard; accepted. □□ **ca•non′i•cal•ly** *adv.*

can•on•ize /kánənīz/ *v.tr.* declare officially to be or regard as a saint. □□ **can•on•i•za′tion** *n.*

can•o•py /kánəpee/ *n.* (*pl.* **-pies**) **1** covering hung or held up over a throne, bed, person, etc. **2** overhanging shelter.

canst /kanst/ *archaic 2nd person sing. present of* CAN¹.

cant¹ /kant/ *n.* **1** insincere pious or moral talk. **2** language peculiar to a class, profession, sect, etc.; jargon.

cant² /kant/ • *n.* **1** slanting surface; bevel. **2** oblique push or movement. **3** tilted or sloping position. • *v.tr.* push or pitch out of level; tilt.

can't /kant/ *contr.* can not.

can•ta•loupe /kánt′lōp/ *n.* variety of melon with orange flesh.

can•tan•ker•ous /kantángkərəs/ *adj.* bad-tempered; quarrelsome. □□ **can•tan′ker•ous•ly** *adv.* **can•tan′ker•ous•ness** *n.*

can•ta•ta /kəntáatə/ *n. Mus.* short composition with vocal solos and usu. chorus and orchestral accompaniment.

can•teen /kanteén/ *n.* **1 a** restaurant for employees in an office or factory, etc. **b** store sell-

ing provisions or liquor in a barracks or camp. **2** water flask.

cant•er /kántər/ • *n.* gentle gallop. • *v.intr.* (of a horse or its rider) go at a canter.

can•ti•cle /kántikəl/ *n.* **1** song or chant with a Biblical text. **2** (also **Can′ticle of Can′ticles**) the Song of Solomon.

can•ti•le•ver /kánt′leevər, -evər/ **1** long bracket or beam, etc., projecting from a wall to support a balcony, etc. **2** beam or girder fixed at only one end. □ **cantilever bridge** bridge made of cantilevers projecting from the piers and connected by girders.

can•to /kántō/ *n.* (*pl.* **-tos**) division of a long poem.

can•ton /kánton/ *n.* **1** subdivision of a country. **2** state of the Swiss confederation. □□ **can•ton•al** /kánt′nəl, kantónəl/ *adj.*

can•tor /kántər/ *n.* liturgical leader in a synagogue or church.

can•vas /kánvəs/ • *n.* **1 a** strong coarse kind of cloth used for sails and tents, etc., and as a surface for oil painting. **b** piece of this. **2** painting on canvas, esp. in oils. • *v.tr.* (**can•vased**, **can•vas•ing**; **can•vassed**, **can•vass•ing**) cover with canvas. □ **under canvas 1** in a tent or tents. **2** with sails spread.

can•vass /kánvəs/ • *v.* **1** *intr.* solicit votes. **2** *tr.* ascertain opinions of. • *n.* canvassing, esp. of electors. □□ **can′vass•er** *n.*

can•yon /kányən/ *n.* deep gorge, often with a stream or river.

cap /kap/ • *n.* **1** covering for the head, often soft and with a visor. **2** device to seal a bottle or protect the point of a pen, lens of a camera, etc. **3** = CROWN *n.* 9b. • *v.tr.* (**capped**, **cap•ping**) **1 a** put a cap on. **b** cover the top or end of. **c** set a limit to (*rate-capping*). **2 a** lie on top of; form the cap of. **b** surpass; excel. □□ **cap′ful** *n.* (*pl.* **-fuls**) **cap′ping** *n.*

cap. *abbr.* **1** capital. **2** capital letter. **3** chapter.

ca•pa•bil•i•ty /káypəbílitee/ *n.* (*pl.* **-ties**) **1** ability; power; condition of being capable. **2** undeveloped or unused faculty.

ca•pa•ble /káypəbəl/ *adj.* **1** competent; able. **2 a** having the ability or fitness, etc., for. **b** susceptible or admitting of (explanation or improvement, etc.). □□ **ca′pa•bly** *adv.*

ca•pa•cious /kəpáyshəs/ *adj.* roomy; able to hold much. □□ **ca•pa′cious•ly** *adv.* **ca•pa′cious•ness** *n.*

ca•pac•i•tance /kəpásit′ns/ *n. Electr.* **1** ability of a system to store an electric charge. **2** ratio of the change in an electric charge in a system to the corresponding change in its electric potential. ¶ Symb.: **C**.

ca•pac•i•tor /kəpásitər/ *n. Electr.* device used to store an electric charge.

ca•pac•i•ty /kəpásitee/ *n.* (*pl.* **-ties**) **1** power of containing, receiving, experiencing, or producing (*capacity for heat, pain,* etc.). **2** maximum amount that can be contained or produced, etc. **2** mental power. **3** position or function (*in a civil capacity*) **4** legal competence. □□ **ca•pac•i•ta•tive** /-táytiv/ *adj.*

ca•par•i•son /kəpárisən/ • *n.* **1** (usu. in *pl.*) horse's trappings. **2** equipment; finery. • *v.tr.* put caparisons on; adorn.

cape¹ /kayp/ *n.* sleeveless cloak.

cape² /kayp/ *n.* **1** headland or promontory. **2** (**the Cape**) a Cape of Good Hope. **b** Cape Cod, Massachusetts.

ca·per¹ /káypər/ • *v.intr.* jump or run playfully. • *n.* **1** playful jump or leap. **2** a prank. **b** *sl.* any activity or occupation. □ **cut a caper** (or **ca·pers**) act friskily. □□ **ca′per·er** *n.*

ca·per² /káypər/ *n.* **1** bramblelike shrub. **2** (in *pl.*) its buds pickled for use as flavoring.

cap·il·lar·y /kápəleree/ • *adj.* **1** of or like a hair. **2** (of a tube) of hairlike internal diameter. **3** of one of the delicate ramified blood vessels intervening between arteries and veins. • *n.* (*pl.* **-ies**) **1** capillary tube. **2** capillary blood vessel. □ **capillary action** rise or depression of a liquid in contact with a solid, owing to surface tension, etc.

cap·i·tal¹ /kápit'l/ • *n.* **1** most important town or city of a country, state, or region. **2** a money or other assets with which a company starts in business. **b** accumulated wealth. **3** capital letter. • *adj.* **1** principal; most important. **2** involving or punishable by death. **3** (of letters of the alphabet) large in size and of the form used to begin sentences and names, etc. □ **capital gain** profit from the sale of investments or property. □□ **cap′i·tal·ly** *adv.*

cap·i·tal² /kápit'l/ *n. Archit.* head of a pillar or column.

Doric

Ionic

Corinthian

CAPITAL

cap·i·tal·ism /kápit'lizəm/ *n.* economic system in which the production and distribution of goods depend on invested private capital and profit making.

cap·i·tal·ist /kápit'list/ • *n.* **1** person using or possessing capital. **2** advocate of capitalism. • *adj.* of or favoring capitalism. □□ **cap·i·tal·is′tic** *adj.* **cap·i·tal·is′ti·cal·ly** *adv.*

cap·i·tal·ize /kápit'līz/ *v.* **1** *tr.* convert into or

provide with capital. **2** *tr.* **a** write (a letter of the alphabet) as a capital. **b** begin (a word) with a capital letter. **3** *intr.* (foll. by *on*) use to one's advantage; profit from. □□ **cap·i·tal·i·za′tion** *n.*

ca·pit·u·late /kəpíchəlayt/ *v.intr.* surrender, esp. on stated conditions. □□ **ca·pit′u·la·tor** *n.* **ca·pit·u·la·to·ry** /-lətáwree/ *adj.*

ca·po /káypō/ *n.* (in full **ca·po·tas·to** /-tástō/) (*pl.* **ca·pos** or **ca·po·tas·tos**) *Mus.* device secured across the neck of a fretted instrument to raise equally the tuning of all strings.

ca·pon /káypon, -pən/ *n.* domestic cock castrated and fattened for eating.

cap·puc·ci·no /kápōōche′enō/ *n.* (*pl.* **-nos**) espresso coffee with milk made frothy with pressurized steam.

ca·price /kəprée's/ *n.* **1 a** unaccountable or whimsical change of mind or conduct. **b** tendency to this. **2** work of lively fancy in painting, drawing, or music.

ca·pri·cious /kəpríshəs, -prée-/ *adj.* subject to caprice; unpredictable. □□ **ca·pri′cious·ly** *adv.* **ca·pri′cious·ness** *n.*

Cap·ri·corn /káprikawrn/ *n.* **1** constellation and tenth sign of the zodiac (the Goat). **2** person born under this sign.

cap·size /kápsīz, -síz/ *v.* **1** *tr.* upset or overturn (a boat). **2** *intr.* be capsized. □□ **cap·siz′al** /-sízəl/ *n.*

cap·stan /kápstən/ *n.* revolving cylinder with a vertical axis, for winding cable, tape, etc.

cap·sule /kápsəl, -sōōl/ *n.* **1** small gelatinous case enclosing a dose of medicine and swallowed with it. **2** detachable compartment of a spacecraft or nose cone of a rocket. **3** enclosing membrane in the body. **4** dry fruit that releases its seeds when ripe. **5** (*attrib.*) concise; highly condensed (*a capsule history*). □□ **cap′su·lar** *adj.* **cap′su·late** *adj.*

cap·sul·ize /kápsəlīz, -syōō-/ *v.tr.* put (information, etc.) in compact form.

Capt. *abbr.* Captain.

cap·tain /káptin/ • *n.* **1** chief, leader, or commander. **2 a** army or air force officer next above lieutenant. **b** navy officer in command of a warship; one ranking below commodore or rear admiral and above commander. • *v.tr.* be captain of; lead. □□ **cap′tain·cy** *n.* (*pl.* **-cies**). **cap′tain·ship** *n.*

cap·tion /kápshən/ • *n.* **1** title or brief explanation appended to an illustration, cartoon, etc. **2** heading of a chapter or article, etc. • *v.tr.* provide with a caption.

---

caption late Middle English (in the sense 'seizing, capture'): from Latin *captio(n-)*, from *capere* 'take, seize.' The early senses 'arrest,' 'warrant for arrest' gave rise to 'statement of where, when, and by whose authority a warrant was issued' (late 17th century): this was usually appended to a legal document, hence the sense 'heading or appended wording' (late 18th century).

---

cap·tious /kápshəs/ *adj.* given to finding fault or raising petty objections. □□ **cap′tious·ly** *adv.* **cap′tious·ness** *n.*

cap·ti·vate /káptivayt/ *v.tr.* charm; fascinate. □□ **cap′ti·vat·ing** *adj.* **cap′ti·vat·ing·ly** *adv.* **cap·ti·va·tion** /-váyshən/ *n.*

cap·tive /káptiv/ • *n.* person or animal that has been taken prisoner or confined. • *adj.* **1**

taken prisoner. **2** kept in confinement or under restraint. □□ **cap·tiv′i·ty** *n.*

cap·tor /káptər, -tawr/ *n.* person who captures.

cap·ture /kápchər/ • *v.tr.* **1** take prisoner; seize. **2** portray in permanent form. **3** cause (data) to be stored in a computer. • *n.* act of capturing. □□ **cap′tur·er** *n.*

cap·y·ba·ra /kápəbaárə/ *n.* very large semi-aquatic rodent native to S. America.

car /kaar/ *n.* **1** automobile. **2** vehicle that runs on rails, esp. a railroad car or a streetcar. **3** passenger compartment of an elevator, cable railway, balloon, etc. □ **car bomb** terrorist bomb concealed in or under a parked car. □□ **car′ful** *n.* (*pl.* **-fuls**).

ca·rafe /kəráf/ *n.* glass container for water or wine.

car·a·mel /kárəmel, -məl, ka'arməl/ *n.* **1 a** sugar or syrup heated until it turns brown, then used as a flavoring or coloring. **b** kind of soft toffee made with sugar, butter, etc., melted and further heated. **2** light-brown color. □□ **car·a·mel·i·za′tion** *n.* **car′a·mel·ize** *v.*

car·a·pace /kárəpays/ *n.* hard upper shell of a turtle or a crustacean.

car·at /kárət/ *n.* unit of weight for precious stones, now equivalent to 200 milligrams.

---

carat from French, from Italian *carato*, from Arabic *k̦īrāț* (a unit of weight), from Greek *keration* 'fruit of the carob' (also denoting a unit of weight), diminutive of *keras* 'horn,' with reference to the elongated seed pod of the carob.

---

car·a·van /kárəvan/ *n.* company of merchants or pilgrims, etc., traveling together, esp. across a desert. □□ **car′a·van·ner** *n.*

car·a·van·sa·ry /kárəvánsəree, -rī/ *n.* (also **car·a·van·se·rai**) Near Eastern inn with a central court.

car·a·vel /kárəvel/ *n.* (also **car·vel** /kaárvəl/) *hist.* small, light, fast ship.

car·a·way /kárəway/ *n.* umbelliferous plant, bearing clusters of tiny white flowers. □ **caraway seed** its fruit used as flavoring and as a source of oil.

car·bide /kaárbīd/ *n.* *Chem.* binary compound of carbon.

car·bine /kaárbeen, -bīn/ *n.* lightweight firearm, usu. a rifle, once for cavalry use.

car·bo·hy·drate /kaárbōhídrayt, -bō-/ *n.* *Biochem.* energy-producing organic compound containing carbon, hydrogen, and oxygen, e.g., starch, glucose, and other sugars.

car·bol·ic /kaarbólik/ *n.* (in full **car·bol′ic ac′id**) phenol.

car·bon /kaárbən/ *n.* **1** nonmetallic element occurring naturally as diamond, graphite, and charcoal, and in all organic compounds. ¶ Symb.: **C. 2 a** = *carbon copy*. **b** = *carbon paper*. □ **carbon copy 1** copy made with carbon paper. **2** person or thing identical or similar to another (*is a carbon copy of his father*). **carbon paper** thin carbon-coated paper used between two sheets of paper when writing to make a copy onto the bottom sheet.

car·bon·ate /kaárbənayt/ • *n.* *Chem.* salt of carbonic acid. • *v.tr.* **1** impregnate with carbon dioxide; aerate. **2** convert into a carbonate. □□ **car·bon·a·tion** /-náyshən/ *n.*

car·bon·ic /kaarbónik/ *adj.* *Chem.* containing carbon. □ **carbonic acid** very weak acid formed from carbon dioxide dissolved in water.

car·bon·if·er·ous /kaárbənífərəs/ *adj.* producing coal.

car·bo·run·dum /kaábərúndəm/ *n.* compound of carbon and silicon used esp. as an abrasive.

car·boy /kaárboy/ *n.* large bottle often held in a frame, used for containing liquids.

car·bun·cle /kaárbungkəl/ *n.* **1** severe abscess in the skin. **2** bright red gem. □□ **car·bun·cu·lar** /-búngkyələr/ *adj.*

car·bu·ret·or /kaárbəráytter, -byə-/ *n.* (also **car′bu·rat·or**) apparatus for mixing fuel and air in an internal combustion engine to make an explosive mixture.

car·cass /kaárkəs/ *n.* **1** dead body of an animal. **2** framework of a building, ship, etc.

car·cin·o·gen /kaarsínəjən, ka'arsinəjen/ *n.* any substance that produces cancer. □□ **car·ci·no·gen·ic** /kaársinəjénik/ *adj.*

car·ci·no·ma /kaársinómə/ *n.* (*pl.* **car·ci·no·mas** or **car·ci·no·ma·ta** /-mətə/) cancer, esp. one arising in epithelial tissue. □□ **car·ci·no′ma·tous** *adj.*

card /kaard/ • *n.* **1** thick, stiff paper or thin pasteboard. **2** flat piece of this, esp. for writing or printing on. **3** rectangular piece of paper or plastic for identity, etc. **4 a** = PLAYING CARD. **b** (in *pl.*) card playing; a card game. **5** program of events. **6** *colloq.* person, esp. an odd or amusing one (*what a card!*). □ **card-carrying** being a registered member of an organization, esp. a political party or labor union. **in the cards** possible or likely. **put** (or **lay**) **one's cards on the table** reveal one's resources, intentions, etc.

card·board /kaárdbawrd/ *n.* pasteboard or stiff paper, esp. for making cards or boxes.

car·di·ac /kaárdeeak/ *adj.* of or relating to the heart.

car·di·gan /kaárdigən/ *n.* sweater fastening down the front.

---

cardigan mid-19th century (Crimean War): named after James Thomas Brudenel, 7th Earl of Cardigan (1797–1868), leader of the famous Charge of the Light Brigade; his troops first wore such garments.

---

car·di·nal /kaárd′nəl/ • *n.* **1** (as a title **Cardinal**) leading dignitary of the RC Church, one of the college electing the pope. **2** small scarlet American songbird. • *adj.* **1** chief; fundamental; on which something hinges. **2** of deep scarlet. □ **cardinal numbers** those denoting quantity (one, two, three, etc.), as opposed to ordinal numbers (first, second, third, etc.). **cardinal points** four main points of the compass (N., S., E., W.). **cardinal virtues** chief moral attributes: justice, prudence, temperance, and fortitude. □□ **car·di·nal·ate** /-nəlayt/ *n.* (in sense 1 of *n.*). **car′di·nal·ly** *adv.* **car′din·al·ship** *n.* (in sense 1 of *n.*).

car·di·o·gram /kaárdeeəgram/ *n.* record of muscle activity within the heart, made by a cardiograph.

car·di·o·graph /kaárdeeəgraf/ *n.* instrument for recording heart muscle activity. □□ **car·di·og·raph·er** /-deeógrəfər/ *n.* **car·di·og′ra·phy** *n.*

car·di·ol·o·gy /ka'ardeeólэjee/ n. branch of medicine concerned with the heart. □□ **car·di·ol'o·gist** n.

car·di·o·pul·mo·nar·y re·sus·ci·ta'tion /kardeeōpŏólmэneree/ n. emergency medical procedures for restoring normal heartbeat and breathing to victims of heart failure, drowning, etc. ¶ Abbr.: **CPR**.

car·di·o·vas·cu·lar /ka'ardeeōváskyэlэr/ adj. of or relating to the heart and blood vessels.

card·sharp /ka'ardshaarp/ n. (also **card'sharp·er**) swindler at card games.

care /kair/ • n. **1** worry; anxiety. **2** occasion for this. **3** serious attention; heed; caution; pains (*assembled with care*). **4** protection; charge. • v.intr. **1** feel concern or interest. **2** wish or be willing to (*do not care to be seen with him*). □ **care for** provide for; look after. **care of** at the address of (*sent it care of his sister*). **have a care 1** take care; be careful. **2** have worries or responsibilities (*don't have a care in the world*). **take care** be careful. **take care of** look after.

ca·reen /kэree'en/ v. **1** tr. turn (a ship) on one side for cleaning, caulking, or repair. **2 a** intr. tilt; lean over. **b** tr. cause to do this. **3** intr. swerve about. □□ **ca·reen'age** n.

ca·reer /kэree'er/ • n. **1** one's advancement through life, esp. in a profession. **2** profession; occupation. • v.intr. **1** move or swerve about wildly. **2** go swiftly.

care·free /káirfree/ adj. free from anxiety or responsibility; lighthearted.

care·ful /káirfŏŏl/ adj. **1** painstaking; thorough. **2** cautious. **3** taking care; not neglecting. □□ **care'ful·ly** adv. **care'ful·ness** n.

care·giv·er /káirgivэr/ n. person who provides care for children, the sick, the elderly, etc.

care·less /káirlis/ adj. **1** not taking care nor paying attention. **2** unthinking; insensitive. **3** lighthearted. □□ **care'less·ly** adv. **care'less·ness** n.

ca·ress /kэrés/ • v.tr. touch or stroke gently or lovingly. • n. loving or gentle touch.

car·et /kárэt/ n. mark (⌃) indicating a proposed insertion in printing or writing.

care·tak·er /káirtaykэr/ n. person employed to look after something, esp. a house in the owner's absence.

care·worn /káirwawrn/ adj. showing the effects of prolonged worry.

car·go /ka'argō/ n. (pl. **-goes** or **-gos**) goods carried on a ship or aircraft.

Car·ib /kárib/ n. **1** aboriginal inhabitant of the southern W. Indies or the adjacent coasts. **2** language of this people.

Car·ib·be·an /káribee'эn, kэribeeэn/ n. part of the Atlantic between the southern W. Indies and Central America.

car·i·bou /káribŏŏ/ n. (pl. same) N. American reindeer.

---

caribou mid-17th century: from Canadian French, from Micmac γalipu, literally 'snowshoveler,' because the caribou scrapes away snow to feed on the vegetation underneath.

---

car·i·ca·ture /kárikэchэr, -chŏŏr/ • n. **1** usu. comic representation of a person by exaggeration of characteristic traits. **2** ridiculously poor imitation or version. • v.tr. make a caricature of. □□ **car·i·ca·tur·al** /-chŏŏrэl/ adj. **car'i·ca·tur·ist** n.

car·ies /káireez/ n. (pl. same) decay of a tooth or bone. □□ **car·i·ous** /káireeэs/ adj.

car·il·lon /kárilon, -lэn/ n. set of bells.

car·ing /káiring/ adj. compassionate.

car·jack·ing /kárjaking/ n. theft of an automobile whose driver is forced to leave the vehicle, kept captive while the thief drives, or forced to drive at gunpoint, etc. □□ **car'jack·er** n.

car·mine /ka'armin, -mīn/ • adj. of a vivid crimson color. • n. this color.

car·nage /ka'arnij/ n. great slaughter, esp. in battle.

car·nal /ka'arnэl/ adj. **1** of the body or flesh; worldly. **2** sensual; sexual. □ **carnal knowledge** *Law* sexual intercourse. □□ **car·nal·i·ty** /-a'alitee/ n. **car'nal·ize** v.tr. **car'nal·ly** adv.

car·na·tion[1] /kaarnáyshэn/ n. variously colored clove-scented flower.

car·na·tion[2] /kaarnáyshэn/ n. rosy pink color.

car·ne·lian /kaarnee'lyэn/ n. (also **cor·ne·lian** /kawr-/) **1** dull red or reddish-white variety of chalcedony. **2** this color.

car·ni·val /ka'arnivэl/ n. **1 a** festivities usual during the period before Lent in Roman Catholic countries. **b** any festivities. **2** merrymaking; revelry. **3** traveling fair or circus.

car·ni·vore /ka'arnivawr/ n. any flesh-eating mammal or plant.

car·niv·o·rous /kaarnívэrэs/ adj. feeding on flesh. □□ **car·niv'or·ous·ly** adv. **car·niv'or·ous·ness** n.

car·ob /kárэb/ n. **1** evergreen tree native to the Mediterranean, bearing edible pods. **2** its bean-shaped edible seed pod sometimes used as a substitute for chocolate.

car·ol /kárэl/ • n. joyous song, esp. a Christmas hymn. • v.intr. sing carols. □□ **car'ol·er** n.

car·o·tene /kárэteen/ n. orange-colored plant pigment found in carrots, tomatoes, etc., acting as a source of vitamin A.

ca·rot·id /kэrótid/ • n. each of the two main arteries carrying blood to the head and neck. • adj. of or relating to either of these arteries.

ca·rouse /kэrówz/ • v.intr. **1** have a noisy or lively drinking party. **2** drink heavily. • n. noisy or lively drinking party. □□ **ca·rous'al** n. **ca·rous'er** n.

car·ou·sel /kárэsél, -zél/ n. **1** merry-go-round. **2** rotating delivery or conveyor system, esp. for passengers' luggage at an airport.

carp[1] /kaarp/ n. (pl. same) freshwater food fish.

carp[2] /kaarp/ v.intr. (usu. foll. by *at*) find fault; complain pettily. □□ **carp'er** n.

car·pal /ka'arpэl/ • adj. of or relating to the bones in the wrist. • n. any of the bones forming the wrist.

car·pel /ka'arpэl/ n. *Bot.* female reproductive organ of a flower. □□ **car'pel·lar·y** adj.

car·pen·ter /ka'arpintэr/ n. person skilled in woodwork, esp. of a structural kind. □□ **car'pen·try** n.

---

carpenter Middle English: from Anglo-Norman French, from Old French *carpentier, charpentier*, from late Latin *carpentarius* (*artifex*) 'carriage(-maker),' from *carpentum* 'wagon,' of Gaulish origin; related to *car*

car·pet /kaárpit/ • *n.* **1 a** thick fabric for covering a floor or stairs. **b** piece of this fabric. **2** expanse or layer resembling a carpet in being smooth, soft, bright, or thick (*carpet of snow*). • *v.tr.* cover with or as with a carpet. □ **on the carpet** *colloq.* being reprimanded. **sweep under the carpet** conceal (a problem or difficulty).

car·pet·bag·ger /kaárpitbagər/ *n.* **1** political candidate who has no local connections. **2** unscrupulous opportunist (orig. a Northerner in the South after the Civil War).

car·pet·ing /kaárpiting/ *n.* **1** material for carpets. **2** carpets collectively.

car·pool /kárpool/ • *n.* (also **car' pool**) **1** arrangement by which a group of commuters travel to and from their destination in a single vehicle. **2** commuters taking part in such an arrangement (*there are four people in our carpool*). • *v.intr.* (also **car'-pool**) participate in or organize a carpool.

car·port /kaárpawrt/ *n.* shelter with a roof and open sides for a car, usu. beside a house.

car·pus /kaárpəs/ *n.* (*pl.* **car·pi** /-pī/) small bones between the forelimb and metacarpus in terrestrial vertebrates, forming the wrist in humans.

car·rel /kárəl/ *n.* small cubicle for a reader in a library.

car·riage /kárij/ *n.* **1** wheeled vehicle, esp. one pulled by horses. **2** carrying part of a machine (e.g., a typewriter). **3** gun carriage. **4** bearing; deportment.

car·ri·er /káreeər/ *n.* **1** person or thing that carries. **2** transport or freight company. **3** person or animal that may transmit a disease or a hereditary characteristic. **4** = *aircraft carrier*. □ **carrier pigeon** pigeon trained to carry messages.

car·ri·on /káree-ən/ *n.* dead putrefying flesh.

car·rot /kárət/ *n.* **1** umbelliferous plant, with a tapering, edible orange-colored root. **2** means of enticement or persuasion. □□ **car'rot·y** *adj.*

car·ry /káree/ • *v.* (**-ries, -ried**) **1** *tr.* support or hold up, esp. while moving. **2** *tr.* convey with one or have on one's person. **3** *tr.* conduct or transmit (*pipe carries water*). **4** *tr.* take (a process, etc.) to a specified point; continue (*carry into effect; carry a joke too far*). **5** *tr.* involve; imply; entail as a feature or consequence (*principles carry consequences*). **6** *tr.* (in reckoning) transfer (a figure) to a column of higher value. **7** *tr.* hold in a specified way (*carry oneself erect*). **8** *tr.* publish or broadcast esp. regularly. **9** *tr.* keep a regular stock of. **10** *intr.* be audible at a distance. **11** *tr.* **a** win victory or acceptance for (a proposal, etc.). **b** gain (a state or district) in an election. **c** *Golf* cause the ball to pass beyond (a bunker, etc.). **12** *tr.* endure the weight of; support. **13** *tr.* be pregnant with. • *n.* (*pl.* **-ries**) **1** act of carrying. **2** *Golf* distance a ball travels in the air. □ **carry away 1** remove. **2** inspire; affect emotionally or spiritually. **3** deprive of self-control (*got carried away*). **carry the day** be victorious or successful. **carry off 1** take away, esp. by force. **2** win (a prize). **3** (esp. of a disease) kill. **4** render acceptable or passable. **carry on 1** continue. **2** engage in (a conversation or a business). **3** *colloq.* behave strangely or excitedly. **4** advance (a process) by a stage. **carry out** put (ideas, instructions,

etc.) into practice. **carry weight** be influential or important.

car·sick /kaársik/ *adj.* affected with nausea caused by the motion of a car. □□ **car'sick·ness** *n.*

cart /kaart/ • *n.* **1** strong vehicle with two or four wheels for carrying loads, usu. drawn by a horse. **2** light vehicle for pulling by hand. • *v.tr.* convey in or as in a cart. □ **cart off** remove, esp. by force. **put the cart before the horse 1** reverse the proper order or procedure. **2** take an effect for a cause. □□ **cart'er** *n.* **cart'ful** *n.* (*pl.* **-fuls**).

carte blanche /kaárt blónsh, blánch/ *n.* full discretionary power given to a person.

car·tel /kaartél/ *n.* informal association of manufacturers or suppliers to maintain prices at a high level. □□ **car·tel·ize** /kaártəlīz/ *v.*

car·ti·lage /kaárt'lij/ *n.* gristle; firm flexible connective tissue. □□ **car·ti·lag·i·noid** /-lájinoyd/ *adj.* **car·ti·lag'i·nous** *adj.*

car·tog·ra·phy /kaartógrəfee/ *n.* science or practice of map drawing. □□ **car·tog'ra·pher** *n.* **car·to·graph·ic** /-təgráfik/ *adj.*

car·ton /kaárt'n/ *n.* light box or container, esp. one made of cardboard.

car·toon /kaartoón/ *n.* **1** humorous drawing in a newspaper, magazine, etc., esp. as a topical comment. **2** sequence of drawings telling a story. **3** animated sequence of these. □□ **car·toon'ist** *n.*

car·touche /kaartoósh/ *n. Archit.* scroll-like ornament, e.g., the volute of an Ionic capital.

car·tridge /kaártrij/ *n.* **1** case containing a charge of propelling explosive for firearms or blasting, with a bullet or shot if for small arms. **2** spool of film, magnetic tape, etc., in a sealed container ready for insertion. **3** ink container for insertion in a pen. □ **cartridge belt** belt with pockets or loops for cartridges (in sense 1).

cart·wheel /kaárt-hweel, -weel/ *n.* **1** wheel of a cart. **2** circular sideways handspring.

carve /kaarv/ *v.tr.* **1** produce or shape (a statue, representation in relief, etc.) by cutting into a hard material (*carved a figure out of rock*). **2** cut patterns, designs, letters, etc., in (hard material). **3** (*absol.*) cut (meat, etc.) into slices for eating. □ **carve out 1** take from a larger whole. **2** establish (a career, etc.) purposefully (*carved out a name for themselves*). □□ **carv'er** *n.*

carv·ing /kaárving/ *n.* carved object, esp. as a work of art.

Cas·a·no·va /kásənóvə/ *n.* man notorious for seducing women.

cas·cade /kaskáyd/ • *n.* **1** small waterfall, esp. one in a series. **2** material, etc., draped in descending folds. • *v.intr.* fall in or like a cascade.

case¹ /kays/ *n.* **1** instance of something occurring. **2** state of affairs, hypothetical or actual. **3 a** instance of a person receiving professional guidance, e.g., from a doctor or social worker. **b** such a person. **4** matter under official investigation, esp. by the police. **5** *Law* cause or suit for trial. **6 a** sum of the arguments on one side, esp. in a lawsuit. **b** set of arguments, esp. in relation to persuasiveness (*have a good case*). **c** valid set of arguments (*have no case*). **7** *Gram.* **a** relation of a word to other words in a sentence. **b** form of a noun, adjective, or pronoun expressing this. □ **in any case** whatever the truth is; whatever may happen. **in case** in the event that; if.

case² /kays/ • *n.* **1** container or covering serving to enclose or contain. **2** container with its contents. • *v.tr.* **1** enclose in a case. **2** *sl.* reconnoiter (a house, etc.), esp. with a view to robbery.

case·ment /káysmənt/ *n.* window or part of a window hinged to open on its outer frame.

case·work /káyswərk/ *n.* social work concerned with family and background. □□ **case'work·er** *n.*

cash /kash/ • *n.* **1** money in coins or bills. **2** (also **cash down**) full payment at the time of purchase, as distinct from credit. • *v.tr.* give or obtain cash for (a note, check, etc.). □ **cash cow** business, product, etc., generating steady profits. **cash flow** movement of money into and out of a business. **cash in 1** obtain cash for. **2** *colloq.* profit (from); take advantage (from). **3** (in full **cash in one's chips**) *colloq.* die. **cash machine** = *automated teller machine.* □□ **cash'a·ble** *adj.* **cash'less** *adj.*

ca·shew /káshō̄o, kashō̄o/ *n.* **1** bushy evergreen tree native to Central and S. America, bearing kidney-shaped nuts. **2** (in full **cashew nut**) edible nut of this tree.

cash·ier /kasheer/ *n.* person dealing with cash transactions in a store, bank, etc. □ **cashier's check** check drawn by a bank on its own funds and signed by a cashier of the bank.

cash·mere /kázhmeer, kásh-/ *n.* **1** fine soft wool, esp. that of a Kashmir goat. **2** material made from this.

cas·ing /káysing/ *n.* **1** protective or enclosing cover or shell. **2** material for this.

ca·si·no /kəseénō/ *n.* (*pl.* **-nos**) place for gambling.

cask /kask/ *n.* **1** large barrellike container made of wood, metal, or plastic, esp. one for alcoholic liquor. **2** its contents.

cas·ket /káskit/ *n.* **1** coffin. **2** small, often ornamental box or chest for jewels, letters, etc.

cas·sa·va /kəsaávə/ *n.* **1** plant with starchy tuberous roots. **2** starch or flour obtained from these roots. Also called **tapioca** or **manioc**.

cas·se·role /kásərōl/ *n.* **1** covered dish for baking. **2** food cooked in a casserole.

cas·sette /kəsét, ka-/ *n.* sealed case containing a length of tape, film, etc., ready for insertion in tape recorder, camera, etc.

cas·si·a /káshə/ *n.* **1** tree bearing leaves from which senna is extracted. **2** cinnamonlike bark of this used as a spice.

cas·sock /kásək/ *n.* long garment worn by clergy, members of choirs, etc. □□ **cas'socked** *adj.*

cas·so·war·y /kásəwairee/ *n.* (*pl.* **-ies**) large flightless Australasian bird.

cast /kast/ • *v.tr.* (*past* and *past part.* **cast**) **1** throw, esp. deliberately or forcefully. **2 a** direct or cause to fall (one's eyes, a glance, light, a shadow, a spell, etc.). **b** express (doubts, aspersions, etc.). **3** throw out (a fishing line) into the water. **4** let down (an anchor, etc.). **5** record, register, or give (a vote). **6 a** shape (molten metal or plastic material) in a mold. **b** make (a product) in this way. **7 a** assign (an actor) to play a particular character. **b** allocate roles in (a play, motion picture, etc.). • *n.* **1** the throwing of a missile, dice, line, etc. **2 a** object of metal, clay, etc., made in a mold. **b** rigid case to support an injured limb. **3** the actors in a play, motion picture, etc. □ **cast aside** give up using; abandon. **cast iron** hard alloy of iron, carbon, and silicon cast in a mold. **cast-iron** *adj.* **1** made of cast iron. **2** hard; unchangeable. **cast off 1** abandon. **2** loosen and throw off (rope, etc.). **cast-off** abandoned; discarded. **cast out** expel.

cas·ta·net /kástənét/ *n.* (usu. in *pl.*) hand-held, concave piece of hardwood, ivory, etc., in pairs, clicked together, esp. by Spanish dancers.

CASTANETS

cast·a·way /kástəway/ • *n.* shipwrecked person. • *adj.* **1** shipwrecked. **2** cast aside; rejected.

caste /kast/ *n.* **1** Hindu hereditary class. **2** more or less exclusive social class. **3** system of such classes.

cas·tel·lat·ed /kástəlaytid/ *adj.* **1** having battlements. **2** castlelike. □□ **cas·tel·la·tion** /-láyshən/ *n.*

cast·er /kástər/ *n.* **1** small swiveled wheel as on furniture. **2** small container with holes in the top for sprinkling the contents. □ **caster action** swiveling of vehicle wheels to ensure stability.

cas·ti·gate /kástigayt/ *v.tr.* rebuke or punish severely. □□ **cas·ti·ga·tion** /-gáyshən/ *n.* **cas'ti·ga·tor** *n.* **cas·ti·ga·to·ry** /-gətáwree/ *adj.*

cast·ing /kásting/ *n.* object made by casting, esp. of molten metal.

cas·tle /kásəl/ *n.* **1** large fortified building or group of buildings; stronghold. **2** *Chess* = ROOK². □ **castles in the air** visionary unattainable scheme; daydream. □□ **cas'tled** *adj.*

cast·off /kástawf/ *n.* cast-off thing, esp. a garment.

cast·or oil /kástər/ *n.* oil from the seeds of a plant, used as a purgative and lubricant.

cas·trate /kástrayt/ *v.tr.* **1** remove the testicles of; geld. **2** deprive of vigor. □□ **cas·tra·tion** /-tráyshən/ *n.* **cas'tra·tor** *n.*

cas·u·al /kázhō̄oəl/ *adj.* **1** accidental; due to chance. **2** not regular nor permanent (*casual work*). **3 a** unconcerned (*was very casual about it*). **b** careless. **4** (of clothes) informal. □□ **cas'u·al·ly** *adv.* **cas'u·al·ness** *n.*

ca·su·al·ty /kázhōōəltee/ *n.* (*pl.* **-ties**) **1** person killed or injured in a war or accident. **2** thing lost or destroyed.

ca·su·ist /kázhōōist/ *n.* person who resolves problems of conscience, duty, etc., with clever but false reasoning. □□ **cas·u·is′tic** *adj.* **cas·u·is′ti·cal** *adj.* **cas·u·is′ti·cal·ly** *adv.* **cas·u·ist·ry** /kázhōōəstree/ *n.*

CAT /kat/ *abbr. Med.* computerized axial tomography.

cat /kat/ *n.* **1** small, soft-furred, four-legged domesticated animal. **2** any wild animal of the same family, e.g., a lion, tiger, or leopard. □ **cat burglar** burglar who enters by climbing to an upper story. **cat-o′-nine-tails** *hist.* rope whip with nine knotted lashes. **cat's cradle** child's game in which a loop of string is held between the fingers and patterns are formed. **cat's-paw** person used as a tool by another. **let the cat out of the bag** reveal a secret, esp. involuntarily. **rain cats and dogs** *colloq.* rain very hard.

cata- /kátə/ *prefix* **1** down; downward. **2** wrongly; badly.

cat·a·clysm /kátəklizəm/ *n.* **1** violent, esp. social or political, upheaval or disaster. **2** a great change. □□ **cat·a·clys·mal** /-klízməl/ *adj.* **cat·a·clys′mic** *adj.* **cat·a·clys′mi·cal·ly** *adv.*

cat·a·comb /kátəkōm/ *n.* (often in *pl.*) underground cemetery, esp. in Rome.

cat·a·falque /kátəfawk, -fawlk/ *n.* framework for supporting the coffin during a funeral.

Cat·a·lan /kát′lan/ • *n.* **1** native of Catalonia in Spain. **2** language of Catalonia. • *adj.* of or relating to Catalonia or its people or language.

cat·a·lep·sy /kát′lepsee/ *n.* trance or seizure with loss of sensation and consciousness. □□ **cat·a·lep·tic** /-léptik/ *adj.* & *n.*

cat·a·log /kát′lawg, -log/ (also **cat·a·logue**) • *n.* ordered list of items often with a description of each. • *v.tr.* (**cat·a·logs, cat·a·loged, cat·a·log·ing; cat·a·logues, cat·a·logued, cat·a·logu·ing**) **1** make a catalog of. **2** enter in a catalog. □□ **cat′a·log·er** *n.* (also **cat′a·logu·er**).

ca·tal·y·sis /kətálisis/ *n.* (*pl.* **ca·tal·y·ses** /-seez/) acceleration of a chemical or biochemical reaction by a catalyst.

cat·a·lyst /kát′list/ *n.* **1** *Chem.* substance that increases the rate of a reaction. **2** person or thing that precipitates a change.

cat·a·lyt·ic /kát′lítik/ *adj. Chem.* relating to or involving catalysis. □ **catalytic converter** device in a motor vehicle for converting pollutant gases into harmless products.

cat·a·ma·ran /kátəmərán/ *n.* **1** boat with twin hulls in parallel. **2** raft of yoked logs or boats.

cat·a·pult /kátəpult, -pōōlt/ • *n.* **1** mechanical device for launching a glider, an aircraft from the deck of a ship, etc. **2** *hist.* military machine for hurling large stones, etc. • *v.* **1** *tr.* **a** hurl from or launch with a catapult. **b** fling forcibly. **2** *intr.* leap or be hurled forcibly.

cat·a·ract /kátərakt/ *n.* **1 a** large waterfall or cascade. **b** downpour; rush of water. **2** *Med.* condition in which the lens of the eye becomes progressively opaque.

ca·tas·tro·phe /kətástrəfee/ *n.* **1** great and usu. sudden disaster. **2** disastrous end; ruin. □□ **cat·a·stroph·ic** /kátəstrófik/ *adj.* **cat·a·stroph′i·cal·ly** *adv.*

cat·a·to·nia /kátətōneeə/ *n.* **1** schizophrenia with intervals of catalepsy and sometimes vio-

---

lence. **2** catalepsy. □□ **cat·a·ton·ic** /-tónik/ *adj.* & *n.*

cat·call /kátkawl/ *n.* shrill whistle of disapproval.

catch /kach/ • *v.* (*past* and *past part.* **caught** /kawt/) **1** *tr.* lay hold of so as to restrain; capture in a trap, in one's hands, etc. **2** *tr.* detect or surprise (esp. a guilty person). **3** *tr.* intercept and hold (a moving thing) in the hands, etc. **4** *tr.* **a** contract (a disease) by infection or contagion. **b** acquire (a quality or feeling). **5** *tr.* **a** reach in time and board (a train, bus, etc.). **b** be in time to see, etc. (a person or thing about to leave or finish). **6** *tr.* apprehend with the mind (esp. a thing occurring quickly or briefly). **7 a** *intr.* become fixed or entangled. **b** *tr.* cause to do this (*caught her tights on a nail*). **8** *tr.* draw the attention of; captivate. **9** *intr.* begin to burn. • *n.* **1** act of catching. **2 a** amount of a thing caught, esp. of fish. **b** thing or person caught or worth catching. **3 a** question, trick, etc., intended to deceive, incriminate, etc. **b** unexpected or hidden difficulty or disadvantage. **4** device for fastening a door or window, etc. □ **catch on** *colloq.* **1** (of a practice, fashion, etc.) become popular. **2** (of a person) understand what is meant. **catch up 1 a** reach a person, etc., ahead. **b** make up arrears (of work, etc.) **2** pick up hurriedly. **3** involve; entangle. □□ **catch′a·ble** *adj.*

catch·all /káchawl/ *n.* (often *attrib.*) **1** something designed to be all-inclusive. **2** container for odds and ends.

catch·ing /káching/ *adj.* infectious; likely to be imitated.

catch·phrase /káchfrayz/ *n.* phrase in frequent use.

catch-22 /káchtwenteetōō/ *n.* (often *attrib.*) *colloq.* circumstance that presents a dilemma because of mutually conflicting or dependent conditions.

catch·word /káchwərd/ *n.* word or phrase in common (often temporary) use; topical slogan.

catch·y /káchee/ *adj.* (**catch·i·er, catch·i·est**) (of a tune) easy to remember; attractive. □□ **catch′i·ly** *adv.* **catch′i·ness** *n.*

cat·e·chism /kátikizəm/ *n.* **1 a** principles of a religion in the form of questions and answers. **b** book containing this. **2** series of questions put to anyone. □□ **cat·e·chis·mal** /-kizməl/ *adj.*

cat·e·chize /kátikīz/ *v.tr.* **1** instruct by means of a catechism. **2** put questions to; examine. □□ **cat′e·chiz·er** *n.*

cat·e·gor·i·cal /kátigáwrikəl, -gór-/ *adj.* (also **cat·e·gor′ic**) unconditional; absolute; explicit. □□ **cat·e·gor′i·cal·ly** *adv.*

cat·e·go·rize /kátigərīz/ *v.tr.* place in a category or categories. □□ **cat·e·go·ri·za′tion** *n.*

cat·e·go·ry /kátigawree, -goree/ *n.* (*pl.* **-ries**) class or division. □□ **cat·e·go·ri·al** /-gáwreeəl/ *adj.*

ca·ter /káytər/ *v.* **1 a** *intr.* provide food. **b** *tr.* provide food and service (*cater a party*). **2** *intr.* provide what is desired or needed by. **3** *intr.* pander to (esp. low tastes).

ca·ter·cor·nered /kátərkáwrnərd/ (also **cat′er·cor′ner, cat·ty·cor′nered** /kátee-/, **kit·ty·cor′ner** /kítee-/) • *adj.* placed or situated diagonally. • *adv.* diagonally.

ca·ter·er /káytərər/ *n.* person who supplies food for social events, esp. professionally.

cat·er·pil·lar /kátərpilər/ *n.* larva of a butterfly or moth.

> **caterpillar** late Middle English: perhaps from a variant of Old French *chatepelose*, literally 'hairy cat,' influenced by obsolete *piller* 'ravager.' The association with 'cat' is found in other languages, e.g., Swiss *teufelskatz* (literally 'devil's cat'), Lombard *gatta* (literally 'cat'). Compare with French *chaton*, English *catkin*, resembling hairy caterpillars.

cat·er·waul /kátərwawl/ • *v.intr.* make the shrill howl of a cat. • *n.* caterwauling noise.

cat·fish /kátfish/ *n.* any of various esp. freshwater fish, usu. having whiskerlike barbels around the mouth.

cat·gut /kátgut/ *n.* material used for surgical sutures, etc., made of animal intestine (but not of the cat).

ca·thar·sis /kətháarsis/ *n.* (*pl.* **ca·thar·ses** /-seez/) **1** emotional release in drama or art. **2** *Psychol.* process of freeing and eliminating repressed emotion.

ca·thar·tic /kətháartik/ • *adj.* **1** effecting catharsis. **2** purgative. • *n.* cathartic drug. □□ **ca·thar·ti·cal·ly** *adv.*

ca·the·dral /kəthéedrəl/ *n.* principal church of a diocese.

cath·e·ter /káthitər/ *n. Med.* tube inserted into a body cavity for introducing or removing fluid. □□ **cath·e·ter·ize** *v.*

cath·ode /káthōd/ *n. Electr.* **1** negative electrode in an electrolytic cell or electronic valve or tube. **2** positive terminal of a primary cell such as a battery (opp. ANODE). □ **cathode ray** beam of electrons emitted from the cathode of a high-vacuum tube. □□ **cath·o·dal** *adj.* **ca·thod·ic** /kəthódik/ *adj.*

cath·o·lic /káthəlik, káthlik/ • *adj.* **1** of interest or use to all; universal. **2** all-embracing; of wide sympathies or interests (*has catholic tastes*). • *n.* (**Catholic**) Roman Catholic. □□ **ca·thol·i·cal·ly** /kəthóliklee/ *adv.* **Ca·thol·i·cism** /kəthólisizəm/ *n.* **cath·o·lic·i·ty** /káthəlísitee/ *n.*

cat·i·on /kátīən/ *n.* positively charged ion; ion that is attracted to the cathode in electrolysis (opp. ANION). □□ **cat·i·on·ic** /-ónik/ *adj.*

cat·kin /kátkin/ *n.* spike of usu. downy or silky flowers hanging from a willow, hazel, etc.

cat·nap /kátnap/ • *n.* short sleep. • *v.intr.* (**-napped, -nap·ping**) have a catnap.

cat·nip /kátnip/ *n.* white-flowered plant that attracts cats.

CAT scan /kat/ *n.* X-ray image made using computerized axial tomography. □□ **CAT scan·ner** *n.*

cat·sup /kátsəp, kéchəp, kách-/ var. of KETCHUP.

cat·tle /kát'l/ *n.pl.* domesticated bovine animals bred for meat and milk.

cat·ty /kátee/ *adj.* (**cat·ti·er, cat·ti·est**) sly; spiteful; deliberately hurtful in speech. □□ **cat'ti·ly** *adv.* **cat'ti·ness** *n.*

CATV *abbr.* community antenna television.

cat·walk /kátwawk/ *n.* narrow footway or platform.

Cau·ca·sian /kawkáyzhən/ • *adj.* **1** of or relating to the white or light-skinned division of mankind. **2** of or relating to the Caucasus. •

n. Caucasian person. □□ **Cau·ca·soid** /káwkəsoyd/ *adj.*

cau·cus /káwkəs/ *n.* meeting of a political party, esp. in a legislature or convention, to decide policy.

cau·dal /káwd'l/ *adj.* of or like a tail. □□ **cau'dal·ly** *adv.*

caught past and past part. of CATCH.

caul·dron /káwldrən/ *n.* (also **cal'dron**) large, deep, bowl-shaped vessel for boiling over an open fire.

cau·li·flow·er /káwliflowr, kól-/ *n.* cabbage with a large flower head of small usu. creamy-white buds. □ **cauliflower ear** ear deformed by injury, as in boxing.

caulk /kawk/ *v.tr.* (also **calk**) stop up (the seams of a boat, etc.) with a pliable sealant. □□ **caulk'er** *n.*

caus·al /káwzəl/ *adj.* **1** of, forming, or expressing a cause or causes. **2** relating to, or of the nature of, cause and effect.

cau·sal·i·ty /kawzálitee/ *n.* the relation of cause and effect.

cau·sa·tion /kawzáyshən/ *n.* **1** act of causing or producing an effect. **2** = CAUSALITY.

caus·a·tive /káwzətiv/ *adj.* **1** acting as cause. **2** (foll. by *of*) producing; having as effect. □□ **caus'a·tive·ly** *adv.*

cause /kawz/ • *n.* **1** person or thing that produces an effect. **2** reason or motive; ground that may be held to justify something (*no cause for complaint*). **3** principle, belief, or purpose (*faithful to the cause*). **4** matter to be settled at law. • *v.tr.* be the cause of; produce; make happen (*caused a commotion*). □□ **caus'a·ble** *adj.* **cause'less** *adj.* **caus'er** *n.*

cause cé·lè·bre /káwz selébrə/ *n.* (*pl.* **causes cé·lè·bres** *pronunc.* same) trial or case that attracts much attention.

cau·se·rie /kōzree, kōzə-/ *n.* (*pl.* **cau·se·ries** *pronunc.* same) informal article or talk, esp. on a literary subject.

cause·way /káwzway/ *n.* raised road or track across low or wet ground or a stretch of water.

caus·tic /káwstik/ • *adj.* **1** corrosive; burning. **2** sarcastic; biting. • *n.* caustic substance. □□ **caus'ti·cal·ly** *adv.* **caus·tic·i·ty** /-tísitee/ *n.*

cau·ter·ize /káwtərīz/ *v.tr. Med.* burn or coagulate (tissue); esp. to stop bleeding. □□ **cau'ter·i·za'tion** *n.*

cau·tion /káwshən/ • *n.* **1** attention to safety; prudence; carefulness. **2** warning. • *v.tr.* warn or admonish.

cau·tion·ar·y /káwshəneree/ *adj.* giving or serving as a warning.

cau·tious /káwshəs/ *adj.* careful; prudent; attentive to safety. □□ **cau'tious·ly** *adv.* **cau'tious·ness** *n.*

cav·al·cade /kávəlkáyd/ *n.* procession or formal company of riders, motor vehicles, etc.

cav·a·lier /kávəleér/ • *n.* courtly gentleman. • *adj.* offhand; supercilious. □□ **cav·a·lier'ly** *adv.*

cav·al·ry /kávəlree/ *n.* (*pl.* **-ries**) (usu. treated as *pl.*) soldiers on horseback or in armored vehicles.

cave /kayv/ • *n.* large hollow in the side of a cliff, hill, etc., or underground. • *v.intr.* explore caves. □ **cave in 1 a** (of a wall, earth over a hollow, etc.) subside; collapse. **b** cause (a wall, earth, etc.) to do this. **2** yield; give up. □□ **cave′ like** *adj.* **cav′er** *n.*

ca·ve·at /kávee-aat, ka'a-, -at/ *n.* warning or proviso.

cave·man /káyvman/ *n.* (*pl.* **-men**) prehistoric human living in a cave.

cav·ern /kávərn/ *n.* cave, esp. a large or dark one. □□ **cav′ern·ous** *adj.* **cav′ern·ous·ly** *adv.*

cav·i·ar /kávee-a'ar/ *n.* (also **cav′i·are**) pickled roe of sturgeon or other large fish, eaten as a delicacy.

cav·il /kávil/ • *v.intr.* make petty objections; carp. • *n.* trivial objection. □□ **cav′il·er** *n.*

cav·ing /káyving/ *n.* exploring caves as a sport or pastime.

cav·i·ty /kávitee/ *n.* (*pl.* **-ties**) **1** hollow within a solid body. **2** decayed part of a tooth.

ca·vort /kəváwrt/ *v.intr. sl.* caper excitedly; gambol; prance.

caw /kaw/ • *n.* harsh cry of a crow, etc. • *v.intr.* utter this cry.

cay·enne /kī-én, kay-/ *n.* (in full **cay·enne′ pep′per**) powdered red pepper.

CB *abbr.* citizens' band.

CCTV *abbr.* closed-circuit television.

CCU *abbr.* **1** cardiac care unit. **2** coronary care unit. **3** critical care unit.

CD *abbr.* **1** compact disc. **2** certificate of deposit.

Cd *symb. Chem.* cadmium.

CDC *abbr.* Centers for Disease Control (and Prevention).

CD-ROM /se'edeeróm/ *abbr. Computing* compact disc read-only memory, a medium for data storage and distribution.

CDT *abbr.* central daylight time.

Ce *symb. Chem.* cerium.

cease /sees/ *v.* stop; bring or come to an end (*ceased breathing*). □ **cease-fire** *n.* **1** order to stop firing. **2** period of truce; suspension of hostilities.

cease·less /se'eslis/ *adj.* without end. □□ **cease′less·ly** *adv.*

ce·cum /se'ekəm/ *n.* (*pl.* **ce·ca** /-kə/) blind-ended pouch at the junction of the small and large intestines. □□ **ce′cal** *adj.*

ce·dar /se'edər/ *n.* **1** spreading evergreen conifer. **2** (in full **cedar wood**) fragrant durable wood of any cedar tree. □□ **ce′darn** *adj. poet.*

cede /seed/ *v.tr.* give up one's rights to or possession of.

ce·dil·la /sidílə/ *n.* mark written under the letter *c*, esp. in French, to show that it is sibilant (as in *façade*).

ceil·ing /se'eling/ *n.* **1** upper interior surface of a room or other similar compartment. **2** upper limit. **3** *Aeron.* maximum altitude a given aircraft can reach.

cel·e·brant /sélibrənt/ *n.* person who performs a rite, esp. a priest at the Eucharist.

cel·e·brate /sélibrayt/ *v.* **1** *tr.* mark with festivities. **2** *tr.* perform publicly and duly (a religious ceremony, etc.). **3** *intr.* engage in festivities. **4** *tr.* (esp. as **celebrated** *adj.*) honor publicly. □□ **cel·e·bra′tion** /-bráyshən/ *n.* **cel′e·bra·tor** *n.* **cel·e·bra·to·ry** /-brətáwree, səlébrətáw-ree/ *adj.*

ce·leb·ri·ty /silébritee/ *n.* (*pl.* **-ties**) **1** well-known person. **2** fame.

cel·er·y /séləree/ *n.* umbelliferous plant, with closely packed succulent leafstalks used as a vegetable.

ce·les·tial /siléschəl/ *adj.* **1** divinely good; sublime. **2** of the sky or heavenly bodies. □□ **ce·les′tial·ly** *adv.*

cel·i·bate /sélibət/ • *adj.* **1** committed to abstention from sexual relations and from marriage. **2** abstaining from sexual relations. • *n.* celibate person. □□ **cel·i·ba·cy** /-bəsee/ *n.*

cell /sel/ *n.* **1** small room, esp. in a prison or monastery. **2** small compartment, e.g., in a honeycomb. **3** *Biol.* the structural and functional, usu. microscopic unit of an organism, consisting of cytoplasm and a nucleus enclosed in a membrane. **4** *Electr.* vessel for containing electrodes within an electrolyte for current generation or electrolysis. □□ **celled** *adj.* (also in *comb.*).

cel·lar /sélər/ *n.* storage room below ground level.

cel·lo /chélō/ *n.* (*pl.* **-los**) bass instrument of the violin family, held between the legs of the seated player. □□ **cel′list** *n.*

cel·lo·phane /séləfayn/ *n. formerly propr.* thin transparent wrapping material made from viscose.

cell·phone /sélfōn/ *n.* portable radiotelephone having access to a cellular telephone system.

cel·lu·lar /sélyələr/ *adj.* consisting of cells; of open texture; porous. □ **cellular telephone** (or **phone**) system of mobile radiotelephone transmission with an area divided into "cells," each served by its own small transmitter. □□ **cel·lu·lar·i·ty** /-láritee/ *n.* **cel′lu·late** *adj.* **cel·lu·la·tion** /-láyshən/ *n.*

cel·lu·lite /sélyəlīt/ *n.* lumpy fat, esp. on the hips and thighs.

cel·lu·loid /sélyəloyd/ *n.* **1** transparent plastic made from camphor and cellulose nitrate. **2** motion-picture film.

cel·lu·lose /sélyəlōs, -lōz/ *n.* **1** carbohydrate forming the main constituent of plant cell walls, used in textile fibers. **2** paint or lacquer containing cellulose acetate or nitrate.

Cel·si·us /sélseeəs/ *adj.* of a scale of temperature on which water freezes at 0° and boils at 100°.

Celt /kelt, selt/ *n.* (also **Kelt**) member of a group of W. European peoples, including inhabitants of Ireland, Wales, Scotland, Cornwall, Brittany, and the Isle of Man.

Celt·ic /kéltik, séltik/ (also **Kelt′ic**) • *adj.* of or relating to the Celts. • *n.* group of languages spoken by Celtic peoples, including Gaelic, Welsh, Cornish, and Breton.

ce·ment /simént/ • *n.* **1** powdery substance made by calcining lime and clay, mixed with water to form mortar or used in concrete. **2** similar substance that hardens and fastens on setting. **3** uniting factor or principle. **4** substance for filling cavities in teeth. • *v.tr.* **1 a** unite with or as with cement. **b** establish or strengthen (a friendship, etc.). **2** apply cement to. □□ **ce·ment′er** *n.*

cem·e·ter·y /sémiteree/ *n.* (*pl.* **-ies**) burial ground.

cen·o·taph /sénətaf/ *n.* tomblike monument, esp. a war memorial, to a person whose body is elsewhere.

Ce·no·zo·ic /se'enəzóik, sén-/ (also **Cai·no·zo·ic** /kīnə-/, **Cae·no·zo·ic** /se'enə-/) *Geol.* • *adj.* of or relating to the most recent era of geological time, marked by the evolution and development of mammals, birds, and flowers. • *n.* this era.

cen·ser /sénsər/ *n.* vessel in which incense is burned.

cen·sor /sénsər/ • *n.* person who examines printed matter, movies, news, etc., to suppress any parts on the grounds of obscenity, security, etc. • *v.tr.* **1** act as a censor of. **2** make deletions or changes in. □□ **cen·so·ri·al** /-sáwreeəl/ *adj.* **cen·so·ri·ous** /-sáwreeəs/ *adj.* **cen′sor·ship** *n.*

¶ Both **censor** and **censure** are both verbs and nouns, but **censor** is used to mean 'to cut unacceptable parts out of a book, movie, etc.' or 'a person who does this,' while **censure** means 'to criticize harshly' or 'harsh criticism:' *The censure of her friends caused her to regret her actions.*

cen·sure /sénshər/ • *v.tr.* criticize harshly; reprove. • *n.* harsh criticism; expression of disapproval. □□ **cen′sur·a·ble** *adj.*

cen·sus /sénsəs/ *n.* (*pl.* **cen·sus·es**) official count of a population or of a class of things.

cent /sent/ *n.* **1** monetary unit valued at one-hundredth of a dollar. **2** coin of this value.

cen·taur /séntawr/ *n. Gk. mythol.* creature with the head, arms, and torso of a man and the body and legs of a horse.

CENTAUR

cen·te·nar·i·an /séntináireeən/ • *n.* person a hundred or more years old. • *adj.* a hundred or more years old.

cen·te·na·ry /senténəree, séntəneree/ • *n.* (*pl.* **-ries**) = CENTENNIAL *n.* • *adj.* **1** of or relating to a centenary. **2** occurring every hundred years.

cen·ten·ni·al /senténeeəl/ • *adj.* **1** lasting for a hundred years. **2** occurring every hundred years. • *n.* **1** hundredth anniversary. **2** celebration of this.

cen·ter /séntər/ • *n.* **1** middle point. **2** pivot or axis of rotation. **3** place or group of buildings forming a central point or a main area for an activity. **4** point of concentration or dispersion; nucleus or source. **5** political party or group holding moderate opinions. • *v.* **1** *intr.* have as its main center. **2** *tr.* place in the center. **3** *tr.* concentrate. □ **center of gravity** (or **mass**) point at which the weight of a body may be considered to act. (often in *comb.*). **cen′ter·most** *adj.* **cen′tric** *adj.*

cen·ter·board /séntərbawrd/ *n.* retractable keel.

cen·ter·fold /séntərfōld/ *n.* printed and usu. illustrated sheet folded to form the center spread of a magazine, etc.

cen·ter·piece /séntərpees/ *n.* **1** ornament for the middle of a table. **2** principal item.

centi- /séntee/ *comb. form* **1** one-hundredth, esp. of a unit in the metric system (*centigram*). **2** hundred. ¶ Abbr.: **c.**

cen·ti·grade /séntigrayd/ *adj.* = CELSIUS.

cen·ti·me·ter /séntimeetər/ *n.* one-hundredth of a meter.

cen·ti·pede /séntipeed/ *n.* arthropod with a wormlike body of many segments each with a pair of legs.

cen·tral /séntrəl/ *adj.* **1** of, at, or forming the center. **2** from the center. **3** chief; essential; most important. □ **Central America** isthmus joining N. and S. America. **central nervous system** *Anat.* brain and spinal cord. **central processor** (or **processing unit**) principal operating part of a computer. □□ **cen·tral·i·ty** /-trálitee/ *n.* **cen′tral·ly** *adv.*

cen·tral·ize /séntrəlīz/ *v.* **1** *tr.* & *intr.* bring or come to a center. **2** *tr.* **a** concentrate (administration) at a single center. **b** subject (a government) to this system. □□ **cen·tral·i·za′tion** *n.*

cen·trif·u·gal /sentrífyəgəl, -trífə-/ *adj.* moving or tending to move from a center (cf. CENTRIPETAL). □ **centrifugal force** apparent force that acts outward on a body moving about a center. □□ **cen·trif′u·gal·ly** *adv.*

cen·tri·fuge /séntrifyōŏj/ *n.* machine with a rapidly rotating device designed to separate liquids from solids or other liquids (e.g., cream from milk).

cen·trip·e·tal /sentrípit'l/ *adj.* moving or tending to move toward a center (cf. CENTRIFUGAL). □ **centripetal force** force acting on a body causing it to move about a center. □□ **cen·trip′e·tal·ly** *adv.*

cen·trist /séntrist/ *n. Polit.* person who holds moderate views. □□ **cen′trism** *n.*

cen·tu·ri·on /sentyŏŏreeən, -tyŏŏr-/ *n.* commander of a century in the ancient Roman army.

cen·tu·ry /sénchəree/ *n.* (*pl.* **-ries**) **1 a** period of one hundred years. **b** any of the centuries calculated from the birth of Christ (*twentieth century* = 1901–2000). **2** company in the ancient Roman army, orig. of 100 men.

¶ In modern use, sense 1b is often considered as, e.g., 1900–1999.

CEO *abbr.* chief executive officer.

ce·phal·ic /sifálik/ *adj.* of or in the head.

ceph·a·lo·pod /séfələpod/ *n.* mollusk having a distinct tentacled head, e.g., octopus, squid, and cuttlefish.

ce·ram·ic /sirámik/ • *adj.* **1** made of (esp.) clay and permanently hardened by heat (*ceramic bowl*). **2** of or relating to ceramics (*ceramic arts*). • *n.* ceramic article or product.

ce·ram·ics /sirámiks/ *n.pl.* **1** ceramic products collectively. **2** (usu. treated as *sing.*) art of making ceramic articles.

ce·re·al /séereeəl/ • *n.* **1 a** grain used for food. **b** any grass producing this, e.g., wheat, corn, rye, etc. **2** breakfast food made from a cereal. • *adj.* of edible grain or products of it.

cer·e·bel·lum /séribéləm/ *n.* (*pl.* **cer·e·bel·lums** or **cer·e·bel·la** /-lə/) part of the brain at the back of the skull.

ce·re·bral /séribrəl, sərée-/ *adj.* **1** of the brain. **2** intellectual rather than emotional. □ **cerebral palsy** *Med.* spastic paralysis from brain damage before or at birth, with jerky or uncontrolled movements. □□ **ce·re′bral·ly** *adv.*

ce·re·brum /séribrəm, sərée-/ *n.* (*pl.* **cer·e·brums** or **cer·e·bra** /-brə/) principal part of the brain in vertebrates, located in the front area of the skull.

cer·e·mo·ni·al /sérimóneeəl/ ● *adj.* **1** with or concerning ritual or ceremony. **2** formal (*a ceremonial bow*). ● *n.* system of rites, etc., to be used esp. at a formal or religious occasion. **2** formalities, esp. of an empty or ritualistic kind. **3** excessively polite behavior. □ **master of ceremonies** (also **MC** or **emcee**) person in charge of a ceremonial or social occasion. **stand on ceremony** insist on the observance of formalities.

ce·rise /sərées, -réez/ ● *adj.* of a light, clear red. ● *n.* this color.

ce·ri·um /séereeəm/ *n. Chem.* silvery metallic element. ¶ Symb.: **Ce.**

cer·tain /sɔrt′n/ ● *adj.* **1 a** confident; convinced. **b** indisputable. **2 a** that may be relied on to happen (*it is certain to rain*). **b** destined (*certain to become a star*). **3** unfailing; reliable. **4** that might be specified, but is not (*a certain lady*). **5** some though not much (*a certain reluctance*). ● *pron.* (as *pl.*) some but not all (*certain of them were wounded*). □ **for certain** without doubt.

cer·tain·ly /sɔrt′nlee/ *adv.* **1** undoubtedly; definitely. **2** (in answer) yes; by all means.

cer·tain·ty /sɔrt′ntee/ *n.* (*pl.* **-ties**) **1** undoubted fact or prospect. **2** absolute conviction. **3** thing or person that may be relied on.

cer·ti·fi·a·ble /sɔrtifíəbəl/ *adj.* **1** able or needing to be certified. **2** *colloq.* insane.

cer·tif·i·cate /sərtifikət/ *n.* formal document attesting a fact, esp. birth, marriage, death, or a medical condition, a level of achievement, etc. □□ **cer·ti·fi·ca·tion** /sɔrtifikáyshən/ *n.*

cer·ti·fy /sɔrtifí/ *v.tr.* (**-fies, -fied**) **1** make a formal statement of; attest; attest to. **2** declare by certificate (*that a person is qualified or competent*) (*certified as a trained bookkeeper*). **3** officially declare insane.

cer·ti·tude /sɔrtitōod, -tyōod/ *n.* feeling of absolute certainty.

ce·ru·le·an /sərōōleeən/ *literary* ● *adj.* deep blue like a clear sky. ● *n.* this color.

cer·vi·cal /sɔrvikəl/ *adj. Anat.* **1** of or relating to the neck (*cervical vertebrae*). **2** of or relating to the cervix.

cer·vix /sɔrviks/ *n.* (*pl.* **cer·vic·es** /-viseez/ or **cer·vix·es**) *Anat.* any necklike structure, esp. the neck of the womb.

Ce·sar·e·an /sizáireeən/ (also **Ce·sar′i·an, Cae·sar′e·an, Cae·sar′i·an**) ● *adj.* (of a birth) effected by cesarean section. ● *n.* cesarean section. □ **cesarean section** (also **C-section**) operation for delivering a child by cutting through the wall of the abdomen.

ce·si·um /séezeeəm/ *n.* soft, silver-white element. ¶ Symb.: **Cs.** □ **cesium clock** atomic clock that uses cesium.

ces·sa·tion /sesáyshən/ *n.* **1** ceasing. **2** pause.

ces·sion /séshən/ *n.* **1** ceding (of rights, property, and esp. of territory by a nation). **2** the territory, etc., so ceded.

cess·pool /séspōol/ *n.* pit for waste or sewage.

ce·ta·cean /sitáyshən/ ● *n.* any marine mammal with dorsal blowhole for breathing, including whales, dolphins, and porpoises. ● *adj.* of cetaceans. □□ **ce·ta·ceous** /-táyshəs/ *adj.*

Cf *symb. Chem.* californium.

cf. *abbr.* compare.

CFA *abbr.* chartered financial analyst.

CFC *abbr. Chem.* chlorofluorocarbon, a compound of carbon, hydrogen, chlorine, and fluorine, used in refrigerants, etc., and thought to be harmful to the ozone layer.

cfm *abbr.* cubic feet per minute.

cfs *abbr.* cubic feet per second.

cg *abbr.* centigram(s).

c.h. *abbr.* (also **C.H.**) **1** clearinghouse. **2** courthouse.

Cha·blis /sháblee, shábleé/ *n.* (*pl.* same /-leez/) type of dry white wine.

cha-cha /cháachaa/ (also **cha-cha-cha** /cháa-chaachaá/) *n.* **1** ballroom dance with a Latin-American rhythm. **2** music for or in the rhythm of a cha-cha.

chafe /chayf/ *v.* **1** make or become sore or damaged by rubbing. **2** make or become annoyed; fret (*was chafed by the delay*).

chaff /chaf/ ● *n.* **1** husks of grain or other seed. **2** chopped hay and straw used as fodder. **3** lighthearted joking. **4** worthless things. ● *v.tr.* tease; banter. □ **separate the wheat from the chaff** distinguish good from bad. □□ **chaff′y** *adj.*

chaf·ing dish /cháyfing/ *n.* **1** cooking pot with an outer pan of hot water, used for keeping food warm. **2** dish with an alcohol lamp, etc., for cooking at table.

cha·grin /shəgrín/ ● *n.* acute vexation or mortification. ● *v.tr.* affect with chagrin.

chain /chayn/ ● *n.* **1 a** connected flexible series of esp. metal links. **b** something resembling this (*formed a human chain*). **2** (in *pl.*) fetters, restraining force. **3** sequence, series, or set (*chain of events; mountain chain*). **4** group of associated restaurants, newspapers, etc. ● *v.tr.* secure or confine with a chain. □ **chain gang** team of convicts chained together and forced to work in the open air. **chain reaction 1** *Physics* self-sustaining nuclear reaction. **2** *Chem.* self-sustaining molecular reaction. **3** series of events, each caused by the previous one. **chain saw** motor-driven saw with teeth on an endless chain.

chair /chair/ ● *n.* **1** separate seat for one person, of various forms, usu. having a back and four legs. **2** professorship. **3 a** chairperson. **b** seat or office of a chairperson (*I'm in the chair*). ● *v.tr.* act as chairperson of or preside over (a meeting).

chair·lift /cháirlift/ *n.* series of chairs on an endless cable for carrying passengers up and down a mountain, etc.

chair·man /cháirmən/ *n.* (*pl.* **-men**; *fem.* **chair·wom·an**, *pl.* **-wom·en**) **1** person chosen to preside over a meeting. **2** permanent president of a committee, board of directors, etc. □□ **chair′man·ship** *n.*

chair·per·son /cháirpərsən/ *n.* chairman or chairwoman.

chaise longue /sháyz lóng, shéz/ *n.* reclining chair with a lengthened seat forming a leg rest.

cha·let /shaláy, shálay/ *n.* **1** small house, bungalow, or hut, esp. with an overhanging roof. **2** Swiss cowherd's hut, or wooden cottage, with overhanging eaves.

chal·ice /chális/ *n.* **1** wine cup used in the Communion service. **2** *literary* goblet.

chalk /chawk/ • *n.* **1** white, soft, earthy limestone. **2** similar substance (calcium sulfate), sometimes colored, used for writing or drawing. • *v.tr.* **1** rub, mark, draw, or write with chalk. **2** (foll. by *up*) **a** write or record with chalk. **b** register (a success, etc.). □□ **chalk·y** /cháwkee/ *adj.* (**chalk·i·er, chalk·i·est**) **chalk′i·ness** *n.*

chal·lenge /chálinj/ • *n.* **1 a** summons to take part in a contest or a trial of strength, etc. **b** summons to prove or justify something. **2** demanding or difficult task. **3** *Law* objection made to a jury member. • *v.tr.* **1 a** invite to take part in a contest, game, debate, duel, etc. **b** invite to prove or justify something. **2** dispute; deny. **3 a** stretch; stimulate (*challenges him to produce his best*). **b** (as **challenging** *adj.*) demanding; stimulatingly difficult. **4** *Law* object to (a jury member, evidence, etc.). **5** (as **challenged** *adj.*) disabled. □□ **chal′lenge·a·ble** *adj.* **chal′leng·er** *n.*

cham·ber /cháymbər/ *n.* **1 a** hall used by a legislative or judicial body. **b** body that meets in it. **2** (in *pl.*) judge's room. **3** enclosed space in machinery, etc. (esp. the part of a gun bore that contains the charge). **4** a cavity in a plant or in the body of an animal. **b** compartment in a structure. **5** *poet.* or *archaic* room, esp. a bedroom. □ **chamber of commerce** association to promote local commercial interests.

cham·ber·lain /cháymbərlin/ *n.* officer managing a royal or noble household.

cham·ber·maid /cháymbərmayd/ *n.* housemaid who cleans bedrooms, esp. in a hotel, etc.

cha·me·le·on /kəméelyən/ *n.* small lizard having the power of changing color. □□ **cha·me·le·on·ic** /-leeónik/ *adj.*

cham·ois /shámee/ *n.* (*pl.* same /-eez/) **1** agile goat antelope native to Europe and Asia. **2** **a** soft leather from sheep, goats, deer, etc. **b** a piece of this or similar soft material used for polishing, etc.

cham·o·mile /kámməmīl, -meel/ *n.* (also **cam′o·mile**) aromatic plant with daisylike flowers. □ **chamomile tea** infusion of its dried flowers used as a tonic.

champ[1] /champ/ *v.* **1** *tr.* & *intr.* munch or chew noisily. **2** *tr.* (of a horse, etc.) work (the bit) noisily between the teeth.

champ[2] /champ/ *n. sl.* champion.

cham·pagne /shampáyn/ *n.* **1** white sparkling wine, originally from Champagne in France. **2** pale cream or straw color.

cham·pi·on /chámpeeən/ • *n.* **1** person, animal, plant, etc., that has defeated or surpassed all rivals in a competition, etc. **2** person who fights or argues for a cause or on behalf of another person. • *v.tr.* support the cause of; defend; argue in favor of.

cham·pi·on·ship /chámpeeənship/ *n.* **1** (often in *pl.*) contest for the position of champion. **2** position of champion.

chance /chans/ • *n.* **1 a** possibility. **b** (often in *pl.*) probability (*the chances are against it*). **2** opportunity (*didn't have a chance to speak*). **3** the way things happen; fortune; luck (*we'll just leave it to chance*). • *adj.* fortuitous; accidental (*a chance meeting*). • *v.* **1** *tr. colloq.* risk (*we'll chance it and go*). **2** *intr.* happen without intention (*I chanced to find it*). □ **by any chance** as it happens; perhaps. **by chance** without design; unintentionally. **chance on** (or **upon**) happen to find, meet, etc. **stand a chance** have a prospect of success, etc.

chan·cel /chánsəl/ *n.* part of a church near the altar.

chan·cel·ler·y /chánsələree, chánslə-/ *n.* (*pl.* **-ies**) **1 a** position, office, staff, department, etc., of a chancellor. **b** official residence of a chancellor. **2** office attached to an embassy or consulate.

chan·cel·lor /chánsələr, chánslər/ *n.* **1** government official of various kinds; head of the government in some European countries, e.g., Germany. **2** chief administrator at certain universities. □□ **chan′cel·lor·ship** *n.*

chan·cer·y /chánsəree/ *n.* (*pl.* **-ies**) **1** (in full **court of chancery**) court of equity. **2** administrative office for a diocese. **3** office attached to an embassy or consulate.

chan·cy /chánsee/ *adj.* (**chanc·i·er, chanc·i·est**) subject to chance; uncertain; risky. □□ **chanc′i·ly** *adv.* **chanc′i·ness** *n.*

chan·de·lier /shándəleér/ *n.* ornamental branched hanging support for several candles or electric lightbulbs.

change /chaynj/ • *n.* **1 a** making or becoming different. **b** alteration or modification. **2 a** money given in exchange for money in larger units or a different currency. **b** money returned as the balance of that given in payment. **3** new experience; variety (*for a change*). **4** substitution of one thing for another (*change of scene*). • *v.* **1** *tr.* & *intr.* undergo, show, or subject to change; make or become different. **2** *tr.* **a** take or use another instead of (*changed trains*). **b** give up or get rid of in exchange (*changed the car for a van*). **3** *tr.* **a** give or get change in smaller denominations for (*can you change a ten-dollar bill?*). **b** exchange (a sum of money) for (*changed his dollars for pounds*). **4** *tr.* & *intr.* put fresh clothes or coverings on (*changed into something loose*). **5** *tr.* give and receive; exchange (*we changed places*). □ **change hands 1** pass to a different owner. **2** substitute one hand for another. **change one's tune 1** voice a different opinion from that expressed previously. **2** change one's style of language or manner. □□ **change′ful** *adj.* **chang′er** *n.*

change·a·ble /cháynjəbəl/ *adj.* **1** irregular; inconstant. **2** that can change or be changed. □□ **change·a·bil′i·ty** *n.* **change′a·ble·ness** *n.* **change′a·bly** *adv.*

change·less /cháynjlis/ *adj.* unchanging.

change·ling /cháynjling/ *n.* child believed to be substituted for another by stealth, esp. in folklore.

change·o·ver /cháynjōvər/ *n.* change from one system or situation to another.

chan·nel /chánəl/ • *n.* **1 a** length of water wider

than a strait, joining two larger areas, esp. seas. **b** (**the Channel**) the English Channel between Britain and France. **2** medium of communication; agency. **3** *Broadcasting* band of frequencies used in radio and television transmission, esp. as used by a particular station. **4** course in which anything moves; direction. **5 a** natural or artificial hollow bed of water. **b** navigable part of a waterway. ● *v.tr.* guide; direct.

chant /chant/ ● *n.* **1** spoken singsong phrase. **2** *Mus.* **a** short musical passage in two or more phrases used for singing unmetrical words, e.g., psalms, canticles. **b** song, esp. monotonous or repetitive. ● *v.* sing or intone (a psalm, etc.).

chan·teuse /shaantöz/ *n.* female singer of popular songs.

chan·ti·cleer /chántiklēer, shán-/ *n.* name given to a domestic cock, esp. in fairy tales, etc.

Cha·nu·kkah var. of HANUKKAH.

cha·os /káyos/ *n.* utter confusion. □ **chaos theory** *Math.* the study of the apparently random behavior of deterministic systems. □□ **cha·ot·ic** /kayótik/ *adj.* **cha·ot´ical·ly** *adv.*

chap¹ /chap/ ● *v.* (**chapped, chap·ping**) **1** *intr.* (esp. of the skin; also of dry ground, etc.) crack in fissures, esp. because of exposure and dryness. **2** *tr.* (of the wind, cold, etc.) cause to chap. ● *n.* (usu. in *pl.*) crack in the skin.

chap² /chap/ *n.* man; boy; fellow.

chap. *abbr.* chapter.

chap·ar·ral /shápərál, cháp-/ *n.* dense, tangled brushwood.

chap·el /chápəl/ *n.* **1** place for private Christian worship in a large church or esp. a cathedral, with its own altar and dedication. **2** place of worship attached to a private house or institution.

chap·er·on /shápərōn/ (also **chap´er·one**) ● *n.* **1** person, esp. an older woman, who ensures propriety by accompanying a young unmarried woman on social occasions. **2** person who takes charge of esp. young people in public. ● *v.tr.* act as a chaperon to. □□ **chap·er·on·age** /shápərōnij/ *n.*

chap·lain /cháplin/ *n.* member of the clergy attached to a private chapel, institution, ship, regiment, etc. □□ **chap´lain·cy** *n.* (*pl.* **-cies**).

chap·let /cháplit/ *n.* **1** garland or circlet for the head. **2** string of 55 beads (one-third of the rosary number) for counting prayers, or as a necklace. □□ **chap´let·ed** *adj.*

chap·ter /cháptər/ *n.* **1** main division of a book. **2** period of time (in a person's life, a nation's history, etc.). **3** local branch of a society.

char /chaar/ *v.* (**charred, char·ring**) **1** make or become black by burning; scorch. **2** burn to charcoal.

char·ac·ter /káriktər/ *n.* **1** collective qualities or characteristics, esp. mental and moral, that distinguish a person or thing. **2 a** moral strength (*has a weak character*). **b** reputation, esp. good reputation. **3 a** person in a novel, play, etc. **b** part played by an actor; role. **4** *colloq.* person, esp. an eccentric or outstanding individual (*he's a real character*). **5** printed or written letter, symbol, or distinctive mark (*Chinese characters*). □□ **char´ac·ter·less** *adj.*

char·ac·ter·is·tic /káriktərístik/ ● *adj.* typical; distinctive (*with characteristic expertise*). ● *n.* distinguishing feature or quality. □□ **char·ac·ter·is´ti·cal·ly** *adv.*

char·ac·ter·ize /káriktərīz/ *v.tr.* **1 a** describe the character of. **b** describe as. **2** be characteristic of. **3** impart character to. □□ **char·ac·ter·i·za´tion** *n.*

cha·rade /shəráyd/ *n.* **1** (usu. in *pl.*, treated as *sing.*) game of guessing a word from a written or acted clue given for each syllable and for the whole. **2** absurd pretense.

char·coal /chaárkōl/ *n.* **1** amorphous form of carbon consisting of a porous black residue from partially burned wood, bones, etc. **b** piece of this used for drawing. **2** drawing in charcoal. **3** (in full **charcoal gray**) dark gray color.

charge /chaarj/ ● *v.* **1** *tr.* **a** ask (an amount) as a price. **b** ask (a person) for an amount as a price. **2** *tr.* **a** debit the cost of to (a person or account). **b** debit (a person or an account). **3** *tr.* **a** accuse (of an offense) (*charged him with theft*). **b** make an accusation that. **4** *tr.* instruct or urge. **5** *tr.* entrust with. **6 a** *intr.*make a rushing attack. **b** *tr.* make a rushing attack on. **7** *tr.* **a** give an electric charge to (a body). **b** store energy in (a battery). **8** *tr.* load or fill, as with fuel, emotion, etc. ● *n.* **1 a** price asked for goods or services. **b** financial liability or commitment. **2** accusation, esp. against a defendant. **3 a** task, duty, or commission. **b** care, custody, responsible possession. **c** person or thing entrusted; minister's congregation. **4 a** impetuous rush or attack, esp. in a battle. **b** signal for this. **5** appropriate amount of material to be put into a receptacle, mechanism, etc. **6 a** property of matter causing electrical phenomena. **b** quantity of this carried by a body. **7** exhortation; directions; orders. □ **charge account** credit account at a store, etc. **charge card** credit card for which the account must be paid in full when a statement is issued. **in charge** having command. **take charge** assume control or direction. □□ **charge´a·ble** *adj.*

char·ger /chaárjər/ *n.* **1** cavalry horse. **2** apparatus for charging a battery. **3** person or thing that charges.

char·i·ot /cháreeət/ *n.* *hist.* two-wheeled vehicle drawn by horses, used in ancient warfare and racing. □□ **char·i·o·teer´** *n.*

CHARIOT

cha·ris·ma /kərízmə/ *n.* (*pl.* **cha·ris·ma·ta** /-mə-tə/) **1** ability to inspire followers with devotion and enthusiasm. **2** attractive aura; great charm. □□ **char·is·mat·ic** /kárizmátik/ *adj.* **char·is·mat´ic·al·ly** *adv.*

char·i·ta·ble /cháritəbəl/ *adj.* **1** generous in giving to those in need. **2** of, relating to, or connected with a charity or charities. **3** apt to judge favorably of persons, acts, and motives. □□ **char´i·ta·ble·ness** *n.* **char´i·ta·bly** *adv.*

char·i·ty /cháritee/ *n.* (*pl.* **-ties**) **1** giving voluntarily to those in need. **2** institution or organization for helping those in need. **3 a** kindness; benevolence. **b** tolerance.

char·la·tan /sháarlətən/ *n.* person falsely claiming a special knowledge or skill. □□ **char′la·tan·ism** *n.* **char′la·tan·ry** *n.*

char·ley horse /cháarlee/ *n. sl.* stiffness or cramp in a thigh.

charm /chaarm/ • *n.* **1 a** power or quality of giving delight or arousing admiration. **b** fascination; attractiveness. **c** (usu. in *pl.*) attractive or enticing quality. **2** trinket on a bracelet, etc. **3 a** object, act, or word(s) supposedly having occult or magic power; spell. **b** thing worn to avert evil, etc.; amulet. • *v.tr.* **1** delight; captivate. **2** influence or protect as if by magic (*leads a charmed life*). **3** gain or influence by charm. □ **like a charm** perfectly; wonderfully. □□ **charm′er** *n.*

charm·ing /cháarming/ *adj.* **1** delightful; attractive; pleasing. **2** (often as *int.*) *iron.* expressing displeasure or disapproval. □□ **charm′ing·ly** *adv.*

chart /chaart/ • *n.* **1** geographical map or plan, esp. for navigation by sea or air. **2** sheet of information in the form of a table, graph, or diagram. **3** (usu. in *pl.*) *colloq.* listing of the currently most popular music recordings. • *v.tr.* make a chart of; map.

charter /cháartər/ • *n.* **1** written grant of rights, by a sovereign or legislature, esp. the creation of a city, company, university, etc. **2** written constitution or description of an organization's functions, etc. • *v.tr.* **1** grant a charter to. **2** hire (an aircraft, ship, etc.). □ **charter member** original member of a society, corporation, etc. □□ **char′ter·er** *n.*

char·treuse /shaartró͞oz, -tró͞os/ *n.* **1** pale green or yellow liqueur made from brandy. **2** pale yellow or pale green color of this.

char·y /cháiree/ *adj.* (**char·i·er, char·i·est**) **1** cautious; wary. **2** sparing; ungenerous. □□ **char′i·ly** *adv.* **char′i·ness** *n.*

chase[1] /chays/ • *v.tr.* **1** pursue in order to catch. **2** drive. **3** *colloq.* **a** try to attain. **b** court persistently and openly. • *n.* **1** pursuit. **2** (prec. by *the*) hunting, esp. as a sport.

chase[2] /chays/ *v.tr.* emboss or engrave (metal).

chas·er /cháysər/ *n. colloq.* drink taken after another of a different kind, e.g., beer after liquor.

chasm /kázəm/ *n.* **1** deep fissure or opening in the earth, rock, etc. **2** wide difference of; a gulf. □□ **chas′mic** *adj.*

chas·sis /shásee, chás-/ *n.* (*pl.* same /-siz/) **1** base frame of a motor vehicle, carriage, etc. **2** frame to carry radio, etc., components.

chaste /chayst/ *adj.* **1** abstaining from extramarital, or from all, sexual intercourse. **2** (of behavior, speech, etc.) pure, virtuous, decent. **3** (of artistic, etc., style) simple; unadorned. □□ **chaste′ly** *adv.* **chaste′ness** *n.*

chast·en /cháysən/ *v.tr.* **1** (esp. as **chastening, chastened** *adjs.*) subdue; restrain. **2** discipline; punish. □□ **chas′ten·er** *n.*

chas·tise /chastíz, chástīz/ *v.tr.* **1** rebuke or reprimand severely. **2** punish, esp. by beating. □□ **chas·tise′ment** *n.* **chas·tis′er** *n.*

chas·ti·ty /chástitee/ *n.* being chaste.

cha·su·ble /cházəbəl, cházyə-, chás-/ *n.* loose, sleeveless, often ornate outer vestment worn by a priest.

chat /chat/ • *v.intr.* (**chat·ted, chat·ting**) talk in a light familiar way. • *n.* informal conversation or talk. □□ **chat′ty** *adj.* (**chat·ti·er, chat·ti·est**) **chat′ti·ly** *adv.* **chat′ti·ness** *n.*

châ·teau /sható/ *n.* (*pl.* **châ·teaus** or **châ·teaux** /-tōz/) large French country house or castle.

chat·e·laine /shát′layn/ *n.* mistress of a large house.

chat·tel /chát′l/ *n.* (usu. in *pl.*) moveable possession; any possession or piece of property other than real estate or a freehold.

chat·ter /chátər/ • *v.intr.* **1** talk quickly, incessantly, trivially, or indiscreetly. **2** (of a bird) emit short, quick notes. **3** (of the teeth) click repeatedly together (usu. from cold). • *n.* chattering talk or sounds. □□ **chat′ter·er** *n.* **chat′ter·y** *adj.*

chat·ter·box /chátərboks/ *n.* talkative person.

chauf·feur /shófər, -fór/ • *n.* person employed to drive a private or rented automobile or limousine. • *v.tr.* drive (a car or a person) as a chauffeur.

chau·vin·ism /shóvinizəm/ *n.* **1** exaggerated or aggressive patriotism. **2** excessive or prejudiced support or loyalty.

chau·vin·ist /shóvinist/ *n.* **1** person exhibiting chauvinism. **2** (in full **male chauvinist**) man showing excessive loyalty to men and prejudice against women. □□ **chau·vin·is′tic** *adj.* **chau·vin·is′ti·cal·ly** *adv.*

cheap /cheep/ • *adj.* **1** low in price; worth more than its cost (*cheap labor*). **2** charging low prices; offering good value (*a cheap restaurant*). **3** of poor quality; inferior. **4** costing little effort and hence of little worth (*a cheap joke*). • *adv.* cheaply (*got it cheap*). □ **dirt cheap** very cheap. **feel cheap** feel ashamed or contemptible. **on the cheap** cheaply. □□ **cheap′ish** *adj.* **cheap′ly** *adv.* **cheap′ness** *n.*

cheap·en /chéepən/ *v.* make or become cheap or cheaper; depreciate; degrade.

cheap·skate /chéepskayt/ *n. colloq.* stingy person.

cheat /cheet/ • *v.* **1** *tr.* deceive; trick. **2** *intr.* gain unfair advantage by deception or breaking rules. • *n.* **1** person who cheats. **2** trick, fraud, or deception. □ **cheat on** *colloq.* be sexually unfaithful to. □□ **cheat′er** *n.* **cheat′ing·ly** *adv.*

check /chek/ • *v.* **1** *tr.* **a** examine the accuracy, quality, or condition of. **b** make sure; verify. **2** *tr.* **a** stop or slow the motion of; curb. **b** *colloq.* find fault with; rebuke. **3** *tr.* *Chess* directly threaten (the opposing king). **4** *intr.* agree or correspond when compared. **5** *tr.* mark with a check mark, etc. **6** *tr.* deposit (luggage, etc.) for storage or dispatch. • *n.* **1** means or act of testing or ensuring accuracy, quality, etc. **2** stopping or slowing of motion. **b** rebuff or rebuke. **c** person or thing that restrains. **3** *Chess* exposure of a king to direct attack. **4** bill in a restaurant. **5** written order to a bank to pay the stated sum from one's account. **6** token of identification for left luggage, etc. **7** crack or flaw in lumber. **8** a pattern of small squares. **b** fabric having this pattern. • *int.* expressing assent or agreement. □ **check in** arrive or register at a hotel, airport, etc. **2** record the arrival of. **check into** register one's arrival at (a hotel, etc.). **check mark** a mark (√) to denote correctness, check items in a been examined or dealt with. **check on** examine carefully; keep a watch on (a person, work done, etc.). **check out 1** leave a hotel, etc., after paying. **2** *colloq.* investigate; examine for authenticity or suitability. **in check** under control; restrained. □□ **check′a•ble** *adj.*

check•er /chékər/ • *n.* **1** person or thing that examines, esp. in a factory, etc. **2** cashier in a supermarket, etc. **3** (often in *pl.*) pattern of squares often alternately colored. **4 a** (in *pl.*) game for two played with 12 pieces each on a checkerboard. **b** pieces used in a game of checkers. • *v. tr.* **1** mark with checkers. **2** (as **checkered** *adj.*) with varied fortunes (*a checkered career*).

check•er•board /chékərbawrd/ *n.* checkered board, identical to a chessboard, used in the game of checkers.

check•ing ac•count /chéking/ *n.* account at a bank against which checks can be drawn by the account depositor.

check•mate /chékmayt/ • *n. Chess* check from which a king cannot escape. • *v. tr.* **1** *Chess* put into checkmate. **2** defeat; frustrate.

check•out /chékowt/ *n.* **1** act of checking out. **2** point at which goods are paid for in a supermarket, etc.

check•point /chékpoynt/ *n.* barrier or gate for inspection.

check•up /chékup/ *n.* thorough (esp. medical) examination.

ched•dar /chédər/ *n.* (in full **ched•dar cheese**) kind of firm smooth cheese orig. made in Cheddar in S. England.

cheek /cheek/ *n.* **1 a** side of the face below the eye. **b** sidewall of the mouth. **2** impertinence; cool confidence. **3** *sl.* either buttock. □ **cheek by jowl** close together; intimate.

cheek•bone /cheekbōn/ *n.* bone below the eye.

cheek•y /cheekee/ *adj.* (**cheek•i•er, cheek•i•est**) impertinent; impudent. □□ **cheek′i•ly** *adv.* **cheek′i•ness** *n.*

cheep /cheep/ • *n.* weak shrill cry of a young bird. • *v. intr.* make such a cry.

cheer /cheer/ • *n.* **1** shout of encouragement or applause. **2** mood; disposition (*full of good cheer*). **3** (in *pl.*; as *int.*) *colloq.* expressing good wishes on parting or before drinking. • *v.* **1** *tr.* **a** applaud with shouts. **b** urge or encourage with shouts. **2** *intr.* shout for joy. **3** *tr.* gladden; comfort.

cheer•ful /cheerfool/ *adj.* **1** in good spirits; noticeably happy. **2** bright; pleasant. □□ **cheer′ful•ly** *adv.* **cheer′ful•ness** *n.*

cheer•lead•er /cheerleedər/ *n.* person who leads cheers of applause, etc., esp. at a sports event.

cheer•less /cheerlis/ *adj.* gloomy; dreary; miserable. □□ **cheer′less•ly** *adv.* **cheer′less•ness** *n.*

cheer•y /cheeree/ *adj.* (**cheer•i•er, cheer•i•est**) lively; in good spirits; genial; cheering. □□ **cheer′i•ly** *adv.* **cheer′i•ness** *n.*

cheese /cheez/ *n.* **1 a** food made from the pressed curds of milk. **2** complete cake of this with rind.

cheese•burg•er /cheezbərgər/ *n.* hamburger with cheese on it.

cheese•cake /cheezkayk/ *n.* **1** rich dessert cake made with cream cheese, etc. **2** *sl.* portrayal of women in a sexually attractive manner.

cheese•cloth /cheezklawth, -kloth/ *n.* thin loosely woven cloth, used orig. for wrapping cheese.

chees•y /cheezee/ *adj.* (**chees•i•er, chees•i•est**) **1** like cheese in taste, smell, appearance, etc. **2** *sl.* inferior; cheap and nasty. □□ **chees′i•ness** *n.*

chee•tah /cheetə/ *n.* swift, spotted leopardlike feline.

chef /shef/ *n.* cook, esp. the chief cook in a restaurant, etc.

chem. *abbr.* **1** chemical. **2** chemist. **3** chemistry.

chem•i•cal /kémikəl/ • *adj.* of, made by, or employing chemistry or chemicals. • *n.* substance obtained or used in chemistry. □ **chemical engineering** design, manufacture, and operation of industrial chemical plants. **chemical warfare** warfare using poison gas and other chemicals. □□ **chem′i•cal•ly** *adv.*

che•mise /shəmeez/ *n. hist.* woman's loose-fitting undergarment or dress hanging straight from the shoulders.

chem•ist /kémist/ *n.* person practicing or trained in chemistry.

chem•is•try /kémistree/ *n.* (*pl.* **-tries**) **1** the study of the elements and the compounds they produce and the reactions they undergo. **2** any complex (esp. emotional) change or process. **3** *colloq.* person's personality or temperament.

che•mo•ther•a•py /keemōthérəpee/ *n.* treatment of disease, esp. cancer, by chemical substances. □□ **che•mo•ther′a•pist** *n.*

che•nille /shəneel/ *n.* **1** tufty, velvety cord or yarn, used in trimming furniture, etc. **2** fabric made from this.

cher•ish /chérish/ *v. tr.* **1** protect or tend (a child, plant, etc.) lovingly. **2** hold dear; cling to (hopes, feelings, etc.).

Cher•o•kee /chérəkee/ *n.* **1 a** N. American people formerly inhabiting much of the southern US. **b** member of this people. **2** language of this people.

che•root /shəroot/ *n.* cigar with both ends open.

cher•ry /chéree/ • *n.* (*pl.* **-ries**) **1** small, soft, round stone fruit. **2** tree bearing this, also grown for its wood and its ornamental flowers. • *adj.* of a light red color. □ **cherry picker** *colloq.* crane for raising and lowering people. **cherry tomato** miniature tomato.

cher•ub /chérəb/ *n.* **1** (*pl.* **cher•u•bim** /-bim/) angelic being, usu. depicted as a winged child or the head of a winged child. **2** beautiful or innocent child. □□ **che•ru•bic** /chiroobik/ *adj.* **che•ru′bi•cal•ly** *adv.*

cher•vil /chárvil/ *n.* umbelliferous plant, with small white flowers, used as an herb.

chess /ches/ *n.* game for two with 16 pieces each, played on a chessboard.

chess•board /chésbawrd/ *n.* checkered board of 64 squares on which chess and checkers are played.

chess•man /chésman, -mən/ *n.* (*pl.* **-men**) any of the 32 pieces with which chess is played.

chest /chest/ *n.* **1** large strong box. **2 a** part of a human or animal body enclosed by the ribs. **b** front surface of the body from neck to waist. **3** small cabinet for medicines, etc. □ **get a thing off one's chest** *colloq.* disclose a fact, secret, etc., to relieve one's anxiety about it.

chest·nut /chésnut/ n. **1 a** glossy, hard, brown edible nut. **b** tree bearing it. **2** = *horse chestnut.* **3** (in full **chestnut wood**) the heavy wood of any chestnut tree. **4** horse of a reddish-brown or yellowish-brown color. **5** *colloq.* stale joke or anecdote. **6** reddish-brown color.

chest·y /chéstee/ adj. (**chest·i·er, chest·i·est**) **1** *colloq.* having a large chest or prominent breasts. **2** *sl.* arrogant. □□ **chest′i·ly** adv. **chest′i·ness** n.

chev·ron /shévrən/ n. **1** V-shaped line or stripe. **2** badge, etc., of such lines or stripes.

CHEVRON

chew /choo/ • v.tr. (also *absol.*) work (food, etc.) between the teeth. • n. **1** act of chewing. **2** something for chewing, esp. a chewy candy. □ **chew the cud** reflect; ruminate. **chew the fat** (or **rag**) *sl.* chat. **chewing gum** flavored gum, for chewing. **chew out** *colloq.* reprimand. □□ **chew′a·ble** adj. **chew′er** n.

chew·y /chooee/ adj. (**chew·i·er, chew·i·est**) **1** needing much chewing. **2** suitable for chewing. □□ **chew′i·ness** n.

Chey·enne /shīán, -én/ n. **1 a** N. American people formerly living between the Missouri and Arkansas rivers. **b** member of this people. **2** language of this people.

chi /kī/ n. twenty-second letter of the Greek alphabet (X, χ).

Chi·an·ti /keeaántee, keeán-/ n. (pl. **Chi·an·tis**) dry, red Italian-style wine.

chi·ar·o·scu·ro /keeaárəskoorō/ n. treatment of light and shade in drawing and painting.

chic /sheek/ • adj. (**chic·er, chic·est**) stylish; elegant. • n. stylishness; elegance. □□ **chic′ly** adv.

chi·ca·ner·y /shikáynəree/ n. (pl. **-ies**) **1** clever but misleading talk; false argument. **2** trickery; deception.

Chi·ca·no /chikaánō/ n. (pl. **-nos;** fem. **chi·ca·na,** pl. **-nas**) American of Mexican origin.

chick /chik/ n. **1** young bird. **2** derog. sl. young woman.

Chick·a·saw /chíkəsaw/ n. **1 a** N. American people native to Mississippi and Alabama. **b** member of this people. **2** language of this people.

chick·en /chíkin/ • n. (pl. same or **chick·ens**) **1** common breed of domestic fowl. **2 a** domestic fowl prepared as food. **b** its flesh. • adj. colloq. cowardly. • v.intr. (foll. by out) colloq. withdraw through fear or lack of nerve. □ **chicken feed 1** food for poultry. **2** colloq. unimportant amount, esp. of money. **chicken pox** infectious

disease, esp. of children, with a rash of small blisters. **chicken wire** light wire netting with a hexagonal mesh.

chick·pea /chíkpee/ n. **1** leguminous plant with pods containing yellow, beaked seeds. **2** this seed used as a vegetable. □□ **gar·ban′zo** (**bean**)

chick·weed /chíkweed/ n. small weed with tiny white flowers.

chic·le /chíkəl/ n. milky juice of the sapodilla tree, used in the manufacture of chewing gum.

chic·o·ry /chíkəree/ n. (pl. **-ries**) **1** blue-flowered plant cultivated for its salad leaves and its root. **2** its root, roasted and ground for use with or instead of coffee.

chide /chīd/ v. (past **chid·ed** or **chid** /chid/; past part. **chid·ed** or **chid** or **chid·den** /chíd′n/) literary scold; rebuke. □□ **chid′er** n. **chid′ing·ly** adv.

chief /cheef/ • n. **1 a** leader or ruler. **b** head of a tribe, clan, etc. **2** head of a department; highest official. • adj. (usu. attrib.) **1** first in position, importance, influence, etc. **2** prominent; leading. □ **chief executive officer** highest ranking executive in a corporation, organization, etc. ¶ Abbr.: **CEO.**

chief·ly /cheeflee/ adv. above all; mainly but not exclusively.

chief·tain /cheeftən/ n. (fem. **chief·tain·ess** /-tənis/) leader of a tribe, clan, etc. □□ **chief′tain·cy** n. (pl. **-cies**). **chief′tain·ship** n.

chif·fon /shifón, shifon/ • n. light, diaphanous fabric of silk, nylon, etc. • adj. **1** made of chiffon. **2** light-textured.

chig·ger /chígər/ n. harvest mite with parasitic larvae.

chi·gnon /sheeenyon, sheenyón/ n. coil or knot of hair worn at the back of the head.

chi·hua·hua /chiwaáwə/ n. **1** very small dog of a smooth-haired, large-eyed breed originating in Mexico. **2** this breed.

chil·blain /chílblayn/ n. painful, itchy swelling of the skin, usu. on a hand, foot, etc., caused by exposure to cold. □□ **chil′blained** adj.

child /chīld/ n. (pl. **chil·dren** /chíldrən/) **1 a** young human being below the age of puberty. **b** unborn or newborn human being. **2** one's son or daughter. **3** descendant, follower, or product (of) (child of God). **4** childish person. □ **child care** care of children, esp. by someone other than a parent. **child's play** easy task. □□ **child′less** adj. **child′less·ness** n.

child·bear·ing /chíldbairing/ n. act of giving birth to a child or children.

child·birth /chíldbərth/ n. act of giving birth to a child.

child·hood /chíldhood/ n. state or period of being a child.

child·ish /chíldish/ adj. **1** of, like, or proper to a child. **2** immature, silly. □□ **child′ish·ly** adv. **child′ish·ness** n.

child·like /chíldlīk/ adj. having the good qualities of a child; as innocence, frankness, etc.

Chil·e·an /chíleeən, chiláyən/ • n. **1** native or national of Chile in S. America. **2** person of Chilean descent. • adj. of or relating to Chile.

chil·i /chílee/ n. (pl. **-ies**) small, hot-tasting dried pod of a certain red pepper, used as a spice. □ **chili con carne** /kon kaárnee/ stew of chili-flavored ground meat and usu. beans.

chill /chil/ • n. **1 a** unpleasant cold sensation;

lowered body temperature. **b** feverish cold. **2** unpleasant coldness (of air, water, etc.). **3** depressing influence (*cast a chill over*). **4** coldness of manner. • *v.* **1** *tr.* & *intr.* make or become cold. **2** *tr.* depress; dispirit. **3** *tr.* cool (food or drink); preserve by cooling. • *adj.* = CHILLY. □ **chill out** become calm or less agitated. □□ **chill′er** *n.* **chill′ing·ly** *adv.*

chill·y /chílee/ *adj.* (**chill·i·er, chill·i·est**) **1** somewhat cold. **2** unfriendly; unemotional. □□ **chill′i·ness** *n.*

chime /chīm/ • *n.* **1 a** set of attuned bells. **b** series of sounds given by this. • *v.* **1** *intr.* (of bells) ring. **2** *tr.* show (the hour) by chiming. □ **chime in** interject a remark. □□ **chim′er** *n.*

chi·me·ra /kīmeérə, kee-/ (also **chi·mae′ra**) *n.* **1** *Gk. mythol.* fire-breathing female monster with a lion's head, a goat's body, and a serpent's tail. **2** fantastic or grotesque product of the imagination. □□ **chi·mer·ic** /-mérik/ *adj.* **chi·mer′i·cal** *adj.* **chi·mer′i·cal·ly** *adv.*

chim·ney /chímnee/ *n.* (*pl.* **-neys**) **1** vertical channel conducting smoke or combustion gases, etc., up and away from a fire, furnace, etc. **2** part of this that projects above a roof. **3** glass tube protecting the flame of a lamp. **4** narrow vertical crack in a rock face.

chim·pan·zee /chímpanze'e, chimpánzee/ *n.* (also *colloq.* **chimp**) small African anthropoid ape.

chin /chin/ *n.* front of the lower jaw. □ **chin-up** exercise in which the chin is raised up to the level of an overhead bar that one grasps. □ **keep one's chin up** *colloq.* remain cheerful, esp. in adversity.

chi·na /chínə/ • *n.* **1** fine white or translucent ceramic ware, porcelain, etc. **2** things made from ceramic, esp. household tableware. • *adj.* made of china.

chin·chil·la /chinchílə/ *n.* **1** S. American small rodent having soft, silver-gray fur. **2** its highly valued fur.

chine /chīn/ *n.* **1** backbone, esp. of an animal. **2** joint of meat containing all or part of this.

Chi·nese /chíne'ez/ • *adj.* **1** of or relating to China. **2** of Chinese descent. • *n.* **1** the Chinese language. **2** (*pl.* same) **a** native or national of China. **b** person of Chinese descent. □ **Chinese lantern** collapsible paper lantern. **Chinese puzzle** very intricate puzzle or problem.

chink[1] /chingk/ *n.* narrow opening; slit.

chink[2] /chingk/ • *v.* **1** *intr.* make a slight ringing sound, as of glasses or coins striking together. **2** *tr.* cause to make this sound. • *n.* this sound.

chi·no /che'enō/ *n.* (*pl.* **-nos**) **1** cotton twill fabric, usu. khaki-colored. **2** (in *pl.*) garment, esp. trousers, made from this.

Chi·nook /shənŏ̄ok, chə-/ *n.* **1 a** N. American people native to the northwestern coast of the US. **b** member of these people. **2** language of this people.

chintz /chints/ *n.* printed, multicolored cotton fabric with a glazed finish.

chintz·y /chíntsee/ *adj.* (**chintz·i·er, chintz·i·est**) **1** like chintz. **2** gaudy; cheap. □□ **chintz′i·ly** *adv.* **chintz′i·ness** *n.*

chip /chip/ • *n.* **1** small piece removed by or in the course of chopping, cutting, or breaking. **2** place where such a chip has been made. **3 a** = *potato chip.* **b** (usu. in *pl.*) = *French fries* (*fish and chips*). **4** counter used in some gambling games

to represent money. **5** *Electronics* = MICROCHIP. • *v.* (**chipped, chip·ping**) **1** *tr.* cut or break (a piece) from a hard material. **2** *intr.* cut pieces off. **3** *intr.* (of stone, china, etc.) be apt to break at the edge (*will chip easily*). □ **chip in** *colloq.* **1** interrupt or contribute abruptly to a conversation. **2** contribute (money or resources). **chip off the old block** child who resembles a parent, esp. in character. **chip on one's shoulder** *colloq.* inclination to feel resentful or aggrieved. **when the chips are down** *colloq.* in times of discouragement or disappointment.

chip·munk /chípmungk/ *n.* small ground squirrel having alternate light and dark stripes.

chip·per /chípər/ *adj. colloq.* **1** cheerful. **2** smartly dressed.

Chip·pe·wa /chípəwaw, -wə, -waa, -way/ *n.* = OJIBWA.

chiro- /kírō/ *comb. form* of the hand.

chi·rog·ra·phy /kīrógrəfee/ *n.* handwriting; calligraphy.

chi·ro·man·cy /kírəmansee/ *n.* palmistry.

chi·rop·o·dy /kirópədee/ = PODIATRY. □□ **chi·rop′o·dist** *n.*

chi·ro·prac·tic /kírəpráktik/ *n.* manipulative treatment of mechanical disorders of the joints, esp. of the spinal column. □□ **chi′ro·prac·tor** *n.*

chirp /chərp/ • *v.* **1** *intr.* (usu. of small birds, grasshoppers, etc.) utter a short, sharp note. **2** *tr.* & *intr.* speak or utter merrily. • *n.* chirping sound. □□ **chirp′er** *n.*

chir·rup /chírəp/ • *v.intr.* (**chir·ruped, chir·rup·ing**) chirp, esp. repeatedly. • *n.* chirruping sound. □□ **chir′rup·y** *adj.*

chis·el /chízəl/ • *n.* hand tool with a squared, beveled blade. • *v.* **1** *tr.* cut or shape with a chisel. **2** *tr.* & *intr.* *sl.* cheat; swindle. □□ **chis′el·er** *n.*

chit /chit/ *n.* note of a sum owed, esp. for food or drink.

chit·chat /chítchat/ *colloq.* • *n.* light conversation; gossip. • *v.intr.* (**-chat·ted, -chat·ting**) talk informally.

chi·tin /kít'n/ *n. Chem.* polysaccharide forming the major constituent in the exoskeleton of insects, etc. □□ **chi′tin·ous** *adj.*

chit·ter·lings /chítlinz/ *n.* (also **chit′lings, chit′lins**) small intestines of pigs, etc., esp. as cooked for food.

chiv·al·rous /shívəlrəs/ *adj.* **1** gallant; honorable; courteous. **2** involving or showing chivalry. □□ **chiv′al·rous·ly** *adv.*

chiv·al·ry /shívəlree/ *n.* **1** medieval knightly system with its religious, moral, and social code. **2** selfless gallantry. □□ **chi′val·ric** *adj.*

chive /chīv/ *n.* plant with onion-flavored tubular leaves.

chla·myd·i·a /kləmídeeə/ *n.* venereal disease caused by a parasitic microorganism.

chlo·ride /kláwrīd/ *n. Chem.* **1** any compound of chlorine with another element or group. **2** any bleaching agent containing chloride.

chlo·ri·nate /kláwrinayt/ *v.tr.* impregnate or treat with chlorine. □□ **chlo·ri·na·tion** /-áyshən/ *n.* **chlo′ri·na·tor** *n.*

chlo·rine /kláwreen/ *n. Chem.* poisonous gaseous element used for purifying water, bleaching, etc. ¶ Symb.: **Cl.**

chlo·ro·fluor·o·car·bon /kláwrōflōˊōrōkaˊarbən, -fláwr-/ see CFC.

chlo·ro·form /kláwrəfawrm/ • *n.* colorless, volatile, sweet-smelling liquid used as a solvent and formerly used as a general anesthetic. ¶ Chem. formula: CHCl₃. • *v.tr.* render (a person) unconscious with this.

chlo·ro·phyll /kláwrəfil/ *n.* green pigment found in most plants. □□ **chlo·ro·phyl·lous** /-fíləs/ *adj.*

chock /chok/ • *n.* block or wedge of wood to check motion, esp. of a cask or a wheel. • *v.tr.* fit or make fast with chocks. □ **chock-full** = CHOCKABLOCK.

chock·a·block /chókəblók/ *adj.* & *adv.* crammed full.

choc·o·late /cháwkələt, cháwklət, chók-/ • *n.* **1 a** food preparation made from roasted and ground cacao seeds, usually sweetened. **b** candy made with this. **c** drink made with chocolate. **2** deep brown color. • *adj.* made from or of chocolate. □□ **choc·o·lat·y** *adj.* (also **choc·o·lat·ey**).

---

chocolate early 17th century (in the sense 'a drink made with chocolate'): from French *chocolat* or Spanish *chocolate*, from Nahuatl *chocolatl* 'food made from cacao seeds,' influenced by unrelated *cacaua-atl* 'drink made from cacao.'

Choc·taw /chóktaw/ *n.* (*pl.* same or **-taws**) **1 a** N. American people originally from Alabama. **b** member of this people. **2** language of this people.

choice /choys/ • *n.* **1 a** act or instance of choosing. **b** thing or person chosen (*not a good choice*). **2** range from which to choose. **3** power or opportunity to choose (*what choice have I?*). • *adj.* of superior quality; carefully chosen. □□ **choice·ly** *adv.*

choir /kwīr/ *n.* **1** group of singers, esp. taking part in church services. **2** part of a cathedral or large church used by the choir and clergy.

choke /chōk/ • *v.* **1** *tr.* hinder or impede the breathing of (a person or animal), esp. by constricting the windpipe or (of gas, smoke, etc.) by being unbreathable. **2** *intr.* suffer a hindrance or stoppage of breath. **3** *tr.* & *intr.* make or become speechless from emotion. **4** *tr.* retard the growth of or kill (esp. plants). **5** *tr.* suppress (feelings) with difficulty. • *n.* valve of an internal combustion engine that controls the intake of air. □ **choke up** become overly anxious or emotionally affected.

chok·er /chókər/ *n.* close-fitting necklace.

cho·ler /kólər/ *n.* poet. anger; irascibility.

chol·er·a /kólərə/ *n.* Med. infectious and often fatal bacterial disease of the small intestine. □□ **chol·e·ra·ic** /-ráyik/ *adj.*

cho·ler·ic /kólərik, kəlérik/ *adj.* irascible; angry. □□ **chol·er·i·cal·ly** *adv.*

cho·les·ter·ol /kəléstərawl, -rōl/ *n.* Biochem. sterol found in most body tissues, including the blood, where high concentrations promote arteriosclerosis.

chomp /chomp/ *v.tr.* = CHAMP¹.

choose /chōōz/ *v.* (*past* **chose** /chōz/; *past part.* **chos·en** /chózən/) **1** *tr.* select out of a greater

number. **2** *intr.* take or select one or another. **3** *tr.* decide; be determined (*chose to stay behind*). **4** *tr.* select as (*was chosen king*). □□ **choos·er** *n.*

choos·y /chōˊōzee/ *adj.* (**choos·i·er**, **choos·i·est**) *colloq.* fastidious. □□ **choos·i·ly** *adv.* **choos·i·ness** *n.*

chop¹ /chop/ • *v.tr.* (**chopped, chop·ping**) **1** cut or fell by a blow, usu. with an ax. **2** cut into small pieces. • *n.* **1** cutting blow. **2** thick slice of meat (esp. pork or lamb) usu. including a rib. □ **chop shop** *colloq.* garage in which stolen cars are dismantled so that the parts can be sold separately.

chop² /chop/ *n.* (usu. in *pl.*) jaw of an animal, etc.

chop·per /chópər/ *n.* **1** person or thing that chops. **2** *colloq.* helicopter.

chop·py /chópee/ *adj.* (**chop·pi·er, chop·pi·est**) (of the sea, etc.) fairly rough. □□ **chop·pi·ly** *adv.* **chop·pi·ness** *n.*

chop·stick /chópstik/ *n.* each of a pair of small thin sticks, used as eating utensils.

chop su·ey /chopsōˊō-ee/ *n.* (*pl.* **-eys**) Chinese-style dish of meat, bean sprouts, bamboo shoots, etc.

cho·ral /káwrəl/ *adj.* of, for, or sung by a choir or chorus. □□ **cho·ral·ly** *adv.*

cho·rale /kərál, -ráal/ *n.* (also **cho·ral**) **1** stately and simple hymn tune; harmonized version of this. **2** choir.

chord¹ /kawrd/ *n.* Mus. group of (usu. three or more) notes sounded together, as a basis of harmony. □□ **chord·al** *adj.*

chord² /kawrd/ *n.* **1** Math. & Aeron., etc., straight line joining the ends of an arc, the wings of an airplane, etc. □ **strike a chord 1** recall something to a person's memory. **2** elicit sympathy. □□ **chord·al** *adj.*

chor·date /káwrdayt/ • *n.* animal possessing a notochord at some stage during its development. • *adj.* of chordates.

chore /chawr/ *n.* tedious or routine task, esp. domestic.

cho·re·o·graph /káwreeəgraf/ *v.tr.* compose the choreography for (a ballet, etc.). □□ **cho·re·og·ra·pher** /-reeógrəfər/ *n.*

cho·re·og·ra·phy /káwreeógrəfee/ *n.* design or arrangement of a ballet or other staged dance. □□ **cho·re·o·graph·ic** /-reeəgráfik/ *adj.* **cho·re·o·graph·i·cal·ly** *adv.*

cho·ris·ter /káwristər, kór-/ *n.* a member of a choir.

chor·tle /cháwrt'l/ • *v.intr.* colloq. chuckle gleefully. • *n.* gleeful chuckle.

cho·rus /káwrəs/ • *n.* (*pl.* **cho·rus·es**) **1** group (esp. a large one) of singers; choir. **2** piece of music composed for a choir. **3** refrain or main part of a popular song. **4** group of singers and dancers performing in concert in a musical comedy, opera, etc. **5** Gk Antiq. **a** in Greek tragedy, a group of performers who comment on the main action. **b** utterance of the chorus. • *v.* (of a group) speak or utter simultaneously.

chose past of CHOOSE.

cho·sen past part. of CHOOSE.

chow /chow/ *n.* **1** *sl.* food. **2** (in full **chow chow**) dog of a Chinese breed with long hair and bluish-black tongue.

chow·der /chówdər/ *n.* rich soup or stew usu. containing fish, clams, or corn with potatoes, onions, etc.

chow mein /chów máyn/ *n.* Chinese-style dish

of fried noodles with shredded meat or shrimp, etc., and vegetables.

Christ /krīst/ *n. Relig.* **1** title, also now treated as a name, given to Jesus of Nazareth. **2** Messiah as prophesied in the Old Testament. □□ **Christ′hood** *n.* **Christ′like** *adj.*

chris·ten /krísən/ *v.tr.* **1** baptize. **2** give a name to. **3** *colloq.* use for the first time. □□ **chris′ten·er** *n.* **chris′ten·ing** *n.*

Chris·ten·dom /krísəndəm/ *n.* Christians worldwide.

Chris·tian /kríśchən/ • *adj.* **1** of Christ's teachings or religion. **2** believing in or following the religion based on the teachings of Jesus Christ. **3** showing the qualities associated with Christ's teachings. **4** *colloq.* (of a person) kind; fair; decent. • *n.* adherent of Christianity. □ **Christian name** forename, esp. as given at baptism. □□ **Chris′tian·ize** *v.* **Chris·tian·i·za′tion** *n.*

Chris·ti·an·i·ty /krícheeániteе/ *n.* **1** Christian religion. **2** being a Christian. **3** = CHRISTENDOM.

Christ·mas /krísmas/ *n.* (*pl.* **Christ·mas·es**) **1** (also **Christmas Day**) annual festival of Christ's birth, celebrated on Dec. 25. **2** season in which this occurs. □ **Christmas club** savings account into which weekly deposits are made to defray the cost of Christmas gifts. □□ **Christ′mas·sy** *adj.*

chro·mat·ic /krōmátik/ *adj.* **1** of or produced by color; in (esp. bright) colors. **2** *Mus.* (of a scale) ascending or descending by semitones. □□ **chro·mat′i·cal·ly** *adv.* **chro·mat·i·cism** /-tisizəm/ *n.*

chro·ma·tin /krómatin/ *n.* material in a cell nucleus that stains with basic dyes and consists of protein, RNA, and DNA.

chrome /krōm/ *n.* **1** chromium, esp. as plating. **2** (in full **chrome yellow**) yellow pigment obtained from lead chromate. □ **chrome steel** hard, fine-grained steel containing much chromium and used for tools, etc.

chro·mi·um /krómeeəm/ *n. Chem.* hard, white metallic element used as a shiny electroplated coating. ¶ Symb.: **Cr.** □ **chromium steel** = *chrome steel.*

chro·mo·some /krómasōm/ *n. Biochem.* threadlike cellular structures that carry the genetic information in the form of genes. □□ **chro·mo·so′mal** *adj.*

chron·ic /krónik/ *adj.* **1** persisting for a long time (usu. of an illness or a personal or social problem). **2** having a chronic complaint. **3** *colloq. disp.* habitual; inveterate (*a chronic liar*). □□ **chron′i·cal·ly** *adv.* **chro·nic·i·ty** /-nísiteе/ *n.* ¶ **Chronic** is often used to mean 'habitual, inveterate,' and is used chiefly of illnesses or other problems, e.g., *More than one million people in the United States have chronic bronchitis.*

chron·i·cle /krónikəl/ • *n.* register of events in order of their occurrence. • *v.tr.* record (events) in the order of their occurrence. □□ **chron′i·cler** *n.*

chro·nol·o·gy /kranólajeе/ *n.* (*pl.* **-gies**) **1** study of historical records to establish the dates of past events. **2 a** arrangement of events, dates, etc., in the order of their occurrence. **b** table or document displaying this. □□ **chron·o·log·i·cal** /krónəlójikal/ *adj.* **chro·nol′o·gist** *n.* **chron·o·log′i·cal·ly** *adv.* **chro·nol′o·gize** *v.tr.*

chro·nom·e·ter /kranómitər/ *n.* time-measuring instrument, esp. one keeping accurate time at all temperatures. □□ **chro·nom·e·try** /kranómitreе/ *n.* **chron·o·met·ric** /krónəmétrik/ *adj.* **chron·o·met′ri·cal** *adj.* **chron·o·met′ri·cal·ly** *adv.*

chrys·a·lis /krísəlis/ *n.* (also **chrys′a·lid**) (*pl.* **chrys·a·lis·es** or **chry·sal·i·des** /krisálideez/) **1** quiescent pupa of a butterfly or moth. **2** hard outer case enclosing it.

chry·san·the·mum /krisánthəməm/ *n.* garden plant of the daisy family having brightly colored flowers.

chub·by /chúbee/ *adj.* (**chub·bi·er, chub·bi·est**) plump and rounded. □□ **chub′bi·ly** *adv.* **chub′bi·ness** *n.*

chuck[1] /chuk/ • *v.tr.* **1** *colloq.* fling or throw carelessly or with indifference. **2** *colloq.* give up; reject; abandon; jilt (*chucked my job*). **3** touch playfully, esp. under the chin. • *n.* playful touch under the chin.

chuck[2] /chuk/ • *n.* **1** cut of beef between the neck and the ribs. **2** device for holding a workpiece in a lathe or a tool in a drill. • *v.tr.* fix (wood, a tool, etc.) to a chuck.

chuck·le /chúkəl/ • *v.intr.* laugh quietly or inwardly. • *n.* quiet or suppressed laugh. □□ **chuck′ler** *n.*

chug /chug/ • *v.intr.* (**chugged, chug·ging**) **1** emit a regular muffled explosive sound, as of an engine running slowly. **2** move with this sound. • *n.* chugging sound.

chum /chum/ *n. colloq.* close friend. □□ **chum′my** *adj.* (**chum·mi·er, chum·mi·est**). **chum′mi·ly** *adv.* **chum′mi·ness** *n.*

chump /chump/ *n. colloq.* foolish person.

chunk /chungk/ *n.* **1** thick, solid slice or piece of something firm or hard. **2** substantial amount or piece.

chunk·y /chúngkeе/ *adj.* (**chunk·i·er, chunk·i·est**) **1** containing or consisting of chunks. **2** short and thick; small and sturdy. **3** (of clothes) made of a thick material. □□ **chunk′i·ness** *n.*

church /chərch/ *n.* **1** building for public (usu. Christian) worship. **2** meeting for public worship in such a building (*go to church*). **3** (**Church**) body of all Christians. **4** (**Church**) clergy or clerical profession. **5** institutionalized religion as a political or social force (*church and state*).

---

church Old English *cir(i)ce, cyr(i)ce,* related to Dutch *kerk* and German *Kirche,* based on medieval Greek *kurikon,* from Greek *kuriakon (dōma)* 'Lord's (house),' from *kurios* 'master or lord.'

---

church·go·er /chərchgōər/ *n.* person who goes to church, esp. regularly. □□ **church′go·ing** *n.* & *adj.*

church·yard /chərchyaard/ *n.* enclosed ground around a church, esp. as used for burials.

churl /chərl/ *n.* ill-bred person.

churl·ish /chərlish/ *adj.* surly; mean. □□ **churl′ish·ly** *adv.* **churl′ish·ness** *n.*

churn /chərn/ • *n.* **1** machine for making butter. • *v.* **1** *tr.* agitate (milk or cream) in a churn. **2** *tr.* produce (butter) in this way. **3** *tr.* upset; agitate. **4** *intr.* (of a liquid) seethe; foam violently (*the churning sea*). □ **churn out** produce routinely or mechanically, esp. in large quantities.

chute[1] /shoōt/ n. sloping channel or slide, for conveying things to a lower level.

chute[2] /shoōt/ n. colloq. parachute. □□ **chut'ist** n.

chut·ney /chútnee/ n. (pl. **-neys**) pungent condiment made of fruits or vegetables, vinegar, spices, sugar, etc.

chutz·pah /khoōtspə/ n. (also **chutz'pa**) sl. shameless audacity; gall.

chyme /kīm/ n. acidic, semisolid, and partly digested food produced by the action of gastric secretion. □□ **chy'mous** adj.

CIA abbr. Central Intelligence Agency.

ciao /chow/ int. colloq. 1 good-bye. 2 hello.

ci·ca·da /sikáydə, -ka'adə/ n. (pl. **ci·ca·das** or **ci·ca·dae** /-dee/) transparent-winged large insect that makes a loud, rhythmic, chirping sound.

cic·a·trix /síkətriks, sikáy-/ n. (also **cic·a·trice** /síkətris/) (pl. **cic·a·tri·ces** /-tríseez/) scar. □□ **cic·a·tri·cial** /-tríshəl/ adj.

-cide /sīd/ suffix forming nouns meaning: 1 person or substance that kills (regicide). 2 killing of (suicide).

ci·der /sídər/ n. usu. unfermented drink made from crushed apples.

ci·de·vant /se'edəvóN/ adj. & adv. that has been (with person's earlier name or status); former or formerly.

ci·gar /siga'ar/ n. tight roll of tobacco leaves for smoking.

cig·a·rette /sígərét/ n. (also **cig·a·ret'**) thin cylinder of finely cut tobacco rolled in paper for smoking. □ **cigarette butt** unsmoked remainder of a cigarette.

cil·i·um /síleeəm/ n. (pl. **cil·ia** /-leeə/) 1 minute hairlike cellular structure. 2 eyelash. □□ **cil'i·ar·y** adj. **cil·i·ate** /-ayt, -ət/ adj. **cil·i·at·ed** adj. **cil·i·a'tion** n.

cinch /sinch/ • n. 1 colloq. a sure thing; certainty. b easy task. 2 firm hold. 3 girth for a saddle or pack. • v.tr. 1 a tighten. b secure a grip on. 2 sl. make certain of.

cin·cho·na /singkónə/ n. a S. American evergreen tree or shrub. b bark of this tree, containing quinine. □□ **cin·chon·ic** /-kónik/ adj. **cin·cho·nine** /síngkəneen/ n.

cinc·ture /síngkchər/ n. literary girdle; belt.

cin·der /síndər/ n. 1 residue of coal or wood, etc., after burning. 2 slag. 3 (in pl.) ashes. □ **cinder block** concrete building block. □□ **cin'der·y** adj.

Cin·der·el·la /síndərélə/ n. person or thing of unrecognized or disregarded merit or beauty.

cin·e·ma /sínəmə/ n. 1 films collectively. 2 production of films as an art or industry; cinematography. □□ **cin·e·mat·ic** /sínəmátik/ adj. **cin·e·mat'i·cal·ly** adv.

cin·e·ma·tog·ra·phy /sínəmətógrəfee/ n. art of making motion pictures. □□ **cin·e·ma·tog'ra·pher** n. **cin·e·mat·o·graph·ic** /-mátəgráfik/ adj. **cin·e·mat·o·graph'i·cal·ly** adv.

cin·na·bar /sínəbaar/ n. 1 bright red mineral form of mercuric sulfide from which mercury is obtained. 2 vermilion.

cin·na·mon /sínəmən/ n. 1 aromatic spice from the peeled, dried, and rolled bark of a SE Asian tree. 2 this tree.

ci·pher /sífər/ n. 1 a secret or disguised way of

writing. b thing written in this way. c key to it. 2 arithmetical symbol (0; zero). 3 person or thing of no importance.

cir. abbr. (also **circ.**) 1 circle. 2 circuit. 3 circular. 4 circulation. 5 circumference.

cir·ca /sórkə/ prep. (preceding a date) about.

cir·ca·di·an /sərkáydeeən/ adj. Physiol. occurring or recurring about once per day.

cir·cle /sórkəl/ • n. 1 a round plane figure whose circumference is everywhere equidistant from its center. b line enclosing a circle. 2 roundish enclosure or structure. 3 persons grouped around a center of interest. 4 set or class or restricted group (literary circles). • v. 1 intr. move in a circle. 2 tr. a revolve around. b form a circle around. □□ **cir'cler** n.

cir·clet /sórklit/ n. 1 small circle. 2 circular band, esp. of gold or jeweled, etc., as an ornament.

cir·cuit /sórkit/ n. 1 line or course enclosing an area; circumference. 2 Electr. a path of a current. b apparatus through which a current passes. 3 journey of a judge or preacher for work in a particular district. □ **circuit breaker** automatic device for stopping the flow of current in an electrical circuit.

cir·cu·i·tous /sərkyoō-itəs/ adj. 1 indirect. 2 going a long way around. □□ **cir·cu'i·tous·ly** adv. **cir·cu'i·tous·ness** n.

cir·cuit·ry /sórkitree/ n. (pl. **-ries**) 1 system of electric circuits. 2 equipment forming this.

cir·cu·lar /sórkyələr/ • adj. 1 a having the form of a circle. b moving or taking place along a circle; indirect; circuitous (circular route). 2 Logic (of reasoning) depending on a vicious circle. • n. letter, leaflet, etc., distributed to a large number of people. □□ **cir·cu·lar·i·ty** /-láritee/ n. **cir'cu·lar·ly** adv.

cir·cu·lar·ize /sórkyələrīz/ v.tr. distribute circulars to. □□ **cir·cu·lar·i·za'tion** n.

cir·cu·late /sórkyəlayt/ v. 1 intr. be in circulation. 2 tr. cause to go around; put into circulation. 3 intr. be actively sociable at a party, gathering, etc. □□ **cir'cu·la·tive** adj. **cir'cu·la·tor** n.

cir·cu·la·tion /sórkyəláyshən/ n. 1 movement within or around, esp. of blood from and to the heart. 2 a transmission or distribution (of news; etc.). b number of copies sold, esp. of journals and newspapers. □ **in** (or **out of**) **circulation** participating (or not participating) in activities, etc.

cir·cu·la·to·ry /sórkyələtawree/ adj. of or relating to the circulation of blood or sap.

circum- /sórkəm/ comb. form round; about; around.

circum. abbr. circumference.

cir·cum·cise /sórkəmsīz/ v.tr. cut off the foreskin or clitoris. □□ **cir·cum·ci·sion** /sórkəmsízhən/ n.

cir·cum·fer·ence /sərkúmfərəns/ n. 1 enclosing boundary, esp. of a circle. 2 distance around. □□ **cir·cum·fer·en·tial** /-fərénshəl/ adj. **cir·cum·fer·en'tial·ly** adv.

cir·cum·flex /sórkəmfleks/ n. mark (ˆ) placed over a vowel in some languages to indicate a contraction or a special quality.

cir·cum·ja·cent /sórkəmjáysənt/ adj. situated around.

cir·cum·lo·cu·tion /sórkəmlōkyoōshən/ n. roundabout expression; evasive talk. □□ **cir·cum·lo·cu'tion·al** adj. **cir·cum·lo·cu'tion·a·ry** adj.

cir·cum·io·cu′tion·ist *n.* **cir·cum·loc·u·to·ry** /-lók-yɔtáwree/ *adj.*

cir·cum·nav·i·gate /sɔ́rkɔmnávigayt/ *v.tr.* sail around (esp. the world). □□ **cir·cum·nav·i·ga·tion** /-gáyshɔn/ *n.* **cir·cum·nav′i·ga·tor** *n.*

cir·cum·scribe /sɔ́rkɔmskrīb/ *v.tr.* **1** enclose or outline. **2** lay down the limits of; confine. □□ **cir·cum·scrib′a·ble** *adj.* **cir′cum·scrib·er** *n.* **cir·cum·scrip·tion** /-skrípshɔn/ *n.*

cir·cum·spect /sɔ́rkɔmspekt/ *adj.* wary; cautious. □□ **cir·cum·spec·tion** /-spékshɔn/ *n.* **cir′cum·spect·ly** *adv.*

cir·cum·stance /sɔ́rkɔmstans/ *n.* **1 a** fact, occurrence, or condition, esp. (in *pl.*) the time, place, occasion, etc., or surroundings of an act or event. **b** (in *pl.*) external conditions. **2** (in *pl.*) one's state of financial or material welfare. **3** ceremony; fuss (*pomp and circumstance*). □ **in** (or **under**) **the** (or **these**) **circumstances** the state of affairs being what it is. **in** (or **under**) **no circumstances** not at all; never. □□ **cir′cum·stanced** *adj.*

cir·cum·stan·tial /sɔ́rkɔmstánshɔl/ *adj.* **1** given in full detail. **2 a** depending on circumstances. **b** adventitious. □□ **cir·cum·stan·ti·al·i·ty** /-sheeálitee/ *n.* **cir·cum·stan′tial·ly** *adv.*

cir·cum·vent /sɔ́rkɔmvént/ *v.tr.* evade (a difficulty); find a way around. □□ **cir·cum·ven·tion** /-vénshɔn/ *n.*

cir·cus /sɔ́rkɔs/ *n.* (*pl.* **cir·cus·es**) **1** traveling show of performing animals, acrobats, clowns, etc. **2** *colloq.* scene of lively action; a disturbance.

cir·rho·sis /sirōsis/ *n.* chronic disease of the liver, a result of alcoholism, hepatitis, etc. □□ **cir·rhot·ic** /sirótik/ *adj.*

cir·rus /síros/ *n.* (*pl.* **cir·ri** /-rī/) *Meteorol.* white wispy cloud, esp. at high altitude. □□ **cir′rose** *adj.* **cir′rous** *adj.*

cis·tern /sístɔrn/ *n.* **1** tank or container for storing water, etc. **2** underground reservoir for rainwater.

cit. *abbr.* **1** citation. **2** cited. **3** citizen.

cit·a·del /sítɔd'l, -del/ *n.* fortress, usu. on high ground protecting or dominating a city.

ci·ta·tion /sītáyshɔn/ *n.* **1** citing of a book or other source; passage cited. **2** mention in an official dispatch. **3** note accompanying an award, describing the reasons for it.

cite /sīt/ *v.tr.* **1** adduce as an instance. **2** quote (a passage, etc.) in support. **3** mention in an official dispatch. **4** summon to appear in a court of law. □□ **cit′a·ble** *adj.*

cit·i·zen /sítizɔn/ *n.* member of a country, state, city, etc. □ **citizen's arrest** arrest by an ordinary person without a warrant. □□ **cit′i·zen·ry** *n.* **cit′i·zen·ship** *n.*

cit·ric /sítrik/ *adj.* derived from citrus fruit. □ **citric acid** sharp-tasting acid found in citrus. □□ **cit′rate** *n.*

cit·ron /sítrɔn/ *n.* **1** shrubby tree bearing large lemonlike fruits with thick fragrant peel. **2** this fruit.

cit·ro·nel·la /sítrɔnélɔ/ *n.* scented oil used in insect repellent, perfume, and soap manufacture.

cit·rus /sítrɔs/ *n.* **1** tree of a group including citron, lemon, lime, orange, and grapefruit. **2** (in full **citrus fruit**) fruit from such a tree. □□ **cit′rous** *adj.*

cit·y /sítee/ *n.* (*pl.* **-ies**) **1** large town. **2** *US* state-chartered municipal corporation occupying a

definite area. □ **city hall** municipal offices or officers. **city slicker** usu. *derog.* **1** smart and sophisticated city dweller. **2** plausible rogue as found in cities. □□ **cit′y·ward** *adj. & adv.* **cit′y·wards** *adv.*

city Middle English: from Old French *cite*, from Latin *civitas*, from *civis* 'citizen.' Originally denoting a town, and often used as a Latin equivalent to Old English *burh* 'borough,' the term was later applied to foreign and ancient cities and to the more important English boroughs. The connection between city and cathedral grew up under the Norman kings, as the episcopal sees (many of which had been established in villages) were removed to the chief borough of the diocese.

cit·y·scape /síteeskayp/ *n.* **1** view of a city (actual or depicted). **2** city scenery.

civ·et /sívit/ *n.* **1** (in full **civet cat**) catlike animal of Central Africa. **2** strong musky perfume obtained from it.

civ·ic /sívik/ *adj.* **1** of a city; municipal. **2** of or proper to citizens (*civic virtues*). □□ **civ′i·cal·ly** *adv.*

civ·ics /síviks/ *n.pl.* (usu. treated as *sing.*) the study of the rights and duties of citizenship.

civ·il /sívɔl/ *adj.* **1** of or belonging to citizens. **2** of ordinary citizens and their concerns, as distinct from military or ecclesiastical matters. **3** polite; obliging; not rude. **4** *Law* concerning private rights and not criminal offenses. □ **civil disobedience** refusal to comply with certain laws or to pay taxes, etc., as a peaceful form of political protest. **civil engineer** engineer who designs or maintains roads, bridges, dams, etc. **civil liberty** freedom of action and speech subject to the law. **civil rights** rights of citizens to political and social freedom and equality. **civil servant** member of the civil service. **civil service** nonelected civilian branches of governmental administration. **civil war** war between citizens of the same country. □□ **civ′il·ly** *adv.*

ci·vil·ian /sivílyɔn/ • *n.* person not in the armed services or the police force. • *adj.* of or for civilians.

ci·vil·i·ty /sivílitee/ *n.* (*pl.* **-ties**) **1** politeness. **2** act of politeness.

civ·i·li·za·tion /sívilɔzáyshɔn/ *n.* **1** advanced stage or system of social development. **2** those peoples of the world regarded as having this. **3** a people or nation (esp. of the past) regarded as an element of social evolution.

civ·i·lize /sívilīz/ *v.tr.* **1** bring out of a less developed stage of society. **2** refine and educate. □□ **civ′i·liz·a·ble** *adj.* **civ′i·liz·er** *n.*

civ·vies /síveez/ *n.pl. sl.* civilian clothes.

Cl *symb. Chem.* chlorine.

cl *abbr.* **1** centiliter(s). **2** class.

clack /klak/ • *v.intr.* make a sharp sound as of boards struck together. • *n.* clacking sound or talk. □□ **clack′er** *n.*

clad /klad/ *adj.* **1** clothed. **2** provided with cladding.

clad·ding /kláding/ *n.* covering or coating.

claim /klaym/ • *v.tr.* **1** demand as one's due or property. **2 a** represent oneself as having or achieving (*claim victory*). **b** assert; contend (*claim that one knows*). **3** have as an achievement or a consequence (*the fire claimed many victims*). **4** (of a thing) deserve (one's attention, etc.). • *n.* **1** demand or request for something considered one's due (*lay claim to*). **2** right or title. **3** contention or assertion. **4** thing claimed. □□ **claim′a·ble** *adj.* **claim′ant** *n.* **claim′er** *n.*

clair·voy·ance /klairvóyəns/ *n.* supposed faculty of perceiving things or events in the future or beyond normal sensory contact. □□ **clair·voy′ant** *n.* & *adj.* **clair·voy′ant·ly** *adv.*

clam /klam/ • *n.* edible bivalve mollusk. • *v.intr.* (**clammed, clam·ming**) **1** dig for clams. **2** (foll. by *up*) *colloq.* refuse to talk.

clam·bake /klámbayk/ *n.* picnic at the seashore typically featuring steamed clams, lobsters, and ears of corn.

clam·ber /klámbər/ • *v.intr.* climb with hands and feet, esp. with difficulty or laboriously. • *n.* difficult climb.

clam·my /klámee/ *adj.* (**clam·mi·er, clam·mi·est**) unpleasantly damp and sticky. □□ **clam′mi·ly** *adv.* **clam′mi·ness** *n.*

clam·or /klámər/ • *n.* **1** loud or vehement shouting or noise. **2** protest; demand. • *v. intr.* make a clamor. □□ **clam′or·ous** *adj.* **clam′or·ous·ly** *adv.* **clam′or·ous·ness** *n.*

clamp /klamp/ • *n.* device, esp. a brace or band of iron, etc., for strengthening other materials or holding things together. • *v.tr.* **1** strengthen or fasten with a clamp. **2** place or hold firmly. □ **clamp down 1** be rigid in enforcing a rule, etc. **2** (foll. by *on*) suppress.

CLAMP

clan /klan/ *n.* **1** group of people with a common ancestor. **2** group with a strong common interest. □□ **clan′nish** *adj.* **clan′nish·ly** *adv.* **clan′nish·ness** *n.*

clan·des·tine /klandéstin/ *adj.* surreptitious; secret. □□ **clan·des′tine·ly** *adv.*

clang /klang/ • *n.* loud, resonant, metallic sound. • *v.* **1** *intr.* make a clang. **2** *tr.* cause to clang.

clan·gor /klánggər/ *n.* **1** prolonged or repeated clanging noise. **2** uproar or commotion. □□ **clan′gor·ous** *adj.* **clan′gor·ous·ly** *adv.*

clank /klangk/ • *n.* sound as of heavy pieces of metal knocking together or a chain rattling. • *v.* **1** *intr.* make a clanking sound. **2** *tr.* cause to clank. □□ **clank′ing·ly** *adv.*

clap /klap/ • *v.* (**clapped, clap·ping**) **1** *intr.* strike the palms of one's hands together as a signal or repeatedly as applause. **2** *tr.* strike (the hands) together in this way. • *n.* **1** act of clapping, esp. as applause. **2** explosive sound, esp. of thunder. **3** slap; pat.

clap·per /klápər/ *n.* tongue or striker of a bell.

clap·trap /kláptrap/ *n.* insincere or pretentious talk.

claque /klak/ *n.* hired applauders.

clar·et /klárət/ *n.* **1** red wine, esp. from Bordeaux. **2** deep purplish-red.

clar·i·fy /klárifī/ *v.* (**-fies, -fied**) make or become clearer. □□ **clar·i·fi·ca′tion** *n.* **clar′i·fi·er** *n.*

clar·i·net /klárinét/ *n.* woodwind instrument with a single-reed mouthpiece. □□ **clar·i·net′ist** *n.* (also **clar·i·net′tist**).

clar·i·on /kláreeən/ *n.* clear, rousing sound.

clar·i·ty /kláritee/ *n.* state or quality of being clear, esp. of sound or expression.

clash /klash/ • *n.* **1** loud, jarring sound as of metal objects being struck together. **2 a** conflict. **b** discord of colors, etc. • *v.* **1 a** *intr.* make a clashing sound. **b** *tr.* cause to clash. **2** *intr.* collide; coincide awkwardly. **3** *intr.* come into conflict or be discordant. □□ **clash′er** *n.*

clasp /klasp/ • *n.* **1** device with interlocking parts for fastening. **2 a** embrace. **b** grasp or handshake. • *v.tr.* **1** fasten with or as with a clasp. **2 a** grasp; hold closely. **b** embrace. □□ **clasp′er** *n.*

class /klas/ • *n.* **1** any set of persons or things grouped together, or graded or differentiated from others. **2** division or order of society. **3** *colloq.* distinction; high quality. **4 a** group of students taught together. **b** occasion when they meet. **c** their course of instruction. **5** *Biol.* grouping of organisms, below a division or phylum. • *v.tr.* assign to a class or category. □ **class-conscious** aware of one's place in a system of social class. **class-consciousness** this awareness.

clas·sic /klásik/ • *adj.* **1 a** of the first class; of acknowledged excellence. **b** remarkably typical; outstandingly important (*a classic case*). **c** having enduring worth; timeless. **2 a** of ancient Greek and Latin literature, or culture. **b** (of style in art, music, etc.) simple, harmonious, well-proportioned. • *n.* **1** classic writer, artist, work, or example. **2 a** ancient Greek or Latin writer. **b** (in *pl.*) the study of ancient Greek and Latin literature and history. **3** follower of classic models. ¶ Traditionally, **classic** means 'typical; excellent as an example; timeless' and **classical** means 'of (esp. Greek or Roman) antiquity.' Thus: *John Ford directed many classic Westerns. The museum was built in the classical style.* Great art is considered *classic*, not *classical*, unless it is created in the forms of antiquity. *Classical music* is formal and sophisticated music adhering to certain stylistic principles, esp. those of the late 18th century, but a *classic folk song* is one that well expresses its culture. A *classical education* exposes a student to *classical* literature, disciplines, and languages (especially Latin and Greek), but the study of Greek and Latin languages and their literature is also referred to as *classics*, as in *he majored in classics at college.*

class·i·cal /klásikəl/ *adj.* **1 a** of ancient Greek or Latin literature or art. **b** (of language) having the form used by the ancient standard authors. **2** (of music) serious or conventional; following traditional principles. **3** restrained in style.

□□ **clas′si·cal·ism** n. **clas′si·cal·ist** n. **clas′si·cal·ly** adv.

clas·si·cism /klásisizəm/ n. 1 the following of a classic style. 2 classical scholarship. □□ **clas′si·cist** n.

clas·si·fy /klásifī/ v.tr. (-fies, -fied) 1 a arrange in classes or categories. b assign (a thing) to a class or category. 2 designate as officially secret. □□ **clas·si·fi′able** adj. **clas·si·fi·ca′tion** n. **clas·si·fi·ca·to·ry** /klásifikətáwree, kləsifi-, klásifikáytəree/ adj. **clas′si·fied** adj. **clas′si·fi·er** n.

class·less /kláslis/ adj. making or showing no distinction of classes (classless society). □□ **class′less·ness** n.

class·mate /klásmayt/ n. person in the same class at school.

class·room /klásroom, -room/ n. room in which a class of students is taught.

class·y /klásee/ adj. (class·i·er, class·i·est) colloq. superior; stylish. □□ **class′i·ly** adv. **class′i·ness** n.

clat·ter /klátər/ n. 1 rattling sound as of many hard objects struck together.

clause /klawz/ n. 1 Gram. distinct part of a sentence, including a subject and predicate. 2 single statement in a treaty, law, bill, or contract. □□ **claus′al** adj.

claus·tro·pho·bi·a /kláwstrəfóbeeə/ n. abnormal fear of confined places. □□ **claus·tro·phobe** /-rəfōb/ n. **claus·tro·pho′bic** adj.

clav·i·chord /klávikawrd/ n. small keyboard instrument with a very soft tone.

clav·i·cle /klávikəl/ n. collarbone. □□ **cla·vic·u·lar** /kləvíkyələr/ adj.

claw /klaw/ • n. 1 a pointed horny nail on an animal's foot. b foot armed with claws. 2 pincers of a shellfish. • v. scratch, maul, or pull with claws or fingernails. □□ **clawed** adj. (also in comb.). **claw′er** n. **claw′less** adj.

clay /klay/ n. 1 stiff, sticky earth, used for making bricks, pottery, ceramics, etc. 2 poet. substance of the human body. □□ **clay′ey** adj. **clay′ish** adj. **clay′like** adj.

clean /kleen/ • adj. 1 free from dirt or contaminating matter; unsoiled. 2 clear; unused or unpolluted; pristine. 3 free from obscenity or indecency. 4 attentive to personal hygiene. 5 complete; clear-cut. 6 streamlined; well-formed. 7 free from any record of a crime, offense, etc. • adv. 1 completely; outright; simply (clean forgot). 2 in a clean manner. • v. make or become clean. □ **clean-cut** 1 sharply outlined. 2 neatly groomed. **clean out** 1 clean or clear thoroughly. 2 sl. empty or deprive (esp. of money). **clean up** 1 a clear (a mess) away. b make (things) neat. c make (oneself) clean. 2 restore order or morality to. 3 sl. acquire as or make a profit. **come clean** colloq. confess everything. □□ **clean′a·ble** adj. **clean′ish** adj. **clean′ness** n.

clean·er /kleénər/ n. 1 person employed to clean the interior of a building. 2 (usu. in pl.) commercial establishment for cleaning clothes. 3 device or substance for cleaning. □ **take to the cleaners** sl. defraud or rob.

clean·ly[1] /kleénlee/ adv. 1 in a clean way. 2 efficiently; without difficulty.

clean·ly[2] /klénlee/ adj. (clean·li·er, clean·li·est) habitually clean; with clean habits. □□ **clean′li·ness** n.

cleanse /klenz/ v.tr. make clean or pure. □□ **cleans′er** /klénzər/ n.

clear /kleer/ • adj. 1 free from dirt or contamination. 2 (of weather, the sky, etc.) not dull or cloudy. 3 transparent. 4 a distinct; easily perceived by the senses. b easily understood (make oneself clear). 5 that discerns or is able to discern readily and accurately (clear-sighted). 6 confident; convinced. 7 free from guilt. 8 without deduction (a clear $1,000). 9 free; unhampered. • adv. 1 clearly. 2 completely (he got clear away). 3 apart; out of contact (keep clear). • v. 1 tr. & intr. make or become clear. 2 tr. free from prohibition or difficulty. 3 tr. free from suspicion or declare (a person) to be innocent. 4 tr. approve (a person) for access to information, etc. 5 tr. pass over or by safely or without touching. 6 tr. make (an amount of money) as a net gain. 7 tr. pass through (a customs office, etc.). □ **clear the air** disperse suspicion, tension, etc. **clear-cut** 1 sharply defined. 2 obvious. **clear out** 1 empty. 2 remove. 3 colloq. go away. **in the clear** free from suspicion or difficulty. □□ **clear′a·ble** adj. **clear′er** n. **clear′ly** adv. **clear′ness** n.

clear·ance /kleérəns/ n. 1 removal of obstructions, etc. 2 clear space allowed for the passing of two objects or two parts in machinery, etc. 3 special authorization or permission. □ **clearance sale** sale to get rid of superfluous stock.

clear·ing /kleéring/ n. area in a forest cleared for cultivation.

clear·ing·house /kleéringhows/ n. 1 bankers' establishment where checks and bills are exchanged and resolved. 2 agency for collecting and distributing information, etc.

cleat /kleet/ n. 1 fixed piece of metal, wood, etc., for fastening ropes to, or to strengthen woodwork, etc. 2 projecting piece to give footing or prevent slipping.

cleav·age /kleévij/ n. 1 hollow between a woman's breasts. 2 division; splitting.

cleave[1] /kleev/ v. (past cleaved or cleft /kleft/ or clove /klōv/; past part. cleaved or cleft or clo·ven /klōvən/) literary 1 tr. chop or break apart; split, esp. along the grain. 2 intr. come apart in this way. □□ **cleav′a·ble** adj.

cleave[2] /kleev/ v.intr. (past cleaved or clove /klōv/ or clave /klayv/) (foll. by to) literary stick fast; adhere.

cleav·er /kleévər/ n. heavy tool for cutting or chopping.

clef /klef/ n. Mus. symbol placed at the beginning of a staff, indicating the pitch of the notes written on it.

cleft[1] /kleft/ adj. split; partly divided. □ **cleft lip** (or **palate**) congenital split in the lip or the roof of the mouth.

cleft[2] /kleft/ n. split; fissure.

cle·ma·tis /klémətis, kləmátis/ n. erect or climbing plant bearing white, pink, or purple flowers and feathery seeds.

clem·ent /klémənt/ adj. 1 mild (clement weather). 2 merciful. □□ **clem·en·cy** /-mənsee/ n.

clem·en·tine /kléməntīn, -teen/ n. small citrus fruit, similar to a tangerine.

clench /klench/ • v.tr. 1 close (teeth or fingers) tightly. 2 grasp firmly. • n. 1 clenching action. 2 clenched state.

clere·sto·ry /kleérstawree/ n. (also **clear′sto·ry**) (pl. **-ries**) upper row of windows in a cathedral or large church.

cler·gy /klɔ́rjee/ *n.* (*pl.* **-gies**) (usu. treated as *pl.*) (usu. prec. by *the*) the body of all persons ordained for religious duties.

cler·gy·man /klɔ́rjeemən/ *n.* (*pl.* **-men**; *fem.* **cler·gy·wom·an**, *pl.* **-wom·en**) member of the clergy.

cler·ic /klérik/ *n.* member of the clergy.

cler·i·cal /klérikəl/ *adj.* **1** of the clergy or clergymen. **2** of or done by a clerk or clerks. □□ **cler′i·cal·ism** *n.* **cler′i·cal·ist** *n.* **cler′i·cal·ly** *adv.*

clerk /klɔrk/ • *n.* **1** person employed to keep records, accounts, etc. **2** secretary, agent, or record keeper of a municipality, court, etc. • *v.intr.* work as a clerk. □□ **clerk′ish** *adj.* **clerk′ly** *adj.* **clerk′ship** *n.*

clev·er /klévər/ *adj.* (**clev·er·er**, **clev·er·est**) skillful; talented; quick; adroit; ingenious; cunning. □□ **clev′er·ly** *adv.* **clev′er·ness** *n.*

---

clever Middle English (in the sense 'quick to catch hold,' only recorded in this period): perhaps of Dutch or Low German origin, and related to CLEAVE². In the late 16th century the term came to mean (probably through dialect use) 'manually skilfull'; the sense 'possessing mental agility' dates from the early 18th century.

---

cli·ché /kleesháy/ *n.* (also **cli·che′**) hackneyed phrase or opinion. □□ **cli·chéd′** *adj.*

click /klik/ • *n.* slight, sharp sound. • *v.* **1** *intr.* make a click. **2** *tr.* cause (one's tongue, heels, etc.) to click. **3** *intr. Computing* press (one of the buttons on a mouse). □□ **click′er** *n.*

cli·ent /klîənt/ *n.* **1** person using the services of a lawyer, architect, social worker, or other professional person. **2** customer. **3** *Computing* desktop computer in a network, capable of obtaining data and applications from a server.

cli·en·tele /klîəntél, kleéon-/ *n.* **1** clients collectively. **2** customers. **3** patrons of a theater, etc.

cliff /klif/ *n.* steep rock face, as at the edge of the sea. □ **cliff-hanger** very suspenseful story, ending, etc. □□ **cliff′like** *adj.*

cli·mac·ter·ic /klīmáktərik, klīmaktérik/ *n.* supposed critical period in life, as menopause.

cli·mate /klîmit/ *n.* **1** prevailing weather conditions. **2** region with particular weather conditions. **3** prevailing opinion or public feeling. □□ **cli·mat·ic** /-mátik/ *adj.* **cli·mat′i·cal** *adj.* **cli·mat′i·cal·ly** *adv.*

cli·max /klîmaks/ *n.* **1** event or point of greatest intensity or interest; culmination or apex. **2** sexual orgasm. □□ **cli·mac·tic** /-máktik/ *adj.*

climb /klīm/ • *v.* **1** *tr. & intr.* ascend, mount, go or come up. **2** *intr.* (of a plant) grow up a wall, tree, trellis, etc., by clinging or twining. **3** *intr.* make progress from one's own efforts. • *n.* **1** ascent by climbing. **2** place, esp. a hill, climbed or to be climbed. □□ **climb′a·ble** *adj.* **climb′er** *n.*

clime /klīm/ *n. literary* **1** region. **2** climate.

clinch /klinch/ • *v.* **1** *tr.* confirm or settle (an argument, bargain, etc.) conclusively. **2** *intr.* embrace. **3** *tr.* secure (a nail or rivet) by driving the point sideways when through. • *n.* **1** clinching action or state. **2** *colloq.* embrace.

clinch·er /klînchər/ *n. colloq.* remark or argument that settles a matter conclusively.

cling /kling/ *v.intr.* (*past* and *past part.* **clung** /klung/) **1** adhere, stick, or hold on. **2** remain persistently or stubbornly faithful (to a friend, habit, idea, etc.). **3** maintain one's grasp; keep hold; resist separation. □□ **cling′er** *n.* **cling′y** *adj.* (**cling·i·er**, **cling·i·est**) **cling′ing·ly** *adv.* **cling′i·ness** *n.*

clin·ic /klinik/ *n.* **1** private or specialized hospital. **2** place or occasion for giving specialist medical treatment or advice. **3** instructional session. □□ **cli·ni·cian** /kliníshən/ *n.*

clin·i·cal /klínikəl/ *adj.* **1** *Med.* of or for the treatment of patients. **2** dispassionate; detached. □□ **clin′i·cal·ly** *adv.*

clink¹ /klingk/ • *n.* sharp ringing sound. • *v.* **1** *intr.* make a clink. **2** *tr.* cause (glasses, etc.) to clink.

clink² /klingk/ *n. sl.* prison (*in the clink*).

clink·er¹ /klíngkər/ *n.* **1** mass of slag or lava. **2** stony residue from burned coal.

clink·er² /klíngkər/ *n. sl.* mistake or blunder.

clip¹ /klip/ • *n.* **1** device for holding things together or for attachment. **2** piece of jewelry fastened by a clip. **3** set of attached cartridges for a firearm. • *v.tr.* (**clipped**, **clip·ping**) fix with a clip.

clip² /klip/ • *v.tr.* (**clipped**, **clip·ping**) **1** cut with shears or scissors, esp. cut short or trim (hair, wool, etc.). **2** trim or remove the hair or wool of. **3** *colloq.* hit smartly. **4** cut short or omit. **5** cut (an extract) from a newspaper, etc. **6** *sl.* swindle; rob. • *n.* **1** act of clipping. **2** *colloq.* smart blow. **3** short sequence from a motion picture. **4** *colloq.* speed, esp. rapid. □ **clip joint** *sl.* club, etc., charging exorbitant prices. □□ **clip′pa·ble** *adj.*

clip·board /klípbawrd/ *n.* small board with a spring clip for holding papers, etc.

clip·per /klípər/ *n.* **1** instrument for clipping hair, hedges, etc. **2** fast sailing ship.

clip·ping /klíping/ *n.* piece clipped or cut from something, esp. from a newspaper.

clique /kleek/ *n.* small exclusive group of people. □□ **cli′quey** *adj.* (**cliqu·i·er**, **cliqu·i·est**). **cli′quish** *adj.* **cli′quish·ness** *n.* **cli′quism** *n.*

cli·to·ris /klítəris, klī́-/ *n.* small erectile part of the female genitals at the upper end of the vulva. □□ **cli′to·ral** *adj.*

cloak /klōk/ • *n.* **1** outdoor overgarment, usu. sleeveless. **2** covering (*cloak of snow*). • *v.tr.* **1** cover with a cloak. **2** conceal; disguise.

clob·ber /klóbər/ *v.tr. sl.* **1** hit; beat up. **2** defeat.

cloche /klōsh/ *n.* (in full **cloche hat**) woman's close-fitting, bell-shaped hat.

CLOCHE

clock /klok/ • n. 1 instrument for measuring and showing time. 2 any measuring device resembling a clock. • v.tr. 1 colloq. attain or register (a stated time, distance, or speed, esp. in a race). 2 time (a race) with a stopwatch.

clock·wise /klókwīz/ adj. & adv. in a curve corresponding in direction to the movement of the hands of a clock.

clock·work /klókwərk/ n. mechanism of or like that of a clock. □ **like clockwork** smoothly; regularly; automatically.

clod /klod/ n. 1 lump of earth, clay, etc. 2 sl. silly or foolish person.

clod·hop·per /klódhopər/ n. (usu. pl.) colloq. large heavy shoe.

clog /klawg, klog/ • n. shoe with a thick wooden sole. • v. (**clogged, clog·ging**) 1 tr. obstruct; choke. 2 intr. become obstructed; choke.

clois·ter /klóystər/ • n. 1 covered walk, often open to a courtyard on one side. 2 monastic life or seclusion. 3 convent or monastery. • v.tr. seclude. □□ **clois′tered** adj. **clois′tral** adj.

clomp var. of CLUMP v. 2.

clone /klōn/ • n. 1 a group of organisms produced asexually from one stock or ancestor. b one such organism. 2 person or thing regarded as identical with another. • v.tr. propagate as a clone. □□ **clon′al** adj.

clonk /klongk, klawngk/ • n. abrupt heavy sound of impact. • v. 1 intr. make such a sound. 2 tr. colloq. hit.

close¹ /klōs/ • adj. 1 situated at only a short distance or interval. 2 a having a strong or immediate relation or connection (close friend). b in intimate association (were very close). c corresponding almost exactly (close resemblance). 3 in or almost in contact (close combat). 4 dense; compact. 5 in which competitors are almost equal (close contest). 6 rigorous (close reasoning). 7 concentrated; searching (close attention). 8 (of air, etc.) stuffy or humid. • adv. at only a short distance or interval (they live close to us). □ **close-knit** tightly bound or interlocked; closely united in friendship. **close shave** colloq. narrow escape. **close-up** 1 photograph, etc., taken at close range. 2 intimate description. □□ **close′ly** adv. **close′ness** n.

close² /klōz/ • v. 1 a tr. shut. b intr. become shut. c tr. block up. 2 tr. & intr. bring or come to an end. 3 intr. end the day's business. 4 tr. & intr. bring or come closer or into contact. • n. conclusion; end. □ **close down** discontinue business. **close in 1** enclose. 2 come nearer. **close up 1** move closer. 2 shut, esp. temporarily. 3 block up. 4 (of an aperture) grow smaller. □□ **clos′a·ble** adj. **clos′er** n.

closed /klōzd/ adj. 1 not giving access; shut. 2 (of a store, etc.) having ceased business. 3 not communicating with others. □ **closed-circuit** (of television) transmitted to a restricted set of receivers.

clos·et /klózit/ • n. 1 small room. 2 storage area. 3 adj. secret; covert (closet drinker). • v.tr. (**clos·et·ed, clos·et·ing**) shut away.

clo·sure /klózhər/ • n. 1 act or process of closing. 2 closed condition.

clot /klot/ • n. thick mass of coagulated liquid, esp. of blood. • v. (**clot·ted, clot·ting**) form into clots.

cloth /klawth, kloth/ n. (pl. **cloths** /kloths,

klothz/) 1 woven or felted material. 2 piece of this. 3 piece of this for a particular purpose. 4 (prec. by the) the clergy.

clothe /klōth/ v.tr. (past and past part. **clothed** or formal **clad**) 1 provide with clothes. 2 cover as with clothes.

clothes /klōz, klōthz/ n.pl. garments worn to cover the body and limbs.

cloth·ier /klótheeər/ n. seller of clothes.

cloth·ing /klóthing/ n. clothes collectively.

clo·ture /klóchər/ • n. legislative procedure for ending debate and taking a vote. • v.tr. apply cloture.

cloud /klowd/ • n. 1 visible mass of condensed watery vapor floating above the ground. 2 mass of smoke or dust. 3 great number of insects, birds, etc. 4 state of gloom, trouble, or suspicion. • v. 1 tr. cover or darken with clouds or gloom or trouble. 2 intr. become overcast or gloomy. □ **on cloud nine** colloq. extremely happy. **under a cloud** out of favor, under suspicion. **with one's head in the clouds** daydreaming; unrealistic. □□ **cloud′less** adj. **cloud′less·ly** adv. **cloud′let** n.

cloud·burst /klówdbərst/ n. sudden violent rainstorm.

cloud·y /klówdee/ adj. (**cloud·i·er, cloud·i·est**) 1 (of the sky or weather) covered with clouds; overcast. 2 not transparent; unclear. □□ **cloud′i·ly** adv. **cloud′i·ness** n.

clout /klowt/ • n. 1 heavy blow. 2 colloq. influence; power. • v.tr. hit hard.

clove¹ /klōv/ n. dried flower bud of a tropical plant used as a pungent aromatic spice.

clove² /klōv/ n. any of the small bulbs making up a compound bulb of garlic, shallot, etc.

clove³ past of CLEAVE¹.

clo·ven /klóv'n/ adj. split; partly divided. □□ **clo·ven-foot·ed** /-fŏŏtid/ adj. **clo·ven-hoofed** /-hŏŏft/ adj.

clo·ver /klóvər/ n. fodder plant. □ **in clover** in ease and luxury.

clown /klown/ • n. 1 comic entertainer, esp. in a pantomime or circus. 2 silly, foolish, or playful person. • v. intr. behave like a clown. □□ **clown′er·y** n. **clown′ish** adj. **clown′ish·ly** adv. **clown′ish·ness** n.

cloy /kloy/ v.tr. (usu. foll. by with) satiate or sicken with an excess of sweetness, richness, etc. □□ **cloy′ing·ly** adv.

club /klub/ • n. 1 heavy stick with a thick end, used as a weapon, etc. 2 headed stick used in golf. 3 a playing card of a suit denoted by a black trefoil. b (in pl.) this suit. 4 association of persons meeting periodically. 5 members' organization or premises. 6 organization offering subscribers certain benefits (book club). • v.tr. (**clubbed, club·bing**) beat with or as with a club. □ **club sandwich** sandwich with two layers of filling between three slices of toast or bread. **club soda** = SODA n. 2. □□ **club′ber** n.

club·foot /klúbfŏŏt/ n. congenitally deformed foot. □□ **club′foot·ed** adj.

club·house /klúbhows/ n. premises used by a club.

cluck /kluk/ • n. guttural cry like that of a hen. • v.intr. emit a cluck or clucks.

clue /klŏŏ/ • n. 1 fact or idea that serves as a

guide, or suggests a line of inquiry, in a problem or investigation. **2** piece of evidence. **3** verbal hint in a crossword. • *v.tr.* (**clues, clued, clue·ing** or **clu·ing**) provide a clue to.

clue·less /klōˊolis/ *adj. colloq.* ignorant; stupid. □□ **clue′less·ly** *adv.* **clue′less·ness** *n.*

clump /klump/ • *n.* cluster or mass. • *v.* **1 a** *intr.* form a clump. **b** *tr.* heap or plant together. **2** *intr.* (also **clomp** /klomp/) walk with heavy tread. □□ **clump′y** *adj.* (**clump·i·er, clump·i·est**).

clum·sy /klúmzee/ *adj.* (**clum·si·er, clum·si·est**) **1** awkward in movement or shape; ungainly. **2** difficult to handle or use. **3** tactless. □□ **clum′si·ly** *adv.* **clum′si·ness** *n.*

clung *past* and *past part.* of CLING.

clunk /klungk/ • *n.* dull sound as of thick pieces of metal meeting. • *v.intr.* make such a sound.

clus·ter /klústər/ • *n.* aggregated or close group or bunch. • *v.* **1** *tr.* bring into a cluster or clusters. **2** *intr.* be or come into a cluster or clusters.

clutch[1] /kluch/ • *v.* **1** *tr.* seize eagerly; grasp tightly. **2** *intr.* snatch suddenly. • *n.* **1 a** tight grasp. **b** grasping. **2** (in *pl.*) cruel or relentless grasp or control. **3 a** (in a vehicle) device for connecting and disconnecting the engine to the transmission. **b** control operating this.

clutch[2] /kluch/ *n.* **1** set of eggs for hatching. **2** brood of chickens.

clut·ter /klútər/ • *n.* **1** crowded and untidy collection of things. **2** untidy state. • *v.tr.* crowd untidily.

Cm *symb. Chem.* curium.

cm *abbr.* centimeter(s).

Cmdr. *abbr.* commander.

CNS *abbr.* central nervous system.

CO *abbr.* **1** Colorado (in official postal use). **2** commanding officer. **3** conscientious objector. **4** carbon monoxide.

Co *symb. Chem.* cobalt.

Co. *abbr.* **1** company. **2** county.

c/o *abbr.* care of.

co- /kō/ *prefix* added to: **1** nouns, with the sense 'joint, mutual, common' (*coauthor*). **2** adjectives and adverbs, with the sense 'jointly, mutually' (*coequal, coequally*). **3** verbs, with the sense 'together with another or others' (*coauthor*).

coach /kōch/ • *n.* **1** bus, usu. comfortably equipped for longer journeys. **2** railroad car. **3** horse-drawn carriage, usu. closed. **4** instructor or trainer in a sport, etc. • *v. tr.* train or teach as a coach.

co·ag·u·late /kō-ágyəlayt/ *v.* **1** change from a fluid to a solid or semisolid state. **2** clot; curdle. **3** set; solidify. □□ **co·ag′u·la·ble** *adj.* **co·ag′u·lant** *n.* **co·ag·u·la·tion** /-láyshən/ *n.* **co·ag·u·la·tive** /-láytiv, -lətiv/ *adj.* **co·ag′u·la·tor** *n.*

coal /kōl/ *n.* **1** hard black mineral used as fuel. **2** red-hot piece of coal, wood, etc., in a fire.

co·a·lesce /kōəlés/ *v.intr.* come together and form one whole. □□ **co·a·les′cence** *n.* **co·a·les′cent** *adj.*

co·a·li·tion /kōəlíshən/ *n. Polit.* temporary alliance for combined action, esp. of political parties. □□ **co·a·li′tion·ist** *n.*

coarse /kawrs/ *adj.* **1** rough or loose in texture or grain; made of large particles. **2** lacking

refinement; crude; obscene. □□ **coarse′ly** *adv.* **coarse′ness** *n.*

coars·en /káwrsən/ *v.* make or become coarse.

coast /kōst/ • *n.* border of the land near the sea; seashore. • *v.intr.* **1** ride or move, usu. downhill, without use of power. **2** make progress without much effort. □ **the coast is clear** there is no danger of being observed or caught. □□ **coast′al** *adj.*

coast·er /kóstər/ *n.* small tray or mat for a bottle or glass.

coast·line /kóstlīn/ *n.* line of the seashore.

coat /kōt/ • *n.* **1** outer garment with sleeves and often extending below the hips. **2** animal's fur, hair, etc. **3** single covering of paint, etc. • *v.tr.* **1 a** provide with a layer or covering. **b** (as **coated** *adj.*) covered with. **2** (of paint, etc.) form a covering to. □ **coat of arms** heraldic bearings or shield of a person, family, or corporation. □□ **coat′ed** *adj.* (also in *comb.*).

coat·ing /kóting/ *n.* thin layer or covering of paint, etc.

coat·tail /kóttayl/ *n.* back flap of a jacket or coat.

coax /kōks/ *v.tr.* **1** persuade (a person) gradually or by flattery. **2** obtain by coaxing. **3** manipulate (a thing) carefully or slowly. □□ **coax′er** *n.* **coax′ing·ly** *adv.*

co·ax·i·al /kō-ákseeəl/ *adj.* **1** having a common axis. **2** *Electr.* (of a cable or line) transmitting by means of two concentric conductors separated by an insulator. □□ **co·ax′i·al·ly** *adv.*

cob /kob/ *n.* **1** = CORN COB. **2** sturdy riding or driving horse with short legs. **3** male swan.

co·balt /kóbawlt/ *n. Chem.* silvery-white, magnetic metallic element. ¶ Symb.: **Co.** □ **cobalt blue 1** pigment containing a cobalt salt. **2** deep-blue color of this.

cob·ble[1] /kóbəl/ • *n.* (in full **cob′ble·stone**) small rounded stone of a size used for paving. • *v.tr.* pave with cobbles.

cob·ble[2] /kóbəl/ *v.tr.* **1** mend or patch up (esp. shoes). **2** (often foll. by *together*) join or assemble roughly.

cob·bler /kóblər/ *n.* **1** person who mends shoes, esp. professionally. **2** deep-dish fruit pie.

co·bra /kóbrə/ *n.* venomous snake of Africa and Asia.

cob·web /kóbweb/ *n.* **1** fine network of threads spun by a spider from a liquid secreted by it. **2** thread of this. □□ **cob′webbed** *adj.*

co·ca /kókə/ *n.* **1** S. American shrub. **2** its dried leaves, chewed as a stimulant.

co·caine /kōkáyn/ *n.* drug derived from coca or prepared synthetically, used as a local anesthetic and as a stimulant.

coc·cyx /kóksiks/ *n.* (*pl.* **coc·cy·ges** /-sijeez/) small triangular bone at the base of the spinal column in humans and some apes. □□ **coc·cyg·e·al** /koksíjeeəl/ *adj.*

cock /kok/ • *n.* **1** male bird, esp. of a domestic fowl. **2 a** firing lever in a gun. **b** cocked position of this (*at full cock*). **3** tap or valve controlling flow. • *v.tr.* **1** turn or move (the eye or ear) attentively or knowingly. **2** set aslant, or turn up the brim of (a hat). **3** raise the cock of (a gun). □ **cock-and-bull story** absurd or incredible account.

cock·ade /kokáyd/ *n.* rosette, etc., worn in a hat as a badge of office or party, or as part of a livery. □□ **cock·ad′ed** *adj.*

cock·a·too /kókətoo/ *n.* crested parrots.

cock·er /kókər/ *n.* (in full **cock'er span'iel**) 1 small spaniel of a breed with a silky coat. 2 this breed.

cock·er·el /kókrəl/ *n.* young cock.

cock-eyed /kókíd/ *adj. colloq.* 1 crooked; askew; not level. 2 (of a scheme, etc.) absurd; not practical.

cock·fight /kókfīt/ *n.* fight between cocks as sport. □□ **cock'fight·ing** *n.*

cock·le /kókəl/ *n.* 1 bivalve edible mollusk. 2 (in full **cock'le·shell**) its shell. □ **warm the cockles of one's heart** make one contented; be satisfying.

cock·ney /kóknee/ *n.* (*pl.* **-neys**) 1 native of London, esp. of the East End. 2 dialect or accent typical of this area. □□ **cock'ney·ism** *n.*

cock·pit /kókpit/ *n.* 1 compartment for the pilot (or the pilot and crew) of an airplane or other craft. 2 place where cockfights are held.

cock·roach /kókrōch/ *n.* flat brown verminous insect.

cock·sure /kókshŏŏr/ *adj.* presumptuously or arrogantly confident. □□ **cock'sure'ly** *adv.* **cock'sure'ness** *n.*

cock·tail /kóktayl/ *n.* 1 usu. alcoholic drink made by mixing various spirits, fruit juices, etc. 2 dish of mixed ingredients (*fruit cocktail*). 3 any hybrid mixture.

cock·y /kókee/ *adj.* (**cock·i·er, cock·i·est**) 1 conceited; arrogant. 2 saucy; impudent. □□ **cock'i·ly** *adv.* **cock'i·ness** *n.*

co·co /kókō/ *n.* (*pl.* **co·cos**) coconut palm.

co·coa /kókō/ *n.* 1 powder made from crushed cacao seeds, often with other ingredients. 2 hot drink made from this. □ **cocoa butter** fatty substance obtained from cocoa beans.

co·co·nut /kókənut/ *n.* (also **co'coa·nut**) large ovate brown seed of the coco, with a hard shell and edible white fleshy lining enclosing a milky juice.

co·coon /kəkoon/ *n.* 1 silky case spun by many insect larvae for protection as pupae. 2 protective covering.

COD *abbr.* 1 cash on delivery. 2 collect on delivery.

cod /kod/ *n.* (*pl.* same) large marine fish used as food. □ **cod-liver oil** oil pressed from the fresh liver of cod, which is rich in vitamins D and A.

co·da /kódə/ *n.* 1 *Mus.* concluding passage of a piece or movement. 2 concluding event or series of events.

cod·dle /kód'l/ *v.tr.* 1 treat as an invalid; protect attentively. 2 cook (an egg) in water below boiling point. □□ **cod'dler** *n.*

code /kōd/ ● *n.* 1 system of words, letters, figures, or symbols, used to represent others for secrecy or brevity. 2 system of laws, etc. 3 standard of moral behavior. ● *v.tr.* put into code.

co·deine /kódeen/ *n.* analgesic alkaloid from morphine.

co·de·pen·den·cy /kōdipéndənsee/ *n.* relationship in which someone is psychologically dependent on a person who has an addiction, as to drugs, gambling, etc. □□ **co·de·pend·ence** *n.* **co·de·pen·dent** *n. & adj.*

co·dex /kódeks/ *n.* (*pl.* **co·di·ces** /kódiseez, kód-/) ancient manuscript text in book form.

cod·fish /kódfish/ *n.* = COD.

cod·ger /kójər/ *n.* (usu. in **old codger**) *colloq.* person, esp. an old or strange one.

cod·i·cil /kódisil/ *n.* addition explaining, modifying, or revoking a will or part of one. □□ **cod·i·cil·la·ry** /kódisiláree/ *adj.*

cod·i·fy /kódifī, kód-/ *v.tr.* (**-fies, -fied**) arrange (laws, etc.) systematically. □□ **cod·i·fi·ca'tion** *n.* **cod'i·fi·er** *n.*

cod·piece /kódpees/ *n. hist.* appendage like a small bag or flap at the front of a man's breeches.

co·ed /kó-ed, -éd/ *colloq.* ● *n.* female student at a coeducational institution. ● *adj.* coeducational.

co·ed·u·ca·tion /kóejŏŏkáyshən/ *n.* education of pupils of both sexes together. □□ **co·ed·u·ca'tion·al** *adj.*

co·ef·fi·cient /kóifíshənt/ *n.* 1 *Math.* quantity placed before and multiplying an algebraic expression (e.g., 4 in $4x$). 2 *Physics* multiplier or factor that measures some property (*coefficient of expansion*).

coe·len·ter·ate /seeléntərayt, -tərit/ *n.* marine animal with a simple tube-shaped or cup-shaped body, e.g., jellyfish.

co·e·qual /kō-éekwəl/ *archaic* or *literary* ● *adj.* equal. ● *n.* equal. □□ **co·e·qual·i·ty** /kó-eekwólitee/ *n.* **co·e'qual·ly** *adv.*

co·erce /kō-órs/ *v.tr.* persuade or restrain by force (*coerced you into signing*). □□ **co·er'ci·ble** *adj.* **co·er·cion** /kō-órzhən, -shən/ *n.* **co·er'cive** *adj.*

co·e·val /kō-éevəl/ ● *adj.* 1 having the same age or date of origin. 2 existing at the same epoch. ● *n.* coeval person; contemporary. □□ **co·e·val·i·ty** /-válitee/ *n.* **co·e'val·ly** *adv.*

co·ex·ist /kóigzíst/ *v.intr.* 1 exist together (in time or place). 2 (esp. of nations) exist in mutual tolerance. □□ **co·ex·ist'ence** *n.* **co·ex·is'tent** *adj.*

co·ex·ten·sive /kóiksténsiv/ *adj.* extending over the same space or time.

cof·fee /káwfee, kófee/ *n.* 1 **a** drink made from the roasted and ground beanlike seeds of a tropical shrub. **b** cup of this. 2 **a** the shrub. **b** its seeds. 3 pale brown color. □ **coffee break** short rest from work. **coffee cake** type of cake or sweetened bread, often served with coffee. **coffee shop** small informal restaurant. **coffee table** small low table.

cof·fee·house /káwfeehows, kóf-/ *n.* place serving coffee and other refreshments, often with informal entertainment.

cof·fer /káwfər, kóf-/ *n.* 1 large strongbox for valuables. 2 (in *pl.*) treasury or store of funds. □□ **cof'fered** *adj.*

cof·fer·dam /káwfərdam, kóf-/ *n.* watertight enclosure pumped dry to permit work below the waterline.

cof·fin /káwfin, kóf-/ *n.* long, narrow, usu. wooden box in which a corpse is buried or cremated.

cog /kawg, kog/ *n.* 1 each of a series of projections on the edge of a wheel or bar transferring motion by engaging with another series. 2 unimportant worker. □□ **cogged** *adj.*

co·gent /kójənt/ *adj.* (of arguments, reasons, etc.) convincing; compelling. □□ **co·gen·cy** /-jənsee/ *n.* **co'gent·ly** *adv.*

cog·i·tate /kójitayt/ *v.* ponder; meditate. □□ **cog·i·ta·tion** /-táyshən/ *n.* **cog'i·ta·tive** *adj.* **cog'i·ta·tor** *n.*

cog·nac /káwnyak, kón-/ *n.* high-quality brandy, properly that distilled in Cognac in W. France.

cog·nate /kógnayt/ • *adj.* 1 related to or descended from a common ancestor. 2 *Philol.* (of a word) having the same derivation. • *n.* cognate word. □□ **cog′nate·ly** *adv.*

cog·ni·tion /kogníshən/ *n.* 1 *Philos.* knowing, perceiving, or conceiving as an act or faculty. 2 a result of this. □□ **cog·ni′tion·al** *adj.* **cog·ni·tive** /kógnitiv/ *adj.*

cog·ni·zance /kógnizəns/ *n.* knowledge or awareness; perception; sphere of one's observation or concern.

cog·ni·zant /kógnizənt/ *adj.* (foll. by *of*) having knowledge or being aware of.

cog·no·men /kognṓmen/ *n.* nickname.

cog·wheel /kóghweel, -weel/ *n.* wheel with cogs.

co·hab·it /kōhábit/ *v.intr.* (**-it·ed, -it·ing**) live together, esp. as an unmarried couple. □□ **co·hab′it·ant** *n.* **co·hab·i·ta′tion** *n.*

co·here /kōhéer/ *v.intr.* 1 (of parts or a whole) stick together; remain united. 2 (of reasoning, etc.) be logical or consistent.

co·her·ent /kōhéerənt, -hér-/ *adj.* 1 intelligible and articulate. 2 (of an argument, etc.) consistent. 3 *Physics* (of waves) having a fixed phase relationship. □□ **co·her·ence** /-rəns/ *n.* **co·her′ency** *n.* **co·her′ent·ly** *adv.*

co·he·sion /kōhéezhən/ *n.* tendency to cohere. □□ **co·he·sive** /-héesiv/ *adj.* **co·he·sive·ly** /-hée-sivlee/ *adv.* **co·he·sive·ness** /-héesivnis/ *n.*

co·hort /kṓhawrt/ *n.* 1 band of warriors. 2 persons banded or grouped together, esp. in a common cause.

coif·fure /kwaafyṓor/ • *n.* hairstyle. • *v.* (also **coif**) provide a coiffure.

coil /koyl/ • *n.* 1 anything arranged in a joined sequence of concentric circles; rope, etc. 2 *Electr.* device consisting of a coiled wire for converting low voltage to high voltage. 3 piece of wire, piping, etc., wound in circles or spirals. • *v.* 1 *tr.* arrange in a series of concentric loops or rings. 2 *tr.* & *intr.* twist or be twisted into a circular or spiral shape. 3 *intr.* move sinuously.

coin /koyn/ • *n.* 1 piece of flat, usu. round metal stamped and issued by authority as money. 2 (*collect.*) metal money. • *v.tr.* 1 make (coins) by stamping. 2 invent or devise (esp. a new word or phrase). □□ **coin′age** *n.*

co·in·cide /kóinsíd/ *v.intr.* 1 occur at or during the same time. 2 occupy the same portion of space. 3 be in agreement.

co·in·ci·dence /kō-ínsidəns/ *n.* 1 a occurring or being together. b instance of this. 2 remarkable concurrence of events or circumstances, apparently by chance.

co·in·ci·den·tal /kō-ínsidént′l/ *adj.* in the nature of or resulting from a coincidence. □□ **co·in·ci·den′tal·ly** *adv.*

co·i·tus /kṓ-itəs, kō-ée-/ *n.* *Med.* sexual intercourse. □□ **co′i·tal** *adj.*

coke¹ /kōk/ *n.* solid substance left after the gases have been extracted from coal.

coke² /kōk/ *n.* *sl.* cocaine.

Col. *abbr.* 1 colonel. 2 Colossians (New Testament).

col- /kol/ *prefix* assim. form of COM- before *l*.

COLA /kṓlə/ *abbr.* cost-of-living adjustment or allowance.

co·la /kṓlə/ *n.* (also **ko′la**) 1 small tree, native to W. Africa, bearing seeds containing caffeine. 2 carbonated drink usu. flavored with these seeds.

col·an·der /kúləndər, kól-/ *n.* perforated vessel used to strain off liquid in cookery.

cold /kōld/ • *adj.* 1 of or at a low or relatively low temperature. 2 not heated. 3 feeling cold. 4 lacking ardor, friendliness, or affection. 5 depressing; uninteresting. 6 a dead. b *colloq.* unconscious. 7 (in games) far from finding what is sought. • *n.* a low temperature, esp. in the atmosphere. b cold weather or environment. 2 infection of the nose or throat, causing sneezing, sore throat, etc. • *adv.* completely; entirely (*stopped cold*). □ **cold cream** ointment for cleansing and softening the skin. **cold cuts** slices of cold cooked meats. **cold feet** *colloq.* loss of nerve. **cold shoulder** intentional unfriendliness. **cold sore** viral inflammation and blisters in and around the mouth. **cold turkey** *sl.* abrupt withdrawal from addictive drugs. **cold war** state of hostility between nations without actual fighting. **in cold blood** without feeling or passion; deliberately. **out in the cold** ignored; neglected. □□ **cold′ish** *adj.* **cold′ly** *adv.* **cold′ness** *n.*

cold-blood·ed /kóldblúdid/ *adj.* 1 having a body temperature varying with that of the environment. 2 callous; deliberately cruel. □□ **cold′-blood′ed·ly** *adv.* **cold′-blood′ed·ness** *n.*

cold-heart·ed /kóldháártid/ *adj.* lacking affection or warmth; unfriendly. □□ **cold′-heart′ed·ly** *adv.* **cold′-heart′ed·ness** *n.*

cole·slaw /kṓlslaw/ *n.* dressed salad of sliced raw cabbage.

co·le·us /kṓleeəs/ *n.* decorative plant with variegated leaves.

col·ic /kólik/ *n.* severe spasmodic abdominal pain. □□ **col′ick·y** *adj.*

col·i·se·um /kóliséeəm/ *n.* large stadium.

co·li·tis /kəlítis/ *n.* inflammation of the lining of the colon.

col·lab·o·rate /kəlábərayt/ *v.intr.* 1 work jointly. 2 cooperate traitorously with an enemy. □□ **col·lab·o·ra·tion** /-ráyshən/ *n.* **col·lab·o·ra′tion·ist** *n.* & *adj.* **col·lab·o·ra·tive** /-ráytiv -rətiv/ *adj.* **col·lab′o·ra·tor** *n.*

col·lage /kəláazh/ *n.* work of art in which various materials are arranged and glued to a backing. □□ **col·lag′ist** *n.*

col·lapse /kəláps/ • *n.* 1 tumbling down or falling in of a structure. 2 sudden failure. 3 physical or mental breakdown. • *v.* 1 a *intr.* undergo or experience a collapse. b *tr.* cause to collapse. 2 *intr. colloq.* lie or sit down and relax. 3 *tr.* & *intr.* fold. □□ **col·lap′si·ble** *adj.* **col·lap·si·bil′i·ty** *n.*

col·lar /kólər/ • *n.* 1 part of a garment, that goes around the neck. 2 band of leather or other material put around an animal's neck. 3 encircling part, device, etc. • *v.tr.* 1 seize (a person) by the collar or neck. 2 capture; apprehend. □□ **col′lared** *adj.* (also in *comb.*). **col′lar·less** *adj.*

col·lar·bone /kólərbōn/ *n.* either of two bones joining the breastbone and the shoulder blades; the clavicle.

col·late /kəláyt, kólayt, kó-/ *v.tr.* 1 compare (texts, statements, etc.). 2 arrange in proper sequence. □□ **col·la′tor** *n.*

col·lat·er·al /kəlátərəl/ • *n.* **1** security pledged as a guarantee for repayment of a loan. **2** person having the same descent as another but by a different line. • *adj.* **1** descended from the same stock but by a different line. **2** side by side; parallel. **3 a** additional but subordinate. **b** contributory. □□ **col·lat′er·al·ly** *adv.*

col·la·tion /kəláyshən, ko-/ *n.* **1** collating. **2** light meal.

col·league /kóleeg/ *n.* fellow official or worker.

col·lect /kəlékt/ • *v.* **1** *tr.* & *intr.* bring or come together; assemble; accumulate. **2** *tr.* systematically seek and acquire, esp. as a hobby. **3** *tr.* obtain (taxes, contributions, etc.). **4** a *refl.* regain control of oneself. **b** *tr.* concentrate (one's thoughts, etc.). **c** *tr.* (as **collected** *adj.*) not perturbed nor distracted. • *adj.* & *adv.* to be paid for by the receiver (of a telephone call, parcel, etc.). □□ **col·lect′a·ble** *adj.* **col·lect′ed·ly** *adv.*

col·lect·i·ble /kəléktibəl/ • *adj.* worth collecting. • *n.* item sought by collectors.

col·lec·tion /kəlékshən/ *n.* **1** collecting or being collected. **2** things collected. **3** money collected, esp. in church or for a charitable cause.

col·lec·tive /kəléktiv/ • *adj.* **1** taken as a whole; aggregate. **2** of or from several or many individuals; common. • *n.* **1** cooperative enterprise. **2** = collective noun. □ **collective bargaining** negotiation of wages, etc., by an organized body of employees. **collective noun** *Gram.* noun that denotes a collection or number of individuals (e.g., *assembly, family, troop*). □□ **col·lec′tive·ly** *adv.* **col·lec′tive·ness** *n.*

col·lec·tiv·ism /kəléktivizəm/ *n.* theory and practice of the collective ownership of land and the means of production. □□ **col·lec′tiv·ist** *n.* **col·lec·tiv·is′tic** *adj.*

col·lec·tor /kəléktər/ *n.* **1** person who collects things of interest as a hobby. **2** person who collects money, etc., due.

col·lege /kólij/ *n.* **1** establishment for further or higher education, sometimes part of a university. **2** establishment for specialized professional education (*naval college*). **3** organized body of persons with shared functions and privileges (*college of cardinals*). □□ **col·le·gi·al** /kəléjəl/ *adj.*

col·le·giate /kəléejət/ *adj.* constituted as or belonging to a college; corporate. □□ **col·le′giate·ly** *adv.*

col·lide /kəlfd/ *v. intr.* come into collision or conflict.

col·lie /kólee/ *n.* longhaired dog orig. of a Scottish breed.

col·lier·y /kólyəree/ *n.* (*pl.* **-ies**) coal mine and its buildings.

col·li·sion /kəlízhən/ *n.* **1** violent impact of a moving body with another or with a fixed object. **2** clashing of opposed interests or considerations.

col·loid /kóloyd/ *n.* **1** *Chem.* substance consisting of ultramicroscopic particles suspended in a liquid or other medium. □□ **col·loi·dal** /kəlóyd′l/ *adj.*

col·lo·qui·al /kəlókweeəl/ *adj.* of ordinary or familiar conversation. □□ **col·lo′qui·al·ism** *n.* **col·lo′qui·al·ly** *adv.*

col·lo·qui·um /kəlókweeəm/ *n.* (*pl.* **col·lo·qui·ums** or **col·lo·qui·a** /-kweeə/) academic conference or seminar.

col·lo·quy /kóləkwee/ *n.* (*pl.* **-quies**) conversation; talk.

col·lude /kəlóód/ *v. intr.* come to an understanding or conspire together. □□ **col·lud′er** *n.* **col·lu·sion** /kəlóózhən/ *n.* **col·lu·sive** /-lóósiv/ *adj.* **col·lu′sive·ly** *adv.*

Colo. *abbr.* Colorado.

co·logne /kəlōn/ *n.* perfumed water for the face, etc.

co·lon[1] /kólən/ *n.* punctuation mark (:), used esp. to set off something to follow.

co·lon[2] /kólən/ *n. Anat.* lower and greater part of the large intestine. □□ **co·lon·ic** /kəlónik/ *adj.*

col·o·nel /kárnəl/ *n.* military officer, just below a brigadier general in rank. □□ **colo′nel·cy** *n.* (*pl.* **-cies**).

---

colonel mid-16th century: from obsolete French *coronel* (earlier form of *colonel*), from Italian *colonnello* 'column of soldiers,' from *colonna* 'column,' from Latin *columna*. The form *coronel*, the source of the modern pronunciation, was usual until the mid-17th century.

---

co·lo·n·i·al /kəlōneeəl/ • *adj.* **1** pertaining to a colony or colonies. **2** (esp. of architecture or furniture) built or in the style of the period in America before independence. • *n.* native or inhabitant of a colony. □□ **co·lo′ni·al·ly** *adv.*

co·lo·ni·al·ism /kəlōneeəlizəm/ *n.* policy of acquiring or maintaining colonies, esp. for economic advantage. □□ **co·lo′ni·al·ist** *n.*

col·o·nize /kólənīz/ *v. tr.* establish a colony or colonies in (a country or area). □□ **col·o·ni·za′tion** *n.* **col′o·niz·er** *n.*

col·on·nade /kólənáyd/ *n.* row of columns, esp. supporting an entablature or roof. □□ **col·on·nad′ed** *adj.*

col·o·ny /kólənee/ *n.* (*pl.* **-nies**) **1** group of settlers or settlement in a new country fully or partly subject to the mother country. **2** people of one nationality, race, occupation, etc., forming a community. **3** *Biol.* collection of animals, plants, etc., connected, in contact, or living close together. □□ **col′o·nist** *n.*

col·o·phon /kóləfon, -fən/ *n.* publisher's identifying device or imprint, as on a title page, etc.

color /kúlər/ • *n.* **1** sensation produced by visible wavelengths of light. **2** one, or any mixture, of the constituents into which light can be separated as in a spectrum or rainbow. **3** coloring substance, esp. paint. **4** use of colors, as in photography and television. **5** pigmentation of the skin, esp. when dark. **6** ruddiness. **7** (*pl.*) appearance or aspect (*see* things in their true colors). **8** (*pl.*) flag, insignia, etc. **9** quality or mood in art, speech, etc. • *v.* **1** *tr.* apply color to. **2** *tr.* influence. **3** *tr.* misrepresent; exaggerate. **4** *intr.* take on color; blush. □ **color-blind 1** unable to distinguish certain colors. **2** ignoring racial prejudice. **color-blindness** condition of being color-blind. **show one's true colors** reveal one's true character or intentions. □□ **col·or·a′tion** *n.*

col·o·ra·tu·ra /kúlərətŏórə, -tyŏór-/ *n.* **1** elaborate ornamentation of a vocal melody. **2** soprano skilled in this.

col·ored /kúlərd/ *adj.* **1** having color(s). **2** often *offens.* wholly or partly of nonwhite descent. ¶ see note at BLACK.

col·or·fast /kúlərfast/ *adj.* dyed in colors that will not fade nor be washed out. □□ **col′or·fast·ness** *n.*

col·or·ful /kúlərfŏŏl/ *adj.* 1 having much or varied color; bright. 2 vivid; lively. □□ **col′or·ful·ly** *adv.*

col·or·ing /kúlaring/ *n.* 1 process of or skill in using color(s). 2 appearance as regards color, esp. complexion.

col·or·ize /kúlərīz/ *v.tr.* add color to (orig. black-and-white film) with computer technology.

col·or·less /kúlərlis/ *adj.* 1 without color. 2 lacking character or interest. 3 dull or pale in hue. □□ **col′or·less·ly** *adv.*

co·los·sal /kəlósəl/ *adj.* 1 huge; gigantic. 2 *colloq.* remarkable; splendid. 3 *Archit.* (of an order) having more than one story of columns.

co·los·sus /kəlósəs/ *n.* (*pl.* **co·los·si** /-sī/ or **co·los·sus·es**) 1 gigantic statue. 2 gigantic or important person or thing.

co·los·to·my /kəlóstəmee/ *n.* (*pl.* **-mies**) *Surgery* operation on the colon to make an artificial anus in the abdominal wall.

colt /kōlt/ *n.* young, uncastrated male horse.

col·um·bine /kóləmbīn/ *n.* garden plant having drooping belled flowers.

col·umn /kóləm/ *n.* 1 *Archit.* upright, usu. cylindrical pillar. 2 column-shaped structure or part. 3 vertical cylindrical mass of liquid or vapor. 4 vertical division of a page, etc., containing a sequence of figures or words. 5 regular newspaper feature devoted to a particular subject. 6 arrangement of troops or ships in successive lines, with a narrow front. □□ **co·lum·nar** /kəlúmnər/ *adj.* **col′umned** *adj.*

col·um·nist /kóləmnist, -mist/ *n.* journalist contributing regularly to a newspaper.

com- /kom, kəm, kum/ *prefix* (also **co-, col-, con-, cor-**) with; together; jointly.

co·ma /kómə/ *n.* prolonged deep unconsciousness.

Co·man·che /kəmánchee/ *n.* 1 a N. American people native to the western plains. b member of this people. 2 language of this people.

co·ma·tose /kómətōs, kóm-/ *adj.* 1 in a coma. 2 lethargic.

comb /kōm/ • *n.* 1 toothed strip of rigid material for grooming hair. 2 tool having a similar design. 3 red, fleshy crest of esp. male fowl. • *v.tr.* 1 groom (hair) with a comb. 2 dress (wool or flax) with a comb. 3 search (a place) thoroughly.

com·bat • *n.* /kómbat, kúm-/ 1 armed conflict; battle. 2 struggle; contest. • *v.* /kəmbát, kómbat/ 1 *intr.* engage in combat. 2 *tr.* engage in combat with. 3 *tr.* oppose. □ **combat fatigue** mental disorder caused by stress in wartime combat.

com·bat·ant /kəmbát′nt, kómbət′nt/ • *n.* person engaged in fighting. • *adj.* 1 fighting. 2 for fighting.

com·bat·ive /kəmbátiv/ *adj.* ready or eager to fight.

com·bi·na·tion /kómbináyshən/ *n.* 1 a combining; process of being combined. 2 combined state (*in combination with*). 3 combined set of things or people. 4 sequence of numbers used

to open a combination lock. □ **combination lock** lock that opens only by a specific sequence of movements.

com·bine • *v.* /kəmbín/ 1 *tr.* & *intr.* join together; unite. 2 *tr.* possess (qualities usually distinct) together. 3 *intr.* form or cause to form a chemical compound. • *n.* /kómbīn/ combination of esp. commercial interests. □ **combine harvester** /kómbīn/ machine that reaps and threshes. **combining form** *Gram.* linguistic element used with another element to form a word (e.g., *bio-* = life, *-graphy* = writing).

com·bo /kómbō/ *n.* (*pl.* **-bos**) *sl.* small jazz or dance band.

com·bus·ti·ble /kəmbústibəl/ • *adj.* capable of or used for burning. • *n.* combustible substance. □□ **com·bus·ti·bil′i·ty** *n.*

com·bus·tion /kəmbúschən/ *n.* 1 burning; consumption by fire. 2 *Chem.* development of light and heat from the chemical combination of a substance with oxygen. □□ **com·bus·tive** /-bústiv/ *adj.*

Comdr. *abbr.* commander.

come /kum/ *v.intr.* (*past* **came** /kaym/; *past part.* **come**) 1 move, be brought toward, or reach a place. 2 reach or be brought to a specified situation or result (*you'll come to no harm; came into prominence*). 3 reach or extend to a specified point. 4 traverse or accomplish (*have come a long way*). 5 occur; happen (*how did you come to break your leg?*). 6 take or occupy a specified position in space or time (*it comes on the third page*). 7 become perceptible or known (*the news comes as a surprise*). 8 be available (*comes in three sizes*). 9 become (*the handle has come loose*). 10 (foll. by *from, of*) a be descended from (*comes from a rich family*). b be the result of (*that comes of complaining*). 11 (in *subj.*) *colloq.* when a specified time is reached (*come next month*). □ **come about** happen; take place. **come across** 1 a be effective or understood. b appear or sound in a specified way (*the ideas came across clearly*). 2 meet or find by chance (*came across an old jacket*). **come along** 1 make progress. 2 (as *imper.*) hurry up. **come around** 1 pay an informal visit. 2 recover consciousness. 3 be converted to another opinion. **come away** become detached or broken off. **come back** 1 return. 2 recur to one's memory. 3 become fashionable or popular again. 4 reply; retort. **come between** 1 interfere with the relationship of. 2 separate; prevent contact between. **come by** 1 pass; go past. 2 call on; visit. 3 acquire; obtain. **come down** 1 lose position or wealth. 2 reach a decision or recommendation (*the report came down against change*). 3 (foll. by *to*) signify; be dependent on (a factor) (*it comes down to who is willing to go*). 4 (foll. by *on*) criticize harshly. 5 (foll. by *with*) begin to suffer from (a disease). **come in** 1 take a specified position in a race, etc. (*came in third*). 2 a have a useful role or function. b prove to be (*came in very handy*). 3 begin speaking, esp. in radio transmission. **come into** receive, esp. as heir. **come off** 1 *colloq.* (of an action) succeed; be accomplished. 2 fare; turn out (*came off badly; came off the winner*). 3 be detached or detachable (from). **come off it** (as *imper.*) *colloq.* expression of disbelief or refusal to accept another's opinion, behavior, etc. **come on 1** advance, esp. to attack. **b** (foll. by *to*) make sexual advances. 2 be heard or seen on television, on the telephone, etc. 3 (as *imper.*) expressing encouragement. **come-on** *n.*

sl. lure or enticement. **come out 1 a** emerge; become known. **b** end; turn out. **2** appear or be published. **3 a** declare oneself; make a decision (*came out in favor of joining*). **b** openly declare that one is a homosexual. **4** turn out in a specified way (esp. the subject of a photograph). **5** (of a stain, etc.) be removed. **come over 1** (of a feeling, etc.) overtake or affect (a person). **2** affect or influence (*I don't know what came over me*). **come through 1** be successful; survive. **2** survive or overcome (a difficulty). **come to 1** recover consciousness. **2** *Naut.* bring a vessel to a stop. **3** reach in total; amount to. **4** have as a destiny; reach (*what is the world coming to?*). **5** be a question of (*when it comes to wine, he is an expert*). **come to pass** happen; occur. **come to rest** cease moving. **come up 1** (of an issue, problem, etc.) arise; present itself. **2** (foll. by *with*) produce (an idea, etc.). **come up against** be faced with or opposed by. **come upon 1** meet or find by chance. **2** attack by surprise. **come what may** no matter what happens.

come·back /kúmbak/ *n.* **1** return to a previous (esp. successful) state. **2** *sl.* retaliation or retort.

co·me·di·an /kəméedeeən/ *n.* humorous entertainer.

co·me·di·enne /kəméedee-én/ *n.* female comedian.

come·down /kúmdown/ *n.* **1** loss of status; decline or degradation. **2** disappointment.

com·e·dy /kómidee/ *n.* (*pl.* **-dies**) **1 a** amusing or satirical play, film, etc. **b** dramatic genre of such works. **2** humor, esp. in a work of art, etc. □□ **co·me·dic** /kəméedik/ *adj.*

come·ly /kúmlee/ *adj.* (**come·li·er, come·li·est**) pleasant to look at; lovely. □□ **come´li·ness** *n.*

co·mes·ti·ble /kəméstibəl/ *n.* (usu. in *pl.*) *formal* or *joc.* food.

com·et /kómit/ *n.* celestial tailed object of ice, dust, and gas, orbiting the sun.

come·up·pance /kumúpəns/ *n. colloq.* one's deserved fate.

com·fort /kúmfərt/ • *n.* **1** consolation; relief in affliction. **2 a** state of physical well-being. **b** (usu. in *pl.*) things that make life easy or pleasant. **3** cause or provider of satisfaction. • *v.tr.* **1** console. **2** make comfortable.

com·fort·a·ble /kúmftəbəl, -fərtəbəl/ *adj.* **1 a** such as to avoid hardship and give comfort. **b** (of a person) relaxing to be with; congenial. **2** free from discomfort. **3** *colloq.* free from (esp. financial) worry. **4** having an easy conscience (*did not feel comfortable about refusing him*).

com·fort·er /kúmfərtər/ *n.* **1** person who comforts. **2** quilt.

com·fy /kúmfee/ *adj.* (**com·fi·er, com·fi·est**) *colloq.* comfortable. □□ **com´fi·ly** *adv.* **com´fi·ness** *n.*

com·ic /kómik/ • *adj.* **1** of, or in the style of, comedy. **2** funny. • *n.* **1** comedian. **2** (*pl.*) comic-strip section of a newspaper. □ **comic book** magazine of comic strips. **comic strip** sequence of drawings in a newspaper, etc., telling a story. □□ **com´i·cal** *adj.* **com´i·cal·ly** *adv.*

com·ing /kúming/ • *attrib.adj.* approaching; next (*this coming Sunday*). • *n.* arrival; approach.

com·i·ty /kómitee/ *n.* (*pl.* **-ties**) courtesy; civility.

comm. *abbr.* **1** commerce. **2** commercial. **3** commissioner. **4** commission. **5** committee. **6** common.

com·ma /kómə/ *n.* **1** punctuation mark (,) indicating pause or division. **2** *Mus.* definite minute interval or difference of pitch.

com·mand /kəmánd/ • *v.tr.* **1** give formal order to. **2** have authority or control over. **3 a** restrain; master. **b** gain or have the use of (skill, resources, etc.). **4** deserve and get (respect, etc.). **5** *Mil.* dominate (a strategic position) from a superior height. • *n.* **1** authoritative order. **2** mastery; possession (*a good command of languages*). **3** exercise of authority, esp. naval or military (*has command of this ship*). **4** *Mil.* **a** body of troops, etc. **b** district under a commander. **5** *Computing* **a** instruction causing a computer to perform a function. **b** signal initiating such an operation. □ **command performance** performance given at the request of a head of state or sovereign.

com·man·dant /kóməndánt, -daánt/ *n.* commanding officer.

com·man·deer /kóməndéer/ *v.tr.* **1** seize for military purposes. **2** take possession of without authority.

com·mand·er /kəmándər/ *n.* person who commands, esp. a naval officer next in rank below captain. □ **commander in chief** supreme commander, esp. of a nation's forces.

com·mand·ing /kəmánding/ *adj.* **1** exalted; impressive. **2** (of a hill, etc.) giving a wide view. **3** substantial (*has a commanding lead*).

com·mand·ment /kəmándmənt/ *n.* divine command. □ **Ten Commandments** divine rules of conduct given by God to Moses (Exod. 20:1–17).

com·man·do /kəmándō/ *n.* (*pl.* **-dos**) *Mil.* member of a unit trained for raids.

com·mem·o·rate /kəmémərayt/ *v.tr.* **1** preserve in memory by ceremony or celebration. **2** be a memorial of. □□ **com·mem·o·ra·tive** /-ráytiv, -rətiv/ *adj.* **com·mem·o·ra·tion** /-ráyshən/ *n.*

com·mence /kəméns/ *v. formal* begin.

com·mence·ment /kəménsmənt/ *n. formal* **1 a** beginning. **2** ceremony of degree conferment.

com·mend /kəménd/ *v.tr.* **1** entrust. **2** praise. **3** recommend.

com·mend·a·ble /kəméndəbəl/ *adj.* praiseworthy.

com·men·da·tion /kómendáyshən/ *n.* **1** act of commending or recommending. **2** praise.

com·men·su·ra·ble /kəménsərəbəl, -shərə-/ *adj.* **1** measurable by the same standard. **2** proportionate.

com·men·su·rate /kəménsərət, -shərət/ *adj.* **1** having the same size, duration, etc. **2** proportionate.

com·ment /kóment/ • *n.* **1 a** remark, esp. critical. **b** criticism. **2 a** explanatory note (e.g., on a written text). **b** written criticism. **3** (of a play, book, etc.) critical illustration (*his art is a comment on society*). • *v.intr.* **1** make (esp. critical) remarks. **2** write explanatory notes.

com·men·tar·y /kómənteree/ *n.* (*pl.* **-ies**) **1** set of critical notes on a text, etc. **2** descriptive spoken account of an event or a performance as it happens.

com·men·ta·tor /kóməntaytər/ *n.* person who provides commentary. □□ **com´men·tate** *v.*

com·merce /kómərs/ *n.* **1** large-scale business transactions. **2** social intercourse.

com·mer·cial /kəmárshəl/ • *adj.* **1** engaged in,

or concerned with, commerce. **2** having profit as a primary aim. • *n.* broadcast advertisement. □□ **com·mer′cial·ism** *n.* **com·mer·cial·i·za′tion** *n.* **com·mer′cial·ize** *v.*

com·min·gle /kəmínggəl/ *v. literary* mingle together.

com·mis·er·ate /kəmízərayt/ *v.intr.* express or feel pity. □□ **com·mis·er·a·tion** /-ráyshən/ *n.* **com·mis·er·a′tive** *adj.* **com·mis′er·a·tor** *n.*

com·mis·sar·y /kómiseree/ *n.* (*pl.* -**ies**) **1** *Mil.* a store for the supply of food, etc., to soldiers. **b** officer responsible for this. **2 a** restaurant in a movie studio, etc. **b** food supplied. **3** deputy or delegate.

com·mis·sion /kəmíshən/ • *n.* **1 a** authority to perform a task or certain duties. **b** person or group entrusted with such authority. **c** instruction or duty given. **2** order for something, esp. a work of art, to be produced. **3** *Mil.* **a** warrant conferring the rank of officer. **b** rank so conferred. **4 a** authority to act as agent for a company, etc., in trade. **b** percentage paid to the agent from profits obtained. **5** act of committing (a crime, sin, etc.). **6** office or department of a commissioner. • *v.tr.* **1** authorize by a commission. **2 a** give (an artist, etc.) a commission for a piece of work. **b** order (a work) to be created. **3** *Naut.* **a** give (an officer) command of a ship. **b** prepare (a ship) for active service. □ **out of commission** not in service.

com·mis·sion·er /kəmíshənər/ *n.* leader appointed by a commission.

com·mit /kəmít/ *v.tr.* (**com·mit·ted, com·mit·ting**) **1** entrust or consign for safekeeping, treatment, etc. **2** perpetrate, do (esp. a crime or blunder). **3** pledge or bind (esp. oneself) to a certain course. **4** (as **committed** *adj.*) **a** morally dedicated; politically aligned. **b** obliged (to take certain action).

com·mit·ment /kəmítmənt/ *n.* **1** obligation that restricts freedom of action. **2** process or instance of committing oneself. **3** dedication.

com·mit·tal /kəmít′l/ *n.* **1** act of committing a person to an institution, esp. prison or a mental hospital. **2** burial.

com·mit·tee *n.* **1** /kəmítee/ body of persons appointed for a specific function by, and usu. out of, a larger body. **2** /kómitèe/ *Law* person entrusted with the charge of another person or another person's property.

com·mode /kəmód/ *n.* **1** chest of drawers. **2** = TOILET 1.

com·mo·di·ous /kəmódeeəs/ *adj.* roomy and comfortable.

com·mod·i·ty /kəmóditee/ *n.* (*pl.* -**ties**) **1** *Commerce* article or raw material that can be bought and sold. **2** useful thing.

com·mo·dore /kómədawr/ *n.* **1** naval officer just above captain. **2** commander of a fleet division. **3** president of a yacht club.

com·mon /kómən/ • *adj.* **1 a** occurring often. **b** overused; trite. **c** ordinary; without special rank. **2** shared by or coming from more than one (*common knowledge*). **3** *derog.* low-class; inferior. **4** familiar. **5** *Math.* belonging to two or more quantities (*common denominator*). • *n.* piece of open public land. □ **common fraction** fraction expressed by numerator and denominator. **common ground** argument accepted by both sides

in a dispute. **common law** law derived from custom and judicial precedent rather than statutes. **common sense** sound practical sense.

com·mon·al·i·ty /kómənálitee/ *n.* (*pl.* -**ties**) **1** sharing of an attribute. **2** common occurrence.

com·mon·er /kómənər/ *n.* one of the common people, as opposed to the aristocracy.

com·mon·place /kómənplays/ • *adj.* lacking originality; trite. • *n.* **1 a** everyday saying; platitude. **b** ordinary topic of conversation. **2** anything usual or trite.

com·mons /kómənz/ *n.pl.* **1** dining hall at a university, etc. **2** *New Eng.* central public park or ground.

com·mon·wealth /kómənwelth/ *n.* **1 a** independent state or community, esp. a democratic republic. **b** designation of four US states (Ky., Mass., Penn., Va.). **2** (**the Commonwealth**) association of the UK with nations previously part of the British Empire. **3** federation of states.

com·mo·tion /kəmóshən/ *n.* **1** confused and noisy disturbance. **2** civil insurrection.

com·mu·nal /kəmyoonəl, kómyə-/ *adj.* relating to or benefiting a community; for common use. □□ **com·mu′nal·ize** *v.* **com·mu′nal·ly** *adv.*

com·mune¹ /kómyoon/ *n.* **1 a** group of people sharing living accommodation, goods, etc. **b** communal settlement. **2 a** smallest French territorial division for administrative purposes. **b** similar division elsewhere.

com·mune² /kəmyoon/ *v.intr.* **1** speak confidentially and intimately. **2** feel in close touch (with nature, etc.).

com·mu·ni·ca·ble /kəmyoonikəbəl/ *adj.* (esp. of disease) able to be passed on. □□ **com·mu·ni·ca·bil′i·ty** *n.* **com·mu′ni·ca·bly** *adv.*

com·mu·ni·cant /kəmyoonikənt/ *n.* person who receives Holy Communion.

com·mu·ni·cate /kəmyoonikayt/ *v.* **1** *tr.* **a** transmit by speaking or writing. **b** transmit (heat, motion, etc.). **c** pass on (an infectious illness). **d** impart (feelings, etc.) nonverbally. **2** *intr.* convey information. **3** *intr.* share a feeling or understanding. □□ **com·mu′ni·ca·tor** *n.*

com·mu·ni·ca·tion /kəmyoonikáyshən/ *n.* **1 a** act of imparting, esp. news. **b** information, etc., communicated. **2** social intercourse. **3** (in *pl.*) science and practice of transmitting information.

com·mu·ni·ca·tive /kəmyoonikáytiv, -kətiv/ *adj.* open; talkative; ready to inform. □□ **com·mu′ni·ca·tive·ly** *adv.*

com·mu·nion /kəmyoonyən/ *n.* **1** sharing, esp. of thoughts, etc.; fellowship. **2** sharing in common (*communion of interests*). **3** (**Communion, Holy Communion**) the Eucharist. **4** Christian denomination (*the Methodist communion*).

com·mu·ni·qué /kəmyoonikáy/ *n.* official communication.

com·mu·nism /kómyənizəm/ *n.* **1** political theory advocating public ownership of property. **2** (usu. **Communism**) communistic form of society, as established in the former USSR.

com·mu·nist /kómyənist/ • *n.* & *adj.* **1** person advocating communism. **2** (**Communist**) member of a Communist party. • *adj.* relating to communism. □□ **com·mu·nis′tic** *adj.*

com·mu·ni·ty /kəmyoonitee/ *n.* (*pl.* -**ties**) **1 a** body of people living in one locale. **b** locality, including its inhabitants. **2** body of people having religion, profession, etc., in common. **3** (prec. by *the*) the public. □ **community college** nonresidential junior college offering college courses to a local community or region. **community service** unpaid work performed in service to the community, esp. as part of a criminal sentence.

com·mu·ta·tive /kəmyóotətiv/ *adj.* **1** relating to or involving substitution. **2** *Math.* unchanged in result by the interchange of the order of quantities.

com·mute /kəmyóot/ ● *v.* **1** *intr.* travel to and from one's daily work. **2** *tr. Law* change (a judicial sentence, etc.) to another less severe. **3** *tr.* change (one kind of payment) for another. **4** *tr.* **a** exchange; interchange (two things). **b** change (to another thing). ● *n.* trip made by one who commutes.

com·mut·er /kəmyóotər/ *n.* person who travels some distance to work.

comp. *abbr.* **1** companion. **2** comparative. **3** compensation. **4** compilation. **5** compiled. **6** compiler. **7** complete. **8** composite. **9** composition. **10** compositor. **11** comprehensive.

com·pact[1] ● *adj.* /kəmpákt, kóm-/ **1** closely or neatly packed together. **2** (of a piece of equipment, a room, etc.) well-fitted and practical though small. **3** (of style, etc.) condensed; brief. **4** (esp. of the human body) small but well-proportioned. ● *v. tr.* /kəmpákt/ **1** join or press firmly together. **2** condense. ● *n.* /kómpakt/ **1** small, flat case for face powder, a mirror, etc. **2** medium-sized automobile. □ **compact disc** /kómpakt/ disc on which information or sound is recorded digitally and reproduced by laser reflection. □□ **com·pact′ly** *adv.* **com·pact′ness** *n.*

com·pact[2] /kómpakt/ *n.* agreement; contract.

com·pan·ion /kəmpányən/ *n.* **1 a** person who accompanies or associates with another. **b** person employed to live with and assist another. **2** handbook on a particular subject. **3** thing that matches another.

com·pan·ion·a·ble /kəmpányənəbəl/ *adj.* friendly; sociable. □□ **com·pan′ion·a·bly** *adv.*

com·pan·ion·ship /kəmpányənship/ *n.* fellowship; friendship.

com·pan·ion·way /kəmpányənway/ *n.* ship's stairway.

com·pa·ny /kúmpənee/ *n.* (*pl.* **-nies**) **1 a** number of people assembled; crowd. **b** guest(s). **2** state of being a companion or fellow; companionship, esp. of a specific kind (*do not care for his company*). **3** commercial business. **4** troupe of entertainers. **5** *Mil.* subdivision of a battalion. □ **be in good company** discover that one's companions, or better people, have done the same as oneself.

com·pa·ra·ble /kómpərəbəl/ *adj.* able or fit to be compared. □□ **com·pa·ra·bil′i·ty** *n.* **com′pa·ra·bly** *adv.*

com·par·a·tive /kəmpárətiv/ ● *adj.* **1** perceptible by comparison; relative. **2** of or involving comparison. **3** *Gram.* (of an adjective or adverb) expressing a higher degree (e.g., *braver, more fiercely*). ● *n. Gram.* comparative expression or word. □□ **com·par′a·tive·ly** *adv.*

com·pare /kəmpáir/ ● *v.* **1** *tr.* express similarities in; liken. **2** *tr.* estimate the similarity of. **3** *intr.* bear comparison. **4** *intr.* be equivalent to. **5** *tr. Gram.* form comparative and superlative degrees of (an adjective or adverb). ● *n.* comparison (*beyond compare*). □ **compare notes** exchange ideas or opinions.

¶ Traditionally, **compare to** is used when similarities are noted in dissimilar things: *He compares life to a box of chocolates.* To **compare with** is to look for either differences or similarities, usually in similar things: *Let's compare the movie with the book on which it was based.* In practice, however, this distinction is rarely maintained. See also note at **contrast.**

com·par·i·son /kəmpárisən/ *n.* **1** comparing. **2** simile or semantic illustration. **3** similarity (*there's no comparison*). **4** (in full **degrees of comparison**) *Gram.* positive, comparative, and superlative forms of adjectives and adverbs. □ **beyond comparison 1** totally different in quality. **2** greatly superior.

com·part·ment /kəmpaártmənt/ *n.* **1** partitioned space within a larger space. **2** watertight division of a ship.

com·part·men·tal /kómpaartmént'l/ *adj.* of or divided into compartments. □□ **com·part·men′tal·ly** *adv.*

com·part·men·tal·ize /kómpaartmént'līz,kómpaart-/ *v. tr.* divide into compartments or categories. □□ **com·part·men·tal·i·za′tion** *n.*

com·pass /kúmpəs, kóm-/ *n.* **1** instrument showing the direction of magnetic north and bearings from it. **2** (often *pl.*) instrument within two hinged legs for taking measurements and describing circles. **3** circumference or boundary.

com·pas·sion /kəmpáshən/ *n.* pity inclining one to be merciful.

com·pas·sion·ate /kəmpáshənət/ *adj.* sympathetic; pitying. □□ **com·pas′sion·ate·ly** *adv.*

com·pat·i·ble /kəmpátəbəl/ *adj.* **1 a** able to co-exist; mutually tolerant. **b** consistent. **2** (of equipment, etc.) able to be used in combination. □□ **com·pat·i·bil′i·ty** *n.* **com·pat′i·bly** *adv.*

com·pa·tri·ot /kəmpáytreeət, -ot/ *n.* fellow countryman.

com·pel /kəmpél/ *v. tr.* (**com·pelled, com·pelling**) **1** force; constrain (*compelled them to admit it*). **2** (as **compelling** *adj.*) rousing strong interest. □□ **com·pel′ling·ly** *adv.*

com·pen·di·ous /kəmpéndeeəs/ *adj.* comprehensive but brief.

com·pen·di·um /kəmpéndeeəm/ *n.* (*pl.* **com·pen·di·ums** or **com·pen·di·a** /-deeə/) concise summary or abridgment.

com·pen·sate /kómpənsayt/ *v.* **1** *tr.* pay. **2** *intr.* make amends. **3** *tr.* counterbalance. **4** *intr.* offset a disability, etc., by development in another direction. □□ **com·pen·sa·to·ry** /-pénsətáwree/ *adj.*

com·pen·sa·tion /kómpensáyshən/ *n.* **1 a** compensating. **b** being compensated. **2** something given as recompense. □□ **com·pen·sa′tion·al** *adj.*

com·pete /kəmpéet/ *v. intr.* **1** contend; vie. **2** take part in a contest.

com·pe·tence /kómpit'ns/ *n.* (also **com·pe·ten·cy** /-tənsee/) **1** ability; being competent. **2** *Law* legal capacity to deal with a matter.

com·pe·tent /kómpit'nt/ *adj.* adequately qualified or skilled. □□ **com·pe′tent·ly** *adv.*

com·pe·ti·tion /kómpətíshən/ *n.* **1** competing. **2** event in which people compete. **3** the others competing; opposition.

com·pet·i·tive /kəmpétitiv/ *adj.* **1** of or involving competition. **2** (of prices, etc.) comparing favorably. **3** driven to win. □□ **com·pet′i·tive·ly** *adv.* **com·pet′i·tive·ness** *n.*

com·pet·i·tor /kəmpétitər/ *n.* person who competes; rival, esp. in business.

com·pile /kəmpíl/ *v.tr.* **1** collect (material) into a list, volume, etc. **2** produce (a volume, etc.) from such material. **3** accumulate (a large number of). □□ **com·pi·la·tion** /kómpiláyshən/ *n.* **com·pil′er** *n.*

com·pla·cent /kəmpláysənt/ *adj.* smugly self-satisfied; content. □□ **com·pla′cence** *n.* **com·pla′cen·cy** *n.* **com·pla′cent·ly** *adv.*

¶ **Complacent** means 'smugly self-satisfied:' *After four consecutive championships the team became complacent.* **Complaisant,** a much rarer word, means 'deferential, willing to please:' *Once released from the pen, the barking dogs become peaceful and complaisant.*

com·plain /kəmpláyn/ *v.intr.* **1** express dissatisfaction. **2 a** say that one is suffering from (an ailment). **b** state a grievance. □□ **com·plain′er** *n.* **com·plain′ing·ly** *adv.*

com·plain·ant /kəmpláynənt/ *n. Law* plaintiff.

com·plaint /kəmpláynt/ *n.* **1** complaining. **2** grievance. **3** ailment.

com·plai·sant /kəmpláysənt/ *adj.* willing to please; acquiescent. □□ **com·plai′sance** *n.*

com·ple·ment ● *n.* /kómpləmənt/ **1** thing that completes; counterpart. **2** full number needed. ● *v.tr.* /kómpliment/ **1** complete. **2** form a complement to. □□ **com·ple·men·tal** /-mént′l/ *adj.*

com·ple·men·ta·ry /kómpliméntəree/ *adj.* **1** forming a complement. **2** (of two or more things) complementing each other. □ **complementary angle** either of two angles making up 90°.

¶ **Complementary** means 'forming a complement or addition, completing': *I purchased a suit with a complementary tie and handkerchief.* It can be confused with **complimentary,** for which one sense is 'given freely, as a courtesy': *You must pay for the suit, but the tie and handkerchief are complimentary.*

com·plete /kəmpléet/ ● *adj.* **1** having all its parts; entire. **2** finished. **3** of the maximum extent (*a complete surprise*). ● *v.tr.* **1** finish. **2** make whole. **3** fill in (a form, etc.). □□ **com·plete′ly** *adv.* **com·plete′ness** *n.* **com·ple·tion** /-plée′shən/ *n.*

com·plex ● *n.* /kómpleks/ **1** building, series of rooms, etc., of related parts. **2** *Psychol.* group of us. repressed feelings or thoughts that influence behavior. **3** preoccupation. ● *adj.* /kəmpléks, kómpleks/ complicated. □ **complex sentence** sentence containing a subordinate clause or clauses. □□ **com·plex·i·ty** /-pléksitee/ *n.* (*pl.* **-ties**)

com·plex·ion /kəmplékshən/ *n.* **1** natural appearance of skin, esp. of the face. **2** aspect; interpretation.

com·pli·ance /kəmplíəns/ *n.* **1** obedience to a request, command, etc. **2** *Mech.* capacity to yield.

com·pli·ant /kəmplíənt/ *adj.* yielding. □□ **com·pli′ant·ly** *adv.*

com·pli·cate /kómplikayt/ *v.* **1** make difficult or complex. **2** (as **complicated** *adj.*) complex.

com·pli·ca·tion /kómplikáyshən/ *n.* **1** involved or confused condition; difficulty. **2** *Med.* condition aggravating a previous one.

com·plic·i·ty /kəmplísitee/ *n.* partnership in wrongdoing.

com·pli·ment ● *n.* /kómplimənt/ **1 a** polite expression of praise. **b** act implying praise. **2** (in *pl.*) formal greetings or praise. ● *v.tr.* /kómpliment/ congratulate; praise.

com·pli·men·ta·ry /kómpliméntəree/ *adj.* **1** expressing a compliment. **2** given free. ¶ See note at COMPLEMENTARY.

com·ply /kəmplí/ *v.intr.* (**-plies, -plied**) act in accordance (with a wish, command, etc.).

com·po·nent /kəmpónənt/ ● *n.* part of a larger whole. ● *adj.* being part of a larger whole. □□ **com·po·nen·tial** /kómpənénshəl/ *adj.*

com·port /kəmpáwrt/ *v.refl.* conduct oneself; behave. □ **comport with** suit; befit. □□ **com·port′ment** *n.*

com·pose /kəmpóz/ *v.tr.* **1** create in music or writing. **2** constitute; make up. **3** arrange artistically. **4 a** (often *refl.*) calm. **b** (as **composed** *adj.*) calm; settled. **5** *Printing* **a** set (type). **b** set (manuscript, etc.) in type. □□ **com·pos′er** *n.*

¶ Both **compose** and **comprise** can be used to mean 'to constitute or make up' but **compose** is preferred in this sense, e.g., *Citizens who have been chosen at random and screened for prejudices compose a jury.* **Comprise** is correctly used to mean 'to be composed of, consist of,' e.g., *Each crew comprises a commander, a gunner, and a driver.* The usage "is comprised of" is avoided by careful speakers and writers.

com·pos·ite /kəmpózit/ ● *adj.* **1** made up of various parts. **2** (of a plant) having a bloom head of many flowers. ● *n.* composite thing or plant.

com·po·si·tion /kómpəzíshən/ *n.* **1 a** putting together; composing. **b** thing so composed, esp. music. **2** constitution of a substance. **3** school essay. **4** artistic arrangement. **5** compound artificial substance. □□ **com·po·si′tion·al** *adj.* **com·po·si′tion·al·ly** *adv.*

com·pos·i·tor /kəmpózitər/ *n.* person who sets type for printing; typesetter.

com·post /kómpōst/ ● *n.* organic fertilizing mixture. ● *v.tr.* **1** treat with compost. **2** make into compost.

com·po·sure /kəmpóz̲h̲ər/ *n.* tranquil manner; calmness.

com·pote /kómpōt/ *n.* fruit preserved or cooked in syrup.

com·pound[1] ● *n.* /kómpownd/ **1** mixture of two or more things. **2** word made up of two or more existing words. **3** substance chemically formed from two or more elements. ● *adj.* /kómpownd/ **1** made up of several ingredients. **2** combined; collective. ● *v.tr.* /kəmpównd/ **1** mix or combine (ingredients, elements, etc.). **2** increase or complicate (difficulties, etc.). **3** make up (a composite whole).

com·pound[2] /kómpownd/ *n.* enclosure or fenced-in space.

com·pre·hend /kómprihénd/ *v.tr.* **1** grasp mentally; understand. **2** include. □□ **com·pre·hen·si·bil·i·ty** /-sibílitee/ *n.* **com·pre·hen′si·ble** *adj.* **com·pre·hen′si·bly** *adv.* **com·pre·hen′sion** *n.*

com·pre·hen·sive /kómprihénsiv/ *adj.* **1** including all or nearly all. **2** (of insurance) providing complete protection. □□ **com·pre·hen′sive·ly** *adv.* **com·pre·hen′sive·ness** *n.*

com·press ● *v.tr.* /kəmprés/ **1** squeeze together. **2** bring into a smaller space or shorter extent. ● *n.* /kómpres/ pad applied to a wound. □□ **com·press·i·ble** /kəmprésəbəl/ *adj.* **com·press·i·bil′i·ty** *n.*

com·pres·sion /kəmpréshən/ *n.* compressing.

com·pres·sor /kəmprésər/ *n.* instrument or device for compressing esp. air or other gases.

com·prise /kəmpríz/ *v.tr.* **1** include. **2** consist of. **3** make up, compose.
¶ See note at COMPOSE.

com·pro·mise /kómprəmīz/ • *n.* **1** mutual settlement of a dispute. **2** intermediate state between conflicting opinions, actions, etc. • *v.* **1 a** *intr.* mutually settle a dispute. **b** *tr.* modify one's opinions, demands, etc. **2** *tr.* bring into disrepute or danger esp. by indiscretion. □□ **com′pro·mis·er** *n.* **com′pro·mis·ing·ly** *adv.*

comp·trol·ler /kəntrólər/ *n.* financial officer.

com·pul·sion /kəmpúlshən/ *n.* **1** constraint; obligation. **2** irresistible urge.

com·pul·sive /kəmpúlsiv/ *adj.* **1** resulting or acting (as if) from compulsion. **2** irresistible.
□□ **com·pul′sive·ly** *adv.* **com·pul′sive·ness** *n.*

com·pul·so·ry /kəmpúlsəree/ *adj.* **1** required by law or a rule. **2** essential. □□ **com·pul′so·ri·ly** *adv.*

com·punc·tion /kəmpúngkshən/ *n.* **1** pricking of the conscience. **2** slight regret; scruple.
□□ **com·punc′tious** /-shəs/ *adj.*

com·pute /kəmpyo͞ot/ *v.* **1** *tr.* reckon or calculate. **2** *intr.* use a computer. □□ **com·put·a·bil′i·ty** *n.* **com·put′a·ble** *adj.* **com·pu·ta·tion** /-táyshən/ *n.* **com·pu·ta′tion·al** *adj.*

com·put·er /kəmpyo͞otər/ *n.* electronic device for storing and processing data. □ **computer virus** hidden code within a computer program intended to corrupt a system.

com·put·er·ize /kəmpyo͞otərīz/ *v.tr.* **1** equip with a computer. **2** store or produce by computer. □□ **com·put·er·i·za′tion** *n.*

com·rade /kómrad, -rid/ *n.* **1** associate or companion. **2** fellow socialist or communist.
□□ **com′rade·ly** *adj.* **com′rade·ship** *n.*

con[1] /kon/ *sl.* • *n.* confidence trick. • *v.tr.* (**conned, con·ning**) swindle; deceive.

con[2] /kon/ • *n.* (usu. in *pl.*) reason against. • *prep.* & *adv.* against.

con[3] /kon/ *n. sl.* convict.

con- /kon, kən/ *prefix* assim. form of COM-.

con·cat·e·nate /konkát′nayt/ • *v.tr.* link together (events, things, etc.). • *adj.* joined; linked. □□ **con·cat·e·na·tion** /-náyshən/ *n.*

con·cave /kónkáyv/ *adj.* curved like the interior of a circle or sphere. □□ **con·cav·i·ty** /-kávitee/ *n.*

con·ceal /kənse͞el/ *v.tr.* **1** keep secret. **2** hide.
□□ **con·ceal′er** *n.* **con·ceal′ment** *n.*

con·cede /kənse͞ed/ *v.tr.* **1 a** admit to be true. **b** admit defeat in. **2** grant (a right, privilege, etc.).

con·ceit /kənse͞et/ *n.* **1** personal vanity; pride. **2** *literary* **a** elaborate metaphoric comparison. **b** fanciful notion.

con·ceit·ed /kənse͞etid/ *adj.* vain; proud.
□□ **con·ceit′ed·ly** *adv.*

con·ceiv·a·ble /kənse͞evəbəl/ *adj.* capable of being grasped or imagined. □□ **con·ceiv′a·bly** *adv.*

con·ceive /kənse͞ev/ *v.* **1** *intr.* become pregnant. **2** *tr.* become pregnant with (a child). **3** *tr.* imagine; formulate.

con·cen·trate /kónsəntrayt/ • *v.* **1** *intr.* focus one's attention. **2** *tr.* bring together to one point. **3** *tr.* make less dilute. • *n.* concentrated substance. □□ **con′cen·tra·tor** *n.*

con·cen·tra·tion /kónsəntráyshən/ *n.* **1** act or instance of concentrating, esp. of mental attention. **2** something concentrated. □ **concentration camp** camp holding political prisoners.

con·cen·tric /kənséntrik/ *adj.* (esp. of circles)

---

having a common center. □□ **con·cen′tri·cal·ly** *adv.* **con·cen·tric·i·ty** /kónsentrísitee/ *n.*

CONCENTRIC CIRCLES

con·cept /kónsept/ *n.* general notion; abstract idea.

con·cep·tion /kənsépshən/ *n.* **1** act or instance of conceiving. **2** idea; plan. □□ **con·cep′tion·al** *adj.*

con·cep·tu·al /kənsépcho͞oəl/ *adj.* of mental conceptions or concepts. □□ **con·cep′tu·al·ly** *adv.*

con·cep·tu·al·ize /kənsépcho͞oəlīz/ *v.tr.* form a concept or idea of. □□ **con·cep·tu·al·i·za′tion** *n.*

con·cern /kənsórn/ • *v.tr.* **1 a** be relevant or important to. **b** relate to; be about. **2** interest or involve oneself. **3** worry; affect. • *n.* **1** anxiety; worry. **2** matter of interest or importance. **3** business; firm.

con·cerned /kənsórnd/ *adj.* **1** involved; interested. **2** troubled; anxious. □□ **con·cern′ed·ly** *adv.*

con·cern·ing /kənsórning/ *prep.* about; regarding.

con·cert /kónsərt/ *n.* **1 a** a musical performance. **b** comedy, etc., stage performance. **2** agreement. **3** combination of voices or sounds.

con·cert·ed /kənsórtid/ *adj.* jointly arranged or planned.

con·cer·ti·na /kónsərte͞enə/ *n.* small accordion-like musical instrument.

CONCERTINA

con·cer·to /kəncháirto͞/ *n.* (*pl.* **con·cer·ti** /-tee/ or **-tos**) *Mus.* composition for solo instrument(s) and orchestra.

con·ces·sion /kənséshən/ *n.* **1 a** a conceding. **b** thing conceded. **2** right to sell goods in a particular territory. □□ **con·ces′sion·ar·y** *adj.* (also **con·ces′sion·al**).

conch /kongk, konch/ *n.* (*pl.* **conchs** /kongks/ or **conches** /kónchiz/) **1** spiral shell of various marine gastropod mollusks. **2** any such gastropod.

CONCH

con·ci·erge /konseeáirzh, káwNsyáirzh/ *n.* **1** hotel worker who arranges special services for guests. **2** porter for an apartment building, etc.

con·cil·i·ate /kənsíleeayt/ *v.tr.* **1** make calm and amenable; pacify. **2** gain (esteem or goodwill). **3** reconcile. □□ **con·cil·i·a·tive** /-sileeətiv, -áytiv/ *adj.* **con·cil·i·a·tor** *n.* **con·cil·i·a·tory** /-sileeətáwree/ *adj.*

con·cise /kənsís/ *adj.* brief but comprehensive. □□ **con·cise·ly** *adv.* **con·cise·ness** *n.*

con·clave /kónklayv, kóng-/ *n.* **1** private meeting. **2** *RC Ch.* assembly of cardinals for the election of a pope.

con·clude /kənklood/ *v.* **1** *tr.* & *intr.* bring or come to an end. **2** *tr.* infer. **3** *tr.* settle (a treaty, etc.).

con·clu·sion /kənklóozhən/ *n.* **1** final result; end. **2** judgment reached by reasoning. **3** summing-up. **4** settling (of peace, etc.).

con·clu·sive /kənklóosiv/ *adj.* decisive; convincing. □□ **con·clu·sive·ly** *adv.* **con·clu·sive·ness** *n.*

con·coct /kənkókt/ *v.tr.* **1** make by mixing ingredients. **2** invent. □□ **con·coc·tion** /-kókshən/ *n.*

con·com·i·tant /kənkómit'nt/ • *adj.* going together; associated. • *n.* accompanying thing. □□ **con·com'i·tance** *n.* **con·com'i·tant·ly** *adv.*

con·cord /kónkawrd, kóng-/ *n.* agreement; harmony.

con·cor·dance /kənkáwrd'ns/ *n.* **1** agreement. **2** book or book part containing an index of important words used in a book or by an author.

con·course /kónkawrs/ *n.* **1** crowd; gathering. **2** large open area in a building for public use.

con·crete /kónkreet, kóng-, konkréet, kong-/ • *adj.* **1 a** existing in a material form. **b** specific; definite. **2** *Gram.* (of a noun) denoting a material object as opposed to a quality, state, action, etc. • *n.* mixture of gravel, sand, cement, and water, used for building. □□ **con·crete'ly** *adv.* **con·crete'ness** *n.*

con·cre·tion /kənkreeshən/ *n.* **1** hard, solid mass. **2** forming of this.

con·cu·bine /kóngkyəbīn/ *n.* **1** mistress. **2** (in some societies) secondary wife.

con·cu·pis·cence /konkyoopisəns/ *n.* lust. □□ **con·cu'pis·cent** *adj.*

con·cur /kənkór/ *v.intr.* (**con·curred, con·cur·ring**) **1** coincide. **2** agree (with).

con·cur·rent /kənkórənt, -kúr-/ *adj.* existing in or operation at the same time or together. □□ **con·cur'rent·ly** *adv.*

con·cus·sion /kənkúshən/ *n.* **1** *Med.* temporary incapacity due to head injury. **2** violent shaking; shock.

con·demn /kəndém/ *v.tr.* **1** express utter disapproval of. **2 a** find guilty; convict. **b** sentence (to). **3** pronounce (a building, etc.) unfit for use. **4** doom or assign (to something unpleasant). □□ **con·dem·na·ble** /-démnəbəl/ *adj.* **con·dem·na·tion** /kóndemnáyshən/ *n.* **con·dem·na·to·ry** /-démnətáwree/ *adj.*

con·den·sa·tion /kóndensáyshən/ *n.* **1** condensing. **2** condensed liquid. **3** abridgment.

con·dense /kəndéns/ *v.* **1** *tr.* make denser or more concentrated. **2** *tr.* express in fewer words. **3** *tr.* & *intr.* reduce or be reduced to a liquid.

con·dens·er /kəndénsər/ *n.* **1** apparatus or vessel for condensing vapor. **2** *Electr.* = CAPACITOR.

con·de·scend /kóndisénd/ *v.intr.* **1** be gracious enough (to do a thing unworthy of one). **2** behave as if one is on equal terms with (an inferior). **3** (as **condescending** *adj.*) patronizing. □□ **con·de·scend'ing·ly** *adv.* **con·de·scen'sion** *n.*

con·dign /kəndín/ *adj.* (of punishment, etc.) severe and well-deserved. □□ **con·dign'ly** *adv.*

con·di·ment /kóndimənt/ *n.* seasoning or relish for food.

con·di·tion /kəndíshən/ • *n.* **1** stipulation; term(s). **2 a** state of fitness. **b** ailment; abnormality. **3** (in *pl.*) circumstances. • *v.tr.* **1 a** bring into a good or desired state. **b** make fit. **2** teach or accustom.

con·di·tion·al /kəndíshənəl/ *adj.* **1** dependent; not absolute. **2** *Gram.* (of a clause, mood, etc.) expressing a condition. □□ **con·di'tion·al·ly** *adv.*

con·di·tion·er /kəndíshənər/ *n.* agent that conditions, as for the hair.

con·do /kóndō/ *n.* (*pl.* **-dos**) *colloq.* condominium.

con·do·lence /kəndóləns/ *n.* (often *pl.*) expression of sympathy (*sent my condolences*).

con·dom /kóndom/ *n.* prophylactic or contraceptive sheath worn on the penis.

con·do·min·i·um /kóndəmíneeəm/ *n.* **1** building or complex containing individually owned apartments. **2** joint sovereignty.

con·done /kəndón/ *v.tr.* forgive or overlook.

con·dor /kóndawr/ *n.* **1** large S. American vulture. **2** smaller vulture of California.

con·du·cive /kəndóosiv, -dyóo-/ *adj.* contributing or helping (toward something).

con·duct • *n.* /kóndukt/ **1** behavior. **2** action or manner of directing or managing. • *v.* /kəndúkt/ **1** *tr.* direct or manage (business, etc.). **2** *tr.* be the conductor of (an orchestra, etc.). **3** *tr.* transmit (heat, electricity, etc.). **4** *refl.* behave. □□ **con·duct·i·ble** /kəndúktibəl/ *adj.* **con·duct·i·bil'i·ty** *n.*

con·duc·tance /kəndúktəns/ *n.* ability to conduct electricity.

con·duc·tion /kəndúkshən/ *n.* transmission of heat, electricity, etc., through a substance. □□ **con·duc·tive** /-tiv/ *adj.* **con·duc·tiv'i·ty** *n.*

con·duc·tor /kəndúktər/ *n.* **1** person who directs an orchestra, choir, etc. **2** official in charge of passengers on a train, etc. **3** thing that conducts heat or electricity.

con·duit /kóndōoit, -dyōoit, -dit/ *n.* **1** channel or pipe conveying liquids. **2** tube protecting electric wires.

cone /kōn/ *n.* **1** solid figure with a circular (or other curved) plane base, tapering to a point. **2** thing or holder of similar shape. **3** dry fruit of a conifer.

con·fec·tion /kənfékshən/ *n.* sweet dish; candy.

con·fec·tion·er /kənfékshənər/ *n.* maker or retailer of confections. □ **confectioners' sugar** fine powdered sugar.

con·fed·er·a·cy /kənfédərəsee/ *n.* (*pl.* **-cies**) **1** league or alliance. **2** (**the Confederacy**) the 11 Southern states that seceded from the US in 1860–61.

con·fed·er·ate • *adj.* /kənfédərət/ allied. • *n.* /kənfédərət/ **1** ally; accomplice. **2** (**Confederate**) supporter of the Confederacy. • *v.* /kənfédərayt/ **1** *tr.* bring into alliance. **2** *intr.* come into alliance.

con·fed·er·a·tion /kənfédəráyshən/ *n.* **1** union or alliance. **2** confederating; being confederated.

con·fer /kənfər/ *v.* (**con·ferred, con·fer·ring**) **1** *tr.* grant or bestow. **2** *intr.* converse; consult. □□ **con·fer′ment** *n.*

con·fer·ence /kónfərəns, -frəns/ *n.* **1** consultation. **2** meeting. □ **conference call** telephone call in which several people are connected.

con·fer·ral /kənfərəl/ *n.* conferring of a degree, honor, etc.

con·fess /kənfés/ *v.* **1 a** *tr.* acknowledge or admit. **b** *intr.* admit (to). **2** *tr.* admit reluctantly. **3 a** *tr.* declare (one's sins) to a priest. **b** *tr.* (of a priest) hear the confession of.

con·fes·sion /kənféshən/ *n.* **1 a** confessing. **b** thing confessed. **2** declaration of one's beliefs. □□ **con·fes′sion·ar·y** *adj.*

con·fes·sion·al /kənféshənəl/ • *n.* enclosed stall in a church in which a priest hears confessions. • *adj.* of confession.

con·fes·sor /kənfésər/ *n.* priest who hears confessions.

con·fet·ti /kənfétee/ *n.* bits of colored paper thrown during celebrations, etc.

con·fi·dant /kónfidánt, -dáant/ *n.* (*fem.* **con·fi·dante**) person trusted with knowledge of one's private affairs.

con·fide /kənfíd/ *v.* **1** *tr.* tell in confidence. **2** *tr.* entrust (an object, a task, etc.) to. **3** *intr.* (foll. by *in*) talk confidentially to.

con·fi·dence /kónfidəns/ *n.* **1** firm trust. **2 a** feeling of reliance or certainty. **b** sense of self-reliance; boldness. **3** something told confidentially. □ **confidence game** swindle in which the victim is persuaded to trust the swindler. **confidence man** swindler in a confidence game.

con·fi·dent /kónfid'nt/ *adj.* feeling or showing confidence. □□ **con′fi·dent·ly** *adv.*

con·fi·den·tial /kónfidénshəl/ *adj.* spoken or written in confidence. □□ **con·fi·den·ti·al·i·ty** /-sheeálitee/ *n.* **con·fi·den′tial·ly** *adv.*

con·fig·u·ra·tion /kənfigyəráyshən/ *n.* arrangement in a particular form.

con·fine • *v.tr.* /kənfín/ **1** keep or restrict (within certain limits, etc.). **2** imprison. • *n.* /kónfín/ (usu. *pl.*) limit; boundary.

con·fine·ment /kənfínmənt/ *n.* **1** confining; being confined. **2** time of childbirth.

con·firm /kənfərm/ *v.tr.* **1** settle the truth or correctness of. **2** make formally valid. **3** encourage (a person) in (an opinion, etc.). **4** administer the religious rite of confirmation to. □□ **con·firm′a·tive** *adj.* **con·firm′a·to·ry** *adj.*

con·fir·ma·tion /kónfərmáyshən/ *n.* **1** confirming; being confirmed. **2** rite confirming a baptized person as a church member.

con·firmed /kənfərmd/ *adj.* firmly settled in some habit or condition (*a confirmed bachelor*).

con·fis·cate /kónfiskayt/ *v.tr.* take or seize by authority. □□ **con·fis·ca·tion** /-káyshən/ *n.* **con′fis·ca·tor** *n.*

con·fla·gra·tion /kónfləgráyshən/ *n.* great and destructive fire.

con·flate /kənfláyt/ *v.tr.* blend or fuse together (esp. two variant texts into one). □□ **con·fla·tion** /-fláyshən/ *n.*

con·flict • *n.* /kónflikt/ **1** state of opposition. **2** fight; struggle. • *v.intr.* /kənflíkt/ clash; be incompatible.

con·flu·ence /kónflōoəns/ *n.* **1** place where two rivers meet. **2** coming together.

con·form /kənfáwrm/ *v.* **1** *intr.* comply with rules or general custom. **2** *tr.* make similar. **3** *intr.* comply with; be in accordance with.

con·form·a·ble /kənfáwrməbəl/ *adj.* **1** similar. **2** consistent. **3** adaptable. □□ **con·form·a·bil′i·ty** *n.* **con·form′a·bly** *adv.*

con·for·ma·tion /kónfawrmáyshən/ *n.* way a thing is formed; shape.

con·form·ist /kənfáwrmist/ • *n.* person who conforms to established practice. • *adj.* conforming; conventional. □□ **con·form′ism** *n.*

con·form·i·ty /kənfáwrmitee/ *n.* **1** accordance with established practice. **2** agreement; suitability.

con·found /kənfównd/ *v.tr.* **1** perplex. **2** confuse (in one's mind).

con·front /kənfrúnt/ *v.tr.* **1 a** face in hostility or defiance. **b** face up to and deal with. **2** present itself to. **3** bring (a person) face to face with. **4** meet or stand facing. □□ **con·fron·ta·tion** /kónfruntáyshən/ *n.* **con·fron·ta′tion·al** *adj.*

Con·fu·cian /kənfyōoshən/ *adj.* of or relating to Confucius, Chinese philosopher d. 479 BC, or his philosophy. □□ **Con·fu′cian·ism** *n.* **Con·fu′cian·ist** *n.*

con·fuse /kənfyōoz/ *v.tr.* **1** perplex; bewilder. **2** mix up in the mind; mistake (one for another). **3** make indistinct (*that point confuses the issue*). □□ **con·fus′ed·ly** *adv.* **con·fus′ing** *adj.* **con·fus′ing·ly** *adv.*

con·fu·sion /kənfyōo<u>zh</u>ən/ *n.* confusing or being confused.

con·fute /kənfyōot/ *v.tr.* prove to be in error. □□ **con·fu·ta·tion** /kónfyootáyshən/ *n.*

Cong. *abbr.* **1** Congress. **2** Congressional. **3** Congregational.

con·ga /kónggə/ *n.* **1** Latin American line dance. **2** tall, narrow drum beaten with the hands.

con·geal /kənjéel/ *v.* **1** make or become semisolid by cooling. **2** coagulate.

con·ge·ni·al /kənjéenyəl/ *adj.* **1** pleasantly sociable. **2** suited or agreeable. □□ **con·ge·ni·al·i·ty** /-jéeneeálitee/ *n.* **con·gen′ial·ly** *adv.*

con·gen·i·tal /kənjénitəl/ *adj.* (esp. of a disease,

defect, etc.) existing from birth. □□ **con·gen′**
i·tal·ly adv.

con·ger /kónggər/ n. large marine eel.

con·ge·ries /kənjeéreez, kónjə-/ n. (pl. same)
disorderly collection; mass or heap.

con·gest /kənjést/ v.tr. (esp. as **congested** adj.)
affect with congestion. □□ **con·ges′tive** adj.

con·ges·tion /kənjés-chən/ n. abnormal accumulation or obstruction.

con·glom·er·ate • adj. /kənglómərət/ gathered
into a rounded mass. • n. /kənglómərət/ **1** heterogeneous mass. **2** group or corporation. • v.
/kənglómərayt/ collect into a coherent mass.
□□ **con·glom·er·a·tion** /-ráyshən/ n.

con·grat·u·late /kəngráchəlayt, -gráj-, kəng-/
v.tr. express pleasure at the good fortune or
excellence of (a person). □□ **con·grat·u·la·to·ry**
/-lətáwree/ adj.

con·grat·u·la·tion /kəngráchəláyshən, -gráj-,
kəng-/ n. **1** congratulating. **2** (usu. pl.) expression of this.

con·gre·gate /kónggrigayt/ v. collect or gather
into a crowd or mass.

con·gre·ga·tion /kónggrigáyshən/ n. **1** gathering of people, esp. for religious worship. **2** body
of persons regularly attending a particular
church, etc.

con·gre·ga·tion·al /kónggrigáyshənəl/ adj. **1** of
a congregation. **2** (**Congregational**) of or adhering to Congregationalism, a Christian denomination of churches that are largely self-
governing. □□ **Con·gre·ga′tion·al·ist** n.

con·gress /kónggris/ n. **1** formal meeting of delegates for discussion. **2** (**Congress**) national legislative body of the US. □□ **con·gres·sion·al**
/kəngréshən'l/ adj.

con·gress·man /kónggrismən/ n. (pl. **-men**; fem.
con·gress·wom·an, pl. **-wom·en**) member of the
US Congress.

con·gru·ent /kónggro+ənt, kəngroo-/ adj. **1** suitable; agreeing. **2** Geom. coinciding when superimposed. □□ **con′gru·ence** n.

con·gru·ous /kónggroōəs/ adj. suitable; fitting.
□□ **con·gru′i·ty** n. **con′gru·ous·ly** adv.

con·ic /kónik/ adj. of a cone. □ **con′i·cal** adj.
con′i·cal·ly adv.

co·ni·fer /kónifər, kó-/ n. any cone-bearing tree
or shrub, usu. evergreen. □□ **co·nif·er·ous** /kə-
nífərəs/ adj.

conj. abbr. conjunction.

con·jec·ture /kənjékchər/ • n. formation of an
opinion on incomplete information. • v. guess.
□□ **con·jec′tur·al** adj.

con·join /kənjóyn/ v. join; combine.

con·joint /kənjóynt/ adj. associated; conjoined.
□□ **con·joint′ly** adv.

con·ju·gal /kónjəgəl/ adj. pertaining to marriage.
□□ **con·ju·gal·i·ty** /-gálitee/ n. **con′ju·gal·ly** adv.

con·ju·gate • v. /kónjəgayt/ **1** tr. Gram. give
the different forms of (a verb). **2** intr. **a** unite.
b become fused. • adj. /kónjəgət, -gayt/ joined
together; fused.

con·ju·ga·tion /kónjəgáyshən/ n. Gram. system
of verbal inflection. □□ **con·ju·ga′tion·al** adj.

con·junct /kənjúngkt/ adj. joined together; associated.

con·junc·tion /kənjúngkshən/ n. **1** joining; connection. **2** Gram. connective word (e.g., and,
but, if). **3** combination (of events or circumstances).

con·junc·ti·va /kónjungktívə, kənjúngktivə/ n.
(pl. **con·junc·ti·vas** or **con·junc·ti·vae** /-vee/)
Anat. mucous membrane of the eye. □□ **con·**
junc·ti′val adj.

con·junc·tive /kənjúngktiv/ adj. **1** serving to
join; connective. **2** Gram. of the nature of a
conjunction.

con·junc·ti·vi·tis /kənjúngktivítis/ n. inflammation of the conjunctiva.

con·jure /kónjər/ v. **1** tr. call upon (a spirit) to
appear. **2** tr. evoke. **3** intr. perform seemingly
magical tricks. □ **conjure up** produce as if by
magic.

conk /kongk/ v.tr. sl. hit on the head, etc. □ **conk**
out 1 (of a machine, etc.) break down. **2** (of a
person) be exhausted and give up; faint.

Conn. abbr. Connecticut.

con·nect /kənékt/ v. **1 a** tr. join (one thing with
another). **b** intr. be joined or joinable. **2** tr. associate mentally or practically. **3** intr. (of a train,
etc.) be timed such that passengers can transfer (to another train, etc.). **4** tr. put into communication. **5** intr. colloq. hit or strike effectively.
□□ **con·nec′tor** n.

con·nec·tion /kənékshən/ n. **1** connecting; being connected. **2** meeting point. **3** link, esp. by
telephone. **4** connecting train, flight, etc. **5** (often in pl.) relevant or helpful acquaintance. **6**
relation of ideas.

con·nec·tive /kənéktiv/ adj. serving or tending
to connect, esp. of body tissue.

conn·ing tow·er /kóning/ n. **1** superstructure of
a submarine containing the periscope. **2** pilot-
house of a warship.

con·nive /kənív/ v.intr. **1** (foll. by at) disregard or
tacitly consent to (a wrongdoing). **2** conspire.

con·nois·seur /kónəsőr/ n. expert judge in matters of taste.

con·note /kənót/ v.tr. imply in addition to the
literal or primary meaning. □□ **con·no·ta′tion** n.
con·no·ta·tive /kónətaytiv, kənótətiv/ adj.
¶ **Connote** means 'suggest': "Mother" connotes
warmth, concern, and security. **Denote** refers to
the literal meaning: "Mother" denotes a female
who has given birth.

con·nu·bi·al /kənoֹobeeəl, kənyoֹo-/ adj. of or
relating to marriage. □□ **con·nu′bi·al·ly** adv.

con·quer /kóngkər/ v.tr. **1 a** overcome militarily. **b** be victorious. **2** overcome (a habit, challenge, etc.) by effort. □□ **con′quer·a·ble** adj.
con′quer·or n.

con·quest /kóngkwest/ n. **1** conquering; being
conquered. **2** something won. **3** person whose
affection has been won.

con·quis·ta·dor /konkwístədawr, kongkeésta-/
n. (pl. **con·quis·ta·dor·es** /-dáwrez/ or **con·quis·**
ta·dors) conqueror, esp. a 16th-c. Spanish conqueror of Mexico and Peru.

con·san·guin·e·ous /kónsanggwíneeəs/ adj.
descended from the same ancestor; akin.
□□ **con·san·guin′i·ty** n.

con·science /kónshəns/ n. moral sense of right
and wrong. □ **in all conscience** by any reasonable
standard.

con·sci·en·tious /kónshee-énshəs/ adj. diligent

and scrupulous. □ **conscientious objector** person who refrains from military service on moral grounds. □□ **con·sci·en′tious·ly** *adv.* **con·sci·en′tious·ness** *n.*

con·scious /kónshəs/ ● *adj.* **1** awake and aware of one's surroundings and identity. **2 a** aware; knowing. **b** intentional. **3** (in *comb.*) aware of; concerned with (*appearance-conscious*). ● *n.* (prec. by *the*) the conscious mind. □□ **con′scious·ly** *adv.* **con′scious·ness** *n.*

con·script ● *v.tr.* /kənskrípt/ summon for compulsory (esp. military) service. ● *n.* /kónskript/ conscripted person. □□ **con·scrip′tion** *n.*

con·se·crate /kónsikrayt/ *v.tr.* **1** make or declare sacred. **2** (foll. by *to*) devote to (a purpose). □□ **con·se·cra·tion** /-kráyshən/ *n.* **con′se·cra·tor** *n.*

con·sec·u·tive /kənsékyətiv/ *adj.* following continuously; in unbroken or logical order. □□ **con·sec′u·tive·ly** *adv.* **con·sec′u·tive·ness** *n.*

con·sen·sus /kənsénsəs/ *n.* general agreement or opinion.

con·sent /kənsént/ ● *v.intr.* express willingness; agree. ● *n.* voluntary agreement; permission.

con·se·quence /kónsikwens, -kwəns/ *n.* **1** result or effect of an action or condition. **2** importance.

con·se·quent /kónsikwənt/ *adj.* following as a result or consequence.

con·se·quen·tial /kónsikwénshəl/ *adj.* **1** following as a consequence. **2** resulting indirectly. **3** significant. □□ **con·se·quen′tial·ly** *adv.*

con·se·quent·ly /kónsikwentlee/ *adv.* & *conj.* as a result; therefore.

con·ser·van·cy /kənsэ́rvənsee/ *n.* (*pl.* **-cies**) **1** body concerned with the preservation of natural resources. **2** official preservation (of forests, etc.).

con·ser·va·tion /kónsərváyshən/ *n.* preservation, esp. of the natural environment. □ **conservation of energy** *Physics* principle that the total quantity of energy of any system not subject to external action remains constant. □□ **con·ser·va′tion·al** *adj.* **con·ser·va′tion·ist** *n.*

con·ser·va·tive /kənsэ́rvətiv/ ● *adj.* **1 a** averse to rapid change. **b** moderate; avoiding extremes. **2** (of an estimate, etc.) purposely low. **3** tending to conserve. ● *n.* conservative person. □□ **con·ser′va·tism** *n.* **con·ser′va·tive·ly** *adv.* **con·ser′va·tive·ness** *n.*

con·ser·va·to·ry /kənsэ́rvətawree/ *n.* (*pl.* **-ries**) **1** greenhouse. **2** music school.

con·serve /kənsэ́rv/ ● *v.tr.* **1** keep from harm or damage, esp. for later use. **2** *Physics* maintain a quantity of (heat, etc.). **3** preserve (food, esp. fruit), usu. with sugar. ● *n.* (also /kónsərv/) fresh fruit jam.

con·sid·er /kənsídər/ *v.tr.* **1** contemplate; weigh and evaluate. **2** examine the merits of. **3** give attention to. **4** take into account. **5** regard as. **6** (as **considered** *adj.*) deliberated. □ **all things considered** taking everything into account.

con·sid·er·a·ble /kənsídərəbəl/ *adj.* **1** much; a lot of. **2** notable; important. □□ **con·sid′er·a·bly** *adv.*

con·sid·er·ate /kənsídərət/ *adj.* thoughtful toward others. □□ **con·sid′er·ate·ly** *adv.*

con·sid·er·a·tion /kənsídəráyshən/ *n.* **1** careful thought. **2** thoughtfulness. **3** fact or thing taken into account. **4** compensation; payment or reward.

con·sid·er·ing /kənsídəring/ ● *prep.* in view of; because of. ● *adv. colloq.* all in all (*not so bad, considering*).

con·sign /kənsín/ *v.tr.* **1** hand over; deliver. **2** assign; commit. **3** transmit or send (goods). □□ **con·sign·ee** /kónsínée/ *n.* **con·sign′or** *n.*

con·sign·ment /kənsínmənt/ *n.* **1** consigning; being consigned. **2** goods consigned. **3** agreement to pay a supplier of goods after the goods are sold.

con·sist /kənsíst/ *v.intr.* be composed; have as ingredients or essential features.

con·sis·ten·cy /kənsístənsee/ *n.* (*pl.* **-cies**) **1** degree of density, viscosity, etc., esp. of liquids. **2** being consistent.

con·sis·tent /kənsístənt/ *adj.* **1** compatible or in harmony. **2** (of a person) constant. □□ **con·sist′ent·ly** *adv.*

con·so·la·tion /kónsəláyshən/ *n.* **1** consoling; being consoled. **2** consoling thing, person, or circumstance.

con·sole[1] /kənsól/ *v.tr.* comfort, esp. in grief or disappointment. □□ **con·sol′a·ble** *adj.* **con·sol′er** *n.* **con·sol′ing·ly** *adv.*

con·sole[2] /kónsól/ *n.* **1** panel for switches, controls, etc. **2** appliance cabinet. **3** cabinet for an organ's keyboards, etc.

con·sol·i·date /kənsólidayt/ *v.* **1** *tr.* & *intr.* make or become strong or solid. **2** *tr.* combine into one whole. □□ **con·sol·i·da·tion** /-dáyshən/ *n.* **con·sol′i·da·tor** *n.*

con·som·mé /kónsəmáy/ *n.* clear soup from meat stock.

con·so·nant /kónsənənt/ ● *n.* **1** speech sound in which the breath is at least partly obstructed. **2** letter(s) representing this. ● *adj.* consistent; in agreement or harmony.

con·sort[1] ● *n.* /kónsawrt/ spouse, esp. of royalty. ● *v.intr.* /kənsórt/ keep company; associate.

con·sort[2] /kónsawrt/ *n. Mus.* group of players, singers, etc.

con·sor·tium /kənsáwrsheeəm, -teeəm/ *n.* (*pl.* **-ti·a** /-sheeə, -teeə/ or **-ti·ums**) association, esp. of several firms.

con·spic·u·ous /kənspíkyŏŏəs/ *adj.* **1** clearly visible; attracting notice. **2** remarkable of its kind. □□ **con·spic′u·ous·ly** *adv.* **con·spic′u·ous·ness** *n.*

con·spir·a·cy /kənspírəsee/ *n.* (*pl.* **-cies**) **1** secret plan to commit a crime; a plot. **2** conspiring.

con·spir·a·tor /kənspírətər/ *n.* person who takes part in a conspiracy. □□ **con·spir·a·to·ri·al** /-táwreeəl/ *adj.*

con·spire /kənspír/ *v.intr.* **1** collude for an unlawful or harmful act. **2** (of events) seem to be working together.

con·sta·ble /kónstəbəl, kún-/ *n.* peace officer, esp. in a small town.

con·stab·u·lar·y /kənstábyəleree/ *n.* (*pl.* **-ies**) constables, collectively.

con·stan·cy /kónstənsee/ *n.* dependability; faithfulness.

con·stant /kónstənt/ ● *adj.* **1** continuous. **2** occurring frequently. **3** faithful; dependable. ● *n.* anything that does not vary. □□ **con′stant·ly** *adv.*

con·stel·la·tion /kónstəláyshən/ *n.* **1** group of associated stars. **2** assemblage of persons, ideas, etc.

consternation ~ content 122

con·ster·na·tion /kónstərnáyshən/ *n.* anxiety; dismay.

con·sti·pate /kónstipayt/ *v.tr.* affect with constipation.

con·sti·pa·tion /kónstipáyshən/ *n.* difficulty in emptying the bowels.

con·stit·u·en·cy /kənstíchoĭoənsee/ *n.* (*pl.* **-cies**) **1** body of voters who elect a representative. **2** area so represented.

con·stit·u·ent /kənstíchoĭoənt/ • *adj.* **1** composing; constituting. **2** able to make or change a constitution. **3** electing. • *n.* **1** member of a constituency. **2** component.

con·sti·tute /kónstitoŏot, tyoŏot/ *v.tr.* **1** be the components or essence of; make up. **2** amount to. **3** give legal or constitutional form to. □□ **con′sti·tu·tor** *n.*

con·sti·tu·tion /kónstitoŏoshən, -tyoŏo-/ *n.* **1** act or method of constituting; composition. **2** body of fundamental governing principles. **3** person's health, strength, etc.

con·sti·tu·tion·al /kónstitoŏoshənəl, -tyoŏo-/ • *adj.* **1** pertaining to a constitution. **2** inherent. • *n.* walk taken regularly for health. □□ **con·sti·tu·tion·al·i·ty** /-álitee/ *n.* **con·sti·tu′tion·al·ly** *adv.*

con·strain /kənstráyn/ *v.tr.* **1** compel. **2 a** confine forcibly. **b** restrict severely. **3** (as **constrained** *adj.*) forced; embarrassed.

con·straint /kənstráynt/ *n.* **1** constraining; being constrained. **2** restriction. **3** self-control.

con·strict /kənstríkt/ *v.tr.* make narrow or tight; compress. □□ **con·stric·tion** /-stríkshən/ *n.* **con·stric′tive** *adj.*

con·stric·tor /kənstríktər/ *n.* **1** snake that kills by compressing. **2** muscle that compresses a part of the body.

con·struct • *v.tr.* /kənstrúkt/ make by fitting together; build. • *n.* /kónstrukt/ thing constructed, esp. by the mind. □□ **con·struc′tor** *n.*

con·struc·tion /kənstrúkshən/ *n.* **1** constructing. **2** thing constructed. **3** interpretation or explanation. **4** particular arrangement of words. □□ **con·struc′tion·al** *adj.*

con·struc·tive /kənstrúktiv/ *adj.* **1** tending to form a basis for ideas. **2** helpful; positive. □□ **con·struc′tive·ly** *adv.*

con·strue /kənstroŏo/ *v.tr.* **1** interpret. **2** analyze the syntax of (a sentence). **3** translate word for word.

con·sul /kónsəl/ *n.* **1** official appointed by a government to protect its citizens and interests in a foreign city. **2** *hist.* either of two chief magistrates in ancient Rome. □□ **con′sul·ar** *adj.* **con′sul·ship** *n.*

con·sul·ate /kónsələt/ *n.* **1** building officially used by a consul. **2** position of consul.

con·sult /kənsúlt/ *v.* **1** *tr.* seek information or advice from. **2** *intr.* solicit counsel. **3** *intr.* give counsel. **4** *tr.* take into account (feelings, interests, etc.). □□ **con·sul·ta·tive** /-súltətiv/ *adj.*

con·sult·ant /kənsúlt'nt/ *n.* person providing professional advice, etc.

con·sul·ta·tion /kónsəltáyshən/ *n.* **1** meeting arranged to consult. **2** act or instance of consulting.

con·sume /kənsoŏom/ *v.tr.* **1** eat or drink. **2** destroy. **3** possess (*consumed with rage*). **4** use up. □□ **con·sum′a·ble** *adj.* & *n.*

con·sum·er /kənsoŏomər/ *n.* person who consumes, esp. one who uses a product or service.

con·sum·er·ism /kənsoŏomərizəm/ *n.* protection or promotion of consumers' interests. □□ **con·sum′er·ist** *adj.* & *n.*

con·sum·mate • *v.tr.* /kónsəmayt/ **1** complete; make perfect. **2** complete (a marriage) by sexual intercourse. • *adj.* /kənsúmit, kónsəmit/ complete; perfect. □□ **con·sum′mate·ly** *adv.* **con·sum·ma·tion** /-máyshən/ *n.* **con·sum·ma′tive** *adj.* **con′sum·ma·tor** *n.*

con·sump·tion /kənsúmpshən/ *n.* **1** consuming; being consumed. **2** purchase and use of goods, etc. **3** amount consumed. **4** *obs.* tuberculosis.

cont. *abbr.* **1** contents. **2** continued.

con·tact • *n.* /kóntakt/ **1** state or condition of touching, meeting, or communicating. **2** person useful to deal with. **3** connection for electric current. **4** *colloq.* contact lens. • *v.tr.* /kóntakt, kəntákt/ get in touch with. □ **contact lens** small lens placed directly on eyeball to correct vision.

con·ta·gion /kəntáyjən/ *n.* **1 a** communication of disease by bodily contact. **b** contagious disease. **2** moral corruption.

con·ta·gious /kəntáyjəs/ *adj.* **1 a** (of a person) likely to transmit disease by contact. **b** (of a disease) transmitted in this way. **2** (of emotions, etc.) likely to spread.

con·tain /kəntáyn/ *v.tr.* **1** hold or be capable of holding within itself. **2** (of measures) be equal to. **3** prevent from moving or extending. **4** control or restrain (feelings, etc.).

con·tain·er /kəntáynər/ *n.* jar, box, etc., for holding things.

con·tain·er·ize /kəntáynəríz/ *v.tr.* pack in or transport by container. □□ **con·tain·er·i·za′tion** *n.*

con·tain·ment /kəntáynmənt/ *n.* prevention of hostile incursion.

con·tam·i·nate /kəntáminayt/ *v.tr.* **1** pollute. **2** infect. □□ **con·tam·i·nant** /-minənt/ *n.* **con·tam·i·na·tion** /-náyshən/ *n.* **con·tam′i·na·tor** *n.*

con·tem·plate /kóntəmplayt/ *v.* **1** *tr.* survey visually or mentally. **2** *tr.* regard (an event) as possible. **3** *tr.* intend. **4** *intr.* meditate. □□ **con·tem·pla·tion** /-pláyshən/ *n.* **con·tem′pla·tive** *adj.*

con·tem·po·ra·ne·ous /kəntémpəráyneeəs/ *adj.* existing or occurring at the same time. □□ **con·tem·po·ra′ne·ous·ly** *adv.*

con·tem·po·rar·y /kəntémpərəree/ • *adj.* **1** living or occurring at the same time. **2** about the same age. **3** modern in style. • *n.* (*pl.* **-ies**) contemporary person or thing.

con·tempt /kəntémpt/ *n.* **1** feeling of scorn or extreme reproach. **2** being so regarded. **3** disrespect shown to a court, etc. □ **beneath contempt** utterly despicable. **hold in contempt** despise.

con·tempt·i·ble /kəntémptibəl/ *adj.* deserving contempt. □□ **con·tempt′i·bly** *adv.*

con·temp·tu·ous /kəntémpchoŏoəs/ *adj.* showing contempt. □□ **con·temp′tu·ous·ly** *adv.*

con·tend /kənténd/ *v.* **1** *intr.* strive; fight. **2** *intr.* compete. **3** *tr.* assert; maintain. □□ **con·tend′er** *n.*

con·tent[1] /kəntént/ • *adj.* **1** satisfied; adequately happy. **2** willing. • *v.tr.* satisfy. • *n.* contented state.

con·tent[2] /kóntent/ *n.* **1** (usu. in *pl.*) what is contained, as in a vessel, book, or house. **2**

con·tent·ed /kənténtid/ *adj.* happy; satisfied. □□ **con·tent′ed·ly** *adv.* **con·tent′ed·ness** *n.*

con·ten·tion /kənténshən/ *n.* **1** dispute or argument; rivalry. **2** point contended.

con·ten·tious /kənténshəs/ *adj.* **1** quarrelsome. **2** likely to cause an argument. □□ **con·ten′tious·ly** *adv.* **con·ten′tious·ness** *n.*

con·tent·ment /kənténtmənt/ *n.* satisfied state; tranquil happiness.

con·test • *n.* /kóntest/ **1** contending; competition. **2** dispute. • *v.tr.* /kəntést, kóntest/ **1** dispute. **2** contend or compete for. □□ **con·test·a·ble** /kəntéstəbəl/ *adj.*

con·test·ant /kəntéstənt/ *n.* person taking part in a contest.

con·text /kóntekst/ *n.* **1** parts that surround and clarify a word or passage. **2** relevant circumstances. □□ **con·tex·tu·al** /kəntéks-chōoəl/ *adj.* **con·tex′tu·al·ize** *v.tr.* **con·tex·tu·al·i·za′tion** *n.* **con·tex′tu·al·ly** *adv.*

con·tig·u·ous /kəntígyōoəs/ *adj.* touching; in contact. □□ **con·tig′u·ous·ly** *adv.*

con·ti·nent[1] /kóntinənt/ *n.* any of earth's main land masses.

con·ti·nent[2] /kóntinənt/ *adj.* **1** able to control one's bowels and bladder. **2** exercising self-restraint. □□ **con′ti·nence** *n.*

con·ti·nen·tal /kóntinént′l/ *adj.* of a continent. □ **continental breakfast** light breakfast of coffee, rolls, etc.

con·tin·gen·cy /kəntínjənsee/ *n.* (*pl.* **-cies**) **1** event that may or may not occur. **2** uncertainty; chance.

con·tin·gent /kəntínjənt/ • *adj.* **1** conditional; dependent (on an uncertain circumstance). **2** that may or may not occur. • *n.* body (of troops, ships, etc.) forming part of a larger group.

con·tin·u·al /kəntínyōoəl/ *adj.* constantly or frequently recurring. □□ **con·tin′u·al·ly** *adv.*
¶ In precise usage, **continual** means 'frequent, repeating at intervals' and **continuous** means 'going on without pause or interruption': *We suffered from the continual attacks of mosquitoes. The waterfall's continuous flow creates an endless roar.*

con·tin·u·ance /kəntínyōoəns/ *n.* **1** continuing in existence or operation. **2** duration. **3** *Law* postponement.

con·tin·u·a·tion /kəntínyōo-áyshən/ *n.* **1** continuing; being continued. **2** part that continues something else.

con·tin·ue /kəntínyōo/ *v.* **1** *tr.* maintain; not stop. **2** *tr.* resume or prolong (a narrative, journey, etc.). **3** *tr.* be a sequel to. **4** *intr.* remain.

con·ti·nu·i·ty /kóntinōoitee, -nyōo-/ *n.* (*pl.* **-ties**) **1** state of being continuous. **2** logical sequence.

con·tin·u·ous /kəntínyōoəs/ *adj.* unbroken; uninterrupted. □□ **con·tin′u·ous·ly** *adv.* /kəntín-yōoəs/ *adj.* unbroken; uninterrupted. □□ **con·tin′u·ous·ly** *adv.*
¶ See note at CONTINUAL.

con·tin·u·um /kəntínyōoəm/ *n.* (*pl.* **con·tin·u·a** /-yōoə/ or **con·tin·u·ums**) thing having a continuous structure.

con·tort /kəntáwrt/ *v.tr.* twist or force out of normal shape. □□ **con·tor′tion** /kəntáwrshən/ *n.*

con·tor·tion·ist /kəntáwrshənist/ *n.* entertainer who adopts contorted postures.

con·tour /kóntŏor/ • *n.* outline. • *v.tr.* mark with contour lines.

contra- /kóntrə/ *comb. form* against; opposite.

con·tra·band /kóntrəband/ • *n.* smuggled goods. • *adj.* forbidden from import or export.

con·tra·cep·tion /kóntrəsépshən/ *n.* prevention of pregnancy esp. by artificial means. □□ **con·tra·cep′tive** *adj.* & *n.*

con·tract • *n.* /kóntrakt/ **1** written or spoken agreement, esp. one enforceable by law. **2** document recording this. • *v.* /kəntrákt, kóntrakt/ **1** *tr.* & *intr.* make or become smaller. **2 a** *intr.* make a contract. **b** *tr.* arrange (work) to be done by contract. **3** *tr.* catch or develop (a disease).

con·trac·tile /kəntrákt′l, -tīl/ *adj.* capable of or producing contraction. □□ **con·trac·til·i·ty** /kóntraktílitee/ *n.*

con·trac·tion /kəntrákshən/ *n.* **1** contracting. **2** *Med.* shortening of the uterine muscles during childbirth. **3** shortened word form (e.g., *it's* for *it is*).

con·trac·tor /kóntraktər, kəntráktər/ *n.* person who makes a contract, as to provide services.

con·trac·tu·al /kəntrákchōoəl/ *adj.* of or in the nature of a contract. □□ **con·trac′tu·al·ly** *adv.*

con·tra·dict /kóntrədíkt/ *v.tr.* **1** deny (a statement). **2** deny a statement made by (a person). **3** be in opposition to or in conflict with. □□ **con·tra·dic·tion** /-díkshən/ *n.* **con·tra·dic·to·ry** /-tawree/ *adj.*

con·tra·dis·tinc·tion /kóntrədistíngkshən/ *n.* distinction made by contrast.

con·trail /kóntrayl/ *n.* condensation trail, esp. from a jet.

con·tral·to /kəntráltō/ *n.* (*pl.* **-tos**) **1** lowest female singing voice. **2** singer with this voice.

con·trap·tion /kəntrápshən/ *n.* machine or device, esp. a strange one.

con·tra·pun·tal /kóntrəpúnt′l/ *adj. Mus.* of or in counterpoint. □□ **con·tra·pun′tal·ly** *adv.* **con·tra·pun′tist** *n.*

con·trar·i·wise /kəntráireewīz/ *adv.* **1** on the other hand. **2** in the opposite way.

con·trar·y /kóntreree/ • *adj.* **1** opposed in nature or tendency. **2** /kəntráiree/ self-willed. **3** (of a wind) unfavorable. **4** opposite in position or direction. • *n.* (*pl.* **-ies**) (prec. by *the*) the opposite. • *adv.* (foll. by *to*) in utter contrast. □□ **con·trar′i·ly** *adv.* **con·trar′i·ness** *n.*

con·trast • *n.* /kóntrast/ **1 a** juxtaposition or comparison showing differences. **b** difference so revealed. **2** thing or person having different qualities. **3** range of color or tone in a picture. • *v.* /kəntrást, kóntrast/ set together so as to reveal a contrast.
¶ **Contrast** means 'note the differences.' **Compare**, though, means 'note the similarities.'

con·tra·vene /kóntrəvéen/ *v.tr.* **1** infringe (a law, etc.). **2** (of things) conflict with. □□ **con·tra·ven′tion** *n.*

con·tre·temps /kóntrətóN/ *n.* awkward or unfortunate occurrence.

con·trib·ute /kəntríbyōot/ *v.tr.* **1** give (money, help, etc.) toward a common purpose. **2** supply (an article, etc.) for publication. □□ **con·trib′u·tor** *n.*

con·tri·bu·tion /kóntribyōoshən/ *n.* **1** act of contributing. **2** thing contributed.

con·trite /kəntrít, kóntrīt/ *adj.* penitent; feeling remorse. □□ **con·trite'ly** *adv.* **con·trite'ness** *n.* **con·tri'tion** *n.*

con·triv·ance /kəntrívəns/ *n.* **1** something contrived, esp. a mechanical device or a plan. **2** act of contriving.

con·trive /kəntrív/ *v.tr.* devise; plan or make resourcefully.

con·trived /kəntrívd/ *adj.* artificial; forced.

con·trol /kəntról/ • *n.* **1** power of directing. **2** power of restraining, esp. self-restraint. **3** means of restraint. **4** (usu. in *pl.*) means of regulating. **5** (usu. in *pl.*) switches, etc., by which a machine is controlled. **6** place where something is overseen. **7** standard of comparison in an experiment. • *v. tr.* (**con·trolled, con·trol·ling**) **1** have control of; regulate. **2** hold in check. □□ **con·trol'la·ble** *adj.* **con·trol·la·bil'i·ty** *n.* **con·trol'la·bly** *adv.*

con·trol·ler /kəntrólər/ *n.* **1** person or thing that controls. **2** person in charge of expenditures.

con·tro·ver·sial /kóntrəvərshəl/ *adj.* causing or subject to controversy. □□ **con·tro·ver'sial·ly** *adv.*

con·tro·ver·sy /kóntrəvərsee/ *n.* (*pl.* **-sies**) prolonged argument or dispute.

con·tro·vert /kóntrəvərt/ *v.tr.* dispute; deny. □□ **con·tro·vert'i·ble** *adj.*

con·tu·ma·cious /kóntoomáyshəs, -tyoo-/ *adj.* stubbornly or willfully disobedient.

con·tu·me·ly /kóntoomələe, -toomlee, -too-, -tyoo-/ *n.* **1** insolent language or treatment. **2** disgrace.

con·tuse /kəntooz, -tyooz/ *v.tr.* bruise. □□ **con·tu·sion** /-zhən/ *n.*

co·nun·drum /kənúndrəm/ *n.* **1** riddle, esp. one with a pun in its answer. **2** puzzling question.

con·ur·ba·tion /kónərbáyshən/ *n.* extended urban area.

con·va·lesce /kónvəlés/ *v.intr.* recover health after illness. □□ **con·va·les'cence** *n.* **con·va·les'cent** *adj.*

con·vec·tion /kənvékshən/ *n.* heat transfer by upward movement of a heated and less dense medium.

con·vene /kənveén/ *v.* **1** *tr.* summon or arrange (a meeting, etc.). **2** *intr.* assemble.

con·ven·ience /kənveényəns/ *n.* **1** state of being convenient; suitability. **2** useful thing. □ **at one's convenience** at a time or place that suits one. **convenience store** store with basic groceries, etc., usu. having extended hours.

con·ven·ient /kənveényənt/ *adj.* serving one's comfort or interests; suitable. □□ **con·ven'ient·ly** *adv.*

con·vent /kónvent, -vənt/ *n.* **1** religious community, esp. of nuns. **2** premises for this.

con·ven·tion /kənvénshən/ *n.* **1** general custom or customary practice. **2** assembly for a common purpose. **3** formal agreement, esp. between nations.

con·ven·tion·al /kənvénshənəl/ *adj.* **1** depending on or according to convention. **2** (of a person) attentive to social conventions. **3** usual; commonplace. **4** (of weapons, etc.) nonnuclear. □□ **con·ven'tion·al·ism** *n.* **con·ven'tion·al·ist** *n.* **con·ven·tion·al·i·ty** /-shənálitee/ *n.* **con·ven'tion·al·ly** *adv.*

con·verge /kənvórj/ *v.intr.* **1** come together or toward the same point. **2** approach from different directions. □□ **con·ver'gence** *n.* **con·ver'gent** *adj.*

con·ver·sant /kənvórsənt, kónvərs-/ *adj.* well acquainted (with).

con·ver·sa·tion /kónvərsáyshən/ *n.* **1** informal spoken communication. **2** instance of this. □□ **con·ver·sa'tion·al** *adj.* **con·ver·sa'tion·al·ist** *n.*

con·verse¹ /kənvórs/ *v.intr.* talk.

con·verse² • *adj.* /kənvórs, kónvərs/ opposite; contrary; reversed. • *n.* /kónvərs/ something opposite or contrary. □□ **con·verse'ly** *adv.*

con·ver·sion /kənvórzhən, -shən/ *n.* converting; being converted.

con·vert • *v.* /kənvórt/ **1 a** *tr.* change in form or function. **b** *intr.* be converted. **2** *tr.* cause (a person) to change beliefs, etc. **3** *tr.* change (money, etc.). **4** *tr.* modify structurally. **5** *tr.* (in certain sports) score an extra point or points. • *n.* /kónvərt/ person converted to a different belief, etc. □□ **con·ver'ter** *n.*

con·vert·i·ble /kənvórtibəl/ • *adj.* that may be converted. • *n.* car with a folding roof. □□ **con·vert·i·bil'i·ty** *n.* **con·vert'i·bly** *adv.*

con·vex /kónveks, kənvéks/ *adj.* curved like the exterior of a circle or sphere (cf. CONCAVE). □□ **con·vex'i·ty** *n.* **con·vex'ly** *adv.*

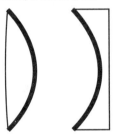

CONVEX AND CONCAVE

con·vey /kənváy/ *v. tr.* **1** transport or carry. **2** communicate or transmit (an idea, meaning, etc.). □□ **con·vey'a·ble** *adj.* **con·vey'or** *n.*

con·vey·ance /kənváyəns/ *n.* **1** conveying; being conveyed. **2** means of transport.

con·vict • *v.tr.* /kənvíkt/ **1** prove to be guilty. **2** declare guilty by legal process. • *n.* /kónvikt/ prison inmate.

con·vic·tion /kənvíkshən/ *n.* **1** convicting; being convicted. **2 a** being convinced. **b** firm belief.

con·vince /kənvíns/ *v.tr.* firmly persuade. □□ **con·vinc'ing** *adj.* **con·vinc'ing·ly** *adv.*

con·viv·i·al /kənvíveeəl/ *adj.* fond of good company; sociable; lively. □□ **con·viv·i·al·i·ty** /-veeálitee/ *n.* **con·viv'i·al·ly** *adv.*

con·vo·ca·tion /kónvəkáyshən/ *n.* **1** act of calling together. **2** large formal gathering, as for giving awards, etc. □□ **con·vo·ca'tion·al** *adj.*

con·voke /kənvók/ *v.tr. formal* call together.

con·vo·lut·ed /kónvəlootid/ *adj.* **1** coiled; twisted. **2** complex. □□ **con'vo·lut·ed·ly** *adv.*

con·vo·lu·tion /kónvəloóshən/ *n.* **1** coiling; twisting. **2** complexity.

con·voy /kónvoy/ *n.* group of ships, vehicles, etc., traveling together or under escort.

con·vulse /kənvúls/ *v.tr.* **1** (usu. *passive*) affect with convulsions. **2** cause to laugh uncontrollably.

con·vul·sion /kənvúlshən/ *n.* **1** (usu. *pl.*) violent body spasm. **2** violent disturbance. **3** (in *pl.*) uncontrollable laughter. □□ **con·vul·sive** /kənvúlsiv/ *adj.* **con·vul'sive·ly** *adv.*

coo /ko͞o/ • *n.* soft murmuring sound as of a dove. • *v.* **1** *intr.* emit a coo. **2** *intr.* & *tr.* talk or say in a soft voice.

cook /ko͝ok/ • *v.* **1** *tr.* prepare (food) by heating it. **2** *intr.* (of food) undergo cooking. **3** *tr. colloq.* falsify (accounts, etc.). • *n.* person who cooks. □ **cook one's goose** ruin one's chances. **cook up** *colloq.* concoct (a story, excuse, etc.). □□ **cook'ing** *n.*

cook·book /ko͝okbo͝ok/ *n.* book of recipes, etc.

cook·er·y /ko͝okəree/ *n.* art or practice of cooking.

cook·ie /ko͝okee/ *n.* (also **cook'y**) (*pl.* **cook·ies**) small sweet cake. □ **that's the way the cookie crumbles** *colloq.* that is how things turn out.

cook·out /ko͝okowt/ *n.* gathering with an open-air cooked meal.

cook·ware /ko͝okwair/ *n.* utensils for cooking, esp. pots, etc.

cool /ko͞ol/ • *adj.* **1** of or at a fairly low temperature. **2** calm; unexcited. **3** lacking enthusiasm. **4** unfriendly. **5** calmly audacious. **6** *sl.* excellent. • *n.* **1** coolness. **2** *sl.* calmness; composure. • *v.* make or become cool. □ **cool it** *sl.* relax; calm down. □□ **cool'ly** *adv.* **cool'ness** *n.*

cool·ant /ko͞olənt/ *n.* cooling agent, esp. fluid.

cool·er /ko͞olər/ *n.* **1** vessel in which a thing is cooled or kept cool. **2** cold drink. **3** *sl.* prison cell.

coo·lie /ko͞olee/ *n. offens.* unskilled native laborer in Asian countries.

coon /ko͞on/ *n.* raccoon.

coop /ko͞op/ • *n.* cage for keeping poultry. • *v.tr.* confine (a person, etc.).

co-op /kó-op/ *n. colloq.* cooperative business, apartment building, etc.

co·op·er·ate /kō-ópərayt/ *v.intr.* **1** work or act together; assist. **2** (of things) concur in producing an effect. □□ **co·op·er·a·tion** /-áyshən/ *n.*

co·op·er·a·tive /kō-ópərətiv, -óprə-/ *adj.* **1** of or affording cooperation. **2** willing to cooperate. **3** (of a business) owned and run jointly by its members, with profits shared. **4** (of an apartment building) with individual units owned by tenants. • *n.* cooperative farm, society, or business. □□ **co·op'er·a·tive·ly** *adv.*

co-opt /kō-ópt/ *v.tr.* appoint to membership of a body by invitation. □□ **co-op·tion** /-ópshən/ *n.* **co-op'tive** *adj.*

co·or·di·nate • *v.* /kō-áwrd'nayt/ **1** *tr.* cause to function together effectively. **2** *intr.* work or act together effectively. • *adj.* /kō-áwrd'nət/ equal in rank or importance. • *n.* /kō-áwrd'nət/ *Math.* value used to fix the position of a point, line, or plane. □□ **co·or·di·na·tion** /-náyshən/ *n.* **co·or'di·na·tor** *n.*

coot /ko͞ot/ *n.* **1** black aquatic bird with upper mandible extended on the forehead. **2** *colloq.* crotchety person.

cop /kop/ • *n.* police officer. • *v.tr.* (**copped**, **cop·ping**) **1** catch or arrest (an offender). **2** take;

seize. □ **cop out** withdraw; renege. **cop a plea** *sl.* = *plea-bargain*.

co·pa·cet·ic /kópəsétik/ *adj. sl.* excellent; in good order.

cope[1] /kōp/ *v.intr.* deal effectively or contend with; manage.

cope[2] /kōp/ *n.* priest's cloaklike vestment.

cop·i·er /kópeeər/ *n.* machine that copies (esp. documents).

co·pi·lot /kópílət/ *n.* second pilot in an aircraft.

cop·ing /kóping/ *n.* top (usu. sloping) course of wall masonry.

co·pi·ous /kópeeəs/ *adj.* **1** abundant. **2** productive. □□ **co'pi·ous·ly** *adv.* **co'pi·ous·ness** *n.*

cop·per /kópər/ • *n.* **1** malleable, red-brown metallic element. ¶ Symb.: **Cu**. **2** bronze coin. • *adj.* made of or colored like copper.

cop·per·head /kópərhed/ *n.* venomous N. American or Australian snake.

co·pra /kóprə/ *n.* dried kernels of the coconut.

copse /kops/ *n.* small dense forest.

cop·ter /kóptər/ *n.* helicopter.

cop·u·la /kópyələ/ *n.* (*pl.* **cop·u·las** or **cop·u·lae** /-lee/) *Gram.* connecting word, esp. a part of the verb *be* connecting subject and predicate. □□ **cop'u·lar** *adj.*

cop·u·late /kópyəlayt/ *v.intr.* have sexual intercourse. □□ **cop·u·la·tion** /-láyshən/ *n.*

cop·u·la·tive /kópyəlaytiv, -lətiv/ *adj.* **1** serving to connect. **2** *Gram.* **a** (of a word) that connects words or clauses linked in sense. **b** connecting a subject and predicate. **3** relating to sexual union. □□ **cop'u·la·tive·ly** *adv.*

cop·y /kópee/ • *n.* (*pl.* **-ies**) **1** thing made to imitate another. **2** issue of a publication. **3** matter to be printed (*scandals make good copy*). • *v.tr.* (**-ies**, **-ied**) **1** make a copy of. **2** do the same as; imitate.

cop·y·cat /kópeekat/ *n. colloq.* imitator.

cop·y·right /kópeerīt/ • *n.* exclusive legal right to print, publish, perform, film, or record material. • *adj.* (of such material) protected by copyright. • *v.tr.* secure copyright for (material).

cop·y·writ·er /kópeerītər/ *n.* person who writes or edits (esp. advertising) copy for publication. □□ **cop'y·writ·ing** *n.*

co·quette /kōkét/ *n.* woman who flirts. □□ **co·quet'tish** *adj.* **co·quet'tish·ly** *adv.* **co·quet'tish·ness** *n.*

cor- /kər/ *prefix* assim. form of COM- before *r*.

cor·al /káwrəl, kór-/ • *n.* **1** hard red, pink, or white calcareous substance secreted by marine polyps. **2** any of these usu. colonial organisms. • *adj.* **1** like coral, esp. in color. **2** made of coral. □ **coral snake** brightly colored poisonous snake of the southeastern US.

cor·bel /káwrbəl, -bel/ • *n.* jutting support of stone, timber, etc. • *v.* (foll. by *out, off*) support or project on corbels.

cord /kawrd/ *n.* **1 a** long, thin, flexible material made from several twisted strands. **b** piece of this. **2** body structure resembling a cord (*spinal cord*). **3 a** ribbed fabric, esp. corduroy. **b** (in *pl.*) corduroy trousers. **4** unit of cut firewood (usu. 128 cu.ft.).

cor·dial /káwrjəl/ • *adj.* heartfelt; warm,

friendly. • *n.* a liqueur. □□ **cor·di·al·i·ty** /-jeeá-litee/ *n.* **cor′dial·ly** *adv.*

cord·ite /káwrdīt/ *n.* smokeless explosive.

cord·less /káwrdlis/ *adj.* (of an electrical appliance, etc.) not connected by wire to an external source of energy, data, etc.

cor·don /káwrd'n/ • *n.* **1** protective line or circle of police, soldiers, guards, etc. **2** ornamental cord or braid. • *v.tr.* enclose or separate with a cordon of police, etc.

cor·du·roy /káwrdəroy/ *n.* **1** thick cotton fabric with velvety ribs. **2** (in *pl.*) corduroy trousers.

core /kawr/ • *n.* **1** central part of various fruits, containing the seeds. **2** central or most important part of anything. **3** central region of the earth. • *v.tr.* remove the core from.

co·re·spon·dent /kó-rispóndənt/ *n.* person cited in a divorce case as having committed adultery with the respondent.

cor·gi /káwrgee/ *n.* (*pl.* **cor·gis**) (in full **Welsh corgi**) short-legged dog with a foxlike head.

co·ri·an·der /káwreeándər/ *n.* **1** aromatic herb of the carrot family. **2** its seeds used for flavoring.

Co·rin·thi·an /kəríntheeən/ *adj. Archit.* of an ornate order characterized by flared capitals with rows of acanthus leaves.

cork /kawrk/ • *n.* **1** buoyant light-brown bark of a S. European oak. **2** bottle stopper, esp. of cork. • *adj.* made of cork. • *v.tr.* stop up, as with a cork.

cork·screw /káwrkskroō/ • *n.* **1** spiral device for extracting corks from bottles. **2** thing with a spiral shape. • *v.* move spirally; twist.

corm /kawrm/ *n. Bot.* underground swollen stem base of some plants, e.g., crocus.

cor·mo·rant /káwrmərənt, -mərant/ *n.* diving black sea bird.

corn[1] /kawrn/ • *n.* **1 a** cereal plant bearing kernels on a long ear (cob). **b** cobs or kernels of this plant. **2** *colloq.* something corny or trite. • *v.tr.* (as **corned**) preserved with salt or brine (*corned beef*).

corn[2] /kawrn/ *n.* tender area of horny skin, esp. on the toe.

corn·ball /kórnbawl/ • *n.* mawkishly sentimental person. • *adj.* = CORNY 1.

corn·cob /káwrnkaab/ *n.* cylindrical center of a corn ear.

cor·ne·a /káwrneeə/ *n.* transparent covering of the front of the eyeball. □□ **cor′ne·al** *adj.*

cor·ner /káwrnər/ • *n.* **1** place where sides or edges meet. **2** projecting angle, esp. where two streets meet. **3** internal space or recess formed by the meeting of two sides, esp. of a room. **4** difficult position. **5** secluded or remote place. **6** monopoly on a stock or commodity. • *v.* **1** *tr.* force into a difficult or inescapable position. **2** *tr.* establish a monopoly in. **3** *intr.* (esp. of or in a vehicle) go around a corner.

cor·ner·stone /káwrnərstōn/ *n.* **1** foundation stone at the corner of a building. **2** indispensable part or basis.

cor·net /kawrnét/ *n.* brass instrument resembling a trumpet but shorter and wider. □□ **cor′net′ist** or **cor·net′tist** *n.*

corn·flow·er /káwrnflowər/ *n.* plant with deep-blue flowers.

cor·nice /káwrnis/ *n.* ornamental molding just below the ceiling.

corn·meal /káwrnmeel/ *n.* coarsely ground corn.

corn·row /kórnrō/ *n.* any of usu. several narrow plaits of hair braided close to the scalp.

corn·starch /káwrnstaarch/ *n.* fine-ground flour from corn.

cor·nu·co·pi·a /káwrnəkópeeə, -nyə-/ *n.* **1** symbol of plenty consisting of a goat's horn overflowing with flowers, fruit, etc. **2** abundant supply. □□ **cor·nu·co′pi·an** *adj.*

corn·y /káwrnee/ *adj.* (**corn·i·er, corn·i·est**) *colloq.* **1** feebly humorous. **2** tritely sentimental. □□ **corn′i·ly** *adv.* **corn′i·ness** *n.*

co·rol·la /kərólə, -ró-/ *n.* petals forming a flower.

cor·ol·lar·y /káwrəleree, kór-/ *n.* (*pl.* **-ies**) **1** proposition that follows from one already proved. **2** natural consequence.

co·ro·na /kərónə/ *n.* (*pl.* **co·ro·nas** or **co·ro·nae** /-nee/) **1** halo around the sun or moon. **2** rarefied gaseous envelope of the sun, seen during a total solar eclipse.

cor·o·nar·y /káwrəneree, kór-/ • *adj. Anat.* resembling or encircling like a crown. • *n.* (*pl.* **-ies**) **1** = *coronary thrombosis*. **2** heart attack. □ **coronary artery** artery supplying blood to the heart. **coronary thrombosis** blockage caused by a blood clot in a coronary artery.

cor·o·na·tion /káwrənáyshən, kór-/ *n.* ceremony of crowning.

cor·o·ner /káwrənər, kór-/ *n.* officer holding inquests on deaths thought to be violent or accidental.

cor·o·net /káwrənit, -nét, kór-/ *n.* small crown or band worn on the head. □□ **cor′o·net·ed** *adj.*

Corp. *abbr.* **1** corporal. **2** corporation.

cor·po·ra *pl.* of CORPUS.

cor·po·ral[1] /káwrpərəl, -prəl/ *n.* noncommissioned officer ranking next below sergeant.

cor·po·ral[2] /káwrpərəl, -prəl/ *adj.* of the human body. □ **corporal punishment** physical punishment. □□ **cor′po·ral·ly** *adv.*

cor·po·rate /káwrpərət, -prit/ *adj.* **1** forming a corporation. **2** forming one body of many individuals.

cor·po·ra·tion /káwrpəráyshən/ *n.* group of people authorized to act as an individual, esp. in business.

cor·po·re·al /kawrpáwreeəl/ *adj.* bodily; physical; material. □□ **cor·po·re·al·i·ty** /-reeálitee/ *n.* **cor·po′re·al·ly** *adv.*

corps /kawr/ *n.* (*pl.* **corps** /kawrz/) **1** military body or subdivision with special duties. **2** body of people engaged in a special activity.

corpse /kawrps/ *n.* dead body.

---

corpse Middle English (denoting the living body of a person or animal): alteration of archaic *corse* by association with Latin *corpus*, a change which also took place in French (Old French *cors* becoming *corps*). The *p* was originally silent, as in French; the final *e* was rare before the 19th century; but now distinguishes *corpse* from *corps*.

---

cor·pu·lent /káwrpyələnt/ *adj.* bulky in body; fat. □□ **cor′pu·lence** *n.*

cor·pus /káwrpəs/ *n.* (*pl.* **cor·po·ra** /káwrpərə/ or **corpuses**) body or collection of writings, texts, etc.

cor·pus·cle /káwrpusəl/ n. minute body in an organism, esp. a red or white cell in the blood of vertebrates. □□ **cor·pus·cu·lar** /kawrpúskyələr/ adj.

corr. abbr. **1** correction. **2** correspondence.

cor·ral /kərál/ • n. pen for cattle, horses, etc. • v.tr. (**cor·ralled, cor·ral·ling**) **1** put or keep in a corral. **2** colloq. gather in; acquire.

cor·rect /kərékt/ • adj. **1** true; right; accurate. **2** proper; in accordance with good standards of taste, etc. • v.tr. **1** set right; amend. **2** mark errors in. **3 a** admonish (a person). **b** punish (a person or fault). **4** counteract (a harmful quality). □□ **cor·rect·ly** adv. **cor·rect·ness** n.

cor·rec·tion /kərékshən/ n. **1 a** correcting. **b** instance of this. **2** thing substituted for what is wrong. **3** program of punishment, esp. of convicted offenders. □□ **cor·rec·tion·al** adj.

cor·rec·tive /kəréktiv/ • adj. serving to correct or counteract something undesired or harmful. • n. corrective measure or thing. □□ **cor·rec·tive·ly** adv.

cor·re·late /káwrəlayt, kór-/ • v. **1** intr. have a mutual relation. **2** tr. bring into a mutual relation. • n. each of two complements. □□ **cor·re·la·tion** n. **cor·re·la·tion·al** adj.

cor·rel·a·tive /kərélətiv/ • adj. **1** having a mutual relation. **2** Gram. used together (as neither and nor). • n. correlative word or thing. □□ **cor·rel·a·tive·ly** adv. **cor·rel·a·tiv·i·ty** n.

cor·re·spond /káwrispónd, kór-/ v.intr. **1 a** be analogous or similar (to). **b** be in agreement with. **2** exchange letters with. □□ **cor·re·spond·ing·ly** adv.

cor·re·spon·dence /káwrispóndəns, kór-/ n. **1** agreement, similarity, or harmony. **2 a** communication by letters. **b** letters.

cor·re·spond·ent /káwrispóndənt, kór-/ n. **1** person who writes letters. **2** reporter or news source. □□ **cor·re·spond·ent·ly** adv.

cor·ri·dor /káwridər, -dor, kór-/ n. **1** passage giving access into rooms, compartments, etc. **2** strip of the territory of one nation passing through that of another.

cor·rob·o·rate /kəróbərayt/ v.tr. confirm or give support to (a statement or belief, etc.). □□ **cor·rob·o·ra·tion** /-ráyshən/ n. **cor·rob·o·ra·tive** /-rətiv, -ráytiv/ adj. **cor·rob·o·ra·tor** n.

cor·rode /kəród/ v. **1 a** tr. wear away, esp. by chemical action. **b** intr. be worn away. **2** tr. destroy gradually. □□ **cor·rod·i·ble** adj.

cor·ro·sion /kərózhən/ n. **1** corroding. **2** damage caused by corroding. □□ **cor·ro·sive** /-siv/ adj. **cor·ro·sive·ly** adv. **cor·ro·sive·ness** n.

cor·ru·gate /káwrəgayt, kór-/ v.tr. (esp. as **corrugated** adj.) form into ridges and grooves. □□ **cor·ru·ga·tion** /-gáyshən/ n.

cor·rupt /kərúpt/ • adj. **1** morally depraved; wicked. **2** influenced by or using bribery or fraudulent activity. **3** (of a text, etc.) harmed by errors or alterations. • v. make or become corrupt. □□ **cor·rup·ter** n. **cor·rupt·i·ble** adj. **cor·rupt·i·bil·i·ty** n. **cor·rup·tive** adj. **cor·rupt·ly** adv. **cor·rupt·ness** n.

cor·rup·tion /kərúpshən/ n. **1** moral deterioration. **2** use of corrupt practices, esp. bribery or fraud. **3** irregular alteration (of a text, language, etc.) from its original state. **4** rot; decay.

cor·sage /kawrsaázh/ n. small bouquet worn by a woman.

cor·sair /káwrsair/ n. **1** pirate ship. **2** pirate.

---

cor·set /káwrsit/ n. closely fitting undergarment worn for support. □□ **cor·set·ed** adj.

cor·tex /káwrteks/ n. (pl. **cor·ti·ces** /-tiseez/ or **cor·tex·es**) outer part of an organ, esp. of the brain (**cerebral cortex**) or kidneys (**renal cortex**). □□ **cor·ti·cal** /káwrtikəl/ adj.

cor·ti·sone /káwrtisōn, -zōn/ n. hormone used esp. against inflammation and allergy.

co·run·dum /kərúndəm/ n. extremely hard crystallized alumina, used esp. as an abrasive or as a gemstone.

cor·us·cate /káwrəskayt, kór-/ v.intr. sparkle. □□ **cor·us·ca·tion** /-káyshən/ n.

cor·vette /kawrvét/ n. small naval escort vessel.

cos[1] /kaws, kos/ n. long-headed variety of lettuce; romaine.

cos[2] /kos, koz/ abbr. cosine.

co·sec /kósek/ abbr. cosecant.

co·se·cant /kóse·ekant, -kənt/ n. Math. ratio of the hypotenuse (in a right triangle) to the side opposite an acute angle.

co·sign /kósīn/ v.tr. sign (a promissory note) jointly with another person. □□ **co·sign·er** n.

co·sig·na·to·ry /kósígnətáwree/ n. (pl. **-ries**) party signing (a treaty, etc.) jointly.

co·sine /kósīn/ n. Math. ratio of the side adjacent to an acute angle (in a right triangle) to the hypotenuse.

cos·met·ic /kozmétik/ • adj. **1** enhancing; beautifying. **2** only superficially improving. **3** (of surgery or a prosthesis) imitating, restoring, or enhancing normal appearance. • n. cosmetic preparation, esp. for the face. □□ **cos·met·i·cal·ly** adv.

cos·me·tol·o·gy /kozmətóləjee/ n. the art and technique of using cosmetics. □□ **cos·me·tol·o·gist** n.

cos·mic /kózmik/ adj. of the universe or cosmos, esp. as distinct from the earth. □□ **cos·mi·cal** adj. **cos·mi·cal·ly** adv.

cos·mog·o·ny /kozmógənee/ n. (pl. **-nies**) **1** origin of the universe. **2** theory about this. □□ **cos·mo·gon·ic** /-məgónik/ adj. **cos·mo·gon·i·cal** adj. **cos·mog·o·nist** /-móg-/ n.

cos·mol·o·gy /kozmóləjee/ n. science or theory of the universe. □□ **cos·mo·log·i·cal** /-məlójikəl/ adj. **cos·mol·o·gist** /-mól-/ n.

cos·mo·naut /kózmənawt/ n. Russian or Soviet astronaut.

cos·mo·pol·i·tan /kózməpólit'n/ • adj. of, from, or knowing many parts of the world. • n. cosmopolitan person. □□ **cos·mo·pol·i·tan·ism** n.

cos·mos /kózmōs, -məs, -mos/ n. the universe, esp. as a well-ordered whole.

Cos·sack /kósak/ n. hist. **1** member of a people of southern Russia. **2** member of a Cossack military unit.

cost /kawst/ • v.tr. (past and past part. **cost**) **1** be obtainable for (a sum); have as a price. **2** involve as a loss or sacrifice (it cost me my job). • n. **1** what a thing costs; price. **2** loss or sacrifice. □ **at all costs** (or **at any cost**) no matter what. **cost-benefit** assessing the cost of an operation and the value of the resulting benefits. **cost-effective** effective or productive in relation to its cost. **cost of living** level of prices, esp. of the basic necessities of life.

costly ~ counterclockwise 128

cost·ly /káwstlee/ *adj.* (**cost·li·er, cost·li·est**) **1** costing much; expensive. **2** of great value. □□ **cost′li·ness** *n.*

cos·tume /kóstoōm, -tyoōm/ • *n.* **1** style of dress, esp. of a particular place, time, or class. **2** set of clothes. **3** clothing for a particular activity or role. • *v.tr.* provide with a costume. □ **costume jewelry** jewelry made of artificial or inexpensive materials.

cot[1] /kot/ *n.* small folding or portable bed.

cot[2] /kot/ *abbr. Math.* cotangent.

co·tan·gent /kōtánjənt/ *n. Math.* ratio of the side adjacent to an acute angle (in a right triangle) to the opposite side.

cote /kōt/ *n.* shelter, esp. for animals or birds.

co·te·rie /kótəree/ *n.* exclusive clique or circle.

co·ter·mi·nous /kōtə́rminəs/ *adj.* having the same boundaries or extent (in space, time, or meaning).

co·til·lion /kətílyən/ *n.* **1** formal ball. **2** ballroom dance resembling a quadrille.

cot·tage /kótij/ *n.* small, simple house, esp. in the country. □ **cottage cheese** soft white cheese made from milk curds. **cottage industry** business activity carried on at home.

cot·ter /kótər/ *n.* **1** securing bolt or wedge. **2** (in full **cotter pin**) split pin that opens after passing through a hole.

cot·ton /kót'n/ • *n.* **1** soft, white fibrous substance covering the seeds of certain plants. **2** such a plant, esp. one cultivated for its fiber or seeds. **3** (*attrib.*) made of cotton. • *v.intr.* (foll. by *to*) be attracted by. □ **cotton candy** fluffy mass of spun sugar. **cotton gin** machine for separating cotton from its seeds. **cotton-picking** *sl.* unpleasant; wretched. □□ **cot′ton·y** *adj.*

cot·ton·mouth /kót'nmowth/ *n.* venomous pit viper of the southeastern US.

cot·ton·tail /kót'ntayl/ *n.* fluffy-tailed N. American rabbit.

cot·ton·wood /kót'nwoōd/ *n.* N. American poplar, having seeds covered in cottony hairs.

cot·y·le·don /kót'leéd'n/ *n.* embryonic leaf in seed-bearing plants.

couch /kowch/ • *n.* upholstered piece of furniture for several people; sofa. • *v.tr.* (foll. by *in*) express in words of a specified kind (*couched in simple language*). □ **couch potato** *sl.* person who likes lazing, esp. watching television.

cou·gar /koōgər/ *n.* puma.

cough /kawf, kof/ • *v.intr.* **1** expel air from the lungs with a sudden, sharp sound. **2** (of an engine, etc.) make a similar sound. • *n.* **1** act of coughing. **2** condition of the respiratory organs causing coughing. □ **cough drop** medicated lozenge to relieve a cough. **cough up** *sl.* bring out or give (money or information) reluctantly.

could *past* of CAN[1].

could·n't /koōd'nt/ *contr.* could not.

cou·lomb /koōlom/ *n. Electr.* unit of electric charge, equal to the quantity of electricity conveyed in one second by a current of one ampere. ¶ Symb.: **C**.

coun·cil /kównsəl/ *n.* advisory, deliberative, or administrative body. □□ **coun·ci·lor** *n.*
¶ See note at COUNSELOR.

coun·cil·man /kównsəlmən/ *n.* (*pl.* **-men**; *fem.*

coun·cil·wom·an, *pl.* **-wom·en**) member of a council.

coun·sel /kównsəl/ • *n.* **1** advice, esp. formally given. **2** (*pl.* same) legal adviser. • *v.tr.* **1** advise (a person). **2** give advice on personal problems, esp. professionally. **3** recommend (a course of action). □□ **coun′sel·ing** *n.*

coun·sel·or /kównsələr, -slər/ *n.* **1** adviser; professional guide. **2** lawyer.
¶ A **counselor** is someone who gives advice or counsel, especially an attorney. A **councilor** is a member of a council, such as a town or city council. Confusion arises because many *counselors* sit on councils, and *councilors* are often called on to give counsel.

count[1] /kownt/ • *v.* **1** *tr.* determine, esp. one by one, the total number of. **2** *intr.* repeat numbers in order. **3 a** *tr.* include. **b** be included. **4** *tr.* consider (a thing or a person) to be (lucky, etc.). **5** *intr.* have value; matter (*his opinion counts for a great deal*). • *n.* **1 a** counting; reckoning. **b** total of a reckoning (*pollen count*). **2** *Law* each charge in an indictment. □ **count one's blessings** be grateful for what one has. **count one's chickens** be hasty in anticipating good fortune. **count down** recite numbers backward to zero. **count on** (or **upon**) depend on. **count out** *colloq.* exclude from. **down for the count 1** *Boxing* defeated by being unable to rise within ten seconds. **2 a** defeated or demoralized. **b** asleep.

count[2] /kownt/ *n.* noble corresponding to a British earl.

count·a·ble /kówntəbəl/ *adj.* that can be counted.

count·down /kówntdown/ *n.* **1** act of counting down. **2** final moments before any significant event.

coun·te·nance /kówntinəns/ • *n.* **1 a** the face. **b** facial expression. **2** composure. • *v.tr.* give approval to (an act, etc.).

count·er[1] /kówntər/ *n.* **1 a** long, flat-topped fixture in a store, etc., across which business is conducted. **b** similar structure used for serving food, etc. **2 a** small disk used in board games. **b** token representing a coin. **3** apparatus used for counting. □ **over the counter 1** (of stock) sold through a broker directly. **2** by ordinary retail purchase. **under the counter** surreptitiously, esp. sold illegally.

count·er[2] /kówntər/ • *v.* **1** *tr.* **a** oppose; contradict. **b** meet by countermove. **2** *intr.* **a** make a countermove. **b** make an opposing statement. **3** *tr. Boxing* give a return blow. • *adv.* in the opposite direction or manner. • *adj.* **1** opposite. **2** duplicate; serving as a check. • *n.* **1** countermove. **2** something opposite. □ **run counter to** act contrary to.

counter- /kówntər/ *comb. form* denoting: **1** retaliation, opposition, or rivalry (*counterthreat*). **2** opposite direction (*counterclockwise*). **3** correspondence (*counterpart*).

coun·ter·act /kówntərákt/ *v.tr.* hinder or neutralize by contrary action. □□ **coun·ter·ac·tion** /-ákshən/ *n.* **coun·ter·ac′tive** *adj.*

coun·ter·at·tack • *n.* /kówntərətak/ attack in reply to an attack. • *v.* /kówntərəták/ attack in reply.

coun·ter·bal·ance • *n.* /kówntərbaləns/ weight or influence balancing another. • *v.tr.* /kówntərbáləns/ act as a counterbalance to.

coun·ter·clock·wise /kówntərklókwīz/ *adv.*

& *adj.* circling in a direction opposite to the movement of the hands of a clock.

coun·ter·cul·ture /kówntərkulchər/ *n.* way of life, etc., opposed to that usually considered normal.

coun·ter·es·pi·o·nage /kówntəréspeeənaazh, -nij/ *n.* action taken to frustrate enemy spying.

coun·ter·feit /kówntərfit/ • *adj.* made in imitation; not genuine; forged. • *n.* forgery; imitation. • *v.tr.* imitate fraudulently; forge. □□ **coun'ter·feit·er** *n.*

coun·ter·in·tel·li·gence /kówntərintélijəns/ *n.* = COUNTERESPIONAGE.

coun·ter·mand • *v.tr.* /kówntərmánd/ revoke (an order or command). • *n.* /kówntərmand/ order revoking a previous one.

coun·ter·meas·ure /kówntərmezhər/ *n.* action taken to counteract a danger, threat, etc.

coun·ter·pane /kówntərpayn/ *n.* bedspread.

coun·ter·part /kówntərpaart/ *n.* **1** complement or equivalent to another. **2** duplicate, esp. of a document.

coun·ter·point /kówntərpoynt/ • *n.* **1** *Mus.* **a** art or technique of combining melodies according to fixed rules. **b** melody played in conjunction with another. **2** contrasting argument, theme, etc., used to set off the main element. • *v.tr.* **1** *Mus.* add counterpoint to. **2** set (an argument, etc.) in contrast to (a main element).

coun·ter·poise • *n.* /kówntərpoyz/ **1** counterbalance. **2** state of equilibrium. • *v.tr.* /kówntərpóyz/ **1** counterbalance. **2** compensate.

coun·ter·pro·duc·tive /kówntərprədúktiv/ *adj.* having the opposite of the desired effect.

coun·ter·rev·o·lu·tion /kówntərévəlóoshən/ *n.* revolution opposing a former one or reversing its results. □□ **coun'ter·rev·o·lu'tion·ar·y** *adj.* & *n.* (*pl.* **-ies**).

coun·ter·sign /kówntərsīn/ • *v.tr.* add a ratifying signature to (a document). • *n.* watchword or password. □□ **coun·ter·sig·na·ture** /-signəchər/ *n.*

coun·ter·sink /kówntərsingk/ *v.tr.* (*past* and *past part.* **-sunk**) **1** enlarge and bevel (the rim of a hole) so that a screw or bolt can be inserted flush with the surface. **2** sink (a screw, etc.) in such a hole.

coun·ter·ten·or /kówntərtenər/ *n.* **1** highest adult male singing voice. **2** singer with this voice.

coun·ter·top /kówntərtop/ *n.* horizontal, flat work surface, as in a kitchen.

coun·ter·vail /kówntərváyl/ *v.* **1** *tr.* counterbalance. **2** *tr.* & *intr.* oppose forcefully and usu. successfully.

coun·ter·weight /kówntərwayt/ *n.* counterbalancing weight.

count·ess /kówntis/ *n.* **1** wife or widow of a count or an earl. **2** woman holding the rank of count or earl.

count·less /kówntlis/ *adj.* too many to be counted.

coun·tri·fied /kúntrifīd/ *adj.* rustic, esp. of manners, appearance, etc.

coun·try /kúntree/ *n.* (*pl.* **-tries**) **1** nation or its territory. **2** (often *attrib.*) rural area. **3** land of a person's birth or citizenship. **4** region associated with a particular person, feature, etc. (*Elvis country; mountain country*). **5** national population, esp. as voters. □ **country and western** popular music originating in the southern US. **country**

club golfing and social club. **country cousin** often *derog.* countrified person.

coun·try·man /kúntreemən/ *n.* (*pl.* **-men**; *fem.* **coun·try·wom·an**, *pl.* **-wom·en**) person of one's own country.

coun·try·side /kúntreesīd/ *n.* **1** rural area. **2** rural areas in general.

coun·try·wide /kúntreewíd/ *adj.* extending throughout a nation.

coun·ty /kówntee/ *n.* (*pl.* **-ties**) **1** political and administrative division of a state, as in the US. **2** administrative divisions of some countries. □ **county seat** administrative capital of a county.

coup /koo/ *n.* (*pl.* **coups** /kooz/) **1** successful stroke or move. **2** = COUP D'ÉTAT.

coup de grâce /koo də graás/ *n.* finishing stroke, esp. to kill a wounded animal or person.

coup d'é·tat /koo daytaá/ *n.* violent or illegal seizure of power.

coupe /koop/ *n.* two-door car with a hard top.

cou·ple /kúpəl/ • *n.* **1 a** two. **b** about two (*a couple of hours*). **2 a** married or engaged pair. **b** pair of partners in a dance, etc. • *v.* **1** *tr.* link together. **2** *tr.* associate in thought or speech. **3** *intr.* copulate.

cou·plet /kúplit/ *n.* two successive lines of verse, usu. rhyming and of the same length.

cou·pling /kúpling/ *n.* link connecting machinery parts, railroad cars, etc.

COUPLING

cou·pon /kóopon, kyóo-/ *n.* **1** discount voucher presented at purchase. **2** detachable ticket or form entitling holder to payment, goods, a discount, services, etc.

cour·age /kərij, kúr-/ *n.* ability to disregard fear; bravery.

cou·ra·geous /kəráyjəs/ *adj.* brave; fearless. □□ **cou·ra'geous·ly** *adv.*

cou·ri·er /kóoreeər, kər-, kúr-/ *n.* special messenger.

course /kawrs/ • *n.* **1** onward movement or progression. **2** direction taken. **3 a** ground on which a race, etc., takes place. **b** series of hurdles, etc., to be crossed in a race, etc. **4** series of lessons, etc., in a particular subject. **5** each successive part of a meal. **6** stretch of land or water. **7** line of conduct. **8** horizontal layer of brick, stone, etc. **9** water channel. • *v.intr.* (esp. of liquid) run, esp. fast. □ **in the course of** during. **matter of course** natural or expected thing. **of course** naturally; as is or was to be expected. **run its course** (esp. of an illness) complete its natural development.

cours·er /káwrsər/ *n. poet.* swift horse.

court /kawrt/ • *n.* **1** (in full **court of law**) a judicial body hearing legal cases. **b** = COURTROOM. **2**

quadrangular area for games. **3** = COURTYARD.
4 milieu or attendants of a sovereign. **5** attention paid to a person for favor. ● *v.tr.* **1** try to win affection or favor of. **2** seek to win (applause, fame, etc.). **3** invite (misfortune) by one's actions (*courting disaster*).

cour·te·ous /kɔ́rteeəs/ *adj.* polite; considerate. □□ **cour'te·ous·ly** *adv.* **cour'te·ous·ness** *n.*

cour·te·san /kɔ́wrtizán/ *n. literary* **1** prostitute, esp. for wealthy clients. **2** mistress of a wealthy man.

cour·te·sy /kɔ́rtisee/ *n.* (*pl.* **-sies**) courteous behavior or act.

court·house /káwrthows/ *n.* **1** judicial building. **2** county administrative building.

cour·ti·er /káwrteeər/ *n.* person who attends or frequents a sovereign's court.

court·ly /káwrtlee/ *adj.* (**court·li·er, court·li·est**) polished or refined in manners. □□ **court'li·ness** *n.*

court-mar·tial /káwrt maárshəl/ ● *n.* (*pl.* **courts-mar·tial**) military judicial court. ● *v.tr.* try by court-martial.

court·room /káwrtrōōm, -rŏŏm/ *n.* room in which a court of law meets.

court·ship /káwrtship/ *n.* **1** process or period of courting with a view to marriage. **2** courting behavior of animals, birds, etc.

court·yard /káwrtyaard/ *n.* area enclosed by walls or buildings.

cous·cous /kōōskōōs/ *n.* N. African dish of semolina steamed over broth, often with meat or fruit added.

cous·in /kúzən/ *n.* **1** (also **first cousin**) child of one's uncle or aunt. **2** person of kindred race or nation. □ **second cousin** child of one's parent's first cousin.

cou·ture /kōōtôōr, -tŷr/ *n.* design and manufacture of fashionable clothes.

cou·tu·ri·er /kōōtōōree-ay, -eeər/ *n.* (*fem.* **cou·tu·ri·ère** /-reeáir/) fashion designer.

co·va·len·cy /kōváylənsee/ *n. Chem.* **1** linking of atoms by a bond of shared electrons. **2** number of pairs of electrons an atom can share with another. □□ **co·va'lent** *adj.*

cove /kōv/ *n.* **1** small, esp. sheltered, bay or creek. **2** sheltered recess.

co·ven /kúvən/ *n.* assembly of witches.

cov·e·nant /kúvənənt/ ● *n.* **1** agreement; contract. **2** *Law* sealed contract, esp. a deed of covenant. **3** (**Covenant**) *Bibl.* agreement between God and the Israelites. ● *v.* agree, esp. by legal covenant. □□ **cov·e·nan·tal** /-nánt'l/ *adj.* **cov'e·nan·tor** *n.*

cov·er /kúvər/ ● *v.tr.* **1** protect or conceal with a cloth, lid, etc. **2** a extend over the surface of. **b** strew thickly or thoroughly. **c** lie over. **3** protect; clothe. **4** include; comprise; deal with. **5** travel (a specified distance). **6** *Journalism* investigate or describe as a reporter. **7** be enough to defray (expenses, etc.). **8** a *refl.* protect oneself. **b** (*absol.*; foll. by *for*) stand in for (*will you cover for me?*). **9** a aim a gun, etc., at. **b** (of a fortress, etc.) command (a territory). **c** protect (an exposed person, etc.) with a gun, etc. ● *n.* **1** something that covers, esp.: **a** lid. **b** binding of a book. **c** envelope or wrapping (*under separate cover*). **d** (in *pl.*) bedclothes. **2** shelter. **3** a pretense; screen. **b** pretended identity. **c** *Mil.*

force protecting an advance party from attack. □ **cover charge** charge levied per head in a restaurant, nightclub, etc. **cover crop** crop grown for protection and enrichment of the soil. **cover girl** female model appearing on magazine covers, etc. **cover letter** explanatory letter sent with an enclosure. **cover story** news story in a magazine, as illustrated on the front cover. **cover up** conceal (circumstances, etc., esp. illicitly). **cover-up** *n.* act of concealing circumstances, esp. illicitly. **take cover** find shelter, esp. against an attack.

cov·er·age /kúvərij/ *n.* **1** area or amount covered. **2** amount of publicity received by a particular story, person, event, etc.

cov·er·all /kúvərawl/ *n.* (usu. in *pl.*) full-length protective garment.

cov·er·let /kúvərlit/ *n.* bedspread.

co·vert /kɔ́vərt, kú-/ ● *adj.* secret or disguised (*covert glance*). ● *n.* shelter, esp. a thicket hiding game. □□ **co·vert'ly** *adv.* **co'vert·ness** *n.*

cov·et /kúvit/ *v.tr.* desire greatly (another's possession, attribute, etc.). □□ **cov'et·a·ble** *adj.*

cov·et·ous /kúvitəs/ *adj.* coveting; grasping. □□ **cov'et·ous·ly** *adv.* **cov'et·ous·ness** *n.*

cov·ey /kúvee/ *n.* (*pl.* **-eys**) **1** brood of partridges. **2** small group of people, etc.

cow¹ /kow/ *n.* **1** grown female of any bovine animal, used esp. as a source of milk and beef. **2** female of other large animals, esp. the elephant, whale, and seal. □ **till the cows come home** *colloq.* an indefinitely long time.

cow² /kow/ *v.tr.* intimidate; dispirit.

cow·ard /kówərd/ *n.* person easily frightened or intimidated.

cow·ard·ice /kówərdis/ *n.* lack of bravery.

cow·ard·ly /kówərdlee/ *adj.* **1** lacking courage. **2** (of an action) done against one who cannot retaliate. □□ **cow'ard·li·ness** *n.*

cow·boy /kówboy/ *n.* **1** (*fem.* **cow·girl**) person who tends cattle. **2** *colloq.* unscrupulous or reckless person in business.

cow·catch·er /kówkachər/ *n.* peaked metal frame at the front of a locomotive for pushing aside obstacles.

cow·er /kowər/ *v.intr.* crouch or shrink in fear.

cow·hand /kówhand/ *n.* = COWBOY 1.

cow·hide /kówhīd/ *n.* **1** cow's hide; leather. **2** whip made from this.

cowl /kowl/ *n.* **1** monk's hooded habit. **2 a** loose hood of a monk's cowl. **b** any such hood. □□ **cowled** *adj.* (in sense 1).

cow·lick /kówlik/ *n.* projecting lock of hair.

cowl·ing /kówling/ *n.* removable cover of a vehicle or aircraft engine.

co·work·er /kɔ́-wɔ́rkər/ *n.* person who works with another.

cow·poke /kówpōk/ *n.* = COWBOY 1.

cow·pox /kówpoks/ *n.* disease of cows, whose virus was formerly used in smallpox vaccination.

cox·comb /kókskōm/ *n.* ostentatiously conceited person.

cox·swain /kóksən, -swayn/ *n.* person who steers and directs the crew, esp. in a rowing boat.

coy /koy/ *adj.* (**coy·er, coy·est**) **1** modestly or affectedly shy. **2** irritatingly reticent. □□ **coy'ly** *adv.* **coy'ness** *n.*

coy·o·te /kīyótee, kíyōt/ *n.* (*pl.* same or **coy·o·tes**) N. American wolflike wild dog.

coz·en /kúzən/ v. literary **1** tr. cheat; defraud. **2** tr. beguile; persuade. **3** intr. act deceitfully. □□ **coz′en·age** n.

co·zy /kózee/ • adj. (**co·zi·er, co·zi·est**) comfortable and warm; snug. • n. (pl. **-zies**) cover to keep something hot, esp. a teapot. □ **cozy up to** colloq. **1** ingratiate oneself with. **2** snuggle up to. □□ **co′zi·ly** adv. **co′zi·ness** n.

cp. abbr. compare.

CPA abbr. certified public accountant.

cpd. abbr. compound.

CPI abbr. consumer price index.

Cpl. abbr. corporal.

CPR abbr. cardiopulmonary resuscitation.

cps abbr. (also **c.p.s.**) **1** Computing characters per second. **2** cycles per second.

CPU abbr. Computing central processing unit.

Cr symb. Chem. chromium.

crab[1] /krab/ • n. **1** crustacean with four pairs of legs and two pincers. **2** (**the Crab**) zodiacal sign or constellation Cancer. **3** (in full **crab louse**) (often in pl.) parasitic louse, infesting hairy parts of the body. **4** irritable person. • v. (**crab·bed, crab·bing**) criticize adversely; grumble. □□ **crab′like** adj.

crab[2] /krab/ n. (in full **crab apple**) **1** small sour, applelike fruit. **2** tree bearing this fruit.

crab·bed /krábid/ adj. **1** irritable. **2** (of handwriting) hard to decipher. □□ **crab′bed·ly** adv. **crab′bed·ness** n.

crab·by /krábee/ adj. (**crab·bi·er, crab·bi·est**) = CRABBED 1. □□ **crab′bi·ly** adv. **crab′bi·ness** n.

crab·grass /krábgras/ n. creeping grass infesting lawns.

crack /krak/ • n. **1 a** sharp, explosive noise. **b** (in a voice) sudden change in pitch. **2** sharp blow. **3** narrow opening; break; partial fracture. **4** colloq. mischievous or malicious remark. **5** colloq. attempt (I'll have a crack at it). **6** exact moment (the crack of dawn). **7** sl. potent crystalline form of cocaine. • v. **1** tr. & intr. break without separating the parts. **2** tr. & intr. make or cause to make a sharp, explosive sound. **3** tr. & intr. break or cause to break with a sharp sound. **4** tr. & intr. give way or cause to give way (under torture, etc.). **5** intr. (of the voice) become dissonant; break. **6** tr. colloq. find a solution to. **7** tr. say (a joke, etc.) in a jocular way. **8** tr. colloq. hit sharply. **9** tr. break (grain) into coarse pieces. • attrib.adj. colloq. excellent; first-rate. □ **crack down on** colloq. take severe measures against. **crack up** colloq. **1** collapse under strain. **2** laugh. **3** repute (not all is cracked up to be). **get cracking** colloq. begin promptly and vigorously.

crack·down /krákdown/ n. colloq. severe measures (esp. against lawbreakers, etc.).

crack·er /krákər/ n. **1** thin, dry biscuit. **2** firework exploding with a sharp noise.

crack·er·jack /krákərjak/ sl. • adj. exceptionally fine or expert. • n. exceptionally fine thing or person.

crack·ers /krákərz/ predic.adj. sl. crazy.

crack·le /krákəl/ • v.intr. make repeated slight cracking sound. • n. **1** such a sound. **2** paintwork, china, or glass decorated with a pattern of minute surface cracks. □□ **crack′ly** adj.

crack·pot /krákpot/ sl. • n. eccentric person. • adj. mad; unworkable (crackpot scheme).

cra·dle /kráyd'l/ • n. **1 a** baby's bed, esp. on

rockers. **b** place in which a thing begins or is nurtured in its infancy (cradle of democracy). **2** supporting structure or framework. • v.tr. contain or shelter as if in a cradle. □ **cradle-robber** (or **-snatcher**) sl. person amorously attached to a much younger person.

craft /kraft/ • n. **1** skill, esp. in practical arts. **2** (esp. in comb.) trade or art. **3** (pl. **craft**) a boat or vessel. **b** aircraft or spacecraft. **4** cunning; deceit. • v.tr. make in a skillful way.

crafts·man /kráftsmən/ n. (pl. **-men**; fem. **crafts·wom·an**, pl. **-wom·en**) skilled worker; artisan. □□ **crafts′man·ship** n.

craft·y /kráftee/ adj. (**craft·i·er, craft·i·est**) cunning; artful; wily. □□ **craft′i·ly** adv. **craft′i·ness** n.

crag /krag/ n. steep or rugged rock.

crag·gy /krágee/ adj. (**crag·gi·er, crag·gi·est**) (of facial features, landscapes, etc.) rugged. □□ **crag′gi·ly** adv. **crag′gi·ness** n.

cram /kram/ v. (**crammed, cram·ming**) **1** tr. **a** fill to bursting; stuff. **b** force (a thing) into. **2** tr. & intr. prepare for an exam by intensive study.

cramp /kramp/ • n. painful involuntary muscle contraction. • v.tr. **1** affect with cramp. **2** confine narrowly. **3** restrict (energies, etc.). **4** (as **cramped** adj.) **a** (of handwriting) small and difficult to read. **b** (of a room, etc.) uncomfortably crowded.

cram·pon /krámpon/ n. (usu. in pl.) spiked plate fixed to a boot for walking on ice, climbing, etc.

cran·ber·ry /kránberee/ n. (pl. **-ries**) **1** N. American evergreen shrub yielding edible small, red, acid berries. **2** berry from this.

crane /krayn/ • n. **1** machine with long hoisting arm. **2** tall wading bird with long legs, long neck, and straight bill. • v.tr. (also absol.) stretch out (one's neck) to see.

cra·ni·um /kráyneeəm/ n. (pl. **cra·ni·ums** or **cra·ni·a** /-neeə/) skull, esp. the part enclosing the brain. □□ **cra′ni·al** adj.

crank /krangk/ • n. **1** part of an axle or shaft bent at right angles for interconverting reciprocal and circular motion. **2 a** eccentric person. **b** bad-tempered person. • v.tr. cause to move by means of a crank. □ **crank up** sl. increase (speed, etc.) by intensive effort.

crank·case /krángk-kays/ n. case enclosing a crankshaft.

crank·shaft /krángkshaft/ n. shaft driven by a crank (see CRANK n. 1).

crank·y /krángkee/ adj. (**crank·i·er, crank·i·est**) ill-tempered; crotchety. □□ **crank′i·ly** adv. **crank′i·ness** n.

cran·ny /kránee/ n. (pl. **-nies**) chink; crevice; crack. □□ **cran′nied** /-need/ adj.

crap /krap/ coarse sl. • n. **1** nonsense; rubbish. **2** feces. • v.intr. (**crapped, crap·ping**) defecate. □ **crap out** be unsuccessful. □□ **crap′py** adj.

crape /krayp/ n. crepe, usu. of black silk, formerly used for mourning.

craps /kraps/ n.pl. gambling game played with dice.

crap·shoot /krápshoot/ n. sl. venture marked by uncertainty.

crap·u·lent /krápyələnt/ adj. suffering the effects of drunkenness. □□ **crap′u·lence** n. **crap′u·lous** adj.

crash /krash/ • v. **1** tr. & intr. make or cause to make a loud smashing noise. **2** tr. & intr. throw, drive, move, or fall with a loud smashing noise. **3** tr. & intr. **a** collide or cause (a vehicle, etc.) to collide violently. **b** fall or cause (an aircraft) to fall and land violently. **4** intr. undergo financial ruin. **5** tr. colloq. enter without permission (crashed the party). **6** intr. Computing (of a system) fail suddenly. **7** intr. sl. sleep, esp. in an improvised setting. • n. **1** loud and sudden smashing noise. **2 a** violent collision, esp. of a vehicle. **b** violent fall and landing of an aircraft. **3** ruin, esp. financial. **4** Computing sudden failure (of a system). • adj. done rapidly or urgently (crash course in first aid). • adv. with a crash (the window went crash). □ **crash-dive 1** intr. (of an aircraft or pilot, etc.) dive and crash. **2** tr. cause to crash-dive. **crash helmet** helmet worn esp. by a motorcyclist to protect the head. **crash-land 1** intr. (of an aircraft or airman) land hurriedly with a crash. **2** tr. cause (an aircraft) to crash-land.

crass /kras/ adj. gross; grossly stupid. □□ **crass′ly** adv. **crass′ness** n.

-crat /krat/ comb. form member or supporter of a particular form of government or rule (autocrat; democrat). □□ **-cratic** /krátik/ (also **-cratical**) comb. form (adj.). **-cratically** comb. form (adv.).

crate /krayt/ • n. **1 a** slatted wooden case for transporting goods. **b** any similar case. **2** sl. old airplane or other vehicle. • v.tr. pack in a crate. □□ **crate′ful** n. (pl. **-fuls**).

cra·ter /kráytər/ • n. **1** mouth of a volcano. **2** bowl-shaped cavity, esp. from a shell or bomb. **3** hollow on the surface of a planet or moon. • v.tr. form a crater in. □□ **cra′ter·ous** adj.

cra·vat /krəvát/ n. **1** scarf worn inside an open-necked shirt. **2** hist. necktie. □□ **cra·vat′ted** adj.

---

cravat mid-17th century: from French cravate, from Cravate 'Croat' (from German Krabat, from Croat Hrvat), because of the scarf worn by Croatian mercenaries in France.

---

crave /krayv/ v. long or beg for.

cra·ven /kráyvən/ adj. cowardly. □□ **cra′ven·ly** adv. **cra′ven·ness** n.

crav·ing /kráyving/ n. strong desire or longing.

craw /kraw/ n. Zool. crop of a bird or insect. □ **stick in one's craw** be unacceptable.

craw·fish /kráwfish/ n. = CRAYFISH.

crawl /krawl/ • v.intr. **1** move slowly, esp.: **a** person on hands and knees; **b** insect, snake, etc., with the body close to the ground. **2** walk or move slowly (the train crawled into the station). **3** colloq. behave obsequiously. **4** be covered or filled with crawling or moving things, people, etc. • n. **1** crawling. **2** slow rate of movement. **3** high-speed overarm swimming stroke. □□ **crawl′ing·ly** adv. **crawl′y** adj. (in sense 4 of v.).

cray·fish /kráyfish/ n. (pl. same) small, lobsterlike freshwater crustacean.

cray·on /kráyon/ • n. stick or pencil of colored wax, chalk, etc. • v.tr. draw with crayons.

craze /krayz/ • v. **1** tr. (usu. as **crazed** adj.) make insane. **2 a** tr. produce fine surface cracks on (pottery glaze, etc.). **b** intr. develop such cracks. • n. fad; rage.

cra·zy /kráyzee/ adj. (**cra·zi·er**, **cra·zi·est**) **1** colloq. insane; mad; foolish. **2** colloq. extremely enthusiastic. □□ **cra′zi·ly** adv. **cra′zi·ness** n.

creak /kreek/ • n. harsh scraping or squeaking sound. • v.intr. **1** make a creak. **2 a** move with a creaking noise. **b** move stiffly. **c** show weakness or frailty under strain. □□ **creak′ing·ly** adv. **creak′y** adj.

cream /kreem/ • n. **1** fatty content of milk. **2** (usu. prec. by the) best part of something. **3** creamlike cosmetic, etc. **4** pale yellow or off-white color. • v. **1** tr. work (butter, etc.) to a creamy consistency. **2** intr. form a cream or scum. **3** tr. colloq. defeat soundly (esp. in a sporting contest). • adj. pale yellow; off-white. □ **cream of tartar** crystallized potassium hydrogen tartrate, used in medicine, baking powder, etc.

cream·er /kréemər/ n. small pitcher for cream.

cream·er·y /kréeməree/ n. (pl. **-ies**) factory or store for dairy products.

cream·y /kréemee/ adj. (**cream·i·er**, **cream·i·est**) **1** like cream. **2** rich in cream. □□ **cream′i·ness** n.

crease /krees/ • n. line caused by folding; wrinkle. • v. **1** tr. make creases in. **2** intr. become creased.

cre·ate /kree-áyt/ v.tr. **1** bring into existence; cause. **2** originate.

cre·a·tion /kree-áyshən/ n. **1** creating; being created. **2 a** (usu. **the Creation**) God's creating of the universe. **b** (usu. **Creation**) everything so created; the universe. **3** product of imagination, art, etc.

cre·a·tion·ism /kree-áyshənizəm/ n. Theol. theory of the origin of life in accordance with the Bible. □□ **cre·a′tion·ist** n.

cre·a·tive /kree-áytiv/ adj. **1** inventive; imaginative. **2** able to create. □□ **cre·a′tive·ly** adv. **cre·a′tive·ness** n. **cre·a·tiv·i·ty** /-aytívitee, -ətiv-/ n.

cre·a·tor /kree-áytər/ n. **1** person who creates. **2** (**the Creator**) God.

crea·ture /kréechər/ n. **1** any living being. **2** person of a specified kind (poor creature). □ **creature comforts** material comforts. **creature of habit** person set in an unvarying routine.

crèche /kresh/ n. representation of a Nativity scene.

cre·dence /kréed'ns/ n. belief. □ **give credence to** believe.

cre·den·tial /kridénshəl/ n. (usu. in pl.) evidence of a person's qualifications, etc., usu. in the form of certificates, references, etc.

cre·den·za /kridénzə/ n. sideboard or cupboard.

cred·i·bil·i·ty /krédibílitee/ n. **1** being credible; believable. **2** reputation; status.

cred·i·ble /krédibəl/ adj. believable; worthy of belief. □□ **cred′i·bly** adv.

cred·it /krédit/ • n. **1** source of honor, pride, etc. **2** acknowledgment of merit. **3** good reputation. **4** a person's financial standing. **b** power to obtain goods, etc., before payment. **5** (usu. in pl.) acknowledgment of a contribution. **6** reputation for solvency and honesty in business. **a** entry in an account of a sum paid into it. **b** sum entered. • v.tr. **1** believe (cannot credit it). **2 a** enter on the credit side of an account. **b** ascribe a good quality or achievement to. □ **do credit to** enhance the reputation of. **on credit** with an arrangement to pay later. **to one's credit** in one's praise, commendation, or defense.

cred·it·a·ble /kréditəbəl/ adj. bringing credit or honor. □□ **cred·it·a·bil´i·ty** n. **cred´it·a·bly** adv.

cred·i·tor /kréditər/ n. person to whom a debt is owed.

cre·do /kréedō, kráy-/ n. (pl. **-dos**) creed.

cred·u·lous /kréjələs/ adj. too ready to believe; gullible. □□ **cre·du·li·ty** /kridóōlitee, -dyōō-/ n. **cred´u·lous·ly** adv. **cred´u·lous·ness** n. ¶ See note at INCREDIBLE.

Cree /kree/ n. (pl. same or **Crees**) **1 a** N. American people of eastern and central Canada. **b** member of this people. **2** language of this people.

creed /kreed/ n. **1** set of principles or beliefs. **2 a** (**the Creed** or **Apostles' Creed**) early statement of the Christian creed, ascribed to the Apostles. **b** formal summary of Christian doctrine (*Nicene Creed*). □□ **creed´al** or **cred´al** adj.

Creek /kreek/ n. **1 a** confederacy of N. American peoples formerly of Alabama and Georgia. **b** member of these peoples. **2** language of these peoples.

creek /kreek, krik/ n. stream. □ **up the creek** sl. in difficulties.

creel /kreel/ n. fisherman's large wicker basket.

creep /kreep/ • v.intr. (*past* and *past part.* **crept** /krept/) **1** move with the body prone and close to the ground. **2** move stealthily or timidly. **3** enter or overcome slowly. **4** colloq. act obsequiously. **5** (of a plant) grow along the ground or up a wall, etc. **6** (of flesh) shiver; shudder. • n. **1** act or instance of creeping. **2** (in pl.; prec. by *the*) colloq. feeling of revulsion or fear. **3** sl. unpleasant person.

creep·y /kréepee/ adj. (**creep·i·er**, **creep·i·est**) colloq. producing a feeling of horror or revulsion. □□ **creep´i·ly** adv. **creep´i·ness** n.

cre·mate /kréemayt, krimáyt/ v.tr. consume (a corpse, etc.) by fire. □□ **cre·ma·tion** /krimáyshən/ n. **cre·ma·tor** n. **cre´ma·to·ry** adj.

cre·ma·to·ri·um /kréemətáwreeəm/ n. (pl. **cre·ma·to·ri·ums** or **cre·ma·to·ri·a** /-reeə/) place for cremating corpses.

crème de la crème /krém də laa krém/ n. best part; elite.

cren·el·late /krénəlayt/ v.tr. provide (a tower, etc.) with battlements. □□ **cren·el·la·tion** /-láyshən/ n.

Cre·ole /krée-ōl/ • n. **1 a** descendant of European (esp. Spanish) settlers in the W. Indies or Central or S. America. **b** white descendant of French settlers, esp. in Louisiana. **c** person of mixed European and black descent. **2** language formed from a European language (esp. English, French, or Portuguese) and another (esp. African) language. • adj. **1** of Creoles. **2** (usu. **creole**) of Creole origin (*creole cooking*).

cre·o·sote /kréeəsōt/ n. distillate of wood or coal tar, used as wood preservative, antiseptic, etc.

crepe /krayp/ n. (also **crêpe**) **1** fine, gauzelike wrinkled fabric. **2** thin pancake, usu. with a filling. **3** hard-wearing wrinkled rubber used for the soles of shoes, etc. □ **crêpe paper** thin crinkled paper. □□ **crep´ey** adj. (also **crep´y**).

crept *past* and *past part.* of CREEP.

cre·scen·do /krishéndō/ • n. (pl. **-dos**) **1** Mus. gradual increase in loudness. **2 a** progress toward a climax. **b** disp. climax. • adv. & adj. increasing in loudness. • v.intr. (**-does**, **-doed**) increase gradually in loudness or intensity.

cres·cent /krésənt/ n. **1** curved sickle shape, as of the waxing or waning moon. **2** anything of this shape.

cress /kres/ n. cruciferous plant with edible leaves.

crest /krest/ • n. **1 a** comb, tuft, etc., on a bird's or animal's head. **b** plume, etc., on a helmet, etc. **2** top of a mountain, wave, roof, etc. **3** heraldic device, as on seals, etc. • v. **1** tr. reach the crest of. **2** intr. (of a wave, etc.) form into a crest. □□ **crest´ed** adj. (also in comb.).

crest·fall·en /kréstfawlən/ adj. dejected; dispirited.

cre·ta·ceous /kritáyshəs/ • adj. **1** of or like chalk. **2** (**Cretaceous**) Geol. of or relating to the last period of the Mesozoic era, with evidence of extensive chalk deposits. • n. (**Cretaceous**) Geol. this era or system.

cre·tin /kréetin/ n. **1** deformed and mentally deficient person. **2** colloq. stupid person. □□ **cre´tin·ism** n. **cre´tin·ize** v.tr. **cre´tin·ous** adj.

cre·vasse /krəvás/ n. deep open crack, esp. in a glacier.

crev·ice /krévis/ n. narrow opening or fissure, esp. in a rock.

crew /krōō/ • n. (often treated as pl.) **1 a** people manning a ship, aircraft, train, etc. **b** these as distinct from the captain or officers. **c** people working together; team. **2** colloq. company of people; gang (*a motley crew*). • v. **1** tr. supply or act as a crew or crew member for. **2** intr. act as a crew or crew member. □ **crew cut** very short haircut. **crew neck** close-fitting round neckline.

crew·el /krōōəl/ n. thin worsted yarn for tapestry and embroidery.

crew·el·work /krōōəlwərk/ n. design in crewel.

crib /krib/ • n. **1** baby's bed with high sides. **2** rack for animal fodder. **3** colloq. furtively used study notes. • v.tr. (also absol.) (**cribbed**, **cribbing**) **1** colloq. copy without acknowledgment. **2** confine in a small space. □ **crib death** = *sudden infant death syndrome*.

crib·bage /kríbij/ n. card game for up to four players. □ **cribbage board** board with pegs for scoring at cribbage.

crick /krik/ n. sudden painful stiffness.

crick·et[1] /kríkit/ n. team game played with ball, bats, and wickets. □ **not cricket** esp. Brit. colloq. underhand behavior.

crick·et[2] /kríkit/ n. grasshopperlike chirping insect.

cried *past* and *past part.* of CRY.

cri·er /krîər/ n. (also **cry´er**) **1** person who cries. **2** official making public announcements, as in a court of law.

crime /krīm/ n. **1 a** offense punishable by law. **b** illegal acts. **2** evil or shameful act.

crim·i·nal /kríminəl/ • n. person guilty of a crime. • adj. **1** of, involving, or concerning crime. **2** guilty of crime. **3** Law relating to or expert in criminal law. **4** colloq. scandalous; deplorable. □□ **crim·i·nal·i·ty** /-nálitee/ n. **crim´i·nal·ly** adv.

crim·i·nol·o·gy /kríminóləjee/ n. study of crime. □□ **crim·i·no·log·i·cal** /-nəlójikəl/ adj. **crim·i·nol´o·gist** n.

crimp /krimp/ • v.tr. **1** compress into small folds.

2 corrugate. **3** make waves in (hair). • *n.* crimped thing or form. □ **put a crimp in** *sl.* thwart. □□ **crimp′er** *n.* **crimp′y** *adj.* **crimp′i•ness** *n.*

crim•son /krímzən/ • *adj.* of a rich, deep red. • *n.* this color.

cringe /krinj/ • *v.intr.* shrink in fear; cower. • *n.* act or instance of cringing. □□ **cring′er** *n.*

crin•kle /kríngkəl/ • *n.* wrinkle; crease. • *v.* **1** *intr.* form crinkles. **2** *tr.* form crinkles in. □ **crinkle-cut** (of vegetables) cut with wavy edges. □□ **crin′kly** *adj.*

crin•o•line /krínəlin/ *n.* **1** stiffened or hooped petticoat. **2** stiff fabric of horsehair, etc., used for linings, hats, etc.

crip•ple /krípəl/ • *n.* usu. *offens.* lame person or animal. • *v.tr.* **1** make a cripple of. **2** disable; impair.

cri•sis /krísis/ *n.* (*pl.* **cri•ses** /-seez/) **1 a** decisive moment. **b** time of danger or great difficulty. **2** turning point.

crisp /krisp/ • *adj.* **1** hard but brittle. **2 a** (of air) bracing. **b** (of a style or manner) lively; brisk and decisive. **c** (of paper) stiff and crackling. • *v.* make or become crisp. □□ **crisp′ly** *adv.* **crisp′ness** *n.*

crisp•er /kríspər/ *n.* refrigerator compartment for produce.

crisp•y /kríspee/ *adj.* (**crisp•i•er, crisp•i•est**) crisp; brittle. □□ **crisp′i•ness** *n.*

criss•cross /krískráws, -krós/ • *n.* pattern of crossing lines. • *adj.* crossing; in cross lines. • *adv.* crosswise; at cross purposes. • *v.* **1** *intr.* a intersect repeatedly. **b** move crosswise. **2** *tr.* mark or make with a crisscross pattern.

cri•te•ri•on /krītéereeən/ *n.* (*pl.* **cri•te•ri•a** /-reeə-/ or **cri•te•ri•ons**) principle or standard that a thing is judged by.
¶ **Criterion** is singular; the plural of this word is usually given as **criteria.** *There are several criteria* is correct usage; "the only criteria" is not.

crit•ic /krítik/ *n.* **1** person who censures or criticizes. **2** person who reviews literary, artistic, etc. works.

crit•i•cal /krítikəl/ *adj.* **1** involving adverse comments; faultfinding. **2** providing textual criticism. **3 a** of or at a crisis. **b** decisive; crucial (*of critical importance*). **4** (of a nuclear reactor) maintaining a self-sustaining chain reaction. □ **critical list** list of critically ill patients. □□ **crit′i•cal•ly** *adv.* **crit′i•cal•ness** *n.*

crit•i•cism /krítisizəm/ *n.* **1 a** finding fault; censure. **b** critical remark, etc. **2 a** work of a critic. **b** judgmental analysis.

crit•i•cize /krítisīz/ *v.tr.* (also *absol.*) **1** find fault with; censure. **2** discuss critically. □□ **crit′i•ciz•able** *adj.* **crit′i•ciz•er** *n.*

cri•tique /kriteék/ • *n.* expression of critical analysis. • *v.tr.* (**cri•tiques, cri•tiqued, cri•ti•qu•ing**) discuss critically.

crit•ter /krítər/ *n.* dial. or joc. creature.

croak /krōk/ • *n.* deep, hoarse sound, as of a frog. • *v.* **1 a** *intr.* utter a croak. **b** *tr.* utter with a croak or in a dismal manner. **2** *sl.* **a** *intr.* die. **b** *tr.* kill.

Croat /kró-at/ • *n.* (also **Cro•a•tian** /krō-áyshən/ **1 a** native of Croatia. **b** person of Croatian descent. **2** Slavic dialect of the Croats. • *adj.* of the Croats or their dialect.

cro•chet /krōsháy/ • *n.* handicraft in which yarn is hooked into a patterned fabric. • *v.* create crochet. □□ **cro•chet′er** *n.*

crock[1] /krok/ *n.* **1** earthenware pot or jar. **2** broken piece of earthenware.

crock[2] /krok/ *n. colloq.* nonsense; exaggeration.

crock•er•y /krókəree/ *n.* earthenware; china dishes, etc.

croc•o•dile /krókədīl/ *n.* **1** large, long-jawed tropical amphibious reptile. **2** leather from its skin. □ **crocodile tears** insincere grief. □□ **croc•o•dil•i•an** /-díleeən/ *adj.*

cro•cus /krókəs/ *n.* (*pl.* **cro•cus•es**) early spring plant growing from a corm and having white, yellow, or purple flowers.

Croe•sus /kreésəs/ *n.* person of great wealth.

crois•sant /krwaasaán, krəsánt/ *n.* crescent-shaped pastry.

Cro-Mag•non /krōmágnən, -mányən/ *adj. Anthropol.* of a tall, broad-faced European race of late Paleolithic times.

crone /krōn/ *n.* withered old woman.

cro•ny /krónee/ *n.* (*pl.* **-nies**) close friend or companion.

crook /krŏok/ • *n.* **1** hooked staff of a shepherd or bishop. **2 a** bend; curve; hook. **b** anything hooked or curved. **3** *colloq.* swindler; criminal. • *v.* bend; curve.

crook•ed /krŏokid/ *adj.* **1 a** not straight or level; bent. **b** deformed. **2** *colloq.* not straightforward; dishonest. □□ **crook′ed•ly** *adv.* **crook′ed•ness** *n.*

croon /krōon/ *v.* hum or sing in a low sentimental voice. □□ **croon′er** *n.*

crop /krop/ • *n.* **1 a** produce of cultivated plants. **b** season's yield of this. **2** group or amount produced or appearing at one time. **3** handle of a whip. **4** predigestive pouch in a bird's gullet. • *v.tr.* (**cropped, crop•ping**) **1 a** cut off. **b** bite off. **2** cut (hair, etc.) short. □ **crop circle** circular depression in a standing crop. **crop-dusting** sprinkling of insecticide or fertilizer, esp. from the air. **crop out** *Geol.* appear at the surface. **crop up** occur unexpectedly.

crop•per /krópər/ *n.* crop-producing plant of specified quality (*a good cropper*). □ **come a cropper** *sl.* fail badly.

cro•quet /krōkáy/ *n.* lawn game with hoops, mallets, and wooden balls.

cro•quette /krōkét/ *n.* fried, breaded ball of mashed potato or ground meat, etc.

cro•sier /krózhər/ *n.* (also **cro′zier**) bishop's hooked staff.

cross /kraws, kros/ • *n.* **1** upright post with a transverse bar, as used for crucifixion. **2 a** (**the Cross**) cross on which Christ was crucified. **b** representation of this. **3** thing or mark like a cross. **4** cross-shaped decoration indicating rank, etc. **5** hybrid. **6** (foll. by *between*) mixture or compromise of two things. **7** trial; affliction. • *v.* **1** *tr.* go across. **2 a** *intr.* intersect; be across. **b** *tr.* cause to do this. **3** *tr.* draw a line or lines across, esp. to delete. **4** *tr.* (often *refl.*) make the sign of the cross on or over. **5** *intr.* **a** pass in opposite or different directions. **b** (of letters, etc.) be sent before receipt of the other. **6** *tr.* a cause to interbreed. **b** cross-fertilize (plants). **7** *tr. sl.* cheat. • *adj.* **1** peevish; angry; contrary. **2** transverse; reaching from side to side. **3** intersecting. □ **at cross purposes** misunderstanding; conflicting. **cross-dress** wear clothing typically worn by the opposite sex. **cross one's fingers** (or **keep one's fingers crossed**) **1** put one finger across another as a sign of hoping for good luck. **2** trust in good luck. **cross one's heart** make a solemn pledge. **cross one's mind** (of a thought, etc.) occur to one. **cross a person's palm** bribe. **cross swords** encounter in opposition. **cross wires** (or **get one's wires crossed**) **1** become wrongly connected by telephone. **2** have a misunderstanding. □□ **cross′ly** *adv.* **cross′ness** *n.*

cross·bar /kráwsbaar, krós-/ *n.* horizontal bar, esp. on a bicycle.

cross·bow /kráwsbō, krós-/ *n.* bow fixed on a wooden stock, with a groove for an arrow. □□ **cross′bow′man** *n.* (*pl.* **-men**).

cross·breed • *n.* /kráwsbreed, krós-/ **1** hybrid breed of animals or plants. **2** individual hybrid. • *v.tr.* /kráwsbrée̱d, krós-/ (*past* and *past part.* **-bred**) produce by crossing.

cross-check • *v.tr.* /kráws-chék, krós-/ check by alternative methods. • *n.* /kráws-chek, krós-/ cross-checking.

cross-coun·try /kráwskúntree, krós-/ *adj.* & *adv.* **1** across open country. **2** not keeping to main roads.

cross·cut • *adj.* /kráwskút, krós-/ cut across the main grain or axis. • *n.* /kráwskut, krós-/ diagonal cut, path, etc.

cross-ex·am·ine /kráwsigzámin, krós-/ *v.tr.* examine (esp. a witness in a court of law) to check or extend testimony already given. □□ **cross-ex·am·in·a′tion** *n.* **cross′-ex·am′in·er** *n.*

cross-eyed /kráwsíd, krós-/ *adj.* having one or both eyes turned inward.

cross-fer·til·ize /kráwsfért′līz, krós-/ *v.tr.* **1** fertilize (an animal or plant) from one of a different species. **2** interchange ideas, etc. □□ **cross′-fer·ti·li·za′tion** *n.*

cross·fire /kráwsfír, krós-/ *n.* (also **cross′ fire**) **1** firing in two crossing directions. **2 a** attack or criticism from several sources. **b** combative exchange of views, etc.

cross·ing /kráwsing, krós-/ *n.* **1** place where things (esp. roads) cross. **2** place for crossing a street, etc. **3** journey across water, mountains, etc.

cross·o·ver /kráwsōvər, krós-/ • *n.* point or place of crossing. • *adj.* having a crossover.

cross·piece /kráwspees, krós-/ *n.* transverse beam or other component of a structure, etc.

cross-ref·er·ence /kráwsréfərəns, krós-/ • *n.* reference from one part of a book, etc., to another. • *v.tr.* provide with cross-references.

cross·road /kráwsrōd, krós-/ *n.* (usu. in *pl.*) intersection of two or more roads. □ **at the crossroads** at a critical point.

cross sec·tion /kráws-sékshən, krós-/ *n.* **1 a** cutting across a solid. **b** plane surface produced in this way. **c** representation of this. **2** representative sample. □□ **cross′-sec′tion·al** *adj.*

cross·walk /kráwswawk, krós-/ *n.* pedestrian crossing.

cross·wind /kráwswind, krós-/ *n.* wind blowing across one's direction of travel.

cross·wise /kráwswīz, krós-/ *adj.* & *adv.* **1** in the form of a cross; intersecting. **2** transverse or transversely.

cross·word /kráwswərd, krós-/ *n.* (also **cross′word puz′zle**) grid of squares and blanks for

words crossing vertically and horizontally to be filled in from clues.

---

crossword, said to have been invented by the journalist Arthur Wynne, whose puzzle (called a 'word cross') first appeared in a Sunday newspaper, the *New York World*, on December 21, 1913.

---

crotch /kroch/ *n.* place where something forks, esp. the legs of the human body or a garment.

crotch·et·y /króchitee/ *adj.* peevish. □□ **crotch′et·i·ness** *n.*

crouch /krowch/ • *v.intr.* lower the body with limbs close to the chest; be in this position. • *n.* crouching; crouching position.

croup /kro͞op/ *n.* inflammation of the larynx and trachea in children, with a hard cough. □□ **croup′y** *adj.*

crou·pi·er /kro͞opeeər, -eeay/ *n.* person in charge of a gaming table.

crou·ton /kro͞oton/ *n.* cube of toasted bread served with soup, etc.

Crow /krō/ *n.* **1 a** N. American people native to eastern Montana. **b** member of this people. **2** language of this people.

crow[1] /krō/ *n.* large black bird having a powerful black beak. □ **as the crow flies** in a straight line. **crow's-foot** (*pl.* **-feet**) (usu. in *pl.*) wrinkle at the outer corner of the eye. **crow's nest** lookout platform at the masthead of a sailing vessel. **eat crow** submit to humiliation.

crow[2] /krō/ • *v.intr.* **1** (of a cock) utter a loud cry. **2** express glee. • *n.* cry of a cock.

crow·bar /króbaar/ *n.* iron bar with a flattened end, used as a lever.

crowd /krowd/ • *n.* **1** large gathering of people. **2** spectators; audience. **3** *colloq.* particular set of people. • *v.* **1 a** *intr.* come together in a crowd. **b** *tr.* cause to do this. **c** *intr.* force one's way. **2** *tr.* **a** (foll. by *into*) force or compress into a confined space. **b** fill or make abundant with. **3** *tr.* come aggressively close to. □ **crowd out** exclude by crowding. □□ **crowd′ed·ness** *n.*

crown /krown/ • *n.* **1** monarch's jeweled headdress. **2** (**the Crown**) a monarch, esp. as head of state. **b** power or authority of the monarchy. **3 a** wreath worn on the head, esp. as an emblem of victory. **b** award or distinction, esp. in sport. **4** crown-shaped device or ornament. **5** top part of a thing, esp. of the head or a hat. **6** highest part. **7 a** part of a tooth projecting from the gum. **b** artificial replacement for this. • *v.tr.* **1** put a crown on. **2** invest with royal authority. **3** be a crown to; rest on top of. **4** (as **crowning** *adj.*) be or cause to be the reward or finishing touch to (*the crowning glory*). **5** promote (a piece in checkers) to king. **6** *sl.* hit on the head. □ **crown prince** male heir to a sovereign throne. **crown princess 1** wife of a crown prince. **2** female heir to a sovereign throne.

cro·zier var. of CROSIER.

CRT *abbr.* cathode-ray tube.

cru·ces *pl.* of CRUX.

cru·cial /kro͞oshəl/ *adj.* **1** decisive; critical. **2** very important. □□ **cru·ci·al·i·ty** /-sheeálitee/ *n.* (*pl.* **-ties**). **cru′cial·ly** *adv.*

¶ **Crucial** is used in formal contexts to mean 'decisive, critical,' e.g., *The testimony of the only* *eyewitness was crucial to the case.* Its broader use to mean 'very important,' as in *It is crucial to get good light for your photographs,* should be restricted to informal contexts.

cru·ci·ble /krō′osibəl/ *n.* **1** melting pot for metals, etc. **2** severe test or trial.

cru·cif·er·ous /krōōsífərəs/ *adj.* of a botanical family having flowers with four petals arranged in a cross.

cru·ci·fix /krōōsifiks/ *n.* image of a cross with a figure of Christ on it.

cru·ci·fix·ion /krōōsifikshən/ *n.* **1** crucifying; being crucified. **2** (**Crucifixion**) crucifixion of Christ.

cru·ci·form /krōōsifawrm/ *adj.* cross-shaped.

cru·ci·fy /krōōsifī/ *v.tr.* (**-fies, -fied**) **1** put to death by fastening to a cross. **2** persecute; torment. **3** *sl.* defeat thoroughly. □□ **cru′ci·fi·er** *n.*

crud /krud/ *n. sl.* **1** deposit of dirt, grease, etc. **2** unpleasant person. **3** nonsense. □□ **crud′dy** *adj.* (**crud·di·er, crud·di·est**).

crude /krōōd/ • *adj.* **1 a** in the natural state; not refined. **b** unpolished; lacking finish. **2 a** rude; blunt. **b** offensive; indecent. **3** inexact; rough (*a crude estimate*). • *n.* natural mineral oil. □□ **crude′ly** *adv.* **crude′ness** *n.* **cru′di·ty** *n.*

cru·di·tés /krōōditáy/ *n.pl.* hors-d'oeuvre of mixed raw vegetables.

cru·el /krōōəl/ *adj.* **1** harsh; severe. **2** causing pain or suffering, esp. deliberately. □□ **cru′el·ly** *adv.* **cru′el·ness** *n.* **cru′el·ty** *n.* (*pl.* **-ties**).

cru·et /krōōit/ *n.* small container (esp. for oil or vinegar) for use at the table.

cruise /krōōz/ • *v.* **1** *intr.* make a journey by sea, esp. for pleasure. **2** *intr.* travel at a moderate or steady speed. **3** *intr.* achieve an objective, win a race, etc., with ease. **4** *intr. & tr. sl.* search for a sexual partner, esp. on streets, in bars, etc. • *n.* cruising voyage. □ **cruise control** device for automatically maintaining the speed of an automobile, etc. **cruise missile** low-flying, self-guiding missile.

cruis·er /krōōzər/ *n.* **1** high-speed warship. **2** police patrol car.

cruis·er·weight /krōōzərwayt/ *n.* weight class in professional boxing between light heavyweight and heavyweight.

crul·ler /krúlər/ *n.* small fried cake made of twisted dough.

crumb /krum/ *n.* **1 a** small fragment, esp. of bread. **b** small particle. **2** *sl.* objectionable person.

crum·ble /krúmbəl/ *v.* **1** *tr. & intr.* break or fall into fragments. **2** *intr.* (of power, reputation, etc.) gradually disintegrate. □□ **crum′bli·ness** /-blee-/ *n.* **crum′bly** *adj.* (**crum·bli·er, crum·bli·est**).

crumb·y /krúmee/ *adj.* (**crumb·i·er, crumb·i·est**) **1** like or covered in crumbs. **2** = CRUMMY.

crum·my /krúmee/ *adj.* (**crum·mi·er, crum·mi·est**) *colloq.* squalid; worthless. □□ **crum′mi·ly** *adv.* **crum′mi·ness** *n.*

crum·ple /krúmpəl/ • *v.* **1** *tr. & intr.* **a** crush or become crushed into creases. **b** ruffle; wrinkle. **2** *intr.* collapse; give way. • *n.* crease or wrinkle. □□ **crum′ply** *adj.*

crunch /krunch/ • *v.tr.* **1** crush noisily with

the teeth. **2** grind under foot, wheels, etc. • *n.* **1** crunching; crunching sound. **2** *colloq.* decisive event; moment of pressure. □□ **crunch′i·ly** *adv.* **crunch′i·ness** *n.* **crunch′y** *adj.* (**crunch·i·er, crunch·i·est**).

cru·sade /krōōsáyd/ • *n.* **1** any of several medieval military expeditions made by Europeans to recover the Holy Land from the Muslims. **2** vigorous campaign in favor of a cause. • *v.intr.* engage in a crusade. □□ **cru·sad′er** *n.*

crush /krush/ • *v.tr.* **1** compress with force or violence, so as to break, bruise, etc. **2** reduce to powder by pressure. **3** crumple. **4** defeat or subdue completely. • *n.* **1** act of crushing. **2** crowded mass of people. **3** drink made from crushed fruit. **4** *colloq.* infatuation.

crust /krust/ • *n.* **1 a** hard outer part of bread. **b** dry scrap of bread. **2** pastry covering of a pie. **3** hard casing of a softer thing. **4** outer portion of the earth. **5** hard residue or deposit. **6** *sl.* impudence. • *v.* **1** cover or become covered with a crust. **2** form into a crust. □□ **crus′tal** *adj.* (in sense 4 of *n.*).

crus·ta·cean /krustáyshən/ • *n.* hard-shelled, esp. aquatic arthropod, e.g., crab, lobster, shrimp. • *adj.* of crustaceans.

crust·y /krústee/ *adj.* (**crust·i·er, crust·i·est**) **1** having a crisp crust. **2** irritable; curt. □□ **crust′i·ly** *adv.* **crust′i·ness** *n.*

crutch /kruch/ *n.* **1** support for walking used by a lame person, usu. with a crosspiece fitting under the armpit. **2** support or object of dependency.

crux /kruks/ *n.* (*pl.* **crux·es** or **cru·ces** /krōōseez/) decisive point at issue.

cry /krī/ • *v.* (**cries, cried**) **1** *intr.* make a loud or shrill sound, esp. to express pain, appeal for help, etc. **2 a** *intr.* shed tears; weep. **b** *tr.* shed (tears). **3** *tr.* say or exclaim loudly or excitedly. **4** *intr.* (of an animal, esp. a bird) make a loud call. • *n.* (*pl.* **cries**) **1** loud shout of grief, pain, joy, etc. **2** loud excited utterance. **3** urgent appeal. **4** spell of weeping. **5 a** public demand. **b** rallying call. **6** call of an animal. □ **cry out for** demand as a self-evident requirement or solution. **far cry 1** long way. **2** very different thing. **for crying out loud** *colloq.* exclamation of surprise or annoyance.

cry·ba·by /krībaybee/ *n.* person who sheds tears or complains frequently.

cry·er var. of CRIER.

cry·ing /krí-ing/ *attrib.adj.* flagrant (*a crying shame*).

cry·o·gen·ics /krīojéniks/ *n.* branch of physics dealing with very low temperatures. □□ **cry·o·gen′ic** *adj.*

crypt /kript/ *n.* underground vault, used usu. for burial.

cryp·tic /kríptik/ *adj.* obscure in meaning; secret; mysterious. □□ **cryp′ti·cal·ly** *adv.*

crypto- /kríptō/ *comb. form* concealed; secret (*crypto-Nazi*).

cryp·to·gram /kríptəgram/ *n.* text written in code.

cryp·tog·ra·phy /kriptógrəfee/ *n.* art of writing or solving ciphers. □□ **cryp·to′gra·pher** *n.* **cryp·to·graph·ic** /-təgráfik/ *adj.* **cryp·to·graph′i·cal·ly** *adv.*

crys·tal /kríst′l/ • *n.* **1 a** clear transparent mineral, esp. rock crystal. **b** piece of this. **2 a** highly transparent glass. **b** articles of this. **3** glass over a watch face. **4**

crystalline piece of semiconductor. **5** substance with a solid internal structure and a solid form enclosed by symmetrical plane faces. ● *adj.* made of, like, or clear as crystal.

crys·tal·line /krístˈlin, -lin/ *adj.* **1** of, like, or clear as crystal. **2** having the structure and form of a crystal. □□ **crys·tal·lin·i·ty** /-línitee/ *n.*

crys·tal·lize /krístˈliz/ *v.* **1** *tr. & intr.* form or cause to form crystals. **2** (of ideas or plans) **a** *intr.* become definite. **b** *tr.* make definite. □□ **crys·tal·li·za′tion** *n.*

Cs *symb. Chem.* cesium.

CST *abbr.* central standard time.

CT *abbr.* Connecticut (in official postal use).

ct. *abbr.* **1** carat. **2** cent.

ctn. *abbr.* **1** carton. **2** cotangent.

Cu *symb. Chem.* copper.

cu. *abbr.* cubic.

cub /kub/ *n.* **1** young of a fox, bear, lion, etc. **2** (in full **cub reporter**) young newspaper reporter.

cub·by /kúbee/ *n.* (*pl.* **-bies**) (in full **cub·by·hole**) small enclosed space, esp. for storage, etc.

cube /kyoob/ ● *n.* **1** solid of six equal square sides. **2** *Math.* product of a number multiplied by its square. ● *v.tr.* **1** find the cube of (a number). **2** cut (food, etc.) into small cubes. □ **cube root** number for which a given number is the cube.

cu·bic /kyóobik/ *adj.* **1** cube-shaped. **2** of three dimensions. **3** involving the cube (and no higher power) of a number.

cu·bi·cal /kyóobikəl/ *adj.* cube-shaped. □□ **cu′bi·cal·ly** *adv.*

cu·bi·cle /kyóobikəl/ *n.* small partitioned space; compartment.

cub·ism /kyóobizəm/ *n.* geometric style in art, esp. painting. □□ **cub′ist** *n. & adj.*

cu·bit /kyóobit/ *n.* ancient measure about the length of a forearm.

cuck·old /kúkōld/ ● *n.* husband of an adulteress. ● *v.tr.* make a cuckold of. □□ **cuck′old·ry** *n.*

cuck·oo /kóokoo/ ● *n.* bird with a characteristic cry, known to lay its eggs in the nests of other birds. ● *predic.adj. sl.* crazy; foolish. □ **cuckoo in the nest** unwelcome intruder.

cu·cum·ber /kyóokumbər/ *n.* long, green, fleshy fruit, used in salads and for pickles.

cud /kud/ *n.* half-digested food returned from the first stomach of ruminants to the mouth for further chewing.

cud·dle /kúdˈl/ ● *v.* **1** *tr.* hug; fondle. **2** *intr.* nestle together; lie close and snug. ● *n.* prolonged hug. □□ **cud′die·some** *adj.* **cud′dly** *adj.* (**cud·dli·er, cud·dli·est**).

cud·gel /kújəl/ ● *n.* short, thick stick used as a weapon. ● *v.tr.* beat with a cudgel.

cue[1] /kyoo/ ● *n.* **1 a** last words of an actor's line as a signal to another to enter or speak. **b** similar signal to a musician, etc. **2 a** stimulus to perception, etc. **b** signal for action. **c** hint on how to behave. ● *v.tr.* (**cues, cued, cu·ing** or **cue·ing**) **1** give a cue to. **2** put (audio equipment) in readiness.

cue[2] /kyoo/ *n. Billiards* long rod for striking the ball. □□ **cue′ist** *n.*

cuff[1] /kuf/ *n.* **1** end part of a sleeve. **2** turned-

up hem on pants. **3** (in *pl.*) *colloq.* handcuffs. □ **off-the-cuff** *colloq.* impromptu. □□ **cuffed** *adj.* (also in *comb.*).

cuff[2] /kuf/ ● *v.tr.* strike with an open hand. ● *n.* such a blow.

cui·sine /kwizéen/ *n.* style or method of cooking.

cul-de-sac /kúldəsak, kōōl-/ *n.* (*pl.* **culs-de-sac** *pronunc.* same) **1** dead-end street. **2** futile course.

cu·li·nar·y /kyóoləneree, kúl-/ *adj.* pertaining to cooking.

cull /kul/ *v.tr.* **1** gather; derive. **2** pick selectively.

cul·mi·nate /kúlminayt/ *v.* **1** *intr.* reach its highest or final point. **2** *tr.* bring to its highest or final point. □□ **cul·mi·na·tion** /-náyshən/ *n.*

cu·lottes /kóolóts, kyóo-/ *n.pl.* skirtlike trousers.

cul·pa·ble /kúlpəbəl/ *adj.* deserving blame. □□ **cul·pa·bil′i·ty** *n.*

cul·prit /kúlprit/ *n.* guilty person.

cult /kult/ *n.* **1** ritualistic religious system. **2 a** devotion to a person or thing (*cult of aestheticism*). **b** popular fashion. **3** (*attrib.*) denoting a fashionable person or thing (*cult film*). □□ **cult′ism** *n.* **cult′ist** *n.*

cul·ti·vate /kúltivayt/ *v.tr.* **1** prepare and use (soil, etc.) for crops or gardening. **2 a** raise (crops). **b** culture (bacteria, etc.). **3 a** (often as **cultivated** *adj.*) improve or develop (the mind, manners, etc.). **b** nurture (a person, friendship, etc.). □□ **cul·ti·va′tion** *n.*

cul·tur·al /kúlchərəl/ *adj.* relating to artistic or intellectual matters or to a specific culture. □□ **cul′tur·al·ly** *adv.*

cul·ture /kúlchər/ ● *n.* **1 a** artistic and intellectual achievement. **b** refined appreciation of this. **2** customs, achievements, etc., of a particular civilization. **3 a** cultivation of plants; rearing of bees, silkworms, etc. **b** cultivation of the soil. **4** quantity of microorganisms and the nutrient material supporting their growth. ● *v.tr.* maintain (bacteria, etc.) in suitable growth conditions. □ **culture shock** disorientation experienced by a person suddenly subjected to an unfamiliar culture. □□ **cul′tured** *adj.*

culture Middle English (denoting a cultivated piece of land): the noun from French *culture* or directly from Latin *cultura* 'growing, cultivation'; the verb from obsolete French *culturer* or medieval Latin *culturare*, both based on Latin *colere* 'tend, cultivate.' In late Middle English the sense was 'the cultivation of the soil' and from this, in the early 16th century, arose the sense 'cultivation (of the mind, faculties, or manners).'

cul·vert /kúlvərt/ *n.* channel carrying water under a road, etc.

cum /kum/ *prep.* (usu. in *comb.*) with; combined with; also used as (*a bedroom-cum-study*).

cum. *abbr.* cumulative.

cum·ber·some /kúmbərsəm/ *adj.* inconvenient in size, weight, or shape; unwieldy.

cum·in /kúmin, kóo-, kyóo-/ *n.* **1** plant with aromatic seeds. **2** these seeds used as flavoring.

cum·mer·bund /kúmərbund/ *n.* waist sash.

cummerbund early 17th century: from Urdu and Persian *kamar-band*, from *kamar* 'waist, loins' and *bandi* 'band.' The sash was formerly worn in the Indian subcontinent by domestic workers and lower-caste office workers.

cu·mu·la·tive /kyo͞omyələtiv, -láytiv/ *adj.* **1** increasing progressively in amount, force, etc. **2** formed by successive additions. □□ **cu′mu·la·tive·ly** *adv.* **cu′mu·la·tive·ness** *n.*

cu·mu·lus /kyo͞omyələs/ *n.* (*pl.* **cu·mu·li** /-lī/) cloud formation of heaped, rounded masses. □□ **cu′mu·lous** *adj.*

cu·ne·i·form /kyo͞oneĕəfawrm, kyo͞oneeə-, kyo͞oni-/ • *adj.* **1** wedge-shaped. **2** of or using wedge-shaped writing, as in ancient Babylonian, etc., inscriptions. • *n.* cuneiform writing.

cun·ning /kúning/ • *adj.* **1** deceitful; clever; crafty. **2** ingenious. **3** attractive; quaint. • *n.* **1** craftiness; skill in deceit. **2** skill; ingenuity. □□ **cun′ning·ly** *adv.*

cup /kup/ • *n.* **1** small bowl-shaped container for drinking from. **2 a** its contents. **b** = CUPFUL. **3** cup-shaped thing. **4** cup-shaped trophy. • *v.tr.* (**cupped, cup·ping**) **1** form (esp. one's hands) into the shape of a cup. **2** take or hold as in a cup. □ **one's cup of tea** *colloq.* what interests or suits one.

cup·board /kúbərd/ *n.* recess or piece of furniture with a door and (usu.) shelves.

cup·cake /kúpkayk/ *n.* small cup-shaped cake.

cup·ful /kúpfo͞ol/ *n.* (*pl.* **-fuls**) amount held by a cup, esp. a half-pint (8-ounce) measure.

Cu·pid /kyo͞opid/ *n.* **1** Roman god of love, represented as a naked winged archer. **2** (also **cupid**) representation of Cupid.

cu·pid·i·ty /kyo͞opíditee/ *n.* greed for gain; avarice.

cu·po·la /kyo͞opələ/ *n.* dome forming or adorning a roof.

cupola

CUPOLA

cu·pric /ko͞oprik, kyo͞o-/ *adj.* of copper.

cu·prous /ko͞oprəs, kyo͞o-/ *adj.* of copper.

cur /kər/ *n.* **1** mongrel. **2** *colloq.* contemptible person.

cur. *abbr.* **1** currency. **2** current.

cur·a·ble /kyo͞orəbəl/ *adj.* that can be cured. □□ **cur·a·bil′i·ty** *n.*

cu·ra·çao /kyo͞orəsô, -sów/ *n.* orange-flavored liqueur.

cu·ra·re /kyo͞oráaree, ko͞o-/ *n.* bitter, poisonous extract of various S. American plants.

cu·rate /kyo͞orət/ *n.* assistant to a parish priest.

cu·ra·tive /kyo͞orətiv/ • *adj.* tending or able to cure. • *n.* curative agent.

cu·ra·tor /kyo͞oráytər, kyo͞orə-/ *n.* keeper or custodian of a museum, etc. □□ **cu·ra·to·ri·al** /kyo͞orətáwreeəl/ *adj.* **cu·ra′tor·ship** *n.*

curb /kərb/ • *n.* **1** check; restraint. **2** street edge or sidewalk border. **3** strap, etc., to restrain a horse. **4** enclosing border. • *v.tr.* restrain.

curd /kərd/ *n.* (often *pl.*) coagulated milk product, often made into cheese.

cur·dle /kərd′l/ *v.* make into or become curds; (of milk) turn sour; congeal. □ **make one's blood curdle** fill one with horror. □□ **cur′dler** *n.*

cure /kyo͞or/ • *v.tr.* **1** restore to health. **2** eliminate (disease, evil, etc.). **3** preserve (meat, fruit, etc.) by salting, drying, etc. • *n.* **1** restoration to health. **2** thing that effects a cure. **3** course of treatment. □ **cure-all** panacea.

cu·rette /kyo͞orét/ *n.* surgeon's scraping instrument.

cur·few /kə́rfyo͞o/ *n.* regulation requiring people to remain indoors between specified hours, usu. at night.

cu·ri·a /kyo͞oreeə/ *n.* (also **Curia**) (*pl.* **cu·ri·ae** /-ree-ee/) the papal court; government departments of the Vatican. □□ **Cu′ri·al** *adj.*

cu·rie /kyo͞oree/ *n.* unit of radioactivity.

cu·ri·o /kyo͞oreeō/ *n.* (*pl.* **-os**) rare or unusual object.

cu·ri·os·i·ty /kyo͞oreeósitee/ *n.* (*pl.* **-ties**) **1** eager desire to know; inquisitiveness. **2** strange, rare, or interesting thing.

cu·ri·ous /kyo͞oreeəs/ *adj.* **1** eager to learn; inquisitive. **2** strange; surprising; odd. □□ **cu′ri·ous·ly** *adv.* **cu′ri·ous·ness** *n.*

cu·ri·um /kyo͞oreeəm/ *n.* artificial radioactive metallic element. ¶ Symb.: **Cm**.

curl /kərl/ • *v.* **1** *tr.* & *intr.* bend or coil into a spiral; form or cause to form curls. **2** *intr.* move in a spiral form. • *n.* **1** lock of curled hair. **2** anything spiral or curved inward. **3 a** curling movement. **b** being curled. □ **make a person's hair curl** *colloq.* shock or horrify a person.

curl·er /kə́rlər/ *n.* pin or roller, etc., for curling the hair.

cur·lew /kə́rlo͞o, -lyo͞o/ *n.* wading bird, usu. with long, slender, bill.

curl·i·cue /kə́rlikyo͞o/ *n.* decorative curl or twist.

curl·ing /kə́rling/ *n.* game played on ice in which round, flat stones are slid across the surface toward a mark.

curl·y /kə́rlee/ *adj.* (**curl·i·er, curl·i·est**) **1** having or arranged in curls. **2** moving in curves. □□ **curl′i·ness** *n.*

cur·mud·geon /kərmújən/ *n.* bad-tempered person. □□ **cur·mud′geon·ly** *adj.*

cur·rant /kə́rənt, kúr-/ *n.* **1** small seedless dried grape. **2 a** any of various shrubs producing red, white, or black berries. **b** such a berry.

cur·ren·cy /kə́rənsee, kúr-/ *n.* (*pl.* **-cies**) **1 a** money in use in a country. **b** other commodity used as money. **2** being current; prevalence.

cur·rent /kə́rənt, kúr-/ • *adj.* belonging to the present time; happening now. • *n.* **1** narrow body of water, air, etc., moving in a definite direction. **2 a** ordered movement of electrically charged particles. **b** quantity representing the intensity of this.

cur·rent·ly /kə́rəntlee, kúr-/ *adv.* at the present time; now.

cur·ric·u·lum /kəríkyələm/ *n.* (*pl.* **cur·ric·u·la** /-lə/ or **cur·ric·u·lums**) subjects in a course of study. □□ **cur·ric′u·lar** *adj.*

cur·ric·u·lum vi·tae /kəríkyələm vítee, veetī/ *n.* (*pl.* **cur·ric·u·la vi·tae**) brief account of one's education, qualifications, etc.

cur·ry[1] /kə́ree, kúree/ ● *n.* (*pl.* **-ries**) dish prepared with curry powder. ● *v.tr.* (**-ries, -ried**) flavor with curry powder. □ **curry powder** usu. hot-tasting preparation of various spices.

cur·ry[2] /kə́ree, kúree/ *v.tr.* (**-ries, -ried**) **1** groom (a horse) with a currycomb. **2** treat (tanned leather) to improve it. **3** thrash. □ **curry favor** ingratiate oneself.

cur·ry·comb /kə́reekōm, kúree-/ *n.* metal serrated device for grooming horses.

curse /kərs/ ● *n.* **1** solemn invocation of supernatural wrath. **2** evil supposedly resulting from a curse. **3** violent exclamation of anger; profane oath. **4** thing that causes evil or harm. ● *v.* **1** *tr.* **a** utter a curse against. **b** (in *imper.*) may God curse. **2** *tr.* afflict (with). **3** *intr.* utter expletive curses.

cursed /kə́rsid, kərst/ *adj.* damnable; abominable. □□ **curs′ed·ly** *adv.* **curs′ed·ness** *n.*

cur·sive /kə́rsiv/ ● *adj.* (of writing) done with joined characters. ● *n.* cursive writing. □□ **cur′sive·ly** *adv.*

cur·sor /kə́rsər/ *n.* Computing positional indicator on a screen.

cur·so·ry /kə́rsəree/ *adj.* hasty; hurried (*cursory glance*). □□ **cur′so·ri·ly** *adv.* **cur′so·ri·ness** *n.*

curt /kərt/ *adj.* rudely brief. □□ **curt′ly** *adv.* **curt′ness** *n.*

cur·tail /kərtáyl/ *v.tr.* cut short; reduce. □□ **cur·tail′ment** *n.*

cur·tain /kə́rtən/ ● *n.* **1** piece of cloth, etc., hung as a screen, esp. at a window. **2 a** rise or fall of a stage curtain. **b** = *curtain call.* **3** partition or cover. **4** (in *pl.*) *sl.* the end. ● *v.tr.* (foll. by *off*) shut off with curtains. □ **curtain call** audience's summons to actor(s) to take a bow.

curt·sy /kə́rtsee/ (also **curt′sey**) ● *n.* (*pl.* **-sies** or **-seys**) woman's or girl's formal greeting or salutation made by bending the knees and lowering the body. ● *v.intr.* (**-sies, -sied** or **-seys, -seyed**) make a curtsy.

---

curtsy early 16th century: variant of COURTESY. Both forms were used to denote the expression of respect or courtesy by a gesture, especially in phrases such as *do courtesy, make courtesy,* and from this arose the current use (late 16th century).

---

cur·va·ceous /kərváyshəs/ *adj.* *colloq.* (esp. of a woman) having a shapely figure.

cur·va·ture /kə́rvəchər/ *n.* curving or degree of curve.

curve /kərv/ ● *n.* **1** line or surface of which no part is straight or flat. **2** curved form or thing. ● *v.* bend or shape to form a curve. □□ **curved** *adj.* **cur′vi·ness** *n.* **curv′y** *adj.* (**curv·i·er, curv·i·est**).

cush·ion /kŏoshən/ ● *n.* **1** bag stuffed with soft material, for sitting or leaning on, etc. **2** pro-

tection against shock. ● *v.tr.* **1** provide or protect with a cushion or cushions. **2** mitigate the adverse effects of. □□ **cush′ion·y** *adj.*

cush·y /kŏoshee/ *adj.* (**cush·i·er, cush·i·est**) *colloq.* easy and pleasant. □□ **cush′i·ness** *n.*

cusp /kusp/ *n.* **1** point or pointed end. **2** point at which two arcs meet.

cus·tard /kústərd/ *n.* pudding or sweet sauce made with milk, eggs, and flavored cornstarch.

cus·to·di·an /kustṓdeeən/ *n.* caretaker, esp. of a public building, etc. □□ **cus·to′di·an·ship** *n.*

cus·to·dy /kústədee/ *n.* **1** guardianship; protective care. **2** imprisonment. □ **take into custody** arrest. □□ **cus·to·di·al** /kustṓdeeəl/ *adj.*

cus·tom /kústəm/ *n.* **1 a** usual behavior. **b** particular, established way of behaving. **2** *Law* established usage having the force of law. **3** (in *pl.*; also treated as *sing.*) **a** duty on imports and exports. **b** officials or area administering this.

cus·tom·ar·y /kústəmeree/ *adj.* usual; in accordance with custom. □□ **cus·tom·ar′i·ly** *adv.*

cus·tom·er /kústəmər/ *n.* **1** person who buys goods or services. **2** person one has to deal with (*tough customer*).

cus·tom·ize /kústəmīz/ *v.tr.* make or modify according to individual requirements.

cut /kut/ ● *v.* (**cut·ting**; *past* and *past part.* **cut**) **1** *tr.* penetrate or wound with a sharp-edged instrument. **2** *tr.* & *intr.* divide or be divided with a knife, etc. **3** *tr.* reduce the length of or detach by cutting. **4** *tr.* reduce (wages, prices, time, etc.) or cease (services, etc.). **5** *tr.* **a** make (a coat, gem, key, record, etc.) by cutting. **b** make (a path, tunnel, etc.) by removing material. **6** *tr.* perform; make (*cut a deal*). **7** *tr.* cross; intersect. **8** *intr.* traverse, esp. as a shorter way. **9** *tr.* refuse to recognize (a person). **10** *tr.* deliberately miss (a class, etc.). **11** *Cards* divide (a deck) into two parts. **12** *tr.* switch off (an engine, etc.). **13** *tr.* dilute. ● *n.* **1** cutting. **2** division or wound made by cutting. **3** stroke with a knife, etc. **4** reduction or excision. **5** wounding remark or act. **6** style in which a garment, the hair, etc., is cut. **7** piece of butchered meat. **8** *colloq.* commission; share of profits. □ **a cut above** *colloq.* noticeably superior to. **be cut out** be suited (*was not cut out to be a teacher*). **cut-and-dried** completely decided; inflexible. **cut corners** do a task, etc., perfunctorily, esp. to save time. **cut a person down to size** *colloq.* deflate a person's pretensions. **cut in 1** interrupt. **2** pull in closely in front of another vehicle. **3** give a share of profits, etc., to. **4** interrupt a dancing couple to take over from one partner. **cut into** interfere with and reduce (*cuts into my free time*). **cut it out** (usu. in *imper.*) *sl.* stop doing that. **cut loose** begin to act freely. **cut the mustard** *sl.* reach the required standard. **cut short** terminate prematurely (*cut short his visit*). **cut one's teeth on** acquire initial practice or experience from (something). **cut a tooth** have it appear through the gum. **cut up 1** criticize severely. **2** behave in a comical or unruly manner.

cu·ta·ne·ous /kyŏotáyneeəs/ *adj.* of the skin.

cut·a·way /kútəway/ *adj.* **1** (of a diagram, etc.) with parts of the interior exposed. **2** (of a coat) with the front below the waist cut away.

cut·back /kútbak/ *n.* cutting back, esp. a reduction in expenditure.

cute /kyo͞ot/ adj. colloq. **1 a** attractive; quaint. **b** affectedly attractive. **2** clever; ingenious. ▫▫ **cute′ly** adv. **cute′ness** n.

cu·ti·cle /kyo͞otikəl/ n. dead skin at the base of a fingernail or toenail.

cut·lass /kútləs/ n. short sword with a slightly curved blade.

cut·ler·y /kútləree/ n. **1** knives, etc., for kitchen use. **2** knives, forks, and spoons for use at table.

cut·let /kútlit/ n. **1** small piece of veal, etc., for frying. **2** flat cake of ground meat, etc.

cut·off /kútawf/ n. **1** point at which something is cut off. **2** device for stopping a flow. **3** shortcut. **4** (pl.) shorts made from jeans, etc.

cut·throat /kút-thrōt/ • n. murderer. • adj. ruthless and intense.

cut·ting /kúting/ • n. piece cut from a plant for propagation. • adj. hostile; wounding. ▫ **cutting edge** forefront; vanguard. ▫▫ **cut′ting·ly** adv.

cut·tle·fish /kút′lfish/ n. mollusk with ten arms that ejects a black fluid when threatened.

cut·worm /kútwərm/ n. caterpillar that eats through stems at ground level.

c.v. abbr. curriculum vitae.

cwt. abbr. hundredweight.

cy·an /sían/ • adj. of a greenish-blue. • n. greenish-blue color.

cy·a·nide /síənīd/ n. highly poisonous substance used in mineral extraction.

cy·a·no·sis /síənōsis/ n. bluish discoloration of the skin due to oxygen-deficient blood. ▫▫ **cy·a·not·ic** /-nótik/ adj.

cyber- prefix relating to electronic communications systems, such as computer networks.

cy·ber·net·ics /síbərnétiks/ n.pl. (usu. treated as sing.) science of communications and control systems in machines and living things. ▫▫ **cy·ber·net′ic** adj. **cy·ber·net·i·cist** /-tisist/ n.

cy·ber·space /síbərspays/ n. environment in which information exchange by computer occurs.

cy·borg /síbawrg/ n. (in science fiction) human being whose biological functions are bionically enhanced.

cy·cla·men /síkləmən, sík-/ n. plant with pink, red, or white flowers.

cy·cle /síkəl/ • n. **1 a** recurrent round or period (of events, phenomena, etc.). **b** time needed for this. **2** Electr. **3** series of related songs, poems, etc. **4** bicycle, tricycle, etc. • v.intr. **1** ride a bicycle, etc. **2** move in cycles.

cy·clic /síklik, sík-/ adj. (also **cy·cli·cal**) /síklikəl, sík-/ **1 a** recurring in cycles. **b** belonging to a chronological cycle. **2** Chem. with constituent atoms forming a ring. ▫▫ **cy′cli·cal·ly** adv.

cy·clist /síklist/ n. rider of a bicycle, etc.

cyclo- /síklō/ comb. form circle, cycle, or cyclic.

cy·clone /síklōn/ n. violent, low-pressure hurricane of limited diameter. ▫▫ **cy·clon·ic** /-klónik/ adj. **cy·clon′i·cal·ly** adv.

cy·clo·tron /síklətron/ n. apparatus for acceleration of charged atomic and subatomic particles revolving in a magnetic field.

cyg·net /sígnit/ n. young swan.

cyl·in·der /sílindər/ n. **1** uniform solid or hollow body with straight sides and a circular cross section. **2** thing of this shape. ▫▫ **cy·lin·dri·cal** /silíndrikəl/ adj. **cy·lin′dri·cal·ly** adv.

cym·bal /símbəl/ n. brass or bronze plate struck to make a ringing sound. ▫▫ **cym′bal·ist** n.

CYMBALS

cyn·ic /sínik/ n. person with little faith in human nature. ▫▫ **cyn′i·cal** adj. **cyn′i·cism** /-nisizəm/ n.

cy·no·sure /sínəsho͞or, sín-/ n. **1** center of attraction or admiration. **2** guiding star.

cy·press /síprəs/ n. conifer with hard wood and dark foliage.

Cy·ril·lic /sirílik/ • adj. of the alphabet used by the Slavic peoples of the Orthodox Church; now used esp. for Russian and Bulgarian. • n. this alphabet.

cyst /sist/ n. sac formed in the body, containing liquid or semiliquid.

cys·tic /sístik/ adj. **1** of the bladder. **2** like a cyst.

cyto- /sítō/ comb. form Biol. cells or a cell.

cy·tol·o·gy /sítóləjee/ n. study of cells. ▫▫ **cy·to·log·i·cal** /sítəlójikəl/ adj. **cy·to·log′i·cal·ly** adv. **cy·tol′o·gist** n.

cy·to·plasm /sítəplazəm/ n. protoplasmic content of a cell apart from its nucleus. ▫▫ **cy·to·plas·mic** /-plázmik/ adj.

czar /zaar/ n. (also **tsar**; fem. **cza·ri′na, tsa·ri′na**) **1** hist. title of the former emperor of Russia. **2** person with great authority. ▫▫ **czar′dom** n. **czar′ism** n. **czar′ist** n.

Czech /chek/ • n. **1** native or national of the Czech Republic. **2** language of the Czech people. • adj. of the Czechs or their language.

Czech·o·slo·vak /chékəslóvak, -vaak/ (also **Czech·o·slo·va·ki·an** /-sləvaákeeən/) • n. native or national of Czechoslovakia, a former nation in central Europe. • adj. of or relating to Czechoslovaks or Czechoslovakia.

Dd

D¹ /dee/ *n.* (also **d**) (*pl.* **Ds** or **D's; d's**) **1** fourth letter of the alphabet. **2** *Mus.* second note of the diatonic scale of C major. **3** (as a Roman numeral) 500.

D² *symb. Chem.* deuterium.

D³ *abbr.* **1** (also **D.**) Democrat. **2** dimension (*3-D*).

d. *abbr.* **1** died. **2** departs. **3** delete. **4** daughter. **5** depth.

'd *v. colloq.* (usu. after pronouns) had; would (*I'd; he'd*).

DA *abbr.* district attorney.

dab /dab/ • *v.* (**dabbed, dab·bing**) **1** *tr.* press (a surface) briefly with a cloth, etc., without rubbing. **2** *tr.* (foll. by *on*) apply (a substance). • *n.* **1** brief application of a cloth, etc., to a surface. **2** small amount applied in this way. □□ **dab′ber** *n.*

dab·ble /dábəl/ *v.intr.* **1** take a casual interest (in an activity, etc.). **2** move the feet, hands, etc., in liquid. □□ **dab′bler** *n.*

da·cha /da'achə/ *n.* country house or cottage in Russia.

dachs·hund /da'aks-hoōnt, da'aksənt/ *n.* dog of a short-legged, long-bodied breed.

Da·cron /dáykron/ *n. propr.* synthetic polyester fiber used in textiles.

dac·tyl /dáktil/ *n.* metrical foot (˘ ˘ ˘) consisting of one long (or stressed) syllable followed by two short (or unstressed). □□ **dac·tyl′ic** *adj.*

dad /dad/ *n. colloq.* father.

dad·dy /dádee/ *n.* (*pl.* **-dies**) *colloq.* father. □ **daddy longlegs** harvestman arachnid.

da·do /dáydō/ *n.* (*pl.* **-dos**) **1** lower part of the wall of a room, visually distinct from the upper part. **2** plinth of a column.

daf·fo·dil /dáfədil/ *n.* **1** bulbous plant with a yellow trumpet-shaped flower. **2** pale-yellow color.

daf·fy /dáfee/ *adj.* (**daf·fi·er, daf·fi·est**) *sl.* = DAFT. □□ **daf′fi·ness** *n.*

daft /daft/ *adj. colloq.* silly; foolish; crazy. □□ **daft′ly** *adv.* **daft′ness** *n.*

dag·ger /dágər/ *n.* **1** short pointed knife for stabbing. **2** *Printing* = OBELUS.

da·go /dáygō/ *n.* (*pl.* **-gos** or **-goes**) *sl. offens.* person of Italian, Spanish, or Portuguese ancestry.

da·guerre·o·type /dəgérətīp/ *n.* photograph taken by an early process using a silvered plate and mercury vapor.

dahl·ia /dályə, da'al-, dáyl-/ *n.* composite garden plant of Mexican origin, cultivated for its many-colored flowers.

dai·ly /dáylee/ • *adj.* done or occurring every day. • *adv.* every day. • *n.* (*pl.* **-lies**) *colloq.* daily newspaper. □ **daily bread** necessary food. **daily dozen** *colloq.* regular exercises.

dain·ty /dáyntee/ • *adj.* (**dain·ti·er, dain·ti·est**) **1** delicately pretty. **2** delicate. **3** (of food) choice. **4** fastidious. • *n.* (*pl.* **-ties**) choice morsel; delicacy. □□ **dain′ti·ly** *adv.* **dain′ti·ness** *n.*

dai·qui·ri /dákəree, dī-/ *n.* cocktail of rum, lime juice, etc.

dair·y /dáiree/ • *n.* (*pl.* **-ies**) **1** place for the storage, processing, and distribution of milk and its products. **2** store where milk and milk products are sold. • *adj.* pertaining to milk and its products (and sometimes eggs).

da·is /dáyis, dī-/ *n.* low platform, usu. at the front of a hall, used to support a table, lectern, etc.

dai·sy /dáyzee/ *n.* (*pl.* **-sies**) small composite plant bearing white-petaled flowers. □ **daisy wheel** disk of spokes extending radially from a hub, each ending in a character, used as a printer in word processors and typewriters. **pushing up daisies** *sl.* dead and buried.

Da·ko·ta /dəkótə/ *n.* **1** N. American people native to the northern Mississippi valley. **2** language of this people. Also called **Lakota** or **Sioux.** □□ **Da·ko′tan** *adj.*

Da·lai La·ma /da'alī la'amə/ *n.* spiritual head of Tibetan Buddhism, formerly also the chief ruler of Tibet (see LAMA).

dale /dayl/ *n.* valley.

dal·li·ance /dáleeəns, -yəns/ *n.* **1** leisurely or frivolous passing of time. **2** act or instance of lighthearted flirting.

dal·ly /dálee/ *v.intr.* (**-lies, -lied**) **1** delay; waste time. **2** flirt; treat frivolously.

Dal·ma·tian /dalmáyshən/ *n.* dog of a large, white, short-haired breed with dark spots.

dam¹ /dam/ • *n.* barrier constructed to hold back water, forming a reservoir or preventing flooding. • *v.tr.* (**dammed, dam·ming**) **1** furnish or confine with a dam. **2** block up; obstruct.

dam² /dam/ *n.* mother, esp. of a four-footed animal.

dam·age /dámij/ • *n.* **1** harm or injury. **2** (in *pl.*) *Law* financial compensation for a loss or injury. **3** (prec. by *the*) *sl.* cost. • *v.tr.* inflict damage on. □□ **dam′ag·ing·ly** *adv.*

dam·ask /dáməsk/ • *n.* **1 a** woven fabric (esp. silk or linen) with a pattern visible on both sides. **b** twilled table linen. **2** tablecloth made of this material. • *adj.* **1** made of or resembling damask. **2** colored like a damask rose, velvety pink or vivid red. • *v.tr.* weave with figured designs. □ **damask rose** sweet-scented variety of rose with very soft petals.

dame /daym/ *n.* **1** (**Dame**) (in the UK) honorific title given to a woman. **2** *sl.* a woman.

dam·mit /dámit/ *int.* damn it.

damn /dam/ • *v.tr.* **1** curse (a person or thing). **2** doom to hell. **3** condemn; censure. **4** (often as **damning** *adj.*) (of evidence, etc.) show or prove to be guilty. • *n.* **1** uttered curse. **2** *sl.* negligible amount (*not worth a damn*). • *adj. & adv. colloq.* = DAMNED. □ **damn with faint praise** commend so unenthusiastically as to imply disapproval. □□ **damn′ing·ly** *adv.*

dam·na·ble /dámnəbəl/ adj. hateful; annoying. □□ **dam'na·bly** adv.

dam·na·tion /damnáyshən/ n. eternal punishment in hell.

damned /damd/ colloq. • adj. damnable. • adv. extremely (damned lovely). □ **do one's damnedest** do one's utmost.

damp /damp/ • adj. slightly wet. • n. moisture, esp. inconvenient or dangerous. • v.tr. 1 make damp; moisten. 2 a take the force or vigor out of. b make (a fire) burn less strongly by reducing the flow of air. □□ **damp'ly** adv. **damp'ness** n.

damp·en /dámpən/ v. 1 tr. & intr. make or become damp. 2 tr. make less forceful or vigorous; choke. □□ **damp'en·er** n.

damp·er /dámpər/ n. 1 person or thing that discourages. 2 metal plate in a flue to control the draft, and so the rate of combustion. □ **put a damper on** take the enjoyment out of.

dam·sel /dámzəl/ n. literary young unmarried woman.

dam·sel·fly /dámzəlflī/ n. (pl. **-flies**) any of various insects like a dragonfly but with its wings folded when resting.

dance /dans/ • v. 1 intr. move about rhythmically, usu. to music, for pleasure or as entertainment. 2 intr. move in a lively way; skip or jump about. 3 tr. a perform (a specified dance). b perform (a specified role) in a ballet, etc. 4 intr. move up and down. • n. 1 piece of dancing; sequence of steps in dancing. 2 social gathering for dancing. 3 piece of music for dancing. 4 lively motion. □□ **dance'a·ble** adj. **danc'er** n.

dan·de·lion /dánd'līən/ n. composite plant with jagged leaves and a yellow flower, then a head of seeds with downy tufts.

dan·der /dándər/ n. colloq. temper; anger; indignation.

dan·dle /dánd'l/ v.tr. dance (a child) on one's knees.

dan·druff /dándruf/ n. dead skin in small scales among the hair.

dan·dy /dándee/ • n. (pl. **-dies**) 1 man unduly devoted to style and fashion. 2 colloq. excellent thing. • adj. (**dan·di·er, dan·di·est**) colloq. splendid; first-rate. □□ **dan'dy·ish** adj. **dan'dy·ism** n.

Dane /dayn/ n. native or national of Denmark. □ **Great Dane** dog of a very large, short-haired breed.

dan·ger /dáynjər/ n. 1 liability or exposure to harm. 2 thing that causes or may cause harm. □ **in danger of** likely to incur or to suffer from.

dan·ger·ous /dáynjərəs/ adj. involving or causing danger. □□ **dan'ger·ous·ly** adv. **dan'ger·ous·ness** n.

dan·gle /dánggəl/ v. 1 intr. be loosely suspended, so as to be able to sway. 2 tr. hold or carry loosely suspended. 3 tr. hold out (hope, temptation, etc.) enticingly. □□ **dan'gler** n.

Dan·ish /dáynish/ • adj. of or relating to Denmark or the Danes. • n. 1 Danish language. 2 (prec. by the; treated as pl.) the Danish people. □ **Danish blue** soft, salty white cheese with blue veins. **Danish pastry** sweetened yeast pastry topped with icing, fruit, nuts, etc.

dank /dangk/ adj. disagreeably damp and cold. □□ **dank'ly** adv. **dank'ness** n.

dap·per /dápər/ adj. 1 neat and precise, esp. in dress or movement. 2 sprightly. □□ **dap'per·ly** adv. **dap'per·ness** n.

dap·ple /dápəl/ • v. 1 tr. mark with spots. 2 intr. be marked in this way. • n. 1 dappled effect. 2 dappled horse.

dare /dair/ • v.tr. 1 have the courage or impudence (to) (I dare not speak; I do not dare to jump). 2 defy or challenge (a person). • n. 1 act of daring. 2 challenge, esp. to prove courage. □ **I daresay** it is probable.

dare·dev·il /dáirdevəl/ • n. recklessly daring person. • adj. recklessly daring. □□ **dare'dev·il·ry** n.

dar·ing /dáiring/ • n. adventurous courage. • adj. adventurous; bold; prepared to take risks. □□ **dar'ing·ly** adv.

dark /daark/ • adj. 1 with little or no light. 2 of deep or somber color. 3 (of a person) with dark coloring. 4 gloomy; depressing; dismal. 5 evil; sinister. 6 sullen; angry. 7 secret; mysterious. • n. 1 absence of light. 2 nightfall. □ **dark chocolate** chocolate without milk. **the Dark Continent** Africa, esp. when little known to Europeans. **dark horse** little-known person who is unexpectedly prominent. **in the dark** lacking information. □□ **dark'ly** adv. **dark'ness** n.

dark·en /dáarkən/ v. 1 tr. make dark or darker. 2 intr. become dark or darker.

dark·room /dáarkrōom, -rŏŏm/ n. room for photographic work, with normal light excluded.

dar·ling /dáarling/ • n. 1 beloved or lovable person or thing. 2 favorite. • adj. 1 beloved; lovable. 2 favorite. 3 colloq. charming or pretty.

darn¹ /daarn/ • v.tr. mend (esp. knitted material) by filling a hole with stitching. • n. darned area in material. □ **darning needle** 1 long needle with a large eye. 2 dragonfly.

darn² /daarn/ v.tr., int., adj., & adv. colloq. = DAMN (in imprecatory senses).

dart /daart/ • n. 1 small pointed missile used as a weapon or in a game. 2 (in pl.; usu. treated as sing.) indoor game of throwing these at a target to score points. 3 sudden rapid movement. 4 tapering tuck stitched in a garment. • v. 1 intr. move or go suddenly or rapidly. 2 tr. direct suddenly (a glance, etc.).

dart·board /dáartbawrd/ n. circular target in darts.

dash /dash/ • v. 1 intr. rush. 2 tr. strike or fling with force, esp. to shatter. 3 tr. frustrate; daunt; dispirit. 4 tr. colloq. (esp. **dash it all**) = DAMN v. 1. • n. 1 rush; sudden advance. 2 horizontal stroke in writing or printing to mark a pause, break in sense, etc. 3 impetuous vigor. 4 showy appearance or behavior. 5 sprinting race. 6 slight admixture. 7 = DASHBOARD. 8 longer signal of the two in Morse code (cf. DOT n. 2). □ **dash off** depart or write hurriedly.

dash·board /dáshbawrd/ n. instrument panel of a vehicle.

dash·ing /dáshing/ adj. 1 spirited; lively. 2 stylish. □□ **dash'ing·ly** adv.

das·tard·ly /dástərdlee/ adj. cowardly; despicable. □□ **das'tard·li·ness** n.

DAT abbr. digital audiotape.

da·ta /dáytə, dátə, dáa-/ n.pl. (also treated as sing., although the singular form is strictly datum) 1 known facts used as a basis for conclusions. 2 quantities or characters operated on by a computer, etc. □ **data capture** entering data into a computer. **data processing** series of operations on data, esp. by a computer. **data processor** machine, esp. a computer, that carries out data processing.

¶ **Data** was originally the plural of the Latin word *datum*, 'something (e.g., a piece of information) given.' **Data** is now used as a singular where it means 'information': *This data was prepared for the conference.* It is used as a plural in technical contexts and when the collection of bits of information is stressed: *All recent data on hurricanes are being compared.*

da·ta·base /dáytəbays, dátə-/ *n.* structured set of data held in a computer.

date[1] /dayt/ • *n.* **1** day of the month, esp. as a number. **2** particular day or year. **3** statement in a document, etc., of the time of composition or publication. **4** period to which a work of art, etc., belongs. **5** *colloq.* **a** appointment, esp. social. **b** person with whom one has a social engagement. • *v.* **1** *tr.* mark with a date. **2** *tr.* assign a date to (an object, etc.). **3** *intr.* have its origins at a particular time. **4** *intr.* be recognizable as from the past. **5** *tr.* indicate as out of date. **6** *colloq.* **a** *tr.* arrange with (a person) to meet socially. **b** *intr.* meet socially by agreement. □ **date rape** sexual assault involving two people who have met socially. **out of date** (*attrib.* **out-of-date**) old-fashioned; obsolete. **to date** until now. **up to date** (*attrib.* **up-to-date**) fashionable; current.

date[2] /dayt/ *n.* **1** oval, single-stoned fruit. **2** (in full **date palm**) tall tree native to W. Asia and N. Africa, bearing this fruit.

---

date Middle English: via Old French from medieval Latin *data*, feminine past participle of *dare* 'give'; from the Latin formula used in dating letters, *data* (*epistola*) '(letter) given or delivered,' to record a particular time or place.

---

dat·ed /dáytid/ *adj.* **1** showing or having a date (*dated letter*). **2** old-fashioned; out-of-date.

date·line /dáytlīn/ *n.* line at the head of a newspaper article showing the date and place of writing.

da·tive /dáytiv/ *Gram.* • *n.* case of nouns and pronouns indicating an indirect object or recipient. • *adj.* of or in the dative.

da·tum /dáytəm, dátəm, dáʾatəm/ *n.* (*pl.* **da·ta**: see DATA as main entry). **1** piece of information. **2** thing known or granted.

daub /dawb/ • *v.tr.* **1** spread (paint, etc.) crudely or roughly. **2** coat (a surface) with paint, etc. **3** (also *absol.*) paint crudely or unskillfully. • *n.* paint, etc., daubed on a surface.

daugh·ter /dáwtər/ *n.* **1** girl or woman in relation to her parents. **2** female descendant. **3** (foll. by *of*) female member of a family, nation, etc. □ **daughter-in-law** (*pl.* **daughters-in-law**) wife of one's son. □□ **daugh·ter·ly** *adj.*

daunt /dawnt/ *v.tr.* discourage; intimidate. □□ **daunt·ing** *adj.* **daunt·ing·ly** *adv.*

daunt·less /dáwntlis/ *adj.* intrepid; persevering. □□ **daunt·less·ly** *adv.* **daunt·less·ness** *n.*

dau·phin /dáwfin, dōfáN/ *n. hist.* eldest son of the king of France.

dav·en·port /dávənpawrt/ *n.* large, heavily upholstered sofa.

daw·dle /dáwd'l/ • *v.* **1** *intr.* **a** walk slowly and idly. **b** delay; waste time. **2** *tr.* (foll. by *away*) waste (time). • *n.* act or instance of dawdling.

dawn /dawn/ • *n.* **1** daybreak. **2** beginning or incipient appearance of something. • *v.intr.* **1** (of a day) begin; grow light. **2** begin to appear or develop.

dawn·ing /dáwning/ *n.* **1** daybreak. **2** beginning of something.

day /day/ *n.* **1** time between sunrise and sunset. **2 a** 24 hours as a unit of time. **b** corresponding period on other planets. **3** daylight (*clear as day*). **4** time in a day during which work is normally done. **5 a** (also *pl.*) period of the past or present (*the old days*). **b** (prec. by *the*) present time (*issues of the day*). **6** prime of a person's life (*in my day*). **7** a point of time (*will do it one day*). **8** day of a particular event. **9** a day's endeavor, esp. as bringing success (*win the day*). □ **all in a day's work** part of normal routine. **call it a day** end a period of activity. **day after day** without respite. **day and night** all the time. **day by day** gradually. **day care** supervision and care, esp. of young children, during the day. **day in, day out** routinely; constantly. **day laborer** unskilled laborer hired by the day. **day of rest** Sabbath. **day-to-day** mundane; routine. **not one's day** day of successive misfortunes for a person. **one of these days** before very long. **one of those days** day when things go badly. **that will be the day** *colloq.* that will never happen.

day·break /dáybrayk/ *n.* first appearance of morning light.

day·dream /dáydreem/ • *n.* pleasant fantasy or reverie. • *v.intr.* indulge in this. □□ **day·dream·er** *n.*

day·light /dáylīt/ *n.* **1** light of day. **2** dawn. **3** visible gap or interval. **4** (usu. in *pl.*) *sl.* one's life or consciousness, esp. as representing vulnerability to fear, etc. (*scared the daylights out of me*). □ **daylight saving** achieving longer evening daylight, esp. in summer, by setting the time an hour ahead of standard time. **see daylight** begin to understand.

day·time /dáytīm/ *n.* part of the day when there is natural light.

daze /dayz/ • *v.tr.* stupefy; bewilder. • *n.* state of bewilderment (*in a daze*). □□ **daz·ed·ly** /-zidlee/ *adv.*

daz·zle /dázəl/ • *v.tr.* **1** blind or confuse temporarily by an excess of light. **2** impress or overpower with knowledge, ability, etc. • *n.* bright confusing light. □□ **daz·zling** *adj.* **daz·zling·ly** *adv.*

Db *symb. Chem.* dubnium.

dB *abbr.* decibel(s).

DBMS *abbr. Computing* database management system.

DC *abbr.* **1** (also **d.c.**) direct current. **2** District of Columbia.

DD *abbr.* doctor of divinity.

D.D.S. *abbr.* **1** doctor of dental science. **2** doctor of dental surgery.

DDT *abbr.* dichlorodiphenyltrichloroethane, a colorless chlorinated hydrocarbon used as an insecticide.

DE *abbr.* Delaware (in official postal use).

de- /dee, di/ *prefix* **1** forming verbs and their derivatives: **a** down; away (*descend*). **b** completely (*denude*). **2** added to form verbs and nouns implying removal or reversal (*decentralize*).

dea·con /déekən/ n. assistant to a priest, minister, etc.

de·ac·ti·vate /deeáktivayt/ v.tr. make inactive or less reactive. □□ **de·ac·ti·va·tion** /-váyshən/ n. **de·ac'ti·va·tor** n.

dead /ded/ • adj. **1** no longer alive. **2** colloq. extremely tired or unwell. **3** benumbed (my fingers are dead). **4** (foll. by to) insensitive to. **5** no longer effective or in use; extinct. **6** inanimate. **7** a lacking force or vigor. **b** (of sound) not resonant. **8** a quiet; lacking activity. **b** motionless; idle. **9** a (of a microphone, etc.) not transmitting sound, esp. because of a fault. **b** (of a circuit, etc.) carrying no current; not connected to a source of electricity. **10** (of the ball in a game) out of play. **11** abrupt; complete; exact (come to a dead stop; dead certainty). • adv. **1** absolutely; exactly (dead on target). **2** colloq. very; extremely (dead easy). • n. (prec. by the) **1** (treated as pl.) those who have died. **2** time of silence or inactivity (dead of night). □ **dead end 1** closed end of a road, passage, etc. **2** (often (with hyphen) attrib.) situation offering no prospects of progress or advancement. **dead heat 1** race in which two or more competitors finish in a tie. **2** result of such a race. **dead letter 1** law or practice no longer observed or recognized. **2** letter that is undeliverable and unreturnable, esp. one with an incorrect address. **dead reckoning** Naut. calculation of a ship's position from the log, compass, etc. **dead to the world** colloq. fast asleep; unconscious.

dead·beat /dédbeet/ n. **1** colloq. penniless person. **2** sl. person constantly in debt.

dead·en /déd'n/ v. **1** tr. & intr. deprive of or lose vitality, force, brightness, sound, feeling, etc. **2** tr. (foll. by to) make insensitive. □□ **dead'en·er** n.

dead·line /dédlīn/ n. time limit.

dead·lock /dédlok/ • n. situation, esp. one involving opposing parties, in which no progress can be made. • v. bring or come to a standstill.

dead·ly /dédlee/ • adj. (**dead·li·er, dead·li·est**) **1** causing or able to cause fatal injury or serious damage. **2** intense; extreme. **3** (of aim, etc.) extremely accurate or effective. **4** deathlike. **5** colloq. dreary; dull. • adv. **1** as if dead. **2** extremely; intensely (deadly serious). □ **deadly nightshade** = BELLADONNA.

dead·pan /dédpan/ adj. & adv. lacking expression or emotion.

dead·wood /dédwŏŏd/ n. **1** dead trees or branches. **2** colloq. useless people or things.

deaf /def/ adj. **1** wholly or partly without hearing. **2** (foll. by to) refusing to listen or comply. □ **fall on deaf ears** to be ignored. **turn a deaf ear** be unresponsive. □□ **deaf'ness** n.

deal /deel/ • v. (past and past part. **dealt** /delt/) **1** intr. **a** (foll. by with) take measures concerning (a problem, etc.), esp. to resolve. **b** (foll. by with) do business with; associate with. **c** (foll. by with) discuss or treat (a subject). **d** behave in a specified way (dealt honorably by them). **2** intr. (foll. by in) to sell or be concerned with commercially. **3** tr. (often foll. by out) distribute to several people, etc. **4** tr. (also absol.) distribute (cards) to players. **5** tr. administer (deal a heavy blow). • n. **1** (usu. **a good** or **great deal**) colloq. large amount. **2** colloq. business arrangement. **3** specified treatment (gave them a bad deal). **4** a distribution of cards by dealing. **b** player's turn to do this. **c** set of hands dealt to players.

deal·er /déelər/ n. **1** person or business dealing in (esp. retail) goods. **2** player dealing in a card game. **3** person who sells illegal drugs. □□ **deal'er·ship** n. (in sense 1).

deal·ings /déelingz/ n.pl. contacts or transactions, esp. in business. □ **have dealings with** associate with.

dealt past and past part. of DEAL.

dean /deen/ n. **1** a college or university official. **b** head of a university faculty or department or of a medical school. **2** head of a cathedral or collegiate church.

dear /deer/ • adj. **1** beloved or esteemed. **2** as a formula of address, esp. beginning a letter (Dear Sir). **3** precious; cherished. **4** (usu. in superl.) earnest; deeply felt. **5** high-priced. • n. (esp. as a form of address) dear person. • adv. at great cost. • int. expressing surprise, dismay, pity, etc. (oh dear!). □ **for dear life** see LIFE. □□ **dear'ly** adv. (esp. in sense 3 of adj.).

dearth /dərth/ n. scarcity or lack, esp. of food.

death /deth/ n. **1** irreversible ending of life. **2** event that terminates life. **3** a being killed or killing. **b** being dead. **4** a destruction or permanent cessation (the death of our hopes). **b** colloq. something terrible or appalling. **5** (usu. **Death**) personification of death, usu. a skeleton. □ **at death's door** close to death. **be the death of 1** cause the death of. **2** be very harmful to. **death trap** colloq. dangerous or unhealthy building, vehicle, etc. **fate worse than death** colloq. disastrous misfortune or experience. □□ **death'less** adj. **death'like** adj.

death·bed /déthbed/ n. bed where a person dies or has died.

death·blow /déthblō/ n. **1** blow or other action that causes death. **2** event, etc., that ends an activity, enterprise, etc.

death·ly /déthlee/ • adj. (**death·li·er, death·li·est**) suggestive of death (deathly silence). • adv. in a deathly way (deathly pale).

deb /deb/ n. colloq. debutante.

de·ba·cle /daybaakəl, -bákel, də-/ n. (also **dé·bâ'cle**) utter defeat, failure, or collapse.

de·bar /deebaár/ v.tr. (**de·barred, de·bar·ring**) exclude; prohibit. □□ **de·bar'ment** n.

de·bark /dibaárk/ v.tr. land from a ship. □□ **de·bar·ka·tion** /-káyshən/ n.

de·base /dibáys/ v.tr. lower in quality, value, or character. □□ **de·base'ment** n. **de·bas'er** n.

de·bat·a·ble /dibáytəbəl/ adj. **1** questionable; subject to dispute. **2** capable of being debated. □□ **de·bat'a·bly** adv.

de·bate /dibáyt/ • v. **1** tr. (also absol.) discuss or dispute, esp. formally. **2** a tr. consider (a matter). **b** intr. consider different sides of a question. • n. **1** formal discussion, esp. in a legislature, etc. **2** discussion. □□ **de·bat'er** n.

de·bauch /dibáwch/ • v.tr. **1** corrupt; pervert. **2** make intemperate or sensually indulgent. • n. bout of sensual indulgence.

deb·au·chee /dibawchée, -shée, déb-/ n. person addicted to excessive sensual indulgence.

de·bauch·er·y /dibáwchəree/ n. excessive sensual indulgence.

de·ben·ture /dibénchər/ n. (in full **de·ben'ture bond**) fixed-interest bond of a company or corporation, backed by general credit rather than specified assets.

de·bil·i·tate /dibílitayt/ *v.tr.* enfeeble; enervate. □□ **de·bil·i·ta·tion** /-táyshən/ *n.*

de·bil·i·ty /dibílitee/ *n.* feebleness, esp. of health.

deb·it /débit/ • *n.* **1** entry in an account recording a sum owed. **2** sum recorded. **3** total of such sums. **4** debit side of an account. • *v.tr.* enter on the debit side of an account. □ **debit card** card issued by a bank allowing the holder to transfer deposited funds electronically, as to make a purchase.

deb·o·nair /débənáir/ *adj.* **1** carefree; selfassured. **2** having pleasant manners.

de·brief /deebréef/ *v.tr. colloq.* interrogate (a diplomat, pilot, etc.) about a mission or undertaking. □□ **de·brief'ing** *n.*

de·bris /dəbrée, day-, débree/ *n.* scattered fragments, esp. of something wrecked or destroyed.

debt /det/ *n.* **1** something owed, esp. money. **2** state of owing (*in debt*).

debt·or /détər/ *n.* person who owes a debt, esp. money.

de·bug /deebúg/ *v.tr.* (**de·bugged, de·bug·ging**) **1** *colloq.* remove concealed listening devices from (a room, etc.). **2** *colloq.* identify and remove defects from (a computer program, etc.).

de·bunk /deebúngk/ *v.tr. colloq.* expose the falseness of (a claim, etc.). □□ **de·bunk'er** *n.*

de·but /daybyōō, dáybyōō/ • *n.* (also **dé·but'**) **1** first public appearance of a performer, show, etc. **2** first appearance of a debutante in society. • *v.* **1** *intr.* make a debut. **2** *tr.* introduce, esp. a performance, etc.

deb·u·tante /débyətaant, dáybyōō-/ *n.* (usu. wealthy) young woman making her social debut.

Dec. *abbr.* December.

deca- /dékə/ *comb. form* (also **dec-** before a vowel) ten or tenfold (*decagon; decaliter*).

dec·ade /dékayd/ *n.* **1** period of ten years. **2** set, series, or group of ten.

dec·a·dence /dékəd'ns/ *n.* **1** moral or cultural deterioration. **2** immoral behavior.

dec·a·dent /dékədənt/ • *adj.* in a state of moral or cultural deterioration. • *n.* decadent person. □□ **dec'a·dent·ly** *adv.*

dec·caf·fein·at·ed /deekáfinaytid/ *adj.* with caffeine removed or reduced.

dec·a·gon /dékəgən/ *n.* plane figure with ten sides and angles. □□ **de·cag·o·nal** /dikágənəl/ *adj.*

de·cal /deékal/ *n.* = DECALCOMANIA 2.

de·cal·co·ma·ni·a /deekálkəmáyneeə/ *n.* **1** process of transferring designs from specially prepared paper to the surface of glass, porcelain, etc. **2** picture or design using this process.

Dec·a·logue /dékəlawg, -log/ *n.* Ten Commandments.

de·camp /dikámp/ *v.intr.* **1** break up or leave a camp. **2** depart suddenly; abscond.

de·cant /dikánt/ *v.tr.* gradually pour off (liquid, esp. wine), esp. without disturbing the sediment.

de·cant·er /dikántər/ *n.* stoppered glass container for wine.

de·cap·i·tate /dikápitayt/ *v.tr.* behead (esp. as a form of capital punishment). □□ **de·cap·i·ta·tion** /-táyshən/ *n.*

de·cath·lon /dikáthlən, -lon/ *n.* athletic contest in which each competitor takes part in ten events. □□ **de·cath·lete** /-leet/ *n.*

de·cay /dikáy/ • *v.* **1 a** *intr.* rot; decompose. **b** *tr.* cause to rot or decompose. **2** *intr. & tr.* decline or cause to decline in quality, power, etc. **3** *intr. Physics* (usu. foll. by *to*) (of a substance, etc.) undergo change by radioactivity. • *n.* **1** rotten state. **2** decline in health, quality, etc. **3** *Physics* change by radioactivity.

de·ceased /diséest/ *formal* • *adj.* dead. • *n.* (usu. prec. by *the*) person who has died, esp. recently.

de·ceit /diséet/ *n.* **1** deception, esp. by concealing the truth. **2** dishonest trick or stratagem. **3** willingness to deceive.

de·ceit·ful /diséetfōōl/ *adj.* using deceit. □□ **de·ceit'ful·ly** *adv.* **de·ceit'ful·ness** *n.*

de·ceive /diséev/ *v.* **1** *tr.* make (a person) believe what is false; mislead purposely. **2** *tr.* be unfaithful to, esp. sexually. **3** *intr.* use deceit. □ **deceive oneself** persist in a mistaken belief. □□ **de·ceiv'er** *n.*

de·cel·er·ate /deesélərayt/ *v.* begin or cause to begin to reduce speed. □□ **de·cel·er·a·tion** /-ráyshən/ *n.*

De·cem·ber /disémbər/ *n.* twelfth month of the year.

de·cen·cy /deésənsee/ *n.* (*pl.* **-cies**) **1** correct and tasteful behavior. **2** (in *pl.*) the requirements of correct behavior.

de·cen·ni·al /diséneeəl/ *adj.* **1** lasting ten years. **2** recurring every ten years. □□ **de·cen'ni·al·ly** *adv.*

de·cent /deésənt/ *adj.* **1 a** conforming with current standards of behavior or propriety. **b** avoiding obscenity. **2** respectable. **3** acceptable; good enough. **4** kind; obliging. □□ **de'cent·ly** *adv.*

de·cen·tral·ize /deeséntrəlīz/ *v.tr.* **1** transfer (power, etc.) from central to local authority. **2** reorganize (a centralized institution, etc.) to give greater local autonomy. □□ **de·cen·tral·i·za'tion** *n.*

de·cep·tion /disépshən/ *n.* **1** deceiving or being deceived. **2** thing that deceives; trick or sham.

de·cep·tive /diséptiv/ *adj.* apt to deceive; misleading. □□ **de·cep'tive·ly** *adv.* **de·cep'tive·ness** *n.*

deci- /désee/ *comb. form* one-tenth, esp. of a metric unit (*deciliter*).

dec·i·bel /désibel/ *n.* unit (one-tenth of a bel) used to measure electrical signals or sound intensities. ¶ Abbr.: **dB.**

de·cide /disíd/ *v.* **1 a** *intr.* resolve after consideration. **b** *tr.* resolve or settle (an issue, etc.). **2** *intr.* give a judgment. □□ **de·cid'a·ble** *adj.*

de·cid·ed /disídid/ *adj.* **1** (usu. *attrib.*) definite; unquestionable. **2** (of a person) resolute, not vacillating.

de·cid·ed·ly /disídidlee/ *adv.* undoubtedly; undeniably.

de·cid·u·ous /disíjōōəs/ *adj.* **1** (of a tree) shedding leaves annually. **2** (of leaves, horns, teeth, etc.) shed periodically.

dec·i·mal /désiməl/ • *adj.* (of a system of numbers, measures, etc.) based on the number ten.

● *n.* decimal fraction. □ **decimal fraction** fraction whose denominator is a power of ten, esp. when expressed positionally by units to the right of a decimal point. **decimal point** period placed before a numerator in a decimal fraction.

dec·i·mate /désimayt/ *v.tr.* destroy a large proportion of. □□ **dec·i·ma·tion** /-máyshən/ *n.*
¶ The usual sense of **decimate** is now 'destroy a large proportion of': *the project would decimate the fragile wetland wilderness.* The original and literal sense is ' kill or remove one in ten of.' In any case, do not use **decimate** to mean 'defeat utterly.'

---

decimate late Middle English: from Latin *decimat-* 'taken as a tenth,' from the verb *decimare*, from *decimus* 'tenth.' In Middle English the term *decimation* denoted the levying of a tithe, and later it denoted the tax imposed by Cromwell on the Royalists (1655). The verb *decimate* originally alluded to the Roman punishment of executing one man in ten of a mutinous legion.

---

de·ci·pher /disīfər/ *v.tr.* **1** convert (text written in code) into an intelligible language. **2** determine the meaning of (anything unclear). □□ **de·ci'pher·a·ble** *adj.*

de·ci·sion /disízhən/ *n.* **1** act or process of deciding. **2** conclusion or resolution reached after consideration. **3** (often foll. by *of*) **a** settlement of a question. **b** formal judgment.

de·ci·sive /disīsiv/ *adj.* **1** that decides an issue; conclusive. **2** (of a person, esp. as a characteristic) able to decide quickly and effectively. □□ **de·ci'sive·ly** *adv.* **de·ci'sive·ness** *n.*

deck /dek/ ● *n.* **1** flooring on a ship. **2** anything resembling a ship's deck, e.g., the floor of a bus. **3** component for playing (disks, tapes, etc.) in sound-reproduction equipment. **4** pack of cards. **5** *sl.* the ground. **6 a** any floor or platform, esp. of a pier for sunbathing. **b** platformlike structure, usu. made of lumber, attached to a house, etc. ● *v.tr.* **1** (often foll. by *out*) decorate; adorn. **2** furnish with or cover as a deck.

-deck·er /dékər/ *comb. form* having a specified number of decks or layers (*double-decker*).

de·claim /dikláym/ *v.* **1** *intr. & tr.* speak rhetorically or affectedly. **2** *intr.* practice oratory or recitation. □□ **de·claim'er** *n.* **de·cla·ma·tion** /dékləmáyshən/ *n.* **de·clam·a·to·ry** /diklámətawree/ *adj.*

dec·la·ra·tion /dékləráyshən/ *n.* **1** declaring. **2** formal, emphatic, or deliberate statement.

de·clare /dikláir/ *v.tr.* **1** announce openly or formally. **2** pronounce (*declared it invalid*). **3** assert emphatically. **4** acknowledge possession of (dutiable goods, etc.). **5** (as **declared** *adj.*) admit to being (*a declared atheist*). **6** *Cards* **a** (also *absol.*) name (the trump suit). **b** announce that one holds (certain combinations of cards, etc.). □□ **de·clar'a·ble** *adj.* **de·clar·a·tive** /-klárətiv/ *adj.* **de·clar'a·tive·ly** *adv.* **de·clar·a·to·ry** /-klárətawree/ *adj.* **de·clar'er** *n.*

dé·clas·sé /dayklasáy/ *adj.* (*fem.* **dé·clas·sée'**) that has fallen in social status.

de·clas·si·fy /deeklásifī/ *v.tr.* (**-fies, -fied**) declare (information, etc.) to be no longer secret. □□ **de·clas·si·fi·ca·tion** /-fikáyshən/ *n.*

de·clen·sion /diklénshən/ *n.* **1** *Gram.* **a** form of a

noun, pronoun, or adjective, by which its grammatical case, number, and gender are identified. **b** class of nouns, etc., with the same inflections. **2** deterioration; declining.

dec·li·na·tion /déklináyshən/ *n.* **1** downward bend or turn. **2** *Astron.* angular distance of a star, etc., north or south of the celestial equator. **3** *Physics* deviation of a compass needle from true north. □□ **dec·li·na'tion·al** *adj.*

de·cline /diklīn/ ● *v.* **1** *intr.* deteriorate; lose strength or vigor. **2 a** *tr.* refuse, esp. formally and courteously. **b** *tr.* turn away from (a challenge, discussion, etc.). **c** *intr.* give or send a refusal. **3** *intr.* slope downward. **4** *intr.* bend down; droop. **5** *tr. Gram.* state the forms of (a noun, pronoun, or adjective). ● *n.* **1** gradual loss of vigor or excellence. **2** decay; deterioration. **3** setting; the last part of the course (of the sun, of life, etc.).

de·cliv·i·ty /diklívitee/ *n.* (*pl.* **-ties**) downward slope, esp. a piece of sloping ground. □□ **de·cliv'i·tous** *adj.*

de·coc·tion /dikókshən/ *n.* **1** boiling down to extract some essence. **2** resulting liquid.

de·code /deekṓd/ *v.tr.* decipher. □□ **de·cod'er** *n.*

dé·col·le·tage /dáykawltáa̯zh/ *n.* low neckline of a woman's dress, etc.

dé·col·le·té /daykawltáy/ ● *adj.* **1** (of a dress, etc.) having a low neckline. **2** (of a woman) wearing a dress with a low neckline. ● *n.* low neckline.

de·com·mis·sion /deekəmíshən/ *v.tr.* **1** close down (a nuclear reactor, etc.). **2** take (a ship) out of service.

de·com·pose /deekəmpṓz/ *v.* **1** *intr.* decay; rot. **2** *tr.* separate (a substance, light, etc.) into its elements. □□ **de·com·po·si·tion** /deekompəzíshən/ *n.*

de·com·pres·sion /deekəmpréshən/ *n.* **1** release from compression. **2** gradual reduction of air pressure on a deep-sea diver. □□ **de·com·press'** *v.*

de·con·ges·tant /deekənjéstənt/ ● *adj.* that relieves (esp. nasal) congestion. ● *n.* medicinal agent that relieves congestion.

de·con·struc·tion /deekənstrúkshən/ *n.* method of critical analysis of philosophical and literary language. □□ **de·con·struc'tion·ism** *n.* **de·con·struc'tion·ist** *adj. & n.*

de·con·tam·i·nate /deekəntáminayt/ *v.tr.* remove contamination from. □□ **de·con·tam·i·na·tion** /-náyshən/ *n.*

de·cor /daykáwr, dáykawr/ *n.* (also **dé·cor'**) furnishing and decoration of a room, stage, etc.

dec·o·rate /dékərayt/ *v.tr.* **1** adorn, beautify. **2** paint, wallpaper, etc. **3** serve as an adornment to. **4** confer an award or distinction on. □□ **dec·o·ra·tive** /dékərətiv, dékərāy-, -əray-/ *adj.* **dec'o·ra·tive·ly** *adv.* **dec'o·ra·tive·ness** *n.*

dec·o·ra·tion /dékəráyshən/ *n.* **1** decorating. **2** thing that decorates. **3** honorary medal, etc. **4** (in *pl.*) flags, etc., put up for a public celebration. □ **Decoration Day** = *Memorial Day.*

dec·o·ra·tor /dékəraytər/ *n.* person who decorates, esp. one who paints or papers houses professionally.

dec·o·rous /dékərəs/ *adj.* having or showing decorum. □□ **dec'o·rous·ly** *adv.* **dec'o·rous·ness** *n.*

de·co·rum /dikáwrəm/ *n.* appropriate or dignified behavior.

de·cou·page /dáykoopáa̯zh/ *n.* (also **dé·cou·**

page′) decoration of surfaces with paper cutouts.

de·coy • *n.* /deékoy, dikóy/ person or thing used as a lure, bait, or enticement. • *v.tr.* /dikóy/ allure or entice, esp. using a decoy.

> **decoy** mid-16th century (earlier as *coy*): from Dutch *de kooi* 'the decoy,' from Middle Dutch *de kouw* 'the cage,' from Latin *cavea* 'cage.' The meaning derives from the practice of using tamed ducks to lead wild ones along channels into captivity.

de·crease • *v.* /dikreés/ make or become smaller or fewer. • *n.* /deékrees/ 1 decreasing. 2 amount by which a thing decreases. □□ **de·creas′ing·ly** *adv.*

de·cree /dikreé/ • *n.* 1 official order. 2 legal judgment or decision, esp. in matrimonial cases. • *v.tr.* ordain by decree.

de·crep·it /dikrépit/ *adj.* 1 weakened or worn out by age or infirmity. 2 dilapidated. □□ **de·crep′i·tude** *n.*

de·crim·i·nal·ize /deekríminəlīz/ *v.tr.* cease to treat (an action, etc.) as criminal. □□ **de·crim·i·nal·i·za′tion** *n.*

de·cry /dikrī/ *v.tr.* (**-cries, -cried**) disparage; belittle.

ded·i·cate /dédikayt/ *v.tr.* 1 devote (esp. oneself) to a special task or purpose. 2 address (a book, etc.) as a compliment to a friend, patron, etc. 3 devote (a building, etc.) to an honored person, cause, etc. 4 (as **dedicated** *adj.*) a (of a person) devoted single-mindedly to a goal, etc. b (of equipment) designed for a specific purpose. □□ **ded′i·ca·tor** *n.* **ded·i·ca·to·ry** /-kətáwree/ *adj.*

ded·i·ca·tion /dédikáyshən/ *n.* 1 dedicating; being dedicated. 2 words with which a book, etc., is dedicated.

de·duce /didoós, -dyoós/ *v.tr.* infer logically. □□ **de·duc′i·ble** *adj.*

de·duct /didúkt/ *v.tr.* subtract, take away, withhold (an amount, portion, etc.).

de·duct·i·ble /didúktibəl/ • *adj.* that may be deducted, esp. from taxable income. • *n.* part of an insurance claim to be paid by the insured.

de·duc·tion /didúkshən/ *n.* 1 a deducting. b amount deducted. 2 a inferring of particular instances from a general law (cf. INDUCTION). b conclusion deduced.

de·duc·tive /didúktiv/ *adj.* of or reasoning by deduction. □□ **de·duc′tive·ly** *adv.*

deed /deed/ • *n.* 1 thing done intentionally or consciously. 2 brave, skillful, or conspicuous act. 3 action. 4 *Law* document used for transferring ownership of property. • *v.tr.* convey or transfer by legal deed.

deem /deem/ *v.tr. formal* regard; consider; judge.

deep /deep/ • *adj.* 1 extending far down or in. 2 a to or at a specified depth (*6 feet deep*). b in a specified number of ranks (*soldiers drawn up six deep*). 3 situated or coming from far down, back, or in (*deep in his pockets; deep sigh*). 4 low-pitched; full-toned (*deep voice*). 5 intense; extreme (*deep disgrace*). 6 heartfelt; absorbing (*deep affection*). 7 fully absorbed or overwhelmed (*deep in debt*). 8 profound; difficult to understand (*deep thought*). n. 1 (prec. by *the*) *poet.* the sea. 2 abyss, pit, or cavity. • *adv.* deeply; far down or in (*read deep into the night*).

□ **deep freeze** 1 refrigerator in which food can be quickly frozen and kept for long periods. 2 suspension of activity. **deep-freeze** *v.tr.* freeze or store (food) in a deep freeze. **deep-fry (-fries, -fried)** fry (food) in fat or oil sufficient to cover it. □□ **deep′ly** *adv. n.*

deep·en /deépən/ *v.* make or become deep or deeper.

deer /deer/ *n.* (*pl.* same) four-hoofed grazing animal, the males of which usu. have antlers.

deer·skin /deérskin/ • *n.* leather from a deer's skin. • *adj.* made from a deer's skin.

de·es·ca·late /dee-éskəlayt/ *v.tr.* reduce the level or intensity of. □□ **de·es·ca·la·tion** /-láyshən/ *n.*

de·face /difáys/ *v.tr.* disfigure. □□ **de·face′ment** *n.*

de fac·to /di fáktō, day/ • *adv.* in fact, whether by right or not. • *adj.* existing in fact (*de facto ruler*). • *n.* (in full **de facto wife** or **husband**) person living with another as if married.

de·fal·ca·tion /deéfalkáyshən, -fawl-/ *n. Law* 1 misappropriation of money. 2 amount misappropriated.

de·fame /difáym/ *v.tr.* libel; slander. □□ **def·a·ma·tion** /défəmáyshən/ *n.* **de·fam·a·to·ry** /difámətawree/ *adj.*

de·fault /difáwlt/ • *n.* 1 failure to appear, pay, or act in some way. 2 preselected option adopted by a computer program when no alternative is specified. • *v.intr.* fail to fulfill an obligation, esp. to pay money or to appear in court. □ **by default** because of a lack of an alternative or opposition.

de·feat /difeét/ • *v.tr.* 1 overcome in battle, contest, etc. 2 frustrate; baffle. 3 reject (a motion, etc.) by voting. • *n.* defeating or being defeated.

de·feat·ism /difeétizəm/ *n.* excessive readiness to accept defeat. □□ **de·feat′ist** *n.* & *adj.*

def·e·cate /défikayt/ *v.intr.* discharge feces from the body. □□ **def·e·ca·tion** /-káyshən/ *n.*

de·fect • *n.* /deéfekt, difékt/ imperfection, shortcoming, blemish. • *v.intr.* /difékt/ leave one's country or cause for another. □□ **de·fec′tion** *n.* **de·fec′tor** *n.*

de·fec·tive /diféktiv/ • *adj.* having a defect or defects; imperfect; faulty. • *n.* often *offens.* mentally defective person. □□ **de·fec′tive·ly** *adv.* **de·fec′tive·ness** *n.*

de·fend /difénd/ *v.tr.* (also *absol.*) 1 resist an attack made on; protect. 2 support or uphold by argument. 3 conduct the defense in a lawsuit. □□ **de·fend′er** *n.*

de·fend·ant /diféndənt, -ant/ *n.* person, etc., sued or accused in a court of law.

de·fense /diféns/ *n.* 1 defending from or resisting attack. 2 means of resisting attack. 3 justification; vindication. 4 defendant's case or counsel in a lawsuit. □ **defense mechanism** 1 body's reaction against disease. 2 usu. unconscious mental process to avoid anxiety. □□ **de·fense′less** *adj.* **de·fense′less·ly** *adv.* **de·fense′less·ness** *n.*

de·fen·si·ble /difénsibəl/ *adj.* 1 justifiable; supportable by argument. 2 able to be easily defended militarily. □□ **de·fen·si·bil′i·ty** *n.* **de·fen′si·bly** *adv.*

de·fen·sive /diffénsiv/ *adj.* **1** done or intended for defense. **2** overreacting to criticism. □□ **de·fen′sive·ly** *adv.* **de·fen′sive·ness** *n.*

de·fer[1] /difór/ *v.tr.* (**de·ferred, de·fer·ring**) postpone. □□ **de·fer′ment** *n.* **de·fer′ral** *n.*

de·fer[2] /difór/ *v.intr.* (**de·ferred, de·fer·ring**) yield or make concessions. □□ **de·fer′rer** *n.*

def·er·ence /défərəns, défrəns/ *n.* **1** courteous regard; respect. **2** compliance. □ **in deference to** out of respect for.

def·er·en·tial /défərénshəl/ *adj.* showing deference; respectful. □□ **def·er·en′tial·ly** *adv.*

de·fi·ance /diffəns/ *n.* open disobedience; bold resistance.

de·fi·ant /diffənt/ *adj.* **1** showing defiance. **2** openly disobedient. □□ **de·fi′ant·ly** *adv.*

de·fi·cien·cy /difishənsee/ *n.* (*pl.* **-cies**) **1** being deficient. **2** lack or shortage. **3** thing lacking.

de·fi·cient /difishənt/ *adj.* **1** incomplete. **2** insufficient.

def·i·cit /défisit/ *n.* **1** amount by which a thing (esp. money) is too small. **2** excess of liabilities over assets.

de·file[1] /diffíl/ *v.tr.* **1** make dirty; pollute; befoul. **2** corrupt. **3** desecrate; profane. □□ **de·file′ment** *n.*

de·file[2] /diffíl/ • *n.* also /deéfíl/ narrow gorge or pass. • *v.intr.* march in file.

de·fine /diffín/ *v.tr.* **1** give the meaning of (a word, etc.). **2** describe or explain the scope of. **3** outline. □□ **de·fin′a·ble** *adj.*

def·i·nite /définit/ *adj.* **1** having exact and discernible limits. **2** clear and distinct; not vague. □ **definite article** see ARTICLE 4. □□ **def′i·nite·ly** *adv.*

def·i·nite·ly /définitlee/ • *adv.* **1** in a definite manner. **2** certainly; without doubt. • *int. colloq.* yes, certainly.

def·i·ni·tion /définíshən/ *n.* **1 a** defining. **b** meaning of a word or nature of a thing. **2** distinctness in outline of an image.

de·fin·i·tive /difinitiv/ *adj.* **1** (of an answer, verdict, etc.) decisive; unconditional; final. **2** (of a book, etc.) most authoritative. □□ **de·fin′i·tive·ly** *adv.*

¶ **Definitive** in the sense 'decisive, unconditional, final' is sometimes confused with **definite**. However, **definite** does not have the connotations of authority: a *definite no* is simply a firm refusal, whereas a *definitive no* is an authoritative judgment or decision that something is not the case.

de·flate /difláyt/ *v.* **1 a** *tr.* let air or gas out of (a tire, balloon, etc.). **b** *intr.* be emptied of air or gas. **2** *tr. & intr.* lose or cause to lose confidence. **3** *Econ.* **a** *tr.* subject (a currency or economy) to deflation. **b** *intr.* pursue a policy of deflation. □□ **de·fla′tor** *n.*

de·fla·tion /difláyshən/ *n.* **1** deflating or being deflated. **2** *Econ.* reduction of money in circulation to increase its value. □□ **de·fla′tion·ar·y** *adj.*

de·flect /diflékt/ *v.* **1** *tr. & intr.* bend or turn aside from a course or purpose. **2 a** *tr.* cause to deviate. **b** *intr.* deviate. □□ **de·flec·tion** /diflékshən/ *n.* **de·flec′tor** *n.*

de·flow·er /diflówr/ *v.tr.* **1** deprive of virginity. **2** ravage; spoil.

de·fo·li·ate /deefóleeayt/ *v.tr.* remove leaves

from, esp. as a military tactic. □□ **de·fo′li·ant** *n. & adj.* **de·fo·li·a′tion** /-áyshən/ *n.*

de·form /difáwrm/ *v.* **1** *tr.* make ugly; deface; misshape. **2** *intr.* undergo deformation. □□ **de·form′a·ble** *adj.* **de·for·ma·tion** /deéfawrmáyshən/ *n.* **de·formed′** *adj.* **de·for′mi·ty** *n.* (*pl.* **-ties**)

de·fraud /difráwd/ *v.tr.* cheat by fraud.

de·fray /difráy/ *v.tr.* pay (a cost or expense). □□ **de·fray′al** *n.*

de·frost /difráwst, -fróst/ *v.* **1** *tr.* remove frost or ice from (esp. a refrigerator, windshield, etc.). **2** unfreeze (frozen food). **3** *intr.* become unfrozen. □□ **de·frost′er** *n.*

deft /deft/ *adj.* neat; dexterous; adroit. □□ **deft′ly** *adv.* **deft′ness** *n.*

de·funct /difúngkt/ *adj.* **1** no longer existing or used. **2** dead or extinct.

de·fuse /deefyóoz/ *v.tr.* **1** remove the fuse from (a bomb, etc.). **2** reduce tensions in (a crisis, difficulty, etc.).

de·fy /diffí/ *v.tr.* (**-fies, -fied**) **1** resist openly; refuse to obey. **2** (of a thing) present insuperable obstacles to (*defies solution*). **3** challenge (a person) to do or prove something.

deg. *abbr.* degree.

de·gen·er·ate • *adj.* /dijénərət/ fallen from former normality or goodness. • *n.* /dijénərət/ degraded person. • *v.intr.* /dijénərayt/ become degenerate. □□ **de·gen′er·a·cy** *n.* **de·gen′er·ate·ly** *adv.*

de·gen·er·a·tion /dijénəráyshən/ *n.* **1** becoming degenerate. **2** *Med.* morbid deterioration of tissue. □□ **de·gen·er·a·tive** /dijénərətiv/ *adj.*

de·grade /digráyd/ *v.tr.* **1** reduce to a lower rank. **2** dishonor; humiliate. □□ **de·grad′a·ble** *adj.* **deg·ra·da·tion** /dégrədáyshən/ *n.* **de·grad′er** *n.*

de·grad·ing /digráyding/ *adj.* humiliating; causing a loss of self-respect. □□ **de·grad′ing·ly** *adv.*

de·gree /digrée/ *n.* **1** stage in scale, series, or process. **2** stage in intensity or amount (*to a degree*). **3** *Math.* unit of measurement of angles or arcs, with 360 degrees comprising a circle. ¶ *Symb.:* °. **4** *Physics* unit of temperature, hardness, etc. **5** *Med.* extent of burns. **6** academic rank. **7** grade of crime. □ **by degrees** gradually. □ **to a degree** *colloq.* considerably.

de·hu·man·ize /deehyóōmənīz/ *v.tr.* **1** deprive of human characteristics. **2** make impersonal. □□ **de·hu·man·i·za′tion** *n.*

de·hu·mid·i·fy /deéhyōōmídifī/ *v.tr.* (**-fies, -fied**) reduce the degree of humidity of; remove moisture from (a gas, esp. air). □□ **de·hu·mid·i·fi·ca′tion** /-fikáyshən/ *n.* **de·hu·mid′i·fi·er** *n.*

de·hy·drate /deéhídrayt/ *v.* **1** *tr.* **a** remove water from (esp. foods). **b** make dry. **2** *intr.* lose water. □□ **de·hy·dra·tion** /-dráyshən/ *n.* **de·hy′dra·tor** *n.*

de·ice /deéís/ *v.tr.* **1** remove ice from. **2** prevent the formation of ice on. □□ **de·ic′er** *n.*

de·i·fy /deéifī, dáyee-/ *v.tr.* (**-fies, -fied**) **1** make a god of. **2** regard or worship as a god. □□ **de·i·fi·ca′tion** /-fikáyshən/ *n.*

deign /dayn/ *v.intr.* think fit; condescend.

de·ism /deéizəm, dáy-/ *n.* reasoned belief in the existence of a god (cf. THEISM). □□ **de′ist** *n.* **de·is′tic** *adj.* **de·is′ti·cal** *adj.*

de·i·ty /deéitee, dáy-/ *n.* (*pl.* **-ties**) **1** god or goddess. **2** divine status, quality, or nature. **3** (**the Deity**) God.

dé·jà vu /dáyzhaa vóō/ *n.* feeling of having already experienced a situation.

de·ject /dijékt/ v.tr. (usu. as **dejected** adj.) make sad or dispirited; depress. □□ **de·ject′ed·ly** adv. **de·jec′tion** n.

de ju·re /dee jŏoree, day jŏoray/ ● adj. rightful. ● adv. rightfully; by right.

Del. abbr. Delaware.

Del·a·ware /déləwair/ n. **1** N. American people native to the northeastern US. **2** language of this people. Also called **Lenape** or **Lenni Lenape.**

de·lay /diláy/ ● v. **1** tr. postpone; defer. **2** tr. make late. **3** intr. be late. ● n. **1** delaying. **2** time lost by inaction. **3** hindrance. □ **delayed-action** (attrib.) (of a bomb, etc.) operating some time after being primed or set. □□ **de·lay′er** n.

de·lec·ta·ble /diléktəbəl/ adj. esp. literary delightful; pleasant. □□ **de·lec·ta·bil·i·ty** /-bílitee/ n. **de·lec′ta·bly** adv.

de·lec·ta·tion /déelektáyshən/ n. literary pleasure; enjoyment.

del·e·gate ● n. /déligət/ **1** elected representative sent to a conference. **2** member of a committee or deputation. ● v.tr. /déligayt/ **1 a** commit (authority, etc.) to an agent or deputy. **b** entrust (a task) to another. **2** send or authorize (a person) as a representative.

del·e·ga·tion /déligáyshən/ n. **1** body of delegates; deputation. **2** delegating or being delegated.

de·lete /dileet/ v.tr. remove (written or printed matter), esp. by striking out. □□ **de·le·tion** /-leeshən/ n.

del·e·te·ri·ous /délitéereeəs/ adj. harmful (to mind or body).

delft /delft/ n. (also **delft′ware** /délftwair/) glazed, usu. blue and white, earthenware, made in Delft in Holland.

del·i /délee/ n. (pl. **del·is**) colloq. a delicatessen.

de·lib·er·ate ● adj. /dilíbərət/ **1 a** intentional. **b** fully considered. **2** slow in deciding; cautious. **3** (of movement, etc.) leisurely and unhurried. ● v. /dilíbərayt/ **1** intr. think carefully. **2** tr. consider; discuss carefully. □□ **de·lib·er·ate·ly** /dilíbərətlee/ adv. **de·lib′er·ate·ness** n. **de·lib′er·a·tive** adj. **de·lib′er·a·tive·ly** adv. **de·lib′er·a·tive·ness** n. **de·lib′er·a·tor** n.

de·lib·er·a·tion /dilibəráyshən/ n. **1** careful consideration. **2** discussion. **3 a** caution and care. **b** (of action or behavior) purposefulness. **c** (of movement) slowness or ponderousness.

del·i·ca·cy /délikəsee/ n. (pl. **-cies**) **1** (esp. in craftsmanship or beauty) fineness or intricacy of structure or texture. **2** susceptibility to injury or disease. **3** quality of requiring discretion or sensitivity. **4** choice food.

del·i·cate /délikət/ adj. **1 a** fine in texture, quality, etc. **b** slender or slight. **c** subtle or subdued. **2 a** (of a person) susceptible to injury or illness. **b** (of a thing) easily spoiled or damaged. **3 a** requiring care; tricky. **b** (of an instrument) highly sensitive. □□ **del′i·cate·ly** adv.

del·i·ca·tes·sen /délikətésən/ n. **1** store selling cooked meats, cheeses, prepared foods, etc. **2** (often attrib.) such foods.

De·li·cious /dilíshəs/ n. red or yellow variety of apple.

de·li·cious /dilíshəs/ adj. highly enjoyable to the taste or smell. □□ **de·li′cious·ly** adv.

de·light /dilít/ ● v. **1** tr. please greatly. **2** intr. take

great pleasure. ● n. **1** great pleasure. **2** something giving pleasure. □□ **de·light′ed** adj. **de·light′ed·ly** adv.

de·light·ful /dilítfŏol/ adj. causing delight. □□ **de·light′ful·ly** adv.

de·lim·it /dilímit/ v.tr. fix the limits or boundary of. □□ **de·lim·i·ta·tion** /-táyshən/ n.

de·lin·e·ate /dilíneeayt/ v.tr. portray by drawing, etc., or in words. □□ **de·lin·e·a·tion** /-áyshən/ n.

de·lin·quent /dilíngkwənt/ ● n. offender. ● adj. **1** guilty of a minor crime or a misdeed. **2** failing in one's duty. **3** in arrears. □□ **de·lin·quen·cy** /dilíngkwənsee/ n. **de·lin′quent·ly** adv.

del·i·quesce /délikwés/ v.intr. become liquid, esp. by absorbing water from the air. □□ **del·i·ques′cence** n. **del·i·ques′cent** adj.

de·lir·i·ous /dilíreeəs/ adj. **1** affected with delirium. **2** wildly excited; ecstatic. □□ **de·lir′i·ous·ly** adv.

de·lir·i·um /dilíreeəm/ n. **1** disorder involving incoherence, hallucinations, etc., caused by intoxication, fever, etc. **2** great excitement; ecstasy. □ **delirium tremens** /treémənz, -menz/ psychosis of chronic alcoholism involving tremors and hallucinations.

de·liv·er /dilívər/ v.tr. **1 a** distribute (letters, goods, etc.) to the addressee or purchaser. **b** hand over. **2** save, rescue, or set free. **3 a** give birth to. **b** assist at the birth of. **4 a** utter or recite (an opinion, speech, etc.) **b** (of a judge) pronounce (a judgment). **5** abandon; resign; hand over (delivered his soul up to God). **6** launch or aim (a blow, ball, or attack).

de·liv·er·ance /dilívərəns/ n. rescuing or being rescued.

de·liv·er·y /dilívəree/ n. (pl. **-ies**) **1 a** delivering of letters, etc. **b** regular distribution of letters, etc. **c** something delivered. **2** childbirth. **3** deliverance. **4** act or style of throwing, esp. a ball. **5** manner or style of giving a speech, etc.

dell /del/ n. small usu. wooded hollow or valley.

del·phin·i·um /delfíneeəm/ n. garden plant with tall spikes of usu. blue flowers.

del·ta /déltə/ n. **1** triangular tract of earth, alluvium, etc., at the mouth of a river. **2** fourth letter of the Greek alphabet (Δ, δ).

del·toid /déltoyd/ ● adj. triangular; like a river delta. ● n. (in full **deltoid muscle**) thick triangular muscle covering the shoulder joint.

de·lude /dilŏod/ v.tr. deceive or mislead.

del·uge /délyŏoj, -yoo_zh_/ ● n. **1** great flood. **2** (**the Deluge**) biblical Flood (Gen. 6–8). **3** great outpouring (of words, paper, etc.). **4** heavy fall of rain. ● v.tr. **1** flood. **2** inundate with a great number or amount.

de·lu·sion /dilŏo_zh_ən/ n. **1** false belief or impression. **2** Psychol. this as a symptom or form of mental disorder. □ **delusions of grandeur** false idea of oneself as being important, noble, famous, etc. □□ **de·lu′sion·al** adj.

de·luxe /dəlúks, lŏoks/ adj. **1** luxurious or sumptuous. **2** of a superior kind.

delve /delv/ v. intr. search or research energetically or deeply.

Dem. abbr. Democrat.

de·mag·ne·tize /deemágnitīz/ v.tr. remove the

magnetic properties of. □□ **de·mag·ne·ti·zation** /-tizáyshən/ n. **de·mag′ne·tiz·er** n.

dem·a·gogue /démagog, -gawg/ n. (also **-gog**) political agitator appealing to mob instincts. □□ **dem·a·gog·ic** /-gójik, -gógik, -gó-/ adj. **dem·a·gogu·er·y** /-gógəree, -gáwg-/ n. **dem·a·go·gy** /-gójee, -gáw-/ n.

de·mand /dimánd/ • n. **1** insistent and peremptory request. **2** Econ. desire for a commodity. **3** urgent claim. • v.tr. **1** ask for (something) insistently and urgently. **2** require or need. **3** insist on. **4** (as **demanding** adj.) requiring skill, effort, etc. □ **in demand** sought after. **on demand** as soon as a demand is made (a check payable on demand). □□ **de·mand′ing·ly** adv.

de·mar·ca·tion /deémaarkáyshən/ n. marking a boundary or limits. □□ **de·mar·cate** /dimaárkayt, deémaar-/ v.tr. **de·mar′ca·tor** n.

de·mean[1] /dimeén/ v.tr. (usu. refl.) lower the dignity of.

de·mean[2] /dimeén/ v.refl. behave (demeaned himself well).

de·mean·or /dimeénər/ n. behavior or bearing.

de·ment·ed /diméntid/ adj. mad; crazy. □□ **de·ment′ed·ly** adv. **de·ment′ed·ness** n.

de·men·tia /diménshə/ n. Med. chronic or persistent insanity marked by memory disorders, impaired reasoning, etc., due to brain disease or injury.

de·mer·it /dimérit/ n. **1** fault. **2** mark given to an offender.

de·mesne /dimáyn, -meén/ n. territory; domain. □ **held in demesne** (of an estate) occupied by the owner.

demi- /démee/ prefix **1** half. **2** partially or imperfectly such.

dem·i·god /démeegod/ n. (fem. **-god·dess** /-godis/) **1** partly divine being. **2** colloq. person of compelling beauty, powers, or personality.

dem·i·john /démeejon/ n. bulbous, narrownecked bottle holding from 3 to 10 gallons and usu. in a wicker cover.

de·mil·i·ta·rize /deemílitəriz/ v.tr. remove military forces from (a frontier, zone, etc.). □□ **de·mil·i·ta·ri·za′tion** n.

dem·i·monde /démeemond, -máwND/ n. **1** class of women considered to be of doubtful social standing and morality. **2** any semi-respectable group.

de·mise /dimíz/ • n. **1** death; termination. **2** Law transfer (of property, title, etc.) by demising. • v.tr. Law **1** convey or grant (an estate) by will or lease. **2** transmit (a title, etc.) by death.

dem·i·tasse /démeetas, -taas/ n. small coffee cup, esp. for strong coffee.

dem·o /démō/ n. (pl. **-os**) colloq. = DEMONSTRATION 3.

de·mo·bi·lize /deemóbiliz/ v.tr. disband (troops, ships, etc.). □□ **de·mo·bi·li·za′tion** n.

de·moc·ra·cy /dimókrəsee/ n. (pl. **-cies**) **1** government by the whole population, usu. through elected representatives. **2** nation or organization so governed.

dem·o·crat /déməkrat/ n. **1** advocate of democracy. **2** (**Democrat**) member of the Democratic party.

dem·o·crat·ic /déməkrátik/ adj. **1** of, like, practicing, advocating, or constituting democracy. **2** favoring social equality. □ **Democratic party** US political party, considered to support social reform and greater federal powers. (cf. Republican party). □□ **dem·o·crat′i·cal·ly** adv.

de·moc·ra·tize /dimókrətīz/ v.tr. make (a nation, institution, etc.) democratic. □□ **de·moc·ra·ti·za′tion** n.

de·mod·u·late /deemójəlayt/ v.tr. Physics extract (a modulating signal). □□ **de·mod·u·la·tion** /-láyshən/ n. **de·mod′u·la·tor** n.

de·mog·ra·phy /dimógrəfee/ n. study of statistics of births, deaths, disease, etc. □□ **de·mog′ra·pher** n. **dem·o·graph·ic** /déməgráfik/ adj. **dem·o·graph′i·cal** adj. **dem·o·graph′i·cal·ly** adv.

de·mol·ish /dimólish/ v.tr. **1 a** pull down (a building). **b** destroy or break. **2** overthrow (an institution). **3** refute. □□ **de·mol′ish·er** n. **dem·o·li·tion** /démǝlishən/ n. **dem·o·li′tion·ist** n.

de·mon /deémǝn/ n. **1** evil spirit or devil. **2** malignant supernatural being; the Devil. **3** (often attrib.) forceful, fierce, or skillful performer. □ **a demon for work** colloq. person who works strenuously. □□ **de·mon·ic** /dimónik/ adj. **de·mon·ize** /deémǝnīz/ v.

de·mo·ni·ac /dimóneeak/ • adj. **1** fiercely energetic or frenzied. **2** of or like demons. • n. person possessed by an evil spirit. □□ **de·mo·ni·a·cal** /deémǝnīǝkəl/ adj. **de·mo·ni′a·cal·ly** adv.

de·mon·stra·ble /dimónstrəbəl/ adj. capable of being shown or proved. □□ **de·mon′stra·bly** adv.

dem·on·strate /démənstrayt/ v. **1** tr. show (feelings, etc.). **2** tr. describe and explain (a proposition, machine, etc.) by experiment, use, etc. **3** tr. logically prove or be proof of. **4** intr. take part in or organize a public demonstration. □□ **dem′on·stra·tor** n.

dem·on·stra·tion /démənstráyshən/ n. **1** showing of feeling, etc. **2** public meeting, march, etc., for political or moral purpose. **3** exhibition or explanation of specimens or experiments as a method of esp. scientific teaching. **4** proof by logic, argument, etc. □□ **dem·on·stra′tion·al** adj.

de·mon·stra·tive /dimónstrətiv/ • adj. **1** showing feelings readily; affectionate. **2** logically conclusive; giving proof (the work is demonstrative of their skill). **3** Gram. (of an adjective or pronoun) indicating the person or thing referred to (e.g., this, that, those). • n. Gram. demonstrative adjective or pronoun. □□ **de·mon′stra·tive·ly** adv. **de·mon′stra·tive·ness** n.

de·mor·al·ize /dimáwrəliz, -mór-/ v.tr. destroy (a person's) morale; make hopeless. □□ **de·mor·al·i·za′tion** n. **de·mor′al·iz·ing** adj. **de·mor′al·iz·ing·ly** adv.

de·mote /dimót/ v.tr. reduce to a lower rank or class. □□ **de·mo′tion** /-móshən/ n.

de·mur /dimór/ • v.intr. (**de·murred, de·mur·ring**) **1** raise objections. **2** Law put in a demurrer. • n. (also **de·mur·ral** /dimórəl/) (usu. in neg.) objection (agreed without demur).

de·mure /dimyóor/ adj. (**de·mur·er, de·mur·est**) **1** composed, quiet, and reserved; modest. **2** coy. **3** decorous. □□ **de·mure′ly** adv. **de·mure′ness** n.

de·mur·rer /dimórər, -múr-/ n. Law objection raised or exception taken.

de·mys·ti·fy /deemístifī/ v.tr. (**-fies, -fied**) **1** clarify (obscure beliefs or subjects, etc.). **2** reduce or remove the mystery from. □□ **de·mys·ti·fi·ca·tion** /-fikáyshən/ n.

de·my·thol·o·gize /deemithólǝjīz/ v.tr. remove mythical elements from (a legend, famous person's life, etc.).

den /den/ n. **1** wild animal's lair. **2** place of crime or vice. **3** homey, informal room.

de·na·ture /deenáychǝr/ v.tr. **1** change the properties of (a protein, etc.) by heat, acidity, etc. **2** make (alcohol) unfit for drinking. □□ **de·na'tur·ant** n. **de·na·tur·a'tion** /deenaychǝráyshǝn/ n.

den·drite /déndrīt/ n. **1 a** stone or mineral with natural treelike or mosslike markings. **b** such marks. **2** Zool. & Anat. branching process of a nerve cell conducting signals to a cell body. □□ **den·drit·ic** /dendrítik/ adj.

den·drol·o·gy /dendrólǝjee/ n. the scientific study of trees. □□ **den·dro·log·i·cal** /-drǝlójikǝl/ adj. **den·drol'o·gist** n.

den·gue /dénggay, -gee/ n. infectious tropical viral disease.

de·ni·al /dinīǝl/ n. **1** denying the truth or existence of. **2** refusal of a request or wish. **3** disavowal of a person as one's leader, etc. **4** = SELF-DENIAL.

de·nier /dényǝr, dǝnyáy, dǝneéer/ n. unit of weight measuring the fineness of silk, nylon, etc.

den·i·grate /dénigrayt/ v.tr. defame or disparage the reputation of (a person); blacken. □□ **den·i·gra·tion** /-gráyshǝn/ n.

den·im /dénim/ n. **1** (often attrib.) usu. blue, hard-wearing, cotton twill used for jeans, overalls, etc. **2** (in pl.) colloq. clothing made of this.

den·i·zen /dénizǝn/ n. **1** inhabitant or occupant. **2** foreigner admitted to certain rights in an adopted country.

de·nom·i·nate /dinóminayt/ v.tr. **1** give a name to. **2** call or describe (a person or thing) as.

de·nom·i·na·tion /dinóminấyshǝn/ n. **1** church or religious sect. **2** class of units of numbers, weights, money, etc. (money of small denominations). **3 a** name or designation, esp. characteristic or class name. **b** class or kind having a specific name. □□ **de·nom·i·na'tion·al** adj.

de·nom·i·na·tor /dinóminaytǝr/ n. Math. number below the line in a fraction; divisor. □ **common denominator 1** common multiple of the denominators of several fractions. **2** common feature of members of a group. **least** (or **lowest**) **common denominator** lowest common multiple as above.

de·note /dinốt/ v.tr. **1** be a sign of; indicate. **2** stand as a name for; signify. □□ **de·no·ta·tion** /deenotáyshǝn/ n. **de·no·ta·tive** /deénotáytiv, dinốtǝtiv/ adj.

¶ See note at CONNOTE.

de·noue·ment /daynoomóN/ n. (also **dé·noue·ment'**) final unraveling of a plot or complicated situation.

de·nounce /dinówns/ v.tr. **1** accuse; condemn. **2** inform against. □□ **de·nounce'ment** n. **de·nounc'er** n.

dense /dens/ adj. **1** closely compacted; thick. **2** crowded together. **3** colloq. stupid. □□ **dense'ly** adv. **dense'ness** n.

den·si·ty /dénsitee/ n. (pl. **-ties**) **1** degree of compactness of a substance. **2** Physics degree of consistency measured by the quantity of mass per unit volume. **3** crowded state. **4** stupidity.

dent /dent/ • n. **1** slight hollow made by a blow

or pressure. **2** noticeable effect (lunch made a dent in our funds). • v.tr. mark with a dent.

dent. abbr. **1** dental. **2** dentist. **3** dentistry.

den·tal /dént'l/ adj. **1** of the teeth or dentistry. **2** Phonet. (of a consonant) produced with the tongue's tip against the upper front teeth (as th) or the ridge of the teeth (as n, s, t). □ **dental floss** thread used to clean between the teeth. **dental hygienist** person trained to clean and examine teeth.

den·ti·frice /déntifris/ n. paste or powder for cleaning teeth.

den·tin /dént'n/ n. (also **den·tine** /-teen/) dense, bony tissue forming the bulk of a tooth.

den·tist /déntist/ n. person qualified to treat diseases and conditions that affect the mouth, jaws, teeth, and their supporting tissues, and to repair and extract teeth. □□ **den'tist·ry** n.

den·ti·tion /dentíshǝn/ n. **1** type, number, and arrangement of teeth. **2** teething.

den·ture /dénchǝr/ n. removable artificial tooth or teeth.

de·nude /dinōod, -nyōod/ v.tr. make naked or bare. □□ **den·u·da·tion** /deenōodáyshǝn, -nyōo-, dényōo-/ n.

de·nun·ci·a·tion /dinúnsee-áyshǝn, -shee-/ n. denouncing (a person, policy, etc.); public condemnation. □□ **de·nun·ci·ate** /-seeayt/ v. **de·nun'ci·a·tor** n.

de·ny /dinī/ v.tr. (**-nies**, **-nied**) **1** declare untrue or nonexistent. **2** repudiate or disclaim. **3** refuse (a person or thing, or something to a person). □ **deny oneself** be abstinent.

de·o·dor·ant /deeốdǝrǝnt/ n. substance applied to the body or sprayed into the air to remove or conceal unpleasant smells.

de·o·dor·ize /deeốdǝrīz/ v.tr. remove or destroy the smell of. □□ **de·o·dor·i·za'tion** n. **de·o'dor·iz·er** n.

de·ox·y·ri·bo·nu·cle·ic ac·id /deéoksee-ríbō-noőkleéik, -kláyik, -nyōo-/ n. see DNA.

de·part /dipaárt/ v. **1** intr. **a** go away; leave. **b** start; set out. **2** intr. diverge; deviate. **3 a** intr. die. **b** tr. formal or literary leave by death (departed this life).

de·part·ed /dipaártid/ • adj. bygone. • n. (prec. by the) euphem. dead person or people (mourn the departed).

de·part·ment /dipaártmǝnt/ n. **1** separate part of a complex whole, esp.: **a** branch of municipal or federal administration. **b** division of a university, school, etc., by subject. **c** section of a large store. **2** colloq. area of special expertise. □ **department store** retail store stocking many varieties of goods by departments. □□ **de·part·men·tal** /deepaartmént'l/ adj. **de·part·men'tal·ize** v. **de·part·men'tal·ly** adv.

de·par·ture /dipaárchǝr/ n. **1** departing. **2** deviation (from the truth, a standard, etc.). **3** (often attrib.) starting of a train, aircraft, etc. **4** new course of action or thought.

de·pend /dipénd/ v.intr. **1** be controlled or determined by. **2 a** be unable to do without. **b** rely on.

de·pend·a·ble /dipéndǝbǝl/ adj. reliable. □□ **de·pend·a·bil'i·ty** n. **de·pend'a·ble·ness** n. **de·pend'a·bly** adv.

de·pend·ence /dipéndǝns/ n. **1** state of being dependent, esp. financially. **2** reliance; trust; confidence.

de·pen·den·cy /dipéndənsee/ *n.* (*pl.* **-cies**) **1** country or province controlled by another. **2** addiction.

de·pen·dent /dipéndənt/ • *adj.* **1** depending, conditional, or subordinate. **2** unable to do without (esp. a drug). **3** *Gram.* (of a clause, phrase, or word) subordinate to a sentence or word. • *n.* person who relies on another, esp. for financial support.

de·pict /dipíkt/ *v.tr.* **1** represent in a drawing, painting, etc. **2** portray in words; describe. □□ **de·pict′er** *n.* **de·pic·tion** /-píkshən/ *n.* **de·pic′tive** *adj.* **de·pic′tor** *n.*

de·pil·a·to·ry /dipílətawree/ • *adj.* that removes unwanted hair. • *n.* (*pl.* **-ries**) depilatory substance.

de·plane /deepláyn/ *v.* disembark from an airplane.

de·plete /dipleét/ *v.tr.* (esp. in *passive*) **1** reduce in numbers or quantity. **2** exhaust. □□ **de·ple·tion** /-pleéshən/ *n.*

de·plor·a·ble /dipláwrəbəl/ *adj.* exceedingly bad. □□ **de·plor′a·bly** *adv.*

de·plore /dipláwr/ *v.tr.* **1** grieve over; regret. **2** find exceedingly bad. □□ **de·plor′ing·ly** *adv.*

de·ploy /diplóy/ *v.* **1** *Mil.* **a** *tr.* cause (troops) to spread out from a column into a line. **b** *intr.* (of troops) spread out in this way. **2** *tr.* use (arguments, forces, etc.) effectively. □□ **de·ploy′ment** *n.*

de·po·lit·i·cize /deépəlítisīz/ *v.tr.* make (a person, an organization, etc.) nonpolitical. □□ **de·po·lit·i·ci·za′tion** *n.*

de·pop·u·late /deepópyəlayt/ *v.* **1** *tr.* reduce the population of. **2** *intr.* decline in population. □□ **de·pop·u·la·tion** /-láyshən/ *n.*

de·port /dipáwrt/ *v.tr.* **1** remove or exile to another country. **2** *refl.* behave (in a specified manner). □□ **de·por·ta·tion** /-táyshən/ *n.*

de·por·tee /deépawrteé/ *n.* deported person.

de·port·ment /dipáwrtmənt/ *n.* bearing or manners.

de·pose /dipóz/ *v.* **1** *tr.* remove from office, esp. dethrone. **2** *intr. Law* bear witness, esp. on oath in court.

de·pos·it /dipózit/ • *n.* **1 a** money in a bank account. **b** anything stored for safekeeping. **2 a** payment made as a first installment on a time-payment purchase or as a pledge for a contract. **b** returnable sum paid on a short-term rental. **3** natural layer of accumulated matter. • *v.tr.* **1** put or lay down. **2** pay (a sum) into a bank account. **3** pay (a sum) as a first installment or as a pledge.

dep·o·si·tion /dépəzíshən/ *n.* **1** deposing, esp. a monarch; dethronement. **2** *Law* **a** process of giving sworn evidence. **b** evidence given under oath; testimony.

de·pos·i·to·ry /dipózitawree/ *n.* (*pl.* **-ries**) **1** storehouse for furniture, etc. **2** store (of wisdom, knowledge, etc.).

de·pot /deépō, dépō/ *n.* **1** storehouse, esp. for military supplies. **2** railroad or bus station.

de·prave /dipráyv/ *v.tr.* corrupt, esp. morally. □□ **dep·ra·va·tion** /déprəváyshən/ *n.* **de·praved′** *adj.* **de·prav·i·ty** /diprávitee/ *n.*

dep·re·cate /déprikayt/ *v.tr.* express disapproval of or a wish against; deplore. □□ **dep′re·cat·ing·ly** *adv.* **dep·re·ca·tion** /-káyshən/ *n.* **dep·re·ca·to·ry** /-kətawree/ *adj.*

¶ **Deprecate** means 'to express disapproval of, to deplore,' e.g., *The mainstream press began by deprecating the politician's attitude towards terrorism,* while **depreciate** (in addition to its financial senses) means 'to disparage or belittle,' e.g., *He is always depreciating his own skills out of a strong sense of humility.*

de·pre·ci·ate /dipreésheeayt/ *v.* **1** *tr. & intr.* lower or diminish in value. **2** *tr.* disparage; belittle.

de·pre·ci·a·tion /dipreésheeáyshən/ *n.* **1** amount of wear and tear (of a property, etc.) for which a reduction may be made in valuation. **2** *Econ.* decrease in the value of a currency. **3** belittlement.

dep·re·da·tion /dépridáyshən/ *n.* (usu. in *pl.*) despoiling, ravaging, or plundering.

de·press /diprés/ *v.tr.* **1** push or pull down; lower. **2** make dispirited or dejected. **3** *Econ.* reduce the activity of (esp. trade). □ **depressed area** area suffering from pronounced economic depression. □□ **de·press′ing** *adj.* **de·press′ing·ly** *adv.*

de·pres·sant /diprésənt/ • *adj.* **1** that depresses. **2** *Med.* sedative. • *n.* **1** *Med.* agent, esp. a drug, that sedates. **2** influence or activity that depresses.

de·pres·sion /dipréshən/ *n.* **1 a** *Psychol.* extreme melancholy, often with physical symptoms. **b** reduction in vitality, vigor, or spirits. **2 a** long period of financial and industrial decline. **b** (**the Depression**) the economic decline of the 1930s. **3** *Meteorol.* lowering of atmospheric pressure. **4** hollow on a surface. **5** pressing down.

de·pres·sive /diprésiv/ • *adj.* **1** tending to depress. **2** *Psychol.* involving or characterized by depression. • *n. Psychol.* person suffering or with a tendency to suffer from depression.

de·prive /diprív/ *v.tr.* **1** strip, dispossess; debar from enjoying. **2** (as **de·prived** *adj.*) **a** (of a child, etc.) suffering from the effects of a poor or loveless home. **b** (of an area) with inadequate housing, facilities, employment, etc. □□ **de·priv′a·ble** *adj.* **de·priv′al** *n.* **dep·ri·va·tion** /déprivάyshən/ *n.*

Dept. *abbr.* department.

depth /depth/ *n.* **1 a** deepness. **b** measurement from the top down, surface inward, or front to back. **2** difficulty; abstruseness. **3** intensity of emotion, color, etc. **4** (in *pl.*) **a** abyss. **b** low, depressed state. **c** lowest or inmost part (*depths of the country*). **5** middle (*in the depth of winter*). □ **depth charge** anti-submarine bomb capable of exploding under water. **in depth** comprehensively, thoroughly, or profoundly. **in-depth** *adj.* thorough. **out of one's depth 1** in water over one's head. **2** engaged in a task or on a subject too difficult for one.

dep·u·ta·tion /dépyootáyshən/ *n.* delegation.

de·pute *v.tr.* /dipyoōt/ (often foll. by *to*) **1** appoint as a deputy. **2** delegate (a task, authority, etc.).

dep·u·tize /dépyətīz/ *v.intr.* create as a deputy.

dep·u·ty /dépyətee/ *n.* (*pl.* **-ties**) person appointed to act for another.

de·rail /diráyl/ *v.tr.* (usu. in *passive*) cause (a train, etc.) to leave the rails. □□ **de·rail′ment** *n.*

de·rail·leur /dəráylər/ *n.* gear-shifting mechanism on a bicycle.

DERAILLEUR

de·range /diráynj/ *v.tr.* **1** throw into confusion; disorganize. **2** (esp. as **deranged** *adj.*) make insane (*deranged by tragic events*). □□ **de·range′ment** *n.*

der·by /dárbee/ *n.* (*pl.* **-bies**) **1** any of several annual horse races, esp. for three-year-olds. **2** sporting contest. **3** bowler hat. □ **Derby Day** day on which the Kentucky Derby is run.

de·reg·u·late /dee-régyəlayt/ *v.tr.* remove regulations or restrictions from. □□ **de·reg·u·la·tion** /-láyshən/ *n.*

DERBY, 3

der·e·lict /dérilikt/ ● *adj.* **1** abandoned; ownerless (esp. of a ship at sea or an empty decrepit property). **2** (esp. of property) ruined; dilapidated. **3** negligent (of duty, etc.). ● *n.* **1** social outcast; person without a home, job, or property. **2** abandoned property, esp. a ship.

der·e·lic·tion /dérilíkshən/ *n.* **1** neglect; failure to carry out obligations. **2** abandoning; being abandoned.

de·ride /diríd/ *v.tr.* mock. □□ **de·rid′ing·ly** *adv.*

de ri·gueur /də rigőr/ *predic.adj.* required by custom or etiquette (*evening dress is de rigueur*).

de·ri·sion /dirízhən/ *n.* ridicule; mockery (*bring into derision*).

de·ri·sive /dirísiv/ *adj.* scoffing; ironical; scornful (*derisive cheers*). □□ **de·ri′sive·ly** *adv.* **de·ri′sive·ness** *n.*

de·ri·so·ry /dirísəree, -zə-/ *adj.* **1** = DERISIVE. **2**

so small or unimportant as to be ridiculous (*derisory offer*).

der·i·va·tion /dériváyshən/ *n.* **1** deriving or being derived. **2** formation or tracing of a word from another or from a root. **3** extraction; descent. □□ **der·i·va′tion·al** *adj.*

de·riv·a·tive /dirívətiv/ ● *adj.* derived from another source; not original. ● *n.* derived word or thing. □□ **de·riv′a·tive·ly** *adv.*

de·rive /dirív/ *v.* **1** *tr.* get, obtain, or form. **2** *intr.* arise from, originate in, be descended or obtained from. **3** *tr.* gather or deduce. **4** *tr.* **a** trace the descent of (a person). **b** show the origin of (a thing). □□ **de·riv′a·ble** *adj.*

der·ma·ti·tis /dármatítis/ *n.* inflammation of the skin.

der·ma·tol·o·gy /dármatólajee/ *n.* the study of skin disorders. □□ **der·ma·to·log·i·cal** /-təlójikəl/ *adj.* **der·ma·tol′o·gist** *n.*

der·mis /dármis/ *n.* (also **der·ma** /dármə/) **1** (in general use) skin. **2** *Anat.* thick layer of living tissue below the epidermis. □□ **der′mal** *adj.*

der·o·gate /dérəgayt/ *v.intr.* (foll. by *from*) *formal* detract from (a merit, a right, etc.). □□ **de·rog·a·tive** /dirógətiv/ *adj.*

de·rog·a·to·ry /dirógətawree/ *adj.* involving disparagement; insulting. □□ **de·rog·a·to′ri·ly** *adv.*

der·rick /dérik/ *n.* **1** pivoting crane for moving or lifting heavy weights. **2** framework over an oil well, etc., holding the drilling machinery.

der·ri·ere /déreeáir/ *n. colloq. euphem.* (also **der·rière′**) buttocks.

der·rin·ger /dérinjər/ *n.* concealable large-bore pistol.

der·vish /dárvish/ *n.* member of an ascetic Muslim fraternity. □ **whirling dervish** dervish performing a wild dance as a religious observance.

de·sal·i·nate /deesálinayt/ *v.tr.* remove salt from (esp. sea water). □□ **de·sal·i·na·tion** /-náyshən/ *n.*

des·cant ● *n.* /déskant/ *Mus.* melody usu. sung or played above a basic melody. ● *v.intr.* /diskánt/ **1** (foll. by *on, upon*) talk lengthily, esp. in praise of. **2** *Mus.* sing or play a descant. □ **descant recorder** most common size of recorder, with a range of two octaves.

de·scend /disénd/ *v.* **1** *tr.* & *intr.* go or come down (a hill, etc.). **2** *intr.* (of a thing) sink; fall (*rain descended heavily*). **3** *intr.* slope downward. **4** *intr.* (usu. foll. by *on*) **a** attack. **b** make an unexpected and usu. unwelcome visit. **5** *intr.* (usu. foll. by *from, to*) (of property, rights, etc.) be passed by inheritance. **6** *intr.* **a** sink in rank, quality, etc. **b** (foll. by *to*) degrade oneself morally to (an unworthy act). □ **be descended from** have as an ancestor. □□ **de·scend′ent** *adj.*

de·scend·ant /diséndənt/ *n.* person or thing descended from another (*a descendant of John Adams*).

de·scent /disént/ *n.* **1** act or way of descending. **2** downward slope. **3** lineage; family origin. **4** decline; fall.

de·scribe /diskríb/ *v.tr.* **1 a** state the characteristics, appearance, etc., of. **b** (foll. by *as*) assert to be (*described him as a habitual liar*). **2** outline; delineate. □□ **de·scrib′a·ble** *adj.* **de·scrib′er** *n.*

de·scrip·tion /diskrípshən/ *n.* **1 a** describing or

being described. **b** representation (of a person, object, etc.), esp. in words. **2** sort, kind, or class (*no food of any description*). □ **answers** (or **fits**) **the description** has the qualities specified. □□ **de·scrip·tive** /-tiv/ *adj.*

de·scry /diskrī/ *v.tr.* (**-scries**, **-scried**) *literary* catch sight of; discern.

des·e·crate /désikrayt/ *v.tr.* violate (a sacred place or thing) with violence, profanity, etc. □□ **des·e·cra·tion** /-kráyshən/ *n.* **des′e·cra·tor** *n.*

de·seg·re·gate /deeségrigayt/ *v.tr.* abolish racial segregation in (schools, etc.). □□ **de·seg·re·ga·tion** /-gáyshən/ *n.*

de·sen·si·tize /deesénsitīz/ *v.tr.* reduce or destroy the sensitiveness of (an allergic person, etc.). □□ **de·sen·si·ti·za′tion** *n.*

de·sert[1] /dizárt/ *v.* **1** *tr.* give up; leave (*deserted the sinking ship*). **2** *tr.* forsake or abandon (a cause, person, etc.) (*deserted his children*). **3** *intr. Mil.* run away (esp. from military service). □□ **de·sert′er** *n.* (in sense 3 of *v.*). **de·ser·tion** /-zárshən/ *n.*

des·ert[2] /dézərt/ ● *n.* dry, barren, often sand-covered area of land; uninteresting or barren subject, period, etc. (*a cultural desert*). ● *adj.* **1** uninhabited; desolate. **2** uncultivated; barren.

de·sert[3] /dizárt/ *n.* **1** (in *pl.*) acts or qualities deserving reward or punishment. **2** such reward or punishment (*his just deserts*).

de·serve /dizárv/ *v.tr.* **1** be worthy of (reward, punishment, etc.) (*deserves to be imprisoned*). **2** (as **deserved** *adj.*) rightfully merited or earned (*a deserved win*). □□ **de·serv·ed·ly** /-vidlee/ *adv.* **de·serving** /dizárving/ *adj.*

des·ic·cate /désikayt/ *v.tr.* dry out (esp. food for preservation). □□ **des·ic·ca·tion** /-káyshən/ *n.* **des′ic·ca·tive** *adj.* **des′ic·ca·tor** *n.*

de·sid·er·a·tum /disídəráytəm, -ráatəm/ *n.* (*pl.* **de·sid·er·a·ta** /-tə/) something lacking but needed or desired.

de·sign /dizín/ ● *n.* **1** plan or sketch for making a building, machine, garment, etc. **2** lines or shapes forming a pattern or decoration. **3** plan, purpose, or intention. **4** arrangement or layout. ● *v.* **1** *tr.* produce a design for. **2** *tr.* intend, plan, or propose. **3** *absol.* be a designer. □ **by design** on purpose. **have designs on** plan to harm or appropriate.

des·ig·nate ● *v.tr.* /dézignayt/ **1** appoint (*designated him as postmaster general*). **2** specify. **3** describe as; style. ● *adj.* /dézignət/ appointed but not yet installed (*bishop designate*). □ **designated driver** member of a group who abstains from alcohol in order to drive the others safely. **designated hitter** *Baseball* batter in the lineup who hits for the pitcher. ¶ Abbr.: **DH.** □□ **des·ig·na·tion** /dézignáyshən/ *n.* **des′ig·na·tor** *n.*

de·sign·ing /dizíning/ *adj.* crafty or scheming. □□ **de·sign′ing·ly** *adv.*

de·sir·a·ble /dizírəbəl/ *adj.* **1** worth having or doing. **2** sexually attractive. □□ **de·sir·a·bil′i·ty** *n.* **de·sir′a·ble·ness** *n.* **de·sir′a·bly** *adv.*

de·sire /dizír/ ● *n.* **1 a** longing or craving. **b** expression of this. **2** lust. **3** something desired. ● *v.tr.* **1** long for; crave. **2** request.

de·sir·ous /dizírəs/ *predic.adj.* **1** ambitious; desiring. **2** wishful; hoping.

de·sist /dizíst/ *v.intr.* (often foll. by *from*) *literary* abstain; cease (*desist from interrupting*).

desk /desk/ *n.* **1** piece of furniture with a writing surface and often drawers. **2** counter in a hotel, bank, etc., which separates the customer from the assistant.

desk·top /désktop/ *n.* **1 a** working surface of a desk. **b** *Computing* working area on a screen for manipulating windows, icons, etc. **2** (*attrib.*) (esp. of a microcomputer) suitable for use on an ordinary desk. □ **desktop publishing** production of printed matter with a desktop computer and printer.

des·o·late ● *adj.* /désələt/ **1** left alone; solitary. **2** (of a building or place) uninhabited; ruined; dreary. **3** forlorn; wretched. ● *v.tr.* /désəlayt/ **1** devastate; lay waste to. **2** (esp. as **desolated** *adj.*) make wretched. □□ **des′o·late·ly** /-lətlee/ *adv.* **des′o·late·ness** *n.*

des·o·la·tion /désəláyshən/ *n.* **1** desolating or being desolated. **2** loneliness, grief, etc. **3** neglected, ruined, barren, or empty state.

de·spair /dispáir/ ● *n.* complete loss or absence of hope. ● *v.intr.* **1** (often foll. by *of*) lose or be without hope. **2** (foll. by *of*) lose hope about. □□ **de·spair′ing·ly** *adv.*

des·patch var. of DISPATCH.

des·per·a·do /déspəraádō/ *n.* (*pl.* **-does** or **-dos**) desperate or reckless person, esp. a criminal.

des·per·ate /déspərət, -prit/ *adj.* **1** reckless or dangerous from despair. **2 a** extremely dangerous or serious. **b** staking all on a small chance. **3** (usu. foll. by *for*) needing or desiring very much. □□ **des′per·ate·ly** *adv.* **des′per·ate·ness** *n.* **des·per·a·tion** /-ráyshən/ *n.*

des·pi·ca·ble /déspikəbəl, dispík-/ *adj.* vile; contemptible, esp. morally. □□ **des′pi·ca·bly** *adv.*

de·spise /dispíz/ *v.tr.* look down on as inferior, worthless, or contemptible.

de·spite /dispít/ *prep.* in spite of.

de·spoil /dispóyl/ *v.tr. literary* plunder; rob; deprive (*despoiled the roof of its lead*). □□ **de·spoil′er** *n.* **de·spo·li·a·tion** /dispóleeáyshən/ *n.*

des·pond·ent /dispóndənt/ *adj.* in low spirits; dejected. □□ **de·spond·ence** /-dəns/ *n.* **de·spond′en·cy** *n.* **de·spond′ent·ly** *adv.*

des·pot /déspət/ *n.* **1** absolute ruler. **2** tyrant. □□ **des·pot·ic** /-spótik/ *adj.* **des·pot′i·cal·ly** *adv.* **des·pot·ism** /-izəm/ *n.*

des·sert /dizárt/ *n.* sweet course of a meal, served at or near the end.

des·ti·na·tion /déstináyshən/ *n.* place to which a person or thing is going.

des·tine /déstin/ *v.tr.* preordain; intend (*destined him for the navy*). □ **be destined to** be fated or preordained to.

des·ti·ny /déstinee/ *n.* (*pl.* **-nies**) **1** predetermined course of events; fate. **2** particular person's fate or lot.

des·ti·tute /déstitoot, -tyoot/ *adj.* **1** completely impoverished. **2** lacking. □□ **des·ti·tu·tion** /-tooshən, -tyoo-/ *n.*

de·stroy /distróy/ *v.tr.* **1** pull or break down; demolish. **2** end the existence of; kill (esp. an animal). **3** make useless; spoil utterly. **4** defeat (*destroyed the enemy*).

de·stroy·er /distróyər/ *n.* **1** person or thing that destroys. **2** *Naut.* fast warship used to protect other ships.

de·struct /distrúkt/ *Astronaut.* ● *v.* **1** *tr.* destroy (one's own rocket, etc.) deliberately, esp. for safety reasons. **2** *intr.* be destroyed in this way. • *n.* act of destructing.

de•struc•tion /distrúkshən/ *n.* **1** destroying or being destroyed. **2** cause of ruin. □□ **de•struct•i•bil•i•ty** /-tibílitee/ *n.* **de•struct′i•ble** *adj.* **de•struc′tive** *adj.* **de•struc′tive•ly** *adv.* **de•struc′tive•ness** *n.*

des•ue•tude /déswitōōd, -tyōōd/ *n.* state of disuse.

des•ul•to•ry /désəltáwree, déz-/ *adj.* **1** going from one subject to another, esp. halfheartedly. **2** disconnected; superficial. □□ **des′ul•to•ri•ly** *adv.* **des′ul•to•ri•ness** *n.*

de•tach /ditách/ *v.tr.* **1** unfasten or disengage and remove. **2** (as **detached** *adj.*) impartial; unemotional (*a detached viewpoint*). □□ **de•tach′a•ble** *adj.* **de•tach•ed•ly** /ditáchidlee/ *adv.*

de•tach•ment /ditáchmənt/ *n.* **1 a** aloofness; indifference. **b** impartiality. **2** detaching or being detached. **3** *Mil.* troops, etc., used for a specific purpose.

de•tail /ditáyl, deétayl/ • *n.* **1** small particular; item; minor element. **2 a** these collectively (*has an eye for detail*). **b** treatment of them (*the detail was insufficient*). **3** *Mil.* small detachment. • *v.tr.* **1** give particulars or circumstances of. **2** *Mil.* assign for special duty. **3** (as **detailed** *adj.*) itemized. □ **in detail** item by item, minutely.

de•tain /ditáyn/ *v.tr.* **1** keep (a person) in custody. **2** keep waiting; delay. □□ **de•tain′ee** *n.* **de•tain′ment** *n.*

de•tect /ditékt/ *v.tr.* discover or perceive. □□ **de•tect′a•ble** *adj.* **de•tect′a•bly** *adv.* **de•tec•tion** /ditékshən/ *n.*

de•tec•tive /ditéktiv/ • *n.* (often *attrib.*) person who investigates crime. • *adj.* serving to detect. □ **private detective** detective carrying out investigations for a private employer.

dé•tente /daytóNt/ *n.* easing of tension, esp. between nations.

de•ten•tion /diténshən/ *n.* detaining or being detained.

de•ter /ditór/ *v.tr.* (**de•terred, de•ter•ring**) discourage or prevent (a person), esp. through fear. □□ **de•ter′ment** *n.*

de•ter•gent /ditórjənt/ • *n.* cleaning agent. • *adj.* cleansing.

de•te•ri•o•rate /ditéereeərayt/ *v.* make or become bad or worse. □□ **de•te•ri•o•ra•tion** /-ráyshən/ *n.*

de•ter•mi•nant /ditórminənt/ • *adj.* serving to determine or define. • *n.* determining factor, element, word, etc.

de•ter•mi•nate /ditórminət/ *adj.* **1** limited. **2** of definite scope or nature.

de•ter•mi•na•tion /ditórmináyshən/ *n.* **1** firmness of purpose. **2** process of deciding, determining, or calculating.

de•ter•mine /ditórmin/ *v.tr.* **1** find out or establish precisely. **2** decide or settle. **3** be a decisive factor in regard to (*demand determines supply*). □ **be determined** be resolved (*was determined not to give up*). □□ **de•ter′min•a•ble** *adj.*

de•ter•mined /ditórmind/ *adj.* **1** showing determination; resolute; unflinching. **2** fixed in scope or character; determinate. □□ **de•ter′mined•ly** *adv.* **de•ter′mined•ness** *n.*

de•ter•rent /ditórənt, -túr-/ • *adj.* that deters. • *n.* dissuading thing or factor. □□ **de•ter•rence** /-rəns/ *n.*

de•test /ditést/ *v.tr.* hate; loathe. □□ **de•test′a•ble** *adj.* **de•test′er** *n.*

de•throne /deethrón/ *v.tr.* remove from the throne; depose. □□ **de•throne′ment** *n.*

det•o•nate /dét′nayt/ *v.* explode with a loud noise. □□ **det•o•na•tion** /dét′náyshən/ *n.* **det′o•na•tive** *adj.* **det•o•na•tor** /dét′naytər/ *n.*

de•tour /deétōōr, ditōór/ • *n.* divergence from a direct or intended route. • *v.* make or cause to make a detour.

de•tox•i•fy /deetóksifí/ *v.tr.* remove the poison from. □□ **de•tox•i•fi•ca•tion** /-fikáyshən/ *n.*

de•tract /ditrákt/ *v.tr.* take away (a part of something); reduce (*self-interest detracted nothing from their victory*). □□ **de•trac•tion** /-trákshən/ *n.* **de•trac′tive** *adj.* **de•trac′tor** *n.*

det•ri•ment /détrimənt/ *n.* **1** harm; damage. **2** something causing this. □□ **det•ri•men•tal** /détrimént′l/ *adj.*

de•tri•tus /ditrítəs/ *n.* **1** gravel, sand, etc., from erosion. **2** debris. □□ **de•tri•tal** /ditrít′l/ *adj.*

deuce /dōōs, dyōōs/ *n.* **1** two on dice or playing cards. **2** *Tennis* score of 40 all, at which two consecutive points are needed to win.

deu•te•ri•um /dōōtéereeəm, dyōō-/ *n.* *Chem.* stable isotope of hydrogen.

deutsche mark /dóychmaark/ *n.* (also **Deutsche•mark** /dóychə maark/) chief monetary unit of Germany.

de•val•ue /deevályōō/ *v.tr.* (**de•val•ues, de•val•ued, de•val•u•ing**) reduce the value of. □□ **de•val•u•a′tion** *n.*

dev•as•tate /dévəstayt/ *v.tr.* **1** cause great destruction to. **2** (often in *passive*) overwhelm with shock or grief. □□ **dev′as•tat•ing** *adj.* **dev′as•tat•ing•ly** *adv.* **dev•as•ta•tion** /-táyshən/ *n.* **dev′as•ta•tor** *n.*

de•vel•op /divéləp/ *v.* **1** *tr.* & *intr.* **a** make or become bigger or fuller, etc. **b** bring or come to an active, visible, or mature state. **2 a** *tr.* begin to exhibit or suffer from. **b** *intr.* come into existence; originate; emerge. **3** *tr.* **a** build on (land). **b** convert (land) to a new use. **4** *tr.* treat (film, etc.) to make the image visible. □ **developing country** poor or undeveloped country that is becoming more advanced economically and socially. □□ **de•vel′op•er** *n.*

de•vel•op•ment /divélǝpmənt/ *n.* **1** developing or being developed. **2** thing that has developed, esp. an event or circumstance (*the latest developments*). **3** full-grown state. **4** developed area of land. □□ **de•vel•op•men•tal** /divelǝpmént′l/ *adj.* **de•vel•op•men′tal•ly** *adv.*

de•vi•ant /deéveeənt/ • *adj.* that deviates from normal, esp. sexually. • *n.* deviant person or thing. □□ **de•vi•ance** /-veeəns/ *n.* **de′vi•an•cy** *n.*

de•vi•ate • *v.intr.* /deéveeayt/ turn aside or diverge (from a course of action, rule, truth, etc.); digress. • *n.* /deéveeət/ deviant, esp. a sexual pervert. □□ **de•vi•a•tion** /-áyshən/ *n.* **de′vi•a•tor** *n.* **de•vi•a•to•ry** /-veeǝtawree/ *adj.*

de•vice /divís/ *n.* **1** thing made or adapted for a particular purpose. **2** plan, scheme, or trick. **3** emblematic or heraldic design. □ **leave a person to his** or **her own devices** leave a person to do as he or she wishes.

device Middle English: from Old French *devis*, based on Latin *divis*-'divided,' from the verb *dividere*. The original sense was 'desire or intention,' found now only in *leave a person to his or her own devices* (which has become associated with sense 2).

dev·il /dévəl/ • *n.* **1** (usu. **the Devil**) (in Christian and Jewish belief) supreme spirit of evil; Satan. **2 a** evil spirit; demon. **b** personified evil. **3 a** wicked or cruel person. **b** mischievous person. **4** *colloq.* person of a specified nature (*lucky devil*). **5** mischievousness (*the devil is in him tonight*). • *v.tr.* (**dev·iled, dev·il·ing; dev·illed, dev·il·ling**) **1** prepare (food) with hot seasoning. **2** harass; worry. □ **between the devil and the deep blue sea** in a dilemma. **a devil of** *colloq.* considerable, difficult, or remarkable (*a devil of a time*). **devil's advocate** person who tests a proposition by arguing against it. **devil's own** *colloq.* very difficult or unusual (*the devil's own job*). **devil take the hindmost** motto of selfish competition. **the devil to pay** trouble to be expected. **go to the devil 1** be damned. **2** (in *imper.*) depart at once. **like the devil** with great energy. **play the devil with** cause severe damage to. **speak of the devil** said when a person appears just after being mentioned. □□ **dev·il·ish** *adj. & adv.*

devil Old English *dēofol* (related to Dutch *duivel* and German *Teufel*), via late Latin from Greek *diabolos* 'accuser, slanderer' (used in Greek to translate Hebrew *śāṭān* 'Satan'), from *diaballein* 'to slander,' from *dia* 'across' + *ballein* 'to throw.'

dev·il·ment /dévəlmənt/ *n.* mischief; wild spirits.

dev·il·ry /dévilree/ *n.* (also **dev·il·try** /-tree/) (*pl.* **-ries**) wickedness; reckless mischief.

de·vi·ous /déeveeəs/ *adj.* **1** (of a person, etc.) not straightforward; underhand. **2** winding; circuitous. □□ **de´vi·ous·ly** *adv.* **de´vi·ous·ness** *n.*

de·vise /divíz/ • *v.tr.* **1** plan or invent carefully. **2** *Law* leave (real estate) by will (cf. BEQUEATH). • *n.* **1** devising. **2** *Law* such a clause in a will. □□ **de·vis´a·ble** *adj.* **de·vi·see** /-zée/ *n.* (in sense 2 of *v.*). **de·vis´er** *n.* **de·vi´sor** *n.* (in sense 2 of *v.*).

de·void /divóyd/ *predic.adj.* (foll. by *of*) lacking or free from (*a book devoid of all interest*).

de·volve /divólv/ *v.* (foll. by *on, upon,* etc.) **1** *tr.* pass (work or duties) to (a deputy, etc.). **2** *intr.* (of work or duties) pass to (a deputy, etc.). □□ **de·volve´ment** *n.*

De·vo·ni·an /divóneeən/ • *adj. Geol.* of or relating to the fourth period of the Paleozoic era. • *n.* this period or system.

de·vote /divót/ *v.tr. & refl.* (foll. by *to*) apply or give over (resources, etc., or oneself) to (a particular activity, purpose, or person) (*devoted himself to his guests*).

de·vot·ed /divótid/ *adj.* very loving or loyal (*a devoted husband*). □□ **de·vot´ed·ly** *adv.* **de·vot´ed·ness** *n.*

dev·o·tee /dévətée, -táy/ *n.* **1** (usu. foll. by *of*) zealous enthusiast or supporter. **2** zealously pious or fanatical person.

de·vo·tion /divóshən/ *n.* **1** enthusiastic loyalty

(to a person or cause); great love. **2** (in *pl.*) prayers. □□ **de·vo´tion·al** *adj.*

de·vour /divówr/ *v.tr.* **1** eat hungrily or greedily. **2** (of fire, etc.) engulf; destroy. □□ **de·vour´ing·ly** *adv.*

de·vout /divówt/ *adj.* **1** earnestly religious. **2** earnestly sincere (*devout hope*). □□ **de·vout´ly** *adv.* **de·vout´ness** *n.*

dew /doo, dyoo/ • *n.* **1** atmospheric vapor condensing on cool surfaces at night. **2** moisture resembling this, e.g., tears. • *v.tr.* wet with or as with dew. □ **dew point** the temperature at which dew forms. □□ **dew·y** /dóo-ee, dyóo-ee/ *adj.* (**dew·i·er, dew·i·est**).

dew·ber·ry /dóoberee, dyóo-/ *n.* (*pl.* **-ries**) bluish fruit like the blackberry.

dew·claw /dóoklaw, dyóo-/ *n.* **1** rudimentary inner toe found on some dogs. **2** false hoof on a deer, etc.

dew·drop /dóodrop, dyóo-/ *n.* drop of dew.

dew·lap /dóolap, dyóo-/ *n.* loose fold of skin hanging from the throat of cattle, dogs, etc.

dex·ter·i·ty /dekstéritee/ *n.* **1** skill in handling. **2** manual or mental adroitness.

dex·ter·ous /dékstrəs, -stərəs/ *adj.* (also **dex·trous**, /-strəs/) having or showing dexterity. □□ **dex´ter·ous·ly** *adv.*

dex·trose /dékstrōs/ *n. Chem.* form of glucose.

DH *abbr. Baseball* designated hitter.

dho·ti /dótee/ *n.* (*pl.* **dho·tis**) loincloth worn by male Hindus.

di-¹ /dī/ *comb. form* twice, two-, double.

di-² /dī, dee/ *prefix* form of DIS- before *l, m, n, r, s* (foll. by a consonant), *v,* usu. *g,* and sometimes *j*.

di-³ /dī/ *prefix* form of DIA- before a vowel.

dia. *abbr.* diameter.

dia- /dīə/ *prefix* (also **di-** before a vowel) **1** through (*diaphanous*). **2** apart (*diacritical*). **3** across (*diameter*).

di·a·be·tes /dīəbéetis, -teez/ *n.* any disorder of the metabolism with excessive thirst, increased urine production, and high blood sugar. □ **diabetes insipidus** rare metabolic disorder due to a pituitary deficiency. **diabetes mellitus** the most common form of diabetes. □□ **di·a·bet·ic** /dīəbétik/ *adj. & n.*

di·a·bol·ic /dīəbólik/ *adj.* (also **di·a·bol·i·cal** /-bólikəl/) **1** of the Devil. **2** devilish; inhumanly cruel or wicked. **3** fiendishly clever or cunning or annoying. □□ **di·a·bol´i·cal·ly** *adv.*

di·a·crit·ic /dīəkritik/ *n.* sign (e.g., an accent, cedilla, etc.) indicating different sounds or values of a letter. □□ **di·a·crit·i·cal** /dīəkritikəl/ *adj.*

di·a·dem /dīədem/ *n.* crown or ornamental headband.

di·aer·e·sis /dī-érəsis/ *n.* (also **di·er´e·sis**) (*pl.* **-ses** /-seez/) mark (as in *naïve*) over a vowel to indicate that it is sounded separately.

diag. *abbr.* **1** diagonal. **2** diagram.

di·ag·nose /dīəgnōs, -nōz/ *v.tr.* make a diagnosis of (a disease, fault, etc.) from its symptoms. □□ **di·ag·nos´a·ble** *adj.*

di·ag·no·sis /dīəgnósis/ *n.* (*pl.* **di·ag·no·ses** /-seez/) **1** identification of a disease, mechanical fault, etc. **2** instance or formal statement of this. □□ **di·ag·nos·tic** /dīəgnóstik/ *adj.* **di·ag·nos´ti·cal·ly** *adv.* **di·ag·nos·ti·cian** /-nostíshən/ *n.*

di·ag·nos·tics /dīəgnóstiks/ *n.* **1** (treated as *pl.*) *Computing* programs used to identify faults in hardware or software. **2** (treated as *sing.*) science or study of diagnosing disease.

di·ag·o·nal /dīágənəl/ • *adj.* **1** crossing a straight-sided figure from corner to corner. **2** slanting; oblique. • *n.* straight line joining two nonadjacent corners. □□ **di·ag′o·nal·ly** *adv.*

di·a·gram /dīəgram/ • *n.* drawing showing the general scheme or outline of an object and its parts. • *v.tr.* (**di·a·gramed, di·a·gram·ing; di·a·grammed, di·a·gram·ming**) represent by means of a diagram. □□ **di·a·gram·mat·ic** /-grəmátik/ *adj.* **di·a·gram·mat′i·cal·ly** *adv.*

di·al /dīəl/ • *n.* **1** face of a clock or watch, marked to show the hours, etc. **2** flat plate with a scale for measuring weight, volume, etc., indicated by a pointer. **3** movable disk on a telephone, with finger holes and numbers for making a call. **4** adjustment control on a radio, appliance, etc. • *v. tr.* (also *absol.*) select (a telephone number) by means of a dial or set of buttons (*dialed 911*). □ **dial tone** sound indicating that a telephone is ready for dialing. □□ **di′al·er** *n.*

di·a·lect /dīəlekt/ *n.* **1** regional form of speech. **2** variety of language with nonstandard vocabulary, pronunciation, or grammar. □□ **di·a·lec·tal** /-lékt'l/ *adj.* **di·a·lec·tol·o·gy** /-tólə̄jee/ *n.* **di·a·lec·tol·o·gist** /-tólə̄jist/ *n.*

di·a·lec·tic /dīəléktik/ • *n.* (often in *pl.*) art of investigating the truth of opinions; testing of truth by discussion. • *adj.* of or relating to logical disputation.

di·a·logue /dīəlawg, -log/ *n.* (also **di′a·log**) **1** conversation. **2** conversation in written form.

di·al·y·sis /dīálisis/ *n.* (*pl.*) (**di·al·y·ses** /-seez/) separation of particles in a liquid by use of a membrane, esp. for purification of blood.

diam. *abbr.* diameter.

di·am·e·ter /dīámitər/ *n.* **1** straight line through the center of a circle or sphere. **2** length of this line. □□ **di·am′e·tral** *adj.*

di·a·met·ri·cal /dīəmétrikəl/ *adj.* (also **di·a·met′ric**) **1** of or along a diameter. **2** (of opposites, etc.) absolute. □□ **di·a·met′ri·cal·ly** *adv.*

di·a·mond /dīmənd, dīə-/ • *n.* **1** precious stone of pure carbon crystallized in octahedrons, etc., the hardest naturally occurring substance. **2** figure shaped like the cross section of a diamond; rhombus. **3 a** playing card of a suit denoted by a red rhombus. **b** (in *pl.*) this suit. **4** *Baseball* the playing field, esp. the infield. • *adj.* **1** made of or set with diamonds or a diamond. **2** rhombus-shaped. □ **diamond jubilee** the 60th (or 75th) anniversary of an event, esp. a sovereign's accession. **diamond wedding** (or **anniversary**) 60th (or 75th) wedding anniversary.

di·a·mond·back /dīməndbak, dīə-/ *n.* **1** edible freshwater terrapin, native to N. America, with diamond-shaped markings on its shell. **2** rattlesnake, native to N. America, with diamond-shaped markings.

di·a·per /dīpər, dīəpər/ *n.* absorbent material wrapped around a baby to retain urine and feces. □ **diaper rash** inflammation of a baby's skin, caused by prolonged contact with a damp diaper.

---

diaper Middle English: from Old French *diapre*, from medieval Latin *diasprum*, from medieval Greek *diaspros* (adjective), from

dia 'across' + *aspros* 'white.' The term seems originally to have denoted a costly fabric, but after the 15th century it was used of a fabric woven with a repeating diamond pattern. This sort of fabric came to be used as a wrap for babies.

---

di·aph·a·nous /dīáfənəs/ *adj.* (of fabric, etc.) light and delicate, and almost transparent. □□ **di·aph′a·nous·ly** *adv.*

di·a·phragm /dīəfram/ *n.* **1** muscular partition separating the thorax from the abdomen in mammals. **2** vibrating disk that produces sound in acoustic systems, etc. **3** device for varying the aperture of a camera lens. **4** contraceptive cap fitting over the cervix. □□ **di·a·phrag·mat·ic** /-fragmátik/ *adj.*

di·a·rist /dīərist/ *n.* person who keeps a diary. □□ **di·a·ris′tic** *adj.*

di·ar·rhe·a /dīəréeə/ *n.* condition of excessively frequent and loose bowel movements. □□ **di·ar·rhe′al** *adj.* **di·ar·rhe′ic** *adj.*

di·a·ry /dīəree/ *n.* (*pl.* **-ries**) **1** daily record of events or thoughts. **2** book for this.

Di·as·po·ra /dīáspərə/ *n.* **1** (prec. *by the*) dispersion of the Jews among the Gentiles mainly in the 8th–6th c. BC. **2** (also **diaspora**) any group of people similarly dispersed.

di·a·stase /dīəstays, -stayz/ *n. Biochem.* enzyme converting starch to sugar. □□ **di·a·sta·sic** /-stáysik, -zik/ *adj.* **di·a·stat·ic** /-státik/ *adj.*

di·as·to·le /dīástəlee/ *n. Physiol.* normal rhythmic expansion of the heart's chambers as they fill with blood (cf. SYSTOLE). □□ **di·as·tol·ic** /dīəstólik/ *adj.*

di·a·tom /dīətom/ *n.* unicellular alga found as plankton and forming fossil deposits. □□ **di·a·to·ma·ceous** /-máyshəs/ *adj.*

di·a·tom·ic /dīətómik/ *adj.* consisting of two atoms.

di·a·ton·ic /dīətónik/ *adj. Mus.* relating to a standard major or minor scale of eight notes.

di·a·tribe /dīətrīb/ *n.* forceful verbal attack or bitter criticism.

dib·ble /dībəl/ *n.* hand tool for making holes in the ground for seeds or young plants.

dibs /dibz/ *n.pl. sl.* rights; claim (*I have dibs on that apple*).

dice /dīs/ • *n.pl.* **1 a** small cubes with faces bearing 1–6 spots used in games of chance. **b** (treated as *sing.*) one of these cubes (see note at DIE²). **2** game played with dice. • *v.tr.* cut (food) into small cubes. □ **no dice** *sl.* no success or prospect of it.

dic·ey /dīsee/ *adj.* (**dic·i·er, dic·i·est**) *sl.* risky; unreliable.

di·chot·o·my /dīkótəmee/ *n.* (*pl.* **-mies**) division into two, esp. a sharply defined one. □□ **di·chot·om·ic** /-kətómik/ *adj.* **di·chot′o·mize** *v.* **di·chot′o·mous** *adj.*

dick /dik/ *n. sl.* detective.

dick·er /díkər/ *v.* **1** *intr.* bargain; haggle. **2** *tr.* barter; exchange. □□ **dick′er·er** *n.*

dick·ey /díkee/ *n.* (also **dick·y**) (*pl.* **-eys** or **-ies**) *colloq.* false shirtfront.

dict. *abbr.* **1** dictionary. **2** dictation.

dic·ta *pl.* of DICTUM.

dic·tate ● *v.* /díktayt, diktáyt/ **1** *tr.* say or read aloud (words to be written down or recorded). **2 a** *tr.* prescribe or lay down authoritatively (terms, etc.). **b** *intr.* lay down the law; give orders. ● *n.* /díktayt/ (usu. in *pl.*) authoritative instruction (*dictates of conscience*). □□ **dic·ta·tion** /diktáyshən/ *n.*

dic·ta·tor /díktaytər, diktáy-/ *n.* **1** ruler with unrestricted authority. **2** person with supreme authority in any sphere. □□ **dic·ta·tor·ship** /diktáytərship/ *n.*

dic·ta·to·ri·al /díktətáwreeəl/ *adj.* **1** of or like a dictator. **2** imperious; overbearing. □□ **dic·ta·to'ri·al·ly** *adv.*

dic·tion /díkshən/ *n.* **1** manner of enunciation in speaking or singing. **2** choice of words.

dic·tion·ar·y /díkshəneree/ *n.* (*pl.* **-ies**) **1** publication that lists (usu. alphabetically) and explains the words of a language or gives equivalents in another language. **2** reference publication on any subject, arranged alphabetically (*dictionary of architecture*). **3** *Computing* ordered list of words, codes, etc., used by a program.

dic·tum /díktəm/ *n.* (*pl.* **dic·ta** /-tə/ or **dic'tums**) **1** formal utterance or pronouncement. **2** saying or maxim.

did *past* of DO¹.

di·dac·tic /dīdáktik/ *adj.* **1** meant to instruct. **2** (of a person) tediously pedantic. □□ **di·dac'ti·cal·ly** *adv.* **di·dac·ti·cism** /-tisizəm/ *n.*

did·dle /díd'l/ *v. colloq.* **1** *tr.* cheat; swindle. **2** *intr.* waste time. □□ **did'dler** *n.*

did·dly /dídlee/ *n.* (also **did·dly squat**) *sl.* slightest amount (*he hasn't done diddly to help us out*).

did·n't /díd'nt/ *contr.* did not.

die¹ /dī/ *v.* (**dies, died, dy·ing** /dí-ing/) **1** *intr.* (of a person, animal, or plant) cease to live; expire. **2** *intr.* **a** come to an end; fade away. **b** cease to function. **c** (of a flame) go out. **3** *intr.* be exhausted or tormented (*nearly died of boredom*). **4** *tr.* suffer (a specified death). □ **be dying** wish for longingly or intently (*am dying to see you*). **die down** become less loud or strong. **die hard** die reluctantly (*old habits die hard*). **die off** die one after another. **die out** become extinct. **never say die** keep up courage, not give in.

die² /dī/ *n.* **1** *sing.* of DICE *n.* 1a.
¶ *Dice* is now standard in general use in this sense. **2** (*pl.* **dies**) engraved stamping device. □ **the die is cast** an irrevocable step has been taken.

die·hard /díhaard/ *n.* conservative or stubborn person.

di·er·e·sis var. of DIAERESIS.

die·sel /deézəl/ *n.* **1** (in full **die·sel engine**) internal combustion engine that burns fuel ignited by compression. **2** vehicle driven by a diesel engine. **3** fuel for a diesel engine. □ **diesel oil** heavy petroleum product used as fuel in diesel engines.

di·et¹ /díət/ ● *n.* **1** kinds of food that a person or animal habitually eats. **2** food to which a person is restricted, esp. for medical reasons or to control weight. ● *v.* **1** *intr.* restrict oneself to small amounts or special kinds of food, esp. to control weight. **2** *tr.* restrict (a person or animal) to a special diet. □□ **di·e·ta·ry** /díəteree/ *adj.* **di'et·er** *n.*

di·et² /díət/ *n.* legislative assembly in certain countries.

di·e·tet·ic /díətétik/ *adj.* of or relating to diet. □□ **di·e·tet'i·cal·ly** *adv.*

di·e·tet·ics /díətétiks/ *n.pl.* (usu. treated as *sing.*) the scientific study of diet and nutrition.

di·e·ti·tian /díətíshən/ *n.* (also **di·e·ti·cian**) expert in dietetics.

dif- /dif/ *prefix* assim. form of DIS- before *f*.

dif·fer /difər/ *v.intr.* **1** be unlike or distinguishable. **2** disagree; be at variance (with a person).

dif·fer·ence /difrəns/ *n.* **1** being different or unlike. **2** distinction. **3** quantity by which amounts differ; deficit (*will have to make up the difference*). **4 a** disagreement, quarrel, or dispute. **b** grounds of disagreement (*put aside their differences*).

dif·fer·ent /difrənt/ *adj.* **1** unlike. **2** distinct; separate. **3** *colloq.* unusual (*wanted to do something different*). **4** of various kinds; assorted; several; miscellaneous (*available in different colors*). □□ **dif'fer·ent·ly** *adv.*
¶ Many traditional critics regard **different than** as an improper substitute for **different from**: *My opinion is quite different from his*. But **different than** now appears widely in good writing, as well as in informal contexts.

dif·fer·en·tial /difərénshəl/ ● *adj.* **1** of, exhibiting, or depending on a difference. **2** varying according to circumstances. ● *n.* **1** difference between individuals or examples of the same kind. **2** (in full **differential gear**) gear allowing a vehicle's driven wheels to revolve at different speeds when in a turn. □ **differential calculus** *Math.* method of calculating rates of change, maximum or minimum values, etc. (cf. INTEGRAL). □□ **dif·fer·en'tial·ly** *adv.*

dif·fer·en·ti·ate /difərénsheeayt/ *v.* **1** *tr.* constitute a difference between or in. **2** *tr.* & *intr.* find differences (between); discriminate. **3** *tr.* & *intr.* make or become different while growing or developing (species, word forms, etc.). □□ **dif·fer·en·ti·a·tion** /-sheeáyshən/ *n.*

dif·fi·cult /difikult, -kəlt/ *adj.* **1 a** needing much effort or skill. **b** troublesome; perplexing. **2** (of a person): **a** not easy to please. **b** uncooperative; troublesome. **3** characterized by hardships or problems (*a difficult period in his life*).

dif·fi·cul·ty /difikultee, -kəl-/ *n.* (*pl.* **-ties**) **1** being difficult. **2 a** difficult thing; problem; hindrance. **b** (often in *pl.*) distress or hardship (*in financial difficulties*).

dif·fi·dent /difidənt/ *adj.* shy; lacking self-confidence. □□ **dif·fi·dence** /-dəns/ *n.* **dif'fi·dent·ly** *adv.*

dif·fuse ● *adj.* /difyo͞os/ **1** (of light, inflammation, etc.) spread out; not concentrated. **2** (of prose, speech, etc.) not concise; long-winded; verbose. ● *v.* /difyo͞oz/ **1** disperse or be dispersed. **2** spread or be spread widely; reach a large area. □□ **dif·fuse'ly** /difyo͞oslee/ *adv.* **dif·fuse'ness**. **dif·fus·i·ble** /difyo͞ozibəl/ *adj.* **dif·fu·sion** /difyo͞ozhən/ *n.* **dif·fu'sive** *adj.*

dig /dig/ ● *v.* (**dig·ging**; *past* and *past part.* **dug** /dug/) **1** *intr.* break up and remove or turn over soil, etc. **2** *tr.* break up the soil of. **3** *tr.* make (a hole, grave, tunnel, etc.) by digging. **4** *tr.* **a** obtain or remove by digging. **b** find or discover after searching. **5** *tr. sl.* like, appreciate, or understand. **6** *tr. sl.* thrust or poke into or down into. **7** *intr.* (usu. foll. by *into*) investigate or study closely; probe. ● *n.* **1** piece of digging. **2** thrust or poke (*a dig in the ribs*). **3** *colloq.* (often foll. by *at*) pointed or critical remark. **4**

archaeological excavation. **5** (in *pl.*) *colloq.* living quarters. □ **dig one's feet** (or **heels** or **toes**) **in** be obstinate. **dig in** *colloq.* begin eating. **dig oneself in 1** prepare a defensive trench or pit. **2** establish one's position. □□ **dig′ger** *n.*

di•gest • *v.tr.* /dijést, dī-/ **1** assimilate (food) in the stomach and bowels. **2** understand and assimilate mentally. **3** reduce to a systematic or convenient form; classify; summarize. • *n.* /dí-jest/ **1** compendium or summary of information; résumé. **2** periodical synopsis of current literature or news. □□ **di•gest′i•ble** *adj.* **di•gest•i•bil′i•ty** *n.*

di•ges•tion /dijés-chən, dī-/ *n.* **1** process of digesting. **2** capacity to digest food. □□ **di•ges•tive** /dijéstiv, dī-/ *adj.* & *n.*

di•git /díjit/ *n.* **1** any numeral from 0 to 9. **2** *Anat.* & *Zool.* finger, thumb, or toe.

dig•i•tal /díjit′l/ *adj.* **1** of or using a digit or digits. **2** (of a clock, watch, etc.) that gives a reading by displayed digits. **3** (of a computer) operating on data represented by digits. **4** (of a recording) with sound electronically represented by digits. □□ **dig′it•al•ly** *adv.*

dig•i•tal•is /díjitális/ *n.* drug prepared from the foxglove, used to stimulate the heart muscle.

dig•i•tize /díjitīz/ *v.tr.* convert (data, etc.) into digital form, esp. for a computer. □□ **dig•i•ti•za′tion** *n.*

dig•ni•fied /dígnifīd/ *adj.* having or expressing dignity; noble or stately in appearance or manner.

dig•ni•fy /dígnifī/ *v.tr.* (**-fies, -fied**) **1** give dignity or distinction to. **2** ennoble. **3** give the appearance of dignity to (*dignified the house with the name of mansion*).

dig•ni•tar•y /dígniteree/ *n.* (*pl.* **-ies**) person of high rank or office.

dig•ni•ty /dígnitee/ *n.* (*pl.* **-ties**) **1** composed and serious manner or style. **2** worthiness; excellence. **3** high or honorable rank or position. **4** high regard. **5** self-respect. □ **beneath one's dignity** not considered worthy enough for one to do.

di•graph /dígraf/ *n.* two letters representing one sound, as in *ph* and *ey*. □□ **di•graph•ic** /-gráfik/ *adj.*

di•gress /dīgrés/ *v.intr.* depart from the main subject in speech or writing. □□ **di•gres•sion** /-gréshən/ *n.*

dike /dīk/ (also **dyke**) • *n.* **1** embankment built to prevent flooding. **2** ditch. **3** causeway. **4** barrier or obstacle; defense. • *v.tr.* provide or defend with a dike or dikes.

di•lap•i•dat•ed /dilápidaytid/ *adj.* in disrepair or ruin.

dil•a•ta•tion /dilətáyshən, dī-/ *n.* widening or expansion of a hollow organ or cavity. □ **dilatation and curettage** operation in which the cervix is expanded and the womb lining scraped off with a curette.

di•late /dīláyt, dílayt/ *v.* **1** *tr.* & *intr.* make or become wider or larger (*dilated pupils*). **2** *intr.* (often foll. by *on, upon*) speak or write at length. □□ **di•la•tion** /-láyshən/ *n.*

dil•a•to•ry /dílətawree/ *adj.* given to or causing delay. □□ **dil′a•to•ri•ly** *adv.* **dil′a•to•ri•ness** *n.*

di•lem•ma /dilémə/ *n.* situation in which a choice has to be made between two equally undesirable alternatives.

¶ **Dilemma** should be used with regard to situations in which a difficult choice has to be made

between undesirable alternatives, as in *You see his dilemma? He would have to give up either his childhood home or his dreams of traveling.* It is imprecise to use **dilemma** to mean simply 'a difficult situation.'

dil•et•tante /dílitáant/ • *n.* (*pl.* **dil′et•tantes** or **dil•et•tan′ti** /-tee/) **1** person who studies a subject or area of knowledge superficially. **2** person who enjoys the arts. • *adj.* not thorough; amateurish. □□ **dil•et•tan′tish** *adj.* **dil•et•tan′tism** *n.*

dil•i•gent /dílijənt/ *adj.* **1** hardworking. **2** showing care and effort. □□ **dil•i•gence** /dílijəns/ *n.* **dil′i•gent•ly** *adv.*

dill /dil/ *n.* herb with aromatic seeds and leaves, used for flavoring and medicinal purposes. □ **dill pickle** pickled cucumber, etc., flavored with dill.

dil•ly•dal•ly /díleedálee/ *v.intr.* (**-lies, -lied**) *colloq.* **1** dawdle; loiter. **2** vacillate.

di•lute /dilo͞ot, dī-/ • *v.tr.* **1** reduce the strength of (a fluid) by adding water, etc. **2** weaken or reduce in effect. • *adj.* also /dī-/ (esp. of a fluid) diluted; weakened. □□ **di•lut′er** *n.* **di•lu•tion** /-lo͞oshən/ *n.*

dim /dim/ • *adj.* (**dim•mer, dim•mest**) **1 a** faintly luminous or visible; not bright. **b** obscure; ill-defined. **2** not clearly perceived or remembered. **3** *colloq.* stupid; slow to understand. • *v.* (**dimmed, dim•ming**) *tr.* & *intr.* make or become dim. □ **dim-witted** *colloq.* stupid. **take a dim view of** *colloq.* disapprove of. □□ **dim′ly** *adv.* **dim′mish** *adj.* **dim′ness** *n.*

dime /dīm/ *n.* US & Can. ten-cent coin. □ **a dime a dozen** very cheap or commonplace. **dime novel** cheap popular novel. **turn on a dime** *colloq.* make a sharp turn in a vehicle.

di•men•sion /diménshən, dī-/ *n.* **1** measurable extent, as length, breadth, etc. **2** (in *pl.*) size; scope; extent. **3** aspect or facet of a situation, etc. □□ **di•men′sion•al** *adj.* (also in *comb.*). **di•men′sion•less** *adj.*

di•min•ish /dimínish/ *v.* **1** *tr.* & *intr.* make or become smaller or less. **2** *tr.* lessen the reputation or influence of (a person). □ **law of diminishing returns** *Econ.* fact that the increase of expenditure, investment, taxation, etc., beyond a certain point ceases to produce a proportionate yield. □□ **di•min′ish•a•ble** *adj.*

di•min•u•en•do /dimínyo͞o-éndō/ *Mus.* • *adv.* gradual decrease in loudness. • *n.* (*pl.* **-dos**) passage played in this way.

dim•i•nu•tion /dimíno͞oshən, -nyo͞o-/ *n.* **1** act or instance of diminishing. **2** amount by which something diminishes.

di•min•u•tive /dimínyətiv/ • *adj.* **1** remarkably small; tiny. **2** *Gram.* (of a word or suffix) implying smallness or affection (e.g., *-let, -kins*). • *n. Gram.* diminutive word or suffix.

dim•mer /dímər/ *n.* device for varying the brightness of an electric light.

dim•ple /dímpəl/ • *n.* small hollow, esp. in the cheeks or chin. • *v.* **1** *intr.* produce or show dimples. **2** *tr.* produce dimples in (a cheek, etc.). □□ **dim′ply** *adj.*

dim sum /dim súm/ *n.* (also **dim sim** /sím/) meal or course of savory Cantonese-style snacks, esp. steamed or fried filled dumplings.

dim•wit /dímwit/ *n. colloq.* stupid person.

din /din/ *n.* prolonged loud and distracting noise.

dine /dīn/ v. **1** intr. eat dinner. **2** tr. give dinner to. □ **dine out** dine away from home. **dining room** room in which meals are eaten.

din·er /dínər/ n. **1** person who dines, esp. in a restaurant. **2** railroad dining car. **3** small restaurant.

di·nette /dīnét/ n. **1** small room or part of a room used for eating meals. **2** (in full **dinette set**) table and chairs designed for such a room.

ding[1] /ding/ • v.intr. make a ringing sound. • n. ringing sound.

ding[2] /ding/ • v.tr. cause surface damage; dent. • n. nick; minor surface damage; dent.

din·ghy /díngee, dínggee/ n. (pl. **-ghies**) small boat for rowing or sailing.

din·go /dínggō/ n. (pl. **-goes**) wild Australian dog.

din·gy /dínjee/ adj. (**din·gi·er, din·gi·est**) dirty-looking; drab; dull-colored. □□ **din′gi·ly** adv. **din′gi·ness** n.

din·ky /díngkee/ adj. (**din·ki·er, din·ki·est**) colloq. small.

din·ner /dínər/ n. **1** main meal of the day, either at midday or in the evening. **2** formal evening meal or banquet. □ **dinner dance** formal dinner followed by dancing. **dinner jacket** man's, usu. black, formal jacket for evening wear. **dinner service** set of usu. matching dishes, etc., for serving a meal.

din·ner·ware /dínərwair/ n. tableware, as plates, glassware, etc.

di·no·saur /dínəsawr/ n. **1** extinct reptile of the Mesozoic era, often of enormous size. **2** large, unwieldy system or organization. □□ **di·no·sau′ri·an** adj. & n.

dint /dint/ n. □ **by dint of** by force or means of.

di·o·cese /díəsis, -sees, -seez/ n. district administered by a bishop. □□ **di·oc·e·san** /dīósisən/ adj.

di·ode /díōd/ n. Electronics semiconductor allowing current flow in one direction only and having two terminals.

di·o·ram·a /díərámə, -ráamə/ n. three-dimensional scenic display with a painted backdrop, viewed through a window, etc. □□ **di·o·ram·ic** /-rámik/ adj.

di·ox·ide /dīóksīd/ n. Chem. oxide containing two atoms of oxygen which are not linked together (carbon dioxide).

DIP /dip/ n. Computing form of integrated circuit. □ **DIP switch** arrangement of miniature switches on an electronic device for selecting various modes of operation.

dip /dip/ • v. (**dipped, dip·ping**) **1** tr. put or let down briefly into liquid, etc.; immerse. **2** intr. a go below a surface or level. **b** (of a level of income, activity, etc.) decline slightly. **3** intr. extend or slope downward. **4** intr. (foll. by into) a read briefly from (a book, etc.). **b** take a cursory interest in (a subject). **5** (foll. by into) a intr. put a hand, ladle, etc., into a container to take something out. **b** tr. put (a hand, etc.) into a container to do this. **6** tr. & intr. lower or be lowered, esp. in salute. • n. **1** dipping or being dipped. **2** liquid or sauce into which something is dipped. **3** brief swim. **4** brief downward slope in a road, skyline, etc. **5** sl. pickpocket.

diph·the·ri·a /difthéereeə, dip-/ n. acute infec-

tious bacterial disease with inflammation, esp. of the throat. □□ **diph·the′ri·al** adj. **diph·the·rit·ic** /-thərítik/ adj. **diph·the·roid** /dífthəroyd, díp-/ adj.

diph·thong /dífthawng, -thong, díp-/ n. speech sound in one syllable in which the articulation begins as for one vowel and moves as for another (as in coin, loud, and side). □□ **diph·thon·gal** /-tháwnggəl, -thóng-/ adj.

dip·lod·o·cus /diplódəkəs, dī-/ n. giant plant-eating dinosaur with a long neck and tail.

di·plo·ma /diplómə/ n. (pl. **di·plo·mas**) certificate of qualification awarded by a college, etc. □□ **di·plo·maed** /-məd/ adj.

di·plo·ma·cy /diplóməsee/ n. **1** management of international relations. **2** adroitness in personal relations; tact.

dip·lo·mat /dípləmat/ n. **1** official representing a country abroad; member of a diplomatic service. **2** tactful person. □□ **dip·lo·mat·ic** /dípləmátik/ adj.

di·pole /dípōl/ n. **1** Physics two equal and oppositely charged or magnetized poles separated by a distance. **2** Chem. molecule charged in this way. **3** aerial consisting of a horizontal metal rod with a connecting wire at its center.

dip·so·ma·ni·a /dipsəmáyneeə/ n. alcoholism. □□ **dip·so·ma·ni·ac** /-máyneeak/ n.

dip·stick /dípstik/ n. rod for measuring the depth of a liquid, esp. in a vehicle's engine.

dip·tych /díptik/ n. **1** painting, esp. an altarpiece, on two hinged, usu. wooden panels which may be closed like a book. **2** ancient writing tablet consisting of two hinged leaves with waxed inner sides.

dire /dīr/ adj. **1 a** calamitous; dreadful. **b** ominous. **2** urgent. □□ **dire′ly** adv. **dire′ness** n.

di·rect /dirékt, dī-/ • adj. **1** extending or moving in a straight line or by the shortest route. **2** straightforward. **b** frank. **3** without intermediaries (direct rule). **4** (of descent) lineal; not collateral. **5** exact; complete; greatest possible (esp. where contrast is implied) (the direct opposite). • adv. in a direct way or manner (dealt with them direct). • v.tr. **1** control; guide; govern the movements of. **2** order or command. **3** tell or show (a person) the way to. **4** (foll. by at, to, toward) **a** point, aim, or cause (a blow or missile) to move in a certain direction. **b** point or address (one's attention, a remark, etc.). **5 a** (also absol.) supervise the performing, staging, etc., of (a movie, play, etc.). **b** supervise the performance of (an actor, etc.). □ **direct access** facility of retrieving data immediately from any part of a computer file. **direct current** electric current flowing in one direction only. ¶ Abbr.: **DC, d.c. direct object** Gram. primary object of the action of a transitive verb. **direct proportion** a relation between quantities whose ratio is constant. □□ **di·rect′ ness** n.

di·rec·tion /dirékshən, dī-/ n. **1** directing; supervision. **2** (usu. in pl.) order or instruction. **3** course or line of movement, sight, etc. **4** tendency or scope of a theme, subject, or inquiry. □□ **di·rec′tion·al** adj. **di·rec·tion·al·i·ty** /-álitee/ n. **di·rec′tion·al·ly** adv. **di·rec′tion·less** adj.

di·rec·tive /diréktiv, dī-/ • n. instruction from an authority. • adj. serving to direct.

di·rect·ly /diréktlee, dī-/ adv. **1 a** at once; without delay. **b** presently; shortly. **2** exactly; im-

mediately (*directly opposite*; *directly after lunch*).
3 in a direct manner.

di·rec·tor /diréktər, dī-/ *n.* **1** person who directs or controls something, esp. a member of the board of a corporation. **2** person who directs a movie, play, etc. □□ **di·rec·to·ri·al** /-táwreeəl/ *adj.* **di·rec′tor·ship** *n.*

di·rec·tor·ate /diréktərət, dī-/ *n.* **1** board of directors. **2** office of director.

di·rec·to·ry /diréktəree, dī-/ *n.* (*pl.* **-ries**) alphabetical or thematic listing of a particular group of individuals (e.g., telephone subscribers) or organizations.

dirge /dərj/ *n.* lament for the dead. □□ **dirge′ful** *adj.*

dir·i·gi·ble /dírijibəl, diríj-/ *n.* rigid-frame airship.

dirk /dərk/ *n.* long dagger.

dirn·dl /dərnd′l/ *n.* **1** Alpine dress with close-fitting bodice, tight waistband, and full skirt. **2** skirt of this kind.

dirt /dərt/ *n.* **1** unclean matter that soils. **2** earth; soil. **3 a** foul or malicious words or talk. **b** scurrilous information; scandal; gossip; the lowdown. **4** person or thing considered worthless. □ **dirt bike** motorcycle designed for use on unpaved roads and tracks. **dirt cheap** *colloq.* extremely cheap. **dirt poor** extremely poor. **dirt track** course made of rolled cinders, soil, etc., for motorcycle racing or flat racing. **treat like dirt** treat (a person) contemptuously; abuse.

dirt·y /dártee/ • *adj.* (**dirt·i·er**, **dirt·i·est**) **1** soiled; unclean. **2** causing dirtiness (*a dirty job*). **3** sordid; lewd; morally illicit or questionable (*dirty joke*). **4** unpleasant; nasty. **5** dishonest; dishonorable; unfair (*dirty play*). **6** (of weather) rough; stormy. **7** (of a color) not pure nor clear; dingy. • *v.* (**-ies**, **-ied**) make or become dirty. □ **dirty dog** *colloq.* scoundrel; despicable person. **dirty linen** (or **laundry**) *colloq.* intimate secrets, esp. of a scandalous nature. **dirty look** *colloq.* look of disapproval, anger, or disgust. **dirty trick 1** dishonorable and deceitful act. **2** (in *pl.*) underhand political activity. **dirty word 1** offensive or indecent word. **2** word for something that is disapproved of (*profit is a dirty word*). **dirty work 1** unpleasant tasks. **2** dishonorable or illegal activity, esp. done clandestinely. □□ **dirt′i·ly** *adv.* **dirt′i·ness** *n.*

dis /dis/ *v.tr. sl.* var. of DISS.

dis- /dis/ *prefix* forming nouns, adjectives, and verbs indicating: **1** negation (*dishonest*). **2** reversal or absence of an action or state (*disengage*; *disbelieve*). **3** removal of a thing or quality (*dismember*, *disable*). **4** separation (*distinguish*; *dispose*). **5** completeness or intensification (*disembowel*; *disgruntled*). **6** expulsion from (*disbar*).

dis·a·bil·i·ty /dísəbílitee/ *n.* (*pl.* **-ties**) **1** physical or mental incapacity. **2** lack of some asset, quality, or attribute, preventing action.

dis·a·ble /disáybəl/ *v.tr.* render unable to function; deprive of an ability. □□ **dis·a′ble·ment** *n.*

dis·a·buse /dísəbyóoz/ *v.tr.* **1** (foll. by *of*) free from a mistaken idea. **2** disillusion; undeceive.

dis·ad·van·tage /dísədvántij/ • *n.* unfavorable circumstance or condition. • *v.tr.* cause disadvantage to. □ **at a disadvantage** in an unfavorable position or aspect. □□ **dis·ad·van·ta·geous** /dísádvəntáyjəs, disad-/ *adj.*

dis·ad·van·taged /dísədvántijd/ *adj.* placed in

unfavorable circumstances (esp. of a person lacking normal opportunities).

dis·af·fect·ed /dísəféktid/ *adj.* **1** disloyal, esp. to one's superiors. **2** estranged; no longer friendly; discontented. □□ **dis·af·fect′ed·ly** *adv.* **dis·af·fec·tion** /dísəfékshən/ *n.*

dis·a·gree /dísəgrée/ *v.intr.* (**-a·grees**, **-a·greed**, **-a·gree·ing**) **1** hold a different opinion. **2** quarrel. **3** (of factors or circumstances) not correspond. **4** have an adverse effect upon (a person's health, digestion, etc.). □□ **dis·a·gree′ment** *n.*

dis·a·gree·a·ble /dísəgrée·əbəl/ *adj.* **1** unpleasant. **2** rude or bad-tempered. □□ **dis·a·gree′a·ble·ness** *n.* **dis·a·gree′a·bly** *adv.*

dis·al·low /dísəlów/ *v.tr.* refuse to allow or accept as valid; prohibit. □□ **dis·al·low′ance** *n.*

dis·ap·pear /dísəpeér/ *v.intr.* **1** cease to be visible. **2** cease to exist or be in circulation or use. □□ **dis·ap·pear′ance** *n.*

dis·ap·point /dísəpóynt/ *v.tr.* **1** (also *absol.*) fail to fulfill a desire or expectation of. **2** frustrate (hopes, plans, etc.). □ **be disappointed** fail to have one's expectation, etc., fulfilled (*was disappointed in you*; *am disappointed to be last*). □□ **dis·ap·point′ed** *adj.* **dis·ap·point′ing** *adj.* **dis·ap·point′ing·ly** *adv.* **dis·ap·point′ment** *n.*

dis·ap·pro·ba·tion /dísáprəbáyshən/ *n.* strong disapproval.

dis·ap·prove /dísəproŏv/ *v.* **1** *intr.* have or express an unfavorable opinion. **2** *tr.* be displeased with. □□ **dis·ap·prov′al** *n.* **dis·ap·prov′ing** *adj.* **dis·ap·prov′ing·ly** *adv.*

dis·arm /disaárm/ *v.* **1** *tr.* take weapons away from (a person, nation, etc.). **2** *intr.* (of a nation, etc.) disband or reduce its armed forces. **3** *tr.* remove the fuse from (a bomb, etc.). **4** *tr.* render harmless. **5** *tr.* charm; mollify; placate. □□ **dis·arm′ing** *adj.* (esp. in sense 5). **dis·arm′ing·ly** *adv.*

dis·ar·ma·ment /disaárməmənt/ *n.* reduction by a nation of its military forces and weapons.

dis·ar·range /dísəráynj/ *v.tr.* bring into disorder. □□ **dis·ar·range′ment** *n.*

dis·ar·ray /dísəráy/ • *n.* (often prec. by *in*, *into*) disorder; confusion (esp. among people). • *v.tr.* throw into disorder.

dis·as·so·ci·ate /dísəsósheeayt, -seeayt/ *v.* = DISSOCIATE. □□ **dis·as·so·ci·a·tion** /-áyshən/ *n.*

dis·as·ter /dizástər/ *n.* **1** great or sudden misfortune. **2** complete failure. □□ **dis·as′trous** *adj.* **dis·as′trous·ly** *adv.*

dis·a·vow /dísəvów/ *v.tr.* disclaim knowledge of, responsibility for, or belief in. □□ **dis·a·vow′al** *n.*

dis·band /disbánd/ *v.* **1** *intr.* (of an organized group, etc.) cease to work or act together. **2** *tr.* cause (such a group) to disband. □□ **dis·band′ ment** *n.*

dis·bar /disbaár/ *v.tr.* (**dis·barred**, **dis·bar·ring**) deprive (an attorney) of the right to practice. □□ **dis·bar′ment** *n.*

dis·be·lieve /dísbileév/ *v.* **1** *tr.* be unable or unwilling to believe (a person or statement). **2** *intr.* have no faith. □□ **dis·be·lief** /-leéf/ *n.* **dis·be·liev′ing** *adj.* **dis·be·liev′ing·ly** *adv.*

dis·burse /disbárs/ *v.* **1** *tr.* expend (money). **2** *intr.* pay money. □□ **dis·burs′al** *n.* **dis·burse′ment** *n.*

disc var. of DISK.

dis·card • *v.tr.* /diskaárd/ **1** reject as unwanted. **2** (also *absol.*) *Cards* remove (a card) from one's hand. • *n.* /dískaard/ (often in *pl.*) discarded item, esp. a card in a card game.

dis·cern /disə́rn/ *v.tr.* perceive clearly with the mind or the senses. □□ **dis·cern'i·ble** *adj.* **dis·cern'i·bly** *adv.*

dis·cern·ing /disə́rning/ *adj.* having or showing good judgment or insight. □□ **dis·cern'ing·ly** *adv.* **dis·cern·ment** /disə́rnmənt/ *n.*

dis·charge • *v.* /dischaárj/ **1** *tr.* release, esp. from a duty, commitment, or confinement. **2** *tr.* dismiss from office, employment, etc. **3** *tr.* **a** fire (a gun, etc.). **b** (of a gun, etc.) fire (a bullet, etc.). **4 a** *tr.* (also *absol.*) pour out or cause to pour out (pus, liquid, etc.) (*the wound was discharging*). **b** *intr.* (foll. by *into*) (of a river, etc.) flow into (esp. the sea). **5** *tr.* **a** carry out; perform (a duty). **b** relieve oneself of (a financial commitment) (*discharged his debt*). **6** *tr. Physics* release an electrical charge from. • *n.* /díschaarj, dischaárj/ **1** discharging or being discharged. **2** dismissal, esp. from the armed services. **3** written certificate of release, etc. **4** an act of firing a gun, etc. **5** matter (pus, liquid, etc.) discharged. **6** *Physics* release of an electric charge. □□ **dis·charge'a·ble** *adj.* **dis·charg'er** *n.* (in sense 6 of *v.*).

dis·ci·ple /disī́pəl/ *n.* **1** follower of a leader, teacher, philosophy, etc. (*a disciple of Zen Buddhism*). **2** early believer in Christ, esp. one of the twelve Apostles.

dis·ci·pli·nar·i·an /dísiplináireeən/ *n.* person who upholds or practices firm discipline.

dis·ci·pline /dísiplin/ • *n.* **1 a** control or order exercised over people or animals, esp. children, prisoners, military personnel, church members, etc. **b** rules used to maintain this control. **c** behavior of groups subjected to such rules (*poor discipline in the ranks*). **2** mental, moral, or physical training. **3** branch of learning. **4** punishment. • *v.tr.* **1** punish. **2** train in obedience; drill. □□ **dis'ci·plin·a·ble** *adj.* **dis'ci·pli·nal** /disiplin'l, disiplín'l/ *adj.* **dis·ci·pli·nar·y** /dísiplineree/ *adj.*

dis·claim /disklaym/ *v.tr.* **1** deny or disown. **2** (often *absol.*) *Law* renounce legal claim to (property, etc.).

dis·claim·er /disklaymər/ *n.* renunciation or disavowal, esp. of responsibility.

dis·close /disklṓz/ *v.tr.* **1** make known. **2** expose to view. □□ **dis·clos'er** *n.* **dis·clo·sure** /disklṓzhər/ *n.*

dis·co /dískō/ *colloq.* • *n.* (*pl.* **-cos**) = DISCOTHEQUE. • *v.intr.* (**-coes, -coed**) **1** attend a discotheque. **2** dance to disco music (*discoed the night away*). □ **disco music** popular dance music characterized by a heavy bass rhythm.

dis·cog·ra·phy /diskógrəfee/ *n.* (*pl.* **-phies**) **1** descriptive catalog of recordings, esp. of a particular performer or composer. **2** the study of recordings. □□ **dis·cog'ra·pher** *n.*

dis·color /diskúlər/ *v.* spoil or cause to spoil the color of; stain; tarnish. □□ **dis·col·or·a'tion** *n.*

dis·com·fit /diskúmfit/ *v.tr.* **1** disconcert or baffle. **2** thwart. □□ **dis·com'fi·ture** *n.*

dis·com·fort /diskúmfərt/ • *n.* **1** lack of ease; slight pain. **2** lack of comfort. • *v.tr.* make uneasy.

dis·com·mode /diskəmṓd/ *v.tr.* inconvenience

(a person, etc.). □□ **dis·com·mo'di·ous** *adj.*

dis·com·pose /dískəmpṓz/ *v.tr.* disturb the composure of; agitate; disturb. □□ **dis·com·po·sure** /-pṓzhər/ *n.*

dis·con·cert /dískənsə́rt/ *v.tr.* **1** (often as **disconcerted** *adj.*) discompose; agitate; fluster. **2** spoil or upset (plans, etc.). □□ **dis·con·cert'ing** *adj.*

dis·con·nect /dískənékt/ *v.tr.* (often foll. by *from*) break the connection or functioning of (things, ideas, etc.). □□ **dis·con·nec·tion** /dískənékshən/ *n.*

dis·con·nect·ed /dískənéktid/ *adj.* **1** separated, not functioning. **2** (of speech, writing, etc.) incoherent and illogical.

dis·con·so·late /diskónsələt/ *adj.* **1** forlorn. **2** unhappy or disappointed. □□ **dis·con'so·late·ly** *adv.*

dis·con·tent /dískəntént/ • *n.* lack of contentment; restlessness, dissatisfaction. • *adj.* dissatisfied. • *v.tr.* (esp. as **discontented** *adj.*) dissatisfy. □□ **dis·con·tent'ment** *n.*

dis·con·tin·ue /dískəntínyōō/ *v.* **1** *intr.* & *tr.* come or bring to an end. **2** *tr.* give up; cease from. □□ **dis·con·tin'u·ance** *n.* **dis·con·tin·u·a'tion** *n.*

dis·con·tin·u·ous /dískəntínyōōəs/ *adj.* lacking continuity in space or time; intermittent. □□ **dis·con·ti·nu·i·ty** /-kontinōō-itee, -nyōō-/ *n.* **dis·con·tin'u·ous·ly** *adv.*

dis·cord • *n.* /dískawrd/ **1** disagreement; strife. **2** harsh noise. **3** *Mus.* lack of harmony. • *v.intr.* /diskáwrd/ **1** (usu. foll. by *with*) disagree; clash. □□ **dis·cor'dance** *n.* **dis·cor'dan·cy** *n.* **dis·cord·ant** /diskáwrd'nt/ *adj.* **dis·cord'ant·ly** *adv.*

dis·co·theque /dískəték/ *n.* club, etc., for dancing to recorded popular music.

dis·count • *n.* /dískownt/ amount deducted from a customary price. • *v.tr.* /diskównt/ **1** disregard as unreliable or unimportant (*discounted his story*). **2** detract from; lessen; deduct (esp. an amount from a bill, etc.). □ **at a discount 1** below the nominal or usual price (cf. PREMIUM). **2** not in demand; depreciated. **discount rate** minimum lending rate. **discount store** store, etc., that sells goods at less than the normal retail price. □□ **dis'count·a·ble** *adj.* **dis'count·er** *n.*

dis·coun·te·nance /diskówntinəns/ *v.tr.* **1** (esp. in *passive*) disconcert (*was discountenanced by his abruptness*). **2** refuse to countenance; show disapproval of.

dis·cour·age /diskə́rij, -kúr-/ *v.tr.* **1** deprive of courage, confidence, or energy. **2** dissuade (*discouraged her from going*). **3** show disapproval of; oppose (*smoking is discouraged*). □□ **dis·cour'age·ment** *n.* **dis·cour'ag·ing·ly** *adv.*

dis·course • *n.* /dískawrs/ *literary* **1** conversation; talk. **2** dissertation or treatise on an academic subject. **3** lecture or sermon. • *v.intr.* /diskórs/ **1** talk; converse. **2** *intr.* speak or write learnedly or at length (on a subject).

dis·cour·te·ous /diskə́rteeəs/ *adj.* impolite; rude. □□ **dis·cour'te·ous·ly** *adv.* **dis·cour'te·ous·ness** *n.* **dis·cour'te·sy** /diskə́rtəsee/ *n.*

dis·cov·er /diskúvər/ *v.tr.* **1** find out or become aware of (*discovered a new entrance*). **2** be the first to find or find out (*who discovered America?*). **3** devise or pioneer (*discover new techniques*). □□ **dis·cov'er·a·ble** *adj.* **dis·cov'er·er** *n.*

dis·cov·er·y /diskúvəree/ *n.* (*pl.* **-ies**) **1** discovering or being discovered. **2** person or thing discovered. •

dis·cred·it /diskrédit/ • n. 1 harm to reputation. 2 person or thing causing this (*he is a discredit to his family*). 3 doubt; disbelief. • v.tr. 1 harm the good reputation of. 2 cause to be disbelieved. 3 refuse to believe.

dis·cred·it·a·ble /diskréditəbəl/ adj. bringing discredit; shameful. □□ **dis·cred′it·a·bly** adv.

dis·creet /diskréet/ adj. (**dis·creet·er, dis·creet·est**) 1 a circumspect in speech or action. b tactful; trustworthy. 2 unobtrusive. □□ **dis·creet′ly** adv. **dis·creet′ness** n.

¶ **Discreet,** meaning 'prudent; cautious,' and **discrete,** meaning 'separate' are different words: *Be discreet and don't give away the surprise. I can see three discrete possibilities causing this problem.*

dis·crep·an·cy /diskrépənsee/ n. (pl. **-cies**) difference; failure to correspond; inconsistency. □□ **dis·crep′ant** adj.

dis·crete /diskréet/ adj. individually distinct; separate; discontinuous. □□ **dis·crete′ly** adv. **dis·crete′ness** n.

dis·cre·tion /diskréshən/ n. 1 being discreet. 2 freedom to act and think as one wishes, usu. within legal limits (*it is within his discretion to leave*). □□ **dis·cre′tion·ary** adj.

dis·crim·i·nate /diskríminayt/ v.intr. 1 make or see a distinction. 2 treat unfavorably, esp. on the basis of race, color, or sex. 3 (esp. as **discriminating** adj.) observe distinction carefully; have good judgment. □□ **dis·crim·i·nate·ly** /-nətlee/ adv. **dis·crim·i·na′tion** n. **dis·crim·i·na·to·ry** /-nətáwree/ adj.

dis·crim·i·nat·ing /diskríminayting/ adj. 1 able to discern, esp. distinctions. 2 having good taste.

dis·cur·sive /diskə́rsiv/ adj. rambling or digressive. □□ **dis·cur′sive·ly** adv. **dis·cur′sive·ness** n.

dis·cus /dískəs/ n. (pl. **dis′cus·es**) heavy disk thrown in competition.

DISCUS THROWER

dis·cuss /diskús/ v.tr. talk or write about; debate. □□ **dis·cuss′a·ble** adj. **dis·cus′sant** n. **dis·cuss′er** n. **dis·cus·sion** /diskúshən/ n.

dis·dain /disdáyn/ • n. scorn; contempt. • v.tr. 1 regard with disdain. 2 think oneself superior to; reject (*disdained to enter; disdained answering*). □□ **dis·dain′ful** adj.

dis·ease /dizéez/ n. 1 unhealthy condition of the body or the mind; illness; sickness. 2 corresponding condition of plants. 3 particular kind of illness.

dis·em·bark /dísimbaárk/ v. put or go ashore or land from a ship or an aircraft. □□ **dis·em·bar·ka′tion** n.

dis·em·bow·el /dísimbówəl/ v.tr. remove the bowels or entrails of. □□ **dis·em·bow′el·ment** n.

dis·en·chant /dísinchánt/ v.tr. disillusion. □□ **dis·en·chant′ing·ly** adv. **dis·en·chant′ment** n.

dis·en·cum·ber /dísinkúmbər/ v.tr. free from encumbrance.

dis·en·fran·chise var. of DISFRANCHISE.

dis·en·gage /dísingáyj/ v. 1 a tr. detach, free, loosen, or separate (parts, etc.) (*disengaged the clutch*). b refl. detach oneself; get loose (*disengaged ourselves from their company*). 2 tr. Mil. remove (troops) from battle. 3 intr. become detached. 4 intr. (as **disengaged** adj.) a unoccupied; free; vacant. b uncommitted, esp. politically. □□ **dis·en·gage′ment** n.

dis·en·tan·gle /dísintánggəl/ v. 1 tr. a unravel; untwist. b free from complications; extricate. 2 intr. become disentangled. □□ **dis·en·tan′gle·ment** n.

dis·fa·vor /disfáyvər/ n. 1 disapproval or dislike. 2 being disliked (*fell into disfavor*).

dis·fig·ure /disfígyər/ v.tr. spoil the appearance of; deform; deface. □□ **dis·fig′ure·ment** n.

dis·fran·chise /dísfránchīz/ v.tr. (also **dis·en·fran·chise** /disinfránchīz/) deprive of the right to vote, be represented, etc. □□ **dis·fran′chise·ment** n.

dis·gorge /disgáwrj/ v.tr. 1 vomit. 2 pour forth; discharge (contents, ill-gotten gains, etc.). □□ **dis·gorge′ment** n.

dis·grace /disgráys/ • n. 1 shame; ignominy. 2 dishonorable, inefficient, or shameful person, thing, state of affairs, etc. • v.tr. bring shame or discredit on. □ **in disgrace** having lost respect or reputation; out of favor. □□ **dis·grace′ful** adj. **dis·grace′ful·ly** adv.

dis·grun·tled /disgrúntld/ adj. discontented; moody; sulky. □□ **dis·grun′tle·ment** n.

dis·guise /disgíz/ • v.tr. alter the appearance, sound, smell, etc., of, so as to conceal the identity; make unrecognizable (*disguised herself as a police officer; disguised the taste by adding sugar*). • n. 1 costume, makeup, action, etc., used to conceal or deceive. 2 act or practice of disguising; concealment of reality. □ **in disguise** 1 wearing a concealing costume, etc. 2 appearing to be the opposite (*a blessing in disguise*).

dis·gust /disgúst/ • n. (usu. foll. by *at, for*) strong aversion; repugnance. • v.tr. cause disgust in (*their behavior disgusts me*). □ **in disgust** as a result of disgust (*left in disgust*). □□ **dis·gust′ed·ly** adv. **dis·gust′ing** adj.

dish /dish/ • n. 1 a shallow, flat-bottomed container for cooking or serving food. b food served in a dish (*all the dishes were delicious*). 2 (in pl.) plates, cooking pots, etc., used for a meal. 3 a dish-shaped receptacle, object, or cavity. b = *satellite dish*. 4 sl. sexually attractive person. • v.tr. put (food) into a dish for serving. □ **dish out** sl. distribute, esp. carelessly or indiscriminately. **dish up 1** serve or prepare to serve (food). 2 colloq. seek to present (facts, argument, etc.) attractively. □□ **dish′ful** n. (pl. **-fuls**). **dish·like** adj.

dis·har·mo·ny /dis-haármənee/ n. lack of harmony; discord. □□ **dis·har·mo·ni·ous** /-mónee-əs/ adj.

dis·heart·en /dis-haʹart'n/ v.tr. cause to lose courage or confidence. □□ **dis·heart'en·ing·ly** adv.

di·shev·eled /dishévəld/ adj. (of the hair, a person, etc.) untidy; ruffled; disordered. □□ **di·shev'el** v. **di·shev'el·ment** n.

dis·hon·est /disónist/ adj. fraudulent or insincere. □□ **dis·hon'est·ly** adv. **dis·hon·es·ty** /disónistee/ n.

dis·hon·or /disónər/ • n. 1 shame or disgrace; discredit. 2 something that causes dishonor (a dishonor to her profession). • v.tr. 1 treat without honor or respect. 2 disgrace.

dis·hon·or·a·ble /disónərəbəl/ adj. 1 causing disgrace. 2 unprincipled. □□ **dis·hon'or·a·ble·ness** n. **dis·hon'or·a·bly** adv.

dish·pan /díshpan/ n. large, deep pan for washing dishes.

dish·wash·er /díshwoshər, -wawshər/ n. 1 machine for automatically washing dishes. 2 person employed to wash dishes.

dis·il·lu·sion /dísilóōzhən/ • n. freedom from illusions; disenchantment. • v.tr. rid of illusions; disenchant. □□ **dis·il·lu'sion·ment** n.

dis·in·cline /dísinklín/ v.tr. 1 make reluctant. 2 (as **disinclined** adj.) unwilling; averse.

dis·in·fect /dísinfékt/ v.tr. cleanse (a wound, a room, clothes, etc.) of infection. □□ **dis·in·fect·ant** /dísinféktənt/ n. & adj. **dis·in·fec·tion** /-fékshən/ n.

dis·in·for·ma·tion /dísinfərmáyshən/ n. false information, intended to mislead.

dis·in·gen·u·ous /dísinjényōōəs/ adj. having secret motives; insincere. □□ **dis·in·gen'u·ous·ly** adv. **dis·in·gen'u·ous·ness** n.

dis·in·her·it /dísinhérit/ v.tr. reject as one's heir; deprive of the right of inheritance. □□ **dis·in·her'i·tance** n.

dis·in·te·grate /disíntigrayt/ v. 1 separate into component parts or fragments. 2 lose or cause to lose cohesion. □□ **dis·in·te·gra'tion** n. **dis·in'te·gra·tor** n.

dis·in·ter /dísintér/ v.tr. (**dis·in·terred, dis·in·ter·ring**) remove (esp. a corpse) from the ground; unearth; exhume. □□ **dis·in·ter'ment** n.

dis·in·ter·est·ed /disíntristid, -intəri-/ adj. 1 not influenced by one's own advantage; impartial. 2 disp. uninterested. □□ **dis·in'ter·est** n. **dis·in'ter·est·ed·ly** adv. **dis·in'ter·est·ed·ness** n. ¶ **Disinterested** means 'not having a personal interest, impartial': A juror must be disinterested in the case being tried. **Uninterested** means 'not interested; indifferent': On the other hand, a juror must not be uninterested.

dis·joint /disjóynt/ • v.tr. 1 take apart at the joints. 2 (as **disjointed** adj.) (esp. of conversation) incoherent; desultory. • adj. (of two or more sets) having no elements in common. □□ **dis·joint'ed·ly** adv. **dis·joint'ed·ness** n.

disk /disk/ n. (also **disc**) 1 a flat thin circular object. b round, or apparently flat surface (the sun's disk). 2 layer of cartilage between vertebrae. 3 a phonograph record. b = compact disc. 4 a (in full **magnetic disk**) round, flat computer storage device. b (in full **optical disk**) smooth nonmagnetic disk with large storage capacity for

data recorded and read by laser. □ **disk** (often **disc**) **brake** brake employing the friction of pads against a disk. **disk drive** Computing mechanism for reading or writing data from a disk on which it is stored digitally. **disk** (also **disc**) **jockey** presenter of a selection of phonograph records, compact discs, etc., of popular music, esp. in a broadcast.

disk·ette /diskét/ n. Computing = floppy disk.

dis·like /dislík/ • v.tr. have an aversion to; not like. • n. 1 feeling of repugnance or not liking. 2 object of dislike. □□ **dis·lik'a·ble** adj. (also **dis·like'a·ble**).

dis·lo·cate /díslōkayt, disló-/ v.tr. 1 disturb the normal connection of (esp. a joint in the body). 2 disrupt; put out of order. 3 displace. □□ **dis·lo·ca·tion** /díslōkáyshən/ n.

dis·lodge /dislój/ v.tr. disturb or move. □□ **dis·lodg'ment** n. (also **dis·lodge'ment**).

dis·loy·al /díslóyəl/ adj. not loyal; unfaithful. □□ **dis·loy'al·ist** n. **dis·loy'al·ly** adv. **dis·loy'al·ty** n.

dis·mal /dízməl/ adj. 1 gloomy; miserable. 2 dreary or somber (dismal brown walls). 3 colloq. feeble or inept (a dismal performance). □□ **dis'mal·ly** adv.

---

dismal late Middle English: from earlier dismal (noun), denoting the two days in each month that in medieval times were believed to be unlucky, from Anglo-Norman French dis mal, from medieval Latin dies mali 'evil days.'

---

dis·man·tle /dismánt'l/ v.tr. take to pieces; pull down.

dis·may /dismáy/ • v.tr. discourage or depress; reduce to despair. • n. 1 anxiety. 2 depression or despair.

dis·mem·ber /dismémbər/ v.tr. 1 remove the limbs from. 2 partition or divide up. □□ **dis·mem'ber·ment** n.

dis·miss /dismís/ v. 1 a tr. send away; cause to leave one's presence. b intr. (of an assembly, etc.) disperse; break ranks. 2 tr. discharge from employment, etc., esp. dishonorably. 3 tr. put out of one's thoughts. 4 tr. treat (a subject) summarily (dismissed his application). 5 tr. Law refuse further hearing to (a case). □□ **dis·mis'sal** n.

dis·mis·sive /dismísiv/ adj. disdainful. □□ **dis·mis'sive·ly** adv. **dis·mis'sive·ness** n.

dis·mount • v. /dismównt/ 1 intr. alight from a horse, bicycle, etc. 2 tr. (usu. in passive) throw from a horse; unseat. • n. /dismównt, dís-/ dismounting.

dis·o·be·di·ent /dísəbeédeeənt/ adj. disobeying; rebellious. □□ **dis·o·be·di·ence** /-deeəns/ n. **dis·o·be'di·ent·ly** adv.

dis·o·bey /dísəbáy/ v.tr. (also absol.) fail or refuse to obey; disregard (orders) (disobeyed his mother). □□ **dis·o·bey'er** n.

dis·o·blige /dísəblíj/ v.tr. 1 refuse to consider the convenience or wishes of. 2 (as **disobliging** adj.) uncooperative.

dis·or·der /disáwrdər/ • n. 1 lack of order; confusion. 2 riot; commotion. 3 Med. ailment or disease. • v.tr. throw into confusion; disarrange.

dis·or·der·ly /disáwrdərlee/ adj. 1 untidy; confused. 2 irregular; unruly; riotous. □□ **dis·or'der·li·ness** n.

dis·or·gan·ize /disáwrgənīz/ v.tr. **1** destroy the system or order of; throw into confusion. **2** (as **disorganized** adj.) lacking organization or system. □□ **dis·or·gan·i·za′tion** n.

dis·o·ri·ent /disáwreeənt/ v.tr. **1** confuse (a person) as to his or her bearings. **2** (often as **disoriented** adj.) confuse (a person).

dis·own /disón/ v.tr. **1** repudiate; disclaim. **2** renounce one's connection with or allegiance to.

dis·par·age /dispárij/ v.tr. **1** criticize; belittle. **2** bring discredit on. □□ **dis·par′age·ment** n. **dis·par′ag·ing·ly** adv.

dis·pa·rate /díspərət, dispár-/ • adj. essentially different; without comparison or relation. • n. (in pl.) things so unlike that there is no basis for their comparison. □□ **dis′pa·rate·ly** adv. **dis′pa·rate·ness** n.

dis·par·i·ty /dispáritee/ n. (pl. **-ties**) inequality; difference; incongruity.

dis·pas·sion·ate /dispáshənət/ adj. free from passion; calm; impartial. □□ **dis·pas′sion·ate·ly** adv. **dis·pas′sion·ate·ness** n.

dis·patch /dispách/ (also **des·patch′**) • v.tr. **1** send off to a destination or for a purpose. **2** perform (business, a task, etc.) promptly; finish off. **3** kill; execute. • n. **1** sending (a messenger, letter, etc.). **2** killing; execution. **3** /also díspach/ **a** official message on state or esp. military affairs. **b** news report. **4** promptness; efficiency (done with dispatch). □□ **dis·patch′er** n.

dis·pel /dispél/ v.tr. (**dis·pelled**, **dis·pel·ling**) dissipate; disperse; scatter. □□ **dis·pel′ler** n.

dis·pen·sa·ble /dispénsəbəl/ adj. **1** able to be done without; unnecessary. **2** that can be given out. □□ **dis·pen·sa·bil′i·ty** n.

dis·pen·sa·ry /dispénsəree/ n. (pl. **-ries**) place where medicines, etc., are dispensed.

dis·pen·sa·tion /díspensáyshən/ n. **1 a** dispensing or distributing. **b** (foll. by with) the state of doing without (a thing). **c** something distributed. **2** exemption from a penalty or duty. **3** the ordering or management of the world by providence. □□ **dis·pen·sa′tion·al** adj.

dis·pense /dispéns/ v. **1** tr. distribute; deal out. **2** tr. administer (a sacrament, justice, etc.). **3** tr. make up and give out (medicine, etc.). **4** intr. (foll. by with) **a** do without; render needless. **b** give exemption from (a rule). □□ **dis·pens′er** n.

dis·perse /dispɔ́rs/ v. **1** intr. & tr. go, send, drive, or distribute in different directions or widely. **2 a** intr. (of people at a meeting, etc.) leave and go their various ways. **b** tr. cause to do this. **3** tr. put in circulation; disseminate. □□ **dis·pers′a·ble** adj. **dis·pers′al** n. **dis·pers′er** n. **dis·pers′i·ble** adj. **dis·per′sion** n. **dis·per′sive** adj.

dis·pir·it /dispírit/ v.tr. **1** (esp. as **dispiriting** adj.) make despondent; discourage. **2** (as **dispirited** adj.) dejected; discouraged. □□ **dis·pir′it·ed·ly** adv. **dis·pir′it·ed·ness** n. **dis·pir′it·ing·ly** adv.

dis·place /displáys/ v.tr. **1** shift from its accustomed place. **2** remove from office. **3** take the place of; oust. □ **displaced person** refugee because of war, persecution, etc.

dis·place·ment /displáysmənt/ n. **1** displacing; being displaced. **2** Physics amount of a fluid displaced by a solid floating or immersed in it (ship with a displacement of 11,000 tons).

dis·play /displáy/ • v.tr. **1** expose to view; exhibit; show. **2** show ostentatiously. **3** allow to appear; reveal; betray. • n. **1** displaying. **2** exhibi-

tion or show. **3** ostentation; flashiness. **4** mating rituals of some birds, fish, etc. **5 a** presentation of signals or data on a visual display unit, etc. **b** information so presented. □□ **dis·play′er** n.

dis·please /displéez/ v.tr. make indignant or angry; offend; annoy. □□ **dis·plea·sure** /displézhər/ n.

dis·port /dispáwrt/ v. frolic; gambol; enjoy oneself (disported on the beach; disported themselves in the ocean).

dis·pos·a·ble /dispózəbəl/ • adj. **1** intended to be used once, then thrown away. **2** that can be disposed of. • n. thing designed to be thrown away after one use. □ **disposable income** income after taxes, etc., available for spending.

dis·pos·al /dispózəl/ n. **1** disposing of something. **2** arrangement, disposition, or placing of something. □ **at one's disposal 1** available. **2** subject to one's orders or decisions.

dis·pose /dispóz/ v. **1** tr. **a** make willing; incline (was disposed to release them). **b** give a tendency to (the wheel was disposed to buckle). **2** tr. (as **disposed** adj.) have a specified mental inclination (usu. in comb.: ill-disposed). **3** intr. determine the course of events (man proposes, God disposes). □ **dispose of 1** deal with. **b** get rid of. **c** finish. **d** kill. **e** distribute; dispense; bestow. **2** sell.

dis·po·si·tion /díspəzíshən/ n. **1 a** natural tendency; inclination. **b** temperament or attitude. **2 a** setting in order. **b** arrangement.

dis·pos·sess /díspəzés/ v.tr. **1** dislodge; oust (a person). **2** (usu. foll. by of) deprive. □□ **dis·pos·ses·sion** /-zéshən/ n.

dis·pro·por·tion /díspropáwrshən/ n. lack of proportion. □□ **dis·pro·por′tion·al** adj. **dis·pro·por′tion·al·ly** adv.

dis·pro·por·tion·ate /díspropáwrshənət/ adj. **1** lacking proportion. **2** relatively too large or small, long or short, etc. □□ **dis·pro·por′tion·ate·ly** adv. **dis·pro·por′tion·ate·ness** n.

dis·prove /disproóv/ v.tr. prove false; refute.

dis·put·a·ble /dispyoótəbəl/ adj. open to question; uncertain. □□ **dis·put′a·bly** adv.

dis·pu·ta·tion /díspyətáyshən/ n. **1 a** disputing; debating. **b** argument; controversy. **2** formal debate.

dis·pu·ta·tious /díspyətáyshəs/ adj. argumentative.

dis·pute /dispyoót/ • v. **1** intr. **a** debate; argue. **b** quarrel. **2** tr. discuss, esp. heatedly. **3** tr. question the truth or correctness or validity of (a statement, alleged fact, etc.). **4** tr. contend for; strive to win (disputed the crown). • n. **1** controversy; debate. **2** quarrel. □ **beyond** (or **past** or **without**) **dispute 1** certainly; indisputably. **2** certain; indisputable. **in dispute 1** being argued about. **2** (of a workforce) involved in industrial action. □□ **dis·pu·tant** /-spyoŏt′nt/ n. **dis·put′er** n.

dis·qual·i·fy /diskwólifī/ v.tr. (**-fies**, **-fied**) **1** debar or pronounce ineligible (disqualified from the race for taking drugs). **2** make or pronounce ineligible or unsuitable (his age disqualifies him for the job). **3** pronounce unqualified (disqualified from practicing as a doctor). □□ **dis·qual·i·fi·ca·tion** /diskwólifikáyshən/ n.

dis·qui·et /diskwíət/ • v.tr. deprive of peace; worry. • n. anxiety; unrest. □□ **dis·qui′et·ing** adj. **dis·qui′et·ing·ly** adv.

dis·qui·si·tion /dískwizíshən/ n. long or elaborate treatise or discourse on a subject. □□ **dis·qui·si′tion·al** adj.

dis·re·gard /dísrigaárd/ • v.tr. **1** pay no attention to; ignore. **2** treat as of no importance. • n. indifference; neglect. □□ **dis·re·gard′ful** adj. **dis·re·gard′ful·ly** adv.

dis·re·pair /dísripáir/ n. poor condition due to neglect.

dis·rep·u·ta·ble /dísrépyətəbəl/ adj. **1** of bad reputation. **2** not respectable in appearance; dirty; untidy. □□ **dis·rep′u·ta·bly** adv.

dis·re·pute /dísripyo͞ot/ n. lack of good reputation or respectability; discredit (esp. *fall into disrepute*).

dis·re·spect /dísrispékt/ n. lack of respect; discourtesy. □□ **dis·re·spect′ful** adj. **dis·re·spect′ful·ly** adv.

dis·robe /disrṓb/ v.tr. & refl. (also absol.) divest (oneself or another) of a garment; undress.

dis·rupt /disrúpt/ v.tr. **1** interrupt the flow or continuity of (a meeting, speech, etc.). **2** separate forcibly; shatter. □□ **dis·rup·tion** /-rúpshən/ n. **dis·rup′tive** adj. **dis·rup′tive·ly** adv.

diss /dis/ v.tr. sl. put (a person) down verbally; bad-mouth.

dis·sat·is·fy /disátisfí/ v.tr. (-fies, -fied) (often as **dissatisfied** adj.) make discontented; fail to satisfy. □□ **dis·sat·is·fac·tion** /-fákshən/ n.

dis·sect /disékt, dī-/ v.tr. **1** cut up, esp. a plant or animal, to examine its parts, structure, etc., or a corpse for a post mortem. **2** analyze; criticize in detail. □□ **dis·sec·tion** /-sékshən/ n.

dis·sem·ble /disémbəl/ v. **1** intr. conceal one's motives; talk or act hypocritically. **2** tr. a disguise or conceal (a feeling, intention, act, etc.). **b** simulate (dissembled grief in public).

dis·sem·i·nate /disémináyt/ v.tr. scatter about; spread (esp. ideas) widely. □□ **dis·sem·i·na·tion** /-náyshən/ n.

dis·sen·sion /disénshən/ n. disagreement.

dis·sent /disént/ • v.intr. **1** disagree. **2** differ, esp. from established or official opinion. • n. **1** difference of opinion. **2** refusal to accept established opinion; nonconformity. □□ **dis·sent′er** n. **dis·sent′ing** adj. **dis·sent′ing·ly** adv.

dis·ser·ta·tion /dísərtáyshən/ n. detailed discourse, esp. one submitted toward a degree or diploma.

dis·serv·ice /dis-sɔ́rvis/ n. ill turn; injury.

dis·si·dent /dísid'nt/ • adj. disagreeing, esp. with an established government, system, etc. • n. dissident person. □□ **dis′si·dence** n.

dis·sim·i·lar /disímilər/ adj. unlike; not similar. □□ **dis·sim·i·lar·i·ty** /-láritee/ n. (pl. -ties).

dis·si·pate /dísipayt/ v. **1 a** tr. cause (a cloud, vapor, fear, darkness, etc.) to disappear or disperse. **b** intr. disperse; scatter; disappear. **2** tr. squander (money, energy, etc.).

dis·si·pa·tion /dísipáyshən/ n. **1** intemperate, dissolute, or debauched living. **2** wasteful expenditure (dissipation of resources).

dis·so·ci·ate /disṓsheeayt, -seeayt/ v. disconnect or become disconnected; separate (dissociated her from their guilt). □ **dissociate oneself from 1** declare oneself unconnected with. **2** de-

cline to support or agree with (a proposal, etc.). □□ **dis·so·ci·a·tive** /-sheeətiv, -seeətiv/ adj.

dis·so·lute /dísəlo͞ot/ adj. lax in morals; licentious.

dis·so·lu·tion /dísəlóoshən/ n. **1** disintegration; decomposition. **2** undoing or relaxing of a bond, esp.: **a** marriage. **b** partnership. **c** alliance. **3** dismissal or dispersal of an assembly, esp. of a parliament. **4** death. **5** bringing or coming to an end; fading away; disappearance.

dis·solve /dizólv/ v. **1** tr. & intr. make or become liquid, esp. by dispersion in a liquid. **2** intr. & tr. disappear or cause to disappear gradually. **3 a** tr. dismiss (an assembly, esp. parliament). **b** intr. (of an assembly) be dissolved (cf. DISSOLUTION 3). **4** tr. annul or put an end to (a partnership, marriage, etc.). **5** intr. (of a person) become enfeebled or emotionally overcome (dissolved into tears). □□ **dis·solv′a·ble** adj.

dis·so·nant /dísonənt/ adj. **1** Mus. harsh-toned; inharmonious. **2** incongruous; clashing. □□ **dis·so·nance** /-nəns/ n.

dis·suade /diswáyd/ v.tr. discourage (a person); persuade against (was dissuaded from his belief). □□ **dis·sua·sion** /-swáyzhən/ n. **dis·sua′sive** adj.

dis·taff /distaf/ n. **1** stick holding wool or flax for spinning by hand. **2** corresponding part of a spinning wheel.

dis·tance /dístəns/ • n. **1** being far off; remoteness. **2** space or interval between two things. **3** distant point or place (came from a distance). **4** avoidance of familiarity; aloofness; reserve (there was a certain distance between them). • v.tr. (often refl.) **1** place far off (distanced the painful memory). **2** leave far behind in a race or competition. □ **go the distance 1** Boxing complete a fight without being knocked out. **2** complete, esp. a hard task; endure an ordeal. **keep one's distance** maintain one's reserve.

dis·tant /dístənt/ adj. **1 a** far away in space or time. **b** (usu. predic.) at a specified distance (three miles distant from them). **2** remote in position, time, resemblance, etc. (a distant prospect; a distant relation; a distant likeness). **3** not intimate; reserved; cool (a distant nod). **4** remote; abstracted (a distant stare). □□ **dis′tant·ly** adv.

dis·taste /dístáyst/ n. dislike; repugnance; aversion, esp. slight (a distaste for polite company). □□ **dis·taste′ful** adj. **dis·taste·ful·ly** adv. **dis·taste′ful·ness** n.

dist. atty. abbr. district attorney.

dis·tem·per /dístémpər/ n. disease of some animals, esp. dogs, causing fever, coughing, and catarrh.

dis·tend /disténd/ v. swell out by pressure from within (distended stomach). □□ **dis·ten·sion** /-ténshən/ n.

dis·till /distíl/ v. **1** tr. Chem. purify (a liquid) by vaporizing it and condensing it. **2** tr. **a** Chem. extract the essence of (a plant, etc.) usu. by heating. **b** extract the essential meaning or implications of (an idea, etc.). **3** tr. make (whiskey, etc.) by distilling raw materials. **4** tr. Chem. drive (the volatile constituent) off or out by heat. **5** tr. come as or give forth in drops; exude. **6** intr. undergo distillation. □□ **dis·til·late** /dístilit, -áyt/ n. **dis·til·la·tion** /dístiláyshən/ n. **dis·till′er** n.

dis·till·er·y /dístiləree/ n. (pl. -ies) place where alcoholic liquor is distilled.

dis·tinct /distíngkt/ adj. **1** not identical; separate; different. **2** clearly perceptible; definite. **3** unmistakable, decided (*had a distinct impression of being watched*). □□ **dis·tinct´ly** *adv.*

dis·tinc·tion /distíngkshən/ *n.* **1 a** discriminating or distinguishing. **b** difference made by distinguishing. **2** thing that differentiates. **3** honor, award, title, etc. **4** distinguished character; excellence; eminence (*a film of distinction*).

dis·tinc·tive /distíngktiv/ *adj.* distinguishing; characteristic. □□ **dis·tinc´tive·ly** *adv.* **dis·tinc´ tive·ness** *n.*

dis·tin·guish /distínggwish/ *v.* **1** *tr.* see or draw distinctions between; differentiate. **2** *tr.* be a mark or property of; characterize (*distinguished by her greed*). **3** *tr.* discern (*could distinguish two voices*). **4** *tr.* make prominent or noteworthy (*distinguished himself by winning*). **5** *intr.* make or point out a difference between. □□ **dis·tin´ guish·a·ble** *adj.*

dis·tin·guished /distínggwisht/ *adj.* **1** eminent; famous. **2** dignified, elegant. □ **Distinguished Flying Cross** US military decoration for heroism or extraordinary achievement in aerial flight. **Distinguished Service Cross** US Army decoration for extraordinary heroism in combat. **Distinguished Service Medal** US military decoration for exceptionally meritorious service in a duty of great responsibility.

dis·tort /distáwrt/ *v.tr.* **1** put out of shape. **2** misrepresent (motives, facts, statements, etc.). □□ **dis·tor´tion** *n.*

distr. *abbr.* **1** distribution. **2** distributor. **3** district.

dis·tract /distrákt/ *v.tr.* **1** draw away the attention of (a person, esp. the mind, etc.). **2** bewilder; perplex. **3** amuse, esp. to take attention from pain or worry. □□ **dis·tract´ed·ly** *adv.* **dis·tract´ ing** *adj.*

dis·trac·tion /distrákshən/ *n.* **1 a** distracting, esp. the mind. **b** thing that distracts; interruption. **2** relaxation; amusement. **3** confusion; madness. □ **to distraction** almost to a state of madness.

dis·trait /distráy/ *adj.* (*fem.* **dis·traite** /-stráyt/) not paying attention; absentminded; distraught.

dis·traught /distráwt/ *adj.* extremely agitated.

dis·tress /distrés/ • *n.* **1** severe pain, sorrow, anguish, etc. **2** poverty. • *v.tr.* **1** subject to distress; exhaust; afflict. **2** cause anxiety to; make unhappy; vex. □ **distress signal** signal from a ship, aircraft, etc., in danger. **in distress 1** suffering or in danger. **2** (of a ship, aircraft, etc.) in danger or damaged. □□ **dis·tress´ful** *adj.*

dis·tressed /distrést/ *adj.* **1** suffering from distress. **2** (of furniture, leather, etc.) aged, damaged, etc., artificially. □ **distressed area 1** region needful of food, shelter, government aid, etc., due to flood, earthquake, hurricane, etc.

dis·tri·bute /distríbyōōt/ *v.tr.* **1** give shares of; deal out. **2** spread about; scatter (*distributed the seeds evenly over the garden*). **3** divide into parts; arrange; classify. □□ **dis·tri·bu·tion** /dístribyōō-shən/ *n.*

dis·trib·u·tor /distríbyətər/ *n.* **1** person or thing that distributes, esp. from a manufacturer to retailers. **2** *Electr.* device in an internal combustion engine for passing current to spark plugs.

dis·trict /dístrikt/ • *n.* **1** (often *attrib.*) territory marked off for special administrative purposes. **2** area that has common characteristics; region (*wine-growing district*). • *v.tr.* divide into dis-

tricts. □ **district attorney** prosecuting officer of a district. **district court 1** (in several US states) court of general jurisdiction. **2** federal trial court in each federal judicial district.

dis·trust /distrúst/ • *n.* lack of trust; doubt; suspicion. • *v.tr.* have no trust in. □□ **dis·trust´ful** *adj.* **dis·trust´ful·ly** *adv.*

dis·turb /distórb/ *v.tr.* **1** break the rest, calm, or quiet of. **2 a** agitate; worry. **b** irritate. **3** move from a settled position. □□ **dis·tur´bing** *adj.*

dis·turb·ance /distárbəns/ *n.* **1** disturbing; being disturbed. **2** tumult; uproar. **3** agitation; worry.

dis·use • *n.* /disyōōs/ **1** lack of use or practice; discontinuance. **2** disused state. • *v.tr.* /disyōōz/ (esp. as **disused** *adj.*) cease to use. □ **fall into disuse** cease to be used.

ditch /dich/ • *n.* **1** long, narrow excavated channel, esp. for drainage. **2** watercourse, stream, etc. • *v.* **1** *intr.* make or repair ditches. **2** *tr.* provide with ditches; drain. **3** *tr.* *sl.* leave in the lurch; abandon. □ **last ditch** see LAST[1].

dith·er /díthər/ • *v.intr.* **1** hesitate; be indecisive. **2** *dial.* tremble; quiver. • *n.* *colloq.* **1** state of agitation or apprehension. **2** state of hesitation; indecisiveness. □□ **dith´er·er** *n.*

dit·zy /dítsee/ *adj.* (also **dit·zy; dit·si·er, dit·si·est; dit·zi·er, dit·zi·est**) *colloq.* silly; scatterbrained. □□ **ditz** *n.*

dit·to /ditō/ • *n.* (*pl.* **-tos**) **1** (in accounts, inventories, lists, etc.) aforesaid; same. **2** *colloq.* (replacing a word or phrase to avoid repetition) the same (*came in late last night and ditto the night before*). • *v.tr.* (**-toes, -toed**) repeat (another's action or words). □ **ditto marks** quotation marks representing 'ditto.'

dit·ty /ditee/ *n.* (*pl.* **-ties**) short simple song.

di·u·ret·ic /dÍəretik/ • *adj.* causing increased output of urine. • *n.* diuretic drug.

di·ur·nal /dÍ-árnəl/ *adj.* **1** of or during the day; not nocturnal. **2** daily; of each day. □□ **di·ur´ nal·ly** *adv.*

div. *abbr.* division.

di·va /déevə/ *n.* (*pl.* **di·vas** or **di·ve** /-vay/) woman opera singer; prima donna.

di·van /diván, dÍ-/ *n.* long, low, backless sofa, often used as a bed.

dive /dÍv/ • *v.* (**dived** or **dove** /dōv/) **1** *intr.* plunge head first into water. **2** *intr.* **a** *Aeron.* (of an aircraft) plunge steeply downward. **b** *Naut.* (of a submarine) submerge. **c** (of a person) plunge downward. **3** *intr.* (foll. by *into*) *colloq.* occupy oneself suddenly and enthusiastically with (a subject, meal, etc.). **4** *tr.* (foll. by *into*) plunge (a hand, etc.) into. • *n.* **1** diving; plunge. **2 a** submerging of a submarine. **b** steep descent of an aircraft. **3** sudden darting movement. **4** *colloq.* disreputable nightclub, bar, etc. □ **dive-bomb** bomb (a target) while diving in an aircraft. **diving bell** open-bottomed box or bell, supplied with air, in which a person can descend into deep water. **diving board** elevated board used for diving from. □□ **div´er** *n.*

di·verge /dÍvórj/ *v.* **1** *intr.* **a** spread out from a point (*diverging rays*). **b** take a different course. **2** *intr.* **a** depart from a set course (*diverged from his parents' wishes*). **b** differ. **3** *tr.* cause to diverge; deflect. □□ **di·ver´gence** *n.* **di·ver´gen·cy** *n.* **di·ver´gent** *adj.* **di·ver´gent·ly** *adv.*

di·vers /dívərz/ *adj.* more than one; sundry; several.

di·verse /dívərs, di-/ *adj.* unlike; varied. □□ **di·verse′ly** *adv.*

di·ver·si·fy /divə́rsifī, dī-/ *v.* (**-fies, -fied**) **1** *tr.* make diverse; vary. **2** *tr. Commerce* spread (investment) over several enterprises or products, esp. to reduce risk. **3** *intr.* esp. *Commerce* (of a firm, etc.) expand the range of products handled. □□ **di·ver·si·fi·ca·tion** /-fikáyshən/ *n.*

di·ver·sion /divə́rzhən, dī-/ *n.* **1** diverting; deviation. **2 a** diverting of attention deliberately. **b** stratagem for this purpose (*created a diversion to secure their escape*). **3** recreation or pastime. □□ **di·ver′sion·ar·y** *adj.*

di·ver·si·ty /divə́rsitee, dī-/ *n.* (*pl.* **-ties**) variety.

di·vert /divə́rt, dī-/ *v.tr.* **1 a** turn aside; deflect. **b** distract (attention). **2** (often as **diverting** *adj.*) entertain; amuse.

di·ver·tic·u·li·tis /dívertíkyəlītis/ *n. Med.* inflammation of a diverticulum.

di·ver·tic·u·lum /dívertíkyələm/ *n.* (*pl.* **di·ver·tic·u·la** /-lə/) *Anat.* blind tube forming at weak points in a cavity or passage, esp. of the alimentary tract.

di·vest /divést, dī-/ *v.tr.* **1** unclothe; strip (*divested himself of his jacket*). **2** deprive; dispossess; free; rid (*cannot divest herself of the idea*). □□ **di·vest′i·ture** *n.* **di·vest′ ment** *n.*

di·vide /divíd/ • *v.* **1** *tr.* & *intr.* separate or be separated into parts; break up; split (*the road divides; divided them into three groups*). **2** *tr.* & *intr.* distribute; deal; share. **3** *tr.* **a** cut off; separate (*divide the sheep from the goats*). **b** mark into parts (*ruler divided into inches*). **c** specify different kinds of; classify (*people can be divided into two types*). **4** *tr.* cause to disagree (*religion divided them*). **5** *Math.* **a** *tr.* find how many times (a number) contains another (*divide 20 by 4*). **b** *intr.* (of a number) be contained in (a number) without a remainder (*4 divides into 20*). • *n.* **1** dividing or boundary line. **2** watershed. □ **divided against itself** formed into factions. **the Great Divide 1** vast continental watershed between two drainage systems, esp. the Rocky Mountains of N. America. **2** boundary between life and death.

div·i·dend /dívidend/ *n.* **1** money to be divided among a number of persons, esp. that paid by a company to shareholders. **2** *Math.* number to be divided. **3** benefit (*their long training paid dividends*).

div·i·na·tion /dívináyshən/ *n.* supposed supernatural insight into the future.

di·vine /divín/ • *adj.* (**di·vin·er, di·vin·est**) **1 a** of, from, or like God or a god. **b** sacred. **2 a** more than humanly excellent. **b** *colloq.* excellent; delightful. • *v.* **1** *tr.* discover by guessing, intuition. **2** *tr.* predict. **3** *intr.* practice divination. • *n.* **1** theologian or clergyman. **2** (**the Divine**) God. □ **divine right of kings** doctrine that kings derive their authority from God. **divining rod** see DOWSE. □□ **di·vine′ ly** *adv.*

di·vin·i·ty /divínitee/ *n.* (*pl.* **-ties**) **1** being divine. **2 a** god; divine being. **b** (as **the Divinity**) God. **3** theology.

di·vis·i·ble /divízibəl/ *adj.* capable of being divided, physically or mentally. □□ **di·vis·i·bil·i·ty** /-bílitee/ *n.*

di·vi·sion /divízhən/ *n.* **1** dividing; being divided. **2** *Math.* dividing one number by another (see also *long division* (see LONG[1])). **3** disagreement or discord (*division of opinion*). **4 a** one of two or more parts into which a thing is divided. **b** point at which a thing is divided. **5** unit of administration or organization. □ **division sign** sign (÷) indicating that one quantity is to be divided by another. □□ **di·vi′sion·al** *adj.*

di·vi·sive /divísiv/ *adj.* tending to divide, esp. in opinion; causing disagreement. □□ **di·vi′sive·ly** *adv.* **di·vi′sive·ness** *n.*

di·vi·sor /divízər/ *n. Math.* number by which another is divided.

di·vorce /diváwrs/ • *n.* **1** legal dissolution of a marriage. **2** severance or separation (*divorce between thought and feeling*). • *v.* **1 a** *tr.* legally dissolve the marriage of. **b** *intr.* separate by divorce. **c** *tr.* end one's marriage with. **2** *tr.* detach; separate (*divorced from reality*).

di·vor·cé /divawrsáy/ *n.* divorced man.

di·vor·cée /divawrsáy/ *n.* divorced woman.

div·ot /dívət/ *n.* piece of turf cut out by a golf stroke.

di·vulge /divúlj, dī-/ *v.tr.* disclose; reveal (a secret, etc.). □□ **di·vul′gence** *n.*

div·vy /dívee/ *v.tr. colloq.* (**-vies, -vied**) share out; divide up.

Dix·ie /díksee/ *n.* southern states of the US.

Dix·ie·land /díkseeland/ *n.* **1** = DIXIE. **2** jazz with a strong, two-beat rhythm and collective improvisation.

diz·zy /dízee/ • *adj.* (**diz·zi·er, diz·zi·est**) **1 a** giddy. **b** confused. **2** causing giddiness (*dizzy heights; dizzy speed*). • *v.tr.* **1** make dizzy. **2** bewilder. □□ **diz′zi·ly** *adv.* **diz′zi·ness** *n.*

DJ *abbr.* **1** disk jockey. **2** district judge.

djel·la·ba /jəláaba/ *n.* (also **djel·la′bah, jel·la′ba**) loose, hooded, usu. woolen cloak worn or as worn by Arab men.

DM *abbr.* (also **D-mark**) deutsche mark.

D.M.D. *abbr.* doctor of dental medicine.

DNA *abbr.* deoxyribonucleic acid, the material that carries genetic information in chromosomes. □ **DNA fingerprinting** identification, esp. in a legal case, by analysis of DNA from body tissue, hair, blood, etc.

do[1] /doo/ • *v.* (*3rd sing. present* **does** /duz/; *past* **did** /did/; *past part.* **done** /dun/) **1** *tr.* perform; carry out; complete (work, etc.) (*did his homework; there's a lot to do*). **2** *tr.* **a** produce; make (*I did a translation*). **b** provide (*do you do lunches?*). **3** *tr.* bestow; grant (*do me a favor*). **4** *intr.* act; behave; proceed (*do as I do*). **5** *tr.* work at; study (*what does your father do?*). **6 a** *intr.* be suitable or acceptable; suffice (*this dress won't do for a wedding*). **b** *tr.* satisfy; be suitable for (*that hotel will do me nicely*). **7** *tr.* deal with; put in order (*the barber will do you next*). **8** *intr.* a fare (*the patients were doing well*). **b** perform (*could do better*). **9** *tr.* **a** solve; work out (*we did the puzzle*). **b** (prec. by *can* or *be able to*) be competent at (*can you do cartwheels?*). **10** *tr.* **a** traverse (a certain distance) (*we did fifty miles today*). **b** travel at a specified speed (*he overtook us doing about eighty*). **11** *tr. colloq.* act or behave like (*did a Houdini*). **12** *intr.* **a** *colloq.* finish (*I'm done in the bathroom*). **b** (as **done** *adj.*) be over (*the day is done*). **13** *tr.* produce or give a performance of (*we've never done Pygmalion*). **14** *tr. colloq.* visit;

see the sights of (*we did all the art galleries*). **15** *tr. colloq.* **a** (often as **done** *adj.*; often foll. by *in*) exhaust; tire out (*the climb has completely done me in*). **b** beat up; defeat; kill. **c** ruin (*now you've done it*). **16** *tr. sl.* undergo (a specified term of imprisonment) (*he did two years for fraud*). **17** *tr. sl.* take (a drug). • *v.aux.* **1** (except with *be, can, may, ought, shall, will*) in questions and negative statements or commands (*do you understand?; I don't smoke; don't be silly*). **2** *ellipt.* or in place of verb (*you know her better than I do*). **3** forming emphasis (*I do want to; they did go*). • *n.* (*pl.* **dos** or **do's**) *colloq.* elaborate event, party, or operation. □ **do away with** *colloq.* **1** abolish. **2** kill. **do in 1** *sl.* **a** kill. **b** ruin; do injury to. **2** *colloq.* exhaust; tire out. **do-it-yourself** *adj.* (of work, esp. building, painting, decorating, etc.) done or to be done by an amateur at home. • *n.* such work. **do over** *colloq.* redecorate, refurbish. **dos and don'ts** rules of behavior. **do up 1** fasten; secure. **2** *colloq.* **a** refurbish; renovate. **b** adorn; dress up. **do with** (prec. by *could*) would be glad to have; would profit by (*I could do with a rest*). **do without** manage without; forgo (also *absol.*: *we shall just have to do without*). □□ **do'a·ble** *adj.*

do² /dō/ *n.* (also **doh**) *Mus.* (in tonic sol-fa) the first and eighth notes of a major scale.

DOA *abbr.* dead on arrival (at a hospital, etc.).

DOB *abbr.* date of birth.

Do·ber·man /dóbərmən/ *n.* (in full **Do'ber·man pin·scher** /pínshər/) large dog of a smooth-coated German breed.

doc /dok/ *n. colloq.* doctor.

do·cent /dósənt/ *n.* well-informed guide, as in a museum.

doc·ile /dósəl/ *adj.* submissive, easily managed. □□ **doc'ile·ly** *adv.* **do·cil·i·ty** /-sílitee/ *n.*

dock¹ /dok/ • *n.* **1** waterway for loading, unloading, and repair of ships. **2** (in *pl.*) docks with wharves and offices; dockyard. **3** ship's berth, wharf. **4** = **dry dock.** • *v.* **1** *tr. & intr.* bring or come into a dock. **2 a** *tr.* join (spacecraft) together in space. **b** *intr.* (of spacecraft) be joined.

dock² /dok/ *n.* enclosure in a criminal court for the accused. □ **in the dock** on trial.

dock³ /dok/ • *v.tr.* **1** cut short (an animal's tail). **2** deduct (a part) from wages, supplies, etc. • *n.* solid, bony part of an animal's tail.

dock·et /dókit/ *n.* **1** schedule of cases in a court of law. **2** list of things to be done.

dock·hand /dókhand/ *n.* longshoreman.

dock·side /dóksīd/ *n.* area adjacent to a dock.

dock·yard /dókyaard/ *n.* area with docks and equipment for building and repairing ships.

doc·tor /dóktər/ • *n.* **1 a** qualified practitioner of medicine; physician. **b** qualified dentist or veterinarian. **2** person who holds a doctorate. • *v. colloq.* **1 a** *tr.* treat medically. **b** *intr.* (esp. as **doctoring** *n.*) practice as a physician. **2** *tr.* fix up (machinery, etc.); mend. **3** *tr.* adulterate. **4** *tr.* tamper with; falsify. □ **Doctor of Philosophy** doctorate in a discipline other than education, law, medicine, or sometimes theology.

doc·tor·al /dóktərəl/ *adj.* of or for a degree of doctor.

doc·tor·ate /dóktərət/ *n.* highest university degree, often honorary.

doc·tri·naire /dóktrináir/ • *adj.* applying theory or doctrine dogmatically; theoretical and impractical. • *n.* pedantic theorist.

doc·trine /dóktrin/ *n.* **1** what is taught; body of instruction. **2 a** religious or political, etc., belief. **b** such principles; dogma. □□ **doc'tri·nal** *adj.*

doc·u·dra·ma /dókyōōdraamə, -dramə/ *n.* television movie based on real events.

doc·u·ment • *n.* /dókyəmənt/ written evidence of events, agreement, ownership, etc. • *v.tr.* /dókyəmənt/ **1** prove by or support with documents. **2** record in a document.

doc·u·men·ta·ry /dókyəméntəree/ • *adj.* **1** consisting of documents (*documentary evidence*). **2** providing a factual record or report. • *n.* (*pl.* **-ries**) documentary film, etc.

doc·u·men·ta·tion /dókyəmentáyshən/ *n.* **1** accumulation, classification, and dissemination of information. **2** material collected or disseminated. **3** collection of documents relating to a process or event, as instructions accompanying a computer program.

DOD *abbr.* Department of Defense.

dod·der /dódər/ *v.intr.* tremble or totter, esp. from age. □□ **dod'der·ing** *adj.*

do·dec·a·gon /dōdékəgon/ *n.* plane figure with twelve sides.

do·dec·a·he·dron /dōdekəhe'edrən/ *n.* solid figure with twelve faces. □□ **do·dec·a·he'dral** *adj.*

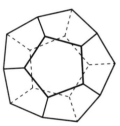

DODECAHEDRON

dodge /doj/ • *v.* **1** *intr.* move quickly to elude a pursuer, blow, etc. (*dodged behind the chair*). **2** *tr.* evade by cunning or trickery. • *n.* **1** quick movement to avoid something. **2** clever trick or expedient. □□ **dodg'er** *n.*

do·do /dódō/ *n.* (*pl.* **-does** or **-dos**) **1** extinct flightless bird. **2** old-fashioned, stupid, or inactive person. □ **as dead as a dodo 1** completely or unmistakably dead. **2** entirely obsolete.

DOE *abbr.* Department of Energy.

doe /dō/ *n.* female deer, reindeer, hare, or rabbit.

do·er /dóoər/ *n.* **1** person who does something. **2** one who acts rather than merely talking or thinking.

does *3rd sing. present* of **DO¹**.

does·n't /dúzənt/ *contr.* does not.

doff /dawf, dof/ *v.tr. literary* take off (one's hat, clothing).

dog /dawg, dog/ • *n.* **1** four-legged, flesh-eating animal of many breeds domesticated and wild, kept as pets or for work or sport. **2 a** *colloq.* despicable person. **b** *colloq.* person or fellow of a specified kind (*lucky dog*). **c** *sl. derog.* unattractive or slovenly woman. **3** mechanical device for gripping. • *v.tr.* (**dogged, dog·ging**) **1** follow closely and persistently; pursue; track. **2** *Mech.* grip with a dog. □ **dog days** hottest period of the year. **dog-eared** (of a book, etc.) with the corners worn or battered with use. **dog-eat-dog** *colloq.* ruthlessly competitive. **dog paddle** elementary swimming stroke like that of a dog. **Dog Star** chief star of the constellation Canis Major or Minor, esp. Sirius. **dog tag 1** usu. metal plate attached to a dog's collar, giving owner's address, etc. **2** identification tag, esp. as worn by a member of the military. **go to the dogs** *sl.* deteriorate, be ruined. **hair of the dog** further alcoholic drink to cure hangover from that drink. **put on the dog** *colloq.* behave pretentiously.

dog·catch·er /dáwgkachər, dóg-/ *n.* official who rounds up and impounds stray dogs in a community.

dog·fight /dáwgfīt, dóg-/ *n.* **1** close combat between fighter aircraft. **2** uproar; rough fight.

dog·fish /dáwgfish, dóg-/ *n.* (*pl.* same or **dog·fish·es**) kind of small shark.

dog·ged /dáwgid, dóg-/ *adj.* tenacious; grimly persistent. □□ **dog′ged·ly** *adv.* **dog′ged·ness** *n.*

dog·ger·el /dáwgərəl, dóg-/ *n.* poor or trivial verse.

dog·gy /dáwgee, dógee/ • *adj.* of or like a dog. • *n.* (also **dog·gie**) (*pl.* **-gies**) pet name for a dog. □ **doggy** (or **doggie**) **bag** bag for putting leftovers in to take home. □□ **dog′gi·ness** *n.*

dog·house /dáwghows, dóg-/ *n.* dog's shelter. □ **in the doghouse** *sl.* in disgrace or disfavor.

do·gie /dógee/ *n.* motherless or neglected calf.

dog·ma /dáwgmə, dóg-/ *n.* **1** principle, tenet, or creed, esp. of a church or political party. **2** arrogant declaration of opinion.

dog·mat·ic /dawgmátik, dog-/ *adj.* **1 a** (of a person) asserting or imposing opinions; arrogant. **b** intolerantly authoritative. **2** of or in the nature of dogma; doctrinal. □□ **dog·mat′i·cal·ly** *adv.*

dog·ma·tism /dáwgmətizəm, dóg-/ *n.* tendency to be dogmatic. □□ **dog′ma·tist** *n.*

do-good·er /doõogoõodər/ *n.* well-meaning but unrealistic philanthropist or reformer.

dog·wood /dáwgwood, dóg-/ *n.* type of flowering tree or shrub.

doi·ly /dóylee/ *n.* (also **doy·ley**) (*pl.* **-lies** or **-leys**) small ornamental mat of paper, lace, etc., on a plate for cakes, etc.

do·ing /doõing/ *n.* **1** (usu. in *pl.*) action; performance of a deed (*it was my doing*). **2** activity; effort (*it takes a lot of doing*).

Dol·by /dólbee/ *n. propr.* electronic noise-reduction system used esp. in tape recording to reduce hiss.

dol·drums /dóldrəmz/ *n.pl.* (usu. prec. by *the*) **1** low spirits. **2** period of inactivity. **3** equatorial ocean region of calms, sudden storms, and light winds.

dole /dōl/ • *n.* **1** (usu. prec. by *the*) unemployment benefits. **2** charitable distribution. • *v.tr.* (usu. foll. by *out*) deal out sparingly. □ **on the dole** *colloq.* receiving welfare, etc., payments from the government.

dole·ful /dólfool/ *adj.* **1** mournful; sad. **2** dreary; dismal. □□ **dole′ful·ly** *adv.* **dole′ful·ness** *n.*

doll /dol/ • *n.* **1** small model of a human figure, as a child's toy. **2** *sl.* young woman, esp. an attractive one. • *v.* (foll. by *up*; often *refl.*) dress up smartly.

dol·lar /dólər/ *n.* chief monetary unit in the US, Canada, and Australia, etc. □ **dollar sign** sign ($) used to indicate currency in dollars.

dollar from early Flemish or Low German *daler*, from German *Taler*, formerly spelled *Thaler*, short for *Joachimsthaler* ('Joachim's valley'), now Jáchymov in the Czech Republic. Originally denoting a German *thaler* coin, the term was later applied to a Spanish coin used in the Spanish American colonies. The Spanish coin was also widely used in the British North American colonies at the time of the Revolutionary War, and its name was adopted as the name of the US monetary unit in the late 18th century.

doll·house /dólhows/ *n.* miniature toy house for dolls.

dol·lop /dóləp/ • *n.* shapeless lump of food, etc. • *v.tr.* (usu. foll. by *out*) serve in large, shapeless quantities.

dol·ly /dólee/ • *n.* (*pl.* **-lies**) **1** child's name for a doll. **2** movable platform for a movie camera. **3** small cart for freight. • *v.* (**-lies, -lied**) *intr.* move a motion-picture or television camera about while shooting.

dol·men /dólmən/ *n.* megalithic tomb with a large, flat stone laid on upright ones.

do·lo·mite /dóləmīt, dól-/ *n.* mineral or rock of calcium magnesium carbonate.

do·lor /dólər/ *n. literary* sorrow; distress. □□ **dol′or·ous** *adj.* **dol′or·ous·ly** *adv.*

dol·phin /dólfin/ *n.* porpoiselike sea mammal having a slender, beaklike snout.

dolt /dōlt/ *n.* stupid person. □□ **dolt′ish** *adj.*

-dom /dəm/ *suffix* forming nouns denoting: **1** state or condition (*freedom*). **2** rank or status (*earldom*). **3** domain (*kingdom*). **4** class of people (or their attitudes, etc.) (*officialdom*).

do·main /dōmáyn/ *n.* **1** area under one rule; realm. **2** sphere of control or influence.

dome /dōm/ • *n.* **1** rounded vault as a roof; large cupola. **2** natural vault or canopy (of the sky, trees, etc.). **3** *Geol.* dome-shaped structure. **4** *sl.* the head. • *v.tr.* (usu. as **domed** *adj.*) cover with or shape as a dome. □□ **dome′like** *adj.*

do·mes·tic /dəméstik/ • *adj.* **1** of the home, household, or family affairs. **2 a** of one's own country. **b** homegrown or homemade. **3** (of an animal) tamed. • *n.* household servant. □□ **do·mes′ti·cal·ly** *adv.*

do·mes·ti·cate /dəméstikayt/ *v.tr.* **1** tame (an animal) to live with humans. **2** accustom to home life and management. □□ **do·mes·ti·ca·tion** /-káyshən/ *n.*

do·mes·tic·i·ty /dóməstísitee/ *n.* **1** being domestic. **2** domestic or home life.

dom·i·cile /dómisīl, -sil, dó-/ (also **dom·i·cil** /-sil/) *n.* dwelling place; one's home; residence. • *v.tr.* (usu. as **domiciled** *adj.*) establish or settle in a place.

dom·i·nant /dóminənt/ • *adj.* dominating; prevailing; most influential. • *n. Mus.* fifth note of the diatonic scale of any key. □□ **dom′i·nance** *n.* **dom′i·nant·ly** *adv.*

dom·i·nate /dóminayt/ *v.* **1** *tr.* & *intr.* command; control (*fear dominated them; dominates over his friends*). **2** *tr.* (of a person, sound, feature of a scene, etc.) be the most influential or conspicuous. **3** *tr.* & *intr.* (of a building, etc.) have a commanding position over; overlook. □□ **dom·i·na′tion** *n.* **dom′i·na·tor** *n.*

dom·i·neer /dómineér/ *v.intr.* (often as **domineering** *adj.*) behave in an arrogant and overbearing way. □□ **dom·i·neer′ing·ly** *adv.*

do·min·ion /dəmínyən/ *n.* **1** sovereignty; control. **2** territory of a sovereign or government; domain.

dom·i·no /dóminō/ *n.* (*pl.* **-noes** or **-nos**) **1 a** small oblong piece marked with 0–6 dots in each half. **b** (in *pl.*, usu. treated as *sing.*) game played with these. **2** mask for the eyes. □ **domino theory** theory that one event will cause similar events, like a row of falling dominoes.

don[1] /don/ *n.* **1** university teacher, esp. a senior member of a college at Oxford or Cambridge. **2** (**Don**) Spanish title of respect.

don[2] /don/ *v.tr.* (**donned, don·ning**) put on (clothing).

do·nate /dónayt, dōnáyt/ *v.tr.* give (money, etc.), esp. voluntarily to charity. □□ **do′na·tor** *n.*

do·na·tion /dōnáyshən/ *n.* **1** donating. **2** thing, esp. money, donated.

done /dun/ *past part.* of DO[1]. *adj.* **1** completed. **2** cooked. **3** *colloq.* socially acceptable (*the done thing*). **4** (often with *in, up*) *colloq.* tired out. □ **be done with** be finished with. **done for** *colloq.* in serious trouble.

Don Juan /don waán, hwaán, jŏoən/ *n.* seducer of women.

don·key /dóngkee, dúng-, dáwng-/ *n.* (*pl.* **-keys**) **1** domestic ass. **2** *colloq.* stupid or foolish person.

don·ny·brook /dóneebrŏok/ *n.* uproar; wild fight.

do·nor /dónər/ *n.* **1** person who gives or donates something (e.g., to a charity). **2** one who provides blood for a transfusion, semen for insemination, or an organ or tissue for transplantation.

don't /dōnt/ *contr.* do not. *n.* prohibition (*dos and don'ts*).
¶ The use of **don't** with *he, she,* or *it* is now generally regarded as uneducated, although it was once standard and is now often employed informally for effect, e.g., "It don't mean a thing."

do·nut var. of DOUGHNUT.

doo·dad /dŏodad/ *n.* **1** fancy article or ornament. **2** gadget.

doo·dle /dŏod'l/ *v.intr.* scribble or draw, esp. absentmindedly. *n.* scrawl or drawing made. □□ **doo′dler** *n.*

doom /dŏom/ *n.* **1 a** grim fate or destiny. **b** death or ruin. **2** condemnation; judgment or sentence. *v.tr.* **1** (usu. foll. by *to*) condemn or destine (*city doomed to destruction*). **2** (esp. as **doomed** *adj.*) consign to misfortune or destruction.

dooms·day /dŏomzday/ *n.* day of the Last Judgment.

door /dawr/ *n.* **1 a** movable barrier for closing and opening an entrance to a building, room, cupboard, etc. **b** this as representing a house, etc. (*lives two doors away*). **2 a** entrance or exit; doorway. **b** means of access. □ **door prize** prize awarded usu. by lottery at a dance, charity event, etc. **door-to-door** (of selling, etc.) done at each house in turn. □□ **doored** *adj.* (also in *comb.*).

door·bell /dáwrbel/ *n.* bell in a house, etc., rung by visitors outside to signal their arrival.

door·knob /dáwrnob/ *n.* knob turned to open a door.

door·man /dáwrman, -mən/ *n.* (*pl.* **-men**) person on duty at the door to a large building.

door·mat /dáwrmat/ *n.* **1** mat at an entrance for wiping shoes. **2** submissive person.

door·step /dáwrstep/ *n.* step leading up to the outer door of a house, etc. □ **on one's** (or **the**) **doorstep** very close.

door·stop /dáwrstop/ *n.* device for keeping a door open or to prevent it from striking a wall, etc., when opened.

door·way /dáwrway/ *n.* opening filled by a door.

doo·zy /dŏozee/ *n.* (*pl.* **doo·zies**) (also **doo′zie**) *colloq.* one that is outstanding of its kind (*a mistake that was a doozy*).

dope /dōp/ *n.* **1** varnish. **2** thick liquid used as a lubricant, etc. **3** substance added to gasoline, etc., to increase its effectiveness. **4 a** *sl.* narcotic; stupefying drug. **b** drug, etc., given to a horse, athlete, etc., to affect performance. **5** *sl.* stupid person. **6** *sl.* information. *v.* **1** *tr.* administer dope to; drug. **2** *tr.* smear; daub; apply dope to. **3** *intr.* take addictive drugs.

dop·e·y /dópee/ *adj.* (also **dop′y**) (**dop·i·er, dop·i·est**) *colloq.* **1 a** half asleep. **b** stupefied by or as if by a drug. **2** stupid; silly. □□ **dop′i·ly** *adv.* **dop′i·ness** *n.*

Dop·pler ra′dar /dóplər/ *n.* radar system to determine velocity and direction, as of storm clouds, etc.

Dor·ic /dáwrik, dór-/ *adj. Archit.* of the oldest, sturdiest, and simplest of the Greek architectural styles. *n. Archit.* Doric order or style.

dork /dawrk/ *n. sl.* dull, slow-witted, or oafish person. □□ **dork′y** *adj.*

dor·mant /dáwrmənt/ *adj.* **1** inactive; sleeping. **2 a** (of a volcano, etc.) temporarily inactive. **b** (of faculties, etc.) in abeyance. **3** (of plants) alive but not growing. □□ **dor′man·cy** *n.*

dor·mer /dáwrmər/ *n.* (in full **dor′mer win′dow**) projecting upright window in a sloping roof.

dormers

DORMER

dor·mi·to·ry /dáwrmitáwree/ *n.* (*pl.* **-ries**) group sleeping area or building, esp. in a school or institution.

dor·mouse /dáwrmows/ *n.* (*pl.* **dor·mice**) small, mouselike hibernating rodent having a long, bushy tail.

dor·sal /dáwrsəl/ *adj. Anat., Zool., & Bot.* of, on, or near the back (cf. VENTRAL). □□ **dor′sal·ly** *adv.*

do·ry /dáwree/ *n.* (*pl.* **-ries**) flat-bottomed fishing boat with high bow and flaring sides.

DOS /dos, daws/ *n. Computing* software operating system for personal computers.

dos·age /dósij/ *n.* **1** giving of a dose. **2** size of a dose.

dose /dōs/ • *n.* **1** single portion of medicine. **2** quantity of something experienced (e.g., work, praise, punishment, etc.). **3** amount of radiation received. **4** *sl.* venereal infection. • *v.tr.* **1** treat (a person or animal) with doses of medicine. **2** give a dose or doses to.

dos·si·er /dósee-ay, dáw-/ *n.* file of specific information about a person, event, or subject.

DOT *abbr.* Department of Transportation.

dot /dot/ • *n.* **1 a** small spot, speck, or mark. **b** such a mark as part of an *i* or *j*, as a diacritical mark, as one of a series of marks to signify omission, or as a period. **c** decimal point. **2** shorter signal of the two in Morse code (cf. DASH *n.* 8). **3** tiny or apparently tiny object (*a dot on the horizon*). • *v.tr.* (**dot·ted**, **dot·ting**) **1 a** mark with a dot or dots. **b** place a dot over (a letter). **2** partly cover as with dots (*an ocean dotted with ships*). □ **dot the i's and cross the t's** *colloq.* **1** be minutely accurate. **2** add final touches to a task, exercise, etc. **dot-matrix printer** *Computing* printer with characters formed from dots. **dotted line** line of dots on a document, esp. to show a place for a signature. **on the dot** exactly on time.

dot·age /dótij/ *n.* feeble-minded senility (*in his dotage*).

do·tard /dótərd/ *n.* senile person.

dote /dōt/ *v.intr.* be excessively fond of. □□ **dot'ing·ly** *adv.*

dou·ble /dúbəl/ • *adj.* **1** consisting of two parts, things, levels, etc. **2** twice as much or many. **3** twice the usual size, quantity, strength, etc. **4** designed for two people (*double bed*). • *adv.* **1** at or to twice the amount, etc. **2** two together. • *n.* **1** double quantity. **2** counterpart; person who looks exactly like another. **3** (*pl.*) game between two pairs of players. • *v.* **1** *tr. & intr.* make or become double; multiply by two. **2** *tr.* amount to twice as much as. **3 a** *tr.* fold or bend (paper, cloth, etc.) over on itself. **b** *intr.* become folded. **4** *intr.* play a twofold role. □ **double agent** one who spies simultaneously for two rival countries, etc. **double back** turn back in the opposite direction. **double-blind** (of a test or experiment) in which neither the tester nor the subject has knowledge of identities, etc., that might lead to bias. **double-cross** deceive or betray (a person one is supposedly helping). **double cross** act of double-crossing. **double-dealer** deceiver. **double-dealing** *n.* deceit, esp. in business. • *adj.* deceitful; practicing deceit. **double-decker** *colloq.* anything consisting of two layers. **double Dutch** synchronized jump-rope game using two ropes. **double eagle** *Golf* score of three strokes under par at any hole. **double play** *Baseball* putting out two runners. **double standard** rule or principle applied more strictly to some people than to others (or to oneself). **double take** delayed reaction to a situation, etc., immediately after one's first reaction. **double-talk** verbal expression that is (usu. deliberately) ambiguous or misleading. **double up 1** be overcome with pain or laughter. **2** share or assign to a room, quarters, etc., with another or others. **on the double** running; hurrying. □□ **dou'bler** *n.* **dou'bly** *adv.*

dou·ble en·ten·dre /dúbəl aantaándrə, dṓblaan taáNdrə/ *n.* **1** word or phrase open to two interpretations, one usu. risqué or indecent. **2** humor using such.

dou·blet /dúblit/ *n.* **1** one of a pair of similar things. **2** *hist.* man's short, close-fitting jacket.

dou·bloon /dublṓn/ *n. hist.* Spanish gold coin.

doubt /dowt/ • *n.* **1** uncertainty; undecided state of mind. **2** inclination to disbelieve. **3** uncertain state of things. **4** lack of full proof. • *v.* **1** *tr.* feel uncertain or undecided about. **2** *tr.* hesitate to believe or trust. **3** *intr.* feel uncertain or undecided. **4** *tr.* call in question. □ **doubting Thomas** skeptical person (after John 20:24–29). **no doubt** certainly; probably. **without doubt** (or **a doubt**) certainly. □□ **doub'ter** *n.* **doubt'ing·ly** *adv.*

doubt·ful /dówtfŏŏl/ *adj.* **1** feeling doubt. **2** causing doubt. **3** unreliable. □□ **doubt'ful·ly** *adv.*

doubt·less /dówtlis/ *adv.* **1** certainly; no doubt. **2** probably. □□ **doubt'less·ly** *adv.*

douche /dŏŏsh/ • *n.* **1** jet of liquid applied to a body part for cleansing or medicinal purposes. **2** device for producing this. • *v.* **1** *tr.* treat with a douche. **2** *intr.* use a douche.

dough /dō/ *n.* **1** thick mixture of flour, etc., and liquid for baking. **2** *sl.* money. □□ **dough'y** *adj.*

dough·boy /dóboy/ *n.* United States infantryman, esp. in World War I.

dough·nut /dónut/ *n.* (also **do'nut**) small fried cake of sweetened dough, usu. ring-shaped.

dough·ty /dówtee/ *adj.* (**dough·ti·er**, **dough·ti·est**) *literary* valiant; stouthearted. □□ **dough'ti·ly** *adv.* **dough'ti·ness** *n.*

Doug·las fir /dúgləs/ *n.* large N. American conifer.

dour /dŏŏr, dowr/ *adj.* severe, stern, or sullenly obstinate in manner or appearance. □□ **dour'ly** *adv.* **dour'ness** *n.*

douse /dows/ *v.tr.* **1 a** throw water over. **b** plunge into water. **2** extinguish (a light).

dove[1] /duv/ *n.* **1** bird with short legs, small head, and large breast. **2** gentle person; advocate of peace.

dove[2] *past* and *past part.* of DIVE.

dove·tail /dúvtayl/ • *n.* mortise and tenon joint shaped like a dove's spread tail. • *v.* **1** *tr.* join

DOVETAIL

by means of a dovetail. **2** *tr. & intr.* fit readily together; combine neatly.

dow·a·ger /dówəjər/ *n.* **1** widow with a title or property from her late husband. **2** dignified elderly woman.

dow·dy /dówdee/ *adj.* (**dow·di·er, dow·di·est**) **1** (of clothes) unattractively dull. **2** dressed dowdily. □□ **dow′di·ly** *adv.* **dow′di·ness** *n.*

dow·el /dówəl/ • *n.* headless peg for holding together components, hanging clothes on, etc. • *v.tr.* fasten with a dowel.

dow·er /dówər/ *n.* **1** widow's share for life of her husband's estate. **2** dowry.

down[1] /down/ • *adv.* (*superl.* **down·most**) **1** into or toward a lower place, esp. to the ground. **2** in a lower place or position (*blinds were down*). **3** to or in a place regarded as lower, esp. southward. **4** in or into a low or weaker position, mood, or condition (*many down with colds*). **5** (of a computer system) not operating. **6** from an earlier to a later time (*customs handed down*). **7** to a finer or thinner consistency or a smaller amount or size. **8** lower in price or value. **9** into a more settled state. **10** in or into recorded or listed form (*copy it down*). **11** (of part of a larger whole) paid. • *prep.* **1** downward along, through, or into. **2** from top to bottom of. **3** along (*cut down the middle*). • *adj.* (*superl.* **down·most**) **1** directed downward. **2** *colloq.* unhappy; depressed. • *v.tr.* **1** knock or bring down. **2** swallow. • *n.* **1** act of putting down. **2** reverse of fortune. **3** *Football* one of a series of plays. □ **be down on** *colloq.* disapprove. **down-and-out** destitute. **down-at-the-heels** shabby; slovenly. **down in the mouth** *colloq.* looking unhappy. **down on one's luck** *colloq.* dispirited by misfortune. **down payment** partial payment at time of purchase. **down-to-earth** practical; realistic. **Down Under** Australia. **down with** *int.* expressing rejection.

down[2] /down/ *n.* **1** fine, soft feathers or hair. **2** fluffy substance. □□ **down′y** *adj.* (**down·i·er, down·i·est**)

down[3] /down/ *n.* open rolling land.

down·beat /dównbeet/ • *n. Mus.* accented beat, usu. the first of the bar. • *adj.* pessimistic; gloomy.

down·cast /dównkast/ *adj.* **1** (of eyes) looking downward. **2** dejected.

down·er /dównər/ *n. sl.* **1** depressant or tranquilizing drug. **2** depressing person or experience; failure.

down·fall /dównfawl/ *n.* **1** fall from prosperity or power. **2** cause of this.

down·grade • *v.tr.* /dówngráyd/ **1** reduce in rank or status. **2** speak disparagingly of. • *n.* /dówngrayd/ **1** descending slope. **2** deterioration.

down·heart·ed /dównháartid/ *adj.* dejected; in low spirits. □□ **down′heart′ed·ly** *adv.*

down·hill • *adv.* /dównhíl/ toward the bottom of an incline. • *adj.* /dównhil/ sloping down; descending. □ **go downhill** *colloq.* decline; deteriorate (in health, state of repair, moral state, etc.).

down·load /dównlód/ *v.tr. Computing* transfer (data) from one storage device or system to another.

down·play /dównpláy/ *v.tr.* minimize the importance of.

down·pour /dównpawr/ *n.* heavy fall of rain.

down·right /dównrīt/ • *adj.* **1** plain; straight-

forward; blunt. **2** utter; complete (*a downright lie*). • *adv.* thoroughly.

down·shift /dównshift/ *v.* shift (a vehicle) into a lower gear.

down·size /dównsīz/ *v.tr.* (**down·sized, down·siz·ing**) (esp. of personnel) reduce in size.

Down's syn·drome /downz/ *n. Med.* (also **Down′ syn′drome**) congenital disorder with mental retardation and physical abnormalities.

down·stage /dównstayj/ *Theatr.* • *n.* frontmost portion of the stage. • *adj. & adv.* at or to the front of the stage.

down·stairs • *adv.* /dównstáirz/ **1** down a flight of stairs. **2** to or on a lower floor. • *adj.* /dównstairz/ situated downstairs. • *n.* /dównstáirz/ a lower floor.

down·state /dównstáyt/ • *adj.* of or in a southern part of a state. • *n.* downstate area. • *adv.* in a downstate area.

down·stream /dównstreém/ • *adv.* in the direction of the flow of a stream, etc. • *adj.* moving downstream.

down·time /dówntīm/ *n.* time during which a machine, esp. a computer, is out of action or unavailable for use.

down·town /dówntówn/ • *adj.* of esp. the central part of a town or city. • *n.* downtown area. • *adv.* in or into a downtown area.

down·trod·den /dówntród′n/ *adj.* oppressed; badly treated.

down·turn /dówntərn/ *n.* decline, esp. economic.

down·ward /dównwərd/ • *adv.* (also **down′ wards**) toward what is lower, inferior, etc. • *adj.* moving, extending, or leading downward. □□ **down′ward·ly** *adv.*

down·wind /dównwínd/ *adj. & adv.* in the direction in which the wind is blowing.

dow·ry /dówree/ *n.* (*pl.* **-ries**) property or money brought by a bride to her husband.

dowse /dowz/ *v.intr.* search for underground water, etc., using a rod that dips when over the right spot. □□ **dows′er** *n.*

dox·ol·o·gy /doksóləjee/ *n.* (*pl.* **-gies**) liturgical formula of praise to God. □□ **dox·o·log·i·cal** /-səlójikəl/ *adj.*

doz. *abbr.* dozen.

doze /dōz/ • *v.intr.* sleep lightly; be half asleep. • *n.* short, light sleep. □ **doze off** fall lightly asleep. □□ **doz′er** *n.*

doz·en /dúzən/ *n.* **1** (*pl.* **doz′en**) twelve, regarded collectively (*two dozen eggs*). **2** set of twelve. **3** (in *pl.*) *colloq.* very many (*made dozens of mistakes*). □ **by the dozen** in large quantities.

DP *abbr.* **1** data processing. **2** displaced person.

DPT *abbr.* (vaccination for) diphtheria, pertussis, and tetanus.

Dr. *abbr.* **1** Doctor. **2** Drive. **3** debtor.

drab /drab/ *adj.* (**drab·ber, drab·best**) **1** dull; uninteresting. **2** of a dull brownish color. □□ **drab′ly** *adv.* **drab′ness** *n.*

drach·ma /drákmə/ *n.* (*pl.* **drach·mas** or **drach·mai** /-mī/ or **drach·mae** /-mee/) **1** chief monetary unit of Greece. **2** silver coin of ancient Greece.

dra·co·ni·an /drəkóneeən, dray-/ *adj.* (also **dra·con·ic** /-kónik/) very harsh or severe (esp. of laws and their application).

draft /draft/ • *n.* **1** preliminary written version

of a speech, document, etc. **2 a** written order for payment by a bank. **b** drawing of money by means of this. **3** military conscription. **4** current of air. **5** pulling; traction. **6** depth of water needed to float a ship. **7** drawing of liquor from a cask, etc. **8 a** single act of drinking. **b** amount thus drunk. **c** a dose of liquid medicine. **9 a** drawing in of a fishing net. **b** the fish taken at one drawing. • *v.tr.* **1** prepare a draft of (a document, etc.). **2** select for a special duty or purpose. **3** conscript for military service. □ **draft horse** horse used for pulling heavy loads. □□ **draft·ee** /-tée/ *n.* **draft′er** *n.*

drafts·man /dráftsmən/ *n.* (*pl.* **-men**) person who makes drawings, plans, or sketches. □□ **drafts′man·ship** *n.*

draft·y /dráftee/ *adj.* (**-i·er, -i·est**) (of a room, etc.) letting in sharp currents of air. □□ **draft′i·ly** *adv.* **draft′i·ness** *n.*

drag /drag/ • *v.* (**dragged, drag·ging**) **1** *tr.* pull along with effort. **2 a** *tr.* allow to trail along the ground. **b** *intr.* trail along the ground. **c** *intr.* (of time, etc.) pass slowly or tediously. **3 a** *intr.* use a grapnel or drag (to find a drowned person or lost object). **b** *tr.* search the bottom of (a river, etc.) with grapnels, nets, or drags. **4** *tr. colloq.* take (an unwilling person to a place, etc.). **5** *intr.* draw on (a cigarette, etc.). • *n.* **1** obstruction to progress. **2** *colloq.* tiresome person, duty, performance, etc. **3** inhalation. **4** *sl.* women's clothes worn by men. **5** *sl.* (in full **drag race**) acceleration race between cars usu. for a short distance. **6** *sl.* street or road (*the main drag*). □ **drag out** protract. **drag queen** *sl.* male transvestite. **drag strip** straight stretch of road for drag racing. **drag up** *colloq.* deliberately mention (an unwelcome subject).

drag·net /drágnet/ *n* **1** net drawn through water or across land to trap fish or game. **2** systematic hunt for criminals, etc.

drag·on /drágən/ *n.* mythical monster, usu. depicted as a fire-breathing, winged reptile.

drag·on·fly /drágənflī/ *n.* (*pl.* **-flies**) insect with a long body and two pairs of transparent wings.

dra·goon /drəgoon/ • *n.* **1** cavalryman. **2** rough, fierce fellow. • *v.tr.* (foll. by *into*) coerce; bully.

drain /drayn/ • *v.* **1** *tr.* draw off liquid from. **2** *tr.* draw off (liquid). **3** *intr.* flow or trickle away. **4** *intr.* become dry as liquid flows away. **5** *tr.* exhaust. **6** *tr.* drink all of; empty. • *n.* **1 a** channel or pipe carrying off liquid. **b** tube for drawing off discharge, etc. **2** constant outflow or expenditure. □ **down the drain** *colloq.* lost; wasted. □□ **drain′er** *n.*

drain·age /dráynij/ *n.* **1** draining. **2** system of drains. **3** what is drained off.

drain·pipe /dráynpīp/ *n.* pipe for carrying off water, etc.

drake /drayk/ *n.* male duck.

dram /dram/ *n.* **1** small drink of liquor. **2** measure of weight (apothecaries' one-eighth ounce; avoirdupois one-sixteenth ounce).

dra·ma /drámə, dra'amə/ *n.* **1** play for stage or broadcasting. **2** art of writing and presenting plays. **3** exciting or emotional event, circumstances, etc. **4** dramatic quality. □□ **dra·mat′ic** *adj.*

dra·mat·ics /drəmátiks/ *n.pl.* (often treated as *sing.*) **1** performance of plays. **2** exaggerated behavior.

dram·a·tist /drámətist, dra'amə-/ *n.* writer of dramas.

dram·a·tize /drámətīz, dra'amə-/ *v.tr.* **1** adapt (a novel, etc.) to a stage play. **2** make a dramatic scene of. **3** express or react to in a dramatic way. □□ **dram·a·ti·za′tion** *n.*

drank *past* of DRINK.

drape /drayp/ • *v.tr.* **1** hang, cover loosely, or adorn with cloth, etc. **2** arrange in folds. • *n.* (in *pl.*) curtains.

dra·per·y /dráypəree/ *n.* (*pl.* **-ies**) clothing or hangings (esp. curtains) arranged in folds.

dras·tic /drástik/ *adj.* having a far-reaching effect; severe. □□ **dras′ti·cal·ly** *adv.*

draught /draft/ esp. *Brit.* = DRAFT.

draw /draw/ • *v.* (*past* **drew** /droo/; *past part.* **drawn** /drawn/) **1** *tr.* pull or cause to move toward or after one. **2** *tr.* pull (a thing) up, over, or across. **3** *tr.* pull (curtains, etc.) open or shut. **4** *tr.* attract; bring; take in (*drew a deep breath*). **5** *intr.* suck smoke from (a cigarette, pipe, etc.). **6** *tr.* take out; remove. **7** *tr.* obtain or take from a source (*draw a salary*). **8** *tr.* produce (a picture) by tracing lines and marks. **9** *tr.* (also *absol.*) finish (a contest or game) with equal scores. **10** *tr.* infer (a conclusion). **11** *tr.* elicit; evoke. **12** *tr.* bring out or extract (liquid). **13** *intr.* (of a chimney, etc.) promote or allow a draft. **14** *intr.* (foll. by *on*) call on (a person, a person's skill, etc.). **15** *tr.* write out or compose (a check, document, etc.). **16** *tr.* formulate or perceive (a comparison or distinction). • *n.* **1** act of drawing. **2** attraction. **3** raffle, lottery, etc. **4** game ending in a tie. **5** act of removing a gun from its holster in order to shoot (*quick on the draw*). □ **draw the line** set a limit (of tolerance, etc.). **draw out 1** prolong. **2** elicit. **draw up 1** draft (a document, etc.). **2** come to a halt.

draw·back /dráwbak/ *n.* disadvantage.

draw·bridge /dráwbrij/ *n.* bridge that may be raised or moved aside.

draw·er *n.* **1** /dráwər/ person or thing that draws. **2** /drawr/ lidless, boxlike storage compartment, sliding in and out of a desk, table, etc. **3** (in *pl.*) /drawrz/ underpants. □□ **draw·er′ful** *n.* (*pl.* **-fuls**).

draw·ing /dráwing/ *n.* **1** the art of representing by line with pencils, crayons, etc. **2** picture produced in this way. □ **back to the drawing board** *colloq.* back to begin afresh (after earlier failure).

draw·ing room /dráwingroom, -room/ *n.* **1** room for receiving guests in a private house. **2** private compartment in a train.

drawl /drawl/ • *v.* **1** *intr.* speak with drawn-out vowel sounds. **2** *tr.* utter in this way. • *n.* drawling utterance.

drawn /drawn/ *past part.* of DRAW. *adj.* **1** looking strained and tense. **2** (of butter) melted.

draw·string /dráwstring/ *n.* string that can be pulled to tighten the mouth of a bag, the waist of a garment, etc.

dray /dray/ *n.* low cart without sides for heavy loads.

dread /dred/ • *v.tr.* **1** fear greatly. **2** look forward to with great apprehension. • *n.* great fear; apprehension. • *adj.* dreaded.

dread·ful /drédfool/ *adj.* **1** terrible; inspiring fear or awe. **2** *colloq.* very bad. □□ **dread′ful·ly** *adv.*

dread·locks /drédloks/ *n.pl.* hair twisted into tight braids hanging down on all sides.

dread·nought /drédnawt/ *n. hist.* battleship greatly superior in armament to all its predecessors.

dream /dreem/ • *n.* **1** pictures or events in the mind of a sleeping person. **2** daydream or fantasy. **3** ideal; aspiration. **4** beautiful or ideal person or thing. • *v.* (*past* and *past part.* **dreamed** or **dreamt** /dremt/) **1** *intr.* experience a dream. **2** *tr.* imagine as in a dream. **3** (usu. with *neg.*) **a** *intr.* contemplate the possibility of (*would not dream of it*). **b** *tr.* think of as a possibility (*never dreamed that he would come*). □ **dream up** imagine; invent. **like a dream** *colloq.* easily; effortlessly. □□ **dream′like** *adj.*

dream·er /dreemar/ *n.* romantic or unpractical person.

dream·land /dreemland/ *n.* ideal or imaginary land.

dream·y /dreemee/ *adj.* (**dream·i·er, dream·i·est**) **1** given to daydreaming; fanciful. **2** dreamlike; vague. **3** *colloq.* delightful; marvelous. □□ **dream′i·ly** *adv.* **dream′i·ness** *n.*

drear·y /dreeree/ *adj.* (**drear·i·er, drear·i·est**) dismal; dull; gloomy. □□ **drear′i·ly** *adv.* **drear′i·ness** *n.*

dredge[1] /drej/ • *v.* **1** *tr.* **a** bring up (lost or hidden material) as if with a dredge. **b** bring up (mud, etc.) from a river, harbor, etc., with a dredge. **2** *intr.* use a dredge. • *n.* apparatus used to scoop from a riverbed or seabed.

dredge[2] /drej/ *v.tr.* sprinkle with flour, sugar, etc.

dregs /dregz/ *n.pl.* **1** sediment; grounds. **2** worthless part.

drench /drench/ *v.tr.* wet thoroughly; soak.

dress /dres/ • *v.* **1 a** *tr.* clothe; array. **b** *intr.* wear clothes, esp. in a specified way (*dresses well*). **2** *intr.* **a** put on clothes. **b** put on formal clothes. **3** *tr.* decorate or adorn. **4** *tr. Med.* treat (a wound) with ointment, etc. **5** *tr.* **a** clean and prepare (poultry, etc.) for cooking or eating. **b** add a dressing to (salad, etc.). **6** *tr.* finish the surface of (fabric, building stone, etc.). **7** *tr.* curry (leather, etc.). **8** *Mil.* **a** *tr.* align (troops, etc.). **b** *intr.* (of troops) come into alignment. • *n.* **1** woman's garment of a bodice and skirt. **2** clothing, esp. a whole outfit. □ **dress code** set of rules for acceptable dress, as at a school, restaurant, etc. **dress down** *colloq.* **1** reprimand or scold. **2** dress casually. **dress out** attire conspicuously. **dress rehearsal** final rehearsal of a play, etc., wearing costume. **dress up 1** dress in fancy dress. **2** disguise (unwelcome facts) by embellishment.

dres·sage /drisáazh, dre-/ *n.* training of a horse in obedience and deportment.

dress·er /drésər/ *n.* **1** chest of drawers. **2** person who assists actors to dress. **3** person who dresses in a specified way (*a snappy dresser*).

dress·ing /drésing/ *n.* **1** in senses of DRESS *v.* **2 a** sauce for salads. **b** stuffing, esp. for poultry. **3** bandage or ointment for a wound. **4** stiffening used to finish fabrics.

dress·y /drésee/ *adj.* (**dress·i·er, dress·i·est**) (of clothes or a person) stylish; elaborate. □□ **dress′i·ness** *n.*

drew *past* of DRAW.

drib·ble /dribal/ • *v.* **1** *intr.* allow saliva to flow from the mouth. **2** *intr. & tr.* flow or allow to flow in drops. **3** *tr. Sports* move (a ball, etc.) with slight touches or taps. • *n.* **1** act of dribbling. **2** trickling flow. □□ **drib′bler** *n.* **drib′bly** *adj.*

dribs and drabs /dríbz ənd drábz/ *n.pl. colloq.* small scattered amounts (*did the work in dribs and drabs*).

dried *past* and *past part.* of DRY.

dri·er[1] *compar.* of DRY.

dri·er[2] /dríər/ *n.* (also **dry′er**) machine for drying hair, laundry, etc.

dri·est *superl.* of DRY.

drift /drift/ • *n.* **1 a** slow movement or variation. **b** such movement caused by a current. **2** intention, meaning, etc., of what is said, etc. **3** mass of windblown snow, etc. **4** deviation of a ship, aircraft, etc., from its course. • *v.* **1** *intr.* be carried by or as if by a current. **2** *intr.* progress passively or aimlessly (*drifted into teaching*). **3** *tr. & intr.* pile or be piled into drifts. □ **drift net** large fishing net allowed to drift with the tide. □□ **drift′age** *n.*

drift·er /driftər/ *n.* aimless or rootless person.

drift·wood /driftwŏod/ *n.* wood afloat or washed ashore.

drill[1] /dril/ • *n.* **1** tool or machine for boring holes. **2 a** military marching. **b** rigorous discipline or methodical instruction. **c** routine procedure in an emergency (*fire drill*). • *v.* **1** *tr.* (also *absol.*) **a** make a hole with a drill through or into. **b** make (a hole) with a drill. **2** *tr. & intr.* undergo discipline by drill. **3** *tr.* impart (knowledge, etc.) by drill. □ **drill press** machine tool for drilling.

DRILL

drill[2] /dril/ • *n.* **1** machine for making furrows, sowing, and covering seed. **2** small furrow. **3** row of plants so sown. • *v.tr.* plant in drills.

drill[3] /dril/ *n.* W. African baboon related to the mandrill.

drill[4] /dril/ *n.* coarse twilled cotton or linen fabric.

dri·ly var. of DRYLY.

drink /dringk/ • *v.* (*past* **drank** /drangk/; *past part.* **drunk** /drungk/) **1 a** *tr.* swallow (liquid). **b** *tr.* swallow the liquid contents of (a vessel). **c** *intr.* swallow liquid. **2** *intr.* take alcohol, esp. to excess. • *n.* **1** liquid for drinking. **2 a** alcoholic liquor. **b** portion, glass, etc., of this. **c** excessive use of alcohol. **3** (as **the drink**) *colloq.* the sea. □ **drink in** listen to eagerly. **drink to** toast (a person, event, etc.). **drink a person under the table** remain sober longer than one's drinking companion. **drink up** drink the whole of. **strong drink** alcoholic liquor. □□ **drink′a·ble** *adj.* **drink′er** *n.*

drip /drip/ • v. (**dripped, drip·ping**) **1** intr. & tr. fall or let fall in drops. **2** intr. be so wet as to shed drops. • n. **1 a** dripping (*steady drip of rain*). **b** drop of liquid. **c** sound of dripping. **2** colloq. dull or ineffective person. □ **drip-dry** v. (**-dries, -dried**) **1** intr. (of fabric, etc.) dry crease-free when hung up to drip. **2** tr. leave (a garment, etc.) hanging up to dry. • adj. able to be drip-dried.

drive /drīv/ • v. (*past* **drove** /drōv/; *past part.* **driv·en** /drívən/) **1** tr. urge in some direction, esp. forcibly. **2** tr. a compel. **b** force into a specified state. **c** urge to overwork. **3 a** tr. operate and direct (a vehicle, etc.). **b** tr. & intr. convey or be conveyed in a vehicle. **c** tr. be competent to drive (a vehicle). **4** tr. (of wind, water, etc.) carry along, propel, or cause to go in some direction. **5** tr. force (a stake, nail, etc.) into place. **6** tr. effect or conclude forcibly (*drove a hard bargain*). **7** tr. set or keep (machinery) going. **8** tr. hit a ball hard, making it go fast or a great distance. • n. **1** journey or excursion in a vehicle. **2 a** motivation and energy. **b** inner urge. **3 a** usu. landscaped street or road. **b** driveway. **4** *Sports* driving stroke of a bat, club, etc. **5** organized effort (*famine-relief drive*). **6** the transmission of power to machinery, wheels, etc. □ **drive at** intend; mean (*what is he driving at?*). **drive-by** (of a crime, etc.) carried out from a moving vehicle. **drive-in** *attrib.adj.* (of a bank, movie theater, etc.) used while sitting in one's car. • n. such a bank, movie theater, etc. **driving rain** excessive downpour. **driving range** area for driving practice. □□ **driv′a·ble** adj.

driv·el /drívəl/ • n. silly nonsense; twaddle. • v. intr. talk drivel. □□ **driv′el·er** n.

driv·en *past part.* of DRIVE.

driv·er /drívər/ n. **1** person who drives a vehicle. **2** *Golf* club for driving from the tee. □ **in the driver's seat** in charge.

drive·way /drívway/ n. usu. private road from a public street, etc., to a house, garage, etc.

driz·zle /drízəl/ • n. very fine rain. • v.intr. (esp. of rain) fall in very fine drops. □□ **driz′zly** adj.

droll /drōl/ adj. **1** quaintly amusing. **2** odd; surprising. □□ **droll′er·y** n. (*pl.* **-ies**). **drol′ly** adv. **droll′ness** n.

-drome /drōm/ *comb. form* forming nouns denoting: **1** place for running, racing, etc. (*aerodrome; hippodrome*). **2** thing that runs or proceeds in a certain way (*palindrome; syndrome*).

drom·e·dar·y /drómideree, drúm-/ n. (*pl.* **-ies**) one-humped camel, bred for riding and racing.

drone /drōn/ • n. **1** nonworking male of certain bees. **2** idler. **3** deep humming sound. **4** monotonous speech or speaker. • v. **1** intr. make a deep humming sound. **2** intr. & tr. speak or utter monotonously.

drool /drōōl/ • v.intr. **1** drivel; slobber. **2** show much pleasure or infatuation. • n. slobbering; driveling.

droop /drōōp/ • v. **1** tr. & intr. sag; hang down; languish. **2** intr. lose heart; be dejected. • n. **1** drooping. **2** loss of spirit or enthusiasm. □□ **droop′y** adj.

drop /drop/ • n. **1 a** globule of liquid. **b** very small amount of liquid. **2 a** abrupt slope. **b** degree of this. **c** act of falling or dropping. **d** fall in prices, temperature, etc. **e** deterioration. **3** globular gemstone, piece of candy, etc. **4** curtain or scenery let down on to a stage. **5** (in *pl.*) liquid medicine used in drops. • v. (**dropped, drop·ping**) **1** intr. & tr. fall or let fall in drops. **2** intr. & tr. relinquish. **3 a** intr. & tr. sink from exhaustion, a wound, etc. die. **4 a** intr. & tr. cease or cause to cease; lapse or let lapse; abandon. **b** tr. colloq. cease to associate with. **5** tr. deposit (a passenger, etc.). **6** tr. & intr. utter or be uttered casually. **7** tr. send casually (*drop me a postcard*). **8 a** intr. & tr. fall or allow to fall in direction, amount, condition, degree, pitch, etc. (*his voice dropped*). **b** intr. (of a person) jump down lightly. **9** tr. colloq. lose (money, esp. in gambling). **10** tr. a omit (*drop this article*). **b** omit (a letter, esp. 'h,' a syllable, etc.) in speech. **11** tr. (as **dropped** adj.) in a lower position than usual (*dropped waist*). **12** tr. give birth to (esp. a lamb, a kitten, etc.). **13** tr. lose (a game, point, etc.). **14** tr. colloq. dismiss or exclude (*was dropped from the team*). □ **at the drop of a hat** given the slightest excuse. **drop in** (or **by**) colloq. visit casually. **drop-leaf** (of a table, etc.) having a hinged flap. **drop off 1** decline gradually. **2** colloq. fall asleep. **3** = sense 5 of v. **drop out** colloq. cease to participate. **ready to drop** extremely tired. □□ **drop′let** n.

drop·out /drópowt/ n. colloq. a person who has dropped out, esp. from school.

drop·per /drópər/ n. device for administering liquid, esp. medicine, in drops.

drop·pings /drópingz/ n.pl. animal dung.

drop·sy /drópsee/ n. (*pl.* **-sies**) = EDEMA.

dro·soph·i·la /drəsófilə/ n. fruit fly used extensively in genetic research.

dross /draws, dros/ n. **1** refuse. **2** scum from melted metals.

drought /drowt/ n. **1** prolonged absence of rain. **2** prolonged lack of something. □□ **drought′y** adj.

drove¹ *past* of DRIVE.

drove² /drōv/ n. **1 a** large number (of people, etc.) moving together. **b** (in *pl.*) colloq. great number. **2** herd or flock driven or moving together.

drown /drown/ v. **1** tr. & intr. kill or be killed by submersion in liquid. **2** tr. submerge; flood; drench (*drowned the fields in six feet of water*). **3** tr. deaden (grief, etc.) with drink (*drowned his sorrows in drink*). **4** tr. make (a sound) inaudible by means of a louder sound.

drowse /drowz/ • v.intr. be lightly asleep. • n. nap.

drow·sy /drówzee/ adj. (**drow·si·er, drow·si·est**) **1** half asleep; dozing. **2** sluggish. □□ **drow′si·ly** adv. **drow′si·ness** n.

drub /drub/ v.tr. (**drubbed, drub·bing**) **1** thump; belabor. **2** beat in a fight. □□ **drub′bing** n.

drudge /druj/ • n. servile worker, esp. at menial tasks. • v.intr. work slavishly. □□ **drudg′er·y** n.

drug /drug/ • n. **1** medicinal substance. **2** (esp. addictive) narcotic, hallucinogen, or stimulant. • v. (**drugged, drug·ging**) **1** tr. add a drug to (food or drink). **2** tr. a administer a drug to. **b** stupefy with a drug. **3** intr. take drugs as an addict.

drug·gist /drúgist/ n. pharmacist.

drug·store /drúgstawr/ n. pharmacy also selling miscellaneous items.

Dru·id /drōóid/ n. member of an ancient Celtic religion. □□ **Dru′id·ism** n. **Dru·id′ic**.

drum /drum/ • n. **1 a** hollow, cylindrical percussion instrument covered at one or both ends.

b percussion section. **c** sound made by or like that of a drum. **2** thing resembling a drum, esp. a container. • *v.* (**•drummed, drum•ming**) **1** *intr.* & *tr.* play a drum. **2** *tr.* & *intr.* beat, tap, or thump (fingers, etc.) continuously (on something). **3** *intr.* (of a bird or an insect) make a loud, hollow noise with quivering wings. □ **drum into** drive (a lesson) into (a person) by persistence. **drum major** leader of a marching band. **drum major-ette** female member of a baton-twirling parading group. **drum out** expel for wrongdoing. **drum up** summon, gather, or call up. □□ **drum′mer** *n.*

drum•stick /drúmstik/ *n.* **1** stick for beating a drum. **2** lower leg of a dressed fowl.

drunk /drungk/ • *adj.* **1** rendered incapable by alcohol. **2** overcome with joy, success, power, etc. • *n.* **1** drunkard. **2** *sl.* drinking bout.

drunk•ard /drúngkərd/ *n.* person who is habitually drunk.

drunk•en /drúngkən/ *adj.* **1** = DRUNK. **2** caused by or exhibiting drunkenness. □□ **drunk′en•ly** *adv.* **drunk′en•ness** *n.*

drupe /droop/ *n.* fleshy stone fruit, e.g., olive or peach. □□ **dru•pa•ceous** /-páyshəs/ *adj.*

dry /drī/ • *adj.* (**dri•er** /drī́ər/; **dri•est** /drī́-ist/) **1** free from moisture, esp.: **a** with moisture having evaporated, drained away, etc. **b** (of the eyes) free from tears. **c** (of a climate, etc.) with insufficient rain. **2** (of wine, etc.) not sweet. **3 a** meager; plain (*dry facts*). **b** uninteresting. **4** (of humor) subtle; ironic. **5** prohibiting the sale of alcohol. • *v.* (**dries, dried**) make or become dry. □ **dry cell** battery cell in which the electrolyte is dry. **dry-clean** clean (clothes, etc.) with solvents and no water. **dry dock** enclosure for the building or repairing of ships. **dry goods** fabric, thread, clothing, etc., esp. as distinct from hardware, groceries, etc. **dry ice** solid carbon dioxide. **dry out 1** become fully dry. **2** (of a drug addict, alcoholic, etc.) undergo treatment for addiction. **dry rot** decay of wood caused by certain fungi. **dry run** *colloq.* rehearsal. **dry up 1** make or become utterly dry. **2** *colloq.* cease talking. **3** (of supplies) run out. □□ **dry′ly, dri′ly** *adv.* **dry′ness** *n.*

dry•ad /drī́ad, drī́əd/ *n.* wood nymph.

dry•wall /drī́wawl/ *n.* = PLASTERBOARD.

DSM *abbr.* Distinguished Service Medal.

DST *abbr.* daylight saving(s) time.

DT *abbr.* (also **DT's** /déeteéez/) delirium tremens.

du•al /dóoəl, dyóoəl/ *adj.* **1** of two; twofold. **2** double (*dual ownership*). □□ **du•al•i•ty** /-álitee/ *n.* **du′al•ize** *v.tr.* **du′al•ly** *adv.*

dub[1] /dub/ *v.tr.* (**dubbed, dub•bing**) **1** make (a person) a knight by touching his shoulders with a sword. **2** give (a person) a name, nickname, etc.

dub[2] /dub/ *v.tr.* (**dubbed, dub•bing**) **1** provide (a movie, etc.) with an alternative soundtrack. **2** add (sound effects or music) to a movie or broadcast. **3** copy (a soundtrack).

dub•ni•um /dóobniəm/ *n. Chem.* artificially produced radioactive element. ¶ Symb.: **Db.**

du•bi•ous /dóobeeəs, dyóo-/ *adj.* **1** hesitating; doubting. **2** questionable. **3** unreliable; suspicious. □□ **du′bi•ous•ly** *adv.*

du•cal /dóokəl, dyóo-/ *adj.* of or like a duke.

du•cat /dúkət/ *n. hist.* former gold coin of Europe.

duch•ess /dúchis/ *n.* **1** duke's wife or widow. **2** woman holding the rank of duke.

duch•y /dúchee/ *n.* (*pl.* **-ies**) territory of a duke or duchess.

duck[1] /duk/ *n.* (*pl.* same or **ducks**) **1** swimming bird, esp. the domesticated mallard or wild duck. **2** its flesh as food. □ **duck soup** *sl.* easy task. **like a duck to water** adapting very readily. **like water off a duck's back** *colloq.* (of remonstrances, etc.) producing no effect.

duck[2] /duk/ • *v.* **1** plunge, dive, or dip under water and emerge. **2** bend quickly, esp. to avoid a blow or being seen. **3** *colloq.* avoid or dodge (*ducked the meeting*). • *n.* quick lowering of the head, etc.

duck[3] /duk/ *n.* **1** strong linen or cotton fabric. **2** (in *pl.*) pants made of this (*white ducks*).

duck•bill /dúkbil/ *n.* (also **duck′-billed plat′ypus**) = PLATYPUS.

duck•ling /dúkling/ *n.* **1** young duck. **2** its flesh as food.

duck•y /dúkee/ *adj. sl.* sweet; pretty; splendid.

duct /dukt/ *n.* channel or tube for conveying fluid, cable, etc.

duc•tile /dúktəl, -tīl/ *adj.* **1** (of metal) capable of being drawn into wire; pliable. **2** (of a substance) easily molded. □□ **duc•til•i•ty** /-tílitee/ *n.*

dud /dud/ *n. sl.* **1** futile or ineffectual person or thing. **2** shell, etc., that fails to explode. **3** (in *pl.*) clothes.

dude /dood, dyood/ *n. sl.* **1** dandy. **2** vacationer on a ranch. **3** fellow; guy.

dudg•eon /dújən/ *n.* resentment. □ **in high dudgeon** very angry or angrily.

due /doo, dyoo/ • *adj.* **1** owing or payable. **2** merited; appropriate. **3** rightful; proper. **4** *predic.* to be ascribed to (a cause, an agent, etc.) (*the discovery was due to Edison*). **5** intended to arrive or occur at a certain time. • *n.* **1** what is owed to a person. **2** (in *pl.*) what one owes. • *adv.* (of a direction) exactly; directly. □ **due process** legal procedures to ensure individual rights. **due to** because of. **in due course 1** at about the appropriate time. **2** in the natural order.

due /doo, dyoo/ • *adj.* **1** owing or payable. **2** merited; appropriate. **3** rightful; proper. **4** *predic.* to be ascribed to (a cause, an agent, etc.) (*the discovery was due to Edison*). **5** intended to arrive or occur at a certain time. • *n.* **1** what is owed to a person. **2** (in *pl.*) what one owes. • *adv.* (of a direction) exactly; directly. □ **due process** legal procedures to ensure individual rights. **due to** because of. **in due course 1** at about the appropriate time. **2** in the natural order.

¶ The use of **due to** meaning 'because of', as in *we were late due to circumstances beyond our control*, is widely used and generally accepted, although some traditionalists hold that **due** is properly a predicate adjective and restrict its use to follow forms of the verb *to be*, e.g., *The collapse was due to flooding.*

du•el /dóoəl, dyóoəl/ • *n.* **1** armed contest between two people, usu. to settle a point of honor. **2** any contest between two. • *v.intr.* fight a duel. □□ **du′el•er** *n.* **du′el•ist** *n.*

---

duel late 15th century: from Latin *duellum*, archaic and literary form of *bellum* 'war,' used in medieval Latin with the meaning 'combat between two persons,' partly influenced by *dualis* 'of two.' The original sense was 'single combat used to decide a judicial dispute'; the sense 'contest to decide a point of honor' dates from the early 17th century.

du·et /dŏo-ét, dyŏo-/ *n. Mus.* **1** performance by two performers. **2** composition for two performers. □□ **du·et′tist** *n.*

duf·fel /dúfəl/ *n.* (also **duf′fle**) coarse woolen cloth with a thick nap. □ **duffel bag** cylindrical canvas, etc., bag used as luggage.

duf·fer /dúfər/ *n. sl.* inefficient, useless, or stupid person.

dug *past* and *past part.* of DIG.

du·gong /dŏogawng, -gong/ *n.* (*pl.* same or **dugongs**) marine mammal of Asian seas and coasts. Also called **sea cow**.

dug·out /dúgowt/ *n.* **1** roofed shelter, esp. for troops or at a baseball field. **2** canoe made from a tree trunk.

duke /dŏok, dyŏok/ *n.* **1 a** person holding the highest hereditary title of nobility. **b** prince ruling a duchy. **2** (usu. in *pl.*) *sl.* hand; fist (*put up your dukes!*).

duke·dom /dŏokdəm, dyŏok-/ *n.* territory ruled by a duke.

dul·cet /dúlsit/ *adj.* (esp. of sound) sweet and soothing.

dul·ci·mer /dúlsimər/ *n.* stringed musical instrument played by being struck with hammers.

dull /dul/ • *adj.* **1** slow to understand; stupid. **2** tedious; boring. **3** (of the weather) overcast; gloomy. **4 a** (esp. of a knife edge, etc.) blunt. **b** (of color, light, sound, etc.) not bright, vivid, or keen. **5** (of pain, etc.) not acute. **6 a** (of a person, an animal, trade, etc.) sluggish; slow-moving. **b** (of a person) listless; depressed. • *v.* make or become dull. □□ **dull′ness** *n.* **dul′ly** *adv.*

dull·ard /dúlərd/ *n.* stupid person.

du·ly /dŏolee, dyŏo-/ *adv.* **1** in due time or manner. **2** rightly; properly; fitly.

dumb /dum/ *adj.* **1** unable to speak; mute. **2** silenced by surprise, shyness, etc. **3** *colloq.* stupid; ignorant. □□ **dumb′ly** /dúmlee/ *adv.* **dumb′ness** *n.*

dumb·bell /dúmbel/ *n.* **1** short bar with a weight at each end, used for muscle-building, etc. **2** *sl.* stupid person.

dumb·found /dúmfownd/ *v.tr.* (also **dumbfound′**) strike dumb; confound; nonplus.

dumb·wait·er /dúmwaytər/ *n.* small elevator for carrying food, plates, etc., between floors.

dum·my /dúmee/ *n.* (*pl.* **-mies**) **1** model of a human, esp.: **a** ventriloquist's doll. **b** figure used to model clothes. **2** imitation or stand-in object. **3** *colloq.* stupid person. **4** *Bridge* partner of the declarer, whose cards are exposed after the first lead. • *adj.* sham; counterfeit. □ **dummy run** trial run; rehearsal. **dummy up** *sl.* keep quiet; give no information.

dump /dump/ • *n.* **1** place for depositing trash, garbage, etc. **2** *colloq.* unpleasant or dreary place. **3** temporary store of ammunition, etc. • *v.tr.* **1** put down firmly or clumsily. **2** deposit or dispose of (rubbish, etc.). **3** *colloq.* abandon; desert. **4** *Mil.* leave (ammunition, etc.) in a dump. **5** *Econ.* send (excess goods) to a foreign market at a low price. **6** *Computing* copy (stored data) to a different location. □ **dump on** *sl.* criticize or abuse; get the better of. **dump truck** truck

with a body that tilts or opens at the back for unloading. □□ **dump′ing** *n.*

dump·ling /dúmpling/ *n.* **1** ball of boiled or steamed dough, usu. eaten with stew, etc. **2** dough filled with fruit, etc.

dumps /dumps/ *n.pl. colloq.* depression (*in the dumps*).

Dump·ster /dúmpstər/ *n. propr.* large trash receptacle designed to be hoisted and emptied into a truck.

dump·y /dúmpee/ *adj.* (**dump·i·er, dump·i·est**) short and stout. □□ **dump′i·ness** *n.*

dun¹ /dun/ • *adj.* dull grayish brown. • *n.* dun color.

dun² /dun/ • *n.* demand for payment. • *v.tr.* (**dunned, dun·ning**) importune for payment of a debt; pester.

dunce /duns/ *n.* ignorant person; dullard.

dune /dŏon, dyŏon/ *n.* bank of sand formed by the wind.

dung /dung/ *n.* excrement of animals; manure.

dun·ga·ree /dúnggəreé/ *n.* **1** coarse cotton cloth. **2** (in *pl.*) pants or overalls made of this.

dun·geon /dúnjən/ *n.* underground prison cell.

dunk /dungk/ *v.tr.* **1** dip (food) into liquid before eating. **2** immerse. □ **dunk shot** basketball shot made by jumping up and thrusting the ball down through the basket.

du·o /dŏo-ō, dyŏo-ō/ *n.* (*pl.* **-os**) **1** pair of performers. **2** duet.

du·o·dec·i·mal /dŏo-ōdésiməl, dyŏo-/ *adj.* relating to a system of numerical notation that has 12 as a base.

du·o·de·num /dŏoədeénəm, dyŏo-, dŏo-ód′-nəm, dyŏo-/ *n.* first part of the small intestine below the stomach. □□ **du·o·de′nal** *adj.*

dupe /dŏop, dyŏop/ • *n.* victim of deception. • *v.tr.* make a fool of; cheat. □□ **dup′a·ble** *adj.* **dup′er** *n.*

du·ple /dŏopəl, dyŏo-/ *adj.* of two parts.

du·plex /dŏopleks, dyŏo-/ • *n.* **1** apartment on two levels. **2** house subdivided for two families. • *adj. Computing* (of a circuit) allowing the transmission of signals in both directions simultaneously.

du·pli·cate • *adj.* /dŏoplikət, dyŏo-/ **1** identical. **2 a** having two identical parts. **b** doubled. • *n.* /dŏoplikət, dyŏo-/ identical thing, esp. a copy. • *v.tr.* /dŏoplikayt, dyŏo-/ **1** make or be an exact copy of. **2** repeat (an action, etc.), esp. unnecessarily. □□ **du·pli·ca·ble** /dŏoplikəbəl, dyŏo-/ *adj.* **du·pli·ca·tion** /-káyshən/ *n.* **dup′li·ca·tor** *n.*

du·plic·i·ty /dŏoplísitee, dyŏo-/ *n.* deceitfulness. □□ **du·plic′i·tous** *adj.*

du·ra·ble /dŏorəbəl, dyŏor-/ *adj.* lasting; hard-wearing. □□ **du·ra·bil′i·ty** *n.*

du·ra ma·ter /dŏorə máytər, maá-, dyŏorə/ *n.* outermost membrane of the brain and spinal cord.

du·ra·tion /dŏoráyshən, dyŏor-/ *n.* length of time for which something continues. □ **for the duration** until the end of something obstructing normal activities, as a war. □□ **du·ra′tion·al** *adj.*

du·ress /dŏorés, dyŏo-/ *n.* **1** coercive circumstances. **2** forcible restraint or imprisonment.

dur·ing /dŏoring, dyŏor-/ *prep.* throughout or at some point in.

du·rum /dŏorəm, dyŏo-/ *n.* hard-seeded wheat used in the manufacture of pasta, etc.

dusk /dusk/ *n.* darker stage of twilight.

dusk·y /dúskee/ *adj.* (**dusk·i·er, dusk·i·est**) shadowy; dim; darkish. □□ **dusk′i·ly** *adv.* **dusk′i·ness** *n.*

dust /dust/ • *n.* **1** finely powdered earth, dirt, etc. **2** dead person's remains. • *v.tr.* **1** clear (furniture, etc.) of dust. **2** sprinkle with powder, dust, sugar, etc. □ **dust bowl** area denuded of vegetation by drought or erosion. **dust devil** whirlwind visible as a column of dust. **dusting powder** talcum powder. **dust jacket** paper cover on a book. **dust off** use and enjoy after a long period of neglect. **when the dust settles** when things quiet down.

dust·pan /dústpan/ *n.* receptacle for (brushed up) dust.

dust·y /dústee/ *adj.* (**dust·i·er, dust·i·est**) **1** full of, covered with, or resembling dust. **2** (of a color) dull or muted. □□ **dust′i·ly** *adv.* **dust′i·ness** *n.*

Dutch /duch/ • *adj.* of the Netherlands. • *n.* **1** language of the Netherlands. **2** (prec. by *the*; treated as *pl.*) people of the Netherlands. □ **Dutch door** door horizontally divided allowing one part to be shut and the other open. **Dutch elm disease** fungus disease affecting elms. **Dutch oven** covered cooking pot for braising, etc. **Dutch treat** outing, etc., at which people pay for themselves. **Dutch uncle** kind but firm adviser. **go Dutch** share expenses.

DUTCH DOOR

du·ti·a·ble /dóoteeəbəl, dyóo-/ *adj.* liable to customs or other duties.

du·ti·ful /dóotifŏŏl, dyóo-/ *adj.* doing one's duty; obedient. □□ **du′ti·ful·ly** *adv.*

du·ty /dóotee, dyóo-/ *n.* (*pl.* **-ties**) **1** moral or legal obligation; responsibility. **2** tax on certain imports, etc. **3** job or function. □ **on** (or **off**) **duty** engaged (or not engaged) in one's work.

du·vet /doováy/ *n.* thick, soft quilt with a detachable cover.

D.V.M. *abbr.* doctor of veterinary medicine.

dwarf /dwawrf/ • *n.* (*pl.* **dwarfs** or **dwarves** /dwawrvz/) **1 a** *offens.* person of abnormally small stature. **b** animal or plant much below

ordinary size. **2** small mythological being with supernatural powers. **3** (in full **dwarf star**) small usu. dense star. • *v.tr.* **1** stunt in growth. **2** cause to seem small or insignificant. □□ **dwarf′·ish** *adj.*

dweeb /dweeb/ *n. sl.* socially inept person.

dwell /dwel/ • *v.intr.* (*past* and *past part.* **dwelled** or **dwelt**) live; reside. • *n.* slight, regular pause in the motion of a machine. □ **dwell on** (or **upon**) linger over; write, brood, or speak at length on. □□ **dwell′er** *n.*

dwell·ing /dwéling/ *n.* house; residence.

DWI *abbr.* driving while intoxicated.

dwin·dle /dwínd'l/ *v.intr.* become gradually less or smaller.

Dy *symb. Chem.* dysprosium.

dye /dī/ • *n.* **1** substance used to change the color of hair, fabric, wood, etc. **2** color produced by this. • *v.tr.* (**dye·ing**) color with dye. □ **dyed-in-the-wool** out-and-out; unchangeable. □□ **dye′a·ble** *adj.*

dy·ing /dī-ing/ *adj.* of, or at the time of, death. □ **to one's dying day** for the rest of one's life.

dy·nam·ic /dīnámik/ *adj.* **1** energetic; active. **2** *Physics* **a** of motive force. **b** of force in actual operation. **3** of dynamics. □□ **dy·nam′i·cal·ly** *adv.*

dy·nam·ics /dīnámiks/ *n.pl.* **1** (usu. treated as *sing.*) the study of motion and its causes. **2** motive forces in any sphere.

dy·na·mism /dínəmizəm/ *n.* energy; dynamic power. □□ **dy′na·mist** *n.*

dy·na·mite /dínəmīt/ • *n.* **1** high explosive containing nitroglycerin. **2** potentially dangerous person, situation, etc. • *v.tr.* charge or shatter with dynamite.

dy·na·mo /dínəmō/ *n.* (*pl.* **-mos**) **1** electric generator. **2** *colloq.* energetic person.

dy·nas·ty /dínəstee/ *n.* (*pl.* **-ties**) **1** line of hereditary rulers. **2** succession of leaders in any field. □□ **dy·nas·tic** /-nástik/ *adj.* **dy·nas′ti·cal·ly** *adv.*

dyne /dīn/ *n. Physics* unit of force that, upon a mass of one gram, increases its velocity by one centimeter per second.

dys- /dis/ *comb. form* bad; difficult.

dys·en·ter·y /dísənteree/ *n.* inflammation of the intestines, causing severe diarrhea. □□ **dys·en·ter′ic** *adj.*

dys·func·tion /dísfúngkshən/ *n.* abnormality or impairment of function. □□ **dys·func′tion·al** *adj.*

dys·lex·i·a /disléksee/ *n.* abnormal difficulty in reading and spelling. □□ **dys·lex′ic** *adj.* & *n.*

dys·pep·si·a /dispépsee/ *n.* indigestion. □□ **dys·pep′tic** *n.*

dys·pro·si·um /disprózeeəm/ *n. Chem.* metallic element of the lanthanide series. ¶ Symb.: **Dy**.

dys·tro·phy /dístrəfee/ *n.* defective nutrition. □ **muscular dystrophy** hereditary progressive weakening of the muscles. □□ **dys·troph·ic** /distrófik, -trô-/ *adj.*

dz. *abbr.* dozen.

Ee

E[1] /ee/ *n.* (also **e**) (*pl.* **Es** or **E's**; **e's**) **1** fifth letter of the alphabet. **2** *Mus.* third note of the diatonic scale of C major.

E[2] *abbr.* (also **E.**) **1** east; eastern. **2** English. **3** energy.

e- /ee, e/ *prefix* form of EX-[1] 1 before some consonants.

ea. *abbr.* each.

each /eech/ • *adj.* every one of two or more persons or things, regarded separately. • *pron.* each person or thing. □ **each and every** every single. **each other** one another (*they wore each other's hats*).
¶ See note at BOTH.

ea·ger /éegər/ *adj.* enthusiastic; keen. □□ **ea′ger·ly** *adv.* **ea′ger·ness** *n.*

ea·gle /éegəl/ *n.* **1 a** large bird of prey with keen vision and powerful flight. **b** this as a symbol, esp. of the US. **2** *Golf* score of two strokes under par at a hole. **3** gold US coin worth ten dollars. □ **eagle-eyed** keen-sighted, watchful. **Eagle Scout** highest Boy Scout rank.

ea·glet /éeglit/ *n.* young eagle.

ear[1] /eer/ *n.* **1** organ of hearing, esp. its external part. **2** faculty for discriminating sounds (*an ear for music*). **3** listening; attention. □ **all ears** listening attentively. **have a person's ear** receive a favorable hearing. **have** (or **keep**) **an ear to the ground** be alert to rumors or the trend of opinion. **in one ear and out the other** heard but disregarded or quickly forgotten. **out on one's ear** dismissed ignominiously. **up to one's ears** *colloq.* deeply involved or occupied. □□ **eared** *adj.*

ear[2] /eer/ *n.* seed-bearing head of a cereal plant.

ear·ache /éerayk/ *n.* pain in the ear.

ear·drum /éerdrum/ *n.* membrane of the middle ear.

ear·ful /éerfŏŏl/ *n.* (*pl.* **-fuls**) *colloq.* **1** prolonged amount of talking. **2** strong reprimand.

earl /ərl/ *n.* British nobleman ranking between marquess and viscount. □□ **earl′dom** *n.*

ear·lobe /éerlōb/ *n.* lower, soft external part of the ear.

ear·ly /ə́rlee/ *adj.* & *adv.* (**ear·li·er, ear·li·est**) **1** before the usual or expected time. **2** a not far on in the day or night, or in time. **b** prompt. **3** not far on in a period or process. □ **early bird** *colloq.* one who arrives, gets up, etc., early. □□ **ear′li·ness** *n.*

ear·mark /éermaark/ • *n.* identifying mark. • *v.tr.* **1** set aside for a special purpose. **2** mark (sheep, etc.) with an earmark.

ear·muff /éermuf/ *n.* cover for the ears, protecting them from cold.

earn /ərn/ *v.tr.* **1** bring in as interest or income. **2** deserve; be entitled to; obtain as reward.

ear·nest /ə́rnist/ *adj.* intensely serious. □ **in earnest** serious(ly), not joking(ly); with determination. □□ **ear′nest·ly** *adv.* **ear′nest·ness** *n.*

earn·ings /ə́rningz/ *n.pl.* money earned.

ear·phone /éerfōn/ *n.* device applied to the ear to receive radio, etc., communications.

ear·ring /éering/ *n.* jewelry worn on the ear.

ear·shot /éershot/ *n.* hearing range.

ear·split·ting /éerspliting/ *adj.* excessively loud.

earth /ərth/ *n.* **1 a** (also **Earth**) the planet on which we live. **b** land and sea, as distinct from sky. **2 a** the ground. **b** soil. **3** *Relig.* this world, as distinct from heaven or hell. □ **come back** (or **down**) **to earth** return to realities. **earth-shattering** *colloq.* having a traumatic or devastating effect. **on earth** *colloq.* **1** existing anywhere (*the happiest man on earth*). **2** as an intensifier (*what on earth?*). □□ **earth′ward** *adj.* & *adv.* **earth′wards** *adv.*

earth·en /ə́rthən/ *adj.* **1** made of earth. **2** made of baked clay.

earth·en·ware /ə́rthənwair/ • *n.* pottery, vessels, etc., made of fired clay. • *adj.* made of fired clay.

earth·ling /ə́rthling/ *n.* inhabitant of earth, esp. in science fiction.

earth·ly /ə́rthlee/ *adj.* **1 a** of the earth; terrestrial. **b** of human life. **2** (usu. with *neg.*) *colloq.* remotely possible (*no earthly use*).

earth·quake /ə́rthkwayk/ *n.* convulsion of the earth's surface due to underground faults or volcanic action.

earth·work /ə́rthwərk/ *n.* **1** artificial bank of earth in fortification, road building, etc. **2** process of excavating soil in civil engineering work.

earth·worm /ə́rthwərm/ *n.* common worm living and burrowing in the ground.

earth·y /ə́rthee/ *adj.* (**earth·i·er, earth·i·est**) **1** of or like earth or soil. **2** somewhat coarse or crude; unrefined (*earthy humor*). **3** down-to-earth. □□ **earth′i·ness** *n.*

ear·wig /éerwig/ *n.* small elongate insect with a pair of terminal appendages in the shape of forceps.

ease /eez/ • *n.* **1** facility; effortlessness. **2** freedom or relief from pain, anxiety, hardship, etc. • *v.* **1** *tr.* **a** relieve from pain, anxiety, etc. **b** help; facilitate. **2** *intr.* **a** become less painful or burdensome. **b** relax. **3 a** *tr.* slacken. **b** *tr.* & *intr.* move or be moved carefully into place.

EASEL

ea·sel /éezəl/ *n.* frame to hold an artist's work, a blackboard, etc.

ease·ment /éezmənt/ n. Law right of way or a similar right over another's land.

eas·i·ly /éezilee/ adv. **1** without difficulty. **2** by far (easily the best). **3** very probably (it could easily snow).

east /eest/ • n. **1 a** point of the horizon where the sun rises at the equinoxes. **b** compass point corresponding to this. **c** direction in which this lies. **2** (usu. **the East**) **a** Asia. **b** formerly Communist nations of eastern Europe. **3** eastern part of a country, town, etc. • adj. **1** toward, at, near, or facing the east. **2** from the east (east wind). • adv. **1** toward, at, or near the east. **2** (foll. by of) further east than.

east·bound /éestbownd/ adj. traveling or leading eastward.

Eas·ter /éestər/ n. festival (held on a Sunday in March or April) commemorating Christ's resurrection.

east·er·ly /éestərlee/ • adj. & adv. **1** in an eastern position or direction. **2** (of a wind) from the east. • n. (pl. **-lies**) such a wind.

east·ern /éestərn/ adj. of or in the east. □ **eastern hemisphere** (also **Eastern Hemisphere**) the half of the earth containing Europe, Asia, Australia, and Africa. **Eastern (standard) time** standard time used in the eastern US and eastern Canada or in eastern Australia. □□ **east·ern·most** adj.

east·ern·er /éestərnər/ (also **East·ern·er**) n. native or inhabitant of the east, esp. in the US.

east·ward /éestwərd/ adj. & adv. (also **east·wards**) toward the east.

eas·y /éezee/ • adj. (**eas·i·er, eas·i·est**) **1** not difficult; achieved without great effort. **2 a** free from pain, discomfort, anxiety, etc. **b** affluent. **3** relaxed and pleasant. **4** compliant. • adv. with ease; in an effortless or relaxed manner. • int. go carefully; move gently. □ **easy chair** large comfortable chair. **easy come easy go** colloq. what is easily obtained is soon lost or spent. **easy does it** colloq. go carefully. **easy on the eye** (or **ear**, etc.) colloq. pleasant to look at (or listen to, etc.). **go easy** (foll. by with, on) be sparing or cautious. **I'm easy** colloq. I have no preference. **of easy virtue** sexually promiscuous. **take it easy 1** proceed carefully. **2** relax; avoid overwork. □□ **eas·i·ness** n.

eas·y·go·ing /éezeegóing/ adj. placid and tolerant.

eat /eet/ v. (past **ate** /ayt/; past part. **eat·en** /éet'n/) **1 a** tr. take into the mouth, chew, and swallow. **b** intr. consume food; have a meal. **2** tr. **a** destroy gradually. **b** begin to consume or diminish (resources, etc.). **3** tr. colloq. trouble; vex (what's eating you?). □ **eat one's hat** colloq. (said as if unlikely to happen) admit being wrong. **eat one's heart out** suffer from excessive longing or envy. **eat out** have a meal away from home, esp. in a restaurant. **eat up 1** consume completely. **2** use rapidly or wastefully (eats up time). **3** encroach upon. **eat one's words** admit that one was wrong. □□ **eat·a·ble** adj. **eat·er** n.

eat·er·y /éetəree/ n. (pl. **-ies**) colloq. informal restaurant.

eats /eets/ n.pl. colloq. food.

eau de co·logne /ódəkəlón/ n. alcohol-based perfume.

eaves /eevz/ n.pl. projecting underside of a pitched roof.

---

eaves·drop /éevzdrop/ v.intr. (**-dropped, -dropping**) listen secretly to a private conversation. □□ **eaves·drop·per** n.

> **eavesdrop** early 17th century: back-formation from eavesdropper (late Middle English) 'a person who listens from under the eaves,' from the obsolete noun eavesdrop 'the ground onto which water drips from the eaves,' probably from Old Norse upsardropi, from ups 'eaves' + dropi 'a drop.'

ebb /eb/ • n. movement of the tide out to sea. • v.intr. **1** flow out to sea; recede. **2** decline. □ **ebb and flow** continuing process of decline and upturn in circumstances.

eb·on·y /ébənee/ • n. (pl. **-ies**) **1** heavy, hard, dark wood. **2** any of various trees producing this. • adj. **1** made of ebony. **2** black like ebony.

e·bul·lient /ibúlyənt, ibóol-/ adj. exuberant. □□ **e·bul·lience** n. **e·bul·lien·cy** n. **e·bul·lient·ly** adv.

EC abbr. European Community.

ec·cen·tric /ikséntrik, ek-/ • adj. **1** odd or capricious in behavior or appearance. **2** not quite concentric nor circular. • n. **1** eccentric person. **2** Mech. disk for changing rotatory into backward-and-forward motion. □□ **ec·cen·tri·cal·ly** adv. **ec·cen·tric·i·ty** /éksentrísitee/ n. (pl. **ties**).

eccl. abbr. **1** ecclesiastic. **2** ecclesiastical.

ec·cle·si·as·tic /iklée'zeeástik/ • n. clergyman. • adj. = ECCLESIASTICAL.

ec·cle·si·as·ti·cal /iklée'zeeástikəl/ adj. of the church or the clergy. □□ **ec·cle·si·as·ti·cal·ly** adv.

ECG abbr. electrocardiogram.

ech·e·lon /éshəlon/ n. **1** level in an organization, in society, etc.; those occupying it. **2** formation of troops, ships, aircraft, etc., in staggered parallel rows.

ech·e·ve·ri·a /échəvərée'ə/ n. succulent plant of the Americas.

e·chi·no·derm /ikínədərm/ n. usu. spiny marine invertebrate, e.g., starfish and sea urchins.

ech·o /ékō/ • n. (pl. **-oes** or **-os**) **1 a** repetition of a sound by reflection of sound waves. **b** sound so produced. **2** reflected radio or radar beam. **3** close imitation or repetition of something already done. • v. (**-oes, -oed**) **1** intr. **a** (of a place) resound with an echo. **b** (of a sound) be repeated; resound. **2** tr. repeat (a sound) by an echo. **3** tr. **a** repeat (another's words). **b** imitate the words, opinions, or actions (of a person). □ **echo sounder** apparatus for determining the depth of the sea by measuring the time taken to receive an echo.

e·cho·ic /ekóik/ adj. Phonet. (of a word) imitating the sound it represents; onomatopoeic. □□ **ech·o·ism** n.

ech·o·lo·ca·tion /ékōlōkáyshən/ n. location of objects by reflected sound.

é·clair /aykláir/ n. small, elongated light pastry filled with whipped cream or custard, etc.

é·clat /aykláa'/ n. **1** brilliant display; dazzling effect. **2** conspicuous success.

ec·lec·tic /ikléktik/ • adj. deriving ideas, style, etc., from various sources. • n. eclectic person. □□ **ec·lec·ti·cal·ly** adv. **ec·lec·ti·cism** /-tisizəm/ n.

e·clipse /iklíps/ ● *n.* **1** obscuring of light from one celestial body by another. **2** loss of light, importance, or prominence. ● *v.tr.* **1** (of a celestial body) obscure the light from or to (another). **2** outshine; surpass.

e·clip·tic /iklíptik/ *n.* sun's apparent path among the stars during the year.

ec·logue /éklawg, -log/ *n.* short pastoral poem.

eco- /ékō, éekō/ *comb. form* ecology, ecological.

ecol. *abbr.* **1** ecological. **2** ecologist. **3** ecology.

E. coli /ée kṓlī/ *n.* any of several, sometimes pathogenic, strains of anaerobic bacteria, occurring in the large intestine of humans and other animals. ¶ Abbr. for *Escherichia coli*.

e·col·o·gy /ikóləjee/ *n.* **1** study of the relations of organisms to one another and to their physical surroundings. **2** study of the interaction of people with their environment. □□ **ec·o·log·i·cal** /ékəlójikəl, éekə-/ *adj.* **ec·o·log′i·cal·ly** *adv.* **e·col′o·gist** *n.*

econ. *abbr.* **1** economics. **2** economy.

ec·o·nom·ic /ékənómik, éekə-/ *adj.* **1** of economics. **2** profitable; cost effective. **3** considered or studied with regard to human needs (*economic geography*).

¶ **Economic** means 'concerning economics': *He's rebuilding a solid economic base for the country's future.* **Economical** is commonly used to mean 'thrifty; avoiding waste': *Small cars should be inexpensive to buy and economical to run.*

---

economic late Middle English: via Old French and Latin from Greek *oikonomikos*, from *oikonomia* (the source of *economy*). Originally a noun, the word denoted household management or a person skilled in this, hence the early sense of the adjective (late 16th century) 'relating to household management.' Modern senses date from the mid-19th century.

---

ec·o·nom·i·cal /ékənómikəl, éekə-/ *adj.* sparing in the use of resources; avoiding waste. □□ **ec·o·nom′i·cal·ly** *adv.*

ec·o·nom·ics /ékənómiks, éekə-/ *n.pl.* (often treated as *sing.*) **1** science of the production and distribution of wealth. **2** application of this to a particular subject.

e·con·o·mist /ikónəmist/ *n.* expert in or student of economics.

e·con·o·mize /ikónəmīz/ *v.intr.* **1** be economical. **2** (foll. by *on*) use sparingly; spend less on. □□ **e·con·o·mi·za′tion** *n.* **e·con′o·miz·er** *n.*

e·con·o·my /ikónəmee/ *n.* (*pl.* **-mies**) **1 a** wealth and resources of a community. **b** particular kind of this (*capitalist economy*). **2 a** careful management of (esp. financial) resources; frugality. **b** instance of this. **3** sparing or careful use.

ec·o·sys·tem /ékōsistəm, éekō-/ *n.* biological community of interacting organisms and their physical environment.

ec·ru /ékrōō, áykrōō/ *n.* color of unbleached linen.

ec·sta·sy /ékstəsee/ *n.* (*pl.* **-sies**) overwhelming joy or rapture. □□ **ec·stat′ic** *adj.* **ec·stat′i·cal·ly** *adv.*

ecto- /éktō/ *comb. form* outside.

ec·to·morph /éktəmawrf/ *n.* person with a lean body type. □□ **ec·to·mor′phic** *adj.*

ec·top·ic /ektópik/ *adj. Med.* in an abnormal position. □ **ectopic pregnancy** pregnancy occurring outside the uterus.

ec·to·plasm /éktəplazəm/ *n.* outer layer of the cytoplasm.

ec·u·men·i·cal /ékyōōménikəl/ *adj.* **1** of or representing the whole Christian world. **2** seeking worldwide Christian unity. □□ **ec·u·men′i·cal·ism** or **ec′u·me·nism** *n.* **ec·u·men′i·cal·ly** *adv.*

ec·ze·ma /éksimə, égzi-, igzée-/ *n.* inflammation of the skin, with itching and discharge.

ed. *abbr.* **1** edited by. **2** edition. **3** editor. **4** education.

-ed[1] /əd, id/ *suffix* forming adjectives: **1** from nouns, meaning 'having, wearing, affected by, etc.' (*talented; trousered; diseased*). **2** from phrases of adjective and noun (*good-humored; three-cornered*).

-ed[2] /əd, id/ *suffix* forming: **1** the past tense and past participle of weak verbs (*needed; risked*). **2** participial adjectives (*escaped prisoner, a pained look*).

E·dam /éedəm, éedam/ *n.* round Dutch cheese, usu. pale yellow with a red rind.

ed·dy /édee/ ● *n.* (*pl.* **-dies**) **1** circular movement of water causing a small whirlpool. **2** similar movement of wind, smoke, etc. ● *v.* (**-dies, -died**) whirl around in eddies.

e·del·weiss /áyd′lvīs/ *n.* white-flowered Alpine plant.

e·de·ma /idéemə/ *n.* accumulation of excess fluid in body tissues. □□ **e·dem·a·tose** /idémətōs, idée-/ *adj.* **e·dem′a·tous** *adj.*

E·den /éedən/ *n.* (also **Garden of Eden**) place of great happiness; paradise (with reference to the abode of Adam and Eve in the biblical account of Creation).

edge /ej/ ● *n.* **1** boundary line or margin of an area or surface. **2** narrow surface of a thin object. **3** meeting line of surfaces. **4 a** sharpened side of the blade. **b** sharpness. **5** area close to a steep drop. **6** edgelike thing. **7** effectiveness, force. **8** advantage. ● *v.* **1** *tr. & intr.* advance gradually or furtively. **2** *tr.* **a** provide with an edge or border. **b** form a border to. □ **on edge 1** tense and irritable. **2** eager; excited. **set a person's teeth on edge** (of a taste, sound, etc.) cause an unpleasant nervous sensation. **take the edge off** make less effective or intense. □□ **edge′less** *adj.* **edg′er** *n.*

---

edge Old English *ecg* 'sharpened side of a blade,' of Germanic origin; related to Dutch *egge* and German *Ecke*, also to Old Norse *eggja*, from an Indo-European root shared by Latin *acies* 'edge' and Greek *akis* 'point.'

---

edge·wise /éjwiz/ *adv.* **1** with edge uppermost or toward the viewer. **2** edge to edge. □ **get a word in edgewise** interject in a conversation dominated by another.

edg·ing /éjing/ *n.* thing forming an edge or border.

edg·y /éjee/ *adj.* (**edg·i·er, edg·i·est**) irritable; nervously anxious. □□ **edg′i·ly** *adv.* **edg′i·ness** *n.*

ed·i·ble /édibəl/ ● *adj.* fit or suitable to be eaten. ● *n.* (in *pl.*) food. □□ **ed·i·bil′i·ty** *n.*

e·dict /éedikt/ *n.* order proclaimed by authority.

ed·i·fice /édifis/ *n.* building, esp. an imposing one.

ed·i·fy /édifī/ *v.tr.* (**-fies, -fied**) improve morally or intellectually. □□ **ed·i·fi·ca'tion** *n.*

---

edify Middle English: from Old French *edifier*, from Latin *aedificare* 'build,' from *aedis* 'dwelling' + *facere* 'make' (the elements in *edifice*). The word originally meant 'construct a building,' also 'strengthen,' hence to 'build up' morally or spiritually.

---

ed·it /édit/ *v.tr.* **1** assemble, prepare, or modify (written material) for publication. **2** be editor of (a newspaper, etc.). **3** take extracts from and collate (movies, etc.) to form a unified sequence. **4** reword; correct.

e·di·tion /idíshən/ *n.* **1** edited or published form of a book, etc. **2** copies of a book, newspaper, etc., issued at one time. **3** particular version or instance of a broadcast. **4** person or thing resembling another.

ed·i·tor /éditər/ *n.* **1** person who edits. **2** person who directs preparation of a newspaper or periodical (or section of one) or a news program. **3** person who selects or commissions material for publication. □□ **ed'i·tor·ship** *n.*

ed·i·to·ri·al /éditáwreeəl/ • *adj.* of editing or editors. • *n.* article giving a newspaper's opinion on a topical issue. □□ **ed·i·to'ri·al·ize** *v.intr.* **ed·i·to'ri·al·ly** *adv.*

-edly /idlee/ *suffix* forming adverbs from verbs, meaning 'in a manner characterized by performance of or undergoing of the verbal action' (*allegedly; disgustedly; hurriedly*).

EDT *abbr.* eastern daylight time.

ed·u·cate /éjəkayt/ *v.tr.* (also *absol.*) **1** give intellectual, moral, or social instruction to. **2** provide education for. □□ **ed·u·ca·ble** /-kəbəl/ *adj.* **ed·u·ca·bil'i·ty** *n.* **ed'u·ca·tive** *adj.* **ed'u·ca·tor** *n.*

ed·u·cat·ed /éjəkaytid/ *adj.* **1** having had an (esp. good) education. **2** resulting from (good) education. **3** based on experience or study (*educated guess*).

ed·u·ca·tion /éjəkáyshən/ *n.* **1** systematic instruction, schooling, etc. **2** particular kind of or stage in education. **3** development of character or mental powers; formative experience. □□ **ed·u·ca'tion·al** *adj.* **ed·u·ca'tion·al·ly** *adv.*

e·duce /idóōs, idyóōs/ *v.tr.* bring out or develop; elicit. □□ **e·duc'i·ble** *adj.* **e·duc·tion** /idúkshen/ *n.* **e·duc'tive** *adj.*

EEC *abbr.* European Economic Community.

EEG *abbr.* electroencephalogram.

eel /eel/ *n.* **1** snakelike fish. **2** evasive person or thing. □□ **eel'like** *adj.* **eel'y** *adj.*

EEOC *abbr.* Equal Employment Opportunity Commission.

e'er /air/ *poet.* var. of EVER.

ee·rie /éeree/ *adj.* (**ee·ri·er, ee·ri·est**) gloomy and strange; weird. □□ **ee'ri·ly** *adv.* **ee'ri·ness** *n.*

ef- /if, ef/ *prefix* assim. form of EX-¹ before *f*.

ef·face /ifáys/ *v.* **1** *tr.* rub or wipe out. **2** *refl.* treat or regard oneself as unimportant (*self-effacing*). □□ **ef·face'ment** *n.*

ef·fect /ifékt/ • *n.* **1** result; consequence. **2** efficacy. **3** impression produced on a spectator, hearer, etc. **4** (in *pl.*) property. **5** (in *pl.*) lighting, sound, etc., used to accompany a movie, etc. **6** physical phenomenon (*Doppler effect*). • *v.tr.* bring about. □ **in effect** for practical purposes; in reality. **take effect** become operative. ¶ See note at AFFECT.

ef·fec·tive /iféktiv/ *adj.* **1** having a definite or desired effect. **2** impressive. **3** actual; existing. **4** operative. □□ **ef·fec'tive·ly** *adv.* **ef·fec'tive·ness** *n.*

ef·fec·tu·al /ifékchōōəl/ *adj.* **1** producing the required result or effect. **2** valid. □□ **ef·fec'tu·al·ly** *adv.*

ef·fec·tu·ate /ifékchōō-ayt/ *v.tr.* effect. □□ **ef·fec·tu·a·tion** /-áyshən/ *n.*

ef·fem·i·nate /iféminət/ *adj.* (of a man) feminine in appearance or manner. □□ **ef·fem·i·na·cy** /-nəsee/ *n.* **ef·fem'i·nate·ly** *adv.*

ef·fer·vesce /éfərvés/ *v.intr.* **1** give off bubbles of gas. **2** be lively. □□ **ef·fer·ves'cence** *n.* **ef·fer·ves'cent** *adj.*

ef·fete /iféet/ *adj.* **1 a** feeble. **b** effeminate. **2** exhausted of its essential quality or vitality. □□ **ef·fete'ness** *n.*

ef·fi·ca·cious /éfikáyshəs/ *adj.* producing the desired effect. □□ **ef·fi·ca'cious·ly** *adv.* **ef·fi·ca·cy** /éfikəsee/ *n.*

ef·fi·cient /ifíshənt/ *adj.* **1** productive with minimum waste or effort. **2** capable; acting effectively. □□ **ef·fi'cien·cy** *n.* **ef·fi'cient·ly** *adv.*

ef·fi·gy /éfijee/ *n.* (*pl.* **-gies**) sculpture or model of a person.

ef·flu·ence /éflōōəns/ *n.* **1** flowing out (of light, electricity, etc.). **2** that which flows out.

ef·flu·ent /éflōōənt/ • *adj.* flowing forth or out. • *n.* waste discharged into a river, etc.

ef·flu·vi·um /iflōōveeəm/ *n.* (*pl.* **ef·flu·vi·a** /-veeə/) unpleasant or noxious odor or vapor.

ef·fort /éfərt/ *n.* **1** physical or mental exertion. **2** determined attempt. **3** force exerted. □□ **ef'fort·less** *adj.* **ef'fort·less·ly** *adv.* **ef'fort·less·ness** *n.*

ef·fron·ter·y /ifrúntəree/ *n.* (*pl.* **-ies**) impudent audacity.

ef·fuse /ifyóōz/ *v.tr.* **1** pour forth (liquid, light, etc.). **2** give out (ideas, etc.). □□ **ef·fu'sive** *adj.* **ef·fu'sive·ly** *adv.* **ef·fu'sive·ness** *n.*

ef·fu·sion /ifyóōzhən/ *n.* **1** outpouring. **2** unrestrained verbiage.

e.g. *abbr.* for example.

e·gal·i·tar·i·an /igálitáireeən/ • *adj.* of or advocating the principle of equal rights and opportunities for all. • *n.* egalitarian person. □□ **e·gal·i·tar'i·an·ism** *n.*

egg¹ /eg/ *n.* **1 a** spheroidal reproductive body produced by females of animals such as birds, reptiles, fish, etc., enclosed in a protective layer and capable of developing into a new individual. **b** egg of the domestic hen, used for food. **2** *Biol.* ovum. **3** *colloq.* person or thing qualified in some way (*a tough egg*). □ **have** (or **put**) **all one's eggs in one basket** *colloq.* risk everything on a single venture. **with egg on one's face** *colloq.* made to look foolish. □□ **egg'y** *adj.* (**egg·i·er, egg·i·est**).

egg² /eg/ *v.tr.* (foll. by *on*) urge.

egg·head /éghed/ *n. colloq.* intellectual.

egg·nog /égnog/ *n.* drink made with eggs, cream, and often alcohol.

egg·plant /égplant/ *n.* plant bearing edible purple or white egg-shaped fruit.

egg·shell /égshel/ *n.* **1** shell of an egg. **2** pale off-white color.

e·go /éegō/ n. (pl. **-gos**) **1** the part of the mind that has self-awareness. **2** self-esteem. □ **ego trip** colloq. activity, etc., devoted entirely to one's own interests or feelings.

e·go·cen·tric /éegōséntrik, égō-/ adj. self-centered. □□ **e·go·cen'tri·cal·ly** adv. **e·go·cen·tric·i·ty** /-trísitee/ n.

e·go·ism /éegōizəm, égō-/ n. **1** self-interest as the foundation of morality. **2** = EGOTISM. □□ **e'go·ist** n. **e·go·is'tic** adj. **e·go·is'ti·cal** adj.
¶ An **egoist** is someone who is self-centered or selfish, as in feelings or actions. An **egotist** is someone who makes these feelings known, as by constant bragging or self-praise.

e·go·ma·ni·a /éegōmáyneeə, égō-/ n. morbid egotism. □□ **e·go·ma'ni·ac** n. **e·go·ma·ni·a·cal** /-mənîəkəl/ adj.

e·go·tism /éegətizəm, égə-/ n. **1** self-conceit. **2** selfishness. □□ **e'go·tist** n. **e·go·tis'tic** adj. **e·go·tis'ti·cal** adj. **e·go·tis'ti·cal·ly** adv.

e·gre·gious /igréejəs/ adj. outstandingly bad; shocking. □□ **e·gre'gious·ly** adv. **e·gre'gious·ness** n.

e·gress /éegres/ n. exit. □□ **e·gres·sion** /-gréshən/ n.

e·gret /éegrit/ n. heron with long white feathers.

E·gyp·tian /ijípshən/ • adj. of Egypt. • n. **1** native of Egypt. **2** language used in ancient Egypt.

eh /ay/ int. colloq. **1** expressing surprise. **2** asking for something to be repeated or explained.

ei·der /ídər/ n. any of various large northern ducks.

ei·der·down /ídərdown/ n. **1** down from the eider duck. **2** quilt stuffed with this.

eight /ayt/ n. **1** one more than seven. **2** symbol for this (8, viii, VIII).

eight·een /áyteén/ n. **1** one more than seventeen. **2** symbol for this (18, xviii, XVIII). □□ **eight'eenth'** adj. & n.

eighth /ayt-th, ayth/ • n. **1** next after seventh. • adj. that is the eighth.

eight·y /áytee/ n. (pl. **-ies**) **1** eight times ten. **2** symbol for this (80, lxxx, LXXX). **3** (in pl.) numbers from 80 to 89, esp. as years. □ **eighty-first**, **-second**, etc. ordinal numbers between eightieth and ninetieth. **eighty-one**, **-two**, etc., cardinal numbers between eighty and ninety. □□ **eight'i·eth** adj. & n.

ein·stein·i·um /ínstíneeəm/ n. artificial radioactive metallic element. ¶ Symb.: **Es**.

ei·ther /éethər, íthər/ • adj. & pron. **1** one or the other of two. **2** each of two. • adv. & conj. **1** as one possibility or alternative. **2** (with neg. or interrog.) any more than the other (I didn't like it either.) □ **either-or** unavoidable choice between alternatives. **either way** in either case.

e·jac·u·late • v.tr. /ijákyəlayt/ **1** exclaim. **2** eject (fluid, etc., esp. semen) from the body. • n. /ijákyəlat/ ejaculated semen. □□ **e·jac·u·la·tion** /-láyshən/ n. **e·jac'u·la·tor** n. **e·jac·u·la·to·ry** /-lətáwree/ adj.

e·ject /ijékt/ v.tr. **1** expel; compel to leave. **2 a** cause (the pilot, etc.) to be propelled from an aircraft, etc., in an emergency. **b** (absol.) (of the pilot, etc.) be ejected in this way (they both ejected at 1,000 feet). **3** cause to be removed. □□ **e·jec'tion** n. **e·jec'tor** n.

eke /eek/ v.tr. (foll. by out) contrive to make (a livelihood) or support (an existence).

EKG abbr. electrocardiogram.

e·lab·o·rate • adj. /ilábərət/ **1** minutely worked out. **2** complicated. • v. /ilábərayt/ **1** tr. work out or explain in detail. **2** intr. go into details (I need not elaborate). □□ **e·lab'o·rate·ly** adv. **e·lab'o·rate·ness** n. **e·lab·o·ra·tion** /-ráyshən/ n. **e·lab'o·ra·tive** adj. **e·lab'o·ra·tor** n.

é·lan /aylóN, aylón/ n. vivacity; dash.

e·land /éelənd/ n. large African antelope.

e·lapse /iláps/ v.intr. (of time) pass by.

e·las·tic /ilástik/ • adj. **1** able to resume its normal bulk or shape after contraction, dilatation, or distortion. **2** springy. • n. elastic cord or fabric. □□ **e·las'ti·cal·ly** adv. **e·las·tic·i·ty** /-lastísitee, eelas-/ n. **e·las·ti·cize** /ilástisīz/ v.tr.

e·late /iláyt/ v.tr. (esp. as **elated** adj.) inspirit; stimulate. □□ **e·lat'ed·ly** adv. **e·lat'ed·ness** n. **e·la·tion** /-láyshən/ n.

el·bow /élbō/ • n. **1** joint between the forearm and the upper arm. **2** elbow-shaped bend. • v.tr. thrust or jostle (a person or oneself). □ **elbow grease** colloq. vigorous polishing; hard work.

el·bow·room /élbōrōōm/ n. plenty of room to move or work in.

el·der[1] /éldər/ • adj. (of persons, esp. when related) senior; of a greater age. • n. **1** older of two (esp. related) persons. **2** (in pl.) persons older and usu. venerable. **3** church official.

el·der[2] /éldər/ n. tree with white flowers and dark berries.

el·der·ber·ry /éldərberee/ n. (pl. **-ries**) berry of the elder.

eld·er·ly /éldərlee/ • adj. rather old; past middle age. • n. (collect.) (prec. by the) elderly people.

eld·est /éldist/ adj. & n. first-born; oldest.

elec. abbr. **1** electric. **2** electrical. **3** electricity.

elect /ilékt/ • v.tr. **1** choose. **2** choose by vote. • adj. **1** chosen. **2** select; choice. **3** (after a noun designating office) chosen but not yet in office (president elect).

e·lec·tion /ilékshən/ n. **1** electing or being elected. **2** instance of this.

e·lec·tion·eer /ilékshəneér/ • v.intr. take part in an election campaign. • n. person who electioneers.

e·lec·tive /iléktiv/ • adj. **1** derived from election. **2** (of a body) having the power to elect. **3** optional. • n. elective course of study. □□ **e·lec'tive·ly** adv.

e·lec·tor /iléktər/ n. **1** person who has the right of voting. **2** member of the electoral college.

e·lec·tor·al /iléktərəl/ adj. relating to electors. □ **electoral college** ad hoc assembly that casts votes for the election of the US president and vice president. □□ **e·lec'tor·al·ly** adv.

e·lec·tor·ate /iléktərət/ n. body of electors.

e·lec·tric /iléktrik/ adj. **1** of, worked by, or charged with electricity; producing electricity. **2** causing or charged with excitement. □ **electric chair** electrified chair used for capital punishment. **electric eel** eellike fish of S. America that stuns prey by electric shock. **electric eye** photoelectric cell operating a relay when light is obscured. □□ **e·lec'tri·cal** adj. **e·lec'tri·cal·ly** adv.

e·lec·tri·cian /ilektríshən, éelek-/ n. person who installs or maintains electrical equipment.

e·lec·tric·i·ty /ilektrísitee, eelek-/ *n.* **1** form of energy resulting from the existence of charged particles (electrons, protons, etc.). **2** science of electricity. **3** supply of electric current. **4** excitement.

e·lec·tri·fy /iléktrifī/ *v.tr.* (**-fies, -fied**) **1** charge with electricity. **2** convert to the use of electric power. **3** cause sudden excitement in. □□ **e·lec·tri·fi·ca'tion** *n.* **e·lec'tri·fi·er** *n.*

electro- /iléktrō/ *comb. form* of, relating to, or caused by electricity (*electrocute; electromagnet*).

e·lec·tro·car·di·o·gram /iléktrōka'ardeeəgram/ *n.* record of the heartbeat traced by an electrocardiograph.

e·lec·tro·car·di·o·graph /iléktrōka'ardeeəgraf/ *n.* instrument recording electric currents generated by a heartbeat.

e·lec·tro·cute /iléktrəkyōōt/ *v.tr.* kill by electric shock. □□ **e·lec·tro·cu·tion** /-kyōoshən/ *n.*

e·lec·trode /iléktrōd/ *n.* conductor through which electricity enters or leaves an electrolyte, gas, vacuum, etc.

e·lec·tro·en·ceph·a·lo·gram /iléktrōinséfələgram/ *n.* record of the brain's activity traced by an electroencephalograph.

e·lec·tro·en·ceph·a·lo·graph /iléktrōinséfələgraf/ *n.* instrument recording electrical activity of the brain.

e·lec·trol·y·sis /ilektrólisis, eelek-/ *n.* **1** *Chem.* decomposition by electric current. **2** destruction of tumors, hair roots, etc., by this process. □□ **e·lec·tro·lyt·ic** /iléktrōlítik/ *adj.* **e·lec·tro·lyt'i·cal** *adj.* **e·lec·tro·lyt'i·cal·ly** *adv.*

elec·tro·lyte /iléktrəlīt/ *n.* **1** substance that conducts electricity when molten or in solution, esp. in a battery. **2** solution of this.

e·lec·tro·lyze /iléktrəlīz/ *v.tr.* subject to or treat by electrolysis. □□ **e·lec'tro·lyz·er** *n.*

e·lec·tro·mag·net /iléktrōmágnit/ *n.* soft metal core made into a magnet by the passage of electricity through a surrounding coil. □□ **e·lec·tro·mag·net'ic** *adj.* **e·lec·tro·mag'net·ism** *n.*

e·lec·tro·mo·tive /iléktrōmótiv/ *adj.* producing or tending to produce an electric current.

e·lec·tron /iléktron/ *n.* stable elementary particle with a charge of negative electricity.

e·lec·tron·ic /iléktrónik, eelek-/ *adj.* **1 a** produced by or involving the flow of electrons. **b** of electrons or electronics. **2** (of a device) using electronic components. **3 a** (of music) produced by electronic means. **b** (of a musical instrument) producing sounds by electronic means. □ **electronic mail** messages distributed by electronic means. Also called **E-mail.**

e·lec·tron·ics /iléktróniks, eelek-/ *n.pl.* (usu. treated as *sing.*) science concerned with the behavior and movement of electrons.

e·lec·tro·plate /iléktrəplayt/ ● *v.tr.* coat by electrolytic deposition with chromium, silver, etc. ● *n.* electroplated articles. □□ **e·lec'tro·plat·er** *n.*

e·lec·tro·shock /iléktrōshok/ *adj.* (of medical treatment) by means of electric shocks.

el·ee·mos·y·nar·y /éləmósineree, -móz-/ éleeə-/ *adj.* **1** of or dependent on alms. **2** charitable. **3** gratuitous.

el·e·gant /éligənt/ *adj.* **1** graceful. **2** tasteful; refined. **3** ingeniously simple. □□ **el'e·gance** *n.* **el'e·gant·ly** *adv.*

el·e·gi·ac /élijī̇̀ək, ileéjeeak/ ● *adj.* **1** used for

elegies. **2** mournful. ● *n.* (in *pl.*) elegiac verses. □□ **el·e·gi'a·cal·ly** *adv.*

el·e·gy /élijee/ *n.* (*pl.* **-gies**) song or poem of lament, esp. for the dead.

elem. *abbr.* elementary.

el·e·ment /élimənt/ *n.* **1** component part; contributing factor or thing. **2** *Chem.* & *Physics* any of the substances that cannot be resolved by chemical means into simpler substances. **3 a** any of the four substances (earth, water, air, and fire) in ancient and medieval philosophy. **b** any of these as a being's natural environment. **4** *Electr.* wire that heats up in an electric appliance. **5** (in *pl.*) atmospheric agencies, esp. wind and storm. **6** (in *pl.*) rudiments of learning. □ **in** (or **out of**) **one's element** in (or out of) one's accustomed or preferred surroundings.

el·e·men·tal /éliment'l/ *adj.* **1** of the elements. **2** of the powers of nature. **3** essential.

el·e·men·ta·ry /éliméntəree, -tree/ *adj.* rudimentary; simple. □ **elementary school** school in which elementary subjects are taught to young children. □□ **el·e·men·tar·i·ly** /-térəlee/ *adv.*

el·e·phant /élifənt/ *n.* (*pl.* same or **el·e·phants**) largest land animal, with a trunk and ivory tusks.

el·e·phan·ti·a·sis /élifəntī́əsis/ *n.* gross enlargement of the body, esp. the limbs, due to lymphatic obstruction.

el·e·phan·tine /élifánteen, -tīn, éləfən-/ *adj.* **1** of elephants. **2 a** huge. **b** clumsy; unwieldy.

elev. *abbr.* elevation.

el·e·vate /élivayt/ *v.tr.* **1** bring to a higher position. **2** exalt in rank, etc. **3** (usu. as **elevated** *adj.*) **a** raise the spirits of; elate. **b** raise morally or intellectually.

el·e·va·tion /élivàyshən/ *n.* **1 a** elevating or being elevated. **b** angle with the horizontal. **c** height above a given level, esp. sea level. **d** raised area. **2** loftiness; grandeur; dignity. **3** diagram showing one side of a building.

el·e·va·tor /élivaytər/ *n.* **1** hoisting machine. **2** *Aeron.* device on an airplane's tail for changing pitch. **3** platform or compartment for raising and lowering persons or things between floors.

el·e·ven /ilévən/ *n.* **1** one more than ten. **2** symbol for this (11, xi, XI).

el·e·venth /ilévənth/ *n.* **1** next after tenth. **2** each of eleven equal parts of a thing. ● *adj.* that is the eleventh. □ **eleventh hour** last possible moment.

elf /elf/ *n.* (*pl.* **elves** /elvz/) mythological being, esp. one that is small and mischievous. □□ **elf'in** *adj.* **elf'ish** *adj.* **elv'ish** *adj.*

e·lic·it /ilísit/ *v.tr.* **1** draw out; evoke (a response, etc.). **2** draw forth (what is latent). □□ **e·lic·i·ta'tion** *n.* **e·lic'i·tor** *n.*

e·lide /ilī́d/ *v.tr.* omit (a vowel or syllable) by elision.

el·i·gi·ble /élijibəl/ *adj.* **1** fit or entitled to be chosen. **2** desirable or suitable, esp. for marriage. □□ **el·i·gi·bil'i·ty** *n.*

e·lim·i·nate /ilíminayt/ *v.tr.* **1 a** remove; get rid of. **b** kill; murder. **2** exclude from consideration. **3** excrete. □□ **e·lim·i·na·tion** /-náyshən/ *n.* **e·lim'i·na·tor** *n.*

e·li·sion /ilízhən/ *n.* **1** omission of a vowel or syllable in pronouncing. **2** omission of a passage in a book, etc.

e·lite /aylée̱t, əlée̱t/ • n. 1 choice part of a body or group. 2 size of letter in typewriting (12 per inch). • adj. exclusive.

e·lit·ism /ayléetizəm, əleet-/ n. advocacy of or reliance on leadership or dominance by a select group. □□ **e·lit′ist** n. & adj.

e·lix·ir /ilíksər/ n. 1 Alchemy a preparation supposedly able to change metals into gold or prolong life. b supposed remedy for all ills. 2 Pharm. aromatic medicinal solution. 3 quintessence of a thing.

E·liz·a·be·than /ilízəbée̱thən/ • adj. of the time of England's Queen Elizabeth I or II. • n. person of the time of Queen Elizabeth I.

elk /elk/ n. (pl. same or **elks**) large deer of N. Europe and Asia.

elk·hound /élkhownd/ n. large Scandinavian hunting dog.

ell /el/ n. 1 right-angled extension to a building. 2 L-shaped thing.

el·lipse /ilíps/ n. closed symmetrical oval figure. □□ **el·lip·tic** /ilíptik/ (also **el·lip′ti·cal**) adj. **el·lip′ti·cal·ly** adv.

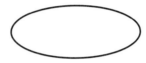

ELLIPSE

el·lip·sis /ilípsis/ n. (pl. **el·lip·ses** /-seez/) 1 omission of words within or at the end of a construction or sense. 2 set of three dots, etc., indicating such.

elm /elm/ n. 1 tall shade tree with rough serrated leaves. 2 its wood.

el·o·cu·tion /éləkyóoshən/ n. art of clear and expressive speech. □□ **el·o·cu′tion·ar·y** adj. **el·o·cu′tion·ist** n.

e·lon·gate /iláwnggayt, -long-/ • v.tr. lengthen; prolong. • adj. long in proportion to width. □□ **e·lon·ga·tion** /-gáyshən/ n.

e·lope /ilóp/ v.intr. run away to wed secretly. □□ **e·lope′ment** n.

el·o·quence /éləkwəns/ n. fluent and effective use of language. □□ **el′o·quent** adj. **el′o·quent·ly** adv.

else /els/ adv. 1 besides (someone else). 2 instead (what else could I say?). 3 otherwise; if not (or else you will be late).

else·where /éls-hwair, -wáir/ adv. in or to some other place.

e·lu·ci·date /ilóosidáyt/ v.tr. throw light on; explain. □□ **e·lu·ci·da′tion** /-dáyshən/ n. **e·lu′ci·da·tive** adj. **e·lu′ci·da·tor** n.

e·lude /ilóod/ v.tr. 1 escape adroitly; dodge. 2 avoid compliance with. □□ **e·lu·sion** /ilóozhən/ n. **e·lu·so·ry** /-lóosəree/ adj.

e·lu·sive /ilóosiv/ adj. 1 difficult to find or catch. 2 difficult to remember. 3 (of an answer, etc.) avoiding the point raised. □□ **e·lu′sive·ly** adv. **e·lu′sive·ness** n.

el·ver /élvər/ n. young eel.

elves pl. of ELF.

em /em/ n. Printing unit of measurement equal to the width of an M.

em- /im, em/ prefix assim. form of EN-[1], EN-[2] before b, p.

'em /əm/ pron. colloq. them (let 'em all come).

e·ma·ci·ate /imáysheeayt/ v.tr. (esp. as **emaciated** adj.) make abnormally thin or feeble. □□ **e·ma·ci·a·tion** /-áyshən/ n.

E-mail /ée̱mayl/ n. (also **e-mail**) = electronic mail.

em·a·nate /émənayt/ v. 1 intr. issue; originate. 2 tr. emit; send forth. □□ **em·a·na·tion** /-náyshən/ n.

e·man·ci·pate /imánsipayt/ v.tr. 1 free from restraint, esp. social or political. 2 cause to be less inhibited. 3 free from slavery. □□ **e·man·ci·pa·tion** /-páyshən/ n. **e·man′ci·pa·tor** n. **e·man′ci·pa·to·ry** adj.

e·mas·cu·late • v.tr. /imáskyəlayt/ 1 deprive of force or vigor. 2 castrate. • adj. /imáskyələt/ effeminate. □□ **e·mas·cu·la·tion** /-láyshən/ n. **e·mas′cu·la·tor** n. **e·mas·cu·la·to·ry** /-lətáwree/ adj.

em·balm /embaám, im-/ v.tr. preserve (a corpse) from decay. □□ **em·balm′er** n.

em·bank·ment /embángkmənt, im-/ n. earth or stone bank for keeping back water, or for carrying a road or railroad.

em·bar·go /embaárgō/ • n. (pl. **-goes**) 1 order forbidding foreign ships access to ports. 2 official suspension of commerce. • v.tr. (**-goes, -goed**) place under embargo.

em·bark /embaárk, im-/ v. 1 tr. & intr. put or go on board a ship or aircraft (to a destination). 2 intr. (foll. by on, upon) engage in an undertaking. □□ **em·bar·ka′tion** n.

em·bar·rass /embárəs, im-/ v.tr. 1 a cause (a person) to feel awkward or ashamed. b (as **embarrassed** adj.) expressing a feeling of awkwardness or self-consciousness. 2 (as **embarrassed** adj.) encumbered with debts. 3 encumber. □□ **em·bar′rass·ing** adj. **em·bar′rass·ing·ly** adv. **em·bar′rass·ment** n.

em·bas·sy /émbəsee/ n. (pl. **-sies**) 1 a residence or offices of an ambassador. b ambassador and staff. 2 deputation to a foreign country.

em·bat·tle /embát′l, im-/ v.tr. 1 set (an army, etc.) in battle array. 2 provide with battlements. 3 (as **embattled** adj.) a prepared or arrayed for battle. b involved in a conflict or difficult undertaking.

em·bed /embéd, im-/ v.tr. (also **im·bed′**) (**-bed·ded, -bed·ding**) fix firmly in; implant.

em·bel·lish /embélish, im-/ v.tr. 1 beautify; adorn. 2 add interest to (a narrative) with fictitious additions. □□ **em·bel′lish·ment** n.

em·ber /émbər/ n. 1 small piece of glowing coal or wood in a dying fire. 2 almost extinct residue of a past activity, feeling, etc.

em·bez·zle /embézəl, im-/ v.tr. divert (money, etc.) fraudulently to one's own use. □□ **em·bez′zle·ment** n. **em·bez′zler** n.

em·bit·ter /embítər, im-/ v.tr. arouse bitter feelings in.

em·bla·zon /embláyzən, im-/ v.tr. 1 portray or adorn conspicuously. 2 adorn (a heraldic shield).

em·blem /émbləm/ n. 1 symbol. 2 heraldic device. □□ **em·blem·at′ic** adj. **em·blem·at′i·cal** adj. **em·blem·at′i·cal·ly** adv.

em·bod·y /embódee, im-/ *v.tr.* (**-ies, -ied**) **1** give a concrete or discernible form to (an idea, concept, etc.). **2** (of a thing or person) be an expression of (an idea, etc.). **3** include; comprise. □□ **em·bod′i·ment** *n.*

em·bold·en /embóldən, im-/ *v.tr.* make bold; encourage.

em·bol·ism /émbəlizəm/ *n.* obstruction of an artery by a clot of blood, air bubble, etc.

em·boss /embós, im-/ *v.tr.* carve or mold in relief.

em·bou·chure /ómbōōshŏŏr/ *n. Mus.* mode of applying the mouth to a brass or wind instrument.

em·brace /embráys, im-/ • *v.tr.* **1 a** hold closely in the arms. **b** (of two people) hold each other closely. **2** clasp; enclose. **3** accept eagerly. **4** adopt (a course of action, etc.). **5** include; comprise. • *n.* act of embracing. □□ **em·brace′a·ble** *adj.*

em·broi·der /embróydər, im-/ *v.tr.* **1** decorate (cloth, etc.) with needlework. **2** embellish (a narrative). □□ **em·broi′der·er** *n.*

em·broi·der·y /embróydəree, im-/ *n.* (*pl.* **-ies**) **1** art of embroidering. **2** embroidered work. **3** embellishment.

em·broil /embróyl, im-/ *v.tr.* involve (a person) in conflict or difficulties. □□ **em·broil′ment** *n.*

em·bry·o /émbreeō/ *n.* (*pl.* **-os**) **1 a** unborn or unhatched offspring. **b** human offspring in the first eight weeks from conception. **2** rudimentary plant in a seed. **3** thing in a rudimentary stage. □□ **em·bry·on·ic** /émbreeónik/ *adj.*

em·bry·ol·o·gy /émbreeóləjee/ *n.* study of embryos. □□ **em·bry·ol′o·gist** *n.*

em·cee /émsée/ • *n.* master of ceremonies. • *v.* (**em·cees, em·ceed**) act as an emcee.

e·mend /iménd/ *v.tr.* edit (a text, etc.) to make corrections. □□ **e·men·da′tion** *n.*

em·er·ald /émərəld, émrəld/ *n.* **1** bright-green precious stone, a variety of beryl. **2** color of this.

e·merge /imárj/ *v.intr.* **1** come up or out into view. **2** come to light; become known, esp. as a result of inquiry, etc. **3** become recognized or prominent. □□ **e·mer′gence** *n.* **e·mer′gent** *adj.*

e·mer·gen·cy /imárjənsee/ *n.* (*pl.* **-cies**) sudden state of danger, etc., requiring immediate action.

e·mer·i·tus /iméritəs/ *adj.* retired and retaining one's title as an honor (*emeritus professor, professor emeritus*).

em·er·y /émaree/ *n.* coarse corundum for polishing metal, etc. □ **emery board** emery-coated strip of thin wood, etc., used as a nail file.

e·met·ic /imétik/ • *adj.* that causes vomiting. • *n.* emetic medicine.

em·i·grate /émigrayt/ *v. intr.* leave one's own country to settle in another. □□ **em′i·grant** *n.* **em·i·gra′tion** /-gráyshən/ *n.*

¶ To **emigrate** is to leave a country, especially one's own, intending to remain away. To **immigrate** is to enter a country, intending to remain there. From the point of view of the receiving country, one might say: *My aunt emigrated from Poland and immigrated into Canada.*

é·mi·gré /émigray/ *n.* (also **e′mi·gré**) emigrant, esp. a political exile.

em·i·nence /éminəns/ *n.* **1** distinction; recognized superiority. **2** piece of rising ground. **3** (**Eminence**) title of address to a cardinal.

187 embody ~ emporium

em·i·nent /éminənt/ *adj.* distinguished; notable; remarkable in degree. □ **eminent domain** right of government to purchase private property for public. □□ **em′i·nent·ly** *adv.*

¶ **Eminent** means 'outstanding; famous': *The book was written by an eminent authority on folk art.* **Imminent** means 'about to happen': *People brushed aside the possibility that war was imminent.* **Immanent**, often used in religious or philosophical contexts, means 'inherent': *He believed in the immanent unity of nature taught by the Hindus.*

e·mir /emeér/ *n.* title of various Muslim rulers. □□ **e·mir·ate** /imeérate, -ayt, aymeér-, émərit/ *n.*

em·is·sar·y /émiseree/ *n.* (*pl.* **-ies**) person sent on a diplomatic mission.

e·mit /imít/ *v.tr.* (**e·mit·ted, e·mit·ting**) send out (heat, sound, light, etc.); discharge. □□ **e·mis·sion** /imíshən/ *n.*

e·mol·lient /imólyənt/ • *adj.* that softens or soothes the skin. • *n.* emollient agent. □□ **e·mol′lience** *n.*

e·mol·u·ment /imólyəmənt/ *n.* fee from employment.

e·mote /imót/ *v.intr.* show excessive emotion.

e·mo·tion /imóshən/ *n.* strong mental or instinctive feeling such as love or fear.

e·mo·tion·al /imóshənəl/ *adj.* **1** of or relating to emotions. **2** liable to excessive emotion. **3** likely to excite emotions. □□ **e·mo′tion·al·ism** *n.* **e·mo′tion·al·ly** *adv.*

em·pa·thize /émpəthīz/ *v.intr.* exercise empathy.

em·pa·thy /émpəthee/ *n.* capacity to identify with a person or object. □□ **em·pa·thet·ic** /-thétik/ *adj.* **em·pa·thet′i·cal·ly** *adv.*

em·per·or /émpərər/ *n.* sovereign of an empire.

em·pha·sis /émfəsis/ *n.* (*pl.* **em·pha·ses** /-seez/) **1** importance or prominence given to a thing. **2** stress laid on a word or words to indicate special meaning or importance.

em·pha·size /émfəsīz/ *v.tr.* put emphasis on.

em·phat·ic /emfátik/ *adj.* **1** forcibly expressive. **2** of words: **a** bearing the stress. **b** used to give emphasis. □□ **em·phat′i·cal·ly** *adv.*

em·phy·se·ma /émfiseémə, -zeémə/ *n.* disease of the lungs causing breathlessness.

em·pire /émpīr/ *n.* **1** extensive group of lands or countries under a single authority. **2** supreme dominion. **3** large commercial organization, etc., directed by one person or group.

em·pir·i·cal /empírikəl, im-/ *adj.* (also **em·pir′ic**) based on observation or experiment, not on theory. □□ **em·pir′i·cal·ly** *adv.* **em·pir·i·cism** /-sizəm/ *n.* **em·pir′i·cist** *n.*

em·place·ment /emplaysmənt, im-/ *n.* **1** putting in position. **2** platform for a gun. **3** situation; position.

em·ploy /emplóy, im-/ *v.tr.* **1** use the services of (a person) in return for payment. **2** use to good effect. **3** keep (a person) occupied. □□ **em·ploy′a·ble** *adj.* **em·ploy·a·bil′i·ty** *n.* **em·ploy′er** *n.*

em·ploy·ee /émployée, -ployeé/ *n.* (also **em·ploy′e**) person employed for wages.

em·ploy·ment /emplóymənt, im-/ *n.* **1** employing or being employed. **2** occupation.

em·po·ri·um /empáwreeəm/ *n.* (*pl.* **-ums** or **em·po·ri·a** /-reeə/) store selling a wide variety of goods.

em·pow·er /empówər, im-/ v.tr. **1** authorize, license. **2** give power to; make able. □□ **em·pow′ er·ment** n.

em·press /émpris/ n. **1** wife or widow of an emperor. **2** woman emperor.

emp·ty /émptee/ • adj. (**emp·ti·er, emp·ti·est**) **1** containing nothing. **2** unoccupied; uninhabited; deserted; unfurnished. **3 a** hollow; insincere. **b** without purpose. **c** vacuous. • v. (**-ties, -tied**) **1** tr. remove the contents of. **2** intr. become empty. **3** intr. (of a river) discharge itself (into the sea, etc.). • n. (pl. **-ties**) colloq. empty bottle, etc. □□ **emp′ti·ly** adv. **emp′ti·ness** n.

EMT abbr. emergency medical technician.

e·mu /eémyōō/ n. large flightless bird of Australia.

em·u·late /émyəlayt/ v.tr. **1** try to equal or excel. **2** imitate. □□ **em·u·la·tion** /-láyshən/ n. **em′u· la·tive** adj. **em′u·la·tor** n.

e·mul·si·fi·er /imúlsifīər/ n. substance that stabilizes an emulsion, esp. a food additive used to stabilize processed foods.

e·mul·si·fy /imúlsifī/ v.tr. (**-fies, -fied**) convert into an emulsion. □□ **e·mul·si·fi·ca′tion** n. **e· mul′si·fi·er** n.

e·mul·sion /imúlshən/ n. fine dispersion of one liquid in another, esp. as paint, medicine, etc. □□ **e·mul·sive** /-siv/ adj.

en /en/ n. Printing unit of measurement equal to half an em.

en-¹ /en, in/ prefix (also **em-** before b, p) forming verbs, = IN-¹: **1** from nouns, meaning 'put into or on' (engulf; entrust; embed). **2** from nouns or adjectives, meaning 'bring into the condition of' (enslave). **3** from verbs: **a** in the sense 'in, into, on' (enfold). **b** as an intensifier (entangle).

en-² /en, in/ prefix (also **em-** before b, p) in; inside (energy).

-en¹ /ən/ suffix forming verbs: **1** from adjectives, usu. meaning 'make or become so or more so' (deepen; fasten; moisten). **2** from nouns (happen; strengthen).

-en² /ən/ suffix (also **-n**) forming adjectives from nouns, meaning **1** made or consisting of (often with extended and figurative senses) (wooden). **2** resembling; of the nature of (golden; silvern).

-en³ /ən/ suffix (also **-n**) forming past participles of strong verbs: **1** as a regular inflection (spoken; sworn). **2** with restricted sense (drunken).

-en⁴ /ən/ suffix forming the plural of a few nouns (children; brethren; oxen).

-en⁵ /ən/ suffix forming diminutives of nouns (chicken; maiden).

en·a·ble /enáybəl/ v.tr. **1** give (a person, etc.) the means or authority. **2** make possible. □□ **en· a′bler** n.

en·act /enákt, in-/ v.tr. **1 a** ordain; decree. **b** make (a bill, etc.) law. **2** play (a part). □□ **en· act′ment** n. **en·ac′tor** n.

e·nam·el /ináməl/ • n. **1** glasslike opaque coating for metal, etc. **2 a** smooth, hard coating. **b** hard gloss paint. **3** hard coating of a tooth. • v.tr. inlay or encrust with enamel.

en·am·or /inámər/ v.tr. (usu. in passive, foll. by of) inspire with love or delight for.

en·camp /enkámp/ v. **1** settle in a military camp. **2** lodge in the open in tents. □□ **en·camp′ment** n.

en·cap·su·late /enkápsəlayt, -syōō-, in-/ v.tr. **1** enclose in or as in a capsule. **2** summarize; express briefly. □□ **en·cap·su·la·tion** /-láyshən/ n.

en·case /enkáys, in-/ v.tr. **1** put into a case. **2** surround as with a case. □□ **en·case′ment** n.

-ence /əns/ suffix forming nouns expressing: **1** quality or state or instance of one (patience). **2** action (reference).

en·ceph·a·li·tis /enséfəlítis/ n. inflammation of the brain. □□ **en·ceph·a·lit·ic** /-lítik/ adj.

en·ceph·a·lo·gram /enséfəlōgram/ n. X-ray of the brain.

en·ceph·a·lo·graph /enséfələgraf/ n. = ELECTROENCEPHALOGRAPH.

en·chant /enchánt, in-/ v.tr. **1** charm; delight. **2** bewitch. □□ **en·chant′ed·ly** adv. **en·chant′ing** adj. **en·chant′ing·ly** adv. **en·chant′ment** n.

en·chi·la·da /énchiláadə/ n. rolled tortilla filled with meat, etc.

en·cir·cle /ensúrkəl, in-/ v.tr. **1** surround. **2** form a circle around. □□ **en·cir′cle·ment** n.

en·clave /énklayv, ón-/ n. **1** territory surrounded by foreign territory. **2** group of people who are culturally, intellectually, or socially distinct from those surrounding them.

en·close /enklóz, in-/ v.tr. **1 a** surround with a wall, fence, etc. **b** shut in. **2** put in a receptacle (esp. an envelope).

en·clo·sure /enklózhər, in-/ n. **1** act of enclosing. **2** enclosed space or area. **3** thing enclosed with a letter. **4** enclosing fence, etc.

en·code /enkód, in-/ v.tr. put into code. □□ **en· cod′er** n.

en·co·mi·um /enkómeeəm/ n. (pl. **en·co·mi·ums** or **en·co·mi·a** /-meeə/) formal or high-flown praise. □□ **en·co·mi·ast** /-ast/ n. **en·co·mi·as′ tic** adj.

en·com·pass /enkúmpəs, in-/ v.tr. **1** surround. **2** contain. □□ **en·com′pass·ment** n.

en·core /óngkawr/ • n. **1** call by an audience for continuation of performance, usu. by applause. **2** such a continuation. • int. also /-kór/ again; once more.

en·coun·ter /enkówntər, in-/ • v.tr. **1** meet unexpectedly. **2** meet as an adversary. **3** meet with; experience (problems, opposition, etc.). • n. **1** meeting by chance. **2** meeting in conflict. □ **en· counter group** group of persons seeking psychological benefit through contact with one another.

en·cour·age /enkɔ́rij, -kúr-, in-/ v.tr. **1** give courage, confidence, or hope to. **2** urge; advise. **3** promote. □□ **en·cour′age·ment** n. **en·cour′ag· ing** adj. **en·cour′ag·ing·ly** adv.

en·croach /enkróch, in-/ v.intr. (foll. by on, upon) intrude. □□ **en·croach′ment** n.

en·crust /enkrúst, in-/ v. **1** cover with a crust. **2** intr. form a crust. □□ **en·crust′ment** n.

en·crypt /enkript, in-/ v.tr. **1** convert (data) into code, esp. to prevent unauthorized access. **2** conceal by this means. □□ **en·cryp·tion** /-krípshən/ n.

en·cum·ber /enkúmbər, in-/ v.tr. **1** be a burden to. **2** hamper; impede. □□ **en·cum′brance** n.

ency. abbr. (also **encyc.**) encyclopedia.

-ency /ənsee/ suffix forming nouns denoting a quality (efficiency; fluency) or state (presidency).

en·cyc·li·cal /ensíklikəl/ • n. papal letter to bishops. • adj. (of a letter) for wide circulation.

en·cy·clo·pe·di·a /ensíkləpeedeeə/ *n.* (also **en·cy·clo·pae′di·a**) publication giving information on many subjects, or on many aspects of one subject.

en·cy·clo·pe·dic /ensíkləpeedik/ *adj.* (also **en·cy·clo·pae′dic**) (of knowledge or information) comprehensive.

end /end/ • *n.* **1 a** extreme limit. **b** extremity. **2** extreme part or surface of a thing. **3 a** conclusion; finish. **b** latter or final part. **c** death; destruction. **d** result; outcome. **4** goal; purpose. **5** piece left over. **6** (prec. by *the*) *colloq.* limit of endurability. **7** part with which a person is concerned (*no problem at my end*). **8** *Football* player at the extremity of the offensive or defensive line. • *v.* **1** *tr.* & *intr.* bring or come to an end. **2** *tr.* destroy. **3** *intr.* (foll. by *in*) result. □ **end it all** (or **end it**) *colloq.* commit suicide. **end of the road** point at which hope has to be abandoned. **end result** final outcome. **end up** reach a specified state, action, or place eventually (*ended up a drunk*). **in the end** finally; after all. **keep one's end up** do one's part. **make ends** (or **both ends**) **meet** live within one's income. **on end 1** upright. **2** continuously (*for three weeks on end*). **put an end to 1** stop (an activity, etc.). **2** abolish; destroy.

en·dan·ger /endáynjər, in-/ *v.tr.* place in danger. □□ **en·dan′ger·ment** *n.*

en·dear /endeér, in-/ *v.tr.* make dear to. □□ **en·dear′ing** *adj.* **en·dear′ing·ly** *adv.* **en·dear′ment** *n.*

en·deav·or /endévər, in-/ • *v.tr.* try earnestly. • *n.* earnest attempt.

en·dem·ic /endémik/ *adj.* regularly or only found among a particular people or in a certain region. □□ **en·dem′i·cal·ly** *adv.*
¶ See note at EPIDEMIC.

end·ing /énding/ *n.* **1** end or final part, esp. of a story. **2** inflected final part of a word.

en·dive /éndīv, óndeev/ *n.* curly-leaved salad green.

end·less /éndlis/ *adj.* **1** infinite; without end. **2** continual. **3** innumerable. **4** (of a belt, chain, etc.) having the ends joined for continuous action over wheels, etc. □□ **end′less·ly** *adv.* **end′less·ness** *n.*

end·most /éndmōst/ *adj.* nearest the end.

endo- /éndō/ *comb. form* internal.

en·do·crine /éndōkrin, -kreen, -krīn/ *adj.* (of a gland) secreting directly into the blood; ductless.

en·do·cri·nol·o·gy /éndōkrinóləjee/ *n.* study of endocrine glands. □□ **en·do·crin·o·log·i·cal** /-nəlójikəl/ *adj.* **en·do·cri·nol·o·gist** /-nól-/ *n.*

en·do·morph /éndōmawrf/ *n.* person with a heavy, rounded body. □□ **en·do·mor′phic** *adj.* **en′do·mor·phy** *n.*

en·dor·phin /endáwrfin/ *n.* peptide neurotransmitter occurring in the brain and having pain-relieving properties.

en·dorse /endáwrs, in-/ *v.tr.* **1** approve. **2** sign or write on (a document), esp. the back of (a bill, check, etc.). □□ **en·dors′a·ble** *adj.* **en·dor·see** /éndorsée/ *n.* **en·dorse′ment** *n.* **en·dors′er** *n.*

en·dow /endów, in-/ *v.tr.* **1** bequeath or give a permanent income to (a person, institution, etc.). **2** provide with talent, ability, etc. □□ **en·dow′er** *n.* **en·dow′ment** *n.*

en·due /endoo, -dyoo, in-/ *v.tr.* (foll. by *with*) invest or provide (a person) with qualities, powers, etc.

en·dur·ance /endoorəns, -dyoor-, in-/ *n.* **1** power or habit of enduring. **2** ability to withstand prolonged strain.

en·dure /endoor, -dyoor, in-/ *v.* **1** *tr.* undergo (a difficulty, etc.). **2** *tr.* tolerate. **3** *intr.* last. □□ **en·dur·a·bil′i·ty** *n.* **en·dur′a·ble** *adj.* **en·dur′ing·ly** *adv.*

end·ways /éndwayz/ *adv.* **1** with end uppermost or foremost. **2** end to end.

en·e·ma /énimə/ *n.* injection of liquid into the rectum, esp. to expel its contents.

en·e·my /énəmee/ *n.* (*pl.* **-mies**) **1** person or group actively hostile to another. **2 a** hostile nation or army. **b** member of this.

en·er·gize /énərjīz/ *v.tr.* **1** infuse energy into. **2** provide energy for the operation of (a device). □□ **en′er·giz·er** *n.*

en·er·gy /énərjee/ *n.* (*pl.* **-gies**) **1** force; vigor; capacity for activity. **2** capacity of matter or radiation to do work. □□ **en·er·get′ic** *adj.* **en·er·get′i·cal·ly** *adv.*

en·er·vate /énərvayt/ *v.tr.* deprive of vigor or vitality. □□ **en·er·va·tion** /-váyshən/ *n.*

en·fee·ble /enfeébəl, in-/ *v.tr.* make feeble. □□ **en·fee′ble·ment** *n.*

en·fi·lade /énfiláyd, -laad/ *n.* gunfire directed along a line from end to end.

en·fold /enfóld, in-/ *v.tr.* **1** wrap; envelop. **2** clasp; embrace.

en·force /enfáwrs, in-/ *v.tr.* **1** compel observance of (a law, etc.). **2** impose (an action, conduct, one's will). □□ **en·force′a·ble** *adj.* **en·force·a·bil′i·ty** *n.* **en·forc′ed·ly** *adv.* **en·force′ment** *n.* **en·forc′er** *n.*

en·fran·chise /enfránchīz, in-/ *v.tr.* **1** give (a person) the right to vote. **2** free (a slave, etc.). □□ **en·fran′chise·ment** *n.*

en·gage /en-gáyj, in-/ *v.* **1** *tr.* hire. **2** *tr.* **a** (usu. in *passive*) occupy. **b** hold fast. **3** *tr.* (usu. in *passive*) bind by a promise, esp. of marriage. **4** *tr.* reserve (a room, seat, etc.). **5 a** *tr.* interlock (parts of a gear, etc.). **b** *intr.* (of a part, gear, etc.) interlock. **6 a** *tr.* & *intr.* come into battle. **b** *tr.* bring (troops) into battle. **7** *intr.* take part (*engage in politics*). □□ **en·gaged′** *adj.*

en·gaged /en-gáyjd, in-/ *adj.* **1** under a promise to marry. **2 a** occupied; busy. **b** reserved; booked.

en·gage·ment /en-gáyjmənt, in-/ *n.* **1** engaging or being engaged. **2** appointment. **3** betrothal. **4** battle. □ **engagement ring** ring given to a woman by her fiancé.

en·gag·ing /en-gáyjing, in-/ *adj.* attractive; charming. □□ **en·gag′ing·ly** *adv.*

en·gen·der /enjéndər, in-/ *v.tr.* give rise to; bring about.

en·gine /énjin/ *n.* **1** mechanical contrivance, esp. as a source of power. **2** locomotive.
¶ An **engine** is a machine that (via combustion) converts fuel into energy, to drive something: *an automobile engine, a steam engine.* **Motor** is also used of a car's engine, but is also used of a wide range of machines that move something, like *electric motors.*

---

engine Middle English (formerly also as *ingine*): from Old French *engin*, from Latin *ingenium* 'talent, device', from *in-* 'in' + *gignere* 'beget.' The original sense was 'inge-

nuity, cunning,' hence 'the product of ingenuity, a plot or snare,' also 'tool, weapon,'
later specifically denoting a large mechanical
weapon; whence a machine (mid-17th century), used commonly later in combinations
such as *steam engine* and *internal-combustion
engine.*

en·gi·neer /énjinéer/ ● n. **1** person qualified in
a branch of engineering. **2 a** person in charge of
engines. **b** operator of an engine, esp. a railroad
locomotive. **3** (foll. by *of*) contriver. ● v. **1** tr.
contrive; bring about. **2** intr. act as an engineer.

en·gi·neer·ing /énjinéering/ n. application of
science to the design, building, and use of machines, etc.

Eng·lish /ínggish/ ● adj. of England or its people or language. ● n. **1** language of England,
now used in the UK, US, Canada, etc. **2** (prec.
by *the*; treated as *pl.*) the people of England. **3**
spin given to a ball. □ **English horn** alto woodwind instrument of the oboe family. **English muffin** flat round bread-dough muffin, usu. served
sliced and toasted. **the Queen's** (or **King's**) **English**
English language as correctly written or spoken
in Britain.

Eng·lish·man /íngglishmən/ n. (*pl.* **-men**; *fem.*
Eng·lish·wom·an /ínglishwŏomən/ *pl.* **-wom·en**)
person who is English by birth or descent.

en·gorge /en-gáwrj, in-/ v.tr. **1** (in *passive*) **a** be
crammed. **b** *Med.* be congested with blood. **2**
devour greedily. □□ **en·gorge′ment** n.

engr. *abbr.* **1** engineer. **2** engraved. **3** engraver. **4**
engraving.

en·grave /en-gráyv, in-/ v.tr. **1** carve (a text or
design) on a hard surface. **2** inscribe (a surface) in this way. **3** impress deeply on a person's
memory, etc. □□ **en·grav′er** n.

en·grav·ing /en-gráyving, in-/ n. print made
from an engraved plate, block, or other surface.

en·gross /en-gróss, in-/ v.tr. absorb the attention of; occupy fully (*engrossed in studying*).
□□ **en·gross′ing** adj.

en·gulf /en-gúlf, in-/ v.tr. flow over and swamp;
overwhelm. □□ **en·gulf′ment** n.

en·hance /enháns, in-/ v.tr. intensify (qualities,
value, etc.); improve (something already of
good quality). □□ **en·hance′ment** n. **en·hanc′er**
n.

e·nig·ma /inígmə/ n. **1** puzzling thing or person.
2 riddle; paradox. □□ **en·ig·mat·ic** /énigmátik/
adj. **en·ig·mat′i·cal** adj. **en·ig·mat′i·cal·ly** adv.

en·join /enjóyn, in-/ v.tr. **1** command; order (a
person). **2** *Law* prohibit (a person) by order.
□□ **en·join′ment** n.

en·joy /enjóy, in-/ v.tr. **1** take pleasure in. **2** have
the use or benefit of. **3** experience. □ **enjoy oneself** experience pleasure. □□ **en·joy′a·ble** adj.
en·joy′er n. **en·joy′ment** n.

en·large /enláarj, in-/ v. **1** tr. & intr. make or become larger or wider. **2** intr. describe in greater
detail. **3** tr. reproduce on a larger scale. □□ **en·
large′ment** n.

en·larg·er /enláarjər, in-/ n. apparatus for enlarging photographs.

en·light·en /enlít'n, in-/ v.tr. **1 a** inform (a person) about a subject. **b** (as **enlightened** adj.)
knowledgeable. **2** (esp. as **enlightened** adj.) free
from prejudice or superstition.

en·light·en·ment /enlít'nmənt, in-/ n. **1**
enlightening; being enlightened. **2** (**the Enlightenment**) the 18th-c. philosophy of reason and
individualism.

en·list /enlíst, in-/ v. **1** intr. & tr. enroll in the
armed services. **2** tr. secure as a means of help or
support. □ **enlisted man** soldier or sailor below
the rank of officer. □□ **en·list′ment** n.

en·liv·en /enlívən, in-/ v.tr. **1** give life or spirit to.
2 make cheerful; brighten (a picture or scene).
□□ **en·liv′en·ment** n.

en masse /on más/ adv. **1** all together. **2** in
a mass.

en·mesh /enmésh, in-/ v.tr. entangle in or as in
a net. □□ **en·mesh′ment** n.

en·mi·ty /énmitee/ n. (*pl.* **-ties**) **1** state of being
an enemy. **2** feeling of hostility.

en·ne·ad /éneead/ n. group of nine.

en·no·ble /enóbəl, in-/ v.tr. make noble; elevate.
□□ **en·no′ble·ment** n.

en·nui /onwée/ n. mental weariness; boredom.

e·nol·o·gy /eenóləjee/ n. the study of wines.
□□ **e·no·log·i·cal** /éenəlójikəl/ adj. **e·nol′o·gist** n.

e·nor·mi·ty /ináwrmitee/ n. (*pl.* **-ties**) **1** extreme
wickedness. **2** great size.
¶ This word is imprecisely used to mean 'great
size,' e.g., *it's difficult to recognize the enormity
of the continent*, but the original and preferred
meaning is 'extreme wickedness,' as in *the enormity of the crime.*

---

enormity late Middle English: via Old
French from Latin *enormitas*, from *enormis*,
from *e-* (variant of *ex-*) 'out of' + *norma* 'pattern, standard.' The word originally meant
'deviation from legal or moral rectitude' and
'transgression.' Current senses have been
influenced by *enormous*.

---

e·nor·mous /ináwrməs/ adj. very large; huge.
□□ **e·nor′mous·ly** adv. **e·nor′mous·ness** n.

e·nough /inúf/ ● adj. as much or as many as required. ● n. amount or quantity that is enough.
● adv. **1** adequately. **2** quite (*oddly enough*).
□ **have had enough of** want no more of; be tired
of.

en·quir·y var. of INQUIRE.

en·quir·y var. of INQUIRY.

en·rage /enráyj, in-/ v.tr. make furious. □□ **en·
rage′ment** n.

en·rap·ture /enrápchər, in-/ v.tr. give intense
delight to.

en·rich /enrích, in-/ v.tr. **1** make rich or richer.
2 increase the strength, value, or contents of.
□□ **en·rich′ment** n.

en·roll /enról, in-/ v. (also **en·rol′**) (**en·rolled**,
en·rol·ling) **1** intr. enlist. **2** tr. **a** write the name of
(a person) on a list. **b** incorporate as a member.
□□ **en·roll·ee** /-lée/ n. **en·roll′er** n. **en·roll′ment**
n. **en·rol′ment** n.

en route /on rŏot/ adv. on the way.

Ens. *abbr.* ensign.

en·sconce /enskóns, in-/ v.tr. establish or settle
comfortably.

en·sem·ble /onsómbəl/ n. **1 a** thing viewed as
the sum of its parts. **b** general effect of this. **2** set
of clothes worn together. **3** group of performers
working together.

en·shrine /enshrín, in-/ v.tr. **1** enclose in a
shrine. **2** preserve or cherish. □□ **en·shrine′ment**
n.

en·shroud /enshrówd, in-/ v.tr. **1** cover with or as with a shroud. **2** cover completely; hide from view.

en·sign /énsin, -sīn/ n. **1** banner or flag, esp. the military or naval flag of a nation. **2** lowest commissioned officer in the US Navy or US Coast Guard.

en·slave /ensláyv, in-/ v.tr. make (a person) a slave. □□ **en·slave′ment** n. **en·slav′er** n.

en·snare /ensnáir, in-/ v.tr. catch in or as in a snare; entrap. □□ **en·snare′ment** n.

en·sue /ensóo, in-/ v.intr. happen afterward or as a result.

en·sure /enshóor, in-/ v.tr. **1** make certain. **2** make safe.
¶ See note at INSURE.

-ent /ənt, ent/ suffix **1** forming adjectives denoting attribution of an action (consequent) or state (existent). **2** forming nouns denoting an agent (coefficient; president).

en·tail /entáyl, in-/ v.tr. **1 a** necessitate or involve unavoidably. **b** give rise to; involve. **2** Law bequeath (property, etc.) so that it remains within a family. □□ **en·tail′ment** n.

en·tan·gle /entánggəl, in-/ v.tr. **1** cause to get caught in a snare or among obstacles. **2** cause to become tangled. **3** involve in difficulties. **4** complicate. □□ **en·tan′gle·ment** n.

en·tente /aanta′ant/ n. friendly relationship between nations.

en·ter /éntər/ v. **1 a** intr. go or come in. **b** tr. go or come into. **c** intr. come on stage. **2** tr. penetrate. **3** tr. write (a name, details, etc.) in a list, book, etc. **4 a** intr. register or announce oneself as a competitor. **b** tr. become a competitor in (an event). **5** tr. **a** become a member of (a society, etc.). **b** enroll in a society, school, etc. **6** tr. present for consideration (entered a protest). **7** intr. (foll. by into) engage in (conversation, an undertaking, etc.). **b** bind oneself by (an agreement, etc.). **8** intr. (foll. by on, upon) undertake; begin to deal with (a subject).

en·ter·prise /éntərprīz/ n. **1** undertaking, esp. a bold or difficult one. **2** initiative. **3** business firm.

en·ter·pris·ing /éntərprīzing/ adj. **1** ready to engage in enterprises. **2** resourceful; imaginative. □□ **en′ter·pris·ing·ly** adv.

en·ter·tain /éntərtáyn/ v.tr. **1** amuse; occupy agreeably. **2 a** receive as a guest. **b** receive guests (they entertain a great deal). **3** consider (an idea, feeling, etc.). □□ **en·ter·tain′er** n. **en·ter·tain′ing** adj.

en·ter·tain·ment /éntərtáynmənt/ n. **1** act or instance of entertaining; process of being entertained. **2** public performance or show. **3** diversions or amusements for guests, etc.

en·thrall /enthráwl, in-/ v.tr. captivate; please greatly. □□ **en·thrall′ment** n.

en·throne /enthrón, in-/ v.tr. place on a throne. □□ **en·throne′ment** n.

en·thuse /enthóoz, in-/ v. colloq. be or make enthusiastic.

en·thu·si·asm /enthóozeeazəm, in-/ n. strong interest; great eagerness. □□ **en·thu′si·ast** n. **en·thu·si·as′tic** adj. **en·thu·si·as′ti·cal·ly** adv.

en·tice /entís, in-/ v.tr. persuade by the offer of pleasure or reward. □□ **en·tice′ment** n. **en·tic′er** n. **en·tic′ing·ly** adv.

en·tire /entír, in-/ adj. whole; complete; unbroken.

en·tire·ly /entírlee, in-/ adv. **1** wholly; completely. **2** solely.

en·tire·ty /entírtee, in-/ n. (pl. -ties) **1** completeness. **2** sum total.

en·ti·tle /entítəl, in-/ v.tr. **1** give just claim or right. **2** give a title to. □□ **en·ti′tle·ment** n.

en·ti·ty /éntitee/ n. (pl. -ties) **1** thing with distinct existence. **2** existence or essential nature of a thing regarded distinctly.

en·tomb /entóom, in-/ v.tr. place in or as in a tomb. □□ **en·tomb′ment** n.

en·to·mol·o·gy /éntəmóləjee/ n. study of insects. □□ **en·to·mo·log′i·cal** /-məlójikəl/ adj. **en·to·mol′o·gist** n.

en·tou·rage /óntoora′azh/ n. people attending an important person.

en·trails /éntraylz, -trəlz/ n.pl. **1** bowels; intestines. **2** innermost parts.

en·trance¹ /éntrəns/ n. **1** going or coming in. **2** door, passage, etc., by which one enters. **3** right of admission. **4** coming of an actor on stage.

en·trance² /entráns, in-/ v.tr. **1** enchant; delight. **2** put into a trance. □□ **en·trance′ment** n. **en·tranc′ing** adj. **en·tranc′ing·ly** adv.

en·trant /éntrənt/ n. person who enters (esp. a competition, profession, etc.).

en·trap /entráp, in-/ v.tr. (**en·trapped, en·trap·ping**) **1** catch in or as in a trap. **2** beguile or trick. □□ **en·trap′per** n.

en·trap·ment /entrápmənt, in-/ n. **1** act or instance of entrapping; process of being entrapped. **2** Law inducement to commit a crime, esp. to secure a prosecution.

en·treat /entreét, in-/ v.tr. ask earnestly; beg. □□ **en·treat′ing·ly** adv. **en·treat′y** n. (pl. -ies).

en·trée /óntray/ n. (also **en′tree**) **1** main dish of a meal. **2** right of admission.

en·trench /entrénch, in-/ v. **1** tr. establish firmly (in a position, office, etc.). **2** intr. (foll. by upon) encroach; trespass. □□ **en·trench′ment** n.

en·tre·pre·neur /óntrəprənóor/ n. person who undertakes a commercial risk for profit. □□ **en·tre·pre·neur′i·al** adj. **en·tre·pre·neur′i·al·ly** adv. **en·tre·pre·neur′ship** n.

en·tro·py /éntrəpee/ n. Physics measure of the disorganization or degradation of the universe. □□ **en·tro·pic** /-trópik/ adj. **en·tro′pi·cal·ly** adv.

en·trust /entrúst, in-/ v.tr. give into the care of another. □□ **en·trust′ment** n.

en·try /éntree/ n. (pl. -tries) **1** going or coming in. **2** liberty to go or come in. **3** place of entrance. **4** item entered (in a diary, list, etc.). **5** registered competitor.

en·twine /entwín, in-/ v. **1** tr. & intr. twine together. **2** tr. interweave.

e·nu·mer·ate /inóomərayt, inyóo-/ v.tr. **1** specify (items) one by one. **2** count. □□ **e·nu′mer·a·ble** adj. **e·nu·mer·a·tion** /-ráyshən/ n. **e·nu′mer·a·tive** /-raytiv, -rətiv/ adj. **e·nu′mer·a·tor** n.

e·nun·ci·ate /inúnseeayt/ v.tr. **1** pronounce clearly. **2** express in definite terms. □□ **e·nun·ci·a·tion** /-áyshən/ n. **e·nun′ci·a·tive** /-seeətiv/ adj. **e·nun′ci·a·tor** n.

e·nu·re·sis /ényooreésis/ n. bedwetting.

en·vel·op /envélap, in-/ v.tr. **1** wrap up or cover completely. **2** completely surround. □□ **en·vel′op·ment** n.

en·ve·lope /énvəlōp, ón-/ n. 1 folded paper container, usu. with a sealable flap, for a letter, etc. 2 wrapper; covering.

en·vi·a·ble /énveeəbəl/ adj. likely to excite envy. □□ **en'vi·a·bly** adv.

en·vi·ous /énveeəs/ adj. feeling or showing envy. □□ **en'vi·ous·ly** adv.

en·vi·ron·ment /envírənmənt, -víərn-, in-/ n. 1 surroundings, esp. as affecting lives. 2 conditions or circumstances of living. □□ **en·vi·ron·men'tal** adj. **en·vi·ron·men·tal·ly** adv.

en·vi·ron·men·tal·ist /envírənméntəlist, -víərn-, in-/ n. person concerned with the protection of the natural environment. □□ **en·vi·ron·men'tal·ism** n.

en·vi·rons /envírənz, -víərnz, in-/ n.pl. surrounding district, esp. around an urban area.

en·vis·age /envízij, in-/ v.tr. have a mental picture of (a thing or conditions not yet existing).

en·vi·sion /envízhən, in-/ v.tr. envisage; visualize.

en·voy /énvoy, ón-/ n. 1 messenger or representative. 2 diplomat ranking below ambassador. □□ **en'voy·ship** n.

en·vy /énvee/ • n. (pl. **-vies**) 1 discontent aroused by another's better fortune, etc. 2 object of this feeling. • v.tr. (**-vies, -vied**) feel envy of (a person, etc.) (I envy you your position). □□ **en'vi·er** n.

en·wrap /enráp, in-/ v.tr. (**-wrapped, -wrap·ping**) wrap or enfold.

en·zyme /énzīm/ n. protein catalyst in a specific biochemical reaction. □□ **en·zy·mat'ic** adj.

e.o.m. abbr. (also **E.O.M.**) end of month.

e·on /éeon/ n. (also **ae·on**) 1 very long or indefinite period. 2 age of the universe. 3 an eternity.

e·o·sin /éeəsin/ n. red fluorescent dyestuff used esp. as a stain in optical microscopy.

-eous /eeəs/ suffix forming adjectives meaning 'of the nature of' (erroneous; gaseous).

EPA abbr. Environmental Protection Agency.

ep·au·let /épəlét/ n. (also **ep'au·lette**) ornamental shoulder piece, esp. on a uniform.

epaulet

EPAULET

é·pée /aypáy, épay/ n. dueling sword, used (with the end blunted) in fencing. □□ **é·pée'ist** n.

e·phem·er·al /ifémərəl/ adj. lasting for only a short time; transitory. □□ **e·phem·er·al·i·ty** /-álitee/ n. **e·phem'er·al·ly** adv.

epi- /épi-/ prefix (usu. **ep-** before a vowel or h) 1 upon (epidermis). 2 above (epicenter). 3 in addition (epilogue).

ep·ic /épik/ • n. 1 long narrative poem of heroic deeds. 2 grand or extended story, film, etc. • adj. 1 of or like an epic. 2 grand; heroic. □□ **ep'i·cal** adj. **ep'i·cal·ly** adv.

ep·i·cene /épiseen/ adj. 1 Gram. denoting either sex without change of gender. 2 having characteristics of both sexes or neither sex.

ep·i·cen·ter /épisentər/ n. 1 Geol. point at which an earthquake reaches the earth's surface. 2 central point of a difficulty. □□ **ep·i·cen·tral** /-séntrəl/ adj.

ep·i·cure /épikyŏor/ n. person with refined tastes, esp. in food and drink.

Ep·i·cu·re·an /épikyŏoree'eən, -kyŏoree-/ • n. 1 disciple of Greek philosopher Epicurus (d. 270 BC), who taught that the highest good is personal happiness. 2 (**epicurean**) devotee of (esp. sensual) enjoyment. • adj. (**epicurean**) characteristic of an epicurean. □□ **Ep·i·cu're·an·ism** n.

ep·i·dem·ic /épidémik/ • n. 1 widespread occurrence of a disease at a particular time. 2 such a disease. • adj. in the nature of an epidemic. □□ **ep·i·dem'i·cal·ly** adv.

¶ A disease that quickly affects a large number of people and then subsides is an **epidemic**: Throughout the Middle Ages, successive epidemics of the plague killed millions. **Epidemic** is also used as an adjective: She studied the causes of epidemic cholera. A disease that is continually present in a one area is **endemic**: Malaria is endemic in hot, moist climates.

ep·i·de·mi·ol·o·gy /épidemeeóləjee/ n. study of epidemic diseases and their control. □□ **ep·i·de·mi·o·log·i·cal** /-meeəlójikəl/ adj. **ep·i·de·mi·ol'o·gist** n.

ep·i·der·mis /épidərmis/ n. outer layer of the skin. □□ **ep·i·der'mal** adj. **ep·i·der'mic** adj. **ep·i·der'moid** adj.

ep·i·du·ral /épidóorəl, -dyŏor-/ • adj. (of an anesthetic) injected around the dura mater of the spinal cord. • n. epidural anesthetic, used esp. in childbirth.

ep·i·glot·tis /épiglótis/ n. flap of cartilage at the root of the tongue, depressed during swallowing to cover the windpipe. □□ **ep·i·glot'tal** adj. **ep·i·glot'tic** adj.

ep·i·gram /épigram/ n. pointed or witty saying. □□ **ep·i·gram·mat·ic** /-grəmátik/ adj. **ep·i·gram·mat'i·cal·ly** adv. **ep·i·gram'ma·tist** /-grámətist/ n. **ep·i·gram'ma·tize** v.

ep·i·graph /épigraf/ n. inscription. □□ **ep·i·graph·ic** /épigráfik/ adj. **ep·i·graph'i·cal** adj. **e·pig·ra·phy** /ipígrəfee/ n.

ep·i·lep·sy /épilepsee/ n. nervous disorder with convulsions and often loss of consciousness.

ep·i·lep·tic /épiléptik/ • adj. relating to epilepsy. • n. person with epilepsy.

ep·i·logue /épilawg, -og/ n. (also **ep'i·log**) concluding narrative part, speech, etc.

ep·i·neph·rine /épinéfrin/ n. (also **ep·i·neph'rin**) 1 hormone secreted by the adrenal glands, affecting circulation and muscular action. 2 natural or synthetic form of this, used as a stimulant. Also called **adrenaline**.

e·piph·a·ny /ipífənee/ n. (pl. **-nies**) 1 (**Epiphany**) a manifestation of Christ to the Magi. b festival of this on January 6. 2 moment of profound insight. □□ **ep·i·phan·ic** /épifánik/ adj.

ep·i·phyte /épifīt/ n. nonparasitic plant growing on another, e.g., a moss. □□ **ep·i·phyt·ic** /-fítik/ adj.

e·pis·co·pa·cy /ipískəpəsee/ n. (pl. **-cies**) **1** government by bishops. **2** (prec. by the) the bishops.

e·pis·co·pal /ipískəpəl/ adj. of or headed by a bishop or bishops. □□ **e·pis′co·pal·ism** n.

E·pis·co·pa·lian /ipískəpáyleeən/ • adj. of or belonging to the Episcopal Church. • n. member of the Episcopal Church. □□ **E·pis·co·pa′lian·ism** n.

e·pis·co·pate /ipískəpət/ n. **1** office or tenure of a bishop. **2** (prec. by the) bishops collectively.

e·pi·si·ot·o·my /ipéezeeótəmee/ n. (pl. **-mies**) incision made at the opening of the vagina to ease childbirth.

ep·i·sode /épisōd/ n. **1** event or period as part of a sequence. **2** dramatic installment. **3** incident or set of incidents in a narrative. □□ **ep·i·sod′ic** /-sódik/ adj. **ep·i·sod′i·cal·ly** adv.

e·pis·tle /ipísəl/ n. **1** formal or joc. letter, esp. a long one on a serious subject. **2** (**Epistle**) any of the letters of the apostles in the New Testament.

e·pis·to·lar·y /ipístəleree/ adj. in the style or form of a letter or letters.

ep·i·taph /épitaf/ n. words written in memory of a person who has died, esp. as a tomb inscription.

ep·i·the·li·um /épithéeleeəm/ n. (pl. **ep·i·the·li·a** /-leeə/ or **ep·i·the·li·ums**) tissue forming the outer layer of the body and lining many hollow structures. □□ **ep·i·the′li·al** adj.

ep·i·thet /épithet/ n. **1** characterizing adjective, etc. **2** such a word as a term of abuse. □□ **ep·i·thet′ic** adj. **ep·i·thet′i·cal** adj. **ep·i·thet′i·cal·ly** adv.

e·pit·o·me /ipítəmee/ n. **1** person or thing embodying a quality, etc. **2** thing representing another in miniature.

e·pit·o·mize /ipítəmīz/ v.tr. perfectly exemplify. □□ **e·pit·o·mi·za′tion** n.

ep·och /épək, éepok/ n. **1** notable period of history. **2** beginning of an era. □□ **ep′och·al** adj.

ep·ode /épōd/ n. lyric poem written in couplets each of a long line followed by a shorter one.

ep·o·nym /épənim/ n. **1** person after whom a discovery, place, etc., is named. **2** the name given.

ep·ox·y /ipóksee/ adj. designating a resin used in adhesives, insulation, coatings, etc.

ep·si·lon /épsilon/ n. fifth letter of the Greek alphabet (Ε, ε).

Ep·som salts /épsəm/ n. magnesium sulfate used as a purgative, etc.

eq·ua·ble /ékwəbəl/ adj. even; not varying; uniform. □□ **eq·ua·bil′i·ty** n. **eq′ua·bly** adv.

e·qual /éekwəl/ • adj. **1** the same in quantity, quality, size, degree, level, etc. **2** evenly balanced. **3** having the same rights or status. • n. person or thing equal to another. • v.tr. **1** be equal to. **2** achieve something that is equal to. □ **equal opportunity** (often in pl.) opportunity to be employed, paid, etc., without discrimination on grounds of sex, race, etc. **equal** (or **equals**) **sign** the symbol =. □□ **e·qual′i·ty** /ikwólitee/ n. **e′qual·ly** adv.

e·qual·ize /éekwəlīz/ v. make or become equal. □□ **e·qual·i·za′tion** n.

e·qua·nim·i·ty /éekwənímitee, ékwə-/ n. mental composure; evenness of temper.

e·quate /ikwáyt/ v. **1** tr. regard as equal or equivalent. **2** intr. be equal or equivalent to. □□ **e·quat′a·ble** adj.

e·qua·tion /ikwáyzhən/ n. **1** equating or making equal; being equal. **2** statement that two mathematical expressions are equal. □□ **e·qua′tion·al** adj.

e·qua·tor /ikwáytər/ n. imaginary line around the earth or other body, equidistant from the poles. □□ **e·qua·to′ri·al** adj.

e·ques·tri·an /ikwéstreeən/ • adj. **1** of horses and horseback riding. **2** on horseback. • n. (fem. **e·ques·tri·enne** /-tree-én/) rider or performer on horseback. □□ **e·ques′tri·an·ism** n.

equi- /éekwee, ékwi/ comb. form equal.

e·qui·dis·tant /éekwidístənt, ékwi-/ adj. at equal distances. □□ **e·qui·dis′tant·ly** adv.

e·qui·lat·er·al /éekwilátərəl, ékwi-/ adj. having all sides equal in length.

e·qui·lib·ri·um /éekwilíbreeəm, ékwi-/ n. (pl. **e·qui·lib·ri·ums** or **e·qui·lib·ri·a** /-reeə/) **1** state of physical balance. **2** state of composure.

e·quine /éekwīn, ékwin/ adj. of or like a horse.

e·qui·nox /éekwinoks, ékwi-/ n. time or date (about March 20 (vernal equinox) and September 22 (autumnal equinox) each year) at which the sun crosses the celestial equator, when day and night are of equal length. □□ **e·qui·noc·tial** /éekwinókshəl, ékwi-/ adj. & n.

e·quip /ikwíp/ v.tr. (**e·quipped, e·quip·ping**) supply with what is needed. □□ **e·quip′per** n.

e·quip·ment /ikwípmənt/ n. **1** necessary articles, clothing, etc., for a purpose. **2** equipping or being equipped.

e·qui·poise /éekwipoyz, ékwi-/ n. **1** equilibrium. **2** counterbalancing thing.

eq·ui·ta·ble /ékwitəbəl/ adj. fair; just. □□ **eq′ui·ta·bly** adv.

eq·ui·ta·tion /ékwitáyshən/ n. horsemanship.

eq·ui·ty /ékwitee/ n. (pl. **-ties**) **1** fairness. **2** net value of property after the deduction of any debts. **3** ownership, as in shares of stock, etc.

e·quiv·a·lent /ikwívələnt/ • adj. **1** equal in value, amount, importance, etc. **2** corresponding. • n. equivalent thing, amount, word, etc. □□ **e·quiv′a·lence** n. **e·quiv′a·len·cy** n. **e·quiv′a·lent·ly** adv.

e·quiv·o·cal /ikwívəkəl/ adj. **1** of double or doubtful meaning. **2** uncertain; questionable. □□ **e·quiv·o·cal·i·ty** /-kálitee/ n. **e·quiv′o·cal·ly** adv.

e·quiv·o·cate /ikwívəkayt/ v.intr. use ambiguity to conceal the truth. □□ **e·quiv′o·ca·cy** n. **e·quiv·o·ca·tion** /-káyshən/ n. **e·quiv′o·ca·tor** n. **e·quiv′o·ca·to·ry** adj.

ER abbr. **1** emergency room. **2** Elizabeth Regina (Queen Elizabeth).

Er symb. Chem. erbium.

-er[1] /ər/ suffix forming nouns from nouns, adjectives, and many verbs, denoting: **1** person, animal, or thing that performs a specified action or activity (cobbler, lover, computer). **2** person or thing that has a specified attribute or form (foreigner). **3** person concerned with a specified thing or subject (geographer). **4** person belonging to a specified place or group (villager).

-er[2] /ər/ suffix forming the comparative of adjectives (wider) and adverbs (faster).

-er³ /ər/ *suffix* used in slang formations usu. distorting the root word (*rugger; soccer*).

-er⁴ /ər/ *suffix* forming iterative and frequentative verbs (*blunder; glimmer; twitter*).

-er⁵ /ər/ *suffix* **1** forming nouns and adjectives through OF or AF, corresponding to: **a** L *-aris* (*sampler*) (cf. -AR¹). **b** L *-arius, -arium* (*butler; carpenter, danger*). **c** (through OF *-eüre*) L *-atura* or (through OF *-eŏr*) L *-atorium*. **2** = -OR ¹, -OR ².

-er⁶ /ər/ *suffix* esp. *Law* forming nouns denoting verbal action or a document effecting this (*disclaimer; misnomer*).
¶ The same ending occurs in *dinner* and *supper*.

ERA *abbr.* **1** *Baseball* earned run average. **2** Equal Rights Amendment.

e·ra /éerə, érə/ *n.* **1** period reckoning from a noteworthy event (*the Christian era*). **2** large distinct period of time, esp. regarded historically (*the pre-Roman era*).

e·rad·i·cate /irádikayt/ *v.tr.* root out; destroy completely. □□ **e·rad´i·ca·ble** *adj.* **e·rad·i·ca·tion** /-káyshən/ *n.* **e·rad´i·ca·tor** *n.*

e·rase /iráys/ *v.tr.* **1** rub out; obliterate. **2** remove recorded material from (a magnetic tape or medium). □□ **e·ras´a·ble** *adj.* **e·ra´sure** *n.*

e·ras·er /iráysər/ *n.* thing that erases, esp. a piece of rubber or plastic used for removing pencil and ink marks.

er·bi·um /ə́rbeeəm/ *n.* soft, silvery, metallic element of the lanthanide series. ¶ Symb.: **Er.**

ere /air/ *prep. & conj. poet.* before (of time) (*ere noon*).

e·rect /irékt/ • *adj.* **1** upright; vertical. **2** enlarged and rigid. • *v.tr.* **1** raise; set upright. **2** build. □□ **e·rect´a·ble** *adj.* **e·rec´tion** *n.* **e·rect´ly** *adv.* **e·rect´ness** *n.* **e·rec´tor** *n.*

e·rec·tile /irékt'l, -tīl/ *adj.* that can be erected or become erect.

erg /ərg/ *n. Physics* unit of work or energy, equal to the work done by a force of one dyne when its point of application moves one centimeter in the direction of the force.

er·go /ə́rgō, ér-/ *adv.* therefore.

er·go·nom·ics /ə́rgənómiks/ *n.* study of the efficiency of persons in their working environment. □□ **er·go·nom´ic** *adj.* **er·gon·o·mist** /ergónəmist/ *n.*

er·got /ə́rgət, -got/ *n.* fungal disease of rye and other cereals.

Er·in /érin/ *n. poet.* Ireland.

er·mine /ə́rmin/ *n.* (*pl.* same or **er·mines**) **1** stoat, esp. when in its white winter fur. **2** its white fur.

erne /ern/ *n.* (also **ern**) *poet.* sea eagle.

e·rode /iród/ *v.* wear away; destroy or be destroyed gradually. □□ **e·rod´i·ble** *adj.*

e·rog·e·nous /irójinəs/ *adj.* (of a part of the body) sensitive to sexual stimulation.

e·ro·sion /iróʒhən/ *n.* **1** wearing away of the earth's surface by the action of water, wind, etc. **2** eroding; process of being eroded. □□ **e·ro´sive** *adj.*

e·rot·ic /irótik/ *adj.* of or causing sexual desire or excitement. □□ **e·rot´i·cal·ly** *adv.*

e·rot·i·ca /irótikə/ *n.pl.* erotic literature or art.

e·rot·i·cism /irótisizəm/ *n.* **1** erotic nature or

character. **2** use of or reponse to erotic images or stimulation.

err /ər, er/ *v.intr.* **1** be mistaken or incorrect. **2** do wrong; sin. □ **err on the right side** act in favor of the least harmful possibility. **err on the side of** act with a specified bias (*errs on the side of generosity*).
¶ Traditionally, **err** rhymes with *her,* though the pronunciation that rhymes with *hair* is now common.

er·rand /érənd/ *n.* short outing for a specific purpose.

er·rant /érənt/ *adj.* **1** deviating from an accepted standard. **2** *literary* traveling in search of adventure (*knight errant*). □□ **er·ran·cy** /-ənsee/ *n.* (in sense 1). **er´rant·ry** *n.* (in sense 2).

er·rat·ic /irátik/ *adj.* **1** inconsistent in conduct, opinions, etc.; unpredictable; eccentric. **2** uncertain in movement. □□ **er·rat´i·cal·ly** *adv.*

er·ra·tum /iráátəm, irát-/ *n.* (*pl.* **er·ra·ta** /-tə/) error in printing or writing.

er·ro·ne·ous /iróneeəs/ *adj.* incorrect; arising from error. □□ **er·ro´ne·ous·ly** *adv.* **er·ro´ne·ous·ness** *n.*

er·ror /érər/ *n.* **1** mistake. **2** moral transgression. □□ **er´ror·less** *adj.*

er·satz /érzaats, -saats, erzáats, -saáts/ *adj.* substitute; imitation.

Erse /ərs/ • *adj.* Gaelic. • *n.* the Gaelic language.

erst·while /ə́rst-hwīl, -wīl/ *adj.* former; previous.

e·ruc·ta·tion /iruktáyshən, éeruk-/ *n.* belching.

er·u·dite /éryədīt, érə-/ *adj.* **1** learned. **2** showing great learning. □□ **er´u·dite·ly** *adv.* **er·u·di·tion** /-díshən/ *n.*

e·rupt /irúpt/ *v.intr.* **1** break out suddenly or dramatically. **2** (of a volcano) become active and eject lava, etc. **3** (of a rash, boil, etc.) appear on the skin. □□ **e·rup·tion** /-rúpshən/ *n.* **e·rup´tive** *adj.*

-ery /əree/ *suffix* forming nouns denoting: **1** class or kind (*greenery; machinery*). **2** employment; state or condition (*dentistry; slavery*). **3** place of work or cultivation or breeding (*brewery; rookery*). **4** behavior (*mockery*). **5** often *derog.* all that has to do with (*knavery*).

e·ryth·ro·cyte /iríthrəsīt/ *n.* red blood cell.

Es *symb. Chem.* einsteinium.

es·ca·late /éskəlayt/ *v.* **1** *intr.* & *tr.* increase or develop (usu. rapidly) by stages. **2** *tr.* cause to become more intense. □□ **es·ca·la·tion** /-láyshən/ *n.*

es·ca·la·tor /éskəlaytər/ *n.* moving staircase consisting of a circulating belt forming steps.

es·ca·pade /éskəpáyd/ *n.* daring or reckless caper.

es·cape /iskáyp/ • *v.* **1** *intr.* get free of restriction, control, a person, etc. **2** *intr.* (of a gas, liquid, etc.) leak. **3** *intr.* succeed in avoiding danger, punishment, etc. **4** *tr.* avoid. **5** *tr.* (of words, etc.) issue unawares from (a person, a person's lips). • *n.* **1** act or instance of escaping. **2** temporary relief from reality or worry. □□ **es·cap´er** *n.*

es·cap·ee /iskaypée/ *n.* person who has escaped.

es·cape·ment /iskáypmənt/ *n.* part of a clock, etc., that connects and regulates the motive power.

es·cap·ism /iskáypizəm/ *n.* tendency to seek distraction and relief from reality, esp. in the arts or through fantasy. □□ **es·cap´ist** *n. & adj.*

es·car·got /eskaargó/ *n.* snail, esp. as prepared for food.

es·carp·ment /iskáarpmənt/ *n.* (also **es·carp´**) *Geol.* long, steep slope at the edge of a plateau, etc.

-esce /es/ *suffix* forming verbs, usu. initiating action (*effervesce; fluoresce*).

-escent /ésənt/ *suffix* forming adjectives denoting the beginning of a state or action (*effervescent; fluorescent*). □□ **-escence** *suffix* forming nouns.

es·cheat /ischéet/ • *n.* reversion of property to the state on the owner's dying without legal heirs. • *v.* **1** *tr.* hand over (property) as an escheat. **2** *intr.* revert by escheat.

es·chew /eschóo/ *v.tr.* avoid; abstain from. □□ **es·chew´al** *n.*

es·cort • *n.* /éskawrt/ **1** one or more persons, vehicles, etc., accompanying a person, vehicle, etc., for protection or as a mark of status. **2** person accompanying a person of the opposite sex socially. • *v.tr.* /iskáwrt/ act as an escort to.

es·cri·toire /éskritwáar/ *n.* writing desk with drawers, etc.

es·crow /éskrō/ *n. Law* **1** money, property, or written bond, kept in the custody of a third party until a specified condition has been fulfilled. **2** status of this (*in escrow*).

es·cutch·eon /iskúchən/ *n.* **1** shield or emblem bearing a coat of arms. **2** protective plate around a keyhole or door handle. □□ **es·cutch´eoned** *adj.*

ESL *abbr.* English as a second language.

e·soph·a·gus /isófəgəs, ee-/ *n.* (*pl.* **e·soph·a·gi** /-gī, -jī/) passage for food from the mouth to the stomach; gullet. □□ **e·soph·a·ge·al** /isófəjeé-əl, eesofájeeəl/ *adj.*

es·o·ter·ic /ésətérik/ *adj.* intelligible only to those with special knowledge. □□ **es·o·ter´i·cal** *adj.* **es·o·ter´i·cal·ly** *adv.* **es·o·ter·i·cism** /-rə-sizəm/ *n.* **es·o·ter´i·cist** *n.*

ESP *abbr.* extrasensory perception.

es·pa·drille /éspədril/ *n.* light canvas shoe with a plaited fiber sole.

es·pal·ier /ispályər, -yay/ *n.* **1** latticework for training branches of a tree or shrub. **2** tree or shrub so trained.

es·pe·cial /ispéshəl/ *adj.* notable; exceptional.

es·pe·cial·ly /ispéshəlee, espésh-/ *adv.* chiefly; much more than in other cases.

Es·pe·ran·to /éspərántō, -ráan-/ *n.* artificial universal language intended for international use.

es·pi·o·nage /éspeeənaazh/ *n.* spying or use of spies.

es·pla·nade /ésplənáad, -náyd/ *n.* long, open level area for walking.

es·pous·al /ispówzəl, -səl/ *n.* **1** espousing of a cause, etc. **2** *archaic* marriage; betrothal.

es·pouse /ispówz/ *v.tr.* **1** adopt or support (a cause, doctrine, etc.). **2** *archaic* (usu. of a man) marry. □□ **es·pous´er** *n.*

es·pres·so /esprésō/ *n.* (also **ex·pres·so** /ekspré-sō/) (*pl.* **-sos**) strong black coffee made under steam pressure.

es·prit /espree/ *n.* sprightliness; wit. □ **esprit de corps** /də káwr/ devotion to and pride in one's group.

es·py /ispí/ *v.tr.* (**-pies, -pied**) *literary* catch sight of; perceive.

Esq. *abbr.* esquire.

-esque /esk/ *suffix* forming adjectives meaning 'in the style of' or 'resembling' (*Schumannesque; statuesque*).

es·quire /éskwīr, iskwír/ *n.* **1** title appended to a man's surname, esp. as a form of address for letters. **2** title placed after the name of an attorney.

es·say • *n.* /ésay/ **1** short piece of writing on a given subject. **2** *formal* attempt. • *v.tr.* /esáy/ *formal* attempt. □□ **es´say·ist** *n.*

es·sence /ésəns/ *n.* **1** fundamental nature, inherent characteristics. **2 a** extract obtained by distillation, etc. **b** perfume. □ **in essence** fundamentally. **of the essence** indispensable; vital.

es·sen·tial /isénshəl/ • *adj.* **1** necessary; indispensable. **2** of or constituting the essence of a person or thing. • *n.* (esp. in *pl.*) basic or indispensable element or thing. □ **essential oil** volatile oil of a plant, etc., with its characteristic odor. □□ **es·sen·ti·al·i·ty** /-sheeálitee/ *n.* **es·sen´tial·ly** *adv.* **es·sen´tial·ness** *n.*

EST *abbr.* **1** eastern standard time. **2** electroshock treatment.

est. *abbr.* **1** established. **2** estimate. **3** estimated.

-est /ist/ *suffix* forming the superlative of adjectives (*widest; nicest; happiest*) and adverbs (*soonest*).

es·tab·lish /istáblish/ *v.tr.* **1** set up on a permanent basis. **2** achieve permanent acceptance for (a custom, belief, etc.). **3** validate; place beyond dispute.

es·tab·lish·ment /istáblishmənt/ *n.* **1** establishing; being established. **2 a** business organization or public institution. **b** site of such. **3** (**the Establishment**) social group or authority exerting influence and resisting change.

es·tate /istáyt/ *n.* **1** property consisting of much land usu. with a large house. **2** person's assets and liabilities, esp. at death.

es·teem /istéem/ • *v.tr.* **1** have a high regard for. **2** *formal* consider. • *n.* high regard; respect; favor.

esteem Middle English (as a noun in the sense 'worth, reputation'): from Old French *estime* (noun), *estimer* (verb), from Latin *aestimare* 'to estimate.' The verb originally meant 'estimate the number, quantity, etc., of something,' also 'value, appraise,' and came to be used figuratively to mean 'assess the merit of.' Current senses date from the 16th century.

es·ter /éstər/ *n.* chemical produced by replacing the hydrogen of an acid by an organic radical.

es·ti·ma·ble /éstiməbəl/ *adj.* worthy of esteem. □□ **es´ti·ma·bly** *adv.*

es·ti·mate • *n.* /éstimət/ **1** approximate judgment, esp. of cost, value, size, etc. **2** statement of approximate charge for work to be undertaken. • *v.tr.* /éstimayt/ **1** form an estimate or opinion of. **2** make a rough calculation. □□ **es·ti·ma·tion** /-máyshən/ *n.* **es´ti·ma·tor** *n.*

Es·to·ni·an /estóneeən/ • *n.* **1 a** native of Estonia. **b** person of Estonian descent. **2** language of Estonia. • *adj.* of Estonia, its people, or language.

es·top /estóp/ *v.tr.* (**es·topped, es·top·ping**) *Law* bar or preclude.

es·trange /istráynj/ v.tr. cause (a person or group) to turn away; alienate. □□ **es·trange′ment** n.

es·tro·gen /éstrəjən/ n. female sex hormone controlling estrus, etc.

es·trus /éstrəs/ n. recurring period of sexual receptivity in many female mammals; heat. □□ **es′trous** adj.

es·tu·ar·y /és-chŏoeree/ n. (pl. **-ies**) tidal course or mouth of a river.

ETA abbr. estimated time of arrival.

e·ta /áytə, éetə/ n. seventh letter of the Greek alphabet (H, η).

et al. /et ál/ abbr. and others.

etc. abbr. = ET CETERA.

et cet·er·a /et sétərə, sétrə/ adv. and the rest; and so on.
¶ Avoid pronouncing this phrase "ek set-uhr-uh"; many regard this as uneducated.

etch /ech/ v. **1 a** tr. reproduce (a picture, etc.) by engraving it on a metal plate with acid. **b** tr. engrave (a plate) in this way. **2** intr. practice this craft. **3** tr. impress deeply (esp. on the mind). □□ **etch′er** n.

etch·ing /éching/ n. **1** print made from an etched plate. **2** art of producing these plates.

ETD abbr. estimated time of departure.

e·ter·nal /itórnəl/ adj. **1** existing always. **2** essentially unchanging (eternal truths). □ **Eternal City** Rome. **eternal triangle** relationship of three people involving sexual rivalry. □□ **e·ter′nal·ly** adv.

e·ter·ni·ty /itórnitee/ n. (pl. **-ties**) **1** infinite (esp. future) time. **2** endless life after death. **3** being eternal.

eth·ane /éthayn/ n. Chem. gaseous hydrocarbon of the alkane series, occurring in natural gas.

eth·a·nol /éthənawl, -nol/ n. Chem. = ALCOHOL 1.

e·ther /éethər/ n. **1** Chem. colorless volatile organic liquid used as an anesthetic or solvent. **2** clear sky; upper regions of air beyond the clouds. **3** medium formerly assumed to permeate space. □□ **e·ther·ic** /eethérik/ adj.

e·the·re·al /itheéreeəl/ adj. **1** light; airy. **2** highly delicate, esp. in appearance. **3** heavenly. □□ **e·the′re·al·ly** adv.

eth·ic /éthik/ n. set of moral principles.

eth·i·cal /éthikəl/ adj. **1** relating to morals, esp. as concerning human conduct. **2** morally correct. □□ **eth′i·cal·ly** adv.

eth·ics /éthiks/ n.pl. (also treated as sing.) **1** science of morals in human conduct. **2 a** moral principles. **b** set of these. □□ **eth·i·cist** /éthisist/ n.

eth·nic /éthnik/ adj. **1** having a common national or cultural tradition. **2** denoting origin by birth or descent rather than nationality. **3** relating to race or culture. □ **ethnic cleansing** euphem. mass expulsion or killing of people from opposing ethnic groups. □□ **eth′ni·cal·ly** adv. **eth·nic·i·ty** /-nísitee/ n.

eth·no·cen·tric /éthnōséntrik/ adj. evaluating other races and cultures by criteria specific to one's own. □□ **eth·no·cen′tri·cal·ly** adv. **eth·no·cen′tric′i·ty** /-trísitee/ n. **eth·no·cen′trism** n.

eth·nol·o·gy /ethnóləjee/ n. comparative study of peoples. □□ **eth·no·log·ic** /-nəlójik/ adj. **eth·no·log′i·cal** adj. **eth·nol′o·gist** n.

e·thos /éethos/ n. characteristic spirit or attitudes of a community, etc.

eth·yl /éthil/ n. (attrib.) Chem. radical derived from ethane by removal of a hydrogen atom (ethyl alcohol).

eth·yl·ene /éthileen/ n. Chem. gaseous hydrocarbon occurring in natural gas and used in the manufacture of polyethylene.

e·ti·ol·o·gy /éeteeóləjee/ n. the science of the causes of disease. □□ **e·ti·o·log·ic** /-teeəlójik/ adj. **e·ti·o·log′i·cal** adj. **e·ti·o·log′i·cal·ly** adv.

et·i·quette /étiket, -kit/ n. conventional rules of social behavior or professional conduct.

E·trus·can /itrúskən/ • adj. of ancient Etruria in Italy. • n. **1** native of Etruria. **2** language of Etruria.

et seq. abbr. (also **et seqq.**) and the following (pages, etc.).

-ette /et/ suffix forming nouns meaning: **1** small (kitchenette). **2** imitation or substitute (leatherette). **3** often offens. female (suffragette).

é·tude /áytŏod, -tyŏod/ n. musical composition designed to improve the technique of the player.

e·tui /etweé/ n. small case for needles, etc.

etym. abbr. **1** etymological. **2** etymology.

et·y·mol·o·gy /étimóləjee/ n. (pl. **-gies**) **1 a** verifiable sources of the formation and development of a word. **b** account of these. **2** study of etymologies. □□ **et·y·mo·log·i·cal** /-məlójikəl/ adj. **et·y·mo·log′i·cal·ly** adv. **et·y·mol′o·gist** n.

Eu symb. Chem. europium.

eu- /yŏo/ comb. form well; easily.

eu·ca·lyp·tus /yŏokəlíptəs/ n. (pl. **eu·ca·lyp·ti** /-tī/ or **eu·ca·lyp·tus·es**) **1** tree of Australasia, cultivated for its wood and the oil from its leaves. **2** this oil used as an antiseptic, etc.

Eu·cha·rist /yŏokərist/ n. **1** Christian sacrament commemorating the Last Supper, in which bread and wine are consecrated and consumed. **2** consecrated elements, esp. the bread. □□ **Eu·cha·ris′tic** adj.

eu·chre /yŏokər/ n. card game for two, three, or four players in which a hand is won by taking three tricks.

eu·clid·e·an /yŏoklídeeən/ adj. (also **Eu·clid′e·an**) relating to Euclid, 3rd-c. BC Greek mathematician, esp. his system of geometry.

eu·gen·ics /yŏojéniks/ n.pl. (also treated as sing.) science of improving the (esp. human) population by controlling inherited characteristics. □□ **eu·gen′ic** adj. **eu·gen′i·cal·ly** adv. **eu·gen·i·cist** /yŏojénisist/ n. **eu′ge·nist** /yŏojinist/ n.

eu·kar·y·ote /yŏokáreeōt/ n. organism consisting of cells in which the genetic material is within a distinct nucleus. □□ **eu·kar·y·ot·ic** /-reeótik/ adj.

eu·lo·gize /yŏoləjīz/ v.tr. praise in speech or writing. □□ **eu·lo·gist** /-jist/ n. **eu·lo·gis′tic** adj. **eu·lo·gis′ti·cal·ly** adv.

eu·lo·gy /yŏoləjee/ n. (pl. **-gies**) speech or writing in praise of a person.

---

eulogy late Middle English (in the sense 'high praise'): from medieval Latin eulogium, eulogia (from Greek eulogia 'praise'), apparently influenced by Latin elogium 'inscription on a tomb' (from Greek elegia 'elegy'). The current sense dates from the late 16th century.

---

eu·nuch /yŏonək/ n. castrated man.

eu·phe·mism /yŏofimizəm/ n. **1** mild or vague expression substituted for a harsher more direct one (e.g., *pass over* for *die*). **2** use of such expressions. □□ **eu′phe·mist** n. **eu·phe·mis′tic** adj. **eu·phe·mis′ti·cal·ly** adv. **eu′phe·mize** v.

eu·pho·ny /yŏofənee/ n. (pl. **-nies**) pleasantness of sound, esp. of a word or phrase; harmony. □□ **eu·phon·ic** /-fónik/ adj. **eu·pho·ni·ous** /-fónee-/ adj. **eu·pho′ni·ous·ly** adv.

eu·pho·ri·a /yŏofáwreeə/ n. intense feeling of well-being. □□ **eu·phor·ic** /-fáwrik, fór-/ adj. **eu·phor′i·cal·ly** adv.

Eur·a·sian /yŏoráyzhən/ • adj. **1** of mixed European and Asian parentage. **2** of Europe and Asia. • n. Eurasian person.

eu·re·ka /yŏoree′ekə/ int. I have found it! (announcing a discovery, etc.).

Euro- /yŏorō/ comb. form Europe; European.

Eu·ro·pe·an /yŏorəpee′eən/ • adj. **1** of or in Europe. **2 a** descended from natives of Europe. **b** originating in or characteristic of Europe. • n. **1** native or inhabitant of Europe. **2** person descended from natives of Europe. □ **European Community** (or **European Economic Community**) confederation of certain European countries as a unit with internal free trade and common external tariffs. **European Union** official name of the European Community from November 1993.

eu·ro·pi·um /yŏorópeeəm/ n. soft, silvery metallic element of the lanthanide series. ¶ Symb.: **Eu**.

Eu·sta·chian tube /yŏostáyshən, -keeən/ n. Anat. tube from the pharynx to the middle ear.

eu·tha·na·sia /yŏothənáyzhə/ n. bringing about of a gentle death in the case of incurable and painful disease.

e·vac·u·ate /iváykŏo-ayt/ v.tr. **1 a** remove (people) from a place of danger. **b** empty or leave (a place). **2** make empty. **3** withdraw from (a place). **4** empty (the bowels, etc.). □□ **e·vac′u·ant** n. & adj. **e·vac·u·a·tion** /-áyshən/ n. **e·vac′u·a·tor** n.

e·vade /iváyd/ v.tr. **1** escape from; avoid, esp. by guile or trickery. **2** avoid doing, answering, etc. □□ **e·vad′a·ble** adj. **e·vad′er** n.

e·val·u·ate /ivályŏo-ayt/ v.tr. **1** assess; appraise. **2** determine the number or amount of. □□ **e·val·u·a·tion** /-áyshən/ n. **e·val′u·a·tive** adj. **e·val′u·a·tor** n.

ev·a·nes·cent /évənésənt/ adj. (of an impression or appearance, etc.) quickly fading. □□ **ev·a·nes′cence** n. **ev·a·nes′cent·ly** adv.

e·van·gel·i·cal /éevanjélikəl, évən-/ • adj. **1** of or according to the teaching of the gospel or the Christian religion. **2** maintaining the doctrine of salvation by faith. • n. believer in this. □□ **e·van·gel′i·cal·ism** n. **e·van·gel′i·cal·ly** adv.

e·van·ge·list /ivánjəlist/ n. **1** any of the writers of the four Gospels (Matthew, Mark, Luke, John). **2** preacher of the gospel. □□ **e·van′ge·lism** n. **e·van·ge·lis′tic** adj.

e·van·ge·lize /ivánjəliz/ v.tr. **1** preach the gospel to. **2** convert to Christianity. □□ **e·van·ge·li·za′tion** n. **e·van′ge·liz·er** n.

e·vap·o·rate /iváporayt/ v. **1** intr. turn from solid or liquid into vapor. **2** intr. & tr. lose or cause to lose moisture as vapor. **3** intr. & tr. disappear or cause to disappear (*our courage evaporated*). □□ **e·vap′o·ra·ble** adj. **e·vap·o·ra·tion** /-ráyshən/ n. **e·vap·o·ra·tive** /-váparətiv, -raytiv/ adj. **e·vap′o·ra·tor** n.

e·va·sion /iváyzhən/ n. **1** evading. **2** evasive answer.

e·va·sive /iváysiv/ adj. **1** seeking to evade. **2** not direct in one's answers, etc. □□ **e·va′sive·ly** adv. **e·va′sive·ness** n.

eve /eev/ n. **1** evening or day before a holiday, etc. **2** time just before anything (*eve of the election*). **3** archaic evening.

e·ven[1] /éevən/ • adj. (**e·ven·er**, **e·ven·est**) **1** level; flat and smooth. **2 a** uniform in quality; constant. **b** equal in amount or value, etc. **c** equally balanced. **3** in the same plane or line. **4** (of a person's temper, etc.) equable; calm. **5 a** (of a number) divisible by two without a remainder. **b** bearing such a number (*no parking on even days*). • adv. **1** not so much as (*never even opened the letter*). **2** used to introduce an extreme case (*it might even cost $100*). **3** in spite of; notwithstanding (*even with the delays, we arrived on time*). • v. make or become even. □ **even now 1** now as well as before. **2** at this very moment. **even so** nevertheless. **even-steven** (or **Steven**) colloq. equal. **get even with** have one's revenge on. **on an even keel 1** (of a ship or aircraft) not listing. **2** (of a plan or person) untroubled. □□ **e′ven·ly** adv.

e·ven[2] /éevən/ n. poet. evening.

e·ven·hand·ed /éevənhándid/ adj. impartial; fair. □□ **e′ven·hand′ed·ly** adv. **e′ven·hand′ed·ness** n.

eve·ning /éevning/ • n. close of the day, esp. from about 6 p.m. to bedtime. • int. courteous greeting or farewell. □ **evening star** planet, esp. Venus, conspicuous in the west after sunset.

e·ven·song /éevənsawng, -song/ n. service of evening prayer.

e·vent /ivént/ n. **1** thing that happens, esp. one of importance. **2** fact or outcome of a thing's occurring. **3** item in a competitive program. □ **in any event** (or **at all events**) whatever happens. **in the event** as it turns (or turned) out. **in the event of** if (a specified thing) happens. **in the event that** if it happens that.

e·vent·ful /ivéntfŏol/ adj. marked by noteworthy events. □□ **e·vent′ful·ly** adv. **e·vent′ful·ness** n.

e·ven·tide /éevəntid/ n. archaic or poet. = EVENING.

e·ven·tu·al /ivénchŏoəl/ adj. occurring in due course; ultimate. □□ **e·ven′tu·al·ly** adv.

e·ven·tu·al·i·ty /ivénchŏo-álitee/ n. (pl. **-ties**) possible event or outcome.

e·ven·tu·ate /ivénchŏo-ayt/ v.intr. formal turn out in a specified way; result. □□ **e·ven·tu·a′tion** /-áyshən/ n.

ev·er /évər/ adv. **1** at all times; always. **2** at any time. **3** (as an emphatic word) in any way; at all. **4** (in comb.) constantly (*ever-present*). **5** (foll. by so) very; very much. □ **ever since** throughout the period since.

ev·er·green /évərgreen/ • adj. retaining green leaves year round. • n. evergreen plant.

ev·er·last·ing /évərlásting/ adj. lasting forever or for a long time. □□ **ev·er·last′ing·ly** adv.

ev·er·more /évərmáwr/ adv. forever; always.

e·vert /ivərt/ v.tr. turn outward or inside out. □□ **e·ver·sion** /-vərzhən/ n.

eve·ry /évree/ adj. **1** each single. **2** each at a specified interval. **3** all possible; the utmost degree of. □ **every now and again** (or **now and then**) from time to time. **every other** each second in a series. **every so often** occasionally. **every which way** *colloq.* **1** in all directions. **2** in a disorderly manner.

eve·ry·bod·y /évreebodee, -budee/ *pron.* every person.

¶ **Everybody,** along with **everyone,,** traditionally used a singular pronoun of reference: *Everybody must sign his* (not *their*) *own name.* Because the use of *his* in this context is now perceived as sexist by some, a second option became popular: *Everybody must sign his or her own name.* But *his or her* is often awkward, and many feel that the plural simply makes more sense: *Everybody must sign their own name.* Although this violates logic, it is standard in British English and informal US usage. In some sentences, only *they* makes grammatical sense: *Everybody agreed to convict the defendant, and they so voted unanimously.*

eve·ry·day /évreedáy/ *adj.* **1** occurring every day. **2** used on ordinary days. **3** commonplace; usual. **4** mundane.

eve·ry·one /évreewun/ *pron.* every person; everybody.

eve·ry·thing /évreething/ *pron.* **1** all things; all the things of a group or class. **2** essential consideration (*speed is everything*).

eve·ry·where /évreehwair, -wair/ *adv.* **1** in every place. **2** *colloq.* in many places.

e·vict /ivíkt/ *v.tr.* expel (a tenant, etc.) by legal process. □□ **e·vic·tion** /-víkshən/ *n.* **e·vic′tor** *n.*

ev·i·dence /évidəns/ ● *n.* **1** available facts, circumstances, etc., determining truth or validity. **2** statements, information, etc., admissible as testimony in a court of law. ● *v.tr.* be evidence of; attest.

ev·i·dent /évidənt/ *adj.* **1** plain or obvious; manifest. **2** seeming; apparent (*his evident anxiety*).

ev·i·dent·ly /évidəntlee, -déntlee/ *adv.* **1** as shown by evidence. **2** seemingly; as it appears.

e·vil /éevəl/ ● *adj.* **1** morally bad; wicked. **2** harmful. **3** disagreeable. ● *n.* **1** evil thing. **2** wickedness. □□ **e′vil·ly** *adv.* **e′vil·ness** *n.*

e·vil·do·er /éevəldōoər/ *n.* person who does evil. □□ **e′vil·do·ing** *n.*

e·vince /ivíns/ *v.tr.* **1** indicate or make evident. **2** show that one has (a quality). □□ **e·vin′ci·ble** *adj.* **e·vin′cive** *adj.*

e·vis·cer·ate /ivísərayt/ *v.tr.* disembowel. □□ **e·vis·cer·a·tion** /-ráyshən/ *n.*

ev·o·ca·tive /ivókətiv/ *adj.* tending to evoke (esp. feelings or memories). □□ **e·voc′a·tive·ly** *adv.* **e·voc′a·tive·ness** *n.*

e·voke /ivók/ *v.tr.* **1** inspire or draw forth (memories, feelings, a response, etc.). **2** summon (a supposed spirit from the dead). □□ **ev·o·ca·tion** /évəkáyshən, éevō-/ *n.* **e·vok′er** *n.*

ev·o·lu·tion /évəlóoshən/ *n.* **1** gradual development. **2** development of species from earlier forms, as an explanation of origins. **3** unfolding of events, etc. □□ **ev·o·lu′tion·ar·y** *adj.*

---

evolution early 17th century: from Latin *evolutio(n-)* 'unrolling,' from the verb *evolvere* (source of *evolve*). Early senses related to physical movement, first recorded in describing a tactical 'wheeling' maneuver in the realignment of troops or ships. Current senses stem from a notion of 'opening out' and 'unfolding,' giving rise to a general sense of 'development.'

---

ev·o·lu·tion·ist /évəlóoshənist/ *n.* person who believes in evolution as explaining the origin of species. □□ **ev·o·lu′tion·ism** *n.* **ev·o·lu·tion·is′tic** *adj.*

e·volve /ivólv/ *v.* **1** *intr.* & *tr.* develop gradually and naturally. **2** *tr.* devise (a theory, plan, etc.). **3** *intr.* & *tr.* unfold. □□ **e·volv′a·ble** *adj.* **e·volve′ment** *n.*

ewe /yōō/ *n.* female sheep.

ew·er /yóōər/ *n.* water jug with a wide mouth.

ex /eks/ *n. colloq.* former husband or wife.

ex-[1] /eks/ *prefix* (also **e-** before some consonants, **ef-** before *f*) **1** forming verbs meaning: **a** out; forth (*exclude*). **b** upward (*extol*). **c** thoroughly (*excruciate*). **d** bring into a state (*exasperate*). **e** remove or free from (*expatriate*). **2** forming nouns meaning 'former' (*ex-convict*).

ex-[2] /eks/ *prefix* out (*exodus*).

ex·ac·er·bate /igzásərbayt/ *v.tr.* **1** make (pain, etc.) worse. **2** irritate. □□ **ex·ac·er·ba·tion** /-báyshən/ *n.*

ex·act /igzákt/ ● *adj.* **1** accurate; correct in all details. **2** precise. ● *v.tr.* **1** enforce payment of (money, etc.). **2** demand; insist on. □□ **ex·ac′ti·tude** *n.* **ex·act′ness** *n.* **ex·ac′tor** *n.*

ex·act·ing /igzákting/ *adj.* **1** making great demands. **2** calling for much effort. □□ **ex·act′ing·ly** *adv.* **ex·act′ing·ness** *n.*

ex·ac·tion /igzákshən/ *n.* **1** exacting; being exacted. **2 a** illegal or exorbitant demand. **b** sum or thing exacted.

ex·act·ly /igzáktlee/ *adv.* **1** accurately; precisely (*worked it out exactly*). **2** in exact terms (*exactly when did it happen?*). **3** (said in reply) quite so. **4** just; in all respects. □ **not exactly** *colloq.* **1** by no means. **2** not precisely.

ex·ag·ger·ate /igzájərayt/ *v.tr.* **1** give an impression of (a thing) as being larger or greater. **2** overdo. □□ **ex·ag′ger·at·ed·ly** *adv.* **ex·ag′ger·at·ing·ly** *adv.* **ex·ag·ger·a·tion** /-ráyshən/ *n.* **ex·ag′ger·a·tor** *n.*

---

exaggerate mid-16th century: from Latin *exaggerat-* 'heaped up,' from the verb *exaggerare*, from *ex-* 'thoroughly' + *aggerare* 'heap up' (from *agger* 'heap'). The word originally meant 'pile up, accumulate,' later 'intensify praise or blame,' 'dwell on a virtue or fault,' giving rise to current senses.

---

ex·alt /igzáwlt/ *v.tr.* **1** raise in rank or power, etc. **2** praise highly. **3** (usu. as **exalted** *adj.*) **a** make lofty or noble. **b** make rapturously excited. □□ **ex·al·ta·tion** /égzawltáyshən/ *n.* **ex·alt′ed·ly** *adv.* **ex·alt′ed·ness** *n.* **ex·alt′er** *n.*

ex·am /igzám/ *n.* = EXAMINATION 3.

ex·am·i·na·tion /igzámináyshən/ *n.* **1** examining; being examined. **2** detailed inspection. **3** test. **4** formal questioning in court.

ex·am·ine /igzámin/ *v.tr.* **1** inquire into the nature or condition, etc., of. **2** look closely at. **3** test by examination. **4** check the health of (a patient). □□ **ex·am′in·a·ble** *adj.* **ex·am·i·nee** /-née/ *n.* **ex·am′in·er** *n.*

ex·am·ple /igzámpəl/ *n.* **1** thing characteristic of its kind or illustrating a rule. **2** model. **3** circumstance or treatment seen as a warning to others. **4** illustrative problem or exercise. □ **for example** by way of illustration.

ex·as·per·ate /igzá'aspərayt/ *v.tr.* irritate intensely. □□ **ex·as´per·at·ing·ly** *adv.* **ex·as·per·a´tion** /-ráyshən/ *n.*

ex ca·the·dra /éks kəthéedrə/ *adj. & adv.* with full authority (esp. of a papal pronouncement).

ex·ca·vate /ékskəvayt/ *v.tr.* **1 a** make (a hole or channel) by digging. **b** dig out material from (the ground). **2** reveal or extract by digging. □□ **ex·ca·va´tion** /-váyshən/ *n.* **ex´ca·va·tor** *n.*

ex·ceed /ikséed/ *v.tr.* **1** be more or greater than. **2** go beyond or do more than is warranted. **3** surpass; excel.

ex·ceed·ing·ly /ikséeding-lee/ *adv.* extremely.

ex·cel /iksél/ *v.* (**ex·celled, ex·cel·ling**) **1** *tr.* be superior to. **2** *intr.* be preeminent.

ex·cel·lence /éksələns/ *n.* outstanding merit or quality.

Ex·cel·len·cy /éksələnsee/ *n.* (*pl.* **-cies**) title used in addressing or referring to certain high officials.

ex·cel·lent /éksələnt/ *adj.* extremely good. □□ **ex´cel·lent·ly** *adv.*

ex·cel·si·or /iksélseeər/ *n.* soft wood shavings used for stuffing, packing, etc.

ex·cept /iksépt/ • *v.tr.* exclude. • *prep.* not including; other than. • *conj.* unless.
¶ See note at ACCEPT.

ex·cept·ing /iksépting/ *prep.* = EXCEPT *prep.*

ex·cep·tion /iksépshən/ *n.* **1** excepting; being excepted. **2** thing to be excepted. **3** instance that does not follow a rule. □ **take exception** object. **with the exception of** except; not including.

ex·cep·tion·a·ble /iksépshənəbəl/ *adj.* open to objection. □□ **ex·cep´tion·a·bly** *adv.*
¶ **Exceptionable** means 'open to objection,' e.g., *There was nothing exceptionable in the evidence,* and is usually found in negative contexts. It is sometimes confused with the much commoner **exceptional,** meaning 'unusual, outstanding.'

ex·cep·tion·al /iksépshənəl/ *adj.* **1** forming an exception. **2** unusual. **3** outstanding. □□ **ex·cep´tion·al·ly** *adv.*

ex·cerpt • *n.* /éksərpt/ extract from a book, film, etc. • *v.tr.* /iksérpt/ take excerpts from (a book, etc.). □□ **ex·cerpt´i·ble** *adj.* **ex·cerp´tion** /-sə́rpshən/ *n.*

ex·cess /iksés, ékses/ • *n.* **1** exceeding. **2** amount by which one thing exceeds another. **3 a** overstepping of accepted limits. **b** (in *pl.*) immoderate behavior. • *attrib.adj.* usu. /ékses/ that exceeds a prescribed amount (*excess weight*). □ **in** (or **to**) **excess** exceeding the proper amount or degree. **in excess of** more than; exceeding. □□ **ex·ces´sive** *adj.* **ex·ces´sive·ly** *adv.* **ex·ces´sive·ness** *n.*

ex·change /ikscháynj/ • *n.* **1** giving of one thing and receiving of another in its place. **2** giving of money for its equivalent in a different currency. **3** part of a telephone number designating a local region. **4** place where merchants, bankers, etc., transact business. **5** short conversation. • *v.* **1** *tr.* give or receive (one thing) in place of another. **2** *tr.* give and receive as equivalents. **3** *intr.* make an exchange. □ **in exchange** as a thing exchanged (for). □□ **ex·change´a·ble** *adj.* **ex·change·a·bil´i·ty** *n.* **ex·chang´er** *n.*

ex·cheq·uer /ikschékər/ *n.* royal or national treasury.

ex·cise¹ /éksīz/ *n.* **1** tax levied on goods produced or sold within the country of origin. **2** tax levied on certain licenses.

ex·cise² /iksíz/ *v.tr.* remove; cut out. □□ **ex·ci·sion** /iksízhən/ *n.*

ex·cit·a·ble /iksítəbəl/ *adj.* easily excited. □□ **ex·cit·a·bil´i·ty** *n.* **ex·cit´a·bly** *adv.*

ex·cite /iksít/ *v.tr.* **1 a** rouse the emotions of (a person). **b** arouse (feelings, etc.). **2** provoke. □□ **ex·cit·ant** /éksit'nt, iksít'nt/ *adj. & n.* **ex·ci·ta·tion** /-sītáyshən/ *n.* **ex·cit´ed·ly** *adv.* **ex·cit´ed·ness** *n.* **ex·cite´ment** *n.*

ex·cit·ing /iksíting/ *adj.* arousing great interest or enthusiasm; stirring. □□ **ex·cit´ing·ly** *adv.*

ex·claim /ikskláym/ *v.* **1** *intr.* cry out suddenly. **2** *tr.* utter by exclaiming.

ex·cla·ma·tion /ékskləmáyshən/ *n.* **1** exclaiming. **2** words exclaimed. □ **exclamation point** punctuation mark (!) indicating exclamation.

ex·clam·a·to·ry /iksklámətawree/ *adj.* of or serving as an exclamation.

ex·clude /iksklóod/ *v.tr.* **1** keep out (a person or thing) from a place, group, privilege, etc. **2** remove from consideration. □□ **ex·clud´a·ble** *adj.* **ex·clud´er** *n.* **ex·clu´sion** *n.*

ex·clu·sive /iksklóosiv/ • *adj.* **1** excluding other things. **2** (*predic.*; foll. by *of*) not including; except for. **3** tending to exclude others, esp. socially; select. **4** high-class. **5** not obtainable or published elsewhere. • *n.* article, etc., published by only one newspaper, etc. □□ **ex·clu´sive·ly** *adv.* **ex·clu´sive·ness** *n.* **ex·clu·siv´i·ty** *n.*

ex·com·mu·ni·cate /ékskəmyóonikayt/ *v.tr.* officially exclude (a person) from membership in and sacraments of the church. □□ **ex·com·mu·ni·ca·tion** /-káyshən/ *n.* *adj.* **ex·com·mu´ni·ca·tor** *n.*

ex·con /ékskón/ *n. colloq.* ex-convict; former prison inmate.

ex·co·ri·ate /ekskáwreeayt/ *v.tr.* **1** strip or peel off (skin). **2** censure severely. □□ **ex·co·ri·a·tion** /-áyshən/ *n.*

ex·cre·ment /ékskrimənt/ *n.* (in *sing.* or *pl.*) feces. □□ **ex·cre·men·tal** /-mént´l/ *adj.*

ex·cres·cence /ikskrésəns/ *n.* **1** abnormal or morbid outgrowth. **2** ugly addition. □□ **ex·cres·cent** /-sənt/ *adj.*

ex·cre·ta /ikskréetə/ *n.pl.* feces and urine.

ex·crete /ikskréet/ *v.tr.* (of an animal or plant) expel (waste matter). □□ **ex·cre·tion** /-kréeshən/ *n.* **ex·cre´tive** *adj.* **ex·cre·to·ry** /ékskrətawree/ *adj.*

ex·cru·ci·ate /ikskróosheeayt/ *v.tr.* (esp. as **excruciating** *adj.*) torment acutely. □□ **ex·cru´ci·at·ing·ly** *adv.*

ex·cul·pate /ékskulpayt, ikskúl-/ *v.tr. formal* free from blame; clear of a charge. □□ **ex·cul·pa·tion** /-páyshən/ *n.* **ex·cul·pa·to·ry** /-kúlpətáwree/ *adj.*

ex·cur·sion /ikskə́rzhən/ *n.* **1** short pleasure trip. **2** digression. □□ **ex·cur´sion·al** *adj.* **ex·cur´sion·ar·y** *adj.* **ex·cur´sion·ist** *n.*

ex·cur·sive /ikskə́rsiv/ *adj.* digressive; diverse. □□ **ex·cur´sive·ly** *adv.* **ex·cur´sive·ness** *n.*

ex·cuse • *v.tr.* /ikskyóoz/ **1** attempt to lessen the blame attaching to (a person, act, or fault). **2** (of a fact or circumstance) serve in mitigation of (a person or act). **3** obtain exemption for (a person or oneself). **4** (foll. by *from*) release (a person) from a duty, etc. **5** forgive. ● *n.* /ikskyoõs/ **1** reason put forward to justify an offense, fault, etc. **2** apology. **3** (foll. by *for*) poor or inadequate example of. □□ **ex·cus´a·ble** *adj.* **ex·cus´a·bly** *adv.*

ex·e·cra·ble /éksikrəbəl/ *adj.* abominable; detestable. □□ **ex´e·cra·bly** *adv.*

ex·e·crate /éksikrayt/ *v.* **1** *tr.* express or feel abhorrence for. **2** *tr.* curse (a person or thing). □□ **ex·e·cra·tion** /-kráyshən/ *n.* **ex´e·cra·tive** *adj.* **ex·e·cra·to·ry** /-krətawree/ *adj.*

ex·e·cute /éksikyoõt/ *v.tr.* **1** carry out a death sentence on. **2** carry out; perform. **3** carry out a design for (a product of art or skill). **4** make valid by signing, sealing, etc. □□ **ex´e·cut·a·ble** *adj.* **ex·e·cu´tion** *n.*

ex·e·cu·tion·er /éksikyóoshənər/ *n.* official who carries out a death sentence.

ex·ec·u·tive /igzékyətiv/ ● *n.* **1** person or body with managerial or administrative responsibility. **2** branch of government concerned with executing laws, agreements, etc. ● *adj.* concerned with executing laws, agreements, etc., or with other administration or management. □□ **ex·ec´u·tive·ly** *adv.*

ex·ec·u·tor /igzékyətər/ *n.* (*fem.* **ex·ec·u·trix** /-triks/, *pl.* **-tri·ces** /-tríseez/ or **-trix·es**) person appointed to fulfill provisions of a will. □□ **ex·ec·u·to·ri·al** /-táwreeəl/ *adj.*

ex·e·ge·sis /éksijeésis/ *n.* (*pl.* **ex·e·ge·ses** /-seez/) critical explanation of a text, esp. of Scripture. □□ **ex·e·gete** /éksijeet/ *n.* **ex·e·get·ic** /-jétik/ *adj.* **ex·e·get´i·cal** *adj.*

ex·em·plar /igzémplər, -plaar/ *n.* **1** model. **2** typical instance.

ex·em·pla·ry /igzémpləree/ *adj.* **1** fit to be imitated; outstandingly good. **2** serving as a warning. **3** illustrative; representative. □□ **ex·em´pla·ri·ness** *n.*

ex·em·pli·fy /igzémplifī/ *v.tr.* (**-fies, -fied**) **1** illustrate by example. **2** be an example of. □□ **ex·em·pli·fi·ca´tion** *n.*

ex·empt /igzémpt/ ● *adj.* free from an obligation imposed on others. ● *v.tr.* (usu. foll. by *from*) free from an obligation. □□ **ex·emp·tion** /-zémpshən/ *n.*

ex·er·cise /éksərsīz/ ● *n.* **1** activity requiring physical effort, done to sustain or improve health. **2** mental or spiritual activity, esp. to develop a skill. **3** task devised as exercise. **4** use or application of a mental faculty, right, etc. **5** (often in *pl.*) military drill or maneuvers. ● *v.* **1** *tr.* use or apply (a faculty, right, etc.). **2** *tr.* perform (a function). **3** *a intr.* do exercises. **b** *tr.* provide with exercise. **4** *tr.* a tax the powers of. **b** perplex; worry. □□ **ex´er·cis·er** *n.*

ex·ert /igzərt/ *v.tr.* **1** exercise; bring to bear (a quality, force, etc.). **2** *refl.* strive. □□ **ex·er·tion** /-zərshən/ *n.*

ex·hale /eks-háyl/ *v.* **1** *tr.* breathe out. **2** *tr. & intr.* give off or be given off in vapor. □□ **ex·ha·la´tion** *n.*

ex·haust /igzáwst/ ● *v.tr.* **1** consume or use up the whole of. **2** (often as **exhausted** *adj.* or **exhausting** *adj.*) tire out. **3** study or expound on (a subject) completely. ● *n.* **1** waste gases, etc., expelled from an engine after combustion. **2** (also **ex·haust´ pipe´**) pipe or system by

which these are expelled. □□ **ex·haust´i·ble** *adj.* **ex·haust·i·bil´i·ty** *n.* **ex·haus´ti·bly** *adv.*

ex·haus·tion /igzáwschən/ *n.* **1** exhausting; being exhausted. **2** total loss of strength. **3** establishing of a conclusion by eliminating alternatives.

ex·haus·tive /igzáwstiv/ *adj.* thorough; comprehensive. □□ **ex·haus´tive·ly** *adv.* **ex·haus´tive·ness** *n.*

ex·hib·it /igzíbit/ ● *v.tr.* **1** show or reveal publicly. **2** display (a quality, etc.). ● *n.* **1** thing or collection displayed. **2** item produced in court as evidence. □□ **ex·hib´i·tor** *n.*

ex·hi·bi·tion /éksibíshən/ *n.* **1** display (esp. public) of works of art, etc. **2** exhibiting; being exhibited.

ex·hi·bi·tion·ism /éksibíshənizəm/ *n.* **1** tendency toward display or extravagant behavior. **2** *Psychol.* compulsion to display one's genitals in public. □□ **ex·hi·bi´tion·ist** *n.* **ex·hi·bi·tion·is´tic** *adj.* **ex·hi·bi·tion·is´ti·cal·ly** *adv.*

ex·hil·a·rate /igzíləráyt/ *v.tr.* (often as **exhilarating** *adj.* or **exhilarated** *adj.*) enliven; raise the spirits of. □□ **ex·hil´a·rant** *adj.* & *n.* **ex·hil´a·rat·ing·ly** *adv.* **ex·hil·a·ra·tion** /-ráyshən/ *n.* **ex·hil´a·ra·tive** *adj.*

ex·hort /igzáwrt/ *v.tr.* urge strongly or earnestly. □□ **ex·hor·ta·tion** /táyshən/ *n.* **ex·hort´a·tive** *adj.* **ex·hort·a·to·ry** /-tətáwree/ *adj.* **ex·hort´ er** *n.*

ex·hume /igzóõm, -zyoõm, eks-hyóõm/ *v.tr.* dig out; unearth (esp. a buried corpse). □□ **ex·hu·ma´tion** *n.*

ex·i·gen·cy /éksijənsee, igzíj-/ *n.* (*pl.* **-cies**) (also **ex´i·gence** /éksijəns/) **1** urgent need or demand. **2** emergency. □□ **ex´i·gent** *adj.*

ex·ig·u·ous /igzígyoõəs, iksig-/ *adj.* scanty; small. □□ **ex·i·gu·i·ty** /éksigyóõitee/ *n.* **ex·ig´u·ous·ly** *adv.* **ex·ig´u·ous·ness** *n.*

ex·ile /éksīl, égzīl/ ● *n.* **1** expulsion from one's native land. **2** long absence abroad. **3** exiled person. ● *v.tr.* (foll. by *from*) send into exile.

ex·ist /igzíst/ *v.intr.* **1** have a place in objective reality. **2** occur; be found. **3** continue in being; live.

ex·is·tence /igzístəns/ *n.* **1** fact or condition of being or existing. **2** the manner of one's existing or living. **3** all that exists. □□ **ex·ist´ent** *adj.*

ex·is·ten·tial /égzisténshəl/ *adj.* **1** of or relating to existence. **2** *Philos.* concerned with human existence as viewed by existentialism. □□ **ex·is·ten´tial·ly** *adv.*

ex·is·ten·tial·ism /égzisténshəlizəm/ *n.* philosophical theory emphasizing the existence of the individual as a free and self-determining agent. □□ **ex·is·ten´tial·ist** *n.*

ex·it /égzit, éksit/ ● *n.* **1** passage or door by which to leave a room, etc. **2** act or right of going out. **3** place to leave a highway. **4** actor's departure from the stage. ● *v.intr.* **1** go out of a room, etc. **2** leave the stage. □ **exit poll** survey of voters leaving voting booths, used to predict an election's outcome, etc.

exo- /éksō/ *comb. form* external.

ex·o·dus /éksədəs/ *n.* **1** mass departure. **2** (**Exodus**) *Bibl.* **a** departure of the Israelites from Egypt. **b** the book of the Old Testament relating this.

ex of·fi·ci·o /éksəfisheeō/ *adv. & adj.* by virtue of one's office.

ex·on·er·ate /igzónərayt/ *v.tr.* **1** free or declare

free from blame, etc. **2** release from a duty, etc. □□ **ex·on·er·a·tion** /-ráyshən/ *n.* **ex·on′er·a·tive** *adj.*

ex·or·bi·tant /igzáwrbit′nt/ *adj.* (of a price, etc.) grossly excessive. □□ **ex·or′bi·tance** *n.* **ex·or′bi·tant·ly** *adv.*

ex·or·cize /éksawrsīz, -sər-/ *v.tr.* **1** expel (a supposed evil spirit) by invocation, etc. **2** free (a person or place) of a supposed evil spirit. □□ **ex·or·cism** /-sizəm/ *n.* **ex·or·cist** *n.*

ex·o·skel·e·ton /éksōskélit′n/ *n.* rigid body covering in certain animals, esp. arthropods. □□ **ex·o·skel′e·tal** *adj.*

ex·o·sphere /éksōsfeer/ *n.* furthermost layer of earth's atmosphere.

ex·ot·ic /igzótik/ • *adj.* **1** introduced from a foreign country. **2** attractively strange or unusual. • *n.* exotic person or thing. □ **exotic dancer** striptease dancer. □□ **ex·ot′i·cal·ly** *adv.* **ex·ot′i·cism** /-tisizəm/ *n.*

ex·pand /ikspánd/ *v.* **1** *tr. & intr.* increase in size or importance. **2** *intr.* give a fuller account. **3** *tr.* set or write out in full. **4** *tr. & intr.* spread out flat. □□ **ex·pand′a·ble** *adj.* **ex·pand′er** *n.* **ex·pan·si·ble** /ikspánsibəl/ *adj.* **ex·pan·si·bil′i·ty** *n.*

ex·panse /ikspáns/ *n.* wide continuous area.

ex·pan·sion /ikspánshən/ *n.* **1** expanding; being expanded. **2** enlargement of the scale or scope of (esp. commercial) operations. □□ **ex·pan′sion·ism** *n.* **ex·pan′sion·ist** *n.* **ex·pan·sion·is′tic** *adj.* (all in sense 2).

ex·pan·sive /ikspánsiv/ *adj.* **1** able or tending to expand. **2** extensive. **3** (of a person, etc.) effusive; open. □□ **ex·pan′sive·ly** *adv.* **ex·pan′sive·ness** *n.*

ex·pa·ti·ate /ikspáysheeayt/ *v.intr.* speak or write at length. □□ **ex·pa·ti·a·tion** /-áyshən/ *n.* **ex·pa′ti·a·to·ry** /-sheeətáwree/ *adj.*

ex·pa·tri·ate • *adj.* /ékspáytreeət/ **1** living abroad. **2** exiled. • *n.* /ekspáytreeət/ expatriate person. • *v.tr.* /ekspáytreeayt/ expel (a person) from his or her native country. □□ **ex·pa·tri·a·tion** /-áyshən/ *n.*

ex·pect /ikspékt/ *v.tr.* **1 a** regard as likely. **b** look for as appropriate or one's due. **2** *colloq.* think; suppose. □ **be expecting** *colloq.* be pregnant.

ex·pec·tan·cy /ikspéktənsee/ *n.* (*pl.* **-cies**) **1** state of expectation. **2** prospect.

ex·pec·tant /ikspéktənt/ *adj.* **1** expecting. **2** (*attrib.*) expecting a baby. □□ **ex·pec′tant·ly** *adv.*

ex·pec·ta·tion /ékspektáyshən/ *n.* **1** expecting or looking forward. **2** thing expected. **3** (foll. by *of*) probability of an event.

ex·pec·to·rant /ikspéktərənt/ • *adj.* causing the coughing out of phlegm, etc. • *n.* expectorant medicine.

ex·pec·to·rate /ikspéktərayt/ *v.tr.* cough or spit out (phlegm, etc.). □□ **ex·pec·to·ra·tion** /-ráyshən/ *n.* **ex·pec′to·ra·tor** *n.*

ex·pe·di·ent /ikspéedeeənt/ • *adj.* advantageous; advisable. • *n.* means of attaining an end. □□ **ex·pe′di·ence** /-əns/ *n.* **ex·pe′di·en·cy** *n.* **ex·pe′di·ent·ly** *adv.*

ex·pe·dite /ékspidīt/ *v.tr.* **1** assist the progress of. **2** accomplish (business) quickly. □□ **ex′pe·dit·er** *n.*

ex·pe·di·tion /ékspidíshən/ *n.* **1** journey or voyage for a particular purpose, esp. exploration. **2**

personnel undertaking this. **3** promptness. □□ **ex·pe·di′tion·ar·y** *adj.* **ex·pe·di′tion·ist** *n.*

ex·pe·di·tious /ékspidíshəs/ *adj.* acting or done with speed and efficiency. □□ **ex·pe·di′tious·ly** *adv.* **ex·pe·di′tious·ness** *n.*

ex·pel /ikspél/ *v.tr.* (**ex·pelled, ex·pel·ling**) **1** deprive of membership, etc. **2** force out; eject. □□ **ex·pel′la·ble** *adj.* **ex·pel·lee** /-leé/ *n.* **ex·pel′ler** *n.*

ex·pend /ikspénd/ *v.tr.* spend or use up (money, time, etc.).

ex·pend·a·ble /ikspéndəbəl/ *adj.* that may be sacrificed or dispensed with; not worth saving. □□ **ex·pend·a·bil′i·ty** *n.* **ex·pend′a·bly** *adv.*

ex·pen·di·ture /ikspéndichər/ *n.* **1** spending or using up. **2** thing (esp. money) expended.

ex·pense /ikspéns/ *n.* **1** cost incurred. **2** amount paid to reimburse this. **3** thing that is a cause of expense. □ **at the expense of** so as to cause damage, discredit, etc., to.

ex·pen·sive /ikspénsiv/ *adj.* costing or charging much. □□ **ex·pen′sive·ly** *adv.*

ex·pe·ri·ence /ikspéereeəns/ • *n.* **1** observation of or practical acquaintance with facts or events. **2** knowledge or skill resulting from this. **3** activity participated in or observed. • *v.tr.* **1** have experience of; undergo. **2** feel. □□ **ex·pe·ri·en′tial** /-énshəl/ *adj.*

ex·pe·ri·enced /ikspéereeənst/ *adj.* **1** having had much experience. **2** skilled from experience (*an experienced driver*).

ex·per·i·ment /ikspérimənt/ • *n.* procedure for testing a hypothesis, etc. • *v.intr.* make an experiment. □□ **ex·per·i·men·ta′tion** *n.* **ex·per′i·ment·er** *n.*

ex·per·i·men·tal /ikspérimént′l/ *adj.* **1** based on or making use of experiment. **2** used in experiments. □□ **ex·per·i·men′tal·ism** *n.* **ex·per·i·men′tal·ist** *n.* **ex·per·i·men′tal·ly** *adv.*

ex·pert /ékspərt/ • *adj.* **1** having special knowledge or skill. **2** involving or resulting from this. • *n.* person having special knowledge or skill. □□ **ex′pert·ly** *adv.* **ex′pert·ness** *n.*

ex·per·tise /ékspərteéz/ *n.* expert skill, knowledge, or judgment.

ex·pi·ate /ékspeeayt/ *v.tr.* **1** pay the penalty for (wrongdoing). **2** make amends for. □□ **ex′pi·a·ble** *adj.* **ex·pi·a·to·ry** /-peeətawree/ *adj.* **ex·pi·a′tion** /-áyshən/ *n.* **ex′pi·a·tor** *n.*

ex·pire /ikspīr/ *v.* **1** *intr.* (of a period of time, validity, etc.) come to an end. **2** *intr.* cease to be valid. **3** *intr.* die. **4** *tr.* exhale. □□ **ex·pi·ra′tion** *n.* **ex·pi′ra·to·ry** *adj.* (in sense 4). **ex·pi′ry** *n.*

ex·plain /iksplávn/ *v.tr.* **1** make clear or intelligible. **2** say by way of explanation. **3** account for (one's conduct, etc.). □ **explain away** minimize the significance of by explanation. **explain oneself** give an account of one's meaning, motives, etc. □□ **ex·plain′a·ble** *adj.* **ex·plain′er** *n.*

ex·pla·na·tion /éksplənáyshən/ *n.* **1** explaining. **2** statement or circumstance that explains something.

ex·plan·a·to·ry /iksplánətawree/ *adj.* serving or intended to serve to explain.

ex·ple·tive /éksplətiv/ *n.* swearword or exclamation.

---

expletive late Middle English (as an adjective): from late Latin *expletivus*, from *explere* 'fill out,' from *ex-* 'out' + *plere* 'fill.' The general noun sense 'word used merely to fill out a sentence' (early 17th century) was applied specifically as an oath or swear word in the early 19th century.

ex·pli·ca·ble /éksplikəbəl, iksplík-/ *adj.* that can be explained.

ex·pli·cate /éksplikayt/ *v.tr.* **1** develop the meaning of (an idea, etc.). **2** explain (esp. a text). □□ **ex·pli·ca·tion** /-káyshən/ *n.* **ex·pli·ca·tive** /éksplikaytiv, iksplíkətiv/ *adj.* **ex'pli·ca·tor** *n.* **ex·pli·ca·to·ry** /éksplikətawree, iksplík-/ *adj.*

ex·plic·it /iksplísit/ *adj.* **1** expressly stated; not merely implied. **2** definite; clear. **3** outspoken. □□ **ex·plic'it·ly** *adv.* **ex·plic'it·ness** *n.*

ex·plode /iksplód/ *v.* **1 a** *intr.* expand suddenly with a loud noise owing to a release of internal energy. **b** *tr.* cause (a bomb, etc.) to explode. **2** *intr.* give vent suddenly to emotion, esp. anger. **3** *intr.* increase suddenly or rapidly. **4** *tr.* show (a theory, etc.) to be false or baseless. **5** *tr.* (as **exploded** *adj.*) (of a drawing, etc.) showing the components of a mechanism somewhat separated. □□ **ex·plod'er** *n.*

explode mid-16th century (in the sense 'reject scornfully, discard'): from Latin *explodere* 'drive out by clapping, hiss off the stage,' from *ex-* 'out' + *plaudere* 'to clap.' Sense 4 is derived from the original sense of the word. Sense 1 (late 18th century) evolved via an old sense 'expel with violence and sudden noise,' perhaps influenced by obsolete *displode* 'burst with a noise.'

ex·ploit • *n.* /éksployt/ daring feat. • *v.tr.* /iksplóyt/ **1** make use of (a resource, etc.). **2** take advantage of (esp. a person) for one's own ends. □□ **ex·ploi·ta'tion** *n.* **ex·ploit'a·tive** *adj.* **ex·ploit'er** *n.* **ex·ploit'ive** *adj.*

ex·plore /ikspláwr/ *v.tr.* **1** travel through (a country, etc.) to learn about it. **2** inquire into. □□ **ex·plo·ra'tion** *n.* **ex·plor'a·tive** *adj.* **ex·plor'a·to·ry** *adj.* **ex·plor'er** *n.*

ex·plo·sion /iksplṓzhən/ *n.* **1** exploding. **2** loud noise caused by this. **3** sudden outbreak of feeling. **4** rapid or sudden increase.

ex·plo·sive /iksplṓsiv/ • *adj.* **1** able, tending, or likely to explode. **2** dangerously tense. • *n.* explosive substance. □□ **ex·plo'sive·ly** *adv.* **ex·plo'sive·ness** *n.*

ex·po·nent /ikspónənt/ *n.* **1** person who promotes an idea, etc. **2** practitioner of an activity, profession, etc. **3** type or representative. **4** *Math.* raised symbol beside a numeral indicating how many times it is to be multiplied by itself (e.g., $2^3 = 2 \times 2 \times 2$).

ex·po·nen·tial /ékspənénshəl/ *adj.* **1** of or indicated by a mathematical exponent. **2** (of an increase, etc.) more and more rapid. □□ **ex·po·nen'tial·ly** *adv.*

ex·port • *v.tr.* /ekspáwrt, éks-/ sell or send to another country. • *n.* /ékspawrt/ **1** exporting. **2** exported article or service. □□ **ex·port'a·ble** *adj.* **ex·port·a·bil'i·ty** *n.* **ex·por·ta'tion** *n.* **ex·port'er** *n.*

ex·pose /ikspóz/ *v.tr.* **1** leave uncovered or unprotected. **2** (foll. by *to*) **a** put at risk of. **b** introduce to (*exposed to the arts*). **3** *Photog.* subject

(film) to light. **4** reveal. **5** exhibit; display. □ **expose oneself** display one's body publicly and indecently. □□ **ex·pos'er** *n.*

ex·po·sé /ekspōzáy/ *n.* revelation of something discreditable.

ex·po·si·tion /ékspəzíshən/ *n.* **1** explanatory account. **2** explanation or commentary. **3** large public exhibition. □□ **ex·po·si'tion·al** *adj.*

ex·pos·tu·late /ikspóschəlayt/ *v.intr.* make a protest; remonstrate. □□ **ex·pos·tu·la'tion** /-láyshən/ *n.*

ex·po·sure /ikspṓzhər/ *n.* **1** exposing; being exposed. **2** condition of being exposed to the elements. **3** *Photog.* **a** exposing film to light. **b** duration of this. □ **exposure meter** *Photog.* a device for measuring the strength of the light to determine the correct duration of exposure.

ex·pound /ikspównd/ *v.tr.* **1** set out in detail. **2** explain or interpret. □□ **ex·pound'er** *n.*

ex·press¹ /iksprés/ *v.tr.* **1** represent or make known in words or by gestures, conduct, etc. **2** communicate. **3** represent by symbols. **4** squeeze out (liquid or air). □□ **ex·press'er** *n.* **ex·press'i·ble** *adj.*

ex·press² /iksprés/ • *adj.* **1** operating at high speed. **2** also /ékspres/ definitely stated. **3 a** done, made, or sent for a special purpose. **b** delivered by a special service. • *adv.* **1** at high speed. **2** by express shipment. • *n.* **1** fast train, etc. **2** service for rapid package delivery. □□ **ex·press'ly** *adv.*

ex·pres·sion /ikspréshən/ *n.* **1** expressing; being expressed. **2 a** word or phrase expressed. **b** manner of expressing. **3** *Math.* collection of symbols expressing a quantity. **4** person's facial appearance, indicating feeling. **5** depiction or conveyance of feeling, movement, etc., in art. □□ **ex·pres'sion·less** *adj.* **ex·pres'sion·less·ly** *adv.*

ex·pres·sion·ism /ikspréshənizəm/ *n.* style of painting, music, drama, etc., seeking to express emotion rather than the external world. □□ **ex·pres'sion·ist** *n.* & *adj.* **ex·pres·sion·is'tic** *adj.* **ex·pres·sion·is'ti·cal·ly** *adv.*

ex·pres·sive /iksprésiv/ *adj.* **1** full of expression. **2** serving to express. □□ **ex·pres'sive·ly** *adv.* **ex·pres'sive·ness** *n.*

ex·press·way /iksprésway/ *n.* high-speed highway.

ex·pro·pri·ate /eksprópreeayt/ *v.tr.* take away (property) from its owner. □□ **ex·pro·pri·a'tion** /-áyshən/ *n.* **ex·pro'pri·a·tor** *n.*

ex·pul·sion /ikspúlshən/ *n.* expelling; being expelled. □□ **ex·pul·sive** /-púlsiv/ *adj.*

ex·punge /ikspúnj/ *v.tr.* erase; remove. □□ **ex·punc·tion** /ikspúngkshən/ *n.* **ex·pung'er** *n.*

ex·pur·gate /ékspərgayt/ *v.tr.* remove objectionable matter from (a book, etc.). □□ **ex·pur·ga'tion** /-gáyshən/ *n.* **ex'pur·ga·tor** *n.*

ex·qui·site /ékskwizit, ikskwízit/ *adj.* **1** extremely beautiful or delicate. **2** keenly felt. **3** highly discriminating (*exquisite taste*). □□ **ex·quis'ite·ly** *adv.* **ex·quis'ite·ness** *n.*

ex·tant /ékstənt, ekstánt/ *adj.* still existing.

ex·tem·po·ra·ne·ous /ikstémpəráyneeəs/ *adj.* spoken or done without preparation. □□ **ex·tem·po·ra'ne·ous·ly** *adv.*

ex·tem·po·re /ikstémpəree/ *adj.* & *adv.* without preparation.

ex·tem·po·rize /ikstémpərīz/ *v.tr.* improvise. □□ **ex·tem·po·ri·za'tion** *n.*

ex·tend /iksténd/ v. **1** tr. & intr. lengthen or make larger in space or time. **2** a tr. stretch or lay out at full length. **b** tr. & intr. (cause to) stretch or span over a period of time. **3** intr. & tr. (foll. by *to*, *over*) reach or encompass. **4** intr. (foll. by *to*) have a certain scope. **5** tr. offer (an invitation, hospitality, etc.). □ **extended family** family that includes nearby relatives. □□ **ex·tend′a·ble** adj. **ex·tend·a·bil′i·ty** n. **ex·tend′ible** adj. **ex·tend·i·bil′i·ty** n. **ex·ten·si·ble** /-sténsibəl/ adj. **ex·ten·si·bil′i·ty** n.

ex·ten·sion /iksténshən/ n. **1** extending; being extended. **2** part enlarging or added on. **3** additional part of anything. □□ **ex·ten′sion·al** adj.

ex·ten·sive /iksténsiv/ adj. **1** covering a large area. **2** far-reaching. □□ **ex·ten′sive·ly** adv. **ex·ten′sive·ness** n.

ex·ten·sor /iksténsər/ n. (in full **extensor muscle**) Anat. muscle that extends or straightens part of the body (cf. FLEXOR).

ex·tent /iksténtt/ n. **1** space over which a thing extends. **2** degree; scope.

ex·ten·u·ate /ikstényōō-ayt/ v.tr. (often as **extenuating** adj.) lessen the seeming seriousness of (guilt or an offense). □□ **ex·ten·u·a·tion** /-áyshən/ n.

ex·te·ri·or /ikstéereeər/ ● adj. **1** of or on the outer side. **2** coming from outside. ● n. **1** outward aspect or surface. **2** outward demeanor.

ex·ter·mi·nate /ikstərminayt/ v.tr. destroy utterly (esp. a living thing). □□ **ex·ter·mi·na·tion** /-náyshən/ n. **ex·ter′mi·na·tor** n.

ex·ter·nal /ikstərnəl/ ● adj. **1** a of or on the outside or visible part. **b** coming or derived from the outside or an outside source. **2** foreign. **3** outside the conscious subject (*the external world*). **4** for use on the outside of the body. ● n. (in pl.) **1** outward features or aspect. **2** external circumstances. **3** inessentials. □□ **ex·ter′nal·ly** adv.

ex·ter·nal·ize /ikstərnəlīz/ v.tr. give or attribute external existence to. □□ **ex·ter·nal·i·za′tion** n.

ex·tinct /ikstíngkt/ adj. **1** that has died out. **2** (of a volcano) that no longer erupts.

ex·tinc·tion /ikstíngkshən/ n. **1** making extinct; becoming extinct. **2** extinguishing; being extinguished. **3** annihilation.

ex·tin·guish /ikstínggwish/ v.tr. **1** cause (a flame, light, etc.) to die out. **2** destroy. □□ **ex·tin′guish·a·ble** adj. **ex·tin′guish·er** n.

ex·tir·pate /ékstərpayt/ v.tr. root out; destroy completely. □□ **ex·tir·pa·tion** /-páyshən/ n. **ex′tir·pa·tor** n.

ex·tol /ikstól/ v.tr. (**extolled, extol·ling**) praise enthusiastically. □□ **ex·tol′ler** n. **ex·tol′ment** n.

ex·tort /ikstáwrt/ v.tr. obtain by coercion. □□ **ex·tor·tion** /ikstáwrshən/ n. act of extorting, esp. money. □□ **ex·tor′tion·ate** adj. **ex·tor′tion·er** n. **ex·tor′tion·ist** n.

ex·tra /ékstrə/ ● adj. additional; more than usual, necessary, or expected. ● adv. **1** more than usually. **2** additionally (*was charged extra*). ● n. **1** extra thing. **2** thing for which an extra charge is made. **3** performer in a minor role.

extra- /ékstrə/ comb. form **1** outside; beyond (*extragalactic*). **2** beyond the scope of (*extracurricular*).

ex·tract ● v.tr. /ikstrákt/ **1** remove or take out. **2** obtain (money, an admission, etc.) by pressure. **3** obtain (a natural resource) from the earth. **4** select (a passage of writing, music, etc.). **5** obtain (juice, etc.) by pressure, distillation, etc. **6**

derive (pleasure, etc.). ● n. /ékstrakt/ **1** short passage from a book, etc. **2** concentrated ingredient. □□ **ex·tract′a·ble** adj. **ex·tract·a·bil′i·ty** n.

ex·trac·tion /ikstrákshən/ n. **1** extracting; being extracted. **2** lineage; descent.

ex·tra·cur·ric·u·lar /ékstrəkəríkyələr/ adj. (of a subject of study) not included in the normal curriculum.

ex·tra·dite /ékstrədīt/ v.tr. hand over (a person accused or convicted of a crime) to the country, state, etc., in which the crime was committed. □□ **ex·tra·di·tion** /ékstrədíshən/ n.

ex·tra·mar·i·tal /ékstrəmárit′l/ adj. (esp. of sexual relations) occurring outside marriage. □□ **ex·tra·mar′i·tal·ly** adv.

ex·tra·ne·ous /ikstráyneeəs/ adj. **1** of external origin. **2** separate; irrelevant; unrelated. □□ **ex·tra′ne·ous·ly** adv. **ex·tra′ne·ous·ness** n.

ex·tra·or·di·nar·y /ikstráwrd′neree, ékstrəáwr-/ adj. **1** unusual or remarkable. **2** unusually great. **3** (of a meeting, official, etc.) additional; special. □□ **ex·tra·or·di·nar′i·ly** adv.

ex·trap·o·late /ikstrápəlayt/ v.tr. calculate or derive approximately from known data, etc. □□ **ex·trap·o·la·tion** /-láyshən/ n. **ex·trap′o·la·tor** n.

ex·tra·sen·so·ry /ékstrəsénsəree/ adj. outside the known senses.

ex·tra·ter·res·tri·al /ékstrətəréstreeəl/ ● adj. outside the earth or its atmosphere. ● n. (in science fiction) being from outer space.

ex·trav·a·gant /ikstrávəgənt/ adj. **1** spending (esp. money) excessively. **2** costing much. **3** unreasonable; absurd. □□ **ex·trav′a·gance** n. **ex·trav′a·gant·ly** adv.

ex·trav·a·gan·za /ikstrávəgánzə/ n. spectacular theatrical production.

ex·treme /ikstréem/ ● adj. **1** of a high or the highest degree (*in extreme danger*). **2** severe. **3** outermost. **4** Polit. on the far left or right of a party. **5** risking life or injury (*extreme sports*). ● n. **1** one or other of two opposite things. **2** highest degree. **3** Math. first or last term of a ratio or series. □ **go to extremes** take an extreme course of action. **go to the other extreme** take an opposite course of action. □□ **ex·treme′ly** adv. **ex·treme′ness** n.

ex·trem·ist /ikstréemist/ n. person with radical views. □□ **ex·trem′ism** n.

ex·trem·i·ty /ikstrémitee/ n. (pl. **-ties**) **1** extreme point; end. **2** (in pl.) the hands and feet. **3** extreme adversity.

ex·tri·cate /ékstrikayt/ v.tr. free or disentangle from a difficulty, etc. □□ **ex′tri·ca·ble** adj. **ex·tri·ca·tion** /-káyshən/ n.

ex·trin·sic /ikstrínsik, -zik/ adj. **1** not inherent or intrinsic. **2** extraneous. **3** from without. □□ **ex·trin′si·cal·ly** adv.

ex·tro·vert /ékstrəvərt/ n. outgoing or sociable person. □□ **ex·tro·ver′sion** /-və́rzhən/ n. **ex′tro·vert·ed** adj.

ex·trude /ikstrōod/ v.tr. thrust or force out as through a die. □□ **ex·tru′sion** /-trōozhən/ n. **ex·tru′sive** /-trōosiv/ adj.

ex·u·ber·ant /igzōobərənt/ adj. **1** lively; high-spirited. **2** (of a plant, etc.) prolific. □□ **ex·u′ber·ance** n. **ex·u′ber·ant·ly** adv.

ex·ude /igzōod, iksōod/ v. **1** tr. & intr. ooze out.

2 *tr.* display (an emotion, etc.) freely. □□ **ex·u·date** /éksyŏŏdayt, éksə-/ *n.* **ex·u·da'tion** *n.* **ex·u'da·tive** *adj.*

ex·ult /igzúlt/ *v.intr.* be joyful. □□ **ex·ul·ta'tion** *n.* **ex·ult'ant** *adj.* **ex·ult'ant·ly** *adv.*

ex·urb /éksərb, égzərb/ *n.* district outside a city or town, esp. a prosperous area beyond the suburbs. □□ **ex·ur'ban** *adj.* **ex·ur·ban·ite** /eksɔ́rbənīt, égzɔ́r-/ *n.*

ex·ur·bi·a /eksɔ́rbeeə, egzɔ́r-/ *n.* the exurbs collectively.

eye /ī/ • *n.* **1** organ of sight. **2** eye characterized by the color of the iris. **3** region around the eye (*eyes red from crying*). **4** (in *sing.* or *pl.*) sight. **5** particular visual faculty. **6** leaf bud of a potato. **7** calm region at the center of a hurricane. **8** hole of a needle, etc. • *v.tr.* (**eyes, eyed, eye·ing** or **ey·ing**) watch or observe closely. □ **all eyes 1** watching intently. **2** general attention (*all eyes were on us*). **before one's** (or **one's very**) **eyes** right in front of one. **eye-catching** *colloq.* striking; attractive. **eye for an eye** retaliation in kind. **eye-opener** *colloq.* **1** enlightening experience. **2** bracing drink, etc. **eye shadow** cosmetic applied to the skin around the eyes. **have one's eye on** wish or plan to procure. **have an eye for** be partial to. **hit a person between the eyes** *colloq.* be very obvious or impressive. **keep an eye on 1** pay attention to. **2** take care of. **keep an eye open** (or **out**) watch carefully. **make eyes at** look flirtatiously at. **my eye** *sl.* nonsense. **open a person's eyes** be enlightening. **see eye to eye** be in agreement.

eye·ball /íbawl/ • *n.* ball of the eye within the lids and socket. • *v. sl.* **1** *tr.* look or stare at. **2** *intr.* look or stare.

eye·brow /íbrow/ *n.* line of hair on the ridge above the eye socket. □ **raise one's eyebrows** show surprise, disbelief, or disapproval.

eye·ful /ífŏŏl/ *n.* (*pl.* **-fuls**) *colloq.* **1** long, steady look. **2** visually striking person or thing.

eye·glass /íglas/ *n.* **1** lens for correcting defective sight. **2** (in *pl.*) pair of these, set into a frame.

eye·lash /ílash/ *n.* each of the hairs growing on the edges of the eyelids. □ **by an eyelash** by a very small margin.

eye·let /ílit/ *n.* **1** small hole for string or rope, etc., to pass through. **2** metal ring reinforcement for this.

eye·lid /ílid/ *n.* either of the skin folds closing to cover the eye.

eye·lin·er /ílīnər/ *n.* cosmetic applied as a line around the eye.

eye·piece /ípees/ *n.* lens or lenses at the end of a microscope, telescope, etc., to which the eye is applied.

eye·sight /ísīt/ *n.* faculty or power of seeing.

eye·sore /ísawr/ *n.* visually offensive or ugly thing.

eye·tooth /ítŏŏth/ *n.* canine tooth in the upper jaw.

eye·wash /íwosh, íwawsh/ *n.* **1** lotion for the eye. **2** *sl.* nonsense; insincere talk.

eye·wit·ness /íwitnis/ *n.* person who saw thing happen.

ey·rie var. of AERIE.

Ff

F¹ /ef/ *n.* (also **f**) (*pl.* **Fs** or **F's; f's**) **1** sixth letter of the alphabet. **2** *Mus.* fourth note of the diatonic scale of C major. **3** grade indicating failure.

F² *abbr.* (also **F.**) **1** Fahrenheit. **2** farad(s). **3** female.

F³ *symb. Chem.* fluorine.

f *abbr.* (also **f.**) **1** female. **2** feminine. **3** following page, etc. **4** *Mus.* forte. **5** folio. **6** focal length (cf. F-NUMBER). **7** filly.

fa /faa/ *n. Mus.* fourth note of a major scale.

FAA *abbr.* Federal Aviation Administration.

fa·ble /fáybəl/ *n.* **1 a** a story, esp. a supernatural one, not based on fact. **b** tale, esp. with animals as characters, conveying a moral. **2** lie. □□ **fa·bler** /fáyblər/ *n.*

fab·ric /fábrik/ *n.* **1** woven material; textile. **2** essential structure.

fab·ri·cate /fábrikayt/ *v.tr.* **1** construct, esp. from prepared components. **2** invent (a story, etc.). □□ **fab'ri·ca·tor** *n.*

fab·ri·ca·tion /fábrikáyshən/ *n.* **1** action or process of manufacturing or constructing something. **2** invention of a lie.

fab·u·lous /fábyələs/ *adj.* **1** incredible; exaggerated; absurd. **2** *colloq.* marvelous (*looking fabulous*). **3** legendary. □□ **fab'u·lous·ly** *adv.* **fab'u·lous·ness** *n.*

fa·çade /fəsaad/ *n.* **1** face of a building, esp. its principal front. **2** outward appearance or front, esp. a deceptive one.

face /fays/ • *n.* **1** front of the head from the forehead to the chin. **2 a** expression of the facial features (*had a happy face*). **b** grimace (*make a face*). **3 a** surface; side. **b** dial of a clock, etc. **4** outward appearance or aspect (*the harsh face of capitalism*). • *v.* **1** *tr. & intr.* look or be positioned toward or in a certain direction (*facing the window*). **2** *tr.* be opposite (*facing page 20*). **3** *tr.* meet resolutely or defiantly; confront (*face one's critics*). **4** *tr.* cover the surface of (a thing) with a coating, extra layer, etc. □ **face-lift 1** (also **face-lifting**) cosmetic surgery to remove wrinkles, etc. **2** procedure to improve the appearance of a thing. **face the music** *colloq.* put up with or stand up to unpleasant consequences, esp. criticism. **face up to** accept bravely; confront; stand up to. **in the face of 1** despite. **2** confronted by. **put one's face on** *colloq.* apply makeup to one's face. **save face** preserve esteem; avoid humiliation. □□ **faced** *adj.* (also in *comb.*). **fac'ing** *adj.* (also in *comb.*).

face·less /fáyslis/ *adj.* **1** without identity; purposely not identifiable. **2** lacking character. **3** without a face. □□ **face'less·ly** *adv.* **face·less·ness** *n.*

fac·et /fásit/ *n.* **1** particular aspect of a thing. **2** one side of a cut gem. □□ **fac'et·ed** *adj.* (also in *comb.*).

facet

FACET

fa·ce·tious /fəseeshəs/ *adj.* **1** characterized by flippant or inappropriate humor. **2** (of a person) intending to be amusing, esp. inappropriately. □□ **fa·ce'tious·ly** *adv.* **fa·ce'tious·ness** *n.*

fa·cial /fáyshəl/ • *adj.* of or for the face. • *n.* beauty treatment for the face. □□ **fa'cial·ly** *adv.*

fa·cile /fásəl, -sil/ *adj.* usu. *derog.* **1** easily achieved but of little value. **2** fluent; ready; glib. □□ **fac'ile·ly** *adv.* **fac'ile·ness** *n.*

fa·cil·i·tate /fəsílitayt/ *v.tr.* ease (a process, etc.). □□ **fa·cil·i·ta·tion** /-táyshən/ *n.* **fa·cil'i·ta·tive** *adj.* **fa·cil'i·ta·tor** *n.*

fa·cil·i·ty /fəsílitee/ *n.* (*pl.* **-ties**) **1** ease. **2** fluency; dexterity; aptitude. **3** (esp. in *pl.*) opportunity, equipment, or resources for doing something. **4** plant, installation, or establishment. **5** *euphem.* (in *pl.*) (public) toilet.

fac·ing /fáysing/ *n.* **1** garment lining. **2** outer layer covering the surface of a wall, etc.

fac·sim·i·le /faksímilee/ *n.* **1** exact copy, esp. of writing, printing, etc. **2 a** production of an exact copy of a document, etc., by electronic scanning and transmission of the resulting data (see also FAX). **b** copy produced in this way. □ **in facsimile** as an exact copy.

fact /fakt/ *n.* **1** thing that is known to have occurred, to exist, or to be true. **2** truth; reality. □ **the facts of life** information about sexual functions and practices.

fac·tion /fákshən/ *n.* small organized dissenting group within a larger one.

fac·tious /fákshəs/ *adj.* of, characterized by, or inclined to faction. □□ **fac'tious·ly** *adv.* **fac' tious·ness** *n.*

fac·ti·tious /faktíshəs/ *adj.* **1** contrived. **2** artificial. □□ **fac·ti'tious·ly** *adv.* **fac·ti'tious·ness** *n.*

fac·toid /fáktoyd/ *n.* **1** simulated or imagined fact. **2** trivial fact or news item.

fac·tor /fáktər/ • *n.* **1** circumstance, fact, or influence contributing to a result. **2** *Math.* whole number, etc., that when multiplied with another produces a given number or expression. ● *v.tr. Math.* resolve into factors or components. □□ **fac′tor·a·ble** *adj.*

fac·to·ri·al /faktáwreeəl/ *Math.* ● *n.* product of a number and all the whole numbers below it (*four factorial = 4 x 3 x 2 x 1*). ¶ Symb.: ! (as in *4!*). ● *adj.* of a factor or factorial. □□ **facto′ri·al·ly** *adv.*

fac·to·ry /fáktəree/ *n.* (*pl.* **-ries**) **1** building or buildings containing equipment for manufacturing machinery or goods. **2** (usu. *derog.*) place producing mass quantities or a low quality of goods, etc. □ **factory farming** system of rearing livestock using industrial or intensive methods. **factory ship** fishing ship with facilities for immediate processing of the catch.

fac·to·tum /faktótəm/ *n.* employee who does all kinds of work.

fac·tu·al /fákchōōəl/ *adj.* based on or concerned with fact. □□ **fac·tu·al·i·ty** /-chōōálitee/ *n.* **fac′tu·al·ly** *adv.*

fac·ul·ty /fákəltee/ *n.* (*pl.* **-ties**) **1** aptitude or ability for a particular activity. **2** inherent mental or physical power. **3** teaching staff.

fad /fad/ *n.* craze; short-lived fashion. □□ **fad′dish** *adj.* **fad′dish·ly** *adv.* **fad′dist** *n.*

fade /fayd/ ● *v.* **1** *intr.* & *tr.* lose or cause to lose color, light, or sound. **2** *intr.* lose freshness or strength; (of flowers, etc.) droop; wither. **3** *tr.* (foll. by *in, out*) *Cinematog.* & *Broadcasting* cause (a photographic image, recorded sound, etc.) to appear or disappear gradually. ● *n.* action or an instance of fading. □ **fade away** *colloq.* languish; grow thin. □□ **fade′less** *adj.* **fad′er** *n.* (in sense 3 of *v.*).

fag·got /fágət/ *n. sl. derog.* male homosexual.

fag·ot /fágət/ ● *n.* **1** bundle of sticks or twigs bound together as fuel. **2** bundle of iron rods for heat treatment. ● *v.tr.* bind in or make into fagots.

Fahr·en·heit /fárənhīt/ *adj.* of a scale of temperature on which water freezes at 32° and boils at 212°.

fa·ience /fī-óNs, fay-/ *n.* decorated and glazed earthenware and porcelain, e.g., delft or majolica.

fail /fayl/ *v.* **1** *intr.* not succeed (*failed to qualify*). **2 a** *tr.* & *intr.* be unsuccessful in (an examination, test, interview, etc.). **b** *tr.* not pass; reject. **3** *intr.* be unable to; neglect to; choose not to (*he failed to appear*). **4** *tr.* disappoint. **5** *intr.* (of supplies, crops, etc.) be or become lacking or insufficient. **6** *intr.* become weaker; cease functioning (*her health is failing*). **7** *intr.* **a** (of an enterprise) collapse; come to nothing. **b** become bankrupt. □ **fail-safe** reverting to a safe condition in the event of a breakdown, etc. **without fail** for certain; whatever happens.

fail·ing /fáyling/ ● *n.* fault; weakness. ● *prep.* in default of; if not.

fail·ure /fáylyər/ *n.* **1** lack of success; failing. **2** unsuccessful person, thing, or attempt. **3** nonperformance; nonoccurrence. **4** breaking down or ceasing to function (*heart failure*). **5** running short of supply, etc. **6** bankruptcy; collapse.

fain /fayn/ *archaic* ● *predic.adj.* (foll. by *to* + infin.) willing under the circumstances to. ● *adv.* gladly (esp. *would fain*).

faint /faynt/ ● *adj.* **1** indistinct; pale; dim; quiet; not clearly perceived. **2** (of a person) weak or

dizzy; inclined to faint. **3** slight; remote; inadequate (*a faint chance*). **4** feeble; halfhearted (*faint praise*). **5** timid (*a faint heart*). ● *v.intr.* lose consciousness. ● *n.* sudden loss of consciousness; fainting. □ **faint-hearted** cowardly; timid. □□ **faint′ly** *adv.* **faint′ness** *n.*

fair[1] /fair/ ● *adj.* **1** just; unbiased; equitable; in accordance with the rules. **2** blond; light or pale. **3 a** of (only) moderate quality or amount; average. **b** considerable; satisfactory (*a fair chance of success*). **4** (of weather) fine and dry; (of the wind) favorable. **5** beautiful; attractive. ● *adv.* in a fair manner (*play fair*). □ **fair game** thing or person one may legitimately pursue, exploit, etc. **fair play** reasonable treatment or behavior. □□ **fair′ish** *adj.* **fair′ness** *n.*

fair[2] /fair/ *n.* **1** gathering of stalls, amusements, etc., for public (usu. outdoor) entertainment. **2** periodic market, often with entertainments. **3** exhibition, esp. commercial.

fair·ing /fáiring/ *n.* **1** streamlining structure added to a ship, aircraft, vehicle, etc. **2** process of streamlining.

fair·ly /fáirlee/ *adv.* **1** in a fair manner. **2** moderately; rather.

fair·way /fáirway/ *n.* part of a golf course between a tee and its green, kept free of rough grass.

fair·y /fáiree/ ● *n.* (*pl.* **-ies**) small imaginary being with magical powers. ● *adj.* of fairies; fairylike; delicate; small. □ **fairy godmother** benefactress. **fairy tale** (or **story**) **1** tale about fairies or other fantastic creatures. **2** incredible story; fabrication. □□ **fair′y·like** *adj.*

fait ac·com·pli /fet aakawNplee′, -komplee′/ *n.* thing that has been done and is past arguing about or altering.

faith /fayth/ *n.* **1** complete trust or confidence. **2** firm belief, esp. without logical proof. **3 a** system of religious belief. **b** belief in religious doctrines. **4** duty or commitment to fulfill a trust, promise, etc.; allegiance (*keep faith*).

faith·ful /fáythfōōl/ *adj.* **1** showing faith. **2** loyal; trustworthy; constant. **3** accurate; true to fact. □□ **faith′ful·ly** *adv.* **faith′ful·ness** *n.*

faith·less /fáythlis/ *adj.* **1** false; unreliable; disloyal. **2** being without religious faith. □□ **faith′less·ly** *adv.* **faith′less·ness** *n.*

fa·ji·tas /faahée′təs, fə-/ *n.pl. Mexican Cookery* thin strips of fried or broiled meat, usu. seasoned.

fake /fayk/ ● *n.* **1** thing or person that is not genuine. **2** trick. **3** *Sport* feint. ● *adj.* counterfeit; not genuine. ● *v.tr.* make a fake or imitation. □□ **fak′er** *n.* **fak′er·y** *n.*

fal·con /fálkən, fáwl-/ *n.* diurnal bird of prey having long pointed wings, and sometimes trained to hunt small game for sport.

fall /fawl/ ● *v.intr.* (*past* **fell** /fel/; *past part.* **fall·en** /fáwlən/) **1** go or come down freely; descend. **2** cease to stand; come to the ground. **3 a** (of hair, clothing, etc.) hang down. **b** (of ground, etc.) slope. **4 a** sink lower. **b** subside. **5** occur (*dark·ness fell*). **6** decline; diminish (*standards have fallen*). **7** (of the face) show dismay or disappointment. **8** lose power, status, esteem, etc. **9** yield to temptation. **10** take or have a particular direction or place (*the accent falls on the first syllable*). **11** (foll. by *under, within*) be classed among. **12** come by chance or duty (*it fell to me to answer*). **13** pass into a specified condition (*fall into decay*). **14** be captured; be defeated. **15** die. **16** (foll. by *on, upon*) **a** attack. **b** meet with. **c** embark on. **17** begin (*fell to wondering*). ● *n.* **1**

act or instance of falling. **2** that which falls or has fallen, e.g., snow, rocks, etc. **3** decline in price, value, demand, etc. **4** overthrow; downfall (*the fall of Rome*). **5 a** succumbing to temptation. **b** (**the Fall**) the biblical sin of Adam and its consequences. **6** (also **Fall**) autumn. **7** (esp. *pl.*) waterfall or cascade. **8** a throw in wrestling. □ **fall apart** (or **to pieces**) **1** break into pieces. **2** be reduced to chaos. **3** lose one's capacity to cope. **fall back** retreat. **fall back on** have recourse to in difficulty. **fall for** *colloq.* **1** be captivated or deceived by. **2** yield to the charms or merits of. **fall guy** *sl.* **1** easy victim. **2** scapegoat. **fall in 1 a** take one's place in military formation. **b** (as *int.*) the order to do this. **2** collapse inward. **falling star** meteor. **fall into place** begin to make sense or cohere. **fall in with 1** meet or become involved with by chance. **2** agree with. **fall short** be or become deficient or inadequate. **fall short of** fail to reach or obtain. **fall through** fail; come to nothing.

fal·la·cy /fáləsee/ *n.* (*pl.* **-cies**) **1** mistaken belief. **2** faulty reasoning; misleading or unsound argument. □□ **fal·la·cious** /fəláyshəs/ *adj.* **fal·la′cious·ly** *adv.*

fal·li·ble /fálibəl/ *adj.* **1** capable of making mistakes. **2** liable to be erroneous. □□ **fal·li·bil′i·ty** *n.* **fal′li·bly** *adv.*

Fal·lo·pi·an tube /fəlópeeən/ *n. Anat.* either of two tubes along which ova travel from the ovaries to the uterus.

fall·out /fáwlowt/ *n.* radioactive nuclear debris.

fal·low /fálō/ *adj.* **1** (of land) plowed and harrowed but left unsown. **2** uncultivated. □□ **fal′low·ness** *n.*

false /fawls/ *adj.* **1** wrong; incorrect. **2 a** spurious; sham; artificial (*false gods*). **b** acting as such; appearing to be such, esp. deceptively (*a false lining*). **3** improperly so called (*false acacia*). **4** deceptive. **5** (foll. by *to*) deceitful, treacherous, or unfaithful. □□ **false′ly** *adv.* **false′ness** *n.* **fal′si·ty** *n.* (*pl.* **-ties**)

false·hood /fáwls-hŏŏd/ *n.* **1** state of being false, esp. untrue. **2** false or untrue thing. **3** a act of lying. **b** a lie or lies.

fal·set·to /fawlsétō/ *n.* (*pl.* **-tos**) male singing voice above the normal range.

fal·si·fy /fáwlsifī/ *v.tr.* (**-fies, -fied**) **1** fraudulently alter or make false (a document, evidence, etc.). **2** misrepresent. □□ **fal′si·fi·a·ble** *adj.* **fal·si·fi·a·bil′i·ty** *n.* **fal·si·fi·ca′tion** *n.*

fal·ter /fáwltər/ *v.* **1** *intr.* stumble; stagger; go unsteadily. **2** *intr.* waver; lose courage. **3** *tr.* & *intr.* stammer; speak hesitatingly. □□ **fal′ter·er** *n.* **fal′ter·ing·ly** *adv.*

fame /faym/ *n.* renown; state of being famous.

famed /faymd/ *adj.* much spoken of (*famed for its good food*).

fa·mil·ial /fəmílyəl, -leeəl/ *adj.* of a family or its members.

fa·mil·iar /fəmílyər/ ● *adj.* **1 a** well known. **b** often encountered or experienced. **2** well acquainted. **3** excessively informal; impertinent. **4** unceremonious; informal. ● *n.* close friend. □□ **fa·mil·i·ar′i·ty** /-eeáritee, -yár-/ *n.* **fa·mil′iar·ly** *adv.*

fa·mil·iar·ize /fəmílyərīz/ *v.tr.* make conversant or well acquainted; make well known. □□ **fa·mil·iar·i·za′tion** *n.*

fam·i·ly /fáMilee/ *n.* (*pl.* **-lies**) **1** set of parents and children, or of relations. **2** descendants of a common ancestor. **3** brotherhood of persons or nations united by political or religious ties. **4**

group of objects distinguished by common features. **5** *Biol.* group of related genera of organisms. □ **family planning** birth control. **family tree** chart showing relationships and lines of descent. **in the** (or **a**) **family way** *colloq.* pregnant.

fam·ine /fámin/ *n.* extreme scarcity, esp. of food.

fam·ish /fámish/ *v.* (usu. in *passive*) **1** reduce or be reduced to extreme hunger. **2** *colloq.* (esp. as **famished** *adj.*) feel very hungry.

fa·mous /fáyməs/ *adj.* **1** celebrated; well known. **2** *colloq.* excellent. □□ **fa′mous·ly** *adv.* **fa′mous·ness** *n.*

fan[1] /fan/ ● *n.* **1** apparatus, usu. with rotating blades, for ventilation, etc. **2** wide, flat device, waved to cool oneself. ● *v.* (**fanned, fan·ning**) **1** *tr.* blow a current of air on, with or as with a fan. **2** *intr.* & *tr.* spread out in the shape of a fan. □□ **fan′like** *adj.* **fan′ner** *n.*

fan[2] /fan/ *n.* devotee; follower. □□ **fan′dom** *n.*

fa·nat·ic /fənátik/ ● *n.* person filled with excessive and often misguided enthusiasm for something. ● *adj.* excessively enthusiastic. □□ **fa·nat′i·cal** *adj.* **fa·nat′i·cal·ly** *adv.* **fa·nat·i·cism** /-tisizəm/ *n.*

---

fanatic mid-16th century (as an adjective): from French *fanatique* or Latin *fanaticus* 'of a temple, inspired by a god,' from *fanum* 'temple.' The adjective originally described behavior or speech that might result from possession by a god or demon.

---

fan·ci·er /fánseeər/ *n.* connoisseur.

fan·ci·ful /fánsifŏŏl/ *adj.* **1** existing only in the imagination. **2** indulging in fancies. □□ **fan′ci·ful·ly** *adv.* **fan′ci·ful·ness** *n.*

fan·cy /fánsee/ ● *n.* (*pl.* **-cies**) **1** individual taste or inclination. **2** whim. **3** supposition. **4** a faculty of imagination. **b** mental image. ● *adj.* (usu. *attrib.*) (**fan·ci·er, fan·ci·est**) **1** ornamental; not plain. **2** capricious; whimsical; extravagant (*at a fancy price*). ● *v.tr.* (**-cies, -cied**) **1** be inclined to suppose. **2** *colloq.* feel a desire for (*do you fancy a drink?*). □ **catch** (or **take**) **the fancy of** please; appeal to. **fancy-free** without (esp. emotional) commitments. □□ **fan′ci·ly** *adv.* **fan′ci·ness** *n.*

fan·dan·go /fandánggō/ *n.* (*pl.* **-goes** or **-gos**) **1** lively Spanish dance for two. **2** music for this.

fan·fare /fánfair/ *n.* **1** short showy or ceremonious sounding of trumpets, bugles, etc. **2** elaborate display.

fang /fang/ *n.* **1** canine tooth, esp. of a dog or wolf. **2** tooth of a venomous snake, by which poison is injected. □□ **fanged** *adj.* (also in *comb.*). **fang′less** *adj.*

fan·ny /fánee/ *n.* (*pl.* **-nies**) *sl.* the buttocks. □ **fanny pack** pouch worn on a belt around the waist or hips.

fan·ta·size /fántəsīz/ *v.* **1** *intr.* have a fantasy or fanciful vision. **2** *tr.* imagine; create a fantasy about. □□ **fan′ta·sist** *n.*

fan·tas·tic /fantástik/ *adj.* (also **fan·tas′ti·cal**) **1** *colloq.* excellent; extraordinary. **2** extravagantly fanciful. **3** grotesque. □□ **fan·tas′ti·cal·ly** *adv.*

fan·ta·sy /fántəsee, -zee/ *n.* (*pl.* **-sies**) **1** faculty of inventing images, esp. extravagant or visionary ones. **2** fanciful mental image; daydream. **3** fiction genre that features supernatural, magical, or otherworldly elements.

far /faar/ ● (**far·ther, far·thest** or **fur·ther, fur·thest**)

● *adv.* **1** at or to or by a great distance (*far off*). **2** a long way (off) in space or time (*are you traveling far?*). **3** to a great extent or degree; by much (*far better*). ● *adj.* **1** remote; distant (*a far cry*). **2** more distant (*the far end of the hall*). **3** extreme (*far right militants*). □ **as far as 1** to the distance of (a place). **2** to the extent that (*travel as far as you like*). **by far** by a great amount. **far cry** a long way. **the Far East** China, Japan, and other countries of E. Asia. **far-fetched** strained; unconvincing. **far-flung 1** extending far; widely distributed. **2** remote; distant. **so far 1** to such an extent or distance; to this point. **2** until now. **so far so good** progress has been satisfactory up to now.

far·ad /fárəd, -ad/ *n. Electr.* unit of capacitance, such that one coulomb of charge causes a potential difference of one volt. ¶ Abbr.: **F.**

far·a·way /fáːrəwáy/ *adj.* **1** remote; long past. **2** (of a look) dreamy. **3** (of a voice) sounding as if from a distance.

farce /faars/ *n.* **1 a** broadly comic dramatic work based on ludicrously improbable events. **b** this branch of drama. **2** absurdly futile proceedings; pretense; mockery.

far·ci·cal /fáːrsikəl/ *adj.* **1** extremely ludicrous or futile. **2** of or like farce. □□ **far·ci·cal·i·ty** /kálitee/ *n.* **far′ci·cal·ly** *adv.*

fare /fair/ ● *n.* **1 a** price a passenger has to pay to be conveyed by bus, train, etc. **b** passenger paying to travel in a public vehicle. **2** food. ● *v.intr.* progress; get on.

fare·well /fáirwél/ ● *int.* good-bye; adieu. ● *n.* leave-taking.

fa·ri·na /fəree′ənə/ *n.* flour or meal of cereal, nuts, or starchy roots. □□ **far·i·na·ceous** /fárináyshəs/ *adj.*

farm /faarm/ ● *n.* **1** area of land and its buildings used under one management for growing crops, rearing animals, etc. **2** place or establishment for breeding a particular type of animal, growing fruit, etc. (*trout farm*). ● *v.* **1 a** *tr.* use (land) for growing crops, rearing animals, etc. **b** *intr.* be a farmer; work on a farm. **2** *tr.* (often foll. by *out*) delegate or subcontract (work) to others. □ **farm hand** worker on a farm. □□ **farm′a·ble** *adj.* **farm′er** *n.* **farm′ing** *n.*

farm·house /fáːrmhows/ *n.* house attached to a farm.

farm·land /fáːrmland/ *n.* land used or suitable for farming.

far·o /fáirō/ *n.* gambling card game.

far·ra·go /fərəágō, -ráy-/ *n.* (*pl.* **-goes**) medley or hodgepodge. □□ **far·rag·i·nous** /-ráajinəs/ *adj.*

far·ri·er /fáreeər/ *n.* smith who shoes horses. □□ **far′ri·er·y** *n.*

far·row /fárō/ ● *n.* **1** litter of pigs. **2** birth of a litter. ● *v.tr.* (also *absol.*) (of a sow) produce (pigs).

far·see·ing /fáːrsée′ing/ *adj.* shrewd in judgment; prescient.

far·sight·ed /fáːrsítid/ *adj.* **1** having foresight; prudent. **2** able to see clearly only what is comparatively distant. □□ **far′sight′ed·ly** *adv.* **far′sight′ed·ness** *n.*

fart /faart/ *coarse* ● *v.intr.* emit intestinal gas from the anus. ● *n.* emission of intestinal gas from the anus.

far·ther /fáːrthər/ (also **fur·ther** /fórthər/) ● *adv.* **1** to or at a more advanced point in space or time (*unsafe to proceed farther*). **2** at a greater distance (*nothing was farther from his thoughts*).

● *adj.* more distant or advanced (*on the farther side*). □□ **far′ther·most** *adj.*

¶ Traditionally, **farther, farthest** were used in referring to physical distance: *The falls were still two or three miles farther up the path.* **Further, furthest** were held to be restricted to figurative or abstract senses: *We decided to consider the matter further.* Although **farther, farthest** are still properly restricted to measurable distances, **further** is now common in both senses: *Put those plants the furthest from the window.*

far·thest /fáːrthist/ (also **furth·est** /fórthist/) ● *adj.* most distant. ● *adv.* to or at the greatest distance.

far·thing /fáːrthing/ *n.* (in the UK) former coin and monetary unit worth a quarter of an old penny.

fas·ces /fáseez/ *n.pl. Rom. Hist.* bundle of rods with a projecting ax blade, symbol of a magistrate's power.

FASCES

fas·cia /fáyshə/ *n.* **1** *Archit.* long flat surface on the architrave in classical architecture. **2** flat surface, usu. of wood, covering the ends of rafters.

fas·ci·nate /fásinayt/ *v.tr.* **1** capture the interest of; attract irresistibly. **2** (esp. of a snake) paralyze (a victim) with fear. □□ **fas′ci·nat·ed** *adj.* **fas′ci·nat·ing** *adj.* **fas′ci·nat·ing·ly** *adv.* **fas·ci·na·tion** /-náyshən/ *n.* **fas′ci·na·tor** *n.*

Fas·cism /fáshizəm/ *n.* extreme totalitarian right-wing nationalist movement or philosophy, as instituted in Italy (1922–43). □□ **Fas′cist** *n.* & *adj.* (also **fas′cist**). **Fa·scis′tic** *adj.* (also **fa·scis′tic**).

fash·ion /fáshən/ ● *n.* **1** current popular custom or style, esp. in dress. **2** manner or style of doing something. ● *v.tr.* make or form. □ **after** (or **in**) **a fashion** as well as is practicable, though not satisfactorily. □□ **fash′ion·er** *n.*

fash·ion·a·ble /fáshənəbəl/ *adj.* **1** following, suited to, or influenced by the current fashion. **2** characteristic of or favored by those who are leaders of social fashion. □□ **fash′ion·a·bly** *adv.*

fast[1] /fast/ ● *adj.* **1** rapid; quick-moving. **2** capable of or intended for high speed (*a fast car*). **3** ahead of the correct time. **4** (of a photographic film) needing only a short exposure. **5** firmly fixed or attached. **6** (of a color) not fading. **7** immoral; dissipated. ● *adv.* **1** quickly; in quick succession. **2** firmly; fixedly; tightly; securely. **3** soundly; completely (*fast asleep*). □ **fast food** food that can be prepared and served quickly and easily, esp. in a snack bar or restaurant.

fast[2] /fast/ ● *v.intr.* abstain from all or some

kinds of food or drink. • *n.* act or period of fasting. □□ **fast′er** *n.*

fast·en /fásən/ *v.tr.* **1** make or become fixed or secure. **2** lock securely; shut in. **3 a** direct (a look, thoughts, etc.) fixedly or intently. **b** focus or direct the attention fixedly upon. □□ **fas′ten·er** *n.*

fast·en·ing /fásəning/ *n.* device that fastens something; fastener.

fas·tid·i·ous /fastídeeəs/ *adj.* **1** very careful in matters of choice or taste; fussy. **2** easily disgusted; squeamish. □□ **fas·tid′i·ous·ly** *adv.* **fas·tid′i·ous·ness** *n.*

fast·ness /fástnis/ *n.* **1** stronghold or fortress. **2** state of being secure.

fat /fat/ • *n.* **1** natural oily or greasy substance occurring esp. in animal bodies. **2** part of anything containing this. **3** overabundance or excess. • *adj.* (**fat·ter**, **fat·test**) **1** corpulent; plump. **2** containing much fat. **3** (of land or resources) fertile; yielding abundantly. **4** thick; substantial. **5** *colloq. iron.* very little; not much (*fat chance*). □ **fat cat** *sl.* **1** wealthy person, esp. as a benefactor. **2** highly paid executive or official. □□ **fat′less** *adj.* **fat′ly** *adv.* **fat′ness** *n.* **fat′tish** *adj.*

fa·tal /fáytəl/ *adj.* **1** causing or ending in death (*fatal accident*). **2** ruinous (*made a fatal mistake*). □□ **fa′tal·ly** *adv.*

fa·tal·ism /fáyt′lizəm/ *n.* **1** belief that all events are predetermined and therefore inevitable. **2** submissive acceptance. □□ **fa′tal·ist** *n.* **fa·tal·is′tic** *adj.* **fa·tal·is′ti·cal·ly** *adv.*

fa·tal·i·ty /fətálətee, fay-/ *n.* (*pl.* **-ties**) **1** occurrence of death by accident or in war, etc. **2** fatal influence.

fate /fayt/ • *n.* **1 a** power regarded as predetermining events unalterably. **2 a** the future regarded as determined by such a power. **b** an individual's appointed lot. **3** death; destruction. • *v.tr.* preordain.

fate·ful /fáytf‍ool/ *adj.* **1** important; decisive. **2** controlled as if by fate. □□ **fate′ful·ly** *adv.* **fate′ful·ness** *n.*

fa·ther /fáathər/ • *n.* **1** male parent. **2** (usu. in *pl.*) progenitor or forefather. **3** originator, designer, or early leader. **4** (also **Father**) (often as a title or form of address) priest. **5** (**the Father**) (in Christian belief) first person of the Trinity. **6** (usu. in *pl.*) elders (*city fathers*). • *v.tr.* **1** beget; be the father of. **2** originate (a scheme, etc.). □ **father figure** older man who is respected like a father. **father-in-law** (*pl.* **fa·thers-in-law**) father of one's husband or wife. □□ **fa′ther·hood** *n.* **fa′ther·less** *adj.* **fa′ther·like** *adj. & adv.*

fa·ther·land /fáathərland/ *n.* one's native country.

fa·ther·ly /fáathərlee/ *adj.* like or of a father. □□ **fa′ther·li·ness** *n.*

fath·om /fáthəm/ • *n.* (*pl.* often **fath·om** when prec. by a number) measure of six feet, esp. used in taking depth soundings. • *v.tr.* **1** grasp or comprehend. **2** measure the depth of. □□ **fath′om·a·ble** *adj.* **fath′om·less** *adj.*

fa·tigue /fətéeg/ • *n.* **1** extreme tiredness. **2** weakness in materials, esp. metal. **3 a** nonmilitary duty in the army. **b** (in *pl.*) clothing worn for this. • *v.tr.* (**fa·tigues**, **fa·tigued**, **fa·tigu·ing**) cause fatigue in. □□ **fat·i·ga·ble** /-gəbəl/ *adj.* **fat·i·ga·bil′i·ty** *n.* **fa·tigue′less** *adj.*

fat·ten /fát′n/ *v.* make or become fat.

fat·ty /fátee/ *adj.* (**fat·ti·er**, **fat·ti·est**) like or containing fat. □ **fatty acid** *Chem.* organic compound that bonds to glycerol to form a fat molecule. □□ **fat′ti·ly** *adv.* **fat′ti·ness** *n.*

fat·u·ous /fáchᴐᴐəs/ *adj.* vacantly silly; purposeless; idiotic. □□ **fa·tu·i·ty** /fətᴐᴐitee, -tyᴐᴐ-/ *n.* (*pl.* **-ties**). **fat′u·ous·ly** *adv.* **fat′u·ous·ness** *n.*

fat·wa /fátwaa/ *n.* (in Islamic countries) authoritative ruling on a religious matter.

fau·cet /fáwsit/ *n.* device by which a flow of liquid from a pipe or vessel can be controlled.

fault /fawlt/ • *n.* **1** defect or imperfection. **2** transgression, offense. **3** *Tennis* service of the ball not in accordance with the rules. **4** responsibility for wrongdoing, error, etc. **5** *Geol.* extended break in the continuity of strata or a vein. • *v.tr.* find fault with; blame. □ **at fault** guilty; to blame. **find fault** (often foll. by *with*) make an adverse criticism; complain. **to a fault** excessively.

fault·find·ing /fáwltfinding/ *n.* continual criticism.

fault·less /fáwltlis/ *adj.* without fault; free from defect or error. □□ **fault′less·ly** *adv.* **fault′less·ness** *n.*

fault·y /fáwltee/ *adj.* (**fault·i·er**, **fault·i·est**) having faults; imperfect; defective. □□ **fault′i·ly** *adv.* **fault′i·ness** *n.*

faun /fawn/ *n.* Roman rural deity with a human face and torso and a goat's horns, legs, and tail.

fau·na /fáwnə/ *n.* (*pl.* **fau·nas** or **fau·nae** /-nee/) animal life of a region or geological period. □□ **fau′nal** *adj.* **fau′nist** *n.* **fau·nis′tic** *adj.*

faux /fō/ *adj.* imitation; counterfeit (*faux emeralds*).

faux pas /fō pa'a/ *n.* (*pl.* same, *pronunc.* /paaz′/) **1** tactless mistake; blunder. **2** social indiscretion.

fa·vor /fáyvər/ • *n.* **1** act of kindness; liking; approval; goodwill; friendly regard (*gained their favor*). **2** esteem. **3** partiality. **4** small present or token given out, as at a party. • *v.tr.* **1** regard or treat with favor or partiality. **2** give support or approval to; promote; prefer. **3 a** be to the advantage of (a person). **b** facilitate (a process, etc.). **4** *colloq.* resemble in features. □□ **fa′vor·er** *n.*

fa·vor·a·ble /fáyvərəbəl/ *adj.* **1 a** well-disposed; propitious. **b** commendatory; approving. **2** giving consent (*a favorable answer*). **3** promising; auspicious. **4** helpful; suitable. □□ **fa′vor·a·ble·ness** *n.* **fa′vor·a·bly** *adv.*

fa·vor·ite /fáyvərit, fáyvrit/ • *adj.* preferred to all others (*my favorite book*). • *n.* **1** particularly favored person. **2** *Sports* competitor thought most likely to win.

fa·vor·it·ism /fáyvəritizəm, fáyvri-/ *n.* unfair partiality.

fawn¹ /fawn/ • *n.* **1** young deer in its first year. **2** light yellowish brown. • *adj.* fawn colored.

fawn² /fawn/ *v.intr.* **1** (of a person) behave servilely; cringe. **2** (of an animal, esp. a dog) show extreme affection. □□ **fawn′er** *n.* **fawn′ing** *adj.* **fawn′ing·ly** *adv.*

fax /faks/ • *n.* **1** facsimile transmission (see FACSIMILE 2). **2** copy produced by this. • *v.tr.* transmit in this way.

faze /fayz/ *v.tr.* (often as **fazed** *adj.*) *colloq.* disconcert; perturb; disorient.

FBI *abbr.* Federal Bureau of Investigation.

FCC *abbr.* Federal Communications Commission.

FDA *abbr.* Food and Drug Administration.

FDIC *abbr.* Federal Deposit Insurance Corporation.

Fe *symb. Chem.* iron.

fe·al·ty /féeəltee/ *n.* (*pl.* **-ties**) **1** *hist.* feudal tenant's or vassal's fidelity to a lord. **2** allegiance.

fear /feer/ • *n.* **1** panic or distress caused by exposure to danger, expectation of pain, etc. **2** cause of fear (*all fears removed*). **3** danger. • *v.* **1 a** *tr.* feel fear about or toward (a person or thing). **b** *intr.* feel fear. **2** *intr.* (foll. by *for*) feel anxiety about. □□ **fear′less** *adj.* **fear′less·ly** *adv.* **fear′less·ness** *n.*

fear·ful /féerfŏŏl/ *adj.* **1** afraid. **2** terrible; awful. □□ **fear′ful·ly** *adv.* **fear′ful·ness** *n.*

fear·some /féersəm/ *adj.* appalling or frightening, esp. in appearance. □□ **fear′some·ly** *adv.* **fear′some·ness** *n.*

fea·si·ble /féezibəl/ *adj.* practicable; possible. □□ **fea·si·bil·i·ty** /féezibílitee/ *n.* **fea′si·bly** *adv.* ¶ The correct meaning of **feasible** is 'practicable' or 'possible,' e.g., *Walking at night was not feasible without the aid of a flashlight.* It should not be used to mean 'likely' or 'probable.'

feast /feest/ • *n.* **1** large or sumptuous meal, esp. with entertainment. **2** gratification to the senses or mind. **3** religious festival. • *v.intr.* partake of a feast; eat and drink sumptuously. □ **feast one's eyes on** take pleasure in beholding. □□ **feast′er** *n.*

feat /feet/ *n.* noteworthy act or achievement.

feath·er /féthər/ • *n.* any of the appendages growing from a bird's skin, with a horny hollow stem and fine strands. • *v.tr.* **1** cover or line with feathers. **2** *Rowing* turn (an oar) so that it passes through the air edgewise. **3** *Aeron. & Naut.* cause (propeller blades) to rotate in such a way as to lessen the air or water resistance. □ **feather in one's cap** achievement to one's credit. **feather one's nest** enrich oneself. **in fine** (or **high**) **feather** *colloq.* in good spirits. □□ **feath′ered** *adj.* (also in *comb.*). **feath′er·less** *adj.* **feath′er·y** *adj.* **feath′er·i·ness** *n.*

feath·er·bed·ding /féthərbeding/ *n.* employment of excess staff, esp. due to union rules.

feath·er·weight /féthərwayt/ *n.* **1** any of various weight classes in certain sports intermediate between bantamweight and lightweight. **2** very light person or thing.

fea·ture /féechər/ • *n.* **1** distinctive or characteristic part of a thing. **2** (usu. in *pl.*) (a distinctive part of) the face. **3** distinctive or regular article in a newspaper or magazine. **4** (in full **fea′ture film**) full-length movie intended as the main at a showing. • *v.* **1** *tr.* make a special display or attraction of; give special prominence to. **2** *tr.* & *intr.* star. □□ **fea′tured** *adj.* (also in *comb.*). **fea′ture·less** *adj.*

Feb. *abbr.* February.

fe·brile /fébral, fée-/ *adj.* of or relating to fever; feverish. □□ **fe·bril·i·ty** /fibrílitee/ *n.*

Feb·ru·ar·y /fébrŏŏeree, fébyŏŏ-/ *n.* (*pl.* **-ies**) second month of the year.

fe·ces /féeseez/ *n.pl.* waste matter discharged from the bowels. □□ **fe·cal** /féekəl/ *adj.*

feck·less /féklis/ *adj.* **1** feeble; ineffective. **2** unthinking; irresponsible. □□ **feck′less·ly** *adv.* **feck′less·ness** *n.*

fe·cund /féekənd, fék-/ *adj.* **1** prolific; fertile. **2** fertilizing. □□ **fe·cun·di·ty** /fikúnditee/ *n.*

fed *past* and *past part.* of FEED. □ **fed up** (often foll. by *with*) discontented; bored.

fed·er·al /fédərəl/ *adj.* **1** of a system of government in which several states or provinces, etc., form a union but remain independent in internal affairs. **2** of such a federation (*federal laws*). □ **Federal Reserve System** national system of reserve cash available to banks. □□ **fed′er·al·ism** *n.* **fed′er·al·ist** *n.* **fed′er·al·ize** *v.tr.* **fed·er·al·i·za′tion** *n.* **fed′er·al·ly** *adv.*

fed·er·ate /fédərayt/ *v.* unite on a federal basis. □□ **fed·er·a·tive** /fédəraytiv, -rətiv/ *adj.*

fed·er·a·tion /fédəráyshən/ *n.* **1** federal system or group. **2** the act or an instance of federating. □□ **fed·er·a′tion·ist** *n.*

fe·do·ra /fidáwrə/ *n.* soft felt hat with a curled brim.

FEDORA

fee /fee/ *n.* **1** payment made for professional advice or services. **2** entrance or access charge.

fee·ble /féebəl/ *adj.* **1** weak; infirm. **2** lacking energy, effectiveness, etc. □□ **fee′ble·ness** *n.* **fee′blish** *adj.* **fee′bly** *adv.*

fee·ble-mind·ed /féebəlmíndid/ *adj.* mentally deficient. □□ **fee′ble-mind′ed·ly** *adv.* **fee′ble-mind′ed·ness** *n.*

feed /feed/ • *v.* (*past* and *past part.* **fed** /fed/) **1** *tr.* **a** supply with food. **b** put food into the mouth of. **2** *tr.* give as food, esp. to animals. **3** *intr.* (esp. of animals, or *colloq.* of people) take food; eat. **4** *tr.* nourish; make grow. **5 a** *tr.* maintain supply of raw material, fuel, etc., to (a fire, machine, etc.). **b** *tr.* supply or send (an electronic signal) for broadcast, etc. **c** *intr.* flow into. **6** *intr.* (foll. by *on*) **a** be nourished by. **b** derive benefit from. **7** *tr.* gratify (vanity, etc.). **8** *tr.* provide (advice, information, etc.) to. • *n.* food, esp. for animals. □□ **feed′a·ble** *adj.* **feed′er** *n.*

feed·back /féedbak/ *n.* **1** information about the result of an experiment, etc.; response. **2** *Electronics* return of a fraction of the output signal to the input.

feel /feel/ • *v.* (*past* and *past part.* **felt** /felt/) **1** *tr.* **a** examine or search by touch. **b** (*absol.*) have the sensation of touch. **2** *tr.* perceive or ascertain by touch. **3** *tr.* experience, exhibit, or be conscious of (an emotion, conviction, etc.). **4** *tr.* have a vague or unreasoned impression. **5**

tr. consider; think. **6** *intr.* seem. **7** *intr.* be consciously; consider oneself (*I feel happy*). **8** *intr.* have sympathy or pity. • *n.* **1** feeling; testing by touch. **2** attendant sensation. **3** sense of touch. □ **feel like** have a wish for; be inclined toward. **feel up to** be ready to face or deal with. **feel one's way** proceed carefully; act cautiously.

feel·er /fee.lər/ *n.* **1** organ in certain animals for sensing or for searching for food. **2** tentative proposal.

feel·ing /feeling/ • *n.* **1 a** capacity to feel; sense of touch. **b** physical sensation. **2 a** emotional reaction. **b** (in *pl.*) emotional susceptibilities or sympathies (*hurt my feelings*). **3** particular sensitivity. **4 a** intuition or notion. **b** general sentiment. **5** readiness to feel sympathy or compassion. **6** emotional commitment or sensibility. • *adj.* sensitive; sympathetic; heartfelt. □□ **feel'ing·less** *adj.* **feel'ing·ly** *adv.*

feet *pl.* of FOOT.

feign /fayn/ *v.tr.* simulate; pretend.

feint /faynt/ • *n.* **1** sham attack or diversionary blow. **2** pretense. • *v.intr.* make a feint.

feld·spar /féldspaar/ *n.* (also **felspar** /félspaar/) *Mineral.* group of aluminum silicates of potassium, sodium, or calcium. □□ **feld·spath·ic** /-spáthik/ *adj.* **feld·spath·oid** /féldspəthoyd, félspə-/ *n.*

fe·lic·i·tate /fəlísitayt/ *v.tr.* congratulate. □□ **fe·lic·i·ta·tion** /-táyshən/ *n.* (usu. in *pl.*).

fe·lic·i·tous /fəlísitəs/ *adj.* strikingly apt; pleasantly ingenious. □□ **fe·lic'i·tous·ly** *adv.* **fe·lic'i·tous·ness** *n.*

fe·lic·i·ty /fəlísitee/ *n.* (*pl.* **-ties**) **1** intense happiness. **2 a** capacity for apt expression. **b** well-chosen phrase.

fe·line /feelīn/ • *adj.* **1** of the cat family. **2** catlike. • *n.* animal of the cat family. □□ **fe·lin·i·ty** /filínitee/ *n.*

fell[1] *past* of FALL *v.*

fell[2] /fel/ *v.tr.* **1** cut down (esp. a tree). **2** strike or knock down (a person or animal). □□ **fell'er** *n.*

fell[3] /fel/ *adj. poet.* or *rhet.* ruthless; destructive. □ **at** (or **in**) **one fell swoop** in a single (orig. deadly) action.

fel·low /félō/ *n.* **1** *colloq.* man or boy. **2** (usu. in *pl.*) comrade. **3** counterpart or match; other of a pair. **4** holder of a fellowship. **5** member of a learned society. **6** (*attrib.*) belonging to the same class or activity.

fel·low·ship /félōship/ *n.* **1** companionship; friendliness. **2** participation; sharing; community of interest. **3** body of associates. **4** financial grant to a scholar.

fel·on /félən/ *n.* person who has committed a felony.

fe·lo·ni·ous /filóneeəs/ *adj.* **1** criminal. **2** *Law* **a** of or involving felony. **b** who has committed felony. □□ **fe·lo'ni·ous·ly** *adv.*

fel·o·ny /félənee/ *n.* (*pl.* **-nies**) serious, often violent, crime.

felt[1] /felt/ • *n.* cloth of matted and pressed fibers of wool, etc. • *v.tr.* make into felt. □□ **felt'y** *adj.*

felt[2] *past* and *pastpart.* of FEEL.

FEMA /feemə/ *abbr.* Federal Emergency Management Agency.

fe·male /feemayl/ • *adj.* **1** of the sex that can bear offspring or produce eggs. **2** (of plants) fruit-bearing. **3** of women or female animals or

female plants. **4** (of a screw, socket, etc.) hollow to receive an inserted part. • *n.* female person, animal, or plant. □□ **fe'male·ness** *n.*

---

female Middle English: from Old French *femelle*, from Latin *femella*, diminutive of *femina* 'a woman.' The change in the ending was due to association with *male*, but the words *male* and *female* are not linked etymologically.

---

fem·i·nine /féminin/ • *adj.* **1** of women. **2** having womanly qualities. **3** *Gram.* of or denoting the gender proper to women's names. • *n.* *Gram.* feminine gender or word. □□ **fem'i·nine·ly** *adv.* **fem'i·nine·ness** *n.* **fem·i·nin·i·ty** /-nínitee/ *n.*

fem·i·nism /féminizəm/ *n.* advocacy of women's rights on the ground of the equality of the sexes. □□ **fem'i·nist** *n.*

femme fa·tale /fém fətál, -ta'al, fay-/ *n.* (*pl.* **femmes fa·tales** *pronunc.* same) seductively attractive woman.

fe·mur /feemər/ *n.* (*pl.* **fe·murs** or **fem·o·ra** /fémərə/) *Anat.* thigh bone. □□ **fem·o·ral** /fémərəl/ *adj.*

fen /fen/ *n.* low marshy or flooded land. □□ **fen'ny** *adj.*

fence /fens/ • *n.* **1** barrier, railing, etc., enclosing an area of ground. **2** *sl.* receiver of stolen goods. • *v.* **1** *tr.* surround with or as with a fence. **2** *tr.* enclose, separate or confine with or as with a fence. **3** *tr.* (also *absol.*) *sl.* deal in (stolen goods). **4** *intr.* practice the sport of fencing; use a sword. **5** *intr.* evade answering. □□ **fence'less** *adj.* **fenc'er** *n.*

fenc·ing /fénsing/ *n.* **1** set or extent of fences. **2** material for making fences. **3** art or sport of swordplay.

fend /fend/ *v.* **1** *intr.* (foll. by *for*) look after (esp. oneself). **2** *tr.* (usu. foll. by *off*) keep away; ward off (an attack, etc.).

fend·er /féndər/ *n.* **1** low frame bordering a fireplace. **2** shieldlike device or enclosure over or around the wheel of a motor vehicle, bicycle, etc.

fen·nel /fénəl/ *n.* yellow-flowered fragrant umbelliferous plant used as flavoring.

fe·ral /feerəl, férəl/ *adj.* **1** (of an animal or plant) wild; untamed; uncultivated. **2** savage; brutal.

fer·ment • *n.* /fərment/ **1** agitation; excitement; tumult. **2 a** fermentation. **b** fermenting agent or leaven. • *v.* /fərmént/ **1** *intr.* & *tr.* undergo or subject to fermentation. **2** *intr.* & *tr.* effervesce or cause to effervesce. **3** *tr.* excite; stir up; foment. □□ **fer·ment'a·ble** *adj.* **fer·ment'er** *n.*

fer·men·ta·tion /fərmentáyshən/ *n.* **1** breakdown of a substance by microorganisms, such as yeasts and bacteria, usu. in the absence of oxygen, esp. of sugar in making alcohol. **2** agitation; excitement. □□ **fer·men·ta·tive** /-méntətiv/ *adj.*

fer·mi·um /fərmeeəm, fér-/ *n.* *Chem.* transuranic radioactive metallic element produced artificially. ¶ Symb.: **Fm**.

fern /fərn/ *n.* (*pl.* same or **ferns**) flowerless plant reproducing by spores and usu. having feathery fronds. □□ **fern'er·y** *n.* (*pl.* **-ies**) **fern'less** *adj.* **fern'y** *adj.*

fe·ro·cious /fərṓshəs/ *adj.* fierce; savage; wildly cruel. ▫▫ **fe·ro′cious·ly** *adv.* **fe·ro′cious·ness** *n.*

fe·roc·i·ty /fərósitee/ *n.* (*pl.* **-ties**) ferocious nature or act.

-ferous /fərəs/ *comb. form* (usu. **-iferous**) forming adjectives with the sense 'bearing,' 'having' (*auriferous*). ▫▫ **-ferously** *suffix* forming adverbs. **-ferousness** *suffix* forming nouns.

fer·ret /férit/ • *n.* **1** small semidomesticated polecat, used in catching rabbits, rats, etc. • *v.* **1** *intr.* hunt with ferrets. **2** *intr.* rummage; search out. ▫▫ **fer′ret·er** *n.* **fer′ret·y** *adj.*

fer·ric /férik/ *adj.* of iron.

Fer·ris wheel /féris/ *n.* carnival ride consisting of a tall revolving vertical wheel with passenger cars.

FERRIS WHEEL

ferro- /férō/ *comb. form Chem.* **1** iron, esp. in ferrous compounds (*ferrocyanide*). **2** (of alloys) containing iron.

fer·rous /férəs/ *adj.* containing iron.

fer·rule /férōōl/ *n.* ring or cap on the end of a stick or tube.

fer·ry /féree/ • *n.* (*pl.* **-ries**) **1** boat or aircraft, etc., for conveying passengers and goods, esp. across water. **2** the service itself or the place where it operates. • *v.* (**-ries, -ried**) **1** *tr.* & *intr.* convey or go in a ferry. **2** *tr.* transport from one place to another, esp. as a regular service. ▫▫ **fer·ry·man** /-mən/ *n.* (*pl.* **-men**)

fer·tile /fərt'l/ *adj.* **1 a** (of soil) producing abundant vegetation or crops. **b** fruitful. **2 a** (of a seed, egg, etc.) capable of becoming a new individual. **b** (of animals and plants) able to reproduce. **3** inventive. ▫▫ **fer·til·i·ty** /-tílitee/ *n.*

fer·til·ize /fərt'līz/ *v.tr.* **1** make (soil, etc.) fertile or productive. **2** cause (an egg, female animal, or plant) to develop or gestate by mating. ▫▫ **fer′ti·liz·a·ble** *adj.* **fer·ti·li·za′tion** *n.*

fer·til·iz·er /fərt'līzər/ *n.* chemical or natural substance added to soil to make it more fertile.

fer·vent /fərvənt/ *adj.* **1** ardent; impassioned; intense (*fervent hatred*). **2** hot; glowing. ▫▫ **fer′ven·cy** *n.* **fer′vent·ly** *adv.*

fer·vid /fərvid/ *adj.* ardent; intense. ▫▫ **fer′vid·ly** *adv.*

fer·vor /fərvər/ *n.* vehemence; passion; zeal.

fes·tal /fést'l/ *adj.* **1** joyous; merry. **2** of or for a festival. **3** of a feast. ▫▫ **fes′tal·ly** *adv.*

fes·ter /féstər/ *v.* **1** *tr.* & *intr.* make or become septic. **2** *intr.* cause continuing annoyance. **3** *intr.* rot; stagnate.

fes·ti·val /féstivəl/ *n.* **1** day or period of celebration, religious or secular. **2** series of cultural events.

fes·tive /féstiv/ *adj.* **1** of or characteristic of a festival. **2** joyous. **3** fond of feasting; jovial. ▫▫ **fes′tive·ly** *adv.* **fes′tive·ness** *n.*

fes·tiv·i·ty /festívitee/ *n.* (*pl.* **-ties**) **1** gaiety; rejoicing. **2 a** festive celebration. **b** (in *pl.*) festive proceedings.

fes·toon /festōn/ • *n.* chain of flowers, leaves, ribbons, etc., hung in a curve as a decoration. • *v.tr.* adorn with or form into festoons; decorate elaborately. ▫▫ **fes·toon′er·y** *n.*

fet·a /fétə/ *n.* crumbly white Greek-style cheese made of sheep's or goat's milk.

fetch /fech/ *v.tr.* **1** go for and bring back (a person or thing). **2** be sold for; realize (a price). ▫▫ **fetch′er** *n.*

fetch·ing /féching/ *adj.* attractive. ▫▫ **fetch′ing·ly** *adv.*

fête /fayt, fet/ • *n.* **1** great entertainment; festival. **2** saint's day. • *v.tr.* honor or entertain lavishly.

fet·id /fétid, feétid/ *adj.* (also **foet′id**) stinking. ▫▫ **fet′id·ly** *adv.* **fet′id·ness** *n.*

fet·ish /fétish/ *n.* **1** *Psychol.* thing abnormally stimulating or attracting sexual desire. **2 a** inanimate object worshiped as magic. **b** thing evoking irrational devotion or respect. ▫▫ **fet′ish·ism** *n.* **fet′ish·ist** *n.* **fet·ish·is′tic** *adj.*

---

fetish early 17th century (originally denoting an object used by the peoples of West Africa as an amulet or charm): from French *fétiche*, from Portuguese *feitiço* 'charm, sorcery' (originally an adjective meaning 'made by art'), from Latin *factitius* (source of *factitious*.)

---

fet·lock /fétlok/ *n.* **1** part of the back of a horse's leg above the hoof where a tuft of hair grows. **2** such a tuft of hair.

fet·ter /fétər/ • *n.* **1 a** shackle for holding a prisoner by the ankles. **b** any shackle or bond. **2** (in *pl.*) captivity. **3** restraint or check. • *v.tr.* **1** put into fetters. **2** restrict.

fet·tle /fét'l/ *n.* condition or trim (*in fine fettle*).

fe·tus /feétəs/ *n.* unborn or unhatched offspring of a mammal, esp. a human one more than eight weeks after conception. ▫▫ **fe′tal** *adj.*

feud /fyōōd/ • *n.* prolonged mutual hostility, esp. between two families, tribes, etc. • *v.intr.* conduct a feud.

feu·dal /fyōōd'l/ *adj.* of, according to, or resembling the feudal system. ▫ **feudal system** medieval social system whereby a vassal held land from a superior in exchange for allegiance and service. ▫▫ **feu′dal·ism** *n.* **feu′dal·ist** *n.* **feu·dal·is′tic** *adj.* **feu′dal·ly** *adv.*

fe·ver /feévər/ *n.* **1 a** abnormally high body temperature, often with delirium, etc. **b** disease characterized by this (*scarlet fever*). **2** nervous excitement; agitation. ▫ **fever pitch** state of extreme excitement. ▫▫ **fe′vered** *adj.*

fe·ver·ish /feévərish/ *adj.* **1** having the symptoms of a fever. **2** excited; restless. ▫▫ **fe′ver·ish·ly** *adv.* **fe′ver·ish·ness** *n.*

few /fyōō/ • *adj.* not many. • *n.* (as *pl.*) **1** (prec.

by *a*) some but not many. **2** not many. **3** (prec. by *the*) **a** the minority. **b** the elect. □ **not a few** considerable number.

¶ **Fewer,** the comparative of *few,* properly refers to a countable quantity: *This has one-third fewer calories than regular sour cream.* Formally, **less** refers to uncountable, mass quantities: *less sand; less water in this glass than that; less time to work with.* Today informal speakers rarely use **fewer** for **less,** but often use **less** where **fewer** has been preferred: *There are less people in the room than there were before lunch.*

fey /fay/ *adj.* **1** strange; otherworldly; elfin; whimsical. **2** clairvoyant. □□ **fey′ly** *adv.* **fey′ ness** *n.*

fez /fez/ *n.* (*pl.* **fez·zes**) flat-topped conical red cap, worn by men in some Muslim countries. □□ **fezzed** *adj.*

FEZ

fi·an·cé /feéonsáy, feeónsay/ *n.* (*fem.* **fi·an·cée** *pronunc.* same) person to whom another is engaged to be married.

fi·as·co /feeáskō/ *n.* (*pl.* **-cos**) ludicrous or humiliating failure or breakdown; ignominious result.

fi·at /fée∂t, -at, -aat, ffat, ffət/ *n.* **1** authorization. **2** decree or order.

fib /fib/ ● *n.* trivial or venial lie. ● *v.intr.* (**fibbed, fib·bing**) tell a fib. □□ **fib′ber** *n.* **fib′ster** *n.*

fi·ber /fíbər/ *n.* **1** *Biol.* threads or filaments forming tissue or textile. **2** piece of glass in the form of a thread. **3** substance formed of fibers or able to be spun, woven, or felted. **4** structure; character. □ **fiber optics** optics employing thin glass fibers, usu. for the transmission of light, esp. modulated to carry signals. □□ **fi′bered** *adj.* (also in *comb.*). **fi′ber·less** *adj.* **fi·bri·form** /fíbrifawrm/ *adj.*

fi·ber·board /fíbərbawrd/ *n.* building material made of wood or other plant fibers compressed into boards.

fi·ber·glass /fíbərglas/ *n.* **1** textile fabric made from woven glass fibers. **2** plastic reinforced by glass fibers.

fi·bril /fíbril, fib-/ *n.* **1** small fiber. **2** subdivision of a fiber. □□ **fi′bril·lar** *adj.* **fi′bril·lar·y** *adj.*

fi·broid /fíbroyd/ *adj.* of, like, or containing fibrous tissue, as some benign tumors.

fi·bro·sis /fíbrósis/ *n.* *Med.* thickening and scarring of connective tissue. □□ **fi·brot·ic** /-brótik/ *adj.*

fib·u·la /fíbyələ/ *n.* (*pl.* **fib·u·lae** /-lee/ or **fib·u·**

las) *Anat.* smaller and outer of the two bones between the knee and the ankle in terrestrial vertebrates. □□ **fib′u·lar** *adj.*

---

fibula late 16th century: from Latin, 'brooch,' perhaps related to *figere* 'to fix.' The bone is so named because the shape it makes with the tibia resembles a clasp, the fibula being the tongue.

-fic /fik/ *suffix* (usu. as **-ific**) forming adjectives meaning 'producing,' 'making' (*prolific; pacific*). □□ **-fically** *suffix* forming adverbs.

FICA /fíkə/ *abbr.* Federal Insurance Contributions Act.

-fication /fikáyshən/ *suffix* (usu. as **-ification** /ifikáyshən/) forming nouns of action from verbs in *-fy* (*acidification*).

fiche /feesh/ *n.* (*pl.* same or **fiches**) microfiche.

fick·le /fíkəl/ *adj.* inconstant or changeable, esp. in loyalty. □□ **fick′le·ness** *n.* **fick′ly** *adv.*

fic·tion /fíkshən/ *n.* **1** invented idea, thing, etc. **2** literature, esp. novels, describing imaginary events and people. □□ **fic′tion·al** *adj.* **fic′tion·al·ize** *v.tr.* **fic·tion·al·i·za′tion** *n.* **fic′tion·al·ly** *adv.*

fic·ti·tious /fiktíshəs/ *adj.* **1** imaginary; unreal. **2** counterfeit; not genuine. □□ **fic·ti′tious·ly** *adv.* **fic·ti′tious·ness** *n.*

fid·dle /fíd′l/ ● *n.* stringed instrument played with a bow, esp. a violin. ● *v.* **1** *intr.* **a** (often foll. by *with*) play restlessly. **b** (often foll. by *about*) move aimlessly. **c** act idly or frivolously. **d** (usu. foll. by *with*) make minor adjustments; tinker. **2 a** *intr.* play the fiddle. **b** *tr.* play (a tune, etc.) on the fiddle. □ **as fit as a fiddle** in very good health. **play second** (or **first**) **fiddle** take a subordinate (or leading) role.

fid·dler /fídlər/ *n.* **1** fiddle player. **2** small N. American crab.

fid·dle·stick /fíd′lstik/ *n.* (in *pl.*; as *int.*) nonsense!

fi·del·i·ty /fidélitee/ *n.* **1** faithfulness; loyalty. **2** strict accuracy. **3** precision in reproduction of sound or video.

fid·get /fíjit/ *v.intr.* move or act restlessly or nervously. □□ **fid′get·y** *adj.* **fidg′et·i·ness** *n.*

fi·du·ci·ar·y /fidoōshee-eree, -shəree, -dyoō-, fī-/ ● *adj.* **1** of a trust, trustee, or trusteeship. **2** held or given in trust. ● *n.* (*pl.* **-ies**) trustee.

fie /fī/ *int.* expressing disgust, shame, etc.

fief /feef/ *n.* land held under the feudal system or in fee.

fief·dom /féefdəm/ *n.* fief.

field /feeld/ ● *n.* **1** area of open land, esp. one used for pasture or crops. **2** area rich in some natural product (*gas field*). **3** piece of land for a specified purpose, esp. **a** an area marked out for a game or sport (*football field*), or **b** an airfield. **4** participants in a contest, race, or sport. **5** expanse of ice, snow, sea, sky, etc. **6** area of activity or study. **7** region in which a force is effective (*magnetic field*). **8** range of perception (*field of view*). **9** (*attrib.*) **a** (of an animal or plant) found in the countryside; wild (*field mouse*). **b** carried out or working in the natural environment (*field test*). **10** background of a picture, coin, flag, etc. ● *v.* **1** *Baseball, etc.* **a** *intr.* act as a fielder. **b** *tr.* catch (and return) (the ball). **2** *tr.* deal with (a succession of questions, etc.). □ **field glasses** binoculars for outdoor use. **play the field** *colloq.* avoid exclusive attachment to one person or activity, etc.

field·er /féeldər/ *n. Baseball* member of the team that is fielding.

field·work /féeldwərk/ *n.* practical work of a surveyor, collector of scientific data, sociologist, etc., conducted in the natural environment. □□ **field′work·er** *n.*

fiend /feend/ *n.* **1** evil spirit; demon. **2** very wicked or cruel person. **3** *sl.* devotee. □□ **fiend′ ish** *adj.* **fiend′ish·ly** *adv.* **fiend′ish·ness** *n.* **fiend′ like** *adj.*

fierce /feers/ *adj.* (**fierc·er, fierc·est**) **1** vehemently aggressive or frightening. **2** eager; intense; ardent. **3** unpleasantly strong or intense. □□ **fierce′ly** *adv.* **fierce′ness** *n.*

fi·er·y /fíree/ *adj.* (**fi·er·i·er, fi·er·i·est**) **1** consisting of or flaming with fire. **2** like fire in appearance; bright red. **3** hot; burning. **4** spirited. □□ **fi′er·i·ly** *adv.* **fi′er·i·ness** *n.*

fi·es·ta /fee-éstə/ *n.* **1** holiday or festivity. **2** religious festival.

fife /fīf/ *n.* kind of small shrill flute used with the drum in military music. □□ **fif′er** *n.*

fif·teen /fíftéen/ • *n.* **1** one more than fourteen. **2** symbol for this (15, xv, XV). **3** size, etc., denoted by fifteen. • *adj.* that amount to fifteen. □□ **fif′teenth′** *adj. & n.*

fifth /fifth/ • *n.* **1** next after fourth. **2** any of five equal parts of a thing. **3** *Mus.* interval or chord spanning five consecutive notes in the diatonic scale (e.g., C to G). **4** (the Fifth) Fifth Amendment to the US Constitution. • *adj.* that is the fifth. □ **take the Fifth** exercise the right guaranteed by the Fifth Amendment to the Constitution of refusing to answer questions in order to avoid incriminating oneself. □□ **fifth′ly** *adv.*

fif·ty /fíftee/ • *n.* (*pl.* **-ties**) **1** product of five and ten. **2** symbol for this (50, l, L). **3** (in *pl.*) numbers from 50 to 59, esp. the years of a century or of a person's life. • *adj.* that amount to fifty. □ **fifty-fifty** *adj.* equal. • *adv.* equally. □□ **fif′ti·eth** *adj. & n. & adv.*

fig /fig/ *n.* **1** soft pear-shaped fruit with many seeds, eaten fresh or dried. **2** (in full **fig tree**) deciduous tree having broad leaves and bearing figs.

fig. *abbr.* figure.

fight /fīt/ • *v.* (*past* and *past part.* **fought** /fawt/) **1** *intr.* **a** contend or struggle in war, battle, single combat, etc. **b** (often foll. by *with*) argue; quarrel. **2** *tr.* contend with (an opponent) in this way. **3** *tr.* engage in (a battle, war, duel, etc.). **4** *tr.* contend about (an issue, an election); maintain (a lawsuit, cause, etc.) against an opponent. **5** *intr.* campaign or strive determinedly to achieve something. **6** *tr.* strive to overcome (disease, fire, fear, etc.). • *n.* **1 a** combat. **b** boxing match. **c** battle; conflict; struggle. **d** argument. **2** power or inclination to fight. □ **fighting chance** opportunity to succeed by great effort. **fight off** repel with effort.

fight·er /fītər/ *n.* **1** person or animal that fights. **2** fast military aircraft designed for attacking other aircraft.

fig·ment /figmənt/ *n.* invented or imaginary thing.

fig·u·ra·tive /fígyərətiv/ *adj.* **1** metaphorical, not literal. **2** characterized by or addicted to figures of speech. **3** of pictorial or sculptural representation. □□ **fig′u·ra·tive·ly** *adv.* **fig′ur· a·tive·ness** *n.*

fig·ure /fígyər/ • *n.* **1** external form or bodily shape. **2 a** person as seen in outline but not identified. **b** person as contemplated mentally. **3** *Geom.* a two-dimensional space enclosed by a line or lines, or a three-dimensional space enclosed by a surface or surfaces; any of the classes of these, e.g., the triangle, the sphere. **4 a** numerical symbol or number, esp. any of the ten in Arabic notation. **b** an amount of money; a value. **5** (in full **figure of speech**) recognized form of rhetorical expression giving variety, force, etc., esp. metaphor or hyperbole. • *v.* **1** *intr.* appear or be mentioned, esp. prominently. **2 a** *tr.* calculate. **b** *intr.* do arithmetic. **3 a** *tr.* understand; ascertain; consider. **b** *intr. colloq.* be likely or understandable. □ **figure on** count on; expect. **figure out 1** work out by arithmetic or logic. **2** estimate. **3** understand. **figure skater** person who practices figure skating. **figure skating** sport of performing jumps, spins, patterns, etc., while ice skating. □□ **fig′ure·less** *adj.*

fig·ure·head /fígyərhed/ *n.* **1** nominal leader. **2** carving, usu. a bust or a full-length figure, at a ship's prow.

fig·u·rine /fígyəréen/ *n.* statuette.

fil·a·ment /fíləmənt/ *n.* **1** threadlike body or fiber. **2** conducting wire or thread with a high melting point in an electric bulb. □□ **fil·a·men· ta·ry** /-méntəree/ *adj.* **fil′a·ment·ed** *adj.* **fil·a· men·tous** /-méntəs/ *adj.*

fil·bert /fílbərt/ *n.* **1** cultivated hazel, bearing edible ovoid nuts. **2** this nut.

filch /filch/ *v.tr.* pilfer; steal. □□ **filch′er** *n.*

file¹ /fīl/ • *n.* **1** folder, box, etc., for holding loose papers. **2** set of papers kept in this. **3** *Computing* collection of (usu. related) data stored under one name. • *v.tr.* **1** place (papers) in a file or among (esp. public) records. **2** submit a petition, application, etc. □□ **fil′er** *n.*

file² /fīl/ • *n.* line of persons or things one behind another. • *v.intr.* walk in a file.

file³ /fīl/ • *n.* tool with a roughened surface or surfaces, usu. of steel, for smoothing or shaping wood, fingernails, etc. • *v.tr.* smooth or shape with a file. □□ **fil′er** *n.*

fi·let /fíláy, filít/ *n.* fillet of meat. □ **filet mignon** /fíláy minyón/ small tender piece of beef from the end of the tenderloin.

fil·i·al /fíleeəl/ *adj.* **1** of or due from a son or daughter. **2** *Biol.* bearing the relation of offspring. □□ **fil′i·al·ly** *adv.*

fil·i·bus·ter /fílibəstər/ • *n.* **1** obstruction of progress in a legislative assembly by prolonged speaking. **2** person who engages in this. • *v.* **1** *intr.* act as a filibuster. **2** *tr.* act in this way against (a motion, etc.).

---

filibuster late 18th century: from French *flibustier*, first applied to pirates who pillaged the Spanish Colonies in the West Indies. In the mid-19th century (via Spanish *filibustero*), the term denoted American adventurers who incited revolution in several Latin American states. The verb was soon extended to describe tactics intended to sabotage legislative proceedings, whence sense 1.

fil·i·gree /fíligree/ n. (also **fil·a·gree** /fílə-/) **1** fine ornamental work of gold or silver or copper wire. **2** anything delicate resembling this. □□ **fil′i·greed** adj.

fil·ing /fíling/ n. (usu. in pl.) particle rubbed off by a file.

Fil·i·pi·no /filipéenō/ • n. (pl. **-nos**; fem. **Fil·i·pi·na** /-nə/, pl. **-nəs**) native or inhabitant of the Philippines, a group of islands in the SW Pacific. • adj. of the Philippines or the Filipinos.

fill /fil/ • v. **1** tr. & intr. make or become full. **2** tr. occupy completely; spread over or through; pervade. **3** tr. drill and put a filling into (a decayed tooth). **4** tr. appoint a person to hold (a vacant post). **5** tr. hold (a position). **6** tr. carry out or supply (an order, commission, etc.). **7** tr. occupy (vacant time). **8** tr. (usu. as **filling** adj.) (esp. of food) satisfy; satiate. • n. **1** as much as one wants or can bear. **2** enough to fill something. □ **fill in 1** add information to complete. **2** fill (a hole, etc.) completely. **3** act as a substitute. **4** colloq. inform (a person) more fully. **fill out 1** enlarge to the required size. **2** become enlarged or plump. **3** add information to complete (a document, etc.).

fill·er /fílər/ n. **1** material or an object used to fill a cavity or increase bulk. **2** item filling space in a newspaper, etc.

fil·let /fílit/ • n. **1** (usu. **fi·let** /fíláy/) **a** fleshy boneless piece of meat from near the loins or the ribs. **b** (in full **fillet steak**) tenderloin. **c** boned longitudinal section of a fish. **2** strip; band. • v.tr. (also /fíláy, filay/) remove bones from (fish or meat). □□ **fil′let·er** n.

fill·ing /fíling/ n. material that fills a cavity, sandwich, pie, etc.

fil·lip /fílip/ • n. **1** stimulus or incentive. **2** flick with finger or thumb. • v. (**fil·liped, fil·lip·ing**) flick.

fil·ly /fílee/ n. (pl. **-lies**) young female horse.

film /film/ • n. **1** thin coating or covering layer. **2** Photog. strip or sheet of plastic or other flexible base coated with light-sensitive emulsion for exposure in a camera. **3** story, episode, etc., on a film, with the illusion of movement; movie. **4** slight veil or haze, etc. • v. **1** tr. (also absol.) make a movie or television film of (a book, etc.). **2** tr. & intr. cover or become covered with or as with a film.

film·mak·er /fílmaykər/ n. person who makes motion pictures.

film·strip /fílmstrip/ n. series of transparencies in a strip for projection as still pictures.

film·y /fílmee/ adj. (**film·i·er, film·i·est**) **1** thin and translucent. **2** covered with or as with a film. □□ **film′i·ly** adv. **film′i·ness** n.

fil·ter /fíltər/ • n. **1** porous device for removing impurities or solid particles from a liquid or gas passed through it. **2** screen or attachment for absorbing or modifying light, X rays, etc. **3** device for suppressing electrical or sound waves of frequencies not required. • v. **1** tr. & intr. pass or cause to pass through a filter. **2** intr. (foll. by through, into, etc.) make way gradually.

filth /filth/ n. **1** repugnant or extreme dirt; excrement; refuse. **2** vileness; corruption; obscenity. □□ **filth′i·ly** adv. **filth′i·ness** n. **filth′y** adj. (**filth·i·er, filth·i·est**)

fil·trate /fíltrayt/ • v.tr. filter. • n. filtered liquid. □□ **fil·tra·tion** /-tráyshən/ n.

fin /fin/ n. **1** organ on various parts of the body of many aquatic vertebrates and some invertebrates, including fish and cetaceans, for propelling, steering, etc. **2** similar projection on an aircraft, car, etc. **3** swimmer's flipper. □□ **fin′less** adj. **finned** adj. (also in comb.).

fi·na·gle /fináygəl/ v. colloq. act or obtain dishonestly or deviously. □□ **fi·na′gler** n.

fi·nal /fín'l/ • adj. **1** situated at the end; coming last. **2** conclusive; decisive. • n. **1** (also in pl.) last or deciding heat or game. **2** examination at the end of an academic course. □□ **fi′nal·ly** adv.

fi·na·le /fináälee, -nálee/ n. last movement or section of a piece of music or drama, etc.

fi·nal·ist /fín'list/ n. competitor in a final.

fi·nal·i·ty /fináalitee, fə-/ n. (pl. **-ties**) **1** quality or fact of being final. **2** belief that something is final.

fi·na·lize /fín'līz/ v.tr. **1** put into final form. **2** bring to an end. **3** approve the final form of. □□ **fi·na·li·za′tion** n.

fi·nance /fínáns, fī-, fínans/ • n. **1** management of (esp. public) money. **2** monetary support for an enterprise. **3** (in pl.) money resources. • v.tr. provide capital for. □□ **fi·nan·cial** /-shəl, fī-/ adj. **fi·nan′cial·ly** adv.

---

finance late Middle English: from Old French, from finer 'make an end, settle a debt,' from fin 'end.' The original sense was 'payment of a debt, compensation, or ransom'; later 'taxation, revenue.' Current senses date from the 18th century, and reflect sense development in French.

---

fi·nan·cier /finənsée′r, fənan-, fínən-/ n. capitalist.

finch /finch/ n. any small seed-eating passerine bird, including crossbills, canaries, and chaffinches.

find /find/ • v.tr. (past and past part. **found** /fownd/) **1 a** discover by chance or effort (found a key). **b** become aware of. **2** succeed in obtaining. **3** seek out and provide or supply. **4** Law (of a jury, judge, etc.) decide and declare (found him guilty). **5** reach by a natural or normal process (water finds its own level). • n. **1** discovery of treasure, minerals, etc. **2** thing or person discovered, esp. when of value. □ **find out 1** discover or detect (a wrongdoer, etc.). **2** get information. **3** discover. □□ **find′a·ble** adj. v.tr. (past and past part. **found** /fownd/) **1 a** discover by chance or effort (found a key). **b** become aware of. **2** succeed in obtaining. **3** seek out and provide or supply. **4** Law (of a jury, judge, etc.) decide and declare (found him guilty). **5** reach by a natural or normal process (water finds its own level). • n. **1** discovery of treasure, minerals, etc. **2** thing or person discovered, esp. when of value. □ **find out 1** discover or detect (a wrongdoer, etc.). **2** get information. **3** discover. □□ **find′a·ble** adj. ¶ See note at LOCATE.

find·ing /fínding/ n. **1** (often in pl.) conclusion reached by an inquiry. **2** (in pl.) small parts or tools used by artisans.

fine¹ /fin/ • adj. **1** of high quality (they sell fine fabrics). **2 a** excellent; of notable merit (a fine painting). **b** good; satisfactory (that will be *fine*). **3** pure; refined. **4** in good health. **5** (of weather, etc.) bright and clear. **6 a** thin; sharp. **b** in small particles. • *adv.* **1** finely. **2** *colloq.* very well (*suits me fine*). □ **fine arts** poetry, music, and esp. painting, sculpture, and architecture. **fine-tune** make small adjustments to. □□ **fine′ly** *adv.* **fine′ness** *n.*

fine² /fīn/ • *n.* sum of money exacted as a penalty. • *v.tr.* punish by a fine (*fined him $5*). □□ **fin·a·ble** /fīnəbəl/ *adj.*

fin·er·y /fīnəree/ *n.* showy dress or decoration.

fi·nesse /finés/ • *n.* **1** refinement. **2** subtle or delicate manipulation. **3** artfulness, esp. in handling a difficulty tactfully. • *v.* use or achieve by finesse.

fin·ger /fínggər/ • *n.* **1** any of the terminal projections of the hand (esp. other than the thumb). **2** part of a glove, etc., intended to cover a finger. **3** finger-like object or structure. • *v.tr.* **1** touch, feel, or handle with the fingers. **2** *Mus.* **a** play (a passage) with fingers used in a particular way. **b** play upon (an instrument) with the fingers. □ **put one's finger on** locate or identify exactly. □□ **fin′gered** *adj.* (also in *comb.*). **fin′ger·less** *adj.*

fin·ger·ing /fínggəring/ *n.* **1** manner or technique of using the fingers, esp. to play an instrument. **2** indication of this in a musical score.

fin·ger·nail /fínggərnayl/ *n.* nail at the tip of each finger.

fin·ger·print /fínggərprint/ • *n.* impression made on a surface by the fine ridges on the fingertips, esp. as used for identifying individuals. • *v.tr.* record the fingerprints of.

fin·ger·tip /fínggərtip/ *n.* tip of a finger. □ **have at one's fingertips** be thoroughly familiar with (a subject, etc.).

fin·i·al /fíneeəl/ *n. Archit.* ornamental top or end of a roof, pediment, gable, tower corner, canopy, etc.

fin·ick·y /fínikee/ *adj.* **1** overly particular; fastidious. **2** detailed. □□ **fin′ick·i·ness** *n.*

fi·nis /fínis, feenée, fínis/ *n.* the end (used esp. at the end of a book, movie, etc.).

fin·ish /fínish/ • *v.* **1** *tr.* **a** bring to an end; come to the end of; complete. **b** *colloq.* kill; overcome completely. **c** consume or get through the whole or the remainder of (food or drink) (*finish your dinner*). **2** *intr.* **a** come to an end; cease. **b** reach the end, esp. of a race. **3** *tr.* treat the surface of (cloth, woodwork, etc.). • *n.* **1** end; last stage; completion. **2** method, material, or texture used for surface treatment of wood, cloth, etc. □ **finish with** have no more to do with; complete one's use of or association with. □□ **fin′ish·er** *n.*

fi·nite /fínīt/ *adj.* **1** limited; not infinite. **2** *Gram.* (of a part of a verb) having a specific number and person. □□ **fi′nite·ly** *adv.* **fi′nite·ness** *n.* **fin·i·tude** /fínitōōd, -tyōōd/ *n.*

Finn /fin/ *n.* native or inhabitant of Finland; person of Finnish descent.

Finn·ish /fínish/ • *adj.* of the Finns or their language. • *n.* language of the Finns.

fiord var. of FJORD.

fir /fər/ *n.* **1** (in full **fir tree**) evergreen coniferous tree with needles borne singly on the stems (cf. PINE¹). **2** wood of the fir. □□ **fir′ry** *adj.*

fire /fīr/ • *n.* **1 a** combustion of substances with oxygen, giving out bright light and heat. **b** flame or incandescence. **2** conflagration; destructive burning (*forest fire*). **3** burning fuel in a fireplace, furnace, etc. **4** fervor; spirit; vivacity. **5** burning heat; fever. • *v.* **1 a** *tr.* discharge (a gun, etc.). **b** *tr.* propel (a missile) from a gun, etc. **c** *tr.* propel (a ball) with force or high speed. **d** *intr.* fire a gun or missile. **e** *tr.* produce (a broadside, salute, etc.) by discharge of guns. **f** *intr.* (of a gun, etc.) be discharged. **2** *tr.* deliver or utter in rapid succession (*fired insults at us*). **3** *tr. sl.* dismiss (an employee). **4** *intr.* (of an engine) undergo ignition. **5** *tr.* stimulate. **6** *tr.* bake or dry (pottery, bricks, etc.). **b** cure (tea or tobacco) by artificial heat. □ **catch fire** begin to burn. **fire department** organized body of firefighters trained and employed to extinguish fires. **fire drill** rehearsal of the procedures to be used in case of fire. **fire engine** vehicle carrying equipment for fighting large fires. **fire escape** emergency staircase or apparatus for escape from a building on fire. **fire extinguisher** apparatus with a jet for discharging liquid chemicals, water, or foam to extinguish a fire. **fire power** destructive capacity of guns, etc. **fire storm** high wind or storm following a very intense fire. **under fire 1** being shot at. **2** being rigorously criticized or questioned. □□ **fire′less** *adj.* **fir′er** *n.*

fire·arm /fíraarm/ *n.* (usu. in *pl.*) gun, esp. a pistol or rifle.

fire·ball /fírbawl/ *n.* **1** large meteor. **2** ball of flame, esp. from an explosion. **3** energetic person.

fire·bomb /fírbom/ *n.* incendiary bomb.

fire·brand /fírbrand/ *n.* **1** piece of burning wood. **2** cause of trouble, esp. a person causing unrest.

fire·break /fírbrayk/ *n.* obstacle to the spread of fire in a forest, etc., esp. an open space.

fire·crack·er /fírkrakər/ *n.* explosive firework.

fire·fly /fírflī/ *n.* (*pl.* **-flies**) soft-bodied beetle that emits phosphorescent light.

fire·fight·er /fírfītər/ *n.* person employed to extinguish fires.

fire·man /fírmən/ *n.* (*pl.* **-men**) **1** member of a fire department. **2** person who tends a furnace.

fire·place /fírplays/ *n. Archit.* **1** place for a domestic fire, esp. a grate or hearth at the base of a chimney. **2** structure surrounding this. **3** area in front of this.

fire·plug /fírplug/ *n.* hydrant for a fire hose.

fire·proof /fírprōōf/ • *adj.* able to resist fire or great heat. • *v.tr.* make fireproof.

fire·side /fírsīd/ *n.* **1** area around a fireplace. **2** a person's home or home life. □ **fireside chat** informal talk.

fire·wa·ter /fírwawtər/ *n. colloq.* strong alcoholic liquor.

fire·wood /fírwōōd/ *n.* wood for use as fuel.

fire·work /fírwərk/ *n.* **1** device containing combustible chemicals that cause explosions or spectacular effects. **2** (in *pl.*) outburst of passion, esp. anger.

fir·ing /fíring/ *n.* **1** discharge of guns. **2** fuel. **3** heating process that hardens clay into pottery. □ **firing line 1** front line in a battle. **2** leading part in an activity, etc.

firm¹ /fərm/ • *adj.* **1 a** of a solid or compact structure. **b** fixed; stable. **2 a** resolute; determined. **b** steadfast; constant. **3** (of an offer, etc.) not liable to cancellation after acceptance. • *adv.*

firmly. • *v.* make or become firm, secure, compact, or solid. □□ **firm′ly** *adv.* **firm′ness** *n.*

firm² /fərm/ *n.* business concern or its partners.

fir·ma·ment /fərməmənt/ *n.* *literary* the sky regarded as a vault or arch. □□ **fir·ma·men′tal** *adj.*

first /fərst/ • *adj.* **1** earliest in time or order. **2** foremost in position, rank, or importance. **3** most willing or likely. **4** basic or evident. • *n.* **1** person or thing first mentioned or occurring. **2** first gear. **3** first place in a race. • *adv.* **1** before any other person or thing. **2** before someone or something else. **3** for the first time. □ **at first** at the beginning. **first aid** emergency medical treatment. **first-born** *adj.* eldest. • *n.* eldest child of a person. **first class 1** set of persons or things grouped together as the best. **2** best accommodation in a train, ship, etc. **3** mail given priority. **first-class** *adj.* **1** belonging to or traveling by first class. **2** of the best quality; very good. • *adv.* by the first class. **first cousin** see COUSIN. **first gear** see GEAR. **First Lady** wife of the US President. **first name** personal name other than a family name. **first person** see PERSON. **first-rate** *adj.* of the highest class; excellent. • *adv.* *colloq.* very well. **2** excellently.

¶ **First, second, third,** etc., are adverbs as well as adjectives: *First, dice three potatoes; second, add the bouillon.* **Firstly, secondly,** etc., are not wrong, but make sure not to mix the two groups: *first, second, third*; not *first, secondly, thirdly.* See also note at FORMER.

first·hand /fərst-hánd/ *attrib. adj. & adv.* from the original source; direct.

first·ly /fərstlee/ *adv.* in the first place; first (cf. FIRST *adv.*).

firth /fərth/ *n.* esp. *Sc.* (also **frith** /frith/) **1** narrow inlet of the sea. **2** estuary.

fis·cal /fískəl/ *adj.* of public revenue; of financial matters. □ **fiscal year** year as reckoned for taxing or accounting. □□ **fis′cal·ly** *adv.*

fish /fish/ • *n.* (*pl.* same or **fish·es**) **1** vertebrate cold-blooded animal with gills and fins living wholly in water. **2** any animal living wholly in water, e.g., cuttlefish, shellfish, jellyfish. **3** flesh of fish as food. **4** (**the Fish** or **Fishes**) zodiacal sign or constellation Pisces. • *v.* **1** *intr.* try to catch fish, esp. with a line or net. **2** *tr.* fish for (a certain kind of fish) or in (a certain stretch of water). **3** *intr.* (foll. by *for*) **a** search for in water or a concealed place. **b** seek by indirect means (*fishing for compliments*). **4** *tr.* (foll. by *up, out,* etc.) bring out with careful or awkward searching. □ **drink like a fish** drink alcoholic beverages excessively. **fish story** *colloq.* exaggerated account. **other fish to fry** other matters to attend to. □□ **fish′like** *adj.*

fish·er·man /físhərmən/ *n.* (*pl.* **-men**) **1** person who catches fish as a livelihood or for recreation. **2** fishing boat.

fish·er·y /físhəree/ *n.* (*pl.* **-ies**) **1** place where fish are caught or reared. **2** industry of catching or rearing fish.

fish·hook /fish-hŏŏk/ *n.* barbed hook for catching fish.

fish·ing /físhing/ *n.* activity of catching fish, esp. for food or as recreation. □ **fishing rod** long tapering, usu. jointed rod to which a fishing line is attached.

fish·net /fishnet/ *n.* (often *attrib.*) open-meshed fabric.

fish·tail /fishtayl/ • *n.* device, etc., shaped like a fish's tail. • *v.intr.* move the tail of a vehicle from side to side.

fish·y /fishee/ *adj.* (**fish·i·er, fish·i·est**) **1** of or like fish. **2** *sl.* of dubious character; questionable; suspect. □□ **fish′i·ly** *adv.* **fish′i·ness** *n.*

fis·sile /físəl, -īl/ *adj.* **1** capable of undergoing nuclear fission. **2** cleavable; tending to split. □□ **fis·sil·i·ty** /-silitee/ *n.*

fis·sion /físhən/ *n.* **1** *Physics* splitting of a heavy atomic nucleus with a release of energy. **2** *Biol.* division of a cell as a mode of reproduction.

fis·sure /físhər/ *n.* opening, usu. long and narrow, made esp. by cracking, splitting, or separation of parts.

fist /fist/ *n.* **1** tightly closed hand. **2** *sl.* handwriting. □□ **fist′ed** *adj.* (also in *comb.*). **fist′ful** *n.* (*pl.* **-fuls**)

fist·i·cuffs /fístikufs/ *n.pl.* fighting with the fists.

fis·tu·la /fischələ/ *n.* (*pl.* **fis·tu·las** or **fis·tu·lae** /-lee/) abnormal or surgically made passage, as between a hollow organ and the body surface. □□ **fis′tu·lar** *adj.* **fis′tu·lous** *adj.*

fit¹ /fit/ • *adj.* (**fit·ter, fit·test**) **1 a** well adapted or suited. **b** qualified; competent; worthy. **c** in a suitable condition; ready. **d** good enough. **2** in good health or athletic condition. **3** proper; becoming; right (*it is fit that*). • *v.tr.* (**fit·ted, fit·ting**) **1 a** (also *absol.*) be of the right shape and size for (*the dress fits her*). **b** make the right size or shape. **2** (usu. foll. by *with*) supply; furnish; equip. **3** be in harmony with; befit; become (*it fits the occasion*). • *n.* way in which a garment, component, etc., fits. □ **fit in 1** be (esp. socially) compatible or accommodating. **2** find space or time for. **fit out** (or **up**) equip. □□ **fit′ly** *adv.* **fit′ness** *n.* **fit′ter** *n.*

fit² /fit/ *n.* **1** sudden seizure of epilepsy, hysteria, apoplexy, fainting, or paralysis, with unconsciousness or convulsions. **2** sudden short bout or burst. □ **by** (or **in**) **fits and starts** spasmodically. **have a fit** *colloq.* be greatly surprised or outraged. **in fits** laughing uncontrollably.

fit·ful /fitfŏŏl/ *adj.* active or occurring spasmodically or intermittently. □□ **fit′ful·ly** *adv.* **fit′ful·ness** *n.*

fit·ting /fiting/ • *n.* **1** process or an instance of having a garment, etc., fitted (*needed several fittings*). **2** (in *pl.*) fixtures and furnishings of a building. • *adj.* proper; becoming; right. □□ **fit′ting·ly** *adv.* **fit′ting·ness** *n.*

five /fiv/ • *n.* **1** one more than four. **2** symbol for this (5, v, V). • *adj.* that amount to five.

fix /fiks/ • *v.* **1** *tr.* make firm or stable; fasten; secure. **2** *tr.* decide; specify (a price, date, etc.). **3** *tr.* repair. **4** *tr.* implant (an idea or memory) in the mind. **5** *tr.* (foll. by *on, upon*) direct (one's eyes, attention, etc.). **6** *tr.* place definitely or permanently. **7** *tr.* determine the exact nature, position, etc., of. **8 a** *tr.* make (eyes, features, etc.) rigid. **b** *intr.* become rigid. **9** *tr.* *colloq.* prepare (food or drink). **10** *tr.* *colloq.* punish; deal with. **11** *tr.* *colloq.* secure or arrange fraudulently. **12** *tr.* castrate or spay (an animal). • *n.* **1** *colloq.* dilemma or predicament. **2** position found by bearings or astronomical observations. **3** *sl.* dose of a narcotic drug. **4** *sl.* bribery. □ **fixed income** income deriving from a pension, investment at fixed interest, etc. **fix up 1** arrange; organize;

prepare. **2** accommodate. **3** provide (a person) with. **4** restore; refurbish. □□ **fix′a·ble** *adj.* **fix·ed·ly** /fíksidlee/ *adv.* **fix·ed·ness** /fíksidnis/ *n.* **fix′er** *n.*

fix·ate /fiksáyt/ *v.tr.* **1** direct one's gaze on. **2** *Psychol.* cause (a person) to become abnormally attached to persons or things.

fix·a·tion /fiksáyshən/ *n.* **1** act or an instance of being fixated. **2** obsession; concentration on a single idea.

fix·a·tive /fíksətiv/ • *adj.* tending to fix or secure. • *n.* substance used to fix colors, hair, perfume, microscopic specimens, etc.

fix·ings /fíksingz/ *n.pl.* **1** apparatus or equipment. **2** trimmings for a dish. **3** trimmings of a dress, etc.

fix·i·ty /fíksitee/ *n.* **1** fixed state. **2** stability; permanence.

fix·ture /fíkschər/ *n.* something fixed in position.

fizz /fiz/ • *v.intr.* **1** make a hissing or spluttering sound. **2** (of a drink) effervesce. • *n.* effervescence.

fiz·zle /fízəl/ • *v.intr.* make a feeble hissing or spluttering sound. • *n.* such a sound. □ **fizzle out** end feebly.

fizz·y /fízee/ *adj.* (**fizz·i·er, fizz·i·est**) effervescent; carbonated. □□ **fizz′i·ly** *adv.* **fizz′i·ness** *n.*

fjord /fyawrd/ *n.* (also **fiord**) long narrow inlet of sea between high cliffs, as in Norway.

FL *abbr.* Florida (in official postal use).

fl. *abbr.* **1** floor. **2** floruit. **3** fluid.

Fla. *abbr.* Florida.

flab /flab/ *n. colloq.* fat; flabbiness.

flab·ber·gast /flábərgast/ *v.tr.* (esp. as **flabbergasted** *adj.*) *colloq.* overwhelm with astonishment; dumbfound.

flab·by /flábee/ *adj.* (**flab·bi·er, flab·bi·est**) **1** (of flesh, etc.) hanging down; limp; flaccid. **2** (of language or character) feeble. □□ **flab′bi·ly** *adv.* **flab′bi·ness** *n.*

flac·cid /flásid, fláksid/ *adj.* limp; flabby; drooping. □□ **flac·cid·i·ty** /-síditee/ *n.* **flac′cid·ly** *adv.*

flag¹ /flag/ • *n.* piece of cloth, usu. oblong or square, used as a country's emblem or as a standard, signal, etc. • *v.* (**flagged, flag·ging**) **1** *intr.* **a** grow tired; lose vigor; lag. **b** hang down; droop; become limp. **2** *tr.* **a** inform (a person) by flag signals. **b** communicate (information) by flagging. □ **flag down** signal to stop. □□ **flag′ger** *n.*

flag² /flag/ *n.* (also **flag′stone**) **1** flat, usu. rectangular stone slab used for paving. **2** (in *pl.*) pavement made of these.

flag³ /flag/ *n.* plant with a bladed leaf, esp. the iris.

flag·el·late /flájəlayt/ *v.tr.* scourge; flog. □□ **flag·el·la·tion** /-láyshən/ *n.* **flag′el·la·tor** *n.*

flag·el·lum /fləjéləm/ *n.* (*pl.* **fla·gel·la** /-lə/) *Biol.* long lashlike appendage found principally on microscopic organisms. □□ **fla·gel·lar** /-lər/ *adj.* **fla·gel·li·form** /-lifawrm/ *adj.*

flag·on /flágən/ *n.* large vessel usu. with a handle, spout, and lid, to hold wine, etc.

flag·pole /flágpōl/ *n.* pole on which a flag may be hoisted.

fla·grant /fláygrənt/ *adj.* glaring; notorious; scandalous. □□ **fla·gran·cy** /-grənsee/ *n.* **fla′grant·ly** *adv.*

flag·ship /flágship/ *n.* **1** ship having an admiral on board. **2** best or most important member, office, etc., of its kind.

flag·stone /flágstōn/ *n.* = FLAG².

flail /flayl/ • *n.* threshing tool consisting of a wooden staff with a short heavy stick swinging from it. • *v.* **1** *tr.* beat. **2** *intr.* wave or swing wildly or erratically.

flair /flair/ *n.* **1** instinct for selecting or performing what is excellent, useful, etc.; a talent (*has a flair for languages*). **2** talent or ability, esp. artistic or stylistic.

flak /flak/ *n.* (also **flack**) **1** antiaircraft fire. **2** adverse criticism; abuse.

flake /flayk/ • *n.* **1 a** small thin light piece of snow. **b** similar flake of another material. **2** thin broad piece of material peeled or split off. **3** *sl.* crazy or eccentric person. • *v.* take off or come away in flakes.

flak·y /fláykee/ *adj.* (**flak·i·er, flak·i·est**) **1** of, like, or in flakes. **2** *sl.* crazy; eccentric. □□ **flak′i·ly** *adv.* **flak′i·ness** *n.*

flam·boy·ant /flambóyənt/ *adj.* **1** ostentatious; showy. **2** floridly decorated. **3** gorgeously colored. □□ **flam·boy′ance** *n.* **flam·boy′an·cy** *n.* **flam·boy′ant·ly** *adv.*

flame /flaym/ • *n.* **1 a** ignited gas. **b** (usu. in *pl.*) visible combustion. **2** brilliant orange-red color. **3 a** strong passion, esp. love. **b** *colloq.* boyfriend or girlfriend. • *v.* burn; blaze. □□ **flame′less** *adj.* **flame′like** *adj.*

fla·men·co /fləméngkō/ *n.* (*pl.* **-cos**) **1** style of Spanish gypsy guitar music. **2** dance performed to this music.

flame·proof /fláymprōōf/ *adj.* (esp. of a fabric) treated so as to be nonflammable.

flame·throw·er /fláymthrōər/ *n.* weapon for throwing a spray of flame.

flam·ing /fláyming/ *adj.* **1** emitting flames. **2** bright colored.

fla·min·go /fləmínggō/ *n.* (*pl.* **-gos** or **-goes**) tall, long-necked, web-footed wading bird with crooked bill and pink, scarlet, and black plumage.

flam·ma·ble /fláməbəl/ *adj.* easily set on fire; inflammable. □□ **flam·ma·bil·i·ty** *n.* ¶ See note at INFLAMMABLE.

flan /flan/ *n.* **1** open pastry case with a savory or sweet filling. **2** custard topped with caramel glaze.

flange /flanj/ *n.* *Engin.* projecting flat rim, etc., used for strengthening or attachment. □□ **flange′less** *n.*

flange

FLANGE

flank /flangk/ • *n.* **1** side of the body between the ribs and the hip. **2** side of a mountain, building, etc. **3** side of an array of troops. • *v.tr.* be situated at both sides of.

flan·nel /flánəl/ *n.* **1** woven wool fabric, usu. napless. **2** (in *pl.*) flannel garments, esp. trousers. □□ **flan′nel·ly** *adj.*

flan·nel·ette /flánəlét/ *n.* napped cotton fabric similar to flannel.

flap /flap/ • *v.* (**flapped, flap·ping**) **1 a** *tr.* move (wings, the arms, etc.) up and down when flying, or as if flying. **b** *intr.* move up and down; beat. **2** *intr.* swing or sway about; flutter. • *n.* **1** piece of cloth, wood, paper, etc., hinged or attached by one side only, e.g., the folded part of an envelope or a table leaf. **2** one up-and-down motion of a wing, an arm, etc. **3** *colloq.* agitation; panic. **4** hinged or sliding section of a wing used to control lift and drag. □□ **flap′py** *adj.*

flap·jack /flápjak/ *n.* pancake.

flap·per /flápər/ *n.* **1** person or thing that flaps. **2** *sl.* (in the 1920s) young unconventional or lively woman.

flare /flair/ • *v.* **1** *intr.* & *tr.* widen, esp. toward the bottom. **2** *intr.* & *tr.* burn suddenly with a bright unsteady flame. **3** *intr.* burst into anger; burst forth. • *n.* **1 a** dazzling irregular flame or light. **b** sudden outburst of flame. **2** signal light, bright light, or firework used as a signal. **3** gradual widening, esp. of a skirt or trousers. □ **flare up** burst into a sudden blaze, anger, activity, etc. **flare-up** *n.* sudden outburst.

flash /flash/ • *v.* **1** *intr.* & *tr.* emit or reflect or cause to emit or reflect light briefly, suddenly, or intermittently; gleam or cause to gleam. **2** *tr.* send or reflect like a sudden flame. **3 a** burst suddenly into view or perception. **b** move swiftly. **4** *tr.* **a** send (news, etc.) by radio, telegraph, etc. **b** signal to (a person) by shining lights or headlights briefly. **5** *tr. colloq.* show ostentatiously. • *n.* **1** sudden bright light or flame, e.g., of lightning. **2** very brief time; an instant. **3 a** brief, sudden burst of feeling (*a flash of hope*). **b** sudden display (of wit, understanding, etc.). **4** breaking news story. **5** *Photog.* = FLASHLIGHT. **6** bright patch of color. □ **flash point 1** temperature at which vapor from oil, etc., will ignite in air. **2** point at which anger, indignation, etc., becomes uncontrollable.

flash·back /fláshbak/ *n.* scene in a movie, novel, etc., set in a time earlier than the main action.

flash·ing /fláshing/ *n.* usu. metallic strip used to prevent water penetration at the junction of a roof with a wall, etc.

flash·light /fláshlīt/ *n.* battery-operated portable light.

flash·y /fláshee/ *adj.* (**flash·i·er, flash·i·est**) showy; gaudy; cheaply attractive. □□ **flash′i·ly** *adv.* **flash′i·ness** *n.*

flask /flask/ *n.* **1** narrow-necked bulbous bottle for wine, etc., or as used in chemistry. **2** pocket-sized beverage container.

---

flask Middle English (in the sense 'cask'): from medieval Latin *flasca*. From the mid-16th century the word denoted a case of horn, leather, or metal for carrying gunpowder. The sense 'glass container' (late 17th century) was influenced by Italian *fiasco*, from medieval Latin *flasco*.

---

flat[1] /flat/ • *adj.* (**flat·ter, flat·test**) **1 a** horizontally level (*a flat roof*). **b** even; smooth; unbroken; (*a flat stomach*). **c** level, shallow (*a flat cap*). **2** unqualified; plain; downright (*a flat denial*). **3** dull; lifeless; monotonous (*spoke in a flat tone*). **4** (of a carbonated drink) having lost its effervescence; stale. **5** *Mus.* **a** below true or normal pitch (*the violins are flat*). **b** half step lower. **6** (of a tire) punctured; deflated. • *adv.* **1** lying at full length; spread out (*lay flat on the floor*). **2** *colloq.* **a** completely; absolutely (*flat broke*). **b** exactly (*five minutes flat*). **3** *Mus.* below the true or normal pitch. • *n.* **1** flat part of anything; something flat (*flat of the hand*). **2** level ground, esp. a plain or swamp. **3** *Mus.* a note lowered a half step below natural pitch. **b** sign (♭) indicating this. **4** *Theatr.* flat section of scenery mounted on a frame. **6** *colloq.* flat tire. □ **flat foot** foot with a less than normal arch. **flat out 1** at top speed. **2** without hesitation or delay. **3** using all one's strength, energy, or resources. □□ **flat′ly** *adv.* **flat′ness** *n.* **flat′tish** *adj.*

flat[2] /flat/ *n.* = APARTMENT.

flat·fish /flátfish/ *n.* any marine fish having both eyes on one side of a flattened body, including sole, turbot, plaice, etc.

flat·foot /flátfŏŏt/ *n.* (*pl.* **-foots** or **-feet**) *sl.* police officer.

flat·foot·ed /flátfŏŏtid/ *adj.* **1** having flat feet. **2** *colloq.* unprepared; off guard. □□ **flat′-foot′ed·ly** *adv.* **flat′-foot′ed·ness** *n.*

flat·i·ron /flátīərn/ *n.* iron heated externally and used for pressing clothes, etc.

flat·ten /flát′n/ *v.* **1** *tr.* & *intr.* make or become flat. **2** *tr. colloq.* **a** humiliate. **b** knock down. □□ **flat′ten·er** *n.*

flat·ter /flátər/ *v.tr.* **1** compliment unduly; overpraise, esp. for gain or advantage. **2** please, congratulate, or delude (oneself, etc.). **3** make (a person) appear to the best advantage (*that blouse flatters you*). **4** make (a person) feel honored. □□ **flat′ter·er** *n.* **flat′ter·ing** *adj.* **flat′ter·ing·ly** *adv.*

flat·ter·y /flátəree/ *n.* (*pl.* **-ies**) **1** exaggerated or insincere praise. **2** act or an instance of flattering.

flat·u·lent /fláchələnt/ *adj.* **1** having or producing intestinal gas. **2** (of speech, etc.) inflated; pretentious. □□ **flat′u·lence** *n.* **flat′u·len·cy** *n.* **flat′u·lent·ly** *adv.*

flat·ware /flátwair/ *n.* **1** forks, knives, spoons, etc. **2** plates, saucers, etc.

flat·worm /flátwərm/ *n.* worm with a flattened body.

flaunt /flawnt/ *v.* display ostentatiously; show off; parade. □□ **flaunt′er** *n.* **flaunt′y** *adj.*

¶ These words are often confused because both suggest arrogance or showing off. However, **flaunt** means 'display ostentatiously,' e.g., *He liked to flaunt his wealth,* while **flout** means 'express contempt for or disobey (laws, convention, etc.),' e.g., *The fine is too low for those who flout the law so egregiously.*

flau·tist /fláwtist, flów-/ *n.* flute player.

fla·vor /fláyvər/ • *n.* **1** distinctive mingled sensation of smell and taste. **2** indefinable characteristic quality. • *v.tr.* give flavor to; season. □□ **fla′vor·ful** *adj.* **fla′vor·less** *adj.* **fla′vor·some** *adj.*

fla·vor·ing /fláyvəring/ *n.* substance used to flavor food or drink.

flaw /flaw/ • *n.* **1** imperfection; blemish. **2** crack or similar fault. • *v.* crack; damage; spoil. □□ **flawed** *adj.* **flaw′less** *adj.* **flaw′less·ly** *adv.* **flaw′less·ness** *n.*

flax /flaks/ *n.* **1** blue-flowered plant, cultivated for its textile fiber and its seeds. **2** dressed or undressed flax fibers.

flax·en /fláksən/ *adj.* **1** of flax. **2** (of hair) pale yellow.

flay /flay/ *v.tr.* **1** strip the skin or hide off, esp. by beating. **2** criticize severely. □□ **flay′er** *n.*

flea /flee/ *n.* small wingless jumping insect that feeds on human and other blood. □ **flea market** market selling secondhand goods, etc.

fleck /flek/ • *n.* **1** small particle or speck, esp. of dust. **2** spot. • *v.tr.* mark with flecks.

fled *past* and *past part.* of FLEE.

fledg·ling /fléjling/ *n.* **1** young bird. **2** inexperienced person.

flee /flee/ *v.* (*past* and *past part.* **fled** /fled/) **1** *intr.* (often foll. by *from, before*) run away. **2** *tr.* run away from; leave abruptly. **3** *intr.* vanish; cease; pass away. □□ **fle·er** /fléeər/ *n.*

fleece /flees/ • *n.* **1** woolly covering of a sheep or a similar animal. **2** soft warm fabric. • *v.tr.* **1** strip (a person) of money, valuables, etc.; swindle. **2** shear (a sheep, etc.). □□ **fleece′a·ble** *adj.* **fleeced** *adj.* (also in *comb.*).

fleec·y /fléesee/ *adj.* (**fleec·i·er, fleec·i·est**) **1** of or like a fleece. **2** covered with a fleece. □□ **fleec′i·ly** *adv.* **fleec′i·ness** *n.*

fleet[1] /fleet/ *n.* **1** warships under one commander. **2** number of vehicles operating under one proprietor.

fleet[2] /fleet/ *adj.* swift; nimble. □□ **fleet′ly** *adv.* **fleet′ness** *n.*

fleet·ing /fléeting/ *adj.* transitory; brief. □□ **fleet′ing·ly** *adv.*

Flem·ish /flémish/ • *adj.* of or relating to Flanders. • *n.* language of Flanders.

flesh /flesh/ *n.* **1 a** soft, esp. muscular, substance between the skin and bones of an animal or human. **b** plumpness; fat. **2** the body as opposed to the mind or the soul, esp. considered as sinful. **3** pulpy substance of a fruit or a plant. **4** (also **flesh′ col·or**) yellowish pink color. **5** animal or human life. □ **flesh and blood** • *n.* **1** the body or its substance. **2** humankind. **3** human nature, esp. as being fallible. • *adj.* actually living, not imaginary or supernatural. **flesh out** make or become substantial. **in the flesh** in bodily form; in person. **one's own flesh and blood** near relatives; descendants. □□ **flesh′less** *adj.*

flesh·ly /fléshlee/ *adj.* (**flesh·li·er, flesh·li·est**) **1** bodily; sensual. **2** mortal; not divine. **3** worldly. □□ **flesh′li·ness** *n.*

flesh·y /fléshee/ *adj.* (**flesh·i·er, flesh·i·est**) **1** plump; fat. **2** of flesh; without bone. **3** pulpy. **4** like flesh. □□ **flesh′i·ness** *n.*

fleur-de-lis /flördəlée/ *n.* (also **fleur-de-lys**) (*pl.* **fleurs-** *pronunc.* same) lily-like emblem used on the former royal arms of France.

flew *past* of FLY[1].

flex /fleks/ *v.* **1** *tr.* & *intr.* bend (a joint, limb, etc.) or be bent. **2** *tr.* & *intr.* move (a muscle) or (of a muscle) be moved to bend a joint. **3** *tr. Geol.* bend (strata).

flex·i·ble /fléksibəl/ *adj.* **1** able to bend without breaking; pliable. **2** adaptable; variable. □□ **flex·i·bil′i·ty** *n.* **flex′i·bly** *adv.*

flex·or /fléksər/ *n.* (in full **flex′or mus′cle**) muscle that bends part of the body.

flex·time /flékstīm/ *n.* (also **flex·i·time** /fléksitīm/) system of flexible working hours.

flick /flik/ • *n.* **1 a** light, sharp, quickly retracted blow with a whip, etc. **b** sudden release of a bent finger or thumb. **2** sudden movement or jerk, esp. of the wrist. **3** *colloq.* **a** a movie. **b** (in *pl.*; prec. by *the*) the movies. • *v.* **1** *tr.* strike or move off with a flick. **2** *intr.* make a flicking movement or sound.

flick·er /flíkər/ • *v.intr.* **1** (of light or flame) shine or burn unsteadily. **2** flutter; quiver; vibrate. **3** (of hope, etc.) waver. • *n.* flickering movement, light, thought, etc.

fli·er /flíər/ *n.* (also **fly′er**) *colloq.* **1** aviator. **2** thing that flies in a specified way (*poor flier*). **3** (*usu.* **fly′er**) small handbill or circular.

flight[1] /flīt/ *n.* **1 a** act or manner of flying. **b** swift movement or passage through the air. **2 a** journey made through the air or in space. **b** timetabled journey made by an airline. **3** series, esp. of stairs. □ **flight attendant** airline employee who attends to passengers' safety and comfort during flights.

flight[2] /flīt/ *n.* fleeing; hasty retreat.

flight·less /flítlis/ *adj.* (of a bird, etc.) naturally unable to fly.

flight·y /flítee/ *adj.* (**flight·i·er, flight·i·est**) **1** frivolous; fickle; changeable. **2** slightly crazy. □□ **flight′i·ly** *adv.* **flight′i·ness** *n.*

flim·sy /flímzee/ *adj.* (**flims·i·er, flims·i·est**) **1** insubstantial; easily damaged. **2** (of an excuse, etc.) unconvincing. **3** (of clothing) thin. □□ **flim′si·ly** *adv.* **flim′si·ness** *n.*

flinch /flinch/ *v.intr.* draw back in fear, etc.; wince. □□ **flinch′er** *n.* **flinch′ing·ly** *adv.*

fling /fling/ • *v.tr.* (*past* and *past part.* **flung** /flung/) **1** throw, rush, or let go of forcefully or hurriedly. **2** put or send suddenly or violently. • *n.* **1** act or instance of flinging; throw; plunge. **2** spell of indulgence or wild behavior (*he's had his fling*). **3** brief or casual romance. **4** impetuous, whirling Scottish dance. □□ **fling′er** *n.*

FLEUR-DE-LIS

flint /flint/ *n.* **1 a** hard gray stone of nearly pure silica. **b** piece of this, esp. as a primitive tool or weapon. **2** piece of hard alloy used to give an igniting spark. □□ **flint′y** *adj.* (**flint·i·er, flint·i·est**). **flint′i·ly** *adv.* **flint′i·ness** *n.*

flip /flip/ • *v.tr.* (**flipped, flip·ping**) **1** flick or toss (a coin, ball, etc.) with a quick movement so that it spins in the air. **2** turn or turn over; flick. • *n*. act of flipping. • *adj. colloq.* glib; flippant. □ **flip one's lid** *sl.* **1** lose self-control. **2** go crazy. **flip through 1** turn over (cards, pages, etc.). **2** look cursorily through (a book, etc.).

flip-flop /flípflòp/ • *n.* **1** usu. rubber sandal with a thong between the toes. **2** esp. sudden change of direction, attitude, policy, etc. • *v.intr.* (**-flopped, -flop·ping**) change direction, attitude, policy, etc., esp. suddenly.

flip·pant /flípənt/ *adj.* treating serious things lightly; disrespectful. □□ **flip′pan·cy** *n.* **flip′ pant·ly** *adv.*

flip·per /flípər/ *n.* **1** broadened limb of a tortoise, penguin, etc., used in swimming. **2** attachment worn on the foot for underwater swimming.

flirt /flərt/ • *v.intr.* **1** behave in a frivolously amorous or sexually enticing manner. **2 a** superficially interest oneself (with an idea, etc.). **b** trifle (with danger, etc.). • *n.* person who indulges in flirting. □□ **flir·ta′tion** *n.* **flir·ta′ tious** *adj.* **flir·ta′tious·ly** *adv.* **flirt′y** *adj.* (**flirt·i·er, flirt·i·est**).

---

flirt mid-16th century: apparently symbolic, the elements *fl-* and *-irt* both suggesting sudden movement; compare with *flick* and *spurt*. The original senses of the verb were 'give someone a sharp blow' and 'sneer or scoff at'; the earliest senses of the noun were 'a joke or gibe' and 'a flighty girl' (defined by lexicographer Samuel Johnson as 'a pert young hussy'), with a notion originally of impertinent behavior, later of playfully amorous behavior.

---

flit /flit/ *v.intr.* (**flit·ted, flit·ting**) move lightly, softly, or rapidly (*flitted from one room to another*). □□ **flit′ter** *n.*

float /flōt/ • *v.* **1 intr.** & *tr.* rest or move or cause (a buoyant object) to rest or move on the surface of a liquid. **2** *intr. colloq.* move in a leisurely or casual way (*floated about humming quietly*). **3** *tr.* **a** bring (a company, scheme, etc.) into being; launch. **b** offer (stock, shares, etc.) on the stock market. **4** *intr.* & *tr.* circulate or cause (a rumor or idea) to circulate. • *n.* **1** thing that floats, esp.: **a** a raft. **b** cork or other buoyant object on a fishing line. **c** floating device on the surface of water, fuel, etc., controlling the flow. **2** platform mounted on a truck or trailer and carrying a display in a parade, etc. □□ **float′a·ble** *adj.* **float·a·bil′i·ty** /-təbílitee/ *n.*

float·ing /flṓting/ *adj.* not settled in a definite place; fluctuating; variable. □ **floating kidney** abnormal condition in which the kidneys are unusually movable. **2** such a kidney. **floating point** *Computing* decimal, etc., point that does not occupy a fixed position in the numbers processed. **floating rib** any of the lower ribs, which are not attached to the breastbone. □□ **float′ing·ly** *adv.*

floc·cu·lent /flókyələnt/ *adj.* **1** like tufts of wool. **2** consisting of or showing tufts; downy. □□ **floc′cu·lence** *n.*

flock /flok/ • *n.* **1 a** number of animals of one kind, esp. birds, feeding or traveling together. **b** number of domestic animals, esp. sheep, goats, or geese, kept together. **2** large crowd of people. **3** Christian congregation or body of believers, esp. in relation to one minister. • *v.intr.* **1** congregate; mass. **2** go together in a crowd; troop.

floe /flō/ *n.* sheet of floating ice.

flog /flawg, flog/ *v.tr.* (**flogged, flog·ging**) beat with a whip, stick, etc. □□ **flog′ger** *n.*

flood /flud/ • *n.* **1 a** overflowing or influx of water, esp. over land; inundation. **b** the water that overflows. **2 a** outpouring of water; torrent (*flood of rain*). **b** something resembling a torrent (*flood of tears*). **c** abundance or excess. **3** inflow of the tide (also in *comb.*: *flood tide*). • *v.* **1 a** cover with or overflow in a flood. **b** overflow as if with a flood. **2** *tr.* irrigate, deluge, or overfill. **3** *intr.* arrive in great quantities (*complaints flooded in*).

flood·gate /flúdgayt/ *n.* **1** gate opened or closed to admit or exclude water, esp. the lower gate of a lock. **2** (usu. in *pl.*) last restraint holding back tears, rain, anger, etc.

flood·light /flúdlīt/ • *n.* large powerful light to illuminate a building, stage, etc. • *v.tr.* illuminate with floodlights.

flood·plain /flúdplayn/ *n.* flat terrain alongside a river that is subject to inundation when the river floods.

flood·wa·ter /flúdwawtər, -wo-/ *n.* water overflowing as the result of a flood.

floor /flawr/ • *n.* **1** lower surface of a room. **2 a** bottom of the sea, a cave, a cavity, etc. **b** any level area. **3** one level of a building; story. **4 a** (in a legislative assembly) the part of the house where members meet. **b** right to speak next in debate (*gave him the floor*). **5** minimum of prices, wages, etc. • *v.tr.* **1** furnish with a floor. **2** bring or knock (a person) down. **3** *colloq.* confound; baffle. **4** *colloq.* overcome. □ **floor show** entertainment presented at a nightclub, etc. **take the floor 1** begin to dance on a dance floor, etc. **2** speak in a debate, at a meeting, etc. □□ **floor′less** *adj.*

floor·ing /fláwring/ *n.* material to make or cover a floor.

flop /flop/ • *v.intr.* (**flopped, flop·ping**) **1** sway about heavily or loosely. **2** sit, kneel, lie, or fall awkwardly or suddenly. **3** *sl.* fail; collapse. **4** make a dull sound as of a soft body landing, or of a flat thing slapping water. • *n.* **1** flopping movement or sound. **2** *sl.* failure.

flop·py /flópee/ • *adj.* (**flop·pi·er, flop·pi·est**) tending to flop; not firm or rigid. • *n.* (*pl.* **-pies**) (in full **flop′py disk**) *Computing* removable disk on flexible magnetic medium for the storage of data. □□ **flop′pi·ly** *adv.* **flop′pi·ness** *n.*

flo·ra /fláwrə/ *n.* (*pl.* **flo·ras** or **flo·rae** /-ree/) plants of a particular region, geological period, or environment.

flo·ral /fláwrəl/ *adj.* **1** of flowers. **2** decorated with or depicting flowers. **3** of flora or floras. □□ **flo′ral·ly** *adv.*

Flor·en·tine /fláwrənteen, -tīn, flór-/ • *adj.* **1** of or relating to Florence in Italy. **2** (**florentine** /-teen/) (of a dish) served on a bed of spinach. • *n.* native or citizen of Florence.

flor·id /fláwrid, flór-/ *adj.* **1** ruddy; flushed (*a florid complexion*). **2** elaborately ornate; ostentatious; showy. □□ **flo·rid′i·ty** *n.* **flor′id·ly** *adv.* **flor′id·ness** *n.*

flor·in /fláwrin, flór-/ *n. hist.* **1 a** British coin of the 19th–20th c. **b** English gold coin of the 14th c. **2** foreign coin, esp. a Dutch guilder.

flo·rist /fláwrist, flór-/ *n.* person who deals in or grows flowers. □□ **flo′ris·try** *n.*

floss /flaws, flos/ • *n.* **1** rough silk enveloping

a silkworm's cocoon. **2** silk thread used in embroidery. **3** = *dental floss*. • *v.tr.* (also *absol.*) clean (teeth) with dental floss.

floss·y /fláwsee, flósee/ *adj.* (**floss·i·er, floss·i·est**) **1** of or like floss. **2** *colloq.* fancy; showy.

flo·ta·tion /flōtáyshən/ *n.* (also **float·a'tion**) **1** process of launching or financing a commercial enterprise. **2** capacity to float.

flo·til·la /flōtílə/ *n.* small fleet of boats or naval vessels.

flot·sam /flótsəm/ *n.* wreckage floating at sea. □ **flotsam and jetsam 1** odds and ends; rubbish. **2** vagrants, etc.

flounce[1] /flowns/ • *v.intr.* go or move with an agitated, violent, or impatient motion. • *n.* flouncing movement.

flounce[2] /flowns/ *n.* wide ornamental strip of material gathered and sewn to a skirt, dress, etc.; frill.

floun·der[1] /flówndər/ *v.intr.* **1** struggle in mud, or as if in mud, or when wading. **2** perform a task badly or without knowledge. □□ **floun'der·er** *n.*

floun·der[2] /flówndər/ *n.* type of edible flatfish.

flour /flowər/ *n.* **1** meal or powder obtained by grinding grain, esp. wheat. **2** any fine powder. □□ **flour'y** *adj.* (**flour·i·er, flour·i·est**). **flour'i·ness** *n.*

flour·ish /flɔ́rish, flúr-/ • *v.* **1** *intr.* **a** grow vigorously; thrive. **b** prosper; be successful. **c** be in one's prime. **2** *tr.* wave (a weapon, one's limbs, etc.) vigorously. • *n.* **1** ostentatious gesture with a weapon, a hand, etc. (*removed his hat with a flourish*). **2** ornamental curving decoration of handwriting. **3** fanfare or ornate musical passage. □□ **flour'ish·er** *n.* **flour'ish·y** *adj.*

> **flourish** Middle English: from Old French *floriss-*, lengthened stem of *florir*, based on Latin *florere*, from *flos, flor-* 'a flower.' The noun senses 'ornamental curve' and 'florid expression' come from an obsolete sense of the verb, 'adorn' (originally with flowers).

flout /flowt/ • *v.tr.* express contempt for (the law, rules, etc.) by word or action; mock; insult. • *n.* flouting speech or act.
¶ See note at FLAUNT.

flow /flō/ • *v.intr.* **1** glide along as a stream. **2** gush out; spring; be spilled. **3** circulate. **4** move smoothly or steadily. **5** (of a garment, hair, etc.) hang easily or gracefully. **6** (often foll. by *from*) result from; be caused by. • *n.* **1 a** flowing movement in a stream. **b** flowing liquid. **c** copious outpouring; stream (*a continuous flow of complaints*). **d** hardened mass that formerly flowed. **2** rise of a tide or a river (*ebb and flow*). □ **flow chart** (or **diagram** or **sheet**) diagram of the movement or action of things or persons engaged in a complex activity.

flow·er /flowər/ • *n.* **1** part of a plant from which the fruit or seed is developed. **2** blossom, esp. on a stem and used in bunches for decoration. **3** plant cultivated or noted for its flowers. • *v.intr.* **1** bloom or blossom. **2** reach a peak. □ **the flower of** the best or best part of. □□ **flow'ered** *adj.* (also in *comb.*). **flow'er·less** *adj.* **flow'er·like** *adj.*

flow·er·pot /flówərpot/ *n.* pot for growing a plant.

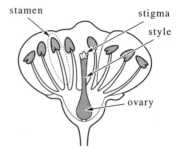

stamen   stigma

style

ovary

FLOWER, 1

flow·er·y /flówəree/ *adj.* **1** florally decorated. **2** (of style, speech, etc.) highly embellished; ornate. □□ **flow'er·i·ness** *n.*

flow·ing /flóing/ *adj.* **1** (of literary style, etc.) fluent; easy. **2** smoothly continuous; not abrupt. **3** (of hair, a garment, a sail, etc.) unconfined. □□ **flow'ing·ly** *adv.*

flown *past part.* of FLY[1].

fl. oz. *abbr.* fluid ounce(s).

flu /floo/ *n. colloq.* influenza.

fluc·tu·ate /flúkchoo-ayt/ *v.intr.* vary irregularly; be unstable; vacillate; rise and fall. □□ **fluc·tu·a·tion** /-áyshən/ *n.*

flue /floo/ *n.* **1** smoke duct in a chimney. **2** channel for conveying heat, esp. a hot-air passage in a wall.

flu·ent /flóoənt/ *adj.* **1** flowing naturally and readily. **2** verbally facile, esp. in a foreign language. □□ **flu'en·cy** *n.* **flu'ent·ly** *adv.*

fluff /fluf/ • *n.* **1** soft, light, feathery material coming off blankets, etc. **2** soft fur or feathers. **3** *sl.* mistake in a performance, etc. • *v.* **1** shake into or become a soft mass. **2** *colloq.* make a mistake in; blunder (*fluffed his opening line*).

fluff·y /flúfee/ *adj.* (**fluff·i·er, fluff·i·est**) **1** of or like fluff. **2** covered in fluff. **3** superficial. □□ **fluff'i·ly** *adv.* **fluff'i·ness** *n.*

flu·gel·horn /flóogəlhawrn/ *n.* valved brass wind instrument like a cornet but with a broader tone.

flu·id /flóoid/ • *n.* substance, esp. a gas or liquid, whose shape is determined by its container. • *adj.* **1** able to flow and alter shape freely. **2** constantly changing. □ **fluid ounce** see OUNCE. □□ **flu·id·i·fy** /-idifī/ *v.tr.* (**-fies, -fied**) **flu·id'i·ty** *n.* **flu'id·ly** *adv.* **flu'id·ness** *n.*

fluke[1] /flook/ *n.* lucky accident. □□ **fluk'y** *adj.* (**fluk·i·er, fluk·i·est**)

fluke[2] /flook/ *n.* **1** parasitic flatworm including liver flukes and blood flukes. **2** flatfish, esp. a flounder.

fluke[3] /flook/ *n.* **1** *Naut.* broad triangular plate on the arm of an anchor. **2** *Zool.* either of the lobes of a whale's tail.

flume /floom/ *n.* **1 a** artificial channel conveying water, etc. **b** water slide into a swimming pool, etc. **2** ravine with a stream.

flum·mox /flúməks/ *v.tr. colloq.* bewilder; disconcert.

flung *past* and *past part.* of FLING.

flunk /flungk/ *colloq.* • *v.* **1** *tr.* **a** fail (an examination, etc.). **b** fail (an examination candidate). **2** *intr.* (often foll. by *out*) fail utterly; give up. • *n.* instance of flunking.

flun·ky /flúngkee/ *n.* (also **flun′key**) (*pl.* **-kies** or **-keys**) usu. *derog.* **1** liveried servant. **2** toady. **3** underling.

flu·o·resce /flo͞orés, flaw-/ *v.intr.* be or become fluorescent.

flu·o·res·cence /flo͞orésəns, flaw-/ *n.* **1** light radiation from certain substances. **2** property of absorbing light of short (invisible) wavelength and emitting light of longer (visible) wavelength.

flu·o·res·cent /flo͞orésənt, flaw-/ *adj.* having or showing fluorescence. □ **fluorescent lamp** (or **bulb**) esp. tubular lamp or bulb giving light by fluorescence.

flu·o·ri·date /flo͞oridayt, fláw-/ *v.tr.* add fluoride to (drinking water, etc.). □□ **fluor·i·da·tion** /flo͞oridáyshən, fláw-/ *n.*

flu·o·ride /flo͞oríd, fláw-/ *n.* any binary compound of fluorine.

flu·o·rine /flo͞oreen, fláw-/ *n.* poisonous pale yellow gaseous element of the halogen group. ¶ Symb.: **F**.

flu·o·rite /flo͞orít, fláw-/ *n.* mineral form of calcium fluoride.

flu·o·ro·car·bon /flo͞orōkaʹarbən, fláw-/ *n.* compound of a hydrocarbon with fluorine atoms.

flur·ry /flə́ree, flúree/ • *n.* (*pl.* **-ries**) **1** gust or squall (esp. of snow). **2** sudden burst of activity. **3** commotion. • *v.tr.* (**-ries**, **-ried**) confuse by haste or noise; agitate.

flush[1] /flush/ • *v.* **1** *intr.* blush; redden. **2** *tr.* (usu. as **flushed** *adj.*) cause to glow, blush, or be elated. **3** *tr.* **a** cleanse (a drain, toilet, etc.) by a rushing flow of water. **b** dispose of (an object) in this way. **4** *intr.* rush out; spurt. • *n.* **1 a** blush. **b** glow of light or color. **2 a** rush of water. **b** cleansing by flushing. **3 a** rush of emotion. **b** elation produced by a victory, etc. **4** freshness; vigor. **5 a** (also **hot flush**) = *hot flash.* **b** feverish temperature. **c** facial redness, esp. caused by fever, alcohol, etc. □□ **flush′er** *n.*

flush[2] /flush/ *adj.* **1** in the same plane; even. **2** *colloq.* having plenty of money. □□ **flush′ness** *n.*

flush[3] /flush/ *n.* hand of cards all of one suit, esp. in poker.

flush[4] /flush/ *v.* **1** *tr.* cause (esp. a game bird) to fly up. **2** *intr.* fly up and away. □ **flush out 1** reveal. **2** drive out.

flus·ter /flústər/ • *v.* make or become nervous or confused. • *n.* confused or agitated state.

flute /flo͞ot/ *n.* **1** high-pitched wind instrument of metal or wood, having holes along it stopped by the fingers or keys. **2** cylindrical groove. □□ **flute′like** *adj.* **flut′ing** *n.* **flut′ist** *n.* (cf. FLAUTIST). **flut′y** *adj.* (in sense 1 of *n.*).

flut·ter /flútər/ • *v.* **1 a** *tr.* flap the wings in flying or trying to fly (*butterflies fluttered in the sunshine*). **b** *tr.* flap (the wings). **2** *intr.* fall with a quivering motion. **3** *intr.* & *tr.* move or cause to move irregularly or tremblingly. **4** *intr.* go about restlessly; flit; hover. **5** *tr.* agitate; confuse. **6** *intr.* (of a pulse or heartbeat) beat feebly or irregularly. • *n.* **1** act of fluttering. **2** tremulous state of excitement. □□ **flut′ter·er** *n.* **flut′ter·y** *adj.*

flu·vi·al /flo͞oveeəl/ *adj.* of or produced by a river or rivers.

flux /fluks/ *n.* **1** process of flowing or flowing out. **2** continuous change (*in a state of flux*). **3** *Metallurgy* substance mixed with a metal, etc., to promote fusion.

fly[1] /flī/ • *v.* (**flies**; *past* **flew** /flo͞o/; *past part.* **flown** /flōn/) **1** *intr.* move through the air under control, esp. with wings. **2** (of an aircraft or its occupants): **a** *intr.* travel through the air or through space. **b** *tr.* traverse (a region or distance) (*flew the Pacific*). **3** *tr.* operate a flying vehicle. **4** *tr.* & *intr.* wave or flutter. **5** *intr.* **a** flee. **b** *colloq.* depart hastily. **6** *intr.* hasten or spring violently. **7** *tr.* flee from. **8** *intr. Baseball* hit a fly ball. • *n.* (*pl.* **-ies**) **1 a** flap on a garment, esp. trousers, to contain or cover a fastening. **b** this fastening. **2** flap at the entrance of a tent. **3** (in *pl.*) space over the proscenium in a theater. **4** *Baseball* batted ball hit high in the air. □ **fly-by-night** *adj.* **1** unreliable. **2** short-lived. • *n.* unreliable person. **fly off the handle** *colloq.* lose one's temper suddenly and unexpectedly. □□ **fly′a·ble** *adj.*

fly[2] /flī/ *n.* (*pl.* **flies**) **1** insect with two usu. transparent wings. **2** natural or artificial fly used as bait in fishing. □ **fly-fish** *v.intr.* fish with a fly. **fly in the ointment** minor irritation that spoils enjoyment.

fly·ing /flī-ing/ • *adj.* **1** fluttering or waving in the air; hanging loose. **2** hasty; brief (*a flying visit*). **3** designed for rapid movement. **4** (of an animal) able to make very long leaps by using winglike membranes, etc. • *n.* flight, esp. in an aircraft. □ **flying buttress** buttress slanting from a separate column, usu. forming an arch with the wall it supports. **flying fish** tropical fish with winglike pectoral fins for gliding through the air. **flying saucer** any unidentified, esp. circular, flying object, popularly supposed to have come from space.

fly·leaf /flīleef/ *n.* (*pl.* **-leaves**) blank leaf at the beginning or end of a book.

fly·pa·per /flīpaypər/ *n.* sticky treated paper for catching flies.

fly·trap /flītrap/ *n.* any of various plants that catch flies, esp. the Venus flytrap.

fly·weight /flīwayt/ *n.* weight class between light flyweight and bantamweight for competitors in certain sports.

fly·wheel /flīhweel, -weel/ *n.* heavy wheel on a revolving shaft used to regulate machinery or accumulate power.

FM *abbr.* **1** frequency modulation. **2** Field Marshal.

Fm *symb. Chem.* fermium.

FNMA /fáneemáy/ *n.* Federal National Mortgage Association.

f-num·ber /éf numbər/ *n.* (also **f-stop**) *Photog.* ratio of the focal length to the effective diameter of a lens.

foal /fōl/ • *n.* young of a horse or related animal. • *v.tr.* (of a mare, etc.) give birth to (a foal).

foam /fōm/ • *n.* **1** mass of small bubbles formed on or in liquid. **2** froth of saliva or sweat. **3** substance resembling these, e.g., rubber or plastic in a cellular mass. • *v.intr.* **1** emit foam; froth. **2** run with foam. □□ **foam′less** *adj.* **foam′y** *adj.* (**foam·i·er, foam·i·est**).

fob[1] /fob/ *n.* **1** (in full **fob chain**) chain of a pocket watch. **2** small pocket. **3** tab on a key ring.

fob[2] /fob/ *v.tr.* (**fobbed, fob·bing**) cheat; deceive. □ **fob off** deceive into accepting something inferior.

fo·cal /fōkəl/ *adj.* of, at, or in terms of a focus.

□ **focal distance** (or **length**) distance between the center of a mirror or lens and its focus. **focal point** = FOCUS *n.* 1.

fo'c's'le var. of FORECASTLE.

fo·cus /fṓkəs/ • *n.* (*pl.* **fo·cus·es** or **fo·ci** /fṓsī/) **1** *Physics* a point at which rays or waves meet after reflection or refraction. **b** the point from which diverging rays or waves appear to proceed. Also called **focal point**. **2 a** *Optics* point at which an object must be situated for an image of it given by a lens or mirror to be well defined (*bring into focus*). **b** adjustment of the eye or a lens necessary to produce a clear image. **c** state of clear definition. **3** center of interest or activity. • *v.* (**fo·cused**, **fo·cus·ing**; **fo·cussed**, **fo·cus·sing**) **1** *tr.* bring into focus. **2** *tr.* adjust the focus of (a lens, the eye, etc.). **3** *tr.* & *intr.* concentrate or be concentrated on. □ **focus group** group that meets to discuss a particular problem, issue, etc. □□ **fo'cus·er** *n.*

fod·der /fódər/ *n.* dried hay, straw, etc., for cattle, horses, etc.

foe /fō/ *n.* enemy or opponent.

fog /fawg, fog/ • *n.* **1** thick cloud of water droplets or smoke suspended in the atmosphere at or near the earth's surface. **2** uncertain or confused position or state. • *v.* (**fogged, fog·ging**) **1** *tr.* cover with or confuse as if with a fog. **2** *intr.* become covered with fog or condensed vapor. □ **in a fog** puzzled; at a loss.

fo·gey var. of FOGY.

fog·gy /fáwgee, fógee/ *adj.* (**fog·gi·er, fog·gi·est**) **1** (of the atmosphere) thick or obscure with fog. **2** of or like fog. **3** vague; confused; unclear. □□ **fog'gi·ly** *adv.* **fog'gi·ness** *n.*

fog·horn /fáwghawrn, fóg-/ *n.* horn warning ships in fog.

fo·gy /fṓgee/ *n.* (also **fo'gey**) (*pl.* **-gies** or **-geys**) dull old-fashioned person (esp. *old fogy*). □□ **fo'gy·ish** *adj.*

foi·ble /fóybəl/ *n.* minor weakness or idiosyncrasy.

foil¹ /foyl/ *v.tr.* frustrate; baffle; defeat.

foil² /foyl/ *n.* **1** metal hammered or rolled into a thin sheet. **2** person or thing setting off another by contrast.

foil³ /foyl/ *n.* light blunt sword used in fencing.

foist /foyst/ *v.tr.* (foll. by *on, upon*) impose (an unwelcome person or thing).

fold¹ /fōld/ • *v.* **1** *tr.* **a** bend or close (a flexible thing) over upon itself. **b** (foll. by *back, over, down*) bend a part of (a flexible thing) in the manner specified (*fold down the flap*). **2** *intr.* become or be able to be folded. **3** *tr.* (foll. by *away, up*) make compact by folding. **4** *intr. colloq.* **a** collapse; disintegrate. **b** (of an enterprise) fail; go bankrupt. **5** *tr. poet.* embrace. **6** *tr.* clasp (the arms); wrap; envelop. • *n.* **1** line made by or for folding. **2** folded part. □□ **fold'a·ble** *adj.*

fold² /fōld/ • *n.* **1** = SHEEPFOLD. **2** body of believers or members of a church. • *v.tr.* enclose (sheep) in a fold.

-fold /fōld/ *suffix* forming adjectives and adverbs from cardinal numbers, meaning: **1** in an amount multiplied by (*repaid tenfold*). **2** consisting of so many parts (*threefold blessing*).

fold·er /fṓldər/ *n.* **1** folding cover or holder for loose papers. **2** folded leaflet.

fo·li·age /fṓleeij/ *n.* leaves; leafage.

fo·lic ac·id /fólik, fṓl-/ *n.* vitamin of the B complex, found in leafy green vegetables, liver, and kidney.

fo·li·o /fṓleeō/ *n.* (*pl.* **-os**) **1** leaf of paper, etc., esp. one numbered only on the front. **2 a** leaf number of a book. **b** page number of a book. **3** sheet of paper folded once, making two leaves of a book. **4** book made of such sheets.

folk /fōk/ *n.* (*pl.* **folk** or **folks**) **1** (treated as *pl.*) people in general or of a specified class (*rich and poor folks alike*). **2** (in *pl.*) (usu. **folks**) one's parents or relatives. **3** (treated as *sing.*) a people. **4** (*attrib.*) of popular origin; traditional (*folk art*). □ **folk dance** dance of traditional origin. **folk singer** singer of folk songs. **folk song** song of popular or traditional origin or style. **folk tale** popular or traditional story.

folk·lore /fṓklawr/ *n.* traditional beliefs and stories of a people; the study of these. □□ **folk'lor·ic** *adj.* **folk'lor·ist** *n.* **folk·lor·is'tic** *adj.*

folk·sy /fṓksee/ *adj.* (**folk·si·er, folk·si·est**) **1** friendly; informal. **2** of or like folk art, culture, etc. □□ **folk'si·ness** *n.*

fol·li·cle /fólikəl/ *n.* **1** small sac or vesicle. **2** small sac-shaped secretory gland or cavity. □□ **fol·lic·u·lar** /folíkyələr/ *adj.* **fol·lic·u·late** /folíkyələt, -layt/ *adj.*

fol·low /fólō/ *v.* **1** *tr.* & *intr.* go or come after (a person or thing proceeding ahead). **2** *tr.* go along (a route, path, etc.). **3** *tr.* & *intr.* come after in order or time (*dessert followed the main course*). **4** *tr.* take as a guide or leader. **5** *tr.* conform to. **6** *tr.* practice (a trade or profession). **7** *tr.* undertake (a course of study, etc.). **8** *tr.* understand. **9** *tr.* maintain awareness of the current state or progress of (events, etc., in a particular sphere). **10** *tr.* provide with a sequel or successor. **11** *intr.* **a** be necessarily true as a result of something else. **b** be a result of. □ **follow through 1** continue (an action, etc.) to its conclusion. **2** *Sports* continue the movement of a stroke after the ball has been struck. **follow-through** *n.* action of following through. **follow up 1** (foll. by *with*) pursue; develop; supplement. **2** make further investigation of. **follow-up** *n.* subsequent or continued action.

fol·low·er /fólōər/ *n.* **1** adherent or devotee. **2** person or thing that follows.

fol·low·ing /fólōing/ • *prep.* after in time; as a sequel to. • *n.* adherents or devotees. • *adj.* that follows or comes after.

fol·ly /fólee/ *n.* (*pl.* **-lies**) **1** foolishness; lack of good sense. **2** foolish act, behavior, idea, etc.

fo·ment /fōmént/ *v.tr.* instigate or stir up (trouble, sedition, etc.). □□ **fo·men·ta·tion** /fōmentáyshən/ *n.* **fo·ment'er** *n.*

fond /fond/ *adj.* **1** (foll. by *of*) having affection or a liking for. **2** affectionate; loving; doting. **3** (of beliefs, etc.) foolishly optimistic or credulous; naive. □□ **fond'ly** *adv.* **fond'ness** *n.*

fon·dant /fóndənt/ *n.* soft creamy candy of flavored sugar.

fon·dle /fónd'l/ *v.tr.* caress. □□ **fon'dler** *n.*

fon·due /fondōó, -dyōó/ *n.* dish of flavored melted cheese.

font¹ /font/ *n.* **1** receptacle in a church for baptismal water. **2** reservoir for oil in a lamp. □□ **font'al** *adj.* (in sense 1).

font² /font/ *Printing* set of type of one face or size.

fon·ta·nel /fóntənél/ *n.* (also **fon·ta·nelle'**)

membranous space in an infant's skull at the angles of the parietal bones.

food /food/ • *n.* **1** nutritious substance, esp. solid in form, ingested to maintain life and growth. **2** mental stimulus. □ **food chain** *Ecol.* series of organisms each dependent on the next for food. **food processor** machine for chopping and mixing food.

food·stuff /foodstuf/ *n.* any substance suitable as food.

fool /fool/ • *n.* **1** person who acts unwisely or imprudently; stupid person. **2** *hist.* jester; clown. **3** dupe. • *v.* **1** *tr.* deceive. **2** *tr.* trick; dupe. **3** *intr.* act in a joking or teasing way. **4** *intr.* behave in a playful or silly way.

fool·har·dy /foolhaardee/ *adj.* (**fool·har·di·er, fool·har·di·est**) rashly or foolishly bold; reckless. □□ **fool'har·di·ly** *adv.* **fool'har·di·ness** *n.*

fool·ish /foolish/ *adj.* lacking good sense or judgment; unwise. □□ **fool'ish·ly** *adv.* **fool'ish·ness** *n.*

fool·proof /foolproof/ *adj.* (of a procedure, mechanism, etc.) incapable of misuse or mistake.

foot /foot/ • *n.* (*pl.* **feet** /feet/) **1 a** lower extremity of the leg below the ankle. **b** part of a sock, etc., covering the foot. **2** lowest or endmost part. **3** step, pace, or tread (*fleet of foot*). **4** (*pl.* **feet** or **foot**) unit of linear measure equal to 12 inches (30.48 cm). **5** *Prosody* a group of syllables (one usu. stressed) constituting a metrical unit. **b** similar unit of speech, etc. • *v. tr.* pay (a bill). □ **foot-and-mouth disease** contagious viral disease of cattle, etc. **have one's** (or **both**) **feet on the ground** be practical. **my foot!** *int.* expressing strong contradiction. **on foot** walking; not riding, etc. **put one's foot down** *colloq.* **1** be firmly insistent or repressive. **2** accelerate a motor vehicle. □□ **foot'ed** *adj.* (also in *comb.*). **foot'less** *adj.*

foot·age /footij/ *n.* **1** length or distance in feet. **2** amount of film made for showing, broadcasting, etc.

foot·ball /footbawl/ *n.* **1** team game played with an inflated oval ball. **2** ball used in this. □□ **foot'ball·er** *n.*

foot·bridge /footbrij/ *n.* bridge for use by pedestrians.

foot·fall /footfawl/ *n.* sound of a footstep.

foot·hill /foot-hil/ *n.* (often in *pl.*) any of the low hills around the base of a mountain.

foot·hold /foot-hōld/ *n.* **1** place, esp. in climbing, where a foot can be supported securely. **2** secure initial position.

foot·ing /footing/ *n.* **1** foothold; secure position (*lost his footing*). **2** basis on which an enterprise is established or operates; relative position or status.

foot·lights /footlīts/ *n.pl.* row of lights along the front of a stage at the level of the actors' feet.

foot·lock·er /footlokər/ *n.* small trunk usu. kept at the foot of a soldier's or camper's bunk.

foot·loose /footloos/ *adj.* free to act as one pleases.

foot·note /footnōt/ *n.* note printed at the foot of a page.

foot·path /footpath/ *n.* trail or path for pedestrians.

foot·print /footprint/ *n.* **1** impression left by a foot or shoe. **2** *Computing* area of desk space,

etc., occupied by a computer or other piece of hardware.

foot·race /foot-rays/ *n.* race run by people on foot.

foot·step /footstep/ *n.* **1** step taken in walking. **2** sound of this. □ **follow** (or **tread**) **in a person's footsteps** do as another person did before.

foot·stool /footstool/ *n.* stool for resting the feet on when sitting.

foot·wear /footwair/ *n.* shoes, socks, etc.

foot·work /footwork/ *n.* use of the feet, esp. skillfully, in sports, dancing, etc.

fop /fop/ *n.* affectedly elegant or fashionable man; dandy. □□ **fop'per·y** *n.* **fop'pish** *adj.* **fop'pish·ly** *adv.* **fop'pish·ness** *n.*

for /fawr, fər/ • *prep.* **1** in the interest or to the benefit of; intended to go to. **2** in defense, support, or favor of. **3** suitable or appropriate to. **4** regarding. **5** representing or in place of. **6** in exchange against. **7** at the price of. **8** as a consequence of. **9 a** with a view to; in the hope or quest of. **b** on account of. **10** to reach; toward (*ran for home*). **11** through or over (a distance or period). **12** as being (*for the last time*). **13** in spite of. **14** considering or making due allowance in respect of. • *conj.* because; since.

for- /fawr, fər/ *prefix* forming verbs and their derivatives meaning: **1** away; off; (*forget*). **2** prohibition (*forbid*). **3** abstention or neglect (*forgo*). **4** excess or intensity (*forlorn*).

for·age /fawrij, fór-/ • *n.* **1** food for horses and cattle. **2** act or an instance of searching for food. • *v.* **1** *intr.* go searching; rummage (esp. for food). **2** *tr.* obtain food from; plunder. □□ **for'ag·er** *n.*

for·ay /fawray, fór-/ • *n.* sudden attack; raid or incursion. • *v.intr.* make or go on a foray.

for·bade (also **for·bad'**) *past* of FORBID.

for·bear[1] /fawrbáir/ *v.* (*past* **for·bore** /-báwr/; *past part.* **for·borne** /-báwrn/-) *literary* abstain or desist (from) (*forbore to mention it*).

for·bear[2] *var.* of FOREBEAR.

for·bear·ance /fawrbáirəns/ *n.* patient self-control; tolerance.

for·bid /fərbíd, fawr-/ *v.tr.* (**for·bid·ding**; *past* **for·bade** /-bád, -báyd/ or **for·bad** /-bád/; *past part.* **for·bid·den** /-bíd'n/) **1** (foll. by *to* + infin.) order not (*I forbid you to go*). **2** refuse to allow. □□ **for·bid·dance** /-dəns/ *n.*

for·bid·ding /fərbíding, fawr-/ *adj.* uninviting; repellent; stern. □□ **for·bid'ding·ly** *adv.*

for·bore *past* of FORBEAR[1].

for·borne *past part.* of FORBEAR[1].

force /fawrs/ • *n.* **1** power; exerted strength or impetus; intense effort. **2** coercion; compulsion. **3 a** military strength. **b** organized body of soldiers, police, etc. **4** binding power; validity. **5** effect; precise significance. **6** mental or moral strength; efficacy. **7** *Physics* influence tending to cause the motion of a body. **8** person or thing regarded as exerting influence. • *v.tr.* **1** compel or coerce (a person). **2** break open or into by force. **3** drive or propel violently or against resistance. **4** impose or press (on a person). **5** cause, produce, or attain by effort (*forced a smile*). **6** strain or increase to the utmost; overstrain. □ **in force 1** valid; effective. **2** in great strength or numbers. □□ **force'a·ble** *adj.* **forc'er** *n.*

forced /fawrst/ *adj.* **1** obtained or imposed by force (*forced entry*). **2** (of a gesture, etc.) affected; unnatural.

force·ful /fáwrsfŏŏl/ *adj.* **1** vigorous; powerful. **2** (of speech) compelling; impressive. □□ **force′ful·ly** *adv.* **force′ful·ness** *n.*

force ma·jeure /fáwrs maᴢhŏr̂/ *n.* unforeseeable course of events excusing a person from the fulfillment of a contract.

for·ceps /fáwrseps/ *n.* (*pl.* same) surgical pincers.

FORCEPS

for·ci·ble /fáwrsibəl/ *adj.* done by or involving force; forceful. □□ **for′ci·ble·ness** *n.* **for′ci·bly** *adv.*

ford /fawrd/ • *n.* shallow water crossing, as in a river. • *v.tr.* cross (water) at a ford. □□ **ford′a·ble** *adj.* **ford′less** *adj.*

fore /fawr/ • *adj.* situated in front. • *n.* front part, esp. of a ship; bow. • *int.* Golf warning to a person in the path of a ball. □ **fore-and-aft** *adj.* (of a sail or rigging) set lengthwise, not on the yards.

fore- /fawr/ *prefix* forming: **1** verbs meaning: **a** in front (*foreshorten*). **b** beforehand (*forewarn*). **2** nouns meaning: **a** situated in front of (*forecourt*). **b** front part of (*forehead*).

fore·arm /fáwraarm/ *n.* part of the arm from the elbow to the wrist or the fingertips.

fore·bear /fáwrbair/ *n.* (also **fore′bear**) (usu. in *pl.*) ancestor.

fore·bode /fawrbŏd/ *v.tr.* **1** betoken; be an advance warning of. **2** have a presentiment of (usu. evil).

fore·bod·ing /fawrbŏding/ *n.* expectation of trouble or evil; presage or omen. □□ **fore·bod′ing·ly** *adv.*

fore·cast /fáwrkast/ • *v.tr.* (*past* and *past part.* -**cast** or -**cast·ed**) predict. • *n.* calculation or estimate of something future, esp. coming weather.□□ **fore′cast·er** *n.*

fore·cas·tle /fŏksəl/ *n.* (also **fo′c's'le**) *Naut.* forward part of a ship where the crew has quarters.

fore·close /fawrklŏz/ *v.tr.* **1** repossess mortgaged property when a loan is not duly repaid. **2** exclude. □□ **fore·clo·sure** /-klŏᴢhər/ *n.*

fore·fa·ther /fáwrfaathər/ *n.* (usu. in *pl.*) ancestor.

fore·fin·ger /fáwrfinggər/ *n.* finger next to the thumb.

fore·foot /fáwrfŏŏt/ *n.* (*pl.* -**feet**) front foot of an animal.

fore·front /fáwrfrunt/ *n.* **1** foremost part. **2** leading position.

fore·go[1] /fáwrgŏ/ (-**goes**; *past* -**went** /-wént/; *past part.* -**gone** /-gón/) precede in place or time.

fore·go[2] var. of FORGO.

fore·go·ing /fáwrgŏing/ *adj.* preceding; previously mentioned.

fore·gone /fáwrgawn, -gón/ *past part.* of FOREGO[1]. • *attrib.adj.* previous; preceding; completed. □ **foregone conclusion** easily foreseen or predictable result.

fore·ground /fáwrgrownd/ *n.* **1** part of a view that is nearest the observer. **2** most conspicuous position.

fore·hand /fáwrhand/ *n.* *Tennis, etc.* **1** stroke played with the palm of the hand facing the opponent. **2** (*attrib.*) (also **fore′hand′ed**) of or made with a forehand.

fore·head /fáwrid, -hed, fór-/ *n.* part of the face above the eyebrows.
¶ Traditionally, **forehead** was pronounced with the stress on the first syllable and with the *h* silent, so that it almost rhymed with *horrid*. But today many pronounce it sounding the *h* and giving the element *head* secondary stress.

for·eign /fáwrin, fór-/ *adj.* **1** of, from, in, or characteristic of a country or a language other than one's own. **2** dealing with other countries (*foreign service*). **3** unfamiliar; strange. **4** coming from outside (*foreign body*). □□ **for′eign·ness** *n.*

for·eign·er /fáwrinər, fór-/ *n.* person born in or coming from a foreign country or place.

fore·leg /fáwrleg/ *n.* each of the front legs of a quadruped.

fore·lock /fáwrlok/ *n.* lock of hair just above the forehead.

fore·man /fáwrmən/ *n.* (*pl.* -**men**) **1** worker supervising others. **2** presiding juror in a legal trial.

fore·mast /fáwrmast, -məst/ *n.* forward mast of a ship.

fore·most /fáwrmŏst/ • *adj.* **1** chief or most notable. **2** first; front. • *adv.* most importantly (*first and foremost*).

fo·ren·sic /fərénsik, -zik/ *adj.* **1** of or used in courts of law. **2** *disp.* of or involving forensic science. □□ **fo·ren′si·cal·ly** *adv.*

fore·play /fáwrplay/ *n.* stimulation preceding sexual intercourse.

fore·run·ner /fáwr-runər/ *n.* **1** predecessor. **2** herald.

fore·see /fáwrsee/ *v.tr.* (*past* -**saw** /-sáw/; *past part.* -**seen** /-seén/) see or be aware of beforehand. □□ **fore·see′a·ble** *adj.* **fore·se·er** /-seéər/ *n.*

fore·shad·ow /fáwrshádŏ/ *v.tr.* be a warning or indication of (a future event).

fore·short·en /fáwrsháwrt'n/ *v.tr.* show or portray (an object) with the apparent shortening due to visual perspective.

fore·sight /fáwrsīt/ *n.* **1** regard or provision for the future. **2** process of foreseeing. □□ **fore·sight·ed** /-sítid/ *adj.* **fore′sight·ed·ly** *adv.* **fore′sight·ed·ness** *n.*

fore·skin /fáwrskin/ *n.* fold of skin covering the end of the penis. Also called **prepuce**.

for·est /fáwrist, fór-/ *n.* large area of trees and undergrowth. • *v.tr.* **1** plant with trees. **2** convert into a forest. □□ **for′est·er** *n.*

fore·stall /fáwrstáwl/ *v.tr.* **1** act in advance of in order to prevent. **2** anticipate. ☐☐ **fore‑stall′er** *n.* **fore‑stall′ment** *n.*

for‑est‑ry /fáwristree, fór‑/ *n.* **1** science or management of forests. **2** wooded country; forests.

fore‑taste ● *n.* /fáwrtayst/ partial enjoyment or suffering in advance. ● *v.tr.* /fáwrtáyst/ taste beforehand.

fore‑tell /fáwrtél/ *v.tr.* (*past* and *past part.* **‑told** /‑tóld/) **1** predict; prophesy. **2** presage. ☐☐ **fore‑tell′er** *n.*

fore‑thought /fáwrthawt/ *n.* **1** care or provision for the future. **2** previous thinking or devising. **3** deliberate intention.

for‑ev‑er /fərévər, fawr‑/ *adv.* continually; persistently.

fore‑warn /fáwrwáwrn/ *v.tr.* warn beforehand. ☐☐ **fore‑warn′er** *n.*

forewent *past* of FOREGO¹, FOREGO².

fore‑wom‑an /fáwrwŏōmən/ *n.* (*pl.* **‑wom‑en**) **1** female worker supervising others. **2** jury spokeswoman.

fore‑word /fáwrwərd/ *n.* introductory remarks at the beginning of a book, often by a person other than the author.

for‑feit /fáwrfit/ ● *n.* **1** penalty. **2** something surrendered as a penalty. ● *adj.* lost or surrendered as a penalty. ● *v.tr.* lose the right to; have to pay as a penalty. ☐☐ **for′feit‑a‑ble** *adj.* **for′feit‑er** *n.* **for‑fei‑ture** /‑fichər/ *n.*

for‑gath‑er /fáwrgáthər/ *v.intr.* (also **fore‑gath′er**) assemble; meet together; associate.

for‑gave *past* of FORGIVE.

forge¹ /fawrj/ ● *v.tr.* **1** make or write in fraudulent imitation. **2** shape (esp. metal) by heating in a fire and hammering. ● *n.* **1** furnace or workshop for melting or refining metal. ☐☐ **forge′a‑ble** *adj.* **forg′er** *n.*

forge² /fawrj/ *v.intr.* move forward gradually or steadily. ☐ **forge ahead 1** take the lead. **2** strive and progress.

forg‑er‑y /fáwrjəree/ *n.* (*pl.* **‑ies**) **1** act or an instance of forging. **2** forged or spurious document; signature, etc.

for‑get /fərgét/ *v.* (**for‑get‑ting**; *past* **for‑got** /‑gót/; *past part.* **for‑got‑ten** /‑gót′n/ or **for‑got**) **1** *tr.* & *intr.* lose the remembrance of. **2** *tr.* overlook; neglect. **3** *tr.* (also *absol.*) cease to think of (*forgive and forget*). ☐ **forget‑me‑not** plant with small yellow‑eyed bright blue flowers. ☐☐ **for‑get′ta‑ble** *adj.* **for‑get′ter** *n.*

for‑get‑ful /fərgétfŏŏl/ *adj.* **1** apt to forget; absent‑minded. **2** forgetting; neglectful. ☐☐ **for‑get′ful‑ly** *adv.* **for‑get′ful‑ness** *n.*

for‑give /fərgív/ *v.tr.* (*past* **for‑gave**; *past part.* **for‑giv‑en**) cease to feel angry or resentful toward; pardon. ☐☐ **for‑giv′a‑ble** *adj.* **for‑giv′a‑bly** *adv.* **for‑give′ness** *n.* **for‑giv′er** *n.*

for‑giv‑ing /fərgíving/ *adj.* inclined readily to forgive. ☐☐ **for‑giv′ing‑ly** *adv.*

for‑go /fáwrgó/ *v.tr.* (also **fore‑go′**) (**‑goes**; *past* **‑went** /‑wént/; *past part.* **‑gone** /‑gáwn, ‑gón/) go without; relinquish.

for‑got *past* of FORGET.

for‑got‑ten *past part.* of FORGET.

fork /fawrk/ ● *n.* **1** instrument with two or more prongs used in eating or cooking. **2** similar much larger instrument used for digging, lifting, etc. **3 a** divergence of anything, e.g., a stick, road, or river, into two parts. **b** place where this occurs. **c** either of the two parts. ● *v.* **1** *intr.* diverge into two parts. **2** *tr.* dig or lift, etc., with

a fork. ☐ **fork out** (or **over** or **up**) *sl.* hand over or pay, usu. reluctantly.

forked /fawrkt/ *adj.* **1** having a fork or forklike end or branches. **2** divergent; cleft. **3** (in *comb.*) having so many prongs (*three‑forked*).

fork‑lift /fáwrklift/ *n.* vehicle with a horizontal fork in front for lifting and carrying loads.

for‑lorn /fawrláwrn/ *adj.* **1** sad and abandoned or lonely. **2** in a pitiful state. ☐☐ **for‑lorn′ly** *adv.* **for‑lorn′ness** *n.*

form /fawrm/ ● *n.* **1** shape; arrangement of parts. **2** person or animal as visible or tangible. **3** mode in which a thing exists or manifests itself. **4** species, kind, or variety. **5** document to be filled in. **6** correct procedure. **7** (of an athlete, horse, etc.) condition of health and training. **8** general state or disposition (*in great form*). **9** *Gram.* one of the ways in which a word may be spelled or pronounced or inflected. **10** arrangement; style. ● *v.* **1** *tr.* make or fashion. **2** *intr.* take a certain shape; be formed. **3** *tr.* make up or constitute. **4** *tr.* train or instruct. **5** *tr.* develop or establish. **6** *tr.* embody; organize. ☐☐ **form′less** *adj.* **form′less‑ly** *adv.*

‑form /fawrm/ *comb. form* (usu. as **‑iform**) forming adjectives meaning having the form of (*cruciform*; *cuneiform*).

for‑mal /fáwrməl/ ● *adj.* **1** in accordance with rules, convention, or ceremony. **2** precise or symmetrical (*formal garden*). **3** prim; stiff in manner. **4** explicit or official (*formal agreement*). ● *n.* **1** evening dress. **2** occasion on which evening dress is worn. ☐☐ **for′mal‑ly** *adv.*

form‑al‑de‑hyde /fawrmáldihīd/ *n.* colorless pungent gas used as a disinfectant and preservative. ¶ Chem. formula: CH_2O. Also called **methanal.**

for‑ma‑lin /fáwrməlin/ *n.* colorless solution of formaldehyde in water used as a preservative for biological specimens, etc.

for‑mal‑ism /fáwrməlizəm/ *n.* **1** excessive adherence to prescribed forms. **2** *derog.* an artist's concentration on form at the expense of content. ☐☐ **for′mal‑ist** *n.* **for‑mal‑is′tic** *adj.*

for‑mal‑i‑ty /fawrmálitee/ *n.* (*pl.* **‑ties**) **1 a** formal, esp. meaningless, procedure or custom. **b** thing done simply to comply with a rule. **2** rigid observance of rules or convention.

for‑mal‑ize /fáwrməlīz/ *v.tr.* **1** give definite shape or legal formality to. **2** make formal. ☐☐ **for‑mal‑i‑za‑tion** /‑lizáyshən/ *n.*

for‑mat /fáwrmat/ ● *n.* **1** shape and size of a book, periodical, etc. **2** style or arrangement. ● *v.tr.* (**for‑mat‑ted, for‑mat‑ting**) arrange or put into a format.

for‑ma‑tion /fawrmáyshən/ *n.* **1** forming. **2** thing formed. **3** particular arrangement, e.g., of troops. ☐☐ **for‑ma′tion‑al** *adj.*

form‑a‑tive /fáwrmətiv/ *adj.* serving to form or fashion; of formation. ☐☐ **form′a‑tive‑ly** *adv.*

for‑mer /fáwrmər/ *attrib.adj.* **1** of the past; earlier; previous. **2** (prec. by *the*) the first or first mentioned of two.
¶ When two previously mentioned items are referred to, the one named first is the **former**, the second the **latter**: *The menu offered coconut‑crusted shrimp and barbecued ribs—the former decidedly sweet, the latter absolutely mild.* If there are three or more, **first, second,** (**etc.**) and **last** should be used, even if all are not mentioned:

Of winter, spring, and summer, I find the last most enjoyable.

for·mer·ly /fáwrmərlee/ *adv.* in the past; in former times.

For·mi·ca /fawrmíkə/ *n. propr.* hard, durable, plastic laminate used for working surfaces, cupboard doors, etc.

for·mi·da·ble /fáwrmidəbəl, *disp.* formídəbəl/ *adj.* 1 inspiring fear or dread. 2 inspiring respect or awe. 3 hard to overcome or deal with. □□ **for'mi·da·ble·ness** *n.* **for'mi·da·bly** *adv.*

for·mu·la /fáwrmyələ/ *n.* (*pl.* **for·mu·las** or (esp. in senses 1, 2) **for·mu·lae** /-lee/) 1 *Chem.* chemical symbols showing the constituents of a substance. 2 *Math.* mathematical rule expressed in symbols. 3 fixed form, esp. of words used on social or ceremonial occasions. 4 a list of ingredients. b infant's liquid food preparation. □□ **for·mu·la·ic** /-láyik/ *adj.* **for·mu·lar·ize** /-lərīz/ *v.tr.* **for'mu·lize** *v.tr.*

for·mu·late /fáwrmyəlayt/ *v.tr.* 1 express in a formula. 2 express clearly and precisely. □□ **for·mu·la·tion** /-láyshən/ *n.*

for·ni·cate /fáwrnikayt/ *v.intr.* (of people not married or not married to each other) have sexual intercourse voluntarily. □□ **for·ni·ca·tion** /-kayshən/ *n.* **for'ni·ca·tor** *n.*

for·sake /fərsáyk, fawr-/ *v.tr.* (*past* **for·sook** /-sŏók/; *past part.* **for·sak·en** /-sáykən/) 1 give up; break off from; renounce. 2 desert; abandon. □□ **for·sak'en·ness** *n.* **for·sak'er** *n.*

for·sooth /fərsŏóth, fawr-/ *adv. archaic* or *joc.* truly; in truth.

for·swear /fáwrswáir/ *v.tr.* (*past* **for·swore** /-swáwr/; *past part.* **for·sworn** /-swáwrn/) 1 renounce. 2 commit perjury.

for·syth·i·a /fawrsítheeə/ *n.* ornamental shrub bearing bright yellow flowers in early spring.

fort /fawrt/ *n.* fortified building or position.

forte[1] /fawrt, fáwrtay/ *n.* person's strong point; a thing in which a person excels.

for·te[2] /fórtay/ *Mus.* • *adj.* performed loudly. • *adv.* loudly.

forth /fawrth/ *adv. archaic* except in set phrases and after certain verbs, esp. *bring, come, go,* and *set.* 1 forward; into view. 2 (often in *comb.*) onward in time (*henceforth*).

forth·com·ing /fáwrthkúming/ *attrib. adj.* 1 coming or available soon. 2 (often in *comb.*) produced when wanted. 3 (of a person) informative; responsive.

forth·right /fáwrthrít/ *adj.* direct and outspoken; straightforward. □□ **forth·right'ly** *adv.* **forth'right·ness** *n.*

forth·with /fáwrthwíth, -wíth/ *adv.* without delay.

for·ti·fy /fáwrtifī/ *v.tr.* (**-fies, -fied**) 1 provide or equip with military defense. 2 strengthen or invigorate physically, mentally, or morally. 3 strengthen (wine) with alcohol. 4 increase the nutritive value of (food, esp. with vitamins). □□ **for'ti·fi·a·ble** *adj.* **for·ti·fi·ca'tion** *n.* **for'ti·fi·er** *n.*

for·tis·si·mo /fawrtísimō/ *Mus.* • *adj.* performed very loudly. • *adv.* very loudly.

for·ti·tude /fáwrtitŏod, -tyŏod/ *n.* courage in pain or adversity.

fort·night /fáwrtnīt/ *n.* period of fourteen days; two weeks. □□ **fort'night·ly** *adj.* & *adv.*

for·tress /fáwrtris/ *n.* fortified building or town.

for·tu·i·tous /fawrtŏóitəs, -tyŏó-/ *adj.* due to or characterized by chance; accidental; casual. □□ **for·tu'i·tous·ly** *adv.* **for·tu'i·tous·ness** *n.* **for·tu'i·ty** *n.*

for·tu·nate /fáwrchənət/ *adj.* 1 favored by fortune; lucky; prosperous. 2 auspicious; favorable. □□ **for'tu·nate·ly** *adv.*

for·tune /fáwrchən/ *n.* 1 a chance or luck as a force in human affairs. b person's destiny. 2 (in *sing.* or *pl.*) good or bad luck that befalls a person or an enterprise. 3 good luck. 4 prosperity; riches. □ **fortune-teller** person who claims to predict future events in a person's life. **fortune-telling** practice of this.

for·ty /fáwrtee/ • *n.* (*pl.* **-ties**) 1 product of four and ten. 2 symbol for this (40, xl, XL). 3 (in *pl.*) numbers from 40 to 49, esp. as years. • *adj.* that amount to forty. □□ **for'ti·eth** *adj.* & *n. adj.* & *adv.*

fo·rum /fáwrəm/ *n.* 1 place, agency, or meeting for public discussion. 2 *hist.* public square in an ancient Roman city.

for·ward /fáwrwərd/ • *adj.* 1 lying in one's line of motion. 2 onward or toward the front. 3 precocious; bold in manner; presumptuous. 4 *Commerce* relating to the future (*forward contract*). • *n.* attacking player positioned near the front of a team in football, hockey, etc. • *adv.* 1 to the front; into prominence. 2 in advance; ahead (*sent them forward*). 3 onward. 4 (also **for'wards**) a toward the front in the direction one is facing. b in the normal direction of motion. • *v.tr.* 1 send (a letter, etc.) on to a further destination. 2 help to advance; promote. □□ **for'ward·er** *n.* **for'ward·ly** *adv.* **for'ward·ness** *n.* (esp. in sense 3 of *adj.*).

for·went *past* of FORGO.

fos·sil /fósəl/ • *n.* 1 remains or impression of a (usu. prehistoric) plant or animal hardened in rock. 2 *colloq.* antiquated or unchanging person or thing. • *adj.* 1 of or like a fossil. 2 antiquated; out of date. □ **fossil fuel** natural fuel such as coal or gas. □□ **fos'sil·ize** *v.* **fos·sil·i·za'tion** *n.*

fos·ter /fáwstər, fós-/ • *v.tr.* 1 a promote the growth or development of. b encourage or harbor (a feeling). 2 (of circumstances) be favorable to. 3 bring up (a child that is not one's own by birth). • *adj.* 1 having a family connection by fostering (*foster child*). 2 concerned with fostering a child (*foster care*). □□ **fos'ter·age** *n.* (esp. in sense 3 of *v.*). **fos'ter·er** *n.*

fought *past* and *past part.* of FIGHT.

foul /fowl/ • *adj.* 1 offensive; loathsome; stinking. 2 dirty; soiled; filthy. 3 *colloq.* revolting; disgusting. 4 noxious. 5 disgustingly abusive or offensive. 6 against the rules. 7 rough; stormy. • *n. Sports* unfair or invalid stroke or action. • *adv.* unfairly. • *v.* 1 *tr.* & *intr.* make or become foul or dirty. 2 a *tr. Sports* commit a foul against (a player). b commit a foul. 3 a *tr.* cause to become entangled or blocked. b *intr.* become entangled. 4 *tr.* bungle. □ **foul mouth** person who uses offensive language. **foul play 1** unfair play in games. 2 treacherous or violent activity, esp. murder. **foul-up** muddle or bungle. □□ **foul'ly** *adv.* **foul'ness** *n.*

found[1] *past* and *past part.* of FIND.

found[2] /fownd/ *v.* 1 *tr.* establish; originate; initiate. 2 a *tr.* construct or base (a story, theory, rule, etc.) on. **b** *intr.* have a basis in. □□ **found′er** *n.* **found′er•ship** *n.*

found[3] /fownd/ *v.tr.* **1 a** melt and mold (metal). **b** fuse (materials for glass). **2** make by founding. □□ **found′er** *n.*

foun•da•tion /fowndáyshən/ *n.* **1 a** solid ground or base on which a building rests. **b** (usu. in *pl.*) lowest load-bearing part of a building. **2** material base. **3** basis or underlying principle. **4 a** establishment (esp. of an endowed institution). **b** such an institution, e.g., a college or hospital. □□ **foun•da′tion•al** *adj.*

found•er /fówndər/ *v.* **1 a** *intr.* (of a ship) fill with water and sink. **b** *tr.* cause (a ship) to founder. **2** *intr.* (of a plan, etc.) fail. **3** *intr.* (of a horse or its rider) fall to the ground, fall from lameness, stick fast in mud, etc.

found•ling /fówndling/ *n.* abandoned infant of unknown parentage.

found•ry /fówndree/ *n.* (*pl.* **-ries**) workshop for or a business of casting metal.

fount /fownt/ *n. poet.* spring or fountain; source.

foun•tain /fówntin/ *n.* **1 a** jet or jets of water made to spout for ornamental purposes or for drinking. **b** structure provided for this. **2** natural spring of water. **3** source. □ **fountain pen** pen with a reservoir or cartridge holding ink. □□ **foun′tained** *adj.* (also in *comb.*).

four /fawr/ • *n.* **1** one more than three. **2** symbol for this (4, iv, IV, iiii, IIII). • *adj.* that amount to four. □ **four-letter word** any of several short words referring to sexual or excretory functions, regarded as coarse or offensive. **four-wheel drive** drive powering all four wheels of a vehicle. **on all fours** on hands and knees.

four•fold /fáwrfold/ *adj. & adv.* **1** four times as much or as many. **2** consisting of four parts. **3** amounting to four.

four•some /fáwrsəm/ *n.* group of four persons.

four•square /fáwrskwáir/ • *adj.* **1** solidly based. **2** steady; resolute. **3** square shaped. • *adv.* steadily; resolutely.

four•teen /fáwrteén/ • *n.* **1** one more than thirteen. **2** symbol for this (14, xiv, XIV). • *adj.* that amount to fourteen. □□ **four′teenth′** *adj. & n.*

fourth /fawrth/ • *n.* **1** next after third. **2** each of four equal parts of a thing; a quarter. **3** (**Fourth**) the Fourth of July. • *adj.* that is the fourth. □ **fourth dimension 1** postulated dimension additional to those determining area and volume. **2** time regarded as equivalent to linear dimensions. **fourth estate** the press; journalism. □□ **fourth′ly** *adv.*

fowl /fowl/ *n.* (*pl.* same or **fowls**) **1** domestic birds, esp. chickens, kept for eggs and flesh. **2** flesh of these birds as food. **3** (in *comb.* or *collect.*) bird (*guineafowl*). □□ **fowl′er** *n.*

Fox /foks/ *n.* **1 a** N. American people native to the northeastern US. **b** member of this people. **2** language of this people.

fox /foks/ • *n.* **1 a** canine animal with a bushy tail and red or gray fur. **b** fur of a fox. **2** cunning or sly person. **3** an attractive young woman or man. • *v.* **1 a** *intr.* act craftily. **b** *tr.* deceive; trick. **2** *tr.* (usu. as **foxed** *adj.*) discolor (the leaves of a book, engraving, etc.) with brownish marks. □ **fox terrier** kind of short-haired terrier. □□ **fox′ing** *n.* (in sense 2 of *v.*). **fox′like** *adj.*

fox•glove /fóksgluv/ *n.* tall plant with erect spikes of purple or white flowers like glove fingers.

fox•hole /fóks-hōl/ *n. Mil.* hole in the ground used as a shelter against enemy fire or as a firing point.

fox•hound /fóks-hownd/ *n.* hound bred and trained to hunt foxes.

fox•trot /fókstrot/ • *n.* **1** ballroom dance with slow and quick steps. **2** music for this. • *v.intr.* (**fox•trot•ted, fox•trot•ting**) perform this dance.

fox•y /fóksee/ *adj.* (**fox•i•er, fox•i•est**) **1** foxlike; sly; cunning. **2** *sl.* sexually attractive. □□ **fox′i•ly** *adv.* **fox′i•ness** *n.*

foy•er /fóyər, fóyay, fwa′ayay/ *n.* entrance hall or other large area in a hotel, theater, etc.

FPO *abbr.* **1** field post office. **2** fleet post office.

fps *abbr.* (also **f.p.s.**) **1** feet per second. **2** foot-pound-second.

Fr *symb. Chem.* francium.

Fr. *abbr.* (also **Fr**) **1** Father. **2** French.

fr. *abbr.* franc(s).

fra•cas /fráykəs/ *n.* (*pl.* same, *pronunc.* /-kaaz/) noisy disturbance or quarrel.

frac•tion /frákshən/ *n.* **1** numerical quantity that is not a whole number (e.g., 0.5, 1/2). **2** small part, piece, or amount. □□ **frac′tion•al** *adj.* **frac′tion•ar•y** *adj.* **frac′tion•ize** *v.tr.*

frac•tious /frákshəs/ *adj.* **1** irritable; peevish. **2** unruly. □□ **frac′tious•ly** *adv.* **frac′tious•ness** *n.*

frac•ture /frákchər/ • *n.* breakage, esp. of a bone. • *v. Med.* undergo or cause to undergo a fracture.

frag•ile /frájil, -jīl/ *adj.* **1** easily broken; weak. **2** delicate; not strong. □□ **frag′ile•ly** *adv.* **fra•gil•i•ty** /frəjílitee/ *n.*

frag•ment • *n.* /frágmənt/ **1** part broken off; a detached piece. **2** isolated or incomplete part (of a book, etc.). • *v.* /fragmént/ break or separate into fragments. □□ **frag•men•tal** /-mént′l/ *adj.* **frag•men•ta′tion** *n.* **frag′ment•ize** *v.tr.*

frag•men•tar•y /frágməntəree/ *adj.* **1** consisting of fragments. **2** disconnected. □□ **frag′men•tar•i•ly** *adv.*

fra•grance /fráygrəns/ *n.* **1** sweetness of smell. **2** sweet scent. □□ **fra′gran•cy** *n.* **fra′grant** *adj.* **fra′grant•ly** *adv.*

frail /frayl/ *adj.* **1** fragile; delicate. **2** in weak health. **3** morally weak. □□ **frail′ly** *adv.* **frail′ness** *n.*

frail•ty /fráyltee/ *n.* (*pl.* **-ties**) **1** condition of being frail. **2** liability to err or yield to temptation. **3** weakness; foible.

frame /fraym/ • *n.* **1** case or border enclosing a picture, window, door, etc. **2** basic rigid supporting structure of anything, e.g., of a building, motor vehicle, or aircraft. **3** (in *pl.*) structure of spectacles holding the lenses. **4** human or animal body structure. **5 a** established order, plan, or system. **b** construction; structure. **6** single image on film, tape, etc. **7** round of play in bowling, etc. • *v.tr.* **1 a** set in a frame. **b** serve as a frame for. **2** construct; devise. **3** adapt; fit. **4** *colloq.* concoct a false charge or evidence against; devise a plot with regard to. **5** articulate (words). □ **frame-up** *colloq.* conspiracy, esp. to make an innocent person appear guilty. □□ **fram′a•ble** *adj.* (also **frame′a•ble**). **frame′less** *adj.* **fram′er** *n.*

frame•work /fráymwərk/ *n.* **1** essential supporting structure. **2** basic system.

franc /frangk/ n. chief monetary unit of France, Belgium, Switzerland, Luxembourg, and several other countries.

fran·chise /fránchīz/ • n. 1 right to vote in elections; citizenship. 2 authorization granted by a company to sell its goods or services in a particular way. • v.tr. grant a franchise to. □□ **fran·chi·see** /-zée/ n. **fran′chis·er** n. (also **fran′chi·sor**).

fran·ci·um /fránseeəm/ n. Chem. radioactive metallic element. ¶ Symb.: **Fr.**

Franco- /frángkō/ comb. form French.

fran·gi·ble /fránjibəl/ adj. breakable; fragile.

Frank /frangk/ n. member of the Germanic nation or coalition that conquered Gaul in the 6th c. □□ **Frank′ish** adj.

frank /frangk/ • adj. 1 candid; outspoken (frank opinion). 2 undisguised; avowed. • v.tr. stamp (a letter) with an official mark to record the payment of postage. • n. franking signature or mark. □□ **frank′a·ble** adj. **frank′er** n. **frank′ly** adv. **frank′ness** n.

Frank·en·stein /frángkənstīn/ n. (in full **Frank′en·stein′s mon′ster**) thing that becomes terrifying to its maker; monster.

frank·furt·er /frángkfərtər/ n. seasoned smoked sausage.

frank·in·cense /frángkinsens/ n. aromatic gum resin used for burning as incense.

Frank·lin stove /frángklin/ n. often freestanding cast-iron stove having the general shape of an open fireplace.

fran·tic /frántik/ adj. 1 wildly excited. 2 hurried or anxious; desperate. □□ **fran′ti·cal·ly** adv. **fran′tic·ly** adv.

frappé /frapáy/ n. drink made with shaved ice.

frat /frat/ n. colloq. student fraternity.

fra·ter·nal /frətə́rnəl/ adj. 1 of a brother or brothers. 2 brotherly. 3 (of twins) developed from separate ova and not necessarily closely similar. □□ **fra·ter′nal·ism** n. **fra·ter′nal·ly** adv.

fra·ter·ni·ty /frətə́rnitee/ n. (pl. **-ties**) 1 male students' society. 2 group or company with common interests, or of the same professional class. 3 being fraternal; brotherliness.

frat·er·nize /frátərnīz/ v.intr. 1 associate with. 2 (of troops) enter into friendly relations with enemy troops or the inhabitants of an occupied country. □□ **frat·er·ni·za′tion** n.

frat·ri·cide /frátrisīd/ n. 1 killing of one's brother or sister. 2 person who does this. □□ **frat·ri·ci·d·al** /-síd′l/ adj.

Frau /frow/ n. (pl. **Frau·en** /frówən/) (often as a title) married or widowed German woman.

fraud /frawd/ n. 1 criminal deception. 2 dishonest artifice or trick. 3 impostor.

fraud·u·lent /fráwjələnt/ adj. of, involving, or guilty of fraud. □□ **fraud′u·lence** n. **fraud′u·lent·ly** adv.

fraught /frawt/ adj. 1 filled or attended with. 2 colloq. causing or affected by great anxiety or distress.

Fräu·lein /fróylīn, frów-/ n. (often as a title or form of address) unmarried (esp. young) German woman.

fray¹ /fray/ v. 1 tr. & intr. wear through or become worn, esp. (of woven material) unweave at the edges. 2 intr. (of nerves, temper, etc.) become strained; deteriorate.

fray² /fray/ n. brawl.

fraz·zle /frázəl/ colloq. • n. worn or exhausted state. • v.tr. (usu. as **frazzled** adj.) wear out; exhaust.

freak /freek/ • n. 1 (also **freak of nature**) monstrosity; abnormally developed individual or thing. 2 colloq. **a** unconventional person. **b** fanatic (health freak). • v. (often foll. by out) colloq. 1 intr. & tr. become or make very angry. 2 intr. & tr. undergo or cause to undergo hallucinations or a strong emotional experience, esp. from use of narcotics. 3 intr. adopt a wildly unconventional lifestyle. □□ **freak′ish** adj. **freak′ish·ly** adv. **freak′ish·ness** n.

freak·y /fréekee/ adj. (**freak·i·er, freak·i·est**) 1 of or like a freak. 2 bizarre; unconventional. □□ **freak′i·ly** adv. **freak′i·ness** n.

freck·le /frékəl/ • n. (often in pl.) light brown spot on the skin. • v. 1 tr. (usu. as **freckled** adj.) spot with freckles. 2 intr. be spotted with freckles. □□ **freck′ly** /fréklee/ adj.

free /free/ • adj. (**fre·er** /fréeər/; **fre·est** /fréeist/) 1 not under the control of another; at liberty. 2 autonomous; democratic. 3 **a** unrestricted; not restrained or fixed. **b** not imprisoned. **c** released from duties, etc. **d** independent. 4 (foll. by of, from) **a** exempt from. **b** not containing (free of preservatives). 5 permitted to (free to choose). 6 **a** costing nothing. **b** not subject to tax, duty, etc. 7 not occupied or in use (the bathroom is free). 8 lavish. 9 frank; unreserved. 10 (of literary style) not observing the strict laws of form. 11 (of a translation) not literal. • adv. 1 in a free manner. 2 without cost or payment. • v.tr. 1 make free; liberate. 2 relieve. 3 disengage; disentangle. □ **free enterprise** system of private business operating free from government control. **free fall 1** part of a parachute descent before the parachute opens. 2 movement of a spacecraft in space without thrust from the engines. **free-for-all** chaotic fight, unrestricted discussion, etc. **free hand** freedom to act at one's own discretion (see also FREEHAND). **free-handed** generous. **free-handedly** generously. **free-handedness** generosity. **free market** market with unrestricted competition. **free speech** right to express opinions freely. **free-standing** not supported by another structure. **free trade** international trade without import or export restrictions. **free verse** verse without a fixed metrical pattern. **free will** power of acting at one's own discretion. □□ **free′ly** adv. **free′ness** n.

¶ **Free** means 'without charge,' and a gift is 'something given without charge.' The expression "free gift" is therefore tautological.

-free /free/ comb. form free of or from (duty-free; trouble-free).

free·bie /fréebee/ n. colloq. thing provided free of charge.

free·boot·er /fréebootər/ n. pirate. □□ **free′boot** v.intr.

free·born /fréebawrn/ adj. inheriting a citizen's rights and liberty.

freed·man /fréedmən/ n. (pl. **-men**) emancipated slave.

free·dom /fréedəm/ n. 1 condition of being free or unrestricted. 2 personal or civic liberty; absence of slave status. 3 power of self-determination; quality of not being controlled by fate or necessity. 4 state of being free to act. 5

condition of being exempt from. **6** unrestricted use of (facilities, etc.).

free·hand /free'hand/ • *adj.* (of a drawing, etc.) done by hand without special instruments. • *adv.* in a freehand manner.

free·hold /free'hōld/ *n.* **1** complete ownership of property for life. **2** such land or property. □□ **free'hold·er** *n.*

free·lance /free'lans/ • *n.* (also **free'lanc·er**) person who, usu. self-employed, offering services on a temporary basis, esp. to several businesses, etc., for particular assignments. • *v.intr.* act as a freelance. • *adv.* as a freelance.

free·load·er /free'lōdər/ *n. sl.* person who eats, drinks, or lives at others' expense; sponger. □□ **free·load** /-lōd/ *v.intr.*

free·style /free'stīl/ *adj.* (of a race or contest) in which all styles are allowed, esp.: **1** *Swimming* in which any stroke may be used. **2** *Wrestling* with few restrictions on the holds permitted.

free·think·er /free'thingkər/ *n.* person who rejects dogma or authority, esp. in religious belief. □□ **free'think'ing** *n.* & *adj.*

free·way /free'way/ *n.* **1** express highway, esp. with controlled access. **2** toll-free highway.

freeze /freez/ • *v.* (*past* **froze** /frōz/; *past part.* **fro·zen** /frōzən/) **1** *tr.* & *intr.* **a** turn or be turned into ice or another solid by cold. **b** make or become rigid from the cold. **2** *intr.* be or feel very cold. **3** *tr.* & *intr.* cover or become covered with ice. **4** *tr.* preserve (food) by refrigeration below the freezing point. **5** *tr.* & *intr.* make or become motionless or powerless through fear, surprise, etc. **6** *tr.* make (credits, assets, etc.) temporarily or permanently unrealizable. **7** *tr.* fix or stabilize (prices, wages, etc.) at a certain level. **8** *tr.* arrest (a movement in a movie, video, etc.) • *n.* **1** period or state of frost. **2** fixing or stabilization of prices, wages, etc. **3** film shot in which movement is arrested by the repetition of a frame. □ **freeze-dry** (**-dries**, **-dried**) freeze and dry by the sublimation of ice in a high vacuum. **freezing point** temperature at which a liquid, esp. water, freezes. □□ **freez'a·ble** *adj.* **fro'zen·ly** *adv.*

---

freeze Old English *frēosan* (in the phrase *hit frēoseth* 'it is freezing, it is so cold that water turns to ice'), of Germanic origin; related to Dutch *vriezen* and German *frieren*, from an Indo-European root shared by Latin *pruina* 'hoar frost' and English *frost.*

---

freez·er /free'zər/ *n.* refrigerated compartment, cabinet, or room for freezing and preserving food.

freight /frayt/ • *n.* **1** transport of goods. **2** goods transported; cargo. **3** charge for transportation of goods. • *v.tr.* **1** transport (goods) as freight. **2** load with freight.

freight·er /fray'tər/ *n.* ship designed to carry freight.

French /french/ • *adj.* **1** of France or its people or language. **2** having the characteristics attributed to the French people. • *n.* **1** language of France. **2** (prec. by *the*; treated as *pl.*) the people of France. □ **French bread** white bread in a long crisp loaf. **French Canadian** *n.* Canadian whose principal language is French. • *adj.* of French-speaking Canadians. **French cuff** double cuff formed by turning back a long cuff

and fastening it. **French door** door with glass panes throughout its length. **French dressing 1** creamy orange salad dressing. **2** salad dressing of vinegar and oil, usu. seasoned. **French fries** (also **French fried potatoes**) strips of potato, deep fried. **French horn** coiled brass wind instrument with a wide bell. **French kiss** openmouthed kiss. **French window** pair of casement windows extending to the floor in an outside wall, serving as both window and door. □□ **French'man** *n.* (*pl.* **-men**) **French'wom·an** *n.* (*pl.* **-wom·en**) **French'ness** *n.*

FRENCH HORN

fre·net·ic /frənétik/ *adj.* **1** frantic; frenzied. **2** fanatic. □□ **fre·net'i·cal·ly** *adv.*

fren·zy /frénzee/ • *n.* (*pl.* **-zies**) wild or delirious excitement, agitation, or fury. • *v.tr.* (**-zies**, **-zied**) (usu. as **frenzied** *adj.*) drive to frenzy; infuriate. □□ **fren'zied·ly** *adv.*

fre·quen·cy /free'kwənsee/ *n.* (*pl.* **-cies**) **1** commonness of occurrence. **2** frequent occurrence. **3** *Physics* rate of recurrence of a vibration, etc. □ **frequency modulation** *Electronics* modulation in which the frequency of the carrier wave is varied. ¶ Abbr.: **FM**.

fre·quent /free'kwənt/ • *adj.* **1** occurring often or in close succession. **2** habitual; constant. • *v.tr.* /also frikwént/ attend or go to habitually. □□ **fre·quen·ta'tion** *n.* **fre·quent·er** /frikwéntər/ *n.* **fre·quent·ly** /free'kwəntlee/ *adv.*

fres·co /frésko/ *n.* (*pl.* **-cos** or **-coes**) painting done in watercolor on wet plaster. □□ **fres'coed** *adj.*

fresh /fresh/ • *adj.* **1** newly made or obtained. **2 a** other; different; new (*start a fresh page*). **b** additional (*fresh supplies*). **3** lately arrived. **4** not stale or musty or faded (*fresh flowers*). **5** (of food) not preserved. **6** not salty (*fresh water*). **7** pure; untainted; refreshing. **8** (of the wind) brisk. **9** *colloq.* impudent. **10** inexperienced. • *adv.* newly; recently (esp. in *comb.*: *fresh-cut*). □□ **fresh'ly** *adv.* **fresh'ness** *n.*

fresh·en /fréshən/ *v.* **1** make or become fresh. **2** (foll. by *up*) wash, change clothes, etc.

fresh·man /fréshmən/ *n.* (*pl.* **-men**) first-year student at a high school, college, or university.

fresh·wa·ter /fréshwawtər, -wotər/ *adj.* not of the sea.

fret¹ /fret/ *v.* (**fret·ted**, **fret·ting**) **1** *intr.* be worried or distressed. **2** *tr.* **a** cause anxiety or distress to. **b** irritate; annoy. **3** *tr.* wear or consume by gnawing or rubbing.

fret² /fret/ *n.* ornamental pattern made of straight lines joined usu. at right angles.

fret³ /fret/ *n.* each of a sequence of bars or ridges

on the fingerboard of a guitar, etc. □□ **fret′less** *adj.*

frets

FRETS, 3

fret·ful /frétfŏŏl/ *adj.* visibly anxious, distressed, or irritated. □□ **fret′ful·ly** *adv.* **fret′ful·ness** *n.*

fret·work /frétwərk/ *n.* ornamental work of interlacing lines.

Freud·i·an /fróydeeən/ *Psychol.* ● *adj.* of or relating to Sigmund Freud or his methods of psychoanalysis. ● *n.* follower of Freud or his methods. □ **Freudian slip** unintentional error regarded as revealing subconscious feelings. □□ **Freud′i·an·ism** *n.*

F.R.G. *abbr.* Federal Republic of Germany.

Fri. *abbr.* Friday.

fri·a·ble /fríəbəl/ *adj.* easily crumbled. □□ **fri·a·bil′i·ty** *n.*

fri·ar /fríər/ *n.* member of any of certain religious orders of men, esp. the four mendicant orders. □□ **fri′ar·ly** *adj.*

fric·as·see /fríkəseé/ ● *n.* dish of stewed or fried pieces of meat served in a thick white sauce. ● *v. tr.* (**fric·as·sees, fric·as·seed**) make a fricassee of.

fric·a·tive /fríkətiv/ *Phonet.* ● *adj.* made by the friction of breath in a narrow opening. ● *n.* consonant made in this way, e.g., *f* and *th*.

fric·tion /fríkshən/ *n.* **1** rubbing of one object against another. **2** the resistance encountered in moving an object. **3** clash of wills, temperaments, or opinions. □□ **fric′tion·al** *adj.* **fric′tion·less** *adj.*

Fri·day /fríday, -dee/ *n.* day of the week following Thursday.

fridge /frij/ *n. colloq.* = REFRIGERATOR.

friend /frend/ *n.* **1** person with whom one enjoys mutual affection and regard. **2** sympathizer, helper. □□ **friend′less** *adj.*

friend·ly /fréndlee/ ● *adj.* (**friend·li·er, friend·li·est**) **1** well-disposed; kindly; cordial. **2** on amicable terms. ● *adv.* in a friendly manner. □□ **friend′li·ness** *n.*

friend·ship /fréndship/ *n.* **1** being friends; relationship between friends. **2** friendly disposition felt or shown.

fri·er var. of FRYER.

frieze /freez/ *n.* horizontal decorative or sculpted band, esp. along a wall near the ceiling.

frig·ate /frígit/ *n.* naval vessel between a destroyer and a cruiser in size.

fright /frīt/ *n.* **1 a** sudden or extreme fear. **b** instance of this (*gave me a fright*). **2** person or thing looking grotesque or ridiculous.

fright·en /frítən/ *v.* **1** *tr.* fill with fright. **2** *tr.* drive or force by fright. □□ **fright′en·ing** *adj.* **fright′en·ing·ly** *adv.*

fright·ful /frítfŏŏl/ *adj.* **1 a** dreadful; shocking; revolting. **b** ugly; hideous. **2** *colloq.* *colloq.* extreme. □□ **fright′ful·ly** *adv.*

frig·id /fríjid/ *adj.* **1** lacking friendliness or enthusiasm. **2** chilling. **3** sexually unresponsive. □□ **fri·gid·i·ty** /-jíditee/ *n.* **frig′id·ly** *adv.* **frig′id·ness** *n.*

fri·jo·les /freehólays/ *n.pl.* beans, esp. in Mexican-style cooking.

frill /fril/ *n.* **1** strip of material with one side gathered or pleated, used as an ornamental edging. **2** (in *pl.*) unnecessary embellishments. □□ **frilled** *adj.* **frill′er·y** /-ləree/ *n.* **frill′i·ness** *n.* **frill′y** *adj.* (**frill·i·er, frill·i·est**)

fringe /frinj/ ● *n.* **1** ornamental bordering of threads left loose or formed into tassels or twists. **2** outer edge or margin; outer limit of an area, population, etc. (often *attrib.: fringe theater*). **3** thing, part, or area of secondary or minor importance. ● *v. tr.* adorn with or serve as a fringe. □ **fringe benefit** employee benefit supplementing a money wage or salary. □□ **fringe′less** *adj.* **fring′y** *adj.*

frip·per·y /frípəree/ *n.* (*pl.* **-ies**) showy, tawdry, or unnecessary finery or ornament, esp. in dress.

Fris·bee /frízbee/ *n. propr.* molded plastic disk for sailing through the air as an outdoor game.

frisk /frisk/ *v. tr. sl.* feel over or search (a person) for a weapon, etc. (usu. rapidly). □□ **frisk′er** *n.*

frisk·y /friskee/ *adj.* (**frisk·i·er, frisk·i·est**) lively; playful. □□ **frisk′i·ly** *adv.* **frisk′i·ness** *n.*

frit·ter¹ /frítər/ *v. tr.* waste (money, time, etc.) triflingly.

frit·ter² /frítər/ *n.* piece of fruit, meat, etc., coated in batter and deep-fried (*apple fritter*).

friv·o·lous /frívələs/ *adj.* **1** paltry; trifling; trumpery. **2** lacking seriousness; given to trifling; silly. □□ **fri·vol·i·ty** /-vólitee/ *n.* (*pl.* **-ties**) **friv′o·lous·ly** *adv.* **friv′o·lous·ness** *n.*

frizz /friz/ ● *v. tr.* form (hair, etc.) into a mass of small curls. ● *n.* **1 a** frizzed hair. **b** row of curls. **2** frizzed state. □□ **friz′zi·ness** *n.* **friz′zy** *adj.* (**friz·zi·er, friz·zi·est**)

friz·zle¹ /frízəl/ *v.* **1** fry, toast, or grill, with a sputtering noise. **2** (often foll. by *up*) burn or shrivel.

friz·zle² /frízəl/ ● *v.* **1** *tr.* form (hair) into tight curls. **2** *intr.* (often foll. by *up*) (of hair, etc.) curl tightly. ● *n.* frizzled hair.

fro /frō/ *adv.* back (now only in *to and fro*: see TO).

frock /frok/ *n.* **1** woman's or girl's dress. **2** monk's or priest's long gown with loose sleeves. **3** smock.

frog¹ /frawg, frog/ *n.* small amphibian having a tailless smooth-skinned body with legs developed for jumping. □ **frog in the** (or **one's**) **throat** *colloq.* hoarseness.

frog² /frawg, frog/ *n.* ornamental coat fastening of a spindle-shaped button and loop. □□ **frogged** *adj.* **frog′ging** *n.*

frog·man /fráwgman, fróg-, -mən/ *n.* (*pl.* **-men**) person equipped with a rubber suit, flippers, and an oxygen supply for underwater swimming.

frol·ic /frólik/ • *v.intr.* (**frol·icked, frol·ick·ing**) play cheerfully. • *n.* **1** cheerful play. **2** merriment. □□ **frol′ick·er** *n.*

frol·ic·some /fróliksəm/ *adj.* merry; playful. □□ **frol′ic·some·ly** *adv.*

from /frum, from, frəm/ *prep.* expressing separation or origin, followed by: **1** person, place, time, etc., that is the starting point (*rain comes from the clouds*). **2** place, object, etc., whose distance or remoteness is reckoned or stated (*ten miles from Los Angeles*). **3 a** source (*dig gravel from a pit*). **b** giver or sender (*presents from their parents*). **4** person or thing avoided, deprived, etc. (*took his gun from him*). **5** reason, cause, or motive (*died from fatigue*). **6** thing distinguished or unlike (*know black from white*). **7** lower limit (*saw from 10 to 20 boats*). **8** state changed for another (*raised the penalty from a fine to imprisonment*). **9** adverb or preposition of time or place (*from long ago*; *from under the bed*).

frond /frond/ *n. Bot.* foliage leaf in various flowerless plants, esp. ferns and palms. □□ **frond′age** *n.* **fron′dose** *adj.*

front /frunt/ • *n.* **1** side or part normally nearer or toward the spectator or the direction of motion. **2** any face of a building, esp. that of the main entrance. **3** *Mil.* **a** foremost line or part of an army, etc. **b** line of battle. **4** sector of activity regarded as resembling a military front. **5** demeanor; bearing (*show a bold front*). **6** forward or conspicuous position (*come to the front*). **7 a** bluff. **b** pretext. **8** person, etc., serving to cover subversive or illegal activities. **9** *Meteorol.* forward edge of an advancing mass of cold or warm air. • *attrib.adj.* **1** of the front. **2** situated in front. • *v.* **1** *intr.* have the front facing or directed forward. **2** *intr. sl.* act as a front or cover for. **3** *tr.* furnish with a front (*fronted with stone*). □ **front office 1** executives or executive branch of an organization. **2** main office. **front runner** contestant most likely to succeed. **front-wheel drive** automobile drive system in which power is transmitted to the front wheels. **in front of 1** ahead of; in advance of. **2** in the presence of; confronting. □□ **front′less** *adj.* **front′ward** *adj.* & *adv.* **front′wards** *adv.*

front·age /frúntij/ *n.* **1** front of a building. **2** land abutting on a street or on water.

fron·tal /frúnt′l/ *adj.* **1** of, at, or on the front (*frontal attack*). **2** of the forehead. □□ **front′al·ly** *adv.*

fron·tier /frúnteér/ *n.* **1 a** the border between two countries. **b** district on each side of this. **2** limits of attainment or knowledge in a subject. **3** borders between settled and unsettled country. □□ **fron·tier′less** *adj.*

fron·tiers·man /frúnteérzmən/ *n.* (*pl.* **-men**) person living in the region of a frontier.

fron·tis·piece /frúntispees/ *n.* illustration facing the title page of a book or of one of its divisions.

frost /frawst, frost/ • *n.* **1** white frozen dew. **2** consistent temperature below freezing point causing frost to form. • *v.* **1** *intr.* become covered with frost. **2** *tr.* **a** cover with or as if with frost, powder, etc. **b** give a roughened or finely granulated surface to (glass, metal). **3** *tr.* decorate (a cake, etc.) with icing. □□ **frost′less** *adj.*

frost·bite /fráwstbīt, fróst-/ *n.* injury to skin due to freezing and often resulting in gangrene.

frost·ing /fráwsting, fróst-/ *n.* icing.

frost·y /fráwstee, fróstee/ *adj.* (**frost·i·er, frost·i·est**) **1** cold with frost. **2** covered with or as with hoarfrost. **3** unfriendly in manner. □□ **frost′i·ly** *adv.* **frost′i·ness** *n.*

froth /frawth, froth/ • *n.* **1** foam. **2 a** idle talk or ideas. **b** anything unsubstantial or of little worth. • *v.intr.* emit or gather froth. □□ **froth′i·ly** *adv.* **froth′i·ness** *n.* **froth′y** *adj.* (**froth·i·er, froth·i·est**).

frown /frown/ • *v.intr.* **1** wrinkle one's brows, esp. in displeasure or deep thought. **2** express disapproval. • *n.* look expressing severity, disapproval, or deep thought. □□ **frown′er** *n.* **frown′ing·ly** *adv.*

frow·zy /frówzee/ *adj.* (also **frow′sy**) (**-zi·er, -zi·est**) slatternly; unkempt; dingy. □□ **frow′zi·ness** *n.*

froze *past* of FREEZE.

fro·zen *past part.* of FREEZE.

fruc·ti·fy /frúktifī, fróok-/ *v.* (**-fies, -fied**) **1** *intr.* bear fruit. **2** *tr.* make fruitful; impregnate.

fruc·tose /frúktōs, fróok-/ *n. Chem.* simple sugar found in honey and fruits. Also called **levulose, fruit sugar.**

fru·gal /fróogəl/ *adj.* **1** sparing; thrifty. **2** meager; slight; costing little. □□ **fru·gal·i·ty** /-gálitee/ *n.* **fru′gal·ly** *adv.* **fru′gal·ness** *n.*

fruit /froot/ • *n.* **1 a** usu. sweet and fleshy edible product of a plant or tree, containing seed. **b** (in *sing.*) these in quantity (*eats fruit*). **2** seed of a plant or tree with its covering, e.g., an acorn, pea pod, cherry, etc. **3** (usu. in *pl.*) vegetables, grains, etc., used for food (*fruits of the earth*). **4** (usu. in *pl.*) the result of action, etc., esp. as financial reward. • *v.* bear or cause to bear fruit. □□ **fruit′ed** *adj.* (also in *comb.*).

fruit·cake /frootkayk/ *n.* cake containing dried fruit.

fruit·ful /frootfŏŏl/ *adj.* **1** producing much fruit; abundant. **2** successful; remunerative. □□ **fruit′ful·ly** *adv.* **fruit′ful·ness** *n.*

fru·i·tion /froo-íshən/ *n.* **1 a** bearing of fruit. **b** production of results. **2** realization of aims or hopes. **3** enjoyment.

fruit·less /frootlis/ *adj.* **1** not bearing fruit. **2** useless; unsuccessful; unprofitable. □□ **fruit′less·ly** *adv.* **fruit′less·ness** *n.*

fruit·y /frootee/ *adj.* (**fruit·i·er, fruit·i·est**) **1** of fruit. **2** tasting or smelling like fruit, esp. (of wine) tasting of the grape. □□ **fruit′i·ly** *adv.* **fruit′i·ness** *n.*

frump /frump/ *n.* dowdy, unattractive, old-fashioned woman. □□ **frump′ish** *adj.* **frump′ish·ly** *adv.*

frump·y /frúmpee/ *adj.* (**frump·i·er, frump·i·est**) dowdy; unattractive. □□ **frump′i·ly** *adv.* **frump′i·ness** *n.*

frus·trate /frústrayt/ *v.tr.* **1** make (efforts) ineffective. **2** prevent (a person) from achieving a purpose. **3** (as **frustrated** *adj.*) **a** discontented because unable to achieve one's desire. **b** sexually unfulfilled. **4** disappoint (a hope). □□ **frus·trat·ed·ly** /-stráytidlee/ *adv.* **frus′trat·er** *n.* **frus′trat·ing·ly** *adv.* **frus·tra·tion** /-tráyshən/ *n.*

fry[1] /frī/ • *v.* (**fries, fried**) cook or be cooked in hot fat. • *n.* (*pl.* **fries**) **1** a French fried potato. **2** social gathering serving fried food.

fry[2] /frī/ *n.pl.* **1** young or newly hatched fishes. **2** young of other creatures produced in large numbers, e.g., bees or frogs. □ **small fry** people of little importance; children.

fry·er /frīər/ *n.* (also **fri′er**) **1** person who fries. **2** vessel for frying, esp. deep frying. **3** young chicken for frying.

FSLIC *abbr.* Federal Savings and Loan Insurance Corporation.

ft. *abbr.* foot, feet.

FTC *abbr.* Federal Trade Commission.

fuch·sia /fyoōshə/ *n.* shrub with drooping red, purple, pink, or white flowers.

fud·dle /fúd′l/ • *v.tr.* confuse or stupefy, esp. with alcoholic liquor. • *n.* **1** confusion. **2** intoxication.

fud·dy-dud·dy /fúdeedúdee/ *sl.* • *adj.* old-fashioned or quaintly fussy. • *n.* (*pl.* **-dies**) fuddy-duddy person.

fudge /fuj/ • *n.* soft toffee-like candy made with milk, sugar, butter, etc. • *v.* **1** *tr.* put together in a makeshift or dishonest way; fake. **2** *tr.* deal with incompetently. **3** *intr.* practice such methods.

---

fudge early 17th century: probably an alteration of obsolete *fadge* 'to fit.' Early usage was as a verb in the sense 'turn out as expected,' also 'merge together': this probably gave rise to its use in candy making. In the late 17th century the verb came to mean 'fit together in a clumsy or underhand manner,' which included facts or figures being cobbled together in a superficially convincing way: this led to the exclamation 'fudge!' and to the verb senses used currently.

---

fueh·rer var. of FÜHRER.

fu·el /fyoōəl/ • *n.* **1** material burned or used as a source of heat or power. **2** food as a source of energy. **3** anything that sustains or inflames emotion or passion. • *v.* (**fu·eled, fu·el·ing**) **1** *tr.* supply with fuel. **2** *intr.* take in or get fuel. □ **fuel injection** direct introduction of fuel into the combustion units of an internal combustion engine. **fuel oil** oil used as fuel in an engine or furnace.

fu·gi·tive /fyoōjitiv/ • *adj.* **1** fleeing. **2** transient; fleeting; of short duration. • *n.* person who flees, esp. from justice, an enemy, danger, or a master. □□ **fu′gi·tive·ly** *adv.*

fugue /fyoōg/ *n.* **1** *Mus.* contrapuntal composition in which a short melody or phrase is introduced by one part and successively taken up and developed by others. **2** *Psychol.* loss of awareness of one's identity, often coupled with flight from one's usual environment. □□ **fu′gal** *adj.*

füh·rer /fyoōrər/ *n.* (also **fueh′rer**) tyrannical leader.

-ful /foōl/ *comb. form* forming: **1** adjectives from nouns, meaning: **a** full of (*beautiful*). **b** having the qualities of (*masterful*). **2** adjectives from adjectives or Latin stems (*direful*). **3** adjectives from verbs, meaning 'apt to,' (*forgetful*). **4** nouns (*pl.* **-fuls**) meaning 'the amount needed to fill' (*handful*).

¶ The combining form **-ful** is used to form nouns

meaning 'the amount needed to fill,' e.g., *cupful, spoonful*. The plural form of such words is -s, (*cupfuls, spoonfuls*, etc.). *Three cups full* would denote the individual cups rather than a quantity measured in cups: *On the sill were three cups full of milk.*

ful·crum /foōlkrəm, fúl-/ *n.* (*pl.* **ful·cra** /-rə/ or **ful·crums**) point against which a lever is placed to get a purchase or on which it turns or is supported.

ful·fill /foōlfil/ *v.tr.* (**ful·filled, ful·fill·ing**) **1** carry out (a prophecy or promise). **2** satisfy (a desire or prayer). **3** perform; carry out (a task). **4** bring to an end; finish; complete. □□ **ful·fill′a·ble** *adj.* **ful·fill′er** *n.* **ful·fill′ment** *n.*

full[1] /foōl/ • *adj.* **1** holding all its limits will allow (*full of water*). **2** having eaten to one's limits or satisfaction. **3** abundant; copious; satisfying; sufficient. **4** having or holding an abundance of. **5** complete (full daylight). **6** (of tone or color) deep and clear. **7** plump; rounded; protuberant (*full figure*). **8** (of clothes) made of much material arranged in folds or gathers. • *adv.* **1** very (*you know full well*). **2** quite; fully (*full six miles*). □ **full-blooded 1** vigorous; hearty; sensual. **2** not hybrid. **full-blown** fully developed; complete. **full-fledged 1** fully developed. **2** of full rank or standing. **full house 1** maximum or large attendance at a theater, etc. **2** *Poker* hand with three of a kind and a pair. **full moon** moon with its whole disk illuminated. **full-scale** not reduced in size; complete. **full-time** *adj.* occupying or using the whole of the available working time. **in full 1** without abridgment. **2** to or for the full amount (*paid in full*). **in full swing** at the height of activity. **in full view** entirely visible. □□ **full′ness** *n.*

full[2] /foōl/ *v.tr.* cleanse and thicken (cloth).

full·back /foōlbak/ *n.* **1** offensive player in the backfield in football. **2** defensive player, or a position near the goal, in soccer, field hockey, etc.

ful·mi·nate /fúlminayt, foōl-/ *v.intr.* **1** express censure loudly and forcefully. **2** explode violently; flash like lightning (*fulminating mercury*). □□ **ful·mi·na·tion** /-náyshən/ *n.* **ful·mi·na·to·ry** /-notáwree/ *adj.*

ful·some /foōlsəm/ *adj.* excessive; cloying. □□ **ful′some·ly** *adv.* **ful′some·ness** *n.*

¶ The earliest recorded use of **fulsome**, in the 13th century, had the meaning 'abundant,' but in modern use this is held by many to be incorrect. The correct current meaning is 'disgusting because overdone; excessive.' The word is still often used to mean 'abundant; copious,' but this use can give rise to ambiguity in such expressions as *fulsome praise*.

fum·ble /fúmbəl/ • *v.* **1** *intr.* use the hands awkwardly; grope about. **2** *tr.* handle or deal with clumsily or nervously. • *n.* act of fumbling. □□ **fum′bler** *n.* **fum′bling·ly** *adv.*

fume /fyoōm/ • *n.* (usu. in *pl.*) exuded gas or smoke or vapor, esp. when harmful or unpleasant. • *v.* **1 a** *intr.* emit fumes. **b** *tr.* give off as fumes. **2** *intr.* be affected by (esp. suppressed) anger (*was fuming at their inefficiency*). □□ **fume′less** *adj.* **fum′ing·ly** *adv.*

fu·mi·gate /fyoōmigayt/ *v.tr.* **1** disinfect or purify with fumes. **2** apply fumes to. □□ **fu·mi·gant** /-gənt/ *n.* **fu·mi·ga·tion** /-gáyshən/ *n.* **fu′mi·ga·tor** *n.*

fun /fun/ • *n.* **1** amusement, esp. lively or playful. **2** source of this. **3** (in full **fun and games**) exciting or amusing goings-on. • *adj. disp. colloq.*

amusing; entertaining; enjoyable (*a fun thing to do*). □ **make fun of** tease; ridicule.

fu·nam·bu·list /fyo͞onámbyəlist/ *n.* tightrope walker.

func·tion /fúngkshən/ • *n.* **1 a** activity proper to a person or institution. **b** mode of action or activity by which a thing fulfills its purpose. **c** official or professional duty. **2** public or social occasion. **3** *Math.* quantity whose value depends on the varying values of others. • *v.intr.* fulfill a function; operate; be in working order. □□ **func′tion·less** *adj.*

func·tion·al /fúngkshənəl/ *adj.* **1** of or serving a function. **2** practical rather than attractive; utilitarian. **3** *Physiol.* (esp. of disease) of or affecting only the functions of an organ, etc., not structural or organic. □□ **func·tion·al·i·ty** /-nálitee/ *n.* **func′tion·al·ly** *adv.*

func·tion·ar·y /fúngkshəneree/ *n.* (*pl.* **-ies**) person who has to perform official functions or duties; an official.

fund /fund/ • *n.* **1** permanently available supply. **2** stock of money, esp. for a specific purpose. **3** (in *pl.*) money resources. • *v.tr.* **1** provide with money. **2** make (a debt) permanent at fixed interest. □ **fund-raiser 1** person who seeks financial support for a cause, enterprise, etc. **2** activity, event, etc., to raise money, as for charity, etc. **fund-raising** seeking of financial support.

fun·da·men·tal /fúndəmént'l/ • *adj.* of, affecting, or serving as a base or foundation; essential; primary. • *n.* (usu. in *pl.*) principle. □□ **fun·da·men′tal·ly** *adv.*

fun·da·men·tal·ism /fúndəméntəlizəm/ *n.* (also **Fun·da·men′tal·ism**) strict maintenance of traditional religious beliefs. □□ **fun·da·men′tal·ist** *n.*

fu·ner·al /fyo͞onərəl/ *n.* burial or cremation of a dead person with its ceremonies. □ **funeral director** undertaker. **funeral parlor** (also **home**) establishment where the dead are prepared for burial or cremation. □□ **fu′ner·ar·y** *adj.*

fu·ne·re·al /fyo͞onéereeəl/ *adj.* **1** of or appropriate to a funeral. **2** gloomy; dismal; dark. □□ **fu·ne′re·al·ly** *adv.*

fun·gi·cide /fúnjisīd, fúnggi-/ *n.* fungus-destroying substance. □□ **fun·gi·cid·al** /-sīd'l/ *adj.*

fun·gus /fúnggəs/ *n.* (*pl.* **fun·gi** /-gī, -jī/ or **fun·gus·es**) any of a group of nonphotosynthetic organisms feeding on organic matter, which include molds, yeast, mushrooms, and toadstools. □□ **fun·gal** /fúnggəl/ *adj.* **fun·gi·form** /fúnjifawrm, fúnggi-/ *adj.* **fun·giv·or·ous** /funjívərəs, funggiv-/ *adj.* **fun′gous** *adj.*

fu·nic·u·lar /fyo͞oníkyələr, fə-/ • *adj.* (of a railway, esp. on a mountainside) operating by cable with ascending and descending cars counterbalanced. • *n.* funicular railway.

funk[1] /fungk/ *n.* fear; panic. □ **in a funk** dejected.

funk[2] /fungk/ *n. sl.* **1** funky music. **2** strong smell.

funk·y /fúngkee/ *adj.* (**funk·i·er, funk·i·est**) *sl.* **1** (esp. of jazz or rock music) earthy, bluesy, with a heavy rhythmical beat. **2** fashionable. **3** odd; unconventional. **4** having a strong smell. □□ **funk′i·ly** *adv.* **funk′i·ness** *n.*

fun·nel /fúnəl/ • *n.* **1** narrow tube or pipe widening at the top, for pouring liquid, powder, etc., into a small opening. **2** metal chimney on a steam engine or ship. • *v.* (**fun·neled, fun·nel·ing;**

fun·nelled, fun·nel·ling) guide or move through or as through a funnel. □□ **fun′nel·like** *adj.*

fun·ny /fúnee/ *adj.* (**fun·ni·er, fun·ni·est**) **1** amusing; comical. **2** strange; perplexing; hard to account for. □ **funny bone** part of the elbow over which the ulnar nerve passes. **funny money** *colloq.* **1** counterfeit money. **2** foreign currency. **3** inflated currency. □□ **fun′ni·ness** *n.*

fur /fər/ • *n.* **1 a** short fine soft hair of certain animals. **b** skin of such an animal with the fur on it; pelt. **2** coat of certain animals as material for making, trimming, or lining clothes. □ **make the fur fly** *colloq.* cause a disturbance; stir up trouble. □□ **fur′less** *adj.*

fur·be·low /fərbilō/ *n.* **1** gathered strip or pleated border of a skirt or petticoat. **2** (in *pl.*) *derog.* showy ornaments.

fur·bish /fərbish/ *v.tr.* **1** remove rust from; polish. **2** give a new look to; renovate. □□ **fur′bish·er** *n.*

fu·ri·ous /fyo͞oreeəs/ *adj.* **1** extremely angry. **2** full of fury. **3** raging; violent; intense. □□ **fu′ri·ous·ly** *adv.*

furl /fərl/ *v.* **1** *tr.* roll up and secure (a sail, umbrella, flag, etc.). **2** *intr.* become furled. □□ **furl′a·ble** *adj.*

fur·long /fərlawng, -long/ *n.* unit of measurement equal to an eighth of a mile or 220 yards.

> **furlong** Old English *furlang*, from *furh* 'furrow' + *lang* 'long.' The word originally denoted the length of a furrow in a common field (formally regarded as a square of ten acres). It was also used as the equivalent of the Roman *stadium*, one eighth of a Roman mile, whence the current sense.

fur·lough /fərlō/ • *n.* leave of absence, esp. granted to a member of the armed services. • *v.tr.* grant furlough to.

furn. *abbr.* **1** furnished. **2** furniture.

fur·nace /fərnis/ *n.* enclosed structure for intense heating.

fur·nish /fərnish/ *v.tr.* **1** provide with furniture. **2** (foll. by *with*) cause to have possession or use of. **3** provide; afford; yield. □□ **fur′nished** *adj.*

fur·nish·ings /fərnishingz/ *n.pl.* furniture and utensils, etc., in a house, room, etc.

fur·ni·ture /fərnichər/ *n.* movable equipment of a house, room, etc., e.g., tables, chairs, and beds. □ **part of the furniture** *colloq.* person or thing taken for granted.

fu·ror /fyo͞orawr, -ər/ *n.* **1** uproar; outbreak of fury. **2** wave of enthusiastic admiration; craze.

fur·ri·er /fəreeər/ *n.* dealer in or dresser of furs.

fur·row /fərō, fúr-/ • *n.* **1** narrow trench made in the ground by a plow. **2** rut, groove, or deep wrinkle. **3** ship's track. • *v.tr.* **1** plow. **2 a** make furrows, grooves, etc., in. **b** mark with wrinkles. □□ **fur·rowed** *adj.* **fur′row·y** *adj.*

fur·ry /fəree, fúree/ *adj.* (**fur·ri·er, fur·ri·est**) **1** of or like fur. **2** covered with or wearing fur. □□ **fur′ri·ness** *n.*

fur·ther /fərthər/ • *adv.* **1** = FARTHER. **2** to a greater extent; more. **3** in addition. • *adj.* **1** = FARTHER. **2** more; additional (*threats of further punishment*). • *v.tr.* promote; favor (a scheme, etc.). □□ **fur′ther·er** *n.* **fur′ther·most** *adj.*

¶ See note at FARTHER.

fur·ther·ance /fɔ́rthərəns/ *n.* furthering or being furthered.

fur·ther·more /fɔ́rthərmáwr/ *adv.* in addition; besides.

fur·thest var. of FARTHEST.

fur·tive /fɔ́rtiv/ *adj.* **1** done by stealth. **2** sly; stealthy. □□ **fur′tive·ly** *adv.* **fur′tive·ness** *n.*

fu·ry /fyŏoree/ *n.* (*pl.* **-ries**) **1 a** wild and passionate anger; rage. **b** fit of rage (*in a blind fury*). **c** impetuosity in battle, etc. **2** violence of a storm, disease, etc. **3** (**Fury**) (usu. in *pl.*) *Gk. mythol.* each of three avenging goddesses.

fuse[1] /fyŏoz/ • *v.* **1** melt with intense heat. **2** blend or amalgamate into one whole by or as by melting. • *n.* device or component for protecting an electric circuit when an excessive current passes through.

fuse[2] /fyŏoz/ *n.* (also **fuze**) device of combustible matter for igniting an explosive. □□ **fuse′less** *adj.*

fu·se·lage /fyŏosəla'azh, -lij, -zə-/ *n.* the body of an airplane.

fus·i·ble /fyŏozibəl/ *adj.* that can be easily fused or melted. □□ **fu·si·bil′i·ty** *n.*

fu·sil·ier /fyŏozilée′r/ *n.* (also **fu·si·leer′**) *hist.* soldier armed with a light musket.

fu·sil·lade /fyŏosiláyd, -la′ad, -zi-/ *n.* **1** continuous discharge of firearms. **2** wholesale execution by this means.

fu·sion /fyŏozhən/ *n.* **1** act or instance of fusing or melting. **2** fused mass. **3** blending of different things into one. **4** coalition. **5** *Physics* = *nuclear fusion.* □□ **fu′sion·al** *adj.*

fuss /fus/ • *n.* **1** excited commotion; bustle. **2** excessive concern about a trivial thing. **3** sustained protest or dispute. • *v.intr.* **1** make a fuss. **2** busy oneself restlessly with trivial things. □ **make a fuss** complain vigorously. **make a fuss over** treat (a person or animal) with great or excessive attention. □□ **fuss′er** *n.*

fuss·budg·et /fúsbujit/ *n.* person who habitually frets over minor matters.

fuss·y /fúsee/ *adj.* (**fuss·i·er, fuss·i·est**) **1** inclined to fuss. **2** full of unnecessary detail or decoration. **3** fastidious. □□ **fuss′i·ly** *adv.* **fuss′i·ness** *n.*

fus·ty /fústee/ *adj.* (**fus·ti·er, fus·ti·est**) **1** musty; moldy. **2** stuffy; close. **3** antiquated. □□ **fus′ti·ly** *adv.* **fus′ti·ness** *n.*

fu·tile /fyŏot′l, -tīl/ *adj.* **1** useless; ineffectual, vain. **2** frivolous; trifling. □□ **fu′tile·ly** *adv.* **fu·til·i·ty** /-tílitee/ *n.*

fu·ton /fŏoton/ *n.* Japanese quilted mattress rolled out on the floor for use as a bed.

fu·ture /fyŏochər/ • *adj.* **1** going or expected to happen or be or become. **2 a** of time to come (*future years*). **b** *Gram.* (of a tense or participle) describing an event yet to happen. • *n.* **1** time to come. **2** what will happen in the future. **3** future condition of a person, country, etc. **4** prospect of success, etc. (*there's no future in it*). **5** *Gram.* future tense. □ **future perfect** *Gram.* tense giving the sense 'will have done'. **future shock** inability to cope with rapid progress. □□ **fu′ture·less** *adj.*

fu·tur·ist /fyŏochərist/ *n.* (often *attrib.*) **1** believer in human progress. **2** student of the future.

fu·tur·is·tic /fyŏochərístik/ *adj.* suitable for the future; ultramodern. □□ **fu·tur·is′ti·cal·ly** *adv.*

fu·tu·ri·ty /fyŏotŏoritee, -tyŏor-, chŏor-/ *n.* (*pl.* **-ties**) **1** future time. **2** (in *sing.* or *pl.*) future events.

fuze var. of FUSE[2].

fuzz /fuz/ *n.* **1** fluff. **2** fluffy or frizzled hair. **3** *sl.* the police.

fuzz·y /fúzee/ *adj.* (**fuzz·i·er, fuzz·i·est**) **1** like fuzz; fluffy. **2** blurred; indistinct. □□ **fuzz′i·ly** *adv.* **fuzz′i·ness** *n.*

FY *abbr.* fiscal year.

-fy /fī/ *suffix* forming: **1** verbs from nouns, meaning: **a** make; produce (*pacify*). **b** make into (*deify*). **2** verbs from adjectives, meaning 'bring or come into such a state' (*solidify*). **3** verbs in causative sense (*horrify*).

FYI *abbr.* for your information.

Gg

G¹ /jee/ *n.* (also **g**) (*pl.* **Gs** or **G's**; **g's**) **1** seventh letter of the alphabet. **2** *Mus.* fifth note in the diatonic scale of C major.

G² *abbr.* (also **G.**) **1** gauss. **2** giga-. **3** gravitational constant.

g *abbr.* (also **g.**) **1** gelding. **2** gram(s). **3** gravity.

GA *abbr.* Georgia (in official postal use).

Ga *symb.* *Chem.* gallium.

Ga. *abbr.* Georgia (US).

gab /gab/ *colloq.* ● *n.* talk; chatter. ● *v.intr.* talk incessantly, trivially, or indiscreetly; chatter. □□ **gab′ber** *n.* **gab′by** *adj.* (**gab·bi·er, gab·bi·est**).

gab·ar·dine /gábərdeén/ *n.* (also **gab′er·dine**) smooth durable twilled cloth, esp. of worsted or cotton.

---

gaberdine early 16th century: from Old French *gauvardine*, earlier *gallevardine*, perhaps from Middle High German *wallevart* 'pilgrimage,' originally 'a garment worn by a pilgrim.' The textile sense is first recorded in the early 20th century.

---

gab·ble /gábəl/ ● *v.intr.* talk inarticulately or too fast. ● *n.* fast unintelligible talk. □□ **gab′bler** *n.*

ga·ble /gáybəl/ *n.* triangular upper part of a wall at the end of a ridged roof. □□ **ga′bled** *adj.* (also in *comb.*).

gable

GABLE

gad /gad/ *v.intr.* (**gad·ded, gad·ding**) (foll. by *about*) go about idly or in search of pleasure.

gad·a·bout /gádəbowt/ *n.* person who gads about.

gad·fly /gádflī/ *n.* (*pl.* **-flies**) **1** cattle-biting fly. **2** irritating or harassing person.

gadg·et /gájit/ *n.* mechanical or electronic device or tool. □□ **gadg·e·teer** /-teér/ *n.* **gadg′et·ry** *n.* **gadg′et·y** *adj.*

gad·o·lin·i·um /gád′líneeəm/ *n.* *Chem.* soft silvery metallic element of the lanthanide series. ¶ Symb.: **Gd.**

Gael·ic /gáylik, gálik/ ● *n.* any of the Celtic languages spoken in Ireland, Scotland, and the Isle of Man. ● *adj.* of or relating to the Celts or the Celtic languages.

gaff /gaf/ *n.* **1** stick with an iron hook for landing large fish. **2** spar to which the head of a fore-and-aft sail is bent.

gaffe /gaf/ *n.* blunder; indiscreet act or remark.

gaf·fer /gáfər/ *n.* **1** old fellow; elderly rustic. **2** *colloq.* chief electrician in a movie or television production unit.

gag /gag/ ● *n.* **1** piece of cloth, etc., thrust into or held over the mouth to prevent speaking. **2** a joke. **3** thing or circumstance restricting free speech. ● *v.* (**gagged, gag·ging**) **1** *tr.* apply a gag to. **2** *tr.* silence; deprive of free speech. **3 a** *intr.* choke or retch. **b** *tr.* cause to do this.

ga·ga /gaágaa/ *adj.* *sl.* **1** infatuated; overly fond. **2** fatuous; slightly crazy.

gage¹ /gayj/ *n.* **1** pledge; thing deposited as security. **2 a** a challenge to fight. **b** symbol of this, esp. a glove thrown down.

gage² var. of GAUGE.
¶ See note at GAUGE.

gag·gle /gágəl/ ● *n.* **1** flock of geese. **2** *colloq.* disorderly group of people. ● *v.intr.* (of geese) cackle.

gai·e·ty /gáyətee/ *n.* (also **gay′e·ty**) **1** state of being lighthearted or merry. **2** merrymaking. **3** bright appearance.

gai·ly /gáylee/ *adv.* in a gay or lighthearted manner.

gain /gayn/ ● *v.* **1** *tr.* obtain or secure. **2** *tr.* acquire; earn. **3** *tr.* obtain as an increment or addition. **4** *intr.* (foll. by *in*) make a specified advance or improvement. **5** *intr.* & *tr.* (of a clock, etc.) display a later time. **6** *intr.* come closer to. **7** *tr.* reach or arrive at (a desired place). ● *n.* **1** something gained, achieved, etc. **2** increase of possessions, etc.; profit, advance, or improvement. **3** acquisition of wealth. **4** increase in amount. □□ **gain′a·ble** *adj.* **gain′er** *n.* **gain′ings** *n.pl.*

gain·ful /gáynfool/ *adj.* **1** (of employment) paid. **2** lucrative; remunerative. □□ **gain′ful·ly** *adv.* **gain′ful·ness** *n.*

gain·say /gáynsáy/ *v.tr.* (*past* and *past part.* **gain·said** /-séd/) deny; contradict. □□ **gain′say·er** *n.*

gait /gayt/ *n.* manner of running or walking.

gai·ter /gáytər/ *n.* covering of cloth, leather, etc., for the leg below the knee. □□ **gait′ered** *adj.*

gal /gal/ *n.* *sl.* girl.

gal. *abbr.* gallon(s).

ga·la /gáylə, gaálə, gálə/ *n.* (often *attrib.*) festive or special occasion (*a gala performance*).

ga·lac·tic /gəláktik/ *adj.* of or relating to a galaxy or galaxies.

gal·ax·y /gáləksee/ *n.* (*pl.* **-ies**) **1** any of many independent systems of stars, gas, dust, etc., held together by gravitational attraction. **2** (often **the Galaxy**) the Milky Way.

---

galaxy late Middle English (originally referring to the Milky Way): via Old French from medieval Latin *galaxia*, from Greek *galaxias* (*kuklos*) 'milky (vault),' from *gala*, *galakt-* 'milk.'

gale /gayl/ *n.* **1** very strong wind. **2** *Naut.* storm. **3** outburst, esp. of laughter.

gall[1] /gawl/ *n.* **1** *sl.* impudence. **2** asperity; rancor. **3** bitterness; anything bitter (*gall and wormwood*). **4** bile.

gall[2] /gawl/ • *n.* sore made by chafing. • *v.tr.* **1** rub sore. **2** vex; annoy; humiliate. □□ **gall' ing·ly** *adv.*

gall[3] /gawl/ *n.* growth produced by insects or fungus, etc., on plants and trees, esp. on oak.

gal·lant • *adj.* /gálənt/ **1** brave; chivalrous. **2** grand; fine; stately. **3** /gálənt, gəlánt, -láant/ markedly attentive to women. • *n.* /gálənt, gəlánt, -láant/ ladies' man. □□ **gal·lant·ly** /gáləntlee/ *adv.*

gal·lant·ry /gáləntree/ *n.* (*pl.* **-ries**) **1** bravery; dashing courage. **2** courtliness; devotion to women. **3** polite act or speech.

gall·blad·der /gáwlbladər/ *n.* (also **gall' blad·der**) *Anat.* organ that stores bile.

gal·le·on /gáleeən/ *n. hist.* **1** ship of war (usu. Spanish). **2** large Spanish merchant ship.

gal·ler·i·a /gálərée·ə / *n.* collection of small shops under a single roof; arcade.

gal·ler·y /gáləree/ *n.* (*pl.* **-ies**) **1** room or building for showing works of art. **2** balcony, esp. in a church, hall, etc. **3 a** highest balcony in a theater. **b** its occupants. **4** portico or colonnade. **5** long narrow room, passage, or corridor. **6** group of spectators. • **play to the gallery** seek to win approval by appealing to popular taste. □□ **gal'ler·ied** *adj.*

gal·ley /gálee/ *n.* (*pl.* **-leys**) **1** *hist.* low flat single-decked vessel using sails and oars, and usu. rowed by slaves or criminals. **2** ship's or aircraft's kitchen. **3** *Printing* (in full **galley proof**) typeset copy before division into pages. □ **galley slave 1** *hist.* person condemned to row in a galley. **2** drudge.

Gal·lic /gálik/ *adj.* **1** French or typically French. **2** of the Gauls; Gaulish. □□ **Gal·li·cize** /-lisīz/ *v.*

gal·li·um /gáleeəm/ *n. Chem.* soft bluish white metallic element. ¶ Symb.: **Ga**.

gal·li·vant /gálivant/ *v.intr. colloq.* **1** gad about. **2** flirt.

gal·lon /gálən/ *n.* **1** measure of capacity equivalent to four quarts (3.785 liters), used for liquids. **2** (usu. in *pl.*) *colloq.* large amount. □□ **gal'lon·age** *n.*

gal·lop /gáləp/ • *n.* fastest pace of a horse or other quadruped, with all the feet off the ground together in each stride. • *v.intr.* (**gal·loped, gal·lop·ing**) **1** (of a horse, etc., or its rider) go at the pace of a gallop. **2** move, talk, etc., very rapidly. □□ **gal'lop·er** *n.*

gal·lows /gálōz/ *n.pl.* (usu. treated as *sing.*) structure, usu. of two uprights and a crosspiece, for the hanging of criminals. □ **gallows humor** grim and ironic humor.

gall·stone /gáwlstōn/ *n.* small hard mass forming in the gallbladder.

ga·lore /gəláwr/ *adv.* in abundance (*decorated with flowers galore*).

ga·losh /gəlósh/ *n.* (usu. in *pl.*) high, waterproof overshoe, usu. of rubber.

ga·lumph /gəlúmf/ *v.intr. colloq.* move noisily or clumsily.

gal·van·ic /galvánik/ *adj.* **1 a** sudden and remarkable (*had a galvanic effect*). **b** stimulating. **2** of or producing an electric current by chemical action. □□ **gal·van'i·cal·ly** *adv.*

gal·va·nize /gálvənīz/ *v.tr.* **1** rouse forcefully, esp. by shock or excitement. **2** coat (iron) with zinc as a protection against rust. □□ **gal·va·ni·za'tion** *n.* **gal'va·niz·er** *n.*

gal·va·nom·e·ter /gálvənómitər/ *n.* instrument for detecting and measuring small electric currents. □□ **gal·va·no·met·ric** /-nəmétrik/ *adj.*

gam·bit /gámbit/ *n.* **1** chess opening in which a player sacrifices a piece or pawn to secure an advantage. **2** opening move in a discussion, etc. **3** trick or device.

gam·ble /gámbəl/ • *v.* **1** *intr.* play games of chance for money, esp. for high stakes. **2** *tr.* bet (a sum of money). **3** *intr.* take great risks in the hope of substantial gain. **4** *intr.* act in the hope or expectation of (*gambled on fine weather*). • *n.* risky undertaking or attempt. □□ **gam'bler** *n.*

gam·bol /gámbəl/ • *v.intr.* (**gam·boled, gam·bol·ing; gam·bolled, gam·bol·ling**) skip or frolic playfully. • *n.* playful frolic.

gam·brel /gámbrəl/ *n.* (in full **gam'brel roof**) gabled roof with each face having two slopes, the lower one steeper. See illus. at ROOF.

game[1] /gaym/ • *n.* **1 a** form or spell of play or sport, esp. a competitive one played according to rules. **b** specific instance of playing such a game; a match. **2** single portion of play forming a scoring unit in some contests. **3** (in *pl.*) meeting for athletic, etc., contests (*Olympic Games*). **4 a** fun; jest. **b** (in *pl.*) jokes; tricks (*none of your games!*). **5** scheme. **6** a policy or line of action. **b** occupation or profession. **7** (*collect.*) **a** wild animals or birds hunted for sport or food. **b** flesh of these. • *adj.* spirited; eager and willing. • *v.intr.* play at games of chance for money; gamble. □ **the game is up** the scheme is revealed or foiled. **game plan 1** winning strategy worked out in advance. **2** plan of campaign, esp. in politics. □□ **game'ly** *adv.* **game'ster** *n.*

game[2] /gaym/ *adj.* (of a leg, arm, etc.) lame; crippled.

game·cock /gáymkok/ *n.* (also **game·fowl** /-fowl/) cock bred and trained for cockfighting.

game·keep·er /gáymkeepər/ *n.* person employed to care for and protect game.

games·man·ship /gáymzmənship/ *n.* art or practice of gaining a psychological advantage over an opponent.

ga·mete /gámeet, gəmée't/ *n. Biol.* mature germ cell able to unite with another in sexual reproduction. □□ **ga·met·ic** /gəmétik/ *adj.*

gam·in /gámin/ *n.* **1** street urchin. **2** impudent boy.

ga·mine /gámeen/ *n.* **1** girl gamin. **2** girl with mischievous or boyish charm.

gam·ma /gámə/ *n.* third letter of the Greek alphabet (Γ, γ). □ **gamma radiation** (or **rays**) electromagnetic radiation of very short wavelength.

gam·ut /gámət/ *n.* whole series or range or scope of anything (*the whole gamut of crime*).

gamut late Middle English (denoting the musical scale of seven hexachords): from medieval Latin *gamma ut*, from *gamma* (taken as the name for a note one tone lower than A of the classical scale) and *ut*, the first of six arbitrary names of the notes forming the hexachord scale, from the initial syllables of words in a Latin hymn: *Ut queant laxis resonare fibris Mira gestorum famuli tuorum, Solve polluti labii reatum, Sancte Iohannes* (a further note, *si*, was added later, from the initial letters of the last two words).

gam·y /gáymee/ *adj.* (**gam·i·er, gam·i·est**) **1** having the flavor or scent of game. **2** scandalous; sensational. □□ **gam'i·ly** *adv.* **gam'i·ness** *n.*

gan·der /gándər/ *n.* **1** male goose. **2** *sl.* a look; a glance.

gang /gang/ *n.* **1 a** band of persons associating, esp. for criminal purposes. **b** *colloq.* such a band pursuing antisocial purposes. **2** set of workers, slaves, or prisoners. □ **gang up** *colloq.* **1** act in concert. **2** combine against.

gang·land /gángland, -lənd/ *n.* the world of organized crime.

gan·gling /gánggling/ *adj.* (of a person) loosely built; lanky.

gan·gli·on /gánggleeən/ *n.* (*pl.* **gan·gli·a** /-leeə/ or **gan·gli·ons**) structure containing an assemblage of nerve cells. □□ **gan·gli·ar** /-gleeər/ *adj.* **gan·gli·on·ic** /-leeónik/ *adj.*

gan·gly /gángglee/ *adj.* (**gan·gli·er, gan·gli·est**) = GANGLING.

gang·plank /gángplangk/ *n.* movable plank usu. with cleats nailed on it for boarding or disembarking from a ship, etc.

gan·grene /gánggreen/ *n.* *Med.* death and decomposition of a part of the body tissue, usu. resulting from obstructed circulation. □□ **gan·gre·nous** /gánggrinəs/ *adj.*

gang·ster /gángstər/ *n.* member of a gang of violent criminals. □□ **gang'ster·ism** *n.*

gang·way /gángway/ *n.* **1** opening in a ship's bulwarks. **2** bridge laid from ship to shore.

gan·net /gánit/ *n.* sea bird that catches fish by plunge-diving.

gant·let var. of GAUNTLET[2].

gan·try /gántree/ *n.* (*pl.* **-tries**) **1** overhead structure supporting a traveling crane, or railroad or road signals. **2** structure supporting a space rocket prior to launching.

GAO *abbr.* General Accounting Office.

gap /gap/ *n.* **1** unfilled space or interval; blank; break in continuity. **2** breach in a hedge, fence, or wall. **3** wide divergence in views, etc. □ **fill** (or **close**, etc.) **a gap** make up a deficiency. □□ **gapped** *adj.* **gap'py** *adj.*

gape /gayp/ • *v.intr.* **1 a** open one's mouth wide. **b** be or become wide open. **2** (foll. by *at*) gaze curiously or wonderingly. **3** split. • *n.* **1** openmouthed stare. **2** yawn. **3** open mouth or beak. **4** a rent or opening. □□ **gap'ing·ly** *adv.*

ga·rage /gəráazh, -ráaj/ • *n.* **1** building or shed for the storage of motor vehicles. **2** establishment selling gasoline, etc., or repairing and selling motor vehicles. • *v.tr.* put or keep (a motor vehicle) in a garage.

garb /gaarb/ • *n.* clothing, esp. of a distinctive kind. • *v.tr.* **1** put (esp. distinctive) clothes on (a person). **2** attire.

gar·bage /gáarbij/ *n.* **1 a** refuse; filth. **b** domes-

tic waste, esp. food wastes. **2** foul or inferior literature, etc. **3** nonsense.

gar·ble /gáarbəl/ *v.tr.* unintentionally distort or confuse (facts, messages, etc.). □□ **gar'bler** *n.*

gar·den /gáard'n/ • *n.* **1** piece of ground used for growing esp. flowers or vegetables. **2** (esp. in *pl.*) ornamental grounds laid out for public enjoyment (*botanical gardens*). • *v.intr.* cultivate or work in a garden. □□ **gar'den·er** *n.* **gar'den·ing** *n.*

gar·de·nia /gaardéenyə/ *n.* tree or shrub with large white or yellow flowers and usu. a fragrant scent.

gar·gan·tu·an /gaargánchoōən/ *adj.* enormous; gigantic.

gar·gle /gáargəl/ • *v.tr.* wash (one's mouth and throat), esp. for medicinal purposes, with a liquid kept in motion by breathing through it. • *n.* liquid used for gargling.

gar·goyle /gáargoyl/ *n.* grotesque carved human or animal face or figure, esp. as a spout from the gutter on a building.

GARGOYLE

gar·ish /gáirish/ *adj.* **1** obtrusively bright; showy. **2** gaudy; over-decorated. □□ **gar'ish·ly** *adv.* **gar'ish·ness** *n.*

gar·land /gáarlənd/ • *n.* wreath of flowers, leaves, etc. • *v.tr.* **1** adorn with garlands. **2** crown with a garland.

gar·lic /gáarlik/ *n.* plant of the onion family with pungent bulb, used as a flavoring in cooking. □□ **gar'lick·y** *adj.*

gar·ment /gáarmənt/ *n.* article of dress.

gar·ner /gáarnər/ *v.tr.* **1** collect. **2** store; deposit.

gar·net /gáarnit/ *n.* vitreous silicate mineral, esp. a transparent deep red kind used as a gem.

gar·nish /gáarnish/ • *v.tr.* **1** decorate or embellish (esp. food). **2** *Law* serve notice on (a person) for the purpose of legally seizing money belonging to a debtor or defendant. • *n.* (also **gar'nish·ing**) decoration or embellishment, esp. to food. □□ **gar'nish·ment** *n.* (in sense 2).

gar·nish·ee /gáarnishée/ *Law* • *n.* a person garnished. • *v.tr.* (**gar·nish·ees, gar·nish·eed**) **1** garnish (a person). **2** attach (money, etc.) by way of garnishment.

ga·rotte var. of GARROTE.

gar·ret /gárit/ *n.* **1** top floor or attic room. **2** attic.

gar·ri·son /gárisən/ • *n.* **1** troops stationed in a fortress, town, etc., to defend it. **2** the building occupied by them. • *v.tr.* provide (a place) with or occupy as a garrison.

gar·rote /gərót/ (also **ga·rotte'**; **gar·rotte'**) • *v.tr.* execute or kill by strangulation, esp. with an iron or wire collar, etc. • *n.* apparatus used for this.

gar·ru·lous /gárələs, gáryə-/ *adj.* 1 talkative, esp. on trivial matters. 2 loquacious; wordy. □□ **gar· ru·li·ty** /gəroʻolitee/ *n.* **gar'ru·lous·ly** *adv.* **gar' ru·lous·ness** *n.*

gar·ter /gaártər/ *n.* band worn to keep a sock or stocking or shirt sleeve up.

gas /gas/ • *n.* (*pl.* **gas·es**) 1 any airlike substance which moves freely to fill any space available, irrespective of its quantity. 2 such a substance used as fuel (also *attrib.*: *gas stove*). 3 nitrous oxide or another gas used as an anesthetic. 4 poisonous gas. 5 *colloq.* **a** gasoline. **b** motor vehicle's accelerator. 6 enjoyable, attractive, or amusing thing or person. • *v.* (**gas·es**, **gassed**, **gas·sing**) 1 *tr.* expose to gas, esp. to kill or make unconscious. 2 *tr. colloq.* fill (the tank of a motor vehicle) with gasoline. □ **gas chamber** room for execution by gas. **gas mask** respirator used as a defense against poison gas.

gas·e·ous /gáseeəs, gáshəs/ *adj.* of or like gas. □□ **gas'e·ous·ness** *n.*

gash /gash/ • *n.* long and deep slash, cut, or wound. • *v.tr.* make a gash in; cut.

gas·ket /gáskit/ *n.* sheet or ring of rubber, etc., shaped to seal the junction of metal surfaces.

gas·o·line /gásəleʻen/ *n.* volatile flammable liquid made from petroleum and used as a fuel.

gasp /gasp/ • *v.* 1 *intr.* catch one's breath with an open mouth as in exhaustion or astonishment. 2 *intr.* (foll. by *for*) strain to obtain by gasping (*gasped for air*). 3 *tr.* utter with gasps. • *n.* convulsive catching of breath. □ **at one's last gasp** 1 at the point of death. 2 exhausted.

gas·sy /gásee/ *adj.* (**gas·si·er**, **gas·si·est**) 1 of or like gas. 2 full of gas. □□ **gas'si·ness** *n.*

gas·tric /gástrik/ *adj.* of the stomach.

gas·tri·tis /gastrítis/ *n.* inflammation of the stomach.

gastro- /gástrō/ *comb. form* (also **gastr-** before a vowel) stomach.

gas·tron·o·my /gastrónəmee/ *n.* the practice, study, or art of eating and drinking well. □□ **gas·tro·nom·ic** /gástrənómik/ *adj.* **gas·tro· nom'i·cal** *adj.* **gas·tro·nom'i·cal·ly** *adv.*

gas·tro·pod /gástrəpod/ *n.* mollusk that moves along by means of a large muscular foot, e.g., a snail, slug, etc.

gate /gayt/ • *n.* 1 barrier, usu. hinged, used to close an entrance through a wall, fence, etc. 2 gateway. 3 means of entrance or exit. 4 numbered place of access to aircraft at an airport. 5 device regulating the passage of water in a lock, etc. 6 **a** number of people entering by payment at the gates of a sports stadium, etc. **b** (in full **gate money**) proceeds taken for admission. • *v.tr.* (as **gated** *adj.*) (of a road) having a gate or gates to control the movement of traffic or animals.

-gate /gayt/ *suffix* forming nouns denoting an actual or alleged scandal comparable in some way to the Watergate scandal of 1972 (*Irangate*).

gate·crash·er /gáytkrashər/ *n.* uninvited guest at a party, etc. □□ **gate'crash** *v.*

gate·fold /gáytfōld/ *n.* page in a book or magazine, etc., that folds out to be larger than the page format.

gate·house /gáyt-hows/ *n.* house standing by a gateway, esp. to a large house or park.

gate·way /gáytway/ *n.* 1 entrance with or opening for a gate. 2 entrance or exit.

gath·er /gáthər/ • *v.* 1 *tr. & intr.* bring or come together; assemble; accumulate. 2 *tr.* acquire by gradually collecting; amass. 3 *tr.* harvest. 4 *tr.* increase (*gather speed*). 6 *tr.* (often foll. by *up*) summon up (one's thoughts, energy, etc.) for a purpose. 7 *tr.* gain or recover (one's breath). 8 *tr.* draw (material, or one's brow) together in folds or wrinkles. • *n.* (in *pl.*) part of a garment that is gathered or drawn in. □□ **gath'er·er** *n.*

gath·er·ing /gáthəring/ *n.* assembly or meeting.

ga·tor /gáytər/ *n.* (also **ga'ter**) *colloq.* alligator.

GATT /gat/ *abbr.* (also **Gatt**) General Agreement on Tariffs and Trade.

gauche /gōsh/ *adj.* 1 lacking ease or grace; socially awkward. 2 tactless. □□ **gauche'ly** *adv.* **gauche'ness** *n.*

gau·che·rie /gōshəree/ *n.* gauche manners or action.

gau·cho /gówchō/ *n.* (*pl.* **-chos**) cowboy from the S. American pampas.

gaud·y /gáwdee/ *adj.* (**gaud·i·er**, **gaud·i·est**) tastelessly or extravagantly bright or showy. □□ **gaud'i·ly** *adv.* **gaud'i·ness** *n.*

gauge /gayj/ (also **gage**) • *n.* 1 standard measure to which certain things must conform, esp.: **a** a measure of the capacity or contents of a barrel. **b** fineness of a textile. **c** diameter of a bullet. **d** thickness of sheet metal. 2 instrument for measuring. 3 distance between a pair of rails or the wheels on one axle. 4 means of estimating; criterion or test. • *v.tr.* 1 measure exactly. 2 estimate or form a judgment of (a person, temperament, situation, etc.). □□ **gauge'a·ble** *adj.* **gaug'er** *n.*

¶ Leaving aside its sense 'pledge', **gage,** meaning 'measure,' is found in some technical writing, but **gauge** is the form used in almost all contexts.

Gaul /gawl/ *n.* native or inhabitant of ancient Gaul.

Gaul·ish /gáwlish/ • *adj.* of or relating to the ancient Gauls. • *n.* their language.

gaunt /gawnt/ *adj.* 1 lean; haggard. 2 grim or desolate in appearance. □□ **gaunt'ly** *adv.* **gaunt' ness** *n.*

gaunt·let[1] /gáwntlit/ *n.* 1 stout glove with a long loose wrist. 2 *hist.* armored glove. 3 the part of a glove covering the wrist. 4 challenge (esp. in **throw down the gauntlet**).

gaunt·let[2] /gáwntlit/ *n.* (also **gant·let** /gánt-/) □ **run the gauntlet** 1 be subjected to harsh criticism. 2 pass between two rows of people and receive punishing blows.

gauze /gawz/ *n.* thin transparent fabric of silk, cotton, etc.

gauz·y /gáwzee/ *adj.* (**gauz·i·er**, **gauz·i·est**) 1 like gauze. 2 flimsy; delicate. □□ **gauz'i·ly** *adv.* **gauz'i·ness** *n.*

gave *past of* GIVE.

gav·el /gávəl/ *n.* small hammer used by an auctioneer, or for calling a meeting, courtroom, etc., to order.

ga·votte /gəvót/ n. **1** old French dance. **2** music for this.

gawk /gawk/ v.intr. colloq. stare stupidly. □□ **gawk′ish** adj.

gawk·y /gáwkee/ adj. (**gawk·i·er, gawk·i·est**) awkward or ungainly. □□ **gawk′i·ly** adv. **gawk′i·ness** n.

gay /gay/ • adj. **1** lighthearted and carefree; mirthful. **2** characterized by cheerfulness or pleasure. **3** a homosexual. **b** intended for or used by homosexuals (gay bar). **4** brightly colored. • n. homosexual, esp. male. □□ **gay′ness** n.

gay·e·ty var. of GAIETY.

gaze /gayz/ • v.intr. look fixedly. • n. intent look. □□ **gaz′er** n.

ga·ze·bo /gəzéebō/ n. (pl. **-bos** or **-boes**) open-sided structure designed to give a wide view.

GAZEBO

ga·zelle /gəzél/ n. any of various graceful soft-eyed antelopes of Asia or Africa.

ga·zette /gəzét/ n. **1** newspaper, esp. the official one of an organization or institution (University Gazette). **2** hist. news sheet; periodical publication giving current events.

---

gazette early 17th century: via French from Italian gazzetta, originally Venetian gazeta de la novità 'a halfpennyworth of news' (because the newssheet sold for a gazeta, a Venetian coin of small value).

---

gaz·et·teer /gázitéer/ n. geographical index or dictionary.

gaz·pa·cho /gəspaáchō/ n. (pl. **-chos**) Spanish soup made with tomatoes, oil, garlic, onions, etc., and served cold.

GB abbr. Great Britain.

Gd symb. Chem. element gadolinium.

GDP abbr. gross domestic product.

Ge symb. Chem. germanium.

gear /geer/ • n. **1** (often in pl.) set of toothed wheels that work together, as in a vehicle. **2** particular setting of these (low gear). **3** equipment or tackle for a special purpose. **4** colloq. **a** clothing, esp. when modern or fashionable. **b** possessions in general. • v. **1** tr. adjust or adapt to. **2** tr. (foll. by up) make ready or prepared. □ **be geared** (or **all geared**) **up** colloq. be ready or enthusiastic.

gear·shift /geérshift/ n. lever used to engage or change gear.

gear·wheel /geérhweel, -weel/ n. **1** toothed wheel in a set of gears. **2** (in a bicycle) cogwheel driven directly by the chain.

geck·o /gékō/ n. (pl. **-os** or **-oes**) tropical lizard.

gee /jee/ int. (also **gee whiz** /wiz/) colloq. mild expression of surprise, discovery, etc.

geek /geek/ n. sl. **1** socially inept person. **2** carnival performer of sensational but disgusting acts.

geese pl. of GOOSE.

gee·zer /geézər/ n. sl. person, esp. an old man.

Gei·ger count·er /gígər/ n. device for measuring radioactivity by detecting and counting ionizing particles.

gei·sha /gáyshə, gée-/ n. (pl. same or **gei·shas**) Japanese hostess trained in entertaining men with dance and song.

gel /jel/ • n. **1** semisolid colloidal suspension or jelly. **2** gelatinous hairstyling preparation. • v.intr. (**gelled, gel·ling**) form a gel. □□ **ge·la′tion** n.

gel·a·tin /jélətin/ n. (also **gel·a·tine** /-teen/) transparent water-soluble protein derived from collagen and used in food preparation, photography, etc. □□ **ge·lat·i·nize** /jilát′nīz/ v. **ge·lat′i·ni·za·tion** n.

ge·lat·i·nous /jilát′nəs/ adj. **1** of or like gelatin. **2** of a jelly-like consistency. □□ **ge·lat′i·nous·ly** adv.

geld /geld/ v.tr. castrate or spay.

geld·ing /gélding/ n. gelded animal, esp. a male horse.

gem /jem/ n. **1** precious stone, esp. when cut and polished. **2** object or person of great beauty or worth. □□ **gem′like** adj. **gem′my** adj.

Gem·i·ni /jéminī, -nee/ n. **1** constellation and third sign of the zodiac (the Twins). **2** person born when the sun is in this sign.

gem·stone /jémstōn/ n. precious stone used as a gem.

Gen. abbr. **1** General. **2** Genesis (Old Testament).

-gen /jən/ comb. form **1** Chem. that which produces (hydrogen; antigen). **2** Bot. growth (endogen; exogen; acrogen).

gen·darme /zhondaárm/ n. police officer, esp. in France.

gen·der /jéndər/ n. **1 a** grammatical classification corresponding to the two sexes and sexlessness. **b** each of these classes of nouns. **2** colloq. a person's sex.

gene /jeen/ n. unit of heredity composed of DNA or RNA and forming part of a chromosome, etc., that determines a particular characteristic of an individual.

ge·ne·al·o·gy /jéeneeáləjee/ n. (pl. **-gies**) **1** descent traced continuously from an ancestor. **2** study of family descent. □□ **ge·ne·a·log·i·cal** /jéeneeəlójikal/ adj. **ge·ne·a·log′i·cal·ly** adv. **ge·ne·al′o·gist** n.

gen·er·al /jénərəl/ • adj. **1 a** completely or almost universal. **b** including or affecting all or nearly all parts or cases of things. **2** prevalent; widespread; usual. **3** not partial, particular, local, or sectional. **4** not limited in application; relating to whole classes or all cases. **5** not restricted, specialized, or detailed (a general idea). • n. **1 a** army officer ranking next above lieutenant general. **b** = brigadier general, lieutenant *general, major general.* **2** commander of an army. **3** tactician or strategist of specified merit (*a great general*). □ **general practitioner** nonspecialist doctor working in the community. **in general 1** as a normal rule; usually. **2** for the most part. □□ **gen·er·al·ist** /jénərəlist/ *n.* **gen′er·al·ness** *n.*

---

general Middle English: via Old French from Latin *generalis*, from *genus*, *gener-* 'class, race, kind.' The noun primarily denotes a person having overall authority: the sense 'army commander' is an abbreviation of *captain general*, from French *capitaine général* 'commander-in-chief.'

---

gen·er·a·lis·si·mo /jénərəlísimō/ *n.* (*pl.* **-mos**) commander of combined military forces in some countries.

gen·er·al·i·ty /jénərálitee/ *n.* (*pl.* **-ties**) **1** statement or principle, etc., having general validity or force. **2** applicability to a whole class of instances. **3** vagueness; lack of detail. **4** (foll. by *of*) the main body or majority.

gen·er·al·ize /jénərəlīz/ *v.* **1** *intr.* speak in general or indefinite terms. **2** *tr.* reduce to a general statement. **3** *tr.* infer (a law or conclusion) by induction. □□ **gen·er·al·i·za′tion** *n.* **gen′er·al·iz·er** *n.*

gen·er·al·ly /jénərəlee/ *adv.* **1** usually; in most cases. **2** in a general sense; without regard to particulars or exceptions.

gen·er·ate /jénərayt/ *v.tr.* **1** bring into existence; produce; evolve. **2** produce (electricity). □□ **gen·er·a·ble** /-rəbəl/ *adj.*

gen·er·a·tion /jénəráyshən/ *n.* **1** all the people born at a particular time, regarded collectively (*my generation*). **2** single step in descent or pedigree. **3** stage in (esp. technological) development (*fourth-generation computers*). **4** average time for a new human generation (about 30 years). **5** production, as of electricity or heat. **6** procreation. □ **Generation X** term used for people born from about 1965 to 1975. □□ **gen·er·a′tion·al** *adj.*

gen·er·a·tive /jénərətiv, -raytiv/ *adj.* **1** of or concerning procreation. **2** able to produce; productive.

gen·er·a·tor /jénəraytər/ *n.* **1** machine for converting mechanical into electrical energy. **2** apparatus for producing gas, steam, etc. **3** person who generates an idea, etc.

ge·ner·ic /jinérik/ *adj.* **1** characteristic of or relating to a class; general, not specific or special. **2** *Biol.* characteristic of or belonging to a genus. **3** (of goods, esp. a drug) having no trade or brand name. □□ **ge·ner′i·cal·ly** *adv.*

gen·er·ous /jénərəs/ *adj.* **1** giving or given freely. **2** magnanimous; noble-minded; unprejudiced. **3** ample; abundant. □□ **gen·er·os·i·ty** /-rósitee/ *n.* **gen′er·ous·ly** *adv.*

gen·e·sis /jénisis/ *n.* **1** origin, or mode of formation or generation, of a thing. **2** (**Genesis**) first book of the Old Testament.

ge·net·ic /jinétik/ *adj.* **1** of genetics or genes. **2** of or in origin. □ **genetic code** *Biochem.* arrangement of genetic information in chromosomes. **genetic engineering** manipulation of DNA to modify hereditary features. **genetic fingerprinting** (or **profiling**) identifying individuals by DNA

patterns from tissue samples. □□ **ge·net′i·cal·ly** *adv.*

ge·net·ics /jinétiks/ *n.pl.* (usu. treated as *sing.*) the study of heredity and the variation of inherited characteristics. □□ **ge·net·i·cist** /-isist/ *n.*

gen·i·al /jeeneeəl/ *adj.* **1** jovial; sociable; kindly; cheerful. **2** (of climate) mild and warm; conducive to growth. **3** cheering; enlivening. □□ **ge·ni·al·i·ty** /-neeálitee/ *n.* **ge′nial·ly** *adv.*

-genic /jénik/ *comb. form* forming adjectives meaning: **1** producing (*carcinogenic; pathogenic*). **2** well suited to (*photogenic; radiogenic*). **3** produced by (*iatrogenic*). □□ **-genically** *suffix* forming adverbs.

ge·nie /jeenee/ *n.* (*pl.* usu. **ge·ni·i** /jeenee-ī/) jinni, goblin, or familiar spirit of Arabian folklore.

gen·i·tal /jénit′l/ • *adj.* of or relating to animal reproduction. • *n.* (in *pl.*) external reproductive organs.

gen·i·ta·li·a /jénitáyleeə/ *n.pl.* genitals.

gen·i·tive /jénitiv/ *Gram.* • *n.* case indicating possession or close association. • *adj.* of or in the genitive. □□ **gen·i·ti·val** /-tívəl/ *adj.* **gen·i·ti′val·ly** *adv.*

ge·ni·us /jeenyəs/ *n.* (*pl.* **gen·ius·es** or **ge·ni·i** /-nee-ī/) **1** (*pl.* **gen·ius·es**) **a** exceptional intellectual or creative power or other natural ability or tendency. **b** person having this. **2** the tutelary spirit of a person, place, institution, etc.

---

genius late Middle English: from Latin, 'attendant spirit present from one's birth, innate ability or inclination,' from the root of *gignere* 'beget.' The original sense 'guardian spirit attendant on a person' gave rise to a sense 'a person's characteristic disposition' (late 16th century), which led to a sense 'a person's natural ability,' and finally 'exceptional natural ability' (mid-17th century).

---

genl. *abbr.* general.

gen·o·cide /jénəsīd/ *n.* deliberate extermination of a people or nation. □□ **gen·o·ci′dal** /-sīd′l/ *adj.*

-genous /jénəs/ *comb. form* forming adjectives meaning 'produced' (*endogenous*).

gen·re /zhónrə/ *n.* kind or style of art, etc. **2** (in full **gen′re paint′ing**) painting of scenes from ordinary life.

gent /jent/ *n. colloq.* (often *joc.*) gentleman.

gen·teel /jenteél/ *adj.* **1** affectedly or ostentatiously refined or stylish. **2** well-bred; refined; upper-class. □□ **gen·teel′ly** *adv.* **gen·teel′ness** *n.*

gen·tian /jénshən/ *n.* mountain plant usu. with vivid blue flowers.

Gen·tile /jéntīl/ • *adj.* not Jewish; heathen. • *n.* person who is not Jewish.

gen·til·i·ty /jentílitee/ *n.* **1** social superiority. **2** good manners; habits associated with the upper class.

gen·tle /jént′l/ *adj.* (**gen·tler**, **gen·tlest**) **1** not rough; mild or kind, esp. in temperament. **2** moderate; not severe or drastic (*gentle rebuke*). **3** (of birth, pursuits, etc.) honorable; refined. □□ **gen′tle·ness** *n.* **gen′tly** *adv.*

gen·tle·man /jént′lmən/ *n.* (*pl.* **-men**) **1** man (in polite or formal use). **2** chivalrous or well-bred man. **3** man of good social position. **4** (in

□□ **gen′tle·man·li·ness** *n.* **gen′tle·man·ly** *adj.*

gen·tri·fi·ca·tion /jéntrifikáyshən/ *n.* social advancement of an urban area by the refurbishing of buildings and arrival of affluent residents who displace poorer inhabitants. □□ **gen·tri·fy** /-fī/ *v.tr.* (**-fies, -fied**).

gen·try /jéntree/ *n.pl.* **1** (in aristocratic societies) people next below the nobility in position and birth. **2** people, esp. a specific group of people (*these gentry*).

gen·u·flect /jényəflekt/ *v.intr.* bend the knee, esp. in worship. □□ **gen·u·flec·tion** /-flékshən/ *n.* **gen′u·flec·tor** *n.*

gen·u·ine /jényōo-in/ *adj.* **1** really coming from its stated, advertised, or reputed source. **2** properly so called; not sham. **3** sincere. □□ **gen′u·ine·ly** *adv.* **gen′u·ine·ness** *n.*

ge·nus /jéenəs/ *n.* (*pl.* **gen·er·a** /jénərə/) **1** *Biol.* taxonomic grouping of organisms, usu. of several species, with common structural characteristics. **2** kind; class.

geo- /jée-ō/ *comb. form* earth.

ge·o·cen·tric /jée-ōséntrik/ *adj.* **1** considered as viewed from the center of the earth. **2** having or representing the earth as the center; not heliocentric. □□ **ge·o·cen′tri·cal·ly** *adv.*

ge·ode /jée-ōd/ *n.* **1** small cavity lined with crystals. **2** rock containing such a cavity. □□ **ge·o·dic** /jee-ódik/ *adj.*

ge·o·de·sic /jée·ədée·zik, -désik/ *adj.* (also **ge·o·det·ic** /-détik/) of or relating to geodesy. □ **geodesic dome** dome constructed as a framework of interlocked polygons.

ge·od·e·sy /jee·ódisee/ *n.* branch of mathematics dealing with the shape and area of the earth. □□ **ge·od′e·sist** *n.*

ge·o·graph·ic /jée·əgráfik/ *adj.* (also **ge·o·graph·i·cal** /-gráfikəl/) of or relating to geography. □ **geographic information system(s)** computerized system utilizing precise locational data for mapping, navigation, etc. Abbr.: **GIS.** □□ **ge·o·graph′i·cal·ly** *adv.*

ge·o·graph·i·cal var. of GEOGRAPHIC.

ge·og·ra·phy /jee·ógrəfee/ *n.* **1** the study of the earth's physical features, resources, and climate, and the physical aspects of its population. **2** main physical features of an area. □□ **ge·og′ra·pher** *n.*

geol. *abbr.* **1** geologic. **2** geological. **3** geologist. **4** geology.

ge·ol·o·gy /jee·óləjee/ *n.* science of the earth, including the composition, structure, and origin of its rocks. □□ **ge·o·log·ic** /jée·əlójik/ *adj.* **ge·o·log′i·cal** *adj.* **ge·o·log′i·cal·ly** *adv.* **ge·ol·o·gist** /-óləjist/ *n.*

geom. *abbr.* **1** geometric. **2** geometrical. **3** geometry.

ge·o·met·ric /jee·əmétrik/ *adj.* (also **ge·o·met′ri·cal**) **1** of, according to, or like geometry. **2** (of a design, architectural feature, etc.) characterized by or decorated with regular lines and shapes. □ **geometric progression** progression of numbers with a constant ratio between each number and the one before (as 1, 3, 9, 27, 81). □□ **ge·o·met′ri·cal·ly** *adv.*

ge·om·e·try /jee·ómitree/ *n.* the study of the properties and relations of points, lines, surfaces, and solids. □□ **ge·om·e·tri·cian** /jée·əmitrishən/ *n.*

ge·o·phys·ics /jée·ōfíziks/ *n.* the physics of the

243   gentrification ~ gerrymander

earth. □□ **ge·o·phys′i·cal** *adj.* **ge·o·phys·i·cist** /-zisist/ *n.*

Geor·gian¹ /jáwrjən/ • *adj.* of or relating to the state of Georgia. • *n.* native of Georgia.

Geor·gian² /jáwrjən/ • *adj.* of or relating to Georgia in the Caucasus. • *n.* **1** native of Georgia; person of Georgian descent. **2** language of Georgia.

ge·o·syn·chro·nous /jée·ōsíngkrənəs/ *adj.* (of an artificial satellite of the earth) moving in an orbit equal to the earth's period of rotation such as to remain in a fixed position above a point on the earth's surface. Also called **geostationary**.

ge·ra·ni·um /jəráyneeəm/ *n.* **1** herb or shrub bearing fruit shaped like the bill of a crane. **2** (in general use) widely cultivated garden plant with red, white, or pink flowers.

ger·bil /jərbil/ *n.* mouselike desert rodent with long hind legs.

ger·i·at·ric /jéreeátrik/ *adj.* **1** of old people. **2** *colloq.* old.

ger·i·at·rics /jéreeátriks/ *n.pl.* (usu. treated as *sing.*) branch of medicine or social science dealing with the health and care of old people. □□ **ger·i·a·tri·cian** /-ətríshən/ *n.*

germ /jərm/ *n.* **1** microorganism, esp. one that causes disease. **2** seed. **3** original idea, etc., from which something may develop; elementary principle. □□ **germ′y** *adj.*

Ger·man /jərmən/ • *n.* **1** native or inhabitant of Germany; person of German descent. **2** language of Germany. • *adj.* of Germany or its people or language. □ **German measles** contagious disease, rubella, with symptoms like mild measles. **German shepherd** breed of large dog bred from the wolfhound.

ger·mane /jərmáyn/ *adj.* (usu. foll. by *to*) relevant (to a subject under consideration). □□ **ger·mane′ly** *adv.* **ger·mane′ness** *n.*

Ger·man·ic /jərmánik/ • *adj.* **1** having German characteristics. **2** *hist.* of the Germans. **3** of the Scandinavians, Anglo-Saxons, or Germans. **4** of the languages or language group called Germanic. • *n.* **1** branch of Indo-European languages including English, German, Dutch, and the Scandinavian languages. **2** the (unrecorded) early language from which other Germanic languages developed.

ger·ma·ni·um /jərmáyneeəm/ *n. Chem.* lustrous brittle semimetallic element. ¶ Symb.: **Ge.**

ger·mi·cide /jərmisīd/ *n.* substance destroying germs, esp. those causing disease. □□ **ger·mi·cid·al** /-síd′l/ *adj.*

ger·mi·nal /jərminəl/ *adj.* **1** relating to or of the nature of a germ or germs. **2** in the earliest stage of development. **3** productive of new ideas. □□ **ger′mi·nal·ly** *adv.*

ger·mi·nate /jərminayt/ *v.* **1 a** *intr.* sprout, bud, or put forth shoots. **b** *tr.* cause to sprout or shoot. **2** *tr.* cause (ideas, etc.) to originate or develop. □□ **ger·mi·na·tion** /-náyshən/ *n.* **ger′mi·na·tor** *n.*

ger·on·tol·o·gy /jarontóləjee/ *n.* the study of old age and aging. □□ **ge·ron·to·log·i·cal** /-təlójikəl/ *adj.* **ger·on·tol′o·gist** *n.*

ger·ry·man·der /jérimándər/ • *v.tr.* manipulate the boundaries of (a constituency, etc.) for political advantage. • *n.* this practice. □□ **ger·ry·man′der·er** *n.*

gerrymander early 19th century: from the name of Governor Elbridge *Gerry* of Massachusetts + (*sala*)*mander*, from the supposed similarity between a salamander and the shape of a new voting district on a map drawn when he was in office (1812), the creation of which was felt to favor his party: the map (with claws, wings, and fangs added), was published in the Boston *Weekly Messenger*, with the title *The Gerry-Mander*.

ger·und /jérənd/ *n. Gram.* verbal noun, in English ending in *-ing* (e.g., *do you mind my asking you?*; *swimming is my favorite exercise*).

Ge·sta·po /gestaápō, -shtaá-/ *n.* German secret police under Nazi rule.

ges·tate /jéstáyt/ *v.tr.* **1** carry (a fetus) in gestation. **2** develop (an idea, etc.).

ges·ta·tion /jestáyshən/ *n.* **1 a** process of carrying or being carried in the womb between conception and birth. **b** this period. **2** private development of a plan, idea, etc.

ges·tic·u·late /jestíkyəlayt/ *v.* **1** *intr.* use gestures instead of or in addition to speech. **2** *tr.* express with gestures. □□ **ges·tic·u·la·tion** /-láyshən/ *n.* **ges·tic′u·la·tive** *adj.* **ges·tic′u·la·tor** *n.* **ges·tic·u·la·to·ry** /-lətáwree/ *adj.*

ges·ture /jés-chər/ • *n.* **1** significant movement of a limb or the body. **2** use of such movements, esp. to convey feeling or as a rhetorical device. **3** action to evoke a response or convey intention, usu. friendly. • *v.* gesticulate. □□ **ges′tur·al** *adj.* **ges′tur·er** *n.*

ge·sund·heit /gəzoöont-hīt/ *int.* expressing a wish of good health, esp. to a person who has sneezed.

get /get/ • *v.* (**get·ting**; *past* **got** /got/; *past part.* **got** or (and in *comb.*) **got·ten** /gót′n/) **1** *tr.* come into the possession of; receive or earn. **2** *tr.* **a** fetch; procure. **b** get hold of (a person). **3** *tr.* go to catch (a bus, train, etc.). **4** *tr.* prepare (a meal, etc.). **5** *intr.* & *tr.* reach or cause to reach a certain state; become or cause to become (*get rich*; *got them ready*). **6** *tr.* contract (a disease, etc.). **7** *tr.* establish contact by telephone or radio. **8** *tr.* experience or suffer; have inflicted on one (*got four years in prison*). **9 a** *tr.* succeed in bringing, placing, etc. (*get it onto the agenda*). **b** *intr.* & *tr.* succeed or cause to succeed in coming or going (*get you there somehow*). **10** *tr.* (prec. by *have*) **a** possess. **b** (foll. by *to* + infin.) be bound or obliged (*have got to see you*). **11** *tr.* induce; prevail upon (*got them to help me*). **12** *tr. colloq.* understand (a person or an argument) (*have you got that?*). **13** *tr. colloq.* punish; retaliate (*I'll get you for that*). **14** *tr. colloq.* **a** annoy. **b** affect emotionally. **c** attract. **15** *tr.* develop an inclination (*getting to like it*). **16** *intr.* begin (*get going*). **17** *tr.* conceive (an idea, etc.). • *n.* **1 a** act of begetting (of animals). **b** an offspring (of animals). □ **get about** (or **around**) **1** travel extensively or fast. **2** manage to walk, etc. (esp. after illness). **3** (of news) be circulated, esp. orally. **get at** **1** reach; get hold of. **2** *colloq.* imply. **get away with** **1** escape blame or punishment for. **2** steal. **get back at** *colloq.* retaliate against. **get by** *colloq.* just manage. **get off** **1** *colloq.* be acquitted; escape with little or no punishment. **2** leave. **3** alight from (a bus, etc.). **get on** **1** make progress. **2** enter (a bus, etc.). **get out** **1** leave or escape. **2** manage to go outdoors. **3** alight from a vehicle. **4** become known. **get out of** avoid or escape (a duty, etc.). **get over** recover from (an illness, upset, etc.). **get through** **1** pass or assist in passing (an examination, etc.). **2** manage; survive. **3** make contact. **4** (foll. by *to*) succeed in making (a person) listen or understand. **get-together** *n. colloq.* social gathering. **get-up** *n. colloq.* style or arrangement of dress, etc., esp. an elaborate one. □□ **get′ta·ble** *adj.*

get·a·way /gétəway/ *n.* escape, esp. after a crime.

gew·gaw /gyoógaw, goó-/ *n.* gaudy plaything or ornament.

gey·ser /gízər/ *n.* intermittently gushing hot spring.

Gha·na·ian /gaáneeən/ • *adj.* of Ghana in W. Africa. • *n.* native or inhabitant of Ghana; person of Ghanaian descent.

ghast·ly /gástlee/ *adj.* (**ghast·li·er**, **ghast·li·est**) **1** horrible; frightful. **2** *colloq.* objectionable; unpleasant. **3** deathlike; pallid. □□ **ghast′li·ness** *n.*

ghee /gee/ *n.* clarified butter, esp. from the milk of a buffalo or cow.

gher·kin /gərkin/ *n.* small variety of cucumber, or a young green cucumber, used for pickling.

ghet·to /gétō/ *n.* (*pl.* **-tos**) **1** part of a city, esp. a slum area, occupied by a minority group or groups. **2** *hist.* Jewish quarter in a city. **3** segregated group or area.

ghost /gōst/ • *n.* **1** supposed apparition of a dead person or animal; disembodied spirit. **2** shadow or mere semblance. **3** secondary or duplicated image produced by defective television reception or by a telescope. • *v.* **1** *intr.* act as ghost writer. **2** *tr.* act as ghost writer of (a work). □ **ghost town** deserted town with few or no remaining inhabitants. □□ **ghost′like** *adj.*

ghost·ly /góstlee/ *adj.* (**ghost·li·er**, **ghost·li·est**) like a ghost; spectral. □□ **ghost′li·ness** *n.*

ghost·write /gόstrīt/ *v.* write on behalf of the credited author of a work. □□ **ghost′writ·er** *n.*

ghoul /gool/ *n.* **1** person morbidly interested in death, etc. **2** evil spirit in Muslim folklore preying on corpses. □□ **ghoul′ish** *adj.* **ghoul′ish·ly** *adv.* **ghoul′ish·ness** *n.*

GI /jeé-í/ *n.* soldier in the US armed forces, esp. the army.

gi·ant /jīənt/ • *n.* **1** imaginary or mythical being of human form but superhuman size. **2** abnormally tall or large person, animal, or plant. **3** person of exceptional ability, integrity, courage, etc. • *attrib.adj.* very large. □□ **gi′ant·ism** *n.* **giant′like** *adj.*

gib·ber /jíbər/ *v.intr.* speak fast and inarticulately.

gib·ber·ish /jíbərish/ *n.* unintelligible or meaningless speech; nonsense.

gib·bet /jíbit/ *n. hist.* **1** gallows. **2** post with an arm on which the bodies of executed criminals were hung up.

gib·bon /gíbən/ *n.* small ape native to SE Asia, having a slender body and long arms.

gib·bous /gíbəs/ *adj.* **1** convex. **2** (of a moon or planet) appearing greater than a semicircle and less than a circle. □□ **gib·bos·i·ty** /-bósitee/ *n.* **gib′bous·ly** *adv.* **gib′bous·ness** *n.*

gibe /jīb/ (also **jibe**) • *v.intr.* (often foll. by *at*) jeer; mock. • *n.* instance of gibing; taunt. □□ **gib′er** *n.*
¶ See note at JIBE.

gib·lets /jíblits/ *n.pl.* liver, gizzard, neck, etc., of a bird.

gid·dy /gídee/ adj. (**gid·di·er, gid·di·est**) 1 having a sensation of whirling and a tendency to fall, stagger, or spin around. 2 mentally intoxicated. b excitable; frivolous. 3 tending to make one giddy. □□ **gid'di·ly** adv. **gid'di·ness** n.

gift /gift/ n. 1 thing given; a present. 2 natural ability or talent. 3 act or instance of giving. □ **gift wrap** (**wrapped, wrap·ping**) wrap attractively as a gift.

gift·ed /gíftid/ adj. exceptionally talented or intelligent. □□ **gift'ed·ly** adv. **gift'ed·ness** n.

gig[1] /gig/ n. 1 light two-wheeled one-horse carriage. 2 light ship's boat for rowing or sailing.

gig[2] /gig/ n. colloq. engagement to play music, etc.

giga- /gígə, jígə/ comb. form denoting a factor of 10⁹.

gig·a·bit /gígəbit, jígə-/ n. Computing unit of information equal to one billion (10⁹) bits.

gig·a·byte /gígəbīt, jígə-/ n. Computing unit of information equal to one billion (10⁹) bytes.

gi·gan·tic /jīgántik/ adj. 1 enormous. 2 like or suited to a giant. □□ **gi·gan·tesque** /-tésk/ adj. **gi·gan'ti·cal·ly** adv.

gig·gle /gígəl/ • v.intr. laugh in half-suppressed spasms, esp. in an affected or silly manner. • n. such a laugh. □□ **gig'gly** adj. (**gig·gli·er, gig·gli·est**). **gig'gli·ness** n.

GIGO /gígō/ n. Computing abbr. for garbage in, garbage out, an informal rule stating that the quality of the data input determines the quality of the results.

gig·o·lo /jígəlō, zhíg-/ n. (pl. **-los**) young man paid by an older woman to be her escort or lover.

gild /gild/ v.tr. (past part. **gild·ed** or as adj. in sense 1 **gilt**) 1 cover thinly with gold. 2 give a specious or false brilliance to. □□ **gild'er** n. **gild'ing** n.

gill[1] /gil/ n. (usu. in pl.) respiratory organ in fishes and other aquatic animals. □□ **gilled** adj. (also in comb.).

gill[2] /jil/ n. unit of liquid measure, equal to a quarter of a pint.

gilt /gilt/ • adj. 1 covered thinly with gold. 2 gold-colored. • n. gilding. □ **gilt-edged** (of securities, stocks, etc.) very reliable.

gim·bals /gímbəlz, jím-/ n.pl. contrivance, usu. of rings and pivots, for keeping a stove or instruments such as a compass and chronometer horizontal at sea, in the air, etc.

gim·crack /jímkrak/ • adj. showy but flimsy and worthless. • n. cheap showy ornament; knick-knack. □□ **gim'crack·er·y** n. **gim'crack·y** adj.

gim·let /gímlit/ n. 1 small tool with a screw tip for boring holes. 2 cocktail, usu. of gin and lime juice.

gim·mick /gímik/ n. colloq. trick or device, esp. to attract attention or publicity. □□ **gim'mick·ry** n. **gim'mick·y** adj.

gin[1] /jin/ n. distilled alcoholic spirit flavored with juniper berries. □ **gin rummy** form of the card game rummy.

gin[2] /jin/ • n. 1 machine for separating cotton from its seeds. 2 snare or trap. 3 kind of crane and windlass. • v.tr. (**ginned, gin·ning**) treat (cotton) in a gin. □□ **gin'ner** n.

gin·ger /jínjər/ • n. 1 a hot spicy root used as a spice or flavoring. b plant having this root. 2 light reddish yellow color. 3 spirit; mettle. • adj. of a ginger color. □ **ginger ale** carbonated

245 giddy ~ give

nonalcoholic clear drink flavored with ginger extract. **ginger beer** carbonated sometimes mildly alcoholic cloudy drink, made from ginger and syrup. □□ **gin'ger·y** adj.

gin·ger·bread /jínjərbred/ n. 1 cake made with molasses or syrup and flavored with ginger. 2 (often attrib.) gaudy, lavish, or superfluous decoration or ornament.

gin·ger·ly /jínjərlee/ • adv. in a careful or cautious manner. • adj. showing great care or caution. □□ **gin'ger·li·ness** n.

ging·ham /ging-əm/ n. plain-woven cotton cloth, esp. striped or checked.

gin·gi·va /jinjívə, jínjivə/ n. (pl. **gin·gi·vae** /-vee/) the gum. □□ **gin·gi·val** /-jívəl, -jívəl/ adj.

gin·gi·vi·tis /jínjivítis/ n. inflammation of the gums.

gink·go /gíngkgō/ n. (also **ging'ko**) (pl. **-gos** or **-goes**) tree with fan-shaped leaves and yellow flowers.

gin·seng /jínseng/ n. 1 medicinal plant found in E. Asia and N. America. 2 root of this.

Gip·sy var. of GYPSY.

gi·raffe /jiráf/ n. (pl. same or **gi·raffes**) ruminant African mammal, with a long neck and forelegs.

---

giraffe late 16th century: from French girafe, Italian giraffa, or Spanish and Portuguese girafa, based on Arabic zarāfa. The animal was known in Europe in the medieval period, and isolated instances of names for it based on the Arabic are recorded in Middle English, when it was commonly called the camelopard.

---

gird /gərd/ v.tr. (past and past part. **gird·ed** or **girt**) 1 encircle or secure with a belt or band. 2 enclose or encircle.

gird·er /górdər/ n. large iron or steel support beam.

gir·dle /górd'l/ • n. 1 belt or cord worn around the waist. 2 woman's corset. 3 thing that surrounds. • v.tr. surround with a girdle.

girl /gərl/ n. 1 female child or youth. 2 colloq. young (esp. unmarried) woman. 3 colloq. girlfriend or sweetheart. 4 derog. female servant. □ **Girl Scout** member of an organization of girls, esp. the Girl Scouts of America, that promotes character, skills, etc. □□ **girl'hood** n. **girl'ish** adj. **girl'ish·ly** adv. **girl'ish·ness** n. □□ **girlish** see YOUNG adj. 3.

girl·friend /górlfrend/ n. 1 regular female companion or lover. 2 female friend.

girt past part. of GIRD.

girth /gərth/ n. 1 distance around a thing. 2 band around the body of a horse to secure the saddle, etc.

GIS abbr. geographic information system(s).

gist /jist/ n. substance or essence of a matter.

give /giv/ • v. (past **gave** /gayv/; past part. **giv·en** /gívən/) 1 tr. transfer the possession of freely; hand over as a present. 2 tr. a bequeath. b transfer temporarily; provide with. c administer (medicine). d deliver (a message). 3 tr. a pay (gave him $30 for the bicycle). b sell (gave him the bicycle for $30) 4 tr. a confer; grant. b bestow. c award. d pledge (gave his word). 5 tr. a perform;

execute. **b** utter (*gave a shriek*). **6** *tr.* yield as a product or result. **7** *intr.* **a** yield to pressure. **b** collapse (*the roof gave under the pressure*). **8** *tr.* devote; dedicate. **9** *tr.* offer; show. **10** *tr.* impart; be a source of. • *n.* capacity to yield; elasticity. □ **give and take** *v.tr.* exchange (words, blows, or concessions). • *n.* exchange of words, etc.; compromise. **give away 1** transfer as a gift. **2** hand over (a bride) ceremonially to a bridegroom. **3** betray or expose to ridicule or detection. **give in** cease fighting; yield. **give off** emit (vapor, etc.). **give or take** *colloq.* more or less. **give out 1** announce; emit. **2** break down from exhaustion, etc. **3** run short. **give rise to** cause. **give up 1** resign; surrender. **2** part with. **3** deliver (a wanted person, etc.). **4** renounce hope of. **5** renounce or cease (an activity). **give way** see WAY. □□ **giv′a·ble, give′a·ble** *adj.* **giv′er** *n.*

giv·en /gívən/ • *adj.* assumed; granted; specified (*a given number of people*). • *n.* known fact or situation.

giz·mo /gízmō/ *n.* (also **gis′mo**) (*pl.* **-mos**) *sl.* gadget.

giz·zard /gízərd/ *n.* second part of a bird's stomach, for grinding food usu. with grit.

gla·cé /glasáy/ *adj.* **1** (of fruit, esp. cherries) candied. **2** (of cloth, leather, etc.) smooth; polished.

gla·cial /gláyshəl/ *adj.* **1** of ice; icy. **2** *Geol.* characterized or produced by ice. **3** *colloq.* exceptionally slow. □ **glacial epoch** period when ice-sheets were exceptionally extensive. □□ **gla′cial·ly** *adv.*

gla·cier /gláyshər/ *n.* mass of land ice formed by the accumulation of snow on high ground.

glad /glad/ *adj.* (**glad·der, glad·dest**) **1** (*predic.*) pleased; willing (*he'll be glad to come*). **2 a** marked by, filled with, or expressing, joy (*a glad expression*). **b** (of news, events, etc.) giving joy (*glad tidings*). □ **glad-hand** *v.tr.* greet cordially or welcome, esp. insincerely. **glad rags** *colloq.* best clothes; evening dress. □□ **glad′ly** *adv.* **glad′ness** *n.*

glad·den /glád′n/ *v.* make or become glad.

glade /glayd/ *n.* open space in a wood or forest.

glad·i·a·tor /gládee-aytər/ *n. hist.* trained fighter at ancient Roman shows. □□ **glad·i·a·tor·i·al** /-deeətáwreeəl/ *adj.*

gla·di·o·lus /gládeeōləs/ *n.* (*pl.* **gla·di·o·li** /-lī/ or **gla·di·o·lus·es**) plant of the lily family with sword-shaped leaves and flower spikes.

Glad·stone bag /gládstōn, -stən/ *n.* suitcase that opens flat into two equal compartments.

glam·or·ize /glámərīz/ *v.tr.* (also **glam′our·ize**) make glamorous or attractive. □□ **glam·or·i·za′tion** *n.*

glam·our /glámər/ (also **glam′or**) *n.* **1** physical or cosmetic attractiveness. **2** excitement; adventure (*the glamour of New York*). □ **glamour girl** (or **boy**) attractive young woman (or man), esp. a model, etc. □□ **glam′or·ous** *adj.* **glam′or·ous·ly** *adv.*

glance /glans/ • *v.intr.* **1** cast a momentary look. **2** (esp. of a weapon) glide or bounce (off an object). **3** (of talk or a talker) pass quickly over a subject(s) (*glanced over the bill*). **4** (of a bright object or light) flash, dart, or gleam; reflect (*the sun glanced off the knife*). • *n.* **1** brief look (*took a glance at the paper*). **2 a** flash or gleam (*a glance of sunlight*). **b** sudden movement producing this. □ **at a glance** immediately upon looking. □□ **glanc′ing·ly** *adv.*

gland /gland/ *n.* **1** organ in an animal that secretes substances. **2** *Bot.* secreting cells on the surface of a plant.

glan·du·lar /glánjələr/ *adj.* of a gland or glands.

glare /glair/ • *v.* **1** *intr.* look fiercely or fixedly. **2** *intr.* shine dazzlingly. **3** *tr.* express (hate, defiance, etc.) by a look. **4** *intr.* be overly conspicuous. • *n.* **1 a** strong fierce light. **b** oppressive public attention (*the glare of fame*). **2** fierce or fixed look (*a glare of defiance*). □□ **glar′y** *adj.*

glar·ing /gláiring/ *adj.* **1** obvious; conspicuous (*a glaring error*). **2** shining oppressively. □□ **glar′ing·ly** *adv.*

glas·nost /glaásnɔst, -nawst/ *n.* (in the former Soviet Union) policy of more open government.

glass /glas/ • *n.* **1** (often *attrib.*) hard, brittle, usu. transparent substance, made by fusing sand with soda and lime, etc. **2** (often *collect.*) object made from glass, esp. a drinking vessel. **3** (in *pl.*) **a** eyeglasses. **b** binoculars; opera glasses. **4** liquid in a glass; a drink (*he likes a glass*). • *v.tr.* (usu. as **glassed** *adj.*) fit with glass; glaze. • *adj.* of or made from glass. □ **glass case** exhibition display case made mostly from glass. **glass ceiling** barrier hindering promotion, esp. of women and minorities, to executive positions. **glass cutter 1** worker who cuts glass. **2** tool used for cutting glass. □□ **glass′ful** *n.* (*pl.* **-fuls**). **glass′like** *adj.*

glass·ware /glásswair/ *n.* articles made from glass, esp. drinking glasses, tableware, etc.

glass·y /glásee/ • *adj.* (**glas·si·er, glas·si·est**) **1** of or resembling glass. **2** (of the eye, expression, etc.) abstracted; dull; fixed (*fixed her with a glassy stare*). • *n.* (also **glas′sie**) glass playing marble. □□ **glass′i·ly** *adv.* **glass′i·ness** *n.*

glau·co·ma /glawkómə, glou-/ *n.* eye condition with increased pressure in the eyeball, causing gradual loss of sight.

glaze /glayz/ • *v.* **1** *tr.* **a** fit (a window, picture, etc.) with glass. **b** provide (a building) with windows. **2** *tr.* cover (pottery, etc.) with a clear, shiny finish. **3** *tr.* cover (pastry, meat, etc.) with a glaze. **4** *intr.* (of the eyes) become fixed or glassy (*his eyes glazed over*). • *n.* **1** vitreous substance used to glaze pottery. **2** shiny coating. □□ **glaz′er** *n.* **glaz′y** *adj.*

gla·zier /gláyzhər/ *n.* person whose trade is glazing windows, etc. □□ **gla′zier·y** *n.*

gleam /gleem/ • *n.* faint or brief light or show (*a gleam of sunlight; not a gleam of hope*). • *v.intr.* **1** emit gleams. **2** shine.

glean /gleen/ *v.tr.* **1** collect (news, facts, gossip, etc.) in small quantities. **2** (also *absol.*) gather (grain, etc.) after the harvest. □□ **glean′er** *n.* **glean′ings** *n.*

glee /glee/ *n.* mirth; delight (*watched the enemy's defeat with glee*). □ **glee club** group that sings choral compositions.

glee·ful /gleéfool/ *adj.* joyful. □□ **glee′ful·ly** *adv.* **glee′ful·ness** *n.*

glen /glen/ *n.* narrow valley.

glide /glīd/ • *v.* **1** *intr.* (of a stream, snake, skater, etc.) move with a smooth continuous motion. **2** *intr.* (of an aircraft, esp. a glider) fly without engine power. **3** *intr.* pass gently and imperceptibly (*night glided into day*). **4** *intr.* move quietly or stealthily. **5** *tr.* cause to glide. • *n.* **1** gliding. **2** *Phonet.* gradually changing sound made in passing from one position of the speech organs to another. **3** gliding dance. **4** flight in a glider. □□ **glid′ing·ly** *adv.*

glid·er /glídər/ • *n.* **1** aircraft that flies without an engine. **2** porch swing with a gliding motion.

glim·mer /glímər/ • *v.intr.* shine faintly or intermittently. • *n.* **1** feeble or wavering light. **2** faint gleam (of hope, understanding, etc.). □□ **glim′ mer·ing·ly** *adv.*

glimpse /glimps/ • *n.* **1** momentary or partial view. **2** faint transient appearance (*glimpses of the truth*). • *v.* **1** *tr.* see faintly or partly (*glimpsed his face in the crowd*). **2** *intr.* cast a passing glance.

glint /glint/ • *v.* flash or cause to flash; glitter; sparkle; reflect (*eyes glinted with amusement*). • *n.* flash; sparkle.

glis·san·do /glisaándō/ *n.* (*pl.* **glis·san·di** /-dee/ or **-dos**) *Mus.* continuous slide of adjacent notes upward or downward.

glis·ten /glísən/ • *v.intr.* shine, esp. like a wet object, snow, etc.; glitter. • *n.* glitter; sparkle.

glitch /glich/ *n. colloq.* sudden irregularity or malfunction.

glit·ter /glítər/ • *v.intr.* **1** shine, esp. with a bright reflected light; sparkle. **2** be showy or ostentatious. • *n.* **1** gleam; sparkle. **2** showiness; splendor. **3** sparkling material as decoration. □□ **glit′ ter·y** *adj.*

glitz /glits/ *n. sl.* showy glamour. □□ **glitz′y** *adj.* (**glitz·i·er, glitz·i·est**)

gloam·ing /glṓming/ *n. poet.* twilight; dusk.

gloat /glōt/ • *v.intr.* consider with lust, greed, malice, triumph, etc. • *n.* **1** gloating. **2** expression of satisfaction. □□ **gloat′ing·ly** *adv.*

glob /glob/ *n.* soft mass or lump.

glob·al /glṓbəl/ *adj.* **1** worldwide (*global conflict*). **2** all-embracing; total. □ **global warming** increase in temperature of the earth's atmosphere caused by the greenhouse effect. □□ **glob′al·ly** *adv.*

globe /glōb/ *n.* **1 a** (prec. by *the*) the earth. **b** planet, star, or sun. **c** spherical body. **2** spherical representation of earth with a map on the surface. □ **globe-trotter** person who travels widely. **globe-trotting** such travel. □□ **globe′like** *adj.*

glob·u·lar /glóbyələr/ *adj.* **1** globe-shaped; spherical. **2** composed of globules. □□ **glob′u· lar·ly** *adv.*

glob·ule /glóbyōōl/ *n.* small round particle; drop.

glock·en·spiel /glókənspeel, -shpeel/ *n.* musical instrument with metal bars, tubes, or bells, played with hammers.

GLOCKENSPIEL

gloom /glōōm/ • *n.* **1** darkness; obscurity. **2** melancholy; despondency. • *v.* **1** *intr.* be melancholy; frown. **2** *intr.* (of the sky, etc.) be dull or threatening. **3** *tr.* make dark or dismal.

gloom·y /glṓomee/ *adj.* (**gloom·i·er, gloom·i·est**) **1** dark; unlighted. **2** depressed; sullen. **3** dismal; depressing. □□ **gloom′i·ly** *adv.* **gloom′i·ness** *n.*

glo·ri·fy /gláwrifī/ *v.tr.* (**-fies, -fied**) **1** exalt; make glorious. **2** transform into something more splendid. **3** extol; praise. **4** (as **glorified** *adj.*) seeming or pretending to be better than in reality (*just a glorified office boy*). □□ **glo·ri·fi·ca′tion** *n.*

glo·ri·ous /gláwreeəs/ *adj.* **1** possessing glory; illustrious. **2** conferring glory; honorable. **3** *colloq.* splendid; magnificent; delightful (*a glorious day*). □□ **glo′ri·ous·ly** *adv.*

glo·ry /gláwree/ • *n.* (*pl.* **-ries**) **1** renown or fame; honor. **2** adoring praise and thanksgiving (*glory to the Lord*). **3** resplendent majesty, beauty, etc. (*the glory of Versailles*). **4** thing that brings renown or praise; distinction. **5** heavenly bliss and splendor. • *v.intr.* pride oneself; exult (*glory in their skill*). □ **glory be! 1** a devout ejaculation. **2** *colloq.* an exclamation of surprise or delight. **go to glory** *sl.* die; be destroyed.

gloss[1] /glaws, glos/ • *n.* **1** surface shine or luster. **2** deceptively attractive appearance. **3** (in full **gloss paint**) paint formulated to give a hard glossy finish. • *v.tr.* make glossy. □ **gloss over 1** seek to conceal beneath a false appearance. **2** conceal or evade by mentioning briefly or misleadingly.

gloss[2] /glaws, glos/ • *n.* **1** explanatory comment inserted between the lines or in the margin of a text. **2** comment, explanation, interpretation, or paraphrase. **3** glossary. • *v.* **1** *tr.* add a gloss to (a text, word, etc.). **2** *intr.* make (esp. unfavorable) comments.

glos·sa·ry /gláwsəree, -glós/ *n.* (*pl.* **-ries**) (also **gloss**) alphabetical list of terms relating to a specific subject or text; brief dictionary.

glos·so·la·li·a /gláwsəláyleeə, glós-/ *n.* = *gift of tongues* (see TONGUE).

gloss·y /gláwsee, glós-/ • *adj.* (**gloss·i·er, gloss· i·est**) **1** shiny; smooth. **2** printed on such paper; expensive and attractive, but sometimes lacking in content. • *n.* (*pl.* **-ies**) *colloq.* glossy magazine or photograph. □□ **gloss′i·ly** *adv.* **gloss′i·ness** *n.*

glot·tal /glót'l/ *adj.* of the glottis. □ **glottal stop** sound produced by the sudden opening or shutting of the glottis.

glot·tis /glótis/ *n.* space between the vocal cords, affecting voice modulation through expansion or contraction.

glove /gluv/ • *n.* **1** hand covering, worn esp. for protection against cold or dirt, usu. with separate fingers. **2** padded protective glove, esp.: **a** boxing glove. **b** *Baseball* fielder's glove. • *v.tr.* cover or provide with a glove(s). □ **glove compartment** recess or cabinet for small articles in the dashboard of a motor vehicle. **throw down** (or **take up**) **the glove** issue (or accept) a challenge. **with the gloves off** mercilessly; unfairly.

glow /glō/ • *v.intr.* **1** emit light and heat without flame; be incandescent. **2 a** (of the body) be heated; sweat. **b** express or feel strong emotion (*glowed with pride*). **3** show a warm color (*the painting glows with warmth*). **4** (as **glowing** *adj.*) expressing pride or satisfaction (*a glowing report*). • *n.* **1** glowing state. **2** bright warm color.

3 feeling of satisfaction or well-being. □□ **glow′ ing·ly** adv.

glow·er /glowər/ • v.intr. stare or scowl, esp. angrily. • n. glowering look. □□ **glow′er·ing·ly** adv.

glow·worm /glṓwərm/ n. beetle whose wingless female emits light from the end of the abdomen.

glu·cose /glṓokōs/ n. **1** simple sugar found in blood, fruit juice, etc. (see DEXTROSE). ¶ Chem. formula: $C_6H_{12}O_6$. **2** syrup containing glucose sugars.

glue /glṓo/ • n. adhesive substance. • v.tr. (**glues, glued, glu·ing** or **glue·ing**) **1** fasten or join with glue. **2** keep or put very close (an eye glued to the keyhole). □□ **glue′like** adj. **glue′y** /glṓo-ee/ adj. (**glu·i·er, glu·i·est**). **glu′ey·ness** n.

glum /glum/ adj. (**glum·mer, glum·mest**) dejected; sullen; displeased. □□ **glum′ly** adv. **glum′ness** n.

glut /glut/ • v.tr. (**glut·ted, glut·ting**) **1** feed (a person, one's stomach, etc.) or indulge (an appetite, a desire, etc.) to the full; satiate. **2** fill to excess. • n. **1** Econ. supply exceeding demand (a glut in the market). **2** full indulgence.

glu·ten /glṓotən/ n. mixture of proteins in cereal grains.

glu·te·us /glṓoteeəs/ n. (pl. **glu·te·i** /-teeī/) any of the three muscles in each buttock. □□ **glu′ te·al** adj.

glu·ti·nous /glṓot′nəs/ adj. sticky; like glue. □□ **glu′ti·nous·ly** adv. **glu′ti·nous·ness** n.

glut·ton /glút′n/ n. **1** greedy eater. **2** colloq. insatiably eager person (a glutton for work). □ **glutton for punishment** person eager to take on hard or unpleasant tasks. □□ **glut′ton·ous** adj. **glut′ ton·ous·ly** adv.

glut·ton·y /glút′nee/ n. habitual greed or excess in eating.

glyc·er·in /glísərin/ n. (also **glyc·er·ol** /glísərawl, -rol/, **glyc′er·ine** /glísəreen/) colorless sweet viscous liquid used as medicine, ointment, etc., and in explosives, etc.

gly·co·gen /glíkəjən/ n. polysaccharide substance in animal tissues that is converted to glucose for energy. □□ **gly·co·gen·ic** /-jénik/ adj.

GM abbr. **1** General Motors. **2** general manager.

gm abbr. gram(s).

G-man /jée′man/ n. (pl. **G-men**) US colloq. federal officer, esp. an FBI agent.

GMT abbr. Greenwich Mean Time.

gnarled /naarld/ adj. (also **gnarl′y** /náarlee/) (of a tree, hands, etc.) knobbly; twisted; rugged.

gnash /nash/ v. **1** tr. grind (the teeth). **2** intr. (of the teeth) strike together; grind.

gnat /nat/ n. **1** small two-winged biting fly. **2** insignificant annoyance.

gnaw /naw/ v. (past part. **gnawed** or **gnawn**) **1 a** tr. bite persistently; wear away by biting. **b** intr. bite; nibble. **2 a** intr. (of pain, fear, etc.) corrode; waste away; consume; torture. **b** tr. corrode, consume, torture, etc., with pain, fear, etc. (was gnawed by doubt). □□ **gnaw′ing** adj. **gnaw′ing·ly** adv.

gneiss /nīs/ n. usu. coarse-grained metamorphic rock.

gnoc·chi /nyáwkee/ n.pl. small Italian dumplings.

gnome /nōm/ n. dwarfish legendary creature or goblin, living under ground.

gnom·ic /nómik/ adj. of, consisting of, or using aphorisms; sententious.

GNP abbr. gross national product.

gnu /nōo, nyōo/ n. antelope, native to S. Africa, with brown stripes on the neck and shoulders. Also called **wildebeest**.

go¹ /gō/ • v.intr. (3rd sing. present **goes** /gōz/; past **went** /went/; past part. **gone** /gon/) **1 a** start moving or be moving; travel; proceed. **b** colloq. expressing annoyance (they've gone and broken it). **2** make a special trip for; participate in; proceed to do (went skiing; often goes running). **3** lie or extend to; lead to (the road goes to the shore; where does that door go?). **4 a** leave; depart (they had to go). **b** colloq. disappear (my bag is gone). **5** move, act, work, etc. (the clock doesn't go). **6 a** make a specified movement (go like this with your foot). **b** make a sound (the gun went bang). **c** colloq. say (so he goes to me "Why didn't you like it?"). **7** be in a specified state (go hungry). **8 a** pass into a specified condition (went mad). **b** colloq. die. **c** proceed or escape in a specified condition (the crime went unnoticed). **9** (of time or distance) pass; elapse; be traversed (ten days to go). **10 a** (of a document, verse, song, etc.) have a specified content or wording; run (the tune goes like this). **b** be suitable; fit; match (the shoes don't go with the hat). **c** be regularly kept or put (the forks go here). **d** find room; fit (it goes in the cupboard). **11 a** turn out; proceed in a certain way (things went well). **b** be successful (make the party go). **c** progress (a long way to go). **12 a** be sold (went cheap). **b** (of money) be spent ($200 went for a new jacket). **13 a** be relinquished, dismissed, or abolished (the car will have to go). **b** fail; decline; give way; collapse (his sight is going). **14** be acceptable or permitted; be accepted without question (what I say goes). **15** be guided by; judge or act on or in harmony with (have nothing to go on; a good rule to go by). **16** attend regularly (goes to church). **17** colloq. proceed (often foolishly) to do (don't go making him angry). **18** act or proceed to a certain point (will go so far and no further). **19** (of a number) be capable of being contained in another (6 goes into 12 twice). **20** be allotted or awarded; pass (first prize went to her). **21** be known or called (goes by the same name). **22** apply to; have relevance for (that goes for me, too). • n. (pl. **goes**) **1** act or instance of going. **2** mettle; spirit; dash; animation (she has a lot of go in her). **3** vigorous activity (it's all go). **4** colloq. success (made a go of it). **5** colloq. turn; attempt (I'll have a go at it). **6** permission; approval; go-ahead (gave us a go on the new project). • adj. colloq. functioning properly (all systems are go). □ **go about 1** busy oneself with; set to work at. **2** make a habit of doing (goes about telling lies). **3** Naut. change to an opposite tack. **go ahead** proceed without hesitation. **go-ahead** n. permission to proceed. • adj. enterprising. **go along with** agree to. **go back on** fail to keep (one's word, promise, etc.). **go-between** intermediary. **go down 1 a** (of an amount) become less (your weight has gone down). **b** subside (the flood went down). **c** decrease in price; lose value. **2 a** (of a ship) sink. **b** (of the sun) set. **3** (usu. foll. by to) be continued to a specified point. **4** deteriorate; fail (of a computer, etc.) cease to function. **5** be recorded in writing. **6** be swallowed. **7** (often foll. by with) be received (in a specified way). **go for 1** go to fetch. **2** be accounted as or achieve (went for nothing). **3** prefer; choose (*that's the one I go for*). **4** *colloq.* strive to attain (*go for it!*). **5** *colloq.* attack (*the dog went for him*). **go in for** take as one's object, style, pursuit, principle, etc. **go into 1** enter (a profession, etc.). **2** take part in; be a part of. **3** investigate. **go off 1** explode. **2 a** leave the stage. **b** leave; depart. **3** sound, as an alarm, siren, etc. **go on 1** continue; persevere (*decided to go on with it*). **2** *colloq.* **a** talk at great length. **b** admonish (*went on and on at him*). **3** proceed (*went on to become a star*). **go out 1** leave a room, house, etc. **2** be broadcast. **3** be extinguished. **4** be courting. **5** cease to be fashionable. **6** (of workers) strike. **go over 1** inspect; rehearse; retouch. **2** (often foll. by *to*) change one's allegiance or religion. **3** (of a play, etc.) be received in a specified way (*went over well in Dallas*). **go through 1** be dealt with or completed. **2** discuss in detail; scrutinize in sequence. **3** perform (a ceremony, a recitation, etc.). **4** undergo. **5** *colloq.* use up; spend (money, etc.). **6** make holes in. **go under** sink; fail; succumb. **on the go** *colloq.* **1** in constant motion. **2** constantly working.

go² /gō/ *n.* Japanese board game of territorial possession and capture.

goad /gōd/ • *n.* **1** spiked stick used for urging cattle forward. **2** anything that incites. • *v.tr.* **1** urge on with a goad. **2** irritate; stimulate (*goaded him into retaliating*).

goal /gōl/ *n.* **1** object of a person's ambition or effort; destination; aim (*fame is his goal; Washington was our goal*). **2 a** *Sports* receiving structure or area at which the ball, puck, etc., is directed for a score. **b** point(s) won (*scored 3 goals*).

goal·keep·er /gṓlkeepər/ *n.* player defending the goal in various sports. □□ **goal′ie** *n.*

goat /gōt/ *n.* **1** hardy, agile short-haired domesticated mammal, having horns and (in the male) a beard, and kept for its milk and meat. **2** lecherous man. **3** (**the Goat**) zodiacal sign or constellation Capricorn. **4** scapegoat. □ **get a person's goat** *colloq.* irritate a person.

goa·tee /gōteé/ *n.* small pointed beard like that of a goat.

goat·herd /gṓt-hərd/ *n.* person who tends goats.

goat·skin /gṓtskin/ *n.* **1** skin of a goat. **2** garment or bottle made of goatskin.

gob /gob/ *sl. n.* **1** lump or clot of slimy matter. **2** (in *pl.*) large amounts (*gobs of cash*)

gob·ble¹ /góbəl/ *v.* eat hurriedly and noisily. □□ **gob′bler** *n.*

gob·ble² /góbəl/ *v.intr.* **1** (of a male turkey) make a characteristic swallowing sound in the throat. **2** make such a sound when speaking, esp. when excited, angry, etc.

gob·ble·dy·gook /góbəldeegōōk/ *n.* (also **gob′ble·de·gook**) *colloq.* pompous or unintelligible jargon.

gob·let /góblit/ *n.* drinking vessel with a foot and a stem, usu. of glass.

gob·lin /góblin/ *n.* mischievous, ugly, dwarflike creature of folklore.

god /god/ *n.* **1 a** (in many religions) superhuman being or spirit worshiped as having power over nature, human fortunes, etc.; deity. **b** image, idol, animal, or other object worshiped as divine or symbolizing a god. **2** (**God**) (in Christian and other monotheistic religions) creator and ruler of the universe; supreme being. **3 a** adored, admired, or influential person. **b** something worshiped like a god (*makes a god of*

success). □□ **god′less** *adj.* **god′less·ness** *n.* **god′ like** *adj.*

god·child /gódchīld/ *n.* person in relation to a godparent.

god·daugh·ter /góddawtər/ *n.* female godchild.

god·dess /gódis/ *n.* **1** female deity. **2** adored woman.

god·fa·ther /gódfaathər/ *n.* **1** male godparent. **2** person directing an illegal organization, esp. the Mafia.

god·for·sak·en /gódfərsaykən/ *adj.* (also **God′ for·sak·en**) devoid of all merit; dismal; dreary.

god·head /gódhed/ *n.* (also **God′head**) **1 a** state of being God or a god. **b** divine nature. **2** deity. **3** (**the Godhead**) God.

god·ly /gódlee/ *adj.* religious; pious; devout. □□ **god′li·ness** *n.*

god·mo·ther /gódmuthər/ *n.* female godparent.

god·par·ent /gódpairənt/ *n.* person who sponsors a child at baptism.

god·send /gódsend/ *n.* unexpected but welcome event or acquisition.

god·son /gódsun/ *n.* male godchild.

go·fer /gṓfər/ *n. sl.* person who runs errands, esp. on a movie set or in an office.

gog·gle /gógəl/ • *v.* **1** *intr.* **a** look with wide-open eyes. **b** (of the eyes) be rolled about; protrude. **2** *tr.* turn (the eyes) sideways or from side to side. • *adj.* (usu. *attrib.*) (of the eyes) protuberant or rolling. • *n.* (in *pl.*) eyeglasses for protecting the eyes from glare, dust, water, etc.

go·ing /gṓing/ • *n.* **1 a** act or process of going. **b** instance of this; departure. **2 a** condition of the ground for walking, riding, etc. **b** progress affected by this (*found the going hard*). • *adj.* **1** in or into action (*set the clock going*). **2** current; prevalent (*the going rate*). □ **get going** start steadily talking, working, etc. (*can't stop him when he gets going*). **going concern** thriving business. **going on fifteen**, etc., approaching one's fifteenth, etc., birthday. **going to** intending or intended to; about to; likely to (*it's going to sink!*).

gold /gōld/ • *n.* **1** yellow, malleable, ductile, high density metallic element resistant to chemical reaction, occurring naturally in quartz veins and gravel, and precious as a monetary medium, in jewelry, etc. ¶ Symb.: **Au**. **2** color of gold. **3 a** coins or articles made of gold. **b** wealth. • *adj.* **1** made wholly or chiefly of gold. **2** colored like gold. □ **gold leaf** gold beaten into a very thin sheet. **gold medal** medal of gold, usu. awarded as first prize. **gold mine 1** place where gold is mined. **2** *colloq.* source of wealth. **gold standard** system valuing currency in terms of gold, for which the currency may be exchanged.

gold·en /gṓldən/ *adj.* **1 a** made or consisting of gold (*golden coin*). **b** yielding gold. **2** colored or shining like gold (*golden hair*). **3** precious; valuable; excellent; important (*a golden memory; a golden opportunity*). □ **golden age 1** supposed past age when people were happy and innocent. **2** period of a nation's greatest prosperity, literary merit, etc. **golden goose** continuing source of wealth or profit. **golden handshake** *colloq.* payment given on layoff or early retirement. **golden jubilee** fiftieth anniversary. **golden mean** principle of moderation, as opposed to excess. **golden**

parachute executive's contract that provides substantial severance pay, etc., upon termination.
golden retriever retriever with a thick, golden-colored coat. **golden rule** basic principle of action, esp. "do unto others as you would have them do unto you." **golden wedding** fiftieth anniversary of a wedding.

gold·en·rod /góldənrod/ n. plant with a rodlike stem and small, bright yellow flower heads.

gold·finch /góldfinch/ n. songbird with a yellow band across each wing.

gold·fish /góldfish/ n. small reddish golden Chinese carp kept for ornament. □ **goldfish bowl 1** globular glass container for goldfish. **2** situation lacking privacy.

gold·smith /góldsmith/ n. worker in gold.

go·lem /góləm/ n. clay figure supposedly brought to life in Jewish legend.

golf /golf, gawlf/ • n. game played on a course set in open country, in which a small hard ball is driven with clubs into a series of 18 or 9 holes with the fewest possible strokes. • v.intr. play golf. □ **golf club 1** club used in golf. **2** premises used by a golf club. □□ **golf′er** n.

gol·ly /gólee/ int. expressing surprise.

go·nad /gónad/ n. animal organ producing gametes, e.g., the testis or ovary. □□ **go·nad·al** /-nádl/ adj.

gon·do·la /góndələ, gondólə/ n. **1** flat-bottomed boat used in Venetian canals, with a high point at each end, worked by one oar at the stern. **2** car suspended from an airship, balloon, or cable.

GONDOLA, 1

gon·do·lier /góndəleé′er/ n. oarsman on a gondola.

gone /gawn, gon/ adj. **1** departed; left. **2 a** lost; hopeless. **b** dead. **3** sl. completely enthralled or entranced, esp. by rhythmic music, drugs, etc.

gon·er /gáwnər, gón-/ n. sl. person or thing that is doomed, ended, irrevocably lost, etc.; dead person.

gong /gawng, gong/ • n. **1** metal disk giving a resonant note when struck. **2** saucer-shaped bell. • v.tr. summon with a gong.

gon·or·rhea /gónəreéə/ n. venereal disease with inflammatory discharge. □□ **gon·or·rhe′al** adj.

goo /goo/ n. **1** sticky or viscous substance. **2** sickening sentiment.

good /good/ • adj. (**bet·ter, best**) **1** having the right or desired qualities; satisfactory; adequate. **2 a** (of a person) efficient; competent (a good driver). **b** (of a thing) reliable; efficient (good brakes). **c** (of health, etc.) strong (good eyesight). **3 a** kind; benevolent (good of you to come). **b** morally excellent; virtuous (a good deed). **c** charitable (good works). **d** well-behaved. **4** enjoyable, agreeable (a good party). **5** thorough; considerable (gave it a good wash). **6** not less than (waited a good hour). **7** valid; sound (a good reason). • n. **1** (only in sing.) that which is good; what is beneficial or morally right (only good can come of it; did it for your own good). **2** (in pl.) **a** movable property or merchandise. **b** (prec. by the) colloq. what one has undertaken to supply (esp. deliver the goods). **3** proof, esp. of guilt. • adv. colloq. well (doing pretty good). □ **as good as** practically (he as good as told me). **for good** (**and all**) finally; permanently. **good for 1** beneficial to; having a good effect on. **2** able to perform; inclined for (good for a ten-mile walk). **3** able to be trusted to pay (is good for $100). **to the good** having as profit or benefit.

¶ The adverb corresponding to the adjective **good** is well: She is a good swimmer who performs well in meets. Confusion sometimes arises because **well** is also an adjective meaning 'healthy, fine,' and **good** is widely accepted as an informal substitute: I feel well (vs. informal "I feel good"). See note at BAD.

good-bye /góodbí/ (also **good-bye′, good-by′** or **good-by′**) • int. expressing good wishes on parting, ending a telephone conversation, etc., or said with reference to a thing gotten rid of or irrevocably lost. • n. (pl. **good-byes**) parting; farewell.

good-hu·mored /góodhyóomərd/ adj. genial; cheerful; amiable. □□ **good′-hu′mored·ly** adv.

good·ly /góodlee/ adj. (**good·li·er, good·li·est**) **1** comely; handsome. **2** of imposing size, etc. □□ **good′li·ness** n.

good-na·tured /góodnáychərd/ adj. kind; patient; easygoing. □□ **good′-na′tured·ly** adv.

good·ness /góodnis/ • n. **1** virtue; excellence, esp. moral. **2** kindness (had the goodness to wait). **3** what is beneficial in a thing (the goodness of fresh air). • int. expressing surprise, anger, etc. (goodness me!).

good·will /góodwíl/ n. **1** kindly feeling. **2** established reputation of a business, etc., as enhancing its value.

good·y /góodee/ • n. (also **good′ie**) (pl. **-ies**) **1** (usu. in pl.) something good or attractive, esp. to eat. **2** = goody-goody n. • int. expressing childish delight. □ **goody-goody** n. smug or obtrusively virtuous person. • adj. obtrusively or smugly virtuous.

goo·ey /góo-ee/ adj. (**goo·i·er, goo·i·est**) sl. **1** viscous; sticky. **2** sentimental. □□ **goo′ey·ness** n. (also **goo′i·ness**).

goof /goof/ sl. • n. **1** foolish or stupid person. **2** mistake. • v. **1** tr. bungle; mess up. **2** intr. blunder; make a mistake. **3** intr. (often foll. by off) idle; waste time.

goof·ball /góofbawl/ n. sl. **1** pill containing a barbiturate or tranquilizer. **2** silly, ridiculous, or inept person.

goof·y /góofee/ adj. (**goof·i·er, goof·i·est**) sl. stupid; silly. □□ **goof′i·ness** n.

goon /goon/ n. sl. **1** stupid or playful person. **2** person hired by racketeers, etc.

goose /goos/ n. (pl. **geese** /gees/) **1 a** large water bird with short legs, webbed feet, and a broad bill. **b** female of this (opp. GANDER). **c** flesh of a goose as food. **2** colloq. simpleton. • v.tr. sl. poke (a person) between the buttocks. □ **goose bumps** (also **goose flesh** or **pimples** or **skin**) bristling state of the skin produced by cold or fright. **goose egg** zero score in a game. **goose**

step military marching step in which the knees are kept stiff.

goose·ber·ry /gŏosberee, -bəree, gŏoz-/ n. (pl. **-ries**) **1** edible yellowish green berry with thin skin enclosing seeds in a juicy flesh. **2** thorny shrub bearing this fruit.

GOP abbr. Grand Old Party (Republican Party).

go·pher /gŏfər/ n. (in full **pock′et go·pher**) burrowing rodent, native to N. America, having external cheek pouches and sharp front teeth; ground squirrel.

Gor·di·an knot /gáwrdeeən/ n. **1** intricate knot. **2** difficult problem or task. □ **cut the Gordian knot** solve a problem by force or by evasion.

gore[1] /gawr/ n. **1** blood shed and clotted. **2** slaughter.

gore[2] /gawr/ v.tr. pierce with a horn, tusk, etc.

gore[3] /gawr/ • n. wedge-shaped piece in a garment, umbrella, etc. • v.tr. shape with a gore.

gorge /gawrj/ • n. **1** narrow opening between hills or a rocky ravine. **2** act of gorging; feast. **3** contents of the stomach. • v. **1** intr. feed greedily. **2** tr. **a** (often refl.) satiate; glut. **b** swallow; devour greedily.

gor·geous /gáwrjəs/ adj. **1** richly colored; sumptuous; magnificent. **2** colloq. very pleasant; splendid (gorgeous weather). **3** colloq. strikingly beautiful. □□ **gor′geous·ly** adv.

gor·gon /gáwrgən/ n. **1** Gk. mythol. each of three snake-haired sisters (esp. Medusa) with the power to turn anyone who looked at them to stone. **2** frightening or repulsive woman. □□ **gor·go·ni·an** /gawrgóneeən/ adj.

Gor·gon·zo·la /gáwrgənzólə/ n. rich cheese with bluish veins.

go·ril·la /gərílə/ n. largest anthropoid ape, native to Central Africa.

> **gorilla** from an alleged African word for a wild or hairy person, found in the Greek account of the voyage of the Carthaginian explorer Hanno in the 5th or 6th century BC; adopted in 1847 as the specific name of the ape.

gorse /gawrs/ n. spiny yellow-flowered shrub native to Europe.

gor·y /gáwree/ adj. (**gor·i·er, gor·i·est**) **1** involving bloodshed; bloodthirsty (a gory film). **2** covered in gore. □□ **gor′i·ly** adv. **gor′i·ness** n.

gosh /gosh/ int. expressing surprise.

gos·ling /gózling/ n. young goose.

gos·pel /góspəl/ n. **1** teaching of Christ. **2** (**Gospel**) **a** record of Christ's life in the first four books of the New Testament. **b** each of these books. **c** portion from one of them read at a service. **3** thing regarded as absolutely true (take my word as gospel). **4** (in full **gos′pel mu·sic**) African-American evangelical religious singing. □ **gospel truth** something considered to be unquestionably true.

gos·sa·mer /gósəmər/ • n. **1** filmy substance of small spiders' webs. **2** delicate filmy material. • adj. light and flimsy.

gos·sip /gósip/ • n. **1 a** unconstrained talk or writing, esp. about persons or social incidents. **b** idle talk; groundless rumor. **2** person who indulges in gossip. • v.intr. (**gos·siped, gos·sip·ing**) talk or write gossip. □□ **gos′sip·mon·ger** n. **gos′sip·y** adj.

got past and past part. of GET.

Goth /goth/ n. **1** member of a Germanic tribe that invaded the Roman Empire in the 3rd–5th c. **2** uncivilized or ignorant person.

Goth·ic /góthik/ • adj. **1** of the Goths. **2** in the style of architecture prevalent in W. Europe in the 12th–16th c., characterized by pointed arches. **3** (of a novel, etc.) with supernatural or horrifying events. **4** barbarous; uncouth. • n. **1** Gothic language. **2** Gothic architecture.

got·ten past part. of GET.

gouache /gwaash, gŏo-aásh/ n. **1** painting in opaque pigments ground in water and thickened with a glue. **2** these pigments. **3** picture painted this way.

Gou·da /gŏodə, gów-/ n. mild Dutch cheese.

gouge /gowj/ • n. **1 a** chisel with a concave blade, used in woodworking, sculpture, and surgery. **b** indentation made with or as with this. **2** colloq. swindle. • v.tr. **1** cut with or as with a gouge. **2** brutally scoop out. **3** colloq. swindle; extort money from.

GOUGE, 1a

gou·lash /gŏolaash, -lash/ n. highly seasoned Hungarian dish of meat and vegetables, usu. flavored with paprika.

gourd /goord/ n. **1 a** fleshy usu. large fruit with a hard skin, often used as containers, ornaments, etc. **b** climbing or trailing plant bearing this fruit. **2** hollow gourd shell used as a drinking vessel, etc. □□ **gourd′ful** n. (pl. **-fuls**).

gour·mand /gŏormaánd/ • n. glutton. • adj. gluttonous; fond of eating, esp. to excess. □□ **gour′mand·ism** n.

gour·met /gŏormáy/ n. connoisseur of good or delicate food.

gout /gowt/ n. inflammation of the smaller joints, esp. the big toe. □□ **gout′y** adj.

gov·ern /gúvərn/ v. **1 a** tr. rule or control (a nation, subject, etc.) with authority; conduct the affairs of. **b** intr. be in government. **2 a** tr. influence or determine (a person or a course of action). **b** intr. be the predominating influence. **3** tr. be a standard or principle for; constitute a law for; serve to decide (a case). **4** tr. check or control (esp. passions and machinery). □□ **gov′ern·a·ble** adj.

gov·er·nance /gúvərnəns/ n. act or manner of governing.

gov·er·ness /gúvərnis/ n. woman employed to teach children in a private household.

gov·ern·ment /gúvərnmənt/ n. **1** act, manner, or system of governing. **2** body of persons governing a nation. □□ **gov·ern·men·tal** /-mént′l/ adj.

gov·er·nor /gúvərnər/ *n.* **1** person who governs; ruler. **2** executive head of each state of the US. **3** *Mech.* automatic regulator controlling the speed of an engine, etc. □□ **gov′er·nor·ship** *n.*

govt. *abbr.* government.

gown /gown/ • *n.* **1** loose flowing garment, esp. a woman's long dress or nightgown. **2** official or academic robe. **3** members of a university as distinct from the permanent residents of the university town. • *v.tr.* (usu. as **gowned** *adj.*) attire in a gown.

goy /goy/ *n.* (*pl.* **goy·im** /góyim/ or **goys**) *sl.* sometimes *derog.* Jewish name for a non-Jew. □□ **goy′ish** *adj.* (also **goy′isch**).

GP *abbr.* **1** general practitioner. **2** Grand Prix.

GPO *abbr.* **1** General Post Office. **2** Government Printing Office.

grab /grab/ • *v.* (**grabbed, grab·bing**) **1** *tr.* **a** seize suddenly. **b** capture; arrest. **2** *tr.* take greedily or unfairly. **3** *tr. sl.* attract the attention of; impress. **4** *intr.* snatch at. • *n.* sudden clutch or attempt to seize. □ **grab bag 1** container from which one removes a mystery gift, as at a party. **2** miscellaneous items. **up for grabs** *sl.* easily obtainable. □□ **grab′ber** *n.*

grace /grays/ • *n.* **1** attractiveness in proportion, manner, movement; elegance. **2** courteous good will (*had the grace to apologize*). **3** attractive feature; accomplishment (*social graces*). **4 a** (in Christian belief) favor of God; divine saving and strengthening influence. **b** state of receiving this. **5** goodwill; favor (*fall from grace*). **6** delay granted as a favor (*a year's grace*). **7** short thanksgiving before or after a meal. **8** (**Grace**) (prec. by *His, Her, Your*) forms of description or address for a duke, duchess, or archbishop. • *v.tr.* **1** lend or add grace to; enhance or embellish. **2** confer honor or dignity on (*graced us with his presence*).

grace·ful /gráysfŏŏl/ *adj.* having or showing grace or elegance. □□ **grace′ful·ly** *adv.* **grace′ful·ness** *n.*

grace·less /gráyslis/ *adj.* lacking grace or elegance or charm.

gra·cious /gráyshəs/ • *adj.* **1** kind; indulgent and beneficent to others. **2** (of God) merciful; benign. **3** elegant; luxurious. • *int.* expressing surprise. □□ **gra′cious·ly** *adv.* **gra′cious·ness** *n.*

gra·date /gráydayt/ *v.* **1** *intr. & tr.* pass or cause to pass by gradations from one shade to another. **2** *tr.* arrange in steps or grades of size, etc.

gra·da·tion /gráydáyshən/ *n.* (usu. in *pl.*) **1** stage of transition or advance. **2 a** certain degree in rank, intensity, merit, divergence, etc. **b** arrangement in such degrees. **3** (of paint, etc.) gradual passing from one shade, tone, etc., to another. □□ **gra·da′tion·al** *adj.*

grade /grayd/ • *n.* **1 a** certain degree in rank, merit, proficiency, quality, etc. **b** class of persons or things of the same grade. **2** mark indicating the quality of a student's work. **3** class in school, concerned with a particular year's work and usu. numbered from the first upward. **4 a** gradient or slope. **b** rate of ascent or descent. • *v.* **1** *tr.* arrange in or allocate to grades; class; sort. **2** *intr.* (foll. by *up, down, off, into*, etc.) pass gradually between grades, or into a grade. **3** *tr.* give a grade to (a student). **4** *tr.* reduce (a road, etc.) to easy gradients. □ **grade crossing**

crossing of a roadway, etc., with a railroad track at the same level. **grade point average** scholastic average obtained by dividing the number of earned grade points by the number of credits taken.

gra·di·ent /gráydeeənt/ *n.* **1** stretch of road, railroad, etc., that slopes. **2** amount of such a slope.

grad·u·al /grájŏŏl/ *adj.* **1** progressing by degrees. **2** not rapid, steep, or abrupt. □□ **grad′u·al·ly** *adv.*

grad·u·al·ism /grájŏŏəlizəm/ *n.* policy of gradual reform. □□ **grad′u·al·ist** *n.* **grad·u·al·is′tic** *adj.*

grad·u·ate • *n.* /grájŏŏət/ **1** person who has been awarded an academic degree (also *attrib.*: *graduate student*). **2** person who has completed a course of study. • *v.* /grájŏŏ-áyt/ **1 a** *intr.* take an academic degree. **b** *tr.* grant an academic degree or certificate of completion of school studies. **2** *intr.* **a** (foll. by *from*) be a graduate of a specified university. **b** be a graduate in a specified subject. **3** *intr.* **a** (foll. by *to*) move up to (a higher status, etc.). **b** (foll. by *as, in*) gain specified qualifications. **4** *tr.* mark out in degrees or parts. **5** *tr.* arrange in gradations; apportion (e.g., tax) according to a scale. □ **graduate school** division of a university for advanced work by graduates. □□ **grad·u·a′tion** /-áyshən/ *n.*

¶ The traditional use is "to be graduated from": *She will be graduated from medical school in June.* It is now more common to say "graduate from": *He will graduate from high school next year.* Avoid using *graduate* as a transitive verb, as in "He graduated high school last week."

graf·fi·ti /grəféetee/ *n.pl.* (*sing.* **graf·fi·to**) writing or drawing scribbled, scratched, or sprayed on a surface.

graft[1] /graft/ • *n.* **1** *Bot.* shoot or scion inserted into a slit of stock, from which it receives sap. **2** *Surgery* tissue, organ, etc., transplanted surgically. • *v.* **1** *tr.* insert (a scion) as a graft. **2** *intr.* insert a graft. **3** *tr. Surgery* transplant (tissue). **4** *tr.* insert or fix (a thing) permanently to another.

graft[2] /graft/ *colloq.* • *n.* practices, esp. bribery, used to secure illicit gains in politics or business. • *v.intr.* seek or make such gains.

gra·ham crack·er /gram, gráyəm/ *n.* crisp, slightly sweet whole-wheat cracker.

Grail /grayl/ *n.* (in full **Ho′ly Grail′**) (in medieval legend) cup or platter used by Christ at the Last Supper.

grain /grayn/ • *n.* **1** fruit or seed of a cereal. **2 a** (*collect.*) wheat or related grass used as food. **b** (*collect.*) their fruit. **c** any cereal crop. **3** small hard particle of salt, sand, etc. **4** smallest unit of weight in the troy system (equivalent to $1/480$ of an ounce) and in the avoirdupois system (equivalent to $1/437.5$ of an ounce). **5** smallest possible quantity (*not a grain of truth in it*). **6 a** roughness of surface. **b** *Photog.* granular appearance on a photograph or negative. **7** texture. **8** pattern of lines of fiber in wood or paper. • *v.tr.* **1** paint in imitation of the grain of wood or marble. **2** give a granular surface to. □ **against the grain** contrary to one's natural inclination or feeling. □□ **grain′y** *adj.*

gram /gram/ *n.* metric unit of mass equal to one-thousandth of a kilogram.

-gram /gram/ *comb. form* forming nouns denoting a thing written or recorded (often in a certain way) (*monogram; telegram*). □□ **-grammatic** /grəmátik/ *comb. form* forming adjectives.

gram·mar /grámər/ *n.* **1** study or rules of a language's inflections, forms, etc. **2** observance or application of such rules (*bad grammar*). **3** book on grammar. □ **grammar school** elementary school. □□ **gram·mar'i·an** *n.* **gram·mat'i·cal** *adj.* **gram·mat'i·cal·ly** *adv.*

gram·o·phone /grámǝfōn/ *n.* = PHONOGRAPH.

gran·a·ry /gránǝree, gráy-/ *n.* (*pl.* **-ries**) storehouse for threshed grain.

grand /grand/ • *adj.* **1 a** magnificent; imposing; dignified. **b** noble. **2** main; of chief importance (*grand staircase; grand entrance*). **3** (**Grand**) of the highest rank (*Grand Cross; Grand Inquisitor*). **4** *colloq.* excellent; enjoyable (*had a grand time*). **5** belonging to high society; wealthy (*the grand folk at the manor*). **6** (in *comb.*) in names of family relationships, denoting the second degree of ascent or descent (*granddaughter*). • *n.* **1** = *grand piano*. **2** (*pl.* same) *sl.* thousand dollars. □ **grand jury** *Law* jury selected to examine the validity of an accusation prior to trial. **grand master 1** chess player of the highest class. **2** head of a military order of knighthood, of Freemasons, etc. **grand piano** large full-toned piano standing on three legs, with horizontal strings. **grand slam 1** *Sports* winning of all of a group of major championships. **2** *Bridge* winning of all 13 tricks. **3** *Baseball* home run with bases loaded. □□ **grand'ly** *adv.* **grand'ness** *n.*

grand·dad·dy /grándadee/ *n.* (also **gran'dad·dy**) (*pl.* **-dies**) **1** *colloq.* grandfather. **2** original and usu. most venerated of its kind (*the granddaddy of symphony orchestras*).

grand·child /gránchīld, gránd-/ *n.* (*pl.* **-children**) child of one's son or daughter.

grand·daugh·ter /gróndawtǝr/ *n.* female grandchild.

gran·dee /grandee/ *n.* **1** highest Spanish or Portuguese nobleman. **2** person of high rank or eminence.

gran·deur /gránjǝr, -jŏŏr/ *n.* **1** majesty; splendor. **2** nobility of character.

grand·fa·ther /gránfaathǝr, gránd-/ *n.* male grandparent. □ **grandfather clock** floor-standing pendulum clock in a tall wooden case. □□ **grand'fa·ther·ly** *adj.*

gran·dil·o·quent /grandílǝkwǝnt/ *adj.* pompous or inflated in language. □□ **gran·dil·o·quence** /-kwǝns/ *n.* **gran·dil'o·quent·ly** *adv.*

gran·di·ose /gróndeeōs/ *adj.* **1** producing or meant to produce an imposing effect. **2** ambitious in scale. □□ **gran'di·ose·ly** *adv.* **gran·di·os·i·ty** /-deeósitee/ *n.*

grand·mo·ther /gránmuthǝr, gránd-/ *n.* female grandparent. □□ **grand'moth·er·ly** *adj.*

grand·pa·rent /gránpairǝnt, gránd-/ *n.* parent of one's father or mother.

grand·son /gránsun, gránd-/ *n.* male grandchild.

grand·stand /gránstand, gránd-/ *n.* main stand for spectators at a racecourse, etc.

grange /graynj/ *n.* **1** country house with farm buildings. **2** (**Grange**) farmer's social organization.

gran·ite /gránit/ *n.* granular igneous rock of quartz, mica, etc., used for building.

gran·ny /gránee/ *n.* (also **gran'nie**) (*pl.* **-nies**) *colloq.* grandmother.

Gran·ny Smith /gránee smíth/ *n.* green variety of apple.

gra·no·la /grǝnṓlǝ/ *n.* breakfast or snack food

consisting of a mixture of rolled oats, nuts, dried fruits, etc.

grant /grant/ • *v.tr.* **1 a** consent to fulfill (a request, wish, etc.) (*granted all he asked*). **b** allow (a person) to have (a thing) (*granted me my freedom*). **2** give (rights, property, etc.) formally; transfer legally. **3** admit as true; concede, esp. as a basis for argument. • *n.* **1** process of granting or thing granted. **2** sum of money officially given, esp. to finance education. □ **take for granted 1** assume something to be true or valid. **2** cease to appreciate through familiarity. □□ **grant·ee** /-tée/ *n.* (esp. in sense 2 of *v.*). **grant'er** *n.* **gran'tor** /-tór/ *n.* (esp. in sense 2 of *v.*).

gran·u·lar /grányǝlǝr/ *adj.* of or like grains or granules. □□ **gran·u·lar·i·ty** /-láritee/ *n.*

gran·u·late /grányǝlayt/ *v.* form into grains (*granulated sugar*). □□ **gran·u·la·tion** /-láyshǝn/ *n.*

gran·ule /grányŏŏl/ *n.* small grain.

grape /grayp/ *n.* **1** berry (usu. green, purple, or black) growing in clusters on a vine, used as fruit and in making wine. **2** (prec. by *the*) *colloq.* wine. □ **grape hyacinth** liliaceous plant with clusters of usu. blue flowers.

grape·fruit /gráypfrŏŏt/ *n.* (*pl.* same) **1** large round yellow citrus fruit. **2** tree bearing this fruit.

grape·vine /gráypvīn/ *n.* **1** vine. **2** *colloq.* means of transmission of rumor (*heard it through the grapevine*).

graph /graf/ • *n.* **1** diagram showing the relation between variable quantities, usu. along two axes. **2** *Math.* collection of points whose coordinates satisfy a given relation. • *v.tr.* plot or trace on a graph. □ **graph paper** paper printed with a network of lines as a basis for drawing graphs.

-graph /graf/ *comb. form* forming nouns and verbs meaning: **1** thing written, drawn, etc., in a specified way (*autograph*). **2** instrument that records (*seismograph; telegraph*).

graph·ic /gráfik/ • *adj.* **1** of or relating to the visual or descriptive arts, esp. writing and drawing. **2** vividly descriptive; conveying all (esp. unwelcome or unpleasant) details; unequivocal. • *n.* product of the graphic arts (cf. GRAPHICS). □ **graphic arts** visual and technical arts involving design, writing, drawing, printing, etc. □□ **graph'i·cal·ly** *adv.*

-graphic /gráfik/ *comb. form* (also **-graphical** /gráfikǝl/) forming adjectives corresponding to nouns in *-graphy.* □□ **-graphically** /gráfiklee/ *comb. form* forming adverbs.

graph·ics /gráfiks/ *n.pl.* (usu. treated as *sing.*) **1** products of the graphic arts. **2** use of diagrams in calculation and design. **3** (in full **com·pu'ter graph'ics**) *Computing* mode of processing and output in which information is in pictorial form.

graph·ite /gráfīt/ *n.* crystalline allotropic form of carbon used as a lubricant, in pencils, etc.

gra·phol·o·gy /grǝfólǝjee/ *n.* the study of handwriting, esp. as a supposed guide to character. □□ **graph·ol'o·gist** *n.*

-graphy /grǝfee/ *comb. form* forming nouns denoting: **1** descriptive science (*geography*). **2** technique of producing images (*photography*). **3** style or method of writing, drawing, etc. (*calligraphy*).

grapnel ~ graze 254

grap·nel /grápnəl/ n. 1 device with iron claws, for dragging or grasping. 2 small anchor with several flukes.

GRAPNEL, 2

grap·ple /grápəl/ • v. 1 intr. fight at close quarters or in close combat. 2 intr. try to manage a difficult problem, etc. 3 tr. a grip with the hands. b seize with or as with a grapnel; grasp. • n. 1 a hold or grip in or as in wrestling. b contest at close quarters. 2 clutching instrument; grapnel. □ **grappling iron** (or **hook**) = GRAPNEL.

grasp /grasp/ • v. 1 tr. a clutch at; seize greedily. b hold firmly; grip. 2 intr. (foll. by at) try to seize. 3 tr. understand or realize (a fact or meaning). • n. 1 firm hold; grip. 2 a mastery or control (a grasp of the situation). b mental hold or understanding (a grasp of the facts). 3 mental agility (a quick grasp).

grasp·ing /gráspiŋ/ adj. avaricious; greedy.

grass /gras/ • n. 1 a small plants with green blades that are eaten by cattle, horses, sheep, etc. b plant that includes cereals, reeds, and bamboos. 2 pasture land. 3 lawn (keep off the grass). 4 sl. marijuana. • v.tr. 1 cover with turf. 2 provide with pasture. □ **grass roots** 1 fundamental level or source. 2 ordinary people, esp. as voters; rank and file of an organization, esp. a political party. □□ **grass'y** adj. (**grass·si·er, grass·si·est**)

grass·hop·per /grás-hoppər/ n. jumping and chirping plant-eating insect.

grass·land /grásland/ n. large open area covered with grass, esp. used for grazing.

grate[1] /grayt/ v. 1 tr. reduce to small particles by rubbing on a serrated surface. 2 intr. rub with a harsh scraping sound. 3 tr. utter in a harsh tone. 4 intr. a sound harshly or discordantly. b have an irritating effect. □□ **grat'er** n.

grate[2] /grayt/ n. metal frame confining fuel in a fireplace.

grate·ful /gráytfŏŏl/ adj. 1 thankful; feeling or showing gratitude (am grateful to you for helping). 2 pleasant, acceptable. □□ **grate'ful·ly** adv. **grate'ful·ness** n.

grat·i·fy /grátifī/ v.tr. (**-fies, -fied**) 1 a please; delight. b please by compliance. 2 indulge in or yield to (a feeling or desire). □□ **grat·i·fi·ca'tion** n.

grat·ing[1] /gráyting/ adj. 1 sounding harsh or discordant (a grating laugh). 2 irritating. □□ **grat'ing·ly** adv.

grat·ing[2] /gráyting/ n. 1 framework of parallel or crossed metal bars. 2 Optics set of parallel wires, lines ruled on glass, etc., for producing spectra by diffraction.

grat·is /grátis, graa-/ adv. & adj. free; without charge.

grat·i·tude /grátitŏŏd, -tyŏŏd/ n. being thankful; appreciation.

gra·tu·i·tous /grətŏŏitəs, tyŏŏ-/ adj. 1 given or done free of charge. 2 uncalled-for (a gratuitous insult). □□ **gra·tu'i·tous·ly** adv. **gra·tu'i·tous·ness** n.

gra·tu·i·ty /grətŏŏitee, -tyŏŏ-/ n. (pl. **-ties**) money given for service; tip.

grave[1] /grayv/ n. 1 a trench for the burial of a corpse. b mound or memorial stone placed over this. 2 (prec. by the) death, esp. as indicating mortal finality. 3 something compared to or regarded as a grave.

grave[2] /grayv/ • adj. 1 a serious; weighty; important (a grave matter). b solemn; somber (a grave look). 2 critical or threatening (grave danger). • n. /graav/ = grave accent. □ **grave accent** /graav, grayv/ mark (`) placed over a vowel to denote pronunciation, length, etc. □□ **grave'ly** adv.

grav·el /grávəl/ • n. mixture of coarse sand and small stones, used for paths, roads, etc. • v.tr. lay or strew with gravel.

grav·el·ly /grávəlee/ adj. 1 of or like gravel. 2 (of a voice) deep and rough sounding.

grave·stone /gráyvstōn/ n. stone marking a grave.

grave·yard /gráyvyaard/ n. burial ground, esp. by a church. □ **graveyard shift** work shift beginning late at night.

grav·i·tate /grávitayt/ v. 1 intr. move or be attracted to. 2 tr. & intr. move or tend by force of gravity toward.

grav·i·ta·tion /grávitáyshən/ n. Physics 1 force of attraction between particles of matter in the universe. 2 effect of this, esp. the falling of bodies to the earth. □□ **grav·i·ta'tion·al** adj.

grav·i·ty /grávitee/ n. 1 a force that attracts a body to the center of the earth or other celestial body. b degree of this measured by acceleration. 2 property of having weight. 3 a importance; seriousness. b solemnity; serious demeanor.

gra·vy /gráyvee/ n. (pl. **-vies**) 1 a juices exuding from meat during and after cooking. b sauce for food, made from these. 2 sl. unearned or unexpected gains, etc. money. □ **gravy boat** vessel for serving gravy. **gravy train** sl. source of easy financial benefit.

gray /gray/ (also **grey**) • adj. 1 of a color intermediate between black and white. 2 a (of the weather, etc.) dull; dismal; overcast. b bleak (of a person) depressed. 3 a (of hair) turning white with age, etc. b (of a person) having gray hair. 4 anonymous; unidentifiable. • n. 1 a gray color or pigment. b gray clothes or material (dressed in gray). 2 gray or white horse. • v. make or become gray. □ **gray area** situation or topic not clearly defined. **gray matter 1** darker tissues of the brain and spinal cord. 2 colloq. intelligence. □□ **gray'ish** adj. **gray'ness** n.

graze[1] /grayz/ v. 1 intr. (of cattle, sheep, etc.)

eat growing grass. **2** *tr.* feed (cattle, etc.) on growing grass.

graze² /grayz/ • *v.* **1** *tr.* rub or scrape (part of the body, esp. the skin). **2 a** *tr.* touch lightly in passing. **b** *intr.* move with a light passing contact. • *n.* abrasion.

grease /grees/ • *n.* **1** oily or fatty matter esp. as a lubricant. **2** melted animal fat. **3** oily matter in unprocessed wool. • *v.tr.* also /greez/ smear or lubricate with grease. □ **grease the palm of** *colloq.* bribe.

grease·paint /gree'spaynt/ *n.* stage makeup for actors.

greas·y /gree'see, gree'zee/ *adj.* (**greas·i·er**, **greas·i·est**) **1 a** of or like grease. **b** smeared or covered with grease. **c** having too much grease. **2 a** slippery. **b** (of a person or manner) unctuous; smooth. **c** objectionable. □□ **greas'i·ly** *adv.* **greas'i·ness** *n.*

great /grayt/ • *adj.* **1 a** of a size, amount, extent, or intensity considerably above the normal or average (*made a great hole; take great care*). **b** reinforcing other words denoting size, quantity, etc. (*a great big hole; a great many*). **2** important; preeminent; worthy. **3** grand; imposing (*a great occasion; the great hall*). **4 a** (esp. of a public or historic figure) distinguished; prominent. **b** (**the Great**) as a title denoting the most important of the name (*Alexander the Great*). **5 a** (of a person) remarkable in ability, character, achievement, etc. (*a great thinker*). **b** (of a thing) outstanding of its kind (*the Great Depression*). **6** (foll. by *at*) competent; skilled; well-informed. **7** *colloq.* **a** very enjoyable or satisfactory; attractive; fine (*had a great time*). **b** (as an exclam.) fine; very good. **8** (in *comb.*) (in names of family relationships) denoting one degree further removed upward or downward (*great-uncle; great-great-grandmother*). • *n.* great or outstanding person or thing. □ **Great Britain** England, Wales, and Scotland. **great circle** see CIRCLE. **Great Dane** see DANE. □□ **great'ly** *adv.* **great'ness** *n.*

grebe /greeb/ *n.* diving bird with a long neck, lobed toes, and almost no tail.

Gre·cian /gree'shən/ *adj.* (of architecture or facial outline) following Greek models or ideals.

Gre·co-Ro·man /gree'kō-rō'mən, grĕkō-/ *adj.* **1** of or relating to the Greeks and Romans. **2** *Wrestling* denoting a style attacking only the upper part of the body.

greed /greed/ *n.* excessive desire, esp. for food or wealth.

greed·y /gree'dee/ *adj.* (**greed·i·er**, **greed·i·est**) **1** having or showing an excessive appetite for food or drink. **2** wanting wealth or pleasure to excess. **3** very keen or eager (*greedy for affection; greedy to learn*). □□ **greed'i·ly** *adv.* **greed'i·ness** *n.*

Greek /greek/ • *n.* **1 a** native or inhabitant of Greece; person of Greek descent. **b** native or citizen of any of the ancient nation-states of Greece. **2** language of Greece. • *adj.* of Greece or its people or language; Hellenic.

green /green/ • *adj.* **1** of the color between blue and yellow in the spectrum; colored like grass, emeralds, etc. **2** covered with leaves or grass. **3** (of fruit, etc., or wood) unripe or unseasoned. **4** not dried, smoked, or tanned. **5** inexperienced; naive; gullible. **6 a** (of the complexion) pale; sickly-hued. **b** jealous; envious. **7** young; flourishing. **8** vegetable (*green salad*). **9** (also **Green**) concerned with or supporting protection of the

environment. • *n.* **1** green color or pigment. **2** green clothes or material (*dressed in green*). **3 a** piece of public or common grassy land (*village green*). **b** grassy area used for a special purpose (*putting green; bowling green*). **4** (in *pl.*) green vegetables. • *v.* make or become green. □ **green** (or **string**) **bean** the green pods of a young kidney bean, eaten as a vegetable. **green belt** area of open land around a city, designated for preservation. **Green Beret** *Mil.* member of the US Army Special Forces. **green card** work and residence permit issued to permanent resident aliens in the US. **green-eyed** jealous. **green-eyed monster** jealousy. **green light 1** signal to proceed on a road, railroad, etc. **2** *colloq.* permission to go ahead with a project. **green pepper** unripe bell or sweet pepper, eaten green as a vegetable. **green thumb** skill in growing plants. □□ **green'ish** *adj.* **green'ly** *adv.* **green'ness** *n.*

green·back /gree'nbak/ *n.* bill of US paper currency.

green·er·y /gree'nəree/ *n.* green foliage or growing plants.

green·gro·cer /gree'ngrōsər/ *n.* retailer of fruit and vegetables.

green·horn /gree'nhawrn/ *n.* inexperienced person.

green·house /gree'nhows/ *n.* structure with sides and roof mainly of glass, for growing plants. □ **greenhouse effect** trapping of the sun's warmth in the earth's lower atmosphere caused by an increase in carbon dioxide.

green·room /gree'nrōom/ *n.* room in a theater for actors and actresses who are off stage.

greens·keep·er /gree'nzkee'pər/ *n.* keeper of a golf course.

green·sward /gree'nswawrd/ *n. archaic* or *literary* expanse of grassy turf.

Green·wich Mean Time /grĕnich, grĭnij/ *n.* (also **Green'wich Time**) local time on the meridian of Greenwich, England, used as an international basis for reckoning time.

green·y /gree'nee/ *adj.* greenish (*greeny-yellow*).

greet /greet/ *v.tr.* **1** address politely or welcomingly on meeting or arrival. **2** receive or acknowledge in a specified way (*was greeted with derision*). **3** (of a sight, sound, etc.) become apparent to or noticed by. □□ **greet'er** *n.*

greet·ing /gree'ting/ *n.* **1** act or instance of welcoming or addressing politely. **2** words, gestures, etc., used to greet a person. **3** (often in *pl.*) expression of goodwill.

gre·gar·i·ous /grigáireeəs/ *adj.* **1** fond of company. **2** living in flocks or communities. □□ **gre·gar'i·ous·ly** *adv.* **gre·gar'i·ous·ness** *n.*

Gre·go·ri·an cal·en·dar /grigáwreeən/ *n.* calendar now in use, introduced in 1582 by Pope Gregory XIII, as a correction of the Julian calendar.

Gre·go·ri·an chant /grigáwreeən/ *n.* plainsong ritual music.

grem·lin /grĕmlin/ *n. colloq.* imaginary mischievous sprite regarded as responsible for mechanical faults, esp. in aircraft.

gre·nade /grináyd/ *n.* small bomb thrown by hand (**hand' gre·nade'**) or shot from a rifle.

grenade mid-16th century (in the sense 'pomegranate'): from French, alteration of

Old French (*pome*)*grenate*, on the pattern of Spanish *granada*. The bomb was so named because of its original shape, supposedly resembling a pomegranate.

grew *past* of GROW.

grey var. of GRAY.

grey·hound /gráyhownd/ *n.* dog of a tall slender breed that is capable of high speed, used in racing and coursing.

grid /grid/ *n.* **1** framework of spaced parallel bars; grating. **2** system of squares printed on a map for reference. **3** network of lines, electrical power connections, gas supply lines, etc. **4** wire network between the filament and the anode of a vacuum tube, etc. **5** arrangement of city streets in a rectangular pattern. □□ **grid′ded** *adj.*

grid·dle /gríd′l/ *n.* circular iron plate placed over a fire or otherwise heated for baking, toasting, etc.

grid·i·ron /grídīərn/ *n.* **1** cooking utensil of metal bars for broiling or grilling. **2** football field (with parallel lines marking the area of play). **3** = GRID 5.

grid·lock /grídlok/ *n.* **1** traffic jam in which vehicular movement is blocked by stoppage of cross traffic. **2** complete standstill in action or progress. □□ **grid′locked** *adj.*

grief /greef/ *n.* **1** deep or intense sorrow or mourning. **2** cause of this. □ **come to grief** meet with disaster.

griev·ance /gréevəns/ *n.* cause for complaint.

grieve /greev/ *v.* **1** *tr.* cause grief or great distress to. **2** *intr.* suffer grief, esp. at another's death.

griev·ous /gréevəs/ *adj.* **1** (of pain, etc.) severe. **2** causing grief. **3** flagrant; heinous. □□ **griev′ous·ly** *adv.*

¶ Do not pronounce this word as though it had an extra syllable, as "gree-vee-uhs."

grif·fin /grífin/ *n.* (also **gryph′on**, **grif′fon**) mythical creature with an eagle's head and wings and a lion's body.

grill /gril/ • *n.* **1** = GRIDIRON 1. **2** food cooked on a grill. **3** (in full **grill′ room**) restaurant serving grilled food. • *v.* **1** *tr.* & *intr.* cook or be cooked under a broiler or on a gridiron. **2** *tr.* & *intr.* subject or be subjected to extreme heat, esp. from the sun. **3** *tr.* subject to severe questioning or interrogation. □□ **grill′ing** *n.* (in sense 3 of *v.*).

grille /gril/ *n.* (also **grill**) **1** grating or latticed screen. **2** metal grid protecting the radiator of a motor vehicle.

grill·work /grílwərk/ *n.* metal fashioned to form a grille.

grim /grim/ *adj.* (**grim·mer**, **grim·mest**) **1** of stern or forbidding appearance. **2** harsh; merciless; severe. **b** resolute (*grim determination*). **3** joyless; sinister (*has a grim truth in it*). **4** unpleasant; unattractive. □□ **grim′ly** *adv.* **grim′ness** *n.*

grim·ace /gríməs, grimáys/ • *n.* distortion of the face made in disgust, etc., or to amuse. • *v. intr.* make a grimace.

grime /grīm/ • *n.* soot or dirt ingrained in a surface. • *v.tr.* blacken with grime; befoul.

grin /grin/ • *v.* (**grin·ned**, **grin·ning**) **1** *intr.* smile broadly, showing the teeth. **2** *tr.* express by grinning (*grinned his satisfaction*). • *n.* act of grinning. □ **grin and bear it** take pain or misfortune stoically.

grind /grīnd/ • *v.* (*past* and *past part.* **ground** /grownd/) **1 a** *tr.* reduce to particles or powder by crushing. **b** *intr.* (of a mill, machine, etc.) move with a crushing action. **2 a** *tr.* reduce, sharpen, or smooth by friction. **b** *tr.* & *intr.* rub or rub together gratingly (*grind one's teeth*). **3** *tr.* oppress. **4** *intr.* **a** work or study hard. **b** produce with effort (*grinding out verses*). **c** (of a sound) continue gratingly. • *n.* **1** act or instance of grinding. **2** *colloq.* hard dull work (*the daily grind*). **3** size of ground particles.

grind·er /gríndər/ *n.* **1** person or thing that grinds, esp. a machine. **2** molar tooth. **3** *US dial.* submarine sandwich.

grind·stone /gríndstōn/ *n.* **1** thick revolving disk used for grinding, sharpening, and polishing. **2** kind of stone used for this. □ **keep one's nose to the grindstone** work hard and continuously.

grip /grip/ • *v.* (**gripped**, **grip·ping**) **1 a** *tr.* grasp tightly. **b** *intr.* take a firm hold. **2** *tr.* (of a feeling or emotion) deeply affect (a person) (*was gripped by fear*). **3** *tr.* compel the attention of (*a gripping story*). • *n.* **1** firm hold; tight grasp. **2** power of holding attention. **3 a** intellectual control. **b** control of a situation or one's behavior, etc. (*lose one's grip*). **4 a** part of a machine that grips. **b** handle. **5** traveling bag. □ **come to grips with** approach purposefully; begin to deal with.

gripe /grīp/ • *v.* **1** *intr. colloq.* complain. **2** *tr.* affect with gastric pain. • *n.* **1** (usu. in *pl.*) colic. **2** *colloq.* **a** complaint. **b** act of griping.

gris·ly /grízlee/ *adj.* (**gris·li·er**, **gris·li·est**) causing horror, disgust, or fear. □□ **gris′li·ness** *n.*

grist /grist/ *n.* grain to grind.

gris·tle /grísəl/ *n.* tough flexible animal tissue; cartilage. □□ **gris′tly** /gríslee/ *adj.*

grit /grit/ • *n.* **1** particles of stone or sand, esp. as irritating or hindering. **2** coarse sandstone. **3** *colloq.* pluck endurance. • *v.* (**grit·ted**, **grit·ting**) **1** *tr.* clench (the teeth). **2** *intr.* make or move with a grating sound. □□ **grit′ty** *adj.* (**grit·ti·er**, **grit·ti·est**) **grit′ti·ness** *n.*

grits /grits/ *n.pl.* coarsely ground hulled grain, esp. hominy.

griz·zled /grízəld/ *adj.* having, or streaked with, gray hair.

griz·zly /grízlee/ • *adj.* (**griz·zli·er**, **griz·zli·est**) gray; grayish; gray-haired. • *n.* (*pl.* **-zlies**) (in full **griz′zly bear**) variety of large brown bear found in N. America.

groan /grōn/ • *v.* **1 a** *intr.* make a deep sound expressing pain, grief, or disapproval. **b** *tr.* utter with groans. **2** *intr.* complain inarticulately. **3** *intr.* (usu. foll. by *under, beneath, with*) be loaded or oppressed. • *n.* sound made in groaning. □□ **groan′er** *n.* **groan′ing·ly** *adv.*

gro·cer /grósər/ *n.* dealer in food and household provisions.

gro·cer·y /grósəree/ *n.* (*pl.* **-ies**) **1** grocer's trade or store. **2** (in *pl.*) provisions, esp. food, sold by a grocer.

grog /grog/ *n.* drink of liquor (orig. rum) and water.

grog·gy /grógee/ *adj.* (**grog·gi·er**, **grog·gi·est**) unsteady; dazed. □□ **grog′gi·ly** *adv.* **grog′gi·ness** *n.*

groin /groyn/ • *n.* **1** depression between the belly and the thigh. **2** *Archit.* **a** edge formed by intersecting vaults. **b** arch supporting a vault. • *v.tr. Archit.* build with groins.

grom·met /grómit/ *n.* (also **grum′met** /grúmit/) metal, plastic, or rubber eyelet placed in a hole to protect or insulate a rope or cable, etc., passed through it.

groom /grōom/ • *n.* **1** = BRIDEGROOM. **2** caretaker of horses. • *v.tr.* **1 a** curry or tend (a horse). **b** give a neat appearance to (a person, etc.). **2** (of an ape, etc.) clean and comb the fur of (its fellow). **3** prepare or train (a person) for a particular purpose (*was groomed for the top job*).

groove /grōov/ • *n.* **1** channel or hollow. **2** established routine or habit. • *v.* **1** *tr.* make a groove or grooves in. **2** *intr. sl.* **a** enjoy oneself. **b** (often foll. by *with*) get on well.

groov·y /grōovee/ *adj.* (**groov·i·er**, **groov·i·est**) *sl.* or *joc.* fashionable and exciting; enjoyable; excellent. □□ **groov′i·ness** *n.*

grope /grōp/ • *v.* **1** *intr.* feel about or search blindly or uncertainly with the hands. **2** *intr.* (foll. by *for, after*) search mentally (*was groping for the answer*). **3** *tr.* feel (one's way) toward something. • *n.* process or instance of groping.

gros·grain /grógrayn/ *n.* corded fabric of silk, rayon, etc.

gross /grōs/ • *adj.* **1** overfed; bloated; repulsively fat. **2** (of a person, manners, or morals) coarse, unrefined, or indecent. **3** flagrant (*gross negligence*). **4** total; without deductions; not net (*gross tonnage*). **5** *sl.* repulsive; disgusting. • *v.tr.* produce or earn as gross profit or income. • *n.* (*pl.* same) amount equal to twelve dozen things. □ **gross domestic product** total value of goods produced and services provided in a country in one year. **gross national product** gross domestic product plus the total of net income from abroad. **gross out** *sl.* disgust, esp. by repulsive or obscene behavior. □□ **gross′ly** *adv.* **gross′ness** *n.*

gro·tesque /grōtésk/ • *adj.* **1** comically or repulsively distorted. **2** incongruous; absurd. • *n.* decorative form interweaving human and animal features. □□ **gro·tesque′ly** *adv.* **gro·tesque′ness** *n.*

---

grotesque mid-16th century (as noun): from French *crotesque* (the earliest form in English), from Italian *grottesca*, from *opera* or *pittura grottesca* 'work or painting in a grotto'; *grotto* here probably denoted the rooms of ancient buildings in Rome that had been revealed by excavations, and that contained murals in a distorted style.

---

grot·to /grótō/ *n.* (*pl.* **-toes** or **-tos**) **1** small, esp. picturesque cave. **2** artificial ornamental cave.

grouch /growch/ *colloq.* • *v.intr.* grumble. • *n.* discontented person. □□ **grouch′y** *adj.*

ground[1] /grownd/ • *n.* **1 a** surface of the earth. **b** part of this specified in some way (*low ground*). **2** substance of the earth's surface; soil; earth (*stony ground; dug deep into the ground*). **3 a** position, area, or distance on the earth's surface. **b** extent of activity, etc., achieved or of a subject dealt with (*the book covers a lot of ground*). **4** (often in *pl.*) foundation, motive, or reason (*there is ground for concern*). **5** designated area (often in *comb.*: *fishing-grounds*). **6** (in *pl.*) land attached to a house, etc. **7** area or basis for consideration, agreement, etc. (*common ground*). **8** (in *pl.*) solid particles, esp. of coffee, forming a residue. **9** *Electr.* connection to the ground

that completes an electrical circuit. • *v.* **1** *tr.* **a** refuse authority for (a pilot or an aircraft) to fly. **b** restrict (esp. a child) from certain activities, places, etc., esp. as a form of punishment. **2 a** *tr.* run (a ship) aground; strand. **b** *intr.* (of a ship) run aground. **3** *tr.* instruct thoroughly (in a subject). **4** *tr.* (often as **grounded** *adj.*) base (a principle, conclusion, etc.) on. **5** *tr. Electr.* connect to the ground. □ **break new** (or **fresh**) **ground** treat a subject previously not dealt with. **get off the ground** *colloq.* make a successful start. **ground control** personnel directing the landing, etc., of aircraft or spacecraft. **ground cover** plants covering the surface of the soil, esp. low-growing spreading plants that inhibit the growth of weeds. **ground floor** floor of a building at ground level. **ground speed** aircraft's speed relative to the ground. **ground swell 1** heavy sea caused by a storm or earthquake. **2** = GROUND-SWELL. **hold one's ground** not retreat or give way. **on the grounds of** because of.

ground[2] *past* and *past part.* of GRIND.

ground·break·ing /grówndbrayking/ *adj.* innovative in character; pioneering (*groundbreaking techniques in communication*).

ground·ing /grównding/ *n.* basic training or instruction.

ground·less /grówndlis/ *adj.* without motive or foundation.

grounds·keep·er /grówndzkeepər, grównz-/ *n.* person who maintains the grounds of a property, as a golf course or park.

ground·swell /grówndswel/ *n.* surge of feeling or support.

ground·water /grówndwáwtər, -wotər/ *n.* water found in soil or in pores, crevices, etc., in rock.

ground·work /grówndwərk/ *n.* **1** preliminary or basic work. **2** foundation or basis.

group /grōop/ • *n.* persons or things located close together, or considered or classed together. • *v.* **1** *tr. & intr.* form or be formed into a group. **2** *tr.* place in a group or groups. **3** *tr.* classify. □ **group therapy** therapy in which patients with a similar condition are brought together to assist one another psychologically. □□ **group′ing** *n.*

group·ie /grōopee/ *n. sl.* ardent follower of touring pop- or rock-music groups, celebrities, or activities.

grouse[1] /grows/ *n.* (*pl.* same) game bird with a plump body and feathered legs.

grouse[2] /grows/ *colloq.* • *v.intr.* grumble or complain pettily. • *n.* complaint.

grout /growt/ • *n.* thin mortar for filling gaps in tiling, etc. • *v.tr.* provide or fill with grout. □□ **grout′er** *n.*

grove /grōv/ *n.* small wood or group of trees.

grov·el /gróvəl/ *v.intr.* (**grov·eled**, **grov·el·ing**; **grov·elled**, **grov·el·ling**) **1** behave obsequiously. **2** lie prone in abject humility. □□ **grov′el·er** *n.* **grov′el·ing** *adj.*

grow /grō/ *v.* (*past* **grew** /grōo/; *past part.* **grown** /grōn/) **1** *intr.* increase in size, height, quantity, degree, etc. **2** *intr.* **a** develop or exist as a living plant or natural product. **b** develop in a specific way or direction (*began to grow sideways*). **c** germinate; sprout; spring up. **3** *intr.* be produced; come naturally into existence; arise. **4** *intr.* (foll. by *on*) become gradually more favored by. **5** *tr.*

growl ~ guffaw 258

a produce (plants, fruit, wood, etc.) by cultivation. **b** bring forth. **c** cause (a beard, etc.) to develop. **6** *tr.* (in *passive*; foll. by *over*, *up*) be covered with a growth. □ **grown-up** *adj.* adult. ● *n.* adult person. **grow up 1** mature. **2** (esp. in *imper.*) begin to behave sensibly. □□ **grow′er** *n.*

growl /growl/ ● *v.* **1** *intr.* **a** (esp. of a dog) make a low guttural sound, usu. of anger. **b** murmur angrily. **2** *intr.* rumble. **3** *tr.* (often foll. by *out*) utter with a growl. ● *n.* **1** growling sound. **2** angry murmur; complaint. **3** rumble.

growth /grōth/ *n.* **1** act or process of growing. **2** increase in size or value. **3** something that has grown or is growing. **4** *Med.* abnormal mass of tissue, as a tumor, wart, etc.

grub /grub/ ● *n.* **1** larva of an insect. **2** *colloq.* food. ● *v.* (**grubbed, grub·bing**) **1** *tr.* & *intr.* dig superficially. **2** *tr.* extract (information, etc.) by searching in books, etc.

grub·by /grúbee/ *adj.* (**grub·bi·er, grub·bi·est**) dirty. □□ **grub′bi·ly** *adv.* **grub′bi·ness** *n.*

grub·stake /grúbstayk/ ● *n.* material or provisions supplied to an enterprise in return for a share in the profits (orig. in prospecting for ore). ● *v.tr.* provide with a grubstake.

grudge /gruj/ ● *n.* persistent feeling of ill will or resentment (*bears a grudge against me*). ● *v.tr.* be resentfully unwilling to give, grant, or allow (a thing). □□ **grudg′ing** *adj.*

gru·el /gróoəl/ *n.* liquid food of oatmeal, etc., chiefly for invalids.

gruel·ing /gróoəling/ *adj.* extremely demanding, severe, or tiring. □□ **gruel′ing·ly** *adv.*

grue·some /gróosəm/ *adj.* horrible; grisly; disgusting. □□ **grue′some·ly** *adv.* **grue′some·ness** *n.*

gruff /gruf/ *adj.* **1 a** (of a voice) low and harsh. **b** (of a person) having a gruff voice. **2** surly. □□ **gruff′ly** *adv.* **gruff′ness** *n.*

grum·ble /grúmbəl/ ● *v.* **1** *intr.* complain peevishly; be discontented. **2** *intr.* a murmur; growl faintly. **b** rumble. **3** *tr.* (often foll. by *out*) utter complainingly. ● *n.* **1** complaint. **2** rumble. □□ **grum′bler** *n.* **grum′bling** *adj.* **grum′bling·ly** *adv.*

grump·y /grúmpee/ *adj.* (**grump·i·er, grump·i·est**) morosely irritable; surly. □□ **grump′i·ly** *adv.* **grump′i·ness** *n.*

grunge /grunj/ *n.* *sl.* **1** grime; dirt. **2** aggressive style of rock music characterized by a raucous guitar sound. **3** style of youthful clothing and appearance marked by studied dishevelment. □□ **grun′gy** *adj.*

grunt /grunt/ ● *n.* **1** low guttural sound made by a pig. **2** similar sound. ● *v.* **1** *intr.* (of a pig) make a grunt or grunts. **2** *intr.* (of a person) make a low inarticulate sound resembling this, esp. to express discontent, dissent, fatigue, etc. **3** *tr.* utter with a grunt.

Gru·yère /gróo-yáir, gree-/ *n.* firm pale cheese made from cow's milk.

gr. wt. *abbr.* gross weight.

Gt. Brit. *abbr.* Great Britain.

gua·ca·mo·le /gwa′akəmṓlee/ *n.* dip or garnish of mashed avocado mixed with chopped onion, tomatoes, chili peppers, and seasoning.

gua·no /gwa′anō/ *n.* (*pl.* **-nos**) *n.* excrement of sea birds, bats, etc., used as fertilizer.

Gua·ra·ni /gwa′ərənee/ *n.* **1 a** member of a S. American Indian people. **b** language of this people. **2** (**guarani**) monetary unit of Paraguay.

guar·an·tee /gárəntee′/ ● *n.* **1 a** formal promise or assurance, esp. of quality or performance. **b** document assuring this. **2** = GUARANTY. ● *v.tr.* (**guar·an·tees, guar·an·teed**) **1 a** give or serve as a guarantee for. **b** assure the permanence, etc., of. **c** provide with a guarantee. **2** give a promise or assurance.

¶ **Guarantee** and **guaranty** are interchangeable for both noun and verb, although the latter is now rare as a verb. **Warranty** is widely used their place. *Warrantee* means ' person to whom a warranty is made'; it is not a spelling variant of *warranty*.

guar·an·tor /gárəntáwr, -tər/ *n.* person who gives a guarantee or guaranty.

guar·an·ty /gárəntee/ *n.* (*pl.* **-ties**) **1** written or other undertaking to answer for the payment of a debt or for the performance of an obligation by another person liable in the first instance. **2** thing serving as security for a guaranty.

guard /gaard/ ● *v.* **1** *tr.* watch over and defend or protect. **2** *tr.* supervise (prisoners, etc.) and prevent from escaping. **3** *tr.* keep (thoughts or speech) in check. **4** *tr.* provide with safeguards. **5** *intr.* take precautions. ● *n.* **1** state of vigilance. **2** person who protects or keeps watch. **3** soldiers, etc., protecting a place or person; escort. **4** part of an army detached for some purpose (*advance guard*). **5** thing that protects or defends. **6** in some sports: **a** protective or defensive player. **b** defensive posture or motion.

guard·ed /gáardid/ *adj.* (of a remark, etc.) cautious; avoiding commitment. □□ **guard′ed·ly** *adv.*

guard·i·an /gáardeeən/ *n.* **1** defender, protector, or keeper. **2** person having legal custody of another, esp. a minor. □□ **guard′i·an·ship** *n.*

gua·va /gwa′avə/ *n.* **1** small tropical American tree bearing an edible pale yellow fruit with pink juicy flesh. **2** this fruit.

gu·ber·na·to·ri·al /gŏobərnətáwreeəl, gyŏo-/ *adj.* of or relating to a governor.

guer·ril·la /gərílə/ *n.* (also **gue·ril′la**) member of a small, independent (usu. political) group taking part in irregular fighting.

guess /ges/ ● *v.* **1** *tr.* (often *absol.*) estimate without calculation or measurement, or on the basis of inadequate data. **2** *tr.* form a hypothesis or opinion about; conjecture; think likely (*cannot guess how you did it*). **3** *tr.* conjecture or estimate correctly (*you have to guess the weight*). **4** *intr.* make a conjecture about. ● *n.* estimate or conjecture.

guess·work /géswərk/ *n.* process of or results got by guessing.

guest /gest/ ● *n.* **1** person invited to visit, have a meal, etc., at the expense of the inviter. **2** person lodging at a hotel, boardinghouse, etc. **3 a** outside performer invited to take part with regular performers. **b** person who takes part by invitation in a radio or television program (often *attrib.*: *guest artist*). ● *v.intr.* be a guest on a radio or television show or in a theatrical performance, etc.

guff /guf/ *n.* *sl.* empty talk; nonsense.

guf·faw /gufáw/ ● *n.* loud or boisterous laugh. ● *v.* **1** *intr.* utter a guffaw. **2** *tr.* say with a guffaw.

guid·ance /gíd'ns/ *n.* **1 a** advice or helpful direction. **b** leadership or direction. **2** guiding or being guided.

guide /gīd/ • *n.* **1** person who leads or shows the way. **2** person who conducts tours, etc. **3** adviser. **4** directing principle (*one's feelings are a bad guide*). **5** book with essential information on a subject, esp. = GUIDEBOOK. **6** thing marking a position. • *v.tr.* **1** act as guide to. **2** be the principle, motive, or ground of (an action, judgment, etc.). **3** direct the affairs of (a government, etc.). □ **guided missile** missile directed to its target by remote control or by equipment within itself. **guide dog** dog trained to guide a blind person.

guide·book /gídbōōk/ *n.* book of information about a place for visitors, tourists, etc.

guide·line /gídlīn/ *n.* principle directing action.

guild /gild/ *n.* **1** association of people for mutual aid or the pursuit of a common goal. **2** medieval association of craftsmen or merchants.

guild·er /gíldər/ *n.* chief monetary unit of the Netherlands.

guile /gīl/ *n.* deceit; cunning or sly behavior. □□ **guile′ful** *adj.* **guile′less** *adj.*

guil·lo·tine /gílətēen, géeə-/ • *n.* machine with a heavy knife blade that drops vertically, used for beheading. • *v.tr.* use a guillotine on.

guilt /gilt/ *n.* **1** fact of having committed a specified or implied offense. **2 a** culpability. **b** feeling of this. □□ **guilt′less** *adj.*

guilt·y /gíltee/ *adj.* (**guilt·i·er**, **guilt·i·est**) **1** responsible for a wrong. **2** affected by guilt (*a guilty conscience*). **3** concerning guilt (*a guilty secret*). **4** having committed a (specified) offense. □□ **guilt′i·ly** *adv.* **guilt′i·ness** *n.*

guin·ea /gínee/ *n.* former British gold coin worth 21 shillings, first coined for the African trade. □ **guinea fowl** African fowl with slate-colored, white-spotted plumage. **guinea pig 1** domesticated S. American rodent, kept as a pet or for research in biology, etc. **2** subject used in an experiment.

guise /gīz/ *n.* **1** assumed appearance; pretense (*in the guise of; under the guise of*). **2** garb.

gui·tar /gitáar/ *n.* usu. six-stringed musical instrument played with the fingers or a plectrum. □□ **gui·tar′ist** *n.*

Gu·ja·ra·ti /gōōjərátee/ • *n.* (*pl.* **Gu·ja·ra·tis**) **1** language of Gujarat in W. India. **2** native of Gujarat. • *adj.* of or relating to Gujarat or its language.

gulch /gulch/ *n.* ravine, esp. one in which a torrent flows.

gulf /gulf/ • *n.* **1** deep ocean inlet with a narrow mouth. **2 (the Gulf) a** Gulf of Mexico. **b** Persian Gulf. **3** deep hollow; chasm or abyss. **4** wide difference of feelings, opinion, etc. • *v.tr.* engulf; swallow up. □ **Gulf Stream** warm ocean current flowing from the Gulf of Mexico toward Europe.

gull¹ /gul/ *n.* long-winged, web-footed sea bird usu. having white plumage with a mantle varying from pearly gray to black, and a bright bill.

gull² /gul/ *v.tr.* (usu. in *passive*; foll. by *into*) dupe; fool.

gul·let /gúlit/ *n.* **1** esophagus. **2** throat.

gul·li·ble /gúlibəl/ *adj.* easily persuaded or deceived; credulous. □□ **gul·li·bil′i·ty** *n.* **gul′lib·ly** *adv.*

gull·y /gúlee/ • *n.* (*pl.* **-ies**) **1** waterworn ravine. **2** deep artificial channel; gutter or drain. • *v.tr.* (**-ies**, **-ied**) **1** form (channels) by water action. **2** make gullies in.

gulp /gulp/ • *v.* **1** *tr.* swallow hastily or greedily. **2** *intr.* swallow with difficulty. **3** *tr.* (foll. by *down, back*) stifle; suppress (esp. tears). • *n.* **1** act of gulping (*drained it at one gulp*). **2** large mouthful of a drink.

gum¹ /gum/ • *n.* **1 a** viscous secretion of some trees and shrubs that hardens on drying but is soluble in water (cf. RESIN). **b** adhesive substance. **2** chewing gum. • *v.tr.* (**gummed**, **gum·ming**) **1** smear or cover with gum. **2** fasten with gum. □ **gum arabic** gum exuded by some kinds of acacia and used as glue and in incense. **gum up 1** (of a mechanism, etc.) become clogged or obstructed with stickiness. **2** *colloq.* interfere with the smooth running of (*gum up the works*). □□ **gum′my** *adj.* (**gum·mi·er**, **gum·mi·est**)

gum² /gum/ *n.* (usu. in *pl.*) firm flesh around the roots of the teeth.

gum·bo /gúmbō/ *n.* (*pl.* **-bos**) soup thickened with okra pods.

gum·drop /gúmdrop/ *n.* soft, flavored candy made with gelatin or gum arabic.

gump·tion /gúmpshən/ *n. colloq.* **1** resourcefulness; initiative. **2** common sense.

gum·shoe /gúmshōō/ *n. sl.* detective.

gun /gun/ • *n.* **1** weapon consisting of a metal tube and with a grip at one end, from which bullets, etc., are propelled with explosive force. **2** device imitative of this, e.g., a starting pistol. **3** device for discharging insecticide, grease, electrons, etc. **4** gunman. • *v.* (**gunned**, **gun·ning**) **1** *tr.* **a** shoot (a person) with a gun. **b** shoot at with a gun. **2** *tr. colloq.* accelerate (an engine or vehicle). **3** *intr.* (foll. by *for*) seek out determinedly to attack or rebuke. □ **go great guns** *colloq.* proceed vigorously or successfully. **stick to one's guns** *colloq.* maintain one's position under attack.

gun·boat /gúnbōt/ *n.* small vessel with heavy guns.

gun·fight /gúnfīt/ *n.* fight with firearms. □□ **gun′fight·er** *n.*

gun·fire /gúnfīr/ *n.* **1** firing of a gun or guns. **2** the noise from this.

gung-ho /gúnghó/ *adj.* enthusiastic; eager.

gunk /gungk/ *n. sl.* viscous or liquid material.

gun·man /gúnmən/ *n.* (*pl.* **-men**) man armed with a gun, esp. in committing a crime.

gun·met·al /gúnmetəl/ *n.* **1** dull bluish gray color. **2** alloy of copper and tin or zinc (formerly used for guns).

gun·nel var. of GUNWALE.

gun·ner /gúnər/ *n.* **1** artillery soldier. **2** *Naut.* warrant officer in charge of a battery, magazine, etc. **3** member of an aircraft crew who operates a gun.

gun·ner·y /gúnəree/ *n.* **1** construction and management of large guns. **2** firing of guns.

gun·ny /gúnee/ *n.* (*pl.* **-nies**) **1** coarse sacking, usu. of jute fiber. **2** sack made of this.

gun·pow·der /gúnpowdər/ *n.* explosive made of saltpeter, sulfur, and charcoal, used in cartridges, fireworks, etc.

gun·run·ner /gúnrunər/ *n.* person engaged in smuggling firearms. □□ **gun′run·ning** *n.*

gun·shot /gúnshot/ *n.* **1** shot fired from a gun. **2** range of a gun (*within gunshot*).

gun·smith /gúnsmith/ *n.* person who makes, sells, and repairs small firearms.

gun·wale /gúnəl/ *n.* (also **gun′nel**) upper edge of the side of a boat or ship.

gup·py /gúpee/ *n.* (*pl.* **-pies**) freshwater fish of the W. Indies and S. America, frequently kept in aquariums, and giving birth to live young.

gur·gle /górgəl/ • *v.* **1** *intr.* make a bubbling sound as of water. **2** *tr.* utter with such a sound. • *n.* gurgling sound.

gu·ru /gŏorŏo/ *n.* **1** Hindu spiritual teacher or head of a religious sect. **2 a** influential teacher. **b** revered mentor.

gush /gush/ • *v.* **1** *tr.* & *intr.* emit or flow in a sudden and copious stream. **2** *intr.* speak or behave effusively. • *n.* **1** sudden or copious stream. **2** effusive or sentimental manner. □□ **gush′ing** *adj.* **gush′y** *adj.*

gush·er /gúshər/ *n.* **1** oil well from which oil flows without being pumped. **2** effusive person.

gus·set /gúsit/ *n.* piece inserted into a garment, etc., to strengthen or enlarge it. □□ **gus′set·ed** *adj.*

gust /gust/ • *n.* **1** sudden strong rush of wind. **2** burst of rain, fire, smoke, or sound. **3** passionate outburst. • *v.intr.* blow in gusts. □□ **gust′y** *adj.*

gus·to /gústō/ *n.* (*pl.* **-toes**) zest; enjoyment or vigor.

gut /gut/ • *n.* **1** intestine. **2** (in *pl.*) the bowel or entrails. **3** (in *pl.*) *colloq.* personal courage. **4** *colloq.* stomach; belly. **5** (in *pl.*) **a** contents. **b** essence, e.g., of an issue or problem. **6 a** material for violin or racket strings or surgical use. **b** material for fishing lines. **7** (*attrib.*) **a** instinctive (*gut reaction*). **b** fundamental (*a gut issue*). • *v.tr.* (**gut·ted**, **gut·ting**) **1** remove or destroy the interior of (a house, etc.). **2** take out the guts of (a fish, etc.). **3** extract the essence of (a book, etc.).

gut·less /gútlis/ *adj. colloq.* lacking courage.

gut·sy /gútsee/ *adj.* (**gut·si·er**, **gut·si·est**) *colloq.* courageous. □□ **gut′si·ness** *n.*

gut·ter /gútər/ • *n.* **1** shallow trough along the eaves of a house, or channel at the side of a street, to carry off rainwater. **2** (prec. by *the*) poor or degraded background or environment. • *v.* **1** *intr.* flow in streams. **2** *tr.* furrow; channel. **3** *intr.* (of a candle) melt away rapidly.

gut·ter·snipe /gútərsnīp/ *n.* street urchin.

gut·tur·al /gútərəl/ • *adj.* **1** throaty; harsh sounding. **2 a** *Phonet.* (of a consonant) produced in the throat or by the back of the tongue and palate. **b** of the throat. • *n. Phonet.* guttural consonant (e.g., *k*, *g*). □□ **gut′tur·al·ly** *adv.*

guy¹ /gī/ *n. colloq.* man; fellow. **2** (usu. in *pl.*) person of either sex.

guy² /gī/ • *n.* rope or chain to secure a tent or steady a load, etc. • *v.tr.* secure with a guy or guys.

guz·zle /gúzəl/ *v.* eat or drink greedily. □□ **guz′zler** *n.*

gybe /jīb/ var. of JIBE².

gym /jim/ *n. colloq.* **1** gymnasium. **2** physical education.

gym·na·si·um /jimnáyzeeəm/ *n.* (*pl.* **gym·na·si·ums** or **gym·na·si·a** /-zeeə/) room or building equipped for indoor sports or training.

gym·nas·tics /jimnástiks/ *n.pl.* (also treated as *sing.*) **1** exercises developing or displaying physical agility and coordination, usu. in competition. **2** other forms of physical or mental agility. □□ **gym′nast** *n.* **gym·nas′tic** *adj.* **gym·nas′ti·cal·ly** *adv.*

gym·no·sperm /jímnəspərm/ *n.* plants having seeds unprotected by an ovary, including conifers, ginkgos, etc. (opp. ANGIOSPERM).

gyn. *abbr.* (also **gynecol.**) **1** gynecological. **2** gynecology.

gy·ne·col·o·gy /gínikóləjee, jínə-/ *n.* the science and medical specialty of the physiological functions and diseases of women and girls, esp. those affecting the reproductive system. □□ **gy·ne·co·log′i·cal** *adj.* **gy·ne·col′o·gist** *n.*

gyp /jip/ *sl.* • *v.tr.* (**gypped**, **gyp·ping**) cheat; swindle. • *n.* act of cheating; swindle.

gyp·sum /jípsəm/ *n.* form of calcium sulfate used to make plaster of Paris and in the building industry.

Gyp·sy /jípsee/ *n.* (also **Gip′sy**) (*pl.* **-sies**) **1** member of a nomadic people of Hindu origin with dark skin and black hair. **2** (**gypsy**) person resembling or living like a Gypsy. □ **gypsy moth** tussock moth of which the larvae are very destructive to foliage.

gy·rate /jírayt/ *v.intr.* (also /jīráyt/) go in a circle or spiral; revolve; whirl. □□ **gy·ra′tion** /-ráyshən/ *n.* **gy′ra·tor** *n.* **gy·ra·to·ry** /-rətáwree/ *adj.*

gy·ro /jírō/ *n.* (*pl.* **-ros**) **1** Greek-style roasted lamb served in pita bread. **2** *colloq.* = GYROSCOPE.

gyro- /jírō/ *comb. form* rotation.

gy·ro·scope /jírəskōp/ *n.* rotating wheel whose axis is free to turn but maintains a fixed direction despite change of position, esp. used for stabilization and with the compass in an aircraft, ship, etc. □□ **gy·ro·scop·ic** /-skópik/ *adj.* **gy·ro·scop′i·cal·ly** *adv.*

GYROSCOPE

Hh

H¹ /aych/ n. (also **h**) (pl. **Hs** or **H's; h's**) **1** eighth letter of the alphabet (see AITCH). **2** anything having the form of an H (esp. in comb.: *H-girder*).

H² symb. Chem. hydrogen.

h. abbr. **1** hecto-. **2** height. **3** horse. **4** hot. **5** hour(s). **6** husband. **7** Planck's constant. **8** Baseball hit; hits.

ha /haa/ int. (also **hah**) expressing surprise, suspicion, triumph, etc. (cf. HA HA).

ha·be·as cor·pus /háybeeəs káwrpəs/ n. writ requiring a person to be brought before a court, esp. to investigate the lawfulness of the detention.

hab·er·dash·er /hábərdashər/ n. dealer in men's clothing. □□ **hab′er·dash·er·y** n. (pl. **-ies**).

ha·bil·i·ment /həbílimənt/ n. (usu. in pl.) clothes.

hab·it /hábit/ n. **1** settled or regular tendency or practice (*has a habit of ignoring me*). **2** practice that is hard to give up. **3** mental constitution or attitude. **4** colloq. addiction. **5 a** dress, esp. of a religious order. **b** (in full **rid′ ing hab·it**) woman's riding dress. □ **habit-forming** addictive.

hab·it·a·ble /hábitəbəl/ adj. suitable for living in. □□ **hab·it·a·bil′i·ty** n.

hab·i·tat /hábitat/ n. natural home of an organism.

hab·i·ta·tion /hábitáyshən/ n. **1** inhabiting. **2** house or home.

ha·bit·u·al /həbícho͞oəl/ adj. **1** done constantly or as a habit. **2** regular; usual. **3** given to a (specified) habit. □□ **ha·bit′ u·al·ly** adv.

ha·bit·u·ate /həbícho͞o-ayt/ v.tr. accustom; make used to something. □□ **ha·bit·u·a·tion** /-áyshən/ n.

ha·bit·u·é /həbícho͞o-áy/ n. habitual visitor or resident.

ha·cek /haáchek/ n. (also **háček**) diacritic (ˇ) placed over letters to modify the sound in Slavic and Baltic languages.

ha·ci·en·da /haásee-éndə/ n. in Spanish-speaking countries, an estate, or specifically the main house of an estate.

hack¹ /hak/ ● v. **1** tr. cut or chop roughly. **2** intr. deliver cutting blows. **3** tr. cut (one's way) through foliage, etc. **4** tr. colloq. gain unauthorized access to (data in a computer). **5** tr. sl. **a** manage. **b** tolerate. **c** (as **hacked off** adj.) annoy; disconcert. ● n. gash or wound, esp. from a kick. □ **hacking cough** short dry frequent cough.

hack² /hak/ ● n. **1 a** horse for ordinary riding. **b** horse let out for hire. **2** person hired to do dull routine work, esp. writing. **3** taxi. ● attrib.adj. **1** used as a hack. **2** typical of a hack. ● v. **1 a** intr. ride on horseback on a road at an ordinary pace. **b** ride (a horse) in this way. **2** tr. make common. **3** drive a taxi.

hack·er /hákər/ n. **1** person or thing that hacks or cuts roughly. **2** colloq. **a** person adept at working with computers. **b** person who gains unauthorized access to computer data. **3** golfer who plays poorly.

hack·le /hákəl/ n. **1** feather(s) on the neck of a domestic fowl, etc. **2** (in pl.) erectile hairs on an animal's back, which rise when it is angry or alarmed. □ **raise one's hackles** cause a person to be angry or indignant.

hack·ney /háknee/ n. (pl. **-neys**) **1** horse for ordinary riding. **2** (attrib.) designating any of various vehicles kept for hire.

hack·neyed /hákneed/ adj. (of a phrase, etc.) made commonplace or trite by overuse.

hack·saw /háksaw/ n. saw with a narrow blade set in a frame, for cutting metal.

had past and past part. of HAVE.

had·dock /hádək/ n. (pl. same) N. Atlantic marine fish used as food.

Ha·des /háydeez/ n. Gk. mythol. the underworld; abode of the spirits of the dead. □□ **Ha·de·an** /-deeən/ adj.

haf·ni·um /háfneeəm/ n. Chem. silvery lustrous metallic element, used in tungsten alloys for filaments, etc. ¶ Symb.: **Hf**.

haft /haft/ ● n. handle of a dagger, knife, etc. ● v.tr. provide with a haft.

hag /hag/ n. **1** ugly old woman. **2** witch.

Hag·ga·dah /həgáadə, -gáwdə, haagaadaá/ n. **1** legend, etc., used to illustrate a point of the Law in the Talmud. **2** book recited at the Passover Seder service.

hag·gard /hágərd/ adj. looking exhausted and distraught, esp. from fatigue, worry, privation, etc. □□ **hag′ gard·ness** n.

hag·gis /hágis/ n. Scottish dish of a sheep's or calf's offal mixed with suet, oatmeal, etc., and boiled in a bag made from the animal's stomach or in an artificial bag.

hag·gle /hágəl/ ● v.intr. (often foll. by about, over) dispute or bargain persistently. ● n. dispute or wrangle. □□ **hag′ gler** n.

hagio- /hágeeō, háyjeeō/ comb. form of saints or holiness.

hah var. of HA.

ha ha /haáhaá/ int. words used in representing laughter.

hai·ku /híkoo/ n. (pl. same) Japanese three-line poem of usu. 17 syllables.

hail¹ /hayl/ ● n. **1** pellets of frozen rain. **2** (foll. by of) barrage or onslaught (of missiles, curses, etc.). ● v. **1** intr. (prec. by it as subject) shower down hail (*it is hailing; if it hails*). **2 a** tr. pour down (blows, words, etc.). **b** intr. come down forcefully.

hail² /hayl/ ● v. **1** tr. greet enthusiastically. **2** tr. signal to or attract the attention of (*hailed a taxi*). **3** tr. acclaim (*hailed him king; was hailed as a prodigy*). **4** intr. originate or come (*she hails from Mexico*). ● n. greeting or act of hailing.

hail·stone /háylstōn/ n. pellet of hail.

hail·storm /háylstorm/ n. **1** period of heavy hail. **2** harsh or sharp criticism.

hair /hair/ n. **1 a** fine threadlike strands growing from the skin of mammals, esp. from the human head. **b** these collectively (*his hair is falling* *out*). **2** anything resembling a hair. **3** elongated cell growing from a plant. **4** very small extent (also *attrib.*: *a hair crack*). □ **get in a person's hair** *colloq.* annoy a person. **hair-raising** alarming; terrifying. **hair's breadth** very small amount or margin. **let one's hair down** *colloq.* abandon restraint; behave freely or wildly. **make a person's hair stand on end** alarm or horrify a person. □□ **hair′less** *adj.* **hair′like** *adj.*

hair·ball /háirbawl/ *n.* (also **hair′ ball**) ball of hair that accumulates in the stomach of a cat, etc., that grooms itself by licking its fur.

hair·brush /háirbrush/ *n.* brush for arranging the hair.

hair·cut /háirkut/ *n.* style or act of cutting the hair.

hair·do /háirdoo/ *n.* (*pl.* **-dos**) *colloq.* style or act of styling hair.

hair·dress·er /háirdresər/ *n.* person who cuts and styles hair, esp. professionally. □□ **hair′ dress·ing** *n.*

hair·line /háirlīn/ *n.* **1** edge of a person's hair, esp. on the forehead. **2** very thin line or crack, etc.

hair·net /háirnet/ *n.* piece of netting for confining the hair.

hair·piece /háirpees/ *n.* quantity or switch of detached hair used to augment a person's natural hair.

hair·pin /háirpin/ *n.* U-shaped pin for fastening the hair. □ **hairpin turn** sharp U-shaped bend in a road.

hair·split·ting /háirspliting/ *adj.* & *n.* quibbling.

hair·style /háirstīl/ *n.* particular way of arranging or dressing the hair. □□ **hair′ styl·ing** *n.* **hair′ styl·ist** *n.*

hair·y /háiree/ *adj.* (**hair·i·er**, **hair·i·est**) **1** made of or covered with hair. **2** having the feel of hair. **3** *sl.* alarmingly unpleasant or difficult. □□ **hair′ i·ness** *n.*

hajj /haj/ *n.* Islamic pilgrimage to Mecca.

hake /hayk/ *n.* marine food fish resembling a cod.

hal·berd /hálbərd/ *n.* (also **hal·bert** /-bərt/) *hist.* combined spear and battle-ax.

HALBERD

hal·cy·on /hálseeən/ *adj.* **1** calm; peaceful (*halcyon days*). **2** (of a period) happy; prosperous.

hale /hayl/ *adj.* strong and healthy (esp. in **hale and hearty**).

half /haf/ • *n.* (*pl.* **halves** /havz/) **1** either of two equal or corresponding parts or groups into which a thing is or might be divided. **2** *Sports* either of two equal periods of play. • *adj.* of an amount or quantity equal to a half, or loosely to a part thought of as a half (*take half the men; spent half the time reading; half a pint; a half pint; half-price*). **2** forming a half (*a half share*). • *adv.* **1** (often in *comb.*) to the extent of half; partly (*only half cooked; half-frozen*). **2** to a certain extent; somewhat (esp. in idiomatic phrases: *half dead; am half inclined to agree*). **3** (in reckoning time) by the amount of half (an hour, etc.) (*half past two*). □ **half-and-half** being half one thing and half another, esp. a liquid of half cream and half milk. **half-baked 1** incompletely considered or planned. **2** (of enthusiasm, etc.) only partly committed. **3** foolish. **half breed** often *offens.* person of mixed race. **half brother** brother with only one parent in common. **half-life** *Physics & Biochem.*, etc., time taken for the radioactivity or some other property of a substance to fall to half its original value. **half-mast** position of a flag halfway down the mast, as a mark of respect for a person who has died. **half sister** sister with only one parent in common. **half-time** *n.* **1** time at which half of a game or contest is completed. **2** short interval at this time. • *adj.* working half the usual hours. **half-truth** statement that (esp. deliberately) conveys only part of the truth. **not half 1** not nearly (*not half long enough*). **2** *colloq.* not at all (*not half bad*).

half·back /háfbak/ *n.* (in some sports) player between the linemen and fullbacks, or behind the forward line.

half·heart·ed /háfha'artid/ *adj.* lacking enthusiasm. □□ **half·heart′ ed·ly** *adv.* **half′ heart′ ed·ness** *n.*

half·pen·ny /háypnee/ *n.* (also **ha′penny**) (*pl.* **-pen·nies** or **-pence** /háypəns/) (in the UK) former coin worth half a penny. ¶ Withdrawn in 1984 (cf. FARTHING).

half·tone /háftōn/ *n.* **1** reproduction printed from a block (produced by photographic means) in which the various tones of gray are produced from small and large black dots. **2** *Mus.* (**half tone**) semitone.

half·way /háfwáy/ • *adv.* **1** at a point equidistant between two others (*we were halfway to Chicago*). **2** to some extent; more or less (*is halfway decent*). • *adj.* situated halfway (*reached a halfway point*). □ **halfway house** facility for assisting ex-prisoners, mental patients, etc., in readjusting to society.

half·wit /háfwit/ *n.* *colloq.* extremely foolish or stupid person. □□ **half′ wit·ted** *adj.*

hal·i·but /hálibət/ *n.* (*pl.* same) large marine flatfish used as food.

hal·i·to·sis /hálitōsis/ *n.* bad breath.

hall /hawl/ *n.* **1 a** space or passage into which the front entrance of a house, etc., opens. **b** corridor or passage in a building. **2** large room or building for meetings, meals, concerts, etc. **3** university residence for students.

hal·le·lu·jah var. of ALLELUIA.

hall·mark /háwlmaark/ • *n.* **1** mark of purity, as

stamped into gold, silver, and platinum. **2** distinctive feature. • *v.tr.* **1** stamp with a hallmark. **2** designate as excellent.

hal·low /hálō/ *v.tr.* **1** make holy; consecrate. **2** honor as holy.

Hal·low·een /hálōwéen/ *n.* (also **Hal·low·e'en'**) eve of All Saints' Day, Oct. 31, esp. as celebrated by children dressing in costumes and collecting treats door-to-door.

hal·lu·ci·nate /həlōo͞sinayt/ *v.* **1** *tr.* produce illusions in the mind of (a person). **2** *intr.* experience hallucinations.

hal·lu·ci·na·tion /həlōo͞sináyshən/ *n.* perception of sights, sounds, etc., not actually present. □□ **hal·lu·ci·na·to·ry** /-sinətáwree/ *adj.*

hal·lu·ci·no·gen /həlōo͞sinəjən/ *n.* drug causing hallucinations. □□ **hal·lu·ci·no·gen·ic** /-jénik/ *adj.*

hall·way /háwlway/ *n.* entrance hall or corridor.

ha·lo /háylō/ • *n.* (*pl.* **-loes, -los**) **1** disk or circle of light shown in art surrounding the head of a sacred person. **2** circle of light around a luminous body, esp. the sun or moon. **3** circle or ring. • *v.tr.* (**-loes, -loed**) surround with a halo.

ha·lo·gen /háləjən/ *n. Chem.* any of the nonmetallic elements: fluorine, chlorine, bromine, iodine, and astatine, which form a salt (e.g., sodium chloride) by simple union with a metal. □□ **ha·lo·gen·ic** /-jénik/ *adj.*

halt[1] /hawlt/ • *n.* stop (usu. temporary) (*come to a halt*). • *v.* stop; come or bring to a halt.

halt[2] /hawlt/ *v.intr.* **1** (esp. as **halting** *adj.*) lack smooth progress. **2** hesitate (*halt between two opinions*). **3** walk hesitatingly. □□ **halt'ing·ly** *adv.*

halt·er /háwltər/ • *n.* **1** bridle and rope for leading or tying up a horse, etc. **2 a** strap around the back of a woman's neck holding her dress top or blouse and leaving her shoulders and back bare. **b** garment held by this. • *v.tr.* put a halter on (a horse, etc.).

halve /hav/ *v.tr.* **1** divide into two halves. **2** reduce by half.

halves *pl.* of HALF.

hal·yard /hályərd/ *n. Naut.* rope or tackle for raising or lowering a sail, flag, etc.

ham /ham/ • *n.* **1** upper part of a pig's leg salted and dried or smoked for food. **2** back of the thigh. **3** *sl.* (often *attrib.*) inexpert or unsubtle actor or piece of acting. **4** (in full **ra'di·o ham**) *colloq.* amateur radio operator. • *v.* (**hammed, ham·ming**) *sl.* overact.

---

ham Old English *ham, hom* (originally denoting the back of the knee), from a Germanic base meaning 'be crooked.' In the late 15th century the term came to denote the back of the thigh, hence that part of the animal used as food.

---

ham·burg·er /hámbərgər/ *n.* patty of ground beef, usu. fried or grilled and eaten in a soft bread roll.

ham·let /hámlit/ *n.* small village.

ham·mer /hámər/ • *n.* **1 a** tool with a heavy metal head used for driving nails, etc. **b** similar contrivance, as for exploding the charge in a gun, striking the strings of a piano, etc. **2 a** metal ball attached to a wire for throwing in an athletic contest. **b** sport of throwing the hammer. **3** bone of the middle ear; malleus. • *v.* **1**

hallow ~ hand

a *tr.* & *intr.* hit or beat with or as with a hammer. **b** *intr.* strike loudly; knock violently (esp. on a door). **2** *tr.* **a** drive in (nails). **b** fasten or secure by hammering (*hammered the lid down*). **3** *tr.* inculcate (ideas, knowledge, etc.) forcefully or repeatedly. **4** *tr. colloq.* utterly defeat; inflict heavy damage on. **5** *intr.* (foll. by *at, away at*) work hard or persistently at. □ **hammer and sickle** symbols of the industrial worker and peasant used as the emblem of the former USSR and of international communism. **hammer out 1** make flat or smooth by hammering. **2** work out the details of (a plan, agreement, etc.) laboriously. **3** play (a tune, esp. on the piano) loudly or clumsily.

ball-peen hammer   sledge hammer

claw hammer   tack hammer

HAMMER, 1a

ham·mer·head /hámərhed/ *n.* **1** striking head of a hammer. **2** shark with a flattened head and eyes in lateral extensions of it.

ham·mer·toe /hámərtō/ *n.* deformed toe bent permanently downward.

ham·mock /hámək/ *n.* bed of canvas or rope network, suspended by cords at the ends.

ham·per[1] /hámpər/ *n.* basket, often with a hinged lid, for laundry, etc.

ham·per[2] /hámpər/ *v.tr.* **1** prevent the free movement or activity of. **2** impede; hinder.

ham·ster /hámstər/ *n.* rodent having a short tail and large cheek pouches, kept as a pet or laboratory animal.

ham·string /hámstring/ *Anat.* • *n.* **1** each of five tendons at the back of the knee in humans. **2** great tendon at the back of the hock in quadrupeds. • *v.tr.* (*past* and *past part.* **ham·strung** or **ham·stringed**) **1** cripple by cutting the hamstrings of (a person or animal). **2** prevent the activity or efficiency of (a person or enterprise).

hand /hand/ • *n.* **1 a** end part of the human arm beyond the wrist, including the fingers and thumb. **b** in other primates, end part of a forelimb, also used as a foot. **2 a** (often in *pl.*) control; management; custody; disposal (*in good hands*). **b** active support. **3** thing compared with a hand or its functions, esp. the pointer of a clock or watch. **4** right or left side or direction.

5 a skill (*a hand for making pastry*). **b** person skillful in some respect. **6** individual's writing or the style of this; signature (*a legible hand; in one's own hand*). (*at first hand*). **8** pledge of marriage. **9** person as a source of manual labor, esp. in a factory, on a farm, or on board ship. **10 a** playing cards dealt to a player. **b** round of play. **11** *colloq.* applause (*got a big hand*). **12** unit of measure of a horse's height, equal to 4 inches (10.16 cm). **13** (*attrib.*) held or done by hand. • *v.tr.* deliver; transfer by hand or otherwise. □ **at hand 1** close by. **2** about to happen. **by hand 1** by a person and not a machine. **2** delivered personally. **hand down 1** pass ownership or use of to another. **2 a** transmit (a decision) from a higher court, etc. **b** express (an opinion or verdict). **hand grenade** see GRENADE. **hand in glove** in collusion or association. **hand in hand** in close association. **hand it to** *colloq.* acknowledge the merit of (a person). **hand-me-down** article of clothing, etc., passed on from another person. **hands down** with no difficulty. **hand-to-hand** (of fighting) at close quarters. **on hand** available. **on the one** (or **the other**) **hand** from one (or another) point of view. **out of hand 1** out of control. **2** peremptorily (*refused out of hand*).

hand·bag /hándbag/ *n.* small bag carried esp. by a woman and used to hold a wallet, cosmetics, etc.

hand·ball *n.* /hándbawl/ game in which a ball is struck with an open hand against a wall.

hand·bill /hándbil/ *n.* printed notice distributed by hand.

hand·book /hándbŏok/ *n.* short manual or guidebook.

hand·cart /hándkaart/ *n.* small cart pushed or drawn by hand.

hand·cuff /hándkuf/ • *n.* (in *pl.*) lockable linked metal rings for securing a person's wrists. • *v.tr.* put handcuffs on.

hand·ful /hándfŏol/ *n.* (*pl.* **-fuls**) **1** quantity that fills the hand. **2** small number or amount. **3** *colloq.* troublesome person or task.

hand·gun /hándgun/ *n.* small firearm fired with one hand.

hand·i·cap /hándeekap/ • *n.* **1 a** disadvantage imposed on a superior competitor to make chances more equal. **b** race, etc., in which this is imposed. **2** number of strokes by which a golfer normally exceeds par for the course. **3** thing that makes progress or success difficult. **4** physical or mental disability. • *v.tr.* (**hand·i·capped, hand·i·cap·ping**) **1** impose a handicap on. **2** place (a person) at a disadvantage. □□ **hand'i·capped** *adj.*

hand·i·craft /hándeekraft/ *n.* work requiring manual and artistic skill.

hand·i·work /hándeewərk/ *n.* work done or a thing made by hand, or by a particular person.

hand·ker·chief /hángkərchif, -cheef/ *n.* (*pl.* **hand·ker·chiefs** or **-chieves** /-cheevz/) cloth for wiping one's nose, etc.

han·dle /hánd'l/ • *n.* **1** part by which a thing is held, carried, or controlled. **2** *colloq.* personal title or nickname. • *v.tr.* **1** touch, feel, operate, or move with the hands. **2** manage or deal with (*knows how to handle people; unable to handle the situation*). **3** deal in (goods). **4** discuss or write about (a subject).

han·dle·bar /hánd'lbaar/ *n.* (often in *pl.*) steering bar of a bicycle, etc., with a handgrip at each end.

han·dler /hándlər/ *n.* **1** person who deals in certain commodities. **2** person who trains and looks after an animal (esp. a working or show dog).

hand·made /hándmáyd/ *adj.* made by hand, not by machine.

hand·out /hándowt/ *n.* **1** something given free to a needy person. **2** statement given to the press, printed information given to a lecture audience, etc.

hand·rail /hándrayl/ *n.* narrow rail for holding as a support.

hand·set /hándset/ *n.* telephone mouthpiece and earpiece forming one unit.

hand·shake /hándshayk/ *n.* clasping of a person's hand as a greeting, etc.

hand·some /hánsəm/ *adj.* (**hand·som·er, hand·som·est**) **1** (of a person) good-looking. **2** (of an object, etc.) imposing; attractive. **3 a** generous; liberal (*a handsome present*). **b** (of a price, fortune, etc.) considerable. □□ **hand'some·ly** *adv.*

hand·spring /hándspring/ *n.* acrobatic flip in which one lands first on the hands and then on the feet.

hand·stand /hándstand/ *n.* balancing on one's hands with the feet in the air or against a wall.

hand·work /hándwərk/ *n.* work done with the hands, esp. as opposed to machinery. □□ **hand'worked** *adj.*

hand·writ·ing /hándríting/ *n.* **1** writing with a pen, pencil, etc. **2** individual's style of writing. □□ **hand·writ·ten** /-rítən/ *adj.*

hand·y /hándee/ *adj.* (**hand·i·er, hand·i·est**) **1** convenient to handle or use; useful. **2** placed or occurring conveniently. **3** clever with the hands. □□ **hand'i·ly** *adv.* **hand'i·ness** *n.*

hand·y·man /hándeeman/ *n.* (*pl.* **-men**) person who does odd jobs.

hang /hang/ • *v.* (*past* and *past part.* **hung** /hung/ except in sense 7) **1** *tr.* secure or cause to be supported from above, esp. with the lower part free. **2** *tr.* set up (a door, gate, etc.) on hinges. **3** *tr.* place (a picture) on a wall or in an exhibition. **4** *tr.* attach (wallpaper) to a wall. **5** *tr. colloq.* blame (a thing) on (a person) (*can't hang that on me*). **6** *tr.* (foll. by *with*) decorate by hanging pictures, etc. (*a hall hung with tapestries*). **7** *tr. & intr.* (*past* and *past part.* **hanged**) suspend or be suspended by the neck, usu. with a noosed rope, until dead. **8** *tr.* let droop (*hang one's head*). **9** *intr.* remain static in the air. **10** *intr.* (often foll. by *over*) be present or imminent (*a hush hung over the room*). • *n.* way a thing hangs or falls. □ **get the hang of** *colloq.* understand the technique or meaning of. **hang around 1** loiter or dally. **2** (foll. by *with*) associate with (a person, etc.). **hang back 1** show reluctance. **2** remain behind. **hang glider** kitelike glider controlled in flight by a person suspended beneath it. **hang in** *colloq.* persist; persevere. **hang on** *colloq.* **1** continue or persevere. **2** cling; retain. **3 a** wait for a short time. **b** (in telephoning) continue to listen during a pause in the conversation. **hang out 1** hang from a clothesline, etc. **2** protrude or cause to protrude downward. **3** lean out of (a window, etc.). **4** *sl.* spend time; frequent. **5** (foll. by *with*) *sl.* accompany; be friends with. **6** loiter; dally. **hang together 1** make sense. **2** remain associated. **hang up 1** hang from a hook, etc. **2** end

a telephone conversation, esp. abruptly (*then he hung up on me*). **3** cause delay or difficulty to. **4** *sl.* be a psychological or emotional obsession or problem to (*is really hung up on her teacher*). **hang-up** *n. sl.* emotional problem or inhibition. **hung jury** jury unable to reach a verdict.
¶ A person suspended by the neck until dead is **hanged**, although **hung** is common in informal usage. Pictures, draperies, decorations, Christmas stockings, and the like are *hung*.

HANG GLIDER

hang·ar /hángǝr/ *n.* building for housing aircraft, etc.

hang·dog /hángdawg, -dog/ *adj.* dejected; shamefaced.

hang·er /hángǝr/ *n.* **1** person or thing that hangs. **2** (in full **coat' hang·er**) shaped piece of wood or plastic, etc., from which clothes may be hung. □ **hanger-on** (*pl.* **hang·ers-on**) follower or dependent, esp. an unwelcome one.

hang·ing /hánging/ ● *n.* **1 a** executing by hanging a person. **b** (*attrib.*) meriting or causing this (*hanging offense*). **2** (usu. in *pl.*) draperies hung on a wall, etc. ● *adj.* that hangs or is hung; suspended.

hang·man /hángmǝn/ *n.* (*pl.* **-men**) **1** executioner who hangs condemned persons. **2** word game for two players, in which the tally of failed guesses is kept by drawing a representation of a figure hanging from a gallows.

hang·nail /hángnayl/ *n.* torn skin near a fingernail.

hang·out /hángowt/ *n. sl.* place frequented by a person.

hang·over /hángōvǝr/ *n.* **1** headache, upset stomach, etc., caused by drinking too much alcohol. **2** survival from the past.

hank /hangk/ *n.* **1** coil or skein of yarn or thread, etc. **2** measure of cloth or yarn, e.g., 840 yds. for cotton yarn and 560 yds. for worsted.

han·ker /hángkǝr/ *v.intr.* long for; crave. □□ **han'ker·ing** *n.*

han·ky-pan·ky /hángkeepángkee/ *n. sl.* **1** naughtiness, esp. sexual misbehavior. **2** dishonest dealing; trickery.

han·som /hánsǝm/ *n.* (in full **han'som cab**) *hist.* two-wheeled horse-drawn carriage, with the driver seated behind.

Ha·nuk·kah /kháʼanǝkǝ, haʼa-/ *n.* (also **Cha'nuk·kah**) Jewish festival of lights, commemorating the purification of the Temple in 165 BC.

hap·haz·ard /hápházǝrd/ ● *adj.* done, etc., by chance; random. ● *adv.* at random. □□ **hap·haz'ard·ly** *adv.*

hap·less /háplis/ *adj.* unlucky. □□ **hap'less·ly** *adv.* **hap'less·ness** *n.*

hap·pen /hápǝn/ *v.intr.* **1** occur. **2** have (good or bad) fortune (*I happened to meet her*). **3** be the (esp. unwelcome) fate or experience of (*what happened to you?*). **4** (foll. by *on*) meet or discover by chance. □ **as it happens** in fact; in reality (*as it happens, it turned out well*).

hap·pen·ing /hápǝning/ ● *n.* **1** event or occurrence. **2** improvised or spontaneous performance. ● *adj. sl.* exciting; trendy.

hap·py /hápee/ *adj.* (**hap·pi·er, hap·pi·est**) **1** feeling or showing pleasure or contentment. **2 a** fortunate; lucky. **b** (of words, behavior, etc.) apt; pleasing. **3** (in *comb.*) *colloq.* inclined to use excessively or at random (*trigger-happy*). □ **happy-go-lucky** cheerfully casual. **happy hour** period of the day when drinks are sold at reduced prices in bars, hotels, etc. □□ **hap'pi·ly** *adv.* **hap'pi·ness** *n.*

ha·ra-ki·ri /hárǝke'eree, haʼaree-/ *n.* (also **ha'ri·ka'ri**) ritual suicide by disembowelment.

ha·rangue /hǝráng/ ● *n.* lengthy and earnest speech. ● *v.tr.* lecture or make a harangue to.

ha·rass /hǝrás, hárǝs/ *v.tr.* **1** trouble and annoy continually. **2** make repeated attacks on. □□ **ha·rass'ment** or **ha'rass·ment** *n.*
¶ Traditionally, the preferred pronunciation stresses the first syllable, as "HAR-uhs," but the pronunciation that puts the stress on the second syllable is more widespread; this is also true for *harassment*.

har·bin·ger /haʼárbinjǝr/ *n.* **1** person or thing that announces or signals the approach of another. **2** forerunner.

har·bor /haʼárbǝr/ ● *n.* **1** place of shelter for ships. **2** shelter; place of refuge or protection. ● *v.tr.* **1** give shelter to (esp. a criminal or wanted person). **2** keep in one's mind, esp. resentfully (*harbor a grudge*).

hard /haard/ ● *adj.* **1** firm and solid. **2 a** difficult to understand or explain (*hard problem*). **b** difficult to accomplish (*hard decision*). **c** not easy (*hard to believe*). **3** difficult to bear (*a hard life*). **4** (of a person) unfeeling; severely critical. **5** severe; harsh (*hard winter; hard frost*). **6 a** enthusiastic; intense (*hard worker, hard fight*). **b** severe; uncompromising (*hard blow; hard bargain*). **7 a** (of liquor) strongly alcoholic. **b** (of drugs) potent and addictive. **8** (of water) containing mineral salts that make lathering difficult. **9** not disputable; reliable (*hard facts; hard data*). **10** *Stock Exch.* (of currency, prices, etc.) not likely to fall in value. **11** *Phonet.* (of a consonant) guttural (as *c* in *cat*, *g* in *go*). ● *adv.* **1** strenuously; intensely; copiously; with one's full effort (*try hard; look hard at; hardworking*). **2** so as to be hard or firm (*hard-baked; the jelly set hard*). **3** *Naut.* fully; to the extreme (*hard to starboard*). □ **be hard on 1** be difficult for. **2** be severe in one's treatment or criticism of. **hard and fast** (of a rule or a distinction made) definite; unalterable; strict. **hard-boiled 1** (of an egg) boiled until the white and yolk are solid. **2** (of a person) tough; shrewd. **hard by** near; close by. **hard copy** printed material produced by computer, usu. on paper. **hard core 1** irreducible nucleus. **2** *colloq.* **a** most active or committed members of a society, etc. **b** conservative or reactionary minority. **hard-core** *adj.* blatant; uncompromising, esp.: **1** (of pornography) explicit; obscene. **2** (of drug addiction) relating to hard drugs, esp. heroin. **hard disk (drive)** *Computing* large-capacity, rigid, usu. magnetic storage disk. **hard hat 1** protective helmet worn on building sites, etc. **2** *colloq.* reactionary person. **hard line** unyielding adherence to a firm policy. **hard-liner** person who adheres rigidly to a policy. **hard-nosed** *colloq.* realistic; uncompromising. **hard-pressed 1** closely pursued. **2** burdened with urgent business. **hard sell** aggressive salesmanship or advertising. **hard up 1** short of money. **2** (foll. *for*) at a loss for; lacking. □□ **hard′ness** *n.*

hard·back /háardbak/ • *adj.* (of a book) bound in stiff covers. • *n.* hardback book.

hard·ball /háardbawl/ • *n.* **1** = BASEBALL. **2** *sl.* uncompromising methods or dealings, esp. in politics or business (*play hardball*). • *v.tr. sl.* pressure or coerce politically.

hard·bit·ten /háardbítən/ *adj. colloq.* tough and cynical.

hard·cov·er /hárdkəvər/ • *adj.* bound between rigid boards covered in cloth, paper, leather, or film (*hardcover edition of the novel*). • *n.* hardcover book.

hard·en /háardən/ *v.* **1** make or become hard or harder. **2** become, or make (one's attitude, etc.), uncompromising or less sympathetic. □□ **hard′en·ing** *n.*

hard·head·ed /háardhédid/ *adj.* practical; not sentimental. □□ **hard′head′ed·ly** *adv.* **hard′head′ed·ness** *n.*

hard·heart·ed /háardhaártid/ *adj.* unfeeling; unsympathetic. □□ **hard′-heart′ed·ly** *adv.* **hard′-heart′ed·ness** *n.*

har·di·hood /háardeehŏŏd/ *n.* boldness; daring.

hard·ly /háardlee/ *adv.* **1** scarcely; only just (*we hardly knew them*). **2** only with difficulty (*could hardly speak*).

hard·ship /háardship/ *n.* **1** severe suffering or privation. **2** circumstance causing this.

hard·top /háardtop/ *n.* **1** automobile without roof supports between the front and back windows. **2** automobile with a rigid (usu. detachable) roof.

hard·ware /háardwair/ *n.* **1** tools and household articles of metal, etc. **2** heavy machinery or armaments. **3** mechanical and electronic components of a computer, etc. (cf. SOFTWARE).

hard·wood /háardwŏŏd/ *n.* wood from a deciduous broad-leaved tree as distinguished from that of conifers.

hard·work·ing /háardwərking/ *adj.* diligent.

hard·y /háardee/ *adj.* (**hard·i·er**, **hard·i·est**) **1** robust; enduring. **2** (of a plant) able to grow in the open air all year. □□ **har′di·ly** *adv.* **har′di·ness** *n.*

hare /hair/ *n.* **1** mammal like a large rabbit, with long ears, short tail, and hind legs longer than forelegs, inhabiting fields, hills, etc. **2** (in full **e·lec′tric hare**) dummy hare propelled by electricity, used in greyhound racing.

hare·brained /háirbraynd/ *adj.* rash; foolish; wild.

hare·lip /háirlíp/ *n.* congenital fissure of the upper lip.

har·em /háirəm, hár-/ *n.* **1** women of a Muslim household, living in a separate part of the house. **2** their quarters.

hark /haark/ *v.intr.* (usu. in *imper.*) *archaic* listen attentively. □ **hark back** revert to a topic discussed earlier.

har·le·quin /háarlikwin/ • *n.* (**Harlequin**) mute character in pantomime, usu. masked and dressed in a diamond-patterned costume. • *adj.* in varied colors.

har·lot /háarlət/ *n. archaic* prostitute. □□ **har′lot·ry** *n.*

harm /haarm/ • *n.* hurt; damage. • *v.tr.* cause harm to. □ **out of harm's way** in safety.

harm·ful /háarmfŏŏl/ *adj.* causing or likely to cause harm. □□ **harm′ful·ly** *adv.* **harm′ful·ness** *n.*

harm·less /háarmlis/ *adj.* **1** not able or likely to cause harm. **2** inoffensive. □□ **harm′less·ly** *adv.* **harm′less·ness** *n.*

har·mon·ic /haarmónik/ • *adj.* of or characterized by harmony; harmonious. • *n. Mus.* overtone accompanying at a fixed interval (and forming a note with) a fundamental. □□ **har·mon′i·cal·ly** *adv.*

har·mon·i·ca /haarmónikə/ *n.* small rectangular wind instrument with reeds played by blowing or sucking air through.

har·mo·ni·ous /haarmṓneeəs/ *adj.* **1** pleasant sounding; tuneful. **2** forming a pleasing or consistent whole. **3** free from disagreement or dissent. □□ **har·mo′ni·ous·ly** *adv.*

har·mo·nize /háarmənīz/ *v.* **1** *tr.* add notes to (a melody) to produce harmony. **2** *tr. & intr.* bring into or be in harmony. **3** *intr.* make or form a pleasing or consistent whole. □□ **har·mo·ni·za′tion** *n.*

har·mo·ny /háarmənee/ *n.* (*pl.* **-nies**) **1** combination of simultaneously sounded musical notes to produce chords. **2** apt or aesthetic arrangement of parts. **3** agreement; concord.

har·ness /háarnis/ • *n.* **1** equipment of straps and fittings by which a horse is fastened to a cart, etc., and controlled. **2** similar arrangement for fastening a thing to a person's body, for restraining a young child, etc. • *v.tr.* **1 a** put a harness on (esp. a horse). **b** attach by a harness. **2** make use of (natural resources), esp. to produce energy.

harp /haarp/ • *n.* upright stringed instrument plucked with the fingers. • *v.intr.* (foll. by *on*) talk repeatedly and tediously about. □□ **harp′ist** *n.*

har·poon /haarpŏŏn/ • *n.* barbed spear with a rope attached, for killing whales, etc. • *v.tr.* spear with a harpoon.

harp·si·chord /háarpsikawrd/ *n.* keyboard instrument in which strings are plucked mechanically. □□ **harp′si·chord·ist** *n.*

har·py /háarpee/ *n.* (*pl.* **-pies**) **1** *Gk. & Rom. mythol.* monster with a woman's head and body and bird's wings and claws. **2** grasping unscrupulous person.

har·ri·dan /hárid′n/ *n.* bad-tempered woman.

har·ri·er /háreeər/ *n.* **1** hound used for hunting hares. **2** cross-country runner.

har·row /hárō/ • *n.* heavy frame with iron teeth dragged over plowed land to break up clods, remove weeds, cover seed, etc. • *v.tr.* **1** draw a harrow over (land). **2** (usu. as **harrowing** *adj.*) distress greatly.

har·ry /háree/ *v.tr.* (**-ries**, **-ried**) **1** ravage or despoil. **2** harass; worry.

harsh /haarsh/ *adj.* **1** unpleasantly rough or sharp, esp. to the senses. **2** severe; cruel. □□ **harsh′ly** *adv.* **harsh′ness** *n.*

har·um-scar·um /háirəmskáirəm/ *colloq.* • *adj.* wild and reckless. • *adv.* in a reckless way.

har·vest /háarvist/ • *n.* **1 a** process of gathering in crops, etc. **b** season of this. **2** season's yield or crop. **3** product or result of any action. • *v. tr.* gather as harvest; reap. □ **harvest moon** full moon nearest to the autumnal equinox (Sept. 22 or 23). □□ **har'ves·ter** *n.*

has *3rd sing. present* of HAVE.

has-been /házbin/ *n. colloq.* person or thing that has lost a former importance or usefulness.

hash[1] /hash/ • *n.* **1** dish of cooked meat and potatoes cut into small pieces and recooked. **2 a** mixture; jumble. **b** mess. • *v. tr.* (often foll. by *out*) settle by conferring or debating.

hash[2] /hash/ *n. colloq.* hashish.

hash·ish /hásheesh, hasheesh/ *n.* resinous product of hemp, smoked or chewed as a narcotic.

has·n't /házənt/ *contr.* has not.

hasp /hasp/ • *n.* hinged metal clasp that fits over a staple and can be secured by a padlock. • *v. tr.* fasten with a hasp.

hasp

HASP

has·si·um /háseeəm/ *n.* radioactive element. ¶ Symb.: **Hs**.

has·sle /hásəl/ *colloq.* • *n.* **1** trouble or inconvenience. **2** argument. • *v.* **1** *tr.* harass; annoy. **2** *intr.* argue; quarrel.

has·sock /hásək/ *n.* **1 a** thick firm cushion for kneeling on, esp. in church. **b** similar cushion used as a footrest, etc. **2** tuft of matted grass, etc.

haste /hayst/ *n.* **1** urgency of movement or action. **2** excessive hurry. □ **make haste** hurry; be quick.

hast·en /háysən/ *v.* **1** *intr.* make haste; hurry. **2** *tr.* bring about sooner.

hast·y /háystee/ *adj.* (**hast·i·er, hast·i·est**) **1** hurried; acting quickly or hurriedly. **2** said, made, or done too quickly or too soon; rash. □□ **hast'i·ly** *adv.* **hast'i·ness** *n.*

hat /hat/ *n.* **1** covering for the head, often with a brim. **2** *colloq.* person's occupation or capacity, esp. one of several (*wearing his managerial hat*). □ **hat trick** *Sports* scoring of three goals, etc., in a single game, etc. **keep it under one's hat** *colloq.* keep it secret. **pass the hat** collect contributions of money. **take one's hat off to** *colloq.* acknowledge admiration for.

hatch[1] /hach/ *n.* **1** opening or door in an aircraft, spacecraft, etc. **2** *Naut.* **a** = HATCHWAY. **b** cover for this (often in *pl.*: *batten the hatches*).

hatch[2] /hach/ • *v.* **1** *intr.* **a** (of a young bird,

267 harum-scarum ~ have

fish, etc.) emerge from the egg. **b** (of an egg) produce a young animal. **2** *tr.* incubate (an egg). **3** *tr.* devise (a plot, etc.). • *n.* **1** act or instance of hatching. **2** brood hatched. □□ **hatch'er·y** *n.*

hatch·back /háchbak/ *n.* car with a sloping back hinged at the top to form a door.

hatch·et /háchit/ *n.* light short-handled ax. □ **hatchet job** *colloq.* fierce destructive critique of a person. **hatchet man** *colloq.* person employed to harm or dismiss another.

hatch·way /háchway/ *n.* opening in a ship's deck for cargo.

hate /hayt/ • *v. tr.* **1** dislike intensely. **2** *colloq.* **a** dislike. **b** be reluctant (to do something) (*I hate to disturb you*). • *n.* **1** hatred. **2** *colloq.* hated person or thing. □ **hate crime** crime motivated by hatred of a person's race, gender, religion, etc.

hate·ful /háytfŏŏl/ *adj.* arousing hatred. □□ **hate'ful·ly** *adv.* **hate'ful·ness** *n.*

ha·tred /háytrid/ *n.* intense dislike or ill will.

hat·ter /hátər/ *n.* maker or seller of hats.

haugh·ty /háwtee/ *adj.* (**haugh·ti·er, haugh·ti·est**) arrogant and disdainful. □□ **haugh'ti·ly** *adv.* **haugh'ti·ness** *n.*

haul /hawl/ • *v. tr.* **1** pull or drag forcibly. **2** transport by truck, cart, etc. • *n.* **1** act or instance of hauling. **2** amount gained or acquired. **3** distance to be traversed (*a short haul*). □□ **haul'er** *n.*

haunch /hawnch/ *n.* **1** fleshy part of the buttock with the thigh, esp. in animals. **2** leg and loin of a deer, etc., as food.

haunt /hawnt/ • *v.* **1** *tr.* (of a ghost) visit (a place) regularly. **2** *tr.* (of a person or animal) frequent (a place). **3** *tr.* (of a memory, etc.) be persistently in the mind of. **4** *intr.* stay habitually. **5** *tr.* trouble; distress (*their shady financial dealings come back to haunt them*). • *n.* (often in *pl.*) place frequented by a person or animal.

haunt·ing /háwnting/ *adj.* (of a memory, melody, etc.) poignant; wistful; evocative. □□ **haunt'ing·ly** *adv.*

Hau·sa /hówzə/ • *n.* (*pl.* same or **Hau·sas**) **1** people of W. Africa and Sudan. **2** Hamitic language of this people. • *adj.* of or relating to this people or language.

haute cui·sine /ṓt kwizeén/ *n.* cooking of a high standard, esp. of the French traditional school.

have /hav/ • *v.* (*3rd sing. present* **has** /haz/; *past* and *past part.* **had** /had/) **1** *tr.* own or be able to use (*has a car; had no time to read; has nothing to wear*). **2** *tr.* hold in a certain relationship (*has a sister*). **3** *tr.* contain as a part or quality (*house has two floors; has green eyes*). **4** *tr.* **a** experience (*had a good time; has a headache*). **b** be subjected to a specified state (*had my car stolen; the book has a page missing*). **c** cause (a person or thing) to be in a particular state or take a particular action (*had him dismissed; had us worried; had my hair cut*). **5** *tr.* **a** engage in (an activity) (*had an argument*). **b** hold (a meeting, party, etc.). **6** *tr.* eat or drink (*had a beer*). **7** *tr.* (usu. in *neg.*) accept or tolerate; permit to (*I won't have it; will not have you say such things*). **8** *tr.* **a** let (a feeling, etc.) be present (*have no doubt; has a lot of sympathy for me*). **b** show or feel (mercy, pity, etc.) (*have pity on him; have mercy!*). **9** *tr.* **a** give birth to (offspring). **b** conceive mentally (an idea, etc.). **10** *tr.* receive; obtain (*not a ticket* *to be had*). **11** *tr. sl.* **a** get the better of (*I had him there*). **b** (usu. in *passive*) cheat; deceive (*you were had*). **12** *aux.* (with *past part.* or *ellipt.*, to form the perfect, pluperfect, and future perfect tenses, and the conditional mood) (*have worked*; *had seen*; *will have been*; *had I known, I would have gone*; *have you met her? yes, I have*). • *n.* (usu. in *pl.*) *colloq.* person who has wealth or resources. □ **have it in for** *colloq.* be hostile or ill-disposed toward. **have it out** (often foll. by *with*) *colloq.* attempt to settle a dispute by discussion or argument. **have-not** (usu. in *pl.*) *colloq.* person lacking wealth or resources. **have on** be wearing (clothes). **have to** be obliged to; must.

ha·ven /háyvən/ *n.* **1** harbor or port. **2** place of refuge.

have·n't /hávənt/ *contr.* have not.

hav·er·sack /hávərsak/ *n.* stout bag for provisions, etc., carried on the back or over the shoulder.

hav·oc /hávək/ *n.* widespread destruction; great confusion or disorder.

Ha·wai·ian /həwíən/ • *n.* **1 a** native or inhabitant of Hawaii, an island or island group (comprising a US state) in the N. Pacific. **b** person of Hawaiian descent. **2** the Malayo-Polynesian language of Hawaii. • *adj.* of or relating to Hawaii or its people or language.

hawk[1] /hawk/ • *n.* **1** diurnal bird of prey having a curved beak, rounded short wings, and a long tail. **2** *Polit.* person who advocates an aggressive or warlike policy, esp. in foreign affairs. • *v.* **1** *intr.* hunt game with a hawk. **2** *intr. & tr.* attack, as a hawk does. **3** *intr.* (of a bird) hunt on the wing for food. □ **hawk-eyed** keen-sighted. □□ **hawk′ish** *adj.* **hawk′ish·ly** *adv.* **hawk′ish·ness** *n.*

hawk[2] /hawk/ *v.tr.* carry about or offer (goods) for sale. □□ **hawk′er** *n.*

hawk[3] /hawk/ *v.* **1** *intr.* clear the throat noisily. **2** *tr.* bring (phlegm, etc.) up from the throat.

haw·ser /háwzər/ *n. Naut.* thick rope or cable for mooring or towing a ship.

haw·thorn /háwthawrn/ *n.* thorny shrub or tree with white, red, or pink blossoms and small dark red fruit.

hay /hay/ • *n.* grass mown and dried for fodder. • *v.* **1** *intr.* make hay. **2** *tr.* put (land) under grass for hay. **3** *tr.* make into hay. □ **hay fever** common allergy with respiratory symptoms, caused by pollen or dust. **make hay (while the sun shines)** seize opportunities for profit or enjoyment.

hay·stack /háystak/ *n.* packed pile of hay.

hay·wire /háywīr/ *adj. colloq.* **1** badly disorganized; out of control. **2** (of a person) badly disturbed; erratic.

haz·ard /házərd/ • *n.* **1** danger or risk. **2** source of this. **3** *Golf* obstruction in playing a shot, e.g., a bunker, water, etc. • *v.tr.* **1** venture on (*hazard a guess*). **2** risk. □□ **haz′ard·ous** *adj.*

haze[1] /hayz/ *n.* **1** thin atmospheric vapor. **2** mental obscurity or confusion.

haze[2] /hayz/ *v.tr.* humiliate (fraternity initiates, etc.).

ha·zel /háyzəl/ *n.* **1** shrub or small tree bearing round brown edible nuts. **2** greenish brown color (esp. of the eyes).

ha·zel·nut /háyzəlnut/ *n.* fruit of the hazel.

haz·y /háyzee/ *adj.* (**haz·i·er**, **haz·i·est**) **1** misty. **2** vague; indistinct. **3** confused; uncertain. □□ **ha′zi·ly** *adv.* **ha′zi·ness** *n.*

H-bomb /áychbom/ *n.* = hydrogen bomb.

hdbk. *abbr.* handbook.

HDTV *abbr.* high-definition television.

He *symb. Chem.* helium.

he /hee/ • *pron.* (*obj.* **him** /him/; *poss.* **his** /hiz/; *pl.* **they** /thay/) **1** the man or boy or male animal previously named or in question. **2** person, etc., of unspecified sex. • *n.* **1** male; man. **2** (in *comb.*) male (*he-goat*). □ **he-man** (*pl.* **-men**) masterful or virile man.

¶ See note at EVERYBODY.

head /hed/ • *n.* **1** upper part of the human body, or foremost or upper part of an animal's body, containing the brain, mouth, and sense organs. **2** a seat of intellect. **b** mental aptitude or tolerance (*good head for business*; *no head for heights*). **3** thing like a head in form or position; top. **4** person in charge. **5** front or forward part of something, e.g., a line. **6** upper end of something, e.g., a table or bed. **7** top or highest part of something, e.g., a page, stairs, etc. **8** individual person or animal regarded as a numerical unit ($10 per head; 20 head of cattle). **9 a** side of a coin bearing the image of a head. **b** (usu. in *pl.*) this side as a choice in a coin toss. **10** source of a river, etc. **11** height or length of a head as a measure. **12** promontory (esp. in place-names) (*Diamond Head*). **13** *Naut.* **a** bow of a ship. **b** ship's latrine. **14** culmination, climax, or crisis. **15** *sl.* habitual taker of drugs; drug addict. • *attrib.adj.* chief or principal (*head gardener*; *head office*). • *v.* **1** *tr.* be the head or front of. **2** *tr.* be in charge of (*headed a small team*). **3 a** *intr.* face or move in a specified direction or toward a specified result (*is heading for trouble*). **b** *tr.* direct in a specified direction. □ **come to a head** reach a crisis. **go to one's head 1** (of liquor) make one dizzy or slightly drunk. **2** (of success) make one conceited. **head off 1** get ahead of so as to intercept. **2** forestall. **head-on 1** with the front foremost (*a head-on crash*). **2** in direct confrontation. **head over heels 1** turning over completely in forward motion as in a somersault, etc. **2** topsy-turvy. **3** utterly; completely (*head over heels in love*). **head shrinker** *sl.* psychiatrist. **head start** advantage granted or gained at an early stage. **head wind** wind blowing from directly in front. **keep one's head** remain calm. **lose one's head** lose self-control; panic. **off the top of one's head** *colloq.* impromptu; without careful thought or investigation. **over one's head 1** beyond one's ability to understand. **2** to a higher authority without one's knowledge or involvement, esp. when one has a right to this.

head·ache /hédayk/ *n.* **1** continuous pain in the head. **2** *colloq.* worrying problem or person. □□ **head′ach·y** *adj.*

head·board /hédbawrd/ *n.* upright panel at the head of a bed.

head·dress /héd-dres/ *n.* ornamental covering for the head.

head·er /hédər/ *n.* **1** *colloq.* headlong fall or dive. **2** *Computing* line(s) of information printed at the top of the page throughout a document.

head·hunt·ing /hédhunting/ *n.* **1** practice among some peoples of collecting heads of dead enemies as trophies. **2** practice of recruiting staff by approaching a person employed elsewhere. □□ **head′ hunt** *v.tr.* (also *absol.*). **head′hunt·er** *n.*

head·ing /héding/ n. **1 a** title at the head of a page, chapter, etc. **b** section of a subject of discourse, etc. **2** course of an aircraft, ship, etc.

head·land /hédlənd/ n. promontory.

head·light /hédlīt/ n. **1** strong light at the front of a motor vehicle or train engine. **2** beam from this.

head·line /hédlīn/ • n. **1** heading at the top of an article or page, esp. in a newspaper. **2** (in *pl.*) most important items in a news bulletin. • *v.tr.* star as a performer. □□ **head′lin·er** n.

head·long /hédlawng, -lóng/ adv. & adj. **1** with head foremost. **2** in a rush.

head·mas·ter /hédmástər/ n. (*fem.* **head·mis·tress** /-místris/) (esp. in private schools) person in charge of a school.

head·phone /hédfōn/ n. (usu. in *pl.*) pair of earphones fitting over the head.

head·quar·ters /hédkwáwrtərz/ n. (as *sing.* or *pl.*) administrative center of an organization.

head·rest /hédrest/ n. support for the head, esp. on a seat.

head·room /hédrŏŏm, -rŏŏm/ n. **1** space or clearance between the top of a vehicle and the underside of a bridge, etc. **2** space above an occupant's head in a vehicle.

head·set /hédset/ n. headphones, often with a microphone attached, used esp. in telephone and radio communications.

head·stone /hédstōn/ n. stone set up at the head of a grave.

head·strong /hédstrawng, -strong/ adj. self-willed, obstinate.

head·wa·ter /hédwawtər, -woter/ n. (in *sing.* or *pl.*) streams flowing at the sources of a river.

head·way /hédway/ n. **1** progress. **2** ship's rate of progress.

head·word /hédwərd/ n. word forming a heading, e.g., of an entry in a dictionary or encyclopedia.

head·y /hédee/ adj. (**head·i·er**, **head·i·est**) **1** (of alcohol) potent; intoxicating. **2** (of success, etc.) apt to cause conceit. □□ **head′i·ly** adv. **head′i·ness** n.

heal /heel/ v. **1** *intr.* become sound or healthy again. **2** *tr.* cause to heal or be healed. **3** *tr.* put right (differences, etc.). □□ **heal′er** n.

health /helth/ n. **1** state of being well in body or mind. **2** person's mental or physical condition (*in poor health*). **3** soundness, esp. financial or moral (*the health of the nation*). □ **health food** food thought to have health-giving or -sustaining qualities. **health maintenance organization** organization that provides medical care to subscribers who have paid in advance, usu. through a health insurance plan.

health·ful /hélthfŏŏl/ adj. conducive to good health; beneficial. □□ **health′ful·ly** adv. **health′ful·ness** n.

health·y /hélthee/ adj. (**health·i·er**, **health·i·est**) **1** having, showing, or promoting good health. **2** indicative of (esp. moral or financial) health. **3** substantial (*a healthy margin*). □□ **health′i·ly** adv. **health′i·ness** n.

heap /heep/ • n. **1** disorderly pile. **2** (esp. *pl.*) *colloq.* large number or amount (*there's heaps of time; a heap of chores to finish*). **3** *sl.* old or dilapidated thing, esp. a motor vehicle or building. • v. **1** *tr.* & *intr.* collect or be collected in a

heap. **2** *tr.* load copiously. **3** *tr.* accord or offer copiously to (*heaped insults on them*).

hear /heer/ v. (*past* and *past part.* **heard** /herd/) **1** *tr.* (also *absol.*) perceive with the ear. **2** *tr.* listen to (*heard them on the radio*). **3** *tr.* judge (a case, etc.). **4** *intr.* be told or informed. **5** *intr.* be contacted by, esp. by letter or telephone. **6** *tr.* grant (a prayer). □ **hear a person out** listen to all that a person says. □□ **hear′er** n.

hear·ing /héering/ n. **1** faculty of perceiving sounds. **2** range of audible sounds (*within hearing*). **3** opportunity to state one's case. **4** preliminary appearance before a court. □ **hearing aid** device to amplify sound, worn by a partially deaf person.

hear·ken /haarkən/ v.intr. *archaic* or *literary* listen (to).

hear·say /héersay/ n. rumor; gossip.

hearse /hers/ n. vehicle for conveying the coffin at a funeral.

heart /haart/ n. **1** hollow muscular organ maintaining the circulation of blood by rhythmic contraction and dilation. **2** region of the heart; the breast. **3 a** center of thought, feeling, and emotion (esp. love). **b** capacity for feeling emotion (*has no heart*). **4 a** courage or enthusiasm (*take heart*). **b** mood or feeling (*change of heart*). **5** central or essential part of something. **6 a** heart-shaped thing. **b** conventional representation of a heart with two equal curves meeting at a point at the bottom and a cusp at the top. **7 a** playing card of a suit denoted by a red figure of a heart. **b** (in *pl.*) this suit. **c** (in *pl.*) card game in which players avoid taking tricks containing a card of this suit. □ **at heart 1** in one's inmost feelings. **2** basically; essentially. **break a person's heart** overwhelm a person with sorrow. **by heart** from memory. **heart attack** sudden occurrence of coronary thrombosis usu. resulting in the death of part of a heart muscle. **heart-rending** very distressing. **heart-to-heart** adj. (of a conversation, etc.) candid; intimate. • n. candid or personal conversation. **take to heart** be much affected or distressed by.

heart·ache /haartayk/ n. mental anguish or grief.

heart·beat /haartbeet/ n. pulsation of the heart.

heart·break /haartbrayk/ n. overwhelming distress. □□ **heart′break·er** n. **heart′break·ing** adj. **heart′bro·ken** adj.

heart·burn /haartbərn/ n. burning sensation in the chest resulting from indigestion; pyrosis.

heart·en /haart′n/ v. make or become more cheerful. □□ **heart′en·ing** adj.

heart·felt /haartfélt/ adj. sincere; deeply felt.

hearth /haarth/ n. **1 a** floor of a fireplace. **b** area in front of a fireplace. **2** this symbolizing the home.

heart·land /haartland/ n. central or vital part of an area.

heart·less /haartlis/ adj. unfeeling; pitiless. □□ **heart′less·ly** adv.

heart·sick /haartsik/ adj. very despondent.

heart·throb /haart-throb/ n. **1** beating of the heart. **2** *colloq.* person for whom one has (esp. immature) romantic feelings.

heart·warm·ing /haartwawrming/ adj. emotionally rewarding or uplifting.

heart·y /haártee/ adj. (**heart·i·er, heart·i·est**) 1 strong; vigorous. 2 spirited. 3 (of a meal or appetite) large. 4 warm; friendly. 5 genuine; sincere. □□ **heart'i·ly** adv. **heart'i·ness** n.

heat /heet/ • n. 1 condition of being hot. 2 Physics a energy arising from the motion of molecules. b amount of this needed to cause a specific process, or evolved in a process (heat of formation; heat of solution). 3 hot weather (succumbed to the heat). 4 a warmth of feeling. b anger or excitement (the heat of the argument). 5 (foll. by of) most intense part or period of an activity (in the heat of battle). 6 (usu. preliminary or trial) round in a race or contest. 7 sl. criticism. • v. 1 tr. & intr. make or become hot or warm. 2 tr. inflame; excite or intensify. □ **heat lightning** flashes of lightning without thunder, as from a distant summer storm. **heat wave** period of very hot weather. **in heat** (of mammals, esp. females) sexually receptive. □□ **heat'ing** n.

heat·ed /heétid/ adj. 1 (of a person, discussion, etc.) angry; impassioned. 2 made hot. □□ **heat'ed·ly** adv.

heat·er /heétər/ n. device for supplying heat.

heath /heeth/ n. 1 area of flattish uncultivated land with low shrubs. 2 plant growing on a heath, esp. heather.

hea·then /heéthən/ • n. 1 person who does not belong to a widely held religion as regarded by those that do. 2 person regarded as lacking culture or moral principles. • adj. 1 of or relating to heathens. 2 having no religion.

heath·er /héthər/ n. 1 evergreen shrub with purple bell-shaped flowers. 2 any of various shrubs growing esp. on moors and heaths. 3 a fabric or yarn of mixed hues supposed to resemble heather. b color of this. □□ **hea'ther·y** adj.

heat·stroke /heétstrōk/ n. severe feverish condition caused by excessive exposure to high temperature.

heat·wave /heétwayv/ n. period of abnormally hot weather.

heave /heev/ • v. (past and past part. **heaved** or esp. Naut. **hove** /hōv/) 1 tr. lift or haul (a heavy thing) with great effort. 2 tr. utter with effort or resignation (heaved a sigh). 3 tr. colloq. throw. 4 intr. rise and fall rhythmically or spasmodically. 5 tr. Naut. haul by rope. 6 intr. retch. • n. 1 instance of heaving. 2 (in pl.) respiratory disease of horses.

heav·en /hévən/ n. 1 place regarded in some religions as the abode of God and of the good after death. 2 place or state of supreme bliss. 3 colloq. something delightful. 4 (the heav'ens) the sky as seen from the earth, esp. at night. □□ **heav'en·ward** adj. & adv.

heav·en·ly /hévənlee/ adj. 1 of heaven; divine. 2 of the heavens or sky. 3 colloq. very pleasing; wonderful.

heav·y /hévee/ • adj. (**heav·i·er, heav·i·est**) 1 of great or exceptionally high weight; difficult to lift. 2 of great density; abundant; considerable (heavy crop). 3 severe; intense (heavy fighting). 4 doing something to excess (heavy drinker). 5 (of machinery, artillery, etc.) very large of its kind; large in caliber, etc. 6 needing much physical effort (heavy work). 7 a (of a person, writing, music, etc.) serious or somber in tone or attitude; dull; tedious. b (of an issue, etc.)

grave; important; weighty. 8 a (of food) hard to digest. b (of a literary work, etc.) hard to read or understand. 9 oppressive; hard to endure (a heavy fate; heavy demands). • n. (pl. **-ies**) 1 colloq. large violent person; thug. 2 villainous role or actor in a play, etc. • adv. heavily (esp. in comb.: heavy-laden). □ **heavy-duty** adj. 1 intended to withstand hard use. 2 serious; grave. **heavy going** slow or difficult progress. **heavy-hearted** sad; doleful. **heavy industry** industry producing metal, machinery, etc. **heavy metal** 1 metal of high density. 2 collog. (often attrib.) highly amplified rock music with a strong beat. □□ **heav'i·ly** adv. **heav'i·ness** n. **heav'y·ish** adj.

heav·y-hand·ed /hévihándid/ adj. 1 clumsy. 2 overbearing; oppressive. □□ **heav'y-hand'ed·ly** adv. **heav'y-hand'ed·ness** n.

heav·y·set /héveesét/ adj. stocky; thickset.

heav·y·weight /héveewayt/ n. 1 a weight class in certain sports, esp. boxing, wrestling, weightlifting, etc. b sports participant of this weight. 2 person, animal, or thing of above average weight. 3 colloq. person of influence or importance.

He·bra·ic /hibráyik/ adj. of Hebrew or the Hebrews.

He·brew /heébroo/ • n. 1 member of a Semitic people orig. centered in ancient Palestine. 2 a language of this people. b modern form of this used esp. in Israel. • adj. 1 of or in Hebrew. 2 of the Hebrews or the Jews.

heck /hek/ int. colloq. mild exclamation of surprise or dismay.

heck·le /hékəl/ v.tr. interrupt and harass (a public speaker, entertainer, etc.); badger. □□ **heck'ler** n.

hec·tare /héktair/ n. metric unit of square measure, equal to 100 ares (2.471 acres or 10,000 square meters).

hec·tic /héktik/ adj. 1 busy and confused; excited. 2 feverish. □□ **hec'ti·cal·ly** adv.

hecto- /héktə/ comb. form hundred, esp. of a unit in the metric system. ¶ Abbr.: **h**.

hec·tor /héktər/ • v.tr. bully; intimidate. • n. bully.

he'd /heed/ contr. 1 he had. 2 he would.

hedge /hej/ • n. 1 fence or boundary of dense bushes or shrubs. 2 protection against possible loss. • v. 1 tr. surround or bound with a hedge. 2 tr. enclose. 3 a tr. reduce one's risk of loss on (a bet or speculation) by compensating transactions. b intr. avoid a definite decision or commitment.

hedge·hog /héjhawg, -hog/ n. 1 small nocturnal insect-eating mammal having a piglike snout and a coat of spines, and rolling itself into a ball for defense. 2 porcupine or other animal similarly covered with spines.

he·do·nism /heéd'nizəm/ n. 1 belief in pleasure as the highest good and the proper aim of humans. 2 behavior based on this. □□ **he'don·ist** n. **he·don·is'tic** adj.

heed /heed/ • v.tr. attend to; take notice of. • n. careful attention. □□ **heed'ful** adj. **heed'less** adj. **heed'less·ly** adv.

hee-haw /heéhaw/ • n. bray of a donkey. • v.intr. emit a braying sound, esp. a braying laugh.

heel[1] /heel/ • n. 1 back part of the foot below the ankle. 2 a part of a sock, etc., covering the heel. b part of a shoe or boot supporting the heel. **3** thing like a heel in form or position. **4** crust end of a loaf of bread. **5** *colloq.* person regarded with contempt or disapproval. **6** (as *int.*) command to a dog to walk close to its owner's heel. • *v.* **1** *tr.* fit or renew a heel on (a shoe or boot). **2** *intr.* touch the ground with the heel, as in dancing. **3** *intr.* (of a dog) follow closely. □ **at** (or **on**) **the heels of** following closely after (a person or event). **down at** (**the**) **heel** see DOWN¹. **kick up one's heels** have fun or go on a spree. **take to one's heels** run away.

heel ² /heel/ • *v.* **1** *intr.* (of a ship, etc.) lean over. **2** *tr.* cause (a ship, etc.) to do this. • *n.* act or amount of heeling.

heft·y /héftee/ *adj.* (**heft·i·er, heft·i·est**) **1** (of a person) big and strong. **2** (of a thing) large; heavy; powerful. □□ **heft'i·ly** *adv.* **heft'i·ness** *n.*

he·ge·mo·ny /hijémənee, héjəmōnee/ *n.* leadership, esp. by one nation over another.

he·gi·ra /hijîrə, héjirə/ *n.* (also **he·ji'ra**) **1** (**Hegira**) **a** Muhammad's flight from Mecca to Medina in AD 622. **b** Muslim era reckoned from this date. **2** general exodus or departure.

heif·er /héfər/ *n.* young cow, esp. one that has not had a calf.

height /hīt/ *n.* **1** measurement from base to top or from head to foot. **2** elevation above ground or a recognized level. **3** considerable elevation. **4** a high place or area. **b** rising ground. **5** top of something. **6 a** most intense part or period. **b** extreme example.
¶ Avoid pronouncing **height** with a *-th* at the end; many regard this as uneducated.

height·en /hītən/ *v.* make or become higher or more intense.

Heim·lich ma·neu·ver /hímlik/ *n.* emergency procedure to aid a choking victim by applying sudden pressure against the victim's upper abdomen to dislodge the object.

hei·nous /háynəs/ *adj.* utterly odious or wicked.

heir /air/ *n.* person entitled to property or rank as the legal successor of its former owner (*heir to the throne*). □ **heir apparent** heir whose claim cannot be set aside by the birth of another heir.

heir·ess /áiris/ *n.* female heir, esp. to great wealth or high title.

heir·loom /áirlōm/ *n.* **1** piece of personal property that has been in a family for several generations. **2** piece of property received as part of an inheritance.

heist /hīst/ *sl.* • *n.* robbery. • *v.tr.* rob.

held *past* and *past part.* of HOLD.

he·li·cal /hélikəl, héeli-/ *adj.* having the form of a helix.

hel·i·ces *pl.* of HELIX.

hel·i·cop·ter /hélikoptər/ • *n.* aircraft without fixed wings, obtaining lift and propulsion from horizontally revolving overhead blades, and capable of moving vertically and horizontally. • *v.* transport or fly by helicopter.

helio- /héeleeō/ *comb. form* sun.

he·li·o·cen·tric /héeleeōséntrik/ *adj.* **1** regarding the sun as center. **2** considered as viewed from the sun's center.

he·li·o·trope /héeleeətrōp/ *n.* **1 a** plant with fragrant purple flowers. **b** scent of these. **2** light purple color. **3** bloodstone.

hel·i·port /hélipawrt/ *n.* place where helicopters take off and land.

he·li·um /héeleeəm/ *n. Chem.* light, inert, gaseous element used in airships and balloons and as a refrigerant. ¶ Symb.: **He**.

he·lix /héeliks/ *n.* (*pl.* **he·li·ces** /-seez, hél-/) spiral curve (like a corkscrew) or a coiled curve (like a watch spring).

hell /hel/ *n.* **1** place regarded in some religions as the abode of the dead, or of condemned sinners and devils. **2** place or state of misery or wickedness. □ **come hell or high water** no matter what the difficulties. **hell of a** *colloq.* very much of a; extremely (*hell of a hot day*).

he'll /heel/ *contr.* he will; he shall.

hel·la·cious /heláyshəs/ *adj. sl.* **1** impressive; terrific; tremendous; remarkable. **2** overwhelmingly powerful, severe, or difficult.

hel·le·bore /hélibawr/ *n.* evergreen plant having large white, green, or purplish flowers, e.g., the Christmas rose.

Hel·le·nism /hélinizəm/ *n.* Greek character or culture (esp. of ancient Greece). □□ **Hel·len·ic** /-lénik/ *adj.* **Hel'len·ist** *n.*

Hel·len·is·tic /hélinístik/ *adj.* of or relating to Greek history, language, and culture from the death of Alexander the Great to the time of Augustus (4th–1st c. BC).

hell·hole /hélhōl/ *n. colloq.* oppressive or unbearable place.

hell·ish /hélish/ *adj.* **1** of or like hell. **2** *colloq.* extremely difficult or unpleasant. □□ **hel'lish·ly** *adv.* **hel'lish·ness** *n.*

hel·lo /heló, hə-/ • *int.* **1 a** expression of informal greeting. **b** used to begin a telephone conversation. **2** cry used to call attention. • *n.* (*pl.* **-los**) cry of "hello."

helm /helm/ • *n.* tiller or wheel for controlling a ship's rudder. • *v.tr.* steer or guide as if with a helm. □ **at the helm** in control; at the head (of an organization, etc.).

hel·met /hélmit/ *n.* protective head covering worn by soldiers, police officers, firefighters, cyclists, etc. □□ **hel'met·ed** *adj.*

helms·man /hélmzmən/ *n.* (*pl.* **-men**) person who steers a vessel.

help /help/ • *v.tr.* **1** provide with the means toward what is needed or sought (*helped me with my work*). **2** (often *absol.*) be of use or service to (a person) (*does that help?*). **3** contribute to alleviating (a pain or difficulty). **4** prevent or remedy (*it can't be helped*). **5** (usu. with *neg.*) **a** *tr.* refrain from (*can't help it*). **b** *refl.* refrain from acting (*couldn't help himself*). **6** *tr.* serve (a person with food) (*shall I help you to more rice?*). • *n.* **1** helping or being helped (*we need your help*). **2** person or thing that helps. **3** domestic servant or employee, or several collectively. **4** remedy or escape. □ **help oneself 1** serve oneself (with food). **2** take without seeking help; take without permission; steal. □□ **help'er** *n.*

help·ful /hélpfool/ *adj.* giving help; useful. □□ **help'ful·ly** *adv.* **help'ful·ness** *n.*

help·ing /hélping/ *n.* portion of food, esp. at a meal.

help·less /hélplis/ *adj.* **1** lacking help or protection; defenseless. **2** unable to act without help. □□ **help'less·ly** *adv.* **help'less·ness** *n.*

help·mate /hélpmayt/ *n.* helpful companion or partner.

hel·ter-skel·ter /héltərskéltər/ • *adv.* in disorderly haste; confusedly. • *adj.* disorderly.

hem[1] /hem/ • *n.* border of cloth, esp. a cut edge turned under and sewn down. • *v.tr.* (**hemmed, hem·ming**) turn and sew the edge of (cloth, etc.). □ **hem in** confine; restrict.

hem[2] /hem, həm/ • *int.* (also **a·hem**′) calling attention or expressing hesitation by a slight cough or clearing of the throat. • *n.* utterance of this. • *v.intr.* (**hemmed, hem·ming**) say *hem*; hesitate in speech. □ **hem and haw** hesitate, esp. in speaking.

he·ma·tol·o·gy /héemətóləjee, hém-/ *n.* the study of the physiology of the blood. □□ **he·ma·tol′o·gist** *n.*

hemi- /hémee/ *comb. form* half.

hem·i·sphere /hémisfeer/ *n.* **1** half a sphere. **2** half of the earth, esp. as divided by the equator (into *northern* and *southern* hemisphere) or by a line passing through the poles (into *eastern* and *western* hemisphere). **3** either lateral half of the brain. □□ **hem·i·spher·ic** /-sféerik, -sférik/ *adj.* **hem·i·spher′i·cal** *adj.*

hem·line /hémlīn/ *n.* lower edge of a skirt, dress, or coat.

hem·lock /hémlok/ *n.* **1** poisonous plant with fernlike leaves and small white flowers. **2** poison made from this.

he·mo·glo·bin /héeməglóbin, hém-/ *n.* oxygen-carrying substance containing iron in red blood cells.

he·mo·phil·i·a /héeməfíleeə, hém-/ *n. Med.* hereditary disorder with a tendency to bleed severely from even a slight injury, through the failure of the blood to clot normally. □□ **he·mo·phil′ic** *adj.*

he·mo·phil·i·ac /héeməfíleeak, -feèlee-, hém-/ *n.* person suffering from hemophilia.

hem·or·rhage /hémərij, hémrij/ • *n.* **1** profuse loss of blood from a ruptured blood vessel. **2** extensive damaging loss suffered by a government, organization, etc., esp. of people or assets. • *v.intr.* undergo a hemorrhage.

hem·or·rhoid /héməroyd/ *n.* (usu. in *pl.*) swollen veins at or near the anus; piles. □□ **hem·or·rhoi′dal** *adj.*

hemp /hemp/ *n.* **1** (in full **In′di·an hemp**′) herbaceous plant, native to Asia. **2** its fiber used to make rope and strong fabrics. **3** narcotic drug made from the hemp plant.

hem·stitch /hémstich/ • *n.* decorative stitch used in sewing hems. • *v.tr.* hem with this stitch.

hen /hen/ *n.* female bird, esp. of a domestic fowl.

hence /hens/ *adv.* **1** from this time (*two years hence*). **2** for this reason (*hence we seem to be wrong*).

hence·forth /hénsfáwrth/ *adv.* (also **hence·for·ward** /-fáwrwórd/) from this time onward.

hench·man /hénchmən/ *n.* (*pl.* **-men**) **1** trusted supporter or attendant. **2** often *derog.* political supporter; partisan.

hen·na /hénə/ *n.* **1** tropical shrub having small pink, red, or white flowers. **2** reddish hair dye made from this.

hen·peck /hénpek/ *v.tr.* (of a woman) constantly harass (a man, esp. her husband).

hep var. of HIP[3].

he·pat·ic /hipátik/ *adj.* of or relating to the liver.

hep·a·ti·tis /hépətîtis/ *n.* inflammation of the liver.

hepta- /héptə/ *comb. form* seven.

hep·ta·gon /héptəgon/ *n.* plane figure with seven sides and angles. □□ **hep·tag·o·nal** /-tágənəl/ *adj.*

hep·tath·lon /heptáthlon, -lən/ *n. Sports* seven-event track and field competition, esp. for women.

her /hər/ • *pron.* **1** *objective case* of SHE (*I like her*). **2** *colloq.* she (*it's her all right; am older than her*). • *poss.pron.* (*attrib.*) of or belonging to her or herself (*her house; her own business*).

her·ald /hérəld/ • *n.* **1** official messenger bringing news. **2** forerunner (*spring is the herald of summer*). • *v.tr.* proclaim the approach of; usher in (*the storm heralded trouble*). □□ **her·ald·ic** /heráldik/ *adj.*

her·ald·ry /hérəldree/ *n.* art or knowledge of coats of arms, genealogies, etc.

herb /ərb, hərb/ *n.* **1** any nonwoody seed-bearing plant. **2** plant with leaves, seeds, or flowers used for flavoring, food, medicine, scent, etc. **3** *sl.* marijuana. □□ **her·ba·ceous** /hərbáyshəs/ *adj.* **herb′al** *adj.* **herb′al·ist** *n.*

her·bi·cide /hˊərbisīd, ˊər-/ *n.* poison used to destroy unwanted vegetation.

her·bi·vore /hˊərbivawr, ˊər-/ *n.* animal that feeds on plants. □□ **her·biv·o·rous** /-bívərəs/ *adj.*

Her·cu·le·an /hˊərkyəleˊeən, -kyóoleeən/ *adj.* having or requiring great strength or effort.

Her·cu·les /hˊərkyəleez/ *n. Gk. & Rom. mythol.* man of exceptional strength and size.

herd /hərd/ • *n.* **1** a number of animals, esp. cattle, feeding, traveling, or kept together. **2** (often *prec.* by the) *derog.* large number of people; crowd; mob (*prefers not to follow the herd*). **3** (esp. in *comb.*) keeper of herds; herdsman (*cowherd*). • *v.* **1** *intr. & tr.* go or cause to go in a herd (*herded the cattle into the field*). **2** *tr.* tend (sheep, cattle, etc.) (*he herds the goats*). □□ **herd′er** *n.*

herds·man /hˊərdzmən/ *n.* (*pl.* **-men**) owner or keeper of herds (of domesticated animals).

here /heer/ • *adv.* **1** in or at or to this place or position (*put it here*). **2** indicating a person's presence or a thing offered (*here is your coat; my son here*). **3** at this point (*here I have a question*). • *n.* this place (*get out of here; lives near here*). • *int.* **1** calling attention: short for *come here, look here*, etc. (*here, where are you going with that?*). **2** indicating one's presence in a roll call: short for *I am here*. □ **neither here nor there** of no importance.

¶ The use of **here** or **there** following a demonstrative, e.g., *this here gadget* or *that there field*, although common in dialect, is not regarded as standard, although a change of position of the words, e.g., *this gadget here, that field there* removes objections.

here·a·bouts /héerəbówts/ *adv.* (also **here′a·bout**) near this place.

here·af·ter /heeráftər/ • *adv.* from now on; in the future. • *n.* **1** the future. **2** life after death.

here·by /heerbí/ *adv.* by this means; as a result of this.

he·red·i·tar·y /hiréditeree/ *adj.* **1** (of disease, instinct, etc.) able to be passed down genetically. **2 a** descending by inheritance. **b** holding a position by inheritance.

he·red·i·ty /hiréditee/ *n.* **1 a** passing on of physical or mental characteristics genetically. **b** these characteristics. **2** genetic constitution.

here·in /heerín/ adv. formal in this matter, book, etc.

her·e·sy /hérəsee/ n. (pl. **-sies**) 1 belief or practice contrary to orthodox doctrine, esp. of the Christian church. 2 nonconforming opinion (it's heresy to suggest that instant coffee is as good as the real thing).

her·e·tic /hérətik/ n. 1 holder of an unorthodox opinion. 2 person believing in or practicing religious heresy. □□ **he·ret·i·cal** /hirétikəl/ adj.

here·to·fore /heertəfáwr/ adv. formal before this time.

here·up·on /heerəpón, -páwn/ adv. after this; in consequence of this.

here·with /heerwíth, -wíth/ adv. with this (esp. of an enclosure in a letter, etc.).

her·i·tage /héritij/ n. 1 anything that is or may be inherited. 2 inherited circumstances, benefits, etc. (heritage of confusion). 3 historic buildings, traditions, etc., deemed valuable.

herk·y-jerk·y /hárkeejárkee/ adj. marked by fitful, spastic, or unpredictable movement or manner.

her·maph·ro·dite /hərmáfrədīt/ • n. person, animal, or plant having both male and female reproductive organs. • adj. combining aspects of both sexes. □□ **her·maph·ro·dit·ic** /-ditik/ adj.

her·met·ic /hərmétik/ adj. 1 with an airtight closure. 2 protected from outside agencies. □□ **her·met·i·cal·ly** adv.

her·mit /hármit/ n. 1 early Christian recluse. 2 any person living in solitude. □ **hermit crab** crab that lives in a cast-off mollusk shell. □□ **her·mit·ic** adj.

her·mit·age /hármitij/ n. 1 hermit's dwelling. 2 monastery. 3 solitary dwelling.

her·ni·a /hárneeə/ n. (pl. **her·ni·as** or **her·ni·ae** /-nee-ee/) protrusion of part of an organ through the wall of the cavity containing it, esp. of the abdomen. □□ **her·ni·at·ed** adj.

he·ro /heerō/ n. (pl. **-roes**) 1 a person noted or admired for nobility, courage, outstanding achievements, etc. (Newton, a hero of science). b great warrior. 2 chief male character in a poem, play, story, etc. 3 dial. = submarine sandwich.

he·ro·ic /hiróik/ • adj. 1 a (of an act or a quality) of or fit for a hero. b (of a person) like a hero. 2 a (of language) grand; high-flown; dramatic. b (of a work of art) heroic in scale or subject; unusually large or impressive. • n. (in pl.) 1 high-flown language or sentiments. 2 unduly bold behavior. □□ **her·o·i·cal·ly** adv.

her·o·in /héróin/ n. highly addictive white crystalline analgesic drug derived from morphine, often used as a narcotic.

her·o·ine /héróin/ n. 1 woman noted or admired for nobility, courage, outstanding achievements, etc. 2 chief female character in a poem, play, story, etc.

her·o·ism /héróizəm/ n. heroic conduct or qualities.

her·on /hérən/ n. large wading bird with long legs and a long S-shaped neck.

her·pes /hárpeez/ n. virus disease causing skin blisters. □ **her·pes zos·ter** /zóstər/ = SHINGLES.

her·pe·tol·o·gy /hárpitóləjee/ n. the study of reptiles. □□ **her·pe·to·log·i·cal** /-təlójikəl/ adj. **her·pe·tol·o·gist** n.

her·ring /héring/ n. N. Atlantic fish used for food.

her·ring·bone /héringbōn/ n. 1 stitch with a zigzag pattern. 2 this pattern, or cloth woven in it.

hers /hərz/ poss.pron. the one(s) belonging to or associated with her (it is hers; hers are over there). □ **of hers** of or belonging to her (friend of hers).

her·self /hərsélf/ pron. 1 a emphat. form of SHE or HER (she herself will do it). b refl. form of HER (she has hurt herself). 2 in her normal state of body or mind (does not feel quite herself).

hertz /hərts/ n. (pl. same) unit of frequency, equal to one cycle per second. ¶ Abbr.: **Hz**.

he's /heez/ contr. 1 he is. 2 he has.

hes·i·tant /hézit'nt/ adj. 1 hesitating; irresolute. 2 (of speech) stammering; faltering. □□ **hes·i·tance** /-təns/ n. **hes·i·tan·cy** n. **hes·i·tant·ly** adv.

hes·i·tate /hézitayt/ v.intr. 1 show or feel indecision or uncertainty; pause in doubt. 2 be reluctant (hesitate to say). 3 stammer or falter in speech. □□ **hes·i·ta·tion** /-táyshən/ n.

hetero- /hétərō/ comb. form other; different.

het·er·o·dox /hétərədoks/ adj. (of a person, opinion, etc.) not orthodox. □□ **het'er·o·dox·y** n.

het·er·o·ge·ne·ous /hétərōjéeneeəs, -nyəs/ adj. 1 diverse in character. 2 varied in content. □□ **het·er·o·ge·ne·i·ty** /-jinéeitee/ n.

het·er·o·sex·u·al /hétərōsékshóoəl/ • adj. feeling or involving sexual attraction to persons of the opposite sex. • n. heterosexual person. □□ **het·er·o·sex·u·al·i·ty** /-álitee/ n. **het·er·o·sex'u·al·ly** adv.

heu·ris·tic /hyŏŏrístik/ • adj. 1 allowing or assisting to discover. 2 Computing proceeding to a solution by trial and error. • n. 1 science of heuristic procedure. 2 heuristic process or method. □□ **heu·ris'ti·cal·ly** adv.

hew /hyōō/ v. (past part. **hewn** /hyōōn/ or **hewed**) 1 tr. a chop or cut (a thing) with an ax, sword, etc. b cut (a block of wood, etc.) into shape. 2 intr. strike cutting blows.

hex /heks/ • v. 1 intr. practice witchcraft. 2 tr. cast a spell on; bewitch. • n. magic spell; curse.

hexa- /héksə/ comb. form six.

hex·a·dec·i·mal /héksədésiməl/ (also **hex**) esp. Computing • adj. of a system of numerical notation that has 16 rather than 10 as a base. • n. hexadecimal system or notation.

hex·a·gon /héksəgon/ n. plane figure with six sides and angles. □□ **hex·ag·o·nal** /-ságənəl/ adj.

hex·a·gram /héksəgram/ n. figure formed by two intersecting equilateral triangles.

hex·am·e·ter /heksámitər/ n. line of verse of six metrical feet.

hey /hay/ int. calling attention or expressing joy, surprise, inquiry, enthusiasm, etc.

hey·day /háyday/ n. time of one's greatest strength, vigor, prosperity, etc.

HF abbr. high frequency.

Hf symb. Chem. hafnium.

Hg symb. Chem. mercury.

hgt. abbr. height.

hgwy. abbr. highway.

HHS abbr. (Department of) Health and Human Services.

HI abbr. Hawaii (in official postal use).

hi /hī/ *int.* expression of greeting or to call attention.

hi·a·tus /hīáytəs/ *n.* (*pl.* **hi·a·tus·es**) break or gap, esp. in a series, account, or chain of proof.

hi·ba·chi /həbáachee/ *n.* portable charcoal-burning grill.

hi·ber·nate /hībərnayt/ *v.intr.* (of some animals) spend the winter in a dormant state. □□ **hi·ber·na′tion** /-náyshən/ *n.*

Hi·ber·ni·an /hībə́rneeən/ *archaic poet.* • *adj.* of Ireland. • *n.* native of Ireland.

hi·bis·cus /hibískəs/ *n.* cultivated tree or shrub with large bright-colored flowers.

hic·cup /híkup/ (also **hic′cough**) • *n.* **1** involuntary spasm of the diaphragm causing a coughlike sound. **2** temporary or minor stoppage or difficulty. • *v.* **1** *intr.* make a hiccup. **2** *tr.* utter with a hiccup.

hick /hik/ *n. colloq.* country dweller; provincial.

hick·o·ry /híkəree/ *n.* (*pl.* **-ries**) **1** N. American tree yielding wood and nutlike edible fruits. **2** the wood of these trees.

hid *past* of HIDE[1].

hid·den *past part.* of HIDE[1].

hide[1] /hīd/ *v.* (*past* **hid** /hid/; *past part.* **hid·den** /hídən/) **1** *tr.* put or keep out of sight (*hid it under the cushion*). **2** *intr.* conceal oneself. **3** *tr.* keep secret (*hid his real motive from her*). **4** *tr.* conceal (*trees hid the house*). □ **hidden agenda** secret motivation; ulterior motive. **hide-and-seek** children's game in which players hide and another searches for them. **hide-out** *colloq.* hiding place. □□ **hid′den** *adj.* **hid′er** *n.*

hide[2] /hīd/ *n.* **1** skin of an animal, esp. when tanned or dressed. **2** *colloq.* human skin (*I'll tan your hide*).

hide·a·way /hídəway/ *n.* hiding place or place of retreat.

hide·bound /hídbownd/ *adj.* **1** narrow-minded; bigoted. **2** (of the law, rules, etc.) constricted by tradition.

---

hidebound mid-16th century (as a noun denoting a condition of cattle): from HIDE[2] + BOUND[4]. The earliest sense of the adjective (referring to cattle) was extended to emaciated human beings, and then applied figuratively in the sense 'narrow, cramped, or bigoted in outlook.'

---

hid·e·ous /hídeeəs/ *adj.* frightful, repulsive, or revolting (*hideous monster*). □□ **hid′e·ous·ly** *adv.* **hid′e·ous·ness** *n.*

hi·er·ar·chy /hī́əraarkee/ *n.* (*pl.* **-chies**) **1** system in which grades of status are ranked one above the other (*ranks third in the hierarchy*). **2** hierarchical system (of government, management, etc.). □□ **hi·er·ar·chi·cal** /-ráarkikəl/ *adj.*

hi·er·o·glyph·ic /hī́rəglifík/ • *adj.* depicted with pictures representing words or sounds, as used for ancient Egyptian. • *n.* (in *pl.*) **1** hieroglyphic writing. **2** *joc.* writing difficult to read.

hi-fi /hī́fī́/ *colloq.* • *adj.* of high fidelity. • *n.* (*pl.* **hi-fis**) set of equipment for high fidelity sound reproduction.

hig·gle·dy-pig·gle·dy /hígəldeepígəldee/ • *adv.* & *adj.* in confusion or disorder. • *n.* state of disordered confusion.

high /hī/ • *adj.* **1 a** of great vertical extent (*high building*). **b** (*predic.*; often in *comb.*) of a specified height (*one inch high; water was waist-high*). **2** far above ground or sea level, etc. (*high altitude*). **3** above the normal level (*high boots; sweater with a high neck*). **4** of exalted, esp. spiritual, quality (*high principles; high art*). **5 a** of exalted rank (*in high society; is high in the government*). **b** important; serious; grave. **6 a** great; intense; extreme; powerful (*high praise; high temperature*). **b** greater than normal (*high prices*). **7** *colloq.* intoxicated. **8** (of a sound or note) of high frequency; shrill; at the top end of the scale. **9** (of a period, an age, a time, etc.) at its peak (*high noon; high summer; High Renaissance*). • *n.* **1** high, or the highest, level or figure. **2** area of high barometric pressure. **3** *sl.* euphoric drug-induced state. • *adv.* **1** far up; aloft (*flew the flag high*). **2** in or to a high degree. **3** at a high price. **4** (of a sound) at or to a high pitch (*sang high*). □ **high and low** everywhere (*searched high and low*). **high beam** full, bright illumination from a motor vehicle's headlight. **high chair** infant's chair with long legs and a tray for meals. **high-class 1** of high quality. **2** characteristic of the upper class. **high fidelity** reproduction of sound with little distortion, giving a result very similar to the original. **high five** gesture in which two people slap each other's raised palm, esp. out of elation. **high-flown** (of language, etc.) extravagant; bombastic. **high frequency** frequency, esp. in radio, of 3 to 30 megahertz. **high jinks** boisterous joking or merrymaking. **high-level 1** (of negotiations, etc.) conducted by high-ranking people. **2** *Computing* (of a programming language) that is not machine-dependent and is usu. at a level of abstraction close to natural language. **high-occupancy vehicle** commuter vehicle carrying several (or many) passengers. ¶ Abbr.: HOV. **high-pitched 1** (of a sound) high. **2** (of a roof) steep. **3** at a high level of energy; intense. **high-powered 1** having great power or energy. **2** important or influential. **high pressure 1** high degree of activity or exertion. **2** condition of the atmosphere with the pressure above average. **high priest 1** chief priest, esp. in early Judaism. **2** head of any cult. **high-rise 1** (of a building) having many stories. **2** such a building. **high school** secondary school. **high sea** (or **seas**) open seas not within any country's jurisdiction. **high-spirited** vivacious; cheerful. **high-strung** very sensitive or nervous. **high tech** *n.* = *high technology.* • *adj.* **1** (of interior design, etc.) imitating styles more usual in industry, etc., esp. using steel, glass, or plastic in a functional way. **2** employing, based on, or involved in high technology. **high technology** advanced technological development, esp. in electronics. **high tide** time or level of the tide at its peak. **high wire** high tightrope.

high·ball /hī́bawl/ *n.* drink of liquor (esp. whiskey) and soda, etc., served with ice in a tall glass.

high·boy /hī́boy/ *n.* tall chest of drawers on legs.

high·brow /hī́brow/ *colloq.* • *adj.* intellectual; cultural. • *n.* intellectual or cultured person.

high·fa·lu·tin /hī́fəlōot′n/ (also **high·fa·lu·ting** /-ing/) *colloq. adj.* absurdly pompous or pretentious.

high-hand·ed /hī́hándid/ *adj.* overbearing. □□ **high′-hand′ed·ly** *adv.* **high′-hand′ed·ness** *n.*

high·land /hī́lənd/ • *n.* (usu. in *pl.*) **1** area of high land. **2** (**the Highlands**) mountainous part of Scotland. • *adj.* of or in a highland or the Highlands. □□ **high′land·er** *n.* (also **High′land·er**).

high·light /hílīt/ • n. 1 (in a painting, etc.) light area, or one seeming to reflect light. 2 moment or detail of vivid interest; outstanding feature. • v.tr. 1 bring into prominence; draw attention to. 2 mark with a highlighter pen.

high·ly /hílee/ adv. 1 in or to a high degree (highly amusing; commend it highly). 2 honorably; favorably (think highly of him).

high-mind·ed /hímíndid/ adj. having high moral principles. □□ **high'-mind'ed·ly** adv. **high'-mind'ed·ness** n.

high·ness /hínis/ n. 1 state of being high (cf. HEIGHT). 2 title used of a prince or princess.

high·way /híway/ n. 1 a public road. b main route (by land or water). 2 direct course of action (highway to success).

high·way·man /híwaymən/ n. (pl. **-men**) hist. robber of passengers, travelers, etc.

hi·jack /híjak/ • v.tr. 1 seize control of (an aircraft in flight, etc.), esp. to force it to a different destination. 2 seize (goods) in transit. • n. instance or act of hijacking. □□ **hi'jack·er** n.

hike /hīk/ • n. 1 long walk, esp. in the country with backpacks, etc. 2 increase (of prices, etc.). • v. 1 intr. go for a hike. 2 tr. pull up (clothing, etc.). 3 tr. increase (prices, etc.). □□ **hik'er** n.

hi·lar·i·ous /hiláireeəs/ adj. 1 exceedingly funny. 2 boisterously merry. □□ **hi·lar'i·ous·ly** adv. **hi·lar'i·ty** n.

hill /hil/ n. 1 naturally raised area of land, lower than a mountain. 2 (often in comb.) heap; mound (anthill; dunghill). 3 sloping piece of road. □□ **hil'li·ness** n. **hill'y** adj.

hill·bil·ly /hílbilee/ n. (pl. **-lies**) colloq., often derog. person from a remote or mountainous area, esp. in the Appalachian mountains of the eastern US.

hill·side /hílsīd/ n. sloping side of a hill.

hill·top /hiltop/ n. summit of a hill.

hilt /hilt/ n. handle of a sword, dagger, tool, etc. □ **up to the hilt** completely.

him /him/ pron. 1 objective case of HE (I saw him). 2 colloq. he (it's him again; taller than him).

Him·a·lay·an /hímaláyan/ adj. of or relating to the Himalaya mountains in Nepal.

him·self /himsélf/ pron. 1 a emphat. form of HE or HIM (he himself will do it). b refl. form of HIM (he has hurt himself). 2 in his normal state of body or mind (does not feel quite himself).

hind /hīnd/ adj. (esp. of parts of the body) at the back (hind leg).

hin·der /híndər/ v.tr. (also absol.) impede; delay; prevent.

Hin·di /híndee/ • n. 1 group of spoken dialects of N. India. 2 literary form of Hindustani, an official language of India. • adj. of or concerning Hindi.

hind·most /híndmōst/ adj. farthest behind; most remote.

hind·quar·ters /híndkwáwrtərz/ n.pl. hind legs and adjoining parts of a quadruped.

hin·drance /híndrəns/ n. 1 hindering; being hindered. 2 thing that hinders.

hind·sight /híndsīt/ n. wisdom after the event (realized with hindsight that they were wrong).

Hin·du /híndoo/ • n. follower of Hinduism. • adj. of or concerning Hindus or Hinduism.

Hin·du·ism /híndooizəm/ n. main religious and social system of India.

Hin·du·sta·ni /híndoostáanee, -stánee/ • n. language based on Western Hindi, a lingua franca in much of India. • adj. of or relating to Hindustan, its people, or its language.

hinge /hinj/ • n. 1 movable joint on which a door, lid, etc., turns or swings. 2 central point or principle on which everything depends. • v. 1 intr. a depend (on a principle, event, etc.) (all hinges on his acceptance). b (of a door, etc.) hang and turn (on a post, etc.). 2 tr. attach with or as if with a hinge.

HINGE, 1

hint /hint/ • n. 1 slight or indirect indication or suggestion (took the hint and left). 2 bit of practical information (handy hints on cooking). 3 trace; suggestion (a hint of perfume). • v.tr. suggest slightly (hinted that they were wrong).

hin·ter·land /híntərland/ n. 1 deserted or uncharted areas beyond a coast or a river's banks. 2 remote area.

hip¹ /hip/ n. 1 projection of the pelvis and upper thigh bone on each side of the body in human beings and quadrupeds. 2 (often in pl.) circumference of the body at the buttocks.

hip² /hip/ n. (also **hep** /hep/) fruit of a rose.

hip³ /hip/ adj. (also **hep** /hep/) (**hip·per**, **hip·pest**) sl. 1 trendy; stylish. 2 understanding; aware.

hip·bone /hípbōn/ n. bone forming the hip, esp. the ilium.

hip·pie /hípee/ n. (also **hip'py**) (pl. **-pies**) colloq. (esp. in the 1960s) person of unconventional appearance, typically with long hair, jeans, beads, etc., often associated with hallucinogenic drugs and a rejection of conventional values.

hip·po /hípō/ n. (pl. **-pos**) colloq. hippopotamus.

hip·po·cam·pus /hípəkámpəs/ n. (pl. **hip·po·cam·pi** /-pī/) 1 marine fish that swims vertically and with a head suggestive of a horse; sea horse. 2 Anat. elongated ridges on the floor of each lateral ventricle of the brain, thought to be the center of emotion and the autonomic nervous system.

Hip·po·crat·ic oath /hípəkrátik/ n. oath taken by doctors affirming their obligations and proper conduct.

hip·po·pot·a·mus /hípəpótəməs/ n. (pl. **hip·po·pot·a·mus·es** or **hip·po·pot·a·mi** /-mī/) large thick-skinned four-legged mammal, native to Africa, inhabiting rivers, lakes, etc.

hip·py var. of HIPPIE.

hire /hīr/ • v.tr. 1 employ (a person) for wages or a fee. 2 pay for the temporary use of (a thing); rent or lease. • n. hiring or being hired. □□ **hir′a·ble** adj. (also **hire′a·ble**). **hir′er** n.

hire·ling /hírling/ n. usu. derog. person who works for hire.

hir·sute /hórsyo͞ot/ adj. 1 hairy; shaggy. 2 untrimmed. □□ **hir·sut′ism** n.

his /hiz/ poss. pron. 1 (attrib.) of or belonging to him or himself (his house; his own business). 2 the one or ones belonging to or associated with him (it is his; his are over there). □ **of his** of or belonging to him (friend of his).

His·pan·ic /hispánik/ • adj. 1 of or being a person of Latin-American or Spanish or Portuguese descent in the US. 2 of or relating to Spain or to Spain and Portugal. 3 of Spanish-speaking countries. • n. person of Spanish descent living in the US.

hiss /his/ • v. 1 intr. make a sharp sibilant sound, esp. as a sign of disapproval or derision (audience booed and hissed; water hissed on the hotplate). 2 tr. express disapproval of by hisses. • n. sharp sibilant sound as of the letter s.

hist. abbr. 1 historian. 2 historical. 3 history.

his·ta·mine /hístəmin, -meen/ n. Biochem. organic compound released by body tissues, etc., as in allergic reactions.

his·tol·o·gy /históləjee/ n. the study of the structure of tissues.

his·to·ri·an /histáwreeən/ n. 1 writer of history, esp. a critical analyst, rather than a compiler. 2 person learned in or studying history (English historian; ancient historian).

his·tor·ic /histáwrik, -stór-/ adj. famous or important in history or potentially so (a historic moment).

¶ **Historic** and historical denote different things. The former means 'important; notable': historic leaders, historic battles. The latter means 'relating to history': historical writings. An event can be either, depending on whether it is viewed as part of history or as extremely important. Note also that both of these words, traditionally preceded by a, are now often used with an: a historic moment, an historic moment.

his·tor·i·cal /histáwrikəl, -stór-/ adj. 1 of or concerning history (historical evidence). 2 (of the study of a subject) showing its development. 3 belonging to the past, not the present. 4 (of a novel, movie, etc.) dealing or professing to deal with historical events. □□ **his·tor′i·cal·ly** adv.

his·to·ric·i·ty /hístərísitee/ n. historical genuineness of an event, etc.

his·to·ri·og·ra·phy /histáwreeógrəfee/ n. 1 writing of history. 2 the study of historical writing. □□ **his·to·ri·og′ra·pher** n. **his·to·ri·o·graph′ic** adj. **his·to·ri·o·graph′i·cal** adj.

his·to·ry /hístəree/ n. (pl. **-ries**) 1 continuous record of important or public events. 2 a study of past events. b accumulation of past events (our nation's history; history of astronomy). c past in general; antiquity. 3 eventful past (this house has a history). 4 account of or research into a past event or events, etc. □ **make history** 1 influence the course of history. 2 do something memorable.

---

history late Middle English (also as a verb): via Latin from Greek historia 'finding out,

narrative, history,' from histōr 'learned, wise man,' from an Indo-European root shared by WIT[2].

---

his·tri·on·ic /hístreeónik/ • adj. theatrical; dramatic. • n. (in pl.) insincere and dramatic behavior designed to impress.

hit /hit/ • v. (**hit·ting**; past and past part. **hit**) 1 tr. a strike with a blow or missile. b (of a moving body) strike. 2 tr. cause to suffer or affect adversely. 3 intr. (often foll. by at, against, upon) direct a blow. 4 tr. knock (hit his head on the door frame). 5 tr. light upon; get at (a thing aimed at) (he's hit the truth at last). 6 tr. colloq. a encounter (hit a snag). b arrive at (hit town). c indulge in, esp. liquor, etc. (hit the bottle). 7 tr. occur forcefully to (the seriousness of the situation hit him later). 8 tr. Sports a propel (a ball, etc.) with a bat, etc. b score (runs, etc.) in this way. • n. 1 a blow; stroke. b collision. 2 shot, etc., that hits its target. 3 colloq. popular success in entertainment. 4 Computing instance of identifying an item of data that matches the requirements of a search. □ **hit and run** 1 cause damage and escape or leave the scene before being discovered. 2 Baseball play in which a base runner begins running to the next base as the pitcher delivers the ball and the batter then tries to hit the thrown ball. **hit it off** agree or be congenial. **hit man** (pl. **hit men**) sl. hired assassin. **hit the nail on the head** state the truth exactly. **hit-or-miss** aimed or done carelessly. **hit the road** (or **trail**) sl. depart. **hit the spot** colloq. be satisfying.

hitch /hich/ • v. 1 a tr. fasten with a loop, hook, etc.; tether (hitched the horse to the cart). b intr. become fastened in this way (the rod hitched in to the bracket). 2 tr. move (a thing) with a jerk; shift slightly (hitched the pillow to a comfortable position). 3 colloq. a intr. = HITCHHIKE. b tr. obtain (a ride) by hitchhiking. • n. 1 temporary obstacle. 2 abrupt pull or push; jerk. 3 a noose or knot of various kinds. b connector assembly between a vehicle and something being towed. 4 colloq. free ride in a vehicle. 5 sl. period of military service. □ **get hitched** colloq. marry.

hitch·hike /hích-hīk/ v.intr. travel by seeking free rides in passing vehicles. □□ **hitch′hiker** n.

hith·er /híthər/ usu. formal or literary adv. to or toward this place. □ **hither and yon** in various directions; to and fro.

hith·er·to /híthərto͞o/ adv. until this time; up to now.

Hit·ler /hítlər/ n. person who embodies the authoritarian characteristics of Adolf Hitler, Ger. dictator d. 1945.

Hit·tite /hítīt/ • n. 1 member of an ancient people of Asia Minor and Syria. 2 extinct language of the Hittites. • adj. of or relating to the Hittites or their language.

HIV abbr. human immunodeficiency virus, any of several retroviruses causing AIDS.

hive /hīv/ • n. 1 a beehive. b bees in a hive. 2 busy swarming place. 3 thing shaped like a hive in being domed. • v. 1 tr. a place (bees) in a hive. b house (people, etc.) snugly. 2 intr. a enter a hive. b live together like bees.

hives /hīvz/ n.pl. allergic skin eruption.

HMO abbr. health maintenance organization.

Ho symb. Chem. holmium.

hoa·gie /hṓgee/ *n.* (also **hoa′gy**) (*pl.* **-gies**) = submarine sandwich.

hoard /hawrd/ • *n.* **1** stock or store (esp. of money or food) laid by. **2** amassed store of facts, etc. • *v.* **1** *tr.* amass and put away; store. **2** *intr.* accumulate more than one's current requirements of food, etc., in a time of scarcity. **3** *tr.* store in the mind. □□ **hoard′er** *n.* **hoard′ing** *n.*

hoarse /hawrs/ *adj.* **1** (of the voice) rough and deep; husky; croaking. **2** having such a voice. □□ **hoarse′ly** *adv.* **hoarse′ness** *n.*

hoar·y /háwree/ *adj.* (**hoar·i·er, hoar·i·est**) **1 a** (of hair) gray or white with age. **b** having such hair; aged. **2** old and trite (*hoary joke*).

hoax /hōks/ • *n.* humorous or malicious deception; practical joke. • *v.tr.* deceive (a person) with a hoax.

hob·ble /hóbəl/ • *v.* **1** *intr.* **a** walk lamely; limp. **b** proceed haltingly (*hobbled lamely to his conclusion*). **2** *tr.* **a** tie the legs of (a horse, etc.) to prevent it from straying. **b** tie (a horse's, etc., legs). **3** *tr.* cause (a person, etc.) to limp. • *n.* **1** uneven or infirm gait. **2** rope, etc., for hobbling a horse, etc.

hob·by /hóbee/ *n.* (*pl.* **-bies**) leisure time activity pursued for pleasure. □□ **hob′by·ist** *n.*

hob·by·horse /hóbeehawrs/ *n.* **1** child's toy consisting of a stick with a horse's head. **2** favorite topic of conversation. **3** rocking horse.

hob·gob·lin /hóbgoblin/ *n.* mischievous imp; bogy.

hob·nail /hóbnayl/ *n.* heavy-headed nail used for boot soles.

hob·nob /hóbnob/ *v.intr.* (**hob·nobbed, hob·nob·bing**) mix socially or informally.

ho·bo /hóbō/ *n.* (*pl.* **-boes** or **-bos**) tramp; vagrant.

hock[1] /hok/ *n.* **1** joint of a quadruped's hind leg between the knee and fetlock. **2** knuckle of pork; lower joint of a ham.

hock[2] /hok/ *colloq.* *v.tr.* pawn; pledge. □ **in hock 1** in pawn. **2** in debt.

hock·ey /hókee/ *n.* team sport played on skates or on a field, with angled sticks and a puck (when played on ice) or ball.

ho·cus-po·cus /hókəspókəs/ • *n.* **1** deception; trickery. **2 a** typical verbal formula used in conjuring. **b** language intended to mystify. • *v.* (**-po·cused, -po·cus·ing; -po·cussed, -po·cus·sing**) **1** *intr.* play tricks. **2** *tr.* play tricks on; deceive.

---

hocus-pocus early 17th century: from *hax pax max Deus adimax*, a pseudo-Latin phrase used as a formula by magicians.

---

hod /hod/ *n.* **1** V-shaped trough on a pole used for carrying bricks, etc. **2** portable receptacle for coal.

hodge·podge /hójpoj/ *n.* confused mixture; jumble.

Hodg·kin's dis·ease /hójkinz/ *n.* malignant disease usu. characterized by enlargement of the lymph nodes.

hoe /hō/ • *n.* long-handled tool with a thin metal blade, used for weeding, etc. • *v.* (**hoes, hoed, hoe·ing**) **1** *tr.* weed (crops); loosen (earth) with a hoe. **2** *intr.* use a hoe.

hog /hawg, hog/ • *n.* **1 a** domesticated pig, esp. reared for slaughter. **b** other pig, e.g., warthog.

2 *colloq.* greedy person. • *v.* (**hogged, hog·ging**) *tr.* *colloq.* take greedily; hoard selfishly. □ **go whole hog** *colloq.* do something completely or thoroughly. □□ **hog′gish** *adj.*

hogs·head /háwgz-hed, hógz-/ *n.* **1** large cask. **2** liquid or dry measure, usu. about 63 gallons.

hog·wash /háwgwosh, -wawsh, hóg-/ *n.* *colloq.* nonsense; rubbish.

hoi pol·loi /hóy pəlóy/ *n.* (often prec. by *the:* see note below) the masses; the common people.
¶ The phrase **hoi polloi** is usually preceded by *the: The hoi polloi grew restless as candidate after candidate spoke.* Strictly speaking, the *the* is unnecessary because *hoi* means 'the' (in Greek). Perhaps because of confusion with *hoity-toity,* **hoi polloi** is sometimes wrongly taken to mean its opposite, 'the few, the elite.'

hoist /hoyst/ • *v.tr.* raise or haul up, esp. with ropes, pulleys, etc. • *n.* **1** act of hoisting; lift. **2** apparatus for hoisting.

hoi·ty-toi·ty /hóyteetóytee/ • *adj.* haughty; petulant; snobbish. • *int.* expressing surprised protest at presumption, etc.

hok·ey /hókee/ *adj.* (also **hok′y**) (**hok·i·er, hok·i·est**) *sl.* sentimental, melodramatic; artificial. □□ **hok′ey·ness** *n.*

ho·kum /hókəm/ *n.* *sl.* **1** sentimental, popular, sensational, or unreal situations, dialogue, etc., in a movie or play, etc. **2** bunkum; rubbish.

hold[1] /hōld/ • *v.* (*past* and *past part.* **held** /held/) **1** *tr.* **a** keep fast; grasp (esp. in the hands or arms). **b** (also *refl.*) keep or sustain in a particular position (*held himself erect*). **c** grasp so as to control (*hold the reins*). **2** *tr.* contain or be capable of containing (*holds two pints*). **3** *tr.* possess, gain, or have, esp.: **a** be the owner or tenant of (land, property, etc.). **b** gain or have gained (a degree, record, etc.). **c** have the position of (a job or office). **d** keep possession of (a place, a person's thoughts, etc.) esp. against attack. **4** *intr.* remain intact (*the roof held under the storm*). **5** *tr.* observe; celebrate; conduct (a meeting, festival, conversation, etc.). **6** *tr.* **a** keep (a person, etc.) in a specified condition, place, etc. (*held her prisoner; held him at arm's length*). **b** detain, esp. in custody. **7** *tr.* **a** engross (*the book held him for hours*). **b** dominate (*held the stage*). **8** *tr.* make (a person, etc.) adhere to (a promise, etc.). **9** *intr.* (of weather) continue as is. **10** *tr.* think; believe (*held that the earth was flat*). **11** *tr.* regard with a specified feeling (*held him in contempt*). **12** *tr.* **a** cease; restrain (*hold your fire*). **b** *colloq.* withhold; not use (*a burger please, and hold the onions!*). **13** *tr.* be able to drink (liquor) without effect. **14** *tr.* (of a judge, a court, etc.) lay down; decide. • *n.* **1** grasp (*catch hold of him*). **2** (often in *comb.*) thing to hold by (*seized the handhold*). **3** (foll. by *on, over*) influence over (*has a strange hold over them*). □ **hold (a thing) against (a person)** regard it as discreditable to. **hold forth** usu. *derog.* speak at length or tediously. **hold the line 1** not yield. **2** maintain a telephone connection. **hold off 1** delay; not begin. **2** keep one's distance. **hold on 1** keep one's grasp on something. **2** wait a moment. **3** (when telephoning) not hang up. **hold out 1** stretch forth (a hand, etc.). **2** offer (an inducement, etc.). **3** maintain resistance. **4** persist or last. **hold out on** *colloq.* refuse something to (a person). **hold up 1 a** support; sustain. **b** maintain (the head, etc.) erect. **c** last; endure.

2 exhibit; display. **3** arrest the progress of; obstruct. **4** stop and rob by force. **hold water** (of reasoning) be sound; bear examination. **take hold** (of a custom or habit) become established. **with no holds barred** with no restrictions; all methods being permitted. □□ **hold´er** n.

hold[2] /hōld/ n. cargo area in a ship or aircraft.

hold·ing /hṓlding/ n. **1 a** land held by lease. **b** tenure of land. **2** stocks, property, etc., held. □ **holding company** company created to hold the shares of other companies, which it then controls.

hold·up /hṓldəp/ n. **1** stoppage or delay. **2** robbery, esp. by the use of threats or violence.

hole /hōl/ • n. **1 a** empty space in a solid body. **b** aperture in or through something. **c** flaw; weakness; gap. **2** animal's burrow. **3 a** colloq. small, mean, or dingy abode. **b** dungeon; prison cell. **4** colloq. awkward situation. **5** Golf **a** receptacle in the ground into which the ball is to be hit. **b** one complete playing area from tee to hole. • v.tr. **1** make a hole or holes in. **2** put into a hole. □ **hole up** colloq. hide oneself. □□ **hol´ey** adj.

-holic comb. form person with a powerful obsession or craving, as chocoholic, one who craves chocolate.

hol·i·day /hóliday/ n. day of festivity or recreation when no work is done, esp. a national or religious festival, etc.

ho·li·ness /hṓleenis/ n. **1** sanctity; being holy. **2** (**Holiness**) title used when referring to or addressing the pope.

ho·lism /hṓlizəm/ n. **1** Philos. theory that certain wholes are greater than the sum of their parts. **2** Med. treating the whole person rather than just the symptoms of a disease. □□ **ho·lis´tic** adj. **ho·lis´ti·cal·ly** adv.

hol·lan·daise sauce /hóləndáyz/ n. creamy sauce of butter, egg yolks, and lemon juice or vinegar, etc.

hol·ler /hólər/ colloq. • v. **1** intr. make a loud cry or noise. **2** tr. shout. • n. loud cry, noise, or shout.

hol·low /hólō/ • adj. **1 a** having a cavity. **b** sunken (hollow cheeks). **2** (of a sound) echoing, low, or muffled. **3** empty; hungry. **4** meaningless (hollow triumph). **5** insincere (hollow laugh; hollow promises). • n. **1** hollow place; hole. **2** valley; basin. • v.tr. make hollow; excavate. □□ **hol´low·ly** adv. **hol´low·ness** n.

hol·low·ware /hólōwair/ n. hollow articles of metal, china, etc., such as pots, kettles, pitchers, etc.

hol·ly /hólee/ n. (pl. **-lies**) evergreen shrub with glossy green leaves and red berries.

hol·ly·hock /hóleehok/ n. tall plant with large showy flowers of various colors.

Hol·ly·wood /hóleewŏŏd/ n. American movie industry or its products, with its center at Hollywood, California.

hol·mi·um /hṓlmeeəm/ n. Chem. soft silvery metallic element of the lanthanide series. ¶ Symb.: **Ho**.

ho·lo·caust /hóləkawst/ n. **1** large-scale destruction, esp. by fire or nuclear war. **2** (**the Holocaust**) mass murder of Jews by the Nazis in World War II.

ho·lo·gram /hóləgram/ n. Physics three-dimensional photographic image made with laser technology.

ho·lo·graph /hóləgraf/ • adj. wholly written by hand by its author. • n. holograph document.

ho·log·ra·phy /həlógrəfee/ n. Physics study or production of holograms. □□ **hol·o·graph·ic** /hóləgráfik/ adj.

hol·ster /hṓlstər/ n. leather case for a pistol or revolver, worn on a belt, etc.

ho·ly /hṓlee/ adj. (**ho·li·er**, **ho·li·est**) **1** morally and spiritually excellent or perfect, and to be revered. **2** belonging to, devoted to, or empowered by, God. **3** consecrated; sacred. □ **holier-than-thou** colloq. self-righteous. **Holy Communion** see COMMUNION. **Holy Father** the Pope. **Holy Ghost** = Holy Spirit. **Holy Grail** see GRAIL. **Holy Land** **1** W. Palestine, esp. Judaea. **2** region similarly revered in non-Christian religions. **Holy See** the papacy or papal court. **Holy Spirit** third person of the Christian Trinity. **holy war** war waged in support of a religious cause. **Holy Week** the week before Easter.

hom·age /hómij/ n. acknowledgment of superiority; respect; dutiful reverence (pay homage to; do homage to).

Hom·burg /hómbərg/ n. man's felt hat with a narrow curled brim and a lengthwise dent in the crown.

home /hōm/ • n. **1 a** place where one lives; fixed residence. **b** dwelling house. **2** members of a family collectively; one's family background (comes from a good home). **3** native land. **4** institution caring for people or animals. **5** place where a thing originates or is native or most common. **6** Baseball home plate. • attrib.adj. **1** of or connected with one's home. **2** carried on or produced in one's own country (home industries; the home market). **3** Sports played on one's own field, etc. (home game; home win). • adv. **1 a** to one's home or country (go home). **b** arrived at home (is he home yet?). **c** at home (stay home). **2 a** to the point aimed at (the thrust went home). **b** as far as possible (drove the nail home; pressed his advantage home). • v. **1** intr. (esp. of a trained pigeon) return home. **2** intr. (of a vessel, missile, etc.) be guided toward a destination or target. □ **at home 1** in one's own house or native land. **2** at ease as if in one's own home (make yourself at home). **3** familiar or well informed. **4** available to callers. **home economics** the study of household management. **home page** Computing introductory document for a site on the World Wide Web. **home plate** Baseball plate beside which the batter stands and which the runner must cross to score a run. □□ **home´like** adj.

home·boy /hómboy/ n. colloq. person from one's own town or neighborhood.

home·com·ing /hṓmkəming/ n. **1** arrival at home. **2** annual reunion of alumni held by some high schools, colleges, etc.

home·grown /hómgrōn/ adj. grown or produced at home.

home·land /hómland/ n. one's native land.

home·less /hómlis/ • adj. lacking a home. • n. (prec. by the) homeless people. □□ **home´less·ness** n.

home·ly /hómlee/ adj. (**home·li·er**, **home·li·est**) **1** (of people or their features) not attractive in appearance; ugly. **2 a** simple; plain. **b** unpretentious. **c** primitive. □□ **home´li·ness** n.

home·made /hómayd/ adj. made at home.

home·maker /hómaykər/ *n.* person who manages a household, esp. as a full-time occupation.

ho·me·op·a·thy /hómeeópəthee/ *n.* treatment of disease by minute doses of drugs that in a healthy person would produce symptoms of the disease. □□ **ho·me·o·path** /-əpáth/ *n.* **ho·me·o·path·ic** /-meeəpáthik/ *adj.*

Ho·mer·ic /hōmérik/ *adj.* **1** of, or in the style of, Homer. **2** of Bronze Age Greece as described in these poems.

home·sick /hómsik/ *adj.* longing for home. □□ **home'sick·ness** *n.*

home·spun /hómspun/ • *adj.* **1** made or spun at home. **2** plain; simple. • *n.* **1** homespun cloth. **2** anything plain or homely.

home·stead /hómsted/ *n.* house and adjoining land.

home·style /hómstīl/ *adj.* (esp. of food) made at home.

home·ward /hómwərd/ • *adv.* (also **home'wards** /-wərdz/) toward home. • *adj.* going toward home.

home·work /hómwərk/ *n.* **1** work to be done at home, esp. by a student. **2** preparatory work or study.

hom·ey /hómee/ *adj.* (also **hom'y**) (**hom·i·er**, **hom·i·est**) suggesting home; cozy. □□ **hom'ey·ness** *n.* (also **hom'i·ness**).

ho·mi·cide /hómisīd, hó-/ *n.* **1** killing of a human being by another. **2** person who kills a human being. □□ **ho·mi·ci'dal** *adj.*

hom·i·ly /hómilee/ *n.* (*pl.* **-lies**) **1** sermon. **2** moralizing discourse. □□ **hom·i·let·ic** /-létik/ *adj.*

hom·i·nid /hóminid/ • *n.* member of the primate family including humans and their fossil ancestors. • *adj.* of this family.

hom·i·noid /hóminoyd/ • *adj.* like a human. • *n.* animal resembling a human.

hom·i·ny /hóminee/ *n.* coarsely ground corn kernels, usu. boiled for food.

homo- /hómō/ *comb. form* same (often opp. HETERO-).

ho·mo·ge·ne·ous /hómɔjéeneeəs, -yəs/ *adj.* **1** of the same kind. **2** consisting of parts all of the same kind; uniform. □□ **ho·mo·ge·ne·i·ty** /-jineéitee/ *n.* **ho·mo·ge'ne·ous·ly** *adv.*

ho·mog·en·ize /həmójiniz/ *v.* **1** *tr.* & *intr.* make or become homogeneous. **2** *tr.* treat (milk) so that the fat droplets are emulsified and the cream does not separate.

hom·o·graph /hómɔgraf, hó-/ *n.* word spelled like another but of different meaning or origin (e.g., POLE¹, POLE²).

ho·mol·o·gous /həmóləgəs/ *adj.* **1 a** having the same relation, relative position, etc. **b** corresponding. **2** *Biol.* (of organs, etc.) similar in position and structure but not necessarily in function.

hom·o·nym /hómɔnim/ *n.* **1** word of the same spelling or sound as another but of different meaning; homograph or homophone. **2** namesake.

ho·mo·pho·bi·a /hómɔfóbeeə/ *n.* hatred or fear of homosexuals. □□ **ho·mo·phobe** /-əfób/ *n.* **ho·mo·pho'bic** *adj.*

ho·mo·phone /hómɔfōn, hó-/ *n.* word sounding the same as another but of different meaning or origin (e.g., *pair, pear*).

Ho·mo sa·pi·ens /hómō sáypee-enz/ *n.* modern humans regarded as a species.

ho·mo·sex·u·al /hómɔséksh∞əl/ • *adj.* feeling or involving sexual attraction only to persons of the same sex. • *n.* homosexual person. □□ **ho·mo·sex·u·al·i·ty** /-sh∞álitee/ *n.*

hom·y var. of HOMEY.

hon·cho /hónchō/ *sl. n.* (*pl.* **-chos**) leader or manager; person in charge.

---

honcho 1940s: from Japanese *hanchō*, 'group leader,' a term brought back to the U.S. by servicemen stationed in Japan during the occupation following World War II.

---

hone /hōn/ • *n.* **1** whetstone, esp. for razors. **2** any stone used for this. • *v.tr.* sharpen on or as on a hone.

hon·est /ónist/ • *adj.* **1** fair and just. **2** free of deceit and untruthfulness; sincere. **3** fairly earned (*an honest living*). **4** (with patronizing effect) blameless but undistinguished. • *adv. colloq.* genuinely; really. □□ **hon'es·ty** *n.*

hon·est·ly /ónistlee/ *adv.* **1** in an honest way. **2** really (*I don't honestly know; honestly, the nerve of them!*).

hon·ey /húnee/ *n.* (*pl.* **-eys**) **1** sweet sticky yellowish fluid made by bees from nectar. **2** color of this. **3** sweetness. **4** person or thing excellent of its kind. **5** (usu. as a form of address) darling; sweetheart.

hon·ey·comb /húneekōm/ • *n.* **1** structure of hexagonal cells of wax, made by bees to store honey and eggs. **2** pattern arranged hexagonally. • *v.tr.* **1** fill with cavities or tunnels; undermine. **2** mark with a honeycomb pattern.

HONEYCOMB, 1

hon·ey·dew /húneedoo, -dyoo/ *n.* **1** melon with smooth pale skin and sweet green flesh. **2** sweet sticky substance found on plants, excreted by aphids, fungi, etc.

hon·eyed /húneed/ *adj.* (also **hon'ied**) **1** of or containing honey. **2** sweet.

hon·ey·moon /húneemoon/ • *n.* **1** vacation taken by a newly married couple. **2** initial period of enthusiasm or goodwill. • *v.intr.* spend a honeymoon. □□ **hon'ey·moon·er** *n.*

hon·ey·suck·le /húneesukəl/ *n.* climbing shrub with fragrant yellow, pink, or red flowers.

honk /hawngk, hongk/ • *n.* **1** cry of a wild goose. **2** sound of a car horn. • *v.* **1** *intr.* emit a honk. **2** *tr.* cause to do this.

honk·y-tonk /háwngkeetawngk, hóngkeetongk/ *n. colloq.* **1** ragtime piano music. **2** cheap or disreputable nightclub, bar, dancehall, etc.

hon·or /ónər/ • *n.* **1** high respect; reputation.

2 adherence to what is right or accepted conduct. **3** nobleness of mind (*honor among thieves*). **4** official award. **5** privilege; special right (*had the honor of being invited*). **6 a** exalted position. **b** (**Honor**) title of a judge, mayor, etc. **7** person or thing that brings honor (*she is an honor to her profession*). **8 a** (of a woman) chastity. **b** reputation for this. **9** (in *pl.*) **a** special distinction in academics. **b** specialized course of degree studies. • *v.tr.* **1** respect highly. **2** confer honor on. **3** accept or pay (a bill or check) when due. **4** acknowledge. □ **do the honors** perform the duties of a host to guests, etc.

hon·or·a·ble /ónərəbəl/ *adj.* **1 a** worthy of honor. **b** bringing honor to its possessor. **c** showing honor; not base. **d** consistent with honor. **2** (**Honorable**) title indicating eminence or distinction, given to certain government officials, members of Congress, etc. □□ **hon′or·a·bly** *adv.*

hon·o·rar·i·um /ónəráireeəm/ *n.* (*pl.* **hon·o·rar·i·ums** or **hon·o·rar·i·a** /-reeə/) fee, esp. a voluntary payment for professional services rendered without the normal fee.

hon·or·ar·y /ónəreree/ *adj.* **1 a** conferred as an honor (*honorary degree*). **b** holding such a title or position (*honorary colonel*). **2** (of an office or its holder) unpaid (*honorary treasurer*).

hon·or·if·ic /ónərífik/ *adj.* **1** conferring honor. **2** (esp. of forms of speech) implying respect. □□ **hon·or·if′i·cal·ly** *adv.*

hooch /hooch/ *n. colloq.* inferior or illicit whiskey.

hood[1] /hood/ • *n.* **1 a** covering for the head and neck, as part of a garment. **b** separate hoodlike garment worn over a university gown to indicate the wearer's degree. **2** cover over the engine of a motor vehicle. **3** canopy to protect users of machinery or to remove fumes, etc. **4** hoodlike part of a cobra, seal, etc. **5** leather covering for a hawk's head. • *v.tr.* cover with a hood.

hood[2] /hood/ *n. sl.* gangster or gunman.

-hood /hood/ *suffix* forming nouns: **1** of condition or state (*childhood; falsehood*). **2** indicating a collection or group (*sisterhood; neighborhood*).

hood·lum /hoodləm, hood-/ *n.* **1** street hooligan. **2** gangster.

hood·wink /hoodwingk/ *v.tr.* deceive; delude.

hoo·ey /hoo-ee/ *n. & int. sl.* nonsense; humbug.

hoof /hoof, hoof/ • *n.* (*pl.* **hoofs** or **hooves** /hoovz/) horny part of the foot of a horse, antelope, etc. • *v.* **1** *tr.* walk. **2** *tr. sl.* kick or shove. □ **hoof it** *sl.* **1** go on foot. **2** dance.

hook /hook/ • *n.* **1 a** bent or curved piece of metal, etc., for catching or hanging things on. **b** fishhook. **2** sharp bend, e.g., in a river. **3 a** *Golf* hooking stroke (see sense 4 of *v.*). **b** *Boxing* short swinging blow with the elbow bent and rigid. • *v.* **1** *tr.* grasp or secure with a hook or hooks. **2 a** *tr.* attach with or as with a hook. **b** *intr.* be or become attached with a hook. **3** *tr.* catch with or as with a hook (*he hooked a fish; she hooked a husband*). **4** *tr.* (also *absol.*) *Golf* strike (the ball) so that it deviates toward the striker. **5** *tr. Boxing* strike (one's opponent) with the elbow bent and rigid. □ **by hook or by crook** by one means or another. **off the hook 1** *colloq.* no longer in difficulty or trouble. **2** (of a telephone receiver) not on its rest, and so preventing incoming calls.

hoo·kah /hookə/ *n.* tobacco pipe with a long tube passing through water to cool the smoke.

hooked /hookt/ *adj.* **1** hook-shaped (*hooked nose*). **2** in senses of HOOK *v.* **3** (of a rug or mat) made by pulling woolen yarn through canvas with a hook. **4** *sl.* captivated or addicted.

hook·er /hookər/ *n. sl.* prostitute.

hook·up /hookəp/ *n.* connection, esp. electronic.

hook·worm /hookwərm/ *n.* **1** nematode worm, with hooklike mouthparts, infesting humans and animals. **2** a disease caused by one of these, often resulting in severe anemia.

hook·y /hookee/ *n.* (also **hook′ey**) □ **play hooky** *sl.* play truant.

hoo·li·gan /hooligən/ *n.* hoodlum; ruffian. □□ **hoo′li·gan·ism** *n.*

hoop /hoop/ • *n.* **1** circular band of metal, wood, etc., esp. as part of a framework. **2** arch through which the balls are hit in croquet; wicket. **3** (*pl.*) game of basketball. • *v.tr.* **1** bind with a hoop or hoops. **2** encircle with or as with a hoop.

hoop·la /hooplaa/ *n.* **1** *sl.* commotion; excitement. **2** noisy publicity; ballyhoo.

hoo·ray /hooráy/ *int.* = HURRAH.

hoot /hoot/ • *n.* **1** owl's cry. **2** sound made by a vehicle's horn or a steam whistle. **3** shout expressing scorn or disapproval. **4** *colloq.* **a** laughter. **b** cause of this. **5** (also **two hoots**) *sl.* anything at all (*don't give a hoot; doesn't matter two hoots*). • *v.* **1** *intr.* **a** utter or make a hoot. **b** (often foll. by *at*) make loud sounds, esp. of scorn or disapproval or *colloq.* merriment (*hooted with laughter*). **2** *tr.* greet or drive away by hooting. **3** *tr.* sound (a vehicle horn or steam whistle).

hooves *pl.* of HOOF.

hop[1] /hop/ • *v.* (**hopped, hop·ping**) **1** *intr.* (of a bird, frog, etc.) spring with two or all feet at once. **2** *intr.* (of a person) jump on one foot. **3** *intr. colloq.* **a** make a quick trip. **b** make a quick change of position or location. **4** *tr. colloq.* **a** jump into (a vehicle). **b** obtain (a ride) in this way. • *n.* **1** hopping movement. **2** *colloq.* informal dance. **3** short journey, esp. a flight.

hop[2] /hop/ *n.* **1** climbing plant cultivated for its cones. **2** (in *pl.*) ripe cones of this, used to flavor beer.

hope /hop/ • *n.* **1** expectation and desire combined, e.g., for a thing (*hope of getting the job*). **2 a** person, thing, or circumstance that gives cause for hope. **b** ground of hope; promise. **3** what is hoped for. • *v.* **1** *intr.* feel hope. **2** *tr.* expect and desire. **3** *tr.* feel fairly confident.

hope·ful /hopfool/ • *adj.* **1** feeling hope. **2** causing or inspiring hope. **3** likely to succeed. • *n.* person likely to succeed.

hope·ful·ly /hopfoolee/ *adv.* **1** in a hopeful manner. **2** it is to be hoped (*hopefully, the car will be ready by then*).

¶ Some object strongly to the use of **hopefully** as a sentence modifier, with the meaning 'it is to be hoped,' e.g., *Hopefully, all the details will be in this evening's newspaper.* However, this usage is not only common but long-established in English, as are similar uses of other sentence-modifying adverbs, such as *regrettably, unfortunately,* and *frankly.*

hope·less /hóplis/ *adj.* **1** feeling no hope. **2** admitting no hope (*a hopeless case*). **3** incompetent (*am hopeless at tennis*). □□ **hope′less·ly** *adv.* **hope′less·ness** *n.*

Ho·pi /hópee/ *n.* **1 a** N. American people native to northeastern Arizona. **b** member of this people. **2** language of this people.

hop·per /hópər/ n. **1** hopping insect. **2 a** container tapering downward (orig. having a hopping motion) through which grain passes into a mill. **b** similar device in various machines.

hop·scotch /hópskoch/ n. children's game of hopping over squares marked on the ground to retrieve a stone.

horde /hawrd/ n. **1** usu. derog. large group. **2** moving swarm or pack (of insects, wolves, etc.).

hore·hound /háwrhownd/ n. **1** plant with a white cottony covering on its stem and leaves. **2** its bitter aromatic juice used against coughs, etc.

ho·ri·zon /hərízən/ n. **1** line at which earth and sky appear to meet. **2** limit of mental perception, experience, interest, etc. □ **on the horizon** (of an event) just imminent or becoming apparent.

hor·i·zon·tal /háwrizónt'l, hór-/ • adj. **1** parallel to the plane of the horizon; at right angles to the vertical (horizontal plane). **2 a** combining firms engaged in the same stage of production (horizontal integration). **b** involving social groups of equal status, etc. • n. horizontal line, plane, etc. □□ **hor·i·zon'tal·ly** adv.

hor·mone /háwrmōn/ n. **1** Biochem. substance produced in an organism and transported in tissue fluids such as blood or sap to stimulate cells or tissues into action. **2** similar synthetic substance. □□ **hor·mon'al** adj.

horn /hawrn/ • n. **1** hard outgrowth, often curved and pointed, on the head of cattle, rhinoceroses, giraffes, and other esp. hoofed mammals, found singly, in pairs, or one in front of another. **2** hornlike projection, or thing shaped like a horn. **3** substance of which horns are made. **4** Mus. **a** = French horn. **b** brass wind instrument. **c** horn player. **5** (often in comb.) device sounding a warning (car horn; foghorn). • v.tr. **1** (esp. as **horned** adj.) provide with horns. **2** gore with horns. □ **horn in** sl. **1** (usu. foll. by on) intrude. **2** interfere. **horn of plenty** cornucopia. **horn-rimmed** (esp. of eyeglasses) having rims made of horn or a similar substance.

horn·blende /háwrnblend/ n. dark brown, black, or green mineral found in rock, and composed of calcium, magnesium, and iron silicates.

hor·net /háwrnit/ n. large wasp with a brown and yellow striped body, and capable of inflicting a serious sting.

horn·pipe /háwrnpīp/ n. **1** lively dance, usu. by one person (esp. associated with sailors). **2** music for this.

horn·y /háwrnee/ adj. (**horn·i·er**, **horn·i·est**) **1** of or like horn. **2** hard; callused (horny-handed). **3** sl. sexually excited or frustrated. □□ **horn'i·ness** n.

ho·rol·o·gy /hawrólajee/ n. art of measuring time or making clocks, watches, etc. □□ **ho·ro·log'i·cal** adj.

hor·o·scope /háwrəskōp, hór-/ n. Astrol. **1** forecast of a person's future based on a diagram showing the relative positions of the stars and planets at that person's birth. **2** such a diagram (cast a horoscope).

hor·ren·dous /həréndəs/ adj. horrifying. □□ **hor·ren'dous·ly** adv.

hor·ri·ble /háwribəl, hór-/ adj. **1** causing or likely to cause horror. **2** colloq. unpleasant; excessive (horrible weather; horrible noise). □□ **hor'ri·bly** adv.

hor·rid /háwrid, hór-/ adj. **1** horrible; revolting. **2**

colloq. unpleasant; disagreeable (horrid weather; horrid children).

hor·rif·ic /hawrífik, hór-/ adj. horrifying. □□ **hor·rif'i·cal·ly** adv.

hor·ri·fy /háwrifī, hór-/ v.tr. (**-fies, -fied**) arouse horror in; shock. □□ **hor'ri·fy·ing** adj.

hor·ror /háwrər, hór-/ n. **1** painful feeling of loathing and fear. **2** intense dislike. **3** person or thing causing horror. • attrib. adj. (of literature, movies, etc.) designed to attract by arousing pleasurable feelings of horror.

hors d'oeuvre /awrdôrvrə, -dörv/ n. (pl. same or **hors d'oeuvres**) appetizer served at the beginning of a meal or (occasionally) in place of or during a meal.

horse /hawrs/ • n. **1 a** solid-hoofed plant-eating quadruped with flowing mane and tail, used for riding and to carry and pull loads. **b** other related four-legged mammals, including asses and zebras. **2** gymnastic apparatus for vaulting. **3** supporting frame esp. with legs (clothes-horse). **4** sl. heroin. • v. intr. (foll. by around) fool around. □ **from the horse's mouth** (of information, etc.) from the person directly concerned or another authoritative source. **horse chestnut 1** large ornamental tree with upright conical clusters of white or pink or red flowers. **2** dark brown fruit of this (like an edible chestnut, but with a coarse bitter taste). **horse race 1** race between horses with riders. **2** colloq. close contest. **horse sense** colloq. plain common sense.

horse·back /háwrsbak/ n. back of a horse, esp. as sat on in riding. □ **on horseback** mounted on a horse.

horse·fly /háwrsflī/ n. (pl. **-flies**) any of various biting dipterous insects troublesome esp. to horses.

horse·hair /háwrs-hair/ n. hair from the mane or tail of a horse, used for padding, etc.

horse·man /háwrsmən/ n. (pl. **-men**) skilled rider of horses.

horse·play /háwrsplay/ n. boisterous play.

horse·pow·er /háwrspowər/ n. (pl. same) **1** unit of power equal to 550 foot-pounds per second (about 750 watts). ¶ Abbr.: **h.p. 2** power of an engine, etc., measured in terms of this.

horse·rad·ish /háwrsradish/ n. **1** plant with long, lobed leaves. **2** pungent root of this scraped or grated as a condiment, often made into a sauce.

horse·shoe /háwrs-shōo/ n. **1** U-shaped iron plate nailed to a horse's hoof for protection. **2** thing of this shape. **3** (pl.) game in which horseshoes are tossed to encircle a stake.

horse·tail /háwrstayl/ n. **1** horse's tail. **2** plant like a horse's tail, with a hollow jointed stem and scale-like leaves.

horse·whip /háwrs-hwip, -wip/ • n. whip for driving horses. • v.tr. (**-whipped, -whip·ping**) beat with a horsewhip.

horse·wom·an /háwrswŏomən/ n. (pl. **-wom·en**) skilled woman rider of horses.

hors·y /háwrsee/ adj. (also **hors'ey**) (**hors·i·er**, **hors·i·est**) **1** of or like a horse. **2** concerned with or devoted to horses or horse racing. **3** colloq. large; clumsy.

hor·ti·cul·ture /háwrtikúlchər/ n. art of garden cultivation. □□ **hor·ti·cul'tur·al** adj. **hor·ti·cul'tur·ist** n.

ho·san·na /hōzánə/ *n. & int.* shout of adoration to God.

hose /hōz/ ● *n.* **1** flexible tube for conveying a fluid. **2** (*collect.*; as *pl.*) stockings and socks. ● *v.tr.* water or spray or drench with a hose.

> **hose** Old English *hosa*, of Germanic origin; related to Dutch *hoos* 'stocking, water-hose' and German *Hosen* 'trousers.' Originally as a singular, it denoted a covering for the leg, sometimes including the foot but sometimes reaching only as far as the ankle.

ho·sier·y /hózhəree/ *n.* stockings and socks.

hosp. *abbr.* **1** hospital. **2** hospice.

hos·pice /hóspis/ *n.* **1** home for people who are terminally ill. **2** lodging for travelers, esp. one kept by a religious order.

hos·pi·ta·ble /hóspitəbəl, hospít-/ *adj.* giving hospitality. □□ **hos′pi·ta·bly** *adv.*

hos·pi·tal /hóspit'l/ *n.* institution providing medical and surgical treatment and nursing care for ill or injured people.

hos·pi·tal·i·ty /hóspitálitee/ *n.* friendly and generous reception and entertainment of guests or strangers.

hos·pi·tal·ize /hóspit'líz/ *v.tr.* send or admit (a patient) to a hospital. □□ **hos·pi·tal·i·za′tion** *n.*

host¹ /hōst/ *n.* **1** large number of people or things. **2** (in full **heav′en·ly host′**) *Bibl.* **a** sun, moon, and stars. **b** angels.

host² /hōst/ ● *n.* **1** person who receives or entertains another as a guest. **2** *Biol.* animal or plant having a parasite. **3** person who introduces and often interviews guests on a show, esp. a television or radio program. ● *v.tr.* act as host to (a person) or at (an event).

host³ /hōst/ *n.* bread consecrated in the Eucharist.

hos·tage /hóstij/ *n.* person seized or held as security for the fulfillment of a condition.

hos·tel /hóst'l/ *n.* inexpensive lodging esp. for travelers, hikers, etc.

hos·tel·ry /hóst'lree/ *n.* (*pl.* **-ries**) inn.

host·ess /hóstis/ *n.* **1** woman who receives or entertains a guest. **2** woman employed to welcome customers at a restaurant, etc.

hos·tile /hóstəl, -tíl/ *adj.* **1** of an enemy. **2** unfriendly; opposed. □□ **hos′tile·ly** *adv.*

hos·til·i·ty /hostílitee/ *n.* (*pl.* **-ties**) **1** being hostile; enmity. **2** (in *pl.*) acts of warfare.

hot /hot/ *adj.* (**hot·ter, hot·test**) **1** having a relatively high temperature. **2** producing the sensation of heat (*hot fever; hot flash*). **3** (of pepper, spices, etc.) pungent; piquant. **4** (of a person) feeling heat. **5 a** ardent; passionate; excited. **b** eager; excited (*in hot pursuit*). **6** (of news, etc.) fresh; recent. **7** (of a competitor) strongly favored to win (*a hot favorite*). **8** *sl.* (of goods) stolen, and hence easily identifiable and difficult to dispose of. **9** live, at a high voltage. □ **hot air** *sl.* empty, boastful, or excited talk. **hot-blooded** ardent; passionate. **hot dog** *n.* **1 a** = FRANKFURTER. **b** frankfurter sandwiched in a soft roll. **2** *sl.* person who is showy or shows off skills. **hot line** direct exclusive line of communication, esp. for emergencies. **hot plate** heated metal plate for cooking food or keeping it hot. **hot potato** *colloq.* controversial or awkward matter or situation. **hot rod** motor vehicle modified to have extra power and speed. **hot seat** *sl.* **1** position of difficult responsibility. **2** electric chair. **hot-tempered** impulsively angry. **hot tub** tub of heated, circulating water for therapy or recreation, usu. able to accommodate several people. **hot under the collar** angry, resentful, or embarrassed. **hot-water bottle** container, usu. made of rubber, filled with hot water, esp. to warm the feet, a bed, etc. □□ **hot′ly** *adv.* **hot′ness** *n.*

hot·bed /hótbed/ *n.* **1** environment promoting the growth of something, esp. something unwelcome (*hotbed of vice*). **2** bed of earth heated by fermenting manure.

hot·cake /hótkayk/ *n.* pancake. □ **like hotcakes** (be sold, etc.) quickly (*the new CD is selling like hotcakes*).

ho·tel /hōtél/ *n.* establishment providing accommodation and meals for payment.

ho·tel·ier /ótelyáy, hōt'leér/ *n.* hotel-keeper.

hot·head /hót-hed/ *n.* impetuous person. □□ **hot′head′ed** *adj.* **hot′head′ed·ness** *n.*

hot·house /hót-hows/ ● *n.* **1** heated building for rearing plants out of season or in a climate colder than is natural for them. **2** environment that encourages the rapid growth or development of something. ● *adj.* (*attrib.*) characteristic of something reared in a hothouse; sheltered; sensitive.

Hou·di·ni /hōōdeénee/ *n.* **1** ingenious escape. **2** person skilled at escaping (for H. Houdini, noted escape artist).

hound /hownd/ ● *n.* **1** dog used for hunting. **2** person keen in pursuit of something (usu. in *comb.*: *newshound*). ● *v.tr.* **1** harass or pursue relentlessly. **2** chase or pursue with a hound.

hour /owr/ *n.* **1** twenty-fourth part of a day and night; 60 minutes. **2** time of day; point in time (*a late hour*). **3** period set aside for some purpose (*lunch hour; keep regular hours*). **4** present time (*question of the hour*). **5** time for action, etc. (*the hour has come*). **6** each time o'clock of a whole number of hours (*buses leave on the hour, on the half hour, at quarter past the hour*). □ **after hours** after closing time.

hour·glass /ówrglas/ ● *n.* reversible device with two connected glass bulbs containing sand that takes a specified time to pass from the upper to the lower bulb. ● *adj.* hourglass-shaped.

HOURGLASS

hour·ly /ówrlee/ • *adj.* **1** done or occurring every hour. **2** reckoned hour by hour (*hourly wage*). • *adv.* **1** every hour. **2** frequently; continually.

house • *n.* /hows/ (*pl.* /hówziz, -siz/) **1 a** building for human habitation. **b** (*attrib.*, often in *comb.*) (of an animal) kept in, frequenting, or infesting houses (*house cat*; *housefly*). **2** building for a special purpose (*opera house*; *summer house*). **3** (often in *comb.*) building for keeping animals or goods (*henhouse*). **4** royal family or dynasty (*House of York*). **5** business or institution. **6 a** legislative or deliberative assembly. **b** building where it meets. **c** (**the House**) the House of Representatives. **7 a** audience in a theater, movie theater, etc. **b** theater. **8** *Astrol.* sign of the zodiac. • *v.tr.* /howz/ **1** provide (a person, a population, etc.) with a house or other accommodation. **2** store (goods, etc.). **3** enclose or encase (a part or fitting). □ **House of Lords** (in the UK) chamber of Parliament composed of peers and bishops. **House of Representatives** lower house of the US Congress and other legislatures. **like a house on fire 1** vigorously; fast. **2** successfully; excellently. **on the house** at the management's expense; free.

house·boat /hówsbōt/ *n.* boat fitted for living in.

house·break·ing /hówsbrayking/ *n.* breaking into a building, esp. in daytime, to commit a crime. □□ **house′break·er** *n.*

house·bro·ken /hówsbrōkən/ *adj.* (of pets) trained to excrete only outdoors or only in proper places.

house·coat /hówskōt/ *n.* woman's informal indoor robe.

house·dress /hówsdres/ *n.* inexpensive dress of simple design suitable for wear while doing housework.

house·fly /hówsflī/ *n.* common fly.

house·hold /hóws-hōld/ *n.* **1** occupants of a house regarded as a unit. **2** house and its affairs. □ **household word** (or **name**) familiar name, person, or thing. □□ **house′hold·er** *n.*

house·hus·band /hóws-həzbənd/ *n.* married man whose main job is managing household duties.

house·keep·er /hówskeepər/ *n.* person employed to manage a household.

house·keep·ing /hówskeeping/ *n.* **1** management of household affairs. **2** operations of maintenance, record keeping, etc., in an organization.

house·maid /hówsmayd/ *n.* female servant in a house.

house·plant /hówsplant/ *n.* plant grown indoors.

house·wares /hówswairz/ *n.pl.* small articles for furnishing a home, such as dishware, glassware, and small appliances.

house·warm·ing /hówswawrming/ *n.* party celebrating a move to a new home.

house·wife /hówswīf/ *n.* (*pl.* **-wives**) woman (usu. married) managing a household. □□ **house′wife·ly** *adj.*

house·work /hówswərk/ *n.* regular housekeeping chores.

hous·ing /hówzing/ *n.* **1 a** dwellings collectively. **b** provision of these. **2** shelter; lodging. **3** rigid casing, esp. for machinery, etc.

HOV *abbr.* high-occupancy vehicle.

hove *past* of HEAVE.

hov·el /húvəl, hóv-/ *n.* small miserable dwelling.

hov·er /húvər, hóvər/ *v.intr.* **1** (of a bird, helicopter, etc.) remain in one place in the air. **2** wait close at hand; linger.

hov·er·craft /húvərkraft, hóv-/ *n.* (*pl.* same) vehicle that travels over land or water on a cushion of air provided by a downward blast.

how /how/ • *interrog. adv.* **1** by what means; in what way (*how do you do it?*). **2** in what condition, esp. of health (*how is the patient?*). **3** to what extent (*how far is it?*; *how did they play?*). • *rel. adv.* in whatever way. • *conj. colloq.* that (*told us how he'd been in Canada*). □ **how about** would you like (*how about a game of chess?*). **how do you do?** formal greeting.

how·dah /hówdə/ *n.* seat for riding on an elephant or camel.

how·ev·er /hówévər/ *adv.* **1 a** in whatever way (*do it however you want*). **b** to whatever extent (*must go however inconvenient*). **2** nevertheless.

how·it·zer /hówitsər/ *n.* short cannon for high-angle firing of shells at low velocities.

howl /howl/ • *n.* **1** long, doleful cry of a dog, wolf, etc. **2** prolonged wailing noise, e.g., as made by a strong wind. **3** loud cry of pain or rage. **4** yell of derision or merriment. • *v.* **1** *intr.* make a howl. **2** *intr.* weep loudly. **3** *tr.* utter (words) with a howl.

howl·er /hówlər/ *n. colloq.* glaring mistake.

how·so·ev·er /hówsō-évər/ *adv.* **1** in whatever way. **2** to whatever extent.

hoy·den /hóyd'n/ *n.* boisterous girl.

h.p. *abbr.* (also **hp**) horsepower.

HQ *abbr.* headquarters.

HR *abbr.* (also **H.R.**) **1** House of Representatives. **2** home run.

hr. *abbr.* hour.

HS *abbr.* high school.

Hs *symb. Chem.* hassium.

HST *abbr.* **1** Hawaii(an) Standard Time.

http *abbr.* (also **HTTP**) *Computing* hypertext transfer protocol, the standard for hypertext data distributed via the World Wide Web.

hub /hub/ *n.* **1** central part of a wheel, rotating on or with the axle. **2** center of interest, activity, etc.

hub·bub /húbub/ *n.* **1** confused noise. **2** disturbance.

hub·by /húbee/ *n.* (*pl.* **-bies**) *colloq.* husband.

hu·bris /hyóóbris/ *n.* arrogant pride or presumption. □□ **hu·bris′tic** *adj.*

huck·le·ber·ry /húkəlberee/ *n.* (*pl.* **-ries**) **1** low-growing N. American shrub. **2** blue or black fruit of this.

huck·ster /húkstər/ • *n.* **1** peddler or hawker. **2** publicity agent, esp. for broadcast material. • *v.* **1** *intr.* bargain; haggle. **2** *tr.* carry on a petty traffic in.

HUD /hud/ *abbr.* (Department of) Housing and Urban Development.

hud·dle /húd'l/ • *v.* **1** *tr. & intr.* crowd together. **2** *intr. & refl.* coil one's body into a small space. • *n.* **1** confused or crowded mass. **2** *colloq.* close or secret conference (esp. in **go into a huddle**). **3** *Football* gathering of the players of one team to receive instructions about the next play.

hue /hyōō/ *n.* **1 a** color or tint. **b** variety or shade of color. **2** attribute of a color by virtue of which it is discernible as red, green, etc.

hue and cry /hyōō/ *n.* loud clamor or outcry.

huff /huf/ • *v.intr.* **1** give out loud puffs of air, steam, etc. **2** bluster loudly or threateningly (*huffing and puffing*). • *n.* fit of petty annoyance. □ **in a huff** annoyed and offended. □□ **huff′y** *adj.*

hug /hug/ • *v.tr.* (**hugged, hug·ging**) **1** squeeze tightly in one's arms, esp. with affection. **2** keep close to (the shore, curb, etc.). • *n.* **1** strong clasp with the arms. **2** squeezing grip in wrestling.

huge /hyōōj/ *adj.* **1** extremely large. **2** (of immaterial things) very great (*a huge success*). □□ **huge′ly** *adv.*

Hu·gue·not /hyōōgənot/ *n. hist.* French Protestant.

huh /hə/ *int.* expressing disgust, surprise, etc.

hu·la /hōōlə/ *n.* (also **hu′la-hu′la**) Polynesian dance with flowing arm and rhythmic hip movements.

hulk /hulk/ *n.* **1** body of a dismantled ship. **2** unwieldy vessel. **3** *colloq.* large clumsy-looking person or thing.

hulk·ing /húlking/ *adj. colloq.* bulky; large and clumsy.

hull[1] /hul/ *n.* body of a ship, airship, flying boat, etc.

hull[2] /hul/ • *n.* **1** outer covering of a fruit, esp. the pod of peas and beans, husk of grain, or calyx of a strawberry. **2** covering. • *v.tr.* remove the hulls from (fruit, etc.).

hul·la·ba·loo /húləbəlōō/ *n.* (*pl.* **hul·la·ba·loos**) uproar; clamor.

hum /hum/ • *v.* (**hummed, hum·ming**) **1** *intr.* make a low steady buzzing sound. **2** *tr.* (also *absol.*) sing (a wordless tune) with closed lips. **3** *intr. colloq.* be active (*really made things hum*). • *n.* humming sound.

hu·man /hyōōmən/ • *adj.* **1** of or belonging to the genus *Homo.* **2** consisting of human beings (*the human race*). **3** of or characteristic of people, esp. as being fallible (*is only human*). **4** showing (esp. the better) qualities of man (*proved to be very human*). • *n.* human being. □ **human being** man or woman or child of the species *Homo sapiens.* **human nature** general characteristics and feelings of human beings. **human rights** rights held to be justifiably belonging to any person.

¶ See note at MAN.

hu·mane /hyōōmáyn/ *adj.* **1** benevolent; compassionate. **2** inflicting the minimum of pain. **3** (of learning) tending to civilize. □□ **hu·mane′ly** *adv.* **hu·mane′ness** *n.*

hu·man·ism /hyōōmənizəm/ *n.* **1** progressive nonreligious philosophy emphasizing human values. **2** (often **Humanism**) literary culture, esp. that of the Renaissance. □□ **hu′man·ist** *n.* **hu·man·is′tic** *adj.*

hu·man·i·tar·i·an /hyōōmánitáireeən/ • *n.* person who seeks to promote human welfare. • *adj.* pertaining to humanitarians. □□ **hu·man·i·tar′i·an·ism** *n.*

hu·man·i·ty /hyōōmánitee/ *n.* (*pl.* **-ties**) **1 a** the human race. **b** being human. **2** humaneness; benevolence. **3** (in *pl.*) learning or literature concerned with human culture.

hu·man·ize /hyōōmənīz/ *v.tr.* **1** make human. **2** make humane. □□ **hu·man·i·za′tion** *n.*

hu·man·kind /hyōōmənkínd/ *n.* human beings collectively.

hu·man·ly /hyōōmənlee/ *adv.* **1** by human means (*I will do it if it is humanly possible*). **2** in a human manner.

hum·ble /húmbəl/ • *adj.* **1** having or showing low self-esteem. **2** of low social or political rank (*humble origins*). **3** (of a thing) of modest pretensions, size, etc. • *v.tr.* **1** make humble; abase. **2** lower the rank or status of. □ **eat humble pie** make a humble apology; accept humiliation. □□ **hum′ble·ness** *n.* **hum′bly** *adv.*

hum·bug /húmbug/ • *n.* **1** deception or lying. **2** impostor. • *v.* (**hum·bugged, hum·bug·ging**) **1** *intr.* be or behave like an impostor. **2** *tr.* deceive; hoax.

hum·ding·er /húmdingər/ *n. sl.* excellent or remarkable person or thing.

hum·drum /húmdrum/ *adj.* **1** commonplace; dull. **2** monotonous.

hu·mer·us /hyōōmərəs/ *n.* (*pl.* **hu·mer·i** /-rī/) bone of the upper arm. □□ **hu′mer·al** *adj.*

hu·mid /hyōōmid/ *adj.* (of the air or climate) warm and damp.

hu·mid·i·fy /hyōōmídifī/ *v.tr.* (**-fies, -fied**) make (air, etc.) humid. □□ **hu·mid·i·fi·ca′tion** *n.* **hu·mid′i·fi·er** *n.*

hu·mid·i·ty /hyōōmíditee/ *n.* (*pl.* **-ties**) **1** humid state. **2** degree of moisture, esp. in the atmosphere.

hu·mil·i·ate /hyōōmílee-ayt/ *v.tr.* injure the dignity or self-respect of. □□ **hu·mil′i·at·ing** *adj.* **hu·mil·i·a′tion** /-áyshən/ *n.*

hu·mil·i·ty /hyōōmílitee/ *n.* humbleness; meekness.

hum·ming·bird /húmingbərd/ *n.* tiny nectar-feeding bird that makes a humming sound with its wings.

hum·mock /húmək/ *n.* hillock, knoll, or hump.

hum·mus /hōōməs/ *n.* dip or appetizer made from ground chickpeas and sesame oil flavored with lemon and garlic.

hu·mon·gous /hyōōmónggəs, -múng-/ *adj.* (also **hu·mun′gous**) *sl.* extremely large or massive.

hu·mor /hyōōmər/ • *n.* **1 a** condition or quality of being amusing. **b** expression of humor in literature, speech, etc. **2** (in full **sense of humor**) ability to perceive or express humor or take a joke. **3** mood or state of mind (*bad humor*). **4** (in full **cardinal humor**) *hist.* each of the four chief fluids (blood, phlegm, choler, melancholy), thought to determine a person's physical and mental qualities. • *v.tr.* gratify or indulge (a person or taste, etc.). □□ **hu′mor·ist** *n.* **hu′mor·less** *adj.* **hu′mor·less·ly** *adv.* **hu′mor·less·ness** *n.*

---

humor Middle English: via Old French from Latin *humor* 'moisture,' from *humere* (source of *humid*). The original sense was 'bodily fluid' (surviving in *aqueous humor* and *vitreous humor*, fluids in the eyeball); it was used specifically for any of the cardinal humors (see sense 4), whence 'mental disposition' (thought to be caused by the relative proportions of the humors). This led, in the 16th century, to the senses 'state of mind, mood' (see sense 3) and 'whim, fancy,' hence *to humor someone* 'to indulge a person's whim.'

hu·mor·ous /hyóōmərəs/ *adj.* **1** showing humor or a sense of humor. **2** facetious; comic. □□ **hu′ mor·ous·ly** *adv.*

hump /hump/ • *n.* **1** rounded protuberance on a camel's back, or as an abnormality on a person's back. **2** rounded raised mass of earth, etc. • *v.tr.* **1** *colloq.* lift or carry (heavy objects, etc.) with difficulty. **2** make hump-shaped. □ **over the hump** over the worst; well begun.

hump·back /húmpbak/ *n.* **1 a** deformed back with a hump. **b** person having this. **2** baleen whale with a dorsal fin forming a hump. □□ **hump′backed** *adj.*

hu·mus /hyóōməs/ *n.* organic constituent of soil, usu. formed by decayed vegetation.

Hun /hun/ *n.* **1** member of a warlike Asiatic nomadic people who ravaged Europe in the 4th–5th c. **2** vandal.

hunch /hunch/ • *v.* **1** *tr.* bend or arch into a hump. **2** *intr.* sit with the body hunched. • *n.* **1** *colloq.* intuitive feeling or conjecture. **2** hump.

hunch·back /húnchbak/ *n.* = HUMPBACK. □□ **hunch′backed** *adj.*

hun·dred /húndrəd/ • *n.* (*pl.* **hun·dreds** or (in sense 1) **hun·dred**) (in *sing.*, prec. by *a* or *one*) **1** product of ten and ten. **2** symbol for this (100, c, C). **3** set of a hundred things. **4** (in *pl.*) the years of a specified century (*the seventeen hundreds*). • *adj.* that amount to a hundred. □□ **hun′dred·fold** *adj. & adv.* **hun′dredth** *adj. & n.*

hun·dred·weight /húndrədwayt/ *n.* (*pl.* same or **-weights**) **1** (in full **short hundredweight**) unit of weight equal to 100 lb. (about 45.4 kg). **2** (in full **metric hundredweight**) unit of weight equal to 50 kg.

hung *past* and *past part.* of HANG.
¶ See note at HANG.

Hun·gar·i·an /hunggáireeən/ • *n.* **1 a** native or inhabitant of Hungary. **b** person of Hungarian descent. **2** Finno-Ugric language of Hungary. • *adj.* of Hungary or its people or language.

hun·ger /húnggər/ • *n.* **1** pain, discomfort, or exhaustion caused by lack of food. **2** strong desire. • *v.intr.* **1** crave or desire. **2** feel hunger. □□ **hun′gry** *adj.* (**hun·gri·er, hun·gri·est**) **hun′ gri·ly** *adv.*

hunk /hungk/ *n.* **1** large piece cut off (*hunk of bread*). **2** *colloq.* sexually attractive man. □□ **hunk′y** *adj.* (**hunk·i·er, hunk·i·est**).

hunt /hunt/ • *v.* **1** *tr.* (also *absol.*) **a** pursue and kill (wild animals, esp. game) for sport or food. **b** (of an animal) chase (its prey). **2** *intr.* seek; search (*hunting for a pen*). • *n.* **1** practice or instance of hunting. **2** search. □□ **hunt′er** *n.* **hunt′ ress** *n.* **hunt′ing** *n.* **hunts·man** /-mən/ *n.* (*pl.* **-men**)

hur·dle /hárd'l/ • *n.* **1** *Track & Field* **a** each of a series of light frames to be cleared by athletes in a race. **b** (in *pl.*) a hurdle race. **2** obstacle or difficulty. • *v.* **1** *Track & Field* **a** *intr.* run in a hurdle race. **b** *tr.* clear (a hurdle). **2** *tr.* overcome (a difficulty). □□ **hur′dler** *n.*

hur·dy-gur·dy /hárdeegárdee/ *n.* (*pl.* **-dies**) **1** musical instrument with a droning sound, played by turning a handle, esp. one with a rosined wheel turned by the right hand to sound the drone strings, and keys played by the left hand. **2** *colloq.* barrel organ.

hurl /hárl/ • *v.tr.* **1** throw with great force. **2** utter (abuse, etc.) vehemently. • *n.* **1** forceful throw. **2** act of hurling.

hur·ly-bur·ly /hárleebárlee/ *n.* boisterous activity; commotion.

---

285   humorous ～ hwy.

Hu·ron /hyóōron, -on/ *n.* **1 a** N. American people native to the northeastern U.S. **b** member of these people. **2** language of this people.

hur·rah /hōōráə/ (also **hur·ray** /hōōráy/) *int. & int.* exclamation of joy or approval.

hur·ri·cane /hárikayn, húr-/ *n.* **1** storm with a violent wind, esp. a cyclone in the W. Atlantic. **2** violent commotion. □ **hurricane lamp** oil lamp designed to resist a high wind.

hur·ry /hóree, húree/ *n.* (*pl.* **-ries**) **1 a** great haste. **b** (with *neg.* or *interrog.*) need for haste (*there is no hurry; what's the hurry?*). **2** eagerness to get a thing done quickly. • *v.* (**-ries, - ried**) **1** *intr.* move or act hastily. **2** *tr.* cause to move or proceed in this way. **3** *tr.* (as **hurried** *adj.*) hasty; done rapidly owing to lack of time. □□ **hur′ried·ly** *adv.*

hurt /hərt/ • *v.* (*past* and *past part.* **hurt**) **1** *tr.* (also *absol.*) cause pain or injury to. **2** *tr.* cause mental pain or distress to. **3** *intr.* suffer pain or harm (*my arm hurts*). • *n.* **1** injury. **2** harm; wrong. • *adj.* expressing emotional pain.

hurt·ful /hártfōōl/ *adj.* causing (esp. mental) hurt. □□ **hurt′ful·ly** *adv.*

hur·tle /hárt′l/ *v.* move or hurl rapidly or noisily.

hus·band /húzbənd/ • *n.* married man, esp. in relation to his wife. • *v.tr.* manage thriftily; use (resources) economically.

> **husband** late Old English (in the senses 'male head of a household' and 'manager, steward,' from Old Norse *húsbóndi* 'master of a house,' from *hús* 'house' + *bóndi* 'occupier and tiller of the soil.' The original sense of the verb was 'till, cultivate.'

hus·band·ry /húzbəndree/ *n.* **1** farming. **2** management of resources.

hush /hush/ • *v.* **1** *tr. & intr.* (often as **hushed** *adj.*) make or become silent or quiet. **2** *tr.* calm; soothe. • *int.* calling for silence. • *n.* expectant stillness or silence. □ **hush puppy** deep-fried ball of cornmeal dough.

hush-hush /húsh-húsh/ *adj. colloq.* highly secret.

husk /husk/ • *n.* **1** dry outer covering of some fruits or seeds. **2** worthless outside part of a thing. • *v.tr.* remove husk(s) from.

husk·y[1] /húskee/ *adj.* (**husk·i·er, husk·i·est**) **1** (of a person or voice) dry in the throat; hoarse. **2** strong; hefty. □□ **husk′i·ly** *adv.* **husk′i·ness** *n.*

husk·y[2] /húskee/ *n.* (*pl.* **-ies**) dog of a powerful breed used in the Arctic for pulling sleds.

hus·sy /húsee, -zee/ *n.* (*pl.* **-sies**) *derog.* impudent or immoral girl or woman.

hus·tings /hústingz/ *n.* political campaigning, esp. appearances and activities involved with a campaign.

hus·tle /húsəl/ • *v.* **1** *tr.* push roughly; jostle. **2** *tr.* force, coerce, or deal with hurriedly or unceremoniously (*hustled them out of the room*). **3** *intr.* push one's way; hurry; bustle. **4** *tr. sl.* obtain by forceful action. **b** swindle. **5** *intr. sl.* engage in prostitution. • *n.* **1 a** act or instance of hustling. **b** forceful or strenuous activity. **2** *colloq.* fraud or swindle. □□ **hus′tler** *n.*

hut /hut/ *n.* small simple or crude house or shelter.

hutch /huch/ *n.* **1** box or cage, usu. with a wire mesh front, for keeping rabbits, etc. **2** cupboard.

hwy. *abbr.* highway.

hy·a·cinth /hīəsinth/ *n.* **1** bulbous plant with clusters of usu. purplish blue, pink, or white bell-shaped fragrant flowers. **2** purplish blue.

hy·brid /hībrid/ • *n.* **1** *Biol.* offspring of two plants or animals of different species or varieties. **2** thing composed of diverse elements, e.g., a word with parts taken from different languages. • *adj.* **1** bred as a hybrid. **2** *Biol.* heterogeneous. **3** of mixed character; derived from incongruous elements or unlike sources. □□ **hy′brid·ism** *n.*

hy·brid·ize /hībridīz/ *v.* **1** *tr.* subject (a species, etc.) to cross-breeding. **2** *intr.* **a** produce hybrids. **b** (of an animal or plant) interbreed. □□ **hy·brid·i·za′tion** *n.*

hy·dra /hīdrə/ *n.* **1** freshwater polyp with tubular body and tentacles around the mouth. **2** something hard to destroy.

hy·dran·gea /hīdráynjə, -dran-/ *n.* shrub with globular clusters of white, pink, or blue flowers.

hy·drant /hīdrənt/ *n.* pipe (esp. in a street) with a nozzle for a hose, for drawing water from a main.

hy·drate /hīdrayt/ • *n. Chem.* compound of water combined with another compound or an element. • *v.tr.* **1 a** combine chemically with water. **b** (as **hydrated** *adj.*) chemically bonded to water. **2** cause to absorb water. □□ **hy·dra·tion** /-dráyshən/ *n.*

hy·drau·lic /hīdráwlik, -drólik/ *adj.* **1** (of water, oil, etc.) conveyed through pipes or channels usu. by pressure. **2** (of a mechanism, etc.) operated by liquid moving in this manner (*hydraulic brakes*). **3** of or concerned with hydraulics (*hydraulic engineer*). □□ **hy·drau′li·cal·ly** *adv.*

hy·drau·lics /hīdráwliks, -dróliks/ *n.pl.* (usu. treated as *sing.*) the science of the conveyance of liquids through pipes, etc., esp. as motive power.

hydro- /hīdrō/ *comb. form* (also **hydr-** before a vowel) **1** having to do with water (*hydroelectric*). **2** *Chem.* combined with hydrogen (*hydrochloric*).

hy·dro·car·bon /hīdrəkáarbən/ *n. Chem.* compound of hydrogen and carbon.

hy·dro·chlo·ric ac·id /hīdrəkláwrik/ *n. Chem.* solution of the colorless gas hydrogen chloride in water. ¶ *Chem.* formula: HCl.

hy·dro·dy·nam·ics /hīdrōdīnámiks/ *n.* the science of forces acting on or exerted by fluids (esp. liquids). □□ **hy·dro·dy·nam′ic** *adj.*

hy·dro·e·lec·tric /hīdrōiléktrik/ *adj.* **1** generating electricity by waterpower. **2** (of electricity) generated in this way. □□ **hy·dro·e·lec·tric·i·ty** /-trisitee/ *n.*

hy·dro·foil /hīdrəfoyl/ *n.* **1** boat with finlike members on struts for lifting its hull out of the water to increase speed. **2** this device.

HYDROFOIL

hy·dro·gen /hīdrəjən/ *n. Chem.* colorless gaseous element, without taste or odor, the lightest element and occurring in water and all organic compounds. ¶ Symb.: **H**. □ **hydrogen bomb** immensely powerful bomb utilizing the explosive fusion of hydrogen nuclei. Also called **H bomb**. **hydrogen peroxide** colorless liquid used as an antiseptic and bleach. ¶ *Chem.* formula: H_2O_2.

hy·drog·e·nate /hīdrójinayt, hídrəjənayt/ *v.tr.* charge with or cause to combine with hydrogen. □□ **hy·drog·en·a·tion** /-áyshən/ *n.*

hy·drol·o·gy /hīdróləjee/ *n.* the science of the properties of water, esp. of its movement in relation to land. □□ **hy·drol′o·gist** *n.*

hy·drol·y·sis /hīdrólisis/ *n.* chemical reaction of a substance with water, usu. resulting in decomposition.

hy·dro·lyze /hīdrəlīz/ *v.* decompose by hydrolysis.

hy·drom·e·ter /hīdrómitər/ *n.* instrument for measuring the density of liquids.

hy·dro·pho·bi·a /hīdrəfōbeeə/ *n.* **1** morbid aversion to water. **2** rabies, esp. in humans. □□ **hy·dro·pho·bic** /-bik/ *adj.*

hy·dro·plane /hīdrəplayn/ • *n.* **1** light fast motorboat designed to skim over water. **2** seaplane. • *v.intr.* **1** (of a boat) skim over the surface of water with its hull lifted. **2** (of a vehicle) glide uncontrollably on a wet road surface.

hy·dro·pon·ics /hīdrəpóniks/ *n.* growing plants in sand, gravel, or liquid, without soil and with added nutrients. □□ **hy·dro·pon′ic** *adj.* **hy·dro·pon′i·cal·ly** *adv.*

hy·dro·sphere /hīdrəsfeer/ *n.* waters of the earth's surface.

hy·dro·ther·a·py /hīdrəthérəpee/ *n.* use of water, esp. swimming, in the treatment of arthritis, paralysis, etc.

hy·drous /hīdrəs/ *adj. Chem. & Mineral.* containing water.

hy·e·na /hī-éenə/ *n.* doglike flesh-eating mammal with hind limbs shorter than forelimbs. □ **laughing hyena** *n.* hyena whose howl is compared to a fiendish laugh.

hyena Middle English: via Latin from Greek *huaina*, feminine of *hus* 'pig.' The transference of the term was probably because the animal's mane was thought to resemble a hog's bristles.

hy·giene /hījeen/ *n.* **1** conditions or practices, esp. cleanliness, conducive to maintaining health. **2** sanitary science. □□ **hy·gi·en·ic** /hījénik, -jéenik/ *adj.* **hy·gi·en′i·cal·ly** *adv.*

hy·gien·ist /hījénist, -jée-, -hījeenist/ *n.* specialist in cleanliness for the preservation of health, esp. (**dental hygienist**) a dental assistant who cleans the teeth.

hy·grom·e·ter /hīgrómitər/ *n.* instrument for measuring humidity.

hy·men /hīmən/ *n. Anat.* membrane at the opening of the vagina.

hymn /him/ • *n.* **1** song of praise, esp. to God in Christian worship. **2** song of praise in honor of a god or other exalted being or thing. • *v.* **1** *tr.* praise or celebrate in hymns. **2** *intr.* sing hymns.

hym·nal /hímnəl/ • *n.* book of hymns. • *adj.* of hymns.

hype /hīp/ *sl.* • *n.* **1** extravagant or intensive publicity promotion. **2** cheating; trick. • *v. tr.* **1** promote (a product) with extravagant publicity. **2** cheat; trick.

hy·per /hípər/ *adj. sl.* excessively excited, nervous, stimulated, etc.

hyper- /hípər/ *prefix* meaning: **1** over; beyond; above (*hyperphysical*). **2** exceeding (*hypersonic*). **3** excessively; above normal (*hyperbole*; *hypersensitive*).

hy·per·ac·tive /hípəráktiv/ *adj.* (of a person, esp. a child) abnormally active. □□ **hy·per·ac·tiv·i·ty** /-tívitee/ *n.*

hy·per·bo·la /hīpə́rbələ/ *n.* (*pl.* **hy·per·bo·las** or **hy·per·bo·lae** /-lee/) *Geom.* plane curve produced when a cone is cut by a plane that makes a larger angle with the base than the side of the cone (cf. ELLIPSE). □□ **hy·per·bol·ic** /-bólik/ *adj.*

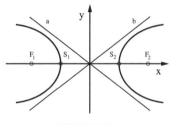

HYPERBOLA

hy·per·bo·le /hīpə́rbəlee/ *n. Rhet.* exaggerated statement not meant to be taken literally. □□ **hy·per·bol·ic** /hīpərbólik/ *adj.* **hy·per·bol´i·cal** *adj.*

hy·per·crit·i·cal /hípərkrítikəl/ *adj.* excessively critical, esp. of small faults. □□ **hy·per·crit´i·cal·ly** *adv.*

hy·per·gly·ce·mi·a /hípərglīsée'meeə/ *n.* excess of glucose in the bloodstream, often associated with diabetes mellitus.

hy·per·sen·si·tive /hípərsénsitiv/ *adj.* abnormally or excessively sensitive. □□ **hy·per·sen·si·tiv·i·ty** /-tívitee/ *n.*

hy·per·ten·sion /hípərténshən/ *n.* **1** abnormally high blood pressure. **2** state of great emotional tension. □□ **hy·per·ten·sive** /-ténsiv/ *adj.*

hy·per·text /hípərtekst/ *n. Computing* computer software that links topics on the screen to related information, graphics, etc., usu. by a point-and-click method.

hy·per·ther·mi·a /hípərthə́rmeeə/ *n. Med.* abnormally high body temperature. □□ **hy·per·ther´mic** *adj.*

hy·per·thy·roid·ism /hípərthíroydizəm/ *n. Med.* overactivity of the thyroid gland, resulting in an increased rate of metabolism. □□ **hy·per·thy´roid** *n. & adj.*

hy·per·ven·ti·la·tion /hípərvént´láyshən/ *n.* abnormally rapid breathing, resulting in an increased loss of carbon dioxide.

hy·phen /hífən/ • *n.* sign (-) used to join words semantically or syntactically (as in *pick-me-up*, *rock-forming*), to indicate the division of a word at the end of a line, or to indicate a missing or implied element (as in *man- and womankind*). • *v. tr.* **1** write (a compound word) with a hyphen. **2** join (words) with a hyphen.

hy·phen·ate /hífənayt/ *v. tr.* = HYPHEN *v.* □□ **hy·phen·a·tion** /-náyshən/ *n.*

hyp·no·sis /hipnṓsis/ *n.* state like sleep in which the subject acts only on external suggestion.

hyp·no·ther·a·py /hípnōthérəpee/ *n.* treatment of disease by hypnosis.

hyp·not·ic /hipnótik/ • *adj.* **1** of or producing hypnosis. **2** (of a drug) soporific. • *n.* **1** thing, esp. a drug, that produces sleep. **2** person under or open to hypnotism. □□ **hyp·not´i·cal·ly** *adv.*

hyp·no·tism /hípnətizəm/ *n.* study or practice of hypnosis. □□ **hyp´no·tist** *n.*

hyp·no·tize /hípnətīz/ *v. tr.* **1** produce hypnosis in. **2** fascinate.

hy·po /hípō/ *n.* (*pl.* **-pos**) *colloq.* = HYPODERMIC *n.*

hypo- /hípō/ *prefix* (usu. **hyp-** before a vowel or *h*) **1** under (*hypodermic*). **2** below normal (*hypoxia*).

hy·po·al·ler·gen·ic /hīpōalərjénik/ *adj.* having little likelihood of causing an allergic reaction (*hypoallergenic foods*).

hy·po·chon·dri·a /hípəkóndreeə/ *n.* abnormal anxiety about one's health. □□ **hy·po·chon·dri·ac** /-ak/ *n.* **hy·po·chon·dri·a·cal** /hípəkondríəkəl/ *adj.*

hy·poc·ri·sy /hipókrisee/ *n.* (*pl.* **-sies**) **1** false claim to virtue; insincerity; pretense. **2** instance of this.

hy·po·crite /hípəkrit/ *n.* person given to hypocrisy. □□ **hy·po·crit´i·cal** *adj.* **hy·po·crit´i·cal·ly** *adv.*

hy·po·der·mic /hípədə́rmik/ • *adj. Med.* **1** of or relating to the area beneath the skin. **2 a** (of a drug, etc., or its application) injected beneath the skin. **b** (of a needle, syringe, etc.) used to do this. • *n.* hypodermic injection or syringe.

hy·po·gly·ce·mi·a /hípōglīsée'meeə/ *n.* deficiency of glucose in the bloodstream. □□ **hy·po·gly·ce·mic** /-mik/ *adj.*

hy·po·ten·sion /hípəténshən/ *n.* abnormally low blood pressure. □□ **hy·po·ten´sive** *adj.*

hy·pot·e·nuse /hīpót´nōōs, -nyōōs/ *n.* side opposite the right angle of a right triangle.

hy·po·thal·a·mus /hípəthálləməs/ *n.* (*pl.* **-mi** /-mī/) *Anat.* region of the brain that controls body temperature, thirst, hunger, etc. □□ **hy·po·thal·a·mic** /-thəlámik/ *adj.*

hy·po·ther·mi·a /hípōthə́rmeeə/ *n. Med.* abnormally low body temperature.

hy·poth·e·sis /hīpóthisis/ *n.* (*pl.* **hy·poth·e·ses** /-seez/) **1** proposition made as a basis for reasoning, without the assumption of its truth. **2** supposition made as a starting point for further investigation from known facts (cf. THEORY). **3** groundless assumption. □□ **hy·poth·e·size** /-sīz/ *v.*

hy·po·thet·i·cal /hípəthétikəl/ *adj.* **1** of or based on or serving as a hypothesis. **2** supposed but not necessarily real or true. □□ **hy·po·thet´i·cal·ly** *adv.*

hy·po·thy·roid·ism /hípōthíroydizəm/ *n. Med.* subnormal activity of the thyroid gland, resulting in cretinism in children, and mental and physical slowing in adults. □□ **hy·po·thy´roid** *n. & adj.*

hys·ter·ec·to·my /hístəréktəmee/ *n.* (*pl.* **-mies**) surgical removal of the uterus.

hys·te·ri·a /histéreeə, -stéer-/ *n.* **1** wild uncontrollable emotion or excitement. **2** functional disturbance of the nervous system, of psycho-neurotic origin.

hys·ter·ic /histérik/ • *n.* **1** (in *pl.*) **a** fit of hysteria. **b** *colloq.* overwhelming mirth or laughter (*we were in hysterics*). **2** hysterical person. • *adj.* = HYSTERICAL.

---

hysteric mid-17th century (as an adjective): via Latin from Greek *husterikos* 'of the womb,' from *hustera* 'womb' (hysteria once being thought to be specific to women and associated with the womb).

---

hys·ter·i·cal /histérikǝl/ *adj.* **1** of or affected with hysteria. **2** morbidly or uncontrolledly emotional. **3** *colloq.* extremely funny. □□ **hys·ter'i·cal·ly** *adv.*

Hz *abbr.* hertz.

Ii

I[1] /ī/ *n.* (also **i**) (*pl.* **Is** or **I's; i's**) ninth letter of the alphabet.

I[2] /ī/ *pron.* (*obj.* **me;** *poss.* **my, mine;** *pl.* **we**) used by a speaker or writer to refer to himself or herself.

I[3] *symb. Chem.* iodine.

I[4] *abbr.* (also **I.**) **1** independent. **2** interstate. **3** Island(s). **4** Isle(s). **5** (as a Roman numeral) 1.

i *abbr.* (also **i.**) **1** incisor. **2** interest. **3** intransitive. **4** island. **5** isle.

IA *abbr.* Iowa (in official postal use).

Ia. *abbr.* Iowa.

-ial /eeəl, (ch)əl/ var. of -AL.

i·amb /íamb/ *n. Prosody* foot consisting of one short (or unstressed) followed by one long (or stressed) syllable.

i·am·bic /īámbik/ *Prosody* • *adj.* of or using iambs. • *n.* (usu. in *pl.*) iambic verse.

-ian /eeən/ *suffix* var. of -AN.

i·bex /íbeks/ *n.* (*pl.* same or **i·bex·es**) wild mountain goat of Europe, N. Africa, and Asia, with a chin beard and curved ridged horns.

ibid. /íbid/ *abbr.* (also **ib.**) in the same book or passage, etc.

-ibility /ibílitee/ *suffix* forming nouns from, or corresponding to, adjectives in *-ible* (*possibility*).

i·bis /íbis/ *n.* (*pl.* same or **i·bis·es**) wading bird with a curved bill, long neck, and long legs.

-ible /ibəl/ *suffix* forming adjectives meaning 'that may or may be' (see -ABLE) (*terrible*).

-ibly /iblee/ *suffix* forming adverbs corresponding to adjectives in *-ible*.

i·bu·pro·fen /íbyōoprófən/ *n.* anti-inflammatory medication used to relieve pain and reduce fever.

-ic /ik/ *suffix* forming adjectives (*Arabic*) and nouns (*critic*).

-ical /ikəl/ *suffix* **1** forming adjectives corresponding to nouns or adjectives, usu. in *-ic* (*classical*). **2** forming adjectives corresponding to nouns in *-y* (*pathological*).

-ically /iklee/ *suffix* forming adverbs corresponding to adjectives in *-ic* or *-ical* (*comically*).

ICBM *abbr.* intercontinental ballistic missile.

ICC *abbr.* **1** Interstate Commerce Commission. **2** International Claims Commission.

ice /īs/ • *n.* **1 a** frozen water. **b** sheet of this. **2** *sl.* diamonds. • *v.* **1** *tr.* mix with or cool in ice. **2** *tr. & intr.* (often foll. by *over, up*) a cover or become covered with ice. **b** freeze. **3** *tr.* cover (a cake, etc.) with icing. □ **ice cap** permanent covering of ice, e.g., in polar regions. **ice cream** sweet creamy frozen food, usu. flavored. **ice cube** small block of ice made in a refrigerator. **ice hockey** form of hockey played on ice. **ice skate** boot with a blade beneath, for skating on ice. **ice-skate** *v.intr.* skate on ice. **ice-skater** person who skates on ice. **on ice 1** performed by skaters. **2** *colloq.* held in reserve; awaiting

further attention. **on thin ice** in a risky situation.

ice·berg /ísbərg/ *n.* large floating mass of ice. □ **iceberg lettuce** type of various crisp roundheaded lettuces. **the tip of the iceberg** small perceptible part of something (esp. a difficulty) the greater part of which is hidden.

ice·box /ísboks/ *n.* refrigerator.

ice·break·er /ísbraykər/ *n.* something that serves to relieve inhibitions, start a conversation, etc.

Ice·land·er /ísləndər/ *n.* **1** native or national of Iceland, an island in the N. Atlantic. **2** person of Icelandic descent.

Ice·land·ic /īslándik/ • *adj.* of or relating to Iceland. • *n.* language of Iceland.

i·chor /íkawr, íkər/ *n.* **1** *Gk. mythol.* fluid flowing like blood in the veins of the gods. **2** *poet.* bloodlike fluid.

ich·thy·ol·o·gy /íktheeóləjee/ *n.* the study of fishes. □□ **ich·thy·o·log·i·cal** /-theeəlójikəl/ *adj.* **ich·thy·ol·o·gist** *n.*

-ician /íshən/ *suffix* forming nouns denoting persons skilled in or concerned with subjects having nouns (usu.) ending in *-ic* or *-ics* (*magician; politician*).

i·ci·cle /ísikəl/ *n.* hanging tapering piece of ice, formed by the freezing of dripping water.

ic·ing /ísing/ *n.* **1** sweet coating on a cake or cookie. **2** formation of ice on a ship or aircraft. □ **icing on the cake** attractive though inessential addition or enhancement.

-icist /isist/ *suffix* = -ICIAN (*classicist*).

-icity /ísitee/ *suffix* forming abstract nouns, esp. from adjectives in *-ic* (*authenticity*).

ick·y /íkkee/ *adj. colloq.* **1** sickly. **2** (as a general term of disapproval) nasty; repulsive.

i·con /íkon/ *n.* **1** (also **i'kon**) devotional painting of Christ or a saint; esp. in the Eastern Church. **2** image or statue. **3** *Computing* symbol or graphic representation that appears on the monitor in a program, option, or window, esp. one of several for selection. □□ **i·con'ic** *adj.*

i·con·o·clast /īkónəklast/ *n.* person who attacks cherished beliefs. □□ **i·con'o·clasm** *n.* **i·con·o·clas'tic** *adj.* **i·con·o·clas'ti·cal·ly** *adv.*

i·co·nog·ra·phy /íkənógrəfee/ *n.* (*pl.* **-phies**) **1** illustration of a subject by drawings or figures. **2 a** the study of portraits, esp. of an individual. **b** the study of artistic images or symbols. **3** treatise on pictures or statuary. □□ **i·co·nog'ra·pher** *n.* **i·con·o·graph·ic** /-nəgráfik/ *adj.* **i·con·o·graph'i·cal** *adj.* **i·con·o·graph'i·cal·ly** *adv.*

-ics /iks/ *suffix* (treated as *sing.* or *pl.*) forming nouns denoting arts or sciences or branches of study or action (*athletics; politics*).

ICU *abbr.* intensive care unit.

i·cy /ísee/ *adj.* (**i·ci·er, i·ci·est**) **1** very cold. **2** covered with or abounding in ice. **3** (of a tone or manner) unfriendly; hostile (*an icy stare*). □□ **i'ci·ly** *adv.* **i'ci·ness** *n.*

ID *abbr.* **1** identification (*ID card*). **2** Idaho (in official postal use).

I'd /īd/ *contr.* **1** I had. **2** I should; I would.

id /id/ *n. Psychol.* inherited instinctive impulses of the individual as part of the unconscious.

i.d. *abbr.* inside diameter.

-ide /īd/ *suffix* (also **-id**) *Chem.* forming nouns denoting: **1** binary compounds of an element (the suffix *-ide* being added to the abbreviated name of the more electronegative element, etc.) (*sodium chloride*; *lead sulfide*; *calcium carbide*). **2** various other compounds (*amide*; *anhydride*; *peptide*; *saccharide*). **3** elements of a series in the periodic table (*actinide*; *lanthanide*).

i·de·a /īdeʹə/ *n.* **1** conception or plan formed by mental effort. **2 a** mental impression or notion; concept. **b** vague belief or fancy. **c** opinion; outlook or point of view. **3** intention, purpose, or essential feature. **4** archetype or pattern. □ **have no idea** *colloq.* **1** not know at all. **2** be completely incompetent. □□ **i·deʹa·less** *adj.*

i·de·al /īdeʹəl/ • *adj.* **1 a** answering to one's highest conception. **b** perfect or supremely excellent. **2 a** existing only in idea. **b** visionary. • *n.* **1** perfect type, or a conception of this. **2 a** actual thing as a standard for imitation. **b** (often in *pl.*) moral principle or standard of behavior. □□ **i·deʹal·ly** *adv.*

i·de·al·ism /īdeʹəlizəm/ *n.* **1** forming or following after ideals, esp. unrealistically (cf. REALISM). **2** representation of things in ideal or idealized form. □□ **i·deʹal·ist** *n.* **i·de·al·isʹtic** *adj.* **i·de·al·isʹti·cal·ly** *adv.*

i·de·al·ize /īdeʹəlīz/ *v.tr.* **1** regard or represent in ideal form or character. **2** exalt in thought to ideal perfection or excellence. □□ **i·de·al·i·zaʹtion** *n.*

i·dée fixe /eeday feʹeks/ *n.* (*pl.* **i·dées fixes** *pronunc.* same) idea that dominates the mind; an obsession.

i·den·ti·cal /īdéntikəl/ *adj.* **1** (of different things) agreeing in every detail. **2** (of one thing viewed at different times) one and the same. **3** (of twins) developed from a single fertilized ovum. □□ **i·denʹti·cal·ly** *adv.*
¶ See note at SAME.

i·den·ti·fi·ca·tion /īdéntifikáyshən/ *n.* **1 a** identifying; recognition; pinpointing. **b** association of oneself with the feelings, etc., of another person or group. **2** means of identifying. **3** (*attrib.*) serving to identify (esp. the bearer) (*identification card*).

i·den·ti·fy /īdéntifī/ *v.tr.* (**-fies, -fied**) **1** establish the identity of; recognize. **2** establish or select. **3** (foll. by *with*) associate inseparably or very closely (with a party, policy, etc.). □□ **i·denʹti·fiʹa·ble** *adj.*

i·den·ti·ty /īdéntitee/ *n.* (*pl.* **-ties**) **1 a** condition of being a specified person or thing. **b** individuality; personality. **2** identification or the result of it (*mistaken identity*). **3** absolute sameness.

id·e·o·gram /īdeeəgram/ *n.* character symbolizing a thing without indicating the sounds in its name (e.g., a numeral, Chinese characters).

id·e·o·logue /īdeeəlawg, -log, ídee-/ *n.* **1** theorist; visionary. **2** adherent of an ideology.

id·e·ol·o·gy /īdeeóləjee, ídee-/ *n.* (*pl.* **-gies**) **1** ideas at the basis of an economic or political

theory. **2** the manner of thinking characteristic of a class or individual. □□ **i·de·o·logʹi·cal** /-əlójikəl/ *adj.* **i·de·o·logʹi·cal·ly** *adv.* **i·de·olʹo·gist** /-deeól-/ *n.*

ides /īdz/ *n.pl.* eighth day after the nones in the ancient Roman calendar (the 15th day of March, May, July, October; the 13th of other months).

id·i·o·cy /īdeeəsee/ *n.* (*pl.* **-cies**) utter foolishness; idiotic behavior or an idiotic action.

id·i·om /īdeeəm/ *n.* **1** phrase established by usage whose meaning is not deducible from the individual words (e.g., *at the drop of a hat*). **2** form of expression peculiar to a language, group, etc. **3** a language of a people or country. **b** specific character of this. **4** characteristic mode of expression in music, art, etc. □□ **id·i·o·matʹic** /īdeeəmátik/ *adj.* **id·i·o·matʹi·cal·ly** *adv.*

id·i·o·syn·cra·sy /īdeeōsíngkrəsee/ *n.* (*pl.* **-sies**) **1** mental constitution, opinion, or mode of behavior peculiar to a person. **2** anything highly individualized. □□ **id·i·o·syn·cratʹic** /-krátik/ *adj.* **id·i·o·syn·cratʹi·cal·ly** *adv.*

id·i·ot /īdeeət/ *n.* **1** *colloq.* stupid person. **2** mentally deficient person incapable of rational conduct. □ **idiot box** *colloq.* television set. □□ **id·i·otʹic** /īdeeótik/ *adj.* **id·i·otʹi·cal·ly** *adv.*

i·dle /īd'l/ • *adj.* (**i·dler, i·dlest**) **1** lazy; indolent. **2** not in use; not working; unemployed. **3** (of time, etc.) unoccupied. **4** having no special basis or purpose. **5** useless. **6** (of an action, thought, or word) ineffective; worthless; vain. • *v.* **1 a** *intr.* (of an engine) run slowly. **b** *tr.* cause (an engine) to idle. **2** *intr.* be idle. **3** *tr.* (foll. by *away*) pass (time, etc.) in idleness. □□ **iʹdle·ness** *n.* **iʹdler** *n.* **iʹdly** *adv.*

i·dol /īd'l/ *n.* **1** image of a deity, etc., as an object of worship. **2** the object of excessive or supreme adulation (*movie idol*).

i·dol·a·try /īdólətree/ *n.* **1** the worship of idols. **2** great adulation.

i·dol·ize /īd'līz/ *v.* **1** *tr.* venerate or love excessively. **2** *tr.* make an idol of. **3** *intr.* practice idolatry. □□ **i·dol·i·zaʹtion** *n.* **iʹdol·iz·er** *n.*

i·dyll /īd'l/ *n.* (also **iʹdyl**) **1** short description in verse or prose of a picturesque scene or incident, esp. in rustic life. **2** episode suitable for such treatment, usu. a love story. □□ **iʹdyl·list** *n.* **iʹdyl·ize** *v.tr.*

i·dyl·lic /īdílik/ *adj.* **1** blissfully peaceful and happy. **2** of or like an idyll. □□ **i·dylʹli·cal·ly** *adv.*

IE *abbr.* **1** Indo-European. **2** industrial engineer(ing).

i.e. *abbr.* that is to say.

-ie /ee/ *suffix* **1** var. of -Y² (*dearie*; *nightie*). **2** archaic var. of -Y¹, -Y³ (*litanie*; *prettie*).

if /if/ • *conj.* **1** introducing a conditional clause: **a** on the condition or supposition that; in the event that (*if he comes I will tell him*). **b** (with past tense) implying that the condition is not fulfilled (*if I knew I would say*). **2** even though (*I'll finish it, if it takes all day*). **3** whenever (*if I am not sure I ask*). **4** whether (*see if you can find it*). **5 a** expressing wish or surprise (*if I could just try!*). **b** expressing a request (*if you wouldn't mind opening the door?*). **6** with implied reservation; perhaps not (*very rarely if at all*). • *n.* condition or supposition (*too many ifs about it*). □ **if only 1** even if for no other reason than (*I'll come if only to see her*). **2** expression of regret (*if only I could swim!*).

if·fy /ífee/ *adj.* (**if·fi·er, if·fi·est**) *colloq.* uncertain; doubtful.

ig·loo /íglōo/ *n.* dome-shaped Eskimo dwelling, esp. one built of snow.

IGLOO

ig·ne·ous /ígneeəs/ *adj.* **1** of fire; fiery. **2** *Geol.* (esp. of rocks) produced by volcanic or magmatic action.

ig·nite /ignít/ *v.* **1** *tr.* set fire to. **2** *intr.* catch fire. **3** *tr.* provoke or excite (feelings, etc.). □□ **ig·nit·a·ble** *adj.* **ig·nit·a·bil·i·ty** *n.* **ig·nit·i·ble** *adj.* **ig·nit·i·bil·i·ty** *n.*

ig·ni·tion /igníshən/ *n.* **1** mechanism for, or action of, starting an internal combustion engine. **2** igniting or being ignited.

ig·no·ble /ignốbəl/ *adj.* (**ig·no·bler, ig·no·blest**) **1** dishonorable; mean; base. **2** of low birth, position, or reputation. □□ **ig·no·bil′i·ty** *n.* **ig·no′bly** *adv.*

ig·no·min·i·ous /ígnəmíneeəs/ *adj.* **1** causing or deserving ignominy. **2** humiliating. □□ **ig·no·min′i·ous·ly** *adv.*

ig·no·mi·ny /ígnəminee/ *n.* dishonor.

ig·no·ra·mus /ígnəráyməs/ *n.* (*pl.* **ig·no·ra·mus·es** or **ig·no·ra·mi**) ignorant person.

---

ignoramus late 16th century (as the endorsement made by a grand jury on an indictment considered backed by insufficient evidence to bring to trial): Latin, literally, 'we do not know' (in legal use 'we take no notice of it'), from *ignorare* (source of *ignore*). The modern sense may derive from the name of a character in George Ruggle's *Ignoramus* (1615), a satirical comedy exposing lawyers' ignorance.

---

ig·no·rance /ígnərəns/ *n.* (often foll. by *of*) lack of knowledge. □□ **ig′no·rant** *adj.* **ig′no·rant·ly** *adv.*

ig·nore /ignáwr/ *v.tr.* **1** refuse to take notice of or accept. **2** intentionally disregard. □□ **ig·nor′er** *n.*

i·gua·na /igwaánə/ *n.* any of various large lizards native to tropical America and the Pacific islands, with a dorsal crest.

IL *abbr.* Illinois (in official postal use).

il- /il/ *prefix* assim. form of IN-[1], IN-[2] before *l*.

il·e·os·to·my /íleeóstəmee/ *n.* (*pl.* **-mies**) surgical operation in which the ileum is brought through the abdominal wall to create an artificial opening for the evacuation of the bowels.

il·e·um /íleeəm/ *n.* (*pl.* **il·e·a** /íleeə/) *Anat.* third and last portion of the small intestine. □□ **il′e·ac** *adj.*

il·i·um /íleeəm/ *n.* (*pl.* **il·i·a** /íleeə/) bone forming the upper part of each half of the pelvis.

ilk /ilk/ *n.* family, class, or set (*not of the same ilk as you*).

Ill. *abbr.* Illinois.

ill. *abbr.* **1** illustrated. **2** illustration. **3** illustrator.

I'll /īl/ *contr.* I shall; I will.

ill /il/ ● *adj.* **1** (usu. *predic.*) out of health; sick (*ill with pneumonia*). **2** (of health) unsound; disordered. **3** wretched; unfavorable (*ill fortune; ill luck*). **4** harmful (*ill effects*). **5** hostile; unkind (*ill feeling*). ● *adv.* **1** badly; wrongly. **2 a** imperfectly (*ill-provided*). **b** scarcely (*can ill afford to do it*). **3** unfavorably (*it would have gone ill with them*). ● *n.* **1** injury; harm. **2** evil. □ **ill-advised 1** (of a person) foolish or imprudent. **2** (of a plan, etc.) not well formed or considered. **ill at ease** embarrassed; uneasy. **ill-bred** badly brought up; rude. **ill-fated** destined to or bringing bad fortune. **ill-favored** unattractive. **ill-gotten** gained by wicked or unlawful means. **ill humor** irritability. **ill-mannered** having bad manners; rude. **ill-natured** churlish; unkind. **ill-tempered** morose; irritable. **ill-treat** (or **-use**) treat badly; abuse. **ill will** bad feeling; animosity.

il·le·gal /ileégəl/ *adj.* **1** not legal. **2** contrary to law. □□ **il·le·gal·i·ty** /-gálitee/ *n.* (*pl.* **-ties**). **il·le′gal·ly** *adv.*

il·leg·i·ble /iléjibəl/ *adj.* not legible. □□ **il·leg·i·bil′i·ty** *n.* **il·leg′i·bly** *adv.*

il·le·git·i·mate ● *adj.* /ilijítimət/ **1** (of a child) born of parents not married to each other. **2** unlawful. **3** improper. ● *n.* /ilijítimət/ person whose position is illegitimate, esp. by birth. ● *v.tr.* /ilijítimayt/ declare or pronounce illegitimate. □□ **il·le·git·i·ma·cy** /-məsee/ *n.* **il·le·git′i·mate·ly** *adv.*

il·lib·er·al /ilíbərəl/ *adj.* **1** intolerant; narrowminded. **2** not generous; stingy. **3** vulgar; sordid. □□ **il·lib·er·al·i·ty** /-álitee/ *n.* (*pl.* **-ties**). **il·lib′er·al·ly** *adv.*

il·lic·it /ilísit/ *adj.* **1** unlawful; forbidden. **2** secret; furtive. □□ **il·li′cit·ly** *adv.* **il·li′cit·ness** *n.*

il·lit·er·ate /ilítərət/ ● *adj.* **1** unable to read. **2** uneducated. ● *n.* illiterate person. □□ **il·lit′er·a·cy** *n.*

ill·ness /ílnis/ *n.* **1** disease. **2** being ill.

il·log·i·cal /ilójikəl/ *adj.* devoid of or contrary to logic. □□ **il·log·i·cal·i·ty** /-kálitee/ *n.* (*pl.* **-ties**). **il·log′i·cal·ly** *adv.*

il·lu·mi·nate /ilōominayt/ *v.tr.* **1** light up; make bright. **2** decorate with lights. **3** decorate (a manuscript, etc.) with gold, silver, etc. **4** help to explain. **5** enlighten spiritually or intellectually. **6** shed luster on. □□ **il·lu′mi·nat·ing** *adj.* **il·lu·mi·na·tion** /-náyshən/ *n.* **il·lu·mi·na·tive** /-náytiv, -nətiv/ *adj.* **il·lu′mi·na·tor** *n.*

il·lu·mi·na·ti /ilōominaátee/ *n.pl.* persons claiming to possess special knowledge or enlightenment.

il·lu·mine /ilōomin/ *v.tr. literary* **1** light up; make bright. **2** enlighten spiritually.

il·lu·sion /ilōōzhən/ *n.* **1** deception; delusion. **2** misapprehension of the true state of affairs. **3 a** faulty perception of an external object. **b** instance of this. **4** figment of the imagination. **5** = *optical illusion*. □□ **il·lu′sion·al** *adj.* **il·lu·sive** /ilōōsiv/ *adj.*

il·lu·sion·ist /ilōōzhənist/ *n.* person who produces illusions; magician.

il·lu·so·ry /ilōosəree; -zəree/ adj. **1** deceptive (esp. as regards value or content). **2** having the character of an illusion. □□ **il·lu′so·ri·ly** adv. **il·lu′so·ri·ness** n.

il·lus·trate /íləstrayt/ v.tr. **1 a** provide (a book, etc.) with pictures. **b** elucidate by drawings or pictures. **2** serve as an example of. **3** explain or make clear, esp. by examples. □□ **il′lus·tra·tor** n.

il·lus·tra·tion /íləstráyshən/ n. **1** drawing or picture in a book, magazine article, etc. **2** explanatory example. **3** act or instance of illustrating. □□ **il·lus′tra·tion·al** adj.

il·lus·tra·tive /ilústrətiv, íləstray-/ adj. (often foll. by of) serving as an explanation or example. □□ **il·lus′tra·tive·ly** adv.

il·lus·tri·ous /ilústreeəs/ adj. distinguished; renowned. □□ **il·lus′tri·ous·ly** adv. **il·lus′tri·ous·ness** n.

I'm /īm/ contr. I am.

im- /im/ prefix assim. form of IN-¹, IN-² before b, m, p.

im·age /ímij/ • n. **1** representation of an object, e.g., a statue. **2** character or reputation of a person or thing as generally perceived. **3** appearance in a mirror, refracted through a lens, etc. **4** semblance; likeness. **5** person or thing that closely resembles another (is the image of his father). **6** simile or metaphor. **7 a** mental representation. **b** idea or conception. • v.tr. make an image of; portray.

im·age·ry /ímijree/ n. **1** figurative illustration, esp. as used by an author. **2** images collectively. **3** statuary; carving. **4** mental images collectively.

i·mag·i·nar·y /imájinéree/ adj. **1** existing only in the imagination. **2** Math. being the square root of a negative quantity. □□ **i·mag′i·nar·i·ly** adv.
¶ **Imaginary** means 'product of the imagination; unreal'; **imaginative** means 'showing imagination; original.' Science fiction deals with imaginary people, places, and events; depending on the writer's ability, it may be more or less imaginative. Historical writing should not be imaginary, but the writer's approach, research, etc., may be quite imaginative.

i·mag·i·na·tion /imájináyshən/ n. **1** mental faculty forming images or concepts of external objects not present to the senses. **2** ability of the mind to be creative or resourceful. **3** process of imagining.

i·mag·i·na·tive /imájinətiv/ adj. having or showing imagination. □□ **i·mag′i·na·tive·ly** adv. **i·mag′i·na·tive·ness** n.
¶ See note at IMAGINARY.

i·mag·ine /imájin/ v.tr. **1 a** form a mental image or concept of. **b** picture to oneself. **2** think or conceive (imagined them to be soldiers). **3** guess. **4** suppose. □□ **i·mag′in·a·ble** adj. **i·mag′in·er** n.

i·mag·in·ings /imájiningz/ n.pl. fancies; fantasies.

i·ma·go /imáygō, imaá-/ n. (pl. **-goes** or **i·ma·gi·nes** /imájineez/) adult insect.

i·mam /imaám/ n. **1** leader of prayers in a mosque. **2** title of various Islamic leaders. □□ **i·mam·ate** /-mayt/ n.

im·bal·ance /imbáləns/ n. **1** lack of balance. **2** disproportion.

im·be·cile /ímbisil, -səl/ • n. **1** person of abnormally weak intellect, esp. an adult with a mental age of about five. **2** colloq. stupid person. • adj. mentally weak; stupid; idiotic. • adj. **im·be·cil′i·ty** n. (pl. **-ties**)

im·bed var. of EMBED.

im·bibe /imbíb/ v.tr. **1** drink (esp. alcoholic liquor). **2 a** absorb or assimilate (ideas, etc.). **b** absorb (moisture, etc.). □□ **im·bib′er** n.

im·bro·glio /imbrólyō/ n. (pl. **-os**) **1** confused or complicated situation. **2** confused heap.

im·bue /imbyōō/ v.tr. (**im·bues, im·bued, im·bu·ing**) **1** inspire or permeate (with feelings, opinions, or qualities). **2** saturate. **3** dye.

IMF abbr. International Monetary Fund.

im·i·tate /ímitayt/ v.tr. **1** follow the example of; copy. **2** mimic. **3** make a copy of. **4** be like. □□ **im′i·ta·ble** adj. **im′i·ta·tor** n.

im·i·ta·tion /ímitáyshən/ • n. **1** imitating or being imitated. **2** a copy. **3** counterfeit; fake.

im·i·ta·tive /ímitaytiv/ adj. **1** imitating; following a model or example. **2** counterfeit. □□ **im′i·ta·tive·ly** adv.

im·mac·u·late /imákyələt/ adj. **1** pure; perfectly clean. **2** perfect. **3** faultless; innocent. □ **Immaculate Conception** RC ch. doctrine that God preserved the Virgin Mary from the taint of original sin from the moment she was conceived. □□ **im·mac′u·late·ly** adv. **im·mac′u·late·ness** n.

im·ma·nent /ímənənt/ adj. **1** indwelling; inherent. **2** (of the Supreme Being) omnipresent (cf. transcendent (TRANSCEND)). □□ **im′ma·nence** n. **im′ma·nen·cy** n.
¶ See note at EMINENT.

im·ma·te·ri·al /ímətéereeəl/ adj. **1** unimportant. **2** incorporeal. □□ **im·ma·te′ri·al·ly** adv.
¶ **Immaterial** and **irrelevant** are familiar in legal, especially courtroom, use. **Immaterial** means 'unimportant because not adding anything to the point.' **Irrelevant,** a much more common word, means 'beside the point, not speaking to the point.' Courts have long since ceased to demand precise distinctions, and evidence is often objected to as "immaterial, irrelevant, and incompetent (offered by a witness who is not qualified to offer it)."

im·ma·ture /ímachóor, -tōōr, -tyōōr/ adj. **1** not mature. **2** emotionally undeveloped. **3** unripe. □□ **im·ma·ture′ly** adv. **im·ma·tu′ri·ty** n.

im·meas·ur·a·ble /imézhərəbəl/ adj. not measurable; immense. □□ **im·mea·sur·a·bil′i·ty** n. **im·mea′sur·a·bly** adv.

im·me·di·ate /imée·deeət/ adj. **1** occurring or done at once. **2** nearest; next; not separated by others. **3** most pressing or urgent. **4** (of a relation or action) having direct effect. **5** (of knowledge, reactions, etc.) gained or exhibited without reasoning. □□ **im·me′di·a·cy** n. **im·me′di·ate·ly** adv. & conj. **im·me′di·ate·ness** n.

im·me·mo·ri·al /ímimáwreeəl/ adj. **1** beyond memory or record. **2** very old.

im·mense /iméns/ adj. **1** immeasurably large; huge. **2** very great; considerable (made an immense difference). **3** colloq. very good. □□ **im·mense′ly** adv. **im·mense′ness** n. **im·men′si·ty** n.

im·merse /imárs/ v.tr. **1 a** dip; plunge. **b** submerge (a person). **2** absorb or involve deeply (in). □□ **im·mer′sion** /imárzhən/ n.

im·mi·grant /ímigrənt/ • n. person who immigrates. • adj. **1** immigrating. **2** of or concerning immigrants.

im·mi·grate /ímigrayt/ v. **1** intr. come as a permanent resident into a country. **2** tr. bring in

(a person) as an immigrant. □□ **im·mi·gra·tion** /-gráyshən/ n.
¶ See note at EMIGRATE.

im·mi·nent /íminənt/ adj. impending; about to happen. □□ **im′mi·nence** n. **im′mi·nent·ly** adv.
¶ See note at EMINENT.

im·mo·bile /imóbəl, -beel, -bīl/ adj. 1 not moving. 2 not able to move or be moved. □□ **im·mo·bil·i·ty** /-bílitee/ n.

im·mo·bi·lize /imóbilīz/ v.tr. 1 make or keep immobile. 2 keep (a limb or patient) still for healing purposes. □□ **im·mo·bi·li·za′tion** n.

im·mod·er·ate /imódərət/ adj. excessive; lacking moderation. □□ **im·mod′er·ate·ly** adv. **im·mod·er·a·tion** /-ráyshən/ n.

im·mod·est /imódist/ adj. 1 lacking modesty; impudent. 2 indecent. □□ **im·mod′est·ly** adv. **im·mod′es·ty** n.

im·mo·late /ímǝlayt/ v.tr. kill or offer as a sacrifice. □□ **im·mo·la·tion** /-láyshən/ n.

im·mor·al /imáwrǝl, imór-/ adj. 1 not conforming to accepted morality (cf. AMORAL). 2 morally wrong (esp. in sexual matters). 3 depraved; dissolute. □□ **im·mo·ral·i·ty** /-álitee/ n. (pl. -ties). **im·mor′al·ly** adv.
¶ **Immoral** means 'failing to adhere to moral standards'; **amoral** means 'without moral standards.' An *immoral* person commits acts that violate society's moral norms; an *amoral* person is someone with no understanding of these norms, no sense of right and wrong.

im·mor·tal /imáwrt′l/ ● adj. 1 a living forever. b divine. 2 unfading. 3 likely or worthy to be famous for all time. ● n. a immortal being. b (pl.) gods of antiquity. 2 person (esp. an author) of enduring fame. □□ **im·mor·tal·i·ty** /-tálitee/ n. **im·mor′tal·ize** v.tr.

im·mov·a·ble /imovábəl/ adj. 1 not able to be moved. 2 steadfast; unyielding. 3 emotionless. 4 not subject to change. 5 motionless. □□ **im·mov·a·bil′i·ty** n. **im·mov′a·bly** adv.

im·mune /imyoon/ adj. 1 a protected against infection through inoculation or inherited or acquired resistance. b relating to immunity (*immune mechanism*). 2 (foll. by *from, to*) exempt from (some undesirable factor or circumstance).

im·mu·ni·ty /imyoonitee/ n. (pl. -ties) 1 Med. ability of an organism to resist infection by means of antibodies and white blood cells. 2 freedom or exemption from an obligation, penalty, etc.

im·mu·nize /imyənīz/ v.tr. make immune, esp. to infection, usu. by inoculation. □□ **im·mu·ni·za′tion** n. **im′mu·niz·er** n.

im·mu·nol·o·gy /ímyənóləjee/ n. scientific study of immunity. □□ **im·mu·no·log·ic** /-nəlójik/ adj. **im·mu·no·log′i·cal** adj. **im·mu·nol·o·gist** /-nóləjist/ n.

im·mu·no·sup·pressed /ímyənōsəprést, imyóō-/ adj. (of an individual) rendered partially or completely unable to react immunologically.

im·mu·no·sup·pres·sion /ímyənōsəpréshən, imyóō-/ n. Biochem. partial or complete suppression of the immune response of an individual, esp. to maintain the survival of an organ after a transplant operation. □□ **im·mu·no·sup·pres·sant** /-présənt/ n. **im·mu·no·sup·pres′sive** adj. & n.

im·mu·no·ther·a·py /ímyənōthérəpee, imyóō-/

293   **imminent ~ impeach**

n. Med. prevention or treatment of disease with substances that simulate the immune response.

im·mure /imyoōr/ v.tr. enclose within walls; imprison.

im·mu·ta·ble /imyoōtəbəl/ adj. unchangeable. □□ **im·mu·ta·bil′i·ty** n. **im·mu′ta·bly** adv.

imp /imp/ n. 1 mischievous child. 2 small devil or sprite.

---

imp Old English *impa*, *impe* 'young shoot, scion,' *impian* 'to graft,' based on Greek *emphuein* 'to implant.' In late Middle English, the noun denoted a descendant, especially of a noble family, and later a child of the devil or a person regarded as such; hence a 'little devil' or mischievous child (sense 1, early 17th century).

---

im·pact ● n. /ímpakt/ 1 forceful contact. 2 strong effect or influence. ● v. /impákt/ 1 tr. press or fix firmly. 2 tr. (as **impacted** adj.) (of a tooth) wedged between another tooth and the jaw. 3 intr. a (foll. by *against, on*) come forcibly into contact with a (larger) body or surface. b (foll. by *on*) have a pronounced effect. □□ **im·pac·tion** /-pákshən/ n.

im·pair /impáir/ v.tr. damage or weaken. □□ **im·pair′ment** n.

im·pa·la /impaálə, -pálə/ n. (pl. same) small antelope of S. and E. Africa.

im·pale /impáyl/ v.tr. transfix or pierce with a sharp instrument. □□ **im·pale′ment** n.

im·pal·pa·ble /impálpəbəl/ adj. 1 not easily grasped by the mind; intangible. 2 imperceptible to the touch. □□ **im·pal·pa·bil′i·ty** n. **im·pal′pa·bly** adv.

im·pan·el /impán′l/ v.tr. officially establish a jury. □□ **im·pan′el·ment** n.

im·part /impaárt/ v.tr. (often foll. by *to*) 1 communicate (news, etc.). 2 give a share of (a thing). □□ **im·part′a·ble** adj.

im·par·tial /impaárshəl/ adj. unprejudiced; fair. □□ **im·par·ti·al·i·ty** /-sheeálitee/ n. **im·par′tial·ly** adv.

im·pass·a·ble /impásəbəl/ adj. that cannot be traversed. □□ **im·pass·a·bil′i·ty** n. **im·pass′a·bly** adv.

im·passe /ímpas/ n. deadlock.

im·pas·si·ble /impásibəl/ adj. 1 impassive. 2 incapable of feeling or emotion. 3 incapable of suffering injury. □□ **im·pas·si·bil′i·ty** n. **im·pas′si·bly** adv.

im·pas·sioned /impáshənd/ adj. deeply felt; ardent.

im·pas·sive /impásiv/ adj. 1 a deficient in or incapable of showing emotion. b serene. 2 without sensation. 3 not subject to suffering. □□ **im·pas′sive·ly** adv. **im·pas′sive·ness** n. **im·pas·siv′i·ty** n.

im·pas·to /impástō, -paás-/ n. Art 1 process of laying on paint thickly. 2 this technique of painting.

im·pa·tient /impáyshənt/ adj. 1 a lacking patience or tolerance. b (of an action) showing a lack of patience. 2 (often foll. by *for*, or *to* + infin.) restlessly eager. 3 (foll. by *of*) intolerant. □□ **im·pa·tience** /-shəns/ n. **im·pa′tient·ly** adv.

im·peach /impeéch/ v.tr. 1 charge (a public official) with misconduct. 2 call in question; disparage. □□ **im·peach′a·ble** adj. **im·peach′ment** n.

im·pec·ca·ble /impékəbəl/ *adj.* faultless; exemplary. □□ **im·pec′ca·bly** *adv.*

im·pe·cu·ni·ous /impikyőőneeəs/ *adj.* having little or no money. □□ **im·pe·cu′ni·ous·ness** *n.*

im·ped·ance /impéed′ns/ *n. Electr.* total effective resistance of a circuit, etc., to alternating current.

¶ Impedance is a specialized electrical term, while impediment is an everyday term meaning 'a hindrance or obstruction,' e.g., *Interpreting his handwriting was an impediment to getting business done.*

im·pede /impéed/ *v.tr.* retard by obstructing; hinder.

im·ped·i·ment /impédimənt/ *n.* **1** hindrance or obstruction. **2** defect in speech. □□ **im·ped·i·men·tal** /-mént′l/ *adj.*
¶ See note at IMPEDANCE.

im·ped·i·men·ta /impédiméntə/ *n.pl.* **1** encumbrances. **2** traveling equipment, esp. of an army.

im·pel /impél/ *v.tr.* (**im·pelled, im·pel·ling**) **1** drive, force, or urge. **2** propel. □□ **im·pel′lent** *adj. & n.* **im·pel′ler** *n.*

im·pend /impénd/ *v.intr.* **1** be about to happen. **2** a (of a danger) be threatening. **b** hang. □□ **im·pend′ing** *adj.*

im·pen·e·tra·ble /impénitrəbəl/ *adj.* **1** not able to be penetrated. **2** inscrutable. **3** inaccessible to ideas, influences, etc. □□ **im·pen·e·tra·bil′i·ty** *n.* **im·pen′e·tra·ble·ness** *n.* **im·pen′e·tra·bly** *adv.*

im·pen·i·tent /impénit′nt/ *adj.* not repentant or penitent. □□ **im·pen′i·tence** *n.* **im·pen′i·tent·ly** *adv.*

im·per·a·tive /impérətiv/ ● *adj.* **1** urgent. **2** obligatory. **3** commanding; peremptory. **4** *Gram.* (of a mood) expressing a command (e.g., *come here!*). ● *n.* **1** *Gram.* the imperative mood. **2** command. □□ **im·per·a·ti·val** /-ətívəl/ *adj.* **im·per′a·tive·ly** *adv.*

im·per·cep·ti·ble /impərséptibəl/ *adj.* **1** not perceptible. **2** very slight, gradual, or subtle. □□ **im·per·cep·ti·bil′i·ty** *n.* **im·per·cep′ti·bly** *adv.*

im·per·fect /impárfikt/ ● *adj.* **1** faulty; incomplete. **2** *Gram.* (of a tense) denoting action in progress but not completed (e.g., *they were singing*). ● *n.* imperfect tense. □□ **im·per′fect·ly** *adv.*

im·per·fec·tion /impərfékshən/ *n.* **1** incompleteness. **2** a faultiness. **b** fault or blemish.

im·pe·ri·al /impéereeəl/ *adj.* **1** of or characteristic of an empire or comparable sovereign state. **2** a of or characteristic of an emperor. **b** supreme in authority. **c** majestic. □□ **im·pe′ri·al·ly** *adv.*

im·pe·ri·al·ism /impéereeəlizəm/ *n.* **1** imperial rule or system. **2** usu. *derog.* policy of acquiring dependent territories or extending a country's influence through foreign trade, etc. □□ **im·pe′ri·al·ist** *n. & adj.* **im·pe·ri·al·is′tic** *adj.* **im·pe·ri·al·is′ti·cal·ly** *adv.*

im·per·il /impéril/ *v.tr.* bring or put into danger.

im·pe·ri·ous /impéereeəs/ *adj.* overbearing; domineering. □□ **im·pe′ri·ous·ly** *adv.* **im·pe′ri·ous·ness** *n.*

im·per·ish·a·ble /impérishəbəl/ *adj.* that cannot perish. □□ **im·per·ish·a·bil′i·ty** *n.* **im·per′ish·a·bly** *adv.*

im·per·ma·nent /impármənənt/ *adj.* not permanent; transient. □□ **im·per′ma·nence** *n.* **im·per′ma·nen·cy** *n.* **im·per′ma·nent·ly** *adv.*

im·per·me·a·ble /impśrmeeəbəl/ *adj.* that cannot be penetrated by fluids. □□ **im·per·me·a·bil′i·ty** *n.*

im·per·mis·si·ble /impərmísibəl/ *adj.* not allowable.

im·per·son·al /impársənəl/ *adj.* **1** having no personality. **2** having no personal feeling or reference. **3** *Gram.* **a** (of a verb) used esp. with *it* as a subject (e.g., *it is snowing*). **b** (of a pronoun) = INDEFINITE. □□ **im·per′son·al·ly** *adv.*

im·per·son·ate /impársənayt/ *v.tr.* **1** pretend to be (another person). **2** act (a character). □□ **im·per·son·a·tion** /-náyshən/ *n.* **im·per′son·a·tor** *n.*

im·per·ti·nent /impárt′nənt/ *adj.* rude or insolent. □□ **im·per′ti·nence** *n.* **im·per′ti·nent·ly** *adv.*

im·per·turb·a·ble /impərtśrbəbəl/ *adj.* not excitable; calm. □□ **im·per·turb·a·bil′i·ty** *n.* **im·per·turb′a·bly** *adv.*

im·per·vi·ous /impárveeəs/ *adj.* **1** not responsive to argument, etc. **2** not affording passage to a fluid. □□ **im·per′vi·ous·ly** *adv.* **im·per′vi·ous·ness** *n.*

im·pe·ti·go /impitígō/ *n.* contagious skin infection forming pustules.

im·pet·u·ous /impéchőős/ *adj.* **1** acting or done rashly or with sudden energy. **2** moving forcefully or rapidly. □□ **im·pet·u·os′i·ty** /-ósitee/ *n.* **im·pet′u·ous·ly** *adv.* **im·pet′u·ous·ness** *n.*

im·pe·tus /impitəs/ *n.* **1** force or energy with which a body moves. **2** driving force or impulse.

im·pi·e·ty /impíətee/ *n. (pl.* **-ies**) **1** lack of piety or reverence. **2** an act, etc., showing this.

im·pinge /impínj/ *v.tr.* **1** make an impact; have an effect. **2** encroach. □□ **im·pinge′ment** *n.* **im·ping′er** *n.*

im·pi·ous /impeeəs, impí-/ *adj.* **1** not pious. **2** wicked; profane. □□ **im′pi·ous·ly** *adv.* **im′pi·ous·ness** *n.*

imp·ish /impish/ *adj.* of or like an imp; mischievous. □□ **imp′ish·ly** *adv.* **imp′ish·ness** *n.*

im·pla·ca·ble /implákəbəl/ *adj.* unable to be appeased. □□ **im·pla·ca·bil′i·ty** *n.* **im·plac′a·bly** *adv.*

im·plant ● *v.tr.* /implánt/ **1** insert or fix. **2** instill (an idea, etc.) in a person's mind. **3** plant. **4** *Med.* **a** insert (tissue, etc.) in a living body. **b** (of a fertilized ovum) become attached to the wall of the womb. ● *n.* /implant/ thing implanted. □□ **im·plan·ta′tion** *n.*

im·plau·si·ble /impláwzibəl/ *adj.* not plausible. □□ **im·plau·si·bil′i·ty** *n.* **im·plau′si·bly** *adv.*

im·ple·ment ● *n.* /implimənt/ **1** tool, instrument, or utensil. **2** (in *pl.*) equipment; articles of furniture, etc. ● *v.tr.* /impliment/ **1** a put (a decision, plan, etc.) into effect. **b** fulfill (an undertaking). **2** complete (a contract, etc.). **3** fill up; supplement. □□ **im·ple·men·ta′tion** *n.*

im·pli·cate ● *v.tr.* /implikayt/ **1** show (a person) to be involved (in a crime, etc.). **2** (in *passive*; often foll. by *in*) be affected or involved. ● *n.* /implikət/ thing implied.

---

implicate late Middle English: from Latin *implicatus* 'folded in,' past participle of *implicare* (source of *imply*). The original sense was 'entwine, entangle.' An early modern sense, synonymous with *imply*, dates from the early 17th century.

im·pli·ca·tion /ímplikáyshən/ *n.* **1** thing implied. **2** act of implicating or implying.

im·plic·it /implísit/ *adj.* **1** implied though not plainly expressed. **2** absolute; unquestioning; unreserved. □□ **im·plic´it·ly** *adv.* **im·plic´it·ness** *n.*

im·plode /implṓd/ *v.* burst or cause to burst inward. □□ **im·plo·sion** /-plṓzhən/ *n.* **im·plo·sive** /-plṓsiv/ *adj.*

im·plore /impláwr/ *v.tr.* **1** entreat (a person). **2** beg earnestly for. □□ **im·plor´ing** *adj.* **im·plor´ing·ly** *adv.*

im·ply /implī́/ *v.tr.* (**-plies, -plied**) **1** strongly suggest the truth or existence of (a thing not expressly asserted). **2** insinuate; hint (*what are you implying?*). **3** signify. □□ **im·plied´** *adj.* ¶ See note at INFER.

> **imply** late Middle English: from Old French *emplier*, from Latin *implicare*, from *in-* 'in' + *plicare* 'to fold' (source of *implicate*). The original sense was 'entwine, entangle'; in the 16th and 17th centuries the word also meant 'employ.'

im·po·lite /ímpəlī́t/ *adj.* ill-mannered; uncivil; rude. □□ **im·po·lite´ly** *adv.* **im·po·lite´ness** *n.*

im·pol·i·tic /impólitik/ *adj.* **1** inexpedient; unwise. **2** not politic. □□ **im·pol´i·tic·ly** *adv.*

im·pon·der·a·ble /impóndərəbəl/ • *adj.* not able to be estimated. • *n.* (usu. in *pl.*) something difficult to assess. □□ **im·pon·der·a·bil´i·ty** *n.* **im·pon´der·a·bly** *adv.*

im·port • *v.tr.* /impáwrt, ím-/ **1** bring in (goods) to a country. **2 a** indicate; signify. **b** make known. • *n.* /ímpawrt/ **1** process of importing. **2 a** imported article. **b** (in *pl.*) amount imported (*imports exceeded $50 billion*). **3** meaning. **4** importance. □□ **im·port´a·ble** *adj.* **im·por·ta´tion** *n.* **im·port´er** *n.* (all in sense 1 of *v.*).

im·por·tant /impáwrt´nt/ *adj.* **1** of great effect or consequence; momentous. **2** having high rank or great authority. □□ **im·por´tance** *n.* **im·por´tant·ly** *adv.*

im·por·tu·nate /impáwrchənət/ *adj.* making persistent requests. □□ **im·por´tu·nate·ly** *adv.* **im·por·tu·ni·ty** /-tōōnátee, -tyōō-/ *n.*

im·por·tune /ímpáwrtōṓn, -tyōṓn, impáwrchən/ *v.tr.* solicit (a person) pressingly.

im·pose /impṓz/ *v.* **1** *tr.* lay (a tax, duty, charge, or obligation) on. **2** *tr.* enforce compliance with. **3** *intr.* & *refl.* (foll. by *on, upon,* or *absol.*) demand the attention or commitment of (a person) (*I do not want to impose on you any longer*). □□ **im·po·si´tion** *n.*

im·pos·ing /impṓzing/ *adj.* impressive or formidable, esp. in appearance. □□ **im·pos´ing·ly** *adv.*

im·pos·si·ble /impósibəl/ *adj.* **1** not possible. **2** (loosely) not easy, convenient, or believable. **3** *colloq.* (of a person) outrageous; intolerable. □□ **im·pos·si·bil´i·ty** *n.* **im·pos´si·bly** *adv.*

im·post /ímpōst/ *n.* tax; duty; tribute.

im·pos·tor /impóstər/ *n.* (also **im·pos´ter**) **1** person who pretends to be someone else. **2** swindler.

im·pos·ture /impós-chər/ *n.* fraudulent deception.

im·po·tent /ímpət´nt/ *adj.* **1 a** powerless. **b** helpless. **c** ineffective. **2 a** (esp. of a male) unable to achieve an erection or orgasm. **b** *colloq.* unable to procreate; infertile. □□ **im´po·tence** *n.* **im´po·ten·cy** *n.* **im´po·tent·ly** *adv.*

im·pound /impównd/ *v.tr.* **1** confiscate. **2** take possession of. **3** shut up (animals) in a pound. □□ **im·pound´a·ble** *adj.* **im·pound´er** *n.* **im·pound´ment** *n.*

im·pov·er·ish /impóvərish/ *v.tr.* (often as **impoverished** *adj.*) **1** make poor. **2** exhaust the strength or natural fertility of. □□ **im·pov´er·ish·ment** *n.*

im·prac·ti·ca·ble /impráktikəbəl/ *adj.* impossible in practice. □□ **im·prac·ti·ca·bil´i·ty** *n.* **im·prac´ti·ca·bly** *adv.*

im·prac·ti·cal /impráktikəl/ *adj.* **1** not practical. **2** not practicable. □□ **im·prac·ti·cal·i·ty** /-kálitee/ *n.* **im·prac´ti·cal·ly** *adv.*

im·pre·ca·tion /ímprikáyshən/ *n.* a curse; malediction.

im·pre·cise /ímprisī́s/ *adj.* not precise. □□ **im·pre·cise´ly** *adv.* **im·pre·ci´sion** /-sízhən/ *n.*

im·preg·na·ble /imprégnəbəl/ *adj.* **1** (of a fortified position) that cannot be taken by force. **2** resistant to attack or criticism. □□ **im·preg·na·bil´i·ty** /-bílitee/ *n.* **im·preg´na·bly** *adv.*

im·preg·nate /imprégnayt/ *v.tr.* **1** fill or saturate. **2** imbue (with feelings, moral qualities, etc.). **3 a** make (a female) pregnant. **b** *Biol.* fertilize an ovum. □□ **im·preg·na·tion** /-náyshən/ *n.*

im·pre·sa·ri·o /ímprisáareeō, -sáir-/ *n.* (*pl.* **-os**) organizer of public entertainments, esp. a theatrical, etc., manager.

im·press • *v.tr.* /imprés/ **1 a** affect or influence deeply. **b** affect (a person) favorably. **2** emphasize (an idea, etc.). **3 a** imprint or stamp. **b** apply (a mark, etc.) with pressure. **4** make a mark or design on (a thing) with a stamp, seal, etc. • *n.* /ímpres/ **1** instance of impressing. **2** mark made by a seal, stamp, etc. **3** characteristic mark or quality. **4** = IMPRESSION. □□ **im·press´i·ble** *adj.*

im·pres·sion /impréshən/ *n.* **1** effect produced (esp. on the mind or feelings). **2** vague notion or belief. **3** imitation of a person or sound, esp. done to entertain. **4 a** impressing of a mark. **b** mark impressed.

im·pres·sion·a·ble /impréshənəbəl/ *adj.* easily influenced. □□ **im·pres·sion·a·bil´i·ty** *n.* **im·pres´sion·a·bly** *adv.*

im·pres·sion·ism /impréshənizəm/ *n.* style or movement in art, music, etc., that seeks to convey a brief impression or emotion without close, realistic detail. □□ **im·pres´sion·ist** *n.* **im·pres·sion·is·tic** /impréshənístik/ *adj.*

im·pres·sive /imprésiv/ *adj.* causing approval or admiration. □□ **im·pres´sive·ly** *adv.* **im·pres´sive·ness** *n.*

im·pri·ma·tur /imprimáatər, -máytər, -tōōr/ *n.* **1** *RC Ch.* official license to print (a religious book, etc.). **2** official approval.

im·print • *v.tr.* /imprínt/ **1** impress or establish firmly, on the mind. **2 a** make a stamp or impression of (a figure, etc.) on a thing. **b** make an impression on (a thing) with a stamp, etc. • *n.* /ímprint/ **1** impression or stamp. **2** printer's or publisher's name, etc., printed in a book.

im·pris·on /imprízən/ *v.tr.* **1** put into prison. **2** confine; shut up. □□ **im·pris´on·ment** *n.*

im·prob·a·ble /impróbəbəl/ *adj.* **1** unlikely. **2** difficult to believe. □□ **im·prob·a·bil´i·ty** *n.* **im·prob´a·bly** *adv.*

im·promp·tu /imprómptōō, -tyōō/ • *adj.* & *adv.*

extempore; unrehearsed. • *n.* extempore performance.

im·prop·er /imprópər/ *adj.* **1 a** unseemly; indecent. **b** not in accordance with accepted rules of behavior. **2** inaccurate; wrong. □□ **im·prop′er·ly** *adv.*

im·pro·pri·e·ty /ímprəprîətee/ *n.* (*pl.* **-ties**) **1** indecency. **2** instance of this. **3** incorrectness. **4** unfitness.

im·prove /impro͞ov/ *v.* **1 a** *tr.* & *intr.* make or become better. **b** *intr.* (foll. by *on*, *upon*) produce something better than. **2** (as **improving** *adj.*) giving moral benefit. □□ **im·prov′a·ble** *adj.* **im·prove′ment** *n.*

improve early 16th century (as *emprowe* or *improwe*): from Anglo-Norman French *emprower* (based on Old French *prou* 'profit,' ultimately from the Latin verb *prodest* 'is of advantage'); *-owe* was changed to *-ove* under the influence of *prove*. The original sense was 'make a profit, increase the value of'; subsequently 'make greater in amount or degree,' which led to sense 1 (early 17th century).

im·prov·i·dent /impróvid'nt/ *adj.* **1** lacking foresight. **2** wasteful. **3** heedless; incautious. □□ **im·prov·i·dence** /-d'ns/ *n.* **im·prov′i·dent·ly** *adv.*

im·pro·vise /ímprəvīz/ *v.tr.* (also *absol.*) **1** compose or perform (music, verse, etc.) extempore. **2** provide or construct (a thing) extempore. □□ **im·pro·vi·sa·tion** /-izáyshən/ *n.* **im·pro·vi·sa′tion·al** *adj.* **im′pro·vi·ser** *n.*

im·pru·dent /impro͞od'nt/ *adj.* rash; indiscreet. □□ **im·pru·dence** /-d'ns/ *n.* **im·pru′dent·ly** *adv.*

im·pu·dent /ímpyəd'nt/ *adj.* impertinent. □□ **im·pu·dence** /-d'ns/ *n.* **im′pu·dent·ly** *adv.*

im·pugn /impyo͞on/ *v.tr.* challenge or call in question (a statement, action, etc.). □□ **im·pugn′a·ble** *adj.*

im·pulse /ímpuls/ *n.* **1** act of impelling; a push. **2** impetus. **3** *Electr.* surge in current or flow. **4** mental incitement. **5** sudden desire or tendency to act without reflection (*did it on impulse*).

im·pul·sion /impúlshən/ *n.* **1** impelling. **2** mental impulse. **3** impetus.

im·pul·sive /impúlsiv/ *adj.* **1** apt to act on impulse. **2** tending to impel. □□ **im·pul′sive·ly** *adv.* **im·pul′sive·ness** *n.*

im·pu·ni·ty /impyo͞onitee/ *n.* exemption from punishment, bad consequences, etc. □ **with impunity** without punishment.

im·pure /impyo͞or/ *adj.* **1** adulterated. **2 a** dirty. **b** ceremonially unclean. **3** unchaste. □□ **im·pure′ly** *adv.* **im·pure′ness** *n.*

im·pu·ri·ty /impyo͞oritee/ *n.* (*pl.* **-ties**) **1** being impure. **2** impure thing or constituent.

im·pute /impyo͞ot/ *v.tr.* (foll. by *to*) attribute (a fault, etc.) to. □□ **im·put′a·ble** *adj.* **im·pu·ta′tion** *n.* **im·pu′ta·tive** *adj.*

IN *abbr.* Indiana (in official postal use).

In *symb. Chem.* indium.

in /in/ • *prep.* **1** expressing inclusion or position within limits of space, time, circumstance, etc. (*in Nebraska; in bed; in the rain*). **2** during the time of. **3** within the time of (*will be back in two hours*). **4 a** with respect to (*blind in one eye*). **b** as a kind of (*the latest thing in luxury*). **5** as a proportionate part of (*one in three failed*). **6** with the form or arrangement of (*packed in tens*). **7** as a member of (*in the army*). **8** concerned with (*is in politics*). **9** as the content of (*there is something in what you say*). **10** within the ability of (*does he have it in him?*). **11** having the condition of; affected by (*in bad health*). **12** having as a purpose (*in reply to*). **13** by means of or using as material (*drawn in pencil*). **14 a** using for expression (*written in French*). **b** (of music) having as its key (*symphony in C*). **15** (of a word) having as a part (*words beginning in un-*). **16** wearing (*in a suit*). **17** with the identity of (*found a friend in Mary*). **18** into (with a verb of motion or change: *put it in the box*). • *adv.* expressing position within limits, or motion to such a position: **1** into a room, house, etc. (*come in*). **2** at home, in one's office, etc. (*is not in*). **3** so as to be enclosed or confined (*locked in*). **4** in a publication (*is the advertisement in?*). **5** in or to the inward side (*rub it in*). **6** in fashion or season (*long skirts are in*). **7** exerting favorable action or influence (*their luck was in*). **8** (of a season, harvest, order, etc.) having arrived or been received. **9** (of the tide) at the highest point. • *adj.* **1** internal; inside. **2** fashionable. **3** confined to a small group (*in-joke*). □ **in on** privy to (a secret, etc.). **ins and outs** all the details. **in that** because; in so far as. **in with** on good terms with.

in. *abbr.* inch(es).

in-¹ /in/ *prefix* (also **il-, im-, ir-**) added to: **1** adjectives, meaning 'not' (*inedible; insane*). **2** nouns, meaning 'without; lacking' (*inaction*).

in·a·bil·i·ty *n.*	in·ar·tis·tic *adj.*
in·ac·ces·si·bil·i·ty *n.*	in·at·ten·tive *adj.*
in·ac·ces·si·bly *adv.*	in·au·di·ble *adj.*
in·ac·cu·ra·cy *adj.*	in·au·di·bly *adv.*
in·ac·cu·rate *adj.*	in·aus·pi·cious *adj.*
in·ac·cu·rate·ly *adv.*	in·aus·pi·cious·ly *adv.*
in·ac·tive *adj.*	in·ca·pa·ble *adj.*
in·ac·tiv·i·ty *n.*	in·cau·tious *adj.*
in·ad·e·qua·cy *n.*	in·ci·vil·i·ty *n.*
in·ad·e·quate *adj.*	in·com·mu·ni·ca·ble *adj.*
in·ad·e·quate·ly *adv.*	in·com·pre·hen·si·ble *adj.*
in·ad·mis·si·ble *adj.*	in·com·pre·hen·si·bly *adv.*
in·an·i·mate *adj.*	in·cor·rect *adj.*
in·ap·pro·pri·ate *adj.*	in·cor·rect·ly *adv.*
in·ap·pro·pri·ate·ly *adv.*	in·cur·a·ble *adj.*
in·apt *adj.*	in·cur·a·bly *adv.*
in·ar·gu·a·ble *adj.*	in·dec·o·rous *adj.*
in·ar·gu·a·bly *adv.*	in·dec·o·rous·ly *adv.*
	in·de·fin·a·ble *adj.*
in·de·fin·a·bly *adv.*	in·ex·pen·sive·ly *adv.*
in·dis·cern·i·ble *adj.*	in·fer·tile *adj.*
in·dis·put·a·ble *adj.*	in·fer·til·i·ty *n.*
in·dis·put·a·bly *adv.*	in·hu·mane *adj.*
in·dis·tinct *adj.*	in·ju·di·cious *adj.*
in·dis·tinct·ly *adv.*	in·op·por·tune *adj.*
in·dis·tin·guish·a·ble *adj.*	in·op·por·tune·ly *adv.*
in·di·vis·i·ble *adj.*	in·sep·a·ra·ble *adj.*
in·ed·i·ble *adj.*	in·sep·a·ra·bly *n.*
in·ed·u·ca·ble *adj.*	in·sig·nif·i·cance *n.*
in·ef·fec·tive *adj.*	in·solv·a·ble *adj.*
in·ef·fec·tive·ly *adv.*	in·suf·fi·cient *adj.*
in·ef·fi·ca·cy *n.*	in·suf·fi·cient·ly *adv.*
in·e·las·tic *adj.*	in·sur·mount·a·ble *adj.*
in·el·i·gi·ble *adj.*	in·sus·cep·ti·ble *adj.*
in·ex·act *adj.*	in·var·i·a·ble *adj.* & *n.*
in·ex·pe·di·ent *adj.*	in·var·i·a·bly *adv.*
in·ex·pe·di·ence *n.*	
in·ex·pen·sive *adj.*	

in-² /in/ *prefix* (also **il-** before *l*, **im-** before *b*, *m*, *p*, **ir-** before *r*) in, on, into, toward, within (*induce*; *influx*; *insight*; *intrude*).

in ab·sen·tia /ín absénshə/ *adv.* in (his, her, or their) absence.

in·ad·ver·tent /ínədvə́rt'nt/ *adj.* **1** (of an action) unintentional. **2 a** not properly attentive. **b** negligent. □□ **in·ad·ver·tence** /-t'ns/ *n.* **in·ad·ver'ten·cy** *n.* **in·ad·ver'tent·ly** *adv.*

in·a·lien·a·ble /ináyleeənəbəl/ *adj.* that cannot be transferred to another. □□ **in·a'lien·a·bly** *adv.*

in·am·o·ra·to /ináməraátō/ *n.* (*pl.* **-os**) (*fem.* **in·am·o·ra·ta** /-tə/) lover.

in·ane /ináyn/ *adj.* **1** silly; senseless. **2** empty; void. □□ **in·ane'ly** *adv.* **in·an·i·ty** /-ánitee/ *n.* (*pl.* **-ties**)

in·ar·tic·u·late /ínaartíkyələt/ *adj.* **1** unable to express oneself clearly. **2** (of speech) indistinctly pronounced. **3** mute. □□ **in·ar·tic'u·late·ly** *adv.* **in·ar·tic'u·late·ness** *n.*

in·as·much /ínəzmúch/ *adv.* (foll. by *as*) **1** since; because. **2** to the extent that.

in·au·gu·ral /ináwgyərəl/ ● *adj.* **1** of inauguration. **2** (of a lecture, etc.) given by a person being inaugurated. ● *n.* an inaugural speech, etc.

in·au·gu·rate /ináwgyərayt/ *v.tr.* **1** admit formally to office. **2** initiate the public use of (a building, etc.). **3** begin; introduce. □□ **in·au·gu·ra·tion** /-ráyshən/ *n.* **in·au'gu·ra·tor** *n.* **in·au·gu·ra·to·ry** /-rətáwree/ *adj.*

in·board /ínbawrd/ ● *adv.* within the sides of or toward the center of a ship, aircraft, or vehicle. ● *adj.* situated inboard.

in·born /ínbáwrn/ *adj.* existing from birth.

in·bred /ínbréd/ *adj.* **1** inborn. **2** produced by inbreeding.

in·breed·ing /ínbreéding/ *n.* breeding from closely related animals or persons. □□ **in'breed** *v.* (*past* and *past part.* **in·bred**).

inc. *abbr.* **1** (esp. **Inc.**) Incorporated. **2** incomplete.

In·ca /ingkə/ *n.* member of a Native American people in Peru before the Spanish conquest. □□ **In'can** *adj.*

in·cal·cu·la·ble /inkálkyələbəl/ *adj.* **1** too great for calculation. **2** unpredictable. □□ **in·cal·cu·la·bil'i·ty** *n.* **in·cal'cu·la·bly** *adv.*

in·can·des·cent /ínkandésənt/ *adj.* **1** glowing with heat. **2** shining brightly. **3** (of artificial light) produced by a glowing filament. □□ **in·can·des'cence** *n.* **in·can·des'cent·ly** *adv.*

in·can·ta·tion /ínkantáyshən/ *n.* **1 a** magical formula. **b** the use of this. **2** spell or charm. □□ **in·can·ta'tion·al** *adj.*

in·ca·pac·i·tate /ínkəpásitayt/ *v.tr.* **1** render incapable or unfit. **2** disqualify. □□ **in·ca·pac·i·ta·tion** /-táyshən/ *n.*

in·ca·pac·i·ty /ínkəpásitee/ *n.* (*pl.* **-ties**) **1** inability. **2** legal disqualification.

in·car·cer·ate /inkaársərayt/ *v.tr.* imprison or confine. □□ **in·car·cer·a·tion** /-ráyshən/ *n.* **in·car'cer·a·tor** *n.*

in·car·nate ● *adj.* /inka'arnət, -nayt/ **1** embodied in human form (*is the devil incarnate*). **2** represented in a recognizable or typical form (*folly incarnate*). ● *v.tr.* /inka'árnayt/ **1** embody in flesh. **2** put (an idea, etc.) into concrete form; realize. **3** (of a person, etc.) be the living embodiment of (a quality).

in·car·na·tion /ínkaarnáyshən/ *n.* **1 a** embodiment in (esp. human) flesh. **b** (**the Incarnation**) *Theol.* the embodiment of God the Son in human flesh as Jesus Christ. **2** living type (of a quality, etc.).

in·cen·di·ar·y /inséndee-eree/ ● *adj.* **1** (of a bomb) designed to cause fires. **2** of or relating to the malicious setting on fire of property. **3** tending to stir up strife. ● *n.* (*pl.* **-ies**) **1** fire bomb or device. **2** arsonist. □□ **in·cen'di·ar·ism** *n.*

in·cense¹ /ínsens/ ● *n.* **1** gum or spice producing a sweet smell when burned. **2** the smoke of this. ● *v.tr.* **1** treat or perfume (a person or thing) with incense. **2** burn incense to (a deity, etc.).

in·cense² /inséns/ *v.tr.* (often foll. by *at*, *with*, *against*) enrage; make angry.

---

incense Middle English (originally as *encense*): from Old French *encens* (noun), *encenser* (verb), from ecclesiastical Latin *incensum* 'something burnt, incense,' neuter past participle of *incendere* 'set fire to,' from *in-* 'in' + *candere* 'to glow.'

---

in·cen·tive /inséntiv/ ● *n.* **1** motive or incitement to action. **2** payment or concession to stimulate greater output by workers. ● *adj.* serving to motivate or incite.

in·cep·tion /insépshən/ *n.* beginning.

in·ces·sant /insésənt/ *adj.* unceasing; continual; repeated. □□ **in·ces'san·cy** *n.* **in·ces'sant·ly** *adv.* **in·ces'sant·ness** *n.*

in·cest /ínsest/ *n.* sexual intercourse between persons regarded as too closely related to legally marry each other.

in·ces·tu·ous /inséschoōəs/ *adj.* **1** involving or guilty of incest. **2** (of human relations generally) excessively restricted or resistant to wider influence. □□ **in·ces'tu·ous·ly** *adv.*

inch /inch/ ● *n.* **1** unit of linear measure equal to one-twelfth of a foot (2.54 cm). **2** small amount (usu. with *neg.*: *would not yield an inch*). ● *v.* move gradually (*inched forward*). □ **every inch** **1** entirely (*every inch a judge*). **2** the whole distance or area (*combed every inch of the garden*). **within an inch of** almost to the point of.

in·cho·ate /inkóit/ *adj.* **1** just begun. **2** undeveloped; rudimentary; unformed. □□ **in·cho'ate·ly** *adv.* **in·cho'ate·ness** *n.* **in·cho'a·tive** *adj.*

¶ **Inchoate** means 'just begun, rudimentary, undeveloped,' e.g., *All was as yet in an inchoate state*, but it is often used incorrectly to mean 'chaotic' or 'incoherent.' The *ch* is pronounced hard, like *k*.

in·ci·dence /ínsidəns/ *n.* **1** fact, manner, or rate of occurrence or action. **2** range, scope, or extent of influence of a thing. **3** *Physics* the falling of a line, or of a thing moving in a line, upon a surface.

¶ **Incidence** and **incidents** sound the same, but **incidence** is more often used in technical contexts, referring to the frequency with which something occurs: *Increased UV is likely to cause increased incidence of skin cancer. Incidents* is simply the plural of *incident*, an event: *The police are supposed to investigate any incidents of domestic violence.* The form "incidences" should be avoided.

in·ci·dent /ínsidənt/ • *n.* **1 a** occurrence. **b** minor event attracting general attention. **2** hostile clash, esp. of warring troops. • *adj.* **1** (often foll. by *to*) apt or liable to happen; naturally attaching. **2** (of light, etc.) falling on or upon.

in·ci·den·tal /ínsidéntəl/ *adj.* **1 a** having a minor role in relation to a more important thing, event, etc. **b** not essential. **c** casual. **2** (foll. by *to*) liable to happen.

in·ci·den·tal·ly /ínsidént'lee/ *adv.* **1** by the way; as an unconnected remark. **2** in an incidental way.

in·cin·er·ate /insínərayt/ *v.tr.* burn to ashes. □□ **in·cin·er·a·tion** /-ráyshən/ *n.* **in·cin'er·a·tor** *n.*

in·cip·i·ent /insípeeənt/ *adj.* **1** beginning. **2** in an initial stage. □□ **in·cip'i·ence** *n.* **in·cip'i·en·cy** *n.* **in·cip'i·ent·ly** *adv.*

in·cise /insíz/ *v.tr.* **1** make a cut in. **2** engrave.

in·ci·sion /insízhən/ *n.* **1** a cut, esp. by a surgeon. **2** act of cutting into a thing.

in·ci·sive /insísiv/ *adj.* **1** mentally sharp. **2** clear and effective. **3** penetrating. □□ **in·ci'sive·ly** *adv.* **in·ci'sive·ness** *n.*

in·ci·sor /insízər/ *n.* cutting tooth, esp. at the front of the mouth.

in·cite /insít/ *v.tr.* urge or stir up. □□ **in·cite'ment** *n.* **in·cit'er** *n.*

in·clem·ent /inklémənt/ *adj.* (of the weather) severe; stormy. □□ **in·clem'en·cy** *n.* (*pl.* **-cies**). **in·clem'ent·ly** *adv.*

in·cli·na·tion /ínklináyshən/ *n.* **1** disposition or propensity. **2** liking or affection. **3** leaning, slope, or slant.

in·cline • *v.* /inklín/ **1** *tr.* **a** make (a person, etc.) willing (*am inclined to think so*). **b** have a tendency (*the door is inclined to bang*). **2** *intr.* **a** be disposed (*I incline to think so*). **b** tend. **3** *intr.* & *tr.* lean or slope. • *n.* /ínklīn/ slope. □□ **in·clin'er** *n.*

in·clude /inklốod/ *v.tr.* **1** comprise or reckon in as part of a whole; place in a class or category. **2** (as **including** *prep.*) if we include (*six members, including the chairperson*). **3** treat or regard as so included. □□ **in·clud'a·ble** *adj.* **in·clud·i·ble** *adj.* **in·clu'sion** /-klốozhən/ *n.*

in·clu·sive /inklốosiv/ *adj.* **1** (often foll. by *of*) including; comprising. **2** including the limits stated (*pages 7 to 26 inclusive*). **3** including all the normal services, etc. (*a hotel offering inclusive terms*). □ **inclusive language** language that is deliberately nonsexist, esp. avoiding the use of masculine pronouns to cover both men and women. □□ **in·clu'sive·ly** *adv.* **in·clu'sive·ness** *n.*

in·cog·ni·to /ínkogneétō, -kógni-/ • *adj.* & *adv.* with one's name or identity kept secret. • *n.* (*pl.* **-os**) **1** person who is incognito. **2** pretended identity of such a person.

in·co·her·ent /ínkōheérənt/ *adj.* **1** unable to speak intelligibly. **2** lacking logic or consistency. □□ **in·co·her'ence** *n.* **in·co·her'en·cy** *n.* (*pl.* **-cies**). **in·co·her'ent·ly** *adv.*

in·come /ínkum/ *n.* money received from one's work, investments, etc.

in·com·ing /ínkuming/ • *adj.* **1** coming in (*incoming telephone calls*). **2** succeeding another (*incoming tenant*). • *n.* **1** (usu. in *pl.*) revenue; income. **2** act of arriving or entering.

in·com·mu·ni·ca·do /ínkəmyōonikaádō/ *adj.* **1** without means of communication. **2** in solitary confinement.

in·com·pa·ra·ble /inkómpərəbəl/ *adj.* without an equal. □□ **in·com·pa·ra·bil'i·ty** *n.* **in·com'pa·ra·ble·ness** *n.* **in·com'pa·ra·bly** *adv.*

in·com·pat·i·ble /ínkəmpátibəl/ *adj.* **1** opposed in character; discordant. **2** inconsistent. **3** unable to live together in harmony. □□ **in·com·pat·i·bil'i·ty** *n.* **in·com·pat'i·bly** *adv.*

in·com·pe·tent /inkómpit'nt/ • *adj.* **1** not able to perform a particular task (*incompetent builder*). **2** showing a lack of skill (*incompetent performance*). • *n.* incompetent person. □□ **in·com·pe·tence** /-t'ns/ *n.* **in·com'pe·ten·cy** *n.* **in·com'pe·tent·ly** *adv.*

in·com·plete /ínkəmpleét/ *adj.* not complete. □□ **in·com·plete'ly** *adv.* **in·com·plete'ness** *n.*

in·con·ceiv·a·ble /ínkənseéevəbəl/ *adj.* **1** unimaginable. **2** *colloq.* very remarkable. □□ **in·con·ceiv'a·bly** *adv.*

in·con·clu·sive /ínkənklốosiv/ *adj.* (of an argument, evidence, or action) not decisive or convincing. □□ **in·con·clu'sive·ly** *adv.* **in·con·clu'sive·ness** *n.*

in·con·gru·ous /inkónggrōoəs/ *adj.* **1** out of place; absurd. **2** disagreeing; out of keeping. □□ **in·con·gru'i·ty** *n.* (*pl.* **-ties**). **in·con'gru·ous·ly** *adv.*

in·con·se·quen·tial /ínkónsikwénshəl, ínkon-/ *adj.* unimportant. □□ **in·con·se·quen·tial·i·ty** /-sheeálitee/ *n.* (*pl.* **-ties**). **in·con·se·quen'tial·ly** *adv.*

in·con·sid·er·a·ble /ínkənsídərəbəl/ *adj.* **1** of small size, value, etc. **2** not worth considering. □□ **in·con·sid'er·a·bly** *adv.*

in·con·sid·er·ate /ínkənsídərət/ *adj.* **1** thoughtless; rash. **2** lacking regard for others. □□ **in·con·sid'er·ate·ly** *adv.* **in·con·sid·er·a·tion** /-ráyshən/ *n.*

in·con·sist·ent /ínkənsístənt/ *adj.* **1** acting at variance with one's own principles or former conduct. **2** not in keeping; incompatible. **3** (of a single thing) incompatible or discordant; having self-contradictory parts. □□ **in·con·sist'en·cy** *n.* (*pl.* **-cies**). **in·con·sist'ent·ly** *adv.*

in·con·sol·a·ble /ínkənsóləbəl/ *adj.* (of a person, grief, etc.) that cannot be comforted. □□ **in·con·sol'a·bly** *adv.*

in·con·spic·u·ous /ínkənspíkyōoəs/ *adj.* not easily noticed. □□ **in·con·spic'u·ous·ly** *adv.* **in·con·spic'u·ous·ness** *n.*

in·con·stant /inkónstənt/ *adj.* **1** fickle; changeable. **2** variable; irregular. □□ **in·con'stan·cy** *n.* (*pl.* **-cies**). **in·con'stant·ly** *adv.*

in·con·test·a·ble /ínkəntéstəbəl/ *adj.* that cannot be disputed. □□ **in·con·test·a·bil'i·ty** *n.* **in·con·test'a·bly** *adv.*

in·con·ti·nent /inkóntinənt/ *adj.* **1** unable to control the bowels or bladder. **2** lacking self-restraint (esp. in sexual desire). □□ **in·con·ti·nence** /-nəns/ *n.* **in·con'ti·nent·ly** *adv.*

in·con·tro·vert·i·ble /ínkontrəvə́rtibəl/ *adj.* indisputable; indubitable. □□ **in·con·tro·vert'i·bly** *adv.*

in·con·ven·ience /ínkənveényəns/ • *n.* **1** lack of comfort or ease. **2** cause or instance of this. • *v.tr.* cause inconvenience to.

in·con·ven·ient /ínkənveényənt/ *adj.* **1** unfavorable to ease or comfort; not convenient. **2** awkward; troublesome. □□ **in·con·ven'ient·ly** *adv.*

in·cor·po·rate ● *v.* /inkáwrpərayt/ **1** *tr.* unite; form into one body. **2** *intr.* become incorporated. **3** *tr.* combine (ingredients) into one substance. **4** *tr.* admit as a member of a company, etc. **5** *tr.* **a** constitute as a legal corporation. **b** (as **incorporated** *adj.*) forming a legal corporation. ● *adj.* /inkáwrpərət/ (of a company, etc.) formed into a legal corporation. □□ **in·cor·po·ra·tion** /-áyshən/ *n.* **in·cor´po·ra·tor** *n.*

in·cor·po·re·al /ínkawrpáwreeəl/ *adj.* **1** not composed of matter. **2** of immaterial beings. □□ **in·cor·po·re·al·i·ty** /-reeálitee/ *n.* **in·cor·po´re·al·ly** *adv.*

in·cor·ri·gi·ble /inkáwrijibəl, -kór-/ *adj.* **1** (of a person or habit) incurably bad or depraved. **2** not readily improved. □□ **in·cor·ri·gi·bil´i·ty** *n.* **in·cor´ri·gi·ble·ness** *n.* **in·cor´ri·gi·bly** *adv.*

in·cor·rupt·i·ble /ínkərúptibəl/ *adj.* **1** that cannot be corrupted, esp. by bribery. **2** that cannot decay; everlasting. □□ **in·cor·rupt·i·bil´i·ty** *n.* **in·cor·rupt´i·bly** *adv.*

in·crease ● *v.* /inkree's/ **1** *tr. & intr.* make or become greater or more numerous. **2** *intr.* advance (in quality, attainment, etc.). **3** *tr.* intensify (a quality). ● *n.* /ínkrees/ **1** growth; enlargement. **2** multiplication. **3** amount or extent of an increase. □□ **in·creas´a·ble** *adj.* **in·creas´er** *n.* **in·creas´ing·ly** *adv.*

in·cred·i·ble /inkrédibəl/ *adj.* **1** not believable. **2** *colloq.* amazing. □□ **in·cred´i·ble·ness** *n.* **in·cred´i·bly** *adv.*

¶ The adjective **incredible** means 'unbelievable' or 'not convincing' and can be applied to a situation, statement, policy, or threat to a person, e.g., *I find this testimony incredible.* **Incredulous** means 'disinclined to believe; skeptical' and is usually applied to a person's attitude, e.g., *You shouldn't wonder that I'm incredulous after all your lies.*

in·cred·u·lous /inkréjələs/ *adj.* (often foll. by *of*) unwilling to believe. □□ **in·cre·du·li·ty** /inkrido͞olitee, -dyo͞o-/ *n.* **in·cred´u·lous·ly** *adv.*

in·cre·ment /ínkrimənt/ *n.* **1** a increase or addition, esp. one of a series on a fixed scale. **b** amount of this. **2** *Math.* a small amount by which a variable quantity increases. □□ **in·cre·ment·al** /-mént´l/ *adj.*

in·crim·i·nate /inkríminayt/ *v.tr.* **1** tend to prove the guilt of (*incriminating evidence*). **2** charge with a crime. □□ **in·crim´i·na·tion** /-náyshən/ *n.* **in·crim´i·na·to·ry** /-nətáwree/ *adj.*

in·crus·ta·tion /ínkrustáyshən/ *n.* **1** encrusting. **2** crust or hard coating. **3** concretion or deposit on a surface.

in·cu·bate /íngkyəbayt/ *v.* **1** *tr.* sit on or artificially heat (eggs) in order to hatch them. **2** *tr.* cause to develop. **3** *intr.* sit on eggs; brood.

in·cu·ba·tion /íngkyəbáyshən/ *n.* **1 a** incubating. **b** brooding. **2** *Med.* period between infection and the appearance of the first symptoms.

in·cu·ba·tor /íngkyəbaytər/ *n.* warming apparatus for protecting a premature baby, hatching eggs, etc.

in·cu·bus /íngkyəbəs/ *n.* (*pl.* **in·cu·bi** /-bī/ or **in·cu·bus·es**) **1** evil spirit supposed to descend on sleeping women. **2** nightmare. **3** person or thing that oppresses like a nightmare.

in·cul·cate /ínkúlkayt/ *v.tr.* urge or impress (a fact, habit, or idea) persistently. □□ **in·cul·ca·tion** /-káyshən/ *n.* **in·cul´ca·tor** *n.*

in·cum·ben·cy /inkúmbənsee/ *n.* (*pl.* **-cies**) office, tenure, or sphere of an incumbent.

in·cum·bent /inkúmbənt/ ● *adj.* **1** (foll. by *on*, *upon*) resting as a duty (*incumbent on you to warn them*). **2** currently holding office. ● *n.* holder of an office or post.

in·cu·nab·u·lum /ínkyənábyələm/ *n.* (*pl.* **in·cu·nab·u·la** /-lə/) **1** book printed before 1501. **2** (in *pl.*) early stages of a thing.

in·cur /inkór/ *v.tr.* (**in·curred, in·cur·ring**) suffer or experience (something unpleasant) as a result of one's own behavior, etc. (*incurred huge debts*). □□ **in·cur´ra·ble** *adj.*

in·cu·ri·ous /inkyo͞oreeəs/ *adj.* lacking curiosity. □□ **in·cu·ri·os·i·ty** /-reeósitee/ *n.* **in·cu´ri·ous·ly** *adv.* **in·cu´ri·ous·ness** *n.*

in·cur·sion /inkórzhən, -shən/ *n.* invasion or attack, esp. when sudden or brief. □□ **in·cur·sive** /-kórsiv/ *adj.*

Ind. *abbr.* **1** Independent. **2** Indiana. **3 a** India. **b** Indian.

in·debt·ed /indétid/ *adj.* owing gratitude or money. □□ **in·debt´ed·ness** *n.*

in·de·cent /indee'sənt/ *adj.* **1** offending decency. **2** unbecoming (*indecent haste*). □□ **in·de´cen·cy** *n.* (*pl.* **-cies**). **in·de´cent·ly** *adv.*

in·de·ci·pher·a·ble /índisífərəbəl/ *adj.* that cannot be deciphered.

in·de·ci·sion /índisízhən/ *n.* lack of decision; hesitation.

in·de·ci·sive /índisísiv/ *adj.* **1** not decisive; hesitating. **2** not conclusive. □□ **in·de·ci´sive·ly** *adv.* **in·de·ci´sive·ness** *n.*

in·deed /indee'd/ ● *adv.* **1** in truth; really; yes; that is so (*they are, indeed, a remarkable family*). **2** expressing emphasis or intensification (*I shall be very glad indeed*). **3** admittedly (*there are indeed exceptions*). **4** in point of fact (*if indeed such a thing is possible*). ● *int.* expressing irony, contempt, incredulity, etc.

indef. *abbr.* indefinite.

in·de·fat·i·ga·ble /índifátigəbəl/ *adj.* unwearying; unremitting. □□ **in·de·fat·i·ga·bil´i·ty** *n.* **in·de·fat´i·ga·bly** *adv.*

in·de·fen·si·ble /índifénsibəl/ *adj.* that cannot be defended or justified. □□ **in·de·fen·si·bil´i·ty** *n.* **in·de·fen´si·bly** *adv.*

in·def·i·nite /indéfinit/ *adj.* **1** vague; undefined. **2** unlimited. **3** *Gram.* not determining the person, etc., referred to. □ **indefinite article** see ARTICLE 4. □□ **in·def´i·nite·ly** *adv.* **in·def´i·nite·ness** *n.*

in·del·i·ble /indélibəl/ *adj.* **1** that cannot be erased or (in abstract senses) removed. **2** (of ink, etc.) that makes indelible marks. □□ **in·del·i·bil´i·ty** *n.* **in·del´i·bly** *adv.*

in·del·i·cate /indélikət/ *adj.* **1** coarse; unrefined. **2** tactless. **3** tending to indecency. □□ **in·del´i·ca·cy** *n.* (*pl.* **-cies**). **in·del´i·cate·ly** *adv.*

in·dem·ni·fy /indémnifī/ *v.tr.* (**-fies, -fied**) **1** protect or secure from harm, a loss, etc. **2** secure against legal responsibility for actions. **3** compensate for a loss. □□ **in·dem·ni·fi·ca´tion** *n.* **in·dem´ni·fi·er** *n.*

in·dem·ni·ty /indémnitee/ *n.* (*pl.* **-ties**) **1** a compensation for loss incurred. **b** sum paid for this, esp. exacted by a victor in war, etc. **2** security against loss. **3** legal exemption from penalties.

in·dent /indént/ ● *v.tr.* **1** start (a line of print

or writing) further from the margin than other lines, e.g., to mark a new paragraph. **2** make or impress marks, notches, etc., in. • *n.* also /índent/ **1** indented line. **2** indentation. □□ **in·dent′ er** *n.*

in·den·ta·tion /índentáyshən/ *n.* **1** indenting or being indented. **2** notch. **3** a zigzag. **4** deep recess in a coastline, etc.

in·den·tion /indénshən/ *n.* **1** the indenting of a line in printing or writing. **2** = INDENTATION.

in·den·ture /indénchər/ • *n.* **1** (usu. in *pl.*) sealed agreement or contract. **2** formal list, certificate, etc. • *v.tr. hist.* bind by indentures, esp. as an apprentice. □□ **in·den′ ture·ship** *n.*

in·de·pend·ence /índipéndəns/ *n.* state of being independent. □ **Independence Day** day celebrating the anniversary of national independence; in the US July 4.

in·de·pen·dent /índipéndənt/ • *adj.* **1 a** not subject to authority or control. **b** self-governing. **2 a** not depending on another person for one's opinion or livelihood. **b** (of income or resources) making it unnecessary to earn one's living. **3** unwilling to be under an obligation to others. **4** *Polit.* (usu. **Independent**) not belonging to or supported by a party. • *n.* (usu. **Independent**) person who is politically independent. □□ **in·de·pen′ dent·ly** *adv.*

in·des·crib·a·ble /indiskríbəbəl/ *adj.* **1** too unusual or extreme to be described. **2** vague; indefinite. □□ **in·des·crib′ a·bly** *adv.*

in·de·struc·ti·ble /índistrúktibəl/ *adj.* unable to be destroyed. □□ **in·de·struc·ti·bil′ i·ty** *n.* **in·de·struc′ ti·bly** *adv.*

in·de·ter·min·a·ble /índitórminəbəl/ *adj.* that cannot be ascertained or settled. □□ **in·de·ter′ min·a·bly** *adv.*

in·de·ter·mi·nate /índitórminət/ *adj.* **1** not fixed in extent, character, etc. **2** left doubtful; vague. □□ **in·de·ter′ mi·nate·ly** *adv.*

in·dex /índeks/ • *n.* (*pl.* **in·dex·es** or esp. in technical use **in·di·ces** /índiseez/) **1** alphabetical list of names, subjects, etc., with references, usu. at the end of a book. **2** (in full **card′ in′ dex**) index with each item entered on a separate card. **3** (in full **in′ dex num′ ber**) number showing the variation of prices or wages as compared with a chosen base period (*Dow-Jones index*). **4 a** pointer, esp. on an instrument. **b** indicator. **c** sign. • *v.tr.* **1** provide with an index. **2** enter in an index. **3** relate (wages, etc.) to a price index. □ **index finger** the forefinger. □□ **in·dex·a′ tion** *n.* **in′ dex·er** *n.*

¶ The plural *indexes* is appropriate for all senses of **index.** In some technical contexts, the plural *indices* is employed.

---

index late Middle English: from Latin *index, indic-* 'forefinger, informer, sign,' from *in-* 'toward' + a second element related to *dicere* 'say' or *dicare* 'make known.' The original sense 'index finger' (with which one points), came to mean 'pointer' (late 16th century), and figuratively something that serves to point to a fact or conclusion; hence a list of topics in a book ("pointing" to their location).

---

in·di·a ink /índeeə/ *n.* (also **In′ dia ink**) black liquid ink.

In·di·an /índeeən/ • *n.* **1 a** native or national of India. **b** person of Indian descent. **2** (in full **A·mer′ i·can In′ di·an**, also called **Na′ tive A·mer′ i·can**) member of the aboriginal peoples of America or their descendants. **3** any of the languages of the aboriginal peoples of America. • *adj.* **1** of or relating to India, or to the subcontinent comprising India, Pakistan, and Bangladesh. **2** of or relating to the aboriginal peoples of America. □ **Indian file** = *single file.* **Indian Ocean** ocean between Africa and Australia. **Indian summer** dry, warm weather in late autumn after a frost.

¶ **Indian,** meaning 'native of America before the arrival of Europeans,' is objected to by many who now favor **Native American.** There are others (including many members ot this ethnic group), however, who see nothing wrong with *Indian* or *American Indian,* which are long-established and often used with pride. The terms *Amerind* and *Amerindian,* once proposed as alternatives to *Indian,* never gained wide use. Newer alternatives, not widely used or established, include *First Nation* (especially Canadian) and the more generic *aboriginal peoples.* It should be noted that *Indian* is held by many not to include some American groups, e.g., Aleuts and Inuit.

in·di·cate /índikayt/ *v.tr.* **1** point out; make known; show. **2** express the presence of. **3** suggest; call for; require. **4** state briefly. **5** (of a gauge, etc.) give as a reading. □□ **in·di·ca·tion** /índikáyshən/ *n.*

in·dic·a·tive /indíkətiv/ • *adj.* **1** serving as an indication. **2** *Gram.* (of a mood) stating a fact. • *n.* *Gram.* indicative mood. □□ **in·dic′ a·tive·ly** *adv.*

in·di·ca·tor /índikaytər/ *n.* **1** person or thing that indicates. **2** device indicating the condition of a machine, etc. **3** recording instrument attached to an apparatus, etc. **4** flashing light on a vehicle to show that it is about to change direction; turn signal.

in·di·ces *pl.* of INDEX.

in·dict /indít/ *v.tr.* accuse (a person) formally by legal process. □□ **in·dict′ a·ble** *adj.* **in·dict′ er** *n.* **in·dict′ ment** *n.*

in·dif·fer·ent /indífrənt/ *adj.* **1** having no partiality for or against; having no interest in or sympathy for. **2** neither good nor bad; average. **3** inferior. □□ **in·dif′ fer·ence** *n.* **in·dif′ fer·ent·ly** *adv.*

in·dig·e·nous /indíjinəs/ *adj.* **1** (esp. of flora or fauna) originating naturally in a region. **2** (of people) born in a region. □□ **in·dig′ e·nous·ly** *adv.*

in·di·gent /índijənt/ *adj.* needy; poor. □□ **in′ di·gence** *n.*

in·di·gest·i·ble /índijéstibəl/ *adj.* difficult or impossible to digest. □□ **in·di·gest′ i·bly** *adv.*

in·di·ges·tion /índijés-chən/ *n.* **1** difficulty in digesting food. **2** pain or discomfort caused by this. □□ **in·di·ges′ tive** *adj.*

in·dig·nant /indígnənt/ *adj.* feeling or showing indignation. □□ **in·dig′ nant·ly** *adv.*

in·dig·na·tion /índignáyshən/ *n.* scornful anger at supposed unjust or unfair conduct or treatment.

in·dig·ni·ty /indígnitee/ *n.* (*pl.* **-ties**) **1** humiliating treatment. **2** a slight or insult. **3** humiliating quality of something (*indignity of my position*).

in·di·go /índigō/ *n.* (*pl.* **-os**) **1** natural blue dye obtained from the indigo plant. **2** (in full **in′ di·go blue**) color between blue and violet in the spectrum.

in·di·rect /índirékt, -dī-/ *adj.* **1** not going straight to the point. **2** (of a route, etc.) not straight. **3** not directly sought (*indirect result*). **4** (of lighting) from a concealed source and diffusely reflected. □ **indirect object** *Gram.* person or thing affected by a verbal action but not primarily acted on (e.g., *him* in *give him the book*). □□ **in·di·rect′ly** *adv.* **in·di·rect′ness** *n.*

in·dis·creet /índiskréet/ *adj.* **1** revealing secrets. **2** injudicious; unwary. □□ **in·dis·creet′ly** *adv.*

in·dis·cre·tion /índiskréshən/ *n.* **1** lack of discretion; indiscreet conduct. **2** indiscreet action, remark, etc.

in·dis·crim·i·nate /índiskríminət/ *adj.* **1** making no distinctions. **2** confused; promiscuous. □□ **in·dis·crim′i·nate·ly** *adv.*

in·dis·pens·a·ble /índispénsəbəl/ *adj.* necessary. □□ **in·dis·pen·sa·bil′i·ty** *n.* **in·dis·pen′sa·bly** *adv.*

in·dis·posed /índispózd/ *adj.* **1** slightly unwell. **2** averse or unwilling. □□ **in·dis·po·si′tion** *n.*

in·dis·sol·u·ble /índisólyəbəl/ *adj.* **1** that cannot be dissolved. **2** lasting. □□ **in·dis·sol·u·bil′i·ty** *n.* **in·dis·sol′u·bly** *adv.*

in·dite /indít/ *v.tr.* formal or joc. put into words; write.

in·di·um /índeeəm/ *n. Chem.* soft, silvery-white metallic element in zinc ores. ¶ Symb.: **In**.

in·di·vid·u·al /índivíjōōəl/ ● *adj.* **1** single. **2** particular; special; not general. **3** having a distinct character. **4** characteristic of a particular person. **5** designed for use by one person. ● *n.* **1** single member of a class. **2** single human being. □ **individual retirement account** savings account that allows tax owed on interest to be deferred.

in·di·vid·u·al·ism /índivíjōōəlizəm/ *n.* **1** being independent and self-reliant. **2** social theory favoring the free action of individuals. □□ **in·di·vid′u·al·ist** *n.* **in·di·vid·u·al·is′tic** *adj.* **in·di·vid·u·al·is′ti·cal·ly** *adv.*

in·di·vid·u·al·i·ty /índivijōō-álitee/ *n.* (*pl.* **-ties**) **1** individual character, esp. when strongly marked. **2** (in *pl.*) individual tastes, etc. **3** separate existence.

in·di·vid·u·al·ize /índivíjōōəlīz/ *v.tr.* **1** give an individual character to. **2** specify. □□ **in·di·vid·u·al·i·za′tion** *n.*

in·di·vid·u·al·ly /índivíjōōəlee/ *adv.* **1** in an individual capacity. **2** distinctively. **3** one by one; not collectively.

Indo- /índō/ *comb. form* Indian; Indian and (*Indo-Iranian*).

in·doc·tri·nate /indóktrinayt/ *v.tr.* teach to accept (esp. partisan or tendentious) ideas uncritically. □□ **in·doc·tri·na′tion** /-náyshən/ *n.* **in·doc′tri·na·tor** *n.*

In·do-Eu·ro·pe·an /índō-yŏorəpéeən/ ● *adj.* **1** of or relating to the family of languages spoken over the greater part of Europe and Asia as far as N. India. **2** of or relating to the hypothetical parent language of this family. ● *n.* **1** Indo-European family of languages. **2** hypothetical parent language of all languages belonging to this family. **3** (usu. in *pl.*) speaker of an Indo-European language.

in·do·lent /índələnt/ *adj.* lazy. □□ **in′do·lence** *n.* **in′do·lent·ly** *adv.*

in·dom·i·ta·ble /indómitəbəl/ *adj.* **1** that cannot be subdued; unyielding. **2** stubbornly persistent. □□ **in·dom·i·ta·bil′i·ty** *n.* **in·dom′i·ta·bly** *adv.*

In·do·ne·sian /índənéezhən, -shən/ ● *n.* **1 a** native or national of Indonesia in SE Asia. **b** person of Indonesian descent. **2** member of the chief pre-Malay population of the E. Indies. **3** language of the group spoken in the E. Indies, esp. the official language of the Indonesian Republic. ● *adj.* of or relating to Indonesia or its people or language.

in·door /índawr/ *adj.* situated, carried on, or used within a building or under cover (*indoor antenna; indoor games*).

in·doors /indáwrz/ *adv.* into or within a building.

in·dorse var. of ENDORSE.

in·du·bi·ta·ble /indōōbitəbəl, -dyōō-/ *adj.* that cannot be doubted. □□ **in·du′bi·ta·bly** *adv.*

in·duce /indōōs, -dyōōs/ *v.tr.* **1** prevail on; persuade. **2** bring about. **3** *Med.* bring on (labor) artificially. **4** *Electr.* produce (a current) by induction. **5** infer; deduce. □□ **in·duc′er** *n.* **in·duc′i·ble** *adj.*

in·duce·ment /indōōsmənt, -dyōōs-/ *n.* **1** attraction that leads one on. **2** thing that induces.

in·duct /indúkt/ *v.tr.* **1** install into a room, office, etc. **2** enlist (a person) for military service. □□ **in·duc·tee′** *n.*

in·duc·tance /indúktəns/ *n. Electr.* property of an electric circuit that causes an electromotive force to be generated by a change in the current flowing.

in·duc·tion /indúkshən/ *n.* **1** act or an instance of inducting or inducing. **2** *Med.* the process of bringing on (esp. labor) by artificial means. **3** *Logic* inference of a general law from particular instances (cf. DEDUCTION). **4** *Electr.* **a** production of an electric or magnetic state by the proximity (without contact) of an electrified or magnetized body. **b** production of an electric current in a conductor by a change of magnetic field. **5** enlistment for military service.

in·due var. of ENDUE.

in·dulge /indúlj/ *v.* **1** *intr.* (often foll. by *in*) take pleasure freely. **2** *tr.* yield freely to (a desire, etc.). **3** *tr.* gratify the wishes of. **4** *intr. colloq.* take alcoholic liquor. □□ **in·dulg′er** *n.*

in·dul·gence /indúljəns/ *n.* **1 a** indulging. **b** state of being indulgent. **2** thing indulged in. **3** *RC Ch.* remission of punishment for sins after absolution. **4** privilege granted.

in·dul·gent /indúljənt/ *adj.* **1** ready to overlook faults, etc. **2** indulging or tending to indulge. □□ **in·dul′gent·ly** *adv.*

in·dus·tri·al /indústreeəl/ ● *adj.* **1** of or relating to industry. **2** designed or suitable for industrial use (*industrial alcohol*). **3** having developed industries (*the industrial nations*). ● *n.* (in *pl.*) shares in industrial companies. □ **industrial park** area of land developed for a complex of factories and other businesses, usu. separate from an urban center. □□ **in·dus′tri·al·ly** *adv.*

in·dus·tri·al·ism /indústreeəlizəm/ *n.* social or economic system in which manufacturing industries are prevalent.

in·dus·tri·al·ist /indústreeəlist/ *n.* person engaged in the management of industry.

in·dus·tri·al·ize /indústreeəlīz/ *v.* **1** *tr.* introduce industries to (a country or region, etc.). **2** *intr.* become industrialized. □□ **in·dus·tri·a·li·za′tion** *n.*

in·dus·tri·ous /indústreeəs/ adj. diligent; hardworking. □□ **in·dus′tri·ous·ly** adv. **in·dus′tri·ous·ness** n.

in·dus·try /índəstree/ n. (pl. **-tries**) **1 a** branch of trade or manufacture. **b** these collectively. **2** concerted or copious activity (the building was a hive of industry). **3** diligence. **4** habitual employment in useful work.

-ine[1] /īn, in/ suffix forming adjectives, meaning 'belonging to, of the nature of' (Alpine; asinine).

-ine[2] /in, een/ suffix forming feminine nouns (heroine).

in·e·bri·ate ● v.tr. /ineébreeayt/ **1** make drunk. **2** excite. ● adj. /ineébreeət/ tending to drink; drunken. ● n. /ineébreeət/ drunkard. □□ **in·e·bri·a·tion** /-áyshən/ n. **in·e·bri·e·ty** /ínibríətee/ n.

in·ef·fa·ble /inéfəbəl/ adj. **1** unutterable; too great for description in words. **2** that must not be uttered. □□ **in·ef·fa·bil′i·ty** n. **in·ef′fa·bly** adv.

in·ef·fec·tu·al /inifékchōoəl/ adj. **1 a** without effect. **b** not producing the desired effect. **2** (of a person) lacking the ability to achieve results. □□ **in·ef·fec·tu·al·i·ty** /-álitee/ n. **in·ef·fec′tu·al·ly** adv. **in·ef·fec′tu·al·ness** n.

in·ef·fi·cient /ínifíshənt/ adj. **1** not efficient. **2** (of a person) not fully capable. □□ **in·ef·fi′cien·cy** n. **in·ef·fi′cient·ly** adv.

in·el·e·gant /inéligənt/ adj. **1** ungraceful. **2 a** unrefined. **b** unpolished. □□ **in·el′e·gance** n. **in·el′e·gant·ly** adv.

in·e·luc·ta·ble /ínilúktəbəl/ adj. **1** unavoidable. **2** inescapable. □□ **in·e·luc′ta·bly** adv.

in·ept /inépt/ adj. **1** unskillful. **2** absurd; silly. **3** out of place. □□ **in·ep′ti·tude** n. **in·ept′ly** adv. **in·ept′ness** n.

in·e·qual·i·ty /ínikwólitee/ n. (pl. **-ties**) **1 a** lack of equality. **b** instance of this. **2** state of being variable. **3** (of a surface) irregularity.

in·ert /inɔ́rt/ adj. **1** without inherent power of action, motion, or resistance. **2** without active chemical or other properties. **3** sluggish; slow. □□ **in·ert′ly** adv. **in·ert′ness** n.

in·er·tia /inɔ́rshə/ n. **1** Physics property of matter by which it continues in its existing state of rest or motion unless an external force is applied. **2** inertness; sloth. □□ **in·er′tial** adj.

in·es·cap·a·ble /íniskáypəbəl/ adj. that cannot be escaped or avoided. □□ **in·es·cap·a·bil′i·ty** n. **in·es·cap′a·bly** adv.

-iness /eenis/ suffix forming nouns corresponding to adjectives in -y (drowsiness; manliness; see -Y[1], -LY[2]).

in·es·ti·ma·ble /inéstiməbəl/ adj. too great, intense, precious, etc., to be estimated. □□ **in·es′ti·ma·bly** adv.

in·ev·i·ta·ble /inévitəbəl/ adj. **1 a** unavoidable. **b** bound to occur. **2** colloq. tiresomely familiar. □□ **in·ev·i·ta·bil′i·ty** n. **in·ev′i·ta·ble·ness** n. **in·ev′i·ta·bly** adv.

in·ex·cus·a·ble /ínikskyóozəbəl/ adj. (of a person, action, etc.) that cannot be excused or justified. □□ **in·ex·cus′a·bly** adv.

in·ex·haust·i·ble /inigzáwstibəl/ adj. **1** that cannot be exhausted or used up. **2** that cannot be worn out. □□ **in·ex·haust′i·bly** adv.

in·ex·o·ra·ble /inéksərəbəl/ adj. **1** relentless. **2** (of a person or attribute) that cannot be persuaded by request or entreaty. □□ **in·ex·o·ra·bil′i·ty** n. **in·ex′o·ra·bly** adv.

in·ex·pe·ri·ence /inikspeéreeəns/ n. lack of experience, or of the resulting knowledge or skill. □□ **in·ex·pe′ri·enced** adj.

in·ex·pert /inékspərt/ adj. unskillful; lacking expertise. □□ **in·ex′pert·ly** adv.

in·ex·pi·a·ble /inékspeeəbəl/ adj. (of an act or feeling) that cannot be expiated or appeased. □□ **in·ex′pi·a·bly** adv.

in·ex·pli·ca·ble /iniksplíkəbəl, inéks-/ adj. that cannot be explained. □□ **in·ex′pli·ca·bly** adv.

in·ex·press·i·ble /iniksprésibəl/ adj. that cannot be expressed in words. □□ **in·ex·press′i·bly** adv.

in·ex·tin·guish·a·ble /ínikstínggwishəbəl/ adj. **1** not quenchable; indestructible. **2** (of laughter, etc.) irrepressible.

in ex·tre·mis /in ekstreémis, -tré-/ adj. **1** at the point of death. **2** in great difficulties.

in·ex·tri·ca·ble /inékstrikəbəl, ínikstrík-/ adj. **1** inescapable. **2** (of a knot, problem, etc.) that cannot be unraveled or solved. **3** intricately confused. □□ **in·ex′tri·ca·bly** adv.

inf. abbr. **1** infantry. **2** inferior. **3** infinitive.

in·fal·li·ble /infálibəl/ adj. **1** incapable of error. **2** unfailing; sure to succeed. □□ **in·fal·li·bil′i·ty** n. **in·fal′li·bly** adv.

in·fa·mous /ínfəməs/ adj. notoriously bad. □□ **in·fa′mous·ly** adv. **in·fa′my** n. (pl. **-mies**)

in·fan·cy /ínfənsee/ n. (pl. **-cies**) **1** early childhood; babyhood. **2** early state in the development of an idea, undertaking, etc. **3** Law the state of being a minor.

in·fant /ínfənt/ n. **1** child during the earliest period of its life. **2** (esp. attrib.) thing in an early stage of its development.

in·fan·ti·cide /infántisīd/ n. **1** killing of an infant. **2** such a practice. **3** person who kills an infant. □□ **in·fan·ti·cid·al** /-síd′l/ adj.

in·fan·tile /ínfəntīl/ adj. **1 a** like or characteristic of a child. **b** childish; immature. **2** in its infancy. □ **infantile paralysis** poliomyelitis. □□ **in·fan·til′i·ty** /-tílitee/ n. (pl. **-ties**)

in·fan·try /ínfəntree/ n. (pl. **-tries**) body of foot soldiers; foot soldiers collectively. □□ **in·fan·try·man** /ínfəntreemən/ n. (pl. **-men**)

in·farct /ínfaarkt/ n. Med. area of dead tissue caused by an inadequate blood supply. □□ **in·farc·tion** /-fáarkshən/ n.

in·fat·u·ate /infáchōo-ayt/ v.tr. inspire with intense, usu. transitory fondness or admiration. □□ **in·fat′u·at·ed** adj. **in·fat·u·a·tion** /-áyshən/ n.

in·fect /infékt/ v.tr. **1** contaminate or affect with harmful organisms or noxious matter. **2** instill bad feeling or opinion into (a person). □□ **in·fec′tor** n.

in·fec·tion /infékshən/ n. **1** infecting or being infected. **2** instance of this; disease.

in·fec·tious /infékshəs/ adj. **1** infecting with disease. **2** transmissible by infection. **3** (of emotions, etc.) quickly affecting others. □□ **in·fec′tious·ly** adv.

in·fe·lic·i·ty /infilísitee/ n. (pl. **-ties**) **1** inapt expression, etc. **2** instance of this.

in·fer /infɔ́r/ v.tr. (**in·ferred, in·fer·ring**) **1** deduce or conclude. **2** disp. imply. □□ **in·fer′a·ble** adj. ¶ **infer** means 'to deduce or conclude,' as in We can infer from the evidence that the car's brakes failed. Its use in place of **imply**, to mean 'to hint or suggest,' is widely considered incorrect.

in·fer·ence /ínfərəns/ n. **1** act of inferring. **2**

thing inferred. □□ **in·fer·en·tial** /-rénshəl/ *adj.* **in·fer·en′tial·ly** *adv.*

in·fe·ri·or /inféereeər/ • *adj.* **1 a** in a lower position. **b** of lower rank, quality, etc. **2** poor in quality. • *n.* person inferior to another. □□ **in·fe·ri·or·i·ty** /inféeree-áwritee, -ór-/ *n.*

in·fer·nal /infэ́rnəl/ *adj.* **1 a** of hell. **b** hellish. **2** *colloq.* detestable. □□ **in·fer′nal·ly** *adv.*

---

infernal late Middle English: from Old French, from Christian Latin *infernalis*, from Latin *infernus* 'below, underground,' used by Christians to mean 'hell,' on the pattern of Latin *inferni* (masculine plural) 'the spirits of the underworld' and *inferna* (neuter plural) 'the lower regions.'

---

in·fer·no /infэ́rnō/ *n.* (*pl.* **-nos**) **1** raging fire. **2** scene of horror or distress. **3** hell.

in·fest /infést/ *v.tr.* (esp. vermin) overrun (a place). □□ **in·fes·ta′tion** *n.*

in·fi·del /infid′l, -del/ • *n.* unbeliever in a particular religion. • *adj.* **1** that is an infidel. **2** of unbelievers.

---

infidel late 15th century: from French *infidèle* or Latin *infidelis*, from *in-* 'not' + *fidelis* 'faithful' (from *fides* 'faith,' related to *fidere* 'to trust'). The word originally denoted a person of a religion other than one's own, specifically a Muslim (to a Christian), a Christian (to a Muslim), or a Gentile (to a Jew).

---

in·fi·del·i·ty /infidélitee/ *n.* (*pl.* **-ties**) **1** unfaithfulness, esp. adultery. **2** instance of this.

in·field /infeeld/ *n.* **1** *Baseball* area enclosed by the three bases and home plate. **2** the four fielders stationed near the bases. □□ **in′field·er** *n.*

in·fight·ing /infĩting/ *n.* **1** hidden conflict within an organization. **2** boxing within arm's length. □□ **in′fight·er** *n.*

in·fil·trate /infiltrayt/ *v.* **1** *tr.* **a** gain entrance or access surreptitiously and by degrees (as spies, etc.). **b** cause to do this. **2** *tr.* permeate by filtration. □□ **in·fil·tra′tion** /-tráyshən/ *n.* **in′fil·tra·tor** *n.*

in·fi·nite /infinit/ *adj.* **1** boundless; endless. **2** very great or many (*infinite resources*). □□ **in′fi·nite·ly** *adv.* **in′fi·nite·ness** *n.*

in·fin·i·tes·i·mal /ínfinitésimal/ *adj.* infinitely or very small. □□ **in·fin·i·tes′i·mal·ly** *adv.* ¶ Although it is widely assumed to refer to large numbers, **infinitesimal** describes only very small size. While there may be an *infinite* number of grains of sand on the beach, a single grain may be said to be *infinitesimal.*

in·fin·i·tive /infinitiv/ *Gram.* • *n.* form of a verb without a particular subject, tense, etc. (e.g., *see* in *we came to see; let him see*). • *adj.* having this form. □□ **in·fin·i·tiv·al** /-tĩvəl/ *adj.* ¶ Writers who maintain that English could be modeled on Latin long ago created the "rule" that the English infinitive must not be split: *to clearly state* was wrong; one must say *to state clearly.* But the Latin infinitive is one word, and cannot be split, so the "rule" is not firmly grounded, and treating two English words as one can lead to awkward, stilted sentences.

in·fin·i·tude /infinitōōd, -tyōōd/ *n.* **1** = INFINITY 1. **2** = INFINITY 2.

in·fin·i·ty /infinitee/ *n.* (*pl.* **-ties**) **1** being infinite. **2** infinite number or extent. **3** infinite distance. **4** *Math.* infinite quantity. ¶ Symb.: ∞

in·firm /infэ́rm/ *adj.* **1** physically weak, esp. through age. **2** (of a person, mind, judgment, etc.) weak; irresolute. □□ **in·firm′i·ty** *n.* (*pl.* **-ties**). **in·firm′ly** *adv.*

in·fir·ma·ry /infэ́rməree/ *n.* (*pl.* **-ries**) **1** hospital. **2** place for those who are ill, as at school, etc.

in fla·gran·te de·lic·to /ín fləgrántee dilíktō/ *adv.* in the very act of committing an offense.

in·flame /infláym/ *v.* **1** *tr.* & *intr.* provoke or become provoked to strong feeling, esp. anger. **2** *Med.* **a** *intr.* become hot, reddened, and sore. **b** *tr.* (esp. as **inflamed** *adj.*) cause inflammation or fever in (a body, etc.); make hot. **3** *tr.* aggravate.

in·flam·ma·ble /infláməbəl/ • *adj.* **1** easily set on fire. **2** easily excited. • *n.* (usu. in *pl.*) flammable substance. □□ **in·flam·ma·bil′i·ty** *n.* **in·flam′ma·bly** *adv.* ¶ Both **inflammable** and **flammable** mean 'easily set on fire or excited.' The opposite is **nonflammable.** Where there is a danger that **inflammable** could be understood to mean its opposite, i.e., 'not easily set on fire,' **flammable** should be used—and is used, as in the labeling of many products—to avoid confusion.

in·flam·ma·tion /infləmáyshən/ *n.* **1** act or instance of inflaming. **2** *Med.* localized physical condition with heat, swelling, redness, and usu. pain.

in·flam·ma·to·ry /inflámətáwree/ *adj.* **1** tending to cause anger, etc. **2** of inflammation.

in·flat·a·ble /infláytəbəl/ • *adj.* that can be inflated. • *n.* inflatable object.

in·flate /infláyt/ *v.tr.* **1** distend with air or gas. **2** puff up (with pride, etc.). **3 a** bring about inflation (of currency). **b** raise (prices) artificially. **4** (as **inflated** *adj.*) (esp. of language, sentiments, etc.) bombastic. □□ **in·flat′ed·ly** *adv.* **in·flat′ed·ness** *n.* **in·flat′er** *n.* **in·fla′tor** *n.*

in·fla·tion /infláyshən/ *n.* **1** act or condition of inflating. **b** instance of this. **2** *Econ.* **a** general increase in prices and fall in the purchasing value of money. **b** increase in available currency regarded as causing this. □□ **in·fla′tion·ar·y** *adj.*

in·flect /inflékt/ *v.* **1** *tr.* change the pitch of (the voice, etc.). **2** *Gram.* **a** *tr.* change the form of (a word) to express tense, gender, number, mood, etc. **b** *intr.* undergo such change. □□ **in·flec′tive** *adj.*

in·flec·tion /inflékshən/ *n.* **1 a** act or condition of inflecting. **b** instance of this. **2** *Gram.* **a** process or practice of inflecting words. **b** inflected form of a word. □□ **in·flec′tion·al** *adj.*

in·flex·i·ble /infléksibəl/ *adj.* **1** unbendable. **2** immovable; obstinate. **3** inexorable. □□ **in·flex·i·bil′i·ty** *n.* **in·flex′i·bly** *adv.*

in·flict /inflíkt/ *v.tr.* **1** deal (a stroke, wound, etc.). **2** (also *refl.*) often *joc.* impose (suffering, oneself, etc.) on.

in·flo·res·cence /inflərésəns/ *n.* **1** *Bot.* **a** complete flower head of a plant. **b** arrangement of this. **2** flowering.

in·flu·ence /inflōōəns/ • *n.* **1** effect a person or thing has on another. **2** moral ascendancy or power. **3** thing or person exercising such power.

• *v.tr.* exert influence on. □ **under the influence** *colloq.* affected by alcoholic drink. □□ **in'flu·enc·er** *n.*

---

influence late Middle English: from Old French, or from medieval Latin *influentia* 'inflow,' from Latin *influere*, from *in-* 'into' + *fluere* 'to flow.' The word originally had the general sense 'an influx, flowing matter,' also specifically (in astrology) 'the flowing in of ethereal fluid (affecting human destiny).' The sense 'imperceptible or indirect action exerted to cause changes' was established in Scholastic Latin by the 13th century, but not recorded in English until the late 16th century.

---

in·flu·en·tial /ínflo͞o-énshəl/ *adj.* having great influence or power. □□ **in·flu·en'tial·ly** *adv.*

in·flu·en·za /ínflo͞o-énzə/ *n.* highly contagious virus infection often occurring in epidemics.

in·flux /ínfluks/ *n.* continual stream of people or things.

in·fo /ínfō/ *n.* *colloq.* information.

in·fo·mer·cial /ínfōmərshəl/ *n.* television program promoting a commercial product.

in·form /infáwrm/ *v.* 1 *tr.* tell. 2 *intr.* (usu. foll. by *against*, *on*) make an accusation. □□ **in·form'ant** *n.* **in·form'er** *n.*

in·for·mal /infáwrməl/ *adj.* 1 without formality. 2 (of language, clothing, etc.) not formal; everyday; normal. □□ **in·for·mal·i·ty** /-málitee/ *n.* (*pl.* **-ties**). **in·for'mal·ly** *adv.*

in·for·mat·ics /infərmátiks/ *n.pl.* (usu. treated as *sing.*) the science of processing data for storage and retrieval; information science.

in·for·ma·tion /ínfərmáyshən/ *n.* 1 **a** something told; knowledge. **b** news. 2 *Computing* data stored or generated by a program. □ **information (super)highway** worldwide computer network offering information, shopping, and other services. □□ **in·for·ma'tion·al** *adj.*

in·for·ma·tive /infáwrmətiv/ *adj.* (also **in·for·ma·to·ry** /infáwrmətawree/) giving information; instructive. □□ **in·for'ma·tive·ly** *adv.*

in·formed /infáwrmd/ *adj.* knowledgeable.

in·fo·tain·ment /infótáynmənt/ *n.* 1 factual information presented in dramatized form on television. 2 television program mixing news and entertainment.

in·fra /ínfrə/ *adv.* (in a book or writing) below; further on.

infra- /ínfrə/ *comb. form* below (opp. SUPRA-).

in·frac·tion /infrákshən/ *n.* esp. Law violation or infringement. □□ **in·fract** /-frákt/ *v.tr.* **in·frac'tor** *n.*

in·fra dig /ínfrə díg/ *predic.adj.* *colloq.* beneath one's dignity.

in·fra·red /ínfrəréd/ *adj.* of or using a wavelength just greater than the red end of the visible spectrum.

in·fra·struc·ture /ínfrəstrukchər/ *n.* basic structural foundations, esp. roads, bridges, sewers, etc.

in·fre·quent /infrée'kwənt/ *adj.* not frequent. □□ **in·fre'quen·cy** *n.* **in·fre'quent·ly** *adv.*

in·fringe /infrínj/ *v.* 1 *tr.* **a** violate (a law, an

oath, etc.). **b** act in defiance of (another's rights, etc.). 2 *intr.* (usu. foll. by *on*, *upon*) encroach; trespass. □□ **in·fringe'ment** *n.* **in·fring'er** *n.*

in·fu·ri·ate *v.tr.* /infyo͞oreeayt/ fill with fury; enrage. □□ **in·fu'ri·at·ing** *adj.* **in·fu'ri·at·ing·ly** *adv.*

in·fuse /infyo͞oz/ *v.tr.* 1 imbue; pervade. 2 steep (herbs, tea, etc.) in liquid to extract the content. 3 instill (grace, spirit, life, etc.). □□ **in·fus'er** *n.* **in·fu'sion** /infyo͞ozhən/ *n.* **in·fu'sive** /-fyo͞osiv/ *adj.*

-ing¹ /ing/ *suffix* forming gerunds and nouns from verbs denoting: 1 **a** verbal action or its result (*asking*). **b** verbal action as described or classified in some way (*tough going*). 2 material associated with a process, etc. (*piping*). 3 occupation or event (*banking*). 4 set or arrangement of (*coloring*).

-ing² /ing/ *suffix* 1 forming the present participle of verbs (*asking*), often as adjectives (*charming*). 2 forming adjectives from nouns (*hulking*) and verbs (*balding*).

in·ge·nious /injée'nyəs/ *adj.* 1 clever at inventing, organizing, etc. 2 (of a machine, etc.) cleverly contrived. □□ **in·ge'ni·ous·ly** *adv.* **in·ge'ni·ous·ness** *n.*

¶ **Ingenuous** and **ingenuous** are sometimes confused. **Ingenious** means 'clever, skillful, or resourceful,' e.g., *an ingenious device*, while **ingenuous** means 'artless' or 'frank,' e.g., *charmed by the ingenuous honesty of the child.*

in·ge·nue /ánzhəno͞o/ *n.* (also **in·gé·nue**) 1 unsophisticated young woman. 2 *Theatr.* **a** such a part in a play. **b** actress who plays this part.

in·ge·nu·i·ty /injíno͞oitee, -nyo͞o-/ *n.* inventiveness; cleverness.

in·gen·u·ous /injényo͞oəs/ *adj.* 1 innocent; artless. 2 open; frank. □□ **in·gen'u·ous·ly** *adv.* **in·gen'u·ous·ness** *n.*

in·gest /injést/ *v.tr.* 1 take in (food, etc.); eat. 2 absorb (facts, knowledge, etc.). □□ **in·ges·tion** /injés-chən/ *n.* **in·ges'tive** *adj.*

in·glo·ri·ous /in-gláwreeəs/ *adj.* 1 shameful; ignominious. 2 not famous. □□ **in·glo'ri·ous·ly** *adv.*

-ingly /inglee/ *suffix* forming adverbs esp. denoting manner of action or nature or condition (*charmingly*).

in·got /ínggət/ *n.* bar of cast metal, esp. of gold, etc.

in·grained /in-gráynd/ *adj.* 1 deeply rooted; inveterate. 2 thorough. 3 (of dirt, etc.) deeply embedded.

in·grate /in-grayt/ *formal or literary* • *n.* ungrateful person. • *adj.* ungrateful.

in·gra·ti·ate /in-gráysheeayt/ *v.refl.* (usu. foll. by *with*) bring oneself into favor. □□ **in·gra'ti·at·ing** *adj.* **in·gra'ti·at·ing·ly** *adv.* **in·gra·ti·a·tion** /-áyshən/ *n.*

in·grat·i·tude /in-grátito͞od, -tyo͞od/ *n.* lack of due gratitude.

in·gre·di·ent /in-grée'deeənt/ *n.* component part or element in a recipe, mixture, or combination.

in·gress /ín-gres/ *n.* 1 act or right of going in or entering. 2 means of entrance. □□ **in·gres·sion** /-gréshən/ *n.*

in·grow·ing /ín-gróing/ *adj.* growing inward, esp. (of a toenail) growing into the flesh. □□ **in'grown** *adj.*

in·gui·nal /ínggwinəl/ *adj.* of the groin. □□ **in'gui·nal·ly** *adv.*

in·hab·it /inhábit/ v.tr. (of a person or animal) dwell in; occupy (a region, town, house, etc.). □□ **in·hab′i·ta·ble** adj. **in·hab′it·ant** n.

in·hal·ant /inháylənt/ n. medicinal preparation for inhaling.

in·hale /inháyl/ v.tr. (often absol.) breathe in (air, gas, tobacco smoke, etc.). □□ **in·ha·la·tion** /-həláyshən/ n.

in·hal·er /inháylər/ n. device for administering an inhalant.

in·here /inhéer/ v.intr. be inherent.

in·her·ent /inhéerənt, inhér-/ adj. **1** existing in something, esp. as a permanent or characteristic attribute. **2** vested in (a person, etc.) as a right or privilege. □□ **in·her′ence** n. **in·her′ent·ly** adv.

in·her·it /inhérit/ v. **1** tr. receive (property, rank, etc.) by legal succession. **2** tr. derive (a quality or characteristic) genetically from one's ancestors. **3** succeed as an heir (a younger son rarely inherits). □□ **in·her′it·a·ble** adj. **in·her′i·tor** n.

in·her·i·tance /inhérit'ns/ n. **1** thing inherited. **2** a act of inheriting. **b** instance of this.

in·hib·it /inhíbit/ v.tr. **1** hinder, restrain, or prevent. **2** (as **inhibited** adj.) subject to inhibition. **3** (usu. foll. by from + verbal noun) forbid or prohibit. □□ **in·hib′i·tive** adj. **in·hib′i·tor** n. **in·hib·i·to·ry** /-itawree/ adj.

in·hi·bi·tion /ínhibishən/ n. **1** Psychol. restraint on the direct expression of an instinct. **2** colloq. emotional resistance to a thought, action, etc. **3** a act of inhibiting. **b** process of being inhibited.

in·hos·pi·ta·ble /ínhospítəbəl, inhóspi-/ adj. **1** not hospitable. **2** (of a region, coast, etc.) not affording shelter, etc. □□ **in·hos′pi·ta·bly** adv.

in-house • adj. /ínhóws/ done or existing within an institution, company, etc. (an in-house project). • adv. /ínhóws/ internally, without outside assistance.

in·hu·man /inhyoˊomən/ adj. **1** (of a person, conduct, etc.) brutal; unfeeling; barbarous. **2** not of a human type. □□ **in·hu·man′i·ty** /ínhyooˊmánitee/ n. (pl. **-ties**). **in·hu′man·ly** adv.

in·im·i·cal /inímikəl/ adj. (usu. foll. by to) **1** hostile. **2** harmful. □□ **in·im′i·cal·ly** adv.

in·im·i·ta·ble /inímitəbəl/ adj. impossible to imitate. □□ **in·im·i·ta·bil′i·ty** n. **in·im′i·ta·bly** adv.

in·iq·ui·ty /iníkwitee/ n. (pl. **-ties**) **1** wickedness; unrighteousness. **2** gross injustice. □□ **in·iq′ui·tous** adj. **in·iq′ui·tous·ly** adv.

in·i·tial /iníshəl/ • adj. of, existing, or occurring at the beginning. • n. **1** = initial letter. **2** (usu. in pl.) the first letter(s) of a (esp. a person's) name or names. • v.tr. mark or sign with one's initials. □ **initial letter** letter at the beginning of a word. □□ **in·i′tial·ly** adv.

in·i·tial·ism /iníshəlizəm/ n. group of initial letters used as an abbreviation for a name or expression (cf. ACRONYM).

in·i·tial·ize /iníshəliz/ v.tr. set or prepare for the start of an operation. □□ **in·i·tial·i·za′tion** n.

in·i·ti·ate • v.tr. /inísheeayt/ **1** begin; set going. **2 a** admit (a person) into a society, an office, a secret, etc., esp. with a ritual. **b** instruct (a person) in science, etc. • n. /inísheeət/ initiated person. • adj. /inísheeət/ (of a person) recently initiated. □□ **in·i·ti·a·tion** /-sheeáyshən/ n. **in·i′ti·a·tor** n. **in·i′ti·a·to·ry** /inisheeətáwree/ adj.

in·i·ti·a·tive /iníshətiv, inísheeətiv/ • n. **1** ability to initiate things; enterprise. **2** origination. **3**

right of citizens outside the legislature to originate legislation. • adj. beginning; originating.

in·ject /injékt/ v.tr. **1** Med. **a** (usu. foll. by into) drive (a solution, medicine, etc.) by or as if by a syringe. **b** (usu. foll. by with) fill (a cavity, etc.) by injecting. **2** place (an object, quality, etc.) into something. □□ **in·ject′a·ble** adj. & n. **in·jec′tor** n.

in·jec·tion /injékshən/ n. **1 a** act of injecting. **b** instance of this. **2** liquid or solution (to be) injected (prepare a morphine injection).

in·junc·tion /injúnkshən/ n. **1** authoritative warning or order. **2** Law judicial order restraining or compelling some action. □□ **in·junc′tive** adj.

in·jure /ínjər/ v.tr. **1** harm; damage. **2** impair. **3** do wrong to. □□ **in′jured** adj. **in′jur·er** n.

in·ju·ri·ous /injōˊoreeəs/ adj. **1** hurtful. **2** (of language) insulting. **3** wrongful. □□ **in·ju′ri·ous·ly** adv. **in·ju′ri·ous·ness** n.

in·ju·ry /ínjəree/ n. (pl. **-ries**) **1 a** physical harm or damage. **b** instance of this. **2** esp. Law a wrongful action. **b** instance of this. **3** damage to one's good name, etc.

in·jus·tice /injústis/ n. **1** lack of fairness. **2** unjust act.

ink /ingk/ • n. **1** colored fluid or paste used for writing, printing, etc. **2** Zool. black liquid ejected by a cuttlefish, octopus, etc. • v.tr. **1** mark with ink. **2** cover (type, etc.) with ink before printing. **3** apply ink to. □ **ink-jet printer** computer-controlled printer in which minute droplets of ink are projected onto the paper.

ink·ling /íngkling/ n. slight knowledge or suspicion; hint.

ink·well /íngkwel/ n. pot for ink usu. in a hole in a desk.

ink·y /íngkee/ adj. (**ink·i·er**, **ink·i·est**) of, as black as, or stained with ink. □□ **ink′i·ness** n.

in·laid past and past part. of INLAY.

in·land /ínlənd, ínland/ • adj. situated in the interior of a country. • n. interior parts of a country. • adv. in or toward the interior of a country. □□ **in′land·er** n.

in-law /ínlaw/ n. (often in pl.) relative by marriage.

in·lay • v.tr. /ínláy/ (past and past part. **in·laid** /ínláyd/) **1 a** embed (a thing in another) so that the surfaces are even. **b** ornament (a thing with inlaid work). **2** (as **inlaid** adj.) (of a piece of furniture, etc.) ornamented by inlaying. • n. /ínlay/ **1** inlaid work. **2** material inlaid. **3** filling shaped to fit a tooth cavity. □□ **in′lay·er** n.

in·let /ínlet, -lit/ n. **1** small arm of the sea, lake, or river. **2** way of entry.

in-line /ínlín/ adj. **1** having parts arranged in a line. **2** constituting an integral part of a continuous sequence of operations or machines. □ **in-line skate** roller skate in which the wheels are fixed in a single line along the sole of the boot. **in-line skater** person who skates wearing in-line skates. **in-line skating** skating with in-line skates as a sport or pastime.

in lo·co pa·ren·tis /in lōkō pəréntis/ adv. in the place or position of a parent.

in·mate /ínmayt/ n. (usu. foll. by of) occupant of a prison, etc.

in me·mo·ri·am /in mimáwreeəm/ • prep. in memory of (a dead person). • n. obituary.

in·most /ínmōst/ adj. 1 most inward. 2 most intimate.

inn /in/ n. 1 small hotel. 2 restaurant or tavern.

□ **inn** Old English (in the sense 'dwelling place, lodging'): of Germanic origin; related to *in*. In Middle English the word was used to translate Latin *hospitium* (source of *hospice*), denoting a house of residence for students: this sense is preserved in the names of some British buildings formerly used for this purpose. The current sense dates from late Middle English.

in·nards /ínərdz/ n.pl. colloq. 1 entrails. 2 works (of an engine, etc.).

in·nate /ináyt, ínayt/ adj. inborn; natural. □□ **in·nate′ly** adv. **in·nate′ness** n.

in·ner /ínər/ adj. 1 inside; interior. 2 (of thoughts, feelings, etc.) deeper; more secret. □ **inner city** central most densely populated area of a city (also (with hyphen) *attrib.*: *innercity housing*). **inner tube** separate inflatable tube inside a pneumatic tire. □□ **in′ner·most** adj.

in·ning /íning/ n. 1 *Baseball* division of a game during which both teams bat. 2 single turn at bat for a team.

inn·keep·er /ínkeepər/ n. person who keeps an inn.

in·no·cent /ínəsənt/ ● adj. 1 free from moral wrong. 2 not guilty (of a crime, etc.). 3 a simple; guileless. b pretending to be guileless. 4 harmless. ● n. innocent person, esp. a young child. □□ **in′no·cence** n. **in′no·cen·cy** n. **in′no·cent·ly** adv.

¶ **Innocent** properly means 'harmless' but has long been extended in general language to mean 'not guilty.' The jury (or judge) in a criminal trial does not, strictly speaking, find a defendant 'innocent.' Rather, a defendant may be *guilty* or *not guilty* of the charges brought. In common use, however, owing perhaps to the concept of the *presumption of innocence*, which instructs a jury to consider a defendant free of wrongdoing until proven guilty on the basis of evidence, 'not guilty' and 'innocent' have come to be thought one and the same.

in·noc·u·ous /inókyōōəs/ adj. 1 harmless. 2 inoffensive. □□ **in·noc′u·ous·ly** adv. **in·noc′u·ous·ness** n.

in·no·vate /ínəvayt/ v.intr. 1 bring in new methods, ideas, etc. 2 make changes. □□ **in·no′va·tion** /-váyshən/ n. **in·no·va′tion·al** adj. **in′no·va·tor** n. **in′no·va·tive** adj. **in′no·va·tive·ness** n.

in·nu·en·do /ínyōō-éndō/ n. (pl. **-dos** or **-does**) 1 allusive remark or hint, usu. disparaging. 2 remark with a double meaning, usu. suggestive.

in·nu·mer·a·ble /inóōmərəbəl, inyōō-/ adj. too many to be counted. □□ **in·nu′mer·a·bly** adv.

in·nu·mer·ate /inóōmərət, inyōō-/ adj. having no knowledge of or feeling for mathematical operations; not numerate. □□ **in·nu′mer·a·cy** n.

in·oc·u·late /inókyəlayt/ v.tr. 1 treat with a vaccine or serum to promote immunity against disease. 2 implant (a disease) by means of vaccine. □□ **in·oc′u·la·ble** adj. **in·oc·u·la′tion** /-láyshən/ n.

in·of·fen·sive /ínəfénsiv/ adj. not objectionable; harmless. □□ **in·of·fen′sive·ly** adv. **in·of·fen′sive·ness** n.

in·op·er·a·ble /inópərəbəl/ adj. 1 *Surgery* that cannot successfully be operated on. 2 that cannot be operated; inoperative. □□ **in·op·er·a·bil′i·ty** n. **in·op′er·a·bly** adv.

in·op·er·a·tive /inópərətiv/ adj. not working or taking effect.

in·or·di·nate /ináwrd′nət/ adj. 1 excessive. 2 intemperate. 3 disorderly. □□ **in·or′di·nate·ly** adv.

in·or·gan·ic /ínawrgánik/ adj. Chem. (of a compound) not organic, usu. of mineral origin (opp. ORGANIC). □ **inorganic chemistry** chemistry of inorganic compounds. □□ **in·or·gan′i·cal·ly** adv.

in·pa·tient /ínpayshənt/ n. patient who stays in the hospital while under treatment.

in·put /ínpōōt/ ● n. 1 what is put in or taken in, or operated on by any process or system. 2 *Electronics* a place where, or a device through which, energy, information, etc., enters a system. b energy supplied to a device or system; electrical signal. 3 information fed into a computer. 4 action or process of putting in or feeding in. 5 contribution of information, etc. ● v.tr. (**in·put·ting**; past and past part. **in·put** or **in·put·ted**) 1 put in. 2 *Computing* supply (data, programs, etc., to a computer, program, etc.). □ **input-** (or **in′put/put′put** *Computing, etc.* of, relating to, or for input and output. □□ **in′put·ter** n.

in·quest /ínkwest, ing-/ n. Law inquiry by a coroner into the cause of a death.

in·qui·e·tude /inkwí-itōōd, -tyōōd/ n. uneasiness.

in·quire /inkwír, ing-/ v. 1 intr. make a formal investigation. 2 tr. ask for information as to (*inquired whether we were coming*). 3 tr. (foll. by *into*) look into. □□ **in·quir′er** n.

in·qui·ry /inkwírée, ing-, ínkwəree, íng-/ n. (pl. **-ries**) 1 investigation, esp. an official one. 2 act of asking.

in·qui·si·tion /ínkwizíshən, íng-/ n. 1 usu. derog. intensive search or investigation. 2 judicial or official inquiry. 3 (**the Inquisition**) RC Ch. hist. ecclesiastical tribunal for the violent suppression of heresy, esp. in Spain. □□ **in·qui·si′tion·al** adj. **in·qui·si·tor** /inkwízitər, ing-/ n.

in·quis·i·tive /inkwízitiv, ing-/ adj. 1 unduly curious. 2 seeking knowledge. □□ **in·quis′i·tive·ly** adv. **in·quis′i·tive·ness** n.

in re /in rée, ráy/ prep. = RE[1].

in·road /ínrōd/ n. 1 (often in pl.) a encroachment. b progress. 2 hostile attack.

INS abbr. Immigration and Naturalization Service.

in·sane /insáyn/ adj. 1 not of sound mind; mad. 2 colloq. extremely foolish. □□ **in·sane′ly** adv. **in·san·i·ty** /-sánitee/ n. (pl. **-ties**)

in·sa·tia·ble /insáyshəbəl/ adj. 1 unable to be satisfied. 2 extremely greedy. □□ **in·sa·tia·bil′i·ty** n. **in·sa′tia·bly** adv.

in·scribe /inskríb/ v.tr. 1 write or carve (words, etc.) on stone, paper, etc. 2 write an informal dedication (to) in (a book, etc.). 3 enter the name of (a person) on a list or in a book. □□ **in·scrib′a·ble** adj. **in·scrib′er** n.

in·scrip·tion /inskrípshən/ n. 1 words inscribed. 2 a act of inscribing. b instance of this. □□ **in·scrip′tion·al** adj. **in·scrip′tive** adj.

in·scru·ta·ble /inskrōōtəbəl/ adj. mysterious; impenetrable. □□ **in·scru·ta·bil′i·ty** n. **in·scru′ta·ble·ness** n. **in·scru′ta·bly** adv.

in·sect /ínsekt/ n. 1 any arthropod having a

head, thorax, abdomen, two antennae, three pairs of thoracic legs, and usu. one or two pairs of thoracic wings. **2** (loosely) any other small segmented invertebrate animal. □□ **in·sec·tile** /-séktəl, -tīl/ *adj.*

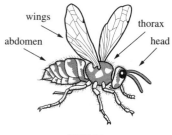

wings

thorax

abdomen

head

INSECT

in·sec·ti·cide /inséktisīd/ *n.* substance used for killing insects. □□ **in·sec·ti·cid′al** *adj.*

in·sec·ti·vore /inséktivawr/ *n.* any animal or plant feeding on insects. □□ **in·sec·ti·vor·ous** /-tívərəs/ *adj.*

in·se·cure /ínsikyóor/ *adj.* **1** lacking confidence. **2 a** unsafe. **b** (of a surface) liable to give way. **c** lacking security. □□ **in·se·cure′ly** *adv.* **in·se·cur′i·ty** *n.*

in·sem·i·nate /inséminayt/ *v.tr.* **1** introduce semen into. **2** sow. □□ **in·sem·i·na·tion** /-náyshən/ *n.* **in·sem′i·na·tor** *n.*

in·sen·sate /insénsayt/ *adj.* **1** without physical sensation. **2** unfeeling. **3** stupid. □□ **in·sen′sate·ly** *adv.*

in·sen·si·ble /insénsibəl/ *adj.* **1 a** unconscious. **b** (of the extremities, etc.) numb. **2** (usu. foll. by *of*, *to*) unaware. **3** callous. **4** too small or gradual to be perceived. □□ **in·sen·si·bil′i·ty** *n.* **in·sen′si·bly** *adv.*

in·sen·si·tive /insénsitiv/ *adj.* **1** unfeeling; boorish; crass. **2** not sensitive to physical stimuli. □□ **in·sen′si·tive·ly** *adv.* **in·sen′si·tive·ness** *n.* **in·sen·si·tiv′i·ty** *n.*

in·sen·ti·ent /insénshənt/ *adj.* not sentient; inanimate. □□ **in·sen′tience** /-shəns/ *n.*

in·sep·a·ra·ble /insépərəbəl/ • *adj.* **1** (esp. of friends) unable or unwilling to be separated. **2** *Gram.* unable to be used as a separate word, e.g., *dis-*, *mis-*, *un-*. • *n.* (usu. in *pl.*) inseparable person or thing, esp. a friend. □□ **in·sep′a·ra·bly** *adv.*

in·sert • *v.tr.* /insárt/ place, fit, or thrust (a thing) into another. • *n.* /ínsərt/ something inserted, e.g., a loose page in a magazine. □□ **in·sert′a·ble** *adj.* **in·sert′er** *n.*

in·ser·tion /insárshən/ *n.* **1** act or instance of inserting. **2** amendment, etc., inserted in writing or printing.

in·set • *n.* /ínset/ **1** an insert. **2** small map, etc., inserted within the border of a larger one. • *v.tr.* /insét/ (**in·set·ting**; *past* and *past part.* **in·set**) **1** put in as an inset. **2** decorate with an inset.

in·shore /ínshawr/ *adv.* & *adj.* at sea but close to the shore.

in·side • *n.* /ínsíd/ **1 a** inner side. **b** inner part; interior. **2** (usu. in *pl.*) *colloq.* **a** stomach and bowels. **b** operative part of a machine, etc. •

adj. /ínsíd/ situated on or in the inside; (of information, etc.) available only to those on the inside. • *adv.* /insíd/ **1** on, in, or to the inside. **2** *sl.* in prison. • *prep.* /insíd/ **1** on the inner side of; within. **2** in less than (*inside an hour*). □ **inside out** with the inner surface turned outward. **know a thing inside out** know a thing thoroughly.

in·sid·er /insídər/ *n.* **1** person who is within a society, organization, etc. (cf. OUTSIDER). **2** person privy to a secret. □ **insider trading** *Stock Exch.* illegal practice of trading while having access to confidential information.

in·sid·i·ous /insídeeəs/ *adj.* **1** proceeding inconspicuously but harmfully. **2** treacherous. □□ **in·sid′i·ous·ly** *adv.* **in·sid′i·ous·ness** *n.*

in·sight /ínsīt/ *n.* **1** capacity of understanding hidden truths, etc. **2** instance of this. □□ **in·sight′ful** *adj.* **in·sight′ful·ly** *adv.*

in·sig·ni·a /insígneeə/ *n.* (treated as *sing.* or *pl.*) **1** badge. **2** distinguishing mark.

¶ **Insignia** is the plural of the Latin word *insigne*, and some traditionalists insist on *insigne* as the singular. **Insignia** and its plural, *insignias*, have long been standard, however.

in·sig·nif·i·cant /insignífikənt/ *adj.* **1** unimportant; trifling. **2** (of a person) undistinguished. **3** meaningless. □□ **in·sig·nif′i·cance** *n.* **in·sig·nif′i·cant·ly** *adv.*

in·sin·cere /ínsinseer/ *adj.* not sincere; not candid. □□ **in·sin·cere′ly** *adv.* **in·sin·cer′i·ty** /-sér-itee/ *n.* (*pl.* **-ties**)

in·sin·u·ate /insínyoo-ayt/ *v.tr.* **1** convey indirectly. **2** (often *refl.*; usu. foll. by *into*) introduce (oneself, a person, etc.) into favor, etc., by subtle manipulation. □□ **in·sin·u·a·tion** /-áyshən/ *n.* **in·sin·u·a·tive** /-yōotiv/ *adj.* **in·sin′u·a·tor** *n.*

in·sip·id /insípid/ *adj.* **1** lacking vigor; dull. **2** lacking flavor. □□ **in·sip·id′i·ty** *n.* **in·sip′id·ly** *adv.* **in·sip′id·ness** *n.*

in·sist /insíst/ *v.tr.* maintain or demand assertively. □□ **in·sist′er** *n.* **in·sist′ing·ly** *adv.*

in·sis·tent /insístənt/ *adj.* **1** insisting. **2** compelling attention; demanding notice. □□ **in·sis′tence** *n.* **in·sis′ten·cy** *n.* **in·sis′tent·ly** *adv.*

in si·tu /in seetoo, sí-/ *adv.* **1** in its place. **2** in its original place.

in·so·bri·e·ty /insəbrí-itee/ *n.* intemperance, esp. in drinking.

in·so·far as /insōfáar az/ *adv.* to the extent that.

in·sole /ínsōl/ *n.* inner sole of a boot or shoe.

in·so·lent /ínsələnt/ *adj.* offensively contemptuous or arrogant; insulting. □□ **in′so·lence** *n.* **in′so·lent·ly** *adv.*

in·sol·u·ble /insólyəbəl/ *adj.* **1** incapable of being solved. **2** incapable of being dissolved. □□ **in·sol·u·bil′i·ty** *n.* **in·sol′u·bly** *adv.*

in·sol·vent /insólvənt/ • *adj.* **1** unable to pay one's debts. **2** relating to insolvency (*insolvent laws*). • *n.* debtor. □□ **in·sol′ven·cy** *n.*

in·som·ni·a /insómneeə/ *n.* habitual sleeplessness; inability to sleep. □□ **in·som·ni·ac** /-neeak/ *n.* & *adj.*

in·so·much /ínsōmúch/ *adv.* **1** to such an extent. **2** (foll. by *as*) inasmuch.

in·sou·ci·ant /insóoseeənt, ANSóosyaàN/ *adj.* carefree; unconcerned. □□ **in·sou′ci·ance** *n.* **in·sou′ci·ant·ly** *adv.*

insp. *abbr.* **1** inspected. **2** inspector.

in·spect /inspékt/ v.tr. **1** look closely at or into. **2** examine (a document, etc.) officially. □□ **in·spec·tion** /-spékshən/ n.

in·spec·tor /inspéktər/ n. **1** person who inspects. **2** police officer usu. ranking just below a superintendent. □□ **in·spec'tor·ate** n. **in·spec·to·ri·al** /-táwreeəl/ adj. **in·spec'tor·ship** n.

in·spi·ra·tion /inspiráyshən/ n. **1 a** creative force or influence stimulating creativity. **b** divine influence, esp. on the writing of Scripture, etc. **2** sudden brilliant idea. **3** inhalation. □□ **in·spi·ra'tion·al** adj.

in·spire /inspír/ v.tr. **1** stimulate creative activity, esp. by supposed divine agency. **2 a** animate (a person) with a feeling. **b** instill (a feeling) into a person, etc. **3** prompt; give rise to. **4** (as **inspired** adj.) **a** (of a work of art, etc.) as if prompted by a supernatural source. **b** (of a guess) intuitive but accurate. **5** inhale. □□ **in·spir·a·to·ry** /-rətáwree/ adj. **in·spir·ed·ly** /-ridlee/ adv. **in·spir' er** n. **in·spir'ing** adj. **in·spir'ing·ly** adv.

inst. abbr. **1** instance. **2** institute. **3** institution. **4** instrument.

in·sta·bil·i·ty /instəbílitee/ n. (pl. **-ties**) **1** lack of stability. **2** Psychol. unpredictability in behavior, etc.

in·stall /instáwl/ v.tr. (**in·stalled, in·stall·ing**) **1** place (equipment, etc.) in position ready for use. **2** place (a person) in an office or rank with ceremony. **3** establish in a place. □□ **in·stal·la' tion** n. **in·stall' er** n.

in·stall·ment /instáwlmənt/ n. **1** any of several usu. equal payments. **2** any of several parts, as of a television or radio serial. □ **installment plan** payment by installments.

in·stance /ínstəns/ ● n. **1** example or illustration of. **2** particular case. ● v.tr. cite (a fact, etc.) as an instance. □ **for instance** as an example.

---

instance Middle English: via Old French from Latin *instantia* 'presence, urgency,' from *instare* 'be present, press upon,' from *in-* 'upon' + *stare* 'to stand.' The original sense was 'urgency, urgent entreaty,' surviving in *at the instance of*. In the late 16th century the word denoted a particular case cited to disprove a general assertion, derived from medieval Latin *instantia* 'example to the contrary' (translating Greek *enstasis* 'objection'); hence the meaning 'single occurrence.'

---

in·stant /ínstənt/ ● adj. **1** occurring immediately. **2 a** (of food, etc.) processed for quick preparation. **b** prepared hastily and with little effort (*I have no instant solution*). **3** urgent; pressing. ● n. **1** precise moment. **2** short space of time. □ **instant replay** immediate repetition of part of a videotaped sports event.

in·stan·ta·ne·ous /ínstəntáyneeəs/ adj. occurring or done in an instant. □□ **in·stan·ta'ne·ous·ly** adv.

in·stant·ly /ínstəntlee/ adv. immediately; at once.

in·stead /instéd/ adv. **1** (foll. by *of*) as an alternative to (*instead of this one*). **2** as an alternative (*took me instead*) (cf. STEAD).

in·step /ínstep/ n. **1** inner arch of the foot between the toes and the ankle. **2** part of a shoe, etc., over or under this.

in·sti·gate /instigayt/ v.tr. **1** bring about by incitement or persuasion. **2** urge on; incite. □□ **in·sti·ga·tion** /-gáyshən/ n. **in'sti·ga·tive** adj. **in'sti·ga·tor** n.

in·still /instíl/ v.tr. (**in·stilled, in·still·ing**) **1** introduce (a feeling, idea, etc.) gradually. **2** put (a liquid) into drops. □□ **in·stil·la'tion** n. **in·still' er** n. **in·still' ment** n.

in·stinct ● n. /ínstingkt/ **1 a** innate pattern of behavior, esp. in animals. **b** innate impulsion. **2** unconscious skill; intuition. ● predic.adj. /instíngkt/ (foll. by *with*) imbued; filled (with life, beauty, etc.). □□ **in·stinc'tive** adj. **in·stinc·tu·al** /-stíngkchōoəl/ adj. **in·stinc'tu·al·ly** adv.

in·sti·tute /ínstitōot, -tyōot/ ● n. **1** society or organization for the promotion of science, education, etc. **2** building used by an institute. ● v.tr. **1** establish; found. **2** initiate (an inquiry, etc.). **3** appoint (a person) as a cleric in a church, etc.

in·sti·tu·tion /ínstitōoshən, -tyōo-/ n. **1** act or an instance of instituting. **2** a society or organization founded esp. for a particular purpose. **b** building used by an institution. **3** established law, practice, or custom. **4** colloq. (of a person, a custom, etc.) familiar object. **5** establishment of a cleric, etc., in a church. □□ **in·sti·tu'tion·al** adj. **in·sti·tu'tion·al·ism** n. **in·sti·tu'tion·al·ly** adv.

in·sti·tu·tion·al·ize /ínstitōoshənəlīz, -tyōo-/ v.tr. **1** place or keep (a person) in an institution. **2** convert into an institution. □□ **in·sti·tu·tion·al·i·za'tion** n.

in·struct /instrúkt/ v.tr. **1** teach (a person) a subject, etc. **2** direct; command. **3** inform (a person) of a fact, etc.

in·struc·tion /instrúkshən/ n. **1** (often in pl.) direction; order. **2** teaching; education. □□ **in·struc'tion·al** adj.

in·struc·tive /instrúktiv/ adj. tending to instruct; enlightening. □□ **in·struc'tive·ly** adv. **in·struc' tive·ness** n.

in·struc·tor /instrúktər/ n. (fem. **in·struc·tress** /-strúktris/) **1** teacher. **2** university teacher below assistant professor.

in·stru·ment /ínstrəmənt/ ● n. **1** tool or implement, esp. for delicate or scientific work. **2** (in full **mu'sic·al in'stru·ment**) device for producing musical sounds. **3 a** thing used in performing an action. **b** person made use of. **4** measuring device, as in an airplane. **5** formal document. ● v.tr. **1** arrange (music) for instruments. **2** equip with instruments (for measuring, recording, controlling, etc.).

in·stru·men·tal /ínstrəmént'l/ ● adj. **1** serving as an instrument or means. **2** (of music) performed on instruments (cf. VOCAL). ● n. piece of music performed by instruments. □□ **in·stru·men'tal·ist** n. **in·stru·men·tal·i·ty** /-méntəlitee/ n. **in·stru·men'tal·ly** adv.

in·stru·men·ta·tion /ínstrəməntáyshən/ n. **1 a** arrangement of music for instruments. **b** instruments used in a piece of music. **2 a** design, provision, or use of instruments in industry, etc. **b** instruments collectively.

in·sub·or·di·nate /ínsəbáwrd'nət/ adj. disobedient; rebellious. □□ **in·sub·or'din·ate·ly** adv. **in·sub·or·di·na·tion** /-náyshən/ n.

in·sub·stan·tial /ínsəbstánshəl/ adj. **1** lacking solidity or substance. **2** not real. □□ **in·sub· stan·ti·al·i·ty** /-sheeálitee/ n. **in·sub·stan'tial·ly** adv.

in·suf·fer·a·ble /insúfərəbəl/ *adj.* **1** intolerable. **2** unbearable.

in·su·lar /ínsələr, ínsyə-/ *adj.* **1 a** of or like an island. **b** separated or remote. **2** narrow-minded. □□ **in′su·lar·ism** *n.* **in·su·lar′i·ty** /-láritee/ *n.* **in′su·lar·ly** *adv.*

in·su·late /ínsəlayt, ínsyə-/ *v.tr.* **1** prevent the passage of electricity, heat, or sound by interposing nonconductors. **2** isolate. □□ **in·su·la·tion** /-láyshən/ *n.* **in′su·la·tor** *n.*

in·su·lin /ínsəlin/ *n. Biochem.* hormone regulating the amount of glucose in the blood, the lack of which causes diabetes.

in·sult • *v.tr.* /insúlt/ **1** speak to or treat with scornful abuse. **2** offend the self-respect or modesty of. • *n.* /ínsult/ insulting remark or action. □□ **in·sult′er** *n.* **in·sult′ing·ly** *adv.*

---

insult mid-16th century (as a verb in the sense 'exult, act arrogantly'): from Latin *insultare* 'jump or trample on,' from *in-* 'on' + *saltare*, from *salire* 'to leap.' The noun (in the early 17th century denoting an attack) is from French *insulte* or ecclesiastical Latin *insultus*. The main current senses date from the 17th century.

---

in·su·per·a·ble /insóōpərəbəl/ *adj.* **1** (of a barrier) impossible to surmount. **2** (of a difficulty, etc.) impossible to overcome. □□ **in·su·per·a·bil′i·ty** *n.* **in·su′per·a·bly** *adv.*

in·sup·port·a·ble /ínsəpáwrtəbəl/ *adj.* **1** unable to be endured. **2** unjustifiable. □□ **in·sup·port′a·bly** *adv.*

in·sur·ance /inshŏŏrəns/ *n.* **1** insuring. **2 a** sum paid for this. **b** sum paid out as compensation for theft, damage, loss, etc. **3** = *insurance policy.* □ **insurance policy** contract of insurance.

in·sure /inshŏŏr/ *v.tr.* purchase or issue an insurance policy. □□ **in·sur′a·ble** *adj.* **in·sur·a·bil′i·ty** *n.*

¶ **Insure** is standard for the sense 'protect against loss' (**assure** was long also used for this). For the nontechnical sense 'make sure,' **insure** and **ensure** are interchangeable: *My telephone call will ensure* (or *insure*) *you an introduction to the director, not a formal interview.*

in·sured /inshŏŏrd/ • *adj.* covered by insurance. • *n.* (usu. prec. by *the*) person, etc., covered by insurance.

in·sur·er /inshŏŏrər/ *n.* person or company offering insurance policies.

in·sur·gent /insúrjənt/ • *adj.* rising in active revolt. • *n.* rebel. □□ **in·sur′gence** *n.* **in·sur′gen·cy** *n.* (*pl.* **-cies**)

in·sur·rec·tion /insərékshən/ *n.* rebellion. □□ **in·sur·rec′tion·ar·y** *adj.* **in·sur·rec′tion·ist** *n.*

in·tact /intákt/ *adj.* **1** entire. **2** untouched. □□ **in·tact′ness** *n.*

in·ta·glio /intályō, -taál-/ • *n.* (*pl.* **-glios**) **1** gem with an incised design (cf. CAMEO). **2** engraved design. • *v.tr.* (**-glioes, -glioed**) engrave (material) with an incised pattern.

in·take /íntayk/ *n.* **1 a** action of taking in. **b** instance of this. **2** number or amount taken in. **3** place where water, fuel, or air is taken in.

in·tan·gi·ble /intánjibəl/ • *adj.* **1** unable to be touched. **2** unable to be grasped mentally. • *n.* thing that cannot be precisely measured or assessed. □□ **in·tan·gi·bil′i·ty** *n.* **in·tan′gi·bly** *adv.*

in·te·ger /íntijər/ *n.* whole number.

in·te·gral /íntigrəl, intégrəl/ *adj.* **1 a** of or necessary to a whole. **b** forming a whole. **c** complete. **2** *Math.* of or denoted by an integer. □□ **in·teg′ral·ly** *adv.*

in·te·grate • *v.* /íntigrayt/ **1** *tr.* **a** combine (parts) into a whole. **b** complete by the addition of parts. **2** *tr. & intr.* bring or come into equal participation in society, a school, etc. **3** *tr.* desegregate, esp. racially (a school, etc.). • *adj.* /íntigrət/ **1** made up of parts. **2** whole; complete. □ **integrated circuit** *Electronics* small chip, etc., of material replacing several separate components in a conventional electrical circuit. □□ **in·teg·ra·ble** /íntigrəbəl/ *adj.* **in·teg·ra·bil′i·ty** *n.* **in·te·gra·tion** /íntigráyshən/ *n.*

in·teg·ri·ty /intégritee/ *n.* **1** moral uprightness; honesty. **2** wholeness; soundness.

in·teg·u·ment /intégyəmənt/ *n.* natural outer covering, as a skin, husk, rind, etc. □□ **in·teg·u·men·tal** /-mént′l/ *adj.* **in·teg·u·men′ta·ry** *adj.*

in·tel·lect /íntilekt/ *n.* **1 a** faculty of reasoning, knowing, and thinking, as distinct from feeling. **b** understanding. **2** clever or knowledgeable person.

in·tel·lec·tu·al /íntilékchŏŏəl/ • *adj.* **1** of or appealing to the intellect. **2** possessing a high level of intelligence. **3** requiring the intellect. • *n.* person possessing a highly developed intellect. □□ **in·tel·lec·tu·al·i·ty** /-chŏŏálitee/ *n.* **in·tel·lec′tu·a·lize** *v.* **in·tel·lec′tu·al·ly** *adv.*

in·tel·li·gence /intélijəns/ *n.* **1 a** intellect; understanding. **b** quickness of understanding. **2 a** collection of information, esp. of military or political value. **b** people employed in this. **c** information; news. □ **intelligence quotient** number denoting the ratio of a person's intelligence to the normal or average.

in·tel·li·gent /intélijənt/ *adj.* **1** having or showing intelligence, esp. of a high level. **2** clever. **3 a** (of a device or machine) able to vary its behavior in response to varying situations, requirements, and past experience. **b** (esp. of a computer terminal) having its own data-processing capability; incorporating a microprocessor. □□ **in·tel′li·gent·ly** *adv.*

in·tel·li·gent·si·a /intélijéntseeə/ *n.* intellectuals, considered as a class.

in·tel·li·gi·ble /intélijibəl/ *adj.* able to be understood. □□ **in·tel·li·gi·bil′i·ty** *n.* **in·tel′li·gi·bly** *adv.*

in·tem·per·ate /intémpərət/ *adj.* **1** immoderate. **2** given to excessive indulgence in alcohol, etc. □□ **in·tem′per·ance** *n.* **in·tem′per·ate·ly** *adv.* **in·tem′per·ate·ness** *n.*

in·tend /inténd/ *v.tr.* **1** have as one's purpose. **2** design or destine for. **3** mean. **4** (foll. by *for*) be meant for a person to have or use, etc. **5** (as **intending** *adj.*) who intends to be.

in·tend·ed /inténdid/ • *adj.* **1** done on purpose. **2** designed; meant. • *n. colloq.* one's fiancé or fiancée.

in·tense /inténs/ *adj.* (**in·tens·er, in·tens·est**) **1** existing in a high degree; violent; forceful. **2** very emotional. **3** (of a feeling, etc.) extreme. □□ **in·tense′ly** *adv.* **in·tense′ness** *n.*

¶ **Intense** is sometimes wrongly used instead of **intensive** to describe a course of study that covers a large amount of material in a short space of time.

in·ten·si·fy /inténsifī/ v. (-fies, -fied) make or become intense or more intense. □□ **in·ten·si·fi·ca'tion** n.

in·ten·si·ty /inténsitee/ n. (pl. -ties) 1 intenseness. 2 esp. Physics measurable amount of some quality, e.g., force, brightness, etc.

in·ten·sive /inténsiv/ adj. 1 thorough; vigorous; directed to a single point, area, or subject. 2 serving to increase production in relation to costs. 3 Gram. (of an adjective, adverb, etc.) expressing intensity, as really in my feet are really cold. □ **intensive care** medical treatment with constant monitoring, etc., of a dangerously ill patient (also (with hyphen) attrib.: intensive-care unit). □□ **in·ten'sive·ly** adv. **in·ten'sive·ness** n.

in·tent /intént/ ● n. intention; purpose. ● adj. 1 (usu. foll. by on) a resolved; determined. b attentively occupied. 2 (esp. of a look) earnest; eager. □ **to** (or **for**) **all intents and purposes** practically; virtually. □□ **in·tent'ly** adv. **in·tent'ness** n.

in·ten·tion /inténshən/ n. 1 thing intended; aim or purpose. 2 intending. □□ **in·ten'tioned** adj. (usu. in comb.).

in·ten·tion·al /inténshənəl/ adj. done on purpose. □□ **in·ten'tion·al·ly** adv.

in·ter /intər/ v.tr. (**in·terred, in·ter·ring**) bury (a corpse, etc.).

inter- /intər/ comb. form 1 between; among (intercontinental). 2 mutually; reciprocally (interbreed).

in·ter·act /íntərákt/ v.intr. act reciprocally; act on each other. □□ **in·ter·ac'tant** adj. & n. **in·ter·ac·tion** /íntərákshən/ n.

in·ter·ac·tive /íntəráktiv/ adj. 1 reciprocally active. 2 (of a computer or other electronic device) allowing a two-way flow of information between it and a user. □□ **in·ter·ac'tive·ly** adv.

in·ter a·li·a /intər áyleeə, aáleeə/ adv. among other things.

in·ter·breed /íntərbreed/ v. (past and past part. -bred /-bréd/) 1 intr. & tr. breed or cause to breed with members of a different race or species to produce a hybrid. 2 tr. breed within one family, etc. (cf. CROSSBREED).

in·ter·cede /íntərseed/ v.intr. intervene on behalf of another; plead. □□ **in·ter·ced'er** n.

in·ter·cept /íntərsépt/ v.tr. 1 seize, catch, or stop (a person or thing) going from one place to another. 2 cut off (light, etc.). □□ **in·ter·cep·tion** /-sépshən/ n. **in·ter·cep·tive** /-séptiv/ adj. **in·ter·cep'tor** n.

in·ter·ces·sion /íntərséshən/ n. 1 interceding. 2 instance of this. 3 prayer. □□ **in·ter·ces'sion·al** adj. **in·ter·ces'sor** n. **in·ter·ces·so·ry** adj.

in·ter·change ● v.tr. /íntərcháynj/ 1 (of two people) exchange (things) with each other. 2 put each of (two things) in the other's place; alternate. ● n. /íntərchaynj/ 1 reciprocal exchange between two people, etc. 2 alternation. 3 road junction designed so that traffic streams do not intersect. □□ **in·ter·change'a·ble** adj. **in·ter·change'a·bly** adv.

in·ter·com /íntərkom/ n. colloq. system of intercommunication by radio or telephone.

in·ter·con·nect /íntərkənékt/ v. connect with each other. □□ **in·ter·con·nec·tion** /-nékshən/ n.

in·ter·con·ti·nen·tal /íntərkóntinént'l/ adj.

connecting or traveling between continents. □□ **in·ter·con·ti·nen'tal·ly** adv.

in·ter·course /íntərkawrs/ n. 1 communication or dealings between individuals, nations, etc. 2 = sexual intercourse.

---

intercourse late Middle English (denoting communication or dealings): from Old French entrecours 'exchange, commerce,' from Latin intercursus, from intercurrere 'intervene,' from inter-'between' + currere 'run.' The specifically sexual use arose in the late 18th century.

---

in·ter·de·nom·i·na·tion·al /íntərdinómináyshənəl/ adj. concerning more than one (religious) denomination. □□ **in·ter·de·nom·i·na'tion·al·ly** adv.

in·ter·de·part·men·tal /íntərdee'epaartmént'l/ adj. concerning more than one department. □□ **in·ter·de·part·men'tal·ly** adv.

in·ter·de·pend /íntərdipénd/ v.intr. depend on each other. □□ **in·ter·de·pend'ence** n. **in·ter·de·pend'en·cy** n. **in·ter·de·pend'ent** adj.

in·ter·dict ● n. /íntərdikt/ formal or authoritative prohibition. ● v.tr. /íntərdíkt/ 1 prohibit (an action). 2 forbid the use of. 3 restrain (a person). 4 (usu. foll. by to) forbid (a thing) to a person. □□ **in·ter·dic·tion** /-díkshən/ n. **in·ter·dic·to·ry** /-díktəree/ adj.

---

interdict Middle English entredite ('forbid a person or place ecclesiastical functions and privileges'), from Old French entredit, from Latin interdictum, past participle of interdicere 'interpose, forbid by decree,' from inter-'between' + dicere 'say.' The spelling was changed in the 16th century by the addition of the c, by association with the Latin form.

---

in·ter·dis·ci·plin·ar·y /íntərdisiplinéree/ adj. of or between more than one branch of learning.

in·ter·est /íntərist, -trist/ ● n. 1 a curiosity; concern. b quality exciting curiosity, etc. c noteworthiness; importance (findings of no particular interest). 2 subject, hobby, etc., in which one is concerned. 3 advantage or profit. 4 money paid for the use of money lent. 5 a financial stake (in an undertaking, etc.). b legal concern, title, or right (in property). 6 party or group having a common interest. 7 self-interest. ● v.tr. 1 excite the curiosity or attention of. 2 cause (a person) to take a personal interest. 3 (as **interested** adj.) not impartial or disinterested (an interested party). □□ **in'ter·est·ed·ly** adv.

in·ter·est·ing /íntristing, -tóresting/ adj. causing curiosity; holding the attention. □□ **in'ter·est·ing·ly** adv.

in·ter·face /íntərfays/ ● n. 1 esp. Physics surface forming a boundary between two regions. 2 point where interaction occurs between two systems, etc. (interface between psychology and education). 3 Computing a apparatus for connecting two pieces of equipment so that they can be operated jointly. b means by which a user interacts with a program or utilizes an application. ● v. connect with.

in·ter·fere /íntərfeer/ v.intr. 1 (usu. foll. by with) a (of a person) meddle; obstruct a process, etc. b (of a thing) be a hindrance. 2 intervene, esp. without invitation or necessity. 3 (foll. by with) euphem. molest or assault sexually. □□ **in·ter·fer'er** n. **in·ter·fer'ing** adj. **in·ter·fer'ing·ly** adv.

in·ter·fer·ence /íntərféerəns/ n. 1 (usu. foll. by *with*) a act of interfering. b instance of this. 2 fading or disturbance of received radio signals.

in·ter·fer·on /íntərféeron/ n. Biochem. any of various proteins that can inhibit the development of a virus in a cell, etc.

in·ter·fuse /íntərfyóoz/ v. 1 tr. a mix (a thing) with; intersperse. b blend (things). 2 intr. (of two things) blend with each other. □□ **in·ter·fu·sion** /-fyóozhən/ n.

in·ter·im /íntərim/ • n. intervening time. • adj. provisional; temporary.

in·te·ri·or /intéereeər/ • adj. 1 inner (opp. EXTERIOR). 2 inland. 3 internal; domestic (opp. FOREIGN). 4 situated further in or within. 5 inward. 6 coming from inside. • n. 1 interior part; inside. 2 interior part of a country or region. 3 domestic affairs of a country. 4 inner nature; the soul. □□ **in·te′ri·or·ize** v.tr. **in·te′ri·or·ly** adv.

interj. abbr. interjection.

in·ter·ject /íntərjékt/ v.tr. 1 utter (words) abruptly or parenthetically. 2 interrupt with. □□ **in·ter·jec·to·ry** /-jéktəree/ adj.

in·ter·jec·tion /íntərjékshən/ n. Gram. exclamation, esp. as a part of speech (e.g., *ah!; dear me!*). □□ **in·ter·jec′tion·al** adj.

in·ter·lace /íntərláys/ v. 1 tr. bind intricately together. 2 intr. cross each other intricately. □□ **in·ter·lace′ment** n.

in·ter·lard /íntərláard/ v.tr. mix (writing or speech) with unusual words or phrases.

in·ter·leave /íntərléev/ v.tr. insert (usu. blank) leaves between the leaves of (a book, etc.).

in·ter·lin·ing /íntərlíning/ n. material used between the fabric (of a garment) and its lining.

in·ter·lock /íntərlók/ v. 1 intr. engage with each other by overlapping. 2 tr. lock or clasp within each other. □□ **in·ter·lock′er** n.

in·ter·loc·u·tor /íntərlókyətər/ n. person who takes part in a conversation. □□ **in·ter·lo·cu·tion** /-ləkyóoshən/ n.

in·ter·loc·u·to·ry /íntərlókyətawree/ adj. 1 of dialogue. 2 Law (of a decree, etc.) given provisionally.

in·ter·lop·er /íntərlópər/ n. 1 intruder. 2 person who interferes in others' affairs, esp. for profit. □□ **in′ter·lope** v.intr.

in·ter·lude /íntərlood/ n. 1 a pause between the acts of a play. b something performed during this pause. 2 intervening time, space, or event that contrasts with what goes before or after.

in·ter·mar·ry /íntərmáree/ v.intr. (**-ries, -ried**) (of races, castes, families, etc.) become connected by marriage. □□ **in·ter·mar·riage** /íntərmárij/ n.

in·ter·me·di·ar·y /íntərméedee-eree/ • n. (pl. **-ies**) intermediate person or thing, esp. a mediator. • adj. acting as mediator; intermediate.

in·ter·me·di·ate • adj. /íntərméedeeət/ coming between two things in time, place, order, character, etc. • n. /íntərméedeeət/ intermediate thing. • v.intr. /íntərméedeeáyt/ act as intermediary. □□ **in·ter·me′di·a·cy** n. **in·ter·me′di·ate·ly** adv. **in·ter·me·di·a·tion** /-deeáyshən/ n. **in·ter·me·di·a·tor** /-deeaytər/ n.

in·ter·ment /íntərmənt/ n. burial of a corpse. ¶ **Interment**, which means 'burial,' should not be confused with *internment*, which means 'imprisonment.'

in·ter·mez·zo /íntərmétsō/ n. (pl. **in·ter·mez·zi** /-see/ or **-zos**) 1 short instrumental movement in a musical work. 2 short, light dramatic or other performance inserted between the acts of a play.

in·ter·mi·na·ble /intórminəbəl/ adj. 1 endless. 2 tediously long. □□ **in·ter′mi·na·bly** adv.

in·ter·min·gle /íntərmínggəl/ v. (often foll. by *with*) mix together; mingle.

in·ter·mis·sion /íntərmíshən/ n. 1 pause or cessation. 2 interval between parts of a play, concert, etc.

in·ter·mit·tent /íntərmít'nt/ adj. occurring at intervals. □□ **in·ter·mit·tence** /-mít'ns/ n. **in·ter·mit′ten·cy** n. **in·ter·mit′tent·ly** adv.

in·tern • n. /íntərn/ recent graduate or advanced medical student living in a hospital and acting as an assistant physician or surgeon. • v. 1 tr. /intórn/ confine; oblige (a prisoner, alien, etc.) to reside within prescribed limits. 2 intr. /íntərn/ serve as an intern. □□ **in′tern·ship** n.

in·ter·nal /intórnəl/ • adj. 1 of or situated on the inside. 2 of the inside of the body (*internal injuries*). 3 of a nation's domestic affairs. 4 used or applying within an organization. 5 a intrinsic. b of the mind or soul. • n. (in pl.) intrinsic qualities. □ **internal combustion engine** engine powered by the explosion of gases or vapor with air in a cylinder. □□ **in·ter·nal·i·ty** /-nálitee/ n. **in·ter′nal·ize** v.tr. **in·ter·nal·i·za′tion** n. **in·ter′nal·ly** adv.

in·ter·na·tion·al /íntərnáshənəl/ adj. 1 existing, involving, or carried on between or among nations. 2 agreed on or used by all or many nations (*international date line*). □□ **in·ter·na·tion·al·i·ty** /-nálitee/ n. **in·ter·na′tion·al·ize** v.tr. **in·ter·na′tion·al·ly** adv.

in·ter·na·tion·al·ism /íntərnáshənəlizəm/ n. the advocacy of a community of interests among nations. □□ **in·ter·na′tion·al·ist** n.

in·ter·ne·cine /íntərnéeseen, -néseen/ adj. mutually destructive.

In·ter·net /íntərnét/ n. communications network enabling the linking of computers worldwide for data interchange.

in·tern·ist /íntórnist/ n. Med. specialist in internal medicine.

in·tern·ment /intórnmənt/ n. confinement; imprisonment.
¶ See note at INTERMENT.

in·ter·per·son·al /íntərpórsənəl/ adj. (of relations) occurring between persons, esp. reciprocally. □□ **in·ter·per′son·al·ly** adv.

in·ter·plan·e·tar·y /íntərplániteree/ adj. between planets.

in·ter·play /íntərplay/ n. reciprocal action.

In·ter·pol /íntərpōl/ n. International Criminal Police Organization.

in·ter·po·late /intórpəlayt/ v.tr. 1 a insert (words) in a book. b make such insertions in (a book, etc.). 2 estimate (values) from known ones in the same range. □□ **in·ter·po·la·tion** /-láyshən/ n. **in·ter′po·la·tive** adj. **in·ter′po·la·tor** n.

in·ter·pose /íntərpóz/ v. 1 tr. place or insert (a thing) between others. 2 tr. say (words) as an interruption. 3 tr. exercise or advance (a veto or objection) so as to interfere. 4 intr. intervene (between parties). □□ **in·ter·po·si′tion** n.

in·ter·pret /intə́rprit/ v. **1** tr. explain the meaning of (words, a dream, etc.). **2** tr. make out or bring out the meaning of (creative work). **3** intr. act as an interpreter. **4** tr. explain or understand (behavior, etc.) in a specified manner. □□ **in·ter′pret·a·ble** adj. **in·ter·pret·a·bil′i·ty** n. **in·ter·pre·ta′tion** n. **in·ter·pre·ta′tion·al** adj. **in·ter·pre·ta·tive** /-táytiv/ adj. **in·ter′pre·tive** adj. **in·ter′pre·tive·ly** adv.

in·ter·pret·er /intə́rpritər/ n. person who interprets, esp. one who translates speech orally.

in·ter·ra·cial /intəráyshəl/ adj. existing between or affecting different races. □□ **in·ter·ra′cial·ly** adv.

in·ter·reg·num /intərégnəm/ n. (pl. **in·ter·reg·nums** or **in·ter·reg·na** /-nə/) interval, esp. when normal government is suspended between successive reigns or regimes.

in·ter·re·late /intəriláyt/ v.tr. relate (two or more things) to each other. □□ **in·ter·re·la·tion** /-láyshən/ n. **in·ter·re·la′tion·ship** n.

in·ter·ro·gate /intérəgayt/ v.tr. ask questions of (a person) esp. closely, thoroughly, or formally. □□ **in·ter·ro·ga·tion** /intérəgáyshən/ n. **in·ter′ro·ga·tor** n.

in·ter·rog·a·tive /intərógətiv/ adj. of, like, or used in questions. □□ **in·ter·rog′a·tive·ly** adv.

in·ter·rog·a·to·ry /intərógətáwree/ adj. of a questioning nature.

in·ter·rupt /intərúpt/ v.tr. **1** break the continuous progress of (an action, speech, a person speaking, etc.). **2** break or suspend the continuity of. □□ **in·ter·rupt′er** n. **in·ter·rup·tion** /-rúpshən/ n. **in·ter·rup′tive** adj.

in·ter·sect /intərsékt/ v. **1** tr. divide (a thing) by crossing it. **2** intr. (of lines, roads, etc.) cross each other.

in·ter·sec·tion /intərsékshən/ n. **1** act of intersecting. **2** place where two roads intersect. □□ **in·ter·sec′tion·al** adj.

in·ter·sperse /intərspə́rs/ v.tr. **1** scatter. **2** (foll. by with) diversify (a thing or things with others so scattered). □□ **in·ter·sper·sion** /-pérzhən/ n.

in·ter·state ● /intərstáyt/ existing or carried on between states, esp. of the US. ● n. /intə́rstayt/ highway that is part of the US Interstate Highway System.

in·ter·stel·lar /intərstélər/ adj. between stars.

in·ter·stice /intə́rstis/ n. **1** intervening space. **2** chink or crevice. □□ **in·ter·sti·tial** /intərstíshəl/ adj.

in·ter·twine /intərtwín/ v. **1** tr. (often foll. by with) entwine (together). **2** intr. become entwined.

in·ter·val /intərvəl/ n. **1** intervening time or space. **2** difference in pitch between two sounds. □ **at intervals** here and there; now and then. □□ **in·ter·val·ic** /-válik/ adj.

in·ter·vene /intərvéen/ v.intr. **1** occur in time between events. **2** interfere; prevent or modify events. **3** be situated between things. □□ **in·ter·ven′er** n. **in·ter·ve′nor** n.

in·ter·ven·tion /intərvénshən/ n. **1** intervening. **2** interference, esp. by a state in another's affairs. **3** mediation.

in·ter·view /intərvyōo/ ● n. **1** usu. in-person examination of an applicant. **2** conversation between a reporter, etc., and a person of public interest, used as a basis of a broadcast or

publication. **3** meeting face to face, esp. for consultation. ● v.tr. hold an interview with. □□ **in·ter·view·ee** /-vyōo-ée/ n. **in′ter·view·er** n.

in·ter·weave /intərwéev/ v.tr. (past **-wove** /-wóv/; past part. **-wo·ven** /-wóvən/) **1** (often foll. by with) weave together. **2** blend intimately.

in·tes·tate /intéstayt/ ● adj. not having made a will before death. ● n. person who has died intestate. □□ **in·tes′ta·cy** n.

in·tes·tine /intéstin/ n. (in sing. or pl.) lower part of the alimentary canal. □□ **in·tes′tin·al** adj.

in·ti·mate[1] /íntimət/ ● adj. **1** closely acquainted; familiar. **2** private and personal. **3** having sexual relations. **4** (of knowledge) detailed; thorough. ● n. very close friend. □□ **in′ti·mate·ly** adv.

in·ti·mate[2] /íntimayt/ v.tr. **1** state or make known. **2** imply; hint. □□ **in′ti·mat·er** n. **in·ti·ma·tion** /-máyshən/ n.

in·tim·i·date /intímidayt/ v.tr. frighten or overawe, esp. to subdue or influence. □□ **in·tim·i·da·tion** /-dáyshən/ n. **in·ti′mi·da·tor** n.

in·to /íntōo/ prep. **1** expressing motion or direction to a point on or within (ran into the house). **2** expressing direction of attention. **3** expressing a change of state (separated into groups). **4** colloq. interested in; knowledgeable about (is really into art).

in·tol·er·a·ble /intólərəbəl/ adj. that cannot be endured. □□ **in·tol′er·a·bly** adv.

in·tol·er·ant /intólərənt/ adj. not tolerant, esp. of views, beliefs, or behavior differing from one's own. □□ **in·tol′er·ance** n. **in·tol′er·ant·ly** adv.

in·to·na·tion /intənáyshən/ n. **1** modulation of the voice; accent. **2** intoning. **3** accuracy of musical pitch. □□ **in·to·na′tion·al** adj.

in·tone /intón/ v.tr. **1** recite (prayers, etc.) with prolonged sounds, esp. in a monotone. **2** utter with a particular tone. □□ **in·ton′er** n.

in to·to /in tótō/ adv. completely.

in·tox·i·cant /intóksikənt/ ● adj. intoxicating. ● n. intoxicating substance.

in·tox·i·cate /intóksikayt/ v.tr. **1** make drunk. **2** excite or elate beyond self-control. □□ **in·tox·i·ca·tion** /-káyshən/ n.

in·tox·i·cat·ing /intóksikayting/ adj. **1** liable to cause intoxication; alcoholic. **2** exhilarating; exciting. □□ **in·tox′i·cat·ing·ly** adv.

intr. abbr. intransitive.

intra- /intrə/ prefix forming adjectives usu. from adjectives, meaning 'on the inside, within' (intramural).

in·trac·ta·ble /intráktəbəl/ adj. **1** hard to control. **2** stubborn. □□ **in·trac·ta·bil′i·ty** n. **in·trac′ta·ble·ness** n. **in·trac′ta·bly** adv.

in·tra·mu·ral /intrəmyōórəl/ adj. **1** situated or done within walls. **2** forming part of normal university or college studies. □□ **in·tra·mu′ral·ly** adv.

in·tra·mus·cu·lar /intrəmúskyələr/ adj. in or into a muscle or muscles.

in·tran·si·gent /intránsijənt, -tránz-/ ● adj. uncompromising; stubborn. ● n. intransigent person. □□ **in·tran′si·gence** n. **in·tran′si·gen·cy** n. **in·tran′si·gent·ly** adv.

in·tran·si·tive /intránsitiv, -tránz-/ adj. Gram. (of a verb or sense of a verb) that does not take a direct object (whether expressed or implied), e.g., look in look at the sky (opp. TRANSITIVE). □□ **in·tran′si·tive·ly** adv. **in·tran·si·tiv′i·ty** /-tívitee/ n.

in·tra·u·ter·ine /íntrəyo͞otərin, -rín/ *adj.* within the uterus. □ **intrauterine device** device inserted into the uterus that provides birth control by preventing implantation. ¶ Abbr.: **IUD**.

in·tra·ve·nous /íntrəve'enəs/ *adj.* in or into a vein or veins. □□ **in·tra·ve'nous·ly** *adv.*

in·trep·id /intrépid/ *adj.* fearless; very brave. □□ **in·tre·pid·i·ty** /-tripíditee/ *n.* **in·trep'id·ly** *adv.*

in·tri·cate /íntrikit/ *adj.* very complicated; perplexingly detailed or obscure. □□ **in'tri·ca·cy** /-kəsee/ *n.* (*pl.* **-cies**). **in'tri·cate·ly** *adv.*

in·trigue ● *v.* /intre'eg/ (**in·trigues, in·trigued, in·trigu·ing**) **1** *intr.* **a** carry on an underhand plot. **b** use secret influence. **2** *tr.* arouse the curiosity of. ● *n.* /intre'eg, ín-/ **1** underhand plot or plotting. **2** secret arrangement. □□ **in·tri'guer** *n.* **in·tri'guing** *adj.* (esp. in sense 2 of *v.*). **in·tri'guing·ly** *adv.*

in·trin·sic /intrínzik/ *adj.* inherent; essential; belonging naturally (*intrinsic value*). □□ **in·trin'si·cal·ly** *adv.*

intro- /íntrō/ *comb. form* into (*introgression*).

intro. *abbr.* **1** introduction. **2** introductory.

in·tro·duce /íntrədo͞os, -dyo͞os/ *v.tr.* **1** (foll. by *to*) make (a person or oneself) known by name to another, esp. formally. **2** announce or present. **3** bring (a custom, idea, etc.) into use. **4** bring (legislation) for consideration. **5** (foll. by *to*) initiate (a person) to a subject. **6** insert. **7** bring in; usher in; bring forward. □□ **in·tro·duc'er** *n.* **in·tro·duc'i·ble** *adj.*

in·tro·duc·tion /íntrədúkshən/ *n.* **1** introducing or being introduced. **2** formal presentation of one person to another. **3** explanatory section at the beginning of a book, etc.

in·tro·duc·to·ry /íntrədúktəree/ *adj.* serving as an introduction; preliminary.

in·tro·spec·tion /íntrəspékshən/ *n.* examination or observation of one's own mental and emotional processes, etc. □□ **in·tro·spec'tive** *adj.* **in·tro·spec'tive·ly** *adv.* **in·tro·spec'tive·ness** *n.*

in·tro·vert ● *n.* /íntrəvərt/ *Psychol.* person predominantly concerned with his or her own thoughts. **2** shy, thoughtful person. ● *adj.* /íntrəvərt/ (also **in·tro·vert'ed** /-tid/) typical or characteristic of an introvert. ● *v.tr.* /íntrəvə́rt/ *Psychol.* direct (one's thoughts or mind) inward. □□ **in·tro·ver·sion** /-və́rzhən, -shən/ *n.* **in·tro·ver·sive** /-və́rsiv/ *adj.* **in'tro·vert·ed** *adj.* **in·tro·ver·tive** /-və́rtiv/ *adj.*

in·trude /intro͞od/ *v.* (foll. by *on, upon, into*) **1** *intr.* come uninvited or unwanted; force oneself abruptly on others. **2** *tr.* thrust or force (something unwelcome) on a person. □□ **in·trud'ing·ly** *adv.* **in·tru·sion** /intro͞ozhən/ *n.*

in·trud·er /intro͞odər/ *n.* person who intrudes, esp. into a building with criminal intent.

in·tru·sive /intro͞osiv/ *adj.* **1** that intrudes or tends to intrude. **2** characterized by intrusion. □□ **in·tru'sive·ly** *adv.* **in·tru'sive·ness** *n.*

in·trust var. of ENTRUST.

in·tu·bate /íntoobayt, -tyo͞o-/ *v.tr. Med.* insert a tube into the trachea for ventilation, usu. during anesthesia. □□ **in·tu·ba·tion** /-báyshən/ *n.*

in·tu·i·tion /íntoo-íshən, -tyo͞o-/ *n.* immediate insight or understanding without conscious reasoning. □□ **in·tu·i'tion·al** *adj.*

in·tu·i·tive /intoo'itiv, -tyo͞o-/ *adj.* of, characterized by, possessing, or perceived by intuition. □□ **in·tu'i·tive·ly** *adv.* **in·tu'i·tive·ness** *n.*

In·u·it /ínyo͞o-it/ *n.* (also **In'nu·it**) (*pl.* same or **In·u·its**) N. American Eskimo.

in·un·date /ínəndayt/ *v.tr.* **1** flood. **2** overwhelm. □□ **in·un·da·tion** /-dáyshən/ *n.*

in·ure /inyo͞or/ *v. tr.* accustom (a person) to something esp. unpleasant. □□ **in·ure'ment** *n.*

in u·ter·o /in yo͞otərō/ *adv.* in the womb; before birth.

in va·cu·o /in váky͞oo-ō/ *adv.* in a vacuum.

in·vade /inváyd/ *v.tr.* **1** enter (a country, etc.) with hostility. **2** swarm into. **3** (of a disease) attack. **4** encroach upon. □□ **in·vad'er** *n.*

in·val·id¹ /ínvəlid/ ● *n.* **1** person enfeebled or disabled by illness or injury. **2** (*attrib.*) **a** of or for invalids. **b** being an invalid (*caring for her invalid mother*). ● *v.* **1** *tr.* disable (a person) by illness. **2** *intr.* become an invalid. □□ **in'va·lid·ism** *n.*

in·val·id² /inválid/ *adj.* not valid. □□ **in·val'id·ly** *adv.*

in·val·i·date /inválidayt/ *v.tr.* **1** make (esp. an argument, etc.) invalid. **2** remove the validity or force of (a treaty, contract, etc.). □□ **in·val·i·da·tion** /-dáyshən/ *n.*

in·val·u·a·ble /invály͞oo-əbəl/ *adj.* above valuation; inestimable. □□ **in·val'u·a·bly** *adv.*

in·va·sion /inváyzhən/ *n.* invading or being invaded. □□ **in·va·sive** /-váysiv/ *adj.*

in·vec·tive /invéktiv/ *n.* **1 a** strongly attacking words. **b** use of such words. **2** abusive rhetoric.

in·veigh /inváy/ *v.intr.* (foll. by *against*) speak or write with strong hostility.

in·vei·gle /inváygəl, -ve'e-/ *v.tr.* entice; persuade by guile. □□ **in·vei'gle·ment** *n.*

in·vent /invént/ *v.tr.* **1** create by thought; originate (a new method, instrument, etc.). **2** concoct (a false story, etc.). □□ **in·vent'a·ble** *adj.* **in·ven'tor** *n.*

in·ven·tion /invénshən/ *n.* **1** process of inventing. **2** thing invented. **3** fictitious story. **4** inventiveness.

in·ven·tive /invéntiv/ *adj.* **1** able to invent; original in devising. **2** showing ingenuity of devising. □□ **in·ven'tive·ly** *adv.* **in·ven'tive·ness** *n.*

in·ven·to·ry /ínvəntáwree/ ● *n.* (*pl.* **-ries**) **1** complete list of goods, etc. **2** goods listed in this. **3** the total of a firm's commercial assets. ● *v.tr.* (**-ries, -ried**) **1** make an inventory of. **2** enter (goods) in an inventory.

in·verse /ínvərs, -və́rs/ ● *adj.* inverted in position, order, or relation. ● *n.* **1** state of being inverted. **2** thing that is the opposite or reverse of another. □ **inverse proportion** (or **ratio**) relation between two quantities such that one increases in proportion as the other decreases. □□ **in·verse'ly** *adv.*

in·ver·sion /invə́rzhən, -shən/ *n.* **1** turning upside down or inside out. **2** reversal of a normal order, position, or relation. □□ **in·ver·sive** /-və́rsiv/ *adj.*

in·vert /invə́rt/ *v.tr.* **1** turn upside down. **2** reverse the position, order, or relation of. □□ **in·vert'er** *n.* **in·vert'i·ble** *adj.* **in·vert·i·bil'i·ty** *n.*

in·ver·te·brate /invə́rtibrət, -brayt/ ● *adj.* **1** (of an animal) not having a backbone. **2** lacking firmness of character. ● *n.* invertebrate animal.

in·vest /invést/ *v.* **1** *tr.* apply or use (money), esp. for profit. **2** *intr.* (foll. by *in*) **a** put money

for profit (into stocks, etc.). **b** *colloq.* buy. **3** *tr.* **a** provide or endue (a person) with qualities, insignia, or rank. **b** attribute or entrust (qualities or feelings to a person). □□ **in•vest′a•ble** *adj.* **in•vest′i•ble** *adj.* **in•ves′tor** *n.*

---

invest mid-16th century (in the senses 'clothe,' 'clothe with the insignia of a rank,' and 'endow with authority'): from French *investir* or Latin *investire*, from *in-* 'into, upon' + *vestire* 'clothe' (from *vestis* 'clothing'). Senses 1 and 2 (early 17th century) are influenced by Italian *investire*, with a similar meaning.

---

in•ves•ti•gate /invéstigayt/ *v.* **1** *tr.* **a** inquire into; examine. **b** make an official inquiry into. **2** *intr.* make a systematic inquiry or search. □□ **in•ves•ti•ga•tion** /invéstigáyshən/ *n.* **in•ves′ti•ga•tive** *adj.* **in•ves′ti•ga•tor** *n.* **in•ves•ti•ga•to•ry** /-gətáwree/ *adj.*

in•ves•ti•ture /invéstichŏŏr, -chər/ *n.* formal investing of a person with honors or rank.

in•vest•ment /invéstmənt/ *n.* **1** investing. **2** money invested. **3** property, etc., in which money is invested.

in•vet•er•ate /invétərət/ *adj.* **1** (of a person) confirmed in a habit, etc. **2 a** (of a habit, etc.) long-established. **b** (of an activity, esp. an undesirable one) habitual. □□ **in•vet•er•a•cy** /-rəsee/ *n.* **in•vet′er•ate•ly** *adv.*

in•vid•i•ous /invídeeəs/ *adj.* likely to excite resentment or indignation. □□ **in•vid′i•ous•ly** *adv.* **in•vid′i•ous•ness** *n.*

in•vig•o•rate /invígərayt/ *v.tr.* give vigor or strength to. □□ **in•vig′or•at•ing** *adj.* **in•vig•or•a•tion** /-ráyshən/ *n.* **in•vig′or•a•tive** *adj.* **in•vig′or•a•tor** *n.*

in•vin•ci•ble /invínsibəl/ *adj.* unconquerable. □□ **in•vin•ci•bil′i•ty** *n.* **in•vin′ci•ble•ness** *n.* **in•vin′ci•bly** *adv.*

in•vi•o•la•ble /invíələbəl/ *adj.* not to be violated or profaned. □□ **in•vi•o•la•bil′i•ty** *n.* **in•vi′o•la•bly** *adv.*

in•vi•o•late /invíələt/ *adj.* not violated or profaned. □□ **in•vi′o•late•ly** *adv.*

in•vis•i•ble /invízibəl/ *adj.* **1** not visible to the eye. **2** artfully concealed so as to be imperceptible. □□ **in•vis•i•bil′i•ty** *n.* **in•vis′i•bly** *adv.*

in•vi•ta•tion /invitáyshən/ *n.* **1 a** inviting or being invited. **b** spoken or written form in which a person is invited. **2** enticing.

in•vite • *v.* /invít/ **1** *tr.* ask (a person) courteously to come or to do something. **2** *tr.* make a formal courteous request for. **3** *tr.* tend to call forth unintentionally (something unwanted). **4 a** *tr.* attract. **b** *intr.* be attractive. • *n.* /invīt/ *colloq.* invitation. □□ **in•vit′er** *n.*

in•vit•ing /invíting/ *adj.* **1** attractive. **2** enticing; tempting. □□ **in•vit′ing•ly** *adv.*

in vi•tro /in véetrō/ *adv. Biol.* taking place in a test tube or other laboratory environment.

in•vo•ca•tion /ínvəkáyshən/ *n.* **1** invoking, esp. in prayer. **2** summoning a source of inspiration, e.g., the Muses. **3** *Eccl.* the words "In the name of the Father," etc., used as the preface to a sermon, etc. □□ **in•vo•ca•to•ry** /invókətáwree/ *adj.*

in•voice /ínvoys/ • *n.* itemized bill for goods or services. • *v.tr.* **1** make an invoice of (goods and services). **2** send an invoice to (a person).

in•voke /invók/ *v.tr.* **1** call on (a deity, etc.) in prayer or as a witness. **2** appeal to (the law, a person's authority, etc.). **3** summon (a spirit) by charms. **4** ask earnestly for (vengeance, help, etc.). □□ **in•vo′ca•ble** *adj.* **in•vok′er** *n.*

in•vol•un•tar•y /invóləntéree/ *adj.* **1** done without the exercise of the will; unintentional. **2** (of a limb, muscle, or movement) not under conscious control. □□ **in•vol•un•tar′i•ly** *adv.*

in•vo•lu•tion /invəlŏŏshən/ *n.* **1** process of involving. **2** entanglement. **3** intricacy. **4** curling inward. □□ **in•vo•lu′tion•al** *adj.*

in•volve /invólv/ *v.tr.* **1** cause (a person or thing) to participate, or share the experience or effect (in a situation, activity, etc.). **2** imply; entail; make necessary. **3** implicate (a person in a charge, crime, etc.). **4** include or affect in its operations. **5** (as **involved** *adj.*) **a** (often foll. by *in*) concerned or interested. **b** complicated in thought or form. □□ **in•volve′ment** *n.*

in•vul•ner•a•ble /invúlnərəbəl/ *adj.* that cannot be wounded or hurt, physically or mentally. □□ **in•vul•ner•a•bil′i•ty** *n.* **in•vul′ner•a•bly** *adv.*

in•ward /ínwərd/ • *adj.* **1** directed toward the inside; going in. **2** situated within. **3** mental; spiritual. • *adv.* (also **in′wards**) **1** toward the inside. **2** in the mind or soul.

in•ward•ly /ínwərdlee/ *adv.* **1** on the inside. **2** in the mind or soul. **3** (of speaking) not aloud; inaudibly.

I/O *abbr. Computing* input/output.

i•o•dide /íədīd/ *n. Chem.* any compound of iodine with another element or group.

i•o•dine /íədīn, -din, -deen/ *n.* **1** *Chem.* element forming black crystals and a violet vapor when heated. ¶ Symb.: **I**. **2** solution of this as a mild antiseptic.

i•on /íən, íon/ *n.* atom or group of atoms that has lost one or more electrons (= CATION), or gained one or more electrons (= ANION). □□ **i•on•ic** /īónik/ *adj.*

-ion *suffix* (usu. as **-sion**, **-tion**, **-xion**; see -ATION, -ITION, -UTION) forming nouns denoting: **1** verbal action (*excision*). **2** instance of this (*suggestion*). **3** resulting state or product (*vexation*; *concoction*).

I•on•ic /īónik/ *adj.* of the order of Greek architecture characterized by a column with scroll shapes on either side of the capital.

i•on•ize /íənīz/ *v.* convert or be converted into an ion or ions. □□ **i•on•iz′a•ble** *adj.* **i•on•i•za′tion** *n.* **i′on•iz•er** *n.*

i•on•o•sphere /īónəsfeer/ *n.* ionized region of the atmosphere above the stratosphere, reflecting radio waves (cf. TROPOSPHERE). □□ **i•on•o•spher•ic** /-sféerik, -sfér-/ *adj.*

i•o•ta /ī-ótə/ *n.* **1** ninth letter of the Greek alphabet (Ι, ι). **2** (usu. with *neg.*) smallest possible amount.

IOU /í-ō-yŏŏ/ *n.* signed document acknowledging a debt.

ip•e•cac /ípikak/ *n.* root of a S. American shrub used as an emetic and purgative.

ips *abbr.* (also **i.p.s.**) inches per second.

ip•so fac•to /ípsō fáktō/ *adv.* **1** by that very fact or act. **2** thereby.

IQ *abbr.* intelligence quotient.

Ir *symb. Chem.* iridium.

ir- /ir/ *prefix* assim. form of IN-[1], IN-[2] before *r*.

IRA *abbr.* **1** individual retirement account. **2** Irish Republican Army.

I·ra·ni·an /iráyneeən/ • *adj.* **1** of or relating to Iran (formerly Persia) in the Middle East. **2** of the Indo-European group of languages including Persian, Pashto, Avestan, and Kurdish. • *n.* native or national of Iran.

I·ra·qi /iráakee/ • *adj.* of or relating to Iraq in the Middle East. • *n.* (*pl.* **I·ra·qis**) **1** native or national of Iraq. **2** form of Arabic spoken in Iraq.

i·ras·ci·ble /irásibəl/ *adj.* irritable; hot-tempered. □□ **i·ras·ci·bil'i·ty** *n.* **i·ras'ci·bly** *adv.*

i·rate /īráyt/ *adj.* angry; enraged. □□ **i·rate'ly** *adv.* **i·rate'ness** *n.*

ire /īr/ *n. literary* anger. □□ **ire'ful** *adj.*

ir·i·des·cent /íridésənt/ *adj.* **1** showing rainbowlike luminous colors. **2** changing color with position. □□ **ir·i·des'cence** *n.* **ir·i·des' cent·ly** *adv.*

i·rid·i·um /irídeeəm/ *n. Chem.* hard, white metallic element of the transition series, used esp. in alloys. ¶ Symb.: **Ir**.

i·ris /fris/ *n.* **1** flat, circular colored membrane behind the cornea of the eye, with a circular opening (pupil) in the center. **2** herbaceous plant of a family with tuberous roots, sword-shaped leaves, and showy flowers.

I·rish /frish/ • *adj.* of or relating to Ireland; of or like its people. • *n.* **1** Celtic language of Ireland. **2** (prec. by *the*; treated as *pl.*) the people of Ireland. □ **Irish coffee** coffee mixed with Irish whiskey and served with cream on top. **Irish Sea** sea between England and Wales and Ireland.

irk /ərk/ *v.tr.* irritate; bore; annoy.

irk·some /ə́rksəm/ *adj.* tedious; annoying; tiresome. □□ **irk'some·ly** *adv.* **irk'some·ness** *n.*

i·ron /fərn/ • *n.* **1** *Chem.* gray metallic element used for tools and implements, and found in some foods. ¶ Symb.: **Fe**. **2** symbol of strength or firmness. **3** implement with a flat base which is heated to smooth clothes, etc. **5** golf club with a metal sloping face. **6** (*pl.*) fetters. • *adj.* **1** made of iron. **2** robust. **3** unyielding; merciless. • *v.tr.* smooth (clothes, etc.) with an iron. □ **Iron Age** *Archaeol.* period following the Bronze Age when iron replaced bronze in the making of implements and weapons. **Iron Curtain** *hist.* notional barrier to the passage of people and information between the former Soviet bloc and the West. □□ **i'ron·er** *n.* **i'ron·ing** *n.* (in sense 1 of *v.*). **i'ron·less** *adj.* **i'ron·like** *adj.*

i·ron·clad • *adj.* **1** clad or protected with iron. **2** impregnable; rigorous. • *n.* /fərnklad/ *hist.* 19th-c. warship protected by iron plates.

i·ron·ic /īrónik/ *adj.* (also **i·ron'i·cal**) using or displaying irony. □□ **i·ron'i·cal·ly** *adv.*

i·ron·stone /fərnstōn/ *n.* kind of hard, white, opaque stoneware.

i·ron·ware /fərnwair/ *n.* articles made of iron.

i·ro·ny /frənee/ *n.* (*pl.* **-nies**) **1** humorous or sarcastic use of language of a different or opposite meaning. **2** ill-timed arrival of an event or circumstance that is in itself desirable.

Ir·o·quois /írəkwoy/ • *n.* (*pl.* same) **1 a** Native American confederacy of five (later six) peoples formerly inhabiting New York State. **b** member of any of these peoples. **2** any of the languages of these peoples. • *adj.* of or relating to

the Iroquois or their languages. □□ **Ir·o·quoi·an** /írəkwóyən/ *n. & adj.*

ir·ra·di·ate /iráydee-áyt/ *v.tr.* **1** subject to radiation. **2** shine upon; light up. **3** throw light on (a subject). □□ **ir·ra·di·a·tion** /iráydee-áyshən/ *n.* **ir·ra·di·a·tive** /-deeətiv/ *adj.*

ir·ra·tion·al /iráshənəl/ *adj.* **1** illogical; unreasonable. **2** not endowed with reason. □□ **ir·ra·tion·al·i·ty** /-álitee/ *n.* **ir·ra'tion·al·ly** *adv.*

ir·rec·on·cil·a·ble /irékənsíləbəl/ *adj.* **1** implacably hostile. **2** (of ideas, etc.) incompatible. □□ **ir·rec·on·cil'a·bly** *adv.*

ir·re·cov·er·a·ble /irikúvərəbəl/ *adj.* that cannot be recovered or remedied. □□ **ir·re·cov' er·a·bly** *adv.*

ir·re·deem·a·ble /iridéeməbəl/ *adj.* **1** that cannot be redeemed. **2** hopeless; absolute. □□ **ir· re·deem'a·bly** *adv.*

ir·re·duc·i·ble /iridóosibəl, -dyóo-/ *adj.* that cannot be reduced or simplified. □□ **ir·re·duc'i· bly** *adv.*

ir·re·fut·a·ble /iréfyətəbəl, irifyóo-/ *adj.* that cannot be refuted. □□ **ir·re·fut·a·bil'i·ty** *n.* **ir· re'fut·a·bly** *adv.*

ir·re·gard·less /irigáardlis/ *disp.* = REGARDLESS. ¶ **Irregardless**, with its illogical negative prefix, is widely heard, perhaps arising under the influence of such perfectly correct forms as *irrespective*. It is avoided by careful users of English. Use **regardless** to mean 'without regard or consideration for' or 'nevertheless': *I go walking every day regardless of season or weather*.

ir·reg·u·lar /irégyələr/ *adj.* **1** not regular; unsymmetrical; varying in form. **2** (of a surface) uneven. **3** contrary to a rule, moral principle, or custom; abnormal. **4** uneven in duration, order, etc. □□ **ir·reg·u·lar·i·ty** /-láritee/ *n.* (*pl.* **-ties**) **ir·reg'u·lar·ly** *adv.*

ir·rel·e·vant /irélivənt/ *adj.* not relevant; not pertinent. □□ **ir·rel'e·vance** *n.* **ir·rel'e·van·cy** *n.* **ir·rel'e·vant·ly** *adv.*
¶ See note at IMMATERIAL.

ir·re·li·gious /irilíjəs/ *adj.* **1** indifferent or hostile to religion. **2** lacking a religion. □□ **ir·re· li'gious·ly** *adv.*

ir·re·me·di·a·ble /irimédeeəbəl/ *adj.* that cannot be remedied. □□ **ir·re·me'di·a·bly** *adv.*

ir·rep·a·ra·ble /irépərəbəl/ *adj.* that cannot be rectified or made good. □□ **ir·rep'a·ra·bly** *adv.*

ir·re·place·a·ble /iripláysəbəl/ *adj.* **1** that cannot be replaced. **2** of which the loss cannot be made good. □□ **ir·re·place'a·bly** *adv.*

ir·re·press·i·ble /iriprésibəl/ *adj.* that cannot be repressed or restrained. □□ **ir·re·press·i·bil'i·ty** *n.* **ir·re·press'i·bly** *adv.*

ir·re·proach·a·ble /iripróchəbəl/ *adj.* faultless; blameless. □□ **ir·re·proach·a·bil'i·ty** *n.* **ir·re· proach'a·bly** *adv.*

ir·re·sist·i·ble /irizístibəl/ *adj.* **1** too strong or convincing to be resisted. **2** delightful; alluring. □□ **ir·re·sist·i·bil'i·ty** *n.* **ir·re·sist'i·bly** *adv.*

ir·res·o·lute /irézəlōot/ *adj.* **1** hesitant; undecided. **2** lacking in resoluteness. □□ **ir·res·o· lute'ly** *adv.* **ir·res·o·lute'ness** *n.* **ir·res·o·lu·tion** /-lóoshən/ *n.*

ir·re·spec·tive /irispéktiv/ *adj.* (foll. by *of*) not taking into account; regardless of. □□ **ir·re· spec'tive·ly** *adv.*

ir·re·spon·si·ble /írispónsibəl/ adj. **1** acting or done without due sense of responsibility. **2** not responsible for one's conduct. □□ **ir·re·spon·si·bil′i·ty** n. **ir·re·spon′si·bly** adv.

ir·re·triev·a·ble /íritreévəbəl/ adj. that cannot be retrieved or restored. □□ **ir·re·triev′a·bly** adv.

ir·rev·er·ent /írévərənt/ adj. lacking reverence. □□ **ir·rev′er·ence** n. **ir·rev′er·ent·ly** adv.

ir·re·vers·i·ble /írivérsibəl/ adj. not reversible or alterable. □□ **ir·re·vers·i·bil′i·ty** n. **ir·re·vers′i·bly** adv.

ir·re·vo·ca·ble /írévəkəbəl, írivók-/ adj. **1** unalterable. **2** gone beyond recall. □□ **ir·re·vo·ca·bil′i·ty** n. **ir·re′vo·ca·bly** adv.

ir·ri·gate /írigayt/ v.tr. **1** water (land) by means of channels. **2** Med. clean (a wound, etc.) with a constant flow of liquid. □□ **ir′ri·ga·ble** adj. **ir·ri·ga·tion** /-gáyshən/ n. **ir′ri·ga·tor** n.

ir·ri·ta·ble /íritəbəl/ adj. **1** easily annoyed. **2** (of an organ, etc.) very sensitive to contact. □□ **ir·ri·ta·bil′i·ty** n. **ir′ri·ta·bly** adv.

ir·ri·tant /írit′nt/ ● adj. causing irritation. ● n. irritant substance. □□ **ir′ri·tan·cy** n.

ir·ri·tate /íritayt/ v.tr. **1** excite to anger; annoy. **2** stimulate discomfort in (a part of the body). □□ **ir′ri·tat·ed·ly** adv. **ir′ri·tat·ing·ly** adv. **ir·ri·ta·tion** /-táyshən/ n. **ir′ri·ta·tive** adj. **ir′ri·ta·tor** n.

ir·rupt /irúpt/ v.intr. (foll. by into) enter forcibly or violently. □□ **ir·rup·tion** /irúpshən/ n.

IRS abbr. Internal Revenue Service.

Is. abbr. **1 a** Island(s). **b** Isle(s). **2** (also **Isa.**) Isaiah (Old Testament).

is 3rd sing. present of BE.

ISBN abbr. international standard book number.

is·chi·um /ískeeəm/ n. (pl. **is·chi·a** /-keeə/) curved bone forming the base of each half of the pelvis. □□ **is′chi·al** adj.

-ise /īz, eez/ suffix forming nouns of quality, state, or function (exercise; expertise; franchise; merchandise).

-ish[1] /ish/ suffix forming adjectives: **1** from nouns, meaning: **a** having the qualities or characteristics of (boyish). **b** of the nationality of (Danish). **2** from adjectives, meaning 'somewhat' (thickish). **3** colloq. denoting an approximate age or time of day (fortyish; six-thirtyish).

-ish[2] /ish/ suffix forming verbs (vanish, finish).

i·sin·glass /ízinglas/ n. **1** gelatin obtained from fish, esp. sturgeon, and used in making jellies, glue, etc. **2** mica.

isl. abbr. island.

Is·lam /íslaam, íz-, isláam, iz-/ n. **1** religion of the Muslims, a monotheistic faith regarded as revealed by Muhammad as the Prophet of Allah. **2** the Muslim world. □□ **Is·lam′ic** adj.

is·land /ílənd/ n. **1** land surrounded by water. **2** anything compared to an island, esp. in being surrounded in some way. **3** detached or isolated thing.

is·land·er /íləndər/ n. native or inhabitant of an island.

isle /īl/ n. poet. island or peninsula, esp. a small one.

is·let /ílit/ n. **1** small island. **2** Anat. portion of tissue structurally distinct from surrounding tissues.

ism /ízəm/ n. colloq. usu. derog. any distinctive but unspecified doctrine or practice with a name ending in -ism.

-ism /ízəm/ suffix forming nouns, esp. denoting: **1** an action or its result (baptism). **2** system, principle, or ideological movement (feminism). **3** state or quality (heroism; barbarism). **4** basis of prejudice or discrimination (racism; sexism). **5** peculiarity in language (Americanism). **6** pathological condition (alcoholism).

isn't /ízənt/ contr. is not.

iso- /ísō/ comb. form equal (isometric).

i·so·bar /ísəbaar/ n. line on a map connecting positions having the same atmospheric pressure. □□ **i·so·bar·ic** /-bárik/ adj.

i·so·late /ísəláyt/ v.tr. **1 a** a place apart or alone; cut off from society. **b** place in quarantine. **2 a** identify and separate for attention. **b** Chem. separate (a substance) from a mixture. □□ **i·so·lat′a·ble** adj. **i′so·lat·ed** adj. **i·so·la′tion** n. **i′so·la·tor** n.

i·so·la·tion·ism /ísəláyshənizəm/ n. policy of holding aloof from the affairs of other countries or groups esp. in politics. □□ **i·so·la′tion·ist** n.

i·so·mer /ísəmər/ n. Chem. one of two or more compounds with the same molecular formula but a different arrangement of atoms and different properties. □□ **i·so·mer·ic** /-mérik/ adj. **i·som·er·ism** /ísómərizəm/ n. **i·som′er·ize** v.

i·so·met·ric /ísəmétrik/ adj. **1** of equal measure. **2** Physiol. (of muscle action) developing tension while the muscle is prevented from contracting. □□ **i·so·met′ri·cal·ly** adv.

i·so·met·rics /ísəmétriks/ n.pl. system of physical exercises in which muscles act against each other or a fixed object.

i·sos·ce·les /īsósileez/ adj. (of a triangle) having two sides equal.

i·so·ton·ic /ísətónik/ adj. **1** having the same osmotic pressure. **2** Physiol. (of muscle action) taking place with normal contraction. □□ **i·so·ton′i·cal·ly** adv.

i·so·tope /ísətōp/ n. Chem. one of two or more forms of an element differing from each other in atomic mass. □□ **i·so·top·ic** /-tópik/ adj. **i·so·top′i·cal·ly** adv.

Is·rae·li /izráylee/ ● adj. of or relating to the modern state of Israel in the Middle East. ● n. native or national of Israel.

Is·ra·el·ite /ízreeəlīt, -rəlīt/ n. hist. native of ancient Israel.

is·sue /íshoō/ ● n. **1 a** giving out or circulation of notes, stamps, etc. **b** quantity of coins, copies of a book, etc., circulated or put on sale at one time. **c** item or amount given out or distributed. **d** each of a regular series of a magazine, etc. (the May issue). **2 a** an outgoing. **b** exit; outlet. **3** point in question; important subject of debate. **4** result. **5** Law children. ● v. (**is·sues, is·sued, is·su·ing**) **1** intr. literary go or come out. **2** tr. **a** publish; put into circulation. **b** supply, esp. officially. **3** intr. **a** be derived or result. **b** end; result. **4** intr. emerge from a condition. □ **at issue 1** in dispute. **2** at variance. **take issue** disagree. □□ **is′su·a·ble** adj. **is′su·ance** n. **is′sue·less** adj. **is′su·er** n.

-ist /ist/ suffix forming personal nouns (and in some senses related adjectives) denoting: **1** an adherent of a system, etc., in -ism: see -ISM 2 (Marxist). **2 a** a member of a profession (pathologist). **b** a person concerned with something (*pharmacist*). **3** a person who uses a thing (*violinist*). **4** a person who does something expressed by a verb in *-ize* (*plagiarist*). **5** a person who subscribes to a prejudice or practices discrimination (*racist*).

isth·mus /ísmǝs/ *n.* narrow piece of land connecting two larger bodies of land.

-istic /ístik/ *suffix* forming adjectives from nouns and other stems generally denoting: of, pertaining to, referring to, or characteristic of that which is denoted by the noun or stem (*stylistic*).

it /it/ *pron.* (*poss.* **its**; *pl.* **they**) **1** thing (or occas. the animal or child) previously named or in question (*took a stone and threw it*). **2** person in question (*Who is it?*). **3** as the subject of an impersonal verb (*it is raining*). **4** as a substitute for a deferred subject or object (*it is silly to talk like that*). **5** as a substitute for a vague object (*run for it!*). **6** as the antecedent to a relative word (*it was an owl I heard*). **7** (in children's games) player who has to catch the others. □ **that's it** *colloq.* that is: **1** what is required. **2** the difficulty. **3** the end; enough.

I·tal·ian /itályǝn/ • *n.* **1** native or national of Italy. **2** language of Italy. • *adj.* of or relating to Italy or its people or language.

I·tal·ian·ate /itályǝnayt/ *adj.* of Italian style or appearance.

i·tal·ic /itálik/ • *adj.* **1** *Printing* slanting type used esp. for emphasis and in foreign words. • *n.* **1** a letter in italic type. **2** this type.

i·tal·i·cize /itálisīz/ *v.tr.* print in italics. □□ **i·tal·i·ci·za′tion** *n.*

itch /ich/ • *n.* **1** irritation in the skin. **2** impatient desire. • *v.intr.* **1** feel an irritation in the skin. **2** (of a person) feel a desire to do something (*itching to tell you*).

itch·y /íchee/ *adj.* (**itch·i·er, itch·i·est**) having or causing an itch. □ **have itchy feet** *colloq.* **1** be restless. **2** have a strong urge to travel. □□ **itch′i·ness** *n.*

it'd /ítǝd/ *contr. colloq.* **1** it had. **2** it would.

-ite¹ /īt/ *suffix* forming nouns meaning 'a person or thing connected with': (*Israelite, Trotskyite, dynamite*).

-ite² /īt, it/ *suffix* **1** forming adjectives (*erudite; favorite*). **2** forming nouns (*appetite*). **3** forming verbs (*expedite; unite*).

i·tem /ítǝm/ *n.* **1 a** any of a number of enumerated things. **b** entry in an account. **2** article, esp. one for sale. **3** piece of news, etc.

i·tem·ize /ítǝmīz/ *v.tr.* state or list item by item. □□ **i·tem·i·za′tion** *n.* **i′tem·iz·er** *n.*

it·er·ate /ítǝrayt/ *v.tr.* repeat; state repeatedly. □□ **it·er·a·tion** /-áyshǝn/ *n.* **it′er·a·tive** *adj.*

-itic /ítik/ *suffix* forming adjectives and nouns corresponding to nouns in *-ite*, *-itis*, etc. (*Semitic; arthritic; syphilitic*).

i·tin·er·ant /ītínǝrǝnt, itín-/ • *adj.* traveling from place to place. • *n.* itinerant person.

i·tin·er·ar·y /ītínǝreree, itín-/ *n.* (*pl.* **-ies**) **1** detailed route. **2** record of travel. **3** guidebook.

-ition /íshǝn/ *suffix* forming nouns, = -ATION (*admonition; perdition; position*).

-itious¹ /íshǝs/ *suffix* forming adjectives corresponding to nouns in *-ition* (*ambitious; supposititious*).

-itious² /íshǝs/ *suffix* forming adjectives meaning 'related to, having the nature of' (*adventitious*).

-itis /ítis/ *suffix* forming nouns, esp.: **1** names of inflammatory diseases (*appendicitis*). **2** *colloq.* with ref. to conditions compared to diseases (*electionitis*).

-itive /ítiv/ *suffix* forming adjectives, = -ATIVE (*positive; transitive*).

it'll /ít'l/ *contr. colloq.* it will; it shall.

-itous /ítǝs/ *suffix* forming adjectives corresponding to nouns in *-ity* (*calamitous; felicitous*).

its /its/ *poss.pron.* of it; of itself (*can see its advantages*).

¶ Although formerly written with an apostrophe, note that **its** is an adjective indicating possession, meaning 'of it, belonging to it'. **It's** is a contraction of 'it is': *It's going to be a good day to tour the city and see its attractions*.

it's /its/ *contr.* **1** it is. **2** it has.

it·self /itsélf/ *pron.* emphatic and refl. form of IT. □ **in itself** viewed in its essential qualities (*not in itself a bad thing*).

it·ty-bit·ty /íteebítee/ *adj.* (also **it·sy-bit·sy** /ítseebítsee/) *colloq.* usu. *derog.* tiny; insubstantial; slight.

-ity /itee/ *suffix* forming nouns denoting: **1** quality or condition (*purity*). **2** instance of this (*humidity*).

IUD *abbr.* intrauterine (contraceptive) device.

IV /īveé/ *abbr.* intravenous(ly).

I've /īv/ *contr.* I have.

-ive /iv/ *suffix* forming adjectives meaning 'tending to, having the nature of,' and corresponding nouns (*suggestive; corrosive; palliative; coercive; talkative*). □□ **-ively** *suffix* forming adverbs. **-iveness** *suffix* forming nouns.

i·vo·ry /ívǝree, ívree/ *n.* (*pl.* **-ries**) **1** hard substance of the tusks of an elephant, etc. **2** color of this. **3** (usu. in *pl.*) piano key or tooth. □ **ivory tower** seclusion or separation from the harsh realities of life. □□ **i′vo·ried** *adj.*

i·vy /ívee/ *n.* (*pl.* **-vies**) climbing evergreen shrub with dark-green, shining five-angled leaves.

-ize /īz/ *suffix* forming verbs, meaning: **1** make or become such (*Americanize; realize*). **2** treat in such a way (*monopolize; pasteurize*). **3 a** follow a special practice (*economize*). **b** have a specified feeling (*sympathize*). □□ **-ization** /-záyshǝn/ *suffix* forming nouns. **-izer** *suffix* forming agent nouns.

J j

J¹ /jay/ *n.* (also **j**) (*pl.* **Js** or **J's**; **j's**) **1** tenth letter of the alphabet.

J² *abbr.* (also **J.**) **1** *Cards* jack. **2** Jewish. **3** joule(s). **4** Judge. **5** Justice.

jab /jab/ • *v.tr.* (**jabbed**, **jab·bing**) **1 a** poke roughly. **b** stab. **2** thrust (a thing) hard or abruptly. • *n.* abrupt blow with one's fist or pointed implement.

jab·ber /jábər/ • *v.* **1** *intr.* chatter volubly. **2** *tr.* utter (words) in this way. • *n.* meaningless jabbering.

ja·bot /zhabó, ja–/ *n.* ornamental frill or ruffle of lace, etc., on the front of a shirt or blouse.

jack /jak/ • *n.* **1** device for lifting heavy objects, esp. vehicles. **2** playing card with a picture of a soldier, page, etc. **3** ship's flag, esp. showing nationality. **4** device to connect an electrical circuit. **5 a** small piece of metal, etc., used with others in tossing games. **b** (in *pl.*) game with a ball and jacks. **6** (**Jack**) familiar form of *John*, esp. typifying the common man or the male of a species. • *v.tr.* **1** raise with or as with a jack (in sense 1). **2** *colloq.* raise, e.g., prices. □ **Jack Frost** frost personified. **jack-in-the-box** toy figure that springs out of a box. **jack-in-the-pulpit** N. American plant having an upright flower spike and an over-arching hoodlike spathe. **jack-of-all-trades** person who can do many different kinds of work. **jack-o'-lantern** lantern made from a pumpkin with holes for facial features.

---

jack late Middle English: from *Jack*, pet form of the given name *John*. The term was used originally to denote an ordinary man (sense 6), also a youth (mid-16th century), hence the 'knave' in cards and 'male animal.' The word also denoted various devices saving human labor, as though one had a helper (senses 1 and 4, and in compounds such as *jackhammer* and *jackknife*); the general sense 'laborer' arose in the early 18th century and survives in *lumberjack, steeplejack*, etc. Since the mid-16th century a notion of 'smallness' has arisen, hence senses 3 and 5.

---

jack·al /jákəl/ *n.* any of various wild doglike mammals found in Africa and S. Asia.

jack·ass /jákas/ *n.* **1** male ass. **2** stupid person.

jack·daw /jákdaw/ *n.* small gray-headed crow.

jack·et /jákit/ *n.* **1 a** sleeved, short outer garment. **b** thing worn esp. around the torso for protection or support (*life jacket*). **2** casing or covering. **3** = *dust jacket*.

jack·ham·mer /ják-hamər/ *n.* pneumatic hammer or drill.

jack·knife /jáknīf/ • *n.* (*pl.* **-knives**) **1** large pocket knife. **2** dive in which the body is first bent at the waist and then straightened. • *v.intr.* (**-knifed**, **-knif·ing**) (of an articulated vehicle) fold against itself in an accidental skidding movement.

jack·pot /jákpot/ *n.* large prize, esp. accumulated in a game or lottery, etc. □ **hit the jackpot** *colloq.* **1** win a large prize. **2** have remarkable luck or success.

jack·rab·bit /jákrabit/ *n.* large prairie hare.

Jac·quard /jákaard, jəkaárd/ *n.* **1** apparatus using perforated cards that record a pattern and are fitted to a loom to mechanize the weaving of figured fabrics. **2** (in full **Jacquard loom**) loom fitted with this. **3** fabric or article made with this.

Ja·cuz·zi /jəkóʊzee/ *n. propr.* large bath with underwater jets of water to massage the body.

jade¹ /jayd/ *n.* **1** hard, usu. green stone used for ornaments, etc. **2** green color of jade.

jade² /jayd/ *n.* **1** inferior or worn-out horse. **2** *derog.* disreputable woman.

jad·ed /jáydid/ *adj.* tired or worn out; surfeited. □□ **jad'ed·ly** *adv.* **jad'ed·ness** *n.*

jag¹ /jag/ • *n.* sharp projection of rock, etc. • *v.tr.* (**jag·ged**, **jag·ging**) **1** cut or tear unevenly. **2** make indentations in. □□ **jag'ger** *n.*

jag² /jag/ *n. sl.* **1** drinking bout; spree. **2** period of indulgence in an activity, emotion, etc.

jag·ged /jágid/ *adj.* **1** unevenly cut or torn. **2** deeply indented; with sharp points. □□ **jag'ged·ly** *adv.* **jag'ged·ness** *n.*

jag·uar /jágwaar/ *n.* large, flesh-eating spotted feline of Central and S. America.

jai a·lai /hí lī, əlí/ *n.* indoor court game similar to handball played with large curved wicker rackets.

jail /jayl/ • *n.* **1** place to which persons are committed by a court for detention. **2** confinement in a jail. • *v.tr.* put in jail.

jail·break /jáylbrayk/ *n.* escape from jail.

jail·er /jáylər/ *n.* person in charge of a jail or of the prisoners in it.

ja·la·pe·ño /halapáynyō, -peén-/ *n.* hot pepper commonly used in Mexican cooking.

JACK-IN-THE-PULPIT

ja·lop·y /jəlópee/ n. (pl. **-ies**) colloq. dilapidated old car.

jal·ou·sie /jáləsee/ n. blind or shutter made of rows of angled slats to keep out rain, etc., and control the influx of light.

jam¹ /jam/ • v. (**jammed, jam·ming**) **1 a** tr. squeeze or wedge into a space. **b** intr. become wedged. **2 a** tr. cause to become wedged or immovable so that it cannot work. **b** intr. become jammed in this way. **3** tr. push or cram together in a compact mass. **4** intr. push or crowd (they jammed onto the bus). **5** tr. **a** block (a passage, road, etc.) by crowding or obstructing. **b** obstruct the exit of (we were jammed in). **6** tr. (usu. foll. by on) apply (brakes, etc.) forcefully or abruptly. **7** tr. make (a radio transmission) unintelligible by interference. **8** intr. colloq. (in jazz, etc.) extemporize with other musicians. • n. **1 a** squeeze or crush. **2** crowded mass (traffic jam). **3** colloq. predicament. **4** stoppage due to jamming. **5** (in full **jam′ ses·sion**) colloq. improvised playing by a group of jazz musicians. □ **jam-packed** colloq. full to capacity. □□ **jam′ mer** n.

jam² /jam/ n. preserve of fruit and sugar.

jamb /jam/ n. Archit. side post or surface of a doorway, window, or fireplace.

jam·ba·lay·a /júmbəlíə/ n. dish of rice with shrimp, chicken, etc.

jam·bo·ree /jámbəree/ n. **1** celebration or merrymaking. **2** large rally of Boy Scouts or Girl Scouts.

Jan. abbr. January.

jan·gle /jánggəl/ • v. **1** intr. & tr. cause (a bell, etc.) to make a harsh metallic sound. **2** tr. irritate (the nerves, etc.) by discord, etc. • n. harsh metallic sound.

jan·i·tor /jánitər/ n. caretaker of a building. □□ **jan·i·to·ri·al** /-táwreeəl/ adj.

Jan·u·ar·y /jányoóeree/ n. (pl. **-ies**) first month of the year.

ja·pan /jəpán/ • n. hard, usu. black varnish, orig. from Japan. • v.tr. (**ja·panned, ja·pan·ning**) **1** varnish with japan. **2** make black and glossy.

Jap·a·nese /jápəne'ez/ • n. (pl. same) **1 a** native or national of Japan. **b** person of Japanese descent. **2** language of Japan. • adj. of or relating to Japan, its people, or its language. □ **Japanese beetle** iridescent green and brown beetle that is a garden and crop pest.

jape /jayp/ • n. practical joke. • v.intr. play a joke. □□ **jap′ er·y** n.

jar¹ /jaar/ n. **1** container of glass, plastic, etc., usu. cylindrical. **2** contents of this. □□ **jar′ ful** n. (pl. **-fuls**).

jar² /jaar/ • v. (**jarred, jar·ring**) **1** intr. (of sound, manner, etc.) sound discordant or grating (on the nerves, etc.). **2 a** tr. strike or cause to strike with vibration or shock. **b** intr. (of a body affected) vibrate gratingly. **3** tr. send a shock through (a part of the body). **4** intr. be at variance; be in conflict. • n. **1** jarring sound or sensation. **2** physical shock or jolt. **3** lack of harmony; disagreement.

jar·di·niere /jaàrd'ne'er, zha̐árdinyáir/ n. (also **jar′ di·nière**) **1** ornamental pot or stand for plants. **2** dish of mixed vegetables.

jar·gon /jaárgən/ n. **1** words or expressions used by a particular group or profession (medical jargon). **2** barbarous or debased language. **3** gibberish. □□ **jar·gon·is′ tic** adj. **jar′ gon·ize** v.

jas·mine /jázmin/ n. (also **jes·sa·mine** /jésəmin/) any of various fragrant ornamental shrubs usu. with white or yellow flowers.

jas·per /jáspər/ n. opaque quartz, usu. red, yellow, or brown.

jaun·dice /jáwndis/ • n. **1** Med. yellowing of the skin or whites of the eyes, often caused by obstruction of the bile duct or by liver disease. **2** envy. • v.tr. **1** affect with jaundice. **2** (esp. as **jaundiced** adj.) affect (a person) with envy, resentment, or jealousy.

jaunt /jawnt/ • n. short excursion for enjoyment. • v.intr. take a jaunt.

jaun·ty /jáwntee/ adj. (**jaunt·i·er, jaunt·i·est**) **1** cheerful and self-confident. **2** sprightly. □□ **jaunt′ i·ly** adv. **jaunt′ i·ness** n.

Jav·a·nese /jávəne'ez, jaà-/ • n. (pl. same) **1 a** native of Java in Indonesia. **b** person of Javanese descent. **2** language of Java. • adj. of or relating to Java, its people, or its language.

jav·e·lin /jávəlin, jávlin/ n. **1** light spear thrown in a competitive sport or as a weapon. **2** such an athletic event.

jaw /jaw/ • n. **1 a** upper or lower bony structure in vertebrates forming the framework of the mouth and containing the teeth. **b** corresponding parts of certain invertebrates. **2 a** (in pl.) mouth with its bones and teeth. **b** narrow mouth of a valley, channel, etc. **c** gripping parts of a tool or machine. • v. colloq. **1** intr. speak, esp. at tedious length. **2** tr. **a** persuade by talking. **b** admonish or lecture.

jaw·bone /jáwbōn/ n. lower jaw in most mammals.

jaw·break·er /jáwbraykər/ n. **1** colloq. word that is very long or hard to pronounce. **2** round, very hard candy.

jay /jay/ n. noisy chattering bird of the crow family with vivid pinkish-brown, blue, black, and white plumage.

jay·walk /jáywawk/ v.intr. cross or walk in the street or road without regard for traffic. □□ **jay′ walk·er** n.

jazz /jaz/ • n. **1** music of American origin characterized by improvisation, syncopation, and usu. a regular or forceful rhythm. **2** sl. pretentious talk or behavior. • v.intr. play or dance to jazz. □ **jazz up** brighten or enliven. □□ **jazz′ er** n.

jazz·y /jázee/ adj. (**jazz·i·er, jazz·i·est**) **1** of or like jazz. **2** vivid; unrestrained; showy. □□ **jazz′ i·ly** adv. **jazz′ i·ness** n.

JCS abbr. (also **J.C.S.**) Joint Chiefs of Staff.

jct. abbr. junction.

jeal·ous /jéləs/ adj. **1** fiercely protective (of rights, etc.). **2** afraid, suspicious, or resentful of rivalry in love. **3** envious or resentful (of a person, etc.). **4** (of inquiry, supervision, etc.) vigilant. □□ **jeal′ ous·ly** adv.

jeal·ou·sy /jéləsee/ n. (pl. **-sies**) **1** jealous state or feeling. **2** instance of this.

jeans /jeenz/ n.pl. casual pants made of denim.

Jeep /jeep/ n. propr. rugged, all-purpose motor vehicle incorporating four-wheel drive.

jeer /jeer/ • v. **1** intr. (usu. foll. by at) scoff derisively. **2** tr. scoff at; deride. • n. a scoff or taunt. □□ **jeer′ ing·ly** adv.

je·had var. of JIHAD.

Je·ho·vah /jəhṓvə/ *n.* Hebrew name of God in the Old Testament.

je·june /jijōōn/ *adj.* **1** intellectually unsatisfying; shallow. **2** puerile. □□ **je·june′ly** *adv.*

je·ju·num /jijōōnəm/ *n. Anat.* small intestine between the duodenum and ileum.

jell /jel/ *v.intr. colloq.* **1 a** set, as jelly. **b** (of ideas, etc.) take a definite form. **2** (of two different things) cohere.

jel·ly /jélee/ • *n.* (*pl.* **-lies**) **1** gelatinous preparation of fruit juice, etc., for use as a jam or a condiment (*grape jelly*). **2** any similar substance. • *v.* (**-lies, -lied**) **1** *intr.* & *tr.* set or cause to set as a jelly; congeal. **2** *tr.* set (food) in a jelly (*jellied eggs*). □ **jelly roll** rolled sponge cake with a jelly filling. □□ **jel′ly·like** *adj.*

jel·ly·fish /jéleefish/ *n.* (*pl.* usu. same) **1** marine coelenterate with a jellylike body and stinging tentacles. **2** *colloq.* feeble person.

jeop·ar·dize /jépərdīz/ *v.tr.* endanger; put into jeopardy.

jeop·ar·dy /jépərdee/ *n.* danger, esp. of severe harm or loss.

jer·e·mi·ad /jérimīad/ *n.* doleful complaint or lamentation.

Jer·e·mi·ah /jérimíə/ *n.* dismal prophet; denouncer of the times.

jerk[1] /jərk/ • *n.* **1** sharp sudden pull, twist, twitch, start, etc. **2** spasmodic muscular twitch. **3** *sl.* fool. • *v.* **1** *intr.* move with a jerk. **2** *tr.* pull, thrust, twist, etc., with a jerk. □□ **jerk′er** *n.*

jerk[2] /jərk/ *v.tr.* cure (beef, etc.) by cutting it in long slices and drying it in the sun.

jer·kin /jə́rkin/ *n.* sleeveless jacket, often of leather.

jer·ky[1] /jə́rkee/ *adj.* (**jerk·i·er, jerk·i·est**) **1** having sudden abrupt movements. **2** spasmodic. □□ **jerk′i·ly** *adv.* **jerk′i·ness** *n.*

jer·ky[2] /jə́rkee/ *n.* meat, esp. beef, cured by jerking.

jer·sey /jə́rzee/ *n.* (*pl.* **-seys**) **1 a** knitted, usu. woolen sweater. **b** knitted fabric. **2** (**Jersey**) light brown dairy cow from Jersey.

jest /jest/ • *n.* **1 a** joke. **b** fun. **2 a** raillery; banter. **b** object of derision (*a standing jest*). • *v.intr.* **1** joke; make jests. **2** fool about; play or act triflingly. □ **in jest** in fun. □□ **jest′ful** *adj.*

---

jest late Middle English: from earlier *gest*, from Old French *geste*, from Latin *gesta* 'actions, exploits,' from *gerere* 'do.' The original sense was 'exploit, heroic deed,' hence 'a narrative of such deeds' (originally in verse); later the term denoted an idle tale, hence a joke (mid-16th century).

---

jest·er /jéstər/ *n.* professional clown at a medieval court, etc.

Jes·u·it /jézhōoit, jézōo-, jézyōo-/ *n.* member of the Society of Jesus, a Roman Catholic order.

Je·sus /jéezəs/ *n.* the name of the source of the Christian religion, d. *c.* AD 30.

jet[1] /jet/ • *n.* **1** stream of water, steam, gas, flame, etc., shot out esp. from a small opening. **2** spout or nozzle for this purpose. **3 a** jet engine. **b** jet plane. • *v.* (**jet·ted, jet·ting**) **1** *intr.* spurt out in jets. **2** *tr.* & *intr. colloq.* send or travel by jet plane. □ **jet lag** extreme tiredness after a long flight across time zones. **jet propulsion** propulsion by the backward ejection of a high-speed jet of gas, etc. **jet set** *colloq.* wealthy people frequently traveling by air, esp. for pleasure. **jet-setter** *colloq.* member of the jet set.

jet[2] /jet/ *n.* **1 a** hard black variety of lignite capable of being carved and highly polished. **b** (*attrib.*) made of this. **2** (in full **jet-black**) deep glossy black color.

jet·sam /jétsəm/ *n.* discarded material washed ashore, esp. that thrown overboard to lighten a ship, etc. (cf. FLOTSAM).

jet·ti·son /jétisən, -zən/ • *v.tr.* **1** throw (esp. heavy material) overboard to lighten a ship, etc. **b** drop (goods) from an aircraft. **2** abandon; get rid of. • *n.* act of jettisoning.

jet·ty /jétee/ *n.* (*pl.* **-ties**) **1** pier or breakwater constructed to protect or defend a harbor, coast, etc. **2** landing pier.

Jew /jōo/ *n.* person of Hebrew descent or whose religion is Judaism. □ **Jew's** (or **Jews'**) **harp** small lyre-shaped musical instrument held between the teeth and struck with the finger.

jew·el /jōoəl/ • *n.* **1 a** precious stone. **b** this used in watchmaking. **2** jeweled personal ornament. **3** precious person or thing. • *v.tr.* (esp. as **jeweled** *adj.*) adorn or set with jewels. □ **jewel box 1** small box in which jewelry is kept. **2** plastic case for a compact disc or CD-ROM. □□ **jew′el·like** *adj.*

jew·el·er /jōoələr/ *n.* maker of or dealer in jewels or jewelry.

jew·el·ry /jōoəlree/ *n.* jewels esp. for personal adornment, regarded collectively. ¶ Avoid pronouncing this word "joo-luh-ree"; many regard this as uneducated.

Jew·ish /jōoish/ *adj.* **1** of or relating to Jews. **2** of Judaism. □□ **Jew′ish·ness** *n.*

Jew·ry /jōoree/ *n.* (*pl.* **-ries**) Jews collectively.

Jez·e·bel /jézəbel/ *n.* shameless or immoral woman.

jg *abbr.* (also **J.G.**) *US Navy* junior grade.

jib /jib/ • *n.* **1** triangular staysail. **2** projecting arm of a crane. • *v.* (**jibbed, jib·bing**) (of a sail, etc.) pull or swing around from one side of the ship to the other; jibe.

jibe[1] /jīb/ • *v.* **1** *intr.* (of a fore-and-aft sail or boom) swing across the vessel. **2** *tr.* cause (a sail) to do this. **3** *intr.* (of a ship or its crew) change course so that this happens. • *n.* change of course causing jibing.

jibe[2] /jīb/ *v.intr.* (usu. foll. by *with*) *colloq.* agree; be in accord. ¶ **Jibe** means 'agree; go together'; **gibe** means 'jeer; deride.' The two words are pronounced identically, but neither should be confused with **jive**, a jazz term applied to a style of music and dance, as well as having the sense 'misleading or pretentious talk.' **Jive** is sometimes informally substituted for **jibe**.

jif·fy /jífee/ *n. colloq.* short time; moment (*in a jiffy*).

jig /jig/ • *n.* **1 a** lively leaping dance. **b** music for this. **2** device that holds a piece of work and guides the tools operating on it. • *v.* (**jigged, jig·ging**) **1** *intr.* dance a jig. **2** *tr.* & *intr.* move quickly and jerkily up and down. **3** *tr.* work on or equip with a jig or jigs.

jig·ger /jígər/ *n.* **1** measure of spirits, etc. **2** small glass holding this.

jig·gle /jígəl/ v. **1** tr. shake lightly; rock jerkily. **2** intr. fidget. □□ **jig′gly** adj.

jig·saw /jígsaw/ n. **1** (in full **jig′saw puz·zle**) picture on board or wood, etc., cut into irregular interlocking pieces to be reassembled. **2** machine saw with a fine blade for cutting on a curve.

ji·had /jiháad/ n. (also **je·had′**) Muslim holy war.

jil·lion /jílyən/ n. colloq. very large indefinite number.

jilt /jilt/ v.tr. abruptly reject or abandon (a lover, etc.).

jim crow /jim krṓ/ n. hist. (also **Jim Crow**) practice of segregating blacks. □□ **jim crow′ism** n.

jim·my /jímee/ • n. (pl. **-mies**) burglar's short crowbar, usu. made in sections. • v.tr. (**-mies**, **-mied**) force open with a jimmy.

jin·gle /jínggəl/ • n. **1** mixed noise as of bells or light metal objects being shaken together. **2 a** repetition of the same sound in words, esp. as an aid to memory or to attract attention. **b** short verse of this kind used in advertising, etc. • v. make or cause to make a jingling sound. □□ **jin′gly** adj. (**jin·gli·er**, **jin·gli·est**).

jin·go /jínggō/ n. (pl. **-goes**) supporter of policy favoring war; blustering patriot. □ **by jingo!** a mild oath. □□ **jin′go·ism** n. **jin′go·ist** n. **jin·go·is′tic** adj.

jin·ni /jínee, jinée/ n. (also **jinn** /jin/) (pl. **jinn** or **jinns**) (in Muslim mythology) intelligent being lower than the angels, able to appear in human and animal forms, and having power over people.

jinx /jingks/ colloq. • n. person or thing that seems to cause bad luck. • v.tr. subject (a person) to an unlucky force.

jit·ter /jítər/ • n.colloq. (**the jitters**) extreme nervousness. • v.intr. be nervous; act nervously. □□ **jit′ter·y** adj. **jit′ter·i·ness** n.

jit·ter·bug /jítərbug/ • n. **1** nervous person. **2** fast acrobatic dance popular in the 1940s. • v.intr. (**-bugged**, **-bug·ging**) dance the jitterbug.

jive /jīv/ • n. **1** jerky lively style of dance esp. popular in the 1950s. **2** music for this. **3** sl. talk or conversation, esp. when misleading or pretentious. • v.intr. **1** dance the jive. **2** play jive music. □□ **jiv′er** n.
¶ See note at JIBE.

job /job/ • n. **1** piece of work to be done. **2** paid position of employment. **3** colloq. anything one has to do. **4** colloq. difficult task (had a job to find them). **5** sl. crime, esp. a robbery. • v. (**jobbed**, **job·bing**) **1 a** intr. do jobs; do piecework. **b** tr. (usu. foll. by out) subcontract. **2 a** intr. deal in stocks. **b** tr. buy and sell (stocks or goods) as a middleman. □ **job action** any action, esp. a strike, taken by employees as a protest. **job lot** miscellaneous group of articles, esp. bought together. **job-sharing** sharing of a full-time job by several part-time employees.

job·ber /jóbər/ n. **1** wholesaler. **2** derog. broker (see BROKER 2). **3** person who jobs.

jock /jok/ n. sl. **1** = JOCKSTRAP. **2** athlete.

jock·ey /jókee/ • n. (pl. **-eys**) rider in horse races, esp. professional. • v. **1** tr. **a** trick or cheat (a person). **b** outwit. **2** tr. draw (a person) by trickery. **3** intr. cheat.

---

jockey late 16th century: diminutive of the given name *Jock*, a nickname for *John*. Originally the name for an ordinary man, lad, or

---

underling, the word came to mean 'mounted courier,' hence the current sense (late 17th century). Another early use, 'horse dealer' (long a byword for dishonesty), probably gave rise to the verb sense 'manipulate,' whereas the verb senses probably relate to the behavior of jockeys maneuvering from an advantageous position during a race.

---

jock·strap /jókstrap/ n. support or protection for the male genitals, worn esp. by athletes.

jo·cose /jōkṓs/ adj. **1** playful in style. **2** fond of joking; jocular. □□ **jo·cose′ly** adv. **jo·cos·i·ty** /-kósitee/ n. (pl. **-ties**).

joc·u·lar /jókyələr/ adj. **1** merry; fond of joking. **2** humorous. □□ **joc·u·lar·i·ty** /-láritee/ n. (pl. **-ties**). **joc′u·lar·ly** adv.

jo·cund /jókənd, jṓ-/ adj. literary merry; cheerful; sprightly. □□ **jo·cun′di·ty** /jəkúnditee/ n. (pl. **-ties**). **jo·cund′ly** adv.

jodh·purs /jódpərz/ n.pl. long breeches for riding, etc., close-fitting from the knee to the ankle.

Joe Blow /jō blṓ/ n. colloq. hypothetical average man.

jog /jog/ • v. (**jogged, jog·ging**) **1** intr. run slowly, esp. as exercise. **2** tr. (of a horse) move at a jog trot. **3** intr. proceed laboriously; trudge. **4** intr. move up and down with an unsteady motion. **5** tr. nudge (a person), esp. to arouse attention. **6** tr. shake with a push or jerk. **7** tr. stimulate (a person's or one's own memory). • n. **1** a shake, push, or nudge. **2** slow walk or trot. □□ **jog′ger** n.

john /jon/ n. sl. toilet or bathroom.

John Bull /jon boŏl/ n. personification of England or the typical Englishman.

joie de vivre /zhwáa də véevrə/ n. feeling of healthy and exuberant enjoyment of life.

join /joyn/ • v. **1** tr. put together; fasten; unite (one or several things or people). **2** tr. connect (points) by a line, etc. **3** tr. become a member of (an association, organization, etc.). **4** tr. take one's place with or in (a company, group, etc.). **5** tr. **a** come into the company of (a person). **b** (foll. by in) take part with (others) in an activity, etc. **c** share the company of for a specified occasion (may I join you for lunch?). **6** intr. (often foll. by in) take part with others in an activity, etc. • n. point, line, or surface at which things are joined. □ **join battle** begin fighting. **join forces** combine efforts. **join hands 1 a** clasp hands. **b** clasp one's hands together. **2** combine in an action. **join up 1** enlist for military service. **2** unite; connect. □□ **join′a·ble** adj.

join·er /jóynər/ n. **1** person who makes furniture and light woodwork. **2** colloq. person who readily joins societies, etc. □□ **join′er·y** n. (in sense 1).

joint /joynt/ • n. **1 a** place at which two or more things are joined. **b** point at which, or a contrivance by which, two parts of an artificial structure are joined. **2** point at which two bones fit together. **3 a** any of the parts into which an animal carcass is divided for food. **b** any of the parts of which a body is made up. **4** sl. place of meeting for drinking, etc. **5** sl. marijuana cigarette. **6** Geol. fissure in a rock. • adj. **1** held or done by, or belonging to, two or more persons, etc. (*joint action*). **2** sharing with another (*joint author*). ● *v.tr.* **1** connect by joints. **2** divide (a body or member) at a joint or into joints. □ **out of joint 1** (of a bone) dislocated. **2** out of order. □□ **joint′less** *adj.* **joint′ly** *adv.*

joist /joyst/ *n.* supporting beams in floors, ceilings, etc. □□ **joist′ed** *adj.*

jo·jo·ba /hōhṓbə/ *n.* plant with seeds yielding an oily extract used in cosmetics, etc.

joke /jōk/ ● *n.* **1 a** thing said or done to excite laughter. **b** witticism or jest. **2** ridiculous thing, person, or circumstance. ● *v.* **1** *intr.* make jokes. **2** *tr.* poke fun at; banter. □ **no joke** *colloq.* serious matter. □□ **jok′ing·ly** *adv.* **jok′i·ly** *adv.*

jok·er /jṓkər/ *n.* **1** person who jokes. **2** *sl.* fellow; man. **3** playing card usu. with a figure of a jester, used in some games.

jol·li·ty /jólitee/ *n.* (*pl.* **-ties**) merrymaking; festiveness.

jol·ly /jólee/ ● *adj.* (**jol·li·er, jol·li·est**) **1** cheerful; merry. **2** festive; jovial. **3** slightly drunk. ● *v.intr.* (**-lies, -lied**) **1** *colloq.* coax or humor in a friendly way. **2** chaff; banter. □ **Jolly Roger** pirates' black flag, usu. with the skull and crossbones. □□ **jol′li·ly** *adv.* **jol′li·ness** *n.*

jolt /jōlt/ ● *v.* **1** *tr.* disturb or shake (esp. in a moving vehicle) with a jerk. **2** *tr.* shock; perturb. **3** *intr.* move along with jerks. ● *n.* **1** such a jerk. **2** surprise; shock.

Jo·nah /jṓnə/ *n.* person who seems to bring bad luck.

jon·quil /jóngkwil/ *n.* narcissus with small fragrant yellow or white flowers.

josh /josh/ *sl.* ● *n.* good-natured or teasing joke. ● *v.* **1** *tr.* tease; banter. **2** *intr.* indulge in ridicule. □□ **josh′er** *n.*

jos·tle /jósəl/ ● *v.* **1** *tr.* push against; elbow. **2** *intr.* (foll. by *with*) struggle roughly. ● *n.* jostling.

jot /jot/ ● *v.tr.* (**jot·ted, jot·ting**) write briefly or hastily. ● *n.* very small amount (*not one jot*).

joule /jōōl/ *n.* unit of work or energy equal to the force of one newton when its point of application moves one meter in the direction of action of the force. ¶ Symb.: **J.**

jour·nal /jə́rnəl/ *n.* **1** newspaper or periodical. **2** daily record of events. **3** book in which transactions are entered. **4** part of a shaft or axle that rests on bearings.

jour·nal·ism /jə́rnəlizəm/ *n.* business or practice of writing and producing newspapers. □□ **jour′ nal·ist** *n.* **jour·nal·is′tic** *adj.*

jour·ney /jə́rnee/ ● *n.* (*pl.* **-neys**) **1** act of going from one place to another. **2** distance traveled in a specified time (*day's journey*). ● *v.intr.* (**-neys, -neyed**) make a journey.

jour·ney·man /jə́rneemən/ *n.* (*pl.* **-men**) **1** qualified mechanic or artisan who works for another. **2** reliable but not outstanding worker.

joust /jowst/ *hist.* ● *n.* combat between two knights on horseback with lances. ● *v.intr.* engage in a joust. □□ **joust′er** *n.*

Jove /jōv/ *n.* (in Roman mythology) Jupiter. □ **by Jove!** exclamation of surprise or approval.

jo·vi·al /jṓveeəl/ *adj.* merry; convivial. □□ **jo·vi· al·i·ty** /-álitee/ *n.* **jo′vi·al·ly** *adv.*

jowl¹ /jowl/ *n.* **1** jaw or jawbone. **2** cheek.

jowl² /jowl/ *n.* loose skin on the throat or neck. □□ **jowl′y** *adj.*

joy /joy/ *n.* **1** pleasure; extreme gladness. **2** thing that causes joy. □□ **joy′less** *adj.* **joy′less·ly** *adv.* **joy′ous** *adj.* **joy′ous·ly** *adv.*

joy·ful /jóyfŏŏl/ *adj.* full of, showing, or causing joy. □□ **joy′ful·ly** *adv.* **joy′ful·ness** *n.*

joy·ride /jóyrīd/ *colloq.* ● *n.* a ride for pleasure in a car, usu. recklessly. ● *v.intr.* (*past* **-rode** /-rōd/; *past part.* **-rid·den** /-rid′n/) go for a joy ride. □□ **joy′rid·er** *n.*

joy·stick /jóystik/ *n.* **1** *colloq.* control column of an aircraft. **2** lever controlling movement of a computer image.

JP *abbr.* **1** justice of the peace. **2** jet propulsion.

Jr. *abbr.* junior.

ju·bi·lant /jŏŏbilənt/ *adj.* exultant; rejoicing. □□ **ju′bi·lance** *n.* **ju′bi·lant·ly** *adv.*

ju·bi·lee /jŏŏbilee/ *n.* **1** time of rejoicing. **2** anniversary, esp. the 25th or 50th.

Ju·da·ism /jŏŏdeeizəm, -day-/ *n.* religion of the Jews, with a belief in one god and a basis in Mosaic and rabbinical teachings. □□ **Ju·da·ic** /-dáyik/ *adj.* **Ju′da·ist** *n.*

Ju·das /jŏŏdəs/ *n.* traitor.

judge /juj/ ● *n.* **1** public officer appointed to hear and try legal cases. **2** person appointed to decide a dispute or contest. **3 a** person who decides a question. **b** person regarded as qualified to decide or pronounce. ● *v.tr.* **1 a** try a legal case. **b** pronounce sentence on. **2** form an opinion about; appraise. **3** act as a judge of. **4** conclude; consider. □□ **judge′like** *adj.* **judge′ship** *n.*

judg·ment /jújmənt/ *n.* (also **judge′ment**) **1** critical faculty; discernment (*an error in judgment*). **2** good sense. **3** opinion or estimate. **4** sentence of a court of justice. □ **against one's better judgment** contrary to what one really feels to be advisable. **judgment by default** see DEFAULT. **Judgment Day** day of the Last Judgment. **Last Judgment** judgment of mankind said to take place at the end of the world.

judg·men·tal /jujmént′l/ *adj.* (also **judge·men′ tal**) **1** making judgments. **2** condemning; critical. □□ **judg·men′tal·ly** *adv.*

ju·di·ca·ture /jŏŏdikəchər/ *n.* **1** administration of justice. **2** jurisdiction. **3** judges collectively.

ju·di·cial /jŏŏdíshəl/ *adj.* **1** of, done by, or proper to a court of law. **2** having the function of judgment (*judicial assembly*). **3** impartial. □□ **ju·di′ cial·ly** *adv.*

¶ **Judicial** means 'relating to judgment and the administration of justice': *judicial robes, the judicial system.* Do not confuse it with **judicious**, which means 'prudent, reasonable': *Getting off the highway the minute you felt tired was a judicious choice.*

ju·di·ci·ar·y /jŏŏdíshee-eree, -díshəree/ *n.* (*pl.* **-ies**) judges of a judicial branch collectively.

ju·di·cious /jŏŏdíshəs/ *adj.* sensible; wise; prudent. □□ **ju·di′cious·ly** *adv.* **ju·di′cious·ness** *n.*

ju·do /jŏŏdō/ *n.* sport derived from jujitsu. □□ **ju′do·ist** *n.*

jug /jug/ *n.* **1** vessel for liquids, with a handle and an opening for pouring. **2** *sl.* prison. □□ **jug′ful** *n.* (*pl.* **-fuls**).

jug·ger·naut /júgərnawt/ *n.* overwhelming force or object.

jug·gle /júgəl/ *v.* **1 a** *intr.* toss objects in the air and catch them, keeping several in the air at the same time. **b** *tr.* perform such feats with. **2** *tr.* deal with (several activities) at once. **3** *intr.* (foll. by *with*) & *tr.* **a** deceive or cheat. **b** rearrange or misrepresent (facts). □□ **jug′gler** *n.*

jug·u·lar /júgyələr/ • *adj.* of the neck or throat. • *n.* = jugular vein. □ **jugular vein** any of several large veins of the neck, which carry blood from the head.

juice /jōōs/ *n.* **1** liquid part of plants or fruits. **2** fluid of animal tissue. **3** essence or spirit of anything. **4** *colloq.* fuel or electricity. **5** *sl.* alcoholic liquor. □□ **juice′less** *adj.*

juic·er /jōōsər/ *n.* **1** device for extracting juice from fruits and vegetables. **2** *sl.* alcoholic.

juic·y /jōōsee/ *adj.* (**juic·i·er, juic·i·est**) **1** full of juice; succulent. **2** *colloq.* interesting; racy; scandalous. **3** *colloq.* profitable. □□ **juic′i·ly** *adv.* **juic′i·ness** *n.*

ju·jit·su /jōōjítsoo/ *n.* (also **jiu·jit′su**) Japanese system of unarmed combat and physical training.

ju·jube /jōōjoob/ *n.* flavored jellylike lozenge or candy.

juke·box /jōōkboks/ *n.* coin-operated machine for playing selected music.

Jul. *abbr.* July.

ju·lep /jōōlip/ *n.* sweet drink, esp. one medicated or with alcohol.

ju·li·enne /jōōlee-én/ *adj.* (esp. of vegetables) cut into thin strips.

Ju·ly /jōōlí/ *n.* (*pl.* **Ju·lys**) seventh month of the year.

jum·ble /júmbəl/ • *v.* **1** *tr.* confuse; mix up. **2** *intr.* move about in disorder. • *n.* confused state or heap. □□ **jumb′ly** *adj.*

jum·bo /júmbō/ *colloq.* • *n.* (*pl.* **-bos**) large animal, person, or thing. • *adj.* very large.

jump /jump/ • *v.* **1** *intr.* move off the ground by sudden muscular effort in the legs. **2** *intr.* move suddenly or hastily. **3** *intr.* jerk; twitch. **4** *intr.* undergo a rapid change, esp. an advance in status. **5** *intr.* change the subject, etc., rapidly. **6 a** *intr.* rise suddenly (*prices jumped*). **b** *tr.* cause to do this. **7** *tr.* **a** pass over (an obstacle, etc.) by jumping. **b** pass over (an intervening thing) to a point beyond. **8** *tr.* pounce on or attack (a person) unexpectedly. • *n.* **1** act of jumping. **2** sudden jerk caused by shock or excitement. **3** abrupt rise in amount, value, status, etc. **4** obstacle to be jumped. **5 a** sudden transition. **b** gap in a series, logical sequence, etc. □ **get** (or **have**) **the jump on** *colloq.* get (or have) an early advantage. **jump at** accept eagerly. **jump down a person's throat** *colloq.* reprimand or contradict a person fiercely. **jump the gun** see GUN. **jump-start** *v.tr.* start (a motor vehicle) by pushing it or with jumper cables. • *n.* jump-starting. **jump to it** *colloq.* act promptly and energetically.

jump·er[1] /júmpər/ *n.* **1** sleeveless one-piece dress worn over a blouse. **2** loose jacket.

jump·er[2] /júmpər/ *n.* **1** person or animal that jumps. **2** *Electr.* short wire used to make or break a circuit. □ **jumper cables** pair of cables attached to a battery and used to start a motor vehicle with a weak or discharged battery.

jump·suit /júmpsoot/ *n.* one-piece garment for the whole body.

jump·y /júmpee/ *adj.* (**jump·i·er, jump·i·est**) **1**

nervous; easily startled. **2** making sudden movements. □□ **jump′i·ly** *adv.* **jump′i·ness** *n.*

Jun. *abbr.* **1** June. **2** Junior.

jun·co /júngkō/ *n.* (*pl.* **-cos** or **-coes**) small American finch.

junc·tion /júngkshən/ *n.* **1** joint; joining point. **2** place where railroad lines or roads meet or cross. **3** joining. □ **junction box** box containing a junction of electric cables, etc.

junc·ture /júngkchər/ *n.* **1** critical convergence of events; critical point of time (*at this juncture*). **2** place where things join. **3** joining.

June /jōōn/ *n.* sixth month of the year. □ **June bug** large brown scarab beetle.

jun·gle /júnggəl/ *n.* **1 a** land with dense vegetation, esp. in the tropics. **b** area of such land. **2** place of bewildering complexity or confusion, or of struggle. **jungle gym** playground structure with bars, ladders, etc., for climbing.

jun·ior /jōōnyər/ • *adj.* **1** (foll. by *to*) inferior in age, standing, or position. **2** the younger (esp. appended to the name of a son with his father's name). • *n.* **1** junior person. **2** one's inferior in length of service, etc. **3** third-year high school or college student. □ **junior college** two-year college. **junior high school** school for grades seven, eight, and sometimes nine.

ju·ni·per /jōōnipər/ *n.* evergreen shrub or tree with prickly leaves and dark purple berrylike cones.

junk[1] /jungk/ • *n.* **1** discarded articles; rubbish. **2** thing of little value. **3** *sl.* narcotic drug. • *v.tr.* discard as junk. □ **junk bond** high-interest bond deemed to be a risky investment. **junk food** food with low nutritional value. **junk mail** unsolicited advertising matter sent through the mail.

junk[2] /jungk/ *n.* flat-bottomed sailing vessel in the China seas.

jun·ket /júngkit/ • *n.* **1** sweetened and flavored curds. **2** pleasure outing. **3** official's tour at public expense. • *v.intr.* feast; picnic. □□ **jun′ket·ing** *n.*

junk·ie /júngkee/ *n.* *sl.* drug addict.

junk·yard /júngkyard/ *n.* yard in which junk is collected and sometimes resold.

jun·ta /hōontə, júntə/ *n.* political or military clique taking power in a coup d'état.

Ju·pi·ter /jōōpitər/ *n.* largest planet of the solar system, fifth from the sun.

Ju·ras·sic /jōōrásik/ *Geol.* • *adj.* of the second period of the Mesozoic era, noted for dinosaurs. • *n.* this era or system.

ju·rid·i·cal /jōōrídikəl/ *adj.* of the law or judicial proceedings. □□ **ju·rid′i·cal·ly** *adv.*

ju·ris·dic·tion /jōōrisdíkshən/ *n.* **1** legal or other authority. **2** extent of this; territory it extends over. □□ **ju·ris·dic′tion·al** *adj.*

ju·ris·pru·dence /jōōrisproōd′ns/ *n.* science or philosophy of law. □□ **ju·ris·pru·dent** /-dənt/ *adj.* & *n.*

ju·rist /jōōrist/ *n.* expert in law.

ju·ror /jōōrər/ *n.* member of a jury.

ju·ry /jōōree/ *n.* (*pl.* **-ries**) **1** body of persons giving a verdict in a court of justice. **2** body of persons awarding prizes in a competition.

ju·ry-rigged /jōōree-rigd/ *adj.* having temporary makeshift rigging or repair.

just /just/ • *adj.* **1** morally right or fair. **2** (of treatment, etc.) deserved (*just reward*). **3** (of feelings, opinions, etc.) valid; well-grounded. **4** right in amount, etc.; proper. • *adv.* **1** exactly (*just what I need*). **2** a little time ago (*have just seen them*). **3** *colloq.* simply; merely (*just good friends*). **4** barely; no more than (*just a minute*). **5** *colloq.* positively (*just splendid*). **6** quite (*not just yet*). □ **just about** *colloq.* almost exactly; almost completely. **just in case** as a precaution. **just so 1** exactly arranged (*everything just so*). **2** exactly as you say. □□ **just′ly** *adv.* **just′ness** *n.*

jus·tice /jústis/ *n.* **1** just conduct. **2** fairness. **3** exercise of authority in the maintenance of right. **4** judicial proceedings. **5** magistrate; judge □ **do justice to** treat fairly; appreciate properly. **do oneself justice** perform in a worthy manner. **justice of the peace** magistrate who hears minor cases, grants licenses, performs marriages, etc.

jus·ti·fy /jústifī/ *v.tr.* (**-fies, -fied**) **1** show the jus-tice or rightness of (a person, act, etc.). **2** demonstrate the correctness of (an assertion, etc.). **3** demonstrate adequate grounds for (conduct, a claim, etc.). **4** vindicate. **5** (as **justified** *adj.*) just; right. **6** *Printing* adjust (a line of type) to fill a space evenly. □□ **jus′ti·fi·a·ble** *adj.* **jus′ti·fi·a·bly** *adv.* **jus·ti·fi·ca′tion** *n.* **jus′ti·fi·er** *n.*

jut /jut/ • *v.intr.* (**jut·ted, jut·ting**) protrude; project. • *n.* projection.

jute /joot/ *n.* **1** rough fiber from the bark of an E. Indian plant, used for sacking, mats, etc. **2** plant yielding this fiber.

ju·ve·nile /joovənīl/ • *adj.* **1 a** youthful. **b** of or for young persons. **2** immature. • *n.* **1** young person. **2** *Commerce* book intended for young people. **3** actor playing a youthful person. □ **juvenile delinquency** offenses committed by minors. **juvenile delinquent** such an offender.

jux·ta·pose /júkstəpōz/ *v.tr.* **1** place (things) side by side. **2** place (a thing) beside another. □□ **jux·ta·po·si·tion** /-pəzíshən/ *n.*

Kk

K[1] /kay/ *n.* (also **k**) (*pl.* **Ks** or **K's**; **k's**) eleventh letter of the alphabet.

K[2] *abbr.* (also **K.**) **1** kelvin(s). **2** King; King's. **3** *Computing* unit of 1,024 (i.e., 2^{10}) bytes or bits, or loosely 1,000. **4** 1,000. **5** *Baseball* strikeout.

K[3] *symb. Chem.* potassium.

k *abbr.* **1** kilo-. **2** knot(s).

ka·bob /kəbób/ *n.* pieces of meat, vegetables, etc., cooked on a skewer.

ka·bu·ki /kəbo͞okee/ *n.* form of traditional Japanese drama.

kai·ser /kízər/ *n. hist.* emperor, esp. of Germany, Austria, or the Holy Roman Empire.

kale /kayl/ *n.* variety of wrinkle-leafed cabbage.

ka·lei·do·scope /kəlídəskōp/ *n.* **1** tube containing mirrors and pieces of colored glass, etc., producing changing patterns when rotated. **2** constantly changing group of bright or interesting objects. □□ **ka·lei·do·scop·ic** /-skópik/ *adj.*

ka·mi·ka·ze /kámika'azee/ • *n. hist.* Japanese aircraft loaded with explosives and deliberately crashed by its pilot onto its target. • *adj.* reckless; dangerous; potentially self-destructive.

Kan. *abbr.* Kansas.

kan·ga·roo /kánggəro͞o/ *n.* Australian marsupial with a long tail and strong hindquarters enabling it to travel by jumping. □ **kangaroo court** improperly constituted or illegal court held by a mob, etc.

Kans. *abbr.* Kansas.

Kan·sa /káanzə, -sə/ *n.* **1 a** N. American people native to eastern Kansas. **b** member of this people **2** language of this people.

ka·o·lin /káyəlin/ *n.* fine, soft, white clay used esp. for porcelain. Also called **china clay.** □□ **ka·o·lin·ic** *adj.*

ka·pok /káypok/ *n.* fibrous, cottonlike substance from a tropical tree, used for stuffing cushions, etc.

Ka·po·si's sar·co·ma /kápəseez, kapó-/ *n. Med.* malignant disease causing skin lesions, often associated with AIDS.

kap·pa /kápə/ *n.* tenth letter of the Greek alphabet (K, κ).

ka·put /kaapo͞ot/ *predic.adj. sl.* broken; ruined; done for.

ka·ra·o·ke /káreeo͞okee, kárə-/ *n.* entertainment in which people sing against prerecorded popular song tracks.

ka·rat /kárət/ *n.* measure of purity of gold, pure gold being 24 karats.

ka·ra·te /kəráatee/ *n.* Japanese system of unarmed combat using the hands and feet as weapons.

kar·ma /ka'armə/ *n. Buddhism & Hinduism* **1** sum of a person's actions in previous lives, viewed as deciding fate in future existences. **2** destiny. □□ **kar'mic** *adj.*

ka·ty·did /káyteedid/ *n.* N. American insect related to the grasshopper.

kay·ak /kíak/ *n.* small, enclosed canoe for one paddler.

KAYAK

ka·zoo /kəzo͞o/ *n.* toy musical instrument into which the player sings or hums.

kc *abbr.* kilocycle(s).

ke·a /ke'eə, káyə/ *n.* colorful parrot of New Zealand.

keel /keel/ • *n.* main lengthwise member along the base of a ship, etc. • *v.* **1** (often foll. by *over*) **a** *intr.* turn over or fall down. **b** *tr.* cause to do this. **2** *tr. & intr.* turn keel upward.

keel·haul /ke'elhawl/ *v.tr.* **1** *hist.* drag (a person) under the keel of a ship and up on the other side as a punishment. **2** scold or rebuke severely.

keen[1] /keen/ *adj.* **1** eager; ardent. **2** (foll. by *on*) fond of; enthusiastic about. **3** (of the senses) sharp. **4 a** (of a person) intellectually acute. **b** (of a remark, etc.) sharp; biting. **5** having a sharp edge or point. **6** (of a sound, light, etc.) penetrating. **7** *colloq.* excellent. □□ **keen'ly** *adv.* **keen'ness** *n.*

keen[2] /keen/ • *n.* Irish funeral song accompanied with wailing. • *v.* **1** *intr.* utter the keen. **2** *tr.* bewail (a person) in this way. **3** *tr.* utter in a wailing tone. □□ **keen'er** *n.*

keep /keep/ • *v.* (*past* and *past part.* **kept** /kept/) **1** *tr.* have continuous charge of; retain possession of. **2** *tr.* retain or reserve for a future occasion. **3** *tr. & intr.* retain or remain in a specified condition, position, etc. (*keep cool; keep off the grass*). **4** *tr.* put or store in a regular place. **5** *tr.* (foll. by *from*) hold back. **6** *tr.* detain (*what kept you?*). **7** *tr.* observe, honor, etc. (a law, custom, etc.). **8** *tr.* own and look after (animals). **9** *tr.* (foll. by *in*) maintain with a supply of. **10** *tr.* manage (business, etc.). **11** *tr.* maintain (a house, accounts, etc.) regularly and in proper order. **12** *tr.* have (a commodity) regularly for sale. **13** *tr.* guard or protect (a person or place). **14** *tr.* preserve in being (*keep order*). **15** *intr.* continue; repeat habitually (*keeps saying that*). **16** *tr.* continue to follow (a way or course). **17** *intr.* remain fresh; not spoil. **18** *tr.* maintain (a person), esp. in return for sexual favors (*a kept woman*). • *n.* **1** maintenance, food, etc. (*hardly earn your keep*). **2** charge or control (*is in your keep*). **3** *hist.* tower or stronghold. □ **for keeps** *colloq.* (esp. of something received or won) permanently; indefinitely. **keep at** persist or cause to persist with. **keep away** prevent from being near. **keep back 1** remain at a distance. **2** retard the progress of. **3** conceal. **4** withhold (*kept back*

§50). **keep down 1** hold in subjection. **2** keep low in amount. **3** lie low; stay hidden. **4** not vomit (food eaten). **keep in mind** take into account having remembered. **keep off 1** cause to stay away from. **2** ward off. **keep on 1** do continually (*kept on laughing*). **2** continue to use or employ. **3** (foll. by *at*) pester. **keep out 1** remain outside. **2** exclude. **keep to 1** adhere to. **2** confine oneself to. **keep to oneself 1** avoid contact with others. **2** refuse to disclose. **keep up 1** maintain (progress, morale, etc.). **2** keep in repair, etc. **3** carry on (a correspondence, etc.). **4** prevent from going to bed. **5** (often foll. by *with*) not fall behind. **keep up with the Joneses** strive to compete socially with one's neighbors.

keep·er /keépər/ *n.* **1** person who keeps or looks after something or someone. **2** custodian; guard. **3** *colloq.* anything worth keeping.

keep·ing /keéping/ *n.* **1** custody; charge (*in safe keeping*). **2** observance.

keep·sake /keépsayk/ *n.* souvenir, esp. of the giver.

kees·hond /káys-hond/ *n.* long-haired Dutch breed of dog.

keg /keg/ *n.* small barrel. □ **keg party** party at which beer is served from a keg.

keis·ter /keéstər/ *n. sl.* buttocks.

kelp /kelp/ *n.* brown seaweed used as a food and mineral source.

kel·vin /kélvin/ *n.* unit of thermodynamic temperature, equal in magnitude to the degree celsius. ¶ Abbr.: **K**. □ **Kelvin scale** scale of temperature with absolute zero as zero.

kempt /kempt/ *adj.* combed; neatly kept.

ken /ken/ *n.* range of sight or knowledge.

ken·do /kéndō/ *n.* Japanese martial art of fencing with bamboo sticks.

ken·nel /kénəl/ • *n.* **1** small shelter for a dog. **2** (often in *pl.*) breeding or boarding place for dogs. • *v.* (**ken·neled**, **ken·nel·ing**; **ken·nelled**, **ken·nel·ling**) **1** *tr.* put into or keep in a kennel. **2** *intr.* live in or go to a kennel.

kep·i /képee, káypee/ *n.* (*pl.* **kep·is**) French military cap with a horizontal peak.

KEPI

kept *past* and *past part.* of KEEP.

ker·a·tin /kérətin/ *n.* fibrous protein in hair, feathers, hooves, claws, horns, etc.

ker·chief /kərchif, -cheef/ *n.* **1** cloth used to cover the head or neck. **2** handkerchief. □□ **ker′chiefed** *adj.*

kerf /kərf/ *n.* slit made by cutting, esp. with a saw.

ker·nel /kərnəl/ *n.* **1** center within the hard shell of a nut, fruit stone, seed, etc. **2** whole seed of a cereal. **3** essence of anything.

ker·o·sene /kérəseen/ *n.* petroleum distillate used as a fuel, solvent, etc.

kes·trel /késtrəl/ *n.* small hovering falcon.

ketch /kech/ *n.* type of two-masted sailboat.

ketch·up /kéchup, káchup/ *n.* (also **cat·sup** /kátsəp/) spicy tomato-based condiment.

ke·tone /keétōn/ *n.* any of a class of organic compounds, including acetone. □□ **ke·ton·ic** /kitónik/ *adj.*

ke·to·sis /keetósis/ *n.* condition of abnormally high levels of ketones in the body, associated with fat metabolism and diabetes.

ket·tle /két'l/ *n.* vessel for boiling or cooking. □ **a fine** (or **pretty**) **kettle of fish** awkward state of affairs. □□ **ket′tle·ful** *n.* (*pl.* **-fuls**).

ket·tle·drum /két'ldrum/ *n.* large bowl-shaped drum.

KETTLEDRUM

Kew·pie /kyóopee/ *n. propr.* small, chubby doll with a curl or topknot.

key¹ /kee/ • *n.* (*pl.* **keys**) **1** instrument, usu. metal, for moving the bolt of a lock to lock or unlock. **2** similar implement for winding a clock, etc. **3** finger-operated button or lever on a piano, flute, typewriter, computer terminal, etc. **4** means of advance, access, etc. **5 a** solution or explanation. **b** word or system for solving a cipher or code. **c** explanatory list of symbols used in a map, table, etc. **6** *Mus.* system of notes related to each other and based on a particular note (*key of C major*). • *adj.* essential; of vital importance. • *v.tr.* (**keys**, **keyed**) **1** fasten with a pin, bolt, etc. **2** enter (data) by means of a keyboard. **3** align or link (one thing to another). **4** regulate the pitch of the strings of (a violin, etc.). □ **key up** make nervous or tense; excite.

key² /kee/ *n.* low-lying island or reef, esp. off Florida.

key·board /keébawrd/ • *n.* **1** set of keys on a typewriter, computer, piano, etc. **2** piano-like electronic musical instrument. • *v.* enter (data) by means of a keyboard. □□ **key′board·er** *n.* **key′board·ist** *n.*

key·hole /keéhōl/ *n.* hole by which a key is put into a lock.

key·note /ke'enōt/ n. **1** (esp. attrib.) prevailing tone or idea (keynote address). **2** Mus. note on which a key is based.

key·pad /ke'epad/ n. small keyboard, etc., on a calculator, telephone, etc.

key·punch /ke'epunch/ • n. device for transferring data by means of punched holes or notches on cards or paper tape. • v.tr. transfer (data) thus. □□ **key'punch·er** n.

key·stone /ke'estōn/ n. **1** central principle of a system, policy, etc. **2** central locking stone of an arch.

key·stroke /ke'estrōk/ n. single depression of a key on a keyboard, esp. as a measure of work.

key·word /ke'eword/ n. **1** key to a cipher, etc. **2 a** word of great significance. **b** significant word used in indexing.

kg abbr. kilogram(s).

KGB /káyjeebe'e/ n. security police of the former USSR.

kha·ki /kákee, ka'a-/ • adj. dull brownish-yellow. • n. (pl. **kha·kis**) **1 a** khaki fabric of twilled cotton or wool. **b** (in pl.) pants or a military uniform made of this fabric. **2** dull brownish-yellow color.

khan /kaan, kan/ n. title of rulers and officials in Central Asia, Afghanistan, etc. □□ **khan'ate** n.

Khmer /kmair/ • n. **1** native of Cambodia. **2** language of this people. • adj. of the Khmers or their language.

kHz abbr. kilohertz.

kib·ble /kibəl/ n. coarsely ground pellets of meal, etc., used as pet food.

kib·butz /kibóots/ n. (pl. **kib·but·zim** /-boõtse'em/) communal, esp. farming, settlement in Israel.

kib·itz /kíbits/ v.intr. colloq. offer unwanted advice, esp. to card players. □□ **kib'itz·er** n.

ki·bosh /kíbosh/ n. sl. nonsense. □ **put the kibosh on** colloq. put an end to; finally dispose of.

kick /kik/ • v. **1** tr. & intr. strike or propel forcibly with the foot or hoof, etc. **2** intr. express annoyance at; rebel against. **3** tr. sl. give up (a habit). **4** tr. expel or dismiss forcibly. **5** refl. be annoyed with oneself. **6** tr. Football score (a goal) by a kick. • n. **1** blow with the foot or hoof, etc. **2** colloq. **a** sharp stimulant effect, esp. of alcohol. **b** (often in pl.) pleasurable thrill (did it for kicks). **3** colloq. temporary interest (on a jogging kick). **4** recoil of a fired gun. □ **kick about** (or **around**) colloq. **1 a** drift idly from place to place. **b** be unused or unwanted. **2 a** treat roughly or scornfully. **b** discuss (an idea) unsystematically. **kick the bucket** sl. die. **kick in 1** knock down (a door, etc.) by kicking. **2** sl. pay one's share. **kick in the pants** (or **teeth**) colloq. humiliating setback. **kick off 1 a** Football, etc. begin or resume play. **b** colloq. begin. **2** remove (shoes, etc.) by kicking. **kick-start** start (a motorcycle, etc.) by the downward thrust of a pedal. **kick up** (or **kick up a fuss**, etc.) create a disturbance. **kick up one's heels** frolic.

kick·back /kíkbak/ n. colloq. **1** recoil. **2** (usu. illegal) payment for collaboration.

kick·off /kíkawf/ n. **1** Football & Soccer kick that starts play. **2** start of a campaign, drive, project, etc.

kick·stand /kíkstand/ n. rod for supporting a bicycle or motorcycle when stationary.

kid[1] /kid/ n. **1** young goat. **2** leather from its skin.

3 colloq. child. **handle with kid gloves** treat carefully. **kid brother** (or **sister**) sl. younger brother (or sister).

¶ **Kid**, meaning 'child,' although widely seen in advertising and other contexts, should be avoided in formal writing.

kid[2] /kid/ v. (**kid·ded, kid·ding**) colloq. **1** tr. & also refl. deceive; trick. **2** tr. & intr. tease (only kidding). □ **no kidding** sl. that is the truth. □□ **kid'der** n. **kid'ding·ly** adv.

kid·die /kídee/ n. (pl. **-dies**) sl. = KID[1] n. 3.

kid·nap /kídnap/ v.tr. (**kid·napped, kid·nap·ping; kid·naped, kid·nap·ing**) **1** abduct (a person, etc.), esp. to obtain a ransom. **2** steal (a child). □□ **kid'nap·per** n.

kid·ney /kídnee/ n. (pl. **-neys**) **1** either of two organs in the abdominal cavity of vertebrates that remove wastes from the blood and excrete urine. **2** animal's kidney as food. □ **kidney bean** red-skinned kidney-shaped bean.

kiel·ba·sa /keelba'asə, kib-/ n. smoked Polish-style sausage.

kill /kil/ • v.tr. **1 a** cause the death of. **b** (absol.) cause death (must kill to survive). **2** destroy; put an end to (feelings, etc.). **3** switch off (a light, engine, etc.). **4** pass (time, or a specified period) usu. while waiting. **5** defeat (legislation, etc.). **6 a** Tennis, etc., hit (the ball) so that it cannot be returned. **b** stop (the ball) dead. **7** render ineffective (taste, sound, color, etc.) (thick carpet killed the sound of footsteps). • n. **1** act of killing. **2** animal or animals killed, esp. by a hunter. **3** colloq. destruction or disablement of an enemy aircraft, submarine, etc. □ **dressed to kill** dressed alluringly or impressively. **in at the kill** present at or benefiting from the successful conclusion of an enterprise. **kill two birds with one stone** achieve two aims at once. **kill with kindness** spoil (a person) with overindulgence.

kill·deer /kíldeer/ n. large American plover.

kill·er /kílər/ n. **1** person, animal, or thing that kills. **2** colloq. **a** impressive, formidable, or excellent thing. **b** decisive blow. □ **killer bee** very aggressive honeybee, orig. from Africa. **killer instinct 1** innate tendency to kill. **2** ruthless streak. **killer whale** voracious cetacean with a prominent dorsal fin.

kill·ing /kíling/ • n. **1 a** causing of death. **b** instance of this. **2** great (esp. financial) success. • adj. colloq. exhausting.

kill·joy /kíljoy/ n. gloomy person, esp. at a party, etc.

kiln /kiln, kil/ n. furnace or oven for burning, baking, or drying, esp. bricks, pottery, etc.

ki·lo /ke'elō/ n. (pl. **-los**) **1** kilogram. **2** kilometer.

kilo- /kílō/ comb. form denoting a factor of 1,000 (esp. in metric units). ¶ Abbr.: **k**, or **K** in Computing.

kil·o·byte /kílabīt/ n. Computing 1,024 (i.e., 2^{10}) bytes as a measure of data storage.

kil·o·cy·cle /kíləsīkəl/ n. former measure of frequency, equivalent to 1 kilohertz. ¶ Abbr.: **kc**.

kil·o·gram /kíləgram/ n. metric unit of mass, approx. 2.205 lb. ¶ Abbr.: **kg**.

kil·o·hertz /kíləhərts/ n. 1,000 hertz; 1,000 cycles per second. ¶ Abbr.: **kHz**.

kil·o·me·ter /kilómitər, kíləmeetər/ n. 1,000 meters (approx. 0.62 miles). ¶ Abbr.: **km**. □□ **kil·o·met·ric** /kíləmétrik/ adj.

kil·o·ton /kílətun/ *n.* unit of explosive power equivalent to 1,000 tons of TNT.

kil·o·watt /kíləwot/ *n.* 1,000 watts. ¶ Abbr.: **kW.**

kil·o·watt-hour /kíləwot-ówr/ *n.* measure of electrical energy equivalent to a power consumption of 1,000 watts for one hour. ¶ Abbr.: **kWh.**

kilt /kilt/ *n.* **1** knee-length skirt, usu. of pleated tartan, traditionally worn by Scottish Highland men. **2** similar garment worn by women.

KILT

kil·ter /kíltər/ *n.* good working order (esp. *out of kilter*).

ki·mo·no /kimốnō/ *n.* (*pl.* **-nos**) **1** long, loose Japanese robe worn with a sash. **2** similar dressing gown.

KIMONO

kin /kin/ • *n.* one's relatives or family. • *predic.adj.* (of a person) related (*we are kin*) (see also AKIN). □ **next of kin** see NEXT.

-kin /kin/ *suffix* forming diminutive nouns (*catkin; manikin*).

kind[1] /kīnd/ *n.* **1** race, species, or natural group of animals, plants, etc. **2** class; type; sort; variety. □ **kind of** *colloq.* to some extent. **in kind 1** in the same form; likewise (*replied in kind*). **2** (of payment) in goods or labor, not money. **nothing of the kind 1** not at all like the thing in question. **2** (expressing denial) not at all. **of a kind 1** *derog.* scarcely deserving the name (*a choir of a kind*). **2** similar in some respect (*they're two of a kind*).

¶ **1. Kind of** is sometimes used to be deliberately vague: *It was kind of a big evening. I was kind of hoping you'd call.* More often, it reveals an inability to speak clearly: *He's kind of, like, awesome, you know?* Used precisely, it means 'sort, type': *A maple is a kind of tree.* **2.** The plural of **kind** often causes difficulty. With *this* or *that*, speaking of one kind, use a singular: *That kind of fabric doesn't need ironing;* with *these* or *those*, speaking of more than one kind, use the plural: *Those kinds of animals ought to be left in the wild.* The same recommendations apply to *sort* and *sorts*.

kind[2] /kīnd/ *adj.* of a friendly, generous, benevolent, or gentle nature.

kin·der·gar·ten /kíndərgaart'n/ *n.* school or class for preschool learning.

kind·heart·ed /kíndha'artid/ *adj.* of a kind disposition. □□ **kind'heart'ed·ly** *adv.* **kind'heart'ed·ness** *n.*

kin·dle /kínd'l/ *v.* **1** *tr.* light or set on fire. **2** *intr.* catch fire. **3** *tr.* arouse; inspire. **4** *intr.* become animated, glow with passion, etc. □□ **kin'dler** *n.*

kin·dling /kíndling/ *n.* small sticks, etc., for lighting fires.

kind·ly[1] /kíndlee/ *adv.* **1** in a kind manner (*spoke kindly*). **2** please (*kindly leave me alone*).

kind·ly[2] /kíndlee/ *adj.* (**kind·li·er, kind·li·est**) **1** kind. **2** (of climate, etc.) pleasant. □□ **kind'li·ness** *n.*

kind·ness /kíndnis/ *n.* **1** being kind. **2** kind act.

kin·dred /kíndrid/ • *n.* one's relations, collectively. • *adj.* related, allied, or similar. □ **kindred spirit** person whose character, etc., has much in common with one's own.

ki·ne·mat·ics /kínimátiks/ *n.pl.* (usu. treated as *sing.*) branch of mechanics concerned with the motion of objects without reference to cause. □□ **ki·ne·mat'ic** *adj.* **ki·ne·mat'i·cal·ly** *adv.*

ki·net·ic /kinétik, kī-/ *adj.* of or due to motion. □□ **ki·net'i·cal·ly** *adv.*

ki·net·ics /kinétiks, kī-/ *n.pl.* = DYNAMICS 1.

kin·folk /kínfōk/ *n.pl.* (also **kin'folks, kins'folk**) relatives.

king /king/ • *n.* **1** male sovereign, esp. a hereditary ruler. **2** person or thing preeminent in a specified field, etc. (*railroad king*). **3** large (or the largest) kind of plant, animal, etc. (*king penguin*). **4** *Chess* piece that must be checkmated for a win. **5** crowned piece in checkers. **6** playing card depicting a king. • *v.tr.* make (a person) king. □ **king cobra** large and venomous hooded Indian snake. **king of (the) beasts** the lion. **king-size** (or **-sized**) larger than normal; very large. **king's ransom** a fortune. □□ **king'ly** *adj.* **king'li·ness** *n.* **king'ship** *n.*

king·dom /kíngdəm/ *n.* **1** territory subject to a king or queen. **2** spiritual reign or sphere attributed to God. **3** domain; sphere. **4** province of nature (*vegetable kingdom*). □ **kingdom come** *colloq.* eternity; the next world.

king·fish·er /kíngfishər/ *n.* long-beaked, brightly colored bird that dives for fish in rivers, etc.

king·pin /kíngpin/ *n.* **1** main or large bolt in a central position. **2** essential person or thing.

kink /kingk/ • *n.* **1 a** twist or bend in wire, etc. **b** tight wave in hair. **2** mental twist or quirk. • *v.* form or cause to form a kink.

kink·y /kíngkee/ *adj.* (**kink·i·er, kink·i·est**) **1** *colloq.* **a** given to or involving abnormal sexual behavior. **b** (of clothing, etc.) bizarre and sexually provocative. **2** eccentric. **3** having kinks. □□ **kink′i·ly** *adv.* **kink′i·ness** *n.*

kins·folk var. of KINFOLK.

kin·ship /kínship/ *n.* **1** blood relationship. **2** sharing of characteristics or origins.

kins·man /kínzmən/ *n.* (*pl.* **-men;** *fem.* **kins·wom·an,** *pl.* **-wom·en**) blood relation or *disp.* relation by marriage.

ki·osk /kéeosk, -ósk/ *n.* **1** open-fronted booth from which food, newspapers, tickets, etc., are sold. **2** columnar structure for posting notices, etc.

Ki·o·wa /kíəwə/ *n.* **1 a** N. American people native to the southwestern US. **b** member of this people. **2** language of this people.

kip·per /kípər/ • *n.* kippered fish, esp. herring. • *v.tr.* cure (herring, etc.) by splitting, salting, and drying.

kirk /kurk/ *n.* Sc. church.

kis·met /kízmet/ *n.* destiny; fate.

kiss /kis/ • *v.* **1** *tr.* touch with the lips, esp. as a sign of love, affection, greeting, or reverence. **2** *absol.* (of two persons) touch each others' lips in this way. **3** *tr.* lightly touch. • *n.* **1** touch with the lips. **2** light touch. **3** droplet-shaped piece of candy, etc. □ **kiss and tell** recount one's sexual exploits. **kissing cousin** distant relative (given a kiss upon meeting). **kiss of death** apparently friendly act that causes ruin. □□ **kiss′a·ble** *adj.*

kit[1] /kit/ *n.* **1** articles, equipment, etc., for a specific purpose. **2** set of parts needed to assemble an item. □ **kit bag** usu. cylindrical bag used for carrying equipment, etc. **the whole kit and caboodle** see CABOODLE.

kit[2] /kit/ *n.* **1** kitten. **2** young fox, badger, etc.

kitch·en /kíchin/ *n.* room or area where food is prepared and cooked. □ **everything but the kitchen sink** everything imaginable. **kitchen cabinet** group of unofficial advisers thought to be unduly influential.

kitch·en·ette /kíchinét/ *n.* small kitchen or cooking area.

kitch·en·ware /kíchinwair/ *n.* utensils used in the kitchen.

kite /kīt/ *n.* **1** light framework with thin covering, flown on a string in the wind. **2** soaring bird of prey with long wings and usu. a forked tail.

kith /kith/ *n.* □ **kith and kin** friends and relations.

kitsch /kich/ *n.* (often *attrib.*) garish, pretentious, or vulgar art.

kit·ten /kít'n/ *n.* young cat, ferret, etc. □ **have kittens** *colloq.* be extremely upset or anxious.

kit·ten·ish /kít'nish/ *adj.* **1** playful; lively. **2** flirtatious. □□ **kit′ten·ish·ly** *adv.*

kit·ty[1] /kítee/ *n.* (*pl.* **-ties**) **1** fund of money for communal use. **2** pool in some card games.

kit·ty[2] /kítee/ *n.* (*pl.* **-ties**) pet name for a kitten or cat.

kit·ty-cor·ner var. of CATERCORNERED.

ki·wi /kéewee/ *n.* (*pl.* **ki·wis**) **1** flightless long-billed New Zealand bird. **2** (**Kiwi**) *colloq.* New Zealander. □ **kiwi fruit** fuzzy-skinned, green-fleshed fruit.

KKK *abbr.* Ku Klux Klan.

klep·to·ma·ni·a /kléptəmáyneeə/ *n.* recurrent urge to steal. □□ **klep·to·ma′ni·ac** *n.* & *adj.*

klutz /kluts/ *n. sl.* **1** clumsy, awkward person. **2** fool. □□ **klutz′y** *adj.*

km *abbr.* kilometer(s).

kmph *abbr.* kilometers per hour.

kmps *abbr.* kilometers per second.

knack /nak/ *n.* **1** acquired faculty of doing a thing. **2** habit of action, speech, etc.

knap·sack /nápsak/ *n.* bag of supplies, etc., carried on the back.

knave /nayv/ *n.* **1** rogue; scoundrel. **2** = JACK *n.* 2. □□ **knav′er·y** *n.* (*pl.* **-ies**). **knav′ish** *adj.* **knav′ish·ly** *adv.*

knead /need/ *v.tr.* **1** prepare dough, paste, etc., by pressing and folding. **2** massage (muscles, etc.) as if kneading. □□ **knead′a·ble** *adj.* **knead′er** *n.*

knee /nee/ • *n.* **1** joint between the thigh and the lower leg in humans and other animals. **2** part of a garment covering the knee. • *v.tr.* (**knees, kneed, knee·ing**) touch or strike with the knee (*kneed him in the groin*). □ **bring a person to his** or **her knees** reduce a person to submission. **knee-deep 1** immersed up to the knees. **2** deeply involved. **knee jerk** reflex kick caused by a blow on the tendon just below the knee. **knee-jerk** (*attrib.*) predictable; automatic.

knee·cap /néekap/ *n.* bone in front of the knee joint; patella.

kneel /neel/ *v.intr.* (*past* and *past part.* **knelt** /nelt/ or **kneeled**) fall or rest on the knees or a knee.

knell /nel/ • *n.* **1** sound of a bell, esp. for a death or funeral. **2** announcement, event, etc., regarded as an ill omen. • *v.* **1** *intr.* (of a bell) ring solemnly. **2** *tr.* proclaim by or as by a knell.

knelt *past* and *past part.* of KNEEL.

knew *past* of KNOW.

knick·ers /níkərz/ *n.pl.* loose-fitting pants gathered at the knee or calf.

KNICKERS

knick·knack /níknak/ *n.* trinket or small, dainty article.

knife /nīf/ • *n.* (*pl.* **knives** /nīvz/) **1** cutting tool, usu. with a sharp-edged blade in a handle. **2** cutting blade in a machine. • *v.tr.* cut or stab with a knife. □ **that one could cut with a knife** *colloq.* (of an accent, atmosphere, etc.) very obvious, oppressive, etc. **under the knife** undergoing surgery. □□ **knife′like** *adj.* **knif′er** *n.*

knight /nīt/ • *n.* **1** man awarded a non-hereditary title (*Sir*) by a sovereign. **2** *hist.* **a** man, usu. noble, raised to honorable military rank. **b** military attendant, esp. of a lady. **3** *Chess* piece usu. shaped like a horse's head. □ **knight-errant 1** medieval knight in search of chivalrous adventures. **2** chivalrous or quixotic man. **knight in shining armor** chivalrous rescuer or helper, esp. of a woman. □□ **knight′hood** *n.* **knight′like** *adj.* **knight′ly** *adj.*

knit /nit/ • *v.* (**knit·ting**; *past* and *past part.* **knit·ted** or (esp. in senses 2–4) **knit**) **1** *tr.* (also *absol.*) make (a garment, etc.) by interlocking loops of yarn with knitting needles or a knitting machine. **2 a** *tr.* contract (the forehead) in vertical wrinkles. **b** *intr.* (of the forehead) contract; frown. **3** *tr.* & *intr.* make or become close or compact (*a close-knit group*). **4** *intr.* (of a broken bone) become joined; heal. • *n.* knitted material or garment. □□ **knit′ter** *n.*

---

knit Old English *cnyttan*, of West Germanic origin; related to German dialect *knütten*, also to KNOT. The original sense was 'tie in or with a knot,' hence 'join, unite' (sense 4); an obsolete Middle English sense 'knot string to make a net' gave rise to sense 1.

---

knit·ting /níting/ *n.* work being knitted.
knives *pl.* of KNIFE.
knob /nob/ *n.* rounded protuberance, esp. at the end or on the surface of a thing as the handle of a door, drawer, etc. □□ **knob′by** *adj.* **knob′like** *adj.*

knock /nok/ • *v.* **1 a** *tr.* strike with an audible sharp blow. **b** *intr.* strike, esp. a door to gain admittance. **2** *tr.* make (a hole, etc.) by knocking. **3** *tr.* drive (a thing, person, etc.) by striking (*knocked her hand away*). **4** *tr. sl.* criticize. **5** *intr.* (of an engine) make a thumping or rattling noise. • *n.* **1** act of knocking. **2** sharp rap, esp. at a door. **3** audible sharp blow. **4** sound of knocking in an engine. □ **knock about** (or **around**) **1** strike repeatedly; treat roughly. **2** wander aimlessly. **3** be present without design (*there's a cup knocking about somewhere*). **knock down 1** strike (esp. a person) to the ground. **2** demolish. **3** (at an auction) sell to a bidder by a knock with a hammer. **4** *colloq.* lower the price of (an article). **knock-kneed** having knock-knees. **knock-knees** condition in which the legs curve inward at the knee. **knock off 1** strike off with a blow. **2** finish work. **3** rapidly produce (a work of art, etc.). **4** deduct (a sum) from a price, etc. **5** *sl.* steal from (*knocked off a liquor store*). **6** *sl.* kill. **knock on** (or **knock**) **wood** knock something wooden with the knuckles to avert bad luck. **knock out 1** make unconscious by a blow on the head. **2** defeat, esp. in competition. **3** *sl.* astonish. **4** (*refl.*) *colloq.* exhaust (*knocked themselves out swimming*). **knock together** assemble hastily or roughly. **knock up 1**

make hastily. **2** damage or mar. **3** *coarse sl.* make pregnant.

knock·er /nókər/ *n.* metal or wooden instrument hinged to a door for knocking.

knock·out /nókowt/ *n.* **1** act of making unconscious by a blow. **2** *Boxing*, etc., blow that knocks an opponent out. **3** *colloq.* outstanding or irresistible person or thing.

knock·wurst /naákwərst/ *n.* variety of thick, seasoned sausage.

knoll /nōl/ *n.* small hill or mound.

knot /not/ • *n.* **1 a** intertwining of rope, string, hair, etc., with another, itself, or something else to join or fasten together. **b** set method of this (*a reef knot*). **c** ribbon, etc., tied as an ornament. **d** tangle in hair, knitting, etc. **2 a** unit of a ship's or aircraft's speed, equivalent to one nautical mile per hour. **b** *colloq.* nautical mile. **3** cluster (*knot of journalists at the gate*). **4** bond or tie, esp. of wedlock. **5** hard lump of body tissue. **6 a** knob in a stem, branch, or root. **b** hard mass in a tree trunk at the intersection with a branch. **c** round cross-grained piece in lumber where a branch has been cut through. **7** difficulty; problem. **8** central point in a problem, plot, etc. • *v.tr.* (**knot·ted, knot·ting**) **1** tie in a knot. **2** entangle. **3** unite closely. □ **knot garden** intricately designed formal garden, esp. of herbs. **tie the knot** get married. □□ **knot′ter** *n.*

KNOT, 1a

knot·hole /nóthōl/ *n.* hole in lumber where a knot has fallen out.

knot·ty /nótee/ *adj.* (**knot·ti·er, knot·ti·est**) **1** full of knots. **2** puzzling (*knotty problem*). □□ **knot′ti·ly** *adv.* **knot′ti·ness** *n.*

know /nō/ • *v.tr.* (*past* **knew** /noō, nyoō/; *past part.* **known** /nōn/) **1 a** have in the mind; have learned; be able to recall (*knows what to do*). **b** (also *absol.*) be aware of (a fact) (*I think she knows*). **c** have a good command of (*knew German*). **2** be acquainted or friendly with. **3 a** recognize; identify (*I knew him at once*). **b** (foll. by *from*) be able to distinguish (*did not know him from Adam*). **4** be subject to (*her joy knew* *no bounds*). **5** have personal experience of (fear, etc.). **6** (as **known** *adj.*) a publicly acknowledged (*a known thief*). **b** *Math.* (of a quantity, etc.) having a value that can be stated. ● *n.* (in phr. **in the know**) *colloq.* well-informed; having special knowledge. □ **all one knows** (or **knows how**) all one can (*did all she knew to stop it*). **before one knows where one is** with baffling speed. **be not to know** be not to be told (*she's not to know about the party*). **don't I know it!** *colloq.* expression of rueful assent. **don't you know** *colloq.* or *joc.* expression used for emphasis (*such a bore, don't you know*). **for all I know** so far as my knowledge extends. **have been known to** be known to have done (*they have been known to forget*). **I knew it!** I was sure that this would happen. **I know what** I have a new idea, suggestion, etc. **know best** be or claim to be better informed, etc., than others. **know better than** (foll. by *that*, or *to* + infin.) be wise, well-informed, or well-mannered enough to avoid (specified behavior, etc.). **know by name** have heard the name of. **know by sight** recognize the appearance (only) of. **know how** know the way to do something. **know-how** *n.* **1** practical knowledge. **2** natural skill or invention. **know-it-all** *colloq.* person who acts as if he or she knows everything. **know of** be aware of (*not that I know of*). **know the ropes** be fully knowledgeable or experienced. **know a thing or two** be experienced or shrewd. **know what's what** have adequate knowledge of the world, life, etc. **not know what hit one** be suddenly injured, killed, disconcerted, etc. **not want to know** refuse to take any notice of. **what do you know** (or **know about that)?** *colloq.* expression of surprise. **you know** *colloq.* expression implying something generally known (*you know, the store on the corner*). **you-know-what** (or **-who**) thing or person unspecified but understood. **you never know** nothing in the future is certain. □□ **know′a·ble** *adj.* **know′er** *n.*

know·ing /nṓing/ ● *n.* state of being aware or informed of any thing. ● *adj.* **1** usu. *derog.* cunning; sly. **2** showing knowledge; shrewd. □□ **know′ing·ly** *adv.*

knowl·edge /nólij/ *n.* **1 a** awareness or familiarity (of a person, fact, or thing) (*have no knowledge of their character*). **b** person's range of information. **2 a** understanding of a subject, language, etc. (*good knowledge of Greek*). **b** sum of what is known (*every branch of knowledge*). □ **to (the best of) my knowledge** so far as I know.

knowl·edge·a·ble /nólijəbəl/ *adj.* well-informed; intelligent. □□ **knowl′edge·a·bly** *adv.*

known *past part.* of KNOW.

knuck·le /núkəl/ ● *n.* **1** bone at a finger joint, esp. that adjoining the hand. **2** knee or ankle joint of an animal, used as food. ● *v.tr.* strike, press, or rub with the knuckles. □ **knuckle down** (often foll. by *to*) apply oneself seriously (to a task, etc.). **knuckle sandwich** *sl.* punch in the mouth. **knuckle under** give in; submit.

---

knuckle Middle English *knokel* (originally denoting the rounded shape when a joint such as the elbow or knee is bent), from Middle Low German, Middle Dutch *knökel*, diminutive of *knoke* 'bone.' In the mid-18th century the verb *knuckle* (*down*) expressed setting the knuckles down to shoot in a game of marbles, hence the notion of applying oneself with concentration.

---

knuck·le·ball /núkəlbawl/ *n.* *Baseball* pitch delivered with the ball held by the knuckles or fingernails such that the ball has minimal spin and moves erratically.

knuck·le·head /núkəlhed/ *n.* *colloq.* slow-witted or stupid person.

knurl /nərl/ *n.* small projecting knob, ridge, etc. □□ **knurl′ed** /nərld/ *adj.*

KO *abbr.* knockout.

ko·a·la /kō-áʼalə/ *n.* Australian bearlike marsupial with thick, gray fur.

kohl·ra·bi /kṓlráʼabee/ *n.* (*pl.* **-bies**) cabbage with an edible turniplike swollen stem.

kook /kook/ *n.* *sl.* crazy or eccentric person. □□ **kook′i·ness** *n.* **kook′y** *adj.* (**kook·i·er**, **kook·i·est**).

kook·a·bur·ra /kookəbə́rə, -búrə/ *n.* Australian kingfisher with a strange laughing cry.

ko·peck /kṓpek, kó-/ *n.* (also **ko′pek**, **co′peck**) Russian coin worth one-hundredth of a ruble.

Ko·ran /kərán, -ráʼan, kaw-/ *n.* the Islamic sacred book. □□ **Ko·ran′ic** *adj.*

Ko·re·an /kəreʼeən, kaw-/ ● *n.* **1** native or national of N. or S. Korea in SE Asia. **2** language of Korea. ● *adj.* of or relating to Korea or its people or language.

ko·sher /kṓshər/ *adj.* **1** (of food, etc.) fulfilling the requirements of Jewish law. **2** *colloq.* correct; genuine; legitimate.

kow·tow /kowtów/ ● *n.* *hist.* Chinese custom of kneeling and touching the ground with the forehead in worship or submission. ● *v.intr.* (usu. foll. by *to*) act obsequiously.

KP *n.* *Mil. colloq.* kitchen police (kitchen duty).

k.p.h. *abbr.* kilometers per hour.

Kr *symb. Chem.* krypton.

kraal /kraal/ *n.* *S.Afr.* **1** village of huts enclosed by a fence. **2** enclosure for cattle or sheep.

krem·lin /krémlin/ *n.* **1** citadel within a Russian city or town. **2** (**the Kremlin**) **a** citadel in Moscow. **b** Russian or former USSR government housed within it.

krill /kril/ *n.* tiny planktonic crustaceans.

kro·na /krṓnə/ *n.* **1** (*pl.* **kro·nor** /krṓnər, -nawr/) chief monetary unit of Sweden. **2** (*pl.* **kro·nur** /krṓnər/) chief monetary unit of Iceland.

kro·ne /krṓnə/ *n.* (*pl.* **kro·ner** /krṓnər/) chief monetary unit of Denmark and of Norway.

Kru·ger·rand /krṓøgərand, -raant/ *n.* (also **kru′ger·rand**) S. African gold coin.

kryp·ton /krípton/ *n.* *Chem.* inert gaseous element used in fluorescent lamps, etc. ¶ Symb.: **Kr.**

KS *abbr.* Kansas (in official postal use).

kt. *abbr.* **1** karat(s). **2** kiloton(s). **3** knots.

ku·dos /kṓdōz, -dōs, -dos, kyṓø-/ *n.* *colloq.* glory; renown.

¶ **Kudos** from Greek, is a singular noun meaning 'praise, honor.' However, because of its *-s* ending, it has come to be used as a plural noun meaning 'compliments, congratulations.' As a result the (etymologically incorrect) singular form *kudo*, also meaning 'praise, honor,' has come into existence.

Ku Klux Klan /kōō kluks klán, kyōō-/ *n.* secret white supremacist society of the US.

kum·quat /kúmkwot/ *n.* (also **cum′quat**) **1** small orangelike fruit. **2** shrub or small tree yielding this.

kung fu /kung fōō, kōōng/ *n.* Chinese martial art similar to karate.

Kurd /kərd/ *n.* Islamic people of Kurdistan (con-tiguous areas of Iraq, Iran, and Turkey). □□ **Kurd′ish** *adj. & n.*

kvetch /kvech/ *sl.* • *n.* objectionable person, esp. a complainer. • *v.* complain; whine. □□ **kvetch′er** *n.*

kW *abbr.* kilowatt(s).

kWh *abbr.* kilowatt-hour(s).

KY *abbr.* Kentucky (in official postal use).

Ky. *abbr.* Kentucky.

Ll

L¹ /el/ *n.* (also **l**) (*pl.* **Ls** or **L's; l's**) **1** twelfth letter of the alphabet. **2** (as a Roman numeral) 50. **3** thing shaped like an L, as a joint connecting two pipes at right angles.

L² *abbr.* (also **L.**) **1** Lake. **2** Latin. **3** large.

l *abbr.* (also **l.**) **1** left. **2** line. **3** liter(s). **4** length.

LA *abbr.* **1** Los Angeles. **2** Louisiana (in official postal use).

La *symb. Chem.* lanthanum.

La. *abbr.* Louisiana.

la /laa/ *n. Mus.* sixth note of a major scale.

lab /lab/ *n. colloq.* laboratory.

la·bel /láybəl/ • *n.* **1** usu. small piece of paper, etc., attached to an object to give information about it. **2** short classifying phrase applied to a person, a work of art, etc. • *v.tr.* (**la·beled, la·bel·ing; la·belled, la·bel·ling**) **1** attach a label to. **2** assign to a category (*labeled them as irresponsible*). □□ **la'bel·er** *n.*

la·bi·al /láybeeəl/ • *adj.* **1 a** of the lips. **b** *Zool.* of, like, or serving as a lip. **2** *Phonet.* requiring partial or complete closure of the lips. • *n.* *Phonet.* labial sound.

la·bi·um /láybeeəm/ *n.* (*pl.* **la·bi·a** /-beeə/) *Anat.* each fold of skin enclosing the vulva.

la·bor /láybər/ • *n.* **1** physical or mental work; exertion. **2** workers, esp. manual, considered as a class or political force. **3** process of childbirth. **4** particular task. • *v.* **1** *intr.* work hard; exert oneself. **2** *intr.* strive for a purpose. **3** *tr.* **a** elaborate needlessly (*I will not labor the point*). **b** (as **labored** *adj.*) done with great effort; not spontaneous. **4** *intr.* (often foll. by *under*) suffer (a disadvantage or delusion) (*labored under universal disapproval*). **5** *intr.* proceed with trouble or difficulty. □ **labor camp** prison camp enforcing hard labor. **Labor Day** first Monday in September (or in some countries May 1), celebrated in honor of working people. **labor-intensive** needing a large workforce. **labor of love** task done for pleasure, not reward. **labor union** association of workers formed to protect and further their rights and interests. **lost labor** fruitless effort.

lab·o·ra·to·ry /lábrətáwree/ *n.* (*pl.* **-ries**) room or building for scientific experiments, research, etc.

la·bor·er /láybərər/ *n.* **1** person doing unskilled, usu. manual, work for wages. **2** person who labors.

la·bo·ri·ous /ləbáwreeəs/ *adj.* **1** needing hard work or toil. **2** (esp. of literary style) showing signs of toil; not fluent. □□ **la·bo'ri·ous·ly** *adv.*

Lab·ra·dor /lábrədawr/ *n.* (in full **Lab'ra·dor re·triev'er**) sporting breed of dog with a black, brown, or golden coat.

lab·y·rinth /lábərinth/ *n.* **1** complicated network of passages, etc. **2** intricate or tangled arrangement. □□ **lab·y·rin·thi·an** /-ríntheeən/ *adj.* **lab·y·rin·thine** /-rínthin, -thīn/ *adj.*

lac /lak/ *n.* resinous secretion of the SE Asian lac insect, used in varnish and shellac.

lace /lays/ • *n.* **1** fine open fabric, made by weaving thread in patterns. **2** cord, etc., passed through eyelets or hooks for fastening shoes, etc. • *v.* **1** *tr.* fasten or tighten with a lace or laces. **2** *tr.* flavor (a drink) with liquor. **3** *tr.* & (foll. by *into*) *intr. colloq.* lash; beat; defeat. **4** *tr.* pass (a shoelace, etc.) through. **5** *tr.* trim with lace.

lac·er·ate /lásərayt/ *v.tr.* mangle or tear (esp. flesh or tissue). □□ **lac·er·a·tion** /-áyshən/ *n.*

lach·ry·mal /lákriməl/ *adj.* (also **lac'ri·mal**) of or for tears.

lach·ry·mose /lákrimōs/ *adj.* *formal* given to weeping; tearful. □□ **lach'ry·mose·ly** *adv.*

lack /lak/ • *n.* (usu. foll. by *of*) want; deficiency (*lack of talent*). • *v.tr.* be without or deficient in (*lacks courage*). □ **for lack of** owing to the absence of (*went hungry for lack of money*). □□ **lack'ing** *adj.*

lack·a·dai·si·cal /lákədáyzikəl/ *adj.* **1** unenthusiastic; listless; idle. **2** feebly sentimental. □□ **lack·a·dai'si·cal·ly** *adv.*

lack·ey /lákee/ *n.* (*pl.* **-eys**) **1** servile follower; toady. **2** footman; manservant.

lack·lus·ter /láklustər/ *adj.* **1** lacking in vitality, etc. **2** dull.

la·con·ic /ləkónik/ *adj.* terse; using few words; concise. □□ **la·con'i·cal·ly** *adv.*

lac·quer /lákər/ • *n.* varnish made of shellac or synthetic substances. • *v.tr.* coat with lacquer.

lac·ri·mal var. of LACHRYMAL.

la·crosse /ləkráws, -krós/ *n.* game like field hockey, but with a ball passed using sticks having a netted pocket.

lac·tate /láktayt/ *v.intr.* (of mammals) secrete milk.

lac·ta·tion /laktáyshən/ *n.* **1** secretion of milk. **2** suckling of young.

lac·te·al /lákteeəl/ *adj.* of milk; milky.

lac·tic /láktik/ *adj. Chem.* of or from milk. □ **lac·tic acid** clear carboxylic acid formed in sour milk or produced in muscle tissues during strenuous exercise.

lac·tose /láktōs/ *n. Chem.* sugar that occurs in milk.

la·cu·na /ləkyo͞onə/ *n.* (*pl.* **la·cu·nae** /-nee/ or **la·cu·nas**) **1** hiatus; gap. **2** missing portion, esp. in a book, etc.

lac·y /láysee/ *adj.* (**lac·i·er, lac·i·est**) of or resembling lace fabric. □□ **lac'i·ly** *adv.* **lac'i·ness** *n.*

lad /lad/ *n.* boy; youth.

lad·der /ládər/ *n.* **1** set of horizontal bars fixed between two uprights and used for climbing up or down. **2** hierarchical structure, esp. as a means of advancement, promotion, etc.

lade /layd/ *v.* (*past part.* **lad·en** /láyd'n/) **1** *tr.* a load (a ship). **b** ship (goods). **2** *intr.* (of a ship) take on cargo. **3** *tr.* (as **laden** *adj.*) loaded; burdened.

la-di-da /laádeedaá/ *adj. colloq.* (also **la'-de-da'**) pretentious or snobbish, esp. in manner or speech.

la·dle /láyd'l/ • *n.* long-handled spoon with a cup-shaped bowl for serving liquids. • *v.tr.* transfer (liquid) with a ladle. □ **ladle out** distribute, esp. lavishly. □□ **la'dle·ful** *n.* (*pl.* **-fuls**). **la'dler** *n.*

la·dy /láydee/ *n.* (*pl.* **-dies**) **1 a** woman regarded as being of superior social status or as having refined manners. **b** (**Lady**) title for certain women of noble rank. **2** woman; female. **3** *colloq.* wife; girlfriend. □ **ladies'** (or **lady's**) **man** man fond of female company; seducer. **ladies' room** women's restroom. **lady-in-waiting** lady attending a queen or princess. **lady-killer** man very attractive to women. **lady of the evening** prostitute. **lady's** (or **lady**) **slipper** orchid with a usu. yellow or pink slipper-shaped lip on its flowers. **old lady** *colloq.* **1** mother. **2** wife; girlfriend. **Our Lady** the Virgin Mary.

---

lady Old English *hlǣfdīge* (denoting a woman to whom homage or obedience is due, such as the wife of a lord or the mistress of a household, also specifically the Virgin Mary), from *hlāf* 'loaf' + a Germanic base meaning 'knead,' related to *dough.*

---

la·dy·bug /láydeebug/ *n.* small beetle, usu. red-orange, with black spots.

la·dy·fin·ger /láydeefinggər/ *n.* finger-shaped sponge cake.

la·dy·like /láydeelīk/ *adj.* like or befitting a lady.

la·dy·ship /láydeeship/ *n.* respectful form of reference or address to a titled lady.

lag /lag/ • *v.intr.* (**lagged, lag·ging**) fall behind; not keep pace. • *n.* delay. □□ **lag'ger** *n.*

la·ger /láʼagər/ *n.* dry, light-colored, mild-flavored beer.

lag·gard /lágərd/ • *n.* dawdler; person who lags behind. • *adj.* dawdling; moving slowly. □□ **lag'gard·ly** *adj. & adv.*

lag·ging /láging/ *n.* material providing heat insulation for a boiler, pipes, etc.

la·goon /ləgốon/ *n.* **1** stretch of salt water separated from the sea by a sandbank, reef, etc. **2** shallow lake near a larger lake or river. **3** artificial pool for sewage, etc.

laid *past* and *past part.* of LAY[1].

lain *past part.* of LIE[1].

lair /lair/ *n.* **1** wild animal's resting place. **2** person's hiding place.

lais·sez-faire /lésayfáir/ *n.* (also **lais·ser-faire**) policy of non-interference, esp. by a government.

la·i·ty /láy-itee/ *n.* lay people, as distinct from the clergy.

lake /layk/ *n.* large body of water surrounded by land. □ **the Great Lakes** the Lakes Superior, Huron, Michigan, Erie, and Ontario, along the US-Canada border.

lal·ly·gag var. of LOLLYGAG.

lam /lam/ *n.* □ **on the lam** *sl.* in flight, esp. from the police.

la·ma /láʼamə/ *n.* Tibetan or Mongolian Buddhist monk.

la·ma·ser·y /láʼaməseree/ *n.* (*pl.* **-ies**) monastery of lamas.

La·maze meth·od /ləmáaz/ *n. Med.* method for childbirth in which breathing exercises and relaxation techniques are used to control pain and facilitate delivery.

lamb /lam/ *n.* **1** young sheep. **2** its flesh as food. **3** mild or gentle person. □ **The Lamb of God** a name for Christ.

lam·ba·da /ləmbáʼadə/ *n.* fast erotic Brazilian dance.

lam·baste /lambáyst/ *v.tr.* (also **lam·bast** /-bást/) *colloq.* **1** thrash; beat. **2** criticize severely.

lamb·da /lámdə/ *n.* **1** eleventh letter of the Greek alphabet (Λ, λ). **2** (as λ) symbol for wavelength.

lam·bent /lámbənt/ *adj.* **1** (of a flame or a light) playing on a surface with a soft radiance but without burning. **2** (of the eyes, sky, etc.) softly radiant. **3** (of wit, etc.) lightly brilliant. □□ **lam'ben·cy** *n.* **lam'bent·ly** *adv.*

lame /laym/ • *adj.* **1** disabled, esp. in the foot or leg; limping. **2 a** (of an excuse, etc.) unconvincing; weak. **b** (of verse, etc.) halting. • *v.tr.* make lame; disable. □ **lame duck** official in the final period of office, after the election of a successor. □□ **lame'ly** *adv.* **lame'ness** *n.*

la·mé /lamáy/ *n.* fabric with gold or silver threads interwoven.

lame·brain /láymbrayn/ *n. colloq.* stupid person. □□ **lame'brain** or **lame'brained** *adj.*

la·ment /ləmént/ • *n.* **1** passionate expression of grief. **2** song or poem of mourning or sorrow. • *v.tr.* (also *absol.*) express or feel grief for or about; regret. □□ **la·men·ta'tion** *n.*

la·men·ta·ble /ləméntəbəl, lámənt-/ *adj.* (of an event, condition, etc.) deplorable; regrettable. □□ **la·men'ta·bly** *adv.*

lam·i·nate • *v.tr.* /láminayt/ **1** overlay with metal plates, a plastic layer, etc. **2** manufacture by placing layer on layer. • *n.* /láminət/ laminated structure, esp. of layers fixed together. • *adj.* /láminət/ in the form of stratified plates or scales. □□ **lam·i·na'tion** /-náyshən/ *n.* **lam'i·na·tor** *n.*

lamp /lamp/ *n.* **1** device for producing a steady light, esp.: **a** electric bulb, and usu. its holder. **b** oil or gas lamp. **2** device producing esp. ultraviolet or infrared radiation.

lamp·black /lámpblak/ *n.* pigment made from soot.

lam·poon /lampốon/ • *n.* satirical attack on a person, etc. • *v.tr.* satirize. □□ **lam·poon'er** *n.* **lam·poon'ist** *n.*

lamp·post /lámp-pōst/ *n.* tall post supporting an outdoor light.

lam·prey /lámpree, -pray/ *n.* (*pl.* **-preys**) eellike fish with a sucker mouth, horny teeth, and a rough tongue.

lamp·shade /lámpshayd/ *n.* translucent cover for a lamp.

LAN /lan/ *abbr.* local area network.

lance /lans/ • *n.* **1** long spear, esp. one used by a horseman. **2** = LANCET. • *v.tr.* **1** prick or cut open with a lancet. **2** pierce with a lance.

lanc·er /lánsər/ *n. hist.* soldier armed with a lance.

lan·cet /lánsit/ *n.* small, two-edged surgical knife with a sharp point.

land /land/ • *n.* **1** solid part of the earth's surface. **2** expanse of country; ground; soil. **3** country; nation; state. **4** estate. • *v.* **1 a** *tr. & intr.* set or go ashore. **b** *intr.* disembark (*landed at the har-*

bor). **2** *tr.* bring (an aircraft, etc.) to the ground or another surface. **3** *intr.* alight on the ground, etc. **4** *tr.* bring (a fish) to land. **5** *tr.* & *intr.* (also *refl.*) *colloq.* bring to, reach, or find oneself in a certain situation, place, or state (*landed in jail*). **6** *tr. colloq.* win or obtain (a prize, job, etc.). □ **land bridge** neck of land joining two large landmasses. **land mine** explosive mine laid in or on the ground.

land·ed /lándid/ *adj.* **1** owning land (*landed gentry*). **2** consisting of, including, or relating to land (*landed property*).

land·fall /lándfawl/ *n.* approach to land, esp. for the first time on a sea or air journey.

land·fill /lándfil/ *n.* **1** waste material, etc., used to landscape or reclaim land. **2** place where garbage is buried.

land·form /lándfawrm/ *n.* natural feature of the earth's surface.

land·ing /lánding/ *n.* **1 a** coming to land. **b** place where ships, etc., land. **2** platform between two flights of stairs, or at the top or bottom of a flight. □ **landing craft** craft designed for putting troops and equipment ashore. **landing gear** undercarriage of an aircraft. **landing strip** airstrip.

land·la·dy /lándlaydee/ *n.* (*pl.* **-dies**) **1** woman who rents land or premises to a tenant. **2** woman who keeps a boardinghouse, an inn, etc.

land·locked /lándlokt/ *adj.* almost or entirely enclosed by land.

land·lord /lándlawrd/ *n.* **1** man who rents land or premises to a tenant. **2** man who keeps a boardinghouse, an inn, etc.

land·lub·ber /lándlubər/ *n.* person unfamiliar with the sea.

land·mark /lándmaark/ *n.* **1 a** conspicuous object in a district, etc. **b** object marking a boundary, etc. **2** prominent and critical event, etc. **3** *attrib.* signifying an important development, etc.

land·mass /lándmas/ *n.* large area of land.

land·own·er /lándōnər/ *n.* owner of land. □□ **land·own·ing** *adj.* & *n.*

land·scape /lándskayp/ • *n.* **1** scenery, as seen in a broad view from one place. **2** picture representing this; this genre of painting. • *v.tr.* (also *absol.*) improve (a piece of land) by planned plantings, etc.

land·slide /lándslīd/ *n.* **1** sliding down of a mass of land from a mountain, cliff, etc. **2** overwhelming victory in an election.

lane /layn/ *n.* **1** narrow road or path. **2** division of a road for a stream of traffic. **3** path regularly followed by a ship, aircraft, etc.

lan·gous·tine /lóngōōstéen, lánggə-/ *n.* any of several varieties of small lobsters, used as food.

lan·guage /lánggwij/ *n.* **1** use of words as a method of human communication. **2** language of a particular community or country, etc. **3 a** faculty of speech. **b** style of expression. **4** system of symbols and rules for writing computer programs. **5** any method of expression (*sign language*). **6** professional or specialized vocabulary. □ **speak the same language** have a similar outlook, manner of expression, etc.

lan·guid /lánggwid/ *adj.* **1** lacking vigor; idle; inert. **2** (of trade, etc.) slow-moving; sluggish. **3** faint; weak. □□ **lan·guid·ly** *adv.* **lan·guid·ness** *n.*

lan·guish /lánggwish/ *v.intr.* **1** lose or lack vi-

tality. **2** droop or pine for. **3** suffer under (esp. depression, confinement, etc.).

lan·guor /lánggər/ *n.* **1** lack of energy; idleness. **2** soft or tender mood or effect. □□ **lan'guor·ous** *adj.* **lan'guor·ous·ly** *adv.*

lan·gur /lunggóor/ *n.* long-tailed Asian monkey.

lank /langk/ *adj.* **1** (of hair, grass, etc.) long, limp, and straight. **2** thin and tall.

lank·y /lángkee/ *adj.* (**lank·i·er**, **lank·i·est**) (of limbs, a person, etc.) ungracefully thin and long or tall. □□ **lank'i·ly** *adv.* **lank'i·ness** *n.*

lan·o·lin /lánəlin/ *n.* fat from sheep's wool used for cosmetics, etc.

lan·tern /lántərn/ *n.* **1** lamp with a transparent case protecting a flame, etc. **2** raised structure on a dome, room, etc., glazed to admit light. □ **lantern fish** marine fish with small light organs on the head and body. **lantern jaws** long thin jaws and chin.

lan·tha·nide /lánthənīd/ *n. Chem.* element of the lanthanide series. □ **lanthanide series** series of 15 metallic elements (from lanthanum to lutetium) having similar chemical properties.

lan·tha·num /lánthənəm/ *n. Chem.* metallic element of the lanthanide series. ¶ Symb.: **La**.

lan·yard /lányərd/ *n.* **1** cord worn around the neck or shoulder to which a knife, etc., may be attached. **2** *Naut.* short line for securing, tightening, etc.

La·o·tian /layóshən, lóushən/ • *n.* **1 a** native or national of Laos in SE Asia. **b** person of Laotian descent. **2** language of Laos. • *adj.* of or relating to Laos or its people or language.

lap¹ /lap/ *n.* front of the body from the waist to the knees of a sitting person. □ **in** (or **on**) **a person's lap** as a person's responsibility. **in the lap of luxury** in extremely luxurious surroundings. **lap robe** blanket, etc., used for warmth, esp. on a journey. □□ **lap'ful** *n.* (*pl.* **-fuls**).

lap² /lap/ • *n.* **1 a** one circuit of a racetrack, etc. **b** section of a journey, etc. **2 a** amount of overlapping. **b** overlapping part. • *v.tr.* (**lapped**, **lap·ping**) **1** lead or overtake (a competitor in a race) by one or more laps. **2** coil, fold, or wrap (a garment, etc.) around. **3** enfold or wrap (a person) in clothing, etc. **4** cause to overlap. □ **lap joint** joining of rails, shafts, etc., by halving the thickness of each at the joint and fitting them together. **lap-weld** *v.tr.* weld with overlapping edges. • *n.* such a weld.

lap³ /lap/ • *v.* (**lapped**, **lap·ping**) **1** *tr.* **a** (also *absol.*) (usu. of an animal) drink (liquid) with the tongue. **b** consume (gossip, praise, etc.) greedily. **2 a** *tr.* (of water) move or beat upon (a shore) with a rippling sound. **b** *intr.* (of waves, etc.) move in ripples; make a lapping sound. • *n.* **1 a** act of lapping. **b** amount of liquid taken up. **2** sound of wavelets.

lap Old English *læppa*, of Germanic origin; related to Dutch *lap*, German *Lappen* 'piece of cloth.' The word originally denoted a fold or flap of a garment (related to *lapel*), later specifically one that could be used as a pocket or pouch, or the front of a skirt when held up to catch or carry something (Middle English), hence the area between the waist and knees as a place where a child could be nursed or an object held.

lap·dog /lápdawg/ n. small pet dog.

la·pel /ləpél/ n. part of a coat, jacket, etc., folded back against the front around the neck opening. □□ **la·pelled'** or **la·peled'** adj.

lap·i·dar·y /lápideree/ • adj. 1 concerned with stone(s). 2 engraved upon stone. • n. (pl. **-ies**) cutter, polisher, or engraver of gems.

lap·is laz·u·li /lápis lázŏŏlee, lázyə-, lázhə-/ n. bright blue semiprecious stone.

Lapp /lap/ • n. 1 member of a Mongol people of N. Scandinavia. 2 language of this people. • adj. of or relating to the Lapps or their language.

lapse /laps/ • n. 1 slight error. 2 weak decline into an inferior state. 3 (foll. by of) passage of time (after a lapse of three years). • v.intr. 1 fail to maintain a position or standard. 2 (foll. by into) fall back into (an inferior or previous state). 3 (of a right or privilege, etc.) become invalid due to disuse, failure to renew, etc.

lap·top /láptop/ n. (often attrib.) portable computer suitable for use while resting on the user's legs.

lap·wing /lápwing/ n. plover with black and white plumage, crested head, and a shrill cry.

lar·board /laárbərd/ n. & adj. Naut. archaic = PORT³.

lar·ce·ny /laársənee/ n. (pl. **-nies**) theft of personal property. □ **grand larceny** Law larceny in which the value of the stolen property exceeds a certain legally established limit. □□ **lar'ce·nist** n. **lar'ce·nous** adj.

larch /laarch/ n. 1 deciduous coniferous tree with bright foliage and tough wood. 2 (in full **larch' wood**) its wood.

lard /laard/ • n. pig fat used in cooking, etc. • v.tr. 1 insert strips of fat or bacon in (meat, etc.) before cooking. 2 (foll. by with) embellish (talk or writing) with foreign or technical terms.

lar·der /laárdər/ n. 1 room or cupboard for storing food. 2 supply of food, esp. for winter.

large /laarj/ • adj. 1 of relatively great size or extent. 2 of the larger kind (large intestine). 3 of wide range; comprehensive. 4 pursuing an activity on a large scale (large farmer). • n. (**at large**) 1 at liberty. 2 as a body or whole (popular with the people at large). 3 without a specific target (scatters insults at large). 4 representing a whole area and not merely a part of it (councilwoman at large). □□ **large'ness** n. **larg'ish** adj.

large·ly /laárjlee/ adv. to a great extent.

lar·gesse /laarzhés/ n. (also **lar·gess'**) 1 money or gifts freely given. 2 generosity; beneficence.

lar·go /laárgō/ Mus. • adv. & adj. in a slow tempo and dignified in style. • n. (pl. **-gos**) largo passage or movement.

lar·i·at /láreeət/ n. 1 lasso. 2 tethering rope.

lark¹ /laark/ n. small bird with tuneful song, esp. the skylark.

lark² /laark/ colloq. • n. frolic; amusing incident. • v.intr. (foll. by about) play tricks; frolic.

lark·spur /laárkspur/ n. plant with a spur-shaped calyx.

lar·va /laárvə/ n. (pl. **lar·vae** /-vee/) stage of development of an insect between egg and pupa. □□ **lar'val** adj.

lar·yn·gi·tis /lárinjítis/ n. inflammation of the larynx.

lar·ynx /láringks/ n. (pl. **la·ryn·ges** /lərínjeez/ or **lar·ynx·es**) hollow organ in the throat holding the vocal cords.

la·sa·gna /ləzaányə/ n. (also **la·sa'gne**) pasta in wide strips, esp. as cooked and served with cheese, tomato sauce, etc.

las·civ·i·ous /ləsíveeəs/ adj. 1 lustful. 2 inciting to or evoking lust. □□ **las·civ'i·ous·ly** adv. **las·civ'i·ous·ness** n.

lase /layz/ v.intr. function as or in a laser.

la·ser /láyzər/ n. device that generates an intense beam of coherent light (acronym of light amplification by stimulated emission of radiation).

lash /lash/ • v. 1 intr. make a sudden whiplike movement. 2 tr. beat with a whip, etc. 3 tr. castigate in words. 4 tr. fasten with a cord, etc. 5 tr. (of rain, etc.) beat forcefully upon. • n. 1 sharp blow by a whip, etc. 2 flexible end of a whip. 3 eyelash. □ **lash out** speak or hit out angrily.

lass /las/ n. girl or young woman.

Las·sa fe·ver /lásə/ n. acute febrile viral disease of tropical Africa.

las·sie /lásee/ n. colloq. = LASS.

las·si·tude /lásitŏŏd, -tyŏŏd/ n. 1 languor; weariness. 2 disinclination to exert or interest oneself.

las·so /lásō, lasŏ'/ • n. (pl. **-sos** or **-soes**) rope with a noose at one end, esp. for catching cattle, etc. • v.tr. (**-soes, -soed**) catch with a lasso. □□ **las'so·er** n.

last¹ /last/ • adj. 1 after all others; coming at or belonging to the end. 2 a most recent. b preceding (got on at the last station). 3 only remaining (our last chance). 4 (prec. by the) least likely. 5 lowest in rank (last place). • adv. 1 after all others. 2 on the most recent occasion. 3 lastly. • n. 1 person or thing that is last. 2 last mention or sight, etc. (shall never hear the last of it). 3 (prec. by the) a end or last moment. b death. □ **at last** (or **long last**) in the end; after much delay. **last-ditch** (of an attempt, etc.) final; desperate. **last name** surname. **last rites** rites for a person about to die. **last straw** slight addition to a burden that makes it finally unbearable. **last word 1** final or definitive statement (always has the last word). **2** latest fashion.

¶ In precise usage, **latest** means 'most recent' and **last** means 'final.' But **last** is commonly used in either case: I read his last novel. The last time she called, she told me about her new job. **Latest** should be used when it is important to distinguish between 'most recent' and 'final': The last day of the school year will be June 18. My latest project is wallpapering my dining room. See also note at FORMER.

last² /last/ v.intr. 1 remain unexhausted or alive for a time. 2 continue for a time.

last³ /last/ n. model for shaping a shoe or boot. □ **stick to one's last** not meddle with what one does not understand.

last·ing /lásting/ adj. 1 continuing; permanent. 2 durable. □□ **last'ing·ly** adv.

last·ly /lástlee/ adv. finally; in the last place.

LATITUDE, 1a

lat. *abbr.* latitude.

latch /lach/ • *n.* **1** fastening for a gate, etc. **2** lock needing a key to be opened from the outside. • *v.* fasten or be fastened with a latch. □ **latch on** (often foll. by *to*) *colloq.* **1** attach oneself (to). **2** understand.

latch·key /láchkee/ *n.* (*pl.* **-keys**) key of an outer door.

late /layt/ • *adj.* **1** after the due, usual, or proper time (*late for dinner*). **2 a** far on in a specified period. **b** far on in development. **3** no longer alive or functioning. **4** of recent date. **5** (as **lat·est**, *prec.* by *the*) fashionable, up to date. • *adv.* **1** after the due or usual time. **2** far on in time. **3** at or till a late hour. □□ **late'ness** *n.*
¶ See note on **latest** at LAST[1].

late·com·er /láytkumər/ *n.* person who arrives late.

la·teen /lətéen/ *adj.* (of a ship) rigged with a triangular sail on a long yard at an angle 45° to the mast.

late·ly /láytlee/ *adv.* not long ago; recently; in recent times.

la·tent /láyt'nt/ *adj.* **1** concealed; dormant. **2** undeveloped. □□ **la'ten·cy** *n.* **la'tent·ly** *adv.*

lat·er·al /látərəl/ *adj.* of, at, toward, or from the side or sides. □ **lateral thinking** solving problems by apparently illogical methods. □□ **lat'er·al·ly** *adv.*

la·tex /láyteks/ *n.* (*pl.* **lat·i·ces** /-tiseez/ or **la·tex·es**) **1** milky fluid of esp. the rubber tree. **2** synthetic product resembling this.

lath /lath/ • *n.* (*pl.* **laths** /laths, laᵗhz/) thin flat strip of wood. • *v.tr.* attach laths to (a wall or ceiling).

lathe /layᵗh/ *n.* machine for shaping wood, metal, etc., by rotating it against a cutting tool.

lath·er /láᵗhər/ • *n.* **1** froth produced by agitating soap, etc., and water. **2** frothy sweat, esp. of a horse. **3** state of agitation. • *v.* **1** *intr.* form a lather. **2** *tr.* cover with lather. **3** *tr. colloq.* thrash. □□ **lath'er·y** *adj.*

Lat·in /lát'n/ • *n.* **1** language of ancient Rome and its empire. **2** person who speaks a language derived from Latin. • *adj.* **1** of or in Latin. **2** of the countries or peoples using languages developed from Latin. □ **Latin America** the parts of Central and S. America where Spanish or Portuguese is the main language. **Latin American** *n.* native of Latin America. • *adj.* of or relating to Latin America.

La·ti·no /lətéenō/ *n.* (*pl.* **La·ti·nos**; *fem.* **La·ti·na** /-nə/, *pl.* **La·ti·nas**) **1** native or inhabitant of

Latin America. **2** person of Spanish-speaking or Latin American descent.

lat·ish /láytish/ *adj. & adv.* fairly late.

lat·i·tude /látitōod, -tyōod/ *n.* **1** *Geog.* **a** angular distance on a meridian north or south of the equator. **b** (usu. in *pl.*) regions or climes. **2** freedom of action or opinion (*was allowed much latitude*). □□ **lat·i·tu·di·nal** /-tóod'nəl, -tyōod-/ *adj.* **lat·i·tu'di·nal·ly** *adv.*

la·trine /lətréen/ *n.* communal toilet, esp. in a camp.

lat·ter /látər/ *adj.* **1** second-mentioned of two. **2** nearer to the end (*latter part of the year*). **3** recent. □ **latter-day** modern; newfangled. **Latter-day Saints** the Mormons.
¶ This word means 'the second-mentioned of two.' Its use to mean 'the last-mentioned of three or more' is common, but considered incorrect by some since *latter* means 'later' rather than 'latest.' *Last* or *last-mentioned* is preferred where three or more things are involved. See note at FORMER.

lat·tice /látis/ *n.* **1** structure of crossed laths with spaces between, used as a screen, fence, etc. **2** = LATTICEWORK. □□ **lat'ticed** *adj.* **lat'tic·ing** *n.*

lat·tice·work /látiswərk/ *n.* laths arranged in lattice formation.

Lat·vi·an /látveeən/ • *n.* **1 a** native of Latvia, a Baltic republic. **b** person of Latvian descent. **2** language of Latvia. • *adj.* of or relating to Latvia or its people or language.

laud /lawd/ *v.tr.* praise or extol.

laud·a·ble /láwdəbəl/ *adj.* commendable; praiseworthy. □□ **laud·a·bil'i·ty** *n.* **laud'a·bly** *adv.*

lau·da·num /láwd'nəm/ *n.* solution prepared from opium.

lau·da·to·ry /láwdətáwree/ *adj.* expressing praise.

laugh /laf/ • *v.* **1** *intr.* make sounds and movements in expressing amusement, scorn, etc. **2** *tr.* express by laughing. **3** *intr.* (foll. by *at*) ridicule; make fun of. • *n.* **1** sound, act, or manner of laughing. **2** *colloq.* comical person or thing. □ **have the last laugh** be ultimately the winner. **laugh off** get rid of (humiliation, etc.) with a jest. **laugh track** recorded laughter added to a comedy show. □□ **laugh'er** *n.*

laugh·a·ble /láfəbəl/ *adj.* ludicrous; amusing. □□ **laugh'a·bly** *adv.*

laugh·ing /láfing/ • *n.* laughter. • *adj.* in senses of LAUGH *v.* □ **laughing gas** nitrous oxide as an anesthetic. **no laughing matter** something serious. □□ **laugh'ing·ly** *adv.*

laugh·ing·stock /láfingstok/ *n.* person or thing ridiculed.

laugh·ter /láftər/ *n.* act or sound of laughing.

launch[1] /lawnch/ • *v.tr.* **1** set (a vessel) afloat. **2** hurl or send forth (a weapon, rocket, etc.). **3** start or set in motion (an enterprise, attack, etc.). **4** formally introduce (a new product). • *n.* act of launching. □ **launching pad 1** = LAUNCHPAD. **2** = SPRINGBOARD 2.

launch[2] /lawnch/ *n.* motorboat, used esp. for pleasure.

launch·pad /láwnchpad/ *n.* platform with a supporting structure, from which rockets are launched.

laun·der /láwndər, laán-/ *v.tr.* **1** wash and iron (clothes, etc.). **2** *colloq.* transfer (funds) to conceal their origin. □□ **laun′der·er** *n.*

Laun·dro·mat /láwndrəmat, laán-/ *n. propr.* establishment with coin-operated washing machines and dryers.

laun·dry /láwndree, laán-/ *n.* (*pl.* **-dries**) **1** place for washing clothes, etc. **2** clothes or linen for laundering or newly laundered. □ **laundry list** *colloq.* lengthy list of items.

lau·re·ate /láwreeət, lór-/ ● *adj.* wreathed with laurel as a mark of honor. ● *n.* person honored for outstanding creative or intellectual achievement (*Nobel laureate*). □□ **lau′re·ate·ship** *n.*

lau·rel /láwrəl, lór-/ *n.* **1** (in *sing.* or *pl.*) wreath of bay leaves as an emblem of victory or poetic merit. **2** (in *pl.*) honor or distinction. **3** evergreen plant with dark-green glossy leaves; bay. □ **rest on one's laurels** be complacent with one's success.

la·va /laávə, lávə/ *n.* matter flowing from a volcano that solidifies as it cools.

la·vage /ləvaázh, lávij/ *n. Med.* washing out of a body cavity with water, etc.

lav·a·to·ry /lávətawree/ *n.* (*pl.* **-ries**) room or compartment with a toilet and wash basin.

lave /layv/ *v.tr. literary* wash; bathe.

lav·en·der /lávindər/ *n.* **1 a** evergreen shrub with purple aromatic flowers. **b** its flowers and stalks dried and used to scent linen, etc. **2** pale purplish-blue color.

lav·ish /lávish/ ● *adj.* **1** abundant; profuse. **2** generous. **3** excessive. ● *v.tr.* (often foll. by *on*) bestow or spend (money, effort, praise, etc.) abundantly. □□ **lav′ish·ly** *adv.* **lav′ish·ness** *n.*

law /law/ *n.* **1 a** rule enacted or customary in a community and recognized as enjoining or prohibiting certain actions. **b** body of such rules. **2** respect for laws (*law and order*). **3** laws collectively as a social system or subject of study. **4** binding force or effect (*their word is law*). **5** (prec. by *the*) **a** the legal profession. **b** *colloq.* the police. **6** regularity in natural occurrences (*law of gravity*). □ **law-abiding** obedient to the laws. **lay down the law** be dogmatic or authoritarian. **take the law into one's own hands** redress a grievance by one's own means, esp. by force.

law·break·er /láwbraykər/ *n.* person who breaks the law. □□ **law′break·ing** *n. & adj.*

law·ful /láwfool/ *adj.* conforming with or recognized by law; not illegal. □□ **law′ful·ly** *adv.* **law′ful·ness** *n.*

law·giv·er /láwgivər/ *n.* person who establishes a set of laws.

law·less /láwlis/ *adj.* **1** having no laws or law enforcement. **2** disregarding laws. **3** unbridled; uncontrolled. □□ **law′less·ly** *adv.* **law′less·ness** *n.*

law·mak·er /láwmaykər/ *n.* legislator.

law·man /láwman/ *n.* (*pl.* **-men**) law-enforcement officer, esp. a sheriff or policeman.

lawn[1] /lawn/ *n.* piece of grass kept mown in a yard, garden, park, etc. □ **lawn tennis** usual form of tennis, played with a soft ball on outdoor grass or a hard court. **lawn mower** machine for cutting the grass on a lawn.

lawn[2] /lawn/ *n.* fine linen or cotton fabric.

law·ren·ci·um /lərénseeəm, law-/ *n. Chem.* artifically made transuranic radioactive metallic element. ¶ Symb.: **Lw.**

law·suit /láwsoot/ *n.* process or instance of making a claim in a court of law.

law·yer /láwyər, lóyər/ *n.* member of the legal profession. □□ **law′yer·ly** *adj.*

lax /laks/ *adj.* **1** lacking care, concern, etc. **2** loose; not compact. □□ **lax′i·ty** *n.* **lax′ly** *adv.* **lax′ness** *n.*

lax·a·tive /láksətiv/ ● *adj.* easing evacuation of the bowels. ● *n.* laxative medicine.

lay[1] /lay/ ● *v.* (*past* and *past part.* **laid** /layd/) **1** *tr.* place on a surface, esp. horizontally or in the proper or specified place. **2** *intr. dial.* or *erron.* lie. **3** *tr.* (often *absol.*) (of a hen bird) produce (an egg). **4** *tr.* attribute or impute (blame, etc.). **5** *tr.* prepare or make ready (a plan or a trap). **6** *tr.* prepare (a table) for a meal. **7** *tr.* put down as a wager; stake. **8** *tr. sl. offens.* have sexual intercourse with. ● *n.* way, position, or direction in which something lies. □ **laid-back** *colloq.* relaxed; unbothered. **laid up** confined to bed or the house. **lay aside 1** put to one side. **2** cease to consider. **3** save (money, etc.) for future needs. **lay bare** expose; reveal. **lay a charge** make an accusation. **lay claim to** claim as one's own. **lay down 1** put on the ground. **2** formulate (a rule or principle). **3** pay or wager (money). **4** store (wine) in a cellar. **5** set down on paper. **6** sacrifice (one's life). **lay one's hands on** locate. **lay hands on 1** seize or attack. **2** place one's hands on or over, esp. in confirmation, or spiritual healing. **lay hold of** seize or grasp. **lay in** provide oneself with a stock of. **lay into** *colloq.* punish or scold severely. **lay it on thick** (or **with a trowel**) *colloq.* flatter or exaggerate grossly. **lay off 1** discharge (workers) temporarily. **2** *colloq.* desist. **lay of the land** current state of affairs. **lay open 1** break the skin of. **2** (foll. by *to*) expose (to criticism, etc.). **lay out 1** spread out; expose to view. **2** prepare (a corpse) for burial. **3** *colloq.* knock unconscious. **4** prepare a layout. **5** expend (money). **lay to rest** bury in a grave. **lay up 1** store; save. **2** put (a ship, etc.) out of service.

¶ **Lay**, 'to put down on a surface,' is a transitive verb, and **lie**, 'to be horizontal,' is intransitive. Avoid the intransitive use of *lay*, as in "I'm going to lay on the grass at lunchtime." Similarly, avoid the transitive use of *lie*, as in "Lie it on the table." These two verbs are often confused, especially because the past of *lie* is *lay*: *We lay on the grass for an hour*. The past of *lay* is *laid*: *I laid down my tools and lay on the grass.*

lay[2] /lay/ *adj.* **1 a** nonclerical. **b** not ordained into the clergy. **2 a** not professionally qualified. **b** of or done by such persons.

lay[3] /lay/ *n.* **1** short poem meant to be sung. **2** song.

lay[4] *past of* LIE[1].

lay·a·bout /láyəbowt/ *n.* habitual loafer or idler.

lay·er /láyər/ ● *n.* **1** thickness of matter, esp. one of several, covering a surface. **2** person or thing that lays. **3** hen that lays eggs. ● *v.tr.* arrange in layers. □□ **lay′ered** *adj.*

lay·ette /layét/ *n.* set of clothing, etc., for a newborn child.

lay·man /láymən/ *n.* (*pl.* **-men**; *fem.* **lay·wom·an**, *pl.* **-wom·en**) **1** nonordained member of a church. **2** person without professional knowledge.

lay·off /láyawf/ *n.* **1** temporary discharge of workers. **2** period when this is in force.

lay·out /láyowt/ *n.* **1** way in which plans, printed matter, etc., are arranged or set out. **2** something arranged or set out in a particular way.

lay·o·ver /láyōvər/ *n.* period of rest before a further stage in a journey, etc.; stopover.

laze /layz/ *v.intr.* spend time lazily or idly.

la·zy /láyzee/ *adj.* (**la·zi·er**, **la·zi·est**) **1** disinclined to work; doing little work. **2** of or inducing idleness. **3** sluggish; slow-moving. □□ **la′zi·ly** *adv.* **la′zi·ness** *n.*

la·zy·bones /láyzeebōnz/ *n.* (*pl.* same) *colloq.* lazy person.

lb. *abbr.* pound (weight).

LC *abbr.* (also **L.C.** or **l.c.**) **1** landing craft. **2** (**LC** or **L.C.**) Library of Congress. **3** lowercase.

LCD *abbr.* **1** liquid crystal display. **2** lowest (or least) common denominator.

LCM *abbr.* lowest (or least) common multiple.

lea /lee, láy/ *n. poet.* (also **ley**) meadow; pasture land.

leach /leech/ *v.* **1** *tr.* make (a liquid) percolate through some material. **2** *tr.* (foll. by *away*, *out*) remove (soluble matter) or be removed in this way. □□ **leach′er** *n.*

lead¹ /leed/ • *v.* (*past* and *past part.* **led** /led/) **1** *tr.* cause to go with one, esp. by guiding or going in front. † *tr.* **a** direct the actions or opinions of. **b** guide by persuasion or example. **3** *tr.* (also *absol.*) provide access to (*the road leads to Atlanta*). **4** *tr.* go through (a life, etc., of a specified kind) (*led a miserable existence*). **5** *tr.* **a** have the first place in. **b** (*absol.*) be ahead in a race or game. **c** (*absol.*) be preeminent in some field. **6** *tr.* be in charge of (*leads a team*). **7** *tr.* **a** direct by example. **b** be the principal player of (a group of musicians). **8** *tr.* (also *absol.*) begin a round of play at cards by playing (a card) or a card of (a particular suit). **9** *intr.* (foll. by *to*) result in. **10** *intr.* (foll. by *with*) (of a newspaper) use a particular item as the main story. • *n.* **1** guidance given by going in front; example. **2 a** leading place; leadership. **b** amount by which a competitor is ahead of the others. **3** clue (*first real lead in the case*). **4** leash. **5 a** chief part in a play, etc. **b** person playing this. **6** (in full **lead story**) item of news given the greatest prominence. **7** *a* act or right of playing first in a game of cards. **b** card led. • *attrib.adj.* leading; principal; first. □ **lead by the nose** cajole (a person) into compliance. **lead-in** *n.* introduction, opening, etc. **2** wire leading in from outside, esp. from an aerial to a receiver or transmitter. **lead off 1** begin. **2** *Baseball* be the first batter in the inning. **lead on** entice deceptively. **lead time** time between the initiation and completion of a production process. **lead up to** precede; prepare for.

lead² /led/ • *n.* **1** *Chem.* heavy, bluish-gray soft ductile metallic element. ¶ Symb.: **Pb**. **2 a** graphite. **b** thin length of this in a pencil. **3** *colloq.* bullets. **4** *Printing* blank space between lines of print. **5** (*attrib.*) made of lead. • *v.tr.* **1** cover, weight, or frame with lead. **2** *Printing* separate lines of (printed matter) with lead strips. **3** add a lead compound to (gasoline, etc.). □ **lead balloon** failure; unsuccessful venture.

lead·en /léd'n/ *adj.* **1** of or like lead. **2** heavy; slow; burdensome (*leaden limbs*). **3** inert; depressing. **4** lead-colored (*leaden skies*). □□ **lead′en·ly** *adv.* **lead′en·ness** *n.*

lead·er /léedər/ *n.* **1** person or thing that leads. **2** person followed by others. □□ **lead′er·ship** *n.*

lead·ing /léeding/ *adj.* chief; most important. □ **leading lady** actress playing the principal part. **leading man** actor playing the principal part. **leading question** question that prompts the answer wanted.

¶ The phrase **leading question**, originally a legal term, means 'a question that prompts the answer wanted,' that 'leads' the answerer to the answer. In common use it has come to mean 'a pointed or loaded question,' 'a question that is awkward to answer,' or even 'the most important question,' but these usages are avoided in precise usage.

leaf /leef/ • *n.* (*pl.* **leaves** /leevz/) **1** each of several flattened usu. green structures of a plant, usu. on the side of a stem or branch. **2** single thickness of paper. **3** very thin sheet of metal, etc. **4** hinged or insertable part of a table, etc. • *v.* **1** *intr.* put forth leaves. **2** *tr.* (foll. by *through*) turn over the pages of (a book, etc.). □□ **leaf′age** *n.* **leafed** *adj.* (also in *comb.*). **leaf′less** *adj.* **leaf′less·ness** *n.* **leaf′like** *adj.* **leaf′y** *adj.* (**leaf·i·er**, **leaf·i·est**).

LEAF, 1

leaf·let /léeflit/ *n.* **1** young leaf. **2** *Bot.* any division of a compound leaf. **3** sheet of paper giving information.

league¹ /leeg/ • *n.* **1** people, countries, groups, etc., combining for a purpose. **2** group of sports teams that compete for a championship. • *v.intr.* (**leagues**, **leagued**, **leagu·ing**) (often foll. by *together*) join in a league. □ **in league** allied; conspiring. **League of Women Voters** nonpartisan organization that promotes voter awareness and participation.

league² /leeg/ *n. archaic* measure of distance, usu. about three miles.

leak /leek/ • *n.* **1 a** hole through which matter, esp. liquid or gas, passes accidentally in or out. **b** matter passing through this. **c** act or instance of leaking. **2** disclosure of secret information. • *v.* **1 a** *intr.* (of liquid, gas, etc.) pass through a leak. **b** *tr.* lose or admit (liquid, gas, etc.) through a leak. **2** *tr.* disclose (secret information). **3** *intr.* (often foll. by *out*) (of secret information) become known. □ **take a leak** *sl.* urinate. □□ **leak′y** *adj.* (**leak·i·er**, **leak·i·est**).

leak·age /léekij/ *n.* **1** action or result of leaking.

2 what leaks in or out. **3** disclosure of secret information.

lean[1] /leen/ • v. (*past* and *past part.* **leaned** /leend, lent/ or **leant** /lent/) **1** tr. & intr. (often foll. by *across, back, over,* etc.) be or place in a sloping position; incline from upright. **2** tr. & intr. (foll. by *against, on, upon*) rest or cause to rest for support against, etc. **3** intr. (foll. by *on, upon*) rely on. **4** intr. (foll. by *to, toward*) be partial to. • n. inclination (*a decided lean to the right*). □ **lean on** colloq. put pressure on (a person) to act in a certain way. **lean-to** (pl. **-tos**) **1** building with its roof leaning against a wall. **2** shed with an inclined roof usu. leaning against trees, posts, etc.

lean[2] /leen/ • adj. **1** thin; having little fat. **2** meager; of poor quality (*lean crop*). • n. lean part of meat. □ **lean years** years of scarcity. □□ **lean′ly** adv. **lean′ness** n.

lean·ing /leening/ n. tendency or partiality.

leap /leep/ • v. (*past* and *past part.* **leaped** /leept, lept/ or **leapt** /lept/) **1** intr. jump or spring forcefully. **2** tr. jump across. • n. forceful jump. □ **by leaps and bounds** with startlingly rapid progress. **leap at 1** rush toward; pounce upon. **2** accept eagerly. **leap of faith** accepting something on the basis of trust no reason. **leap year** year, occurring once in four, with 366 days (adding Feb. 29). □□ **leap′er** n.

leap·frog /leepfrawg, -frog/ • n. game in which players vault with parted legs over others bending down. • v. (**-frogged, -frog·ging**) **1** intr. (foll. by *over*) perform such a vault. **2** tr. vault over in this way. **3** tr. & intr. (of two or more people, vehicles, etc.) overtake alternately.

learn /lərn/ v. (*past* and *past part.* **learned** /lərnd, lərnt/ or **learnt** /lərnt/) **1** tr. gain knowledge of or skill in. **2** tr. memorize. **3** intr. (foll. by *of*) be informed about. **4** tr. (foll. by *that, how,* etc.) become aware of. □□ **learn′a·ble** adj. **learn′er** n. ¶ **Learn** was once commonly used to mean 'teach, impart knowledge,' but today this usage is regarded as uneducated.

learn·ed /lərnid/ adj. **1** having much learning. **2** showing or requiring learning (*a learned work*). □□ **learn′ed·ly** adv. **learn′ed·ness** n.

learn·ing /lərning/ n. knowledge acquired by study. □ **learning curve 1** graph showing time needed to acquire a new skill, knowledge of a subject, etc. **2** time represented by such a graph. **learning disability** disorder that interferes with the learning process.

lease /lees/ • n. agreement by which the owner of property rents it for a specified time. • v. **1** grant or take on a lease. □ **new lease on life** improved prospect of living, or of use after repair. □□ **leas′a·ble** adj. **leas′er** n.

lease·hold /leeshōld/ n. **1** holding of property by lease. **2** property held by lease. □□ **lease′hold·er** n.

leash /leesh/ • n. strap for holding a dog, etc. • v.tr. **1** put a leash on. **2** restrain.

least /leest/ • adj. **1** smallest; slightest. **2** (of a species, etc.) very small (*least tern*). • n. least amount. • adv. in the least degree. □ **at least 1** at any rate. **2** (also **at the least**) not less than. **in the least** (usu. with *neg.*) in the smallest degree (*not in the least offended*). **to say the least** used to imply the moderation of a statement (*that is doubtful to say the least*).

leath·er /lethər/ • n. **1** material made from the skin of an animal by tanning, etc. **2** (*attrib.*) made of leather. • v.tr. beat; thrash. □□ **leath′er·y** adj.

leath·er·back /lethərbak/ n. large marine turtle, having a thick leathery carapace.

leath·er·ette /lethərét/ n. imitation leather.

leath·er·neck /lethərnek/ n. sl. US Marine.

leave[1] /leev/ v. (*past* and *past part.* **left** /left/) **1 a** tr. go away from. **b** intr. depart. **2** tr. cause to or let remain. **3** tr. abandon. **4** tr. have remaining after one's death. □ **leave alone 1** not interfere with. **2** not have dealings with. **leave much** (or **a lot,** etc.) **to be desired** be highly unsatisfactory. **leave off** discontinue. **leave out** omit; not include. **left for dead** abandoned as being beyond rescue. □□ **leav′er** n. ¶ **Leave** means 'go away from': *We left town together.* The common expression, *Leave me alone,* literally means 'leave (me), so that I can be by myself.' **Let** means 'allow.' Thus *Let me be* and *Let me alone* literally mean 'don't bother me.'

leave[2] /leev/ n. **1** permission. **2 a** (in full **leave of absence**) permission to be absent from duty. **b** period for which this lasts. □ **on leave** legitimately absent from duty. **take one's leave** bid farewell. **take one's leave of** bid farewell to.

leav·en /lévən/ • n. **1** substance added to dough to make it ferment and rise. **2** transforming influence. • v.tr. **1** ferment (dough) with leaven. **2 a** permeate and transform. **b** (foll. by *with*) modify with a tempering element.

leaves pl. of LEAF.

leav·ings /leevingz/ n.pl. things left over, esp. as worthless.

Leb·a·nese /lébənéez/ • adj. of or relating to Lebanon in the Middle East. • n. (pl. same) **1** native or national of Lebanon. **2** person of Lebanese descent.

lech /lech/ colloq. v.intr. = LECHER.

lech·er /léchər/ n. person with excessive sexual desire, esp. a man. □□ **lech′er·ous** adj. **lech′er·ous·ly** adv. **lech′er·ous·ness** n. **lech′er·y** n.

lec·i·thin /lésithin/ n. **1** fatty compound found in egg yolk and other living tissue. **2** preparation of this used to emulsify foods, etc.

lec·tern /léktərn/ n. stand for holding a book for a lecturer, etc.

lec·ture /lékchər/ • n. **1** discourse giving information to a class, etc. **2** long reprimand. • v. **1** intr. deliver a lecture or lectures. **2** tr. reprimand. □□ **lec′tur·er** n.

LED abbr. light-emitting diode.

led past and past part. of LEAD[1].

ledge /lej/ n. narrow horizontal or shelflike projection. □□ **ledged** adj.

led·ger /léjər/ n. principal record of the accounts of a business.

lee /lee/ n. **1** shelter. **2** (in full **lee side**) side away from the wind.

leech /leech/ n. **1** bloodsucking worm formerly used medically. **2** person who imposes on others.

leek /leek/ n. plant of the onion family, with overlapping leaves forming a cylindrical bulb.

leer /leer/ • v.intr. look slyly, lasciviously, or maliciously. • n. leering look. □□ **leer′ing·ly** adv.

leer·y /leeree/ adj. (**leer·i·er, leer·i·est**) sl. **1** knowing; sly. **2** (foll. by *of*) wary.

lees /leez/ n.pl. **1** sediment of wine, etc. **2** dregs; refuse.

lee·ward /lee'wərd, *Naut.* lo͞o'ərd/ • *adj.* & *adv.* on or toward the side sheltered from the wind. • *n.* leeward region, side, or direction.

lee·way /lee'way/ *n.* **1** sideways drift of a ship to leeward. **2** allowable scope of action.

left[1] /left/ • *adj.* **1** on or toward the west side of the human body or any object when facing north. **2** (also **Left**) *Polit.* socialistic. • *adv.* on or to the left side. • *n.* **1** left-hand part, region, or direction. **2** (often **Left**) *Polit.* group or section favoring liberalism, social reform, etc. □ **have two left feet** be clumsy. **left bank** bank of a river on the left facing downstream. **left field** *Baseball* part of the outfield beyond third base. **left-hand** *adj.* **1** on or toward the left side of a person or thing (*left-hand drive*). **2** done with the left hand. **3** (of a screw) = LEFT-HANDED 3b. **left wing** liberal or socialist section of a political party. **left-wing** *adj.* liberal; socialist; radical. **left-winger** person on the left wing.

left[2] *past* and *past part.* of LEAVE[1].

left-hand·ed /left-hándid/ *adj.* **1** using the left hand by preference. **2** (of a tool, etc.) made to be used with the left hand. **3 a** turning to the left; toward the left. **b** (of a screw) advanced by turning counterclockwise. **4 a** (of a compliment) ambiguous. **b** of doubtful sincerity. □□ **left-hand'ed·ly** *adv.* **left'-hand'ed·ness** *n.* **left'-hand'er** *n.*

left·ism /léftizəm/ *n. Polit.* principles or policy of the left. □□ **left'ist** *n.* & *adj.*

left·most /léftmōst/ *adj.* furthest to the left.

left·o·ver /léftōvər/ • *adj.* remaining over; not used up or disposed of. • *n.* (in *pl.*) surplus items (esp. of food).

left·y /léftee/ *n.* (*pl.* **-ies**) *colloq.* left-handed person.

leg /leg/ *n.* **1** each of the limbs on which a person or animal walks and stands. **2** leg of an animal or bird as food. **3** part of a garment covering a leg. **4** support of a chair, table, etc. **5** section of a journey, relay race, competition, etc. □ **feel** (or **find**) **one's legs** become able to stand or walk. **give a person a leg up** help a person to mount a horse, etc. **leg it** *colloq.* walk or run fast. **leg-of-mutton sleeve** sleeve that is full and loose on the upper arm but close-fitting on the forearm. **not have a leg to stand on** be unable to support one's argument. **on one's last legs** near death or the end of one's usefulness, etc. □□ **legged** /legd, légid/ *adj.* (also in *comb.*).

leg·a·cy /légəsee/ *n.* (*pl.* **-cies**) **1** gift left in a will. **2** thing handed down by a predecessor.

le·gal /lee'gəl/ *adj.* **1** of or based on law. **2** appointed or required by law. **3** permitted by law. □ **legal age** age at which a person assumes adult rights and privileges by law. **legal aid** state assistance for legal advice or proceedings. **legal holiday** public holiday established by law. **legal tender** currency that cannot legally be refused in payment of a debt. □□ **le'gal·ly** *adv.*

le·gal·ese /lee'gəleez/ *n. colloq.* technical language of legal documents.

le·gal·ism /lee'gəlizəm/ *n.* excessive adherence to law or formula. □□ **le'gal·ist** *n.* **le·gal·is'tic** *adj.* **le·gal·is'ti·cal·ly** *adv.*

le·gal·i·ty /ligálitee, leegál-/ *n.* (*pl.* **-ties**) **1** lawfulness. **2** (in *pl.*) obligations imposed by law.

le·gal·ize /lee'gəliz/ *v.tr.* make lawful. □□ **le·gal·i·za'tion** *n.*

leg·ate /légət/ *n.* **1** member of the clergy

representing the Pope. **2** ambassador or delegate. □□ **leg'ate·ship** *n.*

leg·a·tee /légətee'/ *n.* recipient of a legacy.

le·ga·tion /ligáyshən/ *n.* **1** office and staff of a diplomatic minister. **2** official headquarters of such.

le·ga·to /liga'ātō/ *Mus.* • *adv.* & *adj.* in a smooth flowing manner. • *n.* (*pl.* **-tos**) **1** legato passage. **2** legato playing.

le·ga·tor /ligáytər/ *n.* giver of a legacy.

leg·end /léjənd/ *n.* **1 a** traditional story; myth. **b** such stories collectively. **2** *colloq.* famous or remarkable person or event. **3 a** inscription. **b** caption. **c** wording on a map, etc., explaining the symbols used.

leg·end·ar·y /léjənderee/ *adj.* **1** of or connected with legends. **2** *colloq.* remarkable. □□ **leg·end·ar'i·ly** *adv.*

leg·er·de·main /léjərdəmáyn/ *n.* **1** sleight of hand. **2** trickery.

leg·ging /léging/ *n.* **1** (usu. in *pl.*) covering for the leg from the knee to the ankle. **2** (*pl.*) close-fitting usu. knitted trousers.

leg·gy /légee/ *adj.* (**leg·gi·er**, **leg·gi·est**) **1** long-legged. **2** long-stemmed. □□ **leg'gi·ness** *n.*

leg·horn /léghawrn, -ərn/ *n.* (also **Leg'horn**) bird of a small hardy breed of domestic fowl.

leg·i·ble /léjibəl/ *adj.* clear enough to read; readable. □□ **leg·i·bil'i·ty** *n.* **leg'i·bly** *adv.*

le·gion /lee'jən/ • *n.* **1** division of 3,000–6,000 men in the ancient Roman army. **2** large organized body. • *predic.adj.* great in number. □ **American Legion** association of US ex-servicemen formed in 1919. **foreign legion** body of foreign volunteers in a modern, esp. French, army.

le·gion·naire /lee'jənáir/ *n.* **1** member of a foreign legion. **2** member of the American Legion. □ **legionnaires' disease** form of bacterial pneumonia.

leg·is·late /léjislayt/ *v.intr.* make laws.

leg·is·la·tion /léjisláyshən/ *n.* **1** process of making laws. **2** laws collectively.

leg·is·la·tive /léjislaytiv/ *adj.* of or empowered to make legislation. □□ **leg·is·la'tive·ly** *adv.*

leg·is·la·tor /léjislaytər/ *n.* **1** member of a legislative body. **2** lawgiver.

leg·is·la·ture /léjislaychər/ *n.* legislative body.

le·git /lijít/ *adj. colloq.* legitimate.

le·git·i·mate /lijítimət/ *adj.* **1** (of a child) born of parents married to each other. **2** lawful; proper; regular. **3** logically admissible. **4** relating to serious drama as distinct from musical comedy, revue, etc. □□ **le·git·i·ma·cy** /-məsee/ *n.* **le·git'i·mate·ly** *adv.* **le·git·i·ma·tion** /-máyshən/ *n.*

le·git·i·ma·tize /lijítimətiz/ *v.tr.* = LEGITIMIZE.

le·git·i·mize /lijítimīz/ *v.tr.* **1** make legitimate. **2** serve as a justification for. □□ **le·git·i·mi·za'tion** *n.*

leg·room /légrŌom/ *n.* space for the legs of a seated person.

leg·ume /légyŌom/ *n.* **1** leguminous plant. **2** any edible part of a leguminous plant.

le·gu·mi·nous /ligyŌominəs/ *adj.* of the family of plants with seeds in pods, including peas and beans.

lei /láy-ee, lay/ *n.* Polynesian garland of flowers.

lei·sure /leézhər, lézh-/ *n.* free time, as for recreation. □ **at leisure 1** not occupied. **2** in an unhurried manner. **at one's leisure** when one has time.

lei·sure·ly /leézhərlee, lézh-/ • *adj.* unhurried; relaxed. • *adv.* deliberately, without hurry. □□ **lei′sure·li·ness** *n.*

lei·sure·wear /leézhərwair, lézh-/ *n.* informal clothes, esp. sportswear.

leit·mo·tiv /lítmōteéf/ *n.* (also **leit′mo·tif**) recurrent or main theme.

LEM /lem/ *abbr.* lunar excursion module.

lem·ming /léming/ *n.* small arctic rodent reputed to rush into the sea and drown during mass migration.

lem·on /lémən/ *n.* **1 a** yellow, oval, sour citrus fruit. **b** tree that produces this fruit. **2** pale-yellow color. **3** *colloq.* feeble, unsatisfactory, or disappointing thing, esp. a car. □ **lemon balm** herb with leaves smelling and tasting of lemon. □□ **lem′on·y** *adj.*

lem·on·ade /lémənáyd/ *n.* drink made from lemon juice.

le·mur /leémər/ *n.* long-tailed arboreal primate of Madagascar.

Len·a·pe /lénəpee, lənaápee/ *n.* see DELAWARE.

lend /lend/ *v.tr.* (*past* and *past part.* **lent** /lent/) **1** grant temporary use of (a thing). **2** allow the use of (money) at interest. **3** bestow or contribute (*lend assistance*). □ **lend an ear** (or **one's ears**) listen. **lend itself to** (of a thing) be suitable for. □□ **lend′a·ble** *adj.* **lend′er** *n.* **lend′ing** *n.*
¶ See note at LOAN.

length /lengkth, length/ *n.* **1** extent from end to end. **2** extent in or of time. **3** distance a thing extends (*at arm's length*). **4** length of a horse, boat, etc., as a measure of the lead in a race. □ **at length 1** (also **at great**, etc., **length**) in detail. **2** at last.

length·en /léngkthən, length-/ *v.* make or become longer. □□ **length′en·er** *n.*

length·wise /léngkthwīz, length-/ • *adv.* in a direction parallel with a thing's length. • *adj.* lying or moving lengthwise.

length·y /léngkthee, léngthee/ *adj.* (**length·i·er**, **length·i·est**) **1** of unusual length. **2** (of speech, writing, a speaker, etc.) verbose; tedious. □□ **length′i·ly** *adv.* **length′i·ness** *n.*

le·ni·ent /leényənt/ *adj.* merciful; tolerant; not severe. □□ **le′ni·ence** *n.* **le′ni·en·cy** *n.* **le′ni·ent·ly** *adv.*

le·no /leénō/ *n.* (*pl.* **-nos**) openwork fabric with the warp threads twisted in pairs.

lens /lenz/ *n.* **1** piece of a transparent substance with one or (usu.) both sides curved for concentrating or dispersing light rays, esp. in optical instruments. **2** *Physics* device for focusing or otherwise modifying the direction of movement of light, sound, electrons, etc. □□ **lensed** *adj.* **lens′less** *adj.*

Lent /lent/ *n.* *Eccl.* period of fasting and penitence preceding Easter. □□ **Lent′en** *adj.*

lent *past* and *past part.* of LEND.

-lent /lənt/ *suffix* forming adjectives (*pestilent*; *violent*) (cf. -ULENT).

len·til /léntəl/ *n.* **1** pealike plant. **2** its edible seed.

len·to /léntō/ *Mus.* • *adj.* slow. • *adv.* slowly.

Le·o /leée-ō/ *n.* (*pl.* **-os**) **1** constellation, traditionally regarded as the figure of a lion. **2 a** fifth sign of the zodiac (the Lion). **b** person born under this sign.

le·o·nine /leéənīn/ *adj.* **1** like a lion. **2** of or relating to lions.

leop·ard /lépərd/ *n.* (*fem.* **leop·ard·ess** /-dis/) large African or Asian feline with a black-spotted, yellowish, or all black coat; panther.

le·o·tard /leéətaard/ *n.* **1** close-fitting one-piece garment worn by dancers, acrobats, etc. **2** = TIGHTS.

lep·er /lépər/ *n.* person suffering from leprosy.

lep·i·dop·ter·ous /lépidóptərəs/ *adj.* of the order of insects that includes butterflies and moths. □□ **lep·i·dop′ter·an** *adj.* & *n.* **lep·i·dop′ter·ist** *n.*

lep·re·chaun /léprəkon, -kawn/ *n.* small mischievous sprite in Irish folklore.

lep·ro·sy /léprəsee/ *n.* contagious deforming disease that affects skin and nerves. □□ **lep′rous** *adj.*

les·bi·an /lézbeeən/ • *n.* homosexual woman. • *adj.* of or relating to female homosexuality. □□ **les′bi·an·ism** *n.*

lese-maj·es·ty /leez májistee/ *n.* (also **lèse-majes·té** /layz mázhestay/) **1** treason. **2** insult to a sovereign or ruler. **3** presumptuous conduct.

le·sion /leézhən/ *n.* injury to an organ, etc., affecting its function.

less /les/ • *adj.* **1** smaller in extent, degree, duration, number, etc. **2** of smaller quantity. **3** *disp.* fewer (*eat less cookies*). • *adv.* to a smaller extent. • *n.* smaller amount. • *prep.* minus (*made $1,000 less tax*). □ **much less** with even greater force of denial (*do not suspect him of negligence, much less of dishonesty*).
¶ See note at FEWER.

-less /lis/ *suffix* forming adjectives and adverbs: **1** from nouns, meaning 'not having, without, free from' (*doubtless*). **2** from verbs, meaning 'not affected by or doing the action of the verb' (*tireless*). □□ **-lessly** *suffix* forming adverbs. **-lessness** *suffix* forming nouns.

less·ee /leseé/ *n.* person who holds a property by lease.

less·en /lésən/ *v.* make or become less; diminish.

less·er /lésər/ *adj.* (usu. *attrib.*) not so great as the other or the rest (*lesser evil*; *lesser egret*).

les·son /lésən/ • *n.* **1 a** amount of teaching given at one time. **b** time assigned to this. **2** (in *pl.*; foll. by *in*) systematic instruction (*lessons in French*). **3** thing learned or to be learned by a pupil. **4** experience that serves to warn or encourage (*let that be a lesson to you*). **5** passage from the Bible read aloud during a church service.

les·sor /lésawr/ *n.* person who lets a property by lease.

lest /lest/ *conj.* in order that not; for fear that (*lest we forget*).

let¹ /let/ • *v.* (**let·ting**; *past* and *past part.* **let**) **1** *tr.* **a** allow to. **b** cause to (*let me know*). **2** *tr.* (foll. by *into*) **a** allow to enter. **b** make acquainted with (a secret, etc.). **3** *tr.* rent (rooms, land, etc.). **4** *tr.* allow or cause (liquid or air) to escape (*let blood*). **5** *tr.* award (a contract for work). **6** *aux.* supplying the first and third persons of exhortations (*let us pray*), commands (*let there be light*), assumptions (*let AB be equal to CD*), and permission or challenge (*let him do his worst*).

□ **let alone 1** not to mention (*hasn't got a television, let alone a VCR*). **2** = *let be*. **let be** not interfere with or do. **let down 1** lower. **2** disappoint. **3** lengthen (a garment). **let go 1** release. **2** lose hold of. **3** cease to think or talk about. **let oneself go 1** give way to enthusiasm, impulse, etc. **2** neglect one's appearance or habits. **let in 1** allow to enter (*let the dog in*). **2** (foll. by *on*) allow (a person) to share privileges, information, etc. **let off 1** allow to alight from a vehicle, etc. **2 a** not punish or compel. **b** (foll. by *with*) punish lightly. **let on** *colloq.* **1** reveal a secret. **2** pretend (*let on that he had succeeded*). **let out 1** release. **2** reveal (a secret, etc.). **3** make (a garment) looser. **4** emit (a sound, etc.). **let up** *colloq.* **1** become less intense or severe. **2** relax one's efforts. **to let** for rent.
¶ See note at LEAVE.

let² /let/ *n.* (in tennis, squash, etc.) obstruction of a ball or player, requiring the ball to be served again. □ **without let or hindrance** unimpeded.

-let /lit, lət/ *suffix* forming nouns, usu. diminutives (*droplet; leaflet*) or denoting articles of ornament or dress (*anklet*).

let·down /létdown/ *n.* disappointment.

le·thal /lée̱thəl/ *adj.* causing death. □□ **le'thal·ly** *adv.*

leth·ar·gy /léthərjee/ *n.* **1** lack of energy. **2** *Med.* morbid drowsiness. □□ **le·thar·gic** /lithaárjik/ *adj.* **le·thar'gi·cal·ly** *adv.*

let's /lets/ *contr.* let us (*let's go now*).

let·ter /létər/ • *n.* **1** alphabetic character. **2** written or printed communication, usu. sent by mail. **3** precise terms of a statement. **4** (in *pl.*) **a** literature. **b** erudition. • *v.tr.* inscribe letters on. □ **letter bomb** terrorist explosive device in the form of a mailed package. **letter carrier** one who is employed to deliver mail. **letter-perfect** precise; verbatim. **letter-quality** of the quality of printing suitable for a business letter. **man** (or **woman**) **of letters** scholar or author. **to the letter** with adherence to every detail. □□ **let'ter·er** *n.* **let'ter·less** *adj.*

let·tered /létərd/ *adj.* well-read or educated.

let·ter·head /létərhed/ *n.* **1** printed heading on stationery. **2** stationery with this.

let·ter·ing /létəring/ *n.* **1** process of inscribing letters. **2** letters inscribed.

let·ter·press /létərpres/ *n.* printing from raised type.

let·tuce /létis/ *n.* plant with crisp leaves used in salads.

let·up /létup/ *n. colloq.* **1** reduction in intensity. **2** relaxation of effort.

leu·ke·mi·a /lookee'meeə/ *n.* malignant disease in which too many leukocytes are produced. □□ **leu·ke'mic** *adj.*

leu·ko·cyte /lo͞okəsīt/ *n.* white blood cell. □□ **leu·ko·cyt·ic** /-sítik/ *adj.*

lev·ee /lévee/ *n.* embankment against river floods.

lev·el /lévəl/ • *n.* **1** horizontal line or plane. **2** height or value reached (*eye level; sugar level*). **3** social, moral, or intellectual standard. **4** plane of rank or authority (*discussions at cabinet level*). **5** instrument giving a horizontal line. **6** level surface. **7** floor or story in a building, ship, etc. • *adj.* **1** flat and even. **2** horizontal. **3** even with something else. • *v.* **1** *tr.* make level. **2** *tr.* raze. **3** *tr.* (also *absol.*) aim (a missile or gun). **4** *tr.* (also

absol.) direct (an accusation, etc.). **5** *intr.* (usu. foll. by *with*) *sl.* be frank or honest. □ **do one's level best** *colloq.* do one's utmost. **level off** make or become level or smooth. **on the level** *colloq. adv.* without deception. • *adj.* honest; truthful. **on a level with 1** in the same horizontal plane as. **2** equal with. □□ **lev'el·ly** *adv.* **lev'el·ness** *n.*

lev·el·head·ed /lévəlhédid/ *adj.* mentally well-balanced; sensible. □□ **lev·el·head'ed·ly** *adv.* **lev·el·head'ed·ness** *n.*

lev·er /lévər, lée'v-/ • *n.* **1** bar used to pry. **2** bar pivoted about a fulcrum (fixed point) acted upon by a force (effort) to move a load. **3** handle moved to operate a mechanism. • *v.* **1** *intr.* use a lever. **2** *tr.* lift, move, or act on with a lever.

LEVER, 2

lev·er·age /lévərij, lée'v-/ *n.* **1** action or power of a lever. **2** means of accomplishing a purpose; power; influence. □ **leveraged buyout** buyout of a company by its management using outside capital.

le·vi·a·than /livīəthən/ *n.* **1** *Bibl.* sea monster. **2** anything very large or powerful, esp. a ship.

Le·vis /lée'vīz/ *n.pl. propr.* type of (orig. blue) denim jeans reinforced with rivets.

lev·i·tate /lévitayt/ *v.* **1** *intr.* rise and float in the air (esp. with reference to spiritualism). **2** *tr.* cause to do this. □□ **lev·i·ta·tion** /-táyshən/ *n.* **lev'i·ta·tor** *n.*

lev·i·ty /lévitee/ *n.* lack of serious thought; frivolity.

lev·y /lévee/ • *v.tr.* (**-ies, -ied**) **1** impose or collect payment, etc. **2** enlist or enroll (troops, etc.). **3** proceed to make (war). • *n.* (*pl.* **-ies**) **1 a** collecting of a tax, etc. **b** contribution, tax, etc., levied. **2 a** act of enrolling troops, etc. **b** (in *pl.*) persons enrolled. □□ **lev'i·a·ble** *adj.*

lewd /lo͞od/ *adj.* **1** lascivious. **2** indecent; obscene. □□ **lewd'ly** *adv.* **lewd'ness** *n.*

lex·i·cal /léksikəl/ *adj.* **1** of the words of a language. **2** of or as of a lexicon. □□ **lex'i·cal·ly** *adv.*

lex·i·cog·ra·phy /léksikógrəfee/ *n.* compiling of dictionaries. □□ **lex·i·cog'ra·pher** *n.* **lex·i·co·graph·ic** /-kəgráfik/ *adj.* **lex·i·co·graph'i·cal** *adj.* **lex·i·co·graph'i·cal·ly** *adv.*

lex·i·col·o·gy /léksikóləjee/ *n.* study of the form, history, and meaning of words. □□ **lex·i·co·log·i·cal** /-kəlójikəl/ *adj.* **lex·i·co·log'i·cal·ly** *adv.* **lex·i·col·o·gist** /-kóləjist/ *n.*

lex·i·con /léksikon/ *n.* **1** dictionary. **2** vocabulary of a person, language, branch of knowledge, etc.

Li *symb. Chem.* lithium.

li·a·bil·i·ty /lɪ́əbilitee/ *n.* (*pl.* **-ties**) **1** being liable. **2** troublesome responsibility; handicap. **3** what a person is liable for, esp. (in *pl.*) debts.

li·a·ble /líəbəl/ *predic.adj.* **1** legally bound. **2** (foll. by *to*) subject to (a tax or penalty). **3** (foll. by *to* + infin.) under an obligation. **4** *disp.* (foll. by *to* + infin.) apt; likely (*it is liable to rain*). ¶ **Liable** is commonly used to mean 'likely (to do something undesirable),' e.g., *Without his glasses he's liable to run the car into a tree.* Precisely, however, **liable** means 'legally obligated,' as in *If he runs into another car he may be liable for damages.*

li·aise /lee-áyz/ *v.intr.* (foll. by *with, between*) *colloq.* establish cooperation; act as a link.

li·ai·son /lee-áyzon, lée-ay-/ *n.* **1 a** communication or cooperation. **b** person who initiates such. **2** illicit sexual relationship.

li·ar /líər/ *n.* person who tells a lie or lies, esp. habitually.

Lib. *abbr.* Liberal.

lib /lib/ *n. colloq.* liberation (*women's lib*).

li·ba·tion /lībáyshən/ *n.* **1 a** pouring out of a drink offering to a god. **b** such a drink offering. **2** *joc.* drink.

li·bel /líbəl/ ● *n. Law* **1 a** published false statement damaging to a person's reputation. **2** act of publishing this. ● *v.tr.* (**li·beled, li·bel·ing; li·belled, li·bel·ling**) **1** defame by libelous statements. **2** accuse falsely and maliciously. □□ **li′bel·er** *n.* **li′bel·ous** *adj.*

lib·er·al /líbərəl, líbrəl/ ● *adj.* **1** ample; full; abundant. **2** generous. **3** open-minded. **4** not strict or rigorous. **5** broadening (*liberal studies*). **6** favoring political and social reform. ● *n.* person of liberal views. □ **liberal arts** arts as distinct from science and technology. □□ **lib′er·al·ism** *n.* **lib′er·al·ist** *n.* **lib·er·al·is′tic** *adj.* **lib·er·al′i·ty** *n.* **lib′er·al·ly** *adv.*

> **liberal** Middle English: via Old French from Latin *liberalis*, from *liber* 'free (man).' The original sense was 'suitable for a free man,' then 'suitable for a gentleman' (one not working in a trade), surviving in *liberal arts.* Another early sense, 'generous,' gave rise to an obsolete meaning 'free from restraint,' leading to sense 3 (late 18th century).

lib·er·al·ize /líbərəlīz, líbrə-/ *v.* make or become more liberal or less strict. □□ **lib·er·al·i·za′tion** *n.*

lib·er·ate /líbərayt/ *v.tr.* set free. □□ **lib·er·a·tion** /-áyshən/ *n.* **lib′er·a·tor** *n.*

lib·er·tar·i·an /líbərtáireeən/ ● *n.* **1** advocate of liberty. **2** believer in free will. ● *adj.* believing in free will. □□ **lib·er·tar′i·an·ism** *n.*

lib·er·tine /líbərteen, -tin/ ● *n.* **1** dissolute or licentious person. **2** person who follows his or her own inclinations. ● *adj.* **1** licentious. **2** free-thinking. □□ **lib′er·tin·ism** *n.*

lib·er·ty /líbərtee/ *n.* (*pl.* **-ties**) **1** freedom from captivity, slavery, etc. **2** freedom to do as one pleases. □ **at liberty 1** free. **2** (foll. by *to* + infin.) entitled; permitted. **take liberties 1** behave in an unduly familiar manner. **2** (foll. by *with*) deal freely with rules or facts. **take the liberty** (foll. by *to* + infin., or *of* + verbal noun) presume; venture.

li·bid·i·nous /libídənəs/ *adj.* lustful. □□ **li·bid′i·nous·ly** *adv.*

li·bi·do /libeédō, -bí-/ *n.* (*pl.* **-dos**) *Psychol.* psychic drive or energy, esp. that associated with

sexual desire. □□ **li·bid·i·nal** /libídənəl/ *adj.* **li·bid′i·nal·ly** *adv.*

Li·bra /leébrə, lí-/ *n.* **1** constellation, traditionally regarded as the figure of scales. **2 a** seventh sign of the zodiac (the Balance or Scales). **b** person born under this sign.

li·brar·i·an /lībráireeən/ *n.* person in charge of, or an assistant in, a library. □□ **li·brar′i·an·ship** *n.*

li·brar·y /líbreree/ *n.* (*pl.* **-ies**) **1 a** collection of books. **b** room or building containing such. **2 a** similar collection of films, records, computer software, etc. **b** place where these are kept. ¶ Avoid pronouncing **library** "lie-berry," which many regard as uneducated.

li·bret·to /librétō/ *n.* (*pl.* **-tos** or **li·bret·ti** /-tee/) text of an opera, etc. □□ **li·bret′tist** *n.*

Lib·y·an /líbeeən, líbyən/ ● *adj.* **1** of or relating to modern Libya in N. Africa. **2** of ancient N. Africa west of Egypt. **3** of or relating to the Berber group of languages. ● *n.* **1 a** native or national of modern Libya. **b** person of Libyan descent. **2** ancient language of the Berber group.

lice *pl.* of LOUSE.

li·cense /lísəns/ ● *n.* **1** permit or permission to own or use something, do something, or carry on a business. **2** liberty of action, esp. when excessive. **3** deviation from fact, etc., esp. for effect (*poetic license*). ● *v.tr.* **1** grant a license to. **2** authorize. □ **license plate** usu. metal plate of a motor vehicle that attests to its registration. □□ **li′cens·a·ble** *adj.* **li′cens·er** *n.* **li′cen·sor** *n.*

li·cen·see /lísənsee′/ *n.* holder of a license.

li·cen·ti·ate /lísénsheeət/ *n.* holder of a professional license.

li·cen·tious /lísénshəs/ *adj.* immoral in sexual relations; promiscuous. □□ **li·cen′tious·ly** *adv.* **li·cen′tious·ness** *n.*

li·chee var. of LITCHI.

li·chen /líkən/ *n.* plant composed of a fungus and an alga, growing on rocks, tree trunks, etc.

lic·it /lísit/ *adj.* not forbidden; lawful. □□ **lic′it·ly** *adv.*

lick /lik/ ● *v.* **1** *tr.* pass the tongue over. **2** *tr.* bring into a specified condition by licking (*licked it clean*). **3 a** *tr.* (of a flame, waves, etc.) play lightly over. **b** *intr.* move gently or caressingly. **4** *tr. colloq.* defeat; excel. **5** *tr. colloq.* thrash. ● *n.* **1** act of licking with the tongue. **2** = *salt lick.* **3** *colloq.* small amount (*a lick of paint*). □ **lick and a promise** *colloq.* hasty performance of a task. **lick a person's boots** be servile. **lick one's lips** (or **chops**) **1** look forward with relish. **2** show one's satisfaction. **lick one's wounds** be in retirement after defeat. □□ **lick′er** *n.* (also in *comb.*).

lick·e·ty-split /líkəteesplít/ *adv. colloq.* at full speed; headlong.

lick·ing /líking/ *n. colloq.* **1** thrashing. **2** defeat.

lic·o·rice /líkərish, -ris/ *n.* **1** black root extract used in candy and medicine. **2** leguminous plant from which it is obtained.

lid /lid/ *n.* **1** hinged or removable cover, esp. for a container. **2** = EYELID. □ **put a lid on** be quiet about; keep secret. **take the lid off** *colloq.* expose (a scandal, etc.). □□ **lid′ded** *adj.* (also in *comb.*). **lid′less** *adj.*

lie¹ /lī/ ● *v.intr.* (**ly·ing** /lí-ing/; *past* **lay** /lay/; *past part.* **lain** /layn/) **1** be in or assume a horizontal position. **2** rest flat on a surface. **3** remain undisturbed or undiscussed, etc. (*let matters lie*). **4**

a be kept or remain or be in a specified state or place (*money is lying in the bank*). **b** (of abstract things) exist; reside (*my sympathies lie with the family*). • *n.* **1 a** way, direction, or position in which a thing lies. **b** *Golf* position of a golf ball when about to be struck. **2** place of cover of an animal or a bird. □ **lie ahead** be going to happen; be in store. **lie down** assume a lying position; have a short rest. **lie heavy** cause discomfort or anxiety. **lie in state** be laid in a public place of honor before burial. **lie low 1** keep quiet or unseen. **2** be discreet about one's intentions. **take lying down** (usu. with *neg.*) accept (defeat, rebuke, etc.) without resistance or protest, etc. ¶ See note at LAY[1].

lie[2] /lī/ • *n.* intentionally false statement. • *v.* (**lies, lied, ly·ing** /lī-ing/) **1** *intr.* **a** tell a lie or lies. **b** (of a thing) be deceptive (*the camera cannot lie*). **b** get (oneself) into or out of a situation by lying (*lied my way out of danger*). □ **lie detector** instrument for determining whether a person is telling the truth by testing for certain physiological changes.

liege /leej, leezh/ usu. *hist.* • *adj.* (of a superior) entitled to receive or (of a vassal) bound to give feudal service or allegiance. • *n.* **1** (in full **liege lord**) feudal superior. **2** (usu. in *pl.*) vassal; subject.

lien /leen, lēˈən/ *n. Law* a right over another's property to protect a debt charged on that property.

lieu /lōō/ *n.* □ **in lieu 1** instead. **2** (foll. by *of*) in the place of.

lieut. *abbr.* lieutenant.

lieu·ten·ant /lōōtenˈənt/ *n.* **1** deputy. **2 a** army officer next in rank below captain. **b** naval officer next in rank below lieutenant commander. **3** police officer next in rank below captain. □ **lieutenant colonel** (or **commander** or **general**) officer ranking next below colonel, commander, or general. **lieutenant governor** elected official next in rank to a state's governor. □□ **lieu·ten'an·cy** *n.* (*pl.* **-cies**).

life /līf/ *n.* (*pl.* **lives** /līvz/) **1** capacity for growth, functional activity, and continual change until death. **2** living things (*insect life*). **3** a period during which life lasts; period from birth to the present or from the present to death (*will regret it all my life*). **b** duration of a thing's existence or of its ability to function. **4 a** state of existence as a living individual (*sacrificed their lives*). **b** living person (*many lives were lost*). **5 a** individual's actions or fortunes; manner of one's existence (*start a new life*). **b** particular aspect of this (*love life*). **6** business and pleasures of the world (*best way to see life*). **7** energy; liveliness (*full of life*). **8** biography. **9** *colloq.* sentence of imprisonment for life. □ **come to life 1** emerge from inactivity. **2** (of an inanimate object) assume an imaginary animation. **for dear** (or **one's**) **life** as a matter of extreme urgency (*hanging on for dear life; run for your life*). **for the life of** (foll. by pers. pron.) even if (one's) life depended on it (*can not for the life of me remember*). **large as life** *colloq.* in person, esp. prominently (*stood there large as life*). **larger than life 1** exaggerated. **2** (of a person) having an exuberant personality. **life-and-death** vitally important; desperate (*a life-and-death struggle*). **life belt** buoyant belt for keeping a person afloat. **life buoy** buoyant support for keeping a person afloat. **life cycle** series of changes in the life of an organism. **life expectancy** average period that a person at a

specified age may expect to live. **life insurance** insurance for a sum to be paid on the death of the insured person. **life jacket** buoyant jacket for keeping a person afloat. **life preserver** life jacket, etc. **life raft** inflatable or log, etc., raft for use in an emergency. **life sciences** biology and related subjects. **life sentence** sentence of imprisonment for life. **life-size** (or **-sized**) of the same size as the person or thing represented. **life-support** *adj.* (of equipment) allowing vital functions to continue during severe disablement. **matter of life and** (or **or**) **death** matter of vital importance. **not on your life** *colloq.* most certainly not. **take one's life in one's hands** take a crucial personal risk.

life·blood /līfblud/ *n.* **1** blood, as being necessary to life. **2** vital factor or influence.

life·boat /līfbōt/ *n.* small boat for use in an emergency.

life·guard /līfgaard/ *n.* expert swimmer employed to rescue bathers from drowning.

life·less /līflis/ *adj.* **1** dead. **2** lacking movement or vitality. □□ **life'less·ly** *adv.* **life'less·ness** *n.*

life·like /līflīk/ *adj.* closely resembling the person or thing represented.

life·line /līflīn/ *n.* **1 a** rope, etc., used for life-saving. **b** diver's signaling line. **2** sole means of communication or transport. **3** fold in the palm of the hand, regarded as significant in palmistry.

life·long /līflawng, -long/ *adj.* lasting a lifetime.

lif·er /līfər/ *n. sl.* **1** person serving a life sentence. **2** person committed to a very long career, esp. in the military.

life·sav·er /līfsayvər/ *n.* person or thing that saves one from serious difficulty. □□ **life'sav·ing** *n. & adj.*

life·style /līfstīl/ *n.* way of life of a person or group.

life·time /līftīm/ *n.* **1** duration of a person's life. **2** duration of a thing or its usefulness. **3** *colloq.* long time.

life·work /līfwôrk/ *n.* task, profession, etc., pursued throughout one's lifetime.

lift /lift/ • *v.* **1** *tr.* raise or remove to a higher position. **2** *intr.* go up; be raised. **3** *tr.* elevate to a higher plane of thought or feeling (*the news lifted their spirits*). **4** *intr.* (of a cloud, fog, etc.) rise; disperse. **5** *tr.* remove (a barrier or restriction). **6** *tr.* transport (supplies, troops, etc.) by air. **7** *tr. colloq.* **a** steal. **b** plagiarize (a passage of writing, etc.). • *n.* **1** lifting or being lifted. **2** ride in another person's vehicle. **3 a** *Brit.* = ELEVATOR **3**. **b** apparatus for carrying persons up or down a mountain, etc. (see *ski lift*). **4** transport by air (see AIRLIFT *n.*). **5** upward pressure that air exerts on an airfoil. **6** supporting or elevating influence; feeling of elation. **7** layer of leather, etc., in the heel of a shoe, esp. to increase height. □ **lift a finger** (or **hand**, etc.) (in *neg.*) make the slightest effort (*didn't lift a finger to help*). **lift off** (of a spacecraft or rocket) rise from the launching pad. **lift up one's voice** sing out. □□ **lift'a·ble** *adj.* **lift'er** *n.*

lift·off /liftawf/ *n.* vertical takeoff of a spacecraft or rocket.

lig·a·ment /ligəmənt/ *n.* band of tough, fibrous tissue linking bones.

lig·a·ture /ligəchər/ • *n.* **1** tie, bandage. **2** *Mus.* slur; tie. **3** two or more letters joined, e.g., æ. **4**

bond; thing that unites. • *v.tr.* bind or connect with a ligature.

li·ger /lígər/ *n.* offspring of a male lion and a female tiger.

light¹ /līt/ • *n.* **1** electromagnetic radiation that stimulates sight and makes things visible. **2** source of light, e.g., the sun, a lamp, fire, etc. **3** (often in *pl.*) traffic light. **4 a** flame or spark serving to ignite. **b** device producing this (*have you got a light?*). **5** aspect in which a thing is regarded (*appeared in a new light*). **6 a** mental or spiritual illumination; enlightenment. **b** hope; happy outcome. **7** eminent person (*leading light*). **8** window or opening in a wall to let light in. • *v.* (*past* **lit** /lit/; *past part.* **lit** or (*attrib.*) **light·ed**) **1** *tr.* & *intr.* ignite. **2** *tr.* provide with light or lighting. **3** *intr.* (usu. foll. by *up*) (of the face or eyes) brighten with animation. • *adj.* **1** well provided with light; not dark. **2** (of a color) pale (*light blue*). □ **bring** (or **come**) **to light** reveal or be revealed. **in a good** (or **bad**) **light** giving a favorable (or unfavorable) impression. **in light of** having regard to; drawing information from. **light meter** instrument for measuring light intensity, esp. for correct photographic exposure. **light of one's life** usu. *joc.* a much-loved person. **light up 1** *colloq.* begin to smoke a cigarette, etc. **2** illuminate a scene. **light-year** distance light travels in one year, nearly 6 trillion miles. **lit up** *colloq.* drunk. **out like a light** deeply asleep or unconscious. **throw** (or **shed**) **light on** help to explain. □□ **light'ish** *adj.* **light'ness** *n.*

light² /līt/ • *adj.* **1** not heavy. **2** relatively low in weight, amount, intensity, etc. (*light arms*; *light traffic*). **3** carrying or suitable for small loads (*light aircraft*). **4** (of food) easy to digest. **5** (of entertainment, music, etc.) intended for amusement only; not profound. **6** (of sleep or a sleeper) easily disturbed. **7** easily borne or done (*light duties*). **8** nimble; quick-moving (*light step*). **9 a** unburdened (*light heart*). **b** giddy (*light in the head*). • *adv.* **1** in a light manner (*sleep light*). **2** with a minimum load (*travel light*). • *v.intr.* (*past* and *past part.* **lit** /lit/ or **light·ed**) **1** (foll. by *on*, *upon*) come upon by chance. **2** alight. □ **lighter-than-air** (of an aircraft) weighing less than the air it displaces. **light-fingered** given to stealing. **light-footed** nimble. **light-headed** giddy; delirious. **light-headedness** being light-headed. **light heavyweight** see HEAVY-WEIGHT. **light industry** manufacture of small or light articles. **light into** *colloq.* attack. **light touch** delicate or tactful treatment. **make light of** treat as unimportant. **make light work of** do a thing quickly and easily. □□ **light'ish** *adj.* **light'ly** *adv.* **light'ness** *n.*

---

light Old English *lēoht*, *līht* (noun and adjective), *līhtan* (verb), of Germanic origin; related to Dutch *licht* and German *Licht*, from an Indo-European root shared by Greek *leukos* 'white' and Latin *lux* 'light.'

---

light·bulb /lítbulb/ *n.* glass bulb containing inert gas and a filament, giving light when an electric current is passed through.

light·en¹ /lít'n/ *v.* **1 a** *tr.* & *intr.* make or become lighter in weight. **b** *tr.* reduce the weight or load of. **2** *tr.* bring relief to (the heart, mind, etc.). **3** *tr.* mitigate (a penalty).

light·en² /lít'n/ *v.* **1 a** *tr.* shed light on. **b** *tr.* & *intr.*

make or grow lighter or brighter. **2** *intr.* shine brightly; flash.

light·er¹ /lítər/ *n.* device for lighting cigarettes, etc.

light·er² /lítər/ *n.* boat for transferring goods from a ship.

light·heart·ed /lít-haártid/ *adj.* **1** cheerful. **2** (unduly) casual; thoughtless. □□ **light'heart·ed·ly** *adv.* **light'heart·ed·ness** *n.*

light·house /lít-hows/ *n.* tower or other structure containing a beacon light to warn or guide ships at sea.

light·ing /líting/ *n.* **1** equipment in a room, street, etc., for producing light. **2** arrangement or effect of lights.

light·ning /lítning/ • *n.* flash of bright light produced by an electric discharge between clouds or between clouds and the ground. • *attrib.adj.* very quick (*with lightning speed*). □ **lightning bug** = FIREFLY. **lightning rod** metal rod or wire fixed to a building, mast, etc., to divert lightning.

light·ship /lítship/ *n.* moored or anchored ship with a beacon light.

light·weight /lítwayt/ • *adj.* **1** of below average weight. **2** of little importance or influence. • *n.* **1** lightweight person, animal, or thing. **2 a** weight class in certain sports between featherweight and welterweight. **b** sportsman of this weight.

lig·nite /lígnīt/ *n.* soft brown coal showing traces of plant structure, intermediate between bituminous coal and peat. □□ **lig·nit·ic** /-nítik/ *adj.*

lik·a·ble /líkəbəl/ *adj.* (also **like'a·ble**) pleasant; easy to like. □□ **lik'a·ble·ness** *n.* **lik'a·bly** *adv.*

like¹ /līk/ • *adj.* (**more like**, **most like**) having some or all of the qualities of; alike (*in like manner*). • *prep.* in the manner of; to the same degree as (*acted like an idiot*). • *conj.* *colloq.* *disp.* **1** as (*cannot do it like you do*). **2** as if (*ate like they were starving*). • *n.* counterpart; equal. □ **and the like** and similar things; et cetera (*music, painting, and the like*). **like-minded** having the same tastes, opinions, etc. **like-mindedness** being likeminded. **like so** *colloq.* like this; in this manner. **the likes of** *colloq.* a person such as. **more like it** *colloq.* nearer what is required.

¶ The use of **like** as a conjunction meaning 'as' or 'as if,' e.g., *I don't have a wealthy set of in-laws like you do; They sit up like they're begging for food*, is considered incorrect by many. In more precise use, **like** is a preposition, used before nouns and pronouns: *to fly like a bird; a town like ours.*

like² /līk/ • *v.tr.* **1** find agreeable or enjoyable. **2 a** choose to have; prefer (*like my coffee black*). **b** wish for (*would like tea*). **3** (*prec. by how*) feel about; regard (*how would you like it if it happened to you?*). • *n.* (in *pl.*) things one prefers. □ **I like that!** *iron.* as an exclamation expressing affront.

-like /līk/ *comb. form* forming adjectives from nouns, meaning 'similar to, characteristic of' (*doglike*).

like·a·ble var. of LIKABLE.

like·li·hood /líkleehŏod/ *n.* probability. □ **in all likelihood** very probably.

like·ly /líklee/ • *adj.* **1** probable. **2** reasonably expected (*likely to come*). **3** promising; suitable (*three likely candidates*). • *adv.* probably. □ **as likely as not** probably. **not likely!** *colloq.* certainly not; I refuse. □□ **like'li·ness** *n.*

lik·en /líkən/ *v.tr.* (foll. by *to*) point out the resemblance of.

like·ness /líknis/ *n.* 1 (foll. by *between, to*) resemblance. 2 (foll. by *of*) semblance or guise (*in the likeness of a ghost*). 3 portrait or representation (*is a good likeness*).

like·wise /líkwīz/ *adv.* 1 also. 2 similarly.

lik·ing /líking/ *n.* 1 what one likes; one's taste. 2 regard or fondness (*had a liking for chocolate*).

li·lac /lílək, -lok, -lak/ • *n.* 1 shrub with fragrant pinkish-violet or white blossoms. 2 pale pinkish-violet color. • *adj.* of this color.

lil·li·pu·tian /lílipyốoshən/ (also **Lil·li·pu'tian**) • *n.* diminutive person or thing. • *adj.* diminutive.

lilt /lilt/ • *n.* 1 a light springing rhythm. b tune marked by this. 2 (of the voice) characteristic cadence. • *v.intr.* (esp. as **lilting** *adj.*) move or speak, etc., with a lilt (*lilting melody*).

lil·y /lílee/ *n.* (*pl.* **-ies**) 1 plant with trumpet-shaped flowers on a tall stem. 2 similar plant, as the water lily. □ **lily-livered** cowardly. **lily of the valley** plant with white, bell-shaped, fragrant flowers. **lily pad** floating leaf of a water lily. **lily-white** 1 as white as a lily. 2 faultless. □□ **lil'ied** *adj.*

li·ma bean /líma/ *n.* 1 plant with broad, flat, edible seeds. 2 seed of this plant.

limb¹ /lim/ *n.* 1 arm, leg, or wing. 2 large branch of a tree. □ **out on a limb** 1 isolated; stranded. 2 at a disadvantage. **tear limb from limb** violently dismember. **with life and limb** (esp. escape) without grave injury. □□ **limbed** *adj.* (also in *comb.*). **limb'less** *adj.*

limb² /lim/ *n.* edge of the sun, moon, etc.

lim·ber /límbər/ • *adj.* 1 lithe. 2 flexible. • *v.* 1 *tr.* make limber. 2 *intr.* become limber. □□ **lim'ber·ness** *n.*

lim·bo¹ /límbō/ *n.* (*pl.* **-bos**) 1 (in some Christian beliefs) abode of the souls of unbaptized infants, and of the just who died before Christ. 2 intermediate state or condition.

lim·bo² /límbō/ *n.* (*pl.* **-bos**) W. Indian dance in which the dancer bends backward to pass under a horizontal bar that is progressively lowered.

lime¹ /līm/ • *n.* 1 (in full **quick'lime**) white substance (calcium oxide) obtained by heating limestone. 2 calcium hydroxide obtained by reacting quicklime with water. • *v.tr.* treat with lime. □□ **lim'y** *adj.* **lim·i·er, lim·i·est**).

lime² /līm/ *n.* 1 a citrus fruit like a lemon but green, smaller, and more acid. b tree bearing this. 2 pale green color.

lime·light /límlīt/ *n.* 1 intense white light used formerly in theaters. 2 glare of publicity.

lim·er·ick /límərik, límrik/ *n.* humorous five-line stanza with a rhyme scheme *aabba*.

lime·stone /límstōn/ *n.* rock composed mainly of calcium carbonate.

lim·ey /límee/ *n.* (also **Lim'ey**) (*pl.* **-eys**) *sl. offens.* British person (orig. a sailor).

lim·it /límit/ • *n.* 1 point, line, or level beyond which something does not or may not extend. 2 greatest or smallest amount permissible. • *v.tr.* set or serve as a limit to. □ **off limits** out of bounds. □□ **lim'it·a·ble** *adj.* **lim·i·ta'tion** *n.* **lim'it·er** *n.* **lim'it·less** *adj.*

lim·it·ed /límitid/ *adj.* 1 confined. 2 not great in scope or talents (*limited experience*). 3 a scanty; restricted. b restricted to a few examples (*limited edition*). □□ **lim'it·ed·ness** *n.*

limn /lim/ *v.tr. hist.* illuminate (manuscripts). □□ **lim'ner** /-nər/ *n.*

lim·o /límō/ *n.* (*pl.* **-os**) *colloq.* limousine.

lim·ou·sine /líməzeen/ *n.* large, luxurious automobile, esp. with a chauffeur.

limp¹ /limp/ • *v.intr.* walk lamely. • *n.* lame walk.

limp² /limp/ *adj.* 1 not stiff or firm. 2 without energy or will. □□ **limp'ly** *adv.* **limp'ness** *n.*

lim·pet /límpit/ *n.* marine gastropod that sticks tightly to rocks.

lim·pid /límpid/ *adj.* clear; transparent. □□ **lim·pid'i·ty** *n.* **lim'pid·ly** *adv.* **lim'pid·ness** *n.*

lin·age /líníj/ *n.* number of lines in printed or written matter.

linch·pin /línchpin/ *n.* 1 pin through the end of an axle to keep a wheel on. 2 person or thing vital to an enterprise, etc.

lin·den /líndən/ *n.* tree with heart-shaped leaves and fragrant flowers.

line¹ /līn/ • *n.* 1 continuous mark on a surface. 2 a straight or curved continuous extent of length without breadth. b track of a moving point. 3 contour or outline. 4 limit or boundary. 5 row of persons or things. 6 a row of printed or written words. b portion of verse written in one line. 7 (in *pl.*) words of an actor's part. 8 short letter or note (*drop me a line*). 9 cord, rope, etc. 10 a wire or cable for a telephone or telegraph. b connection by means of this. 11 branch or route of a railroad system, or a whole system under one management. 12 a regular succession of buses, ships, aircraft, etc., plying between certain places. b company conducting this (*shipping line*). 13 lineage. 14 course or manner of procedure, conduct, thought, etc. (*did it along these lines*). 15 course or channel (*lines of communication*). 16 business or occupation. 17 class of commercial goods (*new line of hats*). 18 *colloq.* false or exaggerated account (*gave me a line about missing the bus*). 19 arrangement of soldiers or ships side by side. • *v.* 1 *tr.* mark with lines. 2 *tr. & intr.* stand at intervals along (*crowds lined the route*). □ **bring into line** make conform. **come into line** conform. **end of the line** point at which further effort is unproductive or one can go no further. **in line for** likely to receive. **in the line of** in the course of (esp. duty). **in** (or **out of**) **line with** in (or not in) alignment or accordance with. **lay** (or **put**) **it on the line** speak frankly. **line drive** *Baseball* hard-hit ball that travels nearly parallel to the ground. **line printer** machine that prints output from a computer a line at a time. **line up** 1 arrange or be arranged in a line or lines. 2 have ready (*had a job lined up*). **on the line** 1 at risk (*put my reputation on the line*). 2 speaking on the telephone. **out of line** 1 not in alignment. 2 inappropriate. **step out of line** behave inappropriately.

line² /līn/ *v.tr.* cover the inside surface of (a garment, box, etc.). □ **line one's pocket** (or **purse**) make money, usu. by corrupt means.

lin·e·age /línee-ij/ *n.* lineal descent; ancestry; pedigree.

lin·e·al /líneeəl/ *adj.* 1 in the direct line of descent or ancestry. 2 linear; of or in lines. □□ **lin'e·al·ly** *adv.*

lin·e·a·ment /líneeəmənt/ *n.* (usu. in *pl.*) distinctive feature or characteristic, esp. of the face.

lin·e·ar /líneeər/ *adj.* **1 a** of or in lines. **b** of length (*linear extent*). **2** long and narrow and of uniform breadth. □ **linear equation** equation between two variables that gives a straight line when plotted on a graph. □□ **lin·e·ar·i·ty** /-neéritee/ *n.* **lin′e·ar·ize** *v. tr.* **lin′e·ar·ly** *adv.*

line·man /línmən/ *n.* (*pl.* **-men**) **1 a** person who repairs and maintains telephone or power lines. **b** person who tests the safety of railroad lines. **2** *Football* player on the line of scrimmage.

lin·en /línin/ • *n.* **1** cloth woven from flax. **2** (*collect.*) sheets, towels, tablecloths, etc. • *adj.* made of linen. □ **wash one's dirty linen in public** be indiscreet about one's domestic quarrels, etc.

lin·er[1] /línər/ *n.* ship or aircraft, etc., carrying passengers on a regular line.

lin·er[2] /línər/ *n.* removable lining. □ **liner notes** printed information packaged with cassette tapes, CDs, etc.

lines·man /línzmən/ *n.* (*pl.* **-men**) (in games played on a field or court) official who decides whether a ball has fallen within the playing area.

line·up /línup/ *n.* **1** line of people. **2** list of participants in a game, etc.

-ling /ling/ *suffix* denoting a diminutive (*duckling*).

lin·ger /línggər/ *v. intr.* **1** loiter. **2** dally. **3** (esp. of an illness) be protracted. □□ **lin′ger·er** *n.* **lin′ger·ing** *adj.* **lin′ger·ing·ly** *adv.*

lin·ge·rie /láaNZHəráy, láNZHəreé/ *n.* women's underwear and nightclothes.

lin·go /línggō/ *n.* (*pl.* **-goes**) *colloq.* **1** foreign language. **2** vocabulary of a special subject or group of people.

lin·gua fran·ca /línggwə frángkə/ *n.* (*pl.* **lin·gua fran·cas** or **lin·guae fran·cae** /-gwee frángkee/) common language adopted by speakers with different native languages.

lin·gual /línggwəl/ *adj.* **1** of or formed by the tongue. **2** of speech or languages. □□ **lin′gual·ly** *adv.*

lin·gui·ne /linggweénee/ *n.* (also **lin·gui′ni**) pasta made in slender flattened strips.

lin·guist /línggwist/ *n.* person skilled in languages or linguistics.

lin·guis·tic /linggwístik/ *adj.* of language or the study of languages. □□ **lin·guis′ti·cal·ly** *adv.*

lin·guis·tics /linggwístiks/ *n.* study of language and its structure.

lin·i·ment /línimənt/ *n.* medication rubbed into the skin.

lin·ing /líning/ *n.* material that covers an inside surface.

link /lingk/ • *n.* **1** loop or ring of a chain. **2 a** connecting part; one in a series. **b** state or means of connection. **3** *Computing* connection from one hypertext document to another, activated by clicking on a highlighted word or image on the screen. • *v.* **1** *tr.* connect or join (two things or one to another). **2** *intr.* be joined; attach oneself to (a system, etc.). **3** *tr.* *Computing* activate a connection to (a file, etc.).

link·age /língkij/ *n.* **1** connection. **2** system of links.

links /lingks/ *n. pl.* (treated as *sing.* or *pl.*) golf course.

link·up /língkup/ *n.* act or result of linking up.

lin·net /línit/ *n.* finch with brown and gray plumage.

li·no·le·um /línóleeəm/ *n.* canvas-backed material coated with linseed oil, powdered cork, etc., used esp. as a floor covering.

lin·seed /línseed/ *n.* seed of flax. □ **linseed oil** oil extracted from linseed and used esp. in paint and varnish.

lint /lint/ *n.* fluff. □□ **lint′y** *adj.*

lin·tel /línt'l/ *n.* *Archit.* horizontal supporting piece of wood, stone, etc., across the top of a door or window.

li·on /líən/ *n.* **1** (*fem.* **li·on·ess** /-nis/) large feline of Africa and S. Asia, with a tawny coat and, in the male, a flowing shaggy mane. **2** (**the Lion**) zodiacal sign or constellation Leo. **3** brave or celebrated person. □ **lion's share** largest or best part.

li·on·heart /líənhaart/ *n.* courageous and generous person. □□ **li′on·heart·ed** *adj.*

li·on·ize /líəniz/ *v. tr.* treat as a celebrity. □□ **li·on·i·za′tion** *n.* **li′on·iz·er** *n.*

lip /lip/ *n.* **1** either of the two fleshy parts forming the edges of the mouth opening. **2** edge of a vessel, etc. **3** *colloq.* impudent, talk. □ **curl one's lip** express scorn. **lip service** insincere support, etc. **lip-sync** synchronize lip movements to recorded sound to appear to be singing or talking. □□ **lip′less** *adj.* **lip′like** *adj.* **lipped** *adj.* (also in *comb.*).

lip·gloss /lípglos, -glaws/ *n.* cosmetic preparation for adding shine or color to the lips.

li·pid /lípid/ *n.* *Chem.* any of a group of fatlike substances, including fatty acids, oils, waxes, and steroids.

li·po·suc·tion /lípōsúkshən, líf-/ *n.* surgical removal of excess fat from under the skin by suction.

lip·read·ing /lípreeding/ *n.* (esp. of a deaf person) practice of understanding (speech) from observing a speaker's lip movements. □□ **lip′read** *v.* **lip′read·er** *n.*

lip·stick /lípstik/ *n.* stick of cosmetic for coloring the lips.

li·que·fy /líkwifī/ *v.* (**-fies**, **-fied**) *Chem.* make or become liquid. □□ **li·que·fa·cient** /-fáyshənt/ *adj.* & *n.* **li·que·fac·tion** /-fákshən/ *n.* **li′que·fi·er** *n.*

li·queur /likór, -kyóŏr/ *n.* any of several sweet alcoholic liquors, variously flavored.

liq·uid /líkwid/ • *adj.* **1** having a consistency like that of water or oil. **2** (of sounds) clear and pure; fluent. **3** (of assets) easily converted into cash. • *n.* **1** liquid substance. **2** *Phonet.* sound of *l* or *r*. □ **liquid crystal** turbid liquid with some order in its molecular arrangement. **liquid crystal display** visual display in electronic devices in which liquid crystals respond to signals. □□ **li·quid′i·ty** *n.* **liq′uid·ly** *adv.*

liq·ui·date /líkwidayt/ *v.* **1 a** *tr.* wind up the affairs of (a business) by paying debts and distributing assets. **b** *intr.* (of a company) be liquidated. **2** *tr.* pay off (a debt). **3** *tr.* convert into cash. **4** *tr.* kill. □□ **liq·ui·da·tion** /-dáyshən/ *n.* **liq′ui·da·tor** *n.*

li·quid·i·ty /likwíditee/ *n.* (*pl.* **-ties**) **1** the state of being liquid. **2** availability of liquid assets.

liq·uid·ize /líkwidīz/ *v. tr.* reduce to a liquid state.

liq·uor /líkər/ *n.* **1** alcoholic (esp. distilled) drink. **2** other liquid, esp. that produced in cooking.

li·ra /léerə/ *n.* (*pl.* **li·re** /léere/ or **li·ras**) **1** chief monetary unit of Italy. **2** chief monetary unit of Turkey.

lisle /līl/ *n.* fine cotton thread for stockings, etc.

lisp /lisp/ • *n.* speech in which *s* is pronounced like *th* in *thick* and *z* is pronounced like *th* in *this*. • *v.* speak or utter with a lisp. □□ **lisp′er** *n.* **lisp′ing·ly** *adv.*

lis·some /lísəm/ *adj.* (also **lis′som**) lithe; supple; agile. □□ **lis′some·ly** *adv.* **lis′some·ness** *n.*

list[1] /list/ • *n.* number of items, names, etc., written or printed together as a record. • *v.tr.* **1 a** make a list of. **b** enumerate. **2** enter in a list. □ **list price** price of something as shown in a published list. □□ **list′ing** *n.*

list[2] /list/ • *v.intr.* (of a ship, etc.) lean over to one side. • *n.* process or instance of listing.

lis·ten /lísən/ *v.intr.* **1** make an effort to hear. **2** take notice of; heed. □ **listen in 1** eavesdrop. **2** listen to a radio or television broadcast. □□ **lis′ten·er** *n.*

list·less /lístlis/ *adj.* lacking energy or enthusiasm. □□ **list′less·ly** *adv.* **list′less·ness** *n.*

lit *past* and *past part.* of LIGHT[1], LIGHT[2].

lit·a·ny /lít′nee/ *n.* (*pl.* **-nies**) **1** series of petitions to God with set responses. **2** tedious recital (*a litany of woes*).

li·tchi /léechee/ *n.* (also **li′chee, ly′chee**) **1** sweet, fleshy fruit with a thin, spiny skin. **2** tree bearing this.

li·ter /léetər/ *n.* metric unit of capacity equal to about 1.057 quarts.

lit·er·a·cy /lítərəsee/ *n.* ability to read and write.

lit·er·al /lítərəl/ • *adj.* **1** taking words in their basic sense without metaphor or allegory. **2** following exactly the original wording (*literal translation*). **3** prosaic; matter-of-fact. **4** so called without exaggeration (*literal extermination*). **5** of a letter of the alphabet. **lit′er·al·ize** *v.tr.* **lit′er·al·ly** *adv.* **lit′er·al·ness** *n.*

¶ **Literally** means 'in fact, not figuratively.' Out of exaggeration, though, some speakers (and writers) cannot resist saying things such as, *We were literally scared to death.*

lit·er·ar·y /lítəreree/ *adj.* **1** of, occupied with, or used in formal literature. **2** well informed about literature. □□ **lit′er·ar′i·ness** *n.*

lit·er·ate /lítərət/ • *adj.* able to read and write. • *n.* literate person. □□ **lit′er·ate·ly** *adv.*

li·te·ra·ti /lítəra′atee/ *n.pl.* learned people.

lit·er·a·ture /lítərəchər, -choor/ *n.* **1** written works, esp. those valued for form and style. **2** writings of a country, period, or particular subject. **3** *colloq.* printed matter, leaflets, etc.

-lith /lith/ *suffix* denoting types of stone (*laccolith; monolith*).

lithe /līth/ *adj.* flexible; supple. □□ **lithe′ly** *adv.* **lithe′ness** *n.* **lithe′some** *adj.*

lith·i·um /lítheeəm/ *n. Chem.* soft, silver-white metallic element. ¶ Symb.: **Li.**

lith·o·graph /líthəgraf/ • *n.* lithographic print. • *v.tr.* **1** print by lithography. **2** write or engrave on stone.

li·thog·ra·phy /lithógrəfee/ *n.* process of printing from a plate so treated that ink adheres only to what is to be printed. □□ **li·thog′ra·pher** *n.* **li·tho·graph·ic** /líthəgráfik/ *adj.* **li·tho·graph′i·cal·ly** *adv.*

lith·o·sphere /líthəsfeer/ *n.* layer including the

earth's crust and upper mantle. □□ **lith·o·spher·ic** /-sféerik, -sfér-/ *adj.*

Lith·u·a·ni·an /líthoo-áyneeən/ • *n.* **1 a** native of Lithuania. **b** person of Lithuanian descent. **2** language of Lithuania. • *adj.* of or relating to Lithuania or its people or language.

lit·i·gant /lítigənt/ *n.* a party to a lawsuit.

lit·i·gate /lítigayt/ *v.* **1** *intr.* be a party to a lawsuit. **2** *tr.* contest (a point) in a lawsuit. **lit·i·ga·tion** /-gáyshən/ *n.* **lit′i·ga·tor** *n.*

li·ti·gious /litíjəs/ *adj.* **1** given to litigation. **2** quarrelsome. □□ **li·ti′gious·ly** *adv.* **li·ti′gious·ness** *n.*

lit·mus /lítməs/ *n.* dye that turns red under acid conditions and blue under alkaline conditions. □ **litmus paper** paper stained with litmus, used to test for acids or alkalis. **litmus test 1** test for acids and alkalis using litmus paper. **2** test to establish true character.

lit·ter /lítər/ • *n.* **1 a** refuse, esp. paper, discarded in an open or public place. **b** odds and ends lying about. **2** young animals brought forth at a birth. **3** vehicle containing a couch and carried by people or animals. **4** stretcher for the sick and wounded. **5** straw, etc., as bedding for animals. **6** granulated material for a cat's waste. • *v.tr.* **1** make (a place) untidy with litter. **2** scatter carelessly.

LITTER, 3

lit·ter·bug /lítərbug/ *n.* person who leaves litter in a public place.

lit·tle /lít′l/ • *adj.* (**lit·tler, lit·tlest; less** /les/ or **les·ser** /lésər/; **least** /leest/) **1** small in size, amount, degree, etc. **2 a** short in stature. **b** of short distance or duration. **3** trivial. **4** young or younger (*little boy; my little sister*). **5** paltry; contemptible (*you little sneak*). • *n.* **1** not much; only a small amount (*got very little out of it*). **2** (usu. prec. by *a*) **a** a certain but no great amount (*every little bit helps*). **b** short time or distance (*after a little*). • *adv.* (**less, least**) **1** to a small extent only (*little more than speculation*). **2** not at all; hardly (*they little thought*). **3** (prec. by *a*) somewhat (*is a little deaf*). □ **Little Bear =** *Little Dipper.* **Little Dipper** constellation in Ursa Minor in the shape of a dipper. **little by little** by degrees; gradually. **little finger** smallest finger, at the outer end of the hand. **no little** considerable; a good deal of (*took no little trouble over it*). **not a little** *n.* much; a great deal. • *adv.* extremely (*not a little concerned*). □□ **lit′tle·ness** *n.*

lit·to·ral /lítərəl/ • *adj.* of or on the shore. • *n.* region lying along a shore.

lit·ur·gy /lítərjee/ *n.* (*pl.* **-gies**) prescribed form of public worship. □□ **li·tur′gi·cal** *adj.* **li·tur′gi·cal·ly** *adv.*

liv·a·ble /lívəbəl/ *adj.* (also **live′a·ble**) **1** (of a house, climate, etc.) fit to live in. **2** (of a life) worth living. □□ **liv·a·bil′i·ty** *n.*

live¹ /liv/ *v.intr.* **1** have life; be or remain alive. **2** (foll. by *on, off*) subsist or feed (*lives on fruit*; *lives off the family*). **3** conduct oneself in a specified way (*live quietly*). **4** survive. **5** enjoy life to the fullest. □ **live and let live** condone others' failings so as to be similarly tolerated. **live down** cause (past guilt, embarrassment, etc.) to be forgotten. **live it up** *colloq.* live gaily and extravagantly. **live through** survive. **live to** survive and reach (*lived to a great age*). **live up to** honor; fulfill. **live with 1** share a home with. **2** tolerate.

live² /līv/ *adj.* **1** (*attrib.*) that is alive; living. **2** (of a broadcast) heard or seen at the time of its performance. **3** of current importance (*a live issue*). **4 a** (of coals) glowing. **b** (of a shell) unexploded. **c** (of a wire, etc.) connected to electrical power. □ **live oak** American evergreen tree. **live wire** energetic and forceful person.

live·a·ble var. of LIVABLE.

live·li·hood /lívleehŏŏd/ *n.* means of living; sustenance.

live·long /lívlawng, -long/ *adj.* entire (*the livelong day*).

live·ly /lívlee/ *adj.* (**live·li·er, live·li·est**) **1** full of life; energetic. **2** brisk (*a lively pace*). **3** vivacious; jolly; sociable. **4** bright and vivid. □□ **live′li·ness** *n.*

liv·en /lívən/ *v.* *colloq.* brighten; cheer.

liv·er /lívər/ *n.* **1** large glandular organ in the abdomen of vertebrates. **2** flesh of an animal's liver as food. **3** dark reddish-brown color. □ **liver spots** brownish pigmentation of the skin, esp. of older people.

liv·er·wurst /lívərwərst, -vərst/ *n.* sausage of ground cooked liver, etc.

liv·er·y /lívəree/ *n.* (*pl.* **-ies**) **1** distinctive marking or outward appearance (*birds in their winter livery*). **2 a** place where horses can be hired. **b** company that has vehicles for hire. **3** distinctive uniform of a servant, etc.

---

livery Middle English: from Old French *livree* 'delivered,' feminine past participle of *livrer*, from Latin *liberare* 'liberate' (in medieval Latin 'hand over'). The original sense was 'the dispensing of food, provisions, or clothing to servants'; also 'allowance of provender for horses,' surviving in *livery stable*. Sense 3 arose because medieval nobles provided matching clothes to distinguish their servants from others.

---

lives *pl.* of LIFE.

live·stock /lívstok/ *n.* (usu. treated as *pl.*) animals, esp. on a farm, regarded as an asset.

liv·id /lívid/ *adj.* **1** *colloq.* furiously angry. **2 a** of a bluish leaden color. **b** discolored as by a bruise. □□ **li·vid′i·ty** *n.* **liv′id·ly** *adv.* **liv′id·ness** *n.*

liv·ing /lívíng/ • *n.* **1** livelihood. **2** enjoyment of life. • *adj.* **1** contemporary; now existent

(*greatest living poet*). **2** (of a likeness) exact. **3** (of a language) still in use. □ **living room** room for general day use. **living will** written statement of a person's desire not to be kept alive by artificial means.

liz·ard /lízərd/ *n.* slender reptile having usu. a long tail, four legs, movable eyelids, and a rough or scaly hide.

'll *v.* (usu. after pronouns) shall; will (*I'll*; *that'll*).

lla·ma /laámə, yáa-/ *n.* S. American ruminant, kept as a beast of burden and for its soft, woolly fleece.

lla·no /laánō, yaá-/ *n.* (*pl.* **-nos**) grassy plain or steppe, esp. in S. America.

LLB *abbr.* Bachelor of Laws.

LLD *abbr.* Doctor of Laws.

lo /lō/ *int.* archaic look (*lo and behold!*).

load /lōd/ • *n.* **1** what is carried or is to be carried at one time. **2** burden or commitment of work, responsibility, etc. **3** (in *pl.*) *colloq.* plenty; a lot. **4** amount of power carried by an electric circuit. • *v.* **1** *tr.* put a load on or aboard. **2** *intr.* take a load aboard; pick up a load. **3** *tr.* (often foll. by *with*) **a** add weight to. **b** oppress. **4** *tr.* insert (the required operating medium) in a device, e.g., film in a camera, etc. **5** *tr.* **a** weight with lead. **b** give a bias to (dice, etc.) with weights. □ **get a load of** *sl.* listen attentively to; notice.

load·ed /lōdid/ *adj.* **1** *sl.* **a** wealthy. **b** drunk. **c** drugged. **2** (of dice, etc.) weighted. **3** (of a question or statement) charged with hidden implication.

load·stone var. of LODESTONE.

loaf¹ /lōf/ *n.* (*pl.* **loaves** /lōvz/) **1** unit of baked bread. **2** (often in *comb.*) other food formed in the shape of a bread loaf.

loaf² /lōf/ *v.* *intr.* spend time idly.

loaf·er /lōfər/ *n.* **1** idle person. **2** (**Loaf′er**) *propr.* leather shoe shaped like a moccasin.

loam /lōm/ *n.* fertile soil of clay, sand, and humus. □□ **loam′y** *adj.* **loam′i·ness** *n.*

loan /lōn/ • *n.* **1** thing lent, esp. money. **2** lending or being lent. • *v.tr.* lend. □ **loan shark** *colloq.* person who lends money at exorbitant rates of interest.
¶ Traditionally, **loan** was a noun and **lend** was a verb: *I went to ask for a loan. Can you lend me twenty dollars?* But **loan** is now widely used as a verb, especially in financial contexts.

loath /lōth, lōth/ *predic.adj.* disinclined; reluctant.

loathe /lōth/ *v.tr.* detest. □□ **loath′er** *n.* **loath′ing** *n.*

loath·some /lṓthsəm, lṓth-/ *adj.* arousing hatred or disgust; repulsive. □□ **loath′some·ly** *adv.* **loath′some·ness** *n.*

loaves *pl.* of LOAF¹.

lob /lob/ • *v.tr.* (**lobbed, lob·bing**) hit or throw (a ball, etc.) slowly or in a high arc. • *n.* **1** ball struck in a high arc. **2** stroke producing this result.

lob·by /lóbee/ • *n.* (*pl.* **-bies**) **1** entrance hall. **2** body of persons seeking to influence legislators on behalf of a particular interest (*tobacco lobby*). • *v.tr.* (**-bies, -bied**) **1** solicit the support of (an influential person). **2** (of members of the public) seek to influence (the members of a legislature). □□ **lob′by·er** *n.* **lob′by·ist** *n.*

lobe /lōb/ *n.* **1** roundish and flattish pendulous

part, often one of a pair (*lobes of the brain*). **2** = EARLOBE. □□ **lo'bar** *adj.* **lobed** *adj.*

lo·bel·ia /lōbeّelyə/ *n.* plant with profuse blue, scarlet, white, or purple flowers having a deeply cleft corolla.

lo·bot·o·my /ləbótəmee/ *n.* (*pl.* **-mies**) incision into the frontal lobe of the brain.

lob·ster /lóbstər/ • *n.* edible marine crustacean with stalked eyes and two pincerlike claws. • *v.intr.* catch lobsters. □ **lobster pot** basket in which lobsters are trapped.

lo·cal /lōkəl/ • *adj.* **1** belonging to, peculiar to, or existing in a particular place. **2** of or affecting only a part. **3** (of a train, bus, etc.) stopping at all stations. • *n.* **1** inhabitant of a particular place. **2** local train, bus, etc. **3** local anesthetic. **4** local branch of a labor union. □ **local area network** *Computing* system for linking telecommunications or computer equipment in several offices, a group of buildings, etc. ¶ Abbr.: **LAN**. **local color** characteristics of a place, esp. as depicted in literature, film, etc. □□ **lo'cal·ly** *adv.*

lo·cale /lōkál/ *n.* scene or locality of an event or occurrence.

lo·cal·i·ty /lōkálitee/ *n.* (*pl.* **-ties**) **1** district. **2** site or scene of something.

lo·cal·ize /lōkəlīz/ *v.tr.* restrict or assign to a particular place. □□ **lo·cal·i·za'tion** *n.*

lo·cate /lōkayt, lōkáyt/ *v.tr.* **1** discover the place of. **2** establish in a place. **3** (in *passive*) be situated. ¶ In formal English one should avoid using **locate** to mean merely 'find,' e.g., *It drives him out of his mind when he can't locate something.* In precise usage **locate** means 'fix the position of, put in place,' e.g., *The studio should be located on a north-facing slope.*

> **locate** early 16th century: from Latin *locat-* "placed," from the verb *locare*, from *locus* "place." The original sense was as a legal term meaning 'let out to rent,' later (late 16th century) 'assign to a particular place,' then (particularly in North America) 'establish in a place.' The sense 'discover the exact position of' dates from the late 19th century.

lo·ca·tion /lōkáyshən/ *n.* **1** place. **2** locating. □ **on location** *Cinematog.* in a natural, not a studio setting.

loc. cit. /lók sít/ *abbr.* in the passage already cited.

loch /lok, lokh/ *n.* Sc. **1** lake. **2** narrow inlet of the sea.

lo·ci *pl.* of LOCUS.

lock¹ /lok/ • *n.* **1** mechanism for fastening a door, lid, etc., that requires a key or a combination to work it. **2** section of a canal or river within gates for raising and lowering the water level. **3** mechanism for exploding the charge of a gun. • *v.* **1 a** *tr.* fasten with a lock. **b** *tr.* (foll. by *up*) shut and secure by locking. **2** *tr.* (foll. by *up, in, into*) enclose (a person or thing) by locking or as if by locking. **3** *tr. & intr.* make or become rigidly fixed. **4** *tr. & intr.* become or cause to become jammed or caught. **5** *tr.* entangle; interlock. □ **lock out 1** keep (a person) out by locking the door. **2** (of an employer) submit (employees) to a lockout. **lock, stock, and barrel** *n.* the whole of a thing. • *adv.* completely. **under lock and key** securely locked up. □□ **lock'a·ble** *adj.*

lock² /lok/ *n.* **1** tress of hair. **2** (in *pl.*) the hair of the head.

lock·er /lókər/ *n.* lockable cupboard or compartment, esp. for public use. □ **locker room** room containing lockers, esp. in a sports facility.

lock·et /lókit/ *n.* small ornamental case holding a portrait, lock of hair, etc., and usu. worn on a necklace.

lock·jaw /lókjaw/ *n.* = TRISMUS. ¶ Not in technical use.

lock·out /lókowt/ *n.* employer's exclusion of employees from their workplace until certain terms are agreed to.

lock·smith /lóksmith/ *n.* maker and repairer of locks.

lock·up /lókup/ *n.* holding cell for police suspects.

lo·co /lōkō/ • *adj. sl.* crazy. • *n.* (*pl.* **-cos** or **-coes**) *sl.* crazy person.

lo·co·mo·tion /lōkəmōshən/ *n.* motion or the power of motion from one place to another.

lo·co·mo·tive /lōkəmōtiv/ • *n.* engine for pulling trains. • *adj.* of, relating to, or effecting locomotion (*locomotive power*).

lo·co·weed /lōkōweed/ *n.* poisonous leguminous plant of the southwestern US, causing disease in livestock.

lo·cus /lōkəs/ *n.* (*pl.* **lo·ci** /lōsī, -kee, -kī/) **1** position. **2** *Math.* curve, etc., formed by all points satisfying certain conditions.

lo·cust /lōkəst/ *n.* **1** grasshoppers migrating in swarms and destroying vegetation. **2** cicada. **3** (in full **locust bean**) carob. **4** (in full **locust tree**) N. American flowering tree yielding durable wood.

lo·cu·tion /lōkyōoshən/ *n.* word, phrase, or idiom.

lode /lōd/ *n.* vein of metal ore.

lo·den /lōd'n/ *n.* **1** thick, waterproof woolen cloth. **2** dark green color in which this is often made.

lode·star /lōdstaar/ *n.* **1** star that a ship, etc., is steered by, esp. the pole star. **2 a** guiding principle. **b** object of pursuit.

lode·stone /lōdstōn/ *n.* (also **load'stone**) **1** magnetic oxide of iron. **2** thing that attracts.

lodge /loj/ • *n.* **1** small house occupied by a gatekeeper, gardener, etc. **2** house or hotel in a resort. **3** house occupied in the season for skiing, hunting, etc. **4** members or the meeting place of a branch of a society such as the Freemasons. **5** beaver's or otter's lair. • *v.* **1** *tr.* submit a complaint, etc. **2** *tr. & intr.* make or become fixed or caught. **3** *intr.* reside or live, esp. as a paying guest.

lodg·er /lójər/ *n.* person receiving accommodation in another's house for payment.

lodg·ing /lójing/ *n.* **1** temporary accommodation. **2** (in *pl.*) room or rooms rented for lodging.

lo·ess /lóis, les, lus/ *n.* fertile deposit of fine, wind-blown dust.

loft /lawft, loft/ • *n.* **1** attic. **2** room over a stable, esp. for hay, etc. **3** gallery in a church or hall (*organ loft*). **4** upstairs room. **5** height of an airborne ball. • *v.tr.* send (a ball, etc.) high up.

loft·y /láwftee, lóf-/ *adj.* (**loft·i·er, loft·i·est**) **1** (of things) of imposing height. **2** haughty; aloof. **3** exalted; noble. □□ **loft'i·ly** *adv.* **loft'i·ness** *n.*

log[1] /lawg, log/ • *n.* **1** unhewn piece of a felled tree. **2** device for gauging the speed of a ship. **3** record of events during the voyage of a ship or aircraft. • *v.tr.* (**logged, log·ging**) **1** enter (data) in a logbook. **2** (of a ship, etc.) achieve (a certain distance, speed, etc.). **3** cut into logs. □ **log in** = *log on.* **log on** (or **off**) go through the procedures to begin (or conclude) use of a computer system. **sleep like a log** sleep without stirring.

log[2] /lawg, log/ *n.* logarithm.

lo·gan·ber·ry /lógənberee/ *n.* (*pl.* **-ries**) **1** hybrid of a blackberry and a raspberry. **2** its dark red fruit.

log·a·rithm /láwgərith̬əm, lóg-/ *n.* the power to which a number must be raised to produce a given number (*the logarithm of 1,000 to base 10 is 3*). ¶ Abbr.: **log**. □□ **log·a·rith·mic** /-ríthmik/ *adj.* **log·a·rith'mi·cal·ly** *adv.*

log·book /láwgbŏok, lóg-/ *n.* book containing a detailed record or log.

loge /lōzh/ *n.* (in a theater, etc.) **1** front section of the first balcony. **2** private box or enclosure.

log·ger /láwgər, lóg-/ *n.* lumberjack.

log·ger·head /láwgərhed, lóg-/ *n.* □ **at loggerheads** disagreeing or disputing; at odds.

log·ging /láwging, lóg-/ *n.* cutting and preparing timber.

log·ic /lójik/ *n.* **1 a** science of reasoning. **b** particular scheme of or treatise on this. **2** expected procedure or outcome. □□ **lo·gi·cian** /ləjíshən/ *n.*

-logic /lójik/ *comb. form* (also **-logical** /lójikəl/) forming adjectives corresponding esp. to nouns in *-logy* (*analogic; theological*).

log·i·cal /lójikəl/ *adj.* **1** of logic or formal argument. **2** correctly reasoned. □□ **log·i·cal·i·ty** /-kálitee/ *n.* **log'i·cal·ly** *adv.*

lo·gis·tics /ləjístiks/ *n.pl.* planning for and provision of services and supplies for an operation, program, etc. □□ **lo·gis'tic** *adj.* **lo·gis'ti·cal** *adj.* **lo·gis'ti·cal·ly** *adv.*

log·jam /láwgjam, lóg-/ *n.* **1** crowded mass of logs in a river. **2** deadlock.

lo·go /lōgō/ *n.* (*pl.* **-gos**) *colloq.* = LOGOTYPE.

lo·go·type /láwgətīp, lóg-/ *n.* emblem or trademark of a company, organization, etc.

log·roll·ing /láwgrōling, lóg-/ *n.* **1** *colloq.* exchanging favors, esp. for political gain. **2** sport in which two people stand on and rotate a floating log until one loses by falling off. □□ **log'roll** *v.* **log'roll·er** *n.*

-logy /ləjee/ *comb. form* forming nouns denoting: **1** (usu. as **-ology**) subject of study or interest (*archaeology; zoology*). **2** characteristic of speech or language (*tautology*). **3** discourse (*trilogy*).

loin /loyn/ *n.* **1** (in *pl.*) the part of the body on both sides of the spine between the false ribs and the hipbones. **2** meat from this part of an animal.

loin·cloth /lóynklawth, -kloth/ *n.* cloth worn around the loins, esp. as a sole garment.

loi·ter /lóytər/ *v.intr.* **1** hang around; linger idly. **2** go slowly, with long pauses. □□ **loi'ter·er** *n.*

loll /lol/ *v.* **1** *intr.* stand, sit, or recline in a lazy attitude. **2** *tr. & intr.* (foll. by *out*) hang loosely. □□ **loll'er** *n.*

lol·li·pop /lóleepop/ *n.* hard, usu. round candy on a stick.

lol·ly·gag /lóleegag/ *v.intr.* (also **lal·ly·gag** /láleegag/) (**-gagged, -gag·ging**) *sl.* loiter.

lone /lōn/ *attrib.adj.* **1** (of a person) solitary; without a companion. **2** (of a place) unfrequented; uninhabited. □ **lone wolf** person who prefers to act alone.

lone·ly /lónlee/ *adj.* (**lone·li·er, lone·li·est**) **1** solitary. **2** (of a place) unfrequented. **3** sad because without friends. □ **lonely heart** lonely person (in sense 3). □□ **lone'li·ness** *n.*

lon·er /lónər/ *n.* person or animal that prefers to be alone.

lone·some /lónsəm/ *adj.* **1** solitary. **2** feeling lonely. □ **by** (or **on**) **one's lonesome** all alone. □□ **lone'some·ly** *adv.* **lone'some·ness** *n.*

long[1] /lawng, long/ • *adj.* (**long·er** /láwnggər, lóng-/; **long·est** /láwnggist, lóng-/) **1** measuring much from end to end in space or time. **2** in length or duration (*three miles long; two months long*). **3** consisting of many items or units. **4** seemingly more than the stated amount; tedious (*ten long miles*). **5** elongated. **6** lasting much time (*long friendship*). **7** far-reaching. **8** (of a vowel) having the pronunciation shown in the name of the letter. **9** (of odds or a chance) of low probability. **10** (of stocks) bought with the expectation of a rise in price. **11** (foll. by *on*) *colloq.* well supplied with. • *n.* long interval or period (*will not take long*). • *adv.* (**long·er** /lónggər/; **long·est** /lónggist/) **1** by or for a long time (*long before*). **2** throughout a specified time (*all day long*). □ **as** (or **so**) **long as** provided that. **before long** soon. **in the long run** eventually. **the long and the short of it** **1** all that can or need be said. **2** eventual outcome. **long-distance 1** (of a telephone call, public transport, etc.) between distant places. **2** (of a weather forecast) long-range. **long division** division of numbers with details of the calculations written down. **long-drawn** (or **-drawn-out**) prolonged, esp. unduly. **long face** dismal expression. **long-faced** with a long face. **long haul** prolonged effort or task. **long in the tooth** rather old. **long johns** *colloq.* = *long underwear*. **long jump** track-and-field contest of jumping as far as possible along the ground in one leap. **long-lived** having a long life; durable. **long-playing** (of a phonograph record) playing for about 20–30 minutes on each side. **long-range** extending a long distance or time. **long-running** continuing for a long time. **long shot 1** wild guess or venture. **2** bet at long odds. **3** *Cinematog.* shot including objects at a distance. **long-sleeved** with sleeves reaching to the wrist. **long-standing** that has long existed. **long-suffering** bearing provocation patiently. **long suit** thing at which one excels. **long-term** of or for a long time (*long-term plans*). **long underwear** warm, close-fitting undergarment with ankle-length legs and often a long-sleeved top. **long wave** radio wave of frequency less than 300 kHz. **not by a long shot** by no means. □□ **long'ish** *adj.*

long[2] /lawng, long/ *v.intr.* (foll. by *for* or *to* + infin.) have a strong wish or desire for.

long. *abbr.* longitude.

lon·gev·i·ty /lonjévitee, lawn-/ *n.* long life.

long·hair /láwnghair, lóng-/ *n.* person characterized by the associations of long hair, esp. a hippie or intellectual.

long·hand /láwnghand, lóng-/ *n.* ordinary handwriting.

long·horn /láwnghawrn, lóng-/ *n.* one of a breed of cattle with long horns.

long·ing /láwnging, lóng-/ • *n.* intense desire. • *adj.* having or showing this feeling. □□ **long′ing·ly** *adv.*

lon·gi·tude /lónjitoٚod, -tyoٚod, láwn-/ *n.* angular distance east or west from the prime meridian.

LONGITUDE

lon·gi·tu·di·nal /lónjitoٚod′nəl, -tyoٚod-, láwn-/ *adj.* **1** of or in length. **2** running lengthwise. **3** of longitude. □□ **lon·gi·tu′di·nal·ly** *adv.*

long·shore·man /láwngshawrmən, lóng-/ *n.* (*pl.* **-men**) person employed to load and unload ships.

long·time /láwngtīm, lóng-/ *adj.* that has been such for a long time.

long-wind·ed /láwngwíndid, lóng-/ *adj.* **1** (of speech or writing) tediously lengthy. **2** able to run a long distance without rest. □□ **long-wind′ed·ly** *adv.* **long-wind′ed·ness** *n.*

loo·fah /loٚofə/ *n.* (also **luf·fa** /lúfə/) **1** climbing gourdlike plant. **2** its dried fruit fibers used as a sponge.

look /loٚok/ • *v.* **1 a** *intr.* use one's sight. **b** *tr.* turn one's eyes on; examine. **2** *intr.* **a** make a search. **b** (foll. by *at*) consider; examine (*look at the facts*). **3** *intr.* (foll. by *for*) **a** search for. **b** expect. **4** *intr.* have a specified appearance; seem. **5** *intr.* (foll. by *into*) investigate. • *n.* **1** act of looking; glance (*scornful look*). **2** (in *sing.* or *pl.*) appearance of a face; expression. **3** appearance of a thing (*has a European look*). • *int.* (also **look here!**) calling attention, expressing a protest, etc. □ **look after** take care of. **look one's age** appear to be as old as one really is. **look-alike** person or thing closely resembling another. **look alive** (or **lively**) *colloq.* be brisk and alert. **look as if** suggest by appearance the belief that (*it looks as if he's gone*). **look back 1** turn one's thoughts to (something past). **2** (usu. with *neg.*) cease to progress (*have never looked back*). **look down on** (or **upon** or **look down one's nose at**) regard with contempt or superiority. **look forward to** await with specified feelings. **look in** make a short visit. **look like 1** have the appearance of. **2** threaten or promise (*looks like rain*). **look on** regard (*looks on you as a friend*). **look out 1** (often foll. by *for*) be vigilant or prepared. **2** (foll. by *on, over*, etc.) afford a specified outlook. **look over** inspect; examine. **look-see** *colloq.* quick survey or inspection. **look sharp** act promptly. **look through 1** penetrate (a pretense or pretender) with insight. **2** ignore by pretending not to see. **look up 1** search for

353

(esp. information in a book). **2** *colloq.* go to visit (a person). **3** raise one's eyes. **4** improve, esp. in price, prosperity, or well-being (*things are looking up*). **look up to** respect; venerate. **not like the look of** find alarming or suspicious; distrust. □□ **-looking** *adj.* (in *comb.*).

look·er /loٚokər/ *n. colloq.* an attractive person.

look·ing glass /loٚoking glas/ *n.* mirror.

look·out /loٚokowt/ *n.* **1** watch or looking out. **2 a** post of observation. **b** person or party stationed to keep watch. **3** *colloq.* person's own concern.

loom[1] /loٚom/ *n.* apparatus for weaving.

loom[2] /loٚom/ *v.intr.* **1** appear dimly, esp. as a threatening shape. **2** (of an event or prospect) be ominously close.

loon /loٚon/ *n.* **1** aquatic diving bird. **2** *colloq.* crazy person.

loon·y /loٚonee/ *sl.* • *n.* (*pl.* **-ies**) mad or silly person; lunatic. • *adj.* (**loon·i·er, loon·i·est**) crazy; silly. □ **loony bin** *sl.* psychiatric hospital. □□ **loo′ni·ness** *n.*

loop /loٚop/ • *n.* **1 a** figure produced by a curve, or a doubled thread, etc., that crosses itself. **b** anything forming this figure. **2** contraceptive coil. **3** endless strip of tape or film allowing continuous repetition. **4** *Computing* sequence of instructions that is repeated until a condition is satisfied. • *v.* **1** *tr.* form into a loop. **2** *tr.* fasten with a loop or loops. **3** *intr.* **a** form a loop. **b** move in looplike patterns. **4** *intr.* (also **loop the loop**) *Aeron.* fly in a circle vertically.

loop·hole /loٚop-hōl/ *n.* means of evading a rule, etc., without infringing it.

loop·y /loٚopee/ *adj.* (**loop·i·er, loop·i·est**) *sl.* crazy.

loose /loٚos/ • *adj.* **1** free from bonds or restraint. **2** not tightly held, fixed, etc. **3** slack; relaxed. **4** not compact or dense. **5** inexact. **6** morally lax. • *n.* state of freedom, esp. as an escapee (*on the loose*). • *v.tr.* **1** release; set free. **2** untie (something that constrains). **3** discharge (a missile, etc.). □ **at loose ends** uncertain; disorganized. **loose-leaf** (of a notebook, etc.) with each page separate and removable. **play fast and loose** ignore one's obligations; be unreliable. □□ **loose′ly** *adv.* **loose′ness** *n.*

¶ The adjective **loose**, meaning 'not tight,' should not be confused with the verb **loose**, which means 'let go': *They loosed the reins and let the horse gallop.* This verb in turn should not be confused with the verb **lose**, which means 'be deprived of, fail to keep': *I will lose my keys if I don't mend the hole in my pocket. The neighbors will lose their house if the mortgage is not paid.*

loos·en /loٚosən/ *v.* make or become loose or looser. □□ **loos′en·er** *n.*

loot /loٚot/ • *n.* **1** spoil; booty. **2** *sl.* money. • *v.tr.* plunder. □□ **loot′er** *n.*

lop[1] /lop/ *v.* (**lopped, lop·ping**) **1** *tr.* cut or remove (a part or parts) from a whole, esp. branches from a tree. **2** *tr.* remove (items) as superfluous. **3** *intr.* (foll. by *at*) make lopping strokes on (a tree, etc.). □□ **lop′per** *n.*

lop[2] /lop/ *v.* (**lopped, lop·ping**) hang limply. □ **lop-eared** (of an animal) having drooping ears. □□ **lop′py** *adj.*

lope /lōp/ • *v.intr.* run with a long bounding stride. • *n.* long bounding stride.

lop·sid·ed /lópsídid/ adj. unevenly balanced. □□ **lop′sid·ed·ly** adv. **lop′sid·ed·ness** n.

lo·qua·cious /lōkwáyshəs/ adj. talkative. □□ **lo·qua′cious·ly** adv. **lo·qua′cious·ness** n. **lo·quac·i·ty** /-kwásitee/ n.

lord /lawrd/ • n. **1** master or ruler. **2** hist. feudal superior, esp. of a manor. **3** (in the UK) person with the title Lord, esp. a marquess, earl, viscount, or baron. **4** (**Lord**) (often prec. by the) God or Christ. • int. (**Lord**) expressing surprise, dismay, etc. □ **lord it over** domineer. **lord over** rule over. **Lord's Prayer** prayer taught by Jesus to his disciples. **Lord's Supper** the Eucharist.

lord·ly /láwrdlee/ adj. (**lord·li·er**, **lord·li·est**) **1** haughty; imperious. **2** suitable for a lord. □□ **lord′li·ness** n.

lord·ship /láwrdship/ n. **1** (usu. **Lordship**) title used in addressing or referring to a lord, etc. **2** dominion; rule; ownership.

lore /lawr/ n. traditions and knowledge on a subject.

lor·gnette /lawrnyét/ n. (in sing. or pl.) pair of eyeglasses or opera glasses held by a long handle.

LORGNETTE

lor·i·keet /láwrikeet, lór-/ n. small, brightly colored parrot.

lo·ris /láwris/ n. (pl. same) small, tailless, large-eyed nocturnal lemur of Asia.

lose /lōoz/ v.tr. (past and past part. **lost** /lawst, lost/) **1** be deprived of or cease to have, esp. by negligence. **2** be deprived of (a person, pet, etc.) by death. **3** become unable to follow, grasp, or find. **4** let or have pass from one's control or reach. **5** be defeated in (a game, lawsuit, battle, etc.). **6** evade; get rid of (lost our pursuers). **7** cause (a person) the loss of (will lose you your job). **8** (in passive) disappear; perish. □ **be lost** (or **lose oneself**) **in** be engrossed in. **be lost on** be wasted on; not appreciated by. **be lost without** have great difficulty if deprived of. **get lost** sl. (usu. in imper.) go away. **lose one's cool** colloq. lose one's composure. **lose face** be humiliated. **lose heart** be discouraged. **lose one's nerve** become timid or irresolute. **lose out** (often foll. by on) colloq. not get a fair chance or advantage (in). **lose one's temper** become angry. **losing battle** effort in which failure seems certain. **lost cause** enterprise, etc., with no chance of success. **2** person one can no longer hope to influence. □□ **los′a·ble** adj. **los′er** n. ¶ See note at LOOSE.

loss /laws, los/ n. **1** losing; being lost. **2** person, thing, or amount lost. **3** detriment or disadvantage resulting from losing. □ **at a loss 1** (sold, etc.) for less than was paid for it. **2** puzzled; uncertain. **be at a loss for words** not know what to say. **loss leader** item sold at a loss to attract customers.

lost past and past part. of LOSE.

lot /lot/ • n. **1** colloq. (prec. by a or in pl.) a large number or amount (a lot of people; lots of fun). **b** colloq. much (a lot warmer). **2 a** each of a set of objects used in making a chance selection. **b** this method of deciding (chosen by lot). **c** share or responsibility resulting from it. **3** destiny, fortune, or condition. **4** plot; allotment of land. **5** article or set of articles for sale at an auction, etc. □ **bad lot** person of bad character. **cast** (or **draw**) **lots** decide by lots. **a whole lot** colloq. very much. ¶ Avoid spelling two words as one: "alot," as in I like skating alot.

lo·thar·i·o /lōtháireeō/ n. rake or libertine.

lo·tion /lóshən/ n. medicinal or cosmetic liquid preparation applied externally.

lot·ter·y /lótəree/ n. (pl. **-ies**) **1** game in which numbered tickets are sold and prizes are won by the holders of numbers drawn at random. **2** thing whose success is governed by chance.

lot·to /lótō/ n. **1** game of chance involving the drawing of numbers. **2** lottery.

lo·tus /lótəs/ n. **1** mythological plant inducing luxurious languor when eaten. **2** type of water lily. □ **lotus-eater** person given to indolent enjoyment. **lotus position** cross-legged position of meditation with the feet resting on the thighs.

loud /lowd/ • adj. **1** strongly audible; noisy. **2** (of colors, etc.) gaudy; obtrusive. • adv. loudly. □ **out loud** aloud. **loud′ly** adv. **loud′ness** n.

loud·mouth /lówdmowth/ n. colloq. noisily self-assertive, vociferous person. □□ **loud′mouthed** adj.

loud·speak·er /lówdspeékər/ n. apparatus that converts electrical impulses into sound, esp. music and voice.

Lou Gehr·ig's dis·ease /lōo gérigz/ n. = AMYOTROPHIC LATERAL SCLEROSIS.

lounge /lownj/ • v.intr. **1** recline comfortably; loll. **2** stand or move about idly. • n. **1** place for lounging. **2** waiting room. **3** sofa. □ **lounge lizard** colloq. person who frequents bars, etc. □□ **loung′er** n.

louse /lows/ n. **1** (pl. **lice** /līs/) parasitic insect. **2** sl. (pl. **lous·es**) contemptible person. □ **louse up** sl. botch.

lous·y /lówzee/ adj. (**lous·i·er**, **lous·i·est**) **1** infested with lice. **2** colloq. very bad; disgusting. **3** colloq. well supplied; teeming (with). □□ **lous′i·ly** adv. **lous′i·ness** n.

lout /lowt/ n. boorish person. □□ **lout′ish** adj.

lou·ver /lōovər/ n. each of a set of overlapping slats that admit air and light and exclude rain. □□ **lou′vered** adj.

LOUVER

lov·age /lúvij/ *n.* aromatic herb of the carrot family.

love /luv/ • *n.* **1** deep affection; fondness. **2** sexual passion. **3** sexual relations. **4** beloved one; sweetheart. **5** (in some games) no score; nil. • *v. tr.* **1** feel love or deep fondness for. **2** delight in; admire; greatly cherish. **3** *colloq.* like very much (*loves books*). □ **fall in love** develop a great (esp. sexual) love (for). **for love** for pleasure not profit. **for the love of** for the sake of. **in love** enamored (of). **love affair** romantic relationship between two people; passion for something. **love apple** *archaic* tomato. **love child** child born out of wedlock. **love-hate relationship** intense relationship involving ambivalent feelings. **love life** one's amorous or sexual relationships. **love nest** place of intimate lovemaking. **love seat** small sofa for two. **make love 1** have sexual intercourse (with). **2** *archaic* pay amorous attention (to). **not for love or money** *colloq.* not in any circumstances. □□ **lov'a·ble** *adj.* **love'a·ble** *adj.* **love'less** *adj.*

love·bird /lúvbərd/ *n.* **1** small parrot that seems to be affectionate to its mate. **2** (in *pl.*) pair of overtly affectionate lovers.

love·lorn /lúvlawrn/ *adj.* pining from unrequited love.

love·ly /lúvlee/ • *adj.* (**love·li·er, love·li·est**) **1** exquisitely beautiful. **2** *colloq.* pleasing; delightful. • *n.* (*pl.* **-lies**) *colloq.* pretty woman. □□ **love'li·ness** *n.*

love·mak·ing /lúvmayking/ *n.* **1** amorous sexual activity, esp. sexual intercourse. **2** *archaic* courtship.

lov·er /lúvər/ *n.* **1** person in love with another. **2** person with whom another is having sexual relations. **3** (in *pl.*) couple in love or having sexual relations. **4** person who enjoys something specified (*music lover*).

love·sick /lúvsik/ *adj.* languishing with romantic love. □□ **love'sick·ness** *n.*

lov·ing /lúving/ • *adj.* feeling or showing love; affectionate. • *n.* affection; active love. □ **loving cup** two-handled drinking cup. □□ **lov'ing·ly** *adv.* **lov'ing·ness** *n.*

low¹ /lō/ • *adj.* **1** not high or tall. **2** not elevated. **3** of or in humble rank. **4** small or less than normal amount or extent or intensity. **5** dejected; lacking vigor. **6** not shrill or loud. **7** commonplace. **8** unfavorable (*low opinion*). **9** abject; vulgar. • *n.* **1** low or the lowest level or number. **2** area of low pressure. • *adv.* **1** in or to a low position or state. **2** in a low pitch or tone. □ **low-ball** *n. Cards* a type of poker. • *v.* underestimate or underbid a price (usu. for a service) deliberately. **low beam** automobile headlight providing short-range illumination. **low-class** of low quality or social class. **low comedy** comedy that borders on farce. **low-cut** (of a dress, etc.) made with a low neckline. **low-down** *adj.* abject; mean; dishonorable. • *n. colloq.* relevant information (about). **low-grade** of low quality. **low-key** lacking intensity; restrained. **low-level** *Computing* (of a programming language) close in form to machine language. **low-lying** at low altitude (above sea level, etc.). **low-pitched 1** (of a sound) low. **2** (of a roof) having only a slight slope. **low pressure 1** little demand for activity or exertion. **2** (of atmospheric pressure) below average. **low profile** avoidance of attention or publicity. **low tide** time or level of the tide at its ebb. □□ **low'ish** *adj.* **low'ness** *n.*

low² /lō/ • *n.* sound made by cattle; moo. • *v. intr.* utter this sound.

low·born /lóbawrn/ *adj.* of humble birth.

low·brow /lóbrow/ • *adj.* not intellectual or cultured. • *n.* lowbrow person. □□ **low'browed** *adj.*

low·er /lóər/ • *adj.* (*compar.* of LOW¹). **1** less high in position or status. **2** situated below another part. **3 a** situated on less high land (*Lower Egypt*). **b** situated to the south (*Lower California*). • *adv.* in or to a lower position, status, etc. • *v.* **1** *tr.* let or haul down. **2** *tr.* & *intr.* make or become lower. **3** *tr.* degrade. □ **lower class** working-class people. **lower-class** *adj.* of the lower class. □□ **low'er·most** *adj.*

low·er·case /lóərkays/ • *n.* small letters. • *adj.* of or having small letters.

low·land /lólənd/ • *n.* low-lying country. • *adj.* of or in lowland. □□ **low'land·er** *n.*

low·ly /lólee/ *adj.* (**low·li·er, low·li·est**) humble; unpretentious. □□ **low'li·ness** *n.*

lox¹ /loks/ *n.* liquid oxygen.

lox² /loks/ *n.* smoked salmon.

loy·al /lóyəl/ *adj.* faithful. □□ **loy'al·ly** *adv.* **loy'al·ty** *n.*

loy·al·ist /lóyəlist/ *n.* person who remains loyal to the legitimate sovereign, government, etc. □□ **loy'al·ism** *n.*

loz·enge /lózinj/ *n.* **1** diamond-shaped figure. **2** sweet or medicinal tablet, for dissolving in the mouth.

LP *abbr.* long-playing (phonograph record).

LPG *abbr.* liquefied petroleum gas.

LPN *abbr.* licensed practical nurse.

LSD *abbr.* lysergic acid diethylamide.

Lt. *abbr.* lieutenant.

Ltd. *abbr.* limited.

Lu *symb. Chem.* lutetium.

lub·ber /lúbər/ *n.* clumsy person. □□ **lub'ber·ly** *adj.* & *adv.*

lu·bri·cant /loobrikənt/ • *n.* substance used to reduce friction. • *adj.* lubricating.

lu·bri·cate /loobrikayt/ *v. tr.* **1** apply oil or grease, etc. **2** make slippery. □□ **lu·bri·ca·tion** /-káyshən/ *n.* **lu'bri·ca·tive** *adj.* **lu'bri·ca·tor** *n.*

lu·cid /loosid/ *adj.* **1** expressing or expressed clearly. **2** sane. □□ **lu·cid'i·ty** *n.* **lu'cid·ly** *adv.* **lu'cid·ness** *n.*

Lu·ci·fer /loosifər/ *n.* the devil; Satan.

luck /luk/ *n.* **1** good or bad fortune. **2** circumstances of life (beneficial or not) brought by this. **3** good fortune; success due to chance. □ **no such luck** *colloq.* unfortunately not. □□ **luck'less** *adj.*

luck·i·ly /lúkilee/ *adv.* **1** (qualifying a whole sentence or clause) fortunately (*luckily there was enough food*). **2** in a lucky or fortunate manner.

luck·y /lúkee/ *adj.* (**luck·i·er, luck·i·est**) **1** having or resulting from good luck. **2** bringing good luck. □□ **luck'i·ness** *n.*

lu·cra·tive /lookrətiv/ *adj.* profitable; yielding financial gain. □□ **lu'cra·tive·ly** *adv.* **lu'cra·tive·ness** *n.*

lu·cre /lookər/ *n. derog.* financial profit or gain.

lu·di·crous /lo͞odikrəs/ adj. absurd; ridiculous; laughable. □□ **lu′di·crous·ly** adv. **lu′di·crous·ness** n.

luff /luf/ v.tr. (also absol.) steer (a ship) nearer the wind.

luf·fa var. of LOOFAH.

lug /lug/ • v. (**lugged, lug·ging**) tr. drag or carry with effort. • n. nut that fastens a wheel to an axle.

luge /lo͞ozh/ • n. toboggan ridden in a supine position down a chute. • v.intr. ride on a luge.

Lu·ger /lo͞ogər/ n. type of German automatic pistol.

lug·gage /lúgij/ n. traveler's suitcases, bags, etc.

lug·ger /lúgər/ n. small ship with a quadrilateral sail.

lug·sail /lúgsayl, -səl/ n. sail for a lugger.

lu·gu·bri·ous /lo͞ogo͞obrees, -gyo͞o-/ adj. doleful; mournful; dismal. □□ **lu·gu′bri·ous·ly** adv. **lu·gu′bri·ous·ness** n.

luke·warm /lo͞okwáwrm/ adj. **1** moderately warm; tepid. **2** unenthusiastic; indifferent. □□ **luke′warm′ly** adv. **luke′warm′ness** n.

lull /lul/ • v. **1** tr. soothe or send to sleep. **2** tr. (usu. foll. by into) deceive (a person) into confidence. **3** intr. (of noise, a storm, etc.) abate or fall quiet. • n. calm period.

lul·la·by /lúləbī/ n. (pl. **-bies**) soothing song to send a child to sleep.

lu·lu /lo͞olo͞o/ n. sl. remarkable or excellent person or thing.

lum·ba·go /lumbáygō/ n. rheumatic pain in the lower back.

lum·bar /lúmbər, -baar/ adj. of the lower back area.

lum·ber[1] /lúmbər/ v.intr. move clumsily. □□ **lum′ber·ing** adj.

lum·ber[2] /lúmbər/ • n. **1** timber cut and prepared for use. **2** disused or cumbersome objects. • v.intr. cut and prepare forest timber. □□ **lum′ber·er** n. **lum′ber·ing** n.

lum·ber·jack /lúmbərjak/ n. (also **lum·ber·man** /-mən/, pl. **-men**) one who fells, prepares, or conveys lumber.

lu·mi·nar·y /lo͞omineree/ n. (pl. **-ies**) **1** natural light-giving body. **2** source of intellectual or moral inspiration. **3** celebrity.

lu·mi·nes·cence /lo͞ominésəns/ n. emission of light without heat. □□ **lu·mi·nes′cent** adj.

lu·mi·nous /lo͞ominəs/ adj. **1** shedding light. **2** phosphorescent; visible in darkness (luminous paint). □□ **lu·mi·nos·i·ty** /-nósitee/ n. **lu′mi·nous·ly** adj. **lu′min·ous·ness** n.

lum·mox /lúməks/ n. colloq. clumsy or stupid person.

lump[1] /lump/ • n. **1** compact shapeless mass. **2** tumor; swelling; bruise. **3** heavy, dull, or ungainly person. • v. **1** tr. mass together or group indiscriminately. **2** intr. become lumpy. □ **lump sum 1** sum covering a number of items. **2** money paid down at once. □□ **lump′y** adj.

lump[2] /lump/ v.tr. colloq. put up with ungraciously (like it or lump it).

lu·na·cy /lo͞onəsee/ n. (pl. **-cies**) **1** insanity. **2** great folly.

lu·na moth /lo͞onə/ n. large N. American moth with crescent-shaped spots on pale green wings.

lu·nar /lo͞onər/ adj. of, relating to, or determined by the moon. □ **lunar module** small craft for traveling between the moon and an orbiting spacecraft. **lunar month 1** interval between new moons (about 29 1/2 days). **2** (in general use) four weeks.

lu·nate /lo͞onayt/ adj. crescent-shaped.

lu·na·tic /lo͞onətik/ • n. **1** insane person. **2** someone foolish or eccentric. • adj. mad; foolish. □ **lunatic fringe** extreme or eccentric minority group.

lunch /lunch/ • n. midday meal. • v. intr. eat lunch. □ **out to lunch** sl. unaware; incompetent. □□ **lunch′er** n.

lunch·box /lúnchboks/ n. container for a packed lunch.

lunch·eon /lúnchən/ n. formal lunch. □ **luncheon meat** sliced, cold prepared meats used for sandwiches, etc.

lunch·eon·ette /lúnchənét/ n. restaurant serving light lunches.

lung /lung/ n. either of the pair of respiratory organs in humans and many other vertebrates.

lunge /lunj/ • n. **1** sudden movement forward. **2** basic attacking move in fencing. • v. **1** intr. make or deliver a lunge. **2** tr. drive (a weapon, etc.) violently in some direction.

lu·pine[1] /lo͞opin/ n. plant with long tapering spikes of blue, purple, pink, white, or yellow flowers.

lu·pine[2] /lo͞opīn/ adj. of or like a wolf or wolves.

lu·pus /lo͞opəs/ n. any of various ulcerous skin diseases, esp. tuberculosis of the skin.

lurch[1] /lərch/ • n. stagger; sudden unsteady movement. • v.intr. stagger; move suddenly and unsteadily.

lurch[2] /lərch/ n. □ **leave in the lurch** desert (a friend, etc.) in difficulties.

lure /lo͞or/ • v.tr. **1** entice, usu. by baiting. **2** attract with the promise of a reward. • n. thing used to entice. □□ **lur′ing** adj. **lur′ing·ly** adv.

lu·rid /lo͞orid/ adj. **1** vivid or glowing in color. **2** sensational; horrifying. **3** ghastly; wan (lurid complexion). □□ **lu′rid·ly** adv. **lu′rid·ness** n.

lurk /lərk/ v.intr. **1** linger furtively. **2 a** lie in ambush. **b** hide, esp. for sinister purposes. **3** (as **lurking** adj.) latent (a lurking suspicion). □□ **lurk′er** n.

lus·cious /lúshəs/ adj. **1** richly pleasing to the senses. **2** voluptuously attractive. □□ **lus′cious·ly** adv. **lus′cious·ness** n.

lush[1] /lush/ adj. **1** (of vegetation) luxuriant and succulent. **2** luxurious. □□ **lush′ly** adv. **lush′ness** n.

lush[2] /lush/ n. sl. alcoholic; drunkard.

lust /lust/ • n. **1** strong sexual desire. **2** passionate desire for. • v.intr. have a strong desire. □□ **lust′ful** adj. **lust′ful·ly** adv. **lust′ful·ness** n.

lus·ter /lústər/ n. **1** gloss; brilliance. **2** shining surface. **3** splendor; glory. □□ **lus′trous** adj. **lus′trous·ly** adv. **lus′trous·ness** n.

lust·y /lústee/ adj. (**lust·i·er, lust·i·est**) **1** healthy and strong. **2** vigorous or lively. □□ **lust′i·ly** adv. **lust′i·ness** n.

lute /lo͞ot/ n. guitarlike instrument with a long neck and pear-shaped body.

lu·te·ti·um /lōōteˈeshəm/ *n. Chem.* silvery metallic element of the lanthanide series. ¶ Symb.: **Lu.**

Lu·ther·an /lōōthərən/ • *n.* **1** follower of Martin Luther, German religious reformer d. 1546. **2** member of the Lutheran Church. • *adj.* of or characterized by the theology of Martin Luther. □□ **Lu′ther·an·ism** *n.*

lutz /luts/ *n.* figure skating jump in which the skater jumps from the outside back edge of one skate, rotates in the air, and lands on the outside back edge of the other skate.

Lux·em·bourg·er /lúksəmbərgər/ *n.* **1** native or national of Luxembourg. **2** person who traces descent from Luxembourg.

lux·u·ri·ant /lugzhŏŏreeənt, lukshŏŏr-/ *adj.* **1** profuse in growth; prolific; exuberant. **2** florid; richly ornate. □□ **lux·u′ri·ance** *n.* **lux·u′ri·ant·ly** *adv.*
¶ See note at LUXURIOUS.

lux·u·ri·ate /lugzhŏŏreeayt, lukshŏŏr-/ *v.intr.* **1** (foll. by *in*) enjoy in a luxurious manner. **2** relax in comfort.

lux·u·ri·ous /lugzhŏŏreeəs, lukshŏŏr-/ *adj.* **1** supplied with luxuries. **2** extremely comfortable. □□ **lux·u′ri·ous·ly** *adv.* **lux·u′ri·ous·ness** *n.*
¶ **Luxuriant** and **luxurious** are sometimes confused. **Luxuriant** means 'lush, profuse, or prolific,' e.g., *forests of dark luxuriant foliage; luxuriant black eyelashes.* **Luxurious,** a much commoner word, means 'supplied with luxuries, extremely comfortable,' e.g., *a luxurious mansion.*

lux·u·ry /lúgzhəree, lúkshəree/ *n.* (*pl.* **-ries**) **1** choice or costly surroundings, possessions, etc. **2** (*attrib.*) providing great comfort; expensive (*luxury apartment*).

Lw *symb. Chem.* lawrencium.

-ly[1] /lee/ *suffix* forming adjectives esp. from nouns, meaning: **1** having the qualities of (*princely*). **2** recurring at intervals of (*daily*).

-ly[2] /lee/ *suffix* forming adverbs from adjectives, denoting esp. manner or degree (*boldly; happily; miserably; deservedly*).

ly·chee var. of LITCHI.

Ly·cra /líkrə/ *n. propr.* elastic fiber or fabric used esp. for close-fitting sports clothing.

lye /lī/ *n.* strong alkaline solution, esp. for washing.

ly·ing[1] /lí-ing/ *pres. part.* of LIE[1]. *n.* a place to lie (*a dry lying*).

ly·ing[2] /lí-ing/ *pres. part.* of LIE[2]. *adj.* deceitful; false.

Lyme dis·ease /līm/ *n.* disease transmitted by ticks, characterized by rash, fever, fatigue, and joint pain.

lymph /limf/ *n.* colorless fluid from body tissues. □ **lymph node** (or **gland**) small mass of tissue that conveys lymph. □□ **lym′phoid** *adj.* **lym′phous** *adj.*

lym·phat·ic /limfátik/ *adj.* **1** of, secreting, or conveying lymph. **2** flabby; sluggish.

lym·pho·ma /limfómə/ *n.* (*pl.* **lym·pho·mas** or **lym·pho·ma·ta** /-mətə/) malignant tumor of the lymph nodes.

lynch /linch/ *v.tr.* (of a mob) put (a person) to death without a legal trial. □□ **lynch′er** *n.* **lynch′ing** *n.*

lynx /lingks/ *n.* wild cat with a short tail, spotted fur, and tufted ear tips.

lyre /līr/ *n.* ancient U-shaped harplike instrument.

LYRE

lyre·bird /lírbərd/ *n.* Australian bird, the male of which has a lyre-shaped tail display.

lyr·ic /lírik/ • *adj.* **1** (of poetry) expressing the writer's emotions. **2** meant to be sung; songlike. • *n.* **1** lyric poem. **2** (in *pl.*) words of a song.

lyr·i·cal /lírikəl/ *adj.* **1** = LYRIC *adj.* 1. **2** *colloq.* highly enthusiastic (*wax lyrical about*). □□ **lyr′i·cal·ly** *adv.*

lyr·i·cism /lírisizəm/ *n.* character or quality of being lyric.

lyr·i·cist /lírisist/ *n.* person who writes the words to a song.

ly·ser·gic ac·id /līsárjik/ *n.* crystalline acid. □ **lysergic acid diethylamide** /dī-éthilámīd/ powerful hallucinogenic drug. ¶ Abbr.: **LSD.**

-lysis /lisis/ *comb. form* forming nouns denoting disintegration or decomposition (*electrolysis*).

Mm

M¹ /em/ *n.* (*pl.* **Ms** or **M's; m's**) **1** thirteenth letter of the alphabet. **2** (as a Roman numeral) 1,000.

M² *abbr.* (also **M.**) **1** Master. **2** *Monsieur.* **3** mega-. **4** *Chem.* molar. **5** Mach. **6** *Mus.* major.

m *abbr.* (also **m.**) **1 a** masculine. **b** male. **2** married. **3** mile(s). **4** meter(s). **5** million(s). **6** minute(s). **7** milli-.

MA *abbr.* **1** Master of Arts. **2** Massachusetts (in official postal use).

ma /maa/ *n. colloq.* mother.

ma'am /mam/ *n.* madam.

ma·ca·bre /məkáabər/ *adj.* (also **ma·ca'ber**) grim, gruesome.

mac·ad·am /məkádəm/ *n.* broken stone used for road building. □□ **mac·ad'am·ize** *v.*

mac·a·da·mi·a /mákədáymeeə/ *n.* Australian evergreen tree bearing edible nutlike seeds.

mac·a·ro·ni /mákərónee/ *n.* tubular variety of pasta.

mac·a·roon /mákəróon/ *n.* small light cake or cookie made with egg white, sugar, and ground almonds or coconut.

ma·caw /məkáw/ *n.* long-tailed brightly colored parrot native to S. and Central America.

Mace /mays/ *n. propr.* aerosol spray used to disable an attacker temporarily. □□ **mace** *v.*

mace¹ /mays/ *n.* **1** heavy spiked club used esp. in the Middle Ages. **2** ceremonial staff of office.

mace² /mays/ *n.* fibrous layer between a nutmeg's shell and its husk, dried and ground as a spice.

mac·er·ate /másərayt/ *v.* **1** *tr.* & *intr.* make or become soft by soaking. **2** *intr.* waste away, as by fasting. □□ **mac·er·a·tion** /-ráyshən/ *n.* **mac'er·a·tor** *n.*

Mach /maak, mak/ *n.* (in full **Mach number**) ratio of the speed of a body to the speed of sound in the surrounding medium.

ma·chet·e /məshétee, məchétee/ *n.* heavy knife used in Central America and the W. Indies as a tool and weapon.

Mach·i·a·vel·li·an /mákeeəvéleeən/ *adj.* elaborately cunning; scheming, unscrupulous. □□ **Mach·i·a·vel'li·an·ism** *n.*

mach·i·nate /mákinayt, másh-/ *v.intr.* lay plots; intrigue. □□ **mach·i·na·tion** /-náyshən/ *n.* **mach'i·na·tor** *n.*

ma·chine /məsheen/ ● *n.* **1** apparatus using or applying mechanical power, having several interrelated parts. **2** particular kind of machine, esp. a vehicle or an electrical or electronic apparatus, etc. **3** controlling system of an organization, etc. (*the party machine*). ● *v.tr.* make or operate on with a machine. □ **like mad** *colloq.* automatic gun giving continuous, rapid fire. **machine-readable** in a form that a computer can process. **machine tool** mechanically operated tool.

ma·chin·er·y /məsheenəree/ *n.* (*pl.* **-ies**) **1** machines collectively. **2** components of a machine;

mechanism. **3** means devised or available (*machinery for decision making*).

ma·chin·ist /məsheenist/ *n.* **1** person who operates a machine, esp. a machine tool. **2** person who makes machinery.

ma·chis·mo /məcheezmō, -chízmō/ *n.* exaggeratedly assertive manliness; show of masculinity.

ma·cho /maachō/ *adj.* showily manly or virile.

mack·er·el /mákərəl, mákrəl/ *n.* (*pl.* same or **mack·er·els**) N. Atlantic marine fish used for food.

mack·in·tosh /mákintosh/ *n.* (also **mac'in·tosh**) waterproof, esp. rubberized, coat.

mac·ra·mé /mákrəmáy/ *n.* **1** art of knotting cord or string to make decorative articles. **2** articles made in this way.

macro- /mákrō/ *comb. form* **1** long. **2** large; large-scale.

mac·ro·bi·ot·ic /mákrōbīótik/ ● *adj.* of a diet intended to prolong life, comprising pure vegetable foods, brown rice, etc. ● *n.* (in *pl.*; treated as *sing.*) theory of such a diet.

mac·ro·cosm /mákrōkozəm/ *n.* **1** universe. **2** the whole of a complex structure. □□ **mac·ro·cos·mic** /-kózmik/ *adj.* **mac·ro·cos'mi·cal·ly** *adv.*

ma·cron /máykraan, mák-/ *n.* diacritical mark (‾) over a long or stressed vowel.

mac·ro·scop·ic /mákrəskópik/ *adj.* **1** visible to the naked eye. **2** regarded in terms of large units. □□ **mac·ro·scop'i·cal·ly** *adv.*

mad /mad/ *adj.* (**mad·der, mad·dest**) **1** insane; having a disordered mind. **2** wildly foolish. **3** (often foll. by *about*) wildly excited or infatuated (*is chess-mad*). **4** *colloq.* angry. **5** (of an animal) rabid. □ **like mad** *colloq.* with great energy, intensity, or enthusiasm. □□ **mad'ness** *n.*

mad·am /mádəm/ *n.* **1** polite or respectful form of address or mode of reference to a woman. **2** woman brothel-keeper.

Mad·ame /mədáam, mádəm/ *n.* **1** (*pl.* **Mes·dames** /maydáam, -dám/) title or form of address corresponding to Mrs. or madam. **2** (**madame**) = MADAM 1.

mad·cap /mádkap/ ● *adj.* **1** wildly impulsive. **2** undertaken without forethought. ● *n.* wildly impulsive person.

mad·den /mád'n/ *v.* **1** *tr.* & *intr.* make or become mad. **2** *tr.* irritate intensely. □□ **mad'den·ing** *adj.* **mad'den·ing·ly** *adv.*

mad·der /mádər/ *n.* **1** herbaceous plant with yellowish flowers. **2** red dye obtained from the root of the madder.

made /mayd/ *past* and *past part.* of MAKE.

Ma·dei·ra /mədéerə/ *n.* amber-colored fortified white wine from the island of Madeira off the coast of N. Africa.

Mad·e·moi·selle /mádəməzél, mádmwə-/ *n.* (*pl.* **-s** or **Mes·de·moi·selles** /máydmwə-/) title or form of address used of or to an unmarried woman; Miss.

mad·house /mádhows/ *n.* **1** *archaic* or *colloq.* mental home or hospital. **2** *colloq.* scene of confused uproar.

mad·ly /mádlee/ *adv.* **1** in a mad manner. **2** *colloq.* **a** passionately. **b** extremely.

mad·man /mádmən, -man/ *n.* (*pl.* **-men**) man who is insane or who behaves insanely.

Ma·don·na /mədónə/ *n. Eccl.* **1** (prec. by *the*) name for the Virgin Mary. **2** picture or statue of the Madonna.

ma·dras /mádrəs, mədrás/ *n.* strong, lightweight cotton fabric with colored or white stripes, checks, etc.

mad·ri·gal /mádrigəl/ *n.* usu. 16th-c. or 17th-c. part song for several voices, usu. unaccompanied. □□ **mad'ri·gal·ist** *n.*

mad·wom·an /mádwŏŏmən/ *n.* (*pl.* **-wom·en**) woman who is insane or who behaves insanely.

mael·strom /máylstrəm/ *n.* **1** great whirlpool. **2** state of confusion.

maes·tro /místrō/ *n.* (*pl.* **maes·tri** /-stree/ or **-tros**) (often as a respectful form of address) **1** distinguished musician, esp. a conductor or performer. **2** great performer in any sphere.

Ma·fi·a /ma'afeeə, máf-/ *n.* organized international body of criminals. □□ **Ma·fi·o·so** /-óso/ *n.*

mag·a·zine /mágəze'en/ *n.* **1** periodical publication containing articles, stories, etc. **2** chamber for holding a supply of cartridges in a firearm. **3** similar device feeding a camera, slide projector, etc. **4** military store for arms, ammunition, etc.

---

magazine late 16th century: from French *magasin*, from Italian *magazzino*, from Arabic *makzin*, *makzan* 'storehouse,' from *kazana* 'store up.' The original sense was 'store'; this was often used from the mid-17th century onward in the title of books providing information useful to particular groups of people, and from it arose sense 1 (mid-18th century). Sense 4, a contemporary specialization of the original meaning, gave rise to sense 2 in the mid-18th century.

---

ma·gen·ta /məjéntə/ • *n.* **1** brilliant crimson shade. **2** aniline dye of this color. • *adj.* of or colored with magenta.

mag·got /mágət/ *n.* soft-bodied larva of certain two-winged insects, esp. the housefly or bluebottle. □□ **mag'got·y** *adj.*

ma·gi *pl.* of MAGUS.

mag·ic /májik/ • *n.* **1 a** supposed art of influencing the course of events supernaturally. **b** witchcraft. **2** conjuring tricks. **3** enchanting quality or phenomenon. • *adj.* **1** of or resulting from magic. **2** producing surprising results. □□ **mag'i·cal** *adj.* **mag'i·cal·ly** *adv.*

ma·gi·cian /məjíshən/ *n.* person skilled in magic.

mag·is·te·ri·al /májiste'ereeəl/ *adj.* **1** imperious. **2** of or conducted by a magistrate. □□ **mag·is·te'ri·al·ly** *adv.*

mag·is·trate /májistrayt, -strət/ *n.* **1** civil officer administering the law. **2** official conducting a court for minor cases and preliminary hearings (*magistrates' court*). □□ **mag·is·tra·cy** /májistrəsee/ *n.*

mag·ma /mágmə/ *n.* (*pl.* **mag·ma·ta** /-mətə/ or **mag·mas**) molten rock under the earth's crust,

which forms igneous rock. □□ **mag·mat·ic** /-mátik/ *adj.*

Mag·na Car·ta /mágnə ka'artə/ *n.* (also **Mag'na Char'ta**) charter of liberty and political rights obtained from King John of England in 1215.

mag·nan·i·mous /magnánimas/ *adj.* nobly generous; not petty in feelings or conduct. □□ **mag·na·nim·i·ty** /mágnənímitee/ *n.* **mag·nan'i·mous·ly** *adv.*

mag·nate /mágnayt, -nət/ *n.* wealthy and influential person, esp. in business (*shipping magnate*).

mag·ne·sia /magne'ezhə, -shə, -zyə/ *n.* magnesium oxide used as an antacid and laxative. □□ **mag·ne'sian** *adj.*

mag·ne·si·um /magne'ezeeəm/ *n. Chem.* silvery lightweight metallic element used in alloys. ¶ Symb.: **Mg**.

mag·net /mágnit/ *n.* **1** piece of iron, steel, ore, etc., having properties of attracting or repelling iron. **2** lodestone.

mag·net·ic /magnétik/ *adj.* **1 a** having the properties of a magnet. **b** producing, produced by, or acting by magnetism. **2** very attractive or alluring (*a magnetic personality*). □ **magnetic field** region of variable force around magnets, magnetic materials, or current-carrying conductors. **magnetic resonance imaging** noninvasive diagnostic technique employing a scanner to obtain computerized images of internal body tissue. ¶ Abbr.: **MRI**. **magnetic tape** tape coated with magnetic material for recording sound or pictures or for the storage of information. □□ **mag·net'i·cal·ly** *adv.*

mag·net·ism /mágnitizəm/ *n.* **1 a** magnetic phenomena and their study. **b** property of producing these phenomena. **2** attraction; personal charm.

mag·net·ize /mágnitīz/ *v.tr.* **1** give magnetic properties to. **2** make into a magnet. **3** attract as or like a magnet. □□ **mag·net'iz·a·ble** *adj.* **mag·net·i·za'tion** *n.* **mag'net·iz·er** *n.*

mag·ne·to /magne'etō/ *n.* (*pl.* **-tos**) electric generator using permanent magnets and producing high voltage.

mag·nif·i·cent /magnífisənt/ *adj.* **1** splendid, stately. **2** sumptuously or lavishly constructed or adorned. **3** *colloq.* fine, excellent. □□ **mag·nif'i·cence** *n.* **mag·nif'i·cent·ly** *adv.*

mag·ni·fy /mágnifī/ *v.tr.* (**-fies, -fied**) **1** make (a thing) appear larger than it is, as with a lens. **2** exaggerate. **3** intensify. □□ **mag·ni·fi·ca'tion** *n.* **mag'ni·fi·er** *n.*

mag·ni·tude /mágnitōōd, -tyōōd/ *n.* **1** largeness. **2** size. **3** importance. **4** degree of brightness of a star.

mag·no·lia /magnólyə/ *n.* **1** tree with dark-green foliage and large waxlike flowers. **2** pale creamy-pink color.

mag·num /mágnəm/ *n.* (*pl.* **mag·nums**) wine bottle of about twice the standard size.

mag·num o·pus /mágnəm ópəs/ *n.* **1** great work of art, literature, etc. **2** most important work of an artist, writer, etc.

mag·pie /mágpī/ *n.* **1** kind of crow with a long pointed tail, black-and-white plumage, and noisy behavior. **2** chatterer. **3** person who collects things indiscriminately.

ma·gus /máygəs/ *n.* (*pl.* **ma·gi** /máyjī/) **1** priest of ancient Persia. **2** (**the Magi**) the "wise men" from the East who brought gifts to the infant Christ (Matt. 2:1).

Mag·yar /mágyaar/ • *n.* **1** member of a Ural-Altaic people now predominant in Hungary. **2** language of this people. • *adj.* of or relating to this people or language.

ma·ha·ra·ja /maáhəráajə, -zhə/ *n.* (also **ma·ha·ra'jah**) *hist.* title of some princes of India.

ma·ha·ra·ni /maáhər<aánee/ *n.* (also **ma·ha·ra'nee**) maharaja's wife or widow.

ma·ha·ri·shi /maáhəre'eshi/ *n.* great Hindu sage.

ma·hat·ma /məha'atmə, -hát-/ *n.* **1** (esp. in India) revered person. **2** each of a class of persons in India and Tibet supposed by some to have preternatural powers.

Ma·hi·can /məhe'ekən/ *n.* (also **Mo·hi'can**) **1** N. American people native to the upper Hudson River Valley of New York state. **2** member of this people.

mah-jongg /maajóng, -jáwng, -zhóng, -zháwng/ *n.* (also **mah'jong'**) Chinese game for four resembling rummy and played with 136 or 144 pieces called tiles.

ma·hog·a·ny /məhógənee/ *n.* (*pl.* **-nies**) **1 a** reddish-brown wood used for furniture. **b** color of this. **2** tropical tree yielding this wood.

ma·hout /məhówt/ *n.* (esp. in India) elephant driver.

maid /mayd/ *n.* **1** female domestic servant. **2** *archaic* or *poet.* girl or young woman. □ **maid of honor** principal bridesmaid.

maid·en /máyd'n/ • *n.* *archaic* or *poet.* girl; young unmarried woman. • *adj.* **1** unmarried (*maiden aunt*). **2** first (*maiden voyage*). □ **maiden name** wife's surname before marriage. □□ **maid'en·hood** *n.* **maid'en·ish** *adj.* **maid'en·like** *adj.* **maid'en·ly** *adj.*

maid·en·hair /máyd'nhair/ *n.* (in full **maidenhair fern**) fern with fine hairlike stalks and delicate fronds.

maid·en·head /máyd'nhed/ *n.* **1** virginity. **2** hymen.

maid·serv·ant /máydservənt/ *n.* female domestic servant.

mail¹ /mayl/ • *n.* **1** letters and parcels, etc., conveyed by the postal system. **2** postal system. **3** one complete delivery or collection of mail. • *v.tr.* send by mail. □ **mail carrier** person who delivers mail. **mailing list** list of people to whom advertising matter, information, etc., is to be mailed. **mail order** order for goods sent by mail.

mail² /mayl/ *n.* armor made of rings, chains, or plates, joined together flexibly. □□ **mailed** *adj.*

mail·bag /máylbag/ *n.* large sack or bag for carrying mail.

mail·box /máylboks/ *n.* **1** receptacle for pickup and delivery of mail. **2** computer file in which electronic mail is stored.

mail·man /máylmən/ *n.* (*pl.* **-men**) mail carrier.

maim /maym/ *v.tr.* cripple, disable, mutilate.

main /mayn/ • *adj.* **1** chief in size, importance, etc.; principal (*the main part*). **2** exerted to the full (*by main force*). • *n.* **1** principal duct, etc., for water, sewage, etc. (*water main*). **2** *poet.* ocean or oceans. □ **in the main** for the most part. **main line 1** chief railway line. **2** *sl.* principal vein, esp. as a site for a drug injection (cf. MAINLINE).

main·frame /máynfraym/ *n.* (often *attrib.*) large-scale computer system.

main·land /máynlánd, -lənd/ *n.* large continuous extent of land, excluding neighboring islands, etc. □□ **main'land·er** *n.*

main·line /máynlīn/ *v. sl.* **1** *intr.* take drugs intravenously. **2** *tr.* inject (drugs) intravenously. □□ **main'lin·er** *n.*

main·ly /máynlee/ *adv.* for the most part; chiefly.

main·mast /máynmast, -məst/ *n. Naut.* principal mast of a ship.

main·sail /máynsayl, -səl/ *n. Naut.* **1** (in a square-rigged vessel) lowest sail on the mainmast. **2** (in a fore-and-aft rigged vessel) sail set on the after part of the mainmast.

main·spring /máynspring/ *n.* **1** principal spring of a watch, clock, etc. **2** chief motive power; incentive.

main·stay /máynstay/ *n.* **1** chief support. **2** *Naut.* stay from the maintop to the foot of the foremast.

main·stream /máynstreem/ *n.* (often *attrib.*) prevailing trend in opinion, fashion, etc.

main·tain /mayntáyn/ *v.tr.* **1** cause to continue; keep up (an activity, etc.). **2** support by work, expenditure, etc. **3** assert as true. **4** preserve in good repair. **5** provide means for. □□ **main'tain·er** *n.* **main·tain'a·ble** *adj.* **main·tain·a·bil'i·ty** *n.*

main·te·nance /máyntənəns/ *n.* **1** maintaining or being maintained. **2** provision of the means to support life.

maî·tre d'hô·tel /métrə dōtél, máyt-/ *n.* (*pl.* **maî·tres d'hôtel** *pronunc.* same) (also **maître d'**) headwaiter.

maize /mayz/ *n.* **1** = CORN¹ *n.* 1. **2** yellow.

ma·jes·tic /məjéstik/ *adj.* showing majesty; stately and dignified; grand, imposing. □□ **ma·jes'ti·cal·ly** *adv.*

maj·es·ty /májistee/ *n.* (*pl.* **-ties**) **1** impressive stateliness, dignity, or authority, esp. of bearing, language, the law, etc. **2** (**Majesty**) part of several titles given to a sovereign or a sovereign's wife or widow or used in addressing them.

ma·jol·i·ca /məyólikə, məjól-/ *n.* (also **ma·iol'i·ca**) colorfully decorated earthenware.

ma·jor /máyjər/ • *adj.* **1** important, large, serious, significant. **2** (of an operation) serious. **3** *Mus.* **a** (of a scale) having intervals of a semitone between the third and fourth, and seventh and eighth degrees. **b** (of an interval) greater by a semitone than a minor interval (*major third*). **c** (of a key) based on a major scale. • *n.* **1** army officer next below lieutenant colonel and above captain. **2 a** student's most emphasized subject or course. **b** student specializing in a specified subject. • *v.intr.* (foll. by *in*) study or qualify in as a special subject. □ **major general** officer next below a lieutenant general. □□ **ma'jor·ship** *n.*

ma·jor·do·mo /máyjərdōmō/ *n.* (*pl.* **-mos**) chief steward of a great household.

ma·jor·i·ty /məjáwritee, -jór-/ *n.* (*pl.* **-ties**) **1** (usu. foll. by *of*) greater number or part. **2** *Polit.* number by which the votes cast for one party, candidate, etc., exceed those of the next in rank (*won by a majority of 151*). **3** full legal age (*attained his majority*). **4** rank of major.

¶ **Majority** means more than half: *Fifty-one out of 100 is a majority.* A **plurality** is the largest number among three or more: *If Anne received 50* votes, Barry received 30, and Carlos received 20, then Anne received a plurality, and no candidate won a majority; if Anne got 35 votes, Barry 14, and Carlos 51, then Carlos won both the plurality and the majority.

make /mayk/ • *v.tr.* (*past* and *past part.* **made** /mayd/) **1** construct; create; form from parts or other substances. **2** cause or compel. **3 a** bring about (*made a noise*). **b** cause to become or seem (*made him angry*). **4** compose; prepare (*made her will*). **5** constitute; amount to (*2 and 2 make 4*). **6 a** undertake (*made a promise*). **b** perform (a bodily movement, a speech, etc.). **7** gain; acquire; procure. **8** prepare. **9 a** arrange bedding neatly on (a bed). **b** arrange and ignite materials for (a fire). **10** *colloq.* **a** arrive at (a place) or in time for (a train, etc.). **b** manage to attend. **c** achieve a place in (*made the first team*). **11** enact (a law, etc.). **12** consider to be; estimate as. **13** secure the success of (*it made my day*). **14** accomplish (a distance, speed, score, etc.). **15** form in the mind; (*I make no judgment*). • *n.* **1** type, origin, brand, etc., of manufacture. **2** kind of mental, moral, or physical structure or composition. □ **make away with** = *make off with.* **make-believe 1** pretense. **2** pretended. **make believe** pretend. **make do** manage with the limited or inadequate means available. **make for 1** tend to result in (happiness, etc.). **2** proceed toward (a place). **make it 1** *colloq.* succeed in reaching, esp. in time. **2** *colloq.* be successful. **make off** (or **away**) **with** steal. **make out 1 a** distinguish by sight or hearing. **b** decipher (handwriting, etc.). **2** understand (*can't make him out*). **3** assert; pretend. **4** *colloq.* make progress; fare. **5** write out. **6** *colloq.* engage in sexual play or petting. **make over 1** transfer the possession of. **2** refashion. **make up 1** act to overcome (a deficiency). **2** complete (an amount, a party, etc.). **3** compensate. **4** be reconciled. **5** concoct. **6** apply cosmetics to. **make up one's mind** decide. **make up to** curry favor with. **make water** *colloq.* urinate. **make way 1** allow room for others to proceed. **2** be superseded by. **make one's way** go; prosper. **on the make** *colloq.* **1** intent on gain. **2** looking for sexual partners. □□ **mak'a·ble** *adj.* **mak'er** *n.*

make·shift /máykshift/ • *adj.* temporary; serving for the time being. • *n.* temporary substitute or device.

make·up /máykəp/ *n.* **1** cosmetics for the face, etc., either generally or to create an actor's appearance or disguise. **2** person's character, temperament, etc. **3** composition of a thing.

mak·ing /máyking/ *n.* (in *pl.*) essential qualities or ingredients (*has the makings of a general*). □ **in the making** in the course of being made or formed.

ma·ko /máykō, má·akō/ *n.* (*pl.* **-kos**) type of shark.

mal- /mal/ *comb. form* **1 a** bad, badly (*malpractice*; *maltreat*). **b** faulty, faultily (*malfunction*). **2** not (*maladroit*).

mal·ad·just·ed /máləjústid/ *adj.* **1** not correctly adjusted. **2** (of a person) unable to adapt to or cope with the demands of a social environment. □□ **mal·ad·just'ment** *n.*

mal·a·droit /máladróyt/ *adj.* clumsy; bungling. □□ **mal·a·droit'ly** *adv.* **mal·a·droit'ness** *n.*

mal·a·dy /máladee/ *n.* (*pl.* **-dies**) ailment; disease.

Mal·a·gas·y /máləgásee/ • *adj.* of or relating to Madagascar, an island in the Indian Ocean. • *n.* language of Madagascar.

ma·laise /məláyz/ *n.* **1** nonspecific bodily discomfort. **2** feeling of uneasiness.

mal·a·mute /máləmyōōt/ *n.* (also **mal'e·mute**) any of an Alaskan breed of large sled dogs.

mal·a·prop·ism /máləpropizəm/ *n.* (also **mal·a·prop** /máləprop/) use of a word in mistake for one sounding similar, to comic effect, e.g., *allegory* for *alligator.*

ma·lar·i·a /məláireeə/ *n.* recurrent fever caused by a parasite introduced by the bite of a mosquito. □□ **ma·lar'i·al** *adj.* **ma·lar'i·an** *adj.* **ma·lar'i·ous** *adj.*

ma·lar·key /məlá·arkee/ *n. colloq.* humbug; nonsense.

Ma·lay /máylay, məláy/ • *n.* **1** member of a people predominating in Malaysia and Indonesia. **2** language of this people, the official language of Malaysia. • *adj.* of or relating to this people or this language. □□ **Ma·lay'an** *n.* & *adj.*

Mal·a·ya·lam /máləyaáləm/ *n.* language of S. India.

mal·con·tent /málkəntent/ • *n.* discontented person; rebel. • *adj.* discontented or rebellious.

male /mayl/ • *adj.* **1** of the sex that can beget offspring by fertilization or insemination. **2** of men or male animals, plants, etc.; masculine. **3** (of plants or their parts) containing only fertilizing organs. **4** (of parts of machinery, etc.) designed to enter or fill the corresponding female part (*a male plug*). • *n.* male person or animal. □□ **male'ness** *n.*

mal·e·dic·tion /málidíkshən/ *n.* **1** curse. **2** utterance of a curse. □□ **mal·e·dic'tive** /-tiv/ *adj.* **mal·e·dic·to·ry** /-díktəree/ *adj.*

mal·e·fac·tor /málifaktər/ *n.* criminal; evildoer. □□ **mal·e·fac'tion** *n.*

ma·lev·o·lent /məlévələnt/ *adj.* wishing evil to others. □□ **ma·lev'o·lence** *n.* **ma·lev'o·lent·ly** *adv.*

mal·fea·sance /malfée·zəns/ *n. Law* evildoing. □□ **mal·fea'sant** *n.* & *adj.*

mal·for·ma·tion /málformáyshən/ *n.* faulty or abnormal formation. □□ **mal·formed** /-fáwrmd/ *adj.*

mal·func·tion /málfúngkshən/ • *n.* failure to function normally. • *v.intr.* fail to function normally.

mal·ice /mális/ *n.* **1 a** intention to do evil. **b** desire to tease, esp. cruelly. **2** *Law* wrongful intention. □ **malice aforethought** (or **prepense**) *Law* intention to commit a crime, esp. murder.

ma·li·cious /məlíshəs/ *adj.* characterized by malice, intending to harm. □□ **ma·li'cious·ly** *adv.* **ma·li'cious·ness** *n.*

ma·lign /məlín/ • *adj.* **1** (of a thing) injurious. **2** (of a disease) malignant. **3** malevolent. • *v.tr.* speak ill of; slander. □□ **ma·lign'er** *n.* **ma·lig·ni·ty** /məlígnitee/ *n.* (*pl.* **-ties**). **ma·lign·ly** /-línlee/ *adv.*

ma·lig·nant /məlígnənt/ *adj.* **1 a** (of a disease) very virulent or infectious. **b** cancerous. **2** harmful; feeling or showing intense ill will. □□ **ma·lig'nan·cy** *n.* (*pl.* **-cies**). **ma·lig'nant·ly** *adv.*

ma·lin·ger /məlínggər/ *v.intr.* exaggerate or feign illness in order to escape duty, work, etc. □□ **ma·lin'ger·er** *n.*

mall /mawl/ *n.* **1** sheltered walk or promenade. **2** enclosed shopping center.

mal·lard /málərd/ *n.* (*pl.* same or **mal·lards**) wild duck or drake of the northern hemisphere.

MALLARD

mal·le·a·ble /máleeəbəl/ *adj.* **1** (of metal, etc.) that can be shaped by hammering. **2** adaptable; pliable, flexible. □□ **mal·le·a·bil'i·ty** *n.* **mal'le·a·bly** *adv.*

mal·let /málit/ *n.* **1** hammer, usu. of wood. **2** long-handled wooden hammer for striking a croquet or polo ball.

mal·low /málō/ *n.* plant with hairy stems and leaves and pink or purple flowers.

mal·nour·ished /málnόrisht, -núr-/ *adj.* suffering from malnutrition. □□ **mal·nour'ish·ment** *n.*

mal·nu·tri·tion /málnōōtríshən, -nyōō-/ *n.* dietary condition resulting from the absence of healthful foods.

mal·o·dor·ous /malódərəs/ *adj.* having an unpleasant smell.

mal·prac·tice /malpráktis/ *n.* improper, negligent, or criminal professional conduct, as by a physician.

malt /mawlt/ ● *n.* **1** barley or other grain that is steeped, germinated, and dried, esp. for brewing or distilling and vinegar making. **2** *colloq.* malt whiskey; malt liquor. ● *v. tr.* convert (grain) into malt. □ **malted milk 1** drink combining milk, a malt preparation, and ice cream or flavoring. **2** powdered malt preparation used to make this. **malt liquor** a kind of strong beer. □□ **malt'y** *adj.* (**malt·i·er, malt·i·est**)

Mal·tese /máwlteéz, -teés/ ● *n.* **1** (*pl.* same) native or national of Malta, an island in the W. Mediterranean. **2** language of Malta. ● *adj.* of or relating to Malta.

mal·treat /máltreét/ *v.tr.* ill-treat. □□ **mal·treat'er** *n.* **mal·treat'ment** *n.*

ma·ma /maámə, məmaá/ *n. colloq.* (esp. as a child's term) mother.

mam·ba /maámbə/ *n.* venomous African snake.

mam·bo /maámbō/ *n.* (*pl.* **-bos**) **1** Latin American dance like the rumba. **2** the music for this.

mam·ma /maámə/ *n.* (also **mom'ma**) *colloq.* MAMA.

mam·mal /máməl/ *n.* warm-blooded vertebrate of the class secreting milk for the nourishment of its young. □□ **mam·ma·li·an** /-máyleeən/ *adj.* & *n.* **mam·mal·o·gy** /-mólijee/ *n.*

mam·ma·ry /máməree/ *adj.* of the breasts.

mam·mog·ra·phy /mamógrəfee/ *n. Med.* X-ray technique of diagnosing and locating abnormalities (esp. tumors) of the breasts.

mam·mon /mámən/ *n.* (also **Mam'mon**) wealth regarded as a god or as an evil influence. □□ **mam'mon·ism** *n.* **mam'mon·ist** *n.*

mam·moth /máməth/ ● *n.* large extinct elephant with a hairy coat and curved tusks. ● *adj.* huge.

MAMMOTH

man /man/ ● *n.* (*pl.* **men** /men/) **1** adult human male. **2 a** human being; person (*no man is perfect*). **b** the human race (*man is mortal*). **3** person showing characteristics associated with males (*she's more of a man than he is*). **4 a** worker; employee. **b** manservant or valet. **5** (usu. in *pl.*) soldiers, sailors, etc., esp. nonofficers. **6** any one of a set of pieces used in playing chess, checkers, etc. ● *v.tr.* (**manned, man·ning**) **1** supply with a person or people for work or defense, etc. **2** work or service or defend (*man the pumps*). □ **as one man** in unison; in agreement. **man about town** fashionable man of leisure. **man-hour** (or **-day,** etc.) hour (or day, etc.) regarded in terms of the amount of work that could be done by one person within this period. **man in** (*or* **on**) **the street** ordinary average person. **man-made** artificial; synthetic. **man of letters** scholar; author. **man-of-war** armed ship. **to a man** all without exception. □□ **man'less** *adj.*
¶ Many consider the use of **man** to mean 'human being' or 'the human race' offensive and sexist.

man·a·cle /mánəkəl/ ● *n.* (usu. in *pl.*) **1** handcuff. **2** restraint. ● *v.tr.* fetter with manacles.

man·age /mánij/ *v.* **1** *tr.* organize; regulate; be in charge of. **2** *tr.* succeed in achieving; contrive. **3** *intr.* **a** succeed in one's aim, esp. against heavy odds. **b** meet one's needs with limited resources, etc. **4** *tr.* control. □ **managed care** comprehensive health care administered by a health maintenance organization or similar system.

man·age·a·ble /mánijəbəl/ *adj.* able to be easily managed, controlled, and accomplished, etc. □□ **man·age·a·bil'i·ty** *n.* **man'age·a·bly** *adv.*

man·age·ment /mánijmənt/ *n.* **1** managing or being managed. **2 a** professional administration of business concerns, public undertakings, etc. **b** people engaged in this.

man·ag·er /mánijər/ *n.* **1** person controlling or administering a business or part of a business. **2** person controlling the affairs, training, etc., of a person or team in sports, entertainment, etc. □□ **man·a·ge·ri·al** /mánijeéreeəl/ *adj.* **man·a·ge'ri·al·ly** *adv.* **man'ag·er·ship** *n.*

ma·ña·na /mənyáanə/ • *adv.* in the indefinite future. • *n.* an indefinite future time.

man·a·tee /mánətee/ *n.* large aquatic plant-eating mammal.

MANATEE

man·da·la /mándələ, mún-/ *n.* symbolic circular figure representing the universe in various religions.

man·da·rin /mándərin/ *n.* **1** (**Mandarin**) most widely spoken form of Chinese and official language of China. **2** *hist.* Chinese official in any of nine grades of the pre-Communist civil service. **3 a** party leader. **b** powerful member of the establishment. □□ **man′da·rin·ate** *n.*

man·date /mándayt/ • *n.* **1** official command or instruction by an authority. **2** support given by electors to a government, labor union, etc., for a policy or course of action. **3** commission to act for another. • *v.tr.* instruct (a delegate) to act or vote in a certain way. □□ **man·da′tor** *n.*

man·da·to·ry /mándətáwree/ *adj.* **1** of or conveying a command. **2** compulsory. □□ **man′da·to·ri·ly** *adv.*

man·di·ble /mándibəl/ *n.* **1** jaw, esp. the lower jaw in mammals and fishes. **2** upper or lower part of a bird's beak. **3** either half of the crushing organ in an arthropod's mouthparts. □□ **man·dib′u·lar** *adj.*

man·do·lin /mándəlín/ *n.* musical instrument resembling a lute, having paired metal strings plucked with a plectrum. □□ **man·do·lin′ist** *n.*

MANDOLIN

man·drake /mándrayk/ *n.* poisonous plant having emetic and narcotic properties and possessing a root once thought to resemble the human form.

man·drel /mándrəl/ *n.* **1** shaft in a lathe to which work is fixed while being turned. **2** cylindrical rod around which metal or other material is forged or shaped.

man·drill /mándril/ *n.* large W. African baboon.

mane /mayn/ *n.* long hair on the neck of a horse, lion, etc. □□ **maned** *adj.* (also in *comb.*). **mane′less** *adj.*

ma·nège /manézh/ *n.* (also **ma·nege**) **1** riding school. **2** movements of a trained horse. **3** horsemanship.

ma·neu·ver /mənoovər/ • *n.* **1** planned and controlled movement or series of moves. **2** (in *pl.*) large-scale exercise of troops, warships, etc. **3 a** often deceptive planned or controlled action. **b** skillful plan. • *v.* **1** *intr.* & *tr.* perform or cause to perform a maneuver. **2** *intr.* & *tr.* perform or cause (troops, etc.) to perform military maneuvers. **3 a** *tr.* handle adroitly. **b** *intr.* use artifice. □□ **ma·neu′ver·a·ble** *adj.* **ma·neu·ver·a·bil·i·ty** /-vrəbílitee, -vərə-/ *n.* **ma·neu′ver·er** *n.*

man·ful /mánfool/ *adj.* brave; resolute. □□ **man′ful·ly** *adv.* **man′ful·ness** *n.*

man·ga·nese /mánggənéez/ *n. Chem.* gray metallic transition element used with steel to make alloys. ¶ Symb.: **Mn**.

mange /maynj/ *n.* skin disease in hairy and woolly animals.

man·ger /máynjər/ *n.* long open box or trough in a stable, etc., for horses or cattle to eat from.

man·gle[1] /mánggəl/ *v.tr.* **1** hack, cut, or mutilate by blows, etc. **2** spoil; ruin. □□ **man′gler** *n.*

man·gle[2] /mánggəl/ *n.* machine having two or more cylinders between which clothes, etc., are squeezed and pressed.

man·go /mánggō/ *n.* (*pl.* **-goes** or **-gos**) **1** fleshy yellowish-red fruit. **2** E. Indian evergreen tree bearing this.

man·grove /mánggrōv/ *n.* tropical tree or shrub with many tangled roots above ground.

man·gy /máynjee/ *adj.* (**man·gi·er, man·gi·est**) **1** having mange. **2** squalid; shabby. □□ **man′gi·ly** *adv.* **man′gi·ness** *n.*

man·han·dle /mánhánd'l/ *v.tr. colloq.* handle roughly.

man·hat·tan /manhátən/ *n.* cocktail made of vermouth and whiskey, usu. flavored with bitters.

man·hole /mánhōl/ *n.* covered opening in a floor, pavement, sewer, etc., for workers to gain access.

man·hood /mánhood/ *n.* **1** state of being a man rather than a child or woman. **2 a** manliness; courage. **b** a man's sexual potency. **3** men of a country, etc.

man·hunt /mánhunt/ *n.* search for a person, esp. a criminal.

ma·ni·a /máyneeə/ *n.* **1** *Psychol.* mental illness marked by periods of great excitement and violence. **2** (often foll. by *for*) excessive enthusiasm; obsession (*has a mania for jogging*).

-mania /máyneeə/ *comb. form* **1** *Psychol.* denoting a special type of mental abnormality or obsession (*megalomania*). **2** denoting extreme enthusiasm or admiration (*bibliomania*).

ma·ni·ac /máyneeak/ *n.* **1** *colloq.* person exhibiting extreme symptoms of wild behavior, etc.; madman. **2** *colloq.* obsessive enthusiast. □□ **ma·ni·a·cal** /mənîəkəl/ *adj.* **ma·ni′a·cal·ly** *adv.*

man·ic /mánik/ • *adj.* of or affected by mania. • *n.* person having such a disorder. □ **manic-depressive** *Psychol. adj.* & *n.* affected by or relating to a mental disorder with alternating periods of elation and depression. □□ **man′i·cal·ly** *adv.*

man·i·cure /mánikyoor/ • *n.* cosmetic treatment of the hands and fingernails. • *v.tr.* give a manicure to (the hands or a person). □□ **man′ i·cur·ist** *n.*

man·i·fest[1] /mánifest/ • *adj.* clear or obvious. • *v. tr.* show plainly to the eye or mind. □ **Manifest Destiny** 19th c. doctrine asserting that the United States was destined to expand westward to the Pacific. □□ **man·i·fes·ta′tion** *n.* **man′i·fest·ly** *adv.*

man·i·fest[2] /mánifest/ *n.* cargo or passenger list.

man·i·fes·to /mániféstō/ *n.* (*pl.* **-tos** or **-toes**) public declaration of policy and aims esp. political or social.

man·i·fold /mánifōld/ • *adj. literary* **1** many and various. **2** having various forms, parts, applications, etc. • *n.* **1** manifold thing. **2** *Mech.* pipe or chamber branching into several openings.

man·i·kin /mánikin/ *n.* (also **man′ni·kin**) **1** little man; dwarf. **2** anatomical model of the body.

Ma·nil·a /mənílə/ *n.* (also **Ma·nil′la**) **1** (in full **Manila hemp**) strong fiber of a Philippine tree. **2** (also **ma·nil′a**) strong brown paper made from Manila hemp or other material.

ma·nip·u·late /mənípyəlayt/ *v.tr.* **1** handle, esp. skillfully. **2** manage (a person, situation, etc.) to one's own advantage, esp. unfairly. **3** manually examine and treat (a part of the body). □□ **ma·nip·u·la·ble** /-ləbəl/ *adj.* **ma·nip·u·la·tion** /-láyshən/ *n.* **ma·nip·u·la·tive** /mənípyələtiv/ *adj.* **ma·nip′u·la·tor** *n.*

man·kind *n.* **1** /mánkínd/ human species. **2** /mánkīnd/ male people, as distinct from female.

man·ly /mánlee/ *adj.* (**man·li·er**, **man·li·est**) **1** having qualities regarded as admirable in a man, such as courage, frankness, etc. **2** befitting a man. □□ **man′li·ness** *n.*

man·na /mánə/ *n.* **1** substance miraculously supplied as food to the Israelites in the wilderness (Exod. 16). **2** unexpected benefit (esp. *manna from heaven*).

manned /mand/ *adj.* (of an aircraft, spacecraft, etc.) having a human crew.

man·ne·quin /mánikin/ *n.* **1** fashion model. **2** window dummy.

man·ner /mánər/ *n.* **1** way a thing is done or happens. **2** (in *pl.*) **a** social behavior (*it is bad manners to stare*). **b** polite or well-bred behavior (*he has no manners*). **3** person's outward bearing, way of speaking, etc. **4** style in literature, art, etc. (*in the manner of Rembrandt*). □ **to the manner born** *colloq.* naturally at ease in a specified job, situation, etc. □□ **man′ner·less** *adj.* (in sense 2b).

man·nered /mánərd/ *adj.* **1** (in *comb.*) behaving in a specified way (*ill-mannered*). **2** artificial.

man·ner·ism /mánərizəm/ *n.* **1** habitual gesture or way of speaking, etc.; idiosyncrasy. **2 a** stylistic trick in art, etc. **b** excessive use of these. □□ **man′ner·ist** *n.* **man·ner·is′tic** *adj.*

man·ner·ly /mánərlee/ • *adj.* well-mannered; polite. • *adv.* politely. □□ **man′ner·li·ness** *n.*

man·ni·kin var. of MANIKIN.

man·nish /mánish/ *adj.* **1** usu. *derog.* (of a woman) masculine in appearance or manner. **2** characteristic of a man. □□ **man′nish·ly** *adv.* **man′nish·ness** *n.*

ma·nom·e·ter /mənómitər/ *n.* pressure gauge for gases and liquids. □□ **man·o·met·ric** /mánəmétrik/ *adj.*

man·or /mánər/ *n.* (also **man′or house**) large country house with lands. □□ **ma·no·ri·al** /mənáwreeəl/ *adj.*

man·pow·er /mánpowr/ *n.* number of people available or required for work, service, etc.

man·qué /maaNkáy/ *adj.* (placed after noun) that might have been but is not; unfulfilled (*a comic actor manqué*).

man·sard /mánsaard/ *n.* roof that has four sloping sides, each of which becomes steeper halfway down. See illus. at ROOF.

manse /mans/ *n.* house of a minister, esp. a Presbyterian.

man·ser·vant /mánservənt/ *n.* (*pl.* **men·ser·vants**) male servant.

-manship /mənship/ *suffix* forming nouns denoting skill in a subject or activity (*craftsmanship; gamesmanship*).

man·sion /mánshən/ *n.* large house.

man·slaugh·ter /mánslawtər/ *n. Law* unlawful killing of a human being without malice aforethought.

man·tel·piece /mánt′lpees/ *n.* (also **man·tel**) structure of wood, marble, etc., above and around a fireplace.

man·til·la /mantílə, -te′eə/ *n.* lace scarf worn by Spanish women over the hair and shoulders.

man·tis /mántis/ *n.* (*pl.* same or **man·tis·es**) (in full **praying mantis**) predatory insect that holds its forelegs in a position suggestive of hands folded in prayer.

MANTIS

man·tis·sa /mantísə/ *n.* part of a logarithm after the decimal point.

man·tle /mánt′l/ • *n.* **1** loose sleeveless cloak. **2** covering (*mantle of snow*). **3** lacelike tube fixed around a gas jet to give an incandescent light. **4** region between the crust and the core of the earth. • *v. tr.* clothe; conceal; envelop.

man·tra /mántrə, máan-, mún-/ *n.* **1** word or sound repeated to aid concentration in meditation, orig. in Hinduism and Buddhism. **2** Vedic hymn.

man·u·al /mányōōəl/ • *adj.* **1** of or done with the hands (*manual labor*). **2** (of a machine, etc.) worked by hand, not automatically. • *n.* **1** book of instructions. **2** *Mil.* exercise in handling a rifle, etc. □□ **man′u·al·ly** *adv.*

man·u·fac·ture /mányəfákchər/ • *n.* making of articles, esp. in a factory, etc. • *v.tr.* **1** make (articles), esp. on an industrial scale. **2** invent or fabricate (evidence, a story, etc.). □□ **man· u·fac′tur·er** *n.*

man·u·mit /mányəmít/ *v.tr.* (**man·u·mit·ted, man·u·mit·ting**) *hist.* set (a slave) free. □□ **man·u·mis·sion** /-míshən/ *n.*

ma·nure /mənŏŏr, -nyŏŏr/ • *n.* fertilizer, esp. dung. • *v.tr.* (also *absol.*) apply manure to (land, etc.).

man·u·script /mányəskript/ • *n.* **1** handwritten or typed text. **2** handwritten form. • *adj.* written by hand.

Manx /mangks/ • *adj.* of the Isle of Man. • *n.* **1** former Celtic language of the Isle of Man. **2** (treated as *pl.*) Manx people. □ **Manx cat** breed of tailless cat.

man·y /ménee/ • *adj.* (**more** /mawr/; **most** /mōst/) great in number; numerous. • *n.* (as *pl.*) a large number (*many went*).

Mao·ism /mówizəm/ *n.* Communist doctrines of Mao Zedong (d. 1976), Chinese statesman. □□ **Mao·ist** *n.* & *adj.*

Mao·ri /mówree/ • *n.* (*pl.* same or **Mao·ris**) **1** member of the Polynesian aboriginal people of New Zealand. **2** language of the Maori. • *adj.* of the Maori.

map /map/ • *n.* **1** flat representation of the earth's surface, or part of it. **2** two-dimensional representation of the stars, the heavens, the moon, etc. • *v.tr.* (**mapped, map·ping**) represent on a map. □ **map out** arrange in detail; plan. □□ **map·less** *adj.* **map·per** *n.*

ma·ple /máypəl/ *n.* **1** any of various trees grown for shade, ornament, wood, or its sugar. **2** wood of the maple. □ **maple sugar** sugar produced by evaporating the sap of the sugar maple, etc. **maple syrup** syrup produced from the sap of the sugar maple, etc.

Mar. *abbr.* March.

mar /maar/ *v.tr.* (**marred, mar·ring**) spoil; disfigure.

mar·a·bou /márəbŏŏ/ *n.* (also **mar·a·bout**) **1** large W. African stork. **2** its down as a trimming for hats, etc.

ma·ra·ca /məraákə/ *n.* gourd or gourd-shaped container filled with beans, etc., shaken as a percussion instrument.

mar·a·schi·no /márəske'enŏ, -shée-/ *n.* (*pl.* **-nos**) sweet liqueur made from a Dalmatian cherry. □ **maraschino cherry** cherry with maraschino flavor.

Ma·ra·thi /məraátee, -rátee/ *n.* (also **Mah·rat·ti**) language of central and W. India.

mar·a·thon /márəthon/ *n.* **1** long-distance running race, usu. of 26 miles 385 yards (42.195 km). **2** long-lasting or difficult task, operation, etc. (often *attrib.*: *a marathon shopping expedition*). □□ **mar·a·thon·er** *n.*

ma·raud /məráwd/ *v.* **1** *intr.* make a plundering raid. **2** *tr.* plunder (a place). □□ **ma·raud·er** *n.*

mar·ble /maárbəl/ • *n.* **1** crystalline limestone capable of taking a polish, used in sculpture and architecture. **2** (often *attrib.*) **a** anything made of marble (*marble clock*). **b** anything resembling marble in hardness, coldness, durability, etc. **3 a** small ball of marble, glass, clay, etc., used as a toy. **b** (in *pl.*; treated as *sing.*) game using these. **4** (in *pl.*) *sl.* one's mental faculties. • *v.tr.* **1** (esp. as **marbled** *adj.*) stain or color (paper, soap, etc.) to look like marble. **2** (as **marbled** *adj.*) (of meat) streaked with alternating layers of lean and fat. □□ **mar·bly** *adj.*

March /maarch/ *n.* third month of the year.

march¹ /maarch/ • *v.* **1** *intr.* walk in a military manner with a regular tread. **2** *tr.* cause to march or walk (*marched him out of the room*). **3** *intr.* **a** walk or proceed steadily. **b** (of events, etc.) continue unrelentingly (*time marches on*). • *n.* **1 a** act of marching. **b** uniform step of troops, etc. **2** progress or continuity. **3** piece of music composed to accompany a march. □ **marching orders 1** *Mil.* direction for troops to depart for war, etc. **2** dismissal. □□ **march·er** *n.*

march² /maarch/ *n.* *hist.* (usu. in *pl.*) boundary, frontier.

Mar·di Gras /maárdee graá/ *n.* last day before Lent, celebrated in some places, as New Orleans; Shrove Tuesday.

mare¹ /mair/ *n.* female of any equine animal, esp. the horse. □ **mare's nest** illusory discovery.

ma·re² /maáray/ *n.* (*pl.* **ma·ri·a** /maáreeə/ or **ma·res**) large dark flat area on the moon.

mar·ga·rine /maárjərin/ *n.* butter substitute made from vegetable oils or animal fats with milk, etc.

mar·ga·ri·ta /maargəree'etə/ *n.* cocktail made with tequila, lime or lemon juice, and orange-flavored liqueur.

mar·gin /maárjin/ *n.* **1** edge or border. **2** blank border on each side of the print on a page, etc. **3** amount (of time, money, etc.) by which a thing exceeds, falls short, etc. (*margin of profit*). **4** amount deposited with a stockbroker by the customer when borrowing from the broker to purchase securities. □ **margin of error** allowance for miscalculation. □□ **mar·gin·al** *adj.* **mar·gin·al·ly** *adv.*

mar·gi·na·li·a /maárjináyleeə/ *n.pl.* marginal notes.

mar·gin·al·ize /maárjinəlīz/ *v.tr.* make or treat as insignificant. □□ **mar·gin·al·i·za·tion** *n.*

ma·ri·a·chi /maareeaáchee, mar-/ *n.* **1** Mexican band of strolling musicians. **2** music played by such a band.

mar·i·gold /márigōld/ *n.* plant with bright yellow, orange, or maroon flowers.

ma·ri·jua·na /máriwaánə/ *n.* (also **ma·ri·hua·na**) dried leaves, etc., of hemp, smoked or ingested as a drug.

ma·rim·ba /mərímbə/ *n.* **1** xylophone of Africa and Central America. **2** modern instrument derived from this.

ma·ri·na /məreénə/ *n.* harbor for pleasure yachts, etc.

mar·i·nade /márináyd/ • *n.* **1** mixture of wine, vinegar, oil, spices, etc., in which meat, fish, etc., is soaked before cooking. **2** meat, fish, etc., so soaked. • *v.tr.* = MARINATE.

ma·ri·na·ra /marinaárə/ *adj.* (of a pasta sauce) made with tomatoes, spices, etc., usu. without meat.

mar·i·nate /márinayt/ *v.tr.* soak (meat, fish, etc.) in a marinade. □□ **mar·i·na·tion** /-náyshən/ *n.*

ma·rine /məreén/ • *adj.* **1** of, found in, or produced by the sea. **2** of or relating to shipping or naval matters (*marine insurance*). • *n.* **1** country's shipping, fleet, or navy (*merchant marine*). **2 a** member of the US Marine Corps. **b** member of a body of troops trained to serve on land or sea.

mar·i·ner /márinər/ *n.* sailor.

mar·i·on·ette /máreeənét/ n. puppet worked by strings.

mar·i·tal /márit(ə)l/ adj. of marriage or the relations between husband and wife. □□ **mar'i·tal·ly** adv.

mar·i·time /máritīm/ adj. **1** connected with the sea or seafaring (maritime insurance). **2** living or found near the sea.

mar·jo·ram /máarjərəm/ n. aromatic herb used in cooking.

mark[1] /maark/ • n. **1** trace, sign, stain, etc., on a surface, etc. **2** (esp. in comb.) **a** written or printed symbol (question mark). **b** number or letter denoting excellence, conduct, proficiency, etc. (black mark). **3** sign or indication of quality, character, feeling, etc. **4** target, object, goal, etc. **5** line, etc., indicating a position; marker. **6** (usu. **Mark**) (followed by a numeral) particular design, model, etc., of a car, aircraft, etc. **7** runner's starting point in a race. • v.tr. **1 a** make a mark on (a thing or person), esp. by writing, cutting, scraping, etc. **b** put an identifying mark, initials, name, etc., on. **2** allot marks to; correct (a student's work, etc.). **3** attach a price to. **4** notice or observe (she marked his agitation). **5** characterize (day was marked by storms). □ **beside** (or **off** or **wide of**) **the mark 1** not to the point; irrelevant. **2** not accurate. **make one's mark** attain distinction. **mark down 1** mark (goods, etc.) at a lower price. **2** make a written note of. **mark time 1** Mil. march on the spot, without moving forward. **2** wait. **mark up 1** mark (goods, etc.) at a higher price. **2** mark or correct (text, etc.).

mark[2] /maark/ n. = DEUTSCHE MARK.

mark·down /máarkdown/ n. reduction in price.

marked /maarkt/ adj. **1** having a visible mark. **2** clearly noticeable; evident (a marked difference). **3** (of playing cards) having distinctive marks on their backs to assist cheating. □□ **mark·ed·ly** /-kidlee/ adv. **mark'ed·ness** n.

mark·er /máarkər/ n. **1** stone, post, etc., used to mark a position, etc. **2** person or thing that marks. **3** sl. IOU.

mar·ket /máarkit/ • n. **1** gathering of people for the purchase and sale of provisions, livestock, etc. **2** open space or covered building used for this. **3** demand for a commodity. **4** place or group providing such a demand. **5** conditions as regards, or opportunity for, buying or selling. **6** (prec. by the) trade in a specified commodity (the grain market). • v. tr. offer for sale. □ **market research** study of consumers' needs and preferences. □□ **mar·ket·a·bil'i·ty** n. **mar'ket·a·ble** adj. **mar'ket·er** n.

mar·ket·ing /máarkiting/ n. **1** selling or buying in a market. **2** activity or process involving research, promotion, sales, and distribution of a product or service.

mar·ket·place /máarkitpláys/ n. **1** open space where a market is held in a town. **2** scene of actual dealings. **3** forum or sphere for the exchange of ideas, etc.

mark·ing /máarking/ n. (usu. in pl.) **1** identification mark, esp. a symbol on an aircraft. **2** coloring of an animal's fur, feathers, skin, etc.

marks·man /máarksmən/ n. (pl. **-men**; fem. **-wom·an**, pl. **-wom·en**) person skilled in shooting, esp. with a pistol or rifle. □□ **marks'man·ship** n.

mark·up /máarkup/ n. amount added to cost for profit.

mar·lin /máarlin/ n. large long-nosed marine fish.

mar·ma·lade /máarməlayd/ n. preserve of citrus fruit, usu. bitter oranges, made like jam.

mar·mo·set /máarməset, -zet/ n. small tropical American monkey having a long bushy tail.

mar·mot /máarmot/ n. burrowing rodent with a heavyset body and short bushy tail.

ma·roon[1] /mərṓn/ adj. & n. brownish-crimson.

ma·roon[2] /mərṓn/ v.tr. leave (a person) isolated in a desolate place (esp. an island).

marque /maark/ n. make of a product, as a sports car.

mar·quee /maarkée/ n. projecting roof over an entry.

mar·quess /máarkwis/ n. British nobleman ranking between duke and earl.

mar·que·try /máarkitree/ n. (also **mar'que·te·rie**) inlaid work in wood, ivory, etc.

mar·quis /máarkwis, -kée/ n. nobleman ranking between duke and count.

mar·quise /maarkéez, -kée/ n. **1** wife or widow of a marquis. **2** woman holding the rank of marquis.

mar·riage /márij/ n. **1** legal union of a man and a woman. **2** wedding. **3** intimate union (marriage of true minds). □□ **mar·riage·a·bil'i·ty** n. **mar'riage·a·ble** adj.

mar·ried /máreed/ • adj. **1** united in marriage. **2** of or relating to marriage (married life). • n. (usu. in pl.) married person (young marrieds).

mar·row /márō/ n. soft fatty substance in the cavities of bones.

mar·ry /máree/ v. (**-ries, -ried**) **1** tr. **a** take as one's wife or husband in marriage. **b** join or give in marriage. **2** tr. **a** unite intimately. **b** correlate (things) as a pair. □ **marry off** find a wife or husband for.

Mars /maarz/ n. reddish planet, fourth in order of distance from the sun and next beyond the earth.

marsh /maarsh/ n. low land flooded in wet weather and usu. watery at all times. □ **marsh gas** methane. □□ **marsh'y** adj. (**marsh·i·er, marsh·i·est**). **marsh'i·ness** n.

mar·shal /máarshəl/ • n. **1** officer of a judicial district, similar to a sheriff. **2** head of a fire department. **3** high-ranking officer in the armed forces of certain countries (air marshal). **4** officer arranging ceremonies, controlling procedure at races, etc. • v.tr. arrange (soldiers, facts, one's thoughts, etc.) in due order. □□ **mar'shal·er** n.

> **marshal** Middle English (denoting a high-ranking officer of state): from Old French mareschal 'farrier, commander,' from late Latin mariscalcus, from Germanic elements meaning 'horse' (related to mare) and 'servant.'

marsh·mal·low /máarshmélō, -málō/ n. spongy confection made of sugar, albumen, gelatin, etc.

mar·su·pi·al /maarsoopeeəl/ • n. mammal characterized by being born incompletely developed and usu. carried and suckled in a pouch. • adj. of or like a marsupial.

mart /maart/ n. market.

mar·ten /máart'n/ *n.* weasellike carnivore having valuable fur.

mar·tial /máarshǝl/ *adj.* **1** of or appropriate to warfare. **2** warlike; brave; fond of fighting. □ **martial arts** fighting sports such as judo and karate. **martial law** military government, involving the suspension of ordinary law. □□ **mar′tial·ly** *adv.*

Mar·tian /máarshǝn/ • *adj.* of the planet Mars. • *n.* hypothetical inhabitant of Mars.

mar·tin /máart'n/ *n.* a kind of swallow.

mar·ti·net /máart'nét/ *n.* strict (esp. military or naval) disciplinarian.

mar·ti·ni /maarteénee/ *n.* cocktail made of gin and dry vermouth, often garnished with a green olive, lemon peel, etc.

mar·tyr /máartǝr/ • *n.* **1** person who suffers or is put to death for refusing to renounce a faith or belief. **2** constant sufferer. • *v.tr.* **1** put to death as a martyr. **2** torment. □□ **mar′tyr·dom** *n.*

mar·vel /máarvǝl/ • *n.* wonderful thing or person. • *v.intr.* feel surprise or wonder. □□ **mar′vel·er** *n.*

mar·vel·ous /máarvǝlǝs/ *adj.* **1** astonishing. **2** excellent. □□ **mar′vel·ous·ly** *adv.*

Marx·ism /máarksizǝm/ *n.* anticapitalist political and economic theories of Karl Marx, advocating communism and socialism. □□ **Marx′ist** *n.* & *adj.*

mar·zi·pan /máarzipan/ *n.* paste of ground almonds, sugar, etc., used in confectionery.

mas·car·a /maskárǝ/ *n.* cosmetic for darkening the eyelashes.

mas·cot /maskot/ *n.* person, animal, or thing that is supposed to bring good luck.

mas·cu·line /maskyǝlin/ • *adj.* **1** of or characteristic of men. **2** manly; vigorous. **3** *Gram.* of or denoting the male gender. • *n. Gram.* masculine gender; masculine word. □□ **mas′cu·line·ly** *adv.* **mas·cu·lin′i·ty** *n.*

ma·ser /máyzǝr/ *n.* device for amplifying or generating coherent monochromatic electromagnetic radiation in the microwave range (acronym of *m*icrowave *a*mplification by *s*timulated *e*mission of *r*adiation; cf. LASER).

MASH /mash/ *abbr.* Mobile Army Surgical Hospital.

mash /mash/ • *n.* **1** soft mixture. **2** mixture of boiled grain, bran, etc., given warm to horses, etc. **3** mixture of malt and hot water used in brewing. **4** soft pulp. • *v.tr.* reduce (potatoes, etc.) to a uniform mass by crushing. □□ **mash′er** *n.*

mask /mask/ • *n.* **1** covering for all or part of the face as a disguise or for protection. **2** likeness of a person's face, esp. one made by taking a mold from the face (*death mask*). **3** disguise or pretense (*throw off the mask*). • *v.tr.* **1** cover (the face, etc.) with a mask. **2** disguise or conceal (a taste, one's feelings, etc.). **3** protect from a process. □□ **mask′er** *n.*

mas·och·ism /másǝkizǝm/ *n.* **1** form of (esp. sexual) perversion involving one's own pain or humiliation. **2** *colloq.* enjoyment of what appears to be painful or tiresome. □□ **mas′och·ist** *n.* **mas·och·is′tic** *adj.* **mas·och·is′ti·cal·ly** *adv.*

ma·son /máysǝn/ *n.* **1** person who builds with stone or brick. **2** (**Mason**) Freemason.

Ma·son-Dix·on line /máysǝn-díksǝn/ *n.* bound-

ary between Maryland and Pennsylvania, taken as the northern limit of the slave-owning states before the abolition of slavery.

Ma·son·ic /mǝsónik/ *adj.* of or relating to Freemasons.

ma·son·ry /máysǝnree/ *n.* **1 a** work of a mason. **b** stonework; brickwork. **2** (**Masonry**) Freemasonry.

masque /mask/ *n.* dramatic and musical entertainment esp. of the 16th and 17th c. □□ **mas′quer** *n.*

mas·quer·ade /máskǝráyd/ • *n.* **1** false show or pretense. **2** masked ball. • *v.intr.* (often foll. by *as*) appear in disguise, assume a false appearance. □□ **mas·quer·ad′er** *n.*

Mass. *abbr.* Massachusetts.

mass¹ /mas/ • *n.* **1** coherent body of matter of indefinite shape. **2** dense aggregation of objects (*a mass of fibers*). **3** large number or amount. **4** (prec. by *the*) **a** the majority. **b** (in *pl.*) ordinary people. **5** *Physics* quantity of matter a body contains. **6** (*attrib.*) on a large scale (*mass action*). • *v.* assemble into a mass. □ **mass-market** see MARKET. **mass media** = MEDIA 2. **mass noun** *Gram.* noun that is not countable and cannot be used with the indefinite article or in the plural (e.g., *happiness*). **mass-produce** produce by mass production. **mass production** production of large quantities of a standardized article by a standardized mechanical process. □□ **mass′less** *adj.*

mass² /mas/ *n.* (often **Mass**) celebration of the Eucharist, esp. in the Roman Catholic Church.

mas·sa·cre /másǝkǝr/ • *n.* general slaughter (of persons, occasionally of animals). • *v.tr.* **1** make a massacre of. **2** murder (esp. a large number of people) cruelly or violently.

mas·sage /mǝsaázh, -saáj/ • *n.* rubbing, kneading, etc., of the body with the hands for therapeutic benefit. • *v.tr.* apply massage to. □□ **mas·sag′er** *n.*

mas·seur /masőr/ *n.* (*fem.* **mas·seuse** /masőz/) person who provides massage professionally.

mas·sive /másiv/ *adj.* **1** large and heavy or solid. **2** exceptionally large. **3** substantial; impressive (*a massive reputation*). □□ **mas′sive·ly** *adv.* **mas′sive·ness** *n.*

mast¹ /mast/ *n.* **1** long upright post for supporting a ship's sails. **2** post or latticework upright for supporting a radio or television antenna. **3** flagpole (*half-mast*). □□ **mast′ed** *adj.* (also in *comb.*). **mas′ter** *n.* (also in *comb.*).

mast² /mast/ *n.* fruit of the beech, oak, chestnut, and other forest trees, esp. as food for pigs.

mas·tec·to·my /mastéktǝmee/ *n.* (*pl.* **-mies**) *Surgery* removal of all or part of a breast.

mas·ter /mástǝr/ • *n.* **1** person having control or ownership (*master of the house*). **2** *Naut.* captain of a merchant ship. **3** person who has or gets the upper hand (*we shall see which of us is master*). **4** skilled practitioner (often *attrib.*: *master carpenter*). **5** holder of a university degree orig. giving authority to teach in the university (*Master of Arts; Master of Science*). **6** great artist. **7** *Chess, etc.* player of proven ability at international level. **8** original version (e.g., of a film or audio recording) from which a series of copies can be made. **9** (**Master**) title prefixed to the name of a boy not old enough to be called *Mr.* •

adj. **1** commanding; superior (*a master spirit*).
2 main; principal (*master bedroom*). **3** controlling others (*master plan*). • *v.tr.* **1** overcome; defeat. **2** acquire complete knowledge of or skill in. □ **master key** key that opens several locks, each of which also has its own key. **Master of Ceremonies** see CEREMONY. □□ **mas′ter·dom** *n.* **mas′ter·hood** *n.* **mas′ter·less** *adj.*

mas·ter·ful /mástərfŏŏl/ *adj.* **1** imperious; domineering. **2** masterly. □□ **mas′ter·ful·ly** *adv.* **mas′ter·ful·ness** *n.*

¶ **Masterful** and **masterly** overlap in meaning and are sometimes confused. Leaving aside **masterful**'s meaning of 'domineering,' it also means 'very skillful, masterly.' However, **masterful** used in this sense generally describes a person, e.g., *He has limited talent but he's masterful at exploiting it*, while **masterly** usually describes an achievement or action, e.g., *That was a masterly response to our opponents' arguments*.

mas·ter·ly /mástərlee/ *adj.* very skillful. □□ **mas′ter·li·ness** *n.*

mas·ter·mind /mástərmīnd/ • *n.* **1** person with an outstanding intellect. **2** person directing an intricate operation. • *v.tr.* plan and direct (a scheme or enterprise).

mas·ter·piece /mástərpees/ *n.* **1** outstanding piece of artistry or workmanship. **2** person's best work.

mas·ter·stroke /mástərstrōk/ *n.* outstandingly skillful act of policy, etc.

mas·ter·work /mástərwərk/ *n.* masterpiece.

mas·ter·y /mástəree/ *n.* **1** dominion; sway. **2** comprehensive knowledge or skill.

mast·head /mást-hed/ *n.* **1** highest part of a ship's mast. **2 a** top of a newspaper, etc., at the head of the front or editorial page. **b** printed notice in a newspaper, magazine, etc., giving details of staff, ownership, etc.

mas·ti·cate /mástikayt/ *v.tr.* grind or chew (food) with one's teeth. □□ **mas·ti·ca·tion** /-káyshən/ *n.* **mas′ti·ca·tor** *n.*

mas·tiff /mástif/ *n.* large strong breed of dog.

mas·to·don /mástədon/ *n.* large extinct mammal resembling the elephant.

mas·toid /mástoyd/ • *adj.* shaped like a woman's breast. • *n.* conical prominence on the temporal bone behind the ear.

mas·tur·bate /mástərbayt/ *v.* arouse oneself sexually or cause (another person) to be aroused by manual stimulation of the genitals. □□ **mas·tur·ba·tion** /-báyshən/ *n.* **mas′tur·ba·tor** *n.*

mat[1] /mat/ • *n.* **1** piece of coarse material for wiping shoes on, esp. a doormat. **2** piece of cork, rubber, plastic, etc., for protecting a surface. **3** piece of resilient material for landing on in gymnastics, wrestling, etc. • *v.* (**mat·ted, mat·ting**) **1** *tr.* (esp. as **matted** *adj.*) entangle in a thick mass (*matted hair*). **2** *intr.* become matted.

mat[2] var. of MATTE.

mat[3] /mat/ *n.* = MATRIX.

mat·a·dor /mátədawr/ *n.* bullfighter whose task is to kill the bull.

match[1] /mach/ • *n.* **1** contest or game of skill. **2 a** equal contender. **b** person or thing exactly like or corresponding to another. **3** marriage. • *v.* **1 a** *tr.* be equal to or harmonious with; correspond to. **b** *intr.* correspond; harmonize.

2 *tr.* place in conflict, contest, or competition with. **3** *tr.* find material, etc., that matches (another). **4** *tr.* find a person or thing suitable for another (*matching unemployed workers to available jobs*). □ **match point 1** *Tennis,* etc. **a** the state of a game when one side needs only one more point to win the match. **b** this point. **2** *Bridge* unit of scoring in matches and tournaments. □□ **match′a·ble** *adj.*

match[2] /mach/ *n.* short thin piece of flammable material tipped with a composition that can be ignited by friction.

match·box /máchboks/ *n.* box for holding matches.

match·less /máchlis/ *adj.* without an equal, incomparable. □□ **match′less·ly** *adv.*

match·mak·er /máchmaykər/ *n.* person who tries to arrange an agreement or relationship between two parties, esp. a marriage partnership. □□ **match′mak·ing** *n.*

match·stick /máchstik/ *n.* stem of a match.

mate[1] /mayt/ • *n.* **1** friend or fellow worker. **2 a** each of a pair, esp. of animals, birds, or socks. **b** *colloq.* partner in marriage. **c** (in *comb.*) fellow member or joint occupant of (*roommate*). **3** *Naut.* officer on a merchant ship subordinate to the master. • *v.* **1** *tr.* bring together for marriage or breeding. **2** *intr.* come together for marriage or breeding. □□ **mate′less** *adj.*

mate[2] /mayt/ *n. & v.tr. Chess* = CHECKMATE.

ma·te·ri·al /mətéereeəl/ • *n.* **1** matter from which a thing is made. **2** cloth; fabric. **3** (in *pl.*) things needed for an activity (*building materials*). **4** (in *sing.* or *pl.*) information, etc., to be used in writing a book, etc. (*experimental material*). • *adj.* **1** of matter; corporeal. **2** concerned with bodily comfort, etc. (*material well-being*). **3** important; essential; relevant (*at the material time*). □□ **ma·te·ri·al·i·ty** /-reeálitee/ *n.*

ma·te·ri·al·ism /mətéereeəlizəm/ *n.* **1** tendency to prefer material possessions and physical comfort to spiritual values. **2** *Philos.* theory that nothing exists but matter and its movements and modifications. □□ **ma·te′ri·al·ist** *n.* **ma·te·ri·al·is′tic** *adj.* **ma·te·ri·al·is′ti·cal·ly** *adv.*

ma·te·ri·al·ize /mətéereeəlīz/ *v.* **1** *intr.* become actual fact. **2** *intr. colloq.* appear or be present when expected. **3** *tr.* represent or express in material form. □□ **ma·te·ri·al·i·za′tion** *n.*

ma·te·ri·al·ly /mətéereeəlee/ *adv.* substantially, considerably.

ma·ter·nal /mətérnəl/ *adj.* **1** of or like a mother. **2** motherly. **3** related through the mother (*maternal uncle*). □□ **ma·ter′nal·ism** *n.* **ma·ter·nal·is′tic** *adj.* **ma·ter′nal·ly** *adv.*

ma·ter·ni·ty /mətérnitee/ *n.* **1** motherhood. **2** (*attrib.*) for women during and just after childbirth (*maternity hospital*).

math /math/ *n. colloq.* mathematics.

math·e·mat·i·cal /máthimátikəl/ *adj.* **1** of mathematics. **2** rigorously precise; exact. □□ **math·e·mat′i·cal·ly** *adv.*

math·e·mat·ics /máthimátiks/ *n.pl.* **1** (also treated as *sing.*) abstract science of number, quantity, and space. **2** (as *pl.*) use of mathematics in calculation, etc. □□ **math·e·ma·ti·cian** /-mətíshən/ *n.*

mat·i·née /mat'náy/ *n.* (also **mat·i·nee′**) afternoon performance in a theater, etc. □ **matinée idol** handsome actor admired esp. by women.

mat·ins /mát'nz/ *n.* (as *sing.* or *pl.*) service of morning prayer in churches of the Anglican communion.

ma·tri·arch /máytreeaark/ *n.* female head of a family or tribe. □□ **ma·tri·ar·chal** /-aárkəl/ *adj.* **ma·tri·ar·chy** /-aárkee/ *n.*

ma·tri·ces *pl.* of MATRIX.

mat·ri·cide /mátrisīd, máy-/ *n.* **1** killing of one's mother. **2** person who does this. □□ **mat·ri·ci·d'al** *adj.*

ma·tric·u·late /mətríkyəlayt/ *v.* **1** *intr.* be enrolled at a college or university. **2** *tr.* admit (a student) to membership of a college or university. □□ **ma·tric·u·la·tion** /-láyshən/ *n.*

mat·ri·mo·ny /mátrimōnee/ *n.* (*pl.* **-nies**) **1** rite of marriage. **2** state of being married. □□ **mat·ri·mo·ni·al** /-móneeəl/ *adj.* **mat·ri·mo'ni·al·ly** *adv.*

ma·trix /máytriks/ *n.* (*pl.* **ma·tri·ces** /-triseez/ or **ma·trix·es**) mold in which a thing is cast or shaped.

ma·tron /máytrən/ *n.* **1** married woman, esp. a dignified and sober one. **2** woman supervisor, as in an institution. □ **matron of honor** married woman attending the bride at a wedding. □□ **ma'tron·ly** *adj.*

matte /mat/ (also **matt** or **mat**) • *adj.* (of a color, surface, etc.) dull, without luster. • *n.* (in full **matte paint**) paint formulated to give a dull flat finish.

mat·ter /mátər/ • *n.* **1 a** physical substance in general, as distinct from mind and spirit. **b** that which has mass and occupies space. **2** particular substance (*coloring matter*). **3** thing that is amiss (*what is the matter?*). **4** content as distinct from its manner or form. **5** affair or situation being considered, esp. in a specified way (*a serious matter*). **6** *Physiol.* **a** any substance in or discharged from the body. **b** pus. • *v.intr.* be of importance; have significance. □ **as a matter of fact** in reality (esp. to correct a falsehood or misunderstanding). **no matter 1** regardless of. **2** it is of no importance.

mat·ter-of-fact /mátərəfákt/ *adj.* (see also MATTER). **1** unimaginative; prosaic. **2** unemotional. □□ **mat'ter-of-fact'ly** *adv.* **mat'ter-of-fact'ness** *n.*

mat·ting /máting/ *n.* fabric for mats.

mat·tock /mátək/ *n.* agricultural tool shaped like a pickax, with an adze and a chisel edge as the ends of the head.

MATTOCK

mat·tress /mátris/ *n.* fabric case stuffed with soft, firm, or springy material, or a similar case filled with air or water, used on or as a bed.

ma·ture /məchōōr, -tyōōr, -tōōr/ • *adj.* (**ma·tur·er, ma·tur·est**) **1** with fully developed powers of body and mind; adult. **2** complete in natural development; ripe. **3** (of thought, intentions, etc.) duly careful and adequate. **4** (of a bond, etc.) due for payment. • *v.* **1** *tr.* & *intr.* develop fully; ripen. **2** *intr.* (of a bond, etc.) become due for payment. □□ **ma·ture'ly** *adv.* **ma·ture'ness** *n.* **ma·tu'ri·ty** *n.*

mat·zo /maátsə/ *n.* (also **mat'zoh**; *pl.* **-zos** or **-zohs** or **mat·zoth** /-sōt/) unleavened bread, served esp. at Passover.

maud·lin /máwdlin/ *adj.* weakly or tearfully sentimental, esp. in a tearful and effusive stage of drunkenness.

maul /mawl/ • *v.tr.* **1** beat and bruise. **2** handle roughly or carelessly. • *n.* heavy hammer. □□ **maul'er** *n.*

maun·der /máwndər/ *v.intr.* talk in a rambling manner.

mau·so·le·um /máwsəleéəm/ *n.* large and grand tomb.

mauve /mōv/ • *adj.* pale purple. • *n.* **1** this color. **2** bright but delicate pale purple dye. □□ **mauv'ish** *adj.*

mav·er·ick /mávərik, mávrik/ *n.* **1** unbranded calf or yearling. **2** unorthodox or independent-minded person.

maw /maw/ *n.* **1** stomach of an animal. **2** jaws or throat of a voracious animal.

mawk·ish /máwkish/ *adj.* sentimental in a feeble or sickly way. □□ **mawk'ish·ly** *adv.* **mawk'ish·ness** *n.*

max. *abbr.* maximum.

max·i /máksee/ *n.* (*pl.* **max·is**) *colloq.* maxiskirt or other garment with a long skirt.

maxi- /máksee/ *comb. form* very large or long (*maxicoat*).

max·il·la /maksílə/ *n.* (*pl.* **max·il·lae** /-lee/ or **max·il·las**) **1** jaw or jawbone, esp. the upper jaw in most vertebrates. □□ **max·il·lar·y** /máksəléree/ *adj.*

max·im /máksim/ *n.* general truth or rule of conduct expressed in a sentence.

max·i·mize /máksimīz/ *v.tr.* increase or enhance to the utmost. □□ **max·i·mi·za'tion** *n.* **max'i·miz·er** *n.*

max·i·mum /máksiməm/ • *n.* (*pl.* **max·i·ma** /-mə/) highest possible or attainable amount. • *adj.* that is a maximum. □□ **max'i·mal** *adj.* **max'i·mal·ly** *adv.*

May /may/ *n.* **1** fifth month of the year. **2** (**may**) hawthorn or its blossom. □ **May Day** May 1, esp. as a festival with dancing, or as an international holiday in honor of workers.

may /may/ *v.aux.* (*3rd sing. present* **may**; *past* **might** /mīt/) **1** expressing possibility (*it may be true*). **2** expressing permission (*may I come in?*). **3** expressing a wish (*may he live to regret it*). **4** expressing uncertainty or irony in questions (*who may you be?*).
¶ Traditionalists insist that one should distinguish between **may** (present tense) and **might** (past tense) in expressing possibility: *I may have some dessert after dinner if I'm still hungry. I might*

have known that the highway would be closed because of the storm. In casual use, though, **may** and **might** are generally interchangeable: *They might take a vacation next month. He may have called earlier, but the answering machine was broken.* For **may** vs. **can**, see note at CAN¹.

Ma·ya /maáyə/ *n.* **1** (*pl.* same or **Ma·yas**) member of an ancient native people of Central America. **2** language of this people. □□ **Ma'yan** *adj. & n.*

may·be /máybee/ *adv.* perhaps; possibly.

May·day /máyday/ *n.* international radio distress signal.

may·flow·er /máyflowər/ *n.* any of various flowers that bloom in May.

may·fly /máyflī/ *n.* (*pl.* **-flies**) insect with four delicate wings, the adult of which lives briefly in spring.

may·hem /máyhem/ *n.* violent or damaging action.

may·on·naise /máyənáyz/ *n.* thick creamy dressing made of egg yolks, oil, vinegar, etc.

may·or /máyər, mair/ *n.* chief executive of a city or town. □□ **may'or·al** *adj.*

may·or·al·ty /máyərəltee, máir-/ *n.* (*pl.* **-ties**) **1** office of mayor. **2** mayor's period of office.

may·pole /máypōl/ *n.* (also **Maypole**) decorated pole for dancing around on May Day.

maze /mayz/ *n.* **1** network of paths and hedges designed as a puzzle for those who try to penetrate it. **2** complex network of paths or passages; labyrinth. **3** confusion, confused mass, etc. □□ **ma'zy** *adj.* (**ma·zi·er**, **ma·zi·est**).

ma·zur·ka /məzúrkə/ *n.* **1** lively Polish dance in triple time. **2** music for this.

MB *abbr. Computing* megabyte(s).

MBA *abbr.* Master of Business Administration.

MC *abbr.* **1** master of ceremonies. **2** Member of Congress.

MD *abbr.* **1** Doctor of Medicine. **2** Maryland (in official postal use). **3** Managing Director. **4** muscular dystrophy.

Md *symb. Chem.* mendelevium.

Md. *abbr.* Maryland.

ME *abbr.* **1** Maine (in official postal use). **2** Middle East.

Me. *abbr.* Maine.

me /mee/ *pron. objective case* of I² (*he saw me*).

mead /meed/ *n.* alcoholic drink of fermented honey and water.

mead·ow /médō/ *n.* **1** piece of grassland, esp. one used for hay. **2** piece of low well-watered ground, esp. near a river. □□ **mead'ow·y** *adj.*

mea·ger /méegər/ *adj.* **1** lacking in amount or quality (*a meager salary*). **2** (of a person or animal) lean; thin. □□ **mea'ger·ly** *adv.* **mea'ger·ness** *n.*

meal¹ /meel/ *n.* **1** occasion when food is eaten. **2** the food eaten on one occasion. □ **meal ticket** **1** ticket entitling one to a meal, esp. at a specified place with reduced cost. **2** person or thing that is a source of food or income.

meal² /meel/ *n.* grain or pulse ground to powder.

---

meal Old English *mǣl* (also in the sense 'measure,' surviving in words such as *piecemeal* 'measure taken at one time'), of Ger-

manic origin. The early sense of *meal* involved a notion of 'fixed time'; compare with Dutch *maal* 'meal, (portion of) time' and German *Mal* 'time,' *Mahl* 'meal,' from an Indo-European root meaning 'to measure.'

---

meal·y /méelee/ *adj.* (**meal·i·er**, **meal·i·est**) **1 a** of or like meal; soft and powdery. **b** containing meal. **2** (of a complexion) pale. **3** (of a horse) spotty. **4** (in full **mealy-mouthed**) afraid to use plain expressions. □□ **meal'i·ness** *n.*

mean¹ /meen/ *v.tr.* (*past* and *past part.* **meant** /ment/) **1** have as one's purpose or intention. **2** design or destine for a purpose. **3** intend to convey or indicate or refer to. **4** be of some specified importance to. □ **mean it** not be joking or exaggerating. **mean well** have good intentions.
¶ The difference between *median* and *mean* is most clearly expressed in numbers: **Mean,** or *average,* refers to the result obtained by dividing the sum of a set of quantities by the number of quantities in the set: *The mean or average of 3, 11, 9, and 5 is 28 divided by 4, or 7.* The **median** is the middle number in a sequence or, if the sequence has an even number of quantities, the average between the two middle numbers: *The median of 3, 4, 5, 8, and 14 is 5. The median of 2, 9, 10, and 35 is 9.5, that is, the mean or the average of 9 and 10.*

mean² /meen/ *adj.* **1** not generous or liberal. **2** (of an action) ignoble; small-minded. **3** (of a person's capacity, understanding, etc.) inferior; poor. **4** shabby. **5 a** malicious; ill-tempered. **b** vicious or aggressive in behavior. **6** *colloq.* skillful; formidable. □□ **mean'ly** *adv.* **mean'ness** *n.*

mean³ /meen/ ● *n.* **1** term midway between extremes. **2** *Math.* quotient of the sum of several quantities and their number, the average. ● *adj.* **1** (of a quantity) equally far from two extremes. **2** calculated as a mean.

---

mean Middle English, shortening of Old English *gemǣne,* of Germanic origin, from an Indo-European root shared by Latin *communis* 'common.' The original sense was 'common to two or more persons,' later 'inferior in rank,' leading to senses 3 and 4, from which senses 1 and 2 (which became common in the 19th century) arose.

---

me·an·der /meeándər/ *v.intr.* **1** wander at random. **2** (of a stream) wind about. □□ **me·an'drous** *adj.*

mean·ie /méenee/ *n.* (also **mean'y**) (*pl.* **-ies**) *colloq.* mean, niggardly, or small-minded person.

mean·ing /méening/ ● *n.* **1** what is meant. **2** significance. ● *adj.* expressive; significant. □□ **mean'ing·ly** *adv.*

mean·ing·ful /méeningfŏŏl/ *adj.* **1** full of meaning; significant. **2** *Logic* able to be interpreted. □□ **mean'ing·ful·ly** *adv.* **mean'ing·ful·ness** *n.*

mean·ing·less /méeninglis/ *adj.* having no meaning or significance. □□ **mean'ing·less·ly** *adv.* **mean'ing·less·ness** *n.*

means /meenz/ *n.pl.* **1** (often treated as *sing.*) that by which a result is brought about. **2 a** money resources. **b** wealth. □ **by all means** (or **all manner of means**) certainly. **by means of** by the agency or instrumentality of. **by no means** (or **no manner of means**) not at all; certainly not.

meant *past* and *past part.* of MEAN¹.

mean·time /méentīm/ • *adv.* = MEANWHILE. • *n.* intervening period.

mean·while /méenwīl, -hwīl/ • *adv.* **1** in the intervening period. **2** at the same time. • *n.* intervening period.

mean·y var. of MEANIE.

mea·sles /méezəlz/ *n.pl.* (also treated as *sing.*) acute infectious viral disease marked by red spots on the skin.

mea·sly /méezlee/ *adj.* (**mea·sli·er**, **mea·sli·est**) *colloq.* inferior; contemptible; meager.

meas·ure /mézhər/ • *n.* **1** size or quantity found by measuring. **2** system of measuring (*liquid measure*). **3** instrument for measuring. **4** standard used for valuing. **5** (usu. in *pl.*) suitable action to achieve some end. **6** legislative act. **7** poetical rhythm; meter. **8** *Mus.* bar or the time content of a bar. • *v.* **1** *tr.* ascertain the extent or quantity of (a thing) by comparison with a standard. **2** *intr.* be of a specified size (*it measures six inches*). **3** *tr.* mark (a line, etc., of a given length). **4** *tr.* (foll. by *out*) deal or distribute (a thing) in measured quantities. □ **beyond measure** excessively. **for good measure** as a finishing touch. **measure up** have the necessary qualifications (for). □□ **meas′ur·a·ble** *adj.* **meas′ur·a·bly** *adv.* **meas′ure·less** *adj.*

meas·ured /mézhərd/ *adj.* **1** rhythmical; regular. **2** (of language) carefully considered. □□ **meas′ured·ly** *adv.*

meas·ure·ment /mézhərmənt/ *n.* **1** measuring. **2** amount determined by measuring. **3** (in *pl.*) detailed dimensions.

meat /meet/ *n.* **1** flesh of animals (esp. mammals) as food. **2** (foll. by *of*) essence or chief part of. **3** edible part of nuts, shellfish, etc. □□ **meat′i·ness** *n.* **meat′less** *adj.* **meat′y** *adj.* (**meat·i·er**, **meat·i·est**)

Mec·ca /mékə/ *n.* **1** place one aspires to visit. **2** birthplace of a faith, policy, pursuit, etc.

me·chan·ic /mikánik/ *n.* skilled worker, esp. one who makes or uses or repairs machinery.

me·chan·i·cal /mikánikəl/ *adj.* **1** of machines or mechanisms. **2** working or produced by machinery. **3** (of a person or action) like a machine; automatic; lacking originality. □□ **me·chan′i·cal·ly** *adv.*

me·chan·ics /mikániks/ *n.pl.* (usu. treated as *sing.*) **1** branch of applied mathematics dealing with motion and tendencies to motion. **2** science of machinery. **3** method of construction or routine operation of a thing.

mech·an·ism /mékənizəm/ *n.* **1** structure or adaptation of parts of a machine. **2** system of mutually adapted parts working together. **3** mode of operation of a process.

mech·a·nize /mékənīz/ *v.tr.* **1** give a mechanical character to. **2** introduce machines in. **3** *Mil.* equip with tanks, armored cars, etc. □□ **mech·a·ni·za′tion** *n.* **mech′a·niz·er** *n.*

med·al /méd′l/ *n.* piece of metal, usu. in the form of a disk, struck or cast with an inscription or device to commemorate an event, etc., or awarded as a distinction to a soldier, athlete, etc. □□ **med′aled** *adj.* **me·dal·lic** /midálik/ *adj.*

med·al·ist /méd′list/ *n.* recipient of a (specified) medal.

me·dal·lion /midályən/ *n.* **1** large medal. **2** thing shaped like this, e.g., a decorative panel or tablet, portrait, etc.

med·dle /méd′l/ *v.intr.* (often foll. by *with*, *in*)

interfere in or busy oneself unduly with others' concerns. □□ **med′dler** *n.*

med·dle·some /méd′lsəm/ *adj.* fond of meddling; interfering. □□ **med′dle·some·ly** *adv.* **med′dle·some·ness** *n.*

me·di·a /méedeeə/ *n.pl.* **1** *pl.* of MEDIUM. **2** (usu. prec. by *the*) main means of mass communication (esp. newspapers and broadcasting) regarded collectively. ¶ See note at MEDIUM.

me·di·al /méedeeəl/ *adj.* **1** situated in the middle. **2** of average size. □□ **me′di·al·ly** *adv.*

me·di·an /méedeeən/ • *adj.* situated in the middle. • *n.* **1** *Geom.* straight line drawn from any vertex of a triangle to the middle of the opposite side. **2** *Math.* middle value of a series. **3** (also **median strip**) center divider separating opposing lanes on a divided highway. □□ **me′di·an·ly** *adv.* ¶ See note at MEAN.

me·di·ate *v.* /méedeeayt/ **1** *intr.* intervene (between parties in a dispute) to produce agreement or reconciliation. **2** *tr.* act as an intermediary. □□ **me·di·a′tion** /-áyshən/ *n.* **me′di·a·tor** *n.* **me·di·a·to·ry** /méedeeətáwree/ *adj.*

med·ic /médik/ *n. colloq.* medical practitioner or student, esp. a member of a military medical corps.

Med·i·caid /médikayd/ *n.* federal system of health insurance for those requiring financial assistance.

med·i·cal /médikəl/ *adj.* of medicine. □ **medical examination** examination to determine a person's physical fitness. □□ **med′i·cal·ly** *adv.*

Med·i·care /médikair/ *n.* federal government program of health insurance for persons esp. over 65 years of age.

med·i·cate /médikayt/ *v.tr.* **1** treat medically. **2** impregnate with a medicinal substance. □□ **med·i·ca·tion** /médikáyshən/ *n.* **med·i·ca·tive** /médikáytiv/ *adj.*

me·dic·i·nal /mədísinəl/ *adj.* (of a substance) having healing properties. □□ **me·dic′i·nal·ly** *adv.*

med·i·cine /médisin/ *n.* **1** science or practice of the diagnosis, treatment, and prevention of disease. **2** drug or preparation used for the treatment or prevention of disease. □ **medicine man** person believed to have magical powers of healing, esp. among Native Americans.

me·di·e·val /méedee-ée′vəl, méd-, míd-/ *adj.* **1** of the Middle Ages. **2** *colloq.* old-fashioned; archaic. □□ **me·di·e′val·ism** *n.* **me·di·e′val·ist** *n.* **me·di·e′val·ly** *adv.*

me·di·o·cre /méedeeókər/ *adj.* **1** of middling quality; neither good nor bad. **2** second-rate. □□ **me·di·oc·ri·ty** /-ókritee/ *n.*

med·i·tate /méditayt/ *v.* **1** *intr.* engage in deep thought; reflect. **2** *tr.* plan mentally. □□ **med·i·ta·tion** /-táyshən/ *n.* **med′i·ta·tor** *n.*

med·i·ta·tive /méditaytiv/ *adj.* inclined to meditate. □□ **med′i·ta·tive·ly** *adv.* **med′i·ta·tive·ness** *n.*

Med·i·ter·ra·ne·an /méditəráyneeən/ • *n.* large landlocked sea bordered by S. Europe, SW Asia, and N. Africa. • *adj.* of or characteristic of the Mediterranean or its surrounding region (*Mediterranean climate*).

me·di·um /méedeeəm/ • *n.* (*pl.* **me·di·a** or **me·**

di•ums) **1** middle quality, degree, etc., between extremes. **2** means by which something is communicated. **3** intervening substance through which impressions are conveyed to the senses, etc. **4** material or form used by an artist, composer, etc. **5** (*pl.* **me•di•ums**) person claiming to communicate with the dead. • *adj.* between two qualities, degrees, etc. **me•di•um•is′tic** *adj.* (in sense 5 of *n.*). **me′di•um•ship** *n.* (in sense 5 of *n.*).
¶ The Latin-derived noun **medium**, 'means for distributing information,' is singular. Its plural is **media**: *The newspaper is a powerful advertising medium. The government used all media to reach voters. Some media are more influential than others.* Many speakers now use the plural as singular: *The media is only as good as the integrity of the people who report the stories.*

med•ley /médlee/ *n.* (*pl.* **-leys**) **1** varied mixture. **2** collection of tunes, etc., played as one piece.

me•dul•la /midúlə/ *n.* inner region of certain organs, e.g., the kidney. □ **medulla oblongata** /óblonggáatə/ continuation of the spinal cord within the skull, forming the lowest part of the brain stem.

meek /meek/ *adj.* **1** humble and submissive. **2** piously gentle in nature. □□ **meek′ly** *adv.* **meek′ ness** *n.*

meer•schaum /méershəm, -shawm/ *n.* **1** soft white claylike substance. **2** tobacco pipe with the bowl made from this.

meet /meet/ • *v.* (*past* and *past part.* **met** /met/) **1 a** *tr.* encounter; come face to face with. **b** *intr.* (of two or more people) come into each other's company. **2** *tr.* be present at the arrival of (a person, train, etc.). **3 a** *tr.* come together or into contact with (*where the road meets the river*). **b** *intr.* come together or into contact (*where the sea and the sky meet*). **4 a** *tr.* make the acquaintance of. **b** *intr.* (of two or more people) make each other's acquaintance. **5** *intr.* & *tr.* come together or come into contact with for the purposes of conference, worship, etc. (*the committee meets every week*). **6** *tr.* **a** deal with or answer (*met the proposal with hostility*). **b** satisfy or conform with. **7** *tr.* pay (a bill, etc.). **8** *tr.* & (foll. by *with*) *intr.* experience, encounter, or receive (*met their death*). **9** *tr.* oppose in battle, etc. • *n.* assembly of competitors, etc. □ **meet the eye** (**or the ear**) be visible (or audible). **meet a person halfway** make a compromise. **meet with** receive (a reaction) (*met with the committee's approval*). □□ **meet′er** *n.*

meet•ing /méeting/ *n.* **1** coming together. **2** assembly of people; gathering.

mega- /mégə/ *comb. form* **1** large. **2** one million. ¶ Abbr.: **M.**

meg•a•bucks /mégəbuks/ *n. colloq.* great sums of money.

meg•a•byte /mégəbīt/ *n. Computing* 1,048,576 (i.e., 2^{20}) bytes as a measure of data capacity, or loosely 1,000,000 bytes. ¶ Abbr.: **MB.**

meg•a•hertz /mégəhərts/ *n.* one million hertz. ¶ Abbr.: **MHz.**

meg•a•lith /mégəlith/ *n. Archaeol.* large stone, esp. a prehistoric monument. □□ **meg•a•lith′ic** *adj.*

meg•a•lo•ma•ni•a /mégəlōmáyneeə/ *n.* **1** mental disorder producing delusions of grandeur. **2**

passion for grandiose schemes. □□ **meg•a•lo• ma′ni•ac** *adj.* & *n.* **meg•a•lo•ma•ni•a•cal** /-mənfákəl/ *adj.*

meg•a•lop•o•lis /mégəlópəlis/ *n.* urban area of great extent. □□ **meg•a•lo•pol•i•tan** /-ləpólit′n/ *adj.* & *n.*

meg•a•phone /mégəfōn/ *n.* large funnel-shaped device for amplifying the sound of the voice.

meg•a•ton /mégətun/ *n.* unit of explosive power equal to one million tons of TNT.

meg•a•watt /mégəwot/ *n.* one million watts. ¶ Abbr.: **MW.**

mei•o•sis /mīósis/ *n. Biol.* cell division that results in daughter cells with half the chromosome number of the parent cell. □□ **mei•ot•ic** /mīótik/ *adj.* **mei•ot′i•cal•ly** *adv.*

meit•ne•ri•um /mītnəreeəm/ *n. Chem.* artificially produced chemical element. ¶ Symb.: **Mt.**

mel•a•mine /méləmeen/ *n.* **1** white crystalline compound producing resins. **2** (in full **melamine resin**) plastic made from this and used esp. for laminated coatings.

mel•an•cho•li•a /mélənkóleeə/ *n.* depression; anxiety.

mel•an•chol•y /mélənkolee/ • *n.* (*pl.* **-ies**) **1** pensive sadness. **2** depression. • *adj.* sad; depressing; expressing sadness. □□ **mel•an•chol′ic** *adj.*

Mel•a•ne•sian /mélənéezhən, -shən/ • *n.* **1** member of the dominant Negroid people of Melanesia, an island group in the W. Pacific. **2** language of this people or their language. • *adj.* of or relating to this people or their language.

mé•lange /maylónzh/ *n.* mixture; medley.

mel•a•nin /mélənin/ *n.* dark-brown to black pigment occurring in the hair, skin, and iris of the eye.

mel•a•no•ma /mélənómə/ *n.* malignant tumor of melanin-forming cells, usu. in the skin.

mel•a•to•nin /melətónin/ *n.* hormone that inhibits melanin formation, thought to affect the reproductive cycle.

Mel•ba /mélbə/ *n.* □ **Melba toast** very thin crisp toast.

meld /meld/ *v.* merge; blend; combine.

mel•lif•lu•ous /məliflōoəs/ *adj.* (of a voice or words) pleasing; musical; flowing. □□ **mel•lif′ lu•ence** *n.* **mel•lif′lu•ent** *adj.* **mel•lif′lu•ous•ly** *adv.* **mel•lif′lu•ous•ness** *n.*

mel•low /mélō/ • *adj.* **1** (of sound, color, light) soft and rich; free from harshness. **2** (of character) softened or matured by age or experience. **3** genial; jovial. **4** partly intoxicated. **5** (of wine) well-matured; smooth. • *v.* make or become mellow. □□ **mel′low•ly** *adv.* **mel′low•ness** *n.*

me•lod•ic /məlódik/ *adj.* **1** of or relating to melody. **2** having or producing melody. □□ **me•lod′ i•cal•ly** *adv.*

me•lo•di•ous /məlódeeəs/ *adj.* **1** of, producing, or having melody. **2** sweet-sounding. □□ **me• lo′di•ous•ly** *adv.* **me•lo′di•ous•ness** *n.*

mel•o•dra•ma /mélədraámə, -dramə/ *n.* **1** sensational dramatic piece with crude appeals to the emotions. **2** genre of drama of this type. **3** language, behavior, or an occurrence suggestive of this. □□ **mel•o•dra•mat•ic** /-drəmátik/ *adj.* **mel•o•dra•mat′i•cal•ly** *adv.* **mel•o•dram•a•tist** /-drámətist/ *n.* **mel•o•dram′a•tize** *v.tr.*

mel•o•dy /mélədee/ *n.* (*pl.* **-dies**) **1** arrangement of single notes in a musically expressive succession. **2** principal part in harmonized music; tune.

mel·on /mélən/ n. sweet fruit of various gourds.

melt /melt/ v. **1** intr. become liquefied by heat. **2** tr. change to a liquid condition by heat. **3 a** intr. & tr. dissolve. **b** intr. (of food) be easily dissolved in the mouth. **4** intr. be softened as a result of pity, love, etc. **5** tr. soften (a person, feelings, the heart, etc.). **6** intr. change or merge imperceptibly into. **7** intr. leave or disappear unobtrusively. □ **melting point** temperature at which any given solid will melt. **melting pot** place where races, theories, etc., are mixed. □□ **melt′a·ble** adj. & n. **melt′er** n. **melt′ing·ly** adv.

melt·down /méltdown/ n. **1** melting of a structure, esp. the overheated core of a nuclear reactor. **2** disastrous event.

mem·ber /mémbər/ n. **1** person, animal, plant, etc., belonging to a society, team, taxonomic group, etc. **2** constituent portion of a complex structure. **3 a** any part or organ of the body, esp. a limb. **b** = PENIS. □□ **mem′bered** adj. (also in comb.). **mem′ber·less** adj.

mem·ber·ship /mémbərship/ n. **1** being a member. **2** number of members. **3** body of members.

mem·brane /mémbrayn/ n. **1** any pliable sheetlike structure acting as a boundary, lining, or partition in an organism. **2** thin pliable sheet or skin of various kinds. □□ **mem·bra·nous** /-brənəs/ adj.

me·men·to /miméntō/ n. (pl. **-tos** or **-toes**) object kept as a reminder or a souvenir of a person or an event.

me·men·to mo·ri /məméntō máwree, -rī/ n. (pl. same) warning or reminder of death (e.g., a skull).

mem·o /mémō/ n. (pl. **-os**) colloq. memorandum.

mem·oir /mémwaar/ n. **1** historical account or biography written from personal knowledge or special sources. **2** (in pl.) autobiography. □□ **mem′oir·ist** n.

mem·o·ra·bil·i·a /mémərəbileeə, -bílyə/ n.pl. souvenirs of memorable events.

mem·o·ra·ble /mémərəbəl/ adj. **1** worth remembering, not to be forgotten. **2** easily remembered. □□ **mem·o·ra·bil′i·ty** n. **mem′o·ra·bly** adv.

mem·o·ran·dum /mémərándəm/ n. (pl. **mem·o·ran·da** /-də/ or **mem·o·ran·dums**) **1** note or record made for future use. **2** informal written message, esp. in business, etc.

me·mo·ri·al /məmáwreeəl/ • n. object, institution, or custom established in memory of a person or event. • adj. intending to commemorate a person or thing (memorial service). □ **Memorial Day** holiday on which those who died in war are remembered, usu. the last Monday in May.

mem·o·rize /mémərīz/ v.tr. commit to memory. □□ **mem·o·ri·za′tion** n. **mem′o·riz·er** n.

mem·o·ry /méməree/ n. (pl. **-ries**) **1** mental faculty by which things are recalled. **2** store of things remembered. **3** recollection or remembrance. **4** storage capacity of a computer, etc. **5** reputation of a dead person. **6** length of time over which the memory or memories of any given person or group extends. **7** act of remembering (deed worthy of memory). □ **from memory** without verification in books, etc.

men pl. of MAN.

men·ace /ménis/ • n. **1** threat. **2** joc. pest, nuisance. • v. threaten, esp. in a malignant or hostile manner. □□ **men′ac·er** n. **men′ac·ing** adj. **men′ac·ing·ly** adv.

mé·nage /maynaázh/ n. members of a household.

me·nag·er·ie /mənájəree, -názh-/ n. small zoo.

men·ar·che /menaárkee/ n. onset of first menstruation.

mend /mend/ • v. **1** tr. restore to a sound condition; repair. **2** intr. regain health. **3** tr. improve. • n. darn or repair. □ **mend one′s ways** reform; improve one′s habits. **on the mend** recovering. □□ **mend′a·ble** adj. **mend′er** n.

men·da·cious /mendáyshəs/ adj. lying; untruthful. □□ **men·da′cious·ly** adv. **men·da′cious·ness** n. **men·dac·i·ty** /-dásitee/ n. (pl. **-ties**)

men·de·le·vi·um /méndəlee′veeəm/ n. Chem. artificial transuranic radioactive metallic element. ¶ Symb.: **Md**.

Men·del·ism /méndəlizəm/ n. theory of heredity based on the recurrence of certain inherited characteristics transmitted by genes. □□ **Men·de·li·an** /-dee′leeən/ adj. & n.

men·di·cant /méndikənt/ • adj. **1** begging. **2** (of a friar) living solely on alms. • n. **1** beggar. **2** mendicant friar. □□ **men·di·can·cy** /-kənsee/ n. **men·dic·i·ty** /-dísitee/ n.

men·folk /ménfōk/ n.pl. **1** men in general. **2** the men of one′s family.

me·ni·al /mée′neeəl/ • adj. degrading; servile. • n. domestic servant. □□ **me′ni·al·ly** adv.

men·in·gi·tis /méninjîtis/ n. infection and inflammation of the meninges. □□ **men·in·git·ic** /-jítik/ adj.

me·ninx /mée′ningks/ n. (pl. **me·nin·ges** /mənínjeez/) (usu. in pl.) any of the three membranes that enclose the brain and spinal cord. □□ **me·nin·ge·al** /mínínjeeəl/ adj.

me·nis·cus /mənískəs/ n. (pl. **me·nis·ci** /-nísī/ or **me·nis·cus·es**) **1** Physics curved upper surface of a liquid in a tube. **2** lens that is convex on one side and concave on the other. □□ **me·nis′coid** adj.

men·o·pause /ménəpawz/ n. ceasing of menstruation. □□ **men·o·pau′sal** adj.

me·nor·ah /mənáwrə, -nōrə/ n. seven- or nine-armed candelabrum used in Jewish worship, esp. as a symbol of Judaism.

MENORAH

men·ses /ménseez/ *n.pl.* flow of blood in menstruation.

men·stru·al /ménstrōōəl/ *adj.* of or relating to the menses or menstruation. □ **menstrual cycle** process of ovulation and menstruation in female primates.

men·stru·ate /ménstrōō-ayt/ *v.intr.* discharge blood and other materials from the uterus, usu. at monthly intervals. □□ **men·stru·a·tion** /ménstrōō-áyshən/ *n.*

men·su·ra·tion /ménshəráyshən, -sə-/ *n.* measuring.

mens·wear /ménzwair/ *n.* clothes for men.

-ment /mənt/ *suffix* **1** forming nouns expressing the means or result of the action of a verb (*abridgment; embankment*). **2** forming nouns from adjectives (*merriment; oddment*).

men·tal /mént'l/ *adj.* **1** of, in, or done by the mind. **2** *colloq.* **a** insane. **b** crazy; wild; eccentric (*is mental about pop music*). □ **mental age** degree of mental development compared to chronological age. □□ **men·tal·ly** *adv.*

men·tal·i·ty /mentálitee/ *n.* (*pl.* **-ties**) **1** mental character or disposition. **2** kind or degree of intelligence.

men·thol /ménthawl/ *n.* mint-tasting organic alcohol found in oil of peppermint, etc., used as a flavoring and to relieve local pain. □□ **men·tho·lat·ed** /-thəlaytid/ *adj.*

men·tion /ménshən/ • *v.tr.* **1** refer to briefly. **2** reveal or disclose. • *n.* reference. □ **not to mention** and also. □□ **men·tion·a·ble** *adj.*

men·tor /méntawr/ *n.* experienced and trusted adviser.

men·u /ményōō/ *n.* **1 a** list of dishes available in a restaurant, etc. **b** list of items to be served at a meal. **2** *Computing* list of options showing the commands or facilities available.

me·ow /mee-ów/ • *n.* characteristic cry of a cat. • *v.intr.* make this cry.

mer·can·tile /mórkəntīl/ *adj.* **1** of trade; trading. **2** commercial. **3** mercenary; fond of bargaining.

mer·ce·nar·y /mórsəneree/ • *adj.* primarily concerned with money or other reward (*mercenary motives*). • *n.* (*pl.* **-ies**) hired soldier in foreign service.

mer·cer·ize /mórsərīz/ *v.tr.* treat (cotton) with caustic alkali to strengthen and impart luster. □□ **mer·cer·i·za·tion** *n.*

mer·chan·dise /mórchəndīz/ • *n.* goods for sale. • *v.* **1** *intr.* trade; traffic. **2** *tr.* trade or traffic in. **3** *tr.* **a** put on the market; promote. **b** advertise; publicize (an idea or person). □□ **mer·chan·dis·a·ble** *adj.* **mer·chan·dis·er** *n.*

mer·chant /mórchənt/ *n.* retail trader; dealer; storekeeper. □ **merchant marine** a nation's commercial shipping. **merchant ship** = MERCHANTMAN.

mer·chant·man /mórchəntmən/ *n.* (*pl.* **-men**) ship conveying merchandise.

mer·ci·ful /mórsifŏŏl/ *adj.* having, showing, or feeling mercy. □□ **mer'ci·ful·ly** *adv.* **mer'ci·ful·ness** *n.*

mer·ci·less /mórsilis/ *adj.* **1** pitiless. **2** showing no mercy. □□ **mer'ci·less·ly** *adv.* **mer'ci·less·ness** *n.*

mer·cu·ri·al /mərkyŏŏreeəl/ *adj.* **1** (of a person) sprightly; ready-witted; volatile. **2** of or containing mercury. □□ **mer·cu'ri·al·ism** *n.* **mer·cu·ri·al·i·ty** /-reeálitee/ *n.* **mer·cu'ri·al·ly** *adv.*

mer·cu·ry /mórkyəree/ *n.* **1** *Chem.* silvery-white heavy liquid metallic element used in barometers, thermometers, etc. ¶ Symb.: **Hg**. **2** (**Mercury**) planet nearest to the sun. □□ **mer·cu·ric** /-kyŏŏrik/ *adj.* **mer·cu'rous** *adj.*

mer·cy /mórsee/ *n.* (*pl.* **-cies**) **1** compassion or forbearance shown to enemies or offenders in one's power. **2** quality of compassion. **3** act of mercy. **4** something to be thankful for. □ **at the mercy of** wholly in the power of.

mere /meer/ *attrib.adj.* (**mer·est**) that is solely or no more or better than what is specified. □□ **mere'ly** *adv.*

mer·e·tri·cious /méritríshəs/ *adj.* showily but falsely attractive. □□ **mer·e·tri'cious·ly** *adv.* **mer·e·tri'cious·ness** *n.*

mer·gan·ser /mərgánsər/ *n.* diving fish-eating duck.

merge /mərj/ *v.* **1 a** combine or be combined. **b** join or blend gradually. **2** lose or cause to lose character and identity in (something else).

merg·er /mórjər/ *n.* combining, esp. of two commercial companies, etc., into one.

me·rid·i·an /mərídeeən/ *n.* **1 a** circle of constant longitude, passing through a given place and the terrestrial poles. **b** corresponding line on a map. **2** prime; full splendor.

me·ringue /məráng/ *n.* confection of sugar, egg whites, etc., baked crisp.

me·ri·no /məreénō/ *n.* (*pl.* **-nos**) **1** (in full **merino sheep**) variety of sheep with long fine wool. **2** wool of this sheep, or cloth made from this.

mer·it /mérit/ • *n.* **1** quality of deserving well. **2** excellence; worth. **3** (usu. in *pl.*) **a** thing that entitles one to reward or gratitude. **b** esp. *Law* intrinsic rights and wrongs. • *v.tr.* deserve or be worthy of.

mer·i·toc·ra·cy /méritókrəsee/ *n.* (*pl.* **-cies**) **1** government by persons selected according to merit. **2** group of persons selected in this way. **3** society governed by meritocracy.

mer·i·to·ri·ous /méritáwreeəs/ *adj.* praiseworthy. □□ **mer·i·to'ri·ous·ly** *adv.* **mer·i·to'ri·ous·ness** *n.*

mer·maid /mórmayd/ *n.* imaginary sea creature, with the head and trunk of a woman and the tail of a fish.

mer·ri·ment /mérimənt/ *n.* **1** being merry. **2** mirth; fun.

mer·ry /méree/ *adj.* (**mer·ri·er, mer·ri·est**) **1** joyous. **2** full of laughter or gaiety. □ **make merry** be festive; enjoy oneself. □□ **mer'ri·ly** *adv.* **mer'ri·ness** *n.*

mer·ry-go-round /méreegōrownd/ *n.* **1** revolving machine with wooden horses or other animals, etc., for riding on at an amusement park, etc. **2** cycle of bustling activities.

mer·ry·mak·ing /méreemayking/ *n.* festivity; fun. □□ **mer'ry·mak·er** *n.*

mes·cal /méskal/ *n.* peyote cactus.

mes·ca·line /méskəleen, -lin/ *n.* (also **mes·ca·lin** /-lin/) hallucinogenic alkaloid present in mescal.

mes·dames *pl.* of MADAME.

mes·de·moi·selles *pl.* of MADEMOISELLE.

mesh /mesh/ • n. 1 network fabric or structure. 2 each of the open spaces or interstices between the strands of a net or sieve, etc. 3 (in pl.) a network. b snare. • v.intr. 1 (of the teeth of a wheel) be engaged (with others). 2 be harmonious.

mes·mer·ize /mézmərīz/ v.tr. 1 Psychol. hypnotize. 2 fascinate; spellbind. □□ **mes·mer·ic** /mezmérik/ adj. **mes·mer·ism** /-izəm/ n. **mes'mer·ist** n. **mes·mer·i·za'tion** n. **mes'mer·iz·er** n. **mes'mer·iz·ing·ly** adv.

meso- /mésō, méz-/ comb. form middle; intermediate.

mes·o·morph /mézəmawrf, més-/ n. person with a compact and muscular body. □□ **mes·o·mor'phic** adj.

me·son /mézon, més-, mé'ezon, -son/ n. Physics any of a class of elementary particles believed to participate in the forces that hold nucleons together in the atomic nucleus. □□ **mes·ic** /mézik, més-, mé'ezik, -sik/ adj. **me·son'ic** adj.

mes·o·sphere /mésəsfeer, méz-/ n. region of the atmosphere extending in altitude from 20 to 50 miles.

Mes·o·zo·ic /mésəzō-ik, méz-/ Geol. • adj. of or relating to an era of geological time marked by the development of dinosaurs, and with evidence of the first mammals, birds, and flowering plants. • n. this era.

mes·quite /meskéet/ n. 1 thorny N. American leguminous tree. 2 wood of the mesquite, as used in grilling food.

mess /mes/ • n. 1 dirty or untidy state. 2 state of confusion, embarrassment, or trouble. 3 something causing a mess, e.g., spilled liquid, etc. 4 a soldiers, etc., dining together. b = *mess hall.* c meal taken there. 5 derog. disagreeable concoction. 6 portion of liquid or pulpy food. • v. 1 tr. (often foll. by up) make a mess of; dirty; muddle. 2 intr. (foll. by with) interfere with. □ **mess about** (or **around**) act desultorily. **mess hall** communal, esp. military, dining area. **mess kit** soldier's cooking and eating utensils.

---

mess Middle English: from Old French *mes* 'portion of food,' from Late Latin *missum* 'something put on the table,' past participle of *mittere* 'send, put.' The original sense was 'a serving of food,' also 'a serving of liquid or partly liquid food,' and later 'liquid or mixed food for an animal'; this gave rise, in the early 19th century, to the senses 'unappetizing concoction' and 'predicament,' on which the present senses 1 and 2 are based. In late Middle English there was also a sense 'one of the small groups into which the company at a banquet was divided' (who were served from the same dishes); hence, 'a group who regularly eat together' (recorded in military use from the mid-16th century).

---

mes·sage /mésij/ n. 1 oral or written communication sent by one person to another. 2 central import or meaning of an artistic work, etc. □ **get the message** colloq. understand what is meant.

mes·sen·ger /mésinjər/ n. person who carries a message.

Mes·si·ah /misíə/ n. 1 (also **mes·si'ah**) liberator of an oppressed people or country. 2 a promised deliverer of the Jews. b (usu. prec. by *the*) Christ regarded as this. □□ **Mes·si'ah·ship** n. **Mes·si·an·ic** /méseeánik/ adj. **Mes·si·a·nism** /mesíənizəm/ n.

mes·sieurs pl. of MONSIEUR.

messrs. /mésərz/ pl. of MR.

mess·y /mésee/ adj. (**mess·i·er**, **mess·i·est**) 1 untidy or dirty. 2 causing or accompanied by a mess. 3 difficult to deal with. □□ **mess'i·ly** adv. **mess'i·ness** n.

met past and past part. of MEET.

meta- /métə/ comb. form (usu. **met-** before a vowel or *h*) 1 denoting change of position or condition (*metabolism*). 2 denoting position: **a** behind. **b** after or beyond (*metaphysics*). **c** of a higher or second-order kind (*metalanguage*).

me·tab·o·lism /mətábəlizəm/ n. all the chemical processes that occur within a living organism, resulting in energy production and growth. □□ **met·a·bol·ic** /métəbólik/ adj. **met·a·bol'i·cal·ly** adv.

me·tab·o·lize /mətábəlīz/ v. process or be processed by metabolism. □□ **me·tab'o·liz·a·ble** adj.

met·a·car·pus /métəkáarpəs/ n. (pl. **met·a·car·pi** /-pī/) 1 set of five bones of the hand that connects the wrist to the fingers. 2 this part of the hand. □□ **met·a·car'pal** adj.

met·al /mét'l/ • n. 1 any of a class of chemical elements such as gold, silver, iron, and tin, usu. lustrous ductile solids and good conductors of heat and electricity. 2 alloy of any of these. • adj. made of metal.

met·a·lan·guage /métəlanggwij/ n. language or system used to discuss or analyze another language or system.

me·tal·lic /mətálik/ adj. 1 of, consisting of, or characteristic of metal or metals. 2 sounding like struck metal. 3 having the sheen or luster of metals. □□ **me·tal'li·cal·ly** adv.

met·al·lur·gy /mét'lərjee/ n. science concerned with the production, purification, and properties of metals and their application. □□ **met·al·lur·gic** /mét'lərjik/ adj. **met·al·lur'gi·cal** adj. **met·al·lur'gi·cal·ly** adv. **met·al·lur'gist** n.

met·a·mor·phic /métəmáwrfik/ adj. 1 of metamorphosis. 2 Geol. (of rock) transformed by natural agencies such as heat and pressure. □□ **met·a·mor'phism** n.

met·a·mor·phose /métəmawrfōz/ v.tr. 1 change in form. 2 a turn (into a new form). b change the nature of.

met·a·mor·pho·sis /métəmáwrfəsis / n. (pl. **met·a·mor·pho·ses** /-seez/) 1 change of character, conditions, etc. 2 change of form in an animal, e.g., from a pupa to an insect, etc.

met·a·phor /métəfawr/ n. application of a name or descriptive term or phrase to an object or action to which it is not literally applicable (e.g., *killing him with kindness*). □□ **met·a·phor·ic** /-fáwrik, -fórik/ adj. **met·a·phor·i·cal** /-fáwrikəl, -fórikəl/ adj. **met·a·phor·i·cal·ly** /-fáwriklee, -fóriklee/ adv.

met·a·phys·i·cal /métəfizikəl/ adj. 1 of metaphysics. 2 excessively subtle or theoretical. □□ **met·a·phys'i·cal·ly** adv.

met·a·phys·ics /métəfiziks/ n.pl. (usu. treated as sing.) 1 theoretical philosophy of being and knowing. 2 philosophy of mind. 3 colloq. abstract or subtle talk; mere theory. □□ **met·a·phy·si·cian** /-zíshən/ n.

me·tas·ta·sis /mətástəsis/ n. (pl. **me·tas·ta·ses** /-seez/) *Physiol.* transference of a bodily function, disease, etc., from one part or organ to another. □□ **me·tas'ta·size** v.intr. **met·a·stat·ic** /métəstátik/ adj.

met·a·tar·sus /métəta'arsəs/ n. (pl. **met·a·tar·si** /-sī/) **1** part of the foot between the ankle and the toes. **2** set of bones in this. □□ **met·a·tar'sal** adj.

me·tath·e·sis /mitáthisis/ n. (pl. **me·tath·e·ses** /-seez/) **1** *Gram.* transposition of sounds or letters in a word. **2** *Chem.* interchange of atoms or groups of atoms between two molecules. **3** instance of either of these. □□ **met·a·thet·ic** /métəthétik/ adj. **met·a·thet'i·cal** adj.

mete /meet/ v.tr. *literary* apportion or allot.

me·te·or /meeteeər, -eeawr/ n. **1** small body of matter from outer space that becomes incandescent as a result of friction with the earth's atmosphere. **2** streak of light emanating from a meteor.

me·te·or·ic /meetee-áwrik, -ór-/ adj. **1** of meteors. **2** rapid like a meteor; dazzling; transient. □□ **me·te·or'i·cal·ly** adv.

me·te·or·ite /meeteeərīt/ n. fallen meteor that reaches the earth's surface from outer space. □□ **me·te·or·it·ic** /-rítik/ adj.

me·te·or·oid /meeteeəróyd/ n. any small body moving in the solar system that becomes visible as it passes through the earth's atmosphere as a meteor.

me·te·or·ol·o·gy /meeteeəróləjee/ n. the study of the processes and phenomena of the atmosphere, esp. as a means of forecasting the weather. □□ **me·te·or·o·log·i·cal** /-rəlójikəl/ adj. **me·te·or·o·log'i·cal·ly** adv. **me·te·or·ol'o·gist** n.

me·ter¹ /meetər/ n. basic metric measure of length, equal to about 39.4 inches. □□ **me'ter·age** n.

me·ter² /meetər/ n. **1** poetic rhythm, determined by the number and length of feet in a line. **2** basic pulse and rhythm of a piece of music.

me·ter³ /meetər/ • n. instrument that measures, esp. one for recording a quantity of gas, electricity, postage, etc., supplied, present, or needed. • v.tr. measure by means of a meter.

-meter /mitər, meetər/ comb. form **1** forming nouns denoting measuring instruments (barometer). **2** *Prosody* forming nouns denoting lines of poetry with a specified number of measures (pentameter).

meth·a·done /méthədōn/ n. potent narcotic analgesic drug used esp. as a substitute for morphine or heroin.

meth·ane /méthayn/ n. *Chem.* colorless, odorless, flammable gas, the main constituent of natural gas.

meth·a·nol /méthənawl, -nol/ n. *Chem.* colorless, volatile, flammable liquid, used as a solvent. Also called **methyl alcohol.**

me·thinks /mithíngks/ v.intr. (past **me·thought** /mitháwt/) *archaic* it seems to me.

meth·od /méthəd/ n. **1** special form of procedure esp. in any branch of mental activity. **2** orderliness; regular habits.

me·thod·i·cal /mithódikəl/ adj. (also **me·thod'ic**) characterized by method or order. □□ **me·thod'i·cal·ly** adv.

Meth·od·ist /méthədist/ n. member of any of several Protestant religious bodies (now united) originating in the teachings of John Wesley. □□ **Meth'od·ism** n. **Meth·od·is'tic** adj.

meth·od·ol·o·gy /méthədóləjee/ n. (pl. -gies) system or science of methods. □□ **meth·od·o·log·i·cal** /-dəlójikəl/ adj. **meth·od·o·log'i·cal·ly** adv. **meth·od·ol'o·gist** n.

meth·yl /méthil/ n. *Chem.* univalent hydrocarbon radical CH₃, present in many organic compounds. □ **methyl alcohol** = METHANOL. □□ **me·thyl'ic** adj.

me·tic·u·lous /mətíkyələs/ adj. **1** giving great or excessive attention to details. **2** very careful and precise. □□ **me·tic'u·lous·ly** adv. **me·tic'u·lous·ness** n.

mé·tier /métyáy/ n. (also **me'tier**) **1** one's trade, profession, or department of activity. **2** one's forte.

me·ton·y·my /mitónimee/ n. substitution of the name of an attribute or adjunct for that of the thing meant (e.g., *White House* for *president*). □□ **met·o·nym·ic** /métənímik/ adj. **met·o·nym'i·cal** adj.

met·ric /métrik/ adj. of or based on the meter. □ **metric system** decimal measuring system with the meter, liter, and gram (or kilogram) as units of length, volume, and mass. **metric ton** (or **tonne**) 1,000 kilograms (2,205 lb.).

-metric /métrik/ comb. form (also **-metrical**) forming adjectives corresponding to nouns in -meter and -metry (geometric). □□ **-metrically** comb. form forming adverbs.

met·ri·cal /métrikəl/ adj. **1** of, relating to, or composed in meter (metrical psalms). **2** of or involving measurement (metrical geometry). □□ **met'ri·cal·ly** adv.

met·ro /métró/ n. (pl. **-ros**) subway system, esp. in Paris.

met·ro·nome /métrənōm/ n. *Mus.* instrument marking time at a selected rate by giving a regular tick. □□ **met·ro·nom·ic** /-nómik/ adj.

METRONOME

me·trop·o·lis /mitrópəlis/ n. chief city of a country; capital city. □□ **met·ro·pol·i·tan** /métrəpólit'n/ adj.

-metry /mitree/ comb. form forming nouns denoting procedures and systems corresponding to instruments in -meter (calorimetry; thermometry).

met·tle /mét'l/ n. strength of character; spirit;

courage. □ **on one's mettle** incited to do one's best. □□ **met′tled** adj. (also in comb.). **met′tle·some** adj.

mew /myōō/ • v.intr. (of a cat, gull, etc.) utter its characteristic cry. • n. this sound, esp. of a cat.

mewl /myōōl/ v.intr. **1** cry feebly; whimper. **2** mew like a cat.

mews /myōōz/ n. esp. Brit. set of stables around an open yard or along a lane, now often converted into dwellings.

Mex·i·can /méksikən/ • n. **1** native or national of Mexico, a country in southern N. America. **2** language spoken in Mexico. • adj. of or relating to Mexico or its people.

me·zu·zah /mezōōzə, -zōōzaá/ n. (also **me·zu′za**; pl. **-zas**; also **me·zu·zot** or **me·zu·zoth** /-zōō-zót/) parchment inscribed with religious texts, inserted into a small case, and attached to the doorpost of a Jewish house as a sign of faith.

mez·za·nine /mézəneén/ n. low story between two others (usu. between the first and second floors).

mez·zo /métsō/ Mus. • adv. half; moderately. • n. (in full **mezzo-soprano**) **1** female singing voice between soprano and contralto. **2** singer with this voice.

M.F.A. abbr. Master of Fine Arts.

mfg. abbr. manufacturing.

m.f.n. abbr. most favored nation.

mfr. abbr. **1** manufacture. **2** manufacturer.

Mg symb. Chem. magnesium.

mg abbr. milligram(s).

Mgr. abbr. **1** Manager. **2** Monseigneur. **3** Monsignor.

MHz abbr. megahertz.

MI abbr. Michigan (in official postal use).

mi /mee/ n. Mus. third tone of the diatonic scale.

mi. abbr. mile(s).

MIA abbr. missing in action.

mi·ca /mīkə/ n. any of a group of silicate minerals with a layered structure, esp. muscovite. □□ **mi·ca·ceous** /-káyshəs/ adj.

mice pl. of MOUSE.

Mich. abbr. **1** Michigan. **2** Michaelmas.

Mich·ael·mas /míkəlməs/ n. feast of St. Michael, September 29.

Mick·ey Finn /míkee fin/ (often **Mickey**) n. sl. alcoholic drink adulterated with a narcotic or laxative.

micro- /mīkrō/ comb. form **1** small (microchip). **2** denoting a factor of one millionth (10^{-6}) (microgram). ¶ Symb.: μ.

mi·crobe /mīkrōb/ n. minute living being; microorganism (esp. bacteria causing disease and fermentation). □□ **mi·cro·bi·al** /-krōbeeəl/ adj. **mi·cro·bic** /-krōbik/ adj.

mi·cro·bi·ol·o·gy /mīkrōbīóləjee/ n. scientific study of microorganisms. □□ **mi·cro·bi·o·log·i·cal** /-bīəlójikəl/ adj. **mi·cro·bi·o·log′i·cal·ly** adv. **mi·cro·bi·ol′o·gist** n.

mi·cro·brew·er·y /mīkrōbrōōəree/ n. limited-production brewery, often selling only locally.

mi·cro·chip /mīkrōchip/ n. small piece of semiconductor (usu. silicon) used to carry electronic circuits.

mi·cro·com·put·er /mīkrōkəmpyōōtər/ n. small

computer that contains a microprocessor as its central processor.

mi·cro·cosm /mīkrəkozəm/ n. **1** miniature representation. **2** mankind viewed as the epitome of the universe. **3** any community or complex unity viewed in this way. □□ **mi·cro·cos·mic** /-kózmik/ adj. **mi·cro·cos′mi·cal·ly** adv.

mi·cro·dot /mīkrōdot/ n. microphotograph of a document, etc., reduced to the size of a dot.

mi·cro·ec·o·nom·ics /mīkrō-eékənómiks, -ék-/ n. branch of economics dealing with individual commodities, producers, etc.

mi·cro·e·lec·tron·ics /mīkrō-ílektróniks/ n. design, manufacture, and use of microchips and microcircuits.

mi·cro·fiche /mīkrōfeesh/ n. (pl. same or **mi·cro·fich·es**) flat rectangular piece of film bearing miniaturized photographs of a printed text or document.

mi·cro·film /mīkrəfilm/ • n. length of film bearing miniaturized photographs of documents, etc. • v.tr. photograph (a document, etc.) on microfilm.

mi·cro·light /mīkrōlīt/ n. kind of motorized hang glider.

mi·crom·e·ter /mīkrómitər/ n. gauge for accurately measuring small distances, thicknesses, etc. □□ **mi·crom′e·try** n.

MICROMETER

mi·cron /mīkron/ n. one-millionth of a meter.

Mi·cro·ne·sian /mīkrəneézhən/ • adj. of Micronesia, an island group in the W. Pacific. • n. native of Micronesia.

mi·cro·or·gan·ism /mīkrō-áwrgənizəm/ n. microscopic organism, e.g., algae, bacteria, fungi, protozoa, and viruses.

mi·cro·phone /mīkrəfōn/ n. instrument for converting sound waves into electrical currents. □□ **mi·cro·phon·ic** /-fónik/ adj.

mi·cro·proc·es·sor /mīkrōprósesər/ n. integrated circuit that contains all the functions of a central processing unit of a computer.

mi·cro·scope /mīkrəskōp/ n. instrument magnifying small objects by means of a lens or lenses.

mi·cro·scop·ic /mīkrəskópik/ adj. **1** visible only with a microscope. **2** extremely small. **3** of the microscope. □□ **mi·cro·scop′i·cal** adj. (in sense 4). **mi·cro·scop′i·cal·ly** adv.

mi·cros·co·py /mīkróskəpee/ n. use of the microscope. □□ **mi·cros′co·pist** n.

mi·cro·sec·ond /míkrōsekənd/ n. one-millionth of a second.

mi·cro·sur·ger·y /míkrōsúrjəree/ n. intricate surgery performed using microscopes. □□ **mi·cro·sur·gi·cal** /-súrjikəl/ adj.

mi·cro·wave /míkrəwayv/ • n. 1 electromagnetic wave with a wavelength in the range 0.001–0.3m. 2 (in full **microwave oven**) oven that uses microwaves to cook or heat food quickly. • v.tr. cook in a microwave oven.

mid /mid/ attrib.adj. (usu. in comb.) that is the middle.

Mi·das touch /mídəs/ n. knack for moneymaking.

mid·day /míd-dáy/ n. middle of the day; noon.

mid·dle /míd'l/ • attrib.adj. 1 at an equal distance from the extremities of a thing. 2 (of a member of a group) so placed as to have the same number of members on each side. 3 intermediate in rank, quality, etc. 4 average (of middle height). • n. 1 the middle point or position or part. 2 waist. □ **middle age** period between youth and old age, about 45 to 60. **middle-aged** in middle age. **Middle Ages** period of European history between ancient times and the Renaissance, from c. 476 to 1453. **Middle America 1** middle class in the US, esp. as a conservative political force. 2 US Middle West. **middle class** class of society between the upper and the lower socially, economically, etc. **middle-class** adj. of the middle class. **middle ear** cavity of the central part of the ear behind the eardrum. **Middle East** area covered by countries from Egypt to Iran inclusive. **Middle English** the English language from c. 1150 to 1500. **middle-of-the-road** moderate; avoiding extremes. **middle school** school for children usu. in grades 5 to 8. **Middle West** = MIDWEST.

mid·dle·brow /míd'lbrów/ colloq. adj. claiming to be or regarded as only moderately intellectual.

mid·dle·man /míd'lmán/ n. (pl. **-men**) 1 any of the traders who handle a commodity between its producer and its consumer. 2 intermediary.

mid·dle·weight /míd'lwáyt/ n. weight class in certain sports intermediate between welterweight and light heavyweight.

mid·dling /mídling/ • adj. moderately good (esp. fair to middling). • adv. fairly or moderately. □□ **mid'dling·ly** adv.

midge /mij/ n. colloq. gnatlike insect.

midg·et /míjit/ n. extremely small person or thing.

mid·land /mídlənd/ • n. middle part of a country. • adj. of or in the midland. □□ **mid'land·er** n.

mid·night /mídnít/ n. 12 o'clock at night.

mid·riff /mídrif/ n. 1 region of the front of the body between the thorax and abdomen. 2 diaphragm.

mid·ship·man /mídshípmən/ n. (pl. **-men**) cadet in the US Naval Academy.

mid·ships /mídshíps/ adv. = AMIDSHIPS.

midst /midst/ • prep. poet. amidst. • n. middle (now only in phrases as below). □ **in the midst of** among; in the middle of. **in our** (or **your** or **their**) midst among us (or you or them).

mid·sum·mer /mídsúmər/ n. period of or near the summer solstice, around June 21.

mid·way /mídwáy/ • n. area for concessions and amusements at a carnival, fair, etc. • adv. in or toward the middle of the distance between two points.

Mid·west /mídwést/ n. region of northern US states from Ohio west to the Rocky Mountains.

mid·wife /mídwíf/ n. (pl. **-wives** /-wívz/) person trained to assist at childbirth. □□ **mid·wife·ry** /-wífəree/ n.

mid·win·ter /mídwíntər/ n. period of or near the winter solstice, around Dec. 22.

mien /meen/ n. literary person's look or bearing.

miff /mif/ v.tr. colloq. (usu. in passive) offend.

might[1] /mīt/ past of MAY, used esp.: 1 in reported speech, expressing possibility (said he might come) or permission (asked if I might leave) (cf. MAY 1, 2). 2 expressing a possibility based on a condition not fulfilled (if you'd looked you might have found it). 3 expressing complaint that an obligation or expectation is not or has not been fulfilled (they might have asked). 4 expressing a request (you might call in at the butcher's). 5 colloq. **a** = MAY 1 (it might be true). **b** in tentative questions) = MAY 2 (might I have the pleasure of this dance?). **c** = MAY 4 (who might you be?). ¶ See note at MAY.

might[2] /mīt/ n. strength; power. □ **with might and main** see MAIN.

might·y /mítee/ • adj. (**might·i·er**, **might·i·est**) 1 powerful; strong. 2 massive; bulky. 3 colloq. great; considerable. • adv. colloq. very. □□ **might'i·ly** adv. **might'i·ness** n.

mi·graine /mígrayn/ n. intense headache that often affects vision.

mi·grant /mígrənt/ • adj. that migrates. • n. migrant person or animal.

mi·grate /mígráyt/ v.intr. 1 (of people) move from one place of abode to another, esp. in a different country. 2 (of a bird or fish) change its area of habitation with the seasons. □□ **mi·gra·tion** /-gráyshən/ n. **mi·gra'tion·al** adj. **mi'gra·tor** n. **mi·gra·to·ry** /-grətawree/ adj.

mi·ka·do /mikaádō/ n. (pl. **-dos**) hist. emperor of Japan.

mike /mīk/ n. colloq. microphone.

mil /mil/ n. one-thousandth of an inch.

mi·la·dy /miláydee/ n. (pl. **-dies**) noblewoman or great lady.

Mil·an·ese /mílənéez/ • adj. of or relating to Milan in N. Italy. • n. (pl. same) native of Milan.

milch /milch/ adj. (of a domestic mammal) giving or kept for milk. □ **milch cow** = milk cow.

mild /mīld/ adj. 1 gentle and conciliatory. 2 moderate; not severe. 3 (of food, tobacco, etc.) not sharp or strong in taste, etc. 4 tame; feeble; lacking energy or vivacity. □□ **mild'ish** adj. **mild'ly** adv. **mild'ness** n.

mil·dew /míldoo, -dyoo/ • n. destructive growth of minute fungi on plants, damp paper, leather, etc. • v. taint or be tainted with mildew. □□ **mil'dew·y** adj.

mild·ly /mílodlee/ adv. in a mild fashion. □□ **to put it mildly** as an understatement (implying the reality is more extreme.)

mile /mīl/ n. (also **statute mile**) unit of linear measure equal to 1,760 yards (approx. 1.609 kilometers).

mile·age /mílij/ n. 1 **a** number of miles traveled, used, etc. **b** number of miles traveled by a vehicle per unit of fuel. 2 traveling expenses (per mile). 3 colloq. use; advantage.

mile·post /mílpōst/ n. post or sign giving distance in miles, as along a highway.

mil·er /mílər/ n. colloq. person or horse qualified or trained specially to run a mile.

mile·stone /mílstōn/ n. **1** stone marking a distance in miles. **2** significant event or stage in a life, history, project, etc.

mi·lieu /milyố, méelyō/ n. (pl. **mi·lieus** or **mi·lieux** /-lyốz/) one's environment or social surroundings.

mil·i·tant /mílit'nt/ • adj. **1** combative; aggressively active, esp. in support of a (usu. political) cause. **2** engaged in warfare. • n. militant person. □□ **mil′i·tan·cy** n. **mil′i·tant·ly** adv.

mil·i·ta·rism /mílitərizəm/ n. **1** military spirit. **2** undue prevalence of the military spirit or ideals. □□ **mil′i·ta·rist** n. **mil·i·ta·ris′tic** adj. **mil·i·ta·ris′ti·cal·ly** adv.

mil·i·ta·rize /mílitərīz/ v.tr. **1** equip with military resources. **2** make military or warlike. □□ **mil·i·ta·ri·za′tion** n.

mil·i·tar·y /mílitéree/ • adj. of, relating to, or characteristic of soldiers or armed forces. • n. (as sing. or pl.; prec. by the) members of the armed forces, as distinct from civilians and the police. □ **military police** corps responsible for police and disciplinary duties in the army. □□ **mil·i·tar·i·ly** /-táirəlee/ adv. **mil′i·tar·i·ness** n.

mil·i·tate /mílitayt/ v.intr. (of facts or evidence) have force or effect (against).
¶ **Militate**, a word usually followed by against, means 'have a profound effect or force': Overeagerness on our part would militate against success in negotiation. Do not confuse it with **mitigate**, which means 'make less intense or severe': Tension can lead to headaches unless mitigated by some form of regular relaxation.

mi·li·tia /milíshə/ n. military force, esp. one raised from the civil population and supplementing a regular army in an emergency. □□ **mi·li′tia·man** n. (pl. **-men**).

milk /milk/ • n. **1** opaque white fluid secreted by female mammals for the nourishment of their young. **2** milk of cows, goats, or sheep as food. **3** milklike juice of plants, e.g., in the coconut. • v.tr. **1** draw milk from (a cow, ewe, goat, etc.). **2** exploit (a person or situation). □ **milk cow 1** cow raised for its milk. **2** profitable venture. **milk run** routine expedition or service journey. **milk shake** drink of milk, flavoring, and usu. ice cream, mixed by shaking or blending. **milk tooth** temporary tooth in young mammals. □□ **milk′er** n.

milk·maid /mílkmayd/ n. girl or woman who milks cows or works in a dairy.

milk·man /mílkman/ n. (pl. **-men**) person who sells or delivers milk.

milk·sop /mílksop/ n. spiritless or meek person, esp. a man.

milk·y /mílkee/ adj. (**milk·i·er**, **milk·i·est**) **1** of, like, or mixed with milk. **2** (of a gem or liquid) cloudy; not clear. □ **Milky Way** faintly luminous band of light emitted by countless stars encircling the heavens; the Galaxy. □□ **milk′i·ness** n.

mill¹ /mil/ • n. **1 a** building fitted with a mechanical apparatus for grinding grain. **b** such an apparatus. **2** apparatus for grinding any solid substance to powder or pulp (pepper mill). **3** factory. • v. **1** tr. grind (grain), produce (flour),

---

or hull (seeds) in a mill. **2** tr. produce regular ribbed markings on the edge of (a coin). **3** tr. cut or shape (metal) with a rotating tool. **4** intr. move aimlessly (around). □ **go** (or **put**) **through the mill** undergo (or cause to undergo) intensive work or training, etc. □□ **mill′a·ble** adj.

mill² /mil/ n. one-thousandth of a US dollar.

mil·len·ni·um /miléneeəm/ n. (pl. **mil·len·ni·a** /-neeə/ or **mil·len·ni·ums**) **1** one-thousandth anniversary. **2** a period of 1,000 years. **3** the 1000-year period of Christ's prophesied reign in person on earth (Rev. 20:1–5). □□ **mil·len′ni·al** adj. **mil·len′ni·al·ist** n. & adj.
¶ The spelling of **millennium** is less difficult if one remembers that it comes ultimately from two Latin words containing double letters: mille, 'thousand' and annum 'year.'

mill·er /mílər/ n. person who works or owns a mill.

mil·let /mílit/ n. **1** cereal plant bearing a large crop of small nutritious seeds. **2** seed of this.

milli- /mílee, -i, -ə/ comb. form one thousandth.

mil·li·gram /míligram/ n. one-thousandth of a gram.

mil·li·li·ter /mílileetər/ n. one-thousandth of a liter.

mil·li·me·ter /mílimeetər/ n. one-thousandth of a meter.

mil·li·ner /mílinər/ n. person who makes or sells women's hats. □□ **mil·li·ner·y** /-eree/ n.

mil·lion /mílyən/ n. a thousand thousand. □□ **mil′lion·fold** adj. & adv. **mil′lionth** adj. & n.

mil·lion·aire /mílyənáir/ n. (fem. **mil·lion·air·ess** /-ris/) person who has over one million dollars, pounds, etc.

mil·li·pede /mílipeed/ n. (also **mil′le·pede**) small crawling invertebrate with many legs.

mil·li·sec·ond /mílisekənd/ n. one-thousandth of a second.

mill·race /mílrays/ n. current of water that drives a mill wheel.

mill·stone /mílstōn/ n. **1** each of two circular stones used for grinding grain. **2** heavy burden or responsibility.

mill·wright /mílrīt/ n. person who designs, builds, or operates a mill or milling machinery.

mi·lord /miláwrd/ n. hist. English nobleman.

milt /milt/ n. reproductive gland or sperm of a male fish.

mime /mīm/ • n. **1** acting using only gestures. **2** (also **mime artist**) practitioner of mime. • v. tr. (also absol.) convey by gesture without words. □□ **mim′er** n.

mim·e·o·graph /mímeeəgraf/ • n. **1** (often attrib.) machine that produces copies from a stencil. **2** copy produced in this way. • v.tr. reproduce by this process.

mi·met·ic /mimétik/ adj. relating to or habitually practicing imitation or mimicry. □□ **mi·met′i·cal·ly** adv.

mim·ic /mímik/ • v.tr. (**mim·icked**, **mim·ick·ing**) **1** imitate (a person, gesture, etc.) esp. to entertain or ridicule. **2** copy minutely or servilely. **3** (of a thing) resemble closely. • n. person skilled in imitation. • adj. having an aptitude for mimicry; imitating. □□ **mim′ick·er** n. **mim′ic·ry** n.

mi·mo·sa /mimósə, -zə/ *n.* **1** shrub having globular usu. yellow flowers. **2** acacia plant with showy yellow flowers. **3** cocktail of champagne and orange juice.

min. *abbr.* **1** minute(s). **2** minimum.

min·a·ret /mínərét/ *n.* slender turret connected to a mosque. □□ **min·a·ret´ed** *adj.*

MINARET

min·a·to·ry /mínətáwree/ *adj.* threatening; menacing.

mince /mins/ *v.* **1** *tr.* cut up or grind into very small pieces. **2** *intr.* (usu. as **mincing** *adj.*) speak or walk with an affected delicacy. □ **mince words** (usu. with *neg.*) use polite expressions, etc. □□ **minc´er** *n.* **minc´ing·ly** *adv.* (in sense 2 of *v.*).

mince·meat /mínsmeet/ *n.* mixture of currants, raisins, sugar, apples, candied peel, spices, often suet, and sometimes meat. □ **make mincemeat of** utterly defeat.

mind /mīnd/ • *n.* **1 a** seat of consciousness, thought, volition, and feeling. **b** attention; concentration. **2** intellect; reason. **3** remembrance; memory. **4** one's opinion (*we're of the same mind*). **5** way of thinking or feeling (*shocking to the Victorian mind*). **6** sanity. • *v.tr.* **1** (usu. with *neg.* or *interrog.*) object to (*do you mind if I smoke?*). **2** remember; heed; take care to (*mind you come on time*). **3** have charge of temporarily (*mind the house while I'm away*). **4** apply oneself to; concern oneself with. □ **have (it) in mind** intend. **mind-boggling** *colloq.* overwhelming; startling. **mind-read** discern the thoughts of (another person). **mind reader** person capable of mind reading. **never mind 1** expression used to comfort or console. **2** (also **never you mind**) expression used to evade a question. **3** disregard (*never mind the cost*). **out of one's mind** crazy.

mind·ed /míndid/ *adj.* **1** (in *comb.*) having a specified kind of mind or interest. **2** disposed or inclined.

mind·ful /míndfŏŏl/ *adj.* (often foll. by *of*) taking heed or care; being conscious. □□ **mind´ful·ly** *adv.* **mind´ful·ness** *n.*

mind·less /míndlis/ *adj.* **1** lacking intelligence; stupid. **2** not requiring thought or skill (*totally mindless work*). **3** heedless of (advice, etc.). □□ **mind´less·ly** *adv.* **mind´less·ness** *n.*

mind·set /míndset/ *n.* **1** mental attitude that can influence one's interpretation of events or situations. **2** inclination or a fixed way of thinking.

mine[1] /mīn/ *poss.pron.* the one or ones of or belonging to me (*it is mine*). □ **of mine** of or belonging to me.

mine[2] /mīn/ • *n.* **1** excavation in the earth for extracting metal, coal, salt, etc. **2** abundant source (of information, etc.). **3** military explosive device placed in the ground or in the water. • *v.tr.* **1** obtain (metal, coal, etc.) from a mine. **2** dig in (the earth, etc.) for ore, etc. **3** tunnel. **4** lay explosive mines under or in. □□ **min´ing** *n.*

mine·field /mínfeeld/ *n.* **1** area planted with explosive mines. **2** subject or situation presenting unseen hazards.

min·er /mínər/ *n.* person who works in a mine.

min·er·al /mínərəl/ *n.* **1** any of the species into which inorganic substances are classified. **2** substance obtained by mining. □ **mineral oil** *Pharm.* colorless, odorless, oily liquid obtained from petroleum and used as a laxative, in manufacturing cosmetics, etc. **mineral water** natural or processed water containing some dissolved salts.

min·er·al·o·gy /mínəróləjee/ *n.* scientific study of minerals. □□ **min·er·al·og·i·cal** /-rəlójikəl/ *adj.* **min·er·al´o·gist** *n.*

mine·stro·ne /mínistrónee/ *n.* thick vegetable soup.

mine·sweep·er /mínsweepər/ *n.* ship for clearing away floating and submerged mines.

min·gle /mínggəl/ *v.* **1** *tr.* & *intr.* mix; blend. **2** *intr.* (often foll. by *with*) (of a person) move about; associate. □□ **min´gler** *n.*

min·i /mínee/ *n.* (*pl.* **min·is**) *colloq.* miniskirt, minidress, etc.

mini- /mínee/ *comb. form* miniature.

min·i·a·ture /míneeəchər, mínichər/ • *adj.* **1** much smaller than normal. **2** represented on a small scale. • *n.* **1** any object reduced in size. **2** small-scale minutely finished portrait. □□ **min´i·a·tur·ist** *n.* (in sense 2 of n.).

min·i·a·tur·ize /míneeəchərīz, mínichə-/ *v.tr.* produce in a smaller version; make small. □□ **min·i·a·tur·i·za´tion** *n.*

min·i·bike /míneebīk/ *n.* motorbike designed for off-road use, esp. with elevated handlebars.

min·i·cam /míneekam/ *n.* portable lightweight video camera.

min·i·com·put·er /míneekəmpyŏŏtər/ *n.* computer of medium power.

min·i·ma *pl.* of MINIMUM.

min·i·mal /míniməl/ *adj.* **1** very minute; smallest; least. **2** *Art*, etc. characterized by the use of simple or primary forms or structures, etc. □□ **min´i·mal·ism** *n.* (in sense 2). **min´i·mal·ist** *n.* (in sense 2). **min´i·mal·ly** *adv.* (in sense 1).

min·i·mize /mínimīz/ *v.* **1** *tr.* reduce to, or estimate at, the smallest possible amount or degree. **2** *tr.* estimate or represent at less than the true value or importance. **3** *intr.* attain a minimum value. □□ **min·i·mi·za´tion** *n.* **min´i·miz·er** *n.*

min·i·mum /míniməm/ (*pl.* **min·i·ma** /-mə/) • *n.* least possible or attainable amount. • *adj.* that is a minimum. □ **minimum wage** lowest wage permitted by law.

min·ion /mínyən/ n. derog. servile agent; slave.

min·i·ser·ies /míneeseereez/ n. short series of television programs on a common theme.

min·i·skirt /míneeskərt/ n. very short skirt.

min·is·ter /mínistər/ ● n. **1** member of the clergy. **2** head of a government department (in some countries). **3** diplomatic agent, usu. ranking below an ambassador. ● v. intr. render aid or service to. □□ **min·is·te·ri·al** /-istéereeəl/ adj. **min·is·te´ri·al·ly** adv.

min·is·tra·tion /mínistráyshən/ n. **1** (usu. in pl.) aid or service. **2** supplying (of help, justice, etc.). □□ **min·is·trant** /mínistrənt/ adj. & n.

min·is·try /mínistree/ n. (pl. **-tries**) **1** (prec. by the) vocation office, tenure, or profession of a religious minister. **2** (prec. by the) body of ministers of a government or of a religion. **3** government department headed by a minister. **4** ministering; ministration.

min·i·van /míneeván/ n. vehicle, smaller than a full-sized van, for passengers, cargo, etc.

mink /mingk/ n. **1** semiaquatic stoatlike animal bred for its thick brown fur. **2** this thick brown fur. **3** coat made of this.

Minn. abbr. Minnesota.

min·now /mínō/ n. small freshwater fish.

Mi·no·an /mínóən/ Archaeol. ● adj. of or relating to the Bronze Age civilization centered on Crete (c. 3000–1100 BC). ● n. inhabitant of Minoan Crete or the Minoan world.

mi·nor /mínər/ ● adj. **1** lesser or comparatively small in size or importance (minor poet). **2** Mus. less by a semitone than a corresponding major. ● n. **1** person under the legal age limit or majority. **2** student's subsidiary subject or course. ● v.intr. (foll. by in) (of a student) undertake study in (a subject) as a subsidiary. □ **minor scale** Mus. scale with half steps between the second and third, fifth and sixth, and seventh and eighth degrees.

mi·nor·i·ty /mínáwritee, -nór-/ n. (pl. **-ties**) **1** smaller number or part, esp. within a political party or structure; less than half. **2** relatively small group of people differing from others in race, religion, language, political persuasion, etc. **3** being under full legal age. □ **minority leader** leader of the minority political party in a legislature.

min·ox·i·dil /mənóksədil/ n. drug taken orally to treat hypertension or applied topically to stimulate hair growth.

min·strel /mínstrəl/ n. **1** medieval singer or musician. **2** (usu. in pl.) member of a band of public entertainers with blackened faces, etc., performing songs and music ostensibly of African-American origin.

mint[1] /mint/ n. **1** aromatic plant used for flavoring. **2** peppermint or spearmint candy or lozenge. □ **mint julep** sweet iced alcoholic drink of bourbon flavored with mint. □□ **mint´y** adj. (**mint·i·er**, **mint·i·est**).

mint[2] /mint/ ● n. **1** place where money is coined. **2** vast sum of money. ● v.tr. **1** make (coin) by stamping metal. **2** invent or coin (a word, phrase, etc.). □ **in mint condition** as new. □□ **mint´age** n.

min·u·et /mínyŏo-ét/ n. **1** slow stately dance for two in triple time. **2** Mus. music for this.

mi·nus /mínəs/ ● prep. **1** with the subtraction of (7 minus 4 equals 3). ¶ Symb.: −. **2** (of temperature) below zero (minus 2°). **3** colloq. lacking; deprived of (returned minus their dog). ● adj. negative. ● n. **1** = minus sign. **2** Math. negative quantity. **3** disadvantage. □ **minus sign** the symbol (−) indicating subtraction or a negative value.

mi·nus·cule /mínəskyŏol/ adj. colloq. extremely small or unimportant. □□ **mi·nus·cu·lar** /minúskyŏolər/ adj.
¶ Avoid the common misspelling of **minuscule** as "miniscule."

min·ute[1] /mínit/ n. **1** sixtieth part of an hour. **2** distance covered in one minute (twenty minutes from the station). **3** moment. **4** sixtieth part of an angular degree. **5** (in pl.) official memorandum or brief summary of a meeting, etc. □ **up-to-the-minute** completely up to date.

> **minute** late Middle English (in the singular in the sense 'note or memorandum'): from French minute, from the notion of a rough copy of a manuscript in 'small writing' (Latin scriptura minuta) as distinct from the finished copy in carefully formed book hand.

mi·nute[2] /mīnóot, -yóot/ adj. (**mi·nut·est**) **1** very small. **2** accurate; detailed. □□ **min´ute·ly** adv.

min·ute·man /mínitman/ n. (pl. **-men**) US hist. (also **Min´ute·man**) American militiaman of the Revolutionary War period (ready to march at a minute's notice).

mi·nu·ti·a /minóosheeə, -shə, -nyóo-/ n. (pl. **-ti·ae** /-shee-ee/) (usu. in pl.) precise, trivial, or minor detail.

minx /mingks/ n. pert, sly, or playful girl.

mir·a·cle /mírəkəl/ n. **1** extraordinary event attributed to some supernatural agency. **2** remarkable occurrence. **3** remarkable specimen (the plan was a miracle of ingenuity).

mi·rac·u·lous /mirákyələs/ adj. **1** of the nature of a miracle. **2** supernatural. **3** remarkable; surprising. □□ **mi·rac´u·lous·ly** adv. **mi·rac´u·lous·ness** n.

mi·rage /miráazh/ n. **1** optical illusion caused by atmospheric conditions. **2** illusory thing.

mire /mīr/ ● n. **1** stretch of swampy or boggy ground. **2** mud; dirt. ● v. **1** tr. & intr. plunge or sink in a mire. **2** tr. involve in difficulties.

mir·ror /mírər/ ● n. **1** polished surface, usu. of amalgam-coated glass or metal, which reflects an image. **2** anything reflecting truly or accurately. ● v.tr. reflect as in a mirror.

mirth /mərth/ n. merriment; laughter. □□ **mirth´ful** adj. **mirth´ful·ly** adv. **mirth´ful·ness** n. **mirth´less** adj. **mirth´less·ly** adv. **mirth´less·ness** n.

MIS abbr. Computing management information system.

mis- /mis/ prefix added to verbs, verbal derivatives, and nouns, meaning 'amiss,' 'badly,' 'wrongly,' 'unfavorably,' or having negative force (mislead; misshapen; mistrust; misadventure).

mis·ad·ven·ture /mísədvénchər/ n. bad luck; misfortune.

mis·a·lign /mísəlín/ v.tr. give the wrong alignment to. □□ **mis·a·lign′ment** n.

mis·an·thrope /mísənthrōp, míz-/ n. (also **mis·an·thro·pist** /mísánthrəpist/) person who hates or avoids human society. □□ **mis·an·throp·ic** /-thrópik/ adj. **mis·an·throp′i·cal** adj. **mis·an·throp′i·cal·ly** adv. **mis·an·thro·py** /mísánthrəpee/ n.

mis·ap·ply /mísəplí/ v.tr. (**-plies, -plied**) apply (esp. funds) wrongly. □□ **mis·ap·pli·ca·tion** /mísaplikáyshən/ n.

mis·ap·pre·hend /mísaprihénd/ v.tr. misunderstand. □□ **mis·ap·pre·hen·sion** /-hénshən/ n. **mis·ap·pre·hen′sive** adj.

mis·ap·pro·pri·ate /mísəprṓpreeayt/ v.tr. take for one's own use; embezzle. □□ **mis·ap·pro·pri·a·tion** /-áyshən/ n.

mis·be·got·ten /mísbigót'n/ adj. **1** illegitimate; bastard. **2** contemptible; disreputable.

mis·be·have /mísbiháyv/ v.intr. & refl. (of a person or machine) behave badly. □□ **mis·be·hav′ior** n.

misc. abbr. miscellaneous.

mis·car·riage /mískárij/ n. **1** spontaneous premature abortion. **2** failure (of a plan, system, etc.).

mis·car·ry /mískáree/ v.intr. (**-ries, -ried**) **1** have a miscarriage. **2** (of a business, plan, etc.) fail; be unsuccessful.

mis·cast /mískást/ v.tr. (past and past part. **-cast**) allot an unsuitable part to (an actor).

mis·ce·ge·na·tion /miséjináyshən, mísəjə-/ n. interbreeding of races, esp. of whites and non-whites.

mis·cel·la·ne·ous /mísəláyneeəs/ adj. **1** of mixed composition or character. **2** (foll. by pl. noun) of various kinds. □□ **mis·cel·la′ne·ous·ly** adv.

mis·cel·la·ny /mísəláynee/ n. (pl. **-nies**) mixture; medley, esp. a varied literary collection.

mis·chance /míscháns/ n. **1** bad luck. **2** instance of this.

mis·chief /míschif/ n. **1** pranks; scrapes. **2** playful malice; archness. **3** harm; injury. **4** person or thing responsible for harm or annoyance.

mis·chie·vous /míschivəs/ adj. **1** (of a person) disposed to mischief. **2** (of conduct) playfully malicious. **3** (of a thing) harmful. □□ **mis′chie·vous·ly** adv. **mis′chie·vous·ness** n.
¶ Do not pronounce this word with an extra syllable, "mis-chee-vee-uhs."

mischievous Middle English: from Anglo-Norman French meschevous, from Old French meschever 'come to an unfortunate end.' The early sense was 'unfortunate or calamitous,' later 'having harmful effects'; the sense of 'playfully malicious' dates from the late 17th century.

mis·ci·ble /mísibəl/ adj. (often foll. by with) capable of being mixed. □□ **mis·ci·bil′i·ty** n.

mis·con·ceive /mískənseév/ v. **1** intr. (often foll. by of) have a wrong idea or conception. **2** tr. (as **misconceived** adj.) badly planned, organized, etc. □□ **mis·con·ceiv′er** n. **mis·con·cep·tion** /-sépshən/ n.

mis·con·duct n. /mískóndukt/ **1** improper or unprofessional behavior. **2** bad management.

mis·con·strue /mískənstrṓ/ v.tr. interpret wrongly. □□ **mis·con·struc·tion** /-strúkshən/ n.

mis·count /mískównt/ • v.tr. (also absol.) count wrongly. • n. a wrong count.

mis·cre·ant /mískreeənt/ n. vile wretch; villain.

mis·deal /mísdeél/ • v.tr. (also absol.) (past and past part. **-dealt** /-délt/) make a mistake in dealing (cards). • n. **1** mistake in dealing cards. **2** misdealt hand.

mis·deed /mísdeéd/ n. evil deed; wrongdoing; crime.

mis·de·mean·or /mísdimeénər/ n. **1** offense; misdeed. **2** Law indictable offense, less heinous than a felony.

mis·di·rect /mísdirékt, -dī-/ v.tr. direct (a person, letter, blow, etc.) wrongly. □□ **mis·di·rec·tion** /-rékshən/ n.

mis·do·ing /misdṓing/ n. misdeed.

mi·ser /mízər/ n. person who hoards wealth greedily. □□ **mi′ser·li·ness** n. **mi′ser·ly** adj.

mis·er·a·ble /mízərəbəl/ adj. **1** wretchedly unhappy or uncomfortable. **2** inadequate (miserable hovel); contemptible. **3** causing wretchedness or discomfort (miserable weather). **4** stingy; mean. □□ **mis′er·a·ble·ness** n. **mis′er·a·bly** adv.

mis·er·y /mízəree/ n. (pl. **-ies**) **1** wretched state of mind, or of outward circumstances. **2** thing causing this.

mis·fire /mísfír/ • v.intr. **1** (of a gun, motor engine, etc.) fail to go off or start or function regularly. **2** (of an action, etc.) fail to have the intended effect. • n. such a failure.

mis·fit /mísfit/ n. **1** person unsuited to an environment, occupation, etc. **2** garment, etc., that does not fit.

mis·for·tune /misfáwrchən/ n. bad luck.

mis·giv·ing /misgíving/ n. (usu. in pl.) feeling of mistrust or apprehension.

mis·gov·ern /misgúvərn/ v.tr. govern (a state, a nation, etc.) badly. □□ **mis·gov′ern·ment** n.

mis·guide /misgíd/ v.tr. **1** (as **misguided** adj.) mistaken in thought or action. **2** mislead; misdirect. □□ **mis·guid′ance** n. **mis·guid′ed·ly** adv. **mis·guid′ed·ness** n.

mis·han·dle /mis-hánd'l/ v.tr. **1** deal with incorrectly or ineffectively. **2** handle roughly or rudely; ill-treat.

mis·hap /mís-háp/ n. unlucky accident.

mis·hear /mis-heér/ v.tr. (past and past part. **-heard** /-hérd/) hear incorrectly or imperfectly.

mish·mash /míshmash, -maash/ n. confused mixture.

mis·in·form /mísinfórm/ v.tr. give wrong information to; mislead. □□ **mis·in·for·ma′tion** n.

mis·in·ter·pret /mísintórprit/ v.tr. **1** interpret wrongly. **2** draw a wrong inference from. □□ **mis·in·ter·pre·ta′tion** n. **mis·in·ter′pret·er** n.

mis·judge /mísjúj/ v.tr. (also absol.) **1** judge wrongly. **2** have a wrong opinion of. □□ **mis·judg′ment** n.

mis·lay /misláy/ v.tr. (past and past part. **-laid** /-láyd/) unintentionally put (a thing) where it cannot readily be found.

mis·lead /misleéd/ v.tr. (past and past part. **-led** /-léd/) **1** cause (a person) to go wrong, in conduct, belief, etc. **2** lead astray or in the wrong direction. □□ **mis·lead′er** n.

mis·lead·ing /misleéding/ adj. causing to err or go astray; imprecise. □□ **mis·lead′ing·ly** adv.

mis·man·age /mismánij/ *v.tr.* manage badly or wrongly. □□ **mis·man'age·ment** *n.*

mis·match ● *v.tr.* /mismách/ (usu. as **mismatched** *adj.*) match unsuitably or incorrectly. ● *n.* /mismach/ bad match.

mis·no·mer /misnómər/ *n.* name or term used wrongly.

mi·sog·y·ny /misójinee/ *n.* hatred of women. □□ **mi·sog'y·nist** *n.* **mi·sog'y·nous** *adj.*

mis·place /mispláys/ *v.tr.* **1** put in the wrong place. **2** bestow (affections, confidence, etc.) on an inappropriate object. **3** time (words, actions, etc.) badly. □□ **mis·place'ment** *n.*

mis·print ● *n.* /mísprint/ mistake in printing. ● *v.tr.* /misprínt/ print wrongly.

mis·pri·sion /mispríz̲hən/ *n.* *Law* wrong action or omission.

mis·pro·nounce /misprənówns/ *v.tr.* pronounce (a word, etc.) wrongly. □□ **mis·pro·nun·ci·a·tion** /-nunseeáyshən/ *n.*

mis·quote /mískwót/ *v.tr.* quote wrongly. □□ **mis·quo·ta'tion** *n.*

mis·read /mísréed/ *v.tr.* (*past* and *past part.* -**read** /-réd/) read or interpret (text, a situation, etc.) wrongly.

mis·rep·re·sent /mísreprizént/ *v.tr.* represent wrongly; give a false or misleading account or idea of. □□ **mis·rep·re·sen·ta'tion** *n.* **mis·rep·re·sen'ta·tive** *adj.*

mis·rule /mísro͞ol/ ● *n.* bad government; disorder. ● *v.tr.* govern badly.

Miss. *abbr.* Mississippi.

miss¹ /mis/ ● *v.* **1** *tr.* (also *absol.*) fail to hit, reach, find, catch, see, meet, hear, etc. **2** *tr.* fail to seize (an opportunity, etc.) (*I missed my chance*). **3** *tr.* notice or regret the loss or absence of. **4** *tr.* avoid (*go early to miss the traffic*). **5** *intr.* (of an engine, etc.) fail; misfire. ● *n.* failure to hit, reach, attain, connect, etc. □□ **miss'a·ble** *adj.*

miss² /mis/ *n.* **1** girl or unmarried woman. **2** (**Miss**) a respectful title of an unmarried woman or girl. **b** title of a beauty queen (*Miss World*).

mis·sal /mísəl/ *n.* *RC Ch., Anglican Ch.* **1** book containing the texts used in the service of the Mass. **2** book of prayers, esp. an illuminated one.

mis·shap·en /mís-sháypən/ *adj.* ill-shaped, deformed, distorted. □□ **mis·shap'en·ly** *adv.* **mis·shap'en·ness** *n.*

mis·sile /mísəl/ *n.* object or weapon suitable for throwing or propelling, esp. one directed by remote control or automatically. □□ **mis·sile·ry** /-əlree/ *n.*

miss·ing /mísing/ *adj.* lost; not present.

mis·sion /míshən/ *n.* **1** particular task or goal assigned to or assumed by a person or group. **2** military or scientific operation or expedition. **3** body of persons sent to conduct negotiations, etc., or to propagate a religious faith. **4** missionary post.

mis·sion·ar·y /míshəneree/ ● *adj.* of, concerned with, or characteristic of, religious missions. ● *n.* (*pl.* -**ies**) person doing missionary work.

mis·sis var. of MISSUS.

mis·sive /mísiv/ *n.* letter; message.

mis·spell /mís-spél/ *v.tr.* (*past* and *past part.* -**spelled** or -**spelt**) spell wrongly.

mis·spend /mís-spénd/ *v.tr.* (*past* and *past part.* -**spent** /-spént/) (esp. as **misspent** *adj.*) spend amiss or wastefully.

mis·state /mís-stáyt/ *v.tr.* state wrongly or inaccurately. □□ **mis·state'ment** *n.*

mis·step /mís-stép/ *n.* **1** wrong step or action. **2** faux pas.

mis·sus /mísəz/ *n.* (also **mis'sis**) *sl.* or *joc.* **1** form of address to a woman. **2** a wife. □ **the missus** my or your wife.

mist /mist/ ● *n.* **1 a** water vapor near the ground in minute droplets limiting visibility. **b** condensed vapor obscuring glass, etc. **2** anything resembling or obscuring like mist. ● *v.* cover or become covered with mist or as with mist. □□ **mist'like** *adj.*

mis·take /mistáyk/ ● *n.* **1** incorrect idea or opinion; thing incorrectly done or thought. **2** error of judgment. ● *v.tr.* (*past* **mis·took** /-to͝ok/; *past part.* **mis·tak·en** /-táykən/) **1** misunderstand. **2** wrongly take or identify. **3** choose wrongly. □□ **mis·tak'a·ble** *adj.* **mis·tak'a·bly** *adv.*

mis·tak·en /mistáykən/ *adj.* **1** wrong. **2** misunderstood; incorrect. □□ **mis·tak'en·ly** *adv.*

mis·ter /místər/ *n.* title or form of address for a man.

mis·time /mís-tím/ *v.tr.* say or do at the wrong time.

mis·tle·toe /mísəltō/ *n.* parasitic plant growing on apple and other trees and bearing white glutinous berries.

mis·took *past* of MISTAKE.

mis·treat /místréet/ *v.tr.* treat badly. □□ **mis·treat'ment** *n.*

mis·tress /místris/ *n.* **1** female head of a household. **2** woman in authority. **3** woman (other than his wife) with whom a married man has a (usu. prolonged) sexual relationship.

mis·tri·al /mís-tríəl/ *n.* trial rendered invalid by procedural error.

mis·trust /mís-trúst/ ● *v.tr.* **1** be suspicious of. **2** feel no confidence in. ● *n.* **1** suspicion. **2** lack of confidence.

mis·trust·ful /mís-trústfo͝ol/ *adj.* **1** suspicious. **2** lacking confidence. □□ **mis·trust'ful·ly** *adv.* **mis·trust'ful·ness** *n.*

mist·y /místee/ *adj.* (**mist·i·er, mist·i·est**) **1** of or covered with mist. **2** obscure; vague; dim. □□ **mist'i·ly** *adv.* **mist'i·ness** *n.*

mis·un·der·stand /mísundərstánd/ *v.tr.* (*past* and *past part.* -**un·der·stood** /-sto͝od/) **1** fail to understand correctly. **2** (usu. as **misunderstood** *adj.*) misjudge.

mis·un·der·stand·ing /mísundərstánding/ *n.* **1** failure to understand correctly. **2** slight disagreement or quarrel.

mis·use ● *v.tr.* /mísyo͞oz/ **1** use wrongly; apply to the wrong purpose. **2** ill-treat. ● *n.* /mísyo͞os/ wrong or improper use or application. □□ **mis·us'er** *n.*

mite¹ /mīt/ *n.* small, often parasitic arachnid. □□ **mit'y** *adj.*

mite² /mīt/ *n.* **1** small sum of money. **2** small object or person.

mi·ter /mítər/ ● *n.* **1** tall deeply-cleft headdress worn by bishops, esp. as a symbol of office. **2** joint of two pieces of wood or other ma-

terial at an angle of 90°. • *v.* join with a miter.
□□ **mi′tered** *adj.*

MITER, 1

mit·i·gate /mítigayt/ *v.tr.* make milder or less
intense or severe (*your offer certainly mitigated
their hostility*). □□ **mit′i·ga·ble** *adj.* **mit·i·ga·tion**
/-gáyshən/ *n.* **mit′i·ga·tor** *n.* **mit·i·ga·to·ry** /-gə-
táwree/ *adj.*
¶ See note at MILITATE.

mi·to·sis /mītósis/ *n. Biol.* type of cell division that results in two nuclei each having the
full number of chromosomes. □□ **mi·tot·ic** /-tó-
tik/ *adj.*

mi·tral /mítrəl/ *adj.* of or like a miter. □ **mitral
valve** two-cusped valve between the left atrium
and the left ventricle of the heart.

mitt /mit/ *n.* **1** baseball glove with mittenlike finger section. **2** = MITTEN. **3** *sl.* hand or fist. **4** glove
leaving the fingers and thumb-tip exposed.

mit·ten /mít'n/ *n.* glove with two sections, one
for the thumb and the other for all four fingers.
□□ **mit′tened** *adj.*

mix /miks/ • *v.* **1** *tr.* combine; blend; put together. **2** *tr.* prepare by combining the ingredients **3** *intr.* **a** join, be mixed, or combine, esp.
readily. **b** be compatible. **c** be sociable (*must
learn to mix*). **4** *intr.* (foll. by *in*) participate in.
• *n.* **1 a** mixing; mixture. **b** proportion of materials, etc., in a mixture. **2** ingredients prepared commercially for making a cake, concrete,
etc. **3** merging of film pictures or sound. □ **be
mixed up in** (or **with**) be involved in or with
(esp. something undesirable). **mix up 1** mix thoroughly. **2** confuse; mistake the identity of. **mix-
up** *n.* confusion, misunderstanding, or mistake.
□□ **mix′a·ble** *adj.*

mixed /mikst/ *adj.* **1** of diverse qualities or elements. **2** containing persons from various back-
grounds, both genders, etc. □ **mixed bag** diverse
assortment of things or persons. **mixed blessing** thing having advantages and disadvantages.
mixed-up *colloq.* mentally or emotionally confused; socially ill-adjusted.

mix·er /míksər/ *n.* **1** device for mixing foods,
etc. **2** drink to be mixed with another. **3** *Broadcasting & Cinematog.* device for merging two or
more audio or video input signals.

mix·ture /míks-chər/ *n.* **1** process of mixing or

being mixed. **2** result of mixing; something
mixed; combination of ingredients, qualities,
characteristics, etc.

miz·zen·mast /mízənmast/ *n.* mast next aft of
a ship's mainmast.

ml *abbr.* milliliter(s).

Mlle. *abbr.* (*pl.* **Mlles.**) Mademoiselle.

mm *abbr.* millimeter(s).

MM. *abbr.* Messieurs.

Mme. *abbr.* (*pl.* **Mmes.**) Madame.

MN *abbr.* Minnesota (in official postal use).

Mn *symb. Chem.* manganese.

mne·mon·ic /nimónik/ • *adj.* of or designed to
aid the memory. • *n.* mnemonic device.
□□ **mne·mon′i·cal·ly** *adv.*

MO *abbr.* **1** Missouri (in official postal use). **2**
money order.

Mo *symb. Chem.* molybdenum.

Mo. *abbr.* Missouri.

moan /mōn/ • *n.* **1** long, low plaintive sound. **2**
complaint; grievance. • *v.intr.* **1** make a moan
or moans. **2** *colloq.* complain or grumble.
□□ **moan′er** *n.* **moan′ing·ly** *adv.*

moat /mōt/ *n.* deep defensive ditch around a
castle, town, etc., usu. filled with water.

mob /mob/ • *n.* **1** disorderly crowd; rabble. **2**
(prec. by *the*) usu. *derog.* the populace. **3** =
MAFIA. • *v.tr.* (**mobbed**, **mob·bing**) crowd
around in order to attack or admire. □□ **mob′ber**
n.

mo·bile /móbəl, -beel, -bīl/ • *adj.* **1** movable;
able to move easily. **2** readily changing its expression. **3** transportable in a motor vehicle. **4**
(of a person) able to change his or her social status. • *n.* /-beĕl/ decorative structure that
may be hung so as to turn freely. □ **mobile home**
transportable structure usu. parked and used
as a residence. □□ **mo·bil·i·ty** /mōbílitee/ *n.*

mo·bi·lize /móbilīz/ *v.* **1** *tr.* organize for service
or action (esp. troops in time of war). **2** *intr.*
be organized in this way. □□ **mo′bi·liz·a·ble** *adj.*
mo·bi·li·za′tion *n.* **mo′bi·liz·er** *n.*

mob·ster /móbstər/ *n. sl.* gangster.

moc·ca·sin /mókəsin/ *n.* soft, flat-soled leather
slipper or shoe.

mo·cha /mókə/ *n.* **1** coffee of fine quality. **2** beverage or flavoring made with this, often with
chocolate added.

mock /mok/ • *v.tr.* **1** ridicule; scoff at. **2** mimic
contemptuously. **3** jeer, defy, or delude contemptuously. • *attrib.adj.* sham; imitation; pretended. □ **mock-up** experimental model or rep-
lica of a proposed structure, etc. □□ **mock′a·ble**
adj. **mock′er** *n.* **mock′ing·ly** *adv.*

mock·er·y /mókəree/ *n.* (*pl.* **-ies**) **1** derision; ridicule. **2** absurdly inadequate or futile action, etc.

mock·ing·bird /mókingbərd/ *n.* bird that mimics
the notes of other birds.

mod /mod/ *colloq. adj.* modern, esp. in style
of dress.

mod·al /mód'l/ *adj.* **1** of mode or form. **2** *Gram.*
a of the mood of a verb. **b** (of an auxiliary verb,
e.g., *would*) used to express the mood of another
verb. **3** *Mus.* denoting a style of music using a
particular mode. □□ **mod′al·ly** *adv.*

mode /mōd/ *n.* **1** way or manner in which a
thing is done; method of procedure. **2** prevailing
fashion or custom. **3** *Mus.* any of several types
of scale. **4** *Gram.* = MOOD[2].

mod·el /módʼl/ • *n.* **1** representation in three dimensions of an existing person or thing or of a proposed structure, esp. on a smaller scale (often *attrib.*: *model train*). **2** simplified description of a system, etc., to assist calculations and predictions. **3** particular design or style, esp. of a car. **4** exemplary person or thing. **5** person employed to pose for an artist or photographer or to display clothes, etc., by wearing them. • *v.* **1** *tr.* fashion, shape, or form a model. **2** *a intr.* act or pose as a model. **b** *tr.* display (a garment). □□ **modʹel·er** *n.*

mo·dem /módem/ *n.* device for transmitting data between computers, etc., esp. over a telephone line.

mod·er·ate • *adj.* /mód ərət/ **1** avoiding extremes; temperate in conduct or expression. **2** fairly or tolerably large or good. **3** calm. • *n.* /mód ərət/ person who holds moderate views. • *v.* /mód ərayt/ **1** *tr.* & *intr.* make or become moderate. **2** *tr.* (also *absol.*) act as a moderator of or to. □□ **modʹer·ate·ly** *adv.* **modʹer·ate·ness** *n.* **mod·er·a·tion** /mód əráyshən/ *n.*

mod·er·a·tor /mód əraytər/ *n.* **1** arbitrator or mediator. **2** presiding officer.

mod·ern /mód ərn/ • *adj.* **1** of the present and recent times. **2** in current fashion; not antiquated. • *n.* (usu. in *pl.*) person living in modern times. □ **modern English** English from about 1500 onward. □□ **mo·der·ni·ty** /-dérnitee/ *n.* **modʹern·ly** *adv.* **modʹern·ness** *n.*

mod·ern·ism /mód ərnizəm/ *n.* modern ideas, methods, or practices. □□ **modʹern·ist** *n.* **mod·ern·isʹtic** *adj.* **mod·ern·isʹti·cal·ly** *adv.*

mod·ern·ize /mód ərnīz/ *v.* **1** *tr.* make modern; adapt to modern needs or habits. **2** *intr.* adopt modern ways or views. □□ **mod·ern·i·zaʹtion** *n.* **modʹern·iz·er** *n.*

mod·est /módist/ *adj.* **1** humble; not vain. **2** diffident; bashful; retiring. **3** decorous. **4** restrained; not excessive or exaggerated; unpretentious. □□ **modʹest·ly** *adv.* **modʹes·ty** *n.*

mod·i·cum /módikəm/ *n.* (foll. by *of*) small quantity.

mod·i·fi·er /módifīər/ *n.* **1** person or thing that modifies. **2** *Gram.* a word, esp. an adjective or noun used attributively, that qualifies the sense of another word (e.g., *good* and *family* in *a good family house*).

¶ A modifier is said to be *misplaced* if it has no clear grammatical or logical connection to the part of the sentence which it modifies or describes. Thus, in the sentence *A man of great energy, his works include twenty novels.* the meaning is clear, but the first phrase appears to modify *works.* Careful writers avoid this lapse in syntax, which can cause ludicrous images, especially in the case of **dangling participles** such as the one in the sentence *Filled with wine, the fireworks delighted us.*

mod·i·fy /módifī/ *v.tr.* (**-fies, -fied**) **1** make less severe or extreme. **2** make partial changes in. **3** *Gram.* qualify or expand the sense of (a word, etc.). □□ **modʹi·fi·a·ble** *adj.* **mod·i·fi·caʹtion** *n.*

mod·ish /módish/ *adj.* fashionable; stylish. □□ **modʹish·ly** *adv.* **modʹish·ness** *n.*

mod·u·late /mójələyt/ *v.* **1** *tr.* **a** regulate or adjust. **b** moderate. **2** *tr.* adjust or vary the tone or pitch of (the speaking voice). **3** *tr.* alter the amplitude or frequency of (a wave). **4** *intr.* & *tr.* *Mus.* change or cause to change from one key to another. □□ **mod·u·laʹtion** /-láyshən/ *n.* **modʹu·la·tor** *n.*

---

385   **model ~ mole**

mod·ule /mójōol/ *n.* **1** standardized part or independent self-contained unit of a spacecraft. **3** unit or period of training or education. □□ **modʹu·lar** /-jələr/ *adj.* **mod·u·larʹi·ty** /-jəláritee/ *n.*

mo·dus op·e·ran·di /módəs ópərándee, -dī/ *n.* (*pl.* **mo·di op·e·ran·di** /módee, -dī/) method of working.

mo·dus vi·ven·di /módəs vivéndee, -dī/ *n.* (*pl.* **mo·di vi·ven·di** /módee, -dī/) **1** way of living or coping. **2** arrangement between people who agree to differ.

mo·gul /mógəl/ *n.* *colloq.* important or influential person.

mo·hair /móhair/ *n.* **1** hair of the angora goat. **2** yarn or fabric from this, either pure or mixed with wool or cotton.

Mo·hawk /móhawk/ *n.* **1 a** member of a Native American people of New York State. **b** language of this people. **2** (of a hairstyle) with the head shaved except for a strip of hair from the middle of the forehead to the back of the neck.

Mo·he·gan /mōhéegən/ • *n.* member of a Native American people of Connecticut. • *adj.* of or relating to this people.

Mo·hi·can var. of **Mahican**.

moi·e·ty /móyətee/ *n.* (*pl.* **-ties**) *Law* or *literary* **1** half. **2** each of the two parts into which a thing is divided.

moire /mwaar, mawr/ *n.* (in full **moire antique**) watered fabric, orig. mohair, now usu. silk.

moist /moyst/ *adj.* **1** slightly wet; damp. **2** (of the season, etc.) rainy. □□ **moistʹly** *adv.* **moistʹness** *n.*

moist·en /móysən/ *v.* make or become moist.

mois·ture /móys-chər/ *n.* water or other liquid causing slight dampness. □□ **moisʹture·less** *adj.*

mois·tur·ize /móys-chərīz/ *v.tr.* make less dry (esp. the skin by use of a cosmetic). □□ **moisʹtur·iz·er** *n.*

mo·lar /mólər/ • *adj.* (usu. of a mammal's back teeth) serving to grind. • *n.* molar tooth.

mo·las·ses /məlásiz/ *n.pl.* (treated as *sing.*) uncrystallized syrup extracted from raw sugar during refining.

mold¹ /mōld/ • *n.* **1** hollow container into which a substance is poured or pressed to harden into a required shape. **2** form; shape. **3** *Archit.* molding or group of moldings. **4** frame or template. **5** character or disposition (*in heroic mold*). • *v.tr.* **1** make (an object) in a required shape or from certain ingredients. **2** give a shape to. **3** influence. □□ **moldʹa·ble** *adj.* **moldʹer** *n.*

mold² /mōld/ *n.* woolly or furry growth of minute fungi occurring esp. in moist warm conditions.

mold³ /mōld/ *n.* loose earth, rich in organic matter.

mold·er /móldər/ *v.intr.* decay to dust; deteriorate.

mold·ing /mólding/ *n.* ornamentally shaped plaster or woodwork as an architectural feature.

mold·y /móldee/ *adj.* (**-i·er, -i·est**) **1** covered with mold. **2** stale; out of date. □□ **moldʹi·ness** *n.*

mole¹ /mōl/ *n.* **1** small burrowing insect-eating mammal with dark velvety fur. **2** *colloq.* spy established deep within an organization in a position of trust.

mole[2] /mōl/ *n.* small often dark blemish on the skin.

mole[3] /mōl/ *n.* pier, breakwater, or causeway.

mole[4] /mōl/ *n. Chem.* SI unit of amount of substance equal to the quantity containing as many elementary units as there are atoms in 0.012 kg of carbon 12. □□ **mo′lar** *adj.* **mo·lar·i·ty** /məláritee/ *n.*

mol·e·cule /mólikyōol/ *n.* **1** *Chem.* smallest fundamental unit of an element or compound. **2** small particle. □□ **mo·lec·u·lar** /məlékyələr/ *adj.*

mole·hill /mólhil/ *n.* small mound thrown up by a mole in burrowing.

mole·skin /mólskin/ *n.* **1** skin of a mole used as fur. **2** kind of cotton fustian with its surface shaved before dyeing.

mo·lest /məlést/ *v.tr.* **1** annoy or pester in a hostile or injurious way. **2** attack or interfere with (a person), esp. sexually. □□ **mo·les·ta·tion** /mōlestáyshən, mól-/ *n.* **mo·lest′er** *n.*

mol·li·fy /mólifī/ *v.tr.* (-**fies,** -**fied**) **1** appease. **2** reduce the severity of. □□ **mol·li·fi·ca′tion** *n.* **mol′li·fi·er** *n.*

mol·lusk /móləsk/ *n.* invertebrate with a soft body and usu. a hard shell, e.g., a snail or oyster. □□ **mol·lus·kan** or **mol·lus·can** /məlúskən/ *n.* & *adj.* **mol′lusk·like** *adj.*

mol·ly·cod·dle /móleekodəl/ • *v.tr.* coddle; pamper. • *n.* effeminate man or boy; milksop.

molt /mōlt/ *v.* **1** *intr.* shed feathers, hair, a shell, etc., in the process of renewing plumage, a coat, etc. **2** *tr.* (of an animal) shed (feathers, hair, etc.). □□ **molt′er** *n.*

mol·ten /mōltən/ *adj.* melted, esp. made liquid by heat.

mo·lyb·de·num /məlíbdinəm/ *n. Chem.* silver-white brittle metallic transition element used in steel. ¶ Symb.: **Mo.**

mom /mom/ *n. colloq.* mother. □ **mom-and-pop store** of or pertaining to a small retail business, as a grocery store, owned and operated by members of a family.

mo·ment /mómənt/ *n.* **1** very brief portion of time. **2** exact or particular point of time (*at last the moment arrived*). **3** importance. **4** product of force and the distance from its line of action to a point.

mo·men·tar·y /mómənteree/ *adj.* lasting only a moment. □□ **mo·men·tar·i·ly** /-táirilee/ *adv.* **mo·men·tar′i·ness** *n.*

mo·men·tous /mōméntəs/ *adj.* having great importance. □□ **mo·men′tous·ly** *adv.* **mo·men′tous·ness** *n.*

mo·men·tum /mōméntəm/ *n.* (*pl.* **mo·men·ta** /-tə/) **1** *Physics* quantity of motion of a moving body, the product of its mass and velocity. **2** the impetus gained by movement. **3** strength or continuity derived from an initial effort.

mom·ma /mómə/ *n.* var. of MAMMA.

mom·my /mómee/ *n.* (*pl.* -**mies**) *colloq.* mother.

Mon. *abbr.* Monday.

mon·arch /mónərk, -aark/ *n.* **1** ruler of a country, esp. hereditary, as a king, queen, etc. **2** large orange and black butterfly. □□ **mo·nar·chic** /mənáarkik/ *adj.* **mo·nar′chi·cal** *adj.*

mon·ar·chism /mónərkizəm/ *n.* advocacy of or the principles of monarchy. □□ **mon′ar·chist** *n.*

mon·ar·chy /mónərkee/ *n.* (*pl.* -**chies**) **1** form of government with a monarch at the head. **2** a nation with this. □□ **mo·nar·chi·al** /monáarkeeəl/ *adj.*

mon·as·ter·y /mónəstéree/ *n.* (*pl.* -**ies**) residence of a religious community, esp. of monks living in seclusion.

mo·nas·tic /mənástik/ *adj.* of or relating to monasteries or monks, nuns, etc. □□ **mo·nas′ti·cal·ly** *adv.* **mo·nas·ti·cism** /-tisizəm/ *n.*

Mon·day /múnday, -dee/ *n.* second day of the week, following Sunday.

mon·e·tar·y /móniteree, -mún/ *adj.* **1** of the currency in use. **2** of or consisting of money. □□ **mon·e·tar·i·ly** /-táirəlee/ *adv.*

mon·ey /múnee/ *n.* **1** current medium of exchange in the form of coins and paper currency. **2** (*pl.* -**eys** or -**ies**) (in *pl.*) sums of money. **3** wealth. □ **for my money** in my opinion or judgment; for my preference. **in the money** *colloq.* having or winning a lot of money. **money-grubber** *colloq.* person greedily intent on amassing money. **money-grubbing** *n.* this practice. • *adj.* given to this. **money market** *Stock Exch.* trade in short-term stocks, loans, etc. **money order** order for payment of a specified sum, issued by a bank or post office. □□ **mon′ey·less** *adj.*

mon·ey·bags /múneebagz/ *n.pl.* (treated as *sing.*) *colloq.* usu. *derog.* wealthy person.

mon·eyed /múneed/ *adj.* having much money; wealthy.

mon·ey·mak·er /múneemaykər/ *n.* **1** person who earns much money. **2** thing, idea, etc., that produces much money. □□ **mon′ey·mak·ing** *n.* & *adj.*

mon·ger /múnggər, móng-/ *n.* (usu. in *comb.*) dealer; trader; promoter (*warmonger*).

Mon·go·li·an /monggōleeən/ • *n.* native, inhabitant, or language of Mongolia. • *adj.* of or relating to Mongolia.

mon·gol·ism /mónggəlizəm/ *n.* = DOWN′S SYNDROME.
¶ The term **Down's syndrome** is now preferred.

Mon·gol·oid /mónggəloyd/ • *adj.* **1** characteristic of the Mongolians, esp. in having a broad flat yellowish face. **2** (**mongoloid**) often *offens.* having the characteristic symptoms of Down's syndrome. • *n.* Mongoloid or mongoloid person.

mon·goose /mónggōos/ *n.* (*pl.* **mon·goos·es** or **mon·geese**) small flesh-eating civetlike mammals.

mon·grel /múnggrəl, móng-/ • *n.* dog or other animal or plant of mixed breed. • *adj.* of mixed origin, nature, or character. □□ **mon′grel·ism** *n.* **mon′grel·ize** *v.tr.* **mon·grel·i·za′tion** *n.*

mon·i·ker /mónikər/ *n.* (also **mon′ick·er**) *sl.* name.

mon·i·tor /mónitər/ • *n.* **1** any of various persons or devices for checking or warning about a situation, operation, etc. **2** school pupil with disciplinary or other special duties. **3** cathoderay tube used as a television receiver or computer display device. • *v.tr.* **1** act as a monitor of. **2** maintain regular surveillance over; check. □□ **mon·i·to·ri·al** /-táwreeəl/ *adj.*

monk /mungk/ *n.* member of a religious community of men living under vows. □□ **monk′ish** *adj.*

mon·key /múngkee/ • *n.* (*pl.* -**keys**) **1** any of various primates, including marmosets, baboons, apes, etc. **2** mischievous person, esp. a child (*young monkey*). ● *v.* (*pl.* **-keys, -keyed**) **1** *tr.* mimic or mock. **2** *intr.* tamper; fool around. □ **monkey business** *colloq.* mischief. **monkey wrench** wrench with an adjustable jaw. □□ **mon′key·ish** *adj.*

mon·key·shine /múngkeeshīn/ *n.* (usu. in *pl.*) *colloq.* = monkey business.

mon·o¹ /mónō/ *n. colloq.* infectious mononucleosis.

mon·o² /mónō/ *colloq. adj.* monophonic.

mono- /mónō/ *comb. form* (usu. **mon-** before a vowel) one; alone; single (*monorail*).

mon·o·chro·mat·ic /mónəkrəmátik/ *adj.* **1** *Physics* (of light or other radiation) of a single wavelength or frequency. **2** containing only one color. □□ **mon·o·chro·mat′i·cal·ly** *adv.*

mon·o·chrome /mónəkrōm/ ● *n.* photograph or picture done in one color or different tones of this, or in black and white only. ● *adj.* having or using only one color or in black and white only. □□ **mon·o·chro·mic** /-krómik/ *adj.*

mon·o·cle /mónəkəl/ *n.* single eyeglass. □□ **mon′o·cled** *adj.*

mon·o·clo·nal /mónōklónəl/ *adj.* cloned from one cell.

mon·o·cot·y·le·don /mónəkót′leéd′n/ *n. Bot.* any flowering plant with a single cotyledon. □□ **mon·o·cot·y·le′don·ous** *adj.*

mon·oc·u·lar /mənókyələr/ *adj.* with or for one eye. □□ **mon·oc′u·lar·ly** *adj.*

mo·nog·a·my /mənógəmee/ *n.* practice or state of being married to one person at a time. □□ **mo·nog′a·mist** *n.* **mo·nog′a·mous** *adj.* **mo·nog′a·mous·ly** *adv.*

mon·o·gram /mónəgram/ *n.* two or more letters, esp. a person's initials, interwoven as a device. □□ **mon·o·gram·mat·ic** /-grəmátik/ *adj.* **mon′o·grammed** *adj.*

mon·o·graph /mónəgraf/ *n.* separate treatise on a single subject. □□ **mo·nog·ra·pher** /mənógrəfər/ *n.* **mon·o·graph·ic** /mónəgráfik/ *adj.*

mon·o·lin·gual /mónōlínggwəl/ *adj.* speaking or using only one language.

mon·o·lith /mónəlith/ *n.* **1** single block of stone, esp. shaped into a pillar or monument. **2** massive, immovable, or solidly uniform person or thing. □□ **mon·o·lith′ic** *adj.*

mon·o·logue /mónəlawg, -log/ *n.* **1 a** soliloquy. **b** dramatic composition for one performer. **2** long speech by one person in a conversation, etc. □□ **mon·o·log·ic** /-lójik/ *adj.* **mon·o·log′i·cal** *adj.* **mon·o·log·ist** /mónóləjist/ *n.* (also **-log·uist**).

mon·o·ma·ni·a /mónəmáyneeə/ *n.* obsession of the mind by one idea or interest. □□ **mon·o·ma′ni·ac** *n.* & *adj.* **mon·o·ma·ni·a·cal** /-mənīə-kəl/ *adj.*

mon·o·nu·cle·o·sis /mónōnóōkleeósis, -nyóō-/ *n.* abnormally high proportion of monocytes in the blood.

mon·o·phon·ic /mónəfónik/ *adj.* **1** (of sound reproduction) using only one channel of transmission (cf. STEREOPHONIC). **2** *Mus.* homophonic. □□ **mon·o·phon′i·cal·ly** *adv.*

mo·nop·o·list /mənópəlist/ *n.* person who has or advocates a monopoly. □□ **mo·nop·o·lis′tic** *adj.*

mo·nop·o·lize /mənópəlīz/ *v.tr.* **1** obtain exclusive possession or control of. **2** dominate or prevent others from sharing in. □□ **mo·nop·o·li·za′tion** *n.* **mo·nop′o·liz·er** *n.*

mo·nop·o·ly /mənópəlee/ *n.* (*pl.* **-lies**) **1 a** exclusive possession or control of the trade in a commodity or service. **b** this conferred as a privilege by the government. **2** commodity or service that is subject to a monopoly.

mon·o·rail /mónōrayl/ *n.* railway with a single track.

mon·o·so·di·um glu·ta·mate /mónəsódiəm glóōtəmayt/ *n. Chem.* white crystalline powder used to flavor food. ¶ Abbr.: **MSG.**

mon·o·syl·la·ble /mónəsiləbəl/ *n.* word of one syllable. □□ **mon·o·syl·lab·ic** /-silábik/ *adj.* **mon·o·syl·lab′i·cal·ly** *adv.*

mon·o·the·ism /mónəthee′eizəm/ *n.* doctrine that there is only one God. □□ **mon′o·the·ist** *n.* **mon·o·the·is′tic** *adj.* **mon·o·the·is′ti·cal·ly** *adv.*

mon·o·tone /mónətōn/ ● *n.* **1** sound or utterance continuing or repeated on one note without change of pitch. **2** sameness of style in writing. ● *adj.* without change of pitch.

mo·not·o·nous /mənót′nəs/ *adj.* lacking in variety; tedious through sameness. □□ **mo·not′o·nous·ly** *adv.* **mo·not′o·nous·ness** *n.*

mo·not·o·ny /mənót′nee/ *n.* **1** state of being monotonous. **2** dull or tedious routine.

Mon·sieur /məsyṓ/ *n.* (*pl.* **Mes·sieurs** /mesyṓ/) **1** French title corresponding to Mr. or sir. **2** Frenchman.

Mon·si·gnor /monsee′enyər/ *n.* (*pl.* **Mon·si·gnors** or **Mon·si·gno·ri** /-nyáwree/) title of various Roman Catholic prelates, officers of the papal court, etc.

mon·soon /monsóōn, món-/ *n.* **1** seasonal wind in S. Asia, esp. in the Indian Ocean. **2** rainy season accompanying the summer monsoon. □□ **mon·soon′al** *adj.*

mon·ster /mónstər/ *n.* **1** imaginary creature, usu. large and frightening. **2** inhumanly cruel or wicked person. **3** large, usu. ugly or misshapen animal or thing. **4** (*attrib.*) huge.

mon·strance /mónstrəns/ *n. RC Ch.* vessel in which the consecrated Host is displayed for veneration.

mon·strous /mónstrəs/ *adj.* **1** like a monster; abnormally formed. **2** huge. **3 a** outrageously wrong or absurd. **b** atrocious. □□ **mon·stros·i·ty** /-strósitee/ *n.* **mon′strous·ly** *adv.* **mon′strous·ness** *n.*

Mont. *abbr.* Montana.

mon·tage /montázh, mawN-/ *n.* **1** technique of producing a new composite whole from fragments of pictures, words, music, etc. **2** a composition produced in this way.

month /munth/ *n.* **1** (in full **calendar month**) **a** each of usu. twelve periods into which a year is divided. **b** period of time between the same dates in successive calendar months. **2** period of 28 days or of four weeks. **3** = *lunar month.*

month·ly /múnthlee/ ● *adj.* done, produced, or occurring once a month. ● *adv.* once a month; from month to month. ● *n.* (*pl.* **-lies**) monthly periodical.

mon·u·ment /mónyəmənt/ *n.* **1** anything enduring that serves to commemorate or make celebrated, esp. a structure or building. **2** ancient building or site. **3** typical or outstanding example (*a monument of indiscretion*).

mon·u·men·tal /mónyəmént′l/ *adj.* **1 a** extremely great; stupendous (*a monumental* *achievement*). **b** (of a literary work) massive and permanent. **2** of or serving as a monument. □□ **mon·u·men·tal·i·ty** /-tálitee/ *n.* **mon·u·men′tal·ly** *adv.*

-mony /mōnee/ *suffix* forming nouns, esp. denoting an abstract state or quality (*acrimony*; *testimony*).

moo /mōo/ • *v.intr.* (**moos, mooed**) make the vocal sound of cattle; = LOW² *v.* • *n.* (*pl.* **moos**) this sound.

mooch /mōoch/ *v.tr. colloq.* beg; impose upon. □□ **mooch′er** *n.*

mood¹ /mōod/ *n.* **1** state of mind or feeling. **2** (in *pl.*) fits of melancholy or bad temper.

mood² /mōod/ *n.* *Gram.* form or set of forms of a verb serving to indicate whether it is to express fact, command, wish, etc. (*subjunctive mood*).

mood·swing /mōodswing/ *n.* marked change in temperament, as from euphoria to depression.

mood·y /mōodee/ • *adj.* (**mood·i·er, mood·i·est**) given to changes of mood; gloomy; sullen. • *n. colloq.* bad mood; tantrum. □□ **mood′i·ly** *adv.* **mood′i·ness** *n.*

moon /mōon/ • *n.* **1** the natural satellite of the earth, orbiting it monthly. **2** satellite of any planet. • *v. intr.* behave dreamily or listlessly. □□ **moon′less** *adj.*

---

moon Old English *mōna*, of Germanic origin; related to Dutch *maan* and German *Mond*, also to *month*, from an Indo-European root shared by Latin *mensis* and Greek *mēn* 'month,' and also Latin *metiri* 'to measure' (the moon being used since prehistory to measure time).

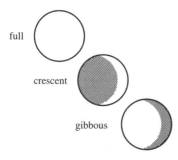

full

crescent

gibbous

MOON (PHASES OF)

---

moon·beam /mōonbeem/ *n.* ray of moonlight.
moon·light /mōonlīt/ • *n.* light of the moon. • *v.intr.* (**-lighted**) *colloq.* have two paid occupations, esp. one by day and one by night. □□ **moon′light·er** *n.*
moon·lit /mōonlit/ *adj.* lighted by the moon.
moon·scape /mōonskayp/ *n.* **1** surface or landscape of the moon. **2** area resembling this; wasteland.
moon·shine /mōonshīn/ *n.* **1** foolish talk or ideas. **2** *sl.* illicitly distilled or smuggled alcoholic liquor. **3** moonlight.
moon·shot /mōonshot/ *n.* launching of a spacecraft to the moon.

moon·stone /mōonstōn/ *n.* feldspar of pearly appearance.
moon·struck /mōonstruk/ *adj.* slightly mad.
Moor /mōor/ *n.* member of a Muslim people inhabiting NW Africa. □□ **Moor′ish** *adj.*
moor¹ /mōor/ *n.* tract of open uncultivated upland, esp. when covered with heather. □□ **moor′ish** *adj.*
moor² /mōor/ *v.tr.* attach (a boat, buoy, etc.) to a fixed object. □□ **moor′age** *n.*
moor·ing /mōoring/ *n.* **1** (often in *pl.*) place where a boat, etc., is moored. **2** (in *pl.*) set of permanent anchors and chains laid down for ships to be moored to.
moose /mōos/ *n.* (*pl.* same) largest variety of N. American deer.
moot /mōot/ • *adj.* (orig. the noun used *attrib.*) debatable; undecided. • *n. Law* discussion of a hypothetical case as an academic exercise.
mop /mop/ • *n.* **1** wad or bundle of cotton or synthetic material fastened to the end of a stick, for cleaning floors, etc. **2** similarly shaped large or small implement for various purposes. **3** thick mass of hair. • *v.tr.* (**mopped, mop·ping**) wipe or clean with or as with a mop. □ **mop up 1** wipe up with or as with a mop. **2** dispatch; make an end of. **3** *Mil.* complete the occupation of (a district, etc.) by capturing or killing enemy troops left there.
mope /mōp/ *v.intr.* be gloomily depressed or listless; behave sulkily. □□ **mop′er** *n.* **mop′i·ly** *adv.* **mop′i·ness** *n.* **mop′y** *adj.* (**mop·i·er, mop·i·est**).
mo·ped /mōped/ *n.* lightweight motorized bicycle with pedals.
mo·raine /məráyn/ *n.* area covered by rocks and debris carried down and deposited by a glacier. □□ **mo·rain′al** *adj.*
mor·al /máwrəl, mór-/ • *adj.* **1 a** concerned with the distinction between right and wrong. **b** concerned with accepted rules and standards of human behavior. **2** virtuous; capable of moral action. **3** founded on moral law. **4** concerned with or leading to a psychological effect associated with confidence in a right action (*moral courage*). • *n.* **1** moral lesson (esp. at the end) of a fable, story, event, etc. **2** (in *pl.*) moral behavior, e.g., in sexual conduct. □□ **mor′al·ly** *adv.*

---

moral late Middle English: from Latin *moralis*, from *mos, mor-* 'custom,' (plural) *mores* 'morals.' As a noun the word was first used to translate Latin *Moralia*, the title of St. Gregory the Great's moral exposition of the biblical Book of Job, and was subsequently applied to the works of various classical writers.

---

mo·rale /mərál/ *n.* mental attitude or bearing of a person or group, esp. as regards confidence, discipline, etc.
mor·al·ist /máwrəlist, mór-/ *n.* person who practices or teaches morality. □□ **mor·al·is′tic** *adj.* **mor·al·is′ti·cal·ly** *adv.*
mor·al·i·ty /mərálitee/ *n.* (*pl.* **-ties**) **1** degree of conformity to moral principles. **2** right moral conduct. **3** particular system of morals (*commercial morality*).
mor·al·ize /máwrəlīz, mór-/ *v.* **1** *intr.* (often foll. by *on*) indulge in moral reflection or talk. **2** *tr.* interpret morally. □□ **mor·al·i·za′tion** *n.* **mor′al·iz·er** *n.* **mor′al·iz·ing·ly** *adv.*

mo·rass /mərás/ *n.* **1** entanglement; disordered situation, esp. one impeding progress. **2** *literary* bog or marsh.

mor·a·to·ri·um /máwrətáwreeəm, mór-/ *n.* (*pl.* **mor·a·to·ri·ums** or **mor·a·to·ri·a** /-reeə/) **1** temporary prohibition or suspension (of an activity). **2 a** legal authorization to debtors to postpone payment. **b** period of this postponement.

mor·bid /máwrbid/ *adj.* **1** unwholesome; macabre. **2** *Med.* of the nature of or indicative of disease. □□ **mor·bid'i·ty** *n.* **mor'bid·ly** *adv.* **mor'bid·ness** *n.*

mor·dant /máwrd'nt/ • *adj.* **1** caustic; biting. **2** serving to fix dye. • *n.* mordant substance (in sense 2 of *adj.*). □□ **mor'dan·cy** *n.* **mor'dant·ly** *adv.*

more /mawr/ • *adj.* greater in quantity or degree; additional. • *n.* greater quantity, number, or amount. • *adv.* **1** to a greater degree or extent. **2** forming the comparative of some adjectives and adverbs. □ **more or less 1** in a greater or less degree. **2** approximately; as an estimate.

more·o·ver /máwrṓvər/ *adv.* further; besides.

mo·res /máwrayz, -reez/ *n.pl.* customs or conventions regarded as essential to or characteristic of a community.

morgue /mawrg/ *n.* **1** mortuary. **2** (in a newspaper office, etc.) room or file of miscellaneous information.

mor·i·bund /máwribund, mór-/ *adj.* **1** at the point of death. **2** lacking vitality. □□ **mor·i·bun'di·ty** *n.*

Mor·mon /máwrmən/ *n.* member of the Church of Jesus Christ of Latter-day Saints. □□ **Mor'mon·ism** *n.*

morn /mawrn/ *n.* *poet.* morning.

morn·ing /máwrning/ *n.* early part of the day, esp. from sunrise to noon. □ **morning glory** twining plant with trumpet-shaped flowers. **morning sickness** nausea felt in the morning in pregnancy.

Mo·roc·can /mərókən/ • *n.* **1** native or national of Morocco in N. Africa. **2** person of Moroccan descent. • *adj.* of or relating to Morocco.

mo·roc·co /mərókō/ *n.* (*pl.* **-cos**) fine flexible leather made (orig. in Morocco) from goatskins tanned with sumac.

mo·ron /máwron/ *n.* **1** *colloq.* very stupid person. **2** adult with a mental age of about 8–12. □□ **mo·ron'ic** *adj.* **mo·ron'i·cal·ly** *adv.*

mo·rose /mərṓs/ *adj.* sullen and ill-tempered. □□ **mo·rose'ly** *adv.* **mo·rose'ness** *n.*

morph /mawrf/ *v.intr.* *Cinematog.* change form or appearance, as from person to animal, by computer-controlled special effects. □□ **morph'ing** *n.*

mor·pheme /máwrfeem/ *n.* *Linguistics* smallest meaningful morphological unit of a language. □□ **mor·phe'mic** *adj.* **mor·phe'mi·cal·ly** *adv.*

mor·phine /máwrfeen/ *n.* narcotic drug from opium used to relieve pain.

mor·phol·o·gy /mawrfóləjee/ *n.* the study of the forms or structures of things. □□ **mor·pho·log·i·cal** /mawrfəlójikəl/ *adj.* **mor·pho·log'i·cal·ly** *adv.* **mor·phol'o·gist** *n.*

mor·row /máwrō, mór-/ *n.* *literary* the following day.

Morse /mawrs/ *n.* (in full **Morse code**) alphabet or code in which letters are represented by combinations of long and short light or sound signals.

mor·sel /máwrsəl/ *n.* mouthful; small piece (esp. of food).

mor·tal /mawrt'l/ • *adj.* **1** subject to death. **2** causing death; fatal. **3** associated with death. **4** intense; very serious; implacable. • *n.* human being. □□ **mor'tal·ly** *adv.*

mor·tal·i·ty /mawrtálitee/ *n.* (*pl.* **-ties**) **1** being subject to death. **2** loss of life on a large scale. **3** death rate.

mor·tar /máwrtər/ *n.* **1** mixture of lime with cement, sand, and water, used in building to bond bricks or stones. **2** short large-bore cannon for firing shells at high angles. **3** vessel in which ingredients are pounded with a pestle. □□ **mor'tar·less** *adj.* (in sense 1).

MORTAR, 3 WITH PESTLE

mor·tar·board /máwrtərbawrd/ *n.* **1** academic cap with a stiff, flat square top. **2** flat board for holding mortar.

MORTARBOARD, 1

mort·gage /máwrgij/ • *n.* **1 a** conveyance of property to a creditor as security for a debt. **b** deed effecting this. **2 a** debt secured by a mortgage. **b** loan resulting in such a debt. • *v.tr.* **1** convey (a property) by mortgage. **2** pledge (oneself, one's powers, etc.). □□ **mort'gage·a·ble** *adj.*

mort·ga·gee /máwrgijée/ *n.* creditor in a mortgage.

mort·ga·gor /máwrgijər/ *n.* (also **mort'gag·er** /-jər/) debtor in a mortgage.

mor·ti·cian /mawrtíshən/ *n.* = UNDERTAKER.

mor·ti·fy /máwrtifī/ *v.* (**-fies, -fied**) **1** *tr.* shame; humiliate. **2** *tr.* bring (the body, the flesh, the passions, etc.) into subjection by self-denial or discipline. **3** *intr.* (of flesh) be affected by gangrene or necrosis. □□ **mor·ti·fi·ca′tion** *n.* **mor′ti·fy·ing** *adj.* **mor′ti·fy·ing·ly** *adv.*

mor·tise /máwrtis/ (also **mor′tice**) • *n.* hole in a framework designed to receive another part, esp. a tenon. • *v.tr.* **1** join securely, esp. by mortise and tenon. **2** cut a mortise in.

mor·tu·ar·y /máwrchoō-eree/ • *n.* (*pl.* -**ies**) room or building in which dead bodies may be kept until burial or cremation. • *adj.* of or concerning death or burial.

Mo·sa·ic /mōzáyik/ *adj.* of Moses (in the Old Testament). □ **Mosaic Law** laws attributed to Moses.

mo·sa·ic /mōzáyik/ *n.* **1 a** picture or pattern produced by an arrangement of small variously colored pieces of glass or stone, etc. **2** (*attrib.*) **a** of or like a mosaic. **b** diversified. □□ **mo·sa·i·cist** /-záyisist/ *n.*

mo·sey /mōzee/ *v.intr.* (-**seys**, -**seyed**) (often foll. by *along*) *sl.* walk in a leisurely or aimless manner.

Mos·lem var. of MUSLIM.
¶ See note at MUSLIM.

mosque /mosk/ *n.* Muslim place of worship.

mos·qui·to /məskeétō/ *n.* (*pl.* -**toes** or -**tos**) insect, the female of which sucks the blood of humans and other animals.

moss /maws/ *n.* small, flowerless plant growing in dense clusters on the surface of the ground, in bogs, on trees, stones, etc. □□ **moss′i·ness** *n.* **moss′like** *adj.* **moss′y** *adj.* (**moss·i·er**, **moss·i·est**)

most /mōst/ • *adj.* **1** existing in the greatest quantity or degree. **2** the majority of. • *n.* **1** greatest quantity or number. **2** the majority. • *adv.* **1** in the highest degree. **2** forming the superlative of some adjectives and adverbs. **3** *colloq.* almost. □ **at most** no more or better than (*this is at most a makeshift*). **make the most of** employ to the best advantage.

-most /mōst/ *suffix* forming superlative adjectives and adverbs from prepositions and other words indicating relative position (*foremost*; *uttermost*).

most·ly /mōstlee/ *adv.* **1** as regards the greater part. **2** usually.

mote /mōt/ *n.* speck of dust.

mo·tel /mōtél/ *n.* roadside hotel for motorists.

moth /mawth, moth-/ *n.* **1** nocturnal insect having a stout body and without clubbed antennae. **2** small insect of this type, the larva of which feeds on cloth, etc. □ **moth-eaten 1** damaged by moths. **2** timeworn. □□ **moth′y** *adj.* (**moth·i·er**, **moth·i·est**)

moth·ball /máwthbawl, móth-/ *n.* ball of naphthalene, etc., placed in stored clothes to keep away moths.

moth·er /múthər/ • *n.* **1** female parent. **2** quality or condition, etc., that gives rise to another. **3** (in full **Mother Superior**) head of a female religious community. • *v.tr.* **1** give birth to; be the mother or origin of. **2** protect as a mother. □ **Mother Goose rhyme** nursery rhyme. **mother-in-law** (*pl.* **moth·ers-in-law**) mother of one's husband or wife. **mother-of-pearl** smooth iridescent inner layer of the shell of some mollusks. **mother tongue** native language. □□ **moth′er·hood** *n.* **moth′er·less** *adj.* **moth′er·like** *adj. & adv.*

moth·er·board /múthərbawrd/ *n.* computer's main circuit board, into which other boards can be plugged or wired.

moth·er·land /múthərland/ *n.* native country.

moth·er·ly /múthərlee/ *adj.* like or characteristic of a mother in affection, care, etc. □□ **moth′er·li·ness** *n.*

mo·tif /mōteéf/ *n.* **1** distinctive feature or dominant idea in artistic or literary composition. **2** *Mus.* short succession of notes producing a single impression, out of which longer passages are developed.

mo·tile /mōt′l, -tīl, -til/ *adj. Zool. & Bot.* capable of motion. □□ **mo·til·i·ty** /-tilitee/ *n.*

mo·tion /mōshən/ • *n.* **1** moving; changing position. **2** gesture. **3** formal proposal put to a committee, legislature, etc. • *v.* **1** *tr.* direct (a person) by a sign or gesture. **2** *intr.* make a gesture directing (*motioned to me to leave*). □ **go through the motions** do something perfunctorily or superficially. **in motion** moving; not at rest. **motion picture** (often (with hyphen) *attrib.*) film or movie with the illusion of movement (see FILM *n.* 3). □□ **mo′tion·less** *adj.*

mo·ti·vate /mōtivayt/ *v.tr.* **1** supply a motive to; be the motive of. **2** stimulate the interest of (a person in an activity). □□ **mo·ti·va·tion** /-váyshən/ *n.* **mo·ti·va′tion·al** *adj.* **mo·ti·va′tion·al·ly** *adv.*

mo·tive /mōtiv/ • *n.* **1** factor or circumstance that induces a person to act in a particular way. **2** = MOTIF. • *adj.* causing or concerned with movement. □□ **mo′tive·less** *adj.*

mot·ley /mótlee/ *adj.* (**mot·li·er**, **mot·li·est**) **1** diversified in color. **2** of varied character (*a motley crew*).

mo·to·cross /mōtōkraws, -kros/ *n.* crosscountry racing on motorcycles.

mo·tor /mótər/ • *n.* **1** thing that imparts motion. **2** engine, esp. one using electricity or internal combustion. • *adj.* **1** giving, imparting, or producing motion. **2** driven by a motor. **3** of or for motor vehicles. **4** *Anat.* relating to muscular movement or the nerves activating it. □ **motor home** vehicle built on a truck frame and outfitted as a residence. **motor pool** vehicles for use by personnel as needed as for a military installation. **motor vehicle** road vehicle powered by an internal-combustion engine.
¶ See note at ENGINE.

mo·tor·bike /mótərbīk/ *n.* **1** lightweight motorcycle. **2** motorized bicycle.

mo·tor·bus /mótərbus/ *n.* = BUS 1.

mo·tor·cade /mótərkayd/ *n.* procession of motor vehicles.

mo·tor·cy·cle /mótərsīkəl/ *n.* two-wheeled motor-driven road vehicle without pedal propulsion. □□ **mo′tor·cy·clist** *n.*

mo·tor·ist /mótərist/ *n.* driver of an automobile.

mo·tor·ize /mótərīz/ *v.tr.* **1** equip (troops, etc.) with motor transport. **2** provide with a motor. □□ **mo·tor·i·za′tion** *n.*

mot·tle /mót′l/ *v.tr.* (esp. as **mottled** *adj.*) mark with spots or smears of color.

mot·to /mótō/ *n.* (*pl.* -**toes** or -**tos**) maxim adopted as a rule of conduct, etc.

mound /mownd/ *n.* heap or pile of earth, stones, etc.

mount[1] /mownt/ • *v.* **1** *tr.* ascend; climb on. **2** *tr.*

a set on horseback. **b** (as **mounted** *adj.*) serving on horseback (*mounted police*). **3** *intr.* increase; accumulate. **4** *tr.* place (an object) on a support or in a backing, frame, etc. **5** *tr.* arrange; organize; set in motion. • *n.* **1** backing, setting, or other support on which a picture, etc., is set for display. **2** horse for riding. □□ **mount′a·ble** *adj.* **mount′er** *n.*

mount² /mownt/ *n. archaic* (*except before a name*) mountain; hill (*Mount Everest; Mount of Olives*).

moun·tain /mównt'n/ *n.* **1** large natural elevation of the earth's surface. **2** large heap or pile; huge quantity. □ **mountain bike** bicycle with a light sturdy frame for riding on mountainous terrain. **mountain goat** white goatlike animal of the Rocky Mountains, etc. **mountain lion** puma. **mountain range** line of mountains connected by high ground. **mountain sickness** sickness caused by the rarefaction of the air at great heights. □□ **moun′tain·y** *adj.*

moun·tain·eer /mównt'néer/ *n.* person skilled in mountain climbing. □□ **moun′tain·eer·ing** *n.*

moun·tain·ous /mównt'nəs/ *adj.* **1** (of a region) having many mountains. **2** huge.

moun·te·bank /mówntibángk/ *n.* **1** swindler; charlatan. **2** clown.

Moun·tie /mówntee/ *n. colloq.* member of the Royal Canadian Mounted Police.

mount·ing /mównting/ *n.* = MOUNT¹ *n.* 1.

mourn /mawrn/ *v.* feel or show deep sorrow or regret for (a dead person, a lost thing, etc.). □□ **mourn′er** *n.*

mourn·ful /máwrnfŏŏl/ *adj.* **1** doleful; sad; expressing mourning. □□ **mourn′ful·ly** *adv.* **mourn′ful·ness** *n.*

mourn·ing /máwrning/ *n.* **1** expression of deep sorrow, esp. for a dead person. **2** solemn clothes worn in mourning.

mouse /mows/ • *n.* (*pl.* **mice** /mīs/) **1** common small rodent. **2** timid or feeble person. **3** *Computing* small hand-held device that controls the cursor on a computer monitor. • *v.intr.* (also /mowz/) hunt for or catch mice. □□ **mouse′like** *adj. & adv.* **mous′er** *n.*

mousse /mŏŏs/ *n.* **1 a** dessert of whipped cream, eggs, etc., usu. flavored with fruit or chocolate. **b** meat or fish purée made with whipped cream, etc. **2** preparation applied to the hair enabling it to be styled more easily.

mous·tache var. of MUSTACHE.

mous·y /mówsee/ *adj.* (**mous·i·er, mous·i·est**) **1** of or like a mouse. **2** shy or timid; ineffectual. **3** nondescript light brown. □□ **mous′i·ly** *adv.* **mous′i·ness** *n.*

mouth • *n.* /mowth/ (*pl.* **mouths** /mow_thz_/) **1** external opening in the head, through which most animals admit food and emit communicative sounds. **2** opening of a container, cave, trumpet, etc. **3** place where a river enters the sea. • *v.* /mowth/ **1** *tr. & intr.* utter or speak solemnly or with affectations; rant; declaim. **2** *tr.* utter very distinctly. **3** *intr.* **a** move the lips silently. **b** grimace. □ **mouth organ** = HARMONICA. □□ **mouthed** /mowthd/ *adj.* (also in *comb.*). **mouth′er** /mówthər/ *n.* **mouth′less** /mówthlis/ *adj.*

mouth·ful /mówthfŏŏl/ *n.* (*pl.* **-fuls**) **1** quantity, esp. of food, that fills the mouth. **2** small quantity. **3** long or complicated word or phrase.

mouth·piece /mówthpees/ *n.* **1** part of a musical instrument, telephone, etc. placed next to or near the mouth. **2** *colloq.* lawyer.

mouth·wash /mówthwosh, -wawsh/ *n.* liquid antiseptic, etc., for rinsing the mouth or gargling.

mouth·wa·ter·ing /mówthwawtəring/ *adj.* having a delicious smell or appearance.

mov·a·ble /mŏŏvəbəl/ (also **move′a·ble**) *adj.* **1** that can be moved. **2** variable in date from year to year. □□ **mov·a·bil′i·ty** *n.* **mov′a·ble·ness** *n.* **mov′a·bly** *adv.*

move /mŏŏv/ • *v.* **1** *intr. & tr.* change one's position, posture, or place, or cause to do this. **2** *tr. & intr.* put or keep in motion; rouse; stir. **3 a** *intr.* make a move in a board game. **b** *tr.* change the position of (a piece) in a board game. **4** *intr.* go; proceed; make progress. **5** *intr.* (foll. by *in*) live or be socially active in (a specified place or group, etc.). **6** *tr.* affect (a person) with emotion. **7** *tr.* stimulate; provoke; prompt or incline. **8 a** *tr.* cause (the bowels) to be evacuated. **b** *intr.* (of the bowels) be evacuated. **9** *tr.* propose in a meeting, deliberative assembly, etc. **10** *intr.* sell; be sold. • *n.* **1** act or instance of moving. **2** change of house, business premises, etc. **3** step taken to secure some action or effect; initiative. **4 a** the changing of the position of a piece in a board game. **b** player's turn to do this. □ **get a move on** *colloq.* **1** hurry up. **2** make a start. □□ **mov′er** *n.*

move·a·ble var. of MOVABLE.

move·ment /mŏŏvmənt/ *n.* **1** moving or being moved. **2** moving parts of a mechanism (esp. a clock or watch). **3 a** body of persons with a common object. **b** campaign undertaken by such a body. **4** (usu. in *pl.*) person's activities and whereabouts, esp. at a particular time. **5** *Mus.* principal division of a longer musical work. **6** progressive development of a poem, story, etc. **7** motion of the bowels.

mov·ie /mŏŏvee/ *n.* esp. *colloq.* **1** motion picture. **2** (**the movies**) a motion-picture industry or medium. **b** the showing of a movie (*going to the movies*).

mov·ie·dom /mŏŏveedəm/ *n.* the movie industry and its associated businesses, personnel, etc.

mow¹ /mō/ *v.tr.* (*past part.* **mowed** or **mown**) cut down (grass, hay, etc.) with a scythe or machine. □ **mow down** kill or destroy randomly or in great numbers. □□ **mow′a·ble** *adj.* **mow′er** *n.*

mow² /mow/ *n. dial.* **1** stack of hay, wheat, etc. **2** place in a barn where hay, etc., is heaped.

MP *abbr.* **1** military police. **2** Member of Parliament.

m.p.g. *abbr.* miles per gallon.

m.p.h. *abbr.* miles per hour.

Mr. /místər/ *n.* (*pl.* **Messrs.**) **1** title for a man. **2** title prefixed to a designation of office, etc. (*Mr. President*).

MRI *abbr.* magnetic resonance imaging.

Mrs. /mísiz/ *n.* (*pl.* same or **Mes·dames**) title for a married woman.

MS *abbr.* **1** Mississippi (in official postal use). **2** Master of Science. **3** multiple sclerosis. **4** (also **ms.**) manuscript.

Ms. /miz/ *n.* title for a married or unmarried woman.

M.Sc. *abbr.* Master of Science.

MSG *abbr.* monosodium glutamate.

Msgr. *abbr.* **1** Monseigneur. **2** Monsignor.

MST *abbr.* Mountain Standard Time.

MT *abbr.* Montana (in official postal use).

Mt *abbr.* meitnerium.

Mt. *abbr.* **1** mount. **2** mountain.

mu /myōō, mōō/ *n.* twelfth Greek letter (M, µ).

much /much/ • *adj.* existing or occurring in a great quantity. • *n.* **1** a great quantity. **2** (usu. in *neg.*) noteworthy or outstanding example (*not much to look at*). • *adv.* **1** in a great degree. **2** for a large part of one's time (*is much away from home*). □□ **much′ly** *adv. joc.*

mu·ci·lage /myōōsilij/ *n.* **1** viscous substance obtained from plants. **2** adhesive gum; glue. □□ **mu·ci·lag·i·nous** /-lájinəs/ *adj.*

muck /muk/ • *n.* **1** farmyard manure. **2** *colloq.* dirt or filth; anything disgusting. • *v.tr.* **1** (usu. foll. by *up*) *colloq.* bungle (a job). **2** make dirty or untidy. □□ **muck′i·ness** *n.* **muck′y** *adj.* (**muck·i·er, muck·i·est**).

muck·rake /múkrayk/ *v.intr.* search out and reveal scandal. □□ **muck′rak·er** *n.* **muck′rak·ing** *n.*

mu·cous /myōōkəs/ *adj.* of or covered with mucus. □ **mucous membrane** mucus-secreting epithelial tissue lining many body cavities and tubular organs. □□ **mu·cos·i·ty** /-kósitee/ *n.*

mu·cus /myōōkəs/ *n.* **1** slimy substance secreted by a mucous membrane. **2** gummy substance found in all plants.

mud /mud/ *n.* wet, soft, earthy matter. □ **fling** (or **sling** or **throw**) **mud** speak disparagingly or slanderously. **one's name is mud** one is unpopular or in disgrace.

mud·dle /múd′l/ *v.tr.* **1** bring into disorder. **2** bewilder; confuse. □ **muddle-headed** confused.

---

muddle late Middle English (in the sense 'wallow in mud'): perhaps from Middle Dutch *moddelen*, derived from *modden* 'dabble in mud' (related to *mud*). The sense 'confuse' was initially associated with alcoholic drink (late 17th century), giving rise to 'busy oneself in a confused way' and 'jumble up' (mid-19th century).

---

mud·dy /múdee/ • *adj.* (**mud·di·er, mud·di·est**) **1** like or covered in mud. **2** turbid; not clear; impure. **3** confused; vague. • *v.tr.* (**-dies, -died**) make muddy. □□ **mud′di·ly** *adv.* **mud′di·ness** *n.*

mu·ez·zin /myōō-ézin, mōō-/ *n.* Muslim crier who proclaims the hours of prayer, usu. from a minaret.

muff¹ /muf/ *n.* fur or other covering for keeping the hands or ears warm.

muff² /muf/ *v.tr.* **1** bungle. **2** miss (a catch, ball, etc.).

muf·fin /múfin/ *n.* small cake or quick bread made from batter or dough and baked in a muffin pan.

muf·fle /múfəl/ *v.tr.* **1** wrap or cover for warmth or to deaden sound. **2** (usu. as **muffled** *adj.*) stifle (an utterance, e.g., a curse). **3** prevent from speaking.

muf·fler /múflər/ *n.* **1** wrap or scarf worn for warmth. **2** noise-reducing device on a motor vehicle's exhaust system.

muf·ti /múftee/ *n.* civilian clothes (*in mufti*).

mug /mug/ • *n.* **1 a** drinking vessel, usu. cylindrical with a handle. **b** its contents. **2** *sl.* face. **3** *sl.* hoodlum or thug. • *v.* (**mugged, mug·ging**) **1** *tr.* rob (a person) with violence, esp. in a public place. **2** *intr. sl.* make faces, esp. before an audience, a camera, etc. □ **mug shot** *sl.* photograph of a face, esp. for official purposes. □□ **mug′ger** *n.* (esp. in sense 1 of *v.*). **mug′ful** *n.* (*pl.* **-fuls**). **mug′ging** *n.* (in sense 1 of *v.*).

mug·gy /múgee/ *adj.* (**mug·gi·er, mug·gi·est**) oppressively damp and warm; humid. □□ **mug′gi·ness** *n.*

mu·ja·hi·din /mōōjaahidéen/ *n.pl.* (also **mu·ja·he·din′, -deen′**) guerrilla fighters in Islamic countries.

mu·lat·to /mōōlátō, -laá-, myōō-/ *n.* (*pl.* **-toes** or **-tos**) person of mixed white and black parentage.

mul·ber·ry /múlberee, -bəree/ *n.* (*pl.* **-ries**) **1** deciduous tree bearing edible dark-red or white berries. **2** its fruit. **3** dark-red or purple color.

mulch /mulch/ • *n.* mixture of straw, leaves, etc., spread around or over a plant to enrich or insulate the soil. • *v.tr.* treat with mulch.

mule¹ /myōōl/ *n.* **1** offspring (usu. sterile) of a male donkey and a female horse. **2** stupid or obstinate person. □□ **mul′ish** *adj.* **mul′ish·ly** *adv.* **mul′ish·ness** *n.*

mule² /myōōl/ *n.* light shoe or slipper without a back.

mu·le·teer /myōōlitéer/ *n.* mule driver.

mull¹ /mul/ *v.* ponder or consider.

mull² /mul/ *v.tr.* warm (wine or cider, etc.) with added sugar, spices, etc.

mul·lah /múlə, mōōl-/ *n.* Muslim learned in Islamic theology and sacred law.

mul·let /múlit/ *n.* any of several kinds of marine fish commonly used as food.

mul·li·ga·taw·ny /múligətáwnee/ *n.* highly seasoned soup orig. from India.

mul·lion /múlyən/ *n.* (also **mun·nion** /mún-/) vertical bar dividing the panes in a window (cf. TRANSOM). □□ **mul′lioned** *adj.*

multi- /múltee, -tī/ *comb. form* many; more than one.

mul·ti·cul·tur·al /múlteekúlchərəl/ *adj.* of or relating to or constituting several cultural or ethnic groups within a society. □□ **mul·ti·cul′tur·al·ism** *n.* **mul·ti·cul′tur·al·ly** *adv.*

mul·ti·far·i·ous /múltifáireeəs/ *adj.* **1** many and various. **2** diverse. □□ **mul·ti·far′i·ous·ly** *adv.* **mul·ti·far′i·ous·ness** *n.*

mul·ti·lat·er·al /múltilátərəl/ *adj.* **1** (of an agreement, treaty, conference, etc.) in which three or more parties participate. **2** having many sides. □□ **mul·ti·lat′er·al·ly** *adv.*

mul·ti·lin·gual /múlteelínggwəl, -tī-/ *adj.* in or using several languages. □□ **mul·ti·lin′gual·ly** *adv.*

mul·ti·me·di·a /múltimée-deeə/ • *attrib. adj.* involving several media. • *n.* combined use of several media, such as film, print, sound, etc.

mul·ti·na·tion·al /múlteenáshənəl, -tī-/ • *adj.* **1** operating in several countries. **2** of several nationalities or ethnic groups. • *n.* multinational company. □□ **mul·ti·na′tion·al·ly** *adv.*

mul·ti·ple /múltipəl/ • *adj.* **1** having several or many parts, elements, or individual components. **2** many and various. • *n.* number that contains another without a remainder (*56 is a* *multiple of 7*). □ **multiple-choice** (of a question in an examination) accompanied by several possible answers from which the correct one has to be chosen. **multiple sclerosis** see SCLEROSIS.

mul·ti·plex /múltipleks/ ● *adj.* **1** manifold; of many elements. **2** involving simultaneous transmission of several messages along a single channel of communication. ● *n.* building that houses several movie theaters □□ **mul'ti·plex·er** *n.* (also **mul'ti·plex·or**).

mul·ti·pli·cand /múltiplikánd/ *n.* quantity to be multiplied by a multiplier.

mul·ti·pli·ca·tion /múltiplikáyshən/ *n.* multiplying. □ **multiplication sign** the symbol (×), to indicate that one quantity is to be multiplied by another, as in *2 × 3 = 6*. □□ **mul·ti·pli·ca·tive** /-plíkətiv/ *adj.*

mul·ti·plic·i·ty /múltiplísitee/ *n.* (*pl.* **-ties**) **1** manifold variety. **2** (foll. by *of*) great number.

mul·ti·pli·er /múltiplīər/ *n.* quantity by which a given number is multiplied.

mul·ti·ply /múltiplī/ *v.* (**-plies, -plied**) **1** *tr.* (also *absol.*) obtain from (a number) another that is a specified number of times its value (*multiply 6 by 4*). **2** *intr.* increase in number.

mul·ti·proc·ess·ing /múlteeprósesing/ *n.* *Computing* processing using two or more processors.

mul·ti·ra·cial /múlteeráyshəl, -tī-/ *adj.* relating to or made up of many human races. □□ **mul·ti·ra'cial·ly** *adv.*

mul·ti·tude /múltitōod, -tyōod/ *n.* great number; crowd.

mul·ti·tu·di·nous /múltitōod'nəs, -tyōod-/ *adj.* **1** very numerous. **2** consisting of many individuals or elements. □□ **mul·ti·tu'di·nous·ly** *adv.* **mul·ti·tu'di·nous·ness** *n.*

mum¹ /mum/ *adj. colloq.* silent (*keep mum*). □ **mum's the word** say nothing.

mum² /mum/ *n.* = CHRYSANTHEMUM.

mum·ble /múmbəl/ ● *v.* speak or utter indistinctly. ● *n.* indistinct utterance. □□ **mum'bler** *n.*

mum·bo jum·bo /múmbōjúmbō/ *n.* (*pl.* **jumbos**) meaningless or ignorant ritual or language.

mum·mer /múmər/ *n.* actor in a traditional mime.

mum·mer·y /múməree/ *n.* (*pl.* **-ies**) **1** ridiculous (esp. religious) ceremonial. **2** performance by mummers.

mum·mi·fy /múmifī/ *v.tr.* (**-fies, -fied**) preserve (a body) as a mummy. □□ **mum·mi·fi·ca'tion** *n.*

mum·my /múmee/ *n.* (*pl.* **-mies**) body of a human being or animal embalmed for burial, esp. in ancient Egypt.

mumps /mumps/ *n.pl.* (treated as *sing.*) infectious viral disease with swelling of the neck and face.

munch /munch/ *v.tr.* eat steadily with a marked action of the jaws.

munch·ies /múncheez/ *n. pl. colloq.* **1** snack foods. **2** urge to snack.

mun·dane /múndáyn/ *adj.* **1** dull; routine. **2** of this world; worldly. □□ **mun·dane'ly** *adv.* **mun·dane'ness** *n.*

mu·nic·i·pal /myōōnísipəl/ *adj.* of or concerning a municipality or its self-government. □ **municipal bond** bond issued by a city, county, state, etc., to finance public projects. □□ **mu·nic'i·pal·ize** *v.tr.* **mu·nic'i·pal·ly** *adv.*

mu·nic·i·pal·i·ty /myōōnísipálitee/ *n.* (*pl.* **-ties**) town or district having local government.

mu·nif·i·cent /myōōnífisənt/ *adj.* splendidly generous; bountiful. □□ **mu·nif'i·cence** *n.* **mu·nif'i·cent·ly** *adv.*

mu·ni·tion /myōōníshən/ *n.* (usu. in *pl.*) military weapons, ammunition, equipment, and stores.

mu·on /myōō-on/ *n. Physics* unstable elementary particle like an electron, but with a much greater mass.

mu·ral /myōōrəl/ ● *n.* painting executed directly on a wall. ● *adj.* **1** of or like a wall. **2** on a wall. □□ **mu'ral·ist** *n.*

mur·der /mórdər/ ● *n.* **1** unlawful premeditated killing of a human being by another. **2** *colloq.* unpleasant, troublesome, or dangerous state of affairs. ● *v.tr.* **1** kill (a human being) intentionally and unlawfully. **2** *colloq.* utterly defeat or spoil by a bad performance, mispronunciation, etc. □□ **mur'der·er** *n.* **mur'der·ess** *n.*

mur·der·ous /mórdərəs/ *adj.* **1** (of a person, weapon, action, etc.) capable of, intending, or involving murder or great harm. **2** *colloq.* extremely troublesome, unpleasant, or dangerous. □□ **mur'der·ous·ly** *adv.*

murk /mərk/ *n.* darkness; poor visibility.

murk·y /mórkee/ *adj.* (**-i·er, -i·est**) **1** dark; gloomy. **2** (of darkness) thick; dirty. **3** suspiciously obscure; shady (*murky past*). □□ **murk'i·ly** *adv.* **murk'i·ness** *n.*

mur·mur /mórmər/ ● *n.* **1** subdued continuous sound, as made by waves, a brook, etc. **2** softly spoken or nearly inarticulate utterance. ● *v.* **1** *intr.* make a murmur. **2** *tr.* utter (words) in a low voice, esp. as a complaint. □□ **mur'mur·er** *n.* **mur'mur·ing·ly** *adv.* **mur'mur·ous** *adj.*

mus·cat /múskat, -kət/ *n.* **1** (also **mus·ca·tel** /múskətél/) sweet fortified white wine made from musk-flavored grapes. **2** this grape.

mus·cle /músəl/ ● *n.* **1** fibrous tissue with the ability to contract, producing movement in or maintaining the position of an animal body. **2** part of an animal body that is composed of muscles. **3** physical power or strength. ● *v.intr.* (usu. foll. by *in*) *colloq.* force oneself on others; intrude. □ **muscle-bound** with muscles stiff and inelastic through excessive exercise or training. □□ **mus'cled** *adj.* (usu. in *comb.*). **mus'cle·less** *adj.*

mus·cu·lar /múskyələr/ *adj.* **1** of or affecting the muscles. **2** having well-developed muscles. □ **muscular dystrophy** see DYSTROPHY. □□ **mus·cu·lar·i·ty** /-láritee/ *n.*

mus·cu·la·ture /múskyələchər/ *n.* muscular system of a body or organ.

mus·cu·lo·skel·e·tal /məskyəlōskélət'l/ *adj.* of or involving both the muscles and the skeleton.

Muse /myōōz/ *n. Gk. & Rom. mythol.* one of the nine goddesses, the daughters of Zeus and Mnemosyne, who inspire poetry, music, drama, etc.

muse /myōōz/ *v. literary* **1** *intr.* (usu. foll. by *on, upon*) ponder; reflect. **2** *tr.* say meditatively.

mu·se·um /myōōzéeəm/ *n.* building used for storing and exhibiting objects of historical, scientific, or cultural interest.

mush¹ /mush/ *n.* **1** soft pulp. **2** feeble sentimentality. **3** boiled cornmeal dish. **4** *sl.* (also /mōōsh/) mouth; face. □□ **mush'y** *adj.* (**mush·i·er, mush·i·est**). **mush'i·ly** *adv.* **mush'i·ness** *n.*

mush[2] /mush/ *v.intr.* **1** (in *imper.*) used as a command to encourage sled dogs. **2** travel across snow with a dogsled.

mush·room /múshrŏom, -rŏom/ • *n.* edible fungus with a stem and domed cap. • *v.intr.* appear or develop rapidly.

mu·sic /myŏozik/ *n.* **1** art of combining vocal or instrumental sounds (or both) to produce beauty of form, harmony, and expression of emotion. **2** sounds so produced. **3** musical compositions. **4** written or printed score of a musical composition. **5** pleasant natural sounds.

mu·si·cal /myŏozikəl/ • *adj.* **1** of or relating to music. **2** melodious; harmonious. **3** fond of or skilled in music. **4** set to or accompanied by music. • *n.* movie or drama that features songs. □□ **mu·si·cal·i·ty** /-kálitee/ *n.* **mu′si·cal·ize** *v.tr.* **mu′si·cal·ly** *adv.* **mu′si·cal·ness** *n.*

mu·si·cian /myŏozíshən/ *n.* person who plays a musical instrument, esp. professionally, or is otherwise musically gifted. □□ **mu·si′cian·ly** *adj.* **mu′si·cian·ship** *n.*

mu·si·col·o·gy /myŏozikóləjee/ *n.* the academic study of music. □□ **mu·si·col′o·gist** *n.* **mu·si·co·log·i·cal** /-kəlójikəl/ *adj.*

musk /musk/ *n.* substance produced by a gland in the male musk deer and used as an ingredient in perfumes. □ **musk deer** small hornless Asian deer. **musk ox** shaggy goat-antelope native to N. America. □□ **musk′y** *adj.* (**musk·i·er, musk·i·est**). **musk′i·ness** *n.*

mus·kel·lunge /múskəlunj/ *n.* large N. American pike.

mus·ket /múskit/ *n. hist.* smooth-bored light gun.

mus·ket·eer /múskiteér/ *n. hist.* soldier armed with a musket.

musk·rat /múskrat/ *n.* **1** large aquatic rodent native to N. America, having a musky smell. **2** fur of this.

Mus·lim /múzlim, mŏoz-, mŏos-/ (also **Mos·lem** /mózləm/) • *n.* follower of the Islamic religion. • *adj.* of or relating to the Muslims or their religion.
¶ **Muslim** is the preferred term for 'follower of Islam,' although *Moslem* is also widely used. Avoid 'Mohammedan.'

mus·lin /múzlin/ *n.* strong, woven cotton fabric.

muss /mus/ *colloq.* • *v.tr.* (often foll. by *up*) disarrange; throw into disorder. • *n.* mess. □□ **muss′y** *adj.*

mus·sel /músəl/ *n.* bivalve mollusk often used for food.

must /must/ • *v.aux.* (*3rd sing. present* **must**; *past* **had to** or in indirect speech **must**) **1** be obliged to. **2** be certain to. **3** ought to. • *n. colloq.* thing that should not be missed.

mus·tache /mústash, məstásh/ *n.* (also **mous′tache**) hair left to grow on a man's upper lip. □□ **mus′tached** *adj.*

mus·tang /mústang/ *n.* small wild horse native to Mexico and California.

mus·tard /mústərd/ *n.* **1** plant with slender pods and yellow flowers. **2** seeds of this which are crushed, made into a paste, and used as a spicy condiment. **3** brownish-yellow color. □ **mustard gas** colorless oily liquid whose vapor is a powerful irritant.

mus·ter /mústər/ • *v.* **1** *tr.* summon. **2** *tr. & intr.* collect, gather together. • *n.* assembly of persons for inspection. □ **pass muster** be accepted as adequate.

must·n't /músənt/ *contr.* must not.

mus·ty /mústee/ *adj.* (**mus·ti·er, mus·ti·est**) **1** moldy; stale. **2** antiquated. □□ **must′i·ly** *adv.* **must′i·ness** *n.*

mu·ta·ble /myŏotəbəl/ *adj. literary* **1** liable to change. **2** fickle. □□ **mu·ta·bil′i·ty** *n.*

mu·ta·gen /myŏotəjən/ *n.* agent promoting mutation. □□ **mu·ta·gen·ic** /-jénik/ *adj.* **mu·ta·gen·e·sis** /-jénisis/ *n.*

mu·tant /myŏot′nt/ • *adj.* resulting from mutation. • *n.* mutant form.

mu·ta·tion /myŏotáyshən/ *n.* **1** change; alteration. **2** genetic, heritable change. **3** mutant. □□ **mu′tate** *v.* **mu·ta′tion·al** *adj.* **mu·ta′tion·al·ly** *adv.*

mute /myŏot/ • *adj.* **1** silent; refraining from speech. **2** (of a person or animal) dumb; speechless. • *n.* **1** dumb person (*a deaf mute*). **2** *Mus.* device for damping the sound of a musical instrument. • *v.tr.* **1** deaden, muffle, or soften the sound, color, etc., of. **2** (as **muted** *adj.*) subdued. □□ **mute′ly** *adv.* **mute′ness** *n.*

mu·ti·late /myŏot′layt/ *v.tr.* **1 a** deprive (a person or animal) of a limb or organ. **b** destroy the use of (a limb or organ). **2** disfigure or destroy, esp. by cutting. □□ **mu·ti·la·tion** /-láyshən/ *n.* **mu·ti·la′tive** *adj.* **mu′ti·la·tor** *n.*

mu·ti·ny /myŏot′nee/ • *n.* (*pl.* **-nies**) open revolt, esp. by soldiers or sailors against their officers. • *v.intr.* (**-nies, -nied**) revolt; engage in mutiny. □□ **mu·ti·neer** /-eér/ *n.* **mu′ti·nous** *adj.* **mu′ti·nous·ly** *adv.*

mutt /mut/ *n.* **1** dog. **2** *sl.* ignorant or blundering person.

mut·ter /mútər/ • *v.* **1** *intr.* speak low in a barely audible manner. **2** *intr.* murmur; grumble. • *n.* **1** muttered words or sounds. **2** muttering. □□ **mut′ter·er** *n.* **mut′ter·ing·ly** *adv.*

mut·ton /mút′n/ *n.* flesh of sheep as food. □□ **mut′ton·y** *adj.*

mu·tu·al /myŏochŏoəl/ *adj.* **1** (of feelings, actions, etc.) experienced or done by each of two or more parties with reference to the other or others (*mutual affection*). **2** *colloq. disp.* common to two or more persons. □ **mutual fund** investment program funded by shareholders that trades in diversified holdings and is professionally managed. □□ **mu·tu·al·i·ty** /-chŏo-álitee, -tyŏo-álitee/ *n.* **mu′tu·al·ly** *adv.*
¶ Traditionalists consider using **mutual** to mean 'common to two or more people,' as in *a mutual friend; a mutual interest*, to be incorrect, holding that the sense of reciprocity is necessary: *mutual respect; mutual need*. However, both senses are well established and acceptable in standard English.

muu·muu /mŏomŏo/ *n.* woman's loose brightly colored dress.

Mu·zak /myŏozak/ *n.* **1** *propr.* system of music transmission for playing in public places. **2** (**muzak**) recorded light background music.

muz·zle /múzəl/ • *n.* **1** projecting part of an animal's face, including the nose and mouth. **2** guard fitted over an animal's nose and mouth to stop it biting or feeding. **3** open end of a firearm. • *v.tr.* **1** put a muzzle on. **2** impose silence upon. □□ **muz′zler** *n.*

MVP *abbr. Sports* most valuable player.

MW *abbr.* megawatt(s).

my /mī/ *poss.pron.* (*attrib.*) of or belonging to me or myself.

my·al·gi·a /mīáljə/ *n.* muscular pain. □□ **my·al'gic** *adj.*

My·ce·nae·an /mīsineéən/ • *adj. Archaeol.* of or relating to the late Bronze Age civilization in Greece (*c.* 1580–1100 BC), depicted in the Homeric poems. • *n.* inhabitant of Mycenae or the Mycenaean world.

my·col·o·gy /mīkólajee/ *n.* **1** the study of fungi. **2** fungi of a particular region. □□ **my·co·log·i·cal** /-kəlójikəl/ *adj.* **my·co·log'i·cal·ly** *adv.* **my·col'o·gist** *n.*

my·e·lin /mí-ilin/ *n.* white substance that forms a sheath around certain nerve fibers. □□ **my·e·li·na'tion** *n.*

my·e·li·tis /mī-ilītis/ *n.* inflammation of the spinal cord.

My·lar /mílaar/ *n. propr.* durable polyester film used for recording tapes, insulation, etc.

my·nah /mínə/ *n.* (also **my'na, mi'na**) any of various SE Asian starlings, esp. those able to mimic the human voice.

my·o·pia /mīópeeə/ *n.* **1** nearsightedness. **2** lack of imagination or intellectual insight. □□ **my·op·ic** /mīópik/ *adj.* **my·op'i·cal·ly** *adv.*

myr·i·ad /míreeəd/ *literary* • *n.* **1** an indefinitely great number. **2** ten thousand. • *adj.* of an indefinitely great number.

myrrh /mər/ *n.* gum resin used, esp. in the Near East, in perfumery, incense, etc. □□ **myrrh'ic** *adj.* **myrrh'y** *adj.*

myr·tle /mə́rtəl/ *n.* **1** evergreen shrub with aromatic foliage and white flowers. **2** = PERIWINKLE[1].

my·self /mīsélf/ *pron.* **1** *emphat. form* of I[2] or ME (*I saw it myself*). **2** *refl. form* of ME (*I was angry with myself*).

mys·te·ri·ous /mistéereeəs/ *adj.* full of or wrapped in mystery. □□ **mys·te'ri·ous·ly** *adv.* **mys·te'ri·ous·ness** *n.*

mys·ter·y /místəree/ *n.* (*pl.* **-ies**) **1** secret, hidden, or inexplicable matter (*the reason remains a mystery*). **2** secrecy or obscurity (*wrapped in mystery*). **3** (in full **mystery story**) fictional work dealing with a puzzling event, esp. a crime.

mys·tic /místik/ • *n.* person who seeks spiritual truths or experiences. • *adj.* **1** mysterious and awe-inspiring. **2** spiritually allegorical or symbolic. **3** occult; esoteric. **4** of hidden meaning. □□ **mys·ti·cism** /-tisizəm/ *n.*

---

mystic Middle English (in the sense 'mystical meaning'): from Old French *mystique*, or via Latin from Greek *mustikos*, from *mustēs* 'initiated person' from *muein* 'close the eyes or lips,' also used to mean 'initiate,' as of initiations into ancient mystery religious. The current sense of the noun dates from the late 17th century.

---

mys·ti·cal /místikəl/ *adj.* of mystics or mysticism. □□ **mys'ti·cal·ly** *adv.*

mys·ti·fy /místifī/ *v.tr.* (**-fies, -fied**) **1** bewilder; confuse. **2** wrap up in mystery. □□ **mys·ti·fi·ca'tion** *n.*

mys·tique /mistéek/ *n.* atmosphere of mystery and veneration attending some activity or person.

myth /mith/ *n.* **1** traditional narrative usu. involving supernatural or imaginary persons and embodying popular ideas on natural or social phenomena, etc. **2** such narratives collectively. **3** widely held but false notion. **4** fictitious person, thing, or idea. **5** allegory (*the Platonic myth*). □□ **myth'ic** *adj.* **myth'i·cal** *adj.* **myth'i·cal·ly** *adv.*

my·thol·o·gy /mithólajee/ *n.* (*pl.* **-gies**) **1** body of myths (*Greek mythology*). **2** the study of myths. □□ **myth·o·log·ic** /-thəlójik/ *adj.* **myth·o·log'i·cal** *adj.* **myth·o·log'i·cal·ly** *adv.* **my·thol'o·gist** *n.* **my·thol'o·gize** *v.*

Nn

N[1] /en/ *n.* (also **n**) (*pl.* **Ns** or **N's; n's**) fourteenth letter of the alphabet. □ **to the nth** (or **nth degree**) **1** *Math.* to any required power. **2** to any extent; to the utmost.

N[2] *abbr.* (also **N.**) **1** north; northern. **2** noon. **3** New.

N[3] *symb. Chem.* nitrogen.

n *abbr.* (also **n.**) **1** born. **2** name. **3** neuter. **4** noon. **5** number. **6** noun.

Na *symb. Chem.* sodium.

N.A. *abbr.* North America.

n/a *abbr.* **1** not applicable. **2** not available.

NAACP /endəbəláyseepee/ *abbr.* National Association for the Advancement of Colored People.

nab /nab/ *v.tr.* (**nabbed, nab·bing**) *sl.* **1** arrest; catch in wrongdoing. **2** seize, grab.

na·bob /náybob/ *n.* wealthy person of influence.

na·cho /naáchō/ *n.* (*pl.* **-chos**) (usu. in *pl.*) tortilla chip, usu. topped with melted cheese, peppers, etc.

na·cre /náykər/ *n.* mother-of-pearl. □□ **na·cre·ous** /náykreeəs/ *adj.*

na·dir /náydər, -deer/ *n.* **1** part of the celestial sphere directly below an observer (opp. ZENITH). **2** lowest point.

NAFTA /náftə/ *abbr.* North American Free Trade Agreement.

nag[1] /nag/ ● *v.* (**nagged, nag·ging**) **1 a** *tr.* persistently annoy, irritate, scold, urge, etc., (a person). **b** *intr.* find fault, complain, or urge, esp. persistently. **2** *intr.* (of a pain) ache dully but persistently. **3 a** *tr.* worry or preoccupy (a person, the mind, etc.) (*his mistake nagged him*). **b** *intr.* (often foll. by *at*) worry or gnaw. ● *n.* persistently nagging person.

nag[2] /nag/ *n. colloq.* horse, esp. an old or worthless one.

Na·hua·tl /naáwaát'l/ ● *n.* **1** member of a group of peoples native to southern Mexico and Central America. **2** language of these peoples. ● *adj.* of the Nahuatl peoples or language.

nai·ad /níad/ *n.* (*pl.* **nai·ads** or **-ades** /níədeez/) *Mythol.* water nymph.

nail /nayl/ ● *n.* **1** small usu. sharpened metal spike with a broadened flat head, driven in with a hammer to join things or to serve as a peg, decoration, etc. (cf. HOBNAIL), or decoration. **2** horny covering at the tip of the human finger or toe. ● *v.tr.* **1** fasten with a nail or nails. **2** fix or keep (a person, attention, etc.) fixed. **3 a** secure, catch, or get hold of (a person or thing). **b** expose or discover (a lie or a liar).

na·ive /naa-éev/ *adj.* (also **na·ïve'**) **1** innocent; unaffected. **2** credulous; simple. □□ **na·ive'ly** *adv.* **na·ive·té** /naa-eevtáy, -éevtáy/ *n.*

na·ked /náykid/ *adj.* **1** without clothes; nude. **2** undisguised (*naked truth*). **3** defenseless. **4** without addition, comment, support, evidence, etc. **5** devoid; without. **6** without leaves, hairs, scales, shell, etc. □□ **na'ked·ly** *adv.* **na'ked·ness** *n.*

nam·by-pam·by /námbeepámbee/ ● *adj.* lacking vigor or drive; weak. ● *n.* (*pl.* **-bies**) timid or weak person.

name /naym/ ● *n.* **1 a** word by which an individual person, animal, place, or thing is known, spoken of, etc. **b** all who go under one name; family, clan, or people in terms of its name (*the Scottish name*). **2** usu. abusive term used of a person, etc. **3** famous person. **4** reputation, esp. a good one. ● *v.tr.* **1** give a name to. **2** call (a person or thing) by the right name (*named the man in the photograph*). **3** mention; specify; cite. **4** nominate, appoint, etc. □ **in name** (or **name only**) as a mere formality; hardly at all (*is the leader in name only*). **in the name of** as representing; by virtue of. □□ **name'a·ble** *adj.*

name·less /náymlis/ *adj.* **1** having or showing no name. **2** inexpressible; indefinable. **3** unnamed; anonymous; by virtue of. **4** too horrific to be named.

name·ly /náymlee/ *adv.* that is to say; in other words.

name·sake /náymsayk/ *n.* person or thing having the same name as another.

nan·ny /nánee/ *n.* (*pl.* **-nies**) **1** child's nursemaid. **2** (in full **nan'ny goat**) female goat.

nano- /nánō, náynō/ *comb. form* denoting a factor of 10^{-9} (*nanosecond*).

nap[1] /nap/ ● *v.intr.* (**napped, nap·ping**) sleep lightly or briefly. ● *n.* short sleep or doze, esp. by day.

nap[2] /nap/ *n.* **1** raised pile on textiles, esp. velvet. **2** soft downy surface.

na·palm /náypaam/ ● *n.* jellied incendiary substance used in bombs. ● *v.tr.* attack with napalm bombs.

nape /nayp/ *n.* back of the neck.

naph·tha /náf-thə, náp-/ *n.* flammable oil obtained by the dry distillation of organic substances such as coal, etc.

naph·tha·lene /náf-thəleen, náp-/ *n.* white crystalline aromatic distillate of coal tar used in mothballs and the manufacture of dyes, etc.

nap·kin /nápkin/ *n.* square piece of linen, paper, etc., used for wiping the lips, fingers, etc., at meals.

narc /nark/ *n.* (also **nark**) *sl.* federal agent or police officer who enforces drug and narcotics laws.

nar·cis·sism /naársisizəm/ *n. Psychol.* excessive or erotic interest in oneself, one's physical features, etc. □□ **nar'cis·sist** *n.* & *adj.* **nar·cis·sis'tic** *adj.*

nar·cis·sus /naarsísəs/ *n.* (*pl.* **nar·cis·si** /-sī/ or **nar·cis·sus·es**) any of several bulbous plants bearing a single flower with an undivided corona, as the daffodil.

nar·co·lep·sy /naárkəlepsee/ *n. Med.* disease with fits of sleepiness and drowsiness. □□ **nar·co·lep·tic** /-léptik/ *adj.* & *n.*

nar·cot·ic /naarkótik/ ● *adj.* **1** (of a substance) inducing drowsiness, sleep, or stupor. **2** (of a drug) affecting the mind. ● *n.* narcotic substance, drug, or influence.

Nar·ra·gan·sett /narəgánsət, -gánt-/ *n.* **1** a N. American people native to Rhode Island. **b** member of this people. **2** language of this people.

nar·rate /nárayt, naráyt/ *v.tr.* (also *absol.*) **1** give a story or account of. **2** provide a spoken accompaniment for (a film, etc.). □□ **nar·ra·tion** /-ráyshən/ *n.* **nar·ra·tor** *n.*

nar·ra·tive /nárətiv/ ● *n.* spoken or written account of connected events in order of happening. ● *adj.* in the form of, or concerned with, narration (*narrative verse*).

nar·row /nárō/ ● *adj.* (**nar·row·er, nar·row·est**) **1 a** of small width. **b** confined or confining. **2** of limited scope. **3** with little margin. ● *n.* (usu. in *pl.*) narrow part of a strait, river, pass, street, etc. ● *v.* **1** *intr.* become narrow; diminish; contract; lessen. **2** *tr.* make narrow; constrict; restrict. □□ **nar'row·ly** *adv.* **nar'row·ness** *n.*

nar·row-mind·ed /nárōmíndid/ *adj.* rigid or restricted in one's views; intolerant. □□ **nar'row·mind'ed·ness** *n.*

nar·whal /naárwəl/ *n.* Arctic white whale, the male of which has a long straight tusk.

nar·y /náiree/ *adj. colloq.* or *dial.* not any; no (*nary a one*).

NASA /násə/ *abbr.* National Aeronautics and Space Administration.

na·sal /náyzəl/ ● *adj.* **1** of, for, or relating to the nose. **2** pronounced or spoken with the breath passing through the nose. ● *n. Phonet.* nasal letter or sound. □□ **na'sal·ize** *v.* **na·sal·i·za'tion** *n.* **na'sal·ly** *adv.*

nas·cent /násənt, náy-/ *adj.* **1** in the act of being born. **2** just beginning to be. □□ **nas'cen·cy** /násənsee, náy-/ *n.*

NASDAQ /názdak, nás-/ *abbr.* National Association of Securities Dealers Automated Quotations.

nas·ty /nástee/ *adj.* (**nas·ti·er, nas·ti·est**) **1 a** highly unpleasant. **b** annoying; objectionable. **2** difficult to negotiate; dangerous; serious. **3** (of a person or animal) ill-natured; offensive. **4 a** obscene. **b** delighting in obscenity. □□ **nas'ti·ly** *adv.* **nas'ti·ness** *n.*

na·tal /náytəl/ *adj.* of or from one's birth.

Natch·ez /náchiz/ *n.* **1 a** N. American people native to Mississippi. **b** member of this people. **2** language of this people.

na·tion /náyshən/ *n.* **1** community of people of mainly common descent, history, language, etc., forming a unified government or inhabiting a territory. **2** tribe or confederation of tribes of Native Americans. □□ **na'tion·hood** *n.*

na·tion·al /náshənəl/ ● *adj.* **1** of or common to a nation or the nation. **2** peculiar to or characteristic of a particular nation. ● *n.* citizen of a specified country. □ **national anthem** patriotic song adopted by a nation. **National Guard** federally subsidized state militia, called into service in cases of emergency. □□ **na'tion·al·ly** *adv.*

na·tion·al·ism /náshənəlizəm/ *n.* **1** patriotic feeling, principles, etc. **2** policy of national independence. □□ **na'tion·al·ist** *n.* & *adj.* **na·tion·al·is'tic** *adj.*

na·tion·al·i·ty /náshənálitee/ *n.* (*pl.* **-ties**) **1 a** status of belonging to a particular nation. **b** nation (*people of all nationalities*). **2** ethnic group forming a part of one or more political nations.

na·tion·al·ize /náshənəlīz/ *v.tr.* **1** take (industry, land, etc.) into government control or ownership. **2 a** make national. **b** make into a nation. □□ **na·tion·al·i·za'tion** *n.*

na·tion·wide /náyshənwíd/ *adj.* & *adv.* extending over the whole nation.

na·tive /náytiv/ ● *n.* **1 a** person born in a specified place. **b** local inhabitant. **2** often *offens.* member of a nonwhite indigenous people, as regarded by the colonial settlers. **3** indigenous animal or plant. ● *adj.* **1** inherent; innate. **2** of one's birth (*native dress*). **3** belonging to a specified place (*the anteater is native to S. America*). **4 a** indigenous. **b** of the natives of a place. **5** in a natural state; unadorned; simple. □ **Native American** member of the indigenous peoples of America or their descendants.

na·tiv·i·ty /nətívitee, nay-/ *n.* (*pl.* **-ties**) **1** (esp. **the Nativity**) **a** the birth of Christ. **b** Christmas. **2** birth.

natl. *abbr.* national.

NATO /náytō/ *abbr.* North Atlantic Treaty Organization.

nat·ty /nátee/ *adj.* (**nat·ti·er, nat·ti·est**) *colloq.* **1** smartly or neatly dressed. **2** trim; smart (*a natty blouse*). □□ **nat'ti·ly** *adv.*

nat·u·ral /náchərəl/ ● *adj.* **1 a** existing in or caused by nature. **b** uncultivated; wild. **2** in the course of nature; not exceptional. **3** (of human nature, etc.) not surprising; to be expected. **4** (of a person or a person's behavior) unaffected, easy, spontaneous. **5 a** (of qualities, etc.) inherent; innate. **b** (of a person) having such qualities (*a natural linguist*). **6** not disguised or altered (as by makeup, etc.). **7** likely by its or their nature to be such (*natural enemies*). **8** *Mus.* **a** (of a note) not sharpened or flatted. **b** (of a scale) not containing sharps or flats. ● *n.* **1** *colloq.* person or thing naturally suitable, adept, expert, etc. **2** *Mus.* **a** sign (♮) denoting a return to natural pitch. **b** natural note. □ **natural gas** flammable mainly methane gas extracted from the earth. **natural history 1** study of animals or plants. **2** aggregate of the facts concerning the flora and fauna, etc., of a particular place or class. **natural law** *Philos.* unchanging moral principles common to all people by virtue of their nature as human beings. **natural numbers** integers 1, 2, 3, etc. **natural resources** materials or conditions occurring in nature and capable of economic exploitation. **natural science** sciences used in the study of the physical world. **natural selection** Darwinian theory of the survival and propagation of organisms best adapted to their environment. □□ **nat'u·ral·ness** *n.*

nat·u·ral·ism /náchərəlizəm/ *n.* **1** realistic representation in art and literature of nature, character, etc. **2 a** *Philos.* theory of the world that excludes the supernatural or spiritual. **b** moral or religious system based on this theory. □□ **nat·u·ral·is'tic** /-ístik/ *adj.*

nat·u·ral·ist /náchərəlist/ *n.* **1** expert in natural history. **2** adherent of naturalism.

nat·u·ral·ize /náchərəlīz/ *v.* **1** *tr.* admit (a foreigner) to citizenship. **2** *tr.* successfully introduce (an animal, plant, etc.) into another region. □□ **nat·u·ral·i·za'tion** *n.*

nat·u·ral·ly /náchərəlee, náchrə-/ *adv.* **1** in a natural manner. **2** as might be expected; of course.

na·ture /náychər/ *n.* **1** innate or essential qualities or character (*is the nature of iron to rust*). **2** (often **Nature**) a physical power causing all material phenomena. **b** these phenomena. **3** kind, sort, or class (*things of this nature*). **4** natural world. □ **by nature** innately.

na·tured /náychərd/ *adj.* (in *comb.*) having a specified disposition (*good-natured*).

naught /nawt/ ● *n.* **1** nothing. **2** zero. ● *adj.* (usu. *predic.*) worthless; useless.

naugh·ty /náwtee/ *adj.* (**naugh·ti·er, naugh·ti·est**) **1** (esp. of children) disobedient; badly behaved. **2** *colloq. joc.* indecent. □□ **naugh′ti·ly** *adv.* **naugh′ti·ness** *n.*

nau·se·a /náwzeeə, -zhə, -seeə, -shə/ *n.* **1** feeling of sickness with an inclination to vomit. **2** loathing; revulsion.

nau·se·ate /náwzeeayt, -zhee-, -see-, -shee-/ *v.* **1** *tr.* affect with nausea (*was nauseated by the smell*). **2** *intr.* feel sick. □□ **nau′se·at·ing** *adj.*
¶ A distinction has traditionally been drawn between **nauseated**, meaning 'affected with nausea,' and **nauseous**, meaning 'causing nausea.' Today, however, the use of **nauseous** to mean 'affected with nausea' is so common that it is generally considered to be standard.

nau·seous /náwshəs, -zeeəs/ *adj.* **1** affected with nausea; sick. **2** causing nausea; offensive to the taste or smell.

nau·ti·cal /náwtikəl/ *adj.* of sailors or navigation; naval; maritime. □ **nautical mile** unit of approx. 2,025 yards (1,852 meters): also called **sea mile.** □□ **naut′i·cal·ly** *adv.*

nau·ti·lus /náwt′ləs/ *n.* (*pl.* **nau·ti·lus·es** or **nau·ti·li** /-lī/) cephalopod with a spiral shell, esp. one having a chambered shell.

NAUTILUS

Nav·a·jo /návəhō, náa-/ *n.* (*pl.* **-jos**) (also **Nav′a·ho**) (*pl.* **-hos**) **1** member of N. American people native to New Mexico and Arizona. **2** language of this people.

na·val /náyvəl/ *adj.* **1** of, in, for, etc., the navy or a navy. **2** of or concerning ships (*a naval battle*).

nave /nayv/ *n.* central part of a church, usu. from the west door to the chancel and excluding the side aisles.

na·vel /náyvəl/ *n.* depression in the center of the belly caused by detachment of the umbilical cord. □ **navel orange** large seedless orange with a navellike formation at the top.

navel Old English *nafela*, of Germanic origin; related to Dutch *navel* and German *Nabel*, from an Indo-European root shared

by Latin *umbo* 'boss (round knob in the middle) of a shield,' *umbilicus* 'navel,' and Greek *omphalos* 'boss, navel.'

nav·i·ga·ble /návigəbəl/ *adj.* **1** (of a river, etc.) affording a passage for ships. **2** (of a ship, etc.) seaworthy. **3** (of a balloon, airship, etc.) steerable. □□ **nav·i·ga·bil′i·ty** *n.*

nav·i·gate /návigayt/ *v.* **1** *tr.* manage or direct the course of (a ship, aircraft, etc.). **2** *tr.* **a** sail on (a sea, etc.). **b** fly through (the air). **3** *intr.* assist the driver by map-reading, etc. **4** *intr.* sail a ship; sail in a ship. □□ **nav′i·ga·tor** *n.*

nav·i·ga·tion /návigáyshən/ *n.* **1** act or process of navigating. **2** method of determining a ship's or aircraft's position and course by geometry, astronomy, radio signals, etc.

na·vy /náyvee/ *n.* (*pl.* **-vies**) **1** (often **the Navy**) **a** a nation's ships of war, including crews, maintenance systems, etc. **b** officers and enlisted personnel of a navy. **2** (in full **na′vy blue′**) dark-blue color. □ **navy bean** small white kidney bean.

nay /nay/ ● *adv.* or rather; and even; and more than that (*impressive, nay, magnificent*). ● *n.* **1** the word 'nay.' **2** negative vote (*counted 16 nays*). □□ **nay′say·er** *n.*

Na·zi /náatsee, nát-/ ● *n.* (*pl.* **Na·zis**) **1** *hist.* member of the German National Socialist party. **2** adherent of this party's tenets. ● *adj.* of Nazis, Nazism, etc. □□ **Na′zism** /náatsizəm, nát-/ *n.*

NB *abbr.* **1** New Brunswick. **2** nota bene.

Nb *symb. Chem.* niobium.

NBC *abbr.* National Broadcasting Company.

NC *abbr.* North Carolina (in official postal use).

NCO *abbr.* noncommissioned officer.

ND *abbr.* North Dakota (in official postal use).

Nd *symb. Chem.* neodymium.

n.d. *abbr.* no date.

N.Dak. *abbr.* North Dakota.

NE *abbr.* **1** Nebraska (in official postal use). **2** northeast. **3** northeastern.

Ne *symb. Chem.* neon.

Ne·an·der·thal /neeándərthawl, -tawl, -taal/ *adj.* (also **Ne·an′der·tal**) of the type of early human widely distributed in Paleolithic Europe.

neap /neep/ *n.* (in full **neap tide**) tide just after the first and third quarters of the moon when there is least difference between high and low water.

Ne·a·pol·i·tan /ne′eəpólitən/ ● *n.* native or citizen of Naples in Italy. ● *adj.* of Naples. □ **Neapolitan ice cream** ice cream made in layers of different colors and flavors.

near /neer/ ● *adv.* **1** to or at a short distance in space or time (*the time drew near; dropped near to them*). **2** closely (*as near as one can guess*). ● *prep.* (compar. & superl. also used) **1** to or at a short distance (in space, time, condition, or resemblance) from. **2** (in *comb.*) **a** that is almost (*near-hysterical*). **b** intended as a substitute for; resembling (*near beer*). ● *adj.* **1** (usu. *predic.*) close to, in place or time (*the man nearest you*). **2 a** closely related. **b** intimate. **3** close; narrow (*near escape*). ● *v.* **1** *tr.* approach; draw near to. **2** *intr.* draw near. □ **the Near East** region comprising the countries of the eastern Mediterranean. **near miss 1** narrowly avoided collision. **2** attempt that is almost but not quite successful. □□ **near′ish** *adj.* **near′ness** *n.*

near·by /neerbí/ ● *adj.* near, in position. ● *adv.* close; not far away.

near·ly /neerlee/ *adv.* **1** almost. **2** closely.

near·sight·ed /neersítid/ *adj.* unable to see distant objects clearly. □□ **near'sight·ed·ness** *n.*

neat /neet/ *adj.* **1** tidy and methodical. **2** elegantly simple. **3** brief, clear, and pointed. **4 a** cleverly executed. **b** deft; dexterous. **5** (of esp. alcoholic liquor) undiluted. **6** *sl.* (as a general term of approval) good, pleasing, excellent. □□ **neat'ly** *adv.* **neat'ness** *n.*

neat·en /néet'n/ *v.tr.* make neat.

Nebr. *abbr.* Nebraska.

neb·u·la /nébyələ/ *n.* (*pl.* **neb·u·lae** /-lee/ or **ne·bu·las**) *Astron.* **1** cloud of gas and dust, glowing or appearing as a dark silhouette against other glowing matter. **2** bright area caused by a galaxy, or a large cloud of distant stars. □□ **neb'u·lar** *adj.*

neb·u·lous /nébyələs/ *adj.* **1** cloudlike. **2 a** formless, clouded. **b** hazy, indistinct, vague (*put forward a few nebulous ideas*). **3** *Astron.* of or like a nebula(e).

nec·es·sar·y /nésəseree/ ● *adj.* **1** requiring to be done, achieved, etc.; requisite; essential. **2** determined, existing, or happening by natural laws, predestination, etc., not by free will; inevitable. ● *n.* (*pl.* **-ies**) (usu. in *pl.*) basic requirements. □□ **nec·es·sar'i·ly** *adv.*

ne·ces·si·tate /nisésitayt/ *v.tr.* make necessary (esp. as a result) (*will necessitate some sacrifice*).

ne·ces·si·ty /nisésitee/ *n.* (*pl.* **-ties**) **1 a** indispensable thing. **b** indispensability. **2** imperative need. **3** want; poverty; hardship. □ **of necessity** unavoidably.

neck /nek/ ● *n.* **1 a** part of the body connecting the head to the shoulders. **b** part of a garment around or close to the neck. **2** something resembling a neck, such as the narrow part of a cavity or vessel, a passage, channel, etc. ● *v.* *colloq.* kiss and caress amorously. □ **neck and neck** running even in a race, etc. **up to one's neck** (often foll. by *in*) *colloq.* very deeply involved; very busy.

neck·er·chief /nékərchif, -cheef/ *n.* square of cloth worn around the neck.

neck·lace /nékləs/ *n.* chain or string of beads, precious stones, links, etc., worn as an ornament around the neck.

neck·line /néklīn/ *n.* edge or shape of the opening of a garment at the neck.

neck·tie /néktī/ *n.* = TIE *n.* 2.

necro- /nékrō/ *comb. form* corpse.

nec·ro·man·cy /nékrōmansee/ *n.* **1** prediction of the future by supposed communication with the dead. **2** witchcraft. □□ **nec'ro·man·cer** *n.*

nec·ro·phil·i·a /nékrəfileeə/ *n.* (also **nec·ro·phil·y** /nikrófilee/) morbid and esp. erotic attraction to corpses. □□ **nec·ro·phile** /nékrəfīl/ *n.* **nec·ro·phil·ic** *adj.* **ne·croph·i·lism** /-krófilizəm/ *n.*

ne·cro·sis /nekrósis/ *n.* *Med.* & *Physiol.* death of tissue caused by disease or injury, esp. as one of the symptoms of gangrene or pulmonary tuberculosis. □□ **ne·crot·ic** /-krótik/ *adj.*

nec·tar /néktər/ *n.* **1** sugary substance produced by plants and made into honey by bees. **2** *Gk.* & *Rom. mythol.* the drink of the gods. **3** drink compared to this. □□ **nec'tar·ous** *adj.*

nec·tar·ine /nektəreén/ *n.* variety of peach with a thin brightly colored smooth skin and firm flesh.

née /nay/ *adj.* (also **nee**) born (*Mrs. Ann Smith, née Jones*).

need /need/ ● *v.tr.* **1** stand in want of; require (*needs a new coat*). **2** be under the necessity or obligation. ● *n.* **1** requirement. **2** circumstances requiring action; necessity. **3** destitution; poverty. **4** crisis; emergency. □ **if need be** if required.

need·ful /néedfool/ *adj.* requisite; necessary. □□ **need'ful·ly** *adv.*

nee·dle /néed'l/ ● *n.* **1 a** very thin small piece of smooth steel, etc., pointed at one end and with a slit (eye) for thread at the other, used in sewing. **b** larger plastic, wooden, etc., slender stick without an eye, used in knitting. **c** slender hooked stick used in crochet. **2** pointer on a dial. **3** end of a hypodermic syringe. **4** pointed rock or peak. **5** leaf of a fir or pine tree. ● *v.tr. colloq.* incite or irritate; provoke (*the silence needled him*).

nee·dle·point /néed'lpoynt/ *n.* decorative needlework or lace made with a needle.

need·less /néedlis/ *adj.* **1** unnecessary. **2** uncalled-for; gratuitous. □□ **need'less·ly** *adv.* **need'less·ness** *n.*

nee·dle·work /néed'lwərk/ *n.* sewing or embroidery.

needs /needz/ *adv. archaic* of necessity (*must needs decide*).

need·y /néedee/ *adj.* (**need·i·er**, **need·i·est**) **1** (of a person) poor; destitute. **2** (of circumstances) characterized by poverty. **3** emotionally impoverished or demanding. □□ **need'i·ness** *n.*

ne'er /nair/ *adv. poet.* = NEVER. □ **ne'er-do-well** *n.* good-for-nothing person. ● *adj.* good-for-nothing.

ne·far·i·ous /nifáireeəs/ *adj.* wicked; iniquitous. □□ **ne·far'i·ous·ly** *adv.* **ne·far'i·ous·ness** *n.*

ne·gate /nigáyt/ *v.tr.* **1** nullify; invalidate. **2** deny.

ne·ga·tion /nigáyshən/ *n.* **1** absence or opposite of something actual or positive. **2** act of denying. □□ **neg·a·to·ry** /négətáwree/ *adj.*

neg·a·tive /négətiv/ ● *adj.* **1** expressing or implying denial, prohibition, or refusal. **2** (of a person or attitude) lacking positive attributes. **3** marked by the absence of qualities (*a negative reaction*). **4** opposite to a thing regarded as positive (*debt is negative capital*). **5** *Algebra* (of a quantity) less than zero, to be subtracted from others or from zero (opp. POSITIVE). **6** *Electr.* **a** of the kind of charge carried by electrons (opp. POSITIVE). **b** containing or producing such a charge. ● *n.* **1** negative statement, reply, or word. **2** *Photog.* **a** image with black and white reversed or colors replaced by complementary ones. **b** developed film or plate bearing such an image. □□ **neg'a·tive·ly** *adv.* **neg·a·tiv'i·ty** *n.*

neg·a·tiv·ism /négətivizəm/ *n.* negative position or attitude; extreme skepticism, criticism, etc.

ne·glect /niglékt/ ● *v.tr.* **1** fail to care for or to do; be remiss about (*neglected their duty*). **2** not pay attention to; disregard (*neglected the obvious warning*). ● *n.* **1** lack of caring; negligence (*the house suffered from neglect*). **2 a** neglecting. **b** being neglected (*the house fell into neglect*). □□ **ne·glect'ful** *adj.* **ne·glect'ful·ly** *adv.*

neg·li·gee /néglizháy/ *n.* (also **neg·li·gée**, **nég·li·gé**) woman's dressing gown of sheer fabric.

neg·li·gence /néglijəns/ *n.* **1** lack of proper care and attention. **2** culpable carelessness. □□ **neg·li·gent** /-jənt/ *adj.* **neg'li·gent·ly** *adv.*

neg·li·gi·ble /néglijibəl/ *adj.* not worth considering; insignificant. □□ **neg′li·gi·bly** *adv.*

ne·go·ti·ate /nigósheeayt, -seeayt/ *v.* **1** *intr.* discuss in order to reach an agreement. **2** *tr.* arrange (an affair) or bring about (a result) by negotiating. **3** *tr.* find a way over, through, etc. (an obstacle, difficulty, etc.). **4** *tr.* convert (a check, etc.) into money. □□ **ne·go·tia·ble** /-shəbəl, -sheeə-/ *adj.* **ne·go·ti·a·tion** /-áyshən/ *n.* **ne·go′ti·a·tor** *n.*

Ne·gro /néegrō/ • *n.* (*pl.* **-groes**) member of a dark-skinned race orig. native to Africa. • *adj.* **1** of black people. **2** (as **negro**) *Zool.* black or dark (*negro ant*). □□ **Ne·groid** /néegroyd/ *adj.* ¶ The term *black* or *African American* is preferred when referring to people.

neigh /nay/ • *n.* high whinnying sound of a horse. • *v.* **1** *intr.* make such a sound. **2** *tr.* say, cry, etc., with such a sound.

neigh·bor /náybər/ • *n.* **1** person or thing near or living next door to or near or nearest another. **2** fellow human being. • *v.* **1** *tr.* border on; adjoin. **2** *intr.* (often foll. by *on, upon*) border; adjoin.

neigh·bor·hood /náybərhood/ *n.* **1 a** district, esp. one forming a community within a town or city. **b** people of a district; one's neighbors. **2** neighborly feeling or conduct. □ **in the neighborhood of** roughly; about (*paid in the neighborhood of $100*).

neigh·bor·ly /náybərlee/ *adj.* characteristic of a good neighbor; friendly; kind. □□ **neigh′bor·li·ness** *n.*

nei·ther /néethər, níth-/ • *adj. & pron.* (foll. by sing. verb) not the one nor the other (of two); not either. • *adv.* **1** not either; not on the one hand (foll. by *nor. neither knowing nor caring*). **2** also not (*if you do not, neither shall I*). • *conj.* archaic nor yet; nor.

nel·son /nélsən/ *n.* wrestling hold in which one arm is passed under the opponent's arm from behind and the hand is applied to the neck (**half nelson**), or both arms and hands are applied (**full nelson**).

nem·a·tode /némətōd/ *n.* parasitic or free-living worm with a slender unsegmented cylindrical shape. Also called **roundworm.**

nem·e·sis /némisis/ *n.* (*pl.* **nem·e·ses** /-seez/) **1** retributive justice. **2 a** downfall caused by this. **b** agent of such a downfall. **3** something that one cannot conquer, achieve, etc.

neo- /née-ō/ *comb. form* **1** new; modern. **2** new form of.

ne·o·clas·si·cal /née-ōklásikəl/ *adj.* (also **ne·o·clas·sic** /-ik/) of or relating to a revival of a classical style in the arts, etc. □□ **ne·o·clas·si·cism** /-sisizəm/ *n.*

ne·o·co·lo·ni·al·ism /née-ō·kəlóneeəlizəm/ *n.* use of economic, political, or other pressures to control or influence other countries, esp. former dependencies.

ne·o·dym·i·um /née·ədímeeəm/ *n. Chem.* silvergray metallic element used in coloring glass, etc. ¶ Symb.: **Nd.**

ne·o·lith·ic /née·əlíthik/ *adj.* of the later Stone Age, when ground or polished stone weapons and implements prevailed.

ne·ol·o·gism /nee-óləjizəm/ *n.* **1** new word or expression. **2** coining or use of new words.

ne·on /née-on/ *n. Chem.* inert gaseous element giving an orange glow when electricity is passed through it (*neon light; neon sign*). ¶ Symb.: **Ne.**

ne·o·phyte /née·ōfīt/ *n.* **1** new convert, esp. to a religious faith. **2** beginner; novice.

ne·o·prene /née-əpreen/ *n.* synthetic rubberlike polymer.

Ne·pal·i /nipáwlee/ • *n.* (*pl.* same as **Ne·pal·is**; also **Ne·pal·ese** /népəleez, -lées/) **1 a** native or national of Nepal in Central Asia. **b** person of Nepali descent. **2** language of Nepal. • *adj.* of Nepal or its language or people.

neph·ew /néfyoo/ *n.* son of one's brother or sister, or of one's brother-in-law or sister-in-law.

ne·phrit·ic /nəfrítik/ *adj.* **1** of or in the kidneys; renal. **2** of or relating to nephritis.

ne·phri·tis /nefrítis/ *n.* inflammation of the kidneys. Also called **Bright's disease.**

ne plus ul·tra /náy ploōs oóltraa, née plus últrə/ *n.* **1** furthest attainable point. **2** culmination, acme, or perfection.

nep·o·tism /népətizəm/ *n.* favoritism to relatives in conferring offices or privileges.

Nep·tune /néptoon, -tyoon/ *n.* **1** eighth planet from the sun. **2** *Gk. mythol.* god of the sea.

nep·tu·ni·um /neptooneeəm, -tyoō-/ *n. Chem.* radioactive transuranic metallic element. ¶ Symb.: **Np.**

nerd /nərd/ *n.* (also **nurd**) *sl.* **1** foolish, feeble, or uninteresting person. **2** person intellectually talented but socially unskilled. □□ **nerd·y** *adj.*

nerve /nərv/ • *n.* **1** fiber or bundle of fibers that transmits impulses of sensation or motion between the brain or spinal cord and other parts of the body. **2 a** coolness in danger; bravery. **b** *colloq.* impudence. **3** (in *pl.*) heightened nervousness or sensitivity; mental or physical stress. • *v.tr.* give strength, vigor, or courage to. □ **get on a person's nerves** irritate a person. **nerve cell** cell transmitting impulses in nerve tissue. **nerve center** center of control. **nerve gas** poisonous gas affecting the nervous system. **nerve-racking** (also **nerve-wrack·ing**) stressful, frightening.

nerve·less /nərvlis/ *adj.* **1** inert; lacking vigor. **2** confident; not nervous. □□ **nerve′less·ly** *adv.* **nerve′less·ness** *n.*

ner·vous /nərvəs/ *adj.* **1** timid or anxious. **2 a** excitable; highly strung. **b** resulting from this (*nervous headache*). **3** affecting or acting on the nerves. □ **nervous breakdown** period of mental illness. **nervous system** the body's network of specialized cells that transmit nerve impulses between parts of the body (cf. *central nervous system*). □□ **ner′vous·ly** *adv.* **ner′vous·ness** *n.*

nerv·y /nárvee/ *adj.* (**nerv·i·er, nerv·i·est**) bold; impudent; pushy.

-ness /nis/ *suffix* forming nouns from adjectives, etc., expressing state or condition, or an instance of this (*happiness*).

nest /nest/ • *n.* **1** structure or place where a bird lays eggs and shelters its young. **2** any creature's breeding place or lair. **3** snug retreat or shelter. **4** group or set of similar objects, often of different sizes and fitting together for storage (*nest of tables*). • *v.* **1** *intr.* use or build a nest. **2** *intr.* (of objects) fit together or one inside another. **3** *tr.* (usu. as **nested** *adj.*) establish in or as in a nest. □ **nest egg** sum of money saved for the future.

nes·tle /nésəl/ *v.* **1** *intr.* settle oneself comfortably. **2** *intr.* press oneself against another in affection, etc. **3** *tr.* push (a head or shoulder, etc.)

affectionately or snugly. **4** *intr.* lie half hidden or embedded.

nest·ling /nésling, nést-/ *n.* bird too young to leave its nest.

net¹ /net/ • *n.* **1** open-meshed fabric of cord, rope, etc. **2** piece of net used esp. to restrain, contain, or delimit, or to catch fish, etc. **3** structure with net used in various games, esp. forming the goal in soccer, hockey, etc., and dividing the court in tennis, etc. **4** = NETWORK. • *v.* (**net·ted, net·ting**) *tr.* cover, confine, or catch with a net.

net² /net/ • *adj.* **1** remaining after all necessary deductions. **2** (of an effect, result, etc.) ultimate, effective. • *v.tr.* (**net·ted, net·ting**) gain or yield as profit, weight, etc. □ **net profit** actual gain after expenses have been paid.

-net /net/ *suffix* forming nouns denoting a relationship to computer networking (*Internet*).

neth·er /néthər/ *adj. archaic* = LOWER 2. □ **nether regions** (or **world**) hell; the underworld.

Neth·er·land·er /néthərlandər/ *n.* **1** native or national of the Netherlands. **2** person of Dutch descent.

net·su·ke /nétsŏŏkee/ *n.* (*pl.* same or **net·su·kes**) carved buttonlike ornament, esp. of ivory or wood.

net·ting /néting/ *n.* **1** netted fabric. **2** piece of this.

net·tle /nét'l/ • *n.* plant with jagged leaves covered with stinging hairs. • *v.tr.* **1** irritate; provoke. **2** sting with nettles.

net·tle·some /nét'lsəm/ *adj.* **1** difficult. **2** annoying.

net·work /nétwərk/ • *n.* **1** arrangement of intersecting horizontal and vertical lines. **2** complex system of railways, roads, people, computers, etc., that interconnect or communicate. **3** group of broadcasting stations connected for simultaneous broadcast of a program. • *v.* **1** *tr.* link (machines, esp. computers) to operate interactively. **2** *intr.* establish a network. **3** *intr.* be a member of a network (esp. people).

neu·ral /nŏŏrəl, nyŏŏr-/ *adj.* of or relating to a nerve or the central nervous system.

neu·ral·gia /nŏŏráljə, nyŏŏ-/ *n.* intense intermittent pain along a nerve, esp. in the head or face. □□ **neu·ral'gic** *adj.*

neu·ri·tis /nŏŏrítis, nyŏŏ-/ *n.* inflammation of a nerve or nerves. □□ **neu·rit·ic** /-rítik/ *adj.*

neuro- /nŏŏrō, nyŏŏrō/ *comb. form* nerve or nerves.

neu·rol·o·gy /nŏŏráləjee, nyŏŏ-/ *n.* study of the nervous system. □□ **neu·ro·log·i·cal** /-rəlójikəl/ *adj.* **neu·rol'o·gist** *n.*

neu·ron /nŏŏron, nyŏŏr-/ *n.* (also **neu·rone** /-ōn/) specialized cell transmitting nerve impulses; nerve cell. □□ **neu·ron'ic** *adj.*

neu·ro·sis /nŏŏrósis, nyŏŏ-/ *n.* (*pl.* **neu·ro·ses** /-seez/) mental illness marked by anxiety, obsessions, compulsive acts, etc., caused by a disorder of the nervous system usu. without organic change.

neu·ro·sur·ger·y /nŏŏrósərjəree, nyŏŏr-/ *n.* surgery performed on the brain or spinal cord. □□ **neu·ro·sur'geon** /-jən/ *n.* **neu·ro·sur'gi·cal** *adj.*

neu·rot·ic /nŏŏrótik, nyŏŏ-/ • *adj.* **1** caused by or relating to neurosis. **2** (of a person) suffering from neurosis. **3** *colloq.* abnormally sensitive or

obsessive. • *n.* neurotic person. □□ **neu·rot'i·cal·ly** *adv.*

neut. *abbr.* neuter.

neu·ter /nŏŏtər, nyŏŏ-/ • *adj.* **1** *Gram.* (of a noun, etc.) neither masculine nor feminine. **2** (of a plant) having neither pistils nor stamen. **3** (of an insect, animal, etc.) sexually undeveloped; castrated or spayed. • *n.* **1** *Gram.* neuter word. **2 a** nonfertile insect. **b** castrated animal. • *v.tr.* castrate or spay.

neu·tral /nŏŏtrəl, nyŏŏ-/ • *adj.* **1** not helping nor supporting either of two sides; impartial. **2** indistinct; vague; indeterminate. **3** (of a gear) in which the engine is disconnected from the driven parts. **4** (of colors) not strong nor positive; gray or beige. **5** *Chem.* neither acid nor alkaline. **6** *Electr.* neither positive nor negative. • *n.* **1 a** neutral nation, person, etc. **b** subject of a neutral nation. **2** neutral gear. □□ **neu·tral·i·ty** /-trálitee/ *n.* **neu'tral·ly** *adv.*

neu·tral·ize /nŏŏtrəlīz, nyŏŏ-/ *v.tr.* **1** make neutral. **2** counterbalance; render ineffective by an opposite force or effect. □□ **neu'tral·iz·er** *n.*

neu·tri·no /nŏŏtree'enō, nyŏŏ-/ *n.* (*pl.* **-nos**) elementary particle with zero electric charge and probably zero mass.

neu·tron /nŏŏtron, nyŏŏ-/ *n.* uncharged elementary particle of about the same mass as a proton. □ **neutron bomb** bomb producing neutrons and little blast, destroying life but not property.

Nev. *abbr.* Nevada.

nev·er /névər/ *adv.* **1** at no time; on no occasion; not ever. **2** not at all. □ **never-never land** imaginary utopian place.

nev·er·more /névərmáwr/ *adv.* at no future time.

nev·er·the·less /névərthəlés/ *adv.* in spite of that; notwithstanding; all the same.

ne·vus /née'vəs/ *n.* (*pl.* **ne·vi** /-vī/) **1** raised red birthmark. **2** = MOLE².

new /nŏŏ, nyŏŏ/ • *adj.* **1 a** of recent origin or arrival. **b** made, invented, discovered, acquired, or experienced recently or now for the first time. **2** in original condition; not worn or used. **3 a** renewed or reformed. **b** reinvigorated. **4** different from a recent previous one. **5** unfamiliar or strange. **6 a** modern. **b** newfangled. **7** advanced in method or theory. • *adv.* (usu. in *comb.*) **1** newly, recently (*new-baked*). **2** anew, afresh. □ **New Age** set of beliefs intended to replace traditional Western Culture, with alternative approaches to religion, medicine, the environment, music, etc. **new moon** moon when first seen as a crescent after conjunction with the sun. **New Testament** part of the Bible concerned with the life and teachings of Christ and his earliest followers. **New World** N. and S. America. **New Year's Day** January 1. **New Year's Eve** December 31. □□ **new'ish** *adj.* **new'ness** *n.*

---

new Old English *nīwe, nēowe*, of Germanic origin; related to Dutch *nieuw* and German *neu*, from an Indo-European root shared by Sanskrit *nava*, Latin *novus*, and Greek *neos* 'new.'

---

new·born /nŏŏbawrn, nyŏŏ-/ *adj.* **1** (of a child, etc.) recently born. **2** spiritually reborn; regenerated.

new·com·er /nóōkumər, nyóō-/ *n.* **1** person who has recently arrived. **2** beginner in some activity.

new·el /nóōəl, nyóō-/ *n.* **1** supporting central post of winding stairs. **2** top or bottom supporting post of a stair rail.

newel post

NEWEL POST

new·fan·gled /nóōfánggəld, nyóō-/ *adj. derog.* different from what one is used to; objectionably new.

New·found·land /nóōfəndlənd, noofówndlənd, nyóō-, -land, -fənd-, nyóō-/ *n.* (in full **New·found·land dog**) very large dog with a thick, usu. black, coarse coat.

new·ly /nóōlee, nyóō-/ *adv.* **1** recently. **2** afresh, anew. **3** in a new or different manner.

news /nóōz, nyóōz/ *n.pl.* (usu. treated as *sing.*) **1** information about important or interesting recent events, esp. when published or broadcast. **2** (prec. by *the*) broadcast report of news. **3** newly received or noteworthy information.

news·cast /nóōzkast, nyóō-/ *n.* radio or television broadcast of news reports. □□ **news'cast·er** *n.*

news·deal·er /nóōzdeelər, nyóōz-/ *n.* person who sells newspapers, magazines, etc.

news·let·ter /nóōzletər, nyóōz-/ *n.* concise periodical of news, events, etc., of special interest.

news·pa·per /nóōzpaypər, nyóōz-, nóōs-, nyóōs-/ *n.* **1** printed publication (usu. daily or weekly) containing news, advertisements, correspondence, etc. **2** newsprint.

news·print /nóōzprint, nyóōz-/ *n.* low-quality paper on which newspapers are printed.

news·stand /nóōzstand, nyóōz-/ *n.* stall for the sale of newspapers, magazines, etc.

news·week·ly /nóōzweeklee, nyóōz-/ *n.* periodical published weekly that summarizes current events.

news·wor·thy /nóōzwərthee, nyóōz-/ *adj.* noteworthy as news.

news·y /nóōzee, nyóō-/ *adj.* (**news·i·er, news·i·est**) *colloq.* full of news.

newt /nóōt, nyóōt/ *n.* small amphibian having a well-developed tail.

New Test. *abbr.* New Testament.

new·ton /nóōt'n, nyóō-/ *n. Physics* SI unit of force that, acting on a mass of one kilogram, increases its velocity by one meter per second every second. ¶ Abbr.: **N.**

New Zea·land·er /nóōzée'eləndər, nyóō-/ *n.* **1** native or national of New Zealand, an island group in the Pacific. **2** person of New Zealand descent.

next /nekst/ • *adj.* **1** being or positioned or living nearest. **2** nearest in order of time. • *adv.* **1** in the nearest place or degree (*put it next to mine*). **2** on the first or soonest occasion. • *n.* next person or thing. □ **next door** in the next house or room. **next to** almost (*next to nothing left*).

nex·us /néksəs/ *n.* (*pl.* same) connected group or series.

Nez Per·cé /náy persáy/ *n.* (also **Nez Per·ce** /néz pórs, nés pérs/) **1 a** N. American people native to the northwest US. **b** member of this people. **2** language of this people.

NH *abbr.* New Hampshire (also in official postal use).

Ni *symb. Chem.* nickel.

ni·a·cin /níəsin/ *n.* = NICOTINIC ACID.

nib /nib/ *n.* pen point.

nib·ble /níbəl/ • *v.* **1** *tr.* & *intr.* **a** take small bites at. **b** eat in small amounts. **c** bite at gently or cautiously or playfully. **2** *intr.* (foll. by *at*) show cautious interest in. • *n.* **1** very small amount of food. **2** *Computing* half a byte, i.e., 4 bits.

nibs /nibz/ *n.* □ **his nibs** *joc. colloq.* mock title used for an important or self-important person.

ni·cad /nícad/ • *adj.* nickel and cadmium. • *n.* nickel and cadmium battery.

nice /nīs/ *adj.* **1** pleasant, satisfactory. **2** (of a person) kind, good-natured. **3** *iron.* bad or awkward (*a nice mess you've made*). **4** fine or subtle (*nice distinction*). **5** fastidious; delicately sensitive. □□ **nice'ly** *adv.* **nice'ness** *n.*

¶ **Nice** originally had a number of meanings, including 'fine, subtle, discriminating'; 'refined in taste, fastidious'; and 'precise, strict': *They are not very nice in regard to the company they keep. She has a nice sense of decorum.* The popular overuse of **nice** to mean 'pleasant, agreeable, satisfactory,' etc., has rendered the word trite: *We had a very nice time. This is a nice room. He's a nice boy.*

---

nice Middle English (in the sense 'stupid'): from Old French, from Latin *nescius* 'ignorant,' from *nescire* 'not know.' Other early senses included 'coy, reserved,' giving rise to 'fastidious, precise, scrupulous': this led both to the sense 'fine, subtle' (regarded by some as the 'correct' sense), and to the main current senses.

---

ni·ce·ty /nísitee/ *n.* (*pl.* **-ties**) **1** subtle distinction or detail. **2** precision, accuracy. **3** (in *pl.*) refinements, trimmings.

niche /nich, neesh/ *n.* **1** shallow recess, esp. in a wall to contain a statue, etc. **2** comfortable or suitable position in life or employment.

nick /nik/ • *n.* small cut or notch. • *v.tr.* make a nick or nicks in. □ **in the nick of time** only just in time.

nick·el /níkəl/ • *n.* **1** *Chem.* malleable silver-white metallic element used in special steels, in magnetic alloys, and as a catalyst. ¶ Symb.: **Ni. 2** five-cent coin. • *v.tr.* coat with nickel. □ **nickel-and-dime** *adj.* involving a small amount of money; insignificant; trivial. • *v.tr.* weaken (one's financial position) by continued small expenses, bills, etc.

nick·el·o·de·on /níkəlṓdeeən/ n. colloq. **1** early movie theater, esp. one with admission priced at 5 cents. **2** jukebox.

nick·name /níknaym/ • n. familiar or humorous name given to a person or thing instead of or as well as the real name. • v.tr. give a nickname to.

nic·o·tine /níkəteen/ n. poisonous alkaloid present in tobacco.

nic·o·tin·ic ac·id /níkətínik/ n. vitamin of the B complex, found in milk, liver, and yeast, a deficiency of which causes pellagra. Also called **niacin.**

nic·ti·tate /níktitayt/ v.intr. close and open the eyes; blink or wink. □ **nictitating membrane** transparent third eyelid in amphibians, birds, etc., that protects the eye without loss of vision.

niece /nees/ n. daughter of one's brother or sister, or of one's brother-in-law or sister-in-law.

nif·ty /níftee/ adj. (**nif·ti·er, nif·ti·est**) colloq. **1** clever; adroit. **2** smart; stylish.

nig·gard·ly /nígərdlee/ • adj. **1** stingy; parsimonious. **2** meager; scanty. • adv. in a stingy or meager manner. □□ **nig′gard·li·ness** n.

nig·gle /nígəl/ v.intr. **1** be overattentive to details. **2** find fault in a petty way. □□ **nig′gling** adj.

nigh /nī/ adv., prep., & adj. archaic or dial. near; nearby.

night /nīt/ n. **1** period of darkness between one day and the next; time from sunset to sunrise. **2** nightfall. **3** darkness of night. □ **night owl** colloq. person active at night.

night·cap /nítkap/ n. **1** hist. cap worn in bed. **2** hot or alcoholic drink taken at bedtime.

night·club /nítklub/ n. club that is open at night and provides refreshment and entertainment.

night·fall /nítfawl/ n. onset of night; end of daylight.

night·gown /nítgown/ n. woman's or child's loose garment worn in bed.

night·hawk /níthawk/ n. nocturnal bird related to the whippoorwill.

night·in·gale /nít′ngayl/ n. small reddish-brown bird, of which the male sings melodiously, esp. at night.

night·life /nítlīf/ n. entertainment available at night in a town.

night·ly /nítlee/ • adj. **1** happening, done, or existing in the night. **2** recurring every night. • adv. every night.

night·mare /nítmair/ n. **1** frightening dream. **2** colloq. terrifying or very unpleasant experience or situation. **3** haunting or obsessive fear. □□ **night′mar·ish** adj.

night·shirt /nítshərt/ n. long shirt worn in bed.

night·spot /nítspot/ n. nightclub.

night·stick /nítstik/ n. policeman's club.

night·time /níttīm/ n. time of darkness.

NIH abbr. National Institutes of Health.

ni·hil·ism /níʼilizəm, née-/ n. rejection of all religious and moral principles. □□ **ni′hil·ist** n. **ni·hil·is′tic** adj.

-nik /nik/ suffix forming nouns denoting a person associated with a specified thing or quality (beatnik; refusenik).

nil /nil/ n. nothing; no number or amount.

nim·ble /nímbəl/ adj. (**nim·bler, nim·blest**) **1** quick and light in movement or action; agile. **2** (of the mind) quick to comprehend; clever; versatile. □□ **nim′bly** adv.

nim·bus /nímbəs/ n. (pl. **nim·bi** /-bī/ or **nim·bus·es**) **1 a** bright cloud or halo investing a deity or person or thing. **b** halo of a saint, etc. **2** Meteorol. rain cloud.

NIMBY /nímbee/ abbr. colloq. not in my backyard.

nin·com·poop /nínkəmpoop/ n. simpleton; fool.

nine /nīn/ • n. **1** one more than eight, or one less than ten. **2** symbol for this (9, ix, IX). • adj. that amount to nine. □□ **ninth** /nīnth/ n. & adj.

nine·fold /nínfōld/ adj. & adv. nine times as much or as many.

nine·teen /níntéen/ • n. **1** one more than eighteen, nine more than ten. **2** symbol for this (19, xix, XIX). • adj. that amount to nineteen. □□ **nine′teenth** n. & adj.

nine·ty /níntee/ n. (pl. **-ties**) **1** product of nine and ten. **2** symbol for this (90, xc, XC). **3** (in pl.) numbers from 90 to 99, esp. years. □□ **nine′ti·eth** n. & adj.

nin·ja /nínjə/ n. person skilled in a Japanese martial art emphasizing stealth.

nin·ny /nínee/ n. (pl. **-nies**) foolish or simple-minded person.

ni·o·bi·um /nīṓbeeəm/ n. Chem. rare gray-blue metallic element used in alloys for superconductors. ¶ Symb.: **Nb.**

nip[1] /nip/ • v.tr. (**nipped, nip·ping**) **1** pinch, squeeze, or bite sharply. **2** remove by pinching, etc. **3** (of the cold, etc.) cause pain or harm to. • n. **1 a** pinch, sharp squeeze. **b** bite. **2** biting cold. □ **nip and tuck** neck and neck. **nip in the bud** suppress or destroy (esp. an idea) at an early stage.

nip[2] /nip/ • n. small quantity of liquor. • v.intr. (**nipped, nip·ping**) drink liquor.

nip·per /nípər/ n. **1** person or thing that nips. **2** claw of a crab, lobster, etc. **3** (in pl.) any tool for gripping or cutting, e.g., forceps or pincers.

nip·ple /nípəl/ n. **1** small projection in which the mammary ducts of either sex of mammals terminate and from which in females milk is secreted for the young. **2** mouthpiece of a feeding bottle or pacifier. **3** device like a nipple in shape or function.

nip·py /nípee/ adj. (**nip·pi·er, nip·pi·est**) colloq. **1** chilly, cold. **2** tending to nip, as a dog.

nir·va·na /nərvaʼanə, neer-/ n. (in Buddhism) perfect bliss attained by the extinction of individuality.

ni·sei /néesay, neesáy/ n. (also **Ni′sei**) American whose parents were immigrants from Japan.

nit /nit/ n. egg or young form of a louse or other parasitic insect.

ni·ter /nítər/ n. saltpeter; potassium nitrate.

nit·pick /nítpik/ v.intr. colloq. find fault in a petty manner. □□ **nit′pick·er** n. **nit′pick·ing** n.

ni·trate /nítrayt/ • n. **1** any salt or ester of nitric acid. **2** potassium or sodium nitrate as a fertilizer. • v.tr. Chem. treat, combine, or impregnate with nitric acid. □□ **ni·tra′tion** /-áyshən/ n.

ni·tric /nítrik/ adj. of or containing nitrogen. □ **nitric acid** colorless corrosive poisonous liquid. ¶ Chem. formula: HNO_3.

nitro- /nítrō/ *comb. form* of or containing nitric acid, niter, or nitrogen.

ni·tro·gen /nítrəjən/ *n. Chem.* colorless, tasteless, odorless gaseous element that forms four-fifths of the atmosphere. ¶ Symb.: **N**. □□ **ni·trog·e·nous** /-trójinəs/ *adj.*

ni·tro·glyc·er·in /nítrōglísərin/ *n.* (also **ni′tro·glyc·er·ine**) explosive yellow liquid made by reacting glycerol with sulfuric and nitric acids.

ni·trous ox·ide /nítrəs/ *n.* colorless gas used as an anesthetic (= *laughing gas*) and as an aerosol propellant. ¶ Chem. formula: N₂O.

nit·ty-grit·ty /níteegrítee/ *n. sl.* realities or practical details of a matter.

nit·wit /nítwit/ *n. colloq.* stupid person.

nix /niks/ *sl.* • *n.* nothing. • *v.tr.* **1** cancel. **2** reject.

NJ *abbr.* New Jersey (in official postal use).

NLRB *abbr.* National Labor Relations Board.

NM *abbr.* New Mexico (in official postal use).

N.Mex. *abbr.* New Mexico.

No *symb. Chem.* nobelium.

No. *abbr.* **1** number. **2** North.

no¹ /nō/ *adj.* **1** not any (*there is no excuse; no two of them are alike*). **2** not a; quite other than (*is no fool; is no part of my plan*). **3** hardly any (*did it in no time*). **4** used elliptically as a slogan, notice, etc., to forbid, reject, or deplore the thing specified (*no parking*). □ **no-brainer** problem, question, examination, etc., that requires very little thought. **no-fault** (of insurance) valid regardless of the allocation of blame for an accident, etc. **no-go** impossible, hopeless. **no man's land 1** *Mil.* space between two opposing armies. **2** area not assigned to any owner. **3** area of uncertainty. **no-no** *colloq.* thing not possible or acceptable. **no-win** of or designating a situation in which success is impossible.

no² /nō/ • *adv.* **1** equivalent to a negative sentence: the answer to your question is negative; your request or command will not be complied with; the statement made or course of action intended or conclusion arrived at is not correct or satisfactory; the negative statement made is correct. **2** (foll. by *compar.*) by no amount; not at all (*no better than before*). • *n.* (*pl.* **noes** or **nos**) **1** utterance of the word *no*. **2** denial or refusal. **3** negative vote.

NOAA /nóə/ *abbr.* National Oceanic and Atmospheric Administration.

No·bel·ist /nōbélist/ *n.* winner of a Nobel prize.

no·bel·i·um /nōbéeleeəm/ *n. Chem.* radioactive metallic element. ¶ Symb.: **No**.

No·bel prize /nóbél/ *n.* any of six international prizes awarded annually for physics, chemistry, physiology or medicine, literature, economics, and the promotion of peace.

no·bil·i·ty /nōbílitee/ *n.* (*pl.* **-ties**) **1** nobleness of character, mind, birth, or rank. **2** class of nobles; aristocracy.

no·ble /nóbəl/ • *adj.* (**no·bler, no·blest**) **1** belonging by rank, title, or birth to the aristocracy. **2** of excellent character; magnanimous. **3** of imposing appearance; splendid. **4** excellent; admirable. • *n.* nobleman or noblewoman. □□ **no′ble·ness** *n.*

no·ble·man /nóbəlmən/ *n.* (*pl.* **-men**) man of noble rank or birth; peer.

no·blesse o·blige /nōblés ōbléezh/ *n.* privilege entails responsibility.

no·ble·wom·an /nóbəlwoomən/ *n.* (*pl.* **-wom·en**) woman of noble rank or birth; peeress.

no·bod·y /nóbodee, -budee, -bədee/ • *pron.* no person. • *n.* (*pl.* **-ies**) person of no importance, authority, or position.

noc·tur·nal /noktárnəl/ *adj.* of or in the night; done or active by night.

noc·turne /nóktərn/ *n. Mus.* short romantic composition, usu. for piano.

nod /nod/ • *v.* (**nod·ded, nod·ding**) **1** *intr.* incline one's head slightly and briefly in greeting, assent, or command. **2** *intr.* let one's head fall forward in drowsiness. **3** *tr.* incline (one's head). **4** *tr.* signify (assent, etc.) by a nod. • *n.* nodding of the head, esp. as a sign to proceed, etc. □ **nod off** *colloq.* fall asleep.

node /nōd/ *n.* **1** *Bot.* **a** part of a plant stem from which leaves emerge. **b** knob on a root or branch. **2** *Anat.* natural swelling in an organ or part of the body. **3** *Physics* point of minimum disturbance in a standing wave system. **4** component in a computer network. □□ **nod′al** *adj.*

nod·ule /nójool/ *n.* **1** small, rounded lump. **2** small swelling or aggregation of cells, e.g., a small tumor, node, or ganglion. □□ **nod·u·lar** /-jələr/ *adj.*

No·el /nō-él/ *n.* **1** Christmas. **2** (also **noel**) Christmas carol.

nog·gin /nógin/ *n.* **1** small mug. **2** *sl.* head.

noise /noyz/ • *n.* **1** sound, esp. a loud or unpleasant or undesired one. **2** irregular fluctuations accompanying a transmitted signal but not relevant to it. • *v. tr.* (usu. in *passive*) make public; spread abroad (a person's fame or a fact).

noise·less /nóyzlis/ *adj.* making little or no noise. □□ **noise′less·ly** *adv.*

noi·some /nóysəm/ *adj.* **1** harmful; noxious. **2** evil-smelling.

¶ **Noisome** means 'bad-smelling.' It has no relation to the word **noise**.

nois·y /nóyzee/ *adj.* (**nois·i·er, nois·i·est**) **1** full of noise. **2** making much noise. □□ **nois′i·ness** *n.*

no·mad /nómad/ • *n.* **1** member of a tribe roaming place to place for pasture. **2** wanderer. • *adj.* **1** living as a nomad. **2** wandering. □□ **no·mad′ic** /-mádik/ *adj.*

nom de plume /nóm də plóom/ *n.* (*pl.* **noms de plume** *pronunc.* same) pen name.

no·men·cla·ture /nómənklaychər, nōménklə-chər/ *n.* **1** person's or community's system of names for things. **2** terminology of a science, etc.

nom·i·nal /nóminəl/ *adj.* **1** existing in name only; not real or actual (*nominal ruler*). **2** (of a sum of money, rent, etc.) virtually nothing; much below the actual value of a thing. **3** of or in names (*nominal and essential distinctions*). **4** of or as or like a noun. □□ **nom′i·nal·ly** *adv.*

nom·i·nate /nóminayt/ *v.tr.* **1** propose (a candidate) for election. **2** appoint to an office. **3** name or appoint (a date or time). □□ **nom·i·na·tion** /-náyshən/ *n.* **nom′i·na·tor** *n.*

nom·i·na·tive /nóminətiv/ • *n. Gram.* **1** case of nouns, pronouns, and adjectives, expressing the subject of a verb. **2** word in this case. • *adj. Gram.* of or in this case.

nom·i·nee /nóminée/ *n.* person who is nominated for an office or as the recipient of a grant, etc.

non- /non/ *prefix* giving the negative sense of words with which it is combined, esp.: **1** not doing or having or involved with (*nonattendance*; *nonpayment*; *nonproductive*). **2 a** not of the kind or class described (*nonalcoholic*; *nonmember*). **b** forming terms used adjectivally (*nonunion*; *nonparty*). **3** lack of (*nonaccess*). **4** (with adverbs) not in the way described (*nonaggressively*). **5** forming adjectives from verbs, meaning "that does not" or "that is not meant to (or to be)" (*nonskid*; *noniron*). **6** used to form a neutral negative sense when a form in *in-* or *un-* has a special sense or (usu. unfavorable) connotation (*noncontroversial*; *noneffective*; *nonhuman*). ¶ The number of words that can be formed with this prefix is unlimited; consequently only a selection, considered the most current or semantically noteworthy, can be given here.

no·na·ge·nar·i·an /nónəjináireeən, nô-/ • *n.* person from 90 to 99 years old. • *adj.* of this age.

no·na·gon /nónəgon/ *n.* plane figure with nine sides and angles.

non·a·ligned /nónəlínd/ *adj.* (of nations, etc.) not aligned with another (esp. major) power. □□ **non·a·lign′ment** *n.*

non·am·big·u·ous /nónambígyōŏəs/ *adj.* not ambiguous. ¶ Neutral in sense: see NON- 6.

non·bel·lig·er·ent /nónbəlíjərənt/ • *adj.* not engaged in hostilities. • *n.* nonbelligerent nation, etc. □□ **non·bel·lig′er·en·cy** *n.*

nonce /nons/ *n.* □ **for the nonce** for the time being; for the present occasion. **nonce word** word coined for one occasion.

non·cha·lant /nónshəlá·ant/ *adj.* calm and casual, unmoved, indifferent. □□ **non·cha·lance′** *n.* **non·cha·lant′ly** *adv.*

non·com /nónkom/ *n. colloq.* noncommissioned officer.

non·com·ba·tant /nónkəmbát′nt, -kómbət′nt/

---

n. person not fighting in a war, esp. a civilian, army chaplain, etc.

non·com·mis·sioned /nónkəmíshənd/ *adj. Mil.* (of an officer) not holding a commission. ¶ Abbr.: **NCO.**

non·com·mit·tal /nónkəmít′l/ *adj.* avoiding commitment to a definite opinion or course of action.

non compos men·tis /nón kompəs méntis/ *adj.* (also **non com′pos**) not in one's right mind.

non·con·duc·tor /nónkəndúktər/ *n.* substance that does not conduct heat or electricity.

non·con·form·ist /nónkənfáwrmist/ *n.* person who does not conform to a prevailing principle. □□ **non·con·form′i·ty** *n.*

non·de·script /nóndiskript/ *adj.* lacking distinctive characteristics; not easily classified.

non·drink·er /nóndríngkər/ *n.* person who does not drink alcoholic liquor.

none /nun/ • *pron.* **1 a** not any of (*none of this concerns me*). **b** not any one of (*none were recovered*). **2** no persons (*none but fools have ever believed it*). • *adj.* (usu. with a preceding noun implied) no; not any (*you have money and I have none*). • *adv.* by no amount; not at all (*am none the wiser*). (*none were recovered*). **2** no persons (*none but fools have ever believed it*). • *adj.* (usu. with a preceding noun implied) no; not any (*you have money and I have none*). • *adv.* by no amount; not at all (*am none the wiser*).

non·en·ti·ty /nonéntitee/ *n.* (*pl.* **-ties**) **1** person or thing of no importance. **2** nonexistent thing, figment.

none·the·less /núnthəlés/ *adv.* nevertheless.

non·e·vent /nónivént/ *n.* unimportant or anti-climactic occurrence.

non·fer·rous /nónférəs/ *adj.* (of a metal) other than iron or steel.

---

non′a·bra′sive *adj.*
non·ab·sor′bent *adj.*
non·ad·dic′tive *adj.*
non·ad·he′sive *adj.*
non·ad·just′a·ble *adj.*
non·ag·gres′sion *n.*
non·al·co·hol′ic *adj.*
non·al·ler′gic *adj.*
non·be·liev′er *n.*
non·black′ *n.*
non·can′cer·ous *adj.*
non-Chris′tian *adj. & n.*
non·cler′i·cal *adj. & n.*
non·com·bus′ti·ble *adj.*
non·com·pli′ance *n.*
non·con·struc′tive *adj.*
non·con·ta′gious *adj.*
non·con·tro·ver′sial *adj.*
non·de·duct′i·ble *adj.*
non·de·nom·i·na′tion·al *adj.*
non·dry′ing *adj.*
non·ef·fec′tive *adj.*
non·es·sen′tial *adj.*
non·ex·ist′ence *n.*
non·ex·ist′ent *adj.*
non·ex·plo′sive *adj. & n.*
non·fat′ten·ing *adj.*
non·flam′ma·ble *adj.*

non·greas′y *adj.*
non·haz′ard·ous *adj.*
non·he·red′i·tar·y *adj.*
non·his·tor′i·cal *adj.*
non·hu′man *adj.*
non·i·den′ti·cal *adj.*
non·in·clu′sive *adj.*
non·in·fec′tious *adj.*
non·in·flect′ed *adj.*
non·in·flam′ma·to·ry *adj.*
non·in·fla′tion·ar·y *adj.*
non·in·te·grat·ed *adj.*
non·in·ter·change′a·ble *adj.*
non·in·ter·fer′ence *n.*
non·in·tox′i·cat·ing *adj.*
non·ir′ri·tat·ing *adj.*
non·lin′e·ar *adj.*
non·mag·net′ic *adj.*
non·ma·lig′nant *adj.*
non·mem′ber *n.*
non·mi′gra·to·ry *adj.*
non·mil′i·tant *adj.*
non·mil′i·tar·y *adj.*
non·nar·cot′ic *adj. & n.*
non·ne·go′ti·a·ble *adj.*
non·ob·jec′tive *adj.*
non·ob·lig′a·to·ry *adj.*
non·ob·serv′ant *adj.*
non·of·fi′cial *adj.*

non·or·gan′ic *adj.*
non·par′ti·san *adj.*
non·pay′ing *adj.*
non·pay′ment *n.*
non·per′ish·a·ble *adj.*
non·poi′son·ous *adj.*
non·po·lit′i·cal *adj.*
non·pol·lut′ing *adj.*
non·po′rous *adj.*
non·prac′tic·ing *adj.*
non·pro·duc′tive *adj.*
non·pro·fes′sion·al *adj. & n.*
non·prof′it·a·ble *adj.*
non·pub′lic *adj.*
non·ra′cial *adj.*
non·re·ac′tive *adj. & n.*
non·re·cip′ro·cal *adj.*
non·re·cip′ro·cat·ing *adj.*
non·re·cur′ring *adj.*
non·re·deem′a·ble *adj.*
non·re·fill′a·ble *adj.*
non·re·new′a·ble *adj.*
non·rep·re·sen·ta′tion·al *adj.*
non·re·sis′tant *adj.*
non·re·turn′a·ble *adj.*
non·rhyth′mic *adj.*
non·sal′a·ried *adj.*

non·sci·en·tif′ic *adj.*
non·sea′son·al *adj.*
non·sec·tar′i·an *adj.*
non·sex′ist *adj.*
non·sex′u·al *adj.*
non′skid′ *adj.*
non·slip′ *adj.*
non·smok′er *n.*
non·smok′ing *adj.*
non·spe·cif′ic *adj.*
non·stain′ing *adj.*
non·stick′ *adj.*
non·swim′mer *n.*
non·tar′nish·ing *adj.*
non·tax′a·ble *adj.*
non·tech′ni·cal *adj.*
non·think′ing *adj.*
non·threat′en·ing *adj.*
non·tox′ic *adj.*
non·trans·fer′a·ble *adj.*
non·us′er *n.*
non·ven′om·ous *adj.*
non·ver′bal *adj.*
non·vir′u·lent *adj.*
non·vo′cal *adj.*
non·vot′er *n.*
non·white′ *n. & adj.*
non·work′ing *adj.*

non·fic·tion /nónfíkshən/ n. literary work other than fiction, including biography and reference books.

non·in·ter·ven·tion /nónintərvénshən/ n. principle or practice of not becoming involved in others' affairs, esp. by one nation in regard to another.

non·pa·reil /nónpərél/ • adj. unrivaled or unique. • n. 1 such a person or thing. 2 candy made from a chocolate disk, decorated with sugar pellets.

non·plus /nonplús/ v.tr. (**non·plussed, non·plus·sing; non·plused, non·plus·ing**) completely perplex.

non·prof·it /nónprófit/ adj. not involving nor making a profit.

non·pro·lif·er·a·tion /nónprəlífəráyshən/ n. prevention of an increase in something, esp. possession of nuclear weapons.

non·res·i·dent /nónrézidənt/ • adj. 1 not residing in a particular place, esp. not residing where one works, seeks office, etc. 2 (of a post) not requiring the holder to reside at the place of work. • n. nonresident person. □□ **non·res·i·den·tial** /-dénshəl/ adj.

non·re·sis·tance /nónrizístəns/ n. practice or principle of not resisting authority.

non·sense /nónsens, -səns/ n. absurd or meaningless words or ideas; foolish or extravagant conduct. □□ **non·sen·si·cal** /-sénsikəl/ adj. **non·sen·si·cal·ly** adv.

non se·qui·tur /non sékwitər/ n. conclusion that does not logically follow from the premises.

non·start·er /nónstaártər/ n. 1 person or animal that does not start in a race. 2 colloq. person or thing that is unlikely to succeed or be effective.

non·stop /nónstóp/ • adj. 1 (of a train, etc.) not stopping at intermediate places. 2 (of a journey, performance, etc.) done without a stop or intermission. • adv. without stopping or pausing.

non·u·nion /nónyoonyən/ adj. 1 not belonging to a labor union. 2 not done or produced by members of a labor union.

non·vi·o·lence /nónvíələns/ n. avoidance of violence, esp. as a principle. □□ **non·vi·o·lent** /-lənt/ adj.

noo·dle¹ /noód'l/ n. strip or ring of pasta.

noo·dle² /noód'l/ n. sl. head.

nook /nook/ n. corner or recess; secluded place. □ **in every nook and cranny** everywhere.

noon /noon/ n. twelve o'clock in the day; midday.

no one /nó wun/ n. no person; nobody.

noose /noos/ • n. 1 loop with a slip knot, tightening when pulled, esp. in a snare, lasso, or hangman's halter. 2 snare or bond. • v.tr. 1 catch with or enclose in a noose; ensnare. 2 a make a noose on (a cord). b (often foll. by around) arrange (a cord) in a noose.

nor /nawr, nər/ conj. 1 and not; and not either (can neither read nor write). 2 and no more; neither ("I cannot go" – "Nor can I").

Nor·dic /náwrdik/ • adj. 1 of the tall blond Germanic people in northern Europe, esp. in Scandinavia. 2 of or relating to Scandinavia or Finland. • n. Nordic person.

nor'east·er /noreéstər/ n. northeaster.

norm /nawrm/ n. 1 standard or pattern or type. 2 customary behavior, etc.

nor·mal /náwrməl/ • adj. 1 conforming to a standard; regular; usual; typical. 2 free from mental or emotional disorder. • n. 1 normal value of a temperature, etc., esp. that of blood. 2 usual state, level, etc. □□ **nor·mal·cy** n. **nor·mal·i·ty** /-máli-tee/ n. **nor·mal·i·za·tion** n. **nor·mal·ize** v.

¶ **Normalcy** has been criticized as an uneducated alternative to **normality**, but actually is a common American usage and can be taken as standard.

nor·mal·ly /náwrməlee/ adv. 1 in a normal manner. 2 usually.

Nor·man /náwrmən/ • n. 1 native or inhabitant of medieval or modern Normandy. 2 people established there in the 10th c., who conquered England in 1066. • adj. 1 of or relating to the Normans. 2 of or relating to the Norman style of architecture. □ **Norman Conquest** conquest of England by William of Normandy in 1066.

nor·ma·tive /náwrmətiv/ adj. of or establishing a norm.

Norse /nawrs/ • n. 1 a Norwegian language. b Scandinavian language group. 2 (prec. by the; treated as pl.) a Norwegians. b Vikings. • adj. of ancient Scandinavia, esp. Norway. □□ **Norse·man** n. (pl. **-men**)

north /nawrth/ • n. 1 a point of the horizon 90° counterclockwise from east. b compass point corresponding to this. 2 (usu. the North) a part of the world or a country or a town lying to the north. b the arctic. • adj. 1 toward, at, near, or facing north. 2 from the north (north wind). • adv. 1 toward, at, or near the north. 2 further north than. □ **North American** adj. of North America. • n. native or inhabitant of North America, esp. a citizen of the US or Canada. **north pole** (also **North Pole**) northernmost point of the earth's axis of rotation. **North Star** polestar.

north·east /nawrtheést/ • n. 1 point of the horizon midway between north and east. 2 direction in which this lies. • adj. of, toward, or coming from the northeast. • adv. toward, at, or near the northeast.

north·east·er /náwrtheéstər, náwreéstər/ n. (also **nor'east·er**) 1 northeast wind. 2 strong storm from the northeast, esp. in New England.

north·er·ly /náwrthərlee/ adj. & adv. 1 in a northern position or direction. 2 (of wind) blowing from the north.

north·ern /náwrthərn/ adj. 1 of or in the north; inhabiting the north. 2 lying or directed toward the north. □ **northern hemisphere** (also **Northern Hemisphere**) the half of the earth north of the equator. **northern lights** aurora borealis. □□ **north·ern·most** adj.

north·er·ner /náwrthərnər/ n. native or inhabitant of the north.

north·west /nawrthwést/ • n. 1 point of the horizon midway between north and west. 2 direction in which this lies. • adj. of, toward, or coming from the northwest. • adv. toward, at, or near the northwest.

Nor·we·gian /nawrweéjən/ • n. 1 a native or national of Norway. b person of Norwegian descent. 2 language of Norway. • adj. of or relating to Norway.

nose /nōz/ • *n.* **1** organ above the mouth of a human or animal, used for smelling and breathing. **2 a** sense of smell. **b** ability to detect a particular thing (*a nose for scandal*). **3** front end or projecting part of a thing, e.g., of a car or aircraft. • *v.* **1** *tr.* **a** perceive the smell of, discover by smell. **b** detect. **2** *intr.* pry or search. **3 a** *intr.* make one's way cautiously forward. **b** *tr.* make (one's or its way). □ **by a nose** by a very narrow margin. **keep one's nose clean** *sl.* stay out of trouble; behave properly. **nose cone** cone-shaped nose of a rocket, etc. **nose job** *sl.* surgery on the nose, esp. for cosmetic reasons; rhinoplasty. **on the nose** *sl.* precisely. **put a person's nose out of joint** *colloq.* embarrass, disconcert, frustrate, or supplant a person. **turn up one's nose** *colloq.* show disdain. **under a person's nose** *colloq.* right before a person. **with one's nose in the air** haughtily.

nose·bleed /nózbleed/ *n.* bleeding from the nose.

nose·dive /nózdīv/ • *n.* **1** steep downward plunge by an airplane. **2** sudden plunge or drop. • *v.intr.* make a nosedive.

nose·gay /nózgay/ *n.* sweet-scented bunch of flowers.

nosh /nosh/ *sl.* • *v.* eat, esp. between meals. • *n.* snack.

nos·tal·gia /nostáljə, -jeeə, nə-/ *n.* **1** sentimental yearning for a period of the past. **2** severe homesickness. □□ **nos·tal'gic** *adj.* **nos·tal'gi·cal·ly** *adv.*

nos·tril /nóstrəl/ *n.* either of two openings in the nose.

nos·trum /nóstrəm/ *n.* **1** quack remedy. **2** panacean plan or scheme, esp. for political or social reform.

nos·y /nózee/ (also **nos'ey**) *adj.* (**nos·i·er**, **nos·i·est**) *colloq.* inquisitive, prying. □□ **nos'i·ly** *adv.* **nos'i·ness** *n.*

not /not/ *adv.* expressing negation, esp.: **1** (also **n't** joined to a preceding verb) following an auxiliary verb or *be* or (in a question) the subject of such a verb (*she isn't there*). **.2** used elliptically for a negative sentence or verb or phrase (*Do you want it? — Certainly not!*). **3** used to express the negative of other words (*not a single one was left*).
¶ Use of **not** with other verbs is now archaic (*fear not*), except with participles and infinitives (*not knowing, I cannot say; we asked them not to come*).

no·ta be·ne /nótə bénay/ *v.* note well (that which follows). ¶ Abbr.: **NB.**

no·ta·ble /nótəbəl/ • *adj.* worthy of note; striking; remarkable; eminent. • *n.* eminent person. □□ **no·ta·bil'i·ty** *n.* **no'ta·bly** *adv.*

no·ta·rize /nótərīz/ *v.tr.* certify (a document) as a notary.

no·ta·ry /nótəree/ *n.* (*pl.* **-ries**) (in full **no'ta·ry pub'lic**) person authorized to perform certain legal formalities, esp. to draw up or certify contracts, deeds, etc. □□ **no·tar·i·al** /nōtáireeəl/ *adj.*

no·ta·tion /nōtáyshən/ *n.* **1** representation of numbers, quantities, musical notes, etc., by symbols. **2** any set of such symbols.

notch /noch/ • *n.* **1** V-shaped indentation on an edge or surface. **2** deep, narrow mountain pass or gap. • *v.tr.* **1** make notches in. **2** (foll. by *up*) record or score with or as with notches.

note /nōt/ • *n.* **1** brief written record as an aid to memory, for use in writing, public speaking, etc. (often in *pl.*: *spoke without notes*). **2** observation, usu. unwritten, of experiences, etc. (*compare notes*). **3** short or informal letter. **4** short annotation or additional explanation in a book, etc.; footnote. **5** written promise of payment. **6** a notice, attention. **b** distinction, eminence. **7 a** written sign representing the pitch and duration of a musical sound. **b** single musical tone of definite pitch. **8** quality or tone of speaking, expressing mood or attitude, etc.; hint or suggestion (*sound a note of warning*). • *v.tr.* **1** observe, notice; give or draw attention to. **2** record as a thing to be remembered or observed. **3** (in *passive*; often foll. by *for*) be famous or well known (*were noted for their generosity*).

note·book /nótbŏŏk/ *n.* small book for making notes. □ **notebook computer** lightweight computer that closes to notebook size.

note·paper /nótpaypər/ *n.* paper for writing notes or letters.

note·wor·thy /nótwərthee/ *adj.* worthy of attention; remarkable.

noth·ing /núthing/ • *n.* **1** not anything. **2** no thing (*can find nothing useful*). **3** person or thing of no importance. **4** nonexistence; what does not exist. **5** (in calculations) no amount (*a third of nothing is nothing*). • *adv.* not at all, in no way. □ **for nothing 1** at no cost; without payment. **2** to no purpose. **nothing doing** *colloq.* **1 a** no prospect of success or agreement. **b** I refuse. **2** nothing is happening.

noth·ing·ness /núthingnis/ *n.* **1** nonexistence. **2** worthlessness, triviality, insignificance.

no·tice /nótis/ • *n.* **1** attention; observation. **2** displayed sheet, etc., bearing an announcement. **3 a** intimation or warning (*give notice*). **b** formal declaration of intention to end an agreement, leave employment, etc. **4** short published review or comment about a new play, book, etc. • *v.tr.* perceive; observe. □ **take notice of 1** observe. **2** act upon.

no·tice·a·ble /nótisəbəl/ *adj.* **1** easily seen or noticed; perceptible. **2** noteworthy. □□ **no'tice·a·bly** *adv.*

no·ti·fy /nótifī/ *v.tr.* (**-fies**, **-fied**) **1** inform or give notice to (a person). **2** make known. □□ **no·ti·fi·ca'tion** *n.*

no·tion /nóshən/ *n.* **1 a** concept or idea. **b** opinion. **c** vague view or understanding. **2** inclination, impulse, or intention. **3** (in *pl.*) small, useful articles, esp. thread, needles, buttons, etc.

no·tion·al /nóshənəl/ *adj.* **1** hypothetical; imaginary. **2** (of knowledge, etc.) speculative. □□ **no'tion·al·ly** *adv.*

no·to·ri·ous /nōtáwreeəs/ *adj.* well-known, esp. unfavorably (*notorious criminal*). □□ **no·to·ri·e·ty** /-tərĪotee/ *n.* **no·to'ri·ous·ly** *adv.*

not·with·stand·ing /nótwithstánding, -with-/ • *prep.* in spite of. • *adv.* nevertheless; all the same.

nou·gat /nŏŏgət/ *n.* chewy candy made from sugar or honey, nuts, egg white, and often fruit pieces.

nought var. of NAUGHT.

noun /nown/ *n.* *Gram.* word (other than a pronoun) used to name a person, place, thing, or concept (*common noun*), or a particular one of these (*proper noun*).

nour·ish /nə́rish, núr-/ *v.tr.* **1 a** sustain with food. **b** enrich. **c** provide with intellectual or emotional sustenance or enrichment. **2** foster or cherish (a feeling, etc.). □□ **nour'ish·ing** *adj.*

nour·ish·ment /nə́rishmənt, núr-/ *n.* sustenance, food.

nou·veau riche /nōovō réesh/ *n.* (*pl.* **nou'veaux riches** *pronunc.* same) person who has recently acquired (usu. ostentatious) wealth.

Nov. *abbr.* November.

no·va /nóvə/ *n.* (*pl.* **no·vas** or **no·vae** /-vee/) star showing a sudden burst of brightness that then subsides.

nov·el[1] /nóvəl/ *n.* fictitious prose story of book length.

---

novel[1] mid-16th century: from Italian *novella* (*storia*) 'new (story),' feminine of *novello* 'new,' from Latin *novellus,* from *novus* 'new.' The word is also found from late Middle English until the 18th century in the sense 'a novelty, a piece of news,' from Old French *novelle,* also from Latin *novellus* and the source of NOVEL[2].

---

nov·el[2] /nóvəl/ *adj.* of a new kind or nature; strange.

nov·el·ette /nóvəlét/ *n.* short novel.

nov·el·ist /nóvəlist/ *n.* writer of novels.

no·vel·la /nəvélə/ *n.* (*pl.* **no·vel·las** or **no·vel·le** /-lee, -lay/) short novel or narrative story; tale.

nov·el·ty /nóvəltee/ *n.* (*pl.* **-ties**) **1** newness. **2** new or unusual thing or occurrence. **3** small toy or decoration, etc. **4** (*attrib.*) having novelty (*novelty toys*).

No·vem·ber /nōvémbər/ *n.* eleventh month of the year.

no·ve·na /nōvéenə, nə-/ *n.* RC Ch. devotion consisting of special prayers or services on nine successive days.

nov·ice /nóvis/ *n.* **1 a** probationary member of a religious order. **b** new convert. **2** beginner; inexperienced person.

no·vi·ti·ate /nōvísheeət, -ayt/ *n.* (also **no·vi'ci·ate**) **1** period of being a novice. **2** religious novice. **3** novices' quarters.

No·vo·caine /nóvəkayn/ *n.* (also **no'vo·caine**) *propr.* local anesthetic derived from benzoic acid.

now /now/ • *adv.* **1** at the present or mentioned time. **2** immediately. **3** under the present circumstances. **4** on this further occasion. **5** (esp. in a narrative) then, next. • *conj.* as a consequence. • *n.* this time; the present. □ **now and again** (or **then**) from time to time; intermittently.

NOW ac·count /now/ *n.* type of savings account against which checks can be written (acronym of *n*egotiable *o*rder of *w*ithdrawal).

now·a·days /nówədayz/ • *adv.* at the present time or age; in these times. • *n.* the present time.

no·where /nóhwair, -wair/ • *adv.* in or to no place. • *pron.* no place. □ **nowhere near** not nearly.

no·wise /nówīz/ *adv.* in no manner; not at all.

nox·ious /nókshəs/ *adj.* harmful, unwholesome.

noz·zle /nózəl/ *n.* spout on a hose, etc., from which a jet issues.

Np *symb. Chem.* neptunium.

NRC *abbr.* Nuclear Regulatory Commission.

ns *abbr.* nanosecond.

NSF *abbr.* **1** National Science Foundation. **2** not sufficient funds.

NT *abbr.* New Testament.

-n't /ənt/ *adv.* (in *comb.*) = NOT (*isn't; mustn't*).

nth see N[1].

nt. wt. *abbr.* net weight.

nu /nōo, nyōo/ *n.* thirteenth letter of the GREEK ALPHABET (N, ν).

nu·ance /nōo-áans, nyōo-/ *n.* subtle shade of meaning, feeling, color, etc.

nub /nub/ *n.* **1** point or gist (of a matter or story). **2** small lump, esp. of coal. □□ **nub'by** *adj.*

nu·bile /nóobīl, -bil, nyōo-/ *adj.* (of a woman) marriageable or sexually attractive. □□ **nu·bil·i·ty** /-bilitee/ *n.*

nu·cle·ar /nóokleear, nyōo-/ *adj.* **1** of, relating to, or constituting a nucleus. **2** using nuclear energy. □ **nuclear energy** energy obtained by nuclear fission or fusion. **nuclear family** a couple and their children, regarded as a basic social unit. **nuclear fission** nuclear reaction in which a heavy nucleus splits, accompanied by the release of energy. **nuclear fusion** nuclear reaction in which atomic nuclei of low atomic number fuse to form a heavier nucleus with the release of energy. **nuclear medicine** *Med.* specialty that uses radioactive materials for diagnosis and treatment. **nuclear physics** physics of atomic nuclei and their interactions, esp. in the generation of nuclear energy. **nuclear power** **1** power generated by a nuclear reactor. **2** country that has nuclear weapons. **nuclear reactor** device in which a nuclear fission chain reaction is used to produce energy.
¶ Although the pronunciation "noo-kyoo-luhr" has been used by many, including presidents, it is still widely regarded as uneducated.

nu·cle·ate /nóokleeayt, nyōo-/ • *adj.* having a nucleus. • *v.* form or form into a nucleus.

nu·cle·ic acid /nōoklée·eik, -klá·yik, nyōo-/ *n.* either of two complex organic molecules (DNA and RNA), present in all living cells.

nu·cle·o·lus /nōoklée·ələs, nyōo-/ *n.* (*pl.* **nu·cle·o·li** /-lī/) dense spherical structure within a nondividing nucleus.

nu·cle·on /nóokleeon, nyōo-/ *n.* *Physics* proton or neutron.

nu·cle·us /nóokleeəs/ *n.* (*pl.* **nu·cle·i** /-lee-ī/) **1 a** central part or thing around which others are collected. **b** kernel of an aggregate or mass. **2** initial part meant to receive additions. **3** *Physics* positively charged central core of an atom. **4** *Biol.* specialized, often central part of a cell, containing the genetic material.

nude /nōod, nyōod/ • *adj.* naked; bare; unclothed. • *n.* **1** painting, sculpture, photograph, etc., of a nude human figure; such a figure. **2** nude person. □□ **nu'di·ty** *n.*

nudge /nuj/ • *v.tr.* **1** prod gently with the elbow to attract attention. **2** give a reminder or encouragement to (a person). • *n.* prod; gentle push.

nud·ist /nŏŏdist, nyŏŏ-/ n. person who advocates or practices going unclothed. □□ **nud′ism** n.

nu·ga·to·ry /nŏŏgətáwree, nyŏŏ-/ adj. 1 futile; trifling; worthless. 2 inoperative; not valid.

nug·get /núgit/ n. 1 lump of gold, etc., as found in the earth. 2 something valuable for its size (*nugget of information*).

nui·sance /nŏŏsəns, nyŏŏ-/ n. person, thing, or circumstance causing trouble or annoyance.

nuke /nŏŏk, nyŏŏk/ colloq. • n. nuclear weapon. • v. tr. colloq. 1 bomb or destroy with nuclear weapons. 2 to cook (something) in a microwave oven.

null /nul/ adj. 1 (esp. **null and void**) invalid. 2 nonexistent; amounting to nothing. 3 without character or expression.

nul·li·fy /núlifī/ v. tr. (**-fies, -fied**) neutralize; invalidate; cancel. □□ **nul·li·fi·ca′tion** n.

num. abbr. 1 number. 2 numerical.

numb /num/ • adj. deprived of feeling or the power of motion (*numb with cold*). • v. tr. 1 make numb. 2 stupefy; paralyze. □□ **numb′ness** n.

num·ber /númbər/ • n. 1 a arithmetical value representing a particular quantity and used in counting and calculating. b word, symbol, or figure representing this; numeral. c arithmetical value showing position in a series. 2 total count or aggregate (*the number of accidents has decreased*). 3 (in pl.) arithmetic. 4 a (in sing. or pl.) quantity or amount; total; count (*large number of people*). b (in pl.) numerical preponderance (*force of numbers*). 5 a person or thing having a place in a series, esp. a single issue of a magazine, an item in a program, etc. b song, dance, musical item, etc. 6 company, collection, group (*among our number*). 7 Gram. classification of words by their singular or plural forms. • v. tr. 1 include. 2 assign a number or numbers to. 3 amount to (a specified number). 4 a count. b comprise (*numbering forty thousand men*). □ **do a number on** sl. injure, cheat, criticize, or humiliate. **have a person's number** colloq. understand a person's real motives, character, etc. **number one** n. colloq. oneself (*always takes care of number one*). • adj. most important (*the number-one priority*).

num·ber·less /númbərlis/ adj. innumerable.

numb·skull var. of NUMSKULL.

nu·mer·a·ble /nŏŏmərəbəl, nyŏŏ-/ adj. that can be counted.

nu·mer·al /nŏŏmərəl, nyŏŏ-/ • n. figure or group of figures denoting a number. • adj. of or denoting a number.

nu·mer·ate • v. /nŏŏmərayt, nyŏŏ-/ = ENUMERATE. • adj. /nŏŏmərət, nyŏŏ-/ acquainted with the basic principles of mathematics. □□ **nu·mer·a·cy** /-əsee/ n.

nu·mer·a·tor /nŏŏməraytər, nyŏŏ-/ n. number above the line in a common fraction showing how many of the parts indicated by the denominator are taken (e.g., 2 in $^2/_3$).

nu·mer·i·cal /nŏŏmérikəl, nyŏŏ-/ adj. (also **nu·mer′ic**) of or relating to a number or numbers. □□ **nu·mer′i·cal·ly** adv.

nu·mer·ol·o·gy /nŏŏməróləjee, nyŏŏ-/ n. (pl. **-gies**) study of the supposed occult significance of numbers.

nu·mer·ous /nŏŏmərəs, nyŏŏ-/ adj. 1 (with pl.)

great in number. 2 consisting of many (*the rose family is a numerous one*).

nu·mi·nous /nŏŏminəs, nyŏŏ-/ adj. 1 indicating the presence of a divinity. 2 spiritual. 3 awe-inspiring.

nu·mis·mat·ics /nŏŏmizmátiks, nyŏŏ-/ n.pl. (usu. treated as *sing.*) study of coins or medals. □□ **nu·mis·mat′ic** adj. **nu·mis·ma·tist** /nŏŏmízmətist, nyŏŏ-/ n.

num·skull /númskul/ n. stupid or foolish person.

nun /nun/ n. member of a community of women living apart under religious vows.

nun·ci·o /núnsheeō/ n. (pl. **-os**) RC Ch. papal ambassador.

nun·ner·y /núnəree/ n. (pl. **-ies**) religious house of nuns; convent.

nup·tial /núpshəl/ • adj. of or relating to marriage or weddings. • n. (usu. in pl.) wedding.

nurd var. of NERD.

nurse /nərs/ • n. 1 person trained to care for the sick or infirm. 2 (formerly) person employed or trained to take charge of young children. • v. 1 a intr. work as a nurse. b tr. attend to (a sick person). 2 tr. & intr. feed or be fed at the breast. 3 tr. hold or treat carefully (*sat nursing my feet*). 4 tr. a foster; promote the development of (the arts, plants, etc.). b harbor or nurture (a grievance, hatred, etc.). 5 tr. consume slowly. □ **nurse-practitioner** registered nurse with advanced training in diagnosing and treating illness.

nurse·maid /nərsmayd/ n. woman in charge of a child or children.

---

nurse late Middle English: contraction of Middle English *nourice*, from Old French, from late Latin *nutricia*, feminine of Latin *nutricius* '(person) who nourishes,' from *nutrix* 'nurse,' from *nutrire* 'nourish.' The verb was originally a contraction of *nourish*, altered in form under the influence of the noun.

---

nur·ser·y /nərsəree/ n. (pl. **-ies**) 1 a room or place equipped for young children. b day-care facility for children. 2 place where plants, trees, etc., are reared for sale or transplantation. □ **nursery rhyme** simple traditional song or story in rhyme for children. **nursery school** school for children from the age of about three to five.

nur·ser·y·man /nərsəreemən/ n. (pl. **-men**) owner of or worker in a plant nursery.

nurs·ing /nərsing/ n. practice or profession of caring for the sick as a nurse. □ **nursing home** facility providing residence and nursing care for the elderly, disabled, etc.

nur·ture /nərchər/ • n. 1 process of bringing up or training (esp. children). 2 nourishment. 3 sociological factors as an influence on or determinant of personality (opp. NATURE). • v. tr. 1 bring up; rear. 2 nourish. □□ **nur′tur·er** n.

nut /nut/ n. 1 a fruit consisting of a hard or tough shell around an edible kernel. b this kernel. 2 pod containing hard seeds. 3 small usu. hexagonal piece of metal, etc., with a threaded hole through it for securing a bolt. 4 sl. a crazy or eccentric person. b obsessive enthusiast or devotee (*health-food nut*). □ **nuts and bolts** colloq. practical details.

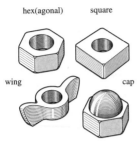

hex(agonal)   square

wing   cap

NUT, 3

nut·case /nútkays/ *n. sl.* crazy or foolish person.

nut·crack·er /nútkrakər/ *n.* device for cracking nuts.

nut·hatch /nút-hach/ *n.* small bird that climbs trees and feeds on nuts, insects, etc.

nut·meg /nútmeg/ *n.* hard aromatic spheroidal seed used as a spice and in medicine.

nu·tri·a /nóotreeə, nyóo-/ *n.* **1** aquatic beaverlike rodent, native to S. America. **2** its skin or fur.

nu·tri·ent /nóotreeənt, nyóo-/ • *n.* substance that provides essential nourishment. • *adj.* nutritious.

nu·tri·ment /nóotrimənt, nyóo-/ *n.* anything nourishing; food.

nu·tri·tion /nootríshən, nyóo-/ *n.* **1** food, nourishment. **2** study of diet and its relation to health. □□ **nu·tri'tion·al** *adj.* **nu·tri'tion·ist** *n.*

nu·tri·tious /nootríshəs, nyóo-/ *adj.* nourishing as food.

nuts /nuts/ • *adj. sl.* crazy, mad. • *int. sl.* expression of contempt (*nuts to you*). □ **be nuts about** *colloq.* be very fond of.

nut·shell /nútshel/ *n.* hard exterior covering of a nut. □ **in a nutshell** in a few words.

nut·ty /nútee/ *adj.* (**nut·ti·er, nut·ti·est**) **1 a** full of nuts. **b** tasting like nuts. **2** *sl.* = NUTS *adj.* □□ **nut'ti·ness** *n.*

nuz·zle /núzəl/ *v.* **1** *tr.* prod or rub gently with the nose. **2** *intr.* (foll. by *into, against, up to*) press the nose gently. **3** *tr.* (also *refl.*) nestle; lie snug.

NV *abbr.* Nevada (in official postal use).

NW *abbr.* **1** northwest. **2** northwestern.

NY *abbr.* New York (in official postal use).

NYC *abbr.* New York City.

ny·lon /nílon/ *n.* **1** synthetic polyamide fibers with tough, lightweight, elastic properties, used in industry and for textiles, etc. **2** nylon fabric. **3** (in *pl.*) stockings of nylon.

nymph /nimf/ *n.* **1** mythological female spirit associated with aspects of nature, esp. rivers and woods. **2** *poet.* beautiful young woman. **3** immature form of some insects.

NYSE *abbr.* New York Stock Exchange.

NZ *abbr.* New Zealand.

Oo

O¹ /ō/ *n.* (also **o**) (*pl.* **Os** or **O's**; **o's**) **1** fifteenth letter of the alphabet. **2** human blood type.

O² *symb. Chem.* oxygen.

O³ /ō/ *int.* **1** var. of OH. **2** prefixed to a name in the vocative (*O God*).

o' /ə/ *prep.* of, on (*o'clock; will-o'-the-wisp*).

-o /ō/ *suffix* forming usu. *sl.* or *colloq.* variants or derivatives (*weirdo; wino*).

oaf /ōf/ *n.* (*pl.* **oafs**) **1** awkward lout. **2** stupid person. □□ **oaf'ish** *adj.* **oaf'ish·ly** *adv.* **oaf'ish·ness** *n.*

oak /ōk/ *n.* **1** tree having lobed leaves and bearing acorns. **2** durable wood of this tree, used esp. for furniture and in building. **3** (*attrib.*) made of oak (*oak table*). □□ **oak'en** *adj.*

oa·kum /ōkəm/ *n.* loose fiber obtained by picking old rope to pieces and used esp. in caulking.

oar /awr/ *n.* pole with a blade used for rowing or steering a boat by leverage against the water.

oar·lock /áwrlok/ *n.* device for holding an oar in position while rowing.

oars·man /áwrzmən/ *n.* (*pl.* **-men**; *fem.* **oars·wom·an**, *pl.* **-wom·en**) rower. □□ **oars'man·ship** *n.*

OAS *abbr.* Organization of American States.

o·a·sis /ō-áysis/ *n.* (*pl.* **o·a·ses** /-seez/) **1** fertile spot in a desert. **2** area or period of calm in the midst of turbulence.

oat /ōt/ *n.* **1** cereal plant, cultivated in cool climates. **2** (in *pl.*) grain yielded by this, used as food. □□ **oat'en** *adj.*

oat·cake /ótkayk/ *n.* thin oatmeal cake.

oath /ōth/ *n.* (*pl.* **oaths** /ōthz, ōths/) **1** solemn declaration (often naming God) as to the truth of something or as a commitment to future action. **2** profane or blasphemous utterance; curse.

oat·meal /ótmeel/ *n.* **1** meal made from ground or rolled oats used esp. in cereal, cookies, etc. **2** cooked breakfast cereal made from this. **3** grayish-fawn color flecked with brown.

ob. *abbr.* he or she died.

ob- /ob/ *prefix* (also **oc-** before *c*, **of-** before *f*, **op-** before *p*) meaning: **1** meeting or facing (*occasion; obvious*). **2** opposition, hostility, or resistance (*obstreperous; opponent; obstinate*). **3** finality or completeness (*obsolete; occupy*).

ob·bli·ga·to /obligaátō/ *n.* (*pl.* **-tos**) *Mus.* complicated accompaniment forming an integral part of a composition.

ob·du·rate /óbdŏŏrit, -dyŏŏr-/ *adj.* **1** stubborn. **2** hardened against persuasion or influence. □□ **ob·du·ra·cy** /-dŏŏrəsee, -dyŏŏr-/ *n.*

o·be·di·ent /ōbeédeeənt/ *adj.* obeying or ready to obey. **2** submissive; dutiful (*obedient to the law*). □□ **o·be'di·ence** *n.* **o·be'di·ent·ly** *adv.*

o·bei·sance /ōbáysəns, ōbée-/ *n.* **1** bow, curtsy, or other respectful or submissive gesture. **2** homage; deference (*pay obeisance*). □□ **o·bei'sant** *adj.*

ob·e·lisk /óbəlisk/ *n.* **1** tapering, usu. four-sided stone pillar set up as a monument or landmark, etc. **2** mountain, tree, etc., of similar shape.

o·bese /ōbées/ *adj.* very fat; corpulent. □□ **o·be'si·ty** *n.*

o·bey /ōbáy/ *v.* **1** *tr.* **a** carry out the command of (*you will obey me*). **b** carry out (a command) (*obey orders*). **2** *intr.* do what one is told to do. **3** *tr.* be actuated by (a force or impulse).

ob·fus·cate /óbfuskayt/ *v.tr.* **1** obscure or confuse. **2** stupefy, bewilder. □□ **ob·fus·ca·tion** /-káyshən/ *n.*

ob-gyn /ōbée-jeewīén/ *abbr.* **1** obstetrician-gynecologist. **2** obstetrics-gynecology.

o·bit·u·ar·y /ōbíchŏŏ-eree/ *n.* (*pl.* **-ies**) **1** notice of a death esp. in a newspaper. **2** account of the life of a deceased person.

obj. *abbr.* **1** object. **2** objective. **3** objection.

ob·ject • *n.* /óbjikt, -jekt/ **1** material thing that can be seen or touched. **2** person or thing to which action or feeling is directed (*the object of our study*). **3** thing sought or aimed at; purpose. **4** *Gram.* noun or its equivalent governed by an active transitive verb or by a preposition. **•** *v.* /əbjékt/ **1** *intr.* express or feel opposition, disapproval, or reluctance; protest. **2** *tr.* state as an objection. □ **object lesson** striking practical example of some principle. □□ **ob·jec'tor** /əbjéktər/ *n.*

ob·jec·ti·fy /əbjéktifī/ *v.tr.* (**-fies, -fied**) present as an object.

ob·jec·tion /əbjékshən/ *n.* **1** expression or feeling of opposition or disapproval. **2** adverse reason or statement.

ob·jec·tion·a·ble /əbjékshənəbəl/ *adj.* **1** open to objection. **2** unpleasant, offensive. □□ **ob·jec'tion·a·bly** *adv.*

ob·jec·tive /əbjéktiv/ **•** *adj.* **1** external to the mind; actually existing. **2** (of a person, writing, art, etc.) dealing with outward things or exhibiting unbiased facts; not subjective. **3** *Gram.* (of a case or word) constructed as or appropriate to the object of a transitive verb or preposition (cf. ACCUSATIVE). **•** *n.* something sought or aimed at; objective point. □□ **ob·jec'tive·ly** *adv.* **ob·jec'tive·ness** *n.* **ob·jec·tiv'i·ty** *n.*

ob·jet d'art /áwbzhay daár/ *n.* (*pl.* **ob·jets d'art** *pronunc.* same) small object of artistic worth.

ob·la·tion /əbláyshən, ob-/ *n. Relig.* thing offered to a divine being.

ob·li·gate /óbligayt/ *v.tr.* (usu. in *passive*; foll. by *to* + *infin.*) bind (a person) legally or morally.

ob·li·ga·tion /obligáyshən/ *n.* **1** constraining power of a law, precept, duty, contract, etc. **2** duty. **3** binding agreement. **4** **a** service or benefit (*repay an obligation*). **b** indebtedness for this.

ob·lig·a·to·ry /əblígətawree/ *adj.* **1** legally or morally binding. **2** compulsory. □□ **ob·lig·a·to'ri·ly** *adv.*

o·blige /əblíj/ *v.tr.* **1** constrain; compel. **2** be binding on. **3 a** make indebted by conferring a favor. **b** gratify (*oblige me by leaving*). **c** perform a service for (often *absol.*: *will you oblige?*). **4** (in *passive*; foll. by *to*) be indebted (*am obliged to you for your help*).

o·blig·ing /əblíjing/ *adj.* courteous, accommodating; ready to do a service or kindness. □□ **o·blig·ing·ly** *adv.*

ob·lique /əbleék/ • *adj.* **1 a** slanting. **b** diverging from a straight line or course. **2** not going straight to the point; indirect. • *n.* oblique muscle. □□ **ob·lique·ly** *adv.* **o·blique·ness** *n.*

ob·lit·er·ate /əblítərayt/ *v.tr.* **1 a** blot out; destroy. **b** leave no clear traces of. **2** deface (a postage stamp, etc.) to prevent further use. □□ **ob·lit·er·a·tion** /-ráyshən/ *n.*

ob·liv·i·on /əblíveeən/ *n.* state of having or being forgotten.

ob·liv·i·ous /əblíveeəs/ *adj.* **1** (often foll. by *of*) forgetful; unmindful. **2** (foll. by *to, of*) unaware of. □□ **ob·liv·i·ous·ly** *adv.* **ob·liv·i·ous·ness** *n.*

ob·long /óblawng/ • *adj.* rectangular with adjacent sides unequal. • *n.* oblong figure or object.

ob·lo·quy /óbləkwee/ *n.* **1** ill spoken of. **2** abuse, detraction.

ob·nox·ious /əbnókshəs/ *adj.* offensive; objectionable; disliked. □□ **ob·nox·ious·ly** *adv.* **ob·nox·ious·ness** *n.*

o·boe /óbō/ *n.* **1** woodwind double-reed instrument of treble pitch and plaintive tone. **2** its player. □□ **o·bo·ist** /óbō-ist/ *n.*

OBOE

ob·scene /əbseén/ *adj.* **1** offensively indecent, esp. by offending accepted sexual morality. **2** *colloq.* highly offensive. □□ **ob·scene·ly** *adv.* **ob·scen·i·ty** /-sén-/ *n.*

ob·scu·ran·tism /əbskyŏ͝orəntizəm, óbskyŏ͝o-rán-/ *n.* opposition to knowledge and enlightenment. □□ **ob·scu·ran·tist** *n.*

ob·scure /əbskyŏ͝or/ • *adj.* **1** not clearly expressed nor easily understood. **2** unexplained; doubtful. **3** dark. **4** indistinct. **5** hidden. **6 a** unnoticed. **b** (of a person) undistinguished; hardly known. • *v.tr.* make obscure, dark, indistinct, or unintelligible. □□ **ob·scure·ly** *adv.* **ob·scu·ri·ty** *n.*

ob·se·quies /óbsikweez/ *n.pl.* funeral rites.

ob·se·qui·ous /əbseékweeəs/ *adj.* servilely obedient or attentive. □□ **ob·se·qui·ous·ly** *adv.* **ob·se·qui·ous·ness** *n.*

ob·serv·ance /əbzérvəns/ *n.* **1** keeping or performing of a law, duty, custom, ritual, etc. **2** ceremony; rite.

ob·serv·ant /əbzérvənt/ *adj.* **1** acute or diligent in taking notice. **2** attentive in esp. religious observances (*an observant Jew*). □□ **ob·serv·ant·ly** *adv.*

ob·ser·va·tion /óbzərváyshən/ *n.* **1** noticing; being noticed. **2** perception. **3** remark, comment, or statement. **4** accurate watching and noting of phenomena as they occur in nature with regard to cause and effect or mutual relations. □□ **ob·ser·va·tion·al** *adj.*

ob·ser·va·to·ry /əbzérvətawree/ *n.* (*pl.* **-ries**) building for astronomical or other observation.

ob·serve /əbzérv/ *v.* **1** *tr.* perceive; become conscious of. **2** *tr.* watch carefully. **3** *tr.* **a** follow or adhere to (a law, command, method, principle, etc.). **b** keep or adhere to (an appointed time). **c** maintain (silence). **d** perform (a rite). **e** celebrate (an anniversary). **4** *tr.* examine and note scientifically. **5** *tr.* say, esp. by way of comment. **6** *intr.* remark. □□ **ob·serv·a·ble** *adj.* **ob·serv·er** *n.*

ob·sess /əbsés/ *v.* (often in *passive*) preoccupy; haunt. □ **obsessive-compulsive** relating to a neurosis characterized by an obsessive thought and compulsive behavior, such as repeated hand washing. □□ **ob·ses·sive** *adj.* & *n.* **ob·ses·sive·ly** *adv.* **ob·ses·sive·ness** *n.*

ob·ses·sion /əbséshən/ *n.* **1** obsessing or being obsessed. **2** persistent idea or thought dominating a person's mind. □□ **ob·ses·sion·al** *adj.* **ob·ses·sion·al·ly** *adv.*

ob·sid·i·an /əbsídeeən/ *n.* dark glassy rock formed from lava.

ob·so·les·cent /óbsəlésənt/ *adj.* becoming obsolete; going out of use or date. □□ **ob·so·les·cence** /-səns/ *n.*

ob·so·lete /óbsəleét/ *adj.* disused; discarded; antiquated.

ob·sta·cle /óbstəkəl/ *n.* person or thing that obstructs progress.

ob·stet·rics /əbstétriks, ob-/ *n.pl.* (usu. treated as *sing.*) branch of medicine concerned with pregnancy and childbirth. □□ **ob·stet·ric** *adj.* **ob·ste·tri·cian** /stətríshən/ *n.*

ob·sti·nate /óbstinət/ *adj.* stubborn, intractable. □□ **ob·sti·na·cy** /nəsee/ *n.* **ob·sti·nate·ly** *adv.*

ob·strep·er·ous /əbstrépərəs/ *adj.* **1** turbulent; unruly. **2** noisy. □□ **ob·strep·er·ous·ly** *adv.* **ob·strep·er·ous·ness** *n.*

ob·struct /əbstrúkt/ *v.tr.* **1** block up. **2** prevent or retard the progress of. □□ **ob·struc·tive** *adj.* **ob·struc·tive·ness** *n.* **ob·struct·or** *n.*

ob·struc·tion /əbstrúkshən/ *n.* **1** blocking; being blocked. **2** obstacle or blockage. **3** retarding of progress by deliberate delays. □□ **ob·struc·tion·ist** *n.* (in sense 3).

ob·tain /əbtáyn/ *v.* **1** *tr.* acquire; secure. **2** *intr.* be prevalent or established or in vogue. □□ **ob·tain·a·ble** *adj.* **ob·tain·ment** *n.*

ob·trude /əbtrŏ͝od/ *v.* **1** *intr.* stick out; push forward. **2** *tr.* thrust forward (oneself, one's opinion, etc.) importunately. □□ **ob·tru·sion** /-trŏ͝o-zhən/ *n.* **ob·tru·sive** /-siv/ *adj.* **ob·tru·sive·ly** *adv.* **ob·tru·sive·ness** *n.*

ob·tuse /əbtŏ͝os, -tyŏ͝os/ *adj.* **1** dull-witted. **2** blunt; not sharp. **3** (of an angle) between 90° and 180°. □□ **ob·tuse·ly** *adv.* **ob·tuse·ness** *n.*

ob·verse /óbvərs/ *n.* **1 a** side of a coin or medal,

etc., bearing the head or principal design. **b** this design (cf. REVERSE). **2** front or proper or top side of a thing. **3** counterpart of a fact or truth.

ob·vi·ate /óbveeayt/ *v.tr.* get around or do away with (a need, inconvenience, etc.). □□ **ob·vi·a·tion** /-áyshən/ *n.*

ob·vi·ous /óbveeəs/ *adj.* easily seen or recognized or understood. □□ **ob'vi·ous·ly** *adv.* **ob'vi·ous·ness** *n.*

oc·a·ri·na /ókəreénə/ *n.* small egg-shaped wind instrument.

OCARINA

oc·ca·sion /əkáyzhən/ ● *n.* **1 a** special or noteworthy event or happening. **b** time of this (*on the occasion of their marriage*). **2** reason, ground(s), or justification. **3** juncture suitable for doing something; opportunity. **4** subordinate or incidental cause (*the assassination was the occasion of the war*). ● *v.tr.* **1** be the cause of. **2** cause (a person or thing to do something). □ **on occasion** now and then; when the need arises.

oc·ca·sion·al /əkáyzhənəl/ *adj.* **1** happening irregularly and infrequently. **2 a** made or meant for, or associated with, a special occasion. **b** (of furniture, etc.) made or adapted for infrequent and varied use. □□ **oc·ca'sion·al·ly** *adv.*

Oc·ci·dent /óksidənt, -dent/ *n. poet.* or *rhet.* **1** (prec. by *the*) West. **2** Europe, America, or both, as distinct from the Orient. □□ **oc·ci·den'tal** *adj. & n.*

oc·ci·put /óksiput/ *n.* back of the head. □□ **oc·cip·i·tal** /-sípit'l/ *adj.*

oc·clude /əklood/ *v.tr.* stop up or close (pores or an orifice). □□ **oc·clu·sion** /əklōozhən/ *n.* **oc·clu·sive** /-siv/ *adj.*

oc·cult /əkúlt, ókult/ *adj.* **1** supernatural; mystical. **2** kept secret; esoteric.

oc·cu·pant /ókyəpənt/ *n.* person who occupies, resides in, or is in a place, etc. □□ **oc'cu·pan·cy** /-pənsee/ *n.* (*pl.* **-cies**)

oc·cu·pa·tion /ókyəpáyshən/ *n.* **1** what occupies one; means of passing one's time. **2** person's employment. **3 a** act of taking or holding possession of (a country, district, etc.) by military force. **b** state or time of this. □□ **oc·cu·pa'tion·al** *adj.*

oc·cu·py /ókyəpī/ *v.tr.* (**pies, pied**) **1** reside in. **2** take up or fill (space or time or a place). **3** hold (a position or office). **4** take military possession of (a country, region, town, strategic position). **5** (usu. in *passive*) keep busy or engaged.

oc·cur /əkər/ *v.intr.* (**oc·curred, oc·cur·ring**) **1** come into being; happen. **2** exist or be encountered. **3** come into the mind of.

oc·cur·rence /əkərəns, əkúr-/ *n.* **1** occurring. **2** incident or event.

o·cean /óshən/ *n.* **1** large expanse of sea, esp. the Atlantic, Pacific, Indian, Arctic, and Antarctic Oceans. **2** (often in *pl.*) very large expanse or quantity of anything (*oceans of time*). □□ **o·ce·an·ic** /ósheeánik/ *adj.*

o·cea·nar·i·um /óshənáireeəm/ *n.* (*pl.* **o·cea·nar·i·ums** or **r·i·a** /reeə/) large seawater aquarium for keeping sea animals.

o·cea·nog·ra·phy /óshənógrəfee/ *n.* the study of the oceans. □□ **o·cea·nog'ra·pher** *n.* **o·cea·no·graph'ic** *adj.* **o·cea·no·graph'i·cal** *adj.*

o·ce·lot /ósilot, ósi-/ *n.* **1** medium-sized feline native to S. and Central America, having a deep yellow or orange coat with black striped and spotted markings. **2** its fur.

o·cher /ókər/ *n.* **1** mineral of clay and ferric oxide, used as a pigment varying from light yellow to brown or red. **2** pale brownish yellow. □□ **o'cher·ous** *adj.*

o'clock /əklók/ *adv.* of the clock (*6 o'clock*).

OCR *abbr.* optical character recognition.

Oct. *abbr.* October.

octa- /óktə/ *comb. form* (**oct-** before a vowel) eight.

oc·ta·gon /óktəgon, -gən/ *n.* plane figure with eight sides and angles. □□ **oc·tag·o·nal** /-tágənəl/ *adj.*

oc·ta·he·dron /óktəheédrən/ *n.* (*pl.* **oc·ta·he·drons** or **oc·ta·he·dra** /-drə/) solid figure contained by eight (esp. triangular) plane faces. □□ **oc·ta·he'dral** *adj.*

OCTAHEDRON

oc·tane /óktayn/ *n.* colorless flammable hydrocarbon present in gasoline. ¶ Chem. formula: C_8H_{18}.

oc·tave /óktiv, -tayv/ *n.* **1** *Mus.* **a** eight notes occupying the interval between (and including) two notes, one having twice or half the frequency of vibration of the other. **b** this interval. **c** each of the two notes at the extremes of this interval. **2** group of eight.

oc·ta·vo /oktáyvo, oktaávō/ *n.* (*pl.* **-vos**) **1** size of book or page given by folding a standard sheet three times to form a quire of eight leaves. **2** book or sheet of this size. ¶ Abbr.: **8vo**.

oc·tet /oktét/ *n.* (also **oc·tette'**) **1** *Mus.* **a** composition for eight voices or instruments. **b** performers of such a piece. **2** group of eight. **3** first eight lines of a sonnet.

octo- /óktō/ *comb. form* (**oct-** before a vowel) eight.

Oc·to·ber /októbər/ *n.* tenth month of the year.

oc·to·ge·nar·i·an /óktəjinaíreeən/ ● *n.* person from 80 to 89 years old. ● *adj.* of this age.

oc·to·pus /óktəpəs/ *n.* (*pl.* **oc·to·pus·es**) cephalopod mollusk having eight suckered arms, a soft saclike body, and strong beaklike jaws.

oc·u·lar /ókyoolər/ adj. of or connected with the eyes or sight; visual.

oc·u·list /ókyəlist/ n. *formerly* **1** ophthalmologist. **2** optometrist.

OD[1] abbr. **1** doctor of optometry. **2** overdraft.

OD[2] /ōdée/ sl. • n. overdose, esp. of a narcotic drug. • v.intr. (**OD's, OD'd, OD'ing**) take an overdose.

o.d. abbr. outside diameter.

odd /od/ adj. **1** strange, remarkable, eccentric. **2** casual, occasional (odd jobs). **3** not normally noticed or considered; unpredictable. **4** additional; besides the calculated amount (a few odd cents). **5 a** (of numbers) not integrally divisible by two. **b** bearing such a number (no parking on odd dates). **6** one item of a pair. **7** (appended to a number, sum, weight, etc.) somewhat more than (forty-odd people). **8** by which a round number, given sum, etc., is exceeded (we have 102 — what shall we do with the odd 2?). □□ **odd′ly** adv. **odd′ness** n.

odd·ball /ódbawl/ n. colloq. **1** eccentric person. **2** (attrib.) strange, bizarre.

odd·i·ty /óditee/ n. (pl. **-ties**) **1** strange person, thing, or occurrence. **2** peculiar trait. **3** state of being odd.

odds /odz/ n.pl. **1** ratio between the amounts staked by the parties to a bet, based on the expected probability either way. **2** balance of probability in favor of or against some result (the odds are that it will rain). □ **odds and ends** miscellaneous articles or remnants. **odds-on** state when success is more likely than failure, esp. as indicated by the betting odds.

ode /ōd/ n. lyric poem, usu. rhymed and in the form of an address, in varied or irregular meter.

o·di·ous /ódeeəs/ adj. hateful; repulsive. □□ **o′di·ous·ly** adv. **o′di·ous·ness** n.

o·di·um /ódeeəm/ n. widespread dislike or disapproval.

o·dom·e·ter /ōdómitər/ n. instrument for measuring the distance traveled by a wheeled vehicle.

o·dor /ódər/ n. **1** property of a substance that has an effect on the nasal sense of smell. **2** quality or trace (odor of intolerance). **3** regard, repute (in bad odor). □□ **o′dor·less** adj. (in sense 1).

o·dor·if·er·ous /ódərifərəs/ adj. diffusing a scent, esp. an agreeable one; fragrant.

od·ys·sey /ódisee/ n. (pl. **-seys**) long adventurous journey.

OED abbr. Oxford English Dictionary.

Oed·i·pus com·plex /édipəs, éedi-/ n. Psychol. (according to Freud, etc.) emotions aroused in a young (esp. male) child by a subconscious sexual desire for the parent of the opposite sex. □□ **Oed′i·pal** adj.

OEM abbr. original equipment manufacturer.

oe·no·phile /éenəfīl/ n. connoisseur of wines.

o'er /ōər/ adv. & prep. poet. = OVER.

oeu·vre /ővrə/ n. works of an author, painter, composer, etc., esp. regarded collectively.

of /uv, ov, əv/ prep. connecting a noun (often a verbal noun) or pronoun with a preceding noun, adjective, adverb, or verb, expressing a wide range of relations broadly describable as follows: **1** origin or cause (paintings of Turner; died of malnutrition). **2** material or substance (house of cards; built of bricks). **3** belonging or connection (thing of the past; articles of clothing). **4** identity or close relation (city of Rome; pound of apples). **5** removal or separation (north of the city; robbed us of $500). **6** reference or direction (beware of the dog; short of money). **7** partition, classification, or inclusion (no more of that; part of the story; this sort of book). **8** description, quality, or condition (person of tact; girl of ten). **9** time in relation to the following hour (quarter of three).

off /awf, of/ adv. **1** away; at or to a distance (is three miles off). **2** out of position; not on or touching or attached (take your coat off). **3** so as to be rid of (sleep it off). **4** so as to be discontinued or stopped (turn off the radio). **5** to the end; so as to be clear (clear off, pay off). **6** situated as regards money, supplies, etc. (is not very well off). **7** (of food, etc.) beginning to decay. • prep. **1 a** from; away or down or up from (fell off the chair). **b** not on (was already off the pitch). **2 a** (temporarily) relieved of or abstaining from (off duty). **b** not achieving or doing one's best in (off one's game). **3** using as a source or means of support (live off the land). **4** leading from; not far from (a street off 1st Avenue). • adj. far, further (the off side of the wall). □ **off and on** intermittently; now and then. **off-color** somewhat indecent. **off-key 1** out of tune. **2** not quite suitable or fitting. **off limits** prohibited. **off-line** Computing (of a computer terminal or process) not directly controlled by or connected to a central processor. **off-load** = UNLOAD. **off-peak** used or for use at times other than those of greatest demand. **off-putting** disconcerting; repellent. **off-road** attrib.adj. (of a vehicle, etc.) designed for rough terrain or for cross-country driving. **off-season** time when business, etc., is slack. **off the wall** crazy; absurd. **off-white** white with a gray or yellowish tinge. ¶ The use of **off of** to mean **off**, e.g., He took the cup off of the table, is nonstandard and to be avoided.

of·fal /áwfəl, óf-/ n. **1** less valuable edible parts of a carcass, esp. the entrails and internal organs. **2** refuse or waste stuff.

off·beat • adj. **1** not coinciding with the beat. **2** eccentric, unconventional. • n. /ófbeet/ any of the unaccented beats in a bar.

of·fend /əfénd/ v. **1** tr. cause offense to; wound the feelings of. **2** tr. displease or anger. **3** intr. do wrong; transgress. □□ **of·fend′er** n. **of·fend′ing** adj.

of·fense /əféns/ n. **1** illegal act; transgression or misdemeanor. **2** wounding of the feelings (no offense was meant). **3** /áwfens, óf-/ aggressive action. **4** /áwfens, óf-/ Sports team in possession of the ball, puck, etc.

---

offense late Middle English: from Old French offens 'misdeed,' from Latin offensus 'annoyance,' reinforced by French offense, from Latin offensa 'a striking against, a hurt, or displeasure'; based on Latin offendere 'strike against.'

---

of·fen·sive /əfénsiv/ • adj. **1** giving or meant or likely to give offense; insulting. **2** disgusting. **3 a** aggressive, attacking. **b** (of a weapon) for attacking. **4** Sports designating the team in possession of the ball, puck, etc. • n. **1** aggressive action or attitude. **2** attack; offensive campaign. □□ **of·fen′sive·ly** adv. **of·fen′sive·ness** n.

of·fer /áwfər, óf-/ • *v.* **1** *tr.* present for acceptance, refusal, or consideration (*offered me a drink*). **2** *intr.* express readiness or show intention (*offered to take the children*). **3** *tr.* provide; give an opportunity for. **4** *intr.* present itself; occur (*as opportunity offers*). **5** *tr.* attempt (*violence, resistance, etc.*). • *n.* **1** expression of readiness to do or give if desired, or to buy or sell. **2** amount offered. **3** proposal (esp. of marriage). **4** bid.

of·fer·ing /áwfəring, óf-/ *n.* **1** contribution or gift, esp. of money to a church. **2** thing offered as a religious sacrifice or token of devotion.

of·fer·to·ry /áwfərtáwree, óf-/ *n.* (*pl.* **-ries**) **1** *Eccl.* offering of the bread and wine at the Eucharist. **2 a** collection of money at a religious service. **b** money collected.

off·hand /áwfhánd, óf-/ • *adj.* curt or casual in manner. • *adv.* without preparation or premeditation. □□ **off′hand′ed** *adj.* **off′hand′ed·ly** *adv.* **off′hand′ed·ness** *n.*

of·fice /áwfis, óf-/ *n.* **1** room or building used as a place of business, esp. for clerical or administrative work. **2** room or place for a particular kind of business. **3** position with duties attached to it. **4** tenure of an official position, esp. that of government. **5** duty attaching to one's position; task or function. **6** (usu. in *pl.*) kindness or attention; service (esp. *through the good offices of*). **7** *Eccl.* form of worship. **8** ceremonial duty.

of·fi·cer /áwfisər, óf-/ *n.* **1** person holding a position of authority or trust, esp. one with a commission in the armed services, etc. **2** policeman or policewoman. **3** holder of a post in a society or business (e.g., the president or secretary). **4** holder of a public, civil, or ecclesiastical office.

of·fi·cial /əfíshəl/ • *adj.* **1** of or relating to an office (see OFFICE *n.* 3, 4) or its tenure or duties. **2** characteristic of officials and bureaucracy. **3** properly authorized. • *n.* person holding office or engaged in official duties. □□ **of·fi′cial·dom** *n.* **of·fi′cial·ly** *adv.*

of·fi·ci·ate /əfísheeáyt/ *v.intr.* **1** act in an official capacity. **2** conduct a religious service. □□ **of·fi·ci·a·tion** /-áyshən/ *n.* **of·fi′ci·a·tor** *n.*

of·fi·cious /əfíshəs/ *adj.* **1** asserting one's authority aggressively; domineering. **2** intrusive; meddlesome. □□ **of·fi′cious·ly** *adv.* **of·fi′cious·ness** *n.*

off·ing /áwfing, óf-/ *n.* more distant part of the sea in view. □ **in the offing** likely to appear or happen soon.

off·screen /áwfskréen, óf-/ • *adj.* not appearing on a movie, television, or computer screen. • *adv.* outside the view presented by a filmed scene.

off·set • *n.* /áwfset, óf-/ **1** compensation; consideration or amount neutralizing the effect of a contrary one. **2** (often *attrib.*) method of printing in which ink is transferred from a plate or stone to a rubber surface and from there to paper, etc. (*offset lithography*). • *v.tr.* /áwfsét, óf-/ (**-set·ting**; *past* and *past part.* **-set**) **1** counterbalance, compensate. **2** print by the offset process.

off·shoot /áwfshōot, óf-/ *n.* **1 a** side shoot or branch. **b** descendant of a family. **2** something derivative.

off·shore /áwfsháwr, óf-/ *adj.* **1** at sea some distance from the shore. **2** (of the wind) blowing seaward. **3** (of goods, funds, etc.) made or registered abroad.

off·side /áwfsíd, óf-/ *adj. Sports* (of a player in a field game or ice hockey) in a position, usu. ahead of the ball, that is not allowed if it affects play.

off·spring /áwfspring, óf-/ *n.* (*pl.* same) children; descendant(s).

off·stage /áwfstayj, óf-/ *adj. & adv. Theatr.* not on the stage and so not visible to the audience.

oft /awft, oft/ *adv. archaic* or *literary* often (usu. in *comb.*: *oft-recurring*).

of·ten /áwfən, áwftən, óf-/ *adv.* (**of·ten·er, of·ten·est**) **1** frequently; many times. **2** at short intervals.
¶ Some speakers sound the *t*, saying "off-ten"; for others, it is silent, as in *soften*. Either pronunciation is acceptable.

o·gle /ṓgəl/ • *v.* **1** *tr.* eye amorously or lecherously. **2** *intr.* look amorously. • *n.* amorous or lecherous look. □□ **o′gler** *n.*

o·gre /ṓgər/ *n.* (*fem.* **o·gress** /ṓgris/) **1** human-eating giant in folklore, etc. **2** terrifying person. □□ **o′gre·ish** *adj.*

OH *abbr.* Ohio (in official postal use).

oh /ṓ/ *int.* (also **O**) expressing surprise, pain, entreaty, etc.

ohm /ṓm/ *n. Electr.* unit of resistance, transmitting a current of one ampere when subjected to a potential difference of one volt. ¶ Symb.: Ω.

oho /ōhṓ/ *int.* expressing surprise or exultation.

-oid /oyd/ *suffix* forming adjectives and nouns, denoting form or resemblance (*asteroid; rhomboid; thyroid*). □□ **-oidal** *suffix* forming adjectives. **-oidally** *suffix* forming adverbs.

oil /oyl/ • *n.* **1** any of various thick, viscous, usu. flammable liquids insoluble in water (see also *mineral oil*). **2** petroleum. **3 a** (usu. in *pl.*) = *oil paint*. **b** *colloq.* picture painted in oil paints. • *v.* **1** *tr.* apply oil to; lubricate. **2** *tr.* impregnate or treat with oil. **3** *tr. & intr.* supply with or take on oil as fuel. □ **oil paint** mix of ground color pigment and oil. **oil painting 1** art of painting in oil paints. **2** picture painted in oil paints. **oil slick** patch of oil, esp. on the sea.

oil·cloth /óylklawth, -kloth/ *n.* **1** fabric waterproofed with oil. **2** canvas coated with oil and used to cover a table or floor.

oil·skin /óylskin/ *n.* **1** cloth waterproofed with oil. **2** (often *pl.*) garment or suit made of this.

oil·stone /óylstōn/ *n.* fine-grained flat stone used with oil for sharpening flat tools, e.g., chisels, planes, etc. (cf. WHETSTONE).

oil·y /óylee/ *adj.* (**oil·i·er, oil·i·est**) **1** of, like, or containing oil. **2** covered or soaked with oil. **3** (of a manner, etc.) fawning, insinuating, unctuous. □□ **oil′i·ness** *n.*

oint·ment /óyntmənt/ *n.* greasy healing or cosmetic preparation for the skin.

O·jib·wa /ōjíbway/ • *n.* **1 a** N. American people native to Canada and the eastern and central northern US. **b** member of this people. **2** language of this people. • *adj.* of or relating to this people or their language. Also called **Chippewa**.

OK[1] /ṓkáy/ (also **o·kay**) *colloq.* • *adj.* (often as *int.*) all right; satisfactory. • *adv.* well; satisfactorily (*that worked out OK*). • *n.* (*pl.* **OKs**) approval, sanction. • *v.tr.* (**OK's, OK'd, OK'ing**) approve, sanction.

OK mid-19th century (originally US): probably an abbreviation of *orl korrect*, humorous form of *all correct*, popularized as a slogan during President Van Buren's re-election campaign of 1840; his nickname *Old Kinderhook* (derived from his New York birthplace) provided the initials.

OK² *abbr.* Oklahoma (in official postal use).

o·key·doke /ṓkeedṓk/ *adj. & adv.* (also **o·key· do·key** /-dṓkee/) *sl.* = OK¹.

Okla. *abbr.* Oklahoma.

ok·ra /ṓkrə/ *n.* **1** plant yielding long ridged seed pods. **2** seed pods eaten as a vegetable and used to thicken soups and stews.

old /ōld/ *adj.* (**old·er, old·est**) (cf. ELDER¹, ELDEST). **1 a** advanced in age. **b** not young or near its beginning. **2** made long ago. **3** long in use. **4** worn or dilapidated or shabby from age or use. **5** having the characteristics (experience, feebleness, etc.) of age. **6** practiced, inveterate. **7** belonging to the past; lingering on; former (*old times*). **8** dating from far back; ancient; primeval (*old friends*). **9** (appended to a period of time) of age (*is four years old*). □ **old age** later part of normal life. **old-boy network** preferment in employment of those from a similar social background, college, etc. **the old country** native country of immigrants, etc. **Old English** English language up to *c.* 1150. **old-fashioned** in or according to a fashion or tastes no longer current; antiquated. **Old Glory** US national flag. **old guard** original or past or conservative members of a group. **old hat** *colloq. adj.* hackneyed. **old lady** *colloq.* one's mother or wife. **old maid 1** *derog.* elderly unmarried woman. **2** prim and fussy person. **3** card game in which players try not to be left with an unpaired queen. **old man** *colloq.* one's husband or father. **old master 1** great artist of former times, esp. of the 13th–17th c. in Europe. **2** painting by such a painter. **Old Norse** Germanic language from which the Scandinavian languages were derived. **old school 1** traditional attitudes. **2** people having such attitudes. **Old Testament** part of the Christian Bible containing the scriptures of the Hebrews. **old-time** belonging to former times. **old-timer** person with long experience or standing. **old wives' tale** foolish or unscientific tradition or belief. **Old World** Europe, Asia, and Africa. □□ **old'ish** *adj.* ¶ Where two, and no more, are involved, they may be **older** and **younger**: *The older of the twins, by ten minutes, is Sam; the younger is Pamela.* Where there are more than two, one may be the **oldest** or **youngest**: *I have four siblings, of whom Jane is the oldest.*

old·en /ṓldən/ *adj.* archaic of old (esp. *in olden times*).

old·ie /ṓldee/ *n. colloq.* old person or thing.

o·le·ag·i·nous /ṓleeájinəs/ *adj.* like or producing oil.

o·le·an·der /ṓleeándər/ *n.* evergreen poisonous shrub native to the Mediterranean and bearing clusters of white, pink, or red flowers.

o·le·o·mar·ga·rine /ṓleeōmárjərin/ *n.* margarine made from vegetable oils.

ol·fac·to·ry /olfáktəree, ōl-/ *adj.* of or relating to the sense of smell.

ol·i·garch /óligaark, óli-/ *n.* member of an oligarchy.

ol·i·gar·chy /óligaarkee, óli-/ *n.* (*pl.* **-chies**) **1** government or nation governed by a small group of people. **2** members of such a government. □□ **ol·i·gar·chic** /-gaárkik/ *adj.* **ol·i·gar' chi·cal** *adj.*

ol·ive /óliv/ • *n.* **1** (in full **ol'ive tree**) evergreen tree having dark-green, lance-shaped leathery leaves with silvery undersides. **2** small oval fruit of this, having a hard stone and bitter flesh, green when unripe and bluish-black when ripe. **3** grayish-green color of an unripe olive. **4** wood of the olive tree. • *adj.* **1** colored like an unripe olive. **2** (of the complexion) yellowish-brown, sallow. □ **olive branch 1** branch of an olive tree as a symbol of peace. **2** gesture of reconciliation or friendship. **olive oil** oil extracted from olives, used esp. in cookery.

O·lym·pi·ad /ōlímpeead/ *n.* **1** period of four years between Olympic games, used by the ancient Greeks in dating events. **2** celebration of the modern or ancient Olympic Games.

O·lym·pi·an /əlímpeeən, ōlím-/ • *adj.* **1** of or associated with Mount Olympus in NE Greece, traditionally the home of the Greek gods. **2** (of manners, etc.) condescending; superior. **3** = OLYMPIC. • *n.* **1** any of the Greek gods regarded as living on Olympus. **2** competitor in the Olympic games.

O·lym·pic /əlímpik, ōlím-/ • *adj.* of or Olympia or the Olympic games. • *n.pl.* (**the O·lym'pics**) Olympic games. □ **Olympic games 1** ancient Greek festival held at Olympia every four years, with athletic, literary, and musical competitions. **2** modern international sports festival usu. held every four years since 1896 in different venues.

O·ma·ha /ṓməhaw, -haa/ • *n.* **1 a** N. American people native to Nebraska. **b** member of this people. **2** language of this people. • *adj.* of or relating to this people or their language.

OMB *abbr.* Office of Management and Budget.

om·buds·man /ómbŏŏdzmən/ *n.* (*pl.* **-men**) official appointed to investigate complaints against public authorities, etc.

o·me·ga /ōmáygə, ṓmeegə, ōmégə/ *n.* **1** last (24th) letter of the Greek alphabet (Ω, ω). **2** last of a series; final development.

om·e·lette /ómlit/ *n.* (also **om'e·let**) beaten eggs cooked in a frying pan and served plain or with a savory or sweet filling.

o·men /ṓmən/ *n.* occurrence or object regarded as portending good or evil.

om·i·cron /ómikron, ṓmi-/ *n.* fifteenth letter of the Greek alphabet (Ο, ο).

om·i·nous /óminəs/ *adj.* **1** threatening. **2** of evil omen. □□ **om'i·nous·ly** *adv.*

o·mis·sion /ōmíshən/ *n.* **1** omitting or being omitted. **2** something omitted or overlooked.

o·mit /ōmít/ *v.tr.* (**o·mit·ted, o·mit·ting**) **1** leave out; not insert or include. **2** leave undone. **3** fail or neglect.

omni- /ómnee/ *comb. form* **1** all. **2** in all ways or places.

om·ni·bus /ómnibəs/ • *n.* = BUS. • *adj.* **1** serving several purposes. **2** comprising several items.

om·nip·o·tent /omnípət'nt/ *adj.* **1** having great or absolute power. **2** having great influence. □□ **om·nip'o·tence** *n.*

om·ni·pres·ent /ómniprézənt/ *adj.* **1** present everywhere. **2** widely or constantly encountered. □□ **om·ni·pres'ence** *n.*

om·ni·scient /omníshənt/ *adj.* knowing everything. □□ **om·ni·science** /-shəns/ *n.*

om·niv·o·rous /omnívərəs/ *adj.* **1** feeding on both plants and flesh. **2** making use of everything available. □□ **om·ni·vore** /ómnivawr/ *n.* **om·niv′o·rous·ly** *adv.*

on /on, awn/ • *prep.* **1** supported by or attached to or covering or enclosing (*sat on a chair; stuck on the wall; rings on her fingers; leaned on his elbow*). **2** (of time) exactly at; during (*on the hour; working on Tuesday*). **3** as a result of (*on further examination I found this*). **4** (so as to be) having membership, etc., of or residence at or in (*she is on the board of directors; lives on the waterfront*). **5** close to (*a house on the sea*). **6** in the direction of. **7** having as a basis or motive (*on good authority; did it on purpose*). **8** concerning (*writes on finance*). **9** using or engaged with (*is on the pill; here on business*). **10** at the expense of (*drinks are on me*). **11** added to (*disaster on disaster*). **12** in a specified manner or style (*on the cheap; on the run*). • *adv.* **1** (so as to be) wearing (*put your boots on*). **2** in the appropriate direction; toward (*look on*). **3** further forward (*is getting on in years*). **4** with continued action or operation (*went plodding on; light is on*). **5** due to take place as planned (*is the party still on?*). • *adj.* Baseball positioned at a base as a runner. □ **be on to** realize the significance or intentions of. **on and off** intermittently. **on and on** continually; at tedious length. **on-line** *Computing* (of equipment or a process) directly controlled by or connected to a central processor. **on-screen** *adj.* appearing in a movie or on television. • *adv.* within the view presented by a filmed scene. **on time 1** punctual; punctually. **2** by means of installment payments (*buying new furniture on time*).

once /wuns/ • *adv.* **1** on one occasion only (*did not once say please; have read it once*). **2** at some time in the past (*could once play chess*). **3** ever or at all (*if you once forget it*). • *conj.* as soon as (*once they have gone we can relax*). • *n.* one time or occasion (*just the once*). □ **at once 1** immediately. **2** simultaneously. **for once** on this (or that) occasion, even if not on any other. **once and for all** conclusively; in conclusion. **once** (or **every once**) **in a while** occasionally. **once-over** *colloq.* **1** rapid inspection. **2** appraising glance. **once upon a time** at some vague time in the past.

on·co·gene /óngkəjeen/ *n.* gene that can transform a cell into a tumor cell.

on·col·o·gy /ongkólǝjee/ *n. Med.* study of tumors.

on·com·ing /ónkuming, áwn-/ *adj.* approaching from the front.

one /wun/ • *adj.* **1** single and integral in number. **2** (with a noun implied) single person or thing of the kind expressed or implied (*one of the best*). **3** particular but undefined, esp. as contrasted with another (*that is one view*). **4** only such (*the one man who can do it*). **5** forming a unity (*one and undivided*). **6** identical; the same. • *n.* **1 a** lowest cardinal number. **b** thing numbered with it. **2** unity; a unit. **3** single thing or person or example (often referring to a noun previously expressed or implied: *the big dog and the small one*). • *pron.* **1** person of a specified kind (*loved ones*). **2** any person. **3** I, me (*one would like to help*). □ **at one** in agreement. **one-horse 1** using a single horse. **2** *colloq.* small, poorly equipped. **one-on-one** of or direct person-to-person conflict. **one-sided** unfair; partial. **one-to-one** with

omniscient ~ ooze

one member of one group corresponding to one of another. **one-track mind** mind preoccupied with one subject. **one up** *colloq.* having a particular advantage. **one-way** allowing movement or travel in one direction only.

O·nei·da /ōnídǝ/ • *n.* **1 a** N. American people native to New York state. **b** member of this people. **2** language of this people. • *adj.* of or relating to this people or their language.

one·ness /wún-nis/ *n.* **1** singleness. **2** uniqueness. **3** agreement. **4** sameness.

on·er·ous /ónǝrǝs, ón-/ *adj.* burdensome. □□ **on′er·ous·ness** *n.*

one·self /wunsélf/ *pron.* reflexive and (in apposition) emphatic form of *one* (*kill oneself; one has to do it oneself*).

one·time /wúntīm/ *adj. & adv.* former.

on·go·ing /ón-gṓing, áwn-/ *adj.* **1** continuing. **2** in progress (*ongoing discussions*).

on·ion /únyǝn/ *n.* **1** plant having a short stem and bearing greenish-white flowers. **2** swollen bulb of this with many concentric skins used in cooking, pickling, etc. □□ **on′ion·y** *adj.*

on·look·er /ónlŏŏkǝr, áwn-/ *n.* spectator. □□ **on′look·ing** *adj.*

on·ly /ónlee/ • *adv.* **1** solely, merely, exclusively. **2** no longer ago than (*saw them only yesterday*). **3** with no better result than (*hurried home only to find her gone*). • *attrib.adj.* **1** existing alone of its or their kind (*their only son*). **2** best or alone worth knowing (*the only place to eat*). • *conj. colloq.* except that; but. □ **only too** extremely (*is only too willing*).

on·o·mas·tics /ónǝmástiks/ *n.pl.* (treated as *sing.*) study of the origin and formation of (esp. personal) proper names.

on·o·mat·o·poe·ia /ónǝmátǝpéeǝ, -máátǝ-/ *n.* formation of a word from a sound associated with what is named (e.g., *cuckoo, sizzle*). □□ **on·o·mat·o·poe′ic** /ono·mat·o·po·et·ic /-pṓē-tik/ *adj.*

on·rush /ónrush, áwn-/ *n.* onward rush.

on·set /ónset, áwn-/ *n.* **1** attack. **2** impetuous beginning.

on·shore /ónsháwr, áwn-/ *adj.* **1** on the shore. **2** (of the wind) blowing from the sea toward the land.

on·slaught /ónslawt, áwn-/ *n.* fierce attack.

on·stage /ónstáyj/ *adj. & adv. Theatr.* on the stage; visible to the audience.

Ont. *abbr.* Ontario.

on·to /óntoo, áwn-/ *prep. disp.* to a position or state on or in contact with (cf. *on to*).

on·tog·e·ny /ontójǝnee/ *n.* life cycle or development of a single organism.

o·nus /ónǝs/ *n.* (*pl.* **o·nus·es**) burden, duty, or responsibility.

on·ward /ónwǝrd, áwn-/ • *adv.* (also **on′wards**) **1** further on. **2** with advancing motion. • *adj.* directed onward.

on·yx /óniks/ *n.* semiprecious variety of agate with colored layers.

oo·dles /ṓod′lz/ *n.pl. colloq.* very great amount.

oops /ŏops, ṓops/ *int. colloq.* expressing surprise or apology, esp. on making an obvious mistake.

ooze¹ /ṓoz/ • *v.* **1** *intr.* trickle or leak slowly

out. **2** *intr.* (of a substance) exude. **3** *tr.* exude
or exhibit (a feeling) liberally (*oozed sympathy*).
● *n.* sluggish flow. □□ **ooz′y** *adj.*

ooze² /ŏoz/ *n.* wet mud or slime, esp. at the
bottom of a river, lake, or estuary. □□ **ooz′y** *adj.*

o·pal /ṓpəl/ *n.* iridescent mineral often used as
a gemstone. □□ **o·pal·es·cence** /ṓpəlésəns/ *n.*
o·pal·es·cent /-sənt/ *adj.*

o·paque /ṓpáyk/ *adj.* (**o·paqu·er**, **o·paqu·est**) **1**
not transmitting light. **2** impenetrable to sight. **3**
obscure; not lucid. **4** obtuse; dull-witted.
□□ **o·pac·i·ty** /ṓpásitee/ *n.* **o·paque′ly** *adv.* **o·**
paque′ness *n.*

op art /op/ *n. colloq.* = optical art.

op. cit. *abbr.* in the work already quoted.

OPEC /ṓpek/ *abbr.* Organization of Petroleum
Exporting Countries.

o·pen /ṓpən/ ● *adj.* **1** not closed nor locked nor
blocked up; allowing access. **2** unenclosed; unconfined; unobstructed. **3** uncovered, exposed.
4 undisguised; public. **5** unfolded or spread out
(*had the map open on the table*). **6** (of a fabric) with gaps or intervals. **7 a** (of a person)
frank and communicative. **b** (of the mind) accessible to new ideas; unprejudiced. **8 a** (of an
exhibition, shop, etc.) accessible to visitors or
customers. **b** (of a meeting) admitting all. **9**
(of a race, competition, scholarship, etc.) unrestricted as to who may compete. **10** (foll. by
to) **a** willing to receive (*is open to offers*). **b** (of
a choice, offer, or opportunity) still available
(*there are three courses open to us*). **c** likely to suffer
from or be affected by (*open to abuse*). ● *v.* **1** *tr.*
& *intr.* make or become open or more open. **2**
a *tr.* change from a closed or fastened position
so as to allow access (*opened the door*). **b** *intr.*
(of a door, lid, etc.) have its position changed
to allow access (*the door opened slowly*). **3** *intr.*
(foll. by *into, on to*, etc.) (of a door, room, etc.)
afford access as specified (*opened on to a large
garden*). **4 a** *tr.* start or establish or get going
(a business, activity, etc.). **b** *intr.* be initiated;
make a start. ● *n.* **1** (prec. by *the*) **a** open space
or country or air. **b** public notice or view; general attention (esp. *into the open*). **2** open championship, competition, or scholarship. □ **open**
air (usu. prec. by *the*) outdoors. **open-and-shut**
(of an argument, case, etc.) straightforward
and conclusive. **open-ended** having no predetermined limit. **open-faced** designating a sandwich
with no covering slice of bread. **open-hearted**
frank and kindly. **open-heart surgery** surgery with
the heart exposed and the blood made to bypass it. **open house 1** welcome or hospitality for
visitors. **2** time when real estate offered for sale
is open to prospective buyers. **open-minded** accessible to new ideas; unprejudiced. **open ques-**
tion undecided matter. □□ **o′pen·er** *n.* **o′pen·ly**
adv. **o′pen·ness** *n.*

o·pen·hand·ed /ṓpənhándid/ *adj.* generous.

o·pen·ing /ṓpəning/ ● *n.* **1** aperture or gap, esp.
allowing access. **2** opportunity. **3** beginning; initial part. ● *adj.* initial; first.

o·pen·work /ṓpənwərk/ *n.* pattern with intervening spaces in metal, leather, lace, etc.

o·pe·ra¹ /ṓpərə, ṓprə/ *n.* **1** dramatic work in one
or more acts, set to music for singers (usu. in
costume) and instrumentalists. **2** this as a genre.
□ **opera glasses** small binoculars for use at the

opera or theater. □□ **op·er·at′ic** /ṓpərátik/ *adj.*
op·er·at′i·cal·ly *adv.*

o·pe·ra² *pl.* of OPUS.

op·er·a·ble /ṓpərəbəl/ *adj.* **1** that can be operated. **2** suitable for treatment by surgery.

op·er·ate /ṓpərayt/ *v.* **1** *tr.* manage; work; control. **2** *intr.* be in action; function. **3** *intr.* (often
foll. by *on*) **a** perform a surgical operation. **b** conduct a military or naval action. **4** *tr.* bring about;
accomplish. □ **operating system** basic software
that enables the running of a computer program.

op·er·a·tion /ṓpərayshən/ *n.* **1 a** action or
method of working or operating. **b** being active
or functioning (*not yet in operation*). **c** scope or
range of effectiveness of a thing's activity. **2**
active process. **3** piece of work, esp. one in a
series (often in *pl.*: *begin operations*). **4** surgery
performed on a patient. **5** strategic movement
of troops, ships, etc., for military action.

op·er·a·tion·al /ṓpərayshənəl/ *adj.* **1 a** of or used
for operations. **b** engaged in operations. **2** able
or ready to function. □□ **op·er·a′tion·al·ly** *adv.*

op·er·a·tive /ṓpərətiv, ṓprə-/ ● *adj.* **1** in operation; having effect. **2** having the principal relevance (*"may" is the operative word*). **3** of or by
surgery. ● *n.* detective; spy.

op·er·a·tor /ṓpəraytər/ *n.* **1** person controlling a
machine, etc. **2** person engaging in business. **3**
colloq. person acting in a specified way (*smooth
operator*).

op·er·et·ta /ṓpərétə/ *n.* **1** one-act or short opera.
2 light opera.

oph·thal·mic /of-thálmik, op-/ *adj.* of or relating
to the eye and its diseases.

oph·thal·mol·o·gy /óf-thalmóləjee, -thə-, op-/
n. scientific study of the eye. □□ **oph·thal·mol′**
o·gist *n.*

o·pi·ate /ṓpeeət/ ● *adj.* **1** containing opium. **2**
narcotic, soporific. ● *n.* **1** drug containing
opium, usu. to ease pain or induce sleep. **2** thing
that soothes or stupefies.

o·pine /ṓpín/ *v.tr.* hold or express as an opinion.

o·pin·ion /əpínyən/ *n.* **1** unproven belief or assessment. **2** view held as probable. **3** what one
thinks about something. **4 a** professional advice.
b *Law* formal statement of reasons for a judgment given.

o·pin·ion·at·ed /əpínyənaytid/ *adj.* conceitedly
assertive or dogmatic in one's opinions.

o·pi·um /ṓpeeəm/ *n.* **1** addictive drug prepared
from the juice of the opium poppy, used as an
analgesic and narcotic. **2** anything regarded as
soothing or stupefying.

o·pos·sum /əpósəm/ *n.* tree-living American
marsupial having a prehensile tail and hind feet
with an opposable thumb.

opp. *abbr.* opposite.

op·po·nent /əpṓnənt/ ● *n.* person who opposes
or belongs to an opposing side. ● *adj.* opposing;
contrary; opposed.

op·por·tune /ṓpərtṓon, -tyṓon/ *adj.* **1** (of a
time) well-chosen or especially favorable. **2** (of
an action or event) well-timed.

op·por·tu·nism /ṓpərtṓonizəm, -tyṓo-/ *n.* adaptation to circumstances, esp. regardless of
principle. □□ **op·por·tun′ist** *n.* & *adj.* **op·por·**
tu·nis′tic *adj.* **op·por·tu·nis′ti·cal·ly** *adv.*

op·por·tu·ni·ty /ṓpərtṓonitee, -tyṓo-/ *n.* (*pl.*
-ties) favorable chance or opening offered by
circumstances.

op·pos·a·ble /əpózəbəl/ *adj. Zool.* (of the thumb in primates) capable of touching the other digits on the same hand.

op·pose /əpóz/ *v.tr.* (often *absol.*) **1** resist; argue against. **2** (foll. by *to*) place in opposition or contrast. □□ **op·pos´er** *n.*

op·po·site /ópəzit/ ● *adj.* **1** (often foll. by *to*) having a position on the other side; facing. **2** (often foll. by *to*, *from*) contrary; diametrically different. ● *n.* anything opposite. ● *adv.* **1** in an opposite position (*the tree stands opposite*). **2** in a complementary role to (another actor, etc.). ● *prep.* in a position opposite to (*opposite the house is a tree*). □ **opposite number** person holding an equivalent position in another group, etc. **the opposite sex** women in relation to men or vice versa.

op·po·si·tion /ópəzíshən/ *n.* **1** resistance, antagonism. **2** being hostile or in conflict or disagreement. **3** contrast or antithesis. **4** group or party of opponents or competitors.

op·press /əprés/ *v.tr.* **1** keep in subservience. **2** govern or treat harshly. □□ **op·pres·sion** /əpréshən/ *n.* **op·pres´sor** *n.*

op·pres·sive /əprésiv/ *adj.* **1** harsh or cruel. **2** (of weather) close and sultry. □□ **op·pres´sive·ly** *adv.* **op·pres´sive·ness** *n.*

op·pro·bri·ous /əpróbreeəs/ *adj.* (of language) severely scornful; abusive.

op·pro·bri·um /əpróbreeəm/ *n.* **1** disgrace. **2** cause of this.

opt /opt/ *v.intr.* decide; make a choice. □ **opt out** (often foll. by *of*) choose not to participate.

op·tic /óptik/ *adj.* of or relating to the eye or vision (*optic nerve*).

op·ti·cal /óptikəl/ *adj.* **1** of sight; visual. **2 a** of or concerning sight or light in relation to each other. **b** belonging to optics. **3** (esp. of a lens) constructed to assist sight. □ **optical art** style of painting that gives the illusion of movement by the precise use of pattern and color. **optical character recognition** identification of printed characters using photoelectric devices. **optical fiber** thin glass fiber through which light can be transmitted. **optical illusion** image that deceives the eye. □□ **op´ti·cal·ly** *adv.*

op·ti·cian /optíshən/ *n.* **1** maker or seller of eyeglasses, contact lenses, etc. **2** person trained in the detection and correction of poor eyesight.

op·tics /óptiks/ *n.pl.* (treated as *sing.*) scientific study of sight and the behavior of light.

op·ti·mal /óptiməl/ *adj.* best or most favorable.

op·ti·mism /óptimizəm/ *n.* **1** inclination to hopefulness and confidence (opp. PESSIMISM). **2** *Philos.* theory that good must ultimately prevail over evil. □□ **op´ti·mist** *n.* **op·ti·mis´tic** *adj.* **op·ti·mis´ti·cal·ly** *adv.*

op·ti·mize /óptimīz/ *v.* **1** *tr.* make the best or most effective use of. **2** *intr.* be an optimist. □□ **op·ti·mi·za´tion** *n.*

op·ti·mum /óptiməm/ ● *n.* (*pl.* **op·ti·ma** /-mə/ or **op·ti·mums**) **1** most favorable conditions (for growth, reproduction, etc.). **2** best possible compromise. ● *adj.* = OPTIMAL.

op·tion /ópshən/ *n.* **1 a** choosing; choice. **b** thing chosen. **2** liberty to choose. **3** *Stock Exch.*, etc., right to buy or sell at a specified price within a set time.

op·tion·al /ópshənəl/ *adj.* not obligatory. □□ **op´tion·al·ly** *adv.*

op·tom·e·try /optómitree/ *n.* practice or profession of testing the eyes for defects in vision and prescribing corrective lenses or exercises. □□ **op·tom´e·trist** /optómitrist/ *n.*

op·u·lent /ópyələnt/ *adj.* **1** wealthy. **2** luxurious. **3** abundant. □□ **op´u·lence** *n.*

o·pus /ópəs/ *n.* (*pl.* **op·er·a** /ópərə/ or **op·us·es**) **1** *Mus.* **a** musical composition. **b** (also **op.**) used before a number given to a composer's work, usu. indicating the order of publication (*Beethoven, op. 15*). **2** any artistic work (cf. MAGNUM OPUS).

OR *abbr.* **1** Oregon (in official postal use). **2** operating room.

or /awr, ər/ *conj.* **1** introducing an alternative (*white or black*). **2** introducing a synonym or explanation of a preceding word, etc. (*suffered from vertigo or dizziness*). **3** otherwise (*run or you'll be late*). □ **or else 1** otherwise (*do it now, or else you will have to do it tomorrow*). **2** *colloq.* expressing a warning or threat (*hand over the money or else*).

-or¹ /ər/ *suffix* forming nouns denoting an agent (*actor, escalator*) or condition (*error, horror*).

-or² /ər/ *suffix* forming nouns denoting state or condition (*error, horror*).

o·ra·cle /áwrəkəl, ór-/ *n.* **1 a** place at which advice or prophecy was sought from the gods in classical antiquity. **b** response given. **c** prophet or prophetess at an oracle. **2** source of wisdom. □□ **or·ac·u·lar** /awrákyələr/ *adj.*

o·ral /áwrəl/ ● *adj.* **1** by word of mouth; spoken; not written (*the oral tradition*). **2** done or taken by mouth (*oral contraceptive*). ● *n. colloq.* spoken examination, test, etc. □□ **o´ral·ly** *adv.*

or·ange /áwrinj, ór-/ ● *n.* **1 a** round juicy citrus fruit with a bright reddish-yellow tough rind. **b** tree or shrub bearing fragrant white flowers and yielding this fruit. **2** reddish-yellow color of an orange. ● *adj.* orange-colored; reddish-yellow.

o·rang·u·tan /awrángətán, əráng-/ *n.* large red long-haired tree-living ape of Borneo and Sumatra, with characteristic long arms and hooked hands and feet.

o·rate /awráyt, áwrayt/ *v.intr.* esp. *joc.* or *derog.* speak, esp. pompously or at length.

o·ra·tion /awráyshən, ōráy-/ *n.* formal speech, etc., esp. when ceremonial.

or·a·tor /áwrətər, ór-/ *n.* **1** person making a speech. **2** eloquent public speaker.

or·a·to·ri·o /áwrətáwreeō, ór-/ *n.* (*pl.* **-os**) semidramatic work for orchestra and voices, esp. on a sacred theme.

or·a·to·ry /áwrətawree, ór-/ *n.* (*pl.* **-ries**) **1** art or practice of formal speaking, esp. in public. **2** exaggerated, eloquent, or highly colored language. □□ **or·a·tor´i·cal** *adj.*

orb /awrb/ *n.* **1** globe surmounted by a cross, esp. carried by a sovereign at a coronation. **2** sphere; globe.

or·bit /áwrbit/ ● *n.* **1 a** curved, usu. closed course of a planet, satellite, etc. **b** one complete passage around a body. **2** range or sphere of action. ● *v.* **1** *intr.* (of a satellite, etc.) go around in orbit. **2** *tr.* move in orbit around. **3** *tr.* put into orbit. □□ **or´bit·al** *adj.* **or´bit·er** *n.* *adj.* **or´bit·er** *n.*

or·ca /áwrkə/ *n.* any of various whales, esp. the killer whale.

orchard ~ organza   420

or·chard /áwrchərd/ *n.* piece of land with fruit trees.

or·ches·tra /áwrkəstrə/ *n.* **1** group of instrumentalists, esp. combining strings, woodwinds, brass, and percussion (*symphony orchestra*). **2 a** (in full **or·ches·tra pit**) part of a theater, etc., where the orchestra plays, usu. in front of the stage. **b** main-floor seating area in a theater. □□ **or·ches′tral** /-késtrəl/ *adj.*

or·ches·trate /áwrkəstrayt/ *v.tr.* **1** arrange or compose for an orchestra. **2** arrange (elements of a situation, etc.) for maximum effect. □□ **or·ches·tra·tion** /-tráyshən/ *n.*

or·chid /áwrkid/ *n.* **1** plant bearing flowers in fantastic shapes and brilliant colors, usu. having one petal larger than the others and variously spurred, lobed, pouched, etc. **2** flower of these plants.

or·dain /awrdáyn/ *v.tr.* **1** confer holy orders on; appoint to the Christian ministry. **2 a** decree (*ordained that he should go*). **b** (of God, fate, etc.) destine; appoint (*has ordained us to die*).

or·deal /awrdeél/ *n.* painful or horrific experience; severe trial.

or·der /áwrdər/ • *n.* **1 a** condition in which every part, unit, etc., is in its right place; tidiness. **b** specified sequence, succession, etc. (*alphabetical order*). **2** (in *sing.* or *pl.*) authoritative command, direction, etc. **3** state of peaceful harmony under a constituted authority. **4** kind; sort (*talents of a high order*). **5 a** direction to a manufacturer, tradesman, waiter, etc., to supply something. **b** goods, etc., supplied. **6** constitution or nature of the world, society, etc. (*the moral order*). **7** *Biol.* taxonomic rank below a class and above a family. **8** (esp. **Order**) fraternity of monks and friars, or formerly of knights, bound by a common rule of life (*the Franciscan Order*). **9 a** any of the grades of the Christian ministry. **b** (in *pl.*) status of a member of the clergy (*Anglican orders*). **10** any of the classical styles of architecture (Doric, Ionic, Corinthian, Tuscan, and Composite). **11** principles of procedure, decorum, etc., accepted by a meeting, legislative assembly, etc., or enforced by its president. • *v.tr.* **1** command; bid; prescribe. **2** command or direct (a person) to a specified destination. **3** direct a manufacturer, waiter, tradesman, etc., to supply (*ordered dinner*). **4** put in order; regulate. □ **in order 1** one after another according to some principle. **2** fit for use. **3** according to the rules (of procedure at a meeting, etc.). **in order that** so that. **in order to** with the purpose of doing. **on the order of** approximately. **on order** (of goods, etc.) ordered but not yet received. **out of order 1** not working properly. **2** not according to the rules (of a meeting, organization, etc.). **3** not in proper sequence.

or·der·ly /áwrd′rlee/ • *adj.* **1** methodically arranged; regular. **2** obedient to discipline; well-behaved. • *n.* (*pl.* **-lies**) **1** hospital attendant with nonmedical duties, esp. cleaning, moving equipment, escorting patients, etc. **2** soldier who carries orders for an officer, etc. □□ **or′der·li·ness** *n.*

or·di·nal /áwrd′nəl/ *n.* (in full **or′di·nal num′ber**) number defining a thing's position in a series, e.g., "first," "second," "third," etc. (cf. CARDINAL).

or·di·nance /áwrd′nəns/ *n.* **1** authoritative order; decree. **2** statute, esp. by a local authority.

or·di·nar·y /áwrd′neree/ *adj.* **1** regular; normal; usual (*in the ordinary course of events*). **2** statute, esp. boring; commonplace (*an ordinary man*). □ **out of the ordinary** unusual. □□ **or·di·nar′i·ly** /-áirəlee/ *adv.* **or·di·nar′i·ness** *n.*

or·di·nate /áwrd′nit/ *n. Math.* straight line from any point parallel to one coordinate axis and meeting the other, usually a coordinate measured parallel to the vertical (cf. ABSCISSA).

or·di·na·tion /áwrd′náyshən/ *n.* **1** conferring holy orders, esp. on a priest or deacon. **2** admission of a priest, etc., to church ministry.

ord·nance /áwrdnəns/ *n.* **1** artillery; military supplies. **2** branch of the armed forces dealing esp. with military stores and materials.

or·dure /áwrjər, -dŏŏr/ *n.* **1** dung. **2** obscenity.

Ore. *abbr.* Oregon.

ore /awr/ *n.* naturally occurring solid material from which metal or other valuable minerals may be extracted.

Oreg. *abbr.* Oregon.

o·reg·a·no /ərégənō, awrég-/ *n.* aromatic herb, the fresh or dried leaves of which are used as a flavoring in cooking. Also called **wild marjoram** (cf. MARJORAM).

or·gan /áwrgən/ *n.* **1 a** usu. large musical instrument having pipes supplied with air from bellows, sounded by keys, and distributed into sets or stops that form partial organs, each with a separate keyboard. **b** smaller instrument without pipes, producing similar sounds electronically. **2** usu. self-contained part of an organism having a special vital function (*vocal organs; digestive organs*). **3** medium of communication, esp. a newspaper, sectarian periodical, etc. □□ **or′gan·ist** *n.*

or·gan·dy /áwrgəndee/ *n.* (also **or′gan·die**) (*pl.* **-dies**) fine translucent cotton muslin, usu. stiffened.

or·gan·elle /áwrgənél/ *n. Biol.* any of various organized or specialized structures that form part of a cell.

or·gan·ic /awrgánik/ *adj.* **1 a** *Physiol.* of a bodily organ(s). **b** *Med.* (of a disease) affecting an organ. **2** (of a plant or animal) having organs or an organized physical structure. **3** *Agriculture* produced without the use of chemical fertilizers, pesticides, etc. (*organic farming*). **4** *Chem.* (of a compound, etc.) containing carbon (opp. INORGANIC). **5** **a** structural; inherent. **b** constitutional; fundamental. **6** organized; systematic (*an organic whole*). □□ **or·gan′i·cal·ly** *adv.*

or·gan·ism /áwrgənizəm/ *n.* **1** living individual consisting of a single cell or of a group of interdependent parts sharing the life processes. **2** individual live plant or animal.

or·ga·ni·za·tion /áwrgənizáyshən/ *n.* **1** organizing; being organized. **2** organized body, esp. a business, government department, charity, etc. □□ **or·ga·ni·za′tion·al** *adj.*

or·gan·ize /áwrgənīz/ *v.tr.* **1** give an orderly structure to; systematize. **2** arrange for or initiate (a plan, etc.). **3** (often *absol.*) **a** enroll (new members) in a labor union, political party, etc. **b** form (a labor union or other political group). □ **organized crime** organization of people who carry out illegal activities for profit. □□ **or′gan·iz·er** *n.*

or·gan·za /awrgánzə/ *n.* thin stiff transparent silk or synthetic dress fabric.

or·gasm /áwrgazəm/ *n.* climax of sexual excitement. □□ **or·gas·mic** /-gázmik/ *adj.*

or·gy /áwrjee/ *n.* (*pl.* **-gies**) **1** wild drunken festivity, esp. one at which indiscriminate sexual activity takes place. **2** excessive indulgence in an activity.

o·ri·el /áwreeəl/ *n.* projecting window of an upper story.

ORIEL

o·ri·ent • *n.* /áwreeənt/ (**the Orient**) countries E. of the Mediterranean, esp. E. Asia. • *v.* /áwree-ent/ **1** *tr.* **a** find the bearings of. **b** bring (oneself, different elements, etc.) into a clearly understood position or relationship; direct. **2** *tr.* **a** place or build (a church, building, etc.) facing toward the East. **b** bury (a person) with the feet toward the East. **3** *intr.* turn eastward or in a specified direction.

o·ri·en·tal /áwree-éntəl/ • *adj.* often offens. **1** (often **Oriental**) of or characteristic of Eastern civilization, etc. **2** of or concerning the East, esp. E. Asia. • *n.* (esp. **Oriental**) native of the Orient.
¶ The term **Oriental**, which has many associations with European empire in Asia, is regarded as offensive by many Asians, especially Asian Americans. **Asian** or, if appropriate, **East Asian** is preferred for reference to people or ethnic groups.

o·ri·en·ta·tion /áwree-entáyshən/ *n.* **1** orienting; being oriented. **2 a** relative position. **b** person's attitude or adjustment in relation to circumstances, esp. politically or psychologically. **3** introduction to a subject or situation; briefing. □□ **o·ri·en·ta'tion·al** *adj.*

o·ri·en·teer·ing /áwree-entéering/ *n.* cross-country race in which participants use a map and a compass to navigate along an unfamiliar course.

or·i·fice /áwrifis, ór-/ *n.* opening, esp. the mouth of a cavity.

orig. *abbr.* **1** original. **2** originally.

o·ri·ga·mi /áwrigáamee/ *n.* Japanese art of folding paper into decorative shapes.

or·i·gin /áwrijin, ór-/ *n.* **1** beginning or starting point; source. **2** (often in *pl.*) person's ancestry (*what are his origins?*).

o·rig·i·nal /əríjinəl/ • *adj.* **1** existing from the beginning; innate. **2** inventive; creative. **3** not derivative or imitative; firsthand. • *n.* **1** original model, pattern, picture, etc., from which another is copied or translated. **2** eccentric or unusual person. □□ **o·rig·i·nal·i·ty** /-nál-/ *n.* **o·rig'i·nal·ly** *adv.*

o·rig·i·nate /əríjinayt/ *v.* **1** *tr.* cause to begin; initiate. **2** *intr.* (usu. foll. by *from, in, with*) have an origin; begin. □□ **o·rig·i·na·tion** /-náyshən/ *n.* **o·rig'i·na·tive** *adj.* **o·rig'i·na·tor** *n.*

O-ring /ó-ring/ *n.* gasket in the form of a ring with a circular cross section.

o·ri·ole /áwreeōl/ *n.* American bird with black and orange plumage in the male.

Or·lon /áwrlon/ *n.propr.* synthetic fiber and fabric for textiles and knitwear.

or·mo·lu /áwrmə lōō/ *n.* **1** (often *attrib.*) gilded bronze or gold-colored alloy of copper, zinc, and tin used to decorate furniture, make ornaments, etc. **2** articles made of or decorated with these.

or·na·ment • *n.* /áwrnəmənt/ **1** thing used to adorn, esp. a trinket, vase, figure, etc. **2** quality or person conferring adornment, grace, or honor (*an ornament to her profession*). • *v.tr.* /áwrnəmənt/ adorn; beautify. □□ **or·na·men'tal** *adj.* **or·na·men·ta'tion** *n.*

or·nate /awrnáyt/ *adj.* elaborately adorned; highly decorated. □□ **or·nate'ly** *adv.* **or·nate'ness** *n.*

or·ner·y /áwrnəree/ *adj. colloq.* cantankerous; unpleasant. □□ **or'ner·i·ness** *n.*

or·ni·thol·o·gy /áwrnithóləjee/ *n.* the scientific study of birds. □□ **or·ni·tho·log·i·cal** /-thəlójikəl/ *adj.* **or·ni·thol'o·gist** *n.*

o·ro·tund /áwrətund/ *adj.* **1** (of the voice) round; imposing. **2** (of writing, style, etc.) pompous; pretentious.

or·phan /áwrfən/ • *n.* (often *attrib.*) **1** child whose parents are dead. **2** young animal that has lost its mother. **3** person or thing bereft of previous protection, support, advantages, etc. • *v.tr.* bereave (a child) of its parents.

or·phan·age /áwrfənij/ *n.* residential institution for orphans.

or·rer·y /áwrəree, ór-/ *n.* (*pl.* **-ies**) clockwork model of the solar system.

ortho- /áwrthō/ *comb. form* **1** straight; rectangular; upright. **2** right; correct.

or·tho·don·tics /áwrthədóntiks/ *n.pl.* (treated as *sing.*) (also **or·tho·don·tia** /-dónshə/) treatment of irregularities in the teeth and jaws. □□ **or·tho·don'tic** *adj.* **or·tho·don'tist** *n.*

or·tho·dox /áwrthədoks/ *adj.* **1** holding correct or currently accepted opinions, esp. on religious doctrine, morals, etc. **2** not independent-minded; unoriginal; unheretical. □ **Orthodox Church** Eastern Christian Church, separated from the Western Christian Church in the 11th c., having the Patriarch of Constantinople as its head, and including the national churches of Russia, Romania, Greece, etc. □□ **or'tho·dox·y** *n.*

or·thog·ra·phy /awrthógrəfee/ n. (pl. **-phies**) **1** correct or conventional spelling. **2** spelling with reference to its correctness (*dreadful orthography*). **3** study or science of spelling. □□ **or·tho·graph·ic** /awrthəgráfik/ adj.

or·tho·pe·dics /àwrthəpe'ediks/ n.pl. (treated as *sing.*) branch of medicine dealing with the correction of deformities of bones or muscles. □□ **or·tho·pe'dic** adj. **or·tho·pe'dist** n.

or·thot·ics /awrtha'atiks/ n. **1** *Med.* science of treating joint, bone, or muscle disorders with mechanical support, braces, etc. **2** devices, such as inserts for athletic shoes, used for such treatment.

-ory /áwree, əree/ suffix forming nouns denoting a place for a particular function (*dormitory; refectory*) or adjectives (and occasionally nouns) relating to or involving a verbal action (*accessory; compulsory; directory*).

OS abbr. **1** old style. **2** ordinary seaman. **3** oculus sinister (left eye). **4** outsize. **5** out of stock.

Os symb. Chem. osmium.

os·cil·late /ósilayt/ v. **1** tr. & intr. **a** swing back and forth like a pendulum. **b** move back and forth between points. **2** intr. vacillate; vary between extremes of opinion, action, etc. □□ **os·cil·la·tion** /-láyshən/ n. **os'·cil·la·tor** n.

os·cil·lo·scope /əsíləskōp/ n. device for viewing oscillations in electrical current, etc., by a display on the screen of a cathode-ray tube.

os·cu·late /óskyəlayt/ v. joc. kiss.

-ose¹ /ōs/ suffix forming adjectives denoting possession of a quality (*grandiose; verbose*). □□ **-ose·ly** suffix forming adverbs. **-ose·ness** suffix forming nouns (cf. -OSITY).

-ose² /ōs/ suffix Chem. forming names of carbohydrates (*cellulose; sucrose*).

OSHA /óshə/ abbr. Occupational Safety and Health Administration.

o·sier /ózhər/ n. willows used in basketwork.

-osis /ósis/ suffix (pl. **-oses** /óseez/) denoting a process or condition (*apotheosis; metamorphosis*), esp. a pathological state (*acidosis; neurosis; thrombosis*).

-osity /ósitee/ suffix forming nouns from adjectives in -ose (see -OSE ¹) and -ous (*verbosity; curiosity*).

os·mi·um /ózmeeəm/ n. Chem. hard, bluish-white element, the heaviest known metal, occurring naturally and used in certain alloys. ¶ Symb.: **Os**.

os·mo·sis /ozmósis, os-/ n. **1** Biochem. passage of a solvent through a semipermeable partition into a more concentrated solution. **2** any process by which something is acquired by absorption. □□ **os·mot·ic** /-mótik/ adj.

os·prey /óspray, -pree/ n. (pl. **-preys**) large bird of prey, with a brown back and white markings, feeding on fish. Also called **fish hawk.**

os·si·fy /ósifī/ v. (**-fies, -fied**) **1** turn into bone; harden. **2** make or become rigid, callous, or unprogressive. □□ **os·si·fi·ca'tion** n.

os·so bu·co /áwsō bōōkō/ n. (also **os'·so buc'co**) shank of veal stewed in wine with vegetables.

os·su·ar·y /óshōōeree, ósyōō-/ n. (pl. **-ies**) receptacle for the bones of the dead.

os·ten·si·ble /osténsibəl/ adj. apparent; professed. □□ **os·ten'·si·bly** adv.

os·ten·sive /osténsiv/ adj. directly demonstrative.

os·ten·ta·tion /óstentáyshən/ n. pretentious display, esp. of wealth and luxury. □□ **os·ten·ta'tious** adj. **os·ten·ta'tious·ly** adv.

osteo- /ósteeō/ comb. form bone.

os·te·o·ar·thri·tis /ósteeōaarthrítis/ n. degenerative disease of joint cartilage. □□ **os·te·o·ar·thrit·ic** /-thrítik/ adj.

os·te·op·a·thy /ósteeópəthee/ n. treatment of disease through manipulation of bones, esp. the spine, displacement of these being the supposed cause. □□ **os·te·o·path** /ósteeəpath/ n.

os·te·o·po·ro·sis /ósteeōpərōsis/ n. condition of brittle bones caused by loss of bony tissue, esp. as a result of hormonal changes, or deficiency of calcium or vitamin D.

os·tra·cize /óstrəsīz/ v.tr. **1** exclude (a person) from a society, favor, common privileges, etc.; refuse to associate with. **2** banish. □□ **os·tra·cism** /-sizəm/ n.

os·trich /óstrich, áw-/ n. **1** large African swift-running flightless bird with long legs and two toes on each foot. **2** person who refuses to accept facts (from the belief that ostriches bury their heads in the sand when pursued).

OT abbr. Old Testament.

o.t. abbr. (also **O.T.**) **1** occupational therapist. **2** occupational therapy. **3** overtime.

OTB abbr. off-track betting.

oth·er /úthər/ • adj. **1** not the same as one or some already mentioned or implied; separate in identity or distinct in kind. **2 a** further; additional. **b** alternative of two (*open your other eye*). • n. or pron. (orig. an ellipt. use of the adj., now with pl. in -s) **1** additional, different, or extra person, thing, example, etc. (see also ANOTHER, *each other*). **2** (in pl.; prec. by *the*) the ones remaining (*where are the others?*). • adv. disp. otherwise (*cannot react other than angrily*). □ **the other day** (or **night** or **week**, etc.) a few days, etc., ago.

oth·er·wise /úthərwīz/ • adv. **1** else; or else; in different circumstances. **2** in other respects (*he is somewhat unkempt, but otherwise very suitable*). **3** in a different way (*could not have acted otherwise*). • adj. (predic.) in a different state (*the matter is quite otherwise*).

oth·er·world·ly /úthərwórldlee/ adj. **1** unworldly; impractical. **2** concerned with life after death, etc.

-otic /ótik/ suffix forming adjectives and nouns corresponding to nouns in -osis, meaning 'affected with or producing or resembling a condition in -osis' or 'a person affected with this' (*narcotic; neurotic; osmotic*). □□ **-o·ti·cal·ly** suffix forming adverbs.

o·ti·ose /ósheeōs, ótee-/ adj. **1** serving no practical purpose; not required. **2** futile.

o·ti·tis /ōtī́tis/ n. inflammation of the ear.

Ot·ta·wa /áatəwə, -waa, -waw/ • n. **1 a** N. American people native to Canada and the Great Lakes region. **b** member of this people. **2** language of this people. • adj. of this people or their language.

ot·ter /ótər/ n. **1** aquatic fish-eating mammal having strong claws and webbed feet. **2** its fur or pelt.

ot·to·man /ótəmən/ *n.* **1** upholstered seat, usu. square and without back or arms. **2** footstool of similar design.

ouch /owch/ *int.* expressing pain or annoyance.

ought /awt/ *v.aux.* (usu. foll. by *to* + infin.; present and past indicated by the following infin.) **1** expressing duty or rightness (*we ought to love our neighbors*). **2** expressing advisability or prudence (*you ought to go for your own good*). **3** expressing esp. strong probability (*he ought to be there by now*).

Oui·ja /wéejə, -jee/ *n.* (in full **Oui′ja board**) *propr.* board game purporting to give advice, etc.

ounce /owns/ *n.* **1 a** unit of weight of one-sixteenth of a pound avoirdupois. ¶ Abbr.: **oz.** **b** unit of one-twelfth of a pound troy. **2** small quantity. □ **fluid ounce** unit of capacity equal to one-sixteenth of a pint.

our /owr, aar/ *poss.pron.* (*attrib.*) **1** of or belonging to us or ourselves (*our house; our own business*). **2** of or belonging to all people (*our children's future*).

ours /owrz, aars/ *poss.pron.* the one or ones belonging to or associated with us (*it is ours; ours are over there*).

our·selves /owrsélvz, aar-/ *pron.* **1 a** *emphat.* form of WE or US (*we ourselves did it; made it ourselves*). **b** *refl.* form of US (*are pleased with ourselves*). **2** in our normal state of body or mind (*not quite ourselves today*).

-ous /əs/ *suffix* forming adjectives meaning 'abounding in, characterized by, of the nature of' (*envious; glorious; mountainous; poisonous*). □□ **-ous·ly** *suffix* forming adverbs. **-ous·ness** *suffix* forming nouns.

oust /owst/ *v.tr.* **1** drive out or expel, esp. by forcing oneself into the place of. **2** dispossess.

oust·er /ówstər/ *n.* **1** ejection as a result of physical action, judicial process, or political upheaval. **2** expulsion.

out /owt/ ● *adv.* **1** away from or not in or at a place, etc. (*keep him out*). **2** (forming part of phrasal verbs) indicating **a** dispersal away from a center, etc. (*hire out*). **b** coming or bringing into the open (*stand out*). **c** need for attentiveness (*look out*). **3 a** not in one's house, office, etc. **b** no longer in prison. **4** to or at an end; completely (*out of bananas*). **5** (of a fire, candle, etc.) not burning. **6** *colloq.* unconscious. **7** (of a party, politician, etc.) not in office. **8** unfashionable. **9** *Sports* (of a batter, base runner, etc.) no longer taking part as such, having been tagged, struck out, caught, etc. **10 a** not worth considering; rejected. **b** not allowed. **11** (of a stain, mark, etc.) not visible; removed. ● *prep.* out of (*looked out the window*). ● *n.* **1** *colloq.* way of escape; excuse. **2** *Baseball* play in which a batter or base runner is retired from an inning. ● *v.* **1** *intr.* come or go out; emerge. **2** *tr. colloq.* expose the homosexuality of (esp. a prominent person). □ **out-and-out** *adj.* thorough; surpassing. ● *adv.* thoroughly; surpassingly. **out for** having one's interest or effort directed to; intent on. **out of 1** from within (*came out of the house*). **2** not within (*I was never out of the city*). **3** from among (*nine people out of ten*). **4** beyond the range of. **5** without or so as to be without (*out of sugar*). **6** from (*get money out of him*). **7** owing to; because of (*asked out of curiosity*). **8** by the use of (material) (*what did you make it out of?*). **9** at a specified distance from (a town, port, etc.) (*seven miles out of Topeka*). **10** beyond

(*something out of the ordinary*). **out to** keenly striving to do.

out- /owt/ *prefix* added to verbs and nouns, meaning: **1** so as to surpass or exceed (*outdo; outnumber*). **2** external; separate (*outline; outhouse*). **3** out of; away from; outward (*outgrowth*).

out·age /ówtij/ *n.* period of time during which a power supply, etc., is not operating.

out·back /ówtbak/ *n.* esp. *Austral.* remote and usu. uninhabited inland districts.

out·bal·ance /ówtbáləns/ *v.tr.* outweigh.

out·board /ówtbawrd/ ● *adj.* **1** (of a motor) attachable to the outside of a boat. **2** (of a boat) having an outboard motor. ● *n.* **1** outboard engine. **2** boat with an outboard engine.

out·break /ówtbrayk/ *n.* **1** sudden eruption of war, disease, rebellion, etc. **2** outcrop.

out·build·ing /ówtbilding/ *n.* detached shed, barn, etc., within the grounds of a main building.

out·burst /ówtbərst/ *n.* **1** verbal explosion of anger, etc. **2** bursting out.

out·cast /ówtkast/ ● *n.* person rejected by his or her home, country, society, etc. ● *adj.* rejected; homeless; friendless.

out·class /ówtklás/ *v.tr.* **1** surpass in quality. **2** defeat easily.

out·come /ówtkum/ *n.* result; visible effect.

out·crop /ówtkrop/ *n.* **1 a** emergence of a stratum, etc., at the surface. **b** stratum, etc., emerging. **2** noticeable manifestation.

out·cry /ówtkrī/ *n.* (*pl.* **-cries**) strong public protest.

out·dat·ed /ówtdáytid/ *adj.* out of date; obsolete.

out·dis·tance /ówtdístəns/ *v.tr.* leave (a competitor) behind completely.

out·do /ówtdóo/ *v.tr.* (*3rd sing. present* **-does**; *past* **-did**; *past part.* **-done**) exceed or excel; surpass.

out·door /ówtdawr/ *adj.* done, existing, or used out of doors.

out·doors /owtdáwrz/ ● *adv.* in or into the open air. ● *n.* the world outside buildings; open air.

out·er /ówtər/ *adj.* **1** outside; external (*pierced the outer layer*). **2** farther from the center or inside. □ **outer space** universe beyond the earth's atmosphere. □□ **out′er·most** *adj.*

out·field /ówtfeeld/ *n.* outer part of a playing area, esp. a baseball field. □□ **out′field·er** *n.*

out·fit /ówtfit/ ● *n.* **1** set of clothes esp. designed to be worn together. **2** set of equipment, etc. **3** *colloq.* group of people regarded as a unit, etc.; team. ● *v.tr.* (also *refl.*) (**-fit·ted**, **-fit·ting**) provide with an outfit, esp. of clothes.

out·fit·ter /ówtfitər/ *n.* **1** business that supplies outdoor equipment, arranges tours, etc. **2** retailer of men's clothing.

out·flank /ówtflángk/ *v.tr.* **1 a** extend one's flank beyond that of (an enemy). **b** outmaneuver (an enemy) in this way. **2** get the better of; confound (an opponent).

out·fox /ówtfóks/ *v.tr. colloq.* outwit.

out·go·ing /ówtgóing/ *adj.* **1** friendly. **2** retiring from office. **3** going out or away.

out·grow /ówtgró/ *v.tr.* (*past* **-grew**; *past part.* **-grown**) **1** grow too big for. **2** leave behind (a childish habit, etc.). **3** grow faster or taller than.

out·growth /ówtgrōth/ *n.* **1** offshoot; natural product. **2** the process of growing out.

out·house /ówt-hows/ *n.* **1** outbuilding used as a toilet, usu. with no plumbing. **2** building, esp. a shed, etc., built next to or on the grounds of a house.

out·ing /ówting/ *n.* pleasure trip; excursion.

out·land·ish /owtlándish/ *adj.* bizarre; strange; unfamiliar. □□ **out·land′ish·ly** *adv.* **out·land′ish·ness** *n.*

out·last /ówtlást/ *v.tr.* last longer than.

out·law /ówtlaw/ • *n.* **1** fugitive from the law. **2** *hist.* person denied protection of the law. • *v.tr.* declare or make illegal.

out·lay /ówtlay/ *n.* what is spent on something.

out·let /ówtlet, -lit/ *n.* **1** means of exit or escape. **2** means of expression (of a talent, emotion, etc.). **3** agency, distributor, or market for goods (*a new retail outlet in China*). **4** electrical power receptacle.

out·line /ówtlīn/ • *n.* **1** rough draft of a diagram, plan, proposal, etc. **2** summary of main features. **3** sketch containing only contour lines. **4** (in *sing.* or *pl.*) lines enclosing or indicating an object. • *v.tr.* **1** draw or describe in outline. **2** mark the outline of.

out·live /ówtlív/ *v.tr.* **1** live longer than (another person). **2** live beyond (a specified date or time).

out·look /ówtlŏŏk/ *n.* **1** prospect for the future. **2** mental attitude.

out·ly·ing /ówtlī-ing/ *adj.* situated far from a center; remote.

out·ma·neu·ver /ówtmənŏ́ŏvər/ *v.tr.* **1** use skill and cunning to secure an advantage over (a person). **2** outdo in maneuvering.

out·mod·ed /ówtmódid/ *adj.* **1** out of fashion. **2** obsolete.

out·pa·tient /ówtpayshənt/ *n.* hospital patient whose treatment does not require overnight hospitalization.

out·place·ment /ówtplaysmənt/ *n.* assistance in finding new employment for workers who have been dismissed.

out·post /ówtpōst/ *n.* **1** detachment set at a distance from the main body of an army, esp. to prevent surprise. **2** distant branch or settlement.

out·put /ówtpŏŏt/ • *n.* **1** product of a process, esp. of manufacture, or of mental or artistic work. **2** quantity or amount of this. **3** printout, results, etc., supplied by a computer. **4** power, etc., delivered by an apparatus. • *v.tr.* (**-put·ting**; *past* and *past part.* **-put** or **-put·ted**) **1** put or send out. **2** (of a computer) supply (results, etc.).

out·rage /ówt-rayj/ • *n.* **1** extreme violation of others' rights, sentiments, etc. **2** gross offense or indignity. **3** fierce resentment. • *v.tr.* **1** subject to outrage. **2** injure, insult, etc., flagrantly.

out·ra·geous /owt-ráyjəs/ *adj.* **1** shocking. **2** grossly cruel. **3** immoral; offensive. □□ **out·ra′geous·ly** *adv.*

ou·tré /ŏŏtráy/ *adj.* unconventional; eccentric.

out·rid·er /ówt-rīdər/ *n.* mounted rider ahead of, or with, a procession, etc.

out·rig·ger /ówt-rigər/ *n.* **1** beam, spar, or framework, rigged out and projecting from or over the side of a boat or canoe to give stability. **2** boat fitted with this.

OUTRIGGER

out·right • *adv.* /owt-rī́t/ **1** altogether; entirely (*proved outright*). **2** without reservation; openly. • *adj.* /ówt-rīt/ **1** downright; direct; complete. **2** undisputed; clear. □□ **out′right·ness** *n.*

out·run /ówt-rún/ *v.tr.* (**-run·ning**; *past* **-ran**; *past part.* **-run**) **1** run faster or farther than. **2** go beyond.

out·sell /ówtsél/ *v.tr.* (*past* and *past part.* **-sold**) **1** sell more than. **2** be sold in greater quantities than.

out·set /ówtset/ *n.* start; beginning.

out·shine /ówtshín/ *v.tr.* (*past* and *past part.* **-shone**) shine brighter than; surpass in ability, excellence, etc.

out·side • *n.* /ówtsíd/ **1** external side or surface; outer parts. **2** external appearance; outward aspect. • *adj.* /ówtsíd/ **1** of, on, or nearer the outside; outer. **2 a** not belonging (*outside help*). **b** not a part of. **3** (of a chance, etc.) remote; very unlikely. **4** (of an estimate, etc.) greatest or highest possible. **5** *Baseball* (of a pitched ball) missing the strike zone by passing home plate on the side away from the batter. • *adv.* /ówtsíd/ **1** on or to the outside. **2** in or to the open air. **3** not within or enclosed or included. • *prep.* /ówtsíd/ **1** not in; to or at the exterior of. **2** external to; not included in; beyond the limits of (*outside the law*).

out·sid·er /ówtsídər/ *n.* **1** nonmember of some circle, party, profession, etc. **2** competitor, applicant, etc., thought to have little chance of success.

out·size /ówtsīz/ *adj.* unusually large.

out·skirts /ówtskərts/ *n.pl.* outer area of a town, etc.

out·smart /ówtsmaart/ *v.tr.* *colloq.* outwit; be cleverer than.

out·spo·ken /ówtspókən/ *adj.* frank in stating one's opinions. □□ **out·spo′ken·ly** *adv.* **out·spo′ken·ness** *n.*

out·spread /ówtspréd/ *adj.* spread out; extended or expanded.

out·stand·ing /ówtstánding/ *adj.* **1 a** conspicuous; eminent, esp. because of excellence. **b** (usu. foll. by *at*, *in*) remarkable in (a specified field). **2** (esp. of a debt) not yet settled (*$200 still outstanding*). □□ **out·stand′ing·ly** *adv.*

out·sta·tion /ówtstayshən/ *n.* remote branch or outpost.

out·strip /ówtstríp/ *v.tr.* (**-stripped**, **-strip·ping**) **1** pass in running, etc. **2** surpass, esp. competitively.

out·take /ówt-tayk/ *n.* length of film or tape rejected in editing.

out·vote /ówtvốt/ v.tr. defeat by a majority of votes.

out·ward /ówt-wǝrd/ • adj. 1 situated on or directed toward the outside. 2 going out. 3 bodily; external; apparent. • adv. (also **out'wards**) in an outward direction. • n. outward appearance of something; exterior. □□ **out'ward·ly** adv.

out·wear /ówt-wáir/ v.tr. (past **-wore**; past part. **-worn**) 1 exhaust; wear out; wear away. 2 live or last beyond the duration of. 3 (as **outworn** adj.) out of date; obsolete.

out·weigh /ówt-wáy/ v.tr. exceed in weight, value, importance, or influence.

out·wit /ówt-wít/ v.tr. (**-wit·ted**, **-wit·ting**) be too clever or crafty for; deceive by greater ingenuity.

o·va pl. of OVUM.

o·val /óvǝl/ • adj. 1 egg-shaped; ellipsoidal. 2 having the outline of an egg; elliptical. • n. egg-shaped or elliptical closed curve.

o·va·ry /óvǝree/ n. (pl. **-ries**) 1 each of the female reproductive organs in which ova are produced. 2 hollow base of the carpel of a flower, containing one or more ovules. □□ **o·var·i·an** /ōváireeǝn/ adj.

o·va·tion /ōváyshǝn/ n. enthusiastic reception, esp. spontaneous and sustained applause.

ov·en /úvǝn/ n. 1 enclosed compartment of brick, stone, or metal for cooking food. 2 chamber for heating or drying.

o·ver /óvǝr/ • adv. expressing movement or position or state above or beyond something stated or implied: 1 outward and downward from a brink or an erect position (knocked the man over). 2 so as to cover or touch a whole surface (paint it over). 3 so as to produce a fold, or reverse a position. 4 a across a street or other space (came over from England). b for a visit, etc. (invited them over). 5 with change from one hand or part to another (went over to the enemy). 6 with motion above something; so as to pass across something (climb over). 7 a from beginning to end (think it over). b again. 8 in excess; more than is right or required. 9 for or until a later time. 10 at an end; settled. • prep. 1 above, in, or to a position higher than; upon. 2 out and down from; down from the edge of. 3 so as to cover (a hat over his eyes). 4 above and across (flew over the North Pole). 5 concerning; while occupied with (laughed over a good joke). 6 a superior to; in charge of. b in preference to. 7 so as to deal with completely (went over the plans). 8 during. 9 beyond; more than. □ **over against** in an opposite situation to; adjacent to, in contrast with. **over and over** repeatedly. **over-the-counter** 1 (of medicine) sold without a prescription. 2 (of stocks, etc.) not

listed on or traded by an organized securities exchange. **over-the-top** colloq. excessive.

---

over Old English ofer, of Germanic origin; related to Dutch over and German über, from an Indo-European word (originally a comparative of the word element represented by -ove in above) that is also the base of Latin super and Greek huper.

---

over- /óvǝr/ prefix added to verbs, nouns, adjectives, and adverbs, meaning: 1 excessively (overheat; overdue). 2 upper; outer; extra (overcoat; overtime). 3 'over' in various senses (overhang; overshadow). 4 completely; utterly (overawe; overjoyed).

over·a·chieve /óvǝrǝcheev/ v. 1 intr. do more than might be expected (esp. scholastically). 2 tr. achieve more than (an expected goal or objective, etc.). □□ **o·ver·a·chieve'ment** n. **o·ver·a·chiev'er** n.

o·ver·act /óvǝrákt/ v. act in an exaggerated manner.

o·ver·all • adj. /óvǝrawl/ 1 from end to end. 2 total; inclusive of all. • adv. /óvǝráwl/ in all parts; taken as a whole. • n. /óvǝrawl/ (in pl.) protective trousers, dungarees, or a combination suit, worn by workmen, etc.

o·ver·arm /óvǝraarm/ adj. & adv. done or made with the arm above the shoulder (pitch it overarm).

o·ver·awe /óvǝr-áw/ v.tr. overcome with awe.

o·ver·bal·ance /óvǝrbálǝns/ v. 1 tr. outweigh. 2 intr. fall over.

o·ver·bear·ing /óvǝrbéring/ adj. 1 domineering; masterful. 2 overpowering.

o·ver·bite /óvǝrbīt/ n. condition in which the teeth of the upper jaw project forward over those of the lower jaw.

o·ver·blown /óvǝrblón/ adj. excessively inflated or pretentious.

o·ver·board /óvǝrbáwrd/ adv. from a ship into the water (fall overboard). □ **go overboard** behave immoderately; go too far.

o·ver·book /óvǝrbŏŏk/ v.tr. (also absol.) make too many bookings for (an aircraft, hotel, etc.).

o·ver·come past of OVERCOME.

o·ver·cast /óvǝrkást/ adj. 1 (of the sky, weather, etc.) covered with cloud; dull and gloomy. 2 (in sewing) edged with stitching to prevent fraying.

o·ver·charge /óvǝrchaárj/ • v.tr. 1 charge too high a price to (a person) or for (a thing). 2

---

o'ver·a·bun'dance n.	o·ver·eat' v.	o'ver·full' adj.	o·ver·sell' v.
o'ver·a·bun'dant adj.	o·ver·em'pha·size· v.	o'ver·gen'er·ous adj.	o'ver·sen'si·tive adj.
o'ver·act'ive adj.	o·ver·en·thu'si·asm n.	o·ver·heat' v.	o'ver·sen'si·tive·ness n.
o·ver·anx'ious adj.	o·ver·en·thu·si·as'tic adj.	o'ver·in·dulge' v.	o'ver·sen·si·tiv'i·ty n.
o·ver·bur'den v.	o·ver·en·thu·si·as'ti·cal·ly adv.	o'ver·in·dul'gence n.	o·ver·spend' v.
o'ver·cau'tious adj.		o'ver·in·dul'gent adj.	o·ver·spill' n. & v.
o'ver·con'fi·dence n.	o·ver·ex·cite' v.	o·ver·in·flate' v.	o·ver·spread' v.
o'ver·con'fi·dent adj.	o'ver·ex·cite'ment n.	o·ver·in·fla'tion n.	o·ver·stim'u·late· v.
o·ver·cook' v.	o·ver·ex·ert' v.	o·ver·par·tic··lar adj.	o·ver·stock' v.
o'ver·crit'i·cal adj.	o'ver·ex·er'tion n.	o·ver·pay' v.	o·ver·sup·ply' v.
o·ver·crowd' v.	o·ver·ex·tend' v.	o·ver·pro·tec'tive adj.	o·ver·tire' v.
o·ver·crowd'ed adj.	o'ver·fa·mil'iar adj.	o·ver·re·fined' v.	o·ver·wind' v.
o·ver·crowd'ing n.	o·ver·feed' v.		
o'ver·ea'ger adj.	o'ver·fond' adj.	o'ver·ripe' adj.	

put exaggerated or excessive detail into (a description, picture, etc.). ● *n.* excessive charge (of explosive, money, etc.).

o·ver·coat /ōvərkōt/ *n.* **1** heavy coat, esp. one worn over indoor clothes for warmth outdoors in cold weather. **2** protective coat of paint, etc.

o·ver·come /ōvərkúm/ *v.* (*past* **-came**; *past part.* **-come**) **1** *tr.* prevail over; master. **2** *tr.* (as **overcome** *adj.*) **a** exhausted; made helpless. **b** (usu. foll. by *with*, *by*) affected by (emotion, etc.). **3** *intr.* be victorious.

o·ver·de·vel·op /ōvərdivélǝp/ *v.tr.* **1** develop too much. **2** *Photog.* treat with developer for too long.

o·ver·do /ōvərdōo/ *v.tr.* (*3rd sing. present* **-does**; *past* **-did**; *past part.* **-done**) **1** carry to excess; take too far (*I think you overdid the sarcasm*). **2** (esp. as **overdone** *adj.*) overcook. □ **overdo it** (or **things**) exhaust oneself.

o·ver·dose /ōvərdōs/ ● *n.* excessive dose (of a drug, etc.). ● *v.* **1** *tr.* give an excessive dose of (a drug, etc.) or to (a person). **2** *intr.* take an excessive dose of (a drug, etc.). **3** *sl.* (usu. foll. by *on*) have or experience an excessive amount of (*we overdosed on movies this weekend*).

o·ver·draft /ōvərdraft/ *n.* **1** deficit in a bank account caused by drawing more money than is credited to it. **2** amount of this.

o·ver·draw /ōvərdráw/ *v.* (*past* **-drew**; *past part.* **-drawn**) **1** *tr.* draw a sum of money in excess of the amount credited to (one's bank account). **2** *intr.* overdraw one's account.

o·ver·drive /ōvərdrīv/ *n.* **1** mechanism in a motor vehicle providing a gear ratio higher than that of the usual gear. **2** state of high activity.

o·ver·dub ● *v.tr.* /ōvərdúb/ (**-dubbed**, **-dub·bing**) (also *absol.*) impose (additional sounds) on an existing recording. ● *n.* /ōvərdub/ overdubbing.

o·ver·due /ōvərdōo, -dyōo/ *adj.* past the time due for payment, arrival, return, etc.

o·ver·es·ti·mate ● *v.tr.* (also *absol.*) /ōvəréstimayt/ form too high an estimate of (a person, ability, cost, etc.). ● *n.* /ōvəréstimit/ too high an estimate. □□ **o·ver·es·ti·ma·tion** /-áyshǝn/ *n.*

o·ver·ex·pose /ōvərikspóz/ *v.tr.* (also *absol.*) **1** expose too much, esp. to the public eye. **2** *Photog.* expose (film) too long. □□ **o·ver·ex·po·sure** /-spózhǝr/ *n.*

o·ver·flow ● *v.* /ōvərflō/ **1** *tr.* flow over (the brim, limits, etc.). **2** *intr.* **a** (of a receptacle, etc.) be so full that the contents overflow it. **b** (of contents) overflow a container. **3** *tr.* (of a crowd, etc.) extend beyond the limits of (a room, etc.). **4** *tr.* flood (a surface or area). **5** *intr.* (of kindness, a harvest, etc.) be very abundant. ● *n.* /ōvərflō/ (also *attrib.*) **1** what overflows or is superfluous. **2** outlet for excess water, etc.

o·ver·grown /ōvərgrón/ *adj.* **1** abnormally large (*overgrown eggplant*). **2** wild; grown over with vegetation (*overgrown pond*).

o·ver·hand /ōvərhand/ *adj. & adv.* **1** (in tennis, baseball, etc.) thrown or played with the hand above the shoulder; overarm. **2** *Swimming* = OVERARM.

o·ver·hang ● *v.* /ōvərháng/ (*past and past part.* **-hung**) project or hang over. ● *n.* /ōvərhang/ **1** overhanging part of a structure or rock formation. **2** amount by which this projects.

o·ver·haul ● *v.tr.* /ōvərháwl/ **1** thoroughly examine and repair as necessary. **2** overtake. ● *n.* /ōvərhawl/ thorough examination, with repairs if necessary.

o·ver·head ● *adv.* /ōvərhéd/ **1** above one's head. **2** in the sky or on the floor above. ● *adj.* /ōvərhed/ **1** placed overhead. **2** (of expenses) arising from general operating costs. ● *n.* /ōvərhed/ overhead expenses.

o·ver·hear /ōvərhéer/ *v.tr.* (*past and past part.* **-heard**) (also *absol.*) hear as an eavesdropper or unintentionally.

o·ver·joyed /ōvərjóyd/ *adj.* filled with great joy.

o·ver·kill /ōvərkil/ ● *n.* **1** amount by which the capacity for destruction exceeds what is necessary for victory or annihilation. **2** excess. ● *v.* kill or destroy to a greater extent than necessary.

o·ver·land /ōvərland, -lənd/ *adj. & adv.* by land.

o·ver·lap ● *v.* /ōvərláp/ (**-lapped**, **-lap·ping**) **1** *tr.* partly cover (another object). **2** *tr.* cover and extend beyond. **3** *intr.* (of two things) partly coincide (*where psychology and philosophy overlap*). ● *n.* /ōvərlap/ **1** extension over. **2** amount of this.

o·ver·lay ● *v.tr.* /ōvərláy/ (*past and past part.* **-laid**) **1** lay over. **2** (foll. by *with*) cover the surface of (a thing) with (a coating, etc.). ● *n.* /ōvərlay/ **1** thing laid over another. **2** (in printing, map reading, etc.) transparent sheet superimposed on another.

o·ver·leaf /ōvərleéf/ *adv.* on the other side of the leaf (of a book).

o·ver·look ● *v.tr.* /ōvərlŏok/ **1** fail to notice; ignore, condone (an offense, etc.). **2** have a view from above. **3** supervise. ● *n.* /óvərlŏok/ commanding position or view.

o·ver·lord /ōvərlawrd/ *n.* supreme lord.

o·ver·ly /ōvərlee/ *adv.* excessively; too.

o·ver·mas·ter /ōvərmástər/ *v.tr.* master completely; conquer.

o·ver·much /ōvərmúch/ ● *adv.* to too great an extent. ● *adj.* excessive.

o·ver·night ● *adv.* /ōvərnít/ **1** for a night. **2** during a night. **3** suddenly; immediately. ● *adj.* /ōvərnīt/ **1** for use overnight (*overnight bag*). **2** done, etc., overnight.

o·ver·pass /ōvərpas/ *n.* road or railroad line that passes over another by means of a bridge.

o·ver·play /ōvərpláy/ *v.tr.* give undue importance to; overemphasize. □ **overplay one's hand** be unduly optimistic about one's capabilities.

o·ver·pop·u·lat·ed /ōvərpópyǝlaytid/ *adj.* having too large a population. □□ **o·ver·pop·u·la·tion** /-láyshǝn/ *n.*

o·ver·pow·er /ōvərpówr/ *v.tr.* **1** subdue. **2** (of heat, emotion, etc.) be too intense for; overwhelm. □□ **o·ver·pow'er·ing** *adj.* **o·ver·pow'er·ing·ly** *adv.*

o·ver·price /ōvərprís/ *v.tr.* price (a thing) too highly.

o·ver·print ● *v.tr.* /ōvərprínt/ **1** print further matter on (a surface already printed, esp. a postage stamp). **2** (also *absol.*) print too many copies of (a work). ● *n.* /ōvərprint/ **1** words, etc., overprinted. **2** overprinted postage stamp.

o·ver·pro·duce /ōvərprǝdōos, -dyōos/ *v.tr.* (usu. *absol.*) **1** produce more of (a commodity) than is wanted. **2** produce to an excessive degree. □□ **o·ver·pro·duc·tion** /-dúkshǝn/ *n.*

o·ver·qual·i·fied /ōvərkwólifīd/ *adj.* too highly qualified (esp. for a particular job, etc.).

o·ver·rate /ōvəráyt/ *v.tr.* assess too highly.

o·ver·reach /ōvəreéch/ *v.tr.* outwit; get the better of by cunning or artifice. □ **overreach oneself** strain oneself or fail by attempting too much.

o·ver·re·act /ōvəreeákt/ *v.intr.* respond more forcibly, etc., than is justified. □□ **o·ver·re·ac·tion** /-ákshən/ *n.*

o·ver·ride ● *v.tr.* /ōvərīd/ (*past* **-rode**; *past part.* **-rid·den**) 1 (often as **overriding** *adj.*) have or claim precedence or superiority over (*an overriding consideration*). 2 a intervene and make ineffective. b interrupt the action of (an automatic device), esp. to take manual control. ● *n.* /ōvərīd/ 1 suspension of an automatic function. 2 device for this.

o·ver·rule /ōvərōōl/ *v.tr.* set aside (a decision, etc.) by exercising a superior authority.

o·ver·run ● *v.tr.* /ōvərún/ (**-run·ning**; *past* **-ran**; *past part.* **-run**) 1 (of pests, weeds, etc.) swarm or spread over. 2 conquer or ravage (territory) by force. 3 (of time, expenditure, etc.) exceed (a fixed limit). ● *n.* /ōvərun/ excess of produced items.

o·ver·seas ● *adv.* /ōvərseéz/ abroad (*was sent overseas for training*). ● *adj.* /ōvərseez/ foreign.

o·ver·see /ōvərseé/ *v.tr.* (**-sees**; *past* **-saw**; *past part.* **-seen**) officially supervise (workers, work, etc.). □□ **o'ver·se·er** *n.*

o·ver·shad·ow /ōvərshádō/ *v.tr.* 1 appear much more prominent or important than. 2 shelter from the sun.

o·ver·shoe /ōvərshōō/ *n.* shoe of rubber, etc., worn over another as protection from wet, cold, etc.

o·ver·shoot /ōvərshōōt/ *v.tr.* (*past* and *past part.* **-shot**) 1 pass or send beyond (a target or limit). 2 (of an aircraft) fly or taxi beyond (the runway) when landing or taking off.

o·ver·sight /ōvərsīt/ *n.* 1 failure to notice something. 2 inadvertent mistake. 3 supervision.

o·ver·sim·pli·fy /ōvərsímplifī/ *v.tr.* (**-fies**, **-fied**) (also *absol.*) distort (a problem, etc.) by stating it in too simple terms. □□ **o·ver·sim·pli·fi·ca'tion** *n.*

o·ver·size /ōvərsīz/ *adj.* (also **-sized** /-sīzd/) of greater than the usual size.

o·ver·sleep /ōvərsleép/ *v.intr.* & *refl.* (*past* and *past part.* **-slept**) sleep beyond the intended time of waking.

o·ver·spe·cial·ize /ōvərspéshəlīz/ *v.intr.* concentrate too much on one aspect or area. □□ **o·ver·spe·cial·i·za'tion** *n.*

o·ver·state /ōvərstáyt/ *v.tr.* 1 state (esp. a case or argument) too strongly. 2 exaggerate. □□ **o·ver·state'ment** *n.*

o·ver·stay /ōvərstáy/ *v.tr.* stay longer than (one's welcome, a time limit, etc.).

o·ver·steer /ōvərsteér/ ● *v.intr.* (of a motor vehicle) tend to turn more sharply than was intended. ● *n.* this tendency.

o·ver·step /ōvərstép/ *v.tr.* (**-stepped**, **-step·ping**) 1 pass beyond (a boundary or mark). 2 violate (certain standards of behavior, etc.).

o·ver·strung *adj.* /ōvərstrúng/ (of a person, disposition, etc.) intensely strained; highly strung.

o·ver·stuff /ōvərstúf/ *v.tr.* 1 stuff more than is necessary. 2 (as **overstuffed** *adj.*) (of furniture) made soft and comfortable by thick upholstery.

o·vert /ōvərt, ōvərt/ *adj.* unconcealed; done openly. □□ **o·vert'ly** *adv.*

o·ver·take /ōvərtáyk/ *v.tr.* (*past* **-took**; *past part.* **-tak·en**) 1 catch up with and pass. 2 (of a storm, misfortune, etc.) come suddenly upon.

o·ver·tax /ōvərtáks/ *v.tr.* 1 make excessive demands on (a person's strength, etc.). 2 tax too heavily.

o·ver·throw ● *v.tr.* /ōvərthrō/ (*past* **-threw**; *past part.* **-thrown**) 1 remove forcibly from power. 2 conquer; overcome. 3 *Baseball* a (of a fielder) throw beyond the intended place. b (of a pitcher) throw too vigorously. ● *n.* /ōvərthrō/ defeat or downfall.

o·ver·time /ōvərtīm/ ● *n.* 1 time worked in addition to regular hours. 2 payment for this. 3 *Sports* additional period of play at the end of a game when the scores are equal. ● *adv.* in addition to regular hours.

o·ver·tone /ōvərtōn/ *n.* 1 *Mus.* any tones above the lowest in a harmonic series. 2 subtle quality or implication (*sinister overtones*).

o·ver·ture /ōvərchər, -chōōr/ *n.* 1 orchestral piece opening an opera, etc. 2 (usu. in *pl.*) a opening of negotiations. b formal proposal or offer (esp. *make overtures to*).

o·ver·turn /ōvərtərn/ *v.* 1 *tr.* cause to turn over; upset. 2 *tr.* reverse; subvert. 3 *intr.* turn over; fall over.

o·ver·use ● *v.tr.* /ōvəryōōz/ use too much. ● *n.* /ōvəryōōs/ excessive use.

o·ver·view /ōvərvyōō/ *n.* general survey.

o·ver·weight /ōvərwáyt/ *adj.* beyond an allowed or suitable weight.

o·ver·whelm /ōvərhwélm, -wélm/ *v.tr.* 1 overpower with emotion. 2 overpower with an excess of business, etc. 3 bury or drown beneath a huge mass; submerge utterly. □□ **o·ver·whelm'ing** *adj.*

o·ver·work /ōvərwərk/ ● *v.* 1 *intr.* work too hard. 2 *tr.* cause (another person) to work too hard. 3 *tr.* weary or exhaust with too much work. 4 *tr.* make excessive use of. ● *n.* excessive work.

o·ver·wrought /ōvəráwt/ *adj.* 1 overexcited; nervous; distraught. 2 too elaborate.

ovi- /ōvee/ *comb. form* egg, ovum.

o·vi·duct /ōvidukt/ *n.* tube through which an ovum passes from the ovary.

o·vine /ōvīn/ *adj.* of or like sheep.

o·vip·a·rous /ōvípərəs/ *adj.* *Zool.* producing young from eggs expelled from the body before they are hatched (cf. VIVIPAROUS).

o·void /ōvoyd/ ● *adj.* (of a solid or of a surface) egg-shaped. ● *n.* ovoid body or surface.

o·vo·vi·vip·a·rous /ōvōvīvípərəs/ *adj.* *Zool.* producing young by means of eggs hatched within the body (cf. OVIPAROUS, VIVIPAROUS). □□ **o·vo·vi·vi·par·i·ty** /-páritee/ *n.*

ov·u·late /ōvyəlayt, óvyə-/ *v.intr.* produce ova or ovules, or discharge them from the ovary. □□ **ov·u·la·tion** /-láyshən/ *n.*

ov·ule /áavyōōl, ōvyōōl/ *n.* part of the ovary of seed plants that contains the germ cell; unfertilized seed. □□ **ov'u·lar** *adj.*

o·vum /ōvəm/ *n.* (*pl.* **o·va** /ōvə/) 1 mature reproductive cell of female animals, produced by the ovary. 2 egg cell of plants.

ow /ow/ *int.* expressing sudden pain.

owe /ō/ *v.tr.* 1 a be under obligation. b (*absol.*,

usu. foll. by *for*) be in debt (*still owe for my car*). **2** (often foll. by *to*) be under obligation to render (gratitude, honor, etc.) (*owe grateful thanks to*). **3** (usu. foll. by *to*) be indebted to a person or thing for (*we owe to Newton the principle of gravitation*).

ow·ing /ṓ-ing/ *predic. adj.* **1** owed; yet to be paid (*the balance owing*). **2** (foll. by *to*) **a** caused by (*the cancellation was owing to ill health*). **b** (as *prep.*) because of (*delayed owing to bad weather*).

owl /owl/ *n.* **1** nocturnal bird of prey with large eyes and a hooked beak. **2** *colloq.* person compared to an owl, esp. in looking solemn or wise. □□ **owl'ish** *adj.*

owl·et /ówlit/ *n.* small or young owl.

own /ōn/ ● *adj.* (prec. by possessive) **1** belonging to oneself or itself. **2** individual; peculiar; particular. ● *v.* **1** *tr.* have as property; possess. **2 a** *tr.* confess; admit as valid, true, etc. (*owns he did not know*). **b** *intr.* (foll. by *up to*) confess to (*owned up to a prejudice*). **3** *tr.* acknowledge. □ **hold one's own** maintain one's position; not be defeated or lose strength. **on one's own 1** alone. **2** independently, without help. □□ **-owned** *adj.* (in *comb.*). **own'er** *n.* **own'er·ship** *n.*

ox /oks/ *n.* (*pl.* **ox·en** /óksən/) **1** large usu. horned domesticated ruminant used for draft, for supplying milk, and for eating as meat. **2** castrated male of a domesticated species of cattle.

ox·bow /óksbō/ *n.* **1** U-shaped collar of an ox yoke. **2** loop formed by a horseshoe bend in a river.

ox·ford /óksfərd/ *n.* **1** low-heeled shoe that laces over the instep. **2** cotton fabric made in a basket weave, used for shirts and sportswear.

ox·ide /óksīd/ *n.* binary compound of oxygen.

ox·i·dize /óksidīz/ *v.* **1** combine or cause to combine with oxygen. **2** cover (metal) or (of metal) become covered with a coating of oxide; make or become rusty. □□ **ox·i·di·za'tion** *n.* **ox'i·diz·er** *n.*

ox·y·a·cet·y·lene /ókseeəsét'leen/ *adj.* of or using a mixture of oxygen and acetylene, esp. in cutting or welding metals.

ox·y·gen /óksijən/ *n. Chem.* colorless, tasteless, odorless gaseous element, occurring naturally in air, water, and most minerals and organic substances, and essential to plant and animal life. ¶ Symb.: **O**. □ **oxygen tent** tentlike enclosure supplying a patient with air rich in oxygen.

ox·y·gen·ate /óksijənayt/ *v. tr.* **1** supply, treat, or mix with oxygen; oxidize. **2** charge (blood) with oxygen by respiration. □□ **ox·y·gen·a·tion** /-náyshən/ *n.*

ox·y·mo·ron /ókseemáwron/ *n. rhet.* figure of speech in which apparently contradictory terms appear in conjunction (e.g., *faith unfaithful kept him falsely true*).

oys·ter /óystər/ *n.* **1** bivalve mollusk, esp. edible kinds, sometimes producing a pearl. **2** something regarded as containing all that one desires (*the world is my oyster*). **3** (in full **oys·ter white**) white color with a gray tinge.

oz. *abbr.* ounce(s).

o·zone /ózōn/ *n.* **1** *Chem.* colorless unstable gas with a pungent odor and powerful oxidizing properties, used for bleaching, etc. ¶ *Chem.* formula: O₃. **2** *colloq.* **a** invigorating air at the seaside, etc. **b** exhilarating influence. □ **ozone-friendly** (of manufactured articles) containing chemicals that are not destructive to the ozone layer. **ozone hole** area of the ozone layer in which depletion has occurred. **ozone layer** layer of ozone in the stratosphere that absorbs most of the sun's ultraviolet radiation.

Pp

P¹ /pee/ *n.* (also **p**) (*pl.* **Ps** or **P's**; **p's**) sixteenth letter of the alphabet.

P² *abbr.* (also **P.**) **1** (on road signs) parking. **2** *Chess* pawn.

P³ *symb. Chem.* phosphorus.

p *abbr.* (also **p.**) **1** page. **2** piano (softly). **3** pico-.

PA *abbr.* **1** Pennsylvania (in official postal use). **2** public address (esp. *PA system*).

Pa *symb. Chem.* protactinium.

pa /paa/ *n. colloq.* father.

p.a. *abbr.* per annum.

PABA /paáabə/ *abbr. Biochem.* PARA-AMINO-BENZOIC ACID.

Pab·lum /pábləm/ *n.* **1** *propr.* bland cereal food for infants. **2** (**pablum**) simplistic or unimaginative writing, ideas, etc.

PAC /pak/ *abbr.* political action committee.

pace /pays/ • *n.* **1 a** single step in walking or running. **b** distance covered in this. **2** speed in walking or running. **3** rate of progression. **4** gait. • *v.* **1** *intr.* **a** walk with a slow or regular pace. **b** (of a horse) = AMBLE. **2** *tr.* traverse or measure by pacing. **3** *tr.* set the pace for. □ **keep pace** advance at an equal rate (as). **put a person through his** (or **her**) **paces** test a person's qualities in action, etc. □□ **paced** *adj.* **pac'er** *n.*

pace·mak·er /páysmaykər/ *n.* **1** device for stimulating heart contractions. **2** competitor who sets the pace in a race.

pace·set·ter /páys-setər/ *n.* leader.

pach·y·derm /pákidərm/ *n.* any thick-skinned mammal, esp. an elephant or rhinoceros.

pach·y·san·dra /pakisándrə/ *n.* low-growing evergreen plant used as a ground cover.

pa·cif·ic /pəsífik/ • *adj.* peaceful; tranquil. • *n.* (**the Pacific**) expanse of ocean between N. and S. America to the east and Asia to the west. □□ **pa·cif'i·cal·ly** *adv.*

pac·i·fi·er /pásifiər/ *n.* **1** person or thing that pacifies. **2** rubber or plastic nipple for a baby to suck on.

pac·i·fism /pásifizəm/ *n.* belief that war and violence are morally unjustified. □□ **pac'i·fist** *n.* & *adj.*

pac·i·fy /pásifī/ *v.tr.* (**-fies, -fied**) **1** appease. **2** bring (a country, etc.) to a state of peace. □□ **pac·i·fi·ca'tion** *n.*

pack¹ /pak/ • *n.* **1 a** collection of things wrapped up or tied together for carrying. **b** = BACKPACK. **2** set of items packaged for use or disposal together. **3** set of playing cards. **4** group or collection, esp. a group of wild animals. • *v.* **1** *tr.* **a** fill (a suitcase, bag, etc.) with clothes and other items. **b** put (things) together in a bag or suitcase. **2** *intr.* & *tr.* crowd or cram; fill tightly. **3** *tr.* cover (a thing) with something pressed tightly around. **4** *tr.* be capable of delivering with force. **5** *intr.* (of animals, etc.) form a pack. □ **pack animal** animal used for carrying packs. **pack ice** area of large crowded pieces of floating ice in the sea. **pack it in** (or **up**) *colloq.* end or stop it. **send packing** *colloq.* dismiss summarily. □□ **pack'a·ble** *adj.* **pack'er** *n.*

pack² /pak/ *v.tr.* select (a jury, etc.) or fill (a meeting) so as to secure a decision in one's favor.

pack·age /pákij/ • *n.* **1 a** bundle of things packed. **b** box, parcel, etc., in which things are packed. **2** (in full **pack'age deal**) set of proposals or items offered or agreed to as a whole. • *v.tr.* make up into or enclose in a package. □ **package store** retail store selling alcoholic beverages in sealed containers. □□ **pack'ag·er** *n.*

pack·ag·ing /pákijing/ *n.* **1** wrapping or container for goods. **2** process of packing goods.

pack·et /pákit/ *n.* **1** small package. **2** (in full **pack'et boat**) *hist.* mail boat or passenger ship.

pack·ing /páking/ *n.* **1** act or process of packing. **2** material used as padding to pack esp. fragile articles.

pact /pakt/ *n.* agreement or a treaty.

pad¹ /pad/ • *n.* **1** piece of soft material used to reduce friction or jarring, fill out hollows, hold or absorb liquid, etc. **2** sheets of blank paper fastened together at one edge, for writing or drawing on. **3** fleshy underpart of an animal's foot or of a human finger. **4** flat surface for helicopter takeoff or rocket launching. **5** *colloq.* apartment or bedroom. **6** floating leaf of a water lily. • *v.tr.* (**pad·ded, pad·ding**) **1** provide with a pad or padding; stuff. **2** lengthen or fill out (a book, etc.) with unnecessary material.

pad² /pad/ • *v.* (**pad·ded, pad·ding**) *intr.* walk with a soft dull steady step. • *n.* sound of soft steady steps.

pad·ding /páding/ *n.* soft material used to pad or stuff with.

pad·dle /pád'l/ • *n.* **1** short broad-bladed oar. **2** paddle-shaped instrument. • *v.* **1** *intr.* & *tr.* move on water or propel a boat by means of paddles. **2** *tr. colloq.* spank. □ **paddle wheel** wheel with radiating paddles around it for propelling a ship. □□ **pad'dler** *n.*

paddle wheel

PADDLE WHEEL

pad·dle·ball /pád'lbawl/ n. ball game played on an enclosed court with short-handled perforated paddles.

pad·dock /pádək/ n. **1** small field, esp. for keeping horses in. **2** turf enclosure at a racecourse.

pad·dy /pádee/ n. (pl. **-dies**) field where rice is grown.

pad·dy wag·on /pádee/ n. colloq. police van for transporting those under arrest.

pad·lock /pádlok/ • n. detachable lock hanging by a pivoted hook on the object fastened. • v.tr. secure with a padlock.

pa·dre /paádray, -dree/ n. **1** clergyman, esp. a priest. **2** chaplain in any of the armed services.

pae·an /pe'eən/ n. song of praise or triumph.

pa·el·la /pī-élə, paa-áyaa/ n. Spanish dish of rice, saffron, chicken, seafood, etc.

pa·gan /páygən/ • n. **1** nonreligious person; pantheist; heathen. **2** person following a polytheistic or pantheistic religion. **3** hedonist. • adj. **1 a** of pagans. **b** irreligious. **2** pantheistic. □□ **pa'gan·ish** adj. **pa'gan·ism** n. **pa'gan·ize** v.

page[1] /payj/ • n. **1 a** leaf of a book, periodical, etc. **b** each side of this. **2** episode; memorable event. • v.tr. paginate.

page[2] /payj/ • n. person employed to run errands, attend to a door, etc. • v.tr. **1** summon by making an announcement or by sending a messenger. **2** summon by a pager.

---

page[2] Middle English (in the sense 'youth, male of uncouth manners'): from Old French, perhaps from Italian paggio, from Greek paidion, diminutive of pais, paid- 'boy.' Early use of the verb (mid-16th century) was in the sense 'follow as or like a page'; its current sense 1 dates from the early 20th century.

---

pag·eant /pájənt/ n. **1** elaborate parade or spectacle. **2** spectacular procession or play illustrating historical events.

pag·eant·ry /pájəntree/ n. (pl. **-ries**) spectacular show; pomp.

pag·er /páyjər/ n. radio device with a beeper, activated from a central point to alert the person wearing it.

pag·i·nate /pájinayt/ v.tr. assign numbers to the pages of a book, etc. □□ **pag·i·na'tion** /-náyshən/ n.

pa·go·da /pəgódə/ n. Hindu or Buddhist temple, esp. a many-tiered tower, in India and the Far East.

paid past and past part. of PAY.

pail /payl/ n. **1** bucket. **2** amount contained in this. □□ **pail'ful** n. (pl. **-fuls**).

pain /payn/ • n. **1** range of unpleasant bodily sensations produced by illness, accident, etc. **2** mental suffering or distress. **3** (in pl.) careful effort (take pains). **4** (also **pain in the neck**, etc.) colloq. troublesome person or thing; nuisance. • v.tr. cause pain to. □ **on** (or **under**) **pain of** with (death, etc.) as the penalty. □□ **pain'ful** adj. **pain'ful·ly** adv. **pain'ful·ness** n.

pain·kill·er /páynkilər/ n. medicine or drug for alleviating pain. □□ **pain'kill·ing** adj.

pain·less /páynlis/ adj. not causing or suffering pain. □□ **pain'less·ly** adv. **pain'less·ness** n.

pain·stak·ing /páynztayking/ adj. careful, industrious, thorough. □□ **pains'tak·ing·ly** adv.

paint /paynt/ • n. **1** coloring matter, esp. in liquid form for imparting color to a surface. **2** this as a dried film or coating (the paint peeled off). • v.tr. **1 a** cover with paint. **b** apply paint of a specified color to. **2** depict (an object, scene, etc.) with paint; produce (a picture) by painting. **3** describe vividly. □□ **paint'a·ble** adj.

paint·er[1] /páyntər/ n. person who paints, esp. an artist or decorator.

paint·er[2] /páyntər/ n. rope attached to the bow of a boat for tying it to a pier, dock, etc.

paint·ing /páynting/ n. **1** process or art of using paint. **2** painted picture.

pair /pair/ • n. **1** set of two persons or things used together or regarded as a unit (a pair of gloves). **2** article (e.g., scissors) consisting of two joined or corresponding parts. **3 a** romantically involved couple. **b** mated couple of animals. **4** two playing cards of the same denomination. • v. **1** arrange or be arranged in couples. **2** mate.

Pais·ley /páyzlee/ n. (also **pais·ley**) (often attrib.) distinctive detailed pattern of curved feather-shaped figures.

Pai·ute /pÍyōot/ n. (also **Piute**) **1 a** N. American people native to the southwestern US. **b** member of this people. **2** language of this people.

pa·ja·mas /pəja'aməz, -jám-/ n.pl. **1** suit of loose pants and jacket for sleeping in. **2** loose pants tied at the waist, worn by both sexes in some Asian countries.

Pa·ki·stan·i /pákistánee, paákistaánee/ • n. **1** native or national of Pakistan. **2** person of Pakistani descent. • adj. of or relating to Pakistan.

pal /pal/ n. colloq. friend or comrade.

pal·ace /pális/ n. **1** official residence of a president or sovereign. **2** mansion; spacious building.

pal·at·a·ble /pálətəbəl/ adj. **1** pleasant to taste. **2** (of an idea, suggestion, etc.) acceptable; satisfactory. □□ **pal·at·a·bil'i·ty** n. **pal'at·a·ble·ness** n. **pal'at·a·bly** adv.

pal·a·tal /pálət'l/ • adj. **1** of the palate. **2** (of a sound) made by placing the surface of the tongue against the hard palate (e.g., y in yes). • n. palatal sound. □□ **pal'a·tal·ize** v.tr. **pal·a·tal·i·za'tion** n. **pal'a·tal·ly** adv.

pal·ate /pálət/ n. **1** structure closing the upper part of the mouth cavity in vertebrates. **2** taste; liking.

pa·la·tial /pəláyshəl/ adj. (of a building) like a palace, esp. spacious and magnificent. □□ **pa·la'tial·ly** adv.

pal·a·tine /pálətīn/ adj. (also **Palatine**) hist. having or subject to authority that elsewhere belongs only to a sovereign.

pa·la·ver /pəlávər, -laávər/ n. tedious fuss and bother.

pale[1] /payl/ • adj. **1** diminished in coloration; of a whitish or ashen appearance. **2** of faint luster; dim. • v. **1** intr. & tr. grow or make pale. **2** intr. become feeble in comparison (with). □□ **pale'ly** adv. **pale'ness** n. **pal'ish** adj.

pale[2] /payl/ n. **1** pointed piece of wood for fencing, etc.; stake. **2** boundary or enclosed area. □ **beyond the pale** outside the bounds of acceptable behavior.

pale·face /páylfays/ n. white person.

paleo- /páyleeō/ comb. form ancient; old; prehistoric.

pa·le·og·ra·phy /páyleeógrəfee/ n. the study of writing and documents from the past. □□ **pa·le·og′ra·pher** n. **pa·le·o·graph·ic** /-leeográfik/ adj. **pa·le·o·graph′i·cal** adj. **pa·le·o·graph′i·cal·ly** adv.

pa·le·o·lith·ic /páyleeəlíthik/ adj. Archaeol. of or relating to the early part of the Stone Age.

pa·le·on·tol·o·gy /páyleeontóləjee/ n. the study of life in the geological past. □□ **pa·le·on·to·log·i·cal** /-təlój-/ adj. **pa·le·on·tol′o·gist** n.

Pa·le·o·zo·ic /páyleeəzóik/ Geol. • adj. of an era of geological time marked by the appearance of marine and terrestrial plants and animals, esp. invertebrates. • n. this era.

Pal·es·tin·i·an /pálistíneeən/ • adj. of or relating to Palestine, a region (in ancient and modern times) on the E. Mediterranean coast. • n. native of Palestine in ancient or modern times.

pal·ette /pálit/ n. 1 thin board or slab or other surface, usu. with a hole for the thumb, on which an artist holds and mixes colors. 2 range of colors, etc., used by an artist.

pal·i·mony /pálimōnee/ n. colloq. allowance made by one member of an unmarried couple to the other after separation.

pa·limp·sest /pálimpsest/ n. writing material or manuscript on which the original writing has been erased for reuse.

pal·in·drome /pálindrōm/ n. word or phrase that reads the same backward as forward (e.g., rotator). □□ **pal·in·drom·ic** /-drómik, -drṓ/ adj. **pa·lin′dro·mist** n.

pal·ing /páyling/ n. 1 fence of pales. 2 pale.

pal·i·sade /pálisáyd/ n. 1 fence of pales or iron railings. 2 (in pl.) line of high cliffs.

pall[1] /pawl/ n. 1 cloth spread over a coffin, hearse, or tomb. 2 dark covering (pall of darkness; pall of smoke).

pall[2] /pawl/ v. 1 intr. (often foll. by on) become uninteresting (to). 2 tr. satiate; cloy.

pal·la·di·um /pəláydeeəm/ n. Chem. white ductile metallic element occurring naturally in various ores and used in chemistry as a catalyst and for making jewelry. ¶ Symb.: Pd.

pall·bear·er /páwlbairər/ n. person helping to carry or officially escorting a coffin at a funeral.

pal·let[1] /pálit/ n. 1 straw mattress. 2 makeshift bed.

pal·let[2] /pálit/ n. 1 = PALETTE. 2 portable platform for transporting and storing loads. □□ **pal′let·ize** v.tr. (in sense 2).

pal·li·ate /páleeayt/ v.tr. 1 alleviate (disease) without curing it. 2 excuse; extenuate. □□ **pal′li·a·tion** /-áyshən/ n. & adj. **pal′li·a·tive** n. & adj. **pal′li·a·tive·ly** adv. **pal′li·a·tor** n.

pal·lid /pálid/ adj. pale, esp. from illness. □□ **pal′lid·ly** adv. **pal′lid·ness** n.

pal·lor /pálər/ n. pallidness; paleness.

palm[1] /paam, paw(l)m/ n. 1 any usu. tropical tree with no branches and a mass of large leaves at the top. 2 leaf of this tree as a symbol of victory. □ **Palm Sunday** Sunday before Easter, celebrating Christ's entry into Jerusalem. □□ **pal·ma′ceous** adj.

palm[2] /paam, paw(l)m/ • n. inner surface of the hand between the wrist and fingers. • v.tr. conceal in the hand. □ **palm off** impose on or dispose of fraudulently. □□ **pal·mar** /pálmər, pa′a(l)-/ adj. **palmed** adj. **palm′ful** n. (pl. **-fuls**).

pal·mate /pálmayt, paál-, paámayt/ adj. 1 shaped like an open hand. 2 having lobes, etc., like spread fingers.

pal·met·to /palmétō/ n. small palm tree.

palm·ist·ry /paámistree/ n. supposed divination from lines and other features on the palm of the hand. □□ **palm′ist** n.

palm·y /paámee/ adj. (**palm·i·er, palm·i·est**) 1 of or like or abounding in palms. 2 triumphant; flourishing.

pal·o·mi·no /páləmeé′enō/ n. golden or tan-colored horse with a light-colored mane and tail.

pal·pa·ble /pálpəbəl/ adj. 1 that can be touched or felt. 2 readily perceived. □□ **pal·pa·bil′i·ty** n. **pal′pa·bly** adv.

pal·pate /pálpáyt/ v.tr. examine (esp. medically) by touch. □□ **pal·pa′tion** /-páyshən/ n.

pal·pi·tate /pálpitayt/ v.intr. 1 pulsate; throb. 2 tremble. □□ **pal′pi·tant** adj. **pal·pi·ta·tion** /-táyshən/ n.

pal·sy /páwlzee/ • n. (pl. **-sies**) paralysis, esp. with involuntary tremors. • v.tr. (**-sies, -sied**) affect with palsy.

pal·try /páwltree/ adj. (**pal·tri·er, pal·tri·est**) worthless; contemptible; trifling. □□ **pal′tri·ness** n.

pam·pas /pámpəs/ n.pl. large treeless plains in S. America.

pam·per /pámpər/ v.tr. overindulge; spoil. □□ **pam′per·er** n.

pam·phlet /pámflit/ • n. small, usu. unbound booklet or leaflet. • v.tr. distribute pamphlets to. □□ **pam·phlet·eer** /-teér/ n. & v.

pan[1] /pan/ • n. 1 vessel of metal, earthenware, etc., usu. broad and shallow, used for cooking, heating, etc. 2 any similar shallow container. • v.tr. (**panned, pan·ning**) 1 colloq. criticize severely. 2 wash (gold-bearing gravel) in a pan. □ **pan out** turn out; work out. □□ **pan′ful** n. (pl. **-fuls**). **pan′like** adj.

pan[2] /pan/ • v. (**panned, pan·ning**) 1 tr. swing (a video or movie camera) horizontally to give a panoramic effect or to follow a moving object. 2 intr. (of a video or movie camera) be moved in this way. • n. panning movement.

pan- /pan/ comb. form 1 all; the whole of. 2 relating to or comprising the whole. (pan-American).

pan·a·ce·a /pánəseé′ə/ n. universal remedy. □□ **pan·a·ce′an** adj.

pa·nache /pənásh, -naásh/ n. assertiveness or flamboyant confidence of style or manner.

pan·a·ma /pánəmaa/ n. hat of strawlike material made from the leaves of a palmlike tropical plant.

Pan·a·ma·ni·an /pánəmáyneeən/ • n. 1 native or national of the Republic of Panama in Central America. 2 person of Panamanian descent. • adj. of or relating to Panama.

pan·cake /pánkayk/ n. 1 thin flat cake of batter usu. fried in a pan or on a griddle. 2 flat cake of makeup, etc.

pan·chro·mat·ic /pánkrōmátik/ adj. Photog. (of film, etc.) sensitive to all visible colors of the spectrum.

pan·cre·as /pángkreeəs/ n. gland near the stomach supplying the duodenum with digestive fluid and secreting insulin. □□ **pan·cre·at·ic** /-kreeá-tik/ adj. **pan·cre·a·ti·tis** /-kreeətítəs/ n.

pan·da /pándə/ *n.* **1** (also **gi′ant pan′da**) large bearlike mammal, native to China and Tibet, having characteristic black and white markings. **2** (also **red′ pan′da**) Himalayan raccoon-like mammal with reddish-brown fur.

pan·dem·ic /pandémik/ *adj.* (of a disease) prevalent over a whole country or the world.

pan·de·mo·ni·um /pándimốneeəm/ *n.* **1** uproar; utter confusion. **2** scene of this.

pan·der /pándər/ • *v.intr.* gratify; indulge. • *n.* (also **pan′der·er**) **1** a go-between in illicit love affairs; procurer. **2** person who encourages licentiousness.

Pan·do·ra's box /pandáwrəz/ *n.* process that once activated will generate many unmanageable problems.

pane /payn/ *n.* single sheet of glass in a window or door.

pan·e·gy·ric /pánijírik, -jírik/ *n.* laudatory discourse; eulogy. □□ **pan·e·gy′ri·cal** *adj.*

pan·el /pánəl/ • *n.* **1 a** distinct, usu. rectangular, section of a surface (e.g., of a wall or door). **b** control panel (see CONTROL *n.* 5). **2** strip of material as part of a garment. **3** group of people gathered to form a team in a broadcast game, for a discussion, etc. **4** list of available jurors; jury. • *v.tr.* fit, cover, or decorate with panels. □ **panel truck** small enclosed delivery truck.

---

panel Middle English: from Old French, literally 'piece of cloth', based on Latin *pannus* '(piece of) cloth.' An early sense, 'piece of parchment,' was extended to mean 'list,' whence the notion 'advisory group.' Sense 1 derives from the late Middle English sense 'distinct (usually framed) section of a surface.'

---

pan·el·ing /pánəling/ *n.* **1** paneled work. **2** wood for making panels.

pan·el·ist /pánəlist/ *n.* member of a panel.

pang /pang/ *n.* (often in *pl.*) sudden sharp pain or painful emotion.

pan·han·dle /pánhand′l/ • *n.* narrow strip of territory extending from one state into another. • *v. colloq.* beg for money in the street. □□ **pan′han·dler** *n.*

pan·ic /pánik/ • *n.* **1** sudden uncontrollable fear or alarm. **2** infectious apprehension or fright esp. in commercial dealings. • *v.* (**pan·icked, pan·ick·ing**) affect or be affected with panic. □ **panic-stricken** (or **-struck**) affected with panic. □□ **pan′ick·y** *adj.*

pan·nier /pányər/ *n.* basket, bag, or box, esp. one of a pair for transporting loads.

pan·o·ply /pánəplee/ *n.* (*pl.* **-plies**) **1** complete or magnificent array. **2** complete suit of armor. □□ **pan′o·plied** *adj.*

pan·o·ra·ma /pánərámə, -ráa-/ *n.* **1** unbroken view of a surrounding region. **2** complete survey or presentation of a subject, sequence of events, etc. **3** continuous passing scene. □□ **pan·o·ram′ic** *adj.* **pan·o·ram′i·cal·ly** *adv.*

pan·sy /pánzee/ *n.* (*pl.* **-sies**) garden plant with flowers of various rich colors.

pant /pant/ • *v.* **1** *intr.* breathe with short quick breaths. **2** *tr.* (often foll. by *out*) utter breath-

lessly. **3** *intr.* yearn or crave. • *n.* panting breath. □□ **pant′ing·ly** *adv.*

pan·ta·loon /pántəlỗon/ *n.* (in *pl.*) *hist.* men's close-fitting breeches fastened below the calf or at the foot.

pan·the·ism /pántheeizəm/ *n.* **1** belief that God is identifiable with the forces of nature and with natural substances. **2** worship that admits or tolerates all gods. □□ **pan′the·ist** *n.* **pan·the·is′tic** *adj.* **pan·the·is′ti·cal** *adj.* **pan·the·is′ti·cal·ly** *adv.*

pan·the·on /pántheeon, -ən/ *n.* **1** building in which illustrious dead are buried or have memorials. **2** the deities of a people collectively. **3** temple dedicated to all the gods, esp. the circular one at Rome. **4** group of esteemed persons.

pan·ther /pánthər/ *n.* **1** leopard, esp. with black fur. **2** cougar.

pant·ies /pánteez/ *n.pl. colloq.* short-legged or legless underpants worn by women and girls.

pan·to·mime /pántəmīm/ • *n.* use of gestures and facial expression to convey meaning without speech, esp. in drama and dance. • *v.* convey meaning without speech using only gestures. □□ **pan·to·mim′ic** /-mímik/ *adj.*

pan·try /pántree/ *n.* (*pl.* **-tries**) small room or cupboard for storage of kitchen supplies, groceries, etc.

pants /pants/ *n.pl.* outer garment reaching from the waist usu. to the ankles, divided into two parts to cover the legs.

pant·suit /pántsễot/ *n.* (also **pants suit**) woman's suit with pants and a jacket.

pan·ty hose /pánteehỗz/ *n.* (usu. treated as *pl.*) usu. sheer one-piece garment combining panties and stockings.

pap /pap/ *n.* **1** soft or semiliquid food for infants or invalids. **2** light or trivial reading matter; nonsense. □□ **pap′py** *adj.*

pa·pa /páapə, pəpáa/ *n.* father (esp. as a child's word).

pa·pa·cy /páypəsee/ *n.* (*pl.* **-cies**) **1** pope's office or tenure. **2** papal system.

pa·pal /páypəl/ *adj.* of a pope or the papacy. □□ **pa′pal·ly** *adv.*

pa·paw var. of PAWPAW.

pa·pa·ya /pəpấə/ *n.* **1** edible yellow fruit with orange flesh. **2** tropical tree bearing this.

pa·per /páypər/ • *n.* **1** material manufactured in thin sheets from the pulp of wood or other fibrous substances, used for writing or drawing or printing on, or as wrapping material, etc. **2** (*attrib.*) **a** made of or using paper. **b** flimsy like paper. **3** = NEWSPAPER. **4** a printed document. **b** (in *pl.*) identification or other legal documents. **5** = WALLPAPER. **6** essay or dissertation. **7** piece of paper. • *v.tr.* **1** apply paper to, esp. decorate (a wall, etc.) with wallpaper. **2** (foll. by *over*) disguise or try to hide. □ **paper clip** clip of bent wire or of plastic for holding several sheets of paper together. **paper tiger** apparently threatening, but ineffectual, person or thing. **paper trail** documentation of transactions, etc. □□ **pa′per·er** *n.* **pa′per·less** *adj.* **pa′per·y** *adj.*

pa·per·back /páypərbak/ (also **pa′per·bound**) • *adj.* (of a book) bound in stiff paper. • *n.* a paperback book.

pa·per·boy /páypərboy/ *n.* (*fem.* **pa·per·girl** /-gərl/) boy or girl who delivers or sells newspapers.

pa·per·weight /páypərwayt/ *n.* small heavy object for keeping loose papers in place.

pa·per·work /páypərwərk/ n. **1** routine clerical or administrative work. **2** documents, esp. for a particular purpose.

pa·pier mâ·ché /páypər məsháy, papyáy/ n. paper pulp used for molding into boxes, trays, etc.

pa·pil·la /pəpílə/ n. (pl. **pa·pil·lae** /-pílee/) small nipplelike protuberance in a part or organ of the body. □□ **pap·il·lar·y** adj. **pap·il·lose** adj.

pa·poose /papŏos, pə-/ n. young Native American child.

pa·pri·ka /pəpréekə, páprikə/ n. **1** Bot. a red pepper. **2** powdery condiment made from it.

Pap smear /pap/ (also **Pap test**) n. test for cervical cancer, etc., done by a cervical smear.

pa·py·rus /pəpírəs/ n. (pl. **pa·py·ri** /-rī/) **1** aquatic plant with dark green stems topped with fluffy inflorescences. **2** writing material prepared in ancient Egypt from the pithy stem of this.

par /paar/ n. **1** average or normal amount, degree, condition, etc. (be up to par). **2** equality; equal footing. **3** Golf number of strokes a skilled player should normally require for a hole or course. **4** Stock Exch. face value of stocks and shares, etc. **5** (in full **par of exchange**) recognized value of one country's currency in terms of another's. □ **par for the course** colloq. what is normal or to be expected.

par- /pər, par, paar/ prefix var. of PARA- before a vowel or h; (paraldehyde; parody; parhelion).

para- /párə/ prefix (also **par-**) **1** beside (paramilitary). **2** beyond (paranormal).

par·a·a·mi·no·ben·zo·ic acid /parə-əméenō-benzóik/ n. Biochem. compound used in suntan lotions and sunscreens to absorb ultraviolet light. ¶ Abbr.: **PABA**.

par·a·ble /párəbəl/ n. **1** narrative of imagined events used to illustrate a moral or spiritual lesson. **2** allegory.

pa·rab·o·la /pərábələ/ n. open plane curve formed by the intersection of a cone with a plane parallel to its side.

par·a·bol·ic /párəbólik/ adj. **1** of or expressed in a parable. **2** of or like a parabola. □□ **par·a·bol·i·cal·ly** adv.

par·a·chute /párəshŏot/ • n. rectangular or umbrella-shaped apparatus allowing a slow and safe descent, esp. from an aircraft. • v. convey or descend by parachute. □□ **par·a·chut·ist** n.

pa·rade /pəráyd/ • n. **1** formal or ceremonial muster of troops for inspection. **2** public procession. **3** ostentatious display. • v. **1 a** tr. march through (streets, etc.) in procession. **b** intr. march ceremonially. **2** tr. display ostentatiously. □□ **pa·rad'er** n.

par·a·digm /párədīm/ n. **1** example or pattern. **2** Gram. representative set of the inflections of a noun, verb, etc. □□ **par·a·dig·mat·ic** /-digmátik/ adj. **par·a·dig·mat·i·cal·ly** adv.

par·a·dise /párədīs/ n. **1** heaven. **2** place or state of complete happiness. **3** (in full **earthly paradise**) abode of Adam and Eve; garden of Eden. □□ **par·a·di·sa'i·cal** /-dəsfəkəl/ adj.

par·a·dox /párədoks/ n. **1 a** seemingly absurd or contradictory statement, even if actually well-founded. **b** self-contradictory or essentially absurd statement. **2** person or thing having contradictory qualities, etc. □□ **par·a·dox'i·cal** adj. **par·a·dox'i·cal·ly** adv.

par·af·fin /párəfin/ n. (also **par'af·fin wax**) waxy

mixture of hydrocarbons used in candles, waterproofing, etc.

par·a·gon /párəgon, -gən/ n. model of excellence.

par·a·graph /párəgraf/ • n. **1** distinct section of a piece of writing, beginning on a new usu. indented line. **2** symbol (usu. ¶) used to mark a new paragraph. **3** short item in a newspaper, usu. of only one paragraph. • v.tr. arrange in paragraphs. □□ **par·a·graph·ic** /-gráfik/ adj.

par·a·keet /párəkeet/ n. small usu. long-tailed parrot.

par·a·le·gal /párəléegəl/ • adj. of auxiliary aspects of the law. • n. person trained in subsidiary legal matters.

par·al·lax /párəlaks/ n. apparent difference in the position or direction of an object caused when the observer's position is changed. □□ **par·al·lac·tic** /-láktik/ adj.

par·al·lel /párəlel/ • adj. **1** side by side and having the same distance continuously between them. **2** precisely similar, analogous, or corresponding; simultaneous. • n. **1** person or thing precisely analogous or equal to another. **2** comparison. **3** (in full **parallel of latitude**) Geog. **a** each of the imaginary parallel circles of constant latitude on the earth's surface. **b** corresponding line on a map (the 49th parallel). • v.tr. **1** be parallel to; correspond to. **2** represent as similar; compare. □□ **par'al·lel·ism** n.

par·al·lel·o·gram /párəléləgram/ n. Geom. four-sided plane rectilinear figure with opposite sides parallel.

pa·ral·y·sis /pərálisis/ n. (pl. **pa·ral·y·ses** /-seez/) **1** impairment or loss of esp. the motor function of the nerves. **2** state of utter powerlessness. □□ **par·a·lyt·ic** /párəlítik/ adj. & n. **par·a·lyt'i·cal·ly** adv.

par·a·lyze /párəlīz/ v.tr. **1** affect with paralysis. **2** render powerless; cripple. □□ **par·a·ly·za'tion** n. **par'a·lyz·ing·ly** adv.

par·a·me·ci·um /párəméeseeəm/ n. freshwater protozoan of a characteristic slipper-like shape covered with cilia.

par·a·med·ic /párəmédik/ n. **1** paramedical worker. **2** person trained in emergency medical procedures.

par·a·med·i·cal /párəmédikəl/ adj. (of services, etc.) supplementing and supporting medical work.

pa·ram·e·ter /pərámitər/ n. **1** Math. quantity constant in the case considered but varying in different cases. **2 a** characteristic or feature. **b** (loosely) constant element or factor, esp. serving as a limit or boundary. □□ **par·a·met·ric** /párəmétrik/ adj. **pa·ram'e·trize** v.tr.

par·a·mil·i·tar·y /párəmíliteree/ adj. (of forces) ancillary to and similarly organized to military forces.

par·a·mount /párəmownt/ adj. supreme; requiring first consideration. □□ **par'a·mount·ly** adv.

par·a·mour /párəmŏor/ n. illicit lover of a married person.

par·a·noi·a /párənóyə/ n. **1** personality disorder esp. characterized by delusions of persecution and self-importance. **2** abnormal tendency to suspect and mistrust others. □□ **par·a·noi'ac** adj. & n. **par·a·noid** /-noyd/ adj. & n.

par·a·nor·mal /párənórməl/ adj. beyond the scope of normal objective investigation or explanation. □□ **par·a·nor′mal·ly** adv.

par·a·pet /párəpit/ n. **1** low wall at the edge of a roof, balcony, etc., or along the sides of a bridge. **2** defense of earth or stone to conceal and protect troops. □□ **par′a·pet·ed** adj.

par·a·pher·na·li·a /párəfərnáylyə/ n.pl. (also treated as sing.) miscellaneous belongings, equipment, accessories, etc.

par·a·phrase /párəfrayz/ • n. free rendering or rewording of a passage. • v.tr. express the meaning of (a passage) in other words. □□ **par·a·phras·tic** /-frástik/ adj.

par·a·ple·gi·a /párəpleéjə/ n. paralysis of the legs and part or the whole of the trunk. □□ **par·a·ple′gic** adj. & n.

par·a·psy·chol·o·gy /párəsīkóləjee/ n. the study of mental phenomena outside the sphere of ordinary psychology. □□ **par·a·psy·cho·log·i·cal** /-síkəlójikəl/ adj. **par·a·psy·chol′o·gist** n.

par·a·quat /párəkwot/ n. quick-acting herbicide, becoming inactive on contact with the soil.

par·a·site /párəsīt/ n. **1** organism living in or on another and benefiting at the expense of the other. **2** person who lives off or exploits another or others. □□ **par·a·sit·ic** /-sitik/ adj. **par·a·sit′i·cal** adj. **par·a·sit′i·cal·ly** adv. **par·a·si·tol·o·gy** /-tóləjee/ n. **par·a·si·tol′o·gist** n.

par·a·sol /párəsawl, -sol/ n. light umbrella used to give shade from the sun.

par·a·sym·pa·the·tic /párəsímpəthétik/ adj. Anat. relating to the part of the autonomic nervous system that controls the slowing of the heartbeat, constriction of the pupils, etc.

par·a·thy·roid /párəthíroyd/ Anat. • n. gland next to the thyroid, secreting a hormone that regulates calcium levels in the body. • adj. of or associated with this gland.

par·a·troops /párətro͞ops/ n.pl. troops equipped to be dropped by parachute from aircraft. □□ **par′a·troop·er** n.

par·boil /paárboyl/ v.tr. partly cook by boiling.

par·cel /paársəl/ • n. **1** goods, etc., wrapped in a package. **2** piece of land. • v.tr. (foll. by out) divide into portions.

parch /paarch/ v. make or become hot and dry.

Par·chee·si /paarcheézee, pər-, -see/ n. propr. board game played with dice.

parch·ment /paárchmənt/ n. **1 a** animal skin, esp. that of a sheep or goat, prepared as a writing or painting surface. **b** manuscript written on this. **2** (in full **vegetable parchment**) high-grade paper made to resemble parchment.

par·don /paárd'n/ • n. **1** act of excusing or forgiving an offense, error, etc. **2** (in full **full pardon**) remission of the legal consequences of a crime or conviction. • v.tr. **1** release from the consequences of an offense, error, etc. **2** forgive; excuse. □□ **par′don·a·ble** adj. **par′don·a·bly** adv.

pare /pair/ v.tr. **1** trim by cutting away the surface or edge. **2** diminish little by little. □□ **par′er** n.

par·ent /páirənt, pár-/ • n. **1** person who has or adopts a child; a father or mother. **2** animal or plant from which others are derived. **3** source, origin, etc. • v.tr. (also absol.) be a parent of. □ **parent company** company of which other companies are subsidiaries. □□ **par·en·tal** /pərént′l/ adj. **pa·ren′tal·ly** adv. **par′ent·hood** n.

par·ent·age /páirəntij, pár-/ n. lineage; descent from or through parents (their parentage is unknown).

pa·ren·the·sis /pərénthəsis/ n. (pl. **pa·ren·the·ses** /-seez/) **1 a** explanatory or qualifying word, clause, or sentence. **b** (in pl.) pair of rounded brackets ( ) used for this in writing or printing. **2** interlude or interval.

par·en·thet·ic /páranthétik/ adj. **1** of or by way of a parenthesis. **2** interposed. □□ **par·en·thet′i·cal** adj. **par·en·thet′i·cal·ly** adv.

par·ent·ing /páirənting, pár-/ n. occupation or concerns of parents.

pa·re·ve /paárəvə, paárvə/ adj. made without milk or meat and thus suitable for kosher use.

par ex·cel·lence /paár eksəlóNs/ adv. as having special excellence; being the supreme example of its kind.

par·fait /paarfáy/ n. **1** rich frozen custard of whipped cream, eggs, etc. **2** layers of ice cream, meringue, etc., served in a tall glass.

pa·ri·ah /pəríə/ n. **1** social outcast. **2** hist. member of a low caste or of no caste in S. India.

pa·ri·e·tal /pəríətəl/ adj. Anat. of the wall of the body or any of its cavities. □ **parietal bone** either of a pair of bones forming the central part of the sides and top of the skull.

par·i·mu·tu·el /párimyoͦochoͦoəl/ n. form of betting in which those backing the first three places divide the losers' stakes.

par·ing /páiring/ n. strip or piece cut off.

par·ish /párish/ n. **1** area having its own church and clergy. **2** county in Louisiana. **3** inhabitants of a parish.

pa·rish·ion·er /pəríshənər/ n. inhabitant or member of a parish.

Pa·ri·sian /pəreé'ezhən, -rízhən, -rízeeən/ • adj. of or relating to Paris in France. • n. native or inhabitant of Paris.

par·i·ty /páritee/ n. **1** equality; equal status or pay. **2** equivalence of one currency with another; being at par.

park /paark/ • n. **1** public land set aside for recreation or as a preserve. **2** gear position or function in an automatic transmission that immobilizes the drive wheels. **3** area devoted to a specified purpose (industrial park). • v. **1** tr. (also absol.) leave (a vehicle) usu. temporarily. **2** tr. colloq. deposit and leave, usu. temporarily. □ **parking meter** coin-operated meter that receives payment for vehicles parked in the street and indicates the time available.

---

park Middle English: from Old French parc, from medieval Latin parricus, of Germanic origin; related to German Pferch 'pen, fold,' also to paddock. The word was originally a legal term designating land held by royal grant for keeping game animals: this was enclosed and therefore distinct from a forest or chase, and (also unlike a forest) had no special laws or officers. A military sense 'space occupied by artillery, wagons, stores, etc., in an encampment' (late 17th century) is the origin of the verb sense (mid-19th century) and of sense 3 (early 20th century).

---

par·ka /paárkə/ n. hooded winter jacket.

Par·kin·son's dis·ease /paárkinsənz/ n. (also

Par′kin·son·ism) progressive disease of the nervous system with tremor, muscular rigidity, and emaciation.

Par·kin·son's law /paárkinsənz/ *n.* facetious notion that work expands so as to fill the time available for its completion.

park·way /paárkway/ *n.* open landscaped highway.

par·lance /paárləns/ *n.* particular idiom.

par·lay /paárlay/ • *v.tr.* use (money won on a bet) as a further stake. • *n.* bet made by parlaying.

par·ley /paárlee/ • *n.* conference for debating points in a dispute, esp. a discussion of terms for an armistice, etc. • *v.intr.* hold a parley.

par·lia·ment /paárləmənt/ *n.* legislature of various countries, as the United Kingdom.

par·lia·men·tar·i·an /paárləmentáireeən/ *n.* 1 member of a parliament. 2 person who is well-versed in parliamentary procedures.

par·lia·men·ta·ry /paárləméntəree, -tree/ *adj.* 1 of or relating to a parliament. 2 enacted or established by a parliament.

par·lor /paárlər/ *n.* 1 sitting room in a private house. 2 store providing specified goods or services (*beauty parlor*).

Par·me·san /paármizaán, -zán, -zən/ *n.* a kind of hard dry cheese made orig. at Parma and used esp. in grated form.

pa·ro·chi·al /pərókeeəl/ *adj.* 1 of or concerning a parish. 2 merely local, narrow, or restricted in scope. □ **parochial school** school run or supported by a church. □□ **pa·ro′chi·al·ism** *n.* **pa·ro′chi·al·ly** *adv.*

par·o·dy /párədee/ • *n.* (*pl.* **-dies**) 1 humorous exaggerated imitation of an author, literary work, style, etc. 2 feeble imitation; travesty. • *v.tr.* (**-dies, -died**) compose a parody of. □□ **pa·rod·ic** /pəródik/ *adj.* **par′o·dist** *n.*

pa·role /pəról/ • *n.* release of a prisoner temporarily for a special purpose or completely before the fulfillment of a sentence, on the promise of good behavior. • *v.tr.* put (a prisoner) on parole. □□ **pa·rol·ee** /-lée/ *n.*

par·ox·ysm /párəksizəm/ *n.* 1 sudden attack or outburst. 2 fit of disease. □□ **par·ox·ys·mal** /-sízməl/ *adj.*

par·quet /paárkáy/ • *n.* 1 flooring of parquetry. 2 main-floor area of a theater. • *v.tr.* furnish (a room) with a parquet floor.

par·quet·ry /paárkitree/ *n.* use of wooden blocks arranged in a pattern to make floors or inlay for furniture.

par·ri·cide /párisīd/ *n.* 1 killing of a near relative, esp. of a parent. 2 act of parricide. 3 person who commits parricide. □□ **par·ri·ci′dal** /-sīd′l/ *adj.*

par·rot /párət/ • *n.* 1 mainly tropical bird with a short hooked bill, often vivid plumage, and the ability to mimic the human voice. 2 person who mechanically repeats the words or actions of another. • *v.tr.* repeat mechanically.

par·ry /páree/ • *v.tr.* (**-ries, -ried**) 1 avert or ward off, esp. with a countermove. 2 deal skillfully with (an awkward question, etc.). • *n.* (*pl.* **-ries**) act of parrying.

parse /paars/ *v.tr.* describe the function and forms (of a sentence or a word in context) grammatically. □□ **pars′er** *n.* esp. Computing.

par·sec /paársek/ *n.* unit of stellar distance, equal to about 3.25 light years (3.08 x 10^{16} meters).

par·si·mo·ny /paársimōnee/ *n.* stinginess. □□ **par·si·mo·ni·ous** /-mōneeəs/ *adj.* **par·si·mo′ni·ous·ly** *adv.*

pars·ley /paárslee/ *n.* biennial herb, with crinkly or flat aromatic leaves, used for seasoning and garnishing food.

pars·nip /paársnip/ *n.* 1 plant with a large pale yellow tapering root. 2 this root eaten as a vegetable.

par·son /paársən/ *n.* 1 rector. 2 any (esp. Protestant) member of the clergy. □□ **par·son·i·cal** /-sónikəl/ *adj.*

par·son·age /paársənij/ *n.* church house provided for a parson.

part /paart/ • *n.* 1 some but not all of a thing or number of things. 2 essential member, constituent, or component. 3 division of a book, broadcast serial, etc. 4 each of several equal portions of a whole (*has 3 parts sugar to 2 parts flour*). 5 a portion allotted; share. b person's share in an action, etc. 6 a character assigned to an actor on stage. b words spoken by an actor on stage. c copy of these. 7 *Mus.* melody, etc., assigned to a particular voice or instrument. 8 each of the sides in an agreement or dispute. 9 (in *pl.*) region or district (*not from these parts*). 10 dividing line in combed hair. • *v.* 1 *tr.* & *intr.* divide or separate into parts. 2 *intr.* leave; say goodbye to. 3 *intr.* (foll. by *with*) give up; hand over. 4 *tr.* comb hair to form a part. • *adv.* to some extent; partly. □ **for one's part** as far as one is concerned. **in part** (or **parts**) to some extent; partly. **part and parcel** an essential part. **part of speech** *n.* each of the categories to which words are assigned in accordance with their grammatical and semantic functions. **part-time** *adj.* occupying or using only part of one's working time. **part-timer** person employed in part-time work. **take part** assist or have a share (in).

par·take /paartáyk/ *v.intr.* (*past* **par·took** /-took/; *past part.* **par·taken** /-táykən/) 1 take a share or part. 2 eat or drink something. □□ **par·tak′a·ble** *adj.* **par·tak′er** *n.*

par·terre /paartáir/ *n.* 1 level space in a garden occupied by flower beds arranged formally. 2 rear seating area of a theater.

par·the·no·gen·e·sis /paárthinōjénisis/ *n.* Biol. reproduction by a female gamete without fertilization. □□ **par·the·no·ge·net·ic** /-jinétik/ *adj.* **par·the·no·ge·net′i·cal·ly** *adv.*

par·tial /paárshəl/ • *adj.* 1 not complete; forming only part. 2 biased; having a liking for. • *n.* denture for replacing one or several, but not all, of the teeth. □□ **par·ti·al·i·ty** /paársheeálitee/ *n.* **par′tial·ly** *adv.*

¶ In the sense 'to some extent, not entirely' traditionalists prefer **partly** to **partially**: *The piece was written partly in poetry. What we decide will depend partly on the amount of the contract.* The form **partial**, however, appears in many phrases as the adjectival form of **part**: *partial blindness, partial denture, partial paralysis, partial payment, partial shade, partial vacuum*, etc. **Partially** is therefore widely used, with the same sense as **partly**: *partially blind in one eye.*

par·tic·i·pate /paartísipayt/ *v.intr.* take a part or share (in). □□ **par·tic·i·pa·tion** /-páyshən/ *n.* **par·tic′i·pant** *n.* **par·tic′i·pa·tor** *n.* **par·tic·i·pa·to·ry** /-pətáwree/ *adj.*

par·ti·ci·ple /páartisipəl/ *n. Gram.* word formed from a verb (e.g., *going, gone, being, been*) and used in compound verb forms (e.g., *is going, has been*) or as an adjective (e.g., *working woman, burned toast*). □□ **par·ti·cip·i·al** /-sípeeəl/ *adj.* **par·ti·cip'i·al·ly** *adv.*
¶ See note at MODIFIER.

par·ti·cle /páartikəl/ *n.* **1** minute portion of matter. **2** least possible amount (*not a particle of sense*). **3** *Gram.* minor part of speech, esp. a short indeclinable one.

par·ti·cle·board /páartikəlbōrd, -bawrd/ *n.* building material made in flat sheets from scrap wood bonded with adhesive.

par·ti·col·ored /páarteekúlərd/ *adj.* of more than one color in patches.

par·tic·u·lar /pərtíkyələr, pətík-/ • *adj.* **1** relating to or considered as one thing or person as distinct from others; individual. **2** more than is usual; special. **3** scrupulously exact; fastidious. • *n.* **1** detail; item. **2** (in *pl.*) points of information; detailed account. □ **in particular** especially; specifically. □□ **par·tic·u·lar·i·ty** /-láritee/ *n.*

par·tic·u·lar·ize /pərtíkyələrīz, pətík-/ *v. tr.* (also *absol.*) **1** name specifically or one by one. **2** specify (items). □□ **par·tic·u·lar·i·za'tion** *n.*

par·tic·u·lar·ly /pərtíkyələrlee, pətík-/ *adv.* **1** especially; very. **2** specifically (*they particularly asked for you*).

par·tic·u·late /pərtíkyəlayt, -lət, paar-/ • *adj.* in the form of separate particles. • *n.* matter in this form.

part·ing /páarting/ *n.* **1** leave-taking or departure. **2** division; separating.

par·ti·san /páartizən/ (also **par·ti·zan**) • *n.* **1** strong, esp. unreasoning, supporter of a party, cause, etc. **2** *Mil.* guerrilla. • *adj.* of or like partisans. □□ **par'ti·san·ship** *n.*

par·ti·tion /paartíshən/ • *n.* **1** division into parts. **2** structure dividing a space into two parts, esp. a light interior wall. • *v. tr.* **1** divide into parts. **2** separate with a partition. □□ **par·ti'tioned** *adj.* **par·ti'tion·er** *n.* **par·ti'tion·ist** *n.*

part·ly /páartlee/ *adv.* to some extent; not entirely.
¶ See note at PARTIAL.

part·ner /páartnər/ • *n.* **1** person who shares or takes part with another or others. **2** companion in dancing. **3** player on the same side in a game. **4** either member of a married or unmarried couple. • *v. tr.* be the partner of. □□ **part'ner·less** *adj.* **part·ner·ship** *n.*

par·took *past* of PARTAKE.

par·tridge /páartrij/ *n.* (*pl.* same or **par·tridg·es**) any of various species of game bird.

par·tu·ri·tion /páartŏŏríshən, -tyŏŏ-, -chŏŏ-/ *n. Med.* act of bringing forth young; childbirth.

par·ty /páartee/ • *n.* (*pl.* **-ties**) **1** social gathering. **2** body of persons engaged in an activity or traveling together (*search party*). **3** group of people united in a cause, opinion, etc., esp. an organized political group. **4** each side in an agreement or dispute. **5** *Law* accessory (to an action). **6** *colloq.* person. • *v.* (**-ties, -tied**) entertain at or attend a party. □ **party line 1** policy adopted by a political party. **2** shared telephone line.

par·ve·nu /páarvənŏŏ/ *n.* (*fem.* **par·ve·nue**) **1** person who has recently gained wealth or position. **2** upstart.

pas·chal /páskəl/ *adj.* **1** of Passover. **2** of Easter.

pa·sha /páashə/ *n.* (also **pa'cha**) *hist.* title (placed after the name) of a Turkish officer of high rank.

pass[1] /pas/ • *v.* (*past part.* **passed**) (see also PAST). **1** *intr.* move onward; proceed past. **2** *tr.* **a** go past; leave (a thing, etc.) on one side or behind in proceeding. **b** overtake, esp. in a vehicle. **3** *intr. & tr.* be transferred or cause to be transferred from one person or place to another. **4** *tr.* surpass; exceed. **5** *intr.* get through. **6** *intr.* be accepted as or known as. **7** *tr.* move; cause to go. **8 a** *intr.* be successful (in school, etc.). **b** *tr.* be successful in (school, etc.). **c** *tr.* judge as satisfactory. **9 a** *tr.* (of a bill) be approved by (a parliamentary process). **b** *tr.* cause or allow (a bill) to proceed to further legislative processes. **c** *intr.* (of a bill or proposal) be approved. **10** *intr.* occur; elapse; happen. **11 a** *intr.* circulate; be current. **b** *tr.* put into circulation. **12** *tr.* spend or use up (a certain time or period). **13** *tr. Sports* send (the ball) to another player of one's own team. **14** *intr.* forgo one's turn or chance in a game, etc. **15** *intr.* come to an end. **16** *tr.* discharge from the body. **17** *tr.* **a** utter (criticism) about. **b** pronounce (judicial sentence) on. • *n.* **1** act or instance of passing. **2** permission giving free entry, access, leave, etc. **3** *Sports* transference of the ball to another player on the same side. □ **in passing** by the way. **2** in the course of conversation, etc. **make a pass at** *colloq.* make amorous or sexual advances to. **pass around 1** distribute. **2** send or give to each of a number in turn. **pass away 1** *euphem.* die. **2** cease to exist; come to an end. **pass the buck** *colloq.* deny or shift responsibility. **pass by 1** go past. **2** disregard; omit. **pass on 1** proceed on one's way. **2** *euphem.* die. **3** transmit to the next person in a series. **pass out 1** become unconscious. **2** distribute. **pass over 1** omit, ignore, or disregard. **2** ignore the claims of (a person). **3** *euphem.* die. **pass up** *colloq.* refuse or neglect (an opportunity, etc.). □□ **pass'er** *n.*

pass[2] /pas/ *n.* narrow passage through mountains.

pass·a·ble /pásəbəl/ *adj.* **1** barely satisfactory; just adequate. **2** (of a road, pass, etc.) that can be passed. □□ **pass'a·bly** *adv.*

pas·sage /pásij/ *n.* **1** process or means of passing; transit. **2** = PASSAGEWAY. **3** liberty or right to pass through. **4** journey by sea or air. **5** transition. **6** short extract from a book, piece of music, etc.

pas·sage·way /pásijway/ *n.* narrow way for passing along, esp. with walls on either side; corridor.

pass·book /pásbŏŏk/ *n.* book issued by a bank, etc., to an account holder for recording deposits and withdrawals.

pas·sé /pasáy/ *adj.* **1** old-fashioned. **2** past its prime.

pas·sen·ger /pásinjər/ *n.* traveler in or on a public or private conveyance (other than the driver, pilot, crew, etc.).

pas·ser·by /pásərbí/ *n.* (*pl.* **pas'sers·by**) person who goes past, esp. by chance.

pas·sim /pásim/ *adv.* (of allusions or references in a published work) to be found at various places throughout the text.

pass·ing /pásing/ • *adj.* **1** in senses of PASS[1]

v. **2** transient; fleeting. **3** cursory; incidental (*a passing reference*). • *n.* **1** in senses of PASS[1] *v.* **2** *euphem.* death. □□ **pass'ing•ly** *adv.*

pas•sion /páshən/ *n.* **1** strong emotion or enthusiasm. **2** emotional outburst. **3** object arousing passion. **4** (**the Passion**) *Relig.* suffering of Christ during his last days. □□ **pas'sion•less** *adj.*

pas•sion•ate /páshənət/ *adj.* **1** dominated by or easily moved to strong feeling, esp. love or anger. **2** showing or caused by passion. □□ **pas'sion•ate•ly** *adv.*

pas•sive /pásiv/ *adj.* **1** suffering action; acted upon. **2** offering no opposition; submissive. **3** not active; inert. **4** *Gram.* designating the voice in which the subject undergoes the action of the verb. □ **passive resistance** nonviolent refusal to cooperate. **passive smoking** involuntary inhaling, of smoke from others' cigarettes, etc. □□ **pas'sive•ly** *adv.* **pas'sive•ness** *n.* **pas•siv'i•ty** *n.*

pass•key /páskee/ *n.* **1** private key to a gate, etc., for special purposes. **2** skeleton key or master key.

Pass•o•ver /pásōvər/ *n.* Jewish spring festival commemorating the liberation of the Israelites from Egyptian bondage.

pass•port /páspawrt/ *n.* **1** official document issued by a government certifying the holder's identity and citizenship, and authorizing travel abroad. **2** (foll. by *to*) thing that ensures admission or attainment (*a passport to success*).

pass•word /páswərd/ *n.* prearranged word or phrase securing recognition, admission, etc.

past /past/ • *adj.* **1** gone by in time. **2** recently completed or gone by (*the past month*). **3** relating to a former time. **4** *Gram.* expressing a past action or state. • *n.* **1 a** past time. **b** past events. **2** person's past life, esp. if discreditable. **3** past tense or form. • *prep.* **1** beyond in time or place. **2** beyond the range, duration, or compass of. • *adv.* so as to pass by (*hurried past*). □ **past master** expert.

pas•ta /paástə/ *n.* **1** dried flour paste used in various shapes in cooking (e.g., spaghetti). **2** cooked dish made from this.

paste /payst/ • *n.* **1** any moist fairly stiff mixture. **2** dough of flour with fat, water, etc. **3** liquid adhesive for sticking paper, etc. **4** hard vitreous composition used in making imitation gems. • *v.tr.* **1** fasten or coat with paste. **2** *sl.* beat or thrash. □□ **past'ing** *n.* (esp. in sense 2 of *v.*).

paste•board /páystbawrd/ *n.* **1** stiff material made by pasting together sheets of paper. **2** (*attrib.*) **a** flimsy. **b** fake.

pas•tel /pastél/ *n.* **1** crayon of powdered pigments bound with a gum solution. **2** work of art in pastel. **3** light and subdued shade of a color. □□ **pas•tel'ist** *n.*

pas•tern /pástərn/ *n.* **1** part of a horse's foot between fetlock and hoof. **2** corresponding part in other animals.

pas•teur•ize /páschərīz, pástyə-/ *v.tr.* sterilize (milk, etc.) by heating. □□ **pas•teur•i•za'tion** *n.* **pas'teur•iz•er** *n.*

pas•tiche /pasteésh/ *n.* literary or artistic work from or imitating various sources.

pas•time /pástīm/ *n.* pleasant recreation or hobby.

pas•tor /pástər/ *n.* priest or minister in charge of a church or a congregation. □□ **pas'tor•ate** *n.* **pas'tor•ship** *n.*

pas•tor•al /pástərəl/ • *adj.* **1** of shepherds or flocks and herds. **2** of or portraying country life. **3** of a pastor. • *n.* pastoral poem, play, picture, etc. □□ **pas'to•ral•ism** *n.* **pas'to•ral•ly** *adv.*

pas•tra•mi /pəstraámee/ *n.* seasoned smoked beef.

pas•try /páystree/ *n.* (*pl.* **-tries**) **1** dough of flour, fat, and water baked and used as a base and covering for pies, etc. **2 a** food, made wholly or partly of this. **b** item of this food.

pas•tur•age /páschərij/ *n.* land for pasture.

pas•ture /páschər/ • *n.* **1** grassland suitable for grazing. **2** herbage for animals. • *v. tr.* put (animals) to pasture.

past•y /páystee/ *adj.* (**past•i•er**, **past•i•est**) unhealthily pale (esp. in complexion). □□ **past'i•ly** *adv.* **past'i•ness** *n.*

pat[1] /pat/ • *v.tr.* (**pat•ted**, **pat•ting**) **1** strike gently with the hand or a flat surface. **2** flatten or mold by patting. • *n.* **1** light stroke or tap, esp. with the hand in affection, etc. **2** sound made by this. **3** small mass (esp. of butter) formed by patting. □ **pat on the back** gesture of approval or congratulation.

pat[2] /pat/ • *adj.* **1** prepared or known thoroughly. **2** apposite or opportune, esp. unconvincingly so. • *adv.* in a pat manner. □ **stand pat** stick stubbornly to one's opinion or decision. □□ **pat'ly** *adv.* **pat'ness** *n.*

patch /pach/ • *n.* **1** piece of material or metal, etc., used to mend a hole or as reinforcement. **2** pad worn to protect an injured eye. **3** dressing, etc., put over a wound. **4** large or irregular distinguishable area on a surface. **5** piece of ground. **6** scrap or remnant. • *v.tr.* **1** repair with a patch or patches. **2** (of material) serve as a patch to. **3** put together, esp. hastily. **4** (foll. by *up*) settle (a quarrel, etc.). □ **patch test** test for allergy by applying to the skin patches containing allergenic substances. □□ **patch'er** *n.*

patch•ou•li /pəchóolee, páchōolee/ *n.* perfume obtained from a strongly scented E. Indian plant.

patch•work /páchwərk/ *n.* **1** sewn work using small pieces of cloth with different designs, forming a pattern. **2** thing composed of various small pieces or fragments.

patch•y /páchee/ *adj.* (**patch•i•er**, **patch•i•est**) **1** uneven in quality. **2** having or existing in patches. □□ **patch'i•ly** *adv.* **patch'i•ness** *n.*

pate /payt/ *n. colloq.* or *joc.* head.

pâ•té /paatáy, pa–/ *n.* rich paste or spread of finely chopped and spiced meat or fish, etc.

pa•tel•la /pətélə/ *n.* (*pl.* **pa•tel•lae** /-lee/) kneecap. □□ **pa•tel'lar** *adj.* **pa•tel•late** /-lət/ *adj.*

pat•ent /pát'nt/ • *n.* **1** official document conferring a right or title, esp. the sole right to make or use or sell some invention. **2** invention or process so protected. • *adj.* **1** /páyt'nt/ obvious; plain. **2** conferred or protected by patent. • *v.tr.* obtain a patent for. □ **patent leather** glossy leather. **patent medicine** trademarked medicine usu. available without prescription. □□ **pa'ten•cy** *n.* **pat'ent•a•ble** *adj.* **pat'ent•ly** *adv.* (/páytəntlee/ in sense 1 of *adj.*).

pa•ter•nal /pətərnəl/ *adj.* **1** fatherly. **2** related through the father. **3** (of a government, etc.)

limiting freedom and responsibility by well-meaning regulations. □□ **pa·ter′nal·ly** adv.

pa·ter·nal·ism /pətɔ́rnəlizəm/ n. policy of governing or behaving in a paternal way. □□ **pa·ter′nal·ist** n. **pa·ter·nal·is′tic** adj. **pa·ter·nal·is′ti·cal·ly** adv.

pa·ter·ni·ty /pətɔ́rnitee/ n. 1 fatherhood. 2 one's paternal origin. 3 the source or authorship of a thing.

path /path/ n. (pl. **paths** /paa<u>th</u>z/) 1 way or track made for or by walking. 2 line along which a person or thing moves (flight path). 3 course of action. □□ **path′less** adj.

pa·thet·ic /pəthétik/ adj. 1 arousing pity, sadness, or contempt. 2 colloq. miserably inadequate.□□ **pa·thet′i·cal·ly** adv.

path·o·gen /páthəjən/ n. agent causing disease. □□ **path·o·gen·ic** /-jeník/ adj.

path·o·log·i·cal /páthəlójikəl/ adj. 1 of pathology. 2 of or caused by a physical or mental disorder (a pathological fear of spiders). □□ **path·o·log′i·cal·ly** adv.

pa·thol·o·gy /pəthólojee/ n. 1 science of bodily diseases. 2 symptoms of a disease. □□ **pa·thol′o·gist** n.

pa·thos /páythos, -thaws, -thōs/ n. quality in speech, writing, events, etc., that evokes pity or sadness.

path·way /páthway/ n. path or its course.

-pathy /pəthee/ comb. form forming nouns denoting: 1 curative treatment (allopathy; homeopathy). 2 feeling (telepathy).

pa·tience /páyshəns/ n. perseverance; ability to endure; forbearance.

pa·tient /páyshənt/ • adj. having or showing patience. • n. person receiving medical treatment. □□ **pa′tient·ly** adv.

pa·ti·na /pəteénə, pát′nə/ n. (pl. **pa·ti·nas**) 1 film, usu. green, formed on old bronze. 2 similar film or gloss on other surfaces. □□ **pat·i·nat·ed** /pát′naytid/ adj. **pat·i·na′tion** n.

pa·ti·o /páteeō/ n. 1 paved usu. roofless area adjoining and belonging to a house. 2 roofless inner court.

pa·tois /patwáa, pátwaa/ n. (pl. same, pronunc. /-waaz/) regional dialect of the common people.

pa·tri·arch /páytreeaark/ n. 1 male head of a family or tribe. 2 Eccl. a chief bishop in the Orthodox Church. b (in the Roman Catholic Church) bishop ranking immediately below the pope. 3 venerable old man. □□ **pa·tri·ar′chal** adj. **pa·tri·ar′chal·ly** adv.

pa·tri·arch·ate /páytreeaárkət, -kayt/ n. office, rank, see, or residence of an patriarch.

pa·tri·ar·chy /páytreeaárkee/ n. (pl. **-chies**) system of society, government, etc., ruled by a man or men and with descent through the male line.

pa·tri·cian /pətríshən/ • n. 1 hist. member of the ancient Roman nobility. 2 aristocrat. • adj. aristocratic; well-bred.

pat·ri·mo·ny /pátrimōnee/ n. (pl. **-nies**) property inherited from one's father or ancestor. □□ **pat·ri·mo′ni·al** adj.

pa·tri·ot /páytreeət, -ot/ n. person who is devoted to and ready to support or defend his or her country. □□ **pa·tri·ot′ic** /-reeótik/ adj. **pa·tri·ot′i·cal·ly** adv. **pa′tri·o·tism** n.

pa·trol /pətról/ • n. 1 act of walking or travel-

ing around an area in order to protect or supervise it. 2 guards, police, troops, etc., sent out to watch or protect. • v. (**pa·trolled, pa·trol·ling**) 1 tr. carry out a patrol of. 2 intr. act as a patrol. □ **patrol car** police car used in patrolling roads and streets. □□ **pa·trol′ler** n.

pa·trol·man /pətrólmən/ n. (pl. **-men**) police officer assigned to or patrolling a specific route.

pa·tron /páytrən/ n. (fem. **pa·tron·ess**) 1 person who gives financial or other support to a person, cause, work of art, etc. 2 habitual customer.□ **patron saint** protecting or guiding saint of a person, place, etc.

pa·tron·age /pátrənij/ n. 1 patron's or customer's support. 2 power to appoint others to government jobs. b distribution of such jobs.

pa·tron·ize /páytrənīz, pát-/ v.tr. 1 treat condescendingly. 2 act as a patron toward (a person, cause, artist, etc.); support; encourage. 3 be a customer of. □□ **pa·tron·i·za′tion** n. **pa′tron·iz·er** n. **pa′tron·iz·ing** adj. **pa′tron·iz·ing·ly** adv.

pat·ro·nym·ic /pátrənímik/ n. name derived from the name of a father or ancestor, e.g., Johnson, O'Brien, Ivanovich.

pat·sy /pátsee/ n. (pl. **-sies**) person who is deceived, ridiculed, tricked, etc.

pat·ter¹ /pátər/ • v. intr. make a rapid succession of taps. • n. rapid succession of taps, short light steps, etc.

pat·ter² /pátər/ • n. rapid speech used by a comedian or salesperson. • v. intr. talk glibly or mechanically.

pat·tern /pátərn/ • n. 1 decorative design. 2 regular or logical form, order, etc. 3 model or design, e.g., of a garment, from which copies can be made. 4 example of excellence; ideal; model (a pattern of elegance). • v.tr. 1 model (a thing) on a design, etc. 2 decorate with a pattern.

pat·ty /pátee/ n. (pl. **-ties**) small flat cake of food.

pau·ci·ty /páwsitee/ n. smallness of number or quantity.

paunch /pawnch/ n. 1 belly or stomach, esp. when protruding. 2 ruminant's first stomach; rumen. □□ **paunch′y** adj. (**paunch·i·er, paunch·i·est**). **paunch′i·ness** n.

pau·per /páwpər/ n. person without means; beggar. □□ **pau′per·ism** /-rizəm/ n. **pau′per·ize** v.tr. **pau·per·i·za′tion** /-rízáysh'n/ n.

pause /pawz/ • n. temporary stop; silence. • v.intr. 1 make a pause; wait. 2 linger over (a word, etc.).

pave /payv/ v.tr. cover (a street, floor, etc.) with paving, etc. □ **pave the way for** prepare for. □□ **pav′er** n. **pav′ing** n.

pave·ment /páyvmənt/ n. paved path, roadway, etc.

pa·vil·ion /pəvílyən/ n. 1 tent, esp. a large one at a show, fair, etc. 2 building or stand used for entertainments, exhibits, etc. 3 detached building that is part of a connected set of buildings, as at a hospital.

Pav·lo·vi·an /pavlóveeən/ adj. of or relating to I. P. Pavlov or his work, esp. on conditioned reflexes.

paw /paw/ • n. 1 foot of an animal having claws or nails. 2 colloq. person's hand. • v. 1 tr. strike or scrape with a paw or foot. 2 intr. scrape the ground with a paw or hoof. 3 tr. colloq. fondle awkwardly or indecently.

pawl /pawl/ n. lever with a catch for the teeth of a wheel or bar.

pawn[1] /pawn/ *n.* **1** *Chess* piece of the smallest size and value. **2** person used by others for their own purposes.

pawn[2] /pawn/ • *v.tr.* **1** deposit an object, esp. with a pawnbroker, as security for money lent. **2** pledge or wager. • *n.* object left as security for money, etc., lent.

pawn·broker /páwnbrókər/ *n.* person who lends money at interest on the security of personal property pawned. □□ **pawn′brok·ing** *n.*

Paw·nee /pawneé, paa-/ *n.* **1 a** N. American people native to Kansas and Nebraska. **b** member of this people. **2** language of this people.

pawn·shop /páwnshop/ *n.* pawnbroker's shop.

paw·paw /páwpaw/ *n.* (also **pa′paw**) N. American tree with purple flowers and edible fruit.

pay /pay/ • *v.tr.* (*past* and *past part.* **paid** /payd/) **1** (also *absol.*) give (a person, etc.) what is due for services done, goods received, debts incurred, etc. **2** give (a sum) for work done, a debt, etc. **3 a** give, bestow, or express. **b** make (a visit). **4** (also *absol.*) be profitable or advantageous. **5** reward or punish. **6** let out (a rope) by slackening it. • *n.* wages. • *adj.* requiring payment of a coin, a set fee, etc., for use. □ **in the pay of** employed by. **pay back 1** repay. **2** punish or be revenged on. **pay dirt 1** *Mineral.* ground worth working for ore. **2** financially promising situation. **pay off 1** dismiss (workers) with a final payment. **2** *colloq.* yield good results; succeed. **3** pay (a debt) in full. **pay phone** coin-operated telephone. □□ **pay·ee** /payeé/ *n.* **pay′er** *n.*

---

pay Middle English (in the sense 'pacify'): from Old French *paie* (noun), *payer* (verb), from Latin *pacare* 'appease,' from *pax, pac-* 'peace.' The notion of 'payment' arose from the sense of 'pacifying' a creditor.

---

pay·a·ble /páyəbəl/ *adj.* that must or may be paid; due.

pay·day /páyday/ *n.* day on which salary or wages are paid.

pay·load /páylōd/ *n.* **1** part of an aircraft's load from which revenue is derived, as paying passengers. **2** explosive warhead carried by an aircraft or rocket.

pay·mas·ter /páymastər/ *n.* official who pays troops, workers, etc.

pay·ment /páymənt/ *n.* **1** act or an instance of paying. **2** amount paid. **3** reward; recompense.

pay·off /páyawf/ *n. sl.* **1** act of payment. **2** climax. **3** final reckoning. **4** *colloq.* bribe; bribery.

pay·o·la /payólə/ *n.* bribe offered in return for unofficial promotion of a product, etc., in the media.

pay·roll /páyrōl/ *n.* list of employees receiving regular pay.

Pb *symb. Chem.* lead.

PBS *abbr.* Public Broadcasting Service.

PC *abbr.* **1** personal computer. **2** politically correct.

PCB *abbr.* **1** *Computing* printed circuit board. **2** *Chem.* polychlorinated biphenyl, any of several toxic aromatic compounds formed as waste in industrial processes.

PCP *n.* **1** *sl.* illicit hallucinogenic drug, phencyclidine hydrochloride (*phenyl cyclohexyl piperidine*). **2** pneumocystis carinii pneumonia.

pct. *abbr.* percent.

PD *abbr.* Police Department.

Pd *symb. Chem.* palladium.

pd. *abbr.* paid.

PDT *abbr.* Pacific Daylight Time.

PE *abbr.* physical education.

pea /pee/ *n.* **1** hardy climbing plant, with seeds growing in pods and used for food. **2** its seed.

peace /pees/ *n.* **1 a** quiet; tranquillity. **b** mental calm; serenity (*peace of mind*). **2** freedom from or the cessation of war. **3** freedom from civil disorder. □ **hold one's peace** keep silent. **peace pipe** tobacco pipe smoked as a token of peace among some Native Americans.

peace·a·ble /peésəbəl/ *adj.* **1** disposed to peace. **2** tranquil; peaceful. □□ **peace′a·ble·ness** *n.* **peace′a·bly** *adv.*

peace·ful /peésfool/ *adj.* **1** characterized by peace; tranquil. **2** not infringing peace. □□ **peace′ful·ly** *adv.* **peace′ful·ness** *n.*

peace·mak·er /peésmaykər/ *n.* person who brings about peace. □□ **peace′mak·ing** *n.* & *adj.*

peace·time /peéstīm/ *n.* period when a country is not at war.

peach /peech/ *n.* **1 a** round juicy fruit with downy cream or yellow skin flushed with red. **b** tree bearing it. **2** yellowish pink color of. **3** *colloq.* **a** person or thing of superlative quality. **b** often *offens.* attractive young woman. □□ **peach′y** *adj.* (**peach·i·er, peach·i·est**). **peach′i·ness** *n.*

pea·cock /peékok/ *n.* male peafowl, having brilliant plumage and an erectile fanlike tail (with eyelike markings).

pea·fowl /peéfowl/ *n.* peacock or peahen.

pea·hen /peéhen/ *n.* female peafowl.

pea·jack·et /peé jakit/ *n.* (also **pea′ coat**) *n.* sailor's short double-breasted woolen overcoat.

peak[1] /peek/ • *n.* **1** projecting usu. pointed part, esp.: **a** the pointed top of a mountain. **b** a mountain with a peak. **c** stiff brim at the front of a cap. **2 a** highest point. **b** time of greatest success. • *v.intr.* reach the highest value, quality, etc. □□ **peaked** *adj.* **peak′i·ness** *n.*

peak[2] /peek/ *v.intr.* **1** waste away. **2** (as **peak·ed** /peékid/ *adj.*) pale; sickly.

peal /peel/ • *n.* **1 a** the loud ringing of a bell or bells, esp. a series of changes. **b** set of bells. **2** loud repeated sound, esp. of thunder, laughter, etc. • *v.* **1** *intr.* sound forth in a peal. **2** *tr.* utter sonorously. **3** *tr.* ring (bells) in peals.

pea·nut /peénut/ *n.* **1** leguminous plant, bearing pods that ripen underground and contain seeds used as food and yielding oil. **2** seed of this plant. **3** (in *pl.*) *colloq.* paltry or trivial thing or amount, esp. of money. □ **peanut butter** paste of ground roasted peanuts.

pear /pair/ *n.* **1** yellowish or brownish green fleshy fruit, tapering toward the stalk. **2** tree bearing it.

pearl /pərl/ • *n.* **1 a** (often *attrib.*) usu. white or bluish gray hard mass formed within the shell of certain oysters highly prized as a gem for its luster (*pearl necklace*). **b** imitation of this. **2** precious thing; finest example. **3** anything resembling a pearl, e.g., a dewdrop, tear, etc. • *v.intr.* fish for pearl oysters. □□ **pearl·er** *n.* **pearl′ly** *adj.*

peas·ant /pézənt/ *n.* **1** small farmer; agricultural worker. **2** *derog.* boorish or unsophisticated person. ▫▫ **peas′ant·ry** *n.* (*pl.* **-ries**).

peat /peet/ *n.* **1** vegetable matter decomposed in water and partly carbonized, used for fuel, in horticulture, etc. **2** a cut piece of this. ▫▫ **peat′y** *adj.*

peat·bog /péetbawg, -bog/ *n.* bog composed of peat.

peat·moss /péetmaws, -mos/ *n.* dried peat from mosses.

peb·ble /pébəl/ *n.* small smooth stone worn by the action of water. ▫▫ **peb′bly** *adj.*

pec /pek/ *abbr.* pectoral (muscle).

pe·can /pikáan, -kán, péekan/ *n.* **1** pinkish brown smooth nut with an edible kernel. **2** hickory of the southern US, producing this.

pec·ca·dil·lo /pékədílō/ *n.* (*pl.* **-loes** or **-los**) trifling offense; venial sin.

peck[1] /pek/ • *v.tr.* **1** strike or bite (something) with a beak. **2** kiss hastily or perfunctorily. **3 a** make (a hole) by pecking. **b** remove or pluck out by pecking. **4** *colloq.* (also *absol.*) eat (food) listlessly; nibble at. • *n.* **1 a** stroke or bite with a beak. **b** mark made by this. **2** hasty or perfunctory kiss. ▫ **pecking order** social hierarchy.

peck[2] /pek/ *n.* dry measure equal to 8 quarts.

pec·tin /péktin/ *n. Biochem.* any of various soluble gelatinous polysaccharides found in ripe fruits, etc., and used as a gelling agent in jams and jellies. ▫▫ **pec′tic** *adj.*

pec·to·ral /péktərəl/ • *adj.* of or worn on the breast or chest. • *n.* (esp. in *pl.*) pectoral muscle or fin.

pec·u·late /pékyəlayt/ *v.* embezzle (money). ▫▫ **pec·u·la·tion** /-láyshən/ *n.* **pec′u·la·tor** *n.*

pe·cu·liar /pikyŏŏlyər/ *adj.* **1** strange; odd; unusual. **2 a** belonging exclusively. **b** belonging to the individual. **3** particular; special. ▫▫ **pe·cu′liar·ly** *adv.*

---

peculiar late Middle English (in the sense 'particular, special'): from Latin *peculiaris* 'of private property,' from *peculium* 'property,' from *pecu* 'cattle' (cattle being a characteristic form of private property in agrarian societies). The sense 'odd' dates from the early 17th century.

---

pe·cu·li·ar·i·ty /pikyŏŏleeáritee/ *n.* (*pl.* **-ties**) **1 a** idiosyncrasy; oddity. **b** instance of this. **2** characteristic or habit.

pe·cu·ni·ar·y /pikyŏŏnee-eree/ *adj.* of, concerning, or consisting of, money (*pecuniary aid*). ▫▫ **pe·cu·ni·ar′i·ly** *adv.*

ped·a·gogue /pédəgog, -gawg/ *n.* schoolmaster or teacher, esp. a pedantic one. ▫▫ **ped·a·gog′ic** /-gójik, -gójik/ *adj.* **ped·a·gog′i·cal** *adj.* **ped·a·gog′i·cal·ly** *adv.* **ped·a·gog′ism** /-gog-/ *n.* (also **ped′a·gogu·ism**)

ped·a·go·gy /pédəgōjee, -gojee/ *n.* science of teaching. ▫▫ **ped·a·gog′ics** /-gójiks, -gójiks/ *n.*

ped·al[1] /péd′l/ • *n.* lever or control operated by foot, esp. in a vehicle, on a bicycle, etc. • *v.* **1** *intr.* operate a cycle, organ, etc., by using the pedals. **2** *tr.* work (a bicycle, etc.) with the pedals.

ped·al[2] /péd′l, pée-/ *adj. Zool.* of the foot or feet.

ped·ant /péd′nt/ *n.* person who insists on strict adherence to formal rules or literal meaning at the expense of a wider view. ▫▫ **pe·dan·tic** /pidántik/ *adj.* **pe·dan′ti·cal·ly** *adv.* **ped′ant·ry** *n.* (*pl.* **-ries**).

ped·dle /péd′l/ *v.* **1** *tr.* **a** sell (goods) while traveling. **b** advocate or promote. **2** *tr.* sell (drugs) illegally. **3** *intr.* engage in selling. ▫▫ **ped·dler** /-dlər/ *n.* **ped′dler·y** *n.*

ped·er·as·ty /pédərastee/ *n.* anal intercourse esp. between a man and a boy. ▫▫ **ped′er·ast** *n.*

ped·es·tal /pédistəl/ *n.* **1** base supporting a column or pillar. **2** stone, etc., base of a statue, etc.

pe·des·tri·an /pidéstreeən/ • *n.* (often *attrib.*) person who is walking. • *adj.* prosaic; dull; uninspired. ▫▫ **pe·des′tri·an·ism** *n.* **pe·des′tri·an·ize** *v.*

pe·di·at·rics /péedeeátriks/ *n.pl.* (treated as *sing.*) branch of medicine dealing with children and their diseases. ▫▫ **pe·di·at′ric** *adj.* **pe·di·a·tri′cian** /-deeətríshən/ *n.*

ped·i·cure /pédikyŏŏr/ *n.* care or treatment of the feet, esp. of the toenails.

ped·i·gree /pédigree/ *n.* **1** (often *attrib.*) recorded line of descent. **2** genealogical table. ▫▫ **ped′i·greed** *adj.*

ped·i·ment /pédimənt/ *n.* triangular front part of a building, esp. over a doorway, etc. ▫▫ **ped·i·men·tal** /-mént′l/ *adj.* **ped′i·ment·ed** *adj.*

PEDIMENT

pe·dom·e·ter /pidómitər/ *n.* instrument for estimating distance traveled on foot by recording the number of steps taken.

pe·dun·cle /pedúngkəl, péedung-/ *n. Bot.* stalk of a flower, fruit, or cluster. ▫▫ **pe·dun·cu·lar** /-kyələr/ *adj.* **pe·dun′cu·late** /-kyələt/ *adj.*

peek /peek/ • *v.intr.* look slyly; peep. • *n.* quick or sly look.

peel /peel/ • *v.* **1** *tr.* **a** strip the skin, rind, bark, wrapping, etc., from. **b** strip (skin, peel, wrapping, etc.) from a fruit, etc. **2** *intr.* **a** become bare of bark, skin, paint, etc. **b** flake off. • *n.* outer covering of a fruit, vegetable, shrimp, etc.; rind. ▫▫ **peel′er** *n.* (in sense 1 of *v.*).

peel·ing /péeling/ *n.* strip of the outer skin of a vegetable, fruit, etc. (*potato peelings*).

peen /peen/ *n.* the wedge-shaped or thin or curved end of a hammer head.

peep[1] /peep/ • *v.intr.* **1** look through a narrow opening; look furtively. **2** come slowly into view; emerge. • *n.* furtive or peering glance. ▫ **peeping Tom** furtive voyeur.

peep[2] /peep/ • *v.intr.* make a shrill feeble sound

as of young birds, mice, etc.; squeak; chirp. •
n. **1** such a sound; cheep. **2** slightest sound or
utterance, esp. of protest, etc.

peep·hole /peep-hōl/ *n.* tiny hole to look
through.

peer[1] /peer/ *v.intr.* look keenly or with difficulty.

peer[2] /peer/ *n.* **1** person who is equal in ability,
standing, rank, or value; a contemporary (*tried
by a jury of his peers*). **2 a** (*fem.* **peer·ess**) member
of the British nobility. **b** noble of any country.
□□ **peer'age** *n.* **peer'less** *adj.*

peeve /peev/ *colloq.* • *v.tr.* (usu. as **peeved** *adj.*)
annoy; vex; irritate. • *n.* **1** cause of annoyance.
2 vexation.

peev·ish /peevish/ *adj.* querulous; irritable.
□□ **pee'vish·ly** *adv.* **pee'vish·ness** *n.*

peg /peg/ • *n.* **1 a** usu. cylindrical pin or bolt
of wood or metal, used for holding, hanging,
or supporting things. **2** small peg, matchstick,
etc., for calculating the scores at cribbage. • *v.tr.*
(**pegged**, **peg·ging**) **1** fix (a thing) with a peg.
2 *Econ.* stabilize (prices, wages, etc.). **3** throw.
□ **peg away** work consistently. **take a person down
a peg or two** humble a person.

peg·board /pégbawrd/ *n.* board having a regular pattern of small holes for pegs, used for
displays, games, etc.

pe·jo·ra·tive /pijáwrətiv, -jór-, péjərə-, pée-/ •
adj. depreciatory. • *n.* depreciatory word.
□□ **pe·jo'ra·tive·ly** *adv.*

Pe·king·ese /peekineez, -ées/ (also **Pe·kin'ese**)
n. (*pl.* same) short-legged lapdog with long hair
and a snub nose.

pe·koe /peekō/ *n.* superior kind of black tea.

pe·lag·ic /pilájik/ *adj.* of or performed on the
open sea.

pelf /pelf/ *n. derog.* or *joc.* money; wealth.

pel·i·can /pélikən/ *n.* large gregarious waterfowl
with a large bill and a pouch in the throat for
storing fish.

pel·la·gra /pilágrə, -láygrə, -laʹa-/ *n.* disease
caused by deficiency of nicotinic acid, characterized by cracking of the skin and often resulting
in insanity. □□ **pel·la'grous** *adj.*

pel·let /pélit/ *n.* **1** small compressed ball of paper, bread, etc. **2** pill. **3** piece of small shot.
□□ **pel'let·ize** *v.tr.*

pell-mell /pélmél/ *adv.* **1** headlong; recklessly
(*rushed pell-mell out of the room*). **2** in disorder
or confusion.

pel·lu·cid /pilóōsid/ *adj.* transparent; clear; not
confused. □□ **pel·lu·cid'i·ty** *n.* **pel·lu'cid·ly** *adv.*

pelt[1] /pelt/ • *v.* **1** *tr.* (usu. foll. by *with*) strike repeatedly with thrown objects. **2** *intr.* fall quickly
and torrentially.

pelt[2] /pelt/ *n.* **1** undressed skin of a fur-bearing
mammal. **2** *joc.* human skin. □□ **pelt'ry** *n.*

pel·vic /pélvik/ *adj.* of or relating to the pelvis.
□ **pelvic girdle** bony or cartilaginous structure
in vertebrates to which the posterior limbs are
attached.

pel·vis /pélvis/ *n.* (*pl.* **pel·vis·es** or **pel·ves** /-
veez/) basin-shaped cavity at the lower end of
the torso of most vertebrates, formed from the
hip bones, sacrum, and other vertebrae.

pen[1] /pen/ • *n.* instrument for writing or drawing with ink. • *v.tr.* (**penned**, **pen·ning**) write.
□ **pen name** literary pseudonym. **pen pal** *colloq.*
friend communicated with by letter only.

pen[2] /pen/ • *n.* small enclosure for cows, sheep,
poultry, etc. • *v.tr.* (**penned**, **pen·ning**) (often
foll. by *in*, *up*) enclose or shut in a pen.

pen[3] /pen/ *n. sl.* = PENITENTIARY *n.*

pe·nal /peenəl/ *adj.* **1** of or concerning punishment or its infliction. **2** (of an offense) punishable, esp. by law. □□ **pe'nal·ly** *adv.*

pe·nal·ize /peenəlīz/ *v.tr.* subject (a person) to
a penalty or comparative disadvantage. □□ **pe·
nal·i·za'tion** *n.*

pen·al·ty /pénəltee/ *n.* (*pl.* **-ties**) **1 a** punishment, esp. a fine, for a breach of law, contract,
etc. **b** fine paid. **2** disadvantage, loss, etc., esp.
as a result of one's own actions (*paid the penalty for his carelessness*). **3** disadvantage imposed
on a competitor or team for a breach of the
rules, etc.

pen·ance /pénəns/ *n.* act of self-punishment as
reparation for guilt, sins, etc.

pen·chant /pénchənt/ *n.* inclination or liking.

pen·cil /pénsil/ *n.* (often *attrib.*) instrument
for writing or drawing, usu. consisting of a thin
rod of graphite, etc., enclosed in a wooden cylinder or metal case. • *v.tr.* (**pen·ciled**, **pen·cil·
ing**; **pen·cilled**, **pen·cil·ling**) **1** tint or mark with
or as if with a pencil. **2** write, esp. tentatively or
provisionally. □□ **pen'cil·er** *n.*

pend·ant /péndənt/ *n.* (also **pend'ent**) hanging
jewel, etc., esp. one attached to a necklace,
bracelet, etc.

pend·ent /péndənt/ *adj.* (also **pend'ant**) **1 a**
hanging. **b** overhanging. **2** undecided; pending.
□□ **pend'den·cy** *n.*

pend·ing /pénding/ • *predic.adj.* awaiting decision or settlement; undecided (*a settlement
was pending*). • *prep.* **1** during (*pending these
negotiations*). **2** until (*pending his return*).

pen·du·lous /pénjələs, péndə-, -dyə-/ *adj.* hanging down; drooping and esp. swinging. □□ **pen'
du·lous·ly** *adv.*

pen·du·lum /pénjələm, péndə-, -dyə-/ *n.* weight
suspended so as to swing freely, esp. a rod with
a weighted end regulating the movement of a
clock's works.

PENDULUM

pen·e·trate /pénitrayt/ v. **1** tr. a find access into or through, esp. forcibly. **b** permeate. **2** tr. see into, find out, or discern (a person's mind, the truth, a meaning, etc.). **3** tr. see through. **4** intr. be absorbed by the mind. **5** tr. (as **penetrating** adj.) a insightful; sensitive. **b** easily heard; piercing. □□ **pen'e·tra·ble** adj. **pen·e·tra·bil'i·ty** n. **pen'e·trant** adj. & n. **pen'e·trat·ing·ly** adv. **pen·e·tra'tion** /-tráyshən/ n. **pen·e·tra·tive** /-trətiv/ adj. **pen'e·tra·tor** n.

pen·guin /pénggwin/ n. flightless sea bird of the southern hemisphere, with wings developed into scaly flippers for swimming underwater.

pen·i·cil·lin /pénisílin/ n. any of various antibiotics produced naturally by molds or synthetically.

pen·in·su·la /pənínsələ, -syələ/ n. piece of land almost surrounded by water. □□ **pen·in'su·lar** adj.

pe·nis /péenis/ n. (pl. **pe·nis·es** or **pe·nes** /-neez/) male organ of copulation and (in mammals) urination. □□ **pe·nile** /-nīl, -nəl/ adj.

pen·i·tent /pénitənt/ • adj. repentant. • n. repentant sinner. □□ **pen'i·tence** n. **pen·i·ten'tial** /-ténshəl/ adj. **pen·i·ten'tial·ly** adv. **pen'i·tent·ly** adv.

pen·i·ten·tia·ry /péniténshəree/ • n. (pl. **-ries**) state or federal prison. • adj. **1** of or concerning penance. **2** of or concerning reformatory treatment.

pen·knife /pén-nīf/ n. pocketknife.

pen·light /pénlīt/ n. pen-sized flashlight.

pen·man·ship /pénmənship/ n. ability in handwriting.

Penn. abbr. (also **Penna.**) Pennsylvania.

pen·nant /pénənt/ n. **1** Naut. long tapering flag. **2** a flag denoting a sports championship, etc. **b** sports championship.

pen·ni·less /pénilis/ adj. having no money; destitute. □□ **pen'ni·less·ly** adv. **pen'ni·less·ness** n.

pen·non /pénən/ n. long narrow flag; pennant. □□ **pen'noned** adj.

Penn·syl·va·nian /pénsilváynyən/ • n. **1** native or inhabitant of Pennsylvania. **2** (prec. by the) Geol. Paleozoic era period from about 310 to 280 million years ago, an age of insect and reptile development. • adj. **1** of or relating to Pennsylvania. **2** Geol. of or relating to the Pennsylvanian period.

pen·ny /pénee/ n. (pl. **-nies**) **1** (in the US, Canada, etc.) one-cent coin. **2** British coin equal to one hundredth of a pound. **3** hist. former British coin equal to one two-hundred-and-fortieth of a pound. □ **penny-pincher** very frugal person. **penny-pinching** n. frugality; cheapness. • adj. frugal.

pen·ny·weight /péneewayt/ n. unit of weight, 24 grains or one twentieth of an ounce troy.

Pe·nob·scot /pənóbskot, -skət/ n. **1** a N. American people native to Maine. **b** member of this people. **2** language of this people.

pe·nol·o·gy /peenóləjee/ n. the study of the punishment of crime and of prison management. □□ **pe·no·log·i·cal** /-nəlójikəl/ adj. **pe·nol'o·gist** n.

pen·sion /pénshən/ • n. regular payment made to the disabled, retirees, etc. • v.tr. grant a pension to. □□ **pen'sion·a·ble** adj. **pen'sion·er** n. **pen'sion·less** adj.

pen·sive /pénsiv/ adj. **1** deep in thought. **2** sorrowfully thoughtful. □□ **pen'sive·ly** adv. **pen'sive·ness** n.

pent /pent/ adj. closely confined; shut in (pent-up feelings).

penta- /péntə/ comb. form five.

pen·ta·cle /péntəkəl/ n. figure used as a symbol, esp. in magic, e.g., a pentagram.

pen·ta·gon /péntəgon/ n. **1** plane figure with five sides and angles. **2** (**the Pentagon**) pentagonal headquarters building of the US Department of Defense, located near Washington, D.C. □□ **pen·tag·o·nal** /-tágənəl/ adj.

pen·ta·gram /péntəgram/ n. five-pointed star.

pen·tam·e·ter /pentámitər/ n. verse of five feet, e.g., English iambic verse of ten syllables.

Pen·ta·teuch /péntətook, -tyook/ n. first five books of the Old Testament. □□ **pen'ta·teuch·al** adj.

pen·tath·lon /pentáthlən, -laan/ n. athletic event comprising five different events for each competitor. □□ **pen·tath'lete** /-táthleet/ n.

Pen·te·cost /péntikawst, -kost/ n. **1** a Whitsunday. **b** festival celebrating the descent of the Holy Spirit on Whitsunday, fifty days after Easter. **2** Jewish harvest festival, on the fiftieth day after the second day of Passover.

Pen·te·cos·tal /péntikóst'l, -káwst'l/ adj. (also **pen'te·cos·tal**) of or designating esp. fundamentalist Christian sects and individuals who emphasize the gifts of the Holy Spirit and express religious feelings by clapping, shouting, dancing, etc. □□ **Pen·te·cos'tal·ism** n. **Pen·te·cos'tal·ist** adj. & n.

pent·house /pént-hows/ n. house or apartment on the roof or the top floor of a tall building.

Pen·to·thal /péntəthawl/ n. propr. intravenous anesthetic, thiopental sodium.

pen·ul·ti·mate /pinúltimət/ adj. & n. last but one.

pen·um·bra /pinúmbrə/ n. (pl. **pen·um·brae** /-bree/ or **pen·um·bras**) **1** a partly shaded region around the shadow of an opaque body, esp. that around the total shadow of the moon or earth in an eclipse. **b** less dark outer part of a sunspot. **2** partial shadow. □□ **pen·um'bral** adj.

pe·nu·ri·ous /pinoŏreeəs, pinyoŏr-/ adj. **1** poor. **2** stingy; grudging. □□ **pe·nu'ri·ous·ly** adv. **pe·nu'ri·ous·ness** n.

pen·u·ry /pényəree/ n. (pl. **-ries**) **1** destitution; poverty. **2** lack; scarcity.

pe·on /pée·on, pée·ən/ n. **1** Spanish American day laborer or farm worker. **2** drudge. **3** hist. worker held in servitude in the southwestern US. □□ **pe'on·age** n.

pe·o·ny /pée·ənee/ n. (pl. **-nies**) herbaceous plant with large globular red, pink, or white flowers.

peo·ple /péepəl/ • n. (usu. as pl.) **1** a persons composing a community, tribe, race, nation, etc. (the American people). **b** group of persons of a usu. specified kind (the chosen people). **2** (prec. by the) the mass of people in a country, etc. **3** parents or other relatives. **4** subjects, armed followers, congregation, etc. **5** persons in general (people do not like rudeness). • v.tr. populate; inhabit.
¶ See note at PERSON.

pep /pep/ *colloq.* • *n.* vigor; go; spirit. • *v.tr.* (**pepped, pep·ping**) (usu. foll. by *up*) fill with vigor. □ **pep talk** usu. short talk intended to enthuse, encourage, etc.

pep·per /pépər/ • *n.* **1** hot aromatic condiment from the dried berries of certain plants. **2** plant with a red, green, or yellow many-seeded fruit grown as a vegetable. • *v.tr.* **1** sprinkle or treat with or as if with pepper. **2** pelt with missiles. □ **pepper mill** device for grinding pepper by hand.

pep·per·corn /pépərkawrn/ *n.* dried pepper berry.

pep·per·mint /pépərmint/ *n.* **1 a** mint plant grown for its strong-flavored oil. **b** this oil. **2** candy flavored with peppermint. □□ **pep'per·mint·y** *adj.*

pep·per·o·ni /pépərōnee/ *n.* spicy sausage seasoned with pepper.

pep·per·y /pépəree/ *adj.* **1** of, like, or containing much pepper. **2** hot-tempered. **3** pungent; stinging. □□ **pep'per·i·ness** *n.*

pep·py /pépee/ *adj.* (**pep·pi·er, pep·pi·est**) *colloq.* vigorous; energetic; bouncy. □□ **pep'pi·ly** *adv.* **pep'pi·ness** *n.*

pep·sin /pépsin/ *n.* enzyme contained in the gastric juice.

pep·tic /péptik/ *adj.* concerning or promoting digestion. □ **peptic ulcer** an ulcer in the stomach or duodenum.

Pe·quot /péekwot/ *n.* **1 a** N. American people native to eastern Connecticut. **b** member of this people. **2** language of this people.

per /pər/ *prep.* **1** for each. **2** by means of; by; through (*per rail*). **3** (in full **as per**) in accordance with.

per- /pər/ *prefix* **1** forming verbs, nouns, and adjectives meaning: through; all over. **2** completely; very.

per·ad·ven·ture /pərədvénchər, pér-/ *archaic* or *joc. adv.* perhaps.

per·am·bu·late /pərámbyəlayt/ *v.* **1** *tr.* walk through, over, or about. **2** *intr.* walk from place to place. □□ **per·am·bu·la·tion** /-láyshən/ *n.* **per·am·bu·la·to·ry** /-lətáwree/ *adj.*

per an·num /pər ánəm/ *adv.* for each year.

per cap·i·ta /pər kápitə/ *adv. & adj.* for each person.

per·ceive /pərseev/ *v.tr.* **1** apprehend, esp. through the sight; observe. **2** apprehend with the mind; understand; regard. □□ **per·ceiv'a·ble** *adj.* **per·ceiv'er** *n.*

per·cent /pərsént/ (also **per cent**) • *adv.* in every hundred. • *n.* **1** percentage. **2** one part in every hundred.

¶ Both spellings, **percent** and **per cent**, are acceptable, but one should be consistent. **Percent** is more common in US usage, and **per cent** is more common in British usage.

per·cent·age /pərséntij/ *n.* **1** rate or proportion percent. **2** proportion. **3** *colloq.* personal benefit or advantage.

per·cen·tile /pərséntīl/ *n. Statistics* one of 99 values of a variable dividing a population into 100 equal groups as regards the value of that variable.

per·cep·ti·ble /pərséptibəl/ *adj.* capable of being perceived. □□ **per·cep·ti·bil'i·ty** *n.* **per·cep'ti·bly** *adv.*

per·cep·tion /pərsépshən/ *n.* **1** act or faculty of

perceiving. **2 a** intuitive recognition of a truth, aesthetic quality, etc. **b** instance of this. □□ **per·cep'tion·al** *adj.* **per·cep·tu·al** /-chōōəl/ *adj.* **per·cep'tu·al·ly** *adv.*

per·cep·tive /pərséptiv/ *adj.* **1** capable of perceiving. **2** sensitive; discerning; observant (*perceptive remark*). □□ **per·cep'tive·ly** *adv.* **per·cep'tive·ness** *n.* **per·cep·tiv'i·ty** *n.*

perch¹ /pərch/ • *n.* **1** bar, branch, etc., used by a bird to rest on. **2** high or precarious place for a person or thing to rest on. • *v.* (usu. foll. by *on*) settle or rest, or cause to settle or rest on or as if on a perch, etc.

perch² /pərch/ *n.* (*pl.* same or **perch·es**) spiny-finned freshwater edible fish.

per·chance /pərcháns/ *adv.* **1** by chance. **2** possibly; maybe.

per·co·late /pérkəlayt/ *v.* **1** *intr.* **a** (of liquid, etc.) filter or ooze gradually. **b** (of an idea, etc.) permeate gradually. **2** *tr.* strain (a liquid, powder, etc.) through a fine mesh, etc. □□ **per·co·la·tion** /-láyshən/ *n.*

per·co·la·tor /pérkəlaytər/ *n.* machine for making coffee by circulating boiling water through ground beans.

per·cus·sion /pərkúshən/ *n.* **1** *Mus.* **a** (often *attrib.*) playing of music by striking instruments with sticks, etc. (*a percussion band*). **b** such instruments collectively. **2** forcible striking of one esp. solid body against another. □ **percussion cap** small amount of explosive powder contained in metal or paper and exploded by striking. □□ **per·cus'sion·ist** *n.* **per·cus'sive** *adj.* **per·cus'sive·ly** *adv.* **per·cus'sive·ness** *n.*

per di·em /pər dée-em, díem/ • *adv. & adj.* for each day. • *n.* allowance or payment for each day.

per·di·tion /pərdíshən/ *n.* eternal death; damnation.

per·e·gri·nate /périgrinayt/ *v.intr.* travel; journey. □□ **per·e·gri·na·tion** /-náyshən/ *n.* **per'e·gri·na·tor** *n.*

per·e·grine /périgrin, -green/ *n.* (in full **per'e·grine fal'con**) widely distributed falcon used for falconry.

pe·remp·to·ry /pərémptəree/ *adj.* **1** admitting no denial or refusal. **2** dogmatic; imperious; dictatorial. □□ **pe·remp'to·ri·ly** *adv.* **pe·remp'to·ri·ness** *n.*

¶ **Peremptory** and **preemptive** can be confused, as both involve stopping something. A **peremptory** act or statement is absolute; it cannot be denied: *Peremptory challenges kept two potential jurors from joining the panel.* A **preemptive** action is one taken before an adversary can act: *Preemptive air strikes stopped the enemy from launching the new warship.*

pe·ren·ni·al /pəréneeəl/ • *adj.* **1** lasting through a year or several years. **2** (of a plant) lasting several years (cf. ANNUAL). **3** lasting a long time or for ever. • *n.* perennial plant. □□ **per·en'ni·al·ly** *adv.*

per·e·stroi·ka /pérestróykə/ *n. hist.* (in the former Soviet Union) reform of the economic and political system.

per·fect • *adj.* /pérfikt/ **1** complete; not deficient. **2 a** faultless (*a perfect diamond*). **b** blameless in morals or behavior. **3 a** very satisfactory (*a perfect evening*). **b** (often foll. by *for*) most

appropriate; suitable. **4** exact; precise (*a perfect circle*). **5** entire; unqualified (*a perfect stranger*). **6** *Gram.* (of a tense) denoting a completed action or event in the past. • *v.tr.* /pərfékt/ **1** make perfect; improve. **2** carry through; complete. • *n.* /pérfikt/ *Gram.* the perfect tense. □ **perfect pitch** = *absolute pitch*. □□ **per·fect′er** *n.* **per·fect′i·ble** *adj.* **per·fect·i·bil′i·ty** *n.* **per′fect·ly** *adv.* **per′fect·ness** *n.*
¶ Literally, **perfect**, **unique**, etc., are absolute words and should not be modified, as they often are in such phrases as "most perfect, quite unique," etc.

per·fec·ta /pərféktə/ *n.* form of betting in which the first two places in a race must be predicted in the correct order.

per·fec·tion /pərfékshən/ *n.* **1** act or process of making perfect. **2** state of being perfect; faultlessness; excellence. **3** perfect person, thing, or example. □ **to perfection** exactly; completely.

per·fec·tion·ism /pərfékshənizəm/ *n.* uncompromising pursuit of excellence. □□ **per·fec′tion·ist** *n. & adj.*

per·fi·dy /pórfidee/ *n.* breach of faith; treachery. □□ **per·fid′i·ous** *adj.* **per·fid′i·ous·ly** *adv.*

per·fo·rate *v.* /pórfərayt/ **1** *tr.* make a hole or holes through; pierce. **2** *tr.* make a row of small holes in (paper, etc.) so that a part may be torn off easily. □□ **per·fo·ra·tion** /-ráyshən/ *n.* **per′fo·ra·tive** *adj.* **per′fo·ra·tor** *n.*

per·force /pərfáwrs/ *adv. archaic* unavoidably; necessarily.

per·form /pərfáwrm/ *v.* **1** *tr.* do; execute. **2** *intr.* act in a play; play an instrument or sing, etc. **3** *intr.* (of a trained animal) execute tricks, etc. **4** *intr.* operate; function. □□ **per·form′a·ble** *adj.* **per·form′er** *n.* **per·form′ing** *adj.*

per·for·mance /pərfáwrməns/ *n.* **1 a** act, process, or manner of performing or carrying out. **b** execution (of a duty, etc.). **2** staging or production (of a drama, piece of music, etc.) (*the afternoon performance*).

per·form·ing arts /pərfáwrming/ *n.pl.* drama, music, and dance, etc.

per·fume /pórfyoom/ • *n.* **1** sweet smell. **2** fluid containing the essence of flowers, etc.; scent. • *v.tr.* (also /pərfyoom/) (usu. as **perfumed** *adj.*) impart a sweet scent to; impregnate with a sweet smell. □□ **per′fum·y** *adj.*

per·fum·er /pərfyoomər/ *n.* maker or seller of perfumes. □□ **per·fum′er·y** *n.* (*pl.* **-ies**).

per·func·to·ry /pərfúngktəree/ *adj.* **1** done merely out of duty; superficial. □□ **per·func′to·ri·ly** *adv.* **per·func′to·ri·ness** *n.*

per·go·la /pórgələ/ *n.* arbor or covered walk, formed of growing plants trained over a trellis.

per·haps /pərháps/ *adv.* it may be; possibly.

peri- /péree/ *prefix* around; about.

per·i·car·di·um /périkárdeeəm/ *n.* (*pl.* **per·i·car·di·a** /-deeə/) membranous sac enclosing the heart. □□ **per·i·car′di·ac** /-deeak/ *adj.* **per·i·car′di·al** *adj.* **per·i·car·di·tis** /-dítis/ *n.*

per·i·gee /périjee/ *n.* point in an orbit where the orbiting body is nearest the center of the body it is orbiting. (opp. APOGEE). □□ **per·i·ge′an** *adj.*

per·i·he·li·on /périhéelyən/ *n.* (*pl.* **per·i·he·li·a** /-lyə/) point of a planet's or comet's orbit nearest the sun's center.

per·il /péril/ *n.* serious and immediate danger.

per·il·ous /périləs/ *adj.* **1** full of risk; dangerous; hazardous. **2** exposed to imminent risk of destruction, etc. □□ **per′il·ous·ly** *adv.* **per′il·ous·ness** *n.*

pe·rim·e·ter /pərímitər/ *n.* **1 a** circumference or outline of a closed figure. **b** length of this. **2** outer boundary of an enclosed area.

per·i·ne·um /périnéeəm/ *n.* region of the body between the anus and the scrotum or vulva. □□ **per·i·ne′al** *adj.*

pe·ri·od /péereeəd/ • *n.* **1** length or portion of time (*periods of rain*). **2** distinct portion of history, a person's life, etc. (*the Federal period*). **3** *Geol.* time forming part of a geological era. **4** interval between recurrences of an event. **5** time allowed for a lesson in school. **6** occurrence of menstruation. **7 a** punctuation mark (.) used at the end of a sentence or an abbreviation. **b** used at the end of a sentence, etc., to indicate finality. • *adj.* characteristic of some past period (*period furniture*).

---

period late Middle English (denoting the time during which something, especially a disease, runs its course): from Old French *periode*, via Latin from Greek *periodos* 'orbit, recurrence, course,' from *peri-* 'around' + *hodos* 'way, course.' The sense 'portion of time' dates from the early 17th century.

---

pe·ri·od·ic /péereeódik/ *adj.* appearing or occurring at regular intervals. □ **periodic table** arrangement of elements in order of increasing atomic number. □□ **pe·ri·od·ic′i·ty** *n.*

pe·ri·od·i·cal /péereeódikəl/ • *n.* newspaper, magazine, etc., issued at regular intervals, usu. monthly or weekly. • *adj.* periodic; occasional. □□ **pe·ri·od′i·cal·ly** *adv.*

per·i·o·don·tics /péreeədóntiks/ *n.pl.* (treated as *sing.*) branch of dentistry concerned with the structures surrounding and supporting the teeth. □□ **per·i·o·don′tal** *adj.* **per·i·o·don′tist** *n.*

per·i·pa·tet·ic /péripətétik/ *adj.* going from place to place; itinerant. □□ **per·i·pa·tet′i·cal·ly** *adv.* **per·i·pa·tet·i·cism** /-tétəsizəm/ *n.*

pe·riph·er·al /pərífərəl/ • *adj.* **1** of minor importance; marginal. **2** of the periphery; on the fringe. **3** (of equipment) used with a computer, etc., but not an integral part of it. • *n.* peripheral device or piece of equipment. □ **peripheral vision 1** area seen around the outside of one's field of vision. **2** ability to perceive in this area. □□ **pe·riph′er·al·ly** *adv.*

pe·riph·er·y /pəríforee/ *n.* (*pl.* **-ies**) **1** boundary of an area or surface. **2** outer or surrounding region.

pe·riph·ra·sis /pərífrəsis/ *n.* (*pl.* **pe·riph·ra·ses** /-seez/) roundabout way of speaking; circumlocution. □□ **per·i·phras·tic** /périfrástik/ *adj.* **per·i·phras′ti·cal·ly** *adv.*

per·i·scope /périskōp/ *n.* apparatus with a tube and mirrors or prisms, by which an observer can see things otherwise out of sight. □□ **per·i·scop·ic** /-skópik/ *adj.* **per·i·scop′i·cal·ly** *adv.*

per·ish /pérish/ *v. intr.* be destroyed; suffer death or ruin.

per·ish·a·ble /périshəbəl/ • *adj.* liable to perish; subject to decay. • *n.* thing, esp. a foodstuff, subject to speedy decay. □□ **per·ish·a·bil′i·ty** *n.* **per′ish·a·ble·ness** *n.*

per·i·to·ne·um /périt'née'əm/ *n.* (*pl.* **per·i·to·ne·ums** or **per·i·to·ne·a** /-nee'ə/) serous membrane lining the cavity of the abdomen. □□ **per·i·to·ne'al** *adj.*

per·i·to·ni·tis /périt'nítis/ *n.* inflammatory disease of the peritoneum.

per·i·wig /périwig/ *n.* esp. *hist.* wig. □□ **per·i·wigged** *adj.*

per·i·win·kle[1] /périwingkəl/ *n.* evergreen trailing plant with blue or white flowers.

per·i·win·kle[2] /périwingkəl/ *n.* intertidal saltwater snail.

per·jure /pórjər/ *v.refl. Law* willfully tell an untruth when under oath. □□ **per'jur·er** *n.*

per·ju·ry /pórjəree/ *n.* (*pl.* **-ries**) *Law* act of willfully telling an untruth when under oath. □□ **per·ju·ri·ous** /-jōoreeəs/ *adj.*

perk[1] /pərk/ *v.tr.* raise (one's head, etc.) briskly. □ **perk up 1** recover confidence, courage, life, or zest. **2** restore confidence or courage or liveliness in. **3** freshen up.

perk[2] /pərk/ *n. colloq.* perquisite.

perk[3] /pərk/ *v. colloq.* **1** *intr.* (of coffee) percolate, make a bubbling sound in the percolator. **2** *tr.* percolate (coffee).

perk·y /pórkee/ *adj.* (**perk·i·er, perk·i·est**) **1** self-assertive; cocky; pert. **2** lively; cheerful. □□ **perk'i·ly** *adv.* **perk'i·ness** *n.*

perm /perm/ ● *n.* permanent wave. ● *v.tr.* give a permanent wave to (a person or a person's hair).

per·ma·frost /pórməfrawst, -frost/ *n.* subsoil that remains frozen throughout the year, as in polar regions.

per·ma·nent /pórmənənt/ ● *adj.* lasting, or intended to last or function, indefinitely. ● *n.* = *permanent wave.* □ **permanent press** process applied to a fabric to make it wrinkle-free. **permanent wave** artificial wave in the hair, intended to last for some time. □□ **per'ma·nence** *n.* **per'ma·nen·cy** *n.* **per'ma·nent·ly** *adv.*

PERISCOPE

per·me·a·ble /pórmeeəbəl/ *adj.* capable of being permeated.

per·me·ate /pórmeeayt/ *v.* **1** *tr.* penetrate throughout; pervade; saturate. **2** *intr.* diffuse it-

self. □□ **per'me·ance** *n.* **per'me·ant** *adj.* **per·me·a·tion** /-áyshən/ *n.* **per'me·a·tor** *n.*

per·mis·si·ble /pərmísibəl/ *adj.* allowable. □□ **per·mis·si·bil'i·ty** *n.* **per·mis'si·bly** *adv.*

per·mis·sion /pərmíshən/ *n.* consent; authorization.

per·mis·sive /pərmísiv/ *adj.* **1** tolerant; liberal. **2** giving permission. □□ **per·mis'sive·ly** *adv.* **per·mis'sive·ness** *n.*

per·mit ● *v.* /pərmít/ (**per·mit·ted, per·mit·ting**) **1** *tr.* give permission or consent to; authorize; allow. **2 a** *tr.* give an opportunity to. **b** *intr.* give an opportunity (*circumstances permitting*). ● *n.* /pórmit/ document giving permission, allowing entry, etc. □□ **per·mit·tee** /pórmitée/ *n.* **per·mit'ter** *n.*

per·mu·ta·tion /pórmyōotáyshən/ *n.* **1** one of the possible ordered arrangements or groupings of a set of numbers, items, etc. **2** any combination or selection of a specified number of things from a larger group. □□ **per·mu·ta'tion·al** *adj.*

per·ni·cious /pərníshəs/ *adj.* destructive; ruinous; fatal. □□ **per·ni'cious·ly** *adv.* **per·ni'cious·ness** *n.*

per·o·ra·tion /pérəráyshən/ *n.* concluding part of a speech, forcefully summing up what has been said.

per·ox·ide /pəróksíd/ ● *n. Chem.* **1 a** = *hydrogen peroxide.* **b** (often *attrib.*) solution of hydrogen peroxide used to bleach the hair or as an antiseptic. **2** compound of oxygen with another element containing the greatest possible proportion of oxygen. ● *v.tr.* bleach (the hair) with peroxide.

per·pen·dic·u·lar /pórpəndíkyələr/ ● *adj.* **1** *Geom.* at right angles (to a given line, plane, or surface). **2** upright; vertical. **3** (of a slope) very steep. ● *n.* perpendicular line, plane, or direction. □□ **per·pen·dic·u·lar·i·ty** /-dikyōoláritee/ *n.* **per·pen·dic'u·lar·ly** *adv.*

per·pe·trate /pórpitrayt/ *v.tr.* commit (a crime, blunder, etc.). □□ **per·pe·tra·tion** /-tráyshən/ *n.* **per'pe·tra·tor** *n.*

¶ To **perpetrate** something is to commit it: *The gang perpetrated outrages against several citizens.* To **perpetuate** something is to cause it to continue or to keep happening: *The stories only serve to perpetuate the myth that the house is haunted.*

perpetrate mid-16th century: from Latin *perpetrat-* 'performed,' from the verb *perpetrare,* from *per-* 'to completion' + *patrare* 'bring about.' In Latin the act perpetrated might be good or bad; in English the verb was first used in statutes referring to crime, hence it acquired a negative association.

per·pet·u·al /pərpéchōoəl/ *adj.* **1** eternal; lasting for ever or indefinitely. **2** continuous; uninterrupted. □□ **per·pet'u·al·ly** *adv.*

per·pet·u·ate /pərpéchōo-ayt/ *v.tr.* **1** make perpetual. **2** preserve from oblivion. □□ **per·pet'u·ance** *n.* **per·pet·u·a·tion** /-áyshən/ *n.* **per·pet'u·a·tor** *n.*

¶ See note at PERPETRATE.

per·pe·tu·i·ty /pórpitōo-itee, -tyōo/ *n.* (*pl.* **-ties**) state or quality of being perpetual. □ **in perpetuity** forever.

per·plex /pərpléks/ *v.tr.* **1** puzzle; bewilder; disconcert. **2** complicate or confuse (a matter).

□□ **per·plex′ed·ly** adv. **per·plex′ing** adj. **per·plex′ing·ly** adv.

per·plex·i·ty /pərpléksitee/ n. (pl. **-ties**) **1** bewilderment. **2** thing which perplexes. **3** state of being complicated.

per·qui·site /pɔ́rkwizit/ n. **1** extra profit or allowance additional to a main income, etc. **2** customary extra right or privilege. **3** incidental benefit attached to employment, etc.

¶ **Perquisite** and **prerequisite** are sometimes confused. **Perquisite** usually means 'an extra allowance or privilege,' e.g., *He had all the perquisites of a movie star, including a stand-in.* **Prerequisite** means 'something required as a precondition,' e.g., *Passing the examination was one of the prerequisites for a teaching position.*

per se /pər sáy/ adv. by or in itself; intrinsically.

per·se·cute /pɔ́rsikyoot/ v.tr. subject to hostility or ill-treatment, esp. on the grounds of political or religious belief. □□ **per·se·cu·tion** /-kyóoshən/ n.**per′se·cu·tor** n. **per·se·cu·to·ry** /-tawree/ adj.

per·se·vere /pɔ́rsiveér/ v.intr. continue steadfastly or determinedly; persist. □□ **per·se·ver′ance** n.

Per·sian /pérzhən, -shən/ • n. **1 a** native or inhabitant of Persia (now Iran). **b** person of Persian descent. **2** language of ancient Persia or modern Iran. **3** (in full **Per′sian cat**) cat of a breed with long silky hair. • adj. of or relating to Persia or its people or language. □ **Persian lamb** tightly curled fur of a young karakul, used in clothing.

per·si·flage /pɔ́rsiflaazh/ n. light raillery; banter.

per·sim·mon /pərsímən/ n. **1** tropical evergreen tree bearing edible tomato-like fruits. **2** fruit of this.

per·sist /pərsíst/ v.intr. **1** continue firmly or obstinately. **2** continue in existence; survive.

per·sist·ent /pərsístənt/ adj. **1** continuing obstinately; persisting. **2** enduring. **3** constantly repeated (*persistent nagging*). □□ **per·sist′ence** n. **per·sist′en·cy** n. **per·sist′ent·ly** adv.

per·snick·e·ty /pərsníkitee/ adj. colloq. **1** fastidious. **2** precise or overprecise.

per·son /pɔ́rsən/ n. **1** individual human being. **2** living body of a human being (*hidden somewhere about your person*). **3** Gram. any of three classes of personal pronouns, verb forms, etc.: the person speaking (**first person**); the person spoken to (**second person**); the person spoken of (**third person**). **4** (in comb.) used to replace -man in words referring to either sex (*salesperson*). □ **in person** physically present.

¶ Some prefer the plural **persons** to **people**, considering the former more formal and specific, and holding **people** to be more general and indefinite. General usage, however, does not support this distinction. In some contexts, **persons**, by pointing to the individual, may sound less friendly than **people**: *The number should not be disclosed to any unauthorized persons.*

per·so·na /pərsónə/ n. (pl. **per·so·nae** /-nee/) aspect of the personality as shown to or perceived by others. □ **persona non grata** /non graátə, graátə/ person not acceptable.

per·son·a·ble /pɔ́rsənəbəl/ adj. pleasing in appearance and behavior. □□ **per′son·a·ble·ness** n. **per′son·a·bly** adv.

per·son·age /pɔ́rsənij/ n. **1** person, esp. of rank or importance. **2** character in a play, etc.

per·son·al /pɔ́rsənəl/ adj. **1** one's own; individual; private. **2** done or made in person (*my personal attention*). **3** directed to or concerning an individual (*personal letter*). **4 a** referring (esp. in a hostile way) to an individual's private life or concerns (*no need to be personal*). **b** close; intimate (*a personal friend*). **5** of the body and clothing (*personal hygiene*). □ **personal computer** computer designed for use by a single individual. **personal pronoun** pronoun replacing the subject, object, etc., of a clause, etc., e.g., *I, we, you, them, us*.

per·son·al·i·ty /pɔ́rsənálitee/ n. (pl. **-ties**) **1** distinctive character or qualities of a person, often as distinct from others (*an attractive personality*). **2** famous person.

per·son·al·ize /pɔ́rsənəlīz/ v.tr. make personal, esp. by marking with one's name, etc. □□ **per·son·al·i·za′tion** n.

per·son·al·ly /pɔ́rsənəlee/ adv. **1** in person. **2** for one's own part. **3** in a personal manner (*took the criticism personally*).

per·son·i·fy /pərsónifī/ v.tr. (**-fies, -fied**) **1** represent (an abstraction or thing) as human. **2** (usu. as **personified** adj.) embody (a quality) in one's own person; exemplify typically. □□ **per·son·i·fi·ca′tion** n. **per·son′i·fi·er** n.

per·son·nel /pɔ́rsənél/ n. body of employees, persons involved in a public undertaking, armed forces, etc.

per·spec·tive /pərspéktiv/ n. **1 a** art of drawing solid objects on a two-dimensional surface to suggest third dimension. **b** picture drawn in this way. **2** apparent relation between visible objects as to position, distance, etc. **3** mental view of the relative importance of things (*keep the right perspective*). **4** geographical or imaginary prospect. □□ **per·spec′ti·val** adj. **per·spec′tive·ly** adv.

per·spi·ca·cious /pɔ́rspikáyshəs/ adj. having mental penetration or discernment. □□ **per·spi·ca′cious·ly** adv. **per·spi·cac′i·ty** /-kásitee/ n.

per·spic·u·ous /pərspíkyooəs/ adj. **1** easily understood; clearly expressed. **2** expressing things clearly. □□ **per·spic·u·i·ty** /pɔ́rspikyoo-itee/ n. **per·spic′u·ous·ly** adv. **per·spic′u·ous·ness** n.

per·spi·ra·tion /pɔ́rspiráyshən/ n. **1** = SWEAT. **2** sweating. □□ **per·spi′ra·to·ry** /pərspīrātawree, pɔ́rspirə-/ adj.

per·spire /pərspír/ v. sweat.

per·suade /pərswáyd/ v.tr. & refl. **1** cause to believe; convince. **2** induce. □□ **per·suad′a·ble** adj. **per·suad·a·bil′i·ty** n. **per·sua′si·ble** adj.

per·sua·sion /pərswáyzhən/ n. **1** persuading. **2** persuasiveness. **3** belief or conviction, or the group holding it.

per·sua·sive /pərswáysiv, -ziv/ adj. able to persuade. □□ **per·sua′sive·ly** adv. **per·sua′sive·ness** n.

pert /pɔrt/ adj. saucy; impudent. □□ **pert′ly** adv. **pert′ness** n.

pert. abbr. pertaining.

per·tain /pərtáyn/ v.intr. **1** (foll. by to) **a** relate or have reference to. **b** belong to as a part or appendage or accessory. **2** (usu. foll. by to) be appropriate to.

per·ti·na·cious /pɔ́rtnáyshəs/ adj. stubborn; persistent; obstinate (in a course of action, etc.). □□ **per·ti·na′cious·ly** adv. **per·ti·nac′i·ty** /-násitee/ n.

per·ti·nent /pə́rt'nənt/ *adj.* **1** relevant. **2** to the point. □□ **per'ti·nence** *n.* **per'ti·nen·cy** *n.* **per'ti·nent·ly** *adv.*

per·turb /pərtə́rb/ *v.tr.* **1** throw into confusion or disorder. **2** disturb mentally; agitate. □□ **per·turb'a·ble** *adj.* **per·tur·ba·tion** /-báyshən/ *n.* **per·tur·ba·tive** /pərtúrbətiv, pə́rtərbáytiv/ *adj.* **per·tur'bing·ly** *adv.*

per·tus·sis /pərtúsis/ *n.* whooping cough.

pe·ruke /pərōok/ *n.* hist. wig.

PERUKE

pe·ruse /pərōoz/ *v.tr.* read or study carefully. □□ **pe·rus'al** *n.* **pe·rus'er** *n.*

Pe·ru·vi·an /pərōveeən/ • *n.* **1** native or national of Peru. **2** person of Peruvian descent. • *adj.* of or relating to Peru.

per·vade /pərváyd/ *v.tr.* spread throughout; permeate. □□ **per·va·sion** /-váyzhən/ *n.*

per·va·sive /pərváysiv, -ziv/ *adj.* **1** pervading. **2** able to pervade. □□ **per·va'sive·ly** *adv.* **per·va'sive·ness** *n.*

per·verse /pərvə́rs/ *adj.* **1** (of a person or action) deliberately or stubbornly departing from what is reasonable or required. **2** persistent in error. **3** wayward; intractable; peevish. **4** perverted; wicked.□□ **per·verse'ly** *adv.* **per·verse' ness** *n.* **per·ver'si·ty** *n.* (*pl.* **-ties**)

per·ver·sion /pərvə́rzhən, -shən/ *n.* **1** act of perverting; state of being perverted. **2 a** preference for an abnormal form of sexual activity. **b** such an activity.

per·vert • *v.tr.* /pərvə́rt/ **1** turn (a person or thing) aside from its proper use or nature. **2** misapply (words, etc.). **3** lead astray from right opinion or conduct. • *n.* /pə́rvərt/ perverted person, esp. sexually. □□ **per·ver·sive** /-və́rsiv/ *adj.* **per·vert'ed·ly** *adv.* **per·vert'er** *n.*

pes·ky /péskee/ *adj.* (**pes·ki·er, pes·ki·est**) *colloq.* troublesome; annoying. □□ **pesk·i·ly** *adv.* **pesk·i·ness** *n.*

pe·so /páysō/ *n.* chief monetary unit of several Latin American countries and of the Philippines.

pes·si·mism /pésimizəm/ *n.* **1** tendency to be gloomy or expect the worst. **2** *Philos.* belief that all things tend to evil. □□ **pes·si·mist** *n.* **pes·si·mis'tic** *adj.* **pes·si·mis'ti·cal·ly** *adv.*

pest /pest/ *n.* **1** troublesome or annoying person or thing; nuisance. **2** destructive animal.

pes·ter /péstər/ *v.tr.* trouble or annoy, esp. with frequent or persistent requests. □□ **pes'ter·er** *n.*

pes·ti·cide /péstisīd/ *n.* substance used for

destroying pests, esp. insects. □□ **pes·ti·cid'al** *adj.*

pes·ti·lence /péstələns/ *n.* fatal epidemic disease; plague.

pes·ti·lent /péstələnt/ *adj.* **1** destructive to life; deadly. **2** harmful or morally destructive. **3** *colloq.* troublesome; annoying. □□ **pes'ti·lent·ly** *adv.*

pes·ti·len·tial /péstəlénshəl/ *adj.* **1** of or relating to pestilence. **2** dangerous; troublesome; pestilent. □□ **pes·ti·len'tial·ly** *adv.*

pes·tle /pésəl/ *n.* **1** club-shaped instrument for pounding substances in a mortar. **2** appliance for pounding, etc.

pes·to /péstō/ *n.* sauce made of fresh chopped basil, garlic, olive oil, and Parmesan cheese, used for pasta, fish, etc.

pet¹ /pet/ • *n.* **1** domestic or tamed animal kept for pleasure or companionship. **2** darling; favorite. • *attrib.adj.* **1** kept as a pet. **2** of or for pet animals. **3** often *joc.* favorite or particular. **4** expressing fondness or familiarity (*pet name*). • *v.tr.* (**pet·ted, pet·ting**) **1** treat as a pet. **2** (also *absol.*) fondle, esp. erotically. □ **pet peeve** *colloq.* something especially annoying to an individual. □□ **pet'ter** *n.*

pet² /pet/ *n.* feeling of petty resentment or ill-humor.

peta- /pétə/ *comb. form* denoting a factor of 10^{15}.

pet·al /pét'l/ *n.* each of the parts of the corolla of a flower. □□ **pet·al·ine** /-līn, -lin/ *adj.* **pe'talled** *adj.* (also in *comb.*). **pet' al·like** *adj.* **pet'al·oid** *adj.*

pe·tard /pitáard/ *n. hist.* **1** small bomb used to blast down a door, etc. **2** kind of firework.

pe·ter /péetər/ *v.intr.* (foll. by *out*) diminish; come to an end.

pe·tite /pəteét/ *adj.* (of a woman) small and trim.

pet·it four /pétee fáwr/ *n.* (*pl.* **pet·its fours** /fórz/) very small fancy frosted cake.

pe·ti·tion /pətíshən/ • *n.* **1** supplication or request. **2** formal written request, esp. one signed by many people. **3** *Law* application to a court for a writ, etc. • *v.* **1** *tr.* make or address a petition to. **2** *intr.* appeal earnestly or humbly. □□ **pe·ti'tion·a·ble** *adj.* **pe·ti·tion'ar·y** *adj.* **pe·ti'tion·er** *n.*

pet·rel /pétrəl/ *n.* sea bird, usu. flying far from land.

Pe·tri dish /péetree/ *n.* shallow covered dish used for the culture of bacteria, etc.

pet·ri·fy /pétrifī/ *v.* (**-fies, -fied**) **1** *tr.* (also as **petrified** *adj.*) paralyze with fear, astonishment, etc. **2** *tr.* change (organic matter) into a stony substance. **3** *intr.* become like stone. □□ **pet·ri·fac·tion** /-fákshən/ *n.*

pet·ro·chem·i·cal /pétrōkémikəl/ *n.* substance industrially obtained from petroleum or natural gas.

pet·ro·dol·lar /pétrōdolər/ *n.* notional unit of currency earned by a petroleum-exporting country.

pet·rol /pétrəl/ *n. Brit.* gasoline.

pe·tro·le·um /pətróleeəm/ *n.* hydrocarbon oil found in the upper strata of the earth, refined for use as fuel, etc. □ **petroleum jelly** (also **pet·ro·la·tum**) translucent solid mixture of hydrocarbons used as a lubricant, ointment, etc.

pet·ti·coat /péteekŏt/ *n.* woman's or girl's skirted undergarment hanging from the waist or shoulders. □□ **pet′ti·coat·ed** *adj.* **pet′ti·coat· less** *adj.*

pet·ti·fog /péteefawg, -fog/ *v.intr.* (**pet·ti·fogged, pet·ti·fog·ging**) 1 practice legal trickery. 2 quibble or wrangle about petty points.□□ **pet′ti· fog·ger** *n.* **pet·ti·fog′ger·y** *n.* **pet′ti·fog·ging** *adj.*

pet·tish /pétish/ *adj.* pccvish; petulant; easily put out. □□ **pet′tish·ly** *adv.* **pet′tish·ness** *n.*

pet·ty /pétee/ *adj.* (**pet·ti·er, pet·ti·est**) 1 unimportant; trivial. 2 mean; small-minded; contemptible. □ **petty cash** money from or for small items of receipt or expenditure. **petty officer** naval NCO. □□ **pet′ti·ly** *adv.* **pet′ti·ness** *n.*

pet·u·lant /péchələnt/ *adj.* peevishly impatient or irritable. □□ **pet′u·lance** *n.* **pet′u·lant·ly** *adv.*

pe·tu·nia /pitōŏnyə, -tyŏŏn-/ *n.* plant with white, purple, red, etc., funnel-shaped flowers.

pew /pyōo/ *n.* (in a church) long bench with a back. □□ **pew·less** *adj.*

pew·ter /pyōŏtər/ *n.* 1 gray alloy of tin with lead, copper, antimony, or various other metals. 2 utensils made of this. □□ **pew′ter·er** *n.*

pey·o·te /payótee/ *n.* 1 type of Mexican cactus; mescal. 2 hallucinogenic drug prepared from this.

Pfc. *abbr.* (also **PFC**) Private First Class.

PG *abbr.* (of movies) classified as suitable for children subject to parental guidance.

pg. *abbr.* page.

PGA *abbr.* Professional Golfers' Association.

PG-13 *abbr.* (of movies) classified as suitable for children under age 13 subject to parental guidance.

pH /pée-áych/ *n. Chem.* numerical scale measuring the relative acidity or alkalinity of a solution.

phag·o·cyte /fágəsīt/ *n.* type of cell capable of engulfing and absorbing foreign matter, esp. a leukocyte ingesting bacteria in the body. □□ **phag·o·cyt·ic** /-sitik/ *adj.*

pha·lanx /fálangks/ *n.* (*pl.* **pha·lanx·es** or **pha· lan·ges** /fəlánjeez/) 1 *Gk. Antiq.* line of battle, esp. a body of Macedonian infantry drawn up in close order. 2 set of people, etc., forming a compact mass, or banded for a common purpose.

phal·lus /fáləs/ *n.* (*pl.* **phal·li** /-lī/ or **phal·lus·es**) 1 (esp. erect) penis. 2 image of this as a symbol of generative power in nature. □□ **phal·lic** /fálik/ *adj.* **phal′li·cal·ly** *adv.* **phal·li·cism** /-lisizəm/ *n.*

phan·tasm /fántazəm/ *n.* illusion; phantom. □□ **phan·tas·mal** /-tázm′l/ *adj.* **phan·tas′mic** /-tázmik/ *adj.*

phan·tas·ma·go·ri·a /fántazməgáwreeə/ *n.* shifting series of real or imaginary figures as seen in a dream. □□ **phan·tas·ma·gor·ic** /-gáwrik, -gór-/ *adj.* **phan·tas·ma·gor′i·cal** *adj.*

phan·tom /fántəm/ *n.* 1 ghost; apparition; specter. 2 mental illusion. *adj.* merely apparent; illusory.

phar. *abbr.* (also **pharm.** or **Pharm.**) 1 pharmaceutical. 2 pharmacist. 3 pharmacy.

Pha·raoh /fáirō, fárō, fáyrō/ *n.* 1 ruler of ancient Egypt. 2 title of this ruler. □□ **Phar·a·on·ic** /fáirayónik/ *adj.*

Phar·i·see /fárisee/ (also **phar′i·see**) *n.* 1 member of an ancient Jewish sect, distinguished by

strict observance of the traditional and written law. 2 self-righteous person; hypocrite. □□ **Phar·i·sa·ic** /fárisáyik/ *adj.* **Phar·i·sa′i·cal** *adj.* **Phar′i·sa·ism** *n.*

phar·ma·ceu·ti·cal /faʹarməsōŏtikəl/ *adj.* of the use or sale of medicinal drugs. *n.* medicinal drug. □□ **phar·ma·ceu′ti·cal·ly** *adv.* **phar· ma·ceu′tics** *n.*

phar·ma·cist /faʹarməsist/ *n.* person qualified to prepare and dispense drugs.

phar·ma·col·o·gy /faʹarməkóləjee/ *n.* the science of the action of drugs on the body. □□ **phar· ma·co·log·i·cal** /-lój-/ *adj.* **phar·ma·co·log′i·cal·ly** *adv.* **phar·ma·col′o·gist** *n.*

phar·ma·co·poe·ia /faʹarməkəpée̊ə/ *n.* 1 book, esp. one officially published, containing a list of drugs with directions for use. 2 stock of drugs. □□ **phar·ma·co·poe′ial** *adj.*

phar·ma·cy /faʹarməsee/ *n.* (*pl.* **-cies**) 1 preparation and (esp. medicinal) dispensing of drugs. 2 drugstore.

phar·ynx /fáringks/ *n.* (*pl.* **pha·ryn·ges** /fərínjeez/) cavity behind the nose and mouth, and connecting them to the esophagus. □□ **pha·ryn′ gal** /-rínggəl/ *adj.* **pha·ryn′ge·al** /fərínjeeəl, -jəl, fárínjée̊al/ *adj.* **phar·yn·gi′tis** /-rinjítis/ *n.*

phase /fayz/ *n.* 1 distinct stage in a process of change or development. 2 each of the aspects of the moon or a planet, according to the amount of its illumination. *v.tr.* carry out (a program, etc.) in phases or stages. □ **phase in** (or **out**) bring gradually into (or out of) use. □□ **pha′sic** *adj.*

Ph.D. *abbr.* Doctor of Philosophy.

pheas·ant /fézənt/ *n.* long-tailed game birds, orig. from Asia.

phe·no·bar·bi·tal /fée̊nōbáʹarbitawl, -tal/ *n.* narcotic and sedative barbiturate drug used esp. to treat epilepsy.

phe·nol /fée̊nawl, -nol/ *n. Chem.* monohydroxyl derivative of benzene used in dilute form as an antiseptic and disinfectant. Also called **carbolic**. □□ **phe·no′lic** /finólik/ *adj.*

phe·nom·e·nal /finóminəl/ *adj.* 1 of the nature of a phenomenon. 2 extraordinary; remarkable; prodigious. □□ **phe·nom′e·nal·ly** *adv.*

phe·nom·e·non /finóminən/ *n.* (*pl.* **phe·nom· e·na** /-nə/) 1 fact or occurrence that appears or is perceived. 2 remarkable person or thing. 3 *Philos.* object of a person's perception; what the senses or the mind notice. ¶ The singular of this Greek word is **phenomenon**, the plural **phenomena**: *Halley's Comet is a rare phenomenon, one of the most spectacular of celestial phenomena.*

pher·o·mone /férəmōn/ *n.* chemical substance secreted and released by an animal for detection and response by another usu. of the same species. □□ **pher·o·mo′nal** *adj.*

phi /fī/ *n.* twenty-first letter of the Greek alphabet (Φ, φ).

phi·al /fíəl/ *n.* = VIAL.

phil- *comb. form* var. of PHILO-.

-phil *comb. form* var. of -PHILE.

phi·lan·der /filándər/ *v.intr.* (often foll. by *with*) flirt or have casual affairs with women; womanize. □□ **phi·lan′der·er** *n.*

phil·an·throp·ic /filənthrópik/ *adj.* loving one's fellow people; benevolent. □□ **phil·an·throp′i· cal·ly** *adv.*

phi·lan·thro·py /filánthrəpee/ *n.* practical benevolence, esp. charity on a large scale. □□ **phi·lan′thro·pist** *n.* **phi·lan′thro·pize** *v.*

phi·lat·e·ly /filát′lee/ *n.* collection and study of postage stamps. □□ **phil·a·tel·ic** /filətélik/ *adj.* **phil·a·tel′i·cal·ly** *adv.* **phi·lat′e·list** *n.*

-phile /fīl/ *comb. form* (also **-phil** /fil/) forming nouns and adjectives denoting fondness for what is specified (*bibliophile; Francophile*).

phil·har·mon·ic /filhaarmónik/ *adj.* fond of music (used characteristically in the names of orchestras, choirs, etc.).

phi·lip·pic /filípik/ *n.* bitter verbal attack or denunciation.

Phi·lis·tine /filisteen, -stīn, filístin, -teen/ • *n.* **1** member of a people opposing the Israelites in ancient Palestine. **2** (usu. **philistine**) person who is hostile or indifferent to culture. • *adj.* hostile or indifferent to culture. □□ **phil′is·tin·ism** *n.*

Phil·lips /filips/ *n.* (usu. *attrib.*) *propr.* denoting a screw with a cross-shaped slot for turning, or a corresponding screwdriver.

philo- /filō/ *comb. form* (also **phil-** before a vowel or *h*) denoting a liking for what is specified.

phil·o·den·dron /filədéndrən/ *n.* (*pl.* **phil·o·den·drons** or **phil·o·den·dra** /-drə/) climbing plant with bright foliage.

phi·lol·o·gy /filólɔjee/ *n.* science of language, esp. in its historical and comparative aspects. □□ **phil·o·lo·gi·an** /-lɔlójeeən/ *n.* **phi·lol′o·gist** *n.* **phil·o·log·i·cal** /-lɔlójikəl/ *adj.* **phil·o·log′i·cal·ly** *adv.*

phi·los·o·pher /filósəfər/ *n.* **1** person engaged or learned in philosophy. **2** person who lives by philosophy.

phil·o·soph·i·cal /filəsófikəl/ *adj.* (also **phil·o·soph′ic**) **1** of or according to philosophy. **2** skilled in or devoted to philosophy. **3** calm in adversity. □□ **phil·o·soph′i·cal·ly** *adv.*

phi·los·o·phize /filósəfīz/ *v.intr.* **1** reason like a philosopher. **2** speculate; theorize. □□ **phi·los′o·phiz·er** *n.*

phi·los·o·phy /filósəfee/ *n.* (*pl.* **-phies**) **1** use of reason and argument in seeking truth and knowledge of reality, esp. of the causes and nature of things and of the principles governing existence. **2** particular system or set of beliefs reached by this; personal rule of life.

phil·ter /fíltər/ *n.* love potion.

phle·bi·tis /flibítis/ *n.* inflammation of the walls of a vein. □□ **phle·bit·ic** /-bítik/ *adj.*

phlegm /flem/ *n.* **1** thick viscous substance secreted by the mucous membranes of the respiratory passages, discharged by coughing. **2 a** calmness. **b** sluggishness. □□ **phlegm′y** *adj.*

---

phlegm Middle English *fleem, fleume,* from Old French *fleume,* from late Latin *phlegma* 'clammy moisture (of the body),' from Greek *phlegma* 'inflammation,' from *phlegein* 'to burn.' The spelling change in the 16th century was due to association with the Latin and Greek forms.

---

phleg·mat·ic /flegmátik/ *adj.* stolidly calm; unexcitable; unemotional. □□ **phleg·mat′i·cal·ly** *adv.*

phlo·em /flóem/ *n. Bot.* tissue conducting food material in plants (cf. XYLEM).

phlox /floks/ *n.* cultivated plant with scented clusters of esp. white, blue, and red flowers.

-phobe /fōb/ *comb. form* forming nouns and adjectives denoting a person with a specified fear or dislike (*xenophobe*).

pho·bi·a /fóbeeə/ *n.* abnormal or morbid fear or aversion. □□ **pho′bic** *adj.* & *n.*

-phobia /fóbeeə/ *comb. form* forming abstract nouns denoting a fear or dislike of what is specified (*agoraphobia; xenophobia*). □□ **-phobic** *comb. form* forming adjectives.

phoe·nix /féeniks/ *n.* mythical bird, the only one of its kind, that burned itself on a funeral pyre and rose from the ashes to live through another cycle.

phone /fōn/ *n.* & *v. colloq.* = TELEPHONE.

pho·neme /fóneem/ *n.* any of the units of sound in a specified language that distinguish one word from another (e.g., *p, b, d, t* as in pad, pat, bad, bat, in English). □□ **pho·ne′mic** *adj.* **pho·ne′mics** *n.*

pho·net·ic /fənétik/ *adj.* **1** representing vocal sounds. **2** (of a system of spelling, etc.) having a direct correspondence between symbols and sounds. **3** of or relating to phonetics. □□ **pho·ne′ti·cal·ly** *adv.* **pho·net′i·cize** /-nétəsīz/ *v.tr.*

pho·net·ics /fənétiks/ *n.pl.* (usu. treated as *sing.*) **1** vocal sounds. **2** the study of these. □□ **pho·ne·ti·cian** /fónitíshən/ *n.*

phon·ic /fónik/ • *adj.* of sound; acoustic; of vocal sounds. • *n.* (in *pl.*) method of teaching reading based on sounds. □□ **phon′i·cal·ly** *adv.*

phono- /fónō/ *comb. form* denoting sound.

pho·no·graph /fónəgraf/ *n.* instrument that reproduces recorded sound by a stylus that is in contact with a rotating grooved disk. ¶ Now more usually called a *record player.*

pho·nol·o·gy /fənólɔjee/ *n.* the study of sounds in a language. □□ **pho·no·log·i·cal** /fónəlójikəl/ *adj.* **pho·no·log′i·cal·ly** *adv.* **pho·nol·o·gist** /fənólɔjist/ *n.*

pho·ny /fónee/ (also **pho·ney**) *colloq.* • *adj.* (**pho·ni·er, pho·ni·est**) **1** sham; counterfeit. **2** fictitious; fraudulent. • *n.* (*pl.* **-nies** or **-neys**) phony person or thing. □□ **pho′ni·ly** *adv.* **pho′ni·ness** *n.*

phos·gene /fósjeen, fóz-/ *n.* colorless poisonous gas (carbonyl chloride), formerly used in warfare.

phos·phate /fósfayt/ *n.* salt or ester of phosphoric acid, esp. used as a fertilizer. □□ **phos·phat·ic** /-fátik/ *adj.*

phos·phor /fósfər/ *n.* synthetic fluorescent or phosphorescent substance esp. used in cathoderay tubes.

phos·pho·res·cence /fósfərésəns/ *n.* **1** radiation similar to fluorescence but detectable after excitation ceases. **2** emission of light without combustion or perceptible heat. □□ **phos′pho·resce** *v.intr.* **phos′pho·res·cent** *adj.*

phos·pho·rus /fósfərəs/ *n. Chem.* nonmetallic element existing in allotropic forms, esp. as a poisonous whitish waxy substance burning slowly at ordinary temperatures and so appearing luminous in the dark. ¶ Symb.: **P.** □□ **phos·phor·ic** /-fórik/ *adj.* **phos′pho·rous** *adj.*

pho·to /fótō/ *n.* = PHOTOGRAPH *n.* □ **photo finish** close finish of a race or contest, esp. one where the winner is only distinguishable on a photograph. **photo opportunity** (also **pho·to-op**) occasion on which celebrities, etc., pose for photographers by arrangement.

photo- /fṓtō/ *comb. form* denoting: **1** light. **2** photography.

pho·to·cop·y /fṓtōkópee/ ● *n.* (*pl.* **-ies**) photographic copy of printed or written material. ● *v.tr.* (**-ies, -ied**) make a photocopy of. □□ **pho'to·cop·i·er** *n.*

pho·to·e·lec·tric /fṓtōiléktrik/ *adj.* marked by or using emissions of electrons from substances exposed to light. □ **photoelectric cell** device using this effect to generate current. □□ **pho·to·e·lec·tric·i·ty** /-trísitee/ *n.*

pho·to·fin·ish·ing /fṓtōfinishing/ *n.* process of developing and printing photographic film.

pho·to·gen·ic /fṓtəjénik/ *adj.* **1** (esp. of a person) having an appearance that looks pleasing in photographs. **2** *Biol.* producing or emitting light. □□ **pho·to·gen'i·cal·ly** *adv.*

pho·to·graph /fṓtəgraf/ ● *n.* picture taken by means of the chemical action of light or other radiation on sensitive film. ● *v.tr.* (also *absol.*) take a photograph of (a person, etc.). □□ **pho·tog·ra·pher** /fətógrəfər/ *n.* **pho·to·graph·i·cal·ly** /-gráfiklee/ *adv.*

pho·to·graph·ic /fṓtōgráfik/ *adj.* **1** of, used in, or produced by photography. **2** having the accuracy of a photograph.

pho·tog·ra·phy /fətógrəfee/ *n.* taking and processing of photographs.

pho·ton /fṓton/ *n.* quantum of electromagnetic radiation energy, proportional to the frequency of radiation.

pho·to·sen·si·tive /fṓtōsénsitiv/ *adj.* reacting chemically, electrically, etc., to light. □□ **pho·to·sen·si·tiv·i·ty** /-tívitee/ *n.*

Pho·to·stat /fṓtəstat/ ● *n. propr.* **1** type of machine for making photocopies. **2** copy made by this means. ● *v.tr.* (**pho·to·stat**) (**-stat·ted, -stat·ting**) make a Photostat of. □□ **pho·to·stat'ic** *adj.*

pho·to·syn·the·sis /fṓtōsínthisis/ *n.* process in which the energy of sunlight is used by organisms, esp. green plants, to synthesize carbohydrates from carbon dioxide and water. □□ **pho·to·syn'the·size** *v.* **pho·to·syn·thet·ic** /-thétik/ *adj.* **pho·to·syn·thet'i·cal·ly** *adv.*

phrase /frayz/ ● *n.* **1** group of words forming a conceptual unit, but not a sentence. **2** idiomatic or short pithy expression. **3** *Mus.* group of notes forming a distinct unit within a larger piece. ● *v.tr.* express in words. □□ **phras'al** *adj.* **phras'ing** *n.*

phra·se·ol·o·gy /fráyzeeóləjee/ *n.* (*pl.* **-gies**) **1** choice or arrangement of words. **2** mode of expression. □□ **phra·se·o·log·i·cal** /-əlójikəl/ *adj.*

phre·nol·o·gy /frinóləjee/ *n. hist.* the study of the shape and size of the cranium as a supposed indication of character and mental faculties. □□ **phren·o·log'i·cal** /-nəlójikəl/ *adj.* **phre·nol'o·gist** *n.*

phy·lac·ter·y /filáktəree/ *n.* (*pl.* **-ies**) small leather box containing Hebrew texts, worn by Jewish men at prayer.

phy·lum /ffləm/ *n.* (*pl.* **phy·la** /-lə/) *Biol.* taxonomic rank below kingdom comprising a class or classes and subordinate taxa.

phys·i·cal /fízikəl/ ● *adj.* **1** of or concerning the body (*physical exercise*). **2** of matter; material

(*both mental and physical force*). **3 a** of, or according to, the laws of nature (*a physical impossibility*). **b** belonging to physics (*physical science*). ● *n.* (in full **physical examination**) medical examination. □ **physical science** sciences used in the study of inanimate natural objects. **physical therapy** *n.* treatment of disease, injury, deformity, etc., by massage, infrared heat treatment, remedial exercise, etc. □□ **phys·i·cal·i·ty** /-kálitee/ *n.* **phys'i·cal·ly** *adv.* **phys'i·cal·ness** *n.*

phy·si·cian /fizíshən/ *n.* medical doctor; M.D.

phys·ics /fíziks/ *n.* science dealing with the properties and interactions of matter and energy. □□ **phys'i·cist** /-zisist/ *n.*

phys·i·og·no·my /fizeeógnəmee, -ónəmee/ *n.* (*pl.* **-mies**) cast or form of a person's features, expression, body, etc. □□ **phys·i·og·nom·ic** /-ognó·mik, -ənómik/ *adj.* **phys·i·og·nom'i·cal** *adj.* **phys·i·og·nom'i·cal·ly** *adv.* **phys·i·og'nom·ist** *n.*

phys·i·og·ra·phy /fizeeógrəfee/ *n.* description of nature, or natural phenomena, or of a class of objects; physical geography. □□ **phys·i·og'ra·pher** *n.* **phys·i·o·graph·ic** /-zeeəgráfik/ *adj.* **phys·i·o·graph'i·cal** *adj.* **phys·i·o·graph'i·cal·ly** *adv.*

phys·i·o·log·i·cal /fizeeəlójikəl/ *adj.* (also **phys·i·o·log'ic**) of or concerning physiology. □□ **phys·i·o·log'i·cal·ly** *adv.*

phys·i·ol·o·gy /fizeeóləjee/ *n.* **1** science of the functions of living organisms and their parts. **2** these functions. □□ **phys·i·ol'o·gist** *n.*

phys·i·o·ther·a·py /fizeeōthérəpee/ *n.* = **physical therapy.**

phy·sique /fizéek/ *n.* bodily structure; build.

pi /pī/ *n.* **1** sixteenth letter of the Greek alphabet (Π, π). **2** (as π) the symbol of the ratio of the circumference of a circle to its diameter (approx. 3.14159).

pia ma·ter /píə máytər, péeə/ *n. Anat.* delicate innermost membrane enveloping the brain and spinal cord.

pi·a·nis·si·mo /péeənisímō/ *Mus.* ● *adj.* performed very softly. ● *adv.* very softly. ● *n.* (*pl.* **-mos** or **pi·a·nis·si·mi** /-mee/) passage to be performed very softly.

pi·a·nist /péeənist, pee-án-/ *n.* player of a piano.

pi·an·o[1] /peeánō, pyánō/ *n.* (*pl.* **-nos**) large musical instrument played by pressing down keys on a keyboard and causing hammers to strike metal strings.

pi·a·no[2] /pyaánō/ ● *adj.* **1** *Mus.* performed softly. **2** subdued. ● *adv.* **1** *Mus.* softly. **2** in a subdued manner. ● *n.* (*pl.* **-nos**) *Mus.* piano passage.

pi·an·o·forte /pyánōfáwrt, -fáwrtee/ *n. Mus.* piano.

pi·az·za /pee-áatsə, -saa/ **1** public square or marketplace. **2** /peeázə, -áazə/ *dial.* veranda of a house.

pi·broch /péebrokh, -brawkh/ *n.* series of esp. martial or funerary variations on a theme for the bagpipes.

pi·ca /píkə/ *n. Printing* **1** unit of type size (¹/₆ inch). **2** size of letters in typewriting (10 per inch).

pic·a·dor /píkədawr/ *n.* matador's mounted assistant who goads the bull with a lance in a bullfight.

pic·a·resque /píkərésk/ *adj.* (of a style of fiction) dealing with the episodic adventures of rogues, etc.

pic·a·yune /píkəyṓon/ *n. adj.* **1** of little value; trivial. **2** mean; contemptible; petty.

pic·ca·lil·li /píkəlilee/ *n.* (*pl.* **pic·ca·lil·lis**) pickle of chopped vegetables, mustard, and hot spices.

pic·co·lo /píkəlō/ *n.* small flute sounding an octave higher than the ordinary one.

pick[1] /pik/ • *v.tr.* **1** choose (*picked a team*). **2** detach or pluck (a flower, fruit, etc.). **3 a** probe with the finger, an instrument, etc., to remove unwanted matter. **b** clear (a bone, carcass, etc.) of scraps of meat, etc. **4** eat (food, a meal, etc.) in small bits. **5** open (a lock) with an instrument other than a key. **6** steal, as from a person's pocket. • *n.* **1** act or instance of picking. **2** a selection or choice. **b** the right to select (*had first pick*). **3** the best (*pick of the bunch*). □ **pick and choose** select fastidiously. **pick at 1** eat (food) without interest. **2** = *pick on* 1 (PICK[1]). **pick off 1** pluck (leaves, etc.) off. **2** shoot (people, etc.) one by one. **3** *Baseball* put out a base runner caught off base. **pick on 1** find fault with; nag at. **2** select, as for special attention. **pick up 1 a** grasp and raise (*picked up his hat*). **b** clean up; straighten up. **2** acquire (*picked up a cold*). **3 a** fetch (a person, animal, or thing) left in another person's charge. **b** stop for and take along with one, esp. in a vehicle. **4** make the acquaintance of (a person) casually, esp. as a sexual overture. **5** recover; prosper; improve. **6** arrest. □□ **pick′a·ble** *adj.* **pick′er** *n.*

pick[2] /pik/ *n.* **1** long-handled tool having a usu. curved iron bar pointed at one or both ends, used for breaking up hard ground, masonry, etc. **2** *colloq.* plectrum.

pick·ax /píkaks/ *n.* (also **pick′axe**) = PICK[2] 1.

pick·et /píkit/ • *n.* **1** person or group of people outside a place of work, intending to persuade esp. workers not to enter during a strike, etc. **2** pointed stake or peg driven into the ground to form a fence, etc. **3** (also **pic·quet, piq·uet**) *Mil.* small body of troops or a single soldier sent out to watch for the enemy. • *v.* **1 a** *tr.* & *intr.* station or act as a picket. **b** *tr.* beset or guard with a picket or pickets. **2** *tr.* secure with stakes. □ **picket line** boundary established by workers on strike. □□ **pick′et·er** *n.*

pick·ings /píkingz/ *n.pl.* **1** perquisites; pilferings (*rich pickings*). **2** remaining scraps; gleanings.

pick·le /píkəl/ • *n.* **1 a** (often in *pl.*) vegetables, esp. cucumbers, preserved in brine, vinegar, mustard, etc. **b** brine, vinegar, etc., in which food is preserved. **2** *colloq.* plight (*a fine pickle we are in!*). • *v.tr.* **1** preserve in pickle. **2** treat with pickle. **3** (as **pickled** *adj.*) *sl.* drunk.

pick·pock·et /píkpókit/ *n.* person who steals from the pockets of others.

pick·up /píkəp/ *n.* **1** *sl.* person met casually, esp. for sexual purposes. **2** small truck with an enclosed cab and open back. **3 a** part of a record player carrying the stylus. **b** detector of vibrations, etc. **4** act of picking up.

pick·y /píkee/ *adj.* (**pick·i·er, pick·i·est**) *colloq.* excessively fastidious; choosy. □□ **pick′i·ness** *n.*

pic·nic /píknik/ • *n.* **1** outing or excursion including a packed meal eaten out of doors. **2** (usu. with *neg.*) *colloq.* something agreeable or easily accomplished, etc. • *v.intr.* (**pic·nicked, pic·nick·ing**) take part in a picnic. □□ **pic′nick·er** *n.* **pic′nick·y** *adj. colloq.*

pico- /peekō, píkō/ *comb. form* denoting a factor of 10^{-12} (*picometer*).

pic·to·graph /píktəgraf/ *n.* (also **pic·to·gram** /píktəgram/) **1** pictorial symbol for a word or phrase. **2** pictorial representation of statistics,

etc., on a chart, graph, etc. □□ **pic·to·graph′ic** *adj.* **pic·tog·ra·phy** /-tógrəfee/ *n.*

pic·to·ri·al /piktáwreeəl/ *adj.* **1** of or expressed in a picture or pictures. **2** illustrated.□□ **pic·to′ri·al·ly** *adv.*

pic·ture /píkchər/ • *n.* **1** (often *attrib.*) painting, drawing, photograph, etc. **2** total visual or mental impression produced; scene (*the picture looks bleak*). **3** movie. **4** person or thing resembling another closely (*the picture of her aunt*). • *v.tr.* **1** represent in a picture. **2** imagine. **3** describe graphically. □ **get the picture** *colloq.* grasp the tendency or drift of circumstances, information, etc. **picture tube** cathode-ray tube of a television set. **picture window** very large window consisting of one pane of glass.

pic·tur·esque /píkchərésk/ *adj.* **1** (of landscape, etc.) beautiful or striking, as in a picture. **2** (of language, etc.) strikingly graphic; vivid. □□ **pic·tur·esque′ly** *adv.* **pic·tur·esque′ness** *n.*

pid·dle /píd'l/ *v.intr.* **1** *colloq.* urinate (used esp. to or by children). **2** work or act in a trifling way. **3** (as **piddling** *adj.*) *colloq.* trivial; trifling. □□ **pid′dler** *n.*

pid·gin /píjin/ *n.* simplified language used for communication between people not having a common language.

pie /pī/ *n.* **1** baked dish of fruit, meat, custard, etc., usu. with a top and base of pastry. **2** anything resembling a pie in form (*mud pie*). □ **easy as pie** very easy. **pie chart** circle divided into sections to represent relative quantities. **pie in the sky** unrealistic prospect of future happiness.

PIE CHART

pie·bald /píbawld/ • *adj.* (usu. of an animal, esp. a horse) having irregular patches of two colors, esp. black and white. • *n.* piebald animal, esp. a horse.

piece /pees/ • *n.* **1 a** distinct portion forming part of or broken off from a larger object. **b** each of the parts of something. **2** coin. **3 a** usu. short literary or musical composition; picture. **b** theatrical play. **4** item. **5** object moved in a board game. **6** definite quantity in which a thing is sold. • *v.tr.* (usu. foll. by *together*) form into a whole; put together; join. □ **go to pieces** collapse emotionally. **piece of cake** see CAKE. **piece of one's mind** sharp rebuke or lecture. **piece work** work paid for by the amount produced. □□ **piec′er** *n.* (in sense 4 of *v.*).

pièce de ré·sis·tance /pyés də rayzéestoNs/ *n.* (*pl.* **pièces de ré·sis·tance** *pronunc.* same) **1** most important or remarkable item. **2** most substantial dish at a meal.

piece·meal /péesmeel/ • *adv.* piece by piece; gradually. • *adj.* partial; gradual; unsystematic.

pied /pīd/ *adj.* parti-colored.

pied-à-terre /pyáydaatáir/ *n.* (*pl.* **pieds-à-terre** *pronunc.* same) usu. small residence for occasional use.

pier /peer/ *n.* 1 structure of iron or wood raised on piles and leading out to sea, a lake, etc., used as a promenade and landing place. 2 a support of an arch or of the span of a bridge; pillar. b solid masonry between windows, etc.

pierce /peers/ *v.* 1 *tr.* a penetrate the surface of. b prick with a sharp instrument, esp. to make a hole in. 2 pass through or into; penetrate. □□ **pierc′er** *n.* **pierc′ing·ly** *adv.*

pie·ro·gi /pərógee, pee-/ *n.* (also **pi·ro′gi**) (*pl.* same or **-gies**) small pastry envelopes filled with mashed potatoes, cabbage, or chopped meat.

pi·e·ty /pí-itee/ *n.* (*pl.* **-ties**) 1 quality of being pious. 2 pious act.

pig /pig/ *n.* 1 omnivorous hoofed bristly mammal, esp. a domesticated kind. 2 flesh of esp. a young or suckling pig as food (*roast pig*). 3 *colloq.* greedy, dirty, obstinate, sulky, or annoying person. 4 oblong mass of metal (esp. iron or lead) from a smelting furnace. □ **buy a pig in a poke** buy, accept, etc., something without knowing its value or esp. seeing it. **pig iron** crude iron from a smelting furnace. **pig out** *sl.* eat gluttonously. □□ **pig′gish** *adj.* **pig′gish·ly** *adv.* **pig′gish·ness** *n.* **pig′let** *n.* **pig′like** *adj.*

pi·geon /píjin/ *n.* large usu. gray and white bird often domesticated and bred and trained to carry messages, etc.; dove. □ **pigeon-toed** (of a person) having the toes turned inward.

pi·geon·hole /píjinhōl/ • *n.* each of a set of compartments in a cabinet or on a wall for papers, letters, etc. • *v.tr.* 1 deposit in a pigeonhole. 2 put aside for future consideration. 3 assign to a preconceived category.

pig·gy /pígee/ • *n.* (also **pig′gie**) *colloq.* little pig. • *adj.* (**pig·gi·er, pig·gi·est**) like a pig. □ **piggy bank** pig-shaped box for coins.

pig·gy·back /pígeebak/ (also **pick′a·back** /píkabak/) • *n.* ride on the back and shoulders of another person. • *adv.* 1 on the back and shoulders of another person. 2 a on the back or top of a larger object. b in addition to; along with.

pig·head·ed /píg-hédid/ *adj.* obstinate. □□ **pig′head·ed·ly** *adv.* **pig′head·ed·ness** *n.*

pig·ment /pígmənt/ *n.* 1 coloring matter used as paint or dye. 2 natural coloring matter of animal or plant tissue, e.g., chlorophyll, hemoglobin. □□ **pig′men·tar·y** *adj.*

pig·men·ta·tion /pígməntáyshən/ *n.* natural coloring of plants, animals, etc.

pig·my var. of PYGMY.

pig·pen /pígpen/ *n.* = PIGSTY.

pig·skin /pígskin/ *n.* 1 hide of a pig. 2 leather made from this. 3 a football.

pig·sty /pígstī/ *n.* (*pl.* **-sties**) 1 pen or enclosure for a pig or pigs. 2 filthy house, room, etc.

pig·tail /pígtayl/ *n.* braid or gathered hank of hair hanging from the back of the head. □□ **pig′tailed** *adj.*

pike[1] /pīk/ *n.* (*pl.* same) large voracious freshwater fish, with a long narrow snout and sharp teeth.

pike[2] /pīk/ *n.* *hist.* infantry weapon with a pointed steel or iron head on a long wooden shaft.

pi·laf /pilaáf, peélaaf/ *n.* (also **pi·laff′**; **pi·law, pi·lau** /-láw, -lów/) dish of spiced rice or wheat with meat, fish, vegetables, etc.

pi·las·ter /pilástər/ *n.* rectangular column, esp. one projecting from a wall. □□ **pi·las′tered** *adj.*

pil·chard /pílchərd/ *n.* small marine fish, of the herring family (see SARDINE).

pile[1] /pīl/ • *n.* 1 heap of things laid or gathered upon one another (*a pile of leaves*). 2 large imposing building (*a stately pile*). 3 *colloq.* a large quantity. b large amount of money. • *v.* 1 *tr.* a heap up. b load. 2 *intr.* crowd hurriedly or tightly. □ **pile it on** *colloq.* exaggerate.

pile[2] /pīl/ *n.* heavy support beam driven vertically into the bed of a river, soft ground, etc. □ **pile driver** machine for driving piles into the ground.

pile[3] /pīl/ *n.* soft projecting surface on velvet, plush, etc., or esp. on a carpet; nap.

piles /pīlz/ *n.pl. colloq.* hemorrhoids.

pile·up /pílup/ *n.* collision of (esp. several) motor vehicles.

pil·fer /pílfər/ *v.tr.* (also *absol.*) steal (objects) esp. in small quantities. □□ **pil′fer·age** *n.* **pil′fer·er** *n.*

pil·grim /pílgrim/ *n.* 1 person who journeys to a sacred place. 2 traveler. 3 (**Pilgrim**) one of the English Puritans who founded the colony of Plymouth, Massachusetts, in 1620.

pil·grim·age /pílgrimij/ *n.* 1 pilgrim's journey. 2 any journey taken for nostalgic or sentimental reasons.

pill /pil/ *n.* 1 a solid medicine formed into a ball or a flat disk for swallowing whole. b (usu. prec. by *the*) *colloq.* contraceptive pill. 2 *sl.* difficult or unpleasant person.

pil·lage /pílij/ • *v.tr.* (also *absol.*) plunder; sack (a place or a person). • *n.* pillaging, esp. in war. □□ **pil′lag·er** *n.*

pil·lar /pílər/ *n.* 1 usu. slender vertical structure of wood, metal, or esp. stone used as a support or for ornament. 2 person regarded as a mainstay or support (*a pillar of strength*). 3 upright mass of air, water, rock, etc. □ **from pillar to post** (driven, etc.) from one place to another; to and fro. □□ **pil′lared** *adj.*

pill·box /pílboks/ *n.* 1 small shallow cylindrical box for holding pills. 2 hat of a similar shape. 3 *Mil.* small partly underground enclosed concrete fort used as an outpost.

pil·lo·ry /píloree/ • *n.* (*pl.* **-ries**) *hist.* wooden framework with holes for the head and hands, enabling the public to assault or ridicule a person so imprisoned. • *v.tr.* (**-ries, -ried**) 1 expose to ridicule. 2 *hist.* put in the pillory.

PILLORY

pil·low /pílō/ • *n.* soft support or cushion, as under the head in sleeping. • *v.tr.* 1 rest on or as if on a pillow. 2 serve as a pillow for (*moss pillowed her head*). □□ **pil′low·y** *adj.*

pil·low·case /pílōkays/ *n.* washable cover for a pillow.

pi·lot /pílət/ • *n.* **1** person who operates the flying controls of an aircraft. **2** person qualified to take charge of a ship entering or leaving a harbor. **3** (usu. *attrib.*) experimental undertaking or test (*a pilot project*). **4** guide. • *v.tr.* **1** act as a pilot on (a ship) or of (an aircraft). **2** conduct, lead, or initiate as a pilot (*piloted the new scheme*). □ **pilot light** small gas burner kept alight to light another. □□ **pi′lot·age** *n.* **pi′lot·less** *adj.*

pi·lot·house /pílət-hows/ *n.* enclosed area on a vessel for the helmsman, etc.

pi·mien·to /piméntō, pímyéntō/ *n.* (also **pi·men′to**) red, ripe bell pepper.

pimp /pimp/ • *n.* man who lives off the earnings of a prostitute or a brothel; pander. • *v.intr.* act as a pimp.

pim·ple /pímpəl/ *n.* **1** small hard inflamed spot on the skin. **2** anything resembling a pimple, esp. in relative size. □□ **pim′pled** *adj.* **pim′ply** *adj.*

PIN /pin/ *n.* personal identification number.

pin /pin/ • *n.* **1 a** small thin pointed piece of esp. steel wire used (esp. in sewing) for holding things in place, attaching one thing to another, etc. **b** small brooch (*diamond pin*). **c** badge fastened with a pin. **2** peg of wood or metal for various purposes. • *v.tr.* (**pinned, pin·ning**) **1 a** fasten with a pin or pins (*pinned up the hem*). **b** transfix with a pin, lance, etc. **2** (usu. foll. by *on*) fix (blame, responsibility, etc.) on a person, etc. **3** seize and hold fast. □ **pin down 1** bind (a person, etc.) to a promise, arrangement, etc. **2** force (a person) to declare his or her intentions. **3** restrict the actions or movement of (an enemy, etc.). **4** specify (a thing) precisely. **pin money** very small sum of money, esp. for spending on inessentials. **pins and needles** tingling sensation in a limb recovering from numbness.

pi·na co·la·da /péenə kəláadə/ *n.* (also **pi·ña co·la·da** /péenyə/) drink made from pineapple juice, rum, and cream of coconut.

pin·a·fore /pínəfawr/ *n.* woman's sleeveless, wraparound, washable covering for the clothes, tied at the back.

pi·ña·ta /peenyáatə/ *n.* decorated container, often of papier mâché, filled with toys, candy, etc., that is used in a game in which attempts are made to break it open with a stick.

pin·ball /pínbawl/ *n.* game in which small metal balls are shot across a board and score points by striking pins with lights, etc.

pince-nez /páNsáy, píns-/ *n.* (*pl.* same) pair of eyeglasses with a nose-clip instead of earpieces.

PINCE-NEZ

pin·cers /pínsərz/ *n.pl.* **1** (also **pair of pin·cers**) gripping tool resembling scissors but with blunt usu. concave jaws. **2** front claws of lobsters and some other crustaceans.

pinch /pinch/ • *v.* **1** *tr.* **a** grip tightly, esp. between finger and thumb. **b** (often *absol.*) (of

a shoe, garment, etc.) constrict painfully. **2** *tr.* (of cold, hunger, etc.) grip painfully (*she was pinched with cold*). **3** *tr. sl.* **a** steal. **b** arrest. • *n.* **1** act of pinching. **2** small amount (*pinch of snuff*). **3** stress or pain caused by poverty, cold, hunger, etc. □ **in a pinch** in an emergency; if necessary.

pinch-hit 1 *Baseball* bat instead of another player. **2** fill in as a substitute, esp. at the last minute.

pin·cush·ion /pínkŏŏshən/ *n.* small cushion for holding pins.

pine[1] /pīn/ *n.* **1** evergreen tree native to northern temperate regions, with needle-shaped leaves. **2** soft timber of this. □□ **pin′er·y** *n.* (*pl.* **-ies**)

pine[2] /pīn/ *v.intr.* **1** decline or waste away, esp. from grief, disease, etc. **2** long eagerly; yearn.

pin·e·al /píneəl, pī-/ *adj.* shaped like a pine cone. □ **pineal gland** (or **body**) pea-sized conical mass of tissue in the brain, secreting a hormonelike substance.

pine·ap·ple /pínapəl/ *n.* **1** tropical plant with a spiral of sword-shaped leaves and a thick stem bearing a large fruit developed from many flowers. **2** fruit of this, consisting of yellow flesh surrounded by a tough segmented skin.

ping /ping/ • *n.* single short high ringing sound. • *v.intr.* **1** make a ping. **2** = KNOCK 5.

Ping-Pong /píngpong/ *n. propr.* = *table tennis.*

pin·head /pínhed/ *n.* **1** flattened head of a pin. **2** very small thing. **3** *colloq.* stupid or foolish person.

pin·hole /pínhōl/ *n.* hole made by or for a pin.

pin·ion[1] /pínyən/ • *n.* outer part of a bird's wing. • *v.tr.* **1** cut off the pinion of (a wing or bird) to prevent flight. **2** bind the arms of (a person).

pin·ion[2] /pínyən/ *n.* **1** small toothed gear engaging with a larger one. **2** toothed spindle engaging with a wheel.

pink[1] /pingk/ • *n.* **1** pale red color (*decorated in pink*). **2** cultivated plant with sweet-smelling white, pink, crimson, etc., flowers. **3** (prec. by *the*) most perfect condition, etc. (*the pink of health*). • *adj.* **1** (often in *comb.*) of a pale red color. **2** esp. *derog.* tending to socialism. □ **in the pink** *colloq.* in very good health. **pink slip** notice of layoff or termination from one's job. □□ **pink′ish** *adj.* **pink′ly** *adv.* **pink′ness** *n.* **pink′y** *adj.*

pink[2] /pingk/ *v.tr.* **1** pierce. **2** cut a scalloped or zigzag edge on. □ **pinking shears** (or **scissors**) dressmaker's serrated shears for cutting a zigzag edge.

PINKING SHEARS

pin·na·cle /pínəkəl/ *n.* **1** culmination or climax. **2** natural peak. **3** small ornamental turret usu. ending in a pyramid or cone, crowning a buttress, roof, etc.

pin·nate /pínayt/ *adj.* (of a compound leaf) having leaflets arranged on either side of the stem. □□ **pin′nat·ed** *adj.* **pin′nate·ly** *adv.* **pin·na·tion** /-náyshən/ *n.*

pin·point /pínpoynt/ ● *n.* **1** point of a pin. **2** something very small or sharp. ● *v.tr.* locate with precision.

pin·prick /pínprik/ *n.* **1** prick caused by a pin. **2** trifling irritation.

pin·stripe /pínstrīp/ *n.* **1** very narrow stripe in cloth. **2** fabric or garment with this.

pint /pīnt/ *n.* measure of capacity for liquids, one half of a quart or 16 fluid ounces (.41 liter). □ **pint-sized** (also **pint-size**) *colloq.* very small, esp. of a person.

pin-up /pínup/ *n.* **1** photograph of a movie star, etc., for display. **2** person in such a photograph.

pin·wheel /pínhweel/ *n.* **1** fireworks device that whirls and emits colored fire. **2** stick with vanes that twirl in the wind.

Pin·yin /pínyín/ *n.* system of romanized spelling for transliterating Chinese.

pi·o·neer /pīəneér/ ● *n.* **1** initiator of a new enterprise, inventor, etc. **2** explorer or settler; colonist. ● *v.* **1 a** *tr.* initiate or originate (an enterprise, etc.). **b** *intr.* act or prepare the way as a pioneer. **2** *tr. Mil.* open up (a road, etc.) as a pioneer. **3** *tr.* go before, lead, or conduct.

pi·ous /pīəs/ *adj.* **1** devout; religious. **2** hypocritically virtuous; sanctimonious. □□ **pi′ous·ly** *adv.* **pi′ous·ness** *n.*

pip[1] /pip/ *n.* seed of an apple, pear, orange, grape, etc.

pip[2] /pip/ *n.* any of the spots on playing cards, dice, or dominos.

pipe /pīp/ ● *n.* **1** tube used to convey water, gas, etc. **2 a** (also **tobacco pipe**) narrow wooden or clay, etc., tube with a bowl at one end containing burning tobacco, etc., for smoking. **b** quantity of tobacco held by this. **3** *Mus.* **a** wind instrument consisting of a single tube. **b** any of the tubes by which sound is produced in an organ. **c** (in *pl.*) = BAGPIPES. **4** tubal organ, vessel, etc., in an animal's body. ● *v.tr.* **1** (also *absol.*) play (a tune, etc.) on a pipe or pipes. **2** convey (oil, water, gas, etc.) by pipes. **3** transmit (music, a radio program, etc.) by wire or cable. □ **pipe cleaner** piece of flexible covered wire for cleaning a tobacco pipe. **pipe down** *colloq.* be quiet or less insistent. **pipe organ** *Mus.* organ using pipes instead of or as well as reeds. □□ **pipe′ful** *n.* (*pl.* **-fuls**). **pipe′less** *adj.*

pipe dream /pīp dreem/ *n.* unattainable or fanciful hope or scheme.

pipe·fit·ter /pípfitər/ *n.* person who installs and repairs pipes.

pipe·fit·ting /pípfiting/ *n.* **1** coupling, elbow, etc., used as a connector in a pipe system. **2** work of a pipefitter.

pipe·line /píplīn/ *n.* **1** long, usu. underground, pipe for conveying esp. oil. **2** channel supplying goods, information, etc. □ **in the pipeline** awaiting completion or processing.

pi·pette /pīpét/ *n.* slender tube for transferring or measuring small quantities of liquids.

pip·ing /pípíng/ *n.* **1** thin pipelike fold used to edge hems or frills on clothing, seams on upholstery, etc. **2** lengths of pipe, or a system of pipes, esp. in domestic use. □ **piping hot** very or suitably hot (esp. as required of food, water, etc.).

pip·it /pípit/ *n.* small bird resembling a lark.

pip·pin /pípin/ *n.* type of apple.

pip·squeak /pípskweek/ *n. colloq.* insignificant or contemptible person or thing.

pi·quant /peékənt, -kaant, peekaánt/ *adj.* **1** agreeably pungent, sharp, or appetizing. **2** pleasantly stimulating, or disquieting, to the mind. □□ **pi′quan·cy** *n.* **pi′quant·ly** *adv.*

pique /peek/ ● *v.tr.* (**pi·ques, piqued, piqu·ing**) **1** wound the pride of; irritate. **2** arouse (curiosity, interest, etc.). ● *n.* ill-feeling; enmity; resentment (*in a fit of pique*).

pi·ra·cy /pírəsee/ *n.* (*pl.* **-cies**) **1** practice or an act of robbery of ships at sea. **2** similar practice or act in other forms, esp. hijacking. **3** infringement of copyright.

pi·ra·nha /pira′anə, -ránə, -ra′anyə, -rányə/ *n.* freshwater predatory fish native to S. America.

pi·rate /pírət/ ● *n.* **1 a** person who commits piracy. **b** ship used by pirates. **2** person who infringes another's copyright or other business rights. ● *v.tr.* reproduce (the work or ideas, etc., of another) without permission. □□ **pi·rat·ic** /-rátik/ *adj.* **pi·rat′i·cal** *adj.* **pi·rat′i·cal·ly** *adv.*

pir·ou·ette /pírōo-ét/ ● *n.* dancer's spin on one foot or the point of the toe. ● *v.intr.* perform a pirouette.

pis·ca·to·ry /pískətawree/ *adj.* of fishermen or fishing.

Pi·sces /píseez/ *n.* **1** constellation and twelfth sign of the zodiac (the Fishes). **2** person born when the sun is in this sign.

pis·tach·i·o /pistásheeō, -sta′asheeō/ *n.* **1** tree bearing small brownish green flowers and ovoid reddish fruit. **2** (in full **pis·tach·i·o nut**) edible pale green seed of this.

pis·til /pístil/ *n.* female organs of a flower, comprising the stigma, style, and ovary. □□ **pis′til·late** /-lət, -layt/ *adj.*

pis·tol /pístəl/ *n.* small hand-held firearm. □ **pistol-whip** (**-whipped, -whip·ping**) beat with a pistol.

---

pistol mid-16th century: from obsolete French *pistole*, from German *Pistole*, from Czech *pišt′ala*, of which the original meaning was 'whistle, fife,' hence 'a firearm' because of the resemblance in shape of the barrel to a fife or pipe.

---

pis·ton /pístən/ *n.* disk or short cylinder fitting closely within a tube in which it moves up and down, as in an internal combustion engine, pump, etc. □ **piston ring** sealing ring on a piston. **piston rod** rod attached to a piston to impart motion.

pit[1] /pit/ ● *n.* **1** usu. large deep hole in the ground. **2** hollow or indentation on a surface. **3** *Theatr.* = orchestra pit. **4** (**the pits**) *sl.* wretched or the worst imaginable place, situation, person, etc. **5** area at the side of a track where racing cars are serviced and refueled. ● *v.tr.* (**pit·ted, pit·ting**) **1** (usu. foll. by *against*) set (one's wits, strength, etc.) in opposition or rivalry. **2** (usu. as **pitted** *adj.*) make pits, esp. scars, in. □ **pit bull**

(**terrier**) strong, compact breed of American dog noted for its ferocity. **pit stop 1** brief stop at the pit by a racing car for servicing or refueling. **2** *colloq.* stop, as during a long journey, for food, rest, etc.

pit² /pit/ • *n.* stone of a fruit. • *v.tr.* (**pit•ted, pit•ting**) remove pits from (fruit).

pi•ta /pe′etə/ *n.* (also **pit′ta**) flat, hollow, unleavened bread that can be split and filled.

pit-a-pat /pítəpát/ (also **pit•ter-pat•ter** /pítərpátər/) • *adv.* **1** with a sound like quick light steps. **2** with a faltering sound (*heart went pit-a-pat*). • *n.* such a sound.

pitch¹ /pich/ • *v.* **1** *tr.* (also *absol.*) erect and fix (a tent, camp, etc.). **2** *tr.* throw. **3** *tr.* express in a particular style or at a particular level. **4** *intr.* fall heavily, esp. headlong. **5** *intr.* (of a ship, aircraft, etc.) plunge in a longitudinal direction (cf. ROLL *v.* 5a). **6 a** *tr. Baseball* deliver (the ball) to the batter. **b** *intr. Baseball* play at the position of pitcher. • *n.* **1** height, degree, intensity, etc. (*the pitch of despair*). **2** degree of a slope, esp. of a roof. **3** *Mus.* that quality of a sound which is governed by the rate of vibrations producing it; degree of highness or lowness of a tone. **4** pitching motion of a ship, etc. **5** delivery of a baseball by a pitcher. **6** *colloq.* salesman's advertising or selling approach. □ **pitched battle 1** vigorous argument, etc. **2** *Mil.* battle planned beforehand and fought on chosen ground. **pitched roof** sloping roof. **pitch in** *colloq.* **1** set to work vigorously. **2** assist; cooperate.

pitch² /pich/ • *n.* sticky resinous black or dark brown substance obtained by distilling tar or turpentine, used for caulking the seams of ships, etc. • *v.tr.* coat or smear with pitch. □ **pitch-black** (or **-dark**) very or completely dark.

pitch•blende /píchblend/ *n.* mineral form of uranium oxide occurring in pitchlike masses and yielding radium.

pitch•er¹ /píchər/ *n.* large jug with a lip and a handle, for holding liquids. □□ **pitch′er•ful** *n.* (*pl.* **-fuls**).

pitch•er² /píchər/ *n.* **1** person or thing that pitches. **2** *Baseball* player who delivers the ball to the batter.

pitch•fork /píchfawrk/ *n.* long-handled two-pronged fork for pitching hay, etc.

pitch•man /píchmən/ *n.* **1** salesperson. **2** person who sells goods from a portable stand, as at a fair or on the street.

pit•e•ous /píteeəs/ *adj.* deserving or causing pity; wretched. □□ **pit′e•ous•ly** *adv.* **pit′e•ous•ness** *n.*

pit•fall /pítfawl/ *n.* **1** unsuspected snare, danger, or drawback. **2** covered pit for trapping animals, etc.

pith /pith/ *n.* **1** spongy white tissue lining the rind of an orange, lemon, etc. **2** essential part. **3** *Bot.* spongy cellular tissue in the stems and branches of plants. **4 a** physical strength; vigor. **b** force; energy. □□ **pith′less** *adj.*

pith•y /píthee/ *adj.* (**pith•i•er, pith•i•est**) **1** (of style, speech, etc.) condensed, terse, and forceful. **2** of, like, or containing much pith. □□ **pith′i•ly** *adv.* **pith′i•ness** *n.*

pit•i•a•ble /píteeəbəl/ *adj.* **1** deserving or causing pity. **2** contemptible. □□ **pit′i•a•ble•ness** *n.* **pit′i•a•bly** *adv.*

pit•i•ful /pítifool/ *adj.* **1** causing pity. **2** contemptible. □□ **pit′i•ful•ly** *adv.* **pit′i•ful•ness** *n.*

pit•i•less /pítilis/ *adj.* showing no pity (*pitiless heat of the desert*). □□ **pit′i•less•ly** *adv.*

pi•ton /pe′eton/ *n.* peg or spike driven into a rock or crack to support a climber or a rope.

pit•tance /pít′ns/ *n.* **1** scanty or meager allowance, remuneration, etc. **2** small number or amount.

pit•ter-pat•ter var. of PIT-A-PAT.

pi•tu•i•tar•y /pito͞o-iteree, -tyo͞o-/ *n.* (*pl.* **-ies**) (also **pi•tu′i•tar•y gland** or **body**) small ductless gland at the base of the brain.

pit•y /pítee/ • *n.* (*pl.* **-ies**) **1** sorrow and compassion aroused by another's condition (*felt pity for the child*). **2** grounds for regret (*what a pity!*). • *v.tr.* (**-ies, -ied**) feel pity for. □□ **pit′y•ing** *adj.* **pit′y•ing•ly** *adv.*

piv•ot /pívət/ • *n.* **1** short shaft or pin on which something turns or oscillates. **2** crucial or essential person, point, etc. • *v.* **1** *intr.* turn on or as if on a pivot. **2** *intr.* hinge on; depend on. **3** *tr.* provide with a pivot. □□ **piv′ot•al** *adj.*

pix•el /píksəl/ *n. Electronics* any of the minute dots, etc., that comprise an image on a display screen.

pix•ie /píksee/ *n.* (also **pix′y**) (*pl.* **-ies**) a being like a fairy.

piz•za /pe′etsə/ *n.* flat round base of dough baked with a topping of tomatoes, cheese, onions, etc.

piz•ze•ri•a /pe′etsəree′ə/ *n.* place where pizzas are made or sold.

piz•zi•ca•to /pítsika′ato/ *Mus.* • *adv.* plucking the strings of a violin, etc., with the finger. • *adj.* (of a note, passage, etc.) performed pizzicato.

pkg. *abbr.* (also **pkge.**) package.

pl. *abbr.* **1** plural. **2** place. **3** plate. **4** esp. *Mil.* platoon.

plac•ard /plákaard, -kərd/ • *n.* large poster, esp. for advertising. • *v.tr.* set up placards on (a wall, etc.).

pla•cate /pláykayt, plák-/ *v.tr.* pacify; conciliate. □□ **pla′cat•ing•ly** *adv.* **pla•ca•tion** /-áyshən/ *n.* **pla′ca•to•ry** /-kətawree/ *adj.*

place /plays/ • *n.* **1 a** a particular portion of space. **b** portion of space occupied by a person or thing. **c** proper or natural position (*take your places*). **2** city, town, village, etc. (*was born in this place*). **3** residence; dwelling. **4** rank; status. **5** space, esp. a seat, for a person (*two places in the coach*). **6** building or area for a specific purpose (*fireplace*). **7** point reached in a book, etc. (*lost my place*). **8** particular spot on a surface, esp. of the skin (*sore place on his wrist*). **9** employment or office. **10** position; rank; prerogative. **11** second finishing position, esp. in a horse race. **12** position of a number in a series indicated in decimal or similar notation. • *v.tr.* **1** put (a thing, etc.) in a particular place or state; arrange. **2** identify, classify, or remember correctly. **3** assign to a particular place; locate. **4** find a job, clerical post, etc., for. **5** assign rank, importance, or worth to. **6** make (an order for goods, etc.). **7** (as **placed** *adj.*) second in a race. □ **go places** *colloq.* be successful. **in place of** in exchange for; instead of. **place mat** small mat on a table underneath a person's plate. **place-name** name of a geographic location, as a city, town, hill, lake, etc. **place setting** set of plates, silverware, etc., for one person at a meal. **put**

a person in his or **her place** deflate or humiliate a person. **take place** occur. **take the place of** be substituted for; replace. □□ **place'less** *adj.* **place'ment** *n.*

pla·ce·bo /pləseˈebō/ *n.* **1 a** pill, medicine, etc., prescribed more for psychological reasons than for any physiological effect. **b** placebo used as a control in testing new drugs, etc.

pla·cen·ta /pləséntə/ *n.* (*pl.* **pla·cen·tae** /-tee/ or **pla·cen·tas**) organ in the uterus of pregnant mammals that nourishes and maintains the fetus. □□ **pla·cen'tal** *adj.*

plac·er /plásər/ *n.* deposit of sand, gravel, etc., in the bed of a stream, etc., containing valuable minerals in particles.

plac·id /plásid/ *adj.* **1** (of a person) not easily aroused or disturbed; peaceful. **2** mild; calm; serene. □□ **pla·cid·i·ty** /pləsíditee/ *n.* **plac'id·ly** *adv.* **plac'id·ness** *n.*

plack·et /plákit/ *n.* opening or slit in a garment.

pla·gia·rism /pláyjərizəm/ *n.* **1** plagiarizing. **2** something plagiarized. □□ **pla'gia·rist** *n.* **pla·gia·ris'tic** *adj.*

pla·gia·rize /pláyjəriz/ *v.tr.* (also *absol.*) **1** take and use (the thoughts, writings, inventions, etc., of another person) as one's own. **2** pass off the thoughts, etc., of (another person) as one's own. □□ **pla'gia·riz·er** *n.*

plague /playg/ • *n.* **1** deadly contagious disease. **2** unusual infestation of a pest, etc. (*a plague of frogs*). **3 a** great trouble. **b** affliction. • *v.tr.* (**plagues, plagued, plagu·ing**) **1** affect with plague. **2** *colloq.* pester or harass continually. □□ **plague'some** *adj.*

plaid /plad/ *n.* **1** any cloth with a tartan pattern. **2** this pattern. □□ **plaid'ed** *adj.*

plain /playn/ • *adj.* **1** clear; evident (*is plain to see*). **2** readily understood; simple (*in plain words*). **3** uncomplicated; unembellished; simple. **4** (esp. of a woman or girl) not good-looking; homely. **5** straightforward. • *adv.* **1** clearly. **2** simply (*that is plain stupid*). • *n.* level tract of esp. treeless country. □□ **plain'ly** *adv.* **plain'ness** *n.*

plain-clothes·man /playnklózmən, klóthz-, -man/ *n.* police officer who wears civilian clothes while on duty.

plain·song /pláynsawng, -song/ *n.* unaccompanied church music sung in unison in medieval modes and in free rhythm.

plaint /playnt/ *n. literary* complaint; lamentation.

plain·tiff /pláyntif/ *n. Law* person who brings a case against another into court (opp. DE-FENDANT).

plain·tive /pláyntiv/ *adj.* **1** expressing sorrow; mournful. **2** mournful-sounding. □□ **plain'tive·ly** *adv.* **plaint'ive·ness** *n.*

plait /playt, plat/ • *n.* **1** = BRAID 2. **2** = PLEAT. • *v.tr.* = BRAID.

plan /plan/ • *n.* **1** method or procedure by which a thing is to be done; design or scheme. **2** drawing or diagram of a structure. **3** map of a town or district. • *v.* (**planned, plan·ning**) **1** *tr.* arrange (a procedure, etc.) beforehand; form a plan. **2** *tr.* **a** design (a building, new town, etc.). **b** make a plan of (an existing building, an area, etc.). **3** *tr.* (as **planned** *adj.*) in accordance with a plan. **4** *intr.* make plans. □□ **plan'ner** *n.* **plan'ning** *n.*

plane¹ /playn/ • *n.* **1** flat surface on which a straight line joining any two points on it would wholly lie. **2** level surface. **3** *colloq.* = AIRPLANE. **4** level of attainment, thought, knowledge, etc. • *adj.* **1** (of a surface, etc.) perfectly level. **2** (of an angle, figure, etc.) lying in a plane.

plane² /playn/ • *n.* tool used to smooth a usu. wooden surface by paring shavings from it. • *v.tr.* smooth (wood, metal, etc.) with a plane.

PLANE²

plane³ /playn/ *n.* (in full **plane tree**) tree with maple-like leaves and bark which peels in uneven patches.

plan·et /plánit/ *n.* **1** celestial body moving in an elliptical orbit around a star. **2** the earth. □□ **plan'e·tar·y** *adj.* **plan·e·tol·o·gy** /-tóləjee/ *n.*

plan·e·tar·i·um /plánitáireeəm/ *n.* (*pl.* **plan·e·tar·i·ums** or **plan·e·tar·i·a** /-reeə/) **1** domed building in which images of stars, planets, constellations, etc., are projected for public entertainment or education. **2** device for such projection.

plan·gent /plánjənt/ *adj.* **1** (of a sound) loud and reverberating. **2** (of a sound) plaintive; sad. □□ **plan'gen·cy** *n.*

plank /plangk/ • *n.* **1** long flat piece of timber used esp. in building, flooring, etc. **2** item of a political or other program. • *v.tr.* **1** provide, cover, or floor, with planks. **2** *colloq.* **a** put (a thing, person, etc.) down roughly or violently. **b** pay (money) on the spot or abruptly.

plank·ing /plángking/ *n.* planks as flooring, etc.

plank·ton /plángktən/ *n.* chiefly microscopic organisms drifting or floating in the sea or fresh water. □□ **plank·ton·ic** /-tónik/ *adj.*

plant /plant/ • *n.* **1 a** living organism usu. containing chlorophyll enabling it to live wholly on inorganic substances and lacking specialized sense organs and the power of voluntary movement. **b** small organism of this kind, as distinguished from a shrub or tree. **2 a** machinery, fixtures, etc., used in industrial processes. **b** factory. • *v.tr.* **1** place (a seed, bulb, or growing thing) in the ground so that it may take root and flourish. **2** put or fix in position. **3** cause (an idea, etc.) to be established esp. in another person's mind. **4** deliver (a blow, kiss, etc.) with a deliberate aim. **5** *colloq.* position or conceal (something incriminating or compromising) for later discovery. □□ **plant'a·ble** *adj.* **plant'let** *n.* **plant'like** *adj.*

plan·tain /plántin/ *n.* **1** kind of banana plant widely grown for its fruit. **2** starchy fruit of this.

plan·ta·tion /plantáyshən/ *n.* **1** estate on which cotton, tobacco, etc., is cultivated. **2** area planted with trees, etc.

plant·er /plántər/ *n.* **1** manager or occupier of a

coffee, cotton, etc., plantation. **2** large container for decorative plants.

plaque /plak/ *n.* **1** ornamental or commemorative tablet. **2** deposit on teeth where bacteria proliferate.

plas·ma /plázmə/ *n.* (also **plasm** /plázəm/) **1** colorless fluid part of blood, lymph, or milk. **2** = PROTOPLASM. **3** gas of positive ions and free electrons in about equal numbers. □□ **plas·mat·ic** /-mátik/ *adj.* **plas´mic** *adj.*

plas·ter /plástər/ • *n.* **1** soft pliable mixture esp. of lime putty with sand or Portland cement, etc., for spreading on walls, ceilings, etc., to form a smooth hard surface when dried. **2** *hist.* curative or protective substance spread on a bandage, etc., and applied to the body (*mustard plaster*). • *v.tr.* **1** cover (a wall, etc.) with plaster or a similar substance. **2** coat thickly or to excess; bedaub. **3** stick or apply (a thing) thickly like plaster. **4** make (esp. hair) smooth with water, gel, etc. □ **plaster of Paris** fine white plaster made of gypsum and used for making plaster casts, etc. □□ **plas´ter·er** *n.* **plas´ter·y** *adj.*

plas·ter·board /plástərbawrd/ *n.* type of board with a center filling of plaster, used for partitions, walls, etc.

plas·tic /plástik/ • *n.* **1** any of a number of synthetic polymeric substances that can be given any required shape. **2** (*attrib.*) made of plastic (*plastic bag*); made of cheap materials. **3** *colloq.* credit card, charge card, etc. • *adj.* capable of being molded; pliant; supple. □ **plastic surgery** process of reconstructing or repairing parts of the body by the transfer of tissue, either in the treatment of injury or for cosmetic reasons. □□ **plas´tic·al·ly** *adv.* **plas·tic·i·ty** /-tísitee/ *n.* **plas·ti·cize** /-tisīz/ *v.tr.* **plas·ti·ci·za´tion** *n.* **plas´ti·ciz·er** *n.*

plate /playt/ • *n.* **1 a** shallow vessel from which food is eaten or served. **b** contents of this. **2** similar vessel used esp. for making a collection in a church, etc. **3** (*collect.*) **a** utensils of silver, gold, or other metal. **b** objects of plated metal. **4** a piece of metal with a name or inscription for affixing to a door, container, etc. **b** = *license plate*. **5** illustration on special paper in a book. **6** thin sheet of metal, glass, etc., coated with a sensitive film for photography. **7** flat thin usu. rigid sheet of metal, etc., often part of a mechanism. **8 a** smooth piece of metal, etc., for engraving. **b** impression made from this. **9** a plastic dental device to hold artificial teeth. **b** *colloq.* denture. **10** *Geol.* each of several rigid sheets of rock thought to form the earth's outer crust. **11** *Baseball* base at which the batter stands and which a runner touches to scores. • *v.tr.* **1** apply a thin coat esp. of silver, gold, or tin to (another metal). **2** cover (esp. a ship) with plates of metal, esp. for protection. □ **plate glass** thick fine-quality glass for storefront windows, etc., orig. cast in plates. **plate tectonics** *Geol.* study of the earth's surface based on the concept of moving plates (see sense 10 of *n.*) forming its structure. □□ **plate´ful** *n.* (*pl.* -fuls). **plate´less** *adj.* **plat´er** *n.*

---

plate Middle English (denoting a flat, thin sheet (usually of metal)): from Old French, from medieval Latin *plata* 'plate armor,' based on Greek *platus* 'flat.' Sense 1 represents Old French *plat* 'platter, large dish,' also 'dish of meat,' a noun use of Old French *plat* 'flat.'

---

pla·teau /plató/ *n.* (*pl.* **pla·teaux** /-tóz/ or **pla·teaus**) **1** area of fairly level high ground. **2** state of little variation after an increase.

plate·let /pláytlit/ *n.* small colorless disk of protoplasm found in blood and involved in clotting.

plat·en /plát'n/ *n.* **1** plate in a printing press which presses the paper against the type. **2** cylindrical roller in a typewriter against which the paper is held.

plat·form /plátfawrm/ *n.* **1** raised level surface, as for a speaker, for freight loading, etc. **2** declared policy of a political party.

plat·i·num /plát'nəm/ *n. Chem.* ductile malleable silvery-white metallic element unaffected by simple acids and fusible only at a very high temperature. ¶ Symb.: **Pt**.

plat·i·tude /plátitōōd, -tyōōd/ *n.* trite or commonplace remark, esp. one solemnly delivered. □□ **plat·i·tu·di·nize** /-tōōd'nīz, -tyōō-/ *v.intr.* **plat·i·tu·di·nous** /-tōōdənəs/ *adj.*

Pla·ton·ic /plətónik/ *adj.* **1** of or associated with the Greek philosopher Plato (d. 347 BC) or his ideas. **2** (**platonic**) (of love or friendship) not sexual. □□ **Pla·ton´i·cal·ly** *adv.*

Pla·to·nism /pláyt'nizəm/ *n.* philosophy of Plato or his followers. □□ **Pla´to·nist** *n.*

pla·toon /plətōōn/ *n.* **1** *Mil.* subdivision of a company. **2** group of persons acting together.

plat·ter /plátər/ *n.* large flat dish or plate, esp. for food.

plat·y·pus /plátipəs/ *n.* Australian aquatic egg-laying mammal having a pliable ducklike bill. Also called **duckbill**.

plau·dit /pláwdit/ *n.* (usu. in *pl.*) tribute; applause.

plau·si·ble /pláwzibəl/ *adj.* **1** (of an argument, statement, etc.) seeming reasonable or probable. **2** (of a person) persuasive but deceptive. □□ **plau·si·bil´i·ty** *n.* **plau´si·bly** *adv.*

play /play/ • *v.* **1** *intr.* occupy or amuse oneself pleasantly or idly. **2** *intr.* act lightheartedly or flippantly (with feelings, etc.). **3** *tr.* **a** perform on or be able to perform on (a musical instrument). **b** perform (a piece of music, etc.). **c** cause (a record, radio, etc.) to produce sounds. **4** *a intr.* perform a role in (a drama, etc.). **b** *tr.* perform (a drama or role) on stage, or in a movie or broadcast. **c** *tr.* give a dramatic performance at (a particular theater or place). **5** *tr.* behave or act as (*play the fool*). **6** *tr.* perform (a trick or joke, etc.) on (a person). **7** *tr.* **a** take part in (a game or recreation). **b** compete with (another player or team) in a game. **c** occupy (a specified position) in a team for a game. **d** assign (a player) to a position. • *n.* **1** recreation or amusement, esp. as the spontaneous activity of children and young animals. **2 a** playing of a game. **b** action or manner of this. **3** dramatic piece for the stage, etc. **4** activity or operation (*brought into play*). **5 a** freedom of movement. **b** space or scope for this. □ **play along** pretend to cooperate. **play around** (or **about**) **1** behave irresponsibly. **2** philander. **play back** play (sounds recorded), esp. to monitor recording quality, etc. **play-by-play** *adj.* pertaining to a description, esp. of a sports event, with continuous commentary. • *n.* such a description (*he called the play-by-play*). **play down** minimize the importance of. **played out** exhausted of energy or usefulness. **play for time** seek to gain time by delaying. **play off** (usu. foll. by *against*) **1** oppose (one person against another), esp. for one's own advantage. **2** play an extra match to decide a draw or tie. **play-off** *Sports* game played to break a tie. **play on words** pun. **play up to** flatter, esp. to win favor. **play with fire** take foolish risks. □□ **play′a•ble** *adj.* **play•a•bil′i•ty** *n.*

play•act /pláyakt/ *v.* **1** *intr.* act in a play. **2** *intr.* behave affectedly or insincerely. **3** *tr.* act (a scene, part, etc.). □□ **play′act•ing** *n.* **play′ac•tor** *n.*

play•back /pláybak/ *n.* act or instance of replaying recorded audio or video from a tape, etc.

play•bill /pláybil/ *n.* poster or program for a play.

play•boy /pláyboy/ *n.* irresponsible pleasure-seeking man.

play•er /pláyər/ *n.* **1** person taking part in a sport or game. **2** person playing a musical instrument. **3** actor.

play•ful /pláyfŏŏl/ *adj.* **1** fond of or inclined to play. **2** done in fun; humorous; jocular. □□ **play′ful•ly** *adv.* **play′ful•ness** *n.*

play•go•er /pláygōər/ *n.* person who goes often to the theater.

play•ground /pláygrownd/ *n.* outdoor area set aside for children to play.

play•house /pláyhows/ *n.* **1** theater. **2** toy house for children to play in.

playing card *n.* each of a set of usu. 52 rectangular cards, divided into four suits and used to play various games.

play•mate /pláymayt/ *n.* child's companion in play.

play•pen /pláypen/ *n.* portable enclosure for young children to play in.

play•thing /pláything/ *n.* toy.

play•wright /pláyrīt/ *n.* person who writes plays.

pla•za /pláazə/ *n.* **1** marketplace or open square (esp. in a town). **2** service and rest area on an expressway.

plea /plee/ *n.* **1** earnest appeal or entreaty. **2** *Law* formal statement by or on behalf of a defendant. **3** excuse. □ **plea bargain** (or **bargaining**) arrangement between prosecutor and defendant whereby the defendant pleads guilty to a lesser charge in the expectation of leniency.

plead /pleed/ *v.* (*past* and *past part.* **plead•ed** or **pled** /pled/) **1** *intr.* make an earnest appeal. **2** *intr. Law* address a court. **3** *tr.* maintain (a cause) esp. in a court. **4** *tr. Law* declare to be one's state as regards guilt in or responsibility for a crime (*plead guilty; plead insanity*). **5** *tr.* offer or allege as an excuse (*pleaded forgetfulness*). □□ **plead′a•ble** *adj.* **plead′er** *n.* **plead′ing** *n.* **plead′ing•ly** *adv.*

pleas•ant /plézənt/ *adj.* (**pleas•ant•er**, **pleas•ant•est**) pleasing to the mind, feelings, or senses. □□ **pleas′ant•ly** *adv.* **pleas′ant•ness** *n.*

pleas•ant•ry /plézəntree/ *n.* (*pl.* **-ries**) pleasant or amusing remark, esp. made in casual conversation.

please /pleez/ *v.* **1** *tr.* (also *absol.*) be agreeable to; give pleasure to. **2** *tr.* (in *passive*) **a** be glad or willing to. **b** derive pleasure or satisfaction (from). **3** *intr.* think fit; have the will or desire (*take as many as you please*). **4** *tr.* (short for

may it please you) used in polite requests (*come in, please*). □ **please oneself** do as one likes. □□ **pleased** *adj.* **pleas′ing** *adj.* **pleas′ing•ly** *adv.*

pleas•ur•a•ble /plézhərəbəl/ *adj.* causing pleasure; agreeable. □□ **pleas′ur•a•ble•ness** *n.* **pleas′ur•a•bly** *adv.*

pleas•ure /plézhər/ *n.* **1** feeling of satisfaction or joy. **2** enjoyment. **3** source of pleasure or gratification. **4** a person's will or desire (*what is your pleasure?*). **5** sensual gratification.

pleat /pleet/ • *n.* fold or crease, esp. a flattened fold in cloth doubled upon itself. • *v.tr.* make a pleat or pleats in.

plebe /pleeb/ *n.* first-year student at a military academy.

ple•be•ian /plibée′ən/ • *n.* commoner, esp. in ancient Rome. • *adj.* **1** uncultured. **2** coarse; ignoble. **4** *formal* a person's will or desire (*what ple•be′ian•ism* *n.*

pleb•i•scite /plébisīt, -sit/ *n.* direct, popular vote on an issue.

---

plebiscite mid-16th century (referring to Roman history): from French *plébiscite*, from Latin *plebiscitum*, from *plebs*, *pleb*- 'the common people' + *scitum* 'decree' (from *sciscere* 'vote for'). The sense 'direct vote of the whole electorate' dates from the mid-19th century.

---

plec•trum /pléktrəm/ *n.* (*pl.* **plec•trums** or **plec•tra** /-trə/) thin flat piece of plastic or horn, etc., held in the hand and used to pluck a string, esp. of a guitar.

pled *past* of PLEAD.

pledge /plej/ • *n.* **1** solemn promise or undertaking. **2** thing given as security for the fulfillment of a contract, the payment of a debt, etc. **3** thing given as a token. • *v.tr.* **1** deposit as security. **2** promise solemnly by the pledge of (one's honor, word, etc.). **3** (often *refl.*) bind by a solemn promise. □□ **pledge′a•ble** *adj.* **pledg′er** *n.* **pled′gor** *n.*

ple•na•ry /plée′ənaree, plén-/ *adj.* **1** entire; unqualified; absolute. **2** (of an assembly) to be attended by all members.

plen•i•po•ten•ti•a•ry /plénipəténshəree, -shee-eree/ • *n.* (*pl.* **-ies**) person (esp. a diplomat) invested with the full power of independent action. • *adj.* having this power.

plen•i•tude /plénitŏŏd, -tyŏŏd/ *n.* **1** fullness; completeness. **2** abundance.

plen•te•ous /plénteeəs/ *adj.* plentiful. □□ **plen′te•ous•ly** *adv.* **plen′te•ous•ness** *n.*

plen•ti•ful /pléntifŏŏl/ *adj.* abundant; copious. □□ **plen′ti•ful•ly** *adv.* **plen′ti•ful•ness** *n.*

plen•ty /pléntee/ • *n.* **1** great or sufficient quantity or number. **2** abundance. • *adv. colloq.* fully; entirely.

ple•o•nasm /plée′ənazəm/ *n.* use of more words than are needed to give the sense (e.g., *see with one's eyes*). □□ **ple•o•nas′tic** /-nástik/ *adj.* **ple•o•nas′ti•cal•ly** *adv.*

pleth•o•ra /pléthərə/ *n.* oversupply; glut; excess. □□ **ple•thor•ic** /plətháwrik, -thór-/ *adj.* **ple•thor′i•cal•ly** *adv.*

pleu•ra /plŏŏrə/ *n.* (*pl.* **pleu•rae** /-ree/) membrane enveloping the lungs. □□ **pleu′ral** *adj.*

pleu•ri•sy /plŏŏrisee/ *n.* inflammation of the pleura, marked by pain in the chest or side, fever, etc. □□ **pleu•rit•ic** /-rítik/ *adj.*

Plex·i·glas /pléksiglas/ *n. propr.* tough, clear thermoplastic used instead of glass.

plex·us /pléksəs/ *n.* (*pl.* same or **plex·us·es**) *Anat.* network of nerves or vessels (*gastric plexus*). □□ **plex′i·form** *adj.*

pli·a·ble /plíəbəl/ *adj.* **1** bending easily; supple. **2** yielding; compliant. □□ **pli·a·bil′i·ty** *n.* **pli′a·ble·ness** *n.* **pli′a·bly** *adv.*

pli·ant /plíənt/ *adj.* = PLIABLE 1. □□ **pli′an·cy** *n.* **pli′ant·ly** *adv.*

pli·ers /plíərz/ *n.pl.* pincers with parallel flat usu. serrated surfaces for holding small objects, bending wire, etc.

PLIERS

plight[1] /plīt/ *n.* condition or state, esp. an unfortunate one.

plight[2] /plīt/ *archaic v.tr.* pledge.

plinth /plinth/ *n.* **1** lower square slab at the base of a column. **2** base supporting a vase or statue, etc.

PLO *abbr.* Palestine Liberation Organization.

plod /plod/ *v.intr.* (**plod·ded, plod·ding**) **1** walk doggedly or laboriously; trudge. **2** (often foll. by *at*) work slowly and steadily. □□ **plod′der** *n.* **plod′ding·ly** *adv.*

plop /plop/ • *n.* **1** sound as of a smooth object dropping into water without a splash. **2** act of falling with this sound. • *v.* (**plopped, plop·ping**) fall or drop with a plop.

plot /plot/ • *n.* **1** defined and usu. small piece of ground. **2** interrelationship of the main events in a play, novel, movie, etc. **3** conspiracy or secret plan. • *v.tr.* (**plot·ted, plot·ting**) **1** make a plan or map of. **2** (also *absol.*) plan or contrive secretly (a crime, conspiracy, etc.). **3** mark (a point or course, etc.) on a chart or diagram. □□ **plot′less** *adj.* **plot′ter** *n.*

plo·ver /plúvər, plố-/ *n.* plump-breasted shorebird, e.g., the lapwing, the sandpiper.

plow /plow/ • *n.* **1** implement for cutting furrows in the soil and turning it up. **2** implement resembling this (*snowplow*). • *v.* **1** *tr.* (also *absol.*) turn up (the earth) with a plow, esp. before sowing. **2** *tr.* **a** furrow or scratch (a surface) as if with a plow. **b** move through or break the surface of (water). **3** *tr.* produce (a furrow, line, or wake) in this way. **4** *intr.* advance laboriously, esp. through work, a book, etc. **5** *intr.* move like a plow steadily or violently. □□ **plow′a·ble** *adj.* **plow′er** *n.*

plow·share /plówshair/ *n.* cutting blade of a plow.

ploy /ploy/ *n. colloq.* cunning maneuver to gain advantage.

pluck /pluk/ • *v.* **1** *tr.* remove by picking or

pulling out or away. **2** *tr.* strip (a bird) of feathers. **3** *intr.* (foll. by *at*) tug or snatch at. **4** *tr.* sound (the string of a musical instrument) with the finger or plectrum, etc. • *n.* **1** courage; spirit. **2** plucking. □□ **pluck′er** *n.* **pluck′less** *adj.*

pluck·y /plúkee/ *adj.* (**pluck·i·er, pluck·i·est**) brave; spirited. □□ **pluck′i·ly** *adv.* **pluck′i·ness** *n.*

plug /plug/ • *n.* **1** piece of solid material fitting tightly into a hole. **2** device fitting into holes in a socket for making an electrical connection. **3** *colloq.* piece of (often free) publicity for an idea, product, etc. **4** cake or stick of tobacco; piece of this for chewing. • *v.* (**plugged, plug·ging**) **1** *tr.* (often foll. by *up*) stop up (a hole, etc.) with a plug. **2** *tr. sl.* shoot or hit (a person, etc.). **3** *tr. colloq.* promote (an idea, product, etc.). **4** *intr. colloq.* work steadily away (at). □□ **plug′ger** *n.*

plum /plum/ *n.* **1 a** oval fleshy fruit with sweet pulp and a flattish stone. **b** tree bearing this. **2** reddish-purple color. **3** something especially prized (often *attrib.: a plum job*).

plum·age /plóómij/ *n.* bird's feathers. □□ **plum′aged** *adj.* (usu. in *comb.*).

plumb /plum/ • *n.* ball of lead or other heavy material, esp. one attached to the end of a line for finding the depth of water or determining the vertical on an upright surface. • *adv.* **1** exactly (*plumb in the center*). **2** vertically. **3** *sl.* quite; utterly (*plumb crazy*). • *adj.* vertical. • *v.tr.* **1** sound or test with a plumb. **2** reach or experience in extremes. **3** learn in detail the facts about (a matter).

PLUMB

plumb·er /plúmər/ *n.* person who fits and repairs the apparatus of a water supply system.

plumb·ing /plúming/ *n.* **1** system or apparatus of water supply, heating, etc., in a building. **2** work of a plumber.

plume /plóóm/ • *n.* **1** feather, esp. a large one used for ornament. **2** ornament of feathers, etc., attached to a helmet or hat or worn in the hair. **3** something resembling this (*plume of smoke*). • *v.tr.* **1** decorate or provide with a plume or plumes. **2** (of a bird) preen (itself or its feathers). □□ **plume′less** *adj.* **plume′like** *adj.* **plum′er·y** *n.* **plum′y** *adj.* (**plum·i·er, plum·i·est**).

plum·met /plúmit/ • *n.* plumb. • *v.intr.* fall or plunge rapidly.

plump ~ poet   460

plump[1] /plump/ • *adj.* having a full rounded shape; fleshy. • *v.* make or become plump. □□ **plump′ish** *adj.* **plump′ly** *adv.* **plump′ness** *n.*

plump[2] /plump/ • *v.* drop or fall abruptly. • *adv. colloq.* directly; bluntly.

plun·der /plúndər/ • *v.tr.* **1** rob; loot. **2** (also *absol.*) steal or embezzle (goods). • *n.* **1** activity of plundering. **2** property acquired by plundering. □□ **plun′der·er** *n.*

plunge /plunj/ • *v.* **1 a** *tr.* thrust forcefully or abruptly. **b** *intr.* dive; propel oneself forcibly. **c** *intr.* & *tr.* enter or cause to enter or embark impetuously. **2** *tr.* immerse completely. **3** *intr.* move suddenly and dramatically downward. • *n.* plunging action or movement; dive. □ **take the plunge** *colloq.* commit oneself to a (usu. risky) course of action.

plung·er /plúnjər/ *n.* **1** part of a mechanism that works with a plunging or thrusting movement. **2** rubber cup on a handle for clearing blocked pipes.

plu·ral /plŏŏrəl/ • *adj.* **1** more than one in number. **2** *Gram.* (of a word or form) denoting more than one. • *n. Gram.* plural word or form. □□ **plu·ral·ly** *adv.*

¶ **1.** The apostrophe is often, but not always, used to form the plural of letters (*r's*) and numbers (*7's*), as well as single words referred to themselves (*four the's in one sentence*). **2.**The regular plurals of abbreviations and acronyms may be spelled by simply adding an *-s: CDs, MiGs.* They may also, especially if periods are involved, employ an apostrophe: *D.D.S.'s.* **3.** The plurals of all proper names should end in *-s* or *-es,* with no apostrophe: *the Smiths, the Joneses, the Rosses.* Exceptions include a few names that would have an *-es* but that would not be pronounced that way: *all the Kings Louis of France.*

plu·ral·ism /plŏŏrəlizəm/ *n.* form of society in which the members of minority groups maintain their independent cultural traditions. □□ **plu′ral·ist** *n.* **plu·ral·is′tic** *adj.* **plu·ral·is′ti·cal·ly** *adv.*

plu·ral·i·ty /plŏŏrálitee/ *n.* (*pl.* **-ties**) **1** state of being plural. **2** large or the greater number. **3** majority that is not absolute.

¶ See note at MAJORITY.

plus /plus/ • *prep.* **1** *Math.* with the addition of. ¶ Symbol: +. **2** *colloq.* with; having gained. • *adj.* **1** (after a number) at least (*fifteen plus*). **2** (after a grade, etc.) somewhat better than. **3** *Math.* positive. **4** having a positive electrical charge. **5** (*attrib.*) additional; extra. • *n.* **1** = *plus sign.* **2** *Math.* additional or positive quantity. **3** advantage. • *conj. colloq. disp.* also; and furthermore (*they arrived late, plus they were hungry*). □ **plus sign** symbol +, indicating addition or a positive value.

¶ The use of **plus** as a conjunction meaning 'and furthermore,' e.g., *plus we will be pleased to give you personal financial advice,* is considered incorrect by many people.

plush /plush/ • *n.* cloth of silk, cotton, etc., with a long soft nap. • *adj.* **1** made of plush. **2** luxurious. □□ **plush′ly** *adv.* **plush′ness** *n.*

Plu·to /plŏŏtō/ *n.* outermost known planet of the solar system.

plu·toc·ra·cy /plŏŏtókrəsee/ *n.* (*pl.* **-cies**) **1 a** government by the wealthy. **b** nation governed in this way. **2** wealthy élite or ruling class.

plu·to·crat /plŏŏtəkrat/ *n.* **plu·to·crat′ic** *adj.* **plu·to·crat′i·cal·ly** *adv.*

plu·to·ni·um /plŏŏtóneeəm/ *n. Chem.* dense silvery radioactive metallic transuranic element. ¶ Symb.: **Pu.**

plu·vi·al /plŏŏveeəl/ *adj.* **1** of rain; rainy. **2** *Geol.* caused by rain. □□ **plu′vi·ous** *adj.* (in sense 1).

ply[1] /plī/ *n.* (*pl.* **plies**) **1** thickness or layer of wood, cloth, etc. (*three-ply*). **2** strand of yarn or rope, etc.

ply[2] /plī/ *v.* (**plies, plied**) **1** *tr.* use or wield vigorously (a tool, weapon, etc.). **2** *tr.* work steadily at (one's business or trade). **3** *tr.* (foll. by *with*) supply (a person) continuously (with food, drink, etc.). **4** *intr.* (of a vehicle, etc.) travel regularly (to and fro).

ply·wood /plíwŏŏd/ *n.* strong thin board consisting of two or more layers glued and pressed together.

Pm *symb. Chem.* promethium.

p.m. *abbr.* between noon and midnight (Latin *post meridiem*).

PMS *abbr.* premenstrual syndrome.

pneu·mat·ic /nŏŏmátik, nyŏŏ-/ *adj.* **1** filled with air or wind. **2** operated by compressed air. □□ **pneu·mat′i·cal·ly** *adv.* **pneu·ma·tic·i·ty** /nŏŏmətisitee, nyŏŏ-/ *n.*

pneu·mo·nia /nŏŏmónyə, nyŏŏ-/ *n.* bacterial inflammation of one lung (**single pneumonia**) or both lungs (**double pneumonia**). □□ **pneu·mon·ic** /-mónik/ *adj.*

PO *abbr.* **1** Post Office. **2** postal order. **3** Petty Officer.

Po *symb. Chem.* polonium.

poach[1] /pōch/ *v.tr.* **1** cook (an egg) without its shell in or over boiling water. **2** cook (fish, etc.) by simmering in a small amount of liquid. □□ **poach′er** *n.*

poach[2] /pōch/ *v.* **1** *tr.* (also *absol.*) catch (game or fish) illegally. **2** *intr.* (often foll. by *on*) trespass or encroach (on another's property, ideas, etc.). □□ **poach′er** *n.*

pock /pok/ *n.* (also **pock·mark**) **1** small pus-filled spot on the skin, esp. caused by chickenpox or smallpox. **2** a mark resembling this. □ **pock-marked** bearing marks resembling or left by such spots. □□ **pock′et·a·ble** *adj.* **pock′et·less** *adj.*

pock·et /pókit/ • *n.* **1** small bag sewn into or on clothing, for carrying small articles. **2** pouchlike compartment or holder. **3** isolated group or area (*pockets of resistance*). **4** (*attrib.*) **a** of a suitable size and shape for carrying in a pocket. **b** small. • *v.tr.* **1** put into one's pocket. **2** appropriate, esp. dishonestly. □ **pocket knife** knife with a folding blade or blades, for carrying in the pocket. **pocket veto** executive veto of a legislative bill by allowing it to go unsigned. □□ **pock′et·a·ble** *adj.* **pock′et·less** *adj.*

pock·et·book /pókitbŏŏk/ *n.* purse or handbag.

pod /pod/ *n.* **1** long seed vessel esp. of a leguminous plant, e.g., a pea. **2** cocoon of a silkworm.

po·di·a·try /pədīətree/ *n. Med.* care and treatment of the foot. □□ **po·di′a·trist** *n.*

po·di·um /pódeeəm/ *n.* (*pl.* **po·di·ums** or **po·di·a** /-deeə/) platform or rostrum.

po·em /póəm/ *n.* metrical composition, usu. concerned with feeling or imaginative description.

po·e·sy /póəzee, -see/ *n. archaic* poetry.

po·et /póit/ *n.* (*fem.* **po′et·ess** /póətis/) **1** writer of poems. **2** person possessing high powers of imagination or expression, etc. □ **poet laureate** poet appointed to write poems for official state occasions.

po·et·ic /pō-étik/ *adj.* (also **po·et′i·cal**) **1** of or like poetry or poets. **2** elevated or sublime in expression. □ **poetic justice** well-deserved unforeseen retribution or reward. **poetic license** writer's or artist's transgression of established rules for effect. □□ **po·et′i·cal·ly** *adv.*

po·et·ics /pō-étiks/ *n.* **1** art of writing poetry. **2** the study of poetry and its techniques.

po·et·ry /póətree/ *n.* **1** art or work of a poet. **2** poems collectively. **3** poetic or tenderly pleasing quality.

po·grom /pógrəm, pəgrúm, -gróm/ *n.* organized massacre (orig. of Jews in Russia).

poign·ant /póynyənt/ *adj.* **1** painfully sharp to the emotions or senses; deeply moving. **2** arousing sympathy. □□ **poign′ance** *n.* **poign′an·cy** *n.* **poign′ant·ly** *adv.*

poin·set·ti·a /poynséteeə, -sétə/ *n.* shrub with large usu. scarlet bracts surrounding small yellow flowers.

point /poynt/ • *n.* **1** sharp or tapered end of a tool, weapon, pencil, etc. **2** tip or extreme end. **3** that which in geometry has position but not magnitude. **4** particular place or position. **5** precise or critical moment. **6** very small mark on a surface. **7** dot or other punctuation mark, esp. = PERIOD. **8** = *decimal point.* **9** stage or degree in progress or increase. **10** of temperature at which a change of state occurs (*freezing point*). **11** single item; detail or particular. **12** unit of scoring in games or of measuring value, etc. **13 a** significant or essential thing. **b** sense or purpose; advantage or value. **14** distinctive feature or characteristic (*it has its points*). **15 a** each of 32 directions marked at equal distances around a compass. **b** corresponding direction toward the horizon. **16** (usu. in *pl.*) electrical contact in the distributor of a motor vehicle. **17** promontory. **18** *Printing* unit of measurement for printed type (in the US 0.351 mm). • *v.* **1 a** *tr.* direct or aim (a finger, weapon, etc.). **b** *intr.* direct attention. **2** *intr.* aim or be directed to. **3** *intr.* indicate; be evidence of (*it all points to murder*). □ **at** (or **on**) **the point of** on the verge of. **beside the point** irrelevant. **point-blank** *adj.* **1** (of a shot) aimed or fired horizontally at a range very close to the target. **2** blunt; direct. • *adv.* **1** at very close range. **2** directly; bluntly. **point of order** parliamentary query as to correct procedure. **point of view 1** position from which a thing is viewed. **2** particular way of considering a matter. **point out** indicate; show; draw attention to. **point up** emphasize; show as important. **to the point** relevant or relevantly. **up to a point** to some extent but not completely.

---

point Middle English: the noun partly from Old French *point*, from Latin *punctum* 'something that is pricked,' giving rise to the senses 'unit, mark, point in space or time'; partly from Old French *pointe*, from Latin *puncta* 'pricking,' giving rise to the senses 'sharp tip, promontory.' The verb derives partly from Old French *pointer* 'sharpen,' but some senses derive from the English noun.

---

point·ed /póyntid/ *adj.* **1** sharpened or tapering to a point. **2** (of a remark, etc.) penetrating; cut-

ting. **3** emphasized; made evident. □□ **point′ed·ly** *adv.* **point′ed·ness** *n.*

point·er /póyntər/ *n.* **1** thing that points, e.g., the index hand of a gauge, etc. **2** rod for pointing to features on a map, chart, etc. **3** *colloq.* hint, clue, or indication. **4** dog of a breed that on scenting game stands rigid looking toward it.

poin·til·lism /pwántilizəm, póyn-/ *n.* *Art* technique of impressionist painting using tiny dots of various pure colors, which become blended in the viewer's eye. □□ **poin′til·list** *n.* & *adj.* **poin·til·list′ic** *adj.*

point·less /póyntlis/ *adj.* lacking force, purpose, or meaning. □□ **point′less·ly** *adv.* **point′less·ness** *n.*

poise /poyz/ • *n.* **1** composure. **2** equilibrium. **3** carriage (of the head, etc.). • *v.* **1** *tr.* balance; hold suspended or supported. **2** *intr.* be balanced; hover in the air, etc.

---

poise late Middle English (in the sense 'weight'): from Old French *pois* (noun), *peser* (verb), from an alteration of Latin *pensum* 'weight,' from the verb *pendere* 'weigh.' From the early senses of 'weight' and 'measure of weight' arose the notion of 'equal weight, balance,' leading to the extended senses 'composure' and 'elegant deportment.'

---

poised /poyzd/ *adj.* **1** composed; self-assured. **2** (often foll. by *for*, or *to* + infin.) ready for action.

poi·son /póyzən/ • *n.* **1** substance causing an organism death or injury, esp. in a small quantity. **2** *colloq.* harmful influence. • *v.tr.* **1** administer poison to. **2** kill, injure, or infect with poison. **3** (esp. as **poisoned** *adj.*) treat something with poison. **4** corrupt; pervert; spoil. □ **poison ivy** climbing plant secreting an irritant oil from its leaves. □□ **poi′son·er** *n.* **poi′son·ous** *adj.* **poi′son·ous·ly** *adv.*

poke¹ /pōk/ • *v.* **1 a** *tr.* thrust or push with the hand, point of a stick, etc. **b** *intr.* be thrust forward. **2** *tr.* thrust the end of a finger, etc., against. **3** *tr.* produce (a hole, etc., in a thing) by poking. **4** *intr.* **a** move or act desultorily. **b** (foll. by *about, into*) pry; search casually. • *n.* thrust; jab. □ **poke fun at** ridicule.

poke² /pōk/ *n.* *dial.* bag or sack.

pok·er¹ /pókər/ *n.* stiff metal rod for stirring an open fire.

pok·er² /pókər/ *n.* card game in which bluff is used as players bet on the value of their hands. □ **poker face 1** impassive countenance appropriate to a poker player. **2** person with this. **poker-faced** having a poker face.

pok·y /pókee/ *adj.* (**pok·i·er, pok·i·est**) **1** (of a room, etc.) small and cramped. **2** slow. □□ **pok′i·ly** *adv.* **pok′i·ness** *n.*

po·lar /pólər/ *adj.* **1** of or near a pole of the earth. **2** having magnetic or electric polarity. **3** directly opposite in character. □ **polar bear** white bear of the Arctic regions.

po·lar·i·ty /pəláritee/ *n.* (*pl.* **-ties**) **1** tendency of a lodestone, magnetized bar, etc., to point with its extremities to the magnetic poles of the earth. **2** condition of having two poles with contrary qualities. **3** state of having two opposite tendencies, opinions, etc. **4** electrical condition of a body (positive or negative).

po·lar·ize /pólərīz/ v. 1 tr. restrict the vibrations of (a transverse wave, esp. light) to one direction. 2 tr. give magnetic or electric polarity. 3 tr. & intr. divide into two opposing groups. □□ **po′ lar·i·za·ble** adj. **po·lar·i·za′tion** n. **po′lar·i·zer** n.

Pole /pōl/ n. 1 native or national of Poland. 2 person of Polish descent.

pole[1] /pōl/ • n. long slender rounded piece of wood or metal. • v. tr. push or propel (a small boat) with a pole. □ **pole vault** n. sport of vaulting over a high bar with the aid of a long flexible pole. • v. intr. take part in this sport. **pole-vaulter** person who pole vaults.

pole[2] /pōl/ n. 1 (in full **north pole, south pole**) **a** each of the two points in the celestial sphere about which the stars appear to revolve. **b** each of the extremities of the axis of rotation of the earth or another body. 2 each of the two opposite points on the surface of a magnet at which magnetic forces are strongest. 3 each of two terminals (positive and negative) of an electric cell or battery, etc. □ **be poles apart** differ greatly, esp. in nature or opinion. □□ **pole′ward** adj. **pole′wards** adj. & adv.

pole·cat /pólkat/ n. 1 skunk. 2 small European brownish black, flesh-eating mammal of the weasel family.

po·lem·ic /pəlémik/ • n. 1 controversial discussion. 2 Polit. verbal or written attack. • adj. (also **po·lem′i·cal**) involving dispute; controversial. □□ **po·lem′i·cal·ly** adv. **po·lem′i·cist** /-misist/ n. **po·lem′i·cize** v. tr.

po·lem·ics /pəlémiks/ n.pl. art or practice of disputation.

pole·star /pólstar/ n. 1 Astron. star now about 1° distant from the celestial north pole. 2 thing serving as a guide.

po·lice /pəlees/ • n. 1 (usu. prec. by the) civil force of a government, responsible for maintaining public order. 2 (as pl.) its members. 3 force with similar functions (transit police). • v. tr. 1 control (a country or area) by means of police. 2 provide with police. 3 keep order in; control; monitor. □ **police officer** policeman or policewoman. **police state** totalitarian country controlled by political police supervising the citizens' activities.

po·lice·man /pəlee′esmən/ n. (pl. **-men**; fem. **po·lice·wom·an**, pl. **-wom·en**) member of a police force.

pol·i·cy[1] /pólisee/ n. (pl. **-cies**) 1 course or principle of action adopted or proposed by a government, party, business, or individual, etc. 2 prudent conduct; sagacity.

pol·i·cy[2] /pólisee/ n. (pl. **-cies**) insurance contract.

pol·i·cy·hold·er /póliseehóldər/ n. person or body holding an insurance policy.

po·li·o·my·e·li·tis /póleeōmf-ilítis/ n. (also **po·li·o**) Med. infectious viral disease that affects the central nervous system and can cause temporary or permanent paralysis.

Po·lish /pólish/ • adj. 1 of or relating to Poland. 2 of the Poles or their language. • n. language of Poland.

pol·ish /pólish/ • v. 1 make or become smooth or glossy esp. by rubbing. 2 (esp. as **polished** adj.) refine or improve; add finishing touches to. • n. 1 substance used for polishing. 2 smoothness or glossiness produced by friction. 3 refinement; elegance. □ **polish off** finish (esp. food) quickly. □□ **pol·ish′able** adj. **pol·ish′er** n.

po·lite /pəlít/ adj. (**po·lit·er**, **po·lit·est**) 1 having good manners; courteous. 2 cultivated; cultured. 3 refined; elegant (polite letters). □□ **po·lite′ly** adv. **po·lite′ness** n.

pol·i·tesse /pólités/ n. formal politeness.

pol·i·tic /pólitik/ • adj. 1 (of an action) judicious; expedient. 2 (of a person) prudent; sagacious. • v. intr. (**pol·i·ticked, pol·i·tick·ing**) engage in politics.

po·lit·i·cal /pəlítikəl/ adj. 1 of or concerning government, or public affairs generally. 2 taking or belonging to a side in politics. 3 concerned with seeking status, authority, etc. (political decision). □ **political action committee** permanent organization that collects and distributes funds for political purposes. ¶ Abbr.: **PAC**. **political correctness** avoidance of forms of expression and action that exclude or marginalize sexual, racial, and cultural minorities; advocacy of this. **politically correct** in conformance with political correctness. **political science** the study of systems of government. □□ **po·lit′i·cal·ly** adv.

pol·i·ti·cian /pólitishən/ n. 1 person engaged in politics, esp. as a practitioner. 2 person skilled in politics. 3 derog. person with self-interested political concerns.

po·lit·i·cize /pəlítisīz/ v. 1 tr. **a** give a political character to. **b** make politically aware. 2 intr. engage in or talk politics. □□ **po·lit′i·ci·za′tion** n.

po·lit·i·co /pəlítikō/ n. (pl. **-cos**) colloq. politician.

pol·i·tics /pólitiks/ n.pl. 1 (treated as sing. or pl.) **a** art and science of government. **b** public life and affairs. 2 (usu. treated as pl.) **a** particular set of ideas, principles, or commitments in politics (what are their politics?). **b** activities concerned with seeking power, status, etc.

pol·i·ty /pólitee/ n. (pl. **-ties**) 1 form or process of civil government or constitution. 2 organized society; state.

pol·ka /pólkə, pókə/ • n. 1 lively dance of Bohemian origin in duple time. 2 music for this. • v. intr. (**pol·kas, pol·kaed** /-kəd/ or **pol·ka′d, pol·ka·ing** /-kəing/) dance the polka. □ **polka dot** round dot as one of many forming a regular pattern on a textile fabric, etc.

poll /pōl/ • n. 1 **a** voting. **b** result of voting or number of votes recorded. 2 survey of opinion. • v. tr. 1 **a** take the vote or votes of. **b** (of a candidate) receive (so many votes). 2 record the opinion of (a person or group). □□ **poll′ster** n.

pol·len /pólən/ n. fine dustlike grains discharged from the male part of a flower containing the gamete that fertilizes the female ovule. □ **pollen count** index of the amount of pollen in the air. □□ **pol·len′less** adj.

pol·li·nate /pólinayt/ v. tr. (also absol.) sprinkle (a stigma) with pollen. □□ **pol·li·na·tion** /-náyshən/ n. **pol′li·na·tor** n.

pol·lute /pəlóōt/ v. tr. 1 contaminate or defile (the environment). 2 make foul or filthy. 3 destroy the purity or sanctity of. □□ **pol·lu′tant** adj. & n. **pol·lut′er** n. **pol·lu′tion** n.

po·lo /pólō/ n. game of Asian origin played on horseback with a long-handled mallet and wooden ball.

po·lo·naise /pólənáyz, pó-/ n. 1 dance of Polish origin in triple time. 2 music for this.

po·lo·ni·um /pəlṓneeəm/ n. Chem. rare radioactive metallic element, occurring naturally in uranium ores. ¶ Symb.: **Po**.

pol·ter·geist /pṓltərgīst/ n. noisy mischievous ghost, esp. one manifesting itself by physical damage.

pol·troon /poltrṓon/ n. spiritless coward. □□ **pol·troon′er·y** n.

poly-[1] /pólee/ comb. form denoting many or much.

poly-[2] /pólee/ comb. form Chem. polymerized (polyester).

pol·y·an·dry /póleeandree/ n. **1** polygamy in which a woman has more than one husband. **2** Bot. state of having numerous stamens. □□ **pol·y·an·drous** /-ándrəs/ adj. ¶ See note at POLYGAMY.

pol·y·chro·mat·ic /póleekrōmátik/ adj. **1** many-colored. **2** (of radiation) containing more than one wavelength. □□ **pol·y·chro·ma·tism** /-krṓmətizəm/ n.

pol·y·chrome /póleekrōm/ • adj. in many colors. • n. work of art in several colors, esp. a colored statue. □□ **pol·y·chrom′ous** adj.

pol·y·es·ter /pólee-éstər/ n. type of synthetic fiber or resin.

pol·y·eth·yl·ene /pólee-éthileen/ n. Chem. plastic polymer of ethylene used for packaging and insulating materials.

po·lyg·a·my /pəlígəmee/ n. practice of having more than one spouse at a time. □□ **po·lyg·a·mist** /-gəmist/ n. **po·lyg′a·mous** adj. ¶ **Polygamy** is having more than one spouse. It may apply to men or women; **polygyny** is specifically the practice of having more than one wife. **Polyandry** is the term for having more than one husband.

pol·y·glot /póleeglot/ • adj. knowing, using, or written in several languages. • n. polyglot person. □□ **pol·y·glot′tal** adj. **pol·y·glot′tic** adj.

pol·y·gon /póleegon/ n. plane figure with many (usu. a minimum of three) sides and angles. □□ **po·lyg·o·nal** /pəlígənəl/ adj.

pol·y·graph /póleegraf/ n. machine designed to detect and record changes in physiological characteristics (e.g., rates of pulse and breathing), used esp. as a lie-detector.

pol·y·he·dron /póleehéedrən/ n. (pl. **pol·y·he·dra** /-drə/) solid figure with many (usu. more than six) faces. □□ **pol′y·he′dral** adj. **pol′y·he′dric** adj.

pol·y·math /póleemath/ n. **1** person of much or varied learning. **2** great scholar. □□ **pol·y·math′ic** adj.

pol·y·mer /pólimər/ n. compound composed of one or more large molecules that are formed from repeated units of smaller molecules.

Pol·y·ne·sian /póleeḗzhən/ • adj. of or relating to Polynesia, a group of Pacific islands including New Zealand, Hawaii, Samoa, etc. • n. **1 a** native of Polynesia. **b** person of Polynesian descent. **2** family of languages including Maori, Hawaiian, and Samoan.

pol·y·no·mi·al /pólinṓmeeəl/ Math. • n. expression of more than two algebraic terms. • adj. of or being a polynomial.

pol·yp /pólip/ n. **1** Zool. individual coelenterate. **2** Med. small usu. benign growth on a mucous membrane.

po·lyph·o·ny /pəlífənee/ n. (pl. **-nies**) Mus. contrapuntal music. □□ **pol·y·phon·ic** /póleefónik/ adj. **pol·y·phon′i·cal·ly** adv. **po·lyph′o·nous** adj.

pol·y·pro·pyl·ene /póleeprṓpileen/ n. Chem. polymer of propylene used for films, fibers, or molding materials.

pol·y·sac·cha·ride /póleesákərīd/ n. any of a group of carbohydrates whose molecules consist of long chains of monosaccharides.

pol·y·sty·rene /póleestíreen/ n. plastic polymer of styrene used for insulation and in packaging.

pol·y·syl·lab·ic /póleesilábik/ adj. **1** (of a word) having many syllables. **2** characterized by the use of words of many syllables. □□ **pol·y·syl′lab′i·cal·ly** adv. **pol·y·syl·la·ble** /-siləbəl/ n.

pol·y·tech·nic /póleetéknik/ • n. institution of higher education offering courses in many esp. vocational or technical subjects. • adj. dealing with or devoted to various vocational or technical subjects.

pol·y·the·ism /póleetheeízəm/ n. belief in or worship of more than one god. □□ **pol·y·the′ist** n. **pol·y·the·is′tic** adj.

pol·y·un·sat·u·rat·ed /póleeunsáchəraytid/ adj. Chem. (of a compound, esp. a fat or oil molecule) containing several double or triple bonds and therefore capable of further reaction.

pol·y·u·re·thane /póleeyŏŏrəthayn/ n. any polymer containing the urethane group, used in adhesives, paints, etc.

pol·y·vi·nyl chlo·ride /póleevínil/ n. polymer of vinyl chloride, easily colored and used for a wide variety of products including pipes, flooring, etc. ¶ Abbr.: **PVC**.

po·made /pomáyd, -maʹad/ n. scented dressing for the hair and the skin of the head.

po·man·der /pṓmandər, pōmán-/ n. **1** ball of mixed aromatic substances. **2** (usu. spherical) container for this.

pome·gran·ate /pómigranit, pómgranit, púm-/ n. **1** orange-sized fruit with a tough reddish outer skin and containing many seeds in a red pulp. **2** tree bearing this.

pom·mel /páməl, póm-/ • n. **1** knob, esp. at the end of a sword hilt. **2** upward projecting front part of a saddle. • v.tr. = PUMMEL.

pomp /pomp/ n. **1** splendid display; splendor. **2** (often in pl.) vainglory (pomps and vanities of this wicked world).

pom·pom /pómpom/ n. (also **pom·pon** /-pon/) ornamental ball or tuft often worn on hats or clothing.

pomp·ous /pómpəs/ adj. self-important; affectedly grand or solemn. □□ **pom·pos·i·ty** /pómpósitee/ n. (pl. **-ties**). **pom′pous·ly** adv. **pomp′ous·ness** n.

pon·cho /póncho/ n. (pl. **-chos**) blanket-like cloak with a slit in the middle for the head.

pond /pond/ n. **1** fairly small body of still water formed naturally or by hollowing or embanking. **2** joc. the sea.

pon·der /póndər/ v. **1** tr. weigh mentally; think over; consider. **2** intr. (usu. foll. by on, over) think; muse.

pon·der·ous /póndərəs/ adj. **1** heavy; unwieldy. **2** laborious. **3** (of style, etc.) tedious. □□ **pon′der·ous·ly** adv. **pon′der·ous·ness** n.

pon·iard /pónyərd/ n. small slim dagger.

pon·tiff /póntif/ n. RC Ch. pope.

pon·tif·i·cal /pontífikəl/ adj. **1** RC Ch. of or befitting a pontiff; papal. **2** pompously dogmatic. □□ **pon·tif′i·cal·ly** adv.

pon·tif·i·cate /pontífikayt/ *v.intr.* **1** be pompously dogmatic. **2** *RC Ch.* officiate as bishop, esp. at Mass.

pon·toon /pontóon/ *n.* **1** flat-bottomed boat. **2** each of several boats, hollow metal cylinders, etc., used to support a temporary bridge. **3** float for a seaplane.

PONTOON, 3

po·ny /pónee/ *n.* (*pl.* **-nies**) **1** horse of any small breed. **2** small drinking glass. **3** (in *pl.*) *sl.* racehorses.

po·ny·tail /póneetayl/ *n.* person's hair drawn back, tied, and hanging down like a pony's tail.

poo·dle /poód'l/ *n.* **1** dog of a breed with a curly coat that is usually clipped. **2** this breed.

pooh-pooh /poópoó/ *v.tr.* express contempt for; ridicule.

pool[1] /pool/ *n.* **1** small body of still water. **2** small shallow body of any liquid. **3** pool for swimming.

pool[2] /pool/ • *n.* **1 a** (often *attrib.*) common supply of persons, vehicles, commodities, etc., for sharing by a group (*car pool*). **b** group sharing duties, etc. **2** collective amount of players' stakes in gambling, etc. **3 a** joint commercial venture. **b** common funding for this. **4** any of several games similar to billiards played on a pool table with usu. 16 balls. • *v.tr.* **1** put (resources, etc.) into a common fund. **2** share (things) in common.

poop[1] /poop/ *n.* stern of a ship; aftermost and highest deck.

poop[2] /poop/ *n.* *sl.* up-to-date or inside information.

poor /poor/ *adj.* **1** lacking adequate money or means to live comfortably. **2 a** deficient in (a possession or quality) (*poor in spirit*). **b** (of soil, ore, etc.) unproductive. **3 a** scanty; inadequate (*a poor crop*). **b** less good than is usual or expected (*poor visibility*). **4** unfortunate (*you poor thing*). □ **poor boy** = *submarine sandwich*.

poor·ly /poórlee/ • *adv.* in a poor manner; badly. • *predic. adj.* unwell.

pop[1] /pop/ • *n.* **1** sudden sharp explosive sound as of a cork when drawn. **2** *colloq.* effervescent soft drink. **3** = *pop fly.* • *v.* (**popped, pop·ping**) **1** *intr.* & *tr.* make or cause to make a pop. **2** *intr.* & *tr.* put or move quickly or suddenly. **3** *intr.* (often foll. by *up*) (of a ball) rise up into the air. □ **pop fly** *Baseball* high fly ball hit esp. to the infield. **pop the question** *colloq.* propose marriage. **pop-up** *adj.* having parts that spring or extend up automatically (*pop-up book*). • *n* = *pop fly.*

pop[2] /pop/ *colloq.* • *adj.* **1** in a popular or modern style. **2** performing popular music, etc. (*pop*

star). • *n.* pop music. □ **pop art** art based on modern popular culture and the mass media. **pop culture** commercial culture based on popular taste.

pop[3] /pop/ *n.* *colloq.* father.

pop. *abbr.* population.

pop·corn /pópkawrn/ *n.* **1** corn whose kernels burst open when heated. **2** these kernels when popped.

pope /pop/ *n.* (as title usu. **Pope**) head of the Roman Catholic Church.

pop·in·jay /pópinjay/ *n.* fop; conceited person.

pop·lar /póplər/ *n.* tree with a usu. rapidly growing trunk and tremulous leaves.

pop·lin /póplin/ *n.* plain woven fabric usu. of cotton, with a corded surface.

pop·o·ver /pópōvər/ *n.* light puffy hollow muffin made from an egg-rich batter.

pop·py /pópee/ *n.* (*pl.* **-pies**) plant with showy often red flowers and a milky sap.

pop·py·cock /pópeekok/ *n.* *sl.* nonsense.

Pop·si·cle /pópsikəl/ *n.* *propr.* flavored ice confection on a stick.

pop·u·lace /pópyələs/ *n.* the common people.

pop·u·lar /pópyələr/ *adj.* **1** liked or admired by many people or by a specified group (*a popular hero*). **2 a** of or carried on by the general public (*popular meetings*). **b** prevalent among the general public (*popular discontent*). **3** adapted to the understanding, taste, or means of the people (*popular science*). □□ **pop′u·lar·ism** *n.* **pop·u·lar·i·ty** /-láritee/ *n.* **pop′u·lar·ly** *adv.*

pop·u·lar·ize /pópyələrīz/ *v.tr.* **1** make popular. **2** cause (a person, principle, etc.) to be generally known or liked. **3** present (a difficult subject) in a readily understandable form. □□ **pop·u·lar·i·za′tion** *n.* **pop′u·lar·iz·er** *n.*

pop·u·late /pópyəlayt/ *v.tr.* **1** inhabit; form the population of (a town, country, etc.). **2** supply with inhabitants.

pop·u·la·tion /pópyəláyshən/ *n.* **1** inhabitants. **2** total number of these or any group of living things.

pop·u·list /pópyəlist/ • *n.* member or adherent of a political party seeking support mainly from the ordinary people. • *adj.* of or relating to such a political party. □□ **pop′u·lism** *n.* **pop·u·lis′tic** *adj.*

pop·u·lous /pópyələs/ *adj.* thickly inhabited. □□ **pop′u·lous·ly** *adv.*

por·ce·lain /páwrsəlin, páwrslin/ *n.* **1** hard vitrified translucent ceramic. **2** objects made of this. □□ **por·cel·a·ne·ous** /páwrsəláyneeəs/ *adj.*

porch /pawrch/ *n.* **1** covered shelter for the entrance of a building. **2** veranda. □□ **porched** *adj.* **porch′less** *adj.*

por·cine /páwrsīn, -sin/ *adj.* of or like pigs.

por·cu·pine /páwrkyəpín/ *n.* rodent having defensive spines or quills.

pore[1] /pawr/ *n.* esp. *Biol.* minute opening in a surface through which gases, liquids, or fine solids may pass.

pore[2] /pawr/ *v.intr.* (foll. by *over*) **1** be absorbed in studying (a book, etc.). **2** meditate on; think intently about.

pork /pawrk/ *n.* **1** the (esp. unsalted) flesh of a pig, used as food. **2** = *pork barrel* □ **pork barrel** *colloq.* government funds as a source of political benefit.

por·ky /páwrkee/ adj. (**por·ki·er, por·ki·est**) **1** colloq. fleshy; fat. **2** of or like pork.

porn /pawrn/ n. colloq. pornography.

por·nog·ra·phy /pawrnógrəfee/ n. **1** explicit description or exhibition of sexual activity in literature, films, etc. **2** literature, etc., characterized by this. □□ **por·nog'ra·pher** n. **por·no·graph·ic** /-nəgráfik/ adj. **por·no·graph'i·cal·ly** adv.

po·rous /páwrəs/ adj. **1** full of pores. **2** letting through air, water, etc. □□ **po·ros·i·ty** /porósitee/ n. **po'rous·ly** adv.

por·phy·ry /páwrfiree/ n. (pl. **-ries**) hard rock quarried in ancient Egypt, composed of crystals of white or red feldspar in a red matrix. □□ **por·phy·rit·ic** /-rítik/ adj.

por·poise /páwrpəs/ n. sea mammal of the whale family with a low triangular dorsal fin and a blunt rounded snout.

por·ridge /páwrij, pór-/ n. dish consisting of oatmeal or another cereal boiled in water or milk.

por·rin·ger /páwrinjər, pór-/ n. small bowl, often with a handle, for soup, stew, etc.

port¹ /pawrt/ n. **1** harbor. **2** town with a harbor. □ **port of call** place where a ship or a person stops on a journey.

port² /pawrt/ n. (in full **port wine**) strong, sweet, dark red (occas. brown or white) fortified wine of Portugal.

port³ /pawrt/ • n. left side (looking forward) of a ship, boat, or aircraft. • v.tr. (also absol.) turn (the helm) to port.

port⁴ /pawrt/ n. **1** opening in the side of a ship for entrance, loading, etc. **2** porthole.

por·ta·ble /páwrtəbəl/ • adj. easily movable; convenient for carrying. • n. portable object, e.g., a radio, typewriter, etc. □□ **por·ta·bil'i·ty** n. **por'ta·bly** adv.

por·tage /páwrtij, -tá'azh/ • n. **1** carrying of boats or goods between two navigable waters. **2** place at which this is necessary. • v.tr. convey (a boat or goods) over a portage.

por·tal /páwrt'l/ n. doorway or gate, etc., esp. a large and elaborate one.

port·cul·lis /pawrtkúlis/ n. strong heavy grating lowered to block a gateway in a fortress, etc.

PORTCULLIS

por·tend /pawrténd/ v.tr. **1** foreshadow as an omen. **2** give warning of.

por·tent /páwrtent/ n. omen; sign of something

to come, esp. something of a momentous or calamitous nature.

por·ten·tous /pawrténtəs/ adj. **1** like or serving as a portent. **2** pompously solemn. □□ **por·ten'tous·ly** adv.

por·ter¹ /páwrtər/ n. **1** person employed to carry luggage, etc., at an airport, hotel, etc. **2** dark brown bitter beer. □□ **por'ter·age** n.

por·ter² /páwrtər/ n. gatekeeper or doorkeeper.

por·ter·house steak /páwrtərhows/ n. thick steak cut from the thick end of a sirloin.

port·fo·li·o /pawrtfṓleeō/ n. (pl. **-os**) **1** case for keeping loose sheets of paper, drawings, etc. **2** range of investments held by a person, a company, etc. **3** office of a minister of state. **4** samples of an artist's work.

port·hole /páwrt-hōl/ n. (esp. glassed-in) aperture in a ship's or aircraft's side for the admission of light.

por·ti·co /páwrtikō/ n. (pl. **-coes** or **-cos**) roof supported by columns usu. attached as a porch to a building.

PORTICO

por·tion /páwrshən/ • n. **1** part or share. **2** amount of food allotted to one person. **3** one's destiny or lot. • v.tr. **1** divide (a thing) into portions. **2** (foll. by out) distribute.

Port·land ce·ment /páwrtlənd/ n. cement manufactured from chalk and clay.

port·ly /páwrtlee/ adj. (**port·li·er, port·li·est**) corpulent; stout. □□ **port'li·ness** n.

port·man·teau /pawrtmántō, pawrtmantó/ n. (pl. **port·man·teaus** or **port·man·teaux** /-tōz, -tóz/) leather trunk for clothes, etc., opening into two equal parts. □ **portmanteau word** word blending the sounds and combining the meanings of two others, e.g., motel from motor and hotel.

por·trait /páwrtrit, -trayt/ n. **1** representation of a person or animal, esp. of the face, made by drawing, painting, photography, etc. **2** verbal picture; graphic description. **3** (in graphic design, etc.) format in which the height of an illustration, etc., is greater than the width (cf. LANDSCAPE).

por·trait·ist /páwrtritist/ n. person who makes portraits.

por·trai·ture /páwrtrichər/ n. the making of portraits.

por·tray /pawrtráy/ v.tr. **1** make a likeness of. **2** describe graphically. □□ **por·tray'able** adj. **por·tray'al** n. **por·tray'er** n.

Por·tu·guese /páwrchəgeéz, -geés/ • n. (pl.

same) **1 a** native or national of Portugal. **b** person of Portuguese descent. **2** language of Portugal. ● *adj.* of or relating to Portugal or its people or language.

pose /pōz/ ● *v.* **1** *intr.* assume a certain attitude of body, esp. when being photographed or being painted for a portrait. **2** *intr.* (foll. by *as*) pretend to be (another person, etc.) (*posing as a celebrity*). **3** *intr.* behave affectedly in order to impress others. **4** *tr.* put forward or present (a question, etc.). ● *n.* **1** an attitude of body or mind. **2** affectation; pretense.

po·seur /pōzŕ/ *n.* (*fem.* **po·seuse** /pōzŕz/) person who poses for effect or behaves affectedly.

posh /posh/ *colloq. adj.* elegant; stylish. □□ **posh'ly** *adv.* **posh'ness** *n.*

posh early 20th century: perhaps from slang *posh*, denoting a dandy. There is no evidence to support the popular etymology that *posh* is formed from the initials of *port out starboard home* (referring to the more comfortable staterooms out of the heat of the sun, on ships between England and India).

pos·it /pózit/ *v.tr.* **1** assume as a fact; postulate. **2** put in place or position.

po·si·tion /pəzíshən/ ● *n.* **1** place occupied by a person or thing. **2** placement or arrangement. **3** proper place (*in position*). **4** advantage (*jockey for position*). **5** viewpoint. **6** person's situation in relation to others. **7** rank; status. **8** paid employment. ● *v.tr.* place in position. □ **in a position to** able to. □□ **po·si'tion·al** *adj.* **po·si'tion·er** *n.*

pos·i·tive /pózitiv/ ● *adj.* **1** explicit; definite. (*positive proof*). **2** (of a person) convinced, confident, or overconfident in his or her opinion. **3 a** constructive; directional (*positive thinking*). **b** optimistic. **4** marked by the presence rather than absence of qualities or (esp. *Med.*) symptoms. **5** esp. *Philos.* dealing only with matters of fact; practical. **6** tending toward increase or progress. **7** greater than zero. **8** *Electr.* of, containing, or producing the kind of electrical charge produced by rubbing glass with silk; absence of electrons. **9** (of a photographic image) showing lights and shades or colors true to the original. ● *n.* positive photograph, quantity, etc. □□ **pos'i·tive·ly** *adv.* **pos'i·tive·ness** *n.* **pos·i·tiv·i·ty** /pózitívitee/ *n.*

positive late Middle English: from Old French *positif*, *-ive* or Latin *positivus*, from *posit-* 'placed,' from the verb *ponere*. The original sense referred to laws as being formally 'laid down,' which gave rise to the sense 'explicitly laid down and admitting no question,' hence 'very sure, convinced.'

pos·i·tron /pózitron/ *n. Physics* elementary particle with a positive charge equal to the negative charge of an electron and having the same mass as an electron.

poss. *abbr.* **1** possession. **2** possessive. **3** possible. **4** possibly.

pos·se /pósee/ *n.* **1** strong force or company or assemblage. **2** (in full **pos·se co·mi·ta·tus** /kómitáytəs/) summoned body of law enforcers.

pos·sess /pəzés/ *v.tr.* **1** hold as property; own.

2 have a faculty, quality, etc. **3** occupy; dominate the mind of. (*possessed by fear*). □□ **pos·ses'sor** *n.*

pos·ses·sion /pəzéshən/ *n.* **1** possessing or being possessed. **2** thing possessed. **3** holding or occupancy. **4** (in *pl.*) property, wealth, subject territory, etc. □□ **pos·ses'sion·less** *adj.*

pos·ses·sive /pəzésiv/ ● *adj.* **1** a desire to possess or retain what one already owns. **2** jealous and domineering. **3** *Gram.* indicating possession. ● *n.* (in full **possessive case**) *Gram.* case of nouns and pronouns expressing possession. □□ **pos·ses'sive·ly** *adv.* **pos·ses'sive·ness** *n.*

¶ **1.** Form the possessive of all singulars by adding *-'s*: *Ross's, Fox's, Reese's.* A few classical and other foreign names are traditional exceptions to this rule, e.g., *Jesus', Euripides',* which take an apostrophe only. **2.** Form the possessive of plurals by adding an apostrophe to the plural form: *the Rosses' house, the Perezes' car.* See also note at ITS.

pos·si·bil·i·ty /pósibílitee/ *n.* (*pl.* **-ties**) **1** state or fact of being possible. **2** thing that may exist or happen. **3** (usu. in *pl.*) potential (esp. *have possibilities*).

pos·si·ble /pósibəl/ *adj.* **1** capable of existing, happening, being done, etc. **2** potential (*possible way of doing it*).

pos·si·bly /pósiblee/ *adv.* **1** perhaps. **2** in accordance with possibility (*cannot possibly refuse*).

pos·sum /pósəm/ *n. colloq.* = OPOSSUM. □ **play possum 1** pretend to be asleep or unconscious. **2** feign ignorance.

post[1] /pōst/ ● *n.* **1** piece of timber or metal set upright in the ground, etc., used as a support, marker, etc. **2** pole, etc., marking the start or finish of a race. ● *v.tr.* **1** attach (a paper, etc.) in a prominent place. **2** announce or advertise by placard or in a published text.

post[2] /pōst/ ● *n.* mail. ● *v.tr.* (esp. as **posted** *adj.*) supply a person with information (*keep me posted*). □ **post exchange** *Mil.* store at a military base, etc. **post-haste** with great speed. **Post Office 1** public department or corporation responsible for postal services. **2** (**post office**) room or building where postal business is carried on.

post[3] /pōst/ ● *n.* **1** place where a soldier is stationed or which he or she patrols. **2** place of duty. **3 a** position taken up by a body of soldiers. **b** force occupying this. **4** job. ● *v.tr.* place or station (soldiers, an employee, etc.).

post- /pōst/ *prefix* after in time or order (*postwar*).

post·age /póstij/ *n.* amount charged for sending a letter, etc., by mail. □ **postage stamp** official stamp affixed to a letter, etc., indicating the amount of postage paid.

post·al /póst'l/ *adj.* of or by mail.

post·card /póstkaard/ *n.* card for sending by mail.

post·er /póstər/ *n.* **1** placard in a public place. **2** large printed picture. □ **poster paint** gummy opaque paint.

pos·te·ri·or /posteéreeər, pō-/ ● *adj.* **1** later; coming after in series, order, or time. **2** at the back. ● *n.* buttocks. □□ **pos·te·ri·or·i·ty** /-áwritee, -ór-/ *n.* **pos·te'ri·or·ly** *adv.*

pos·ter·i·ty /postéritee/ *n.* **1** all succeeding generations. **2** descendants of a person.

post·grad·u·ate /pōstgrájōoət/ *adj.* **1** (of a course of study) carried on after taking a high school or college degree. **2** of or relating to postgraduate students.

post·hu·mous /póschəməs/ adj. **1** occurring after death. **2** (of a child) born after the death of its father. **3** (of a book, etc.) published after the author's death. □□ **post'hu·mous·ly** adv.

post·man /póstmən/ n. (pl. **-men**; fem. **post·wom·an**, pl. **-wom·en**) person employed to deliver and collect letters, etc.

post·mark /póstmaark/ • n. official dated postage cancellation mark stamped on a letter. • v.tr. mark (an envelope, etc.) with this.

post·mas·ter /póstmástər/ n. person in charge of a post office.

post·mod·ern /póstmódərn/ adj. (in literature, architecture, the arts, etc.) denoting a movement reacting against modern tendencies, esp. by drawing attention to former conventions. □□ **post'mod'ern·ism'** n. **post'mod'ern·ist** n. & adj.

post·mor·tem /póstmáwrtəm/ • n. **1** (in full **postmortem examination**) examination made after death, esp. to determine its cause. **2** colloq. discussion analyzing the course and result of a game, election, etc. • adv. & adj. after death.

post·na·tal /póstnáyt'l/ adj. characteristic of or relating to the period after childbirth.

post·paid /póstpáyd/ adj. on which postage has been paid.

post·pone /póstpón, pəspón/ v.tr. cause or arrange (an event, etc.) to take place at a later time. □□ **post·pon'able** adj. **post·pone'ment** n. **post·pon'er** n.

post·script /póstskript, póskript/ n. additional paragraph or remark, usu. at the end of a letter, introduced by 'P.S.'

pos·tu·late • v.tr. /póschəlayt/ **1** assume as a necessary condition, esp. as a basis for reasoning; take for granted. **2** claim. • n. /póschələt/ **1** thing postulated. **2** fundamental prerequisite or condition. □□ **pos·tu·la·tion** /-láyshən/ n.

pos·ture /póschər/ • n. **1** bodily carriage or bearing. **2** mental or spiritual attitude or condition. **3** condition or state (of affairs, etc.) (in more diplomatic postures). • v. **1** intr. assume a mental or physical attitude, esp. for effect. **2** tr. pose (a person). □□ **pos'tur·al** adj. **pos'tur·er** n.

po·sy /pózee/ n. (pl. **-sies**) small bunch of flowers.

pot[1] /pot/ • n. **1** vessel, usu. rounded, for holding liquids or solids or for cooking in. **2** contents of a pot. **3** total amount of the bet in a game, etc. **4** colloq. large sum (pots of money). • v.tr. (**pot·ted**, **pot·ting**) place in a pot. □ **go to pot** colloq. deteriorate; be ruined. **pot roast** a piece of meat cooked slowly in a covered dish. **pot-roast** v.tr. cook (a piece of meat) in this way. □□ **pot'ful** n. (pl. **-fuls**).

pot[2] /pot/ n. sl. marijuana.

po·ta·ble /pótəbəl/ adj. drinkable. □□ **po·ta·bil'i·ty** n.

pot·ash /pótash/ n. alkaline potassium compound.

po·tas·si·um /pətáseeəm/ n. Chem. soft silvery white metallic element. ¶ Symb.: **K**. □□ **po·tas'sic** adj.

po·ta·to /pətáytō/ n. (pl. **-toes**) **1** starchy plant tuber that is cooked and used for food. **2** plant bearing this.

pot·bel·ly /pótbelee/ n. (pl. **-lies**) **1** protruding

stomach. **2** person with this. **3** small bulbous stove. □□ **pot'bel'lied** adj.

pot·boil·er /pótboylər/ n. work of literature or art done merely to make the writer or artist a living.

po·tent /pót'nt/ adj. **1** powerful; strong. **2** (of a reason) cogent; forceful. **3** (of a male) capable of sexual erection or orgasm. □□ **po'tence** n. **po'ten·cy** n. **po'tent·ly** adv.

po·ten·tate /pót'ntayt/ n. monarch or ruler.

po·ten·tial /pəténshəl/ • adj. capable of coming into being or action; latent. • n. **1** capacity for use or development; possibility. **2** usable resources. **3** Physics quantity determining the energy of mass in a gravitational field or of charge in an electric field. □□ **po·ten·ti·al·i·ty** /-sheeálitee/ n. **po·ten'tial·ly** adv.

poth·er /póthər/ n. noise; commotion; fuss.

pot·herb /pótərb, -hərb/ n. any herb grown in a kitchen garden or a pot.

pot·hole /pót-hōl/ n. **1** deep hole, as in rock. **2** hole in a road surface.

po·tion /póshən/ n. a liquid medicine, drug, poison, etc.

pot·luck /pótlək/ n. **1** whatever (hospitality, food, etc.) is available. **2** meal to which each guest brings a dish to share.

pot·pour·ri /pópoōree'/ n. **1** mixture of dried petals and spices used to perfume a room, etc. **2** musical or literary medley.

pot·sherd /pótshərd/ n. shard of pottery, esp. one found on an archaeological site.

pot·shot /pótshót/ n. **1** random shot. **2** shot aimed at an animal, etc., within easy reach. **3** shot at a game bird, etc., merely to provide a meal.

pot·tage /pótij/ n. archaic soup; stew.

pot·ter /pótər/ n. maker of ceramic vessels. □ **potter's field** burial place for paupers, strangers, etc. **potter's wheel** horizontal revolving disk to carry clay for making pots.

POTTER'S WHEEL

pot·ter·y /pótəree/ n. (pl. **-ies**) **1** vessels, etc., made of fired clay. **2** potter's work. **3** potter's workshop.

pot·ty /pótee/ n. (pl. **-ties**) colloq. small pot for toilet-training a child.

pouch /powch/ • n. **1** small bag or detachable outside pocket. **2** pocketlike receptacle of kangaroos, etc. • v.tr. put or make into a pouch. □□ **pouched** adj. **pouch'y** adj.

poul·tice /póltis/ • *n.* soft medicated and usu. heated mass applied to the body for relieving soreness and inflammation. • *v.tr.* apply a poultice to.

poul·try /póltree/ *n.* domestic fowls (ducks, geese, turkeys, chickens, etc.), esp. as a source of food.

pounce /powns/ • *v.intr.* **1** spring or swoop, esp. as in capturing prey. **2** (often foll. by *on*, *upon*) make a sudden attack. • *n.* act or an instance of pouncing. □□ **pounc'er** *n.*

pound[1] /pownd/ *n.* **1** unit of weight equal to 16 oz. avoirdupois or 12 oz. troy. ¶ Abbr.: **lb. 2** (in full **pound sterling**) (*pl.* same or **pounds**) chief monetary unit of the UK and several other countries. □ **pound sign 1** the sign #. **2** the sign £, representing pound sterling. □□ **pound'age** *n.*

pound[2] /pownd/ *v.* **1** *tr.* crush or beat with repeated heavy blows. **2** *intr.* deliver heavy blows or gunfire. **3** *intr.* (of the heart) beat heavily. □□ **pound'er** *n.*

pound[3] /pownd/ *n.* enclosure where stray animals or officially removed vehicles are kept until redeemed.

pour /pawr/ *v.* **1** *intr.* & *tr.* flow or cause to flow, esp. downward. **2** *tr.* dispense (a drink) by pouring. **3** *intr.* (of rain, or with *it* as subject) fall heavily. **4** *intr.* come or go in profusion or rapid succession (*letters poured in*). □□ **pour'a·ble** *adj.* **pour'er** *n.*

pout /powt/ • *v.* **1** *intr.* push the lips forward as an expression of displeasure or sulking. **2** *tr.* push (the lips) forward in pouting. • *n.* **1** such an action or expression. **2** (**the pouts**) a fit of sulking. □□ **pout'er** *n.* **pout'ing·ly** *adv.* **pout'y** *adj.*

pov·er·ty /póvərtee/ *n.* **1** being poor; need. **2** scarcity or lack. □ **poverty-stricken** extremely poor.

POW *abbr.* prisoner of war.

pow·der /pówdər/ • *n.* **1** substance in the form of fine dry particles. **2** medicine or cosmetic in this form. **3** = GUNPOWDER. • *v.tr.* **1** apply powder to. **2** (esp. as **powdered** *adj.*) reduce to a fine powder (*powdered milk*). □ **powder puff** soft pad for applying powder to the skin. **powder room** women's toilet. □□ **pow'der·y** *adj.*

pow·er /pówər/ • *n.* **1** the ability to do or act (*will do all in my power*). **2** particular faculty of body or mind (*powers of persuasion*). **3** government, influence, or authority; control (*the party in power*). **4** authorization; delegated authority (*police powers*). **5** influential person, body, government, etc. **6** vigor; energy. **7** active property or function (*heating power*). **8** mechanical or electrical energy as distinct from hand labor (often *attrib.*: *power tools; power steering*). **9** a public supply of (esp. electrical) energy. **b** particular source or form of energy (*hydroelectric power*). **10** *Physics* rate of energy output. **11** product obtained when a number is multiplied by itself a certain number of times (*2 to the power of 3 = 8*). **12** magnifying capacity of a lens. • *v.tr.* supply with mechanical or electrical energy. □ **power of attorney** see ATTORNEY. **power plant 1** facility producing esp. electrical power. **2** source of power, as an engine. **the powers that be** those in authority. □□ **pow'ered** *adj.* (also in *comb.*).

pow·er·boat /pówərbōt/ *n.* powerful motorboat.

pow·er·ful /pówərfŏŏl/ *adj.* having much power or influence. □□ **pow'er·ful·ly** *adv.* **pow'er·ful·ness** *n.*

pow·er·house /pówərhows/ *n.* **1** = *power plant.* **2** *colloq.* person or thing of great energy.

pow·er·less /pówərlis/ *adj.* **1** without power or strength. **2** wholly unable. □□ **pow'er·less·ly** *adv.* **pow'er·less·ness** *n.*

pow·wow /pów-wów/ • *n.* a meeting for discussion (orig. among Native Americans). • *v.tr.* hold a powwow.

pox /poks/ *n.* **1** any virus disease producing a rash of pimples that leave pockmarks on healing. **2** *colloq.* = SYPHILIS.

pp *abbr.* pianissimo.

pp. *abbr.* pages.

ppd. *abbr.* **1** postpaid. **2** prepaid.

p.p.m. *abbr.* parts per million.

PPS *abbr.* additional postscript.

PR *abbr.* **1** public relations. **2** Puerto Rico.

Pr *symb. Chem.* praseodymium.

pr. *abbr.* pair.

prac·ti·ca·ble /práktikəbəl/ *adj.* **1** that can be done or used. **2** possible in practice. □□ **prac·ti·ca·bil'i·ty** *n.* **prac'ti·ca·bly** *adv.* ¶ See note at PRACTICAL.

prac·ti·cal /práktikəl/ *adj.* **1** of or concerned with practice or use rather than theory. **2** useful; functional. **3** (of a person) inclined to action rather than speculation; able to make things function well. **4** so in practice or effect. **5** feasible; concerned with what is actually possible (*practical politics*). □ **practical joke** humorous trick played on a person. □□ **prac·ti·cal·i·ty** /-kálitee/ *n.* (*pl.* **-ties**). ¶ **Practical** and **practicable** are sometimes confused. **Practical** means 'concerning practice,' that is, 'useful; functional.' **Practicable** comes from *practice able*, meaning 'able to be practiced,' or 'able to be done; possible.' Some things—especially ideas—can be both: Nuclear rockets may be both practical (that is, there is something to be gained from developing them) and practicable (that is, they may be possible).

prac·ti·cal·ly /práktiklee/ *adv.* **1** virtually; almost (*practically nothing*). **2** in a practical way.

prac·tice /práktis/ • *n.* **1** habitual action or performance. **2** habit or custom (*has been my regular practice*). **3 a** repeated exercise in an activity requiring the development of skill. **b** session of this. **4** action or execution as opposed to theory. **5** the professional work or business of a doctor, lawyer, etc. • *v.* **1** *tr.* perform habitually; carry out in action. **2** *tr.* & *intr.* do repeatedly as an exercise to improve a skill; exercise oneself in or on (*an activity requiring skill*). **3** *tr.* (as **practiced** *adj.*) experienced, expert. **4** *tr.* pursue or be engaged in (a profession, religion, etc.). □□ **prac'tic·er** *n.*

prac·ti·tio·ner /praktíshənər/ *n.* person practicing a profession, esp. medicine (*general practitioner*).

prae·to·ri·an guard /preetáwreeən/ (also **pre·to·ri·an**) *Rom.Hist.* bodyguard of the Roman emperor.

prag·mat·ic /pragmátik/ *adj.* dealing with matters with regard to their practical requirements or consequences. □□ **prag·mat'i·cal·ly** *adv.*

prag·ma·tism /prágmətizəm/ *n.* **1** pragmatic attitude or procedure. **2** philosophy that evaluates assertions solely by their practical consequences and bearing on human interests. □□ **prag'ma·tist** *n.* **prag·ma·tis'tic** *adj.*

prai·rie /práiree/ *n.* large area of usu. treeless grassland esp. in central N. America. □ **prairie dog** N. American rodent living in burrows and making a barking sound.

praise /prayz/ ● *v.tr.* **1** express warm approval or admiration of. **2** glorify (God) in words. ● *n.* praising; commendation (*won high praise*). □□ **praise'ful** *adj.* **prais'er** *n.*

praise·wor·thy /práyzwərthee/ *adj.* worthy of praise; commendable. □□ **praise'wor·thi·ly** *adv.* **praise'wor·thi·ness** *n.*

pra·line /práaleen, práy-/ *n.* any of several candies made with almonds, pecans, or other nuts and sugar.

prance /prans/ ● *v.intr.* **1** (of a horse) raise the forelegs and spring from the hind legs. **2** walk or behave in an arrogant manner. ● *adj.* prancing. □□ **pranc'er** *n.*

prank /prangk/ *n.* practical joke; piece of mischief. □□ **prank'ish** *adj.*

prank·ster /prángkstər/ *n.* person fond of playing pranks.

pra·se·o·dym·i·um /práyzeeōdímeeəm, práysee-/ *n. Chem.* soft silvery metallic element of the lanthanide series, occurring naturally in various minerals. ¶ Symb.: **Pr.**

prate /prayt/ ● *v.* **1** *intr.* chatter; talk too much. **2** *intr.* talk foolishly or irrelevantly. **3** *tr.* tell or say in a prating manner. ● *n.* prating; idle talk. □□ **prat'er** *n.* **prat'ing** *adj.*

prat·tle /prát'l/ ● *v.* chatter or say in a childish or inconsequential way. ● *n.* **1** childish chatter. **2** inconsequential talk. □□ **prat'tler** *n.* **prat'tling** *adj.*

prawn /prawn/ *n.* edible shrimplike shellfish.

pray /pray/ *v.* **1** *intr.* say prayers (to God, etc.); make devout supplication. **2 a** *tr.* entreat; beseech. **b** *tr. & intr.* ask earnestly (*prayed to be released*). **3** *tr.* (as *imper.*) old-fashioned please (*pray tell me*). □ **praying mantis** see MANTIS.

prayer /prair/ *n.* **1 a** solemn request or thanksgiving to God. **b** formula used in praying (*the Lord's prayer*). **c** act of praying (*be at prayer*). **2** entreaty to a person. □ **prayer book** book of set prayers. □□ **prayer'ful** *adj.*

pre- /pree/ *prefix* before (in time, place, order, degree, or importance).

preach /preech/ *v.* **1 a** *intr.* deliver a sermon. **b** *tr.* deliver (a sermon); proclaim or expound. **2** *intr.* give moral advice in an obtrusive way. **3** *tr.* advocate or inculcate (a quality or practice, etc.). □□ **preach'a·ble** *adj.* **preach'er** *n.*

pre·am·ble /pree-ámbəl/ *n.* **1** preliminary statement or introduction. **2** introductory part of a constitution, statute, or deed, etc.

Pre·cam·bri·an /préekámbreeən/ *Geol.* ● *adj.* of or relating to the earliest era of geological time. ● *n.* this era.

pre·can·cer·ous /preekánsrəs, -kántsər-/ *adj.* having the tendency to develop into a cancer. □□ **pre·can'cer·ous·ly** *adv.*

pre·car·i·ous /prikáireeəs/ *adj.* **1** uncertain; dependent on chance (*makes a precarious living*). **2** insecure; perilous (*precarious health*). □□ **pre·car'i·ous·ly** *adv.* **pre·car'i·ous·ness** *n.*

pre·cau·tion /prikáwshən/ *n.* **1** action taken beforehand to avoid risk or ensure a good result. **2** caution exercised beforehand; prudent foresight. □□ **pre·cau'tion·ary** *adj.*

pre·cede /priseéd/ *v.tr.* (often as **preceding** *adj.*) come or go before in time, order, importance, etc.

prec·e·dence /présidəns, priseéd'ns/ *n.* (also **prec'e·den·cy**) priority in time, order, or importance, etc.

prec·e·dent ● *n.* /présidənt/ previous case or legal decision, etc., taken as a guide for subsequent cases or as a justification. ● *adj.* /priseéd'nt, présidənt/ preceding in time, order, importance, etc.

pre·cept /preésept/ *n.* rule or guide, esp. for conduct. □□ **pre·cep'tive** /-séptiv/ *adj.*

pre·cep·tor /priséptər/ *n.* (*fem.* **pre·cep·tress** /-tris/) teacher or instructor. □□ **pre·cep·to·ri·al** /préeseptawreeəl/ *adj.*

pre·ces·sion /priséshən/ *n.* □ **pre·ces·sion of the e·qui·nox·es** **1** slow retrograde motion of equinoctial points along the ecliptic. **2** resulting earlier occurrence of equinoxes in each successive sidereal year.

pre·cinct /preésingkt/ *n.* **1** enclosed or specially designated area. **2** (in *pl.*) environs. **3** official district, esp. for police or electoral purposes.

pre·ci·os·i·ty /présheeósitee/ *n.* overrefinement in art or language, esp. in the choice of words.

pre·cious /préshəs/ *adj.* **1** of great value or worth. **2** beloved; much prized (*precious memories*). **3** affectedly refined. □ **precious metals** gold, silver, and platinum. □□ **pre'cious·ly** *adv.* **pre'cious·ness** *n.*

prec·i·pice /présipis/ *n.* **1** vertical or steep face of a rock, cliff, mountain, etc. **2** dangerous situation.

pre·cip·i·tate ● *v.tr.* /prisípitayt/ **1** hasten the occurrence of; cause to occur prematurely. **2** throw down headlong. **3** *Chem.* cause (a substance) to be deposited in solid form from a solution. **4** *Physics* **a** cause (dust, etc.) to be deposited from the air on a surface. **b** condense (vapor) into drops and so deposit it. ● *adj.* /prisípitət/ **1** headlong; violently hurried (*precipitate departure*). **2** (of a person or act) hasty; rash; inconsiderate. ● *n.* /prisípitət/ *Chem.* substance precipitated from a solution. □□ **pre·cip'i·tate·ly** /-sípitətlee/ *adv.* **pre·cip·i·tate·ness** /-sípitətnəs/ *n.* **pre·cip'i·ta·tor** *n.*
¶ The adjective **precipitate** means 'sudden, hasty'; *a precipitate decision, precipitate flight by the fugitive*. **Precipitous** means 'steep': *precipitous slope of the mountain, precipitous decline in stock prices.*

***

precipitate early 16th century: from Latin *praecipitat-* 'thrown headlong,' from the verb *praecipitare,* from *praeceps, praecip(it)-* 'headlong,' from *prae* 'before' + *caput* 'head.' The original sense of the verb was 'hurl down, send violently'; hence 'cause to move rapidly,' which gave rise to sense 1 (early 17th century).

***

pre·cip·i·ta·tion /prisípitáyshən/ *n.* **1** act of precipitating or the process of being precipitated. **2** rash haste. **3** a rain or snow, etc., falling to the ground. **b** quantity of this.

pre·cip·i·tous /prisípitəs/ *adj.* **1 a** of or like a precipice. **b** dangerously steep. **2** = PRECIPITATE *adj.* □□ **pre·cip'i·tous·ly** *adv.* **pre·cip'i·tous·ness** *n.*
¶ See note at PRECIPITATE.

pré·cis /práysee/ n. (pl. same /-seez/) summary; abstract.

pre·cise /prisís/ adj. **1 a** accurately expressed. **b** definite; exact. **2** scrupulous in being exact. □□ **pre·cise′ness** n.

pre·cise·ly /prisíslee/ adv. in a precise manner; exactly.

pre·ci·sion /prisízhən/ n. **1** accuracy. **2** (attrib.) marked by or adapted for precision (precision timing). □□ **pre·ci′sion·ism** n. **pre·ci′sion·ist** n.

pre·clude /priklóod/ v.tr. **1** prevent. **2** make impossible. □□ **pre·clu·sion** /-klóōzhən/ n. **pre·clu·sive** /-klóōsiv/ adj.

pre·co·cious /prikóshəs/ adj. **1** (of a person, esp. a child) prematurely developed in some faculty or characteristic. **2** (of an action, etc.) indicating such development. □□ **pre·co′cious·ly** adv. **pre·coc·i·ty** /-kósitee/ n.

pre·cog·ni·tion /preékognishən/ n. (supposed) foreknowledge, esp. of a supernatural kind. □□ **pre·cog·ni·tive** /-kógnitiv/ adj.

pre·con·ceive /preékənseév/ v.tr. (esp. as **preconceived** adj.) form (an idea or opinion, etc.) beforehand.

pre·con·cep·tion /preékənsépshən/ n. **1** preconceived idea. **2** prejudice.

pre·con·di·tion /preékəndishən/ n. prior condition, that must be fulfilled before other things can be done.

pre·cur·sor /prikúrsər, preékər-/ n. **1 a** forerunner. **b** person who precedes in office, etc. **2** harbinger.

pred. abbr. predicate.

pre·date /preédáyt/ v.tr. exist or occur at a date earlier than.

pred·a·tor /prédətər/ n. animal naturally preying on others.

pred·a·to·ry /prédətawree/ adj. **1** (of an animal) preying naturally upon others. **2** plundering or exploiting others. □□ **pred·a·to′ri·ly** adv.

pre·de·cease /preédiseés/ ● v.tr. die earlier than (another person). ● n. death preceding that of another.

pre·de·ces·sor /prédisesər, preé-/ n. person or thing coming before, as a former holder of an office or position.

pre·des·tine /preédéstin/ v.tr. **1** determine beforehand. **2** ordain in advance by divine will or as if by fate. □□ **pre·des·ti·na′tion** n.

pre·de·ter·mine /preéditórmin/ v.tr. **1** determine or decree beforehand. □□ **pre·de·ter′mi·na·ble** adj. **pre·de·ter′mi·nate** adj. **pre·de·ter·mi·na′tion** n.

pre·dic·a·ment /pridíkəmənt/ n. difficult, unpleasant, or embarrassing situation.

pred·i·cate ● v.tr. /prédikayt/ **1** assert or affirm as true or existent. **2** found or base (a statement, etc.) on. ● n. /-kət/ Gram. & Logic what is said about the subject of a sentence or proposition, etc. (e.g., went home in John went home). □□ **pred′i·ca′tion** /-káyshən/ n.

pred·i·ca·tive /prédikaytiv/ adj. **1** Gram. (of an adjective or noun) forming or contained in the predicate, as old in the dog is old. **2** that predicates. □□ **pred′i·ca·tive·ly** adv.

pre·dict /pridíkt/ v.tr. foretell; prophesy. □□ **pre·dic′tive** adj. **pre·dic′tive·ly** adv. **pre·dic′tor** n.

pre·dict·a·ble /pridíktəbəl/ adj. that can be predicted or is to be expected. □□ **pre·dict·a·bil′i·ty** n. **pre·dict′a·bly** adv.

pre·dic·tion /pridíkshən/ n. **1** art of predicting or process of being predicted. **2** thing predicted; forecast.

pred·i·lec·tion /prédlékshən, preé-/ n. (often foll. by for) preference or special liking.

pre·dis·pose /preédispóz/ v.tr. **1** influence favorably in advance. **2** (foll. by to, or to + infin.) render liable or inclined beforehand. □□ **pre·dis·po·si·tion** /-pəzíshən/ n.

pre·dom·i·nant /pridóminənt/ adj. **1** predominating. **2** being the strongest or main element. □□ **pre·dom′i·nance** n. **pre·dom′i·nant·ly** adv.

pre·dom·i·nate /pridóminayt/ v.intr. **1** (foll. by over) have or exert control. **2** be superior. **3** be the strongest or main element; preponderate (garden in which dahlias predominate).

pree·mie /preémee/ n. colloq. infant born prematurely.

pre·em·i·nent /pree-éminənt/ adj. **1** surpassing others. **2** outstanding. □□ **pre·em′i·nence** n. **pre·em′i·nent·ly** adv.

pre·empt /pree-émpt/ v.tr. **1 a** forestall. **b** acquire or appropriate in advance. **2** obtain by preemption. □□ **pre·emp′tor** n. **pre·emp′to·ry** adj.

pre·emp·tion /pree-émpshən/ n. acquisition by one person or party before the opportunity is offered to others.

pre·emp·tive /pree-émptiv/ adj. **1** preempting. **2** (of military action) intended to prevent attack by disabling the enemy. ¶ See note at PEREMPTORY.

preen /preen/ v.tr. & refl. **1** (of a bird) straighten (the feathers or itself) with its beak. **2** (of a person) primp or admire (oneself, one's hair, clothes, etc.). □□ **preen′er** n.

pre·fab /preéfáb/ n. colloq. prefabricated building.

pre·fab·ri·cate /preéfábrikayt/ v.tr. manufacture sections of (a building, etc.) prior to their assembly on a site. □□ **pre·fab·ri·ca·tion** /-brikáyshən/ n.

pref·ace /préfəs/ ● n. introduction to a book. ● v.tr. **1** (foll. by with) introduce or begin (a speech or event). **2** provide (a book, etc.) with a preface. □□ **pre·fa·to·ri·al** /-fətáwreeəl/ adj. **pref′a·to·ry** adj.

pre·fect /preéfekt/ n. administrator; overseer. □□ **pre·fec·to·ri·al** /-táwreeəl/ adj.

pre·fec·ture /preéfekchər/ n. administrative district. □□ **pre·fec·tur·al** /prifékchorəl/ adj.

pre·fer /prifór/ v.tr. (**preferred, preferring**) **1** choose; like better. **2** submit (information, an accusation, etc.) for consideration. **3** promote or advance (a person).

pref·er·a·ble /préfərəbəl/ disp. prifér-/ adj. **1** to be preferred. **2** more desirable. □□ **pref′er·a·bly** adv.

pref·er·ence /préfərəns, préfrəns/ n. **1** act or an instance of preferring or being preferred. **2** thing preferred. **3** favoring of one person, etc., before others. □□ **pref·er·en·tial** /-énshəl/ adj. **pref·er·en′tial·ly** adv.

pre·fer·ment /prifórmənt/ n. promotion to a higher office.

pre·fig·ure /preéfigyər/ v.tr. **1** represent beforehand by a figure or type. **2** imagine beforehand. □□ **pre·fig·u·ra′tion** n. **pre·fig′ur·a·tive** adj.

pre·fix /préefiks/ • *n.* element at the beginning of a word to adjust or qualify its meaning (e.g., *ex-, non-, re-*). • *v.tr.* **1** add as an introduction. **2** join (a word or element) as a prefix. □□ **pre·fix·ion** /-fíkshən/ *n.*

preg·nan·cy /prégnənsee/ *n.* (*pl.* **-cies**) condition or instance of being pregnant.

preg·nant /prégnənt/ *adj.* **1** having a child or young developing in the uterus. **2** full of meaning; significant or suggestive (*a pregnant pause*). □□ **preg′nant·ly** *adv.* (in sense 2).

pre·hen·sile /preehénsəl, -sīl/ *adj.* *Zool.* (of a tail or limb) capable of grasping.

pre·his·tor·ic /preehistáwrik, -stór-/ *adj.* **1** of or relating to the period before written records. **2** *colloq.* utterly out of date. □□ **pre·his·tor′i·cal·ly** *adv.* **pre·his·to·ry** /-hístəree/ *n.*

pre·judge /preejúj/ *v.tr.* form a premature judgment on (a person, issue, etc.). □□ **pre·judg′ment** *n.*

prej·u·dice /préjədis/ • *n.* **1 a** preconceived opinion. **b** bias or partiality. **2** detriment. • *v.tr.* **1** impair the validity or force of (a right, claim, statement, etc.). **2** (esp. as **prejudiced** *adj.*) cause (a person) to have a prejudice.

prej·u·di·cial /préjədíshəl/ *adj.* causing prejudice; detrimental. □□ **prej·u·di′cial·ly** *adv.*

pre·lim·i·nar·y /prilíminəree/ • *adj.* introductory; preparatory. • *n.* (*pl.* **-ies**) (usu. in *pl.*) **1** preliminary action or arrangement (*dispense with the preliminaries*). **2** preliminary trial or contest.

prel·ude /prélyōōd, práylōōd, pree-/ *n.* (often foll. by *to*) **1** action, event, or situation serving as an introduction. **2** beginning introductory part of a poem, etc. **3 a** introductory piece of music to a fugue, suite, or an act of an opera. **b** short piece of music of a similar type.

pre·ma·ture /preemǝchŏŏr, -tyŏŏr, -tŏŏr/ *adj.* **1** occurring or done before the usual or proper time; too early (*premature decision*). **2** (of a baby) born (esp. three or more weeks) before the end of the full term of gestation. □□ **pre·ma·ture′ly** *adv.*

pre·med·i·tate /preeméditayt/ *v.tr.* (often as **premeditated** *adj.*) think out or plan (an action) beforehand (*premeditated murder*). □□ **pre·med·i·ta′tion** *n.*

pre·men·stru·al /preeménstrōōəl/ *adj.* of, occurring, or experienced before menstruation. □ **premenstrual syndrome** physical and psychological symptoms experienced by some women prior to menstruation. □□ **pre·men′stru·al·ly** *adv.*

pre·mier /prəmeér, -myeér, preemeer/ • *n.* prime minister or other head of government in certain countries. • *adj.* first in importance, order, or time.

pre·miere /prəmeér, -myáir/ (also **pre·mière**) • *n.* first performance or showing. • *v.tr.* give a premiere of.

prem·ise /prémis/ *n.* **1** *Logic* previous statement from which another is inferred. **2** (in *pl.*) house or building with its grounds and appurtenances.

pre·mi·um /preemeeəm/ *n.* **1** amount to be paid for a contract of insurance. **2** sum added to interest, wages, price, etc. **3** reward or prize. **4** (*attrib.*) (of a commodity) of best quality and therefore more expensive. □ **at a premium 1** highly valued. **2** scarce and in demand.

prem·o·ni·tion /prémǝníshǝn, pree-/ *n.* forewarning; presentiment. □□ **pre·mon·i·to·ry** /primónitawree/ *adj.*

pre·oc·cu·py /pree-ókyəpī/ *v.tr.* (**-pies, -pied**) **1** (of a thought, etc.) dominate or engross the mind of (a person). **2** (as **preoccupied** *adj.*) mentally distracted. **3** occupy beforehand. □□ **pre·oc·cu·pa′tion** *n.*

pre·or·dain /preeawrdáyn/ *v.tr.* ordain or determine beforehand.

prep /prep/ *colloq.* *n.* • *n.* **1** preparation (esp. of a patient before surgery). **2** student in a preparatory school. • *v.tr.* prepare (a person) for an examination, etc. □ **prep school** = *preparatory school.*

prep. *abbr.* preposition.

pre·paid *past* and *past part.* of PREPAY.

prep·a·ra·tion /prépəráyshǝn/ *n.* **1** preparing; being prepared. **2** (often in *pl.*) something done to make ready. **3** specially prepared substance, esp. a food or medicine.

pre·par·a·to·ry /pripárǝtawree, -páir-, prépərə-/ • *adj.* serving to prepare; introductory. • *adv.* in a preparatory manner. □ **preparatory school** usu. private school preparing pupils for college.

pre·pare /pripáir/ *v.* **1** *tr.* make or get ready for use, consideration, etc. **2** *tr.* make ready or assemble (food, a meal, etc.). **3 a** *tr.* make (a person or oneself) ready or disposed in some way. **b** *intr.* get ready (*prepare to jump*). □□ **pre·par′er** *n.*

pre·par·ed·ness /pripáiridnis/ *n.* readiness, esp. for war.

pre·pay /preepáy/ *v.tr.* (*past* and *past part.* **prepaid**) pay (a charge) in advance. □□ **pre·pay′a·ble** *adj.* **pre·pay′ment** *n.*

pre·pon·der·ant /pripóndǝrǝnt/ *adj.* predominant; preponderating. □□ **pre·pon′der·ance** *n.* **pre·pon′der·ant·ly** *adv.*

pre·pon·der·ate /pripóndǝrayt/ *v.intr.* (often foll. by *over*) **1** be greater in influence, quantity, or number. **2** predominate.

prep·o·si·tion /prépǝzíshǝn/ *n.* *Gram.* word governing (and usu. preceding) a noun or pronoun and expressing a relation to another word or element, as in: "the man *on* the platform," "came *after* dinner," "what did you do it *for*?" □□ **prep′o·si′tion·al** *adj.* **prep′o·si′tion·al·ly** *adv.*

¶ Many sentences and clauses in English end with prepositions, and this has been true through the language's history. The "rule" that forbids placing a preposition at the end of a clause or sentence should be disregarded.

pre·pos·sess /preepǝzés/ *v.tr.* **1** (usu. in *passive*) (of an idea, feeling, etc.) take possession of (a person); imbue. **2 a** prejudice (usu. favorably). **b** (as **prepossessing** *adj.*) attractive; appealing. □□ **pre·pos·ses′sion** /-zéshǝn/ *n.*

pre·pos·ter·ous /pripóstǝrǝs/ *adj.* utterly absurd; outrageous. □□ **pre·pos′ter·ous·ly** *adv.*

prep·py /prépee/ (also **prep′pie**) *colloq.* • *n.* (*pl.* **-pies**) person attending an expensive private school. • *adj.* (**prep·pi·er, prep·pi·est**) **1** like a preppy. **2** neat and fashionable.

pre·req·ui·site /preerékwizit/ • *adj.* required as a precondition. • *n.* prerequisite thing.
¶ See note at PERQUISITE.

pre·rog·a·tive /prirógətiv/ *n.* right or privilege exclusive to an individual or class.

pres·age /présij/ • *n.* **1** omen or portent. **2** presentiment or foreboding. • *v.tr.* (also /prisáyj/) portend; foreshadow.

Pres·by·te·ri·an /prézbite'ereeən/ • *adj.* (of a church) governed by elders all of equal rank. • *n.* member of a Presbyterian Church. □□ **Pres'by·te'ri·an·ism'** *n.*

pre·school /preéskōol/ *adj.* of or relating to the time before a child is old enough to go to school. □□ **pre'school·er** *n.*

pre·scient /préshənt, -eeənt, pré-/ *adj.* having foreknowledge or foresight. □□ **pre'science** *n.* **pre'scient·ly** *adv.*

pre·scribe /priskríb/ *v.tr.* **1 a** advise the use of (a medicine, etc.). **b** recommend. **2** lay down or impose authoritatively. □□ **pre·scrib'er** *n.*

¶ **Prescribe** and **proscribe** are sometimes confused, but they are nearly opposite in meaning. **Prescribe** means 'to advise the use of' or 'impose authoritatively,' whereas **proscribe** means 'to denounce or ban.' Examples of each are as follows: *Our teacher prescribed topics to be covered. The doctor prescribed a painkiller. The principal proscribed tabloid newspapers from the school library. A totalitarian regime may prescribe some books and proscribe others.*

pre·scrip·tion /priskrípshən/ *n.* **1** act or an instance of prescribing. **2 a** doctor's (usu. written) instruction for the preparation and use of a medicine. **b** medicine prescribed.

pre·scrip·tive /priskríptiv/ *adj.* **1** prescribing. **2** *Linguistics* concerned with or laying down rules of usage. □□ **pre·scrip'tive·ly** *adv.* **pre·scrip'tive·ness** *n.* **pre·scrip'tiv·ism** *n.* **pre·scrip'tiv·ist** *n. & adj.*

pres·ence /prézəns/ *n.* **1** being present. **2** place where a person is. **3** person's appearance or bearing, esp. when imposing. **4** person or thing that is present (*there was a presence in the room*). □ **presence of mind** calmness and self-command in sudden difficulty, etc.

pres·ent[1] /prézənt/ • *adj.* **1** (usu. *predic.*) being in the place in question. **2 a** now existing, occurring, or being such. **b** now being considered or discussed, etc. (*in the present case*). **3** *Gram.* expressing an action, etc., now going on or habitually performed. • *n.* (prec. by *the*) **1** the time now passing (*no time like the present*). **2** *Gram.* present tense. □ **at present** now. **present-day** *adj.* of this time; modern.

pre·sent[2] /prizént/ *v.tr.* **1** introduce, offer, or exhibit. **2 a** offer, give, or award as a gift. **b** make available to; cause to have (*presented them with a new car*). **3** put (a form of entertainment) before the public. **4** introduce (*may I present my fiancé?*). **5** (of an idea, etc.) offer or suggest itself. □ **present arms** hold a rifle, etc., vertically in front of the body as a salute. □□ **pre·sent'er** *n.* (in sense 3 of *v.*).

pres·ent[3] /prézənt/ *n.* gift; thing given or presented.

pre·sent·a·ble /prizéntəbəl/ *adj.* **1** of good appearance; fit to be presented. **2** fit for presentation. □□ **pre·sent·a·bil'i·ty** *n.* **pre·sent'a·bly** *adv.*

pre·sen·ta·tion /prézəntáyshən, preézen-/ *n.* **1 a** presenting; being presented. **b** thing presented. **2** manner or quality of presenting. **3** demonstration or display; lecture. □□ **pre·sen·ta'tion·al** *adj.*

pre·sen·ti·ment /prizéntimənt, -séntimənt/ *n.* vague expectation; foreboding (esp. of misfortune).

pres·ent·ly /prézəntlee/ *adv.* **1** soon; after a short time. **2** at the present time; now.

¶ In *The pain will lessen presently*, the meaning of **presently** is 'soon'; in *Limited resources are presently available*, the meaning is 'at this moment.' Both senses are widely used.

pres·er·va·tion /prézərváyshən/ *n.* **1** preserving or being preserved. **2** state of being well or badly preserved.

pre·ser·va·tive /prizə́rvətiv/ • *n.* substance for preserving perishable foods, wood, etc. • *adj.* tending to preserve.

pre·serve /prizə́rv/ • *v.tr.* **1 a** keep safe or free from harm, decay, etc. **b** keep alive (a name, memory, etc.). **2** maintain or retain. **3** treat or refrigerate (food) to prevent decomposition or fermentation. • *n.* (in *sing.* or *pl.*) **1** preserved fruit; jam. **2** place where game or fish, etc., are preserved. **3** sphere or area of activity regarded as a person's own. □□ **pre·serv'a·ble** *adj.* **pre·serv'er** *n.*

pre·shrunk /preéshrúngk/ *adj.* (of a fabric or garment) treated so that it shrinks during manufacture and not in use.

pre·side /prizíd/ *v.intr.* **1** be chairperson or president of a meeting, etc. **2** exercise control or authority.

pres·i·den·cy /prézidənsee/ *n.* (*pl.* **-cies**) office, term, or function of president.

pres·i·dent /prézidənt/ *n.* **1** elected head of a republican government. **2** head of a college, university, company, society, etc. □□ **pres·i·den·tial** /-dénshəl/ *adj.* **pres·i·den'tial·ly** *adv.*

press[1] /pres/ • *v.* **1** *tr.* apply steady force to (a thing in contact). **2** *tr.* **a** compress or squeeze a thing to flatten, shape, or smooth it. **b** squeeze (a fruit, etc.) to extract its juice. **c** manufacture (a record, etc.) by molding under pressure. **3** *intr.* be urgent; demand immediate action. **4** *intr.* (foll. by *for*) make an insistent demand. **5** *intr.* form a crowd. **6** *intr.* (foll. by *on, forward*, etc.) hasten insistently. **7** *tr.* (of an enemy, etc.) bear heavily on. **8** *tr.* urge or entreat. **9** *tr.* insist on. • *n.* **1** act or instance of pressing. **2** device for compressing, flattening, shaping, extracting juice, etc. **3** = *printing press.* **4** (prec. by *the*) **a** art or practice of printing. **b** newspapers, journalists, etc., generally or collectively. **5** publicity. **6** (**Press**) **a** printing house or establishment. **b** publishing company. **7 a** crowding. **b** crowd (of people, etc.). **8** the pressure of affairs. □ **be pressed for** have barely enough (time, etc.). **press agent** person employed to obtain publicity. **press conference** interview given to a number of journalists. **press release** official statement issued to newspapers.

press[2] /pres/ *v.tr.* **1** *hist.* force to serve in the army or navy. **2** bring into use as a makeshift (*was pressed into service*).

press·ing /présing/ *adj.* urgent. □□ **press'ing·ly** *adv.*

pres·sure /préshər/ • *n.* **1 a** exertion of continuous force on or against a body by another in contact with it. **b** force exerted. **c** amount of this. **2** urgency (*work under pressure*). **3** affliction or difficulty (*under financial pressure*). **4** constraining influence (*if pressure is brought to bear*). • *v.tr.* **1** coerce. **2** persuade. □ **pressure**

cooker airtight pot for cooking quickly under steam pressure. **pressure group** group formed to influence public policy.

pres·sur·ize /préshəriz/ v.tr. **1** (esp. as **pressurized** adj.) maintain normal atmospheric pressure in (an aircraft cabin, etc.) at a high altitude. **2** raise to a high pressure. □□ **pres·sur·i·za′tion** n.

pres·ti·dig·i·ta·tor /préstidíjitaytər/ n. formal magician. □□ **pres·ti·dig·i·ta′tion** n.

pres·tige /prestéezh/ n. **1** respect, reputation, or influence derived from achievements, power, associations, etc. **2** (attrib.) having or conferring prestige.

---

prestige mid-17th century (in the sense 'illusion, magic trick'): from French, literally 'illusion, glamour', from late Latin praestigium 'illusion,' from Latin praestigiae (plural) 'magic tricks.' The transference of meaning occurred by way of the sense 'dazzling influence, glamour,' used with negative intent.

---

pres·ti·gious /prestéejəs, -stíj-/ adj. having or showing prestige. □□ **pres·ti′gious·ly** adv. **pres·ti′gious·ness** n.

pres·to /préstō/ adv. **1** Mus. in quick tempo. **2** (in a magician's formula in performing a trick) look!

pre·sum·a·bly /prizóoməblee/ adv. as may reasonably be presumed.

pre·sume /prizóom/ v. **1** tr. suppose to be true; take for granted. **2** tr. (often foll. by to + infin.) **a** dare. **b** venture (may I presume to ask?). **3** intr. be presumptuous. □□ **pre·sum′a·ble** adj. **pre·sum′ed·ly** adv.

pre·sump·tion /prizúmpshən/ n. **1** arrogance; presumptuous behavior. **2 a** act of presuming a thing to be true. **b** thing that is or may be presumed to be true.

pre·sump·tive /prizúmptiv/ adj. giving reasonable grounds for presumption. □□ **pre·sump′tive·ly** adv.

pre·sump·tu·ous /prizúmpchōoəs/ adj. unduly or overbearingly confident and presuming. □□ **pre·sump′tu·ous·ly** adv. **pre·sump′tu·ous·ness** n.

pre·sup·pose /préesəpóz/ v.tr. **1** assume beforehand. **2** require as a precondition; imply. □□ **pre·sup·po·si′tion** n.

pre·tend /priténd/ v. **1** tr. claim or assert falsely so as to deceive. **2** tr. imagine to oneself in play (pretended to be monsters). **3** intr. (foll. by to) **a** lay claim to (a right or title, etc.). **b** profess to have (a quality, etc.).

pre·tend·er /priténdər/ n. **1** person who claims a throne or title, etc. **2** person who pretends.

pre·tense /préetens, priténs/ n. **1** pretending; make-believe. **2** false show of intentions or motives (under false pretenses). **3** (foll. by to) claim, esp. a false or ambitious one. **4** display; ostentation.

pre·ten·sion /priténshən/ n. **1 a** assertion of a claim. **b** justifiable claim. **2** pretentiousness.

pre·ten·tious /priténshəs/ adj. **1** making an excessive claim to great merit or importance. **2** ostentatious. □□ **pre·ten′tious·ly** adv. **pre·ten′tious·ness** n.

pret·er·it /prétərit/ (also **pret′er·ite**) Gram. • adj. expressing a past action or state. • n. preterit tense or form.

pre·ter·nat·u·ral /préetərnáchərəl/ adj. outside the ordinary course of nature; supernatural. □□ **pre·ter·nat′u·ral·ly** adv.

pro·text /préetekst/ n. **1** ostensible or alleged reason or intention. **2** excuse offered.

pret·ti·fy /pritifí/ v.tr. (**-fies**, **-fied**) make pretty, esp. in an affected way. □□ **pret′ti·fi·er** n.

pret·ty /prítee/ • adj. (**pret·ti·er**, **pret·ti·est**) **1** attractive in a fine or charming way. **2** fine or good of its kind (a pretty wit). • adv. colloq. fairly; moderately; considerably. • v.tr. (**-ties**, **-tied**) (often foll. by up) make pretty or attractive. □□ **pret′ti·ly** adv. **pret′ti·ness** n. **pret′ty·ish** adj.

---

pretty Old English prættig; related to Middle Dutch pertich 'brisk, clever,' obsolete Dutch prettig 'humorous, sporty,' from a West Germanic base meaning 'trick.' The sense development 'deceitful, cunning, clever, skillful, admirable, pleasing' has parallels in adjectives such as fine, nice, etc.

---

pret·zel /prétsəl/ n. crisp or chewy knot-shaped or stick-shaped bread, usu. salted.

pre·vail /priváyl/ v.intr. **1** be victorious or gain mastery. **2** be the more usual or predominant. **3** exist or occur in general use or experience; be current. **4** (foll. by on, upon) persuade. □□ **pre·vail′ing·ly** adv.

prev·a·lent /prévələnt/ adj. **1** generally existing or occurring. **2** predominant. □□ **prev′a·lence** n. **prev′a·lent·ly** adv.

pre·var·i·cate /privárikayt/ v.intr. **1** speak or act evasively or misleadingly. **2** quibble; equivocate. □□ **pre·var·i·ca·tion** /-rikáyshən/ n. **pre·var′i·ca·tor** n.

¶ **Prevaricate** means 'to act or speak evasively,' e.g., When the teacher asked what I was reading, I knew I would have to prevaricate or risk a detention. It is sometimes confused with **procrastinate,** which means 'to postpone or put off an action,' e.g., He procrastinated until it was too late.

pre·vent /privént/ v.tr. stop from happening or doing something; hinder; make impossible. □□ **pre·vent′a·ble** adj. (also **pre·vent′i·ble**). **pre·vent′er** n. **pre·ven·tion** /-vénshən/ n.

pre·ven·tive /privéntiv/ (also **pre·ven·ta·tive** /privéntətiv/) • adj. serving to prevent, esp. preventing disease. • n. preventive agent, measure, drug, etc. □□ **pre·ven′tive·ly** adv. ¶ Avoid adding an unnecessary syllable to **preventive.** The variant "preventative" is considered uneducated by many.

pre·view /préevyoo/ • n. showing of a movie, play, exhibition, etc., before it is seen by the general public. • v.tr. see or show in advance.

pre·vi·ous /préeveeəs/ • adj. coming before in time or order. • adv. (foll. by to) before. □□ **pre′vi·ous·ly** adv.

prey /pray/ • n. **1** animal that is hunted or killed by another for food. **2** person or thing that is influenced by or vulnerable to (something undesirable) (prey to morbid fears). • v.intr. (foll. by on, upon) **1** seek or take as prey. **2** (of a disease, emotion, etc.) exert a harmful influence. □□ **prey′er** n.

price /prīs/ • n. **1** amount of money or goods for which a thing is bought or sold. **2** what is or must be given, done, sacrificed, etc., to obtain or achieve something. • v.tr. fix or find the price or value of (a thing for sale). □ **at a price** at a high cost. □□ **priced** *adj.* (also in *comb.*). **pric′er** *n.*

price·less /prɪ́slis/ *adj.* **1** invaluable. **2** *colloq.* very amusing or absurd. □□ **price′less·ly** *adv.* **price′less·ness** *n.*

pric·ey /prɪ́see/ *adj.* (also **pric′y**) (**pric·i·er**, **pric·i·est**) *colloq.* expensive. □□ **pric′i·ness** *n.*

prick /prik/ • *v.tr.* **1** pierce slightly; make a small hole in. **2** trouble mentally. • *n.* **1** act or instance of pricking. **2** small hole or mark made by pricking. **3** pain. □ **prick up one's ears 1** (of a dog, etc.) make the ears erect when on the alert. **2** (of a person) become suddenly attentive.

prick·er /prɪ́kər/ *n.* **1** one that pricks, as an animal or plant. **2** small thorn or other sharp pointed outgrowth.

prick·le /prɪ́kəl/ • *n.* **1** small thorn. **2** hard pointed spine of a hedgehog, etc. **3** prickling sensation. • *v.* affect or be affected with a sensation as of pricking.

prick·ly /prɪ́klee/ *adj.* (**prick·li·er**, **prick·li·est**) **1** having prickles. **2** (of a person) ready to take offense. □ **prickly heat** itchy inflammation of the skin. **prickly pear 1** cactus bearing large pearshaped prickly fruits. **2** its fruit. □□ **prick′li·ness** *n.*

pricy var. of PRICEY.

pride /prīd/ • *n.* **1 a** elation or satisfaction at achievements, qualities, or possessions, etc., that do one credit. **b** object of this feeling. **2** high or overbearing opinion of one's worth or importance. **3** self-respect. **4** group or company (of animals, esp. lions). • *v.refl.* (foll. by *on*, *upon*) be proud of. □ **take pride** (or **a pride**) **in 1** be proud of. **2** maintain in good condition or appearance. □□ **pride′ful** *adj.* **pride′ful·ly** *adv.* **pride′less** *adj.*

priest /preest/ *n.* **1** ordained minister of hierarchical Christian churches. **2** official minister of a non-Christian religion. □□ **priest′hood** *n.* **priest′like** *adj.*

priest·ess /preéstis/ *n.* female priest of a non-Christian religion.

priest·ly /preéstlee/ *adj.* of or associated with priests. □□ **priest′li·ness** *n.*

prig /prig/ *n.* self-righteous or moralistic person. □□ **prig′gish** *adj.* **prig′gish·ly** *adv.* **prig′gish·ness** *n.*

prim /prim/ *adj.* (**prim·mer**, **prim·mest**) **1** stiffly formal and precise. **2** prudish. □□ **prim′ly** *adv.* **prim′ness** *n.*

pri·ma bal·le·ri·na /preémə/ *n.* chief female dancer in a ballet or ballet company.

pri·ma·cy /prɪ́məsee/ *n.* (*pl.* **-cies**) **1** preeminence. **2** office of an ecclesiastical primate.

pri·ma don·na /preémə/ *n.* (*pl.* **pri·ma don·nas**) **1** chief female singer in an opera or opera company. **2** temperamentally self-important person. □□ **pri′ma don′na-ish** *adj.*

pri·ma fa·cie /prɪ́mə fáyshee, -shee-ee, shə, preémə/ *adj.* (of evidence) based on the first impression.

pri·mal /prɪ́məl/ *adj.* **1** primitive; primeval. **2** chief; fundamental. □□ **pri′mal·ly** *adv.*

pri·mar·y /prɪ́meree, -məree/ • *adj.* **1 a** of the first importance; chief. **b** fundamental; basic. **2** earliest; original. **3** designating any of the colors

red, green, and blue, or (for pigments) red, blue, and yellow. • *n.* (*pl.* **-ies**) **1** thing that is primary. **2** (in full **primary election**) preliminary election to appoint delegates or to select candidates. □ **primary school** = *elementary school.* □□ **pri·mar·i·ly** /prīmérilee/ *adv.*

pri·mate /prɪ́mayt/ *n.* **1** member of the highest order of mammals, including lemurs, apes, monkeys, and human beings. **2** archbishop. □□ **pri·ma·tial** /-máyshəl/ *adj.* **pri·ma·tol·o·gy** /-mətóləjee/ *n.* (in sense 1)

pri·ma·ver·a /preéməvairə/ *adj.* (of pasta, seafood, etc.) made with or containing an assortment of vegetables.

prime¹ /prīm/ • *adj.* **1** chief; most important. **2** (esp. of beef) first-rate; excellent. **3** primary; fundamental. **4** *Math.* (of a number) divisible only by itself and 1 (e.g., 2, 3, 5, 7, 11). • *n.* **1** state of the highest perfection (*prime of life*). **2** the best part. □ **prime minister** head of an elected parliamentary government. **prime time** time at which a radio or television audience is largest.

prime² /prīm/ *v.tr.* **1** prepare (a thing) for use or action. **2** prepare for firing or detonation. **3** pour (liquid) into a pump to prepare it for working. **4** prepare (wood, etc.) for painting by applying a substance that prevents paint from being absorbed. **5** equip (a person) with information, etc.

prim·er¹ /prɪ́mər/ *n.* substance used to prime wood, etc.

prim·er² /prɪ́mər, prɪ́mər/ *n.* **1** elementary textbook for teaching children to read. **2** introductory book.

pri·me·val /prīmeévəl/ *adj.* **1** of or relating to the earliest age of the world. **2** ancient; primitive. □□ **pri·me′val·ly** *adv.*

prim·i·tive /primitiv/ • *adj.* **1** at an early stage of civilization. **2** undeveloped; crude; simple (*primitive methods*). • *n.* primitive person or thing. □□ **prim′i·tive·ly** *adv.* **prim′i·tive·ness** *n.*

pri·mo·gen·i·ture /prɪ́mōjénichər/ *n.* **1** fact or condition of being the firstborn child. **2** (in full **right of primogeniture**) right of inheritance of the firstborn. □□ **pri·mo·gen′i·tal** *adj.*

pri·mor·di·al /prīmáwrdeeəl/ *adj.* **1** existing at or from the beginning; primeval. **2** original; fundamental. □□ **pri·mor′di·al·ly** *adv.*

primp /primp/ *v.tr.* **1** make (the hair, one's clothes, etc.) neat or overly tidy. **2** *refl.* groom (oneself) painstakingly.

prim·rose /prɪ́mrōz/ *n.* **1 a** plant bearing pale yellow flowers. **b** flower of this. **2 a** pale yellow color. □ **primrose path** pursuit of pleasure, esp. with disastrous consequences.

prince /prins/ *n.* **1** male member of a royal family other than a reigning king. **2** ruler of a small nation. **3** nobleman in some countries. **4** (as a courtesy title in some connections) a duke, marquess, or earl. **5** chief or greatest (*the prince of novelists*). □ **Prince of Wales** the heir apparent to the British throne, as a title. □□ **prince′like** *adj.*

prince·ly /prɪ́nslee/ *adj.* (**prince·li·er**, **prince·li·est**) **1** of or worthy of a prince. **2 a** generous; splendid. **b** (of a sum of money) substantial. □□ **prince′li·ness** *n.*

prin·cess /prɪ́nses/ *n.* **1** wife of a prince. **2** female member of a royal family other than a reigning queen.

prin·ci·pal /prɪ́nsipəl/ • *adj.* **1** (usu. *attrib.*) first in rank or importance; chief. **2** main; leading. • *n.* **1** head, ruler, or superior. **2** head of a school. **3** leading performer. **4** capital sum as distinguished from interest or income. □ **principal parts** *Gram.* parts of a verb from which all other parts can be deduced.

¶ **Principal** means 'important; person in charge': *the high school principal.* It also means 'a capital sum': *the principal would be repaid in five years.* **Principle** means 'rule, basis for conduct': *Her principles kept her from stealing despite her poverty.*

prin·ci·pal·i·ty /prínsipálitee/ *n.* (*pl.* **-ties**) **1** nation ruled by a prince. **2** government of a prince.

prin·ci·pal·ly /prínsiplee/ *adv.* for the most part; chiefly.

prin·ci·ple /prínsipəl/ *n.* **1** fundamental truth or law as the basis of reasoning or action. **2 a** personal code of conduct. **b** (in *pl.*) such rules of conduct. **3** general law in physics, etc. **4** law of nature or science. □ **in principle** as regards fundamentals but not necessarily in detail. **on principle** on the basis of a moral attitude (*I refuse on principle*).

¶ See note at PRINCIPAL.

prin·ci·pled /prínsipəld/ *adj.* based on or having (esp. praiseworthy) principles of behavior.

print /print/ *n.* **1** indentation or residual mark (*fingerprint*). **2 a** printed lettering or writing. **b** words in printed form. **3** picture or design printed from a block or plate. **4** *Photog.* picture produced on paper from a negative. **5** printed cotton fabric. • *v.tr.* **1** produce or cause (a book, picture, etc.) to be produced by applying inked types, blocks, or plates, to paper, vellum, etc. **2** express or publish in print. **3** (often foll. by *on, in*) impress or stamp. **4** (often *absol.*) write (words or letters) without joining, in imitation of typography. **5** *Photog.* produce (a photograph) from a negative. **6** (usu. foll. by *out*) (of a computer, etc.) produce output in printed form. □ **in print** (of a book, etc.) available from the publisher. **out of print** no longer available from the publisher. □□ **print'a·ble** *adj.* **print'less** *adj.* (in sense 1 of *n.*).

print·er /príntər/ *n.* **1** person who prints books, magazines, advertising matter, etc. **2** owner of a printing business. **3** device that prints, esp. as part of a computer system.

print·ing /príntíng/ *n.* **1** production of printed books, etc. **2** single impression of a book. **3** printed letters or writing imitating them. □ **printing press** machine for printing from types or plates, etc.

print·out /príntowt/ *n.* computer output in printed form.

pri·or /príər/ • *adj.* **1** earlier. **2** coming before in time, order, or importance. • *adv.* (foll. by *to*) before. • *n.* superior officer of a religious house or order. □□ **pri·or·ate** /-rət/ *n.* **pri·or·ess** /príəris/ *n.*

pri·or·i·ty /prīáwritee, -ór-/ *n.* (*pl.* **-ties**) **1** precedence in rank, etc. **2** interest having prior claim to consideration. □□ **pri·or'i·tize** *v.tr.* **pri·or·i·ti·za'tion** *n.*

pri·o·ry /príəree/ *n.* (*pl.* **-ries**) monastery governed by a prior or a convent governed by a prioress.

prism /prízəm/ *n.* **1** solid geometric figure whose two ends are similar, equal, and parallel rectilinear figures, and whose sides are parallelograms.

2 transparent body in this form, usu. triangular, that separates white light into a spectrum of colors. □□ **pris·mat·ic** /-mátik/ *adj.* **pris·mat'i·cal·ly** *adv.*

PRISM, 1

pris·on /prízən/ *n.* **1** place of confinement for convicted criminals or persons awaiting trial. **2** custody; confinement. □ **prison camp 1** camp for prisoners of war or political prisoners. **2** minimum-security prison.

pris·on·er /príznər/ *n.* **1** person kept in prison. **2** person or thing confined by illness, another's grasp, etc.

pris·sy /prísee/ *adj.* (**pris·si·er, pris·si·est**) prim; prudish. □□ **pris'si·ly** *adv.* **pris'si·ness** *n.*

pris·tine /prísteen, pristéen/ *adj.* **1** in its original condition; unspoiled. **2** *disp.* spotless; fresh as if new.

pri·va·cy /prívəsee/ *n.* **1 a** state of being private and undisturbed. **b** person's right to this. **2** freedom from intrusion or public attention. **3** avoidance of publicity.

pri·vate /prívət/ • *adj.* **1** belonging to an individual; one's own; personal (*private property*). **2** confidential (*private talks*). **3** kept or removed from public knowledge or observation. **4** not open to the public. **5** secluded. **6** (of a person) not holding public office or an official position. • *n.* **1** soldier with a rank below corporal. **2** (in *pl.*) *colloq.* genitals. □ **in private** privately. **private detective** detective engaged privately, outside an official police force. **private enterprise** business or businesses not under government control. **private eye** *colloq.* private detective. **private parts** genitals. **private sector** the part of the economy free of direct government control. □□ **pri'vate·ly** *adv.*

pri·va·tion /prīváyshən/ *n.* lack of the comforts or necessities of life (*suffered many privations*).

pri·vat·ize /prívətīz/ *v.tr.* make private, esp. transfer (a business, etc.) to private as distinct from government control or ownership. □□ **pri·va·ti·za'tion** *n.*

priv·et /prívit/ *n.* deciduous or evergreen shrub bearing small white flowers and much used for hedges.

priv·i·lege /prívilij, prívlij/ • *n.* **1** right, advantage, or immunity. **2** special benefit or honor (*a privilege to meet you*). • *v.tr.* invest with a privilege. □□ **priv'i·leged** *adj.*

priv·y /prívee/ • *adj.* **1** (foll. by *to*) sharing in the secret of (a person's plans, etc.). **2** *archaic* hidden; secret. • *n.* (*pl.* **-ies**) toilet, esp. an outhouse. □□ **priv'i·ly** *adv.*

prize¹ /prīz/ • *n.* **1** something that can be won

in a competition, lottery, etc. **2** reward given as a symbol of victory or superiority. **3** something worth striving for. **4** (*attrib.*) supremely excellent or outstanding of its kind. ● *v.tr.* value highly. □ **prize money** money offered as a prize.

prize² /prīz/ (also **prise**) *v.tr.* force open or out by leverage.

prize·fight /prízfīt/ *n.* boxing match fought for prize money. □□ **prize'fight'er** *n.*

prize·win·ner /prízwínər/ *n.* winner of a prize. □□ **prize'win'ning** *adj.*

pro¹ /prō/ *colloq. n.* (*pl.* **pros**) professional.

pro² /prō/ ● *adj.* for; in favor. ● *n.* (*pl.* **pros**) reason or argument for or in favor. ● *prep.* in favor of. □ **pro bono** pertaining to a service, esp. legal work, for which no fee is charged. **pro-choice** in favor of the right to legal abortion. **pro-life** opposed to the right to legal abortion. **pros and cons** reasons for and against a proposition, etc.

pro- /prō/ *prefix* **1** favoring or supporting (*pro-government*). **2** acting as a substitute or deputy for (*proconsul*). **3** forward (*produce*). **4** forward and downward (*prostrate*). **5** onward (*progress*). **6** in front of (*protect*).

pro·ac·tive /prō-áktiv/ *adj.* (of a person, policy, etc.) taking the initiative. □□ **pro·ac'tion** *n.* **pro·ac'tive·ly** *adv.*

prob. *abbr.* **1** probable. **2** probably. **3** problem.

prob·a·bil·ism /próbəbəlizəm/ *n.* **1** *Philos.* doctrine that probability is the basis for belief and action since certainty is impossible. **2** *RC Ch.* ethical theory that it is allowable to follow any one of many conflicting opinions even though an opposing one may be more probable.

prob·a·bil·i·ty /próbəbílitee/ *n.* (*pl.* **-ties**) **1** being probable. **2** likelihood of something happening. **3** probable or most probable event (*probability is that they will come*). **4** *Math.* extent to which an event is likely to occur, measured by the ratio of the favorable cases to the whole number of cases possible. □ **in all probability** most probably.

prob·a·ble /próbəbəl/ ● *adj.* expected to happen or prove true; likely. ● *n.* probable candidate, member of a team, etc. □□ **prob'a·bly** *adv.*

pro·bate /próbayt/ *v.tr.* establish the validity of (a will).

pro·ba·tion /prəbáyshən/ *n.* **1** *Law* system of suspending the sentence of a criminal offender subject to a period of good behavior under supervision. **2** period of testing, as for a new employee. □ **probation officer** official supervising offenders on probation. □□ **pro·ba'tion·al** *adj.* **pro·ba'tion·ary** *adj.*

pro·ba·tion·er /prōbáyshənər/ *n.* person on probation, a newly appointed nurse, teacher, etc.

probe /prōb/ ● *n.* **1** penetrating investigation. **2** small device for measuring, testing, etc. **3** blunt surgical exploratory instrument. **4** (in full **space probe**) unmanned exploratory spacecraft. ● *v.tr.* **1** examine or inquire into closely. **2** explore with a probe. □□ **probe'a·ble** *adj.* **prob'er** *n.* **prob'ing·ly** *adv.*

pro·bi·ty /próbitee, prób-/ *n.* uprightness; honesty.

prob·lem /próbləm/ *n.* **1** doubtful or difficult matter requiring a solution (*the problem of ventilation*). **2** something hard to understand, accomplish, or deal with.

prob·lem·at·ic /próbləmátik/ *adj.* (also **prob·lem·at'i·cal**) **1** difficult; posing a problem. **2** doubtful or questionable. □□ **prob·lem·at'i·cal·ly** *adv.*

pro·bos·cis /prōbósis/ *n.* **1** long flexible trunk or snout of some mammals, e.g., an elephant or tapir. **2** elongated mouth parts of some insects.

pro·ce·dure /prəséejər/ *n.* **1** way of proceeding, esp. a mode of conducting business or a legal action. **2** mode of performing a task. **3** series of actions conducted in a certain order or manner. □□ **pro·ce'dur·al** *adj.* **pro·ce'dur·al·ly** *adv.*

pro·ceed /prōséed/ *v.intr.* **1** go forward or on further; make one's way. **2** continue; go on with an activity. **3** (of an action) be carried on or continued. **4** adopt a course of action. **5** go on to say.

pro·ceed·ing /prōséeding, prə-/ *n.* **1** action or piece of conduct. **2** (in *pl.*) (in full **legal proceedings**) lawsuit. **3** (in *pl.*) published report of discussions or a conference.

pro·ceeds /próseedz/ *n.pl.* profits.

pro·cess¹ /próses, prō-/ ● *n.* **1** course of action or proceeding, esp. as a series of stages. **2** progress or course (*in process of construction*). **3** natural evolution or change (*process of growing old*). **4** summons or writ. **5** *Anat., Zool., & Bot.* natural appendage or outgrowth on an organism. ● *v.tr.* **1** handle or deal with by a particular process. **2** treat (food, esp. to prevent decay) (*processed cheese*). □□ **pro'cess·a·ble** *adj.*

pro·cess² /prəsés/ *v.intr.* walk in procession.

pro·ces·sion /prəséshən/ *n.* **1** number of people or vehicles, etc., moving forward in orderly or ceremonial succession. **2** movement of such a group.

pro·ces·sion·al /prəséshənəl/ *adj.* **1** of processions. **2** used, carried, or sung in processions.

pro·ces·sor /prósesər, prō-/ *n.* machine that processes things, esp.: **1** = *central processor*. **2** = *food processor*.

pro·claim /prōkláym, prə-/ *v.tr.* **1** announce or declare publicly or officially. **2** declare (a person) to be (a king, traitor, etc.). □□ **pro·claim'er** *n.* **proc·la·ma·tion** /prókləmáyshən/ *n.*

pro·cliv·i·ty /prōklívitee/ *n.* (*pl.* **-ties**) tendency or inclination.

pro·cras·ti·nate /prōkrástinayt/ *v.* **1** *intr.* defer action. **2** *tr.* defer or delay, esp. intentionally or habitually. □□ **pro·cras·ti·na·tion** /-náyshən/ *n.* **pro·cras'ti·na·tor** *n.*

pro·cre·ate /prókreeayt/ *v.tr.* (often *absol.*) produce (offspring) naturally. □□ **pro·cre·ant** /prókreeənt/ *adj.* **pro·cre·a'tive** *adj.* **pro·cre·a'tion** *n.* **pro'cre·a·tor** *n.*

Pro·crus·te·an /prōkrústeeən/ *adj.* seeking to enforce uniformity by forceful or ruthless methods.

proc·tor /próktər/ *n.* supervisor of students in an examination, etc. □□ **proc·to·ri·al** /-táwreeəl/ *adj.*

pro·cure /prōkyŏŏr, prə-/ *v.tr.* **1** obtain, esp. by care or effort; acquire. **2** bring about. **3** obtain (people) for prostitution. □□ **pro·cur'a·ble** *adj.* **pro·cure'ment** *n.*

pro·cur·er /prōkyŏŏrər, prə-/ *n.* pimp.

prod /prod/ ● *v.tr.* (**prod·ded, prod·ding**) **1** poke with the finger or a pointed object. **2** stimulate to action. ● *n.* **1** poke or thrust. **2** stimulus to action. □□ **prod'der** *n.*

prod·i·gal /pródigəl/ • *adj.* **1** recklessly wasteful. **2** (foll. by *of*) lavish. • *n.* prodigal person. □□ **prod·i·gal·i·ty** /-gálitee/ *n.* **prod′i·gal·ly** *adv.*

pro·di·gious /prədíjəs/ *adj.* **1** marvelous or amazing. **2** enormous. □□ **pro·di′gious·ly** *adv.*

prod·i·gy /pródijee/ *n.* (*pl.* **-gies**) **1** person endowed with exceptional qualities or abilities, esp. a precocious child. **2** marvelous, esp. extraordinary, thing.

pro·duce • *v.tr.* /prədōos, -dyōos/ **1** bring forward for consideration, inspection, or use. **2** manufacture (goods) from raw materials, etc. **3** bear or yield (offspring, fruit, a harvest, etc.). **4** bring into existence. **5** cause or bring about. **6** supervise the production of (a movie, broadcast, etc.). • *n.* /pródōos, -dyōos, prō-/ **1** what is produced, esp. agricultural products. **2** fruits and vegetables collectively. □□ **pro·duc·i·ble** /-sib′l/ *adj.*

pro·duc·er /prədōosər, -dyōo-/ *n.* **1** *Econ.* person who produces goods or commodities. **2** person generally responsible for the production of a movie, play, broadcast, etc.

prod·uct /pródukt/ *n.* **1** thing or substance produced by natural process or manufacture. **2** result. **3** *Math.* quantity obtained by multiplying quantities together.

pro·duc·tion /prədúkshən/ *n.* **1** producing or being produced, esp. in large quantities (*go into production*). **2** total yield. **3** thing produced, esp. a movie, broadcast, play, etc. □□ **pro·duc′tion·al** *adj.*

pro·duc·tive /prədúktiv/ *adj.* **1** of or engaged in the production of goods. **2** producing much. **3** (foll. by *of*) producing or giving rise to. □□ **pro·duc′tive·ly** *adv.* **pro·duc′tive·ness** *n.*

pro·duc·tiv·i·ty /próduktívitee, prō-/ *n.* **1** capacity to produce. **2** effectiveness of productive effort, esp. in industry. **3** production per unit of effort.

Prof. *abbr.* Professor.

pro·fane /prōfáyn, prə-/ • *adj.* **1** not sacred; secular. **2 a** irreverent; blasphemous. **b** vulgar; obscene. • *v.tr.* **1** treat (a sacred thing) with irreverence or disregard. **2** violate or pollute (something entitled to respect). □□ **pro·fa·na·tion** /prófənáyshən/ *n.* **pro·fane′ly** *adv.* **pro·fan′er** *n.*

pro·fan·i·ty /prōfánitee, prə-/ *n.* (*pl.* **-ties**) **1** profane act. **2** profane language; blasphemy.

pro·fess /prəfés, prō-/ *v.tr.* **1** claim openly to have (a quality or feeling). **2** declare (*profess ignorance*). **3** affirm one's faith in or allegiance to.

pro·fessed· /prəfést, prō-/ *adj.* **1** self-acknowledged. **2** alleged; ostensible. □□ **pro·fess·ed·ly** /-fésidlee/ *adv.*

pro·fes·sion /prəféshən/ *n.* **1** work that involves some branch of advanced learning or science. **2** people engaged in a profession. **3** declaration or avowal.

---

profession Middle English (denoting the vow made on entering a religious order): via Old French from Latin *professio(n-)*, from *profiteri* 'declare publicly' (source of *profess*). Sense 1 derives from the notion of an occupation that one 'professes' to be skilled in.

---

pro·fes·sion·al /prəféshənəl/ • *adj.* **1** of or belonging to or connected with a profession. **2 a** skillful. **b** worthy of a professional (*professional*

conduct). **3** engaged in a specified activity as one's main paid occupation. • *n.* a professional person. □□ **pro·fes′sion·al·ism′** *n.* **pro·fes′sion·al·ly** *adv.*

pro·fes·sor /prəfésər/ *n.* **1 a** (often as a title) university academic of the highest rank. **b** university teacher. **2** person who professes a religion. □□ **pro·fes·so·ri·al** /prófisáwreeəl/ *adj.* **pro·fes·so′ri·al·ly** *adv.* **pro·fes′sor·ship** *n.*

prof·fer /prófər/ *v.tr.* (esp. as **proffered** *adj.*) offer.

pro·fi·cient /prəfishənt/ *adj.* (often foll. by *in, at*) adept; expert. □□ **pro·fi·cien·cy** /-shənsee/ *n.* **pro·fi′cient·ly** *adv.*

pro·file /prófil/ • *n.* **1 a** outline (esp. of a human face) as seen from one side. **b** representation of this. **2** short biographical or character sketch. • *v.tr.* represent or describe by a profile. □ **keep a low profile** remain inconspicuous. □□ **pro′filer** *n.*

prof·it /prófit/ • *n.* **1** advantage or benefit. **2** financial gain; excess of returns over expenditures. • *v.* **1** *tr.* (also *absol.*) be beneficial to. **2** *intr.* obtain an advantage or benefit. □ **at a profit** with financial gain. □□ **prof·it·a·bil′i·ty** *n.* **prof′·it·a·ble** *adj.* **prof′it·a·bly** *adv.* **prof′it·less** *adj.*

prof·i·teer /prófitéer/ • *v.intr.* make or seek to make excessive profits, esp. illegally. • *n.* person who profiteers.

prof·li·gate /prófligət/ • *adj.* **1** licentious; dissolute. **2** recklessly extravagant. • *n.* profligate person. □□ **prof·li·ga·cy** /-gəsee/ *n.* **prof′li·gate·ly** *adv.*

pro for·ma /prō fáwrmə/ *adv. & adj.* as or being a matter of form; for the sake of form.

pro·found /prəfównd, prō-/ *adj.* (**pro·found·er, pro·found·est**) **1** having or demanding great knowledge or insight. **2** deep; intense; unqualified (*profound indifference*). **3** deeply felt. □□ **pro·found′ly** *adv.* **pro·found′ness** *n.* **pro·fun·di·ty** /-fúnditee/ *n.* (*pl.* **-ties**).

pro·fuse /prəfyōos, prō-/ *adj.* **1** lavish; extravagant. **2** exuberantly plentiful; abundant (*a profuse variety*). □□ **pro·fuse′ly** *adv.* **pro·fuse′ness** *n.* **pro·fu·sion** /-fyōozhən/ *n.*

pro·gen·i·tor /prōjénitər/ *n.* **1** ancestor. **2** predecessor. □□ **pro·gen·i·to·ri·al** /-táwreeəl/ *adj.*

prog·e·ny /prójinee/ *n.* **1** offspring of a person or other organism. **2** descendant or descendants.

pro·ges·ter·one /prōjéstərōn/ *n.* steroid hormone that stimulates the preparation of the uterus for pregnancy.

prog·no·sis /prognósis/ *n.* (*pl.* **prog·no·ses** /-seez/) forecast, as of a process or the course of a disease.

prog·nos·tic /prognóstik/ • *n.* **1** advance indication or omen, esp. of the course of a disease, etc. **2** prediction; forecast. • *adj.* foretelling; predictive. □□ **prog·nos′ti·cal·ly** *adv.*

prog·nos·ti·cate /prognóstikayt/ *v.tr.* foretell; foresee). prophesy. □□ **prog·nos·ti·ca·tion** /káyshən/ *n.* **prog·nos·ti·ca·tive** /-kətiv/ *adj.* **prog·nos′ti·ca·tor** *n.*

pro·gram /prógram, -grəm/ • *n.* **1** list of a series of events, performers, etc., at a public function, etc. **2** radio or television broadcast. **3** plan of future events. **4** course or series of studies, lectures, etc.; syllabus. **5** series of coded instructions to control the operation of a computer or other machine. ● *v.tr.* (**pro·grammed, pro·gram·ming; pro·gramed, pro·gram·ing**) 1 make a program of. 2 express (a problem) or instruct (a computer) by means of a program. □□ **pro·gram′ma·ble** *adj.* **pro·gram·mat′ic** *adj.* **pro·gram·mat′i·cal·ly** *adv.* **pro′gram·mer** (or **pro′gram·er**) *n.*

prog·ress ● *n.* /prógres/ 1 forward or onward movement toward a destination. 2 advance; improvement. ● *v.intr.* /prəgrés/ 1 move or be moved forward or onward; continue. 2 advance, develop, or improve (*science progresses*). □ **in progress** developing; going on.

pro·gres·sion /prəgréshən/ *n.* 1 progressing (*mode of progression*). 2 succession; series. □□ **pro·gres′sion·al** *adj.*

pro·gres·sive /prəgrésiv/ ● *adj.* 1 moving forward. 2 proceeding step-by-step; cumulative. 3 a favoring or implementing rapid progress or social reform. b modern. 4 (of disease, violence, etc.) increasing in severity or extent. 5 *Gram.* (of an aspect) expressing an action in progress, e.g., *am writing, was writing*. ● *n.* (also **Progressive**) advocate of progressive political policies. □□ **pro·gres′sive·ly** *adv.* **pro·gres′sive·ness** *n.* **pro·gres′siv·ism** *n.*

pro·hib·it /prōhíbit/ *v.tr.* 1 forbid. 2 prevent. □□ **pro·hib′it·er, pro·hib′i·tor** *n.*

pro·hi·bi·tion /próhibíshən, próibíshən/ *n.* 1 forbidding or being forbidden. 2 *Law* edict or order that forbids. 3 (usu. **Prohibition**) period (1920–33) in the US when the manufacture and sale of alcoholic beverages was prohibited by law. □□ **pro·hi·bi′tion·ist** *n.*

pro·hib·i·tive /prōhíbitiv/ *adj.* 1 prohibiting. 2 (of prices, taxes, etc.) extremely high. □□ **pro·hib′i·tive·ly** *adv.* **pro·hib′i·tive·ness** *n.*

proj·ect ● *n.* /prójekt/ 1 plan; scheme. 2 extensive undertaking, academic assignment, etc. ● *v.* /prəjékt/ 1 *intr.* protrude; jut out. 2 *tr.* throw. 3 *tr.* extrapolate (results, etc.); forecast. 4 *tr.* cause (light, shadow, images, etc.) to fall on a surface. 5 *tr.* cause (a sound, esp. the voice) to be heard at a distance. 6 *tr.* (often *refl.* or *absol.*) express or promote forcefully or effectively. 7 *tr. Psychol.* a (also *absol.*) attribute (an emotion, etc.) to an external object or person, esp. unconsciously. b (*refl.*) project (oneself) into another's feelings, the future, etc.

---

project late Middle English (in the sense 'preliminary design, tabulated statement'): from Latin *projectum* 'something prominent,' neuter past participle of *projicere* 'throw forth,' from *pro-* 'forth' + *jacere* 'to throw.' Early senses of the verb were 'plan,' devise' and 'cause to move forward.'

---

pro·jec·tile /prəjéktəl, -tīl/ *n.* 1 missile, esp. fired by a rocket. 2 bullet, shell, etc.

pro·jec·tion /prəjékshən/ *n.* 1 projecting or being projected. 2 thing that projects or obtrudes. 3 presentation of an image, etc., on a surface or screen. 4 forecast. 5 a mental image viewed as an objective reality. b unconscious transfer of feelings, etc., to external objects or persons. 6 representation on a plane surface of any part of the surface of the earth. □□ **pro·jec′tion·ist** *n.* (in sense 3).

pro·jec·tor /prəjéktər/ *n.* apparatus for projecting slides or movies onto a screen.

pro·lapse /prólaps/ ● *n.* (also **pro·lap·sus** /-lápsəs/) forward or downward displacement of a part or organ. ● *v.intr.* undergo prolapse.

pro·le·tar·i·at /prólitáireeət/ *n.* 1 the working class. 2 esp. *derog.* lowest, esp. uneducated, class. □□ **pro·le·tar′i·an** *adj.* **pro·le·tar′i·an·ism** *n.*

pro·lif·er·ate /prəlífərayt/ *v.* 1 *intr.* reproduce; increase rapidly in numbers. 2 *tr.* produce (cells, etc.) rapidly. □□ **pro·lif·er·a′tion** /-fəráyshən/ *n.*

pro·lif·ic /prəlífik/ *adj.* 1 producing many offspring or much output. 2 (often foll. by *of*) abundantly productive. □□ **pro·lif′i·ca·cy** *n.* **pro·lif′i·cal·ly** *adv.*

pro·lix /prōlíks, prólíks/ *adj.* (of speech, writing, etc.) lengthy; tedious. □□ **pro·lix′i·ty** *n.* **pro·lix′ly** *adv.*

pro·logue /prólawg, -log/ *n.* (also **pro′log**) 1 preliminary speech, poem, etc., esp. of a play. 2 introductory event.

pro·long /prəláwng, -lóng/ *v.tr.* extend in time or space. □□ **pro′lon·ga′tion** *n.* **pro·long′ed·ly** *adv.* **pro·long′er** *n.*

prom /prom/ *n. colloq.* school or college formal dance.

prom·e·nade /prómənáyd, -naád/ ● *n.* 1 outing for display or pleasure. 2 paved public walk. ● *v.* 1 *intr.* make a promenade. 2 *tr.* make a promenade through (a place).

Pro·me·the·an /prəmée′theeən/ *adj.* daring or inventive.

pro·me·thi·um /prəmée′theeəm/ *n. Chem.* radioactive metallic element of the lanthanide series. ¶ Symb.: **Pm**.

prom·i·nent /próminənt/ *adj.* 1 jutting out; projecting. 2 conspicuous. 3 distinguished; important. □□ **prom′i·nence** *n.* **prom′i·nency** *n.* **prom′i·nent·ly** *adv.*

pro·mis·cu·ous /prəmískyōōəs/ *adj.* 1 having frequent and diverse sexual relationships, esp. transient ones. 2 random or indiscriminate. □□ **prom·is·cu·i·ty** /prómiskyōoitee/ *n.* **pro·mis′cu·ous·ly** *adv.*

prom·ise /prómis/ ● *n.* 1 assurance that one will or will not undertake a certain action, behavior, etc. 2 potential for achievement. ● *v.tr.* 1 make (a person) a promise. 2 a afford expectations of (*promises to be a good cook*). b seem likely to (*is promising to rain*). 3 *colloq.* assure. □ **the promised land** 1 *Bibl.* Canaan (Gen. 12:7, etc.). 2 any desired place, esp. heaven. □□ **prom′is·er** *n.*

prom·is·ing /prómising/ *adj.* likely to turn out well; hopeful; full of promise (*promising start*). □□ **prom′is·ing·ly** *adv.*

prom·is·so·ry /prómisawree/ *adj.* conveying a promise. □ **promissory note** signed document containing a written promise to pay a stated sum.

pro·mo /prómō/ *colloq. n.* (pl. **-mos**) 1 publicity blurb or advertisement. 2 trailer for a television program, etc.

prom·on·to·ry /próməntawree/ *n.* (pl. **-ries**) point of high land jutting out into the sea, etc.; headland.

pro·mote /prəmōt/ *v.tr.* 1 raise (a person) to a higher office, rank, grade, etc. 2 encourage (a cause, process, desired result, etc.). 3 publicize and sell (a product). □□ **pro·mot′a·ble** *adj.* **pro·mot·a·bil′i·ty** *n.* **pro·mo·tion** /-mōshən/ *n.* **pro·mo′tion·al** *adj.*

pro·mot·er /prəmōtər/ *n.* 1 person who promotes. 2 person who finances, organizes, etc., a sporting event, show, etc.

prompt /prompt/ • *adj.* made, done, etc., readily or at once. • *adv.* punctually. • *v.tr.* **1** incite; urge (*prompted them to action*). **2** assist (an actor or hesitating speaker) with a cue or suggestion. **3** give rise to; inspire. • *n.* **1** something that prompts. **2** *Computing* indication or sign on a computer screen to show that the system is waiting for input. □□ **prompt′ing** *n.* **promp′ti·tude** *n.* **prompt′ly** *adv.* **prompt′ness** *n.*

prompt·er /prómptər/ *n.* person or thing prompts actors, etc.

pro·mul·gate /prómǝlgayt/ *v.tr.* **1** make known to the public; disseminate; promote. **2** proclaim (a decree, news, etc.). □□ **prom·ul·ga·tion** /-gáyshǝn/ *n.* **prom′ul·ga·tor** *n.*

prone /prōn/ *adj.* **1 a** lying face downward. **b** lying flat; prostrate. **2** (usu. foll. by *to*, or *to* + infin.) disposed or liable. □□ **prone′ness** /prónnis/ *n.*

prong /prong/ *n.* each of two or more projections at the end of a fork, etc. □□ **pronged** *adj.* (also in *comb.*).

pro·noun /prónown/ *n. Gram.* word used instead of and to indicate a noun already mentioned or known, esp. to avoid repetition (e.g., *we, their, this, ourselves*).

pro·nounce /prǝnówns/ *v.tr.* **1** (also *absol.*) utter or speak (words, sounds, etc.) in a certain way. **2** utter or deliver (a judgment, sentence, curse, etc.) officially or formally. **3** state as being one's opinion. □□ **pro·nounce′a·ble** *adj.* **pro·nounce′ment** *n.* **pro·nounc′er** *n.*

pro·nounced /prǝnównst/ *adj.* strongly marked; decided (*pronounced flavor*). □□ **pro·nounc·ed·ly** /-nównsidlee/ *adv.*

pron·to /próntō/ *adv. colloq.* promptly; quickly.

pro·nun·ci·a·tion /prǝnúnseeáyshǝn/ *n.* **1** way in which a word is pronounced, esp. with reference to a standard. **2** act of pronouncing. **3** way of pronouncing words, etc.

proof /prōof/ • *n.* **1** facts, evidence, argument, etc., establishing or helping to establish a fact. **2** demonstration; proving. **3** test or trial (*put them to the proof*). **4** standard of strength of distilled alcoholic spirits. **5** *Printing* trial impression before final printing. **6** stage in the resolution of a mathematical or philosophical problem. **7** photographic print made for selection, etc. • *adj.* impervious to penetration, ill effects, etc. (*proof against the harshest weather*). □□ **proof′less** *adj.*

proof·read /prōofreed/ *v.tr.* (*past* and *past part.* **-read** /-red/) read (esp. printer's proofs) and mark any errors. □□ **proof′read′er** *n.* **proof′-read·ing** *n.*

prop¹ /prop/ • *n.* **1** rigid, esp. separate, support. **2** person who supplies support, assistance, comfort, etc. • *v.tr.* (**propped, prop·ping**) (often foll. by *against, up*, etc.) support with or as if with a prop.

prop² /prop/ *n. Theatr. colloq.* = PROPERTY 3.

prop³ /prop/ *n. colloq.* aircraft propeller.

pro·pa·gan·da /própǝgándǝ/ *n.* **1** organized program of publicity, selected information, etc., used to propagate a doctrine, etc. **2** usu. *derog.* ideas, etc., so propagated. □□ **prop·a·gan′dist** *n.* **pro·pa·gan′dize** *v.*

prop·a·gate /própǝgayt/ **1** *tr.* **a** breed (a plant, animal, etc.) from the parent stock. **b** (of a plant, animal, etc.) reproduce itself. **2 a** *tr.* disseminate (a statement, belief, theory, etc.). **b** *intr.* grow

more widespread or numerous. □□ **prop·a·ga·tion** /-gáyshǝn/ *n.* **prop′a·ga·tive** *adj.* **prop′a·ga·tor** *n.*

pro·pane /própayn/ *n.* gaseous hydrocarbon of the alkane series used as bottled fuel. ¶ Chem. formula: C_3H_8.

pro·pel /prǝpél/ *v.tr.* (**pro·pelled, pro·pel·ling**) **1** drive or push forward. **2** urge on; encourage. □□ **pro·pel′lant** *n.* **pro·pel·lent** *n. & adj.*

pro·pel·ler /prǝpélǝr/ *n.* revolving shaft with blades, esp. for propelling a ship or aircraft.

aircraft   marine

PROPELLER

pro·pen·si·ty /prǝpénsitee/ *n.* (*pl.* **-ties**) inclination or tendency (*has a propensity for wandering*).

prop·er /própǝr/ *adj.* **1 a** accurate; correct. **b** fit; suitable; right (*at the proper time*). **2** decent; respectable, esp. excessively so. **3** belonging or relating (*respect proper to them*). **4** (usu. placed after noun) strictly so called; real; genuine (*this is the crypt, not the cathedral proper*). □ **proper noun** (or **name**) *Gram.* name used for an individual person, place, animal, country, title, etc., e.g., Jane, London, Everest. □□ **prop′er·ness** *n.*

prop·er·ly /própǝrlee/ *adv.* **1** fittingly; suitably. **2** accurately; correctly (*properly speaking*). **3** rightly (*he very properly refused*). **4** with decency; respectably (*behave properly*).

prop·er·tied /própǝrteed/ *adj.* having property, esp. land.

prop·er·ty /própǝrtee/ *n.* (*pl.* **-ties**) **1 a** something owned; a possession, esp. a house, land, etc. **b** possessions collectively. **2** attribute, quality, or characteristic. **3** movable object used on a theater stage, in a movie, etc.

proph·e·cy /prófisee/ *n.* (*pl.* **-cies**) **1 a** prophetic utterance, esp. Biblical. **b** prediction of future events. **2** faculty, practice, etc., of prophesying (*the gift of prophecy*).
¶ Note that **prophesy** is the verb, **prophecy** the noun.

proph·e·sy /prófisī/ *v.* (**-sies, -sied**) **1** *tr.* (usu. foll. by *that, who*, etc.) foretell (an event, etc.). **2** *intr.* speak as a prophet; foretell future events. □□ **proph′e·si·er** *n.*

proph·et /prófit/ *n.* (*fem.* **proph·et·ess** /-tis/) **1** religious seer or interpreter. **2 a** person who foretells events. **b** spokesman; advocate.

pro·phet·ic /prǝfétik/ *adj.* **1** (often foll. by *of*) containing a prediction; predicting. **2** of a prophet. □□ **pro·phet′i·cal** *adj.* **pro·phet′i·cal·ly** *adv.*

pro·phy·lac·tic /prófiláktik, próf-/ • *adj.* tending to prevent disease. • *n.* **1** preventive medicine or action. **2** condom.

pro·phy·lax·is /prōfiláksis, próf-/ *n.* (*pl.* **pro·phy·lax·es** /-seez/) preventive treatment against disease.

pro·pin·qui·ty /prəpíngkwitee/ *n.* **1** nearness in space; proximity. **2** close kinship. **3** similarity.

pro·pi·ti·ate /prōpísheeayt/ *v.tr.* appease (an offended person, etc.). □□ **pro·pi·ti·a·tion** /-áyshən/ *n.* **pro·pi′ti·a·tor** *n.*

pro·pi·ti·a·to·ry /prōpísheeətawree, -píshə-/ *adj.* serving or intended to propitiate.

pro·pi·tious /prəpíshəs/ *adj.* **1** favorable. **2** (of the weather, etc.) suitable. □□ **pro·pi′tious·ly** *adv.* **pro·pi′tious·ness** *n.*

prop·jet /própjet/ *n.* jet airplane powered by turboprops.

pro·po·nent /prəpónənt/ *n.* person advocating a motion, theory, or proposal.

pro·por·tion /prəpáwrshən/ • *n.* **1 a** comparative part or share. **b** comparative ratio (*proportion of births to deaths*). **2** correct or pleasing relation of things or parts of a thing. **3** (in *pl.*) dimensions; size (*large proportions*). **4** *Math.* equality of ratios between two pairs of quantities, e.g., 3:5 and 9:15. • *v.tr.* make proportional. □□ **pro·por′tioned** *adj.* (also in *comb.*). **pro·por′tion·less** *adj.* **pro·por′tion·ate** *adj.* **pro·por′tion·ate·ly** *adv.* ¶ Except in certain long-established phrases, such as *proportional representation, proportional* and *proportionate* may be used interchangeably.

pro·por·tion·al /prəpáwrshənəl/ *adj.* in due proportion; comparable. □□ **pro·por·tion·al·i·ty** /-nálitee/ *n.* **pro·por′tion·al·ly** *adv.*

pro·pos·al /prəpózəl/ *n.* **1 a** act or an instance of proposing something. **b** course of action, etc., so proposed (*the proposal was never carried out*). **2** offer of marriage.

pro·pose /prəpóz/ *v.* **1** *tr.* (also *absol.*) put forward for consideration or as a plan. **2** *tr.* intend; purpose. **3** *intr.* make an offer of marriage. **4** *tr.* nominate. □□ **pro·pos′er** *n.*

prop·o·si·tion /própəzíshən/ • *n.* **1** statement or assertion. **2** scheme proposed; proposal. **3** *Logic* statement subject to proof or disproof. **4** *colloq.* problem (*difficult proposition*). **5** *Math.* formal statement of a theorem or problem. **6** *colloq.* sexual proposal. • *v.tr. colloq.* make a proposal (esp. of sexual intercourse) to. □□ **prop·o·si′tion·al** *adj.*

pro·pound /prəpównd/ *v.tr.* offer for consideration; propose. □□ **pro·pound′er** *n.*

pro·pri·e·tar·y /prəprīəteree/ *adj.* **1** of, holding, or concerning property, or relating to a proprietor (*proprietary rights*). **2** held in private ownership.

pro·pri·e·tor /prəprīətər/ *n.* (*fem.* **pro·pri·e·tress**) owner of a business, hotel, etc. □□ **pro·pri·e·to·ri·al** /-táwreeəl/ *adj.* **pro·pri·e·to′ri·al·ly** *adv.* **pro·pri′e·tor·ship** *n.*

pro·pri·e·ty /prəprī-itee/ *n.* (*pl.* **-ties**) **1** fitness; rightness. **2** correctness of behavior or morals. **3** (in *pl.*) details or rules of correct conduct.

pro·pul·sion /prəpúlshən/ *n.* **1** driving or pushing forward. **2** impelling influence. □□ **pro·pul·sive** /-púlsiv/ *adj.*

pro ra·ta /prō ráytə, ráatə/ • *adj.* proportional. • *adv.* proportionally.

pro·rate /próráyt/ *v.tr.* allocate or distribute pro rata. □□ **pro·ra′tion** *n.*

pro·sa·ic /prōzáyik/ *adj.* **1** like prose; lacking poetic beauty. **2** unromantic; dull; commonplace (*took a prosaic view of life*). □□ **pro·sa′i·cal·ly** *adv.*

pro·sce·ni·um /prəséeneeəm/ *n.* (*pl.* **pro·sce·ni·ums** or **pro·sce·ni·a** /-neeə/) vertical arched opening to the stage.

pro·scribe /prəskríb/ *v.tr.* **1** banish; exile. **2** put (a person) outside the protection of the law. **3** reject or denounce. □□ **pro·scrip·tion** /-skrípshən/ *n.* **pro·scrip·tive** /-skríptiv/ *adj.* ¶ See note at PRESCRIBE.

prose /prōz/ *n.* ordinary form of the written or spoken language (opp. POETRY, VERSE).

pros·e·cute /prósikyoot/ *v.tr.* **1** (also *absol.*) **a** institute legal proceedings against (a person). **b** institute a prosecution with reference to (a claim, crime, etc.). **2** carry on (a trade, pursuit, etc.). □□ **pros·e·cut′a·ble** *adj.* **pros·e·cu·tion** /-kyóoshən/ *n.* **pros′e·cu·tor** *n.* **pros·e·cu·to·ri·al** /-táwreeəl/ *adj.*

pros·e·lyte /prósilīt/ • *n.* person converted, esp. recently, from one opinion, creed, party, etc., to another. • *v.tr.* = PROSELYTIZE. □□ **pros·e·ly·tism** /-səlitizəm/ *n.*

pros·e·lyt·ize /prósilitīz/ *v.tr.* (also *absol.*) convert (a person or persons) from one belief, etc., to another, esp. habitually. □□ **pros′e·lyt·iz·er** *n.*

pros·o·dy /prósədee/ *n.* versification; study of meter, rhyme, etc. **2** the study of speech rhythms. □□ **pro·sod·ic** /prəsódik/ *adj.* **pros′o·dist** *n.*

pros·pect /próspekt/ • *n.* **1 a** (often in *pl.*) expectation, esp. of success in a career, etc. **b** something anticipated. **2** extensive view of landscape, etc. (*striking prospect*). **3** possible or probable customer, subscriber, etc. • *v.* (usu. foll. by *for*) explore (a region) for gold, etc. □□ **pros′pec·tor** *n.*

---

prospect late Middle English (as a noun denoting the action of looking toward a distant object): from Latin *prospectus* 'view,' from *prospicere* 'look forward,' from *pro-* 'forward' + *specere* 'to look.' Early use, referring to a view or landscape, gave rise to the meaning 'mental picture' (mid-16th century), whence 'anticipated event.'

---

pro·spec·tive /prəspéktiv/ *adj.* expected; future (*prospective bridegroom*). □□ **pro·spec′tive·ly** *adv.*

pro·spec·tus /prəspéktəs/ *n.* printed document advertising or describing a school, commercial enterprise, etc.

pros·per /próspər/ *v.intr.* succeed; thrive.

pros·per·i·ty /prospéritee/ *n.* state of being prosperous; wealth or success.

pros·per·ous /próspərəs/ *adj.* successful; rich; thriving. □□ **pros′per·ous·ly** *adv.* **pros′per·ous·ness** *n.*

pros·tate /próstayt/ *n.* (in full **prostate gland**) gland surrounding the neck of the bladder in male mammals and releasing part of the semen. □□ **pros·tat′ic** /-státik/ *adj.*

pros·the·sis /prósthéesis/ *n.* (*pl.* **pros·the·ses** /-seez/) artificial part supplied to replace a missing body part. □□ **pros·thet′ic** /-thétik/ *adj.* **pros·thet′i·cal·ly** *adv.*

pros·ti·tute /próstitoot, -tyoot/ • *n.* person who engages in sexual activity for payment. •

v.tr. **1** make a prostitute of (esp. oneself). **2** misuse (one's talents, skills, etc.) for money. □□ **pros·ti·tu·tion** /-tōoshən/ *n.* **pros'ti·tu·tor** *n.*

pros·trate /próstrayt/ • *adj.* **1 a** lying face downward, esp. in submission. **b** lying horizontally. **2** overcome, esp. by grief, exhaustion, etc. • *v.tr.* **1** lay (a person, etc.) flat on the ground. **2** (*refl.*) throw (oneself) down in submission, etc. **3** overcome; make weak. □□ **pros·tra·tion** /prostráyshən/ *n.*

pros·y /prózee/ *adj.* (**pros·i·er, pros·i·est**) tedious; commonplace; dull (*prosy talk*). □□ **pros' i·ly** *adv.* **pros'i·ness** *n.*

Prot. *abbr.* Protestant.

prot·ac·tin·i·um /prótaktíneeəm/ *n. Chem.* radioactive metallic element. ¶ Symb.: **Pa.**

pro·tag·o·nist /prōtágənist/ *n.* **1** chief person in a drama, story, etc. **2** advocate or champion of a cause.

¶ The correct meaning of **protagonist** is 'chief or leading person,' e.g., *The novelist's first challenge is to create a protagonist the reader can identify with.* However, it is also used, usually with *of* or *for*, to mean 'a supporter or champion of a cause, etc.,' e.g., *Protagonists of peace rallied at the Capitol.*

pro·te·an /prōteeən, -te'ən/ *adj.* **1** variable; taking many forms. **2** (of an artist, writer, etc.) versatile.

pro·tect /prətékt/ *v.tr.* keep (a person, thing, etc.) safe; defend; guard (*goggles protected her eyes from dust*).

pro·tec·tion /prətékshən/ *n.* **1 a** protecting or being protected; defense. **b** thing, person, or animal that provides protection. **2** *colloq.* **a** immunity from molestation obtained by payment to organized criminals, etc. **b** (in full **protection money**) payment, as bribes, made to police, etc., for overlooking criminal activities. □□ **pro·tec' tion·ist** *n.*

pro·tec·tive /prətéktiv/ *adj.* protecting. □□ **pro· tec'tive·ly** *adv.* **pro·tec'tive·ness** *n.*

pro·tec·tor /prətéktər/ *n.* **1** person who protects. **2** guardian or patron. □□ **pro·tec'tor·al** *adj.*

pro·tec·tor·ate /prətéktərət/ *n.* **1** nation that is controlled and protected by another. **2** this relation.

pro·té·gé /prótizhay, prōtizháy/ *n.* (*fem.* **pro·té· gée** *pronunc.* same) person under the protection, patronage, tutelage, etc., of another.

pro·tein /prōteen/ *n.* any of a group of organic compounds composed of amino acids and forming an essential part of all living organisms. □□ **pro·tein·a·ceous** /-teenáyshəs/ *adj.*

pro tem /prō tém/ *adj. & adv. colloq.* = PRO TEMPORE.

pro tem·po·re /prō témpəree/ *adj. & adv.* for the time being.

Prot·er·o·zo·ic /prótərəzóik, prō-/ *Geol.* • *adj.* of or relating to the later part of the Precambrian era. • *n.* this time.

pro·test • *n.* /prótest/ statement or act of dissent or disapproval. • *v.* /prətést, prō-/ **1** *intr.* make a protest. **2** *tr.* affirm (one's innocence, etc.) solemnly. **3** *tr.* object to (a decision, etc.). □ **under protest** unwillingly. □□ **pro·test' er** *n.* **pro·test'ing·ly** *adv.* **pro·tes'tor** *n.*

Prot·es·tant /prótistənt/ • *n.* member or follower of a Christian Church separated from the Roman Catholic Church after the Reforma-

tion. • *adj.* of the Protestant Churches or their members, etc. □□ **Prot'es·tant·ism** *n.* **Prot'es· tant·ize** *v.*

pro·tes·ta·tion /prótistáyshən, prōte-/ *n.* **1** strong affirmation. **2** protest.

proto- /prótō/ *comb. form* first (*prototype*).

pro·to·col /prótəkawl, -kol/ *n.* **1** official formality and etiquette. **2** original draft of a diplomatic document, esp. of the terms of a treaty. **3** formal statement of a transaction.

---

protocol late Middle English (denoting the original notation of an agreement, forming the legal authority for future dealings relating to it): from Old French *prothocole*, via medieval Latin from Greek *prōtokollon* 'first page, flyleaf,' from *prōtos* 'first' + *kolla* 'glue.' Sense 1 derives from French *protocole*, the collection of set forms of etiquette to be observed by the French head of state, and the name of the government department responsible for this (in the 19th century).

---

pro·to·lan·guage /prótōlanggwij/ *n.* language from which other languages are believed to have been derived.

pro·ton /prótɔn/ *n. Physics* stable elementary particle with a positive electric charge, occurring in all atomic nuclei. □□ **pro·ton·ic** /prətónik/ *adj.*

pro·to·plasm /prótəplazəm/ *n.* material comprising the living part of a cell. □□ **pro·to·plas· mal** /-plazməl/ *adj.* **pro·to·plas·mat·ic** /-mátik/ *adj.* **pro'to·plas'mic** *adj.*

pro·to·type /prótətīp/ *n.* **1** original as a pattern for imitations, improved forms, etc. **2** trial model or preliminary version. □□ **pro·to·typ· ic** /-típik/ *adj.* **pro·to·typ'i·cal** *adj.* **pro·to·typ'i· cal·ly** *adv.*

pro·to·zo·an /prótəzóən/ • *n.* (also **pro·to· zo·on** /-zó-on/) (*pl.* **pro·to·zo·a** /-zóə/ or **pro· to·zo·ans**) unicellular microscopic organism. • *adj.* (also **pro·to·zo·ic** /-zó-ik/) of or of this group. □□ **pro'to·zo'al** *adj.*

pro·tract /prōtrákt, prə-/ *v.tr.* **1** prolong or lengthen. **2** (as **protracted** *adj.*) of excessive length or duration. **3** draw (a plan, etc.) to scale. □□ **pro·tract'ed·ly** *adv.* **pro·tract'ed·ness** *n.*

pro·trac·tor /prōtráktər, prə-/ *n.* instrument for measuring angles, usu. in the form of a graduated semicircle.

PROTRACTOR

pro·trude /prōtrōod/ *v.* **1** *intr.* project. **2** *tr.* thrust or cause to thrust forth. □□ **pro·tru·sion** /-trōozhən/ *n.* **pro·tru'sive** *adj.*

pro·tu·ber·ant /prōtōobərənt, -tyōo-, prə-/ *adj.* bulging out; prominent (*protuberant eyes*). □□ **pro·tu'ber·ance** *n.*

proud /prowd/ *adj.* **1** feeling greatly honored or pleased. **2 a** haughty; arrogant. **b** (often in *comb.*) having a proper pride; satisfied. **3** (of an occasion, etc.) justly arousing pride. (*a proud day for us*). **4** (of a thing) imposing; splendid. □□ **proud′ly** *adv.* **proud′ness** *n.*

prove /proov/ *v.* (*past part.* **proved** or **prov·en**) **1** *tr.* demonstrate the truth of by evidence or argument. **2** *intr.* **a** be found (*it proved to be untrue*). **b** emerge as (*will prove the winner*). **3** *tr.* *Math.* test the accuracy of (a calculation). □ **prove oneself** show one's abilities, courage, etc. □□ **prov′a·ble** *adj.* **prov·a·bil′i·ty** *n.* **prov′a·bly** *adv.*

prov·e·nance /próvinəns/ *n.* origin or place of origin.

Pro·ven·çal /próvonsáal, próv-/ • *adj.* of Provence, a former province of SE France. • *n.* **1** native of Provence. **2** language of Provence.

prov·en·der /próvindər/ *n.* animal fodder.

prov·erb /próvərb/ *n.* short pithy saying in general use, held to embody a general truth.

pro·ver·bi·al /prəvə́rbeeəl/ *adj.* **1** as well-known as a proverb; notorious (*his proverbial honesty*). **2** of or referred to in a proverb (*proverbial ill wind*). □□ **pro·ver′bi·al·ly** *adv.*

pro·vide /prəvíd/ *v.* **1** *tr.* supply; furnish. **2** *intr.* **a** make due preparation. **b** prepare for the maintenance of a person, etc. **3** *tr.* stipulate in a will, statute, etc. □□ **pro·vid′er** *n.*

pro·vid·ed /prəvídid/ on the condition or understanding (that).

prov·i·dence /próvidəns/ *n.* **1** protective care of God or nature. **2** (**Providence**) God in this aspect. **3** timely care or preparation; foresight; thrift.

prov·i·dent /próvidənt, -dent/ *adj.* having or showing foresight; thrifty. □□ **prov′i·dent·ly** *adv.*

prov·i·den·tial /próvidénshəl/ *adj.* **1** of or by divine foresight or interposition. **2** opportune; lucky. □□ **prov′i·den′tial·ly** *adv.*

prov·ince /próvins/ *n.* **1** principal administrative division of some countries. **2** (**the provinces**) whole of a country outside major cities, esp. regarded as uncultured, unsophisticated, etc. **3** field, area or sphere of action.

pro·vin·cial /prəvínshəl/ • *adj.* **1** of a province or provinces. **2** unsophisticated or uncultured. • *n.* **1** inhabitant of a province or the provinces. **2** unsophisticated or uncultured person. □□ **pro·vin′cial·ism** *n.* **pro·vin·ci·al·i·ty** /-sheeálitee/ *n.* **pro·vin′cial·ly** *adv.*

pro·vi·sion /prəvízhən/ • *n.* **1** act or an instance of providing (*made no provision for his future*). **2** (in *pl.*) food, drink, etc., esp. for an expedition. **3 a** legal or formal statement providing for something. **b** clause of this. • *v.tr.* supply with provisions. □□ **pro·vi′sion·er** *n.*

pro·vi·sion·al /prəvízhənəl/ *adj.* providing for immediate needs only; temporary. □□ **pro·vi′sion·al·ly** *adv.*

pro·vi·so /prəvízō/ *n.* (*pl.* **-sos**) **1** stipulation. **2** clause of stipulation or limitation in a document.

prov·o·ca·tion /próvəkáyshən/ *n.* **1** act or instance of provoking; state of being provoked. **2** cause of annoyance.

pro·voc·a·tive /prəvókətiv/ • *adj.* **1** tending to provoke, esp. anger or sexual desire. **2** intention-

ally annoying. • *n.* provocative thing. □□ **pro·voc′a·tive·ly** *adv.* **pro·voc′a·tive·ness** *n.*

pro·voke /prəvók/ *v.tr.* **1** rouse or incite. **2** call forth; instigate; cause. **3** irritate or anger. □□ **pro·vok′a·ble** *adj.* **pro·vok′ing·ly** *adv.*

pro·vo·lo·ne /próvəlónee/ *n.* medium hard Italian cheese.

pro·vost /próvōst, próvəst/ *n.* high administrative officer of a church or university. □ **provost marshal** /próvō/ head of military police force or detail.

prow /prow/ *n.* bow of a ship adjoining the stem.

prow·ess /prówis/ *n.* **1** skill; expertise. **2** valor; gallantry.

prowl /prowl/ • *v.* **1** *tr.* roam (a place) in search or as if in search of prey, plunder, etc. **2** *intr.* move about like a hunter. • *n.* act or an instance of prowling. □□ **prowl′er** *n.*

prox·i·mate /próksimət/ *adj.* **1** nearest or next before or after. **2** approximate. □□ **prox′i·mate·ly** *adv.*

prox·im·i·ty /proksímitee/ *n.* nearness in space, time, etc.

prox·y /próksee/ *n.* (*pl.* **-ies**) (also *attrib.*) **1** authorization given to a substitute or deputy (*a proxy vote*). **2** person authorized to act as a substitute, etc.

prude /prood/ *n.* person having or affecting an attitude of extreme propriety or modesty, esp. in sexual matters. □□ **prud′er·y** *n.* (*pl.* **-ies**). **prud′ish** *adj.* **prud′ish·ly** *adv.* **prud′ish·ness** *n.*

pru·dent /prood′nt/ *adj.* **1** (of a person or conduct) careful to avoid undesired consequences; circumspect. **2** discreet. □□ **pru′dence** *n.* **pru′dent·ly** *adv.*

pru·den·tial /proodénshəl/ *adj.* of, involving, or marked by prudence (*prudential motives*). □□ **pru·den′tial·ly** *adv.*

prune[1] /proon/ *n.* dried plum.

prune[2] /proon/ *v.tr.* **1** trim (a tree, etc.) by cutting away dead or overgrown branches, etc. **2 a** (often foll. by *of*) clear (a book, etc.) of superfluous matter. **b** remove (superfluous matter). □□ **prun′er** *n.*

pru·ri·ent /próoreeənt/ *adj.* **1** having an unhealthy obsession with sexual matters. **2** encouraging such an obsession. □□ **pru′ri·ence** *n.* **pru′ri·en·cy** *n.* **pru′ri·ent·ly** *adv.*

Prus·sian /prúshən/ • *adj.* of or relating to Prussia, a former German kingdom, or relating to its rigidly militaristic tradition. • *n.* native of Prussia.

pry[1] /prī/ *v.intr.* (**pries, pried**) (usu. foll. by *into*) inquire presumptuously. □□ **pry′ing** *adj.* **pry′ing·ly** *adv.*

pry[2] /prī/ *v.tr.* (**pries, pried**) = PRIZE[2].

PS *abbr.* **1** postscript. **2** private secretary.

psalm /saam/ *n.* (also **Psalm**) sacred songs esp. from the Book of Psalms (Old Testament). □□ **psalm′ist** *n.*

psal·ter /sáwltər/ *n.* **1** the Book of Psalms. **2** copy of the Psalms, esp. for liturgical use.

p's and q's *n.* □ **mind one's p's and q's 1** attend to one's own conduct and manners. **2** attend to one's own accuracy in work.

PSAT *abbr.* Preliminary Scholastic Assessment Test.

pseud. *abbr.* pseudonym.

pseudo- /sōōdō/ *comb. form* (also **pseud-** before a vowel) **1** false; not genuine (*pseudointellectual*). **2** resembling or imitating (often in technical applications) (*pseudomalaria*).

pseu·do·nym /sōōdənim/ *n.* fictitious name, esp. one assumed by an author.

psf *abbr.* (also **p.s.f.**) pounds per square foot.

psi /sī, psī/ *n.* twenty-third letter of the Greek alphabet (Ψ, ψ).

p.s.i. *abbr.* pounds per square inch.

pso·ri·a·sis /sərīəsis/ *n.* skin disease marked by red scaly patches.

psst /pst/ *int.* (also **pst**) whispered exclamation seeking to attract a person's attention surreptitiously.

PST *abbr.* Pacific Standard Time.

psych /sīk/ *v.tr. colloq.* (also **psyche**) **1** prepare (oneself or another person) mentally for an ordeal, etc. **2** (often foll. by *out*) influence a person psychologically, esp. negatively; intimidate; frighten.

psych. /sīk/ (also **psychol.**) *abbr.* **1** psychological. **2** psychology.

psy·che /sīkee/ *n.* **1** soul; spirit. **2** mind.

psy·che·del·ic /sīkidélik/ • *adj.* **1 a** expanding the mind's awareness, etc., esp. through the use of hallucinogenic drugs. **b** (of a drug) producing hallucinations. **2** *colloq.* hallucinatory in effect, color, design, etc. • *n.* hallucinogenic drug. □□ **psy·che·del'i·cal·ly** *adv.*

psy·chi·a·try /sīkīətree/ *n.* the study and treatment of mental disease. □□ **psy·chi·at·ric** /-keeátrik/ *adj.* **psy·chi·at'ri·cal** *adj.* **psy·chi·at'ri·cal·ly** *adv.* **psy·chi·a·trist** /-kīətrist/ *n.*

psy·chic /sīkik/ • *adj.* **1** (of a person) considered to have occult powers, such as telepathy, clairvoyance, etc. **2** of the soul or mind. • *n.* person considered to have psychic powers; medium. □□ **psy'chi·cal** *adj.* **psy'chi·cal·ly** *adv.*

psy·cho /sīkō/ *colloq.* • *n.* (*pl.* **-chos**) psychopath. • *adj.* psychopathic.

psycho- /sīkō/ *comb. form* relating to the mind or psychology.

psy·cho·a·nal·y·sis /sīkōənálisis/ *n.* therapeutic method of treating mental disorders by discussion and analysis of repressed fears and conflicts. □□ **psy·cho·an·a·lyze** /-ánəlīz/ *v.* **psy·cho·an·a·lyst** /-ánəlist/ *n.* **psy·cho·an·a·lyt'ic** *adj.* **psy·cho·an·a·lyt'i·cal·ly** *adv.*

psy·cho·bab·ble /sīkōbabəl/ *n. colloq. derog.* jargon used in popular psychology. □□ **psy'cho·bab·bler** *n.*

psy·cho·log·i·cal /sīkəlójikəl/ *adj.* **1** of, or arising in the mind. **2** of psychology. **3** *colloq.* (of an ailment, etc.) imaginary. □ **psychological warfare** campaign directed at reducing an opponent's morale. □□ **psy·cho·log'i·cal·ly** *adv.*

psy·chol·o·gy /sīkóləjee/ *n.* (*pl.* **-gies**) **1** scientific study of the human mind. **2** treatise on or theory of this. **3** mental characteristics, etc., of a person, group, situation, etc. □□ **psy·chol'o·gist** *n.* **psy·chol'o·gize** *v.*

psy·cho·path /sīkəpath/ *n.* **1** person suffering from chronic mental disorder esp. with abnormal or violent social behavior. **2** mentally or emotionally unstable person. □□ **psy·cho·path'ic** *adj.* **psy·cho·path'i·cal·ly** *adv.*

psy·cho·pa·thol·o·gy /sīkōpəthóləjee/ *n.* **1** scientific study of mental disorders. **2** mentally or

behaviorally disordered state. □□ **psy·cho·path·o·log·i·cal** /-pathəlójikəl/ *adj.*

psy·cho·sis /sīkósis/ *n.* (*pl.* **psy·cho·ses** /-seez/) severe mental derangement with loss of contact with external reality.

psy·cho·so·mat·ic /sīkōsəmátik/ *adj.* (of an illness, etc.) mental, not physical, in origin. □□ **psy·cho·so·mat'i·cal·ly** *adv.*

psy·cho·ther·a·py /sīkōthérəpee/ *n.* the treatment of mental disorder by psychological means. □□ **psy·cho·ther·a·peu·tic** /-pyōōtik/ *adj.* **psy·cho·ther'a·pist** *n.*

psy·chot·ic /sīkótik/ • *adj.* of or characterized by a psychosis. • *n.* psychotic person. □□ **psy·chot'i·cal·ly** *adv.*

PT *abbr.* **1** physical therapy. **2** physical training.

Pt *symb. Chem.* platinum.

pt. *abbr.* **1** part. **2** pint. **3** point. **4** port.

PTA *abbr.* Parent-Teacher Association.

ptar·mi·gan /taармigən/ *n.* grouse with black or gray plumage in the summer and white in the winter.

pter·o·dac·tyl /térədáktil/ *n.* large extinct flying reptile.

pto·maine /tōmayn/ *n.* any of various amine compounds, some toxic, in putrefying animal and vegetable matter.

Pu *symb. Chem.* plutonium.

pub /pub/ *n. colloq.* tavern or bar.

pub. *abbr.* (also **publ.**) **1** public. **2** publication. **3** published. **4** publisher. **5** publishing.

pu·ber·ty /pyōōbərtee/ *n.* period during which adolescents reach sexual maturity.

pu·bes /pyōōbeez/ *n.* (*pl.* same) **1** lower part of the abdomen at the front of the pelvis. **2** pubic hair.

pu·bes·cence /pyōōbésəns/ *n.* **1** time when puberty begins. **2** *Bot.* soft down on plants. **3** *Zool.* soft down on various parts of animals, esp. insects. □□ **pu·bes'cent** *adj.*

pu·bic /pyōōbik/ *adj.* of or relating to the pubes or pubis.

pu·bis /pyōōbis/ *n.* (*pl.* **pu·bes** /-beez/) either of a pair of bones forming the two sides of the pelvis.

pub·lic /públik/ • *adj.* **1** of the people as a whole. **2** open to or shared by all. **3** done or existing openly (*public protest*). **4** (of a service, funds, etc.) provided by, concerning, or serving government (*public records*). • *n.* **1** (as *sing.* or *pl.*) community in general, or members of the community. **2** specified section of the community (*reading public*). □ **go public** become a public company or corporation. **in public** openly; publicly. **public-address system** loudspeakers, microphones, amplifiers, etc., used in addressing large audiences. **public health** provision of adequate sanitation, drainage, etc., by government. **public relations** professional maintenance of a favorable public image, esp. by a company, famous person, etc. **public school 1** *US* free, government-supported school. **2** *Brit.* private boarding school. **public sector** government-controlled part of an economy, industry, etc. **public utility** organization supplying water, gas, etc., to the community. □□ **pub'lic·ly** *adv.*

pub·li·can /públikən/ *n.* **1** *Rom.Hist.* & *Bibl.* tax collector. **2** *Brit.* keeper of a pub.

pub·li·ca·tion /públikáyshən/ *n.* **1 a** preparation and issuing of a book, newspaper, etc. **b** book, etc., so issued. **2** making something publicly known.

pub·li·cist /públisist/ *n.* publicity or public relations agent.

pub·lic·i·ty /publísitee/ *n.* **1 a** advertising. **b** material or information used for this. **2** public exposure.

pub·li·cize /públisīz/ *v.tr.* advertise; make publicly known.

pub·lish /públish/ *v.tr.* **1** (also *absol.*) prepare and issue (a book, newspaper, etc.) for public sale. **2** make generally known. □□ **pub′lish·a·ble** *adj.*

pub·lish·er /públishər/ *n.* **1** person or esp. a company that produces and distributes copies of books, etc., for sale.

puce /pyōos/ *adj. & n.* dark red or purplish brown.

puck[1] /puk/ *n.* rubber disk used in ice hockey.

puck[2] /puk/ *n.* mischievous or evil sprite. □□ **puck′ish** *adj.* **puck′ish·ly** *adv.*

puck·er /púkər/ • *v.* gather or cause to gather into wrinkles, folds, or bulges (*puckered her eyebrows*). • *n.* such a wrinkle, bulge, fold, etc. □□ **puck′er·y** *adj.*

pud·ding /pōoding/ *n.* any of various dessert dishes, usu. containing flavoring, sugar, milk, etc.

pud·dle /púd′l/ *n.* small pool, esp. of rainwater. □□ **pud′dler** *n.* **pud′dly** *adj.*

pu·den·dum /pyōodéndəm/ *n.* (*pl.* **pu·den·da** /-də/) (usu. in *pl.*) genitals, esp. of a woman.

pudg·y /pú}ee/ *adj.* (**pudg·i·er, pudg·i·est**) *colloq.* (esp. of a person) plump; slightly overweight. □□ **pudge** *n.* **pudg′i·ly** *adv.* **pudg′i·ness** *n.*

pueb·lo /pwéblō/ *n.* (*pl.* **-los**) settlement of multistoried adobe houses built by the Native Americans of the southwestern United States.

pu·er·ile /pyōoəril, pyōoril, -rīl/ *adj.* trivial; childish; immature. □□ **pu′er·ile·ly** *adv.* **pu·er·il·i·ty** /-rílitee/ *n.* (*pl.* **-ties**)

Puer·to Ri·can /pwértō reékən, páwrtə/ • *n.* **1** native of Puerto Rico, an island of the West Indies. **2** person of Puerto Rican descent. • *adj.* of or relating to Puerto Rico.

puff /puf/ • *n.* **1 a** short quick blast of breath, wind, vapor, etc. **b** sound of or like this. **2** draw of smoke from a cigarette, pipe, etc. **3** light pastry containing jam, cream, etc. **4** extravagantly enthusiastic review of a book, etc., esp. in a newspaper. **5** = *powder puff.* • *v.* **1** *intr.* emit a puff of air or breath; blow with short blasts. **2** *intr.* (of a person smoking, a steam engine, etc.) emit or move with puffs. **3** *intr.* breathe hard; pant. **4** *intr. & tr.* (usu. foll. by *up, out*) become or cause to become inflated; swell (*his eye was inflamed and puffed up*). **5** *tr.* (usu. as **puffed up** *adj.*) elate; make proud or boastful. **6** *tr.* advertise or promote (goods, a book, etc.) with exaggerated or false praise. □ **puff pastry** light flaky pastry.

puff·ball /púfbawl/ *n.* ball-shaped fungus emitting clouds of spores.

puf·fin /púfin/ *n.* northern seabird with a large head, brightly colored triangular bill, and black and white plumage.

puff·y /púfee/ *adj.* (**puff·i·er, puff·i·est**) **1** swollen, esp. of the face, etc. **2** fat. **3** gusty. □□ **puff′i·ly** *adv.* **puff′i·ness** *n.*

pug /pug/ *n.* (in full **pugdog**) dog of a dwarf breed with a broad flat nose and deeply wrinkled face. □ **pug nose** a short squat or snub nose. **pug-nosed** having such a nose.

pu·gil·ist /pyōojilist/ *n.* boxer, esp. a professional. □□ **pu′gil·ism** *n.* **pu·gil·is′tic** *adj.*

pug·na·cious /pugnáyshəs/ *adj.* quarrelsome; disposed to fight. □□ **pug·na′cious·ly** *adv.* **pug·nac·i·ty** /-násitee/ *n.*

puke /pyōok/ *v. sl.* vomit. □□ **puk′ey** *adj.*

pul·chri·tude /púlkritōod, -tyōod/ *n. literary* beauty. □□ **pul·chri·tu·di·nous** /-tōodinəs, -tyōod-/ *adj.*

pule /pyōol/ *v.intr.* cry querulously or weakly; whimper.

pull /pōol/ • *v.* **1** *tr.* exert force upon (a thing) tending to move it to oneself or the origin of the force (*stop pulling my hair*). **2** *tr.* cause to move in this way. **3** *intr.* exert a pulling force. **4** *tr.* extract; pluck out. **5** *tr.* damage (a muscle, etc.) by abnormal strain. **6** *tr.* (foll. by *on*) bring out (a weapon). **7** *intr.* (foll. by *at*) tear or pluck at. **8** *intr.* inhale deeply; draw or suck (on a pipe, etc.). **9** *tr.* remove (a plant) by the root. • *n.* **1** act of pulling. **2** force exerted by this. **3** influence; advantage. **4** something that attracts or draws attention. **5** deep draft of esp. liquor. □ **pull back** retreat or cause to retreat. **pull in 1** arrive, esp. at a destination. **b** restrain; tighten. **2** (of a bus, train, etc.) arrive to take passengers. **3** earn or acquire. **4** *colloq.* arrest. **pull a person's leg** deceive a person playfully. **pull off 1** remove by pulling. **2** succeed in achieving or winning. **pull out 1** take out by pulling. **2** depart. **3** withdraw from an undertaking. **4** (of a bus, train, etc.) leave with its passengers. **5** (of a vehicle) move onto the road and accelerate. **pull over** (of a vehicle) move to the side of or off the road. **pull one's punches** avoid using one's full force. **pull strings** exert (esp. clandestine) influence. **pull together** work in harmony. **pull up 1** stop or cause to stop moving. **2** pull out of the ground. **3** draw closer to or even with, as in a race. **pull one's weight** do one's fair share of work. □□ **pull′er** *n.*

pul·let /pōolit/ *n.* young hen, esp. one less than one year old.

pul·ley /pōolee/ *n.* (*pl.* **-leys**) grooved wheel or set of wheels for a rope, etc., to pass over, set in a block and used for changing the direction of a force.

Pull·man /pōolmən/ *n.* railroad sleeping car.

pull·o·ver /pōolōvər/ *n.* garment put on over the head and covering the top half of the body.

pul·mo·nar·y /pōolməneree, púl-/ *adj.* **1** of or relating to the lungs. **2** having lungs or lunglike organs. □□ **pul·mo·nate** /-nayt, -nət/ *adj.*

pulp /pulp/ • *n.* **1** soft fleshy part of fruit, etc. **2** soft shapeless mass derived from rags, wood, etc., used in papermaking. • *v.* **1** *tr.* reduce to pulp. **2** *intr.* become pulp. □□ **pulp′er** *n.* **pulp′less** *adj.* **pulp′y** *adj.* **pulp′i·ness** *n.*

pul·pit /pōolpit, púl-/ *n.* **1** raised enclosed platform in a church, etc., from which the preacher delivers a sermon. **2** (prec. by *the*) preachers or preaching collectively.

pul·sar /púlsaar/ *n. Astron.* cosmic source of regular and rapid pulses of radiation, e.g., a rotating neutron star.

pul·sate /púlsayt/ v.intr. **1** expand and contract rhythmically; throb. **2** vibrate; quiver; thrill. □□ **pul·sa·tion** /-sáyshən/ n. **pul'sa·tor** n. **pul·sa·to·ry** /púlsətawree/ adj.

pulse /puls/ • n. **1 a** rhythmical throbbing of the arteries, esp. as felt in the wrists, temples, etc. **b** each successive beat of the arteries or heart. **2** throb or thrill of life or emotion. **3** latent feeling. **4** single vibration of sound, electric current, light, etc. **5** rhythmical beat, esp. of music. • v.intr. pulsate. □□ **pulse'less** adj.

pul·ver·ize /púlvərīz/ v. **1** tr. reduce to fine particles. **2** intr. be reduced to dust. **3** colloq. tr. **a** demolish. **b** defeat utterly. □□ **pul'ver·i·za'tion** n. **pul'ver·iz·er** n.

pu·ma /pyoomə, poo-/ n. large American wild cat. Also called **cougar, panther, mountain lion.**

pum·ice /púmis/ n. (in full **pumice stone**) **1** light porous volcanic rock often used as an abrasive in cleaning or polishing substances. **2** piece of this used for removing callused skin, etc.

pum·mel /púmǝl/ v.tr. (also **pom·mel**) strike repeatedly, esp. with the fist.

pump[1] /pump/ • n. **1** machine for raising or moving liquids, compressing gases, inflating tires, etc. • v. **1** tr. raise or remove (liquid, gas, etc.) with a pump. **2** tr. (often foll. by up) fill (a tire, etc.) with air. **3** intr. work a pump. **4** tr. question (a person) persistently to obtain information. **5** tr. move vigorously up and down. **pump iron** (also **pump up**) colloq. exercise with weights.

pump[2] /pump/ n. low-cut shoe without ties, straps, etc.

pum·per·nick·el /púmpərnikǝl/ n. type of dark rye bread.

pump·kin /púmpkin, púng-/ n. rounded orange edible gourd of a vine.

pun /pun/ • n. humorous use of a word to suggest different meanings, or of words of the same sound and different meanings. • v.intr. (**punned, pun·ning**) (foll. by on) make a pun or puns with (words). □□ **pun'ning·ly** adv. **pun'ster** n.

punch[1] /punch/ • v.tr. **1** strike bluntly, esp. with a closed fist. **2 a** pierce a hole in (metal, paper, a ticket, etc.) as or with a punch. **b** pierce (a hole) by punching. • n. **1** blow with a fist. **2** colloq. vigor; momentum. □ **punch-drunk** stupefied from or as though from a series of heavy blows. **punch line** words giving the point of a joke or story. □□ **punch'er** n.

punch[2] /punch/ n. tool or machine for punching holes in or impressing a design or stamping a die on a material.

punch[3] /punch/ n. drink of fruit juices, sometimes mixed with wine or liquor, served cold or hot.

punch·y /púnchee/ adj. (**punch·i·er, punch·i·est**) **1** having punch or vigor; forceful. **2** = *punch-drunk* (**PUNCH**[1]).

punc·til·i·o /pungktileeo/ n. (pl. **-os**) **1** delicate point of ceremony or honor. **2** etiquette.

punc·til·i·ous /pungktileeəs/ adj. **1** attentive to formality or etiquette. **2** precise in behavior. □□ **punc·til'i·ous·ly** adv. **punc·til'i·ous·ness** n.

punc·tu·al /púngkchooǝl/ adj. observant of the appointed time; prompt. □□ **punc·tu·al·i·ty** /-álitee/ n. **punc'tu·al·ly** adv.

punc·tu·ate /púngkchoo-ayt/ v.tr. **1** insert punctuation marks in. **2** interrupt at intervals. **3** emphasize.

punc·tu·a·tion /púngkchoo-áyshən/ n. **1** system or arrangement of marks used to punctuate a written passage. **2** practice or skill of punctuating. □ **punctuation mark** any of the marks (e.g., period and comma) used in writing to separate sentences, etc., and to clarify meaning.

punc·ture /púngkchər/ • n. **1** piercing, as of a tire. **2** hole made in this way. • v. **1** tr. make a puncture in. **2** intr. become punctured. **3** tr. prick, pierce, or deflate.

pun·dit /púndit/ n. often iron. learned expert or teacher. □□ **pun'dit·ry** n.

pun·gent /púnjənt/ adj. **1** having a sharp or strong taste or smell. **2** (of remarks) penetrating; biting; caustic. **3** Biol. having a sharp point. □□ **pun'gen·cy** n. **pun'gent·ly** adv.

pun·ish /púnish/ v.tr. **1** cause (an offender) to suffer for an offense. **2** inflict a penalty for (an offense). **3** a tax severely. **b** hurt, abuse, or treat improperly. □□ **pun'ish·a·ble** adj. **pun'ish·er** n. **pun'ish·ing** adj. (in sense 3a).

pun·ish·ment /púnishmənt/ n. **1** act or instance of punishing; condition of being punished. **2** loss or suffering inflicted in this. **3** colloq. severe treatment or suffering.

pu·ni·tive /pyoonitiv/ adj. (also **pu·ni·to·ry** /-tawree/) inflicting or intended to inflict punishment. □□ **pu'ni·tive·ly** adv.

punk /pungk/ n. **1 a** worthless person or thing (often as a general term of abuse). **b** nonsense. **2** (in full **punk rock**) loud fast-moving form of rock music with crude and aggressive effects. **3** hoodlum or ruffian. □□ **punk'y** adj.

punt[1] /punt/ • n. flat-bottomed boat, square at both ends, propelled by a long pole. • v. **1** tr. propel (a punt) with a pole. **2** intr. & tr. travel or convey in a punt. □□ **punt'er** n.

punt[2] /punt/ • v.tr. kick (a football) after it has dropped from the hands and before it reaches the ground. • n. such a kick. □□ **punt'er** n.

pu·ny /pyoonee/ adj. (**pu·ni·er, pu·ni·est**) **1** undersized. **2** weak; feeble. **3** petty. □□ **pu'ni·ly** adv. **pu'ni·ness** n.

pup /pup/ n. **1** young dog. **2** young wolf, rat, seal, etc. □ **pup tent** small two-person tent.

pu·pa /pyoopə/ n. (pl. **pu·pae** /-pee/) insect in the stage of development between larva and imago. □□ **pu'pal** adj.

pu·pil[1] /pyoopəl/ n. person who is taught by another.

pu·pil[2] /pyoopəl/ n. dark circular opening in the center of the iris of the eye. □□ **pu'pil·lar** adj. **pu'pil·lar·y** adj.

pup·pet /púpit/ n. **1** small figure moved by various means as entertainment. **2** person controlled by another. □□ **pup'pet·ry** n.

pup·py /púpee/ n. (pl. **-pies**) **1** young dog. **2** conceited or arrogant young man. □ **puppy love** infatuation, esp. among adolescents. □□ **pup'py·hood** n. **pup'py·ish** adj.

pur·blind /pórblind/ adj. **1** partly blind. **2** obtuse; dim-witted. □□ **pur'blind·ness** n.

pur·chase /pórchis/ • v.tr. **1** buy. **2** obtain or achieve at some cost. • n. **1** buying. **2** something bought. **3** firm hold on a thing to move it or to prevent it from slipping; leverage. □□ **pur'chas·a·ble** adj. **pur'chas·er** n.

pure /pyoor/ adj. **1** unmixed; unadulterated. **2**

chaste. **3** not morally corrupt. **4** guiltless. **5** (of a subject of study) abstract; not applied. □□ **pure′ness** n.

pure·bred /pyŏ́orbred/ • adj. belonging to a recognized breed of unmixed lineage. • n. purebred animal.

purée /pyŏoráy, pyŏoée/ • n. smooth pulp of vegetables, fruit, etc. • v.tr. (**pu·rées, pu·réed**) make a purée of.

pure·ly /pyŏ́orlee/ adv. **1** in a pure manner. **2** merely; solely; exclusively.

pur·ga·tive /pɔ́rgətiv/ • adj. **1** serving to purify. **2** strongly laxative. • n. **1** purgative thing. **2** laxative.

pur·ga·to·ry /pɔ́rgətawree/ • n. (pl. **-ries**) **1** condition or supposed place of spiritual cleansing, esp. (RC Ch.) of those dying in the grace of God but having to expiate venial sins, etc. **2** place or state of temporary suffering or expiation. • adj. purifying. □□ **pur·ga·to·ri·al** /-táwreeəl/ adj.

purge /pərj/ • v.tr. **1** make physically or spiritually clean. **2** remove by cleansing. **3** rid (an organization, party, etc.) of persons regarded as undesirable. **4** empty (the bowels). • n. **1** act of purging. **2** purgative. □□ **purg′er** n.

pu·ri·fy /pyŏ́orifi/ v.tr. (**-fies, -fied**) **1** (often foll. by of, from) cleanse or make pure. **2** make ceremonially clean. **3** clear of extraneous elements. □□ **pu·ri·fi·ca′tion** n. **pu·rif·i·ca·to·ry** /-rífəkətáwree/ adj. **pu′ri·fi·er** n.

pu·rist /pyŏ́orist/ n. stickler for or advocate of scrupulous purity, esp. in language or art. □□ **pur′ism** n. **pu·ris′tic** adj.

pu·ri·tan /pyŏ́orit′n/ • n. **1** (**Puritan**) hist. member of a group of English Protestants who sought to simplify and regulate forms of worship. **2** person practicing extreme strictness in religion or morals. • adj. **1** hist. of the Puritans. **2** scrupulous and austere in religion or morals. □□ **pu′ri·tan·ism** n.

pu·ri·tan·i·cal /pyŏoritánikəl/ adj. often derog. strictly religious or moral in behavior. □□ **pu·ri·tan′i·cal·ly** adv.

pu·ri·ty /pyŏ́oritee/ n. pureness; cleanness.

purl[1] /pərl/ • n. **1** type of inverted knitting stitch. **2** chain of minute loops ornamenting edges of lace, etc. • v.tr. (also absol.) knit with a purl stitch.

purl[2] /pərl/ v.intr. (of a brook, etc.) flow with a swirling motion and babbling sound.

pur·loin /pərlóyn/ v.tr. literary steal; pilfer. □□ **pur·loin′er** n.

pur·ple /pɔ́rpəl/ • n. **1** color intermediate between red and blue. **2** purple robe, esp. as the dress of an emperor or senior magistrate. **3** (prec. by the) position of rank, authority, or privilege. • adj. of a purple color. □ **purple passage** (or **prose** or **patch**) overly ornate or elaborate literary passage. □□ **pur′plish** adj.

pur·port • v.tr. /pərpáwrt/ **1** profess; be intended to seem. **2** (of a document or speech) have as its meaning; state. • n. /pɔ́rpawrt/ ostensible meaning; sense or tenor. □□ **pur·port′ed·ly** adv.

pur·pose /pɔ́rpəs/ • n. **1** object to be attained; thing intended. **2** intention to act. **3** resolution; determination. • v.tr. have as one's purpose; design; intend. □ **on purpose** intentionally. **to no**

purpose with no result or effect. □□ **pur′pose·ful** adj. **pur′pose·ful·ly** adv. **pur′pose·ful·ness** n.

pur·pos·ive /pɔ́rpəsiv, pərpó-/ adj. **1** having or serving a purpose. **2** done with a purpose. **3** resolute; purposeful. □□ **pur′pos·ive·ly** adv. **pur′pos·ive·ness** n.

purr /pər/ • v.intr. **1** (of a cat) make a low vibratory sound expressing contentment. **2** (of machinery, etc.) make a similar sound. • n. purring sound.

purse /pərs/ • n. **1** small pouch for carrying money on the person. **2** handbag. **3** money; funds. **4** sum as a present or prize in a contest. • v.tr. pucker or contract (the lips). □ **hold the purse strings** have control of expenditure.

purs·er /pɔ́rsər/ n. officer on a ship who keeps accounts, esp. the head steward in a passenger vessel.

pur·su·ance /pərsŏóəns/ n. (foll. by of) carrying out or observance (of a plan, idea, etc.).

pur·su·ant /pərsŏóənt/ • adj. pursuing. • adv. (foll. by to) conforming to or in accordance with. □□ **pur·su′ant·ly** adv.

pur·sue /pərsŏó/ v.tr. (**pur·sues, pur·sued, pur·su·ing**) **1** follow with intent to overtake or capture or do harm to. **2** continue or proceed along (a route or course of action). **3** follow or engage in (study or other activity). **4** proceed in compliance with (a plan, etc.). **5** seek after; aim at. **6** continue to investigate or discuss (a topic). **7** seek the attention or acquaintance of (a person) persistently. □□ **pur·su′er** n.

pur·suit /pərsŏót/ n. **1** act or an instance of pursuing. **2** occupation or activity pursued. □ **in pursuit of** pursuing.

pu·ru·lent /pyŏ́orələnt, pyŏ́oryə-/ adj. of, containing, or discharging pus. □□ **pu′ru·lence** n. **pu′ru·len·cy** n. **pu′ru·lent·ly** adv.

pur·vey /pərváy/ v.tr. **1** provide or supply (articles of food) as one's business. **2** intr. (often foll. by for) **a** make provision. **b** act as supplier. □□ **pur·vey′ance** n. **pur·vey′or** n.

pur·view /pɔ́rvyŏo/ n. **1** scope or range of a document, scheme, etc. **2** range of physical or mental vision.

pus /pus/ n. thick yellowish or greenish liquid produced from infected tissue.

push /pŏosh/ • v. **1** tr. exert a force on (a thing) to move it or cause it to move away. **2** intr. exert such a force (do not push). **3** intr. & tr. **a** thrust forward or upward. **b** project or cause to project (pushes out new roots). **4** intr. move forward or make (one's way) by force or persistence. **5** intr. exert oneself, esp. to surpass others. **6** tr. urge, impel, or press (a person) hard. **7** tr. pursue or demand persistently (pushed for reform). **8** tr. promote. **9** tr. colloq. sell (a drug) illegally. • n. **1** act or instance of pushing; shove or thrust. **2** force exerted in this. **3** vigorous effort. **4** enterprise; determination to succeed. □ **push around** colloq. bully. **push button** button to be pushed esp. to operate an electrical device. **push one's luck 1** take undue risks. **2** act presumptuously. **push-up** exercise in which the body, extended and prone, is raised upward by pushing down with the hands until the arms are straight.

push·er /pŏoshər/ n. **1** colloq. illegal seller of drugs. **2** colloq. pushing or pushy person. **3** thing for pushing.

push·ing /pŏoshing/ adj. **1** pushy. **2** colloq. having nearly reached (a specified age).

push·o·ver /pŏoshōvər/ n. colloq. **1** something

that is easily done. **2** person easily overcome, persuaded, etc.

push·y /pŏoshee/ *adj.* (**push·i·er, push·i·est**) *colloq.* excessively self-assertive. □□ **push′i·ly** *adv.* **push′i·ness** *n.*

pu·sil·lan·i·mous /pyŏosilánimǝs/ *adj.* lacking courage; timid. □□ **pu·sil·la·nim·i·ty** /-lǝnímitee/ *n.* **pu·sil·lan′i·mous·ly** *adv.*

puss·y /pŏosee/ *n.* (*pl.* **-ies**) (also **puss; puss′y·cat**) *colloq.* cat. □ **pussy willow** willow with furry catkins.

puss·y·foot /pŏoseefŏot/ *v.intr.* **1** move stealthily or warily. **2** act cautiously or noncommittally. □□ **puss′y·foot′er** *n.*

pus·tule /púschŏol/ *n.* pimple containing pus. □□ **pus′tu·lar** *adj.* **pus′tu·lous** *adj.*

put /pŏot/ • *v.* (**put·ting;** *past* and *past part.* **put**) **1** *tr.* move to or cause to be in a specified place or position. **2** *tr.* bring into a specified condition, relation, or state. **3** *tr.* **a** impose or assign. **b** (foll. by *on, to*) impose or enforce the existence of (*put a stop to it*). **4** *tr.* **a** cause (a person) to go or be, habitually or temporarily (*put them at their ease*). **b** *refl.* imagine (oneself) in a specified situation (*put yourself in my shoes*). **5** *tr.* express in a specified way (*to put it mildly*). **6** *tr.* (foll. by *at*) estimate (an amount, etc.) (*put the cost at $50*). **7** *tr.* (foll. by *into*) express or translate in (words, or another language). **8** *tr.* (foll. by *into*) invest. **9** *tr.* (foll. by *on*) wager. **10** *tr.* (foll. by *to*) submit for consideration or attention (*put it to a vote*). **11** *tr.* throw (esp. a shot or weight) as sport. **12** *intr.* (of a ship, etc.) proceed in a specified direction. • *n.* **1** a throw of the shot or weight. **2** *Stock Exch.* option of selling stock or a commodity at a fixed price at a given date. • *adj.* stationary; fixed (*stay put*). □ **put across 1** make acceptable or effective. **2** express in an understandable way. **3** (often in **put it** (or **one**) **across**) achieve by deceit. **put away 1** put (a thing) back in the place where it is normally kept. **2** set (money, etc.) aside for future use. **3** *a* imprison. **b** commit to a mental institution. **4** consume (food and drink), esp. in large quantities. **put down 1** suppress by force. **2** *colloq.* snub or humiliate. **3** record or enter in writing. **4** enter the name of (a person) on a list. **5** attribute (*put it down to bad planning*). **6** put (an old or sick animal) to death. **7** preserve or store (eggs, etc.) for future use. **8** pay as a deposit. **put off 1** postpone. **2** evade (a person). **3** hinder or dissuade. **put on 1** clothe oneself with. **2** turn on (an electrical device, light, etc.). **3** stage (a play, show, etc.). **4 a** pretend to be affected by (an emotion). **b** assume; take on (a character or appearance). **5** increase one's weight by (a specified amount). **6** (foll. by *to*) make aware of or put in touch with (*put us on to their new accountant*). **put-on** *n. colloq.* deception or hoax. **put out 1 a** (often as *adj.*) disconcert or annoy. **b** (often *refl.*) inconvenience (*don't put yourself out*). **2** extinguish (a fire or light). **put up 1** build or erect. **2** can; preserve (food) for later use. **3** take or provide accommodation for (*put me up for the night*). **4** engage in (a fight, struggle, etc.) as a form of resistance. **5** offer. **6 a** present oneself for election. **b** propose for election. **7** provide (money) as a backer. **8** display (a notice). **put upon** *colloq.* take advantage of (a person). **put up with** endure; tolerate; submit to. □□ **put′ter** *n.*

pu·ta·tive /pyŏotǝtiv/ *adj.* reputed; supposed (*his putative father*). □□ **pu′ta·tive·ly** *adv.*

pu·tre·fy /pyŏotrifī/ *v.* (**-fies, -fied**) become or

---

487   pushy ~ pyrotechnics

make putrid; go bad. □□ **pu·tre·fa·cient** /-fáyshǝnt/ *adj.* **pu·tre·fac·tion** /-fákshǝn/ *n.* **pu·tre·fac·tive** /-fáktiv/ *adj.*

pu·tres·cent /pyŏotrésǝnt/ *adj.* **1** in the process of rotting. **2** of or accompanying this process. □□ **pu·tres′cence** *n.*

pu·trid /pyŏotrid/ *adj.* **1** decomposed; rotten. **2** foul; noxious. □□ **pu′trid·ly** *adv.*

putsch /pŏoch/ *n.* sudden revolution; violent uprising.

putt /put/ • *v.tr.* strike (a golf ball) gently on a putting green. • *n.* putting stroke. □ **putting green** (in golf) area of close-cropped grass around a hole. □□ **putt′ter** *n.*

put·ter /pútǝr/ *v.intr.* **1** work or occupy oneself in a desultory but pleasant manner. **2** go slowly; dawdle; loiter. □□ **put′ter·er** *n.*

put·ty /pútee/ • *n.* (*pl.* **-ties**) soft, pliable mixture used for fixing panes of glass, filling holes in woodwork, etc. • *v.tr.* (**-ties, -tied**) cover, fix, join, or fill up with putty.

putz /puts/ • *n. sl.* simple-minded foolish person. • *v.intr. sl.* (usu. foll. by *around*) move (about) or occupy oneself in an aimless or idle manner.

puz·zle /púzǝl/ • *n.* **1** difficult or confusing problem; enigma. **2** problem or toy designed to test knowledge or ingenuity. • *v.* **1** *tr.* confound or disconcert mentally. **2** *intr.* be perplexed (about). **3** *tr.* (usu. as **puzzling** *adj.*) require much thought to comprehend. □□ **puz′zle·ment** *n.* **puz′zling·ly** *adv.*

puz·zler /púzlǝr/ *n.* difficult question or problem.

Pvt. *abbr.* private.

PX *abbr.* post exchange.

pyg·my /pígmee/ *n.* (also **pig′my**) (*pl.* **-mies**) **1** member of a small people of equatorial Africa and parts of SE Asia. **2** very small person, animal, or thing. □□ **pyg·mae·an** /pigmeéǝn, pígmee-/ *adj.* (also **pyg′me·an**).

py·lon /pílon/ *n.* tall structure erected as a support (esp. for electric power cables) or boundary or decoration.

py·or·rhe·a /pīǝreéǝ/ *n.* gum disease causing shrinkage of the gums, loosening of the teeth, and discharge of pus.

pyr·a·mid /pírǝmid/ *n.* **1** monumental structure, usu. of stone, with a square base and sloping sides meeting centrally at an apex, esp. an ancient Egyptian royal tomb. **2** solid of this type with a base of three or more sides. □□ **py·ram·i·dal** /-rámid'l/ *adj.* **py·ram′i·dal·ly** *adv.* **pyr·a·mid′ic** *adj.* (also **pyr·a·mid′i·cal**). **pyr·a·mid′i·cal·ly** *adv.*

pyre /pīr/ *n.* heap of combustible material, esp. a funeral pile for burning a corpse.

Py·rex /píreks/ *n. propr.* hard heat-resistant type of glass, often used for cookware.

py·rite /pírīt/ *n.* = PYRITES.

py·rites /pīríteez, pírīts/ *n.* (in full **iron pyrites**) yellow lustrous form of iron disulfide. □□ **py·rit·ic** /-rítik/ *adj.* **py·ri·tous** /pírítǝs/ *adj.*

pyro- /pírō/ *comb. form* **1** denoting fire. **2** *Mineral.* denoting a mineral, etc., altered by heat or fiery in color.

py·ro·ma·ni·a /pírōmáyneeǝ/ *n.* obsessive desire to set fire to things. □□ **py·ro·ma′ni·ac** *n.*

py·ro·tech·nics /pírōtékniks/ *n.pl.* **1** art of making fireworks. **2** display of fireworks. **3** any brilliant display. □□ **py′·ro·tech′·nic** *adj.* **py·ro·tech′·ni·cal** *adj.*

pyr·rhic /pírik/ *adj.* (of a victory) won at too great a cost.

Py·thag·o·re·an the·o·rem /pīthágəreʹeən/ *n.* theorem that the square of the hypotenuse of a right triangle is equal to the sum of the squares of the other two sides.

py·thon /píthon, -thən/ *n.* large tropical constricting snake.

pyx /piks/ *n.* (also **pix**) *Eccl.* vessel in which the consecrated bread of the Eucharist is kept.

Qq

Q[1] /kyoo/ n. (also **q**) (pl. **Qs** or **Q's**; **q's**) seventeenth letter of the alphabet.

Q[2] abbr. (also **Q.**) **1** question. **2** Queen, Queen's.

qb abbr. quarterback.

QED abbr. QUOD ERAT DEMONSTRANDUM.

qt. abbr. quart(s).

qty. abbr. quantity.

qua /kwaa/ conj. in the capacity of; as being.

quack[1] /kwak/ ● n. harsh sound made by ducks. ● v.intr. **1** utter this sound. **2** colloq. talk loudly and foolishly.

quack[2] /kwak/ n. unqualified practitioner, esp. of medicine. □□ **quack'er•y** n. **quack'ish** adj.

quad /kwod/ n. colloq. quadrangle.

quad•ran•gle /kwódranggəl/ n. **1** four-sided plane figure, esp. a square or rectangle. **2** four-sided courtyard. □□ **quad•ran'gu•lar** adj.

quad•rant /kwódrənt/ n. **1** quarter of a circle's circumference. **2** quarter of a circle enclosed by two radii at right angles. **3** instrument for taking angular measurements.

qua•drat•ic /kwodrátik/ adj. Math. **1** involving the second and no higher power of an unknown quantity or variable (quadratic equation). **2** square.

quadri- /kwódree/ (also **quadr-** or **quadru-**) comb. form denoting four.

quad•ri•ceps /kwódriseps/ n. Anat. four-part muscle at the front of the thigh.

quad•ri•lat•er•al /kwódrilátərəl/ ● adj. having four sides. ● n. four-sided figure.

QUADRILATERALS

qua•drille /kwodríl/ n. **1** square dance containing usu. five figures. **2** music for this.

quad•ri•ple•gia /kwódriplé'ejeeə, -jə/ n. Med. paralysis of all four limbs. □□ **quad•ri•ple'gic** adj. & n.

quad•ru•ped /kwódrəped/ n. four-footed animal, esp. a mammal. □□ **quad•ru•ped•al** /-roo-pid'l/ adj.

qua•dru•ple /kwodróōpəl, -drúp-, kwódroōpəl/ ● adj. **1** fourfold. **2** having four parts. ● n. fourfold number or amount. ● v. multiply by four. □□ **qua•drup'ly** adv.

qua•dru•plet /kwodróōplit, -drúp-, kwódroōplit/ n. each of four children born at one birth.

qua•dru•pli•cate ● adj. /kwodróōplikət/ **1** fourfold. **2** of which four copies are made. ● v.tr. /-kayt/ multiply by four. □ **in quadruplicate** in four identical copies.

quag•mire /kwágmīr, kwóg-/ n. **1** soft boggy or marshy area that gives way underfoot. **2** hazardous situation.

quail[1] /kwayl/ n. (pl. same or **quails**) small game bird related to the partridge.

quail[2] /kwayl/ v.intr. flinch; be apprehensive with fear.

quaint /kwaynt/ adj. piquantly or attractively odd or old-fashioned. □□ **quaint'ly** adv. **quaint'ness** n.

> **quaint** Middle English: from Old French cointe, from Latin cognitus 'ascertained,' past participle of cognoscere 'to know, understand.' The original sense was 'wise, clever,' also 'marked by ingenuity or cunning; intricate,' hence 'out of the ordinary,' giving rise to the current sense (late 18th century)

quake /kwayk/ ● v.intr. shake; tremble. ● n. colloq. earthquake. □□ **quak'y** adj. (**quak•i•er, quak•i•est**).

Quak•er /kwáykər/ n. member of the Society of Friends, a Christian movement devoted to peaceful principles and eschewing formal ritual. □□ **Quak'er•ish** adj. **Quak'er•ism** n.

qual•i•fi•ca•tion /kwólifikáyshən/ n. **1** act or instance of qualifying. **2** (often in pl.) quality, skill, or accomplishment fitting a person for a position or purpose. **3** thing that modifies or limits.

qual•i•fy /kwólifī/ v. (**-fies, -fied**) **1** tr. make competent or fit for a position or purpose. **2** tr. make legally entitled. **3** intr. satisfy conditions or requirements. **4** tr. add reservations to; modify or make less absolute (a statement or assertion). □□ **qual'i•fi•er** n.

qual•i•ta•tive /kwólitaytiv/ adj. concerned with or depending on quality. □□ **qual'i•ta•tive•ly** adv.

qual•i•ty /kwólitee/ n. (pl. **-ties**) **1** degree of excellence. **2** general excellence. **3** distinctive attribute or faculty. **4** relative nature or kind or character of a thing. □ **quality control** system of maintaining standards in manufactured products.

qualm /kwaam, kwawm/ n. **1** misgiving; uneasy doubt esp. about one's own conduct. **2** scruple of conscience. **3** momentary faint or sick feeling.

quan•da•ry /kwóndəree, -dree/ n. (pl. **-ries**) **1** state of perplexity. **2** difficult situation; practical dilemma.

quan•ti•fy /kwóntifī/ v.tr. (**-fies, -fied**) **1** determine the quantity of. **2** measure or express as a quantity. □□ **quan'ti•fi•a•ble** adj. **quan•ti•fi•ca'tion** n. **quan'ti•fi•er** n.

quan•ti•ta•tive /kwóntitaytiv/ adj. pertaining to quantity. □□ **quan'ti•ta•tive•ly** adv.

quan•ti•ty /kwóntitee/ n. (pl. **-ties**) **1** property of

things that is measurable. **2** amount; number.
3 specified or considerable portion or number
or amount. **4** (in *pl.*) large amounts or numbers
(*quantities of food*). **5** *Math.* value, component,
etc., that may be expressed in numbers.

quan·tum /kwóntəm/ *n.* (*pl.* **quan·ta** /-tə/) **1**
Physics discrete quantity of radiant energy. **2**
required or allowed amount. □ **quantum jump**
(or **leap**) **1** sudden large increase or advance.
2 *Physics* abrupt transition in an atom or molecule from one quantum state to another. **quantum mechanics** (or **theory**) *Physics* system or
theory using the assumption that energy exists
in discrete units.

quar·an·tine /kwáwrənteen, kwór-/ • *n.* **1** isolation imposed on persons or animals to prevent infection or contagion. **2** period of this. •
v.tr. put in quarantine.

quark /kwawrk, kwaark/ *n.* *Physics* any of several
postulated components of elementary particles.

quar·rel /kwáwrəl, kwór-/ • *n.* **1** usu. verbal
contention or altercation. **2** occasion of complaint or dispute. • *v.intr.* **1** find fault. **2** dispute;
break off friendly relations. □□ **quar'rel·er** *n.*

quar·rel·some /kwáwrəlsəm, kwór-/ *adj.* given
to quarreling. □□ **quar'rel·some·ly** *adv.* **quar'
rel·some·ness** *n.*

quar·ry[1] /kwáwree, kwór-/ • *n.* (*pl.* **-ries**) place
from which stone, etc., may be extracted. • *v.tr.*
(**-ries, -ried**) extract (stone) from a quarry.

quar·ry[2] /kwáwree, kwór-/ • *n.* (*pl.* **-ries**) **1** object of pursuit by a bird of prey, hunters, etc. **2**
intended victim or prey.

---

quarry[2] Middle English: from Old French
cuiree, an alteration, influenced by *cuir*
'leather' and *curer* 'clean, disembowel,'
which is based on Latin *cor* 'heart.' Originally the term denoted the parts of a deer
that, after a hunt, were placed on the hide
and given as a reward to the hounds.

---

quart /kwawrt/ *n.* **1** liquid measure equal to a
quarter of a gallon; two pints (.95 liter). **2** unit
of dry measure, equivalent to one thirty-second
of a bushel (1.1 liter).

quar·ter /kwáwrtər/ • *n.* **1** each of four equal
parts into which a thing is or might be divided.
2 period of three months. **3 a** 25 cents. **b** coin
of this denomination. **4** district or section. **5**
source of supply (*help from any quarter*). **6** (in
pl.) **a** lodgings; abode. **b** *Mil.* living accommodation of troops, etc. **7** mercy offered or granted
to an enemy in battle, etc., on condition of
surrender. • *v.tr.* **1** divide into quarters. **2 a** put
(troops, etc.) into quarters. **b** station or lodge
in a specified place.

quar·ter·back /kwáwrtərbak/ *Football n.* player
who directs offensive play.

quar·ter·deck /kwáwrtərdek/ *n.* part of a ship's
upper deck near the stern, usu. reserved for
officers.

quar·ter·fi·nal /kwáwrtərfínˈl/ *Sports n.* match
or round immediately preceding a semifinal.

quar·ter·ly /kwáwrtərlee/ • *adj.* produced, payable, or occurring once every quarter of a year.
• *adv.* once every quarter of a year. • *n.* (*pl.*
-lies) quarterly journal.

quar·ter·mas·ter /kwáwrtərmastər/ *n.* **1** army
officer in charge of quartering, rations, etc. **2**

naval petty officer in charge of steering, signals, etc.

quar·tet /kwawrtét/ *n.* **1** *Mus.* **a** composition for
four performers. **b** the performers. **2** any group
of four.

quar·to /kwáwrtō/ *n.* (*pl.* **-tos**) *Printing* **1** size
given by folding a (usu. specified) sheet of pa-
per twice. **2** book consisting of sheets folded in
this way. ¶ Abbr.: **4to.**

quartz /kwawrts/ *n.* mineral form of silica that
crystallizes as hexagonal prisms.

qua·sar /kwáyzaar, -zər, -saar, -sər/ *n.* *Astron.*
starlike celestial object having a spectrum with
a large red shift.

quash /kwosh/ *v.tr.* **1** annul; reject as not valid,
esp. by a legal procedure. **2** suppress; crush (a
rebellion, etc.).

quasi- /kwáyzī, kwáazee/ *comb. form* **1** seemingly;
not really (*quasi-scientific*). **2** almost (*quasi-
independent*).

qua·ter·na·ry /kwótərneree, kwətórnəree/ •
adj. **1** having four parts. **2** (**Quaternary**) *Geol.* of
the most recent period in the Cenozoic era. •
n. (**Quaternary**) *Geol.* this period.

quat·rain /kwótrayn/ *n.* stanza of four lines.

qua·ver /kwáyvər/ • *v.* **1** *intr.* (esp. of a voice
or musical sound) vibrate; shake; tremble. **2** *tr.*
sing or say with a quavering voice. • *n.* **1** trill in
singing. **2** tremble in speech. □□ **qua'ver·ing·ly**
adv. **qua'ver·y** *adj.*

quay /kee, kay/ *n.* solid, stationary, artificial landing place for loading and unloading ships.
□□ **quay'age** *n.*

quea·sy /kwéezee/ *adj.* (**-si·er, -si·est**) **1 a** (of a
person) feeling nausea. **b** (of a person's stomach) easily upset; weak of digestion. **2** (of the
conscience, etc.) overscrupulous; tender.
□□ **quea'si·ly** *adv.* **quea'si·ness** *n.*

Quech·ua /kéchwə, -waa/ *n.* **1** member of a central Peruvian native people. **2** S. American native language widely spoken in Peru and neighboring countries. □□ **Quech'uan** *adj.*

queen /kween/ *n.* **1** (as a title usu. **Queen**) female sovereign. **2** (in full **queen consort**) king's
wife. **3** woman, country, or thing preeminent of
its kind (*tennis queen*). **4** fertile female among
ants, bees, etc. **5** most powerful piece in chess. **6**
playing card with a picture of a queen. □ **queen
bee 1** fertile female in a hive. **2** chief or controlling woman in an organization or social group.
□□ **queen'less** *adj.* **queen'like** *adj.*

queen·ly /kwéenlee/ *adj.* (**queen·li·er, queen·
li·est**) **1** fit for or appropriate to a queen. **2**
majestic. □□ **queen'li·ness** *n.*

queer /kweer/ • *adj.* **1** strange; odd; eccentric.
2 *derog. sl.* homosexual. • *n. derog. sl.* homosexual. • *v.tr. sl.* spoil; put out of order. □□
queer'ish *adj.* **queer'ly** *adv.* **queer'ness** *n.*

quell /kwel/ *v.tr.* **1** crush or put down (a rebellion, etc.). **2** suppress (fear, anger, etc.).
□□ **quell'er** *n.* (also in *comb.*).

quench /kwench/ *v.tr.* **1** satisfy (thirst) by drinking. **2** extinguish (a fire or light, etc.). **3** cool,
esp. with water. □□ **quench'a·ble** *adj.* **quench'er**
n. **quench'less** *adj.*

quer·u·lous /kwérələs, kwéryə-/ *adj.*
complaining; peevish. □□ **quer'u·lous·ly** *adj.*
quer'u·lous·ness *n.*

que·ry /kwéeree/ • *n.* (*pl.* **-ries**) **1** question. **2**
question mark. • *v.tr.* (**-ries, -ried**) **1** ask or
inquire. **2** call (a thing) in question.

quest /kwest/ *n.* search or the act of seeking. □□ **quest′er** *n.* **quest′ing·ly** *adv.*

ques·tion /kwéschən/ • *n.* **1** sentence worded or expressed so as to seek information. **2** doubt or dispute about a matter **3** matter to be discussed or decided or voted on. **4** problem requiring an answer or solution. • *v.tr.* **1** ask questions of; interrogate. **2** throw doubt upon; raise objections to. □ **call in** (or **into**) **question** make a matter of dispute; query. **in question** that is being discussed or referred to. **out of the question** too impracticable, etc., to be worth discussing; impossible. **question mark** punctuation mark (?) indicating a question. □□ **ques′tion·er** *n.* **ques′tion·ing·ly** *adv.* **ques′tion·less** *adj.*

ques·tion·a·ble /kwéschənəbəl/ *adj.* doubtful as regards truth, quality, honesty, wisdom, etc. □□ **ques′tion·a·ble·ness** *n.* **ques′tion·a·bly** *adv.*

ques·tion·naire /kwéschənáir/ *n.* written series of questions, esp. for statistical study.

queue /kyōō/ • *n.* **1** line or sequence of persons, vehicles, etc., awaiting their turn. **2** pigtail or braid of hair. • *v.intr.* (**queues, queued, queu·ing** or **queue·ing**) esp. *Brit.* line (up).

quib·ble /kwíbəl/ • *n.* **1** petty objection; trivial point of criticism. **2** play on words; pun. **3** evasion; insubstantial argument which relies on an ambiguity, etc. • *v.intr.* use quibbles. □□ **quib′bler** *n.* **quib′bling** *adj.* **quib′bling·ly** *adv.*

quiche /keesh/ *n.* unsweetened custard pie with a savory filling.

quick /kwik/ • *adj.* **1** taking only a short time. **2** arriving after a short time; prompt. **3** with only a short interval (*in quick succession*). **4** lively; intelligent; alert. **5** (of a temper) easily roused. **6** *archaic* alive (*the quick and the dead*). • *adv.* quickly. • *n.* **1** soft flesh below the nails, or the skin, or a sore. **2** seat of feeling or emotion (*cut to the quick*). □ **quick-tempered** quick to lose one's temper; irascible. □□ **quick′ly** *adv.* **quick′ness** *n.*

---

quick Old English *cwic, cwicu* 'alive, animated, alert' (hence the sense in the biblical phrase "the quick and the dead"), of Germanic origin; related to Dutch *kwiek* 'sprightly' and German *keck* 'saucy,' from an Indo-European root shared by Latin *vivus* 'alive' and Greek *bios* 'life.'

---

quick·en /kwíkən/ *v.* **1** *tr.* & *intr.* make or become quicker; accelerate. **2** *tr.* give life or vigor to; rouse.

quick·ie /kwíkee/ *n. colloq.* thing done or made quickly.

quick·lime /kwíklīm/ *n.* = LIME¹ *n.* 1.

quick·sand /kwíksand/ *n.* **1** loose wet sand that sucks in anything placed or falling into it. **2** bed of this.

quick·sil·ver /kwíksilvər/ *n.* mercury.

quick-wit·ted /kwíkwítid/ *adj.* quick to grasp a situation, make repartee, etc. □□ **quick′-wit′ted·ness** *n.*

quid pro quo /kwíd prō kwó/ *n.* **1** thing given as compensation. **2** return made (for a gift, favor, etc.).

qui·es·cent /kwiésənt, kwee-/ *adj.* **1** inert. **2** silent; dormant. □□ **qui·es′cence** *n.* **qui·es′cent·ly** *adv.*

qui·et /kwíət/ • *adj.* (**qui·et·er, qui·et·est**) **1** with little or no sound or motion. **2** of gentle or peaceful disposition. **3** unobtrusive; not

---

491   quest ~ quiz

overt. **4** undisturbed; uninterrupted. **5** enjoyed in quiet (*a quiet smoke*). **6** tranquil; not anxious or remorseful. • *n.* **1** silence; stillness. **2** undisturbed state; tranquillity. • *v.* **1** *tr.* soothe; make quiet. **2** *intr.* (often foll. by *down*) become quiet or calm. □□ **qui′et·ly** *adv.* **qui′et·ness** *n.*

qui·e·tude /kwí-itōōd, -tyōōd/ *n.* state of quiet.

qui·e·tus /kwī-éetəs/ *n.* **1** something which quiets or represses. **2** discharge or release from life; death; final riddance.

quill /kwil/ *n.* **1** large feather in a wing or tail. **2** hollow stem of this. **3** (in full **quill pen**) pen made of a quill. **4** (usu. in *pl.*) spine of a porcupine.

quilt /kwilt/ • *n.* bedcovering made of padding enclosed between layers of cloth, etc., and kept in place by patterned stitching. • *v.tr.* make quilts. □□ **quilt′er** *n.* **quilt′ing** *n.*

quince /kwins/ *n.* **1** hard acidic pear-shaped fruit used chiefly in preserves. **2** tree bearing this fruit.

qui·nine /kwínīn, kwín-/ *n.* **1** alkaloid found esp. in cinchona bark. **2** bitter drug containing this, used as a tonic and to reduce fever.

quin·tes·sence /kwintésəns/ *n.* purest and most perfect, or most typical, form, manifestation, or embodiment of some quality or class. □□ **quin·tes·sen′tial** /kwíntisénshəl/ *adj.* **quin·tes·sen′tial·ly** *adv.*

quin·tet /kwintét/ *n.* **1** *Mus.* **a** composition for five. **b** the performers. **2** any group of five.

quin·tu·ple /kwintōōpəl, -tyōō-, -túpəl, kwíntə-pəl/ • *adj.* fivefold; consisting of five parts. • *n.* fivefold number or amount. • *v.* multiply by five.

quin·tu·plet /kwintúplit, -tōō-, -tyōō-, kwíntə-/ *n.* each of five children born at one birth.

quip /kwip/ • *n.* clever saying; epigram. • *v.intr.* (**quipped, quip·ping**) make quips. □□ **quip′ster** *n.*

quire /kwīr/ *n.* 25 (also 24) sheets of paper.

quirk /kwərk/ *n.* **1** peculiarity of behavior. **2** trick of fate; freak. □□ **quirk′ish** *adj.* **quirk′y** *adj.* (**quirk·i·er, quirk·i·est**) **quirk′i·ly** *adv.* **quirk′i·ness** *n.*

quis·ling /kwízling/ *n.* traitorous collaborator.

quit /kwit/ *v.tr.* (**quit·ting**; *past* and *past part.* **quit** or **quit·ted**) **1** (also *absol.*) give up; let go; abandon (a task, etc.). **2** cease; stop (*quit grumbling*). **3** leave or depart from.

quite /kwīt/ *adv.* **1** completely; entirely. **2** rather; to some extent. □ **quite a few** *colloq.* a fairly large number of.

quits /kwits/ *predic.adj.* on even terms by retaliation or repayment (*then we'll be quits*). □ **call it quits** agree not to proceed further in a quarrel, etc.

quit·ter /kwítər/ *n.* **1** person who gives up easily. **2** shirker.

quiv·er¹ /kwívər/ • *v.intr.* tremble or vibrate with a slight rapid motion. • *n.* quivering motion or sound. □□ **quiv′er·ing·ly** *adv.* **quiv′er·y** *adj.*

quiv·er² /kwívər/ *n.* case for holding arrows.

quix·ot·ic /kwiksótik/ *adj.* **1** extravagantly and romantically chivalrous. **2** visionary; pursuing lofty but unattainable ideals. **3** *derog.* foolhardy. □□ **quix·ot′i·cal·ly** *adv.*

quiz /kwiz/ • *n.* (*pl.* **quiz·zes**) **1** quick or informal test. **2** (also **quiz show**) test of knowledge, esp. as a form of entertainment. • *v.tr.* (**quizzed**, **quiz•zing**) examine by questioning.

quiz•zi•cal /kwízikəl/ *adj.* **1** expressing or done with mild or amused perplexity. **2** strange; comical. □□ **quiz′zi•cal•ly** *adv.*

quod e•rat de•mon•stran•dum /kwod érət démənstrándəm, éraat démōnstra'andōōm/ (esp. at the conclusion of a proof, etc.) which was the thing to be proved. ¶ Abbr.: **QED**.

quod vi•de /kwod vé′eday, vídee/ which see (in cross-references, etc.). ¶ Abbr.: **q.v.**

quoin /koyn, kwoin/ *n.* **1** external angle of a building. **2** cornerstone. **3** wedge.

quoit /koyt, kwoit/ *n.* **1** ring of rope or metal, etc., thrown to encircle a peg. **2** (in *pl.*) game using these.

quon•dam /kwóndəm, -dam/ *predic.adj.* that once was; sometime; former.

Quon•set hut /kwónsit/ *n. propr.* prefabricated metal building with a semicylindrical corrugated roof.

QUONSET HUT

quo•rum /kwáwrəm/ *n.* minimum number of members that must be present to constitute a valid meeting.

quo•ta /kwótə/ *n.* **1** share that an individual person, group, or company is bound to contribute to or entitled to receive from a total. **2** number of goods, people etc., stipulated or permitted.

quot•a•ble /kwótəbəl/ *adj.* worth, or suitable for, quoting.

quo•ta•tion /kwōtáyshən/ *n.* **1** act or an instance of quoting or being quoted. **2** passage or remark quoted. **3** *Stock Exch.* amount stated as the current price of stocks or commodities. **4** contractor's estimate. □ **quotation mark** raised marks, single (' ') or double (" "), used to mark a quoted passage, for emphasis, etc.

quote /kwōt/ • *v.tr.* **1** cite or appeal to (an author, book, etc.) in confirmation of some view. **2** repeat or copy out a passage from. **3** (as *int.*) (in dictation, reading aloud, etc.) indicate the presence of opening quotation marks (*he said, quote, "I shall stay"*). **4** state the price of. • *n. colloq.* **1** passage quoted. **2** price quoted. **3** (usu. in *pl.*) quotation marks.

quoth /kwōth/ *v.tr.* (only in 1st and 3rd person) *archaic* said.

quo•tid•i•an /kwotídeeən/ *adj.* **1** daily; of every day. **2** commonplace; trivial.

quo•tient /kwóshənt/ *n.* result of a division.

q.v. *abbr.* quod vide.

qwerty /kwə́rtee/ *attrib.adj.* denoting the standard keyboard on English-language typewriters, word processors, etc.

Rr

R[1] /aar/ *n.* (also **r**) (*pl.* **Rs** or **R's**; **r's**) eighteenth letter of the alphabet.

R[2] *abbr.* **1** (also **R.**) river. **2** *Chess* rook. **3** (of movies) classified as prohibited to children under age 17 unless accompanied by an adult.

r. *abbr.* (also **r**) **1** right. **2** recto. **3** run(s). **4** radius.

Ra *symb. Chem.* radium.

rab·bet /rábit/ • *n.* step-shaped channel, etc., cut into wood, etc., usu. to receive the edge or tongue of another piece. • *v.tr.* **1** join or fix with a rabbet. **2** make a rabbet in.

rab·bi /rábī/ *n.* (*pl.* **rabbis**) **1** Jewish scholar or teacher, esp. of the law. **2** Jewish religious leader. □□ **rab·bin·i·cal** /rəbínikəl/ *adj.*

rab·bit /rábit/ *n.* **1** long-eared, burrowing, plant-eating mammal related to the hare. **2** its fur. □ **rabbit ears** television antenna consisting of two movable rods, usu. on top of the set. **rabbit punch** chopping blow to the nape of the neck.

rab·ble /rábəl/ *n.* **1** disorderly crowd; mob. **2** contemptible or inferior set of people. □ **rabble-rouser** person who stirs up the rabble or a crowd.

ra·bid /rábid/ *adj.* **1** furious; violent. **2** fanatical. **3** affected with rabies; mad. □□ **ra·bid·i·ty** *n.* **ra·bid·ly** *adv.* **ra·bid·ness** *n.*

ra·bies /ráybeez/ *n.* contagious and fatal viral disease, esp. of dogs, cats, raccoons, etc., transmissible through saliva to humans; hydrophobia.

rac·coon /rakó̄on/ *n.* **1** N. American nocturnal mammal with a bushy, ringed tail and masklike band across the eyes. **2** its fur.

race[1] /rays/ • *n.* **1** contest of speed between runners, horses, vehicles, etc. **2** contest between persons to be first to achieve something. **3 a** strong sea or river current. **b** channel with a swift current. **4** each of two grooved rings in a ball bearing or roller bearing. • *v.* **1** *intr.* take part in a race. **2** *tr.* have a race with. **3** *tr.* cause to race. **4 a** *intr.* go at full or excessive speed. **b** *tr.* cause to do this. □□ **rac·er** *n.*

race[2] /rays/ *n.* **1** each of the major divisions of humankind, having distinct physical characteristics. **2** fact or concept of division into races. **3** genus, species, breed, or variety of animals or plants. □ **race relations** relations between members of different races, usu. in the same country.

race·horse /ráys-hors/ *n.* horse bred or kept for racing.

ra·ceme /rayse'em, rə–/ *n. Bot.* flower cluster with separate flowers attached by short stalks at equal distances along the stem.

race·track /ráystrak/ *n.* track for horse, automobile, etc.

ra·cial /ráyshəl/ *adj.* **1** of or concerning race. **2** on the grounds of or connected with difference in race (*racial discrimination*). □□ **ra·cial·ly** *adv.*

rac·ism /ráysizəm/ *n.* **1** belief in the superiority of a particular race; prejudice based on this. **2** antagonism toward other races. □□ **rac·ist** *n. & adj.*

rack[1] /rak/ • *n.* **1** framework usu. with rails, bars, etc., for holding things. **2** cogged or toothed bar or rail engaging with a wheel or pinion, etc. **3** *hist.* instrument of torture used to stretch the victim's limbs. • *v.tr.* **1** (of disease or pain) inflict suffering on. **2** place in or on a rack. □ **on the rack** in distress or under strain. **rack one's brains** make a great mental effort. **rack up** accumulate or achieve (a score, etc.).

rack[2] /rak/ *n.* destruction (esp. *rack and ruin*).

rack[3] /rak/ *n.* cut of lamb, etc., including the front ribs.

rack·et[1] /rákit/ *n.* (also **rac·quet**) hand-held implement with a round or oval frame strung with catgut, nylon, etc., used in tennis, squash, etc.

rack·et[2] /rákit/ *n.* **1** uproar; din. **2** *sl.* scheme for obtaining money, etc., by fraudulent and often violent means. **3** *colloq.* line of business.

rack·e·teer /rákite'er/ *n.* person who operates an illegal business, as gambling, extortion, etc. □□ **rack·et·eer·ing** *n.*

ra·con·teur /rákontór/ *n.* (*fem.* **ra·con·teuse** /–tőz/) teller of interesting anecdotes.

rac·quet var. of RACKET[1].

rac·quet·ball /rákitbawl/ *n.* racket game played on a four-walled court.

rac·y /ráysee/ *adj.* (**rac·i·er**, **rac·i·est**) **1** lively and vigorous in style. **2** risqué; suggestive. **3** of distinctive quality (*racy flavor*). □□ **rac·i·ly** *adv.* **rac·i·ness** *n.*

rad[1] /rad/ *n.* unit of absorbed dose of ionizing radiation.

rad[2] /rad/ • *n. sl.* political radical. • *adj. sl.* wonderful; terrific.

ra·dar /ráydaar/ *n.* system for detecting the direction, range, or presence of objects by reflection of transmitted radio waves (acronym of *radio detecting* and *ranging*).

ra·di·al /ráydeeəl/ • *adj.* **1** of or in rays. **2 a** arranged like rays or radii. **b** having spokes or radiating lines. **3** (of a tire) having fabric layers laid radially at right angles to the center of the tread. • *n.* radial tire. □□ **ra·di·al·ly** *adv.*

ra·di·ant /ráydeeənt/ *adj.* **1** emitting rays of light or energy. **2** (of eyes or looks) beaming with joy, hope, or love. **3** (of beauty) splendid or dazzling. □ **radiant heat** heat transmitted by radiation. □□ **ra·di·ance** *n.* **ra·di·ant·ly** *adv.*

ra·di·ate *v.* /ráydeeayt/ **1** *intr.* **a** emit rays of light, heat, etc. **b** (of light or heat) be emitted in rays. **2** *tr.* emit (light, heat, or sound) from a center. **3** *tr.* transmit or demonstrate (joy, etc.). **4** *intr. & tr.* diverge or cause to diverge or spread from a center.

ra·di·a·tion /ráydeeáyshən/ *n.* **1** radiating; being radiated. **2** *Physics* **a** emission of energy as electromagnetic waves or as moving particles. **b** energy thus transmitted. **3** (in full **ra·di·a·tion ther·a·py**) treatment of disease using radiation, such as X rays or ultraviolet light. □□ **ra·di·a·tion·al** *adj.* **ra·di·a·tion·al·ly** *adv.*

ra·di·a·tor /ráydeeaytər/ *n.* **1** person or thing

that radiates. **2** device through which hot water or steam circulates to heat a room, etc. **3** engine-cooling device in a motor vehicle, etc.

rad·i·cal /rádikəl/ • *adj.* **1** primary; fundamental. **2** far-reaching; thorough. **3** representing or holding extreme political views; revolutionary. **4** *Math.* of the root of a number or quantity. • *n.* **1** person holding radical views or belonging to a radical party. **2** *Chem.* **a** atom with one or more unpaired electrons. **b** element or atom normally forming part of a compound and remaining unaltered during ordinary chemical changes. **3** *Math.* quantity forming or expressed as the root of another. □ **radical sign** √ , √ ³, etc., indicating the square, cube, etc., root of the number following. □□ **rad′i·cal·ism** *n.* **rad′i·cal·ly** *adv.*

ra·dic·chi·o /rədéekeeō/ *n.* (*pl.* **–os**) variety of chicory with dark red leaves.

rad·i·ces *pl.* of RADIX.

ra·di·i *pl.* of RADIUS.

ra·di·o /ráydeeō/ • *n.* (*pl.* **–os**) **1** (often *attrib.*) **a** transmission and reception of sound messages, etc., by electromagnetic waves of radio frequency. **b** apparatus for this. **2** sound broadcasting (*prefers the radio*). • *v.* (**–oed**) **1** *tr.* **a** send (a message) by radio. **b** send a message to (a person) by radio. **2** *intr.* communicate or broadcast by radio. □ **radio frequency** frequency band of telecommunication, ranging from 10⁴ to 10¹¹ or 10¹² Hz. **radio star** small star, etc., emitting strong radio waves. **radio telescope** directional aerial system for collecting and analyzing radiation in the radio-frequency range from stars, etc.

radio- /ráydeeō/ *comb. form* **1** denoting radio or broadcasting. **2** connected with radioactivity. **3** connected with rays or radiation.

ra·di·o·ac·tive /ráydeeō-áktiv/ *adj.* of or exhibiting radioactivity. □□ **ra·di·o·ac′tive·ly** *adv.*

ra·di·o·ac·tiv·i·ty /ráydeeō-aktívitee/ *n.* spontaneous disintegration of atomic nuclei, with emission of radiation or particles.

ra·di·ol·o·gy /ráydeeóləjee/ *n.* the study of X rays and other high-energy radiation, esp. as used in medicine. □□ **ra·di·o·log·ic** /–deeəlójik/ *adj.* **ra·di·o·log′i·cal** *adj.* **ra·di·ol′o·gist** *n.*

ra·di·om·e·ter /ráydeeómitər/ *n.* instrument for measuring the intensity or force of radiation. □□ **ra·di·om′e·try** *n.*

RADIOMETER

ra·di·os·co·py /ráydeeóskəpee/ *n.* examination by X rays, etc., of objects opaque to light. □□ **ra·di·o·scop·ic** /–deeəskópik/ *adj.*

ra·di·o·ther·a·py /ráydeeōthérəpee/ *n.* radiation therapy (see RADIATION). □□ **ra·di·o·ther·a·peu·tic** /–pyóótik/ *adj.* **ra·di·o·ther′a·pist** *n.*

rad·ish /rádish/ *n.* **1** plant with a fleshy pungent root. **2** this root, eaten esp. raw.

ra·di·um /ráydeeəm/ *n.* *Chem.* radioactive metallic element orig. obtained from pitchblende, etc. ¶ Symb.: **Ra**.

ra·di·us /ráydeeəs/ *n.* (*pl.* **ra·di·i** /–dee-ī/ or **ra·di·us·es**) **1** *Math.* **a** straight line from the center to the circumference of a circle or sphere. **b** length of this. **2** distance from a center (*within a radius of 20 miles*). **3 a** thicker and shorter of the two bones in the human forearm. **b** corresponding bone in a vertebrate's foreleg or a bird's wing.

RADIUS, 1a

ra·dix /ráydiks/ *n.* (*pl.* **rad·i·ces** /–diseez/ or **ra·dix·es**) *Math.* number or symbol used as the basis of a numeration scale (e.g., ten in the decimal system).

ra·don /ráydon/ *n.* *Chem.* gaseous radioactive inert element arising from the disintegration of radium. ¶ Symb.: **Rn**.

RAF *abbr.* (in the UK) Royal Air Force.

raf·fi·a /ráfeeə/ *n.* **1** palm tree native to Madagascar, having very long leaves. **2** fiber from its leaves used for weaving, tying plants, etc.

raf·fish /ráfish/ *adj.* **1** disreputable; rakish. **2** tawdry. □□ **raf′fish·ly** *adv.* **raf′fish·ness** *n.*

raf·fle /ráfəl/ • *n.* fund-raising lottery with prizes. • *v.tr.* (often foll. by *off*) sell by means of a raffle.

raft¹ /raft/ • *n.* **1** flat floating structure of logs or other materials for conveying persons or things. **2** lifeboat or small (often inflatable) boat. • *v.* **1** *tr.* cross (water) on a raft. **2** *intr.* (often foll. by *across*) work a raft (across water, etc.).

raft² /raft/ *n.* *colloq.* large collection.

raft·er /ráftər/ *n.* each of the sloping beams forming the framework of a roof.

rag¹ /rag/ *n.* **1** torn, frayed, or worn piece of woven material. **2** (in *pl.*) old or worn clothes. **3** *derog.* newspaper. □ **in rags 1** much torn. **2** in old torn clothes. **rag bag 1** bag for scraps of fabric, etc. **2** miscellaneous collection. **rag doll** stuffed doll made of cloth. **rag paper** paper made from cotton or linen pulp. **rags to riches** poverty to affluence.

rag² /rag/ *v.tr.* (**rag·ged, rag·ging**) **1** tease; play rough jokes on. **2** scold; reprove severely.

rag³ /rag/ *n.* *Mus.* ragtime composition or tune.

rag·a·muf·fin /rágəmufin/ n. child in ragged dirty clothes.

rage /rayj/ • n. **1** fierce or violent anger. **2** fit of this. **3** violent action of a natural force. **4** temporary enthusiasm; fad. • v.intr. **1** be full of anger. **2** speak furiously or madly. **3** (of wind, battle, fever, etc.) be violent; be at its height; continue unchecked. □ **all the rage** popular; fashionable.

rag·ged /rágid/ adj. **1** torn; frayed. **2** in ragged clothes. **3** with a broken or jagged outline or surface. **4** lacking finish, smoothness, or uniformity. **5** exhausted (esp. *be run ragged*). □ **run ragged** exhaust; wear out. □□ **rag′ged·ly** adv. **rag′ged·ness** n. **rag′ged·y** adj.

rag·lan /ráglən/ n. (often *attrib.*) overcoat without shoulder seams, the sleeves running up to the neck.

ra·gout /ragóō/ n. meat stewed with vegetables and highly seasoned.

rag·pick·er /rágpikər/ n. collector and seller of rags.

rag·tag /rágtag/ adj. motley.

rag·time /rágtīm/ n. form of highly syncopated early jazz, esp. for the piano.

rag·weed /rágweed/ n. any of various plants with allergenic pollen.

rah /raa/ int. *colloq.* expression of encouragement, approval, etc., esp. to a team or a player.

raid /rayd/ • n. rapid surprise attack, esp.: **1** in warfare. **2** to commit a crime or do harm. **3** by police, etc., to arrest suspects or seize illicit goods. • v.tr. make a raid on. □□ **raid′er** n.

rail¹ /rayl/ • n. **1** level or sloping bar or series of bars: **a** used to hang things on. **b** as the top of a banister. **c** forming part of a fence or barrier. **2** steel bar or continuous line of bars laid on the ground, usu. as a railroad. **3** (often *attrib.*) railroad (*send it by rail*). • v.tr. **1** furnish with a rail or rails. **2** enclose with rails.

rail² /rayl/ v.intr. complain using abusive language; rant. □□ **rail′er** n. **rail′ing** n. & adj.

rail³ /rayl/ n. wading bird often inhabiting marshes.

rail·ing /ráyling/ n. **1** fence or barrier made of rails. **2** material for these.

rail·ler·y /ráyləree/ n. (*pl.* **–ies**) good-humored ridicule.

rail·road /ráylrōd/ • n. **1** track or set of tracks of steel rails upon which trains run. **2** such a system. • v.tr. rush or coerce (a person or thing) (*railroaded me into going*).

rail·way /ráylway/ n. = RAILROAD.

rai·ment /ráymənt/ n. *archaic* clothing.

rain /rayn/ • n. **1 a** condensed atmospheric moisture falling in drops. **b** fall of such drops. **2** (in *pl.*) **a** rainfalls. **b** (prec. by *the*) rainy season. **3** rainlike falling of liquid, particles, objects, etc. • v. **1** intr. (prec. by *it* as subject) rain falls (*if it rains*). **2 a** intr. fall like rain. **b** tr. (prec. by *it* as subject) send in large quantities (*it rained blood*). **3** tr. lavishly bestow. **4** intr. (of the sky, etc.) send down rain. □ **rain check 1** ticket given for later use when an outdoor event is canceled by rain. **2** promise that an offer will be maintained though deferred. **rain date** date on which an event postponed by rain is held. **rain forest** luxuriant tropical forest with heavy rainfall. **rain gauge** instrument measuring rainfall. **rain out** (esp. in *passive*) cause (an event, etc.) to be canceled because of rain. □□ **rain′y** adj. (**rain·i·er**, **rain·i·est**).

rain·bow /ráynbō/ • n. arch of colors formed by reflection, refraction, and dispersion of the sun's rays in rain or mist. • adj. many-colored. □ **rainbow trout** large Pacific coast trout of N. America.

rain·coat /ráynkōt/ n. waterproof or water-resistant coat.

rain·drop /ráyndrop/ n. single drop of rain.

rain·fall /ráynfawl/ n. **1** fall of rain. **2** quantity of rain falling within a given area in a given time.

rain·proof /ráynprōof/ adj. resistant to rainwater.

rain·storm /ráynstawrm/ n. storm with heavy rain.

rain·water /ráynwawtər, –wotər/ n. water obtained from collected rain, as distinct from a well, etc.

raise /rayz/ • v.tr. **1** put or take into a higher position. **2** cause to rise, stand, or be vertical. **3** increase the amount, value, or strength of. **4** construct or build. **5** levy, collect, or bring together (*raise money*). **6** cause to be heard or considered (*raise an objection*). **7** bring into being; arouse (*raise hopes*). **8** bring up; educate. **9** breed; grow (*raise vegetables*). **10** (foll. by *to*) *Math.* multiply a quantity to a specified power. **11** *Cards* bet more than (another player). **12** remove (a barrier, etc.). • n. **1** *Cards* increase in a stake or bid. **2** increase in salary. □ **raise the devil** *colloq.* make a disturbance. **raise from the dead** restore to life. **raise hell** *colloq.* make a disturbance.

rai·sin /ráyzən/ n. partially dried grape. □□ **rai′sin·y** adj.

rai·son d'ê·tre /ráyzon détrə/ n. (*pl.* **raisons d'être** *pronunc.* same) purpose or reason for a thing's existence.

raj /raaj/ n. (prec. by *the*) *hist.* British sovereignty in India.

ra·ja /ráajə/ n. (also **ra′jah**) *hist.* **1** Indian king or prince. **2** petty dignitary or noble in India.

rake¹ /rayk/ • n. implement consisting of a pole with a toothed crossbar at the end, used for gathering loose material, smoothing soil, etc. • v. **1** tr. collect or make smooth with or as with a rake. **2** intr. use a rake. **3** tr. direct gunfire along (a line) from end to end. **4** tr. scratch or scrape. □ **rake in** *colloq.* amass (profits, etc.). **rake up** (or **over**) revive the unwelcome memory of. □□ **rak′er** n.

rake² /rayk/ n. dissolute man of fashion.

rake³ /rayk/ • v. set or be set at a sloping angle. • n. raking position or build.

rak·ish /ráykish/ adj. dashing; jaunty. □□ **rak′ish·ly** adv. **rak′ish·ness** n.

rale /raal/ n. abnormal rattling sound from the lungs.

ral·ly /rálee/ • v. (**–lies**, **–lied**) **1** tr. & intr. bring or come together as support for or action. **2** tr. revive (courage, etc.). **3** intr. recover after illness, etc.; revive. **4** intr. (of share prices, etc.) increase after a fall. • n. (*pl.* **–lies**) **1** rallying or being rallied. **2** mass meeting for a cause. **3** (in tennis, etc.) extended exchange of strokes. □□ **ral′li·er** n.

RAM /ram/ abbr. *Computing* random-access memory; internally stored software or data that is directly accessible.

ram /ram/ • *n.* **1** male sheep. **2** (**the Ram**) zodiacal sign or constellation Aries. • *v.tr.* (**rammed, ram·ming**) **1** force or squeeze into place by pressure. **2** beat or drive by heavy blows. **3** (of a ship, vehicle, etc.) strike violently; crash against. □ **ram home** stress forcefully (an argument, lesson, etc.).

Ram·a·dan /rámədan, ramədaʹan/ *n.* ninth month of the Muslim year, with strict fasting from sunrise to sunset.

ram·ble /rámbəl/ • *v.intr.* **1** walk for pleasure. **2** talk or write disconnectedly. • *n.* walk taken for pleasure. □□ **ram′bling** *adj.*

ram·bler /rámblər/ *n.* **1** person who rambles. **2** straggling or climbing rose.

ram·bunc·tious /rambúngkshəs/ *adj. colloq.* **1** uncontrollably exuberant. **2** unruly. □□ **ram·bunc′tious·ly** *adv.* **ram·bunc′tious·ness** *n.*

ram·e·kin /rámikin/ *n.* small dish for baking and serving an individual portion of food.

ram·i·fi·ca·tion /rámifikáyshən/ *n.* **1** subdivision of a complex structure or process. **2** consequence.

ramp /ramp/ *n.* **1** slope, esp. joining two levels of ground, floor, etc. **2** movable stairs for entering or leaving an aircraft.

ram·page • *v.intr.* /rámpayj/ **1** rush wildly or violently about. **2** rage; storm. • *n.* /rámpayj/ wild or violent behavior. □ **on the rampage** rampaging. □□ **ram′pag·er** *n.*

ram·pant /rámpənt/ *adj.* **1** unchecked; flourishing excessively. **2** violent or fanatical. □□ **ram′pan·cy** *n.* **ram′pant·ly** *adv.*

ram·part /rámpaart/ *n.* **1** defensive wall with a broad top and usu. a stone parapet. **2** walkway on top of such a wall.

ram·rod /rámrod/ *n.* **1** rod for ramming down the charge of a muzzle-loading firearm. **2** thing that is very straight or rigid.

ram·shack·le /rámshakəl/ *adj.* tumbledown; rickety.

ran *past* of RUN.

ranch /ranch/ • *n.* farm where animals are bred, such as cattle, sheep, etc. **2** (in full **ranch house**) single-story or split-level house. • *v.intr.* farm on a ranch. □□ **ranch′er** *n.*

ran·cid /ránsid/ *adj.* smelling or tasting like rank, stale fat. □□ **ran·cid′i·ty** *n.*

ran·cor /rángkər/ *n.* inveterate bitterness; malignant hate. □□ **ran′cor·ous** *adj.* **ran′cor·ous·ly** *adv.*

rand /rand, raant/ *n.* chief monetary unit of South Africa.

R & B *abbr.* rhythm and blues.

R & D *abbr.* research and development.

ran·dom /rándəm/ *adj.* made, done, etc., without method or conscious choice. □ **at random** without aim or purpose. **random-access** *Computing* (of a memory or file) having all data directly accessible, so it need not be read sequentially. □□ **ran′dom·ly** *adv.* **ran′dom·ness** *n.*

R and R *abbr.* **1** rescue and resuscitation. **2** rest and recreation (or recuperation or relaxation).

ran·dy /rándee/ *adj.* (**ran·di·er, ran·di·est**) lustful. □□ **ran′di·ly** *adv.* **ran′di·ness** *n.*

rang *past* of RING[2].

range /raynj/ • *n.* **1 a** region between limits of variation; extent; scope. **b** such limits. **2** distance attainable by a gun or projectile. **3** row, series, etc., esp. of mountains. **4** open or enclosed area with targets for shooting. **5** cooking stove. **6** nonstop distance that can be covered by a vehicle, aircraft, etc. **7** distance between a camera and the subject to be photographed. **8** large area of open land for grazing or hunting. • *v.* **1** *intr.* reach; lie spread out; extend. **2** *tr.* (usu. in *passive* or *refl.*) place or arrange in a row or ranks or in a specified situation, order, etc. (*trees ranged in ascending order of height*). **3** *intr.* rove; wander. □ **range finder** instrument for estimating the distance of an object, esp. one to be shot at or photographed.

rang·er /ráynjər/ *n.* **1** keeper of a national park or forest. **2** member of a body of armed men. **3** wanderer.

rang·y /ráynjee/ *adj.* (**rang·i·er, rang·i·est**) tall and slim.

ra·ni /ráanee/ *n.* (also **ra′nee**) *hist.* raja's wife or widow; Hindu queen.

rank[1] /rangk/ • *n.* **1 a** position in a hierarchy. **b** high social position. **c** place in a scale. **2** row or line. **3** row of soldiers drawn up abreast. **4** order; array. • *v.* **1** *intr.* have rank or place (*ranks next to the chief of staff*). **2** *tr.* classify; grade. □ **close ranks** maintain solidarity. **pull rank** use one's superior rank to gain advantage, coerce another, etc. **rank and file** ordinary undistinguished people. **the ranks** the common soldiers, i.e., privates and corporals.

rank[2] /rangk/ *adj.* **1** too luxuriant; choked with or apt to produce weeds or excessive foliage. **2 a** foul-smelling. **b** loathsome; corrupt. **3** flagrant; complete. □□ **rank′ness** *n.*

ran·kle /rángkəl/ *v.intr.* (of envy, disappointment, etc., or their cause) cause persistent annoyance or resentment.

ran·sack /ránsak/ *v.tr.* **1** pillage or plunder (a house, country, etc.). **2** thoroughly search. □□ **ran′sack·er** *n.*

ran·som /ránsəm/ • *n.* **1** money demanded or paid for the release of a captive. **2** liberation of a captive in return for this. • *v.tr.* buy the freedom or restoration of; redeem.

rant /rant/ • *v.* speak loudly, bombastically, violently, or theatrically. • *n.* piece of ranting.

rap /rap/ • *n.* **1** smart, slight blow. **2** sharp tapping sound. **3** *sl.* blame; punishment. **4** a rhythmic monologue recited to music. **b** (in full **rap′ mu·sic**) style of pop music with words recited rather than sung. • *v.* (**rapped, rap·ping**) **1** *tr.* strike smartly. **2** *intr.* knock; make a sharp tapping sound. **3** *tr.* criticize adversely. **4** *intr. sl.* talk. □ **beat the rap** escape punishment. **take the rap** suffer the consequences, esp. for a crime, etc., committed by another. □□ **rap′per** *n.*

ra·pa·cious /rəpáyshəs/ *adj.* grasping; predatory. □□ **ra·pa′cious·ly** *adv.* **ra·pa′cious·ness** *n.* **ra·pac·i·ty** /rəpásitee/ *n.*

rape[1] /rayp/ • *n.* **1** act of forcing a person to have sexual intercourse. **2** violent assault; forcible interference. • *v.tr.* commit rape on. □□ **rap′ist** *n.*

rape[2] /rayp/ *n.* plant grown as food for livestock and for its seed, from which oil is made.

rap·id /rápid/ • *adj.* **1** quick; swift; brief. **2** (of a slope) descending steeply. • *n.* (usu. in *pl.*) steep descent in a riverbed, with a swift current. □ **rapid eye movement** type of jerky movement of the eyes during dreaming. **rapid-fire**

(*attrib.*) fired, asked, etc., in quick succession. □□ **ra·pid′i·ty** *n.* **rap′id·ly** *adv.* **rap′id·ness** *n.*

ra·pi·er /ráypeeər, ráypyər/ *n.* light slender sword for thrusting.

rap·ine /rápin, –īn/ *n. rhet.* plundering; robbery.

rap·port /rapáwr/ *n.* relationship or communication, esp. when useful and harmonious.

rap·proche·ment /raprōshmóN/ *n.* resumption of harmonious relations, esp. between nations.

rap·scal·lion /rapskályən/ *n.* rascal; scamp; rogue.

rapt /rapt/ *adj.* **1** fully absorbed or intent. **2** carried away with joyous feeling or lofty thought. □□ **rapt′ly** *adv.* **rapt′ness** *n.*

rap·tor /ráptər/ *n.* bird of prey, e.g., an owl, falcon, or eagle. □□ **rap·to·ri·al** /–táwreeəl/ *adj.*

rap·ture /rápchər/ *n.* **1** ecstatic delight. **2** (in *pl.*) great pleasure or enthusiasm or the expression of it. □□ **rap′tur·ous** *adj.* **rap′tur·ous·ly** *adv.*

rare[1] /rair/ *adj.* (**rar·er, rar·est**) **1** seldom done or found or occurring; uncommon; unusual. **2** exceptionally good (*had a rare time*). **3** of less than the usual density (*rare atmosphere of the mountain*). □ **rare earth** lanthanide element. □□ **rare′ness** *n.*

rare[2] /rair/ *adj.* (**rarer, rarest**) (of meat) cooked lightly, so as to be still red inside.

rare·bit /ráirbit/ *n.* = *Welsh rabbit.*

rar·e·fy /ráirifī/ *v.* (**–fies, –fied**) (esp. as **rarefied** *adj.*) make or become less dense or solid (*rarefied air*). □□ **rar·e·fac·tion** /–fákshən/ *n.* **rar·e·fac′tive** *adj.*

rare·ly /ráirlee/ *adv.* **1** seldom; not often. **2** exceptionally.

rar·ing /ráiring/ *adj.* (foll. by *to* + infin.) *colloq.* enthusiastic; eager (*raring to go*).

rar·i·ty /ráiritee/ *n.* (*pl.* **–ties**) **1** rareness. **2** uncommon thing.

ras·cal /ráskəl/ *n.* dishonest or mischievous person. □□ **ras′cal·ly** *adj.*

rash[1] /rash/ *adj.* reckless; impetuous; hasty. □□ **rash′ly** *adv.* **rash′ness** *n.*

rash[2] /rash/ *n.* **1** eruption of the skin in spots or patches. **2** sudden widespread appearance.

rash·er /ráshər/ *n.* thin slice of bacon or ham.

rasp /rasp/ • *n.* **1** coarse kind of file. **2** rough grating sound. • *v.* **1** *tr.* scrape with or as with a rasp. **2** a *intr.* make a grating sound. **b** *tr.* say gratingly. □□ **rasp′ing·ly** *adv.* **rasp′y** *adj.*

rasp·ber·ry /rázberee/ *n.* (*pl.* **–ries**) **1** a bramble having stoneless, usu. red berries. **b** this berry. **2** *colloq.* sound made with the lips expressing dislike, derision, or disapproval.

Ras·ta·far·i·an /ráastəfáareeən, rástəfáir–/ • *n.* member of a sect regarding Ethiopian emperor Haile Selassie (d. 1975, entitled *Ras Tafari*) as God. • *adj.* of or relating to this sect. □□ **Ras·ta·far′i·an·ism** *n.*

rat /rat/ • *n.* **1 a** rodent like a large mouse. **b** any similar rodent. **2** *colloq.* deserter; turncoat. **3** *colloq.* unpleasant person. **4** (in *pl.*) *sl.* exclamation of contempt, annoyance, etc. • *v.intr.* (**rat·ted, rat·ting**) *colloq.* (foll. by *on*) **1** betray; let down. **2** inform on. □ **rat race** hectic work routine; struggle to succeed.

ra·ta·tou·ille /rátətŏó-ee, ráataa–/ *n.* dish made of stewed eggplant, onions, tomatoes, zucchini, and peppers.

ratch·et /ráchit/ *n.* **1** set of teeth on the edge of a bar or wheel with a catch permitting motion in one direction only. **2** (in full **ratchet wheel**) wheel with a rim so toothed.

RATCHET

rate[1] /rayt/ • *n.* **1** numerical proportion expressed in units (*rate of 50 miles per hour*) or as the basis of calculating (*rate of taxation*). **2** fixed or appropriate charge, cost, or value (*postal rates*). **3** pace of movement or change. **4** class or rank (*first-rate*). • *v.* **1** *tr.* **a** estimate the worth or value of. **b** assign a value to. **2** *tr.* consider; regard as. **3** *intr.* (foll. by *as*) rank or be rated. **4** *tr.* be worthy of; deserve. □ **at any rate** in any case; whatever happens. **at this rate** if this example is typical.

rate[2] /rayt/ *v.tr.* scold angrily.

rath·er /ráthər/ *adv.* **1** by preference (*would rather stay*). **2** as a more likely alternative (*is stupid rather than honest*). **3** more precisely (*a book, or rather, a pamphlet*). **4** slightly; to some extent (*rather drunk*).

rat·i·fy /rátifī/ *v.tr.* (**–fies, –fied**) confirm or accept by formal consent, signature, etc. □□ **rat·i·fi·ca′tion** *n.* **rat′i·fi·er** *n.*

rat·ing /ráyting/ *n.* **1** placing in a rank or class. **2** estimated standing of a person as regards credit, etc. **3** rank on a ship, in the military, etc. **4** relative popularity of a broadcast program as determined by the estimated size of the audience.

ra·ti·o /ráysheeō, ráyshō/ *n.* (*pl.* **–os**) quantitative relation between two comparable magnitudes (*a ratio of three to two*).

ra·tion /ráshən, ráy–/ • *n.* **1** official allowance of food, clothing, etc., in a time of shortage. **2** (usu. in *pl.*) fixed daily allowance of food, esp. in the armed forces. **3** (in *pl.*) provisions. • *v.tr.* **1** limit (persons or provisions) to a fixed ration. **2** distribute (food, etc.) in fixed quantities.

ra·tion·al /ráshənəl/ *adj.* **1** of or based on reason. **2** sensible; sane. **3** endowed with reason. **4** *Math.* (of a quantity or ratio) expressible as a ratio of whole numbers. □□ **ra·tion·al·i·ty** /–nálitee/ *n.* **ra′tion·al·ly** *adv.*

ra·tion·ale /ráshənál/ *n.* fundamental reason; logical basis.

ra·tion·al·ism /ráshənəlizəm/ *n.* practice of treating reason as the basis of knowledge and belief. □□ **ra′tion·al·ist** *n.*

ra·tion·al·ize /ráshənəlīz/ *v.* offer a rational but specious explanation of (one's behavior or attitude). □□ **ra·tion·al·i·za′tion** *n.*

rat·line /rátlin/ *n.* (also **rat′lin**) (usu. in *pl.*)

any of the small lines fastened across a ship's shrouds like ladder rungs.

rat·tan /rətán/ • *n.* East Indian climbing palm with long, thin, jointed pliable stems, used for furniture, etc.

rat·tle /rát'l/ • *v.* **1 a** *intr.* give out a rapid succession of short, sharp, hard sounds. **b** *tr.* make (a window, etc.) do this. **2** *intr.* move with a rattling noise. **3 a** *tr.* (usu. foll. by *off*) say or recite rapidly. **b** *intr.* (usu. foll. by *on*) talk in a lively thoughtless way. **4** *tr. colloq.* disconcert; alarm. • *n.* **1** rattling sound. **2** device or plaything made to rattle. **3** set of horny rings in a rattlesnake's tail. □ **rattle the saber** threaten war.

rat·tle·snake /rát'lsnayk/ *n.* poisonous American snake with rattling horny rings in its tail.

rat·tling /rátling/ • *adj.* **1** that rattles. **2** brisk; vigorous (*rattling pace*). • *adv.* remarkably (*rattling good story*).

rat·ty /rátee/ *adj.* (**rat·ti·er**, **rat·ti·est**) *colloq.* shabby; seedy. □□ **rat'ti·ness** *n.*

rau·cous /ráwkəs/ *adj.* harsh sounding; loud and hoarse. □□ **rau'cous·ly** *adv.* **rau'cous·ness** *n.*

raun·chy /ráwnchee/ *adj.* (**raun·chi·er**, **raun·chi·est**) *colloq.* **1** coarse; earthy. **2** grubby. □□ **raun'chi·ly** *adv.* **raun'chi·ness** *n.*

rav·age /rávij/ • *v.* devastate; plunder. • *n.* **1** the act or an instance of ravaging; devastation; damage. **2** (usu. in *pl.*) destructive effect (*the ravages of winter*).

rave /rayv/ • *v.intr.* **1** talk wildly or furiously in or as in delirium. **2** speak with rapturous admiration (about). • *n.* (usu. *attrib.*) *colloq.* highly enthusiastic review of a film, play, etc.

rav·el /rávəl/ *v.* **1** *tr.* & *intr.* entangle or become entangled or knotted. **2** *tr.* confuse or complicate (a question or problem). **3** *tr.* disentangle; separate into threads.

ra·ven /ráyvən/ • *n.* large glossy blue-black crow with a hoarse cry. • *adj.* glossy black.

rav·en·ing /rávəning/ *adj.* voraciously seeking prey.

rav·en·ous /rávənəs/ *adj.* **1** very hungry. **2** voracious. **3** rapacious. □□ **rav'en·ous·ly** *adv.* **rav'en·ous·ness** *n.*

ra·vine /rəveén/ *n.* deep narrow gorge. □□ **ra·vined'** *adj.*

rav·ing /ráyving/ • *n.* (usu. in *pl.*) wild or delirious talk. • *adj.* **1** delirious; frenzied. **2** remarkable; intensive (*a raving beauty*) • *adv.* wildly (*raving mad*). □□ **rav'ing·ly** *adv.*

rav·i·o·li /ráveeólee/ *n.* small pasta envelopes containing cheese, ground meat, etc.

rav·ish /rávish/ *v.tr.* **1** rape (a woman). **2** enrapture. **3** carry off by force. □□ **rav'ish·er** *n.* **rav'ish·ment** *n.*

rav·ish·ing /rávishing/ *adj.* entrancing; delightful; very beautiful. □□ **rav'ish·ing·ly** *adv.*

raw /raw/ *adj.* **1** uncooked. **2** in the natural state; not processed or manufactured. **3** inexperienced; untrained. **4 a** having the flesh exposed. **b** sensitive to the touch from being exposed. **5** (of the atmosphere, day, etc.) chilly and damp. **6 a** crude; coarse. **b** brutal. □ **in the raw 1** in its natural state. **2** naked. **raw deal** harsh or unfair treatment. **raw material** that from which the process of manufacture makes products. **raw si·enna** brownish-yellow earth used as a pigment.

raw umber umber in its natural state, dark yellow in color. □□ **raw'ish** *adj.* **raw'ly** *adv.* **raw'ness** *n.*

raw·boned /ráwbōnd/ *adj.* gaunt and bony.

raw·hide /ráwhīd/ *n.* **1** untanned hide. **2** rope or whip of this.

ray[1] /ray/ *n.* **1** narrow beam of light from a small or distant source. **2** straight line in which radiation travels to a given point. **3** (in *pl.*) radiation of a specified type (*X rays*). **4** promising trace (*ray of hope*). **5** any of a set of radiating lines, parts, or things. □□ **rayed** *adj.*

ray[2] /ray/ *n.* marine fish with a broad flat body and a long slender tail.

ray·on /ráyon/ *n.* textile fiber or fabric made from cellulose.

raze /rayz/ *v.tr.* completely destroy; tear down.

ra·zor /ráyzər/ *n.* instrument with a sharp blade used in cutting hair, esp. from the skin. □ **razor's edge 1** keen edge. **2** critical situation. **razor wire** wire with sharpened projections, often coiled atop walls for security.

ra·zor·back /ráyzərbak/ *n.* wild hog with a sharp ridged back.

razz /raz/ *v.tr. sl.* tease; ridicule.

raz·zle-daz·zle /rázəldázəl/ *n. sl.* **1** glamorous excitement; bustle. **2** extravagant publicity.

razz·ma·tazz /rázmətáz/ *n.* (also **razz·za·ma·tazz** /rázəmə–/) *colloq.* **1** = RAZZLE-DAZZLE. **2** insincere actions; double-talk.

Rb *symb. Chem.* rubidium.

RC *abbr.* Roman Catholic.

RD *abbr.* Rural Delivery.

Rd. *abbr.* Road (in names).

RDA *abbr.* **1** recommended daily allowance. **2** recommended dietary allowance.

Re *symb. Chem.* rhenium.

re[1] /ray, ree/ *prep.* **1** in the matter of (as the first word in a heading). **2** *colloq.* about; concerning.

re[2] /ray/ *n. Mus.* **1** second note of a major scale. **2** the note D in the fixed-do system.

re- /ree, ri, re/ *prefix* **1** attachable to almost any verb or its derivative, meaning: **a** once more; afresh; anew (*readjust*). **b** back; with return to a previous state (*reassemble*). ¶ A hyphen is sometimes used when the word begins with *e* (*re-enact*), or to distinguish the compound from a more familiar one-word form (*re-form* = form again). **2** (also **red-** before a vowel, as in *redolent*) in verbs and verbal derivatives denoting: **a** in return; mutually (*react*). **b** opposition (*repel*). **c** behind or after (*remain*). **d** retirement or secrecy (*recluse*). **e** off; away; down (*recede; repress*). **f** frequentative or intensive force (*redouble; refine*). **g** negative force (*recant*).

reach /reech/ • *v.* **1** *intr.* & *tr.* stretch out; extend. **2** *intr.* stretch out the hand, etc.; make a reaching motion or effort. **3** *tr.* get as far as (*reached Chicago at noon*). **4** *tr.* get to or attain (*temperature reached 90°*). **5** *tr.* make contact with the hand, etc., or by telephone, etc. **6** *tr.* hand; pass (*reach that book for me*). • *n.* **1** extent to which a hand, etc., can be reached out, influence exerted, motion carried out, etc. **2** act of reaching out. **3** continuous extent, esp. of a river. □□ **reach'a·ble** *adj.*

re·act /reéakt/ *v.intr.* **1** respond (to a stimulus, etc.). **2** tend in a reverse or contrary direction. **3** *Chem. & Physics* (of a substance or particle) be the cause of activity or interaction with another (*nitrous oxide reacts with the metal*).

re·ac·tion /reeákshən/ n. **1** reacting; response. **2** bodily response to a drug, etc. **3** response in a reverse or contrary way. **4** interaction of substances undergoing chemical change. □□ **re·ac′tion·ist** n. & adj.

re·ac·tion·ar·y /reeákshəneree/ ● adj. tending to oppose (esp. political) change and advocate return to a former system. ● n. (pl. **-ies**) reactionary person.

re·ac·ti·vate /reeáktivayt/ v.tr. restore to a state of activity; bring into action again. □□ **re·ac·ti·va·tion** /–váyshən/ n.

re·ac·tive /reeáktiv/ adj. **1** showing reaction. **2** reacting rather than initiating. □□ **re·ac·tiv′i·ty** n.

re·ac·tor /reeáktər/ n. **1** person or thing that reacts. **2** (in full **nu′cle·ar re·ac′tor**) apparatus or structure in which a controlled nuclear chain reaction releases energy.

read /reed/ ● v. (past and past part. **read** /red/) **1** tr. (also absol.) reproduce mentally or vocally written or printed words. **2** tr. convert or be able to convert (characters, symbols, etc.) into the intended words or meaning. **3** tr. interpret mentally. **4** tr. find (a thing) stated in print, etc. **5** tr. assume as intended or deducible (read too much into it). **6** tr. (of a recording instrument) show (a specified figure, etc.) (the thermometer reads 20°). **7** intr. convey meaning in a specified manner when read (it reads persuasively). **8** tr. Computing access (data), as to copy or display. **9** tr. understand or interpret by hearing words or seeing signs, gestures, etc. ● n. **1** period of reading. **2** colloq. book, etc., as regards its readability (is a good read). □ **read a person like a book** understand a person's motives, etc. **read between the lines** look for or find hidden meaning. **read lips** = lipread (LIPREADING). **read-only** Computing (of a memory) able to be read at high speed but not

capable of being changed by program instructions. **read up** make a special study of (a subject). **read-write** Computing capable of reading existing data and accepting alterations or further input.

read·a·ble /reédəbəl/ adj. **1** able to be read. **2** interesting or pleasant to read. □□ **read·a·bil′i·ty** n. **read′a·bly** adv.

read·er /reédər/ n. **1** person who reads. **2** book of extracts for learning, esp. a language. **3** person appointed to read aloud, esp. in church.

read·er·ship /reédərship/ n. readers of a newspaper, etc.

read·i·ly /réd′lee/ adv. **1** without reluctance; willingly. **2** without difficulty or delay.

read·ing /reéding/ n. **1 a** act of reading. **b** matter to be read. **2** (in comb.) used for reading (reading room). **3** literary knowledge. **4** entertainment at which a play, poems, etc., are read. **5** figure, etc., shown by a recording instrument. **6** interpretation.

read·out /reédowt/ n. **1** display of information, as on a gauge, etc. **2** information displayed.

read·y /rédee/ ● adj. (**read·i·er, read·i·est**) **1** with preparations complete (dinner is ready). **2** in a fit state (are you ready?). **3** willing, inclined, or resolved (ready for anything). **4** within reach; easily secured (ready cash). **5** immediate; unqualified (found ready acceptance). **6** (foll. by to + infin.) about to do something (a bud just ready to burst). ● adv. beforehand; immediately usable (ready-to-eat). ● v.tr. (**-ies, -ied**) make ready; prepare. □ **at the ready** ready for action. **ready-made 1** (esp. of clothes) made in a standard size, not to measure. **2** already available; convenient (ready-made excuse). □□ **read′i·ness** n.

re·a·gent /ree-áyjənt/ n. Chem. substance used

re·ab·sorb′ v.	re·as·sign′ v.	re·es·tab′lish·ment n.	re·oc·cur′ v.
re·ac·cept′ v.	re·as·sign′ment n.	re·e·val′u·ate· v.	re·o′pen v.
re·ac·cus′tom v.	re·a·wak′en v.	re·ex·am′ine v.	re·or·ga·nize· v.
re·ac·quaint′ v.	re·bind′ v.	re·ex·am·i·na′tion v.	re·pop′u·late· v.
re·ac·quire v.	re·build′ v.	re·fo′cus v.	re·pro′cess v.
re·ad·apt′ v.	re·charge′ v. & n.	re·for′mat v.	re·pro′gram v.
re·ad·ap·ta′tion n.	re·charge′a·ble adj.	re·for′mu·late v.	re·pro·gram′ma·ble adj.
re·ad·dress′ v.	re·clas′si·fy v.	re·for·mu·la′tion n.	re·pub′lish v.
re·ad·just′ v.	re·clas·si·fi·ca′tion n.	re·fur′nish v.	re·read′ v.
re·ad·just′ment n.	re·com·mence′ v.	re·grow′ v.	re·re·cord′ v.
re·ad·mit′ v.	re·com·mence′ment n.	re·heat′ v.	re·re·lease′ v.
re·ad·mis′sion n.	re·con·nect′ v.	re·im·pose′ v.	re·route′ v.
re·a·dopt′ v.	re·con·nec′tion n.	re·in·fect′ v.	re·sched′ule v.
re·af·firm′ v.	re·con·vene′ v.	re·in·oc′u·late· v.	re·seal′ v.
re·af·fir·ma′tion n.	re·con·vert′ v.	re·in·sert′ v.	re·seal′a·ble v.
re·a·lign′ v.	re·con·ver′sion n.	re·in·ter′pret v.	re·sell′ v.
re·a·lign′ment n.	re·de·fine′ v.	re·in·ter·pre·ta′tion n.	re·set′tle v.
re·al′lo·cate v.	re·dis·cov′er v.	re·in·vest′ v.	re·shape′ v.
re·al·lo·ca′tion n.	re·dis·trib′ute v.	re·in·vest′ment n.	re·state′ v.
re·ap·pear′ v.	re·dis·tri·bu′tion n.	re·is′sue v. & n.	re·stock′ v.
re·ap·pear′ance n.	re·draft′ v.	re·kin′dle v.	re·string′ v.
re·ap·ply′ v.	re·draw′ v.	re·learn′ v.	re·style′ v.
re·ap·pli·ca′tion n.	re·e·lect′ v.	re·light′ v.	re·tell′ v.
re·ap·point′ v.	re·e·lec′tion n.	re·load′ v.	re·type′ v.
re·ap·point′ment n.	re·em·bark′ v.	re·name′ v.	re·up·hol′ster v.
re·arm′ v.	re·e·merge′ v.	re·ne·go′ti·ate· v.	re·use′ v. & n.
re·ar′ma·ment n.	re·em′pha·size· v.	re·ne·go·ti·a′tion n.	re·vis′it v.
re·as·sem′ble v.	re·em·ploy′ v.	re·nom′i·nate· v.	re·vi′tal·ize· v.
re·as·sem′bly n.	re·em·ploy′ment n.	re·num′ber v.	re·wire′ v.
re·as·sess′ v.	re·en′ter v.	re·oc′cu·py v.	
re·as·sess′ment n.	re·es·tab′lish v.	re·oc·cu·pa′tion n.	

to cause a reaction, esp. to detect another substance.

re·al /reel/ • *adj.* **1** actually existing or occurring. **2** genuine; rightly so called; not artificial. **3** *Law* consisting of immovable property such as land or houses (*real estate*). **4** appraised by purchasing power (*real value*). • *adv. colloq.* really; very. □ **for real** *colloq.* as a serious or actual concern. **real estate** property, esp. land and buildings. **real life** that lived by actual people, as distinct from fiction, drama, etc. **real time** actual time during which a process or event occurs. **real-time** (*attrib.*) *Computing* (of a system) in which the response is ongoing and occurs during the actual time of an event. □□ **real′ness** *n.*

re·al·ism /reeəlizəm/ *n.* **1** practice of regarding things in their true nature and dealing with them as they are. **2** fidelity to nature in representation. □□ **re′al·ist** *n.*

re·al·is·tic /reeəlistik/ *adj.* **1** regarding things as they are. **2** based on facts rather than ideals. □□ **re·al·is′ti·cal·ly** *adv.*

re·al·i·ty /reeálitee/ *n.* (*pl.* **-ties**) **1** what is real or existent or underlies appearances. **2** the real nature (of). **3** real existence; state of being real. □ **in reality** in fact.

re·al·ize /reeəlīz/ *v.tr.* **1** (also *absol.*) be fully aware of; conceive as real. **2** (also *absol.*) understand clearly. **3** present as real. **4** convert into actuality (*realized a childhood dream*). **5** obtain, as profit. □□ **re·al·iz′a·ble** *adj.* **re·al·i·za′tion** *n.* **re′al·iz·er** *n.*

re·al·ly /reeəlee, reelee/ *adv.* **1** in reality. **2** positively (*really useful*). **3** indeed; truly. **4** (often in *interrog.*) an expression of mild protest or surprise.

realm /relm/ *n.* **1** kingdom. **2** domain.

Re·al·tor /reeəltər/ *n. propr.* real estate agent who is a member of the National Association of Realtors.

re·al·ty /reeəltee/ *n.* real estate.

ream¹ /reem/ *n.* **1** twenty quires (or 500 sheets) of paper. **2** (in *pl.*) large quantity (*wrote reams about it*).

ream² /reem/ *v.tr.* widen (a hole in metal, etc.) with a borer.

re·an·i·mate /ree-ánimayt/ *v.tr.* **1** restore to life. **2** restore to activity or liveliness. □□ **re·an·i·ma′tion** /-máyshən/ *n.*

reap /reep/ *v.tr.* **1** cut or gather (esp. grain) as a harvest. **2** harvest the crop of (a field, etc.). **3** receive as the consequence of one's own or others' actions.

reap·er /reepər/ *n.* **1** person who reaps. **2** machine for reaping. □ **the reaper** (or **grim reaper**) death personified.

rear¹ /reer/ • *n.* **1** back part of anything. **2** space behind, or position at the back of, anything. **3** *colloq.* buttocks. • *adj.* at the back. □ **bring up the rear** come last. **rear admiral** naval officer ranking below vice admiral. **rear guard 1** body of troops detached to protect the rear, esp. in retreats. **2** defensive or conservative element in an organization, etc.

rear² /reer/ *v.* **1** *tr.* **a** bring up and educate (children). **b** breed and care for (animals). **c** cultivate (crops). **2** *intr.* (of a horse, etc.) raise itself on its hind legs. **3** *tr.* set upright; build. □□ **rear′er** *n.*

rear·most /reermōst/ *adj.* furthest back.

re·ar·range /reeeəráynj/ *v.tr.* arrange again in a different way. □□ **re·ar·range′ment** *n.*

rear·ward /reerwərd/ • *adj.* to the rear. • *adv.* (also **rear′wards**) toward the rear.

rea·son /reezən/ • *n.* **1** motive, cause, or justification. **2** fact adduced or serving as this. **3** intellectual faculty by which conclusions are drawn from premises. **4** sanity (*has lost his reason*). **5** sense; moderation. • *v.* **1** *intr.* form or try to reach conclusions by connected thought. **2** *intr.* use an argument (with) by way of persuasion. **3** *tr.* conclude or assert in argument. □ **stand to reason** be evident or logical. **listen to reason** be persuaded to act sensibly. □□ **rea′son·ing** *n.*

¶ **Reason** means 'cause or basis,' and it is redundant to say "the reason is because"; the preferred usage is *the reason is that*: The reason the car won't start is that (not *because*) the battery cable came loose.

rea·son·a·ble /reezənəbəl/ *adj.* **1** having sound judgment. **2** not absurd. **3 a** not excessive; inexpensive. **b** tolerable; fair. □□ **rea′son·a·ble·ness** *n.* **rea′son·a·bly** *adv.*

re·as·sure /reeəshoor/ *v.tr.* **1** restore confidence to; dispel the apprehensions of. **2** confirm in an opinion or impression. □□ **re·as·sur′ance** *n.* **re·as·sur′ing** *adj.* **re·as·sur′ing·ly** *adv.*

re·bate /reebayt/ • *n.* partial refund. • *v.tr.* pay back as a rebate. □□ **re·bat′a·ble** *adj.* **re·bat′er** *n.*

reb·el • *n.* /rébəl/ person who fights against or resists established authority. • *adj.* /rébəl/ (*attrib.*) **1** rebellious. **2** of rebels. **3** in rebellion. • *v.intr.* /ribél/ (**re·belled, re·bel·ling**) **1** act as a rebel; revolt. **2** feel or display repugnance.

re·bel·lion /ribélyən/ *n.* open resistance to authority, esp. organized armed resistance to an established government.

re·bel·lious /ribélyəs/ *adj.* **1** tending to rebel. **2** in rebellion. **3** (of a thing) unmanageable. □□ **re·bel′lious·ly** *adv.* **re·bel′lious·ness** *n.*

re·birth /reebérth/ *n.* **1** new incarnation. **2** spiritual enlightenment. **3** revival. □□ **re·born** /reebáwrn/ *adj.*

re·bound • *v.intr.* /ribównd/ spring back after impact. • *n.* /reebownd/ **1** act of rebounding; recoil. **2** reaction after a strong emotion. □ **on the rebound** while still recovering from an emotional shock, esp. rejection by a lover. □□ **re·bound′er** *n.*

re·buff /ribúf/ • *n.* **1** rejection of another's advances, help, sympathy, request, etc. **2** repulse; snub. • *v.tr.* give a rebuff to.

re·buke /ribyóók/ • *v.tr.* reprove sharply; subject to protest or censure. • *n.* rebuking or being rebuked; reproof. □□ **re·buk′er** *n.* **re·buk′ing·ly** *adv.*

re·bus /reebəs/ *n.* representation of a word or phrase by pictures, etc., suggesting its parts.

re·but /ribút/ *v.tr.* (**re·but·ted, re·but·ting**) **1** refute or disprove (evidence or a charge). **2** force or turn back; check. □□ **re·but′ment** *n.* **re·but′ta·ble** *adj.* **re·but′tal** *n.*

rec. *abbr.* **1** receipt. **2** record. **3** recreation.

re·cal·ci·trant /rikálsitrənt/ • *adj.* **1** obstinately disobedient. **2** objecting to restraint. • *n.* recalcitrant person. □□ **re·cal′ci·trance** *n.* **re·cal′ci·trant·ly** *adv.*

re·call /rikáwl/ • *v.tr.* **1 a** summon to return. **b**

(of a product) request return to fix a defect. **2** recollect; remember. **3** bring back to memory; serve as a reminder of. **4** revoke or annul (an action or decision). **5** take back (a gift). ● *n.* (also /reˊekawl/) **1** act or instance of recalling. **2** act of remembering. **3** ability to remember. □□ **re·callˊa·ble** *adj.*

re·cant /rikánt/ *v.* **1** *tr.* withdraw and renounce (a former belief, etc.) as erroneous or heretical. **2** *intr.* disavow a former opinion. □□ **re·can·taˊtion** *n.* **re·cantˊer** *n.*

re·cap /reˊekap/ *colloq.* ● *v.* (**re·capped, re·cap·ping**) recapitulate. ● *n.* recapitulation.

re·ca·pit·u·late /reˊekəpíchəlayt/ *v.tr.* go briefly through again; summarize. □□ **re·ca·pit·u·la·tive** /–ələtiv/ *adj.* **re·ca·pit·u·la·to·ry** /–lətáwree/ *adj.*

re·ca·pit·u·la·tion /reˊekəpíchəláyshən/ *n.* **1** act of recapitulating. **2** *Mus.* section in which themes are restated.

re·cede /riseˊed/ *v.intr.* **1** go or shrink back or further off. **2** diminish; fade. **3** slope backward (*a receding chin*).

re·ceipt /riseˊet/ *n.* **1** receiving or being received. **2** written acknowledgment of payment. **3** (usu. in *pl.*) amount of money, etc., received.

re·ceive /riseˊev/ *v.tr.* **1** take or accept. **2** acquire; be provided with. **3** accept delivery of (something sent). **4** have conferred or inflicted on one. **5** admit; provide accommodation for (*received many visitors*). **6** (of a receptacle) be able to hold. **7** greet or welcome, esp. in a specified manner. **8** convert (broadcast signals) into sound or pictures. □□ **re·ceivˊa·ble** *adj.*

re·ceiv·er /riseˊevər/ *n.* **1** person or thing that receives. **2** telephone earpiece. **3** person appointed by a court to receive funds, administer property of a bankrupt, etc. **4** radio or television receiving apparatus. **5** *Football* offensive player eligible to catch a forward pass.

re·ceiv·er·ship /riseˊevərship/ *n.* state of being dealt with by a receiver.

re·cent /reˊesənt/ ● *adj.* **1** not long past. **2** not long established; lately begun. **3** (**Recent**) *Geol.* of the most recent epoch of the Quaternary period. ● *n. Geol.* this epoch. □□ **reˊcent·ly** *adv.*

re·cep·ta·cle /riséptəkəl/ *n.* **1** containing vessel, place, or space.

re·cep·tion /risépshən/ *n.* **1** receiving or being received. **2** manner in which a person or thing is received. **3** social occasion for receiving guests. **4** (also **re·cepˊtion desk**) arrival area at a hotel, office, etc. **5 a** receiving of broadcast signals. **b** quality of this.

re·cep·tion·ist /risépshənist/ *n.* person employed to receive guests, answer the telephone, etc.

re·cep·tive /riséptiv/ *adj.* able or quick to receive impressions or ideas. □□ **re·cepˊtive·ly** *adv.* **re·cep·tiv·i·ty** /reˊeseptívitee/ *n.*

re·cess /reˊeses, risés/ ● *n.* **1** space set back in a wall. **2** (often in *pl.*) remote or secret place. **3** temporary cessation from proceedings, school, etc. ● *v.* **1** *tr.* make a recess in. **2** *tr.* place in a recess. **3 a** *intr.* take a recess; adjourn. **b** *tr.* order a recess.

re·ces·sion /riséshən/ *n.* **1** temporary decline in economic activity or prosperity. **2** receding or withdrawal from a place or point. □□ **re·cesˊsion·ar·y** *adj.*

re·ces·sion·al /riséshənəl/ *n.* hymn sung while the clergy and choir withdraw after a service.

re·ces·sive /risésiv/ *adj.* **1** tending to recede. **2** *Genetics* appearing in offspring only when not masked by an inherited dominant characteristic. □□ **re·cesˊsive·ly** *adv.* **re·cesˊsive·ness** *n.*

re·cher·ché /rəsháirsháy/ *adj.* **1** carefully sought out; rare; exotic. **2** far-fetched; obscure.

re·cid·i·vist /risídivist/ *n.* person who relapses into crime, etc. □□ **re·cidˊi·vism** *n.* **re·cid·i·visˊtic** *adj.*

rec·i·pe /résipee/ *n.* **1** statement of ingredients and procedure required for preparing cooked food. **2** device for achieving something.

re·cip·i·ent /risípeeənt/ *n.* person who receives something.

re·cip·ro·cal /risíprəkəl/ ● *adj.* **1** in return (*reciprocal greeting*). **2** mutual. ● *n. Math.* expression or function so related to another that their product is one (e.g., $\frac{1}{2}$ is the reciprocal of 2). □□ **re·cip·ro·calˊi·ty** /–kálitee/ *n.* **re·cipˊro·cal·ly** *adv.*

re·cip·ro·cate /risíprəkayt/ *v.* **1** *tr.* return or requite (affection, etc.). **2** *intr.* (foll. by *with*) offer or give something in return. **3** *tr.* interchange. **4 a** *intr.* (of a part of a machine) move backward and forward. **b** *tr.* cause to do this. □□ **re·cip·ro·ca·tion** /–káyshən/ *n.* **re·cipˊro·ca·tor** *n.*

rec·i·proc·i·ty /résiprósitee/ *n.* **1** condition of being reciprocal. **2** mutual action. **3** give and take, esp. of privileges.

re·cit·al /risítˊl/ *n.* **1** reciting or being recited. **2** performance by a solo instrumentalist, dancer, or singer or by a small group. **3** detailed account; narrative.

rec·i·ta·tion /résitáyshən/ *n.* **1** reciting. **2** thing recited.

rec·i·ta·tive /résitəteˊev/ *n.* musical declamation in the narrative and dialogue parts of opera and oratorio.

re·cite /risít/ *v.* **1** *tr.* repeat aloud or declaim (a poem or passage) from memory. **2** *intr.* give a recitation. **3** *tr.* enumerate. □□ **re·citˊer** *n.*

reck·less /réklis/ *adj.* heedless; rash. □□ **reckˊless·ly** *adv.* **reckˊless·ness** *n.*

reck·on /rékən/ *v.* **1** *tr.* count; compute. **2** *tr.* consider or regard. **3** *tr.* be of the considered opinion. **4** *intr.* (foll. by *with*) take into account. **5** *dial.* think; suppose (*I reckon I'll stay*). □ **to be reckoned with** of considerable importance; not to be ignored.

---

reckon Old English (*ge*)*recenian* 'recount, relate,' of West Germanic origin; related to Dutch *rekenen* and German *rechnen* 'to count (up).' Early senses included 'give an account of items received' and 'mention things in order,' which gave rise to the notion of 'calculation' and hence of 'coming to a conclusion.'

---

re·claim /rikláym/ *v.tr.* **1** seek the return of (one's property, rights, etc.). **2** bring under cultivation, esp. after being under water. **3** win back. **b** tame; civilize. □□ **re·claimˊa·ble** *adj.* **re·claimˊer** *n.* **rec·la·ma·tion** /rékləmáyshən/ *n.*

re·cline /riklín/ *v.* **1** *intr.* assume or be in a horizontal or leaning position. **2** *tr.* cause to recline or move from the vertical. □□ **re·clinˊa·ble** *adj.*

re·clin·er /riklínər/ n. comfortable chair for reclining in.

rec·luse /réklo͞os, riklo͞os/ n. person given to or living in seclusion or isolation; hermit. □□ **re·clu·sion** /riklo͞ozhən/ n. **re·clu′sive** adj.

rec·og·ni·tion /rékəgníshən/ n. recognizing or being recognized.

re·cog·ni·zance /rikógnizəns, –kónə–/ n. Law a charge to observe some condition, e.g., to appear when summoned.

rec·og·nize /rékəgnīz/ v.tr. **1** identify as already known. **2** realize or discover the nature of. **3** realize or admit. **4** acknowledge the existence, validity, etc., of. **5** show appreciation of; reward. □□ **rec·og·niz′a·ble** adj. **rec·og·niz·a·bil′i·ty** n. **rec·og·niz′a·bly** adv. **rec′og·niz·er** n.

re·coil /rikóyl/ • v.intr. **1** suddenly move or spring back in fear, horror, or disgust. **2** shrink mentally in this way. **3** (of a gun) be driven backward by its discharge. • n. (also /ré′koyl/) act or sensation of recoiling.

rec·ol·lect /rékəlékt/ v.tr. **1** remember. **2** succeed in remembering; call to mind. □□ **rec·ol·lec·tion** /–lékshən/ n.

re·com·bi·nant /reekómbinənt/ Biol. • adj. (of a gene, etc.) formed by recombination. • n. recombinant organism or cell. □ **recombinant DNA** DNA that has been recombined using constituents from different sources.

rec·om·mend /rékəménd/ v.tr. **1** suggest as fit for some purpose or use. **2** advise as a course of action, etc. **3** make acceptable or desirable. □□ **rec·om·men·da′tion** n.

rec·om·pense /rékəmpens/ • v.tr. **1** make amends to (a person) or for (a loss, etc.). **2** reward or punish (a person or action). • n. **1** reward; requital. **2** retribution.

rec·on·cile /rékənsīl/ v.tr. **1** make friendly again after an estrangement. **2** make acquiescent or contentedly submissive to (something disagreeable). **3** settle (a quarrel, etc.). **4** make or show to be compatible. □□ **rec·on·cil′a·ble** adj. **rec′on·cile·ment** n. **rec′on·cil·er** n. **rec·on·cil·i·a·to·ry** /–sileeáyshən/ n. **rec·on·cil·i·a·to·ry** /–sileeə-tawree/ adj.

rec·on·dite /rékəndīt, rikón–/ adj. **1** (of a subject or knowledge) abstruse; little known. **2** (of an author or style) obscure. □□ **re′con·dite·ly** adv. **re′con·dite·ness** n.

re·con·di·tion /réekəndíshən/ v.tr. **1** overhaul; refit; renovate. **2** make usable again. □□ **re·con·di′tion·er** n.

re·con·nais·sance /rikónisəns/ n. survey of a region, esp. to locate an enemy or ascertain strategic features.

re·con·noi·ter /réekənóytər, rékə–/ v. make a reconnaissance.

re·con·sid·er /réekənsídər/ v. consider again, esp. for a possible change of decision. □□ **re·con·sid·er·a′tion** n.

re·con·sti·tute /réekónstito͞ot, –tyo͞ot/ v.tr. **1** reconstruct; reorganize. **2** restore dried food, etc., by adding water. □□ **re·con·sti·tu′tion** /–to͞o-shən/ n.

re·con·struct /réekənstrúkt/ v.tr. **1** build again. **2** recall or reenact past events, etc., by assembling the evidence for them. □□ **re·con·struct′i·ble** adj. (also **re·con·struct′a·ble**). **re·con·struc·tion** /–strúkshən/ n. **re·con·struc′tive** adj.

re·cord • n. /rékərd/ **1 a** evidence or information constituting an (esp. official) account of something that has occurred, been said, etc. **b** document preserving this. **2** state of being set down or preserved in writing, etc. **3** (in full **pho′no·graph rec′ord**) disk carrying recorded sound in grooves on each surface, for reproduction by a record player. **4** official report of legal proceedings. **5 a** facts known about a person's past. **b** list of a person's previous criminal convictions. **6** best performance or most remarkable event of its kind. • v.tr. /rikáwrd/ **1** set down in writing, etc., for later reference. **2** convert (sound, a broadcast, etc.) into permanent form for later reproduction. □ **break** (or **beat**) **the record** outdo all previous performances, etc. **for the record** as an official statement, etc. **go on record** state one's opinion or judgment openly or officially. **off the record** unofficially; confidentially. **record player** apparatus for reproducing sound from phonograph records. □□ **re·cord′a·ble** adj.

---

record Middle English: from Old French record 'remembrance,' from recorder 'bring to remembrance,' from Latin recordari 'remember,' based on cor, cord- 'heart.' The noun was earliest used in law to denote the fact of something being written down as evidence. The verb originally meant 'narrate orally or in writing,' also 'repeat so as to commit to memory.'

---

re·cord·er /rikáwrdər/ n. **1** apparatus for recording, esp. a tape recorder. **2** keeper of records. **3** wind instrument like a flute but blown through the end.

re·cord·ing /rikáwrding/ n. **1** process by which audio or video signals are recorded for later reproduction. **2** material or a program recorded.

re·count[1] /rikównt/ v.tr. **1** narrate. **2** tell in detail.

re·count[2] • v. /ré′kównt/ tr. count again. • n. /ré′kownt/ recounting, esp. of votes in an election.

re·coup /riko͞op/ v.tr. recover or regain (a loss). □□ **re·coup′a·ble** adj. **re·coup′ment** n.

re·course /ré′kawrs, rikáwrs/ n. **1** resorting to a possible source of help. **2** person or thing resorted to. □ **have recourse to** turn to (a person or thing) for help.

re·cov·er /rikúvər/ v. **1** tr. regain possession, use, or control of. **2** intr. return to health, consciousness, or to a normal state or position. **3** tr. obtain or secure by legal process. **4** tr. retrieve or make up for (a loss, setback, etc.). **5** tr. retrieve; salvage. □□ **re·cov′er·a·ble** adj. **re·cov·er·a·bil′i·ty** n. **re·cov′er·y** n.

rec·re·ant /rékreeənt/ literary • adj. craven; cowardly. • n. coward. □□ **rec′re·an·cy** n. **rec′re·ant·ly** adv.

rec·re·a·tion /rékree-áyshən/ n. **1** process or means of refreshing or entertaining oneself. **2** pleasurable activity. □□ **rec·re·a′tion·al** adj. **rec·re·a′tion·al·ly** adv.

re·crim·i·nate /rikríminayt/ v.intr. make mutual or counter accusations. □□ **re·crim·i·na·tion** /–náyshən/ n. **re·crim·i·na·to·ry** /–nətawree/ adj.

re·cruit /rikro͞ot/ • n. **1** newly enlisted serviceman or servicewoman. **2** new member; beginner. • *v.* **1** *tr.* enlist (a person) as a recruit. **2** *tr.* form (an army, etc.) by enlisting recruits. **3** *intr.* get or seek recruits. □□ **re·cruit′ment** *n.*

rec·ta *pl.* of RECTUM.

rec·tal /réktəl/ *adj.* of or by means of the rectum. □□ **rec′tal·ly** *adv.*

rec·tan·gle /réktanggəl/ *n.* plane figure with four straight sides and four right angles. □□ **rec·tan′gu·lar** *adj.*

rec·ti·fy /réktifī/ *v.tr.* (**–fies, –fied**) **1** adjust; make right. **2** convert (alternating current) to direct current. □□ **rec·ti·fi′a·ble** *adj.* **rec·ti·fi·ca′tion** *n.* **rec′ti·fi·er** *n.*

rec·ti·lin·e·ar /réktilíneeər/ *adj.* (also **rec·ti·lin·e·al** /–eeəl/) **1** bounded or characterized by straight lines. **2** in or forming a straight line. □□ **rec·ti·lin·e·ar·i·ty** /–neeáritee/ *n.* **rec·ti·lin′e·ar·ly** *adv.*

rec·ti·tude /réktitōōd, –tyōōd/ *n.* **1** moral uprightness. **2** correctness.

rec·to /réktō/ *n.* (*pl.* **–tos**) **1** right-hand page of an open book. **2** front of a printed leaf.

rec·tor /réktər/ *n.* **1** clergy member in charge of a church or religious institution. **2** head of some schools, universities, and colleges.

rec·to·ry /réktəree/ *n.* (*pl.* **–ries**) rector's house.

rec·tum /réktəm/ *n.* (*pl.* **rectums** or **recta** /–tə/) final section of the large intestine, terminating at the anus.

re·cum·bent /rikúmbənt/ *adj.* lying down; reclining.□□ **re·cum′ben·cy** *n.* **re·cum′bent·ly** *adv.*

re·cu·per·ate /rikōōpərayt/ *v.* **1** *intr.* recover from illness, exhaustion, loss, etc. **2** *tr.* regain (health, a loss, etc.). □□ **re·cu·per·a′tion** /–ráyshən/ *n.* **re·cu·per·a′tive** /–rətiv/ *adj.*

re·cur /rikár/ *v.intr.* (**re·curred, re·cur·ring**) **1** occur again; be repeated. **2** come back to one's mind.

¶ **Recur** and **recurrence** are generally regarded as better than *reoccur* and *reoccurrence*.

re·cur·rent /rikárənt, –kúr–/ *adj.* recurring; happening repeatedly. □□ **re·cur′rence** *n.* **re·cur′rent·ly** *adv.*

re·cy·cle /réesíkəl/ *v.tr.* convert (waste) to reusable material. □□ **re·cy′cla·ble** *adj.*

red /red/ • *adj.* **1** of a color like blood. **2** flushed in the face with shame, anger, etc. **3** (of the eyes) bloodshot or red-rimmed. **4** (of the hair) reddish-brown; tawny. **5** *colloq.* communist; socialist. • *n.* **1** red color or pigment. **2** *colloq.* communist; socialist. **3** debit side of an account (*in the red*). □ **red-blooded** virile; vigorous. **red carpet** privileged treatment of a visitor. **red cell** (or **cor′pus·cle**) erythrocyte. **Red Cross** international relief organization. **red dwarf** old, relatively cool star. **red-eye** **1** late-night or overnight flight. **2** *sl.* cheap whiskey. **red-faced** embarrassed; ashamed. **red flag** warning of danger. **red giant** relatively cool giant star. **red-handed** in the act of committing a crime, doing wrong, etc. **red herring** misleading clue. **red hot 1** *colloq.* hot dog. **2** small, red candy with a strong cinnamon flavor. **red-hot 1** heated until red. **2** (of news) fresh; completely new. **red-letter day** day that is pleasantly noteworthy or memorable. **red light 1** signal to stop on a road, etc. **2** warning or refusal. **red-light district** district containing many brothels. **red meat** meat that is red when raw, esp. beef. **red tape** excessive bureaucracy or formality, esp. in public business. □□ **red′dish** *adj.* **red′ness** *n.*

red Old English *rēad*, of Germanic origin; related to Dutch *rood* and German *rot*, from an Indo-European root shared by Latin *rufus*, *ruber*, Greek *eruthros*, and Sanskrit *rudhira* 'red.'

red·cap /rédkap/ *n.* baggage porter.

red·coat /rédkōt/ *n.* *hist.* British soldier (so called from the scarlet uniform of most regiments).

red·den /réd′n/ *v.* make or become red.

re·dec·o·rate /réedékərayt/ *v.tr.* decorate (a room, etc.) again or differently. □□ **re·dec·o·ra′tion** /–ráyshən/ *n.*

re·deem /rideém/ *v.tr.* **1** recover by a stipulated payment. **2** make a single payment to discharge (a regular charge or obligation). **3** convert (tokens or bonds, etc.) into goods or cash. **4** deliver from sin and damnation. **5** make up for; compensate for. **6** *refl.* save (oneself) from blame. □□ **re·deem′a·ble** *adj.*

re·deem·er /rideémər/ *n.* person who redeems. □ **the Redeemer** Christ.

re·demp·tion /ridémpshən/ *n.* **1** redeeming; being redeemed. **2** thing that redeems. □□ **re·demp·tive** /–tiv/ *adj.*

re·de·vel·op /réedivéləp/ *v.tr.* develop anew (esp. an urban area). □□ **re·de·vel′op·er** *n.* **re·de·vel′op·ment** *n.*

red·head /rédhed/ *n.* person with red hair.

red·neck /rédnek/ *n.* *derog.* working-class, politically conservative or reactionary white person.

re·do /réedōo/ *v.tr.* (*3rd sing. present* **re·does**; *past* **re·did**; *past part.* **re·done**) **1** do again or differently. **2** redecorate.

red·o·lent /réd′lənt/ *adj.* **1** strongly suggestive or smelling of. **2** fragrant. □□ **red′o·lence** *n.* **red′o·lent·ly** *adv.*

re·dou·ble /réedúbəl/ *v.* make or grow greater or more intense or numerous.

re·doubt /ridówt/ *n.* *Mil.* outwork or fieldwork without flanking defenses.

re·doubt·a·ble /ridówtəbəl/ *adj.* formidable, esp. as an opponent. □□ **re·doubt′a·bly** *adv.*

re·dound /ridównd/ *v.intr.* **1** make a great contribution to (one's credit or advantage, etc.). **2** come back or recoil (upon).

re·dress /ridrés/ • *v.tr.* remedy or rectify (a wrong, grievance, etc.). • *n.* (also /réedres/) **1** reparation for a wrong. **2** (foll. by *of*) redressing (a grievance, etc.). □□ **re·dress′er** *n.* (also **re·dres′sor**).

re·duce /ridōós, –dyōós/ *v.* **1** *tr.* & *intr.* make or become smaller or less. **2** *tr.* bring by force or necessity (to some undesirable state or action) (*reduced them to tears*). **3** *tr.* convert to another (esp. simpler) form (*reduced it to a powder*). **4** *tr.* convert (a fraction) to the form with the lowest terms. **5** *tr.* simplify. **6** *tr.* make lower in status, rank, price, etc. **7** *intr.* lessen one's weight or size. □ **reduced circumstances** poverty after relative prosperity. □□ **re·duc′er** *n.* **re·duc′i·ble** *adj.* **re·duc·i·bil′i·ty** *n.* **re·duc′tion** *n.*

reduce late Middle English: from Latin *reducere*, from *re-* 'back, again' + *ducere* 'bring, lead.' The original sense was 'bring back' (hence 'restore'); from this developed the senses 'bring to a different state' and then 'bring to a simpler or lower state' (hence sense 3); and finally 'diminish in size or amount' (sense 1, dating from the late 18th century).

re·dun·dant /ridúndənt/ *adj.* **1** superfluous. **2** that can be omitted without any loss of significance. □□ **re·dun′dan·cy** *n.* (*pl.* **–cies**). **re·dun′dant·ly** *adv.*

re·du·pli·cate /ridŏoplikayt, –dyŏo–/ *v.tr.* **1** make double. **2** repeat. □□ **re·du·pli·ca′tion** /–káyshən/ *n.*

red·wood /rédwŏod/ *n.* very large Californian conifer yielding red wood.

reed /reed/ *n.* **1 a** water or marsh plant with a firm stem. **b** tall straight stalk of this. **2 a** the vibrating, sound-producing part of the mouthpiece of some wind instruments. **b** (esp. in *pl.*) reed instrument. □ **reed organ** keyboard instrument with the sound produced by metal reeds.

reed·y /reédee/ *adj.* (**reed·i·er, reed·i·est**) **1** full of reeds. **2** like a reed. **3** (of a voice) like a reed instrument in tone; not full. □□ **reed′i·ness** *n.*

reef¹ /reef/ *n.* ridge of rock, coral, etc., at or near the surface of the sea.

reef² /reef/ *Naut.* ● *n.* part of a sail, folded and tied to reduce the surface area in a high wind. ● *v.tr.* take in a reef or reefs of (a sail).

reef·er /reéfər/ *n.* **1** *sl.* marijuana cigarette. **2** thick close-fitting double-breasted jacket.

reek /reek/ ● *v.intr.* **1** smell strongly and unpleasantly. **2** have unpleasant or suspicious associations (*reeks of corruption*). ● *n.* foul or stale smell.

reel /reel/ ● *n.* **1** cylindrical device on which film, wire, etc., are wound. **2** quantity wound on a reel. **3** device for winding and unwinding a line as required, esp. in fishing. **4** revolving part in various machines. **5 a** lively folk dance. **b** music for this. ● *v.* **1** *tr.* wind (fishing line, etc.) on a reel. **2** *tr.* (foll. by *in, up*) draw (fish, etc.) with a reel. **3** *intr.* stand or move unsteadily. **4** *intr.* be shaken mentally or physically. □ **reel off** say or recite very rapidly and without apparent effort. □□ **reel′er** *n.*

re·en·act /reéinákt/ *v.tr.* act out (a past event). □□ **re·en·act′ ment** *n.*

re·en·try /reé–éntree/ *n.* (*pl.* **–tries**) act of entering again, esp. (of a spacecraft, missile, etc.) into the earth's atmosphere.

ref /ref/ *n. colloq.* referee in sports.

re·fec·to·ry /riféktəree/ *n.* (*pl.* **–ries**) dining room, esp. in a monastery or college.

re·fer /rifər/ *v.* (**re·ferred, re·fer·ring**) **1** *tr.* send on or direct (a person, or a question for decision). **2** *intr.* appeal or have recourse (to some authority or source of information) (*referred to his notes*). **3** *tr.* send (a person) to a medical specialist, etc. **4** *intr.* make an allusion or direct the hearer's attention (*did not refer to our problems*). **5** *intr.* (of a statement, etc.) pertain (*this paragraph refers to last year*). □□ **re·fer·a·ble** /rifèrəbəl, réfər–/ *adj.* **re·fer′ral** *n.* **re·fer′rer** *n.*

ref·er·ee /réfəreé/ ● *n.* **1** umpire, esp. in football or boxing. **2** person consulted in a dispute,

etc. ● *v.* (**ref·er·ees, ref·er·eed**) **1** *intr.* act as referee. **2** *tr.* be the referee of (a game, etc.).

ref·er·ence /réfərəns, réfrəns/ ● *n.* **1** referring of a matter to some authority. **2 a** direction to a book, passage, etc. **b** book or passage so cited. **3 a** written testimonial supporting an applicant for employment, etc. **b** person giving this. ● *v.tr.* provide (a book, etc.) with references to authorities. □ **reference book** book intended to be consulted for information on individual matters. **with** (or **in**) **reference to** regarding; as regards; about. **without reference to** not taking account of. □□ **ref·er·en′tial** /réfərénshəl/ *adj.*

ref·er·en·dum /réfəréndəm/ *n.* (*pl.* **ref·er·en·dums** or **ref·er·en·da** /–də/) direct popular vote on a political question.

re·fill ● *v.tr.* /reéfil/ fill again. ● *n.* /reéfil/ **1** new filling. **2** material for this. □□ **re·fill′a·ble** *adj.*

re·fine /rifín/ *v.* **1** *tr.* free from impurities or defects. **2** *tr.* & *intr.* make or become more polished, elegant, or cultured. □□ **re·fin′a·ble** *adj.* **re·fined′** *adj.* **re·fine′ ment** *n.*

re·fin·er·y /rifínəree/ *n.* (*pl.* **–ies**) plant where oil, etc., is refined.

re·fit ● *v.* /reéfit/ (**re·fit·ted, re·fit·ting**) make or become fit or serviceable again by renewal, repairs, etc. ● *n.* /reéfit/ refitting. □□ **re·fit′ ment** *n.*

refl. *abbr.* **1** reflex. **2** reflexive.

re·flect /riflékt/ *v.* **1** *tr.* (of a surface or body) throw back (heat, light, sound, etc.). **2** *tr.* (of a mirror) show an image of. **3** *tr.* testify to (*their behavior reflects a wish to succeed*). **4** *tr.* (of an action, result, etc.) show or bring (credit, discredit, etc.). **5 a** *intr.* meditate. **b** *tr.* consider.

re·flec·tion /riflékshən/ *n.* **1** reflecting; being reflected. **2 a** reflected light, heat, or color. **b** reflected image. **3** reconsideration (*on reflection*). **4** discredit or thing bringing discredit. **5** idea arising in the mind; comment. □□ **re·flec′ tion·al** *adj.*

re·flec·tive /rifléktiv/ *adj.* **1** reflecting. **2** (of mental faculties) concerned in reflection or thought. **3** thoughtful; given to meditation. □□ **re·flec′ tive·ly** *adv.* **re·flec′ tive·ness** *n.*

re·flec·tor /rifléktər/ *n.* **1** piece of glass or metal, etc., for reflecting light in a required direction. **2 a** telescope, etc., using a mirror to produce images. **b** the mirror itself.

re·flex /reéfleks/ ● *adj.* **1** (of an action) independent of will, as an automatic response to the stimulation of a nerve. **2** (of an angle) exceeding 180°. ● *n.* reflex action.

re·flex·ive /rifléksiv/ *Gram.* ● *adj.* **1** (of a word or form) referring back to the subject of a sentence (esp. of a pronoun, e.g., *myself*). **2** (of a verb) having a reflexive pronoun as its object (as in *to wash oneself*). ● *n.* reflexive word or form, esp. a pronoun. □□ **re·flex′ ive·ly** *adv.* **re·flex′ ive·ness** *n.*

re·for·est /reéfáwrist, fór–/ *v.tr.* replant former forest land with trees. □□ **re·for·es·ta·tion** /–stáyshən/ *n.*

re·form ● *v.* **1** *tr.* & *intr.* make or become better by the removal of faults and errors. **2** *tr.* abolish or cure (an abuse or malpractice). ● *n.* **1** removal of faults or abuses, esp. moral, political, or social. **2** improvement. □ **reform school** institution for the reform of young offenders. □□ **re·form′a·ble** *adj.*

ref·or·ma·tion /réfərmáyshən/ *n.* reforming or

being reformed, esp. a radical change for the better in political, religious, or social affairs. □ **the Reformation** *hist.* 16th-c. movement for the reform of abuses in the Roman Catholic Church.

re·for·ma·to·ry /rifáwrmətawree/ *n.* (*pl.* **–ries**) = reform school.

re·form·er /rifáwrmər/ *n.* person who advocates or brings about (esp. political or social) reform.

re·fract /rifrákt/ *v.tr.* (of water, air, glass, etc.) deflect (a ray of light, etc.) at a certain angle when it enters obliquely from another medium. □□ **re·frac′tion** *n.* **re·frac′tive** *adj.*

re·frac·tor /rifráktər/ *n.* **1** refracting medium or lens. **2** telescope using a lens to produce an image.

re·frac·to·ry /rifráktəree/ *adj.* stubborn; unmanageable; rebellious. □□ **re·frac′to·ri·ly** *adv.*

re·frain¹ /rifráyn/ *v.intr.* (foll. by *from*) avoid doing (an action).

re·frain² /rifráyn/ *n.* **1** recurring phrase or lines, esp. at the ends of stanzas. **2** music accompanying this.

re·fresh /rifrésh/ *v.tr.* **1** give fresh spirit or vigor to. **2** revive or stimulate (the memory). □□ **re·fresh′er** *n.* **re·fresh′ing** *adj.* **re·fresh′ing·ly** *adv.*

re·fresh·ment /rifréshmənt/ *n.* **1** refreshing or being refreshed in mind or body. **2** (usu. in *pl.*) food or drink that refreshes.

re·frig·er·ant /rifríjərənt/ ● *n.* substance used for refrigeration. ● *adj.* cooling.

re·frig·er·ate /rifríjərayt/ *v.* **1** *tr.* & *intr.* make or become cool or cold. **2** *tr.* subject (food, etc.) to cold in order to freeze or preserve it. □□ **re·frig·er·a·tion** /-ráyshən/ *n.* **re·frig·er·a·tive** /-rətiv/ *adj.*

re·frig·er·a·tor /rifríjəraytər/ *n.* cabinet or room in which food, etc., is kept cold.

ref·uge /réfyōōj/ *n.* **1** shelter from pursuit, danger, or trouble. **2** person or place, etc., offering this.

ref·u·gee /réfyōōjée/ *n.* person taking refuge, esp. in a foreign country, from war, persecution, or natural disaster.

re·fund ● *v.* /rifúnd/ *tr.* (also *absol.*) **1** pay back (money or expenses). **2** reimburse (a person). ● *n.* /réefund/ **1** act of refunding. **2** sum refunded. □□ **re·fund′a·ble** *adj.*

re·fur·bish /rifərbish/ *v.tr.* **1** brighten up. **2** restore and redecorate. □□ **re·fur′bish·ment** *n.*

re·fuse¹ /rifyōōz/ *v.tr.* **1** withhold acceptance of or consent to. **2** indicate unwillingness or inability. **3** (often with double object) not grant (a request) made by (a person). □□ **re·fus′a·ble** *adj.* **re·fus′al** *n.*

re·fuse² /réfyōōs/ *n.* items rejected as worthless; waste.

re·fute /rifyōōt/ *v.tr.* **1** prove the falsity or error of (a statement, etc.). **2** rebut by argument. □□ **re·fut′a·ble** *adj.* **re·fu·ta·tion** /réfyōōtáyshən/ *n.* **re·fut′er** *n.*
¶ Strictly speaking, **refute** means 'to prove (a person or statement) to be wrong,' e.g., *No amount of research can refute the claim.* However, it is sometimes used to mean simply 'to deny or repudiate.' This usage is considered incorrect by some.

re·gain /rigáyn/ *v.tr.* obtain possession or use of after loss.

re·gal /réegəl/ *adj.* **1** royal; of or by a monarch or monarchs. **2** fit for a monarch; magnificent; majestic. □□ **re′gal·ly** *adv.*

re·gale /rigáyl/ *v.tr.* **1** entertain lavishly with feasting. **2** entertain or divert (with talk, etc.). □□ **re·gale′ment** *n.*

re·ga·li·a /rigáylyə/ *n.pl.* **1** insignia of royalty. **2** elaborate clothes, accouterments, etc.; trappings; finery.

re·gard /rigáard/ ● *v.tr.* **1** gaze on steadily (usu. in a specified way) (*regarded them suspiciously*). **2** heed; take into account. **3** think of in a specified way (*I regard them kindly*). ● *n.* **1** gaze; steady or significant look. **2** attention or care. **3** esteem; kindly feeling. **4** respect; point attended to. **5** (in *pl.*) expression of friendliness in a letter, etc.; compliments (*sent my best regards*). □ **as regards** about; concerning; in respect of. **in** (or **with**) **regard to** as concerns; in respect of.

re·gard·ing /rigáarding/ *prep.* about; concerning; in respect of.

re·gard·less /rigáardlis/ ● *adj.* without regard or consideration for (*regardless of cost*). ● *adv.* no matter what (*carried on regardless*). □□ **re·gard′less·ly** *adv.*
¶ See note at IRREGARDLESS.

re·gat·ta /rigáatə, –gátə/ *n.* sporting event consisting of a series of boat or yacht races.

re·gen·cy /réejənsee/ *n.* (*pl.* **–cies**) office of regent.

re·gen·er·ate ● *v.* /rijénərayt/ **1** *tr.* & *intr.* generate again. **2** *tr.* improve the moral condition of. **3** *tr.* impart new, more vigorous, and spiritually greater life to. **4** *intr.* & *tr.* *Biol.* regrow or cause (new tissue) to regrow. ● *adj.* /rijénərət/ spiritually born again; reformed. □□ **re·gen·er·a·tion** /-jenəráyshən/ *n.* **re·gen·er·a·tive** /-rətiv/ *adj.* **re·gen′er·a·tive·ly** *adv.* **re·gen′er·a·tor** *n.*

re·gent /réejənt/ ● *n.* **1** person appointed to rule when a monarch is a minor or is absent or incapacitated. **2** member of a governing body, as of a university. ● *adj.* (placed after noun) acting as regent (*prince regent*).

reg·gae /régay/ *n.* W. Indian style of music with a strongly accented subsidiary beat.

reg·i·cide /réjisīd/ *n.* **1** person who kills or takes part in killing a king. **2** act of killing a king. □□ **reg·i·cid′al** *adj.*

re·gime /rayzhéem/ *n.* (also **ré·gime′**) **1 a** system of government. **b** *derog.* particular government. **2** = REGIMEN.

reg·i·men /réjimen/ *n.* prescribed course of exercise, way of life, and diet.

reg·i·ment ● *n.* /réjimənt/ **1** military unit below division level. **2** large array or number. ● *v.tr.* /réjiment/ **1** organize (esp. oppressively) in groups or according to a system. **2** form into a regiment. □□ **reg·i·ment′al** *adj.* **reg′i·ment·ed** *adj.* **reg·i·men·ta′tion** *n.*

re·gion /réejən/ *n.* **1** geographical area or division (*mountainous region*). **2** part of the body (*lumbar region*). **3** sphere or realm (*region of metaphysics*). □ **in the region of** approximately. □□ **re′gion·al** *adj.* **re′gion·al·ly** *adv.*

reg·is·ter /réjistər/ ● *n.* **1** official list, e.g., of births, marriages, property transactions, etc. **2** book in which items are recorded for reference. **3 a** range of a voice or instrument. **b** part of this range (*lower register*). **4** machine in a store, etc., usu. with a drawer for money, for recording sales, etc. **5** *Linguistics* each of several forms of a language (colloquial, literary, etc.) used in particular circumstances. • *v.* **1** *tr.* set down (a name, fact, etc.) formally; record in writing. **2** *tr.* make a mental note of. **3** *tr.* enter or cause to be entered in a particular register. **4** *tr.* (of an instrument) record automatically; indicate. **5 a** *tr.* express (an emotion) facially or by gesture (*registered surprise*). **b** *intr.* (of an emotion) show in a person's face or gestures. □ **registered nurse** state-certified nurse. □□ **reg′is·tra·ble** *adj.*

reg·is·trar /réjistraár/ *n.* **1** official responsible for keeping a register. **2** enrollment administrator in a university, etc.

reg·is·tra·tion /réjistráyshən/ *n.* **1** registering; being registered. **2** certificate, etc., that attests to this.

reg·is·try /réjistree/ *n.* (*pl.* **-tries**) **1** place where registers or records are kept. **2** registration.

re·gress • *v.* /rigrés/ **1** *intr.* move backward, esp. return to a former state. **2** *intr.* & *tr. Psychol.* return or cause to return mentally to a former stage of life. • *n.* /réegres/ act or an instance of going back. □□ **re·gres·sion** /–grés-shən/ *n.* **re·gres′sive** *adj.* **re·gres′sive·ly** *adv.*

re·gret /rigrét/ • *v.tr.* (**re·gret·ted, re·gret·ting**) feel or express sorrow, repentance, or distress over (an action or loss, etc.). • *n.* **1** feeling of sorrow, repentance, disappointment, etc., over an action or loss, etc. **2** (often in *pl.*) an (esp. polite or formal) expression of disappointment or sorrow at an occurrence, inability to comply, etc. □ **give** (or **send**) **one's regrets** formally decline an invitation. □□ **re·gret′ful** *adj.* **re·gret′ful·ly** *adv.* **re·gret′ta·ble** *adj.* **re·gret′ta·bly** *adv.*

re·group /réegroop/ *v.* group or arrange again or differently. □□ **re·group′ment** *n.*

reg·u·lar /régyələr/ • *adj.* **1** conforming to a rule or principle; systematic. **2 a** harmonious; symmetrical (*regular features*). **b** (of a surface, etc.) smooth; level; uniform. **3** acting, done, or recurring uniformly or calculably in time or manner; habitual; constant. **4** *Gram.* (of a noun, verb, etc.) following the normal type of inflection. **5** *colloq.* complete; absolute (*a regular hero*). **6** *Geom.* (of a figure) having all sides and all angles equal. **7** (of forces or troops, etc.) proper or full-time (*regular soldiers*). **8** (of a person) defecating or menstruating at predictable times. • *n.* **1** regular soldier. **2** *colloq.* regular customer, visitor, etc. □□ **reg·u·lar·i·ty** /–láritee/ *n.* **reg′u·lar·ize** *v.tr.* **reg·u·lar·i·za′tion** *n.* **reg′u·lar·ly** *adv.*

reg·u·late /régyəlayt/ *v.tr.* **1** control by rule. **2** subject to restrictions. **3** adapt to requirements. **4** alter the speed of (a machine or clock) so that it may work accurately. □□ **reg·u·la·tive** /–lətiv/ *adj.* **reg′u·la·tor** *n.* **reg·u·la·to·ry** /–lətáwree/ *adj.*

reg·u·la·tion /régyəláyshən/ *n.* **1** regulating; being regulated. **2** prescribed rule. **3** (*attrib.*) in accordance with regulations; of the correct type, etc. (*regulation uniform*).

re·gur·gi·tate /rigərjitayt/ *v.* **1** *tr.* bring (swallowed food) up again to the mouth. **2** *tr.* cast or pour out again (*regurgitate the facts*). **3** *intr.* be brought up again; gush back. □□ **re·gur·gi·ta·tion** /–táyshən/ *n.*

re·hab /réehab/ *n. colloq.* rehabilitation.

re·ha·bil·i·tate /réehəbílitayt/ *v.tr.* **1** restore to effectiveness or normal life by training, etc., esp. after imprisonment or illness. **2** restore to former privileges, proper condition, etc. □□ **re·ha·bil·i·ta·tion** /–táyshən/ *n.* **re·ha·bil′i·ta·tive** *adj.*

re·hash • *v.tr.* /réehásh/ put (old material) into a new form without significant change or improvement. • *n.* /réehash/ **1** material rehashed. **2** rehashing.

re·hears·al /rihərsəl/ *n.* **1** act or instance of rehearsing. **2** trial performance or practice of a play, recital, etc.

re·hearse /rihərs/ *v.* **1** *tr.* practice (a play, recital, etc.) for later public performance. **2** *intr.* hold a rehearsal. **3** *tr.* train (a person) by rehearsal. **4** *tr.* recite or say over.

Reich /rīkh/ *n.* the former German state, esp. the Third Reich (1933–45).

reign /rayn/ • *v.intr.* **1** be king or queen. **2** prevail (*confusion reigns*). **3** (as **reigning** *adj.*) (of a winner, champion, etc.) currently holding the title, etc. • *n.* **1** sovereignty; rule. **2** period during which a sovereign rules.

re·im·burse /réeimbərs/ *v.tr.* **1** repay (a person who has expended money). **2** repay (a person's expenses). □□ **re·im·burs′a·ble** *adj.* **re·im·burse′ment** *n.* **re·im·burs′er** *n.*

rein /rayn/ • *n.* (in *sing.* or *pl.*) **1** long narrow strap with each end attached to the bit, used to guide or check a horse, etc. **2** means of control or guidance. • *v.tr.* **1** check or manage with reins. **2** hold (in) as with reins. **3** govern; restrain; control. □ **give free rein to** remove constraints from; allow full scope to. **keep a tight rein on** allow little freedom to.

re·in·car·na·tion /réeinkaarnáyshən/ *n.* rebirth of a soul in a new body. □□ **re·in·car·nate** /–kaʹarnayt/ *v.tr.* **re·in·car·nate** /–kaʹarnət/ *adj.*

rein·deer /ráyndeer/ *n.* (*pl.* same or **reindeers**) subarctic deer of which both sexes have large antlers.

re·in·force /réeinfáwrs/ *v.tr.* strengthen or support, esp. with additional personnel, material, etc. □ **reinforced concrete** concrete with metal bars or wire, etc., embedded to increase its strength. □□ **re·in·force′ment** *n.* **re·in·forc′er** *n.*

re·in·state /réeinstáyt/ *v.tr.* **1** replace in a former position. **2** restore (a person, etc.) to former privileges. □□ **re·in·state′ment** *n.*

re·in·sure /réeinshoōr/ *v.* insure again (esp. by transferring risk to another insurer). □□ **re·in·sur′ance** *n.* **re·in·sur′er** *n.*

REIT /reet/ *abbr.* real estate investment trust.

re·it·er·ate /rée-ítərayt/ *v.tr.* say or do again or repeatedly. □□ **re·it·er·a·tion** /–ráyshən/ *n.* **re·it·er·a·tive** /–raytiv, –rətiv/ *adj.*

re·ject • *v.tr.* /rijékt/ **1** put aside or send back as not to be used or complied with, etc. **2** refuse to accept or believe in. **3** rebuff or snub (a person). **4** cast up again; vomit. **5** *Med.* show an immune response to (a transplanted organ or tissue) so that it fails to survive. • *n.* /réejekt/ thing or person rejected as unfit or below standard. □□ **re·ject′er** /rijéktər/ *n.* (also **re·jec′tor**) **re·jec·tion** /–jékshən/ *n.*

re·joice /rijóys/ *v.intr.* feel great joy; be glad. □□ **re·joic′ing·ly** *adv.*

re·join[1] /réejóyn/ *v.* **1** *tr.* & *intr.* join together again; reunite. **2** *tr.* join (a companion, etc.) again.

re·join² /rijóyn/ v. **1** tr. say in answer; retort. **2** intr. Law reply to a charge or pleading in a lawsuit. □□ **re·join′der** n.

re·ju·ve·nate /rijǒovinayt/ v.tr. make (as if) young again. □□ **re·ju·ve·na·tion** /–náyshən/ n. **re·ju′ve·na·tor** n.

rel. abbr. **1** relating. **2** relative. **3** religion. **4** religious.

re·lapse /riláps/ • v.intr. fall back or sink again (into a worse state after improvement). • n. (also /réelaps/) relapsing, esp. a deterioration in a patient's condition after partial recovery.

re·late /riláyt/ v. **1** tr. narrate or recount. **2** tr. (in passive; often foll. by to) be connected by blood or marriage. **3** tr. connect (two things) in thought or meaning. **4** intr. have reference (to). **5** intr. **a** bring oneself into relation (to). **b** feel sympathetic (to). □□ **re·lat′a·ble** adj.

re·lat·ed /riláytid/ adj. connected.

re·la·tion /riláyshən/ n. **1 a** what one person or thing has to do with another. **b** way in which one person stands or is related to another. **2** relative. **3** (in pl.) **a** dealings (with others). **b** sexual intercourse. **4** = RELATIONSHIP. □ **in relation to** as regards. □□ **re·la′tion·al** adj.

re·la·tion·ship /riláyshənship/ n. **1** fact or state of being related. **2** colloq. **a** connection or association (good working relationship). **b** emotional (esp. sexual) association between two people.

rel·a·tive /rélətiv/ • adj. **1** considered in relation to something else (relative velocity). **2** implying comparison or contextual relation ("heat" is a relative word). **3** comparative (their relative advantages). **4** having mutual relations; corresponding in some way; related to each other. **5** (foll. by to) having reference or relating (the facts relative to the issue). **6** Gram. (of a word, esp. a pronoun) referring to an expressed or implied antecedent. • n. **1** person connected by blood or marriage. **2** species related to another by common origin. **3** Gram. relative word, esp. a pronoun. □□ **rel′a·tive·ly** adv.

rel·a·tiv·i·ty /rélətívitee/ n. **1** being relative. **2** Physics **a** (special theory of relativity) theory based on the principle that all motion is relative and that light has constant velocity. **b** (general theory of relativity) theory extending this to gravitation and accelerated motion.

re·lax /riláks/ v. **1** tr. & intr. make or become less stiff, rigid, tense, or formal. **2** intr. cease work or effort. **3** tr. (as relaxed adj.) at ease; unperturbed. □□ **re·lax·a′tion** n. **re·lax′er** n.

re·lax·ant /riláksənt/ • n. drug, etc., that relaxes and reduces tension. • adj. causing relaxation.

re·lay /réelay/ • n. **1** fresh set of people, material, etc. **2** = relay race. **3** device activating an electric circuit, etc., in response to changes affecting itself. **4 a** device to receive, reinforce, and transmit a message, broadcast, etc. **b** relayed message or transmission. • v.tr. (also /riláy/) receive (a message, broadcast, etc.) and transmit it to others. □ **relay race** team race in which each member in turn covers part of the distance.

re·lease /rileés/ • v.tr. **1** set free; liberate. **2** allow to move from a fixed position. **3** make (information, a film, etc.) publicly available. • n. **1** liberation from restriction, duty, or difficulty. **2** handle or catch that frees a mechanism. **3** document or item of information made available for publication (press release). **4 a** film, record, etc., that is released. **b** releasing or being released in this way. □□ **re·leas′a·ble** adj.

rel·e·gate /réligayt/ v.tr. **1** consign or dismiss to an inferior position. **2** banish. □□ **rel·e·ga·tion** /–gáyshən/ n.

re·lent /rilént/ v.intr. abandon a harsh intention; yield to compassion; relax severity.

re·lent·less /riléntlis/ adj. **1** unrelenting. **2** oppressively constant. □□ **re·lent′less·ly** adv. **re·lent′less·ness** n.

rel·e·vant /rélivənt/ adj. bearing on or having reference to the matter in hand. □□ **rel′e·vance** n. **rel′e·van·cy** n. **rel′e·vant·ly** adv.

re·li·a·ble /rilfəbəl/ adj. dependable; of sound and consistent character or quality. □□ **re·li·a·bil′i·ty** n. **re·li′a·bly** adv.

re·li·ance /rilfəns/ n. trust; confidence. □□ **re·li′ant** adj.

rel·ic /rélik/ n. **1** object interesting because of its age or association. **2** part of a deceased holy person's remains, etc., kept out of reverence. **3** surviving custom or belief, etc., from a past age. **4** memento or souvenir. **5** (in pl.) fragments, ruins, etc.

re·lief /rileéf/ n. **1 a** alleviation of or deliverance from pain, distress, anxiety, etc. **b** feeling accompanying such deliverance. **2** assistance (esp. financial) given to those in need. **3 a** replacing of a person or persons on duty. **b** person or persons replacing others in this way. **4 a** method of molding, carving, or stamping in which the design stands out from the surface. **b** piece of sculpture, etc., in relief. **5** vividness; distinctness (in sharp relief). **6** reinforcement or rescue (of a place). □ **relief map** map indicating hills and valleys by shading, etc.

re·lieve /rileév/ v.tr. **1** bring or give relief to. **2** mitigate the tedium or monotony of. **3** release (a person) from a duty by acting as or providing a substitute. **4** (foll. by of) take (a burden or responsibility) away from (a person). □ **relieve oneself** urinate or defecate. □□ **re·liev′a·ble** adj. **re·lieved′** adj. **re·liev′er** n.

re·li·gion /rilíjən/ n. **1** belief in a personal God or gods entitled to obedience and worship. **2** expression of this in worship. **3** particular system of faith and worship. **4** thing that one is devoted to.

re·lig·i·os·i·ty /rilijeeósitee/ n. condition of being religious or excessively religious.

re·li·gious /rilíjəs/ adj. **1** devoted to religion; pious; devout. **2** of or concerned with religion. **3** of or belonging to a monastic order. **4** scrupulous; conscientious. □□ **re·li′gious·ly** adv.

re·lin·quish /rilíngkwish/ v.tr. **1** surrender or resign (a right or possession). **2** give up or cease from (a habit, plan, etc.). **3** relax hold of (an object held). □□ **re·lin′quish·ment** n.

rel·ish /rélish/ • n. **1** great liking or enjoyment. **2 a** appetizing flavor. **b** attractive quality. **3** condiment eaten with plainer food to add flavor. • v.tr. **1** get pleasure out of; enjoy greatly. **2** anticipate with pleasure.

---

relish Middle English: alteration of obsolete *reles*, from Old French *reles* 'remainder,' from *relaisser* 'to release.' The early noun sense was 'odor, taste' giving rise to 'appetizing flavor, piquant taste' (mid-17th century), and hence sense 3 (late 18th century).

re·live /reelív/ v.tr. live (an experience, etc.) over again, esp. in the imagination.

re·lo·cate /reelókayt/ v. 1 tr. locate in a new place. 2 tr. & intr. move to a new place. □□ **re·lo·ca·tion** /–káyshən/ n.

re·luc·tant /rilúktənt/ adj. unwilling or disinclined. □□ **re·luc′tance** n. **re·luc′tant·ly** adv.

re·ly /rilí/ v.intr. (**–lies, –lied**) (foll. by on, upon) depend on with confidence or assurance.

REM /rem/ abbr. rapid eye movement.

re·main /rimáyn/ v.intr. 1 be left over after others or other parts have been removed, used, etc. 2 stay; be left behind (remained at home). 3 continue to be (remained calm). 4 (as **remaining** adj.) left behind; unused.

re·main·der /rimáyndər/ • n. 1 part remaining or left over. 2 remaining persons or things. 3 number left after division or subtraction. 4 copies of a book left unsold. • v.tr. dispose of (a remainder of books) at a reduced price.

re·mains /rimáynz/ n.pl. 1 what remains after other parts have been removed or used, etc. 2 relics of antiquity, esp. of buildings. 3 dead body.

re·make • v.tr. /reemáyk/ (past and past part. **re·made**) make again or differently. • n. /reemáyk/ thing that has been remade, esp. a movie.

re·mand /rimánd/ v.tr. return (a prisoner) to custody, esp. to allow further inquiries to be made.

re·mark /rimaark/ • v. 1 tr. **a** say by way of comment. **b** take notice of. 2 intr. make a comment. • n. 1 written or spoken comment; anything said. 2 noticing or noting (worthy of remark).

re·mark·a·ble /rimaarkəbəl/ adj. worth notice; exceptional; striking. □□ **re·mark′a·ble·ness** n. **re·mark′a·bly** adv.

re·match /reemach/ n. return match or game.

re·me·di·al /rimeedeeəl/ adj. 1 affording or intended as a remedy. 2 (of teaching) for those in need of improvement in a particular discipline. □□ **re·me′di·al·ly** adv.

rem·e·dy /rémidee/ • n. (pl. **–dies**) 1 medicine or treatment. 2 means of counteracting or removing something undesirable. • v.tr. (**–dies, –died**) rectify; make good.

re·mem·ber /rimémbər/ v.tr. 1 keep in the memory; not forget. 2 bring back into one's thoughts. 3 convey greetings from (one person) to (another) (remember me to your mother).

re·mem·brance /rimémbrəns/ n. 1 remembering; being remembered. 2 memory; recollection. 3 keepsake; souvenir. 4 (in pl.) greetings conveyed through a third person.

re·mind /rimínd/ v.tr. cause (a person) to remember or think of (something or someone).

re·mind·er /rimíndər/ n. 1 thing that reminds, esp. a memo or note. 2 memento.

rem·i·nisce /réminís/ v.intr. indulge in reminiscence.

rem·i·nis·cence /réminísəns/ n. 1 remembering things past. 2 (in pl.) collection in literary form of incidents and experiences that a person remembers.

rem·i·nis·cent /réminísənt/ adj. 1 (foll. by of) tending to remind one of or suggest. 2 concerned with reminiscence. □□ **rem·i·nis′cent·ly** adv.

re·miss /rimís/ adj. careless of duty; lax; negligent.

re·mis·sion /rimíshən/ n. 1 forgiveness (of sins, etc.). 2 remitting of a debt or penalty, etc. 3 diminution of force, effect, or degree (esp. of disease or pain). □□ **re·mis·sive** /–mísiv/ adj.

re·mit v. /rimít/ (**re·mit·ted, re·mit·ting**) 1 tr. cancel or refrain from exacting or inflicting (a debt, punishment, etc.). 2 intr. & tr. abate or slacken; cease partly or entirely. 3 tr. send (money, etc.) in payment. 4 tr. refer (a matter for decision, etc.) to some authority. 5 tr. pardon (sins, etc.). □□ **re·mit·ta·ble** /–mítəbəl/ adj. **re·mit′tal** n. **re·mit′ter** n.

re·mit·tance /rimít′ns/ n. 1 payment sent, esp. by mail. 2 sending money.

rem·nant /rémnənt/ n. 1 small remaining quantity. 2 piece of leftover cloth, etc.

re·mod·el /reem ódl/ v.tr. 1 model again or differently. 2 reconstruct.

re·mon·strate /rémənstrayt, rimón–/ v. 1 intr. (foll. by with) make a protest; argue forcibly. 2 tr. urge protestingly. □□ **re·mon′strance** n. **re·mon′strant** adj. **re·mon·stra·tion** /rémənstráyshən/ n. **re·mon·stra·tive** /rimónstrətiv/ adj. **re·mon′stra·tor** n.

re·morse /rimáwrs/ n. 1 deep regret for a wrong committed. 2 compassion (esp. in without remorse). □□ **re·morse′ful** adj. **re·morse′ful·ly** adv. **re·morse′less** adj.

re·mote /rimót/ adj. (**re·mot·er, re·mot·est**) 1 far away in place or time. 2 isolated; secluded. 3 distantly related (remote ancestor). 4 slight; faint (not the remotest chance). 5 aloof; not friendly. □ **remote control** control of an apparatus from a distance by means of signals transmitted from a radio or electronic device. □□ **re·mote′ly** adv. **re·mote′ness** n.

re·move /rimóov/ v.tr. 1 take off or away from the place occupied. 2 get rid of; eliminate (will remove all doubts). 3 take away. 4 dismiss (from office, etc.). 5 (in passive; foll. by from) distant or remote in condition (not far removed from anarchy). 6 (as **removed** adj.) (esp. of cousins) separated by a specified number of steps of descent (a first cousin twice removed = a grandchild of a first cousin). □□ **re·mov′a·ble** adj. **re·mov·a·bil′i·ty** n. **re·mov′al** n.

re·mu·ner·ate /rimyóonərayt/ v.tr. serve as or provide recompense for (toil, etc.) or to (a person). □□ **re·mu·ner·a·tion** /–ráyshən/ n. **re·mu·ner·a·tive** /–rətiv, –raytiv/ adj.

Ren·ais·sance /rénəsaans, –zaáns/ n. 1 revival of art and literature in the 14th–16th c. 2 period of this. 3 culture and style of art, architecture, etc., developed during this era. 4 (**renaissance**) any similar revival.

re·nal /reenəl/ adj. of or concerning the kidneys.

re·nas·cent /rinásənt, rináy–/ adj. springing up anew; being reborn. □□ **re·nas′cence** n.

rend /rend/ v. (past and past part. **rent** /rent/) tr. tear or wrench forcibly.

rend·er /réndər/ v.tr. 1 cause to be or become (rendered us helpless). 2 give or pay (money, service, etc.), esp. in return or as a thing due (render thanks). 3 **a** give (assistance). **b** show (obedience, etc.). **c** do (a service, etc.). 4 **a** represent or portray. **b** perform; execute. 5 translate. 6 melt (fat, etc.). □□ **ren′der·ing** n.

ren·dez·vous /róndayvōo, –də–/ • *n.* (*pl.* same /–vōoz/) **1** agreed or regular meeting place. **2** meeting by arrangement. • *v.intr.* (**ren·dez·vouses** /–vōoz/; **ren·dez·voused** /–vōod/; **ren·dez·vous·ing** /–vōoing/) meet at a rendezvous.

ren·di·tion /rendíshən/ *n.* interpretation or rendering, esp. artistic.

ren·e·gade /rénigayd/ • *n.* person who deserts a party or principles. • *adj.* traitorous; heretical.

re·nege /riníg, –nég, –néeg/ *v.* **1** *intr.* go back on one's word, etc. **2** *tr.* deny; renounce. □□ **re·neg′er** *n.*

re·new /rinōo, –nyōo/ *v.tr.* **1** revive; restore. **2** reinforce; resupply; replace. **3** reestablish; resume. **4** (also *absol.*) grant or be granted a continuation of (a license, lease, etc.). □□ **re·new′a·ble** *adj.* **re·new′al** *n.* **re·new′er** *n.*

ren·net /rénit/ *n.* preparation made from the stomach membrane of a calf or from certain fungi, used in making cheese.

re·nounce /rinówns/ *v.tr.* **1** formally abandon (a claim, right, etc.). **2** repudiate; reject. □□ **re·nounce′a·ble** *adj.* **re·nounce′ment** *n.*

ren·o·vate /rénəvayt/ *v.tr.* restore to good condition; repair. □□ **ren·o·va′tion** /–váyshən/ *n.* **ren′o·va·tor** *n.*

re·nown /rinówn/ *n.* fame; high distinction. □□ **re·nowned′** *adj.*

rent[1] /rent/ • *n.* **1** tenant's periodical payment to an owner for the use of land or premises. **2** payment for the use of a service, equipment, etc. • *v.* **1** *tr.* take, occupy, or use at a rent. **2** *tr.* let or hire (a thing) for rent. **3** *intr.* (foll. by *for, at*) be let or hired out at a specified rate. □□ **rent′er** *n.*

rent[2] /rent/ *n.* **1** large tear in a garment, etc. **2** cleft; fissure.

rent[3] *past* and *past part.* of REND.

rent·al /rént′l/ *n.* **1** amount paid or received as rent. **2** act of renting. **3** rented house, etc.

re·nun·ci·a·tion /rinúnseeáyshən/ *n.* **1** renouncing or giving up. **2** self-denial.

re·o·ri·ent /rée-áwree-ent, –óree-ent/ *v.tr.* **1** give a new direction or outlook to (ideas, a person, etc.); redirect (a thing). **2** help (a person) find his or her bearings again. **3** (*refl.*) adjust oneself to.

re·o·ri·en·tate /rée-áwreeəntayt, –óreeən–/ *v.tr.* = REORIENT. □□ **re·o·ri·en·ta′tion** /–táyshən/ *n.*

Rep. *abbr.* **1** Representative. **2** Republican. **3** Republic.

rep[1] /rep/ *n. colloq.* representative, esp. a salesperson.

rep[2] /rep/ *n. colloq.* repertory theater or company.

repaid *past* and *past part.* of REPAY.

re·pair[1] /ripáir/ • *v.tr.* **1** restore to good condition after damage or wear. **2** set right or make amends for (loss, wrong, etc.). • *n.* **1** restoring to sound condition (*in need of repair*). **2** result of this (*the repair is hardly visible*). **3** relative condition for working or using (*in good repair*). □□ **re·pair′a·ble** *adj.* **re·pair′er** *n.*

re·pair[2] /ripáir/ *v.intr.* (foll. by *to*) resort; have recourse to, go (*repaired to Spain*).

re·pair·man /ripáirmən/ *n.* (*pl.* **–men**) person who repairs machinery, etc.

rep·a·ra·ble /répərəbəl, ripáirəbəl/ *adj.* (of a

loss, etc.) that can be made good. □□ **rep·a·ra·bil′i·ty** *n.* **rep′a·ra·bly** *adv.*

rep·a·ra·tion /répəráyshən/ *n.* **1** making amends. **2** (esp. in *pl.*) compensation for war damage. □□ **re·par·a·tive** /ripáirətiv/ *adj.*

rep·ar·tee /répaartée, –táy/ *n.* **1** practice or faculty of making witty retorts. **2** witty banter.

re·past /ripást/ *n.* **1** meal. **2** food and drink for a meal.

re·pa·tri·ate • *v.* /réepáytreeayt/ **1** *tr.* restore (a person) to his or her native land. **2** *intr.* return to one's own native land. • *n.* /–treeət/ person who has been repatriated. □□ **re·pa·tri·a·tion** /–áyshən/ *n.*

re·pay /réepáy/ *v.tr.* (*past* and *past part.* **repaid**) **1** pay back (money). **2** make repayment to (a person). **3** requite (a service, action, etc.). □□ **re·pay′a·ble** *adj.* **re·pay′ment** *n.*

re·peal /ripéel/ • *v.tr.* revoke or annul (a law, etc.). • *n.* repealing. □□ **re·peal′a·ble** *adj.*

re·peat /ripéet/ • *v.* **1** *tr.* say or do over again. **2** *tr.* recite, rehearse, report, or reproduce (something from memory). **3** a *intr.* recur; appear again. **b** *refl.* recur in the same or a similar form (*history repeats itself*). • *n.* **1** a repeating. **b** thing repeated (often *attrib.*: *repeat performance*). **2** repeated broadcast. □ **repeating decimal** decimal fraction in which the same figures repeat indefinitely. □□ **re·peat′a·ble** *adj.* **re·peat·a·bil′i·ty** *n.* **re·peat′ed·ly** *adv.*

re·pel /ripél/ *v.tr.* (**re·pelled, re·pel·ling**) **1** drive back; ward off. **2** refuse admission or acceptance to. **3** be repulsive or distasteful to. □□ **re·pel′lent** *adj.* & *n.* **re·pel′ler** *n.*

¶ **Repellent** and **repulsive** are very close in meaning, but the latter, perhaps because of its sound, is felt to express stronger feeling.

re·pent /ripént/ *v.* **1** *intr.* feel deep sorrow about one's actions, etc. **2** *tr.* (also *absol.*) wish one had not done; resolve not to continue (a wrongdoing, etc.). □□ **re·pent′ance** *n.* **re·pent′ant** *adj.* **re·pent′er** *n.*

re·per·cus·sion /réepərkúshən, répər–/ *n.* **1** indirect effect or reaction. **2** recoil after impact. **3** echo. □□ **re·per·cus′sive** /–kúsiv/ *adj.*

rep·er·toire /répərtwaar/ *n.* stock of pieces, etc., that a performer, etc. is prepared to perform.

rep·er·to·ry /répərtawree/ *n.* (*pl.* **–ries**) **1** = REPERTOIRE. **2** performance of various plays for short periods by one company. **3** a repertory company. **b** repertory theaters collectively. **4** store or collection, esp. of information, instances, etc. □ **repertory company** theatrical company that performs plays from a repertoire.

rep·e·ti·tion /répitíshən/ *n.* **1** repeating or being repeated. **2** thing repeated. □□ **rep·e·ti′tious** *adj.* **rep·e·ti′tious·ly** *adv.* **re·pet′i·tive** *adj.* **re·pet′i·tive·ly** *adv.*

re·place /ripláys/ *v.tr.* **1** put back in place. **2** take the place of; succeed; be substituted for. **3** provide a substitute for. □□ **re·place′a·ble** *adj.* **re·place′ment** *n.* **re·plac′er** *n.*

re·play • *v.tr.* /reepláy/ play (a match, recording, etc.) again. • *n.* /réeplay/ act or instance of replaying a match, recording, or recorded incident in a game, etc.

re·plen·ish /riplénish/ *v.tr.* **1** fill up again. **2** renew (a supply, etc.). □□ **re·plen′ish·ment** *n.*

re·plete /ripleét/ *adj.* **1** filled or well-supplied. **2** stuffed; gorged; sated. □□ **re·plete′ness** *n.* **re·ple·tion** /–pleéshən/ *n.*

rep·li·ca /réplikə/ *n.* **1 a** exact copy. **b** (of a person) exact likeness. **2** copy or model, esp. on a smaller scale. □□ **rep′li·cate** *v.* **rep·li·ca′tion** *n.*

re·ply /riplí/ • *v.* (**–plies, –plied**) **1** *intr.* make an answer; respond in word or action. **2** *tr.* say in answer. • *n.* (*pl.* **–plies**) **1** act of replying. **2** what is replied; response. □□ **re·pli′er** *n.*

re·port /ripáwrt/ • *v.* **1** *tr.* **a** give an account of. **b** state as fact or news. **c** relate as spoken by another. **2** *tr.* make an official or formal statement about. **3** *tr.* name or specify (an offender or offense). **4** *intr.* present oneself as having returned or arrived. **5** *intr.* make or send in a report. **6** *intr.* be responsible (to a supervisor, etc.). **7** *intr.* (usu. foll. by *on*) act as a journalist. • *n.* **1** account given or opinion formally expressed after investigation or consideration. **2** account of an event, esp. for publication or broadcast. **3** common talk; rumor. **4** way a person or thing is spoken of. **5** periodical statement on (esp. a student's) work, conduct, etc. **6** sound of an explosion. □ **report card** official report of a student's grades, progress, etc. □□ **re·port′ed·ly** *adv.*

re·port·age /ripáwrtij, répawrta'azh/ *n.* **1** reporting of news, etc. **2** factual presentation in a book, etc.

re·port·er /ripáwrtər/ *n.* person employed to report news, etc., for newspapers or broadcasts.

---

report late Middle English: from Old French *reporter* (verb), *report* (noun), from Latin *reportare* 'bring back,' from *re-* 'back' + *portare* 'carry.' The sense 'give an account' gave rise to 'submit a formal report' and hence 'inform an authority of one's presence' (sense 4, mid-19th century) and 'be accountable for one's activities (to a superior)' (sense 6, late 19th century).

---

re·pose¹ /ripóz/ • *n.* **1** cessation of activity. **2** sleep. **3** peaceful state; tranquillity. • *v.* **1** *intr.* & *refl.* lie down in rest. **2** *intr.* lie, be lying, or be laid, esp. in sleep or death.

re·pose² /ripóz/ *v.tr.* (foll. by *in*) place (trust, etc.) in.

re·pos·i·to·ry /ripózitawree/ *n.* (*pl.* **–ries**) **1** place where things are stored, esp. a warehouse or museum. **2** receptacle. **3** book, person, etc., regarded as a store of information, etc.

re·pos·sess /reépəzés/ *v.tr.* regain possession of (esp. property or goods on which repayment of a debt is in arrears). □□ **re·pos·ses·sion** /–zéshən/ *n.* **re·pos·ses′sor** *n.*

place where things are stored, esp. a warehouse or museum. **2** receptacle. **3** book, person, etc., regarded as a store of information, etc.

re·pos·sess /reépəzés/ *v.tr.* regain possession of (esp. property or goods on which repayment of a debt is in arrears). □□ **re·pos·ses·sion** /–zéshən/ *n.* **re·pos·ses′sor** *n.*

rep·re·hend /réprihénd/ *v.tr.* rebuke; blame; find fault with. □□ **rep·re·hen·sion** /–henshən/ *n.*

rep·re·hen·si·ble /réprihénsibəl/ *adj.* deserving censure; blameworthy. □□ **rep·re·hen·si·bil′i·ty** *n.* **rep·re·hen′si·bly** *adv.*

rep·re·sent /réprizént/ *v.tr.* **1** stand for or cor-

respond to. **2** be a specimen or example of. **3** symbolize. **4** describe; depict; delineate. **5** be a substitute or deputy for; be entitled to act or speak for. **6** be elected as a member of a legislature, etc. □□ **rep·re·sent′a·ble** *adj.*

rep·re·sen·ta·tion /réprizentáyshən/ *n.* **1** representing or being represented. **2** thing that represents another. **3** (esp. in *pl.*) allegation or opinion. □□ **rep·re·sen·ta′tion·al** *adj.*

rep·re·sen·ta·tive /réprizéntətiv/ • *adj.* **1** typical of a class or as a specimen (*representative sample*). **2 a** consisting of elected deputies, etc. **b** based on representation by such deputies (*representative government*). **3** serving as a portrayal or symbol (of). • *n.* **1** sample, specimen, or typical embodiment. **2** agent, spokesperson, etc. **3** legislative delegate, deputy, etc.

re·press /riprés/ *v.tr.* **1** check; restrain; keep under (control); quell. **2** *Psychol.* actively exclude (an unwelcome thought) from conscious awareness. □□ **re·press′er** *n.* (also **re·pres′sor**). **re·pres′si·ble** *adj.* **re·pres·sion** /–préshən/ *n.* **re·pres′sive** *adj.* **re·pres′sive·ly** *adv.*

re·prieve /ripreév/ • *v.tr.* **1** remit or postpone the execution of (a condemned person). **2** give respite to. • *n.* **1 a** reprieving or being reprieved. **b** warrant for this. **2** respite.

---

reprieve late 15th century (as the past participle *repryed*): from Anglo-Norman French *repris* (source of *reprise*), past participle of *reprendre*, from Latin *re-* 'back' + *prehendere* 'seize.' The insertion of *-v-* (16th century) remains unexplained. Sense development has undergone a reversal, from the early meaning 'send back to prison,' via 'postpone (a legal process),' to the current sense 'rescue from impending punishment.'

---

rep·ri·mand /réprimand/ • *n.* official or sharp rebuke. • *v.tr.* administer this.

re·print *v.tr.* /reéprínt/ print again. • *n.* /reé-print/ **1** reprinting of a book, etc. **2** book, etc., reprinted.

re·pri·sal /riprízəl/ *n.* (act of) retaliation.

re·prise /ripreéz/ *n.* **1** repeated passage in music. **2** repeated item in a musical program.

re·proach /ripróch/ • *v.tr.* express disapproval to (a person) for a fault, etc. • *n.* **1** rebuke or censure. **2** thing that brings disgrace or discredit. **3** disgraced or discredited state. □ **above** (or **beyond**) **reproach** perfect. □□ **re·proach′a·ble** *adj.* **re·proach′er** *n.* **re·proach′ful** *adj.* **re·proach′ful·ly** *adv.* **re·proach′ing·ly** *adv.*

rep·ro·bate /réprəbayt/ • *n.* unprincipled or immoral person. • *adj.* immoral.

re·pro·duce /reéprədoõs, –dyoõs/ *v.* **1** *tr.* produce a copy or representation of. **2** *tr.* cause to be seen or heard, etc., again (*reproduce the sound exactly*). **3** *intr.* produce further members of the same species by natural means. **4** *refl.* produce offspring. □□ **re·pro·duc′er** *n.* **re·pro·duc′i·ble** *adj.* **re·pro·duc·i·bil′i·ty** *n.*

re·pro·duc·tion /reéprədúkshən/ *n.* **1** reproducing or being reproduced. **2** copy; (*attrib.*) imitation. □□ **re·pro·duc′tive** *adj.* **re·pro·duc′tive·ly** *adv.*

re·proof / riproõf/ *n.* **1** blame. **2** rebuke.

re·prove /riproõv/ *v.tr.* rebuke (a person, a person's conduct, etc.). □□ **re·prov′er** *n.* **re·prov′ing·ly** *adv.*

rep·tile /réptīl/ *n.* **1** cold-blooded scaly animal of the class including snakes, lizards, crocodiles, turtles, tortoises, etc. **2** mean, groveling, or repulsive person. □□ **rep·til·i·an** /–tílleeən, –tílyən/ *adj. & n.*

re·pub·lic /ripúblik/ *n.* nation in which power is held by the people or their elected representatives.

re·pub·li·can /ripúblikən/ • *adj.* **1** of or constituted as a republic. **2** characteristic of a republic. **3** advocating or supporting republican government. • *n.* **1** person advocating or supporting republican government. **2** (**Republican**) supporter of the Republican party. □ **Republican party** one of the two main US political parties, favoring a lesser degree of central power. □□ **re·pub'li·can·ism** *n.*

re·pu·di·ate /ripyōodeeayt/ *v.tr.* **1 a** disown; disavow; reject. **b** refuse dealings with. **c** deny. **2** refuse to recognize or obey (authority or a treaty). **3** refuse to discharge (an obligation or debt). □□ **re·pu·di·a·tion** /–áyshən/ *n.* **re·pu'di·a·tor** *n.*

re·pug·nance /ripúgnəns/ *n.* (also **re·pug'nan·cy**) **1** antipathy; aversion. **2** inconsistency or incompatibility of ideas, etc. □□ **re·pug'nant** *adj.*

re·pulse /ripúls/ • *v.tr.* **1** drive back by force of arms. **2** a rebuff. **b** refuse. **3** be repulsive to. • *n.* repulsing or being repulsed.

re·pul·sion /ripúlshən/ *n.* **1** aversion; disgust. **2** *Physics* tendency of bodies to repel each other.

re·pul·sive /ripúlsiv/ *adj.* **1** causing aversion or loathing; disgusting. **2** *Physics* exerting repulsion. □□ **re·pul'sive·ly** *adv.* **re·pul'sive·ness** *n.*

rep·u·ta·ble /répyətəbəl/ *adj.* of good repute; respectable. □□ **rep'u·ta·bly** *adv.*

rep·u·ta·tion /répyətáyshən/ *n.* **1** what is generally said or believed about a person's or thing's character or standing (*a reputation for dishonesty*). **2** good repute; respectability.

re·pute /ripyōot/ • *n.* reputation. • *v.tr.* (as **reputed** *adj.*) be generally considered; be said to be. □ **house of ill repute** brothel. □□ **re·put'ed·ly** *adv.*

re·quest /rikwést/ • *n.* **1** act of asking for something. **2** thing asked for. **3** demand (*in great request*). • *v.tr.* **1** ask to be given or allowed or favored with. **2** ask a person to do something. **3** ask (that). □ **by** (or **on**) **request** in response to an expressed wish. □□ **re·quest'er** *n.*

re·qui·em /rékweeəm, réekwee–/ *n.* **1** (**Requiem**) (also *attrib.*) esp. *RC Ch.* Mass for the repose of the souls of the dead. **2** music for this.

re·quire /rikwír/ *v.tr.* **1** need; depend on. **2** lay down as an imperative (*required by law*). **3** command; instruct; insist on. □□ **re·quir'er** *n.* **re·quire'ment** *n.*

req·ui·site /rékwizit/ • *adj.* required by circumstances; necessary. • *n.* thing needed (for some purpose).

req·ui·si·tion /rékwizíshən/ • *n.* **1** official order for supplies. **2** formal demand or request. **3** being called or put into service. • *v.tr.* demand the use or supply of, esp. by requisition order. □□ **req·ui·si'tion·er** *n.*

re·quite /rikwít/ *v.tr.* **1** make return for (a service). **2** reward or avenge (a favor or injury). □□ **re·quit'al** *n.*

re·run • *v.tr.* /rée-rún/ (**re·run·ning**; *past* **re·ran**; *past part.* **re·run**) run (a race, broadcast, etc.) again. • *n.* /rée-run/ **1** act of rerunning. **2** television program, etc., shown again.

re·sale /réesáyl/ *n.* sale of a thing previously bought.

re·scind /risínd/ *v.tr.* abrogate; revoke; cancel. □□ **re·scind'a·ble** *adj.* **re·scind'ment** *n.* **re·scis·sion** /–sízhən/ *n.*

res·cue /réskyōo/ • *v.tr.* (**res·cues, res·cued, res·cu·ing**) save or set free from danger, harm, etc. • *n.* rescuing or being rescued. □□ **res'cu·a·ble** *adj.* **res'cu·er** *n.*

re·search /risərch, réesərch/ • *n.* systematic investigation into and study of materials, sources, etc., in order to establish facts and reach new conclusions. • *v.* **1** *tr.* do research into or for. **2** *intr.* make researches. □ **research and development** work directed toward the innovation, introduction, and improvement of products and processes. □□ **re·search'a·ble** *adj.* **re·search'er** *n.*

re·sem·blance /rizémbləns/ *n.* likeness; similarity.

re·sem·ble /rizémbəl/ *v.tr.* be like; have a similarity to.

re·sent /rizént/ *v.tr.* feel indignation at; be aggrieved by. □□ **re·sent'ful** *adj.* **re·sent'ful·ly** *adv.* **re·sent'ment** *n.*

res·er·va·tion /rézərváyshən/ *n.* **1** reserving or being reserved. **2** thing booked, e.g., a room in a hotel. **3** express or tacit limitation to an agreement, etc. (*had reservations about the plan*). **4** area of land reserved for a particular group, as a tract federally designated for Native Americans.

re·serve /rizərv/ • *v.tr.* **1** put aside; keep back for a later occasion or special use. **2** order to be specially retained or allocated for a particular person or at a particular time. **3** retain or secure (*reserve the right to*). • *n.* **1** thing reserved for future use; extra amount. **2** self-restraint; reticence; lack of cordiality. **3** (in *sing.* or *pl.*) assets kept readily available. **4** (in *sing.* or *pl.*) standby or supplemental troops. **5** = RESERVIST. **6** substitute player on a team. **7** land reserved for special use, esp. as a habitat. □ **in reserve** unused and available if required. □□ **re·serv'a·ble** *adj.* **re·serv'er** *n.*

re·served /rizərvd/ *adj.* **1** reticent; uncommunicative. **2** set apart; destined for some use or fate. □□ **re·serv'ed·ly** *adv.* **re·serv'ed·ness** *n.*

re·serv·ist /rizərvist/ *n.* member of the reserve forces.

res·er·voir /rézərvwaar/ *n.* **1** large lake used as a source of water supply. **2** receptacle for or of fluid. **3** reserve or supply esp. of information.

re·set /réesét/ *v.tr.* (**re·set·ting**; *past* and *past part.* **re·set**) set (a broken bone, gems, a mechanical device, etc.) again or differently. □□ **re·set'ta·ble** *adj.*

re·side /rizíd/ *v.intr.* **1** have one's home; dwell permanently. **2** (of power, a right, etc.) rest or be vested in. **3** (foll. by *in*) (of a quality) be present or inherent in.

res·i·dence /rézidəns/ *n.* **1** act of residing. **2** place where a person resides; abode. □ **in residence** dwelling at a specified place, esp. for the performance of duties.

res·i·den·cy /rézidənsee/ *n.* (*pl.* **–cies**) **1** = RESIDENCE 1, 2. **2** period of hospital staff training for a physician.

res·i·dent /rézidənt/ • *n.* **1** permanent inhabitant. **2** medical graduate engaged in specialized practice under supervision in a hospital. ● *adj.* **1** residing; in residence. **2** having quarters at one's workplace, etc. (*resident housekeeper*). **3** located in; inherent. **4** (of birds, etc.) nonmigratory.

res·i·den·tial /rèzidénshəl/ *adj.* **1** suitable for or occupied by private houses (*residential area*). **2** pertaining to or used as a residence (*residential hotel*). □□ **res·i·den′tial·ly** *adv.*

re·sid·u·al /rizíjŏŏəl/ ● *adj.* **1** left as a residue. **2** *Math.* resulting from subtraction. ● *n.* **1** residual quantity. **2** (in *pl.*) pay to performers for reruns of taped shows, etc. □□ **re·sid′u·al·ly** *adv.*

res·i·due /rézidŏŏ, –dyŏŏ/ *n.* what is left over or remains; remainder.

re·sign /rizín/ *v.* **1** *intr.* give up office, one's employment, etc. **2** *tr.* surrender; hand over (a right, charge, task, etc.). **3** *refl.* reconcile (oneself) to the inevitable.

res·ig·na·tion /rèzignáyshən/ *n.* **1** resigning, esp. from one's job or office. **2** document, etc., conveying this. **3** uncomplaining endurance of a sorrow or difficulty.

re·signed /rizínd/ *adj.* having resigned oneself; submissive, acquiescent. □□ **re·sign·ed·ly** /–zínidlee/ *adv.* **re·sign′ed·ness** *n.*

re·sil·ient /rizílyənt/ *adj.* **1** resuming its original shape after bending, compression, etc. **2** readily recovering from a setback. □□ **re·sil′ience** *n.* **re·sil′ien·cy** *n.* **re·sil′ient·ly** *adv.*

res·in /rézin/ *n.* **1** adhesive substance secreted by some plants. **2** (in full **syn·thet′ic res′in**) organic compound made by polymerization, etc., and used in plastics, etc. □□ **res′in·ous** *adj.*

re·sist /rizíst/ ● *v.* **1** *tr.* withstand the action or effect of. **2** *tr.* abstain from (pleasure, temptation, etc.). **3** *tr.* strive against; refuse to comply with (*resist arrest*). **4** *intr.* offer opposition; refuse to comply. ● *n.* protective coating of a resistant substance. □□ **re·sist′ant** *adj.* **re·sist′er** *n.* **re·sist′i·ble** *adj.* **re·sist·i·bil′i·ty** *n.*

re·sis·tance /rizístəns/ *n.* **1** resisting; refusal to comply. **2** power of resisting (*resistance to wear and tear*). **3** ability to withstand disease. **4** impeding or stopping effect exerted by one thing on another. **5** *Physics* property or measure of hindering the conduction of electricity, heat, etc. **6** (in full **re·sist′ance move′ment**) secret organization resisting authority, esp. in an occupied country.

re·sis·tor /rizístər/ *n. Electr.* device having resistance to the passage of an electrical current.

res·o·lute /rézəlŏŏt/ *adj.* determined; firm of purpose. □□ **res·o·lute′ly** *adv.* **res·o·lute′ness** *n.*

res·o·lu·tion /rézəlŏŏshən/ *n.* **1** resolute temper or character. **2** thing resolved on; intention (*New Year's resolutions*). **3** formal expression of opinion or intention by a legislative body, etc. **4** solving of a problem, doubt, or question. **5** separation into components. **6** optical clarity or sharpness.

re·solve /rizólv/ ● *v.* **1** *intr.* make up one's mind; decide firmly. **2** *tr.* (of an assembly or meeting) pass a resolution by vote. **3** *intr.* & *tr.* separate or cause to separate into constituent parts. **4** *tr.* solve; explain; settle (doubt, argument, etc.). ● *n.* firm mental decision or intention. □□ **re·solv′a·ble** *adj.* **re·solv·a·bil′i·ty** *n.* **re·solv′er** *n.*

re·solved /rizólvd/ *adj.* resolute; determined.

res·o·nant /rézənənt/ *adj.* **1** (of sound) echoing; resounding. **2** (of a body, room, etc.) tending to reinforce or prolong sounds. **3** (of a place) resounding. □□ **res′o·nance** *n.* **res′o·nant·ly** *adv.*

res·o·nate /rézənayt/ *v.intr.* produce or show resonance; resound. □□ **res′o·na·tor** *n.*

re·sorb /risáwrb, –záwrb/ *v.tr.* absorb again. □□ **re·sorb′ence** *n.* **re·sorb′ent** *adj.* **re·sorp·tion** /–sáwrpshən, –záwrp–/ *n.*

re·sort /rizáwrt/ ● *n.* **1** place frequented for recreation, health, etc. **2 a** thing to which one has recourse; expedient; measure. **b** recourse (to). ● *v.intr.* turn (to) as an expedient (*resorted to threats*). □ **as a last resort** when all else has failed.

re·sound /rizównd/ *v.intr.* **1** (of a place) ring or echo. **2** *intr.* produce echoes; go on sounding.

re·sound·ing /rizównding/ *adj.* **1** in senses of RESOUND. **2** unmistakable; emphatic (*a resounding success*). □□ **re·sound′ing·ly** *adv.*

re·source /rée'sawrs, –zawrs, risáwrs, –záwrs/ *n.* **1** expedient or device. **2** (usu. in *pl.*) means available; asset. **3** (in *pl.*) country's collective wealth. **4** (often in *pl.*) skill in devising expedients. □□ **re·source′ful** *adj.* **re·source′ful·ly** *adv.* **re·source′ful·ness** *n.*

re·spect /rispékt/ ● *n.* **1** deferential esteem felt or shown toward a person or quality. **2** heed or regard. **3** aspect, particular, etc. **4** reference; relation (*morality that has no respect to religion*). **5** (in *pl.*) greetings; polite messages (*give them my respects*). ● *v.tr.* **1** regard with deference, esteem, or honor. **2 a** avoid interfering with, harming, etc. **b** treat with consideration. □ **with all due respect** mollifying formula preceding an expression of one's disagreement with another's views. **with respect to** regarding. □□ **re·spect′er** *n.*

re·spect·a·ble /rispéktəbəl/ *adj.* **1** decent and proper in appearance and behavior. **2** fairly competent (*a respectable effort*). **3** reasonably good in condition, appearance, number, size, etc. (*a respectable salary*). □□ **re·spect·a·bil′i·ty** *n.* **re·spect′a·bly** *adv.*

re·spect·ful /rispéktfŏŏl/ *adj.* showing deference (*stood at a respectful distance*). □□ **re·spect′ful·ly** *adv.* **re·spect′ful·ness** *n.*

re·spect·ing /rispékting/ *prep.* with regard to; concerning.

re·spec·tive /rispéktiv/ *adj.* concerning or appropriate to each of several individually (*go to your respective places*). □□ **re·spec′tive·ly** *adv.*

res·pi·ra·tion /réspiráyshən/ *n.* **1 a** breathing. **b** single breath. **2** *Biol.* in organisms, absorption of oxygen and release of energy and carbon dioxide.

res·pi·ra·tor /réspiraytər/ *n.* **1** apparatus worn over the face to purify, warm, etc., inhaled air. **2** *Med.* apparatus for maintaining artificial respiration.

re·spire /rispír/ *v.* **1** *tr.* & *intr.* breathe. **2** *intr.* inhale and exhale air. **3** *intr.* (of a plant) carry out respiration. □□ **res·pi·ra·to·ry** /réspərətawree, rispírə–/ *adj.*

res·pite /réspit/ *n.* **1** interval of rest or relief. **2** delay permitted before discharge of obligation or suffering of penalty.

re·splen·dent /rispléndənt/ *adj.* brilliant; dazzlingly or gloriously bright. □□ **re·splen′dence** *n.* **re·splen′den·cy** *n.* **re·splen′dent·ly** *adv.*

re·spond /rispónd/ *v.* **1** *intr.* answer; reply. **2** *intr.*

react. **3** *intr.* show sensitiveness (to) by behavior or change (*does not respond to kindness*).

re·spon·dent /rispóndənt/ *n.* defendant, esp. in an appeal or divorce case.

re·sponse /rispóns/ *n.* **1** answer given in word or act; reply. **2** feeling, movement, change, etc., caused by a stimulus or influence. **3** (often in *pl.*) *Eccl.* any part of the liturgy said or sung in answer to the priest.

re·spon·si·bil·i·ty /rispónsibílitee/ *n.* (*pl.* **–ties**) **1 a** being responsible. **b** authority and obligation. **2** person or thing for which one is responsible.

re·spon·si·ble /rispónsibəl/ *adj.* **1** liable to be called to account (to a person or for a thing). **2** morally accountable for one's actions; capable of rational conduct. **3** of good credit, position, or repute; respectable. **4** being the primary cause. **5** involving responsibility. □□ **re·spon′si·bly** *adv.*

re·spon·sive /rispónsiv/ *adj.* **1** responding readily (to some influence). **2** sympathetic. **3** answering. □□ **re·spon′sive·ly** *adv.* **re·spon′sive·ness** *n.*

rest[1] /rest/ • *v.* **1** *intr.* cease, abstain, or be relieved from exertion, action, etc. **2** *intr.* be still or asleep, esp. to refresh oneself or recover strength. **3** *tr.* give relief or repose to; allow to rest. **4** *intr.* lie (on); be supported (by). **5** *intr.* depend; be based; rely. **6** *intr.* (of a look) light (upon) or be steadily directed (on). **7** *tr.* place for support. **8** *intr.* be left without further investigation or discussion (*let the matter rest*). **9** *intr.* a lie in death. **b** lie buried (in a churchyard, etc.). **10** *tr.* (as **rested** *adj.*) refreshed by resting. • *n.* **1** repose or sleep. **2** cessation of exertion, activity, etc. **3** period of resting. **4** support for holding or steadying something. **5** *Mus.* **a** interval of silence. **b** sign denoting this. □ **at rest** not moving; not troubled; dead. **lay to rest** inter (a corpse). **rest area** = *rest stop.* **rest one's case** conclude one's argument, etc. **rest** (or **God rest**) **his** (or **her**) **soul** may God grant his (or her) soul repose. **rest home** place where old or frail people can be cared for. **rest room** public toilet. **rest stop** area for travelers to stop for rest, refreshment, etc.

rest[2] /rest/ • *n.* (prec. by *the*) the remaining part or parts; the others; the remainder. • *v.intr.* **1** remain in a specified state (*rest assured*). **2** be left in the hands or charge of (*final arrangements rest with you*).

res·tau·rant /réstərənt, –raant, réstraant/ *n.* public premises where meals or refreshments may be had.

res·tau·ra·teur /réstərətör/ *n.* restaurant owner or manager.
¶ Despite its close relation to *restaurant*, there is no *n* in **restaurateur**, either in its spelling or in its pronunciation.

rest·ful /réstfool/ *adj.* **1** favorable to quiet or repose. **2** undisturbed. □□ **rest′ful·ly** *adv.* **rest′ful·ness** *n.*

res·ti·tu·tion /réstitooshən, –tyoo–/ *n.* **1** restoring of a thing to its proper owner. **2** reparation.

res·tive /réstiv/ *adj.* **1** fidgety; restless. **2** unmanageable; rejecting control. □□ **res′tive·ly** *adv.* **res′tive·ness** *n.*

rest·less /réstlis/ *adj.* **1** finding or affording no rest. **2** uneasy; agitated. **3** constantly in motion; fidgety. □□ **rest′less·ly** *adv.* **rest′less·ness** *n.*

res·to·ra·tion /réstəráyshən/ *n.* **1** restoring or

being restored. **2** model or representation of the supposed original form of a thing. **3** (**Restoration**) *hist.* **a** (prec. by *the*) reestablishment of England's monarchy in 1660. **b** (often *attrib.*) literary period following this (*Restoration comedy*).

re·stor·a·tive /ristáwrətiv, –stór–/ • *adj.* tending to restore health or strength. • *n.* restorative medicine, food, etc. (*needs a restorative*). □□ **re·stor′a·tive·ly** *adv.*

re·store /ristáwr/ *v.tr.* **1** bring back to the original state by rebuilding, repairing, etc. **2** bring back to health, etc. **3** give back to the original owner. **4** reinstate. **5** replace; put back; bring back. □□ **re·stor′a·ble** *adj.* **re·stor′er** *n.*

re·strain /ristráyn/ *v.tr.* **1** check or hold in; keep in check or under control or within bounds. **2** repress; keep down. **3** confine; imprison. □□ **re·strain′a·ble** *adj.* **re·strain′er** *n.*

re·straint /ristráynt/ *n.* **1** restraining or being restrained. **2** controlling agency or influence. **3** self-control; moderation. **4** reserve of manner. **5** confinement, esp. because of insanity.

re·strict /ristríkt/ *v.tr.* **1** confine; bound; limit. **2** withhold from general circulation or disclosure. □□ **re·strict′ed·ly** *adv.* **re·strict′ed·ness** *n.* **re·stric′tion** *n.*

re·stric·tive /ristríktiv/ *adj.* imposing restrictions. □ **restrictive clause** *Gram.* relative clause, usu. without surrounding commas. □□ **re·stric′tive·ly** *adv.* **re·stric′tive·ness** *n.*

re·sult /rizúlt/ • *n.* **1** consequence, issue, or outcome of something. **2** satisfactory outcome (*gets results*). **3** end product of calculation. **4** (in *pl.*) list of scores or winners, etc., in an examination or sporting event. • *v.intr.* **1** arise as the actual or follow as a logical consequence. **2** have a specified end or outcome (*resulted in a large profit*). □□ **re·sult′ant** *adj.*

re·sume /rizoom/ • *v.* **1** *tr.* & *intr.* begin again or continue after an interruption. **2** *tr.* & *intr.* begin to speak, work, or use again; recommence. **3** *tr.* get back; take back (*resume one's seat*). • *n.* = RÉSUMÉ. □□ **re·sum′a·ble** *adj.*

ré·su·mé /rézoomay/ *n.* (also **resumé, resume**) summary, esp. of a person's employment history.

re·sump·tion /rizúmpshən/ *n.* resuming. □□ **re·sump′tive** /–tiv/ *adj.*

re·sur·face /réesórfis/ *v.* **1** *tr.* lay a new surface on (a road, etc.). **2** *intr.* rise or arise again; turn up again.

re·sur·gent /risórjənt/ *adj.* **1** rising or arising again. **2** tending to rise again. □□ **re·sur′gence** *n.*

re·sur·rect /rézərékt/ *v.* **1** *tr.* *colloq.* revive the practice, use, or memory of. **2** *tr.* & *intr.* raise or rise from the dead.

re·sur·rec·tion /rézərékshən/ *n.* **1** rising from the dead. **2** (**Resurrection**) **a** Christ's rising from the dead. **b** rising of the dead at the Last Judgment. **3** revival after disuse, inactivity, or decay. □□ **re·sur·rec′tion·al** *adj.*

re·sus·ci·tate /risúsitayt/ *v.* **1** revive from unconsciousness or apparent death. **2** restore to vogue, vigor, or vividness. □□ **re·sus·ci·ta·tion** /–táyshən/ *n.* **re·sus·ci·ta′tive** *adj.* **re·sus′ci·ta·tor** *n.*

re·tail /réetayl/ • *n.* sale of goods in small quantities to the public. • *adj. & adv.* by retail; at a retail price. • *v.* (also /ritáyl/) **1** *tr.* sell (goods) in retail trade. **2** *intr.* (of goods) be sold in this way (*retails at $4.95*). □□ **re′tail•er** *n.*

re•tain /ritáyn/ *v.tr.* **1 a** keep possession of; not lose. **b** not abolish, discard, nor alter. **2** keep in one's memory. **3** keep in place; hold fixed. **4** secure the services of (a person, esp. an attorney) with a preliminary payment. □□ **re•tain′a•ble** *adj.*

re•tain•er /ritáynər/ *n.* **1** person or thing that retains. **2** fee for retaining an attorney, etc. **3** faithful servant (esp. *old retainer*).

re•take • *v.tr.* /reetáyk/ (*past* **re′took**; *past part.* **re•tak′en**) **1** take again. **2** recapture. • *n.* /reé-tayk/ **1** act of filming a scene or recording music, etc., again. **2** scene or recording obtained in this way.

re•tal•i•ate /ritáleeayt/ *v.* repay an injury, insult, etc., in kind; attack in return. □□ **re•tal•i•a•tion** /–áyshən/ *n.* **re•tal′i•a•tor** *n.* **re•tal•i•a•to•ry** /–táleeətáwree/ *adj.*

re•tard /ritaárd/ *v.tr.* **1** make slow or late. **2** delay the progress or accomplishment of. □□ **re•tard′ant** *adj. & n.* **re•tar•da•tion** /reétaardáyshən/ *n.*

re•tard•ed /ritaárdid/ *adj.* backward in mental or physical development.

retch /rech/ *v.intr.* make a motion of vomiting esp. involuntarily and without effect.

re•ten•tion /riténshən/ *n.* **1 a** retaining; being retained. **b** memory. **2** failure to evacuate urine or another secretion. □□ **re•ten•tive** /–tiv/ *adj.* **re•ten′tive•ly** *adv.*

ret•i•cence /rétisəns/ *n.* **1** personal hesitancy or avoidance; reluctance. **2** disposition to silence. □□ **ret′i•cent** *adj.* **ret′i•cent•ly** *adv.*

re•tic•u•late • *v.* /ritíkyəlayt/ divide or be divided in fact or appearance into a network. • *adj.* /–yələt, –layt/ reticulated. □□ **re•tic′u•late•ly** *adv.* **re•tic•u•la•tion** /–láyshən/ *n.*

ret•i•na /rét′nə/ *n.* (*pl.* **ret′i•nas, ret•i•nae** /–nee/) layer at the back of the eyeball sensitive to light. □□ **ret′i•nal** *adj.*

ret•i•nue /rét′noo, –yoo/ *n.* body of attendants accompanying an important person.

re•tire /ritír/ *v.* **1 a** *intr.* leave office or employment, esp. because of age. **b** *tr.* cause (a person) to do this. **2** *intr.* withdraw; go away; retreat. **3** *intr.* seek seclusion or shelter. **4** *intr.* go to bed. **5** *intr. & tr. Baseball* (of a batter or side) put out. □□ **re•tired′** *adj.* **re•tir•ee′** *n.* **re•tire′ment** *n.* **re•tir′er** *n.*

re•tir•ing /ritíring/ *adj.* fond of seclusion. □□ **re•tir′ing•ly** *adv.*

re•took *past* of RETAKE.

re•tort¹ /ritáwrt/ • *n.* incisive or witty or angry reply. • *v.* **1** *tr.* say by way of a retort. **2** *intr.* make a retort.

re•tort² /ritáwrt, reétawrt/ *n.* vessel with a long downward-turned neck used in distilling liquids.

re•touch /reétúch/ *v.tr.* improve (a picture, photograph, etc.) by minor alterations.

re•trace /reetráys/ *v.tr.* **1** go back over (one's steps, etc.). **2** trace back to a source or beginning.

re•tract /ritrákt/ *v.* **1** *tr.* (also *absol.*) withdraw (a statement or undertaking). **2** *tr. & intr.* draw

or be drawn back or in. □□ **re•tract′a•ble** *adj.* **re•trac′tion** *n.* **re•trac′tive** *adj.*

re•trac•tile /ritráktil, –tīl/ *adj.* capable of being retracted. □□ **re•trac•til•i•ty** /–tílitee/ *n.*

re•tread • *v.tr.* /reétréd/ (*past* **re•trod′**; *past part.* **re•trod′den**) **1** tread (a path, etc.) again. **2** put a fresh tread on (a tire). • *n.* /reétred/ retreaded tire.

re•treat /ritreét/ • *v.* **1** *intr.* (esp. of military forces) go back; retire. **2** *intr.* (esp. of features) recede. • *n.* **1 a** act of retreating. **b** *Mil.* signal for this. **2** withdrawal into privacy or security. **3** place of shelter, seclusion, or meditation. **4** *Mil.* bugle call at sunset.

re•trench /ritrénch/ *v.* **1** *tr.* reduce the amount of (costs). **2** *intr.* cut down expenses. □□ **re•trench′ment** *n.*

ret•ri•bu•tion /rétribyooshən/ *n.* requital, usu. for evil done; vengeance. □□ **re•trib•u•tive** /ritríbyətiv/ *adj.* **re•trib•u•to•ry** /ritríbyətawree/ *adj.*

re•trieve /ritreév/ *v.tr.* **1 a** regain possession of. **b** recover by investigation or effort of memory. **2** obtain (information stored in a computer, etc.). **3** (of a dog) find and bring in (killed or wounded game, etc.). **4** rescue (esp. from a bad state). □□ **re•triev′a•ble** *adj.* **re•triev′al** *n.*

re•triev•er /ritreévər/ *n.* **1** dog of a breed used for retrieving game. **2** this breed.

ret•ro /rétrō/ *adj.* reviving or harking back to the past.

retro- /rétrō/ *comb. form* **1** denoting action back or in return. **2** *Anat. & Med.* denoting location behind.

ret•ro•ac•tive /rétrō-áktiv/ *adj.* (esp. of legislation) having retrospective effect. □□ **ret•ro•ac′tive•ly** *adv.* **ret•ro•ac•tiv•i•ty** /–tívitee/ *n.*

ret•ro•fit /rétrōfit/ *v.tr.* (**–fit•ted**, **–fit•ting**) modify machinery, vehicles, etc.) to incorporate changes and developments introduced after manufacture.

ret•ro•grade /rétrəgrayd/ • *adj.* **1** directed backward; retreating. **2** reverting esp. to an inferior state; declining. **3** inverse; reversed (*retrograde order*). • *v.intr.* **1** move backward; recede. **2** decline; revert.

ret•ro•gress /rétrəgrés/ *v.intr.* **1** move backward. **2** deteriorate. □□ **ret•ro•gres•sion** /–gréshən/ *n.* **ret•ro•gres′sive** *adj.* **ret•ro•gres′sive•ly** *adv.*

ret•ro•rock•et /rétrō-rókit/ *n.* auxiliary rocket for slowing down a spacecraft, etc.

ret•ro•spect /rétrəspekt/ *n.* regard or reference to previous conditions. □ **in retrospect** when looked back on. □□ **ret•ro•spec•tion** /–spékshən/ *n.*

ret•ro•spec•tive /rétrəspéktiv/ • *adj.* **1** looking back on or dealing with the past. **2** (of an exhibition, recital, etc.) showing an artist's development over his or her lifetime. • *n.* retrospective exhibition, recital, etc. □□ **ret•ro•spec′tive•ly** *adv.*

ret•ro•vi•rus /rétrōvīrəs/ *n. Biol.* any of a group of RNA viruses that form DNA during the replication of their RNA.

re•try /reétrī/ *v.tr.* (**–tries**, **–tried**) try (a defendant or lawsuit) a second or further time. □□ **re•tri′al** *n.*

re•turn /ritórn/ • *v.* **1** *intr.* come or go back. **2** *tr.* bring or put or send back. **3** *tr.* pay back or reciprocate; give in response. **4** *tr.* yield (a profit). **5** *tr.* say in reply; retort. **6** *tr.* (in tennis, etc.) hit or send (the ball) back. **7** *tr.* reelect to political office, etc. • *n.* **1** coming or going back. **2 a** giving, sending, putting, or paying back. **b** thing given or sent back. **3** key on a computer or typewriter to start a new line. **4** (in *sing.* or *pl.*) proceeds or profit of an undertaking. **5** formal report compiled or submitted by order (*tax return*). □ **in return** as an exchange or reciprocal action. **many happy returns (of the day)** greeting on a birthday, etc. □□ **re·turn′a·ble** *adj.*

re·turn·ee /rítərnéé/ *n.* person who returns home from abroad, esp. after war service.

re·un·ion /reeyóonyən/ *n.* **1** reuniting; being reunited. **2** social gathering of people formerly associated.

Rev. *abbr.* **1** Reverend. **2** Revelation (New Testament).

rev /rev/ *colloq.* • *n.* (in *pl.*) number of revolutions of an engine per minute. • *v.* (**revved, rev·ving**) **1** *intr.* (of an engine) revolve; turn over. **2** *tr.* (also *absol.*; often foll. by *up*) cause (an engine) to run quickly.

re·vamp /réevámp/ *v.tr.* renovate; revise; improve.

re·veal /rivéel/ *v.tr.* **1** display or show; allow to appear. **2** disclose; divulge; betray (*revealed his plans*). **3** *tr.* (in *refl.* or *passive*) come to sight or knowledge. □□ **re·veal′ing·ly** *adv.*

rev·eil·le /révəlee/ *n.* military wake-up signal.

rev·el /révəl/ • *v.intr.* **1** have a good time; be extravagantly festive. **2** take keen delight (in). • *n.* (in *sing.* or *pl.*) reveling. □□ **rev′el·er** *n.* **rev′el·ry** *n.* (*pl.* **–ries**).

rev·e·la·tion /révəláyshən/ *n.* **1 a** revealing, esp. by divine or supernatural agency. **b** knowledge disclosed in this way. **2** striking disclosure. **3** (**Revelation**) last book of the New Testament. □□ **rev·e·la′tion·al** *adj.*

re·venge /rivénj/ • *n.* **1** retaliation for an offense or injury. **2** desire for this; vindictive feeling. **3** (in games) win after an earlier defeat. • *v.* **1** *tr.* (in *refl.* or *passive*) inflict retaliation for an offense. **2** *intr.* take vengeance. □□ **re·venge′ful** *adj.* **re·venge′ful·ly** *adv.* **re·veng′er** *n.*

rev·e·nue /révənoo, –nyoo/ *n.* **1 a** income, esp. of a large amount. **b** (in *pl.*) items constituting this. **2** government's income from which public expenses are met.

re·ver·ber·ate /rivárbərayt/ *v.* **1 a** *intr.* (of sound, light, or heat) be returned, echoed, or reflected repeatedly. **b** *tr.* return (a sound, etc.) in this way. **2** *intr.* (of a story, rumor, etc.) be heard much or repeatedly. □□ **re·ver′ber·ant** *adj.* **re·ver′ber·ant·ly** *adv.* **re·ver·ber·a′tion** /–ráyshən/ *n.* **re·ver·ber·a·tive** /–rətiv/ *adj.* **re·ver′ber·a·tor** *n.* **re·ver·ber·a·to·ry** /–rətawree/ *adj.*

re·vere /rivéer/ *v.tr.* hold in deep or religious respect. □□ **rev′er·ence** *n.* **rev′er·ent** *adj.* **rev·er·en·tial** /–énshəl/ *adj.* **rev·er·en′tial·ly** *adv.*

rev·er·end /révərənd, révrənd/ • *adj.* (esp. as the title of a clergyman) deserving reverence. • *n. colloq.* clergyman.

rev·er·ie /révəree/ *n.* spell of abstracted musing.

re·verse /rivárs/ • *v.* **1** *tr.* turn the other way around or up or inside out. **2** *tr.* change to the opposite character or effect (*reversed the decision*). **3** *intr.* & *tr.* travel or cause to travel backward. **4** revoke or annul (a decree, etc.). • *adj.* **1** backward or upside-down. **2** opposite or contrary in

character or order; inverted. • *n.* **1** opposite or contrary (*the reverse is the case*). **2** occurrence of misfortune; defeat. **3** reverse gear or motion. **4** reverse side. □ **reverse the charges** make the recipient of a telephone call responsible for payment. □□ **re·ver′sal** *n.* **re·vers′er** *n.* **re·vers′i·ble** *adj.* **re·vers·i·bil′i·ty** *n.* **re·vers′i·bly** *adv.*

re·vert /rivárt/ *v.intr.* **1** (foll. by *to*) return to a former state, practice, opinion, etc. **2** (of property, an office, etc.) return by reversion. □□ **re·ver′sion** *n.* **re·ver′sion·a·ry** *adj.*

re·view /rivyóo/ • *n.* **1** general survey or assessment of a subject or thing. **2** survey of the past. **3** revision or reconsideration. **4** display and formal inspection of troops, etc. **5** criticism of a book, play, etc. **6** periodical with critical articles on current events, the arts, etc. • *v.tr.* **1** survey or look back on. **2** reconsider or revise. **3** hold a review of (troops, etc.). **4** write a review of (a book, play, etc.). **5** view again. □□ **re·view′a·ble** *adj.* **re·view′er** *n.*

re·vile /rivíl/ *v.* **1** *tr.* abuse; criticize abusively. **2** *intr.* talk abusively; rail. □□ **re·vile′ment** *n.* **re·vil′er** *n.* **re·vil′ing** *n.*

re·vise /rivíz/ *v.tr.* **1** examine and improve or amend (esp. written or printed matter). **2** consider and alter (an opinion, etc.). □□ **re·vis′a·ble** *adj.* **re·vis′er** *n.* **re·vi·sion** /–vízhən/ *n.* **re·vi′so·ry** *adj.*

re·vi·sion·ism /rivízhənizəm/ *n.* departure from or modification of accepted doctrine, theory, view of history, etc. □□ **re·vi′sion·ist** *n.* & *adj.*

re·viv·al /rivívəl/ *n.* **1** reviving; being revived. **2** new production of an old play, etc. **3** reawakening of religious fervor. □□ **re·viv′al·ism** *n.* **re·viv′al·ist** *n.* **re·viv·al·is′tic** *adj.*

re·vive /rivív/ *v.* **1** come or bring back to consciousness, life, or strength. **2** come or bring back to existence, use, notice, etc. □□ **re·viv′a·ble** *adj.*

re·viv·i·fy /rivívifī/ *v.tr.* (**–fies, –fied**) restore to animation, activity, vigor, or life. □□ **re·viv·i·fi·ca′tion** *n.*

re·voke /rivók/ *v.tr.* rescind, withdraw, or cancel (a decree or promise, etc.). □□ **re·vo′ca·ble** /révəkəbəl/ *adj.* **re·vo·ca·bil′i·ty** /révəkəbílitee/ *n.* **rev·o·ca·tion** /révəkáyshən/ *n.* **re·vok′er** *n.*

re·volt /rivólt/ • *v.* **1** *intr.* rise in rebellion. **2 a** *tr.* affect with strong disgust (*was revolted by the thought of it*). **b** *intr.* feel strong disgust. • *n.* act of rebelling.

re·volt·ing /rivólting/ *adj.* disgusting; horrible. □□ **re·volt′ing·ly** *adv.*

rev·o·lu·tion /révəlóoshən/ *n.* **1** forcible overthrow of a government or social order. **2** any fundamental change or reversal of conditions. **3** revolving. **4** completion of an orbit or rotation. **5** cyclic recurrence. □□ **rev·o·lu′tion·ar·y** *adj.* & *n.* **rev·o·lu′tion·ism** *n.* **rev·o·lu′tion·ist** *n.*

rev·o·lu·tion·ize /révəlóoshənīz/ *v.tr.* introduce fundamental change to.

re·volve /rivólv/ *v.* **1** *intr.* & *tr.* turn or cause to turn around, esp. on an axis; rotate. **2** *intr.* move in a circular orbit. **3** *tr.* ponder (a problem, etc.).

re·volv·er /rivólvər/ *n.* pistol with revolving chambers enabling several shots to be fired without reloading.

re·vue /rivyóo/ *n.* theatrical entertainment of a series of short usu. satirical sketches and songs.

re·vul·sion /rivúlshən/ *n.* abhorrence; sense of loathing.

re·ward /riwáwrd/ • *n.* **1 a** return or recompense for service or merit. **b** requital for good or evil; retribution. **2** sum offered for the detection of a criminal, restoration of lost property, etc. • *v.tr.* give a reward to (a person) or for (a service, etc.).

re·ward·ing /riwáwrding/ *adj.* (of an activity, etc.) worthwhile; satisfying. □□ **re·ward′ing·ly** *adv.*

re·wind /re͞eẃind/ • *v.tr.* (*past* and *past part.* **re·wound**) wind (a film, tape, etc.) back to the beginning. • *n.* function on a tape deck, camera, etc., to rewind (tape, film, etc.). □□ **re·wind′er** *n.*

re·word /re͞ewə́rd/ *v.tr.* change the wording of.

re·work /re͞ewə́rk/ *v.tr.* revise; refashion; remake.

re·write • *v.tr.* /re͞erít/ (*past* **re·wrote**; *past part.* **re·writ·ten**) write again, esp. differently. • *n.* /re͞erít/ **1** rewriting. **2** thing rewritten.

Reye's syn·drome /rīz, ráz/ *n. Med.* acute, often fatal brain disease of children, associated with aspirin use.

Rf *symb. Chem.* rutherfordium.

RFD *abbr.* rural free delivery.

Rh[1] *symb. Chem.* rhodium.

Rh[2] see RH FACTOR.

rhap·so·dize /rápsədīz/ *v.intr.* talk or write rhapsodies.

rhap·so·dy /rápsədee/ *n.* (*pl.* **–dies**) **1** enthusiastic, ecstatic, or extravagant utterance or composition. **2** piece of music in one extended movement, usu. emotional in character. □□ **rhap·sod·ic** /rapsódik/ *adj.* **rhap·sod′i·cal** *adj.*

rhe·a /re͞eə/ *n.* small, flightless ostrichlike bird of South America.

rhe·ni·um /re͞eneeəm/ *n. Chem.* rare metallic element of the manganese group. ¶ Symb.: **Re**.

rhe·o·stat /re͞eəstat/ *n. Electr.* device used to control a current by varying the resistance. □□ **rhe·o·stat′ic** *adj.*

rhe·sus /re͞esəs/ *n.* (in full **rhe′sus mon′key**) small monkey common in N. India. □ **rhesus factor** = RH FACTOR.

rhet·o·ric /rétərik/ *n.* **1** art of effective or persuasive speaking or writing. **2** language designed to persuade or impress. □ **rhetorical question** question asked not for information but for an effect, e.g., *who cares?* for *nobody cares.* □□ **rhe·tor′i·cal** *adj.* **rhe·tor′i·cal·ly** *adv.*

rheu·ma·tism /ro͞omətizəm/ *n.* disease marked by inflammation and pain in the joints, muscles, or fibrous tissue, esp. rheumatoid arthritis. □□ **rheu·mat′ic** *adj.* **rheu·mat′i·cal·ly** *adv.*

rheu·ma·toid /ro͞omətoyd/ *adj.* having the character of rheumatism. □ **rheumatoid arthritis** chronic progressive disease causing inflammation and stiffening of the joints.

Rh fac·tor *Physiol.* antigen occurring in the red blood cells of most humans.

rhine·stone /rínstōn/ *n.* imitation gemstone.

rhi·ni·tis /rīnítis/ *n.* inflammation of the mucous membrane of the nose.

rhi·no /rínō/ *n.* (*pl.* same or **–nos**) *colloq.* rhinoceros.

rhi·noc·er·os /rīnósərəs/ *n.* (*pl.* same or **rhi·noc′er·os·es**) large thick-skinned ungulate of Africa and S. Asia, with one or two horns on the nose.

rhi·zome /rízōm/ *n.* underground rootlike stem bearing both roots and shoots.

rho /rō/ *n.* seventeenth letter of the Greek alphabet (P, ρ).

rho·di·um /rṓdeeəm/ *n. Chem.* hard white metallic element of the platinum group. ¶ Symb.: **Rh**.

rho·do·den·dron /rṓdədéndrən/ *n.* evergreen shrub with large clusters of trumpet-shaped flowers.

rhom·boid /rómboyd/ • *adj.* (also **rhom·boid·al** /–bóyd′l/) like a rhombus. • *n.* quadrilateral of which only the opposite sides and angles are equal.

RHOMBOID

rhom·bus /rómbəs/ *n.* (*pl.* **rhom·bus·es** or **rhom·bi** /–bī/) *Geom.* parallelogram with oblique angles and equal sides.

RHOMBUS

rhu·barb /ro͞obaarb/ *n.* **1 a** plants producing long fleshy dark-red stalks used cooked as food. **b** stalks of this. **2** *sl.* heated dispute.

rhubarb late Middle English (denoting the rootstock of other plants of this genus used medicinally): from Old French *reubarbe,* from a shortening of medieval Latin *rheubarbarum,* an alteration (by association with *rheum* 'rhubarb') of *rhabarbarum* 'foreign rhubarb,' from Greek *rha* (also meaning 'rhubarb') + *barbaros* 'foreign.'

rhyme /rīm/ • *n.* **1** identity of sound between words or the endings of words, esp. in verse. **2** (in *sing.* or *pl.*) verse or poem having rhymes. **3** word providing a rhyme. • *v.* **1** *intr.* **a** (of words or lines) produce a rhyme. **b** (foll. by *with*) act as a rhyme (with another). **2** *intr.* make or write rhymes; versify. □ **rhyme or reason** sense; logic. □□ **rhym′er** *n.*

rhythm /rítͪəm/ *n.* **1** measured regular flow of verse or prose determined by the length of stress and syllables. **2** pattern of accent and duration of notes in music. □ **rhythm and blues** popular music with a blues theme and a strong rhythm. **rhythm method** birth control by avoiding sexual intercourse when ovulation is likely to occur. □□ **rhyth′mic** *adj.* **rhyth′mi·cal** *adj.* **rhyth′mi·cal·ly** *adv.* **rhythm′less** *adj.*

RI *abbr.* Rhode Island (also in official postal use).

rib /rib/ • *n.* **1** each of the curved bones joined in pairs to the spine and protecting the chest. **2** supporting ridge, timber, rod, etc. • *v.tr.* (**ribbed**, **rib′bing**) **1** provide with ribs. **2** *colloq.* make fun of; tease. □ **rib cage** wall of bones formed by the ribs. □□ **ribbed** *adj.* **rib′bing** *n.* **rib′less** *adj.*

> **rib** Old English *rib*, *ribb* (in sense 1), of Germanic origin; related to Dutch *rib(be)* and German *Rippe*. Sense 1 of the verb dates from the mid-16th century; the sense 'make fun of' arises from a US slang usage in the sense 'to fool, dupe' (1930s).

rib·ald /ríbəld/ • *adj.* coarsely or disrespectfully humorous; scurrilous.

rib·bon /ríbən/ *n.* **1** narrow strip or band of fabric, used esp. for trimming or decoration. **2** long, narrow strip of anything (*typewriter ribbon*). **3** (in *pl.*) ragged strips. □□ **rib′boned** *adj.*

ri·bo·fla·vin /ríbōfláyvin/ *n.* vitamin of the B complex, found in liver, milk, eggs, etc. Also called **vitamin B₂**.

ri·bo·nu·cle·ic ac·id /ríbənōōkléeik, –kláyik, –nyōō–/ *n.* nucleic acid in living cells, involved in protein synthesis. ¶ *Abbr.*: **RNA**.

rice /rīs/ • *n.* **1** cereal grass cultivated in marshes, esp. in Asia. **2** grains of this, used as food. • *v.tr.* sieve (cooked potatoes, etc.) into thin strings. □□ **ric′er** *n.*

rich /rich/ • *adj.* **1** having much wealth. **2** splendid; costly; elaborate. **3** copious; abundant; fertile. **4** (of food or diet) containing much fat, spice, etc. **5** (of the fuel mixture in an engine) containing a high proportion of fuel. **6** (of color or sound or smell) mellow and deep; strong and full. **7** highly amusing. • *n.* (**the rich**) (used with a *pl. v.*) wealthy persons, collectively. □□ **rich′ly** *adv.* **rich′ness** *n.*

rich·es /ríchiz/ *n.pl.* abundant means; valuable possessions.

Rich·ter scale /ríktər/ *n.* scale of 0 to 10 for representing the strength of an earthquake.

rick·ets /ríkits/ *n.* (treated as *sing.* or *pl.*) bone-softening disease of children, caused by a deficiency of vitamin D.

rick·et·y /ríkitee/ *adj.* **1** insecure; shaky. **2** suffering from rickets. □□ **rick′et·i·ness** *n.*

rick·sha /ríkshaw/ *n.* (also **rick′shaw**) light, two-wheeled hooded vehicle drawn by one or more persons.

RICKSHA

---

ric·o·chet /ríkəshay, ríkəsháy/ • *n.* action of a projectile, esp. a shell or bullet, in rebounding off a surface. • *v.intr.* (**ric·o·cheted** /–shayd/; **ric·o·chet·ing** /–shaying/) (of a projectile) make a ricochet.

ri·cot·ta /rikótə, –káwtaa/ *n.* soft Italian cheese resembling cottage cheese.

rid /rid/ *v.tr.* (**rid·ding**; *past* and *past part.* **rid**) free (a person or place) of something unwanted. □ **be** (or **get**) **rid of** dispose of.

rid·dance /rídəns/ *n.* getting rid of something. □ **good riddance** welcome relief from an unwanted person or thing.

rid·dle¹ /ríd'l/ • *n.* **1** question or statement testing ingenuity in divining its answer or meaning. **2** puzzling fact, thing, or person. • *v.intr.* speak in riddles. □□ **rid′dler** *n.*

rid·dle² /ríd'l/ • *v.tr.* **1** make many holes in, esp. with gunshot. **2** (in *passive*) spread through; permeate (*riddled with errors*). **3** pass through a riddle. • *n.* coarse sieve.

ride /rīd/ • *v.* (*past* **rode** /rōd/; *past part.* **rid·den** /ríd'n/) **1** *tr. & intr.* travel or be carried on (a bicycle, etc.) or in (a vehicle). **2** *tr. & intr.* sit on and control or be carried by (a horse, etc.). **3** *tr.* be carried or supported by (*the ship rides the waves*). **4** *tr.* traverse. **5** *intr.* lie at anchor; float buoyantly. **6** *tr.* give a ride to (*rode the child on his back*). **7** (as **ridden** *adj.*) infested or afflicted (often in *comb.*: *rat-ridden cellar*). • *n.* **1** journey or spell of riding. **2** amusement for riding on at a carnival, etc. □ **let ride** leave to a natural course. **ride out** come safely through (a storm, danger, etc.). **ride shotgun** *colloq.* ride in the front passenger seat of a vehicle. **ride up** (of a garment, etc.) work upward out of place. **take for a ride 1** *colloq.* hoax or deceive. **2** *sl.* abduct in order to murder. □□ **rid′a·ble** *adj.*

rid·er /rídər/ *n.* **1** person who rides (esp. a horse). **2** addition to a document. □□ **rid′er·less** *adj.*

ridge /rij/ • *n.* **1** line of the junction of two surfaces sloping upward toward each other. **2** long, narrow hilltop, mountain range, or watershed. **3** any narrow elevation. • *v.tr.* mark with ridges. □□ **ridg′y** *adj.*

ridge·pole /ríjpōl/ *n.* horizontal roof pole.

rid·i·cule /rídikyōōl/ • *n.* derision; mockery. • *v.tr.* ridicule.

ri·dic·u·lous /ridíkyələs/ *adj.* **1** deserving or inviting ridicule. **2** unreasonable; absurd. □□ **ri·dic′u·lous·ly** *adv.* **ri·dic′u·lous·ness** *n.*

rid·ing /ríding/ *n.* **1** in senses of RIDE *v.* **2** practice or skill of riding horses.

rife /rīf/ *predic.adj.* **1** of common occurrence; widespread. **2** (foll. by *with*) abounding with; teeming with. □□ **rife′ness** *n.*

riff /rif/ *n.* short repeated phrase in jazz, etc.

rif·fle /rífəl/ • *v.* **1** *tr.* **a** turn (pages) in quick succession. **b** shuffle (playing cards). **2** *intr.* (often foll. by *through*) leaf quickly (through pages). • *n.* **1** act or instance of riffling. **2** patch of waves or ripples on water.

riff·raff /rífraf/ *n.* rabble; disreputable persons.

ri·fle¹ /rífəl/ • *n.* gun with a long, rifled barrel, esp. one fired from shoulder level. • *v.tr.* make spiral grooves in (a gun barrel) to make a bullet spin. □ **rifle range** place for rifle practice.

ri·fle² /rífəl/ *v.tr. &* (foll. by *through*) *intr.* search and rob.

ri·fle·man /rífəlmən/ *n.* (*pl.* **–men**) 1 soldier armed with a rifle. 2 person skilled in shooting a rifle.

ri·fling /rífling/ *n.* grooves in a gun barrel.

rift /rift/ • *n.* 1 crack; split; opening. 2 disagreement; breach. • *v.tr.* tear or burst apart.

rig[1] /rig/ • *v.tr.* (**rigged, rig·ging**) 1 provide (a sailing ship) with sails, rigging, etc. 2 fit out; equip. 3 (foll. by *up*) set up as a makeshift. 4 assemble. • *n.* 1 arrangement of a vessel's masts, sails, etc. 2 equipment for a special purpose. 3 tractor-trailer. □□ **rigged** *adj.* (also in *comb.*).

rig[2] /rig/ • *v.tr.* (**rigged, rig·ging**) manage or conduct fraudulently (*rigged the election*). • *n.* trick or dodge. □□ **rig′ger** *n.*

rig·ger /rígər/ *n.* 1 person who rigs or who arranges rigging. 2 worker on an oil rig.

rig·ging /ríging/ *n.* vessel's spars, ropes, etc.

right /rīt/ • *adj.* 1 just; morally or socially correct. 2 true; not mistaken. 3 suitable; preferable. 4 sound or normal; healthy; satisfactory. 5 on or toward the east side of the human body or of anything when facing north. 6 (of a side of fabric, etc.) meant for display or use. • *n.* 1 that which is correct or just. 2 justification or fair claim. 3 legal or moral authority to act. 4 right-hand part, region, or direction. 5 (often **Right**) conservative political group. • *v.tr.* 1 (often *refl.*) restore to a proper, straight, or vertical position. 2 correct or avenge (mistakes, wrongs, etc.). • *adv.* 1 straight (*go right on*). 2 *colloq.* immediately (*I'll be right back*). 3 a (foll. by *to, around, through,* etc.) all the way (*sank right to the bottom*). b (foll. by *off, out,* etc.) completely (*came right off its hinges*). 4 exactly; quite (*right in the middle*). 5 properly; correctly; satisfactorily (*if I remember right*). 6 on or to the right side. • *int. colloq.* expressing agreement or assent. □ **as right as rain** perfectly sound and healthy. **in one's own right** through one's own position or effort, etc. **right angle** angle of 90°. **right away** immediately. **right-hand** *adj.* 1 on or toward the right side of a person or thing. 2 done with the right hand. **right-handed** 1 using the right hand by preference. 2 (of a tool, etc.) made to be used with the right hand. **right-minded** (or **–thinking**) having sound views and principles. **right of way** 1 right established by usage to pass over another's ground. 2 right of one vehicle to proceed before another. **right on!** *colloq.* expression of strong approval or encouragement. **right-to-die** pertaining to the avoidance of using artificial life support in case of severe illness or injury. **right-to-life** pertaining to the movement opposing abortion. **right-to-work** pertaining to legislation outlawing obligatory union membership. **right wing** conservative section of a political party or system. **right-wing** *adj.* conservative or reactionary. **right-winger** person on the right wing. □□ **right′a·ble** *adj.* **right′ly** *adv.* **right′ness** *n.*

right·eous /ríchəs/ *adj.* morally right; virtuous; law-abiding. □□ **right′eous·ly** *adv.* **right′eous·ness** *n.*

right·ful /rítfool/ *adj.* 1 legitimate. 2 equitable; fair. □□ **right′ful·ly** *adv.*

right·ism /rítizəm/ *n. Polit.* principles or policy of the right. □□ **right′ist** *n.* & *adj.*

right·most /rítmōst/ *adj.* furthest to the right.

right·size /rítsīz/ *v. tr.* reduce staff to reach the optimum size.

rig·id /ríjid/ *adj.* 1 not flexible; unbendable. 2 inflexible; harsh. □□ **ri·gid′i·ty** *n.* **rig′id·ly** *adv.* **rig′id·ness** *n.*

rig·ma·role /rígmərōl/ (also **rig·a·ma·role** /rígə-/) *n.* 1 lengthy, complicated procedure. 2 rambling or meaningless talk.

rig·or /rígər/ *n.* severity; strictness. □ **rigor mortis** stiffening of the body after death. □□ **rig′or·ous** *adj.* **rig′or·ous·ly** *adv.* **rig′or·ous·ness** *n.*

rile /rīl/ *v.tr. colloq.* anger; irritate.

rill /ril/ *n.* small stream.

rim /rim/ • *n.* 1 a edge or border. b margin or verge, esp. of something circular. 2 part of eyeglasses frame surrounding the lenses. 3 outer edge of a wheel, holding the tire. • *v.tr.* (**rimmed, rim·ming**) provide with a rim; edge. □□ **rim′less** *adj.* **rimmed** *adj.* (also in *comb.*).

rime /rīm/ *n.* light covering of frost.

rind /rīnd/ *n.* tough outer skin of fruit, vegetables, cheese, etc.

ring[1] /ring/ • *n.* 1 circular band, usu. of metal, worn on a finger. 2 circular band of any material. 3 circular line or band around an object. 4 enclosure for a circus performance, boxing, etc. 5 people or things in a circle. 6 group of people combined illicitly for profit, etc. • *v.tr.* 1 make or draw a circle around. 2 put a ring through the nose of (a pig, bull, etc.). □ **ring finger** finger next to the little finger, esp. of the left hand. **run rings around** *colloq.* outclass or outwit (another person). □□ **ringed** *adj.* (also in *comb.*).

ring[2] /ring/ • *v.* (*past* **rang** /rang/; *past part.* **rung** /rung/) 1 *intr.* give a clear resonant or vibrating sound of or as of a bell. 2 *tr.* make (esp. a bell) ring. 3 *tr.* call by telephone. 4 *intr.* (of a place) resound with a sound (*theater rang with applause*). 5 *intr.* (of the ears) be filled with a sensation of ringing. 6 *intr.* convey a specified impression (*words rang hollow*). • *n.* 1 ringing sound or tone. 2 act or sound of ringing a bell. 3 telephone call. 4 specified feeling conveyed by words (*a melancholy ring*). □ **ring up** record (an amount, etc.) on a cash register. □□ **ringed** *adj.* (also in *comb.*). **ring′er** *n.* **ring′ing** *adj.* **ring′ing·ly** *adv.*

ring·er /ríngər/ *n. sl.* 1 a athlete or horse entered in a competition by fraudulent means, esp. as a substitute. b person's double, esp. an impostor. 2 bell ringer. □ **be a dead ringer for** resemble (a person) exactly.

ring·lead·er /ríngleedər/ *n.* leading instigator of a crime, etc.

ring·let /ringlit/ *n.* curly lock of hair.

ring·mas·ter /ríngmastər/ *n.* director of a circus performance.

ring·side /ríngsīd/ *n.* (often *attrib.*) area beside a boxing ring, circus ring, etc.

ring·worm /ríngwərm/ *n.* fungous infections of the skin causing circular inflamed patches.

rink /ringk/ *n.* 1 area of ice for skating. 2 enclosed area for roller-skating.

ring·mas·ter /ríngmastər/ *n.* director of a circus performance.

ring·side /ríngsīd/ *n.* (often *attrib.*) area beside a boxing ring, circus ring, etc.

ring·worm /ríngwərm/ *n.* fungous infections of the skin causing circular inflamed patches.

rink /ringk/ *n.* 1 area of ice for skating. 2 enclosed area for roller-skating.

rinse /rins/ • *v.tr.* **1** wash lightly. **2** put (clothes, etc.) through clean water to remove soap or detergent. **3** treat (hair) with a rinse. • *n.* **1** rinsing. **2** solution for cleansing the mouth. **3** temporary hair tint. □□ **rins′er** *n.*

ri·ot /rī́ət/ • *n.* **1 a** disturbance of the peace by a crowd. **b** (*attrib.*) involved in suppressing riots (*riot police*). **2** uncontrolled revelry. **3** lavish display or sensation (*riot of emotion*). **4** *colloq.* very amusing thing or person. • *v.intr.* engage in a riot. □ **read the Riot Act** put a firm stop to insubordination, etc. **run riot 1** throw off all restraint. **2** (of plants) grow or spread uncontrolled. □□ **ri′ot·er** *n.* **ri′ot·ous** *adj.*

RIP *abbr.* may he or she or they rest in peace (acronym of Latin *requiescat* (pl. *requiescant*) *in pace*).

rip[1] /rip/ • *v.* (**ripped, rip·ping**) **1** *tr.* tear or cut (a thing) quickly or forcibly away or apart. **2** *tr.* make a tear in. **3** *intr.* come violently apart; split. **4** *intr.* rush along. • *n.* **1** long tear. **2** act of ripping. □ **let rip** *colloq.* act or proceed without restraint. **rip cord** cord for releasing a parachute from its pack. **rip into** attack (a person) verbally. **rip off** *colloq.* defraud; steal. **rip-off** *n.* *colloq.* fraud; swindle.

rip[2] /rip/ *n.* stretch of rough water in the sea or in a river, caused by the meeting of currents.

ri·par·i·an /rīpáireeən/ *adj.* of or on a riverbank.

ripe /rīp/ *adj.* **1** (of grain, fruit, cheese, etc.) ready to be reaped, picked, or eaten. **2** mature; fully developed. **3** (of a person's age) advanced. **4** fit or ready (*land ripe for development*). □□ **ripe′ly** *adv.* **ripe′ness** *n.*

rip·en /rī́pən/ *v.* make or become ripe; mature.

ri·poste /ripóst/ *n.* quick retort.

rip·ple /rípəl/ • *n.* **1** ruffling of the water's surface. **2 a** gentle lively sound, e.g., of laughter or applause. **b** brief wave of emotion, etc. (*a ripple of interest*). • *v.* **1 a** *intr.* form or flow in ripples. **b** *tr.* cause to do this. **2** *intr.* show or sound like ripples. □□ **rip′ply** *adj.*

rip-roar·ing /ríprawring/ *adj.* **1** wildly noisy or boisterous. **2** excellent; first-rate. □□ **rip-roar′ing·ly** *adv.*

rip·saw /rípsaw/ *n.* saw for sawing wood along the grain.

rip·snort·er /rípsnawrtər/ *n.* *colloq.* energetic, remarkable, or excellent person or thing. □□ **rip·snort′ing** *adj.* **rip·snort′ing·ly** *adv.*

rip·tide /ríptīd/ *n.* disturbance in the sea where opposing tidal currents meet.

rise /rīz/ • *v.intr.* (*past* **rose** /rōz/; *past part.* **ris·en** /rízən/) **1** come up or go up. **2** grow, project, expand, or incline upward; become higher. **3** appear above the horizon. **4 a** get up from lying, sitting, or kneeling. **b** get out of bed. **5** come to life again (*rise from the ashes*). **6** (of dough) swell by the action of yeast, etc. **7** rebel. **8** originate; have as its source. • *n.* **1** rising. **2** upward slope; hill. **3** increase. **4** increase in status or power. **5** origin. □ **get a rise out of** *colloq.* provoke a reaction from (a person). **rise above 1** be superior to (petty feelings, etc.). **2** show dignity or strength in the face of (difficulty, poor conditions, etc.).

ris·er /rī́zər/ *n.* **1** person who rises; e.g. from bed. **2** vertical section between the treads of a staircase.

ris·i·ble /rízibəl/ *adj.* laughable; ludicrous.

ris·ing /rī́zing/ • *adj.* **1** increasing (*rising costs*). **2** advancing to maturity or high standing (*ris-*

ing young lawyer). • *n.* revolt; insurrection; uprising.

risk /risk/ • *n.* **1** chance or possibility of danger, loss, injury, etc. **2** person or thing regarded in relation to risk (*is a poor risk*). • *v.tr.* **1** expose to risk. **2** accept the chance of. □□ **risk′i·ly** *adv.* **risk′i·ness** *n.* **risk′y** *adj.*

ris·qué /riskáy/ *adj.* slightly indecent.

rite /rīt/ *n.* religious or solemn observance, act, or procedure. □ **rite of passage** (often in *pl.*) event marking a stage of life, e.g., marriage.

rit·u·al /ríchōōəl/ • *n.* **1** prescribed order of performing rites. **2** procedure regularly followed. • *adj.* of or done as a ritual or rites. □□ **rit′u·al·ism** *n.* **rit′u·al·ist** *n.* **rit·u·al·is′tic** *adj.* **rit·u·al·is′ti·cal·ly** *adv.* **rit·u·al·i·za′tion** *n.* **rit′u·al·ize** *v.* **rit′u·al·ly** *adv.*

ritz·y /rítsee/ *adj.* (**ritz·i·er, ritz·i·est**) *colloq.* **1** high-class; luxurious. **2** ostentatiously smart. □□ **ritz′i·ly** *adv.* **ritz′i·ness** *n.*

riv. *abbr.* river.

ri·val /rī́vəl/ • *n.* **1** person competing with another. **2** person or thing that equals another in quality. • *v.tr.* **1** be the rival of. **2** seem or claim to be as good as. □□ **ri′val·ry** *n.* (*pl.* **-ries**).

rive /rīv/ *v.tr* (*past* **rived**; *past part.* **riv·en** /rívən/) split or tear apart violently.

riv·er /rívər/ *n.* **1** copious natural stream of water flowing to the sea, a lake, etc. **2** copious flow (*river of lava*). □ **sell down the river** *colloq.* betray or let down.

riv·er·side /rívərsīd/ *n.* ground along a riverbank.

riv·et /rívit/ • *n.* bolt for joining parts with its headless end being beaten out or pressed down when in place. • *v.tr.* **1 a** join or fasten with rivets. **b** fix; make immovable. **2 a** direct intently (one's eyes or attention, etc.). **b** (esp. as **riveting** *adj.*) engross (a person or the attention). □□ **riv′et·er** *n.*

riv·u·let /rívyəlit/ *n.* small stream.

rm. *abbr.* room.

RN *abbr.* registered nurse.

Rn *symb. Chem.* radon.

RNA *abbr.* ribonucleic acid.

roach /rōch/ *n.* **1** *colloq.* cockroach. **2** *sl.* butt of a marijuana cigarette.

road /rōd/ *n.* **1** path or way with a prepared surface, used by vehicles, pedestrians, etc. **2** one's way or route. **3** (usu. in *pl.*) anchorage near the shore. □ **one for the road** *colloq.* final (esp. alcoholic) drink before departure. **on the road** traveling, esp. as a firm's representative. **road hog** *colloq.* reckless or inconsiderate motorist. **road show** performance given by a touring company. **the road to** way of getting to or achieving (*road to ruin*).

road·bed /rṓdbed/ *n.* foundation of a railroad, road, etc.

road·block /rṓdblok/ *n.* barrier on a road, esp. one set up to stop and examine traffic.

road·house /rṓdhows/ *n.* inn or club on a major road.

road·run·ner /rṓdrunər/ *n.* fast-running species of cuckoo of Mexican and US deserts.

road·side /rṓdsīd/ *n.* strip of land beside a road.

road·ster /rṓdstər/ *n.* open car without rear seats.

road·way /ródway/ *n.* road, esp. the part for traffic.

road·work /ródwərk/ *n.* **1** construction or repair of roads. **2** athletic exercise or training involving running on roads.

roam /rōm/ *v.* **1** *intr.* ramble; wander. **2** *tr.* travel unsystematically over, through, or about. □□ **roam'er** *n.*

roan /rōn/ • *adj.* (of esp. a horse) having a coat thickly interspersed with another color. • *n.* roan animal.

roar /rawr/ • *n.* **1** loud, deep, hoarse sound. **2** loud laugh. • *v.* **1** *intr.* utter or make a roar. **2** *intr.* travel in a vehicle at high speed. **3** *tr.* say, sing, or utter in a loud tone. □□ **roar'er** *n.*

roar·ing /ráwring/ *adj.* in senses of ROAR *v.* □ **roaring forties** stormy ocean tracts between lat. 40° and 50° S. **roaring twenties** decade of the 1920s (with ref. to its postwar buoyancy).

roast /rōst/ • *v.* **1** *tr.* cook (food, esp. meat) in an oven or by open heat. **2** *tr.* expose to great heat. **3** *tr.* **a** criticize severely. **b** honor at a roast (sense n. 4). **4** *intr.* undergo roasting. • *attrib.adj.* roasted. • *n.* **1** roast meat. **2** piece of meat for roasting. **3** party where roasted food is eaten. **4** banquet at which the honoree is subjected to good-natured ridicule.

roast·er /róstər/ *n.* **1** person or thing that roasts. **2** something fit for roasting, e.g., a fowl, a potato, etc.

roast·ing /rósting/ • *adj.* very hot. • *n.* **1** in senses of ROAST *v.* **2** severe criticism or denunciation.

rob /rob/ *v.tr.* (**robbed, rob·bing**) **1** take unlawfully from, esp. by force or threat. **2** deprive of what is due or normal (*was robbed of my sleep*). **3** (*absol.*) commit robbery. **4** *colloq.* cheat; swindle. □□ **rob'ber** *n.* **rob'ber·y** *n.* (*pl.* **–ies**). ¶ In law, to **rob** is to take something from someone by causing fear of harm, whether or not actual harm occurs. The term is widely, but incorrectly, used to mean simple *theft*,, e.g.: *Our house was robbed while we were away.*

robe /rōb/ • *n.* **1** long, loose outer garment. **2** (often in *pl.*) long outer garment worn as an indication of rank, office, profession, etc. • *v.* **1** *tr.* clothe in a robe; dress. **2** *intr.* put on one's robes or vestments.

rob·in /róbin/ *n.* (also **rob'in red'breast**) red-breasted thrush.

ro·bot /róbot/ *n.* **1** machine with a human appearance or functioning like a human. **2** person who works mechanically but insensitively. □□ **ro·bot'ic** *adj.* **ro'bot·ize** *v.tr.*

ro·bot·ics /rōbótiks/ *n.pl.* the study of robots; art or science of their design and operation.

ro·bust /rōbúst/ *adj.* **1** strong and sturdy, esp. in physique or construction. **2** (of wine, etc.) full-bodied. □□ **ro·bust'ly** *adv.* **ro·bust'ness** *n.*

rock¹ /rok/ *n.* **1** hard material of the earth's crust. **2** *Geol.* any natural material, hard or soft (e.g., clay), consisting of one or more minerals. **3** stone of any size. **4** firm and dependable support or protection. □ **between a rock and a hard place** forced to choose between two unpleasant alternatives. **on the rocks** *colloq.* **1** short of money. **2** broken down. **3** (of a drink) served over ice cubes. **rock-bottom** (of prices, etc.) the very lowest. **rock candy** sugar crystallized in large masses onto a string or stick. **rock garden** garden in which rocks are a chief feature. **rock salt** common salt as a solid mineral.

rock² /rok/ • *v.* **1** *tr.* move gently to and fro; set or maintain such motion. **2** *intr.* be in such motion. **3 a** *intr.* sway from side to side; shake; reel. **b** *tr.* cause to do this. • *n.* **1** rocking movement. **2** = *rock and roll.* □ **rock and** (or **rock 'n'**) **roll** popular music originating in the 1950s, characterized by a heavy beat and simple melodies, often with a blues element. **rock the boat** *colloq.* disturb the equilibrium of a situation. **rocking chair** chair mounted on rockers or springs for gently rocking in. **rocking horse** toy horse on rockers or springs for a child to rock on.

rock·a·bil·ly /rókəbilee/ *n.* music combining elements of rock and roll and hillbilly music.

rock·er /rókər/ *n.* **1** person or thing that rocks. **2** curved bar, etc., on which something can rock. **3** rocking chair. **4 a** devotee of rock music. **b** performer of rock music. □ **off one's rocker** *sl.* crazy.

rock·et /rókit/ • *n.* **1** cylindrical projectile that can be propelled to a great height or distance by combustion of its contents. **2** engine using a similar principle. **3** rocket-propelled missile, spacecraft, etc. • *v.intr.* **1** move rapidly upward or away. **2** increase rapidly (*prices rocketed*).

rock·et·ry /rókitree/ *n.* science or practice of rocket propulsion.

rock·y¹ /rókee/ *adj.* (**rock·i·er, rock·i·est**) **1** of or like rock. **2** full of rock or rocks. □□ **rock'i·ness** *n.*

rock·y² /rókee/ *adj.* (**rock·i·er, rock·i·est**) *colloq.* unsteady; tottering. □□ **rock'i·ly** *adv.* **rock'i·ness** *n.*

ro·co·co /rəkōkō/ • *adj.* **1** of a late baroque style of decoration. **2** (of literature, music, architecture, etc.) highly ornamented; florid. • *n.* rococo style.

rod /rod/ *n.* **1** slender straight bar, esp. of wood or metal. **2** cane for flogging. **3** = *fishing rod.* **4** measure of length equal to 5½ yards. □□ **rod'less** *adj.* **rod'like** *adj.*

rode *past of* RIDE.

ro·dent /ród'nt/ *n.* mammal with strong incisors, e.g., rat, mouse, squirrel, beaver, porcupine.

ro·de·o /ródeeō, rōdáyō/ *n.* (*pl.* **–os**) exhibition of cowboys' skills in handling animals.

roe¹ /rō/ *n.* fish eggs.

roe² /rō/ *n.* (*pl.* same or **roes**) (also **roe deer**) small European and Asian deer.

roe·buck /róbuk/ *n.* (*pl.* same or **roe'bucks**) male roe deer.

roent·gen /réntgən, –jən, rúnt–/ *n.* unit of radiation produced by X rays, etc.

rog·er /rójər/ *int.* **1** your message has been received and understood (used in radio communication, etc.). **2** *sl.* I agree.

rogue /rōg/ *n.* **1** dishonest or unprincipled person. **2** *joc.* mischievous person. **3** (usu. *attrib.*) **a** wild animal driven away or living apart from others. **b** stray, irresponsible, or undisciplined person or thing. □ **rogues' gallery** collection of photographs of known criminals, etc., used for identification of suspects. □□ **ro'guer·y** *n.* **ro'guish** *adj.* **ro'guish·ly** *adv.* **ro'guish·ness** *n.*

roil /royl/ *v.tr.* **1** make (a liquid) turbid by agitating it. **2** = RILE.

rois·ter /róystər/ *v.intr.* (esp. as **roistering** *adj.*) be uproarious. □□ **rois'ter·er** *n.* **rois'ter·ing** *n.* **rois'ter·ous** *adj.*

role /rōl/ *n.* (also **rôle**) **1** actor's part in a play, motion picture, etc. **2** function. □ **role model** person looked to by others as an example.

roll /rōl/ • *v.* **1 a** *intr.* move or go in some direction by turning on an axis. **b** *tr.* cause to do this. **2 a** *intr.* move or advance on or (of time, etc.) as if on wheels, etc. **b** *tr.* cause to do this. **3 a** *tr.* turn over and over on itself to form a more or less cylindrical or spherical shape (*rolled a newspaper*). **b** *tr.* form a cylinder or ball. **4** *intr.* & *tr.* rotate. **5** *intr.* **a** (of a moving vehicle) sway to and fro sideways. **b** walk unsteadily. **6** *intr.* show or go with an undulating surface (*rolling hills*; *waves roll in*). **7** *intr.* & *tr.* sound or utter with a vibratory or trilling effect. **8** *tr.* throw (dice). **9** *tr.* *sl.* rob (esp. a helpless victim). • *n.* **1** rolling motion or gait. **2** rolling. **3** rhythmic sound of thunder, etc. **4** complete revolution of an aircraft, etc. **5** cylinder formed by turning material over and over on itself **6** small portion of bread individually baked. **7 a** official list or register. **b** total numbers on this. □ **on a roll** *sl.* experiencing a bout of success or progress. **roll back** cause (esp. prices) to decrease. **roll call** calling out a list of names to establish who is present. **rolled gold** thin coating of gold applied to a baser metal by rolling. **rolled into one** combined in one person or thing. **roll in 1** arrive in great numbers or quantity. **2** wallow or luxuriate in. **rolling pin** cylinder for rolling out pastry, dough, etc. **rolling stone** person who is unwilling to settle down. **roll-top desk** desk with a flexible cover sliding in curved grooves. **roll with the punches** withstand adversity, difficulties, etc. □□ **roll′a•ble** *adj.*

roll·a·way /rôləway/ *adj.* (of a bed, etc.) that can be removed on wheels or casters.

roll·er /rólər/ *n.* **1** revolving cylinder for smoothing, spreading, crushing, stamping, hanging a cloth on, etc., used alone or in a machine. **2** small cylinder on which hair is rolled for setting. **3** long, swelling wave. □ **roller bearing** bearing like a ball bearing but with small cylinders instead of balls. **roller coaster** *n.* amusement ride consisting of an elevated track with cars that rise and plunge steeply. **roller skate** see SKATE[1].

Rol·ler·blade /rólərblayd/ • *n.propr.* (usu. *pl.*) in-line skates. • *v.intr.* use Rollerblades.

roll·ick /rólik/ *v.intr.* (esp. as **rollicking** *adj.*) be jovial or exuberant.

roll·over /rólōvər/ *n.* *Econ.* extension or transfer of a debt or other financial relationship.

ro·ly-po·ly /róleepólee/ *adj.* pudgy; plump.

ROM /rom/ *n.* *Computing* read-only memory; memory not capable of being changed by program instruction.

Rom. *abbr.* **1** Roman. **2** Romania. **3** Romans (New Testament).

ro·maine /rōmáyn/ *n.* long-leafed lettuce.

Ro·man /rómən/ • *adj.* **1** of ancient or modern Rome, its territory, people, etc. **2** of papal Rome, esp. = ROMAN CATHOLIC. **3** (**roman**) (of type) plain and upright, used in ordinary print. **4** based on the ancient Roman alphabet. • *n.* **1** native or inhabitant of Rome. **2** (**roman**) roman type. □ **Roman candle** firework discharging colored balls and sparks. **Roman Empire** *hist.* that established by Augustus in 27 BC, including much of Europe, N Africa, and SW Asia. **Roman holiday** enjoyment derived from others' discomfiture. **Roman numeral** any of the Roman letters representing numbers: I = 1, V = 5, X = 10, L = 50, C = 100, D = 500, M = 1000.

Ro·man Cath·o·lic /rómən/ • *adj.* of the part of the Christian Church acknowledging the pope as its head. • *n.* member of this Church. □□ **Ro′man Ca·thol′i·cism** *n.*

ro·mance /rōmáns/ • *n.* (also *disp.* /rómans/) **1** atmosphere, attitude or tendency characterized by a sense of remoteness from or idealization of everyday life. **2 a** love affair. **b** sentimental or idealized love. **3** literary genre with romantic love or highly imaginative unrealistic episodes. • *adj.* (**Romance**) of any of the languages descended from Latin (French, Italian, Spanish, etc.). • *v.tr.* court; woo.

Ro·ma·ni·an /rōmáyneeən/ (also **Rumanian** /rōō–/) • *n.* **1 a** native or national of Romania. **b** person of Romanian descent. **2** language of Romania. • *adj.* of Romania, its people, or its language.

Ro·ma·no /rōmaáanō/ *n.* strong-tasting hard cheese.

Ro·mansh /rōmánsh, –maánsh/ *n.* Rhaeto-Romanic dialect, esp. as spoken in Switzerland.

ro·man·tic /rōmántik/ • *adj.* **1** of, characterized by, or suggestive of romance. **2** inclined toward or suggestive of love. **3** (of a person) imaginative; visionary; idealistic. **4 a** (of style in art, music, etc.) concerned more with feeling and emotion than with form and aesthetic qualities. **b** (also **Romantic**) of the 18th–19th c. movement or style in the European arts. **5** impractical; fantastic. • *n.* **1** romantic person. **2** romanticist. □□ **ro·man′ti·cal·ly** *adv.*

ro·man·ti·cism /rōmántisizəm/ *n.* (also **Romanticism**) adherence to a romantic style in art, music, etc. □□ **ro·man′ti·cist** *n.* (also **Romanticist**).

ro·man·ti·cize /rōmántisīz/ *v.* **1** *tr.* make or render romantic or unreal (*romanticized account of war*). **2** *intr.* indulge in romantic thoughts or actions. □□ **ro·man·ti·ci·za′tion** *n.*

Rom·a·ny /rómənee, rṓ–/ *n.* language of the Gypsies.

Ro·me·o /rómeeō/ *n.* (*pl.* **–os**) passionate male lover or seducer.

romp /romp/ • *v.intr.* play energetically. • *n.* **1** spell of romping. **2** *colloq.* easy win.

romp·er /rómpər/ *n.* (usu. in *pl.*) one-piece garment, esp. for a child, that covers the trunk and has short pants.

rood /rōōd/ *n.* crucifix.

roof /rōōf, rŏŏf/ *n.* (*pl.* **roofs**) **1** upper covering of a building. **2** top of any enclosed space. • *v.tr.* cover with or as with a roof. □ **go through**

gambrel

gable

mansard

ROOF

the roof *colloq.* (of prices, etc.) reach extreme or unexpected heights. **hit** (or **go through** or **raise**) **the roof** *colloq.* become very angry. **raise the roof 1** create a noisy racket. **2** protest noisily. □□ **roofed** *adj.* (also in *comb.*). **roof′er** *n.*

roof·ing /róofing, ro͞of-/ *n.* material for constructing a roof.

roof·top /róoftop, ro͞of-/ *n.* top of a house.

rook[1] /ro͝ok/ • *n.* black European and Asiatic bird of the crow family. • *v.tr.* **1** charge (a customer) extortionately. **2** win money from (a person), esp. by swindling.

rook[2] /ro͝ok/ *n.* chess piece with its top in the shape of a battlement; castle.

rook·er·y /ro͝okəree/ *n.* (*pl.* **–ies**) colony of certain birds (esp. rooks or penguins) or seals.

rook·ie /ro͝okee/ *n. sl.* **1** new recruit. **2** *Sports* first-year player.

room /ro͞om, ro͝om/ • *n.* **1** space for or occupied by something; capacity. **2** part of a building enclosed by walls, floor, and ceiling. • *v.intr.* lodge; board. □ **rooming house** house with rented rooms for lodging. **room service** (in a hotel, etc.) service of food or drink taken to a guest's room. □□ **–roomed** *adj.* (in *comb.*). **room′er** *n.* **room′ful** *n.* (*pl.* **–fuls**).

room·mate /ro͞om-mayt, ro͝om-/ *n.* person occupying the same room, apartment, etc., as another.

room·y /ro͞omee, ro͝o-/ *adj.* (**room·i·er**, **room·i·est**) having much room; spacious. □□ **room′i·ly** *adv.* **room′i·ness** *n.*

roost /ro͞ost/ • *n.* branch or perch for a bird, esp. to sleep. • *v.intr.* settle for rest or sleep. □ **come home to roost** (of a scheme, etc.) recoil unfavorably upon the originator. **rule the roost** be in charge (esp. of others).

roost·er /ro͞ostər/ *n.* male domestic chicken; cock.

root[1] /ro͞ot, ro͝ot/ • *n.* **1** part of a plant normally below the ground, conveying nourishment from the soil. **2** (in *pl.*) attachment, esp. to one's place of origin. **3** embedded part of a hair, tooth, nail, etc. **4** basic cause, source, or origin. **5** *Math.* number that when multiplied by itself a specified number of times gives a specified number or quantity (*cube root of eight is two*). **6** core of a word, without prefixes, suffixes, etc. • *v.* **1 a** *intr.* take root or grow roots. **b** *tr.* cause to do this. **2** *tr.* fix firmly; establish. **3** *tr.* (foll. by *out*) **a** drag or dig up by the roots. **b** find and get rid of. □ **put down roots** become settled or established. **root beer** carbonated drink made from an extract of roots. **root canal** *Dentistry* surgery to remove the diseased nerve of a tooth. **take root 1** begin to grow and draw nourishment from the soil. **2** become fixed or established. □□ **root′ed·ness** *n.* **root′less** *adj.* **root′let** *n.*

root[2] /ro͞ot, ro͝ot/ *v.* **1 a** *intr.* (of an animal, esp. a pig) turn up the ground with the snout, beak, etc., in search of food. **b** *tr.* (foll. by *up*) turn up (the ground) by rooting. **2 a** *intr.* rummage. **b** *tr.* find or extract by rummaging. **3** *intr.* (foll. by *for*) *sl.* encourage by applause or support. □□ **root′er** *n.* (in sense 3).

rope /rōp/ • *n.* **1** stout cord made by twisting together strands of hemp, nylon, wire, etc. **2** onions, garlic bulbs, pearls, etc., strung together. **3** (in *pl.*, prec. by *the*) conditions in some sphere

of action (*show a person the ropes*). • *v.tr.* **1** fasten, secure, or catch with rope. **2** (usu. foll. by *off*, *in*) enclose with rope. □ **give a person plenty of** (or **enough**) **rope** (**to hang himself** or **herself**) give a person enough freedom of action to bring about his or her own downfall. **rope in** (or **into**) persuade to take part in (*was roped into doing the laundry*).

Roque·fort /rókfərt/ *n. propr.* soft blue cheese made from sheep's milk.

ror·qual /ráwrkwəl/ *n.* any of various whales having a dorsal fin. Also called **finback, fin whale**.

Ror·schach test /ráwrshaak/ *n. Psychol.* personality test based on interpretation of inkblots.

ro·sa·ceous /rōzáyshəs/ *adj. Bot.* of the large plant family that includes the rose.

ro·sa·ry /rózəree/ *n.* (*pl.* **–ries**) **1** *RC Ch.* repeated sequence of prayers, usu. said while counting them on a string of beads. **2** string of beads used for this.

rose[1] /rōz/ • *n.* **1** prickly bush or shrub bearing usu. fragrant red, pink, yellow, or white flowers. **2** this flower. **3** light crimson color; pink. • *adj.* rose-colored. □ **rose water** perfume made from roses. **rose window** circular window with roselike tracery. **see** (or **look**) **through rose-colored glasses** regard (circumstances, etc.) with unfounded favor or optimism.

rose[2] *past* of RISE.

ro·sé /rōzáy/ *n.* light pink wine.

ro·se·ate /rózeeət, –ayt/ *adj.* rose-colored (*roseate tern*).

rose·bud /rózbud/ *n.* bud of a rose.

rose·mary /rózmairee, –mɔree/ *n.* evergreen fragrant shrub used as an herb.

ro·sette /rōzét/ *n.* rose-shaped ornament of ribbon.

rose·wood /rózwo͝od/ *n.* any of several fragrant close-grained woods used in making furniture.

Rosh Ha·sha·nah /ráwsh həshǎwnə, –shaʹá–, haashaanáʹa, rōsh/ *n.* (also **Rosh Ha·sha′na**) the Jewish New Year.

ros·in /rózin/ • *n.* resin, esp. in solid form. • *v.tr.* rub (esp. the bow of a violin, etc.) with rosin. □□ **ros′in·y** *adj.*

ros·ter /róstər/ *n.* list or plan of turns of duty, players available, etc.

ros·trum /róstrəm/ *n.* (*pl.* **ros·tra** /–strə/ or **ros·trums**) platform for public speaking, conducting an orchestra, etc.

---

rostrum mid-16th century: from Latin, literally 'beak' (from *rodere* 'gnaw,' the source of *rodent*). The word was originally used (at first in the plural *rostra*) to denote a place in the Forum in ancient Rome that was decorated with the beaks or prows of captured warships and was used as a platform for public speakers.

---

ros·y /rózee/ *adj.* (**ros·i·er**, **ros·i·est**) **1** pink; red. **2** optimistic; hopeful. □□ **ros′i·ly** *adv.* **ros′i·ness** *n.*

rot /rot/ • *v.intr.* (**rot·ted**, **rot·ting**) **1** decompose; decay. **2** gradually perish; waste away. • *n.* **1** process or state of rotting. **2** *sl.* nonsense.

ro·ta·ry /rótəree/ • *adj.* acting by rotation (*rotary drill*). • *n.* (*pl.* **–ries**) **1** rotary machine. **2** traffic circle.

ro·tate /rṓtayt/ v. **1** intr. & tr. move around an axis or center; revolve. **2 a** tr. take or arrange in rotation. **b** intr. act or take place in rotation (the chairmanship will rotate). □□ **ro'tat·a·ble** adj. **ro·ta'tion** n. **ro·ta·tive** /rṓtaytiv/ adj. **ro'ta·tor** n. **ro·ta·to·ry** /rṓtətawree/ adj.

ROTC /rṓtsee/ abbr. Reserve Officers Training Corps.

rote /rōt/ n. (usu. prec. by by) mechanical or habitual repetition (with ref. to acquiring knowledge).

rot·gut /rótgut/ n. inferior whiskey.

ro·tis·ser·ie /rōtísəree/ n. rotating spit for roasting and barbecuing meat.

ro·tor /rṓtər/ n. **1** rotary part of a machine. **2** rotary airfoil on a helicopter.

ro·to·til·ler /rṓtətilər/ n. machine with a rotating blade for breaking up or tilling the soil. □□ **ro'to·till** v.tr.

rot·ten /rót'n/ adj. (**rot·ten·er, rot·ten·est**) **1** rotting or rotted. **2** morally, socially, or politically corrupt. **3** sl. **a** disagreeable; unpleasant. **b** (of a plan, etc.) ill-advised; unsatisfactory (rotten idea). **c** ill (feel rotten today). □□ **rot'ten·ly** adv. **rot'ten·ness** n.

Rott·wei·ler /rótwīlər/ n. **1** dog of a tall black-and-tan breed. **2** this breed.

ro·tund /rōtúnd/ adj. plump; round. □□ **ro·tun'di·ty** n. **ro·tund'ly** adv.

ro·tun·da /rōtúndə/ n. circular building, hall, or room, esp. one with a dome.

rou·é /r‍oo-áy/ n. debauchee, esp. an elderly one; rake.

rouge /r‍oozh/ • n. **1** red cosmetic for coloring the cheeks. **2** reddish metal polish. • v. **1** tr. color with rouge. **2** intr. apply rouge.

rough /ruf/ • adj. **1** uneven; bumpy; not smooth. **2** hairy; shaggy; coarse in texture. **3** not mild, quiet, nor gentle; boisterous; coarse. **4** harsh; insensitive. **5** unpleasant; severe; demanding. **6** hard or unfair toward. **7** incomplete; rudimentary; approximate. • adv. in a rough manner. n. **1** hard aspect of life; hardship (take the rough with the smooth). **2** Golf rough ground. **3** unfinished or natural state. • v.tr. **1** (foll. by up) ruffle (feathers, hair, etc.). **2** (foll. by out) shape, sketch, or plan roughly. □ **rough-and-ready** crude but effective. **rough-and-tumble** irregular; scrambling; disorderly. **diamond in the rough** person of good nature but rough manners. **rough draft** first or original draft (of a story, report, document, etc.). **rough-hewn** uncouth; unrefined. **rough it** do without basic comforts. **rough up** sl. treat (a person) with violence. □□ **rough'ly** adv. **rough'ness** n.

rough·age /rúfij/ n. coarse, fibrous material in food.

rough·en /rúfən/ v. make or become rough.

rough·house /rúfhows/ sl. • n. disturbance or row; boisterous play. • v. **1** tr. handle (a person) roughly. **2** intr. make a disturbance.

rough·neck /rúfnek/ n. colloq. **1** rough or rowdy person. **2** worker on a drill rig.

rough·shod /rúfshod/ adj. (of a horse) having shoes with nail heads projecting to prevent slipping. □ **ride roughshod over** treat inconsiderately or arrogantly.

rou·lette /r‍oolét/ n. gambling game in which a ball is dropped on to a revolving numbered wheel.

round /rownd/ • adj. **1** shaped like a circle, sphere, or cylinder; convex; circular; curved. **2** entire; complete. **3** candid; outspoken. **4** (usu. attrib.) (of a number) expressed for convenience as a whole number (spent $297.32, or in round figures $300). • n. **1** round object or form. **2 a** recurring series of activities, functions, etc. **b** fixed route for deliveries, etc. **3** single provision of drinks, etc., to each member of a group. **4 a** ammunition to fire one shot. **b** act of firing this. **5** set, series, or sequence of actions in turn, esp. **a** one spell of play in a game, etc. **b** one stage in a competition. **6** song overlapping at intervals. • adv. = AROUND adv. 5-12. • prep. = AROUND prep. 5-12. • v. **1 a** tr. give a round shape to. **b** intr. assume a round shape. **2** tr. double or pass around (a corner, cape, etc.). **3** tr. express (a number) approximately for brevity (also foll. by down when the number is decreased and up when it is increased). □ **make one's rounds** take a customary route for inspection, etc. **make the rounds** (of news, etc.) be passed on from person to person, etc. **round robin 1** petition, esp. with signatures written in a circle to conceal the order of writing. **2** tournament in which each competitor plays in turn against every other. **round table** assembly for discussion, esp. at a conference (often attrib.: round-table talks). **round trip** trip to one or more places and back again. **round up** collect or bring together. □□ **round'ish** adj. **round'ness** n.

round·a·bout /równdəbowt/ adj. circuitous; indirect.

roun·de·lay /równdilay/ n. short simple song with a refrain.

round·house /równdhows/ n. circular repair shed for railroad locomotives, built around a turntable.

round·ly /równdlee/ adv. **1** bluntly; in plain language (was roundly criticized). **2** in a thoroughgoing manner (go roundly to work).

round·up /równdup/ n. **1** systematic rounding up of people or things. **2** summary of facts or events.

round·worm /równdwərm/ n. worm, esp. a nematode, with a rounded body.

rouse /rowz/ v. **1 a** tr. bring out of sleep; wake. **b** intr. cease to sleep; wake up. **2 a** tr. stir up; make active or excited. **b** intr. become active. **3** tr. provoke to anger (is terrible when roused). **4** tr. evoke (feelings). □□ **rous'a·ble** adj. **rous'er** n. **rous'ing** adj. **rous'ing·ly** adv.

roust·a·bout /rówstəbowt/ n. **1** laborer on an oil rig. **2** unskilled or casual laborer, as in a circus.

rout[1] /rowt/ • n. **1** disorderly retreat. **2** heavy defeat. • v.tr. put to flight; defeat utterly.

rout[2] /rowt/ v. **1** intr. & tr. = ROOT[2]. **2** tr. cut a groove, or any pattern not extending to the edges, in (a wooden or metal surface). □ **rout out** force out of bed, a hiding place, etc. □□ **rout'er** n.

route /r‍oot, rowt/ • n. way or course taken (esp. regularly). • v.tr. send, forward, or direct by a particular route.

rou·tine /r‍ooteen/ • n. **1** regular course or procedure. **2** set sequence in a dance, comedy act, etc. • adj. **1** performed as part of a routine. **2** of a customary or standard kind. □□ **rou·tine'ly** adv.

rove /rōv/ *v.* **1** *intr.* wander without a settled destination; roam. **2** *intr.* (of eyes) look in changing directions. **3** *tr.* wander over or through. □□ **rov′er** *n.*

row[1] /rō/ *n.* **1** line of persons or things. **2** line of seats across a theater, etc. □ **hard** (or **tough**) **row to hoe** difficult task. **in a row 1** forming a row. **2** *colloq.* in succession (*two Sundays in a row*).

row[2] /rō/ • *v.* **1** *tr.* propel (a boat) with oars. **2** *tr.* convey (a passenger) in this way. **3** *intr.* propel a boat in this way. • *n.* excursion in a rowboat. □□ **row′er** *n.*

row[3] /row/ *colloq.* • *n.* commotion; quarrel. • *v.intr.* make or engage in a row.

row·boat /rōbōt/ *n.* small boat propelled by oars.

row·dy /rówdee/ • *adj.* (**row·di·er, row·di·est**) noisy and disorderly. • *n.* (*pl.* **–dies**) rowdy person. □□ **row′di·ly** *adv.* **row′di·ness** *n.* **row′dy·ism** *n.*

row·el /rówəl/ *n.* spiked revolving disk at the end of a spur.

roy·al /róyəl/ • *adj.* **1** of, suited to, or worthy of a king or queen; majestic. **2** in the service or under the patronage of a king or queen. • *n.* *colloq.* member of the royal family. □ **royal blue** deep vivid blue. **royal family** family to which a sovereign belongs. **royal jelly** substance secreted by honeybee workers and fed by them to future queen bees. □□ **roy′al·ly** *adv.*

roy·al·ist /róyəlist/ *n.* supporter of monarchy. □□ **roy′al·ism** *n.*

roy·al·ty /róyəltee/ *n.* (*pl.* **–ties**) **1** office, dignity, or power of a king or queen; sovereignty. **2** royal person(s). **3** percentage of profit from a patent, song, book, etc., paid to the creator.

---

royalty late Middle English: from Old French *roialte*, from *roial* (as in *royal*). The sense 'royal right (especially over minerals)' (late 15th century) developed into the sense 'payment made by a mining company to the site owner' (mid-19th century), which was then transferred to payments for the permission to hold patents and issue published materials; this permission was originally granted by a monarch.

---

rpm. *abbr.* (also **r.p.m.**) revolutions per minute.

rps *abbr.* (also **r.p.s.**) revolutions per second.

RR *abbr.* **1** railroad. **2** rural route.

RSV *abbr.* Revised Standard Version (of the Bible).

RSVP *abbr.* (in an invitation, etc.) please answer, (French *répondez s'il vous plaît*).

rt. *abbr.* right.

rte. *abbr.* route.

Ru *symb. Chem.* ruthenium.

rub /rub/ • *v.* (**rubbed, rub·bing**) **1** *tr.* move one's hand or another object with firm pressure over the surface of. **2** *tr.* apply (one's hand, etc.) in this way. **3** *tr.* clean, polish, make dry, chafe, make sore, etc., by rubbing. **4** *tr.* apply (polish, ointment, etc.) by rubbing. **5** *intr.* (foll. by *against, on*) move with contact or friction.

• *n.* **1** spell or instance of rubbing. **2** impediment or difficulty (*there's the rub*). □ **rub away** remove by rubbing. **rub elbows with** associate or come into contact with (another person), esp. socially. **rub it in** (or **rub a person's nose in it**) emphasize or repeat an embarrassing fact, etc. **rub off 1** (usu. foll. by *on*) be transferred by contact (*some of his attitudes have rubbed off on me*). **2** remove by rubbing. **rub out 1** erase with an eraser. **2** *sl.* kill; eliminate. **rub the wrong way** irritate.

rub·ber[1] /rúbər/ *n.* **1** tough elastic substance made from the latex of plants or synthetically. **2** *colloq.* condom. **3** (in *pl.*) galoshes. □ **rubber band** loop of rubber for holding papers, etc., together. **rubber plant 1** evergreen plant with dark-green shiny leaves, often cultivated as a houseplant. **2** (also **rubber tree**) any of various tropical trees yielding latex. **rubber stamp** device for inking and imprinting on a surface. **rubber-stamp** *v.tr.* **1** use a rubber stamp. **2** approve automatically. □□ **rub′ber·y** *adj.* **rub′ber·i·ness** *n.*

---

rubber mid-16th century: from the verb RUB + -ER[1]. The original sense was 'an implement (such as a hard brush) used for rubbing and cleaning.' Because an early use of the elastic substance (previously known as *caoutchouc*) was to rub out pencil marks, *rubber* gained the sense 'eraser' in the late 18th century. The sense was subsequently (mid-19th century) generalized to refer to the substance in any form or use, at first often differentiated as *India rubber*.

---

rub·ber[2] /rúbər/ *adj.* designating the deciding game or match in a series.

rub·ber·ize /rúbərīz/ *v.tr.* treat or coat with rubber.

rub·ber·neck /rúbərnek/ *colloq.* • *n.* person, esp. a tourist, who stares inquisitively or stupidly. • *v.intr.* act in this way.

rub·bish /rúbish/ *n.* **1** waste material; debris; refuse; litter. **2** worthless material or articles; junk. **3** (often as *int.*) nonsense. □□ **rub′bish·y** *adj.*

rub·ble /rúbəl/ *n.* rough fragments of stone, brick, etc. □□ **rub′bly** *adj.*

rube /rōōb/ *n. colloq.* country bumpkin.

ru·bel·la /rōōbélə/ *n.* German measles.

ru·bi·cund /rōōbikund/ *adj.* ruddy; reddish.

ru·bid·i·um /rōōbídeeəm/ *n. Chem.* soft silvery metallic element. ¶ Symb.: **Rb**.

ru·ble /rōōbəl/ *n.* chief monetary unit of Russia, the USSR (*hist.*), and some other former republics of the USSR.

ru·bric /rōōbrik/ *n.* **1** heading or passage in red or special lettering. **2** explanatory words. □□ **ru′bri·cal** *adj.*

---

rubric late Middle English *rubrish* (originally referring to a heading, section of text, etc., written in red for distinctiveness), from Old French *rubriche*, from Latin *rubrica* (*terra*) 'red (earth or ocher as writing material),' from the base of *rubeus* 'red'; the later spelling is influenced by the Latin form.

---

ru·by /rōōbee/ • *n.* (*pl.* **–bies**) **1** rare precious stone varying from deep crimson or purple to

pale rose. **2** glowing, purple-tinged red color. •
adj. of this color.

ruck·sack /rúksak, rŏŏk–/ = BACKPACK *n.*

ruck·us /rúkəs/ *n.* fracas or commotion.

rud·der /rúdər/ *n.* **1** flat piece hinged vertically
to the stern of a ship for steering. **2** vertical airfoil pivoted from the stabilizer of an aircraft, for
controlling horizontal movement.

RUDDER, 2

rud·dy /rúdee/ *adj.* (**rud·di·er**, **rud·di·est**) **1** (of a
person or complexion) freshly or healthily red.
2 reddish. □□ **rud′di·ly** *adv.* **rud′di·ness** *n.*

rude /rŏŏd/ *adj.* **1** impolite; offensive. **2** roughly
made or done (*rude shelter*). **3** primitive. **4**
abrupt; startling (*rude awakening*). **5** *colloq.* indecent; lewd. □□ **rude′ly** *adv.* **rude′ness** *n.*

ru·di·ment /rŏŏdimənt/ *n.* **1** (in *pl.*) elements
or first principles of a subject. **2** (in *pl.*) imperfect beginning of something yet to develop.
□□ **ru·di·men′ta·ry** *adj.*

rue[1] /rŏŏ/ *v.tr.* (**rues**, **rued**, **ru·ing**) repent of.
□□ **rue′ful** *adj.* **rue′ful·ly** *adv.* **rue′ful·ness** *n.*

rue[2] /rŏŏ/ *n.* perennial evergreen shrub with
bitter strong-scented leaves.

ruff /ruf/ *n.* **1** projecting, starched, frilly collar
of the 16th c. **2** projecting or colored ring of
feathers or hair around a bird's or animal's neck.

RUFF, 1

ruf·fi·an /rúfeeən/ *n.* violent, lawless person.
□□ **ruf′fi·an·ism** *n.*

ruf·fle /rúfəl/ • *v.tr.* **1** disturb the smoothness
or tranquillity of. **2** upset the calmness of (a
person). **3** gather (lace, etc.) into a ruffle. • *n.*
frill of lace, etc.

ru·fous /rŏŏfəs/ *adj.* (esp. of animals) reddish-
brown.

rug /rug/ *n.* floor covering of shaggy material or
thick pile. □ **pull the rug (out) from under** deprive
of support; weaken; unsettle.

rug·by /rúgbee/ *n.* team game played with an oval
ball that may be kicked, carried, and passed.

rug·ged /rúgid/ *adj.* **1** rough; uneven; wrinkled. **2**
unpolished; lacking refinement. **3** robust;
sturdy. □□ **rug′ged·ly** *adv.* **rug′ged·ness** *n.*

ru·in /rŏŏin/ • *n.* **1** destroyed or wrecked state.
2 utter destruction. **3** (in *sing.* or *pl.*) remains of
a destroyed building, etc. **4** cause of ruin (*will
be the ruin of us*). • *v.tr.* **1** bring to ruin. **2** (esp.
as **ruined** *adj.*) reduce to ruins. □□ **ru·in·a′tion**
n. **ru′in·ous** *adj.* **ru′in·ous·ly** *adv.*

rule /rŏŏl/ • *n.* **1** principle to which an action
conforms or is required to conform. **2** custom;
standard. **3** government; dominion. **4** straight
measure; ruler. • *v.* **1** *tr.* dominate; keep under
control. **2** *tr. & intr.* have sovereign control of.
3 *tr.* pronounce authoritatively. **4** *tr.* make parallel lines across (paper). □ **as a rule** usually.
rule of thumb rule based on experience or practice rather than theory. **rule out** exclude; pronounce irrelevant or ineligible. **rule the roost** be
in control.

rul·er /rŏŏlər/ *n.* **1** person exercising government
or dominion. **2** straight usu. graduated strip of
wood, metal, etc., used to draw lines or measure
distance. □□ **rul′er·ship** *n.*

rul·ing /rŏŏling/ • *n.* authoritative decision or
announcement. • *adj.* dominant; prevailing
(*ruling prices*).

rum /rum/ *n.* spirit distilled from sugar cane or
molasses.

Ru·ma·ni·an var. of ROMANIAN.

rum·ba /rúmbə, rŏŏm–/ • *n.* **1** Cuban dance. **2**
music for it. • *v.tr.* (**rum·bas**, **rum·baed** /–bəd/,
rum·ba·ing /–bə-ing/) dance the rumba.

rum·ble /rúmbəl/ • *v.intr.* **1** make a continuous
deep resonant sound as of distant thunder. **2**
move with a rumbling noise. **3** engage in a street
fight, esp. as part of a gang. • *n.* **1** rumbling
sound. **2** *sl.* street fight between gangs. □ **rumble seat** uncovered folding seat in the rear of an
automobile. □□ **rum′bler** *n.*

ru·mi·nant /rŏŏminənt/ • *n.* cud-chewing animal. • *adj.* **1** of ruminants. **2** contemplative.

ru·mi·nate /rŏŏminayt/ *v.tr. & intr.* (foll. by *over, on,*
etc.) *intr.* meditate; ponder. **2** *intr.* (of ruminants) chew the cud. □□ **ru·mi·na·tion** /–náy-
shən/ *n.* **ru·mi·na·tive** /–nətiv/ *adj.* **ru′mi·na·
tive·ly** *adv.* **ru′mi·na·tor** *n.*

rum·mage /rúmij/ • *v.tr. & intr.* (foll. by *in, through,
among*) *intr.* search, esp. unsystematically. • *n.* **1**
instance of rummaging. **2** things found by rummaging. □ **rummage sale** sale of miscellaneous
usu. secondhand articles, esp. for charity.
□□ **rum′mag·er** *n.*

---

rummage late 15th century: from Old
French *arrumage*, from *arrumer* 'stow (in
a hold),' from Middle Dutch *ruim* 'room.'
In early use the word referred to the arranging of items such as casks in the hold
of a ship, giving rise (early 17th century)
to the verb sense 'make a search of (a vessel).'

---

rum·my[1] /rúmee/ *n.* any of various card games in
which the players try to form sets and sequences
of cards.

rum·my[2] /rúmee/ *n. sl.* drunkard or sot.

ru·mor /róómər/ • *n.* general talk or hearsay of doubtful accuracy. • *v.tr.* (usu. in *passive*) report by way of rumor (*it is rumored that you are leaving*).

rump /rump/ *n.* hind part of a mammal or bird, esp. the buttocks.

rum·ple /rúmpəl/ *v.* make or become creased or ruffled. □□ **rum′ply** *adj.*

rum·pus /rúmpəs/ *n. colloq.* disturbance; brawl; uproar.

run /run/ • *v.* (**run·ning**; *past* **ran** /ran/; *past part.* **run**) **1** *intr.* go with quick steps on alternate feet. **2** *intr.* flee. **3** *intr.* go hurriedly, briefly, etc. **4** *intr.* **a** advance by or as by rolling or on wheels, or smoothly or easily. **b** be in action or operation (*left the engine running*). **5** *intr.* be current or operative (*the lease runs for 99 years*). **6** *intr.* (of a play, etc.) be staged or presented. **7** *intr.* extend; have a course, order, or tendency. **8 a** *intr.* compete in a race. **b** *intr.* finish a race in a specified position. **c** *tr.* compete in (a race). **9** *intr.* seek election (*ran for president*). **10** *tr.* cause (water, etc.) to flow. **11** *intr.* spread rapidly. **12** *tr.* traverse (a course, race, or distance). **13** *tr.* perform (an errand). **14** *tr.* publish (an article, etc.) in a periodical. **15 a** *tr.* cause (a machine or vehicle, etc.) to operate. **b** *intr.* (of a mechanism, etc.) move or work freely. **16** *tr.* direct or manage (a business, etc.). **17** *tr.* own and use (a vehicle) regularly. **18** *tr.* transport in a vehicle (*shall I run you to the post office?*). **19** *tr.* smuggle (guns, etc.). **20** *intr.* (of a dyed color) spread. **21 a** *intr.* (of a thought, the eye, the memory, etc.) pass quickly (*ideas ran through my mind*). **b** *tr.* cause (one's eye) to look cursorily. **c** *tr.* pass (a hand, etc.) rapidly over. **22** *intr.* (of hosiery) unravel along a line from a snag. **23** *intr.* exude liquid matter. • *n.* **1** running. **2** short excursion. **3** distance traveled. **4** general tendency. **5** regular route. **6** spell or course (*run of bad luck*). **7** high general demand. **8** quantity produced in one period of production. **9** average type or class. **10** *Baseball* point scored by a runner reaching home plate. **11** (foll. by *of*) free use of or access to (*had the run of the house*). **12 a** enclosure for domestic animals. **b** range of pasture. **13** line of unraveled stitches, esp. in hosiery. **14** (**the runs**) *colloq.* attack of diarrhea. □ **on the run 1** escaping. **2** hurrying about. **run across** happen to meet. **run against** oppose, as in an election. **run along** *colloq.* depart. **run around** *sl.* engage in sexual relations (esp. casually or illicitly). **run away with** win (a prize, etc.) easily. **run down 1** knock down. **2** (of an unwound clock, etc.) stop. **3** become feeble from overwork or underfeeding. **4** discover after a search. **5** disparage. **run-down 1** decayed after prosperity. **2** enfeebled through overwork, etc. **run dry** cease to flow; be exhausted. **run for it** seek safety by fleeing. **run in** *colloq.* arrest. **run-in** *n.* quarrel. **run into 1** collide with. **2** encounter. **run into the ground** *colloq.* bring to exhaustion, disrepair, etc. **run its course** follow its natural progress. **run low** (or **short**) become depleted; have too little (*ran short of gas*). **run off 1** flee. **2** produce (copies, etc.) on a machine. **3** flow or cause to flow away. **run off at the mouth** *sl.* talk incessantly. **run-of-the-mill** ordinary. **run on** talk incessantly. **run out 1** come to an end; become used up. **2** (foll. by *of*) exhaust one's stock of. **3** expel;

drive out (*ran him out of town*). **run out on** *colloq.* desert (a person). **run over 1** overflow. **2** study or repeat quickly. **3** (of a vehicle or its driver) knock down or crush. **run ragged** exhaust (a person). **run the show** *colloq.* dominate in an undertaking, etc. **run a temperature** be feverish. **run through** examine or rehearse briefly. **run-through** rehearsal. **run up** accumulate (a debt, etc.) quickly. **run up against** meet with (a difficulty or difficulties).

run·a·bout /rúnəbowt/ *n.* light car, boat, or aircraft.

run·a·round /rúnərownd/ *n.* (esp. as *give a person the runaround*) deceit or evasion.

run·a·way /rúnəway/ *n.* **1** fugitive. **2** animal or vehicle that is running out of control. **3** (*attrib.*) that is running away or out of control (*runaway inflation*).

run·down /rúndown/ *n.* summary or brief analysis.

rune /roon/ *n.* **1** letter of the earliest Germanic alphabet. **2** mark of mysterious or magic significance. □□ **ru′nic** *adj.*

RUNES, 2

rung¹ /rung/ *n.* **1** step of a ladder. **2** strengthening crosspiece in a chair, etc. □□ **runged** *adj.* **rung′less** *adj.*

rung² *past part.* of RING².

run·nel /rúnəl/ *n.* brook.

run·ner /rúnər/ *n.* **1** person, horse, etc., that runs, esp. in a race. **2** creeping plant stem that can take root. **3** rod, groove, or blade on which a thing (e.g., a sled) slides. **4** messenger, scout, etc. □ **runner-up** (*pl.* **runners-up**) competitor or team taking second place.

run·ning /rúning/ • *n.* **1** action of runners in a race, etc. **2** management; operation. • *adj.* **1** continuous (*running battle*). **2** consecutive (*three days running*). **3** done with a run (*running jump*). □ **in** (or **out of**) **the running** (of a competitor) with a good (or poor) chance of winning. **running light** navigational light displayed by a ship, aircraft, etc., during darkness. **running mate** candidate for a secondary position in an election.

run·ny /rúnee/ *adj.* (**run·ni·er, run·ni·est**) **1** tending to run or flow. **2** excessively fluid.

run·off /rúnawf/ *n.* **1** additional election, race, etc., after a tie. **2** surface water not absorbed by the ground.

runt /runt/ *n.* **1** smallest animal in a litter. **2** weakling; undersized person. □□ **runt'y** *adj.*

run·way /rúnway/ *n.* **1** surface along which aircraft take off and land. **2** narrow walkway extending out from a stage into an auditorium.

ru·pee /roopee, roopee/ *n.* chief monetary unit of India, Pakistan, etc.

rup·ture /rúpchər/ • *n.* **1** breaking; breach. **2** abdominal hernia. • *v.* **1** *tr.* break or burst (a cell or membrane, etc.). **2** *intr.* undergo a rupture. □□ **rup'tur·a·ble** *adj.*

ru·ral /roorəl/ *adj.* in, of, or suggesting the country. □ **rural free delivery** (also **rural delivery service**) postal delivery to mailboxes in rural areas. □□ **ru'ral·ly** *adv.*

ruse /rooz/ *n.* stratagem; trick.

rush¹ /rush/ • *v.* **1** *intr.* go, move, or act precipitately or with great speed. **2** *tr.* move or transport with great haste. **3** *intr.* (foll. by *at*) **a** move suddenly toward. **b** begin impetuously. **4** *tr.* perform or deal with hurriedly (*don't rush your dinner*). **5** *tr.* force (a person) to act hastily. **6** *tr.* attack or capture by sudden assault. • *n.* **1** rushing. **2** great activity; commotion. **3** (*attrib.*) done with great haste or speed (*a rush job*). **4** sudden migration of large numbers. □ **rush hour** time each day when traffic is heaviest. □□ **rush'er** *n.* **rush'ing·ly** *adv.*

rush² /rush/ *n.* marsh plant with slender stems, used for making chair seats, baskets, etc. □□ **rush'y** *adj.*

rusk /rusk/ *n.* slice of bread rebaked as a light biscuit.

rus·set /rúsit/ • *adj.* reddish-brown. • *n.* **1** reddish-brown color. **2** russet-colored fruit (esp. apple) or vegetable (esp. potato). □□ **rus' set·y** *adj.*

Rus·sian /rúshən/ • *n.* **1** native or national of Russia or the former Soviet Union. **2** language of Russia. • *adj.* of Russia, its people, or their language. □ **Russian roulette** act of daring in which one squeezes the trigger of a revolver held to one's head with one chamber loaded, having first spun the chamber.

rust /rust/ • *n.* **1** reddish corrosive coating formed on iron, steel, etc., by oxidation, esp. when wet. **2** fungal plant disease with rust-colored spots. **3** impaired state due to disuse or

inactivity. • *v.* **1** *tr.* & *intr.* affect or be affected with rust. **2** *intr.* lose quality or efficiency by disuse or inactivity.

rus·tic /rústik/ • *adj.* **1** having the characteristics of or associations with the country or country life. **2** unsophisticated. **3** rude; rough. • *n.* country person. □□ **rus'ti·cal·ly** *adv.* **rus·tic·i·ty** /-tísitee/ *n.*

rus·ti·cate /rústikayt/ *v.* **1** *intr.* retire to or live in the country. **2** *tr.* make rural. □□ **rus·ti·ca·tion** /-káyshən/ *n.*

rus·tle /rúsəl/ • *v.* **1** *intr.* & *tr.* make or cause to make a gentle sound as of dry, blown leaves. **2** *tr.* (also *absol.*) steal (cattle or horses). • *n.* rustling sound. □ **rustle up** *colloq.* produce quickly when needed. □□ **rus'tler** *n.* (esp. in sense 2 of *v.*).

rust·proof /rústproof/ • *adj.* not susceptible to corrosion by rust. • *v.tr.* make rustproof.

rust·y /rústee/ *adj.* (**rust·i·er, rust·i·est**) **1** rusted or affected by rust. **2** impaired by neglect. **3** rust-colored. □□ **rust'i·ly** *adv.* **rust'i·ness** *n.*

rut¹ /rut/ • *n.* **1** deep track made by the passage of wheels. **2** established (esp. tedious) procedure. • *v.tr.* (**rut·ted, rut·ting**) mark with ruts. □ **in a rut** following a fixed (esp. tedious or dreary) pattern of behavior. □□ **rut'ty** *adj.*

rut² /rut/ • *n.* periodic sexual excitement of male deer and other animals. • *v.intr.* (**rut·ted, rut·ting**) be affected with rut.

ru·ta·ba·ga /rootəbáygə/ *n.* large yellow-fleshed turnip.

ru·the·ni·um /roothee'neeəm/ *n. Chem.* rare hard white metallic element. ¶ Symb.: **Ru**.

ruth·er·for·di·um /rúthərfáwrdeeəm/ *n. Chem.* artificially made transuranic metallic element. ¶ Symb.: **Rf**.

ruth·less /roothlis/ *adj.* having no pity nor compassion. □□ **ruth'less·ly** *adv.* **ruth'less·ness** *n.*

RV *abbr.* **1** Revised Version (of the Bible). **2** recreational vehicle.

-ry /ree/ *suffix* = -ERY (*infantry; rivalry*).

rye /rī/ *n.* **1 a** cereal plant. **b** grain of this used for bread and fodder. **2** (in full **rye whis'key**) whiskey distilled from fermented rye.

Ss

S[1] /es/ *n.* (also **s**) (*pl.* **Ss** or **S's**; **s's** /ésiz/) **1** nineteenth letter of the alphabet. **2** S-shaped object or curve.

S[2] *abbr.* (also **S.**) **1** Saint. **2** society. **3** south, southern.

S[3] *symb. Chem.* sulfur.

s. *abbr.* **1** second(s). **2** singular. **3** son. **4** succeeded.

-s' *suffix* denoting the possessive case of plural nouns and sometimes of singular nouns ending in *s* (*the boys' shoes*; *Charles' book*).

's *abbr.* **1** is; has (*he's*). **2** us (*let's*). **3** *colloq.* does (*what's he say?*).

-s[1] /s; z after a vowel sound or voiced consonant, e.g., *ways, bags*/ *suffix* denoting the plurals of nouns.

-s[2] /s; z after a vowel sound or voiced consonant, e.g., *ties, begs*/ *suffix* forming the 3rd person sing. present of verbs.

-s[3] /s; z after a vowel sound or voiced consonant, e.g., *besides*/ *suffix* **1** forming adverbs (*afterwards*; *besides*; *mornings*). **2** forming possessive pronouns (*hers*; *ours*).

-s[4] /s after a vowel sound or voiced consonant/ *suffix* forming nicknames or pet names (*Fats*; *Cutes*).

-'s[1] /s; z/ *suffix* denoting the possessive case of singular nouns and of plural nouns not ending in *-s* (*John's book*; *book's cover*; *children's shoes*).

-'s[2] /s; z after a vowel sound or voiced consonant/ *suffix* denoting the plural of a letter or symbol (*S's*; *8's*).

SA *abbr.* **1** Salvation Army. **2** South Africa. **3** South America.

Sab·bath /sábəth/ *n.* religious day of rest kept by Christians on Sunday and Jews on Saturday.

sab·bat·i·cal /səbátikəl/ ● *adj.* **1** of the Sabbath. **2** (of leave) granted at intervals from one's usual work, as to a teacher for study or travel. ● *n.* period of sabbatical leave.

sa·ber /sáybər/ *n.* **1** curved cavalry sword. **2** tapered fencing sword. □ **saber rattling** display or threat of military force.

Sa·bin vac·cine /sáybin/ *n.* oral vaccine giving immunity against poliomyelitis.

sa·ble /sáybəl/ *n.* **1** small, brown-furred mammal of N. Europe and N. Asia. **2** its skin or fur.

sa·bot /sabó, sábō/ *n.* shoe hollowed out from a block of wood.

sab·o·tage /sábətaazh/ ● *n.* deliberate damage to productive capacity, esp. as a political act. ● *v.tr.* commit sabotage on. □□ **sab·o·teur'** *n.*

SAC /sak/ Strategic Air Command.

sac /sak/ *n.* membranous bag in an animal or plant.

sac·cha·rin /sákərin/ *n.* sugar substitute.

sac·cha·rine /sákərin, –reen, –rīn/ *adj.* **1** sugary. **2** unpleasantly overpolite, sentimental, etc.

sac·er·do·tal /sásərdótəl, sák–/ *adj.* of priests or the priestly office. □□ **sac·er·do'tal·ly** *adv.*

sa·chem /sáychəm/ *n.* supreme leader of some Native American tribes.

sa·chet /sasháy/ *n.* small bag or packet containing dry perfume, etc.

sack[1] /sak/ ● *n.* **1 a** large, strong bag for storing or conveying goods. **b** quantity contained in a sack. **2** (prec. by *the*) *colloq.* dismissal from employment. **3** (prec. by *the*) *sl.* bed. ● *v.tr.* **1** put into a sack or sacks. **2** *colloq.* dismiss from employment. □□ **sack'ful** *n.* (*pl.* **–fuls**).

sack[2] /sak/ ● *v.tr.* plunder and destroy (a captured town, etc.). ● *n.* such sacking.

sack·cloth /sák-klawth, -kloth/ *n.* **1** coarse fabric of flax or hemp. **2** clothing for mourning (esp. *sackcloth and ashes*).

sac·ra·ment /sákrəmənt/ *n.* symbolic Christian ceremony, e.g., baptism and the Eucharist. □□ **sac·ra·ment'al** *adj.*

---

sacrament Middle English: from Old French *sacrement*, from Latin *sacramentum* 'solemn oath' (from *sacrare* 'to hallow,' from *sacer* 'sacred'), used in Christian Latin as a translation of Greek *mustērion* 'mystery.'

---

sa·cred /sáykrid/ *adj.* **1 a** dedicated to a god. **b** connected with religion. **2** safeguarded or required by religion, reverence, or tradition. □ **sacred cow** *colloq.* hallowed idea or institution. □□ **sa'cred·ly** *adv.* **sa'cred·ness** *n.*

sac·ri·fice /sákrifīs/ ● *n.* **1 a** voluntary giving up of something valued. **b** thing given up. **c** the loss entailed. **2 a** slaughter of an animal or person or surrender of a possession, as an offering to a deity. **b** animal, person, or thing offered. ● *v.tr.* give up (a thing) as a sacrifice. □□ **sac·ri·fi·cial** /–físhəl/ *adj.* **sac·ri·fi'cial·ly** *adv.*

sac·ri·lege /sákrilij/ *n.* violation or misuse of what is regarded as sacred. □□ **sac·ri·le·gious** /–líjəs/ *adj.* **sac·ri·le'gious·ly** *adv.*

sac·ro·il·i·ac /sákrōíleeak, sákrō–/ *n.* juncture of the sacrum and the ilium bones of the pelvis.

sac·ro·sanct /sákrōsangkt/ *adj.* (of a person, place, law, etc.) most sacred; inviolable. □□ **sac·ro·sanc·ti·ty** /–sángktitee/ *n.*

sac·rum /sáykrəm, sák–/ *n.* (*pl.* **sac'ra** /–krə/ or **sac'rums**) *Anat.* triangular bone formed from fused vertebrae and situated between the two hipbones of the pelvis.

sad /sad/ *adj.* (**sad·der, sad·dest**) **1** unhappy; feeling sorrow or regret. **2** causing sorrow. **3** regrettable. **4** shameful; deplorable. □ **sad sack** *colloq.* inept person, esp. a soldier. □□ **sad'ly** *adv.* **sad'ness** *n.*

---

sad Old English *sæd* 'sated, weary,' also 'weighty, dense,' of Germanic origin; related to Dutch *zat* and German *satt*, from an Indo-European root shared by Latin *satis* 'enough.' The original meaning was replaced in Middle English by the senses 'steadfast, firm' and 'serious, sober,' and later 'sorrowful.'

sad·den /sád'n/ *v.* make or become sad.

sad·dle /sád'l/ • *n.* **1** seat of leather, etc., fastened on a horse, etc., for riding. **2** seat on a bicycle, etc. **3** cut of meat consisting of the two loins. • *v.tr.* **1** put a saddle on (a horse, etc.). **2** (foll. by *with*) burden (a person). □ **in the saddle 1** mounted. **2** in office or control. **saddle shoes** laced shoes with yokes that contrast in color with the rest of the upper. **saddle stitch** stitch of thread or a wire staple passed through a magazine or booklet at its folded spine.

SADDLE, 1

sad·dle·bag /sád'lbag/ *n.* **1** each of a pair of bags laid across a horse, etc. **2** bag attached to a bicycle saddle, etc.

Sad·du·cee /sájəsee, sádyə–/ *n.* member of an ancient fundamentalist Jewish sect. □□ **Sad·du·ce·an** /–se'eən/ *adj.*

sa·dism /sáydizəm, sád–/ *n.* pleasure derived from inflicting cruelty on others. □□ **sa'dist** *n.* **sa·dis·tic** /sədístik/ *adj.* **sa·dis'ti·cal·ly** *adv.*

sa·do·mas·o·chism /sáydōmásəkizəm, sádō–/ *n.* combination of sadism and masochism in one person. □□ **sa·do'mas'o·chist** *n.* **sa·do·mas·o·chis·tic** /–kístik/ *adj.*

sa·fa·ri /səfaáree/ *n.* (*pl.* **sa·fa·ris**) expedition, esp. in E. Africa, to hunt or observe animals.

safe /sayf/ • *adj.* **1** free of danger or injury. **2** secure; not risky. **3** reliable; certain. **4** (also **safe and sound**) uninjured. • *n.* strong, lockable cabinet, etc., for valuables. □ **safe-conduct 1** privilege of immunity from arrest or harm. **2** document securing this. **safe-deposit box** secured box (esp. in a bank vault) for storing valuables. **safe house** place of refuge for spies, etc. **safe sex** sexual activity in which precautions are taken against sexually transmitted diseases. □□ **safe'ly** *adv.* **safe'ness** *n.*

safe·crack·er /sáyfkrakər/ *n.* person who breaks open and robs safes.

safe·guard /sáyfgaard/ • *n.* proviso, stipulation, quality, or circumstance that tends to prevent something undesirable. • *v.tr.* guard; protect.

safe·keep·ing /sáyfkeeping/ *n.* preservation in a safe place.

safe·ty /sáyftee/ *n.* (*pl.* **–ties**) **1** being safe. **2** (*attrib.*) designating an item for preventing injury (*safety lock*). □ **safety belt** = *seat belt.* **safety-deposit box** = *safe-deposit box.* **safety first** motto advising caution. **safety match** match igniting only on a specially prepared surface. **safety pin** doubled pin with a guarded point. **safety razor** razor with a guard to prevent cutting the skin. **safety valve 1** automatic valve relieving excessive pressure. **2** means of giving harmless vent to excitement, etc.

saf·flow·er /sáflowr/ *n.* thistlelike plant yielding a red dye and edible oil.

saf·fron /sáfrən/ • *n.* **1** bright yellow-orange food coloring and flavoring made from dried crocus stigmas. **2** color of this. • *adj.* saffron-colored.

sag /sag/ • *v.intr.* (**sagged, sag·ging**) **1** sink or subside, esp. unevenly. **2** bulge or curve downward in the middle. **3 a** fall in price. **b** (of a price) fall. • *n.* state or extent of sagging. □□ **sag'gy** *adj.*

sa·ga /saágə/ *n.* **1** long, heroic story of achievement, esp. medieval Icelandic or Norwegian. **2** any long, involved story.

sa·ga·cious /səgáyshəs/ *adj.* showing insight, good judgment, or wisdom. □□ **sa·ga'cious·ly** *adv.* **sa·gac'i·ty** /səgásitee/ *n.*

sage[1] /sayj/ *n.* aromatic herb with dull grayish-green leaves. □□ **sag'y** *adj.*

sage[2] /sayj/ • *n.* wise person. • *adj.* of or indicating profound wisdom. □□ **sage'ly** *adv.*

sage·brush /sáyjbrush/ *n.* shrubby aromatic plant of western N. America.

Sag·it·tar·i·us /sájitáireeəs/ *n.* **1** constellation and ninth sign of the zodiac (the Archer). **2** person born under this sign. □□ **Sag·it·tar'i·an** *adj. & n.*

sa·go /sáygō/ *n.* (*pl.* **–gos**) **1** edible starch made from the sago palm. **2** (in full **sago palm**) tropical palm from which sago is made.

sa·gua·ro /səgwaárō, səwaárō/ *n.* (*pl.* **–ros**) giant cactus of Mexico and the SW United States.

sa·hib /saab, saáhib/ *n. hist.* (in India) form of address to European men.

said *past* and *past part.* of SAY.

sail /sayl/ • *n.* **1** piece of material extended on rigging to catch the wind and propel a vessel. **2** ship's sails collectively. **3** voyage or excursion in a sailing ship, etc. **4** wind-catching apparatus of a windmill. • *v.* **1** *intr.* travel on water by the use of sails or engine power. **2** *tr.* **a** navigate (a ship, etc.). **b** travel on (a sea). **3** *tr.* set (a toy boat) afloat. **4** *intr.* glide or move smoothly. **5** *intr. colloq.* succeed easily (*sailed through the exams*). □ **sail into** *colloq.* attack physically or verbally. **under sail** with sails set. □□ **sail'a·ble** *adj.* **sailed** *adj.* (also in *comb.*). **sail'less** *adj.*

sail·board /sáylbáwrd/ *n.* board with a mast and sail, used in windsurfing. □□ **sail'board·er** *n.* **sail'board·ing** *n.*

sail·boat /sáylbōt/ *n.* boat driven by sails.

sail·cloth /sáylklawth, –kloth/ *n.* canvas or canvaslike material for sails, upholstery, tents, etc.

sail·fish /sáylfish/ *n.* large marine fish with a large dorsal fin.

sail·or /sáylər/ *n.* **1** seaman or mariner, esp. one below the rank of officer. **2** person who enjoys boating. □□ **sail'or·ly** *adj.*

sail·plane /sáylplayn/ *n.* glider designed for sustained flight.

saint /saynt/ • *n.* **1** holy or (in some churches) canonized person regarded as having a place in heaven. **2** very virtuous person. • *v.tr.* (as **sainted** *adj.*) sacred; of a saintly life. □□ **saint'hood** *n.* **saint'like** *adj.* **saint'ly** (**saint·li·er, saint·li·est**) *adj.*

St. Ber·nard /bərnaárd/ *n.* very large dog of a breed orig. kept in the Alps for rescue.

sake[1] /sayk/ *n.* **1** benefit; advantage. **2** cause; purpose.

sa·ke[2] /saákee, –ke/ *n.* Japanese rice wine.

sa·laam /səlaám/ *n.* esp. Islamic greeting with a low bow and the right palm on the forehead.

sal·a·ble /sáyləbəl/ *adj.* (also **sale′a·ble**) fit to be sold; finding purchasers. □□ **sal·a·bil′i·ty** *n.*

sa·la·cious /səláyshəs/ *adj.* **1** lustful; lecherous. **2** (of writings, pictures, talk, etc.) tending to cause sexual desire. □□ **sa·la′cious·ly** *adv.* **sa·la′cious·ness** *n.* **sa·lac′i·ty** /səlásitee/ *n.*

sal·ad /sáləd/ *n.* mixture of usu. cold vegetables, eggs, meats, pasta, etc., often with dressing. □ **salad days** period of youthful inexperience. **salad dressing** mixture of oil, vinegar, etc., used in a salad.

sal·a·man·der /sáləmandər/ *n.* tailed newtlike amphibian.

sa·la·mi /səlaámee/ *n.* (*pl.* **sa·la·mis**) highly seasoned orig. Italian sausage often flavored with garlic.

sal·a·ry /sáləree/ ● *n.* (*pl.* **–ries**) fixed regular wages. ● *v.tr.* (**–ries, –ried**) (usu. as **salaried** *adj.*) pay a salary to.

sale /sayl/ *n.* **1** exchange of a commodity for money, etc.; act or instance of selling. **2** amount sold. **3** event at which goods are sold, esp. at reduced prices. □ **for** (or **up for**) **sale** offered for purchase. **on sale** available for purchase, esp. at a reduced price.

sale·a·ble var. of SALABLE.

sales·clerk /sáylzklərk/ *n.* salesperson in a retail store.

sales·girl /sáylzgərl/ *n.* saleswoman.

sales·la·dy /sáylzlaydee/ *n.* (*pl.* **–dies**) saleswoman.

sales·man /sáylzmən/ *n.* (*pl.* **–men;** *fem.* **sales·wom·an,** *pl.* **–wom·en**) person employed to sell goods or services.

sales·man·ship /sáylzmənship/ *n.* **1** skill in selling. **2** techniques used in selling.

sales·per·son /sáylzpersən/ *n.* salesman or saleswoman.

sales·room /sáylzroŏm, –roŏm/ *n.* room for the display and purchase of items, esp. at an auction.

sal·i·cyl·ic ac·id /sálisílik/ *n.* chemical used as a fungicide and in aspirin and dye. □□ **sa·lic·y·late** /səlísilayt/ *n.*

sa·lient /sáylyənt/ ● *adj.* **1** prominent; conspicuous. **2** (of a fortification) pointing outward. ● *n.* salient angle or part of a fortification. □□ **sa′li·ence** *n.* **sa′li·en·cy** *n.* **sa′li·ent·ly** *adv.*

sa·line /sáyleen, –līn/ ● *adj.* containing or like salt. ● *n.* saline solution. □□ **sa·lin·i·ty** /səlínitee/ *n.* **sal·i·ni·za·tion** /sálinizáyshən/ *n.*

sa·li·va /səlīvə/ *n.* liquid secreted into the mouth by glands. □□ **sa·li·var·y** /sáliveree/ *adj.*

sal·i·vate /sálivayt/ *v.intr.* secrete saliva. □□ **sal·i·va·tion** /–váyshən/ *n.*

sal·low /sálō/ *adj.* (**sal·low·er, sal·low·est**) (of the skin or complexion, or of a person) of a sickly yellow or pale brown. □□ **sal′low·ness** *n.*

sal·ly /sálee/ (*pl.* **–lies**) ● *n.* **1** sudden charge;

---

sortie. **2** going forth; excursion. **3** witticism; piece of banter. ● *v.intr.* (**–lies, –lied**) (usu. foll. by *out, forth*) go for a walk, set out on a journey, etc.

salm·on /sámən/ ● *n.* (*pl.* same or **salm′ons**) edible fish with characteristic pink flesh. ● *adj.* of the color of salmon flesh. □□ **salm′on·y** *adj.*

sal·mo·nel·la /sálmənélə/ *n.* (*pl.* **sal·mo·nel·lae** /–lee/) bacterium causing food poisoning.

sa·lon /səlón, saláwN/ *n.* **1** reception room. **2** room or establishment of a hairdresser, beautician, etc. **3** *hist.* meeting of eminent people in the home of a lady of fashion.

sa·loon /səloŏn/ *n.* bar; tavern.

sal·sa /saálsə/ *n.* **1** dance music of Cuban origin, with jazz and rock elements. **2** dance performed to this music. **3** spicy sauce made from tomatoes, chilies, onions, etc.

SALT /sawlt/ *abbr.* Strategic Arms Limitation Talks (or Treaty).

salt /sawlt/ ● *n.* **1** (also **common salt**) sodium chloride, esp. mined or evaporated from seawater. **2** chemical compound formed from the reaction of an acid with a base. **3** piquancy; pungency; wit. **4** (in *sing.* or *pl.*) a substance resembling salt in taste, form, etc. (*bath salts*). **b** substance used as a laxative. **5** (also **old salt**) experienced sailor. ● *adj.* **1** impregnated with, containing, or tasting of salt. **2** (of a plant) growing in the sea or in salt marshes. ● *v.tr.* **1** cure or preserve with salt or brine. **2** season with salt. **3** make (a narrative, etc.) piquant. **4** sprinkle (the ground, etc.) with salt, esp. in order to melt snow, etc. □ **salt away** *sl.* stash money, etc.; save. **salt the books** *sl.* show receipts as larger than they really have been. **salt lick** place where animals go to lick salt. **salt a mine** *sl.* introduce extraneous ore, material, etc., to make the source seem rich. **salt of the earth** person or people of great worthiness, reliability, honesty, etc. (Matt. 5:13). **take with a grain of salt** regard as exaggerated; believe only part of. **worth one's salt** efficient; capable.

salt·cel·lar /sáwltselər/ *n.* vessel holding salt for table use.

sal·tine /sawltéen/ *n.* lightly salted, square, flat cracker.

salt·pe·ter /sáwltpeetər/ *n.* potassium nitrate, used in preserving meat and in gunpowder.

salt·shak·er /sáwltshaykər/ *n.* container of salt for sprinkling.

salt·wa·ter /sáwltwawtər/ *adj.* **1** of or living in the sea. **2** pertaining to or made with salt water.

salt·y /sáwltee/ *adj.* (**salt·i·er, salt·i·est**) **1** tasting of, containing, or preserved with salt. **2** racy; risqué. □□ **salt′i·ness** *n.*

sa·lu·bri·ous /səloŏbreeəs/ *adj.* **1** health-giving; healthy. **2** (of surroundings, etc.) pleasant; agreeable. □□ **sa·lu′bri·ous·ly** *adv.* **sa·lu′bri·ous·ness** *n.*

sa·lu·ki /səloŏkee/ *n.* (*pl.* **sa·lu·kis**) **1** tall, swift, slender dog of a silky-coated breed. **2** this breed.

sal·u·tar·y /sályəteree/ *adj.* **1** producing good effects; beneficial. **2** health-giving.

sal·u·ta·tion /sályətáyshən/ *n.* expression of greeting, spoken or written. □□ **sal·u·ta′tion·al** *adj.*

sa·lu·ta·to·ry /səloŏtətawree/ ● *adj.* of salutation. ● *n.* (*pl.* **–ries**) oration, esp. as given by the second-ranking member of a graduating class. □□ **sa·lu·ta·to·ri·an** /–táwreeən/ n. (in sense of n.).

sa·lute /səlóŏt/ • n. **1** gesture of respect, homage, greeting, etc. **2** Mil. & Naut. prescribed gesture or use of weapons or flags as a sign of respect or recognition. **3** ceremonial discharge of a gun or guns. • v. **1 a** tr. make a salute to. **b** intr. perform a salute. **2** tr. greet. □□ **sa·lut′er** n.

sal·vage /sálvij/ • n. **1** rescue of property, from the sea, fire, etc. **2** property saved in this way. **3 a** saving and use of waste materials. **b** materials salvaged. • v.tr. save from a wreck, fire, adverse circumstances, etc. □□ **sal′vage·a·ble** adj. **sal′vag·er** n.

sal·va·tion /salváyshən/ n. **1** saving or being saved. **2** deliverance from sin and damnation. **3** person or thing that saves.

salve /sav, saav/ • n. **1** healing ointment. **2** thing that is soothing or consoling. • v.tr. soothe.

sal·ver /sálvər/ n. metal serving tray.

sal·vo /sálvō/ n. (pl. **–voes** or **–vos**) simultaneous firing of artillery.

SAM abbr. surface-to-air missile.

Sa·mar·i·tan /səmárit′n/ n. (in full **good Samaritan**) charitable or helpful person (Luke 10:33, etc.). □□ **Sa·mar′i·tan·ism** n.

sa·mar·i·um /səmáireeəm/ n. Chem. soft, silvery metallic element of the lanthanide series. ¶ Symb.: **Sm**.

sam·ba /sámbə, saám–/ • n. **1** ballroom dance of Brazilian and African origins. **2** music for this. • v.intr. (**sam·bas, sam·baed** /–bəd/, **sam·ba·ing** /–bə–ing/) dance the samba.

same /saym/ • adj. **1** identical; not different. **2** unvarying; uniform. **3** just mentioned. • pron. (prec. by the) the same thing or person (asked for the same). • adv. (usu. prec. by the) similarly; in the same way (we all feel the same). □ **all** (or **just**) **the same 1** emphatically the same. **2** in spite of changed conditions. **at the same time 1** simultaneously. **2** notwithstanding. **be all** (or **just**) **the same to** expression of indifference or impartiality (it's all the same to me what we do). **same here** colloq. the same applies to me. **the same to you!** may you do, have, find, etc., the same thing. □□ **same′ness** n. ¶ Do not use **same** in place of identical when referring to objects. You and your friend may have bought identical sweaters, but if you bought the same sweater, you will be sharing one clothing item between the two of you.

Sa·mo·an /səmóən/ • n. **1** native of Samoa, a group of islands in the Pacific. **2** language of this people. • adj. of or relating to Samoa or its people or language.

sam·o·var /sáməvaar/ n. Russian urn for making tea.

Sam·o·yed /sámɔyed, səmóyed/ n. **1** dog of a white Arctic breed. **2** this breed.

sam·pan /sámpan/ n. small boat used in the Far East.

sam·ple /sámpəl/ • n. **1** (also attrib.) small representative part or quantity. **2** illustrative or typical example. • v.tr. take, give, or try samples of.

sam·pler /sámplər/ n. **1** person who samples. **2** collection of representative items, etc. **3** piece of embroidery worked in various stitches as a specimen of proficiency.

Sam·son /sámsən/ n. person of great strength.

sam·u·rai /sámōōrī, sáa–/ n. (pl. same) member of a former military caste in Japan.

sanc·ti·fy /sángktifī/ v.tr. (**–fies, –fied**) **1** treat as holy. **2** free from sin. □□ **sanc·ti·fi·ca′tion** n. **sanc′ti·fi·er** n.

sanc·ti·mo·ni·ous /sángktimóneeəs/ adj. making a show of sanctity or piety. □□ **sanc·ti·mo′ni·ous·ly** adv. **sanc·ti·mo′ni·ous·ness** n. **sanc′ti·mo·ny** n.

sanc·tion /sángkshən/ • n. **1** approval or encouragement given to an action, etc., by custom or tradition. **2** confirmation of a law, etc. **3** penalty for disobeying a law or rule. **4** (esp. in pl.) esp. economic action by a nation to coerce another to conform to norms of conduct. • v.tr. **1** authorize, countenance, or agree to (an action, etc.). **2** ratify; make binding. □□ **sanc′tion·able** adj.

¶ **Sanction** is confusing because it has two meanings that are almost opposite, depending on whether you are discussing domestic or foreign relations. In domestic terms, **sanction** means 'approval; permission': Voters gave the measure their sanction. In foreign affairs, **sanction** means 'penalty; deterrent': International sanctions against the republic go into effect in January.

sanc·ti·ty /sángktitee/ n. (pl. **–ties**) holiness; sacredness; inviolability.

sanc·tu·ar·y /sángkchōōeree/ n. (pl. **–ies**) **1** holy place; church, temple, etc. **2** place of refuge for birds, wild animals, etc. **3 a** immunity from arrest. **b** the right to offer this.

---

sanctuary Middle English (in sense 1): from Old French sanctuaire, from Latin sanctuarium, from sanctus 'holy.' The early sense 'a church or other sacred place where a fugitive was immune, by the law of the medieval church, from arrest' gave rise to senses 2 and 3.

---

sanc·tum /sángktəm/ n. (pl. **sanc·tums** or **sanc·ta** /–tə/) **1** holy place. **2** colloq. study; den.

SAMOVAR

sand /sand/ • n. **1** loose grains resulting from the erosion of rocks and found on the seashore, riverbeds, deserts, etc. **2** (in pl.) grains of sand. **3** (in pl.) expanse of sand. • v.tr. smooth with sandpaper. □ **sand dollar** round, flat sea urchin.

sand dune mound or ridge of sand formed by the wind. **sands are running out** allotted time is nearly at an end. □□ **sand′er** *n.*

san·dal /sánd'l/ *n.* shoe with an openwork upper or no upper, attached to the foot usu. by straps.

san·dal·wood /sánd'lwŏŏd/ *n.* scented wood of an Asian tree.

sand·bag /sándbag/ ● *n.* bag filled with sand used for fortifications, ballast, etc. ● *v.tr.* (**–bagged, –bag·ging**) **1** barricade or defend with sandbags. **2** fell with a blow from a sandbag. **3** coerce. □□ **sand′bag·ger** *n.*

sand·bar /sándbaar/ *n.* bank of sand at the mouth of a river or on the coast.

sand·blast /sándblast/ ● *v.tr.* roughen, treat, or clean with a jet of sand driven by compressed air or steam. ● *n.* this jet. □□ **sand′blast·er** *n.*

sand·box /sándboks/ *n.* box of sand for children to play in.

sand·hog /sándhawg, –hog/ *n.* person who works underwater laying foundations, constructing tunnels, etc.

sand·lot /sándlot/ *n.* piece of unoccupied sandy land used for children's games.

sand·man /sándman/ *n.* personification of tiredness causing children's eyes to smart toward bedtime.

sand·pa·per /sándpaypər/ ● *n.* paper with an abrasive coating for smoothing or polishing. ● *v.tr.* smooth with sandpaper.

sand·pip·er /sándpīpər/ *n.* wading shore bird with a piping call.

sand·stone /sándstōn/ *n.* sedimentary rock of consolidated sand.

sand·storm /sándstawrm/ *n.* storm of wind with clouds of sand.

sand·wich /sándwich, sán–/ ● *n.* two or more slices of bread with a filling of meat, cheese, etc. ● *v.tr.* **1** put (a thing, statement, etc.) between two of another character. **2** squeeze in between others (*sat sandwiched in the middle*).

sand·y /sándee/ *adj.* (**sand·i·er, sand·i·est**) **1** having the texture of sand. **2** having much sand. **3** yellowish-red. □□ **sand′i·ness** *n.*

sane /sayn/ *adj.* **1** of sound mind; not mad. **2** (of views, etc.) moderate; sensible. □□ **sane′ly** *adv.* **sane′ness** *n.*

sang *past* of SING.

sang·froid /saaⁿfrwaá/ *n.* composure, coolness, etc., in danger or under agitating circumstances.

san·gri·a /sanggreéə/ *n.* drink of red wine with lemonade, fruit, spices, etc.

san·gui·nar·y /sánggwəneree/ *adj.* bloody; bloodthirsty. □□ **san·gui·nar·i·ly** /–nérəlee/ *adv.*

san·guine /sánggwin/ *adj.* **1** optimistic; confident. **2** (of the complexion) florid; ruddy. □□ **san′guine·ly** *adv.* **san′guine·ness** *n.*

san·i·tar·i·um /sánitáireeəm/ *n.* (*pl.* **san·i·tar·i·ums** or **san·i·tar·i·a** /–reeə/) **1** establishment for the restoration of health. **2** health resort.

san·i·tar·y /sániteree/ *adj.* **1** of conditions that affect health, esp. with regard to dirt and infection. **2** hygienic; free from or designed to kill germs, infection, etc. □ **sanitary engineer** person dealing with systems needed to maintain public health. **sanitary napkin** absorbent pad used during menstruation. □□ **san·i·tar·i·an** /–áireeən/ *n.* & *adj.* **san·i·tar′i·ly** *adv.*

san·i·ta·tion /sánitáyshən/ *n.* **1** sanitary conditions. **2** maintenance or improving of these. **3** disposal of sewage and refuse.

san·i·tize /sánitīz/ *v.tr.* **1** make sanitary; disinfect. **2** render (information, etc.) more acceptable by removing improper or disturbing material. □□ **san′i·tiz·er** *n.*

san·i·ty /sánitee/ *n.* **1** state of being sane. **2** tendency to avoid extreme views.

sank *past* of SINK.

sans /sanz, soN/ *prep.* without.

San·skrit /sánskrit/ ● *n.* ancient and sacred language of the Hindus in India. ● *adj.* of or in this language.

sans ser·if /sansérif/ (also **sans-ser′if**) *Printing* ● *n.* form of type without serifs. ● *adj.* without serifs.

San·ta Claus /sántə klawz/ *n.* (also *colloq.* **Santa**) legendary person said to bring children Christmas presents.

sap[1] /sap/ ● *n.* **1** vital juice circulating in plants. **2** vigor; vitality. ● *v.tr.* (**sapped, sap·ping**) drain of sap.

sap[2] /sap/ *v.tr.* (**sapped, sap·ping**) undermine; weaken.

sap[3] /sap/ *n. sl.* foolish person.

sap·id /sápid/ *adj.* **1** having an agreeable flavor; palatable. **2** (of talk, writing, etc.) not vapid. □□ **sa·pid′i·ty** *n.*

sa·pi·ent /sáypeeənt/ *adj.* wise. □□ **sa′pi·ence** *n.* **sa′pi·ent·ly** *adv.*

sap·ling /sápling/ *n.* **1** young tree. **2** youth.

sap·phire /sáfīr/ ● *n.* **1** transparent, bright blue precious stone. **2** its color. ● *adj.* of sapphire blue.

sap·py /sápee/ *adj.* (**sap·pi·er, sap·pi·est**) **1** full of sap. **2** overly emotional or sentimental. □□ **sap′pi·ly** *adv.* **sap′pi·ness** *n.*

sap·ro·phyte /sáprəfīt/ *n.* plant or microorganism living on dead or decayed organic matter. □□ **sap·ro·phyt·ic** /–fitik/ *adj.*

Sar·a·cen /sárəsən/ *hist.* ● *n.* Arab or Muslim at the time of the Crusades. ● *adj.* of the Saracens.

sar·casm /saárkazəm/ *n.* **1** bitter or wounding remark. **2** taunt, esp. one ironically worded. □□ **sar·cas·tic** /–kástik/ *adj.* **sar·cas′ti·cal·ly** *adv.*

sar·co·ma /saarkómə/ *n.* (*pl.* **sar·co·mas** or **sar·co·ma·ta** /–mətə/) malignant tumor of connective tissue. □□ **sar·co·ma·to·sis** /–mətósis/ *n.*

sar·coph·a·gus /saarkófəgəs/ *n.* (*pl.* **sar·coph·a·gi** /–gī, –jī/) stone coffin.

sar·dine /saardeén/ *n.* small, edible fish, usu. sold tightly packed in cans.

sar·don·ic /saardónik/ *adj.* **1** grimly jocular. **2** bitterly mocking or cynical. □□ **sar·don′i·cal·ly** *adv.*

sa·ri /saáree/ *n.* (also **sa′ree**) (*pl.* **sa·ris** or **sa·rees**) length of cloth draped around the body, traditionally worn by women of India.

sa·rong /səráwng, –róng/ *n.* Malay and Javanese garment of a long strip of cloth wrapped around the body and tucked around the waist or under the armpits.

sar·sa·pa·ril·la /sáspərilə, saárs–/ *n.* preparation of the dried roots of various plants, used to flavor a carbonated drink.

sar·to·ri·al /saartáwreeəl/ adj. of men's clothes or tailoring. □□ **sar·to′ri·al·ly** adv.

s.a.s.e. abbr. self-addressed stamped envelope.

sash[1] /sash/ n. long strip or loop of cloth, etc., worn over one shoulder or around the waist. □□ **sashed** adj.

sash[2] /sash/ n. frame holding the glass in a fixed or sliding window. □□ **sashed** adj.

sa·shay /sasháy/ v.intr. colloq. walk or move ostentatiously, casually, or diagonally.

sass /sas/ colloq. • n. impudence; disrespectful mannerism or speech. • v.tr. be impudent to.

sas·sa·fras /sásəfras/ n. **1** small tree native to N. America. **2** medicinal preparation from its leaves or bark.

SAT abbr. propr. **1** Scholastic Assessment Test. **2** (formerly) Scholastic Aptitude Test.

Sat. abbr. Saturday.

Sa·tan /sáyt'n/ n. the Devil; Lucifer.

sa·tan·ic /sətánik, say–/ adj. **1** of, like, or befitting Satan. **2** diabolical; hellish. □□ **sa·tan′i·cal·ly** adv.

Sa·tan·ism /sáyt′nizəm/ n. **1** worship of Satan. **2** pursuit of evil. □□ **Sa′tan·ist** n.

satch·el /sáchəl/ n. bag, usu. with a shoulder strap, for carrying books, etc.

sate /sayt/ v.tr. **1** gratify fully. **2** overfill.

sa·teen /sateén/ n. glossy, satinlike cotton fabric.

sat·el·lite /sát′līt/ • n. **1** celestial body orbiting the earth or another planet. **2** artificial body placed in orbit around the earth or another planet. **3** small country controlled by another. • adj. transmitted by satellite (satellite communications). □ **satellite dish** concave dish-shaped antenna for receiving broadcasting signals transmitted by satellite.

sa·ti·e·ty /sətī́-itee/ n. **1** being glutted or overfilled. **2** feeling of having too much of something. **3** (foll. by of) cloyed dislike of.

sat·in /sát′n/ • n. fabric with a glossy surface on one side. • adj. smooth as satin. □□ **sat′in·ized** adj. **sat′in·y** adj.

sat·in·wood /sát′nwōōd/ n. kind of yellow, glossy timber.

sat·ire /sátīr/ n. **1** use of ridicule, irony, sarcasm, etc., to expose folly or vice or to lampoon an individual. **2** work using this. □□ **sa·tir·ic** /sətírik/ adj. **sa·tir′i·cal** adj. **sa·tir′i·cal·ly** adv. **sat·i·rist** /sátərist/ n.

sat·i·rize /sátirīz/ v.tr. assail or describe with satire. □□ **sat·i·ri·za′tion** n.

sat·is·fac·tion /sátisfákshən/ n. **1** satisfying or being satisfied. **2** thing that satisfies. **3** thing that settles an obligation or pays a debt. **4** atonement; compensation.

sat·is·fac·to·ry /sátisfáktəree/ adj. adequate; causing or giving satisfaction. □□ **sat·is·fac′to·ri·ly** adv.

sat·is·fy /sátisfī/ v. (**–fies, –fied**) **1** tr. **a** meet the expectations or desires of; comply with (a demand). **b** be adequate. **2** tr. meet (an appetite or want). **3** tr. pay (a debt or creditor). **4** tr. provide with adequate information or proof; convince. □□ **sat′is·fi·a·ble** adj. **sat′is·fy·ing** adj.

sa·trap /sátrap, sáy–/ n. **1** provincial governor in the ancient Persian empire. **2** subordinate, often despotic ruler.

sat·u·rate /sáchərayt/ v.tr. **1** fill with moisture.

2 fill to capacity. **3** cause (a substance, etc.) to absorb, hold, etc., as much as possible of another substance, etc. □□ **sat·u·ra·ble** /–rəbəl/ adj. **sat·u·rant** /–rənt/ n. & adj. **sat·u·ra·tion** /sáchəráyshən/ n.

Sat·ur·day /sátərday, –dee/ n. seventh day of the week, following Friday.

Sa·turn /sátərn/ n. sixth planet from the sun, with a system of broad flat rings circling it. □□ **Sa·tur·ni·an** /satórneeən/ adj.

sat·ur·nine /sátərnīn/ adj. **1** of a sluggish, gloomy temperament. **2** (of looks, etc.) dark and brooding.

sa·tyr /sáytər, sát–/ n. **1** Gk. & Rom. mythol. woodland god with some manlike and goatlike features. **2** lustful or sensual man.

sauce /saws/ n. **1** liquid or semisolid preparation taken as a relish with food; the liquid constituent of a dish. **2** something adding piquancy or excitement. **3** colloq. impudence; impertinence. □□ **sauce′less** adj.

sauce·pan /sáwspan/ n. cooking pan, usu. with a lid and a long handle. □□ **sauce′pan·ful** n. (pl. **–fuls**).

sau·cer /sáwsər/ n. shallow circular dish for holding a cup. □□ **sau′cer·ful** n. (pl. **–fuls**). **sau′cer·less** adj.

sau·cy /sáwsee/ adj. (**sau·ci·er, sau·ci·est**) impudent. □□ **sau′ci·ly** adv. **sau′ci·ness** n.

Sau·di /sówdee, sáw–/ (also **Sau·di A·ra·bi·an** /əráybeeən/) • n. (pl. **Saudis**) **1** native or national of Saudi Arabia. **2** person of Saudi descent. • adj. of or relating to Saudi Arabia.

sau·er·kraut /sówərkrowt/ n. chopped pickled cabbage.

sau·na /sáwnə, sow–/ n. **1** Finnish-style steam bath. **2** building used for this.

saun·ter /sáwntər/ • v.intr. walk slowly; stroll. • n. a leisurely ramble. □□ **saun′ter·er** n.

sau·ri·an /sáwreeən/ adj. of or like a lizard.

sau·sage /sáwsij/ n. seasoned ground meat, often in a tube-shaped edible casing.

sau·té /sōtáy, saw–/ • adj. quickly cooked or browned in a little hot fat. • v.tr. (**sau·te′ed** or **sau·téd**) cook in this way.

sav·age /sávij/ • adj. **1** fierce; cruel. **2** wild; primitive. **3** colloq. angry; bad-tempered. • n. **1** derog. member of a primitive tribe. **2** cruel or barbarous person. • v.tr. **1** (esp. of a dog, wolf, etc.) attack and bite or trample. **2** (of a critic, etc.) attack fiercely. □□ **sav′age·ly** adv. **sav′age·ry** n. (pl. **–ries**).

sa·van·na /səvánə/ n. (also **sa·van′nah**) grassy plain in tropical and subtropical regions.

sa·vant /savaánt, sávənt/ n. (fem. **sa·vante**) learned person.

save[1] /sayv/ • v. **1** tr. (often foll. by from) rescue, preserve, protect, or deliver from danger, harm, etc. **2** tr. keep for future use. **3** tr. (often refl.) **a** relieve (another person or oneself) from spending (money, time, trouble, etc.). **b** obviate a need. **4** tr. preserve from damnation. **5** tr. & refl. preserve (one's strength, health, etc.). • n. Ice hockey, soccer, etc. prevention of an opponent's scoring, etc. □□ **sav′a·ble** adj. (also **save′a·ble**) **sav′er** n..

save[2] /sayv/ archaic or formal • prep. except; but. • conj. unless; but; except.

sav·ing /sáyving/ • *adj.* (often in *comb.*) making economical use of (*labor-saving*). • *n.* **1** anything saved. **2** an economy. **3** (usu. in *pl.*) money saved. • *prep.* except. □ **savings and loan association** banking institution that accepts funds deposited at interest and lends funds for mortgages. **savings bank** bank receiving deposits at interest and returning the profits to the depositors.
¶ Use **savings** in the modifying position (*savings bank, savings bond*) and when referring to money saved in a bank: *Your savings are fully insured.* When speaking of an act of saving, as when one obtains a discount on a purchase, the preferred form is **saving**: *With this coupon you will receive a saving* (not *savings*) *of $3.*

sav·ior /sáyvyər/ *n.* (also **sav'iour**) **1** person who saves from danger, destruction, etc. **2** (**Savior**) (prec. by *the, our*) Christ.

sa·voir faire /sávwaa fáir/ *n.* the ability to act suitably in any situation; tact.

sa·vor /sáyvər/ • *n.* characteristic taste, flavor, etc. • *v.* **1** *tr.* **a** appreciate and enjoy the taste of (food). **b** enjoy or appreciate (an experience, etc.). **2** *intr.* (foll. by *of*) suggest by taste, smell, etc. (*savors of mushrooms*). □□ **sa'vor·less** *adj.*

sa·vor·y[1] /sáyvəree/ *n.* (*pl.* **–ries**) aromatic herb used esp. in cooking.

sa·vor·y[2] /sáyvəree/ *adj.* **1** having an appetizing taste or smell. **2** pleasant; acceptable. □□ **sa'vor·i·ly** *adv.* **sa'vor·i·ness** *n.*

sav·vy /sávee/ • *n.* knowingness; shrewdness; understanding. • *adj.* (**sav·vi·er, sav·vi·est**) knowing; wise.

saw[1] /saw/ • *n.* hand tool having a toothed blade or disk used to cut hard materials. • *v.* (*past part.* **sawed** or **sawn** /sawn/) **1** *tr.* cut (wood, etc.) with a saw. **2** *intr.* use a saw. **3** *intr.* move with a sawing motion. □□ **saw'like** *adj.*

saw[2] *past* of SEE[1].

saw[3] /saw/ *n.* proverb; maxim (*that's just an old saw*).

saw·dust /sáwdust/ *n.* powdery particles of wood produced in sawing.

saw·horse /sáwhawrs/ *n.* rack supporting wood for sawing.

saw·mill /sáwmil/ *n.* factory in which wood is sawed mechanically into planks or boards.

sawn *past part.* of SAW[1].

saw·tooth /sáwtooth/ *adj.* (also **saw·toothed** /–tootht/) (esp. of a roof, wave, etc.) shaped like the teeth of a saw.

saw·yer /sáwyər/ *n.* person who saws lumber professionally.

sax /saks/ *n.* colloq. = SAXOPHONE. □□ **sax'ist** *n.*

Sax·on /sáksən/ *n.* **1** *hist.* **a** member of the Germanic people that conquered parts of England in 5th– 6th c. **b** (usu. **Old Sax'on**) language of the Saxons. **2** = ANGLO-SAXON.

sax·o·phone /sáksəfōn/ *n.* keyed brass reed instrument. □□ **sax·o·phon·ic** /–fónik/ *adj.* **sax·o·phon·ist** /–sófənist, –sofōnist/ *n.*

say /say/ • *v.* (*3rd sing. present* **says** /sez/; *past and past part.* **said** /sed/) **1** *tr.* **a** utter (specified words); remark. **b** express. **2** *tr.* **a** state; promise. **b** have specified wording; indicate. **3** *tr.* (in

passive; usu. foll. by *to* + infin.) be asserted or described. **4** *tr.* repeat (a lesson, etc.); recite. **5** *tr.* Art, etc., convey (inner meaning or intention). • *n.* **1 a** opportunity for stating one's opinion, etc. **b** stated opinion. **2** share in a decision. □ **say-so 1** power of decision. **2** mere assertion. **that is to say 1** in other words. **2** or at least. □□ **say'a·ble** *adj.* **say'er** *n.*

say·ing /sáying/ *n.* **1** act or instance of saying. **2** maxim, proverb, adage, etc. □ **go without saying** be too well known or obvious to need mention.

SBA *abbr.* Small Business Administration.

Sb *symb.* Chem. the element antimony.

SC *abbr.* South Carolina (also in official postal use).

Sc *symb.* Chem. the element scandium.

s.c. *abbr.* small capitals.

scab /skab/ • *n.* **1** dry rough crust formed over a healing cut, sore, etc. **2** *colloq. derog.* person who refuses to strike or join a trade union, or who tries to break a strike by working. • *v.intr.* (**scabbed, scab·bing**) **1** act as a scab. **2** form a scab; heal over. □□ **scabbed** *adj.* **scab'by** *adj.* (**scab·bi·er, scab·bi·est**). **scab'bi·ness** *n.* **scab'like** *adj.*

scab·bard /skábərd/ *n.* *hist.* sheath for a sword, etc.

sca·bies /skáybeez/ *n.* contagious skin disease causing severe itching (cf. ITCH).

sca·brous /skábrəs, skáy–/ *adj.* **1** having a rough surface; scaly. **2** indecent; salacious. □□ **scab' rous·ly** *adv.* **scab'rous·ness** *n.*

scaf·fold /skáfəld, –fōld/ • *n.* **1** *hist.* raised wooden platform for the execution of criminals, esp. by hanging. **2** = SCAFFOLDING. • *v.tr.* attach scaffolding to (a building). □□ **scaf'fold·er** *n.*

scaf·fold·ing /skáfōlding, –fōlding/ *n.* temporary structure formed of poles, planks, etc., erected by workers and used by them while building or repairing a house, etc.

scal·a·wag /skáləwag/ *n.* (also **scal'ly·wag**) scamp; rascal.

scald /skawld/ • *v.tr.* **1** burn (the skin, etc.) with hot liquid or steam. **2** heat (esp. milk) to near boiling point. **3** clean with boiling water. • *n.* burn, etc., caused by scalding. □□ **scald'er** *n.*

scale[1] /skayl/ • *n.* **1** each of the small, thin, bony or horny overlapping plates protecting the skin of fish and reptiles. **2** deposit formed in a kettle, boiler, etc. • *v.* **1** *tr.* remove scale(s). **2** *intr.* form, come off in, or drop scales.

scale[2] /skayl/ *n.* **1 a** (often in *pl.*) weighing device. **b** (also **scale'pan**) each of the dishes on a simple scale balance. **2** (**the Scales**) zodiacal sign or constellation Libra. □ **tip** (or **turn**) **the scales** be the decisive factor.

scale[3] /skayl/ • *n.* **1** graded classification system. **2 a** (often *attrib.*) Geog. & Archit. ratio of size in a map, model, picture, etc. **b** relative dimensions or degree (*generosity on a grand scale*). **3** Mus. arrangement of all the notes in any system of music in ascending or descending order. **4 a** set of marks on a line used in measuring. **b** piece of metal, apparatus, etc., on which these are marked. • *v.tr.* climb (a wall, height, etc.) □ **scale down** reduce in size. **scale up** increase in size. □□ **scal'er** *n.*

---

scale late Middle English (in the senses 'ladder' and 'climb with a scaling ladder'): from Latin *scala* 'ladder' (the verb via Old

French *escaler* or medieval Latin *scalare*), from the base of Latin *scandere* 'to climb.'

sca·lene /skáyleen/ *adj.* (esp. of a triangle) having unequal sides.

scal·lion /skályən/ *n.* any long-necked onion with a small bulb.

scal·lop /skáləp, skól–/ (also **scol'lop** /skól–/) • *n.* **1** bivalve mollusk much prized as food. **2** (in full **scal'lop shell**) single shell of a scallop, with a toothed edge. **3** (in *pl.*) ornamental edging cut in material in imitation of a scallop edge. • *v.tr.* (**scal·loped, scal·lop·ing**) ornament (an edge or material) with scallops or scalloping. □□ **scal'lop·er** *n.* **scal'lop·ing** *n.* (in sense 3 of *n.*).

SCALLOP, 2

scalp /skalp/ • *n.* **1** skin covering the top of the head, with the hair, etc., attached. **2 a** *hist.* scalp of an enemy cut or torn away as a trophy by a Native American. **b** trophy or symbol of triumph, conquest, etc. • *v.tr.* **1** *hist.* take the scalp of (an enemy). **2** *colloq.* resell (shares, tickets, etc.) at a high or quick profit. □□ **scalp'er** *n.*

scal·pel /skálpəl/ *n.* surgeon's sharp knife.

scam /skam/ *n. sl.* trick or swindle; fraud.

scam·per /skámpər/ • *v.intr.* run quickly. • *n.* act or instance of scampering.

scam·pi /skámpee/ *n.pl.* large shrimp, esp. sautéed in garlic butter.

scan /skan/ • *v.* (**scanned, scan·ning**) **1** *tr.* look at intently or quickly. **2** *intr.* (of a verse, etc.) be metrically correct (*this line doesn't scan*). **3** *tr.* resolve (a picture) into its elements of light and shade in a prearranged pattern. • *n.* **1** scanning. **2** image obtained by scanning or with a scanner. □□ **scan'na·ble** *adj.*

scan·dal /skánd'l/ *n.* **1** thing or a person causing general public outrage or indignation. **2** outrage, etc., so caused. **3** malicious gossip □□ **scan'dal·ous** *adj.* **scan'dal·ous·ly** *adv.*

---

scandal Middle English (in the sense 'one who discredits religion (by reprehensible behavior)'): from Old French *scandale*, from ecclesiastical Latin *scandalum* 'cause of offense,' from Greek *skandalon* 'snare, stumbling block.'

---

scan·dal·ize /skándəlīz/ *v.tr.* offend morally; shock.

scan·dal·mon·ger /skánd'lmɒnggər, –mɒnggər/ *n.* person who spreads malicious scandal.

Scan·di·na·vi·an /skándináyveeən/ • *n.* **1 a** native or inhabitant of Scandinavia (Denmark, Norway, Sweden, and sometimes Finland and Iceland). **b** person of Scandinavian descent. **2** family of languages of Scandinavia. • *adj.* of or relating to Scandinavia or its people or languages.

scan·di·um /skándeeəm/ *n. Chem.* metallic element occurring naturally in lanthanide ores. ¶ Symb.: **Sc.**

scan·ner /skánər/ *n.* **1** device for obtaining an electronic image of something. **2** device for monitoring radio frequencies, esp. police or emergency frequencies.

scan·sion /skánshən/ *n.* metrical scanning of verse.

scant /skant/ *adj.* barely sufficient; deficient. □□ **scant'ly** *adv.* **scant'ness** *n.*

scant·y /skántee/ *adj.* (**scant·i·er, scant·i·est**) **1** of small extent or amount. **2** barely sufficient. □□ **scant'i·ly** *adv.* **scant'i·ness** *n.*

scape·goat /skáypgōt/ • *n.* person blamed for others. • *v.tr.* make a scapegoat of. □□ **scape'goat·er** *n.*

scap·u·la /skápyələ/ *n.* (*pl.* **scap·u·lae** /–lee/ or **scap·u·las**) shoulder blade.

scar /skaar/ • *n.* usu. permanent mark on the skin from a healed wound, burn, or sore. •. *v.* (**scarred, scar·ring**) **1** *tr.* (esp. as **scarred** *adj.*) mark with a scar. **2** *intr.* form a scar. □□ **scar'less** *adj.*

scar·ab /skárəb/ *n.* **1** sacred dung beetle of ancient Egypt. **2** ancient Egyptian gem cut in the form of a beetle.

scarce /skairs/ *adj.* **1** (usu. *predic.*) insufficient for the demand; scanty. **2** rare. □ **make oneself scarce** *colloq.* keep out of the way. □□ **scarce'ness** *n.*

scarce·ly /skáirslee/ *adv.* **1** hardly; barely; only just. **2** surely not.

scar·ci·ty /skáirsitee/ *n.* (*pl.* **–ties**) lack or inadequacy, esp. of food.

scare /skair/ • *v.* **1** *tr.* frighten, esp. suddenly. **2** *tr.* (as **scared** *adj.*) frightened; terrified. **3** *tr.* (usu. foll. by *away*, *off*, etc.) drive away by frightening. • *n.* **1** sudden attack of fright. **2** alarm. □□ **scar'er** *n.*

scare·crow /skáirkrō/ *n.* human figure dressed in old clothes and set up in a field to scare birds away.

scarf[1] /skaarf/ *n.* (*pl.* **scarfs** or **scarves** /skaarvz/) square, triangular, or long, narrow strip of material worn around the neck, over the shoulders, or tied around the head for warmth or ornament. □□ **scarfed** *adj.*

scarf[2] /skaarf/ • *v.tr.* join the beveled ends of lumber, etc., by bolting, gluing, etc. • *n.* joint made by scarfing.

scar·i·fy /skárifī, skáir–/ *v.tr.* (**–fies, –fied**) make superficial incisions in. □□ **scar·i·fi·ca'tion** *n.*

scar·let /skáarlit/ • *n.* brilliant red color tinged with orange. • *adj.* of a scarlet color. □ **scarlet fever** infectious bacterial fever with a scarlet rash.

scarp /skaarp/ *n.* steep slope.

scar·y /skáiree/ *adj.* (**scar·i·er, scar·i·est**) *colloq.* frightening. □□ **scar'i·ly** *adv.*

scat[1] /skat/ *colloq.* • *v.intr.* (**scat·ted, scat·ting**) depart quickly. • *int.* go!

scat[2] /skat/ • *n.* improvised jazz singing using sounds imitating instruments, instead of words. • *v.intr.* (**scat·ted, scat·ting**) sing scat.

scathe /skayth/ v. (as **scathing** adj.) witheringly scornful.

scat·ter /skátər/ • v. **1** tr. throw here and there; strew. **2** tr. & intr. disperse or cause (hopes, clouds, etc.) to disperse. **3** tr. (as **scat·tered** adj.) not clustered together. • n. (also **scat·ter·ing**) **1** act or instance of scattering. **2** small amount scattered. □□ **scat'ter·er** n.

scat·ter·brain /skátərbrayn/ n. person lacking concentration. □□ **scat'ter·brained** adj.

scav·enge /skávinj/ v. **1** tr. & intr. search for and collect (discarded items). **2** tr. feed on carrion, refuse, etc.

scav·en·ger /skávinjər/ n. **1** person who seeks and collects discarded items. **2** animal feeding on carrion, refuse, etc.

sce·nar·i·o /sináreeō, –naáreeō/ n. (pl. **–os**) **1** outline of the plot of a play, film, opera, etc. **2** postulated sequence of future events. □□ **sce·nar'ist** n. (in sense 1).
¶ The proper meaning of this word is 'an outline of a plot' or 'a postulated sequence of events.' It should not be used loosely to mean 'situation,' e.g., a nightmare scenario.

scene /seen/ n. **1** place where events occur. **2 a** incident in real life, fiction, etc. **b** description or representation of an incident, etc. **3** public display of emotion, temper, etc. **4** portion of a play in a fixed setting. **5** piece of scenery used in a play. **6** landscape or a view. **7** colloq. area of action or interest; milieu. □ **behind the scenes 1** Theatr. offstage. **2** unknown to the public; secret(ly).

sce·ner·y /seénəree/ n. **1** natural features of a landscape. **2** Theatr. painted representations of landscape, rooms, etc., used as the background in a play, etc.

sce·nic /seénik/ adj. **1 a** picturesque. **b** of natural scenery. **2** (of a picture, etc.) representing an incident. **3** Theatr. of or on the stage. □□ **sce'ni·cal·ly** adv.

scent /sent/ • n. **1** distinctive, esp. pleasant, smell. **2 a** perceptible scent trail left by an animal. **b** sense of smell. **3** = PERFUME 2. • v. **1** tr. **a** discern by scent. **b** sense the presence of. **2** tr. make fragrant. **3** tr. (as **scented** adj.) having esp. a pleasant smell (scented soap).

scep·ter /séptər/ n. staff as a symbol of sovereignty. □□ **scep'tered** adj.

sch. abbr. **1** school. **2** scholar.

sched·ule /skéjōol, –ŏŏəl/ • n. **1 a** list or plan of intended events, times, etc. **b** plan of work. **2** list of rates or prices. **3** timetable. • v.tr. include in a schedule. □□ **sched'ul·er** n.

---

schedule late Middle English (in the sense 'scroll, explanatory note, appendix'): from Old French cedule, from late Latin schedula 'slip of paper,' diminutive of scheda, from Greek skhedē 'papyrus leaf.' The verb dates from the mid-19th century.

---

sche·mat·ic /skimátik, skee–/ • adj. **1** of or concerning a scheme or diagram. **2** representing objects by symbols, etc. • n. diagram, esp. of an electronic circuit. □□ **sche·mat'i·cal·ly** adv.

scheme /skeem/ • n. **1 a** systematic plan or arrangement. **b** proposed or operational systematic arrangement (color scheme). **2** cunning plot.

• v. plan, esp. secretly or deceitfully. □□ **schem'er** n. **schem'ing** adj. & n.

---

scheme mid-16th century (denoting a figure of speech): from Latin schema, from Greek. An early sense included 'horoscope, representation of the position of celestial objects,' giving rise to 'diagram, design,' whence the current senses. The unfavorable notion 'plot' arose in the early 18th century.

---

scher·zo /skáirtsō/ n. (pl. **–zos**) Mus. vigorous, light, or playful composition, usu. as a movement in a symphony, sonata, etc.

schism /sízəm, skíz–/ n. division of a group (esp. religious) into opposing sects or parties usu. over doctrine. □□ **schis·mat·ic** /sizmátik, skiz–/ adj. & n.

schist /shist/ n. layered crystalline rock.

schiz·o·phre·ni·a /skítsəfreéneeə, –fréneeə/ n. mental disease marked by a breakdown in the relation between thoughts, feelings, and actions, frequently accompanied by delusions and retreat from society. □□ **schiz·o·phren·ic** /–frénik/ adj. & n.

schle·miel /shləmeél/ n. colloq. foolish or unlucky person.

schlep /shlep/ (also **schlepp**) colloq. • v. (**schlepped**, **schlep·ping**) **1** tr. carry; drag. **2** intr. go or work tediously or effortfully. • n. (also **schlep·per**) person or thing that is tedious, awkward, or slow.

schlock /shlok/ n. colloq. inferior goods; trash.

schmaltz /shmaalts/ n. colloq. sentimentality, esp. in music, etc. □□ **schmaltz'y** adj. (**schmaltz·i·er**, **schmaltz·i·est**).

schmuck /shmuk/ n. sl. foolish or contemptible person.

schnapps /shnaaps/ n. any of various alcoholic drinks, often flavored.

schnau·zer /shnówzər/ n. **1** dog of a German breed with a close wiry coat and heavy whiskers around the muzzle. **2** this breed.

schnit·zel /shnítsəl/ n. veal cutlet.

schol·ar /skólər/ n. **1** learned person; academic. **2** pupil. □□ **schol'ar·ly** adj. **schol'ar·li·ness** n.

schol·ar·ship /skólərship/ n. **1 a** academic achievement; learning of a high level. **b** standards of a good scholar. **2** payment from the funds of a school, university, local government, etc., to maintain a student in full-time education, awarded on the basis of scholarly achievement.

scho·las·tic /skəlástik/ adj. of or concerning schools, education, etc. □□ **scho·las'ti·cal·ly** adv. **scho·las·ti·cism** /–tisizəm/ n.

school[1] /skōol/ • n. **1** educational institution. **2 a** buildings used by such an institution. **b** pupils, teachers, etc. **c** time of teaching, or the teaching itself (no school today). **3** university division. **4 a** group of artists, etc., whose works share distinctive characteristics. **b** group of people sharing a cause, principle, method, etc. (school of thought). • v.tr. **1** educate. **2** discipline; train; control. **3** (as **schooled** adj.) (foll. by in) educated or trained (schooled in humility).

school[2] /skōol/ • n. group of fish, porpoises, whales, etc. • v.intr. form schools.

school·boy /skōolboy/ n. boy attending school.

school·child /skōolchīld/ n. child attending school.

school·girl /skōolgərl/ n. girl attending school.

school·house /skoolhows/ n. building used as a school.

school·ing /skooling/ n. education, esp. at school.

school·marm /skoolmaarm/ n. **1** old-fash. (also **school·ma'am**/–maam/) female schoolteacher. **2** colloq. formal, rule-conscious person. □□ **school'marm·ish** adj.

school·mas·ter /skoolmastər/ n. head or assistant male teacher. □□ **school'mas·ter·ly** adj.

school·mis·tress /skoolmistris/ n. head or assistant female teacher.

school·room /skoolroom, –room/ n. room used for lessons.

school·teach·er /skoolteechər/ n. teacher in a school. □□ **school'teach·ing** n.

schoo·ner /skoonər/ n. **1** fore-and-aft rigged ship with two or more masts, the foremast being smaller than the other masts. **2** very tall beer glass.

schuss /shoos/ • n. straight downhill run on skis. • v.intr. make a schuss.

schwa /shwaa/ n. Phonet. **1** indistinct unstressed vowel sound as in a moment ago. **2** symbol /ə/ representing this.

sci·at·ic /sīatik/ adj. of the hip or its nerves.

sci·at·i·ca /sīatikə/ n. neuralgia of the hip and thigh.

sci·ence /sīəns/ n. **1** branch of knowledge involving systematized observation and experimentation. **2 a** systematic and formulated knowledge, esp. on a specified subject. **b** pursuit or principles of this. **3** skillful technique. □ **science fiction** fiction based on imagined future scientific discoveries, frequently dealing with space travel, life on other planets, etc.

sci·en·tif·ic /sīəntifik/ adj. **1 a** (of an investigation, etc.) according to the systematic methods of science. **b** systematic; accurate. **2** used in, engaged in, or relating to science. □□ **sci·en·tif'·i·cal·ly** adv.

sci·en·tist /sīəntist/ n. expert in a science.

sci-fi /sīfī/ n. (often attrib.) colloq. science fiction.

scim·i·tar /símitər, –taar/ n. Oriental curved sword.

scin·til·la /sintílə/ n. **1** trace. **2** spark.

scin·til·late /síntilayt/ v.intr. **1** (esp. as **scintillating** adj.) talk cleverly or wittily; be brilliant. **2** sparkle; twinkle. □□ **scin·til·la·tion** /–láyshən/ n.

sci·on /sīən/ n. **1** descendant. **2** (also **ci·on**) shoot of a plant, etc., esp. for grafting or planting. **2** descendant.

scis·sors /sízərz/ n.pl. (also **pair of scis'sors** sing.) manual cutting instrument having two pivoted blades with finger and thumb holes in the handles.

scle·ro·sis /sklərósis/ n. **1** abnormal hardening of body tissue (see also ARTERIOSCLEROSIS, ATHEROSCLEROSIS). **2** (in full **mul·ti·ple scle·ro·sis**) chronic and progressive disease of the nervous system. □□ **scle·rot·ic** /sklərótik/ adj.& n.

scoff /skof/ • v.intr. (usu. foll. by at) speak derisively; mock; be scornful. • n. mocking words; taunt. □□ **scoff'er** n. **scoff'ing·ly** adv.

scold /skōld/ • v. **1** tr. rebuke. **2** intr. find fault noisily. • n. archaic nagging or grumbling woman. □□ **scold'er** n. **scold'ing** n.

sconce /skons/ n. wall bracket for candles or electric lights.

---

sconce late Middle English (originally denoting a portable lantern with a screen to protect the flame): shortening of Old French esconse 'lantern,' or from medieval Latin sconsa, from Latin absconsa (laterna) 'dark (lantern),' from abscondere 'to hide.'

---

scone /skon, skōn/ n. biscuitlike cake, esp. served with tea.

scoop /skoop/ • n. **1** any of various objects resembling a spoon, esp.: **a** short-handled deep shovel used for transferring grain, sugar, etc. **b** long-handled ladle used for transferring liquids. **c** excavating part of a digging machine, etc. **2** quantity taken up by a scoop. **3** scooping movement. **4** exclusive news item. • v.tr. **1** (usu. foll. by out) hollow out with or as if with a scoop. **2** (usu. foll. by up) lift with or as if with a scoop. **3** precede (a rival newspaper, etc.) with news. □□ **scoop'er** n. **scoop'ful** n. (pl. **–fuls**).

scoot /skoot/ colloq. v.intr. dart away quickly.

scoot·er /skootər/ n. **1** child's toy consisting of a footboard on two wheels and a long steering handle. **2** (in full **motor scooter**) light two-wheeled motorized bicycle with a shieldlike protective front.

scope /skōp/ n. **1** range; opportunity. **2** reach of mental activity, observation, or outlook.

-scopy /skəpee/ comb. form indicating viewing or observation, usu. with an instrument ending in -scope (microscopy).

scor·bu·tic /skawrbyóotik/ • adj. relating to, resembling, or affected with scurvy. • n. person affected with scurvy. □□ **scor·bu'ti·cal·ly** adv.

scorch /skawrch/ • v. **1** tr. **a** burn or discolor the surface of with dry heat. **b** affect with the sensation of burning. **2** intr. become discolored, etc., with heat. **3** tr. (as **scorch·ing** adj.) colloq. **a** (of the weather) very hot. **b** (of criticism, etc.) stringent; harsh. • n. mark made by scorching. □ **scorched earth policy** destroying anything that might be of use to an invading enemy force. □□ **scorch'er** n. **scorch'ing·ly** adv.

score /skawr/ • n. **1 a** number of points made by a player, team, etc., in some games. **b** total number of points, etc., at the end of a game. **2** (pl. same as **scores**) twenty or a set of twenty. **3** (in pl.) a great many. **4 a** reason or motive (rejected on the score of absurdity). **b** topic; subject (no worries on that score). **5** Mus. **a** copy of a composition showing all the vocal and instrumental parts arranged one below the other. **b** music for a film or play. **6** notch, line, etc., cut or scratched into a surface. • v. **1** tr. win or gain (a goal, run, success, etc.). **2** intr. **a** make a score in a game. **b** keep the tally of points, runs, etc., in a game. **3** tr. mark with notches, incisions, lines, etc. **4** tr. Mus. orchestrate or arrange (a piece of music).

score·board /skáwrbawrd/ n. board for publicly displaying the score in a game or match.

scorn /skawrn/ • n. **1** disdain; contempt; derision. **2** object of contempt, etc. (the scorn of all onlookers). • v.tr. **1** hold in contempt. **2** (often foll. by to + infin.) abstain or refuse to do as unworthy. □□ **scorn'er** n. **scorn'ful** adj. **scorn'ful·ly** adv. **scorn'ful·ness** n.

Scor·pi·o /skáwrpeeō/ *n.* (*pl.* **–os**) **1** constellation and eighth sign of the zodiac (the Scorpion). **2** person born under this sign. □□ **Scor′pi·an** *adj.* & *n.*

scor·pi·on /skáwrpeeən/ *n.* **1** arachnid with lobsterlike pincers and a jointed stinging tail. **2** (**the Scor·pi·on**) zodiacal sign or constellation Scorpio.

SCORPION, 1

Scot /skot/ *n.* **1 a** native of Scotland. **b** person of Scottish descent. **2** *hist.* member of a Gaelic people that migrated from Ireland to Scotland around the 6th century.

Scotch /skoch/ • *adj.* var. of SCOTTISH or SCOTS. • *n.* **1** var. of SCOTTISH or SCOTS. **2** (in full **Scotch whiskey**) whiskey distilled in Scotland, esp. from malted barley.
¶ In Scotland the terms **Scots** and **Scottish** are preferred to **Scotch**, and they mean the same (e.g., *a Scots/Scottish accent, miner, farmer,* etc.) **Scotch** is used in various compound nouns such as *Scotch broth, egg, fir, mist, terrier,* and *whisky.* Similarly, **Scotsman** and **Scotswoman** are preferred to **Scotchman** and **Scotchwoman.**

scotch /skoch/ *v.tr.* **1** put an end to; frustrate. **2** *archaic* wound without killing.

Scots /skots/ • *adj.* **1** = SCOTTISH *adj.* **2** in the dialect, accent, etc., of (esp. Lowlands) Scotland. • *n.* **1** = SCOTTISH *n.* **2** form of English spoken in (esp. Lowlands) Scotland.

Scots·man /skótsmən/ *n.* (*pl.* **–men**; *fem.* **Scots·wom·an**, *pl.* **–wom·en**) **1** native of Scotland. **2** person of Scottish descent.

Scot·tie /skótee/ *n. colloq.* **1** (also **Scot′tie dog**) = *Scottish terrier.* **2** Scot.

Scot·tish /skótish/ • *adj.* of or relating to Scotland or its inhabitants. • *n.* (prec. by *the*; treated as *pl.*) the people of Scotland (see also SCOTS). □ **Scottish terrier 1** small terrier of a rough-haired short-legged breed. **2** this breed. □□ **Scot′tish·ness** *n.*

scoun·drel /skówndrəl/ *n.* unscrupulous villain; rogue.

scour¹ /skowr/ • *v.tr.* **1 a** cleanse or brighten by rubbing, esp. with soap, chemicals, sand, etc. **b** (usu. foll. by *away, off,* etc.) clear (rust, stains, reputation, etc.) by rubbing, hard work, etc. **2** clear out (a pipe, channel, etc.) by flushing through. • *n.* scouring; state of being scoured, esp. by a swift water current. □□ **scour′er** *n.*

scour² /skowr/ *v.tr.* **1** *tr.* hasten over (an area, etc.) searching thoroughly (*scoured the newspaper*). **2** *intr.* range hastily, esp. in search or pursuit.

scourge /skərj/ • *n.* **1** whip used for punishment, esp. of people. **2** anything regarded as a cause of suffering (*scourge of famine*). • *v.tr.* **1** whip. **2** punish harshly; oppress. □□ **scourg′er** *n.*

scout /skowt/ • *n.* **1** person, esp. a soldier, sent ahead to get information about the enemy's position, strength, etc. **2** = *talent scout.* **3** (**Scout**) Boy Scout or Girl Scout. • *v.* **1** *intr.* act as a scout. **2** *intr.* (foll. by *about, around*) make a search. **3** *tr.* (often foll. by *out*) *colloq.* explore to get information about (territory, etc.). □□ **scout′er** *n.* **scout′ing** *n.*

scout·mas·ter /skówtmastər/ *n.* person in charge of a group of Scouts.

scow /skow/ *n.* flat-bottomed boat for freight, etc.

scowl /skowl/ • *n.* frowning or sullen expression. • *v.intr.* make a scowl or frown. □□ **scowl′er** *n.*

scrab·ble /skrábəl/ • *v.intr.* scratch or grope to find or collect or hold on to something. • *n.* act of scrabbling.

scrag·gly /skráglee/ *adj.* sparse and irregular.

scram /skram/ *v.intr.* (**scrammed, scram·ming**) (esp. in *imper.*) *colloq.* go away.

scram·ble /skrámbəl/ • *v.* **1** *intr.* make one's way over rough ground, rocks, etc., by clambering, crawling, etc. **2** *intr.* (foll. by *for, at*) struggle with competitors (for a thing or share). **3** *intr.* move with difficulty or awkwardly. **4** *tr.* **a** mix together indiscriminately. **b** jumble or muddle. **5** *tr.* cook (beaten eggs). **6** *tr.* make (a broadcast transmission or telephone conversation) unintelligible. **7** *intr.* move hastily. **8** *intr.* (of fighter aircraft or their pilots) take off quickly for action. • *n.* **1** act of scrambling. **2** difficult climb or walk. **3** (foll. by *for*) eager struggle or competition. **4** emergency takeoff by fighter aircraft.

scram·bler /skrámblər/ *n.* device for scrambling telecommunications signals.

scrap¹ /skrap/ • *n.* **1** small detached piece; fragment. **2** rubbish or waste material. **3** (in *pl.*) **a** odds and ends. **b** bits of uneaten food. • *v.tr.* (**scrapped, scrap·ping**) discard as useless.

scrap² /skrap/ *colloq.* • *n.* fight or rough quarrel. • *v.tr.* (**scrapped, scrap·ping**) (often foll. by *with*) have a scrap. □□ **scrap′per** *n.*

scrap·book /skrápbŏŏk/ *n.* book of blank pages for sticking cuttings, drawings, etc., in.

scrape /skrayp/ • *v.* **1** *tr.* **a** move a hard or sharp edge across (a surface), esp. to make smooth. **b** apply (a hard or sharp edge) in this way. **2** *tr.* (foll. by *away, off,* etc.) remove (a stain, projection, etc.) by scraping. **3** *tr.* **a** rub (a surface) harshly against another. **b** scratch or damage by scraping. **4** *tr.* move with a sound of scraping. **b** *intr.* emit or produce such a sound. **c** *tr.* produce such a sound from. **5** *intr.* move or pass along while almost touching close or surrounding obstacles, etc. (*the car scraped through the narrow lane*). **6** *tr.* just manage to achieve (a living, an examination pass, etc.). **7** *intr.* **a** barely manage. **b** pass an examination, etc., with difficulty. **8** *tr.* amass with difficulty. • *n.* **1** act or sound of scraping. **2** abrasion. **3** *colloq.* awkward predicament. □□ **scrap′er** *n.*

scrap·py /skrápee/ *adj.* (**scrap·pi·er, scrap·pi·est**) **1** consisting of scraps. **2** carelessly arranged or put together. **3 a** argumentative. **b** (of a fighter) wiry and aggressive. □□ **scrap′pi·ly** *adv.* **scrap′pi·ness** *n.*

scratch /skrach/ • v.tr. **1** score or mark the surface of with a sharp object. **2** scrape, esp. with the nails to relieve itching. **3** cancel or strike (out) with a pencil, etc. **4** withdraw (a competitor, candidate, etc.). • n. **1** mark or wound made by scratching. **2** sound of scratching. **3** colloq. superficial wound. • adj. **1** collected by chance. **2** heterogeneous (a scratch crew). □ **from scratch 1** from the beginning. **2** without help or advantage. **up to scratch** up to the required standard. □□ **scratch′er** n. **scratch′i•ly** adv. **scratch′i•ness** n. **scratch′y** adj.

scrawl /skrawl/ • v. write in a hurried untidy way. • n. piece of hurried writing. □□ **scrawl′y** adj.

scraw•ny /skráwnee/ adj. (**scraw•ni•er, scraw•ni•est**) lean; skinny. □□ **scrawn′i•ness** n.

scream /skreem/ • n. **1** loud, high-pitched, piercing cry of fear, pain, etc. **2** act of emitting a scream. **3** colloq. irresistibly funny occurrence or person. • v. **1** intr. emit a scream. **2** tr. speak or sing (words, etc.) in a screaming tone. **3** intr. laugh uncontrollably.

screech /skreech/ • n. harsh, high-pitched scream. • v. utter with or make a high-pitched noise. □□ **screech′er** n. **screech′y** adj. (**screech•i•er, screech•i•est**).

screed /skreed/ n. long usu. tiresome piece of writing or speech.

screen /skreen/ • n. **1** fixed or movable upright partition for separating, concealing, or sheltering. **2** thing used to conceal or shelter. **3 a** blank surface on which a photographic image is projected. **b** (prec. by the) movies or the motion-picture industry. **4** frame with fine wire netting to keep out flies, mosquitoes, etc. **5** large sieve or riddle. • v.tr. **1** shelter; hide. **2 a** show (a film, etc.). **b** broadcast (a television program). **3** sift (grain, coal, etc.) through a screen. □ **screen test** audition for a part in a motion picture. □□ **screen′er** n.

screen•play /skréenplay/ n. script of a motion picture or television show.

screen•writ•er /skréenrītər/ n. person who writes screenplays.

screw /skrōō/ • n. **1** thin metal cylinder or cone with a spiral ridge or thread running around the outside (**male screw**) or the inside (**female screw**). **2** (in full **screw propeller**) propeller with twisted blades acting like a screw on the water or air. • v. **1** tr. fasten or tighten with a screw or screws. **2** tr. turn (a screw). **3** intr. twist or turn around like a screw. **4** tr. (foll. by out of) extort (consent, money, etc.) from (a person). □ **have a screw loose** colloq. be slightly crazy. **put the screws on** colloq. pressure; intimidate. **screw up 1** contract or contort (one's face, etc.). **2** contract and crush into a tight mass (piece of paper, etc.). **3** summon up (one's courage, etc.). **4** sl. bungle.

screw•ball /skrōōbawl/ sl. • n. **1** Baseball pitch thrown with spin opposite that of a curveball. **2** crazy or eccentric person. • adj. crazy.

screw•driv•er /skrōōdrīvər/ n. tool with a shaped tip to fit into the head of a screw to turn it.

screw•y /skrōō-ee/ adj. (**screw•i•er, screw•i•est**) sl. **1** crazy or eccentric. **2** absurd. □□ **screw′i•ness** n.

scrib•ble /skríbəl/ • v. write carelessly or hurriedly. • n. scrawl. □□ **scrib′bler** n. **scrib′bly** adj.

scribe /skrīb/ n. **1** ancient or medieval copyist of manuscripts. **2** writer, esp. a journalist.

scrim /skrim/ n. open-weave fabric for lining or upholstery, etc.

scrim•mage /skrímij/ • n. **1** rough or confused struggle; brawl. **2** Football a single play from the snap of the ball till the ball is dead. **3** Sports practice game. • v. intr. engage in a scrimmage. □□ **scrim′mag•er** n.

scrimp /skrimp/ v. **1** intr. be sparing or parsimonious. **2** tr. use sparingly. □□ **scrimp′y** adj.

scrip /skrip/ n. **1** provisional certificate of money subscribed to a bank or company, etc., entitling the holder to a formal certificate and dividends. **2** (collect.) such certificates.

script /skript/ • n. **1** handwriting; written characters. **2** type imitating handwriting. **3** alphabet or system of writing (Russian script). **4** text of a play, film, or broadcast. • v.tr. write a script for (a motion picture, etc.).

scrip•ture /skrípchər/ n. **1** sacred writings. **2** (**Scripture** or **the Scriptures**) the Bible.

script•writ•er /skrípt-rītər/ n. person who writes scripts for a motion picture, broadcast, etc. □□ **script′writ•ing** n.

scrod /skrod/ n. young cod or haddock, esp. as food.

scrof•u•la /skrófyələ/ n. archaic disease with glandular swellings, prob. a form of tuberculosis. Also called **king's evil**. □□ **scrof′u•lous** adj.

scroll /skrōl/ • n. **1** roll of parchment or paper esp. with writing on it. **2** ornamental design or carving imitating a roll of parchment. • v.tr. move (a display on a computer screen) vertically.

scro•tum /skrōtəm/ n. (pl. **scro•ta** /-tə/ or **scro•tums**) pouch of skin containing the testicles. □□ **scro′tal** adj.

scrounge /skrownj/ colloq. • v. **1** tr. obtain (things) illicitly or by cadging. **2** intr. search about to find something at no cost. • n. act of scrounging. □□ **scroung′er** n.

scrub¹ /skrub/ • v. (**scrubbed, scrub•bing**) **1** tr. rub hard so as to clean. **2** intr. use a brush in this way. **3** tr. colloq. scrap or cancel. **4** tr. use a chemical process to remove impurities from (gas, etc.). • n. scrubbing or being scrubbed. □□ **scrub′ber** n.

scrub² /skrub/ n. **1 a** brushwood or stunted forest growth. **b** area of land covered with this. **2** Sports colloq. team or player not of the first class. □□ **scrub′by** adj.

scruff /skruf/ n. back of the neck.

scruff•y /skrúfee/ adj. (**scruff•i•er, scruff•i•est**) colloq. shabby; slovenly; untidy. □□ **scruff′i•ly** adv. **scruff′i•ness** n.

scrump•tious /skrúmpshəs/ adj. colloq. **1** delicious. **2** giving pleasure; delightful. □□ **scrump′tious•ly** adv. **scrump′tious•ness** n.

scrunch /skrunch/ • v. **1** make or become crushed or crumpled. **2** make or cause to make a crunching sound. • n. act or instance of scrunching.

scru•ple /skrōōpəl/ • n. (in sing. or pl.) moral concern; doubt caused by this. • v.intr. (foll. by to) be reluctant because of scruples.

scru•pu•lous /skrōōpyələs/ adj. **1** conscientious

or thorough. **2** careful to avoid doing wrong. □□ **scru·pu·los·i·ty** /–lósitee/ *n.* **scru′pu·lous·ly** *adv.* **scru′pu·lous·ness** *n.*

scru·ti·nize /skro͞ot′nīz/ *v.tr.* look closely at; examine with close scrutiny. □□ **scru′ti·niz·er** *n.*

scru·ti·ny /skro͞ot′nee/ *n.* (*pl.* **–nies**) **1** critical gaze. **2** close examination.

scu·ba /sko͞obə/ *n.* (*pl.* **scu·bas**) gear that provides an air supply from a portable tank for swimming underwater (acronym for *self-contained underwater breathing apparatus*).

scuff /skuf/ • *v.* **1** *tr.* graze or brush against. **2** *tr.* mark or wear down (shoes) in this way. **3** *intr.* walk with dragging feet; shuffle. • *n.* mark of scuffing.

scuf·fle /skúfəl/ • *n.* confused struggle or disorderly fight at close quarters. • *v.intr.* engage in a scuffle.

scull /skul/ • *n.* **1** either of a pair of small oars used by a single rower. **2** oar placed over the stern of a boat to propel it, usu. by a twisting motion. **3** racing rowboat. • *v.tr.* propel (a boat) with sculls.

scul·ler·y /skúləree/ *n.* (*pl.* **–ies**) small kitchen or room at the back of a house for washing dishes, etc.

sculpt /skulpt/ *v.* (also **sculp**) sculpture.

sculp·tor /skúlptər/ *n.* (*fem.* **sculp·tress** /–tris/) artist who makes sculptures.

sculp·ture /skúlpchər/ • *n.* **1** art of making three-dimensional or relief forms. **2** work of sculpture. • *v.* **1** *tr.* represent in sculpture. **2** *intr.* practice sculpture. □□ **sculp′tur·al** *adj.* **sculp′tur·al·ly** *adv.* **sculp·tur·esque′** *adj.*

scum /skum/ • *n.* **1** layer of dirt, froth, etc., at the top of liquid. **2** most worthless part of something. **3** *colloq.* worthless person or group. • *v.* (**scummed, scum·ming**) **1** *tr.* remove scum from; skim. **2** *tr.* be or form a scum on. **3** *intr.* (of a liquid) develop scum. □□ **scum′my** *adj.* (**scum·mi·er, scum·mi·est**) *adj.*

scum·bag /skúmbag/ *n. sl.* worthless despicable person.

scup·per /skúpər/ *n.* hole at the edge of a boat's deck to allow water to run off.

scur·ri·lous /skɔ́riləs, skúr–/ *adj.* grossly or indecently abusive. □□ **scur′ril·ous·ly** *adv.* **scur′ril·ous·ness** *n.*

scur·ry /skɔ́ree, skúree/ • *v.intr.* (**–ries, –ried**) run or move hurriedly; scamper. • *n.* (*pl.* **–ries**) **1** act or sound of scurrying. **2** bustle; haste.

scur·vy /skúrvee/ *n.* disease caused by a deficiency of vitamin C.

scut·tle[1] /skút′l/ *n.* receptacle for carrying and holding a small supply of coal.

scut·tle[2] /skút′l/ • *v.intr.* **1** scurry. **2** run away; flee from danger or difficulty. • *n.* hurried gait.

scut·tle[3] /skút′l/ • *n.* hole with a lid in a ship's deck or side. • *v.tr.* let water into (a ship) to sink it.

scut·tle·butt /skút′lbut/ *n.* **1** water cask on the deck of a ship, for drinking from. **2** *colloq.* rumor; gossip.

scuz·zy /skúzee/ *adj. sl.* abhorrent or disgusting.

scythe /sīth/ • *n.* mowing and reaping implement with a long curved blade swung over the

ground by a long pole with two short handles projecting from it. • *v.tr.* cut with a scythe.

SCYTHE

SD *abbr.* South Dakota (in official postal use).

S.Dak. *abbr.* South Dakota.

SE *abbr.* **1** southeast. **2** southeastern.

Se *symb. Chem.* selenium.

sea /see/ *n.* **1** expanse of salt water that covers most of the earth's surface. **2** any part of this. **3** particular (usu. named) tract of salt water partly or wholly enclosed by land (*North Sea*). **4** large inland lake (*Sea of Galilee*). **5** waves of the sea; their motion or state (*choppy sea*). **6** (foll. by *of*) vast quantity or expanse. □ **at sea 1** in a ship on the sea. **2** (also **all at sea**) perplexed; confused. **sea horse** small upright marine fish with a head like that of a horse. **sea legs** ability to keep one's balance and avoid seasickness when at sea. **sea lion** large-eared seal.

sea·bed /seebed/ *n.* ground under the sea; ocean floor.

sea·board /seebawrd/ *n.* **1** seashore or coastal region. **2** the line of a coast.

sea·borg·i·um /seebáwrgeeəm/ *n. Chem.* artificially produced element, atomic number 106. Symb.: **Sg**.

sea·coast /seekōst/ *n.* land adjacent to the sea.

sea·far·er /seefairər/ *n.* **1** sailor. **2** traveler by sea. □□ **sea′far·ing** *adj. & n.*

sea·food /seefo͞od/ *n.* edible sea fish or shellfish.

sea·go·ing /seegōing/ *adj.* (of ships) fit for crossing the sea.

sea·gull /seegul/ *n.* = GULL[1].

seal[1] /seel/ • *n.* **1** piece of wax, lead, paper, etc., with a stamped design, attached to a document as a guarantee of authenticity or security. **2** engraved piece of metal, gemstone, etc., for stamping a design on a seal. **3** substance or device to close a gap. **4** act or gesture regarded as a guarantee. **5** decorative adhesive stamp. • *v.tr.* **1** close securely. **2** stamp or fasten with a seal. **3** fix a seal to. **4** certify as correct with a seal or stamp. **5** confine or fasten securely. □□ **seal′a·ble** *adj.*

seal[2] /seel/ • *n.* fish-eating amphibious sea mammal with flippers and webbed feet. • *v.intr.* hunt for seals. □□ **seal′er** *n.*

seal·ant /seelənt/ *n.* material for sealing.

seal·skin /seelskin/ *n.* **1** skin or prepared fur of a seal. **2** garment made from this.

seam /seem/ • *n.* **1** line where two edges join,

esp. of cloth or boards. **2** fissure between parallel edges. **3** wrinkle. **4** stratum of coal, etc. • *v.tr.* join with a seam. □□ **seam′er** *n.* **seam′less** *adj.*

sea·man /se͞emən/ *n.* (*pl.* **-men**) sailor, esp. one below the rank of officer. □□ **sea′man·like** *adj.* **sea′man·ly** *adj.*

sea·man·ship /se͞emənship/ *n.* skill in managing a ship or boat.

seam·stress /se͞emstris/ *n.* woman who sews professionally.

seam·y /se͞emee/ *adj.* (**seam·i·er, seam·i·est**) unpleasant; disreputable. □□ **seam′i·ness** *n.*

se·ance /sáyoNs/ *n.* (also **séance**) meeting at which spiritualists attempt to make contact with the dead.

sea·plane /se͞eplayn/ *n.* aircraft designed to take off from and land and float on water.

sea·port /se͞epawrt/ *n.* town with a harbor for seagoing ships.

sear /seer/ *v.tr.* **1 a** scorch; cauterize; brand. **b** (as **searing** *adj.*) burning (*searing pain*). **2** brown (meat) quickly at a high temperature.

search /sərch/ • *v.* **1** *tr.* look through or go over thoroughly to find something. **2** *tr.* examine or feel over (a person) to find anything concealed. **3** *tr.* a probe. **b** examine or question (one's mind, conscience, etc.) thoroughly. **4** *intr.* (often foll. by *for*) make a search or investigation. **5** *intr.* (as **searching** *adj.*) (of an examination) thorough. • *n.* **1** searching. **2** investigation. □□ **search′a·ble** *adj.* **search′er** *n.* **search′ing·ly** *adv.*

search·light /sərchlīt/ *n.* **1** powerful outdoor electric light with a concentrated directional beam. **2** beam from this.

sea·scape /se͞eskayp/ *n.* picture or view of the sea.

sea·shell /se͞eshel/ *n.* shell of a saltwater mollusk.

sea·shore /se͞eshawr/ *n.* land next to the sea.

sea·sick /se͞esik/ *adj.* nauseated from the motion of the sea. □□ **sea′sick·ness** *n.*

sea·side /se͞esīd/ *n.* seacoast, esp. as a vacation resort.

sea·son /se͞ezən/ • *n.* **1** each of the four divisions of the year (spring, summer, autumn, and winter). **2** time of year characterized by climatic or other features (*dry season*). **3** time of year when something is plentiful, active, etc. **4** proper or suitable time. • *v.* **1** *tr.* flavor (food) with salt, herbs, etc. **2** *tr.* & *intr.* **a** make or become suitable or in the desired condition, esp. by exposure to the air or weather. **b** (usu. as **seasoned** *adj.*) make or become experienced. □ **in season 1** (of food) available in plenty and in good condition. **2** (of an animal) in heat. **3** timely. **season ticket** ticket entitling the holder to any number of journeys, admittances, etc., in a given period. □□ **sea′son·er** *n.*

sea·son·a·ble /se͞ezənəbəl/ *adj.* **1** suitable to or usual in the season. **2** opportune. **3** meeting the needs of the occasion. □□ **sea′son·a·ble·ness** *n.* **sea′son·a·bly** *adv.*

¶ **Seasonable** means 'usual or suitable for the season' or 'opportune,' e.g., *Although seasonable, the April weather was not warm enough for a picnic.* **Seasonal** means 'of, depending on, or varying with the season,' e.g., *Seasonal changes in labor requirements draw migrant workers to the area in spring and fall.*

sea·son·al /se͞ezənəl/ *adj.* of, depending on, or varying with the season. □□ **sea′son·al·ly** *adv.*

sea·son·ing /se͞ezəning/ *n.* spice or flavoring added to food.

seat /seet/ • *n.* **1** thing made or used for sitting on. **2** buttocks. **3** part of a garment covering the buttocks. **4** part of a chair, etc., on which the sitter's weight directly rests. **5** place for one person to sit. **6** *Polit.* right to occupy a seat, esp. as a member of Congress, etc. **7** site or location of something specified (*seat of learning*). • *v.tr.* **1** cause to sit. **2 a** provide seating for. **b** provide with seats. **3** (as **seated** *adj.*) sitting. **4** put or fit in position. □ **seat belt** belt securing a person in the seat of a car, aircraft, etc.

seat·ing /se͞eting/ *n.* **1** seats collectively. **2** sitting accommodation.

sea·ward /se͞ewərd/ • *adv.* (also **sea′wards** /-wərdz/) toward the sea. • *adj.* going or facing toward the sea. • *n.* such a direction or position.

sea·way /se͞eway/ *n.* **1** inland waterway open to seagoing ships. **2** ship's progress. **3** ship's path across the sea.

sea·weed /se͞eweed/ *n.* algae growing in the sea.

sea·wor·thy /se͞ewərthee/ *adj.* (esp. of a ship) fit to put to sea. □□ **sea′wor·thi·ness** *n.*

se·ba·ceous /sibáyshəs/ *adj.* of or relating to oily secretions or fat.

seb·or·rhe·a /sébəre͞eə/ *n.* excessive discharge from the sebaceous glands.

SEC *abbr.* Securities and Exchange Commission.

Sec. *abbr.* secretary.

sec /sek/ *n. colloq.* (in phrases) a second (of time).

sec. *abbr.* second(s).

se·cant /se͞ekant, -kənt/ *Math. n.* **1** line cutting a curve at one or more points. **2** the ratio of the hypotenuse to the shorter side adjacent to an acute angle (in a right triangle). Abbr.: **sec.**

se·cede /sise͞ed/ *v.intr.* (usu. foll. by *from*) withdraw formally from an organization. □□ **se·ced′er** *n.*

se·ces·sion /siséshən/ *n.* **1** act or instance of seceding. **2** (**Secession**) *hist.* the withdrawal of eleven southern states from the US Union in 1860–61, leading to the Civil War. □□ **se·ces′sion·ism** *n.* **se·ces′sion·ist** *n.*

se·clude /sikloo͞d/ *v.tr.* (also *refl.*) **1** keep (a person or place) away from company. **2** (esp. as **secluded** *adj.*) hide or screen from view.

se·clu·sion /sikloo͞zhən/ *n.* **1** secluded state; retirement. **2** secluded place. □□ **se·clu′sion·ist** *n.* **se·clu′sive** /-kloo͞siv/ *adj.*

sec·ond[1] /sékənd/ • *n.* **1** position in a sequence corresponding to that of the number 2 in the sequence 1–2. **2** runner-up. **3** second (and next to lowest) in a sequence of gears. **4** another person or thing in addition to one previously mentioned or considered. **5** (in *pl.*) inferior goods. **6** (in *pl.*) *colloq.* a second helping. **7** assistant to a boxer, etc. • *adj.* **1** next after first. **2** additional. **3** subordinate; inferior. • *v.tr.* support; back up. □ **second-guess** *colloq.* judge or criticize with hindsight. **second lieutenant** lowest-ranked commissioned officer of the army, air force, or marines. **second nature** acquired tendency that has become instinctive (*is second nature to him*). **second person** *Gram.* see PERSON. **second-rate** mediocre; inferior. **second string** alternative available in case of need. **second thoughts**

revised opinion or resolution. **second wind 1** recovery of normal breathing during exercise after initial breathlessness. **2** renewed energy to continue an effort.
¶ See notes at FIRST and FORMER.

sec·ond[2] /sékənd/ *n.* **1** sixtieth of a minute of time or angular distance. ¶ Symb.: ″. **2** *colloq.* very short time (*wait a second*). □ **second hand** hand in some watches and clocks, recording seconds.

sec·ond·ar·y /sékənderee/ ● *adj.* **1** coming after or next below what is primary. **2** derived from or depending on or supplementing what is primary. **3** (of education, a school, etc.) for those who have had primary education, usu. from 11 to 18 years. ● *n.* (*pl.* **–ies**) secondary thing. □□ **sec·ond·ar′i·ly** *adv.*

sec·ond·hand /sékəndhánd/ ● *adj.* **1 a** (of goods) having had a previous owner; not new. **b** (of a store, etc.) where such goods can be bought. **2** (of information, etc.) accepted on another's authority and not from original investigation. ● *adv.* **1** on a secondhand basis. **2** indirectly.

sec·ond·ly /sékəndlee/ *adv.* **1** furthermore; in the second place. **2** as a second item.

se·cre·cy /séekrisee/ *n.* **1** keeping of secrets as a fact, habit, or faculty. **2** state in which all information is withheld.

se·cret /séekrit/ ● *adj.* **1** kept or meant to be kept private, unknown, or hidden. **2** acting or operating secretly. ● *n.* **1** thing to be kept secret. **2** thing known only to a few. **3** valid but not commonly known or recognized method of achieving or maintaining something (*what's their secret?*). □ **secret agent** spy. **Secret Service** branch of the US Treasury Department charged with apprehending counterfeitors and with providing security for the president and certain other officials and their families. □□ **se′cret·ly** *adv.*

sec·re·tar·i·at /sékritáireeət/ *n.* administrative office or department, esp. a governmental one.

sec·re·tar·y /sékriteree/ *n.* (*pl.* **–ies**) **1** employee who assists with correspondence, records, makes appointments, etc. **2** official appointed by a society, etc., to conduct its correspondence, keep its records, etc. □□ **sec·re·tar·i·al** /-táireeəl/ *adj.*

se·crete[1] /sikréet/ *v.tr. Biol.* (of a cell, organ, etc.) produce by secretion. □□ **se·cre′tor** *n.*

se·crete[2] /sikréet/ *v.tr.* conceal; put into hiding.

se·cre·tion /sikréeshən/ *n.* **1** *Biol.* **a** process by which substances are produced and discharged from a cell for a function in the organism or for excretion. **b** secreted substance. **2** act or instance of concealing.

se·cre·tive /séekritiv, səkrée–/ *adj.* inclined to make secrets; uncommunicative. □□ **se′cre·tive·ly** *adv.* **se′cre·tive·ness** *n.*

sect /sekt/ *n.* **1** group subscribing to (sometimes unorthodox) religious, political, or philosophical doctrines. **2** religious denomination.

sec·tar·i·an /sektáireeən/ ● *adj.* **1** of or concerning a sect. **2** bigoted or narrow-minded in following the doctrines of one's sect. ● *n.* **1** member of a sect. **2** bigot. □□ **sec·tar′i·an·ism** *n.*

sec·tion /sékshən/ ● *n.* **1** part cut off or separated from something. **2** each of the parts into which a thing is divided (actually or conceptually) or divisible or out of which a structure can be fitted together. **3** distinct group or subdivision of a larger body of people. **4** esp. Surgery separation by cutting. **5 a** cutting of a solid by a plane. **b** resulting figure. ● *v.tr.* arrange in or divide into sections.

sec·tion·al /sékshənəl/ *adj.* **1** made in sections. **2** local rather than general. □□ **sec′tion·al·ism** *n.* **sec′tion·al·ist** *n.* & *adj.* **sec′tion·al·ize** *v.tr.* **sec′tion·al·ly** *adv.*

sec·tor /séktər/ *n.* **1** distinct part of an enterprise, society, the economy, etc. **2** *Mil.* subdivision of an area. **3** plane figure enclosed by two radii of a circle, ellipse, etc., and the arc between them.

sec·u·lar /sékyələr/ *adj.* **1** not spiritual nor sacred. **2** (of education, etc.) not concerned with religion nor religious belief. □□ **sec′u·lar·ism** *n.* **sec′u·lar·ize** *v.tr.* **sec·u·lar·i·za′tion** *n.* **sec′u·lar·ly** *adv.*

se·cure /sikyŏŏr/ ● *adj.* **1** untroubled by danger or fear. **2** safe. **3** reliable; certain not to fail. **4** fixed or fastened. ● *v.tr.* **1** make secure or safe. **2** fasten, close, or confine securely. **3** succeed in obtaining. □□ **se·cur′a·ble** *adj.* **se·cure′ly** *adv.* **se·cure′ment** *n.*

se·cu·ri·ty /sikyŏŏritee/ *n.* (*pl.* **–ties**) **1** secure condition or feeling. **2** thing that guards or guarantees. **3** thing deposited or pledged as a guarantee of a loan, etc. **4** (often in *pl.*) certificate attesting credit or the ownership of stock, bonds, etc.

secy. *abbr.* secretary.

se·dan /sidán/ *n.* enclosed automobile for four or more people.

se·date[1] /sidáyt/ *adj.* tranquil and dignified; equable; serious. □□ **se·date′ly** *adv.* **se·date′ness** *n.*

se·date[2] /sidáyt/ *v.tr.* put under sedation.

se·da·tion /sidáyshən/ *n.* state of rest or sleep, produced by a sedative drug.

sed·a·tive /sédətiv/ ● *n.* calming drug, influence, etc. ● *adj.* calming; soothing; inducing sleep.

sed·en·tar·y /séd'nteree/ *adj.* **1** sitting. **2** (of work, etc.) done while sitting and with little physical exercise.

sedge /sej/ *n.* grasslike plant usu. growing in wet areas. □□ **sedg′y** *adj.*

sed·i·ment /sédimənt/ *n.* **1** matter that settles to the bottom of a liquid; dregs. **2** *Geol.* matter deposited by water or wind. □□ **sed·i·men·ta·ry** /-méntəree/ *adj.* **sed·i·men·ta′tion** *n.*

se·di·tion /sidíshən/ *n.* conduct or speech inciting to rebellion. □□ **se·di′tious** *adj.* **se·di′tious·ly** *adv.*

se·duce /sidóŏs, –dyóŏs/ *v.tr.* **1** entice into sexual activity or wrongdoing. **2** tempt (*seduced by the smell of coffee*). □□ **se·duc′er** *n.* **se·duc′i·ble** *adj.* **se·duc·tion** /sidúkshən/ *n.* **se·duc′tive** *adj.* **se·duc′tive·ly** *adv.* **se·duc·tress** /sidúktris/ *n.*

sed·u·lous /séjələs/ *adj.* persevering; diligent; painstaking. □□ **se·du·li·ty** /sidóŏlitee, –dyŏŏ–/ *n.* **sed′u·lous·ly** *adv.* **sed′u·lous·ness** *n.*

se·dum /séedəm/ *n.* plant with fleshy leaves and star-shaped yellow, pink, or white flowers.

see[1] /see/ *v.* (*past* **saw** /saw/; *past part.* **seen** /seen/) **1** *tr.* discern by use of the eyes. **2** *intr.* have or use the power of discerning objects with the eyes. **3** *tr.* understand. **4** *tr.* learn; find out. **5** *tr.* meet and recognize. **6** *tr.* **a** meet socially. **b**

meet regularly as a boyfriend or girlfriend. **7 a** *intr.* wait until one knows more. **b** *tr.* consider; decide (on). **8** *tr.* experience. **9** *intr.* ensure. **10** *tr.* **a** (in gambling, esp. poker) equal (a bet). **b** equal the bet of (a player). □ **see about 1** attend to. **2** consider; look into. **see through 1** not be deceived by; detect the true nature of. **2** penetrate visually. **see-through** *adj.* (esp. of clothing) translucent. **see to** = *see about.*

see² /see/ *n.* office or jurisdiction of a bishop or archbishop.

seed /seed/ • *n.* **1 a** flowering plant's unit of reproduction capable of developing into another such plant. **b** seeds collectively. **2** semen; milt. **3** fundamental or underlying cause. **4** descendants. • *v.* **1** *tr.* place seeds in. **2** *intr.* sow seeds. **3** *intr.* produce or drop seed. □ **go** (or **run**) **to seed 1** cease flowering as seed develops. **2** become degenerate; unkempt, etc. **seed money** money allocated to initiate a project. □□ **seed′less** *adj.*

seed·ling /séedling/ *n.* plant raised from seed.

seed·y /séedee/ *adj.* (**seed·i·er, seed·i·est**) **1** full of seed. **2** going to seed. **3** shabby looking. □□ **seed′i·ly** *adv.* **seed′i·ness** *n.*

see·ing /séeing/ *conj.* considering that; inasmuch as; because.

seek /seek/ *v.* (*past* and *past part.* **sought** /sawt/) **1 a** *tr.* make a search or inquiry for. **b** *intr.* (foll. by *for, after*) make a search or inquiry. **2** *tr.* **a** try or want to find or get. **b** ask for (*sought help from him*). **3** *tr.* endeavor. □□ **seek′er** *n.* (also in *comb.*).

seem /seem/ *v.intr.* **1** give the impression of being (*seems ridiculous*). **2** appear to be.

seem·ing /séeming/ *adj.* apparent but perhaps not real (*with seeming sincerity*). □□ **seem′ing·ly** *adv.*

seem·ly /séemlee/ *adj.* (**seem·li·er, seem·li·est**) conforming to propriety or good taste; decorous; suitable. □□ **seem′li·ness** *n.*

seen *past part.* of SEE¹.

seep /seep/ *v.intr.* ooze out; percolate slowly. □□ **seep′age** *n.*

seer /séeər, seer/ *n.* prophet; visionary.

seer·suck·er /séersukər/ *n.* material of linen, cotton, etc., with a puckered surface.

see·saw /séesaw/ • *n.* **1 a** long plank balanced on a central support for children to sit on at each end and move up and down by pushing the ground with their feet. **b** game played on this. **2** up-and-down or to-and-fro motion. • *v.intr.* **1** play on a seesaw. **2** move up and down as on a seesaw. **3** vacillate in policy, emotion, etc. • *adj. & adv.* with up-and-down or backward-and-forward motion.

seethe /seeth/ *v.intr.* **1** boil; bubble over. **2** be very agitated, esp. with anger. □□ **seeth′ing·ly** *adv.*

seg·ment /ségmənt/ • *n.* **1** each part into which a thing is or can be divided. **2** *Geom.* part of a figure cut off by a line or plane intersecting it, esp.: **a** part of a circle enclosed between an arc and a chord. **b** part of a line included between two points. **c** part of a sphere cut off by any plane not passing through the center. • *v.* (usu. /-mént/) divide into segments. □□ **seg·men·tal** /-mént′l/ *adj.* **seg·men·tal·ly** /-mént′lee/ *adv.* **seg·men·tar·y** /ségməntairee/ *adj.* **seg·men·ta·tion** /-táyshən/ *n.*

seg·re·gate /ségrigayt/ *v.tr.* **1** isolate. **2** enforce

racial segregation on (persons) or in (a community, etc.). □□ **seg′re·ga·ble** *adj.* **seg′re·ga·tive** *adj.*

seg·re·ga·tion /ségrigáyshən/ *n.* **1** enforced separation of racial groups in a community, etc. **2** act or instance of segregating; state of being segregated. □□ **seg·re·ga′tion·al** *adj.* **seg·re·ga′tion·ist** *n. & adj.*

se·gue /ségway/ esp. Mus. • *v.intr.* (**se·gues, se·gued, se·gue·ing**) go on without a pause. • *n.* uninterrupted transition from one song or melody to another.

sei·gneur /saynyór/ *n.* (also **sei′gnior** /sáynyawr/) feudal lord; lord of a manor. □□ **sei·gneu′ri·al** *adj.* **sei·gnio·ri·al** /-nyáwreeəl/ *adj.*

seine /sayn/ *n.* fishing net for encircling fish, usu. hauled ashore.

seis·mic /sízmik/ *adj.* of or relating to an earthquake or earthquakes. □□ **seis′mal** *adj.* **seis′mi·cal** *adj.* **seis′mi·cal·ly** *adv.*

seis·mo·graph /sízməgraf/ *n.* instrument that records the force, direction, etc., of earthquakes. □□ **seis·mo·graph′ic** *adj.* **seis·mo·graph′i·cal** *adj.*

seis·mol·o·gy /sízmóləjee/ *n.* the study of earthquakes. □□ **seis·mo·log′i·cal** /-məlójikəl/ *adj.* **seis·mo·log′i·cal·ly** *adv.* **seis·mol′o·gist** *n.*

seize /seez/ *v.* **1** *tr.* take hold of forcibly or suddenly. **2** *tr.* take possession of forcibly. **3** *tr.* **a** take possession of (contraband goods, etc.) by warrant or legal right; confiscate; impound. **b** arrest or apprehend (a person). **4** *tr.* affect suddenly. **5** *tr.* take advantage of (an opportunity). **6** *tr.* comprehend quickly or clearly. **7** *intr.* **a** take hold forcibly or suddenly. **b** take advantage eagerly. **8** *intr.* (of a moving part in a machine) become jammed. □□ **seiz′a·ble** *adj.* **seiz′er** *n.* **sei′zure** *n.*

sel·dom /séldəm/ • *adv.* rarely; not often. • *adj.* rare.

se·lect /silékt/ • *v.tr.* choose, esp. as the best or most suitable. • *adj.* **1** chosen for excellence or suitability; choice. **2** (of a society, etc.) exclusive. □□ **se·lec′ta·ble** *adj.*

se·lec·tion /silékshən/ *n.* **1** selecting or being selected. **2** selected person or thing. □□ **se·lec′tive** *adj.* **se·lec′tive·ly** *adv.* **se·lec·tiv·i·ty** /sílektívitee, sél-/, **se·lec′tiv·i·ty** /-n.*

se·le·ni·um /sileéneeəm/ *n. Chem.* nonmetallic element. ¶ Symb.: **Se**.

self /self/ • *n.* (*pl.* **selves** /selvz/) **1** individuality; essence; personality. **2** person or thing as the object of introspection or reflexive action (*the consciousness of self*). **3 a** one's own interests or pleasure. **b** concentration on these (*self is a bad guide to happiness*). • *adj.* of the same color as the rest or throughout.

self- /self/ *comb. form* expressing reflexive action: **1** of or directed toward oneself or itself (*self-respect*). **2** by oneself or itself, esp. without external agency (*self-evident*). **3** on, in, for, or relating to oneself or itself (*self-confident*).

self-a·base·ment /sélfəbáysmənt/ *n.* self-humiliation; cringing.

self-a·buse /sélfəbyoos/ *n.* **1** the reviling of oneself. **2** masturbation.

self-ad·dressed /sélfədrést/ *adj.* (of an envelope, etc.) having one's own address on for return communication.

self-aggrandizement ~ self-reliance 544

self·ag·gran·dize·ment /sélfəgrándizmənt/ *n.* process of enriching oneself or making oneself powerful. □□ **self·ag·gran·diz·ing** /–grándīzing/ *adj.*

self·ap·point·ed /sélfəpóyntid/ *adj.* designated so by oneself; not authorized by another.

self·a·ware /sélfəwáir/ *adj.* conscious of one's character, feelings, motives, etc. □□ **self′-a·ware′ness** *n.*

self·cen·tered /sélfséntərd/ *adj.* preoccupied with one's own personality or affairs. □□ **self′-cen′tered·ly** *adv.* **self′-cen′tered·ness** *n.*

self·clean·ing /sélfkléening/ *adj.* (esp. of an oven) cleaning itself when heated, etc.

self·con·fessed /sélfkənfést/ *adj.* openly admitting oneself to be (*a self-confessed thief*).

self·con·scious /sélfkónshəs/ *adj.* socially inept through embarrassment or shyness. □□ **self′-con′scious·ly** *adv.* **self′-con′scious·ness** *n.*

self·con·tained /sélfkəntáynd/ *adj.* **1** (of a person) uncommunicative or reserved; independent; self-possessed. **2** complete in itself. □□ **self′-con·tain′ment** *n.*

self·con·trol /sélfkəntról/ *n.* power of controlling one's external reactions, emotions, etc.; equanimity. □□ **self′-con·trolled′** *adj.*

self·de·cep·tion /sélfdisépshən/ *n.* deceiving oneself esp. concerning one's true feelings, etc. □□ **self·de·ceit** /–deseet/ *n.* **self·de·ceiv·er** /–deseevər/ *n.* **self·de·ceiv·ing** /–deseeving/ *adj.* **self′-decep′tive** *adj.*

self·de·feat·ing /sélfdifeeting/ *adj.* (of an action, etc.) doomed to failure because of internal inconsistencies.

self·de·fense /sélfdiféns/ *n.* **1** aggressive act, speech, etc., intended as defense. **2** skills for defending oneself. □□ **self′-de·fen′sive** *adj.*

self·de·ni·al /sélfdiníəl/ *n.* negation of one's interests, needs, or wishes, esp. in favor of those of others; self-control; forbearance. □□ **self′-de·ny′ing** *adj.*

self·de·struct /sélfdistrúkt/ • *v.intr.* (of a spacecraft, bomb, etc.) explode or disintegrate automatically, esp. when preset to do so. • *adj.* enabling a thing to self-destruct.

self·de·ter·mi·na·tion /sélfditərmináyshən/ *n.* **1** nation's right to determine its own government, etc. **2** ability to act with free will. □□ **self·de·ter·mined** /–tórmind/ *adj.* **self·de·ter·min·ing** /–tórmining/ *adj.*

self·dis·ci·pline /sélfdísiplin/ *n.* ability to apply oneself; self-control. □□ **self·dis′ciplined** *adj.*

self·ef·fac·ing /sélfifáysing/ *adj.* retiring; modest; timid. □□ **self′-ef·face′ment** *n.* **self′-ef·fac′ing·ly** *adv.*

self·em·ployed /sélfimplóyd/ *adj.* working for oneself, as a contractor or owner of a business, etc. □□ **self′-em·ploy′ment** *n.*

self·es·teem /sélfisteem/ *n.* **1** good opinion of oneself; self-confidence. **2** unduly high regard for oneself; conceit.

self·ev·i·dent /sélfévidənt/ *adj.* obvious; without the need of evidence or further explanation. □□ **self-ev′i·dence** *n.* **self-ev′i·dent·ly** *adv.*

self·ex·am·i·na·tion /sélfigzámináyshən/ *n.* **1** study of one's own conduct, etc. **2** examining of one's body for signs of illness, etc.

self·ex·plan·a·to·ry /sélfiksplánətawree/ *adj.* easily understood; not needing explanation.

self·ex·pres·sion /sélfikspréshən/ *n.* artistic or free expression. □□ **self′-ex·pres′sive** *adj.*

self·ful·fill·ing /sélf-foolfiling/ *adj.* (of a prophecy, etc.) bound to come true as a result of its being made.

self·help /sélfhélp/ *n.* theory that individuals should provide for their own support and improvement in society.

self·im·age /sélfimij/ *n.* one's own idea or picture of oneself.

self·in·dul·gent /sélfindúljənt/ *adj.* indulging or tending to indulge oneself in pleasure, idleness, etc. □□ **self′-in·dul′gence** *n.* **self′-in·dul′gent·ly** *adv.*

self·in·ter·est /sélfintrist, –tərist/ *n.* one's personal interest or advantage. □□ **self·in′ter·est·ed** *adj.*

self·ish /sélfish/ *adj.* concerned chiefly with one's own personal profit or pleasure. □□ **self′-ish·ly** *adv.* **self′ish·ness** *n.*

self·know·ledge /sélfnólij/ *n.* understanding of oneself, one's motives, etc.

self·less /sélflis/ *adj.* unselfish. □□ **self′less·ly** *adv.* **self′less·ness** *n.*

self·made /sélfmáyd/ *adj.* **1** successful or rich by one's own effort. **2** made by oneself.

self·pit·y /sélfpítee/ *n.* extreme sorrow for one's own troubles, etc. □□ **self·pit′y·ing** *adj.* **self·pit′y·ing·ly** *adv.*

self·por·trait /sélfpáwrtrit/ *n.* portrait or description of an artist, writer, etc., by himself or herself.

self·pos·sessed /sélfpəzést/ *adj.* habitually exercising self-control; poised; composed. □□ **self·pos·ses′sion** /–zéshən/ *n.*

self·pres·er·va·tion /sélfprézərváyshən/ *n.* **1** preservation of one's own life, safety, etc. **2** this as a basic instinct of human beings and animals.

self·pro·pelled /sélfprəpéld/ *adj.* (esp. of a motor vehicle, etc.) moving or able to move without external propulsion. □□ **self′-pro·pel′ling** *adj.*

self·reg·u·lat·ing /sélfrégyəlayting/ *adj.* regulating oneself or itself without intervention. □□ **self·reg·u·la·tion** /–láyshən/ *n.* **self·reg·u·la·to·ry** /–lətawree/ *adj.*

self·re·li·ance /sélfrilíəns/ *n.* reliance on one's

self′-ab·sorp′tion *n.*
self′-ab·sorbed′ *adj.*
self′-ad·just′ing *adj.*
self′-as·ser′tion *n.*
self′-as·sured′ *adj.*
self′-com·pla′cent *adj.*
self′-con′fi·dence *n.*
self′-con′fi·dent *adj.*

self-cri′ti·cal *adj.*
self-cri′ti·cism *n.*
self-de·lu′sion *n.*
self′-doubt′ *n.*
self-ed′u·cat·ed *adj.*
self′-fer·ti·li·za′tion *n.*
self-gov′ern·ment *n.*
self-gov′ern·ing *adj.*
self′-im·posed′ *adj.*

self′-im·prove′ment *n.*
self′-in·crim·i·na′tion *n.*
self′-in·duced′ *adj.*
self′-in·flict′ed *adj.*
self′-jus·ti·fi·ca′tion *n.*
self′-love′ *n.*
self′-mo′ti·vat·ed *adj.*
self′-mo·ti·va′tion *n.*
self′-per·pet′u·at·ing *adj.*

self′-pol·li·na′tion *n.*
self′-pol′li·nat·ing *adj.*
self′-pro·claimed′ *adj.*
self′-pro·tec′tion *n.*
self′-re·proach′ *n.*
self′-sus·tain′ing *adj.*

own resources, etc.; independence. □□ **self'-re•li'ant** *adj.* **self'-re•li'ant•ly** *adv.*

self-re•spect /sélfrispékt/ *n.* respect for oneself. □□ **self'-re•spect'ing** *adj.*

self-re•straint /sélfristráynt/ *n.* = SELF-CONTROL. □□ **self'-re•strained'** *adj.*

self-right•eous /sélfríchəs/ *adj.* smugly sure of one's rectitude, correctness, etc. □□ **self-right' eous•ly** *adv.* **self-right' eous•ness** *n.*

self-sac•ri•fice /sélfsákrifīs/ *n.* negation of one's own interests, wishes, etc., in favor of those of others. □□ **self-sac'ri•fic•ing** *adj.*

self•same /sélfsaym/ *adj.* (prec. by *the*) very same (*the selfsame village*).

self-seek•ing /sélfseéking/ *adj. & n.* seeking one's own welfare before that of others. □□ **self'-seek'er** *n.*

self-ser•vice /sélfsɔ́rvis/ • *adj.* **1** (of a store, restaurant, gas station, etc.) where customers serve themselves. **2** (of a machine) serving goods after the insertion of coins. • *n. colloq.* self-service store, gas station, etc.

self-start•er /sélfstaártər/ *n.* **1** electric appliance for starting an engine. **2** ambitious person who needs no external motivation.

self-styled /sélfstīld/ *adj.* called so by oneself.

self-suf•fi•cient /sélfsəfíshənt/ *adj.* **1 a** needing nothing; independent. **b** (of a person, nation, etc.) able to supply one's own needs. **2** arrogant. □□ **self'-suf•fi' cien•cy** *n.* **self'-suf•fi' cient•ly** *adv.*

self-sup•port•ing /sélfsəpáwrting/ *adj.* capable of maintaining oneself financially. □□ **self'-sup•port'** *n.*

self-taught /sélftáwt/ *adj.* self-educated.

self-willed /sélfwíld/ *adj.* obstinately pursuing one's own wishes. □□ **self-will'** *n.*

self-worth /sélfwɔ́rth/ *n.* = SELF-ESTEEM 1.

sell /sel/ • *v.* (*past* and *past part.* **sold** /sōld/) **1** *tr.* make over or dispose of in exchange for money. **2** *tr.* offer for sale. **3** *intr.* (of goods) be purchased (*will never sell*). **4** *intr.* have a specified price. **5** *tr.* cause to be sold (*the author's name alone will sell many copies*). • *n. colloq.* manner of selling (*soft sell*). □ **sell-by date** latest recommended date for sale, esp. of perishable food. **sell off** sell the remainder of (goods) at reduced prices. **sell out 1** sell all one's stock, shares, etc. **2** betray. **b** be treacherous or disloyal. □□ **sell'a•ble** *adj.* **sell'er** *n.*

sell-out /sélowt/ *n.* **1** commercial success, esp. the selling of all tickets for a show. **2** betrayal.

selt•zer /séltsər/ *n.* soda water.

sel•vage /sélvij/ *n.* (also **sel'vedge**) edging that prevents cloth from unraveling.

se•man•tic /simántik/ *adj.* relating to meaning in language; relating to the connotations of words. □□ **se•man'ti•cal•ly** *adv.*

se•man•tics /simántiks/ *n.pl.* (usu. treated as *sing.*) branch of linguistics concerned with meaning. □□ **se•man•ti•cist** /-tisist/ *n.*

sem•a•phore /sémɔfawr/ • *n.* **1** *Mil.*, etc., system of signaling with the arms or two flags. **2** railroad signaling apparatus consisting of a post with a movable arm or arms, etc. • *v.* signal or send by semaphore. □□ **sem•a•phor'ic** *adj.*

sem•blance /sémblɔns/ *n.* **1** outward or superficial appearance of something (*semblance of anger*). **2** resemblance.

se•men /seémən/ *n.* reproductive fluid of males.

se•mes•ter /siméstər/ *n.* half of an academic year.

sem•i /sémī, sémee/ *n.* (*pl.* **sem•is**) *colloq.* SEMITRAILER.

semi- /sémee, sémī/ *prefix* **1** half (*semicircle*). **2** partly. **3** almost (*a semismile*). **4** occurring or appearing twice in a specified period (*semiannual*).

sem•i•cir•cle /sémeesɔrkəl, sémī-/ *n.* half of a circle or of its circumference. □□ **sem•i•cir•cu•lar** /sémeesɔ́rkyəlɔr, sémī-/ *adj.*

sem•i•co•lon /sémikōlən/ *n.* punctuation mark (;) of intermediate value between a comma and a period.

sem•i•con•duc•tor /sémeekəndúktər, sémī-/ *n.* substance that has conductivity intermediate between insulators and metals. □□ **sem•i•con•duct'ing** *adj.*

sem•i•con•scious /sémeekónshəs, sémī-/ *adj.* partly or imperfectly conscious.

sem•i•fi•nal /sémeefīnəl, sémī-/ *n.* match or round immediately preceding the final. □□ **sem•i•fi'nal•ist** *n.*

sem•i•nal /séminəl/ *adj.* **1** of seed, semen, or reproduction. **2** germinal. **3** rudimentary; undeveloped. **4** (of ideas, etc.) providing the basis for future development. □ **seminal fluid** semen. □□ **sem'i•nal•ly** *adv.*

sem•i•nar /séminaar/ *n.* **1** small class at a university, etc., for discussion and research. **2** conference of specialists.

sem•i•nar•y /sémineree/ *n.* (*pl.* **–ies**) **1** training college for priests, rabbis, etc. **2** place of education or development. □□ **sem•i•nar•i•an** /-náireeən/ *n.*

Sem•i•nole /sémənōl/ *n.* **1 a** N. American people native to Florida. **b** member of this people. **2** language of this people.

se•mi•ot•ics /seémeeótiks, sém-/ *n.* study of signs and symbols in various fields, esp. language. □□ **se•mi•ot'ic** *adj.* **se•mi•ot'i•cal** *adj.* **se•mi•o•ti•cian** /-tishən/ *n.*

sem•i•per•me•a•ble /sémeepɔ́rmeeəbəl, sémī-/ *adj.* (of a membrane, etc.) allowing certain substances to pass through.

sem•i•pre•cious /sémeepréshəs, sémī-/ *adj.* (of a gem) less valuable than a precious stone.

sem•i•pro•fes•sion•al /sémeeprəféshənəl, sémī-/ • *adj.* **1** receiving payment for an activity but not relying on it for a living. **2** involving semiprofessionals. • *n.* semiprofessional musician, sportsman, etc.

sem•i•skilled /sémeeskild, sémī-/ *adj.* (of work or a worker) having or needing some training.

Sem•ite /sémīt/ *n.* member of the peoples supposed to be descended from Shem, son of Noah (Gen. 10:21 ff.), including esp. the Jews, Arabs, Assyrians, and Phoenicians. □□ **Sem•i•tism** /sémitizəm/ *n.*

Se•mit•ic /simítik/ *adj.* **1** of or relating to the Semites, esp. the Jews. **2** of or relating to the languages of the family including Hebrew and Arabic.

sem•i•tone /sémeetōn, sémī-/ *n. Mus.* half a tone.

sem•i•trail•er /sémeetráylər, sémī-/ *n.* trailer

having wheels at the back but supported at the front by a towing vehicle.

sen. *abbr.* **1 a** senator. **b** senate. **2** senior.

sen·ate /sénit/ *n.* **1** legislative body. **2** (**Senate**) upper and smaller assembly in the US, France, and other countries, in the states of the US, etc.

sen·a·tor /sénǝtǝr/ *n.* member of a senate. □□ **sen·a·to·ri·al** /–táwreeǝl/ *adj.*

send /send/ *v.tr.* (*past* and *past part.* **sent** /sent/) **1 a** order or cause to go or be conveyed. **b** propel; cause to move (*sent him flying*). **c** cause to go or become (*send to sleep*). **d** dismiss with or without force (*sent her away*). **2** *sl.* put into ecstasy. □ **send away for** send an order to a dealer for (goods). **send for 1** summon. **2** order by mail. **send off 1** get (a letter, parcel, etc.) dispatched. **2** attend the departure of (a person) as a sign of respect, etc. **send-off** *n.* demonstration of goodwill, etc., at the departure of a person, the start of a project, etc. □□ **send·a·ble** *adj.* **send·er** *n.*

Sen·e·ca /sénikǝ/ *n.* **1 a** N. American people native to western New York. **b** member of this people. **2** language of this people. □□ **Sen·e·can** *adj.*

se·nile /seénīl/ • *adj.* **1** of or characteristic of old age. **2** having the weaknesses or diseases of old age. • *n.* senile person. □□ **se·nil·i·ty** /sinílitee/ *n.*

se·nior /seényǝr/ • *adj.* **1** more or most advanced in age or standing. **2** of high or highest position. **3** (placed after a person's name) senior to a relative of the same name. **4** of the final year at a university, high school, etc. • *n.* **1** person of advanced age or comparatively long service, etc. **2** one's elder, or one's superior in length of service, membership, etc. **3** senior student. □ **senior citizen** elderly person, esp. a retiree. □□ **sen·ior·i·ty** /seényáwritee, –yor–/ *n.*

sen·na /sénǝ/ *n.* **1** cassia tree. **2** laxative prepared from the dried pod of this.

se·ñor /senyáwr/ *n.* (*pl.* **se·ñor·es** /–rez/) title used of or to a Spanish-speaking man.

se·ño·ra /senyáwrǝ/ *n.* title used of or to a Spanish-speaking married woman.

se·ño·ri·ta /sényǝreétǝ/ *n.* title used of or to a Spanish-speaking unmarried woman.

sen·sa·tion /sensáyshǝn/ *n.* **1** feeling in one's body detected by the senses. **2 a** intense interest, etc., esp. among a large group of people. **b** person, event, etc., causing such interest.

sen·sa·tion·al /sensáyshǝnǝl/ *adj.* **1** causing or intended to cause great public excitement, etc. **2** dazzling; wonderful. □□ **sen·sa′tion·al·ism** *n.* **sen·sa′tion·al·ize** *v.tr.* **sen·sa′tion·al·ly** *adv.*

sense /sens/ • *n.* **1 a** any of the five bodily faculties by which sensation is roused (*dull sense of smell*). **b** sensitiveness of all or any of these. **2** ability to perceive or feel. **3** consciousness; intuitive awareness. **4** quick or accurate appreciation, understanding, or instinct. **5** common sense. **6 a** meaning of a word. **b** intelligibility or coherence. • *v.tr.* **1** perceive by a sense or senses. **2** be vaguely aware of.

sense·less /sénslis/ *adj.* **1** unconscious. **2** wildly foolish. **3** without meaning or purpose. **4** incapable of sensation. □□ **sense′less·ly** *adv.* **sense′less·ness** *n.*

sen·si·bil·i·ty /sénsibilitee/ *n.* (*pl.* **–ties**) **1** ca-

pacity to feel. **2** sensitiveness. **3** (in *pl.*) emotional capacities or feelings.

sen·si·ble /sénsibǝl/ *adj.* **1** having or showing wisdom or common sense. **2 a** perceptible by the senses. **b** great enough to be perceived. **3** (of clothing, etc.) practical and functional. **4** (foll. by *of*) aware. □□ **sen′si·ble·ness** *n.* **sen′si·bly** *adv.*

sen·si·tive /sénsitiv/ • *adj.* **1** acutely affected by external stimuli or mental impressions; having sensibility. **2** (of a person) easily offended. **3** (of an instrument, film, etc.) responsive to or recording slight changes. **4** (of a topic, etc.) requiring tactful treatment or secrecy. • *n.* person who is sensitive (esp. to supposed occult influences). □□ **sen′si·tive·ly** *adv.* **sen′si·tive·ness** *n.* **sen·si·tiv·i·ty** /sénsitívitee/ *n.*

sen·si·tize /sénsitīz/ *v.tr.* make sensitive. □□ **sen·si·ti·za′tion** *n.* **sen′si·tiz·er** *n.*

sen·sor /sénsǝr/ *n.* device for the detection or measurement of a physical property to which it responds.

sen·so·ry /sénsǝree/ *adj.* of sensation or the senses. □□ **sen′so·ri·ly** *adv.*

sen·su·al /sénshōōǝl/ *adj.* **1 a** of or depending on the senses only and not on the intellect or spirit; carnal; fleshly. **b** given to the pursuit of sensual pleasures or the gratification of the appetites. **2** of sense or sensation; sensory. □□ **sen′su·al·ism** *n.* **sen′su·al·ist** *n.* **sen·su·al·i·ty** /sénshōō-álitee/ *n.* **sen′su·al·ly** *adv.*

sent *past* and *past part.* of SEND.

sen·tence /séntǝns/ • *n.* **1** set of words complete in itself as the expression of a thought, containing or implying a subject and predicate, and conveying a statement, question, exclamation, or command. **2 a** decision of a court of law, esp. the punishment allotted to a person convicted in a criminal trial. **b** declaration of this. • *v.tr.* **1** declare the sentence of (a convicted criminal, etc.). **2** (foll. by *to*) declare (such a person) to be condemned to a specified punishment.

sen·ten·tious /sénténshǝs/ *adj.* **1** pompously moralizing. **2** affectedly formal. **3** aphoristic; given to the use of maxims. □□ **sen·ten′tious·ly** *adv.* **sen·ten′tious·ness** *n.*

sen·tient /sénshǝnt/ *adj.* having the power of perception by the senses. □□ **sen′tience** *n.* **sen′tient·ly** *adv.*

sen·ti·ment /séntimǝnt/ *n.* **1** mental feeling. **2 a** what one feels. **b** verbal expression of this. **3** mawkish tenderness.

sen·ti·men·tal /séntimént′l/ *adj.* **1** of or characterized by sentiment. **2** showing or affected by emotion rather than reason. □□ **sen·ti·men′tal·ism** *n.* **sen·ti·men′tal·ist** *n.* **sen·ti·men·tal·i·ty** /–tálitee/ *n.* **sen·ti·men′tal·ize** *v.* **sen·ti·men′tal·ly** *adv.*

sen·ti·nel /séntinǝl/ *n.* sentry; lookout.

sen·try /séntree/ *n.* (*pl.* **–tries**) soldier standing guard.

se·pal /seépǝl/ *n. Bot.* division or leaf of the calyx.

sep·a·ra·ble /sépǝrǝbǝl/ *adj.* able to be separated. □□ **sep·a·ra·bil′i·ty** *n.* **sep′a·ra·ble·ness** *n.* **sep′a·ra·bly** *adv.*

sep·a·rate • *adj.* /sépǝrǝt, séprǝt/ forming a unit by itself; physically disconnected, distinct, or individual. • *n.* /sépǝrǝt, séprǝt/ (in *pl.*) separate articles of clothing suitable for wearing together in various combinations. • v. /séparayt/ 1 tr. make separate; sever. 2 tr. prevent union or contact of. 3 intr. go different ways; disperse. 4 tr. divide or sort (milk, ore, fruit, etc.) into constituent parts or sizes. □□ **sep′a·rate·ly** adv. **sep′a·rate·ness** n. **sep·a·ra·tive** /–rətiv/ adj.

sep·a·ra·tion /sépəráyshən/ n. 1 separating or being separated. 2 (in full **judicial separation** or **legal separation**) arrangement by which a husband and wife remain married but live apart.

sep·a·rat·ist /sépərətist, séprə–/ n. person who favors separation, esp. political independence. □□ **sep′a·ra·tism** n.

sep·a·ra·tor /sépəraytər/ n. machine for separating, e.g., cream from milk.

se·pi·a /seepeeə/ n. 1 dark reddish-brown color or paint. 2 brown tint used in photography.

sep·sis /sépsis/ n. 1 state of being septic. 2 blood poisoning.

Sept. abbr. 1 September. 2 Septuagint.

Sep·tem·ber /septémbər/ n. ninth month of the year.

sep·tet /septét/ n. (also **sep·tette′**) 1 Mus. a composition for seven performers. **b** the performers. 2 any group of seven.

sep·tic /séptik/ adj. contaminated with bacteria from a festering wound, etc.; putrefying. □ **septic tank** tank in which the organic matter in sewage is disintegrated through bacterial activity.

sep·ti·ce·mi·a /séptiseémeeə/ n. blood poisoning. □□ **sep·ti·ce′mic** adj.

sep·tu·a·ge·nar·i·an /sépchoōojináireeən, –toō–, –tyoō–/ • n. person from 70 to 79 years old. • adj. of this age.

Sep·tu·a·gint /séptoōəjint, –tyoō–/ n. Greek version of the Old Testament including the Apocrypha.

sep·tum /séptəm/ n. (pl. **sep·ta** /–tə/) Anat. partition such as that between the nostrils.

sep·ul·cher /sépəlkər/ n. (also **sep′ul·chre**) tomb or burial place. □□ **sepulchral** /sipúlkrəl/ adj.

seq. abbr. (pl. **seqq.**) the following.

se·quel /seékwəl/ n. 1 what follows (esp. as a result). 2 novel, motion picture, etc., that continues the story of an earlier one.

se·quence /seékwəns/ • n. 1 succession. 2 order of succession. 3 set of things belonging next to one another. 4 part of a motion picture, etc., dealing with one scene or topic. • v.tr. arrange in a definite order. □□ **se·quen·tial** /sikwénshəl/ adj. **se·quen′tial·ly** adv.

se·ques·ter /sikwéstər/ v.tr. (esp. as **sequestered** adj.) seclude; isolate; set apart.

se·quin /seékwin/ n. circular spangle for attaching to clothing as an ornament. □□ **se′ quined** adj.

se·quoi·a /sikwóyə/ n. Californian evergreen coniferous tree of very great height.

se·ragl·io /sərályō, –ra̓al–/ n. (pl. **–ios**) harem.

se·ra·pe /səra̓apee/ n. shawl or blanket worn as a cloak by Spanish Americans.

ser·aph /sérəf/ n. (pl. **ser·a·phim** /–fim/ or **ser·aphs**) angelic being of the highest order of the celestial hierarchy. □□ **se·raph·ic** /səráfik/ adj. **se·raph′i·cal·ly** adv.

Ser·bi·an /sórbeeən/ • n. 1 dialect of the Serbs

(cf. SERBO-CROAT). 2 native or inhabitant of Serbia. • adj. of or relating to the Serbs or their dialect.

Ser·bo-Cro·at /sórbōkrôat/ (also **Ser·bo-Cro·a·tian** /–krō–áyshən/) • n. main official language of the former Yugoslavia, combining Serbian and Croatian dialects. • adj. of or relating to this language.

ser·e·nade /sérənáyd/ • n. piece of music sung or played at night, esp. by a lover under his lady's window. • v.tr. sing or play a serenade to. □□ **ser·e·nad′er** n.

ser·en·dip·i·ty /sérəndípitee/ n. faculty of making happy discoveries by accident. □□ **ser·en·dip′i·tous** adj. **ser·en·dip′i·tous·ly** adv.

se·rene /sireén/ adj. (**se·ren·er**, **se·ren·est**) 1 **a** clear and calm. **b** unruffled. 2 placid; tranquil; unperturbed. □□ **se·rene′ly** adv. **se·ren·i·ty** /sirénitee/ n.

serf /sərf/ n. hist. agricultural laborer not allowed to leave the land. □□ **serf′dom** n.

serge /sərj/ n. durable twilled worsted, etc., fabric.

ser·geant /sa̓arjənt/ n. 1 noncommissioned army, marine, or air force officer next below warrant officer. 2 police officer ranking below captain. **sergeant major** Mil. highest-ranking noncommissioned officer. □□ **ser′gean·cy** n. (pl. **–cies**).

se·ri·al /seéreeəl/ • n. 1 story, play, etc., published, broadcast, or shown in regular installments. 2 periodical. • adj. 1 of or in or forming a series. 2 (of a story, etc.) in the form of a serial. □ **serial number** number showing the position of an item in a series. □□ **se′ri·al·ly** adv.

se·ri·al·ize /seéreeəlīz/ v.tr. publish or produce in installments. □□ **se·ri·al·i·za′tion** n.

se·ries /seéreez/ n. (pl. same) 1 number of things of which each is similar to the preceding or in which each successive pair are similarly related; sequence, succession, order, row, or set. 2 set of successive games between the same teams. 3 set of related but individual programs.

ser·if /sérif/ n. slight projection extending from the main part of a letter, as in T contrasted with T (cf. SANS SERIF).

se·ri·ous /seéreeəs/ adj. 1 thoughtful; earnest; sober. 2 important; demanding consideration. 3 not slight nor negligible. 4 sincere; not ironic nor joking. □□ **se′ri·ous·ly** adv. **se′ri·ous·ness** n.

ser·mon /sórmən/ n. 1 spoken or written discourse on a religious or moral subject, esp. a discourse based on a text or passage of Scripture and delivered in church. 2 piece of admonition or reproof; lecture. □□ **ser′mon·ize** v. **ser′mon·iz·er** n.

se·rous /seérəs/ adj. of or like or producing serum; watery. □ **serous gland** (or **membrane**) gland (or membrane) with a serous secretion.

ser·pent /sórpənt/ n. 1 usu. literary a snake, esp. large. **b** scaly limbless reptile. 2 sly or treacherous person.

ser·pen·tine /sórpəntīn/ adj. 1 of or like a serpent. 2 coiling; tortuous; sinuous; meandering; writhing. 3 cunning; subtle; treacherous.

ser·rate • v.tr. /seráyt/ (usu. as **serrated** adj.) provide with a sawlike edge. • adj. /sérayt/ esp. Anat., Bot., & Zool. notched like a saw. □□ **ser·ra·tion** /–ráyshən/ n.

ser·ried /sḗreed/ *adj.* (of ranks of soldiers, rows of trees, etc.) pressed together; without gaps.

se·rum /sḗerəm/ *n.* (*pl.* **se·ra** /–rə/ or **se·rums**) **1** liquid that separates from a clot when blood coagulates used esp. in inoculations. **2** watery fluid in animal bodies.

ser·vant /sɔ́rvənt/ *n.* **1** person employed to do domestic duties. **2** devoted follower; person willing to serve another.

serve /sɔrv/ • *v.* **1** *tr.* do a service for (a person, community, etc.). **2** *tr.* (also *absol.*) be a servant to. **3** *intr.* carry out duties. **4** *intr.* **a** be employed in (an organization, the armed forces, etc.). **b** be a member of the armed forces. **5 a** *tr.* be useful; meet the needs of. **b** *intr.* meet requirements; perform a function. **6** *intr.* act as a waiter. **7** *tr.* attend to (a customer). **8** *tr.* deliver (a subpoena, etc.) to (someone). **9** *tr. Tennis,* etc. deliver (a ball, etc.) to begin or resume play. • *n. Tennis,* etc. act or instance of serving □ **serve a person right** be a person's deserved punishment or misfortune.

serv·er /sɔ́rvər/ *n.* **1** person who serves. **2** *Eccl.* person assisting the celebrant at a service, esp. the Eucharist. **3** *Computing* computer that manages data access to clients on a network.

serv·ice /sɔ́rvis/ • *n.* **1** helping or doing work for another or for a community, etc. **2** work done in this way. **3** assistance or benefit given. **4** supplying of a public need, e.g., water, gas, etc. **5** employment as a servant. **6** state or period of employment. **7** public department or organization (*civil service*). **8** (in *pl.*) the armed forces. **9** ceremony of worship. **10** maintenance of a machine, etc. **11** assistance or advice given to customers after the sale of goods. **12 a** serving of food, drinks, etc. **b** extra charge nominally made for this. **13** set of dishes, etc., for serving meals. **14** *Tennis,* etc. **a** act or instance of serving. **b** person's turn to serve. • *v.tr.* **1** provide a service. **2** maintain or repair (a car, machine, etc.). □ **at a person's service** ready to serve a person. **in service 1** employed as a servant. **2** available for use. **service industry** one providing services not goods. **service station** place for servicing cars, selling fuel, etc.

serv·ice·a·ble /sɔ́rvisəbəl/ *adj.* **1** useful or usable. **2** able to render service. **3** durable but plain. □□ **serv·ice·a·bil′i·ty** *n.* **serv′ice·a·bly** *adv.*

serv·ice·man /sɔ́rvismən/ *n.* (*pl.* **–men**) **1** man serving in the armed forces. **2** man providing service or maintenance.

serv·ice·wom·an /sɔ́rviswoomən/ *n.* (*pl.* **–women**) woman serving in the armed forces.

ser·vile /sɔ́rvīl/ *adj.* **1** of or like a slave. **2** slavish; fawning; completely dependent. □□ **ser′vile·ly** *adv.* **ser·vil·i·ty** /–vílitee/ *n.*

serv·ing /sɔ́rving/ *n.* quantity of food served to one person.

ser·vi·tude /sɔ́rvitood, –tyood/ *n.* **1** slavery. **2** subjection (esp. involuntary); bondage.

ser·vo /sɔ́rvō/ *n.* (*pl.* **–vos**) in full **ser′vo·mech·a·n·ism**) powered mechanism for automatic control of electrical, hydraulic, etc., devices.

ses·a·me /sésəmee/ *n. Bot.* **1** E. Indian plant with seeds used as food and yielding an edible oil. **2** its seeds.

ses·qui·cen·ten·ni·al /séskwisenténeeəl/ • *n.* one-hundred-and-fiftieth anniversary. • *adj.* of or relating to a sesquicentennial.

ses·sion /séshən/ *n.* **1** assembly of a deliberative or judicial body to conduct its business. **2** single meeting for this purpose. **3** period during which such meetings are regularly held. **4** academic year.

set[1] /set/ *v.* (**set·ting;** *past* and *past part.* **set**) **1** *tr.* put, lay, or stand (a thing) in a certain position or location. **2** *tr.* **a** fix ready or in position. **b** dispose suitably for use, action, or display. **3** *tr.* **a** adjust (a clock or watch) to show the right time. **b** adjust (an alarm clock) to sound at the required time. **4** *tr.* insert (a jewel) in a ring, framework, etc. **5** *tr.* lay (a table) for a meal. **6** *tr.* arrange (the hair) while damp so that it dries in the required style. **7** *intr.* & *tr.* harden or solidify. **8** *intr.* (of the sun, moon, etc.) appear to move below the horizon. **9** *tr.* represent (a story, etc.) as happening in a certain time or place. **10** *tr.* assign (*set them an essay*). **11** *tr.* exhibit as a model. **12** *tr.* initiate; lead. **13** *tr.* establish (a record, etc.). **14** *tr.* **a** put parts of (a broken or dislocated bone, limb, etc.) into the correct position for healing. **b** deal with (a fracture or dislocation) in this way. **15** *tr.* (in full **set to music**) provide (words, etc.) with music for singing. **16** *tr.* (often foll. by *up*) *Printing* **a** arrange or produce (type or film, etc.) as required. **b** arrange the type or film, etc., for (a book, etc.). **17** *tr.* **a** cause (a hen) to sit on eggs. **b** place (eggs) for a hen to sit on. □ **set about** begin. **set down 1** record in writing. **2** land an aircraft. **set forth 1** begin a journey. **2** make known. **set on** (or **upon**) **1** attack violently. **2** cause or urge to attack. **set out 1** begin a journey. **2** (foll. by *to* + infin.) intend. **set up 1** place in position or view. **2** organize or start (a business, etc.). **3** establish.

¶ **Set** means 'to place or put': *Set the flowers on top of the piano.* **Sit** means 'to be seated': *Sit in this chair while I check the light meter.*

set[2] /set/ *n.* **1** group of linked, related, or similar persons or things. **2** collection of implements, vessels, etc., regarded collectively and needed for a specified purpose. **3** radio or television receiver. **4** (in tennis, etc.) group of games counting as a unit toward a match. **5** setting, including stage furniture, etc., for a play, etc.

set[3] /set/ *adj.* **1** in senses of SET[1]. **2** determined in advance. **3** fixed. **4** prepared for action. □ **set screw** screw for adjusting or clamping parts of a machine.

set·back /sétbak/ *n.* **1** reversal or arrest of progress. **2** relapse.

set·tee /setée/ *n.* seat (usu. upholstered), with a back and usu. arms, for more than one person.

set·ter /sétər/ *n.* **1** dog of a large, long-haired breed trained to stand rigid when scenting game. **2** this breed.

set·ting /séting/ *n.* **1** position or manner in which a thing is set. **2** immediate surroundings (of a house, etc.). **3** surroundings of any object regarded as its framework; the environment of a thing. **4** place and time, scenery, etc., of a story, drama, etc. **5** mounting in which a jewel is set. **6** set of cutlery and other accessories for one person at a table.

set·tle /sét'l/ *v.* **1** *tr.* & *intr.* establish or become established in an abode or way of life. **2** *intr.* & *tr.* **a** cease or cause to cease from wandering, disturbance, movement, etc. **b** adopt a regular or secure style of life. **c** apply oneself (to work, etc.). **3 a** *intr.* sit or come down to stay for some time. **b** *tr.* cause to do this. **4** *tr.* & *intr.* bring to or attain fixity, certainty, composure, or quietness. **5** *tr.* determine or decide or agree upon. **6** *tr.* resolve (a dispute, etc.). **7** *tr.* terminate (a lawsuit) by mutual agreement. **8** *tr.* pay (a debt, an account, etc.). **9** *intr.* (as **settled** *adj.*) not likely to change for a time. **10** *tr.* colonize. **11** *intr.* subside. □□ **set´tler** *n.*

set·tle·ment /sét´lmənt/ *n.* **1** settling; being settled. **2 a** colonization of a region. **b** place occupied by settlers. **3** agreement.

set·up /setup/ *n.* **1** arrangement or organization. **2** manner, structure, or position of this. **3** *colloq.* trick or conspiracy, esp. to make an innocent person appear guilty.

sev·en /sévən/ *n.* **1** one more than six. **2** symbol for this (7, vii, VII). □□ **sev´enth** *adj.* & *n.*

sev·en·teen /sévəntéen/ *n.* **1** one more than sixteen. **2** symbol for this (17, xvii, XVII). □□ **sev´en·teenth´** *adj.* & *n.*

sev·en·ty /sévəntee/ *n.* (*pl.* **–ties**) **1** seven times ten. **2** symbol for this (70, lxx, LXX). **3** (in *pl.*) the numbers from 70 to 79, esp. the years of a century or of a person's life. □□ **sev´en·ti·eth** *adj.* & *n.* **sev´en·ty·fold** *adj.* & *adv.*

sev·er /sévər/ *v.* **1** divide, break, or make separate, esp. by cutting. **2** part; divide (*severed our friendship*). □□ **sev´er·a·ble** *adj.*

sev·er·al /sévrəl/ • *adj.* **1** more than two but not many. **2** separate or respective. • *n.* some; a few. □□ **sev´er·al·ly** *adv.*

sev·er·ance /sévərəns, sévrəns/ *n.* act or instance of severing. □ **severance pay** amount paid to an employee on the early termination of a contract.

se·vere /siveér/ *adj.* **1** rigorous, strict, and harsh. **2** serious; critical. **3** vehement or forceful. **4** unadorned; plain in style. □□ **se·vere´ly** *adv.* **se·ver·i·ty** /–véritee/ *n.*

sew /sō/ *v.tr.* (*past part.* **sewn** /sōn/ or **sewed**) fasten, join, etc., by making stitches with a needle and thread or a sewing machine. □ **sew up 1** join or enclose by sewing. **2** *colloq.* (esp. in *passive*) satisfactorily conclude. **3** obtain exclusive use of. □□ **sew´er** *n.*

sew·age /sóoij/ (also **sew·er·age** /sóowərij/) *n.* waste matter conveyed in sewers.

sew·er /sóoər/ *n.* conduit, usu. underground, for carrying off drainage water and sewage.

sew·er·age /sóoərij/ *n.* **1** system of or drainage by sewers. **2** = SEWAGE.

sew·ing /sóing/ *n.* piece of material or work to be sewn.

sew·ing ma·chine /sóing/ *n.* machine for sewing or stitching.

sex /seks/ • *n.* **1** either of the main divisions (male and female) into which living things are placed on the basis of their reproductive functions. **2** sexual instincts, desires, etc., or their manifestation. **3** *colloq.* sexual intercourse. • *adj.* of or relating to sex (*sex education*). • *v.tr.* **1** determine the sex of. **2** (as **sexed** *adj.*) **a** having a sexual appetite (*highly sexed*). **b** having sexual characteristics. □ **sex appeal** sexual attractiveness. **sex chromosome** chromosome determining the sex of an organism. **sex symbol** person widely noted for sex appeal.

sex·a·ge·nar·i·an /séksəjináireeən/ • *n.* person from 60 to 69 years old. • *adj.* of this age.

sex·ism /séksizəm/ *n.* prejudice or discrimination, esp. against women, on the grounds of sex. □□ **sex´ist** *adj.* & *n.*

sex·ol·o·gy /seksólojee/ *n.* study of sexual life or relationships, esp. in human beings. □□ **sex·o·log·i·cal** /séksəlójikəl/ *adj.* **sex·ol´o·gist** *n.*

sex·tant /sékstənt/ *n.* instrument for measuring the angular distance of objects by means of mirrors.

SEXTANT

sex·tet /sekstét/ *n.* (also **sex·tette´**) **1** *Mus.* composition for six voices or instruments. **2** performers of such a piece. **3** any group of six.

sex·ton /sékstən/ *n.* person who looks after a church and churchyard.

sex·tu·plet /sekstúplit, –tŏŏ–, –tyŏŏ–, sékstŏŏ–, tyŏŏ–/ *n.* each of six children born at one birth.

sex·u·al /sékshŏŏəl/ *adj.* of or relating to sex, or to the sexes or the relations between them. □ **sexual intercourse** insertion of a man's erect penis into a woman's vagina, usu. followed by the ejaculation of semen. □□ **sex·u·al·i·ty** /–álitee/ *n.* **sex´u·al·ly** *adv.*

sex·y /séksee/ *adj.* (**sex·i·er**, **sex·i·est**) **1** sexually attractive or stimulating. **2** sexually aroused. □□ **sex´i·ly** *adv.* **sex´i·ness** *n.*

Sg *abbr.* SEABORGIUM.

Sgt. (also **SGT**) *abbr.* Sergeant.

shab·by /shábee/ *adj.* (**shab·bi·er**, **shab·bi·est**) **1** in bad repair or condition; faded and worn. **2** contemptible; dishonorable. □□ **shab´bi·ly** *adv.* **shab´bi·ness** *n.*

shack /shak/ • *n.* roughly built hut or cabin. • *v.intr.* (foll. by *up*) *sl.* cohabit, esp. as lovers.

shack·le /shákəl/ • *n.* **1** metal loop or link, closed by a bolt, to connect chains, etc. **2** fetter enclosing the ankle or wrist. **3** (usu. in *pl.*) restraint or impediment. • *v.tr.* fetter; impede; restrain.

shad /shad/ *n.* (*pl.* same or **shads**) *Zool.* edible marine fish spawning in fresh water.

shade /shayd/ • *n.* **1** comparative darkness (and usu. coolness) caused by shelter from direct light. **2** area so sheltered. **3** color, esp. as distinguished from one nearly like it. **4** slight amount. **5** screen excluding or moderating light. **6** (in *pl.*) *colloq.* sunglasses. **7** *literary* ghost. • *v.tr.* **1** screen from light. **2** cover, moderate, or exclude the light of. **3** darken, esp. with parallel pencil lines to represent shadow, etc. □□ **shade′less** *adj.*

shad·ing /sháyding/ *n.* representation of light and shade, e.g., by penciled lines, on a map or drawing.

shad·ow /shádō/ • *n.* **1** shade; patch of shade projected by a body intercepting light. **2** slightest trace; weak or insubstantial remnant. **3** shaded part of a picture. **4** gloom or sadness. • *v.tr.* **1** cast a shadow over. **2** secretly follow and watch. □□ **shad′ow·er** *n.* **shad′ow·less** *adj.* **shad′ow·y** *adj.*

shad·ow·box /shádōboks/ *v.intr.* box against an imaginary opponent as a form of training. □□ **shad′ow·box·ing** *n.*

shad·y /sháydee/ *adj.* (**shad·i·er, shad·i·est**) **1** giving shade. **2** situated in shade. **3** (of a person or behavior) disreputable; of doubtful honesty. □□ **shad′i·ly** *adv.* **shad′i·ness** *n.*

shaft /shaft/ • *n.* **1 a** arrow or spear. **b** long slender stem of these. **2** remark intended to hurt or provoke. **3** (foll. by *of*) bolt (of lightning). **4** stem or handle of a tool, implement, etc. **5** long narrow space, usu. vertical, for access to a mine, for ventilation, etc. **6** long and narrow part transmitting motion between other parts. **7** central stem of a feather. • *v.tr. colloq.* treat unfairly.

shag[1] /shag/ *n.* **1** rough growth or mass of hair, carpet pile, etc. **2** coarse kind of cut tobacco.

shag[2] /shag/ *v.tr.* (**shagged, shag·ging**) *Baseball* catch and return (fly balls) during practice.

shag·gy /shágee/ *adj.* (**shag·gi·er, shag·gi·est**) **1** hairy; rough-haired. **2** unkempt. □□ **shag′gi·ly** *adv.* **shag′gi·ness** *n.*

shah /shaa/ *n. hist.* title of the former monarch of Iran.

shake /shayk/ • *v.* (*past* **shook** /shŏŏk/; *past part.* **shak·en** /sháykən/) **1** *tr. & intr.* move forcefully or quickly up and down or to and fro. **2 a** *intr.* tremble or vibrate markedly. **b** *tr.* cause to do this. **3** *tr.* **a** agitate or shock. **b** *colloq.* upset the composure of. **4** *intr. colloq.* shake hands. • *n.* **1** shaking; being shaken. **2** (in *pl.*; prec. by *the*) fit of or tendency to trembling or shivering. **3** = *milk shake.* **4** shingle made by splitting sections from a log. □ **no great shakes** *colloq.* not very good or significant. **shake down 1** settle or cause to fall by shaking. **2** settle down; break in. **3** *sl.* extort money from. **shake hands** (often foll. by *with*) clasp right hands at meeting or parting, in reconciliation or congratulation, etc. **shake off** get rid of (something unwanted). **shake up 1** mix (ingredients) by shaking. **2** make uncomfortable. **3** rouse from lethargy, apathy, conventionality, etc. **n.** upheaval or drastic reorganization. □□ **shak′a·ble** *adj.* (also **shake′a·ble**).

shake·down /sháykdown/ *n.* **1** extortion. **2** *sl.* thorough search. **3** (*attrib.*) *colloq.* denoting a voyage, flight, etc., to test a new ship or aircraft and its crew.

shak·er /sháykər/ *n.* **1** person or thing that shakes. **2** container for shaking together the ingredients of cocktails, etc. **3** (**Shaker**) member of an American religious sect living simply, in celibate mixed communities. □□ **Shak′er·ism** *n.* (in sense 3).

Shake·spear·e·an /shaykspe′ereeən/ (also **Shake·spear′i·an**) • *adj.* **1** of or relating to William Shakespeare, English dramatist d. 1616. **2** in the style of Shakespeare. • *n.* student of Shakespeare's works, etc.

shak·y /sháykee/ *adj.* (**shak·i·er, shak·i·est**) **1** unsteady; trembling. **2** unsound; infirm. **3** unreliable. □□ **shak′i·ly** *adv.* **shak′i·ness** *n.*

shale /shayl/ *n.* soft rock of consolidated mud or clay that splits easily. □□ **shal′y** *adj.*

shall /shal, shəl/ *v.aux.* (*3rd sing. present* **shall**; *past* **should** /shŏŏd, shəd/) (foll. by infin. without *to*, or *absol.*; present and past only in use) **1** (in the 1st person) expressing the future tense (*I shall return soon*) or (with *shall* stressed) emphatic intention (*I shall have a party*). **2** (in the 2nd and 3rd persons) expressing strong assertion or command rather than a wish (cf. **WILL**[1]) (*you shall not catch me again*). ¶ **Shall** and **should** were traditionally used after *I* or *we*, and **will** and **would** after other pronouns, to express the ordinary future. **Shall** was sometimes also used to indicate an order: *You shall disperse or be arrested.* **Should** is still heard, especially in British English, in first-person conditional sentences: *I should like to visit America.* But these distinctions are all but lost in today's speech and writing.

shal·lot /shálət, shəlót/ *n.* onionlike plant with a cluster of small edible bulbs.

shal·low /shálō/ • *adj.* **1** of little depth. **2** superficial; trivial. • *n.* (often in *pl.*) shallow place. □□ **shal′low·ly** *adv.* **shal′low·ness** *n.*

shalt /shalt/ *archaic* 2nd person sing. of **SHALL**.

sham /sham/ • *v.* (**shammed, sham·ming**) **1** *intr.* feign; pretend. **2** *tr.* pretend to be. • *n.* **1** imposture; pretense. **2** person or thing pretending or pretended to be what he or she or it is not. • *adj.* counterfeit. □□ **sham′mer** *n.*

sham·ble /shámbəl/ • *v.intr.* walk or run with a shuffling or awkward gait. • *n.* shambling gait.

sham·bles /shámbəlz/ *n.pl.* (usu. treated as *sing.*) **1** *colloq.* mess or muddle (*the room was a shambles*). **2** butcher's slaughterhouse. **3** scene of carnage.

shame /shaym/ • *n.* **1** distress or humiliation caused by consciousness of one's guilt or folly. **2** capacity for experiencing this feeling, esp. as imposing a restraint on behavior (*has no sense of shame*). **3** state of disgrace, discredit, or intense regret. **4 a** person or thing that brings disgrace, etc. **b** thing or action that is wrong or regrettable. • *v.tr.* **1** bring shame on; make ashamed. **2** force by shame. □ **put to shame** disgrace or humiliate by revealing superior qualities, etc. □□ **shame′ful** *adj.* **shame′ful·ly** *adv.*; **shame′ful·ness** *n.*

shame·faced /sháymfáyst/ *adj.* **1** showing shame. **2** bashful; diffident.

shame·less /sháymlis/ *adj.* **1** having or showing no shame. **2** impudent. □□ **shame′less·ly** *adv.* **shame′less·ness** *n.*

sham·poo /shampŏŏ/ • *n.* **1** substance used to wash hair, a car, a carpet, etc. **2** act or instance of cleaning with shampoo. • *v.tr.* (**sham·poos, sham·pooed**) wash with shampoo.

sham·rock /shámrok/ *n.* plant with trifoliate leaves; national emblem of Ireland.

shang·hai /shanghí/ *v.tr.* (**shang·hais, shang·haied, shang·hai·ing**) trick or force (a person) into working.

shank /shangk/ *n.* **1 a** the leg. **b** lower part of the leg. **2** lower part of an animal's foreleg, esp. as a cut of meat. **3** shaft or stem. **4** long narrow part of a tool, etc., joining the handle to the working end. □□ **shanked** adj. (also in comb.).

shan·ty /shántee/ n. (pl. **–ties**) hut or cabin.

shape /shayp/ • n. **1** total effect produced by the outlines of a thing. **2** external form or appearance. **3** specific form or guise. **4** person or thing as seen, esp. indistinctly (shape emerged from the mist). • v. **1** tr. give a certain shape or form to; fashion. **2** tr. adapt or make conform. **3** intr. give signs of a future shape or development. □ **shape up** show promise; make good progress. □□ **shap′a·ble** adj. (also **shape′a·ble**). **shaped** adj. **shape′less** adj. (also in comb.). **shape′less·ly** adv. **shape′less·ness** n. **shap′er** n.

shape·ly /sháyplee/ adj. (**shape·li·er**, **shape·li·est**) **1** well formed. **2** of pleasing shape. □□ **shape′li·ness** n.

shard /shaard/ n. **1** broken piece of pottery, etc. **2** = POTSHERD.

share¹ /shair/ • n. **1** portion that a person receives from or gives to a common amount. **2 a** part contributed by an individual to an enterprise or commitment. **b** part received by an individual from this. • v. **1** tr. get or have or give a share of. **2** tr. use or benefit from jointly with others. **3** intr. have a share; be a sharer (shall I share with you?). **4** intr. (foll. by in) participate. □□ **share′a·ble** adj. (also **shar′a·ble**). **shar′er** n.

share² /shair/ n. = PLOWSHARE.

share·hold·er /sháirhōldǝr/ n. owner of shares in a company.

share·ware /sháirwair/ n. Computing software distributed free.

shark¹ /shaark/ n. large, usu. voracious marine fish with a long body and prominent dorsal fin.

shark² /shaark/ n. colloq. swindler; profiteer.

shark·skin /sha′arkskin/ n. **1** skin of a shark. **2** smooth, dull-surfaced fabric.

sharp /shaarp/ • adj. **1** having an edge or point able to cut or pierce. **2** tapering to a point or edge. **3** abrupt; steep. **4** well-defined; clean-cut. **5** a severe or intense. **b** (of food, etc.) pungent. **c** (of a frost) severe; hard. **6** (of a voice or sound) shrill and piercing. **7** (of words, etc.) harsh or acrimonious (had a sharp tongue). **8** acute; quick to comprehend. **9** quick to take advantage; artful. **10** vigorous or brisk. **11** Mus. (**C**, **F**, etc., **sharp**) semitone higher than C, F, etc. **12** colloq. stylish. • n. **1** Mus. **a** note raised a semitone above natural pitch. **b** the sign (♯) indicating this. **2** colloq. swindler; cheat. • adv. **1** punctually. **2** suddenly. **3** Mus. above true pitch. □ **sharp-witted** keenly perceptive or intelligent. □□ **sharp′ly** adv. **sharp′ness** n.

sharp·en /sha′arpǝn/ v. make or become sharp. □□ **sharp′en·er** n.

sharp·er /sha′arpǝr/ n. swindler, esp. at cards.

sharp·shoot·er /sha′arpshōōtǝr/ n. skilled marksman. □□ **sharp′shoot·ing** n. & adj.

shat·ter /shátǝr/ v. **1** tr. & intr. break suddenly in pieces. **2** tr. severely damage or utterly destroy. **3** tr. greatly upset. **4** tr. (usu. as **shattered** adj.) exhaust. □□ **shat′ter·ing** adj. **shat′ter·ing·ly** adv. **shat′ter·proof** adj.

shave /shayv/ • v.tr. (past part. **shaved** or (as adj.) **shav·en**) **1** remove (bristles or hair) with a razor. **2** reduce by a small amount. **3** pass close to without touching; miss narrowly. • n. **1** shav-

ing or being shaved. **2** narrow miss or escape = close shave (see CLOSE¹).

shav·er /sháyvǝr/ n. **1** thing that shaves. **2** colloq. young lad.

shav·ing /sháyving/ n. **1** thin strip cut off of wood, etc. **2** (attrib.) used in shaving the face (shaving cream).

shawl /shawl/ n. piece of fabric, usu. rectangular, worn over the shoulders or head. □□ **shawled** adj.

Shaw·nee /shawne′e, shaa–/ n. **1 a** N. American people native to the central Ohio valley. **b** member of this people. **2** language of this people.

she /shee/ • pron. (obj. **her**; poss. **her**; pl. **they**) **1** woman or girl or female animal previously named or in question. **2** thing regarded as female, e.g., vehicle or ship. • n. **1** female; woman. **2** (in comb.) female (she-goat). ¶ See note at EVERYBODY.

sheaf /sheef/ • n. (pl. **sheaves** /sheevz/) group of things laid lengthwise together and usu. tied, esp. grain stalks, etc. • v.tr. (also **sheave** /sheev/) make into sheaves.

shear /sheer/ • v.tr. (past **sheared**, archaic **shore** /shor/; past part. **shorn** /shorn/ or **sheared**) **1** cut with scissors or shears, etc. **2** remove by cutting. **3** clip the wool off (a sheep, etc.). • n. (in pl.) (also **pair of shears** sing.) large clipping or cutting instrument shaped like scissors. □□ **shear′er** n.

sheath /sheeth/ n. (pl. **sheaths** /sheethz, sheeths/) **1** close-fitting cover for the blade of a knife or sword. **2** condom. **3** Bot., Anat., & Zool. enclosing case or tissue. **4** woman's close-fitting dress. □□ **sheath′less** adj.

sheathe /sheeth/ v.tr. **1** put into a sheath. **2** encase; protect with a sheath.

she·bang /shibáng/ n. sl. (esp. the whole shebang) everything.

shed¹ /shed/ n. one-story structure usu. of wood for storage or shelter for animals, etc., or as a workshop.

shed² /shed/ v.tr. (**shed·ding**; past and past part. **shed**) **1** let or cause to fall off (trees shed their leaves). **2** take off (clothes). **3** cause to fall or flow (shed blood). **4** disperse; diffuse; radiate (shed light). □□ **shed′der** n.

she'd /sheed/ contr. **1** she had. **2** she would.

sheen /sheen/ n. **1** gloss or luster. **2** radiance; brightness.

sheep /sheep/ n. (pl. same) **1** ruminant mammal with a thick woolly coat, esp. kept in flocks for its wool or meat. **2** bashful, timid, or silly person.

sheep·dog /shee′pdawg, –dog/ n. **1** dog trained to guard and herd sheep. **2 a** dog of various breeds suitable for this. **b** any of these breeds.

sheep·fold /shee′pfōld/ n. enclosure for sheep.

sheep·ish /shee′pish/ adj. **1** bashful; shy; reticent. **2** embarrassed through shame. □□ **sheep′ish·ly** adv. **sheep′ish·ness** n.

sheep·skin /shee′pskin/ n. **1** garment or rug of sheep's skin with the wool on. **2** leather from sheep's skin used in bookbinding.

sheer¹ /sheer/ • adj. **1** unqualified; absolute (sheer luck). **2** (of a cliff or ascent, etc.) perpendicular. **3** (of a textile) diaphanous. • adv. **1** directly; outright. **2** perpendicularly. □□ **sheer′ly** adv. **sheer′ness** n.

sheer[2] /sheer/ • *v.intr.* swerve or change course. • *n. Naut.* deviation from a course.

sheet[1] /sheet/ *n.* **1** large rectangular piece of cotton or other fabric, used for bedclothes. **2 a** broad usu. thin flat piece of material (e.g., paper or metal). **b** (*attrib.*) made in sheets (*sheet iron*). **3** wide continuous surface or expanse of water, ice, flame, falling rain, etc. **4** set of unseparated postage stamps. □ **sheet metal** metal formed into thin sheets. **sheet music** music published on unbound pages.

sheet[2] /sheet/ *n.* rope attached to the lower corner of a sail for securing or controlling it.

sheet·ing /she'eting/ *n.* fabric for making bed linens.

sheikh /sheek, shayk/ *n.* (also **sheik**) chief or head of an Arab tribe, family, or village. □□ **sheikh′dom** *n.*

shek·el /shékəl/ *n.* **1** chief monetary unit of modern Israel. **2** *hist.* silver coin and unit of weight in ancient Israel, etc. **3** (in *pl.*) *colloq.* money; riches.

shelf /shelf/ *n.* (*pl.* **shelves** /shelvz/) **1** flat piece of wood or metal, etc., projecting from a wall, or as part of a unit, used to support books, etc. **2** flat-topped recess in a wall, etc., used for supporting objects. □ **on the shelf** postponed, as a plan or project. **shelf life** amount of time for which a stored item of medicine, food, etc., remains usable. □□ **shelved** /shelvd/ *adj.* **shelf′ful** *n.* (*pl.* **-fuls**).

shell /shel/ • *n.* **1** hard outer case of many marine mollusks, tortoises, eggs, nuts, etc. **2** explosive projectile for use in a gun or mortar. **3** any of several things resembling a shell in being an outer case, esp.: **a** a light racing boat. **b** walls of an unfinished or gutted building, ship, etc. • *v.* **1** *tr.* remove the shell or pod from. **2** *tr.* bombard with shells. **3** *intr.* (of a seed, etc.) be released from a shell. □ **shell out** *colloq.* pay out (money). **shell shock** nervous breakdown resulting from exposure to battle. **shell-shocked** suffering from shell shock. □□ **shelled** *adj.* **shell′-less** *adj.* **shell′-like** *adj.*

she'll /sheel, shil/ *contr.* she will; she shall.

shel·lac /shəlák/ • *n.* lac resin used for making varnish. • *v.tr.* (**shel·lacked, shel·lack·ing**) **1** varnish with shellac. **2** *sl.* defeat or thrash soundly.

shell·fish /shélfish/ *n.* **1** edible aquatic shelled mollusk, e.g., oyster, mussel, etc. **2** crustacean, e.g., crab, shrimp, etc.

shel·ter /shéltər/ • *n.* **1** protection from danger, bad weather, etc. **2 a** place of refuge. **b** animal sanctuary. • *v.* **1** *tr.* serve as shelter to; protect. **2** *intr. & refl.* find refuge; take cover.

shelve /shelv/ *v.tr.* **1** put (books, etc.) on a shelf. **2 a** abandon or defer (a plan, etc.). **b** remove (a person) from active work, etc. **3** fit (a cupboard, etc.) with shelves. □□ **shelv′er** *n.* **shelv′ing** *n.*

shelves *pl.* of SHELF.

she·nan·i·gan /shinánigən/ *n.* (esp. in *pl.*) *colloq.* high-spirited or dubious behavior.

shep·herd /shépərd/ • *n.* **1** (*fem.* **shep·herd·ess** /shépərdis/) person employed to tend sheep. **2** member of the clergy, etc., who cares for and guides a congregation. • *v.tr.* **1 a** tend (sheep, etc.) as a shepherd. **b** guide (followers, etc.). **2** marshal or drive (a crowd, etc.) like sheep.

sher·bet /shórbət/ *n.* fruit-flavored ice confection.
¶ Avoid the pronunciation "sher-bert." **Sherbet** has only one *r*, in the first syllable.

sher·iff /shérif/ *n.* civil law-enforcement officer.

Sher·pa /shórpə/ *n.* (*pl.* same or **Sher·pas**) **1** a Himalayan people living on the borders of Nepal and Tibet, and skilled in mountaineering. **2** member of this people.

sher·ry /shéree/ *n.* (*pl.* **-ries**) fortified wine orig. from S. Spain.

she's /sheez/ *contr.* **1** she is. **2** she has.

Shi·a /shée∂/ *n.* one of the two main branches of Islam.

shib·bo·leth /shíbəleth/ *n.* long-standing formula, doctrine, phrase, etc., held to be true by a party or sect.

shield /sheeld/ • *n.* **1 a** esp. *hist.* piece of armor held in front of the body for protection when fighting. **b** thing serving to protect. **2** shield-shaped trophy, protective screen on machinery, etc. • *v.tr.* protect or screen. □□ **shield′less** *adj.*

shi·er *compar.* of SHY[1].

shi·est *superl.* of SHY[1].

shift /shift/ • *v.* **1** *intr. & tr.* change or move or cause to change or move from one position to another. **2** *intr.* manage as best one can. **3 a** *tr.* change (gear) in a vehicle. **b** *intr.* change gear. • *n.* **1 a** act or instance of shifting. **b** substitution of one thing for another; rotation. **2 a** relay of workers. **b** time for which they work. **3 a** device, stratagem, or expedient. **b** dodge, trick, or evasion. **4 a** woman's straight unwaisted dress. **b** *archaic* loose-fitting undergarment. **5** (in full **shift key**) key on a keyboard used to switch between lowercase and uppercase, etc. **6** gear lever in a motor vehicle. □□ **shift′a·ble** *adj.* **shift′er** *n.*

shift·less /shíftlis/ *adj.* lacking resourcefulness; lazy; inefficient. □□ **shift′less·ly** *adv.* **shift′less·ness** *n.*

shift·y /shíftee/ *adj.* *colloq.* (**shift·i·er, shift·i·est**) evasive; deceitful. □□ **shift′i·ly** *adv.* **shift′i·ness** *n.*

shill /shil/ *n.* person employed to decoy or entice others into buying, gambling, etc.

shil·le·lagh /shiláylee, -lə/ *n.* = CUDGEL.

shil·ling /shíling/ *n. hist.* former British coin and monetary unit worth one-twentieth of a pound or twelve pence.

shil·ly-shal·ly /shíleeshálee/ *v.intr.* (**-lies, -lied**) be undecided; vacillate.

shim /shim/ • *n.* thin strip of material used in machinery, etc., to make parts fit. • *v.tr.* (**shimmed, shim·ming**) fit or fill up with a shim.

shim·mer /shímər/ • *v.intr.* shine with a tremulous or faint diffused light. • *n.* such a light. □□ **shim′mer·ing·ly** *adv.* **shim′mer·y** *adj.*

shin /shin/ • *n.* **1** front of the leg below the knee. **2** cut of beef from the lower foreleg. • *v.tr. & intr.* (usu. foll. by *up, down*) *intr.* (**shinned, shin·ning**) climb quickly by clinging with the arms and legs.

shin·bone /shínbōn/ = TIBIA.

shin·dig /shíndig/ *n. colloq.* festive, esp. noisy, party.

shine /shīn/ • *v.* (*past* and *past part.* **shone** /shon/ or **shined**) **1** *intr.* emit or reflect light; be bright; glow. **2** *intr.* (of the sun, a star, etc.) be visible.

3 *tr.* cause (a lamp, etc.) to shine. **4** *tr.* (*past and past part.* **shined**) polish. **5** *intr.* be brilliant; excel. ● *n.* **1** light; brightness, esp. reflected. **2** high polish; luster. □□ **shin'ing·ly** *adv.*

shin·er /shínər/ *n. colloq.* black eye.

shin·gle /shínggəl/ ● *n.* **1** rectangular tile used on roofs, spires, or esp. walls. **2 a** shingled hair. **b** act of shingling hair. **3** small signboard, esp. of a doctor, lawyer, etc. ● *v.tr.* **1** roof or clad with shingles. **2** cut hair very short.

shin·gles /shínggəlz/ *n.pl.* (usu. treated as *sing.*) acute painful viral inflammation of the nerve ganglia, with a skin eruption often forming a girdle around the middle of the body.

Shin·to /shíntō/ *n.* official religion of Japan, incorporating the worship of ancestors and nature spirits. □□ **Shin'to·ism** *n.* **Shin'to·ist** *n.*

shin·y /shínee/ *adj.* (**shin·i·er, shin·i·est**) **1** having a shine. **2** (of clothing, esp. the seat of pants, etc.) having the nap worn off. □□ **shin'i·ly** *adv.* **shin'i·ness** *n.*

ship /ship/ ● *n.* **1** large seagoing vessel. **2** aircraft. **3** spaceship. ● *v.* (**shipped, ship·ping**) **1** *tr.* put, take, or send as in a ship, etc. **2** *tr.* **a** take in (water) over the side of a ship, boat, etc. **b** take (oars) from the rowlocks and lay them inside a boat. **3** *intr.* embark. □□ **ship'pa·ble** *adj.*

-ship /ship/ *suffix* forming nouns denoting: **1** quality or condition (*hardship*). **2** status, office, or honor (*authorship*). **3** tenure (*chairmanship*). **4** skill (*workmanship*). **5** collective individuals of a group (*membership*).

ship·board /shípbawrd/ *n.* (usu. *attrib.*) used or occurring on board a ship.

ship·build·er /shípbildər/ *n.* person, company, etc., that constructs ships. □□ **ship'build·ing** *n.*

ship·mate /shípmayt/ *n.* fellow member of a ship's crew.

ship·ment /shípmənt/ *n.* **1** amount of goods shipped; consignment. **2** act or instance of shipping goods, etc.

ship·per /shípər/ *n.* person or company that sends or receives goods.

ship·ping /shíping/ *n.* **1** act or instance of shipping goods, etc. **2** ships, esp. the ships of a country, port, etc.

ship·shape /shípshayp/ *adv. & predic.adj.* in good order; trim and neat.

ship·wreck /shíprek/ ● *n.* **1 a** destruction of a ship by a storm, foundering, etc. **b** ship so destroyed. **2** (often foll. by *of*) destruction of hopes, dreams, etc. ● *v.* **1** *tr.* inflict shipwreck on (a ship, a person's hopes, etc.). **2** *intr.* suffer shipwreck.

ship·wright /shíprīt/ *n.* **1** shipbuilder. **2** ship's carpenter.

ship·yard /shípyaard/ *n.* place where ships are built, repaired, etc.

shire /shīr/ *n.* county in Great Britain.

shirk /shərk/ ● *v.tr.* (also *absol.*) avoid (duty, work, responsibility, fighting, etc.). ● *n.* (also **shirk'er**) person who shirks.

shirr /shər/ ● *n.* two or more rows of gathered threads in a garment. ● *v.tr.* **1** gather (material) with parallel threads. **2** bake (eggs) without shells. □□ **shirr'ing** *n.*

shirt /shərt/ *n.* upper-body garment, often having a collar and sleeves.

shirt Old English *scyrte*, of Germanic origin; related to Old Norse *skyrta* (source of *skirt*), Dutch *schort*, German *Schürze* 'apron,' also to *short*; probably from a base meaning 'short garment.'

shirt·tail /shə́rttayl/ *n.* lower curved part of a shirt below the waist.

shirt·waist /shə́rtwayst/ *n.* woman's dress with a bodice like a shirt.

shish ke·bab /shísh kibób/ *n.* pieces of marinated meat and vegetables grilled and served on skewers.

shiv·er¹ /shívər/ ● *v.intr.* **1** tremble with cold, fear, etc. **2** shudder. ● *n.* **1** momentary shivering movement. **2** (in *pl.*) attack of shivering (*got the shivers in the dark*). □□ **shiv'er·er** *n.* **shiv'er·ing·ly** *adv.* **shiv'er·y** *adj.*

shi·ver² /shívər/ ● *n.* (esp. in *pl.*) small piece or splinter. ● *v.* break into shivers.

shoal¹ /shōl/ ● *n.* **1** great number of fish swimming together. **2** multitude. ● *v.intr.* (of fish) form shoals.

shoal² /shōl/ ● *n.* **1** area of shallow water. **2** submerged sandbank visible at low water. ● *v.intr.* (of water) get shallower. ● *adj.* archaic (of water) shallow.

shock¹ /shok/ ● *n.* **1** violent collision, impact, tremor, etc. **2** sudden and disturbing effect on the emotions, etc. **3** acute state of prostration following a wound, pain, etc., esp. when much blood is lost. ● *v.tr.* **1 a** horrify; outrage. **b** cause shock. **2** affect with an electric or pathological shock. □□ **shock'a·ble** *adj.*

shock² /shok/ ● *n.* group of usu. twelve sheaves of grain stood up with their heads together in a field. ● *v.tr.* arrange (grain) in shocks.

shock³ /shok/ *n.* unkempt or shaggy mass of hair.

shock·er /shókər/ *n. colloq.* **1** shocking, horrifying, etc., person or thing. **2** *hist.* sordid or sensational novel, etc.

shock·ing /shóking/ ● *adj.* causing indignation or disgust. ● *adv. colloq.* shockingly. □ **shocking pink** vibrant shade of pink. □□ **shock'ing·ly** *adv.*

shock·proof /shókprōof/ *adj.* resistant to the effects of (esp. physical) shock.

shod *past* and *past part.* of SHOE.

shod·dy /shódee/ ● *adj.* (**shod·di·er, shod·di·est**) **1** trashy; shabby; poorly made. **2** counterfeit. ● *n.* (*pl.* **–dies**) **1** inferior cloth made partly from the shredded fiber of old woolen cloth. **2** such fiber. □□ **shod'di·ly** *adv.* **shod'di·ness** *n.*

shoe /shōo/ ● *n.* **1** outer foot coverings having a sturdy sole and not reaching above the ankle. **2** metal rim nailed to the hoof of a horse, etc.; horseshoe. **3** (also **brake shoe**) part of a brake that presses against a wheel rim or drum. ● *v.tr.* (**shoes, shoe·ing**; *past* and *past part.* **shod** /shod/) **1** fit (esp. a horse, etc.) with a shoe or shoes. **2** (as **shod** *adj.*) (in *comb.*) having shoes, etc., of a specified kind (*dry-shod; roughshod*). □ **shoe tree** shaped block for keeping a shoe in shape when not worn. □□ **shoe'less** *adj.*

shoe·horn /shóohawrn/ *n.* curved piece of horn, metal, etc., for easing one's heel into a shoe.

shoe·lace /shóolays/ *n.* cord for lacing up shoes.

shoe·mak·er /shóomaykər/ *n.* maker of boots and shoes. □□ **shoe'mak·ing** *n.*

shoe·string /shōostring/ *n.* **1** shoelace. **2** *colloq.* small, esp. inadequate amount of money. **3** (*attrib.*) barely adequate; precarious (*shoestring majority*).

sho·far /shōfər, shawfaár/ *n.* (*pl.* **sho·froth** /shōfrōt/) ram's-horn trumpet used by Jews in religious ceremonies.

sho·gun /shōgən, –gun/ *n. hist.* any of a succession of Japanese hereditary commanders in chief and virtual rulers before 1868. □□ **sho·gun·ate** /–nət, –nayt/ *n.*

shone *past* and *past part.* of SHINE.

shoo /shōo/ ● *int.* exclamation used to frighten away birds, children, etc. ● *v.* (**shoos, shooed**) **1** *intr.* utter the word "shoo!" **2** *tr.* (usu. foll. by *away*) drive (birds, etc.) away by shooing.

shook /shŏok/ ● *past* of SHAKE. ● *predic. adj. colloq.* (foll. by *up*) emotionally or physically disturbed; upset.

shoot /shōot/ ● *v.* (*past* and *past part.* **shot** /shot/) **1** *tr.* **a** cause (a gun, bow, etc.) to fire. **b** discharge (a bullet, arrow, etc.) from a gun, bow, etc. **c** kill or wound (a person, animal, etc.) with a bullet, arrow, etc. **2** *intr.* discharge a gun, etc., esp. in a specified way (*shoots well*). **3** *tr.* send out, discharge, etc., esp. swiftly (*shot a glance at his neighbor*). **4** *intr.* come or go swiftly or vigorously. **5** *intr.* **a** (of a plant, etc.) put forth buds, etc. **b** (of a bud, etc.) appear. **6** *tr.* film or photograph. **7** *tr. Basketball, etc.* **a** score (a goal). **b** take a shot at (the goal). **8** *intr.* (of a pain) pass with a stabbing sensation. **9** *tr.* (foll. by *up*) *sl.* inject, esp. oneself with (a drug). ● *n.* **1** act or instance of shooting. **2** young branch or new growth of a plant. **3** hunting party, etc. ● *int. colloq.* **1** demand for a reply, information, etc. **2** *euphem.* exclamation of disgust, anger, etc. □ **shoot-out** *colloq.* decisive gunfight; showdown. □□ **shoot′er** *n.* **shoot′ing** *n. & adj.*

shop /shop/ ● *n.* **1** place for the retail sale of goods or services; store. **2** place for manufacture or repair; workshop. **3** *colloq.* institution, establishment, place of business, etc. ● *v.* (**shopped, shop·ping**) **1** *intr.* go to buy goods. **2** = *window-shop*. □ **shop around** look for the best bargain. □□ **shop′per** *n.*

shop·keep·er /shópkeepər/ *n.* owner and manager of a store. □□ **shop′keep·ing** *n.*

shop·lift·er /shópliftər/ *n.* person who steals goods while appearing to shop. □□ **shop′lift** *v.* **shop′lift·ing** *n.*

shop·ping /shóping/ *n.* **1** (often *attrib.*) purchase of goods, etc. **2** goods purchased (*put the shopping on the table*). □ **shopping center** area or complex of stores, with associated facilities.

shop·worn /shópwawrn/ *adj.* **1** (of an article) soiled or faded by display in a shop. **2** (of a person, idea, etc.) grubby; tarnished; no longer fresh or new.

shore¹ /shawr/ *n.* land that adjoins the sea or a large body of water. □□ **shore′less** *adj.* **shore′ward** *adj. & adv.* **shore′wards** *adv.*

shore² /shawr/ ● *v.tr.* (often foll. by *up*) support with or as if with a shore or shores; hold up. ● *n.* prop or beam set obliquely against a ship, wall, tree, etc., as a support. □□ **shor′ing** *n.*

shore·line /sháwrlīn/ *n.* line along which a stretch of water, esp. a sea or lake, meets the shore.

shorn *past part.* of SHEAR.

short /shawrt/ ● *adj.* **1 a** measuring little; not long from end to end. **b** not long in duration. **2** of small height; not tall. **3 a** (usu. foll. by *of, on*) deficient; scanty. **b** *colloq.* having little money. **c** not far-reaching. **4** a concise; brief. **b** curt; uncivil. **5** (of the memory) unable to remember distant events. **6** (of paper) crumbling; flaky. **7** esp. *Stock Exch.* (of stocks, etc.) sold or selling when the amount is not in hand, with reliance on getting the deficit in time for delivery. ● *adv.* **1** abruptly. **2** rudely; uncivilly. ● *n.* **1** short circuit. **2** short movie. ● *v.* short-circuit. □ **be caught short 1** be put at a disadvantage. **2** be unprepared. **for short** as a short name (*Tom for short*). **short circuit** electric circuit through small resistance, esp. instead of the resistance of a normal circuit. **short-circuit** *v.* **1** cause a short circuit (in). **2** shorten or avoid by taking a more direct route, etc. **short cut 1** route shortening the distance traveled. **2** quick way of accomplishing something. **short for** abbreviation for. **short-list** *v.tr.* put on a shortlist. **short-lived** ephemeral; not long-lasting. **short-order a** prepared or provided quickly, esp. simple restaurant fare. **b** pertaining to one who provides this (*a short-order cook*). **short story** story with a fully developed theme but shorter than a novella. **short-winded** easily becoming breathless. □□ **short′ish** *adj.* **short′ness** *n.*

short·age /sháwrtij/ *n.* deficiency; lack.

short·bread /sháwrtbred/ *n.* crisp, rich, crumbly type of cookie made with butter, flour, and sugar.

short·cake /sháwrtkayk/ *n.* cake, pastry or biscuit with fruit and whipped cream.

short·change /sháwrtcháynj/ *v.tr.* rob or cheat by giving insufficient money as change.

short·com·ing /sháwrtkuming/ *n.* failure to come up to a standard; defect.

short·en /sháwrt'n/ *v.* become or make shorter or short; curtail.

short·en·ing /sháwrt'ning, sháwrtning/ *n.* fat used for making pastry, bread, etc.

short·fall /sháwrtfawl/ *n.* deficit below what was expected.

short·hand /sháwrt-hand/ *n.* **1** (often *attrib.*) method of rapid writing in abbreviations and symbols, esp. for taking dictation. **2** abbreviated mode of expression.

short·hand·ed /shawrt-hánded/ *adj.* understaffed.

short·horn /sháwrt-horn/ *n.* **1** animal of a breed of cattle with short horns. **2** this breed.

short·list /sháwrtlist/ *n.* selective list of candidates from which a final choice is made.

short·ly /sháwrtlee/ *adv.* **1** soon. **2** briefly. **3** curtly.

shorts /shawrts/ *n.pl.* **1** pants reaching only to the knees or higher. **2** underpants.

short·sight·ed /sháwrtsíftid/ *adj.* **1** = NEARSIGHTED. **2** lacking imagination or foresight. □□ **short′sight′ed·ly** *adv.* **short′sight′ed·ness** *n.*

short·stop /sháwrtstop/ *n.* baseball fielder positioned between second and third base.

short·wave /sháwrtwáyv/ *n.* radio that receives long-distance signals carried by waves shorter than those used for commercial broadcasts.

short·y /sháwrtee/ *n.* (also **short′ie**) (*pl.* **–ies**) *colloq.* person or garment shorter than average.

Sho·sho·ne /shəshốn, –shốnee/ *n.* (also **Sho· sho'ni**) **1 a** N. American people native to the western US. **b** member of this people. **2** language of this people.

shot¹ /shot/ *n.* **1** firing of a gun, cannon, etc. **2** attempt to hit by shooting or throwing, etc. **3 a** single nonexplosive missile for a cannon, gun, etc. **b** (*pl.* same or **shots**) small lead pellet used in quantity in a single charge or cartridge in a shotgun. **c** (as *pl.*) these collectively. **4 a** photograph. **b** film sequence photographed continuously by one camera. **5 a** stroke or kick in a ball game. **b** *colloq.* an attempt to guess or do something (*let her have a shot at it*). **6** *colloq.* person having a specified skill with a gun, etc. **7** heavy ball thrown by a shot-putter. **8** launch of a space rocket (*a moonshot*). **9** *colloq.* **a** drink of liquor. **b** hypodermic injection. □ **shot put** athletic contest in which a heavy metal ball is thrown a great distance. **shot-putter** athlete who puts the shot. □□ **shot'proof** *adj.*

shot² /shot/ *past* and *past part.* of SHOOT. ● *adj.* **1** (of colored material) woven so as to show different colors at different angles. **2** *colloq.* exhausted; finished.

shot·gun /shótgun/ *n.* smoothbore gun for firing small shot.

should /shŏŏd/ *v.aux.* (*3rd sing.* **should**) *past* of SHALL, used esp.: **1 a** to express a duty, obligation, or likelihood; ought to (*you should be more careful*). **b** (in the 1st person) to express a tentative suggestion (*I should like to say something*). **2** forming an indefinite clause (*if you should see him*). ¶ See note at SHALL.

shoul·der /shốldər/ ● *n.* **1 a** part of the body at which the arm, foreleg, or wing is attached. **b** (in full **shoul'der joint**) the end of the upper arm joining with the clavicle and scapula. **c** either of the two projections below the neck from which the arms hang. **2** upper foreleg and shoulder blade of a pig, lamb, etc., when butchered. **3** (often in *pl.*) **a** the upper part of the back and arms. **b** this part of the body regarded as capable of bearing a burden or blame, providing comfort, etc. **4** strip of land next to a paved road. ● *v.* **1 a** *tr.* push with the shoulder. **b** *intr.* make one's way by jostling. **2** *tr.* take on (a burden, etc.). □ **shoulder blade** *Anat.* either of the large flat bones of the upper back; the scapula. □□ **shoul'dered** *adj.* (also in *comb.*).

shouldn't /shŏŏd'nt/ *contr.* should not.

shout /showt/ ● *v.* **1** *intr.* speak or cry loudly. **2** *tr.* say or express loudly. ● *n.* **1** loud cry. □□ **shout' er** *n.*

shove /shuv/ ● *v.* **1** *tr.* push vigorously. **2** *intr.* make one's way by pushing. **3** *tr.* *colloq.* put somewhere (*shoved it in the drawer*). ● *n.* act of shoving. □ **shove off 1** start from the shore in a boat. **2** *sl.* depart; go away (*told him to shove off*).

shov·el /shúvəl/ ● *n.* spadelike tool with raised sides for shifting quantities of earth, snow, etc. ● *v.tr.* **1** shift or clear (coal, etc.) with or as if with a shovel. **2** *colloq.* move (esp. food) in large quantities or roughly (*shoveled peas into his mouth*). □□ **shov'el·ful** *n.* (*pl.* **–fuls**).

show /shō/ ● *v.* (*past part.* **shown** /shōn/ or **showed**) **1** *intr.* & *tr.* be, allow, or cause to be visible; manifest. **2** *tr.* offer, exhibit, or produce for scrutiny, etc. **3** *tr.* indicate or reveal (one's feelings). **4** *intr.* (of feelings, etc.) be manifest. **5** *tr.* **a** demonstrate. **b** cause (a person) to under-

stand. **6** *tr.* conduct or lead. **7** *intr.* finish third in a race. ● *n.* **1** act or instance of showing; state of being shown. **2 a** spectacle, display, exhibition, etc. **b** collection of things, etc., shown for public entertainment or in competition (*flower show*). **3 a** play, etc., esp. a musical. **b** entertainment program on television, etc. **c** any public entertainment or performance. **4** outward appearance or display. □ **show off 1** display to advantage. **2** *colloq.* act pretentiously. **show-off** *n.* *colloq.* person who shows off. **show up 1** make or be conspicuous or clearly visible. **2** expose (a fraud, impostor, inferiority, etc.). **3** *colloq.* appear; arrive.

show·case /shốkays/ ● *n.* **1** glass case used for exhibiting goods, etc. **2** event, etc., for presenting (esp. attractively) to general attention. ● *v.tr.* display in or as if in a showcase.

show·down /shốdown/ *n.* final test or confrontation; decisive situation.

show·er /shówər/ ● *n.* **1** brief fall of esp. rain, hail, sleet, or snow. **2 a** brisk flurry of bullets, dust, etc. **b** similar flurry of gifts, honors, etc. **3** a cubicle, bath, etc., in which one bathes under a spray of water. **b** apparatus used for this. **c** act of bathing in a shower. **4** party for giving presents to a prospective bride, expectant mother, etc. ● *v.* **1** *tr.* **a** discharge (water, missiles, etc.) in a shower. **b** make wet with (or as if with) a shower. **2** *intr.* bathe in a shower. **3** *tr.* lavishly bestow (gifts, etc.). **4** *intr.* descend in a shower. □□ **show'er·y** *adj.*

show·girl /shốgərl/ *n.* actress who sings and dances in musicals, variety shows, etc.

show·ing /shốing/ *n.* **1** act or instance of showing. **2** usu. specified quality of performance.

show·man /shốmən/ *n.* (*pl.* **–men**) **1** proprietor or manager of a circus, etc. **2** person skilled in self-advertisement or publicity. □□ **show' man·ship** *n.*

shown *past part.* of SHOW.

show·piece /shốpees/ *n.* **1** item presented for exhibition or display. **2** outstanding specimen.

show·place /shốplays/ *n.* house, etc., that tourists go to see.

show·room /shốrōōm, –rŏŏm/ *n.* room used to display goods for sale.

show·stop·per /shốstopər/ *n.* *colloq.* act or performance receiving prolonged applause.

show·y /shốee/ *adj.* (**show·i·er, show·i·est**) **1** brilliant; gaudy, esp. vulgarly so. **2** striking. □□ **show'i·ly** *adv.* **show'i·ness** *n.*

shrank *past* of SHRINK.

shrap·nel /shrápnəl/ *n.* **1** fragments of an exploded artillery shell, bomb, etc. **2** artillery shell designed to scatter metal fragments.

shred /shred/ ● *n.* **1** scrap, fragment, or bit. **2** least amount. ● *v.tr.* (**shred·ded, shred·ding**) tear or cut into shreds. □□ **shred'der** *n.*

shrew /shrōō/ *n.* **1** small, usu. insect-eating, mouselike mammal with a long pointed snout. **2** bad-tempered or scolding woman. □□ **shrew' ish** *adj.* (in sense 2).

shrewd /shrōōd/ *adj.* astute; clever and judicious □□ **shrewd'ly** *adv.* **shrewd'ness** *n.*

---

shrewd Middle English (in the sense 'evil in nature or character'): from *shrew* in the sense 'evil person or thing,' or as the past participle of obsolete *shrew* 'to curse.' The word developed the sense 'cunning,' and gradually a favorable connotation during the 16th century.

shriek /shreek/ • *v.* **1** *intr.* **a** utter a shrill screeching sound. **b** (foll. by *of*) provide a clear or blatant indication of. **2** *tr.* **a** utter (sounds or words) by shrieking (*shrieked his name*). **b** indicate clearly or blatantly. • *n.* high-pitched piercing cry or scream. □□ **shriek′er** *n.*

shrift /shrift/ *n.* □ **short shrift** curt or dismissive treatment.

shrike /shrīk/ *n.* bird of prey with a strong hooked and toothed bill. Also called **butcher-bird**.

shrill /shril/ • *adj.* **1** piercing and high-pitched in sound. **2** *derog.* (esp. of a protester) sharp; unrestrained; unreasoning. • *v.* **1** *intr.* (of a cry, etc.) sound shrilly. **2** *tr.* (of a person, etc.) utter or send out (a complaint, etc.) shrilly. □□ **shrill′ly** *adv.* **shrill′ness** *n.*

shrimp /shrimp/ • *n.* **1** (*pl.* same or **shrimps**) small (esp. marine) edible crustaceans. **2** *colloq.* often *derog.* very small slight person. • *v.intr.* go catching shrimps. □□ **shrimp′er** *n.*

shrine /shrīn/ • *n.* **1 a** chapel, church, altar, etc., sacred to a saint, holy person, relic, etc. **b** tomb of a saint, etc. **c** casket, esp. containing sacred relics. **2** place associated with or containing memorabilia of a particular event, etc. • *v.tr. poet.* enshrine.

shrink /shringk/ • *v.* (*past* **shrank** /shrangk/; *past part.* **shrunk** /shrungk/ or (esp. as *adj.*) **shrunken** /shrúngkən/) **1** *tr.* & *intr.* make or become smaller, esp. from moisture, heat, or cold. **2** *intr.* (usu. foll. by *from*) **a** retire; recoil; flinch; cower. **b** be averse from doing. **3** (as **shrunk′en** *adj.*) (esp. of a face, person, etc.) having grown smaller, esp. because of age, illness, etc. • *n.* **1** act or instance of shrinking; shrinkage. **2** *sl.* psychiatrist (from "headshrinker"). □ **shrink-wrap** *v.tr.* (**-wrapped, -wrap·ping**) enclose (an article) in film that shrinks tightly on to it. • *n.* plastic film used to shrink-wrap. □□ **shrink′a·ble** *adj.* **shrink′er** *n.* **shrink′proof** *adj.*

shrink·age /shríngkij/ *n.* **1** a process or fact of shrinking. **b** degree or amount of shrinking. **2** allowance made for loss due to wastage, theft, etc.

shrive /shrīv/ *v.tr.* (*past* **shrove** /shrōv/; *past part.* **shriv·en** /shrívən/) *Eccl. archaic* **1** (of a priest) hear the confession of, assign penance to, and absolve. **2** (*refl.*) (of a penitent) submit oneself to a priest for confession, etc.

shriv·el /shrívəl/ *v.* contract or wither into a wrinkled, folded, rolled-up, contorted, or dried-up state.

shroud /shrowd/ • *n.* **1** sheetlike garment for wrapping a corpse for burial. **2** anything that conceals. **3** (in *pl.*) *Naut.* ropes supporting the mast or topmast. • *v.tr.* **1** clothe (a body) for burial. **2** cover, conceal, or disguise. □□ **shroud′less** *adj.*

Shrove Tues·day /shrōv/ *n.* the day before Ash Wednesday.

shrub /shrub/ *n.* any woody plant smaller than a tree; bush. □□ **shrub′by** *adj.*

shrub·ber·y /shrúbəree/ *n.* (*pl.* **–ies**) **1** area planted with shrubs. **2** shrubs, collectively.

shrug /shrug/ • *v.* (**shrugged, shrug·ging**) **1** *intr.* slightly and momentarily raise the shoulders to express indifference, helplessness, contempt, etc. **2** *tr.* **a** raise (the shoulders) in this way. **b** shrug the shoulders to express (indifference, etc.) (*shrugged his consent*). • *n.* act or instance of shrugging. □ **shrug off** dismiss as unimportant.

shtick /shtik/ *n. sl.* theatrical routine, gimmick, etc.

shuck /shuk/ • *n.* **1** husk or pod. **2** shell of an oyster or clam. **3** (in *pl.*) *colloq.* expression of contempt or regret or self-deprecation in response to praise. • *v.tr.* **1** remove the shucks of; shell. **2** peel off or remove. □□ **shuck′er** *n.*

shud·der /shúdər/ • *v.intr.* **1** shiver, esp. convulsively, from fear, cold, repugnance, etc. **2** feel strong repugnance. • *n.* act or instance of shuddering. □□ **shud′der·ing·ly** *adv.* **shud′der·y** *adj.*

shuf·fle /shúfəl/ • *v.* **1** drag (the feet) in walking. **2** *tr.* rearrange or intermingle (playing cards, papers, etc.). **3** *intr.* **a** equivocate; prevaricate. **b** fidget. • *n.* **1** shuffling movement. **2** act or instance of shuffling cards. **3** general change of relative positions. **4** piece of equivocation. **5** quick alternation of the position of the feet in dancing. □□ **shuf′fler** *n.*

shuf·fle·board /shúfəlbawrd/ *n.* game played by pushing disks with a long-handled cue over a marked surface.

shun /shun/ *v.tr.* (**shunned, shun·ning**) avoid; keep clear of.

shunt /shunt/ • *v.* **1** *intr.* & *tr.* redirect or cause (a train) to be redirected, esp. onto a siding. **2** *tr. Electr.* provide (a current) with a shunt. **3** *tr.* **a** postpone or evade. **b** divert (a decision, etc.) on to another person, etc. • *n.* **1** act or instance of shunting. **2** *Electr.* bypass for diverting current. **3** *Surgery* bypass for the circulation of the blood. □□ **shunt′er** *n.*

shush /shoosh, shush/ • *int.* = HUSH *int.* • *v.* **1** *intr.* call for silence by saying *shush*. **2** *tr.* make or attempt to make silent.

shut /shut/ *v.* (**shut·ting**; *past and past part.* **shut**) **1** *tr.* **a** move (a door, window, lid, etc.) to block an aperture. **b** close (a room, window, box, eye, mouth, etc.) by moving a door, etc. **2** *intr.* become or be capable of being closed. **3** *tr.* fold or contract (a book, hand, telescope, etc.). **4** *tr.* (usu. foll. by *in, out*) keep (a person, sound, etc.) in or out of a room, etc. □ **shut down 1** stop (a factory, nuclear reactor, etc.) from operating. **2** (of a factory, etc.) stop operating. **shut-eye** *colloq.* sleep. **shut-in** invalid confined to home, bed, etc. **shut off 1** stop the flow of (water, gas, etc.). **2** separate from society, etc. **shut out 1** exclude. **2** prevent (an opponent) from scoring. **shut up 1** close all doors and windows. **2** imprison. **3** (esp. in *imper.*) *colloq.* stop talking.

shut·down /shútdown/ *n.* closure of a factory, etc.

shut·ter /shútər/ • *n.* **1** person or thing that shuts. **2 a** movable, often louvered, cover for a window. **b** structure of slats on rollers used for the same purpose. **3** device that exposes the film in a camera. • *v.tr.* put up the shutters of.

shut·tle /shút'l/ • *n.* **1** bobbin with two pointed ends used for carrying the weft thread across between the warp threads in weaving. **2** train, bus, etc., going back and forth over a short route continuously. **3** = SHUTTLECOCK. **4** = *space shuttle*. • *v.* **1** move or cause to move back and forth like a shuttle. **2** transport by or travel in a shuttle.

shut·tle·cock /shút'lkok/ *n.* device struck in badminton.

shy /shī/ • *adj.* (**shy·er, shy·est** or **shi·er, shi·est**) **1 a** diffident or uneasy in company; timid. **b** (of an animal, bird, etc.) easily startled; timid. **2** avoiding; wary of. **3** (in *comb.*) showing fear of or distaste for (*gun-shy*). • *v.intr.* (**shies, shied**) **1** (esp. of a horse) start suddenly aside in fright. **2** (usu. foll. by *away from, at*) avoid. • *n.* sudden startled movement. □□ **shy'er** *n.* **shy'ly** *adv.* **shy'ness** *n.*

shy·ster /shíster/ *n. colloq.* unscrupulous lawyer.

Si *symb. Chem.* silicon.

Si·a·mese /sīəmeéz/ • *n.* (*pl.* same) **1 a** native of Siam (now Thailand) in SE Asia. **b** language of Siam. **2** (in full **Si·a·mese cat'**) **a** cat of a cream-colored short-haired breed with a brown face and ears and blue eyes. **b** this breed. • *adj.* of or concerning Siam, its people, or language. □ **Siamese twins** twins born joined at any part of the body.

sib·i·lant /síbilənt/ • *adj.* **1** (of a letter or set of letters, as *s, sh*) sounded with a hiss. • *n.* sibilant letter or sound. □□ **sib'i·lance** *n.*

sib·ling /síbling/ *n.* brother or sister.

sib·yl /síbil/ *n.* pagan prophetess. □□ **sib·yl·line** /síbilīn, –leen/ *adj.*

sic[1] /sik/ *v.tr.* (**sicced, sic'cing**; also **sicked** /sikt/, **sick'ing**) (usu. in *imper.*) urge (a dog) to attack.

sic[2] /sik, seek/ *adv.* (usu. in brackets) used, spelled, etc., as written.

sick /sik/ *adj.* **1** (often in *comb.*) vomiting or tending to vomit (*seasick*). **2** ill; affected by illness. **3 a** esp. mentally perturbed. **b** pining; longing (*lovesick*). **4** (often foll. by *of*) *colloq.* **a** disgusted. **b** angry (*am sick of being teased*). **5** *colloq.* (of humor, etc.) jeering at misfortune, etc.; morbid. □ **sick leave** leave granted because of illness. □□ **sick'ish** *adj.*

sick·bay /síkbay/ *n.* **1** part of a ship used as a hospital. **2** any room, etc., for sick people.

sick·bed /síkbed/ *n.* invalid's bed.

sick·en /síkən/ *v.tr.* **1** affect with loathing or disgust. **2** (as **sickening** *adj.*) loathsome; disgusting. □□ **sick'en·ing·ly** *adv.*

sick·le /síkəl/ *n.* **1** short-handled tool with a semicircular blade, used for cutting grain, lopping, or trimming. **2** anything sickle-shaped, esp. the crescent moon. □ **sickle cell** sickle-shaped blood cell, esp. as found in a type of severe hereditary anemia.

SICKLE

557   **shuttlecock ~ sideways**

sick·ly /síklee/ *adj.* (**sick·li·er, sick·li·est**) **1 a** of weak health; apt to be ill. **b** faint or pale. **2** causing ill health. **3** sentimental or mawkish. □□ **sick'li·ness** *n.*

sick·ness /síknis/ *n.* **1** state of being ill; disease. **2** nausea.

side /sīd/ • *n.* **1 a** each of the surfaces bounding an object. **b** inner or outer surface. **c** such a surface as distinct from the top or bottom, front or back. **2 a** half of a person or animal that is on the right or the left, esp. of the torso. **b** left or right half or a specified part of a thing, etc. **c** (often in *comb.*) a position next to a person or thing (*seaside*). **d** direction. **3** either surface of a thing having two surfaces. **4** any of several aspects of a question, character, etc. **5** each of two sets of opponents in war, politics, games, etc. **6 a** part or region near the edge and remote from the center. **b** (*attrib.*) subordinate, peripheral, or detached part. **7** each of the bounding lines of a plane figure **8** line of hereditary descent through the father or the mother. • *v.intr.* (usu. foll. by *with*) be on the same side as a disputant, etc. (*sided with his father*). □ **on the side 1** as a sideline. **2** secretly or illicitly. **3** as a side dish. **side arm** pistol or other weapon worn at the belt. **side dish** extra dish subsidiary to the main course. **take sides** support one cause, etc., in a dispute. □□ **side'less** *adj.*

side·board /sídbawrd/ *n.* flat-topped cupboard for dishes, table linen, decanters, etc.

side·burns /sídbərnz/ *n.pl. colloq.* hair grown by a man down the sides of his face.

side·car /sídkaar/ *n.* **1** small car for a passenger attached to the side of a motorcycle. **2** cocktail of orange liqueur, lemon juice, and brandy.

side·kick /sídkik/ *n. colloq.* close associate.

side·light /sídlīt/ *n.* incidental information, etc.

side·line /sídlīn/ • *n.* **1** work, etc., done in addition to one's main activity. **2** (usu. in *pl.*) **a** line bounding the side of a football field, tennis court, etc. **b** space next to these where spectators, etc., sit. • *v.tr.* remove (a player) from a team through injury, suspension, etc.

side·long /sídlawng, –long/ • *adj.* oblique. • *adv.* obliquely.

si·de·re·al /sīdeéreeəl/ *adj.* of the constellations or fixed stars.

side·sad·dle /sídsad'l/ • *n.* saddle having supports for both feet on the same side of the horse. • *adv.* riding in this position on a horse.

side·show /sídshō/ *n.* minor show or attraction in an exhibition or entertainment.

side·split·ting /sídspliting/ *adj.* causing violent laughter.

side·step /sídstep/ • *n.* step taken sideways. • *v.tr.* (**–stepped, –step·ping**) **1** avoid by stepping sideways. **2** evade. □□ **side'step·per** *n.*

side·swipe /sídswīp/ • *n.* glancing blow on or from the side. • *v.tr.* hit with or as if with a sideswipe.

side·track /sídtrak/ *v.tr.* **1** shunt. **2 a** postpone, evade, or divert consideration of. **b** divert (a person) from considering, etc.

side·walk /sídwawk/ *n.* paved track for pedestrians.

side·wall /sídwawl/ *n.* part of a tire between the tread and the wheel rim.

side·ways /sídwayz/ • *adv.* **1** to or from a side.

2 with one side facing forward. ● *adj.* to or from a side. □□ **side′wise** *adv.* & *adj.*

sid·ing /sīding/ *n.* **1** short track at the side of a railroad line, used for switching trains. **2** material for the outside of a building, e.g., clapboards, shingles, etc.

si·dle /sīd′l/ ● *v.intr.* walk in a timid, furtive, stealthy, or cringing manner. ● *n.* act or instance of sidling.

SIDS /sids/ *abbr.* sudden infant death syndrome; crib death.

siege /seej/ *n.* **1** military action of surrounding and blockading a town, building, etc. **2** period during which a siege lasts. □ **lay siege to** esp. Mil. conduct the siege of.

si·er·ra /seeéra/ *n.* long jagged mountain chain.

si·es·ta /seeésta/ *n.* afternoon sleep or rest esp. in hot countries.

sieve /siv/ ● *n.* utensil having a perforated or meshed bottom for separating solids or coarse material from liquids or fine particles. ● *v.tr.* **1** sift. **2** examine (evidence, etc.) to select or separate. □□ **sieve′like** *adj.*

sift /sift/ *v.tr.* **1** sieve (material) into finer and coarser parts. **2** (usu. foll. by *from, out*) separate (finer or coarser parts) from material. **3** examine (evidence, facts, etc.). □□ **sift′er** *n.* (also in *comb.*).

sigh /sī/ ● *v.intr.* **1** emit a long, deep, audible breath expressive of sadness, weariness, relief, etc. **2** (foll. by *for*) yearn for (a lost person or thing). **3** (of the wind, etc.) make a sound like sighing. ● *n.* act or instance of sighing.

sight /sīt/ ● *n.* **1 a** faculty of seeing. **b** act or instance of seeing; state of being seen. **2** thing seen. **3** range of vision. **4** (usu. in *pl.*) noteworthy features of a town, etc. **5 a** device on a gun or optical instrument for assisting the precise aim or observation. **b** aim or observation so gained. **6** *colloq.* person or thing having a ridiculous, repulsive, or disheveled appearance ● *v.tr.* **1** get sight of, esp. by approaching (*they sighted land*). **2** observe (esp. aircraft, animals, etc.) (*sighted buffalo*). **3** aim (a gun, etc.). □ **at** (or **on**) **sight** as soon as seen (*liked him on sight*).

sight-read (*past* and *past part.* **–read** /–red/) read and perform (music) at sight. □□ **sight′er** *n.*

sight·ed /sītid/ *adj.* **1** not blind. **2** (in *comb.*) having a specified kind of sight (*farsighted*).

sight·less /sītlis/ *adj.* blind. □□ **sight′less·ly** *adv.* **sight′less·ness** *n.*

sight·ly /sītlee/ *adj.* attractive to the sight. □□ **sight′li·ness** *n.*

sight·se·er /sītseeor/ *n.* person who visits places of interest; tourist. □□ **sight′see** *v.* **sight′see·ing** *n.*

sig·ma /sígma/ *n.* eighteenth letter of the Greek alphabet (Σ, σ, or, when final, ς).

sign /sīn/ ● *n.* **1** thing indicating a quality, state, etc.; thing perceived as indicating a future state or occurrence (*violence is a sign of weakness*). **b** portent. **2** mark, symbol, etc. **3** gesture or action conveying information, an order, etc. **4** signboard or signpost. **5** any of the twelve divisions of the zodiac. ● *v.* **1** tr. **a** write (one's name, initials, etc.). **b** sign (a document) as authorization. **2** *intr.* & *tr.* communicate by gesture, esp. using sign language. **3** tr. & *intr.* engage or be engaged by signing a contract, etc. (see also *sign on, sign up*). **4** tr. mark with a sign (esp. with the sign of the cross in baptism). □ **sign away** convey (one's right, property, etc.) by signing a deed, etc. **sign for** acknowledge receipt of by signing. **sign language** system of communication by hand gestures, used esp. by the hearing impaired. **sign of the cross** Christian sign made in blessing or prayer, by tracing a cross with the hands. **sign off 1** end work, broadcasting, a letter, etc. **2** acknowledge by signature. **sign on 1** agree to a contract, employment, etc. **2** begin work, broadcasting, etc. **3** employ (a person). **sign up 1** engage or employ (a person). **2** enlist in the armed forces. **3 a** commit (another person or oneself) by signing, etc. **b** enroll. □□ **sign′a·ble** *adj.* **sign′er** *n.*

sig·nal /sígnal/ ● *n.* **1 a** usu. prearranged sign conveying information, guidance, etc. **b** message made up of such signs (*signals made with flags*). **2** immediate cause of action, etc. **3** *Electr.* **a** electrical impulse or impulses or radio waves transmitted as a signal. **b** sequence of these. ● *v.* **1** *intr.* make signals. **2** tr. **a** (often foll. by *to* + infin.) make signals to; direct. **b** transmit by signal; announce. □□ **sig′nal·er** *or* **sig′nal·ler** *n.*

sig·nal·man /sígnalmən/ *n.* (*pl.* **–men**) operator of signals, as in the army or on a railroad.

sig·na·to·ry /sígnatawree/ ● *n.* (*pl.* **–ries**) party or esp. a nation that has signed an agreement or esp. a treaty. ● *adj.* having signed such an agreement, etc.

sig·na·ture /sígnachər/ *n.* **1 a** person's name, initials, or mark used in signing. **b** act of signing a document, etc. **2** *Mus.* **a** group of sharps or flats indicating the key. **b** notation showing tempo. **3** *Printing* section of a book made from one folded sheet.

sign·board /sínbawrd/ *n.* board displaying a name, symbol, etc.

sig·net /sígnit/ *n.* small seal, as on a ring.

sig·nif·i·cant /signífikənt/ *adj.* **1** having a meaning; indicative. **2** noteworthy; important; consequential. □ **significant other** spouse or lover. □□ **sig·nif′i·cance** *n.* **sig·nif′i·cant·ly** *adv.*

sig·ni·fy /sígnifī/ *v.* (**–fies, –fied**) **1** tr. be a sign or indication of. **2** tr. mean. **3** tr. make known. **4** *intr.* be of importance; matter. □□ **sig·ni·fi·ca′tion** *n.* **sig′ni·fier** *n.*

si·gnor /seenyáwr/ *n.* (*pl.* **si·gno·ri** /–nyóree/) **1** title or form of address used of or to an Italian-speaking man, corresponding to Mr. or sir. **2** Italian man.

si·gno·ra /seenyáwrə/ *n.* **1** title or form of address used of or to an Italian-speaking married woman, corresponding to Mrs. or madam. **2** married Italian woman.

si·gno·ri·na /seényəreénə/ *n.* **1** title or form of address used of or to an Italian-speaking unmarried woman. **2** Italian unmarried woman.

sign·post /sínpōst/ *n.* **1** post with a sign indicating direction. **2** means of guidance; indication.

si·lage /sīlij/ *n.* green fodder stored in a silo.

si·lence /sīləns/ ● *n.* **1** absence of sound. **2** abstinence from speech or noise. **3** avoidance of mentioning a thing, betraying a secret, etc. ● *v.tr.* make silent, esp. by coercion or superior argument.

si·lenc·er /sīlənsər/ *n.* device for reducing the noise emitted by a gun, etc.

si·lent /sīlənt/ *adj.* **1** not speaking; not uttering or making or accompanied by any sound. **2** (of an agreement) unspoken; unrecorded. □ **silent partner** non-working financial partner. □□ **si′lent·ly** *adv.*

sil·hou·ette /síloo-ét/ • *n.* **1** representation of a person or thing showing the outline only, usu. in solid black on white or cut from paper. **2** dark shadow or outline against a lighter background. • *v.tr.* represent or (usu. in *passive*) show in silhouette.

SILHOUETTE

sil·i·ca /sílikə/ *n.* silicon dioxide, occurring as quartz, etc. □ **silica gel** hydrated silica in a hard granular form used as a desiccant.

sil·i·cate /sílikayt, –kət/ *n.* compound of a metal with silicon and oxygen.

sil·i·con /sílikən, –kon/ *n. Chem.* nonmetallic element occurring widely in silica and silicates. ¶ Symb.: **Si.**

sil·i·cone /sílikōn/ *n.* any organic compound of silicon.

silk /silk/ *n.* **1** fine, strong, soft lustrous fiber produced by silkworms. **2** thread or cloth from this □ **silk-screen printing** process in which ink is pressed through a silk stencil bearing a design to the surface below. □□ **silk′like** *adj.*

silk·worm /sílkwərm/ *n.* caterpillar that spins its cocoon of silk.

silk·y /sílkee/ *adj.* (**silk·i·er, silk·i·est**) **1** like silk in smoothness, softness, fineness, or luster. **2** suave; insinuating. □□ **silk′i·ly** *adv.* **silk′i·ness** *n.*

sill /sil/ *n.* slab of stone, wood, or metal at the foot of a window or doorway.

sil·ly /sílee/ • *adj.* (**sil·li·er, sil·li·est**) **1** lacking sense; foolish; imprudent; unwise. **2** weak-minded. • *n.* (*pl.* **–lies**) *colloq.* foolish person. □□ **sil′li·ness** *n.*

si·lo /síló/ • *n.* (*pl.* **–los**) **1** pit or airtight structure in which green crops are stored for fodder. **2** pit or tower for the storage of grain, cement, etc. **3** underground storage chamber for a guided missile. • *v.tr.* (**–oes, –oed**) make silage of.

silt /silt/ • *n.* sediment deposited by water in a channel, harbor, etc. • *v.* choke or be choked with silt. □□ **silt′y** *adj.*

sil·ver /sílvər/ • *n. Chem.* **1** grayish-white, lustrous, precious metallic element. ¶ Symb.: **Ag. 2** color of silver. **3** silver coins. **4** household cutlery. • *adj.* **1** made wholly or chiefly of silver. **2** colored like silver. • *v.tr.* coat or plate with

silver. □ **silver jubilee** 25th anniversary. **silver lining** consolation or hopeful feature in misfortune. **silver medal** medal of silver, usu. awarded as second prize. **silver plate** vessels, spoons, etc., plated with silver. **silver screen** (usu. prec. by *the*) motion pictures collectively.

sil·ver·fish /sílvərfish/ *n.* (*pl.* same or **–fish·es**) silvery wingless insect.

sil·ver·smith /sílvərsmith/ *n.* worker in silver; manufacturer of silver articles. □□ **sil′ver·smith·ing** *n.*

sil·ver·ware /sílvərwair/ *n.* **1** articles of or coated with silver. **2** tableware of any metal.

sim·i·an /símeeən/ • *adj.* **1** of or concerning the anthropoid apes. **2** like an ape or monkey. • *n.* ape or monkey.

sim·i·lar /símilər/ *adj.* **1** like; alike. **2** (often foll. by *to*) having a resemblance. **3** of the same kind, nature, or amount. □□ **sim·i·lar·i·ty** /–láritee/ *n.* (*pl.* **–ties**). **sim′i·lar·ly** *adv.*

sim·i·le /símilee/ *n.* comparison of one thing with another of a different kind, as an illustration or ornament (e.g., *as brave as a lion*).

si·mil·i·tude /símilitood, –tyood/ *n.* likeness, guise, or outward appearance.

sim·mer /símər/ • *v.* **1** *intr.* & *tr.* be or keep bubbling or boiling gently. **2** *intr.* be in a state of suppressed anger or excitement. • *n.* simmering condition. □ **simmer down** become calm or less agitated.

si·mo·ny /símonee, sím–/ *n.* buying or selling of ecclesiastical privileges, e.g., pardons or benefices.

sim·per /símpər/ • *v.* **1** *intr.* smile in a silly or affected way. **2** *tr.* express by or with simpering. • *n.* such a smile. □□ **sim′per·ing·ly** *adv.*

sim·ple /símpəl/ *adj.* **1** easily understood or done. **2** not complicated or elaborate; without luxury or sophistication. **3** not compound. **4** absolute; unqualified; straightforward. **5** foolish or ignorant; gullible; feeble-minded.

sim·ple-mind·ed /simpəlmíndid/ *adj.* **1** natural; unsophisticated. **2** feeble-minded. □□ **sim′ple-mind′ed·ly** *adv.* **sim′ple-mind′ed·ness** *n.*

sim·ple·ton /símpəltən/ *n.* fool.

sim·plic·i·ty /simplísitee/ *n.* fact or condition of being simple.

sim·pli·fy /símplifi/ *v.tr.* (**–fies, –fied**) make simple or simpler. □□ **sim·pli·fi·ca′tion** *n.*

sim·plis·tic /simplístik/ *adj.* **1** excessively or affectedly simple. **2** oversimplified so as to conceal or distort difficulties. □□ **sim·plis′ti·cal·ly** *adv.*

sim·ply /símplee/ *adv.* **1** in a simple manner. **2** absolutely; without doubt. **3** merely.

sim·u·late /símyəlayt/ *v.tr.* **1 a** pretend to have or feel (an attribute or feeling). **b** pretend to be. **2** imitate or counterfeit. **3** (as **simulated** *adj.*) made to resemble the real thing. □□ **sim·u·la′tion** /–láyshən/ *n.* **sim′u·la·tor** *n.*

si·mul·ta·ne·ous /síməltáyneeəs, sím–/ *adj.* occurring or operating at the same time. □□ **si·mul·ta′ne·ous·ly** *adv.*

sin[1] /sin/ • *n.* **1 a** breaking of divine or moral law, esp. by a conscious act. **b** such an act. **2** offense against good taste or propriety, etc. • *v.intr.* (**sinned, sin·ning**) **1** commit a sin. **2** (foll. by *against*) offend. □□ **sin′ful** *adj.* **sin′**

ful·ly adv. **sin′ful·ness** n. **sin′less** adj. **sin′less·ly** adv. **sin′less·ness** n. **sin′ner** n.

sin[2] /sīn/ abbr. sine.

since /sins/ • prep. throughout or during the period after (must have happened since yesterday). • conj. 1 during or in the time after (has not spoken since the dog died). 2 because; inasmuch as. • adv. 1 from that time or event until now. 2 ago.

sin·cere /sinséer/ adj. (**sin·cer·er**, **sin·cer·est**) 1 free from pretense or deceit. 2 genuine; honest; frank. □□ **sin·cere′ly** adv. **sin·cer·i·ty** /–séritee/ n.

sine /sīn/ n. Math. ratio of the side opposite a given angle (in a right triangle) to the hypotenuse.

si·ne·cure /sínikyoor, sín–/ n. position that requires little or no work but usu. yields profit or honor.

si·ne qua non /sínay kwaa nón/ n. indispensable condition or qualification.

sin·ew /sínyoo/ n. 1 tough fibrous tissue uniting muscle to bone; tendon. 2 (in pl.) muscles; bodily strength; wiriness. □□ **sin′ew·less** adj. **sin′ew·y** adj.

sing /sing/ • v. (past **sang** /sang/; past part. **sung** /sung/) 1 intr. utter musical sounds, esp. words with a set tune. 2 tr. utter or produce by singing. 3 intr. (of the wind, a kettle, etc.) make humming, buzzing, or whistling sounds. 4 intr. sl. turn informer. • n. act or spell of singing. □□ **sing′a·ble** adj. **sing′er** n.

singe /sinj/ • v. (**singe·ing**) burn superficially or lightly. • n. superficial burn.

sin·gle /singgəl/ • adj. 1 one only. 2 united or undivided. 3 a designed or suitable for one person (single room). b used or done by one person, etc. 4 consisting of or involving only one part, fold, etc. 5 (foll. by out) choose as an example or as distinguishable or to serve some purpose. 2 intr. Baseball hit a single. □ **single-breasted** (of a coat, etc.) having only one set of buttons and buttonholes, not overlapping. **single file** line of people or things arranged one behind another. **single-handed** adv. 1 without help from another. 2 with one hand. • adj. 1 done, etc., single-handed. 2 for one hand. **single-handedly** in a single-handed way. **single-minded** having or intent on only one purpose. **single parent** person bringing up a child or children without a partner. □□ **sin′gle·ness** n. **sin′gly** adv.

sin·gle·ton /singgəltən/ n. 1 Cards one card only of a suit, esp. as dealt to a player. 2 single person or thing.

sing·song /síngsawng, –song/ • adj. uttered with a monotonous rhythm or cadence. • n. singsong manner. • v. (past and past part. **sing·songed**) speak or recite in a singsong manner.

sin·gu·lar /síngyələr/ • adj. 1 unique; much beyond the average; extraordinary. 2 eccentric or strange. 3 Gram. (of a word or form) denoting a single person or thing. • n. Gram. 1 singular word or form. 2 singular number. □□ **sin·gu·lar·i·ty** /–láritee/ n. (pl. **–ties**). **sin′gu·lar·ly** adv.

Sin·ha·lese /sínhəléez, sínə–/ (also **Sin·gha·lese**)

sin·is·ter /sínistər/ adj. 1 suggestive of evil; looking malignant or villainous. 2 wicked or criminal (a sinister motive). 3 ominous.

sink /singk/ • v.intr. (past **sank** /sangk/ or **sunk** /sungk/; past part. **sunk** or **sunk·en**) 1 fall or come slowly downward. 2 disappear below the horizon. 3 a go or penetrate below the surface esp. of a liquid. b (of a ship) go to the bottom of the sea, etc. 4 settle down comfortably (sank into a chair). 5 a gradually lose strength or value or quality, etc.; decline. b (of the voice) descend in pitch or volume. c (of a sick person) approach death. • n. 1 basin with a water supply and outflow pipe. 2 place where foul liquid collects. 3 place of vice or corruption. □ **sink in** 1 (also sink into) penetrate or make its way in. 2 become gradually comprehended. **sinking fund** money set aside for the gradual repayment of a debt. □□ **sink′a·ble** adj. **sink′age** n.

sink·er /síngkər/ n. 1 weight used to sink a fishing line or sounding line. 2 Baseball pitch that curves sharply downward.

Sino- /sínō/ comb. form Chinese; Chinese and (Sino-American).

sin·u·ous /sínyooəs/ adj. with many curves; tortuous; undulating. □□ **sin′u·ous·ly** adv. **sin′u·ous·ness** n.

si·nus /sínəs/ n. cavity of bone or tissue, esp. in the skull connecting with the nostrils.

si·nus·i·tis /sínəsítis/ n. inflammation of a nasal sinus.

-sion /shən, zhən/ suffix forming nouns (see -ION) from Latin participial stems in -s- (mansion; mission; persuasion).

Sioux /soo/ n. (pl. same) 1 a group of native N. American peoples. Also called **Dakota**. b member of these peoples. 2 language of this group. □□ **Siou·an** /sóoən/ adj. & n.

sip /sip/ • v. (**sipped**, **sip·ping**) drink in small amounts or by spoonfuls. • n. 1 small mouthful of liquid. 2 act of taking this. □□ **sip′per** n.

si·phon /sífən/ (also **sy′phon**) • n. 1 tube for conveying liquid from a container to a lower level by atmospheric pressure. 2 (in full **si′phon bot′tle**) aerated-water bottle from which liquid is forced out through a tube by the pressure of gas. • v. 1 conduct or flow through a siphon. 2 divert or set aside (funds, etc.). □□ **si′phon·age** n.

sir /sər/ n. 1 polite form of address or reference to a man. 2 (Sir) titular prefix to the forename of a knight or baronet.

sire /sīr/ • n. 1 male parent of an animal, esp. a stallion. 2 archaic respectful form of address, now esp. to a king. 3 archaic poet. father or male ancestor. • v.tr. (esp. of a stallion) beget.

si·ren /sírən/ n. 1 device for making a loud prolonged signal or warning sound. 2 Gk. mythol. woman or winged creature whose singing lured unwary sailors onto rocks. 3 dangerously fascinating woman; temptress.

sir·loin /sárloyn/ n. choicer part of a loin of beef.

si·roc·co /sirókō/ n. (pl. **–cos**) hot Saharan wind that blows over S. Europe.

sir·up var. of SYRUP.

sis /sis/ n. colloq. sister.

si·sal /sísəl/ *n.* **1** fiber made from a Mexican agave. **2** this plant.

sis·sy /sísee/ *colloq.* • *n.* (*pl.* **–sies**) effeminate or cowardly person. • *adj.* (**sis·si·er, sis·si·est**) effeminate; cowardly. □□ **sis′si·fied** *adj.* **sis′sy·ish** *adj.*

sis·ter /sístər/ *n.* **1** woman or girl in relation to sons and other daughters of her parents. **2 a** (often as a form of address) close female friend or associate. **b** female fellow member of a labor union, class, etc. **3** nun. **4** (*attrib.*) of the same type or design or origin, etc. □ **sister-in-law** (*pl.* **sisters-in-law**) **1** sister of one's spouse. **2** wife of one's brother. **3** wife of one's brother-in-law. □□ **sis′ter·hood** *n.* **sis′ter·less** *adj.* **sis′ter·ly** *adj.* **sis′ter·li·ness** *n.*

Sis·y·phe·an /sisiféeən/ *adj.* (of toil) endless and fruitless like that of Sisyphus in Greek mythology (whose task in Hades was to push uphill a stone that at once rolled down again).

sit /sit/ *v.* (**sit·ting**; *past* and *past part.* **sat** /sat/) **1** *intr.* rest the buttocks on the ground or a raised seat, etc., with the torso upright. **2** *tr.* cause to sit; place in a sitting position. **3** *intr.* **a** (of a bird) perch or remain on its nest to hatch its eggs. **b** (of an animal) rest with the hind legs bent and the body close to the ground. **4** *intr.* (of a committee, etc.) be in session. **5** *intr.* pose (for a portrait). **6** *intr.* act as a babysitter. □ **sit down 1** sit after standing. **2** cause to sit. **sit-down** *adj.* (of a meal) eaten sitting at a table. **sit-down strike** strike in which workers refuse to leave their place of work. **sit in 1** occupy a place as a protest. **2** (foll. by *for*) take the place of. **3** (foll. by *on*) be present as a guest or observer at (a meeting, etc.). **sit-in** *n.* protest involving sitting in. **sit out 1** take no part in (a dance, etc.). **2** stay till the end of (esp. an ordeal). **sit tight** *colloq.* remain firmly in one's place. **sit up 1** rise from a lying to a sitting position. **2** sit firmly upright. **3** go to bed later than the usual time. **sit-up** *n.* physical exercise in which a person sits up without raising the legs from the ground. □□ **sit′ter** *n.*
¶ See note at SET.

si·tar /sitaár, sítaar/ *n.* long-necked E. Indian lute with movable frets. □□ **si·tar·ist** /sitaárist/ *n.*

sit·com /sítkom/ *n. colloq.* situation comedy.

site /sīt/ • *n.* place; location. • *v.tr.* locate or place.

sit·ting /síting/ • *n.* **1** continuous period of being engaged in an activity (*finished the book in one sitting*). **2** session. **3** session in which a meal is served (*dinner will be served in two sittings*). • *adj.* **1** having sat down. **2** (of an animal or bird) not running or flying. **3** (of a hen) engaged in hatching. □ **sitting duck** (or **target**) *colloq.* vulnerable person or thing. **sitting room 1** living room. **2** space enough to accommodate seated persons.

sit·u·ate /síchoo-ayt/ *v.tr.* **1** put in a certain position or circumstances. **2** establish or indicate the place of; put in a context.
¶ See note at LOCATE.

sit·u·a·tion /síchoo-áyshən/ *n.* **1** place and its surroundings. **2** circumstances; position; state of affairs. **3** employee's job. □ **situation comedy** television comedy in which the humor derives from the situations the characters are placed in. □□ **sit·u·a′tion·al** *adj.*

six /siks/ *n.* **1** one more than five, or four less than ten. **2** symbol for this (6, vi, VI). □ **at**

sixes and sevens in confusion or disagreement.
six-gun = *six-shooter.* **six-pack** package of six cans or bottles, as of beer, soft drink, etc. **six-shooter** revolver with six chambers.

six·teen /síksteén/ *n.* **1** one more than fifteen, or six more than ten. **2** symbol for this (16, xvi, XVI). □□ **six′teenth** *adj. & n.*

sixth /siksth/ • *n.* **1** next after fifth. **2** each of six equal parts of a thing. • *adj.* that is the sixth. □ **sixth sense** supposed faculty giving intuitive or extrasensory knowledge.

six·ty /síkstee/ *n.* (*pl.* **–ties**) **1** six times ten. **2** symbol for this (60, lx, LX). **3** (in *pl.*) numbers from 60 to 69, esp. the years of a century or of a person's life. □□ **six′ti·eth** *adj. & n.* **six′ty·fold** *adj. & adv.*

siz·a·ble /sízəbəl/ *adj.* (also **size′a·ble**) large or fairly large. □□ **siz′a·bly** *adv.*

size[1] /sīz/ • *n.* **1** relative dimensions; magnitude. **2** each of the classes, usu. numbered, into which similar things are divided according to size. • *v.tr.* sort or group in sizes or according to size. □ **size up 1** estimate the size of. **2** *colloq.* form a judgment of. □□ **sized** *adj.* (also in *comb.*). **siz′er** *n.*

size[2] /sīz/ • *n.* gelatinous solution used in glazing paper, stiffening textiles, etc. • *v.tr.* glaze, stiffen, etc.

siz·zle /sízəl/ • *v.intr.* **1** sputter or hiss, esp. in frying. **2** *colloq.* be in a state of great heat or excitement, etc. • *n.* **1** sizzling sound. **2** *colloq.* state of great heat or excitement. □□ **siz′zler** *n.* **siz′zling** *adj. & adv.*

SJ *abbr.* Society of Jesus (Jesuit).

skate[1] /skayt/ • *n.* **1** metal blade, usu. attached to a boot, for gliding on ice. **2** (in full **roller skate**) metal frame with small wheels, fitted to shoes for riding on a hard surface. • *v.* **1** *intr.* move on skates. **2** *tr.* perform (a specified figure) on skates. □□ **skat′er** *n.*

skate[2] /skayt/ *n.* (*pl.* same or **skates**) large, flat, raylike marine fish used as food.

skate·board /skáytbawrd/ • *n.* short narrow board on roller-skate wheels for riding on while standing. • *v.intr.* ride on a skateboard. □□ **skate′board·er** *n.*

ske·dad·dle /skidád′l/ *colloq.* • *v.intr.* run away; depart quickly; flee. • *n.* hurried departure or flight.

skeet /skeet/ *n.* shooting sport in which a clay target is thrown from a trap to simulate the flight of a bird.

skein /skayn/ *n.* **1** loosely-coiled bundle of yarn or thread. **2** flock of wild geese, etc., in flight.

skel·e·ton /skélit′n/ *n.* **1 a** hard internal or external framework of bones, cartilage, woody fiber, etc., supporting or containing the body of an animal or plant. **b** dried bones of a human being or other animal fastened together in the same relative positions as in life. **2** supporting framework or structure of a thing. □ **skeleton key** key designed to fit many locks by having the interior of the bit hollowed. □□ **skel′e·tal** *adj.* **skel′e·tal·ly** *adv.* **skel′e·ton·ize** *v.tr.*

skep·tic /sképtik/ *n.* person inclined to doubt all accepted opinions; cynic. □□ **skep′ti·cal** *adj.* **skep′ti·cal·ly** *adv.* **skep·ti·cism** /–tisizəm/ *n.*

sketch /skech/ • *n.* **1** a rough or unfinished

drawing or painting. **2** rough draft or general outline. **3** very short play, usu. humorous and limited to one scene. • *v.* **1** *tr.* make or give a sketch of. **2** *intr.* draw sketches. **3** *tr.* (often foll. by *in, out*) indicate briefly or in outline.

sketch·y /skéchee/ *adj.* (**sketch·i·er, sketch·i·est**) **1** giving only a slight or rough outline, like a sketch. **2** *colloq.* unsubstantial or imperfect, esp. through haste. □□ **sketch′i·ly** *adv.* **sketch′i·ness** *n.*

skew /skyoo/ • *adj.* oblique; slanting. • *n.* slant. • *v.* **1** *tr.* make skew. **2** *tr.* distort. **3** *intr.* move obliquely.

skew·er /skyóōər/ • *n.* long pin designed for holding meat compactly together while cooking. • *v.tr.* fasten together or pierce with or as with a skewer.

ski /skee/ • *n.* (*pl.* **skis** or **ski**) **1** each of a pair of long narrow pieces of wood, etc., for traveling over snow. **2** = *water ski.* • *v.* (**skis, skied** /skeed/; **ski·ing**) **1** *intr.* travel on skis. **2** *tr.* ski at (a place). □ **ski lift** device for carrying skiers up a slope, usu. on seats hung from an overhead cable. □□ **ski′a·ble** *adj.* **ski′er** *n.*

skid /skid/ • *v.* (**skid·ded, skid·ding**) **1** *intr.* (of a vehicle, a wheel, or a driver) slide on slippery ground, esp. sideways or obliquely. **2** *tr.* cause (a vehicle, etc.) to skid. • *n.* **1** act or instance of skidding. **2** strong base for supporting heavy objects during moving. **3** braking device. **4** runner beneath an aircraft for use when landing. □ **on the skids** *colloq.* about to be discarded or defeated. **put the skids under** *colloq.* hasten the downfall or failure of. **skid row** *colloq.* part of a town frequented by vagrants, alcoholics, etc.

skiff /skif/ *n.* light rowboat or scull.

skill /skil/ *n.* expertness; practiced ability; facility in an action; dexterity or tact. □□ **skilled** *adj.* **skill′ful** *adj.* **skill′ful·ly** *adv.* **skill′ful·ness** *n.*

skil·let /skílit/ *n.* frying pan.

skim /skim/ • *v.* (**skimmed, skim·ming**) **1** *tr.* take a floating layer from the surface of (a liquid). **2** *tr.* **a** keep touching lightly or nearly touching (a surface) in passing over. **b** deal with or treat (a subject) superficially. **3** *intr.* go or glide lightly. **4 a** *tr.* read superficially; look over cursorily. **b** *intr.* read or look over cursorily. • *n.* act or instance of skimming. □ **skim** (or **skimmed**) **milk** milk from which the cream has been removed. □□ **skim′mer** *n.*

skimp /skimp/ • *v.tr.* be stingy. • *adj.* scanty.

skimp·y /skímpee/ *adj.* (**skimp·i·er, skimp·i·est**) meager; not ample or sufficient. □□ **skimp′i·ly** *adv.* **skimp′i·ness** *n.*

skin /skin/ • *n.* **1** flexible continuous covering of a human or other animal body. **2** skin of a flayed animal with or without the hair, etc. **3** outer layer or covering, esp. of a plant, fruit, or sausage. • *v.tr.* (**skinned, skin·ning**) **1** remove the skin from. **2** *sl.* fleece or swindle. □ **skin-deep** superficial; not deep or lasting. **skin diver** person who swims underwater without a diving suit, usu. with scuba, flippers, etc. □□ **skin′less** *adj.* **skin′like** *adj.* **skinned** *adj.* (also in *comb.*)

skin-flint /skínflint/ *n.* miserly person.

skin·head /skínhed/ *n.* youth with close-cropped hair, esp. one of an aggressive gang.

skin·ny /skínee/ *adj.* (**skin·ni·er, skin·ni·est**) thin

or emaciated. □ **skinny-dipping** *colloq.* swimming in the nude. □□ **skin′ni·ness** *n.*

skin·tight /skíntit/ *adj.* (of a garment) very close-fitting.

skip /skip/ • *v.* (**skipped, skip·ping**) **1** *intr.* **a** move along lightly, esp. with alternate hops. **b** jump lightly from the ground, esp. so as to clear a jump rope. **c** jump about; gambol. **2** *intr.* move quickly from one point, subject, etc., to another. **3** *tr.* omit in dealing with a series or in reading (*skip every tenth row*). **4** *tr. colloq.* not participate in. **5** *tr. colloq.* leave hurriedly. • *n.* **1** skipping movement or action. **2** *Computing* action of passing over part of a sequence of data or instructions.

skip·per /skípər/ • *n.* **1** sea captain, esp. the master of a small trading or fishing vessel. **2** captain of an aircraft. • *v.tr.* act as captain of.

skir·mish /skёrmish/ • *n.* minor battle. • *v.intr.* engage in a skirmish. □□ **skir′mish·er** *n.*

skirt /skərt/ • *n.* **1** woman's outer garment hanging from the waist. **2** part of a coat, etc., that hangs below the waist. • *v.tr.* **1** go along or around or past the edge of. **2** avoid. □□ **skirt′ed** *adj.* (also in *comb.*). **skirt′less** *adj.*

skit /skit/ *n.* light, usu. short, piece of satire or burlesque.

skit·tish /skítish/ *adj.* **1** lively; playful. **2** (of a horse, etc.) nervous; inclined to shy. □□ **skit′tish·ly** *adv.* **skit′tish·ness** *n.*

skiv·vy /skívee/ *n.* (*pl.* **–vies**) *sl.* (in *pl.*) men's underwear of T-shirt and shorts.

skul·dug·ger·y /skuldúggəree/ *n.* (also **skull·dug′ger·y**) trickery; unscrupulous behavior.

skulk /skulk/ *v.intr.* move stealthily, lurk, or keep oneself concealed. □□ **skulk′er** *n.*

skull /skul/ *n.* **1** bony case of the brain of a vertebrate. **2** the head as the seat of intelligence. □□ **skulled** *adj.* (also in *comb.*).

skull·cap /skúlkap/ *n.* small, close-fitting, peakless cap.

skunk /skunk/ • *n.* **1** black cat-sized mammal with white stripes on the back that emits a powerful stench as a defense. **2** *colloq.* thoroughly contemptible person. • *v.tr. sl.* defeat soundly.

sky /ski/ *n.* (*pl.* **skies**) (in *sing.* or *pl.*) atmosphere and outer space seen from the earth. □ **sky-high** *adv.* & *adj.* very high.

sky·box /skíboks/ *n.* elevated enclosure in a sports stadium containing plush seating, food services, and other amenities.

sky·cap /skíkap/ *n.* airport porter.

sky·div·ing /skídiving/ *n.* sport of performing acrobatic maneuvers under free fall with a parachute. □□ **sky′dive** *v.intr.* **sky′div′er** *n.*

sky·jack /skíjak/ *sl.* • *v.tr.* hijack (an aircraft). • *n.* act of skyjacking. □□ **sky′jack·er** *n.*

sky·light /skílit/ *n.* window in a roof or ceiling.

sky·line /skílin/ *n.* outline of buildings, etc., defined against the sky.

sky·rock·et /skírokkit/ • *n.* fireworks rocket. • *v.intr.* (esp. of prices, etc.) rise very rapidly.

sky·scrap·er /skískraypər/ *n.* very tall building.

sky·ward /skíwərd/ • *adv.* (also **sky·wards** /–wərdz/) toward the sky. • *adj.* moving skyward.

sky·writ·ing /skíriting/ *n.* writing traced in the sky by an airplane's smoke trails.

slab /slab/ • *n.* flat, broad, fairly thick piece of solid material. • *v.tr.* (**slabbed, slab·bing**) remove slabs from (a log or tree) to prepare it for sawing into planks.

slack /slak/ • *adj.* **1** (of rope, etc.) not taut. **2** inactive or sluggish. **3** negligent or remiss. **4** (of tide, etc.) neither ebbing nor flowing. • *n.* **1** slack part of a rope. **2** slack period. **3** (in *pl.*) informal trousers. • *v.* **1** *tr.* & *intr.* slacken. **2** *tr.* loosen (rope, etc.). □□ **slack′ly** *adv.* **slack′ness** *n.*

slack·en /slákən/ *v.* make or become slack.

slack·er /slákər/ *n.* shirker; indolent person.

slag /slag/ *n.* refuse left after smelting. □□ **slag′gy** *adj.* (**slag·gi·er, slag·gi·est**).

slain *past part.* of SLAY.

slake /slayk/ *v.tr.* **1** satisfy (thirst, desire, etc.). **2** disintegrate (quicklime) by combination with water.

sla·lom /slaáləm/ *n.* ski race down a zigzag obstacle course.

slam[1] /slam/ • *v.* (**slammed, slam·ming**) **1** *tr.* & *intr.* shut forcefully and loudly. **2** *intr.* move violently. **3** *tr. sl.* criticize severely. • *n.* sound or action of slamming.

slam[2] /slam/ *n. Cards* winning of every trick in a game. □ **grand slam 1** *Bridge* winning of 13 tricks. **2** winning of all of a group of championships or matches in a sport. **small** (or **little**) **slam** *Bridge* winning of 12 tricks.

slan·der /slándər/ • *n.* **1** malicious, false, and injurious statement spoken about a person. **2** uttering of such statements. • *v.tr.* utter slander about. □□ **slan′der·er** *n.* **slan′der·ous** *adj.* **slan′der·ous·ly** *adv.*

slang /slang/ *n.* words, phrases, and uses that are regarded as very informal or taboo or are peculiar to a specified profession, class, etc. (*racing slang*). □□ **slang′i·ly** *adv.* **slang′i·ness** *n.* **slang′y** *adj.* (**slang·i·er, slang·i·est**).

slant /slant/ • *v.* **1** *intr.* slope; lie or go at an angle. **2** *tr.* cause to do this. **3** *tr.* (often as **slanted** *adj.*) present (information), esp. in a biased or unfair way. • *n.* **1** slope; oblique position. **2** point of view, esp. a biased one. • *adj.* sloping; oblique.

slap /slap/ • *v.* (**slapped, slap·ping**) **1** *tr.* & *intr.* strike with the palm or a flat object, so as to make a similar noise. **2** *tr.* lay forcefully (*slapped the money on the table*). **3** *tr.* put hastily or carelessly. • *n.* **1** blow with the palm or a flat object. **2** rebuke; insult.

slap·dash /slápdash/ • *adj.* hasty and careless. • *adv.* in a slapdash manner.

slap·hap·py /sláp-hápee/ *adj. colloq.* **1** cheerfully casual or flippant. **2** punch-drunk.

slap·stick /slápstik/ *n.* **1** boisterous knockabout comedy. **2** flexible divided lath used by a clown.

slash /slash/ • *v.* **1** *intr.* make a sweeping cut or cuts with a knife, etc. **2** *tr.* make such a cut or cuts at. **3** *tr.* reduce (prices, etc.) drastically. • *n.* **1 a** slashing cut or stroke. **b** wound or slit made by this. **2** oblique stroke; solidus. □□ **slash′er** *n.*

slat /slat/ *n.* thin, narrow piece of wood, etc.

slate /slayt/ • *n.* **1** fine-grained, esp. bluish-gray, rock easily split into flat smooth plates. **2** piece of this used as roofing material or for writing on. **3** color of slate. **4** list of nominees for office, etc. • *v.tr.* **1** cover with slates esp. as roofing. **2** nominate for office, etc. • *adj.* made of slate. □□ **slat′y** *adj.*

slath·er /sláth̲ər/ *v.tr. colloq.* spread thickly.

slat·tern /slátərn/ *n.* slovenly woman.

slaugh·ter /sláwtər/ • *n.* **1** killing of animals for food. **2** killing of many people or animals at once or continuously; carnage; massacre. • *v.tr.* **1** kill (people) in a ruthless manner or on a great scale. **2** kill for food; butcher. □□ **slaugh′ter·er** *n.*

slaugh·ter·house /sláwtərhows/ *n.* **1** place for the slaughter of animals as food. **2** place of carnage.

Slav /slaav/ • *n.* member of a group of peoples in Central and Eastern Europe speaking Slavic languages. • *adj.* **1** of or relating to the Slavs. **2** Slavic. □□ **Slav′ism** *n.*

slave /slayv/ • *n.* **1** person who is the legal property of and has to serve another. **2** drudge; hard worker. **3** helpless victim of some dominating influence (*slave to duty*). • *v. intr.* work very hard. □ **slave driver 1** overseer of slaves. **2** person who works others hard. **slave trade** *hist.* dealing in slaves.

sla·ver[1] /sláyvər/ *n. hist.* ship or person engaged in the slave trade.

sla·ver[2] /slávər/ • *n.* **1** saliva running from the mouth. **2 a** fulsome or servile flattery. **b** drivel; nonsense. • *v.intr.* drool; dribble.

slav·er·y /sláyvəree, sláyvree/ *n.* **1** condition of a slave. **2** drudgery. **3** custom of having slaves.

Slav·ic /slaávik/ • *adj.* **1** of or relating to the group of Indo-European languages including Russian, Polish, and Czech. **2** of or relating to the Slavs. • *n.* Slavic language group.

slav·ish /sláyvish/ *adj.* **1** like slaves. **2** without originality. □□ **slav′ish·ly** *adv.* **slav′ish·ness** *n.*

slay /slay/ *v.tr.* (*past* **slew** /sloŏ/; *past part.* **slain** /slayn/) **1** *literary* or *joc.* kill. **2** *sl.* overwhelm, esp. with laughter. □□ **slay′er** *n.*

sleaze /sleez/ *colloq. n.* **1** sleaziness. **2** person of low moral standards.

slea·zy /sléezee/ *adj.* (**slea·zi·er, slea·zi·est**) **1** squalid; tawdry. **2** slatternly. **3** (of textiles, etc.) flimsy. □□ **slea′zi·ly** *adv.* **slea′zi·ness** *n.*

sled /sled/ • *n.* **1** vehicle on runners for use on snow. **2** toboggan. • *v.intr.* (**sled·ded, sled·ding**) ride on a sled.

sledge /slej/ • *n.* large, heavy sled. • *v.* travel or convey by sledge.

sledge·ham·mer /sléjhamər/ *n.* heavy, long-handled hammer used to break stone, etc.

sleek /sleek/ • *adj.* **1** (of hair, fur, skin, etc.) smooth and glossy. **2** looking well-fed and comfortable. • *v.tr.* make sleek, esp. by stroking or pressing down. □□ **sleek′ly** *adv.* **sleek′ness** *n.*

sleep /sleep/ • *n.* **1** naturally recurring condition of suspended consciousness, with the eyes closed and the muscles relaxed. **2** state like sleep, such as rest, quiet, etc. • *v.* (*past* and *past part.* **slept** /slept/) **1** *intr.* **a** be in a state of sleep. **b** fall asleep. **2** *tr.* provide sleeping accommodation for. **3** *intr.* have sexual intercourse (with). □ **put to sleep 1** anesthetize. **2** kill (an animal) mercifully. **sleeping bag** padded bag to sleep in esp. when camping, etc. **sleeping car** railroad car with berths; Pullman. **sleeping sickness** tropical disease causing extreme lethargy. □□ **sleep′less** *adj.* **sleep′less·ly** *adv.* **sleep′less·ness** *n.*

sleep·er /sléepər/ *n.* **1** person or animal that sleeps. **2** railroad tie or similar supporting beam. **3 a** sleeping car. **b** berth in this.

sleep·walk /sleepwawk/ *v.intr.* walk or perform other actions while asleep. □□ **sleep'walk·er** *n.* **sleep'walk·ing** *n.*

sleep·y /sleepee/ *adj.* (**sleep·i·er, sleep·i·est**) **1** drowsy; ready for sleep. **2** quiet; inactive. □□ **sleep'i·ly** *adv.* **sleep'i·ness** *n.*

sleet /sleet/ • *n.* snow and rain falling together. • *v.intr.* (prec. by *it* as subject) sleet falls (*it is sleeting*). □□ **sleet'y** *adj.*

sleeve /sleev/ *n.* **1** part of a garment that covers an arm. **2** cover of a phonograph record. **3** tube enclosing a rod or smaller tube. □ **up one's sleeve** concealed but in reserve. □□ **sleeved** *adj.* (also in *comb.*). **sleeve'less** *adj.*

sleigh /slay/ • *n.* = SLED. • *v.intr.* travel on a sleigh.

sleight /slīt/ *n.* □ **sleight of hand 1** dexterity, esp. in conjuring or fencing. **2** display of dexterity.

slen·der /sléndər/ *adj.* (**slen·der·er, slen·der·est**) **1 a** of small girth or breadth. **b** gracefully thin. **2** relatively small or scanty; inadequate. □□ **slen'der·ly** *adv.* **slen'der·ness** *n.*

slept *past* and *past part.* of SLEEP.

sleuth /slᵒᵒth/ *colloq. n.* detective.

slew¹ /slᵒᵒ/ (also **slue**) • *v.* turn or swing forcibly to a new position. • *n.* such a change of position.

slew² *past* of SLAY.

slew³ /slᵒᵒ/ *n. colloq.* large number or quantity.

slice /slīs/ • *n.* **1** thin piece or wedge cut off or out. **2** share; part. **3** *Golf & Tennis* slicing stroke. • *v.* **1** *tr.* cut into slices. **2** *tr.* cut (a piece) off. **3** *intr.* cut (as) with a knife. **4** *tr.* **a** *Golf* strike (the ball) so that it deviates away from the striker. **b** (in other sports) propel (the ball) forward at an angle. □□ **slice'a·ble** *adj.* **slic'er** *n.* (also in *comb.*).

slick /slik/ • *adj. colloq.* **1 a** skillful or efficient. **b** superficially or pretentiously smooth and dexterous. **c** glib. **2 a** sleek; smooth. **b** slippery. • *n.* patch of oil, etc., esp. on the sea. • *v.tr. colloq.* **1** make sleek or smart. **2** flatten (one's hair, etc.). □□ **slick'ly** *adv.* **slick'ness** *n.*

slick·er /slíkər/ *n.* **1** *colloq.* usu. *derog.* **a** plausible rogue. **b** (in full **city slicker**) smart and sophisticated city dweller. **2** raincoat of smooth material.

slide /slīd/ • *v.* (*past* and *past part.* **slid** /slid/) **1 a** *intr.* move along a smooth surface with continuous contact. **b** *tr.* cause to do this (*slide the drawer into place*). **2** *intr.* move quietly; glide. • *n.* **1 a** act or instance of sliding. **b** decline. **2** inclined plane down which children, goods, etc., slide. **3 a** piece of glass holding an object for a microscope. **b** mounted transparency viewed with a projector. □ **let things slide** be negligent; allow deterioration. **slide rule** ruler with a sliding central strip, graduated logarithmically for making rapid calculations. **sliding scale** scale of fees, taxes, wages, etc., that varies according to some standard. □□ **slid'er** *n.*

slight /slīt/ • *adj.* **1 a** inconsiderable; of little significance. **b** barely perceptible. **c** inadequate; scanty. **2** slender; frail-looking. • *v.tr.* treat disrespectfully; neglect. • *n.* failure to show due respect. □□ **slight'ing·ly** *adv.* **slight'ish** *adj.* **slight'ly** *adv.* **slight'ness** *n.*

slim /slim/ • *adj.* (**slim·mer, slim·mest**) **1 a** of

long, narrow shape. **b** gracefully thin. **2** slight; insufficient. • *v.* (**slimmed, slim·ming**) **1** *intr.* become slimmer by dieting, exercise, etc. **2** *tr.* make slim or slimmer. □□ **slim'ly** *adv.* **slim'mer** *n.* **slim'ming** *n. & adj.* **slim'mish** *adj.* **slim'ness** *n.*

slime /slīm/ • *n.* thick slippery or sticky substance. • *v.tr.* cover with slime. □□ **slim'i·ly** *adv.* **slim'i·ness** *n.* **slim'y** *adj.* (**slim·i·er, slim·i·est**).

sling /sling/ • *n.* **1** strap, etc., to support or raise a hanging weight. **2** bandage looped around the neck to support an injured arm. **3** straplike device for flinging a stone or other missile. • *v.tr.* (*past* and *past part.* **slung** /slung/) **1** *colloq.* throw. **2** suspend with a sling.

sling·shot /slíngshot/ *n.* forked stick, etc., with elastic for shooting stones, etc.

slink /slingk/ *v.intr.* (*past* and *past part.* **slunk** /slungk/) move in a stealthy or guilty manner.

slink·y /slíngkee/ *adj.* (**slink·i·er, slink·i·est**) **1** stealthy. **2** (of a garment) close-fitting and flowing; sinuous. **3** gracefully slender. □□ **slink'i·ly** *adv.* **slink'i·ness** *n.*

slip¹ /slip/ • *v.* (**slipped, slip·ping**) **1** *intr.* slide unintentionally, esp. for a short distance; lose one's footing or balance. **2** *intr.* go or move with a sliding motion. **3** *intr.* escape by being slippery or hard to hold. **4** *intr.* **a** go unobserved or quietly. **b** (foll. by *by*) (of time) go by rapidly or unnoticed. **5** *intr.* **a** make a careless or casual mistake. **b** fall below standard. **6** *tr.* (foll. by *on, off*) pull (a garment) hastily on or off. **7** *tr.* escape from; give the slip to. • *n.* **1** act or instance of slipping. **2** accidental or slight error. **3 a** petticoat. **b** pillowcase. **4** bay in a dock for mooring a vessel. □ **let slip** utter inadvertently. **slip-on** *adj.* (of shoes or clothes) that can be easily slipped on and off. • *n.* slip-on shoe or garment. **slipped disk** disk between vertebrae. **slip up** *colloq.* make a mistake.

slip² /slip/ *n.* **1** small piece of paper. **2** cutting taken from a plant for grafting or planting; scion. □ **slip of a** small and slim.

slip³ /slip/ *n.* clay in a creamy mixture with water, for decorating earthenware.

slip·cov·er /slípkəvər/ • *n.* **1** removable fabric covering for usu. upholstered furniture. **2** jacket or slipcase for a book. • *v.tr* cover with a slipcover.

slip·knot /slípnot/ *n.* knot that can be undone by a pull.

slip·page /slípij/ *n.* act, amount, or instance of slipping.

slip·per /slípər/ *n.* **1** light, loose, comfortable indoor shoe. **2** light slip-on shoe for dancing, etc.

slip·per·y /slípəree/ *adj.* **1** difficult to hold. **2** (of a surface) causing sliding or slipping by its smoothness or slickness. **3** unreliable; unscrupulous. □□ **slip'per·i·ness** *n.*

slip·shod /slípshod/ *adj.* **1** careless; unsystematic. **2** slovenly.

slip-up /slípəp/ *n.* mistake; blunder.

slit /slit/ • *n.* straight, narrow incision or opening. • *v.tr.* (**slit·ting**; *past* and *past part.* **slit**) **1** make a slit in. **2** cut into strips. □□ **slit'ter** *n.*

slith·er /slíthər/ • *v.intr.* slide unsteadily. • *n.* instance of slithering. □□ **slith'er·y** *adj.*

sli·ver /slívər/ • *n.* long, thin piece cut or split off; splinter. • *v.* **1** break off as a sliver. **2** break or form into slivers.

slob /slob/ *n. colloq.* lazy, untidy person. □□ **slob'bish** *adj.*

slob·ber /slóbər/ • *v.intr.* **1** slaver. **2** show excessive sentiment. • *n.* saliva running from the mouth; slaver. □□ **slob′ber·y** *adj.*

sloe /slō/ *n.* **1** = BLACKTHORN. **2** its small bluish-black fruit with a sharp sour taste.

slog /slog/ • *v.intr.* (**slogged, slog·ging**) walk or work doggedly. • *n.* hard steady work or walking. □□ **slog′ger** *n.*

slo·gan /slógən/ *n.* **1** short catchy phrase used in advertising, etc. **2** party cry; watchword or motto.

sloop /slo͞op/ *n.* one-masted, fore-and-aft-rigged vessel.

slop /slop/ • *v.* (**slopped, slop·ping**) **1** *intr.* spill or flow over the edge of a vessel. **2** *tr.* allow to do this. • *n.* **1** liquid spilled or splashed. **2** (in *pl.*) dirty waste water. **3** (in *sing.* or *pl.*) unappetizing, weak, liquid food.

slope /slōp/ • *n.* **1** inclined position, state, or direction. **2** piece of rising or falling ground. **3** difference in level between the two ends or sides of a thing. • *v.* **1** *intr.* have or take a slope; slant. **2** *tr.* cause to slope.

slop·py /slópee/ *adj.* (**slop·pi·er, slop·pi·est**) **1 a** (of the ground) full of puddles. **b** (of food, etc.) watery and disagreeable. **2** unsystematic; careless. **3** weakly emotional; maudlin. □□ **slop′pi·ly** *adv.* **slop′pi·ness** *n.*

slosh /slosh/ *v.* **1** *intr.* splash or flounder about; move with a splashing sound. **2** *tr. colloq.* pour (liquid) clumsily.

sloshed /slosht/ *adj. sl.* drunk.

slot /slot/ • *n.* **1** slit in a machine for a coin. **2** allotted place in an arrangement or schedule. • *v.* (**slot·ted, slot·ting**) **1** *tr.* & *intr.* place or be placed into or as if into a slot. **2** *tr.* provide with slots. □ **slot machine** gambling machine worked by the insertion of a coin in a slot.

sloth /slawth, slōth/ *n.* **1** laziness or indolence. **2** slow-moving nocturnal mammal of S. America that hangs upside down in trees. □□ **sloth′ful** *adj.* **sloth′ful·ly** *adv.* **sloth′ful·ness** *n.*

slouch /slowch/ • *v.intr.* stand, move, or sit in a drooping fashion. • *n.* **1** slouching posture or movement. **2** *sl.* incompetent or indifferent worker. □□ **slouch′y** *adj.* (**slouch·i·er, slouch·i·est**).

slough[1] /slow, slo͞o (for 2)/ *n.* **1** swamp; miry place. **2** marshy pond, backwater, etc. **3** state of hopeless depression.

slough[2] /sluf/ • *n.* **1** part that an animal casts or molts, esp. a snake's cast skin. **2** dead tissue that drops off from living flesh, etc. • *v.* **1** *tr.* cast off as a slough. **2** *intr.* (often foll. by *off*) drop off as a slough.

Slo·vak /slóvaak, –vak/ • *n.* **1** member of a Slavic people inhabiting Slovakia in central Europe, formerly part of Czechoslovakia and now an independent republic. **2** West Slavic language of this people. • *adj.* of or relating to this people or language.

slov·en /slúvən/ *n.* person who is habitually untidy or careless. □□ **slov′en·ly** *adj.* & *adv.* **slov′en·li·ness** *n.*

slow /slō/ • *adj.* **1 a** taking a relatively long time to do a thing. **b** not quick; acting or moving or done without speed. **2** gradual. **3** not conducive to speed. **4** (of a clock, etc.) showing a time earlier than is the case. **5** (of a person)

565   slobber ~ sly

not understanding or learning readily. **6** slack or sluggish. **7** *Photog.* (of a film) needing long exposure. • *adv.* (often in *comb.*) slowly (*slow-moving traffic*). • *v.* (usu. foll. by *down, up*) **1** *intr.* & *tr.* reduce one's speed or the speed of (a vehicle, etc.). **2** *intr.* reduce one's pace of life. □ **slow motion** speed of a film in which actions, etc., appear much slower than usual. □□ **slow′ish** *adj.* **slow′ly** *adv.* **slow′ness** *n.*

slow·down /slódown/ *n.* deliberate slowing down of productivity.

SLR *abbr. Photog.* single-lens reflex.

sludge /sluj/ *n.* **1** thick, greasy mud or sediment. **2** sewage. □□ **sludg′y** *adj.*

slue var. of SLEW[1].

slug[1] /slug/ *n.* **1** small shell-less mollusk destructive to plants. **2 a** bullet. **b** missile for an airgun. **3** shot of liquor. **4** counterfeit coin.

slug[2] /slug/ • *v.tr.* (**slugged, slug·ging**) strike with a hard blow. • *n.* hard blow. □□ **slug′ger** *n.*

slug·gard /slúgərd/ *n.* lazy, sluggish person. □□ **slug′gard·ly** *adj.* **slug′gard·li·ness** *n.*

slug·gish /slúgish/ *adj.* slow-moving; indolent. □□ **slug′gish·ly** *adv.* **slug′gish·ness** *n.*

sluice /slo͞os/ • *n.* **1** (also **sluice gate, sluice valve**) sliding gate, etc., for controlling the flow of water, etc. **2** water so regulated. **3** artificial channel with a sluice gate, esp. one for washing ore. **4** act or instance of rinsing. • *v.tr.* **1** provide or wash with a sluice or sluices. **2** rinse, pour, or throw water freely upon.

slum /slum/ • *n.* **1** overcrowded and squalid back street, district, etc., usu. in a city. **2** house or building unfit for human habitation. • *v.intr.* (**slummed, slum·ming**) **1** live in slumlike conditions. **2** visit slums, as out of curiosity. □□ **slum′my** *adj.* (**slum·mi·er, slum·mi·est**). **slum′mi·ness** *n.*

slum·ber /slúmbər/ *poet. rhet. v.* & *n.* sleep. □□ **slum′ber·er** *n.* **slum′ber·ous** *adj.*

slump /slump/ • *n.* sudden fall in prices and trade. • *v.intr.* **1** undergo a slump; fail. **2** sit or fall heavily or limply. **3** lean or subside.

slung *past* and *past part.* of SLING.

slunk *past* and *past part.* of SLINK.

slur /slər/ • *v.* (**slurred, slur·ring**) **1** *tr.* & *intr.* pronounce indistinctly so that the sounds run into one another. **2** *tr. Mus.* **a** perform (notes) legato. **b** mark (notes) with a slur. **3** *tr.* put a slur on (a person or a person's character). **4** *tr.* (usu. foll. by *over*) pass over (a fact, fault, etc.) lightly. • *n.* **1** imputation of wrongdoing. **2** act or instance of slurring. **3** *Mus.* curved line joining notes to be slurred.

slurp /slərp/ • *v.tr.* eat or drink noisily. • *n.* sound of this.

slur·ry /slúree/ *n.* (*pl.* **–ries**) thin, semiliquid mud, cement, etc.

slush /slush/ *n.* **1** thawing, muddy snow. **2** silly sentiment. □ **slush fund** reserve fund, esp. for political bribery. □□ **slush′y** *adj.* (**slush·i·er, slush·i·est**). **slush′i·ness** *n.*

slut /slut/ *n. derog.* **1** slovenly woman. **2** prostitute. □□ **slut′tish** *adj.* **slut′tish·ness** *n.*

sly /slī/ *adj.* (**sli·er, sli·est** or **sly·er, sly·est**) **1** cunning; crafty; wily. **2 a** (of a person) practicing secrecy or stealth. **b** (of an action, etc.) done, etc., in secret. **3** mischievous; knowing; insinuating. □ **on the sly** secretly; covertly. □□ **sly′ly** *adv.* (also **sli•ly**). **sly′ness** *n.*

smack[1] /smak/ • *n.* **1** sharp slap or blow. **2** hard hit in baseball, etc. **3** loud kiss. **4** loud, sharp sound. • *v.* **1** *tr.* slap. **2** *tr.* part (one's lips) noisily in eager anticipation of food. **3** *tr.* & *intr.* move, hit, etc., with a smack. • *adv. colloq.* **1** with a smack. **2** suddenly; directly; violently. **3** exactly.

smack[2] /smak/ • *v.intr.* **1** have a flavor of; taste of. **2** suggest the presence or effects of. • *n.* **1** flavor. **2** barely discernible quality.

smack[3] /smak/ *n.* single-masted sailboat.

smack[4] /smak/ *n. sl.* heroin.

smack•er /smákər/ *n. sl.* **1** loud kiss. **2** resounding blow. **3** (usu. *pl.*) *sl.* dollar bill.

small /smawl/ • *adj.* **1** not large or big. **2** slender; thin. **3** not great in importance, amount, number, strength, or power. **4** petty; mean. **5** young. • *n.* slenderest part of something (esp. small of the back). • *adv.* into small pieces. □ **feel** (or **look**) **small** be humiliated. **small arms** portable firearms. **small fry** *colloq.* **1** young child or children. **2** insignificant things or people. **small print** inconspicuous and usu. unfavorable limitations, etc., in a contract. **small talk** light social conversation. **small-time** *colloq.* unimportant or petty. □□ **small′ish** *adj.* **small′ness** *n.*

small-mind•ed /smáwlmíndid/ *adj.* petty; narrow in outlook. □□ **small′-mind′ed•ly** *adv.* **small′-mind′ed•ness** *n.*

small•pox /smáwlpoks/ *n. hist.* acute contagious viral disease, with fever and pustules, usu. leaving permanent scars.

smart /smaart/ • *adj.* **1** clever; ingenious; quick-witted. **2** well-groomed; neat. **3** in good repair. **4** stylish; fashionable. **5** quick; brisk. **6** painfully severe. • *v.intr.* **1** feel or give pain. **2** (of an insult, grievance, etc.) rankle. **3** (foll. by *for*) suffer the consequences of. • *n.* sharp pain. • *adv.* smartly; in a smart manner. □ **smart aleck** *colloq.* person displaying ostentatious or smug cleverness. **smart-ass** *sl.* = SMART ALECK. **smart bomb** bomb that can be guided directly to its target by use of radio waves, television, or lasers. □□ **smart′ing•ly** *adv.* **smart′ly** *adv.* **smart′ness** *n.*

smart•en /smaárt'n/ *v.* make or become smart.

smash /smash/ • *v.* **1** *tr.* & *intr.* **a** break into pieces; shatter. **b** bring or come to sudden destruction, defeat, or disaster. **2** *tr.* move with great force and impact. **3** *tr.* (as **smashed** *adj.*) *sl.* intoxicated. • *n.* **1** act or instance of smashing; violent fall, collision, or disaster. **2** sound of this. **3** (in full **smash hit**) very successful play, song, performer, etc.

smash•ing /smáshing/ *adj. colloq.* superlative; excellent; wonderful; beautiful. □□ **smash′ing•ly** *adv.*

smash•up /smáshəp/ *n. colloq.* violent collision.

smear /smeer/ • *v.tr.* **1** daub or mark with a greasy or sticky substance. **2** smudge. **3** defame; slander. • *n.* **1** act or instance of smearing. **2** *Med.* **a** material smeared on a microscopic slide, etc., for examination. **b** specimen taken from this. □□ **smear′er** *n.* **smear′y** *adj.* (**smear•i•er, smear•i•est**).

smell /smel/ • *n.* **1** faculty of perceiving odors. **2** quality perceived by this. **3** unpleasant odor.

4 act of inhaling to ascertain smell. • *v.* (*past* and *past part.* **smelled** or **smelt** /smelt/) **1** *tr.* perceive or examine by smell. **2** *intr.* emit odor. **3** *tr.* perceive; detect. **4** *intr.* have or use a sense of smell. □ **smelling salts** ammonium carbonate mixed with scent to be sniffed as a restorative in faintness, etc. □□ **smell′a•ble** *adj.* **smell′er** *n.* **smell′-less** *adj.*

smell•y /smélee/ *adj.* (**smell•i•er, smell•i•est**) having a strong or unpleasant smell. □□ **smell′i•ness** *n.*

smelt[1] /smelt/ *v.tr.* **1** separate metal from (ore) by melting. **2** extract or refine (metal) in this way. □□ **smelt′er** *n.*

smelt[2] *past* and *past part.* of SMELL.

smelt[3] /smelt/ *n.* (*pl.* same or **smelts**) small edible green and silver fish.

smid•gen /smíjən/ *n.* (also **smid′gin**) *colloq.* small bit.

smile /smīl/ • *v.* **1** *intr.* relax the features into a pleased or kind or gently skeptical expression, with the lips parted and the corners of the mouth turned up. **2** *tr.* express by smiling (*smiled their consent*). **3** (foll. by *on, upon*) encourage. • *n.* **1** act or instance of smiling. **2** smiling expression or aspect. □□ **smile′less** *adj.* **smil′er** *n.* **smil′ing•ly** *adv.*

smirch /smərch/ • *v.tr.* mark, soil, or discredit. • *n.* spot or stain.

smirk /smərk/ • *n.* affected, conceited, or silly smile. • *v.intr.* make such a smile. □□ **smirk′er** *n.* **smirk′ing•ly** *adv.* **smirk′y** *adj.* **smirk′i•ly** *adv.*

smite /smīt/ *v.tr.* (*past* **smote** /smōt/; *past part.* **smit•ten** /smit'n/) *archaic* or *literary* **1** hit. **2** chastise; defeat. **3** (in *passive*) **a** have a sudden strong effect on. **b** infatuate; fascinate. □□ **smit′er** *n.*

smith /smith/ • *n.* **1** (esp. in *comb.*) worker in metal (*goldsmith*). **2** blacksmith. • *v.tr.* make or treat by forging.

smith•er•eens /smíthəreenz/ *n.pl.* small fragments (*smash into smithereens*).

smith•y /smíthee/ *n.* (*pl.* –**ies**) blacksmith's workshop; forge.

smit•ten *past part.* of SMITE.

smock /smok/ • *n.* loose shirtlike garment for protecting the clothing. • *v.tr.* adorn with smocking.

smock•ing /smóking/ *n.* ornamental effect on cloth made by gathering the material tightly and embroidering in a decorative pattern.

smog /smog, smawg/ *n.* fog intensified by smoke. □□ **smog′gy** *adj.* (**smog•gi•er, smog•gi•est**).

smoke /smōk/ • *n.* **1** visible vapor from a burning substance. **2** act of smoking tobacco. **3** *colloq.* cigarette or cigar. • *v.* **1** *intr.* emit smoke or visible vapor. **2** *tr.* **a** inhale and exhale the smoke of a cigarette, etc. **b** *intr.* do this habitually. **3** *tr.* preserve by the action of smoke. □ **smoke out** drive out by means of smoke. **smoke screen 1** cloud of smoke diffused to conceal (esp. military) operations. **2** ruse for disguising one's activities. □□ **smok′a•ble** *adj.* (also **smoke′a•ble**). **smoke′less** *adj.* **smok′er** *n.* **smok′i•ly** *adv.* **smok′i•ness** *n.* **smok′y** *adj.* (**smok•i•er, smok•i•est**)

smoke•stack /smókstak/ *n.* chimney.

smol•der /smóldər/ • *v.intr.* **1** burn slowly without a flame. **2** (of emotions, etc.) exist in a suppressed state. **3** (of a person) show silent anger, hatred, etc. • *n.* smoldering fire.

smooch /smōoch/ *colloq.* • *n.* kiss. • *v.intr.* kiss.

□□ **smooch′er** *n.* **smooch′y** *adj.* (**smooch·i·er,** **smooch·i·est**).

567   **smooth ~ sneer**

smooth /smo͞oth/ • *adj.* **1** having an even and regular surface. **2** not wrinkled, pitted, scored, or hairy. **3** (of a journey, etc.) untroubled by difficulties. **4** suave; conciliatory. **5** (of movement, etc.) not suddenly varying; not jerky. • *v.* **1** *tr.* & *intr.* make or become smooth. **2 a** *tr.* reduce or get rid of (differences, faults, difficulties, etc.). **b** *intr.* (of difficulties, etc.) become less obtrusive. • *n.* **1** smoothing touch or stroke. **2** easy part of life (*take the rough with the smooth*). • *adv.* smoothly. □ **smooth-tongued** insincerely flattering. □□ **smooth′a·ble** *adj.* **smooth′er** *n.* **smooth′ish** *adj.* **smooth′ly** *adv.* **smooth′ness** *n.*

smooth·ie /smo͞othee/ *n. colloq.* person who is smooth (see SMOOTH *adj.* 4).

smor·gas·bord /smáwrgəsbawrd/ *n.* buffet offering a variety of hot and cold meats, salads, hors d'oeuvres, etc.

smote *past* of SMITE.

smoth·er /smúthər/ *v.tr.* **1** suffocate; stifle. **2** overwhelm with (kisses, kindness, etc.). **3** cover entirely in or with. **4** extinguish (a fire) by covering it.

smudge /smuj/ • *n.* **1** blurred or smeared spot, stain or mark; blot. **2** stain or blot on a person's character, etc. • *v.* **1** *tr.* make a smudge on. **2** *intr.* become smeared or blurred. **3** *tr.* smear or blur the lines of (writing, drawing, etc.). □□ **smudge′less** *adj.* **smudg′i·ly** *adv.* **smudg′i·ness** *n.* **smudg′y** *adj.* (**smudg·i·er, smudg·i·est**).

smug /smug/ *adj.* (**smug·ger, smug·gest**) self-satisfied; complacent. □□ **smug′ly** *adv.* **smug′ness** *n.*

smug·gle /smúgəl/ *v.tr.* **1** import or export (goods) illegally, esp. without payment of customs duties. **2** convey secretly. **3** (foll. by *away*) put into concealment; hide. □□ **smug′gler** *n.* **smug′gling** *n.*

smut /smut/ *n.* **1** small flake of soot, etc. **2** spot or smudge made by this. **3** obscene or lascivious talk, pictures, or stories. **4** fungal disease of cereals. □□ **smut′ty** *adj.* (**smut·ti·er, smut·ti·est**) (esp. in sense 3 of *n.*). **smut′ti·ly** *adv.* **smut′ti·ness** *n.*

Sn *symb. Chem.* tin.

snack /snak/ • *n.* **1** light, casual, or hurried meal. **2** small amount of food eaten between meals. • *v.intr.* eat a snack. □ **snack bar** place where snacks are sold.

snaf·fle /snáfəl/ • *n.* (in full **snaf′fle bit**) bridle bit without a curb. • *v.tr.* put a snaffle on.

snag /snag/ • *n.* **1** unexpected obstacle or drawback. **2** jagged or projecting point. **3** tear in material, etc. • *v.tr.* (**snagged, snag·ging**) catch or tear on a snag. □□ **snagged** *adj.* **snag′gy** *adj.*

snail /snayl/ *n.* slow-moving mollusk with a spiral shell. □□ **snail′like** *adj.*

snake /snayk/ • *n.* **1 a** long, limbless reptile. **b** limbless lizard or amphibian. **2** (also **snake in the grass**) treacherous person or secret enemy. **3** plumber's snakelike device for clearing obstructed pipes. • *v.intr.* move or twist like a snake. □ **snake charmer** person appearing to make snakes move by music, etc. □□ **snake′like** *adj.*

snak·y /snáykee/ *adj.* **1** of or like a snake. **2** winding; sinuous. **3** showing coldness, ingratitude, treachery, or guile. □□ **snak′i·ly** *adv.* **snak′i·ness** *n.*

snap /snap/ • *v.* (**snapped, snap·ping**) **1** *intr.* & *tr.* break suddenly or with a snap. **2** *intr.* & *tr.* emit or cause to emit a sudden sharp crack. **3 a** *intr.* (often foll. by *at*) speak irritably or spitefully (to a person). **b** *tr.* say irritably or spitefully. **4** *intr.* (often foll. by *at*) (esp. of a dog, etc.) make a sudden audible bite. **5** *tr.* & *intr.* move quickly. **6** *tr.* take a snapshot of. **7** *tr.* *Football* put (the ball) into play on the ground by a quick backward movement. • *n.* **1** act or sound of snapping. **2** (often in *comb.*) crisp cookie (*gingersnap*). **3** snapshot. **4** (in full **cold snap**) sudden brief spell of cold weather. **5** vigor or liveliness; zest. **6** *sl.* easy task (*it was a snap*). **7** fastener for clothing, etc., that closes with a snapping sound. **8** *Football* beginning of a play, when the ball is passed quickly back. • *adv.* with the sound of a snap. • *adj.* made or done on the spur of the moment. □□ **snap′pa·ble** *adj.* **snap′per** *n.* **snap′ping·ly** *adv.* **snap′pish** *adj.*

snap·drag·on /snápdragən/ *n.* plant with a bag-shaped flower like a dragon's mouth.

snap·py /snápee/ *adj.* (**snap·pi·er, snap·pi·est**) *colloq.* **1** brisk; full of zest. **2** neat and elegant. **3** irritable; ill-tempered. □ **make it snappy** be quick. □□ **snap′pi·ly** *adv.* **snap′pi·ness** *n.*

snap·shot /snápshot/ *n.* casual photograph.

snare /snair/ • *n.* **1** trap for catching birds or animals. **2** trick or temptation. **3** (in *sing.* or *pl.*) *Mus.* twisted strings of gut, hide, or wire stretched across the lower head of a snare drum. **4** (in full **snare drum**) small, double-headed drum fitted with snares. • *v.tr.* **1** catch (a bird, etc.) in a snare. **2** ensnare; lure or trap (a person). □□ **snar′er** *n.* (also in *comb.*).

snarl¹ /snaarl/ • *v.intr.* **1** (of a dog) growl with bared teeth. **2** (of a person) speak cynically or angrily. • *n.* act or sound of snarling. □□ **snarl′er** *n.* **snarl′ing·ly** *adv.* **snarl′y** *adj.* (**snarl·i·er, snarl·i·est**).

snarl² /snaarl/ • *v.* **1** *tr.* twist; entangle; hamper the movement of (traffic, etc.). **2** *intr.* become entangled, congested, or confused. • *n.* knot or tangle.

snatch /snach/ • *v.tr.* **1** seize quickly, eagerly, or unexpectedly. **2** steal (a wallet, handbag, etc.) by grabbing. **3** *sl.* kidnap. **4** (foll. by *at*) **a** try to seize. **b** take (an offer, etc.) eagerly. • *n.* **1** act of snatching. **2** fragment. **3** short spell of activity, etc. □□ **snatch′er** *n.* (esp. in sense 3 of *n.*).

snaz·zy /snázee/ *adj.* (**snaz·zi·er, snaz·zi·est**) *sl.* smart or attractive, esp. in an ostentatious way. □□ **snaz′zi·ly** *adv.* **snaz′zi·ness** *n.*

sneak /sneek/ • *v.* **1** *intr.* & *tr.* go or convey furtively; slink. **2** *tr. sl.* steal unobserved; make off with. **3** *intr.* (as **sneaking** *adj.*) **a** furtive; undisclosed. **b** troubling. • *n.* mean-spirited, underhanded person. • *adj.* acting or done without warning; secret. □□ **sneak′i·ly** *adv.* **sneak′ing·ly** *adv.* **sneak′i·ness** *n.* **sneak′y** *adj.* (**sneak·i·er, sneak·i·est**).

sneak·er /sne͞ekər/ *n.* rubber-soled shoe for sport or casual wear.

sneer /sneer/ • *n.* derisive smile or remark. • *v.* **1** *intr.* smile derisively. **2** *tr.* say sneeringly. **3** *intr.* (often foll. by *at*) comment on derisively, esp. covertly or ironically. □□ **sneer′er** *n.* **sneer′ing·ly** *adv.*

sneeze /sneez/ • *n.* **1** sudden involuntary expulsion of air from the nose and mouth. **2** sound of this. • *v.intr.* make a sneeze. □ **not to be sneezed at** considerable; notable. □□ **sneez′er** *n.* **sneez′y** *adj.*

snick·er /sníkər/ *v.* & *n.* = SNIGGER *v.* □□ **snick′er·ing·ly** *adv.*

snide /snīd/ *adj.* **1** sneering; slyly derogatory. **2** mean; underhanded. □□ **snide′ly** *adv.* **snide′ness** *n.*

sniff /snif/ • *v.* **1** *intr.* draw up air audibly through the nose. **2** *tr.* (often foll. by *up*) draw in (a scent, drug, liquid, or air) through the nose. **3** *tr.* draw in the scent of (food, flowers, etc.) through the nose. • *n.* **1** act or sound of sniffing. **2** amount sniffed up. □ **sniff at 1** try the smell of; show interest in. **2** show contempt for. **sniff out** detect. □□ **sniff′er** *n.* **sniff′ing·ly** *adv.*

snif·fle /snífəl/ • *v.intr.* sniff slightly or repeatedly. • *n.* **1** act of sniffling. **2** (in *sing.* or *pl.*) cold in the head causing a running nose and sniffling. □□ **snif′fler** *n.* **sniff′ly** *adj.*

snif·ter /sníftər/ *n.* **1** balloon glass for brandy. **2** *sl.* small drink of alcohol.

SNIFTER

snig·ger /snígər/ • *n.* half-suppressed secretive laugh. • *v.intr.* utter such a laugh. □□ **snig′ger·er** *n.* **snig′ger·ing·ly** *adv.*

snip /snip/ • *v.tr.* (**snipped, snip·ping**) cut with scissors, esp. in small, quick strokes. • *n.* **1** act of snipping. **2** piece snipped off. **3** *sl.* something easily achieved. **4** (in *pl.*) hand shears for metal cutting (*tin snips*). □□ **snip′ping** *n.*

snipe /snīp/ • *n.* (*pl.* same or **snipes**) wading bird with a long, straight bill. • *v.* **1** *intr.* fire shots from hiding, usu. at long range. **2** *tr.* kill by sniping. **3** *intr.* (foll. by *at*) make a sly critical attack. □□ **snip′er** *n.*

snip·pet /snípit/ *n.* **1** small piece cut off. **2** (usu. in *pl.*; often foll. by *of*) scrap or fragment (of information).

snip·py /snípee/ *adj.* (**snip·pi·er, snip·pi·est**) (also **snip′pet·y**) *colloq.* faultfinding and snappish. □□ **snippily** *adv.* **snippiness** *n.*

snit /snit/ *n.* rage; sulk.

snitch /snich/ *sl.* • *v.* **1** *tr.* steal. **2** *intr.* inform on a person. • *n.* informer.

sniv·el /snívəl/ • *v.intr.* **1** weep with sniffling. **2** run at the nose. **3** show weak or tearful sentiment. • *n.* **1** running mucus. **2** hypocritical talk; cant. □□ **sniv′el·er** *n.* **sniv′el·ing** *adj.* **sniv′el·ing·ly** *adv.*

snob /snob/ *n.* **1** person who despises those considered socially, intellectually, etc., inferior. **2** person who behaves with servility to social superiors. □□ **snob′ber·y** *n.* (*pl.* **-ies**). **snob′bish** *adj.* **snob′bish·ly** *adv.* **snob′bish·ness** *n.* **snob′by** *adj.* (**snob·bi·er, snob·bi·est**).

snood /snōod/ *n.* ornamental hairnet usu. worn at the back of the head.

snooker /snōokər, snŏok-/ • *n.* a game similar to pool in which the players use a cue ball (white) to pocket the other balls (15 red and 6 colored) in a set order. • *v.tr.* (esp. as **snookered** *adj.*) *sl.* defeat;thwart.

snoop /snōop/ *colloq.* • *v.intr.* pry. • *n.* **1** act of snooping. **2** person who snoops; detective. □□ **snoop′er** *n.* **snoop′y** *adj.*

snoot /snōot/ *n. sl.* the nose.

snooze /snōoz/ *colloq.* • *n.* short sleep, esp. in the daytime. • *v.intr.* take a snooze. □□ **snooz′er** *n.* **snooz′y** *adj.* (**snooz·i·er, snooz·i·est**).

snore /snawr/ • *n.* snorting or grunting sound in breathing during sleep. • *v.intr.* make this sound. □□ **snor′er** *n.*

SNORKEL, 1

snor·kel /snáwrkəl/ • *n.* **1** breathing tube for an underwater swimmer. **2** device for supplying air to a submerged submarine. • *v.intr.* use a snorkel. □□ **snor′kel·er** *n.*

snort /snawrt/ • *n.* **1** explosive sound made by the sudden forcing of breath through the nose. **2** *colloq.* small drink of liquor. **3** *sl.* inhaled dose of a (usu. illegal) powdered drug. • *v.* **1** *intr.* make a snort. **2** *tr. sl.* inhale (esp. cocaine or heroin). **3** *tr.* express (defiance, etc.) by snorting.

snot /snot/ *n. sl.* **1** nasal mucus. **2** term of contempt.

snot·ty /snótee/ *adj.* (**snot·ti·er, snot·ti·est**) *sl.* **1** running or foul with nasal mucus. **2** *colloq.* contemptible. **3** *colloq.* supercilious; conceited. □□ **snot′ti·ly** *adv.* **snot′ti·ness** *n.*

snout /snowt/ *n.* **1** projecting nose and mouth of an animal. **2** *derog.* person's nose. □□ **snout′ed** *adj.* (also in *comb.*). **snout′like** *adj.* **snout′y** *adj.*

snow /snō/ • *n.* **1** frozen atmospheric vapor falling to earth in light white flakes. **2** fall or layer of this. **3** *sl.* cocaine. • *v.* **1** *intr.* (prec. by *it* as subject) fall as snow (*it is snowing*). **2** *tr. sl.* deceive or charm with plausible words. □ **be snowed under** be overwhelmed, esp. with work. □□ **snow′less** *adj.* **snow′like** *adj.*

snow·ball /snóbawl/ • *n.* **1** snow pressed together into a ball, esp. for throwing in play. **2** anything that increases rapidly like a snowball rolled on snow. • *v.* **1** *intr.* & *tr.* throw or pelt with snowballs. **2** *intr.* increase rapidly.

snow·blow·er /snóblōər/ *n.* machine that clears snow by blowing it to the side of the road, etc.

snow·board /snṓbawrd/ *n.* board similar to a wide ski, ridden over snow in an upright or surfing position. □□ **snow′board·er** *n.*

snow·bound /snṓbownd/ *adj.* prevented by snow from going out or traveling.

snow·drift /snṓdrift/ *n.* bank of snow heaped up by the action of the wind.

snow·drop /snṓdrop/ *n.* bulbous plant with white drooping flowers in the early spring.

snow·fall /snṓfawl/ *n.* **1** fall of snow. **2** *Meteorol.* amount of snow that falls on one occasion.

snow·flake /snṓflayk/ *n.* each of the flakes of ice crystals in which snow falls.

snow·man /snṓman/ *n.* (*pl.* **-men**) figure resembling a human, made of compressed snow.

snow·mo·bile /snṓməbeel, –mō–/ *n.* motor vehicle, esp. with runners or revolving treads, for traveling over snow.

snow·plow /snṓplow/ *n.* device, or a vehicle equipped with one, for clearing roads of thick snow.

snow·shoe /snṓshoo/ *n.* racket-shaped attachment to a boot for walking on snow without sinking in. □□ **snow·sho′er** *n.*

SNOWSHOES

snow·storm /snṓstawrm/ *n.* heavy fall of snow, esp. with a high wind.

snow·y /snṓee/ *adj.* (**snow·i·er, snow·i·est**) **1** of or like snow. **2** with much snow. □□ **snow′i·ly** *adv.*

snub /snub/ • *v.tr.* (**snubbed, snub·bing**) rebuff or humiliate. • *n.* act of snubbing; rebuff. • *adj.* short and blunt in shape. □□ **snub′ber** *n.*

snuff¹ /snuf/ • *n.* charred part of a candlewick. • *v.tr.* trim the snuff from (a candle). □ **snuff out 1** extinguish by snuffing. **2** kill; put an end to.

snuff² /snuf/ *n.* powdered tobacco or medicine taken by sniffing. □ **up to snuff** *colloq.* up to standard.

snuff·box /snúfboks/ *n.* small box for holding snuff.

snug /snug/ *adj.* (**snug·ger, snug·gest**) **1** cozy; comfortable; sheltered. **2** close-fitting. □□ **snug′ly** *adv.* **snug′ness** *n.*

snug·gle /snúgəl/ *v.* (usu. foll. by *down, up, together*) settle or draw into a warm comfortable position.

so¹ /sō/ • *adv.* **1** to such an extent. **2** (foll. by *that* or *as* + clause) to the degree or in the manner implied (*so expensive that few can afford it*). **3** (adding emphasis) to that extent; in that or a similar manner (*I want to leave and so does she*). **4** very (*I am so glad*). **5** (with verb of saying or thinking, etc.) as previously mentioned or described (*I think so*). • *conj.* **1** with the result that (*there was none left, so we had to go without*). **2** in order that (*came home early so that I could see you*). **3** and then; as the next step. □ **and so on** (or **forth**) **1** and others of the same kind. **2** and in other similar ways. **so as to** in order to. **so-called** commonly designated or known as, often incorrectly. **so long!** *colloq.* good-bye. **so-so** *adj.* (usu. *predic.*) indifferent; not very good. • *adv.* indifferently. **so what?** *colloq.* why should that be considered significant?

so² var. of SOL.

soak /sōk/ • *v.* **1** *tr.* & *intr.* make or become thoroughly wet through saturation with or in liquid. **2** *tr.* (foll. by *in, up*) **a** absorb (liquid). **b** acquire (knowledge, etc.) copiously. **3** *intr.* (of liquid) make its way or penetrate by saturation. **4** *tr. colloq.* overcharge. • *n.* soaking. □□ **soak′age** *n.* **soak′er** *n.* **soak′ing** *n.* & *adj.*

so-and-so /sṓəndsō/ *n.* (*pl.* **so-and-sos**) **1** particular person or thing not needing to be specified (*told me to do so-and-so*). **2** *colloq.* person disliked or regarded with disfavor.

soap /sōp/ • *n.* **1** cleansing agent yielding lather when rubbed in water. **2** *colloq.* = soap opera. • *v.tr.* apply soap to. □ **soap opera** broadcast melodrama, usu. serialized in many episodes. □□ **soap′i·ly** *adv.* **soap′i·ness** *n.* **soap′less** *adj.* **soap′like** *adj.* **soap′y** *adj.* (**soap·i·er, soap·i·est**).

soap·box /sṓpboks/ *n.* makeshift stand for a public speaker.

soap·stone /sṓpstōn/ *n.* talc in the form of stone.

soar /sawr/ *v.intr.* **1** fly or rise high. **2** reach a high level. **3** fly without using power. □□ **soar′er** *n.* **soar′ing·ly** *adv.*

sob /sob/ • *v.* (**sobbed, sob·bing**) **1** *intr.* draw breath in convulsive gasps usu. with weeping. **2** *tr.* utter with sobs. • *n.* convulsive drawing of breath, esp. in weeping. □ **sob sister** journalist who writes or edits sentimental stories. □□ **sob′ber** *n.* **sob′bing·ly** *adv.*

so·ber /sṓbər/ • *adj.* (**so·ber·er, so·ber·est**) **1** not affected by alcohol. **2** not given to excessive drinking of alcohol. **3** moderate; tranquil; sedate; serious. **4** (of a color, etc.) quiet and inconspicuous. • *v.* (often foll. by *down, up*) make or become sober. □□ **so′ber·ing·ly** *adv.* **so′ber·ly** *adv.*

so·bri·e·ty /səbrī-itee/ *n.* state of being sober.

so·bri·quet /sṓbrikay, –ket/ *n.* (also **sou·bri·quet** /soo–/) **1** nickname. **2** assumed name.

Soc. *abbr.* **1** Socialist. **2** Society.

soc·cer /sókər/ *n.* game played by two teams of eleven players with a round ball that cannot be touched with the hands during play except by the goalkeepers.

so·cia·ble /sṓshəbəl/ *adj.* liking the society of other people; gregarious; friendly. □□ **so·cia·bil′i·ty** *n.* **so′cia·ble·ness** *n.* **so′cia·bly** *adv.*

so·cial /sṓshəl/ • *adj.* **1** of or relating to society or its organization. **2** concerned with the mutual relations of human beings or of classes of human beings. **3** living in organized communities. **4** needing companionship; gregarious; interdependent. • *n.* social gathering, esp. one organized by a club, congregation, etc. □ **social disease** venereal disease. **social science** study of human society and social relationships. **social scientist** student of or expert in the social sciences. **social security** (usu. **Social Security**) federal program of assistance to the elderly, disabled, etc. **social services** services provided by the government, esp. education, health, and housing. **social work** work of benefit to those in need of help or welfare, esp. done by specially trained personnel. **social worker** person trained to do social work. □□ **so′cial•ly** *adv.*

so•cial•ism /sṓshəlizəm/ *n.* **1** political and economic theory of social organization advocating state ownership and control of the means of production, distribution, and exchange. **2** policy or practice based on this theory. □□ **so′cial•ist** *n.* & *adj.* **so•cial•is′tic** *adj.*

so•cial•ite /sṓshəlīt/ *n.* person prominent in fashionable society.

so•cial•ize /sṓshəlīz/ *v.* **1** *intr.* act in a sociable manner. **2** *tr.* make social. **3** *tr.* organize on socialistic principles. □□ **so•cial•i•za′tion** *n.*

so•ci•e•ty /səsíətee/ *n.* (*pl.* **–ties**) **1** sum of human conditions and activity regarded as a whole functioning interdependently. **2** social community. **3** a social mode of life. **b** customs and organization of an ordered community. **4** socially advantaged or prominent members of a community. **5** companionship; company. **6** association; club. □ **Society of Friends** see QUAKER. **Society of Jesus** see JESUIT. □□ **so•ci′e•tal** *adj.* (esp. in sense 1). **so•ci′e•tal•ly** *adv.*

so•ci•ol•o•gy /sṓseeóləjee, sṓshee–/ *n.* the study of society and social problems. □□ **so•ci•o•log′i•cal** /–əlójikəl/ *adj.* **so•ci•o•log′i•cal•ly** *adv.* **so•ci•ol′o•gist** *n.*

so•ci•o•path /sṓseeopáth, sṓshee–/ *n. Psychol.* person who is an antisocial psychopath. □□ **so•ci•o•path′ic** *adj.*

sock[1] /sok/ *n.* (*pl.* **socks** or *colloq.* **sox** /soks/) short knitted covering for the foot, usu. not reaching the knee.

sock[2] /sok/ *colloq.* • *v.tr.* hit forcefully. • *n.* hard blow.

sock•et /sókit/ *n.* hollow for something to fit into.

So•crat•ic /səkrátik, sō–/ *adj.* of or relating to the Greek philosopher Socrates (d. 399 BC) or his philosophy, esp. the method associated with him of seeking the truth by a series of questions and answers.

sod /sod/ *n.* **1** turf or a piece of turf. **2** surface of the ground.

so•da /sṓdə/ *n.* **1** sodium bicarbonate. **2 a** (also **so′da pop**) sweet effervescent soft drink. **b** (in full **soda water**) preparation of effervescent water used in mixed drinks, etc. **c** soda water, ice cream, and flavoring combined as a sweet drink. □ **soda fountain** counter for preparing and serving sodas, sundaes, and ice cream.

sod•den /sódən/ *adj.* saturated with liquid; soaked through; soggy. □□ **sod′den•ly** *adv.*

so•di•um /sṓdeeəm/ *n. Chem.* soft silver white reactive metallic element. ¶ Symb.: **Na.** □ **sodium bicarbonate** white soluble powder used in the manufacture of fire extinguishers and efferves-

cent drinks. **sodium chloride** common salt. **sodium hydroxide** deliquescent compound that is strongly alkaline and used in the manufacture of soap and paper.

sod•om•y /sódəmee/ *n.* sexual intercourse involving anal or oral copulation. □□ **sod′om•ite** *n.* **sod′om•ize** *v.tr.*

so•fa /sṓfə/ *n.* long upholstered seat with a back and arms. □ **sofa bed** sofa that can be converted into a bed.

sof•fit /sófit/ *n.* underside of an architrave, arch, etc.

soft /sawft, soft/ • *adj.* **1** lacking hardness or firmness; yielding to pressure; easily cut. **2** (of cloth, etc.) smooth; not rough or coarse. **3** (of air, etc.) mellow; mild. **4** (of water) free from mineral salts. **5** (of a light or color, etc.) not brilliant or glaring. **6** gentle and pleasing. **7** (of an outline, etc.) not sharply defined. **8** gentle; conciliatory; complimentary; amorous. **9** compassionate; sympathetic. **10** *colloq.* (of a job, etc.) easy. **11** (of drugs) mild; not likely to cause addiction. **12** *Stock Exch.* (of currency, prices, etc.) likely to fall in value. • *adv.* softly (*play soft*). □ **soft-boiled** (of an egg) lightly boiled with the yolk soft or liquid. **soft drink** nonalcoholic usu. effervescent drink. **soft palate** rear part of the palate. **soft pedal** pedal on a piano that makes the tone softer. **soft-pedal** *v.* refrain from emphasizing; be restrained (about). **soft sell** restrained, low key or subtly persuasive salesmanship. **soft soap** *colloq.* persuasive flattery. **soft-soap** *v.tr. colloq.* persuade (a person) with flattery. **soft-spoken** speaking with a gentle voice. **soft touch** *colloq.* gullible person, esp. over money. □□ **soft′ish** *adj.* **soft′ly** *adv.* **soft′ness** *n.*

soft•ball /sáwftbawl, sóft–/ *n.* **1** ball like a baseball but larger and pitched underhand. **2** form of baseball using this.

soft-cov•er /sáwftcəvər, sóft–/ • *adj.* (of a book) bound in flexible covers. • *n.* softcover book.

soft•en /sáwfən, sófən/ *v.* make or become soft or softer. □□ **soft′en•er** *n.*

soft-heart•ed /sáwft-haártid, sóft–/ *adj.* tender; compassionate; easily moved. □□ **soft-heart′ed•ness** *n.*

soft•ware /sáwftwair, sóft–/ *n.* programs for a computer.

soft•y /sáwftee, sóftee/ *n.* (also **soft′ie**) (*pl.* **soft′ies**) *colloq.* weak or silly or softhearted person.

sog•gy /sógee/ *adj.* (**sog•gi•er, sog•gi•est**) sodden; saturated; dank. □□ **sog′gi•ly** *adv.* **sog′gi•ness** *n.*

soil[1] /soyl/ *n.* **1** upper layer of earth in which plants grow. **2** ground belonging to a nation; territory (*on British soil*). □□ **soil′less** *adj.*

soil[2] /soyl/ • *v.tr.* **1** make dirty; smear or stain with dirt. **2** tarnish; defile; bring discredit to. • *n.* **1** dirty mark. **2** filth; refuse.

soi•rée /swaaráy/ *n.* evening party.

so•journ /sṓjərn/ • *n.* temporary stay. • *v.intr.* stay temporarily. □□ **so′journ•er** *n.*

sol /sol/ *n.* (also **so** /sō/) *Mus.* fifth note of a major scale.

sol•ace /sóləs/ • *n.* comfort. • *v.tr.* give solace to.

so•lar /sṓlər/ *adj.* of, relating to, or reckoned by the sun (solar time). □ **solar battery** (or **cell**) device converting solar radiation into electricity. **solar plexus** complex of radiating nerves at the pit of the stomach. **solar system** the sun and the celestial bodies whose motion it governs.

so·lar·i·um /səláireeəm/ *n.* (*pl.* **so·lar·i·ums** or **so·lar·i·a** /–reeə/) room with sun lamps or extensive areas of glass for sunbathing.

sold past and past part. of SELL.

sol·der /sódər/ • *n.* **1** fusible alloy used to join less fusible metals or wires, etc. **2** cementing or joining agency. • *v.tr.* join with solder. □□ **sol′der·er** *n.*

sol·dier /sóljər/ • *n.* **1** person serving in or having served in an army. **2** (in full **com′mon sol′dier**) enlisted person in an army. • *v.intr.* serve as a soldier (*was off soldiering*). □ **soldier of fortune** mercenary; adventurer. **soldier on** *colloq.* persevere doggedly. □□ **sol′dier·ly** *adj.*

sole[1] /sōl/ • *n.* **1** undersurface of the foot. **2** part of a shoe, sock, etc., under the foot (esp. excluding the heel). • *v.tr.* provide (a shoe, etc.) with a sole. □□ **–soled** *adj.* (in comb.).

sole[2] /sōl/ *n.* flatfish used as food.

sole[3] /sōl/ *adj.* (attrib.) one and only; single; exclusive. □□ **sole′ly** *adv.*

sol·e·cism /sólisizəm/ *n.* mistake of grammar or idiom. □□ **sol′e·cist** *n.* **sol′e·cis′tic** *adj.*

sol·emn /sóləm/ *adj.* **1** serious and dignified. **2** formal. **3** mysteriously impressive. **4** serious or cheerless in manner; grave; sober. □□ **sol′emn·ly** *adv.* **sol′emn·ness** *n.*

so·lem·ni·ty /səlémnitee/ *n.* (*pl.* **–ties**) **1** being solemn. **2** rite or celebration; piece of ceremony.

sol·em·nize /sóləmnīz/ *v.tr.* **1** duly perform (a ceremony, esp. of marriage). **2** celebrate (a festival, etc.). **3** make solemn. □□ **sol·em·ni·za′tion** *n.*

so·le·noid /sólənoyd, sól–/ *n.* cylindrical coil of wire acting as a magnet when charged.

so·lic·it /səlísit/ *v.* **1** *tr.* & (foll. by *for*) *intr.* ask repeatedly or earnestly for or seek or invite (business, etc.). **2** *tr.* accost as a prostitute. □□ **so·lic·i·ta′tion** *n.*

so·lic·i·tor /səlísitər/ *n.* **1** person who solicits. **2** canvasser. **3** chief law officer of a city, county, etc.

so·lic·i·tous /səlísitəs/ *adj.* **1** showing interest or concern. **2** eager; anxious. □□ **so·lic′i·tous·ly** *adv.*

so·lic·i·tude /səlísitōod, –tyōod/ *n.* being solicitous.

sol·id /sólid/ • *adj.* (**sol·id·er**, **sol·id·est**) **1** firm and stable in shape; not liquid or fluid (*solid food*). **2** of a single material throughout, not hollow or containing cavities (*solid sphere*). **3** of the same substance throughout (*solid silver*). **4** of strong material or construction or build; not flimsy or slender, etc. **5** three dimensional. **6** sound; reliable. **7** uninterrupted; continuous. **8** unanimous; undivided. • *n.* **1** solid substance or body. **2** (in *pl.*) solid food. □ **solid-state** *adj.* using semiconductors instead of vacuum tubes. □□ **sol′id·ly** *adv.*

sol·i·dar·i·ty /sólidáritee/ *n.* unity or agreement of feeling or action, esp. among individuals with a common interest.

so·lid·i·fy /səlídifī/ *v.* (**–fies**, **–fied**) make or become solid. □□ **so·lid·i·fi·ca′tion** *n.* **so·lid′i·fi·er** *n.*

so·lid·i·ty /səlíditee/ *n.* state of being solid; firmness.

sol·i·dus /sólidəs/ *n.* (*pl.* **sol·i·di** /–dī/) virgule (/).

so·lil·o·quy /səlíləkwee/ *n.* (*pl.* **–quies**) **1** act of talking when alone or regardless of any hearers, esp. in drama. **2** part of a play involving this. □□ **so·lil′o·quist** *n.* **so·lil′o·quize** *v.intr.*

sol·i·taire /sólitáir/ *n.* **1** diamond or other gem set by itself. **2** any of several card games for one player.

sol·i·tar·y /sóliteree/ *adj.* **1** living alone; not gregarious. **2** secluded or unfrequented. **3** single or sole (*solitary instance*). □□ **sol·i·tar′i·ly** *adv.*

sol·i·tude /sólitōod, –tyōod/ *n.* **1** state of being solitary. **2** lonely place.

so·lo /sólō/ • *n.* **1** (*pl.* **–los** or **so·li** /–lee/) vocal or instrumental piece or passage, or dance, performed by one person with or without accompaniment. **2** (*pl.* **–los**) **a** unaccompanied flight by a pilot in an aircraft. **b** anything done by one person unaccompanied. • *v.intr.* (**–loes**, **–loed**) perform a solo. • *adv.* unaccompanied; alone. □□ **so′lo·ist** *n.*

sol·stice /sólstis, sól–, sáwl–/ *n.* time or date, about June 21 (*summer solstice*) and December 22 (*winter solstice*), at which the sun's path is farthest from the equator. □□ **sol·sti′tial** /–stíshəl/ *adj.*

sol·u·ble /sólyəbəl/ *adj.* **1** that can be dissolved, esp. in water. **2** that can be solved. □□ **sol·u·bil′i·ty** *n.*

so·lute /sólyōot, sólōot/ *n.* dissolved substance.

so·lu·tion /səlōoshən/ *n.* **1** act or a means of solving a problem or difficulty. **2 a** conversion of a solid or gas into a liquid by mixture with a liquid. **b** mixture produced by this.

solve /solv/ *v.tr.* answer or effectively deal with (a problem or difficulty). □□ **solv′a·ble** *adj.* **solv′er** *n.*

sol·vent /sólvənt/ • *adj.* **1** able to dissolve or form a solution with something. **2** having enough money to meet one's liabilities. • *n.* solvent liquid, etc. □□ **sol′ven·cy** *n.* (in sense 2).

So·ma·li /sōmáalee, sə–/ • *n.* **1** (*pl.* same or **So·ma′lis**) member of a Hamitic Muslim people of Somalia in NE Africa. **2** the Cushitic language of this people. • *adj.* of or relating to this people or language. □□ **So·ma′li·an** *adj.*

so·mat·ic /sōmátik, sə–/ *adj.* of or relating to the body, esp. as distinct from the mind. □□ **so·mat′i·cal·ly** *adv.*

som·ber /sómbər/ *adj.* dark; gloomy; dismal. □□ **som′ber·ly** *adv.* **som′ber·ness** *n.*

som·bre·ro /sombráirō/ *n.* (*pl.* **–ros**) broad-brimmed felt or straw hat worn esp. in Mexico and the southwest US.

some /sum/ • *adj.* **1** unspecified amount or number of (*some apples*). **2** that is unknown or unnamed (*some day*). **3** denoting an approximate number (*some twenty minutes*). **4** considerable (*went to some trouble*). **5** at least a small amount of (*have some consideration*). • *pron.* some number or amount (*I have some already*). • *adv. colloq.* to some extent (*do it some more*).

-some[1] /səm/ *suffix* forming adjectives meaning: **1** productive of (*fearsome*). **2** characterized by being (*litheome*).

-some[2] /səm/ *suffix* forming nouns from numerals, meaning 'a group of (so many)' (*four-some*).

-some³ /sōm/ *comb. form* denoting a portion of a body, esp. of a cell (*chromosome; ribosome*).

some·bod·y /súmbodee, –budee, –bədee/ • *pron.* some person. • *n.* (*pl.* **–ies**) person of importance.

some·day /súmday/ *adv.* at some time in the future.

some·how /súmhow/ *adv.* for some unstated reason or way.

some·one /súmwun/ *n.* & *pron.* = SOMEBODY.

some·place /súmplays/ *adv. colloq.* = SOME-WHERE.

som·er·sault /súmərsawlt/ (also **sum'mer·sault**) • *n.* leap or roll in which a person turns head over heels and lands on the feet. • *v.intr.* perform a somersault.

some·thing /súmthing/ *n.* & *pron.* 1 some unspecified or unknown thing (*something has happened*). 2 unexpressed quantity, quality, or extent (*something of a fool*). 3 *colloq.* notable person or thing. □ **something else** 1 something different. 2 *colloq.* something exceptional.

some·time /súmtīm/ • *adv.* 1 at some unspecified time. 2 formerly. • *attrib.adj.* former (*some-time mayor*).

some·times /súmtīmz/ *adv.* at some times; occasionally.

some·what /súmhwut, –hwot, –hwət, –wut, –wot, –wət/ *adv.* to some extent.

some·where /súmhwair, –wair/ • *adv.* in or to some place. • *pron.* some unspecified place.

som·nam·bu·lism /somnámbyəlizəm/ *n.* sleepwalking. □□ **som·nam'bu·list** *n.*

som·no·lent /sómnələnt/ *adj.* 1 sleepy; drowsy. 2 inducing drowsiness. 3 *Med.* in a state between sleeping and waking. □□ **som'no·lence** *n.* **som'no·lent·ly** *adv.*

son /sun/ *n.* 1 boy or man in relation to his parents. 2 male descendant. □ **son-in-law** (*pl.* **sons-in-law**) husband of one's daughter. □□ **son'less** *adj.* **son'ship** *n.*

so·nar /sónaar/ *n.* 1 system for the underwater detection of objects by reflected sound. 2 apparatus for this.

so·na·ta /sənaàtə/ *n.* composition for one or two instruments, usu. in several movements.

song /sawng, song/ *n.* 1 words set to music or meant to be sung. 2 singing or vocal music. 3 musical cry of some birds. □ **for a song** *colloq.* very cheaply. **song and dance** *colloq.* fuss or commotion. □□ **song'less** *adj.*

song·bird /sáwngbərd, sóng–/ *n.* bird with a musical call.

son·ic /sónik/ *adj.* of or relating to or using sound or sound waves. □ **sonic barrier** = *sound barrier* (see SOUND¹). **sonic boom** loud explosive noise made when an aircraft surpasses the speed of sound.

son·net /sónit/ *n.* poem of 14 lines using any of a number of rhyme schemes and usu. having ten syllables per line.

son·ny /súnee/ *n. colloq.* familiar form of address to a young boy.

son·o·gram /sónəgram/ *n. Med.* image produced by ultrasound waves, used for diagnostic purposes.

so·no·rous /sónərəs, sənáwrəs/ *adj.* 1 having a loud, full, or deep sound; resonant. 2 (of a speech, style, etc.) imposing; grand. □□ **so·nor·i·ty** /sənáwritee/ *n.* **so'no·rous·ly** *adv.* **so'no·rous·ness** *n.*

soon /soon/ *adv.* 1 in a short time. 2 quickly; before long. 3 readily or willingly (*would as soon stay behind*). □ **sooner or later** at some future time; eventually. □□ **soon'ish** *adv.*

soot /soot/ *n.* black powdery deposit from smoke.

soothe /sooth/ *v.tr.* 1 calm (a person or feelings). 2 soften or mitigate (pain). □□ **sooth'er** *n.* **sooth'ing** *adj.* **sooth'ing·ly** *adv.*

sooth·say·er /soothsayər/ *n.* diviner or seer.

soot·y /sootee/ *adj.* (**soot·i·er, soot·i·est**) 1 covered with or full of soot. 2 like soot; black. □□ **soot'i·ly** *adv.* **soot'i·ness** *n.*

SOP *abbr.* (also **S.O.P.**) standard operating procedure.

sop /sop/ • *n.* 1 piece of bread, etc., dipped in gravy, etc. 2 thing given or done to pacify or bribe. • *v.* (**sopped, sop·ping**) 1 *intr.* be drenched. 2 *tr.* (foll. by *up*) absorb (liquid) in a towel, etc. 3 *tr.* wet thoroughly; soak.

soph. /sof/ *abbr.* sophomore.

soph·ism /sófizəm/ *n.* false argument, esp. one intended to deceive.

soph·ist /sófist/ *n.* one who reasons with clever but fallacious arguments. □□ **so·phis'tic** *adj.* **so·phis'ti·cal** *adj.*

so·phis·ti·cate • *v.tr.* /səfístikayt/ 1 make educated, cultured, or refined. 2 make highly developed or complex. • *n.* /səfístikət/ sophisticated person. □□ **so·phis·ti·ca·tion** /–káyshən/ *n.*

so·phis·ti·cat·ed /səfístikaytid/ *adj.* 1 (of a person) educated and refined; worldly-wise. 2 (of a thing, idea, etc.) highly developed and complex.

soph·ist·ry /sófistree/ *n.* (*pl.* **–ries**) 1 use of sophisms. 2 a sophism.

soph·o·more /sófəmawr, sófmawr/ *n.* second year college or high school student. □□ **soph·o·mor'ic** *adj.*

sop·o·rif·ic /sópərífik/ • *adj.* inducing sleep. • *n.* soporific drug or influence. □□ **sop·o·rif·er·ous** /–rífərəs/ *adj.* **sop·o·rif'i·cal·ly** *adv.*

sop·py /sópee/ *adj.* (**sop·pi·er, sop·pi·est**) 1 *colloq.* a silly or foolish in a feeble or self-indulgent way. b mawkishly sentimental. 2 soaked with water.

so·pran·o /səpránō, –praá–/ *n.* (*pl.* **–os** or **so·pran·i** /–nee/) 1 a highest pitched singing voice. b female or boy singer with this voice. c a part written for it. 2 a instrument of a high or the highest pitch in its family. b its player.

sor·bet /sawrbáy, sáwrbit/ *n.* sweetened frozen confection, usu. with fruit flavoring.

sor·cer·er /sáwrsərər/ *n.* (*fem.* **sor·cer·ess** /–ris/) magician; wizard. □□ **sor'cer·y** *n.* (*pl.* **–ies**).

sor·did /sáwrdid/ *adj.* 1 dirty or squalid. 2 ignoble, mean, or mercenary. □□ **sor'did·ly** *adv.* **sor'did·ness** *n.*

sore /sawr/ • *adj.* 1 (of a part of the body) painful. 2 (of a person) suffering pain. 3 angry or vexed. 4 grievous or severe (*in sore need*). • *n.* sore place on the body. □ **sore point** subject causing distress or annoyance. □□ **sore'ness** *n.*

sore·ly /sáwrlee/ *adv.* extremely; badly (*am sorely tempted*).

sor·ghum /sáwrgəm/ *n.* tropical cereal grass.

so·ror·i·ty /səráwritee, –rór–/ *n.* (*pl.* **–ties**) female students' society in a university or college, usu. for social purposes.

sor·rel /sáwrəl, sór–/ • *adj.* of a light reddish-brown color. • *n.* **1** this color. **2** sorrel animal, esp. a horse.

sor·row /sáwrō, sór–/ • *n.* **1** mental distress caused by loss or disappointment, etc. **2** cause of sorrow. • *v.intr.* **1** feel sorrow. **2** mourn. □□ **sor'row·er** *n.* **sor'row·ing** *adj.*

sor·row·ful /sáwrōfŏŏl, sór–/ *adj.* **1** feeling or showing sorrow. **2** distressing; lamentable. □□ **sor'row·ful·ly** *adv.* **sor'row·ful·ness** *n.*

sor·ry /sáwree, sór–/ *adj.* (**sor·ri·er, sor·ri·est**) **1** (*predic.*) pained or regretful or penitent. **2** (*predic.*; foll. by *for*) feeling pity or sympathy for. **3** wretched; in a poor state. □□ **sor'ri·ly** *adv.*

sort /sawrt/ • *n.* **1** group of things, etc., with common attributes; class or kind. **2** (foll. by *of*) roughly of the kind specified (*is some sort of doctor*). • *v.tr.* arrange systematically or according to type, class, etc. □ **of a sort** (or **of sorts**) *colloq.* not fully deserving the name (*a holiday of sorts*). **out of sorts** slightly unwell. **sort of** *colloq.* as it were; to some extent. □□ **sort'a·ble** *adj.* **sort'er** *n.* **sort'ing** *n.*
¶ See note at KIND.

sor·tie /sáwrtee, sawrtée/ *n.* **1** sally, esp. from a besieged garrison. **2** operational flight by a single military aircraft.

SOS /ésō-és/ *n.* (*pl.* **SOSs**) international code signal of extreme distress, used esp. by ships at sea.

sot /sot/ *n.* habitual drunkard.

sot·to vo·ce /sótō vóchee, sáwt–tō váwche/ *adv.* in an undertone or aside.

sou·bri·quet var. of SOBRIQUET.

souf·flé /sŏŏfláy/ *n.* light dish usu. made with flavored egg yolks added to stiffly beaten egg whites and baked.

sought past and past part. of SEEK.

soul /sōl/ *n.* **1** spiritual or immaterial part of a human being, often regarded as immortal. **2** moral or emotional or intellectual nature of a person or animal. **3** personification or pattern of something (*the very soul of discretion*). **4** an individual (*not a soul in sight*). **5** animating or essential part. **6** African-American culture, music, ethnic pride, etc. □ **soul mate** person ideally suited to another. **soul music** a kind of music incorporating elements of rhythm and blues and gospel music, popularized by African Americans.

soul·ful /sólfŏŏl/ *adj.* having or expressing or evoking deep feeling. □□ **soul'ful·ly** *adv.* **soul'ful·ness** *n.*

soul·less /sól-lis/ *adj.* **1** lacking sensitivity or noble qualities. **2** having no soul. □□ **soul'less·ly** *adv.* **soul'less·ness** *n.*

sound[1] /sownd/ • *n.* **1** sensation caused in the ear by the vibration of air or other medium. **2** vibrations causing this sensation. **3** what is or may be heard. **4** idea or impression conveyed by words (*don't like the sound of that*). • *v.* **1** *intr.* & *tr.* emit or cause to emit sound. **2** *tr.* utter or pronounce (*sound a note of alarm*). **3** *intr.* convey an impression when heard (*you sound worried*). □ **sound barrier** high resistance of air to objects moving at speeds near that of sound. **sound bite** short extract from a recorded interview, chosen for its pungency or appropriateness. **sound effect**

573   sorghum ~ south

sound other than speech or music made artificially for use in a play, movie, etc. □□ **sound'less** *adj.* **sound'less·ly** *adv.* **sound'less·ness** *n.*

sound[2] /sownd/ • *adj.* **1** healthy; not diseased, injured, or rotten. **2** (of an opinion or policy, etc.) correct; orthodox; well-founded; judicious; legally valid. **3** financially secure. **4** restful; undisturbed. • *adv.* soundly (*sound asleep*). □□ **sound'ly** *adv.* **sound'ness** *n.*

sound[3] /sownd/ *v.tr.* **1** test the depth or quality of the bottom of (the sea or a river, etc.). **2** (often foll. by *out*) inquire (esp. cautiously or discreetly) into the opinions or feelings of (a person). □□ **sound'er** *n.*

sound[4] /sownd/ *n.* **1** narrow passage of water connecting two seas or a sea with a lake, etc. **2** arm of the sea.

sound·ing /sównding/ *n.* **1** measurement of the depth of water. **2** (in *pl.*) waters close to shore. □ **sounding board 1** canopy over a pulpit, etc., to direct sound toward the congregation. **2** person, etc., used as a trial audience.

sound·proof /sówndprŏŏf/ • *adj.* impervious to sound. • *v.tr.* make soundproof.

sound·track /sówndtrak/ *n.* the sound element of a movie, television broadcast, etc.

soup /sŏŏp/ • *n.* liquid dish made by boiling meat, fish, or vegetables, etc., in stock or water. • *v.tr.* (usu. foll. by *up*) *colloq.* **1** increase the power and efficiency of (an engine). **2** enliven. □ **in the soup** *colloq.* in difficulties.

soup·çon /sŏŏpsáwn, sŏŏpsón/ *n.* small quantity; dash.

soup·y /sŏŏpee/ *adj.* (**soup·i·er, soup·i·est**) **1** of or resembling soup. **2** *colloq.* sentimental. □□ **soup'i·ly** *adv.* **soup'i·ness** *n.*

sour /sowr/ • *adj.* **1** acid in taste or smell. **2** (of food, esp. milk or bread) bad because of fermentation. **3** (of a person, temper, etc.) harsh; morose; bitter. **4** (of a thing) unpleasant; distasteful. • *v.* make or become sour (*soured the cream*). □ **sour grapes** resentful disparagement of something one cannot personally acquire. □□ **sour'ish** *adj.* **sour'ly** *adv.* **sour'ness** *n.*

source /sawrs/ *n.* **1** place, person, or thing from which something issues or originates. **2** person or document, etc., providing evidence (*reliable sources of information*).

sour·puss /sówrpŏŏs/ *n. colloq.* ill-tempered person.

souse /sows/ • *v.* **1** *tr.* put (pickles, fish, etc.) in brine. **2** *tr.* & *intr.* plunge into liquid. **3** *tr.* (usu. foll. by *in*) soak (a thing) in liquid. • *n.* **1 a** pickling brine made with salt. **b** pickled food. **2** a dip, plunge, or drenching in water.

south /sowth/ • *n.* **1** point of the horizon 90° clockwise from east. **2** compass point corresponding to this. **3** direction in which this lies. **4** (usu. **the South**) **a** part of the world or a country or a town lying to the south. **b** southern states of the US, especially those that were part of the Confederacy. • *adj.* **1** toward, at, near, or facing the south. **2** coming from the south (*south wind*). • *adv.* **1** toward, at, or near the south. **2** (foll. by *of*) further south than. □ **South African** *adj.* of or relating to the republic of South Africa. • *n.* **1** native or inhabitant of South Africa. **2** person of South African descent. **South American** *adj.* of or relating to South

America. • *n.* native or inhabitant of South America. **southeast** *n.* **1** point midway between south and east. **2** direction in which this lies. • *adj.* of, toward, or coming from the southeast. • *adv.* of, toward, or coming from the southeast. **southeasterly** *adj. & adv.* = *southeast.* **southeastern** lying on the southeast side. **south pole** see POLE². **South Sea** southern Pacific Ocean. **southwest** *n.* **1** point midway between south and west. **2** direction in which this lies. • *adj.* of, toward, or coming from the southwest. • *adv.* toward, at, or near the southwest. **southwesterly** *adj. & adv.* = *southwest.* **southwestern** lying on the southwest side.

south·east·er /sówtheéstər, sou-eéstər/ *n.* southeast wind.

south·er·ly /súthərlee/ • *adj. & adv.* **1** in a southern position or direction. **2** (of a wind) blowing from the south. • *n.* (*pl.* **–lies**) southerly wind.

south·ern /súthərn/ *adj.* esp. Geog. of, toward, or in the south. □ **southern hemisphere** the half of the earth below the equator. □□ **south′ern·er** *n.* **south′ern·most** *adj.*

south·paw /sówthpaw/ *colloq.* • *n.* left-handed person, esp. as a pitcher in baseball. • *adj.* left-handed.

south·ward /sówthwərd/ • *adj. & adv.* (also **south′wards**) toward the south. • *n.* southward direction or region.

south·west·er /sówthwéstər, sow-wéstər/ *n.* southwest wind.

sou·ve·nir /soõvəneér/ *n.* (often foll. by *of*) memento of an occasion, place, etc.

sou′west·er /sow-wéstər/ *n.* **1** = SOUTHWESTER. **2** waterproof hat with a broad flap covering the neck.

sov·er·eign /sóvrin/ • *n.* **1** supreme ruler, esp. a monarch. **2** *Brit. hist.* gold coin nominally worth £1. • *adj.* **1** supreme. **2** possessing independent authority (*a sovereign state*). □□ **sov′er·eign·ty** *n.* (*pl.* **–ties**).

so·vi·et /sóveeət, sóv-/ • *n.* (in the former USSR) **1** elected local, district, or national council. **2** (**Soviet**) citizen of the USSR. **3** revolutionary council of workers, peasants, etc., before 1917. • *adj.* (usu. **Soviet**) of or concerning the former Soviet Union.

sow¹ /sō/ *v.tr.* (*past* **sowed** /sōd/; *past part.* **sown** /sōn/ or **sowed**) **1** (also *absol.*) **a** scatter or put (seed) on or in the earth. **b** (often foll. by *with*) plant (a field, etc.) with seed. **2** initiate; arouse. □□ **sow′er** *n.* **sow′ing** *n.*

sow² /sow/ *n.* female adult pig, esp. after farrowing.

sox *colloq. pl.* of SOCK¹.

soy /soy/ *n.* (also **soy·a** /sóyə/) **1** (also **soy sauce**) sauce from pickled soya beans. **2** (in full **soy bean**) = *soya bean.*

soy·a /sóyə/ *n.* (in full **soy′a bean**) **1 a** leguminous plant, cultivated for the edible oil and flour it yields, and used as a replacement for animal protein in certain foods. **b** seed of this. **2** (also **soya sauce**) = SOY 1.

spa /spaa/ *n.* place or resort with facility offering use of exercise equipment, steam baths, etc.

space /spays/ • *n.* **1 a** continuous unlimited area

or expanse which may or may not contain objects, etc. **b** interval between points or objects. **c** empty area; room. **2** = *outer space.* **3** place, seat, berth, etc., made available (*no space on the bus*). **4** interval of time. • *v.tr.* set or arrange at intervals. □ **space age** era when space travel has become possible. **space shuttle** a spacecraft for repeated use. **space station** artificial satellite used as a base for operations in space. **space-time** (or **space-time continuum**) fusion of the concepts of space and time, esp. as a four-dimensional continuum. □□ **spac′er** *n.*

space·craft /spáyskraft/ *n.* vehicle for traveling in space.

space·man /spáysman/ *n.* (*pl.* **–men;** *fem.* **space·wom·an,** *pl.* **–wom·en**) astronaut.

space·ship /spáys-ship/ *n.* spacecraft.

space·suit /spáys-soõt, –syoõt/ *n.* garment designed to allow an astronaut to survive in space.

space·y /spáysee/ *adj.* (also **spac′y**) (**spac·i·er, spac·i·est**) *sl.* **1** seemingly out of touch with reality; disoriented. **2** being in a confused or dazed state because of the influence of mind-altering drugs.

spa·cial var. of SPATIAL.

spa·cious /spáyshəs/ *adj.* having ample space; covering a large area; roomy. □□ **spa′cious·ly** *adv.* **spa′cious·ness** *n.*

spade¹ /spayd/ • *n.* tool used for digging or cutting the ground, etc., with a sharp-edged metal blade and a long handle. • *v.tr.* dig over (ground) with a spade. □ **call a spade a spade** speak plainly or bluntly. □□ **spade′ful** *n.* (*pl.* **–fuls**).

spade² /spayd/ *n.* **1** playing card of a suit denoted by black inverted heart-shaped figures with small stalks. **2** (in *pl.*) this suit. □ **in spades** *sl.* to a high degree; with great force.

spade·work /spáydwərk/ *n.* hard or routine preparatory work.

spa·ghet·ti /spəgétee/ *n.* pasta made in long thin strings.

span /span/ • *n.* **1** full extent from end to end in space or time. **2** each arch or part of a bridge between piers or supports. **3** maximum distance between the tips of the thumb and little finger (approx. 9 inches). • *v.* (**spanned, span·ning**) **1** *tr.* stretch from side to side of; extend across. **2** bridge (a river, etc.).

span·drel /spándril/ *n. Archit.* space between an arch and a cornice or exterior wall.

SPANDREL

span·gle /spánggəl/ • *n.* **1** sequin. **2** a small sparkling object. • *v.tr.* (esp. as **spangled** *adj.*) cover with or as with spangles (*spangled costume*). □□ **span·gly** /spángglee/ *adj.*

Span·iard /spányərd/ n. **1** native or inhabitant of Spain in southern Europe. **2** person of Spanish descent.

span·iel /spányəl/ n. **1** dog of any of various breeds with a long silky coat and drooping ears. **2** any of these breeds.

Span·ish /spánish/ • adj. of or relating to Spain or its people or language. • n. **1** language of Spain and Spanish America. **2** (prec. by the; treated as pl.) the people of Spain. □ **Spanish America** those parts of America orig. settled by Spaniards, including Central and South America and part of the West Indies.

spank /spangk/ • v.tr. slap, esp. on the buttocks, with the open hand. • n. slap, esp. on the buttocks.

spank·ing /spángking/ • adj. **1** brisk or lively. **2** colloq. striking; excellent. • adv. colloq. very; exceedingly (spanking clean). • n. slapping on the buttocks.

spar[1] /spaar/ n. stout pole, esp. as a ship's mast, etc.

spar[2] /spaar/ v.intr. (**sparred, spar·ring**) **1** make the motions of boxing without landing heavy blows. **2** argue.

spare /spair/ • adj. **1** extra. **2** lean; thin. **3** scanty; frugal; not copious (spare diet). • n. **1** spare part. **2** Bowling knocking down of all the pins with the first two balls. • v.tr. **1** afford to give or do without (can spare you a couple). **2 a** abstain from killing, hurting, wounding, etc. **b** abstain from inflicting or causing; relieve from (spare my blushes). **3** be frugal or grudging of. □□ **spare'ly** adv. **spare'ness** n. **spar'er** n.

spare·ribs /spáir-ríbs/ n. closely trimmed ribs of esp. pork.

spar·ing /spáiring/ adj. **1** inclined to save; economical. **2** restrained; limited. □□ **spar'ing·ly** adv.

spark /spaark/ • n. **1** fiery particle thrown off from a fire. **2** particle of a quality, etc. (not a spark of life). **3** flash of light between electric conductors, etc. **4** flash of wit, etc. • v. **1** intr. emit sparks of fire or electricity. **2** tr. stir into activity; initiate (a process) suddenly. □ **spark plug** device for firing the explosive mixture in an internal combustion engine. □□ **spark'less** adj. **spark'y** adj.

spar·kle /spaárkəl/ • v.intr. **1** emit or seem to emit sparks; glitter; scintillate. **2** (of wine, etc.) effervesce. • n. **1** gleam or spark. **2** vivacity; liveliness. □□ **spark'ly** adj.

spar·kler /spaárklər/ n. **1** handheld sparkling firework. **2** colloq. diamond or other gem.

spar·row /spárō/ n. small brownish-gray bird.

sparse /spaars/ adj. thinly dispersed or scattered; not dense. □□ **sparse'ly** adv. **sparse'ness** n. **spar'si·ty** n.

Spar·tan /spaárt'n/ • adj. **1** of Sparta in ancient Greece. **2** rigorous; frugal; austere. • n. citizen of Sparta.

spasm /spázəm/ n. **1** sudden involuntary, convulsive muscular contraction. **2** colloq. brief spell of an activity.

spas·mod·ic /spazmódik/ adj. **1** of, caused by, or subject to, a spasm or spasms. **2** occurring or done by fits and starts (spasmodic efforts). □□ **spas·mod'i·cal·ly** adv.

spas·tic /spástik/ • adj. of or afflicted with

spasms. • n. offens. person suffering from cerebral palsy. □□ **spas'ti·cal·ly** adv. **spas·tic'i·ty** /–tísitee/ n.

spat[1] past and past part. of SPIT[1].

spat[2] /spat/ n. **1** (usu. in pl.) hist. short gaiter covering a shoe. **2** cover for an aircraft wheel.

spat[3] /spat/ n. colloq. petty quarrel.

spate /spayt/ n. large or excessive amount.

spathe /spayth/ n. Bot. large bract or pair of bracts enveloping a spadix or flower cluster.

spa·tial /spáyshəl/ adj. (also **spa'cial**) of or concerning space. □□ **spa·ti·al·i·ty** /–sheeálitee/ n. **spa'tial·ly** adv.

spat·ter /spátər/ • v. **1** tr. **a** splash (a person, etc.). **b** scatter or splash (liquid, mud, etc.). **2** intr. (of rain, etc.) fall here and there. • n. **1** splash; drop. **2** quick pattering sound.

spat·u·la /spáchələ/ n. broad-bladed flat implement used for spreading, lifting, stirring, mixing (food), etc.

spawn /spawn/ • v. **1 a** tr. (also absol.) (of a fish, frog, mollusk, or crustacean) produce (eggs). **b** intr. be produced as eggs or young. **2** tr. produce or generate, esp. in large numbers. • n. eggs of fish, frogs, etc. □□ **spawn'er** n.

spay /spay/ v.tr. sterilize (a female animal) by removing the ovaries.

SPCA abbr. Society for the Prevention of Cruelty to Animals.

speak /speek/ v. (past **spoke** /spōk/; past part. **spok·en** /spōkən/) **1** intr. make articulate verbal utterances. **2** tr. utter (words, the truth, etc.). **3** intr. **a** (foll. by to, with) hold a conversation. **b** (foll. by of) mention in writing, etc. **c** (foll. by for) articulate the feelings of (another person, etc.) in speech or writing. **4** intr. make a speech. **5** tr. use or be able to use (a specified language). □ **speak out** speak loudly or freely; give one's opinion. **speak up** = speak out. **speak volumes** (or **well**, etc.) **for 1** be abundant evidence of. **2** place in a favorable light. □□ **speak'a·ble** adj.

speak·eas·y /spéekeezee/ n. (pl. **-ies**) illicit liquor store or drinking club during Prohibition in the US.

speak·er /spéekər/ n. **1** person who speaks, esp. in public. **2** person who speaks a specified language (esp. in comb.: French speaker). **3** (**Speaker**) presiding officer in a legislative assembly, esp. the US House of Representatives. **4** = LOUDSPEAKER.

speak·er·phone /spéekərfōn/ n. telephone equipped with a microphone and loudspeaker, allowing it to be used without picking up the handset.

spear /speer/ • n. **1** weapon with a pointed usu. steel tip and a long shaft. **2** pointed stem of asparagus, etc. • v.tr. pierce or strike with or as if with a spear (speared an olive).

spear·head /spéerhed/ • n. **1** point of a spear. **2** individual or group chosen to lead a thrust or attack. • v.tr. act as the spearhead of (an attack, etc.).

spear·mint /spéermint/ n. common garden mint used in flavoring.

spec[1] /spek/ n. colloq. commercial speculation or venture. □ **on spec** in the hope of success; as a gamble.

spec[2] /spek/ *n. colloq.* specification.

spe·cial /spéshəl/ • *adj.* **1 a** particularly good; exceptional. **b** peculiar; specific. **2** for a particular purpose. **3** denoting education for children with particular needs, e.g., the disabled. • *n.* special edition of a newspaper, dish on a menu, etc. □ **special delivery** delivery of mail in advance of the regular delivery. **special edition** extra edition of a newspaper including later news than the ordinary edition. **special effects** movie or television illusions created by props, camera work, etc. □□ **spe′cial·ly** *adv.* **spe′cial·ness** *n.*

spe·cial·ist /spéshəlist/ *n.* person who is trained in a particular branch of a profession, esp. medicine. □□ **spe′cial·ism** *n.*

spe·cial·ize /spéshəlīz/ *v.* **1** *intr.* **a** be or become a specialist. **b** devote oneself to an area of interest, skill, etc. **2** *tr.* adapt for a particular purpose. □□ **spe·cial·i·za′tion** *n.*

spe·cial·ty /spéshəltee/ *n.* (*pl.* –**ties**) special pursuit, product, operation, etc., to which a company or a person gives special attention.

spe·cie /spéeshee, –see/ *n.* coin as opposed to paper money.

spe·cies /spéesheez, –seez/ *n.* (*pl.* same) **1** class of things having some characteristics in common. **2** *Biol.* category in the system of classification of living organisms consisting of similar individuals capable of exchanging genes or interbreeding. **3** kind or sort.

spe·cif·ic /spisífik/ • *adj.* **1** clearly defined; definite. **2** relating to a particular subject; peculiar (*a style specific to that*). • *n.* specific aspect or factor (*shall we discuss specifics?*). □ **specific gravity** the ratio of the density of a substance to the density of a standard, as water for a liquid and air for a gas. □□ **spe·cif′i·cal·ly** *adv.* **spec·i·fic·i·ty** /spésifisitee/ *n.*

spec·i·fi·ca·tion /spésifikáyshən/ *n.* **1** act of specifying. **2** (esp. in *pl.*) detailed description of the construction, workmanship, materials, etc., of work done or to be done.

spec·i·fy /spésifī/ *v.tr.* (–**fies**, –**fied**) **1** name or mention expressly or as a condition. **2** include in specifications. □□ **spec′i·fi·er** *n.*

spec·i·men /spésimən/ *n.* **1** individual or part taken as an example of a class or whole. **2** *Med.* sample of fluid or tissue for testing.

spe·cious /spéeshəs/ *adj.* plausible but wrong. □□ **spe·ci·os·i·ty** /–sheeósitee/ *n.* **spe′cious·ly** *adv.* **spe′cious·ness** *n.*

speck /spek/ *n.* **1** small spot or stain. **2** particle. • *v.tr.* (esp. as **specked** *adj.*) mark with specks. □□ **speck′less** *adj.*

speck·le /spékəl/ • *n.* speck, esp. one of many. • *v.tr.* (esp. as **speckled** *adj.*) mark with speckles or patches.

specs /speks/ *n.pl. colloq.* pair of eyeglasses.

spec·ta·cle /spéktəkəl/ *n.* **1** public show, ceremony, etc. **2** anything attracting public attention.

spec·ta·cles /spéktəkəlz/ *n.pl. old-fashioned* or *joc.* eyeglasses.

spec·tac·u·lar /spektákyələr/ • *adj.* striking; amazing; lavish. • *n.* spectacular show. □□ **spec·tac′u·lar·ly** *adv.*

spec·ta·tor /spéktaytər/ *n.* person who looks on at a show, game, incident, etc.

spec·ter /spéktər/ *n.* **1** ghost. **2** haunting presentiment.

spec·tral /spéktrəl/ *adj.* **1 a** of or relating to specters or ghosts. **b** ghostlike. **2** of a spectrum. □□ **spec′tral·ly** *adv.*

spec·trom·e·ter /spektrómitər/ *n.* instrument used for the measurement of observed spectra. □□ **spec·tro·met·ric** /spéktrəmétrik/ *adj.* **spec·trom·e·try** /–trómitree/ *n.*

spec·tro·scope /spéktrəskōp/ *n.* instrument for producing and recording spectra for examination. □□ **spec·tro·scop·ic** /–skópik/ *adj.* **spec·tro·scop′i·cal** *adj.* **spec·tros·co·py** /–tróskəpee/ *n.*

spec·trum /spéktrəm/ *n.* (*pl.* **spec·tra** /–trə/) **1** band of colors, as seen in a rainbow, etc. **2** distribution of visible electromagnetic radiation arranged in a progressive series according to wavelength. **3** entire range or a wide range of anything arranged by degree or quality, etc.

spec·u·late /spékyəlayt/ *v.* **1** *intr.* form a theory or conjecture. **2** *tr.* conjecture; consider. **3** *intr.* invest in stocks, etc., in the hope of gain but with the possibility of loss. □□ **spec·u·la·tion** /–láyshən/ *n.* **spec′u·la·tor** *n.*

spec·u·la·tive /spékyələtiv, –lay–/ *adj.* **1** of speculation. **2** (of a business investment) involving the risk of loss (*a speculative builder*). □□ **spec′u·la·tive·ly** *adv.*

spec·u·lum /spékyələm/ *n.* (*pl.* **spec·u·la** /–lə/ or **spec·u·lums**) **1** *Surgery* instrument for dilating the cavities of the human body for inspection. **2** mirror, usu. of polished metal, esp. in a reflecting telescope.

sped *past* and *past part.* of SPEED.

speech /speech/ *n.* **1** faculty, act, or manner of speaking. **2** formal public address. **3** language of a nation, region, group, etc. □□ **speech′ful** *adj.*

speech·less /spéechlis/ *adj.* **1** temporarily unable to speak. **2** mute. □□ **speech′less·ly** *adv.* **speech′less·ness** *n.*

speed /speed/ • *n.* **1** rapidity of movement. **2** rate of progress or motion over a distance in time. **3** arrangement of gears yielding a specific ratio in a bicycle or automobile transmission. **4** *Photog.* **a** sensitivity of film to light. **b** light-gathering power of a lens. **c** duration of an exposure. **5** *sl.* amphetamine drug. • *v.* (*past* and *past part.* **sped** /sped/) **1** *intr.* go fast. **2** (*past* and *past part.* **speed·ed**) *intr.* travel at an illegal or dangerous speed. **3** *tr.* send fast or on its way. □ **speed bump** raised ridge across a roadway to force slow travel. **speed up** move or work at greater speed. □□ **speed′er** *n.*

speed·boat /spéedbōt/ *n.* high-speed motorboat.

speed·om·e·ter /spidómitər/ *n.* instrument on a motor vehicle, etc., indicating its speed to the driver.

speed·way /spéedway/ *n.* racetrack used for automobiles, motorcycles, etc.

speed·y /spéedee/ *adj.* (**speed·i·er**, **speed·i·est**) **1** moving quickly; rapid. **2** done without delay; prompt (*speedy answer*). □□ **speed′i·ly** *adv.* **speed′i·ness** *n.*

spe·le·ol·o·gy /spéeleeóləjee/ *n.* the study of caves. □□ **spe·le·o·log·i·cal** /–leeəlójikəl/ *adj.* **spe·le·ol′o·gist** *n.*

spell[1] /spel/ *v.tr.* (*past* and *past part.* **spelled** or **spelt**) **1** write or name correctly the letters that form (a word, etc.). **2 a** (of letters) form (a word, etc.). **b** result in; involve (*spell ruin*). □ **spell out 1** make out (words, writing, etc.) letter by letter. **2** explain in detail. □□ **spell'a·ble** *adj.*

spell[2] /spel/ *n.* **1** form of words used as a magical charm or incantation. **2** attraction or fascination exercised by a person, activity, quality, etc.

spell[3] /spel/ • *n.* **1** short or fairly short period (*a cold spell in April*). **2** turn of work (*did a spell of woodwork*). • *v.tr.* relieve or take the place of (a person) in work, etc.

spell·bind /spélbīnd/ *v.tr.* (*past* and *past part.* **spell'bound**) bind with or as if with a spell; cast a spell on or over. □□ **spell'bind·er** *n.* **spell' bind·ing·ly** *adv.*

spel·ler /spélər/ *n.* **1** person who spells, esp. in a specified way (*is a poor speller*). **2** book on spelling.

spel·ling /spéling/ *n.* **1** writing or naming the letters of a word, etc. **2** way a word is spelled. **3** ability to spell. □ **spelling bee** spelling competition.

spe·lunk·er /spilúngkər, speélung–/ *n.* person who explores caves, esp. as a hobby. □□ **spe' lunk·ing** *n.*

spend /spend/ *v.tr.* (*past* and *past part.* **spent** /spent/) **1** pay out (money). **2 a** use or consume (time or energy). **b** use up; exhaust; wear out. □□ **spend'a·ble** *adj.* **spend'er** *n.*

spend·thrift /spéndthrift/ • *n.* extravagant person; prodigal. • *adj.* extravagant; prodigal.

sperm /spərm/ *n.* (*pl.* same or **sperms**) **1** = SPERMATOZOON. **2** male reproductive fluid containing spermatozoa; semen. □ **sperm whale** large whale yielding valuable oil.

sper·ma·to·zo·on /spərmátəzō-on, –ən, spórmə–/ *n.* (*pl.* **sper·ma·to·zo·a** /–zōə/) mature motile sex cell in animals. □□ **sper·ma·to· zo'an** *adj.*

sper·mi·cide /spórmisīd/ *n.* substance able to kill spermatozoa. □□ **sper·mi·cid'al** *adj.*

spew /spyōō/ *v.* **1** *tr.* & *intr.* vomit. **2** (often foll. by *out*) **a** *tr.* expel (contents) rapidly and forcibly. **b** *intr.* (of contents) be expelled in this way. □□ **spew'er** *n.*

SPF *abbr.* sun protection factor.

sp. gr. *abbr.* specific gravity.

sphere /sfeer/ *n.* **1** solid figure, or its surface, with every point on its surface equidistant from its center. **2** object having this shape; ball or globe. **3** field of action, influence, etc. □□ **spher·i·cal** /–ikəl, sfér–/ *adj.*

spher·oid /sféeroyd/ *n.* spherelike but not perfectly spherical body. □□ **sphe·roi'dal** *adj.*

sphinc·ter /sfíngktər/ *n.* *Anat.* ring of muscle surrounding and serving to guard or close an opening or tube, esp. the anus.

sphinx /sfingks/ *n.* **1** (**Sphinx**) *Gk. mythol.* winged monster of Thebes, having a woman's head and a lion's body. **2** *Antiq.* **a** any of several ancient Egyptian stone figures having a lion's body and a human or animal head. **b** (**the Sphinx**) the huge stone figure of a sphinx near the Pyramids at Giza. **3** enigmatic or inscrutable person.

sphyg·mo·ma·no·me·ter /sfigmōmənómitər/ *n.* instrument for measuring blood pressure.

spice /spīs/ • *n.* **1** aromatic or pungent vegetable substance used to flavor food. **2** interest-

ing or piquant quality. • *v.tr.* flavor with spice. □□ **spic'y** *adj.*

spick-and-span /spík ənd spán/ (also **spic'-and- span'**) *adj.* **1** fresh and new. **2** neat and clean.

spi·der /spídər/ *n.* **1** arachnid, many species of which spin webs for the capture of insects as food. **2** frying pan, esp. one with legs or feet.

spi·der·y /spídəree/ *adj.* elongated and thin.

spiel /speel, shpeel/ *sl. n.* glib speech or story, esp. a salesman's patter. □□ **spiel'er** *n.*

spiff·y /spífee/ *adj.* (**spif·fi·er, spif·fi·est**) *sl.* stylish; smart. □□ **spif'fi·ly** *adv.*

spig·ot /spígət/ *n.* **1** small peg or plug, esp. in a cask. **2** faucet.

spike[1] /spīk/ • *n.* **1 a** sharp point. **b** pointed piece of metal, esp. the top of an iron railing, etc. **2 a** any of several metal points set into the sole of a running shoe to prevent slipping. **b** (in *pl.*) pair of running shoes with spikes. **3** large stout nail. • *v.tr.* **1 a** fasten or provide with spikes. **b** fix on or pierce with spikes. **2** (of a newspaper editor, etc.) reject (a story), esp. by filing it on a spike. **3** *colloq.* lace (a drink) with alcohol, a drug, etc. **4** make useless; put an end to; thwart (an idea, etc.). □□ **spik'i·ly** *adv.* **spik'i·ness** *n.* **spik'y** *adj.* (**spik·i·er, spik·i·est**)

spike[2] /spīk/ *n.* *Bot.* flower cluster formed of many flower heads attached closely on a long stem. □□ **spike'let** *n.*

spill[1] /spil/ • *v.* (*past* and *past part.* **spilled** or **spilt**) **1** *intr.* & *tr.* fall or run or cause (a liquid, powder, etc.) to fall or run out of a vessel, esp. unintentionally. **2 a** *tr.* & *intr.* throw (a person, etc.) from a vehicle, saddle, etc. **b** *intr.* (esp. of a crowd) tumble out quickly from a place, etc. **3** *tr.* *sl.* disclose (information, etc.). • *n.* **1** spilling or being spilled. **2** tumble or fall, esp. from a horse, etc. □ **spill the beans** *colloq.* divulge information, etc., esp. unintentionally or indiscreetly. **spill blood** be guilty of bloodshed. □□ **spill'age** /spílij/ *n.* **spill'er** *n.*

spill·way /spílway/ *n.* passage for surplus water from a dam.

spin /spin/ • *v.* (**spin·ning;** *past* and *past part.* **spun** /spun/) **1** *intr.* & *tr.* turn or cause to turn or whirl around quickly. **2** *tr.* (also *absol.*) **a** draw out and twist (wool, cotton, etc.) into threads. **b** make (yarn) in this way. **3** *tr.* (of a spider, silkworm, etc.) make (a web, gossamer, a cocoon, etc.) by extruding a fine viscous thread. **4** *tr.* tell or write (a story, essay, article, etc.). **5** *intr.* (of a person's head, etc.) be dizzy through excitement, astonishment, etc. • *n.* **1** spinning motion; whirl. **2** aircraft's diving descent combined with rotation. **3** revolving motion through the air, esp. in a rifle bullet or in a ball. **4** *colloq.* brief drive, esp. in a car. **5** emphasis; interpretation. □ **spin doctor** political operative who attempts to influence press coverage of events. **spin off 1** throw off by centrifugal force in spinning. **2** create or establish as a by-product or derivative endeavor. □□ **spin'ner** *n.*

spi·na bi·fi·da /spínə bífidə/ *n.* congenital defect of the spine.

spin·ach /spínich, –nij/ *n.* dark green vegetable with edible leaves.

spi·nal /spín'l/ *adj.* of or relating to the spine. □ **spinal column** spine. **spinal cord** cylindrical structure of the central nervous system enclosed in the spine.

spin·dle /spínd'l/ n. **1 a** pin in a spinning wheel used for twisting and winding the thread. **b** small bar with tapered ends used for the same purpose in hand spinning. **2** pin or axis that revolves or on which something revolves. **3** turned piece of wood used as a banister, chair leg, etc.

spin·dly /spíndlee/ adj. (**spin·dli·er, spin·dli·est**) long or tall and thin; thin and weak.

spine /spīn/ n. **1** series of vertebrae extending from the skull to the small of the back; backbone. **2** Zool. & Bot. any hard pointed process or structure. **3** sharp ridge or projection. **4** part of a book's jacket or cover that encloses the fastened edges of the pages. □ **spine-chilling** (esp. of a story, etc.) frightening. **spine-tingling** thrilling; pleasurably exciting. □□ **spined** adj.

spine·less /spínlis/ adj. **1** having no spine; invertebrate. **2** lacking resolve; weak. □□ **spine′less·ly** adv. **spine′less·ness** n.

spin·et /spínit, spinét/ n. Mus. small upright piano.

spin·ner·et /spínəret/ n. spinning organ in a spider, etc.

spin·ning /spíning/ n. the act or an instance of spinning. □ **spinning jenny** hist. machine for spinning with more than one spindle at a time. **spinning wheel** household machine for spinning yarn or thread with a spindle driven by a wheel attached to a crank or treadle.

spin·ster /spínstər/ n. **1** unmarried woman. **2** woman, esp. elderly, thought unlikely to marry. □□ **spin′ster·hood** n. **spin′ster·ish** adj.

spin·y /spínee/ adj. (**spin·i·er, spin·i·est**) **1** full of spines; prickly. **2** perplexing; troublesome; thorny. □□ **spin′i·ness** n.

spi·ral /spírəl/ ● adj. coiled in a plane or as if around a cylinder or cone. ● n. **1** plane or three-dimensional spiral curve. **2** spiral thing. **3** progressive rise or fall. ● v.intr. **1** move in a spiral course. **2** esp. Econ. (of prices, wages, etc.) rise or fall, esp. rapidly. □□ **spi′ral·ly** adv.

spire /spīr/ n. tapering cone- or pyramid-shaped structure built esp. on a church tower.

spi·re·a /spíreéə/ n. (also **spi·rae′a**) shrub with clusters of small white or pink flowers.

spir·it /spírit/ ● n. **1** vital animating essence of a person or animal; soul. **2** ghost. **3** prevailing mental or moral condition or attitude; mood; tendency (public spirit). **4** (in pl.) strong distilled liquor. **5 a** person's mental or moral nature or qualities, usu. specified (unbending spirit). **b** person viewed as possessing these (is an ardent spirit). **c** (in full **high spirit**) courage; energy; vivacity. **6** real meaning (spirit of the law). ● v.tr. (usu. foll. by away, off, etc.) convey rapidly and secretly by or as if by spirits.

spir·it·ed /spíritid/ adj. full of spirit; animated, lively, brisk, or courageous. □□ **spir′it·ed·ly** adv. **spir′it·ed·ness** n.

spir·it·less /spíritlis/ adj. lacking courage, vigor, or vivacity. □□ **spir′it·less·ly** adv.

spir·i·tu·al /spírichōōəl/ ● adj. **1** of or concerning the spirit as opposed to matter. **2** religious; divine; inspired. ● n. religious song derived from the musical traditions of African-American people. □□ **spir·i·tu·al·i·ty** /-chōō-álitee/ n. **spir′i·tu·al·ly** adv. **spir′i·tu·al·ness** n.

spir·i·tu·al·ism /spírichōōəlizəm/ n. belief that the spirits of the dead can communicate with the living, esp. through mediums. □□ **spir′i·tu·al·ist** n.

spir·i·tu·ous /spírichōōəs/ adj. **1** containing much alcohol. **2** distilled, as whiskey, rum, etc.

spi·ro·chete /spírōkeet/ n. (also **spi′ro·chaete**) any of various flexible spiral-shaped bacteria.

spit¹ /spit/ ● v. (**spit·ting**; past and past part. **spat** /spat/ or **spit**) **1** intr. **a** eject saliva from the mouth. **b** do this as a sign of hatred or contempt (spat at him). **2** tr. (usu. foll. by out) **a** eject (saliva, blood, food, etc.) from the mouth (spit the meat out). **b** utter (oaths, threats, etc.) vehemently. **3** intr. (of a fire, pen, pan, etc.) send out sparks, ink, hot fat, etc. ● n. **1** spittle. **2** the act or an instance of spitting. □ **spit and polish** military cleaning and polishing. **spitting distance** very short distance. **spitting image** (foll. by of) colloq. the exact double of (another person or thing). □□ **spit′ter** n.

spit² /spit/ ● n. **1** rod on which meat is skewered before being roasted on a fire, etc. **2** small point of land projecting into the sea. ● v.tr. (**spit·ted, spit·ting**) **1** thrust a spit through. **2** pierce or transfix with a sword, etc.

spit·ball /spítbawl/ n. **1** ball of chewed paper, etc., used as a missile. **2** baseball moistened by the pitcher to affect its flight. □□ **spit′ball·er** n.

spite /spīt/ ● n. feeling of ill will; malice. ● v.tr. thwart; mortify; annoy (does it to spite me). □ **in spite of** notwithstanding.

spite·ful /spítfōōl/ adj. motivated by spite; malevolent. □□ **spite′ful·ly** adv. **spite′ful·ness** n.

spit·fire /spítfīr/ n. person with a fiery temper.

spit·tle /spít'l/ n. saliva.

spit·toon /spitōōn/ n. vessel to spit into.

splash /splash/ ● v. **1** intr. & tr. spatter or cause (liquid) to spatter in small drops. **2** tr. cause (a person) to be spattered with liquid, etc. (splashed them with mud). **3** intr. **a** (of a person) cause liquid to spatter (was splashing about in the bath). **b** move while spattering liquid, etc. **4** tr. display (news) prominently. ● n. **1** act or instance of splashing. **2** quantity of liquid splashed. **3** spot or patch of dirt, etc., splashed on to a thing. □ **make a splash** attract much attention. □□ **splash′y** adj. (**splash·i·er, splash·i·est**).

splash·down /spláshdown/ n. landing of a spacecraft in the sea.

splat¹ /splat/ n. flat piece of thin wood in the center of a chair back.

splat² /splat/ colloq. ● n. sharp cracking or slapping sound. ● adv. with a splat. ● v. (**splat·ted, splat·ting**) fall or hit with a splat.

splat·ter /splátər/ v. splash, esp. with a continuous noisy action.

splay /splay/ ● v.tr. spread out. ● adj. **1** wide and flat. **2** turned outward.

spleen /spleen/ n. **1** abdominal organ involved in maintaining the proper condition of blood in most vertebrates. **2** moroseness. □□ **spleen′ful** adj.

splen·did /spléndid/ adj. **1** magnificent; sumptuous. **2** dignified; impressive. **3** excellent; fine. □□ **splen′did·ly** adv.

splen·dor /spléndər/ n. **1** great or dazzling brightness. **2** magnificence; grandeur.

sple·net·ic /splinétik/ adj. ill-tempered; peevish. □□ **sple·net′i·cal·ly** adv.

splice /splīs/ • v.tr. **1** join the ends of (ropes) by interweaving strands. **2** join (pieces of timber, tape, film, etc.) in an overlapping position. **3** (esp. as **spliced** adj.) colloq. join in marriage. • n. joint made by splicing. □□ **splic′er** n.

splint /splint/ • n. **1** strip of rigid material used for holding a broken bone, etc., when set. **2** rigid or flexible strip of esp. wood used in basketwork, etc. • v.tr. secure (a broken limb, etc.) with a splint or splints.

splin·ter /splíntər/ • v. break into fragments. • n. small thin sharp-edged piece broken off from wood, glass, etc. □□ **splin′ter·y** adj.

split /split/ • v. (**split·ting**; past and past part. **split**) **1** intr. & tr. **a** break or cause to break forcibly into parts, esp. with the grain or into halves. **b** divide into parts; esp. equal shares. **2** tr. & intr. remove or be removed by breaking, separating, or dividing. **3** intr. & tr. **a** separate esp. through discord. **b** quarrel or cease association. **4** intr. & tr. sl. leave, esp. suddenly. **5** intr. (as **splitting** adj.) very painful; acute. • n. **1** act or result of splitting. **2** separation into parties; schism. **3** (in pl.) athletic feat of leaping in the air or sitting down with the legs at right angles to the body in front and behind, or at the sides with the trunk facing forward. □ **split infinitive** infinitive with an adverb, etc., inserted between to and the verb, e.g., seems to really like it. **split-level** (of a building) having a room or rooms a fraction of a story higher than other parts. **split pea** dried pea split in half for cooking. **split personality** alteration or dissociation of personality occurring in some mental illnesses, esp. schizophrenia and hysteria. □□ **split′ter** n.

splotch /sploch/ • n. & v.tr. colloq. • n. daub, blot, or smear. • v.tr. make a splotch on. □□ **splotch′y** adj.

splurge /splərj/ colloq. • n. **1** ostentatious display or effort. **2** instance of sudden great extravagance. • v.intr. spend large sums of money.

splut·ter /splútər/ • v. **1** intr. **a** speak in a hurried, vehement, or choking manner. **b** emit spitting sounds. **2** tr. speak rapidly or incoherently. • n. rapid, incoherent speech. □□ **splut′ter·er** n. **splut′ter·ing·ly** adv.

spoil /spoyl/ • v. (past and past part. **spoiled** or **spoilt**) **1** tr. **a** damage; diminish the value of. **b** reduce a person's enjoyment, etc., of. **2** tr. overindulge (esp. a child, pet, etc.). **3** intr. (of food) go bad; decay. **4** tr. literary plunder or deprive (a person of a thing) by force or stealth. • n. **1** (usu. in pl.) plunder. **2** esp. joc. profit or advantages gained by succeeding to public office, high position, etc. □□ **spoil′age** n. **spoil′er** n.

spoke[1] /spōk/ n. each of the bars running from the hub to the rim of a wheel.

spoke[2] past of SPEAK.

spo·ken /spōkən/ past part. of SPEAK. adj. (in comb.) speaking in a specified way (well-spoken). □ **spoken for** claimed.

spokes·man /spōksmən/ n. (pl. **-men**; fem. **spokes·wom·an**, pl. **-wom·en**) person speaking for a group, etc.

spokes·per·son /spōkspərsən/ n. (pl. **-per·sons** or **-peo·ple**) spokesman or spokeswoman.

spo·li·a·tion /spōleeáyshən/ n. plunder or pillage.

spon·dee /spóndee/ n. Prosody metrical foot consisting of two long (or stressed) syllables. □□ **spon·da·ic** /-dáyik/ adj.

sponge /spunj/ • n. **1** any aquatic animal with pores in its body wall and a rigid internal skeleton. **2 a** skeleton of a sponge, esp. the soft light elastic absorbent kind used in bathing, etc. **b** piece of porous rubber or plastic, etc., used similarly. **3** thing of spongelike absorbency or consistency. **4** (also **sponger**) person who lives off another's means. • v. **1** tr. wipe, clean, or absorb with or as with a sponge. **2** intr. live as a parasite. □ **sponge cake** very light cake with a spongelike consistency. □□ **sponge′a·ble** adj. **sponge′like** adj. **spon′gi·form** adj. (esp. in senses 1, 2).

spong·y /spúnjee/ adj. (**spong·i·er**, **spong·i·est**) **1** like a sponge. **2** (of metal) finely divided and loosely coherent. □□ **spong′i·ly** adv. **spong′i·ness** n.

spon·sor /spónsər/ • n. **1** person who supports an activity; backer. **2** business organization that promotes a broadcast program in return for advertising time. **3** Eccles. godparent at baptism or esp. a person who presents a candidate for confirmation. • v.tr. be a sponsor for. □□ **spon·so·ri·al** /sponsáwreeəl/ adj. **spon′sor·ship** n.

spon·ta·ne·ous /spontáyneeəs/ adj. **1** acting or done or occurring without external cause. **2** instinctive; automatic; natural. □ **spontaneous combustion** ignition of a mineral or vegetable substance from internal heat. □□ **spon·ta·ne·i·ty** /spóntənéeitee, –náyitee/ n. **spon·ta′ne·ous·ly** adv.

spoof /spoof/ n. & v. colloq. **1** parody. **2** hoax.

spook /spook/ • n. colloq. ghost. • v. sl. **1** tr. frighten; unnerve; alarm. **2** intr. take fright; become alarmed.

spook·y /spookee/ adj. (**spook·i·er**, **spook·i·est**) **1** colloq. ghostly; eerie. **2** sl. nervous; easily frightened. □□ **spook′i·ly** adv. **spook′i·ness** n.

spool /spool/ • n. **1** reel for winding magnetic tape, yarn, etc. **2** revolving cylinder of an angler's reel. • v.tr. wind on a spool.

spoon /spoon/ • n. **1 a** utensil consisting of an oval or round bowl and a handle for conveying food (esp. liquid) to the mouth, for stirring, etc. **b** spoonful. • v. **1** tr. take (liquid, etc.) with a spoon. **2** colloq. intr. behave in an amorous way, esp. foolishly. □□ **spoon′er** n. **spoon′ful** n. (pl. **-fuls**).

spoon·bill /spoonbil/ n. large wading bird having a bill with a very broad flat tip.

spoo·ner·ism /spoonərizəm/ n. transposition, usu. accidental, of the initial letters, etc., of two or more words, e.g., you have hissed the mystery lectures for you have missed the history lectures.

spoon·feed /spoonfeed/ v.tr. (past and past part. **-fed**) **1** feed with a spoon. **2** provide help, information, etc., to (a person) without requiring any effort on the recipient's part.

spo·rad·ic /spərádik, spaw–/ adj. occurring only here and there or occasionally; separate; scattered. □□ **spo·rad′i·cal·ly** adv.

spore /spawr/ n. **1** specialized reproductive cell of many plants and microorganisms. **2** these collectively.

sport /spawrt/ • n. **1 a** game or competitive activity, esp. an outdoor one involving physical exertion, e.g., baseball, football, racing, hunting. **b** (usu. in pl.) such activities collectively (*world of sports*). **2** amusement; diversion; fun. **3** *colloq.* fair or generous person. **4** plaything or laughingstock (*was the sport of Fortune*). • *v.* **1** *intr.* **a** divert oneself; take part in a pastime. **b** frolic; gambol. **2** *tr.* wear, exhibit, or produce, esp. ostentatiously. □ **in sport** jestingly. **make sport of** make fun of; ridicule. **sports car** low-built fast car. **sports coat** (or **jacket**) man's jacket for informal wear. **sport utility vehicle** passenger vehicle with a light-truck chassis and four-wheel drive. □□ **sport′er** *n.*

sport·ing /spáwrting/ *adj.* **1** interested in sports (*sporting man*). **2** sportsmanlike; generous (*sporting offer*). **3** concerned about, active in, or involved in sports (*sporting dog*). □ **sporting chance** some possibility of success. □□ **sport′ing·ly** *adv.*

sport·ive /spáwrtiv/ *adj.* playful.

sports·man /spáwrtsmən/ *n.* (*pl.* **–men**; *fem.* **sports·wom·an**, *pl.* **–wom·en**) **1** person who takes part in sports. **2** person who behaves fairly and generously. □□ **sports′man·like** *adj.* **sports′man·ly** *adj.* **sports′man·ship** *n.*

sports·wear /spáwrtswair/ *n.* clothes worn for sports or for casual use.

sport·y /spáwrtee/ *adj.* (**sport·i·er**, **sport·i·est**) *colloq.* **1** fond of sports. **2** rakish; showy. □□ **sport′i·ly** *adv.* **sport′i·ness** *n.*

spot /spot/ • *n.* **1 a** small roundish part of the surface of a thing distinguished by color, texture, etc. **b** blemish; defect. **2** particular place; definite locality. **3** = SPOTLIGHT. **4** *colloq.* awkward or difficult situation (esp. in *in a* (tight, etc.) spot). • *v.* (**spot·ted**, **spot·ting**) **1** *tr.* **a** *colloq.* identify; recognize; catch sight of. **b** watch for and take note of (trains, talent, etc.). **2** *tr.* & *intr.* mark or become marked with spots. □ **on the spot 1** at the scene of an action or event. **2** *colloq.* in a position such that response or action is required. □□ **spot′ter** *n.*

spot·less /spótlis/ *adj.* immaculate; absolutely clean or pure. □□ **spot′less·ly** *adv.* **spot′less·ness** *n.*

spot·light /spótlīt/ • *n.* **1** beam of light directed on a small area. **2** lamp projecting this. **3** full attention or publicity. • *v.tr.* (*past* and *past part.* **–light·ed** or **–lit**) **1** direct a spotlight on. **2** draw attention to.

spot·ty /spótee/ *adj.* (**spot·ti·er**, **spot·ti·est**) **1** marked with spots. **2** patchy; irregular. □□ **spot′ti·ly** *adv.* **spot′ti·ness** *n.*

spouse /spows, spowz/ *n.* husband or wife.

spout /spowt/ • *n.* **1** projecting tube or lip through which a liquid, etc., is poured from a teapot, kettle, pitcher, etc., or issues from a fountain, pump, etc. **2** jet or column of liquid, grain, etc. • *v.* **1** discharge or issue forcibly in a jet. **2** utter (verses, etc.) or speak in a declamatory manner; speechify. □□ **spout′er** *n.* **spout′less** *adj.*

sprain /sprayn/ • *v.tr.* wrench (an ankle, wrist, etc.) so as to cause pain and swelling. • *n.* such a wrench.

sprang *past* of SPRING.

sprat /sprat/ *n.* small European herring-like fish, much used as food.

sprawl /sprawl/ • *v.* **1 a** *intr.* sit or lie or fall with limbs flung out or in an ungainly way. **b** *tr.* spread (one's limbs) in this way. **2** *intr.* (of

handwriting, a plant, a town, etc.) be of irregular or straggling form. • *n.* sprawling movement, position, or mass. □□ **sprawl′ing·ly** *adv.*

spray[1] /spray/ • *n.* **1** water or other liquid flying in small drops. **2** device for creating this. • *v.tr.* (also *absol.*) **1** throw (liquid) in the form of spray. **2** sprinkle (an object) with small drops or particles. □ **spray gun** gunlike device for spraying paint, etc. □□ **spray′a·ble** *adj.* **spray′er** *n.*

spray[2] /spray/ *n.* sprig of flowers or leaves.

spread /spred/ • *v.* (*past* and *past part.* **spread**) **1** *tr.* **a** open or extend the surface of. **b** cause to cover a larger surface. **c** display to the eye or the mind. **2** *intr.* have a wide or increasing extent (*spreading trees*). **3** *intr.* & *tr.* become or make widely known, felt, etc. (*rumors are spreading*). **4** *tr.* lay (a table). • *n.* **1** act or an instance of spreading. **2** extent of spreading. **3** diffusion (*spread of learning*). **4** increased bodily girth (*middle-aged spread*). **5** difference between two rates, prices, scores, etc. **6** *colloq.* elaborate meal. **7** food for spreading on bread, etc. **8** bedspread. **9** printed matter spread across more than one column. **10** ranch or farm with extensive land. □ **spread eagle** in the shape of an eagle with legs and wings extended. **spread-eagle** *v.tr.* (usu. as **spread-eagled** *adj.*) place in a position with limbs extended. □□ **spread′a·ble** *adj.* **spread′er** *n.*

spread·sheet /sprédsheet/ *n.* computer program allowing manipulation of esp. tabulated numerical data.

spree /spree/ *colloq. n.* **1** lively extravagant outing (*shopping spree*). **2** bout of fun or drinking, etc.

sprig /sprig/ *n.* small branch or shoot.

spright·ly /sprítlee/ *adj.* (**spright·li·er**, **spright·li·est**) vivacious; lively; brisk. □□ **spright′li·ness** *n.*

spring /spring/ • *v.* (*past* **sprang** /sprang/ also **sprung** /sprung/; *past part.* **sprung**) **1** *intr.* jump; move rapidly or suddenly (*sprang from his seat*). **2** *intr.* move rapidly as from a constrained position or by the action of a spring. **3** *intr.* originate or arise (*springs from an old family*). **4** *intr.* come into being; appear, esp. suddenly (*a breeze sprang up*). **5** *tr.* produce or develop or make known suddenly or unexpectedly (*loves to spring surprises*). **6** *tr. sl.* contrive the escape or release of. • *n.* **1** jump (*took a spring*). **2** recoil, e.g., of a bow. **3** elasticity. **4** resilient device usu. of bent or coiled metal used esp. to drive clockwork or for cushioning in furniture or vehicles. **5 a** season in which vegetation begins to appear, first season of the year. **b** early stage of life, etc. **6** place where water, oil, etc., wells up from the earth. □ **spring fever** restless or lethargic feeling sometimes associated with spring. □□ **spring′less** *adj.* **spring′like** *adj.*

spring·board /spríngbawrd/ *n.* **1** springy board giving impetus in leaping, diving, etc. **2** point of departure.

spring·y /springee/ *adj.* (**spring·i·er**, **spring·i·est**) resilient; bouncy; elastic. □□ **spring′i·ly** *adv.* **spring′i·ness** *n.*

sprin·kle /springkəl/ • *v.tr.* **1** scatter in small drops or particles. **2** subject to sprinkling with liquid, etc. **3** distribute in small amounts. • *n.* **1** light shower. **2** = SPRINKLING. □□ **sprin′kler** *n.*

sprin·kling /springkling/ *n.* sparse number or amount.

sprint /sprint/ • *v.* **1** *intr.* run a short distance at full speed. **2** *tr.* run (a specified distance) in this way. ● *n.* **1** such a run. **2** similar short spell of maximum effort in cycling, swimming, auto racing, etc. □□ **sprint′er** *n.*

sprite /sprīt/ *n.* elf, fairy, or goblin.

spritz·er /sprítsər/ *n.* mixture of wine and soda water.

sprock·et /sprókit/ *n.* each of several teeth on a wheel engaging with links of a chain.

SPROCKET

sprout /sprowt/ ● *v.* **1** *tr.* put forth; produce (shoots, hair, etc.). **2** *intr.* begin to grow; put forth shoots. ● *n.* shoot of a plant.

spruce[1] /sprōōs/ ● *adj.* neat in dress and appearance; smart. ● *v.* (also *refl.*; usu. foll. by *up*) make or become neat and fashionable.

spruce[2] /sprōōs/ *n.* **1** conifer with dense foliage. **2** wood of this tree used as timber.

sprung *past. and past part.* of SPRING.

spry /sprī/ *adj.* (**spry·er, spry·est**) active; lively. □□ **spry′ly** *adv.* **spry′ness** *n.*

spud /spud/ *n. sl.* potato.

spume /spyōōm/ *n. & v.intr.* froth; foam. □□ **spum′y** *adj.* (**spum·i·er, spum·i·est**).

spun *past and past part.* of SPIN.

spunk·y /spúngkee/ *adj.* (**spunk·i·er, spunk·i·est**) *colloq.* brave; spirited. □□ **spunk′i·ly** *adv.*

spur /spər/ ● *n.* **1** device with a small spike or a spiked wheel worn on a rider's heel for urging a horse forward. **2** stimulus or incentive. **3** spur-shaped thing, esp.: **a** projection from a mountain or mountain range. **b** branch road or railway. ● *v.tr.* (**spurred, spur·ring**) **1** prick (a horse) with spurs. **2** incite; stimulate. □ **on the spur of the moment** on a momentary impulse; impromptu. □□ **spur′less** *adj.*

spu·ri·ous /spyōōreeəs/ *adj.* not genuine; not being what it purports to be. □□ **spu′ri·ous·ly** *adv.* **spu′ri·ous·ness** *n.*

spurn /spərn/ *v.* reject with disdain; treat with contempt. □□ **spurn′er** *n.*

spurt /spərt/ ● *v.* **1 a** *intr.* gush out in a jet or stream. **b** *tr.* cause (liquid, etc.) to do this. **2** *intr.* make a sudden effort. ● *n.* **1** sudden gushing out; jet. **2** short sudden effort or increase of pace, esp. in racing.

sput·nik /spōōtnik, spút–/ *n.* each of a series of Russian artificial satellites launched from 1957.

sput·ter /spútər/ ● *v.* **1** *intr.* emit spitting sounds. **2** *intr.* speak in a hurried or vehement fashion. **3** *tr.* emit with a spitting sound. **4** *tr.* speak or utter rapidly or incoherently. ● *n.* sputtering. □□ **sput′ter·er** *n.*

spu·tum /spyōōtəm/ *n.* (*pl.* **spu·ta** /–tə/) **1** sa-

liva; spittle. **2** expectorated matter, usu. a sign of disease.

spy /spī/ ● *n.* (*pl.* **spies**) **1** person who secretly collects and reports information on the activities, movements, etc., of an enemy, competitor, etc. **2** person who keeps watch on others, esp. furtively. ● *v.* (**spies, spied**) **1** *tr.* discern; see. **2** *intr.* act as a spy. □□ **spy′ing** *n.*

spy·glass /spíglas/ *n.* small telescope.

sq. *abbr.* square.

squab /skwob/ *n.* young pigeon or other bird.

squab·ble /skwóbəl/ ● *n.* petty or noisy quarrel. ● *v.intr.* engage in a squabble. □□ **squab′bler** *n.*

squad /skwod/ *n.* **1** small group of people sharing a task, etc.; esp. of soldiers or policemen. **2** *Sports* team. □ **squad car** police car.

squad·ron /skwódrən/ *n.* unit of aircraft, warships, etc.

squal·id /skwólid/ *adj.* **1** filthy. **2** mean or poor. □□ **squa·lid′i·ty** *n.* **squal′id·ly** *adv.* **squal′id·ness** *n.*

squall /skwawl/ ● *n.* **1** sudden or violent wind, esp. with rain or snow or sleet. **2** discordant cry; scream (esp. of a baby). ● *v.intr.* utter a squall; scream. □□ **squal′ly** *adj.*

squa·lor /skwólər/ *n.* state of being filthy or squalid.

squan·der /skwóndər/ *v.tr.* spend (money, time, etc.) wastefully. □□ **squan′der·er** *n.*

square /skwair/ ● *n.* **1** equilateral rectangle. **2** open (usu. four-sided) area surrounded by buildings. **3** product of a number multiplied by itself (*81 is the square of 9*). **4** L-shaped or T-shaped instrument for obtaining or testing right angles. **5** *sl.* conventional or old-fashioned person. ● *adj.* **1** having the shape of a square. **2** having or in the form of a right angle (*table with square corners*). **3** angular and not round. **4** designating the area of a square whose side is the length of the unit specified (*square mile*). **5** level; parallel. **6** at right angles. **7** equal; settled. **8** fair and honest. **9** *sl.* conventional or old-fashioned. ● *adv.* squarely. ● *v.* **1** *tr.* make square. **2** *tr.* multiply (a number) by itself (*3 squared is 9*). **3** *tr. & intr.* reconcile (*the results do not square with your conclusions*). **4** *tr.* settle or pay (a bill, etc.). **5** *tr.* place (one's shoulders, etc.) squarely facing forward. □ **square dance** dance with usu. four couples facing inward from four sides. **square meal** substantial and satisfying meal. **square off** assume the attitude of a boxer. **square root** number that multiplied by itself gives a specified number. □□ **square′ly** *adv.* **square′ness** *n.* **squar′ish** *adj.*

squash[1] /skwosh/ ● *v.* **1** *tr.* crush or squeeze flat or into pulp. **2** *intr.* make one's way by squeezing. **3** *tr.* dismiss (a proposal, etc.). ● *n.* game played with rackets and a small ball against the walls of a closed court. □□ **squash′y** *adj.* (**squash·i·er, squash·i·est**). **squash′i·ly** *adv.* **squash′i·ness** *n.*

squash[2] /skwosh/ *n.* (*pl.* same or **squash·es**) plant with gourdlike fruit that may be used as a vegetable.

squat /skwot/ ● *v.* (**squat·ted, squat·ting**) **1** *intr.* sit on one's heels or on the ground, etc., with the knees drawn up. **2 a** *intr.* act as a squatter. **b** *tr.* occupy (a building) as a squatter. ● *adj.* (**squat·ter, squat·test**) (of a person, etc.) short and thick; dumpy. ● *n.* squatting posture.

squat·ter /skwótər/ *n.* person who takes unauthorized possession of unoccupied premises.

squaw /skwaw/ *n.* often *offens.* Native American woman or wife.

squawk /skwawk/ • *n.* **1** loud harsh cry, esp. of a bird. **2** complaint. • *v.* utter with or make a squawk. □□ **squawk′er** *n.*

squeak /skweek/ • *n.* **1** short shrill cry or sound. **2** (also **nar′row squeak**) narrow escape. • *v.* **1** *intr.* make a squeak. **2** *tr.* utter (words) shrilly. **3** *intr.* (foll. by *by, through*) *colloq.* pass narrowly. □□ **squeak′er** *n.* **squeak′i·ly** *adv.* **squeak′i·ness** *n.* **squeak′y** *adj.* (**squeak·i·er, squeak·i·est**).

squeal /skweel/ • *n.* prolonged shrill sound, esp. a cry of a child or a pig. • *v.* **1** *intr.* make a squeal. **2** *tr.* utter (words) with a squeal. **3** *intr. sl.* turn informer. □□ **squeal′er** *n.*

squeam·ish /skwée′mish/ *adj.* **1** easily nauseated or disgusted. **2** fastidious; sensitive. □□ **squeam′ish·ly** *adv.* **squeam′ish·ness** *n.*

squee·gee /skwée′jee/ *n.* rubber-edged implement often set on a long handle and used for cleaning windows, etc.

squeeze /skweez/ • *v.tr.* **1 a** exert pressure on. **b** reduce the size of or alter the shape of by squeezing. **2** force (a person or thing) into or through a small or narrow space. **3 a** harass by exactions; bring pressure to bear on. **b** obtain (money, etc.) by extortion, entreaty, etc. **4** press or hold closely as a sign of sympathy, affection, etc. • *n.* **1** squeezing; being squeezed. **2** close embrace. **3** crowd or crowded state; crush. **4** small quantity produced by squeezing (*a squeeze of lemon*). **5** *Econ.* restriction on borrowing, investment, etc., in a financial crisis. □ **put the squeeze on** *colloq.* coerce or pressure (a person). □□ **squeez′a·ble** *adj.* **squeez′er** *n.*

squelch /skwelch/ • *v.* **1** *intr.* **a** make a sucking sound as of treading in thick mud. **b** move with a squelching sound. **2** *tr.* suppress; silence. • *n.* instance of squelching. □□ **squelch′er** *n.* **squelch′y** *adj.*

squib /skwib/ *n.* **1** small hissing firework that finally explodes. **2** short satirical composition; lampoon.

squid /skwid/ *n.* ten-armed cephalopod used as bait or food.

squig·gle /skwígəl/ • *n.* short curly line, esp. in handwriting or doodling. • *v.* make such lines. □□ **squig′gly** *adj.*

squint /skwint/ • *v.intr.* **1** have the eyes turned in different directions; have a squint. **2** look obliquely or with half closed eyes. • *n.* **1** = STRABISMUS. **2** stealthy or sidelong glance. □□ **squint′er** *n.* **squint′y** *adj.*

squire /skwīr/ • *n.* **1** country gentleman, esp. the chief landowner in a country district. **2** *hist.* knight's attendant. • *v.tr.* (of a man) attend upon or escort (a woman).

squirm /skwərm/ • *v.intr.* **1** wriggle; writhe. **2** show or feel embarrassment. • *n.* squirming movement. □□ **squirm′er** *n.* **squirm′y** *adj.* (**squirm·i·er, squirm·i·est**).

squir·rel /skwə́rəl, skwúr–/ • *n.* **1** tree-dwelling rodent with a bushy tail. **2** fur of this animal. • *v.tr.* hoard.

squirt /skwərt/ • *v.* **1** *tr.* eject (liquid or powder) in a jet. **2** *intr.* be discharged in this way. **3** *tr.* splash with liquid or powder ejected by squirting. • *n.* **1 a** jet of water, etc. **b** small quantity produced by squirting. **2** *colloq.* insignificant but presumptuous person. □□ **squirt′er** *n.*

squish /skwish/ • *n.* slight squelching sound. • *v.intr.* move with a squish. □□ **squish′y** *adj.* (**squish·i·er, squish·i·est**).

Sr *symb. Chem.* strontium.

Sr. *abbr.* **1** Senior. **2** Señor. **3** Signor. **4** *Eccl.* Sister.

Sri Lank·an /shree lángkən, sree/ • *n.* **1** native or inhabitant of Sri Lanka (formerly Ceylon), an island in the Indian Ocean. **2** person of Sri Lankan descent. • *adj.* of or relating to Sri Lanka or its people.

SRO *abbr.* standing room only.

SS *abbr.* **1** steamship. **2** *hist.* Nazi special police force.

SSA *abbr.* Social Security Administration.

SSS *abbr.* Selective Service System.

SST *abbr.* supersonic transport.

St. *abbr.* **1** Street. **2** Saint.

stab /stab/ • *v.* (**stabbed, stab·bing**) **1** *tr.* pierce or wound with a knife, etc. **2** *intr.* aim a blow with or as if with such a weapon. **3** *intr.* cause a sensation like being stabbed. • *n.* **1 a** instance of stabbing. **b** blow or thrust with a knife, etc. **2** wound made in this way. **3** sharp pain. **4** *colloq.* attempt; try. □□ **stab′ber** *n.*

sta·bil·i·ty /stəbílitee/ *n.* quality or state of being stable.

sta·bi·lize /stáybilīz/ *v.* make or become stable. □□ **sta·bi·li·za′tion** *n.*

sta·bi·liz·er /stáybilīzər/ *n.* device or substance used to keep something stable, esp. in a ship or aircraft.

sta·ble¹ /stáybəl/ *adj.* (**sta·bler, sta·blest**) **1** firmly fixed or established. **2** (of a person) well-adjusted; sane; reliable; sensible. □□ **sta′ble·ness** *n.* **sta′bly** *adv.*

sta·ble² /stáybəl/ • *n.* **1** building for keeping horses. **2** establishment where racehorses are trained. **3** persons, products, etc., having a common origin or affiliation. • *v.tr.* put or keep in a stable. □□ **sta′ble·ful** *n.* (*pl.* **–fuls**).

stac·ca·to /stəkaátō/ esp. *Mus. adv. & adj.* with each sound or note sharply detached or separated from the others.

stack /stak/ • *n.* **1** pile or heap, esp. in orderly arrangement. **2** stacked pile of hay, straw, etc. **3** *colloq.* large quantity. **4** = SMOKESTACK. **5** (also **stacks**) part of a library where books are compactly stored. • *v.tr.* **1** pile in a stack or stacks. **2 a** arrange (cards) secretly for cheating. **b** manipulate (circumstances, etc.) to one's advantage. □□ **stack′a·ble** *adj.* **stack′er** *n.*

sta·di·um /stáydeeəm/ *n.* (*pl.* **sta·di·ums** or **sta·di·a** /–deeə/) athletic or sports arena with tiers of seats for spectators.

staff /staf/ • *n.* **1** (*pl.* **staffs** or **staves** /stayvz/) **a** stick or pole for use in walking or climbing or as a weapon. **b** stick or pole as a sign of office or authority. **2 a** body of persons employed in a business, etc. **b** those in authority within an organization, esp. the teachers in a school. **c** *Mil., etc.* body of officers. **3** (also **stave**; *pl.* **staffs** or **staves**) *Mus.* set of usu. five parallel lines on or between which a note is placed to indicate its pitch. • *v.tr.* provide (an institution, etc.) with staff. □□ **staffed** *adj.* (also in *comb.*).

stag /stag/ • *n.* adult male deer. • *adj.* for men only, as a party, etc.

stage /stayj/ • *n.* 1 point or period in a process or development (*is in the larval stage*). 2 a raised floor or platform, esp. one on which plays, etc., are performed. b (prec. by *the*) theatrical profession. c scene of action. 3 a regular stopping place on a route. b distance between two stopping places. 4 *Astronaut.* section of a rocket with a separate engine. • *v.tr.* 1 present (a play, etc.) on stage. 2 arrange the occurrence of (*staged a comeback*). □ **stage fright** nervousness on facing an audience.

stage·coach /stáyjkōch/ *n.* *hist.* large enclosed horse-drawn coach running regularly by stages between two places.

stage·craft /stáyjkraft/ *n.* theatrical skill or experience.

stage·hand /stáyjhand/ *n.* person handling scenery, etc., during a performance on stage.

stag·fla·tion /stagfláyshən/ *n.* *Econ.* state of inflation without a corresponding increase of demand and employment.

stag·ger /stágər/ • *v.* 1 a *intr.* walk unsteadily; totter. b *tr.* cause to totter. 2 *tr.* shock; confuse. 3 *tr.* arrange (events, hours of work, etc.) so that they do not coincide. 4 *tr.* arrange (objects) so that they are not in line. • *n.* 1 tottering movement. 2 (in *pl.*) disease of the brain and spinal cord, esp. in horses and cattle, causing staggering. □□ **stag′ger·er** *n.*

stag·ger·ing /stágəring/ *adj.* 1 astonishing; bewildering. 2 that staggers. □□ **stag′ger·ing·ly** *adv.*

stag·nant /stágnənt/ *adj.* 1 (of liquid) motionless; having no current. 2 (of life, action, the mind, etc.) showing no activity; dull; sluggish. □□ **stag′nan·cy** *n.*

stag·nate /stágnayt/ *v.intr.* be or become stagnant. □□ **stag·na·tion** /–náyshən/ *n.*

staid /stayd/ *adj.* of quiet and steady character; sedate. □□ **staid′ly** *adv.* **staid′ness** *n.*

stain /stayn/ • *v.* 1 *tr.* & *intr.* discolor or be discolored by the action of liquid sinking in. 2 *tr.* damage (a reputation, character, etc.). 3 *tr.* color (wood, glass, etc.) by a process other than painting or covering the surface. 4 *tr.* impregnate (a specimen) for microscopic examination with coloring matter. • *n.* 1 discoloration; spot; mark. 2 a blot or blemish. b damage to a reputation, etc. 3 substance used in staining. □ **stained glass** dyed or colored glass, esp. in a lead framework in a window (also (with hyphen) *attrib.*: *stained-glass window*). □□ **stain′a·ble** *adj.* **stain′er** *n.*

stain·less steel /stáynlis steel/ *n.* steel alloy not liable to rust or tarnish under ordinary conditions.

stair /stair/ *n.* 1 each of a set of fixed indoor steps. 2 (usu. in *pl.*) set of esp. indoor steps (*passed him on the stairs*).

stair·case /stáirkays/ *n.* 1 flight of stairs and the supporting structure. 2 part of a building containing a staircase.

stair·way /stáirway/ *n.* flight of stairs; staircase.

stair·well /stáirwel/ *n.* shaft in which a staircase is built.

stake¹ /stayk/ • *n.* 1 stout, sharpened stick or post driven into the ground as a support,

boundary mark, etc. 2 *hist.* post to which a person was tied to be burned alive. • *v.tr.* 1 fasten, secure, or support with a stake or stakes. 2 (foll. by *off*, *out*) mark off (an area) with stakes. 3 establish (a claim). □ **stake out** *colloq.* place under surveillance.

stake² /stayk/ • *n.* 1 sum of money, etc., wagered. 2 interest or concern, esp. financial. 3 (in *pl.*) prize money, esp. in a horse race. • *v.tr.* 1 wager. 2 *colloq.* support, esp. financially. □ **at stake** risked; to be won or lost. □□ **stak′er** *n.*

stake·out /stáykowt/ *n.* *colloq.* period of surveillance.

sta·lac·tite /stəláktīt, stálək–/ *n.* deposit of calcium carbonate having the shape of a large icicle hanging from the roof of a cave, cliff overhang, etc.

sta·lag·mite /stəlágmīt, stálag–/ *n.* deposit of calcium carbonate in the shape of a large inverted icicle rising from the floor of a cave, etc.

stale /stayl/ • *adj.* (**stal·er**, **stal·est**) 1 not fresh; musty; insipid. 2 trite or unoriginal. • *v.* make or become stale. □□ **stale′ness** *n.*

stale·mate /stáylmayt/ • *n.* 1 *Chess* position counting as a draw, in which a player cannot move except into check. 2 deadlock; drawn contest. • *v.tr.* 1 *Chess* bring (a player) to a stalemate. 2 bring to a standstill.

stalk¹ /stawk/ *n.* main stem of a plant; leaf, flower, fruit, etc. □□ **stalked** *adj.* (also in *comb.*).

□□ **stalk′y** *adj.* **stalk²** /stawk/ • *v.* 1 a *tr.* pursue stealthily. b *intr.* steal up to game under cover. 2 *intr.* stride; walk in a stately or haughty manner. • *n.* 1 stalking of game. 2 imposing gait. □□ **stalk′er** *n.* (also in *comb.*).

stall¹ /stawl/ • *n.* 1 trader's stand or booth in a market, etc. 2 compartment for one animal in a stable, etc. 3 fixed, usu. partly enclosed, seat in the choir or chancel of a church. 4 compartment for one person in a shower, toilet, etc. 5 loss of engine power. • *v.* 1 *intr.* (of a vehicle or its engine) stop or lose power because of an overload on the engine or an inadequate supply of fuel to it. 2 *tr.* cause to stall.

stall² /stawl/ *v.* 1 *intr.* play for time when being questioned, etc. 2 *tr.* delay; obstruct; block.

stal·lion /stályən/ *n.* uncastrated adult male horse.

stal·wart /stáwlwərt/ • *adj.* 1 strongly built; sturdy. 2 courageous; resolute; determined. • *n.* stalwart person, esp. a loyal partisan. □□ **stal′wart·ly** *adv.*

sta·men /stáymən/ *n.* male fertilizing organ of a flowering plant, including the anther containing pollen.

stam·i·na /stáminə/ *n.* physical or mental endurance.

stam·mer /stámər/ • *v.* 1 *intr.* speak with halting articulation, esp. with pauses or rapid repetitions of the same syllable. 2 *tr.* utter (words) in this way (*stammered out an excuse*). • *n.* 1 tendency to stammer. 2 instance of stammering. □□ **stam′mer·er** *n.* **stam′mer·ing·ly** *adv.*

stamp /stamp/ • *v.* 1 a *tr.* bring down (one's foot) heavily on the ground, etc. b *tr.* crush or flatten in this way. c *intr.* walk with heavy steps. 2 *tr.* a impress (a pattern, mark, etc.) on a surface. b impress (a surface) with a pattern, etc. 3

tr. affix a postage or other stamp to. **4** *tr.* assign a specific character to; characterize; mark out (*stamps the story an invention*). ● *n.* **1** instrument for stamping. **2** mark or pattern made by this; esp. as an official authorization or certification. **3** small adhesive piece of paper indicating that a price, fee, or tax has been paid, esp. a postage stamp. **4 a** heavy downward blow with the foot. **b** sound of this. **5 a** characteristic mark or impression (*bears the stamp of genius*). **b** character; kind. □ **stamp out 1** produce by cutting out with a die, etc. **2** put an end to; crush; destroy. □□ **stamp′er** *n.*

stam·pede /stampe′ed/ ● *n.* **1** sudden flight or hurried movement of animals or people. **2** spontaneous response of many persons to a common impulse. ● *v.* **1** *intr.* take part in a stampede. **2** *tr.* cause to do this. □□ **stam·ped′er** *n.*

stance /stans/ *n.* **1** attitude or position of the body, esp. when hitting a ball, etc. **2** standpoint; attitude of mind.

stanch /stawnch, stanch, staanch/ *v.tr.* (also **staunch**) **1** restrain the flow of (esp. blood). **2** restrain the flow from (esp. a wound).

stan·chion /stánshən, –chən/ *n.* **1** post or pillar; upright support; vertical strut. **2** upright bar, pair of bars, or frame for confining cattle in a stall.

stand /stand/ ● *v.* (*past* and *past part.* **stood** /sto͞od/) **1** *intr.* have or take or maintain an upright position, esp. on the feet or a base. **2** be situated (*here once stood a village*). **3** *intr.* be of a specified height. **4** *intr.* be in a specified condition (*stands accused*). **5** *tr.* place or set in an upright or specified position (*stood it against the wall*). **6** *intr.* **a** move to and remain in a specified position (*stand aside*). **b** take a specified attitude (*stand aloof*). **7** *intr.* remain valid or unaltered. **8** *tr.* endure; tolerate. **9** *tr.* provide at one's own expense (*stood him a drink*). ● *n.* **1** cessation from motion or progress; a stoppage. **2** resistance to attack or compulsion (esp. *make a stand*). **3** rack, set of shelves, etc. **4** small open-fronted structure for a trader outdoors or in a market, etc. **5** standing place for vehicles. **6 a** (usu. in *pl.*) a raised structure to sit or stand on. **b** witness box. **7 a** *Theatr., etc.* each halt made on a tour to give one or more performances. **b** *Sports* each place in which a traveling team plays one or more games (*two-game stand in Boston*). **8** group of growing plants (*stand of trees*). □ **as it stands 1** in its present condition. **2** in the present circumstances. **stand back 1** withdraw; take up a position further from the front. **2** withdraw psychologically in order to take an objective view. **stand by 1** look on without interfering. **2** uphold; support (a person). **3** adhere to (terms or promises). **4** wait; stand ready for. **stand a chance** see CHANCE. **stand for 1** represent; signify; imply (*"US" stands for "United States"*). **2** (often with *neg.*) *colloq.* endure; tolerate; acquiesce in. **stand one's ground** maintain one's position, not yield. **stand-in** *n.* deputy or substitute. **stand off** move or keep away; keep one's distance. **stand out 1** be prominent or conspicuous or outstanding. **2** (usu. foll. by *against, for*) hold out; persist in opposition or support or endurance. **stand pat** see PAT[2]. **stand to** be likely or certain to (*stands to lose everything*). **stand up 1 a** rise to one's feet. **b** come to or remain in or place in a standing position. **2** (of an argument, etc.) be

valid. **3** *colloq.* fail to keep an appointment with. **stand up for 1** support; side with; maintain (a person or cause). **2** serve as best man, maid of honor, or other attendant in a wedding. **stand up to 1** meet or face (an opponent) courageously. **2** be resistant to the harmful effects of (wear, use, etc.). □□ **stand′er** *n.*

stan·dard /stándərd/ ● *n.* **1** object or quality or measure serving as a basis or example or principle by which others are judged. **2** the degree of excellence, etc., required for a particular purpose. **3** distinctive flag. **4** upright support. **5** tune or song of established popularity. ● *adj.* **1** serving or used as a standard. **2** of a normal or prescribed but not exceptional quality or size, etc. **3** having recognized and permanent value; authoritative. **4** (of language) conforming to established educated usage (*Standard English*). □ **standard-bearer 1** soldier who carries a standard. **2** prominent leader in a cause. **standard of living** degree of material comfort available to a person or class or community. **standard time** uniform time for places in approximately the same longitude, established in a country or region by law or custom.

stand·ard·ize /stándərdīz/ *v.tr.* cause to conform to a standard. □□ **stand·ard·i·za′tion** *n.*

stand·by /stándbī/ *n.* (*pl.* **stand·bys**) **1** person or thing ready if needed in an emergency, etc. **2** readiness for duty (*on standby*).

stand·ing /stánding/ ● *n.* **1** esteem or repute, esp. high; status; position. **2** duration (*long standing*). ● *adj.* **1** upright. **2** established; permanent (*standing rule*). **3** (of a jump, start, race, etc.) performed from rest or from a standing position. **4** (of water) stagnant.

stand·off·ish /stándáwfish, –óf–/ *adj.* cold or distant in manner. □□ **stand·off′ish·ly** *adv.* **stand·off′ish·ness** *n.*

stand·pipe /stándpīp/ *n.* vertical pipe extending from a water supply.

stand·point /stándpoynt/ *n.* point of view.

stand·still /stándstil/ *n.* stoppage; inability to proceed.

stank *past* of STINK.

stan·za /stánzə/ *n.* basic metrical unit in a poem or verse, typically of four or more lines.

sta·ple[1] /stáypəl/ ● *n.* U-shaped metal bar or piece of wire with pointed ends for driving into and holding together papers, etc. ● *v.tr.* provide or fasten with a staple. □□ **sta′pler** *n.*

sta·ple[2] /stáypəl/ ● *n.* **1** principal or important article of commerce. **2** chief element or main component. **3** fiber of cotton or wool, etc., as determining its quality (*cotton of fine staple*). ● *adj.* **1** main or principal (*staple commodities*). **2** important as a product or an export.

star /staar/ ● *n.* **1** celestial body appearing as a luminous point in the night sky. **2** large naturally luminous gaseous body such as the sun is. **3** celestial body regarded as influencing a person's fortunes, etc. **4** thing resembling a star in shape or appearance. **5** figure or object with radiating points esp. as a decoration or mark of rank, or to show a category of excellence (*five-star hotel*). **6 a** famous or brilliant person; principal performer. **b** (*attrib.*) outstanding (*star pupil*). ● *v.* (**starred, star·ring**) **1** *tr.* (of a movie, etc.) feature as a principal performer. **2** *intr.* (of a performer) be featured in a movie, etc. □ **Star of David** two interlaced equilateral triangles used as a Jewish and Israeli symbol. **Stars and Stripes** national flag of the US. **star-spangled** (esp. of the US national flag) covered or glittering with stars. □□ **star′dom** n. **star′less** adj. **star′like** adj.

star·board /staárbərd/ Naut. & Aeron. n. right-hand side (looking forward) of a ship, boat, or aircraft.

starch /staarch/ • n. 1 polysaccharide obtained chiefly from cereals and potatoes. 2 preparation of this for stiffening fabric before ironing. 3 stiffness of manner; formality. • v.tr. stiffen (clothing) with starch. □□ **starch′er** n.

starch·y /staárchee/ adj. (**starch·i·er, starch·i·est**) of, like, or containing much starch. □□ **starch′i·ly** adv. **starch′i·ness** n.

stare /stair/ • v.intr. look fixedly with eyes open, esp. as the result of curiosity, surprise, horror, etc. (stared in amazement). • n. staring gaze. □□ **star′er** n.

star·fish /staárfish/ n. echinoderm with five or more radiating arms.

star·gaz·er /staárgayzər/ n. colloq. usu. derog. or joc. astronomer or astrologer.

stark /staark/ • adj. 1 desolate; bare (stark landscape). 2 sharply evident; brutally simple (in stark contrast). 3 downright; sheer (stark madness). • adv. completely; wholly (stark naked). □□ **stark′ly** adv. **stark′ness** n.

star·let /staárlit/ n. 1 promising young performer, esp. a woman. 2 little star.

star·light /staárlīt/ n. light of the stars.

star·ling /staárling/ n. small gregarious partly migratory bird with blackish-brown speckled iridescent plumage.

star·lit /staárlit/ adj. 1 lighted by stars. 2 with stars visible.

star·ry /staáree/ adj. (**star·ri·er, star·ri·est**) 1 covered with stars. 2 like a star. □ **starry-eyed** colloq. visionary; enthusiastic but impractical. **star′ri·ness** n.

start /staart/ • v. 1 tr. & intr. begin; commence. 2 tr. set in motion or action. 3 intr. set oneself in motion or action. 4 intr. begin a journey, etc. 5 a intr. (of a machine) begin operating. b tr. cause to begin operating. 6 tr. a cause or en-able (a person) to make a beginning. b cause (a person) to begin (doing something). 7 intr. make a sudden movement from surprise, pain, etc. 8 intr. spring out, up, etc. • n. 1 beginning. 2 place from which a race, etc., begins. 3 sudden movement of surprise, pain, etc.

start·er /staártər/ n. 1 person or thing that starts. 2 esp. automatic device for starting the engine of a motor vehicle, etc. 3 person giving the signal for the start of a race.

star·tle /staárt'l/ v.tr. shock; surprise.

star·tling /staártling/ adj. 1 surprising. 2 alarming (startling news). □□ **star′tling·ly** adv.

starve /staarv/ v. 1 intr. die of hunger; suffer from malnourishment. 2 tr. cause to die of hunger or suffer from lack of food. 3 intr. colloq. (esp. as **starved** or **starving** adj.) feel very hungry. 4 tr. feel a strong need or craving for. 5 tr. deprive of. 6 tr. compel by starving. □□ **star·va′tion** n.

stash /stash/ colloq. • v.tr. 1 conceal; put in a safe or hidden place. 2 hoard. • n. 1 hiding place. 2 thing hidden.

stat. abbr. 1 at once. 2 statistics. 3 statute.

state /stayt/ • n. 1 existing condition or position of a person or thing. 2 colloq. a excited,

anxious, or agitated mental condition. b untidy condition. 3 a political community under one government. b this as part of a federal republic. c (**the States**) US. 4 (also **State**) civil government. • v.tr. 1 express in speech or writing. 2 specify. 3 Mus. introduce (a theme, etc.). □ **in state** with all due ceremony. **state of the art** 1 the current stage of development of a practical or technological subject. 2 (usu. **state-of-the-art**) (attrib.) using the latest techniques or equipment (state-of-the-art weaponry). □□ **stat′a·ble** adj. **stat′ed·ly** adv. **state′hood** n.

state·hood /stáyt-hŏŏd/ n. condition or status of being a state, esp. a state of the United States.

state·less /stáytlis/ adj. 1 (of a person) having no nationality or citizenship. 2 without a state. □□ **state′less·ness** n.

state·ly /stáytlee/ adj. (**state·li·er, state·li·est**) dignified; imposing; grand. □□ **state′li·ness** n.

state·ment /stáytmənt/ n. 1 stating or being stated; expression in words. 2 thing stated. 3 formal account of facts. 4 record of transactions in a bank account, etc. 5 formal notification of an amount due.

state·room /stáytrŏŏm, –rŏŏm/ n. private compartment in a passenger ship or train.

states·man /stáytsmən/ n. (pl. **-men**; fem. **states·wom·an**, pl. **-wom·en**) distinguished and capable politician or diplomat. □□ **states′man·like** adj. **states′man·ship** n.

stat·ic /státik/ • adj. 1 stationary; not acting or changing; passive. 2 Physics concerned with bodies at rest or forces in equilibrium (opp. DYNAMIC). • n. electrical disturbances in the atmosphere or the interference with telecommunications caused by this. □ **static electricity** electricity not flowing as a current as that produced by friction. □□ **stat′i·cal·ly** adv.

sta·tion /stáyshən/ • n. 1 a regular stopping place on a railroad, bus, route, etc. b building at this. 2 place or building, etc., where a person or thing stands or is placed. 3 establishment involved in radio or television broadcasting. 4 military or naval base. 5 position in life; rank or status. • v.tr. 1 assign a station to. 2 put in position. □ **station wagon** car with passenger seating and storage or extra seating area in the rear, accessible by a rear door.

sta·tion·ar·y /stáyshəneree/ adj. 1 remaining in one place. 2 not meant to be moved. 3 not changing.

¶ Be careful to distinguish **stationary** 'not moving, fixed' from **stationery** 'writing paper and other supplies.'

sta·tion·er /stáyshənər/ n. person who sells stationery.

sta·tion·er·y /stáyshəneree/ n. 1 writing materials such as pens, paper, etc. 2 writing paper, esp. with matching envelopes.

sta·tis·tic /stətístik/ n. statistical fact or item.

sta·tis·tics /stətístiks/ n.pl. 1 (usu. treated as sing.) science of collecting and analyzing numerical data. 2 any systematic collection or presentation of such facts. □□ **sta·tis′ti·cal** adj. **sta·tis′ti·cal·ly** adv. **stat·is·ti·cian** /státistíshən/ n.

stat·u·ar·y /stáchŏŏeree/ • adj. of or for statues (statuary art). • n. (pl. **-ies**) statues collectively.

stat·ue /stáchŏŏ/ n. sculptured figure of a person or animal, esp. life-size or larger.

stat·u·esque /stáchoo-ésk/ adj. like, or having the dignity or beauty of, a statue. □□ **stat·u·esque′ness** n.

stat·u·ette /stáchoo-ét/ n. small statue.

stat·ure /stáchər/ n. **1** height of a (esp. human) body. **2** degree of eminence, social standing, or advancement (recruit someone of his stature). □□ **stat′ured** adj. (also in comb.).

sta·tus /stáytəs, stát–/ n. **1** rank; social position; relative importance (not sure of their status in the hierarchy). **2** prestige. **3** state of affairs. □ **status symbol** possession, etc., taken to indicate a person's high status.

sta·tus quo /stáytəs kwó, státəs/ n. existing state of affairs.

stat·ute /stáchoot/ n. **1** written law passed by a legislative body. **2** rule of a corporation, founder, etc., intended to be permanent.

stat·u·to·ry /stáchətawree/ adj. required, permitted, or enacted by statute. □□ **stat·u·to′ri·ly** adv.

staunch[1] /stawnch, staanch/ adj. **1** trustworthy; loyal. **2** (of a ship, joint, etc.) strong, watertight, airtight, etc. □□ **staunch′ly** adv. **staunch′ness** n.

staunch[2] var. of STANCH.

stave /stayv/ • n. **1** each of the curved pieces of wood forming the sides of a cask, barrel, etc. **2** = STAFF n. 3. **3** stanza; verse. • v.tr. (past and past part. **stove** /stov/ or **staved**) **1** break a hole in. **2** crush or knock out of shape. □ **stave in** crush by forcing inward. **stave off** avert or defer (danger, etc.).

STAVE, 1

stay[1] /stay/ • v. **1** intr. continue to be in the same place or condition; not depart or change. **2** intr. have temporary residence. **3** archaic or literary **a** tr. stop or check. **b** intr. (esp. in imper.) pause. **4** tr. postpone (judgment, decision, execution, etc.). • n. **1 a** act or an instance of staying. **b** duration of this (just a ten-minute stay). **2** suspension or postponement of a sentence, judgment, etc. (stay of execution). **3** prop or support. □ **staying power** endurance; stamina. **stay put** colloq. remain where it is placed or where one is. **stay up** not go to bed (until late). □□ **stay′er** n.

stay[2] /stay/ n. **1** Naut. rope or guy supporting a mast, spar, flagstaff, etc. **2** supporting cable on an aircraft, etc.

STD abbr. sexually transmitted disease.

std. abbr. standard.

stead /sted/ n. □ **in a person's** (or **thing's**) **stead** as a substitute; instead of him or her or it. **stand a person in good stead** be advantageous or serviceable to him or her.

stead·fast /stédfast/ adj. constant; firm; unwavering. □□ **stead′fast·ly** adv. **stead′fast·ness** n.

stead·y /stédee/ • adj. (**stead·i·er, stead·i·est**) **1** firmly fixed or supported unwavering. **2** uniform and regular. **3 a** constant in mind or conduct. **b** persistent. **4** (of a person) serious and dependable. **5** regular; established (steady girlfriend). • v. (**–ies, –ied**) make or become steady (steady the boat). • adv. steadily (hold it steady). • n. (pl. **–ies**) colloq. regular boyfriend or girlfriend. □ **go steady** colloq. have as a regular boyfriend or girlfriend. **steady state** unvarying condition, esp. in a physical process. □□ **stead′i·er** n. **stead′i·ly** adv. **stead′i·ness** n.

steak /stayk/ n. thick slice of meat (esp. beef) or fish, often cut for grilling, frying, etc.

steal /steel/ • v. (past **stole** /stol/; past part. **sto·len** /stólən/) **1** tr. (also absol.) take (another person's property) illegally or without right or permission, esp. in secret. **2** tr. obtain surreptitiously or by surprise (stole a kiss). **3** tr. gain insidiously or artfully. **4** intr. move, esp. silently or stealthily. **5** tr. Baseball run to (a base) while the pitcher is in the act of delivery. • n. colloq. unexpectedly easy task or good bargain. □ **steal the show** outshine other performers, esp. unexpectedly. **steal a person's thunder** use another person's words, ideas, etc., without permission and without giving credit. □□ **steal′er** n. (also in comb.). **steal′ing** n.

stealth /stelth/ • n. secrecy; secret procedure. • adj. Mil. Aeron. designed to avoid detection by radar.

stealth·y /stélthee/ adj. (**stealth·i·er, stealth·i·est**) done with stealth; furtive. □□ **stealth′i·ly** adv. **stealth′i·ness** n.

steam /steem/ • n. **1** vapor from heated water. **2 a** power obtained from steam. **b** colloq. power or energy generally. • v. **1** tr. **a** cook (food) in steam. **b** treat with steam. **2** intr. give off steam. **3** intr. **a** move under steam power (the ship steamed down the river). **b** (foll. by ahead, away, etc.) colloq. proceed or travel fast or with vigor. **4** tr. & intr. **a** cover or become covered with condensed steam. **b** (as **steamed up** adj.) colloq. angry or excited. □ **steam engine 1** engine which uses steam to generate power. **2** locomotive powered by this. **steam iron** electric iron that emits steam.

steam·boat /steémbot/ n. boat propelled by a steam engine.

steam·er /steémər/ n. **1** vessel propelled by steam, esp. a ship. **2** vessel for steaming food in.

steam·roll·er /steémrolər/ • n. **1** heavy slow-moving vehicle with a roller, used to flatten newly laid asphalt, etc. **2** crushing power or force. • v.tr. **1** crush forcibly or indiscriminately. **2** force (a measure, etc.) through a legislature.

steam·ship /steémship/ n. ship propelled by a steam engine.

steam·y /steémee/ adj. (**steam·i·er, steam·i·est**) **1** like or full of steam. **2** colloq. erotic; salacious. □□ **steam′i·ly** adv. **steam′i·ness** n.

steed /steed/ n. archaic or poet. horse.

steel /steel/ • n. **1** alloy of iron and carbon with other elements increasing strength and malleability, much used for making tools, weapons, etc. **2** strength; firmness (*nerves of steel*). **3** (not in *pl.*) *literary* sword. • *adj.* of or like steel. • *v.tr.* & *refl.* harden or make resolute. □ **steel wool** abrasive substance consisting of a mass of fine steel shavings. □□ **steel'i•ness** *n.* **steel'y** *adj.* (**steel•i•er, steel•i•est**).

steel•works /steelwǝrks/ *n.pl.* (usu. treated as *sing.*) place where steel is manufactured. □□ **steel'work•er** *n.*

steel•yard /steelyaard/ *n.* balance with a graduated arm along which a weight is moved.

STEELYARD

steep[1] /steep/ *adj.* **1** sloping sharply. **2** (of a rise or fall) rapid. **3** (*predic.*) *colloq.* exorbitant; unreasonable (esp. *a bit steep*). □□ **steep'en** *v.* **steep'ly** *adv.* **steep'ness** *n.*

steep[2] /steep/ *v.tr.* soak or bathe in liquid. □ **steep in 1** pervade or imbue with. **2** make deeply acquainted with (a subject, etc.).

stee•ple /steepǝl/ *n.* tall tower, esp. one surmounted by a spire, above the roof of a church. □□ **stee'pled** *adj.*

stee•ple•chase /steepǝlchays/ *n.* race with ditches, hedges, etc., to jump. □□ **stee'ple•chas•er** *n.* **stee'ple•chas•ing** *n.*

stee•ple•jack /steepǝljak/ *n.* person who climbs tall chimneys, steeples, etc., to do repairs, etc.

steer[1] /steer/ *v.* **1** *tr.* guide (a vehicle, aircraft, ship, etc.) by a wheel, etc. **2** *tr.* direct (one's course). **3** *intr.* direct one's course in a specified direction. **4** *tr.* guide the movement or trend of. □ **steer clear of** avoid. **steering wheel** wheel by which a vehicle, etc., is steered. □□ **steer'a•ble** *adj.* **steer'er** *n.* **steer'ing** *n.* (esp. in sense 1 of *v.*).

steer[2] /steer/ *n.* castrated male bovine that is raised for beef.

steer•age /steerij/ *n.* **1** act of steering. **2** part of a ship allotted to passengers traveling at the cheapest rate.

steg•o•sau•rus /stegǝsáwrǝs/ *n.* plant-eating dinosaur with a double row of large bony plates along the spine.

ste•la /steelǝ/ *n.* (*pl.* **ste•lae** /-lee/) *Archaeol.* upright slab or pillar usu. inscribed and sculpted, esp. as a gravestone.

stel•lar /stélǝr/ *adj.* of a star or stars. □□ **stel'li•form** *adj.*

stem[1] /stem/ • *n.* **1** main body or stalk of a plant, fruit, flower, leaf, etc. **2** stem-shaped part of an object: **a** slender part of a wineglass. **b** tube of a tobacco pipe. **c** vertical stroke in a letter or musical note. **3** *Gram.* root or main part of a noun, verb, etc., to which inflections are added. **4** *Naut.* main upright timber or metal piece at the bow of a ship (*from stem to stern*). • *v.intr.* (**stemmed, stem•ming**) spring or originate from. □□ **stem'less** *adj.* **stem'like** *adj.* **stem'med** *adj.* (also in *comb.*).

stem[2] /stem/ *v.tr.* (**stemmed, stem•ming**) check or stop.

stench /stench/ *n.* offensive or foul smell.

sten•cil /sténsil/ • *n.* **1** thin sheet of plastic, metal, card, etc., in which a pattern or lettering is cut, used to produce a corresponding pattern on the surface beneath it by applying ink, paint, etc. **2** pattern so produced. • *v.tr.* (**sten•ciled, sten•cil•ing; sten•cilled, sten•cil•ling**) **1** produce (a pattern) with a stencil. **2** decorate or mark (a surface) in this way.

ste•nog•ra•phy /stǝnógrǝfee/ *n.* shorthand or the art of writing this. □□ **ste•nog'ra•pher** *n.* **sten•o•graph•ic** /sténǝgráfik/ *adj.*

sten•to•ri•an /stǝntáwreeǝn/ *adj.* (of a voice) loud and powerful.

step /step/ • *n.* **1 a** complete movement of one leg in walking or running. **b** distance covered by this. **2** unit of movement in dancing. **3** measure taken, esp. one of several. **4** surface of a stair, stepladder, etc.; tread. **5** short distance. **6** footfall. **7** manner of walking, etc. **8** degree in the scale of promotion, advancement, or precedence. **9** stepping (or not stepping) in time with others or music (esp. *in* or out of step). • *v.intr.* (**stepped, step•ping**) **1** lift and set down one's foot or alternate feet in walking. **2** come or go in a specified direction by stepping. **3** make progress in a specified way. □ **step aerobics** exercise regimen using a step-climbing motion. **step-by-step** gradually; cautiously. **step down** resign. **step in 1** enter. **2** intervene to help or hinder. **step on it** *colloq.* accelerate. **step out 1** leave a room, house, etc. **2** be active socially. **stepping-stone 1** raised stone, usu. one of a set in a stream, muddy place, etc., to help in crossing. **2** means of progress. **step up** increase; intensify. □□ **step'like** *adj.* **stepped** *adj.*

step- /step/ *comb. form* denoting a relationship like the one specified but resulting from a parent's remarriage.

step•broth•er /stépbruthǝr/ *n.* son of a stepparent by a union other than with one's father or mother.

step•child /stépchīld/ *n.* child of one's husband or wife by a previous marriage.

step•daugh•ter /stépdawtǝr/ *n.* female stepchild.

step•fa•ther /stépfaathǝr/ *n.* male stepparent.

step•lad•der /stéplǝdǝr/ *n.* short ladder with flat steps and a folding support.

step•moth•er /stépmuthǝr/ *n.* female stepparent.

step•par•ent /stép-pairǝnt/ *n.* mother's or father's later husband or wife.

steppe /step/ *n.* level grassy unforested plain.

step•sis•ter /stépsistǝr/ *n.* daughter of a stepparent by a union other than with one's father or mother.

step·son /stépsun/ n. male stepchild.

-ster /stər/ suffix denoting a person engaged in or associated with a particular activity or thing (gangster, youngster).

ste·re·o /stéreeō, stéereeō/ • n. (pl. **–os**) **1 a** stereophonic record player, tape recorder, etc. **b** stereophonic sound reproduction. • adj. **1** = STEREOPHONIC. **2** = stereoscopic (see STEREOSCOPE).

stereo- /stéreeō, stéereeō/ comb. form solid; having three dimensions.

ster·e·o·phon·ic /stéreeōfónik, stéereeō–/ adj. (of sound reproduction) using two or more channels giving the effect of naturally distributed sound. □□ **ster·e·o·phon′i·cal·ly** adv.

ster·e·o·scope /stéreeəskōp, stéereeə–/ n. device for producing a three-dimensional effect by viewing together two slightly different photographs of the same object. □□ **ster·e·o·scop·ic** /–skópik/ adj. **ster·e·o·scop′i·cal·ly** adv. **ster·e·os·co·py** /–reeóskəpee/ n.

ster·e·o·type /stéreeətīp, stéeree–/ • n. **1** a person or thing that conforms to a widely accepted type. **b** such a type, idea, or attitude. **2** printing plate cast from a mold of composed type. • v.tr. **1** (esp. as **stereotyped** adj.) standardize; cause to conform to a type. **2 a** print from a stereotype. **b** make a stereotype of. □□ **ster·e·o·typ·ic** /–típik/ adj. **ster·e·o·typ′i·cal** adj. **ster·e·o·typ′i·cal·ly** adv.

ster·ile /stérəl, –īl/ adj. **1** not able to produce seeds or fruit or (of an animal) young; barren. **2** unfruitful; unproductive (sterile discussions). **3** free from living microorganisms, etc. □□ **ster′ile·ly** adv. **ste·ril·i·ty** /stərílitee/ n.

ster·il·ize /stérilīz/ v.tr. **1** make sterile. **2** deprive of the power of reproduction. □□ **ster·i·li·za′tion** n. **ster′i·liz·er** n.

ster·ling /stə́rling/ • adj. **1** of or in British money (pound sterling). **2** (of a person or qualities, etc.) of solid worth; genuine; reliable. • n. **1** = sterling silver. **2** British money (paid in sterling). □ **sterling silver** silver of 92¹/₂% purity.

stern¹ /stərn/ adj. severe; grim; strict; authoritarian (stern treatment). □□ **stern′ly** adv. **stern′ness** n.

stern² /stərn/ n. **1** rear part of a ship or boat. **2** any rear part. □□ **sterned** adj. (also in comb.). **stern′most** adj. **stern′ward** adj. & adv. **stern′wards** adv.

ster·num /stə́rnəm/ n. (pl. **ster·nums** or **ster·na** /–nə/) breastbone.

ster·oid /stéeroyd, stér–/ n. Biochem. any of a group of organic compounds including many hormones, alkaloids, and vitamins. □□ **ster·oi·d·al** /–róyd'l/ adj.

ste·rol /stéerawl, –ol, stér–/ n. Chem. any of a group of naturally occurring steroid alcohols.

ster·to·rous /stə́rtərəs/ adj. (of breathing, etc.) labored and noisy.

stet /stet/ v.intr. (**stet·ted**, **stet·ting**) (usu. as an instruction written on printed text, etc.) ignore or cancel the correction or alteration; let the original form stand.

steth·o·scope /stéthəskōp/ n. instrument used in listening to the action of the heart, lungs, etc.

Stet·son /stétsən/ n. propr. felt hat with a very wide brim and a high crown.

ste·ve·dore /stéevədawr/ n. person employed in loading and unloading ships.

stew /stoo, styoo/ • v. **1** tr. & intr. cook by long simmering. **2** intr. colloq. fret or be anxious. • n. **1** dish of stewed meat, etc. **2** colloq. agitated or angry state (be in a stew).

stew·ard /stoo̅o̅rd, styoo̅–/ • n. **1** passengers' attendant on a ship or aircraft or train. **2** person responsible for supplies of food, etc., for a college or club, etc. **3** property manager. • v.tr. act as a steward of. □□ **stew′ard·ship** n.

stew·ard·ess /stoo̅o̅rdis, styoo̅–/ n. female steward, esp. on a ship or aircraft.

stick¹ /stik/ n. **1 a** short slender branch or length of wood. **b** this trimmed for use as a support or weapon. **2** implement used to propel the ball in hockey or polo, etc. **3** gear lever. **4** slender piece, often of a group or set, e.g., celery, dynamite, deodorant, etc. □□ **stick′like** adj.

stick² /stik/ v. (past and past part. **stuck** /stuk/) **1** tr. (foll. by in, into, through) insert or thrust (a thing or its point) (stuck a finger in my eye). **2** tr. stab. **3** tr. & intr. (foll. by in, into, on, etc.) fix or be fixed on a pointed end or thing. **4** tr. & intr. fix or become or remain fixed by or as by adhesive, etc. (stick a label on it). **5** intr. endure; make a continued impression (the name stuck). **6** intr. not open, release, etc.; jam. **7** colloq. **a** tr. put in a specified position or place. **b** intr. remain in a place (stuck indoors). □ **be stuck with** colloq. be unable to get rid of. **stick around** colloq. linger; remain. **stick by** (or **with**) stay loyal or close to. **stick-in-the-mud** colloq. unprogressive or old-fashioned person. **stick it out** colloq. put up with or persevere with a burden, etc., to the end. **stick one's neck out** expose oneself to censure, etc., by acting or speaking boldly. **stick out** protrude or cause to protrude. **stick to 1** remain close to or fixed on or to. **2** keep to (a subject, etc.) (stick to the point). **stick up 1** be or make erect or protruding upward. **2** fasten to an upright surface. **3** colloq. rob or threaten with a gun. **stick-up** n. colloq. armed robbery. **stick up for** support or defend.

stick·ball /stíkbawl/ n. form of baseball played with a stick or broom handle and a rubber ball.

stick·er /stíkər/ n. adhesive label or notice, etc. □ **sticker shock** colloq. surprise reaction at a higher-than-expected retail price.

stick·ler /stíklər/ n. (foll. by for) person who insists on something (stickler for accuracy).

stick·y /stíkee/ adj. (**stick·i·er**, **stick·i·est**) **1** tending or intended to stick or adhere. **2** glutinous; viscous. **3** humid. **4** difficult; awkward.□□ **stick′i·ly** adv. **stick′i·ness** n.

stiff /stif/ • adj. **1** rigid; not flexible. **2** hard to bend or move or turn, etc. **3** needing strength or effort (stiff climb). **4** severe or strong (stiff penalty). **5** formal; constrained. **6** (of a muscle, person, etc.) aching when used, owing to previous exertion, injury, etc. **7** (of an alcoholic drink) strong. **8** (predic.) colloq. to an extreme degree (bored stiff). • n. sl. **1** corpse. **2** foolish or useless person. □ **stiff-necked** obstinate or haughty. **stiff upper lip** determination; fortitude. □□ **stiff′ish** adj. **stiff′ly** adv. **stiff′ness** n.

stiff·en /stífən/ v. make or become stiff. □□ **stiff′en·er** n. **stiff′en·ing** n.

sti·fle /stífəl/ v. **1** tr. suppress. **2** intr. & tr. experience or cause to experience constraint of breathing (*stifling heat*). **3** *tr.* kill by suffocating. □□ **sti·fler** /stíflər/ *n.* **sti'fling·ly** *adv.*

stig·ma /stígmə/ *n.* (*pl.* **stig·mas** or esp. in sense 3 **stig·ma·ta** /–mətə, –maátə/) **1** mark or sign of disgrace or discredit. **2** part of a pistil that receives the pollen in pollination. **3** (in *pl.*) *Eccl.* (in Christian belief) marks corresponding to those left on Christ's body by the Crucifixion, said to have appeared on the bodies of St. Francis of Assisi and others.

stig·ma·tize /stígmətīz/ *v.tr.* (often foll. by *as*) describe as unworthy or disgraceful. □□ **stig·ma·ti·za'tion** *n.*

stile /stīl/ *n.* arrangement of steps allowing people but not animals to climb over a fence or wall.

sti·let·to /stilétō/ *n.* (*pl.* **–tos**) **1** short dagger with a thick blade. **2** (in full **stiletto heel**) **a** long tapering heel of a woman's shoe. **b** shoe with such a heel.

still¹ /stil/ • *adj.* **1** not or hardly moving. **2** with little or no sound; calm and tranquil (*a still evening*). • *n.* **1** deep silence (*still of the night*). **2** static photograph, esp. a single shot from a movie or videotape. • *adv.* **1** without moving (*stand still*). **2** even now or at a particular time (*why are you still here?*). **3** nevertheless. **4** (with *compar.*, etc.) even; yet; increasingly (*still greater efforts*). • *v.* make or become still. □ **still life** (*pl.* **still lifes**) painting or drawing of inanimate objects such as fruit or flowers. □□ **still'ness** *n.*

still² /stil/ *n.* apparatus for distilling alcohol, etc.

still·birth /stílbərth/ *n.* birth of a dead child.

still·born /stílbawrn/ *adj.* **1** born dead. **2** abortive.

stilt /stilt/ *n.* **1** either of a pair of poles with supports for the feet for walking with the body elevated. **2** each of a set of piles or posts supporting a building, etc.

stilt·ed /stíltid/ *adj.* (of a literary style, etc.) stiff and unnatural; bombastic. □□ **stilt'ed·ly** *adv.* **stilt'ed·ness** *n.*

stim·u·lant /stímyələnt/ *n.* stimulating substance or influence.

stim·u·late /stímyəlayt/ *v.tr.* **1** act as a stimulus to. **2** animate; excite; arouse. □□ **stim'u·lat·ing** *adj.* **stim·u·la·tion** /–láyshən/ *n.* **stim'u·la·tive** *adj.* **stim'u·la·tor** *n.*

stim·u·lus /stímyələs/ *n.* (*pl.* **stim·u·li** /–lī/) **1** thing that rouses to activity or energy. **2** stimulating or rousing effect.

sting /sting/ • *n.* **1** sharp wounding organ of an insect, snake, nettle, etc. **2 a** act of inflicting a wound with this. **b** the wound itself or the pain caused by it. **3** painful quality or effect. **4** pungency; sharpness; vigor (*sting in the voice*). **5** *sl.* swindle. • *v.* (*past* and *past part.* **stung** /stung/) **1 a** *tr.* wound or pierce with a sting. **b** *intr.* be able to sting. **2** *intr. & tr.* feel or cause to feel a tingling physical or sharp mental pain. **3** *tr.* (foll. by *into*) incite by a strong or painful mental effect (*stung into replying*). **4** *tr.* *sl.* swindle. □□ **sting'er** *n.* **sting'ing·ly** *adv.* **sting'less** *adj.* **sting'like** *adj.*

sting·ray /stíng-ray/ *n.* broad flatfish having a long poisonous serrated spine at the base of its tail.

stin·gy /stínjee/ *adj.* (**stin·gi·er, stin·gi·est**) ungenerous; mean. □□ **stin'gi·ly** *adv.* **stin'gi·ness** *n.*

stink /stingk/ • *v.* (*past* **stank** /stangk/ or **stunk** /stungk/; *past part.* **stunk**) **1** *intr.* emit a strong offensive smell. **2** *tr.* (often foll. by *up*) fill (a place) with a stink. • *n.* **1** strong or offensive smell. **2** *colloq.* fuss.

stink·er /stíngkər/ *n.* **1** person or thing that stinks. **2** *sl.* objectionable person or thing. **3** *sl.* difficult task.

stink·ing /stíngking/ • *adj.* **1** that stinks. **2** *sl.* very objectionable. • *adv.* *sl.* extremely and usu. objectionably. □□ **stink'ing·ly** *adv.*

stint /stint/ • *v.* **1** *tr.* supply (food or aid, etc.) in an ungenerous amount or grudgingly. **2** *intr.* (foll. by *on*) be grudging or mean about. • *n.* **1** limitation of supply or effort (*without stint*). **2** allotted amount of work (*do one's stint*). □□ **stint'er** *n.* **stint'less** *adj.*

sti·pend /stípend/ *n.* fixed regular allowance or salary.

stip·ple /stípəl/ • *v.* draw or paint or engrave, etc., with dots instead of lines. • *n.* **1** stippling. **2** effect of stippling. □□ **stip'pler** *n.* **stip'pling** *n.*

stip·u·late /stípyəlayt/ *v.tr.* demand or specify as part of an agreement. □□ **stip·u·la·tion** /–láyshən/ *n.* **stip'u·la·tor** *n.*

stir¹ /stər/ • *v.* (**stirred, stir·ring**) **1** *tr.* move an implement around and around in (a liquid, etc.) to mix the ingredients or constituents. **2 a** *tr.* cause to move, esp. slightly. **b** *intr.* be or begin to be in motion. **3** *intr.* rise from sleep. **4** *tr.* arouse or inspire or excite (the emotions, a person, etc.). • *n.* **1** act of stirring. **2** commotion or excitement. □ **stir up** **1** incite (trouble, etc.). **2** stimulate; excite; arouse. □□ **stir'rer** *n.*

stir² /stər/ *n.* *sl.* prison (esp. in stir).

stir-fry /stárfrī/ • *v.tr.* (**–fries, –fried**) fry rapidly while stirring and tossing. • *n.* food cooked this way.

stir·ring /stáring/ *adj.* **1** stimulating; exciting; arousing. **2** actively occupied (*lead a stirring life*). □□ **stir'ring·ly** *adv.*

stir·rup /stárəp, stír–/ *n.* each of a pair of devices attached to each side of a horse's saddle, in the form of a loop with a flat base to support the rider's foot.

stitch /stich/ • *n.* **1** (in sewing or knitting or crocheting, etc.) single pass of a needle or the thread or loop, etc., resulting from this. **2** least bit of clothing (*hadn't a stitch on*). **3** acute pain in the side. *v.tr.* sew; make stitches (in). □ **in stitches** *colloq.* laughing uncontrollably. □□ **stitch'er** *n.* **stitch'er·y** *n.*

stoat /stōt/ *n.* carnivorous mammal of the weasel family, having brown fur in the summer turning mainly white in the winter. Also called **ermine.**

stock /stok/ • *n.* **1** store of goods, etc., ready for sale or distribution, etc. **2** supply; quantity. **3** equipment or raw material for manufacture or trade, etc. **4** farm animals or equipment. **5 a** capital of a business company. **b** shares in this. **6** one's reputation or popularity. **7** line of ancestry. **8** liquid made by stewing bones, vegetables, fish, etc., as a basis for soup, gravy, sauce, etc. **9** plant into which a graft is inserted. **10** (in *pl.*) *hist.* wooden frame with holes for the feet and occas. the hands and head, in which offenders were locked as a public punishment. **11** base or support or handle for an implement or machine. **12** butt of a rifle, etc. • *adj.* **1**

kept in stock and so regularly available (*stock sizes*). **2** hackneyed; conventional (*stock answer*). • *v.tr.* **1** have or keep (goods) in stock. **2** supply. □ **stock car** specially modified production car for use in racing. **stock exchange 1** place where stocks and shares are bought and sold. **2** dealers working there. **stock-in-trade 1** requisites of a trade or profession. **2** ready supply of characteristic phrases, attitudes, etc. **stock market** = *stock exchange*. **stock-still** without moving. **stock up 1** provide with or get stocks or supplies. **2** (foll. by *with*, *on*) get in or gather a stock of (food, fuel, etc.). □□ **stock'er** *n.* **stock'less** *adj.*

stock·ade /stokáyd/ • *n.* **1** line or enclosure of upright stakes. **2** military prison. • *v.tr.* fortify with a stockade.

stock·brok·er /stókbrōkər/ *n.* dealer in shares of stock. □□ **stock'brok·er·age** *n.* **stock'brok·ing** *n.*

stock·hold·er /stók-hōldər/ *n.* owner of stocks or shares. □□ **stock'hold·ing** *n.*

stock·ing /stóking/ *n.* knitted fabric covering for the leg and foot. □□ **stock'inged** *adj.* (also in *comb.*). **stock'ing·less** *adj.*

stock·pile /stókpīl/ • *n.* accumulated stock of goods, materials, weapons, etc., held in reserve. • *v.tr.* accumulate a stockpile of. □□ **stock'pil·er** *n.*

stock·room /stókrōōm, –rōŏm/ *n.* room for storing goods.

stock·tak·ing /stóktayking/ *n.* **1** making an inventory of stock. **2** review of one's position and resources.

stock·y /stókee/ *adj.* (**stock·i·er**, **stock·i·est**) short and strongly built; thickset. □□ **stock'i·ly** *adv.* **stock'i·ness** *n.*

stock·yard /stókyaard/ *n.* enclosure with pens, etc., for the sorting or temporary keeping of cattle.

stodg·y /stójee/ *adj.* (**stodg·i·er**, **stodg·i·est**) dull; uninteresting; old-fashioned. □□ **stodg'i·ly** *adv.* **stodg'i·ness** *n.*

Sto·ic /stóik/ • *n.* **1** member of the ancient Greek school of philosophy that taught control of one's feelings and passions. **2** (**stoic**) stoical person. • *adj.* **1** of or like the Stoics. **2** (**stoic**) = STOICAL.

sto·i·cal /stóikəl/ *adj.* having or showing great self-control in adversity. □□ **sto'i·cal·ly** *adv.*

Sto·i·cism /stóisizəm/ *n.* **1** philosophy of the Stoics. **2** (**stoicism**) stoical attitude.

stoke /stōk/ *v.tr.* feed and tend (a fire or furnace, etc.).

STOL *abbr. Aeron.* short take-off and landing.

stole[1] /stōl/ *n.* **1** woman's long scarf, worn around the shoulders. **2** strip of silk, etc., worn over the shoulders as a vestment by a priest.

stole[2] *past of* STEAL.

sto·len *past part. of* STEAL.

stol·id /stólid/ *adj.* **1** lacking or concealing emotion or animation. **2** not easily excited or moved. □□ **sto·lid·i·ty** /–líditee/ *n.* **stol'id·ly** *adv.* **stol'id·ness** *n.*

stom·ach /stúmək/ • *n.* **1 a** internal organ in which food is digested. **b** any of several such organs in animals. **2** lower front of the body. **3** appetite or inclination. • *v.tr.* **1** find sufficiently palatable to swallow or keep down. **2** endure (usu. with *neg.*: *cannot stomach it*). □□ **stom'ach·ful** *n.* (*pl.* **–fuls**).

stomp /stomp/ • *v.intr.* tread or stamp heavily. • *n.* lively jazz dance with heavy stamping. □□ **stomp'er** *n.*

stone /stōn/ • *n.* **1 a** solid nonmetallic mineral matter, of which rock is made. **b** small piece of this. **2** precious stone, esp. used in jewelry. **3** a thing resembling stone in hardness or form, e.g., the hard case of the kernel in some fruits. **b** *Med.* (often in *pl.*) hard mass forming in certain body organs. **4** (*pl.* same) *Brit.* unit of weight equal to 14 lb. (6.35 kg). • *v.tr.* pelt with stones. □ **leave no stone unturned** try all possible means. **Stone Age** prehistoric period when weapons and tools were made of stone. **stone's throw** short distance. □□ **stoned** *adj.* (also in *comb.*). **stone'less** *adj.* **ston'er** *n.*

stoned /stōnd/ *adj. sl.* under the influence of alcohol or drugs.

stone·ma·son /stónmaysən/ *n.* person who cuts, prepares, and builds with stone. □□ **stone·ma'son·ry** *n.*

stone·wall /stónwawl/ *v.* obstruct (discussion or investigation) or be obstructive with evasive answers or denials, etc. □□ **stone'wall·er** *n.* **stone'wall·ing** *n.*

stone·ware /stónwair/ *n.* ceramic ware that is impermeable and partly vitrified but opaque.

stone·washed /stónwawsht, –wosht/ *adj.* (esp. of denim) washed with abrasives to produce a worn or faded look.

stone·work /stónwərk/ *n.* walls, etc., made of stone; masonry. □□ **stone'work·er** *n.*

ston·y /stónee/ *adj.* (**ston·i·er**, **ston·i·est**) **1** full of stones (*stony soil*). **2** a hard; rigid. **b** cold; unfeeling; uncompromising (*stony stare*). □□ **ston'i·ly** *adv.* **ston'i·ness** *n.*

stood *past and past part. of* STAND.

stooge /stōōj/ *colloq. n.* **1** butt or foil, esp. for a comedian; straight man. **2** assistant or subordinate, esp. for routine or unpleasant work.

stool /stōōl/ *n.* **1** single seat without a back or arms. **2** = FOOTSTOOL. **3** (usu. in *pl.*) = FECES. □ **stool pigeon** police informer or decoy.

stoop[1] /stōōp/ • *v.* **1** *tr.* bend (one's head or body) forward and downward. **2** *intr.* carry one's head and shoulders bowed forward. **3** *intr.* (often foll. by *down*) lower the body by bending forward, sometimes also bending at the knee. **4** *intr.* condescend. **5** *intr.* descend or lower oneself to (some conduct) (*has stooped to crime*). • *n.* stooping posture.

stoop[2] /stōōp/ *n.* porch or small veranda or set of steps in front of a house.

stop /stop/ • *v.* (**stopped**, **stop·ping**) **1** *tr.* a put an end to (motion, etc.); completely check the progress or motion or operation of. **b** effectively hinder or prevent. **c** discontinue (an action or sequence of actions). **2** *intr.* come to an end. **3** *intr.* cease from motion or speaking or action. **4** *tr.* defeat. **5** *intr.* stay for a short time. **6** *tr.* block or close up (a hole or leak, etc.). • *n.* **1** stopping; being stopped. **2** place designated for a bus or train, etc., to stop. **3** device for stopping motion at a particular point. **4 a** (in an organ) row of pipes of one character. **b** knob, etc., operating these. □ **stop at nothing** be ruthless. □□ **stop'less** *adj.* **stop'pa·ble** *adj.*

stop·cock /stópkok/ *n.* externally operated valve

regulating the flow of a liquid or gas through a pipe, etc.

stop·gap /stópgap/ *n.* (often *attrib.*) temporary substitute.

stop·o·ver /stópōvər/ *n.* break in one's journey.

stop·page /stópij/ *n.* **1** condition of being blocked or stopped. **2** stopping or interruption of work in a factory, etc.

stop·per /stópər/ • *n.* plug for closing a bottle, etc. • *v.tr.* close or secure with a stopper.

stop·watch /stópwoch/ *n.* watch with a mechanism for recording elapsed time, used to time races, etc.

stor·age /stáwrij/ *n.* **1 a** storing of goods, etc. **b** space available for storing. **2** cost of storing. **3** electronic retention of data in a computer, etc. □ **storage battery** (or **cell**) battery (or cell) for storing electricity.

store /stawr/ • *n.* **1** quantity of something kept available for use. **2** (in *pl.*) **a** articles for a particular purpose accumulated for use. **b** supply of these or the place where they are kept. **3** retail outlet or shop. • *v.tr.* **1** put (furniture, etc.) in storage. **2** accumulate for future use. **3** stock or provide with something useful. **4** enter or retain (data) for retrieval. □ **in store 1** kept in readiness. **2** coming in the future. **3** (foll. by *for*) destined or intended. **set store by** consider important. □□ **stor′a·ble** *adj.* **stor′er** *n.*

store·house /stáwrhows/ *n.* place where things are stored.

store·keep·er /stáwrkeepər/ *n.* store owner or manager.

store·room /stáwr-rōōm, -rŏŏm/ *n.* storage room.

sto·ried /stáwreed/ *adj.* *literary* celebrated in or associated with stories or legends.

stork /stawrk/ *n.* long-legged large wading bird with white plumage, black wingtips, and a long reddish beak.

storm /stawrm/ • *n.* **1** violent disturbance of the atmosphere with strong winds and usu. with thunder and rain or snow, etc. **2** violent political, etc., disturbance. **3** (foll. by *of*) outbreak of applause, indignation, hisses, etc. **4** direct assault by troops on a fortified place. • *v.* **1** *intr.* rage; bluster. **2** *intr.* move violently or angrily (*stormed out*). **3** *tr.* attack or capture by storm. □ **storm petrel** = *stormy petrel*. **storm trooper 1** *hist.* member of the Nazi political militia. **2** member of the shock troops. **take by storm 1** capture by direct assault. **2** rapidly captivate. □□ **storm′less** *adj.* **storm′proof** *adj.*

storm·y /stáwrmee/ *adj.* (**storm·i·er, storm·i·est**) **1** of or affected by storms. **2** full of angry feeling or outbursts; tempestuous (*stormy meeting*). □ **stormy petrel 1** small black and white petrel of the North Atlantic. **2** person causing unrest. □□ **storm′i·ly** *adv.* **storm′i·ness** *n.*

sto·ry¹ /stáwree/ *n.* (*pl.* **–ries**) **1** account of imaginary or past events; narrative, tale, or anecdote. **2** history of a person or institution, etc. **3** (in full **story line**) narrative or plot of a novel or play, etc. **4** facts or experiences that deserve narration. **5** *colloq.* fib or lie.

sto·ry² /stáwree/ *n.* (*pl.* **–ries**) horizontal division of a building, from floor to ceiling in each. □□ **–sto·ried** (in *comb.*).

sto·ry·board /stáwreebawrd/ *n.* displayed sequence of pictures, etc., outlining the plan of a movie, etc.

sto·ry·tell·er /stáwreetelər/ *n.* **1** person who tells stories. **2** *colloq.* liar. □□ **sto′ry·tell·ing** *n.* & *adj.*

stout /stowt/ • *adj.* **1** somewhat fat; corpulent; bulky. **2** thick; strong. **3** brave; resolute. • *n.* strong, dark brown beer. □□ **stout′ish** *adj.* **stout′ly** *adv.* **stout′ness** *n.*

stout·heart·ed /stówt-hártəd/ *adj.* courageous. □□ **stout′heart·ed·ly** *adj.*

stove¹ /stōv/ *n.* closed apparatus burning fuel or electricity for heating or cooking.

stove² *past* and *past part.* of STAVE *v.*

stove·pipe /stóvpīp/ *n.* pipe conducting smoke and gases from a stove to a chimney. □ **stovepipe hat** *colloq.* tall silk hat.

stow /stō/ *v.tr.* pack (goods, etc.) tidily and compactly. □ **stow away 1** place (a thing) where it will not cause an obstruction. **2** be a stowaway on a ship, etc.

stow·a·way /stóəway/ *n.* person who hides on board a ship or aircraft, etc., to get free passage.

stra·bis·mus /strəbízməs/ *n.* *Med.* cross eyes; squint. □□ **stra·bis′mal** *adj.* **stra·bis′mic** *adj.*

strad·dle /strád'l/ *v.* **1** *tr.* **a** sit or stand across (a thing) with the legs wide apart. **b** be situated across or on both sides of. **2** *intr.* sit or stand in this way. □□ **strad′dler** *n.*

strafe /strayf/ *v.tr.* harass with gunfire.

strag·gle /strágəl/ *v.intr.* **1** lack or lose compactness or tidiness. **2** be or become dispersed or sporadic. **3** trail behind others in a march or race, etc. □□ **strag′gler** *n.* **strag′gly** *adj.* (**strag·gli·er, strag·gli·est**).

straight /strayt/ • *adj.* **1** extending uniformly in the same direction; without a curve or bend, etc. **2** successive; uninterrupted (*three straight wins*). **3** in proper order or condition; level (*put things straight*). **4** honest; candid. **5 a** unmodified. **b** (of a drink) undiluted. **6** *colloq.* **a** (of a person, etc.) conventional or respectable. **b** heterosexual. **7** direct; undeviating. • *n.* **1** straight condition. **2** sequence of five cards in poker. **3** *colloq.* **a** conventional person. **b** heterosexual. • *adv.* **1** in a straight line; direct; without deviation or hesitation or circumlocution. **2** correctly. □ **straight man** comedian's set-up man or foil. **straight off** *colloq.* without hesitation. **straight up** *colloq.* **1** truthfully; honestly. **2** (of liquor) without ice. □□ **straight′ly** *adv.* **straight′ness** *n.*

straight·a·way /stráytəway/ *n.* straight part of a course, track, road, etc.

straight·en /stráyt'n/ *v.* **1** make or become straight. **2** (foll. by *up*) stand erect after bending. □□ **straight′en·er** *n.*

straight·for·ward /stráytfáwrwərd/ *adj.* **1** honest or frank. **2** (of a task, etc.) uncomplicated. □□ **straight·for′ward·ly** *adv.* **straight·for′ward·ness** *n.*

strain¹ /strayn/ • *v.* **1** *tr.* & *intr.* stretch tightly; make or become taut or tense. **2** *tr.* exercise (oneself, one's senses, a thing, etc.) intensely or excessively; press to extremes. **3** *intr.* strive intensely. **4** *intr.* (foll. by *at*) tug; pull. **5** *tr.* distort from the true intention or meaning. **6** *tr.* overwhelm or injure by overuse or excessive demands. **7** *tr.* clear (a liquid) of solid matter by passing it through a sieve, etc.; filter. • *n.* **1 a** act or an instance of straining. **b** force exerted in this. **2** injury caused by straining a muscle, etc. **3 a** severe demand on physical strength or resources. **b** exertion needed to meet this. **4** (in *sing.* or *pl.*) snatch or spell of music or poetry. **5** tone or tendency in speech or writing (*more in the same strain*). □□ **strain′a·ble** *adj.*

strain[2] /strayn/ *n.* **1** breed or stock of animals, plants, etc. **2** moral tendency as part of a person's character.

strained /straynd/ *adj.* **1** constrained; forced; artificial. **2** (of a relationship) mutually distrustful or tense.

strain·er /stráynər/ *n.* device for straining liquids, etc.

strait /strayt/ *n.* **1** (in *sing.* or *pl.*) narrow passage of water connecting two seas or large bodies of water. **2** (usu. in *pl.*) difficulty; distress. □□ **strait′ly** *adv.* **strait′ness** *n.*

strait·ened /stráyt'nd/ *adj.* characterized by poverty.

strait·jack·et /stráytjakit/ *n.* **1** strong garment with long arms for confining a violent person. **2** restrictive measures.

strait·laced /stráytláyst/ *adj.* puritanical.

strand[1] /strand/ • *v.* **1** *tr.* & *intr.* run aground. **2** *tr.* (as **stranded** *adj.*) in difficulties, esp. without money or means of transport. • *n. rhet.* or *poet.* shoreline, beach.

strand[2] /strand/ *n.* **1** each of the threads or wires twisted around each other to make a rope or cable. **2** single thread or strip of fiber. **b** constituent filament. **3** lock of hair. **4** element or strain in any composite whole.

strange /straynj/ *adj.* **1** unusual; peculiar; surprising; eccentric; novel. **2** unfamiliar; alien; foreign. **3** not at ease; out of one's element (*felt strange in such company*). □□ **strange′ly** *adv.* **strange′ness** *n.*

strang·er /stráynjər/ *n.* **1** person new to a particular place or company. **2** person one does not know. **3** person entirely unaccustomed to (a feeling, experience, etc.).

stran·gle /stránggəl/ *v.tr.* **1** squeeze the windpipe or neck of, esp. so as to kill. **2** hamper or suppress. □□ **stran′gler** *n.*

stran·gle·hold /stránggəlhōld/ *n.* **1** illegal throttling hold in wrestling. **2** deadly grip. **3** complete and exclusive control.

stran·gu·late /stránggyəlayt/ *v.tr. Surgery* prevent circulation through (a vein, intestine, etc.) by compression.

stran·gu·la·tion /stránggyəláyshən/ *n.* **1** act of strangling or the state of being strangled. **2** the act of strangulating.

strap /strap/ • *n.* **1** strip of leather, etc., often with a buckle or other fastening for holding things together, etc. **2** thing like this for keeping a garment in place. • *v.tr.* (**strapped, strap·ping**) secure or bind with a strap.

strap·ping /stráping/ *adj.* (esp. of a person) large and sturdy.

stra·ta *pl.* of STRATUM.
¶ See note at STRATUM.

strat·a·gem /strátəjəm/ *n.* **1** cunning plan or scheme, esp. for deceiving an enemy. **2** trickery.

stra·te·gic /strətée jik/ *adj.* **1** of or serving the ends of strategy; useful or important with regard to strategy. **2** (of materials) essential in fighting a war. **3** (of bombing or weapons) done or for use as a longer-term military objective. □□ **stra·te′gi·cal** *adj.* **stra·te′gi·cal·ly** *adv.* **stra·te′gics** *n.pl.* (usu. treated as *sing.*).

strat·e·gy /strátijee/ *n.* (*pl.* **–gies**) **1** art of war or military deployment. **2** plan of action or policy in business or politics, etc. (*economic strategy*). □□ **strat′e·gist** *n.*

strat·i·fy /strátifī/ *v.tr.* (**–fies, –fied**) **1** (esp. as **stratified** *adj.*) arrange in strata. **2** construct in layers, social grades, etc. □□ **strat·i·fi·ca′tion** *n.*

strat·o·sphere /strátəsfeer/ *n.* layer of atmospheric air above the troposphere extending to about 30 miles above the earth's surface. □□ **strat·o·spher′ic** *adj.*

stra·tum /stráytəm, strát–/ *n.* (*pl.* **stra·ta** /–tə/ or **stratums**) **1** esp. *Geol.* or *Archaeol.* layer or set of layers of any deposited substance. **2** atmospheric layer. **3** social class. □□ **stra′tal** *adj.*
¶ The singular is *stratum*, 'a layer.' The plural, **strata**, is sometimes mistaken for singular.

straw /straw/ *n.* **1** dry cut stalks of grain for use as fodder or as material for packing, etc. **2** single stalk or piece of straw. **3** thin tube for sucking a drink from a glass, etc. **4** pale yellow color. □ **straw vote** (or **poll**) unofficial ballot as a test of opinion.

straw·ber·ry /stráwberee/ *n.* (*pl.* **–ries**) **1** plant with white flowers, trifoliate leaves, and runners. **2** pulpy red edible fruit of this, having a seed-studded surface.

stray /stray/ • *v.intr.* **1 a** wander from the right place or from one's companions, etc.; go astray. **b** digress. **2** deviate morally. • *n.* person or thing that has strayed, esp. a domestic animal. • *adj.* **1** strayed or lost. **2** isolated; found or occurring occasionally (*hit by a stray bullet*). □□ **stray′er** *n.*

streak /streek/ • *n.* **1** long thin usu. irregular line or band, esp. of color. **2** strain or element in a person's character. **3** spell or series (*winning streak*). • *v.* **1** *tr.* mark with streaks. **2** *intr.* move very rapidly. **3** *intr. colloq.* run naked in a public place. □□ **streak′er** *n.* **streak′ing** *n.*

streak·y /stréekee/ *adj.* (**streak·i·er, streak·i·est**) full of streaks. □□ **streak′i·ly** *adv.* **streak′i·ness** *n.*

stream /streem/ • *n.* **1** flowing body of water, esp. a small river. **2** flow of a fluid, a mass of people, questions, etc. **3** current; direction (*against the stream*). • *v.intr.* **1** flow or move as a stream. **2** run with liquid.

stream·er /stréemər/ *n.* **1** long narrow flag. **2** long narrow strip of ribbon or paper.

stream·line /stréemlīn/ *v.tr.* **1** give (a vehicle, etc.) the form which presents the least resistance to motion. **2** make simple or more efficient or better organized. **3** (as **streamlined** *adj.*) **a** aerodynamic. **b** having a simplified and more efficient structure or organization.

street /street/ *n.* **1 a** public road in a city, town, or village. **b** this with the houses and other buildings on each side. **2** persons who live or work on a particular street. □ **on the streets 1** living by prostitution. **2** homeless.

street·car /stréetkaar/ *n.* commuter vehicle that operates on rails in city streets.

street·walk·er /stréetwawkər/ *n.* prostitute seeking customers on the street. □□ **street′walk·ing** *n.* & *adj.*

street·wise /ˈstreetwīz/ n. familiar with the ways of modern urban life.

strength /strengkth, strength, strenth/ n. **1** being strong; degree or manner of this. **2 a** person or thing affording strength. **b** positive attribute. **3** number of persons present or available. **4** full complement. □ **in strength** with the force of large numbers. **on the strength of** on the basis of.

strength·en /ˈstrengkthən, ˈstren–/ v. make or become stronger. □□ **strength'en·er** n.

stren·u·ous /ˈstrényōōəs/ adj. **1** requiring or using great effort. **2** energetic. □□ **stren'u·ous·ly** adv. **stren'u·ous·ness** n.

strep·to·coc·cus /ˌstréptəˈkókəs/ n. (pl. **strep·to·coc·ci** /–ˈkóksī, –ˈkókī/) bacterium of a type often causing infectious diseases. □□ **strep·to·coc'cal** adj.

strep·to·my·cin /ˌstréptəˈmīsin/ n. antibiotic effective against many disease-producing bacteria.

stress /stres/ • n. **1** pressure; tension. **2** physical or mental strain or distress. **3 a** emphasis. **b** accentuation; emphasis laid on a syllable or word. • v.tr. **1** emphasize. **2** subject to stress. □ **stressed out** lethargic owing to long-term stress. □□ **stress'less** adj.

stress·ful /ˈstrésfŏŏl/ adj. causing stress; mentally tiring. □□ **stress'ful·ly** adv. **stress'ful·ness** n.

stretch /strech/ • v. **1** tr. & intr. draw or be drawn or admit of being drawn out into greater length or size. **2** tr. & intr. make or become taut. **3** tr. & intr. place or lie at full length or spread out. **4** tr. (also absol.) **a** extend (an arm, leg, etc.). **b** (often refl.) thrust out one's limbs and tighten one's muscles after being relaxed. **5** intr. have a specified length or extension; extend. **6** tr. strain; exaggerate (stretch the truth). • n. **1** continuous extent or expanse or period. **2** stretching or being stretched. **3** (attrib.) elastic (stretch fabric). **4** colloq. period of imprisonment, military service, etc. **5** straight side of a racetrack. □ **at a stretch** in one continuous period. **stretch a point** agree to something not normally allowed. □□ **stretch'a·ble** adj. **stretch·a·bil'i·ty** n. **stretch'y** adj. **stretch'i·ness** n.

stretch·er /ˈstréchər/ n. framework of two poles with canvas, etc., between, for carrying a person in a lying position.

strew /strŏŏ/ v.tr. (past part. **strewn** or **strewed**) **1** scatter or spread about over a surface. **2** (usu. foll. by with) spread (a surface) with scattered things. □□ **strew'er** n.

stri·ate /ˈstrīət/ adj. (also **stri·at·ed** /ˈstrīaytid/) Anat., Zool., Bot., & Geol. marked with parallel lines, ridges, etc. □□ **stri·a'tion** /strīˈayshən/ n.

strick·en /ˈstrikən/ adj. affected or overcome with illness or misfortune, etc. (stricken with measles).

strict /strikt/ adj. **1** precisely limited or defined; undeviating. **2** requiring complete compliance or exact performance (gave strict orders). □□ **strict'ly** adv. **strict'ness** n.

stric·ture /ˈstríkchər/ n. **1** (usu. in pl.) critical or censorious remark. **2** restriction.

stride /strīd/ • v. (past **strode** /strōd/; past part. **strid·den** /ˈstrid'n/) **1** intr. & tr. walk with long firm steps. **2** tr. cross with one step. **3** tr. bestride; straddle. • n. **1 a** single long step. **b** length of this. **2** person's gait as determined by the length of stride. **3** (usu. in pl.) progress (great strides). **4** settled rate of progress (get into one's stride). □ **take in one's stride** manage without difficulty. □□ **strid'er** n.

stri·dent /ˈstrīd'nt/ adj. loud and harsh. □□ **stri'den·cy** n. **stri'dent·ly** adv.

strife /strīf/ n. conflict; struggle.

strike /strīk/ • v. (past **struck** /struk/; past part. **struck** or archaic **strick·en** /ˈstrikən/) **1 a** tr. subject to an impact. **b** tr. deliver (a blow) or inflict a blow on; hit. **2** tr. come or bring sharply into contact with (ship struck a rock). **3** tr. propel or divert with a blow (struck the ball into the pond). **4** intr. (foll. by at) try to hit. **5** tr. ignite (a match) or produce (sparks, etc.) by rubbing. **6** tr. make (a coin) by stamping. **7** tr. produce (a musical note) by striking. **8 a** tr. (also absol.) (of a clock) indicate (the time) with a chime, etc. **b** intr. (of time) be indicated in this way. **9** tr. **a** attack or affect suddenly. **b** (of a disease) afflict. **10** tr. cause to become suddenly (struck dumb). **11** tr. reach or achieve (strike a balance). **12** tr. agree on (a bargain). **13** tr. assume (an attitude) suddenly and dramatically. **14** tr. **a** discover or find. **b** find (oil, etc.) by drilling. **15** occur to or appear to (strikes me as silly). **16 a** intr. (of employees) engage in a strike. **b** tr. act in this way against (an employer). **17 a** tr. lower or take down (a flag, tent, stage set, etc.). **b** intr. signify surrender by striking a flag. • n. **1** act or instance of striking. **2** organized refusal by employees to work until some grievance is remedied. **3** sudden find or success (lucky strike). **4** an attack, esp. from the air. **5** Baseball pitched ball counted against a batter, either for failure to hit it fair or because it passes through the strike zone. □ **on strike** taking part in an industrial, etc., strike. **strike home 1** deal an effective blow. **2** have an intended effect (my words struck home). **strike out 1** hit out. **2** act vigorously. **3** delete (an item or name, etc.). **4** Baseball **a** dismiss (a batter) by means of three strikes. **b** be dismissed in this way. **c** sl. fail. **strike up 1** start (an acquaintance, conversation, etc.) off-handedly or casually. **2** (also absol.) begin playing (a tune, etc.). □□ **strik'a·ble** adj. **strik'er** n.

strike·break·er /ˈstrīkbraykər/ n. person working or employed in place of strikers. □□ **strike'break** v.intr.

strik·ing /ˈstrīking/ adj. impressive; attracting attention. □□ **strik'ing·ly** adv.

string /string/ • n. **1** twine or narrow cord. **2** piece of this. **3** length of catgut or wire, etc., on a musical instrument, producing a note by vibration. **4 a** (in pl.) stringed instruments in an orchestra, etc. **b** (attrib.) relating to or consisting of stringed instruments (string quartet). **5** (in pl.) condition; complication (offer has no strings). • v.tr. (past and past part. **strung** /strung/) **1** supply with a string or strings. **2** thread (beads, etc.) on a string. **3** arrange in or as a string. □ **string along** colloq. **1** deceive. **2** keep company (with). **string out** extend; prolong (esp. unduly). **string up 1** hang up on strings, etc. **2** kill by hanging. □□ **string'less** adj. **string'like** adj.

stringed /stringd/ adj. (of musical instruments) having strings (also in comb.: twelve-stringed guitar).

strin·gent /ˈstrínjənt/ adj. (of rules, etc.) strict; precise. □□ **strin'gen·cy** n. **strin'gent·ly** adv.

string·er /ˈstríngər/ n. **1** longitudinal structural member in a framework, esp. of a ship or aircraft. **2** colloq. newspaper correspondent not on the regular staff.

string·y /stríngee/ adj. (**string·i·er, string·i·est**) (of food, etc.) fibrous; like string. □□ **string′i·ly** adv. **string′i·ness** n.

strip[1] /strip/ • v. (**stripped, strip·ping**) **1** tr. remove the clothes or covering from. **2** intr. undress oneself. **3** tr. deprive (a person) of property or titles. **4** tr. leave bare. **5** tr. remove the accessory fittings of or take apart (a machine, etc.). **6** tr. tear the thread from (a screw). **7** tr. tear the teeth from (a gearwheel). • n. act of stripping, esp. of undressing in striptease. □ **strip mine** mine worked by removing the material that overlies the ore, etc. **strip search** n. search of a person involving the removal of all clothes. • v.tr. search in this way.

strip[2] /strip/ n. long narrow piece (*strip of land*).

stripe /strīp/ n. **1** long narrow band or strip differing in color or texture from the surface on either side of it (*black with a red stripe*). **2** Mil. chevron, etc., denoting military rank. **3** category of character, opinion, etc. (*man of that stripe*).

striped /strīpt/ adj. marked with stripes (also in comb.: *red-striped*).

strip·ling /strípling/ n. youth not yet fully grown.

strip·per /strípər/ n. **1** person or thing that strips something. **2** striptease performer.

strip·tease /stríptèez/ n. entertainment in which the performer slowly and erotically undresses. □□ **strip·teas′er** n.

strive /strīv/ v.intr. (*past* strove /strōv/; *past part.* striv·en /strívən/) **1** try hard. **2** struggle or contend. □□ **striv′er** n.

strobe /strōb/ n. colloq. stroboscope.

stro·bo·scope /strṓbəskōp/ n. **1** Physics instrument for determining speeds of rotation, etc., by shining a bright light at intervals so that a rotating object appears stationary. **2** lamp made to flash intermittently. □□ **stro·bo·scop·ic** /-skópik/ adj.

strode past of STRIDE.

stroke /strōk/ • n. **1** act of striking; blow or hit. **2** sudden disabling attack caused esp. by thrombosis. **3 a** action or movement esp. as one of a series. **b** slightest such action (*stroke of work*). **4** whole of the motion (of a wing, oar, etc.) until the starting position is regained. **5** mode of moving the arms and legs in swimming. **6** specially successful or skillful effort (*a stroke of diplomacy*). **7** mark made by the movement in one direction of a pen or pencil or paintbrush. **8** sound made by a striking clock. **9** act or a spell of stroking. • v.tr. **1** caress lightly. **2** act as the stroke of (a boat or crew). **3** colloq. flatter; seek to influence by flattery.

stroll /strōl/ • v.intr. saunter or walk in a leisurely way. • n. short leisurely walk (*go for a stroll*).

stroll·er /strṓlər/ n. **1** person who strolls. **2** folding chair on wheels, for pushing a child in.

strong /strawng, strong/ • adj. (**strong·er** /stráwnggər, stróng-/; **strong·est** /stráwnggist, stróng-/) **1** having the power of resistance; not easily damaged, overcome, or disturbed. **2** healthy. **3** capable of exerting great force or of doing much; muscular; powerful. **4** forceful or powerful in effect (*strong wind*). **5** decided or firmly held (*strong views*). **6** (of an argument, etc.) convincing or striking. **7** intense; concentrated. **8** for-

midable (*strong candidate*). **9** (of a group) having a specified number (*200 strong*). **10** Gram. forming inflections by change of vowel within the stem (e.g., *swim, swam*). • adv. strongly. □ **come on strong** act aggressively. **strong-arm** using force (*strong-arm tactics*). □□ **strong′ly** adv.

strong·box /stráwngboks, stróng-/ n. strongly made small chest for valuables.

strong·hold /stráwnghōld, stróng-/ n. **1** fortified place. **2** secure refuge. **3** center of support for a cause, etc.

strong·room /stráwngrōom, -rŏom, stróng-/ n. room designed to protect valuables against fire and theft.

stron·ti·um /strónteeəm/ n. Chem. soft silver white metallic element occurring naturally in various minerals. ¶ Symb.: **Sr**. □ **strontium 90** radioactive isotope of strontium.

strop /strop/ • n. device, esp. a strip of leather, for sharpening razors. • v.tr. (**stropped, strop·ping**) sharpen on or with a strop.

strove past of STRIVE.

struck past and past part. of STRIKE.

struc·ture /strúkchər/ • n. **1 a** constructed unit, esp. a building. **b** way in which a building, etc., is constructed. **2** framework. • v.tr. give structure or shape to; organize; frame. □□ **struc′tur·al** adj. **struc′tured** adj. (also in comb.). **struc′ture·less** adj.

stru·del /strōōd′l/ n. confection of thin pastry rolled up around a filling and baked (*apple strudel*).

strug·gle /strúgəl/ • v.intr. **1** make forceful or violent efforts to get free of restraint or constriction. **2** try hard under difficulties. **3** (foll. by *with, against*) contend; fight. **4** make one's way with difficulty (*struggled to my feet*). **5** (esp. as **struggling** adj.) have difficulty in gaining recognition or a living. • n. **1** act or spell of struggling. **2** hard or confused contest. **3** determined effort under difficulties. □□ **strug′gler** n.

strum /strum/ • v.tr. (**strummed, strum·ming**) **1** play on (a stringed or keyboard instrument), esp. carelessly or unskillfully. **2** play (a tune, etc.) in this way. • n. sound made by strumming. □□ **strum′mer** n.

strung past and past part. of STRING.

strut /strut/ • n. **1** bar forming part of a framework and designed to resist compression. **2** strutting gait. • v.intr. (**strut·ted, strut·ting**) walk with a pompous or affected stiff erect gait. □□ **strut′ter** n. **strut′ting·ly** adv.

strych·nine /stríknīn, -nin, -neen/ n. vegetable alkaloid, bitter and highly poisonous, formerly used as a stimulant and (in small amounts) a medication. □□ **strych′nic** adj.

stub /stub/ • n. **1** shortened remnant of a pencil, cigarette, etc., after use. **2** part of a check, receipt, etc., retained as a record. **3** stump. • v.tr. (**stubbed, stub·bing**) **1** strike (one's toe) against something. **2** extinguish (a cigarette) by pressure.

stub·ble /stúbəl/ n. **1** cut stalks of cereal plants left sticking up after the harvest. **2 a** cropped hair or cropped beard. **b** short growth of unshaven hair. □□ **stub′bled** adj. **stub′bly** adj.

stub·born /stúbərn/ adj. obstinate; inflexible. □□ **stub′born·ly** adv. **stub′born·ness** n.

stub·by /stúbee/ adj. (**stub·bi·er, stub·bi·est**) short and thick. □□ **stub′bi·ly** adv. **stub′bi·ness** n.

stuc·co /stúkō/ • *n.* (*pl.* **–coes** or **–cos**) plaster or cement for coating walls. • *v.tr.* (**–coes, –coed**) coat with stucco.

stuck *past* and *past part.* of STICK[2].

stuck-up /stúk úp/ *adj.* conceited.

stud[1] /stud/ • *n.* **1** large-headed nail, boss, or knob, esp. for ornament. **2** double button for a collar, shirt front, etc. • *v.tr.* (**stud·ded, stud·ding**) **1** set with or as with studs. **2** (as **studded** *adj.*) (foll. by *with*) thickly set or strewn.

stud[2] /stud/ *n.* **1** (in full **stud horse**) stallion. **2** *colloq.* young man (esp. one noted for sexual prowess). **3** (in full **stud poker**) form of poker in which some cards are dealt face up. □ **at stud** (of a male horse) hired out for breeding.

stu·dent /sto͞od′nt, styo͞od–/ *n.* person who is studying, esp. at school, college, etc.

stu·di·o /sto͞odeeō, styo͞od–/ *n.* (*pl.* **–os**) **1** workroom of a painter or photographer, etc. **2** place where movies, recordings, or broadcast programs are made. □ **studio couch** couch that can be converted into a bed.

stu·di·ous /sto͞odeeəs, styo͞od–/ *adj.* **1** assiduous in study. **2** painstaking. □□ **stu′di·ous·ly** *adv.* **stu′di·ous·ness** *n.*

stud·y /stúdee/ • *n.* (*pl.* **–ies**) **1** acquisition of knowledge, esp. from books. **2** (in *pl.*) pursuit of academic knowledge. **3** room used for reading, writing, etc. **4** piece of work, esp. a drawing, done for practice or as an experiment (*a study of a head*). **5** thing worth observing closely (*your face was a study*). **6** thing that has been or deserves to be investigated. • *v.* (**–ies, –ied**) **1** *tr.* make a study of; investigate or examine (a subject) (*study law*). **2** *intr.* apply oneself to study. **3** *tr.* scrutinize or earnestly contemplate (*studied their faces*). **4** *tr.* learn (one's role, etc.). **5** *tr.* (as **studied** *adj.*) deliberate; affected.

stuff /stuf/ • *n.* **1** material; fabric. **2** unspecified content, things, etc. **3** particular knowledge or activity (*know one's stuff*). • *v.* **1** *tr.* pack (a receptacle) tightly. **2** *tr.* (foll. by *in, into*) force or cram (a thing). **3** *tr.* fill out the skin of (a preserved animal or bird, etc.) to restore the original shape. **4** *tr.* fill (poultry, vegetables, etc.) with a mixture, esp. before cooking. **5 a** *tr.* & *refl.* fill (a person or oneself) with food. **b** *tr.* & *intr.* eat greedily. **6** *tr.* (usu. in *passive*) block up (a person's nose, etc.). □ **stuffed shirt** *colloq.* pompous person. □□ **stuf′fer** *n.* (also in *comb.*).

stuff·ing /stúfing/ *n.* **1** padding used to stuff cushions, etc. **2** mixture used to stuff food, esp. before cooking.

stuff·y /stúfee/ *adj.* (**stuff·i·er, stuff·i·est**) **1** (of a room, etc.) lacking fresh air. **2** (of a person's nose, etc.) stuffed up. **3** dull and conventional. □□ **stuff′i·ly** *adv.* **stuff′i·ness** *n.*

stul·ti·fy /stúltifī/ *v.tr.* (**–fies, –fied**) make ineffective, useless, or futile, esp. as a result of tedious routine (*stultifying boredom*). □□ **stul·ti·fi·ca′tion** *n.* **stul′ti·fi·er** *n.*

stum·ble /stúmbəl/ • *v.intr.* **1** involuntarily lurch forward or have a partial fall. **2** walk with repeated stumbles. **3** make a mistake or repeated mistakes in speaking, etc. **4** (foll. by *on, upon, across*) find by chance (*stumbled on an abandoned well*). • *n.* act of stumbling. □ **stumbling block** obstacle. □□ **stum′bler** *n.* **stum′bling·ly** *adv.*

stump /stump/ • *n.* **1** projecting remnant of a cut or fallen tree. **2** similar remnant cut off

595   stucco ~ stylus

or worn down. • *v.tr.* **1** (of a question, etc.) be too hard for; puzzle. **2** (also *absol.*) travel through (a state, etc.) making political speeches. □□ **stump′y** *adj.* (**stump·i·er, stump·i·est**)

stun /stun/ *v.tr.* (**stunned, stun·ning**) **1** knock senseless; stupefy. **2** bewilder or shock. **3** (of a sound) deafen temporarily.

stung *past* and *past part.* of STING.

stunk *past* and *past part.* of STINK.

stun·ning /stúning/ *adj.* *colloq.* extremely impressive or attractive. □□ **stun′ning·ly** *adv.*

stunt[1] /stunt/ *v.tr.* **1** retard the growth or development of. **2** dwarf; cramp. □□ **stunt′ed·ness** *n.*

stunt[2] /stunt/ *n.* **1** something unusual done to attract attention. **2** trick or daring maneuver.

stu·pe·fy /sto͞opifī, styo͞o–/ *v.tr.* (**–fies, –fied**) **1** make stupid or insensible. **2** stun with astonishment. □□ **stu·pe·fa·cient** /–fáyshənt/ *adj.* & *n.* **stu·pe·fac·tion** /–fákshən/ *n.* **stu′pe·fy·ing** *adj.* **stu′pe·fy·ing·ly** *adv.*

stu·pen·dous /sto͞opéndəs, styo͞o–/ *adj.* amazing or prodigious, esp. in terms of size or degree. □□ **stu·pen′dous·ly** *adv.* **stu·pen′dous·ness** *n.*

stu·pid /sto͞opid, styo͞o–/ (**stu·pid·er, stu·pid·est**) *adj.* **1** unintelligent; slow-witted; foolish. **2** typical of stupid persons. **3** uninteresting or boring. □□ **stu·pid·i·ty** /–píditee/ *n.* (*pl.* **–ties**) **stu′pid·ly** *adv.*

stu·por /sto͞opər, styo͞o–/ *n.* dazed, torpid, or helplessly amazed state. □□ **stu′por·ous** *adj.*

stur·dy /stórdee/ *adj.* (**stur·di·er, stur·di·est**) **1** robust; strongly built. **2** vigorous (*sturdy resistance*). □□ **stur′di·ly** *adv.* **stur′di·ness** *n.*

stur·geon /stórjən/ *n.* large sharklike fish used as food and a source of caviar and isinglass.

stut·ter /stútər/ • *v.intr.* stammer, esp. by involuntarily repeating the first consonants of words. • *n.* act or habit of stuttering. □□ **stut′ter·er** *n.* **stut′ter·ing·ly** *adv.*

sty[1] /stī/ *n.* (*pl.* **sties**) **1** pen or enclosure for pigs. **2** *colloq.* filthy room or dwelling.

sty[2] /stī/ *n.* (also **stye**) (*pl.* **sties** or **styes**) inflamed swelling on the edge of an eyelid.

style /stīl/ • *n.* **1** kind or sort, esp. in regard to appearance and form (*elegant style of house*). **2** manner of writing or speaking or performing. **3** distinctive manner of a person or school or period. **4 a** superior quality or manner (*do it in style*). **b** fashion in dress, etc. • *v.tr.* **1** design or make, etc., in a particular (esp. fashionable) style. **2** designate in a specified way.

styl·ish /stīlish/ *adj.* **1** fashionable; elegant. **2** having a superior quality, manner, etc. □□ **styl′ish·ly** *adv.* **styl′ish·ness** *n.*

styl·ist /stīlist/ *n.* **1 a** designer of fashionable styles, etc. **b** hairdresser. **2** stylish writer or performer.

sty·lis·tic /stīlístik/ *adj.* of or concerning esp. literary style. □□ **sty·lis′ti·cal·ly** *adv.*

styl·ize /stīlīz/ *v.tr.* (esp. as **stylized** *adj.*) paint, draw, etc., in a conventional nonrealistic style. □□ **styl·i·za′tion** *n.*

sty·lus /stīləs/ *n.* (*pl.* **–li** /–lī/ or **–luses**) **1** needle following a groove in a phonograph record and transmitting the recorded sound for reproduction. **2** pointed writing tool.

sty·mie /stímee/ (also **sty′my**) • *n.* (*pl.* **–mies**) *Golf* situation where an opponent's ball lies between the player and the hole. • *v.tr.* (**sty·mies, sty·mied, sty·my·ing** or **sty·mie·ing**) obstruct; thwart.

styp·tic /stíptik/ • *adj.* (of a drug, etc.) that checks bleeding. • *n.* styptic drug or substance.

sty·rene /stíreen/ *n. Chem.* liquid hydrocarbon easily polymerized and used in making plastics, etc.

Sty·ro·foam /stírəfōm/ *n. propr.* brand of expanded rigid lightweight polystyrene plastic.

sua·sion /swáyzhən/ *n. formal* persuasion as opposed to force (*moral suasion*). □□ **sua′sive** /swáysiv/ *adj.*

suave /swaav/ *adj.* smooth; polite; sophisticated. □□ **suave′ly** *adv.* **suave′ness** *n.* **suav·i·ty** /–vitee/ *n.* (*pl.* **–ties**)

sub /sub/ *colloq.* • *n.* **1** submarine. **2** subscription. **3** substitute. • *v.intr.* (**subbed, sub·bing**) (usu. foll. by *for*) act as a substitute for a person.

sub- /sub, səb/ *prefix* **1** at or to or from a lower position (*subordinate*; *submerge*; *subtract*). **2** secondary or inferior position (*subclass*; *subtotal*). **3** nearly; more or less (*subarctic*).

sub·a·tom·ic /súbətómik/ *adj.* occurring in or smaller than an atom.

sub·com·mit·tee /súbkəmitee/ *n.* committee formed from another committee for a specialized task.

sub·com·pact /səbkómpakt/ *n. & adj.* car that is smaller than a compact.

sub·con·scious /súbkónshəs/ • *adj.* of or concerning the part of the mind which is not fully conscious but influences actions, etc. • *n.* this part of the mind. □□ **sub·con′scious·ly** *adv.* **sub·con′scious·ness** *n.*

sub·con·ti·nent /súbkóntinənt/ *n.* extensive landmass, smaller than a continent. □□ **sub·con·ti·nent·al** /–nént′l/ *adj.*

sub·con·tract • *v.tr.* /súbkəntrákt/ employ a firm, etc., to do (work) as part of a larger project. • *n.* /súbkóntrakt/ secondary contract. □□ **sub·con·trac·tor** /–kóntraktər/ *n.*

sub·cul·ture /súbkulchər/ *n.* distinct cultural group within a larger culture. □□ **sub·cul·tur·al** /–kúlchərəl/ *adj.*

sub·cu·ta·ne·ous /súbkyōōtáyneeəs/ *adj.* under the skin. □□ **sub·cu·ta′ne·ous·ly** *adv.*

sub·di·vide /súbdivíd/ *v.tr.* divide again after a first division. □□ **sub·di·vi·sion** /súbdivízhən/ *n.*

sub·due /səbdóō, –dyóō/ *v.tr.* (**sub·dues, sub·dued, sub·du·ing**) **1** conquer, subjugate, or tame. **2** (as **subdued** *adj.*) softened; lacking in intensity; toned down (*subdued light*).

sub·head /súbhed/ *n.* (also **sub′head·ing**) subordinate heading or title in a chapter, article, etc.

sub·hu·man /súbhyōōmən/ *adj.* (of behavior, intelligence, etc.) less than human.

subj. *abbr.* **1** subject. **2** subjective. **3** subjunctive.

sub·ject • *n.* /súbjikt/ **1** matter, theme, etc., to be discussed, described, represented, dealt

with, etc. **2** field of study. **3** *Gram.* noun or its equivalent about which a sentence is predicated and with which the verb agrees. **4** any person living under a government. **5** person or animal undergoing treatment, examination, or experimentation. • *adj.* /súbjikt/ **1** owing obedience to a government, colonizing power, force, etc. **2** (foll. by *to*) liable, exposed, or prone to (*subject to infection*). **3** under the power or authority of. • *adv.* /súbjikt/ (foll. by *to*) conditionally upon (*subject to your consent, I propose to try again*). • *v.tr.* /səbjékt/ (foll. by *to*) make liable; expose; treat (*subjected us to hours of waiting*). □□ **sub·jec·tion** /səbjékshən/ *n.* **sub·ject·less** /súbjiktlis/ *adj.*

sub·jec·tive /səbjéktiv/ *adj.* **1** (of art, literature, written history, a person's views, etc.) personal; not impartial or literal. **2** esp. *Philos.* of the individual consciousness or perception; imaginary, partial, or distorted. □□ **sub·jec′tive·ly** *adv.* **sub·jec′tive·ness** *n.* **sub·jec·tiv′i·ty** *n.*

sub·join /súbjóyn/ *v.tr.* add or append (an illustration, anecdote, etc.) at the end.

sub·ju·gate /súbjəgayt/ *v.tr.* bring into subjection; subdue; vanquish. □□ **sub·ju·ga·tion** /–gáyshən/ *n.* **sub′ju·ga·tor** *n.*

sub·junc·tive /səbjúngktiv/ *Gram.* • *adj.* (of a mood) denoting what is imagined or wished or possible (e.g., *if I were you; be that as it may*). • *n.* **1** the subjunctive mood. **2** a verb in this mood.

sub·lease • *n.* /súbleess/ lease of a property by a tenant to a subtenant. • *v.tr.* /súbleéss/ lease to a subtenant.

sub·let • *n.* /súblet/ = SUBLEASE *n.* • *v.tr.* /súblét/ (**–let·ting;** *past* and *past part.* **–let**) = SUBLEASE *v.*

sub·li·mate *v.* /súblimayt/ **1** *tr. & intr.* divert (the energy of a primitive impulse, esp. sexual) into a culturally more acceptable activity. **2** *tr. & intr. Chem.* convert (a substance) from the solid state directly to its vapor by heat, and usu. allow it to solidify again. **3** *tr.* refine; purify; idealize. □□ **sub·li·ma·tion** /–máyshən/ *n.*

sub·lime /səblím/ • *adj.* (**sub·lim·er, sub·lim·est**) **1** of the most exalted, grand, or noble kind; awe-inspiring (*sublime genius*). **2** arrogantly unruffled; extreme (*sublime ignorance*). • *v. Chem.* = SUBLIMATE *v.* 2. □□ **sub·lime′ly** *adv.* **sub·lim·i·ty** /–límitee/ *n.*

sub·li·mi·nal /səblíminəl/ *adj. Psychol.* (of a stimulus, etc.) below the threshold of sensation or consciousness. □□ **sub·lim′in·al·ly** *adv.*

sub·ma·chine gun /súbməsheén/ • *n.* hand-held lightweight machine gun.

sub·ma·rine /súbməreén/ • *n.* vessel, esp. an armed warship, capable of operating under water. • *adj.* existing, occurring, done, or used under the surface of the sea (*submarine cable*). □ **submarine sandwich** sandwich made with a long bread roll. □□ **sub·mar·i·ner** /–mareénər, səbmárinər/ *n.*

sub·merge /səbmérj/ *v.tr.* place, go, or dive under water. □□ **sub·mer′gence** *n.* **sub·mer·sion** /–mórzhən, –shən/ *n.*

sub′base·ment *n.*	sub′class *n.*
sub′branch *n.*	sub′clause *n.*
sub·cat′e·go·ry *n.*	sub·cra′ni·al *adj.*
sub·cat′e·go·rize *v.*	sub·fam·i·ly *n.*
sub·cat·e·go·ri·za′tion *n.*	sub′form *n.*
sub·ge′nus *n.*	sub·sec′tion *n.*
sub·group′ *n.*	sub·spe′cies *n.*
sub′king·dom *n.*	sub·ze′ro *adj.*
sub·or′der *n.*	
sub·phy′lum *n.*	

sub·mers·i·ble /səbmərsibəl/ • *n.* submarine operating under water for short periods. • *adj.* capable of submerging.

sub·mis·sion /səbmíshən/ *n.* **1 a** submitting or being submitted. **b** anything that is submitted. **2** submissiveness.

sub·mis·sive /səbmísiv/ *adj.* humble; obedient. □□ **sub·mis´sive·ly** *adv.* **sub·mis´sive·ness** *n.*

sub·mit /səbmít/ *v.* (**sub·mit·ted, sub·mit·ting**) **1** (usu. foll. by *to*) *intr.* cease resistance; give way; yield. **2** *tr.* present for consideration. **3** *tr.* subject (a person or thing) to an operation, process, treatment, etc. □□ **sub·mit´ter** *n.*

sub·nor·mal /súbnáwrməl/ *adj.* (esp. as regards intelligence) below or less than normal. □□ **sub·nor·mal·i·ty** /–málitee/ *n.*

sub·or·di·nate • *adj.* /səbáwrd'nət/ of inferior importance or rank; secondary; subservient. • *n.* /səbáwrd'nət/ person working under another. • *v.tr.* /səbáwrd'nayt/ (usu. foll. by *to*) make or treat as subordinate. □ **subordinate clause** clause modifying or dependent on a main clause. □□ **sub·or´di·nate·ly** *adv.* **sub·or·di·na·tion** /–náyshən/ *n.*

sub·orn /səbáwrn/ *v.tr.* induce by bribery, etc., to commit perjury, etc. □□ **sub·or·na´tion** *n.* **sub·orn´er** *n.*

sub·plot /súbplot/ *n.* subordinate plot in a play, etc.

sub·poe·na /səpéenə/ • *n.* writ ordering a person to appear in court. • *v.tr.* (*past* and *past part.* **sub·poe·naed**) serve a subpoena on.

sub ro·sa /sub rózə/ *adj.* & *adv.* in secrecy or confidence.

sub·scribe /səbskríb/ *v.* **1** *tr.* & *intr.* contribute (a specified sum) or make or promise a contribution to a fund, project, charity, etc., esp. regularly. **2** *intr.* express one's agreement with an opinion, resolution, etc. (*cannot subscribe to that*). **3** *tr.* & *intr.* arrange to receive a periodical, cable television service, etc., regularly. □□ **sub·scrib´er** *n.*

sub·script /súbskript/ • *adj.* written or printed below the line. • *n.* subscript number or symbol.

sub·scrip·tion /səbskrípshən/ *n.* **1** subscribing. **2** agreement to take and pay for usu. a specified number of issues of a newspaper, magazine, etc.

sub·se·quent /súbsikwənt/ *adj.* (usu. foll. by *to*) following a specified event, etc., in time, esp. as a consequence. □□ **sub´se·quent·ly** *adv.*

sub·ser·vi·ent /səbsərveeənt/ *adj.* **1** servile. **2** subordinate. □□ **sub·ser´vi·ence** *n.* **sub·ser´vi·ent·ly** *adv.*

sub·set /súbset/ *n.* **1** secondary part of a set. **2** *Math.* a set, all the elements of which are contained in another set.

sub·side /səbsíd/ *v.intr.* **1** become tranquil; abate (*excitement subsided*). **2** (of water, etc.) sink. □□ **sub·sid·ence** /–síd'ns, súbsíd'ns/ *n.*

sub·sid·i·ar·y /səbsídee–airee/ • *adj.* **1** supplementary; auxiliary. **2** (of a company) controlled by another. • *n.* (*pl.* **–ies**) subsidiary thing, person, or company.

sub·si·dize /súbsidíz/ *v.tr.* **1** pay a subsidy to. **2** reduce the cost of by subsidy. □□ **sub·si·di·za´tion** *n.* **sub´si·diz·er** *n.*

sub·si·dy /súbsidee/ *n.* (*pl.* **–dies**) grant of money, esp. by the government.

sub·sist /səbsíst/ *v.intr.* **1** keep oneself alive; be

---

kept alive. **2** remain in being; exist. □□ **sub·sist´ent** *adj.*

sub·sis·tence /səbsístəns/ *n.* **1** state or an instance of subsisting. **2 a** means of supporting life; livelihood. **b** minimal level of existence or the income providing this.

sub·soil /súbsoyl/ *n.* soil immediately under the surface soil.

sub·son·ic /súbsónik/ *adj.* relating to speeds less than that of sound. □□ **sub·son´i·cal·ly** *adv.*

subst. *abbr.* **1** substantive. **2** substitute.

sub·stance /súbstəns/ *n.* **1** particular kind of material having uniform properties. **2** reality; solidity. **3** content or essence as opposed to form, etc. **4** wealth and possessions.

sub·stand·ard /súbstándərd/ *adj.* of less than the required or normal quality or size; inferior.

sub·stan·tial /səbstánshəl/ *adj.* **1 a** of real importance, value, or validity. **b** large. **2** solid; stout (*substantial house*). **3** commercially successful; wealthy. **4** essential; true in large part. **5** having substance; real. □□ **sub·stan´tial·ly** *adv.*

sub·stan·ti·ate /səbstánsheeayt/ *v.tr.* prove the truth of (a charge, claim, etc.). □□ **sub·stan·ti·a·tion** /–áyshən/ *n.*

sub·stan·tive /súbstəntiv/ • *adj.* (also /səbstántiv/) having separate and independent existence. • *n. Gram.* = NOUN. □□ **sub·stan·ti·val** /–tívəl/ *adj.* **sub·stan´tive·ly** *adv.* esp. *Gram.*

sub·sti·tute /súbstitōōt, –tyōōt/ • *n.* (also *attrib.*) person or thing acting or serving in place of another. • *v.* act or cause to act as a substitute. □□ **sub·sti´tut´a·ble** *adj.* **sub·sti·tu·tion** /–tōōshən, –tyōō–/ *n.* **sub´sti·tu·tive** *adj.*

sub·strate /súbstrayt/ *n.* **1** = SUBSTRATUM. **2** surface to be painted, printed, etc., on.

sub·stra·tum /súbstraytəm, –strát–/ *n.* (*pl.* **sub·stra·ta** /–tə/ or **substratums**) underlying layer or substance.

sub·struc·ture /súbstrukchər/ *n.* underlying or supporting structure. □□ **sub·struc´tur·al** *adj.*

sub·sume /səbsōōm, –syōōm/ *v.tr.* include (an instance, idea, category, etc.) in a rule, class, category, etc. □□ **sub·sum´a·ble** *adj.*

sub·ter·fuge /súbtərfyōōj/ *n.* **1** evasive or conspiratorial lying or deceit. **2** statement, etc., used for such a purpose.

sub·ter·ra·ne·an /súbtəráyneeən/ *adj.* underground; concealed.

sub·text /súbtekst/ *n.* underlying theme.

sub·ti·tle /súbtīt'l/ • *n.* **1** secondary or additional title of a book, etc. **2** caption at the bottom of a movie, etc. page translating dialogue. • *v.tr.* provide with a subtitle or subtitles.

sub·tle /sút'l/ *adj.* (**sub·tler, sub·tlest**) **1** evasive or mysterious; hard to grasp (*subtle charm*). **2** (of scent, color, etc.) faint; delicate (*subtle perfume*). **3 a** perceptive (*subtle senses*). **b** ingenious (*subtle device*). □□ **sub´tle·ness** *n.* **sub´tle·ty** *n.* **sub´tly** *adv.*

sub·to·tal /súbtōt'l/ *n.* total of one part of a group of figures to be added.

sub·tract /səbtrákt/ *v.tr.* (often foll. by *from*) deduct (a part, quantity, or number) from another. □□ **sub·tract´er** *n.* **sub·trac·tion** /–trákshən/ *n.* **sub·trac´tive** *adj.*

sub·trop·ics /súbtrópiks/ *n.pl.* regions adjacent

to or bordering on the tropics. □□ **sub·trop'i·cal** adj.

sub·urb /súbərb/ n. outlying district of a city. □□ **sub·ur·ban** /səbə́rbən/ adj.

sub·ur·bi·a /səbə́rbeeə/ n. often derog. suburbs, their inhabitants, and their way of life.

sub·ver·sive /səbvə́rsiv/ • adj. seeking to subvert (esp. a government). • n. subversive person. □□ **sub·ver·sion** /–və́rzhən, –shən/ n. **sub·ver'sive·ly** adv. **sub·ver'sive·ness** n.

sub·vert /səbvə́rt/ v.tr. esp. Polit. overturn, overthrow, or upset (religion, government, morality, etc.). □□ **sub·vert'er** n.

sub·way /súbway/ n. underground, usu. electrically powered commuter railroad.

suc- /suk, sək/ prefix assim. form of SUB- before c.

suc·ceed /səkse'ed/ v. **1** intr. have success; be successful. **2 a** tr. follow in order. **b** intr. come next. **3** intr. come by an inheritance, office, title, or property (succeeded to the throne). **4** tr. take over an office, property, inheritance, etc., from (succeeded his father).

suc·cess /səksés/ n. **1** accomplishment of an aim; favorable outcome. **2** attainment of wealth, fame, or position. **3** thing or person that turns out well.

suc·cess·ful /səksésfŏŏl/ adj. having success; prosperous. □□ **suc·cess'ful·ly** adv. **suc·cess'ful·ness** n.

suc·ces·sion /səkséshən/ n. **1 a** process of following in order; succeeding. **b** series or sequence. **2 a** succeeding to a throne, office, inheritance, etc. **b** those having such a right. □ **in succession** one after another. □□ **suc·ces'sion·al** adj.

suc·ces·sive /səksésiv/ adj. following one after another; continuing; consecutive. □□ **suc·ces'sive·ly** adv. **suc·ces'sive·ness** n.

suc·ces·sor /səksésər/ n. (often foll. by to) person or thing that succeeds another.

suc·cinct /səksíngkt/ adj. briefly expressed; terse; concise. □□ **suc·cinct'ly** adv. **suc·cinct' ness** n.

suc·cor /súkər/ • n. aid; assistance, esp. in time of need. • v.tr. give succor to.

suc·cu·lent /súkyələnt/ • adj. **1** juicy; palatable. **2** Bot. (of a plant, its leaves, or stems) thick and fleshy. • n. Bot. succulent plant. □□ **suc'cu·lence** n. **suc'cu·lent·ly** adv.

suc·cumb /səkúm/ v.intr. **1** surrender; be overcome. **2** die.

such /such/ adj. **1** of the kind or degree indicated (such people; people such as these). **2** so great; in such high degree (not such a fool as to believe them). **3** of a more than normal kind or degree (such crude language). • pron. such a person; such a thing. □ **as such** as being what has been indicated or named (there is no theater as such). **such as** for example.

such·like /súchlīk/ colloq. • adj. of such a kind. • n. things, people, etc., of such a kind.

suck /suk/ • v. **1** tr. draw (a fluid) into the mouth by suction. **2** tr. (also absol.) draw fluid from (a thing) in this way. **3** tr. roll the tongue around (a candy, etc.). **4** tr. engulf, smother, or drown in a sucking movement. **5** intr. sl. be or seem very unpleasant, contemptible, or unfair. • n. act or instance of sucking. □ **suck in**

1 absorb. **2** involve (a person) in an activity, etc., esp. against his or her will. **suck up 1** colloq. behave obsequiously. **2** absorb.

suck·er /súkər/ n. **1** sl. **a** gullible person. **b** (foll. by for) person especially susceptible to. **2 a** rubber cup, etc., that adheres to a surface by suction. **b** similar organ of an organism. **3** Bot. shoot springing from a root, stem, or axil.

suck·le /súkəl/ v. **1** tr. **a** feed (young) from the breast or udder. **b** nourish (suckled his talent). **2** intr. feed by sucking the breast, etc. □□ **suck'ler** n.

suck·ling /súkling/ n. unweaned child or animal.

su·crose /sŏ́ŏkrōs/ n. Chem. sugar from sugar cane, sugar beet, etc.

suc·tion /súkshən/ n. **1** act or instance of sucking. **2 a** production of a partial vacuum by the removal of air, etc., in order to force in liquid, etc., or procure adhesion. **b** force produced by this process (suction keeps the lid on).

sud·den /súd'n/ adj. occurring or done unexpectedly or without warning; abrupt; hurried; hasty (sudden storm). □ **all of a sudden** suddenly. **sudden death** colloq. decision in a tied game, etc., dependent on one move, card, toss of a coin, etc. **sudden infant death syndrome** Med. death of a seemingly healthy infant from an unknown cause; crib death. □□ **sud'den·ly** adv. **sud'den·ness** n.

suds /sudz/ n.pl. froth of soap and water. □□ **suds'y** adj.

sue /sŏŏ/ v. (**sues, sued, su·ing**) **1** tr. (also absol.) Law institute legal proceedings against (a person). **2** intr. Law make application to a court of law for redress. **3** intr. make entreaty to a person for a favor. □□ **su·er** n.

suede /swayd/ n. (often attrib.) **1** leather with the flesh side rubbed to a nap. **2** cloth resembling suede.

su·et /sŏ́ŏ-it/ n. hard white fat from the kidneys or loins of cattle, etc., used in cooking, etc. □□ **su·et·y** adj.

suf- /suf, səf/ prefix assim. form of SUB- before f.

suf·fer /súfər/ v. **1** intr. undergo pain, grief, damage, etc. **2** tr. undergo, experience, or be subjected to (pain, loss, grief, defeat, change, etc.) (suffered banishment). **3** tr. tolerate (does not suffer fools gladly). **4** tr. archaic allow. □□ **suf'fer·a·ble** adj. **suf'fer·er** n. **suf'fer·ing** n.

suf·fer·ance /súfərəns, súfrəns/ n. tacit consent.

suf·fice /səfís/ v. **1** intr. be enough or adequate. **2** tr. satisfy.

suf·fi·cien·cy /səfíshənsee/ n. (pl. **–cies**) adequate amount.

suf·fi·cient /səfíshənt/ adj. sufficing; adequate; enough (is sufficient for a family). □□ **suf·fi'cient·ly** adv.

suf·fix /súfiks/ n. verbal element added at the end of a word to form a derivative (e.g., –ation, –fy, –ing, –itis).

suf·fo·cate /súfəkayt/ v. **1** tr. choke or kill by stopping breathing, esp. by pressure, fumes, etc. **2** tr. produce a choking or breathlessness in. **3** intr. be or feel suffocated. □□ **suf'fo·cat·ing** adj. **suf'fo·cat·ing·ly** adv. **suf·fo·ca·tion** /–káyshən/ n.

suf·fra·gan /súfrəgən/ n. bishop appointed to help a diocesan bishop.

suf·frage /súfrij/ n. right to vote in political elections. □□ **suf'fra·gist** n.

suf·fra·gette /súfrəjét/ n. hist. woman seeking the right to vote through organized protest.

suf·fuse /səfyóoz/ v.tr. (of color, moisture, etc.) overspread throughout. □□ **suf·fu·sion** /–fyóo-zhən/ n.

Su·fi /sóofee/ n. (pl. **Su·fis**) Muslim ascetic and mystic. □□ **Su'fic** adj. **Su'fism** n.

sug- /sug, səg/ prefix assim. form of SUB- before g.

sug·ar /shóogər/ • n. **1** sweet crystalline substance obtained from various plants, esp. the sugar cane and sugar beet, used in cooking, etc.; sucrose. **2** Chem. soluble usu. sweet-tasting crystalline carbohydrate, e.g., glucose. • v.tr. sweeten or coat with sugar. □ **sugar beet** beet from which sugar is extracted. **sugar cane** Bot. tropical grass from which sugar is made. **sugar-coated 1** (of food) enclosed in sugar. **2** made superficially attractive. **sugar daddy** sl. older man who lavishes gifts on a younger partner. □□ **sug'ar·less** adj.

sug·ar·y /shóogəree/ adj. **1** containing or resembling sugar. **2** excessively sweet or esp. sentimental. □□ **sug'ar·i·ness** n.

sug·gest /səgjést, səjést/ v.tr. **1** propose (a theory, plan, or hypothesis). **2 a** evoke, etc. (this poem suggests peace). **b** hint at. □□ **sug·gest'er** n.

sug·gest·i·ble /səgjéstəbəl, səjés–/ adj. **1** capable of being suggested. **2** easily swayed.

sug·ges·tion /səgjéschən, səjés–/ n. **1** suggesting or being suggested. **2** theory, plan, etc., suggested (made a helpful suggestion). **3** slight trace; hint.

sug·ges·tive /səgjéstiv, səjés–/ adj. **1** conveying a suggestion; evocative. **2** (esp. of a remark, joke, etc.) indecent; improper; racy. □□ **sug·ges'tive·ly** adv. **sug·ges'tive·ness** n.

su·i·cid·al /sóoisíd'l/ adj. **1** inclined to commit suicide. **2** of suicide. **3** self-destructive; rash. □□ **su·i·cid'al·ly** adv.

su·i·cide /sóoisīd/ n. **1 a** intentional killing of oneself. **b** person who commits suicide. **2** self-destructive action or course (political suicide).

su·i ge·ne·ris /sóo-ī jénəris, sóo-ee, sóo-ee gé-n–/ adj. of its own kind; unique.

suit /sóot/ • n. **1** set of dress clothes of matching material, usu. of a jacket and trousers, or a jacket and a skirt; (esp. in comb.) set of clothes for a special occasion, etc. (playsuit). **2** any of the four sets (spades, hearts, diamonds, clubs) in a pack of cards. **3** lawsuit. **4** courting a woman (paid suit to her). • v.tr. **1** go well with (a person's figure, features, etc.). **2** (also absol.) meet the demands or requirements of; satisfy. **3** make fitting; accommodate. □ **suit oneself** do as one chooses.

---

suit Middle English: from siute, and suite, via Old French from a feminine past participle of an alteration of Latin sequi 'follow.' Early senses included 'attendance at a court' and 'legal process.' The notion of 'make agreeable or appropriate' dates from the late 16th century.

---

suit·a·ble /sóotəbəl/ adj. (usu. foll. by to, for) well fitted for the purpose; appropriate. □□ **suit·a·bil'i·ty** n. **suit'a·ble·ness** n. **suit'a·bly** adv.

suit·case /sóotkays/ n. usu. oblong case with a handle for carrying clothes, etc. □□ **suit'case·ful** n. (pl. **–fuls**).

suite /sweet/ n. **1** set of things belonging together, esp.: **a** set of rooms in a hotel, etc. **b** furniture intended for the same room. **2** Mus. set

of instrumental compositions to be played as a unit. **3** set of people in attendance; retinue.

suit·or /sóotər/ n. **1** man seeking to marry a specified woman; wooer. **2** plaintiff or petitioner in a lawsuit.

sul·fa /súlfə/ n. any anti-bacterial sulfonamide drug.

sul·fate /súlfayt/ n. salt or ester of sulfuric acid.

sul·fide /súlfīd/ n. Chem. binary compound of sulfur.

sul·fite /súlfīt/ n. Chem. salt or ester of sulfurous acid.

sul·fon·a·mide /sulfónəmīd/ n. any of a class of antibiotic drugs containing sulfur.

sul·fur /súlfər/ n. Chem. pale yellow nonmetallic element burning with a blue flame and a suffocating smell. ¶ Symb.: **S**. □ **sulfur dioxide** colorless pungent gas formed by burning sulfur in air and used as a food preservative. □□ **sul·fur·ous** /–fərəs, –fyóor–/ adj. **sul'fur·y** adj.

sul·fu·ric ac·id /sulfyóorik/ adj. dense, oily, colorless, highly corrosive acid.

sulk /sulk/ • v.intr. be sulky. • n. period of sullen, esp. resentful, silence. □□ **sulk'er** n.

sulk·y /súlkee/ adj. (**sulk·i·er**, **sulk·i·est**) sullen, morose, or silent, esp. from resentment. □□ **sulk'i·ly** adv. **sulk'i·ness** n.

sul·len /súlən/ adj. **1** morose; resentful; sulky. **2** dismal; melancholy (sullen sky). □□ **sul'len·ly** adv. **sul'len·ness** n.

sul·ly /súlee/ v.tr. (**–lies, –lied**) disgrace; tarnish.

sul·tan /súlt'n/ n. Muslim sovereign. □□ **sul·tan·ate** /–nayt/ n.

sul·ta·na /sultánə, –táanə/ n. **1** seedless raisin. **2** mother, wife, concubine, or daughter of a sultan.

sul·try /súltree/ adj. (**sul·tri·er, sul·tri·est**) **1** (of the atmosphere or the weather) hot or oppressive; close. **2** (of a person, etc.) passionate; sensual. □□ **sul'tri·ly** adv. **sul'tri·ness** n.

sum /sum/ • n. **1** total resulting from addition. **2** particular amount of money. **3** arithmetical problem. • v.tr. (**summed, sum·ming**) find the sum of. □ **sum up 1** (esp. of a judge) recapitulate or review the evidence in a case, etc. **2** form or express an idea of the character of (a person, situation, etc.). **3** collect into or express as a total or whole.

su·mac /sóomak, shóo–/ n. (also **su'mach**) **1** shrub having reddish cone-shaped fruits used as a spice in cooking. **2** dried and ground leaves of this used in tanning and dyeing.

sum·ma·rize /súmərīz/ v.tr. make or be a summary of; sum up. □□ **sum·ma·ri·za'tion** n. **sum'ma·riz·er** n.

sum·ma·ry /súməree/ • n. (pl. **–ries**) brief account. • adj. dispensing with needless details or formalities; brief. □□ **sum·mar·i·ly** /səmáirilee/ adv.

sum·ma·tion /səmáyshən/ n. **1** finding of a total or sum; an addition. **2** summing-up. □□ **sum·ma'tion·al** adj.

sum·mer /súmər/ • n. warmest season of the year. • v.intr. pass the summer. □ **summer solstice** see SOLSTICE. □□ **sum'mer·less** adj. **sum'mer·y** adj.

sum·mer·time /súmərtīm/ n. season or period of summer.

sum·mit /súmit/ *n.* **1** highest point; apex. **2** highest degree. **3** (in full **sum·mit meet·ing, talks,** etc.) discussion between heads of government. □□ **sum′mit·less** *adj.*

sum·mon /súmən/ *v.tr.* **1** call upon to appear, esp. at a court of law. **2** call upon (*summoned her to assist*). **3** call together. □ **summon up** gather (courage, spirits, resources, etc.). □□ **sum′mon·er** *n.*

sum·mons /súmənz/ *n.* (*pl.* **sum·mons·es**) authoritative or urgent call to attend on some occasion or do something.

su·mo /so͞omō/ *n.* (*pl.* **–mos**) style of Japanese wrestling practiced by very heavy competitors.

sump /sump/ *n.* pit, well, hole, etc., to collect liquid.

sump·tu·ous /súmpcho͞oəs/ *adj.* rich; lavish; costly. □□ **sump′tu·ous·ly** *adv.* **sump′tu·ous·ness** *n.*

Sun. *abbr.* Sunday.

sun /sun/ • *n.* **1** star around which the earth orbits and from which it receives light and warmth. **2** any similar star. • *v.* (**sunned, sun·ning**) *refl.* bask in the sun. □ **sun lamp** lamp giving ultraviolet rays for an artificial suntan, therapy, etc. □□ **sun′less** *adj.* **sun′proof** *adj.*

sun·bathe /súnbayth/ *v.intr.* bask in the sun, esp. to tan the body. □□ **sun′bath·er** *n.*

sun·beam /súnbeem/ *n.* ray of sunlight.

sun·burn /súnbərn/ • *n.* reddening and inflammation of the skin caused by overexposure to the sun. • *v.intr.* **1** suffer from sunburn. **2** (as **sunburned** or **sunburnt** *adj.*) suffering from sunburn; brown or tanned.

sun·dae /súnday, –dee/ *n.* dish of ice cream with fruit, nuts, syrup, etc.

Sun·day /súnday, –dee/ *n.* first day of the week, the Christian sabbath and day of worship.

sun·der /súndər/ *v. archaic* or *literary* separate; sever.

sun·dial /súndīəl/ *n.* instrument showing the time by the shadow of a pointer cast by the sun onto a graduated disk.

SUNDIAL

sun·down /súndown/ *n.* sunset.

sun·dry /súndree/ • *adj.* various; several. • *n.* (*pl.* **–dries**) (in *pl.*) items or oddments not mentioned individually.

sun·fish /súnfish/ *n.* almost spherical fish, esp. a large ocean variety.

sun·flow·er /súnflówər/ *n.* very tall plant with large, showy, golden-rayed flowers.

sung *past part.* of SING.

sun·glass·es /súnglasiz/ *n.* glasses tinted to protect the eyes from sunlight or glare.

sunk *past* and *past part.* of SINK.

sunk·en /súngkən/ *adj.* **1** at a lower level; submerged. **2** (of the eyes, cheeks, etc.) hollow; depressed.

sun·light /súnlīt/ *n.* light from the sun.

sun·lit /súnlit/ *adj.* illuminated by sunlight.

Sun·ni /so͞onee/ • *n.* (*pl.* same or **Sun·nis**) adherent of one of the two main branches of Islam. • *adj.* (also **Sun′nite**) of or relating to Sunnis.

sun·ny /súnee/ *adj.* (**sun·ni·er, sun·ni·est**) **1** bright with or warmed by sunlight. **2** cheery and bright in temperament. □□ **sun′ni·ly** *adv.* **sun′ni·ness** *n.*

sun·rise /súnrīz/ *n.* **1** sun's rising. **2** time of this.

sun·roof /súnro͞of/ *n.* section of an automobile roof that can be slid open.

sun·set /súnset/ • *n.* **1** sun's setting. **2** time of this. • *adj.* pertaining to a law or government program subject to review for its continuation.

sun·shine /súnshīn/ *n.* **1 a** light of the sun. **b** area lit by the sun. **2** good weather. **3** cheerfulness.

sun·spot /súnspot/ *n.* one of the dark patches, lasting for varying periods, observed on the sun's surface.

sun·stroke /súnstrōk/ *n.* acute prostration or collapse from the excessive heat of the sun.

sun·tan /súntan/ • *n.* brownish coloring of skin caused by exposure to the sun. • *v.intr.* (**–tanned, –tan·ning**) color the skin with a suntan.

sun·up /súnup/ *n.* sunrise.

sup /sup/ *v.intr.* (**supped, sup·ping**) *archaic* eat supper.

sup- /sup, səp/ *prefix* assim. form of SUB- before *p.*

su·per /so͞opər/ • *adj. colloq.* (also as *int.*) exceptional; splendid. • *n. colloq.* superintendent.

super- /so͞opər/ *comb. form* forming nouns, adjectives, and verbs, meaning: **1** above, beyond, or over in place or time or conceptually (*superstructure; supernormal*). **2** to a great or extreme degree (*superabundant*). **3** extra good or large of its kind (*supertanker*). **4** of a higher kind (*superclass*).

su·per·a·bun·dant /so͞opərəbúndənt/ *adj.* abounding beyond what is normal or right. □□ **su·per·a·bun′dance** *n.* **su·per·a·bun′dant·ly** *adv.*

su·per·an·nu·ate /so͞opərányo͞oayt/ *v.tr.* **1** retire (a person) with a pension. **2** dismiss or discard as too old for use, work, etc. **3** (as **superannuated** *adj.*) too old for work or use; obsolete. □□ **su·per·an·nu·a′tion** *n.*

su·perb /so͞opərb/ *adj.* **1** splendid; grand (*superb courage*). **2** *colloq.* excellent; fine. □□ **su·perb′ly** *adv.* **su·perb′ness** *n.*

su·per·charge /so͞opərchaarj/ *v.tr.* **1** charge (the atmosphere, etc.) with energy, emotion, etc. **2** use a supercharger on (an internal combustion engine).

su·per·charg·er /so͞opərchaarjər/ *n.* device supplying air or fuel under pressure to an internal combustion engine for added power.

su·per·cil·i·ous /so͞opərsíleəs/ *adj.* contemptuous; haughty. □□ **su·per·cil′i·ous·ly** *adv.* **su·per·cil′i·ous·ness** *n.*

su·per·con·duc·tiv·i·ty /so͞opərkónduktívitee/ *n. Physics* property of zero electrical resistance in some substances at very low absolute temperatures. □□ **su·per·con·duct·ing** /–kəndúkting/ *adj.* **su·per·con·duc′tive** *adj.*

su·per·con·duc·tor /sōōpərkəndúktər/ *n. Physics* substance having superconductivity.

su·per·e·go /sōōpəre′egō, –égō/ *n.* (*pl.* **–gos**) *Psychol.* part of the mind that acts as a conscience.

su·per·er·o·ga·tion /sōōpərérəgáyshən/ *n.* doing more than duty requires. □□ **su·per·e·rog·a·to·ry** /–irógətawree/ *adj.*

su·per·fi·cial /sōōpərfíshəl/ *adj.* **1** of or on the surface; lacking depth (*superficial wounds*). **2** swift or cursory. **3** apparent but not real (*superficial resemblance*). **4** (esp. of a person) shallow. □□ **su·per·fi·ci·al·i·ty** /–sheeálitee/ *n.* (*pl.* **–ties**). **su·per·fi′cial·ly** *adv.*

su·per·flu·i·ty /sōōpərflōōitee/ *n.* (*pl.* **–ties**) **1** state of being superfluous. **2** superfluous amount or thing.

su·per·flu·ous /sōōpə́rflōōəs/ *adj.* more than enough; redundant; needless. □□ **su·per′flu·ous·ly** *adv.* **su·per′flu·ous·ness** *n.*

superhighway /sōōpərhīway/ *n.* multilane, limited-access divided highway for fast travel.

su·per·hu·man /sōōpərhyōōmən/ *adj.* **1** beyond normal human capability. **2** above what is human. □□ **su·per·hu′man·ly** *adv.*

su·per·im·pose /sōōpərimpóz/ *v.tr.* lay (a thing) on something else. □□ **su·per·im·po·si·tion** /–pəzíshən/ *n.*

su·per·in·tend /sōōpərinténd/ *v.* supervise; direct. □□ **su·per·in·tend′ence** *n.* **su·per·in·tend′en·cy** *n.*

su·per·in·tend·ent /sōōpərinténdənt/ *n.* **1** person who superintends; director. **2** caretaker of a building.

su·pe·ri·or /sōōpe′ereeər/ ● *adj.* **1** in a higher position; of higher rank. **2 a** above the average in quality, etc. (*made of superior leather*). **b** supercilious; haughty. **3** better or greater in some respect. **4** *Printing* (of figures or letters) placed above the line. ● *n.* **1** person superior to another in rank, character, etc. (*is her superior in courage*). **2** (*fem.* also **superioress** /–ris/) *Eccl.* head of a monastery or other religious institution (*Mother Superior*).

su·pe·ri·or·i·ty /sōōpe′eree-áwritee, –ór–/ *n.* state of being superior.

su·per·la·tive /sōōpə́rlətiv/ ● *adj.* **1** of the highest quality or degree (*superlative wisdom*). **2** *Gram.* (of an adjective or adverb) expressing the highest degree of a quality (e.g., *bravest, most fiercely*). ● *n.* **1** *Gram.* superlative expression or form of an adjective or adverb. **2** exaggerated or excessive statement, comment, expression, etc. □□ **su·per′la·tive·ly** *adv.* **su·per′la·tive·ness** *n.*

su·per·man /sōōpərman/ *n.* (*pl.* **–men**) *colloq.* man of exceptional strength or ability.

su·per·mar·ket /sōōpərmaarkit/ *n.* large self-service store selling foods, household goods, etc.

su·per·nat·u·ral /sōōpərnáchərəl/ ● *adj.* attributed to or thought to reveal some force above the laws of nature; magical; mystical. ● *n.* (*prec.* by *the*) supernatural, occult, or magical forces, effects, etc. □□ **su·per·nat′u·ral·ism** *n.* **su·per·nat′u·ral·ist** *n.* **su·per·nat′u·ral·ly** *adv.*

su·per·no·va /sōōpərnóvə/ *n.* (*pl.* **–no·vae** /–vee/ or **–no·vas**) *Astron.* star that suddenly increases very greatly in brightness because of an explosion ejecting most of its mass.

su·per·nu·mer·ar·y /sōōpərnōōməreree, –ny-ōō–/ ● *adj.* in excess of the normal number; extra. ● *n.* (*pl.* **–ies**) **1** extra or unwanted person or thing. **2** actor without a speaking part; extra.

su·per·pow·er /sōōpərpowr/ *n.* extremely powerful nation.

su·per·script /sōōpərskript/ ● *adj.* written or printed above the line. ● *n.* superscript number or symbol.

su·per·sede /sōōpərse′ed/ *v.tr.* **1 a** adopt or appoint another person or thing in place of. **b** set aside; cease to employ. **2** (of a person or thing) take the place of. □□ **su·per·sed′ence** *n.*

su·per·son·ic /sōōpərsónik/ *adj.* designating or having a speed greater than that of sound. □□ **su·per·son′i·cal·ly** *adv.*

su·per·star /sōōpərstaar/ *n.* extremely famous or renowned actor, movie star, athlete, etc. □□ **su′per·star·dom** *n.*

su·per·sti·tion /sōōpərstíshən/ *n.* **1** credulity regarding the supernatural. **2** irrational fear of the unknown. **3** practice, opinion, or religion based on these tendencies. □□ **su·per·sti′tious** *adj.* **su·per·sti′tious·ly** *adv.*

su·per·struc·ture /sōōpərstrukchər/ *n.* **1** part of a building above its foundations. **2** structure built on top of something else. □□ **su·per·struc′tur·al** *adj.*

su·per·vene /sōōpərve′en/ *v.intr.* occur as an interruption in or a change from some state. □□ **su·per·ven′ient** *adj.* **su·per·ven·tion** /–vénshən/ *n.*

su·per·vise /sōōpərvíz/ *v.tr.* superintend; oversee. □□ **su·per·vi·sion** /–vízhən/ *n.* **su′per·vi·sor** *n.* **su′per·vi′so·ry** *adj.*

su·pine /sōōpín/ *adj.* **1** lying face upward. **2** inert; indolent. □□ **su·pine′ly** *adv.* **su·pine′ness** *n.*

sup·per /súpər/ *n.* light evening meal. □□ **sup′per·less** *adj.*

sup·plant /səplánt/ *v.tr.* dispossess and take the place of, esp. by underhand means. □□ **sup·plant′er** *n.*

sup·ple /súpəl/ *adj.* (**sup·pler**, **sup·plest**) **1** flexible; pliant; easily bent. **2** compliant; avoiding overt resistance; artfully or servilely submissive. □□ **sup′ple·ness** *n.*

sup·ple·ment ● *n.* /súplimənt/ **1** thing or part added to improve or provide further information. **2** separate section of a newspaper or periodical. ● *v.tr.* also /súpliment/ provide a supplement for. □□ **sup·ple·men·tal** /–mént′l/ *adj.* **sup·ple·men′tal·ly** *adv.* **sup·ple·men·ta·tion** /–mentáyshən/ *n.*

sup·pli·ant /súpleeənt/ ● *adj.* supplicating. ● *n.* supplicating person. □□ **sup·pli′ant·ly** *adv.*

sup·pli·cate /súplikayt/ *v.* **1** *tr.* petition humbly to (a person) or for (a thing). **2** *intr.* make a petition. □□ **sup′pli·cant** *adj.* & *n.* **sup·pli·ca·tion** /–áyshən/ *n.*

sup·ply /səplí/ ● *v.tr.* (**–plies**, **–plied**) **1** provide or furnish (a thing needed). **2** provide (a person, etc., with a thing needed). **3** meet or make up for (a deficiency or need, etc.). ● *n.* (*pl.* **–plies**) **1** providing what is needed. **2** stock, store, amount, etc. **3** (in *pl.*) provisions; equipment. □□ **sup·pli′er** *n.*

sup·port /səpáwrt/ • *v.tr.* 1 carry all or part of the weight of. 2 keep from falling or sinking or failing. 3 provide for (a family, etc.). 4 give strength to; encourage. 5 bear out; substantiate. 6 give help or countenance to; further. 7 speak in favor of. • *n.* 1 supporting or being supported. 2 person or thing that supports. □□ **sup·port′a·ble** *adj.* **sup·port′er** *n.*

sup·port·ive /səpáwrtiv/ *adj.* providing support or encouragement. □□ **sup·port′ive·ly** *adv.* **sup·port′ive·ness** *n.*

sup·pose /səpṓz/ *v.tr.* 1 assume, be inclined to think. 2 take as a possibility or hypothesis. 3 require as a condition (*design in creation supposes a creator*). 4 (in *passive*) **a** be expected or required (*was supposed to write to you*). **b** (with *neg.*) not have to; not be allowed to. □□ **sup·pos′a·ble** *adj.*

sup·pos·ed·ly /səpṓzidlee/ *adv.* as is generally supposed.

sup·po·si·tion /súpəzíshən/ *n.* 1 fact or idea, etc., supposed. 2 act or an instance of supposing. □□ **sup·po·si′tion·al** *adj.*

sup·pos·i·to·ry /səpṓzitawree/ *n.* (*pl.* **–ries**) medical preparation that is inserted in the rectum or vagina.

sup·press /səprés/ *v.tr.* 1 put an end to, esp. forcibly. 2 prevent from being done, seen, heard, or known. □□ **sup·pres·sion** /préshən/ *n.* **sup·pres′sor** *n.*

sup·pu·rate /súpyərayt/ *v.intr.* 1 form pus. 2 fester. □□ **sup·pu·ra·tion** /ráyshən/ *n.* **sup·pu·ra·tive** /rətiv/ *adj.*

supra- /sóóprə/ *prefix* 1 above. 2 beyond; transcending.

su·pra·na·tion·al /sóóprənáshənəl/ *adj.* transcending national limits.

su·prem·a·cy /sóópréməsee/ *n.* (*pl.* **–cies**) being supreme.

su·preme /sóópreém/ *adj.* 1 highest in authority or rank. 2 greatest; most important. 3 (of a penalty or sacrifice, etc.) involving death. □ **Supreme Court** highest judicial court in a nation, etc. □□ **su·preme′ly** *adv.* **su·preme′ness** *n.*

Supt. *abbr.* Superintendent.

sur-[1] /sər/ *prefix* = SUPER- (*surcharge*; *surrealism*).

sur-[2] /sər/ *prefix* assim. form of SUB- before *r*.

sur·charge • *n.* /sə́rchaarj/ additional charge or payment. • *v.tr.* /sə́rchaarj, –cha′arj/ exact a surcharge from.

surd /sərd/ • *adj. Math.* (of a number) irrational. • *n. Math.* surd number, esp. the root of an integer.

sure /shŏŏr/ • *adj.* 1 having or seeming to have adequate reason for a belief or assertion. 2 convinced. 3 confident. 4 reliable or unfailing (*there is one sure way to find out*). 5 certain. 6 undoubtedly true or truthful. • *adv. colloq.* certainly. □ **make sure** make or become certain; ensure. **sure-fire** *colloq.* certain to succeed. **sure-footed** never stumbling or making a mistake. **to be sure** 1 it is undeniable or admitted. 2 it must be admitted. □□ **sure′ness** *n.*
¶ Unless intending an informal effect, do not use **sure** when the adverb **surely** is meant: *It surely was foolhardy to take on all these problems yourself. I surely was happy to see them again.*

sure·ly /shŏŏrlee/ *adv.* 1 with certainty. 2 as an appeal to likelihood or reason. 3 with safety; securely.

sur·e·ty /shŏŏritee/ *n.* (*pl.* **ties**) 1 person who takes responsibility for another's debt, obligation, etc. 2 certainty.

surf /sərf/ • *n.* 1 swell of the sea breaking on the shore or reefs. 2 foam produced by this. • *v.intr.* 1 ride the surf, with or as with a surfboard. 2 switch freely between different television channels or Internet sites. □□ **surf′er** *n.*

sur·face /sə́rfis/ • *n.* 1 **a** outside of a material body. **b** area of this. 2 any of the limits terminating a solid. 3 upper boundary of a liquid or of the ground, etc. 4 outward or superficial aspect of anything. 5 *Geom.* set of points that has length and breadth but no thickness. • *v.* 1 *tr.* give the required surface to (a road, paper, etc.). 2 *intr. & tr.* rise or bring to the surface. 3 *intr.* become visible or known. □□ **sur·faced** *adj.* (usu. in *comb.*). **surf′fac·er** *n.*

surf·board /sə́rfbawrd/ *n.* long narrow board used in surfing.

sur·feit /sə́rfit/ • *n.* 1 excess, esp. in eating or drinking. 2 feeling of satiety or disgust resulting from this. • *v.* 1 *tr.* overfeed. 2 *intr.* overeat. 3 *intr. & tr.* (foll. by *with*) be or cause to be wearied through excess.

surg. *abbr.* 1 surgeon. 2 surgery. 3 surgical.

surge /sərj/ • *n.* 1 sudden rush. 2 swell of the waves at sea. 3 heavy forward or upward motion. 4 rapid increase in price, activity, etc. 5 sudden marked increase in voltage. • *v.intr.* 1 (of the sea, etc.) swell. 2 move suddenly and powerfully forward. 3 increase suddenly.

sur·geon /sə́rjən/ *n.* medical practitioner qualified to practice surgery.

sur·ger·y /sə́rjəree/ *n.* (*pl.* **–ies**) medical treatment of injuries or disorders by incision, manipulation or alteration of organs, etc., with the hands or with instruments.

sur·gi·cal /sə́rjikəl/ *adj.* 1 of or used by surgeons or in surgery. 2 extremely precise. □□ **sur′gi·cal·ly** *adv.*

sur·ly /sə́rlee/ *adj.* (**sur·li·er, sur·li·est**) bad-tempered and unfriendly; churlish. □□ **sur′li·ness** *n.*

sur·mise /sərmíz/ • *n.* conjecture. • *v.* 1 *tr.* infer doubtfully. 2 *tr.* suspect the existence of. 3 *intr.* make a guess.

---

surmise late Middle English (denoting a formal legal allegation): from Anglo-Norman French and Old French *surmise*, feminine past participle of *surmettre* 'accuse,' from late Latin *supermittere* 'throw upon, put in afterwards,' from *super-* 'over' + *mittere* 'send.'

---

sur·mount /sərmównt/ *v.tr.* 1 overcome or get over (a difficulty or obstacle). 2 cap or crown. □□ **sur·mount′a·ble** *adj.*

sur·name /sə́rnaym/ *n.* family or last name.

sur·pass /sərpás/ *v.tr.* 1 outdo; be greater or better than. 2 (as **surpassing** *adj.*) preeminent. □□ **sur·pass′ing·ly** *adv.*

sur·plice /sə́rpliss/ *n.* loose white linen vestment worn over a cassock by clergy and choristers. □□ **sur′pliced** *adj.*

sur·plus /sə́rpləs, –plus/ • *n.* 1 amount left over. 2 excess of revenue over expenditure. • *adj.* exceeding what is needed or used.

sur·prise /sərpríz/ • *n.* 1 unexpected or astonishing event or circumstance. 2 emotion caused by this. 3 catching or being caught unawares.

● *v.tr.* **1** turn out contrary to the expectations of (*your answer surprised me*). **2** (usu. in *passive*) shock; scandalize (*I am surprised at you*). **3** capture or attack by surprise. **4** come upon (a person) unawares. □□ **sur·pris·ed·ly** /–prízidlee/ *adv.* **sur·pris′ing** *adj.* **sur·pris′ing·ly** *adv.*

sur·re·al /sәréeәl/ *adj.* **1** having the qualities of surrealism. **2** strange; bizarre. □□ **sur·re′al·ly** *adv.*

sur·re·al·ism /sәréeәlizәm/ *n.* 20th-c. movement in art and literature aiming at expressing the subconscious mind, e.g., by the irrational juxtaposition of images. □□ **sur′re·al·ist** *n.* & *adj.* **sur·re·al·is′tic** *adj.* **sur·re·al·is′ti·cal·ly** *adv.*

sur·ren·der /sәréndәr/ ● *v.* **1** *tr.* hand over; relinquish. **2** *intr.* submit, esp. to an enemy. **3** *intr.* & *refl.* (foll. by *to*) give oneself over to a habit, emotion, influence, etc. **4** *tr.* abandon (hope, etc.). ● *n.* act or an instance of surrendering.

sur·rep·ti·tious /sәrәptíshәs/ *adj.* done by stealth; clandestine. □□ **sur·rep·ti′tious·ly** *adv.*

sur·ro·gate /sә́rәgәt, –gayt, sú́r–/ *n.* **1** substitute. **2** judge in charge of probate, inheritance, and guardianship. □ **surrogate mother** woman who bears a child on behalf of another woman, usu. from her own egg fertilized by the other woman's partner. □□ **sur′ro·ga·cy** *n.*

sur·round /sәrównd/ *v.tr.* come or be all around; encircle; enclose. □□ **sur·round′ing** *adj.*

sur·round·ings /sәrówndingz/ *n.pl.* things in the neighborhood of, or conditions affecting, a person or thing.

sur·tax /sә́rtaks/ *n.* additional tax.

sur·veil·lance /sәrváylәns/ *n.* close observation, esp. of a suspected person.

sur·vey ● *v.tr.* /sәrváy/ **1** take or present a general view of. **2** examine the condition of (a building, etc.). **3** determine the boundaries, extent, ownership, etc., of (a district, etc.). ● *n.* /sә́rvay/ **1** general view or consideration. **2 a** act of surveying opinions, etc. **b** result or findings of this, esp. in a written report. **3** inspection or investigation. **4** map or plan made by surveying.

sur·vey·or /sәrváyәr/ *n.* person who surveys land and buildings, esp. professionally.

sur·viv·al /sәrvívәl/ *n.* **1** surviving. **2** relic.

sur·vive /sәrvív/ *v.* **1** *intr.* continue to live or exist; be still alive or existent. **2** *tr.* live or exist longer than. **3** *tr.* remain alive in spite of (a danger, accident, etc.). □□ **sur·vi′vor** *n.*

sus- /sus, sәs/ *prefix* assim. form of SUB- before *c, p, t.*

sus·cep·ti·bil·i·ty /sәséptibílitee/ *n.* (*pl.* **–ties**) **1** state of being susceptible. **2** (in *pl.*) person's sensitive feelings.

sus·cep·ti·ble /sәséptibәl/ *adj.* **1** impressionable; sensitive. **2** (*predic.*) **a** (foll. by *to*) liable or vulnerable. **b** (foll. by *of*) allowing; admitting (*facts not susceptible of proof*). □□ **sus·cep′ti·bly** *adv.*

su·shi /sóoshee/ *n.* Japanese dish of balls of cold rice flavored and garnished, esp. with raw fish or shellfish.

sus·pect ● *v.tr.* /sәspékt/ **1** have an impression of the existence or presence of. **2** believe tentatively, without clear ground. **3** be inclined to think. **4** mentally accuse. **5** doubt the genuineness or truth of. ● *n.* /súspekt/ person under suspicion. ● *adj.* /súspekt/ subject to or deserving suspicion.

sus·pend /sәspénd/ *v.tr.* **1** hang up. **2** keep inoperative or undecided for a time; defer. **3** bar temporarily from a school, function, office, privilege, etc. **4** (as **suspended** *adj.*) (of particles or a body in a fluid) sustained somewhere between top and bottom. □ **suspended animation** temporary deathlike condition. □□ **sus·pens·i·ble** /sәspénsibәl/ *adj.*

sus·pend·ers /sәspéndәrz/ *n. pl.* straps worn across the shoulders and supporting trousers, a skirt, etc.

sus·pense /sәspéns/ *n.* state of anxious uncertainty or expectation. □□ **sus·pense′ful** *adj.*

sus·pen·sion /sәspénshәn/ *n.* **1** suspending or being suspended. **2** means by which a vehicle is supported on its axles. **3** substance consisting of particles suspended in a medium. □ **suspension bridge** bridge with a roadway suspended from cables supported by structures at each end.

SUSPENSION BRIDGE

sus·pi·cion /sәspíshәn/ *n.* **1** feeling or thought of a person who suspects. **2** suspecting or being suspected. **3** slight trace of.

sus·pi·cious /sәspíshәs/ *adj.* **1** prone to or feeling suspicion. **2** prompting suspicion (*suspicious lack of surprise*). □□ **sus·pi′cious·ly** *adv.*

sus·tain /sәstáyn/ *v.tr.* **1** support, bear the weight of, esp. for a long period. **2** encourage; support. **3** (of food) give nourishment to. **4** endure; stand; bear up against. **5** undergo or suffer (defeat or injury, etc.). **6** (of a court, etc.) uphold or decide in favor of (an objection, etc.). **7** corroborate. **8** maintain. □□ **sus·tain′a·ble** *adj.* **sus·tain′er** *n.* **sus·tain′ment** *n.*

sus·te·nance /sústinәns/ *n.* **1 a** nourishment; food. **b** process of nourishing. **2** means of support; livelihood.

su·ture /sóochәr/ *n.* **1** *Surgery* joining of the edges of a wound or incision by stitching. **2** thread or wire used for this. □□ **su′tured** *adj.*

SUV *abbr.* sport utility vehicle.

svelte /svelt/ *adj.* slender; graceful.

SW *abbr.* **1** southwest. **2** southwestern.

swab /swob/ ● *n.* **1** mop. **2 a** absorbent pad used in surgery. **b** specimen of a secretion taken with a swab for examination. ● *v.tr.* (**swabbed, swab·bing**) **1** clean with a swab. **2** (foll. by *up*) absorb (moisture) with a swab.

swad·dle /swód'l/ *v.tr.* swathe (esp. an infant) tightly.

swag /swag/ *n.* ornamental display of flowers, drapery, etc., hanging decoratively in a curve.

swag·ger /swágər/ • v.intr. walk or behave arrogantly. • n. swaggering gait or manner. □ **swagger stick** short cane carried by a military officer. □□ **swag′ger·er** n. **swag′ger·ing·ly** adv.

Swa·hi·li /swaaheé́elee/ n. (pl. same) 1 member of a Bantu people of Zanzibar and adjacent coasts. 2 their language, widely spoken in E. Africa.

swain /swayn/ n. 1 archaic country youth. 2 poet. young male lover or suitor.

swal·low[1] /swólō/ • v. 1 tr. cause or allow (food, etc.) to pass down the throat. 2 intr. perform the muscular movement of the esophagus required to do this. 3 tr. accept meekly or credulously. 4 tr. repress (swallow one's pride). 5 tr. engulf or absorb. • n. 1 act of swallowing. 2 amount swallowed in one action. □□ **swal′low·er** n.

swal·low[2] /swólō/ n. migratory swift-flying insect-eating bird with a forked tail and long pointed wings.

swam past of SWIM.

swa·mi /swaámee/ n. (pl. **swa·mis**) Hindu male religious teacher.

swamp /swaamp/ • n. piece of waterlogged ground. • v. 1 a tr. overwhelm, flood, or soak with water. b intr. become swamped. 2 tr. overwhelm with an excess or large amount of something. □□ **swamp′y** adj. (**swamp·i·er**, **swamp·i·est**).

swan /swon/ n. large, usu. white, water bird having a long flexible neck and webbed feet. □ **swan song** person's last work or act before death or retirement, etc. □□ **swan′like** adj. & adv.

swank /swangk/ colloq. • n. ostentation; swagger. • adj. = SWANKY.

swank·y /swángkee/ adj. (**swank·i·er**, **swank·i·est**) ostentatiously stylish or showy. □□ **swank′i·ly** adv. **swank′i·ness** n.

swap /swop/ (also **swop**) • v. (**swapped**, **swapping**) exchange or barter (one thing for another). • n. 1 act of swapping. 2 thing swapped. □□ **swap′per** n.

swarm /swaarm/ • n. 1 cluster of bees leaving the hive with the queen to establish a new colony. 2 large cluster of insects, birds, or people. 3 (in pl.; foll. by of) great numbers. • v.intr. 1 move in or form a swarm. 2 (of a place) be overrun, crowded, or infested.

swarth·y /swáwrthee/ adj. (**swarth·i·er**, **swarth·i·est**) dark; dark-complexioned. □□ **swarth′i·ness** n.

swash /swosh/ v. intr. (of water, etc.) wash about; make the sound of washing or rising and falling.

swash·buck·ler /swóshbuklər/ n. swaggering adventurer, esp. in a novel, movie, etc. □□ **swash′buck·ling** adj. & n.

swas·ti·ka /swóstika/ n. 1 ancient symbol formed by an equal-armed cross with each arm continued at a right angle. 2 this with clockwise continuations as the symbol of Nazi Germany.

swat /swot/ • v.tr. (**swat·ted**, **swat·ting**) 1 crush (a fly, etc.) with a sharp blow. 2 hit hard and abruptly. • n. swatting blow.

swatch /swoch/ n. sample, esp. of cloth or fabric.

swath /swoth, swawth/ n. 1 ridge of cut grass or grain, etc. 2 space left clear by a mower, etc. 3 broad strip.

swathe /swoth, swayth/ • v.tr. bind or enclose in bandages or garments, etc. • n. bandage or wrapping.

sway /sway/ • v. 1 intr. & tr. lean or cause to lean unsteadily in different directions alternately. 2 intr. oscillate irregularly; waver. 3 tr. a control the motion or direction of. b have influence or rule over. • n. 1 rule, influence, or government (hold sway). 2 swaying motion or position.

swear /swair/ v. (past **swore** /swor/; past part. **sworn** /sworn/) 1 tr. a (often foll. by to + infin. or that + clause) state or promise solemnly or on oath. b take (an oath). 2 tr. colloq. insist (swore he had not seen it). 3 tr. cause to take an oath. 5 intr. a appeal to as a witness in taking an oath (swear by Almighty God). b colloq. have or express great confidence in. 6 intr. admit the certainty of (could not swear to it). □ **swear off** colloq. promise to abstain from (drink, etc.). □□ **swear′er** n.

sweat /swet/ • n. 1 moisture exuded through the pores of the skin, esp. from heat or nervousness. 2 state or period of sweating. 3 colloq. drudgery; effort. • v. (past and past part. **sweat** or **sweat·ed**) 1 intr. exude sweat. 2 intr. be terrified, suffering, etc. 3 intr. (of a wall, etc.) exhibit surface moisture. 4 intr. drudge; toil. 5 tr. emit (blood, gum, etc.) like sweat. 6 tr. cause to drudge or toil. □ **no sweat** colloq. there is no need to worry. **sweat blood** colloq. 1 work strenuously. 2 be extremely anxious. **sweat it out** colloq. endure a difficult experience to the end.

sweat·band /swétband/ n. band of absorbent material inside a hat or around a wrist, etc., to soak up sweat.

sweat·er /swétər/ n. knitted garment for the upper body, usu. worn over a shirt, etc.

sweat·pants /swétpants/ n.pl. loose pants of absorbent cotton material worn for exercise, etc.

sweat·shirt /swétshərt/ n. pullover shirt of absorbent material.

sweat·y /swétee/ adj. (**sweat·i·er**, **sweat·i·est**) 1 sweating; covered with sweat. 2 causing sweat. □□ **sweat′i·ly** adv. **sweat′i·ness** n.

Swede /sweed/ n. 1 native or national of Sweden. 2 person of Swedish descent.

Swed·ish /sweédish/ • adj. of or relating to Sweden or its people or language. • n. language of Sweden.

sweep /sweep/ • v. (past and past part. **swept** /swept/) 1 tr. clean or clear with or as with a broom. 2 intr. clean a room, etc., in this way. 3 tr. collect or remove (dirt, etc.) by sweeping. 4 tr. a push with or as with a broom. b dismiss abruptly. 5 tr. carry or drive along with force. 6 tr. remove or clear forcefully. 7 tr. traverse swiftly or lightly. 8 intr. a glide swiftly; speed along. b go majestically. 9 tr. win every game, etc., in (a series). • n. 1 act or motion of sweeping. 2 range or scope. □ **make a clean sweep of** completely abolish or expel. □□ **sweep′er** n.

sweep·ing /sweéping/ • adj. 1 wide in range or effect (sweeping changes). 2 taking no account of particular cases or exceptions (sweeping statement). • n. (in pl.) dirt, etc., collected by sweeping. □□ **sweep′ing·ly** adv.

sweep·stake /sweépstayk/ n. 1 form of gambling in which all competitors' stakes are paid to the winners. 2 race with betting of this kind. 3 prize or prizes won in a sweepstake.

sweet /sweet/ • adj. 1 tasting of sugar. 2 fragrant. 3 melodious or harmonious. 4 highly gratifying or attractive. **5** amiable; pleasant; charming. **6** (foll. by *on*) *colloq.* fond of; in love with. • *n.* **1** something sweet. **2** sweetness. **3** (usu. *pl.*) candy. □ **sweet pea** any dwarf or climbing plant with fragrant flowers. **sweet pepper** see PEPPER. **sweet potato 1** tropical climbing plant with sweet tuberous roots used for food. **2** root of this. **sweet talk** *colloq.* flattery; blandishment. **sweet-talk** *v.tr. colloq.* flatter in order to persuade. **sweet tooth** liking for sweet-tasting foods. □□ **sweet′ly** *adv.*

sweet·bread /sweétbred/ *n.* pancreas or thymus of an animal, esp. as food.

sweet·bri·er /sweétbriər/ *n.* wild rose of Europe and central Asia with small fragrant pink flowers.

sweet·en /sweét'n/ *v.* **1** make or become sweet or sweeter. **2** make agreeable or less painful. □ **sweeten the pill** see PILL. □□ **sweet′en·ing** *n.*

sweet·en·er /sweét'nər/ *n.* **1** substance used to sweeten food or drink. **2** *colloq.* bribe or inducement.

sweet·heart /sweét-haart/ *n.* **1** lover or darling. **2** term of endearment (esp. as a form of address).

sweet·meat /sweétmeet/ *n.* **1** candy. **2** small fancy cake.

sweet·ness /sweétnis/ *n.* being sweet; fragrance.

swell /swel/ • *v.* (*past part.* **swol·len** /swólən/ or **swelled**) **1** *intr.* & *tr.* grow or cause to grow bigger or louder or more intense. **2** *intr.* & *tr.* rise or raise up. **3** *intr.* bulge. **4** *intr.* (of the heart, etc.) feel full of joy, pride, relief, etc. **5** *intr.* (foll. by *with*) be hardly able to restrain (pride, etc.). • *n.* **1** act or state of swelling. **2** heaving of the sea with waves that do not break. **3** crescendo. **4** *colloq.* stylish person. • *adj. colloq.* fine; splendid; excellent.

swell·ing /sweling/ *n.* abnormal protuberance.

swel·ter /sweltər/ • *v.intr.* (usu. as **sweltering** *adj.*) be uncomfortably hot. • *n.* sweltering atmosphere or condition. □□ **swel′ter·ing·ly** *adv.*

swept *past* and *past part.* of SWEEP.

swerve /swərv/ • *v.* change or cause to change direction, esp. abruptly. • *n.* swerving movement. □□ **swerv′er** *n.*

swift /swift/ • *adj.* **1** quick; rapid. **2** prompt. • *n.* swift-flying insect-eating bird with long wings. □□ **swift′ly** *adv.* **swift′ness** *n.*

swig /swig/ *colloq.* • *v.* (**swigged, swig·ging**) drink in large swallows. • *n.* swallow of drink, esp. a large amount. □□ **swig′ger** *n.*

swill /swil/ • *v.* drink greedily. • *n.* **1** mainly liquid refuse as pig food. **2** inferior liquor. □□ **swill′er** *n.*

swim /swim/ • *v.* (**swim·ming;** *past* **swam** /swam/; *past part.* **swum** /swum/) **1** *intr.* propel the body through water with limbs, fins, or tail. **2** *tr.* **a** traverse (a stretch of water or its distance) by swimming. **b** use (a swimming stroke). **3** *intr.* have a dizzy effect or sensation. **4** *intr.* (foll. by *in, with*) be flooded. • *n.* spell or act of swimming. □□ **swim′ma·ble** *adj.* **swim′mer** *n.*

swim·ming·ly /swiminglee/ *adv.* with easy progress.

swim·suit /swimsoot/ *n.* garment worn for swimming.

swin·dle /swind'l/ • *v.tr.* cheat (a person) of money, possessions, etc. • *n.* act of swindling. □□ **swin′dler** *n.*

swine /swin/ *n.* (*pl.* same) **1** pig. **2** *colloq.* (*pl.*

---

swine or **swines**) contemptible person. □□ **swin′ish** *adj.* (esp. in sense 2). **swin′ish·ly** *adv.*

swing /swing/ • *v.* (*past* and *past part.* **swung** /swung/) **1 a** *intr.* & *tr.* move or cause to move with a to-and-fro or curving motion; sway. **b** hang so as to be free to sway. **c** oscillate or cause to oscillate. **2** *intr.* & *tr.* revolve or cause to revolve. **3** *intr.* move by gripping something and leaping, etc. **4** *intr.* go with a swinging gait (*swung out of the room*). **5** *intr.* (foll. by *around*) move around to the opposite direction. **6** *intr.* change from one opinion or mood to another. **7** *intr.* (foll. by *at*) attempt to hit. **8 a** *intr.* play music with a swing rhythm. **b** *tr.* play (a tune) with swing. **9** *colloq.* (of a party, etc.) be lively, successful, etc. **10** *tr.* have a decisive influence on (esp. voting, etc.). **11** *tr. colloq.* deal with or achieve; manage. **12** *intr. colloq.* **a** enjoy oneself. **b** be promiscuous. • *n.* **1** act, motion, or extent of swinging. **2** swinging or smooth gait or rhythm or action. **3** seat slung by ropes, etc., for swinging on or in. **4 a** rhythmic jazz or dance music. **b** the rhythmic feeling of this. □□ **swing′er** *n.* (esp. in sense 12 of *v.*).

swipe /swip/ *colloq.* • *v.* **1** *tr.* & (often foll. by *at*) *intr.* hit hard and recklessly. **2** *tr.* steal. • *n.* reckless hard hit or attempted hit. □□ **swip′er** *n.*

swirl /swərl/ • *v.* move or flow or carry along with a whirling motion. • *n.* **1** swirling motion. **2** twist or curl, esp. as part of a pattern or design. □□ **swirl′y** *adj.*

swish /swish/ • *v.* **1** *tr.* swing (a scythe or stick, etc.) audibly through the air, grass, etc. **2** *intr.* move with or make a swishing sound. • *n.* swishing action or sound.

Swiss /swis/ • *adj.* of Switzerland in Western Europe or its people. • *n.* (*pl.* same) **1** native or inhabitant of Switzerland. **2** person of Swiss descent. □ **Swiss cheese** hard cheese with large holes that form during ripening.

switch /swich/ • *n.* **1** device for making and breaking the connection in an electric circuit. **2** a transfer, changeover, or deviation. **b** exchange. **3** slender flexible shoot cut from a tree. **4** tapering rod. **5** device at the junction of railroad tracks for transferring a train from one track to another. • *v.* **1** *tr.* turn (an electrical device) on or off. **2** *intr.* change or transfer position, subject, etc. **3** *tr.* change or transfer. **4** *tr.* exchange. **5** *tr.* beat or flick with a switch. □□ **switch′er** *n.*

switch·back /swichbak/ *n.* (often *attrib.*) railroad or road with alternate sharp ascents and descents.

switch·board /swichbawrd/ *n.* apparatus for varying connections between electric circuits, esp. in telephony.

swiv·el /swivəl/ • *n.* coupling between two parts enabling one to revolve without turning the other. • *v.* turn on or as on a swivel.

swiz·zle stick /swizəl/ *n.* rod used for stirring drinks.

swol·len *past part.* of SWELL.

swoon /swoon/ *literary* • *v.intr.* faint. • *n.* occurrence of fainting.

swoop /swoop/ • *v.intr.* **1** descend rapidly like a bird of prey. **2** make a sudden attack. • *n.* swooping or snatching movement or action.

swop var. of SWAP.

sword /sawrd/ *n.* weapon usu. of metal with a

long blade and hilt with a handguard. □□ **sword′like** adj.

sword·fish /sáwrdfish/ n. large marine fish with an extended swordlike upper jaw.

swords·man /sáwrdzmən/ n. (pl. **–men**) person of (usu. specified) skill with a sword. □□ **swords′man·ship** n.

swore past of SWEAR.

sworn /swawrn/ **1** past part. of SWEAR. **2** adj. bound by or as by an oath (sworn enemies).

swum past part. of SWIM.

swung past and past part. of SWING.

syb·a·rite /síbərīt/ n. person who is self-indulgent or devoted to sensuous luxury.

syc·a·more /síkəmawr/ n. **1** plane tree of N. America or its wood. **2** (in full **syc′a·more ma′ple**) large Eurasian maple or its wood.

syc·o·phant /síkəfant, síkə–/ n. flatterer; toady. □□ **syc′o·phan·cy** n. **syc·o·phan·tic** /–fántik/ adj. **syc·o·phan′ti·cal·ly** adv.

syl·lab·ic /silábik/ adj. of, relating to, or based on syllables. □□ **syl·lab′i·cal·ly** adv.

syl·lab·i·ca·tion /sílabikáyshən/ n. (also **syl·lab·i·fi·ca′tion**) division into or articulation by syllables. □□ **syl·lab′i·fy** v.tr. (**–fies, –fied**).

syl·la·ble /síləbəl/ n. **1** unit of pronunciation forming the whole or a part of a word and usu. having one vowel sound. **2** character or characters representing a syllable. □□ **syl′la·bled** adj. (also in comb.).

syl·la·bus /síləbəs/ n. (pl. **syl·la·bus·es** or **syl·la·bi** /–bī/) program or outline of a course of study, teaching, etc.

syl·lo·gism /síləjizəm/ n. reasoning in which a conclusion is drawn from two given or assumed propositions. □□ **syl·lo·gis′tic** adj. **syl·lo·gis′ti·cal·ly** adv.

sylph /silf/ n. **1** elemental spirit of the air. **2** slender graceful woman or girl. □□ **sylph′like** adj.

syl·van /sílvən/ adj. (also **sil·van**) **1 a** of the woods. **b** having woods; wooded. **2** rural.

sym. abbr. **1** symbol. **2** symphony.

sym- /sim/ prefix assim. form of SYN- before b, m, p.

sym·bi·o·sis /símbee-ṓsis, –bī–/ n. (pl. **sym·bi·o·ses** /–seez/) **1** close coexistence and interaction of two different organisms, usu. to the advantage of both. **2** mutually advantageous association. □□ **sym·bi·ot·ic** /–bīótik/ adj. **sym·bi·ot′i·cal·ly** adv.

sym·bol /símbəl/ n. **1** thing conventionally regarded as typifying, representing, or recalling something. **2** representative mark, sign, logo, etc. □□ **sym·bol·ic** /–bólik/ adj. **sym·bol′i·cal·ly** adv. **sym·bol·o·gy** /–bóləjee/ n.

sym·bol·ism /símbəlizəm/ n. **1 a** use of symbols to represent ideas. **b** symbols collectively. **2** artistic and poetic movement or style using symbols and indirect suggestion to express ideas, emotions, etc. □□ **sym′bol·ist** n. **sym·bol·is′tic** adj.

sym·bol·ize /símbəlīz/ v.tr. **1** be a symbol of. **2** represent by means of symbols. □□ **sym·bol·i·za′tion** n.

sym·me·try /símitree/ n. (pl. **–tries**) **1** correct or beautiful proportion of parts; balance; harmony. **2** repetition of exactly similar parts facing each other or a center. □□ **sym·met·ric** /simétrik/ adj. **sym·met′ri·cal** adj. **sym·met′ri·cal·ly** adv.

sym·pa·thet·ic /símpəthétik/ adj. **1** of, showing, or expressing sympathy. **2** pleasant; likable. **3** inclined to favor. □□ **sym·pa·thet′i·cal·ly** adv.

sym·pa·thize /símpəthīz/ v.intr. (often foll. by with) **1** feel or express sympathy. **2** agree. □□ **sym′pa·thiz·er** n.

sym·pa·thy /símpəthee/ n. (pl. **–thies**) **1 a** state of being simultaneously affected with the same feeling as another. **b** capacity for this. **2** (in sing. or pl.) compassion or commiseration; condolences. **3** (in sing. or pl.) agreement in opinion or desire.

sym·pho·ny /símfənee/ n. (pl. **–nies**) **1** elaborate composition usu. for full orchestra, and in several movements. **2** interlude for orchestra alone in a large-scale vocal work. **3** = symphony orchestra. □ **symphony orchestra** large orchestra suitable for playing symphonies, etc. □□ **sym·phon·ic** /–fónik/ adj. **sym·phon·i·cal·ly** /–fóniklee/ adv.

sym·po·si·um /simpṓzeeəm/ n. (pl. **sym·po·si·ums** or **sym·po·si·a** /–zeeə/) **1** conference or meeting to discuss a particular subject. **2** collection of essays or papers for this purpose.

symp·tom /simptəm/ n. **1** Med. physical or mental sign of disease. **2** sign of the existence of something.

symp·tom·at·ic /símptəmátik/ adj. serving as a symptom. □□ **symp·to·mat′i·cal·ly** adv.

syn. abbr. **1** synonym. **2** synonymous. **3** synonymy.

syn- /sin/ prefix connoting 'with; together; at the same time' (in words of Greek origin).

syn·a·gogue /sínəgog/ n. **1** house of worship where a Jewish assembly or congregation meets for religious observance and instruction. **2** assembly itself. □□ **syn·a·gog·al** /–gógəl/ adj. **syn·a·gog·i·cal** /–gójikəl/ adj.

syn·apse /sínaps, sináps/ n. Anat. junction of two nerve cells.

sync /singk/ (also **synch**) colloq. • n. synchronization. • v. synchronize. □ **in** (or **out of**) **sync** harmonizing or agreeing well (or badly).

syn·chron·ic /singkrónik/ adj. describing a subject as it exists at one point in time. □□ **syn·chron′i·cal·ly** adv.

syn·chro·nize /síngkrənīz/ v. **1** intr. be simultaneous. **2** tr. cause to occur at the same time. **3** tr. make the sound and picture of (a movie, etc.), coincide. **4 a** tr. cause (clocks, etc.) to show a standard or uniform time. **b** intr. (of clocks, etc.) be synchronized. □□ **syn·chro·ni·za′tion** n. **syn′chro·niz·er** n.

syn·chro·nous /síngkrənəs/ adj. existing or occurring at the same time. □□ **syn′chro·nous·ly** adv.

syn·cline /síngklīn/ n. rock bed forming a trough. □□ **syn·cli′nal** adj.

syn·co·pate /síngkəpayt/ v.tr. **1** Mus. displace the beats or accents in (a passage) so that strong beats become weak and vice versa. **2** shorten (a word) by dropping interior sounds or letters, as symbology for symbology. □□ **syn·co·pa·tion** /–páyshən/ n. **syn′co·pa·tor** n.

synd. abbr. **1** syndicate. **2** syndicated.

syn·di·cate • n. /síndikət/ **1** combination of individuals or businesses to promote a common interest. **2** agency supplying features, columns, etc. to newspapers, etc. • v.tr. /síndikayt/ **1** form into a syndicate. **2** publish (material) through a syndicate. □□ **syn·di·ca′tion** /–káyshən/ n.

syn·drome /síndrōm/ *n.* **1** group of concurrent symptoms of a disease. **2** characteristic combination of opinions, emotions, behavior, etc. □□ **syn·drom·ic** /–drómik/ *adj.*

syn·ec·do·che /sinékdəkee/ *n.* figure of speech in which a part is made to represent the whole or vice versa (e.g., *new faces at the meeting*). □□ **syn·ec·doch·ic** /–dókik/ *adj.*

syn·er·gism /sínərjizəm/ *n.* (also **syn·er·gy** /sínərjee/) combined effect of drugs, organs, etc., that exceeds the sum of their individual effects. □□ **syn·er·get·ic** /–jétik/ *adj.* **syn·er′gic** *adj.* **syn′er·gist** *n.* **syn·er·gis′tic** *adj.* **syn·er·gis′ti·cal·ly** *adv.*

syn·od /sínəd/ *n.* **1** church council of delegated clergy and sometimes laity. **2** governing body in certain Christian churches.

syn·o·nym /sínənim/ *n.* word or phrase that means the same as another (e.g., *shut* and *close*). □□ **syn·o·nym′ic** *adj.* **syn·o·nym′i·ty** *n.*

syn·on·y·mous /sinóniməs/ *adj.* **1** having the same meaning. **2** (of a name, idea, etc.) suggestive of or associated with another. □□ **syn·on′y·mous·ly** *adv.* **syn·on′y·mous·ness** *n.*

syn·op·sis /sinópsis/ *n.* (*pl.* **syn·op·ses** /–seez/) summary; outline; brief general survey. □□ **syn·op′size** *v.tr.*

syn·o·vi·a /sinōveeə, sī–/ *n.* *Physiol.* viscous fluid lubricating joints and tendon sheaths. □□ **syn·o′vi·al** *adj.*

syn·tax /síntaks/ *n.* **1** grammatical arrangement of words. **2** rules for or analysis of this. □□ **syn·tac·tic** /–táktik/ *adj.* **syn·tac′ti·cal·ly** *adv.*

syn·the·sis /sínthisis/ *n.* (*pl.* **syn·the·ses** /–seez/) **1** combining of elements into a whole. **2** *Chem.* artificial production of compounds from their constituents.

syn·the·size /sínthisīz/ *v.tr.* **1** make a synthesis of. **2** combine into a coherent whole.

syn·the·siz·er /sínthisīzər/ *n.* electronic console or keyboard, producing a variety of instrumental sounds.

syn·thet·ic /sinthétik/ • *adj.* **1** made by chemical synthesis, esp. to imitate a natural product. **2** affected; insincere. • *n.* synthetic substance. □□ **syn·thet′i·cal·ly** *adv.*

syph·i·lis /sífilis/ *n.* contagious venereal disease. □□ **syph·i·lit·ic** /–lítik/ *adj.*.

Syr·i·an /séereeən/ • *n.* native or inhabitant of Syria; person of Syrian descent. • *adj.* of or relating to Syria.

sy·ringe /sirínj/ • *n.* device for sucking in and ejecting liquid in a fine stream. • *v.tr.* sluice or spray with a syringe.

SYRINGE

syr·up /sírəp, sə́r–/ *n.* **1** sweet sauce of sugar dissolved in water. **2** any thick, esp. sweet liquid. **3** excessive sweetness of style or manner. □□ **syr′up·y** *adj.*

sys·tem /sístəm/ *n.* **1 a** complex whole; set of connected things or parts. **b** organized arrangement; network. **2 a** set of organs in the body with a common structure or function (*digestive system*). **b** human or animal body as a whole. **3** method; scheme of procedure or classification. **4** orderliness. **5** (prec. by *the*) prevailing political or social order. □ **get a thing out of one's system** *colloq.* be rid of a preoccupation or anxiety.

sys·tem·at·ic /sìstəmátik/ *adj.* **1** methodical; according to a system. **2** regular; deliberate. □□ **sys·tem·at′i·cal·ly** *adv.*

sys·tem·a·tize /sístəmətīz/ *v.tr.* **1** make systematic. **2** devise a system for. □□ **sys·tem·a·ti·za′tion** *n.* **sys′tem·a·tiz·er** *n.*

sys·tem·ic /sistémik/ *adj.* of or concerning the whole body. □□ **sys·tem′i·cal·ly** *adv.*

sys·to·le /sístəlee/ *n.* normal rhythmic contraction of the heart. □□ **sys·tol·ic** /sistólik/ *adj.*

Tt

T¹ /tee/ *n.* (also **t**) (*pl.* **Ts** or **T's**; **t's**) **1** twentieth letter of the alphabet. **2** T-shaped thing (esp. *attrib.*: *T-joint*). □ **to a T** exactly; to perfection.

T² *abbr.* **1** tera–. **2** tesla. **3** tablespoon. **4** temperature.

T³ *symb. Chem.* tritium.

t. *abbr.* **1** ton(s). **2** teaspoon. **3** temperature.

Ta *symb. Chem.* tantalum.

tab¹ /tab/ • *n.* **1** small flap or strip attached for grasping, fastening, or hanging up, or for identification. **2** *colloq.* bill; check (*picked up the tab*). • *v.tr.* (**tabbed, tab·bing**) provide with a tab or tabs. □ **keep tabs on** *colloq.* **1** have under observation.

tab² /tab/ *n.* device on a computer keyboard or typewriter for advancing to a sequence of set positions.

Ta·bas·co /təbáskō/ *n. propr.* pungent hot pepper sauce.

tab·by /tábee/ *n.* (*pl.* **–bies**) **1** gray, orange, or brownish cat with dark stripes. **2** any domestic cat, esp. female.

tab·er·na·cle /tábərnakəl/ *n.* **1** *hist.* tent used as a sanctuary by the Israelites during the Exodus. **2** *Eccl.* niche or receptacle esp. for the Eucharistic elements. **3** large place of worship.

ta·bla /táablə, túb–/ *n. Ind. Mus.* pair of small drums played with the hands.

ta·ble /táybəl/ • *n.* **1** flat surface with one or more legs, used for eating, working at, etc. **2 a** food provided in a household (*keeps a good table*). **b** group seated for dinner, etc. **3** set of facts or figures in columns, etc. (*a table of contents*). • *v.tr.* postpone consideration of (a matter). □ **table tennis** indoor game played with paddles and a ball bounced on a table divided by a net. **turn the tables** reverse circumstances to one's advantage. **under the table** *colloq.* **1** drunk. **2** (esp. of a payment) covertly; secretly. □□ **ta′ble·ful** *n.* (*pl.* **–fuls**). **ta′bling** *n.*

tab·leau /tabló, táblō/ *n.* (*pl.* **tab·leaux** /–lōz/) **1** picturesque presentation. **2** silent and motionless group of people arranged to represent a scene.

ta·ble·cloth /táybəlklawth, –kloth/ *n.* cloth spread over the top of a table, esp. for meals.

ta·ble·land /táybəl-land/ *n.* plateau.

ta·ble·spoon /táybəlspoon/ *n.* **1** large spoon for serving food. **2** unit of measure equal to 15 ml. or ¹/₂ fl. oz. □□ **ta′ble·spoon·ful** *n.* (*pl.* **–fuls**).

tab·let /táblit/ *n.* **1** solid dose of a medicine, etc. **2** flat slab of stone or wood, usu. inscribed. **3** writing pad.

tab·loid /tábloyd/ *n.* small-sized, usu. sensationalized newspaper.

ta·boo /təbṓo, ta–/ • *n.* **1** ritual isolation of a person or thing apart as sacred or accursed. **2** prohibition imposed by social custom. • *adj.* avoided or prohibited, esp. by social custom (*taboo words*). • *v.tr.* (**ta·boos, ta·booed**) **1** put under taboo. **2** exclude or prohibit by authority or social influence.

tab·u·lar /tábyələr/ *adj.* of or arranged in tables or lists.

ta·bu·late /tábyəlayt/ *v.tr.* arrange (figures or facts) in tabular form. □□ **tab·u·la·tion** /–láyshən/ *n.* **tab′u·la·tor** *n.*

ta·chom·e·ter /təkómitər, ta–/ *n.* instrument measuring velocity or rate of rotation of a shaft, esp. of a vehicle.

tac·it /tásit/ *adj.* understood or implied without being stated (*tacit consent*). □□ **tac′it·ly** *adv.*

tac·i·turn /tásitərn/ *adj.* saying little; uncommunicative. □□ **tac·i·tur′ni·ty** *n.* **tac′i·turn·ly** *adv.*

tack¹ /tak/ • *n.* **1** small sharp broad-headed nail. **2** = THUMBTACK. **3** long stitch for fastening fabrics, etc., lightly or temporarily together. **4** direction or temporary change of direction in sailing to take advantage of a side wind, etc. **5** course of action or policy. • *v.* **1** *tr.* fasten with tacks. **2** *tr.* stitch lightly together. **3** *tr.* (foll. by *to, on*) annex (a thing). **4** *intr.* **a** change a ship's course by turning its head to the wind. **b** make a series of tacks. **5** *intr.* change one's conduct or policy, etc. □□ **tack′er** *n.*

tack² /tak/ *n.* saddle, bridle, etc., of a horse.

tack·le /tákəl/ • *n.* **1** equipment for a task or sport (*fishing tackle*). **2** mechanism, esp. of ropes, pulley blocks, etc., for lifting weights, etc. **3** act of tackling in football, etc. **4** *Football* **a** either of two linemen. • *v.tr.* **1** try to deal with (a problem or difficulty). **2** grapple with (an opponent). **3** enter into discussion with. **4** *Football* stop (a player with the ball). **5** secure by means of tackle. □ **tackle block** pulley over which a rope runs. □□ **tack′ler** *n.* **tack′ling** *n.*

tack·y¹ /tákee/ *adj.* (**tack·i·er, tack·i·est**) (of glue, paint, etc.) still slightly sticky after application. □□ **tack′i·ness** *n.*

tack·y² /tákee/ *adj.* (**tack·i·er, tack·i·est**) *colloq.* **1** showing poor taste or style. **2** shoddy; seedy. □□ **tack′i·ly** *adv.* **tack′i·ness** *n.*

ta·co /táakō/ *n.* (*pl.* **–cos**) tortilla filled with meat, cheese, lettuce, tomatoes, etc.

tact /takt/ *n.* adroitness in dealing with others, esp. in delicate situations; intuitive social grace. □□ **tact′ful** *adj.* **tact′ful·ly** *adv.* **tact′ful·ness** *n.*

tac·tic /táktik/ *n.* tactical maneuver. □□ **tac′ti·cal** *adj.* **tac′ti·cal·ly** *adv.*

tac·tics /táktiks/ *n.pl.* **1** (also treated as *sing.*) disposition of armed forces, esp. in war. **2** procedure to achieve an end. □□ **tac·ti·cian** /taktíshən/ *n.*

tac·tile /táktəl, –tīl/ *adj.* **1** of the sense of touch. **2** perceived by touch. **3** tangible. □□ **tac·til·i·ty** /–tílitee/ *n.*

tact·less /táktlis/ *adj.* having or showing no tact. □□ **tact′less·ly** *adv.* **tact′less·ness** *n.*

tad /tad/ *n. colloq.* small amount (often used adverbially: *a tad salty*).

tad·pole /tádpōl/ *n.* larva of an amphibian, esp. a frog or toad.

tae kwon do /tī kwón dó/ *n.* martial art similar to karate.

taf·fe·ta /táfitə/ *n.* fine lustrous silk or silklike fabric.

taf·fy /táfee/ *n.* (*pl.* **–fies**) chewy boiled sugar or molasses candy.

tag[1] /tag/ • *n.* **1** label, esp. attached to an object. **2** metal or plastic point at the end of a lace, etc. **3** epithet; nickname. **4** loose or ragged end of anything. • *v.tr.* (**tagged, tag·ging**) **1** provide with a tag or tags. **2** join; attach. □ **tag along** go along or accompany passively.

tag[2] /tag/ • *n.* children's chasing game. • *v.tr.* (**tagged, tag·ging**) touch in or as in a game of tag.

Ta·ga·log /təgaálog, –lawg/ • *n.* **1** member of the principal people of the Philippine Islands. **2** language of this people. • *adj.* of or relating to this people or language.

Ta·hi·tian /təhee'eshən/ • *n.* **1** native or inhabitant of Tahiti. **2** language of Tahiti. • *adj.* of or relating to Tahiti or its people or language.

t'ai chi ch'uan /tī chee chwaán/ *n.* (also **t'ai chi**) Chinese martial art and system of calisthenics consisting of sequences of very slow controlled movements.

---

t'ai chi ch'uan Chinese, literally 'great ultimate boxing', from *tái* 'extreme' + *ji* 'limit' + *quán* 'fist, boxing.' In Taoism *t'ai chi* denoted the ultimate point, both source and limit, of the life force; t'ai chi ch'uan, believed to have been developed by a Taoist priest, is intended as a spiritual as well as physical exercise.

---

tail /tayl/ • *n.* **1** hindmost part of an animal, esp. extending beyond the rest of the body. **2 a** thing like a tail, esp. a rear extension. **b** rear of a procession, etc. **3** rear part of an airplane, rocket, or vehicle. **4** luminous trail following a comet. **5** part of a shirt or coat below the waist at the back. **6** (in *pl.*) *colloq.* **a** tailcoat. **b** evening dress including this. **7** (in *pl.*) reverse of a coin. **8** *colloq.* person following another. **9** buttocks. • *v. tr.* & (foll. by *after*) *intr. colloq.* shadow or follow closely. □ **tail wind** wind blowing in the direction of travel of a vehicle or aircraft, etc. **with one's tail between one's legs** in a state of dejection or humiliation. □□ **tailed** *adj.* (also in *comb.*). **tail'less** *adj.*

tail·back /táylbak/ *n.* *Football* offensive player positioned behind the quarterback.

tail·coat /táylkōt/ *n.* man's formal coat with a long divided flap at the back.

tail·gate /táylgayt/ • *n.* hinged or removable flap or door at the rear of a motor vehicle. • *v. colloq.* **1** *intr.* drive too closely behind another vehicle. **2** *tr.* follow (a vehicle) too closely. □□ **tail'gat·er** *n.*

tail·light /táyl-līt/ *n.* rear light of a vehicle.

tai·lor /táylər/ • *n.* maker or fitter of clothes. • *v.tr.* **1** make (clothes) as a tailor. **2** make or adapt for a special purpose. □ **tailor-made** *adj.* **1** made to order by a tailor. **2** made or suited for a particular purpose (*a job tailor-made for me*). □□ **tai'lor·ing** *n.*

tai·lored /táylərd/ *adj.* (of clothing) well or closely fitted.

tail·pipe /táylpīp/ *n.* rear exhaust pipe.

tail·spin /táylspin/ • *n.* **1** spin by an aircraft with the tail spiraling. **2** chaos or panic; rapid decline. • *v.intr.* (**–spin·ning**; *past* and *past part.* **–spun**) perform a tailspin.

taint /taynt/ • *n.* spot or trace of decay, infection, corruption, etc. • *v.* **1** *tr.* affect with a taint. **2** *tr.* (foll. by *with*) affect slightly. **3** *intr.* become tainted.

take /tayk/ • *v.* (**took** /t\u014dok/; **tak·en** /táykən/) **1** *tr.* lay hold of; get into one's hands. **2** *tr.* acquire; capture; earn; win. **3** *tr.* get by purchase, hire, or formal agreement. **4** *tr.* (in a recipe) use. **5** *tr.* occupy (*take a chair*). **6** *tr.* make use of (*take precautions*). **7** *tr.* consume as food or medicine. **8** *intr.* be effective (*inoculation did not take*). **9** *tr.* **a** require or use up (*these things take time*). **b** hold (*takes three quarts*). **10** *tr.* carry; convey (*bus will take you*). **11** *tr.* **a** remove; steal. **b** annihilate (*took her own life*). **c** (often foll. by *for*) *sl.* swindle. **12** *tr.* **a** experience (*take pleasure*). **b** exert (*take courage*). **13** *tr.* find out and note (*took my temperature*). **14** *tr.* understand (*I take your point*). **15** *tr.* treat or regard in a specified way (*took it badly*). **16** *tr.* (foll. by *for* or *to be*) regard as being (*do you take me for an idiot?*). **17** *tr.* **a** accept (*take the offer*). **b** submit to (*take a joke*). **18** *tr.* choose; assume (*took responsibility*). **19** *tr.* derive (*takes its name from the inventor*). **20** *tr.* (foll. by *from*) subtract (*take 3 from 9*). **21** *tr.* make; undertake; perform (*take notes*; *take an oath*). **22** *tr.* teach; be taught or examined in (a subject). **23** *tr.* make (a photograph). **24** *tr.* use as an instance (*take Napoleon*). **25** *tr. Gram.* have or require as part of a construction (*this verb takes an object*). **26** *tr.* (in *passive*; foll. by *by*, *with*) be attracted or charmed by. • *n.* **1** amount taken or caught in one session or attempt, etc. **2** film sequence photographed continuously at one time. **3** money received by a business, esp. at a theater for seats. □ **have what it takes** *colloq.* have the necessary qualities, etc., for success. **on the take** *sl.* accepting bribes. **take after** resemble (a parent, etc.). **take away 1** remove or carry elsewhere. **2** subtract. **take back 1** retract (a statement). **2** convey (a person or thing) to his or her or its original position. **3** carry in thought to a past time. **take a bath** *sl.* lose money. **take the cake** *colloq.* be the most remarkable. **take down 1** write down (spoken words). **2** remove by separating into pieces. **3** humiliate. **take five** (or **ten**) take a break, esp. from work. **take from** diminish; weaken; detract from. **take heart** be encouraged. **take the heat** endure criticism, punishment, etc. **take home** earn. **take-home pay** pay received after taxes, etc. **take in 1** accept as a boarder, etc. **2** make (a garment, etc.) smaller. **3** cheat. **4** include. **5** *colloq.* visit (a place) on the way to another (*shall we take in the White House?*). **6** attend; watch (*take in a show*). **7** arrest. **take it 1** assume (*I take it that you have finished*). **2** see TAKE *v.* 15. **take it from me** (or **take my word for it**) I can assure you. **take it or leave it** (esp. in *imper.*) accept it or not. **take it out** relieve one's frustration by attacking or treating harshly. **take off 1** deduct. **2** depart, esp. hastily. **3** become airborne. **4** (of a scheme, enterprise, etc.) become successful. **5** have (a period) away from work. **take on 1** undertake (work, etc.). **2** engage (an employee). **3** be willing or ready to meet (an adversary, etc.). **4** acquire (a new meaning, etc.). **take out 1** remove; extract. **2** escort; date. **3** buy (food) for eating elsewhere. **4** *sl.* murder or destroy. **take-out** *adj.* (of food) bought cooked for eating elsewhere. • *n.* this food. **take over 1** succeed to the management or ownership of. **2** take control. **take that!** an exclamation accompanying a blow, etc. **take one's time** not hurry. **take to 1** begin or fall into the habit of (*took to drink*). **2** form a liking for. **3** make for (*took to the hills*). **take up 1** become interested or engaged in (a pursuit, etc.). **2** occupy (time or space). **3** begin (residence, etc.). **4** accept (an offer, etc.). **5** shorten (a garment). **6** absorb (*sponges take up water*). **7** pursue (a matter, etc.) further. **take a person up on** accept (a person's offer, etc.). **take up with** begin to associate with. □□ **tak′a•ble** *adj.* (also **take′a•ble**). **tak′er** *n.*

take•off /táykawf/ *n.* **1** act of becoming airborne. **2** *colloq.* act of mimicking.

take•o•ver /táykōvər/ *n.* assumption of control (esp. of a business).

tak•ing /táyking/ *adj.* attractive; captivating.

talc /talk/ • *n.* **1** talcum powder. **2** magnesium silicate used as a lubricant, etc. • *v.tr.* (**talcked, talck•ing**) treat (a surface) with talc.

tal•cum /tálkəm/ *n.* (in full **tal′cum pow′der**) powdered talc for toilet and cosmetic use, usu. perfumed.

tale /tayl/ *n.* **1** narrative or story, esp. fictitious. **2** gossip. **3** lie; falsehood.

tal•ent /tálənt/ *n.* **1** special aptitude or faculty. **2** high mental ability. **3** person or persons of talent. **4** ancient weight and unit of currency, esp. Greek. □ **talent scout** person looking for talented performers, esp. in sports and entertainment. □□ **tal′ent•ed** *adj.* **tal′ent•less** *adj.*

tal•is•man /tálizmən/ *n.* (*pl.* **tal•is•mans**) ring, stone, etc., supposed to have magic powers, esp. of bringing good luck. □□ **tal•is•man•ic** /–mánik/ *adj.*

talk /tawk/ • *v.* **1** *intr.* converse or communicate by spoken words. **2** *intr.* (foll. by *about*) (in *imper.*) *colloq.* as an emphatic statement (*talk about expense!*). **3** *tr.* express; utter; discuss (*talking nonsense*). **4** *tr.* use (a language) in speech (*talking Spanish*). **5** *intr.* reveal secrets. **6** *intr.* gossip (*people will talk*). **7** *intr.* have influence (*money talks*). • *n.* **1** conversation; talking. **2** particular mode of speech (*baby talk*). **3** address or lecture. **4 a** rumor or gossip (*talk of a merger*). **b** its theme (*the talk of the town*). **c** empty words (*mere talk*). **5** (often in *pl.*) discussions; negotiations. □ **now you're talking** *colloq.* I like what you say, suggest, etc. **talk back** reply defiantly. **talk big** *colloq.* boast. **talk down** denigrate; belittle. **talk down to** patronize or condescend to. **talk of 1** discuss; mention. **2** express some intention of (*talked of moving*). **talk over** discuss at length. **talk shop** talk about one's occupation, etc. **talk show** television or radio program featuring guest speakers. **talk through one's hat** *colloq.* **1** exaggerate. **2** bluff. **3** talk wildly or nonsensically. **talk to** reprove or scold (a person). **talk up** discuss (a subject) in order to arouse interest in it. □□ **talk′er** *n.*

talk•a•tive /táwkətiv/ *adj.* fond of or given to talking.

talk•ie /táwkee/ *n.* (esp. *hist.*) movie with a soundtrack.

tall /tawl/ • *adj.* **1** of more than average height. **2**

of a specified height (*about six feet tall*). **3** *colloq.* extravagant or excessive (*tall story*). • *adv.* as if tall; proudly (*sit tall*). □ **tall order** exorbitant or unreasonable demand. □□ **tall′ish** *adj.*

tall•boy /táwlboy/ *n.* tall chest of drawers.

tal•low /tálō/ *n.* hard (esp. animal) fat melted down to make candles, soap, etc. □□ **tal′low•ish** *adj.* **tal′low•y** *adj.*

tal•ly /tálee/ • *n.* (*pl.* **–lies**) **1** reckoning of a debt or score. **2** total score or amount. **3** mark registering the number of objects delivered or received. **4** ticket or label for identification. • *v.* (**–lies, –lied**) (often foll. by *with*) **1** *intr.* agree; correspond. **2** *tr.* record or reckon by tally. □□ **tal′li•er** *n.*

tal•ly-ho /táleehô/ • *int.* huntsman's cry on sighting a fox. • *n.* (*pl.* **–hos**) utterance of this. • *v.* (**–hoes, –hoed**) **1** *intr.* utter a cry of "tallyho." **2** *tr.* indicate (a fox) or urge (hounds) with this cry.

Tal•mud /taálmŏŏd, –məd, tál–/ *n.* body of Jewish civil and ceremonial law and tradition. □□ **Tal•mud•ic** /–mŏŏdik, myŏŏ–/ *adj.* **Tal•mud′i•cal** *adj.* **Tal′mud•ist** *n.*

tal•on /tálən/ *n.* claw, esp. of a bird of prey. □□ **tal′oned** *adj.*

ta•lus /táyləs, tál–/ *n.* (*pl.* **ta•li** /–lī/) *Anat.* ankle bone supporting the tibia.

tam /tam/ *n.* tam-o'-shanter.

ta•ma•le /təmaálee/ *n.* Mexican food of seasoned meat and corn flour steamed or baked in corn husks.

tam•a•rind /támərind/ *n.* **1** tropical evergreen tree. **2** its edible fruit.

tam•bou•rine /támbəreén/ *n.* percussion instrument consisting of a hoop with parchment stretched over one side and jingling disks around the hoop. □□ **tam•bou•rin′ist** *n.*

TAMBOURINE

tame /taym/ • *adj.* **1** (of an animal) domesticated; not wild or shy. **2** insipid; dull. **3** (of a person) amenable and submissive. • *v.tr.* **1** make tame; domesticate. **2** subdue; curb. □□ **tam′a•ble** *adj.* **tame′ly** *adv.* **tame′ness** *n.* **tam′er** *n.* (also in *comb.*).

Tam•il /támil, túm–, taá–/ • *n.* **1** member of a people of South India and Sri Lanka. **2** language of this people. • *adj.* of this people or their language. □□ **Tam•il′ian** *adj.*

tam-o'-shanter /táməshántər/ *n.* round woolen or cloth beret of Scottish origin.

tamp /tamp/ *v.tr.* ram down tightly by a series of taps. □□ **tam′per** *n.* **tamp′ing** *n.*

tam•per /támpər/ *v.intr.* (foll. by *with*) **1** meddle with or make unauthorized changes in. **2** exert a secret or corrupt influence upon; bribe. □□ **tam′per•er** *n.* **tam′per•proof** *adj.*

tam·pon /támpon/ *n.* plug of soft material used to absorb fluid, esp. blood.

tan¹ /tan/ • *n.* **1** brown skin color from exposure to ultraviolet light. **2** yellowish-brown color. • *adj.* yellowish-brown. • *v.* (**tanned, tan·ning**) **1** *tr. & intr.* make or become brown by exposure to ultraviolet light. **2** *tr.* convert (raw hide) into leather. **3** *tr. sl.* beat; whip. □□ **tan′na·ble** *adj.* **tan′ning** *n.* **tan′nish** *adj.*

tan² /tan/ *abbr.* tangent.

tan·a·ger /tánəjər/ *n.* small American bird, the male usu. having brightly-colored plumage.

tan·dem /tándəm/ *n.* set of two with one following the other. □ **in tandem** one behind another.

tan·door·i /tandŏoree/ *n.* spicy Indian food cooked over charcoal in a clay oven.

tang /tang/ *n.* **1** strong taste or smell. **2** characteristic quality. **3** projection on a blade fitting into a handle.

tan·ge·lo /tánjəlō/ *n.* (*pl.* **-los**) hybrid of tangerine and grapefruit.

tan·gent /tánjənt/ *n.* **1** straight line, curve, or surface that meets a curve but does not intersect it. **2** ratio of the sides opposite and adjacent to an angle in a right triangle. □ **on a tangent** diverging from a previous course of action or thought, etc. □□ **tan′gen·cy** *n.*

TANGENT, 1

tan·gen·tial /tanjénshəl/ *adj.* **1** of or along a tangent. **2** divergent. **3** peripheral. □□ **tan·gen′tial·ly** *adv.*

tan·ger·ine /tánjəreén/ *n.* **1** small sweet orange-colored citrus fruit with a thin skin. **2** deep orange-yellow color.

tan·gi·ble /tánjəbəl/ *adj.* **1** perceptible by touch. **2** definite; clearly intelligible; not elusive (*tangible proof*). □□ **tan·gi·bil′i·ty** *n.* **tan′gi·ble·ness** *n.* **tan′gi·bly** *adv.*

tan·gle /tánggəl/ • *v.* **1 a** *tr.* intertwine (threads, hairs, etc.) in a confused mass; entangle. **b** *intr.* become tangled. **2** *intr.* (foll. by *with*) *colloq.* become involved (esp. in conflict) with. • *n.* **1** confused mass of intertwined threads, etc. **2** confused or complicated state.

tan·go /tánggō/ • *n.* (*pl.* **-gos**) **1** slow S. American ballroom dance. **2** music for this. • *v.intr.* (**-goes, -goed**) dance the tango.

tan·gram /tánggram/ *n.* Chinese puzzle square cut into seven pieces to be combined into various figures.

tang·y /tángee/ *adj.* (**tang·i·er, tang·i·est**) having a strong usu. spicy tang. □□ **tang′i·ness** *n.*

tank /tangk/ • *n.* **1** large container usu. for liquid or gas. **2** heavy armored fighting vehicle moving on a tracked carriage. **3** *colloq.* prison cell or holding cell. • *v.* **1** *tr.* fill the tank of (a vehicle,

etc.) with fuel. **2** *intr. & colloq. tr.* (in *passive*) become drunk. □ **tank top** sleeveless, close-fitting, collarless upper garment. □□ **tank′ful** *n.* (*pl.* **-fuls**).

tan·kard /tángkərd/ *n.* tall mug with a handle and sometimes a hinged lid, esp. for beer.

tank·er /tángkər/ *n.* ship, aircraft, or truck for carrying liquids or gases in bulk.

tan·ner /tánər/ *n.* person who tans hides.

tan·ner·y /tánəree/ *n.* (*pl.* **-ies**) place where hides are tanned.

tan·nic /tánik/ *adj.* astringent; tasting of tannin. □ **tannic acid** organic compound of a yellowish color used as a mordant and astringent.

tan·sy /tánzee/ *n.* (*pl.* **-sies**) plant with yellow button-like flowers and aromatic leaves.

tan·ta·lize /tántəlīz/ *v.tr.* torment or tease by the sight or promise of what is unobtainable. □□ **tan·ta·li·za′tion** *n.* **tan′ta·liz·er** *n.* **tan′ta·liz·ing·ly** *adv.*

tan·ta·lum /tántələm/ *n. Chem.* rare hard white metallic element.¶ Symb.: **Ta**. □□ **tan·tal·ic** /-tálik/ *adj.*

tan·ta·mount /tántəmownt/ *predic.adj.* equivalent (to).

tan·tra /tántrə, tún-/ *n.* any of a class of Hindu or Buddhist mystical and magical writings.

tan·trum /tántrəm/ *n.* outburst of bad temper or petulance.

Tao·ism /tówizəm, dów-/ *n.* Chinese philosophy advocating humility and religious piety. □□ **Tao′ist** *n.* **Tao·is′tic** *adj.*

tap¹ /tap/ • *n.* **1** = FAUCET. **2** wiretapping. • *v.tr.* (**tapped, tap·ping**) **1 a** provide (a cask) with a tap. **b** let out (liquid) by means of, or as if by means of, a tap. **2** draw sap from (a tree) by cutting into it. **3** obtain information or supplies from. **4** install a secret listening device. □ **on tap** *colloq.* ready for immediate use. **tap root** tapering root growing vertically downward. **tap water** water from a piped supply. □□ **tap′pa·ble** *adj.*

tap² /tap/ • *v.* (**tapped, tap·ping**) **1** *intr.* (foll. by *at, on*) strike a gentle but audible blow. **2** *tr.* strike lightly (*tapped me on the shoulder*). **3** *intr.* = tap-dance. • *n.* **1 a** light blow; rap. **b** sound of this. **2 a** = *tap dance n.* **b** metal attachment on a tap dancer's shoe. **3** (in *pl.*, usu. treated as *sing.*) military bugle call. □ **tap dance** *n.* rhythmic dance performed wearing shoes with metal taps. **tap-dance** *v.intr.* perform a tap dance. □□ **tap′ danc·er** *n.* **tap′ danc·ing** *n.* **tap′per** *n.*

tape /tayp/ • *n.* **1** narrow strip of woven material for tying up, fastening, etc. **2 a** this across the finishing line of a race. **b** similar strip for marking off an area. **3** (in full **ad·he′sive tape**) strip of adhesive plastic, etc., for fastening, masking, etc. **4 a** = *magnetic tape.* **b** tape recording. **5** = *tape measure.* • *v.tr.* **1** tie up, join, seal, mark off, etc., with tape. **2** record on magnetic tape. □ **tape deck** device for playing and recording magnetic tape. **tape measure** strip of tape or flexible metal marked for measuring lengths. **tape-record** record (sounds) on magnetic tape. **tape recorder** apparatus for recording and replaying sounds on magnetic tape. **tape recording** recording on magnetic tape. □□ **tape′a·ble** *adj.*

ta·per /táypər/ • *n.* **1** wick coated with wax, etc.,

for lighting fires, candles, etc. **2** slender candle.
● *v.* **1** diminish or reduce in thickness toward one end. **2** make or become gradually less.

tap·es·try /tápistree/ *n.* (*pl.* **–tries**) thick fabric in which colored weft threads are woven to form pictures or designs.

tape·worm /táypwərm/ *n.* parasitic intestinal flatworm with a segmented body.

tap·i·o·ca /tápeeókə/ *n.* starchy substance in hard white grains, obtained from cassava and used for puddings, etc.

ta·pir /táypər, təpe'er/ *n.* nocturnal hoofed mammal of Central and S. America and Malaysia, with a short flexible snout.

tap·pet /tápit/ *n.* lever or projecting part in machinery giving intermittent motion.

tap·room /táprōōm, -rŏŏm/ *n.* barroom.

tar[1] /taar/ ● *n.* **1** dark, thick, flammable liquid distilled from wood, coal, etc., used as a preservative of wood and iron, in making roads, etc. **2** similar substance formed in the combustion of tobacco, etc. ● *v.tr.* (**tarred, tar·ring**) cover with tar. □ **tar and feather** smear with tar and then cover with feathers as a punishment. **tarred with the same brush** having the same faults.

tar[2] /taar/ *n. colloq.* sailor.

tar·an·tel·la /tárəntélə/ *n.* **1** whirling S. Italian dance. **2** music for this.

ta·ran·tu·la /təránchələ/ *n.* **1** large, hairy tropical spider. **2** large black S. European spider.

tar·dy /taardee/ *adj.* (**tar·di·er, tar·di·est**) **1** slow to act, come, or happen. **2** delaying; delayed. □□ **tar′di·ly** *adv.* **tar′di·ness** *n.*

tare[1] /tair/ *n.* **1** vetch, esp. as a weed or fodder. **2** (in *pl.*) *Bibl.* injurious grain weed (Matt. 13:24–30).

tare[2] /tair/ *n.* **1** allowance made for the weight of the packing or wrapping around goods. **2** weight of a vehicle without its fuel or load.

tar·get /taargit/ ● *n.* **1** mark fired or aimed at, esp. an object marked with concentric circles. **2** person or thing aimed or fired at. **3** (also *attrib.*) objective (*target date*). **4** butt for criticism, abuse, etc. ● *v.tr.* **1** identify or single out (a person or thing) as an object of attention or attack. **2** aim or direct (*target our efforts*). □□ **tar′get·a·ble** *adj.*

tar·iff /tárif/ *n.* **1** table of fixed charges. **2** duty on a particular class of goods.

Tar·mac /taarmak/ ● *n. propr.* **1** = TARMACADAM. **2** surface made of this, e.g., a runway. ● *v.tr.* (**tarmac**) (**tar·macked, tar·mack·ing**) apply tarmacadam to.

tar·mac·ad·am /taarməkádəm/ *n.* material of stone or slag bound with tar, used in paving roads, etc.

tarn /taarn/ *n.* small mountain lake.

tar·na·tion /taarnáyshən/ *int.* esp. *dial. sl.* damn; blast.

tar·nish /taarnish/ ● *v.* **1** *tr.* lessen or destroy the luster of (metal, etc.). **2** *tr.* sully. **3** *intr.* (of metal, etc.) lose luster. ● *n.* **1** loss of luster, esp. as a film on a metal's surface. **2** blemish; stain. □□ **tar′nish·a·ble** *adj.*

ta·ro /taarō, tárō/ *n.* (*pl.* **–ros**) tropical plant with edible tuberous roots.

ta·rot /tárō, tərō/ *n.* **1** (in *sing.* or *pl.*) pack of

mainly picture cards used in fortune-telling. **2** any card from a fortune-telling pack.

tar·pau·lin /taarpáwlin, taarpə-/ (also *colloq.* **tarp**) *n.* **1** heavy-duty waterproof cloth, esp. of canvas or plastic. **2** sheet or covering of this.

tar·pon /taarpon/ *n.* **1** large silvery tropical Atlantic fish. **2** similar Pacific fish.

tar·ra·gon /tárəgən/ *n.* bushy herb with leaves used as a flavoring.

tar·ry /táree/ *v.intr.* (**–ries, –ried**) linger; stay; wait. □□ **tar′ri·er** *n.*

tar·sus /taarsəs/ *n.* (*pl.* **tar·si** /-sī, –see/) bones of the ankle and upper foot. □□ **tar′sal** *adj.*

tart[1] /taart/ *n.* small pie containing jam, etc. □□ **tart′let** *n.*

tart[2] /taart/ *n. sl.* prostitute; promiscuous woman. □□ **tart′y** *adj.* (**tart′i·er, tart′i·est**).

tart[3] /taart/ *adj.* **1** sharp or acid in taste. **2** (of a remark, etc.) cutting; bitter. □□ **tart′ly** *adv.* **tart′ness** *n.*

tar·tan /taart'n/ *n.* **1** plaid pattern, esp. denoting a Scottish Highland clan. **2** woolen fabric woven in this pattern.

Tar·tar /taartər/ (also **Ta·tar** /taatər/ except in sense 2 of *n.*) ● *n.* **1 a** member of a group of Central Asian peoples including Mongols and Turks. **b** Turkic language of these peoples. **2** (**tartar**) violent-tempered or intractable person. ● *adj.* **1** of Tartars. **2** of Central Asia east of the Caspian Sea. □ **tartar sauce** sauce of mayonnaise and chopped pickles, etc. □□ **Tar·tar·i·an** /-táireeən/ *adj.*

tar·tar /taartər/ *n.* **1** hard deposit that forms on the teeth. **2** deposit that forms a hard crust in wine.

task /task/ ● *n.* piece of work to be done. ● *v.tr.* make great demands on (a person's powers, etc.). □ **take to task** rebuke; scold. **task force 1** *Mil.* armed force organized for a special operation. **2** unit specially organized for a task.

task·mas·ter /táskmastər/ *n.* (*fem.* **task·mis·tress** /-mistris/) person who makes others work hard.

Tas·ma·ni·an /tazmáyneeən/ ● *n.* **1** native of Tasmania. **2** person of Tasmanian descent. ● *adj.* of or relating to Tasmania. □ **Tasmanian devil** nocturnal, badgerlike carnivorous marsupial of Tasmania.

tas·sel /tásəl/ *n.* **1** decorative tuft of loosely hanging threads or cords. **2** tassellike flowerhead of some plants, esp. corn. □□ **tas′seled** *adj.*

taste /tayst/ ● *n.* **1 a** sensation caused in the mouth by contact of the taste buds with a substance. **b** faculty of perceiving. **2** small sample of food or drink. **3** slight experience (*taste of success*). **4** liking or predilection (*expensive tastes*). **5** aesthetic discernment in art, conduct, etc. ● *v.* **1** *tr.* sample the flavor of (food, etc.). **2** *tr.* (also *absol.*) perceive the flavor of (*cannot taste with a cold*). **3** *tr.* (esp. with *neg.*) eat or drink a small portion of (*had not tasted food for days*). **4** *tr.* experience (*never tasted failure*). **5** *intr.* have a specified flavor (*tastes of onions*). □ **taste bud** cells or nerve ending on the surface of the tongue by which things are tasted. □□ **taste′a·ble** *adj.* **tast′er** *n.*

taste·ful /táystfŏŏl/ *adj.* having, or done in, good taste. □□ **taste′ful·ly** *adv.* **taste′ful·ness** *n.*

taste·less /táystlis/ *adj.* **1** lacking flavor. **2** having, or done in, bad taste. □□ **taste′less·ly** *adv.* **taste′less·ness** *n.*

tast·y /táystee/ adj. (**tast·i·er, tast·i·est**) (of food) pleasing in flavor; appetizing. □□ **tast′i·ly** adv. **tast′i·ness** n.

tat¹ /tat/ v. (**tat·ted, tat·ting**) **1** intr. do tatting. **2** tr. make by tatting.

tat² see TIT².

Ta·tar var. of TARTAR.

tat·er /táytər/ n. sl. = POTATO.

tat·ter /tátər/ n. (usu. in pl.) rag; irregularly torn cloth or paper, etc. □ **in tatters** colloq. (of a negotiation, etc.) ruined; demolished. □□ **tat′ tered** adj.

tat·ting /táting/ n. **1** kind of knotted lace used as trim, etc. **2** process of making this.

tat·tle /tát′l/ v. **1** intr. chatter; gossip. **2** tr. reveal (secrets).

tat·tle·tale /tát′ltayl/ n. one who tells tales or informs.

tat·too¹ /tatóo/ n. **1** evening drum or bugle signal recalling soldiers to quarters. **2** rhythmic tapping or drumming.

tat·too² /tatóo/ • v.tr. **1** mark (skin) indelibly by puncturing it and inserting pigment. **2** make (a design) in this way. • n. such a design. □□ **tat·too′er** n. **tat·too′ist** n.

tau /tow, taw/ n. nineteenth letter of the Greek alphabet (T, τ).

taught past and past part. of TEACH.

taunt /tawnt/ • n. insult; provocation. • v.tr. insult; reproach (a person) contemptuously. □□ **taunt′er** n. **taunt′ing·ly** adv.

taupe /tōp/ adj. & n. dark, brownish gray.

Tau·rus /táwrəs/ n. **1** constellation and second sign of the zodiac (the Bull). **2** person born under this sign. □□ **Tau′re·an** adj. & n.

taut /tawt/ adj. **1** (of a rope, muscles, etc.) tight; not slack. **2** (of nerves) tense. **3** (of a ship, etc.) in good condition. □□ **taut′en** v. **taut′ly** adv. **taut′ness** n.

tau·tol·o·gy /tawtóləjee/ n. (pl. **-gies**) saying of the same thing twice in different words, esp. as a fault of style (e.g., arrived one after the other in succession). □□ **tau·to·log′ic** /-t′lójik/ adj. **tau·to·log′i·cal** adj. **tau·to·log′i·cal·ly** adv. **tau·tol′o·gist** n. **tau·tol′o·gize** v.intr. **tau·tol·o·gous** /-ləgəs/ adj.

tav·ern /távərn/ n. inn or bar.

taw·dry /táwdree/ adj. (**taw·dri·er, taw·dri·est**) **1** showy but worthless. **2** gaudy; vulgar. □□ **taw′ dri·ly** adv. **taw′dri·ness** n.

---

tawdry early 17th century: short for tawdry lace, a fine silk lace or ribbon worn as a necklace in the 16th–17th centuries, a contraction of St. Audrey's lace: Audrey was a later form of Etheldrida (died 679), patron saint of the English city of Ely, where tawdry laces, along with cheap imitations and other cheap finery, were traditionally sold at a fair.

---

taw·ny /táwnee/ adj. (**taw·ni·er, taw·ni·est**) orangish or yellowish brown. □□ **taw′ni·ness** n.

tax /taks/ • n. **1** government revenue compulsorily levied on individuals, property, or businesses. **2** strain; heavy demand; burdensome obligation. • v.tr. **1** impose a tax on. **2** deduct tax from (income, etc.). **3** make heavy demands on (a person's powers or resources, etc.) □□ **tax′a·ble** adj. **tax′er** n.

tax·a pl. of TAXON.

tax·a·tion /taksáyshən/ n. imposition or payment of tax.

tax·i /táksee/ • n. (pl. **taxis**) (in full **tax′i·cab**) automobile licensed for hire and usu. fitted with a meter. • v. (**tax·is, tax·ied, taxi·i·ing** or **tax·y·ing**) **1 a** intr. (of an aircraft or pilot) move along the ground before takeoff or after landing. **b** tr. cause (an aircraft) to taxi. **2** intr. & tr. go or convey in a taxi.

tax·i·der·my /táksidərmee/ n. art of preparing, stuffing, and mounting the skins of animals. □□ **tax′i·der·mist** n.

tax·i·me·ter /tákseemeetər/ n. device fitted to a taxi, recording distance traveled and fare payable.

tax·on /tákson/ n. (pl. **tax·a** /táksə/) any taxonomic group.

tax·on·o·my /taksónəmee/ n. classification of living and extinct organisms. □□ **tax·o·nom′ic** /-sənómik/ adj. **tax·o·nom′i·cal** adj. **tax·o·nom′ i·cal·ly** adv. **tax·on′o·mist** n.

tax·pay·er /tákspayər/ n. person who pays taxes.

TB abbr. **1** tubercle bacillus. **2** tuberculosis.

Tb symb. Chem. terbium.

T-bone /teébon/ n. T-shaped bone, esp. in steak from the thin end of a loin.

tbs. abbr. (also **tbsp.**) tablespoon.

Tc symb. Chem. technetium.

TD abbr. **1** touchdown. **2** Treasury Department.

Te symb. Chem. tellurium.

te var. of TI.

tea /tee/ n. **1 a** (in full **tea plant**) evergreen shrub or small tree of Asia. **b** its dried leaves. **2** drink made by infusing tea leaves in boiling water. **3** infusion of herbal or other leaves. **4** afternoon party, reception, or light meal at which tea is served. □ **tea and sympathy** colloq. hospitable behavior toward a troubled person. **tea bag** small porous bag of tea leaves for infusion. **tea ball** ball of perforated metal to hold tea leaves for infusion. **tea rose** hybrid rose shrub with a tealike scent.

teach /teech/ v.tr. (past and past part. **taught** /tawt/) **1 a** give systematic information to (a person) or about (a subject or skill). **b** (absol.) practice this professionally. **c** enable (a person) to learn by instruction and training (taught me how to dance). **2** advocate as a moral, etc., principle (taught me tolerance). **3** (foll. by to + infin.) impress upon by example or punishment (will teach you not to laugh). □□ **teach′a·ble** adj.

teach·er /teéchər/ n. person who teaches, esp. in a school.

teach·ing /teéching/ n. **1** profession of a teacher. **2** (often in pl.) what is taught; doctrine.

tea·cup /teékup/ n. **1** cup from which tea, etc., is drunk. **2** amount held by this. □□ **tea′cup·ful** n. (pl. **-fuls**).

teak /teek/ n. **1** large deciduous tree of India and SE Asia. **2** its hard durable wood.

teal /teel/ n. (pl. same) **1** small freshwater duck. **2** dark, greenish blue color.

team /teem/ • n. **1** set of players forming one side in a game, debate, etc. **2** two or more persons working together. **3** set of draft animals. • v. join in a team or in common action.

team·mate /téemmayt/ n. member of the same team.

team·ster /téemstər/ n. driver of a truck or a team of animals.

team·work /téemwərk/ n. combined action; co-operation.

tea·pot /téepot/ n. pot with a handle, spout, and lid, for brewing and pouring tea.

tear¹ /tair/ • v. (past **tore** /tor/; past part. **torn** /torn/) 1 tr. pull apart or to pieces with some force. 2 tr. make a hole or rent in by tearing. 3 tr. & intr. pull violently (tore off the cover). 4 tr. violently disrupt or divide (torn by conflicting emotions). 5 intr. colloq. go hurriedly. 6 intr. undergo tearing (the curtain tore down the middle). • n. 1 hole or split caused by tearing. 2 torn part of cloth, etc. 3 sl. spree; drinking bout. □ **be torn between** have difficulty in choosing between. **tear apart** 1 search (a place) exhaustively. 2 criticize forcefully. 3 distress deeply. **tear into** 1 attack verbally; reprimand. 2 start (an activity) vigorously. **tear oneself away** leave reluctantly. **tear one's hair out** behave with extreme desperation or anger. □□ **tear′a·ble** adj. **tear′er** n.

tear² /teer/ n. 1 drop of clear salty liquid secreted by glands in the eye. 2 tearlike thing; drop. □ **in tears** crying; shedding tears. **tear gas** gas that disables by causing severe irritation to the eyes. □□ **tear′like** adj.

tear·ful /téerfool/ adj. 1 crying or inclined to cry. 2 sad (tearful event). □□ **tear′ful·ly** adv. **tear′ful·ness** n.

tear·jerk·er /téerjərkər/ n. colloq. sentimental story, film, etc.

tea·room /téeroom, -room/ n. small restaurant or café where tea, etc. is served.

tease /teez/ • v.tr. (also absol.) 1 a make fun of playfully, unkindly, or annoyingly. b tempt or allure, esp. sexually. 2 pick (wool, hair, etc.) into separate fibers. 3 dress (cloth) esp. with teasels. • n. 1 colloq. person fond of teasing. 2 instance of teasing. □□ **teas′er** n. **teas′ing·ly** adv.

tea·sel /téezəl/ (also **tea′zel, tea′zle**) • n. 1 plant with large prickly heads that are dried and used to raise the nap on woven cloth. 2 device used as a substitute for teasels. • v.tr. dress (cloth) with teasels. □□ **tea′sel·er** n.

tea·spoon /téespoon/ n. 1 spoon for stirring tea, etc. 2 amount held by this, approx. 1/6 fl. oz. □□ **tea′spoon·ful** n. (pl. **-fuls**).

teat /teet/ n. mammary nipple, esp. of an animal.

tech /tek/ n. colloq. 1 technician. 2 technical college.

tech·ne·tium /teknéeshəm, –sheeəm/ n. Chem. artificially produced radioactive metallic element. ¶ Symb.: **Tc**.

tech·ni·cal /téknikəl/ adj. 1 of the mechanical arts and applied sciences (technical college). 2 of a particular subject, etc., or its techniques. 3 (of a drug, discourse, etc.) using technical language. 4 due to mechanical failure. 5 strictly or legally interpreted. □ **technical knockout** ruling by the referee that a boxer has lost on the grounds of a contestant's inability to continue, the opponent being declared the winner. □□ **tech′ni·cal·ly** adv.

tech·ni·cal·i·ty /téknikálitee/ n. (pl. **-ties**) 1 being technical. 2 technical expression. 3 technical point or detail.

tech·ni·cian /teknishən/ n. person skilled in artistic, scientific, mechanical, etc., technique.

Tech·ni·col·or /téknikulər/ n. propr. process of color cinematography.

tech·nique /teknéek/ n. 1 mechanical skill; applicable method. 2 manner of artistic execution in music, painting, etc.

tech·noc·ra·cy /teknókrəsee/ n. (pl. **-cies**) rule or control by technical experts. □□ **tech′no·crat** n. **tech·no·crat′ic** adj.

tech·nol·o·gy /teknóləjee/ n. (pl. **-gies**) 1 study or use of the mechanical arts and applied sciences. 2 these subjects collectively. □□ **tech·no·log′i·cal** adj. **tech·no·log′i·cal·ly** adv. **tech·nol′o·gist** n.

tec·ton·ic /tektónik/ adj. 1 Geol. relating to deformation of the earth's crust or to structural changes caused by this. 2 of building or construction. □□ **tec·ton′i·cal·ly** adv.

tec·ton·ics /tektóniks/ n.pl. (usu. treated as sing.) study of the earth's large-scale structural features.

ted·dy /tédee/ n. (pl. **-dies**) (in full **ted′dy bear**) stuffed toy bear.

te·di·ous /téedeeəs/ adj. tiresomely long; wearisome. □□ **te′di·ous·ly** adv. **te′di·ous·ness** n.

te·di·um /téedeeəm/ n. state of being tedious; boredom.

tee /tee/ • n. Golf 1 cleared space from which a golf ball is struck at the beginning of play for each hole. 2 small wood or plastic support for a golf ball. • v.tr. (**tees, teed**) Golf place (a ball) on a tee. □ **tee off** 1 Golf play a ball from a tee. 2 colloq. start; begin.

tee-hee /teehée/ (also **te-hee**) • n. 1 titter. 2 restrained or contemptuous laugh. • v.intr. (**tee-hees, tee-heed**) titter or laugh in this way.

teem /teem/ v.intr. 1 be abundant. 2 be full of or swarming (teeming with ideas).

teen /teen/ • adj. = TEENAGE. • n. = TEENAGER.

-teen /teen/ suffix forming numerals from 13 to 19.

teen·age /téenayj/ adj. of or characteristic of teenagers. □□ **teen′aged** adj.

teen·ag·er /téenayjər/ n. person from 13 to 19 years of age.

teens /teenz/ n.pl. years of age from 13 to 19.

teen·sy /téensee/ adj. (**teen·si·er, teen·si·est**) colloq. = TEENY. □ **teensy-weensy** = teeny-weeny.

tee·ny /téenee/ adj. (**tee·ni·er, tee·ni·est**) colloq. tiny. □ **teeny-weeny** very tiny.

tee·ny·bop·per /téeneebopər/ n. colloq. young teenager, usu. a girl, who follows the latest fashions.

tee·pee var. of TEPEE.

tee-shirt var. of T-SHIRT.

tee·ter /téetər/ v.intr. totter; move unsteadily.

teeth pl. of TOOTH.

teethe /teeth/ v.intr. grow or cut teeth, esp. baby teeth. □□ **teeth′ing** n.

tee·to·tal /téetótl/ adj. of or advocating total abstinence from alcohol. □□ **tee·to′tal·er** n. (also **tee·to′tal·ler**) **tee·to′tal·ism** n.

Tef·lon /téflon/ n. propr. nonstick coating for kitchen utensils, etc.

tel. abbr. 1 telephone. 2 telegraph.

tele- /télee/ comb. form 1 at or to a distance (telekinesis). 2 television (telecast). 3 by telephone (teleconference).

tel·e·cast /télikast/ • *n.* television broadcast. • *v.tr.* transmit by television. □□ **tel'e·cast·er** *n.*

tel·e·com·mu·ni·ca·tion /télikəmyŏonikáyshən/ *n.* **1** communication over a distance by cable, telegraph, telephone lines, etc. **2** (usu. in *pl.*) technology using these means.

tel·e·com·mute /télikəmyŏot/ *v.intr.* (**tel·e·com·mut·ed, tel·e·com·mut·ing**) work, esp. at home, communicating electronically with one's employer, etc., by computer, fax, and telephone.

tel·e·con·fer·ence /télikónfərəns, –frəns/ *n.* conference with participants linked by telecommunication devices. □□ **tel'e·con·fer·enc·ing** *n.*

tel·e·gram /téligram/ *n.* message sent by telegraph.

tel·e·graph /téligraf/ • *n.* **1** system or device for transmitting messages or signals over a distance esp. by making and breaking an electrical connection. **2** (*attrib.*) used in this system (*telegraph pole*). • *v.tr.* **1** send a message to by telegraph. **2** send by telegraph. **3** give advance indication of. □□ **te·leg·ra·pher** /tilégrəfər, téligrafər/ *n.* **tel·e·graph'ic·al·ly** *adv.* **te·leg·ra·phy** /təlógrəfee/ *n.*

tel·e·ki·ne·sis /télikineésis, –kī/ *n.* supposed paranormal force moving objects at a distance. □□ **tel·e·ki·net·ic** /–nétik/ *adj.*

tel·e·mar·ket·ing /télimaárkiting/ *n.* marketing by unsolicited telephone calls. □□ **tel'e·mar·ket·er** *n.*

te·lep·a·thy /təlépəthee/ *n.* supposed paranormal communication of thoughts. □□ **tel·e·path·ic** /télipáthik/ *adj.* **tel·e·path'i·cal·ly** *adv.* **te·lep'a·thist** *n.*

tel·e·phone /télifōn/ • *n.* **1** apparatus for transmitting and receiving sound (esp. speech) over a distance by using optical or electrical signals. **2** system of communication using a network of telephones. • *v.* **1** *tr.* speak to or send (a message) by telephone. **2** *intr.* make a telephone call. □ **telephone booth** public booth, etc., with a telephone. □□ **tel·e·phon·ic** /–fónik/ *adj.* **tel·e·phon'i·cal·ly** *adv.*

te·leph·o·ny /təléfənee/ *n.* use or system of telephones.

tel·e·pho·to /télifōtō/ *n.* (*pl.* **–tos**) (in full **tel'e·pho'to lens**) lens used in telephotography.

tel·e·pho·tog·ra·phy /télifótógrəfee/ *n.* photographing of distant objects with a system of magnifying lenses. □□ **tel·e·pho·to·graph·ic** /–fōtəgráfik/ *adj.*

Tel·e·Promp·Ter /télipromptər/ *n. propr.* device used in television and filmmaking to display a speaker's script.

tel·e·scope /téliskōp/ • *n.* **1** optical instrument using lenses or mirrors to magnify distant objects. **2** = *radio telescope.* • *v.* **1** *tr.* press or drive (sections of a tube, etc.) together so that one slides into another. **2** *intr.* be capable of closing in this way. **3** *tr.* compress in space or time. □□ **tel·e·scop·ic** /téliskópik/ *adj.* **tel·e·scop'i·cal·ly** *adv.*

tel·e·thon /télithon/ *n.* exceptionally long television program, esp. to raise money for a charity.

Tel·e·type /télitīp/ *n. propr.* telegraphic apparatus for direct exchange of printed messages.

tel·e·van·ge·list /tələvánjəlist/ *n.* evangelical minister whose religious messages and services are broadcast regularly on television.

tel·e·vise /téliyvīz/ *v.tr.* transmit by television.

tel·e·vi·sion /téliyvízhən/ *n.* **1** system for reproducing on a screen visual images transmitted (usu. with sound) by radio waves. **2** (in full **tel'e·vi·sion set**) device with a screen for receiving these signals. **3** television broadcasting.

tel·ex /téleks/ (also **Telex**) • *n.* system of telegraphy for printed messages using a public telecommunications network. • *v.tr.* communicate by telex.

tell /tel/ *v.* (*past* and *past part.* **told** /tōld/) **1** *tr.* relate in speech or writing. **2** *tr.* express in words (*tell me what you want*). **3** *tr.* reveal or signify to (a person) (*your face tells me everything*). **4** *intr.* **a** divulge information, etc.; reveal a secret. **b** (foll. by *on*) *colloq.* inform against. **5** *tr.* instruct; order (*tell them to wait*). **6** *tr.* assure (*it's true, I tell you*). **7** *tr.* decide; predict; distinguish (*cannot tell what might happen*). **8** *intr.* produce a noticeable effect or influence. □ **tell apart** distinguish between. **tell off** *colloq.* reprimand; scold. **tell tales** report a discreditable fact about another. **there is no telling** it is impossible to know. □□ **tell'a·ble** *adj.*

tell·er /télər/ *n.* **1** person employed to receive and pay out money in a bank, etc. **2** person who tells esp. stories (*teller of tales*).

tell·ing /téling/ *adj.* **1** having a marked effect; striking. **2** significant. □□ **tell'ing·ly** *adv.*

tell·tale /téltayl/ *n.* **1** person who reveals secrets about another. **2** (*attrib.*) that reveals or betrays (*telltale smile*). **3** device for automatic indicating, monitoring, or registering of a process, etc.

tel·lu·ri·um /telŏoreeəm/ *n. Chem.* rare lustrous silver-white element used in semiconductors. ¶ Symb.: **Te**. □□ **tel·lu·ride** /télyərīd/ *n.* **tel·lu·rite** /télyərīt/ *n.* **tel'lu·rous** *adj.* **tel·lu'ric** *adj.*

te·mer·i·ty /timéritee/ *n.* **1** rashness. **2** audacity; impudence.

temp /temp/ *colloq.* • *n.* temporary employee. • *v.intr.* work as a temp.

temp. /temp/ *abbr.* **1** temperature. **2** temporary.

tem·per /témpər/ • *n.* **1** mood; mental disposition. **2** irritation; anger (*fit of temper*). **3** tendency to have fits of anger. **4** composure; calmness (*lose one's temper*). **5** hardness or elasticity of metal. • *v.tr.* **1** bring (metal or clay) to a proper hardness or consistency. **2** moderate (*temper justice with mercy*). □□ **tem'per·a·ble** *adj.* **tem'pered** *adj.*

---

temper Old English *temprian* 'bring something into the required condition by mixing it with something else,' from Latin *temperare* 'mingle, restrain oneself.' Sense development was probably influenced by Old French *temprer* 'to temper, moderate.' The noun originally denoted a correct or proportionate mixture of elements or qualities, also the combination of the four bodily humors, believed in medieval times to be the basis of temperament, hence sense 1 (late Middle English).

---

tem·per·a /témpərə/ *n.* method of painting using an emulsion, e.g., of pigment with egg, esp. on canvas.

tem·per·a·ment /témprəmənt/ *n.* person's or animal's nature and character.

tem·per·a·men·tal /témprəmént'l/ *adj.* **1** of

temperament. **2** moody; unreliable. □□ **tem·per·a·men′tal·ly** adv.

tem·per·ance /témpərəns, témprəns/ n. **1** moderation, esp. in eating and drinking. **2** abstinence from alcohol.

tem·per·ate /témpərət, témprət/ adj. **1** avoiding excess. **2** moderate. **3** (of a region or climate) mild. □□ **tem′per·ate·ly** adv. **tem′per·ate·ness** n.

tem·per·a·ture /témprichər/ n. **1** measured or perceived degree of heat or cold of a body, thing, region, etc. **2** body temperature above normal (have a temperature).

tem·pest /témpist/ n. **1** violent storm. **2** violent agitation. □□ **tem·pes·tu·ous** /–péschōōəs/ adj. **tem·pes′tu·ous·ly** adv. **tem·pes′tu·ous·ness** n.

tem·plate /témplit, –playt/ n. piece of thin board or metal plate used as a pattern in cutting, drilling, etc.

tem·ple[1] /témpəl/ n. building for the worship of a god or gods.

tem·ple[2] /témpəl/ n. flat part of either side of the head between the forehead and the ear.

tem·po /témpō/ n. (pl. **–pos** or **tem·pi** /–pee/) **1** speed at which music is or should be played. **2** rate of motion or activity.

tem·po·ral /témpərəl, témprəl/ adj. **1** worldly as opposed to spiritual; secular. **2** of time. **3** of the temples of the head (temporal artery). □□ **tem′po·ral·ly** adv.

tem·po·rar·y /témpəréree/ • adj. lasting or meant to last only for a limited time. • n. (pl. **–ies**) person employed temporarily. □□ **tem·po·rar·i·ly** /–pəráirilee/ adv.

tem·po·rize /témpəriz/ v.intr. **1** avoid committing oneself so as to gain time. **2** comply temporarily; adopt a time-serving policy. □□ **tem·po·ri·za′tion** n. **tem′po·riz·er** n.

tempt /tempt/ v.tr. **1** entice or incite (a person) to do a wrong or forbidden thing. **2** allure; attract. **3** risk provoking (fate, etc.). □□ **tempt′a·ble** adj. **tempt′er, tempt′ress** n.

temp·ta·tion /temptáyshən/ n. **1** tempting; being tempted; incitement esp. to wrongdoing. **2** attractive thing or course of action.

tempt·ing /témpting/ adj. attractive; inviting. □□ **tempt′ing·ly** adv.

tem·pu·ra /tempŏŏrə/ n. Japanese dish of fish, shellfish, or vegetables, dipped in batter and deep-fried.

ten /ten/ n. **1** one more than nine. **2** symbol for this (10, x, X). **3** ten-dollar bill.

---

ten Old English *tēn*, of Germanic origin; related to Dutch *tien* and German *zehn*, from an Indo-European root shared by Sanskrit *daśa*, Greek *deka*, and Latin *decem*.

---

ten·a·ble /ténəbəl/ adj. maintainable or defensible against attack or objection (tenable position). □□ **ten·a·bil′i·ty** n. **ten′a·ble·ness** n.

te·na·cious /tináyshəs/ adj. **1** keeping a firm hold. **2** (of memory) retentive. **3** persistent; resolute. □□ **te·na′cious·ly** adv. **te·na′cious·ness** n. **te·nac·i·ty** /tinásitee/ n.

ten·an·cy /ténənsee/ n. (pl. **–cies**) **1** status of a tenant; possession as a tenant. **2** duration of this.

ten·ant /ténənt/ n. **1** person who rents land or property from a landlord. **2** occupant of a place.

tend[1] /tend/ v.intr. **1** be apt or inclined (to). **2** be moving; hold a course (tends to the same conclusion).

tend[2] /tend/ v. **1** tr. take care of; look after. **2** intr. (foll. by to) give attention to.

ten·den·cy /téndənsee/ n. (pl. **–cies**) leaning; inclination.

ten·den·tious /tendénshəs/ adj. derog. (of writing, etc.) calculated to promote a particular cause or viewpoint; having an underlying purpose. □□ **ten·den′tious·ly** adv. **ten·den′tious·ness** n.

ten·der[1] /téndər/ adj. (**tend·er·er, ten·der·est**) **1** easily cut or chewed; not tough. **2** susceptible to pain or grief (tender heart). **3** sensitive; delicate; fragile. **4** loving; affectionate. **5** requiring tact or careful handling (tender subject). **6** (of age) immature (of tender years). □ **tender-hearted** easily moved by pity, etc. **tender mercies** iron. attention or treatment which is not in the best interests of its recipient. □□ **ten′der·ly** adv. **ten′der·ness** n.

tend·er[2] /téndər/ • v. **1** tr. offer; present (one's services, payment, resignation, etc.). **2** intr. make a tender for the supply of a thing or the execution of work. • n. offer, esp. in writing, to execute work or supply goods at a fixed price.

tend·er[3] /téndər/ n. **1** person who looks after people or things. **2** vessel attending a larger one. **3** car coupled to a steam locomotive to carry fuel, water, etc.

ten·der·foot /téndərfŏŏt/ n. newcomer or novice.

ten·der·ize /téndəriz/ v.tr. make tender, esp. make (meat) tender by beating, etc. □□ **ten′der·iz·er** n.

ten·der·loin /téndərloyn/ n. tender cut of beef or pork loin.

ten·don /téndən/ n. cord of strong tissue attaching a muscle to a bone, etc.

ten·dril /téndril/ n. slender leafless shoots by which some climbing plants cling.

ten·e·ment /ténimənt/ n. overcrowded or run-down apartment house.

ten·et /ténit/ n. doctrine; dogma; principle.

ten·fold /ténfōld/ adj. & adv. **1** ten times as much or as many. **2** consisting of ten parts.

Tenn. abbr. Tennessee.

ten·nis /ténis/ n. game in which two or four players strike a ball with rackets over a net stretched across a court. □ **tennis elbow** inflammation of the elbow caused by overuse.

ten·on /ténən/ n. projecting piece of wood made for insertion into a cavity (esp. a mortise) in another piece.

ten·or /ténər/ n. **1 a** male singing voice between baritone and alto or countertenor. **b** singer with this voice. **2** general purport or drift. **3** prevailing course, esp. of a person's life or habits.

ten·pins /ténpinz/ n. (usu. treated as sing.) bowling game using ten pins.

tense[1] /tens/ • adj. **1** stretched tight; strained. **2** causing tenseness (tense moment). • v. make or become tense. □□ **tense′ly** adv. **tense′ness** n. **ten′si·ty** n.

tense[2] /tens/ n. Gram. form taken by a verb to indicate the time (also the continuance or completeness) of the action, etc. (present tense; imperfect tense).

ten·sile /ténsəl, –sīl/ *adj.* **1** of tension. **2** capable of being stretched. □□ **ten·sil·i·ty** /tensílitee/ *n.*

ten·sion /ténshən/ *n.* **1** stretching; being stretched; tenseness. **2** mental strain or excitement. **3** strained (political, social, etc.) state or relationship. **4** stress produced by forces pulling apart. **5** electromagnetic force (*high tension; low tension*).

ten·sor /ténsər/ *n.* muscle that tightens or stretches a part.

tent /tent/ *n.* **1** portable shelter or dwelling of canvas, cloth, etc., supported by poles and ground pegs. **2** tentlike enclosure.

ten·ta·cle /téntəkəl/ *n.* long, slender, flexible appendage of an (esp. invertebrate) animal, used for feeling, grasping, or moving. □□ **ten'ta·cled** *adj.* (also in *comb.*).

ten·ta·tive /téntətiv/ *adj.* **1** experimental. **2** hesitant; not definite (*tentative suggestion*). □□ **ten'ta·tive·ly** *adv.* **ten'ta·tive·ness** *n.*

ten·ter·hook /téntərhoŏk/ *n.* hook to which cloth is fastened for stretching. □ **on tenterhooks** in a state of anxiety or uncertainty.

tenth /tenth/ • *n.* **1** next after ninth. **2** each of ten equal parts of a thing. • *adj.* that is the tenth. □□ **tenth'ly** *adv.*

ten·u·ous /tényŏoəs/ *adj.* **1** slight; insubstantial. **2** (of a distinction, etc.) oversubtle. **3** thin; slender; small. **4** rarefied. □□ **ten'u·ous·ly** *adv.* **ten'u·ous·ness** *n.*

ten·ure /tényər/ *n.* **1** right or title under which (esp. real) property is held. **2** period of this. **3** guaranteed permanent employment, esp. as a teacher or professor. □□ **ten'ured** *adj.*

te·pee /téepee/ *n.* (also **tee'pee**) conical tent orig. used by Native Americans.

TEPEE

tep·id /tépid/ *adj.* **1** slightly warm. **2** unenthusiastic. □□ **te·pid'i·ty** *n.* **tep'id·ly** *adv.* **tep'id·ness** *n.*

te·qui·la /tekéelə/ *n.* Mexican liquor made from an agave.

tera- /térə/ *comb. form* denoting a factor of 10^{12}.

ter·bi·um /tớrbeeəm/ *n. Chem.* silvery metallic element of the lanthanide series. ¶ Symb.: **Tb**.

ter·cen·te·nar·y /tớrsenténəree, tərséntineree/ • *n.* (*pl.* **ies**) **1** three-hundredth anniversary. **2** celebration of this. • *adj.* of this anniversary.

ter·cen·ten·ni·al /tớrsenténeeəl/ • *adj.* **1** occurring every three hundred years. **2** lasting three hundred years. • *n.* tercentenary.

ter·i·ya·ki /tereeyókee/ *n.* usu. grilled dish of meat, poultry, or fish that has been marinated in soy sauce.

term /tərm/ • *n.* **1** word for a definite concept, esp. specialized. **2** (in *pl.*) language used; mode of expression (*in no uncertain terms*). **3** (in *pl.*) relationship (*on familiar terms*). **4** (in *pl.*) a stipulations (*cannot accept your terms*). **b** charge; price (*his terms are $20 a lesson*). **5** limited, usu. specified, period (*term of five years*). **6** *Math.* each of the two in a ratio, series, or expression. **7** completion of a normal length of pregnancy. • *v. tr.* call; assign a term to (*the music termed classical*). □ **bring to terms** cause to accept conditions. **come to terms with 1** reconcile oneself to (a difficulty, etc.). **2** conclude an agreement with. **in terms of 1** in the language peculiar to. **2** by way of. **on terms** on terms of friendship or equality.

ter·ma·gant /tớrməgənt/ • *n.* overbearing woman; virago. • *adj.* violent; turbulent; shrewish.

ter·mi·na·ble /tớrminəbəl/ *adj.* that may be terminated.

ter·mi·nal /tớrminəl/ • *adj.* **1 a** (of a disease) fatal. **b** (of a patient) dying. **c** *colloq.* ruinous; very great (*terminal laziness*). **2** of or forming a limit or terminus. • *n.* **1** terminating thing; extremity. **2** terminus for planes, trains, or long-distance buses. **3** point of connection for closing an electric circuit. **4** apparatus for transmission of messages between a user and a computer, communications system, etc. □ **terminal velocity** velocity of a falling body such that the resistance of the air, etc., prevents further increase of speed under gravity. □□ **ter'mi·nal·ly** *adv.*

ter·mi·nate /tớrminayt/ *v.* **1** *tr. & intr.* bring or come to an end. **2** *intr.* (foll. by *in*) (of a word) end in (a specified letter, syllable, etc.). □□ **ter·mi·na'tion** *n.* **ter'mi·na·tor** *n.*

ter·mi·nol·o·gy /tớrminóləjee/ *n.* (*pl.* **–gies**) **1** system of specialized terms. **2** science of the proper use of terms. □□ **ter·mi·nol'o·gist** *n.*

ter·mi·nus /tớrminəs/ *n.* (*pl.* **ter·mi·ni** /–nī/ or **ter·mi·nus·es**) end of a bus route, pipeline, etc.; end point.

ter·mite /tớrmīt/ *n.* antlike social insect destructive to wood.

tern /tərn/ *n.* marine bird like a gull but usu. smaller and with a long forked tail.

terp·si·cho·re·an /tớrpsikəréeən, –kάwreeən/ *adj.* of dancing.

terr. *abbr.* **1** terrace. **2** territory.

ter·race /térəs/ • *n.* **1** flat area formed on a slope and used for cultivation. **2** patio. • *v. tr.* form into or provide with a terrace or terraces.

ter·ra-cot·ta /térəkótə/ *n.* **1** unglazed usu. brownish red earthenware. **2** its color.

ter·ra fir·ma /térə fə́rmə/ *n.* dry land; firm ground.

ter·rain /teráyn/ *n.* tract of land as regarded by the physical geographer or the military tactician.

ter·ra·pin /térəpin/ *n.* N. American edible freshwater turtle.

ter·rar·i·um /teráireeəm/ *n.* (*pl.* **ter·rar·i·ums** or **ter·rar·i·a** /–reeə/) usu. glass enclosure for plants or small land animals.

ter·res·tri·al /təréstreeəl/ • *adj.* **1** of or on the earth; earthly. **2** of or on dry land. • *n.* inhabitant of the earth.

ter·ri·ble /téribəl/ adj. **1** colloq. very great or bad (terrible bore). **2** colloq. very incompetent (terrible at tennis). **3** causing terror; awful; dreadful. **4** (predic.) colloq. full of remorse; sorry (I felt terrible). □□ **ter′ri·ble·ness** n.

ter·ri·bly /téribleé/ adv. **1** colloq. very; extremely (terribly nice). **2** in a terrible manner.

ter·ri·er /téreeər/ n. small dog of various breeds originally used to ferret out game.

ter·rif·ic /tərifik/ adj. **1** colloq. **a** huge; intense. **b** excellent (did a terrific job). **2** causing terror. □□ **ter·rif′i·cal·ly** adv.

ter·ri·fy /térifi/ v.tr. (**-fies**, **-fied**) fill with terror. □□ **ter′ri·fi·er** n. **ter′ri·fy·ing** adj. **ter′ri·fy·ing·ly** adv.

ter·ri·to·ri·al /téritáwreeəl/ adj. **1** of territory or a district. **2** tending to defend one's territory. □□ **ter·ri·to′ri·al·ly** adv.

ter·ri·to·ry /téritawree/ n. (pl. **-ries**) **1** extent of land under a ruler, nation, city, etc. **2** (**Territory**) division of a country, esp. one not yet having full rights. **3** sphere of action or thought; province. **4** designated business or sales area. **5** human's or animal's defended space or area.

ter·ror /térər/ n. **1** extreme fear. **2 a** terrifying person or thing. **b** (also **holy terror**) colloq. formidable person; troublesome person or thing. **3** use of organized intimidation. □ **reign of terror** period of remorseless repression, esp. during the French Revolution 1793–94. **terror-stricken** (or **-struck**) affected with terror.

ter·ror·ist /térərist/ n. (also attrib.) person who uses violent methods of coercing a government or community. □□ **ter′ror·ism** n. **ter·ror·is′tic** adj.

> **terrorist** late 18th century: from French *terroriste*, from Latin *terror* (source of *terror*). The word was originally applied to supporters of the Jacobins in the French Revolution, who advocated repression and violence in pursuit of the principles of democracy and equality.

ter·ror·ize /térəriz/ v.tr. **1** fill with terror. **2** use terrorism against. □□ **ter·ror·i·za′tion** n. **ter′ror·iz·er** n.

ter·ry /téree/ • n. (pl. **-ries**) pile fabric with the loops uncut, used esp. for towels. • adj. of this fabric.

terse /ters/ adj. (**ters·er**, **ters·est**) **1** (of language) brief; concise. **2** curt; abrupt. □□ **terse′ly** adv. **terse′ness** n.

ter·ti·ar·y /tə́rshee-eree, –shəri/ • adj. **1** third in order or rank, etc. **2** (**Tertiary**) Geol. of the first period in the Cenozoic era. • n. (**Tertiary**) Geol. Tertiary period.

tes·la /téslə/ n. unit of magnetic flux density.

tes·sel·lat·ed /tésəlaytid/ adj. **1** of or resembling mosaic. **2** Bot. & Zool. regularly checkered. □□ **tes·sel·la′tion** n.

test /test/ • n. **1** critical examination or trial of a person's or thing's qualities. **2** means of so examining. **3** oral or written examination. • v.tr. **1** cause to undergo a test. **2** try severely. **3** Chem. examine by means of a reagent. □ **test pattern** still television picture designed for use in judging the quality and position of the image. **test pilot** pilot who tests the performance of

aircraft. **test tube** thin glass tube closed at one end used for chemical tests, etc. **test-tube baby** colloq. baby conceived by in vitro fertilization. □□ **test′a·ble** adj. **test·a·bil′i·ty** n. **test′er** n.

Test. abbr. Testament.

tes·ta·ment /téstəmənt/ n. **1** will (esp. last will and testament). **2** evidence; proof (testament to his loyalty). **3** Bibl. **a** covenant; dispensation. **b** (**Testament**) division of the Christian Bible (see Old Testament, New Testament). □□ **tes·ta·men′ta·ry** adj.

tes·tate /téstayt/ • adj. having left a valid will at death. • n. testate person. □□ **tes·ta·cy** /–təsee/ n. (pl. **–cies**).

tes·ta·tor /téstaytər, testáytər/ n. (fem. **tes·ta·trix** /testáytriks/) (esp. deceased) person who has made a will.

tes·tes pl. of TESTIS.

tes·ti·cle /téstikəl/ n. male organ that produces spermatozoa, etc., esp. one of a pair in the scrotum of a man and most mammals. □□ **tes·tic·u·lar** /–stikyələr/ adj.

tes·ti·fy /téstifi/ v. (**-fies**, **-fied**) **1** intr. (of a person or thing) bear witness (testified to the facts). **2** intr. give evidence. **3** tr. affirm; declare (testified that she had lied). □□ **tes′ti·fi·er** n.

tes·ti·mo·ni·al /téstimóneeəl/ n. **1** statement of character, conduct, or qualifications. **2** gift presented to a person (esp. in public) as a mark of esteem, gratitude, etc.

tes·ti·mo·ny /téstimōnee/ n. (pl. **-nies**) **1** witness's statement under oath. **2** declaration or statement of fact. **3** evidence (produce testimony).

tes·tis /téstis/ n. (pl. **tes·tes** /–teez/) Anat. & Zool. testicle.

tes·tos·ter·one /testóstərōn/ n. sex hormone formed in the testicles.

tes·ty /téstee/ adj. (**tes·ti·er**, **tes·ti·est**) irritable; touchy. □□ **tes′ti·ly** adv. **tes′ti·ness** n.

tet·a·nus /tét'nəs/ n. bacterial disease causing painful spasm of the voluntary muscles.

tête-à-tête /táytaatáyt, tétaatét/ • n. private conversation between two persons. • adv. together in private (dined tête-à-tête).

teth·er /téthər/ • n. rope, etc., confining an animal. • v.tr. tie (an animal) with a tether. □ **at the end of one's tether** having reached the limit of one's patience, resources, abilities, etc.

tetra- /tétrə/ comb. form (also **tetr-** before a vowel) four.

tet·ra·cy·cline /tétrəsíkleen, –klin/ n. antibiotic with a molecule of four rings.

Tet·ra·gram·ma·ton /tétrəgrámətɒn/ n. Hebrew name of God written in four letters, articulated as Yahweh, etc.

tet·ra·he·dron /tétrəhee′edrən/ n. (pl. **tet·ra·he·**

TETRAHEDRON

dra /–drə/ or **tet·ra·he·drons**) four-sided solid; triangular pyramid. ▫▫ **tet·ra·he′dral** *adj.*

te·tral·o·gy /tetráləjee, –tról–/ *n.* (*pl.* **–gies**) group of four related literary or operatic works.

te·tram·e·ter /tetrámitər/ *n. Prosody* verse of four measures.

tet·ra·pod /tétrəpod/ *n. Zool.* animal with four feet. ▫▫ **tet·ra·pod·ous** /titrápədəs/ *adj.*

te·trarch /tétraark/ *n.* **1** *Rom.Hist.* **a** governor of a fourth part of a country or province. **b** subordinate ruler. **2** one of four joint rulers. ▫▫ **te′trarch·ate** *n.* **te·trar′chi·cal** *adj.* **te′trar·chy** *n.* (*pl.* **–chies**).

Teu·ton /tóōt'n, tyóōtən/ *n.* member of a Teutonic nation, esp. a German.

Teu·ton·ic /tōōtónik, tyōō–/ *adj.* **1** of the Germanic peoples or languages. **2** German.

Tex. *abbr.* Texas.

Tex·an /téksən/ • *n.* native or inhabitant of Texas. • *adj.* of or relating to Texas.

Tex-Mex /téksméks/ *adj.* combining cultural elements from Texas and Mexico, as in cooking, music, etc.

text /tekst/ *n.* **1** main body of a book as distinct from notes, etc. **2** original words of an author or document. **3** passage from Scripture, esp. as the subject of a sermon. **4** subject; theme. **5** textbook.

text·book /tékstbōōk/ • *n.* book for use in studying, esp. a standard account of a subject. • *attrib.adj.* **1** exemplary; accurate. **2** instructively typical. ▫▫ **text′book·ish** *adj.*

tex·tile /tékstīl/ • *n.* **1** any woven material. **2** any cloth. • *adj.* **1** of weaving or cloth (*textile industry*). **2** woven (*textile fabrics*).

tex·tu·al /tékschōōəl/ *adj.* of, in, or concerning a text. ▫▫ **tex′tu·al·ly** *adv.*

tex·ture /tékschər/ • *n.* **1** feel or appearance of a surface or substance. **2** arrangement of threads, etc., in textile fabric. **3** quality or style of music, writing, etc., resulting from composition. • *v.tr.* (usu. as **textured** *adj.*) provide with a texture. ▫▫ **tex′tur·al** *adj.* **tex′tur·al·ly** *adv.*

Th *symb. Chem.* thorium.

Th. *abbr.* Thursday.

-th /th/ *suffix* (also **-eth** /ith/) forming ordinal and fractional numbers from *four* onward (*fourth*; *thirtieth*).

Thai /tī/ • *n.* (*pl.* same or **Thais**) **1 a** native or inhabitant of Thailand in SE Asia. **b** person of Thai descent. **2** language of Thailand. • *adj.* of or relating to Thailand or its people or language.

thal·a·mus /tháləməs/ *n.* (*pl.* **thal·a·mi** /–mī/) *Anat.* either of two masses of gray matter in the forebrain, serving as relay stations for sensory tracts. ▫▫ **tha·lam·ic** /thəlámik, thálomik/ *adj.*

tha·lid·o·mide /thəlídəmīd/ *n.* sedative drug found to cause fetal malformation when taken early in pregnancy.

thal·li·um /tháleeəm/ *n. Chem.* rare soft white metallic element. ¶ Symb.: **Tl.** ▫▫ **thal′lic** *adj.* **thal′lous** *adj.*

than /than, thən/ *conj.* **1** introducing a comparison (*you are older than he*). **2** introducing an element of difference (*anyone other than me*).

thane /thayn/ *n. hist.* former English or Scottish noble rank.

thank /thangk/ • *v.tr.* **1** express gratitude to.

2 hold responsible (*you can thank yourself for that*). • *n.* (in *pl.*) **1** gratitude. **2** expression of gratitude (*give thanks*). **3** thank you. ▫ **thank goodness** (or **God** or **heavens**, etc.) *colloq.* an expression of relief or pleasure. **2** an expression of pious gratitude. **thanks to** as the (good or bad) result of (*thanks to my foresight*). **thank you** polite formula expressing gratitude.

thank·ful /thángkfŏōl/ *adj.* **1** grateful; pleased. **2** (of words or acts) expressive of thanks. ▫▫ **thank′ful·ness** *n.*

thank·ful·ly /thángkflis/ *adv.* **1** in a thankful manner. **2** *disp.* fortunately (*thankfully, nobody was hurt*).

thank·less /thángklis/ *adj.* **1** not expressing or feeling gratitude. **2** (of a task, etc.) giving no pleasure. ▫▫ **thank′less·ly** *adv.* **thank′less·ness** *n.*

thanks·giv·ing /thángksgíving/ *n.* **1** expression of gratitude, esp. as a prayer. **2** (**Thanksgiving** or **Thanksgiving Day**) national holiday for giving thanks, the fourth Thursday in November in the US.

that /that/ • *demons.pron.* (*pl.* **those** /thōz/) **1** person or thing indicated, named, or understood (*who is that in the yard?*). **2** (contrasted with *this*) the further or less immediate or obvious, etc., of two (*this is much heavier than that*). **3** action, behavior, or circumstances just observed or mentioned (*don't do that again*). **4** (esp. in relative constructions) the one, the person, etc., specified in some way (*those who have cars*). **5** (*pl.* **that**) used instead of *which* or *whom* to introduce a defining clause (*there is nothing here that matters*). • *demons.adj.* (*pl.* **those** /thōz/) **1** designating the person or thing indicated, named, understood, etc. (cf. sense 1 of *pron.*) (*look at that dog*). **2** contrasted with *this* (cf. sense 2 of *pron.*) (*this is heavier than that one*). • *adv.* **1** to such a degree; so (*have done that much*). **2** *colloq.* very (*not that good*). **3** at which, on which, etc. (*the day that I first met her*). • *conj.* introducing a subordinate clause indicating: **1** statement or hypothesis (*they say that he is better*). **2** purpose (*we live that we may eat*). **3** result (*am so sleepy that I cannot think*). ▫ **all that** very (*not all that good*). **and all that** and so forth. **that is** (or **that is to say**) formula introducing or following an explanation of a preceding word or words. **that's** *colloq.* you are (*that's a good boy*). **that's that** formula concluding a narrative or discussion or indicating completion of a task. **that will do** no more is needed or desirable.

¶ See note at WHICH.

thatch /thach/ • *n.* roofing material of straw, reeds, palm leaves, or similar material. • *v.tr.* (also *absol.*) cover with thatch. ▫▫ **thatch′er** *n.*

thaw /thaw/ • *v.* **1** *intr.* (of a frozen thing) pass into a liquid or unfrozen state. **2** *intr.* become warm enough to melt ice, etc. **3** *intr.* become genial, etc. **4** *tr.* cause to thaw. **5** *tr.* make cordial. • *n.* **1** thawing. **2** warmth of weather that thaws.

the /before a vowel *thee*, before a consonant *thə*, when stressed *thee*/ • *adj.* (called the definite article) **1** denoting one or more persons or things already mentioned, under discussion, implied, or familiar (*gave the man a wave*). **2** describing as unique (*the president*). **3 a** (foll. by defining adj.) which is, who are, etc. (*the* embarrassed *Mr. Smith*). **b** (foll. by adj. used *absol.*) denoting a class described (*from the sublime to the ridiculous*). **4** best known (with the stressed: *no relation to the Hemingway*). **5** indicating a following defining clause or phrase (*the best I can do*). **6** speaking generically (*plays the harp well*). • *adv.* (preceding comparatives in expressions of proportional variation) in or by that (or such a) degree (*the more the merrier*).

theat. *abbr.* **1** theater. **2** theatrical.

the·a·ter /thе́eətər/ *n.* (esp. *Brit.* **the′a·tre**) **1** a building or outdoor area for dramatic performances. **b** (in full **mov′ie the·ater**) building for showing movies. **2** writing and production of plays. **3** room or hall for lectures, etc., with seats in tiers. **4** scene or field of action (*theater of war*). □ **theater-goer** frequenter of theaters. **theater-in-the-round** performance on a stage surrounded by spectators.

the·at·ric /theeátrik/ • *adj.* = THEATRICAL. • *n.* (in *pl.*) theatrical actions.

the·at·ri·cal /theeátrikǝl/ • *adj.* **1** of or for the theater; of acting or actors. **2** calculated for effect; showy. • *n.* (in *pl.*) dramatic performances (*amateur theatricals*). □□ **the·at′ri·cal·ism** *n.* **the·at·ri·cal·i·ty** /-kálitee/ *n.* **the·at′ri·cal·ly** *adv.*

thee /thee/ *pron. objective case of* THOU¹.

theft /theft/ *n.* act of stealing.

their /thair/ *poss.pron.* (*attrib.*) of or belonging to them.

¶ **Their** is a possessive pronoun; **there** is an adverb meaning 'at that place'; and **they′re** is a contraction of 'they are': *They're having a party at their camp next week; why don't we drive there?*

theirs /thairz/ *poss.pron.* the one or ones belonging to or associated with them (*theirs are over here*). □ **of theirs** of or belonging to them (*friend of theirs*).

the·ism /thе́eizəm/ *n.* belief in gods or a god. □□ **the′ist** *n.* **the·is′tic** *adj.*

them /them, thǝm/ • *pron.* **1** objective case of THEY (*I saw them*). **2** *colloq.* they (*it's them again*). • *adj. sl.* or *dial.* those (*them bones*).

theme /theem/ *n.* **1** subject, topic, or recurrent focus. **2** *Mus.* prominent melody in a composition. **3** school exercise, esp. an essay, on a given subject. □ **theme park** amusement park organized around a unifying idea. **theme song 1** recurrent melody in a musical. **2** signature tune. □□ **the·mat·ic** /-mátik/ *adj.* **the·mat′i·cal·ly** *adv.*

them·selves /themsélvz, thǝm-/ *pron.* **1 a** *emphat. form* of THEY or THEM. **b** *refl. form* of THEM. **2** in their normal state of body or mind (*are quite themselves again*).

then /then/ • *adv.* **1** at that time. **2 a** next; after that. **b** and also. **3 a** in that case (*then you should have said so*). **b** (implying grudging or impatient concession) if you must have it so. **c** used parenthetically to resume a narrative, etc. (*finally, then, he knocked on the door*). • *adj.* such at the time in question (*the then senator*). • *n.* that time (*until then*). □ **then and there** immediately and on the spot.

thence /thens/ *adv.* **1** from that place. **2** for that reason.

thence·forth /thénsfáwrth/ *adv.* from that time onward.

thence·for·ward /thénsfáwrwǝrd/ *adv. formal* thenceforth.

theo- /thе́e-ō/ *comb. form* God or gods.

the·o·cen·tric /thе́eǝséntrik/ *adj.* having God or a god as its center.

the·oc·ra·cy /theeókrǝsee/ *n.* (*pl.* **-cies**) form of government by God or a god directly or through a priestly order, etc. □□ **the·o·crat** /thе́eǝkrat/ *n.* **the·o·crat′ic** *adj.* **the·o·crat′i·cal·ly** *adv.*

the·od·o·lite /theeód′līt/ *n.* surveying instrument for measuring angles with a rotating telescope. □□ **the·od·o·lit·ic** /-lítik/ *adj.*

theol. *abbr.* **1** theological. **2** theology.

the·o·lo·gian /thе́eǝlójǝn/ *n.* person trained in theology.

the·ol·o·gy /theeólǝjee/ *n.* (*pl.* **-gies**) study or system of theistic (esp. Christian) religion. □□ **the·o·log·i·cal** /thе́eǝlójikǝl/ *adj.* **the·o·log′i·cal·ly** *adv.* **the·ol′o·gist** *n.*

the·o·rem /thе́eǝrǝm, theérǝm/ *n.* esp. Math. **1** general proposition not self-evident but proved by reasoning. **2** rule in algebra, etc., esp. one expressed by symbols or formulae.

the·o·ret·ic /theeǝrétik/ • *adj.* = THEORETICAL.

the·o·ret·i·cal /theeǝrétikǝl/ *adj.* **1** concerned with knowledge but not with its practical application. **2** based on theory rather than experience. □□ **the·o·ret′i·cal·ly** *adv.*

the·o·rist /thе́eǝrist, theérist/ *n.* holder or inventor of a theory or theories.

the·o·rize /thе́eǝrīz, theérīz/ *v.intr.* evolve or indulge in theories. □□ **the′o·riz·er** *n.*

the·o·ry /thе́eǝree, theéree/ *n.* (*pl.* **-ries**) **1** supposition or system of ideas explaining something, esp. one based on general principles. **2** speculative (esp. fanciful) view. **3** sphere of abstract knowledge (*works well in theory, but not in practice?*). **4** exposition of the principles of a science, etc. **5** *Math.* collection of propositions.

the·os·o·phy /theeósǝfee/ *n.* (*pl.* **-phies**) any of various philosophies professing to achieve knowledge of God by spiritual ecstasy, direct intuition, or special individual relations, esp. a modern movement following Hindu and Buddhist teachings and seeking universal brotherhood. □□ **the·o·soph·i·cal** /-sóf-/ *adj.* **the·o·soph′i·cal·ly** *adv.* **the·os′o·phist** *n.*

ther·a·peu·tic /thérǝpyо́otik/ *adj.* **1** of, for, or contributing to the cure of disease. **2** healing; soothing. □□ **ther·a·peu′ti·cal·ly** *adv.*

ther·a·peu·tics /thérǝpyо́otiks/ *n.pl.* (usu. treated as *sing.*) branch of medicine concerned with cures and remedies.

ther·a·py /thérǝpee/ *n.* (*pl.* **-pies**) nonsurgical treatment of physical or mental disorders. □□ **ther′a·pist** *n.*

there /thair/ • *adv.* **1** in, at, or to that place or position (*lived there for years*). **2** at that point (in speech, performance, writing, etc.). **3** in that respect (*I agree with you there*). **4** used for emphasis in calling attention (*you there!*). **5** used to indicate the fact or existence of something (*there is a house on the corner*). • *n.* that place (*lives near there*). • *int.* **1** expressing confirmation, triumph, dismay, etc. (*there! what did I tell you?*). **2** used to soothe a child, etc. (*there, there, now*). □ **so there** *colloq.* that is my final decision (whether you like it or not). **there you are** (or **go**) *colloq.* **1** this is what you wanted, etc. **2** expressing confirmation, triumph, resignation, etc.

¶ See notes at HERE and THEIR.

there·abouts /ᵗẖáirəbówts/ *adv.* (also **there'a·bout**) **1** near that place. **2** near that number, quantity, etc.

there·af·ter /ᵗẖáiráftər/ *adv.* after that.

there·by /ᵗẖáirbí/ *adv.* by that means; as a result of that.

there·fore /ᵗẖáirfawr/ *adv.* for that reason; consequently.

there·in /ᵗẖáirín/ *adv.* **1** in that place, etc. **2** in that respect.

there·of /ᵗẖáirúv, -óv/ *adv.* of that or it.

there·to /ᵗẖáirtóō/ *adv.* **1** to that or it. **2** in addition; to boot.

there·up·on /ᵗẖáirəpón, -páwn/ *adv.* **1** in consequence of that. **2** soon or immediately after that.

ther·mal /ᵗẖórməl/ • *adj.* **1** of, for, or producing heat. **2** promoting the retention of heat (*thermal underwear*). • *n.* rising current of heated air. □ **British thermal unit** amount of heat needed to raise 1 lb. of water at maximum density through one degree Fahrenheit, equivalent to 1.055 x 10^3 joules. □□ **ther'mal·ly** *adv.*

thermo- /ᵗẖórmō/ *comb. form* denoting heat.

ther·mo·dy·nam·ics /ᵗẖórmōdīnámiks/ *n.pl.* (usu. treated as *sing.*) science of the relations between heat and other forms of energy. □□ **ther·mo·dy·nam'ic** *adj.* **ther·mo·dy·nam'i·cal·ly** *adv.*

ther·mom·e·ter /ᵗẖərmómitər/ *n.* instrument for measuring temperature, esp. a graduated glass tube containing mercury or alcohol.

ther·mo·nu·cle·ar /ᵗẖórmōnóōkleeər, -nyóō-/ *adj.* **1** relating to nuclear reactions that occur only at very high temperatures. **2** (of weapons) using thermonuclear reactions.

ther·mo·plas·tic /ᵗẖórmōplástik/ • *adj.* (of a substance) that becomes plastic on heating and hardens on cooling. • *n.* thermoplastic substance.

ther·mos /ᵗẖórməs/ *n.* (in full **ther'mos bot·tle** or **flask**) *propr.* bottle, etc., with a double wall enclosing a vacuum, used to keep liquids hot or cold.

ther·mo·stat /ᵗẖórməstat/ *n.* device that automatically regulates or responds to temperature. □□ **ther·mo·stat'ic** *adj.* **ther·mo·stat'i·cal·ly** *adv.*

the·sau·rus /thisáwrəs/ *n.* (*pl.* **the·sau·ri** /-rī/ or **the·sau·rus·es**) book that categorizes or lists synonyms and related concepts.

these *pl.* of THIS.

the·sis /ᵗẖéesis/ *n.* (*pl.* **the·ses** /-seez/) **1** proposition to be maintained or proved. **2** dissertation, esp. by a candidate for a degree.

thes·pi·an /ᵗẖéspeeən/ • *adj.* of drama. • *n.* actor or actress.

the·ta /ᵗẖáytə, ᵗẖée-/ *n.* eighth letter of the Greek alphabet (Θ, ϑ).

they /ᵗẖay/ *pron.* (*obj.* **them**; *poss.* **their, theirs**) **1** *pl.* of HE, SHE, IT. **2** people in general (*they say we are wrong*). **3** those in authority (*they have raised the fees*).
¶ See note at EVERYBODY.

they'd /ᵗẖayd/ *contr.* **1** they had. **2** they would.

they'll /ᵗẖayl/ *contr.* **1** they will. **2** they shall.

they're /ᵗẖair/ *contr.* they are.
¶ See note at THEIR.

they've /ᵗẖayv/ *contr.* they have.

thi·a·mine /ᵗẖíəmin, -meen/ *n.* (also **thi'a·min**) vitamin of the B complex, found in unrefined

cereals, beans, and liver, a deficiency of which causes beriberi. Also called **vitamin B₁**.

thick /ᵗẖik/ • *adj.* **1 a** of great or specified extent between opposite surfaces (*thick wall*). **b** of large diameter. **2** (of a line, etc.) broad; not fine. **3** arranged closely; crowded together; dense. **4** densely covered or filled (*air thick with snow*). **5 a** firm in consistency; containing much solid matter. **b** made of thick material. **6** muddy; cloudy; impenetrable by sight (*thick darkness*). **7** *colloq.* stupid; dull. **8 a** (of a voice) indistinct. **b** (of an accent) pronounced; exaggerated. **9** *colloq.* intimate or very friendly (esp. thick as thieves). • *n.* thick part of anything. • *adv.* thickly (*snow was falling thick*. □ **in the thick of 1** at the busiest part of. **2** heavily occupied with. **thick-skinned** not sensitive to reproach or criticism. **through thick and thin** in spite of all difficulties. □□ **thick'ish** *adj.* **thick'ly** *adv.*

thick·en /ᵗẖíkən/ *v.* **1** *tr.* make or become thick or thicker. **2** *intr.* become more complicated (*the plot thickens*). □□ **thick'en·er** *n.*

thick·et /ᵗẖíkit/ *n.* tangle of shrubs or trees.

thick·head·ed /ᵗẖík-hedíd/ *n. adj. colloq.* stupid. □□ **thick'head·ed·ness** *n.*

thick·ness /ᵗẖíknis/ *n.* **1** being thick. **2** extent to which a thing is thick. **3** layer of material (*three thicknesses of cardboard*).

thick·set /ᵗẖíksét/ *adj.* **1** heavily or solidly built. **2** set or growing close together.

thief /ᵗẖeef/ *n.* (*pl.* **thieves** /ᵗẖeevz/) person who steals, esp. secretly.

thieve /ᵗẖeev/ *v.* **1** *intr.* be a thief. **2** *tr.* steal (a thing). □□ **thiev'ish** *adj.* **thiev'ish·ly** *adv.* **thiev'ish·ness** *n.*

thiev·er·y /ᵗẖéevəree/ *n.* act or practice of stealing.

thieves *pl.* of THIEF.

thigh /ᵗẖī/ *n.* part of the leg between the hip and the knee.

thim·ble /ᵗẖímbəl/ *n.* metal or plastic cap worn to protect the finger and push the needle in sewing. □□ **thim'ble·ful** (*pl.* **-fuls**) *n.*

thin /ᵗẖin/ • *adj.* (**thin·ner, thin·nest**) **1** having opposite surfaces close together; of small thickness. **2** (of a line, etc.) narrow or fine. **3** made of thin material. **4** lean; not plump. **5** not dense or copious (*thin hair*). **6** of slight consistency. **7** weak; lacking an important ingredient (*thin blood; thin voice*). **8** (of an excuse, etc.) flimsy or transparent. • *adv.* thinly (*cut the bread very thin*). • *v.* (**thinned, thin·ning**) **1** *tr.* & *intr.* make or become thin or thinner. **2** *tr.* & *intr.* make or become less dense or crowded or numerous. **3** *tr.* remove some of a crop to improve the growth of the rest. □ **thin air** state of invisibility or nonexistence (*vanished into thin air*). **thin on top** balding. **thin-skinned** sensitive to reproach or criticism. □□ **thin'ly** *adv.* **thin'ness** *n.* **thin'nish** *adj.*

thine /ᵗẖīn/ *poss.pron. archaic* or *dial.* **1** (*predic.* or *absol.*) of or belonging to thee. **2** (*attrib.* before a vowel) = THY.

thing /ᵗẖing/ *n.* **1** entity, idea, action, etc., that is or may be thought about or perceived. **2** inanimate material object. **3** unspecified item (*a few things to buy*). **4** act, idea, or utterance (*silly thing to do*). **5** event (*unfortunate thing to happen*). **6** *colloq.* **a** one's special interest (*not my* *thing*). **b** obsession, fear, or prejudice (*have a thing about spiders*). **7** *colloq.* fashion (*latest thing in footwear*). **8** (in *pl.*) personal belongings or clothing (*where are my things?*). **9** (in *pl.*) affairs in general (*not in the nature of things*). **10** (in *pl.*) circumstances; conditions (*things look good*). □ **do things to** *colloq.* affect remarkably. **make a thing of** *colloq.* cause a fuss about. **one** (or **just one**) **of those things** *colloq.* something unavoidable or to be accepted.

thing·a·ma·bob /thíngəməbob/ *n.* (also **thing·a·ma·jig** /thíngəməjig/) *colloq.* person or thing whose name one has forgotten or does not know, etc.

think /thingk/ *v.* (*past* and *past part.* **thought** /thawt/) **1** *tr.* (foll. by *that* + clause) be of the opinion. **2** *tr.* (foll. by *that* + clause or *to* + infin.) judge or consider (*is thought to be a fraud*). **3** *intr.* exercise the mind (*let me think*). **4** *tr.* (foll. by *of* or *about*) consider; imagine. **5** *tr.* have a half-formed intention (*I think I'll stay*). **6** *tr.* (foll. by *to* + infin.) remember (*did not think to lock the door*). □ **think again** revise one's plans or opinions. **think out loud** (or **aloud**) utter one's thoughts as soon as they occur. **think back** to recall (a past event or time). **think better of** change one's mind after reconsideration. **think for oneself** have an independent mind or attitude. **think little** (or **nothing**) **of** consider to be insignificant or unremarkable. **think much** (or **highly**) **of** have a high opinion of. **think out** consider carefully. **think over** reflect upon in order to reach a decision. **think tank** body of experts providing advice and ideas on specific national or commercial problems. **think through** reflect fully upon (a problem, etc.). **think twice** use careful consideration, avoid hasty action, etc. **think up** *colloq.* devise. □□ **think′er** *n.*

think·ing /thíngking/ • *adj.* using thought or rational judgment. • *n.* opinion or judgment. □ **put on one's thinking cap** *colloq.* meditate on a problem.

thin·ner /thínər/ *n.* volatile liquid used to dilute paint, etc.

third /thərd/ • *n.* **1** next after second. **2** each of three equal parts of a thing. • *adj.* that is the third. □ **third-class** *adj.* lower quality; inferior. **third degree** long and severe questioning, esp. by police to obtain information or a confession. **third-degree** *Med.* denoting burns of the most severe kind, affecting lower layers of tissue. **third person** *Gram.* see PERSON. **third-rate** inferior; very poor in quality. **Third World** (usu. prec. by *the*) developing countries of Asia, Africa, and Latin America. □□ **third′ly** *adv.*
¶ See note at FIRST.

thirst /thərst/ • *n.* **1** need to drink liquid; feeling of discomfort caused by this. **2** strong desire; craving (*thirst for power*). • *v.intr.* **1** feel thirst. **2** have a strong desire. □□ **thirst′y** *adj.* **thirst′i·ly** *adv.* **thirst′i·ness** *n.*

thir·teen /thárteé′en/ • *n.* **1** one more than twelve, or three more than ten. **2** symbol for this (13, xiii, XIII). • *adj.* that amount to thirteen. □□ **thir′teenth** *adj.* & *n.*

thir·ty /thártee/ *n.* (*pl.* **-ties**) **1** product of three and ten. **2** symbol for this (30, xxx, XXX). **3** (in *pl.*) numbers from 30 to 39, esp. the years of a century or of a person's life. □ **thirty-first, -second,** etc., ordinal numbers between thirtieth and fortieth. **thirty-one, -two,** etc., cardinal numbers between thirty and forty. □□ **thir′ti·eth** *adj.* & *n.*

this /this/ • *demons.pron.* (*pl.* **these** /theez/) **1** person or thing close at hand or indicated or already named or understood (*this is my cousin*). **2** (contrasted with *that*) person or thing nearer to hand or more immediately in mind. • *demons.adj.* (*pl.* **these** /theez/) **1** designating the person or thing close at hand, etc. (cf. senses 1, 2 of *pron.*). **2** (of time): the present or current (*am busy all this week*). **3** *colloq.* (in narrative) designating a person or thing previously unspecified (*then up came this policeman*). • *adv.* to this degree or extent (*knew him when he was this high*). □ **this and that** *colloq.* various unspecified things.

this·tle /thísəl/ *n.* prickly plant, usu. with globular heads of purple flowers.

THISTLE

thith·er /thíthər, thi–/ *adv. archaic* to or toward that place.

tho′ var. of THOUGH.

thong /thong/ *n.* narrow strip of hide or leather.

tho·rax /tháwraks, thór–/ *n.* (*pl.* **tho·rax·es** or **tho·ra·ces** /tháwrəseez/) *Anat.* & *Zool.* part of the trunk between the neck and the abdomen. □□ **tho·rac·ic** /thawrásik/ *adj.*

tho·ri·um /tháwreeəm, thór–/ *n. Chem.* radioactive metallic element. ¶ Symb.: **Th.**

thorn /thawrn/ *n.* **1** sharp-pointed projection on a plant. **2** thorn-bearing shrub or tree. □ **thorn in one's side** (or **flesh**) constant annoyance.

thorn·y /tháwrnee/ *adj.* (**thorn·i·er, thorn·i·est**) **1** having many thorns. **2** (of a subject) hard to handle without offense; problematic. □□ **thorn′i·ly** *adv.* **thorn′i·ness** *n.*

thor·ough /thúrō/ *adj.* **1** complete and unqualified; not superficial. **2** acting or done with great care and completeness. **3** absolute (*thorough nuisance*). □□ **thor′ough·ly** *adv.* **thor′ough·ness** *n.*

thor·ough·bred /thórōbred, thórə–, thúr–/ • *adj.* of pure breeding. • *n.* thoroughbred animal, esp. a horse.

thor·ough·fare /thórōfair, thórə–, thúr–/ *n.* road or path open at both ends, esp. for traffic.

thor·ough·go·ing /thórōgóing, thórə–, thúr–/ *adj.* complete; uncompromising; not superficial.

those *pl.* of THAT.

thou[1] /thow/ *pron. archaic* or *dial.* (*obj.* **thee**

/_thee_/; *poss.* **thy** or **thine**; *pl.* **ye** or **you**) second person singular pronoun.

thou[2] /thow/ *n.* (*pl.* same or **thous**) *colloq.* thousand.

though /_th_ō/ • *conj.* **1** in spite of being; despite the fact that. **2** (introducing a possibility) even if (*ask him, though he may refuse*). **3** and yet; nevertheless. • *adv. colloq.* however; all the same (*I wish you had told me, though*).

thought[1] /thawt/ *n.* **1** process or power of thinking; the faculty of reason. **2** way of thinking associated with a particular time, people, etc. (*medieval European thought*). **3** reflection; consideration; regard. **4** idea or piece of reasoning produced by thinking. **5** (usu. in *pl.*) what one is thinking; one's opinion.

thought[2] *past* and *past part.* of THINK.

thought·ful /tháwtfŏŏl/ *adj.* **1** engaged in or given to meditation. **2** (of a book, writer, remark, etc.) giving signs of serious thought. **3** considerate. □□ **thought′ful·ly** *adv.* **thought′ful·ness** *n.*

thought·less /tháwtlis/ *adj.* **1** careless of consequences or of others' feelings. **2** due to lack of thought. □□ **thought′less·ly** *adv.* **thought′less·ness** *n.*

thou·sand /thówzənd/ • *n.* (*pl.* **thou·sands** (in sense 1) **thou·sand**) (in *sing.* prec. by *a* or *one*) **1** product of a hundred and ten. **2** symbol for this (1,000; m; M). **3** (in *sing.* or *pl.*) *colloq.* large number. • *adj.* that amount to a thousand. □□ **thou′sand·fold** *adj.* & *adv.* **thou′sandth** *adj.* & *n.*

thrall /thrawl/ *n. literary* **1** slave. **2** bondage; slavery (*in thrall*). □□ **thrall′dom** *n.* (also **thral′dom**).

thrash /thrash/ • *v.* **1** *tr.* beat or whip severely. **2** *tr.* defeat thoroughly in a contest. **3** *intr.* (of a paddlewheel, branch, etc.) act like a flail; deliver repeated blows. **4** *intr.* (foll. by *about, around*) move or fling the limbs about violently or in panic. **5** *tr.* = THRESH 1. • *n.* act of thrashing. □ **thrash out** discuss to a conclusion. □□ **thrash′ing** *n.*

thrash·er /tháshər/ *n.* long-tailed N. American thrushlike birds.

thread /thred/ • *n.* **1 a** spun cotton, silk, glass, etc.; yarn. **b** length of this. **2** thin cord of twisted yarns used esp. in sewing and weaving. **3** continuous aspect of a thing (*the thread of life*). **4** spiral ridge of a screw. **5** (in *pl.*) *sl.* clothes. • *v.tr.* **1** pass a thread through (a needle). **2** put (beads) on a thread. **3** insert (a strip of film, tape, etc.) into equipment. **4** make (one's way) carefully through a crowded place, etc. □ **hang by a thread** be in a precarious state, position, etc. □□ **thread′er** *n.* **thread′like** *adj.*

thread·bare /thrédbair/ *adj.* **1** (of cloth) with the nap worn and the thread visible. **2** (of a person) wearing such clothes. **3 a** hackneyed. **b** feeble (*threadbare excuse*).

threat /thret/ *n.* **1** declaration of an intention to punish or hurt. **2** imminence of something undesirable (*threat of war*). **3** person or thing as a likely cause of harm, etc.

threat·en /thrét′n/ *v.tr.* **1 a** make a threat or threats against. **b** constitute a threat to. **2 b** be a sign of (something undesirable). **3** (also *absol.*) present imminent danger of (*clouds were threatening rain*). □□ **threat′en·er** *n.* **threat′en·ing** *adj.* **threat′en·ing·ly** *adv.*

thou ~ throne

three /three/ • *n.* **1 a** one more than two, or seven less than ten. **b** symbol for this (3, iii, III). • *adj.* that amount to three. □ **three-dimensional** having or appearing to have length, breadth, and depth. **three-ring circus 1** circus with three rings for simultaneous performances. **2** extravagant display. **the three Rs** reading, writing (*joc.* 'riting), and arithmetic (*joc.* 'rithmetic).

three·fold /thréefōld/ *adj.* & *adv.* **1** three times as much or as many. **2** consisting of three parts.

three·score /thréeskáwr/ *n. archaic* sixty.

three·some /thréesəm/ *n.* group of three persons.

thren·o·dy /thrénədee/ *n.* (also **thre·node** /thrénōd/) (*pl.* **–dies** or **thre·nodes**) song of lamentation or mourning.

thresh /thresh/ *v.* **1** *tr.* beat out or separate grain from (wheat, etc.). **2** *intr.* = THRASH *v.* 4. **3** *tr.* (foll. by *over*) analyze (a problem, etc.) in search of a solution. □ **thresh out** = *thrash out.* □□ **thresh′er** *n.*

thresh·old /thréshōld, thrésh-hōld/ *n.* **1** strip of wood or stone forming the bottom of a doorway. **2** point of entry or beginning (*threshold of a new century*). **3** limit (*pain threshold*).

threw *past* of THROW.

thrice /thris/ *adv. archaic* or *literary* **1** three times. **2** (esp. in *comb.*) highly (*thrice-blessed*).

thrift /thrift/ *n.* frugality. □ **thrift shop** store selling secondhand items.

thrift·y /thríftee/ *adj.* (**thrift·i·er, thrift·i·est**) economical; frugal. □□ **thrift′i·ly** *adv.* **thrift′i·ness** *n.*

thrill /thril/ • *n.* **1** a wave or nervous tremor of emotion or sensation (*thrill of joy*). **b** thrilling experience. **2** throb; pulsation. • *v.* **1** *intr.* & *tr.* feel or cause to feel a thrill. **2** *intr.* quiver or throb with or as with emotion. □ **thrills and spills** excitement of potentially dangerous activities. □□ **thrill′ing** *adj.* **thrill′ing·ly** *adv.*

thrill·er /thrílər/ *n.* exciting or sensational story or play, etc., esp. one involving crime or espionage.

thrive /thrīv/ *v.intr.* (*past* **throve** /thrōv/ or **thrived**; *past part.* **thriven** /thrívən/ or **thrived**) **1** prosper; flourish. **2** grow rich. **3** grow vigorously.

throat /thrōt/ *n.* **1 a** windpipe or gullet. **b** front part of the neck. **2** narrow passage, entrance, or exit. □ **cut one's own throat** bring about one's own downfall. **ram down a person's throat** force (a thing) on a person's attention. □□ **–throat′ed** *adj.* (in *comb.*).

throat·y /thrōtee/ *adj.* (**throat·i·er, throat·i·est**) (of a voice) hoarsely resonant. □□ **throat′i·ly** *adv.* **throat′i·ness** *n.*

throb /throb/ • *v.intr.* (**throbbed, throb·bing**) **1** pulsate, esp. with more than the usual force or rapidity. **2** vibrate with a persistent rhythm or with emotion. • *n.* **1** throbbing. **2** (esp. violent) pulsation.

throe /thrō/ *n.* (usu. in *pl.*) **1** violent pang, esp. of childbirth or death. **2** anguish. □ **in the throes of** struggling with the task of.

throm·bo·sis /thrombósis/ *n.* (*pl.* **throm·bo·ses** /–seez/) coagulation of the blood in a blood vessel or organ. □□ **throm·bot·ic** /–bótik/ *adj.*

throne /thrōn/ *n.* **1** chair of state for a sovereign, bishop, etc. **2** sovereign power (*came to the throne*).

throng /thrawng, throng/ ● *n.* crowd, esp. of people. ● *v.* **1** *intr.* come in great numbers. **2** *tr.* flock into or crowd around; fill with or as with a crowd.

throt·tle /thrót'l/ ● *n.* **1** valve controlling flow of fuel, steam, etc., in an engine. **2** lever or pedal operating this. ● *v.tr.* **1** choke; strangle. **2** prevent the utterance, etc., of. **3** control (an engine or steam, etc.) with a throttle.

through /throo/ (also **thru**) ● *prep.* **1 a** from end to end or from side to side of. **b** going in one side or end and out the other. **2** between or among. **3** from beginning to end of (*read through the letter*). **4** because of (*lost it through carelessness*). **5** up to and including (*Monday through Friday*). ● *adv.* through a thing; from side to side, end to end, or beginning to end. ● *attrib.adj.* (of traffic) going through a place to its destination. □ **be through** *colloq.* **1** have finished. **2** cease to have dealings. **3** have no further prospects (*is through as a politician*). **through and through** thoroughly; completely.

through·out /throo-ówt/ ● *prep.* right through; from end to end of. ● *adv.* in every part or respect.

through·put /throópoͦot/ *n.* amount of material put through a process, esp. in manufacturing or computing.

through·way /throó-way/ *n.* (also **thru'way**) thoroughfare, esp. a highway.

throve *past of* THRIVE.

throw /throͦ/ ● *v.tr.* (*past* **threw** /throͦo/; *past part.* **thrown** /throͦn/) **1** propel with force through the air. **2** force violently into a specified position or state. **3** compel suddenly to be in a specified condition (*thrown out of work*). **4** turn or move (part of the body) quickly or suddenly (*threw an arm out*). **5** project or cast (light, a shadow, etc.). **6 a** bring to the ground in wrestling. **b** (of a horse) unseat (its rider). **7** *colloq.* disconcert (*the question threw me*). **8 a** cast (dice). **b** obtain (a specified number) by throwing dice. **9** extend or provide (*threw a bridge across the river*). **10** operate (a switch or lever). **11** have (a fit or tantrum, etc.). **12** give (a party). **13** *colloq.* lose (a contest or race, etc.) intentionally. ● *n.* **1** act of throwing or being thrown. **2** distance a thing is or may be thrown. **3** light cover for furniture, etc. **4** (prec. by *a*) *sl.* each; per item (*sold at $10 a throw*). □ **throw away** **1** discard as useless or unwanted. **2** waste or fail to make use of (an opportunity, etc.). **throw down the gauntlet** (or **glove**) issue a challenge. **throw good money after bad** incur further loss in a hopeless attempt to recoup a previous loss. **throw one's hand in** **1** abandon one's chances in a card game, esp. poker. **2** give up; withdraw from a contest. **throw in** **1** interpose (a word or remark). **2** include at no extra cost. **throw in the towel** admit defeat. **throw off** **1** discard. **2** write or utter in an offhand manner. **3** confuse or distract (a person) from the matter in hand. **4** emit. **throw oneself at** seek blatantly as a spouse or sexual partner. **throw oneself into** engage vigorously in. **throw out** **1** put out forcibly or suddenly. **2** discard as unwanted. **throw over** desert or abandon. **throw stones** cast aspersions. **throw together** **1** assemble hastily. **2** bring into casual contact. **throw up** **1** *colloq.* vomit. **2** erect hastily. **throw one's weight around** (or **about**) *colloq.* act with unpleasant

self-assertiveness. □□ **throw'a·ble** *adj.* **throw'er** *n.* (also in *comb.*).

throw·a·way /thróͦway/ ● *adj.* **1** meant to be thrown away after (one) use. **2** (of lines, etc.) deliberately underemphasized. ● *n.* thing to be thrown away after (one) use.

throw·back /thróbak/ *n.* **1** reversion to ancestral character. **2** instance of this.

thru var. of THROUGH.

thrum /thrum/ ● *v.* (**thrummed, thrum·ming**) **1** *tr.* play (a stringed instrument) monotonously or unskillfully. **2** *intr.* drum idly. ● *n.* **1** such playing. **2** resulting sound.

thrush[1] /thrush/ *n.* any of various songbirds.

thrush[2] /thrush/ *n.* fungal disease, esp. one marked by whitish vesicles in the mouth and throat.

thrust /thrust/ ● *v.* (*past* and *past part.* **thrust**) **1** *tr.* push with a sudden impulse or with force. **2** *tr.* (foll. by *on, upon*) impose (a thing) forcibly. **3** *intr.* stab; lunge suddenly. ● *n.* **1** sudden or forcible push or lunge. **2** propulsive force developed by a jet or rocket engine. **3** military offensive. **4** stress between the parts of an arch, etc. **5** chief theme or gist of remarks, etc.

thru·way var. of THROUGHWAY.

thud /thud/ ● *n.* low dull sound as of a blow on a nonresonant surface. ● *v.intr.* (**thud·ded, thud·ding**) make or fall with a thud. □□ **thud'ding·ly** *adv.*

---

thud late Middle English (originally Scots): probably from Old English *thyddan* 'to thrust, push'; related to *thoden* 'violent wind.' The noun is recorded earlier, denoting a sudden blast or gust of wind, later the sound of a thunderclap, whence a dull heavy sound. The verb dates from the early 16th century.

---

thug /thug/ *n.* vicious ruffian. □□ **thug'ger·y** *n.* **thug'gish** *adj.* **thug'gish·ly** *adv.* **thug'gish·ness** *n.*

thu·li·um /thoóleeəm, thyoͦo–/ *n. Chem.* soft metallic element of the lanthanide series. ¶ Symb.: **Tm.**

thumb /thum/ ● *n.* **1** short thick finger on the human hand, set apart from the other four. **2** part of a glove, etc., for a thumb. ● *v.* **1** *tr.* wear or soil (pages, etc.) with a thumb (*well-thumbed book*). **2** *intr.* turn over pages with or as with a thumb. **3** *tr.* request or obtain (a lift) by signaling with a raised thumb. □ **all thumbs** clumsy with one's hands. **thumb one's nose** **1** put one's thumb up to one's nose with fingers extended up, a gesture of contempt. **2** display contempt or disdain. **thumbs-down** indication of rejection or failure. **thumbs-up** indication of satisfaction or approval. **under a person's thumb** completely dominated by a person. □□ **thumbed** *adj.* (also in *comb.*)

thumb·nail /thúmnayl/ *n.* **1** nail of a thumb. **2** (*attrib.*) concise (*thumbnail sketch*).

thumb·print /thúmprint/ *n.* impression of a thumb, esp. as used for identification.

thumb·screw /thúmskroͦo/ *n.* **1** instrument of torture for crushing the thumbs. **2** screw with a flattened head for turning with the thumb and forefinger.

thumb·tack /thúmtak/ *n.* tack with a flat head, pressed in with the thumb.

thump /thump/ • v. **1** tr. beat or strike heavily, esp. with the fist. **2** intr. throb strongly. **3** intr. (foll. by at, on, etc.) deliver blows (thumped on the door). **4** intr. tread heavily. • n. **1** heavy blow. **2** sound of this. □□ **thump′er** n.

thun·der /thúndər/ • n. **1** loud noise heard after a lightning flash and due to the expansion of rapidly heated air. **2** resounding, loud, deep noise. • v. **1** intr. produce sounds of thunder (it is thundering). **2** intr. make a noise like thunder. **3** tr. utter (approval, disapproval, etc.) loudly. **4** intr. (foll. by against, etc.) make violent threats, etc., against. □ **steal a person's thunder** spoil the effect of another's idea, action, etc., by expressing or doing it first. □□ **thun′der·er** n.

thun·der·bolt /thúndərbōlt/ n. **1** flash of lightning with a simultaneous crash of thunder. **2** unexpected occurrence or item of news.

thun·der·clap /thúndərklap/ n. crash of thunder.

thun·der·cloud /thúndərklowd/ n. cumulus cloud charged with electricity and producing thunder and lightning.

thun·der·head /thúndərhed/ n. rounded cumulus cloud projecting upward and heralding a thunderstorm.

thun·der·ous /thúndərəs/ adj. **1** like thunder. **2** very loud. □□ **thun′der·ous·ly** adv. **thun′der·ous·ness** n.

thun·der·show·er /thóndərshowər/ n. brief rain shower accompanied by thunder and sometimes lightning.

thun·der·storm /thúndərstawrm/ n. storm with thunder and lightning and usu. heavy rain or hail.

thun·der·struck /thúndərstruk/ adj. amazed; surprised.

Thur. abbr. Thursday.

Thurs. abbr. Thursday.

Thurs·day /thórzda/, –dee/ n. fifth day of the week, following Wednesday.

thus /thus/ adv. **1 a** in this way. **b** as indicated. **2 a** accordingly. **b** as a result or inference. **3** to this extent; so.
¶ There is never a need to expand the adverb **thus** to "thusly."

thwart /thwawrt/ • v.tr. frustrate or foil (a person or purpose, etc.). • n. rower's seat.

thy /thī/ poss.pron. (attrib.) (also **thine** /thīn/ before a vowel) of or belonging to thee.

thyme /tīm/ n. any of several aromatic herbs used for flavoring.

thy·mi pl. of THYMUS.

thy·mus /thíməs/ n. (pl. -mus·es or -mi /–mī/) Anat. lymphoid organ situated in the neck of vertebrates.

thy·roid /thíroyd/ n. (in full **thy′roid gland**) **1** large ductless gland in the neck of vertebrates, secreting a hormone that regulates growth and development. **2** extract prepared from the thyroid gland of animals and used in treating goiter, etc.

thy·self /thīsélf/ pron. archaic emphat. & refl. form of THOU[1], THEE.

Ti symb. Chem. titanium.

ti /tee/ n. (also **te**) seventh note of a major scale.

ti·ar·a /teeárə, –áarə, –áirə/ n. **1** jeweled ornamental band worn on the front of a woman's hair. **2** three-crowned diadem worn by a pope.

Ti·bet·an /tibét′n/ • n. **1 a** native of Tibet. **b**

person of Tibetan descent. **2** language of Tibet. • adj. of or relating to Tibet or its language.

tib·i·a /tíbeeə/ n. (pl. **tib·i·ae** /–bee-ee/) Anat. inner of two bones extending from the knee to the ankle. □□ **tib′i·al** adj.

tic /tik/ n. **1** habitual spasmodic contraction of the muscles, esp. of the face. **2** behavioral quirk.

tick[1] /tik/ • n. slight recurring click, esp. that of a watch or clock. • v. **1** intr. **a** (of a clock, etc.) make ticks. **b** (foll. by away) (of time, etc.) pass. **2** intr. (of a mechanism) function (see how it ticks). □ **tick off** sl. annoy; anger. **tick-tack-toe** (also **tic-tac-toe**) game of marking Xs or Os in a nine-square grid. **what makes a person tick** colloq. person's motivation.

tick[2] /tik/ n. parasitic arachnid on the skin of warm-blooded vertebrates.

tick[3] /tik/ n. **1** cover of a mattress or pillow. **2** = TICKING.

tick·er /tíkər/ n. colloq. **1** heart. **2** machine that receives and prints telegraphed messages onto paper tape. □ **ticker tape 1** paper strip from a ticker. **2** this or similar material thrown from windows, etc., to greet a celebrity.

tick·et /tíkit/ • n. **1** written or printed piece of paper or card entitling the holder to admittance, travel by public transport, etc. **2** notification of a traffic offense, etc. **3** label giving price, etc. **4** list of a political party's candidates. **5** (prec. by the) colloq. what is correct or needed. • v.tr. attach or serve a ticket to. □□ **tick′et·ed** adj.

tick·ing /tíking/ n. stout usu. striped material used to cover mattresses, etc.

tick·le /tíkəl/ • v. **1 a** tr. apply light touches or strokes to (a person, etc.) so as to produce laughter and spasmodic movement. **b** intr. feel this sensation (my foot tickles). **2** tr. excite agreeably; amuse. • n. **1** act of tickling. **2** tickling sensation. □ **tickled pink** (or **to death**) colloq. extremely amused or pleased. □□ **tick′ler** n. **tick′ly** adj.

---

tickle Middle English (in the sense 'be delighted or thrilled,' surviving in tickled pink): perhaps a frequentative of TICK[1], or an alteration of Scots and dialect kittle 'to tickle,' of Germanic origin and related to Dutch kittelen and German kizzeln.

---

tick·lish /tíklish/ adj. **1** sensitive to tickling. **2** (of a matter or person) requiring careful handling. □□ **tick′lish·ly** adv. **tick′lish·ness** n.

tid·al /tíd′l/ adj. relating to, like, or affected by tides. □ **tidal wave 1** = TSUNAMI **2** widespread manifestation of feeling, etc. □□ **tid′al·ly** adv.

tid·bit /tídbit/ n. **1** small morsel. **2** choice item of news, etc.

tid·dly·winks /tídleewingks/ n. game played by flicking counters into a cup, etc.

tide /tīd/ n. **1 a** periodic rise and fall of the sea due to the attraction of the moon and sun. **b** water as affected by this. **2** time or season (usu. in comb.: Yuletide). **3** marked trend of opinion, fortune, or events. □ **tide over** enable (a person) to deal with a difficult period, etc.

tide·ta·ble /tídtaybəl/ n. table indicating the times of high and low tides at a place.

tide·wa·ter /tídwawtər/, –wotər/ n. **1** water

brought by or affected by tides. **2** (*attrib.*) affected by tides (*tidewater region*).

ti·dings /tídingz/ *n.* (as *sing.* or *pl.*) news; information.

ti·dy /tídee/ ● *adj.* (**ti·di·er, ti·di·est**) **1** neat; orderly. **2** *colloq.* considerable (*tidy sum*). ● *v.tr.* (**–dies, –died**) (also *absol.*) put in good order; make tidy. □□ **ti′di·ly** *adv.* **ti′di·ness** *n.*

tie /tī/ ● *v.* (**ty·ing**) **1** *tr.* **a** attach or fasten with string, cord, etc. **b** link conceptually. **2** *tr.* **a** form (a string, ribbon, shoelace, necktie, etc.) into a knot or bow. **b** form (a knot or bow) in this way. **3** *tr.* restrict (a person) as to conditions, place, etc. (*tied to his job*). **4** *intr.* achieve the same score or place as another competitor. ● *n.* **1** cord, line, etc., used for fastening. **2** strip of material worn around the collar and tied in a knot at the front. **3** bond (*family ties*). **4** draw, dead heat, or equality of score among competitors. **5** beam laid horizontally as a support for railroad rails. □ **fit to be tied** *colloq.* very angry. **tie down** = TIE *v.* **3** above. **tie-dye** method of producing irregular dyed patterns by tying string, etc., to the fabric. **tie in** (foll. by *with*) bring into or have a close association or agreement. **tie-in** *n.* connection or association. **tie the knot** *colloq.* get married. **tie up 1** bind securely with cord, etc. **2** invest or reserve (capital, etc.) so that it is not immediately available for use. **3** secure (a boat, animal, etc.). **4** complete (an undertaking, etc.). **5** (usu. in *passive*) fully occupy (a person).

tie·pin /típin/ *n.* ornamental pin for holding a tie in place.

tier /teer/ *n.* vertical or sloped row, rank, or unit of structure. □□ **tiered** *adj.* (also in *comb.*).

tiff /tif/ *n.* slight or petty quarrel.

ti·ger /tígər/ *n.* **1** large Asian feline with a yellowish brown coat with black stripes. **2** domestic cat with similar striping. **3** fierce, energetic, or formidable person. □ **tiger-eye** (or **tiger's-eye**) lustrous, yellowish brown, striped gem. **tiger lily** tall garden lily with dark-spotted orange flowers.

tight /tīt/ ● *adj.* **1** closely held, drawn, fastened, etc. **2** too closely fitting. **3** impermeable; impervious, esp. (in *comb.*) to a specified thing (*watertight*). **4** tense; stretched. **5** *colloq.* drunk. **6** *colloq.* stingy. **7** (of money or materials) not easily obtainable. **8 a** (of precautions, etc.) stringent. **b** presenting difficulties (*tight situation*). **9** *colloq.* friendly; close. ● *adv.* tightly (*hold tight!*). □ **tight-fisted** stingy. **tight-lipped** secretive; taciturn. □□ **tight′ly** *adv.* **tight′ness** *n.*

tight·en /tít'n/ *v.* make or become tighter.

tight·rope /títrōp/ *n.* rope stretched tightly high above the ground, on which acrobats perform.

tights /tīts/ *n.pl.* thin but not sheer close-fitting wool or nylon, etc., garment covering the legs and lower body.

tight·wad /títwod/ *n. colloq.* person who is miserly or stingy.

ti·gress /tígris/ *n.* **1** female tiger. **2** fierce or passionate woman.

tike var. of TYKE.

til·de /tíldə/ *n.* mark (~), put over a letter, e.g., over a Spanish *n* when pronounced *ny* (as in *señor*).

tile /tīl/ ● *n.* **1** thin slab of concrete, baked clay,

etc., used for roofing, paving, etc. **2** similar slab of glazed pottery, cork, linoleum, etc., for covering a floor, wall, etc. **3** thin flat piece used in a game (esp. mah-jongg). ● *v.tr.* cover with tiles. □□ **til′er** *n.*

til·ing /tíling/ *n.* **1** process of fixing tiles. **2** area of tiles.

till[1] /til/ ● *prep.* **1** up to or as late as (*wait till six o'clock*). **2** up to the time of (*waited till the end*). ● *conj.* **1** up to the time when (*wait till I return*). **2** so long that (*laughed till I cried*). ¶ See note at UNTIL.

till[2] /til/ *n.* drawer for money in a store, bank, etc.

till[3] /til/ *v.tr.* cultivate (land). □□ **till′a·ble** *adj.* **till′er** *n.*

till·age /tílij/ *n.* **1** preparation of land for bearing crops. **2** tilled land.

till·er /tílər/ *n.* horizontal bar fitted to the head of a boat's rudder to turn it in steering.

tilt /tilt/ ● *v.* **1 a** *intr.* & *tr.* assume or cause to assume a sloping position; heel over. **b** lean or cause to lean toward one side of an opinion, action, etc. **2** *intr.* (foll. by *at*) strike, thrust, or run at with a weapon. **3** *intr.* (foll. by *with*) engage in a contest. ● *n.* **1** tilting. **2** sloping position. **3** inclination or bias. **4** (of medieval knights, etc.) charging with a lance against an opponent or at a mark. □ **full** (or **at full**) **tilt 1** at full speed. **2** with full force. □□ **tilt′er** *n.*

tim·ber /tímbər/ *n.* **1** standing trees suitable for lumber. **2** (esp. as *int.*) warning cry that a tree is about to fall. **3** piece of wood or beam, esp. as the rib of a vessel. □ **timber wolf** large N. American gray wolf. □□ **tim′ber·ing** *n.*

tim·ber·line /tímbərlīn/ *n.* line or level above which no trees grow.

tim·bre /támbər, tánbrə/ *n.* distinctive character of a musical sound or voice apart from its pitch and intensity.

Tim·buk·tu /tímbuktŏo/ *n. colloq.* any distant or remote place.

time /tīm/ ● *n.* **1** indefinite continued progress of existence, events, etc., in past, present, and future, regarded as a whole. **2** progress of this as affecting persons or things (*stood the test of time*). **3** portion of time; period (*prehistoric times*). **4** allotted or available portion of time (*no time to visit*). **5** point of time, esp. in hours and minutes (*the time is 7:30*). **6** (prec. by *a*) indefinite period (*waited for a time*). **7** particular reckoning of time (*in record time; eight o'clock Eastern time*). **8** occasion (*last time*). **9** opportune occasion or moment (*shall we set a time?*). **10** (in *pl.*) expressing multiplication (*five times six is thirty*). **11** (in *sing.* or *pl.*) **a** the conditions of life or of a period (*hard times*). **b** (prec. by *the*) the present age, or that being considered. **12** *colloq.* prison sentence (*is doing time*). **13** period of apprenticeship or military service. **14** date or expected date of childbirth or death. **15** any of several rhythmic patterns of music. ● *v.tr.* **1** choose the time for. **2** do at a chosen or correct time. **3** arrange the time of arrival of. **4** ascertain the time taken by. **5** regulate the duration or interval of. □ **against time** with utmost speed. **ahead of time** earlier than expected. **ahead of one's time** having ideas too advanced to be accepted by one's contemporaries. **all the time 1** throughout. **2** constantly. **at one time 1** in a known but unspecified past period. **2** simultaneously. **at the same time 1** simultaneously. **2** nevertheless. **for**

the time being until some other arrangement is made. **have no time for 1** be unable or unwilling to spend time on. **2** dislike. **have the time 1** be able to spend the time needed. **2** know from a watch, etc., what time it is. **in no** (or **less than no**) **time 1** very soon. **2** very quickly. **in time 1** punctual. **2** eventually. **3** in accordance with a given rhythm or tempo. **know the time of day** be well informed. **lose no time** act immediately. **on** (also **in**) **one's own time** outside working hours. **pass the time of day** *colloq.* exchange a greeting or casual remarks. **time after time** repeatedly; on many occasions. **time and** (or **time and time**) **again** on many occasions. **time and a half** rate of payment for work at one and a half times the normal rate. **time bomb** bomb designed to explode at a preset time. **time capsule** box, etc., containing objects typical of the present time, buried for discovery in the future. **time clock** clock with a device for recording workers' hours of work. **time exposure** exposure of photographic film for longer than the maximum normal shutter setting. **time-honored** esteemed by tradition or through custom. **time immemorial** longer time than anyone can remember or trace. **time off** time for rest or recreation, etc. **time of one's life** occasion of exceptional enjoyment. **time out** brief intermission in a game, etc. **time-share** share in a property under a time-sharing arrangement. **time-sharing** use of a vacation home at agreed different times by several joint owners. **time warp** imaginary distortion of space in relation to time. **time was** there was a time (*time was when I could do that*). **time zone** range of longitudes where a common standard time is used.

time·keep·er /tímkeepər/ *n.* **1** person who records time, esp. of workers or in a game. **2** watch or clock as regards accuracy. □□ **time′keep·ing** *n.*

time·less /tímlis/ *adj.* not affected by the passage of time; eternal. □□ **time′less·ly** *adv.* **time′less·ness** *n.*

time·ly /tímlee/ *adj.* (**time·li·er, time·li·est**) opportune; coming at the right time. □□ **time′li·ness** *n.*

time·piece /tímpees/ *n.* clock or watch.

tim·er /tímər/ *n.* **1** person or device that measures or records time taken. **2** automatic mechanism for activating a device, etc., at a preset time.

time·ta·ble /tímtaybəl/ *n.* list of times on a schedule, esp. arrivals and departures of buses, trains, etc.

tim·id /tímid/ *adj.* easily frightened; apprehensive; shy. □□ **ti·mid′i·ty** *n.* **tim′id·ly** *adv.* **tim′id·ness** *n.*

tim·ing /tíming/ *n.* **1** way an action or process is timed. **2** regulation of the opening and closing of valves in an internal combustion engine.

tim·o·rous /tímərəs/ *adj.* timid; fearful. □□ **tim′or·ous·ly** *adv.* **tim′or·ous·ness** *n.*

tim·pa·ni /tímpənee/ *n.pl.* (also **tym′pa·ni**) kettledrums. □□ **tim′pa·nist** *n.*

tin /tin/ • *n.* **1** *Chem.* silvery white metallic element used esp. in alloys and to form tin plate. ¶ Symb.: **Sn**. **2** = *tin plate.* • *v.tr.* (**tinned, tin·ning**) cover or coat with tin. □ **tin can** tin-plated container, esp. an empty one. **tin foil** foil made of tin, aluminum, or tin alloy, used for wrapping food. **Tin Pan Alley** the world of composers and publishers of popular music. **tin plate** sheet iron or sheet steel coated with tin. **tin-plate** *v.tr.* coat with tin.

tinc·ture /tíngkchər/ • *n.* **1** slight flavor or trace. **2** tinge (of a color). **3** medicinal solution (of a drug) in alcohol (*tincture of quinine*). • *v.tr.* **1** color slightly; tinge, flavor. **2** (often foll. by *with*) affect slightly (with a quality).

tin·der /tíndər/ *n.* dry substance that readily catches fire from a spark.

tin·der·box /tíndərboks/ *n.* **1** *hist.* box containing tinder, flint, and steel, for kindling fires. **2** potentially explosive or violent person, place, situation, etc.

tine /tīn/ *n.* prong, tooth, or point of a fork, comb, antler, etc. □□ **tined** *adj.* (also in *comb.*).

tinge /tinj/ • *v.tr.* (**tinge·ing** or **ting·ing**) **1** color slightly. **2** affect slightly. • *n.* **1** tendency toward or trace of some color. **2** slight admixture of a feeling or quality.

tin·gle /tínggəl/ • *v. intr.* feel or cause to feel a slight prickling, stinging, or throbbing sensation. • *n.* tingling sensation. □□ **tin′gly** *adj.*

tin·ker /tíngkər/ • *n.* itinerant mender of kettles, pans, etc. • *v. intr.* (foll. by *at, with*) work or repair in an amateurish or desultory way. □□ **tin′ker·er** *n.*

tin·kle /tíngkəl/ • *v.* **1** *intr. & tr.* make or cause to make a succession of short light ringing sounds. **2** *intr. colloq.* urinate. • *n.* tinkling sound.

tin·ni·tus /tíniŧəs, tíni-/ *n.* *Med.* ringing in the ears.

tin·ny /tínee/ *adj.* (**tin·ni·er, tin·ni·est**) **1** of or like tin. **2** flimsy; insubstantial. **3** (of sound) thin and metallic. □□ **tin′ni·ly** *adv.* **tin′ni·ness** *n.*

tin·sel /tínsəl/ *n.* **1** glittering metallic strips, threads, etc., used as decoration. **2** superficial brilliance or splendor. □□ **tin′seled** *adj.*

tint /tint/ • *n.* **1** light or delicate variety of a color. **2** tendency toward or admixture of a different color (*red with a blue tint*). **3** hair dye. • *v.tr.* apply a tint to; color. □□ **tint′er** *n.*

tin·tin·nab·u·la·tion /tíntinábyəláyshən/ *n.* ringing or tinkling of bells.

ti·ny /tínee/ *adj.* (**ti·ni·er, ti·ni·est**) very small or slight. □□ **ti′ni·ness** *n.*

-tion /shən/ *suffix* forming nouns of action, condition, etc. (see -ION, -ATION, -ITION, -UTION).

tip¹ /tip/ • *n.* **1** extremity or end, esp. of a small or tapering thing. **2** small piece or part attached to the end of a thing. • *v.tr.* (**tipped, tip·ping**) provide with a tip. □ **on the tip of one's tongue** about to be said, esp. after difficulty in recalling to mind. **tip of the iceberg** small evident part of something much larger.

tip² /tip/ • *v.* (**tipped, tip·ping**) **1** *intr.* lean or slant. **2** *tr.* cause to do this. • *n.* slight push or tilt. □ **tip the balance** make the critical difference.

tip³ /tip/ • *v.* (**tipped, tip·ping**) **1** *tr.* make a small present of money to, esp. for a service given. **2** *tr.* strike or touch lightly. • *n.* **1** small gift of money, esp. for a service given. **2** piece of private or special information, esp. regarding betting or investment. **3** small or casual piece of advice. □ **tip off** give (a person) helpful information or warning. **tip-off** hint or warning, etc. □□ **tip′per** *n.*

tip·ple /típəl/ *v. intr.* drink intoxicating liquor habitually. □□ **tip′pler** *n.*

tip·sy /típsee/ *adj.* (**tip·si·er, tip·si·est**) slightly intoxicated. □□ **tip′si·ly** *adv.* **tip′si·ness** *n.*

tiptoe ~ today 628

tip·toe /típtō/ • n. tips of the toes. • v.intr. (**tip·toes, tip·toed, tip·toe·ing**) walk on tiptoe, or very stealthily. • adv. (also **on tiptoe**) with the heels off the ground.

tip·top /típtóp/ colloq. • adj. & adv. highest in excellence. • n. highest point of excellence.

ti·rade /tírayd, tīráyd/ n. long vehement denunciation or declamation.

tire[1] /tīr/ v. 1 tr. & intr. make or grow weary. 2 tr. bore. 3 tr. (in passive; foll. by of) have had enough of (tired of arguing).

tire[2] /tīr/ n. rubber covering, usu. inflatable, that fits around a wheel rim.

tired /tīrd/ adj. 1 weary; ready for sleep. 2 hackneyed. □□ **tired′ly** adv. **tired′ness** n.

tire·less /tírlis/ adj. having inexhaustible energy. □□ **tire′less·ly** adv. **tire′less·ness** n.

tire·some /tírsəm/ adj. wearisome; tedious. □□ **tire′some·ly** adv. **tire′some·ness** n.

'tis /tiz/ archaic it is.

tis·sue /tíshoō/ n. 1 any coherent mass of specialized cells of which animals or plants are made. 2 = tissue paper. 3 disposable piece of thin, soft, absorbent paper for wiping, drying, etc. 4 fine, gauzy fabric. □ **tissue paper** thin, soft paper for wrapping, etc.

tit[1] /tit/ n. any of various small birds.

tit[2] /tit/ n. □ **tit for tat** /tat/ blow for blow; retaliation.

Ti·tan /tīt'n/ n. (often **titan**) person of very great strength, intellect, or importance.

ti·tan·ic /tītánik/ adj. gigantic; colossal. □□ **ti·tan′i·cal·ly** adv.

ti·ta·ni·um /tītáyneeəm, tee–/ n. Chem. gray metallic element. ¶ Symb.: **Ti**.

tithe /tīth/ n. one tenth of the annual product of land or labor, formerly taken as a church tax. • v. intr. pay tithes. □□ **tith′ing** n.

tit·il·late /tít'layt/ v.tr. 1 excite pleasantly. 2 tickle. □□ **tit′il·lat·ing·ly** adv. **tit·il·la·tion** /–láyshən/ n.

ti·tle /tít'l/ • n. 1 name of a book, work of art, etc. 2 heading of a chapter, document, etc. 3 book, etc., regarded in terms of its title (published 20 new titles). 4 caption or credit in a movie, broadcast, etc. 5 nomenclature indicating a person's status (e.g., professor, queen) or used as a form of address (e.g., Mr.). 6 championship. 7 Law a right to ownership of property with or without possession. **b** (foll. by to) just or recognized claim. • v.tr. give a title to. □ **title role** part in a play, etc., that gives its name (e.g., Othello).

ti·tled /tít'ld/ adj. having a title of nobility or rank.

tit·mouse /títmows/ n. (pl. **tit·mice** /–mīs/) any of various small birds.

tit·ter /títər/ • v.intr. laugh furtively; giggle. • n. furtive laugh.

tit·tle /tít'l/ n. 1 small stroke or dot. 2 particle.

tit·u·lar /tíchələr/ adj. 1 of or relating to a title. 2 in name or title only (titular ruler). □□ **tit′u·lar·ly** adv.

tiz·zy /tízee/ n. (pl. **–zies**) colloq. state of nervous agitation (in a tizzy).

TKO abbr. Boxing technical knockout.

Tl symb. Chem. thallium.

TLC abbr. colloq. tender loving care.

Tlin·git /tlíngkət, –gət, klíng–/ n. 1 a N. American people native to southern Alaska. **b** member of this people. 2 language of this people.

TM abbr. transcendental meditation.

Tm symb. Chem. thulium.

TN abbr. Tennessee (in official postal use).

TNT abbr. trinitrotoluene, a high explosive.

to /tōō; tə (when unstressed)/ • prep. 1 introducing a noun expressing: **a** what is reached, approached, or touched (fell to the ground). **b** what is aimed at (throw it to me). **c** as far as (went on to the end). **d** what is followed (made to order). **e** what is considered or affected (am used to that). **f** what is caused or produced (turn to stone). **g** what is compared (won by three to two). **h** what is increased (add it to mine). **i** what is involved or composed as specified (there is nothing to it). 2 introducing the infinitive: **a** as a verbal noun (to get there). **b** expressing purpose, consequence, or cause (we eat to live). **c** as a substitute for to + infinitive (wanted to come but was unable to). • adv. 1 in the normal or required position or condition (come to; heave to). 2 (of a door) in a nearly closed position. □ **to and fro** backward and forward.

toad /tōd/ n. 1 froglike amphibian breeding in water but living chiefly on land. 2 repulsive or detestable person. □□ **toad′ish** adj.

toad·stool /tódstōōl/ n. poisonous mushrooms.

toad·y /tódee/ • n. (pl. **–ies**) sycophant. • v.tr. & (foll. by to) intr. (**–ies, –ied**) behave servilely to; fawn upon. □□ **toad′y·ish** adj. **toad′y·ism** n.

toast /tōst/ • n. 1 sliced bread browned on both sides by radiant heat. 2 a person or thing in whose honor a company is requested to drink. **b** call to such a drink or an instance of it. • v. 1 tr. cook or brown by radiant heat. 2 intr. (of bread, etc.) become brown in this way. 3 tr. warm (one's feet, oneself, etc.) at a fire, etc. 4 tr. drink to the health or in honor of (a person or thing).

---

toast late Middle English (as a verb in the sense 'burn as the sun does, parch'): from Old French toster 'roast,' from Latin torrere 'parch.' Sense 2 derives from the practice of placing a small piece of toasted bread, flavored with spices, into a drink such as wine, later associated with the practice of toasting a woman in whose honor a company was requested to drink.

---

toast·er /tóstər/ n. electrical device for making toast.

toast·mas·ter /tóstmastər/ n. (fem. **toast·mis·tress** /–mistris/) person who announces toasts at a public occasion.

to·bac·co /təbákō/ n. (pl. **–cos**) 1 plant with narcotic leaves used for smoking, chewing, or snuff. 2 its leaves, esp. as prepared for smoking.

to·bog·gan /təbógən/ • n. narrow, runnerless sled curled up at the front, for use on snow. • v.intr. ride on a toboggan. □□ **to·bog′gan·er** n. **to·bog′gan·ing** n. **to·bog′gan·ist** n.

to·coph·er·ol /tōkófərawl, –rol/ n. any of several closely related vitamins, found in wheat germ oil, egg yolk, and leafy vegetables. Also called **vitamin E**.

to·day /tədáy/ • adv. 1 on this present day. 2 nowadays. • n. 1 this present day. 2 modern times.

tod·dle /tód'l/ • v.intr. walk with short unsteady steps. • n. toddling walk.

tod·dler /tódlər/ n. child who is just beginning to walk.

tod·dy /tódee/ n. (pl. **–dies**) drink of liquor with hot water, sugar, etc.

to-do /tədōō/ n. commotion or fuss.

toe /tō/ • n. **1** any of the five digits of the foot. **2** part of footwear that covers the toes. • v. (**toes, toed, toe·ing**) **1** tr. touch (a starting line, etc.) with the toes. **2** intr. (foll. by *in*, *out*) converge (or diverge) slightly at the front. □ **on one's toes** alert. **toe the line** conform, esp. unwillingly or under pressure. □□ **toed** adj. (also in *comb.*). **toe′less** adj.

toe·nail /tónayl/ n. nail at the tip of each toe.

tof·fee /táwfee, tóf–/ n. firm or hard candy made by boiling sugar, butter, etc.

to·fu /tófōō/ n. curd made from mashed soy beans.

tog /tog/ n. colloq. (usu. in pl.) item of clothing.

to·ga /tógə/ n. hist. ancient Roman citizen's loose flowing outer garment. □□ **to′gaed** adj.

TOGA

to·geth·er /təgéthər/ • adv. **1** in company or conjunction (*walking together*). **2** simultaneously (*both shouted together*). **3** one with another (*were talking together*). **4** so as to unite (*tied them together*). **5** into company or companionship. • adj. colloq. well organized or controlled. □ **together with** as well as.

to·geth·er·ness /təgéthərnis/ n. **1** being together. **2** feeling of comfort from being together.

tog·gle /tógəl/ • n. **1** pin or other crosspiece put through the eye of a rope, a link of a chain, etc., to keep it in place. **2** *Computing* switch action that is operated the same way but with opposite effect on successive occasions. □ **toggle switch** electric switch with a lever to be moved usu. up and down.

toil /toyl/ • v.intr. **1** work laboriously or incessantly. **2** make slow painful progress. • n. prolonged or intensive labor; drudgery. □□ **toil′er** n.

---

toil Middle English (in the senses 'strife' and 'contend verbally'): from Old French *tooillier* (verb), *tooil* (noun) 'confusion,' from Latin

tudiculare 'stir about,' from *tudicula* 'machine for crushing olives,' related to *tundere* 'crush.'

toi·let /tóylit/ n. **1 a** fixture, as in a bathroom, etc., for defecating and urinating. **b** lavatory. **2** process of washing oneself, dressing, etc. □ **toilet paper** (or **tissue**) paper for cleaning oneself after excreting. **toilet water** diluted perfume.

---

toilet mid-16th century: from French *toilette* 'cloth, wrapper,' diminutive of *toile*. The word originally denoted a cloth used as a wrapper for clothes, or occasionally a cloth placed around the shoulders during hairdressing; hence, the articles needed for washing and dressing or the process involved (sense 2). In the US the word came to denote a dressing-room, especially one with washing facilities, hence, a bathroom (early 20th century).

---

toi·let·ry /tóylitree/ n. (pl. **–ries**) (usu. in pl.) any of various articles or cosmetics used in washing, dressing, etc.

toi·lette /twaalét/ n. = TOILET 2.

toil·some /tóylsəm/ adj. involving toil; laborious.

to·ken /tókən/ n. **1** thing serving as a symbol, reminder, or mark (*token of affection*). **2** anything used to represent something else, esp. a metal disk, etc., used instead of money. **3** (*attrib.*) **a** nominal or perfunctory (*token effort*). **b** chosen by tokenism to represent a particular group (*token woman on the committee*). □ **by the same token 1** similarly. **2** moreover.

to·ken·ism /tókənizəm/ n. **1** esp. *Polit.* granting of minimum concessions, esp. to appease radical demands, etc. **2** making only a token effort.

told past and past part. of TELL.

tol·er·a·ble /tólərəbəl/ adj. **1** endurable. **2** fairly good. □□ **tol′er·a·bly** adv.

tol·er·ance /tólərəns/ n. **1** willingness or ability to tolerate; forbearance. **2** capacity to tolerate. **3** allowable variation in any measurable property.

tol·er·ant /tólərənt/ adj. **1** disposed to tolerate. **2** (foll. by *of*) enduring or patient. □□ **tol′er·ant·ly** adv.

tol·er·ate /tólərayt/ v.tr. **1** allow the existence or occurrence of without interference. **2** endure (suffering, etc.). **3** be able to take (a drug, radiation, etc.) without harm. □□ **tol·er·a·tion** /–áyshən/ n. **tol′er·a·tor** n.

toll¹ /tōl/ n. **1** charge to use a bridge, road, etc. **2** cost or damage caused by a disaster, etc. **3** charge for a long distance telephone call. □ **take its toll** be accompanied by loss, injury, etc.

toll² /tōl/ • v. **1 a** intr. (of a bell) sound with slow, uniform strokes. **b** tr. ring (a bell) in this way. **2** tr. strike (the hour). • n. **1** tolling. **2** stroke of a bell.

toll·booth /tólbōōth/ n. booth on toll road, bridge, etc., from which tolls are collected.

Tol·tec /tóltek, tól–/ n. **1 a** N. American people that flourished in Mexico before the Aztecs. **b** member of this people. **2** language of this people.

tom /tom/ n. male animal, esp. a cat (in full **tom′cat**) or a turkey.

tom·a·hawk /tómǝhawk/ *n.* Native American war ax.

to·ma·to /tǝmáytō, –maʹa–/ *n.* (*pl.* **–toes**) glossy red or yellow, pulpy edible fruit. **2** plant bearing this. □□ **to·ma·to·ey** *adj.*

tomb /tōōm/ *n.* **1** burial vault. **2** grave.

tom·boy /tómboy/ *n.* girl who behaves in a traditionally boyish way. □□ **tom·boy·ish** *adj.* **tom·boy·ish·ness** *n.*

tomb·stone /tōōmstōn/ *n.* stone over a grave, usu. with an epitaph.

tome /tōm/ *n.* large heavy book or volume.

tom·fool·er·y /tómfōōlǝree/ *n.* (*pl.* **–ies**) foolish behavior.

tom·my gun /tómee/ *n.* type of submachine gun.

tom·my·rot /tómeerot/ *n. sl.* nonsense.

to·mog·ra·phy /tǝmógrǝfee/ *n.* method of radiography displaying details in a selected plane within the body.

to·mor·row /tǝmáwrō, –mór–/ • *adv.* **1** on the day after today. **2** at some future time. • *n.* **1** the day after today. **2** the near future.

tom-tom /tómtom/ *n.* **1** early drum beaten with the hands. **2** tall drum used in jazz bands, etc.

ton /tun/ *n.* **1** (in full **short ton**) unit of weight equal to 2,000 lb. (907.19 kg). **2** (in full **long ton**) unit of weight equal to 2,240 lb. (1016.05 kg). **3** = *metric ton.* **4** (in full **dis·place'ment ton**) unit of measurement of a ship's weight or volume. **5** (usu. in *pl.*) *colloq.* large number or amount (*tons of money*). □ **weigh a ton** *colloq.* be very heavy.

ton·al /tōnǝl/ *adj.* **1** of or relating to tone or tonality. **2** (of a fugue, etc.) having repetitions of the subject at different pitches in the same key. □□ **ton'al·ly** *adv.*

to·nal·i·ty /tōnálitee/ *n.* (*pl.* **–ties**) **1** *Mus.* a relationship between the tones of a musical scale. **b** observance of a single tonic key as the basis of a composition. **2** color scheme of a picture.

tone /tōn/ • *n.* **1** musical or vocal sound, esp. with reference to its pitch, quality, and strength. **2** (often in *pl.*) expressive vocal manner or quality. **3** manner of expression in writing or speaking. **4** *Mus.* musical sound, esp. of a definite pitch and character. **5 a** general coloration or contrast in a picture. **b** tint or shade of a color. **6** prevailing attitude or sentiment. **7** proper firmness of bodily organs. • *v.tr.* **1** give the desired tone to. **2** modify the tone of. □ **tone arm** movable arm supporting the pickup of a record player. **tone-deaf** unable to perceive differences of musical pitch accurately. **tone down** make or become softer in tone. **tone up** make or become stronger in tone. □□ **tone'less** *adj.* **tone'less·ly** *adv.*

ton·er /tónǝr/ *n.* black or colored powder used in photocopiers, etc., to make letters, images, etc. on paper.

tongs /tawngz, tongz/ *n.pl.* (also **pair of tongs** *sing.*) instrument with two arms for grasping and holding.

tongue /tung/ • *n.* **1** fleshy muscular organ in the mouth used in tasting, licking, and swallowing, and (in humans) for speech. **2** tongue of an ox, etc., as food. **3** faculty of or tendency in speech (*a sharp tongue*). **4** particular language (*the German tongue*). **5** thing like a tongue in shape or position, esp.: **a** a long

low promontory. **b** a strip of leather, etc., under the laces in a shoe. **c** a projecting strip on a board, etc., fitting into the groove of another. • *v.* (**tongues, tongued, tongu·ing**) **1** *tr.* produce staccato, etc., effects with (a flute, etc.) by means of tonguing. **2** *intr.* use the tongue in this way. □ **gift of tongues** power of speaking in unknown languages, as one of the gifts of the Holy Spirit (Acts 2). **tongue-and-groove** applied to boards in which a tongue along one edge fits into a groove along the edge of the next. **tongue-in-cheek** *adj.* ironic; slyly humorous. • *adv.* insincerely or ironically. **tongue-lashing** severe scolding. **tongue-tied** too shy, embarrassed, or surprised to speak. **tongue twister** sequence of words difficult to pronounce quickly and correctly. **with one's tongue hanging out** eagerly or expectantly. □□ **tongued** *adj.* (also in *comb.*). **tongue'less** *adj.*

ton·ic /tónik/ • *n.* **1** invigorating medicine. **2** anything serving to invigorate. **3** = *tonic water.* **4** *Mus.* keynote. • *adj.* invigorating. □ **tonic water** carbonated water containing quinine. □□ **ton'i·cal·ly** *adv.*

to·night /tǝnít/ • *adv.* on the present or approaching evening or night. • *n.* the evening or night of the present day.

ton·nage /túnij/ *n.* **1** ship's internal cubic capacity or freight-carrying capacity. **2** charge per ton on freight or cargo.

tonne /tun/ *n.* = *metric ton.*

ton·sil /tónsǝl/ *n.* either of two small organs, one on each side of the root of the tongue.

ton·sil·lec·to·my /tónsilléktǝmee/ *n.* (*pl.* **–mies**) surgical removal of the tonsils.

ton·sil·li·tis /tónsilítis/ *n.* inflammation of the tonsils.

ton·so·ri·al /tonsáwreeǝl/ *adj.* usu. *joc.* of or relating to a barber or hairdressing.

ton·sure /tónshǝr/ • *n.* **1** shaving of the crown of the head or the entire head, esp. of a person entering a monastic order. **2** bare patch made in this way. • *v.tr.* give a tonsure to.

too /tōō/ *adv.* **1** to a greater extent than is desirable, permissible, etc. (*too large*). **2** *colloq.* extremely (*too kind*). **3** in addition (*are they coming, too?*). **4** moreover (*consider, too, the time of year*). □ **none too** barely or not at all (*feeling none too good*).

took *past of* TAKE.

tool /tōōl/ • *n.* **1** implement used to carry out mechanical functions manually or by machine. **2** thing used in an occupation or pursuit (*tools of one's trade*). **3** person used as a mere instrument by another. • *v.tr.* **1** dress (stone) with a chisel. **2** impress a design on (leather). **3** (foll. by *along, around*, etc.) *sl.* drive or ride, esp. in a casual or leisurely manner. □□ **tool'er** *n.*

tool·mak·er /tōōlmaykǝr/ *n.* person who makes precision tools. □□ **tool'mak·ing** *n.*

toot /tōōt/ • *n.* **1** short sharp sound as made by a horn. **2** *sl.* drinking session; binge. • *v.* **1** *tr.* sound (a horn, etc.) with a short sharp sound. **2** *intr.* give out such a sound. □□ **toot'er** *n.*

tooth /tōōth/ • *n.* (*pl.* **teeth** /teeth/) **1** each of a set of hard, bony, enamel-coated structures in the jaws of most vertebrates, used for biting and chewing. **2** toothlike part or projection, e.g., the cog of a gearwheel, point of a saw or comb, etc. **3** (in *pl.*) force; effectiveness (*penalties give the contract teeth*). □ **armed to the teeth** completely and elaborately armed. **fight tooth and nail** fight very fiercely. **get** (or **sink**) **one's teeth into** devote oneself seriously to. **in the teeth of 1** in spite of (opposition or difficulty, etc.). **2** contrary to (instructions, etc.). **3** directly against (the wind, etc.). □□ **toothed** *adj.* (also in *comb.*). **tooth′less** *adj.* **tooth′like** *adj.*

tooth·ache /tŏŏthayk/ *n.* pain in a tooth or teeth.

tooth·brush /tŏŏthbrush/ *n.* brush for cleaning the teeth.

tooth·paste /tŏŏthpayst/ *n.* paste for cleaning the teeth.

tooth·pick /tŏŏthpik/ *n.* small sharp instrument for removing food lodged between the teeth.

tooth·some /tŏŏthsəm/ *adj.* **1** delicious. **2** attractive. □□ **tooth′some·ly** *adv.* **tooth′some·ness** *n.*

tooth·y /tŏŏthee/ *adj.* (**tooth·i·er, tooth·i·est**) having large, numerous, or prominent teeth.

too·tle /tŏŏt'l/ *v.intr.* **1** toot gently or repeatedly. **2** *colloq.* move casually or aimlessly. □□ **too′tler** *n.*

top[1] /top/ • *n.* **1** highest point or part. **2** highest rank or place. **3** upper part or surface. **4** garment for the upper part of the body. **5** lid of a jar, saucepan, etc. **6** utmost degree; height (*at the top of his voice*). **7** (in *pl.*) *colloq.* person or thing of the best quality (*tops at swimming*). • *adj.* **1** highest in position (*top shelf*). **2** highest in degree or importance (*top speed*). • *v.tr.* (**topped, top·ping**) **1** provide with a top, cap, etc. **2** be higher or better than; surpass (*topped the list*). □ **on top** in a superior position; above. **on top of 1** fully in command of. **2** in close proximity to. **3** in addition to. **on top of the world** *colloq.* exuberant. **top banana 1** *Theatr. sl.* comedian who tops the bill of a show. **2** *sl.* head of an organization, etc. **top brass** esp. Mil. *colloq.* highest ranking officers, etc. **top dog** *colloq.* victor or master. **top drawer** *colloq.* high social position or origin. **top-drawer** *colloq.* of high social standing; of the highest level or quality. **top-notch** *colloq.* first rate. **top off 1** put an end or the finishing touch to (a thing). **2** fill up, esp. a container already partly full. **top secret** of the highest secrecy. □□ **top′most** *adj.*

top[2] /top/ *n.* twirling toy that spins on a point.

to·paz /tṓpaz/ *n.* transparent or translucent mineral, usu. yellow, used as a gem.

top·coat /tópkōt/ *n.* **1** overcoat. **2** outer coat of paint, etc.

top-heav·y /tóphévee/ *adj.* **1** disproportionately heavy at the top. **2** (of an organization, etc.) having a disproportionately large number of people in administrative positions. □□ **top′-heav·i·ness** *n.*

to·pi·ar·y /tópee-eree/ • *adj.* of or formed by clipping shrubs, trees, etc., into ornamental shapes. • *n.* (*pl.* **–ies**) topiary art.

top·ic /tópik/ *n.* subject of a discourse, conversation, argument, etc.

top·i·cal /tópikəl/ *adj.* **1** dealing with the news, current affairs, etc. **2** (of medicine, etc.) applied to or affecting a part of the body. □□ **top·i·cal·i·ty** /-kálitee/ *n.* **top′i·cal·ly** *adv.*

top·knot /tópnot/ *n.* knot, tuft, crest, or bow worn or growing on the head.

top·less /tóplis/ *adj.* **1** without a top. **2 a** (of clothes) having no upper part. **b** (of a person) barebreasted. **c** (of a place) where women go or work topless. □□ **top′less·ness** *n.*

top·mast /tópmast/ *n. Naut.* mast next above the lower mast.

to·pog·ra·phy /təpógrəfee/ *n.* **1** detailed description, mapping, etc., of the features of a town, district, etc. **2** such features. □□ **to·pog′ra·pher** *n.* **top·o·graph·ic** /tópəgráfik/ *adj.* **top·o·graph′i·cal** *adj.* **top·o·graph′i·cal·ly** *adv.*

top·ping /tóping/ *n.* thing that tops another thing, as on cake, ice cream, pizza, etc.

top·ple /tópəl/ *v.* (usu. foll. by *over, down*) **1** fall or cause to fall as if top-heavy. **2** overthrow.

top·sail /tópsayl, –səl/ *n.* square sail next above the lowest; fore-and-aft sail on a gaff.

top·side /tópsīd/ *n.* side of a ship above the waterline.

top·soil /tópsoyl/ *n.* top layer of soil.

top·spin /tópspin/ *n.* spinning motion imparted to a ball in tennis, etc., by hitting it forward and upward.

top·sy-tur·vy /tópseetɔ́rvee/ *adv. & adj.* **1** upside down. **2** in utter confusion.

toque /tōk/ *n.* woman's small brimless hat.

tor /tor/ *n.* hill or rocky peak.

torch /tawrch/ • *n.* **1** thing lit for illumination. **2** source of heat, illumination, or enlightenment (*torch of freedom*). • *v.tr. sl.* set alight with or as with a torch. □ **carry a torch for** suffer from unrequited love for. **torch song** popular song of unrequited love.

tore *past of* TEAR[1].

tor·e·a·dor /táwreeədor/ *n.* bullfighter, esp. on horseback.

to·ri·i /táwree-ee/ *n.* (*pl.* same) gateway of a Shinto shrine, with two uprights and two crosspieces.

TORII

tor·ment • *n.* /táwrment/ **1** severe physical or mental suffering. **2** cause of this. • *v.tr.* /tawrmént/ **1** subject to torment. **2** tease or worry excessively. □□ **tor·men′tor** *n.*

torn *past part.* of TEAR[1].

tor·na·do /tawrnáydō/ *n.* (*pl.* **–does**) violent, usu. localized storm with whirling winds in a funnel-shaped cloud.

tor·pe·do /tawrpéedō/ • *n.* (*pl.* **–does**) cigarshaped, self-propelled, underwater explosive missile. • *v.tr.* (**–does, –doed**) **1** destroy or attack with a torpedo. **2** destroy (a policy, institution, plan, etc.).

tor·pid /táwrpid/ *adj.* **1** sluggish; inactive; dull; apathetic. **2** (of a hibernating animal) dormant. □□ **tor·pid′i·ty** *n.* **tor′pid·ly** *adv.* **tor′pid·ness** *n.*

tor·por /táwrpər/ *n.* torpidity. □□ **tor·por·if·ic** /–pərífik/ *adj.*

torque /tawrk/ *n. Mech.* moment of a system of forces tending to cause rotation.

tor·rent /táwrənt, tór–/ *n.* **1 a** rushing stream of liquid. **2** (usu. in *pl.*) great downpour of rain. **3** violent or copious flow. □□ **tor·ren·tial** /tərénshəl/ *adj.* **tor·ren'tial·ly** *adv.*

tor·rid /táwrid, tór–/ *adj.* **1 a** (of the weather) very hot and dry. **b** (of land, etc.) parched by such weather. **2** passionate; intense. □ **torrid zone** the part of the earth between the Tropics of Cancer and Capricorn. □□ **tor'rid·ly** *adv.* **tor'rid·ness** *n.*

tor·sion /táwrshən/ *n.* twisting, esp. of one end of a body while the other is held fixed.

tor·so /táwrsō/ *n.* (*pl.* **–sos** or **tor·si**) **1** trunk of the human body. **2** statue of this.

tort /tawrt/ *n. Law* breach of duty (other than under contract) leading to liability for damages.

torte /táwrt/ *n.* elaborate sweet cake.

tor·ti·lla /tawrtéeyə/ *n.* thin, flat, orig. Mexican corn or wheat bread eaten with or without a filling.

tor·toise /táwrtəs/ *n.* turtle, esp. a land turtle. □□ **tor'toise·like** *adj. & adv.*

tor·toise·shell /táwrtəs-shel/ • *n.* yellowish brown, mottled or clouded outer shell of some turtles, used for jewelry, etc. • *adj.* having the coloring or appearance of tortoiseshell.

tor·tu·ous /táwrchŏŏəs/ *adj.* **1** full of twists and turns. **2** devious; circuitous. □□ **tor·tu·os·i·ty** /–ósitee/ *n.* (*pl.* **–ties**) **tor'tu·ous·ly** *adv.* **tor'tu·ous·ness** *n.*

¶ **Tortuous** means 'full of twists and turns' or 'devious; circuitous,' e.g., *The path was tortuous and strewn with boulders.* **Torturous** is derived from *torture* and means 'involving torture; excruciating,' e.g., *I found the concert torturous because of the music's volume.*

tor·ture /táwrchər/ • *n.* **1** infliction of severe bodily pain, esp. as a punishment or a means of persuasion. **2** severe physical or mental suffering. • *v.tr.* subject to torture. □□ **tor'tur·er** *n.* **tor'tur·ous** *adj.* **tor'tur·ous·ly** *adv.*

To·ry /táwree/ • *n.* (*pl.* **–ries**) **1** esp. *Brit. colloq.* a supporter or member of the Conservative party. **2** *Hist.* member of the British party that gave rise to the Conservative party (opp. WHIG). **3** colonist loyal to the English during the American Revolution. • *adj. colloq.* of or characteristic of Conservatives or the Conservative party. □□ **To'ry·ism** *n.*

toss /taws, tos/ • *v.* **1** *tr.* throw up (a ball, etc.). **2** *tr. & intr.* roll about, throw, or be thrown, restlessly or from side to side. **3** *tr.* throw (a thing) lightly or carelessly. **4** *tr.* **a** throw (a coin) into the air to decide a choice, etc., by the side on which it lands. **b** (also *absol.*) settle a question or dispute with (a person) in this way (*tossed him for the armchair*). **5** *tr.* prepare (salads, etc.) by mixing or shaking. • *n.* **1** act of tossing (a coin, etc.). **2** fall, esp. from a horse. □ **toss-up** *n.* **1** doubtful matter; even chance (*it's a toss-up whether he wins*). **2** tossing of a coin. □□ **toss'er** *n.*

tot /tot/ *n.* small child.

to·tal /tót'l/ • *adj.* **1** complete; comprising the whole. **2** absolute (*in total ignorance*). • *n.* total number or amount. • *v.* (**to·taled, to·tal·ing;**

to·talled, to·tal·ling) **1** *tr.* **a** amount in number to (*they totaled 131*). **b** find the total of (things, a set of numbers, etc.). **2** *intr.* (foll. by *to, up to*) amount to. **3** *tr. sl.* demolish. □□ **to'tal·ly** *adv.*

to·tal·i·tar·i·an /tōtálitáireeən/ • *adj.* of a dictatorial government requiring complete subservience. • *n.* person advocating such a system. □□ **to·tal·i·tar'i·an·ism** *n.*

to·tal·i·ty /tōtálitee/ *n.* complete amount.

tote /tōt/ *v.tr. colloq.* carry; convey. □ **tote bag** open-topped bag for shopping, etc. □□ **tot'er** *n.* (also in *comb.*).

to·tem /tótəm/ *n.* **1** natural object or animal adopted by Native American people as an emblem of a clan or individual. **2** image of this. □ **totem pole** pole on which totems are carved or hung. □□ **to·tem·ic** /–témik/ *adj.* **to'tem·ism** *n.*

TOTEM POLE

tot·ter /tótər/ • *v.intr.* **1** stand or walk unsteadily or feebly. **2 a** shake as if about to collapse. **b** (of a system of government, etc.) be about to fall. • *n.* unsteady or shaky movement. □□ **tot'ter·er** *n.* **tot'ter·y** *adj.*

tou·can /tóokan/ *n.* tropical American fruit-eating bird with an immense beak and brightly colored plumage.

touch /tuch/ • *v.* **1** *tr.* come into or be in physical contact with (another thing). **2** *tr.* bring the hand, etc., into contact with. **3 a** *intr.* (of two things, etc.) be in or come into contact. **b** *tr.* bring (two things) into contact (*they touched hands*). **4** *tr.* rouse tender or painful feelings in (*touched by his appeal*). **5** *tr.* strike lightly. **6** *tr.* (usu. with *neg.*) **a** disturb or harm (*don't touch my things*). **b** have any dealings with (*won't touch that subject*). **c** consume; make use of (*dare not touch alcohol; need not touch your savings*). **7** *tr.* concern. **8** *tr.* (usu. with *neg.*) approach in excellence, etc. (*can't touch him for style*). **9** *tr.* (as **touched** *adj.*) slightly mad. • *n.* **1** act of touching. **2 a** faculty of perception through physical contact, esp. with the fingers. **b** qualities of an object, etc., as perceived in this way (*soft touch* *of silk*). **3** small amount; slight trace. **4 a** manner of playing keys or strings. **b** response of the keys or strings. **c** distinguishing style of workmanship, writing, etc. **5** *sl.* act of asking for and getting money, etc., from a person. □ **easy touch** *sl.* person who readily parts with money. **finishing touch** (or **touch´es**) final details completing and enhancing a piece of work, etc. **in touch** (often foll. by *with*) **1** in communication. **2** up to date, esp. regarding news, etc. **3** aware. **lose touch 1** cease to be informed. **2** cease to be in contact. **lose one's touch** not show one's customary skill. **out of touch 1** not in correspondence. **2** not up to date. **3** lacking in awareness (*out of touch with his son's beliefs*). **soft touch** = *easy touch* (above). **touch and go** risky. **touch base** (**with**) make contact with. **touch down** (of an aircraft or spacecraft) make contact with the ground in landing. **touch football** football with touching in place of tackling. **touch-me-not** any of various plants with ripe seed capsules bursting open when touched. **touch off 1** explode by touching with a match, etc. **2** initiate (a process) suddenly. **touch on** (or **upon**) **1** refer to or mention casually. **2** verge on (*touches on impudence*). **touch-tone** of or relating to a tone dialing telephone system. **touch-type** type without looking at the keys. **touch typing** this skill. **touch typist** person who touch-types. **touch up** give finishing touches to or retouch. □□ **touch´a·ble** *adj.* **touch´er** *n.*

touch·down /túchdown/ *n.* **1** act of landing by an aircraft. **2** *Football* act or instance of scoring by crossing the goal line.

tou·ché /tōōsháy/ *int.* **1** acknowledgment of a hit by a fencing opponent. **2** acknowledgment of a justified accusation, witticism, or point made in reply to one's own.

touch·ing /túching/ *adj.* moving; pathetic. □□ **touch´ing·ly** *adv.*

touch·stone /túchstōn/ *n.* **1** dark schist or jasper used for testing alloys by marking it with them. **2** criterion.

touch·y /túchee/ *adj.* (**touch·i·er, touch·i·est**) **1** apt to take offense; overly sensitive. **2** not to be touched without danger; ticklish; risky; awkward. □□ **touch´i·ly** *adv.* **touch´i·ness** *n.*

tough /tuf/ • *adj.* **1** hard to break, cut, tear, or chew. **2** able to endure hardship; hardy. **3** unyielding; difficult. **4** *colloq.* **a** acting sternly. **b** (of circumstances, luck, etc.) severe; hard. **5** *colloq.* criminal or violent (*tough guys*). • *n.* tough person, esp. a hoodlum. □ **tough it out** *colloq.* endure or withstand difficult conditions. □□ **tough´en** *v.* **tough´en·er** *n.* **tough´ly** *adv.* **tough´ness** *n.*

tou·pee /tōōpáy/ *n.* hairpiece to cover a bald spot.

tour /tōōr/ • *n.* **1** pleasure journey from place to place. **2** term of military or diplomatic duty. **3** series of performances, games, etc., at different places. • *v.* **1** *intr.* make a tour (*toured through Italy*). **2** *tr.* make a tour of (a country, etc.). □ **on tour** (esp. of a team, theater company, etc.) touring.

tour de force /tōōr də fáwrs/ *n.* feat of strength or skill.

tour·ism /tōōrizəm/ *n.* tourist booking and travel.

tour·ist /tōōrist/ *n.* person traveling for pleasure (often *attrib.*: *tourist accommodations*).

tour·ma·line /tōōrməlin, –leen/ *n.* mineral of

various colors used in electrical and optical instruments and as a gemstone.

tour·na·ment /tōōrnəmənt, tór–/ *n.* **1** large contest of many rounds. **2** *hist.* pageant with jousting.

tour·ney /tōōrnee, tór–/ *n.* tournament.

tour·ni·quet /tərnikit, tōōr–/ *n.* device for stopping arterial blood flow.

tou·sle /tówzəl/ *v.tr.* make (esp. the hair) untidy; rumple.

tout /towt/ • *v.* **1** *tr.* & *intr.* solicit patronage persistently. **2** *intr.* **a** spy out the movements and condition of racehorses in training. **b** offer racing tips for profit. • *n.* person who touts. □□ **tout´er** *n.*

---

tout Old English *tȳtan* 'look out,' of Germanic origin; related to Dutch *tuit* 'spout, nozzle.' The Old English meaning gave rise to the sense 'be on the lookout'; hence 'be on the lookout for customers, solicit' (mid-18th century), also 'watch, spy on' (early 19th century).

---

tow /tō/ • *v.tr.* pull along by a rope, etc. • *n.* towing; being towed. □ **have in tow 1** be towing. **2** be accompanied by and often in charge of (a person).

toward /tawrd, təwáwrd, twawrd/ (also **towards** /tawrdz, təwáwrdz, twawrdz/) *prep.* **1** in the direction of (*set out toward town*). **2** as regards; in relation to (*attitude toward death*). **3** as a contribution to; for (*toward your expenses*). **4** near (*toward the end of our journey*).

tow·el /tówəl/ • *n.* piece of absorbent cloth or paper used for drying after washing. • *v.* **1** *tr.* (often *refl.*) wipe or dry with a towel. **2** *intr.* wipe or dry oneself with a towel. □□ **tow´el·ing** *n.*

tow·er /tówər/ • *n.* **1** tall structure, often part of a church, castle, etc. **2** fortress, etc., with a tower. **3** tall structure housing machinery, etc. (*cooling tower; control tower*). • *v.intr.* **1** reach or be high or above; be superior. **2** (as **towering** *adj.*) **a** high; lofty (*towering intellect*). **b** violent (*towering rage*).

tow·head /tóhed/ *n.* person with very light blond hair. □□ **tow´head·ed** *adj.*

town /town/ *n.* **1 a** defined area between a village and a city in size. **b** densely populated area, esp. as opposed to the country. **2** central business area in a neighborhood (*going into town*). □ **go to town** *colloq.* act with energy or enthusiasm. **on the town** *colloq.* enjoying the entertainments of a town; celebrating. **town hall** building for the administration of local government. **town house 1** town residence, esp. of a person with a house in the country. **2** house in a development.

town·ie /tównee/ *n. colloq.* person living in a town, esp. as opposed to a student, etc.

towns·folk /tównzfōk/ *n.* inhabitants of a town.

town·ship /tównship/ *n.* division of a county in some states, having limited corporate powers.

towns·peo·ple /tównzpeepəl/ *n.pl.* inhabitants of a town.

tox·e·mi·a /tokseémeeə/ *n.* blood poisoning.

tox·ic /tóksik/ *adj.* **1** of poison. **2** poisonous. □□ **tox·ic·i·ty** /–sísitee/ *n.*

tox·i·col·o·gy /tóksikóləjee/ *n.* scientific study

of poisons. □□ **tox·i·co·log·i·cal** /–kəlójikəl/ adj. **tox·i·col'o·gist** n.

tox·in /tóksin/ n. poison produced by a living organism.

toy /toy/ • n. **1** plaything. **2** thing regarded as providing amusement. **3** (usu. attrib.) diminutive breed of dog, etc. • v.intr. (usu. foll. by with) **1** trifle; amuse oneself; flirt. **2** move a thing idly.

tp. abbr. **1** (also **t.p.**) title page. **2** township. **3** troop.

tpk. abbr. turnpike.

trace[1] /trays/ • v.tr. **1 a** observe, or find vestiges or signs of by investigation. **b** follow or mark the track or position of. **c** follow to its origins (can trace my family to the 12th century). **2** copy (a drawing, etc.) by drawing over its lines on superimposed translucent paper. **3** mark out, often laboriously (traced out a plan). **4** pursue one's way along (a path, etc.). • n. **1 a** indication of something having existed; vestige. **b** very small quantity. **2** track; footprint. □ **trace element 1** chemical element occurring in minute amounts. **2** chemical element required only in minute amounts by living organisms for normal growth. □□ **trace'a·ble** adj. **trace·a·bil'i·ty** n.

trace[2] /trays/ n. each of two straps, chains, or ropes by which a horse draws a vehicle.

trac·er /tráysər/ n. **1** person or thing that traces. **2** bullet, etc., that is visible in flight because of flames, etc., emitted. **3** radioactive isotope that can be followed through the body by the radiation it produces.

trac·er·y /tráysəree/ n. (pl. **-ies**) **1** ornamental stone openwork, esp. in the upper part of a Gothic window. **2** fine decorative pattern.

tra·che·a /tráykeeə/ n. (pl. **tra·che·ae** /–kée-ee/ or **tra·che·as**) windpipe. □□ **tra'che·al** adj.

tra·che·ot·o·my /traykeeótəmee/ n. (pl. **-mies**) incision in the trachea to remove an obstruction.

trac·ing /tráysing/ n. **1** copy of a drawing, etc., made by tracing. **2** act of tracing. □ **tracing paper** translucent paper for tracing.

track /trak/ • n. **1** mark or marks left by a person, animal, or thing in passing. **2** rough path, esp. one beaten by use. **3** continuous line of railroad rails. **4** a racecourse. **b** prepared course for runners, etc. **c** various sports performed on a track, as running or hurdles. **5** section of a record, compact disc, etc., containing one song, etc. **6** line of travel or motion. **7** line of reasoning or thought. • v.tr. **1** follow the track of. **2** trace (a course, development, etc.). **3** make a track with (dirt, etc.) from the feet. □ **in one's tracks** colloq. where one stands (stopped him in his tracks). **keep** (or **lose**) **track of** follow (or fail to follow) the course of. **make tracks** colloq. go or run away. **off the track** away from the subject. **on the wrong side of the tracks** colloq. in an inferior or dubious part of town. **on the wrong** (or **right**) **track** following the wrong (or right) line of inquiry. **track down** reach or capture by tracking. **track record** person's past performance.

tract[1] /trakt/ n. **1** region or area of indefinite, esp. large, extent. **2** Anat. bodily organ or system (respiratory tract).

tract[2] /trakt/ n. pamphlet, esp. political or religious.

trac·ta·ble /tráktəbəl/ adj. easily handled; manageable. □□ **trac·ta·bil'i·ty** n.

trac·tion /trákshən/ n. **1** act of drawing or pulling a thing over a surface. **2** therapeutic pulling on a limb, muscle, etc. **3** gripping power on a surface.

trac·tor /tráktər/ n. vehicle used for hauling machinery, heavy loads, etc. □ **tractor-trailer** truck consisting of a tractor or cab unit attached to a trailer.

trade /trayd/ • n. **1 a** buying and selling. **b** this between nations, etc. **c** business conducted for profit (esp. as distinct from a profession). **d** business of a specified nature or time (tourist trade). **2** skilled professional craft. **3** transaction, esp. a swap. **4** (usu. in pl.) = trade wind. • v. **1** intr. engage in trade; buy and sell. **2** tr. **a** exchange in commerce; barter (goods). **b** exchange (insults, blows, etc.). **3** intr. have a transaction with a person for a thing. □ **trade deficit** extent by which a country's imports exceed its exports. **trade in** exchange (esp. a used car, etc.) in part payment for another. **trade-in** n. thing exchanged in this way. **trade off** exchange, esp. as a compromise. **trade-off** n. such an exchange. **trade on** take advantage of (a person's reputation, etc.). **trade secret 1** secret device or technique used esp. in a trade. **2** joc. any secret. **trade wind** wind blowing continually toward the equator and deflected westward. □□ **trad'a·ble**, **trade'a·ble** adj.

trade·mark /tráydmaark/ n. **1** device, word, or words, secured by law or custom as representing a company, product, etc. **2** distinctive characteristic, etc.

trad·er /tráydər/ n. person, ship, etc., engaged in trade.

trades·man /tráydzmən/ n. (pl. **-men**; fem. **trades·wom·an**, pl. **-wom·en**) person engaged in trading or a trade.

trad·ing /tráyding/ n. act of engaging in trade. □ **trading post** store, etc., in a remote or unsettled region.

tra·di·tion /trədíshən/ n. **1 a** custom, opinion, or belief handed down to posterity. **b** this process of handing down. **2** valued convention or observance. **3** artistic, literary, etc., principles based on experience and practice. □□ **tra·di'tion·al** adj. **tra·di'tion·al·ly** adv.

tra·di·tion·al·ism /trədíshənəlizəm/ n. respect for tradition, esp. in religion. □□ **tra·di'tion·al·ist** n.

tra·duce /trədoos, –dyoos/ v.tr. speak ill of; misrepresent. □□ **tra·duce'ment** n. **tra·duc'er** n.

traf·fic /tráfik/ • n. **1** (often attrib.) vehicles moving on a public highway, in the air, or at sea. **2** trade, esp. illegal. **3** comings and goings. **4** dealings between people, etc. **5 a** transmitted messages. **b** volume of these. • v. (**traf·ficked**, **traf·fick·ing**) **1** intr. (usu. foll. by in) deal in something, esp. illegally. **2** tr. deal in; barter. □ **traffic circle** road junction at which traffic moves in one direction around a central island. **traffic jam** traffic at a standstill. **traffic light** (or **traf'fic sig·nal**) signal with colored lights to control road traffic. □□ **traf'fick·er** n.

tra·ge·di·an /trəjeedeeən/ n. **1** writer of tragedies. **2** actor in tragedy.

trag·e·dy /trájidee/ n. (pl. **-dies**) **1** serious accident, crime, disaster, etc.; great misfortune. **2 a** play dealing with tragic events and with an unhappy ending, esp. concerning the downfall of the protagonist. **b** tragic plays as a genre.

trag·ic /trájik/ *adj.* **1** sad; calamitous; greatly distressing. **2** of tragedy. □□ **trag′i·cal·ly** *adv.*

trag·i·com·e·dy /trájikómidee/ *n.* (*pl.* **–dies**) play or situation having a mixture of comedy and tragedy. □□ **trag·i·com′ic** *adj.*

trail /trayl/ • *n.* **1** track left by a moving thing, person, etc. **2** beaten path or track, esp. through a wild region. **3** part dragging behind a thing or person (*trail of smoke*). • *v.* **1** *tr. & intr.* draw or be drawn along behind, esp. on the ground. **2** *intr.* walk wearily (behind); lag. **3** *tr.* follow the trail of; pursue. **4** *intr.* be losing in a contest. **5** *intr.* (usu. foll. by *off*) peter out. **6** *intr.* **a** (of a plant, etc.) grow or hang over a wall, along the ground, etc. **b** (of a garment, etc.) hang loosely.

trail·blaz·er /tráylblayzər/ *n.* **1** person who marks a new trail or track through wild country. **2** pioneer. □□ **trail′blaz·ing** *n.*

trail·er /tráylər/ *n.* **1** scenes from a movie, etc., used to advertise it in advance. **2** vehicle towed by another. **3** mobile home. □ **trailer park** place where trailers are parked as dwellings.

train /trayn/ • *v.* **1 a** *tr.* teach (a person, animal, oneself, etc.) a specified skill, esp. by practice. **b** *intr.* undergo this process. **2** *tr. & intr.* bring or come into a state of physical fitness by exercise, diet, etc. **3** *tr.* cause (a plant) to grow in a required shape. **4** (usu. as **trained** *adj.*) make (the mind, eye, etc.) discerning through practice. **5** *tr.* point or aim (a gun, camera, etc.). • *n.* **1** series of railroad cars drawn by an engine. **2** thing dragged along behind or forming the back part of a dress, robe, etc. **3** succession or series of people, things, events, etc. □ **train of thought** sequence or direction in one's thinking process. □□ **train·ee** /–née/ *n.* **train′ing** *n.*

train·er /tráynər/ *n.* **1** person who prepares horses, athletes, etc., for competition. **2** aircraft or simulator used to train pilots.

traipse /trayps/ *v.intr. colloq.* tramp or trudge wearily.

trait /trayt/ *n.* distinguishing feature or characteristic.

trait late 15th century (as a rare usage denoting arrows or other missiles): from French, from Latin *tractus* 'drawing, draft.' An early sense was 'stroke of the pen or pencil,' giving rise to the notion of 'a trace,' hence the current sense 'a characteristic' (mid-18th century).

trai·tor /tráytər/ *n.* (*fem.* **trai·tress** /–tris/) person who is treacherous or disloyal, esp. to his or her country. □□ **trai′tor·ous** *adj.* **trai′tor·ous·ly** *adv.*

tra·jec·to·ry /trəjéktəree/ *n.* (*pl.* **–ries**) path of an object moving under given forces.

tram·mel /tráməl/ • *n.* **1** (usu. in *pl.*) impediment; hindrance. **2** triple dragnet for fish. • *v.tr.* confine; hamper.

tramp /tramp/ • *v.* **1** *intr.* **a** walk heavily and firmly. **b** go on foot, esp. a distance. **2** *tr.* cross on foot, esp. wearily or reluctantly. **3** *tr.* tread on; trample; stamp on. • *n.* **1** itinerant vagrant or beggar. **2** sound of a person, or esp. people, walking, marching, etc., or of horses' hooves. **3** long walk. **4** *sl. derog.* promiscuous woman. **5** (also **tramp steam·er**) merchant ship that takes on any cargo available.

tram·ple /trámpəl/ *v.tr.* **1** tread underfoot. **2** crush in this way.

tram·po·line /trámpəleen/ • *n.* strong fabric sheet connected by springs to a horizontal frame, used for gymnastic jumping. • *v.intr.* use a trampoline. □□ **tram·po·lin′ist** *n.*

trance /trans/ *n.* **1 a** sleeplike state without response to stimuli. **b** hypnotic or cataleptic state. **2** state of rapture; ecstasy.

tran·quil /trángkwil/ *adj.* calm; serene; unruffled. □□ **tran·quil′li·ty** *n.* **tran′quil·ly** *adv.*

tran·quil·ize /trángkwilīz/ *v.tr.* make tranquil, esp. by a drug, etc.

tran·quil·iz·er /trángkwilīzər/ *n.* drug used to diminish anxiety.

trans- /trans, tranz/ *prefix* **1** across; beyond (*transcontinental*). **2** on or to the other side of (*transatlantic*). **3** into another state or place (*transform*).

trans. *abbr.* **1** transaction. **2** transfer. **3** transitive. **4** (also **transl.**) translated; translation; translator. **5** transmission. **6** transportation.

trans·act /tranzákt, –sákt/ *v.tr.* perform or carry through (business). □□ **trans·ac′tor** *n.*

trans·ac·tion /tranzákshən, –sák–/ *n.* **1 a** business agreement; deal. **b** management of business, etc. **2** (in *pl.*) published reports of the proceedings of a learned society.

trans·at·lan·tic /tránzətlántik, trans–/ *adj.* **1** beyond the Atlantic Ocean. **2** crossing the Atlantic (*a transatlantic flight*).

tran·scend /transénd/ *v.tr.* **1** be beyond the range or grasp of (human experience, reason, belief, etc.). **2** excel; outdo; surpass. □□ **tran·scend′ence** *n.* **tran·scend′en·cy** *n.* **tran·scend′ent** *adj.* **tran·scend′ent·ly** *adv.*

tran·scen·den·tal /tránsendént'l/ *adj.* **1** = *transcendent* (TRANSCEND). **2 a** not based on experience; a priori. **b** innate in the mind. **3** visionary; abstract. □ **transcendental meditation** method of detaching oneself from anxiety, etc., by meditation. □□ **tran·scen·den′tal·ism** *n.* **tran·scen·den′tal·ly** *adv.*

trans·con·ti·nen·tal /tránzkontinént'l/ *adj.* (of a railroad, etc.) extending across a continent.

tran·scribe /transkrīb/ *v.tr.* **1** make a copy of, esp. in writing. **2** transliterate. **3** write out (shorthand, notes, etc.) **4** arrange (music) for a different instrument, etc. □□ **tran·scrib′er** *n.* **tran·scrip′tion** /–skrípshən/ *n.*

tran·script /tránskript/ *n.* written or recorded copy.

trans·duc·er /tranzdóosər, –dyóo–, trans–/ *n.* device for converting a nonelectrical signal into an electrical one, e.g., pressure into voltage.

tran·sect /transékt/ *v.tr.* cut across or transversely. □□ **tran·sec′tion** /–sékshən/ *n.*

tran·sept /tránsept/ *n.* either arm of a cross-shaped church at right angles to the nave (*north transept; south transept*).

trans·fer • *v.* /transfér/ (**trans·ferred, trans·fer·ring**) *tr.* (often foll. by *to*) **a** convey, remove, or hand over. **b** make over the possession of (property, rights, etc.) to a person. **2** *tr. & intr.* change or move to another group, club, department, etc. **3** *intr.* change from one station, route, etc., to another on a journey. **4** *tr.* convey (a drawing, etc.) from one surface to another. • *n.* /tránsfər/ **1** transferring or being transferred. **2** design, etc., conveyed or to be conveyed from one surface to another. **3 a** conveyance of property, a right, etc. **b** document effecting this. **4**

ticket for transferring during travel. □□ **trans·fer'a·ble** adj.

trans·fer·ence /transfórəns, tránsfər–/ n. 1 transferring; being transferred. 2 Psychol. redirection of childhood emotions to a new object, esp. to a psychoanalyst.

trans·fig·ure /transfigyər/ v.tr. change in form or appearance, esp. so as to elevate or idealize. □□ **trans·fig·u·ra'tion** n.

trans·fix /transfiks/ v.tr. 1 pierce with a sharp implement or weapon. 2 paralyze with horror or astonishment.

trans·form /transfáwrm/ v. 1 tr. make a thorough or dramatic change in the form, appearance, character, etc., of. 2 intr. (often foll. by into, to) undergo such a change. □□ **trans·for·ma'tion** n.

trans·form·er /transfáwrmər/ n. apparatus for reducing or increasing the voltage of an electrical current.

trans·fuse /transfyóoz/ v.tr. 1 permeate. 2 a transfer (blood) from one person or animal to another. b inject (liquid) into a blood vessel to replace lost fluid. □□ **trans·fu·sion** /–fyóo-zhən/ n.

trans·gress /tranzgrés/ v.tr. (also absol.) go beyond the bounds or limits set by (a commandment, law, etc.); violate. □□ **trans·gres·sion** /–gréshən/ n. **trans·gres'sor** n.

tran·sient /tránzhənt, –shənt, –zeeənt/ • adj. of short duration; passing. • n. temporary visitor, worker, etc. □□ **tran'sience** n.

tran·sis·tor /tranzístər/ n. 1 semiconductor device with three connections, capable of amplification in addition to rectification. 2 (in full **tran·sis'tor ra'di·o**) portable radio with transistors.

transit /tránzit, –sit/ n. 1 going, conveying, or being transported, esp. over a distance. 2 passage; route. 3 apparent passage of a celestial body across the meridian of a place or across the sun or a planet. □ **in transit** while going or being conveyed.

tran·si·tion /tranzíshən, –síshən/ n. passing or change from one place, state, condition, style, etc., to another.

tran·si·tive /tránzitiv, –si–/ adj. Gram. (of a verb or sense of a verb) that takes a direct object (whether expressed or implied), e.g., saw in saw the donkey, saw that she was ill.

tran·si·to·ry /tránzitawree/ adj. not permanent; transient; passing. form. 4 tr. interpret **tran'si·to·ri·ly** adv. **tran'si·to·ri·ness** n.

trans·late /tránzláyt, tráns–/ v. 1 tr. (also absol.) express the sense of (a word, text, etc.) in another language. 2 intr. be translatable (does not translate well). 3 tr. express (an idea, book, etc.) in another, esp. simpler, form. 4 tr. interpret (translated his silence as dissent). □□ **trans·lat'a·ble** adj. **trans·la·tion** /–láyshən/ n. **trans·la'tor** n.

trans·lit·er·ate /tranzlítərayt, trans–/ v.tr. represent (a word, etc.) in the closest corresponding characters of a different language. □□ **trans·lit·er·a·tion** /–ráyshən/ n.

trans·lu·cent /tranzlóosənt, trans–/ adj. allowing light to pass through; semitransparent. □□ **trans·lu'cence** n. **trans·lu'cen·cy** n. **trans·lu'cent·ly** adv.

trans·mi·grate /tranzmígrayt, tráns–/ v.intr. 1 (of the soul) pass into a different body at death. 2 migrate. □□ **trans·mi·gra·tion** /–gráyshən/ n.

trans·mis·sion /tranzmíshən, trans–/ n. 1 transmitting; being transmitted. 2 broadcast program. 3 mechanism by which power is transmitted from an engine to the axle in a vehicle.

trans·mit /tranzmít, trans–/ v.tr. (**trans·mit·ted, trans·mit·ting**) 1 a pass or hand on; transfer. b communicate. 2 allow to pass through; conduct. 3 broadcast (a radio or television program). □□ **trans·mit'ta·ble** adj. **trans·mit'tal** n.

trans·mit·ter /tránzmítər, trans–/ n. 1 person or thing that transmits. 2 equipment used to transmit radio or other electronic signals.

trans·mog·ri·fy /tranzmógrifī, trans–/ v.tr. (**–fies, –fied**) joc. transform, esp. in a magical or surprising manner. □□ **trans·mog·ri·fi·ca'tion** n.

trans·mute /tranzmyóot, trans–/ v.tr. 1 change the form, nature, or substance of. 2 Alchemy hist. subject (base metals) to transmutation. □□ **trans·mut'a·ble** adj. **trans·mut·a·bil'i·ty** n. **trans·mu·ta'tion** n.

trans·oce·an·ic /tránzósheeánik, tráns–/ adj. 1 beyond the ocean. 2 crossing the ocean (transoceanic flight).

tran·som /tránsəm/ n. 1 horizontal bar of wood or stone across a window or the top of a door. 2 (in full transom window) window above a door or larger window.

trans·par·en·cy /tranzpárənsee, –páirənsee, trans–/ n. (pl. –cies) 1 being transparent. 2 photograph, picture, inscription, etc., made visible by a light behind it.

trans·par·ent /tranzpáirənt, –párənt, trans–/ adj. 1 allowing light to pass through; clear and usu. colorless. 2 a (of a disguise, pretext, etc.) easily seen through. b (of a motive, quality, etc.) evident; obvious. 3 easily understood; frank; open. □□ **trans·par'ent·ly** adv.

tran·spire /transpír/ v. 1 intr. (usu. prec. by it as subject) turn out; prove to be the case (it transpired he knew nothing about it). 2 intr. occur; happen. 3 tr. & intr. emit (vapor, sweat, etc.), or be emitted, through the skin, lungs, or leaves. □□ **tran·spi·ra'tion** n.

trans·plant • v.tr. /tranzplánt, trans–/ 1 plant in or move to another place. 2 Surgery transfer (living tissue or an organ) to another part of the body or to another body. • n. /tránzplant, tráns–/ 1 Surgery a transplanting of an organ or tissue. b such an organ, etc. 2 thing, esp. a plant, transplanted. □□ **trans·plan·ta'tion** n.

trans·pon·der /tranzpóndər, trans–/ n. device for receiving a radio signal and automatically transmitting a different signal.

trans·port • v.tr. /tranzpáwrt, trans–/ 1 take or carry to another place. 2 (as **transported** adj.) affected with strong emotion. • n. /tránzpawrt, tráns–/ 1 system or vehicle for conveyance. 2 ship, aircraft, etc., used to carry soldiers, stores, etc. 3 (esp. in pl.) vehement emotion (transports of joy). □□ **trans·port'a·ble** adj. **trans·port'er** n.

trans·por·ta·tion /tránzpərtáyshən, tráns–/ n. 1 conveying; being conveyed. 2 a system of conveying. b means of this.

trans·pose /tranzpóz, trans–/ v.tr. 1 a cause (two or more things) to change places. b change the position of (a thing) in a series. 2 change the order or position of (words or a word) in a sentence. 3 Mus. write or play in a different key. □□ **trans·pos'er** n. **trans·po·si'tion** n.

trans·sex·u·al /tránsékshооэl/ • *adj.* having the physical characteristics of one sex but psychological identification with the other. • *n.* **1** transsexual person. **2** person whose sex has been changed by surgery. □□ **trans·sex′u·al·ism** *n.*

trans·ship /tranz-shíp, trans-/ *v.tr.* (**-shipped, -ship·ping**) transfer from one ship or form of transport to another. □□ **trans·ship′ment** *n.*

tran·sub·stan·ti·a·tion /tránsəbstánsheeáy-shən/ *n. Theol. & RC Ch.* conversion of the Eucharistic elements wholly into the body and blood of Christ.

trans·verse /tránzvэrs, tráns-/ *adj.* crosswise. □□ **trans·verse′ly** *adv.*

trans·ves·tite /tranzvéstīt, trans-/ *n.* person who derives pleasure from wearing clothes of the opposite sex. □□ **trans·ves′tism** *n.*

trap /trap/ • *n.* **1** device, often baited, for catching animals. **2** trick betraying a person into speech or an act. **3** arrangement to catch an unsuspecting person. **4** device for hurling an object such as a clay pigeon into the air to be shot at. **5** curve in a downpipe, etc., that fills with liquid and forms a seal against the upward passage of gases. **6** *Golf* bunker. **7** two-wheeled carriage. **8** = TRAPDOOR. **9** *sl.* mouth (esp. *shut one's trap*). **10** (esp. in *pl.*) *colloq.* percussion instrument, esp. in a jazz band. • *v.tr.* (**trapped, trap·ping**) **1** catch (an animal) in a trap. **2** catch (a person) by means of a trick, etc. **3** stop and retain in or as in a trap.

TRAP, 5

trap·door /trápdáwr/ *n.* hinged door in a horizontal surface.

tra·peze /trapéez/ *n.* crossbar suspended by ropes used as a swing for acrobatics, etc.

tra·pe·zi·um /trapéezeeam/ *n.* (*pl.* **tra·pe·zi·a** /-zeeə/ or **tra·pe·zi·ums**) quadrilateral with no two sides parallel.

trap·e·zoid /trápizoyd/ *n.* quadrilateral with only one pair of sides parallel. □□ **trap·e·zoi′dal** *adj.*

trap·per /trápər/ *n.* person who traps wild animals, esp. to obtain furs.

trap·pings /trápingz/ *n.pl.* **1** ornamental accessories. **2** harness of a horse, esp. when ornamental.

Trap·pist /trápist/ *n.* monk of an order vowed to silence.

trash /trash/ • *n.* **1** worthless material; rubbish. **2** worthless person or persons. • *v.tr. colloq.* wreck; vandalize; discard.

trash·y /tráshee/ *adj.* (**trash·i·er, trash·i·est**) worthless; poorly made. □□ **trash′i·ness** *n.*

trau·ma /trówma, tráw-/ *n.* (*pl.* **trau·ma·ta** /-mə-tə/ or **trau·mas**) **1** physical injury. **2** physical shock following this. **3** profound emotional shock. □□ **trau′ma·tize** *v.tr.* **trau·ma·ti·za′tion** *n.*

trau·mat·ic /trəmátik, trow-, traw-/ *adj.* **1** of or causing trauma. **2** *colloq.* distressing (*traumatic experience*). □□ **trau·mat′i·cal·ly** *adv.*

trav. *abbr.* **1** travel. **2** traveler.

tra·vail /trəváyl, trávayl/ *n.* **1** painful or laborious effort. **2** pangs of childbirth.

trav·el /trával/ • *v.* **1** *intr.* go from one place to another; make a journey, esp. of some length or abroad. **2** *tr.* **a** journey along or through (a country). **b** cover (a distance) in traveling. **3** *intr.* move or proceed as specified (*light travels faster than sound*). **4** *intr. colloq.* move quickly. **5** *intr.* (of a machine or part) move or operate in a specified way. • *n.* **1 a** traveling, esp. in foreign countries. **b** (often in *pl.*) time or occurrence of this (*returned from their travels*). **2** range, rate, or mode of motion of a part in machinery. □□ **trav′el·er** *n.* **trav′el·ing** *adj.*

trav·eled /trávəld/ *adj.* experienced in traveling (also in *comb.*: *much traveled*).

trav·e·logue /trávəlog/ *n.* (also **trav′e·log**) movie or illustrated lecture about travel.

tra·verse /trávərs, trəvэ́rs/ • *v. tr.* travel or lie across (*traversed the country*). • *n.* **1** traversing. **2** thing that crosses another. □□ **tra·vers′al** *n.* **tra·vers′er** *n.*

trav·es·ty /trávistee/ • *n.* (*pl.* **–ties**) grotesque misrepresentation or imitation (*travesty of justice*). • *v.tr.* (**-ties, -tied**) make or be a travesty of.

trawl /trawl/ • *v.* **1** *intr.* fish with a trawl or seine. **2** *tr.* catch by trawling. • *n.* **1** act of trawling. **2** (in full **trawl net**) large wide-mouthed fishing net dragged by a boat along the sea bottom.

trawl·er /tráwlər/ *n.* boat used for trawling.

tray /tray/ *n.* **1** flat board, usu. with a raised rim, for carrying dishes, etc. **2** shallow lidless box for small articles, papers, etc.

treach·er·ous /tréchərəs/ *adj.* **1** guilty of or involving treachery. **2** (of the weather, ice, the memory, etc.) unreliable; hazardous. □□ **treach′er·ous·ly** *adv.* **treach′er·ous·ness** *n.*

treach·er·y /tréchəree/ *n.* (*pl.* **–ies**) violation of faith or trust; betrayal.

trea·cle /tréekəl/ *n.* **1** esp. *Brit.* molasses. **2** cloying sentiment. □□ **trea′cly** *adj.*

tread /tred/ • *v.* (**trod** /trod/; **trod·den** /tród′n/ or **trod**) **1** *intr.* set down one's foot; walk; step. **2** *tr.* walk upon. **3** *tr.* perform (steps, etc.) by walking. • *n.* **1** manner or sound of walking. **2** top surface of a step or stair. **3** surface pattern on a tire. **4** shoe part that rests on the ground. □ **tread the boards** be an actor; appear on the stage. **tread water** maintain an upright position in the water by moving the feet and hands.

trea·dle /trédəl/ *n.* lever worked by the foot and imparting motion to a machine.

tread·mill /trédmil/ *n.* **1** device for producing motion by the weight of persons or animals stepping on the inner surface of a revolving upright wheel. **2** monotonous routine work.

trea·son /tréezən/ *n.* betrayal of one's nation. □□ **trea′son·a·ble** *adj.* **trea′son·ous** *adj.*

treas·ure /tré<u>zh</u>ər/ • *n.* **1 a** precious metals or gems. **b** hoard of these. **c** accumulated wealth. **2** thing valued for its rarity, workmanship, associations, etc. **3** *colloq.* much loved or highly valued person. • *v.tr.* value highly. □ **treasure trove** discovered treasure of unknown ownership.

treas·ur·er /tré<u>zh</u>ərər/ *n.* person in charge of the funds of an organization, etc.

treas·ur·y /tré<u>zh</u>əree/ *n.* (*pl.* **–ies**) **1** place or building where treasure is stored. **2** funds or revenue of a nation, institution, or society. **3** (**Treasury**) **a** department managing the public revenue of a country. **b** offices and officers of this.

treat /treet/ • *v.* **1** *tr.* act or behave toward or deal with in a certain way. **2** *tr.* apply a process to (*treat with acid*). **3** *tr.* apply medical care or attention to. **4** *tr.* present or deal with (a subject) in literature or art. **5** *tr.* pay for food, drink, entertainment, etc. **6** *intr.* negotiate terms (with a person). **7** *intr.* discuss. • *n.* **1** delightful event or circumstance. **2** meal, entertainment, etc., paid for by another. □□ **treat′a·ble** *adj.* **treat′er** *n.* **treat′ing** *n.*

trea·tise /tréetis/ *n.* written work dealing formally and systematically with a subject.

treat·ment /tréetmənt/ *n.* **1** process or manner of behaving toward or dealing with a person or thing. **2** medical care or attention. **3** manner of treating a subject in literature or art.

trea·ty /tréetee/ *n.* (*pl.* **–ties**) formal agreement between nations.

tre·ble /trébəl/ • *adj.* threefold; triple. • *n. Mus.* = SOPRANO. • *v.* make or become three times as much or many; increase threefold. □ **treble clef** *Mus.* clef placing G above middle C on the second lowest line of the staff.

tree /tree/ • *n.* **1** branched perennial plant with a woody, self-supporting main stem or trunk. **2** piece or frame of wood, etc., for various purposes (*shoe tree*). **3** = *family tree.* • *v.tr.* **1** force to take refuge in a tree. **2** put into a difficult position. □ **tree line** = TIMBERLINE. **up a tree** cornered; nonplussed. □□ **tree′less** *adj.*

trek /trek/ • *v.intr.* (**trekked, trek·king**) travel or make one's way arduously. • *n.* **1** journey or walk made by trekking. **2** organized migration of a body of persons. □□ **trek′ker** *n.*

trel·lis /trélis/ *n.* lattice of light wooden or metal bars, esp. as a support for climbing plants.

trem·a·tode /trémətōd, trée–/ *n.* type of parasitic flatworm.

trem·ble /trémbəl/ • *v.intr.* **1** shake involuntarily from weakness, etc. **2** be in a state of extreme apprehension. **3** quiver. • *n.* trembling; quiver. □□ **trem′bly** *adj.*

tre·men·dous /triméndəs/ *adj.* **1** awe inspiring; overpowering. **2** *colloq.* remarkable; considerable; excellent. □□ **tre·men′dous·ly** *adv.*

trem·o·lo /trémələ/ *n. Mus.* tremulous effect in music.

trem·or /trémər/ *n.* **1** shaking; quivering. **2** thrill. **3** slight earthquake.

trem·u·lous /trémyələs/ *adj.* trembling. □□ **trem′u·lous·ly** *adv.* **trem′u·lous·ness** *n.*

trench /trench/ *n.* **1** long, narrow, usu. deep ditch. **2** *Mil.* this dug by troops as a shelter from enemy fire. □ **trench coat** loose belted raincoat.

tren·chant /trénchənt/ *adj.* (of style or language, etc.) incisive; terse; vigorous. □□ **tren′chan·cy** *n.* **tren′chant·ly** *adv.*

tren·cher·man /trénchərmən/ *n.* (*pl.* **–men**) person who eats well, or in a specified manner.

trend /trend/ *n.* general direction and tendency (esp. of events, fashion, or opinion).

trend·set·ter /tréndsetər/ *n.* person who leads the way in fashion, etc. □□ **trend′set·ting** *adj.*

trend·y /tréndee/ *adj. colloq.* (**trend·i·er, trend·i·est**) often *derog.* fashionable. □□ **trend′i·ly** *adv.* **trend′i·ness** *n.*

trep·i·da·tion /trépidáyshən/ *n.* fear; anxiety.

tres·pass /tréspəs, –pas/ • *v.intr.* **1** make an unlawful or unauthorized intrusion (esp. on land or property). **2** encroach (*trespass on your hospitality*). • *n. Law* act of trespassing. □□ **tres′pass·er** *n.*

tress /tres/ *n.* **1** long lock of human hair. **2** (in *pl.*) head of hair.

tres·tle /trésəl/ *n.* **1** supporting structure for a table, etc., usu. consisting of a bar with two divergent pairs of legs. **2** open braced framework to support a bridge, etc.

trey /tray/ *n.* the three on dice or cards.

tri– /trī/ *comb. form* three or three times.

tri·ad /tríad/ *n.* group of three (esp. notes in a chord).

tri·age /tree-aázh, trée-aa<u>zh</u>/ *n.* assignment of priorities for treatment of wounds, illnesses, etc.

trial /tríəl/ *n.* **1** judicial examination and determination of issues between parties by a judge with or without a jury. **2** tryout; test. **3** affliction (*trials of old age*). □ **on trial 1** being tried in a court of law. **2** to be proved or tested. **trial and error** repeated (usu. unsystematic) attempts continued until successful. **trial run** preliminary operational test.

tri·an·gle /tríanggəl/ *n.* **1** plane figure with three sides and angles. **2** three things not in a straight line, with imaginary lines joining them. **3** implement of this shape. **4** triangular steel musical instrument struck with a small steel rod. **5** situation, esp. an emotional relationship, involving three people. □□ **tri·an′gu·lar** *adj.*

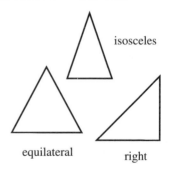

isosceles

equilateral   right

TRIANGLES

tri·an·gu·late *v.tr.* /tríánggyəlayt/ measure and map (an area) by dividing it into triangles. □□ **tri·an·gu·la·tion** /–láyshən/ *n.*

Tri·as·sic /tríásik/ *Geol.* • *adj.* of the earliest period of the Mesozoic era. • *n.* this period.

tri·ath·lon /trīáthlən, –lon/ *n.* three-event competition, usu. comprising running, swimming, and bicycling. □□ **tri·ath·lete** /–leet/ *n.*

trib. *abbr.* **1** tribunal. **2** tribune. **3** tributary.

tribe /trīb/ *n.* **1** group of (esp. primitive) families or communities, usu. linked by cultural ties and having a recognized leader. **2** any similar natural or political division. □□ **trib′al** *adj.* **trib′al·ism** *n.*

tribes·man /trībzmən/ *n.* (*pl.* **–men**) member of a tribe.

trib·u·la·tion /tríbyəláyshən/ *n.* great affliction.

tri·bu·nal /trībyōōnəl, tri–/ *n.* **1** board appointed to adjudicate in some matter. **2** court of justice. **3** seat or bench for a judge or judges.

trib·une /tríbyōōn, tribyōōn/ *n.* **1** popular leader. **2** official in ancient Rome chosen by the people to protect their interests.

trib·u·tar·y /tríbyəteree/ • *n.* (*pl.* **–ies**) **1** river or stream flowing into a larger river or lake. **2** *hist.* person or nation paying or subject to tribute. • *adj.* **1** (of a river, etc.) that is a tributary. **2** *hist.* **a** paying tribute. **b** serving as tribute.

trib·ute /tríbyōōt/ *n.* **1** thing said, done, or given as a mark of respect or affection. **2** *hist.* periodic payment by one nation or ruler to another.

trice /trīs/ *n.* □ **in a trice** in a moment; instantly.

tri·ceps /tríseps/ *adj.* muscle (esp. in the upper arm) with three points of attachment at one end.

tri·cer·a·tops /tríserətops/ *n.* dinosaur with three sharp horns on the forehead and a wavy neck crest.

trich·i·no·sis /tríkinósis/ *n.* disease caused by hairlike worms, ingested in undercooked meat.

trick /trik/ • *n.* **1** action or scheme to fool, outwit, or deceive. **2** illusion (*trick of the light*). **3** special technique; knack. **4** feat of skill or dexterity. **5** practical joke. **6 a** cards played in one round of a card game. **b** point gained in this. **7** (*attrib.*) done to deceive or mystify (*trick photography*; *trick question*). • *v. tr.* **1** deceive by a trick; outwit. **2** swindle (*tricked out of their savings*). □ **do the trick** *colloq.* achieve the required result. **how′s tricks?** *colloq.* how are you?

trick·er·y /tríkəree/ *n.* (*pl.* **–ies**) deception; use of tricks.

trick·le /tríkəl/ • *v.* **1** *intr.* & *tr.* flow or cause to flow in drops or a small stream. **2** *intr.* come or go slowly or gradually (*information trickles out*). • *n.* trickling flow.

trick·ster /tríkstər/ *n.* deceiver; rogue.

trick·y /tríkee/ *adj.* (**trick·i·er, trick·i·est**) **1** requiring care and adroitness. **2** crafty; deceitful. □□ **trick′i·ly** *adv.* **trick′i·ness** *n.*

tri·col·or /tríkulər/ • *n.* flag of three colors, esp. the French national flag of blue, white, and red. • *adj.* (also **tri′col·ored**) having three colors.

tri·corn /tríkawrn/ (also **tri′corne**) • *adj.* (of a hat) having a brim turned up on three sides. • *n.* tricorn hat.

tri·cot /treékō/ *n.* knitted fabric.

tri·cy·cle /trísikəl/ *n.* three-wheeled pedal-driven vehicle.

tri·dent /tríd′nt/ *n.* three-pronged spear.

tried *past* and *past part.* of TRY.

tri·en·ni·al /trī-éneeəl/ *adj.* lasting or recurring every three years. □□ **tri·en′ni·al·ly** *adv.*

tri·fec·ta /trīféktə/ *n.* form of betting in which

the first three places in a race must be predicted in the correct order.

tri·fle /trífəl/ • *n.* **1** thing of slight value or importance. **2 a** small amount, esp. of money. **b** (*prec. by a*) somewhat (*a trifle annoyed*). • *v. intr.* **1** talk or act frivolously. **2** (foll. by *with*) treat or deal with frivolously.

tri·fling /trífling/ *adj.* **1** unimportant; petty. **2** frivolous.

tri·fo·cal /trífókəl/ • *adj.* having three focuses, esp. of a lens with different focal lengths. • *n.* (in *pl.*) trifocal eyeglasses.

tri·fo·ri·um /trīfáwreeəm/ *n.* (*pl.* **tri·fo·ri·a** /–reeə/) upper gallery or arcade in a church.

trig /trig/ *n. colloq.* trigonometry.

trig·ger /trígər/ • *n.* **1** movable device for releasing a spring or catch and so setting off a mechanism (esp. that of a gun). **2** event, occurrence, etc., that sets off a chain reaction. • *v. tr.* set (an action or process) in motion; precipitate. □ **trigger-happy** apt to shoot without or with slight provocation. □□ **trig′gered** *adj.*

trig·o·nom·e·try /trígənómitree/ *n.* branch of mathematics dealing with the relations of the sides and angles of triangles and with the relevant functions of angles. □□ **trig·o·no·met·ric** /–nəmétrik/ *adj.* **trig·o·no·met′ri·cal** *adj.*

tri·lat·er·al /trīlátərəl/ *adj.* **1** of, on, or with three sides. **2** involving three parties, countries, etc.

trill /tril/ • *n.* **1** quavering sound, esp. a rapid alternation of sung or played notes. **2** bird's warbling. **3** pronunciation of *r* with a vibration of the tongue. • *v.* **1** *intr.* produce a trill. **2** *tr.* warble (a song) or pronounce (*r*, etc.) with a trill.

tril·lion /trílyən/ *n.* (*pl.* same or **tril·lions**) a million million (1,000,000,000,000 or 10^{12}). □□ **tril′lionth** *adj.* & *n.*

tri·lo·bite /tríləbīt/ *n.* kind of three-lobed fossil marine arthropod.

tril·o·gy /tríləjee/ *n.* (*pl.* **–gies**) group of three related literary or operatic works.

trim /trim/ • *v. tr.* (**trimmed, trim·ming**) **1** make neat or of the required size or form, esp. by cutting. **2** cut off (unwanted parts). **3** ornament; decorate. **4** adjust the balance of (a ship or aircraft) by arranging its cargo, etc. **5** arrange (sails) to suit the wind. • *n.* **1** state of readiness or fitness (*in perfect trim*). **2** ornament; decorative material. **3** cutting of a person's hair. • *adj.* **1** neat, slim, or tidy. **2** in good order; well arranged or equipped. □□ **trim′ly** *adv.* **trim′ness** *n.*

tri·ma·ran /trímərən/ *n.* vessel like a catamaran, with three hulls side by side.

tri·mes·ter /tríméstər/ *n.* period of three months, esp. of human gestation or as a college or university term.

trim·e·ter /trímitər/ *n. Prosody* verse of three measures.

trim·ming /tríming/ *n.* **1** ornamentation or decoration. **2** (in *pl.*) *colloq.* usual accompaniments, esp. of the main course of a meal. **3** (in *pl.*) pieces cut off in trimming.

tri·ni·tro·tol·u·ene /trīnítrōtólyōōeen/ *n.* (also **tri·ni·tro·tol·u·ol** /–tólyōō-awl, –ōl/) = TNT.

trin·i·ty /trínitee/ *n.* (*pl.* **–ties**) **1** state of being three. **2** group of three. **3** (**Trinity** or **Holy Trinity**) *Theol.* the three persons of the Christian Godhead (Father, Son, and Holy Spirit).

trin·ket /tríngkit/ *n.* trifling ornament, esp. a piece of jewelry. □□ **trin′ket·ry** *n.*

tri·o /treé-ō/ *n.* (*pl.* **–os**) **1** group of three. **2** *Mus.* a composition for three performers. **b** group of three performers.

trip /trip/ • *v.* (**tripped, trip·ping**) **1** *intr.* **a** move with quick light steps. **b** (of a rhythm, etc.) run lightly. **2** *tr.* & *intr.* **a** stumble or cause to stumble, esp. by catching the feet. **b** (foll. by *up*) make or cause to make a slip or blunder. **3** *tr.* release (part of a machine) suddenly by knocking aside a catch, etc. **4** *intr. colloq.* have a hallucinatory experience caused by a drug. • *n.* **1** journey or excursion, esp. for pleasure. **2** **a** stumble; blunder. **b** tripping or being tripped up. **3** nimble step. **4** *colloq.* hallucinatory experience caused by a drug. □ **trip the light fantastic** *joc.* dance. **trip wire** wire stretched close to the ground, operating an alarm, etc., when disturbed.

tri·par·tite /trīpa′ártīt/ *adj.* **1** consisting of three parts. **2** shared by or involving three parties.

tripe /trīp/ *n.* **1** first or second stomach of a ruminant, esp. an ox, as food. **2** *colloq.* nonsense; rubbish.

tri·ple /trípəl/ • *adj.* **1** consisting of three usu. equal parts or things; threefold. **2** involving three parties. **3** three times as much or many. • *n.* **1** threefold number or amount. **2** set of three. **3** *Baseball* hit on which the batter reaches third base. • *v.* **1** multiply by three. **2** hit a triple. □ **triple crown** winning of all three of a group of important events in horse racing, etc. **triple jump** athletic contest comprising a hop, step, and jump.

trip·let /tríplit/ *n.* **1** each of three children or animals born at one birth. **2** set of three things, esp. of equal notes played in the time of two.

trip·li·cate • *adj.* /tríplikət/ **1** existing in three examples or copies. **2** having three corresponding parts. **3** tripled. • *n.* /tríplikət/ each of a set of three copies or corresponding parts. • *v. tr.* /tríplikayt/ **1** make in three copies. **2** multiply by three. □□ **trip·li·ca·tion** /–káyshən/ *n.*

tri·pod /trípod/ *n.* three-legged stand for a camera, etc.

trip·tych /tríptik/ *n.* picture or relief carving on three usu. hinged panels.

tri·sect /trīsékt/ *v. tr.* divide into three (usu. equal) parts. □□ **tri·sec·tion** /–sékshən/ *n.* **tri·sec′tor** *n.*

tris·mus /trízməs/ *n. Med.* variety of tetanus with spasm of the jaw muscles causing the mouth to remain tightly closed; lockjaw.

trite /trīt/ *adj.* (of a phrase, opinion, etc.) hackneyed; worn out by constant repetition. □□ **trite′ly** *adv.* **trite′ness** *n.*

tri·ti·um /tríteeəm/ *n. Chem.* radioactive isotope of hydrogen with a mass about three times that of ordinary hydrogen. ¶ Symb.: **T**.

tri·umph /tríəmf, –umf/ • *n.* **1 a** state of victory or success. **b** great success or achievement. **2** supreme example (*a triumph of engineering*). • *v. intr.* **1** gain a victory; be successful. **2** (often foll. by *over*) exult.

tri·um·phal /trīúmfəl/ *adj.* of or used in or celebrating a triumph.

¶ **Triumphant,** the more common of these words, means 'victorious' or 'exultant,' e.g., *She led an arduous campaign to its triumphant conclusion,* or *He returned triumphant with a patent for his device.* **Triumphal** means 'used in or celebrating a triumph,' e.g., *a triumphal arch, a triumphal parade.*

tri·um·phant /trīúmfənt/ *adj.* **1** victorious; successful. **2** exultant. □□ **tri·um′phant·ly** *adv.*

tri·um·vi·rate /trīúmvirət/ *n.* ruling group of three persons.

tri·va·lent /trīváylənt/ *adj. Chem.* having a valence of three. □□ **tri·va′lence** *n.* **tri·va′len·cy** *n.*

triv·et /trívit/ *n.* tripod or bracket for a hot pot, kettle, or dish to stand on.

triv·i·a /tríveeə/ *n. pl.* trifles or trivialities.

triv·i·al /tríveeəl/ *adj.* of small value or importance; trifling. □□ **triv·i·al·i·ty** /–veeálitee/ *n.* (*pl.* **–ties**) **triv′i·al·ly** *adv.*

triv·i·al·ize /tríveeəlīz/ *v. tr.* make trivial or apparently trivial; minimize. □□ **triv·i·al·i·za′tion** *n.*

tro·che /trókee/ *n.* small medicated tablet or lozenge.

tro·chee /trókee/ *n. Prosody* foot consisting of one long followed by one short syllable.

trod *past* and *past part.* of TREAD.

trod·den *past part.* of TREAD.

trog·lo·dyte /tróglədīt/ *n.* cave dweller, esp. of prehistoric times. □□ **trog·lo·dyt·ic** /–dítik/ *adj.*

troi·ka /tróykə/ *n.* **1 a** Russian vehicle with a team of three horses abreast. **b** this team. **2** group of three people, esp. as an administrative council.

Tro·jan /trójən/ • *adj.* of ancient Troy in Asia Minor. • *n.* native or inhabitant of Troy. □ **Trojan Horse 1** hollow wooden horse used by the Greeks to enter Troy. **2** person or device secreted, intended to bring about ruin.

troll[1] /trōl/ *n.* (in Scandinavian folklore) fabled being, esp. a giant or dwarf dwelling in a cave.

troll[2] /trōl/ *v.* fish by drawing bait along in the water.

trol·ley /trólee/ *n.* **1** (in full **trol′ley wheel**) wheel attached to a pole, etc., used to carry current from an overhead electric wire to drive a vehicle. **2** = *trolley car.* □ **off one's trolley** *sl.* crazy. **trolley car** electric streetcar using a trolley wheel.

trol·lop /tróləp/ *n.* **1** disreputable woman. **2** prostitute.

trom·bone /trombón/ *n.* brass wind instrument with a sliding tube. □□ **trom·bon′ist** *n.*

trompe-l'œil /troNplóyə, trámpláy, –loi/ *n.* still life painting, etc., designed to give an illusion of reality.

-tron /tron/ *suffix Physics* forming nouns denoting: **1** elementary particle (*positron*). **2** particle accelerator.

troop /troōp/ • *n.* **1** assembled company; assemblage of people or animals. **2** (in *pl.*) soldiers; armed forces. **3** cavalry unit under a captain. **4** unit of Girl Scouts, Boy Scouts, etc. • *v. intr.* come together or move in large numbers.

troop·er /troōpər/ *n.* **1** soldier in a cavalry or armored unit. **2** mounted or state police officer.

trop. *abbr.* **1** tropic. **2** tropical.

tro·phy /trófee/ *n.* (*pl.* **–phies**) **1** cup, statuette, etc., awarded as a prize in a contest. **2** memento or souvenir taken in hunting, war, etc.

trop·ic /trópik/ • *n.* **1** parallel of latitude 23°27′ north (**tropic of Cancer**) or south (**tropic of Capricorn**) of the Equator. **2** (**the Tropics**) warmweather region between the tropics of Cancer and Capricorn. □□ **trop′i·cal** *adj.*

tro·po·sphere /trópəsfeer, trō′–/ *n.* lowest layer of atmosphere air extending upward from the earth's surface. □□ **tro·po·spher′ic** *adj.*

trot /trot/ • *v.* (**trot·ted, trot·ting**) **1** *intr.* run at a moderate pace. **2** *intr.* (of a horse) proceed at a steady pace faster than a walk, lifting each diagonal pair of legs alternately. • *n.* **1** action or exercise of trotting. **2** (**the trots**) *sl.* diarrhea.

troth /trawth, trōth/ *n. archaic* **1** faith; loyalty. **2** truth. □ **plight** (or **plight**) **one's troth** pledge one's word esp. in marriage or betrothal.

trou·ba·dour /trŏŏbədawr/ *n.* **1** French medieval lyric poet singing of courtly love. **2** singer or poet.

trou·ble /trúbəl/ • *n.* **1** difficulty or distress; vexation; affliction. **2 a** inconvenience; unpleasant exertion; bother. **b** cause of this. **3** perceived failing (*that's the trouble with you*). **4** dysfunction (*engine trouble*). **5** strife; disturbance. • *v.* **1** *tr.* cause distress or anxiety to; disturb. **2** *tr.* afflict; cause pain, etc., to. **3** *tr. & intr.* (often *refl.*) subject or be subjected to inconvenience or unpleasant exertion (*sorry to trouble you*).

trou·ble·mak·er /trúbəlmaykər/ *n.* person who habitually causes trouble. □□ **trou′ble·mak·ing** *n.*

trou·ble·shoot·er /trúbəlshōōtər/ *n.* **1** mediator in a dispute. **2** person who corrects faults in machinery, etc. □□ **trou′ble·shoot·ing** *n.*

trou·ble·some /trúbəlsəm/ *adj.* causing trouble; vexing.

trough /trawf, trof/ *n.* **1** long, narrow, open receptacle for water, animal feed, etc. **2** channel or hollow like this. **3** elongated region of low barometric pressure.

trounce /trowns/ *v.tr.* **1** defeat heavily. **2** beat; thrash. □□ **trounc′er** *n.* **trounc′ing** *n.*

troupe /trŏŏp/ *n.* company of actors or acrobats, etc.

troup·er /trŏŏpər/ *n.* **1** member of a theatrical troupe. **2** staunch reliable person, esp. during difficult times.

trou·sers /trówzərz/ *n.pl.* **1** = PANTS. **2** (**trouser**) (*attrib.*) designating part of this (*trouser leg*).

trous·seau /trŏŏsō, trōōsṓ/ *n.* (*pl.* **trous·seaus** or **trous·seaux** /–sōz/) bride's collection of clothes, linens, etc.

trout /trowt/ *n.* (*pl.* same or **trouts**) food fish related to salmon.

trove /trōv/ *n.* = treasure trove.

trow·el /trówəl/ *n.* **1** small flat-bladed tool used to spread mortar, etc. **2** scoop for lifting plants or earth.

troy /troy/ *n.* (in full **troy weight**) system of weights used for precious metals and gems.

tru·ant /trŏŏənt/ • *n.* **1** child who stays away from school without permission. **2** person missing from work, etc. • *adj.* shirking; idle; wandering. □□ **tru′an·cy** *n.*

truce /trŏŏs/ *n.* temporary agreement to cease hostilities.

truck[1] /truk/ • *n.* **1** vehicle for carrying loads. **2** handcart. • *v.* **1** *tr.* convey on or in a truck. **2** *intr.* drive a truck. □□ **truck′er** *n.*

truck[2] /truk/ *n.* dealings. □ **have no truck with** avoid dealing with.

truck·le /trúkəl/ • *n.* (in full **truck′le bed**) = *trundle bed.* • *v.intr.* (foll. by *to*) submit obsequiously. □□ **truck′ler** *n.*

tru·cu·lent /trúkyələnt/ *adj.* **1** aggressively defiant. **2** fierce; savage. □□ **truc′u·lence** *n.* **truc′u·lent·ly** *adv.*

trudge /truj/ • *v.* **1** *intr.* go on foot, esp. laboriously. **2** *tr.* traverse (a distance) in this way. • *n.* trudging walk.

true /trŏŏ/ • *adj.* **1** in accordance with fact or reality. **2** genuine; authentic. **3** loyal; faithful. **4** accurately conforming (to a standard or expectation, etc.) (*true to form*). **5** correctly positioned or balanced; upright; level. **6** exact; accurate (*true aim*). • *adv.* accurately. • *v.tr.* (**trues, trued, true·ing** or **tru·ing**) bring (a tool, wheel, frame, etc.) into the position required. □ **come true** actually happen. **true-blue** *adj.* extremely loyal or orthodox.

truf·fle /trúfəl/ *n.* **1** edible, rich-flavored underground fungus. **2** candy made of chocolate covered with cocoa, etc.

tru·ism /trŏŏizəm/ *n.* obviously true or hackneyed statement.

tru·ly /trŏŏlee/ *adv.* **1** sincerely; genuinely. **2** really; indeed. **3** faithfully; loyally. **4** accurately.

trump /trump/ • *n.* **1** playing card of a suit ranking above the others. **2** this suit. • *v.* **1 a** *tr.* defeat (a card or its player) with a trump. **b** *intr.* play a trump card when another suit has been led. **2** *tr. colloq.* gain a surprising advantage over. □ **trump card 1** card belonging to a trump suit. **2** *colloq.* surprise move to gain an advantage. **trump up** fabricate or invent (an accusation, etc.).

trum·per·y /trúmpəree/ *n.* (*pl.* **–ies**) **1** worthless finery. **2** worthless article; junk.

trum·pet /trúmpit/ • *n.* **1** brass instrument with a flared bell and a bright penetrating tone. **2** trumpet-shaped thing (*ear trumpet*). **3** sound of or like a trumpet. • *v.* **1** *intr.* **a** blow a trumpet. **b** (of an enraged elephant, etc.) make a trumpetlike cry. **2** *tr.* proclaim loudly (a person's or thing's merit). □□ **trum′pet·er** *n.*

trun·cate /trúngkayt/ *v.tr.* cut the top or the end from; shorten. □□ **trun·ca·tion** /–káyshən/ *n.*

trun·cheon /trúnchən/ *n.* short club carried esp. by a police officer.

trun·dle /trúnd′l/ *v.* roll or move heavily or noisily, esp. on or as on wheels. □ **trundle bed** wheeled bed stored under a larger bed.

trunk /trungk/ *n.* **1** main stem of a tree. **2** body apart from the limbs and head. **3** main part of any structure. **4** large box with a hinged lid for luggage, storage, etc. **5** usu. rear storage compartment of an automobile. **6** elephant's elongated prehensile nose. **7** (in *pl.*) men's shorts worn for swimming, etc. □ **trunk line** main line of a railroad, etc.

truss /trus/ • *n.* **1** framework supporting a roof, bridge, etc. **2** surgical appliance worn to support a hernia. • *v.tr.* **1** tie up (a fowl) for cooking.

2 support (roof, bridge, etc.) with a truss or trusses.

TRUSS, 1

trust /trust/ • *n.* **1** firm belief in the reliability, truth, or strength, etc., of a person or thing. **2** confident expectation. **3** responsibility (*in a position of trust*). **4** commercial credit. **5** *Law* **a** arrangement whereby a person or group manages property on another's behalf. **b** property so held. **6** body of trustees. **7** association of companies for reducing competition, etc. • *v.* **1** *tr.* place trust in; believe in. **2** *tr.* (foll. by *with*) allow to have or use (a thing) (*trust them with my books*). **3** *tr.* have faith, confidence, hope that a thing will take place. **4** *intr.* (foll. by *in*) place reliance in (*we trust in you*). **5** *intr.* (foll. by *to*) place (esp. undue) reliance on (*trust to luck*). □ **in trust** *Law* held on the basis of trust (see sense 5 of *n.*).

trus·tee /trustée/ *n.* **1** *Law* person managing property in trust. **2** member of an administrative board. □□ **trust·ee′ship** *n.*

trust·ful /trústfŏŏl/ *adj.* full of trust or confidence. □□ **trust′ful·ly** *adv.* **trust′ful·ness** *n.*

trust·ing /trústing/ *adj.* having trust; trustful. □□ **trust′ing·ly** *adv.*

trust·wor·thy /trústwurthee/ *adj.* deserving of trust; reliable. □□ **trust′wor·thi·ness** *n.*

trust·y /trústee/ *adj.* (**trust·i·er, trust·i·est**) *archaic* or *joc.* trustworthy (*a trusty steed*).

truth /trooth/ *n.* (*pl.* **truths** /troothz, trooths/) **1** quality or a state of being true. **2** what is true.

truth·ful /troothfŏŏl/ *adj.* **1** speaking the truth. **2** (of a story, etc.) true. □□ **truth′ful·ly** *adv.* **truth′ful·ness** *n.*

try /trī/ • *v.* (**tries, tried**) **1** *intr.* make an effort with a view to success. **2** *tr.* make an effort to achieve (*tried my best*). **3** *tr.* test by use or experiment. **4** *tr.* tax (*tries my patience*). **5** *tr.* examine the effectiveness of for a purpose (*try cold water*). **6** *tr.* ascertain the state of fastening of (a door, window, etc.). **7** *tr.* **a** investigate and decide (a case or issue) judicially. **b** subject (a person) to trial (*tried for murder*). **8** *intr.* aim; strive (*try for a gold medal*). • *n.* (*pl.* **tries**) effort to accomplish something. □ **tried and true** proved reliable by experience. **try on for size** try out or test for suitability. **try one's hand** see how skillful one is, esp. at the first attempt.

try·ing /trí-ing/ *adj.* annoying; hard to endure.

tryst /trist/ *n.* meeting, esp. a secret one of lovers.

tsar var. of CZAR.

tsa·ri·na var. of *czarina* (CZAR).

tset·se /tsétsee, tét–, tsé′etsee, tée–/ *n.* African fly that feeds on blood and transmits sleeping sickness.

TSH *abbr.* thyroid-stimulating hormone.

T-shirt /tée′short/ *n.* (also **tee shirt**) short-sleeved, collarless casual top having the form of a T when spread out.

tsp. *abbr.* (*pl.* **tsps.**) teaspoon; teaspoonful.

T square /tée skwair/ *n.* T-shaped instrument for drawing or testing right angles.

T SQUARE

tsu·na·mi /tsŏŏnaámee/ *n.* (*pl.* **tsu·na·mis**) long, high sea wave caused by underwater earthquakes, etc.

Tswa·na /tswaánə, swaá–/ *n.* (also **Set·swa·na** /setswaánə/) Bantu language used in Botswana and neighboring areas of South Africa.

tub /tub/ *n.* **1** open, flat-bottomed, usu. round container for various purposes. **2** tub-shaped carton. **3** *colloq.* clumsy, slow boat.

tu·ba /tŏŏbə, tyŏŏ–/ *n.* (*pl.* **tu·bas**) low-pitched brass wind instrument.

tub·by /túbee/ *adj.* (**tub·bi·er, tub·bi·est**) short and fat. □□ **tub′bi·ness** *n.*

tube /tŏŏb, tyŏŏb/ *n.* **1** long, hollow cylinder. **2** pliable cylinder sealed at one end for holding a semiliquid substance (*tube of toothpaste*). **3** hollow, cylindrical organ in the body. **4** (prec. by *the*) *colloq.* television. **5** = *inner tube.* □□ **tube′like** *adj.*

tu·ber /tŏŏbər, tyŏŏ–/ *n.* thick, rounded part of a stem or rhizome, usu. found underground, e.g., a potato. □□ **tu′ber·ous** *adj.*

tu·ber·cle /tŏŏbərkəl, tyŏŏ–/ *n.* small, rounded swelling on the body or in an organ, esp. as characteristic of tuberculosis. □□ **tu·ber′cu·lar** *adj.* **tu·ber′cu·lous** *adj.*

tu·ber·cu·lo·sis /tŏŏbərkyəlósis, tyŏŏ–/ *n.* infectious disease characterized by tubercles, esp. in the lungs.

tub·ing /tŏŏbing, tyŏŏ–/ *n.* **1** length of tube. **2** quantity of tubes.

tu·bu·lar /tŏŏbyələr, tyŏŏ–/ *adj.* **1** tube-shaped. **2** having or consisting of tubes.

tu·bule /tŏŏbyŏŏl, tyŏŏ–/ *n.* small tube in a plant or animal body.

tuck /tuk/ • *v.tr.* **1** draw, fold, or turn the outer or end parts of (cloth or clothes, etc.) close together so as to be held; thrust in the edge of (a thing). **2** draw together into a small space (*tucked its head under its wing*). **3** stow (*tucked it in a corner*). **4** make a stitched fold in (material, a garment, etc.). • *n.* flattened, usu. stitched fold in material, etc.

tuck·er /túkər/ *v.tr.* (esp. in *passive*; often foll. by *out*) *colloq.* tire; exhaust.

-tude /tood, tyood/ *suffix* forming abstract nouns (*altitude*).

Tu·dor /toodər, tyoo–/ *adj.* **1** of the royal family of England 1485–1603 or this period. **2** of the architectural style of this period.

Tues. *abbr.* (also **Tue.**) Tuesday.

Tues·day /toozday, –dee, tyoo–/ *n.* third day of the week, following Monday.

tuft /tuft/ *n.* bunch or collection of threads, grass, feathers, hair, etc., held or growing together at the base. □□ **tuft′ed** *adj.* **tuft′y** *adj.*

tug /tug/ • *v.* (**tugged, tug·ging**) **1** *tr. & intr.* pull hard or violently; jerk. **2** *tr.* tow (a ship, etc.) with a tugboat. • *n.* **1** hard, violent, or jerky pull. **2** sudden strong emotion. **3** = TUGBOAT. □ **tug-of-war 1** trial of strength between two sides pulling against each other on a rope. **2** decisive or severe contest.

tug·boat /túgbōt/ *n.* small, powerful boat for towing or pushing ships, barges, etc.

tu·i·tion /too-íshən, tyoo–/ *n.* **1** teaching. **2** fee for this.

tu·lip /toolip, tyoo–/ *n.* **1** bulbous spring-flowering plant with showy cup-shaped flowers. **2** its flower.

tulle /tool/ *n.* soft fine silk, etc., net for veils and dresses.

tum·ble /túmbəl/ • *v.* **1** *tr. & intr.* fall or cause to fall suddenly, clumsily, or headlong. **2** *intr.* fall rapidly in amount, etc. (*prices tumbled*). **3** *intr.* roll or toss to and fro. **4** *intr.* move or rush in a headlong or blundering manner. **5** *intr.* perform acrobatic feats, esp. somersaults. • *n.* **1** sudden or headlong fall. **2** somersault or other acrobatic feat.

---

tumble Middle English (also in the sense 'dance with contortions'): of Germanic origin; related to German *taumeln* 'be giddy, stagger,' Swedish *tumla* 'tumble down'; related to Old English *tumbian* 'to dance.' The sense was probably influenced by Old French *tomber* 'to fall.' The noun dates from the mid-17th century.

---

tum·ble·down /túmbəldown/ *adj.* falling or fallen into ruin.

tum·bler /túmblər/ *n.* **1** drinking glass. **2** acrobat. **3** pivoted piece in a lock that holds the bolt until lifted by a key or a combination.

tum·ble·weed /túmbəlweed/ *n.* plant whose globular bush breaks off in late summer and is tumbled about by the wind.

tum·brel /túmbrəl/ *n.* (also **tum·bril** /–ril/) *hist.* open cart in which condemned persons were taken to the guillotine during the French Revolution.

tu·mes·cent /toomésənt, tyoo–/ *adj.* swelling. □□ **tu·mes′cence** *n.*

tu·mid /toomid, tyoo–/ *adj.* **1** swollen; inflated. **2** (of a style, etc.) inflated; bombastic. □□ **tu·mid′i·ty** *n.* **tu′mid·ly** *adv.*

tum·my /túmee/ *n.* (*pl.* **–mies**) *colloq.* stomach.

tu·mor /toomər, tyoo–/ *n.* swelling, esp. from an abnormal growth of tissue. □□ **tu′mor·ous** *adj.*

tu·mult /toomult, tyoo–/ *n.* **1** uproar or din, esp. of a disorderly crowd. **2** angry demonstration; riot. **3** emotional agitation.

tu·mul·tu·ous /toomúlchooəs, tyoo–/ *adj.* noisily vehement; uproarious; agitated. □□ **tu·mul′tu·ous·ly** *adv.*

tun /tun/ *n.* large beer or wine cask.

tu·na /toonə, tyoo–/ *n.* (*pl.* same or **tu·nas**) **1** large edible marine fish. **2** (in full **tu′na fish**) its flesh as food.

tun·dra /túndrə/ *n.* vast, level, treeless Arctic region usu. with underlying permafrost.

tune /toon, tyoon/ • *n.* melody. • *v.* **1** *tr.* put (a musical instrument) in tune. **2 a** *tr.* adjust (a radio, etc.) to the frequency of a signal. **b** *intr.* (foll. by *in*) adjust a radio receiver to the required signal (*tuned in to the news*). **3** *tr.* adjust (an engine, etc.) to run smoothly and efficiently. □ **in tune 1** having the correct pitch. **2** harmonizing (with one's associates, surroundings, etc.). **to the tune of** *colloq.* to the considerable amount of. **tuned in 1** (of a radio, etc.) adjusted to a particular frequency, station, etc. **2** *colloq.* up to date; aware of what is going on. □□ **tun′a·ble** *adj.* (also **tune′a·ble**).

tune·ful /toonfool, tyoo–/ *adj.* melodious; musical. □□ **tune′ful·ly** *adv.* **tune′ful·ness** *n.*

tune·less /toonlis, tyoo–/ *adj.* **1** unmelodious; unmusical. **2** out of tune. □□ **tune′less·ly** *adv.* **tune′less·ness** *n.*

tun·er /toonər, tyoo–/ *n.* **1** person who tunes musical instruments, esp. pianos. **2** device for tuning a radio receiver.

tung·sten /túngstən/ *n. Chem.* dense metallic element with a very high melting point. ¶ Symb.: **W.**

tu·nic /toonik, tyoo–/ *n.* **1** blouselike garment extending to the hips, sometimes belted. **2** loose, often sleeveless garment, esp. as worn in ancient Greece and Rome.

tun·ing /tooning, tyoo–/ *n.* process of putting a musical instrument in tune. □ **tuning fork** two-pronged steel fork that gives a particular note when struck.

TUNING FORK

tun·nel /túnəl/ • *n.* **1** underground passage dug through a hill or under a road, river, etc., esp. for a railroad or road. **2** underground passage dug by an animal. • *v.* **1** *intr.* make a tunnel through. **2** *tr.* make (one's way) by tunneling. □ **tunnel vision 1** vision that is normal only in a small central area. **2** *colloq.* inability to grasp a situation's wider implications. □□ **tun′nel·er** *n.*

tu·pe·lo /toopilō, tyoo–/ *n.* (*pl.* **–los**) **1** any of various Asian and N. American deciduous trees with colorful foliage and growing in swamps. **2** its wood.

Tupi ~ turn 644

Tu·pi /toˈopee/ • *n.* (*pl.* same or **Tu·pis**) **1** member of a Native American people native to the Amazon valley. **2** their language. • *adj.* of this people or language.

tur·ban /ˈtərbən/ *n.* **1** man's headdress of fabric wound around a cap or the head, worn esp. by Muslims and Sikhs. **2** woman's headdress resembling this. □□ **tur′baned** *adj.*

tur·bid /ˈtərbid/ *adj.* **1** muddy; thick; not clear. **2** (of a style, etc.) confused; disordered. □□ **tur·bid′i·ty** *n.*

¶ **Turbid** is used of a liquid or color to mean 'muddy, not clear,' or of literary style, etc., to mean 'confused,' e.g., *the turbid utterances and twisted language of Carlyle.* **Turgid** means 'swollen, inflated, enlarged.' When used of literary style it means 'pompous, bombastic': *Communications from headquarters were largely turgid exercises in self-congratulation.*

tur·bine /ˈtərbin, -bīn/ *n.* rotary motor driven by a flow of water, steam, gas, wind, etc.

turbo- /ˈtərbō/ *comb. form* turbine.

tur·bo·charg·er /ˈtərbōˌchaarjər/ *n.* supercharger driven by a turbine powered by the engine's exhaust gases.

tur·bo·jet /ˈtərbōjet/ *n.* **1** jet engine in which the jet also operates a turbine-driven air compressor. **2** aircraft powered by this.

tur·bo·prop /ˈtərbōprop/ *n.* **1** jet engine in which a turbine is used as in a turbojet and also to drive a propeller. **2** aircraft powered by this.

tur·bot /ˈtərbət/ *n.* any of various flatfishes prized as food.

tur·bu·lent /ˈtərbyələnt/ *adj.* **1** disturbed; in commotion. **2** (of a flow of air, etc.) varying irregularly. **3** tumultuous; riotous. □□ **tur′bu·lence** *n.* **tur′bu·lent·ly** *adv.*

tu·reen /tooˈreen, tyoo-/ *n.* deep covered dish for soup, etc.

turf /tərf/ • *n.* **1 a** layer of grass, etc., with earth and its roots. **b** piece of this. **2** slab of peat. **3** (prec. by *the*) **a** horse racing generally. **b** general term for racetracks. **4** *sl.* person's territory or sphere of influence. • *v.tr.* cover (ground) with turf.

tur·gid /ˈtərjid/ *adj.* **1** swollen; inflated. **2** (of language) pompous; bombastic. □□ **tur·gid′i·ty** *n.*

Turk /tərk/ *n.* **1 a** native or inhabitant of Turkey. **b** person of Turkish descent. **2** member of a Central Asian people from whom the Ottomans derived.

tur·key /ˈtərkee/ *n.* **1** large bird orig. of N. America, wild or bred for food. **2** its flesh as food. **3** *sl.* theatrical failure; flop. □ **talk turkey** *colloq.* talk frankly; get down to business.

Tur·kish /ˈtərkish/ • *adj.* of Turkey, the Turks, or their language. • *n.* this language. □ **Turkish bath** hot-air or steam bath followed by washing, massage, etc. **Turkish towel** thick towel made of cotton terry cloth.

tur·mer·ic /ˈtərmərik/ *n.* **1** E. Indian plant of the ginger family. **2** its powdered rhizome used for yellow dye or as a spice, esp. in curry powder.

tur·moil /ˈtərmoyl/ *n.* **1** confusion; agitation. **2** din and bustle.

turn /tərn/ • *v.* **1** *tr.* & *intr.* move around a point or axis; give or receive a rotary motion. **2** *tr.* & *intr.* change in position; invert; reverse. **3 a** *tr.* give a new direction to. **b** *intr.* take a new direction. **4** *tr.* aim in a certain way (*turned the hose on*

them). **5** *tr.* & *intr.* (foll. by *into*) change in nature, form, or condition (*turned into a dragon*). **6** *intr.* (foll. by *to*) **a** set about (*turned to doing the ironing*). **b** have recourse to (*turned to me for help*). **c** go on to consider next (*we'll now turn to your report*). **7** *tr.* & *intr.* become or cause to become (*turned sour*). **8 a** *tr.* & *intr.* (foll. by *against*) make or become hostile to (*turned them against us*). **b** *intr.* (foll. by *on, upon*) become hostile to; attack (*suddenly turned on them*). **9** *intr.* change color. **10** *intr.* (of milk, etc.) become sour. **11** *intr.* (of the stomach) be nauseated. **12** *tr.* move to the other side of; go around (*turned the corner*). **13** *tr.* pass the age of (*he has turned 40*). **14** *tr.* **a** perform (a somersault, etc.) with rotary motion. **b** twist (an ankle) out of position; sprain. **15** *tr.* make (a profit). **16** *tr.* shape (an object) on a lathe. **17** *tr.* give an (esp. elegant) form to (*turn a compliment*). **18** *tr.* & *intr.* (of the tide) change or cause to change direction. • *n.* **1** turning; rotary motion. **2** change of direction or tendency (*sudden turn to the left*). **3** point at which a turning or change occurs. **4** change of direction of the tide. **5** tendency or disposition (*mechanical turn of mind*). **6** opportunity or obligation, etc., that comes successively (*my turn to read*). **7** short walk or ride (*take a turn around the block*). **8** short performance. **9** service of a specified kind (*did me a good turn*). **10** momentary nervous shock (*gave me quite a turn*). □ **at every turn** continually; at each new stage, etc. **by turns** in rotation; alternately. **in turn** in succession. **out of turn 1** when it is not one's turn. **2** inappropriately (*speak out of turn*). **take turns** act alternately. **to a turn** (esp. cooked) perfectly. **turn back 1** begin or cause to retrace one's steps. **2** fold back. **turn the corner** pass the critical point in an illness, difficulty, etc. **turn down 1** reject (a proposal, application, etc.). **2** reduce the volume or strength of (sound, heat, etc.) by turning a knob, etc. **3** fold down. **turn in 1** hand in; deliver. **2** achieve or register (a performance, score, etc.). **3** *colloq.* go to bed. **4** fold or incline inward. **turn off 1 a** stop the flow or operation of (water, electricity, etc.) by tap, switch, etc. **b** operate (a tap, switch, etc.) to achieve this. **2 a** enter a side road. **b** (of a side road) lead off from another road. **3** *colloq.* cause to lose interest. **turn on 1 a** start the flow or operation of (water, electricity, etc.) by a tap, switch, etc. **b** operate (a tap, switch, etc.) to achieve this. **2** *colloq.* stimulate the interest of, esp. sexually. **3** *tr.* & *intr.* *colloq.* intoxicate or become intoxicated with drugs. **turn-on** *n.* *colloq.* person or thing that causes (esp. sexual) arousal. **turn one's stomach** make one nauseous or disgusted. **turn out 1** expel. **2** extinguish (an electric light, etc.). **3** produce (goods, etc.). **4** *colloq.* assemble; attend a meeting, etc. **5** prove to be the case; result (*how things turn out*). **turn over 1** reverse the position of (*turn over the page*). **2** upset; fall or cause to fall over. **3 a** cause (an engine) to run. **b** (of an engine) start running. **4** consider thoroughly. **5** (foll. by *to*) transfer or delegate. **6** do business to the amount of. **turn over a new leaf** improve one's conduct or performance. **turn the other cheek** respond meekly to insult or abuse. **turn signal** flashing light on an automobile that indicates that the vehicle is about to turn or change lanes. **turn tail** run away. **turn the tide** reverse the trend of events. **turn up 1** increase the volume or strength of (sound, heat, etc.) by turning a knob, etc. **2** discover; reveal. **3** be found, esp. by chance. **4** arrive. **5** shorten (a garment). **turn up one's nose** (or **turn one's nose up**) react with disdain.

turn·a·bout /tɔ́rnəbowt/ *n.* **1** act of turning about. **2** abrupt change of policy, etc.

turn·a·round /tɔ́rnərownd/ *n.* **1** = TURNABOUT. **2** space needed for a vehicle to turn around.

turn·buck·le /tɔ́rnbukəl/ *n.* device for tightly connecting parts of a metal rod or wire.

TURNBUCKLE

turn·coat /tɔ́rnkōt/ *n.* person who changes sides in a conflict, dispute, etc.

turn·ing /tɔ́rning/ *n.* □ **turning point** point at which a decisive change occurs.

tur·nip /tɔ́rnip/ *n.* **1** plant with a large white globular root. **2** its root as a vegetable. □□ **tur'nip·y** *adj.*

turn·key /tɔ́rnkee/ • *n.* jailer. • *adj.* (of a process, etc.) fully ready for operation.

turn·off /tɔ́rnof/ *n.* **1** turning off a main road. **2** *colloq.* something that repels or causes a loss of interest.

turn·out /tɔ́rnowt/ *n.* **1** number of people attending a meeting, etc. **2** quantity of goods produced in a given time. **3** set or display of equipment, clothes, etc.

turn·o·ver /tɔ́rnōvər/ *n.* **1** act of turning over. **2** amount of money taken in a business. **3** rate at which people enter and leave employment, etc. **4** small pastry made by folding crust over a filling. **5** rate at which goods are sold and replaced.

turn·pike /tɔ́rnpīk/ *n.* highway on which a toll is usu. charged.

turn·stile /tɔ́rnstīl/ *n.* gate with revolving arms, allowing people through singly.

turn·ta·ble /tɔ́rntaybəl/ *n.* circular revolving plate on which records are played.

tur·pen·tine /tɔ́rpəntīn/ *n.* resin secreted by several trees and used in various commercial preparations.

tur·pi·tude /tɔ́rpitōōd, –tyōōd/ *n.* depravity; wickedness.

tur·quoise /tɔ́rkwoyz, –koyz/ • *n.* **1** semiprecious stone, usu. opaque and greenish blue or blue. **2** greenish blue color. • *adj.* of this color.

tur·ret /tɔ́rit, túr–/ *n.* **1** small tower, esp. decorating a building. **2** low, flat, usu. revolving armored tower for a gun and gunners in a ship, aircraft, fort, or tank. **3** rotating holder for tools in a lathe, etc. □□ **tur'ret·ed** *adj.*

tur·tle /tɔ́rt'l/ *n.* **1** terrestrial or aquatic reptile encased in a shell of bony plates, and having flippers or webbed toes. **2** flesh of the turtle, esp. used for soup. □ **turn turtle** capsize.

tur·tle·dove /tɔ́rt'lduv/ *n.* wild dove noted for its soft cooing and affection for its mate.

tur·tle·neck /tɔ́rt'lnek/ *n.* **1** high, close-fitting, turned over collar on a garment. **2** such a garment.

Tus·ca·ro·ra /təskərórə, –ráwr–/ *n.* **1 a** N. American people native to N. Carolina and later to New York. **b** member of this people. **2** language of this people.

tusk /tusk/ *n.* long, pointed tooth, esp. protruding from a closed mouth, as in the elephant, walrus, etc. □□ **tusked** *adj.* (also in *comb.*).

tus·sle /túsəl/ • *n.* scuffle. • *v.intr.* engage in a tussle.

tus·sock /túsək/ *n.* clump of grass, etc. □□ **tus'sock·y** *adj.*

tu·te·lage /tōōt'lij, tyōō–/ *n.* **1** guardianship. **2** being under this. **3** instruction.

tu·te·lar·y /tōōt'lairee, tyōō–/ *adj.* **1** serving as guardian. **2** giving protection.

tu·tor /tōōtər, tyōō–/ • *n.* private teacher. • *v.* **1** *tr.* act as a tutor to. **2** *intr.* work as a tutor. **tu'tor·ship** *n.*

tu·to·ri·al /tōōtáwreeəl, tyōō–/ • *adj.* of a tutor or tuition. • *n.* period of individual instruction.

tut·ti /tōōtee/ *Mus.* • *adv.* with all voices or instruments together. • *n.* such a passage.

tut·ti-frut·ti /tōōteefrōōtee/ *n.* ice cream flavored with mixed fruits.

tu·tu /tōōtōō/ *n.* ballet dancer's short skirt of stiffened frills.

tux /tuks/ *n.* *colloq.* = TUXEDO.

tux·e·do /tukséedō/ *n.* (*pl.* **–dos** or **–does**) **1** man's short black formal jacket. **2** suit of clothes including this.

TV *abbr.* television.

TVA *abbr.* Tennessee Valley Authority.

twad·dle /twód'l/ *n.* silly writing or talk.

twain /twayn/ *adj. & n. archaic* two.

twang /twang/ • *n.* **1** sound made by the plucked string of a musical instrument or bow. **2** nasal quality of a voice. • *v.* emit or cause to emit this sound. □□ **twang'y** *adj.*

'twas /twuz, twoz/ *archaic* it was.

tweak /tweek/ • *v.tr.* pinch and twist sharply. • *n.* instance of tweaking.

tweed /tweed/ *n.* **1** rough-surfaced woolen cloth, usu. of mixed colors. **2** (in *pl.*) clothes made of tweed.

tweet /tweet/ • *n.* chirp of a small bird. • *v.intr.* make a chirping noise.

tweet·er /twéetər/ *n.* loudspeaker for high frequencies.

tweeze /tweez/ *v.tr.* pluck out with tweezers.

tweez·ers /twéezərz/ *n.pl.* small pair of pincers for picking up small objects, plucking out hairs, etc.

twelfth /twelfth/ • *n.* **1** next after eleventh. **2** each of twelve equal parts of a thing. • *adj.* that is the twelfth.

twelve /twelv/ *n.* **1** one more than eleven. **2** symbol for this (12, xii, XII).

twelve·fold /twélvfōld/ *adj. & adv.* **1** twelve times as much or as many. **2** consisting of twelve parts.

twen·ty /twéntee/ *n.* (*pl.* **–ties**) **1** product of two and ten. **2** symbol for this (20, xx, XX). **3** (in *pl.*) numbers from 20 to 29, esp. the years of a century or of a person's life. □ **twenty-twenty** (or **20/20**) **1** vision of normal acuity. **2**

colloq. denoting clear perception or hindsight. □□ **twen′ti·eth** *adj.* & *n.*

'twere /twər/ *archaic* it were.

twerp /twərp/ *n.* (also **twirp**) *sl.* stupid or objectionable person.

twice /twīs/ *adv.* **1** two times; on two occasions. **2** in double degree or quantity (*twice as good*).

twid·dle /twid′l/ • *v.* **1** *tr.* & *intr.* twirl, adjust, or play randomly or idly. **2** *intr.* move twirlingly. • *n.* act of twiddling. □ **twiddle one's thumbs 1** make one's thumbs rotate around each other. **2** have nothing to do. □□ **twid′dler** *n.* **twid′dly** *adj.*

twig /twig/ *n.* small branch or shoot of a tree or shrub. □□ **twig′gy** *adj.*

twi·light /twīlīt/ *n.* **1** light from the sky when the sun is below the horizon, esp. in the evening. **2** period of this. **3** faint light. **4** period of decline or destruction.

twi·lit /twīlit/ *adj.* dimly illuminated by or as by twilight.

twill /twil/ *n.* fabric so woven as to have a surface of diagonal parallel ridges. □□ **twilled** *adj.*

'twill /twil/ *archaic* it will.

twin /twin/ • *n.* **1** each of a closely related or associated pair, esp. of children or animals born at one birth. **2** exact counterpart of a person or thing. **3** (**the Twins**) zodiacal sign or constellation Gemini. • *adj.* forming, or being one of, such a pair (*twin brothers*). • *v.* (**twinned, twin·ning**) **1** *tr.* **a** join intimately together. **b** (foll. by *with*) pair. **2** *intr.* bear twins. □ **twin bed** each of a pair of single beds. □□ **twin′ning** *n.*

twine /twīn/ • *n.* **1** strong string of twisted strands of fiber. **2** coil; twist. • *v.* **1** *intr.* coil; wind. **2** *intr.* & *refl.* (of a plant) grow in this way. □□ **twin′er** *n.*

twinge /twinj/ *n.* sharp momentary local pain or pang.

twin·kle /twingkəl/ • *v.intr.* **1** (of a star, light, etc.) shine with rapidly intermittent gleams. **2** (of the eyes) sparkle. **3** (of the feet) move lightly and rapidly. • *n.* **1** sparkle or gleam of the eyes. **2** slight flash of light; glimmer. **3** short, rapid movement. □□ **twin′kler** *n.* **twin′kling** *n.*

twirl /twərl/ • *v.* spin, swing, or twist quickly and lightly around. • *n.* **1** twirling motion. **2** flourish made with a pen. □□ **twirl′er** *n.* **twirl′y** *adj.*

twirp var. of TWERP.

twist /twist/ • *v.* **1 a** *tr.* change the form of by rotating one end and not the other, or the two ends in opposite directions. **b** *intr.* undergo such a change. **c** *tr.* wrench or pull out of shape with a twisting action (*twisted my ankle*). **2** *tr.* wind (strands, etc.) around each other. **3 a** *tr.* give a spiral form to. **b** *intr.* take a spiral form. **4** *tr.* (foll. by *off*) break off by twisting. **5** *tr.* misrepresent the meaning of (words). **6 a** *intr.* take a winding course. **b** *tr.* make (one's way) in a winding manner. **7** *intr.* dance the twist. • *n.* **1** act of twisting. **2** twisted state. **3** thing formed by twisting. **4** point at which a thing twists or bends. **5** unexpected turn in a story, etc. **6** curled peel of lemon, etc., to flavor a drink. **7** (prec. by *the*) dance with a twisting movement, popular in the 1960s. □ **twist a person's arm** *colloq.* apply coercion, esp. by moral pressure. □□ **twist′y** *adj.* (**twist·i·er, twist·i·est**).

twist·er /twistər/ *n.* *colloq.* tornado, waterspout, etc.

twit¹ /twit/ *n.* *sl.* silly or foolish person.

twit² /twit/ *v.tr.* (**twit·ted, twit·ting**) reproach or taunt, usu. good-humoredly.

twitch /twich/ • *v.* **1** *intr.* (of features, muscles, etc.) move or contract spasmodically. **2** *tr.* pull sharply at. • *n.* **1** sudden involuntary contraction or movement. **2** sudden pull or jerk.

twit·ter /twitər/ • *v.* **1** *intr.* (of or like a bird) emit a succession of light tremulous sounds. **2** *tr.* utter or express in this way. • *n.* **1** act of twittering. **2** *colloq.* tremulously excited state. □□ **twit′ter·y** *adj.*

two /tōō/ • *n.* **1** one more than one. **2** symbol for this (2, ii, II). • *adj.* that amount to two. □ **in two** in or into two pieces. **put two and two together** infer from known facts. **that makes two of us** *colloq.* that is true of me also. **two-bit** *colloq.* cheap; petty. **two-dimensional 1** having or appearing to have length and breadth but no depth. **2** lacking depth or substance; superficial. **two-faced 1** having two faces. **2** insincere; deceitful. **two-ply** of two strands, webs, or thicknesses. **two-step** dance in march or polka time. **two-time** *colloq.* **1** be unfaithful to (a lover). **2** swindle. **two-timer** *colloq.* one who two-times. **two-tone** having two colors or sounds. **two-way 1** involving two ways or participants. **2** (of a radio) capable of transmitting and receiving signals.

two·fold /tōōfōld/ *adj.* & *adv.* **1** twice as much or as many. **2** consisting of two parts.

two·some /tōōsəm/ *n.* two persons together.

'twould /twŏŏd/ *archaic* it would.

twp. *abbr.* township.

TX *abbr.* Texas (in official postal use).

-ty¹ /tee/ *suffix* forming nouns denoting quality or condition (*cruelty; plenty*).

-ty² /tee/ *suffix* denoting tens (*twenty; thirty; ninety*).

ty·coon /tīkōōn/ *n.* business magnate.

ty·ing *pres. part.* of TIE.

tyke /tīk/ *n.* (also **tike**) small child.

tym·pa·ni var. of TIMPANI.

tym·pa·num /timpənəm/ *n.* (*pl.* **tym·pa·nums** or **tym·pa·na** /-nə/) **1** middle ear. **2** eardrum. □□ **tym·pan′ic** *adj.*

type /tīp/ • *n.* **1** class; kind; sort. **2** person, thing, or event exemplifying a group or class. **3** (in *comb.*) made of, resembling, or functioning as (*ceramic-type material*). **4** *colloq.* person, esp. of a specified character (*quiet type; not my type*). **5** object, conception, or work serving as a model for subsequent artists. **6** *Printing* **a** piece of metal, etc., with a raised letter or character on its upper surface for printing. **b** kind or size of such pieces (*printed in large type*). • *v.* **1** *tr.* & *intr.* write with a typewriter or keyboard. **2** *tr.* esp. Biol. & Med. assign to a type; classify. **3** *tr.* = TYPECAST.

a   **a**   *a*

roman   boldface   italic

TYPE, 6b

type·cast /típkast/ v.tr. (past and past part. **–cast**) assign (an actor or actress) repeatedly to the same type of role.

type·face /típfays/ n. Printing **1** set of type or characters in one design. **2** inked surface of type.

type·script /típskript/ n. typewritten document.

type·set·ter /típsetər/ n. Printing **1** person who composes type. **2** composing machine. □□ **type′set·ting** n.

type·writ·er /típrītər/ n. machine with keys for producing printlike characters on paper inserted around a roller.

type·writ·ten /típrit'n/ adj. produced with a typewriter.

ty·phoid /tífoyd/ n. (in full **ty′phoid fe′ver**) infectious bacterial fever attacking the intestines.

ty·phoon /tīfo͞on/ n. violent hurricane in E. Asia.

ty·phus /tífəs/ n. infectious fever with a purple rash, headaches, and usu. delirium. □□ **ty′phous** adj.

typ·i·cal /típikəl/ adj. **1** serving as a characteristic example; representative. **2** characteristic; to be expected. □□ **typ·i·cal·i·ty** /–kálitee/ n. **typ′i·cal·ly** adv.

typ·i·fy /típifī/ v.tr. (**–fies, –fied**) **1** be typical of.

2 represent by or as a type or symbol. □□ **typ·i·fi·ca′tion** n. **typ′i·fi·er** n.

typ·ist /típist/ n. person who types.

ty·po /típō/ n. (pl. **–pos**) colloq. typographical error.

ty·pog·ra·phy /tīpógrəfee/ n. **1** printing as an art. **2** style and appearance of printed matter. □□ **ty·pog′ra·pher** n. **ty·po·graph′i·cal** adj. **ty·po·graph′i·cal·ly** adv.

ty·ran·ni·cal /tiránikəl/ adj. despotic. □□ **ty·ran′ni·cal·ly** adv.

tyr·an·nize /tírənīz/ v.tr. & (foll. by over) intr. treat despotically or cruelly.

ty·ran·no·sau·rus /tiránəsáwrəs/ n. (also **ty·ran′no·saur**) carnivorous dinosaur with short front legs and a long well-developed tail.

tyr·an·ny /tírənee/ n. (pl. **–nies**) **1** cruel and arbitrary use of authority. **2** rule by a tyrant. □□ **tyr′an·nous** adj. **tyr′an·nous·ly** adv.

ty·rant /tírənt/ n. **1** oppressive or cruel ruler. **2** person exercising power arbitrarily or cruelly.

ty·ro /tírō/ n. (pl. **–ros**) beginner; novice.

Uu

U[1] /yōō/ *n.* (also **u**) (*pl.* **Us** or **U's; u's**) **1** twenty-first letter of the alphabet. **2** U-shaped object or curve.

U[2] *abbr.* (also **U.**) university.

U[3] *symb. Chem.* uranium.

-ubility /yōōbílitee/ *suffix* forming nouns from, or corresponding to, adjectives in *-uble* (*solubility*; *volubility*).

u·biq·ui·tous /yōōbíkwitəs/ *adj.* **1** present everywhere or in several places simultaneously. **2** often encountered. □□ **u·biq'ui·tous·ly** *adv.* **u·biq'ui·tous·ness** *n.* **u·biq'ui·ty** *n.*

-uble /yəbəl/ *suffix* forming adjectives meaning 'that may or must be' (see ABLE) (*soluble*; *voluble*).

-ubly /yəblee/ *suffix* forming adverbs corresponding to adjectives in *-uble.*

U-boat /yōōbōt/ *n. hist.* German submarine.

ud·der /údər/ *n.* baglike mammary gland of cattle, sheep, etc., with several teats.

UFO /yōō-ef-ó, yōōfó/ *n.* (also **ufo**) (*pl.* **UFOs** or **ufos**) unidentified flying object.

u·fol·o·gy /yōōfóləjee/ *n.* the study of UFOs. □□ **u·fol'o·gist** *n.*

ugh /əkh, ug, ukh/ *int.* expressing disgust or horror.

ug·ly /úglee/ *adj.* (**ug·li·er, ug·li·est**) **1** unpleasing or repulsive to see or hear. **2** unpleasantly suggestive (*ugly rumors are about*). **3** threatening; dangerous (*the sky has an ugly look*). **4** morally repulsive (*ugly vices*). □□ **ug'li·ly** *adv.* **ug'li·ness** *n.*

UHF *abbr.* ultrahigh frequency.

UK *abbr.* United Kingdom.

Ukrai·ni·an /yōōkráyneeən/ • *n.* **1** native of Ukraine. **2** language of Ukraine. • *adj.* of or relating to Ukraine or its people or language.

u·ku·le·le /yōōkəláylee/ *n.* small, four-stringed Hawaiian guitar. (orig. Portuguese) guitar.

-ular /yələr/ *suffix* forming adjectives, sometimes corresp. to nouns in *-ule* (*pustular*) but often without diminutive force (*angular, granular*). □□ **-ularity** /-láritee/ *suffix* forming nouns.

ul·cer /úlsər/ *n.* **1** open sore on or in the body, often forming pus. **2 a** moral blemish. **b** corroding or corrupting influence, etc. □□ **ul·cered** *adj.* **ul'cer·ous** *adj.*

ul·cer·ate /úlsərayt/ *v.* form into or affect with an ulcer. □□ **ul'cer·a·ble** *adj.* **ul·cer·a·tion** /-ráyshən/ *n.* **ul'cer·a·tive** *adj.*

-ule /əl, yōōl/ *suffix* forming diminutive nouns (*capsule*; *globule*).

-ulent /yələnt/ *suffix* forming adjectives meaning 'abounding in; full of' (*fraudulent*). □□ **-ulence** *suffix* forming nouns.

ul·na /úlnə/ *n.* (*pl.* **ul·nae** /-nee/) the thinner and longer of the two forearm bones (cf. RADIUS 3). □□ **ul'nar** *adj.*

-ulous /yələs/ *suffix* forming adjectives (*fabulous*; *populous*).

ul·ster /úlstər/ *n.* long, loose overcoat of rough cloth.

ult. *abbr.* **1** ultimo. **2** ultimate.

ul·te·ri·or /ultéreeər/ *adj.* existing in the background; hidden; secret (esp. ulterior motive). □□ **ul·te'ri·or·ly** *adv.*

ul·ti·mate /últimət/ • *adj.* **1** last or last possible; final. **2** fundamental; primary (*ultimate truths*). **3** maximum (*ultimate tensile strength*). • *n.* **1** best achievable or imaginable. **2** final or fundamental fact or principle. □□ **ul'ti·mate·ly** *adj.* **ul'ti·mate·ness** *n.*

ul·ti·ma·tum /últimáytəm/ *n.* (*pl.* **ul·ti·ma·tums** or **ul·ti·ma·ta** /-tə/) final demand or statement of terms in negotiations.

ul·ti·mo /últimō/ *adj. Commerce* of last month (*the 28th ultimo*).

ul·tra /últrə/ *adj.* favoring extreme views or measures, esp. in religion or politics.

ultra- /últrə/ *comb. form* **1** beyond; on the other side of. **2** extreme(ly), excessive(ly) (*ultraconservative*; *ultramodern*).

ul·tra·high /últrəhí/ *adj.* **1** (of a frequency) in the range 300 to 3,000 megahertz. **2** extremely high (*ultrahigh prices*).

ul·tra·ma·rine /últrəməreéen/ • *n.* brilliant blue pigment or color. • *adj.* **1** of this color. **2** *archaic* situated beyond the sea.

ul·tra·mon·tane /últrəmontáyn/ *adj.* situated on the other side of the mountains (esp. the Alps) from the point of view of the speaker.

ul·tra·son·ic /últrəsónik/ *adj.* of or involving sound waves with a frequency above the upper limit of human hearing. □□ **ul·tra·son'i·cal·ly** *adv.*

ul·tra·sound /últrəsownd/ *n.* ultrasonic waves, esp. as used in medicine.

ul·tra·vi·o·let /últrəvíələt/ *adj. Physics* **1** having a wavelength (just) beyond the violet end of the visible spectrum. **2** of or using such radiation.

ul·u·late /úlyəlayt, yōōl-/ *v.intr.* howl; wail; make a hooting cry. □□ **ul'u·lant** *adj.* **ul·u·la·tion** /-láyshən/ *n.*

um /um, əm/ *int.* expressing hesitation or a pause in speech.

um·bel /úmbəl/ *n. Bot.* flower cluster in which stalks nearly equal in length spring from a common center and form a flat or curved surface, as in parsley. □□ **um'bel·lar** *adj.* **um·bel·lif·er·ous** /-íferəs/ *adj.*

um·ber /úmbər/ • *n.* natural pigment or color like ocher but darker and browner. • *adj.* **1** of this color. **2** dark; dusky.

um·bil·i·cal /umbílikəl/ *adj.* of, situated near, or affecting the navel. □ **umbilical cord** flexible, cordlike structure attaching a fetus to the placenta.

um·bil·i·cus /umbílikəs/ *n.* (*pl.* **um·bil·i·ci** /-bílisī/ or **um·bil·i·cus·es**) *Anat.* navel.

um·bra /úmbrə/ *n.* (*pl.* **um·bras** or **um·brae**

/–bree/) *Astron.* **1** total shadow usu. cast on the earth by the moon during a solar eclipse. **2** dark central part of a sunspot. □□ **um′bral** *adj.*

um·brage /úmbrij/ *n.* offense; sense of slight or injury.

um·brel·la /umbrélə/ *n.* **1** light, portable device for protection against rain, strong sun, etc., consisting of a usu. circular canopy of cloth mounted by means of a collapsible metal frame on a central stick. **2** protection or patronage. **3** coordinating or unifying agency (*umbrella organization*). □□ **um·brel·laed** /–ləd/ *adj.* **um·brel′la·like** *adj.*

u·mi·ak / oomeeak/ *n.* Inuit skin-and-wood open boat propelled with paddles.

um·laut / oomlowt/ *n.* **1** mark (¨) used over a vowel, esp. in Germanic languages, to indicate a vowel change. **2** such a vowel change.

ump /ump/ *n. colloq.* umpire.

um·pire /úmpīr/ • *n.* person chosen to enforce the rules and settle disputes esp. in various sports. • *v.* act as umpire.

ump·teen /úmpteen/ *sl.* • *adj.* indefinitely many; a lot of. • *pron.* indefinitely many. □□ **ump′teenth′** *adj.*

UN *abbr.* United Nations.

un-¹ /un/ *prefix* **1** added to adjectives and participles and their derivative nouns and adverbs, meaning: **a** not: denoting the absence of a quality or state (*unusable*; *unhappiness*). **b** reverse of, usu. with an implication of approval or disapproval (*unselfish*; *unscientific*). **2** (less often) added to nouns, meaning 'a lack of' (*unrest*; *untruth*).

un-² /un/ *prefix* added to verbs and (less often) nouns, forming verbs denoting: **1** reversal or cancellation of an action or state (*undress*; *unsettle*). **2** deprivation or separation (*unmask*). **3** release from (*unburden*). **4** causing to be no longer (*unman*).

'un /ən/ *pron. colloq.* one (*that's a good 'un*).

un·a·bat·ed /únəbáytid/ *adj.* not abated; undiminished. □□ **un·a·bat′ed·ly** *adv.*

un·a·bridged /únəbríjd/ *adj.* (of a text, etc.) complete; not abridged.

un·ac·a·dem·ic /únakədémik/ *adj.* **1** not academic (esp. not scholarly or theoretical). **2** (of a person) not suited to academic study.

un·ac·com·pa·nied /únəkúmpəneed/ *adj.* **1** not accompanied. **2** *Mus.* without accompaniment.

---

un·a·bashed′ *adj.*
un·ab′ le *adj.*
un·ac·cept′a·ble *adv.*
un·ac·cept′a·bly *adv.*
un·a·chiev′a·ble *adj.*
un·ac·knowl′edged *adj.*
un·ac·quaint′ed *adj.*
un·af·fil′i·at·ed *adj.*
un·a·fraid′ *adj.*
un·aid′ ed *adj.*
un·al′ter·a·ble *adj.*
un·al′ter·a·bly *adv.*
un·al′tered *adj.*
un·am·bi·gu′i·ty *n.*
un·am·big′u·ous *adj.*
un·am·big′u·ous·ly *adv.*
un·am·bi′tious *adj.*
un·an·nounced′ *adj.*
un·an′swered *adj.*
un·an·tic′i·pat·ed *adj.*
un·ap·peal′ing *adj.*
un·ap·peal′ing·ly *adv.*
un·ap′pe·tiz·ing *adj.*
un·ap·pre′ci·at·ed *adj.*
un·ap·pre′cia·tive *adj.*
un·ap·proved′ *adj.*
un·ar′gu·a·ble *adj.*
un·asked′ *adj.*
un·as·sail′a·ble *adj.*
un·as·sist′ed *adj.*
un·at·tain′a·ble *adj.*
un·at·trac′tive *adj.*
un·at·trac′tive·ly *adv.*
un·au′thor·ized *adj.*
un·a·vail′a·ble *adj.*
un·a·vail·a·bil′i·ty *n.*
un·a·void′a·ble *adj.*
un·a·void′a·bly *adv.*
un·bear′a·ble *adj.*
un·bear′a·bly *adv.*
un·beat′a·ble *adj.*
un·bi′ased *adj.*
un·bleached′ *adj.*
un·blem′ished *adj.*

un·bound′ *adj.*
un·break′a·ble *adj.*
un·buck′le *v.*
un·but′ton *v.*
un·ceas′ing *adj.*
un·ceas′ing·ly *adv.*
un·cen′sored *adj.*
un·chal′lenged *adj.*
un·change′a·ble *adj.*
un·changed′ *adj.*
un·chang′ing *adj.*
un·chap′er·oned· *adj.*
un·char·ac·ter·is′tic *adj.*
un·char·ac·ter·is′ti·cal·ly *adv.*
un·checked′ *adj.*
un·civ′i·lized *adj.*
un·claimed′ *adj.*
un·claimed′ *adj.*
un·clas′si·fied *adj.*
un·clean′ *adj.*
un·clear′ *adj.*
un·cloud′ed *adj.*
un·clut′tered *adj.*
un·combed′ *adj.*
un·com·plain′ing *adj.*
un·com·plain′ing·ly *adv.*
un·com·plet′ed *adj.*
un·com′pli·cat·ed *adj.*
un·com·pli·men′ta·ry *adj.*
un·com·pre·hend′ing *adj.*
un·con·cealed′ *adj.*
un·con·fined′ *adj.*
un·con·firmed′ *adj.*
un·con′quer·a·ble *adj.*
un·con′quered *adj.*
un·con·strained′ *adj.*
un·con·tam′i·nat·ed *adj.*
un·con·test′ed *adj.*
un·con·trol′la·ble *adj.*
un·con·trol′la·bly *adv.*
un·con·trolled′ *adj.*
un·con·vinced′ *adj.*
un·con·vin′cing *adj.*
un·con·vin′cing·ly *adv.*
un·cooked′ *adj.*

un·co·op′er·a·tive *adj.*
un·cor·rob′o·rat·ed *adj.*
un·crit′i·cal *adj.*
un·cross′ *v.*
un·cul′ti·vat·ed *adj.*
un·cured′ *adj.*
un·dam′aged *adj.*
un·dat′ed *adj.*
un·daunt′ed *adj.*
un·de·clared′ *adj.*
un·de·feat′ed *adj.*
un·de·fend′ed *adj.*
un·de·fined′ *adj.*
un·de·mand′ing *adj.*
un·de·mo·cra′tic *adj.*
un·de·pend′a·ble *adj.*
un·de·served′ *adj.*
un·de·serv′ed·ly *adv.*
un·de·serv′ing *adj.*
un·de·tect′a·ble *adj.*
un·de·tect′a·bly *adv.*
un·de·tect′ed *adj.*
un·de·ter′mined *adj.*
un·de·terred′ *adj.*
un·de·vel′oped *adj.*
un·di·gest′ed *adj.*
un·dig′ni·fied· *adj.*
un·di·lut′ed *adj.*
un·di·min′ished *adj.*
un·dip·lo·mat′ic *adj.*
un·dis′ci·plined *adj.*
un·dis·closed′ *adj.*
un·dis·co′vered *adj.*
un·dis·guised′ *adj.*
un·dis·mayed′ *adj.*
un·dis·put′ed *adj.*
un·dis·tin′guished *adj.*
un·dis·turbed′ *adj.*
un·di·vid′ed *adj.*
un·dressed′ *adj.*
un·drink′a·ble *adj.*
un·eat′en *adj.*
un·ec·o·nom′ic *adj.*
un·ec·o·nom′i·cal *adj.*
un·ec·o·nom′i·cal·ly *adv.*

un·ed′it·ed *adj.*
un·ed′u·cat·ed *adj.*
un·em·phat′ic *adj.*
un·en·cum′bered *adj.*
un·end′ing *adj.*
un·en·dur′a·ble *adj.*
un·en·dur′a·bly *adv.*
un·en·light′ened *adj.*
un·en·thu·si·as′tic *adj.*
un·en·thu·si·as′ti·cal·ly *adv.*
un·en′vi·a·ble *adj.*
un·e·vent′ful *adj.*
un·e·vent′ful·ly *adv.*
un·ex·plain′a·ble *adj.*
un·ex·plain′a·bly *adv.*
un·ex·plained′ *adj.*
un·ex·plored′ *adj.*
un·ex·posed′ *adj.*
un·ex·pressed′ *adj.*
un·fad′ing *adj.*
un·fal′ter·ing *adj.*
un·fa·mil′iar *adj.*
un·fa·mil·i·ar′i·ty *n.*
un·fash′ion·a·ble *adj.*
un·fash′ion·a·bly *adv.*
un·fas′tened *adj.*
un·fath′o·ma·ble *adj.*
un·fa′vor·a·ble *adj.*
un·fa′vor·a·bly *adv.*
un·fit′ *adj.*
un·flat′ter·ing *adj.*
un·flat′ter·ing·ly *adv.*
un·flinch′ing *adj.*
un·flinch′ing·ly *adv.*
un·fore·see′a·ble *adj.*
un·fore·seen′ *adj.*
un·for·giv′a·ble *adj.*
un·for·giv′a·bly *adv.*
un·for·giv′en *adj.*
un·for·giv′ing *adj.*
un·for·got′ten *adj.*
un·ful·filled′ *adj.*
un·fur′nished *adj.*
un·gen′tle·man·ly *adj.*
un·grace′ful *adj.*

un·ac·com·plished /únəkómplisht/ *adj.* **1** not accomplished; uncompleted. **2** lacking accomplishments.

un·ac·count·a·ble /únəkówntəbəl/ *adj.* **1** unable to be explained. **2** unpredictable or strange in behavior. **3** not responsible. □□ **un·ac·count·a·bil´i·ty** *n.* **un·ac·count´a·ble·ness** *n.* **un·ac·count´a·bly** *adv.*

un·ac·count·ed /únəkówntid/ *adj.* of which no account is given.

un·ac·cus·tomed /únəkústəmd/ *adj.* **1** (usu. foll. by *to*) not accustomed. **2** not customary; unusual (*unaccustomed silence*). □□ **un·ac·cus´tomed·ly** *adv.*

un·a·dorned /únədáwrnd/ *adj.* not adorned; plain.

un·a·dul·ter·at·ed /únədúltəraytid/ *adj.* **1** not adulterated; pure; concentrated. **2** sheer; complete; utter.

un·ad·vis·a·ble /únədvízəbəl/ *adj.* **1** not open to advice. **2** (of a thing) inadvisable.

un·ad·vised /únədvízd/ *adj.* **1** indiscreet; rash. **2** not having had advice. □□ **un·ad·vis´ed·ly** /–zídlee/ *adv.* **un·ad·vis´ed·ness** *n.*

un·af·fect·ed /únəféktid/ *adj.* **1** (usu. foll. by *by*) not affected. **2** free from affectation; genuine; sincere. □□ **un·af·fect´ed·ly** *adv.* **un·af·fect´ed·ness** *n.*

un·a·lien·a·ble /únáyleeənəbəl/ *adj.* *Law* = IN·ALIENABLE.

un·a·ligned /únəlínd/ *adj.* **1** = NONALIGNED. **2** not physically aligned.

un·a·live /únəlív/ *adj.* **1** lacking in vitality. **2** (foll. by *to*) not fully susceptible or awake to.

un·al·loyed /únəlóyd, únál–/ *adj.* **1** not alloyed; pure. **2** complete; utter (*unalloyed joy*).

un·A·mer·i·can /únəmérikən/ *adj.* **1** not in accordance with American characteristics, etc. **2** contrary to the interests of the US. □□ **un·A·mer´i·can·ism** *n.*

u·nan·i·mous /yōōnánimǝs/ *adj.* **1** all in agreement (*the committee was unanimous*). **2** (of an opinion, vote, etc.) held or given by general consent (*the unanimous choice*). □□ **u´na·nim´i·ty** /–nənímitee/ *n.* **u·nan´i·mous·ly** *adv.*

un·an·swer·a·ble /únánsərəbəl/ *adj.* **1** unable to be refuted. **2** unable to be answered (*an unanswerable question*). □□ **un·an´swer·a·bly** *adv.*

un·ap·proach·a·ble /únəpróchəbəl/ *adj.* **1** not

un·grace´ful·ly *adv.*	un·lace´ *v.*
un·gram·mat´i·cal *adj.*	un·li´censed *adj.*
un·gram·mat´i·cal·ly *adv.*	un·lined´ *adj.*
un·grate´ful *adj.*	un·list´ed *adj.*
un·grate´ful·ly *adv.*	un·lit´ *adj.*
un·grudg´ing *adj.*	un·made´ *adj.*
un·grudg´ing·ly *adv.*	un·man´age·a·ble *adj.*
un·ham´pered *adj.*	un·man´age·a·bly *adv.*
un·harmed´ *adj.*	un·man´ly *adj.*
un·help´ful *adj.*	un·marked´ *adj.*
un·help´ful·ly *adv.*	un·mar´ried *adj.*
un·hes´i·tat·ing *adj.*	un·matched´ *adj.*
un·hes·i·tat´ing·ly *adv.*	un·mer´it·ed *adj.*
un·hin´dered *adj.*	un·mind´ful *adj.*
un·hook´ *v.*	un·named´ *adj.*
un·hoped´ -for· *adj.*	un·need´ed *adj.*
un·hur´ried *adj.*	un·no´tice·a·ble *adj.*
un·hurt´ *adj.*	un·no´tice·a·bly *adv.*
un·i·den´ti·fi·a·ble *adj.*	un·no´ticed *adj.*
un·i·den´ti·fied· *adj.*	un·ob·jec´tion·a·ble *adj.*
un·i·ma´gi·na·ble *adj.*	un·o·blig´ing *adj.*
un·im·paired´ *adj.*	un·ob·ser´vant *adj.*
un·im·ped´ed *adj.*	un·ob·served´ *adj.*
un·im·por´tant *adj.*	un·ob·struct´ed *adj.*
un·im·pres´sive *adj.*	un·ob·tain´a·ble *adj.*
un·im·proved´ *adj.*	un·oc´cu·pied· *adj.*
un·in·cor´po·rat·ed *adj.*	un·of·fi´cial *adj.*
un·in·formed´ *adj.*	un·of·fi´cial·ly *adv.*
un·in·hab´it·a·ble *adj.*	un·o´pened *adj.*
un·in·hab´it·ed *adj.*	un·op·posed´ *adj.*
un·in·hib´it·ed *adj.*	un·or´tho·dox· *adj.*
un·in´jured *adj.*	un·paid´ *adj.*
un·in·sured´ *adj.*	un·paint´ed *adj.*
un·in·tel´li·gi·ble *adj.*	un·par´don·a·ble *adj.*
un·in·tend´ed *adj.*	un·par´don·a·bly *adv.*
un·in·ten´tion·al *adj.*	un·pat·ri·o´tic *adj.*
un·in·ten´tion·al·ly *adv.*	un·paved´ *adj.*
un·in·ter·rupt´ed *adj.*	un·per·turbed´ *adj.*
un·just´ *adj.*	un·planned´ *adj.*
un·just´ly *adv.*	un·pol´ished *adj.*
un·jus·ti·fi´a·ble *adj.*	un·pol·lut´ed *adj.*
un·jus·ti·fi´a·bly *adv.*	un·pre·dict´a·ble *adj.*
un·jus´ti·fied· *adj.*	un·pre·dict·a·bil´i·ty *n.*
un·la´beled *adj.*	un·pre·dict´a·bly *adv.*
	un·pre·dict´ed *adj.*

un·pre´ju·diced *adj.*	un·sink´a·ble *adj.*
un·pre·med´i·tat·ed *adj.*	un·skill´ful *adj.*
un·pre·pared´ *adj.*	un·sliced´ *adj.*
un·pro·duct´ive *adj.*	un·sold´ *adj.*
un·prof´it·a·ble *adj.*	un·solved´ *adj.*
un·pro·nounce´a·ble *adj.*	un·spe·cif´ic *adj.*
un·pro·pi´tious *adj.*	un·spe´ci·fied· *adj.*
un·pro·tect´ed *adj.*	un·spec·tac´u·lar *adj.*
un·pro·voked´ *adj.*	un·spec·tac´u·lar·ly *adv.*
un·pub´lished *adj.*	un·spoiled´ *adj.*
un·pun´ished *adj.*	un·sports´man·like· *adj.*
un·quench´a·ble *adj.*	un·stat´ed *adj.*
un·re·a·list´ic *adj.*	un·stop´pa·ble *adj.*
un·re·a·list´i·cal·ly *adv.*	un·sub·stan´ti·at·ed *adj.*
un·re·a·liz´a·ble *adj.*	un·suc·cess´ful *adj.*
un·re´a·lized· *adj.*	un·suc·cess´ful·ly *adv.*
un·rec·og·niz´a·ble *adj.*	un·suit´a·ble *adj.*
un·rec´on·ciled· *adj.*	un·suit·a·bil´i·ty *n*
un·re·cord´ed *adj.*	un·suit´a·ble *adj.*
un·re·fined´ *adj.*	un·suit´a·bly *adv.*
un·reg´is·tered *adj.*	un·sul´lied *adj.*
un·re·hearsed´ *adj.*	un·su·per·vised´ *adj.*
un·re·lated´ *adj.*	un·sup·port´ed *adj.*
un·re·pent´ant·ly *adv.*	un·sure´ *adj.*
un·re·spon´sive *adj.*	un·sur·passed´ *adj.*
un·re·strained´ *adj.*	un·sus·pect´ed *adj.*
un·re·strict´ed *adj.*	un·sus·pect´ing *adj.*
un·safe´ *adj.*	un·sweet´ened *adj.*
un·said´ *adj.*	un·test´ed *adj.*
un·salt´ed *adj.*	un·tir´ing *adj.*
un·san´i·tar·y *adj.*	un·trained´ *adj.*
un·sat·is·fac´to·ry *adj.*	un·treat´ed *adj.*
un·sat·is·fac´to·ri·ly *adv.*	un·trust´wor·thy *adj.*
un·scarred´ *adj.*	un·trust´wor·thi·ness *n.*
un·sche´duled *adj.*	un·us´a·ble *adj.*
un·sea´soned *adj.*	un·var´y·ing *adj.*
un·see´ing *adj.*	un·want´ed *adj.*
un·self·con´scious *adj.*	un·wa´ver·ing *adj.*
un·self·con´scious·ly *adv.*	un·wa´ver·ing·ly *adv.*
un·self·con´scious·ness *n.*	un·wel´come *adj.*
un·self´ish *adj.*	un·work´a·ble *adj.*
un·self´ish·ly *adv.*	un·work´a·bly *adv.*
un·self´ish·ness *n.*	un·zip´ *v.*
un·sen·ti·men´tal *adj.*	
un·signed´ *adj.*	

approachable; remote; inaccessible. **2** (of a person) unfriendly. □□ **un·ap·proach·a·bil′i·ty** *n.* **un·ap·proach′a·bly** *adv.*

un·ap·pro·pri·at·ed /únəprópreeaytid/ *adj.* **1** not allocated or assigned. **2** not taken into possession by anyone.

un·apt /únápt/ *adj.* **1** (usu. foll. by *for*) not suitable. **2** (usu. foll. by *to* + infin.) not apt. □□ **un·apt′ly** *adv.* **un·apt′ness** *n.*

un·armed /únáarmd/ *adj.* not armed; without weapons.

un·ar·tic·u·lat·ed /únaartíkyəlaytid/ *adj.* not articulated or distinct.

un·ar·tis·tic /únaartístik/ *adj.* not artistic, esp. not concerned with art. □□ **un·ar·tis′ti·cal·ly** *adv.*

un·a·shamed /únəsháymd/ *adj.* **1** feeling no guilt; shameless. **2** blatant; bold. □□ **un·a·sham′ed·ly** *adv.* **un·a·sham′ed·ness** *n.*

un·as·sum·ing /únəso͝oming/ *adj.* not pretentious or arrogant; modest. □□ **un·as·sum′ing·ly** *adv.*

un·at·tached /únətácht/ *adj.* **1** not attached, esp. to a particular body, organization, etc. **2** not engaged or married.

un·at·tend·ed /únəténdid/ *adj.* **1** not attended. **2** (of a person, vehicle, etc.) not accompanied; alone; uncared for.

un·at·trib·ut·a·ble /únətríbyətəbəl/ *adj.* (esp. of information) that cannot or may not be attributed to a source, etc. □□ **un·at·trib′ut·a·bly** *adv.*

un·a·vail·ing /únəváyling/ *adj.* not availing; achieving nothing; ineffectual. □□ **un·avail′ing·ly** *adv.*

un·a·ware /únəwáir/ • *adj.* **1** not aware; ignorant (*unaware of her presence*). **2** (of a person) insensitive; unperceptive. • *adv.* = UNAWARES. □□ **un·a·ware′ness** *n.*

un·a·wares /únəwáirz/ *adv.* **1** unexpectedly (*met them unawares*). **2** inadvertently (*dropped it unawares*).

un·bal·ance /únbáləns/ *v.tr.* **1** upset the physical or mental balance of (*unbalanced by the blow; the shock unbalanced him*). **2** (as **unbalanced** *adj.*) **a** not balanced. **b** (of a mind or a person) unstable or deranged.

un·bear·a·ble /únbáirəbəl/ *adj.* not bearable. □□ **un·bear′a·bly** *adv.*

un·be·com·ing /únbikúming/ *adj.* **1** not flattering a person. **2** not fitting; unsuitable. □□ **un·be·com′ing·ly** *adv.*

un·be·known /únbinón/ *adj.* (also **un·be·knownst** /–nónst/) without the knowledge of (*was there all day unbeknown to us*).

un·be·lief /únbilee͡f/ *n.* lack of belief, esp. in religious matters. □□ **un·be·liev·er** /–lee͡vər/ *n.* **un·be·liev′ing** *adj.*

un·be·liev·a·ble /únbilee͡vəbəl/ *adj.* not believable; incredible. □□ **un·be·liev′a·bly** *adv.*

un·bend /únbénd/ *v.* (*past* and *past part.* **un·bent**) **1** *tr.* & *intr.* straighten. **2** *intr.* relax from strain or severity; become affable.

un·bend·ing /únbénding/ *adj.* **1** inflexible. **2** firm; austere (*unbending rectitude*).

un·blink·ing /únblíngking/ *adj.* **1** not blinking. **2** steadfast; not hesitating. **3** stolid; cool. □□ **un·blink′ing·ly** *adv.*

un·bolt /únbólt/ *v.tr.* release (a door, etc.) by drawing back the bolt.

un·born /únbáwrn/ *adj.* **1** not yet born (*an unborn child*). **2** never to be brought into being (*unborn hopes*).

un·bos·om /únbo͝ozəm/ *v.tr.* **1** disclose (thoughts, etc.). **2** (*refl.*) unburden (oneself) of one's thoughts, etc.

un·bound·ed /únbówndid/ *adj.* infinite (*unbounded optimism*).

un·bri·dle /únbri͡d'l/ *v.tr.* **1** remove a bridle from (a horse). **2** remove constraints from (one's tongue, a person, etc.). **3** (as **unbridled** *adj.*) unconstrained (*unbridled insolence*).

un·bro·ken /únbrókən/ *adj.* **1** not broken. **2** not tamed (*unbroken horse*). **3** not interrupted (*unbroken sleep*). **4** not surpassed (*unbroken record*).

un·bur·den /únbúrd'n/ *v.tr.* **1** relieve of a burden. **2** (esp. *refl.*) relieve (oneself, one's conscience, etc.) by confession, etc.

un·called /únkáwld/ *adj.* not summoned or invited. □ **uncalled-for** (of an opinion, action, etc.) impertinent or unnecessary (*an uncalled-for remark*).

un·can·ny /únkánee/ *adj.* (**un·can·ni·er**, **un·can·ni·est**) seemingly supernatural; mysterious. □□ **un·can′ni·ly** *adv.*

un·cared-for /únkáirdfawr/ *adj.* disregarded; neglected.

un·car·ing /únkáiring/ *adj.* lacking compassion for others.

un·cer·e·mo·ni·ous /únserimóneeəs/ *adj.* **1** informal. **2** abrupt; discourteous. □□ **un·cer·e·mo′ni·ous·ly** *adv.*

un·cer·tain /únsə́rt'n/ *adj.* **1** not certainly knowing or known (*the result is uncertain*). **2** unreliable (*his aim is uncertain*). **3** changeable; erratic (*uncertain weather*). □ **in no uncertain terms** clearly and forcefully. □□ **un·cer′tain·ly** *adv.* **un·cer′tain·ty** *n.*

un·char·i·ta·ble /úncháritəbəl/ *adj.* censorious; severe in judgment. □□ **un·char′i·ta·bly** *adv.*

un·chart·ed /úncháartid/ *adj.* not mapped or surveyed.

un·chris·tian /únkríschən/ *adj.* **1** contrary to Christian principles, esp. uncaring or selfish. **2** not Christian.

un·ci·al /únsheeəl, únshəl/ • *adj.* of or written in rounded, unjoined letters found in manuscripts of the 4th–8th c., from which modern capitals are derived. • *n.* **1** uncial letter. **2** uncial style or manuscript.

uncial

UNCIAL

un·civ·il /únsívil/ *adj.* ill-mannered; impolite. □□ **un·civ′il·ly** *adv.*

un·cle /úngkəl/ *n.* **1 a** brother of one's father or mother. **b** aunt's husband. **2** *colloq.* name given by children to a male family friend. □ **Uncle Sam** *colloq.* federal government personified (*will fight for Uncle Sam*). **Uncle Tom** *derog.* black person considered to be servile, cringing, etc. (from the hero of H. B. Stowe's *Uncle Tom's Cabin*, 1852).

un·clean /únkleén/ *adj.* **1** not clean. **2** religiously impure. **3** *Bibl.* (of a spirit) wicked.

un·clear /únkleér/ *adj.* **1** not clear or easy to understand; obscure. **2** (of a person) doubtful; uncertain (*I'm unclear as to what you mean*). □□ **un·clear′ly** *adv.*

un·cloud·ed /únklówdid/ *adj.* **1** not clouded; clear; bright. **2** untroubled (*unclouded serenity*).

un·coil /únkóyl/ *v.* unwind.

un·com·fort·a·ble /únkúmftəbəl, –kúmfərtə–/ *adj.* **1** not comfortable. **2** uneasy; disquieting (*uncomfortable silence*). □□ **un·com′fort·a·bly** *adv.*

un·com·mit·ted /únkəmítid/ *adj.* **1** not committed. **2** unattached to any specific political cause or group.

un·com·mon /únkómən/ *adj.* **1** unusual; remarkable. **2** remarkably great, etc. (*uncommon fear of spiders*). □□ **un·com′mon·ly** *adv.* **un·com·mon·ness** /–mən-nis/ *n.*

un·com·mu·ni·ca·tive /únkəmyoónikətiv/ *adj.* not wanting to communicate; taciturn.

un·com·pro·mis·ing /únkómprəmīzing/ *adj.* unwilling to compromise; stubborn; unyielding. □□ **un·com′pro·mis·ing·ly** *adv.*

un·con·cern /únkənsə́rn/ *n.* indifference; apathy. □□ **un·con·cerned′** *adj.* **un·con·cern′ed·ly** /–nidleé/ *adv.*

un·con·di·tion·al /únkəndíshənəl/ *adj.* not subject to conditions; complete (*unconditional surrender*). □□ **un·con·di′tion·al·ly** *adv.*

un·con·di·tioned /únkəndíshənd/ *adj.* **1** not subject to conditions or to an antecedent condition. **2** (of behavior, etc.) not determined by conditioning; natural.

un·con·nec·ted /únkənéktid/ *adj.* **1** not physically joined. **2** not connected or associated. **3** (of speech, etc.) disconnected; not joined in order or sequence (*unconnected ideas*).

un·con·scion·a·ble /únkónshənəbəl/ *adj.* **1 a** having no conscience. **b** contrary to conscience. **2** excessive (*an unconscionable length of time*). □□ **un·con′scion·a·bly** *adv.*

un·con·scious /únkónshəs/ • *adj.* not conscious (*unconscious of any change*; *fell unconscious on the floor*). • *n.* that part of the mind that is inaccessible to the conscious mind but that affects behavior, emotions, etc. □□ **un·con′scious·ly** *adv.* **un·con′scious·ness** *n.*

un·con·sti·tu·tion·al /únkonstitoóshənəl, –tyoó–/ *adj.* not in accordance with the political constitution or with procedural rules. □□ **un·con·sti·tu′tion·al·ly** *adv.*

un·con·ven·tion·al /únkənvénshənəl/ *adj.* unusual; unorthodox. □□ **un·con·ven·tion·al·i·ty** /–nálitee/ *n.* **un·con·ven′tion·al·ly** *adv.*

un·co·or·di·nat·ed /únkō-áwrd′naytid/ *adj.* **1** not coordinated. **2** (of a person's movements, etc.) clumsy.

un·cork /únkáwrk/ *v.tr.* **1** draw the cork from (a bottle). **2** allow (feelings, etc.) to be vented.

un·count·ed /únkówntid/ *adj.* **1** not counted. **2** very many; innumerable.

un·cou·ple /únkúpəl/ *v.tr.* **1** release from couplings. **2** unfasten.

un·couth /únkoóth/ *adj.* (of a person, manners, appearance, etc.) lacking in ease and polish; uncultured; rough (*uncouth voices*; *behavior was uncouth*).

un·cov·er /únkúvər/ *v.* **1** *tr.* **a** remove a cover or covering from. **b** make known; disclose. **2** *intr.* remove one's hat, cap, etc. **3** *tr.* (as **uncovered** *adj.*) **a** not covered by a roof, clothing, etc. **b** not wearing a hat.

unc·tion /úngkshən/ *n.* **1 a** anointing with oil, etc., as a religious rite. **b** oil, etc., so used. **2 a** soothing words or thought. **b** excessive or insincere flattery. **3 a** anointing for medical purposes. **b** ointment so used.

unc·tu·ous /úngkchoóəs/ *adj.* **1** (of behavior, speech, etc.) unpleasantly flattering; oily. **2** (esp. of minerals) having a greasy or soapy feel; oily. □□ **unc′tu·ous·ly** *adv.*

un·cut /únkút/ *adj.* **1** not cut. **2** (of a book, film, etc.) complete; uncensored. **3** (of a stone, esp. a diamond) not shaped by cutting.

un·de·cid·ed /úndisídid/ *adj.* **1** not settled or certain. **2** hesitating; irresolute.

un·de·mon·stra·tive /úndimónstrətiv/ *adj.* not expressing feelings, etc., outwardly; reserved.

un·de·ni·a·ble /úndiníəbəl/ *adj.* **1** unable to be disputed; certain. **2** excellent (*of undeniable character*). □□ **un·de·ni′a·bly** *adv.*

un·der /úndər/ • *prep.* **1 a** in or to a position lower than; below; beneath (*fell under the table*). **b** on the inside of (a surface, etc.) (*vest under his jacket*). **2 a** inferior to; less than (*a captain is under a major*; *is under 18*). **b** at or for a lower cost than (*under $20*). **3 a** subject to; controlled by (*lives under oppression*; *the country prospered under him*). **b** undergoing (*is under repair*). **c** classified or subsumed in (*that book goes under biology*). **4** at the foot of or sheltered by (*hid under the wall*; *under the cliff*). **5** powered by (sail, steam, etc.). • *adv.* **1** in or to a lower position or condition (*kept him under*). **2** *colloq.* in a state of unconsciousness (*put her under for the operation*). • *adj.* lower (*the under jaw*). □ **under the sun** anywhere in the world. **under way** in motion; in progress. □□ **un′der·most** *adj.*

under- /úndər/ *prefix* in senses of UNDER: **1** below; beneath (*underground*). **2** lower in status; subordinate (*undersecretary*). **3** insufficiently; incompletely (*undercook*; *underdeveloped*).

un·der·a·chieve /úndərəcheév/ *v.intr.* do less well than might be expected (esp. scholastically). □□ **un·der·a·chiev′er** *n.*

un·der·act /úndərákt/ *v.* **1** *tr.* act (a part, etc.) with insufficient force. **2** *intr.* act a part in this way.

un·der·age /úndəráyj/ *adj.* not old enough, esp. not yet of adult status.

un·der·arm /úndəráarm/ • *adj.* & *adv.* **1** *Sports* with the arm below shoulder level. **2** under the arm. **3** in the armpit. • *n.* armpit.

un·der·bel·ly /úndərbélee/ *n.* (*pl.* **–lies**) underside of an animal, vehicle, etc., esp. as an area vulnerable to attack.

un·der·bid /úndərbíd/ *v.tr.* (**–bid·ding**; *past* and *past part.* **–bid**) **1** make a lower bid than. **2** (also *absol.*) *Bridge*, etc., bid less on (one's hand) than warranted. □□ **un′der·bid·der** *n.*

un·der·brush /úndərbrúsh/ *n.* undergrowth in a forest.

un·der·car·riage /úndərkárij/ *n.* **1** wheeled, retractable structure beneath an aircraft used for landing, etc. **2** supporting frame of a vehicle.

un·der·charge /úndərcháarj/ *v.tr.* **1** charge too little for (a thing) or to (a person). **2** give too little charge to (a gun, battery, etc.).

un·der·class /úndərklás/ *n.* subordinate social class.

un·der·clothes /úndərklóz, –klóthz/ *n.pl.* clothes worn under others, esp. next to the skin.

un·der·coat /úndərkót/ • *n.* **1** layer of paint under a topcoat. **2** animal's under layer of hair or down. • *v.tr.* seal the underpart of a car against rust, etc., with an undercoat. □□ **un′ der·coat·ing** *n.*

un·der·cov·er /úndərkúvər/ *adj.* (usu. *attrib.*) **1** surreptitious. **2** spying, esp. by infiltration (*undercover agent*).

un·der·cur·rent /úndərkə́rənt, –kúr–/ *n.* **1** current below the surface. **2** underlying, often contrary, feeling, activity, or influence (*undercurrent of protest*).

un·der·cut /úndərkút/ *v.tr.* (**–cut·ting**; *past* and *past part.* **–cut**) **1** sell or work at a lower price than. **2** cut away the part below or under (a thing). **3** render unstable or less firm; undermine.

un·der·de·vel·oped /úndərdivéləpt/ *adj.* **1** not fully developed; immature. **2** (of a country, etc.) below its potential economic level. □□ **un·der· de·vel′ op·ment** *n.*

un·der·dog /úndərdawg, –dog/ *n.* **1** oppressed person. **2** person whose loss in a contest, etc., is expected.

un·der·done /úndərdún/ *adj.* (of food) not sufficiently cooked.

un·der·em·ployed /úndərimplóyd/ *adj.* having employment inadequate to one's abilities, education, etc. □□ **un·der·em·ploy′ ment** *n.*

un·der·es·ti·mate • *v.tr.* /úndəréstimayt/ form too low an estimate of. • *n.* /úndəréstimət/ estimate that is too low. □□ **un·der·es·ti·mation** /–máyshən/ *n.*

un·der·ex·pose /úndərikspóz/ *v.tr. Photog.* expose (film) for too short a time. □□ **un·der·ex· po·sure** /–pózhər/ *n.*

un·der·foot /úndərfŏŏt/ *adv.* **1** under one's feet. **2** in the way.

un·der·gar·ment /úndərgaarmənt/ *n.* piece of underwear.

un·der·go /úndərgó/ *v.tr.* (*3rd sing. present* **–goes**; *past* **–went**; *past part.* **–gone**) be subjected to; suffer; endure.

un·der·grad·u·ate /úndərgrájŏŏət/ *n.* student at a college or university who has not yet taken a degree.

un·der·ground • *adv.* /úndərgrównd/ **1** beneath the ground. **2** in or into secrecy or hiding. • *adj.* /úndərgrownd/ **1** situated underground. **2** secret; subversive. **3** unconventional; experimental (*underground press*). • *n.* /úndərgrownd/ **1** secret subversive group or activity. **2** *Brit.* subway system.

un·der·growth /úndərgróth/ *n.* dense growth of shrubs, etc., esp. under large trees.

un·der·hand • *adj.* /úndərhánd/ **1** secret; deceptive; crafty. **2** *Sports* underarm. • *adv.* /úndərhánd/ in an underhand manner.

un·der·lie /úndərlí/ *v.tr.* (**–ly·ing**; *past* **–lay**; *past part.* **–lain**) **1** (also *absol.*) lie under (a stratum, etc.). **2** (also *absol.*) (esp. as **underlying** *adj.*) be the basis of (a doctrine, law, conduct, etc.). **3** exist beneath the superficial aspect of.

un·der·line *v.tr.* /úndərlín/ **1** draw a line under. **2** emphasize; stress.

un·der·ling /úndərling/ *n.* usu. *derog.* subordinate.

un·der·ly·ing *pres. part.* of UNDERLIE.

un·der·mine /úndərmín/ *v.tr.* **1** injure, weaken, or wear out secretly or insidiously. **2** wear away the base of (*rivers undermine their banks*). **3** make an excavation under.

un·der·neath /úndərnéeth/ • *prep.* **1** at or to a lower place than, below. **2** on the inside of, within. • *adv.* **1** at or to a lower place. **2** inside. • *n.* lower surface or part. • *adj.* lower.

un·der·pants /úndərpánts/ *n.pl.* undergarment covering the lower part of the torso.

un·der·pass /úndərpás/ *n.* road, etc., passing under a railroad, another road, etc.

un·der·pay /úndərpáy/ *v.tr.* (*past* and *past part.* **–paid**) pay too little to (a person) or for (a thing). □□ **un·der·pay′ ment** *n.*

un·der·pin /úndərpín/ *v.tr.* (**–pinned**, **–pin·ning**) **1** support from below with masonry, etc. **2** support; strengthen.

un·der·play /úndərpláy/ *v.* **1** *tr.* play down the importance of. **2** *intr.* & *tr. Theatr.* underact.

un·der·pop·u·lat·ed /úndərpópyəláytid/ *adj.* having an insufficient or very small population.

un·der·priv·i·leged /úndərprívilijd, –prívlijd/ *adj.* not enjoying the normal standard of living or rights in a society.

un·der·rate /úndəráyt/ *v.tr.* have too low an opinion of.

un·der·score *v.tr.* /úndərskáwr/ = UNDERLINE *v.*

un·der·sea /úndərsée/ *adj.* below the sea or its surface.

un·der·sec·re·tar·y /úndərsékrəteree/ *n.* (*pl.* **–ies**) subordinate official, esp. a junior minister or senior civil servant.

un·der·sell /úndərsél/ *v.tr.* (*past* and *past part.* **–sold**) sell at a lower price than (another seller).

un·der·shirt /úndərshə́rt/ *n.* undergarment worn under a shirt.

un·der·shoot /úndərshŏŏt/ *v.tr.* (*past* and *past part.* **–shot**) **1** land short of (a runway, etc.). **2** shoot short of or below.

un·der·shorts /úndərsháwrts/ *n.* short underpants; trunks.

un·der·shot /úndərshót/ *adj.* (of a waterwheel) turned by water flowing under it.

un·der·side /úndərsíd/ *n.* lower or under side or surface.

un·der·signed /úndərsínd/ *adj.* whose signature is appended (*we, the undersigned, wish to state . . .*).

un·der·skirt /úndərskərt/ *n.* skirt worn under another; petticoat.

un·der·staffed /úndərstáft/ *adj.* having too few staff.

un·der·stand /úndərstánd/ *v.* (*past* and *past part.* **–stood** /–stŏŏd/) **1** *tr.* perceive the meaning of (words, a person, a language, etc.) (*understood you perfectly; cannot understand French*). **2** *tr.* perceive the significance or explanation or cause of (*do not understand why he came*). **3** *tr.* sympathize with; know how to deal with (*understand your difficulty; cannot understand him at all*). **4** *tr.* **a** infer esp. from information received; take as implied; take for granted (*I understand that it begins at noon*). **b** (*absol.*) believe or assume from knowledge or inference (*he is coming tomorrow, I understand*). **5** *tr.* supply (a word) mentally (*the verb may be either expressed or understood*). □□ **un·der·stand′a·ble** *adj.* **un·der·stand′a·bly** *adv.*

un·der·stand·ing /úndərstánding/ • *n.* **1 a** ability to understand or think; intelligence. **b** power of apprehension; power of abstract thought. **2** individual's perception of a situation, etc. **3** agreement, esp. informally (*had an understanding with the rival company*). **4** sympathy or tolerance. • *adj.* **1** having understanding or insight or good judgment. **2** sympathetic. □□ **un·der·stand′ing·ly** *adv.*

un·der·state /úndərstáyt/ *v.tr.* (often as **understated** *adj.*) **1** express in greatly restrained terms. **2** represent as being less than it actually is. □□ **un·der·state′ment** *n.*

un·der·stood *past* and *past part.* of UNDERSTAND.

un·der·stud·y /úndərstúdee/ esp. *Theatr.* • *n.* (*pl.* **–ies**) person ready to act at short notice in the absence of another. • *v.tr.* (**–ies, –ied**) **1** study (a role, etc.) as an understudy. **2** act as an understudy to (a person).

un·der·take /úndərtáyk/ *v.tr.* (*past* **–took**; *past part.* **–tak·en**) **1** bind oneself to perform; make oneself responsible for; engage in; enter upon (work, an enterprise, a responsibility). **2** accept an obligation; promise. **3** guarantee; affirm.

un·der·tak·er /úndərtaykər/ *n.* person whose business is to make arrangements for funerals.

un·der·tak·ing /úndərtáyking/ *n.* **1** work, etc., undertaken; enterprise (*a serious undertaking*). **2** pledge or promise.

un·der·things /úndərthingz/ *n.pl. colloq.* underclothes.

un·der·tone /úndərtón/ *n.* **1** subdued tone of sound or color. **2** underlying quality. **3** undercurrent of feeling.

un·der·tow /úndərtó/ *n.* current below the surface of the sea moving in the opposite direction to the surface current.

un·der·val·ue /úndərvályōo/ *v.tr.* (**–val·ues, –val·ued, –val·u·ing**) **1** value insufficiently. **2** underestimate. □□ **un·der·val·u·a′tion** *n.*

un·der·wa·ter /úndərwáwtər, –wótər/ • *adj.* situated or done under water. • *adv.* in and covered by water.

un·der·wear /úndərwáir/ *n.* underclothes.

un·der·weight /úndərwáyt/ *adj.* weighing less than is normal or desirable.

un·der·whelm /úndərhwélm, –wélm/ *v.tr. joc.* fail to impress.

un·der·world /úndərwórld/ *n.* **1** those who live by organized crime and immorality. **2** mythical abode of the dead under the earth.

un·der·write /úndər-rít/ *v.* (*past* **–wrote**; *past part.* **–writ·ten**) **1 a** *tr.* sign and accept liability under (an insurance policy, etc.). **b** *tr.* accept (liability) in this way. **c** *intr.* practice (marine) insurance. **2** *tr.* undertake to finance or support. **3** *tr.* engage to buy all the unsold stock in (a company, etc.). □□ **un′der·writ·er** *n.*

un·de·signed /úndizínd/ *adj.* unintentional.

un·de·sir·a·ble /úndizírəbəl/ • *adj.* objectionable; unpleasant. • *n.* undesirable person. □□ **un·de·sir·a·bil′i·ty** *n.*

un·did *past* of UNDO.

un·dies /úndeez/ *n.pl. colloq.* (esp. women's) underclothes.

un·dif·fer·en·ti·at·ed /úndifərénsheeaytid/ *adj.* not differentiated; amorphous.

un·do /úndōo/ *v.tr.* (*3rd sing. present* **–does**; *past* **–did**; *past part.* **–done**) **1** unfasten or untie (a coat, button, package, etc.). **2** annul; cancel (*cannot undo the past*). **3** ruin the prospects, reputation, or morals of.

un·doc·u·ment·ed /úndókyəmentid/ *adj.* **1** not having the appropriate document. **2** not supported by written evidence.

un·do·ing /úndōoing/ *n.* **1** ruin or cause of ruin. **2** reversing what has been done. **3** opening or unfastening.

un·done /úndún/ *adj.* **1** not done; incomplete (*left the job undone*). **2** not fastened (*left the buttons undone*). **3** ruined.

un·doubt·ed /úndówtid/ *adj.* certain; not questioned. □□ **un·doubt′ed·ly** *adv.*

un·dreamed /úndreémd, úndrémt/ *adj.* (also **un·dreamt** /úndrémt/) not dreamed or thought of or imagined.

un·dress /úndrés/ • *v.* **1** *intr.* take off one's clothes. **2** *tr.* take the clothes off (a person). • *n.* **1** ordinary dress as opposed to full dress or uniform. **2** casual or informal dress.

un·due /úndōo, –dyōo/ *adj.* excessive; disproportionate. □□ **un·du′ly** *adv.*

un·du·late /úndyú/ • *v.* /únjəlayt, –dyə–, –də–/ have or cause to have a wavy motion or look. • *adj.* /únjələt, –dyə–, –də–/ wavy (*leaves with undulate margins*). □□ **un·du·la′tion** /–láyshən/ *n.*

un·dy·ing /úndí-ing/ *adj.* **1** immortal. **2** never-ending (*undying love*). □□ **un·dy′ing·ly** *adv.*

un·earned /únórnd/ *adj.* not earned. □ **unearned income** income from investments, etc., as opposed to salary, etc.

un·earth /únórth/ *v.tr.* discover by searching, digging, or rummaging.

un·earth·ly /únórthlee/ *adj.* **1** supernatural; mysterious. **2** *colloq.* absurdly early or inconvenient (*unearthly hour*). □□ **un·earth′li·ness** *n.*

un·ease /únéez/ *n.* lack of ease; discomfort; distress.

un·eas·y /únéezee/ *adj.* (**un·eas′i·er, un·eas′i·est**) **1** nervous; anxious. **2** disturbing (*had an uneasy suspicion*). □□ **un·eas′i·ly** *adv.* **un·eas′i·ness** *n.*

un·e·mo·tion·al /únimóshənəl/ *adj.* not emotional; lacking emotion.

un·em·ploy·a·ble /únimplóyəbəl/ *adj.* unfit for paid employment. □□ **un·em·ploy·a·bil′i·ty** *n.*

un·em·ployed /únimplóyd/ *adj.* **1** out of work. **2** not in use. □□ **un·em·ploy′ment** *n.*

un·e·qual /únéekwəl/ *adj.* **1** not equal. **2** of varying quality. **3** unfair (*an unequal bargain*). □□ **un·e′qual·ly** *adv.*

un·e·qualed /únéekwəld/ *adj.* superior to all others.

un·e·quiv·o·cal /únikwívəkəl/ *adj.* not ambiguous; plain; unmistakable. □□ **un·e·quiv′o·cal·ly** *adv.*

un·err·ing /únéring/ *adj.* not erring; true; certain. □□ **un·err′ing·ly** *adv.* **un·err′ing·ness** *n.*

UNESCO /yōonéskō/ *abbr.* United Nations Educational, Scientific, and Cultural Organization.

un·eth·i·cal /únéthikəl/ *adj.* not ethical, esp. unscrupulous in business or professional conduct. □□ **un·eth′i·cal·ly** *adv.*

un·e·ven /únéevən/ *adj.* **1** not level or smooth. **2** not uniform. **3** (of a contest) unequal. □□ **un·e'ven·ly** *adv.* **un·e'ven·ness** *n.*

un·ex·am·pled /únigzámpəld/ *adj.* without precedent.

un·ex·cep·tion·a·ble /úniksépshənəbəl/ *adj.* entirely satisfactory. □□ **un·ex·cep'tion·a·bly** *adv.* ¶ See note at EXCEPTIONABLE.

un·ex·cep·tion·al /úniksépshənəl/ *adj.* not out of the ordinary; usual; normal. □□ **un·ex·cep'tion·al·ly** *adv.*

un·ex·pect·ed /únikspéktid/ *adj.* not expected; surprising. □□ **un·ex·pect'ed·ly** *adv.* **un·ex·pect'ed·ness** *n.*

un·ex·pur·gat·ed /únékspərgaytid/ *adj.* (esp. of a text) complete.

un·fail·ing /únfáyling/ *adj.* **1** not failing. **2** not running short. **3** constant. **4** reliable. □□ **un·fail'ing·ly** *adv.*

un·fair /unfáir/ *adj.* **1** not equitable or honest (*obtained by unfair means*). **2** not impartial or according to the rules. □□ **un·fair'ly** *adv.* **un·fair'ness** *n.*

un·faith·ful /únfáythfŏŏl/ *adj.* **1** not faithful, esp. adulterous. **2** not loyal. **3** treacherous. □□ **un·faith'ful·ly** *adv.* **un·faith'ful·ness** *n.*

un·fas·ten /únfásən/ *v.* **1** *tr.* & *intr.* make or become loose. **2** *tr.* open the fastening(s) of. **3** *tr.* detach.

un·feel·ing /únfééling/ *adj.* unsympathetic; harsh. □□ **un·feel'ing·ly** *adv.*

un·feigned /únfáynd/ *adj.* genuine; sincere.

un·fin·ished /únfínisht/ *adj.* not finished; incomplete.

un·fit·ting /únfíting/ *adj.* not suitable; unbecoming. □□ **un·fit'ting·ly** *adv.*

un·fix /únfíks/ *v.tr.* **1** release or loosen. **2** detach.

un·flag·ging /únflágíng/ *adj.* tireless; persistent. □□ **un·flag'ging·ly** *adv.*

un·flap·pa·ble /únflápəbəl/ *adj.* *colloq.* imperturbable; calm. □□ **un·flap·pa·bil'i·ty** *n.* **un·flap'pa·bly** *adv.*

un·fold /únfŏld/ *v.* **1** *tr.* open the fold(s) of; spread out. **2** *tr.* reveal (thoughts, etc.). **3** *intr.* become opened out. **4** *intr.* develop.

un·forced /únfáwrst/ *adj.* **1** easy; natural. **2** not compelled or constrained.

un·for·get·ta·ble /únfərgétəbəl/ *adj.* that cannot be forgotten; memorable; wonderful (*an unforgettable experience*). □□ **un·for·get'ta·bly** *adv.*

un·formed /únfáwrmd/ *adj.* **1** not formed. **2** shapeless. **3** not developed.

un·for·tu·nate /únfáwrchənət/ • *adj.* **1** having bad fortune; unlucky. **2** unhappy. **3** regrettable. **4** disastrous. • *n.* unfortunate person. □□ **un·for'tu·nate·ly** *adv.*

un·found·ed /únfówndid/ *adj.* having no foundation (*unfounded hopes*; *unfounded rumor*).

un·friend·ly /únfréndlee/ *adj.* (**un·friend'li·er**, **un·friend'li·est**) not friendly. □□ **un·friend'li·ness** *n.*

un·fun·ny /únfúnee/ *adj.* (**un·fun·ni·er**, **un·fun·ni·est**) not amusing (though meant to be). □□ **un·fun'ni·ly** *adv.*

un·furl /únfárl/ *v.* **1** *tr.* spread out a sail, etc.). **2** *intr.* become spread out.

un·gain·ly /úngáynlee/ *adj.* awkward; clumsy. □□ **un·gain'li·ness** *n.*

un·god·ly /úngódlee/ *adj.* **1** impious; wicked. **2** *colloq.* outrageous (*ungodly hour*). □□ **un·god'li·ness** *n.*

un·gov·ern·a·ble /úngúvərnəbəl/ *adj.* uncontrollable; violent. □□ **un·gov·ern·a·bil'i·ty** *n.* **un·gov'ern·a·bly** *adv.*

un·gra·cious /úngráyshəs/ *adj.* not kindly or courteous; unkind. □□ **un·grac'ious·ly** *adv.* **un·gra'cious·ness** *n.*

un·guard·ed /úngáardid/ *adj.* **1** incautious; thoughtless (*unguarded remark*). **2** not guarded. □□ **un·guard'ed·ly** *adv.* **un·guard'ed·ness** *n.*

un·guent /únggwənt/ *n.* soft substance used as ointment or for lubrication.

un·gu·late /úngyələt, –layt/ • *adj.* hoofed. • *n.* hoofed mammal.

un·hal·lowed /únhálōd/ *adj.* **1** not consecrated. **2** not sacred; unholy; wicked.

un·hand /únhánd/ *v.tr. rhet.* or *joc.* **1** take one's hands off (a person). **2** release from one's grasp.

un·hap·py /únhápee/ *adj.* (**un·hap·pi·er**, **un·hap·pi·est**) **1** miserable. **2** unsuccessful; unfortunate. **3** disastrous. □□ **un·hap'pi·ly** *adv.* **un·hap'pi·ness** *n.*

un·health·y /únhélthee/ *adj.* (**un·health·i·er**, **un·health·i·est**) **1** not in good health. **2 a** (of a place, etc.) harmful to health. **b** unwholesome. **c** *sl.* dangerous to life. □□ **un·health'i·ly** *adv.* **un·health'i·ness** *n.*

un·heard /únhárd/ *adj.* **1** not heard. **2** (usu. **unheard-of**) unprecedented; unknown.

un·hinge /únhínj/ *v.tr.* **1** take (a door, etc.) off its hinges. **2** (esp. as **unhinged** *adj.*) unsettle or disorder (a person's mind, etc.), make (a person) crazy.

un·hitch /únhích/ *v.tr.* **1** release from a hitched state. **2** unhook; unfasten.

un·ho·ly /únhŏlee/ *adj.* (**un·ho'li·er**, **un·ho'li·est**) **1** impious; wicked. **2** *colloq.* dreadful; outrageous (*made an unholy ordeal out of nothing*). □□ **un·ho'li·ness** *n.*

uni- /yŏŏni/ *comb. form* one; having or consisting of one.

u·ni·cam·er·al /yŏŏnikámərəl/ *adj.* with a single legislative chamber.

UNICEF /yŏŏnisef/ *abbr.* United Nations Children's (orig. International Children's Emergency) Fund.

u·ni·cel·lu·lar /yŏŏnisélyələr/ *adj.* (of an organism, organ, tissue, etc.) consisting of a single cell.

u·ni·corn /yŏŏnikawrn/ *n.* mythical animal with a horse's body and a single straight horn.

u·ni·cy·cle /yŏŏnisīkəl/ *n.* single-wheeled cycle, esp. as used by acrobats. □□ **u'ni·cy·clist** *n.*

u·ni·form /yŏŏnifawrm/ • *adj.* **1** not changing in form or character; unvarying (*present a uniform appearance*; *of uniform size*). **2** conforming to the same standard, rules, or pattern. • *n.* distinctive clothing worn by members of the same body, e.g., by soldiers, police, and schoolchildren. □□ **u'ni·formed** *adj.* **u·ni·for'mi·ty** *n.* **u'ni·form·ly** *adv.*

u·ni·fy /yŏŏnifī/ *v.tr.* (also *absol.*) (**–fies**, **–fied**) reduce to unity or uniformity. □□ **u·ni·fi·ca'tion** *n.* **u'ni·fi·er** *n.*

u·ni·lat·er·al /yŏŏnilátərəl/ *adj.* **1** performed by

or affecting only one person or party (*unilateral disarmament*). **2** one-sided. □□ **u·ni·lat′er·al·ly** *adv.*

un·i·mag·i·na·tive /únimájinətiv/ *adj.* lacking imagination; stolid; dull. □□ **un·i·mag′i·na·tive·ly** *adv.*

un·im·peach·a·ble /únimpéechəbəl/ *adj.* beyond reproach or question. □□ **un·im·peach′a·bly** *adv.*

un·i·ni·ti·at·ed /únınísheeaytid/ *adj.* not initiated; not admitted or instructed.

un·in·spired /úninspírd/ *adj.* **1** not inspired. **2** (of oratory, etc.) commonplace.

un·in·ter·est·ed /únıntrəstid, –tóristid, –tərəs–/ *adj.* **1** not interested. **2** unconcerned; indifferent. □□ **un·in′ter·est·ed·ly** *adv.*
¶ See note at DISINTERESTED.

un·in·vit·ing /úninvíting/ *adj.* unattractive; repellent. □□ **un·in·vit′ing·ly** *adv.*

u·nion /yōōnyən/ *n.* **1** uniting; being united. **2 a** whole resulting from the combination of parts or members. **b** political unit formed in this way, esp. (**Union**) the US (esp. as distinct from the Confederacy during the Civil War), the UK, or South Africa. **3** = *labor union.* **4** marriage. **5** concord; agreement (*lived together in perfect union*). **6** *Math.* totality of the members of two or more sets. □ **Union Jack** national flag of the United Kingdom formed by the union of the crosses of St. George, St. Andrew, and St. Patrick.

u·nion·ize /yōōnyənīz/ *v.* bring or come under labor-union organization or rules. □□ **un·ion·i·za′tion** *n.*

u·nique /yōōnéek/ *adj.* **1** of which there is only one; unequaled; having no like, equal, or parallel (*this vase is considered unique*). **2** *disp.* unusual; remarkable (*the most unique man I ever met*). □□ **u·nique′ly** *adv.* **u·nique′ness** *n.*
¶ See note at PERFECT.

u·ni·sex /yōōniseks/ *adj.* (of clothing, hairstyles, etc.) designed to be suitable for both sexes.

u·ni·son /yōōnisən/ *n.* **1** *Mus.* coincidence in pitch of sounds or notes. **2** agreement; concord (*acted in perfect unison*).

u·nit /yōōnit/ *n.* **1 a** individual thing, person, or group regarded as single and complete. **b** each of the (smallest) separate individuals or groups into which a complex whole may be analyzed (*the family as the unit of society*). **2** quantity as a standard in terms of which other quantities may be expressed (*unit of heat; mass per unit volume*). **3** device with a specified function forming part of a complex mechanism. **4** group of buildings, wards, etc., as in a hospital. **5** the number 'one'. □ **unit cost** cost of producing one item. **unit price** price charged for each unit of goods supplied.

un·i·tard /yōōnətaard/ *n.* one-piece leotard that covers the legs as well as the torso.

U·ni·tar·i·an /yōōnitáireeən/ • *n.* **1** person who believes that God is not a Trinity but one being. **2** member of a religious body maintaining this and advocating freedom from formal dogma or doctrine. • *adj.* of or relating to the Unitarians. □□ **U·ni·tar′i·an·ism** *n.*

u·ni·tar·y /yōōniteree/ *adj.* **1** of a unit or units. **2** marked by unity or uniformity.

u·nite /yōōnít/ *v.* **1** join together; combine. **2** join in marriage. **3** form or cause to form a physical or chemical whole (*oil will not unite with water*).

u·ni·ty /yōōnitee/ *n.* (*pl.* **–ties**) **1** oneness; being

one, single, or individual; being formed of parts that constitute a whole (*disturbs the unity of the idea; national unity*). **2** harmony or concord between persons, etc. **3** thing forming a complex whole (*a person regarded as a unity*). **4** *Math.* the number 'one,' the factor that leaves unchanged the quantity on which it operates.

Univ. *abbr.* University.

u·ni·va·lent /yōōniváylənt/ *adj. Chem.* having a valence of one.

u·ni·valve /yōōnivalv/ *Zool.* • *adj.* having one valve. • *n.* univalve mollusk.

u·ni·ver·sal /yōōnivórsəl/ • *adj.* of, belonging to, or done, etc., by all; applicable to all cases (*met with universal approval*). • *n.* **1** *Logic* universal proposition. **2** *Philos.* **a** term or concept of general application. **b** nature or essence signified by a general term. □ **universal joint** (or **coupling**) joint or coupling that can transmit rotary power by a shaft at any angle. **Universal Product Code** bar code on products that can be read by an electronic scanner, usu. providing price and product identification. □□ **u·ni·ver·sal·i·ty** /–sálitee/ *n.* **u·ni·ver′sal·ize** *v.tr.* **u·ni·ver′sal·ly** *adv.*

u·ni·verse /yōōnivərs/ *n.* **1 a** all existing things; the cosmos. **b** sphere of existence, influence, activity, etc. **2** all humankind. **3** *Statistics & Logic* all the objects under consideration.

u·ni·ver·si·ty /yōōnivórsitee/ *n.* (*pl.* **–ties**) educational institution designed for instruction, examination, or both, of students in many branches of advanced learning, conferring degrees in various faculties, and often embodying colleges and similar institutions.

un·kempt /únkémpt/ *adj.* **1** untidy; of neglected appearance. **2** disheveled. □□ **un·kempt′ly** *adv.* **un·kempt′ness** *n.*

un·kind /únkínd/ *adj.* **1** not kind. **2** harsh; cruel. **3** unpleasant. □□ **un·kind′ly** *adv.* **un·kind′ness** *n.*

un·know·a·ble /ún-nóəbəl/ • *adj.* that cannot be known. • *n.* **1** unknowable thing. **2** (**the Unknowable**) the postulated absolute or ultimate reality.

un·know·ing /ún-nóing/ *adj.* not knowing; ignorant; unconscious. □□ **un·know′ing·ly** *adv.*

un·known /ún-nón/ • *adj.* not known; unfamiliar (*his purpose was unknown to me*). • *n.* **1** unknown thing or person. **2** unknown quantity (*equation in two unknowns*). □ **Unknown Soldier** unidentified soldier killed in war, given burial with special honors in a national memorial.

un·law·ful /únláwfŏŏl/ *adj.* illegal; not permissible. □□ **un·law′ful·ly** *adv.* **un·law′ful·ness** *n.*

un·lead·ed /únlédid/ *adj.* **1** (of gasoline, etc.) without added lead. **2** not covered, weighted, or framed with lead.

un·learn /únlórn/ *v.tr.* (*past* and *past part.* **un·learned** or **un·learnt**) **1** discard from one's memory. **2** rid oneself of (a habit, false information, etc.).

un·learn·ed /únlórnid/ *adj.* not well educated; untaught; ignorant.

un·leash /únléesh/ *v.tr.* release from a leash or restraint.

un·leav·ened /únlévənd/ *adj.* made without yeast or other raising agent.

un·less /únlés, ən–/ *conj.* if not; except when (*shall go unless I hear from you; always walked unless I had a bicycle*).

un·let·tered /únlétərd/ *adj.* **1** illiterate. **2** not well educated.

un·like /únlík/ • *adj.* **1** not like; different from (*is unlike both his parents*). **2** uncharacteristic of (*such behavior is unlike him*). **3** dissimilar; different. • *prep.* differently from (*acts quite unlike anyone else*).

un·like·ly /únlíklee/ *adj.* (**un·like·li·er, un·like·li·est**) **1** improbable (*unlikely tale*). **2** not expected (*he's unlikely to be available*). **3** unpromising (*unlikely candidate*). □□ **un·like′li·hood** *n.* **un·like′li·ness** *n.*

un·lim·it·ed /únlímitid/ *adj.* without limit; unrestricted; very great in number or quantity (*unlimited possibilities; unlimited expanse of sea*). □□ **un·lim′it·ed·ness** *n.*

un·load /únlṓd/ *v.tr.* **1** (also *absol.*) remove a load from (a vehicle, etc.). **2** remove the charge from (a firearm, etc.). **3** *colloq.* get rid of. **4** (often foll. by *on*) *colloq.* **a** divulge (information). **b** (also *absol.*) give vent to (feelings). □□ **un·load′er** *n.*

un·lock /únlók/ *v.tr.* **1 a** release the lock of (a door, box, etc.). **b** release or disclose by unlocking. **2** release thoughts, feelings, etc., from (one's mind, etc.).

un·looked-for /únlŏŏktfawr/ *adj.* unexpected; unforeseen.

un·loose /únlṓs/ *v.tr.* (also **un·loos′en**) loose; set free.

un·luck·y /únlúkee/ *adj.* (**un·luck′i·er, un·luck′i·est**) **1** not fortunate or successful. **2** wretched. **3** bringing bad luck. **4** ill-judged. □□ **un·luck′i·ly** *adv.* **un·luck′i·ness** *n.*

un·make /únmáyk/ *v.tr.* (*past* and *past part.* **un·made**) undo the making of; destroy; depose; annul.

un·man /únmán/ *v.tr.* (**un·manned, un·man·ning**) deprive of supposed manly qualities (e.g., self-control, courage); cause to weep, etc.; discourage.

un·mask /únmásk/ *v.* **1** *tr.* **a** remove the mask from. **b** expose the true character of. **2** *intr.* remove one's mask. □□ **un·mask′er** *n.*

un·men·tion·a·ble /únménshənəbəl/ • *adj.* that cannot (properly) be mentioned. • *n.* **1** (in *pl.*) *joc.* undergarments. **2** person or thing not to be mentioned. □□ **un·men′tion·a·bly** *adv.*

un·mer·ci·ful /únmɔ́rsifŏŏl/ *adj.* merciless. □□ **un·mer′ci·ful·ly** *adv.*

un·mis·tak·a·ble /únmistáykəbəl/ *adj.* that cannot be mistaken or doubted; clear. □□ **un·mis·tak′a·bly** *adv.*

un·mit·i·gat·ed /únmítigaytid/ *adj.* **1** not mitigated or modified. **2** absolute; unqualified (*an unmitigated disaster*). □□ **un·mit′i·gat·ed·ly** *adv.*

un·mor·al /únmáwrəl, -mór-/ *adj.* not concerned with morality (cf. IMMORAL). □□ **un·mo·ral·i·ty** /-rálitee/ *n.* **un·mor′al·ly** *adv.*

un·moved /únmṓovd/ *adj.* **1** not moved. **2** not changed in one's purpose. **3** not affected by emotion. □□ **un·mov′a·ble** *adj.* (also **un·move′a·ble**).

un·nat·u·ral /ún·náchərəl/ *adj.* **1** contrary to nature; not normal. **2 a** lacking natural feelings. **b** extremely cruel or wicked. **3** artificial. **4** affected. □□ **un·nat′u·ral·ly** *adv.*

un·nec·es·sar·y /únnésəseree/ *adj.* **1** not necessary. **2** more than is necessary (*with unnecessary care*). □□ **un·nec·es·sar′i·ly** *adv.*

un·nerve /ún·nɔ́rv/ *v.tr.* deprive of strength or resolution. □□ **un·nerv′ing·ly** *adv.*

un·num·bered /ún·númbərd/ *adj.* **1** not marked with a number. **2** not counted. **3** countless.

657   unlike ~ unquote

un·ob·tru·sive /únəbtrṓosiv/ *adj.* not making oneself or itself noticed. □□ **un·ob·tru′sive·ly** *adv.* **un·ob·tru′sive·ness** *n.*

un·or·gan·ized /únáwrgənīzd/ *adj.* **1** not organized (cf. DISORGANIZE). **2** not represented by a labor union.

un·pack /únpák/ *v.tr.* **1** (also *absol.*) open and remove the contents of (a package, luggage, etc.). **2** take (a thing) out from a package, etc. □□ **un·pack′er** *n.*

un·pal·at·a·ble /únpálətəbəl/ *adj.* **1** not pleasant to taste; inedible. **2** (of an idea, suggestion, etc.) disagreeable; distasteful. □□ **un·pal·at·a·bil′i·ty** *n.*

un·par·al·leled /únpárəleld/ *adj.* having no parallel or equal.

un·pleas·ant /únplézənt/ *adj.* not pleasant; disagreeable. □□ **un·pleas′ant·ly** *adv.* **un·pleas′ant·ness** *n.*

un·plug /únplúg/ *v.tr.* (**un·plugged, un·plug·ging**) **1** disconnect (an electrical device) by removing its plug from the socket. **2** unstop.

un·plumbed /únplúmd/ *adj.* **1** not plumbed. **2** not fully explored or understood. □□ **un·plumb′a·ble** *adj.*

un·pop·u·lar /únpópyələr/ *adj.* not popular; not liked by the public or by people in general. □□ **un·pop·u·lar·i·ty** /-láritee/ *n.* **un·pop′u·lar·ly** *adv.*

un·prac·ticed /únpráktist/ *adj.* **1** not experienced or skilled. **2** not put into practice.

un·prec·e·dent·ed /únprésidentid/ *adj.* **1** having no precedent; unparalleled. **2** novel. □□ **un·prec′e·dent·ed·ly** *adv.*

un·pre·pos·sess·ing /únpreepəzésing/ *adj.* unattractive.

un·pre·ten·tious /únpriténshəs/ *adj.* not making a great display; simple; modest. □□ **un·pre·ten′tious·ly** *adv.* **un·pre·ten′tious·ness** *n.*

un·prin·ci·pled /únprínsipəld/ *adj.* lacking or not based on sound moral principles.

un·print·a·ble /únpríntəbəl/ *adj.* that cannot be printed, esp. because too indecent or libelous or blasphemous. □□ **un·print′a·bly** *adv.*

un·pro·fes·sion·al /únprəféshənəl/ *adj.* **1** contrary to professional standards of behavior, etc. **2** not belonging to a profession; amateur. □□ **un·pro·fes′sion·al·ly** *adv.*

un·prompt·ed /únprómptid/ *adj.* spontaneous.

un·qual·i·fied /únkwólifīd/ *adj.* **1** not competent (*unqualified to give an answer*). **2** not legally or officially qualified (*unqualified practitioner*). **3** complete (*unqualified success*).

un·ques·tion·a·ble /únkwéschənəbəl/ *adj.* that cannot be disputed or doubted. □□ **un·ques′tion·a·bly** *adv.*

un·ques·tioned /únkwéschənd/ *adj.* **1** not disputed or doubted; definite; certain. **2** not interrogated.

un·ques·tion·ing /únkwéschəning/ *adj.* **1** asking no questions. **2** done, etc., without asking questions. □□ **un·ques′tion·ing·ly** *adv.*

un·qui·et /únkwíət/ *adj.* **1** restless; agitated. **2** perturbed; anxious. □□ **un·qui′et·ly** *adv.* **un·qui′et·ness** *n.*

un·quote /únkwót/ *v.tr.* (as *int.*) (in reading aloud, etc.) indicate the presence of closing quotation marks (cf. QUOTE *v.* 3).

un·rav·el /únrávəl/ v. **1** tr. cause to be no longer raveled, tangled, or intertwined. **2** tr. probe and solve (a mystery, etc.). **3** tr. undo (a fabric, esp. a knitted one). **4** intr. become disentangled or unknitted.

un·read /únréd/ adj. **1** (of a book, etc.) not read. **2** (of a person) not well-read.

un·read·a·ble /únréedəbəl/ adj. **1** too dull or too difficult to be worth reading. **2** illegible. □□ **un·read·a·bil′i·ty** n. **un·read′a·bly** adv.

un·real /únréeəl/ adj. **1** not real. **2** imaginary; illusory. **3** sl. incredible. □□ **un·re·al·i·ty** /–reeálitee/ n. **un·re′al·ly** adv.

un·rea·son /únréezən/ n. lack of reasonable thought or action.

un·rea·son·a·ble /únréezənəbəl/ adj. **1** going beyond the limits of what is reasonable or equitable (unreasonable demands). **2** not guided by or listening to reason. □□ **un·rea′son·a·ble·ness** n. **un·rea′son·a·bly** adv.

un·re·gen·er·ate /únrijénərət/ adj. not regenerate; obstinately wrong or bad. □□ **un·re·gen′er·a·cy** n. **un·re·gen′er·ate·ly** adv.

un·re·lent·ing /únrilénting/ adj. **1** not relenting or yielding. **2** unmerciful. □□ **un·re·lent′ing·ly** adv.

un·re·li·a·ble /únrilíəbəl/ adj. not reliable; erratic. □□ **un·re·li·a·bil′i·ty** n. **un·re·li′a·bly** adv.

un·re·lieved /únrileevd/ adj. **1** lacking the relief given by contrast or variation. **2** not aided or assisted.

un·re·mit·ting /únrimíting/ adj. never relaxing or slackening; incessant. □□ **un·re·mit′ting·ly** adv. **un·re·mit′ting·ness** n.

un·re·quit·ed /únrikwítid/ adj. (of love, etc.) not returned. □□ **un·re·quit′ed·ly** adv.

un·re·served /únrizórvd/ adj. **1** not reserved (unreserved seats). **2** without reservations; absolute (unreserved confidence). □□ **un·re·serv′ed·ly** adv.

un·re·solved /únrizólvd/ adj. **1 a** uncertain how to act; irresolute. **b** undecided. **2** (of questions, etc.) undetermined; undecided; unsolved.

un·rest /únrést/ n. restlessness; disturbance; agitation.

un·right·eous /únríchəs/ adj. not righteous; unjust; wicked; dishonest. □□ **un·right′eous·ly** adv. **un·right′eous·ness** n.

un·ri·valed /únrívəld/ adj. having no equal; peerless.

un·roll /únról/ v. **1** open out from a rolled-up state. **2** display or be displayed in this form.

un·ruf·fled /únrúfəld/ adj. **1** not agitated or disturbed; calm. **2** not physically ruffled.

un·rul·y /únróolee/ adj. (**un·rul·i·er, un·rul·i·est**) not easily controlled or disciplined; disorderly. □□ **un·rul′i·ness** n.

un·sad·dle /únsád′l/ v.tr. **1** remove the saddle from (a horse, etc.). **2** dislodge from a saddle.

un·sat·u·rat·ed /únsáchəraytid/ adj. **1** Chem. (of a compound, esp. a fat or oil) having double or triple bonds in its molecule and therefore capable of further reaction. **2** not saturated. □□ **un·sat·u·ra·tion** /–ráyshən/ n.

un·sa·vor·y /únsáyvəree/ adj. **1** disagreeable; disgusting. **2** morally offensive. □□ **un·sa′vor·i·ness** n.

un·scathed /únskáythd/ adj. without suffering any injury.

un·schooled /únskóold/ adj. **1** uneducated; untaught. **2** untrained; undisciplined.

un·sci·en·tif·ic /únsīəntífik/ adj. not in accordance with scientific principles. □□ **un·sci·en·tif′i·cal·ly** adv.

un·scram·ble /únskrámbəl/ v.tr. restore from a scrambled state, esp. interpret (a scrambled transmission, etc.). □□ **un·scramb′ler** n.

un·screw /únskróo/ v. **1** tr. & intr. unfasten or be unfastened by removing a screw or screws or by twisting like a screw. **2** tr. loosen (a screw).

un·script·ed /únskríptid/ adj. (of a speech, etc.) delivered without a prepared script.

un·scru·pu·lous /únskróopyələs/ adj. having no scruples; unprincipled. □□ **un·scru′pu·lous·ly** adv. **un·scru′pu·lous·ness** n.

un·seal /únséel/ v.tr. break the seal of; open (a letter, receptacle, etc.).

un·sea·son·a·ble /únséezənəbəl/ adj. **1** not appropriate to the season. **2** untimely; inopportune. □□ **un·sea′son·a·bly** adv.

un·seat /únséet/ v.tr. **1** remove from a seat, esp. in an election. **2** dislodge from a seat, esp. on horseback.

un·seem·ly /únséemlee/ adj. (**un·seem·li·er, un·seem·li·est**) **1** indecent. **2** unbecoming. □□ **un·seem′li·ness** n.

un·seen /únséen/ adj. **1** not seen. **2** invisible.

un·self·ish /únsélfish/ adj. mindful of others' interests. □□ **un·self′ish·ly** adv. **un·self′ish·ness** n.

un·set·tle /únsét′l/ v. **1** tr. disturb the settled state or arrangement of; discompose. **2** tr. derange. **3** intr. become unsettled. □□ **un·set′tling** adj.

un·set·tled /únsét′ld/ adj. **1** not (yet) settled. **2** liable to change or open to change or further discussion. **3** (of a bill, etc.) unpaid.

un·shak·a·ble /únsháykəbəl/ adj. (also **un·shake·able**) firm; obstinate. □□ **un·shak·a·bil′i·ty** n. **un·shak′a·bly** adv.

un·shrink·ing /únshrínking/ adj. unhesitating; fearless. □□ **un·shrink′ing·ly** adv.

un·sight·ly /únsítlee/ adj. unpleasant to look at; ugly. □□ **un·sight′li·ness** n.

un·skilled /únskíld/ adj. lacking or not needing special skill or training.

un·so·lic·it·ed /únsəlísitid/ adj. not asked for; given or done voluntarily.

un·so·phis·ti·cat·ed /únsəfístikaytid/ adj. **1** artless; simple; natural; ingenuous. **2** not adulterated or artificial. □□ **un·so·phis′ti·cat·ed·ly** adv.

un·sought /únsáwt/ adj. **1** not searched out or sought for. **2** unasked; without being requested.

un·sound /únsównd/ adj. **1** unhealthy; diseased. **2** rotten; weak. **3 a** ill-founded; fallacious. **b** unorthodox; heretical. □□ **un·sound′ly** adv. **un·sound′ness** n.

un·spar·ing /únspáiring/ adj. **1** lavish; profuse. **2** merciless. □□ **un·spar′ing·ly** adv.

un·speak·a·ble /únspéekəbəl/ adj. **1** that cannot be expressed in words. **2** indescribably bad or objectionable. □□ **un·speak′a·ble·ness** n. **un·speak′a·bly** adv.

un·sta·ble /únstáybəl/ adj. (**un·sta·bler, un·sta·blest**) **1** not stable. **2** changeable. **3** showing a tendency to sudden mental or emotional changes. □□ **un·sta′ble·ness** n. **un·sta′bly** adv.

un·stead·y /únstédee/ *adj.* (**un·stead·i·er, un·stead·i·est**) **1** not steady or firm. **2** changeable; fluctuating. **3** not uniform or regular. □□ **un·stead'i·ly** *adv.* **un·stead'i·ness** *n.*

un·stint·ing /únstínting/ *adj.* ungrudging; lavish. □□ **un·stint'ing·ly** *adv.*

un·stop /únstóp/ *v.tr.* (**un·stopped, un·stop·ping**) **1** free from obstruction. **2** remove the stopper from.

un·stressed /únstrést/ *adj.* **1** (of a word, syllable, etc.) not pronounced with stress. **2** not subjected to stress.

un·string /únstríng/ *v.tr.* (*past* and *past part.* **un·strung**) **1** remove or relax the string(s) of (a bow, harp, etc.). **2** remove from a string. **3** (esp. as **unstrung** *adj.*) unnerve.

un·struc·tured /únstrúkchərd/ *adj.* **1** not structured. **2** informal.

un·stud·ied /únstúdeed/ *adj.* easy; natural; spontaneous.

un·sub·stan·tial /únsəbstánshəl/ *adj.* having little or no solidity, reality, or factual basis. □□ **un·sub·stan·tial·i·ty** /–sheeálitee/ *n.* **un·sub·stan'tial·ly** *adv.*

un·suit·ed /únsoótid/ *adj.* **1** (usu. foll. by *for*) not fit for a purpose. **2** (usu. foll. by *to*) not adapted.

un·sung /únsúng/ *adj.* **1** not celebrated; unknown. **2** not sung.

un·swerv·ing /únswərving/ *adj.* **1** steady; constant. **2** not turning aside. □□ **un·swerv'ing·ly** *adv.*

un·tan·gle /úntánggəl/ *v.tr.* disentangle.

un·tapped /úntápt/ *adj.* not (yet) tapped or used.

un·taught /úntáwt/ *adj.* **1** not instructed by teaching; ignorant. **2** not acquired by teaching; natural; spontaneous.

un·ten·a·ble /únténəbəl/ *adj.* not tenable; that cannot be defended. □□ **un·ten·a·bil'i·ty** *n.* **un·ten'a·bly** *adv.*

un·think·a·ble /únthíngkəbəl/ *adj.* **1** that cannot be imagined or grasped by the mind. **2** *colloq.* highly unlikely or undesirable. □□ **un·think'a·bly** *adv.*

un·think·ing /únthíngking/ *adj.* **1** thoughtless. **2** unintentional; inadvertent. □□ **un·think'ing·ly** *adv.*

un·ti·dy /úntídee/ *adj.* (**un·ti·di·er, un·ti·di·est**) not neat or orderly. □□ **un·ti'di·ly** *adv.* **un·ti'di·ness** *n.*

un·tie /úntí/ *v.tr.* (*pres. part.* **un·ty·ing**) **1** undo (a knot, the cords of a package, etc.). **2** release from bonds or attachment.

un·til /əntíl, un–/ *prep. & conj.* till; before; up to the time that.
¶ **Until** is more formal than **till**, and is more usual at the beginning of a sentence, e.g., *Until the 1920s it was quite unusual for women to wear short hair.* **'Til** is considered incorrect in standard English and should be avoided.

un·time·ly /úntímlee/ *adj.* **1** inopportune. **2** (of death) premature. □□ **un·time'li·ness** *n.*

un·to /úntoo, úntə/ *prep. archaic* = TO *prep.* (in all uses except as the sign of the infinitive); (*do unto others; faithful unto death; take unto oneself*).

un·told /úntóld/ *adj.* **1** not told. **2** not (able to be) counted or measured (*untold misery*).

un·touch·a·ble /úntúchəbəl/ • *adj.* that may

not or cannot be touched. • *n.* member of a hereditary Hindu group held to defile members of higher castes on contact. □□ **un·touch·a·bil'i·ty** *n.* **un·touch'a·ble·ness** *n.*

un·touched /úntúcht/ *adj.* **1** not touched. **2** not affected physically. **3** not affected by emotion.

un·to·ward /úntáwrd, –təwáwrd/ *adj.* **1** inconvenient; unlucky. **2** awkward. **3** unseemly. □□ **un·to·ward'ly** *adv.* **un·toward'ness** *n.*

un·tram·meled /úntráməld/ *adj.* unhampered.

un·tried /úntríd/ *adj.* **1** not tried or tested. **2** inexperienced.

un·trou·bled /úntrúbəld/ *adj.* not troubled; calm; tranquil.

un·true /úntroó/ *adj.* **1** not true; contrary to what is the fact. **2** (often foll. by *to*) not faithful or loyal. **3** deviating from an accepted standard. □□ **un·tru'ly** *adv.*

un·truth /úntroóth/ *n.* (*pl.* **un·truths** /–troóthz, –troóths/) **1** state of being untrue; falsehood. **2** false statement (*told me an untruth*). □□ **un·truth'ful** *adj.* **un·truth'ful·ly** *adv.* **un·truth'ful·ness** *n.*

un·tu·tored /úntoótərd, –tyoó–/ *adj.* uneducated; untaught.

un·twist /úntwíst/ *v.* open from a twisted or spiraled state.

un·used *adj.* **1** /únyoózd/ **a** not in use. **b** never having been used. **2** /únyoóst/ (foll. by *to*) not accustomed.

un·u·su·al /únyoózhooəl/ *adj.* **1** not usual. **2** exceptional; remarkable. □□ **un·u'su·al·ly** *adv.*

un·ut·ter·a·ble /únútərəbəl/ *adj.* inexpressible; beyond description (*unutterable torment*). □□ **un·ut'ter·a·bly** *adv.*

un·var·nished /únváarnisht/ *adj.* **1** not varnished. **2** plain and straightforward (*the unvarnished truth*).

un·veil /únváyl/ *v.* **1** *tr.* remove a veil from. **2** *tr.* remove a covering from (a statue, plaque, etc.) as part of the ceremony of the first public display. **3** *tr.* disclose; reveal; make publicly known. **4** *intr.* remove one's veil.

un·voiced /únvóyst/ *adj.* **1** not spoken. **2** *Phonet.* not voiced.

un·war·rant·ed /únwáwrəntid, –wór–/ *adj.* **1** unauthorized. **2** unjustified.

un·wary /únwáiree/ *adj.* **1** not cautious. **2** (often foll. by *of*) not aware of possible danger, etc. □□ **un·war'i·ly** *adv.* **un·war'i·ness** *n.*

un·washed /únwósht, –wáwsht/ *adj.* not washed or clean. □ **the great unwashed** *colloq.* the masses; the common people.

un·wea·ry·ing /únweéreeing/ *adj.* **1** persistent. **2** not causing or producing weariness. □□ **un·wea'ry·ing·ly** *adv.*

un·well /únwél/ *adj.* not in good health; (somewhat) ill.

un·whole·some /únhólsəm/ *adj.* **1** not promoting, or detrimental to, physical or moral health. **2** unhealthy-looking. □□ **un·whole'some·ly** *adv.* **un·whole'some·ness** *n.*

un·wield·y /únweéldee/ *adj.* (**un·wield·i·er, un·wield·i·est**) cumbersome, or hard to manage, owing to size, shape, etc. □□ **un·wield'i·ness** *n.*

un·will·ing /únwíling/ *adj.* not willing or inclined; reluctant. □□ **un·will'ing·ly** *adv.* **un·will'ing·ness** *n.*

un·wind /únwínd/ v. (past and past part. **un·wound'** /-wównd/) **1 a** tr. draw out (a thing that has been wound). **b** intr. become drawn out after being wound. **2** intr. & tr. colloq. relax.

un·wise /únwíz/ adj. foolish; imprudent. □□ **un·wise'ly** adv.

un·wit·ting /únwíting/ adj. **1** unaware (unwitting offender). **2** unintentional. □□ **un·wit'ting·ly** adv. **un·wit'ting·ness** n.

un·wont·ed /únwáwntid, –wón–, –wún–/ adj. not customary or usual. □□ **un·wont'ed·ly** adv. **un·wont'ed·ness** n.

un·world·ly /únwórldlee/ adj. **1** spiritual. **2** naive. □□ **un·world'li·ness** n.

un·wor·thy /únwúrthee/ adj. (**un·wor·thi·er**, **un·wor·thi·est**) **1** (often foll. by of) not worthy or befitting the character of a person, etc. **2** discreditable; unseemly. **3** contemptible; base. □□ **un·wor'thi·ly** adv. **un·wor'thi·ness** n.

un·wrap /únráp/ v. (**un·wrapped**, **un·wrap·ping**) **1** tr. remove the wrapping from. **2** tr. open or unfold. **3** intr. become unwrapped.

un·writ·ten /únrít'n/ adj. **1** not written. **2** (of a law, etc.) resting originally on custom or judicial decision, not on statute.

un·yield·ing /únyéelding/ adj. **1** not yielding to pressure, etc. **2** firm; obstinate. □□ **un·yield'ing·ly** adv. **un·yield'ing·ness** n.

up /up/ • adv. **1** at, in, or toward a higher place or position (jumped up in the air; what are they doing up there?). **2** to or in a place regarded as higher, esp. northward (up in New England). **3** colloq. ahead, etc., as indicated (went up front). **4 a** to or in an erect position or condition (stood it up). **b** to or in a prepared or required position (wound up the watch). **c** in or into a condition of efficiency, activity, or progress (stirred up trouble; the house is up for sale). **5** in a stronger or winning position or condition (our team was three goals up). **6** (of a computer, machine, etc.) running and available for use. **7** to the place or time in question or where the speaker, etc., is (a child came up to me; has been fine up till now). **8** at or to a higher price or value (our costs are up). **9 a** completely or effectually (burn up; eat up; use up). **b** more loudly or clearly (speak up). **10** completed; past (time is up). **11** into a compact, accumulated, or secure state (pack up; save up; tie up). **12 a** awake. **b** out of bed (are you up yet?). **13** (of the sun, etc.) having risen. **14** happening, esp. unusually or unexpectedly (something is up). **15** (usu. foll. by on) informed about. **16** Baseball at bat (he struck out his last time up). • prep. **1** upward along, through, or into (climbed up the ladder). **2** from the bottom to the top of. **3** along (walked up the road). **4 a** at or in a higher part of (is situated up the street). **b** toward the source of (a river). • adj. (often in comb.) directed upward (upstroke). • n. spell of good fortune. • v. (**upped, up·ping**) **1** intr. colloq. begin abruptly to say or do something (upped and hit him). **2** tr. increase or raise, esp. abruptly (upped all their prices). □ **on the up and up** colloq. honest(ly); on the level. **up against 1** close to. **2** colloq. confronted with (up against a problem). **up and about** (or **doing**) having risen from bed; active. **up-and-coming** colloq. making good progress and likely to succeed. **up and down 1** in every direction. **2** colloq. in varying health or spirits. **up for** available for or being

considered for (office, etc.). **up-front** adv. (usu. **up front**) **1** at the front; in front. **2** (of payments) in advance. • adj. **1** honest; open; frank. **2** (of payments) made in advance. **3** at the front or most prominent. **ups and downs** mixed fortune. **up to 1** until (up to the present). **2** less than or equal to (adds up to $10). **3** incumbent on (it is up to you to say). **4** capable of or fit for (am not up to a long walk). **5** occupied or busy with (what have you been up to?).

up- /up/ prefix in senses of UP, added: **1** as an adverb to verbs and verbal derivations, = 'upward' (update). **2** as a preposition to nouns forming adverbs and adjectives (up-country; upland). **3** as an adjective to nouns (upland; upstroke).

up·beat /úpbeet/ • n. unaccented beat in music. • adj. colloq. optimistic or cheerful.

up·braid /upbráyd/ v.tr. chide or reproach (a person). □□ **up·braid'ing** n.

up·bring·ing /úpbringing/ n. care and education of a child.

UPC abbr. = Universal Product Code (UNIVERSAL).

up·chuck /úpchuk/ v. sl. vomit.

up·com·ing /úpkúming/ adj. forthcoming; about to happen.

up·date • v.tr. /úpdáyt/ bring up to date. • n. /úpdayt/ **1** updating. **2** updated information, etc. □□ **up·dat'er** n.

up·end /upénd/ v. set or rise up on end.

up·grade • v.tr. /úpgráyd/ **1** raise in rank, etc. **2** improve (equipment, etc.). • n. /úpgrayd/ **1** upgrading. **2** improvement. **3** upward slope. □□ **up'grad·er** n.

up·heav·al /upheévəl/ n. violent or sudden change or disruption.

up·hill /úphíl/ • adv. up a hill, slope, etc. • adj. **1** sloping up; ascending. **2** arduous; difficult (an uphill task).

up·hold /úphóld/ v.tr. (past and past part. **up·held** /-héld/) **1** confirm. **2** support (a person, practice, etc.). □□ **up·hold'er** n.

up·hol·ster /uphólstər, əpól–/ v.tr. provide (furniture) with upholstery. □□ **up·hol'ster·er** n.

up·hol·ster·y /uphólstəree, əpól–/ n. **1** covering, padding, springs, etc., for furniture. **2** upholsterer's work.

up·keep /úpkeep/ n. **1** maintenance in good condition. **2** cost or means of this.

up·land /úplənd/ • n. the higher or inland parts of a country. • adj. of or relating to these parts.

up·lift • v.tr. /úplíft/ **1** raise; lift up. **2** elevate morally or spiritually. • n. /úplift/ colloq. morally or spiritually elevating influence. □□ **up·lift'er** n. **up·lift'ing** adj. (esp. in sense 2 of v.).

up·mar·ket /úpmaárkit/ adj. & adv. = UPSCALE.

up·on /əpón, əpán/ prep. = ON. ¶ Upon is sometimes more formal, and is preferred in once upon a time and upon my word, and in uses such as row upon row of seats and Christmas is almost upon us.

up·per[1] /úpər/ • adj. **1** higher in place; situated above (upper lip). **2** higher in rank or dignity, etc. (upper class). • n. part of a boot or shoe above the sole. □ **on one's uppers** colloq. extremely short of money. **upper class** highest class of society. **upper crust** colloq. high society. **upper hand** dominance or control. **upper house** the higher house in a legislature, e.g., the U.S. Senate.

up·per² /úpər/ *n. sl.* stimulant drug, esp. an amphetamine.

up·per·case /úpərkáys/ • *adj.* (of letters) capital. • *n.* capital letters. • *v.tr.* set or print in uppercase.

up·per·cut /úpərkut/ • *n.* upward blow delivered with the arm bent. • *v.tr.* hit with an uppercut.

up·per·most /úpərmōst/ • *adj.* (also **up·most** /úpmōst/) **1** highest. **2** predominant. • *adv.* at or to the uppermost position.

up·pi·ty /úpitee/ *adj. colloq.* arrogant; snobbish.

up·right /úprīt/ • *adj.* **1** erect; vertical (*an upright posture*). **2** (of a piano) with vertical strings. **3** honorable or honest. • *adv.* vertically. • *n.* **1** post or rod fixed upright, esp. as a structural support. **2** upright piano. □□ **up'right·ly** *adv.* **up'right·ness** *n.*

up·ris·ing /úprīzing/ *n.* rebellion or revolt.

up·roar /úprawr/ *n.* tumult; violent disturbance.

up·roar·i·ous /upráwreeəs/ *adj.* **1** very noisy. **2** provoking loud laughter. □□ **up·roar'i·ous·ly** *adv.*

up·root /úprŏŏt, rŏŏt/ *v.tr.* **1** pull (a plant, etc.) up from the ground. **2** displace. **3** eradicate; destroy. □□ **up·root'er** *n.*

up·scale /úpskáyl/ *adj. & adv.* toward or relating to the more affluent or upper sector of society or the market.

up·set • *v.* /úpsét/ (**up'set·ting**; *past* and *past part.* **up'set**) **1 a** *tr.* & *intr.* overturn or be overturned. **b** *tr.* overcome; defeat. **2** *tr.* disturb the composure or digestion of. **3** *tr.* disrupt. • *n.* /úpset/ **1** condition of upsetting or being upset (*a stomach upset*). **2** surprising result in a game, etc. • *adj.* /úpsét/ disturbed (*upset stomach*). □□ **up·set'ter** *n.* **up·set'ting·ly** *adv.*

up·shot /úpshot/ *n.* outcome or conclusion.

up·side down /úpsīd dówn/ • *adv.* **1** with the upper part where the lower part should be; inverted. **2** in or into total disorder. • *adj.* (also **up'side-down'** *attrib.*) inverted.

up·si·lon /úpsilon, yŏŏp–/ *n.* twentieth letter of the Greek alphabet (Υ, υ).

up·stage /úpstáyj/ • *adj. & adv.* nearer the back of a stage. • *v.tr.* divert attention from (a person) to oneself; outshine.

up·stairs /úpstáirz/ • *adv.* to or on an upper floor. • *adj.* (also **up'stair**) situated upstairs. • *n.* upper floor.

up·stand·ing /úpstánding/ *adj.* **1** standing up. **2** honest.

up·start /úpstaart/ • *n.* newly successful, esp. arrogant, person. • *adj.* of or characteristic of an upstart.

up·state /úpstáyt/ • *n.* part of a state remote from its large cities, esp. the northern part. • *adj.* of or relating to this part. • *adv.* in or to this part. □□ **up'stat'er** *n.*

up·stream /úpstréem/ • *adv.* against the flow of a stream, etc. • *adj.* moving upstream.

up·surge /úpsərj/ *n.* upward surge; rise (esp. in feelings, etc.).

up·swing /úpswing/ *n.* upward movement or trend.

up·take /úptayk/ *n.* **1** *colloq.* understanding; comprehension (esp. *quick* or *slow on the uptake*). **2** taking up.

up·thrust /úpthrust/ *n.* **1** upward thrust. **2** *Geol.* = UPHEAVAL.

up·tight /úptít/ *adj. colloq.* **1** nervously tense or angry. **2** rigidly conventional.

up·town /úptówn/ • *adj.* **1** of or in the residential part of a town or city. **2** of affluent or sophisticated people. • *adv.* in or into this part. • *n.* this part. □□ **up'town'er** *n.*

up·turn • *n.* /úptərn/ upward trend; improvement. • *v.tr.* /úptúrn/ turn up or upside down.

up·ward /úpwərd/ • *adv.* (also **up'wards**) toward what is higher, superior, larger in amount, or more important. • *adj.* moving, extending, pointing, or leading upward. □ **upward of** more than (*found upward of forty specimens*).

up·ward·ly /úpwərdlee/ *adv.* in an upward direction. □ **upwardly mobile** able or aspiring to advance socially or professionally.

up·wind /úpwínd/ *adj. & adv.* against the direction of the wind.

u·ra·ni·um /yŏŏráyneeəm/ *n. Chem.* radioactive, gray, dense metallic element, capable of nuclear fission and used as a source of nuclear energy. ¶ Symb.: **U.** □□ **u·ran·ic** /–ránik/ *adj.*

U·ra·nus /yŏŏrənəs, yŏŏráynəs/ *n.* seventh planet from the sun.

ur·ban /śrbən/ *adj.* of, living in, or situated in a town or city (*an urban population*) (opp. RURAL).

ur·bane /ərbáyn/ *adj.* courteous; suave; elegant and refined in manner. □□ **ur·bane'ly** *adv.* **ur·ban·i·ty** /ərbánitee/ *n.*

ur·ban·ize /śrbənīz/ *v.tr.* **1** make urban. **2** destroy the rural quality of (a district). □□ **ur·ban·i·za'tion** *n.*

ur·chin /śrchin/ *n.* mischievous child, esp. young and raggedly dressed.

Ur·du /ŏŏrdŏŏ, śr–/ *n.* language related to Hindi but with many Persian words, used in Pakistan and India.

-ure /ər/ *suffix* forming: **1** nouns of action or process (*seizure*). **2** nouns of result (*scripture*). **3** collective nouns (*nature*).

u·re·a /yŏŏréeə/ *n. Biochem.* soluble, nitrogenous compound contained esp. in urine. □□ **u·re'al** *adj.*

u·re·ter /yŏŏréetər/ *n.* duct by which urine passes from the kidney to the bladder.

u·re·thane /yŏŏríthayn/ *n. Chem.* crystalline amide, ethyl carbamate, used in plastics and paints.

u·re·thra /yŏŏréethrə/ *n.* (*pl.* **u·re'thras** or **u·re'thrae** /–ree/) duct by which urine is discharged from the bladder.

urge /ərj/ • *v.tr.* **1** drive forcibly; impel (*urged the horses forward*). **2** encourage or entreat earnestly or persistently (*urged them to go*). **3** advocate (an action or argument, etc.) emphatically (to a person). • *n.* **1** urging impulse or tendency. **2** strong desire.

ur·gent /śrjənt/ *adj.* **1** requiring immediate action or attention. **2** persistent in demand. □□ **ur'gen·cy** *n.* **ur'gent·ly** *adv.*

u·ric /yŏŏrik/ *adj.* of or relating to urine.

u·ri·nal /yŏŏorinəl/ *n.* place or receptacle for urination by men.

u·ri·nal·y·sis /yŏŏorinálisis/ *n.* (*pl.* **u·ri·nal'y·ses** /–seez/) chemical analysis of urine, esp. for diagnostic purposes.

u·ri·nate /yŏŏrinayt/ *v.intr.* discharge urine. □□ **u·ri·na·tion** /–náyshən/ *n.*

u·rine /yŏŏrin/ *n.* pale-yellow fluid secreted as waste from the blood by the kidneys, stored in the bladder, and discharged through the urethra. □□ **u′ri·na·ry** *adj.*

urn /ərn/ *n.* **1** vase with a foot and usu. a rounded body, esp. for storing the ashes of the dead. **2** large vessel with a tap, in which tea or coffee, etc., is made or kept hot. □□ **urn′ful** *n.* (*pl.* **–fuls**).

u·ro·gen·i·tal /yŏŏrəjénit′l/ *adj.* of or relating to urinary and genital products or organs.

u·rol·o·gy /yŏŏrólōjee/ *n.* scientific study of the urinary system. □□ **u·ro·log′ic** /–rəlójik/ *adj.* **u·rol′o·gist** *n.*

ur·sine /ə́rsīn/ *adj.* of or like a bear.

US or U.S. *abbr.* United States (of America).

us /us, əs/ *pron.* **1** *objective case* of WE (*they saw us*). **2** *colloq.* = WE (*it's us again*). **3** *colloq.* = ME (*give us a kiss*).

USA *abbr.* **1** United States of America. **2** United States Army.

us·a·ble /yŏŏzəbəl/ *adj.* (also **use′a·ble**) that can be used. □□ **us·a·bil′i·ty** *n.* **us′a·ble·ness** *n.*

USAF *abbr.* United States Air Force.

us·age /yŏŏsij/ *n.* **1** use; treatment (*damaged by rough usage*). **2** habitual or customary practice, esp. as creating a right, obligation, or standard.

¶ **Usage** means 'manner of use; practice,' while **use** means the 'act of employing.' In discussions of writing, **usage** is the term for normal or prescribed practice: *Standard usage calls for a plural.* In describing particular examples, however, employ **use**: *The use of the plural with this noun is incorrect.*

U.S.C. *abbr. Law* United States Code.

USCG *abbr.* United States Coast Guard.

use • *v.tr.* /yŏŏz/ **1 a** cause to act or serve for a purpose; bring into service (*rarely uses the car*). **b** consume or take (alcohol, a drug, etc.), esp. habitually. **2** treat (a person) in a specified manner (*they used him shamefully*). **3** exploit for one's own ends (*they are just using you; used his position*). **4** (in *past* /yŏŏst/; foll. by *to* + infin.) did or had in the past (but no longer) as a customary practice or state (*I used to be an archaeologist; it did not use to rain so often*). **5** (as **used** *adj.*) secondhand. **6** (as **used** /yŏŏst/ *predic. adj.*) (foll. by *to*) familiar by habit; accustomed (*not used to hard work*). • *n.* /yŏŏs/ **1** using or being used (*put it to good use; worn and polished with use*). **2** right or power of using (*lost the use of my right arm*). **3 a** ability to be used (*a flashlight would be of use*). **b** purpose for which a thing can be used (*it's no use talking*). **4** custom or usage (*long use has reconciled me to it*). □ **have no use for 1** be unable to find a use for. **2** dislike or be impatient with. **use up** consume completely; use the whole of. □□ **us′er** *n.*

¶ See note at USAGE.

use·ful /yŏŏsfŏŏl/ *adj.* **1 a** of use; serviceable. **b** producing or able to produce good results (*gave me some useful hints*). **2** *colloq.* highly creditable or efficient (*a useful performance*). □□ **use′ful·ly** *adv.* **use′ful·ness** *n.*

use·less /yŏŏslis/ *adj.* **1** serving no purpose; unavailing (*protest is useless*). **2** *colloq.* feeble or ineffectual (*a useless gadget*). □□ **use′less·ly** *adv.* **use′less·ness** *n.*

us·er-friend·ly /yŏŏzər-fréndlee/ *adj.* esp. *Computing* (of a machine or system) designed to be easy to use.

ush·er /úshər/ • *n.* person who shows people to their seats in a theater, church, etc. • *v.tr.* **1** act as usher to. **2** announce or show in, etc. (*ushered us into the room*).

USIA *abbr.* United States Information Agency.

USMC *abbr.* United States Marine Corps.

USN *abbr.* United States Navy.

USO *abbr.* United Service Organizations.

USPS *abbr.* United States Postal Service.

USS *abbr.* United States Ship.

USSR *abbr. hist.* Union of Soviet Socialist Republics.

usu. *abbr.* **1** usual. **2** usually.

u·su·al /yŏŏzhŏŏəl/ *adj.* **1** customary; habitual (*the usual formalities; it is usual to tip them; forgot my keys as usual*). **2** (prec. by *the, my,* etc.) *colloq.* person's usual drink, etc. □□ **u′su·al·ly** *adv.*

u·surp /yŏŏzə́rp, –sə́rp/ *v.* **1** *tr.* seize or assume (a throne or power, etc.) wrongfully. **2** *intr.* (foll. by *on, upon*) encroach. □□ **u·sur·pa′tion** *n.* **u·surp′er** *n.*

u·su·ry /yŏŏzhəree/ *n.* **1** lending of money at an exorbitant or illegal rate of interest. **2** interest at this rate. □□ **u′su·rer** *n.* **u·su·ri·ous** /–zhŏŏreeəs/ *adj.*

UT *abbr.* Utah (in official postal use).

Ute /yŏŏt/ *n.* (*pl.* same or **Utes**) **1 a** N. American people native to the Colorado, New Mexico, Utah, and Arizona area. **b** member of this people. **2** language of this people.

u·ten·sil /yŏŏténsəl/ *n.* implement or vessel, esp. for domestic use (*cooking utensils*).

u·ter·us /yŏŏtərəs/ *n.* (*pl.* **u·ter·i** /–rī/) the womb. □□ **u·ter·ine** /–in, –īn/ *adj.*

u·til·i·tar·i·an /yŏŏtílitáireeən/ *adj.* **1** designed to be useful rather than attractive; severely practical. **2** of utilitarianism.

u·til·i·tar·i·an·ism /yŏŏtílitáireeənizəm/ *n.* doctrine that actions are right if they are useful or benefit a majority.

u·til·i·ty /yŏŏtílitee/ *n.* (*pl.* **–ties**) **1** being useful or profitable. **2** useful thing. **3** = *public utility.* □ **utility room** room equipped with appliances for washing, ironing, and other domestic work.

u·ti·lize /yŏŏt′līz/ *v.tr.* make practical use of; use effectively. □□ **u′ti·liz·a·ble** *adj.* **u·ti·li·za′tion** *n.* **u·ti·liz·er** *n.*

-ution /ŏŏshən/ *suffix* forming nouns, = -ATION (*solution*).

ut·most /útmōst/ • *adj.* furthest, extreme, or greatest (*showed the utmost reluctance*). • *n.* utmost point or degree, etc.

U·to·pi·a /yŏŏtōpeeə/ *n.* imagined perfect place or state of things. □□ **U·to′pi·an** *adj.* & *n.*

ut·ter[1] /útər/ *attrib.adj.* complete; total; absolute (*utter misery; saw the utter absurdity of it*). □□ **ut′ter·ly** *adv.*

ut·ter[1] /útər/ *attrib.adj.* complete; total; absolute (*utter misery; saw the utter absurdity of it*). □□ **ut′ter·ly** *adv.*

ut·ter[2] /útər/ *v.tr.* **1** emit audibly. **2** express in words. □□ **ut′ter·a·ble** *adj.* **ut′ter·er** *n.*

ut·ter·ance /útərəns/ *n.* **1** act of uttering. **2** thing spoken. **3 a** power of speaking. **b** manner of speaking.

ut·ter·most /útərmōst/ *adj.* furthest; extreme.

U-turn /yo͞otərn/ *n.* **1** turning of a vehicle so as to face in the opposite direction. **2** reversal of policy.

UV *abbr.* ultraviolet.

u·vu·la /yo͞ovyələ/ *n.* (*pl.* **u·vu·las** *or* **u·vu·lae** /–lee/) fleshy extension of the soft palate hanging above the throat. □□ **u'vu·lar** *adj.*

ux·o·ri·al /uksáwreeəl, ugzáwr–/ *adj.* of or relating to a wife.

ux·o·ri·ous /uksáwreeəs, ugzáwr–/ *adj.* greatly or excessively fond of one's wife. □□ **ux·o'ri·ous·ly** *adv.* **ux·o'ri·ous·ness** *n.*

Uz·bek /o͞ozbek–, úz–/ *n.* (also **Uz·beg** /–beg/) **1** member of a Turkic people living mainly in Uzbekistan, a country of south central Asia. **2** language of this people.

V v

V¹ /vee/ *n.* (also **v**) (*pl.* **Vs** or **V's**; **v's**) **1** twenty-second letter of the alphabet. **2** V-shaped thing. **3** (as a Roman numeral) five.

V² *abbr.* (also **V.**) volt(s).

V³ *symb. Chem.* vanadium.

v. *abbr.* **1** verse. **2** verso. **3** versus. **4** very. **5** *vide*.

VA *abbr.* **1** Veterans Administration. **2** Virginia (in official postal use).

Va. *abbr.* Virginia.

va·can·cy /váykənsee/ *n.* (*pl.* **-cies**) **1** being vacant or empty. **2** unoccupied position or job (*there are three vacancies for computer specialists*). **3** available room in a hotel, etc.

va·cant /váykənt/ *adj.* **1** not filled nor occupied; empty. **2** not mentally active; showing no interest. □□ **va'cant·ly** *adv.*

va·cate /váykayt, vaykáyt/ *v.tr.* **1** leave vacant or cease to occupy (a room, etc.). **2** give up (a post, etc.).

va·ca·tion /vaykáyshən, və-/ • *n.* time of rest, recreation, etc., esp. spent away from home. • *v.intr.* take a vacation, esp. away from home for pleasure and recreation. □□ **va·ca'tion·er** *n.*

vac·ci·nate /váksinayt/ *v.tr.* inoculate to immunize against a disease. □□ **vac·ci·na'tion** *n.*

vac·cine /vákse'en/ *n.* antigenic preparation used to stimulate the production of antibodies and procure immunity from disease.

vac·il·late /vásilayt/ *v.intr.* **1** fluctuate; be irresolute. **2** move from side to side. □□ **vac·il·la·tion** /-láyshən/ *n.* **vac'il·la·tor** *n.*

va·cu·i·ty /vakyóōətee, və-/ *n.* **1** state of being vacuous. **2** something, such as a comment, that is senseless or inane. **3** empty space.

vac·u·ole /vákyōō-ōl/ *n. Biol.* tiny space in the cytoplasm of a cell containing air, fluid, etc. □□ **vac·u·o·lar** /vakyōō-ólər, vákyooolər/ *adj.* **vac·u·o·la'tion** *n.*

vac·u·ous /vákyōōəs/ *adj.* **1** lacking expression. **2** unintelligent. **3** empty. □□ **va·cu·i·ty** /vəkyóō-itee/ *n.* **vac'u·ous·ly** *adv.*

vac·u·um /vákyōōəm, -yōōm, -yəm/ • *n.* (*pl.* **vac·u·ums** or **vac·u·a** /-yōōə/) **1** space entirely devoid of matter. **2** space from which the air has been completely or partly removed by a pump, etc. **3** absence of the normal or previous content, activities, etc. **4** (*pl.* **vac·u·ums**) *colloq.* vacuum cleaner. • *v. colloq.* **1** *tr.* clean with a vacuum cleaner. **2** *intr.* use a vacuum cleaner. □ **vacuum cleaner** apparatus for removing dust, etc., by suction. **vacuum-packed** sealed after partial removal of air. **vacuum tube** *Electronics* tube with a near-vacuum that regulates electric current.

vag·a·bond /vágəbond/ • *n.* **1** wanderer, esp. an idle one. **2** *colloq.* rascal. • *adj.* wandering. □□ **vag'a·bond·age** *n.*

va·ga·ry /váygəree/ *n.* (*pl.* **-ries**) caprice; eccentric idea or act (*the vagaries of Fortune*). □□ **va·gar'i·ous** /vəgáireəs/ *adj.*

va·gi·na /vəjīnə/ *n.* (*pl.* **va·gi·nas** or **va·gi·nae** /-nee/) canal between the uterus and vulva in female mammals. □□ **vag·i·nal** /vájin'l/ *adj.* **vag·i·ni·tis** /vájinītis/ *n.*

va·grant /váygrənt/ • *n.* **1** person without a home or work. **2** wanderer or vagabond. • *adj.* wandering or roving (*a vagrant musician*). □□ **va·gran·cy** /-grənsee/ *n.* **va'grant·ly** *adv.*

vague /vayg/ *adj.* **1** uncertain or ill-defined (*gave a vague answer*). **2** (of a person or mind) imprecise; inexact in thought, expression, or understanding. □□ **vague'ly** *adv.* **vague'ness** *n.*

vain /vayn/ *adj.* **1** excessively proud or conceited, esp. about one's own attributes. **2** empty; trivial (*vain boasts*). **3** useless; futile. □ **in vain** without success (*it was in vain that we protested*). □□ **vain'ly** *adv.* **vain'ness** *n.*

vain·glo·ry /vayngláwree/ *n. literary* boastfulness; extreme vanity. □□ **vain·glo'ri·ous** *adj.* **vain·glo'ri·ous·ly** *adv.*

val·ance /váləns, váyl-/ *n.* short curtain around the frame or canopy of a bed, above a window, or under a shelf. □□ **val'anced** *adj.*

VALANCE

vale /vayl/ *n. archaic* or *poet.* (except in place-names) valley (*Vale of the White Horse*).

val·e·dic·tion /válidíkshən/ *n.* **1** bidding farewell. **2** words used in this.

val·e·dic·to·ri·an /válidiktáwreeən/ *n.* person who gives a valedictory, esp. the highest-ranking member of a graduating class.

val·e·dic·to·ry /válidíktəree/ • *adj.* serving as a farewell. • *n.* (*pl.* **-ries**) farewell address.

va·lence /váyləns/ *n. Chem.* combining power of an atom measured by the number of hydrogen atoms it can displace or combine with.

val·en·tine /váləntīn/ *n.* **1** card or gift sent as a mark of love or affection on St. Valentine's Day (Feb. 14). **2** sweetheart chosen on this day.

va·let /valáy, válit, -lay/ • *n.* **1** gentleman's personal attendant. **2** hotel, etc., employee with similar duties. **3** standing rack for holding one's suit, coat, etc. • *v.* **1** *intr.* work as a valet. **2** *tr.* act as a valet to.

val·e·tu·di·nar·i·an /válitōōd'náireeən,

–tyŏod–/ • *n.* person of poor health or unduly anxious about health. • *adj.* of poor health. □□ **val·e·tu·di·nar'i·an·ism** *n.*

Val·hal·la /valhálə, vaalha'alə/ *n.* (in Norse mythology) palace in which the souls of slain heroes feasted for eternity.

val·iant /vályənt/ *adj.* brave; courageous. □□ **val'iant·ly** *adv.*

val·id /válid/ *adj.* **1** (of a reason, objection, etc.) sound or defensible. **2 a** legally acceptable (*valid passport*). **b** not having reached its expiration date. □□ **va·lid'i·ty** *n.* **val'id·ly** *adv.*

val·i·date /válidayt/ *v.tr.* make valid; ratify. □□ **val·i·da·tion** /–dáyshən/ *n.*

val·ise /vəlee's/ *n.* small suitcase; traveling bag.

Val·i·um /váleeəm/ *n. propr.* drug (diazepam) used as a tranquilizer.

Val·kyr·ie /valkee'ree, válkiree/ *n.* (in Norse mythology) maidens who selected heroes destined to be slain in battle and escorted them to Valhalla.

val·ley /válee/ *n.* (*pl.* **–leys**) low area between hills and usu. with a stream flowing through it.

val·or /válər/ *n.* courage, esp. in battle. □□ **val'or·ous** *adj.*

val·u·a·ble /vályŏoəbəl, vályə–/ • *adj.* of great value, price, or worth. • *n.* (usu. in *pl.*) valuable thing. □□ **val'u·a·bly** *adv.*

val·u·a·tion /vályŏo-áyshən/ *n.* **1** estimation (esp. by a professional) of a thing's worth. **2** worth estimated. □□ **val'u·ate** *v.tr.*

val·ue /vályŏo/ • *n.* **1** worth, desirability, or utility (*the value of regular exercise*). **2** worth as estimated. **3** amount of money or goods for which a thing can be exchanged in the open market. **4** ability of a thing to serve a purpose or cause an effect (*news value; nuisance value*). **5** (in *pl.*) one's principles or standards; one's judgment of what is valuable or important in life. **6** *Mus.* duration of a note. **7** *Math.* amount denoted by an algebraic term. • *v.tr.* (**val'ues, val·ued, val·u·ing**) **1** estimate the value of (esp. professionally) (*valued the property at $200,000*). **2** have a high or specified opinion of (*a valued friend*). □ **value-added tax** tax on the amount by which the value of an article has been increased at each stage of its production. **value judgment** subjective estimate of quality, etc. □□ **val'ue·less** *adj.*

VALVE, 1

valve /valv/ *n.* **1** device controlling the flow of fluid through a pipe, etc. **2** *Anat.* & *Zool.* part of an organ, etc., allowing a flow of blood, etc., in one direction only. **3** device to vary the effective length of the tube in a brass musical instrument. **4** each of the two shells of an oyster, mussel, etc. □□ **val·vate** /–vayt/ *adj.* **valved**

adj. (also in *comb.*). **valve'less** *adj.* **val'vu·lar** *adj.*

va·moose /vamŏos, və–/ *v.intr.* (esp. as *int.*) *sl.* depart hurriedly.

vamp[1] /vamp/ • *n.* **1** upper front part of a boot or shoe. **2** improvised musical accompaniment. • *v.* **1** *tr.* & *intr.* improvise a musical accompaniment (to). **2** *tr.* improvise (a musical accompaniment).

vamp[2] /vamp/ *colloq.* • *n.* woman who uses sexual attraction to exploit men. • *v. intr.* act as a vamp.

vam·pire /vámpīr/ *n.* **1** supposedly reanimated corpse that sucks the blood of sleeping persons. **2** person who preys ruthlessly on others. **3** (in full **vam'pire bat**) tropical (esp. South American) bloodsucking bat.

van[1] /van/ *n.* **1** covered vehicle for conveying goods, etc., esp. a large truck or trailer (*moving van*). **2** smaller such vehicle, similar to a panel truck and used esp. for carrying passengers, etc.

van[2] /van/ *n.* **1** = VANGUARD. **2** forefront (*in the van of progress*).

va·na·di·um /vənáydeeəm/ *n. Chem.* hard, gray, metallic element used for strengthening some steels. ¶ Symb.: **V**.

van·dal /vánd'l/ *n.* person who willfully or maliciously damages property. □□ **van'dal·ism** *n.* **van'dal·ize** *v.*

VANDYKE BEARD

Van·dyke beard /vandík/ *n.* neat, pointed beard.

vane /vayn/ *n.* **1** (in full **weather vane**) revolving pointer on a barn roof or other high place to show the direction of the wind (cf. WEATHERCOCK). **2** blade of a propeller, windmill, etc. □□ **vaned** *adj.* **vane'less** *adj.*

VANE, 1 (WEATHER VANE)

van·guard /vángaard/ *n.* **1** foremost part of an advancing army, etc. **2** leaders of a movement, etc.

va·nil·la /vənílə/ *n.* **1 a** tropical climbing orchid with fragrant flowers. **b** (in full **va·nil′la bean**) fruit of these. **2** substance obtained from the vanilla bean or synthesized and used to flavor ice cream, chocolate, etc.

van·ish /vánish/ *v.intr.* **1** disappear. **2** cease to exist. □ **vanishing point** point at which receding parallel lines viewed in perspective appear to meet.

van·i·ty /vánitee/ *n.* (*pl.* **–ties**) **1** conceit about one's appearance or attainments. **2** futility or unsubstantiality (*the vanity of human achievement*). **3** ostentatious display. **4** dressing table. □ **vanity bag** (or **case**) bag or case for carrying a small mirror, makeup, etc.

van·quish /vángkwish/ *v.tr. literary* conquer or overcome. □□ **van′quish·a·ble** *adj.* **van′quish·er** *n.*

van·tage /vántij/ *n.* (also **van′tage point**) place affording a good view or prospect.

vap·id /vápid/ *adj.* insipid; lacking interest; flat; dull. □□ **va·pid′i·ty** *n.* **vap′id·ly** *adv.* **vap′id·ness** *n.*

va·por /váypər/ *n.* **1** moisture or another substance diffused or suspended in air, e.g., mist or smoke. **2** *Physics* gaseous form of a substance (cf. GAS). □ **vapor trail** trail of condensed water from an aircraft or rocket at high altitude, seen as a white streak against the sky. □□ **va′por·ous** *adj.* **va′por·ous·ly** *adv.* **va′por·y** *adj.*

va·por·ize /váypərīz/ *v.* convert or be converted into vapor. □□ **va′por·iz·a·ble** *adj.* (also **va′por·a·ble**). **va·por·i·za′tion** *n.* **va′por·i·zer** *v.*

va·ri·a·ble /váireeəbəl/ • *adj.* **1** changeable; adaptable. **2** apt to vary; not constant (*variable fortunes*). **3** *Math.* (of a quantity) indeterminate; able to assume different numerical values. • *n.* variable thing or quantity. □□ **var·i·a·bil′i·ty** *n.* **var′i·a·bly** *adv.*

var·i·ance /váireeəns/ *n.* **1** difference of opinion; dispute; lack of harmony (*a theory at variance with all known facts*). **2** discrepancy. **3** officially allowed exception to regulations, zoning laws, etc.

var·i·ant /váireeənt/ • *adj.* **1** differing in form or details from the main one (*variant spelling*). **2** having different forms. • *n.* variant form, spelling, type, etc.

var·i·a·tion /váireeáyshən/ *n.* **1** varying. **2** departure from a former or normal condition, action, or amount, or from a standard or type (*prices are subject to variation*). **3** extent of this. **4** thing that varies. **5** *Mus.* theme in a changed or elaborated form. □□ **var·i·a′tion·al** *adj.*

var·i·col·ored /váirikúlərd, vári–/ *adj.* of various colors.

var·i·cose /várikōs/ *adj.* permanently and abnormally dilated (*varicose veins*). □□ **var·i·cos′i·ty** /–kósitee/ *n.*

var·ied /váireed/ *adj.* showing variety. □□ **var′ied·ly** *adv.*

var·i·e·gat·ed /váirigaytid, váireeə–, vár–/ *adj* **1** with irregular patches of different colors. **2** *Bot.* (of plants) having leaves of two or more colors. □□ **var·i·e·ga′tion** /–gáyshən/ *n.*

va·ri·e·tal /vərίət'l/ *adj.* (of wine) made from a single designated variety of grape. □□ **va·ri′e·tal·ly** *adv.*

va·ri·e·ty /vərίətee/ *n.* (*pl.* **–ties**) **1** diversity; absence of uniformity (*not enough variety in our lives*). **2** quantity or collection of different things (*for a variety of reasons*). **3** different form of a thing, quality, etc. **4** *Biol.* subspecies.

var·i·ous /váireeəs/ *adj.* **1** different; diverse. **2** more than one; several. □□ **var′i·ous·ly** *adv.*

var·let /vaárlit/ *n.* **1** *archaic* or *joc.* rascal. **2** *hist.* knight's attendant. □□ **var′let·ry** *n.*

var·mint /vaármint/ *n. dial.* objectionable person or animal.

var·nish /vaárnish/ • *n.* **1** resinous solution used to give a hard shiny transparent coating. **2** external appearance or display without an underlying reality. • *v.tr.* **1** apply varnish to. **2** gloss over (a fact). □□ **var′nish·er** *n.*

var·si·ty /vaársitee/ *n.* (*pl.* **–ties**) principal team representing a high school, college, etc., in a sport.

var·y /váiree/ *v.* (**–ies, –ied**) **1** *tr.* make different; modify; diversify. **2** *intr.* **a** undergo change; become or be different. **b** be of different kinds (*his mood varies*).

vas·cu·lar /váskyələr/ *adj.* of or containing vessels for conveying blood or sap, etc. (*vascular tissue*). □□ **vas′cu·lar·ly** *adv.*

vas def·er·ens /vas défərenz/ *n.* (*pl.* **va·sa def·er·en·ti·a** /váysə déforénsheeə/) *Anat.* sperm duct from the testicle to the urethra.

vase /vays, vayz, vaaz/ *n.* vessel used as an ornament or container, esp. for flowers. □□ **vase′ful** *n.* (*pl.* **–fuls**).

va·sec·to·my /vəséktəmee/ *n.* (*pl.* **–mies**) surgical removal of part of each vas deferens for sterilization.

Vas·e·line /vásileén/ *n. propr.* type of petroleum jelly used as an ointment, lubricant, etc.

vas·o·mo·tor /váyzōmótər/ *adj.* causing constriction or dilatation of blood vessels.

vas·sal /vásəl/ *n.* **1** *hist.* feudal land tenant. **2** humble dependent. □□ **vas′sal·age** *n.*

vast /vast/ *adj.* immense; huge. □□ **vast′ly** *adv.* **vast′ness** *n.*

VAT /vat, vee-aytée/ *abbr.* value-added tax.

vat /vat/ *n.* large tank or other vessel, esp. for holding liquids. □□ **vat′ful** *n.* (*pl.* **–fuls**).

Vat·i·can /vátikən/ *n.* seat of the Roman Catholic Church in Rome, Italy.

vaude·ville /váwdvil, váwdə–/ *n.* stage show of dances, songs, comedy acts, etc. □□ **vaude·vil′li·an** /–vílyən/ *adj.* & *n.*

vault /vawlt/ • *n.* **1** arched roof. **2** vaultlike covering (*the vault of heaven*). **3** underground chamber: **a** as a place of storage. **b** as a place of interment. **4** act of vaulting. • *v.* **1** *intr.* leap, esp. using the hands or a pole. **2** *tr.* spring over (a gate, etc.) in this way. **3** *tr.* (esp. as **vaulted**) make in the form of a vault. □□ **vault′er** *n.*

vault·ing /váwlting/ *n.* **1** arched work in a vaulted roof or ceiling. **2** gymnastic exercise in which participants vault over obstacles. □ **vaulting horse** padded rectangular apparatus to be vaulted over by gymnasts.

vaunt /vawnt/ *literary* • *v.* **1** *intr.* boast; brag. **2** *tr.* boast of. • *n.* boast. □□ **vaunt′er** *n.* **vaunt′ing·ly** *adv.*

VCR *abbr.* videocassette recorder.

VD *abbr.* venereal disease.

VDT *abbr.* video display terminal.

've *abbr.* (chiefly after pronouns) = HAVE (*I've*; *they've*).

veal /veel/ *n.* calf's flesh as food.

vec·tor /véktər/ *n.* **1** *Math.* & *Physics* quantity having direction as well as magnitude (*radius vector*). **2** carrier of disease. □□ **vec·to·ri·al** /‑táwreeəl/ *adj.*

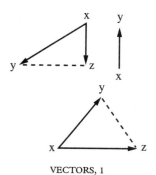

VECTORS, 1

Ve·da /váydə, vée‑/ *n.* (in *sing.* or *pl.*) most ancient Hindu scriptures. □□ **Ve'dic** *adj.*

vee·jay /vée'jay/ *n.* video jockey.

veer /veer/ • *v.intr.* **1** change direction. **2** change in course, opinion, conduct, emotions, etc. • *n.* change of direction.

veg /vej/ *v.* = VEGETATE 1.

veg·an /véjən, vée'gən/ • *n.* person who does not eat or use animal products. • *adj.* using or containing no animal products.

veg·e·ta·ble /véjtəbəl, véjitəbəl/ • *n.* **1** *Bot.* herbaceous plant used for food, e.g., a cabbage, potato, turnip, bean, etc. **2** *colloq.* a person who is incapable of normal intellectual activity, esp. through brain injury, etc. **b** dull or inactive person. • *adj.* **1** of, derived from, relating to, or comprising plant life. **2** of or relating to vegetables as food.

veg·e·tar·i·an /véjitáireeən/ • *n.* person who abstains from eating meat or fish. • *adj.* excluding animal food, esp. meat (*vegetarian diet*). □□ **veg·e·tar'i·an·ism** *n.*

veg·e·tate /véjitayt/ *v.intr.* **1** **a** live an uneventful or monotonous life. **b** spend time lazily or passively. **2** grow as plants do. □□ **veg'e·ta·tive** *adj.*

veg·e·ta·tion /véjitáyshən/ *n.* plants collectively; plant life. □□ **veg·e·ta'tion·al** *adj.*

veg·gie /véjee/ *n.* *colloq.* **1** vegetable. **2** vegetarian.

ve·he·ment /vée'əmənt/ *adj.* showing or caused by strong feeling; forceful; ardent. □□ **ve'he·mence** *n.* **ve'he·ment·ly** *adv.*

ve·hi·cle /vée'ikəl/ *n.* **1** conveyance for transporting people, goods, etc., esp. on land. **2** medium for thought, feeling, or action (*the stage is the best vehicle for their talents*). **3** liquid, etc., as a medium for suspending pigments, drugs, etc. □□ **ve·hic·u·lar** /veehíkyələr/ *adj.*

veil /vayl/ • *n.* **1** piece of usu. transparent fabric attached to a woman's hat, etc. **2** part of a nun's headdress. **3** thing that conceals (*under the veil of friendship; a veil of mist*). • *v.tr.* **1** cover with a veil. **2** (esp. as **veiled** *adj.*) partly conceal

(*veiled threats*). □ **take the veil** become a nun. □□ **veil'less** *adj.*

vein /vayn/ *n.* **1 a** any of the tubes by which blood is conveyed to the heart (cf. ARTERY). **b** (in general use) any blood vessel. **2** rib of an insect's wing or of a leaf. **3** streak of a different color in wood, marble, cheese, etc. **4** fissure in rock filled with ore. **5** distinctive character or tendency; mood (*spoke in a sarcastic vein*). □□ **vein'less** *n.* **vein'like** *adj.* **vein'y** *adj.* (**vein·i·er**, **vein·i·est**).

Vel·cro /vélkrō/ *n.* *propr.* fastener for clothes, etc., consisting of two strips of nylon fabric, one looped and one burred, which adhere when pressed together. □□ **Vel'croed** *adj.*

veld /velt, felt/ *n.* (also **veldt**) *S.Afr.* open country; grassland.

vel·lum /véləm/ *n.* **1 a** fine parchment orig. calfskin. **b** manuscript on this. **2** smooth writing paper imitating vellum.

ve·loc·i·rap·tor /velósiraptər/ *n.* small carnivorous bipedal dinosaur.

ve·loc·i·ty /vilósitee/ *n.* (*pl.* **ties**) speed, esp. of an inanimate object in a given direction.

ve·lo·drome /véladrōm/ *n.* arena or building with a track for cycling.

ve·lour /vəlŏŏr/ *n.* (also **ve·lours'**) plushlike woven fabric.

ve·lum /vée'ləm/ *n.* (*pl.* **ve·la** /‑lə/) *Biol.* & *Anat.* membrane, membranous covering, or flap.

vel·vet /vélvit/ • *n.* **1** woven fabric of silk, cotton, etc., with a thick short pile. **2** furry skin on a deer's growing antler. • *adj.* of, like, or soft as velvet. □□ **vel'vet·ed** *adj.* **vel'vet·y** *adj.*

vel·ve·teen /vélvitée'n/ *n.* cotton fabric with a pile like velvet.

ve·nal /vée'nəl/ *adj.* able to be bribed or corrupted. □□ **ve·nal'i·ty** /‑nálitee/ *n.* **ve'nal·ly** *adv.*

¶ **Venal** and **venial** are sometimes confused. **Venal** means 'corrupt, able to be bribed, or involving bribery,' e.g., *Local customs officials are notoriously venal, and smuggling thrives.* **Venial** is used among Christians to describe a certain type of sin and means 'pardonable, excusable, not mortal,' e.g., *Purgatory, to Catholics, was an intermediate stage in which those who had committed venial sins might earn their way into heaven.*

vend /vend/ *v.tr.* offer (small wares) for sale. □ **vending machine** machine that dispenses small articles for sale when a coin or token is inserted. □□ **ven'dor** *n.*

ven·det·ta /vendétə/ *n.* **1** blood feud. **2** prolonged bitter quarrel.

ve·neer /vinéer/ • *n.* **1** thin covering of fine wood, etc. **2** deceptive outward appearance of a good quality, etc. • *v.tr.* **1** apply a veneer to (wood, furniture, etc.). **2** disguise (an unattractive character, etc.) with a more attractive manner, etc.

ven·er·a·ble /vénərəbəl/ *adj.* entitled to respect on account of character, age, associations, etc. □□ **ven·er·a·bil'i·ty** *n.* **ven'er·a·ble·ness** *n.* **ven'er·a·bly** *adv.*

ven·er·ate /vénərayt/ *v.tr.* regard with deep respect. □□ **ven·er·a·tion** /‑ráyshən/ *n.* **ven'er·a·tor** *n.*

ve·ne·re·al /vinéereeəl/ *adj.* of sexual desire or intercourse. □ **venereal disease** any of various diseases contracted by sexual intercourse with an infected person. □□ **ve·ne're·al·ly** *adv.*

ve·ne·tian blind /vinéeshən/ *n.* window blind of adjustable horizontal slats to control the light.

ven·geance /vénjəns/ *n.* punishment inflicted for wrong to oneself or to a person, etc., whose cause one supports. □ **with a vengeance** in a higher degree than was expected or desired; in the fullest sense.

venge·ful /vénjfŏŏl/ *adj.* vindictive; seeking vengeance. □□ **venge'ful·ly** *adv.* **venge'ful·ness** *n.*

ve·ni·al /véeneeəl/ *adj.* (of a sin or fault) pardonable; not mortal. □□ **ve·ni·al·i·ty** /–neeálitee/ *n.* **ve'ni·al·ly** *adv.*
¶ See note at VENAL.

ven·i·son /vénisən, –zən/ *n.* deer's flesh as food.

Venn di·a·gram /ven/ *n.* diagram of usu. circular areas representing mathematical sets, the areas intersecting where they have elements in common.

ven·om /vénəm/ *n.* 1 poisonous fluid of snakes, scorpions, etc., usu. transmitted by a bite or sting. 2 malignity. □□ **ven'om·ous** *adj.* **ven'om·ous·ly** *adv.*

ve·nous /véenəs/ *adj.* of, full of, or contained in veins. □□ **ve·nos·i·ty** /vinósitee/ *n.* **ve'nous·ly** *adv.*

vent[1] /vent/ • *n.* 1 opening allowing the passage of air, etc. 2 outlet; free expression (*gave vent to their indignation*). • *v.* 1 *tr.* **a** make a vent in. **b** provide (a machine) with a vent. 2 *tr.* give free expression to (*vented my anger on the cat*). 3 *tr.* & *intr.* discharge. □ **vent one's spleen on** scold or ill-treat without cause. □□ **vent'less** *adj.*

vent[2] /vent/ *n.* slit in a garment, esp. in the lower edge of the back of a coat.

ven·ti·late /vént'layt/ *v.tr.* 1 cause air to circulate freely in (a room, etc.). 2 air (a question, grievance, etc.). 3 *Med.* **a** oxygenate (the blood). **b** admit or force air into (the lungs). □□ **ven·ti·la·tion** /–láyshən/ *n.*

ven·ti·la·tor /véntilaytər/ *n.* 1 appliance or aperture for ventilating a room, etc. 2 *Med.* = RESPIRATOR 2.

ven·tral /véntrəl/ *adj.* *Anat.* & *Zool.* of or on the abdomen (cf. DORSAL). □□ **ven'tral·ly** *adv.*

ven·tri·cle /véntrikəl/ *n.* *Anat.* hollow part of an organ, esp. in the brain or heart. □□ **ven·tric·u·lar** /–tríkyələr/ *adj.*

ven·tril·o·quism /ventrílakwizəm/ *n.* skill of speaking without moving the lips, esp. as entertainment. □□ **ven·tril'o·quist** *n.* **ven·tril'o·quize** *v.intr.*

ven·ture /vénchər/ • *n.* 1 risky undertaking. 2 commercial speculation. • *v.* 1 *intr.* dare; not be afraid (*did not venture to stop them*). 2 *intr.* dare to go (out), esp. outdoors. 3 *tr.* dare to put forward (an opinion, suggestion, etc.). 4 **a** *tr.* expose to risk; stake (a bet, etc.). **b** *intr.* take risks. 5 *intr.* dare to engage in, etc. (*ventured on a longer journey*).

ven·ture·some /vénchərsəm/ *adj.* 1 disposed to take risks. 2 risky. □□ **ven'ture·some·ly** *adv.* **ven'ture·some·ness** *n.*

ven·ue /vényŏŏ/ *n.* 1 place for a sports event, meeting, concert, etc. 2 *Law hist.* place where a jury must be gathered and a cause tried (orig. the neighborhood of the crime, etc.).

Ve·nus /véenəs/ *n.* 1 planet second from the sun in the solar system. 2 *poet.* **a** (*pl.* **Ve'nus·es**) beautiful woman. **b** sexual love; amorous influences or desires. □□ **Ve·nu·si·an** /vinŏ́oshən, –sheeən, –zeeən, –nyŏ́o–/ *adj.* & *n.*

ve·ra·cious /vəráyshəs/ *adj.* 1 speaking the truth. 2 (of a statement, etc.) true. □□ **ve·ra'cious·ly** *adv.* **ve·rac'i·ty** *n.*

ve·ran·da /vərándə/ *n.* = PORCH[2].

verb /vərb/ *n.* *Gram.* word used to indicate an action, state, or occurrence (e.g., *hear, become, happen*).

ver·bal /vɔ́rbəl/ • *adj.* 1 of words (*made a verbal distinction*). 2 oral; not written (*gave a verbal statement*). 3 *Gram.* of or in the nature of a verb (*verbal inflections*). 4 talkative. • *n.* *Gram.* 1 = verbal noun. 2 word(s) functioning as a verb. □ **verbal noun** *Gram.* noun derived from a verb (e.g., *smoking* in *smoking is forbidden*: see -ING[1]). □□ **ver'bal·ly** *adv.*

ver·bal·ize /vɔ́rbəliz/ *v.* 1 *tr.* express in words. 2 *intr.* be verbose. □□ **ver·bal·i·za'tion** *n.* **ver'bal·i·zer** *n.*

ver·ba·tim /vərbáytim/ *adv.* & *adj.* in exactly the same words; word for word (*copied it verbatim*).

ver·be·na /vərbéenə/ *n.* plant bearing clusters of fragrant flowers.

ver·bi·age /vɔ́rbeeij/ *n.* needless accumulation of words.

ver·bose /vərbɔ́s/ *adj.* using more words than are needed. □□ **ver·bose'ly** *adv.* **ver·bos·i·ty** /–bósitee/ *n.*

ver·dant /vɔ́rd'nt/ *adj.* 1 green, esp. bright and fresh-colored. 2 (of a person) unsophisticated. □□ **ver·dan·cy** /–d'nsee/ *n.* **ver'dant·ly** *adv.*

ver·dict /vɔ́rdikt/ *n.* 1 decision on an issue of fact in a civil or criminal cause or an inquest. 2 decision; judgment.

ver·di·gris /vɔ́rdigrees, –gris, –gree/ *n.* green substance that forms on copper and its alloys.

ver·dure /vɔ́rjər/ *n.* 1 green vegetation. 2 the greenness of this. □□ **ver'dured** *adj.*

verge[1] /vərj/ *n.* 1 edge or border. 2 extreme limit beyond which something happens (*on the verge of tears*).

verge[2] /vərj/ *v.intr.* 1 incline downward or in a specified direction (*the now verging sun; verge to a close*). 2 (foll. by *on*) border on; approach closely (*verging on the ridiculous*).

ver·i·fy /vérifi/ *v.tr.* (**-fies, -fied**) establish the truth or correctness of by examination (*must verify the statement; verified my figures*). □□ **ver·i·fi'a·ble** *adj.* **ver·i·fi'a·bly** *adv.* **ver·i·fi·ca'tion** *n.* **ver'i·fi·er** *n.*

ver·i·ly /vérilee/ *adv.* archaic really; truly.

ver·i·si·mil·i·tude /vérisimílitŏŏd, –tyŏŏd/ *n.* appearance of being true or real.

ver·i·ta·ble /véritəbəl/ *adj.* real; rightly so called (*a veritable feast*). □□ **ver'i·ta·bly** *adv.*

ver·i·ty /véritee/ *n.* (*pl.* **-ties**) 1 true statement, esp. one of fundamental import. 2 truth.

ver·mi·cel·li /vɔ́rmichélee/ *n.* pasta made in long slender threads.

ver·mi·cide /vɔ́rmisid/ *n.* substance that kills worms.

ver·mic·u·lite /vərmíkyəlit/ *n.* hydrous silicate mineral used as an insulation material and as a medium for plant growth.

ver·mi·form /vɔ́rmifawrm/ *adj.* worm-shaped. □ **vermiform appendix** see APPENDIX 1.

ver·mil·ion /vərmílyən/ • *n*. **1** cinnabar. **2 a** brilliant red pigment made by grinding this or artificially. **b** color of this. • *adj*. of this color.

ver·min /vərmin/ *n*. (usu. treated as *pl*.) **1** mammals, insects, and birds injurious to game, crops, etc. **2** vile persons. □□ **ver′min·ous** *adj*.

ver·mouth /vərmóoth/ *n*. wine flavored with aromatic herbs.

ver·nac·u·lar /vərnákyələr/ • *n*. **1** language or dialect of a particular country. **2** language of a particular clan or group. **3** plain, everyday speech. • *adj*. (of language) native; not foreign or formal. □□ **ver·nac′u·lar·ism** *n*. **ver·nac′u·lar·ly** *adv*.

ver·nal /vərnəl/ *adj*. of, in, or appropriate to spring (*vernal breezes*). □ **vernal equinox** see EQUINOX. □□ **ver′nal·ly** *adv*.

ver·ni·er /vərneeər/ *n*. small, movable graduated scale for obtaining fractional parts on a fixed scale of a barometer, etc.

ver·sa·tile /vərsət'l, –tīl/ *adj*. **1** turning easily or readily from one subject or occupation to another; capable of dealing with many subjects (*a versatile mind*). **2** (of a device, etc.) having many uses. □□ **ver·sa·til′i·ty** /–tilitee/ *n*.

verse /vərs/ • *n*. **1 a** poetry. **b** particular type of this (*English verse*). **2** stanza of a poem or song. **3** each of the short numbered divisions of the Bible or other scripture. • *v.tr*. (usu. *refl*.; foll. by *in*) instruct; make knowledgeable.

versed /vərst/ *predic.adj*. (foll. by *in*) experienced or skilled in; knowledgeable about.

ver·si·fy /vərsifī/ *v*. (**–fies, –fied**) **1** *tr*. turn into or express in verse. **2** *intr*. compose verses. □□ **ver·si·fi·ca′tion** *n*. **ver′si·fi·er** *n*.

ver·sion /vərzhən, –shən/ *n*. **1** account of a matter from a particular point of view (*told them my version of the incident*). **2** book, etc., in a particular edition or translation (*Authorized Version*). **3** form or variant of a thing as performed, adapted, etc. □□ **ver′sion·al** *adj*.

ver·so /vərsō/ *n*. (*pl*. **–sos**) **1 a** left-hand page of an open book. **b** back of a printed leaf (opp. RECTO). **2** reverse of a coin.

ver·sus /vərsəs, –səz/ *prep*. against. ¶ Abbr.: **v., vs.**

ver·te·bra /vərtibrə/ *n*. (*pl*. **ver·te·brae** /–bray, –bree/) each segment of the backbone. □□ **ver′te·bral** *adj*.

ver·te·brate /vərtibrət, –brayt/ • *n*. animal having a spinal column, including mammals, birds, reptiles, amphibians, and fishes. • *adj*. of or relating to the vertebrates.

ver·tex /vərteks/ *n*. (*pl*. **ver·ti·ces** /–tiseez/ or **ver·tex·es**) **1** highest point; top or apex. **2** *Geom*. **a** each angular point of a polygon, etc. **b** meeting point of lines that form an angle.

ver·ti·cal /vərtikəl/ • *adj*. **1** at right angles to a horizontal plane; perpendicular. **2** in a direction from top to bottom. **3** of or at the vertex or highest point. • *n*. vertical line or plane. □□ **ver·ti·cal·i·ty** /–kálitee/ *n*. **ver′ti·cal·ly** *adv*.

ver·tig·i·nous /vərtijinəs/ *adj*. of or causing vertigo. □□ **ver·tig′i·nous·ly** *adv*.

ver·ti·go /vərtigō/ *n*. condition with a sensation of whirling and a tendency to lose balance; dizziness; giddiness.

verve /vərv/ *n*. enthusiasm; vigor.

ver·y /véree/ • *adv*. **1** in a high degree (*did it very easily; had a very bad cough*). **2** in the fullest

sense (foll. by *own* or superl. adj.: *at the very latest; my very own room*). • *adj*. **1** (usu. prec. by *the, this, his*, etc.) actual; truly such (emphasizing identity, significance, or extreme degree: *the very thing we need; those were his very words*). **2** mere; sheer (*the very idea of it was horrible*). □ **not very 1** in a low degree. **2** far from being.

ves·i·cle /vésikəl/ *n*. **1** *Anat., Zool.,* & *Bot*. small bladder, bubble, or hollow structure. **2** *Med*. blister. □□ **ve·sic·u·lar** /–síkyələr/ *adj*. **ve·sic·u·late** /–síkyəlayt/ *adj*. **ve·sic·u·la·tion** /–láyshən/ *n*.

ves·pers /véspərz/ *n*. evening prayer service.

ves·sel /vésəl/ *n*. **1** hollow receptacle esp. for liquid, e.g., a cask, cup, pot, bottle, or dish. **2** ship or boat, esp. a large one. **3 a** *Anat*. duct or canal, etc., holding or conveying blood or other fluid, esp. = *blood vessel*. **b** *Bot*. woody duct carrying or containing sap, etc.

vest /vest/ • *n*. waist-length close-fitting, sleeveless garment, often worn under a suit jacket, etc. • *v*. **1** *tr*. (esp. in *passive*; foll. by *with*) bestow (powers, authority, etc.) on (a person). **2** *intr*. (foll. by *in*) (of property, a right, etc.) come into the possession of (a person). □ **vested interest 1** *Law* interest (usu. in land or money held in trust) recognized as belonging to a person. **2** personal interest in a state of affairs, usu. with an expectation of gain. **vest-pocket** small enough to fit into a pocket.

ves·tal /vést'l/ *adj*. chaste; pure. □ **vestal virgin** *Rom. Antiq*. virgin consecrated to the goddess Vesta, vowed to chastity, and charged with maintaining the sacred fire burning on the goddess's altar.

ves·ti·bule /véstibyool/ *n*. hall or lobby next to the outer door of a building.

ves·tige /véstij/ *n*. **1** trace or sign (*vestiges of an earlier civilization; found no vestige of their presence*). **2** slight amount; particle (*without a vestige of clothing*). **3** atrophied part or organ of an animal or plant. □□ **ves·tig·i·al** /–tijeeəl, –jəl/ *adj*.

vest·ment /véstmənt/ *n*. official robes, esp. those worn by clergy, choristers, etc., during divine service.

ves·try /véstree/ *n*. (*pl*. **–tries**) **1** chasuble; church room or building for keeping vestments in. **2** *hist*. **a** meeting of parishioners for parochial business. **b** parishioners meeting this way. □□ **ves′tral** *adj*.

vet[1] /vet/ • *n*. *colloq*. veterinarian. • *v.tr*. (**vet·ted, vet·ting**) make a critical examination of (a scheme, work, candidate, etc.).

vet[2] /vet/ *n*. *colloq*. veteran.

vetch /vech/ *n*. plant of the pea family largely used for silage or fodder.

vet·er·an /vétərən/ *n*. **1** person with long experience in esp. military service or an occupation (*war veteran; veteran marksman*). **2** ex-serviceman; ex-servicewoman. □ **Veteran's Day** US holiday on November 11 honoring all veterans.

vet·er·i·nar·i·an /vétərináireeən, vétrə–/ *n*. doctor who practices veterinary medicine or surgery.

vet·er·i·nar·y /vétərineree, vétrə–/ *adj*. of or for diseases and injuries of animals, or their treatment.

ve·to /véetō/ • *n*. (*pl*. **–toes**) **1 a** right to reject a bill, resolution, etc. **b** such a rejection. **2** prohibition (*put one's veto on a proposal*). ● *v.tr.* (**–toes**, **–toed**) **1** exercise a veto against (a measure, etc.). **2** forbid authoritatively. □□ **ve'to·er** *n.*

vex /veks/ *v.tr.* **1** anger by a petty annoyance; irritate. **2** *archaic* grieve; afflict. □□ **vex'er** *n.* **vex'ing** *adj.* **vex'ing·ly** *adv.*

vex·a·tion /veksáyshən/ *n.* **1** vexing; being vexed. **2** annoying or distressing thing. □□ **vex·a·tious** /–áyshəs/ *adj.*

vexed /vekst/ *adj.* **1** irritated; angered. **2** (of a problem, issue, etc.) difficult and much discussed; problematic. □□ **vex'ed·ly** *adv.*

VF *abbr.* (also **V.F.**) **1** video frequency. **2** visual field.

VHF *abbr.* very high frequency.

VI *abbr.* Virgin Islands.

vi·a /ví'ə, ví'ə/ *prep.* by way of; through.

vi·a·ble /ví'əbəl/ *adj.* **1** (of a plan, etc.) feasible; practicable esp. from an economic standpoint. **2** (of a fetus or newborn child) capable of maintaining life. □□ **vi·a·bil'i·ty** *n.* **vi'a·bly** *adv.*

vi·a·duct /ví'ədukt/ *n.* **1** long bridge esp. a series of arches, carrying a road or railroad across a valley, etc. **2** such a road or railroad.

vi·al /ví'əl/ *n.* small vessel esp. for medicines. □□ **vi'al·ful** *n.* (*pl.* **–fuls**).

vi·and /ví'ənd/ *n. formal* **1** article of food. **2** (in *pl.*) provisions; victuals.

vibes /víbz/ *n.pl. colloq.* **1** = VIBRATION 2. **2** = VIBRAPHONE.

vi·brant /ví'brənt/ *adj.* **1** vibrating. **2** (of a person or thing) thrilling; quivering (*vibrant with emotion*). **3** (of sound) resonant. **4** (of color) vivid. □□ **vi·bran·cy** /–rənsee/ *n.* **vi'brant·ly** *adv.*

vi·bra·phone /ví'brəfōn/ *n.* percussion instrument of tuned metal bars with motor-driven resonators and metal tubes giving a vibrato effect. □□ **vi'bra·phon·ist** *n.*

vi·brate /ví'brayt/ *v.* **1** *intr.* & *tr.* move or cause to move continuously and rapidly to and fro; oscillate. **2** *intr.* (of a sound) throb; continue to be heard. **3** *intr.* (foll. by *with*) quiver; thrill (*vibrating with passion*). **4** *intr.* (of a pendulum) swing to and fro. □□ **vi'bra·tor** *n.* **vi·bra·to·ry** /–brətawree/ *adj.*

vi·bra·tion /víbráyshən/ *n.* **1** vibrating; oscillation. **2** (in *pl.*; also **vibes**) characteristic atmosphere or feeling in a place, regarded as communicable to people present in it. □□ **vi·bra'tion·al** *adj.*

vi·bra·to /vibra'tō/ *n. Mus.* rapid slight variation in pitch in singing or playing an instrument, producing a tremulous effect (cf. TREMOLO).

vi·bur·num /víbárnəm, vee–/ *n. Bot.* any of various shrubs usu. with white flowers, of the honeysuckle family.

vic·ar /víkər/ *n.* **1** (in the Church of England) parish priest receiving a stipend rather than tithes (cf. RECTOR). **2** *RC Ch.* deputy of a bishop.

vic·ar·age /víkərij/ *n.* residence of a vicar.

vi·car·i·ous /víkáreeəs/ *adj.* **1** experienced in the imagination through another person (*vicarious pleasure*). **2** acting or done for another (*vicarious suffering*). **3** deputed; delegated (*vicarious authority*). □□ **vi·car'i·ous·ly** *adv.* **vi·car'i·ous·ness** *n.*

vice[1] /vís/ *n.* **1 a** evil or immoral conduct. **b** particular form of this, esp. prostitution, drugs, etc. **2** defect of character or behavior (*drunkenness was not among his vices*). □ **vice squad** police department enforcing laws against prostitution, drug abuse, etc. □□ **vice'less** *adj.*

vice[2] /víssee, –sə/ *prep.* in the place of; in succession to.

vice- /vís/ *comb. form* forming nouns meaning: **1** as a substitute or deputy for (*vice chancellor*). **2** next in rank to (*vice admiral*).

vice pres·i·dent /vís-prézidənt, –dent/ *n.* official ranking below and deputizing for a president. □□ **vice' pres'i·den·cy** *n.* (*pl.* **–cies**). **vice' pres·i·den·tial** /–dénshəl/ *adj.*

vice·roy /vísroy/ *n.* sovereign's deputy ruler in a colony, province, etc.

vi·ce ver·sa /víssə vársə, vís/ *adv.* with the order of the terms changed; the other way around (*from left to right or vice versa*).

vi·chys·soise /vísheeswáaz, vee–/ *n.* creamy soup of leeks and potatoes, usu. served chilled.

vi·cin·i·ty /visinitee/ *n.* (*pl.* **–ties**) **1** surrounding district. **2** (foll. by *to*) nearness or closeness of place or relationship.

vi·cious /víshəs/ *adj.* **1** bad-tempered; spiteful. **2** violent. **3** of the nature of or addicted to vice. **4** (of language or reasoning, etc.) faulty or unsound. □ **vicious circle** self-perpetuating, harmful sequence of cause and effect. □□ **vi'cious·ly** *adv.* **vi'cious·ness** *n.*

vi·cis·si·tude /visísitōōd, –tyōōd/ *n.* change of circumstances, esp. variation of fortune.

vic·tim /víktim/ *n.* **1** person injured or killed as a result of an event or circumstance. **2** person or thing injured or destroyed in pursuit of an object or in gratification of a passion, etc. **3** prey; dupe (*fell victim to a con man*).

vic·tim·ize /víktimīz/ *v.tr.* make (a person, etc.) a victim. □□ **vic·tim·i·za'tion** *n.* **vic'tim·i·zer** *n.*

vic·tor /víktər/ *n.* winner in battle or in a contest.

Vic·to·ri·an /viktáwreeən/ ● *adj.* **1** of the time of Queen Victoria. **2** prudish; morally strict. ● *n.* person of this time. □□ **Vic·to'ri·an·ism** *n.*

vic·to·ri·ous /viktáwreeəs/ *adj.* **1** conquering; triumphant. **2** marked by victory (*victorious day*). □□ **vic·to'ri·ous·ly** *adv.*

vic·to·ry /víktəree/ *n.* (*pl.* **–ries**) defeat of an enemy or an opponent.

vict·ual /vít'l/ *n.* (usu. in *pl.*) food, provisions, esp. as prepared for use. □□ **vict'ual·less** *adj.*

vi·cu·ña /víkōōnə, –nyə, –kyōō–, vi–/ *n.* (also **vi·cu'na**) **1** S. American mammal, related to the llama, with fine silky wool. **2** its wool or an imitation.

vi·de·li·cet /vidéliset, vī–/ *adv.* = VIZ.

vid·e·o /vídeeō/ ● *adj.* **1** relating to the recording, reproducing, or broadcasting of visual images, and usu. sound, on magnetic tape. **2** relating to the broadcasting of television pictures. ● *n.* (*pl.* **–os**) **1** such recording, reproducing, or broadcasting. **2** *colloq.* = *videocassette recorder.* **3** a movie, etc., on videotape. ● *v.tr.* (**–oes**, **–oed**) make a video recording of. □ **video display terminal** *Computing* monitor. **video game** game played by electronically manipulating images produced by a computer program on a television screen. **video jockey** person who introduces music videos, as on television.

vid·e·o·cas·sette /vídeeōkasét, –kəsét/ *n.* cassette of videotape. □ **videocassette recorder** apparatus for recording and playing videotapes.

vid·e·o·tape /vídeeōtayp/ • *n.* magnetic tape for recording moving pictures and sound. • *v.tr.* record on this. □ **videotape recorder** = *videocassette recorder.*

vie /vī/ *v.intr.* (**vy·ing**) (often foll. by *with*) compete; strive for superiority (*vied with each other for recognition*).

Vi·en·nese /veéənéez/ • *adj.* of, relating to, or associated with Vienna in Austria. • *n.* (*pl.* same) native or citizen of Vienna.

Vi·et·nam·ese /vee-étnəméez/ • *adj.* of or relating to Vietnam in SE Asia. • *n.* (*pl.* same) **1** native or national of Vietnam. **2** language of Vietnam.

view /vyoo/ • *n.* **1** range of vision (*came into view*). **2** what is seen from a particular point; scene or prospect (*room with a view*). **3** inspection by the eye or mind. **4 a** opinion (*holds strong views on morality*). **b** manner of considering a thing (*took a long-term view of it*). • *v.* **1** *tr.* look at; survey visually; inspect (*we are going to view the house*). **2** *tr.* examine; survey mentally (*different ways of viewing a subject*). **3** *tr.* consider (*does not view the matter in the same light*). **4** *intr.* watch. **5** *tr.* see. □ **have in view 1** have as one's object. **2** bear (a circumstance) in mind. **in view of** considering. **with a view to** with the hope or intention of. □ **view'a·ble** *adj.*

view·er /vyoóər/ *n.* **1** person who views. **2** device for looking at film transparencies, etc.

view·er·ship /vyoóərship/ *n.* viewing audience, especially of a television program.

view·find·er /vyoófīndər/ *n.* device on a camera showing the area covered by the lens in taking a photograph.

view·point /vyoópoynt/ *n.* point of view.

vig·il /víjil/ *n.* **1** keeping awake during the night, etc., esp. to keep watch or pray (*keep vigil*). **2** *Eccl.* eve of a festival or holy day.

vig·i·lance /víjiləns/ *n.* watchfulness; caution. □ **vig'i·lant** *adj.*

vig·i·lan·te /víjilántee/ *n.* member of a self-appointed group maintaining order.

vi·gnette /vinyét/ *n.* **1** short description or character sketch. **2** illustration or design, esp. on a book's title page without a definite border. **3** photograph showing only the head and shoulders with the background shaded off. **4** brief scene in a movie, etc. □ **vi·gnet'tist** *n.*

vig·or /vígər/ *n.* **1** physical strength or energy. **2** healthy growth. **3 a** mental strength. **b** forcefulness. □ **vig'or·ous** *adj.* **vig'or·ous·ly** *adv.*

Vi·king /víking/ • *n.* of the Scandinavian seafaring pirates and traders who raided and settled in parts of NW Europe in the 8th–11th c. • *adj.* of the Vikings or their time.

vile /vīl/ *adj.* **1** disgusting. **2** morally base; depraved. **3** *colloq.* abominably bad (*vile weather*). □ **vile'ly** *adv.* **vile'ness** *n.*

vil·i·fy /vílifī/ *v.tr.* (**–fies, –fied**) defame; speak evil of. □ **vil·i·fi·ca'tion** *n.* **vil'i·fi·er** *n.*

vil·la /vílə/ *n.* country house, esp. a luxurious one.

vil·lage /vílij/ *n.* **1 a** group of houses and associated buildings, larger than a hamlet and smaller than a town, esp. in a rural area. **b** inhabitants of a village regarded as a community. **2** small municipality with limited corporate powers. □ **vil'lag·er** *n.*

vil·lain /vílən/ *n.* **1** person guilty or capable of

great wickedness. **2** (in a play, etc.) character whose evil actions or motives are important in the plot. □□ **vil'lain·ous** *adj.* **vil'lain·y** *n.*

vil·lein /vílin, –ayn, viláyn/ *n. hist.* feudal tenant entirely subject to a lord or attached to a manor. □□ **vil'lein·age** /vílinij/ *n.*

vil·lus /víləs/ *n.* (*pl.* **vil·li** /–lī/) **1** *Anat.* each of the short, fingerlike processes on some membranes, esp. on the mucous membrane of the small intestine. **2** *Bot.* (in *pl.*) long, soft hairs covering fruit, flowers, etc. □□ **vil·lous** /–əs/ *adj.*

vim /vim/ *n. colloq.* vigor.

vin·ai·grette /vínigrét/ *n.* salad dressing of oil, vinegar, and seasoning.

vin·di·cate /víndikayt/ *v.tr.* **1** clear of blame or suspicion. **2** establish the existence, merits, or justice of (one's courage, conduct, assertion, etc.). **3** justify. □□ **vin·di·ca'tion** /–káyshən/ *n.* **vin·dic·a·tive** /vindíkətiv, víndikaytiv/ *adj.* **vin'di·ca·tor** *n.*

vin·dic·tive /vindíktiv/ *adj.* **1** tending to seek revenge. **2** spiteful. □□ **vin·dic'tive·ly** *adv.* **vin·dic'tive·ness** *n.*

vine /vīn/ *n.* **1** climbing or trailing woody-stemmed plant, esp. one bearing grapes. **2** stem of this. □□ **vin'y** *adj.*

vin·e·gar /vínigər/ *n.* sour liquid obtained from wine, cider, etc., by fermentation and used as a condiment or for pickling. □□ **vin'e·gar·ish** *adj.* **vin'e·gar·y** *adj.*

vine·yard /vínyərd/ *n.* plantation of grapevines, esp. for wine-making.

vi·no /veénō/ *n. sl.* wine, esp. a red Italian wine.

vin·tage /víntij/ • *n.* **1 a** season's produce of grapes. **b** wine from this. **2** wine of high quality from a particular year and district. **3 a** year, etc., when a thing was made, etc. **b** thing made, etc., in a particular year, etc. • *adj.* **1** of high quality, esp. from the past or characteristic of the best period of a person's work. **2** of a past season.

vint·ner /víntnər/ *n.* wine merchant.

vi·nyl /vínəl/ *n.* plastic made by polymerization.

vi·ol /vīəl/ *n.* medieval stringed musical instrument, played with a bow and held vertically on the knees or between the legs.

vi·o·la /vee-ólə/ *n.* **1 a** instrument larger than the violin and of lower pitch. **b** viola player. **2** viol.

vi·o·late /vīəlayt/ *v.tr.* **1** disregard; fail to comply with (an oath, treaty, law, etc.). **2** treat (a sanctuary, etc.) profanely or with disrespect. **3** disturb (a person's privacy, etc.). **4** rape. □□ **vi'o·la·ble** *adj.* **vi·o·la·tion** /–láyshən/ *n.* **vi'o·la·tor** *n.*

vi·o·lence /vīələns/ *n.* **1** being violent. **2** violent conduct or treatment. **3** *Law* a unlawful exercise of physical force. **b** intimidation by the exhibition of this.

vi·o·lent /vīələnt/ *adj.* **1** involving or using great physical force (*violent person; violent storm*). **2 a** intense; vehement; passionate; furious (*violent contrast; violent dislike*). **b** vivid (*violent colors*). **3** resulting from or caused by violence. □□ **vi'o·lent·ly** *adv.*

vi·o·let /vīələt/ • *n.* **1** plant, esp. the sweet violet, with usu. purple, blue, or white flowers. **2** bluish-purple color seen at the end of the spectrum opposite red. • *adj.* of this color.

vi·o·lin /vīəlín/ *n.* **1** musical instrument with four strings of treble pitch played with a bow. **2** violin player. □□ **vi·o·lin′ist** *n.*

VIOLIN

vi·o·lon·cel·lo /veˊeələnchélō, vĭ–/ *n.* (*pl.* **–los**) *formal* = CELLO. □□ **vi·o·lon·cel′list** *n.*

VIP *abbr.* very important person.

vi·per /vípər/ *n.* **1** small venomous snake, esp. the common viper (see ADDER). **2** treacherous person. □□ **vi′per·ous** *adj.*

vi·ra·go /viraˊagō, –ráygō/ *n.* (*pl.* **–gos**) fierce or abusive woman.

vi·ral /vírəl/ *adj.* of or caused by a virus. □□ **vi′ral·ly** *adv.*

vir·e·o /víreeō/ *n.* (*pl.* **–os**) small American songbird.

vir·gin /vórjin/ • *n.* **1** person who has never had sexual intercourse. **2** (**the Virgin**) Christ's mother, the Blessed Virgin Mary. **3** (**the Virgin**) zodiacal sign or constellation Virgo. • *adj.* **1** that is a virgin. **2** of or befitting a virgin (*virgin modesty*). **3** not yet used, penetrated, or tried (*virgin soil*). **4** undefiled; spotless. □□ **vir′gin·al** *adj.* **vir·gin′i·ty** *n.*

Vir·gin·ia creep·er /vərjínyə/ *n.* ornamental N. American vine.

Vir·gin·ia reel /vərjínyə/ *n.* country dance done by partners in two facing rows.

Vir·go /vórgō/ *n.* (*pl.* **–gos**) **1** constellation and sixth sign of the zodiac (the Virgin). **2** person born under this sign.

vir·gule /vórgyōōl/ *n.* **1** slanting line used to mark division of words or lines. **2** = SOLIDUS.

vir·ile /vírəl, –īl/ *adj.* **1** of a man; having masculine vigor or strength. **2** of or having procreative power. **3** of a man as distinct from a woman or child. □□ **vi·ril·i·ty** /virílitee/ *n.*

vi·rol·o·gy /vīróləjee/ *n.* the scientific study of viruses. □□ **vi·ro·log·i·cal** /–rəlójikəl/ *adj.* **vi·ro·log′i·cal·ly** *adv.* **vi·rol′o·gist** *n.*

vir·tu·al /vórchōōəl/ *adj.* that is such for practical purposes though not in name or according to strict definition (*is the virtual manager of the business*). □ **virtual reality** generation by computer software of an image or environment that appears real to the senses. □□ **vir·tu·al·i·ty** /–álitee/ *n.* **vir′tu·al·ly** *adv.*

vir·tue /vórchōō/ *n.* **1** moral excellence; goodness. **2** particular form of this (*patience is a virtue*). **3** chastity. **4** good quality (*has the virtue of being adjustable*). **5** efficacy; inherent power (*no*

virtue in such drugs). □ **by** (or **in**) **virtue of** on the strength or ground of (*got the job by virtue of his experience*). □□ **vir′tue·less** *adj.*

vir·tu·o·so /vórchōō-ósō, –zō/ *n.* (*pl.* **vir·tu·o·si** /–see, –zee/ or **–sos**) **1** person highly skilled in the technique of a fine art, esp. music. **2** (*attrib.*) displaying the skills of a virtuoso. □□ **vir·tu·os·i·ty** /–ósitee/ *n.*

vir·tu·ous /vórchōōəs/ *adj.* **1** possessing or showing moral rectitude. **2** chaste. □□ **vir′tu·ous·ly** *adv.* **vir′tu·ous·ness** *n.*

vir·u·lent /víryələnt, víra–/ *adj.* **1** strongly poisonous. **2** (of a disease) violent or malignant. **3** bitterly hostile (*virulent animosity*). □□ **vir′u·lence** *n.* **vir′u·lent·ly** *adv.*

vi·rus /vírəs/ *n.* **1** microscopic organism often causing diseases. **2** *Computing* = computer virus.

vi·sa /veˊezə/ *n.* endorsement on a passport, etc., esp. allowing the holder to enter or leave a country.

vis·age /vízij/ *n. literary* face. □□ **vis′aged** *adj.* (also in *comb.*).

vis·à·vis /veˊezaavee/ • *prep.* **1** in relation to. **2** opposite to. • *adv.* facing one another.

¶ **Vis-à-vis** means 'face to face.' Avoid using it to mean 'about, concerning,' e.g., "He wanted to talk to us vis-à-vis next weekend." In the sense 'in contrast, comparison, or relation to,' however, **vis à vis** is generally acceptable: *Let us consider government regulations vis-à-vis employment rates.*

vis·cer·a /vísərə/ *n.pl.* interior organs of the body (e.g., brain, heart, liver), esp. in the abdomen (e.g., the intestines).

vis·cer·al /vísərəl/ *adj.* **1** of the viscera. **2** feelings rather than reasoning. □□ **vis′cer·al·ly** *adv.*

vis·cid /vísid/ *adj.* glutinous; sticky. □□ **vis·cid′i·ty** *n.*

vis·cose /vískōs/ *n.* cellulose in a highly viscous state, used for making rayon.

vis·count /víkownt/ *n.* British nobleman ranking between an earl and a baron.

vis·count·ess /víkowntəs/ *n.* **1** viscount's wife or widow. **2** woman holding the rank of viscount in her own right.

vis·cous /vískəs/ *adj.* **1** glutinous; sticky. **2** semi-fluid. **3** *Physics* not flowing freely. □□ **vis′cous·ly** *adv.* **vis·cos′i·ty** /viskósitee/ *n.*

vise /vīs/ *n.* instrument, esp. attached to a workbench, with two movable jaws holding an object so as to leave the hands free to work on it. □□ **vise′like** *adj.*

VISE

Vish·nu /víshnōō/ *n.* Hindu god regarded by his worshipers as the supreme deity and savior, by others as the second member of a triad with Brahma and Siva. □□ **Vish′nu•ism** n.

vis•i•bil•i•ty /vízibilitee/ n. **1** being visible. **2** range or possibility of vision as determined by the light and atmosphere (*visibility was 50 yards*).

vis•i•ble /vízibəl/ adj. **1** that can be seen by the eye. **2** that can be perceived or ascertained (*has no visible means of support; spoke with visible impatience*). □□ **vis′i•ble•ness** n. **vis′i•bly** adv.

vi•sion /vízhən/ n. **1** act or faculty of seeing (*impaired his vision*). **2 a** thing or person seen in a dream or trance. **b** supernatural or prophetic apparition. **3** thing or idea perceived vividly in the imagination (*romantic visions of youth*). **4** imaginative insight. **5** statesmanlike foresight; sagacity in planning. **6** person, etc., of unusual beauty. □□ **vi′sion•less** adj.

vi•sion•ar•y /vízhəneree/ • adj. **1** given to seeing visions; indulging in fanciful theories. **2** of a vision or the imagination. **3** not practicable. • n. (pl. **–ies**) visionary person.

vis•it /vízit/ • v. **1** tr. (also absol.) go or come to see (a person, place, etc.) as an act of friendship or ceremony, on business or for a purpose, or from interest. **2** tr. reside temporarily with (a person) or at (a place). **3** intr. be a visitor. **4** tr. (of a disease, calamity, etc.) come upon; attack. • n. **1 a** act of visiting; call on a person or at a place. **b** temporary stay with a person or at a place. **2** (foll. by to) occasion of going to a doctor, dentist, etc. **3** formal or official call. **4** chat. □□ **vis′i•tor** n.

vis•i•tant /vízit′nt/ n. visitor, esp. a supernatural one.

vis•i•ta•tion /vízitáyshən/ n. **1** official visit of inspection. **2** divine punishment. **3** legally permitted visits, as to one's children after a divorce.

vi•sor /vízər/ n. **1 a** movable part of a helmet covering the face. **b** projecting front part of a cap. **2** shield (fixed or movable) to protect the eyes from unwanted light, esp. at the top of a vehicle windshield. □□ **vi′sored** adj. **vi′sor•less** adj.

VISTA /vístə/ abbr. Volunteers in Service to America.

vis•ta /vístə/ n. **1** long, narrow view as between rows of trees. **2** mental view of a series of events. □□ **vis′taed** adj.

vis•u•al /vízhōōəl/ • adj. of or used in seeing. • n. (usu. in pl.) visual image or display; picture. □□ **vis′u•al•ly** adv.

vis•u•al•ize /vízhōōəlīz/ v.tr. imagine visually. □□ **vis•u•al•i•za′tion** n.

vi•tal /vít′l/ • adj. **1** of or essential to organic life. **2** essential. **3** full of life or activity. **4** fatal to life or to success, etc. • n. (in pl.) the body's vital organs, e.g., the heart and brain. □ **vital signs** pulse rate, rate of respiration, and body temperature considered as signs of life. **vital statistics** number of births, marriages, and deaths, etc. □□ **vi′tal•ly** adv.

vi•tal•i•ty /vītálitee/ n. **1** liveliness; animation. **2** (of an institution, language, etc.) ability to endure and to perform its functions.

vi•tal•ize /vít′līz/ v.tr. **1** endow with life. **2** infuse with vigor. □□ **vi•tal•i•za′tion** n.

vit•a•min /vítəmin/ n. any of various organic compounds essential for many living organisms to maintain normal health and development.

vi•ti•ate /vísheeayt/ v.tr. **1** impair; corrupt; debase. **2** make invalid or ineffectual. □□ **vi•ti•a•tion** /–sheeáyshən/ n. **vi′ti•a•tor** n.

vit•i•cul•ture /vítikulchər/ n. cultivation of grapevines; study of this. □□ **vit•i•cul′tur•al** adj. **vit•i•cul′tur•ist** n.

vit•re•ous /vítreeəs/ adj. of or like glass. □ **vitreous humor** (or **body**) Anat. transparent jellylike tissue filling the eyeball. □□ **vit′re•ous•ness** n.

vit•ri•fy /vitrifī/ v. (**–fies**, **–fied**) convert or be converted into glass or a glasslike substance, esp. by heat. □□ **vit•ri•fac•tion** /–fákshən/ n. **vit′ri•fi•a•ble** adj. **vit•ri•fi•ca′tion** n.

vit•ri•ol /vítreeōl, –əl/ n. **1** sulfuric acid or a sulfate, orig. one of glassy appearance. **2** caustic or hostile speech, criticism, or feeling. □□ **vit•ri•ol•ic** /–ólik/ adj.

vi•tu•per•ate /vītōōpərayt, –tyōō, vi–/ v. revile; abuse. □□ **vi•tu•per•a•tion** /–ráyshən/ n. **vi•tu•per•a•tive** /–rətiv, –ráytiv/ adj.

vi•va /véevə/ • int. long live. • n. cry of this as a salute, etc.

vi•va•ce /viva′achay/ adv. Mus. in a lively brisk manner.

vi•va•cious /vivá yshəs/ adj. lively; sprightly; animated. □□ **vi•va′cious•ly** adv. **vi•va′cious•ness** n. **vi•vac•i•ty** /vivásitee/ n.

viv•id /vívid/ adj. **1** (of color) strong; intense (*vivid green*). **2** (of a mental faculty, impression, or description) clear; lively; graphic (*vivid imagination; vivid recollection of the scene*). □□ **viv′id•ly** adv. **viv′id•ness** n.

viv•i•fy /vivifī/ v.tr. (**–fies**, **–fied**) enliven; animate; make lively or living. □□ **viv•i•fi•ca′tion** n.

vi•vip•a•rous /vīvípərəs, vi–/ adj. Zool. bringing forth live young. □□ **vi•vip′a•rous•ly** adv.

viv•i•sec•tion /vívisékshən/ n. surgery on living animals for purposes of scientific research. □□ **viv′i•sect** v. **viv•i•sec′tion•al** adj. **viv•i•sec′tion•ist** n. **viv•i•sec•tor** /–sektər/ n.

vix•en /víksən/ n. **1** female fox. **2** spiteful woman. □□ **vix′en•ish** adj. **vix′en•ly** adv.

viz. /viz/ adv. (usu. introducing a gloss or explanation) namely; that is to say; in other words. Abbr. of **videlicet**.

vi•zier /vizéer, víziər/ n. hist. high official in the Ottoman Empire. □□ **vi•zier•i•al** /vizéereeəl/ adj. **vi•zier′ship** n.

VJ abbr. video jockey.

V.M.D. abbr. doctor of veterinary medicine.

voc. abbr. **1** vocational. **2** vocative.

vocab. abbr. vocabulary.

vo•cab•u•lar•y /vōkábyəleree/ n. (pl. **–ies**) **1** words used by a particular language, individual, book, branch of science, etc., or by a particular author. **2** list of these, arranged alphabetically with definitions or translations.

vo•cal /vókəl/ • adj. **1** of or uttered by the voice (*vocal communication*). **2** outspoken (*was very vocal about her rights*). **3** (of music) written for or produced by the voice. • n. (in sing. or pl.) sung part of a musical composition. □ **vocal cords** folds of the lining membrane of the larynx near the opening of the glottis, with edges vibrating in the air stream to produce the voice. □□ **vo•cal′i•ty** /vōkálitee/ n. **vo′cal•ly** adv.

vo•cal•ist /vókəlist/ n. singer, esp. of jazz or popular songs.

vo•cal•ize /vókəlīz/ v. **1** tr. form (a sound), utter (a word), or sing. **2** intr. utter a vocal sound. □□ **vo•cal•i•za′tion** n. **vo′cal•iz•er** n.

vo·ca·tion /vōkáyshən/ *n.* **1** strong feeling of fitness for a particular career (in religious contexts, a divine call). **2 a** person's employment. **b** trade or profession. □□ **vo·ca′tion·al** *adj.*

voc·a·tive /vókətiv/ *Gram.* • *n.* case of nouns used in addressing a person or thing. • *adj.* of or in this case.

vo·cif·er·ate /vōsífərayt/ *v.* **1** *tr.* utter (words, etc.) noisily. **2** *intr.* shout; bawl. □□ **vo·cif·er·a·tion** /–ráyshən/ *n.*

vo·cif·er·ous /vōsífərəs/ *adj.* **1** noisy; clamorous. **2** insistent. □□ **vo·cif′er·ous·ly** *adv.* **vo·cif′er·ous·ness** *n.*

vod·ka /vódkə/ *n.* alcoholic spirit distilled from rye, etc.

vogue /vōg/ *n.* **1** prevailing fashion. **2** popularity (*has had a great vogue*). □ **in vogue** in fashion. □□ **vogu′ish** *adj.*

voice /voys/ • *n.* **1 a** sound formed in the larynx and uttered by the mouth, esp. by a person. **b** ability to produce this (*has lost her voice*). **2 a** spoken or written words (*esp. give voice*). **b** opinion so expressed. **c** right to express an opinion (*I have no voice in the matter*). **d** medium for expression. **3** *Gram.* set of verbal forms showing the relation of the subject to the action (*active voice; passive voice*). **4** *Mus.* **a** vocal part in a composition. **b** vocal ability, esp. in singing. • *v.tr.* **1** express (*the letter voices our opinion*). **2** (esp. as **voiced** *adj.*) *Phonet.* utter with vibration of the vocal cords (e.g., *b, d, g, v, z*). □ **voice box** larynx. **voice mail** automatic telephone answering system that records messages from callers. **voice-over** narration in a movie, etc., not accompanied by a picture of the speaker. **with one voice** unanimously. □□ **–voiced** *adj.*

void /voyd/ • *adj.* **1 a** empty; vacant. **b** (foll. by *of*) lacking; free from (*a style void of affectation*). **2** esp. Law invalid; not binding (*null and void*). **3** useless; ineffectual. • *n.* empty space; vacuum (*cannot fill the void made by death*). • *v.tr.* **1** render invalid. **2** (also *absol.*) excrete. □□ **void′a·ble** *adj.*

voile /voyl, vwaal/ *n.* thin, semitransparent dress material of cotton, wool, or silk.

vol. *abbr.* volume.

vol·a·tile /vólət'l, –tī/ *adj.* **1** evaporating rapidly (*volatile salts*). **2** changeable; fickle. **3** apt to break out into violence. □□ **vol·a·til·i·ty** /–tílitee/ *n.*

vol·can·ic /volkánik/ *adj.* of, like, or produced by a volcano. □□ **vol·can′i·cal·ly** *adv.*

vol·ca·no /volkáynō/ *n.* (*pl.* **–noes**) mountain from which lava, cinders, steam, gases, etc., escape through openings in the earth's crust.

vole /vōl/ *n.* small plant-eating rodent.

vo·li·tion /vəlíshən/ *n.* **1** exercise of the will. **2** power of willing. □□ **vo·li′tion·al** *adj.* **vo·li′tion·al·ly** *adv.* **vol·i·tive** /vólitiv/ *adj.*

vol·ley /vólee/ • *n.* (*pl.* **–leys**) **1 a** simultaneous discharge of a number of weapons. **b** bullets, etc., discharged in a volley. **2** torrent of oaths, etc. **3** *Tennis* return of a ball in play before it touches the ground. **4** *Soccer* kicking of a ball in play before it touches the ground. • *v.* (**–leys, –leyed**) **1** *tr.* (also *absol.*) *Tennis & Soccer* return or send (a ball) by a volley. **2** *tr.* & *absol.* discharge (bullets, abuse, etc.) in a

volley. **3** *intr.* (of bullets, etc.) fly in a volley. □□ **vol′ley·er** *n.*

vol·ley·ball /vóleebawl/ *n.* game for two teams of six hitting a large ball by hand over a net.

volt /vōlt/ *n.* unit of electromotive force, the difference of potential that would carry one ampere of current against one ohm resistance. ¶ *Abbr.*: **V.**

volt·age /vóltij/ *n.* electromotive force expressed in volts.

vol·ta·ic /voltáyik/ *adj. archaic* of electricity from a primary battery; galvanic (*voltaic battery*).

volt-me·ter /vóltmeētər/ *n.* instrument for measuring an electric charge.

volt·me·ter /vóltmeetər/ *n.* instrument for measuring electric potential in volts.

vol·u·ble /vólyəbəl/ *adj.* speaking or spoken at length. □□ **vol·u·bil′i·ty** *n.* **vol′u·ble·ness** *n.* **vol′u·bly** *adv.*

vol·ume /vólyoom/ *n.* **1** single book forming part or the whole of a work. **2 a** solid content; bulk. **b** space occupied by a gas or liquid. **3** quantity or power of sound. □□ **vol′umed** *adj.* (also in *comb.*).

vo·lu·mi·nous /vəloóminəs/ *adj.* **1** large in volume; bulky. **2** (of drapery, etc.) loose and ample. **3** (of a writer) producing many books. □□ **vo·lu′mi·nous·ly** *adv.* **vo·lu′mi·nous·ness** *n.*

vol·un·ta·rism /vóləntərizəm/ *n.* principle of relying on voluntary action rather than compulsion.

vol·un·tar·y /vólənteree/ • *adj.* **1** done, acting, or able to act of one's own free will; not compulsory. **2** unpaid. **3** supported by voluntary contributions. **4** brought about, produced, etc., by voluntary action. **5** controlled by the will. • *n.* (*pl.* **–ies**) **1** organ solo played before or after a church service. □□ **vol·un·tar′i·ly** *adv.*

vol·un·teer /vólənteer/ • *n.* **1** person who voluntarily undertakes a task or enters military service. • *v.* **1** *tr.* undertake or offer voluntarily. **2** *intr.* make a voluntary offer of one's services; be a volunteer.

vo·lup·tu·ar·y /vəlúpchooeree/ *n.* (*pl.* **–ies**) person given up to luxury and sensual pleasure.

vo·lup·tu·ous /vəlúpchooəs/ *adj.* **1** of, tending to, occupied with, or derived from sensuous or sensual pleasure. **2** full of sexual promise, esp. through shapeliness or fullness. □□ **vo·lup′tu·ous·ly** *adv.* **vo·lup′tu·ous·ness** *n.*

vo·lute /vəlóot/ *n. Archit.* spiral-shaped ornamental scroll. □□ **vo·lut′ed** *adj.*

vom·it /vómit/ • *v.tr.* **1** eject (matter) from the stomach through the mouth. **2** (of a volcano, etc.) eject violently; belch (forth). • *n.* matter vomited from the stomach. □□ **vom′it·er** *n.*

voo·doo /voódoo/ • *n.* **1** religious witchcraft, esp. as practiced in the W. Indies. **2** object used in voodoo practice. • *v.tr.* affect by voodoo; bewitch. □□ **voo′doo·ism** *n.* **voo′doo·ist** *n.*

vo·ra·cious /vawráyshəs, və–/ *adj.* **1** greedy in eating; ravenous. **2** very eager. □□ **vo·ra′cious·ly** *adv.* **vo·ra′cious·ness** *n.* **vo·rac·i·ty** /vərásitee/ *n.*

vor·tex /váwrteks/ *n.* (*pl.* **vor·ti·ces** /–tiseez/ or **vor·tex·es**) **1** whirlpool or whirlwind. **2** any whirling motion or mass. **3** thing viewed as swallowing up or engrossing. □□ **vor·ti·cal**

/-tikəl/ *adj.* **vor'ti·cal·ly** *adv.* **vor·tic·i·ty** /vortísitee/ *n.* **vor·ti·cose** /-tikōs/ *adj.*

vo·ta·ry /vótəree/ *n.* (*pl.* **-ries**; *fem.* **vo·ta·ress**) **1** person vowed to religious service. **2** devoted follower, adherent, or advocate of a person, system, occupation, etc. □□ **vo'ta·rist** *n.*

vote /vōt/ • *n.* **1** formal expression of choice or opinion by a ballot, show of hands, etc. **2** right to vote. **3** opinion expressed by a majority of votes. **4** votes given by or for a particular group. • *v.* **1** *intr.* give a vote. **2** *tr.* enact or resolve by vote. □ **vote with one's feet** *colloq.* indicate an opinion by one's presence or absence. □□ **vot'a·ble** *adj.* **vote'less** *adj.* **vot'er** *n.*

vo·tive /vótiv/ *adj.* offered or consecrated in fulfillment of a vow.

vouch /vowch/ *v. intr.* (foll. by *for*) answer for; be surety for.

vouch·er /vówchər/ *n.* **1** document exchangeable for goods or services. **2** receipt.

vouch·safe /vówchsáyf/ *v.tr. formal* condescend to grant.

vow /vow/ • *n. Relig.* solemn promise, esp. in the form of an oath to God. • *v.tr.* promise solemnly.

vow·el /vówəl/ *n.* **1** speech sound made with vibration of the vocal cords but without audible friction. **2** letter representing this, as *a, e, i, o, u.* □□ **vow'eled** *adj.* (also in *comb.*). **vow'el·less** *adj.*

vox po·pu·li /vóks pópyəlee, -lī/ *n.* public opinion.

voy·age /vóyij/ • *n.* journey, esp. a long one by sea or in space. • *v.intr.* make a voyage. □□ **voy'ag·er** *n.*

vo·ya·geur /vwa'ayaazhόr/ *n. hist.* French Canadian explorer or trader in colonial N. America.

voy·eur /vwaayόr/ *n.* person who obtains sexual

gratification from observing others' sexual actions or organs. □□ **vo·yeur'ism** *n.* **voy·eur·is'tic** *adj.* **voy·eur·is'ti·cal·ly** *adv.*

VP *abbr.* VICE PRESIDENT.

VS *abbr.* veterinary surgeon.

vs. *abbr.* **1** versus. **2** verse.

VT *abbr.* Vermont (in official postal use).

Vt. *abbr.* Vermont.

VTOL /véetol/ *abbr.* vertical takeoff and landing.

vul·can·ize /vúlkənīz/ *v.tr.* treat (rubber, etc.) with sulfur at a high temperature to increase its strength. □□ **vul·can·i·za'tion** *n.* **vul'can·iz·er** *n.*

vul·gar /vúlgər/ *adj.* **1 a** of or characteristic of the common people. **b** coarse in manners; low. **2** common; prevalent. □□ **vul·gar·i·ty** /-gárity/ *n.* **vul'gar·ly** *adv.*

vul·gar·i·an /vulgáireeən/ *n.* vulgar (esp. rich) person.

vul·gar·ism /vúlgərizəm/ *n.* word or expression in coarse or uneducated use.

vul·gar·ize /vúlgərīz/ *v.tr.* **1** make vulgar. **2** popularize. □□ **vul·gar·i·za'tion** *n.*

Vul·gate /vúlgayt, -gət/ *n.* 4th-Century Latin version of the Bible.

vul·ner·a·ble /vúlnərəbəl/ *adj.* **1** easily wounded or harmed. **2** (foll. by *to*) exposed to damage by a weapon, criticism, etc. □□ **vul·ner·a·bil'i·ty** *n.* **vul'ner·a·ble·ness** *n.* **vul'ner·a·bly** *adv.*

vul·pine /vúlpīn/ *adj.* **1** of or like a fox. **2** crafty; cunning.

vul·ture /vúlchər/ *n.* **1** large carrion-eating bird of prey. **2** rapacious person. □□ **vul·tur·ine** /-rīn/ *adj.* **vul'tur·ous** *adj.*

vul·va /vúlvə/ *n.* (*pl.* **vul·vas**) *Anat.* external female genitals.

vy·ing *pres. part.* of VIE.

Ww

W[1] /dúbəlyo͞o/ *n.* (also **w**) (*pl.* **Ws** or **W's; w's**) twenty-third letter of the alphabet.

W[2] *abbr.* (also **W.**) **1** watt(s). **2** West; Western. **3** women's (size). **4** Welsh.

W[3] *symb. Chem.* tungsten.

w. *abbr.* **1** warden. **2** wide(s). **3** with. **4** wife. **5** watt(s).

WA *abbr.* **1** Washington (state) (in official postal use). **2** Western Australia.

Wac /wak/ *n.* member of the US Army's Women's Army Corps.

wack·o /wákō/ (also **whack'o**) *sl.* ● *adj.* crazy. ● *n.* (*pl.* **–os** or **–oes**) crazy person.

wack·y /wákee/ (also **whack'y**) *sl.* ● *adj.* (**wack·i·er, wack·i·est**) crazy. ● *n.* (*pl.* **–ies**) crazy person. □□ **wack'i·ly** *adv.* **wack'i·ness** *n.*

wad /wod/ ● *n.* **1** lump of soft material. **2** disk of felt, etc., keeping powder or shot in place in a gun. **3** number of bills of currency or documents placed together. **4** (in *sing.* or *pl.*) large quantity, esp. of money. ● *v.tr.* (**wad·ded, wad·ding**) **1** stop up or keep in place with a wad. **2** press (cotton, etc.) into a wad or wadding.

wad·ding /wóding/ *n.* soft, pliable material of cotton, etc., used for stuffing, etc., or to pack fragile articles.

wad·dle /wód'l/ ● *v.intr.* walk with short steps and a swaying motion. ● *n.* waddling gait. □□ **wad'dler** *n.*

wade /wayd/ *v.intr.* **1** walk through water, mud, etc., esp. with difficulty. **2** make one's way with difficulty. **3** (foll. by *through*) read (a book, etc.) in spite of its dullness, etc. **4** (foll. by *into*) *colloq.* attack vigorously. □□ **wad'a·ble** *adj.* (also **wade'a·ble**).

wad·er /wáydər/ *n.* **1** long-legged wading bird. **2** (in *pl.*) high waterproof boots, or a waterproof garment for the legs and body, worn in fishing, etc.

wa·di /waádee/ *n.* (also **wa'dy**) (*pl.* **wa·dis** or **wa·dies**) rocky watercourse in N. Africa, etc., dry except in the rainy season.

wa·fer /wáyfər/ *n.* **1** very thin, light, crisp sweet cake, cookie, or biscuit. **2** thin disk of unleavened bread used in the Eucharist. □ **wafer-thin** very thin. □□ **wa'fer·y** *adj.*

waf·fle[1] /wófəl/ *colloq.* ● *n.* verbose but aimless, misleading, or ignorant talk or writing. ● *v.intr.* indulge in waffle. □□ **waf'fler** *n.* **waf'fly** *adj.*

waf·fle[2] /wófəl/ *n.* small, crisp batter cake with an indented lattice pattern. □ **waffle iron** utensil, usu. of two shallow metal pans hinged together, for cooking waffles.

waft /woft, waft/ ● *v.* convey or travel easily as through air or over water. ● *n.* **1** whiff or scent. **2** transient sensation of peace, joy, etc.

wag[1] /wag/ ● *v.* (**wagged, wag·ging**) shake or wave rapidly to and fro. ● *n.* wagging motion.

wag[2] /wag/ *n.* facetious person; joker.

wage /wayj/ ● *n.* **1** (in *sing.* or *pl.*) fixed regular payment to an employee, esp. to a manual or unskilled worker. **2** return; recompense. ● *v.tr.* carry on (a war, etc.).

wa·ger /wáyjər/ *n.* & *v.* = BET.

wag·gish /wágish/ *adj.* playful; facetious. □□ **wag'gish·ly** *adv.* **wag'gish·ness** *n.*

wag·gle /wágəl/ *v. colloq.* wag[1].

wag·gly /wáglee/ *adj.* unsteady.

wag·on /wágən/ *n.* **1** four-wheeled vehicle for heavy loads. **2** = station wagon. □ **on the wagon** *sl.* teetotal.

waif /wayf/ *n.* **1** homeless and helpless person, esp. an abandoned child. **2** ownerless object or animal. □□ **waif'ish** *adj.*

wail /wayl/ ● *n.* prolonged and plaintive loud, high-pitched cry of pain, grief, etc. ● *v.intr.* **1** utter a wail. **2** lament or complain persistently or bitterly. □□ **wail'er** *n.* **wail'ing·ly** *adv.*

wain /wayn/ *n. archaic* wagon.

wain·scot /wáynskət, –skot, –skōt/ ● *n.* wooden paneling on the lower part of an interior wall. ● *v.tr.* panel with wainscot.

wain·scot·ing /wáynskōting, –skot–, –skə–/ *n.* **1** wainscot. **2** material for this.

wain·wright /wáynrīt/ *n.* wagon builder or repairer.

waist /wayst/ *n.* **1 a** part of the human body below the ribs and above the hips. **b** circumference of this. **2** similar narrow part in the middle of a violin, hourglass, etc. **3 a** part of a garment encircling or covering the waist. **b** blouse or bodice. □□ **waist'ed** *adj.* (also in *comb.*). **waist'less** *adj.*

waist·band /wáystband/ *n.* strip of cloth forming the waist of a garment.

waist·line /wáystlīn/ *n.* outline or size of a person's body at the waist.

wait /wayt/ ● *v.* **1** *intr.* **a** defer action or departure for a specified time or until some event occurs. **b** be expectant or on the watch. **2** *tr.* await. **3** *tr.* defer (an activity). **4** *intr.* **a** (in full **wait at** or **on tables**) serve food, drinks, etc. **b** act as an attendant to. ● *n.* period of waiting. □ **wait and see** await the progress of events. **wait up** (often foll. by *for*) not go to bed until a person arrives or an event happens.

wait·er /wáytər/ *n.* person who serves at table in a hotel or restaurant, etc.

wait·ing /wáyting/ *n.* in senses of WAIT *v.* □ **waiting game** abstention from early action in a contest, etc., so as to act more effectively later.

wait·per·son /wáytpərsən/ *n.* waiter or waitress.

wait·ress /wáytris/ *n.* woman who serves at table in a hotel or restaurant, etc.

waive /wayv/ *v.tr.* refrain from insisting on or using (a right, claim, opportunity, legitimate plea, rule, etc.).

¶ **Waive**, meaning 'surrender,' and the related noun, *waiver*, should not be confused with **wave**, 'a back-and-forth or up-and-down motion,' or with **waver** 'to go back and forth, vacillate': *He* *waived potential rights in the case by by signing the waiver. She waved the papers at her friends across the room. Just as we were all ready to go, he wavered and said he wasn't sure whether he should go.*

waiv·er /wáyvər/ n. Law act or an instance of waiving.

wake[1] /wayk/ • v. (past **woke** /wōk/ or **waked**; past part. **wok·en** /wōkən/ or **waked**) **1** cease or cause to cease to sleep. **2** become or cause to become alert, attentive, or active. **3** intr. (archaic except as **waking** adj. & n.) be awake. **4** tr. evoke (an echo). • n. watch beside a corpse before burial. □□ **wak′er** n.

wake[2] /wayk/ n. **1** track left on the water's surface by a moving ship. **2** turbulent air left behind a moving aircraft, etc. □ **in the wake of** following; as a result of.

wake·ful /wáykfool/ adj. **1** unable to sleep. **2** (of a night, etc.) passed with little or no sleep. **3** vigilant. □□ **wake′ful·ly** adv. **wake′ful·ness** n.

wak·en /wáykən/ v. make or become awake.

wale /wayl/ • n. **1** = WEAL[1]. **2** ridge on corduroy. • v.tr. mark with wales; thrash; whip.

walk /wawk/ • v. **1** intr. **a** (of a person or other biped) progress by lifting and setting down each foot in turn, never having both feet off the ground at once. **b** progress with similar movements (walked on his hands). **c** (of a quadruped) go with the slowest gait. **2** intr. travel or go on foot. **3** tr. **a** tread the floor or surface of. **b** traverse or cover (a specified distance) on foot. **4** tr. cause to walk with one. **5** Baseball **a** intr. reach first base on balls. **b** tr. allow to do this. • n. **1** **a** act of walking; the ordinary human gait. **b** slowest gait of an animal. **c** person's manner of walking. **2** **a** distance walked. **b** excursion on foot. **3** place, track, or route intended or suitable for walking. **4** Baseball four pitched balls advancing a batter to base. □ **walk all over** colloq. **1** defeat easily. **2** take advantage of. **walk away** (or **off**) **with** colloq. **1** steal. **2** win easily. **walk of life** occupation, profession, or calling. **walk on air** see AIR. **walk out 1** depart suddenly or angrily. **2** cease work, esp. to go on strike. **walk out on** desert; abandon.

walk·er /wáwkər/ n. **1** one who walks. **2** **a** wheeled or footed framework in which a baby can learn to walk. **b** tubular metal frame with rubberized ferrules, used by disabled or elderly people to help them walk.

walk·ie-talk·ie /wáwkeetáwkee/ n. two-way radio carried on the person, esp. by police officers, etc.

Walk·man /wáwkmən/ n. (pl. **–mans**) propr. type of small portable stereo equipment with headphones.

walk·out /wáwkowt/ n. sudden angry departure, esp. as a protest or strike.

walk·way /wáwkway/ n. passage or path (esp. raised) for walking.

wall /wawl/ • n. vertical structure of usu. brick or stone, esp. enclosing, protecting, or dividing a space or supporting a roof. • v.tr. (esp. as **walled** adj.) surround, block off, or protect with a wall. □ **go to the wall** be defeated or ruined. **off the wall** sl. unorthodox; unconventional. **up the wall** colloq. crazy or furious. **wall-to-wall** (of a carpet) fitted to cover a whole room, etc. **2** colloq. ubiquitous. □□ **wall′ing** n. **wall′-less** adj.

wal·la·by /wólləbee/ n. (pl. **–bies**) small kangaroo.

wall·board /wáwlbawrd/ n. type of wall covering made from wood pulp, plaster, etc.

wal·let /wólit/ n. usu. pocket-size case for holding paper money, etc.

wall·eye /wáwlī/ n. **1** **a** eye with a streaked or opaque white iris. **b** eye squinting outward. **2** (also **wall′ eyed pike**) American perch with large prominent eyes. □□ **wall′ eyed** adj.

wall·flow·er /wáwlflowr/ n. colloq. woman sitting out at a dance for lack of partners.

Wal·loon /woloon/ n. **1** member of a French-speaking people inhabiting S. and E. Belgium and neighboring France. **2** French dialect spoken by this people. • adj. of or concerning the Walloons or their language.

wal·lop /wóləp/ sl. • v.tr. thrash; beat. • n. heavy blow. □□ **wal′lop·er** n. **wal′lop·ing** n.

wal·low /wólō/ • v.intr. **1** (esp. of an animal) roll about in mud, etc. **2** (usu. foll. by in) indulge in unrestrained pleasure, misery, etc. • n. **1** act or instance of wallowing. **2** place used for wallowing. □□ **wal′low·er** n.

wall·pa·per /wáwlpaypər/ • n. decorative paper for pasting on to interior walls. • v.tr. (often absol.) decorate with wallpaper.

Wall Street /wáwl/ n. U.S. financial world and investment market.

wal·nut /wáwlnut/ n. **1** tree with aromatic leaves and drooping catkins. **2** edible nut of this tree. **3** its timber.

wal·rus /wáwlrəs, wól–/ n. large, amphibious, long-tusked arctic mammal related to the seal and sea lion.

waltz /wawlts, wawls/ • n. **1** ballroom dance in triple time performed by couples. **2** music for this. • v. **1** intr. dance a waltz. **2** intr. (often foll. by in, out, around, etc.) colloq. move lightly, casually, etc. □ **waltz′er** n.

wam·pum /wómpəm/ n. beads made from shells and strung together for use as money, decoration, etc., by N. American Indians.

wan /won/ adj. pale; exhausted, weak; worn. □□ **wan′ly** adv. **wan′ness** n.

wand /wond/ n. **1** stick used by a magician for effect. **2** staff symbolizing some officials' authority. **3** handheld electronic device which can be passed over a bar code to read the data this represents.

wan·der /wóndər/ v. **1** intr. go from place to place aimlessly. **2** intr. **a** wind about; diverge; meander. **b** stray from a path, etc. **3** intr. talk or think incoherently. □□ **wan′der·er** n. **wan′der·ing** n. (esp. in pl.).

wan·der·lust /wóndərlust/ n. eagerness for traveling or wandering.

wane /wayn/ • v.intr. **1** (of the moon) decrease in apparent size after the full moon (cf. WAX[2]). **2** decrease in power, vigor, etc. • n. process of waning. □ **on the wane** declining.

wan·gle /wánggəl/ colloq. • v.tr. obtain (a favor, etc.) by scheming, etc. • n. act or instance of wangling. □□ **wan′gler** n.

wan·na·be /wónəbee/ n. sl. **1** avid fan who tries to emulate the person he or she admires. **2** anyone who would like to be someone or something else.

want /wont, wawnt/ • v. **1** tr. **a** desire; wish for possession of; need. **b** need or desire (a person, esp. sexually). **2** *intr.* lack. **3** *tr.* be without or fall short of. **4** *tr.* (as **wanted** *adj.*) (of a suspected criminal, etc.) sought by the police. • *n.* **1 a** lack, deficiency. **b** poverty; need. **2** craving. □ **want ad** classified newspaper advertisement, esp. for something sought. □□ **want′er** *n.*

---

want Middle English: the noun from Old Norse *vant*, neuter of *vanr* 'lacking'; the verb from Old Norse *vanta* 'be wanting.' The notions of 'lack' and 'need' became complemented by the notion of 'desire' (i.e., to satisfy the need).

---

want·ing /wónting, wáwn–/ *adj.* **1** lacking not equal to requirements. **2** absent; not supplied.

wan·ton /wóntən/ • *adj.* **1** licentious; lewd. **2** capricious; arbitrary. **3** luxuriant; unrestrained. • *n. literary* immoral or licentious person, esp. a woman. □□ **wan′ton·ly** *adv.* **wan′ton·ness** *n.*

wa·pi·ti /wópitee/ *n.* N. American deer; elk.

war /wawr/ • *n.* **1 a** armed hostilities, esp. between nations; conflict. **b** specific period or instance of this. **2** (as **the war**) most recent major war. **3 a** hostility or contention between people, groups, etc. **b** sustained campaign against crime, disease, poverty, etc. • *v.intr.* (**warred, war·ring**) make war. □ **at war** engaged in a war. **go to war** declare or begin a war. □□ **war′ring** *adj.*

---

war late Old English *werre*, from an Anglo-Norman French variant of Old French *guerre*, from a Germanic base shared by *worse.* Curiously, in early historic times, no Germanic nation had a word in living use properly expressing the sense 'war,' except in poetry, proverbs, and compound personal names. The root *werr-* meant 'strife, struggle.'

---

war·ble /wáwrbəl/ • *v.* **1** *intr.* & *tr.* sing in a gentle, trilling manner. **2** *tr.* speak or utter in a warbling manner. • *n.* warbled song or utterance.

war·bler /wáwrblər/ *n.* person, bird, etc., that warbles.

ward /wawrd/ • *n.* **1** division of a hospital, prison, etc. **2** administrative division of a city or town, esp. an electoral district. **3 a** minor under the care of a guardian or a court. **b** (in full **ward of the court**) minor or mentally deficient person placed under the protection of a court. **4** (in *pl.*) corresponding notches and projections in a key and a lock. **5** *archaic* guardian's control. • *v.tr. archaic* guard; protect. □ **ward heeler** party worker in elections, etc. **ward off 1** parry (a blow). **2** avert (danger, etc.).

-ward /wərd/ *suffix* (also **–wards**) added to nouns of place or destination and to adverbs of direction and forming: **1** adverbs meaning 'toward the place, etc.' (*moving backward*). **2** adjectives meaning 'turned or tending toward' (*downward look*). **3** (less commonly) nouns meaning 'the region toward or about' (*look to the eastward*).

war·den /wáwrd′n/ *n.* **1** chief administrator of a prison. **2** supervising official (*game warden*).

ward·er /wáwrdər/ *n.* guard; caretaker.

ward·robe /wáwrdrōb/ *n.* **1** large cupboard for storing clothes. **2** person's entire stock of clothes. **3** costume department or costumes of a theater, a movie company, etc.

ward·room /wáwrdrōōm, –rŏŏm/ *n.* mess in a warship for commissioned officers.

ware /wair/ *n.* (often in *comb.*) **1** things of the same kind made usu. for sale (*chinaware; hardware*). **2** (usu. in *pl.*) articles for sale. **3** ceramics, etc., of a specified material, factory, or kind (*Wedgwood ware; delftware*).

ware·house /wáirhows/ • *n.* building in which goods are stored. • *v.tr.* (also /–howz/) store, esp. temporarily, in a repository.

war·fare /wáwrfair/ *n.* campaigning or engaging in war.

war·head /wáwrhed/ *n.* explosive head of a missile, torpedo, or similar weapon.

war·horse /wáwrhawrs/ *n. colloq.* veteran soldier, politician, etc.

war·like /wáwrlīk/ *adj.* **1** hostile. **2** soldierly.

war·lock /wáwrlok/ *n. archaic* sorcerer or wizard.

war·lord /wáwrlawrd/ *n.* military commander, esp. in a warlike nation.

warm /wawrm/ • *adj.* **1** of or at a fairly high temperature. **2** (clothes, etc.) affording warmth. **3** a sympathetic; friendly. **b** enthusiastic. **4** *colloq.* **a** close to the object, etc., sought. **b** near to guessing. **5** *Hunting* (of a scent) fresh and strong. • *v.* **1** *tr.* make warm. **b** make cheerful. **2** *intr.* **a** warm oneself. **b** (often foll. by *to*) become animated or sympathetic. □ **warm-blooded** having blood that maintains a warm temperature. **warmed-up** (or **-over**) **1** (of food, etc.) reheated. **2** secondhand. **warm front** advancing mass of warm air. **warm up 1** prepare for a contest, performance, etc., by practicing. **2** (of a room, etc.) become warmer. **3** (of a person) become enthusiastic, etc. **4** (of an engine, etc.) reach a temperature for efficient working. **5** reheat (food). **warm-up** *n.* period of preparatory exercise for a contest or performance. □□ **warm′er** *n.* (also in *comb.*). **warm′ish** *adj.* **warm′ly** *adv.* **warm′ness** *n.* **warmth** *n.*

warm·heart·ed /wáwrmhaártid/ *adj.* kind; friendly. □□ **warm′heart′ed·ly** *adv.* **warm′heart′ed·ness** *n.*

war·mon·ger /wáwrmunggər, –mong–/ *n.* person who seeks to bring about or promote war. □□ **war′mon·ger·ing** *n.* & *adj.*

warn /wawrn/ *v.tr.* **1 a** inform of danger, etc. **b** advise; inform. **2** admonish. □□ **warn′er** *n.*

warn·ing /wáwrning/ *n.* anything that serves to warn. □ **warning track** (or **path**) *Baseball* dirt strip that borders the outfield just inside the fence. □□ **warn′ing·ly** *adv.*

warp /wawrp/ • *v.* **1** make or become twisted out of shape. **2** make or become perverted or strange. • *n.* **1** a state of being warped, esp. of lumber. **b** perversion, bitterness, etc., of the mind or character. **2** lengthwise threads in a loom. □□ **warp′age** *n.* (esp. in sense 1 of *v.*).

war·path /wáwrpath/ *n.* **1** warlike expedition of N. American Indians. **2** *colloq.* hostile course or attitude (*is on the warpath again*).

war·rant /wáwrənt, wór–/ • *n.* **1** authorization; justification. **2** written authorization allowing police to search premises, arrest a suspect, etc. • *v.tr.* **1** justify. **2** guarantee or attest to. □ **warrant officer** officer ranking between commissioned officers and NCOs. □□ **war′rant·er** *n.* **war′ran·tor** *n.*

war·ran·ty /wáwrəntee, wór–/ *n.* (*pl.* **-ties**) guarantee of the ownership or quality of a thing sold,

etc., often accepting responsibility for defects or repairs.
¶ See note at GUARANTEE.

war·ren /wáwrən, wór–/ n. **1** network of interconnecting rabbit burrows. **2** densely populated or labyrinthine building or district.

war·ri·or /wáwreeər, wór–/ n. person experienced or distinguished in fighting.

war·ship /wáwrship/ n. armored ship used in war.

wart /wawrt/ n. **1** small, hard, round growth on the skin. **2** protuberance on the surface of a plant, etc. □□ **wart′y** adj.

wart·hog /wáwrt-hog/ n. African wild pig.

war·y /wáiree/ adj. (**war·i·er, war·i·est**) **1** on one's guard; circumspect. **2** cautious. □□ **war′i·ly** adv. **war′i·ness** n.

was 1st & 3rd sing. past of BE.

Wash. abbr. Washington.

wash /wosh, wawsh/ • v. **1** tr. cleanse with liquid, esp. water. **2** tr. remove (a stain) in this way. **3** intr. wash oneself. **4** intr. wash clothes, etc. **5** intr. (foll. by off, out) (of a stain, etc.) be removed by washing. **6** tr. poet. moisten; water. **7** tr. (of a river, etc.) touch (a coast, etc.). **8** tr. (of moving liquid) carry along in a specified direction (a wave washed him overboard). **9** intr. sweep, move, or splash. **10** tr. sift (ore) by the action of water. **11** tr. **a** brush a thin coat of watery paint or ink over. **b** coat (inferior metal) with gold, etc. • n. **1** act or instance of washing. **2** clothes for washing or just washed. **3** visible or audible motion of agitated water or air, esp. due to the passage of a ship or aircraft. **4** liquid to spread over a surface to cleanse, heal, or color. **5** thin coating of watercolor, wall paint, or metal. □ **come out in the wash** colloq. be resolved in the course of time. **wash-and-wear** adj. (of a fabric or garment) not requiring ironing. **wash down 1** wash completely. **2** (usu. foll. by with) accompany or follow (food) with a drink. **washed out 1** faded. **2** pale. **3** colloq. limp; enfeebled. **washed up** sl. defeated, having failed. **wash one's hands of** renounce responsibility for. **wash-out** n. **1** colloq. fiasco; complete failure. **2** breach in a road, railroad track, etc., caused by flooding. □□ **wash·a·bil′i·ty** n. **wash′a·ble** adj.

wash·board /wóshbawrd, wáwsh–/ n. ribbed board of wood or sheet of corrugated zinc on which clothes are scrubbed.

wash·cloth /wóshkloth, wáwsh–/ n. cloth for washing the face or body.

wash·er /wóshər, wáwsh–/ n. **1** person or machine that washes. **2** flat ring of rubber, metal, leather, etc., inserted at a joint to tighten and prevent leakage. **3** similar ring placed under the head of a screw, etc., to disperse its pressure.

wash·er·wom·an /wóshərwoomən, wáwsh–/ n. (pl. **–wom·en**) (also **wash′wom·an**) woman whose occupation is washing clothes; laundress.

wash·ing /wóshing, wáwsh–/ n. quantity of clothes for washing or just washed. □ **washing machine** machine for washing clothes and linen, etc.

wash·room /wóshroom, –room, wáwsh–/ n. bathroom.

wash·stand /wóshstand, wáwsh–/ n. piece of furniture to hold a washbowl, pitcher, soap, etc.

was·n't /wúzənt, wóz/ contr. was not.

WASP /wosp/ n. (also **Wasp**) usu. derog. white Anglo-Saxon Protestant. □□ **Wasp′y** adj.

wasp /wosp/ n. stinging insect with black and yellow stripes and a very thin waist. □□ **wasp′like** adj.

wasp·ish /wóspish/ adj. irritable; petulant; sharp in retort. □□ **wasp′ish·ly** adv. **wasp′ish·ness** n.

was·sail /wósəl, wósayl, wosáyl/ archaic • n. **1** festive occasion. **2** spiced ale or cider with which toasts were formerly drunk. • v.intr. make merry; celebrate with drinking. □□ **was′sail·er** n.

> **wassail** Middle English (as a salutation): from Old Norse ves heill, corresponding to the Old English greeting wæs hæil 'be in (good) health!' (source of HAIL[2]). No trace has been found of the use of drinking formulas in Old English, Old Norse or other Teutonic languages; wassail and the reply drinkhail 'drink good health') were probably introduced by Danish-speaking inhabitants of England, the use then spreading to the native population. By the 12th century, the usage was considered, by the Normans, characteristic of Englishmen.

wast·age /wáystij/ n. **1** amount wasted. **2** loss by use, wear, or leakage. **3** Commerce loss of employees other than by layoffs.

waste /wayst/ • v. **1** tr. use to no purpose or extravagantly. **2** tr. fail to use. **3** tr. & intr. wear gradually away; make or become weak. **4** tr. **a** devastate. **b** sl. murder; kill. **5** intr. be expended without useful effect. • adj. **1** superfluous. **2** not inhabited or cultivated. • n. **1** act or instance of wasting. **2** waste material or food. **3** waste region. □ **go** (or **run**) **to waste** be wasted. **lay waste** ravage; devastate. □□ **waste′less** adj.

waste·bas·ket /wáystbaskit/ n. receptacle for wastepaper.

waste·ful /wáystfool/ adj. **1** extravagant. **2** causing or showing waste. □□ **waste′ful·ly** adj. **waste′ful·ness** n.

waste·land /wáystland/ n. **1** unproductive or useless area of land. **2** place or time considered spiritually or intellectually barren.

waste·pa·per /wáystpaypər/ n. spoiled, valueless, or discarded paper. □ **wastepaper basket** = WASTEBASKET.

wast·rel /wáystrəl/ n. good-for-nothing person.

watch /woch/ • v. **1** tr. keep the eyes fixed on. **2** tr. **a** keep under observation. **b** monitor carefully. **3** intr. (often foll. by for) be in an alert state; be vigilant. **4** intr. (foll. by over) look after; take care of. • n. **1** small portable timepiece for carrying on one's person. **2** state of alert or constant observation or attention. **3** Naut. **a** four-hour period of duty. **b** ship's crew on watch. **4** guard; security officer. □ **watch it** (or **oneself**) colloq. be careful. **watch out 1** (often foll. by for) be on one's guard. **2** as a warning of immediate danger. □□ **watch′a·ble** adj. **watch′er** n. (also in comb.).

watch·band /wóchband/ n. strap or bracelet for fastening a watch on the wrist.

watch·dog /wóchdawg, dog/ • n. **1** dog kept to guard property, etc. **2** person or body monitoring others' rights, etc. • v.tr. (**–dogged, –dog·ging**) maintain surveillance over.

watch·ful /wóchfool/ adj. **1** on the watch. **2**

showing vigilance. □□ **watch′ful•ly** adv. **watch′ ful•ness** n.

watch•man /wóchmən/ n. (pl. **–men**) person employed to look after an empty building, etc., at night.

watch•tow•er /wóchtowr/ n. tower from which observation can be kept.

watch•word /wóchwərd/ n. phrase summarizing a guiding principle.

wa•ter /wáwtər, wót–/ • n. **1** colorless, transparent, odorless, tasteless liquid compound of oxygen and hydrogen. ¶ Chem. formula: H_2O. **2** liquid consisting chiefly of this and found in seas, lakes, rivers, and rain. **3** expanse of water. **4** (in pl.) part of a sea or river. **5** (often as **the waters**) mineral water at a spa, etc. **6** state of a tide. • v. **1** tr. sprinkle or soak with water. **2** tr. supply (a plant or animal) with water. **3** intr. (of the mouth or eyes) secrete water. **4** tr. (as **watered** adj.) (of silk, etc.) having irregular wavy glossy markings. **5** intr. take in a supply of water. □ **make one's mouth water** cause one's saliva to flow; stimulate one's appetite or anticipation. **water bed** mattress filled with water. **water buffalo** common domestic E. Indian buffalo. **water chestnut** nutlike tuber from a sedge used esp. in Chinese cooking. **water lily** aquatic plant with broad flat floating leaves and flowers. **water main** main pipe in a water-supply system. **water moccasin** venomous snake of the southern US; cottonmouth. **water pipe 1** pipe for conveying water. **2** hookah. **water polo** ball game played by swimmers. **water rat** aquatic rodent. **water-repellent** not easily penetrated by water. **water ski** each of a pair of skis for skimming the surface of the water when towed by a motorboat. **water table** level below which the ground is saturated with water. **water tower** tower with an elevated tank to store and distribute water. **water wings** inflatable floats fixed on the arms of a person learning to swim. □□ **wa′ter•er** n. **wa′ter•less** adj.

wa•ter•col•or /wáwtərkúlər, wótər–/ n **1** pigment diluted with water. **2** picture painted with this. □□ **wa′ter•col•or•ist** n.

wa•ter•course /wáwtərkawrs, wótər–/ n. **1** brook, stream, or artificial water channel. **2** bed along which this flows.

wa•ter•cress /wáwtərkres, wótər–/ n. pungent edible plant growing in running water.

wa•ter•fall /wáwtərfawl, wótər–/ n. stream or river flowing over a precipice or down a steep hillside.

wa•ter•fowl /wáwtərfowl, wótər–/ n. (usu. collect. as pl.) birds frequenting water, esp. swimming game birds.

wa•ter•front /wáwtərfrunt, wótər/ n. part of a town or city adjoining a river, lake, harbor, etc.

wa•ter•line /wáwtərlīn, wótər–/ n. line along which the surface of water touches a ship's side.

wa•ter•logged /wáwtərlawgd, –logd, wótər–/ adj. saturated or filled with water.

Wa•ter•loo /wáwtərlōō, wótər–/ n. decisive defeat or contest.

wa•ter•man /wáwtərmən, wótər–/ n. (pl. **–men**) person who earns a living on the water, esp. a fisherman, etc.

wa•ter•mark /wáwtərmaark, wótər–/ • n. faint identifying design in some paper. • v.tr. mark with this.

wa•ter•mel•on /wáwtərmelən, wótər–/ n. large, smooth, green melon with sweet, juicy red pulp.

wa•ter•pow•er /wáwtərpowr, wótər–/ n. mechanical force derived from the weight or motion of water.

wa•ter•proof /wáwtərprōōf, wótər–/ • adj. impervious to water. • v.tr. make waterproof.

wa•ter•shed /wáwtərshed, wótər–/ n. **1** line of separation between waters flowing to different rivers, basins, or seas. **2** turning point in affairs.

wa•ter•spout /wáwtərspowt, wótər–/ n. gyrating column of water and spray formed by a whirlwind between sea and cloud.

wa•ter•tight /wáwtərtīt, wótər–/ adj. **1** closely fastened or fitted to prevent the passage of water. **2** (of an argument, etc.) unassailable.

wa•ter•way /wáwtərway, wótər–/ n. navigable channel.

wa•ter•works /wáwtərwərks, wótər–/ n. **1** establishment for managing a water supply. **2** colloq. shedding of tears.

wa•ter•y /wáwtəree, wótər–/ adj. **1** containing too much water. **2** too thin in consistency. **3** of or consisting of water. **4** (of the eyes) suffused or running with water. **5** (of conversation, style, etc.) vapid; uninteresting. □□ **wa′ter•i•ness** n.

WATS /wots/ abbr. Wide-Area Telecommunications Service.

watt /wot/ n. the SI unit of electrical power, equivalent to one joule per second. ¶ Symb.: **W**.

watt•age /wótij/ n. amount of electrical power expressed in watts.

wat•tle¹ /wót'l/ • n. interlaced rods and split rods used for fences, etc. • v.tr. make of wattle.

wat•tle² /wót'l/ n. loose fleshy appendage on the head or throat of a turkey or other birds. □□ **wat′tled** adj.

WATTLE

wave /wayv/ • v. **1 a** intr. (often foll. by to) move a hand, etc., to and fro in greeting or as a signal. **b** tr. move (a hand, etc.) in this way. **2 a** intr. show a sinuous or sweeping motion as of a flag, tree, or a wheat field in the wind. **b** tr. impart a waving motion to. **3** tr. tell or direct (a person) by waving. **4** tr. express (a greeting, etc.) by waving. **5** tr. give an undulating form to (hair, etc.). **6** intr. (of hair, etc.) be wavy. • n. **1** ridge of water between two depressions. **2** such a ridge curling into an arched form and breaking on the shore. **3** fluctuating motion, etc. **4** gesture of waving. **5** undulating form, as in the hair. **6** Physics a disturbance of the particles of a fluid medium for the propagation or direction of

motion, heat, light, sound, etc. **b** single curve in the course of this motion. □ **make waves** *colloq.* cause trouble. □□ **wave′less** *adj.* **wave′like** *adj.* & *adv.*
¶ See note at WAIVE.

wave·form /wáyvfawrm/ *n. Physics* curve showing the shape of a wave at a given time.

wave·length /wáyvlengkth, –length, –lenth/ *n.* **1** distance between successive crests of a wave. ¶ Symb.: λ. **2** *colloq.* particular mode or range of thinking.

wave·let /wáyvlit/ *n.* small wave on water.

wa·ver /wáyvər/ *v.intr.* **1** be or become unsteady. **2** be irresolute. **3** (of a light) flicker. □□ **wa′ver·er** *n.* **wa′ver·ing·ly** *adv.*
¶ See note at WAIVE.

wav·y /wáyvee/ *adj.* (**wav·i·er, wav·i·est**) having waves or alternate contrary curves. □□ **wav′i·ly** *adv.* **wav′i·ness** *n.*

wax[1] /waks/ • *n.* **1** sticky, plastic, yellowish substance secreted by bees as the material of honeycomb cells; beeswax. **2** this used for candles, modeling, etc. **3** any similar substance, e.g., earwax. • *v.tr.* cover or treat with wax. □ **wax bean** yellow-podded snap bean. **wax paper** (also **waxed paper**) paper waterproofed with a layer of wax. □□ **wax′er** *n.* **wax′i·ly** *adv.* **wax′i·ness** *n.* **wax′y** *adj.* (**wax·i·er, wax·i·est**).

wax[2] /waks/ *v.intr.* **1** (of the moon between new and full) increasing in apparent size. **2** become larger or stronger. **3** pass into a specified state or mood. □ **wax and wane** undergo alternate increases and decreases.

wax·en /wáksən/ *adj.* of, consisting of, or like wax.

wax·wing /wákswing/ *n.* any of various birds with small tips like red sealing wax to some wing feathers.

wax·work /wákswərk/ *n.* **1** object, esp. a lifelike dummy, modeled in wax. **2** (in *pl.*) exhibition of wax dummies.

way /way/ • *n.* **1** road, track, path, etc. **2** course or route for reaching a place. **3** place of passage into a building, through a door, etc. **4 a** method or plan for attaining an object. **b** the ability to obtain one's object. **5 a** person's desired or chosen course of action. **b** custom or manner of behaving. **6** normal course of events. **7** traveling distance. **8** unimpeded opportunity of advance. **9** impetus; progress. **10** specified direction. **11** (in *pl.*) parts into which a thing is divided. **12** specified condition. **13** respect (*useful in some ways*). **14 a** (in *pl.*) structure of lumber, etc., down which a new ship is launched. **b** parallel rails, etc., as a track for the movement of a machine. • *adv. colloq.* far. □ **by the way** incidentally. **by way of 1** by means of. **2** as a form of. **3** passing through. **give way 1 a** make concessions. **b** yield. **2** (of a structure, etc.) collapse. **go out of one's way** make a special effort. **lead the way** act as guide or leader. **way-out** *colloq.* **1** unusual; eccentric. **2** excellent. **ways and means** methods of achieving something, esp. of raising government revenue.

-way /way/ *suffix* = -WAYS.

way·far·er /wáyfairər/ *n.* traveler, esp. on foot. □□ **way′far·ing** *n.*

way·lay /wáylay/ *v.tr.* (*past* and *past part.* **way·laid**) **1** lie in wait for. **2** stop to rob or interview. □□ **way′lay·er** *n.*

-ways /wayz/ *suffix* forming adjectives and adverbs of direction or manner (*sideways*).

way·side /wáysīd/ *n.* side of a road.

way·ward /wáywərd/ *adj.* childishly self-willed or perverse. □□ **way′ward·ly** *adv.* **way′ward·ness** *n.*

we /wee/ *pron.* (*obj.* **us**; *poss.* **our, ours**) **1** (*pl.* of I[2]) used by and with reference to more than one person. **2** used for or by a royal person, an editor, etc., when speaking.

weak /week/ *adj.* **1** deficient in strength, power, vigor, or number. **2** easily led. **3** unconvincing. **4** (of a syllable, etc.) unstressed. **5** *Gram.* (of a verb) forming inflections by the addition of a suffix to the stem. □ **weak-kneed** *colloq.* lacking resolution. **weak-minded 1** mentally deficient. **2** lacking in resolution. **weak moment** time when one is unusually compliant or temptable. □□ **weak′ish** *adj.*

weak·en /wéekən/ *v.* **1** *tr.* & *intr.* make or become weak or weaker. **2** *intr.* relent; give way; succumb to temptation, etc. □□ **weak′en·er** *n.*

weak·ling /wéekling/ *n.* feeble person or animal.

weak·ly /wéeklee/ • *adv.* in a weak manner. • *adj.* (**weak·li·er, weak·li·est**) sickly; not robust. □□ **weak′li·ness** *n.*

weak·ness /wéeknis/ *n.* **1** being weak. **2** weak point. **3** self-indulgent liking.

weal[1] /weel/ • *n.* ridge raised on the flesh by a stroke of a rod or whip. • *v.tr.* mark with a weal.

weal[2] /weel/ *n. literary* welfare; prosperity; good fortune.

wealth /welth/ *n.* **1** riches. **2** state of being rich. **3** abundance.

wealth·y /wélthee/ *adj.* (**wealth·i·er, wealth·i·est**) having an abundance, esp. of money. □□ **wealth′i·ly** *adv.* **wealth′i·ness** *n.*

wean /ween/ *v.tr.* **1** accustom (an infant or other young mammal) to food other than (esp. its mother's) milk. **2** disengage (from a habit, etc.).

weap·on /wépən/ *n.* **1** thing designed or used or usable for inflicting bodily harm. **2** means for trying to gain the advantage in a conflict. □□ **weap′oned** *adj.* (also in *comb.*). **weap′on·less** *adj.*

weap·on·ry /wépənree/ *n.* weapons collectively.

wear /wair/ • *v.* (*past* **wore** /wawr/; *past part.* **worn** /wawrn/) **1** *tr.* have on one's person as clothing or an ornament, etc. **2** *tr.* be dressed habitually in. **3** *tr.* exhibit or present (a facial expression, etc.). **4** *tr. a* injure the surface of, or partly obliterate or alter, by rubbing, stress, or use. **b** *intr.* undergo such injury or change. **5** *tr.* & *intr.* (foll. by *off, away*) rub or be rubbed off. **6** *tr.* & *intr.* exhaust. **7** *tr.* (foll. by *down*) overcome by persistence. **8** *intr.* endure continued use or life. • *n.* **1** wearing or being worn. **2** (often in *comb.*) things worn; clothing (*sportswear*). **3** (in full **wear and tear**) damage sustained from continuous use. □ **wear off** lose effectiveness or intensity. **wear out** use or be used until no longer usable. □□ **wear′a·ble** *adj.* **wear·a·bil′i·ty** /–wáirəbilitee/ *n.* **wear′er** *n.* **wear′ing** *adj.* **wear′ing·ly** *adv.*

wea·ri·some /wéereesəm/ *adj.* tedious; tiring by monotony or length. □□ **wea′ri·some·ly** *adv.* **wea′ri·some·ness** *n.*

wea·ry /wéeree/ • *adj.* (**wea·ri·er, wea·ri·est**) **1** very tired. **2** impatient of. **3** tiring or tedious. • *v.* (**-ries, -ried**) make or grow weary. □□ **wea′ri·less** *adj.* **wea′ri·ly** *adv.* **wea′ri·ness** *n.* **wea′ry·ing·ly** *adv.*

wea·sel /wéezəl/ • *n.* small, flesh-eating mammal related to the stoat and ferret. • *v.intr.* **1**

equivocate or quibble. **2** (foll. by *on, out*) default on an obligation. □□ **wea′sel·ly** *adj.*

weath·er /wéthər/ ● *n.* state of the atmosphere at a place and time as regards heat, cloudiness, dryness, sunshine, wind, and rain, etc. ● *v.* **1** *tr.* expose to or affect by atmospheric changes. **2 a** *tr.* discolor or partly disintegrate (rock or stones) by exposure to air. **b** *intr.* be discolored or worn in this way. **3** *tr.* come safely through (a storm, difficult period, etc.). **4** *tr.* (of a ship or its crew) get to the windward of (a cape, etc.). □ **under the weather** *colloq.* indisposed or out of sorts; drunk. **weather-beaten** affected by exposure to the weather. **weather strip** (or **stripping**) piece of material used to proof a door or window against rain or wind. **weather-strip** install a weather strip. **weather vane** see VANE.

weath·er·cock /wéthərkok/ *n.* weather vane in the form of a cock.

weath·er·man /wéthərman/ *n.* (*pl.* **–men**) meteorologist, esp. one who broadcasts a weather forecast.

weath·er·proof /wéthərproof/ ● *adj.* resistant to the effects of bad weather, esp. rain. ● *v.tr.* make weatherproof. □□ **weath′er·proofed** *adj.*

weave[1] /weev/ ● *v.* (*past* **wove** /wōv/; *past part.* **wo·ven** /wóvən/ or **wove**) **1** *tr.* form (fabric) by interlacing long threads in two directions. **2** *intr.* **a** make fabric in this way. **b** work at a loom. **3** *tr.* make (a basket or wreath, etc.) by interlacing rushes or flowers, etc. **4** *tr.* make (facts, etc.) into a story or connected whole. ● *n.* style of weaving. □□ **weav′er** *n.*

weave[2] /weev/ *v.intr.* move repeatedly from side to side.

web /web/ *n.* **1 a** woven fabric. **b** amount woven in one piece. **2** connected series (*web of lies*). **3** cobweb, gossamer, or similar product of a spinning creature. **4** membrane between the toes of a swimming animal or bird. **5** large roll of paper used in printing. □ **web-footed** having the toes connected by webs. □□ **webbed** *adj.*

web·bing /wébing/ *n.* strong, narrow, closely woven fabric used for belts, etc.

we·ber /wébər, váybər/ *n.* the SI unit of magnetic flux. ¶ Abbr.: **Wb**.

Web site /wébsīt/ *n.* *Computing* location that maintains one or more pages on the World Wide Web.

Wed. *abbr.* Wednesday.

wed /wed/ *v.* (**wed·ding;** *past* and *past part.* **wed·ded** or **wed**) **1** usu. *formal* or *literary* **a** *tr.* marry. **b** *tr.* join in marriage. **2** *tr.* unite. **3** *tr.* (as **wedded** *adj.*) of or in marriage. **4** *tr.* (as **wedded** *adj.*) (foll. by *to*) obstinately attached.

we'd /weed/ *contr.* **1** we had. **2** we should; we would.

wed·ding /wéding/ *n.* marriage ceremony.

wedge /wej/ ● *n.* **1** piece of wood or metal, etc., tapering to a sharp edge, driven between two objects or parts to secure or separate them. **2** anything resembling a wedge. ● *v.tr.* **1** secure or fasten by means of a wedge. **2** force open or apart with a wedge. **3** pack or thrust (a thing or oneself) tightly in or into. □□ **wedge′like** *adj.* **wedge′wise** *adv.*

wed·lock /wédlok/ *n.* married state.

Wednes·day /wénzday, –dee/ *n.* fourth day of the week, following Tuesday.

wee /wee/ *adj.* (**we·er** /wéeər/; **we·est** /wéeist/) little; tiny.

weed /weed/ ● *n.* **1** plant growing where it is not wanted. **2** *sl.* **a** marijuana. **b** tobacco. ● *v.* **1** *tr.* a clear (an area) of weeds. **b** remove unwanted parts from. **2** *tr.* (foll. by *out*) sort out (inferior or unwanted persons, etc.) for removal. □□ **weed′er** *n.* **weed′less** *adj.*

weeds /weedz/ *n.pl.* (in full **widow's weeds**) deep mourning worn by a widow.

weed·y /wéedee/ *adj.* (**weed·i·er, weed·i·est**) **1** having many weeds. **2** of or like a weed. □□ **weed′i·ness** *n.*

week /week/ *n.* **1** period of seven days reckoned usu. from and to midnight on Saturday–Sunday. **2** period of seven days reckoned from any point (*stay for a week*). **3** six days between Sundays. **4 a** Monday to Friday. **b** normal amount of work done in this period.

week·day /wéekday/ *n.* day other than Sunday or other than at a weekend (often *attrib.*: *a weekday afternoon*).

week·end /wéekénd/ ● *n.* **1** Saturday and Sunday. **2** this period extended slightly esp. for a vacation, etc. ● *v.intr.* spend a weekend.

week·ly /wéeklee/ ● *adj.* done, produced, or occurring once a week. ● *adv.* once a week. ● *n.* (*pl.* **–lies**) weekly newspaper or periodical.

weep /weep/ *v.* (*past* and *past part.* **wept** /wept/) **1** *intr.* shed tears. **2** *tr.* & (foll. by *for*) *intr.* bewail; lament over. **3 a** *intr.* be covered with or send forth drops. **b** *intr.* & *tr.* exude liquid. **4** *intr.* (as **weeping** *adj.*) (of a tree) having drooping branches. □□ **weep′er** *n.* **weep′ing·ly** *adv.* **weep′y** *adj.* (**weep·i·er, weep·i·est**).

wee·vil /wéevil/ *n.* destructive beetle feeding esp. on grain, cotton, etc. □□ **wee′vil·y** *adj.*

weft /weft/ *n.* threads woven across a warp to make fabric.

weigh /way/ *v.* **1** *tr.* find the weight of. **2** *tr.* balance in the hands to guess or as if to guess the weight of. **3** compare. **4** *tr.* be equal to (a specified weight). **5** *intr.* exert an influence. **6** *intr.* (often foll. by *on*) be heavy or burdensome (to). □ **weigh anchor** see ANCHOR. **weigh down 1** bring or keep down. **2** be oppressive. □□ **weigh′a·ble** *adj.* **weigh′er** *n.*

---

weigh Old English *wegan*, of Germanic origin; related to Dutch *wegen* 'weigh,' German *bewegen* 'move,' from an Indo-European root shared by Latin *vehere* 'convey.' Early senses included 'transport from one place to another' and 'raise up' (as in *weigh anchor*).

---

weight /wayt/ ● *n.* **1** *Physics* force experienced by a body as a result of the earth's gravitation. **2** heaviness of a body. **3** quantitative expression of a body's weight. **4** body of a known weight for use in weighing. **5** heavy body, esp. used in a mechanism, etc. **6** load or burden. **7 a** influence; importance. **b** preponderance. ● *v.tr.* **1 a** attach a weight to. **b** hold down with a weight. **2** impede or burden.

weight·less /wáytlis/ *adj.* not apparently acted on by gravity. □□ **weight′less·ly** *adv.* **weight′less·ness** *n.*

weight·lift·ing /wáytlifting/ *n.* sport or exercise of lifting heavy weights. □□ **weight′lift·er** *n.*

weight·y /wáytee/ *adj.* (**weight·i·er, weight·i·est**) **1** heavy. **2** momentous. **3** (of utterances, etc.)

deserving careful consideration. **4** influential; authoritative. □□ **weight′i•ly** *adv.* **weight′i•ness** *n.*

weir /weer/ *n.* **1** dam built across a river to raise the level of water upstream or regulate its flow. **2** enclosure of stakes, etc., set in a stream as a trap for fish.

weird /weerd/ • *adj.* **1** uncanny; supernatural. **2** *colloq.* queer; incomprehensible. □□ **weird′ly** *adv.* **weird′ness** *n.*

weird•o /we′erdō/ *n.* (*pl.* **–os**) *colloq.* odd or eccentric person.

welch var. of WELSH.

wel•come /wélkəm/ • *n.* act of greeting or receiving gladly; kind or glad reception. • *int.* expressing such a greeting. • *v.tr.* receive with a welcome. • *adj.* **1** received with pleasure. **2 a** allowed or invited. **b** *iron.* gladly given (an unwelcome task, thing, etc.) (*here's my work and you are welcome to it*). □□ **wel′come•ly** *adv.* **wel′come•ness** *n.* **wel′com•er** *n.* **wel′com•ing•ly** *adv.*

weld /weld/ • *v.tr.* **1 a** hammer or press (heated pieces of metal) into one piece. **b** join by fusion with an electric arc, etc. **c** form by welding into some article. **2** unite; join. • *n.* welded joint. □□ **weld′a•ble** *adj.* **weld•a•bil′i•ty** *n.* **weld′er** *n.*

wel•fare /wélfair/ *n.* **1** well-being; happiness; health and prosperity. **2** financial support given by a government to the unemployed, disadvantaged, etc.

wel•kin /wélkin/ *n. poet.* sky; the upper air.

well¹ /wel/ • *adv.* (**better, best**) **1** in a satisfactory way. **2** in the right way. **3** with some distinction. **4** in a kind way. **5 a** thoroughly; carefully. **b** intimately; closely. **6** with approval; favorably. **7** probably; reasonably. **8** to a considerable extent. • *adj.* (**better, best**) **1** in good health. **2 a** satisfactory. **b** advisable. • *int.* expressing surprise, resignation, insistence, etc. □ **as well as** in addition to. **leave** (or **let**) **well enough alone** avoid needless change or disturbance. **well-advised** prudent. **well-appointed** having all the necessary equipment. **well-balanced** sane; sensible. **well-being** state of being well, healthy, contented, etc. **well-bred** having or showing good breeding or manners. **well-disposed** (often foll. by *toward*) having a good disposition or friendly feeling (for). **well-done 1** (of meat, etc.) thoroughly cooked. **2** (of a task, etc.) performed well (also as *int.*). **well-founded** based on good evidence. **well-groomed** with carefully tended hair, clothes, etc. **well-grounded 1** = *well-founded.* **2** having good knowledge of the groundwork of a subject. **well-heeled** *colloq.* wealthy. **well-informed** having much knowledge or information about a subject. **well-intentioned** having or showing good intentions. **well-known 1** known to many. **2** known thoroughly. **well-meaning** (or **-meant**) well-intentioned. **well-off 1** wealthy. **2** in a fortunate situation. **well-preserved** see PRESERVE. **well-read** knowledgeable through much reading. **well-rounded 1** complete and symmetrical. **2** having or showing a fully developed personality, ability, etc. **well-spoken** articulate or refined in speech. **well-to-do** prosperous. **well-worn 1** much worn by use. **2** (of a phrase, etc.) trite. ¶ See note at GOOD.

well² /wel/ • *n.* **1** shaft sunk into the ground to obtain water, oil, etc. **2** enclosed space like a well shaft. **3** source. **4** = INKWELL. **5** *archaic* water spring or fountain. • *v.intr.* spring as from a fountain.

we'll /weel, wil/ *contr.* we shall; we will.

well•born /wélbáwrn/ *adj.* of a good or esteemed family.

well•head /wélhed/ *n.* source, esp. of a spring or stream.

well•ness /wélnis/ *n.* healthful condition through proper diet, exercise, and preventive medicine.

well•nigh /wélnī/ *adv. archaic* or *rhet.* almost.

Welsh /welsh/ • *adj.* of or relating to Wales or its people or language. • *n.* **1** Celtic language of Wales. **2** (prec. by *the*; treated as *pl.*) the people of Wales. □ **Welsh rabbit** (or **rarebit** by folk etymology) dish of melted cheese, etc., on toast. □□ **Welsh′man** *n.* (*pl.* **–men**). **Welsh′wom•an** *n.* (*pl.* **–wom•en**).

welsh /welsh/ *v.intr.* (also **welch** /welch/) evade an obligation, debt, promise, etc. □□ **welsh′er** *n.*

welt /welt/ *n.* **1** leather rim sewn around the edge of a shoe upper for the sole to be attached to. **2** = WEAL¹. **3** trimming.

wel•ter /wéltər/ • *v.intr.* roll; wallow. • *n.* **1** state of general confusion. **2** disorderly mixture or contrast of beliefs, policies, etc.

wel•ter•weight /wéltərwayt/ *n.* **1** weight class in certain sports intermediate between lightweight and middleweight. **2** athlete of this weight.

wen /wen/ *n.* benign tumor on the skin, esp. of the scalp.

wench /wench/ *n.* **1** *joc.* girl or young woman. **2** *archaic* prostitute. □□ **wench′er** *n.*

wend /wend/ *v. literary* or *archaic* go. □ **wend one's way** make one's way.

went *past* of GO¹.

wept *past* of WEEP.

were *2nd sing. past, pl. past,* and *past subj.* of BE.

we're /weer/ *contr.* we are.

were•n't /wərnt, wərənt/ *contr.* were not.

were•wolf /we′erwŏŏlf, wáir–/ *n.* (also **wer•wolf** /wŏr–/) (*pl.* **–wolves**) mythical being who at times changes from a person to a wolf.

west /west/ • *n.* **1 a** point of the horizon where the sun sets at the equinoxes. **b** compass point corresponding to this. **c** direction in which this lies. **2** (usu. **the West**) **a** European civilization. **b** the nations of western Europe and N. America. **c** western part of a country, etc., esp. the American West. • *adj.* **1** toward, at, near, or facing west. **2** from the west. • *adv.* **1** toward, at, or near the west. **2** (foll. by *of*) further west than. □ **West Indies** islands of Central America, including Cuba and the Bahamas.

west•er•ly /wéstərlee/ • *adj. & adv.* **1** in a western position or direction. **2** (of a wind) blowing from the west. • *n.* (*pl.* **–lies**) wind blowing from the west.

west•ern /wéstərn/ • *adj.* **1** of or in the west. **2** lying or directed toward the west. **3** (**Western**) of or relating to the West (see WEST *n.* 2). • *n.* movie or novel about cowboys in western N. America. □ **western hemisphere** the half of the earth containing the Americas. □□ **west′ern•most** *adj.*

west•ern•er /wéstərnər/ *n.* native or inhabitant of the West.

west•ern•ize /wéstərnīz/ *v.tr.* (also **Wes′ter•nize**) influence with or convert to the ideas and customs, etc., of the West. □□ **west•ern•i•za′tion** *n.*

west•ward /wéstwərd/ • *adj. & adv.* (also **west′wards**) toward the west. • *n.* westward direction or region.

wet /wet/ • *adj.* (**wet·ter, wet·test**) **1** soaked, covered, or dampened with water or other liquid. **2** rainy. **3** not yet dried. **4** *sl.* allowing sales of liquor. • *v. tr.* (**wet·ting**; *past* and *past part.* **wet** or **wet·ted**) **1** make wet. **2** urinate in or on. • *n.* **1** liquid that wets something. **2** rainy weather. □ **wet behind the ears** immature; inexperienced. **wet nurse** woman employed to suckle another's child. **wet-nurse 1** act as a wet nurse to. **2** *colloq.* treat as if helpless. **wet suit** close-fitting rubber garment worn by skin divers, etc., to keep warm. □□ **wet′ly** *adv.* **wet′ness** *n.* **wet′ta·ble** *adj.* **wet′ting** *n.* **wet′tish** *adj.*

wet·back /wétbak/ *n. offens.* illegal immigrant from Mexico to the US.

wet·lands /wétləndz/ *n.pl.* swamps and other damp areas of land.

we've /weev/ *contr.* we have.

whack /hwak, wak/ *colloq.* • *v. tr.* strike or beat forcefully. • *n.* sharp or resounding blow. □ **have a whack at** *sl.* attempt. **out of whack** *sl.* out of order; malfunctioning. □□ **whack′er** *n.* **whack′ing** *n.*

whale¹ /hwayl, wayl/ *n.* (*pl.* same or **whales**) large marine mammal having a streamlined body and horizontal tail, and breathing through a blowhole on the head. □ **a whale of a** *colloq.* exceedingly good or fine, etc. **whale oil** oil from the blubber of whales.

whale² /hwayl, wayl/ *v.tr. colloq.* beat; thrash.

whale·bone /hwáylbōn, wáyl–/ *n.* elastic horny substance growing in thin parallel plates in the upper jaw of some whales.

whal·er /hwáylər, wáyl–/ *n.* **1** whaling ship. **2** seaman engaged in whaling.

wham /hwam, wam/ *colloq.* • *int.* expressing the sound of a forcible impact. • *n.* such a sound. • *v.* (**whammed, wham·ming**) **1** *intr.* make such a sound or impact. **2** *tr.* strike forcibly.

wham·my /hwámee, wám–/ *n.* (*pl.* **–mies**) *colloq.* evil or unlucky influence.

wharf /hwawrf, wawrf/ • *n.* (*pl.* **wharves** /wawrvz/ or **wharfs**) level quayside area to which a ship may be moored to load and unload. • *v. tr.* moor (a ship) at a wharf.

what /hwot, wot, hwut, wut/ • *interrog. adj.* **1** asking for a choice from an indefinite number or for a statement of amount, number, or kind. **2** *colloq.* = WHICH. • *adj.* (usu. in exclam.) how great or remarkable (*what luck!*). • *rel. adj.* whatever (*will give you what help I can*). • *pron.* (corresp. to the functions of the *adj.*) **1** what thing or things? **2** (asking for a remark to be repeated) = what did you say? **3** how much (*what you must have suffered!*). **4** (as *rel. pron.*) that or those which (*what followed was worse*). • *adv.* to what extent (*what does it matter?*). □ **what about** what is the news or position or your opinion of.

what·ev·er /hwotévər, wot–, hwut, wut–/ *adj.* & *pron.* **1** = WHAT (in relative uses) with the emphasis on indefiniteness. **2** though anything (*we are safe whatever happens*). **3** (with *neg.* or *interrog.*) at all; of any kind (*there is no doubt whatever*).

what·not /hwótnot, wót–, hwút–, wút–/ *n.* **1** indefinite or trivial thing. **2** stand with shelves for small objects.

what·so·ev·er /hwótsō-évər, wót–, hwút–, wút–/ *adj.* & *pron.* = WHATEVER.

wheat /hweet, weet/ *n.* **1** cereal plant bearing dense four-sided seed spikes. **2** its grain, used in making flour, etc. □ **wheat germ** embryo of the wheat plant, extracted as a source of vitamins. □□ **wheat′en** *adj.*

whee·dle /hweédəl, weédəl/ *v. tr.* coax, influence, or get by flattery or endearments. □□ **whee′dler** *n.* **whee′dling** *adj.* **whee′dling·ly** *adv.*

wheel /hweel, weel/ • *n.* **1** circular frame or disk that revolves on an axle. **2** wheellike thing. **3** motion as of a wheel. **4** (in *pl.*) *sl.* car. • *v.* **1 a** turn on an axis or pivot. **b** swing around in line with one end as a pivot. **2 a** *intr.* change direction or face another way. **b** *tr.* cause to do this. **3** *tr.* push or pull (a wheeled thing). □ **at the wheel1** driving a vehicle. **2** directing a ship. **3** in control of affairs. **wheeler-dealer** *colloq.* person who wheels and deals. □□ **wheeled** *adj.* (also in *comb.*). **wheel′less** *adj.*

wheel·bar·row /hweélbarō, weél–/ *n.* small cart with one wheel and two shafts for carrying garden loads, etc.

WHEELBARROW

wheel·base /hweélbays, weél–/ *n.* distance between the front and rear axles of a vehicle.

wheel·chair /hweélchair, weél–/ *n.* chair on wheels for an invalid or disabled person.

wheel·house /hweélhows, weel–/ *n.* = PILOT-HOUSE.

wheel·ie /hweélee, weé–/ *n. sl.* stunt of riding a bicycle or motorcycle with the front wheel off the ground.

wheel·wright /hweélrīt, weél–/ *n.* person who makes or repairs, esp. wooden, wheels.

wheeze /hweez, weez/ • *v.* **1** *intr.* breathe with an audible whistling sound. **2** *tr.* utter in this way. • *n.* sound of wheezing. □□ **wheez′er** *n.* **wheez′i·ly** *adv.* **wheez′i·ness** *n.* **wheez′ing·ly** *adv.* **wheez′y** *adj.* (**wheez·i·er, wheez·i·est**).

whelk /hwelk, welk/ *n.* edible marine mollusk having a spiral shell.

WHELK

whelm /hwelm, welm/ *v.tr. poet.* **1** engulf. **2** overwhelm.

whelp /hwelp, welp/ • *n.* **1** young dog; puppy. **2** *archaic* cub. **3** ill-mannered child or youth. • *v.tr.* give birth to (a whelp or whelps).

when /hwen, wen/ • *adv.* **1** at what time? **2** on what occasion? **3** (time) at or on which (*there are times when I could cry*). • *conj.* **1** at the or any time that; as soon as (*come when you like*). **2** although. **3** after which; and then; but just then (*was nearly asleep when the bell rang*). • *pron.* what time? (*till when can you stay?*). • *n.* time; occasion (*have finally decided on the where and when*).

whence /hwens, wens/ *formal* • *adv.* from what place? • *conj.* **1** to the place from which. **2** (often prec. by *place*, etc.) from which (*source whence these errors arise*). **3** and thence (*whence it follows that*).

when·ev·er /hwenévər, wen–/ *conj. & adv.* **1** at whatever time; on whatever occasion. **2** every time that.

when·so·ev·er /hwénsō-évər, wén–/ *conj. & adv. formal* = WHENEVER.

where /hwair, wair/ • *adv.* **1** in or to what place or position? (*where is the milk?*). **2** in what respect? (*where does the argument lead?*). **3** in what book, etc.?; from whom? (*where did you read that?*). **4** in or to which (*places where they meet*). • *conj.* wherever (*go where you like*). • *pron.* what place? • *n.* place; scene of something (see WHEN *n.*).

where·a·bouts • *adv.* /hwáirəbówts, wáir–/ approximately where? (*whereabouts are they?*). • *n.* /hwáirəbowts, wáir–/ (as *sing.* or *pl.*) person's or thing's location.

where·as /hwairáz, wair–/ *conj.* **1** in contrast or comparison with the fact that. **2** (esp. in legal preambles) taking into consideration the fact that.

where·by /hwairbí, wair–/ *conj.* by what or which means.

where·fore /hwáirfawr, wáir–/ • *adv. archaic* **1** for what reason? **2** for which reason. • *n.* reason.

where·in /hwairín, wair–/ *formal conj.* in what or which place or respect.

where·of /hwairúv, –óv, wair–/ *formal conj.* of what or which (*the means whereof*).

where·up·on /hwáirəpón, –páwn, wáir–/ *conj.* immediately after which.

wher·ev·er /hwairévər, wair–/ • *adv.* in or to whatever place. • *conj.* in every place that.

where·with·al /hwáirwiṯhawl, –wiṯh–, wáir–/ *n. colloq.* money, etc., needed for a purpose (*has not the wherewithal to do it*).

wher·ry /hwéree, wéree/ *n.* (*pl.* **–ries**) light rowboat usu. for carrying passengers.

whet /hwet, wet/ *v.tr.* (**whet·ted, whet·ting**) **1** sharpen (a tool). **2** stimulate (the appetite or a desire, etc.). □□ **whet′ter** *n.* (also in *comb.*).

wheth·er /hwéṯhər, wéṯh–/ *conj.* introducing the first or both of alternative possibilities (*I do not know whether they have arrived or not*).

whet·stone /hwétstōn, wét–/ *n.* abrasive stone used with water to sharpen tools.

whew /hwyōō/ *int.* expressing surprise, consternation, or relief.

whey /hway, way/ *n.* watery liquid left when milk forms curds.

which /hwich, wich/ • *adj.* **1** asking for choice from a definite set of alternatives (*which John do you mean?*). **2** being the one just referred to (*ten years, during which time they admitted nothing*). • *pron.* **1** which person or persons. **2** which thing or things. **3** used in place of *that* after *in* or *that* (*the house in which I was born*).
¶ **Which** should be employed only for nonrestrictive (or nonessential) clauses: The horse, which is in the paddock, is six years old (the *which-* clause contains a nonessential fact, noted in passing; the horse would be six years old wherever it was). A *that-*clause is restrictive (or essential), as it identifies a particular thing: The horse that is in the paddock is six years old (not any horse, but the one in the paddock).

which·ev·er /hwichévər, wích–/ *adj. & pron.* **1** any which (*whichever one you like*). **2** no matter which (*whichever one wins, they both get a prize*).

whiff /hwif, wif/ • *n.* **1** puff or breath of air, smoke, etc. **2** odor. • *v.* **1** *tr. & intr.* blow or puff lightly (*while I want to believe it, I cannot*). **3** *tr.* get a slight smell of. **4** *intr. Baseball* strike out by swinging and missing on the third strike. **5** *tr. Baseball* strike out a batter in this way.

Whig /hwig, wig/ *n. hist.* **1** *Polit.* member of a British reformist party before the 19th c. **2 a** American colonist supporting the American Revolution. **b** member of an American political party in the 19th c. □□ **Whig′ger·y** *n.* **Whig′gish** *adj.* **Whig′gism** *n.*

while /hwīl, wīl/ • *n.* period of time (*waited a while*). • *conj.* **1** during the time that. **2** although (*while I want to believe it, I cannot*). • *v.tr.* (foll. by *away*) pass (time, etc.) in a leisurely or interesting manner. • *adv.* (prec. by *time*, etc.) during which (*the summer while I was abroad*). □ **worth one's while** worth the time or effort spent.

whim /hwim, wim/ *n.* sudden fancy; caprice.

whim·per /hwímpər, wím–/ • *v.* **1** *intr.* make feeble, querulous, or frightened sounds. **2** *tr.* utter whimperingly. • *n.* whimpering sound. □□ **whim′per·er** *n.* **whim′per·ing·ly** *adv.*

whim·si·cal /hwímzikəl, wím–/ *adj.* **1** capricious. **2** fantastic. **3** odd or quaint; fanciful; humorous. □□ **whim·si·cal·i·ty** /–kálitee/ *n.* **whim′si·cal·ly** *adv.* **whim′si·cal·ness** *n.*

whim·sy /hwímzee, wím–/ *n.* (also **whim′sey**) (*pl.* **–sies** or **–seys**) WHIM.

whine /hwīn, wīn/ • *n.* **1** complaining, long-drawn wail as of a dog. **2** similar shrill, prolonged sound. **3** querulous tone or complaint. • *v.* **1** *intr.* emit or utter a whine. **2** *intr.* complain in a querulous tone. **3** *tr.* utter in a whining tone. □□ **whin′er** *n.* **whin′ing·ly** *adv.* **whin′y** *adj.* (**whin·i·er, whin·i·est**).

whin·ny /hwínee, wín–/ • *n.* (*pl.* **–nies**) gentle or joyful neigh. • *v.intr.* (**–nies, –nied**) give a whinny.

whip /hwip, wip/ • *n.* **1** lash attached to a stick for urging on animals or punishing, etc. **2** legislative member of a political party appointed to control discipline, tactics, etc. • *v.* (**whipped, whip·ping**) **1** *tr.* beat or urge on with a whip. **2** *tr.* beat (cream or eggs, etc.) into a froth. **3** *tr. & intr.* take or move suddenly, unexpectedly, or rapidly. **4** *tr. sl.* **a** excel. **b** defeat. **5** *tr.* bind with spirally wound twine. **6** *tr.* sew with overcast stitches. □ **whip hand 1** hand that holds the whip (in riding, etc.). **2** (usu. prec. by *the*) advantage or control in any situation. **whip up 1** excite or stir up (feeling, etc.). **2** prepare (a meal, etc.) hurriedly. □□ **whip′less** *adj.* **whip′like** *adj.* **whip′per** *n.* **whip′ping** *n.*

whip·cord /hwípkawrd, wíp–/ *n.* **1** tightly twisted cord. **2** close-woven worsted fabric.

whip·lash /hwíplash, wíp–/ *n.* **1** flexible end of a whip. **2** (in full **whiplash injury**) injury to the neck caused by a jerk of the head, esp. as in a motor vehicle accident.

whip·per·snap·per /hwípərsnapər, wíp–/ *n.* **1** small child. **2** insignificant but presumptuous (esp. young) person.

whip·pet /hwípit, wíp–/ *n.* crossbred dog of the greyhound type used for racing.

whip·ping /hwíping, wíp–/ *n.* □ **whipping boy** scapegoat.

whip·poor·will /hwípərwil, wíp–/ *n.* nocturnal N. American bird, named for its call.

whir /hwər, wər/ (also **whirr**) • *n.* continuous rapid buzzing or softly clicking sound. • *v.intr.* (**whirred, whir·ring**) make this sound.

whirl /hwərl, wərl/ • *v.* **1** *tr.* & *intr.* swing around and around; revolve rapidly. **2** *tr.* & *intr.* send or travel swiftly in an orbit or a curve. **3** *intr.* **a** (of the brain, etc.) seem to spin around. **b** (of thoughts, etc.) be confused. • *n.* **1** whirling movement. **2** state of intense activity. **3** state of confusion. □ **give it a whirl** try; attempt. □□ **whirl′er** *n.* **whirl′ing·ly** *adv.*

whirl·i·gig /hwərligig, wərl–/ *n.* spinning or whirling toy.

whirl·pool /hwərlpōol, wərl–/ *n.* powerful circular eddy in the sea, etc., often causing suction to its center.

whirl·wind /hwərlwind, wərl–/ *n.* **1** mass or column of air whirling rapidly in a funnel shape over land or water. **2** confused tumultuous process. **3** (*attrib.*) very rapid (*a whirlwind romance*).

whisk /hwisk, wisk/ • *v.* **1** *tr.* **a** brush with a sweeping movement. **b** take with a sudden motion. **2** *tr.* whip (cream, eggs, etc.). **3** *tr.* & *intr.* convey or go (esp. out of sight) lightly or quickly. • *n.* **1** whisking action or motion. **2** utensil for whisking eggs or cream, etc. **3** (in full **whisk broom**) small short-handled broom.

whisk·er /hwískər, wís–/ *n.* **1** (usu. in *pl.*) hair growing on a man's face, esp. on the cheeks. **2** each of the bristles on the face of a cat, etc. **3** *colloq.* very small distance. □□ **whisk′ered** *adj.* **whisk′er·y** *adj.*

whis·key /hwískee, wís–/ *n.* (also **whis′ky**) (*pl.* **–keys** or **–kies**) alcoholic liquor distilled esp. from grain, such as corn or malted barley. ¶ Note that the British and Canadian spelling is without the *e*, so that properly one would write of *Scotch whisky* or *Canadian whisky*, but *Kentucky bourbon whiskey*.

whis·per /hwíspər, wís–/ • *v.* **1 a** *intr.* speak very softly without vibration of the vocal cords. **b** *intr.* & *tr.* talk or say in a barely audible tone. **2** *intr.* speak privately or conspiratorially. **3** *intr.* rustle or murmur. • *n.* **1** whispering speech or sound. **2** thing whispered. □□ **whis′per·er** *n.* **whis′per·ing** *n.*

whist /hwist, wist/ *n.* card game usu. for four players.

whis·tle /hwísəl, wís–/ • *n.* **1** clear shrill sound made by forcing breath through a small hole between nearly closed lips. **2** similar sound made by a bird, the wind, a missile, etc. **3** instrument used to produce such a sound. • *v.* **1** *intr.* emit a whistle. **2 a** *intr.* give a signal or express surprise or derision by whistling. **b** *tr.* summon or give a signal to (a dog, etc.) by whistling. **3** *tr.* produce (a tune) by whistling. □ **whistle-stop 1** small, unimportant town on a railroad line. **2** politician's brief pause for a campaign speech on tour.

whis·tle·blow·er /hwísəlblōər, wí–/ *n. colloq.* one who publicizes wrongdoing in a workplace or organization.

whit /hwit, wit/ *n.* particle; least possible amount.

white /hwīt, wīt/ • *adj.* **1** resembling a surface reflecting sunlight without absorbing any of the visible rays; of the color of milk or fresh snow. **2** approaching such a color; pale esp. in the face. **3 a** having light-colored skin. **b** of or relating to white people. **4** lacking or having lost color. • *n.* **1** white color or pigment. **2** innocent. **3** visible part of the eyeball around the iris. **4** member of a light-skinned race. □ **white cell** (or **blood cell** or **corpuscle**) leukocyte. **white-collar** (of a worker) clerical; professional. **white elephant** useless possession. **white flag** symbol of surrender. **white goods 1** domestic linen. **2** large domestic electrical appliances. **white heat 1** the temperature at which metal emits white light. **2** state of intense passion or activity. **White House** official residence of the US president and offices of the executive branch of government in Washington D.C. **white lie** harmless or trivial untruth. **white light** colorless light, e.g., ordinary daylight. **white meat** poultry, veal, rabbit, and pork. **white noise** noise containing many frequencies with equal intensities. **white-out** dense blizzard allowing no visibility. **white sale** sale of household linen. **white tie** man's white bow tie as part of full evening dress. **white water** rapids; foamy stretch of water. □□ **white′ly** *adv.* **white′ness** *n.* **whit′ish** *adj.*

white·cap /hwítkap, wít–/ *n.* white-crested wave.

white·head /hwít-hed, wít–/ *n. colloq.* white or white-topped skin pustule.

whit·en /hwítən, wít–/ *v.* make or become white. □□ **white′en·er** *n.* **whit′en·ing** *n.*

white·wall /hwítwawl, wít–/ *n.* tire having a white band encircling the outer sidewall.

white·wash /hwítwosh, –wawsh, wít–/ • *n.* **1** solution of lime or whiting for whitening walls, etc. **2** means employed to conceal mistakes or faults. • *v.tr.* **1** cover with whitewash. **2** attempt by concealment to clear the reputation of. □□ **white′wash·er** *n.*

whith·er /hwíthər, wíth–/ *archaic* • *adv.* to what place, position, or state? • *conj.* to which place; to whatever place.

whit·ing[1] /hwíting, wí–/ *n.* small, white-fleshed fish used as food.

whit·ing[2] /hwíting, wí–/ *n.* ground chalk used in whitewashing, etc.

Whit·sun·day /hwítsúnday, wít–/ *n.* seventh Sunday after Easter, commemorating Pentecost (Acts 2).

whit·tle /hwítəl, wítəl/ *v.* **1** *tr.* & (foll. by *at*) *intr.* carve or pare (wood, etc.) with a knife. **2** *tr.* reduce by repeated subtractions.

whiz /hwiz, wiz/ (also **whizz**) *colloq.* • *n.* (*pl.* **whiz·zes**) **1** sound made by an object moving through the air at great speed. **2** (also **wiz** /wiz/) *colloq.* genius; expert. • *v.intr.* (**whizzed, whiz·zing**) move with or make a whiz. □ **whiz kid** *colloq.* brilliant or highly successful young person.

WHO *abbr.* World Health Organization.

who /hoō/ *pron.* (*obj.* **whom** /hoōm/ or *colloq.* **who**; *poss.* **whose** /hoōz/) **1 a** what or which person or persons? (*who called?*). **b** what sort of person or persons? (*who am I to object?*). **2** (a person) that (*anyone who wishes can come*).

¶ **Whom**, the objective case of **who**, is properly used where the word functions as an object: *Our mayor is the one whom you mean. To whom is the package addressed?* In informal usage, **who** often serves in all cases ("Who did you see?"), but in formal writing it is best to maintain the distinction.

whoa /wō/ *int.* command to stop or slow a horse, etc.

who'd /hoōd/ *contr.* **1** who had. **2** who would.

who·dun·it /hoōdúnit/ *n.* (also **who·dun'nit**) *colloq.* story or play about the detection of a crime, etc., esp. murder.

who·ev·er /hoō-évər/ *pron.* (*obj.* **whom·ev·er** /hoōm–/ or *colloq.* **who·ev·er**; *poss.* **whos·ev·er** /hoōz–/) **1** the or any person or persons who. **2** though anyone. **3** *colloq.* (as an intensive) who.

whole /hōl/ • *adj.* **1** uninjured; unbroken; intact; undiminished. **2** not less than; all there is of. **3** with no part removed. • *n.* **1** thing complete in itself. **2** all there is of a thing. **3** all members, etc., of. □ **as a whole** as a unity; not as separate parts. **on the whole** taking everything relevant into account. **whole number** number without fractions; integer. **whole-wheat** made of wheat with none of the bran or germ removed. □□ **whole'ness** *n.*

whole·heart·ed /hólha'artid/ *adj.* **1** completely devoted. **2** done with all possible effort or sincerity. □□ **whole'heart'ed·ly** *adv.* **whole'heart'ed·ness** *n.*

whole·sale /hólsayl/ • *n.* selling of things in large quantities to be retailed by others. • *adj.* & *adv.* **1** by wholesale. **2** on a large scale. • *v.tr.* sell wholesale. □□ **whole'sal·er** *n.*

whole·some /hólsəm/ *adj.* **1** promoting or indicating physical, mental, or moral health. **2** prudent. □□ **whole'some·ly** *adv.* **whole'some·ness** *n.*

whol·ly /hólee/ *adv.* **1** entirely; without limitation. **2** purely; exclusively.

whom *objective case* of WHO.

¶ See note at WHO.

whom·ev·er *objective case* of WHOEVER.

whom·so·ev·er *objective case* of WHOSOEVER.

whoop /hoōp, hwoōp, woōp/ • *n.* **1** loud cry of or as of excitement, etc. **2** long, rasping, indrawn breath in whooping cough. • *v.intr.* utter a whoop. □ **whooping cough** infectious bacterial disease, esp. of children, with a series of short, violent coughs followed by a whoop.

whop·per /hwópər, wóp–/ *n. sl.* **1** something big of its kind. **2** great lie.

whop·ping /hwóping, wóp–/ *adj. sl.* huge (*whopping lie*).

whore /hawr/ • *n.* prostitute. • *v.intr.* seek or chase after whores. □□ **whor'er** *n.*

whorl /hwawrl, wawrl, hwərl, wərl/ *n.* **1** ring of leaves, etc., around a stem. **2** one turn of a spiral. **3** complete circle in a fingerprint. □□ **whorled** *adj.*

whose /hoōz/ • *pron.* of or belonging to which person (*whose is this book?*). • *adj.* of whom or which (*whose book is this?*).

¶ It is not necessary to avoid using **whose** in referring to things rather than people. *I admired the houses, whose windows glowed in the sunset* is perfectly acceptable. To say *I admired the houses, the windows of which glowed in the sunset* is more awkward.

who·so·ev·er /hoōsō-évər/ *pron.* (*obj.* **whom·so·ev·er** /hoōm–/; *poss.* **whose·so·ev·er** /hoōz–/) *archaic* = WHOEVER.

why /hwī, wī/ • *adv.* **1 a** for what reason or purpose (*why did you do it?*). **b** on what grounds (*why do you say that?*). **2** for which (*reasons why I did it*). • *int.* expressing: **1** surprised discovery or recognition (*why, it's you!*). **2** impatience (*why, of course I do!*). **3** reflection (*why, yes, I think so*). **4** objection (*why, what is wrong with it?*). • *n.* (*pl.* **whys**) reason or explanation (esp. whys and wherefores).

WI *abbr.* **1** Wisconsin (in official postal use). **2** West Indies. **3** West Indian.

Wich·i·ta /wichitaw/ *n.* **1 a** N. American people native to Kansas. **b** member of this people. **2** language of this people.

wick /wik/ • *n.* **1** strip or thread of fibrous or spongy material feeding a flame with fuel in a candle, lamp, etc. **2** *Surgery* gauze strip inserted in a wound to drain it. • *v.tr.* draw (moisture) away by capillary action.

wick·ed /wikid/ *adj.* (**wick·ed·er, wick·ed·est**) **1** sinful; iniquitous. **2** spiteful. **3** playfully malicious. **4** *colloq.* very bad. **5** *sl.* excellent. □□ **wick'ed·ly** *adv.* **wick'ed·ness** *n.*

wick·er /wikər/ *n.* braided twigs, etc., as material for chairs, baskets, mats, etc.

wick·er·work /wikərwərk/ *n.* **1** wicker. **2** things made of wicker.

wick·et /wikit/ *n.* **1** small door or gate, esp. beside or in a larger one. **2** aperture in a door or wall, usu. closed with a sliding panel. **3** croquet hoop.

wide /wīd/ • *adj.* **1 a** having sides far apart; broad; not narrow. **b** considerable; more than is needed (*wide margin*). **2** in width (*foot wide*). **3** extending far. **4** not restricted; loose. **5** open to the full extent. **6 a** not within a reasonable distance of. **b** at a considerable distance from. **7** (in *comb.*) extending over the whole of (*nationwide*). • *adv.* **1** widely. **2** to the full extent. **3** far from the target, etc. □ **wide awake 1** fully awake. **2** *colloq.* wary; knowing. **wide-eyed** surprised or naive. □□ **wide'ness** *n.* **wid'ish** *adj.*

wide·ly /wídlee/ *adv.* **1** to a wide extent; far apart. **2** extensively. **3** by many people. **4** considerably; to a large degree.

wid·en /wíd'n/ *v.* make or become wider. □□ **wid'en·er** *n.*

wide·spread /wídspréd/ *adj.* widely distributed.

wid·geon /wíjən/ *n.* (also **wi'geon**) species of wild duck.

wid·get /wíjit/ *n. colloq.* any gadget or device.

wid·ow /wídō/ • *n.* **1** woman who has lost her husband by death and has not married again. **2** woman whose husband is often away on or preoccupied with a specified activity (*golf widow*). • *v.tr.* **1** make into a widow or widower. **2** (as **widowed** *adj.*) bereft by the death of a spouse. □□ **wid'ow·hood** *n.*

widow Old English *widewe, widuwe*, from an Indo-European root meaning 'be empty, be separated'; related to Sanskrit *vidh* 'be destitute,' Latin *viduus* 'bereft, widowed,' and Greek *ēitheos* 'unmarried man.'

wid·ow·er /wídōər/ *n.* man who has lost his wife by death and has not married again.

width /width, witth, with/ *n.* **1** measurement from side to side. **2** large extent. **3** strip of material of full width. □□ **width′ways** *adv.* **width′wise** *adv.*

wield /weeld/ *v.tr.* **1** hold and use. **2** exert or command. □□ **wield′er** *n.*

wie·ner /wéenər/ *n.* = FRANKFURTER.

wife /wīf/ *n.* (*pl.* **wives** /wīvz/) married woman, esp. in relation to her husband. □□ **wife′hood** *n.* **wife′less** *adj.* **wife′like** *adj.* **wife′ly** *adj.* **wife′li·ness** *n.*

wig /wig/ *n.* artificial head of hair. □□ **wigged** *adj.* (also in *comb.*). **wig′less** *adj.*

wig·eon var. of WIDGEON.

wig·gle /wígəl/ *colloq.* • *v.* move or cause to move quickly from side to side, etc. • *n.* act of wiggling. □□ **wig′gler** *n.*

wig·wag /wígwag/ *v.intr.* (**wig·wagged, wig·wag·ging**) *colloq.* **1** move lightly to and fro. **2** wave flags in this way in signaling.

wig·wam /wígwom/ *n.* Native American hut or tent.

wild /wīld/ • *adj.* **1** in its original natural state; not domesticated nor cultivated. **2** not civilized; barbarous. **3** unrestrained; disorderly. **4** tempestuous. **5** intensely eager. **b** (foll. by *about*) *colloq.* enthusiastically devoted to. **6** haphazard; ill-aimed. • *adv.* in a wild manner. • *n.* wild tract. □ **wild card 1** playing card having a rank chosen by the player holding it. **2** *Computing* character that will match any character or sequence of characters. **wild-goose chase** foolish or hopeless quest. **wild rice** N. American aquatic grass with edible grains. **Wild West** western US before the establishment of law and order. □□ **wild′ish** *adj.* **wild′ly** *adv.* **wild′ness** *n.*

wild·cat /wíldkat/ • *n.* **1** hot-tempered or violent person. **2** any of various smallish undomesticated cats, as the lynx, bobcat, etc. **3** exploratory oil well. • *adj.* **1** reckless; financially unsound. **2** (of a strike) sudden and unofficial.

wil·de·beest /wíldəbeest, víl-/ *n.* = GNU.

wil·der·ness /wíldərnis/ *n.* desert; uncultivated and uninhabited region.

wild·fire /wíldfīr/ *n. hist.* **1** rapidly spreading fire. **2** combustible liquid, esp. Greek fire, formerly used in warfare. **3** = WILL-O′-THE-WISP.

wild·fowl /wíldfowl/ *n.* (*pl.* same) game bird.

wild·life /wíldlīf/ *n.* wild animals collectively.

wile /wīl/ • *n.* (usu. in *pl.*) stratagem; trick or cunning procedure. • *v.tr.* lure or entice.

will[1] /wil/ *v.aux.* & *tr.* (*3rd sing. present* **will**; *past* **would** /wŏŏd/) **1** (in the 2nd and 3rd persons, and often in the 1st: see SHALL) expressing the future tense in statements, commands, or questions (*you will regret this*). **2** (in the 1st person) expressing intention (*I will return soon*). **3** expressing desire, consent, or inclination (*will you have a sandwich?*). **4** expressing ability or capacity (*jar will hold a quart*). **5** expressing habitual or inevitable tendency (*accidents will*

happen). **6** expressing probability or expectation (*that will be my wife*). ¶ See note at SHALL.

will[2] /wil/ • *n.* **1** faculty by which a person decides what to do. **2** self-control; willpower. **3** strong desire or intention. **4** power of effecting one's intentions or dominating others. **5** directions (usu. written) in legal form for the disposition of one's property after death. • *v.tr.* **1** intend; desire. **2** exercise willpower. **3** bequeath by the terms of a will. □ **at will** whenever one pleases. □□ **willed** *adj.* (also in *comb.*).

will·ful /wílfŏŏl/ *adj.* **1** intentional; deliberate. **2** obstinate; headstrong. □□ **will′ful·ly** *adv.* **will′ful·ness** *n.*

wil·lies /wíleez/ *n.pl. colloq.* nervous discomfort.

will·ing /wíling/ *adj.* **1** ready to consent or undertake. **2** given or done, etc., by a willing person. □□ **will′ing·ly** *adv.* **will′ing·ness** *n.*

will-o′-the-wisp /wíləthəwisp/ *n.* **1** phosphorescent light seen on marshy ground. **2** elusive person. **3** delusive hope or plan.

wil·low /wílō/ *n.* tree, usu. near water, yielding wood and pliant branches for furniture, baskets, etc.

wil·low·y /wílō-ee/ *adj.* lithe and slender.

will·pow·er /wílpowr/ *n.* control exercised by deliberate purpose over impulse; self-control.

wil·ly-nil·ly /wíleenílee/ • *adv.* whether one likes it or not. • *adj.* existing or occurring willy-nilly.

wilt /wilt/ • *v.* **1** *intr.* wither; droop. **2** *intr.* lose one's energy. **3** *tr.* cause to wilt. • *n.* plant disease causing wilting.

wil·y /wílee/ *adj.* (**wil·i·er, wil·i·est**) full of wiles; crafty; cunning. □□ **wil′i·ness** *n.*

wimp /wimp/ *n. colloq.* feeble or ineffectual person. □□ **wimp′ish** *adj.* **wimp′ish·ly** *adv.* **wimp′ish·ness** *n.* **wimp′y** *adj.*

wim·ple /wímpəl/ • *n.* headdress also covering the neck and the sides of the face, worn by some nuns. • *v.* arrange or fall in folds.

win /win/ • *v.* (**win·ning;** *past and past part.* **won** /wun/) **1** *tr.* acquire or secure as a result of a fight, contest, bet, effort, etc. **2** *tr.* be victorious in. **3** *intr.* be the victor. • *n.* victory in a game, etc. □□ **win′na·ble** *adj.*

wince /wins/ • *n.* start or involuntary shrinking movement showing pain or distress. • *v.intr.* give a wince. □□ **winc′er** *n.* **winc′ing·ly** *adv.*

winch /winch/ • *n.* **1** crank of a wheel or axle. **2** windlass. • *v.tr.* lift with a winch. □□ **winch′er** *n.*

wind[1] /wind/ • *n.* **1** air in more or less rapid natural motion. **2 a** breath. **b** power of breathing. **3** mere empty words. **4** gas generated in the bowels, etc. **5** wind instruments of an orchestra collectively. **6** scent carried by the wind, indicating the presence or proximity of an animal, etc. • *v.tr.* **1** exhaust the wind of by exertion or a blow. **2** renew the wind of by rest (*stopped to wind the horses*). **3** detect the presence of by a scent. □ **get wind of 1** smell out. **2** begin to suspect. **in the wind** happening or about to happen. **wind instrument** musical instrument in which sound is produced by a current of air, esp. the breath. **wind sock** canvas cylinder or cone on a mast to show the direction of the wind at an airfield, etc. **wind tunnel** tunnellike device to produce an air stream past models of aircraft, etc., for the study of wind effects on them. □□ **wind′less** *adj.*

wind² /wīnd/ • v. (past and past part. **wound** /wownd/) **1** intr. go in a circular, spiral, curved, or crooked course. **2** tr. make (one's way) by such a course. **3** tr. wrap closely; surround with or as with a coil. **4 a** tr. coil. **b** intr. coil into a ball. **5** tr. wind up (a clock, etc.). • n. bend or turn in a course.

wind·bag /wíndbag/ n. colloq. person who talks a lot but says little of any value.

wind·break /wíndbrayk/ n. row of trees or a fence or wall, etc., serving to break the force of the winds.

wind·break·er /wíndbraykər/ n. wind-resistant outer jacket.

wind·burn /wíndbərn/ n. inflammation of the skin caused by exposure to the wind.

wind·chill /wíndchil/ n. cooling effect of wind blowing on a surface.

wind·fall /wíndfawl/ n. **1** fruit blown to the ground by the wind. **2** unexpected good fortune.

wind·jam·mer /wíndjamər/ n. merchant sailing ship.

wind·lass /wíndləs/ • n. machine with a horizontal axle for hauling or hoisting. • v.tr. hoist or haul with a windlass.

wind·mill /wíndmil/ n. mill worked by the action of the wind on its sails.

win·dow /wíndō/ n. **1 a** opening in a wall, etc., usu. with glass in fixed, sliding, or hinged frames, to admit light or air, etc., and allow the occupants to see out. **b** glass filling this opening. **2** gap. **3** windowlike opening. **4** Comp. on-screen display selected to show a particular category or part of the data. □ **window box** box placed on an outside windowsill for growing flowers. **window dressing 1** display in a store window, etc. **2** adroit presentation of facts, etc., to give a deceptively favorable impression. **window-shop** (**-shopped, -shop·ping**) look at goods displayed in store windows, usu. without buying anything. **window-shopper** person who window-shops. □□ **win′dowed** adj. (also in comb.). **win′dow·less** adj.

win·dow·pane /wíndōpayn/ n. pane of glass in a window.

win·dow·sill /wíndōsil/ n. sill below a window.

wind·pipe /wíndpīp/ n. air passage from the throat to the lungs; trachea.

wind·shield /wíndsheeld/ n. shield of glass at the front of a motor vehicle. □ **windshield wiper** rubber blade on an arm, moving in an arc, to keep a windshield clear of rain, etc.

wind·surf·ing /wíndsərfing/ n. sport of riding on water on a sailboard. □□ **wind′surf** v.intr. **wind′surf·er** n.

wind·up /wíndup/ n. **1** conclusion; finish. **2** Baseball motions made by a pitcher, esp. arm swinging, in preparation for releasing a pitch.

wind·ward /wíndwərd/ • adj. & adv. on the side from which the wind is blowing (opp. LEEWARD). • n. windward direction.

wind·y /wíndee/ adj. (**wind·i·er, wind·i·est**) **1** stormy with wind. **2** exposed to the wind; wind-swept. **3** colloq. wordy; verbose. □□ **wind′i·ly** adv. **wind′i·ness** n.

wine /wīn/ • n. **1** fermented grape juice as an alcoholic drink. **2** fermented drink resembling this made from other fruits, etc. **3** dark-red color of red wine. • v. **1** intr. drink wine. **2** tr. entertain with wine. □□ **wine′less** adj. **win′y** adj. (**win·i·er, win·i·est**).

689   **wind ~ wire**

win·er·y /wínəree/ n. (pl. **-ies**) establishment where wine is made.

wing /wing/ • n. **1** each of the limbs or organs by which a bird, bat, or insect is able to fly. **2** winglike structure forming a supporting part of an aircraft. **3** part of a building, etc., extended in a certain direction. **4** section of a political party in terms of the extremity of its views. **5** flank of a battle array. **6 a** air force unit of several squadrons or groups. **b** (in pl.) pilot's badge in the air force, etc. • v. **1** intr. & tr. travel or traverse on wings or in an aircraft. **2** tr. wound in a wing or an arm. **3** tr. equip with wings. **4** tr. enable to fly; send in flight. □ **on the wing** flying or in flight. **take under one's wing** treat as a protégé. **take wing** fly away; soar. **wing nut** nut with projections for the fingers. □□ **winged** adj. (also in comb.). **wing′less** adj. **wing′let** n. **wing′like** adj.

wingspan /wíngspan/ n. measurement across the wings from tip to tip.

wink /wingk/ • v. **1 a** tr. close and open (one eye or both eyes) quickly. **b** intr. close and open an eye. **2** intr. (often foll. by at) wink one eye as a signal of friendship or greeting or to convey a message to a person. **3** intr. (of a light, etc.) twinkle; shine or flash intermittently. • n. **1** act or instance of winking. **2** colloq. short sleep. □ **wink at 1** purposely avoid seeing. **2** connive at (a wrongdoing, etc.). □□ **wink′er** n.

win·ner /wínər/ n. person, racehorse, etc., that wins.

win·ning /wíning/ • adj. **1** having or bringing victory or an advantage. **2** attractive; persuasive. • n. (in pl.) money won. □□ **win′ning·ly** adv. **win′ning·ness** n.

win·now /wínō/ v.tr. **1** blow (grain) free of chaff, etc. **2** get rid of (chaff, etc.) from grain. **3** sift; separate; examine. □□ **win′now·er** n. (in senses 1, 2).

wi·no /wínō/ n. (pl. **-nos**) sl. alcoholic.

win·some /wínsəm/ adj. attractive; engaging. □□ **win′some·ly** adv. **win′some·ness** n.

win·ter /wíntər/ • n. **1** coldest season of the year, in the northern hemisphere from December to February and in the southern hemisphere from June to August. **2** Astron. period from the winter solstice to the vernal equinox. **3** bleak or lifeless period or region, etc. (esp. of a person's age: a man of fifty winters). • adj. characteristic of or suitable for winter. • v.intr. pass the winter. □ **winter solstice** see SOLSTICE. □□ **win′ter·er** n. **win′ter·less** adj.

win·ter·green /wíntərgreen/ n. evergreen plant with red berries, source of all aromatic flavoring oil.

win·ter·ize /wíntərīz/ v.tr. adapt for operation or use in cold weather. □□ **win·ter·i·za′tion** n.

win·ter·time /wíntərtīm/ n. season of winter.

win·try /wíntree/ adj. (also **win·ter·y** /-təree/) (**win·tri·er, win·tri·est**) **1** characteristic of winter. **2** (of a smile, greeting, etc.) lacking warmth or enthusiasm. □□ **win′tri·ly** adv. **win′tri·ness** n.

wipe /wīp/ • v.tr. **1** clean or dry by rubbing. **2** rub (a cloth) over a surface. **3 a** spread or remove by wiping. **b** remove or eliminate completely. • n. **1** act of wiping. **2** piece of material for wiping. □ **wipe out 1** destroy; annihilate. **2** sl. murder. **wiped out** adj. sl. tired out; exhausted. □□ **wipe′a·ble** adj. **wip′er** n.

wire /wīr/ • n. **1 a** metal drawn out into a thread

or thin flexible rod. **b** piece of this. **c** (*attrib.*) made of wire. **2** telegram or cablegram. ● *v.tr.* **1** provide, attach, fasten, strengthen, etc., with wire. **2** *Electr.* install electrical circuits in. **3** *colloq.* telegraph. **wire service** business that gathers news and distributes it to subscribers, usu. newspapers. □□ **wir′er** *n.*

wire·haired /wírhaird/ *adj.* (esp. of a dog) having stiff or wiry hair.

wire·less /wírlis/ *adj.* operating without wires, esp. by electromagnetic waves.

wire·tap /wírtap/ *v.* (**–tapped, –tap·ping**) **1** *intr.* connect a listening device to (a telephone or telegraph line, etc.) to listen to a call or transmission. **2** *tr.* obtain (information, etc.) by wiretapping. □□ **wire′tap·per** *n.* **wire′tap·ping** *n.*

wir·ing /wíring/ *n.* system or installation of wires providing electrical circuits.

wir·y /wíree/ *adj.* (**wir·i·er, wir·i·est**) **1** tough and flexible as wire. **2** (of a person) thin and sinewy. □□ **wir′i·ly** *adv.* **wir′i·ness** *n.*

Wis. *abbr.* Wisconsin.

wis·dom /wízdəm/ *n.* **1** state of being wise. **2** experience and knowledge together with the power of applying them. **3** sagacity; prudence; common sense. **4** wise sayings, thoughts, etc. □ **wisdom tooth** each of four hindmost molars not usu. cut before 20 years of age.

wise[1] /wíz/ ● *adj.* **1** having, showing, or dictated by wisdom. **2** prudent; sensible. **3** having knowledge. **4** suggestive of wisdom. **5** *colloq.* **a** crafty. **b** having (usu. confidential) information (about). ● *v.* (foll. by *up*) *colloq.* **1** become aware of. **2** inform (a person about). □ **wise guy** *colloq.* know-it-all. □□ **wise′ly** *adv.*

wise[2] /wíz/ *n. archaic* way, manner, or degree (*in solemn wise*). □ **in no wise** not at all.

-wise /wíz/ *suffix* forming adjectives and adverbs of manner (*crosswise; lengthwise*) or respect (*moneywise*) (cf. **-WAYS**).

wise·a·cre /wízaykər/ *n.* person who affects a wise manner; wise guy.

wise·crack /wízkrak/ *colloq.* ● *n.* smart pithy remark. ● *v.intr.* make a wisecrack. □□ **wise′crack·er** *n.*

wish /wish/ ● *v.* **1** *intr.* (often foll. by *for*) have or express a desire or aspiration for. **2** *tr.* have as a desire or aspiration. **3** *tr.* want or demand. **4** *tr.* express one's hopes for. ● *n.* **1 a** desire, request, or aspiration. **b** expression of this. **2** thing desired. □□ **wish′er** *n.* (in sense 4 of *v.*); (also in *comb.*).

wish·bone /wíshbōn/ *n.* forked bone between the neck and breast of a fowl.

wish·ful /wíshfŏŏl/ *adj.* desiring. □□ **wish′ful·ly** *adv.* **wish′ful·ness** *n.*

wish·y-wash·y /wísheewóshee, –wáwshee/ *adj.* **1** feeble, insipid, or indecisive in quality or character. **2** weak; watery.

wisp /wisp/ *n.* **1** small, bundle or twist of straw, etc. **2** small, separate quantity of smoke, hair, etc. **3** small, thin person, etc. □□ **wisp′y** *adj.* (**wisp·i·er, wisp·i·est**) **wisp′i·ly** *adv.* **wisp′i·ness** *n.*

wis·te·ri·a /wistéereeə/ *n.* (also **wis·tar·i·a** /–stáiriə/) climbing plant with hanging racemes of blue, purple, or white flowers.

wist·ful /wístfŏŏl/ *adj.* yearningly or mournfully expectant. □□ **wist′ful·ly** *adv.* **wist′ful·ness** *n.*

wit[1] /wit/ *n.* **1** (in *sing.* or *pl.*) intelligence; quick understanding. **2 a** quick, unexpected, and humorous combining or contrasting of ideas or expressions. **b** power of giving intellectual pleasure by this. **3** person possessing such a power. □ **at one's wit's** (or **wits'**) **end** utterly at a loss or in despair. □□ **wit′ted** *adj.* (in sense 1); (also in *comb.*).

wit[2] /wit/ *v.* (*1st & 3rd sing. present* **wot** /wot/; *past* and *past part.* **wist**) *archaic* know. □ **to wit** namely.

witch /wich/ *n.* **1** sorceress, esp. a woman supposed to have dealings with the devil or evil spirits. **2** hag. **3** fascinating girl or woman. □ **witch doctor** tribal magician of primitive people. **witch hazel 1** American shrub with bark yielding an astringent lotion. **2** this lotion. **witch·hunt** campaign directed against a particular group of those holding unpopular or unorthodox views, esp. communists. □□ **witch′ing** *adj.* **witch′like** *adj.*

witch·craft /wíchkraft/ *n.* use of magic; sorcery.

witch·er·y /wíchəree/ *n.* **1** WITCHCRAFT. **2** power exercised by beauty or eloquence or the like.

with /with, with/ *prep.* expressing: **1** instrument or means used (*cut with a knife*). **2** association or company (*lives with his mother*). **3** cause (*shiver with fear*). **4** possession (*vase with handles*). **5** circumstances (*sleep with the window open*). **6** manner (*behaved with dignity*). **7** reference or regard (*how are things with you?*). □ **with-it** *adj. colloq.* in step with the times, fashion, etc. **with that** thereupon.

with·al /witháwl, with–/ *archaic adv.* moreover; as well; at the same time.

with·draw /withdráw, with–/ *v.* (*past* **with·drew** /–drŏŏ/; *past part.* **with·drawn** /–dráwn/) **1** *tr.* pull or take aside or back. **2** *tr.* discontinue; cancel; retract. **3** *tr.* remove; take away. **4** *tr.* take (money) out of an account. **5** *intr.* retire or go away; move away or back. **6** *intr.* (as **withdrawn** *adj.*) abnormally shy and unsociable. □□ **with·draw′er** *n.*

with·draw·al /withdráwəl, with–/ *n.* **1** act or instance of withdrawing or being withdrawn. **2** process of ceasing to take addictive drugs.

withe /with, with, with/ *n.* tough, flexible shoot, esp. of willow, used for binding, basketwork, etc.

with·er /withər/ *v.* **1** *tr.* & *intr.* make or become dry and shriveled. **2** *tr.* & *intr.* deprive of or lose vigor, vitality, freshness, or importance. **3** *tr.* **a** blight with scorn, etc. **b** (as **withering** *adj.*) scornful (*withering look*). □□ **with′er·ing·ly** *adv.*

with·ers /withərz/ *n.pl.* ridge between a horse's shoulder blades.

with·hold /with-hóld, with–/ *v.tr.* (*past* and *past part.* **–held** /–héld/) **1** hold back; restrain. **2** refuse to give, grant, or allow. **3** deduct, esp. from a paycheck. □□ **with·hold′er** *n.*

with·in /within, with–/ ● *adv. archaic* or *literary* **1** inside; internally. **2** indoors. **3** in spirit (*make me pure within*). ● *prep.* **1** inside; enclosed or contained by. **2 a** not beyond or exceeding. **b** not transgressing. **3** not further off than. ● *n.* inside part of a building, etc.

with·out /withówt, with–/ ● *prep.* **1** not having, feeling, or showing. **2** with freedom from. **3** in the absence of. **4** with neglect or avoidance of. **5** *archaic* outside. ● *adv. archaic* or *literary* **1** outside. **2** out of doors. ● *n.* outside part of a building, etc. ● *conj. dial.* unless (*the dog won't eat without you give him some meat*).

with·stand /withstánd, with–/ v. (past and past part. **–stood** /–sto͞od/) **1** tr. oppose; hold out against. **2** intr. make opposition; offer resistance. □□ **with·stand′er** n.

wit·less /wítlis/ adj. **1** foolish; stupid. **2** crazy. □□ **wit′less·ly** adv. **wit′less·ness** n.

wit·ness /wítnis/ • n. **1** EYEWITNESS. **2 a** person giving sworn testimony. **b** person attesting another's signature to a document. **3** testimony; confirming evidence; confirmation. • v. **1** tr. be a witness of (an event, etc.). **2** tr. be witness to the authenticity of. **3** tr. & intr. give or serve as evidence or an indication of. □ **bear witness to** (or **of**) attest the truth of.

wit·ti·cism /wítisizəm/ n. witty remark.

wit·ty /wítee/ adj. (**wit·ti·er, wit·ti·est**) showing verbal wit. □□ **wit′ti·ly** adv. **wit′ti·ness** n.

wives pl. of WIFE.

wiz·ard /wízərd/ n. **1** sorcerer; magician. **2** person of remarkable powers; genius. □□ **wiz′ard·ly** adj. **wiz′ard·ry** n.

wiz·ened /wízənd/ adj. (also **wiz′en**) shriveled-looking.

wob·ble /wóbəl/ • v. **1 a** intr. sway or vibrate unsteadily from side to side. **b** tr. cause to do this. **2** intr. stand or go unsteadily; stagger. **3** intr. waver; vacillate. **4** intr. (of the voice or sound) quaver; pulsate. • n. **1** wobbling movement. **2** instance of vacillation or pulsation. □□ **wob′bler** n. **wob′bli·ness** n. **wob′bly** adj. (**wob·bli·er, wob·bli·est**).

woe /wō/ n. archaic or literary **1** affliction; bitter grief. **2** (in pl.) calamities; troubles.

woe·be·gone /wóbigon, –gawn/ adj. dismal-looking.

woe·ful /wófool/ adj. **1** sorrowful. **2** causing sorrow or affliction. **3** wretched. □□ **woe′ful·ly** adv. **woe′ful·ness** n.

wok /wok/ n. bowl-shaped metal pan used in esp. Chinese cooking.

woke past of WAKE¹.

wok·en past part. of WAKE¹.

wolf /woolf/ • n. (pl. **wolves** /woolvz/) **1** wild, flesh-eating mammal related to the dog, and hunting in packs. **2** sl. man given to seducing women. • v.tr. (often foll. by down) devour (food) greedily. □ **cry wolf** raise repeated false alarms (so that a genuine one is disregarded). □□ **wolf′ish** adj. **wolf′ish·ly** adv. **wolf′like** adj. & adv.

wolf·hound /woolfhownd/ n. borzoi or other dog of a kind used orig. to hunt wolves.

wolf·ram /woolfrəm/ n. TUNGSTEN.

wol·ver·ine /woolvəreen/ n. voracious carnivorous mammal of the weasel family.

wom·an /wooman/ n. (pl. **wom·en** /wímin/) **1** adult human female. **2** the female sex. **3** (prec. by the) emotions or characteristics traditionally associated with women (brought out the woman in him). **4** (comb. form) woman of a specified nationality, profession, skill, etc. (Englishwoman; horsewoman; congresswoman). □ **women's lib** colloq. = women's liberation. **women's liberation** liberation of women from inequalities and subservient status in relation to men, and elimination of attitudes causing these. □□ **wom′an·less** adj. **wom′an·like** adj.

wom·an·hood /woomanhood/ n. **1** female maturity. **2** womanly instinct. **3** womankind.

wom·an·ish /wooménish/ adj. usu. derog. (of

a man) effeminate; unmanly. □□ **wom′an·ish·ly** adv. **wom′an·ish·ness** n.

wom·an·ize /woomanīz/ v. **1** intr. chase after women; philander. **2** tr. make womanish. □□ **wom′an·iz·er** n.

wom·an·kind /woomankīnd/ n. (also **wom·en·kind** /wímin–/) women in general.

wom·an·ly /woomanlee/ adj. having or showing qualities traditionally associated with women; not masculine nor girlish. □□ **wom′an·li·ness** n.

womb /woom/ n. organ of conception and gestation in a woman and other female mammals; uterus. □□ **womb′like** adj.

wom·bat /wómbat/ n. burrowing, plant-eating Australian marsupial resembling a small bear, with short legs.

wom·en pl. of WOMAN.

wom·en·folk /wíminfōk/ n. **1** women in general. **2** the women in a family.

wom·en·kind var. of WOMANKIND.

won past and past part. of WIN.

won·der /wúndər/ • n. **1** emotion excited by what is unexpected, unfamiliar, or inexplicable. **2** strange or remarkable person or thing; specimen, event, etc. **3** (attrib.) having marvelous or amazing properties, etc. (wonder drug). • v. **1** intr. be filled with wonder. **2** tr. be surprised to find. **3** tr. desire or be curious to know. □□ **won′der·er** n.

won·der·ful /wúndərfool/ adj. very remarkable or admirable. □□ **won′der·ful·ly** adv. **won′der·ful·ness** n.

won·der·land /wúndərland/ n. **1** enchanted place. **2** land of surprises or marvels.

won·der·ment /wúndərmənt/ n. surprise; awe.

won·drous /wúndrəs/ poet. • adj. wonderful. • adv. archaic or literary wonderfully (wondrous kind). □□ **won′drous·ly** adv. **won′drous·ness** n.

wont /wōnt, wawnt, wunt/ • predic.adj. archaic or literary accustomed (as we were wont to say). • n. formal or joc. what is customary; one's habit (as is my wont).

won't /wōnt/ contr. will not.

wont·ed /wóntid, wáwn–, wún–/ attrib.adj. habitual; accustomed; usual.

woo /woo/ v.tr. (**woos, wooed**) **1** court; seek the love of. **2** try to win. **3** seek the favor or support of. □□ **woo′a·ble** adj. **woo′er** n.

wood /wood/ n. **1 a** hard fibrous material that forms the main substance of the trunk or branches of a tree or shrub. **b** this cut for lumber, fuel, etc. **2** (in sing. or pl.) growing trees densely occupying a tract of land. **3** wooden-headed golf club. □ **out of the woods** (or **wood**) out of danger or difficulty. **wood alcohol** methanol. **wood pulp** wood fiber reduced to pulp as raw material for paper. □□ **wood′ed** adj. **wood′less** adj.

wood·bine /woodbīn/ n. **1** wild honeysuckle. **2** Virginia creeper.

wood·chuck /woodchuk/ n. reddish-brown and gray N. American marmot.

wood·cock /woodkok/ n. (pl. same) game bird related to the snipe.

wood·craft /woodkraft/ n. **1** skill in woodwork. **2** knowledge of woodland, esp. in camping, scouting, etc.

wood·cut /woodkut/ n. **1** relief cut on a block of wood. **2** print made from this.

wood·cut·ter /wo͝odkutər/ *n.* person who cuts wood.

wood·en /wo͝od'n/ *adj.* **1** made of or like wood. **2 a** stiff, clumsy. **b** expressionless. □□ **wood'en·ly** *adv.* **wood'en·ness** *n.*

wood·land /wo͝odlənd/ *n.* wooded country, woods (often *attrib.: woodland scenery*). □□ **wood'land·er** *n.*

wood·peck·er /wo͝odpekər/ *n.* bird that taps tree trunks with its beak in search of insects.

wood·pile /wo͝odpīl/ *n.* pile of wood, esp. for fuel.

wood·shed /wo͝odshed/ *n.* shed where wood for fuel is stored.

woods·man /wo͝odzmən/ *n.* (*pl.* **–men**) person who lives in or is familiar with woodland.

wood·sy /wo͝odzee/ *adj.* like or characteristic of woods.

wood·wind /wo͝odwind/ *n.* (often *attrib.*) **1** (*collect.*) wind instruments that were orig. made mostly of wood, e.g., flute and clarinet. **2** (usu. in *pl.*) individual instrument of this kind or its player (*the woodwinds are out of tune*).

wood·work /wo͝odwərk/ *n.* **1** making of things in wood. **2** things made of wood, esp. paneling, moldings, etc. □□ **wood'work·er** *n.* **wood'work·ing** *n.*

wood·y /wo͝odee/ *adj.* (**wood·i·er, wood·i·est**) **1** wooded; abounding in woods. **2** like or of wood (*woody tissue*). □□ **wood'i·ness** *n.*

woof[1] /wo͝of/ • *n.* gruff bark of a dog. • *v.intr.* give a woof.

woof[2] /wo͝of, wo͞of/ *n.* = WEFT.

woof·er /wo͝ofər/ *n.* loudspeaker designed to reproduce low frequencies (cf. TWEETER).

wool /wo͝ol/ *n.* **1** fine, soft, wavy hair from the fleece of sheep, goats, etc. **2 a** yarn produced from this hair. **b** cloth or clothing made from it. **3** woollike substances (*steel wool*). □□ **wool'like** *adj.*

wool·en /wo͝olən/ (also **wool'len**) • *adj.* made of wool. • *n.* (in *pl.*) woolen garments.

wool·ly /wo͝olee/ (also **wool'y**) *adj.* (**wool·li·er, wool·li·est**) **1** bearing or naturally covered with wool or woollike hair. **2** resembling or suggesting wool (*woolly clouds*). **3** vague or confused. □□ **wool'li·ness** *n.*

woo·zy /wo͝ozee/ *adj.* (**woo·zi·er, woo·zi·est**) *colloq.* **1** dizzy or unsteady. **2** slightly drunk. □□ **woo'zi·ly** *adv.* **woo'zi·ness** *n.*

word /wərd/ • *n.* **1** sound or combination of sounds forming a meaningful element of speech, writing, or printing. **2** speech, esp. as distinct from action. **3** one's promise or assurance. **4** (in *sing.* or *pl.*) remark or conversation. **5** (in *pl.*) text of a song or an actor's part. **6** (in *pl.*) angry talk. **7** news; intelligence; message. **8** command. • *v.tr.* put into words; select words to express. □ **in other words** expressing the same thing differently. **in so many words** explicitly or bluntly. **in a** (or **one**) **word** briefly. **the Word** (or **Word of God**) the Bible. **word of honor** promise or assurance. **word of mouth** speech (only). **word-of-mouth** verbal; unwritten. **word processor** computer software program for electronically storing text entered from a keyboard, incorporating corrections, and providing a printout. □□ **word'age** *n.* **word'less** *adj.* **word'less·ly** *adv.* **word'less·ness** *n.*

word·ing /wərding/ *n.* **1** form of words used. **2** way in which something is expressed.

word·play /wərdplay/ *n.* witty use of words, esp. punning.

word·y /wərdee/ *adj.* (**word·i·er, word·i·est**) using or expressed in too many words; verbose. □□ **word'i·ly** *adv.* **word'i·ness** *n.*

wore *past* of WEAR.

work /wərk/ • *n.* **1** application of mental or physical effort to a purpose; use of energy. **2 a** task to be undertaken. **b** materials for this. **3** thing done or made by work; result of an action. **4** employment or occupation. **5 a** literary or musical composition. **b** (in *pl.*) all such by an author or composer, etc. **6** (in *pl.*) operative part of a clock or machine. **7** (in *pl.*) *colloq.* all that is available; everything needed. **8** (in *pl.*) operations of building or repair. **9** (in *pl.*; often treated as *sing.*) factory. **10** (usu. in *pl.*) *Theol.* meritorious act. • *v.* (*past* and *past part.* **worked** or (esp. as *adj.*) **wrought**) **1** *intr.* do work; be engaged in bodily or mental activity. **2** *intr.* **a** be employed in certain work. **b** (foll. by *with*) be the coworker of (a person). **3** *intr.* (foll. by *in*) be a craftsman (in a material). **4** *intr.* operate or function, esp. effectively. **5** *tr.* carry on, manage, or control. **6** *tr.* **a** cause to toil (*works the staff very hard*). **b** cultivate (land). **7** *tr.* bring about; produce as a result. **8** *tr.* knead; bring to a desired shape or consistency. **9** *tr.* do, or make by, needlework, etc. **10** *tr.* & *intr.* (cause to) make (one's way) gradually or with difficulty. **11** *intr.* gradually become (loose, etc.) by constant movement. **12** *tr.* artificially excite (*worked themselves into a rage*). **13** *tr.* **a** purchase with one's labor instead of money. **b** obtain by labor the money for. **14** *intr.* (foll. by *on, upon*) have influence. **15** *intr.* ferment. □ **at work** in action. **work off** get rid of by work or activity. **work out 1** solve or calculate. **2** have a result. **3** provide for the details of. **4** engage in physical exercise or training. **work over 1** examine thoroughly. **2** *colloq.* treat with violence. **work sheet 1** paper for recording work done or in progress. **2** paper listing questions or activities for students, etc., to work through. **work up 1** develop or advance gradually. **2** elaborate or excite by degrees. □□ **work'less** *adj.*

work·a·ble /wərkəbəl/ *adj.* **1** that can be worked or will work. **2** that is practicable; feasible. □□ **work·a·bil'i·ty** *n.* **work'a·ble·ness** *n.* **work'a·bly** *adv.*

work·a·day /wərkəday/ *adj.* ordinary; everyday; practical.

work·a·hol·ic /wərkəhólik/ *n.* *colloq.* person addicted to working.

work·bench /wərkbench/ *n.* bench for doing mechanical or practical work, esp. carpentry.

work·day /wərkday/ *n.* day on which work is usually done.

work·er /wərkər/ *n.* **1** person who works, esp. a manual or industrial employee. **2** neuter bee or ant.

work·force /wərkfawrs/ *n.* **1** workers engaged or available in an industry, etc. **2** number of such workers.

work·horse /wərk-hawrs/ *n.* horse, person, or machine that performs hard work.

work·ing /wərking/ • *adj.* **1** engaged in work. **2** functioning or able to function. • *n.* activity of work. □ **working class** class of people who are employed for wages, esp. in manual or industrial work. **working-class** *adj.* of the working class.

work·load /wórklōd/ *n.* amount of work to be done.

work·man /wórkmən/ *n.* (*pl.* **-men**) person employed to do manual labor.

work·man·like /wórkmənlīk/ *adj.* characteristic of a good workman; showing practiced skill.

work·man·ship /wórkmənship/ *n.* degree of skill in doing a task or of finish in the product made.

work·out /wórkowt/ *n.* session of physical exercise or training.

work·place /wórkplays/ *n.* place at which a person works.

work·shop /wórkshop/ *n.* **1** room or building in which goods are manufactured. **2** meeting for concerted discussion or activity.

work·sta·tion /wórkstayshən/ *n.* **1** location of a stage in a manufacturing process. **2** computer terminal or the desk, etc., where this is located.

world /wərld/ *n.* **1 a** the earth, or a planetary body like it. **b** its countries and their inhabitants. **c** all people; the earth as known or in some particular respect. **2** the universe or all that exists; everything. **3** secular interests and affairs. **4** human affairs; active life. **5** a specified class, time, domain, or sphere of activity (*world of baseball*). **6** vast amount. □ **world-class** of a quality or standard regarded as high throughout the world. **World Series** the championship for U.S. major-league baseball teams. **world-weary** weary of the world and life in it. **World Wide Web** global computer network for exchange of text, hypertext, graphics, audio, etc. ¶ Abbr.: **WWW**.

world·ly /wórldlee/ *adj.* (**world·li·er, world·li·est**) **1** temporal or earthly. **2** sophisticated. □ **worldly-wise** having worldly wisdom. □□ **world´li·ness** *n.*

world·wide /wórldwīd/ • *adj.* affecting, occurring, or known in all parts of the world. • *adv.* throughout the world.

worm /wərm/ • *n.* **1** any of various types of creeping or burrowing invertebrate animals with long, slender bodies and no limbs. **2** long, slender larva of an insect. **3** (in *pl.*) intestinal or other internal parasites. **4** insignificant or contemptible person. **5** spiral part of a screw. • *v.* **1** *intr.* & *tr.* (often *refl.*) move with a crawling motion. **2** *intr.* & *refl.* insinuate oneself into a person's favor, confidence, etc. **3** *tr.* (foll. by *out*) obtain by cunning persistence. **4** *tr.* rid of intestinal worms. □ **worm gear** arrangement of a toothed wheel worked by a revolving spiral. □□ **worm´er** *n.* **worm´i·ness** *n.* **worm´like** *adj.* **worm·y** *adj.*

WORM GEAR

worm·wood /wórmwŏŏd/ *n.* **1** woody plant with a bitter aromatic taste. **2** bitter mortification or a source of this.

worn /wawrn/ *past part.* of WEAR. • *adj.* **1** damaged by use or wear. **2** looking tired and exhausted. **3** (in full **well-worn**) (of a joke, etc.) stale; often heard.

wor·ri·some /wóreesəm, wúr–/ *adj.* causing or apt to cause worry or distress. □□ **wor´ri·some·ly** *adv.*

wor·ry /wóree, wúr–/ • *v.* (**-ries, -ried**) **1** *intr.* give way to anxiety. **2** *tr.* harass; be a trouble or anxiety to. **3** *tr.* (of a dog, etc.) shake or pull about with the teeth. **4** (as **worried** *adj.*) **a** uneasy; troubled in the mind. **b** suggesting worry (*worried look*). • *n.* (*pl.* **-ries**) **1** thing that causes anxiety. **2** disturbed state of mind; anxiety. □□ **wor´ried·ly** *adv.* **wor´ri·er** *n.* **wor´ry·ing·ly** *adv.*

wor·ry·wart /wóreewawrt, wúr–/ *n. colloq.* person who habitually worries unduly.

worse /wərs/ • *adj.* (*compar.* of BAD) **1** more bad. **2** (*predic.*) in or into worse health or a worse condition. • *adv.* (*compar.* of BADLY) more badly or more ill. • *n.* **1** worse thing or things. **2** worse condition (*change for the worse*). □ **none the worse** (often foll. by *for*) not adversely affected (by). **worse off** in a worse (esp. financial) position.

wors·en /wórsn/ *v.* make or become worse.

wor·ship /wórship/ • *n.* **1 a** homage or reverence paid to a deity. **b** acts, rites, or ceremonies of worship. **2** adoration or devotion (*worship of wealth*). • *v.* (**wor·shiped, wor·ship·ing; wor·shipped, wor·ship·ping**) **1** *tr.* adore as divine; honor with religious rites. **2** *tr.* idolize. **3** *intr.* attend public worship. □□ **wor´ship·er** *n.* (or **wor´ship·per**).

worst /wərst/ • *adj.* (*superl.* of BAD) most bad. • *adv.* (*superl.* of BADLY) most badly. • *n.* worst part, event, circumstance, or possibility. • *v. tr.* get the better of; defeat. □ **at worst** (or **the worst**) in the worst possible case. **if worst comes to worst** if the worst happens.

wors·ted /wŏŏstid, wór–/ *n.* **1** fine smooth yarn spun from combed long, stapled wool. **2** fabric made from this.

wort /wərt, wawrt/ *n.* infusion of malt which after fermentation becomes beer.

worth /wərth/ • *predic. adj.* **1** of a value equivalent to. **2** such as to justify or repay; deserving. **3** possessing or having property amounting to. • *n.* **1** what a person or thing is worth; the (usu. specified) merit of. **2** equivalent of money in a commodity. □ **for what it is worth** without a guarantee of its truth or value.

worth·less /wórthlis/ *adj.* without value or merit. □□ **worth´less·ly** *adv.* **worth´less·ness** *n.*

worth·while /wórth-hwíl, wíl/ *adj.* worth the time or effort spent; of value or importance. □□ **worth´while·ness** *n.*

¶ **Worth while** (two words) is used only in the predicate, e.g., *Nobody thought it worth while to call the police,* and means 'worth the time or effort.' **Worthwhile** (one word) also has this meaning, but can be used both predicatively and attributively, e.g., *Would this investment be worthwhile?* (predicative), or *He was a worthwhile candidate for the office* (attributive).

wor·thy /wórthee/ • *adj.* (**wor·thi·er, wor·thi·**

est) **1** estimable; deserving respect. **2** entitled to. **3** deserving. • *n.* (*pl.* **–thies**) worthy person. □□ **wor'thi·ly** *adv.* **wor'thi·ness** *n.*

-worthy /wərthee/ *comb. form* forming adjectives meaning: **1** deserving of. **2** suitable for.

would /wŏŏd, when unstressed wəd/ *v.aux.* (*3rd sing.* **would**) *past* of WILL¹, used esp.: **1 a** in reported speech (*he said he would be home by evening*). **b** to express the conditional mood (*they would have been killed if they had gone*). **2** to express habitual action (*would wait every evening*). **3** to express a question or polite request (*would you come in, please?*). **4** to express consent (*they would not help*). □ **would-be** often *derog.* desiring or aspiring to be.
¶ See note at SHALL.

would·n't /wŏŏd'nt/ *contr.* would not.

wound¹ /wŏŏnd/ • *n.* **1** injury done to living tissue by a cut or blow, etc. **2** injury to a person's reputation or a pain inflicted on a person's feelings. • *v.tr.* inflict a wound on. □□ **wound'ing·ly** *adv.* **wound'less** *adj.*

wound² *past* and *past part.* of WIND².

wove *past* of WEAVE¹.

wo·ven *past part.* of WEAVE¹.

wow /wow/ • *int.* expressing astonishment or admiration. • *n. sl.* sensational success. • *v.tr. sl.* impress or excite greatly.

w.p.m. *abbr.* words per minute.

wrack /rak/ *n.* = RACK².

wraith /rayth/ *n.* ghost. □□ **wraith'like** *adj.*

wran·gle /ránggəl/ • *n.* noisy argument, altercation, or dispute. • *v.* **1** *intr.* engage in a wrangle. **2** *tr.* herd (cattle).

wran·gler /rángg   lər/ *n.* cowboy.

wrap /rap/ • *v.tr.* (**wrapped, wrap·ping**) **1** envelop in folded or soft encircling material. **2** arrange or draw (a pliant covering) around. • *n.* **1** shawl, scarf, etc. **2** material used for wrapping. □ **under wraps** in secrecy. **wrapped up in** engrossed or absorbed in. **wrap up** finish off.

wrap·a·round /rápərownd/ • *adj.* **1** (esp. of clothing) designed to wrap around. **2** curving or extending around at the edges. • *n.* anything that wraps around.

wrap·per /rápər/ *n.* **1** that which wraps; cover. **2** loose enveloping robe or gown.

wrap·ping /ráping/ *n.* (esp. in *pl.*) material used to wrap. □ **wrapping paper** strong or decorative paper for wrapping packages.

wrasse /ras/ *n.* any of several species of bright-colored marine fish with thick lips and strong teeth.

wrath /rath, roth, rawth/ *n. literary* extreme anger. □□ **wrath'ful** *adj.* **wrath'ful·ly** *adv.* **wrath'ful·ness** *n.*

wreak /reek/ *v.tr.* **1** express (vengeance or one's anger, etc.). **2** cause (damage, etc.). □□ **wreak'er** *n.*

wreath /reeth/ *n.* (*pl.* **wreaths** /reethz, reeths/) **1** flowers or leaves fastened in a ring. **2** curl or ring of smoke or cloud.

wreathe /reeth/ *v.* **1** *tr.* encircle as, with, or like a wreath. **2** *intr.* (of smoke, etc.) move in the shape of wreaths. **3** *tr.* form into a wreath.

wreck /rek/ • *n.* **1** destruction or disablement, esp. of a ship or automobile. **2** ship or automobile, etc., that has suffered a wreck. **3** greatly damaged thing. **4** *colloq.* dilapidated car. • *v.* **1**
tr. cause the wreck of. **2** *tr.* completely ruin (hopes, chances, etc.). **3** *intr.* suffer a wreck. **4** *tr.* (as **wrecked** *adj.*) involved in a shipwreck.

wreck·age /rékij/ *n.* **1** wrecked material. **2** remnants of a wreck. **3** action of wrecking.

wreck·er /rékər/ *n.* **1** person or thing that wrecks or destroys. **2** esp. *hist.* person on the shore who tries to bring about a shipwreck in order to plunder or profit by the wreckage. **3** person who removes wrecks or breaks them up for spares and scrap. **4** vehicle used to remove disabled cars, etc.

wren /ren/ *n.* small, usu. brown, songbird having an erect tail.

wrench /rench/ • *n.* **1** violent twist or oblique pull or tearing off. **2** tool for gripping and turning nuts, etc. **3** painful uprooting or parting. • *v.tr.* **1 a** twist or pull violently around or sideways. **b** injure (a limb, etc.) by undue straining; sprain. **2** pull off with a wrench. **3** distort (facts) to suit a theory, etc.

socket

allen

open-end

adjustable

WRENCH, 2

wrest /rest/ • *v.tr.* **1** wrench away from a person's grasp. **2** obtain by effort or with difficulty.

wres·tle /résəl/ • *n.* **1** contest in which two opponents grapple and try to throw each other to the ground, esp. as an athletic sport. **2** hard struggle. • *v.* **1** *intr.* take part in a wrestle. **2** *tr.* fight (a person) in a wrestle. **3** *intr.* struggle; contend. □□ **wres'tler** *n.* **wres'tling** *n.*

wretch /rech/ *n.* **1** unfortunate or pitiable person. **2** reprehensible or contemptible person.

wretch·ed /réchid/ *adj.* (**wretch·ed·er, wretch·ed·est**) **1** unhappy or miserable. **2** of bad quality or no merit; contemptible. **3** unsatisfactory; displeasing. □□ **wretch'ed·ly** *adv.* **wretch'ed·ness** *n.*

wrig·gle /rígəl/ • *v.* **1** *intr.* twist or turn with short, writhing movements. **2** *intr.* make wriggling motions. **3** *tr. & intr.* move or go in this way. **4** *intr.* practice evasion. • *n.* act of wriggling. □□ **wrig'gler** *n.* **wrig'gly** *adj.* (**wrig·gli·er, wrig·gli·est**).

wright /rīt/ *n.* (usu. in *comb.*) maker or builder (*playwright; wheelwright*).

wring /ring/ • *v.tr.* (*past* and *past part.* **wrung** /rung/) **1 a** squeeze tightly. **b** squeeze and twist, esp. to remove liquid. **2** distress or torture. **3** extract by squeezing. **4** obtain by pressure or importunity; extort. • *n.* act of wringing; squeeze.

wring·er /ríngər/ n. 1 device for wringing water from washed clothes, etc. 2 difficult ordeal (*that exam put me through the wringer*).

wrin·kle /ríngkəl/ • n. 1 slight crease in the skin such as is produced by age. 2 similar mark in another flexible surface. • v. 1 tr. make wrinkles in. 2 intr. form wrinkles; become marked with wrinkles. □□ **wrin′kly** adj. (**wrin·kli·er, wrin·kli·est**).

wrist /rist/ n. 1 joint connecting the hand with the forearm. 2 part of a garment covering the wrist.

wrist·watch /rístwoch/ n. small watch worn on the wrist.

writ /rit/ n. legal document commanding or forbidding action.

write /rīt/ v. (*past* **wrote** /rōt/; *past part.* **writ·ten** /rít'n/) 1 intr. mark paper or some other surface by means of a pen, pencil, etc., with symbols, letters, or words. 2 tr. form or mark (such symbols, etc.). 3 tr. fill or complete (a form, check, etc.). 4 tr. put (data) into a computer store. 5 tr. compose. 6 intr. (foll. by *to*) write and send a letter (to a recipient). □ **write-in** n. candidate whose name is written on a ballot by a voter. **write off 1** cancel the record of (a bad debt, etc.); acknowledge the loss of. 2 dismiss as insignificant. **write-off** n. thing written off. **write out** write in full or in finished form. **write up** write a full account of. **write-up** n. colloq. written or published account; review.

writ·er /rítər/ n. person who writes, esp. as a profession; author.

writhe /rīth/ • v. 1 intr. twist or roll oneself about in or as if in acute pain. 2 intr. suffer severe mental discomfort or embarrassment. 3 tr. twist (one's body, etc.) about. • n. act of writhing.

writ·ing /ríting/ n. 1 group or sequence of letters or symbols. 2 = HANDWRITING. 3 (usu. in pl.) author's works.

writ·ten *past part.* of WRITE.

wrong /rawng, rong/ • adj. 1 mistaken; not true; in error. 2 unsuitable; less or least desirable. 3 contrary to law or morality. 4 amiss; out of order. • adv. in a wrong manner or direction;

with an incorrect result. • n. 1 what is morally wrong. 2 injustice. • v. tr. 1 treat unjustly; do wrong to. 2 mistakenly attribute bad motives to; discredit. □ **in the wrong** responsible for a quarrel, mistake, or offense. **wrong side out** inside out. □□ **wrong′ly** adv.

wrong·do·er /ráwngdōoər, róng–/ n. person who behaves immorally or illegally. □□ **wrong′do·ing** n.

wrong·ful /ráwngfool, róng–/ adj. 1 characterized by unfairness or injustice. 2 contrary to law. □□ **wrong′ful·ly** adv. **wrong′ful·ness** n.

wrong·head·ed /ráwnghedid, róng–/ adj. perverse and obstinate. □□ **wrong′head·ed·ly** adv. **wrong′head·ed·ness** n.

wrote *past* of WRITE.

wrought /rawt/ archaic *past* and *past part.* of WORK. • adj. (of metals) beaten out or shaped by hammering. □ **wrought iron** tough malleable form of iron.

wrung *past* and *past part.* of WRING.

wry /rī/ adj. (**wry·er, wry·est; wri·er, wri·est**) 1 distorted. 2 contorted in disgust, disappointment, or mockery. 3 (of humor) dry and mocking. □□ **wry′ly** adv. **wry′ness** n.

wt. abbr. weight.

wuss /woos/ n. colloq. person seen as a coward or weakling. □□ **wuss′y** adj.

WV abbr. West Virginia (in official postal use).

W.Va. abbr. West Virginia.

WW abbr. World War (I, II).

WWW abbr. World Wide Web.

WY abbr. Wyoming (in official postal use).

Wyo. abbr. Wyoming.

WYSIWYG /wíziwig/ adj. (also **wysiwyg**) *Computing* denoting the representation of text on-screen in a form exactly corresponding to its appearance on a printout (acronym of *what you see is what you get*).

Xx

X[1] /eks/ *n.* (also **x**) (*pl.* **Xs** or **X's**; **x's**) twenty-fourth letter of the alphabet.

X[2] **1** *Rom. num.* ten. **2** extra. **3** extraordinary. **4** cross-shaped symbol esp. used to indicate position (*X marks the spot*) or incorrectness or to symbolize a kiss or a vote, or as the signature of a person who cannot write. **5** (in full **X-rated**) (of a movie) classified as suitable for adults only.

x *symb.* **1** excess. **2** *Math.* unknown quantity or variable. **3** *Math.* horizontal-axis coordinate.

-x /z/ *suffix* forming the plural of many nouns ending in *–u* taken from French (*beaux*; *tableaux*).

X chro·mo·some /éks krṓməsōm/ *n.* sex chromosome of which the number in female cells is twice that in male cells.

Xe *symb. Chem.* xenon.

xe·non /zénon, zḗe–/ *n. Chem.* heavy, colorless, odorless inert gaseous element. ¶ Symb.: **Xe**.

xe·no·pho·bi·a /zénəfṓbeeə, zéenə–/ *n.* deep dislike of foreigners. □□ **xe·no·phobe** /zénəfōb, zéenə–/ *n.* **xe·no·pho'bic** *adj.*

xe·rog·ra·phy /zeerógrəfee/ *n.* dry copying process in which black or colored powder adheres to electrically charged parts of a surface. □□ **xe·ro·graph·ic** /–rəgráfik/ *adj.* **xe·ro·graph'i·cal·ly** *adv.*

Xe·rox /zéeroks/ ● *n. propr.* **1** machine for copying by xerography. **2** copy thus made. ● *v.tr.* (**xerox**) reproduce by this process.

xi /zī, sī, ksee/ *n.* fourteenth letter of the Greek alphabet (Ξ, ν).

-xion /kshən/ *suffix* forming nouns (see -ION) from Latin participial stems ending in -*x* (*fluxion*).

X·mas /krísməs, éksməs/ *n. colloq.* = CHRISTMAS.

X ray /éksray/ (also **x-ray**) ● *n.* **1** (in *pl.*) electromagnetic radiation of short wavelength, able to pass through opaque bodies. **2** photograph made by X rays. ● *v.tr.* photograph, examine, or treat with X rays. ● *adj.* by, like, or of X rays.

xy·lem /zíləm/ *n. Bot.* woody tissue.

xy·lo·phone /zíləfōn/ *n.* musical instrument of graduated wooden or metal bars struck with small wooden hammers. □□ **xy·lo·phon·ic** /–fónik/ *adj.* **xy·lo·phon·ist** /–fōn–/ *n.*

Yy

Y¹ /wī/ *n.* (also **y**) (*pl.* **Ys** or **Y's**; **y's**) twenty-fifth letter of the alphabet.

Y² *abbr.* (also **Y.**) **1** yen. **2** = YMCA, YWCA.

Y³ *symb. Chem.* yttrium.

y *symb. Math.* **1** vertical-axis coordinate. **2** unknown quantity or variable.

y. *abbr.* **1** yard(s). **2** year(s).

-y¹ /ee/ *suffix* forming adjectives: **1** from nouns and adjectives, meaning: full of; having the quality of (*messy*). **2** from verbs, meaning 'inclined to,' 'apt to' (*runny*).

-y² /ee/ *suffix* (also **-ey, -ie**) forming diminutives, pet names, etc. (*nightie; Mickey*).

-y³ /ee/ *suffix* forming nouns denoting: state, condition, or quality (*modesty*).

yacht /yot/ • *n.* **1** sailing vessel for racing, for cruising, etc., esp. for pleasure. • *v.intr.* race or cruise in a yacht. □□ **yacht'ing** *n.*

yachts·man /yótsmən/ *n.* (*pl.* **–men**; *fem.* **yachts·wom·an**, *pl.* **–wom·en**) person who sails yachts.

ya·hoo /yaáhoo/ *n.* coarse, bestial person.

Yah·weh /yaáway, –we/ *n.* (also **Yah·veh** /–vay, –ve/) = JEHOVAH.

yak /yak/ *n.* long-haired, humped Tibetan ox.

yam /yam/ *n.* **1 a** tropical or subtropical climbing plant. **b** edible starchy tuber of this. **2** sweet potato.

yam·mer /yámər/ *colloq.* or *dial.* • *n.* **1** lament, wail, or grumble. **2** voluble talk. • *v.intr.* **1** utter a yammer. **2** talk volubly. □□ **yam'mer·er** *n.*

yang /yang/ *n.* (in Chinese philosophy) active male principle of the universe (cf. YIN).

Yank /yangk/ *n. colloq.* American.

yank /yangk/ *colloq.* • *v.tr.* pull with a jerk. • *n.* sudden hard pull.

Yan·kee /yángkee/ • *n. colloq.* **1** inhabitant of the U.S. **2** inhabitant of New England or one of the other northern states. **3** *hist.* Union soldier in the American Civil War. • *adj.* characteristic of the Yankees.

yap /yap/ • *v.intr.* (**yapped, yap·ping**) **1** bark shrilly. **2** *colloq.* talk noisily, foolishly, or complainingly. • *n.* **1** sound of yapping. **2** *sl.* mouth. □□ **yap'per** *n.*

yard¹ /yaard/ *n.* **1** unit of linear measure equal to 3 feet (0.9144 meter). **2** this length of material. **3** square or cubic yard, esp. (in building) of sand, etc. **4** spar slung across a mast for a sail to hang from.

yard² /yaard/ *n.* **1** piece of ground, esp. attached to a building or used for a particular purpose. **2** lawn and garden area of a house.

yard·age /yaárdij/ *n.* number of yards of material, etc.

yard·arm /yaárdaarm/ *n.* outer extremity of a ship's yard.

yard·stick /yaárdstik/ *n.* **1** standard used for comparison. **2** measuring rod a yard long, usu. divided into inches, etc.

yar·mul·ke /yaármɔlkə, yaáməl–/ *n.* (also **yar'mul·ka**) skullcap worn by Jewish men.

yarn /yaarn/ • *n.* **1** spun thread, esp. for knitting, weaving, etc. **2** *colloq.* long or rambling story or discourse. • *v.intr. colloq.* tell yarns.

yaw /yaw/ • *v.intr.* (of a ship or aircraft, etc.) fail to hold a straight course; go unsteadily. • *n.* yawing of a ship, etc., from its course.

yawl /yawl/ *n.* two-masted sailing vessel with aftermast set astern of the rudder.

yawn /yawn/ • *v.* **1** *intr.* (as a reflex) open the mouth wide and inhale, esp. when sleepy or bored. **2** *intr.* gape; be wide open. **3** *tr.* utter or say with a yawn. • *n.* act of yawning. □□ **yawn'er** *n.* **yawn'ing·ly** *adv.*

yaws /yawz/ *n.pl.* (usu. treated as *sing.*) contagious tropical skin disease with large red swellings.

Yb *symb. Chem.* ytterbium.

Y chro·mo·some /wí-krómɔsōm/ *n.* sex chromosome occurring only in male cells.

yd. *abbr.* (*pl.* **yds.**) yard (measure).

ye¹ /yee/ *pron. archaic pl.* of THOU¹.

ye² /yee/ *adj. pseudo-archaic* = THE (*ye olde tea shoppe*).

yea /yay/ *formal* • *adv.* **1** yes. **2** indeed. • *n.* "yes" vote or voter.

yeah /yeə/ *adv. colloq.* yes.

year /yeer/ *n.* **1** (also **astronomical year, equinoctial year, natural year, solar year, tropical year**) time occupied by the earth in one revolution around the sun, 365 days, 5 hours, 48 minutes, and 46 seconds in length. **2** (also **calendar year, civil year**) period of 365 days (**common year**) or 366 days (see *leap year*) from Jan. 1 to Dec. 31. **3** a period of the same length as this starting at any point (*four years ago*). **b** such a period in terms of a particular activity, etc., occupying its duration (*school year*). **4** (in *pl.*) age or time of life. **5** (usu. in *pl.*) *colloq.* very long time.

year·book /yeerbŏŏk/ *n.* annual publication dealing with events or aspects of the (usu. preceding) year.

year·ling /yeerling/ • *n.* **1** animal between one and two years old. **2** racehorse in the calendar year after the year of foaling. • *adj.* year old (*yearling heifer*).

year·ly /yeerlee/ • *adj.* **1** done, produced, or occurring once a year. **2** of or lasting a year. • *adv.* once a year; from year to year.

yearn /yərn/ *v.intr.* **1** have a strong emotional longing. **2** be filled with compassion or tenderness. □□ **yearn'er** *n.* **yearn'ing** *n.* & *adj.* **yearn'ing·ly** *adv.*

yeast /yeest/ *n.* grayish-yellow fungous substance obtained esp. from fermenting malt liquors and used as a fermenting agent, to raise bread, etc. □□ **yeast'less** *adj.* **yeast'like** *adj.*

yeast·y /yeestee/ *adj.* (**yeast·i·er, yeast·i·est**) **1** frothy or tasting like yeast. **2** in a ferment. **3** light and superficial. □□ **yeast'i·ly** *adv.* **yeast'i·ness** *n.*

yell /yel/ • *n.* **1** loud sharp cry of pain, anger, etc. **2** shout. • *v.* utter with or make a yell.

yel·low /yélō/ • *adj.* **1** of the color between green and orange in the spectrum, as of lemons, egg yolks, or gold. **2** having a yellow skin or complexion. **3** *colloq.* cowardly. **4** (of newspapers, etc.) unscrupulously sensational. ● *n.* yellow color or pigment. ● *v.* make or become yellow. □ **yellow fever** tropical virus disease with fever and jaundice. **yellow jacket** any of various wasps or hornets with yellow and black bands. **Yellow Pages** (or **yellow pages**) telephone directory of classified business listings, on yellow paper. □□ **yel′low·ish** *adj.* **yel′low·ly** *adv.* **yel′low·ness** *n.* **yel′low·y** *adj.*

yelp /yelp/ ● *n.* sharp, shrill cry of or as of a dog in pain or excitement. ● *v.intr.* utter a yelp. □□ **yelp′er** *n.*

yen[1] /yen/ *n.* (*pl.* same) chief monetary unit of Japan.

yen[2] /yen/ *colloq. n.* longing or yearning.

yeo·man /yṓmən/ *n.* (*pl.* **–men**) **1** esp. *hist.* man holding and cultivating a small landed estate. **2** in the US Navy, petty officer performing clerical duties on board ship. □□ **yeo′man** (or **yeo′man's**) **service** efficient or useful help in need.

yeo·man·ry /yṓmənree/ *n.* (*pl.* **–ries**) body or class of yeomen.

yep /yep/ *adv.* & *n.* (also **yup** /yup/) *colloq.* = YES.

yes /yes/ ● *adv.* **1** indicating affirmation, consent, assent, etc. **2** (in answer to a summons or address) an acknowledgment of one's presence. ● *n.* utterance of the word *yes.* □ **yes?** **1** indeed? **2** what do you want? **yes-man** (*pl.* **–men**) *colloq.* weakly acquiescent person.

yes·ter·day /yéstərday/ ● *adv.* **1** on the day before today. **2** in the recent past. ● *n.* **1** day before today. **2** the recent past.

yes·ter·year /yéstəryeer/ *n. literary* **1** last year. **2** the recent past.

yet /yet/ ● *adv.* **1** as late as; until; now or then. **2** (with *neg.* or *interrog.*) so soon as; by; now or then. **3** again; in addition. **4** still (*I will do it yet*). **5** even (*a yet more difficult task*). **6** nevertheless. ● *conj.* but nevertheless.

yew /yōō/ *n.* **1** dark-leaved evergreen coniferous tree with red berrylike cones. **2** its wood.

yield /yeeld/ ● *v.* **1** *tr.* produce or return as a fruit, profit, or result. **2** *tr.* give up; surrender. **3** *intr.* submit; defer to. **4** *intr.* (foll. by *to*) give right of way to (other traffic, etc.). ● *n.* amount yielded or produced. □□ **yield′er** *n.*

yield·ing /yéelding/ *adj.* **1** compliant; submissive. **2** (of a substance) able to bend; not stiff nor rigid. □□ **yield′ing·ly** *adv.*

yin /yin/ *n.* (in Chinese philosophy) passive female principle of the universe (cf. YANG).

YIN AND YANG

yip /yip/ ● *v.intr.* (**yipped**, **yip·ping**) = YELP *v.* ● *n.* = YELP *n.*

yip·pee /yíppée/ *int.* expressing delight or excitement.

YMCA *abbr.* Young Men's Christian Association.

YMHA *abbr.* Young Men's Hebrew Association.

yo·del /yṓd'l/ ● *v.* sing with melodious inarticulate sounds and frequent changes between falsetto and the normal voice. ● *n.* yodeling cry. □□ **yo′del·er** *n.*

yo·ga /yṓgə/ *n.* Hindu system of philosophic meditation and exercise. □□ **yo·gic** /yṓgik/ *adj.*

yo·gi /yṓgee/ *n.* teacher of yoga. □□ **yo′gism** *n.*

yo·gurt /yṓgərt/ *n.* (also **yo′ghurt**) semisolid sourish food prepared from milk fermented by added bacteria.

yoke /yōk/ ● *n.* **1** wooden crosspiece fastened over the necks of two oxen, etc., and attached to the plow or wagon to be drawn. **2** (*pl.* same or **yokes**) pair (of oxen, etc.). **3** object like a yoke in form or function, e.g., wooden shoulderpiece for carrying a pair of pails, etc. **4** dominion or servitude. **5** bond of union, esp. that of marriage. ● *v.* **1** *tr.* put a yoke on. **2** *tr.* couple or unite (a pair). **3** *tr.* (foll. by *to*) link (one thing) to (another).

yo·kel /yṓkəl/ *n.* country bumpkin.

yolk /yōk/ *n.* yellow internal part of an egg. □□ **yolked** *adj.* (also in *comb.*). **yolk′less** *adj.* **yolk′y** *adj.*

Yom Kip·pur /yawm kípər, keepṓōr, yōm, yom/ *n.* most solemn holy day of the Jewish year; Day of Atonement.

yon /yon/ *literary & dial.* ● *adj.* & *adv.* yonder. ● *pron.* yonder person or thing.

yon·der /yóndər/ ● *adv.* over there; at some distance in that direction. ● *adj.* situated yonder.

yoo-hoo /yṓōhōō/ *int.* used to attract a person's attention.

yore /yawr/ *n. literary* long ago. □ **of yore** formerly.

you /yōō/ *pron.* (*obj.* **you**; *poss.* **your**, **yours**) **1** person or persons addressed. **2** (as *int.* with a noun) in an exclamatory statement (*you fools!*). **3** (in general statements) one; a person; people.

you'd /yōōd/ *contr.* **1** you had. **2** you would.

you'll /yōōl, yŏŏl/ *contr.* you will; you shall.

young /yung/ ● *adj.* (**young·er** /yúnggər/; **young·est** /yúnggist/) **1** not far advanced in life, development, or existence; not yet old. **2** immature; inexperienced. **3** of or characteristic of youth. ● *n.* offspring. □□ **young′ish** *adj.* **young′ling** *n.*

young·ster /yúngstər/ *n.* child or young person.

your /yŏŏr, yawr/ *poss.pron.* of or belonging to you.

you're /yŏŏr, yawr/ *contr.* you are.

yours /yŏŏrz, yawrz/ *poss.pron.* **1** the one or ones belonging to you. **2** introducing a formula ending a letter (*yours truly*).

your·self /yŏŏrsélf, yawr–/ *pron.* (*pl.* **your·selves** /–sélvz/) **1 a** *emphat. form* of YOU. **b** *refl. form* of YOU. **2** in your normal state of body or mind (*are quite yourself again*).

youth /yōōth/ *n.* (*pl.* **youths** /yōōthz/) **1** being young; period between childhood and adult age. **2** vigor, enthusiasm, inexperience, or other characteristic of this period. **3** young person. **4** (*pl.*) young people collectively.

youth·ful /yōōthfŏŏl/ *adj.* young or having the characteristics of youth. □□ **youth′ful·ly** *adv.* **youth′ful·ness** *n.*

you've /yōōv, yŏŏv/ *contr.* you have.

yowl /yowl/ • *n.* loud, wailing cry. • *v.intr.* utter a yowl.

yo-yo /yóyō/ • *n.* (*pl.* **yo-yos**) **1** *propr.* toy consisting of a pair of disks that can be made to fall and rise on a string. **2** thing that repeatedly falls and rises. • *v.intr.* (**yo-yoes, yo-yoed, yo-yoing**) **1** play with a yo-yo. **2** move up and down; fluctuate.

yr. *abbr.* (*pl.* **yrs.**) **1** year(s). **2** yours. **3** younger.

yt·ter·bi·um /itə́rbeeəm/ *n. Chem.* silvery metallic element of the lanthanide series. Symb.: **Yb.**

yt·tri·um /ítreeəm/ *n. Chem.* grayish metallic element resembling the lanthanides. ¶ Symb.: **Y.**

yu·an /yoo-áan, yö-/ *n.* (*pl.* same) chief monetary unit of China.

yuc·ca /yúkə/ *n.* N. American white-flowered liliaceous plant with swordlike leaves.

yuck /yuk/ *int. sl.* expression of strong distaste or disgust.

yuck·y /yúkee/ *adj.* (**–i·er, –i·est**) *sl.* **1** messy; repellent. **2** sickly; sentimental.

Yu·go·slav /yóogəslaav/ (also **Jugoslav**) *hist.* •

n. **1** native or national of the former republic of Yugoslavia. **2** person of Yugoslav descent. • *adj.* of or relating to Yugoslavia or its people. □□ **Yu·go·sla'vi·an** *adj. & n.*

yule /yool/ *n.* (in full **yule'tide**) *archaic* Christmas festival.

Yu·ma /yóomə/ *n.* **1 a** N. American people native to Arizona. **b** member of this people. **2** language of this people.

yum·my /yúmee/ *adj.* (**yum·mi·er, yum·mi·est**) *colloq.* tasty; delicious.

yup var. of YEP.

yup·pie /yúpee/ (also **yup'py**; *pl.* **–pies**) *colloq.,* usu. *derog.* • *n.* young, ambitious professional person working in a city. • *adj.* characteristic of a yuppie or yuppies. (from *y*oung *u*rban *p*rofessional.)

YWCA *abbr.* Young Women's Christian Association.

YWHA *abbr.* Young Women's Hebrew Association.

Zz

Z /zee/ *n.* (also **z**) (*pl.* **Zs** or **Z's**; **z's**) twenty-sixth letter of the alphabet.

z *symb.* **1** *Math.* unknown quantity or variable. **2** *Math.* coordinate of the third-dimensional axis. **3** *Chem.* (usu. **Z**) atomic number.

zag /zag/ • *n.* sharp change of direction in a zigzag course. • *v.intr.* (**zagged, zag·ging**) move in one of the two directions in a zigzag course.

za·ny /záynee/ • *adj.* (**za·ni·er, za·ni·est**) comically idiotic; crazily ridiculous. • *n.* buffoon or jester. □□ **za′ni·ly** *adv.* **za′ni·ness** *n.*

zap /zap/ *sl.* • *v.* (**zapped, zap·ping**) **1** *tr.* a kill or destroy. **b** hit forcibly. **c** send an electric current, radiation, etc., through (someone or something). **2** *intr.* move quickly. **3** *tr. Computing* erase or change (an item in a program). **4** *tr.* heat or cook (food) by microwave. **5** *tr.* change (television channels) by remote control. • *n.* strong emotional effect. • *int.* expressing the sound or impact of a bullet, ray gun, etc., or any sudden event.

zap·per /zápər/ *n. colloq.* hand-held remote-control device for changing television channels, adjusting volume, etc.

Zarathustrian var. of ZOROASTRIAN.

zeal /zeel/ *n.* **1** earnestness or fervor. **2** hearty and persistent endeavor. □□ **zeal·ous** /zéləs/ *adj.* **zeal′ous·ly** *adv.* **zeal′ous·ness** *n.*

zeal·ot /zélət/ *n.* extreme partisan; fanatic. □□ **zeal′ot·ry** *n.*

ze·bra /zeebrə/ *n.* (*pl.* same or **zebras**) black and white striped African quadruped related to the ass and horse. □□ **ze·brine** /-brīn/ *adj.*

ze·bu /zeebōō/ *n.* humped ox of India, E. Asia, and Africa.

zed /zed/ *n. Brit.* the letter Z.

Zen /zen/ *n.* form of Mahayana Buddhism emphasizing the value of meditation and intuition. □□ **Zen′ist** *n.* (also **Zennist**).

ze·nith /zeénith/ *n.* **1** part of the sky directly above an observer (opp. NADIR). **2** any peak or highest point.

zeph·yr /zéfər/ *n. literary* mild gentle breeze.

zep·pe·lin /zépəlin/ *n. hist.* German large dirigible airship of the early 20th c., orig. for military use.

ze·ro /zeérō/ • *n.* (*pl.* **-ros**) **1 a** the figure 0; naught. **b** no quantity or number; nil. **2** point on the scale from which a positive or negative quantity is reckoned. **3** no; not any. **4** lowest or earliest point. • *v.tr.* (**-roes, -roed**) **1** adjust (an instrument, etc.) to zero point. **2** set the sights of (a gun) for firing. □ **zero in on** **1** take aim at. **2** focus one's attention on. **zero-sum** (of a political situation, etc.) system in which gains and losses are equal.

zest /zest/ *n.* **1** piquancy; stimulating flavor or quality. **2 a** keen enjoyment or interest. **b** relish. **c** gusto. **3** a scraping of orange or lemon peel as flavoring. □□ **zest′ful** *adj.* **zest′ful·ly** *adv.* **zest′i·ness** *n.* **zest′y** *adj.* (**zest·i·er, zest·i·est**).

ze·ta /záytə, zée-/ *n.* sixth letter of the Greek alphabet (Z, ζ).

zig·gu·rat /zígərat/ *n.* rectangular stepped pyramidal tower in ancient Mesopotamia, surmounted by a temple.

zig·zag /zígzag/ • *n.* **1** line or course having abrupt alternate right and left turns. **2** (often in *pl.*) each of these turns. • *adj.* having the form of a zigzag. • *adv.* with a zigzag course. • *v.intr.* (**zig·zagged, zig·zag·ging**) move in a zigzag course. □□ **zig·zag′ged·ly** *adv.*

zilch /zilch/ *n. sl.* nothing.

zil·lion /zílyən/ *n. colloq.* indefinite large number. □□ **zil′lionth** *adj. & n.*

zinc /zingk/ *n. Chem.* white metallic element used as a component of brass, in galvanizing, in electric batteries, and in printing plates. ¶ Symb.: **Zn**. □□ **zinced** or **zincked** *adj.*

zing /zing/ *colloq.* • *n.* vigor; energy. • *v.intr.* move swiftly or with a shrill sound. □□ **zing′er** *n.* **zing′y** *adj.* (**zing·i·er, zing·i·est**).

zin·ni·a /zíneeə/ *n.* composite plant with showy rayed flowers of various colors.

Zi·on /zíən/ *n.* (also **Sion** /síən/) **1** hill of Jerusalem on which the city of David was built. **2** the Jewish people or religion. **3** (in Christian thought) the kingdom of God in heaven.

Zi·on·ism /zíənizəm/ *n.* movement (orig.) for the re-establishment and (now) the development of a Jewish nation in what is now Israel. □□ **Zi′on·ist** *n.*

zip /zip/ • *n.* **1** light fast sound, as of a bullet passing through air. **2** energy; vigor. • *v.* (**zipped, zip·ping**) **1** *tr. & intr.* (often foll. by *up*) fasten with a zipper. **2** *intr.* move with zip or at high speed.

zip code /zip/ *n.* (also **ZIP code**) assigned numeric postal code to speed the sorting and delivering mail.

zip·per /zípər/ • *n.* fastening device of two flexible strips with interlocking projections closed or opened by pulling a slide along them. • *v.tr.* (often foll. by *up*) fasten with a zipper. □□ **zip′pered** *adj.*

zip·py /zípee/ *adj.* (**zip·pi·er, zip·pi·est**) *colloq.* **1** bright; fresh; lively. **2** fast; speedy. □□ **zip′pi·ly** *adv.* **zip′pi·ness** *n.*

zir·con /zárkon/ *n.* zirconium silicate of which some translucent varieties are cut into gems.

zir·co·ni·um /zərkóneeəm/ *n. Chem.* gray metallic element. ¶ Symb.: **Zr**.

zit /zit/ *n. sl.* pimple.

zith·er /zíthər/ *n.* musical instrument consisting of a flat wooden sound box with numerous strings stretched across it, placed horizontally and played with the fingers and a plectrum. □□ **zith′er·ist** *n.*

Zn *symb. Chem.* zinc.

zo·di·ac /zódeeak/ *n.* **1** imaginary belt of the heavens including all apparent positions of the sun, moon, and planets divided into twelve equal parts (**signs of the zodiac**) named for constellations: Aries, Taurus, Gemini, Cancer, Leo,

Virgo, Libra, Scorpio, Sagittarius, Capricorn(us), Aquarius, Pisces. **2** diagram of these signs. □□ **zo·di·a·cal** /–díakəl/ adj.

zom·bie /zómbee/ n. **1** colloq. dull or apathetic person. **2** corpse said to be revived by witchcraft.

zone /zōn/ • n. **1** area having particular features, properties, purpose, or use (danger zone). **2** well-defined region of more or less beltlike form. **3** (in full **time zone**) range of longitudes where a common standard time is used. **4** Geog. latitudinal division of the earth (see FRIGID, TEMPERATE, TORRID). • v.tr. **1** encircle as or with a zone. **2** assign as or to a particular area. □□ **zon′al** adj. **zon′ing** n. (in sense 2 of v.).

zonked /zongkt/ adj. sl. (often foll. by out) exhausted; intoxicated.

zoo /zoō/ n. park with a collection of animals for exhibition or study.

zool. abbr. **1** zoological. **2** zoology.

zo·ol·o·gy /zō-óləjee/ n. the scientific study of animals. □□ **zo·o·log·i·cal** /–lój–/ adj. **zo·ol′o·gist** n.

zoom /zoōm/ • v. **1** intr. move quickly, esp. with a buzzing sound. **2 a** intr. cause an airplane to climb at high speed and a steep angle. **b** tr. cause (an airplane) to do this. **3 a** intr. (of a camera) close up rapidly from a long shot to a close-up. **b** tr. cause (a lens or camera) to do this. • n. **1** airplane's steep climb. **2** zooming camera shot. □ **zoom lens** lens allowing a camera to zoom by varying the focal length.

zo·o·phyte /zóəfīt/ n. plantlike animal, esp. a coral, sea anemone, or sponge. □□ **zo·o·phyt·ic** /–fítik/ adj.

Zo·ro·as·tri·an /záwrō-ástreeən/ (also **Zar·a·thus·tri·an** /zárəthoōóstreeən/) • adj. of or relating to Zoroaster (or Zarathustra) of Persia, or the dualistic religious system taught by him in the 6th c. BC. • n. follower of Zoroaster. □□ **Zo·ro·as′tri·an·ism** n.

Zr symb. Chem. zirconium.

zuc·chi·ni /zoōkeénee/ n. (pl. same or **zuc·chi·nis**) green variety of smooth-skinned summer squash.

Zu·lu /zoōloō/ • n. **1** member of a black South African people orig. inhabiting Zululand and Natal. **2** language of this people. • adj. of or relating to this people or language.

Zu·ni /zoōnee/ n. (also **Zu·ñi** /zoōnyee/) **1 a** N. American people native to New Mexico. **b** member of this people. **2** language of this people.

zwie·back /zwíbak, –baak, zweé–, swí–, sweé–/ n. a kind of rusk or sweet cake toasted in slices.

zy·gote /zígōt, zíg–/ n. Biol. cell formed by the union of two gametes. □□ **zy·got·ic** /–gótik/ adj. **zy·got′i·cal·ly** adv.

zy·mur·gy /zímərjee/ n. the branch of applied chemistry dealing with the use of fermentation in brewing, etc.

Biographical Entries

Aar·on /áirən/, **Hank** (**Henry Louis**) 1934–   ; U.S. baseball player.

Ab·e·lard /ábəlaard/, **Peter** 1079–1142; French theologian and philosopher.

A·bra·ham /áybrəham/ Hebrew patriarch.

A·che·be /aacháybay/, **Chinua** (born **Albert Chinualumgu**) 1930–   ; Nigerian author.

Ach·e·son /áchəsən/, **Dean Gooderham** 1893–1971; U.S. secretary of state (1949–53).

Ad·ams /ádəmz/, **Ansel Easton** 1902–84; U.S. photographer.

Ad·ams family of U.S. politicians, including: **1 John** 1735–1826; 2nd president of the U.S. (1797–1801); father of: **2 John Quincy** 1767–1848; 6th president of the U.S. (1825–29).

Ad·ams, Samuel 1722–1803; U.S. patriot.

Ad·dams /ádəmz/, **Jane** 1860–1935; U.S. social worker.

Ad·di·son /ádəsən/, **Joseph** 1672–1719; English author.

A·de·nau·er /aàd-nowər, áad–/, **Konrad** 1876–1967; chancellor of West Germany (1949–63).

Ad·ler /ádlər/, **Alfred** 1870–1937; Austrian psychiatrist.

Ael·fric /álfrik/ c. 955–c. 1020; English abbot, author, and grammarian.

Aes·chy·lus /éskələs/ c. 525–c. 456 B.C.; Greek playwright.

Ae·sop /eésaap, –səp/ 6th cent. B.C.; Greek writer of fables.

Ag·as·siz /ágəsee/, (**Jean**) **Louis** 1807–73; U.S. naturalist, born in Switzerland.

Ag·new /ágnoo/, **Spiro Theodore** 1918–96; U.S. vice president (1969–73); resigned.

Ai·ken /áykən/, **Conrad Potter** 1889–1973; U.S. poet.

Ak·bar /ákbər, –baar/, **Jalaludin Muhammad** 1542–1605; Mogul emperor of India (1556–1605).

Akh·na·ton /aaknaàtən/ see *Amenhotep IV* (AMENHOTEP).

A·ki·hi·to /aakiheètō/ 1933–   ; emperor of Japan (1989–   ).

Al·a·ric /álərik/ c. 370–410; king of the Visigoths (395–410); captured Rome (410).

Al·bee /áwlbee, ál–/, **Edward** 1928–   ; U.S. playwright.

Al·bright /áwlbrīt/, **Madeleine** 1937–   ; U.S. secretary of state (1997–   ), born in Czechoslovakia.

Al·ci·bi·a·des /alsəbíədeez/ c. 450–404 B.C.; Athenian general and statesman.

Al·cott /áwlkət, ál–, –kaat/, **Louisa May** 1832–88; U.S. novelist.

Al·cuin /álkwin/ c. 735–804; English theologian.

Al·ex·an·der /aligzándər/ (called **"the Great"**) 356–323 B.C.; king of Macedonia (336–323 B.C.); conqueror of the Persian Empire.

Al·ex·an·der name of three czars of Russia: **1 Alexander I** 1777–1825; reigned 1801–25. **2 Alexander II** (called **"the Liberator"**) 1818–81; reigned 1855–81; father of: **3 Alexander III** 1845–94; reigned 1881–94.

Al·fred /álfrəd/ (called **"the Great"**) 849–899; Anglo-Saxon king (871–899).

A·li /aalee, aleè/, **Muhammad** (born **Cassius Marcellus Clay, Jr.**) 1942–   ; U.S. boxer.

A·li·ghie·ri /aləgyéree/, **Dante** see DANTE.

Al·len /álən/, **Ethan** 1738–89; American Revolutionary War soldier.

Al·len, Woody (born **Allen Stewart Konigsberg**) 1935–   ; U.S. film director, author, and actor.

All·en·de Gos·sens /aayénday gáwsens/, **Salvador** 1908–73; Chilean political leader.

A·ma·ti /əmaàtee, aa–/ family of Italian violinmakers, including: **1 Andrea** c. 1520–c. 1580; grandfather of: **2 Nicolò** 1596–1684.

A·men·ho·tep /aamənhótep/ (also **Am·e·no′phis**) name of four kings of Egypt: **1 Amenhotep I** reigned 1546–1526 B.C. **2 Amenhotep II** reigned 1450–1425 B.C. **3 Amenhotep III** reigned 1417–1379 B.C.; built capital city of Thebes. **4 Amenhotep IV** (also **Akh·na′ton; Ikh·na′ton**) reigned 1379–1362 B.C.

A·min /aameén/, **Idi** 1925–   ; president of Uganda (1971–79); exiled (1979).

An·ax·ag·o·ras /anakságərəs/ c. 500–c. 428 B.C.; Greek philosopher.

An·der·sen /ándərsən, aàn–/, **Hans Christian** 1805–75; Danish author.

An·der·son /ándərsən/, **Marian** 1902–93; U.S. contralto.

An·der·son, Maxwell 1888–1959; U.S. playwright.

An·der·son, Sherwood 1876–1941; U.S. author.

Andrew ~ Ayer

An·drew /ándrōō/, **St.** died c. 60; apostle of Jesus; patron saint of Scotland.

An·dro·pov /andrópawf/, **Yuri** 1914–84; Soviet politician.

An·ge·lou /aˊanjəlōō, –lō/, **Maya** 1928– ; U.S. novelist and poet.

An·nan /aˊanaan/, **Kofi** 1938– ; Ghanaian secretary-general of the United Nations (1997–).

Anne /an/ 1665–1714; queen of England (1702–14).

Anne Bol·eyn see BOLEYN, ANNE.

Anne of Cleves /kleevz/ 1515–57; 4th wife of Henry VIII.

An·nen·berg /ánənbərg/, **Walter** 1908– ; U.S. publisher and philanthropist.

A·nou·ilh /aanóʊbee/, **Jean** 1910–87; French playwright.

An·selm /ánselm/, **St.** c. 1033–1109; English theologian.

An·tho·ny /ánthənee/, **Susan B(rownell)** 1820–1906; U.S. suffragist.

An·to·ni·nus Pi·us /antənínəs píəs/ 86–161; Roman emperor (137–161).

An·to·ny /ántənee/, **Mark** (Latin name **Mar'cus An·to'ni·us**) c. 83–30 B.C.; Roman general and political leader.

Ap·ol·lo·ni·us /apəlóneeəs/ **of Rhodes** /rōdz/ 3rd cent. B.C.; Greek poet.

A·pu·lei·us /apyəláyəs/ 2nd cent.; Roman author.

A·qui·nas /əkwínəs/, **St. Thomas** 1225–74; Italian philosopher and theologian.

Ar·a·fat /árəfat/, **Yasser** 1929– ; Palestinian political leader.

Ar·i·os·to /aaree-aˊastō, –óstō/, **Ludovico** 1474–1533; Italian poet.

Ar·is·ti·des /arəstídeez/ (called **"the Just"**) fl. 5th cent. B.C.; Athenian statesman and general.

Ar·is·toph·a·nes /arəstaˊafəneez/ c. 450–c. 385 B.C.; Greek comic playwright.

Ar·is·tot·le /árəstaat'l, arəstaˊat'l/ 384–322 B.C.; Greek philosopher.

Arm·strong /aˊarmstrawng/, **(Daniel) Louis** (called **"Satchmo"**) 1900–71; U.S. jazz trumpeter and bandleader.

Arm·strong, Neil Alden 1930– ; U.S. astronaut; first to walk on the moon (1969).

Ar·nold /aˊarnəld/, **Benedict** 1741–1801; American Revolutionary War general; turned traitor (1779).

Ar·nold, Matthew 1822–88; English poet and essayist.

Arou·et /áawə/, **François-Marie** see VOLTAIRE.

Ar·ta·xerx·es /aartəzárkseez/ name of three kings of Persia: **1 Artaxerxes I** reigned 464–424 B.C.; son of Xerxes I. **2 Artaxerxes II** reigned 404–358 B.C.; father of: **3 Artaxerxes III** reigned 358–338 B.C.

Ar·thur /aˊarthər/ 5th cent. or 6th cent.; legendary king of Britain. □□ **Ar·thu'ri·an** adj.

Ar·thur, Chester Alan 1830–86; 21st president of the U.S. (1881–85).

Ashe /ash/, **Arthur Robert** 1943–93; U.S. tennis player.

As·i·mov /ázəmawf, –mawv/, **Isaac** 1920–92; U.S. scientist and author, born in Russia.

As·sad /aasaˊad/, **Hafiz al-** 1928– ; president of Syria (1971–).

A·staire /əstáir/, **Fred** (born **Frederick Austerlitz**) 1899–1987; U.S. dancer, singer, and actor.

As·tor /ástər/, **John Jacob** 1763–1848; U.S. capitalist, born in Germany.

As·tu·ri·as /aastóoreeəs, –tyoo-/, **Miguel Angel** 1899–1974; Guatemalan author.

A·ta·türk /átətərk/, **Kemal** (born **Mustafa Kemal**) 1881–1938; president of Turkey (1923–38).

At·ti·la /ətílə, át'lə/ 406–453; king of the Huns (434–453).

Att·lee /átlee/, **Clement Richard** 1883–1967; prime minister of Great Britain (1945–51).

At·tucks /átəks/, **Crispus** c. 1723–70; American patriot; killed in the Boston Massacre.

At·wood /átwōōd/, **Margaret** 1939– ; Canadian author and critic.

Au·den /áwd'n/, **W(ystan) H(ugh)** 1907–73; U.S. poet, born in England.

Au·du·bon /áwdəbaan, –bən/, **John James** 1785–1851; U.S. naturalist and artist.

Au·gus·tine /áwgusteen, awgústən/ name of two saints: **1** (called **St. Augustine of Hippo**) 354–430; early Christian author. **2** (also known as **Aus'tin**) died c. 604; first archbishop of Canterbury. □□ **Au·gus·tin'i·an** adj.

Au·gus·tus /awgústəs/ (also known as **Oc·ta'vi·an**) 63 B.C.–A.D. 14; first Roman emperor.

Aung San Suu Kyi /ówng saˊan sóo cheˊe/ 1945– ; Burmese political leader.

Au·re·li·us, Marcus see MARCUS AURELIUS.

Aus·ten /áwstən/, **Jane** 1775–1817; English novelist.

Aus·tin /áwstən/, **Stephen Fuller** 1793–1836; Texas pioneer and colonizer.

A·ver·ro·ës /əvéró-eez, avəró-/ c. 1126–98; Islamic philosopher, born in Spain.

A·vi·cen·na /avəsénə/ 980–1037; Islamic philosopher and physician, born in Persia.

Ayer /áyər/, **A(lfred) J(ules)** 1910–89; British philosopher.

Ba·ber /baábər/ (also **Ba'bar; Ba'bur**) 1483–1530; founder of the Mogul Empire.

Bach /baa<u>kh</u>, baak/ family of German composers, including: **1 Johann Sebastian** 1685–1750; father of: **2 Wilhelm Friedemann** 1710–84; **3 C(arl) P(hilipp) E(manuel)** 1714–88; **4 Johann Christoph Friedrich** 1732–95; and **5 Johann Christian** 1735–82.

Ba·con /báykən/, **Francis** 1561–1626; English statesman and philosopher.

Ba·con, Roger c. 1214–94; English scientist and philosopher.

Ba·den-Pow·ell /bayd'n póəl, pówəl/, (**Lord**) **Robert Stephenson Smyth** 1857–1941; English general; founder of the Boy Scouts (1908).

Bal·an·chine /bálənsheén/, **George** 1904–83; U.S. choreographer and ballet dancer, born in Russia.

Bal·boa /balbóə/, **Vasco Núñez de** 1475–1517; Spanish explorer of America.

Bald·win /báwldwin/, **James** 1924–87; U.S. author.

Bald·win, Stanley 1867–1947; prime minister of Great Britain (1923–29; 1935–37).

Bal·four /bálfər, –fawr/, **Arthur James** 1848–1930; British statesman.

Ball /bawl/, **Lucille Désirée** 1911–1989; U.S. comedienne.

Bal·ti·more, Lord see CALVERT, GEORGE.

Bal·zac /báwlzak, bál–/, **Honoré de** 1799–1850; French novelist.

Bar·ba·ros·sa /baarbərósə/ see FREDERICK I.

Bar·nard /baárnərd/, **Christiaan Neethling** 1922– ; South African physician; performed first human heart transplant (1967).

Bar·num /baárnəm/, **P(hineas) T(aylor)** 1810–91; U.S. showman.

Bar·rett /bárit/, **Elizabeth** see BROWNING, ELIZABETH BARRETT.

Bar·rie /báree/, (**Sir**) **J(ames) M(atthew)** 1860–1937; Scottish author.

Bar·ry·more /bárimawr/ family of U.S. actors, including three siblings: **1 Lionel** 1878–1954; **2 Ethel** 1879–1959; and **3 John** 1882–1942.

Barth /baarth/, **John** 1930– ; U.S. author.

Barth /baart/, **Karl** 1886–1968; Swiss Protestant theologian.

Barthes /baart/, **Roland** 1915–80; French author and critic.

Bar·tók /baártaak, –tawk/, **Béla** 1881–1945; Hungarian composer.

Bar·ton /baárt'n/, **Clara** 1821–1912; U.S. health worker; founded the American Red Cross (1881).

Ba·rysh·ni·kov /bəríshnikawf/, **Mikhail**

1948– ; U.S. ballet dancer and choreographer, born in Latvia.

Ba·sie /báysee/, **Count** (**William**) 1904–84; U.S. jazz pianist, bandleader, and composer.

Ba·tis·ta /bəteéstə/, **Fulgencio** 1901–73; president of Cuba (1940–44; 1954–59).

Bau·de·laire /bōd'lair/, **Charles** 1821–67; French poet and critic.

Beards·ley /beérdzlee/, **Aubrey Vincent** 1872–98; English artist.

Be·a·trix /báyətriks/ 1938– ; queen of the Netherlands (1980–).

Beau·mar·chais /bōmaarsháy/, **Pierre Augustin Caron de** 1732–99; French playwright.

Beau·mont /bómaant/, **Francis** 1584–1616; English playwright.

Beauvoir, Simone de see DE BEAUVOIR, SIMONE.

Beck·et /békit/, **St. Thomas à** c. 1118–70; archbishop of Canterbury; murdered for opposing King Henry II.

Beck·ett /békit/, **Samuel Barclay** 1906–89; Irish author.

Bede /beed/, **St.** (called **"the Venerable Bede"**) c. 673–735; English theologian and historian.

Bee·cher /beéchər/, **Henry Ward** 1813–87; U.S. abolitionist.

Beer·bohm /beérbōm/, (**Sir**) **Max** (**Henry Maximilian**) 1872–1956; English caricaturist and critic.

Bee·tho·ven /báytōvən/, **Ludwig van** 1770–1827; German composer.

Be·gin /bəgeén, báygin/, **Menachem** 1913–92; Israeli political leader.

Be·han /beéən/, **Brendan** 1923–64; Irish playwright and poet.

Bell /bel/, **Alexander Graham** 1847–1922; U.S. inventor of the telephone, born in Scotland.

Bel·li·ni /beleénee/ family of Italian artists, including: **1 Jacopo** c. 1400–70; father of: **2 Gentile** c. 1429–1507; and **3 Giovanni** c. 1430–1516.

Bel·low /bélō/, **Saul** 1915– ; U.S. novelist, born in Canada.

Ben·e·dict /bénədikt/, **St.** c. 480–c. 550; Italian monk; founded Western monasticism.

Be·nét /bənáy/, **Stephen Vincent** 1898–1943; U.S. poet.

Ben-Gu·ri·on /ben gŏŏreeən/, **David** (born David Gruen) 1886–1973; prime minister of Israel (1948–53; 1955–63), born in Poland.

Ben·ny /bénee/, **Jack** (born **Benjamin Kubelsky**) 1894–1974; U.S. comedian.

Ben·tham /bénthəm/, **Jeremy** 1748–1832; English philosopher and jurist.

Ben·ton /bént'n/ **1 Thomas Hart** 1782–1858; U.S. politician; great-uncle of: **2 Thomas Hart** 1889–1975; U.S. artist.

Bent·sen /béntsən/, **Lloyd Millard** 1921– ; U.S. politician.

Benz /benz, bents/, **Karl Friedrich** 1844–1929; German automotive engineer.

Berg·son /bérgsən/, **Henri** 1859–1941; French philosopher.

Ber·ing /beéring, bér–/, **Vitus Jonassen** 1681–1741; Danish explorer.

Berke·ley /baárklee, bə́r–/, **George** 1685–1753; Irish philosopher and bishop.

Ber·lin /bərlín/, **Irving** (born **Israel Isidore Baline**) 1888–1989; U.S. composer, born in Russia.

Ber·li·oz /bérlee-ōz/, **Hector Louis** 1803–69; French composer.

Ber·na·dette /bərnədét/, **St.** (born **Marie-Bernarde Soubirous**) 1844–79; French peasant girl who had visions of the Virgin Mary at Lourdes.

Ber·nard /bərnaárd/ **of Clair·vaux** /klairvó/ 1090–1153; French theologian.

Bern·hardt /bə́rnhaart/, **Sarah** (born **Henriette Rosine Bernard**) 1844–1923; French actress.

Ber·ni·ni /bərneénee/, **Gianlorenzo** 1598–1680; Italian artist and architect.

Bern·stein /bə́rnstīn, –steen/, **Leonard** 1918–90; U.S. composer and conductor.

Ber·ry /béree/, **Chuck** (**Charles Edward**) 1931– ; U.S. rock and roll musician.

Bes·se·mer /bésimər/, (**Sir**) **Henry** 1813–98; English engineer and inventor.

Be·thune /bəthoón, –yoón/, **Mary McLeod** 1875–1955; U.S. educator.

Bet·je·man /béchəmən/, (**Sir**) **John** 1906–84; English poet.

Beyle /bel/, **Marie Henri** see STENDHAL.

Bhut·to /boótō/ **1 Zulfikar Ali** 1928–79; president (1971–73) and prime minister (1973–77) of Pakistan; father of: **2 Benazir** 1953– ; prime minister of Pakistan (1988–91; 1993–96).

Bierce /beers/, **Ambrose Gwinnett** 1842–c. 1914; U.S. author.

Bi·ko /beékō/, **Stephen** 1946–77; South African civil rights activist.

Bis·marck /bízmaark/, **Otto Eduard Leopold von** (called **"the Iron Chancellor"**) 1815–98; chancellor of the German Empire (1871–90).

Bi·zet /beezáy/, **Georges Alexandre César Léopold** 1838–75; French composer.

Black /blak/, **Shirley Temple** 1928– ; U.S. actress and diplomat.

Blair /blair/, **Tony** (**Anthony Charles Lynton**) 1953– ; prime minister of Great Britain (1997–).

Blake /blayk/, **William** 1757–1827; English artist and poet.

Bligh /blī/, **William** 1754–1817; British naval officer.

Bo·ad·i·ce·a /bōədəseéə/ (also **Bou·dic'ca**) died 62; warrior queen of the ancient Britons.

Boc·cac·ci·o /bəkaácheeō, –chō/, **Giovanni** 1313–75; Italian poet.

Bo·e·thi·us /bō-eétheeəs/, **Anicius Manlius Severinus** c. 480–524; Roman philosopher.

Bo·gart /bógaart/, **Humphrey De Forest** 1899–1957; U.S. actor.

Bohr /bawr/, **Niels Henrik David** 1885–1962; Danish nuclear physicist.

Bol·eyn /boólín, boólən/, **Anne** 1507–36; 2nd wife of King Henry VIII of England; mother of Queen Elizabeth I; beheaded.

Bol·i·var /bōleévaar, baáləvər/, **Simón** (called **"the Liberator"**) 1783–1830; Venezuelan patriot and liberator of South America.

Bo·na·parte /bónəpaart/ see NAPOLEON I; NAPOLEON III.

Boone /boōn/, **Daniel** c. 1735–1820; American pioneer.

Boor·stin /boórstin/, **Daniel J**(**oseph**) 1914– ; U.S. author.

Booth /boōth/, **John Wilkes** 1838–65; U.S. actor; assassin of President Abraham Lincoln (1865).

Bor·ges /báwrhays/, **Jorge Luis** 1899–1986; Argentine author.

Bor·gi·a /báwrjə, –_zh_ə/ **1 Cesare** 1476–1507; Italian cardinal and militarist; brother of: **2 Lucrezia** 1480–1519; Italian patron of the arts.

Born /bawrn/, **Max** 1882–1970; German physicist.

Bosch /baash, bawsh/, **Hieronymus** c. 1450–1516; Dutch artist.

Bos·well /baázwel, –wəl/, **James** 1740–95; Scottish author; biographer of Samuel Johnson.

Bot·ti·cel·li /baatəchélee/, **Sandro** 1445–1510; Italian artist.

Bou·dic·ca /boōdíkə/ see BOADICEA.

Bou·lez /boōléz/, **Pierre** 1925– ; French conductor and composer.

Bourke-White /boórk wīt/, **Margaret** 1906–71; U.S. photojournalist.

Bou·tros-Gha·li /boótrōs gaalee/, **Boutros** 1922– ; Egyptian statesman; secretary-general of the United Nations (1992–96).

Brad·bur·y /brádberee, –bəree/, **Ray**(**mond Douglas**) 1920– ; U.S. science-fiction author.

Brad·ford /brádfərd/, **William** 1590–1657; English Puritan governor of Plymouth colony in Massachusetts.

Brad·ley /brádlee/, **Omar Nelson** 1893–1981; U.S. general.

Bra·dy /bráydee/, **Mathew B.** 1823–96; U.S. Civil War photographer.

Brahe /braa, braahee/, **Tycho** 1546–1601; Danish astronomer.

Brahms /braamz/, **Johannes** 1833–97; German composer.

Bran·deis /brándīs/, **Louis Dembitz** 1856–1941; U.S. Supreme Court justice (1916–39).

Bran·do /brándō/, **Marlon** 1924– ; U.S. actor.

Brandt /braant, brant/, **Willy** (born **Karl Herbert Frahm**) 1913–92; German politician.

Braun /brown/, **Wernher von** 1912–77; U.S. rocket scientist, born in Germany.

Brecht /bre<u>kh</u>t, brekt/, **Bertolt** 1898–1956; German playwright and poet.

Breu·ghel see BRUEGEL, PIETER.

Brey·er /bríər/, **Stephen Gerald** 1938– ; U.S. Supreme Court justice (1994–).

Brezh·nev /bré<u>zh</u>nef, –nyəf/, **Leonid** 1906–83; Soviet political leader.

Bridg·es /bríjiz/, **Robert** 1844–1930; English poet and critic.

Brit·ten /brít'n/, (**Edward**) **Benjamin** 1913–76; English composer.

Brod·sky /braádskee, braát–/, **Joseph** 1940–1996; U.S. poet, born in Russia.

Bron·të /braántee, braántay/ family of English novelists; three sisters: **1 Charlotte** 1816–55; **2 Emily Jane** 1818–48; and **3 Anne** 1820–49.

Brown /brown/, **John** 1800–59; U.S. radical abolitionist.

Brown·ing /brówning/ two English poets: **1 Elizabeth Barrett** 1806–61; wife of: **2 Robert** 1812–89.

Bruce /broōs/, **Robert the** see ROBERT I.

Brue·gel /bróygəl/ (also **Breu'ghel; Brue'ghel**), **Pieter** c. 1525–69; Flemish artist.

Bru·nel·les·chi /broōn'léskee/ (also **Bru·nel·les'co**), **Filippo** 1377–1446; Italian architect.

Bru·tus /broōtəs/, **Marcus Junius** 85–42 B.C.; Roman senator; an assassin of Julius Caesar.

Bry·an /bríən/, **William Jennings** 1860–1925; U.S. lawyer, politician, and orator.

Bry·ant /bríənt/, **William Cullen** 1794–1878; U.S. poet.

Bryn·ner /brínər/, **Yul** 1915–85; U.S. actor, born in Russia.

Bu·ber /boōbər/, **Martin** 1878–1965; Israeli philosopher, born in Austria.

Bu·chan·an /byoōkánən/, **James** 1791–1868; 15th president of the U.S. (1857–61).

Buck /buk/, **Pearl S(ydenstricker)** 1892–1973; U.S. author.

Buck·ley /búklee/, **William F(rank)** 1925– ; U.S. political commentator and author.

Bud·dha /boōdə, boōdə/ (born **Siddhartha Gautama**) c. 563–c. 483 B.C.; Indian philosopher; founder of Buddhism.

Bult·mann /boōltmaan, –mən/, **Rudolf Karl** 1884–1976; German theologian.

Bunche /bunch/, **Ralph Johnson** 1904–71; U.S. diplomat.

Bu·nin /boōnyeen/, **Ivan Alekseyevich** 1870–1953; Russian author and poet.

Bun·yan /búnyən/, **John** 1628–88; English author.

Bur·bank /bárbangk/, **Luther** 1849–1926; U.S. horticulturalist.

Bur·ger /bárgər/, **Warren Earl** 1907–95; Chief Justice of the U.S. (1969–86).

Burke /bərk/, **Edmund** 1729–97; British author and politician.

Bur·nett /bərnét, bárnət/, **Frances (Eliza) Hodgson** 1849–1924; U.S. novelist, born in England.

Burns /bərnz/, **George** 1895–1996; U.S. entertainer.

Burns, Robert 1759–96; Scottish poet.

Burn·side /bárnsīd/, **Ambrose Everett** 1824–81; Union general in the American Civil War.

Burr /bər/, **Aaron** 1756–1836; vice president of the U.S. (1801–05).

Bur·roughs /báröz/, **Edgar Rice** 1875–1950; U.S. author.

Bur·ton /bárt'n/, **Richard** (born **Richard Jenkins**) 1925–84; Welsh actor.

Bur·ton, (Sir) Richard Francis 1821–90; English explorer and anthropologist.

Bush /boōsh/, **George Herbert Walker** 1924– ; 41st president of the U.S. (1989–93).

But·ler /bútlər/, **Samuel** 1612–80; English poet.

But·ler, Samuel 1835–1902; English novelist.

Byrd /bərd/, **Richard Evelyn** 1888–1957; U.S. polar explorer.

By·ron /bírən/, (**Lord**) **George Gordon** 1788–1824; English poet.

Cab·ot /kábət/, **John** (Italian name **Giovanni Caboto**) 1425–c. 1498; Italian explorer.

Ca·bri·ni /kəbreénee/, **St. Frances Xavier** (called **"Mother Cabrini"**) 1850–1917; U.S. nun, born in Italy.

Cad·il·lac /kád'l-ak, kaadeeyaák/, **Antoine de la Mothe** c. 1656–1730; French explorer.

Cae·sar /séezər/, (**Gaius**) **Julius** 100–44 B.C.; Roman general and statesman; assassinated.

Cag·ney /kágnee/, **James** 1904–86; U.S. actor.

Cal·der /káwldər/, **Alexander Milne** 1898–1976; U.S. sculptor, born in Scotland.

Cal·houn /kalhóon/, **John C**(**aldwell**) 1782–1850; U.S. politician.

Ca·li·gu·la /kəlígyələ/ (born **Gaius Caesar**) 12–41; Roman emperor (37–41).

Cal·las /kálɔs, kaál–/, **Maria** (born **Maria Anna Sofia Cecilia Kalogeropoulos**) 1923–77; U.S. operatic soprano.

Cal·vert /kálvɔrt/ family of English colonial administrators of Maryland, including: **1** (**Lord**) **George** (**1st Baron Baltimore**) c. 1580–1632; father of: **2 Cecilius** (**2nd Baron Baltimore**) 1605–75; established Maryland colony; **3 Leonard** 1606–47; and **4 Charles** (**3rd Baron Baltimore**) 1637–1715; son of Cecilius Calvert.

Cal·vin /kálvɔn/, **John** 1509–64; French Protestant theologian.

Ca·mus /kamóo, kaamý/, **Albert** 1913–60; French author.

Ca·na·let·to /kan'létō/ (born **Giovanni Antonio Canale**) 1697–1768; Italian artist.

Ca·no·va /kɔnóvɔ/, **Antonio** 1757–1822; Italian sculptor.

Ca·nute /kɔnóot, –nyóot/ (also **Cnut; Knut**) died 1035; Danish king of England (1017–35), Denmark (1018–35), and Norway (1028–35).

Ca·pet /kaapáy, káypɔt/, **Hugh** (**Hugo**) 938–996; king of France (987–996).

Ca·pone /kɔpón/, **Al**(**phonse**) (called **"Scarface"**) 1899–1947; U.S. gangster, born in Italy.

Ca·po·te /kɔpótee/, **Truman** 1924–84; U.S. author.

Ca·ra·vag·gio /kaarɔvaájō, –jeeō/, **Michelangelo Merisi da** 1573–1610; Italian artist.

Car·lyle /kaarlíl, kaár–/, **Thomas** 1795–1881; Scottish historian and political philosopher.

Car·mi·chael /kaármīkɔl/, **Hoagy** (**Hoagland Howard**) 1899–1981; U.S. jazz pianist, singer, and composer.

Car·ne·gie /kaárnɔgee, kaarnégee/, **Andrew** 1835–1919; U.S. industrialist and philanthropist, born in Scotland.

Car·o·lus Mag·nus /kárɔlɔs mágnɔs/ see CHARLEMAGNE.

Car·rac·ci /kaaraáchee/ family of Italian artists, including: **1 Ludovico** 1555–1619; cousin of two brothers: **2 Agostino** 1557–1602; and **3 Annibale** 1560–1609.

Car·re·ras /kɔréraas/, **José** 1946– ; Spanish operatic tenor.

Car·roll /kárɔl/, **Lewis** (pseudonym of **Charles Lutwidge Dodgson**) 1832–98; English author and logician.

Car·son /kaársɔn/, **Kit** (**Christopher**) 1809–68; U.S. frontiersman.

Car·son, **Rachel Louise** 1907–64; U.S. zoologist and ecologist.

Car·ter /kaártɔr/, **Jimmy** (**James Earl**) 1924– ; 39th president of the U.S. (1977–81).

Car·tier /kaartyáy, kaártee-ay/, **Jacques** 1491–1557; French explorer.

Ca·ru·so /kɔróosō, –zō/, **Enrico** 1873–1921; Italian operatic tenor.

Car·ver /kaárvɔr/, **George Washington** 1864–1943; U.S. botanist and educator.

Ca·sals /kɔsaálz/, **Pablo** 1876–1973; Spanish cellist and composer.

Cas·a·no·va /kasɔnóvɔ, kaz–/, **Giovanni Jacopo** 1725–98; Italian adventurer.

Cash /kash/, **Johnny** 1932– ; U.S. country music singer and songwriter.

Cas·satt /kɔsát/, **Mary Stevenson** 1845–1926; U.S. artist.

Cas·sius /káshɔs/, **Gaius** died 42 B.C.; Roman general; an assassin of Julius Caesar.

Cas·tro /kástrō/, **Fidel** 1927– ; Cuban revolutionary; president of Cuba (1976–).

Cath·er /káthɔr/, **Willa Sibert** 1876–1974; U.S. novelist.

Cath·er·ine II /káthɔrɔn, káthrɔn/ (called **"the Great"**) 1729–96; empress of Russia (1762–96), born in Germany.

Ca·the·rine de Méd·i·cis /maydeesées, méd–/ (Italian name **Ca·te·ri·na de' Med·i·ci** /kaatayreénaa dɔ médɔchee, madeéchee/) 1519–89; queen of Henry II of France, born in Florence.

Cath·er·ine of Ar·a·gon /aírɔgon/ 1485–1536; 1st wife of Henry VIII; mother of Mary I.

Ca·to /káytō/, **Marcus Porcius** (called **"the Elder"** and **"the Censor"**) 234–149 B.C.; Roman statesman, orator, and author.

Catt /kat/, **Carrie Chapman Lane** 1859–1947; U.S. suffragist.

Ca·tul·lus /kɔtúlɔs/, **Gaius Valerius** c. 84–c. 54 B.C.; Roman poet.

Ca·vour /kɔvóor/, **Camillo Benso** 1810–61; Italian statesman.

Ceau·ses·cu /chowshéshkōo/, **Nicolae** 1918–89; president of Romania (1967–89); executed.

Cel·li·ni /chɔleénee/, **Benvenuto** 1500–71; Italian artisan.

Cer·van·tes /sɔrvánteez, servaántays/ (**Saa·ve'dra**), **Miguel de** 1547–1616; Spanish author.

Cé·zanne /sayzáan/, **Paul** 1839–1906; French artist.

Cha·gall /shəgáal/, **Marc** 1887–1985; French artist, born in Russia.

Chal·lans /chálənz/ **Mary** see RENAULT, MARY.

Cham·ber·lain /cháymbərlən/, (**Arthur**) **Neville** 1869–1940; prime minister of Great Britain (1937–40).

Cham·plain /shampláyn/, **Samuel de** 1567–1635; French explorer and colonial statesman in Canada.

Chan·dler /chándlər/, **Raymond Thornton** 1888–1959; U.S. novelist.

Cha·nel /shənél/, **Coco** (**Gabrielle Bonheur**) 1883–1971; French fashion designer.

Chap·lin /cháplən/, **Charlie** (**Sir Charles Spencer**) 1889–1977; English film actor and director.

Char·le·magne /shaárləmayn/ (called **Carolus Magnus** or **Charles the Great**) 742–814; king of the Franks (768–814); Holy Roman Emperor (800–814).

Charles[1] /chaarlz/ name of two British kings: **1 Charles I** 1600–49; reigned 1625–49. **2 Charles II** 1630–85; reigned 1660–85.

Charles[2] name of four kings of Spain, including: **1 Charles I** 1500–58; reigned 1516–56; (as **Charles V**) Holy Roman Emperor (1519–56). **2 Charles II** 1661–1700; reigned 1665–1700.

Charles (**Prince of Wales**) 1948– ; heir apparent to the throne of the United Kingdom.

Charles Mar·tel /maartél/ c. 688–741; ruler of the Franks (714–741).

Chase /chays/, **Salmon P**(**ortland**) 1808–73; Chief Justice of the U.S. (1864–73).

Cha·teau·bri·and /shaatōbree-aáN/, **François-René** (**Vicomte de**) 1768–1848; French author and diplomat.

Chau·cer /cháwsər/, **Geoffrey** c. 1342–1400; English poet.

Chee·ver /cheévər/, **John** 1912–82; U.S. author.

Che·khov /chékawf, –awv/, **Anton Pavlovich** 1860–1904; Russian author.

Che·ops /keéaaps/ (also **Khu'fu**) fl. early 26th cent. B.C.; Egyptian king; built the pyramid at Giza.

Ches·ter·ton /chéstərtən/, **G**(**ilbert**) **K**(**eith**) 1874–1936; English author and critic.

Chiang Kai-shek /cháng kíshék/ 1887–1975; president of China (1928–31; 1943–49) and Taiwan (1950–75).

Chi·rac /shiraák, –rák/, **Jacques** 1932– ; prime minister (1974–76; 1986–88) and president (1995–) of France.

Chi·ri·co /keérikō, kir–/, **Giorgio de** 1888–1978; Italian artist, born in Greece.

Chom·sky /chaámskee/, (**Avram**) **Noam** 1928– ; U.S. linguist.

Cho·pin /shópan, shōpáN/, **Frédéric François** 1810–49; French composer, born in Poland.

Chou En-lai /jṓ énlf/ (also **Zhou En-lai'**) 1898–1976; Chinese political leader.

Chré·tien de Troyes /kraytyáN də trwaá/ 12th cent.; French poet.

Chris·tie /krístee/, (**Dame**) **Agatha Mary Clarissa Miller** 1890–1976; English author.

Church /chərch/, **Frederick Edwin** 1826–1900; U.S. artist.

Church·ill /chə́rchil/, **John** (**1st Duke of Marlborough**) 1650–1722; British military commander.

Church·ill, (**Sir**) **Winston Leonard Spencer** 1874–1965; British statesman; prime minister of Great Britain (1940–45; 1951–55).

Cic·e·ro /sísərō/, **Marcus Tullius** 106–43 B.C.; Roman statesman and author.

Cid /síd/, **El** (born **Rodrigo Díaz de Vivar**) c. 1043–99; Spanish military hero.

Clap·ton /kláptən/, **Eric** 1945– ; British guitarist and composer.

Clark /klaark/, **1 George Rogers** 1752–1818; U.S. frontiersman and soldier; brother of: **2 William** 1770–1838; U.S. explorer (with Meriwether Lewis) of the North American continent (1804–06).

Clarke /klaark/, **Arthur C**(**harles**) 1917– ; English science-fiction author.

Claude Lor·rain /klṓd lawrén/ (born **Claude Gellée**) 1600–82; French landscape artist.

Clau·di·us /kláwdeeəs/ 10 B.C.–A.D. 54; Roman emperor (41–54).

Clau·se·witz /klówzəvits/, **Karl von** 1780–1831; Prussian military theorist.

Cla·vell /kləvél/, **James** 1924–94; U.S. author.

Clay /klay/, **Henry** 1777–1852; U.S. politician.

Clay, Cassius see ALI, MUHAMMAD.

Cle·men·ceau /klemənsṓ/, **Georges Eugène Benjamin** 1841–1929; French political leader.

Clem·ens /klémənz/, **Samuel Langhorne** see TWAIN, MARK.

Cle·o·pat·ra /kleeōpátrə/ (**Cleopatra VII**) 69–30 B.C.; queen of Egypt (47–30 B.C.).

Cleve·land /kleévlənd/, (**Stephen**) **Grover** 1837–1908; 22nd and 24th president of the U.S. (1885–89; 1893–97).

Clin·ton /klínt'n/, **1 Bill** (**William Jefferson**) 1946– ; 42nd president of the U.S. (1993–); husband of: **2 Hillary Rodham** 1947– ; U.S. lawyer.

Clin·ton, DeWitt 1769–1828; governor of

New York (1817–23; 1825–28); promoter of the Erie Canal.

Clo·vis /klóvəs/ 465–511; king of the Franks (481–511).

Cnut /kəno͝͞ot, –nyo͝͞ot/ see CANUTE.

Co·chise /kōcheės/ c. 1812–74; Apache Indian chief.

Coc·teau /kaaktó/, **Jean** 1889–1963; French playwright and film director.

Co·dy /kódee/, **William Frederick** (called **"Buffalo Bill"**) 1846–1917; U.S. army scout and showman.

Co·han /kóhan/, **George M(ichael)** 1878–1942; U.S. songwriter and theatrical producer.

Cole /cōl/, **Nat King** (born **Nathaniel Adams Coles**) 1919–65; U.S. popular singer and pianist.

Cole, Thomas 1801–48; U.S. artist.

Cole·ridge /kólrij, kólərij/, **Samuel Taylor** 1772–1834; English poet, critic, and philosopher.

Co·lette /kəlét/ (born **Sidonie Gabrielle Claudine Colette**) 1873–1954; French novelist.

Colt /kōlt/, **Samuel** 1814–62; U.S. inventor; patented the Colt revolver (1836).

Co·lum·ba /kəlúmbə/, **St.** c. 521–597; Irish abbot and missionary.

Co·lum·bus /kəlúmbəs/, **Christopher** 1451–1506; Spanish explorer, born in Italy; initiated colonization of America by Europeans (1492).

Comte /kōnt/, **Auguste** 1798–1857; French philosopher.

Con·fu·cius /kənfyo͝oshəs/ (also **K'ung Fu-tzu**) 551–479 B.C.; Chinese philosopher. □□ **Con·fu′cian** adj.

Con·greve /kaán-greev, kaáng–/, **William** 1670–1729; English playwright.

Con·ner·y /kaánəree/, **Sean** (born **Thomas Connery**) 1930– ; Scottish actor.

Con·rad /kaánrad/, **Joseph** 1857–1924; British novelist, born in Poland.

Con·sta·ble /kaánstəbəl/, **John** 1776–1837; English artist.

Con·stan·tine /kaánstənteen, –tīn/ (called **"the Great"**) c. 274–337; Roman emperor (306–337); adopted and sanctioned Christianity.

Cook /kook/, **(Captain) James** 1728–79; English explorer of the Pacific.

Cool·idge /koólij/, **(John) Calvin** 1872–1933; 30th president of the U.S. (1923–29).

Coop·er /koópər, ko͝opər/, **James Fenimore** 1789–1851; U.S. novelist.

Co·per·ni·cus /kəpórnikəs/, **Nicolaus** 1473–

1543; Polish astronomer; set forth the heliocentric theory of the solar system.

Cop·land /kóplənd/, **Aaron** 1900–90; U.S. composer.

Cop·ley /kaáplee/, **John Singleton** 1738–1815; U.S. artist.

Cor·day d'Ar·mont /kawrdáy daarmóN/, **(Marie-Anne) Charlotte** 1768–93; French patriot and political assassin.

Cor·i·o·la·nus /kawreeəláynəs/, **Gaius** (or **Gnaeus**) **Marcius** 6th cent.–5th cent. B.C.; legendary Roman general.

Cor·neille /kawrnáy/, **Pierre** 1606–84; French playwright.

Corn·wal·lis /kawrnwáwləs/, **Charles** (**1st Marquis**) 1738–1805; British general; surrendered at Yorktown (1781), ending American Revolutionary War.

Co·ro·na·do /kawrənaádō/, **Francisco Vásquez de** 1510–54; Spanish explorer in North America.

Co·rot /kawró/, **(Jean-Baptiste) Camille** 1796–1875; French artist.

Cor·reg·gio /kəréjō, –jeeō/, **Antonio Allegri da** c. 1489–1534; Italian artist.

Cor·tés /kawrtéz, kawrtés/ (also **Cor·tez′**), **Hernando** 1485–1547; Spanish conquistador; conqueror of Mexico.

Cos·by /kózbee/, **Bill** (**William Henry**) 1937– ; U.S. entertainer.

Cou·pe·rin /ko͝op(ə)ráN/, **François** 1668–1733; French composer.

Cow·ard /kówərd/, **(Sir) Noel Peirce** 1899–1973; English playwright, actor, and composer.

Cow·per /koópər, ków–/, **William** 1731–1800; English poet.

Crane /krayn/, **Stephen** 1871–1900; U.S. author.

Cran·mer /kránmər/, **Thomas** 1489–1556; English leader of Protestant Reformation.

Cras·sus /krásəs/, **Marcus Licinius** c. 115–53 B.C.; Roman politician; financier of First Triumvirate.

Cra·zy Horse /kráyzee hawrs/ c. 1849–77; Sioux chief of Oglala tribe; led Sioux uprising (1876–77).

Crick /krik/, **Francis Harry Compton** 1916– ; English biophysicist.

Crock·ett /kraákit/, **Davy** (**David**) 1786–1836; U.S. frontiersman.

Croe·sus /kreésəs/ died 546 B.C.; Lydian king of legendary wealth.

Crom·well /kraámwel, –wəl/, **Oliver** 1599–1658; English soldier and political leader.

Cro·nin /krónən/, **A(rchibald) J(oseph)** 1896–1981; Scottish novelist.

Cron·kite /krónkīt/, **Walter Leland, Jr.** 1916– ; U.S. broadcast journalist.

Cum·mings /kúmingz/, **Edward Estlin** (known as **"e e cummings"**) 1894–1962; U.S. poet.

Cu·rie /kyo͞oreé, kyo͞oree/ two French physicists and chemists: **1 Pierre** 1859–1906; codiscovered radium and polonium with his wife: **2 Marie** (born **Maria Sklowdowska**) 1867–1934; born in Poland.

Cur·tiss /kʉ́rtəs/, **Glenn Hammond** 1878–1930; U.S. inventor and aviation pioneer.

Cus·ter /kʉ́stər/, **George Armstrong** 1839–76; U.S. cavalry commander.

Cym·be·line /símbəleen/ died c. 42; British chieftain of Catuvellauni tribe.

Cyr·a·no de Ber·ge·rac /seérənō də bérzhərak/, **Savinien de** 1619–55; French soldier and author.

Cyr·il /seérəl/, **St.** (called **"the Apostle of the Slavs"**) 826–869; Greek missionary; inventor of the Cyrillic alphabet.

Cy·rus the Great /síərəs/ died 529 B.C.; king of Persia (559–529 B.C.).

Dahl /daal/, **Roald** 1916–90; British author.

Da·lai La·ma /daálī laamə, –lee/ title of the leader of Tibetan Buddhism.

Da·li /daálee/, **Salvador** 1904–89; Spanish surrealist artist.

Da·na /dáynə/, **Richard Henry** 1815–82; U.S. adventurer, author, and lawyer.

d'An·nun·zio /daanoóntsee-ō/, **Gabriele** 1863–1938; Italian novelist, playwright, and poet.

Dan·te /daántay, dántee/ (surname **Alighieri**) 1265–1321; Italian poet.

Dan·ton /daaNtóN/, **Georges-Jacques** 1759–94; French revolutionary leader.

Dare /dar, der/, **Virginia** 1587–?; first child born in W hemisphere of European parents.

Da·ri·us I /dəríəs/ (called **"the Great"**) c. 550–486 B.C.; king of Persia (521–486 B.C.).

Dar·row /dárō/, **Clarence Seward** 1857–1938; U.S. lawyer.

Dar·win /daárwin/, **Charles Robert** 1809–82; English naturalist; promulgated theory of evolution.

Dau·det /dōdáy/, **Alphonse** 1840–97; French author.

Dau·mier /dōmyáy/, **Honoré** 1808–78; French artist.

Da·vid /dáyvid/ died c. 970 B.C.; biblical king of Israel.

Da·vid /daaveéd/, **Jacques-Louis** 1748–1825; French artist.

da Vin·ci, Leonardo see LEONARDO DA VINCI.

Da·vis /dáyvəs/, **Jefferson** 1808–89; president of the Confederate States of America (1861–65).

Da·yan /dī-aán, daa-yaán/, **Moshe** 1915–81; Israeli politician and military commander.

de Beau·voir /də bōvwaár/, **Simone** 1908–86; French playwright and novelist.

Debs /debz/, **Eugene Victor** 1855–1926; U.S. labor leader.

De·bus·sy /debyo͞oseé, dáybyo͞o–/, (**Achille**) **Claude** 1862–1918; French composer.

de Fal·la, Manuel see FALLA, MANUEL DE.

De·foe /difó/, **Daniel** 1660–1731; English novelist and journalist.

De·gas /daygaá/, (**Hilaire-Germain**) **Edgar** 1834–1917; French artist.

de Gaulle /də gól, gáwl/, **Charles André Joseph Marie** 1890–1970; French general and statesman.

de Klerk /də klérk, klárk/, **F**(**rederik**) **W**(**illem**) 1936– ; president of South Africa (1989–94).

de Koo·ning /də koóning/, **Willem** 1904–97; U.S. artist, born in the Netherlands.

De·la·croix /delakrwaá/, (**Ferdinand Victor**) **Eugène** 1798–1863; French artist.

de la Mare /del ə már, mér/, **Walter John** 1873–1956; English poet and novelist.

De·li·us /deéleeəs/, **Frederick Theodore Albert** 1862–1934; English composer.

De·moc·ri·tus /dimaákrətəs/ c. 460–c. 370 B.C.; Greek philosopher.

De·mos·the·nes /dimaásthəneez/ 384–322 B.C.; Athenian orator and statesman.

Demp·sey /démpsee/, **Jack** (**William Harrison**) (called **"the Manassa Mauler"**) 1895–1983; U.S. boxer.

Deng Xiao·ping /dúng shówpíng/ (also **Teng Hsiao-p'ing**) 1904–97; Chinese political leader.

De Quin·cey /də kwínsee/, **Thomas** 1785–1859; English essayist and critic.

de Sade, Marquis see SADE, DONATIEN.

Des·cartes /daykaárt/, **René** 1596–1650; French philosopher and mathematician.

de So·to /də sótō/, **Hernando** 1496–1542; Spanish explorer in Central and North America.

De Va·le·ra /devəlérə, –lírə/, **Eamon** 1882–1975; Irish political leader, born in U.S.

Dew·ey /do͞obee, d(y)o͞o–/, **John** 1859–1952; U.S. philosopher and educator.

Dew·ey, Melvil 1851–1931; U.S. librarian; developed decimal system for book classification (1876).

Di·a·ghi·lev /dee-aágəlef/, **Sergei Pavlovich** 1872–1929; Russian ballet impresario.

Di·an·a /dīánə/ (**Princess of Wales**) (born Diana Frances Spencer) 1961–97; divorced wife of Charles, Prince of Wales.

Di·as /deéəs, deéaash/ (also **Di′az**), **Bartolomeu** c. 1450–1500; Portuguese explorer.

Dick·ens /díkənz/, **Charles John Huffam** 1812–70; English novelist.

Dick·in·son /díkinsən/, **Emily Elizabeth** 1830–86; U.S. poet.

Di·de·rot /deédərō/, **Denis** 1713–84; French philosopher, encyclopedist, and critic.

Di·Mag·gi·o /dimájeeō/, **Joe** (**Joseph Paul**) 1914– ; U.S. baseball player.

Di·o·cle·tian /dīəkleéshən/ 245–313; Roman emperor (284–305).

Di·og·e·nes /dī-aájəneez/ c. 400–c. 325 B.C.; Greek philosopher.

Di·o·ny·si·us I /dīənísheeəs, –níseeəs/ (called "**the Elder**") c. 430–367 B.C.; tyrant of Syracuse.

Dis·ney /díznee/, **Walt** (**Walter Elias**) 1901–66; U.S. animator, film producer, and theme-park creator.

Dis·rae·li /dizráylee/, **Benjamin** (**1st Earl of Beaconsfield**) 1804–81; prime minister of Great Britain (1868; 1874–80).

Dodg·son /daájsən/, **Charles Lutwidge** see CARROLL, LEWIS.

Dole /dōl/ **1 Robert Joseph** 1923– ; U.S. politician; husband of: **2 Elizabeth Hanford** 1936– ; U.S. public official.

Do·min·go /dəmíng-gō/, **Placido** 1941– ; Spanish operatic tenor.

Dom·i·nic /daáminik/, **St.** c. 1170–1221; Spanish cleric; founder of Dominican religious order.

Do·mi·tian /dəmíshən/ 51–96; Roman emperor (81–96).

Don·a·tel·lo /daanətélō/ (born **Donato de Betto di Bardi**) 1386–1466; Italian sculptor.

Don·i·zet·ti /donizétee, dōnə(d)zétee/, **Gaetano** 1797–1848; Italian composer.

Donne /dún/, **John** 1572–1631; English poet and priest.

Dos Pas·sos /dəs pásəs/, **John** 1896–1970; U.S. novelist.

Do·sto·ev·sky /daastəyéfskee, –yév–/ (also **Do·sto·yev·sky**), **Fyodor Mikhailovich** 1821–81; Russian author.

Doug·las /dúgləs/, **Stephen A(rnold)** 1813–61; U.S. political leader and orator.

Doug·lass /dúgləs/, **Frederick** (born **Frederick Augustus Washington Bailey**) c. 1817–95; U.S. abolitionist, author, and orator.

Doyle /doyl/, (**Sir**) **Arthur Conan** 1859–1930; Scottish author.

Dra·co /dráykō/ 7th cent. B.C.; Athenian lawgiver.

Drake /drayk/, (**Sir**) **Francis** c. 1540–96; English explorer; circumnavigated the world (1577–80).

Drei·ser /drízər/, **Theodore** 1871–1945; U.S. novelist.

Drey·fus /drífəs/, **Alfred** 1859–1935; French army officer; falsely convicted of treason.

Dry·den /dríd'n/, **John** 1631–1700; English poet.

Dub·ček /doóbchek/, **Alexander** 1921–92; Czech political leader.

Du Bois /doō bóys/, **W(illiam) E(dward) B(urghardt)** 1868–1963; U.S. sociologist and educator.

Du·champ /dy shaáN/, **Marcel** 1887–1968; U.S. artist, born in France.

Du·de·vant /doódəvaaN/, **Amandine-Aurore-Lucile Dupin** see SAND, GEORGE.

Du·fy /dyfeé/, **Raoul** 1877–1953; French artist.

Dul·les /dúləs/, **John Foster** 1888–1959; U.S. secretary of state (1953–59).

Dumas /d(y)ōōmaá/ two French playwrights and novelists: **1 Alexandre** (called "**Dumas père**") 1802–70; father of: **2 Alexandre** (called "**Dumas fils**") 1824–95.

Du Mau·ri·er /də máwree-ay, dyōō–/, two English literary figures: **1 George Louis Palmella Busson** 1834–96; novelist and illustrator, born in France; grandfather of: **2** (**Dame**) **Daphne** 1907–89; novelist.

Dun·can /dúngkən/, **Isadora** 1878–1927; U.S. dancer.

Duns Sco·tus /duns skótəs/, **John** c. 1265–1308; Scottish theologian.

du Pont /doōpónt/, **Eleuthère Irénée** 1771–1834; U.S. industrialist, born in France.

Du·rant /dəránt/ two U.S. historians: **1 Will(iam James)** 1885–1981; husband of: **2 Ariel** (born **Ida Kaufman**) 1898–1981.

Dü·rer /doórər, dyoō–/, **Albrecht** 1471–1528; German artist.

Durey /dyré/, **Louis-Edmond** 1888–1979; French composer.

Durk·heim /dyrkém, dərkhīm/, **Émile** 1858–1917; French sociologist.

Du·va·lier /doōvaalyáy/, **François** (called "**Papa Doc**") 1907–71; president of Haiti (1957–71).

Dvo·řák /dváwrzhaak/, **Antonin Leopold** 1841–1904; Czech composer.

Dyl·an /dílən/, **Bob** (born **Robert Allen Zimmerman**) 1941– ; U.S. folk-rock singer and songwriter.

Ear·hart /érhaart, eér–/, **Amelia Mary** 1898–1937?; U.S. aviator.

East·man /eėstmən/, **George** 1854–1932; U.S. inventor and philanthropist; invented Kodak box camera (1888).

Eco /ékō/, **Umberto** 1932– ; Italian novelist and scholar.

Ed·dy /édee/, **Mary** (**Morse**) **Baker** 1821–1910; U.S. founder of the Christian Science Church.

E·den /eėd'n/, (**Sir**) (**Robert**) **Anthony** 1897–1977; prime minister of Great Britain (1955–57).

Ed·i·son /édisən/, **Thomas Alva** 1847–1931; U.S. inventor.

Ed·ward /édwərd/ name of eight British kings, including: **1 Edward I** 1239–1307; reigned 1272–1307. **2 Edward VII** 1841–1910; eldest son of Queen Victoria; reigned 1901–10. **3 Edward VIII** 1894–1972; reigned 1936; abdicated, became Duke of Windsor.

Ed·wards /édwərdz/, **Jonathan** 1703–58; American theologian and clergyman.

Eich·mann /íkmən, íkhmaan/, (**Karl**) **Adolf** 1906–62; German Nazi officer; executed as a war criminal.

Eif·fel /ífəl/, **Alexandre Gustave** 1832–1923; French engineer; designer of the Eiffel Tower.

Ein·stein /ínstīn/, **Albert** 1879–1955; U.S. physicist, born in Germany; promulgated theory of relativity.

Ei·sen·how·er /ízənhowər/, **Dwight David** (called **"Ike"**) 1890–1969; U.S. general and 34th president of the U.S. (1953–61).

Ei·sen·staedt /ízənstat/, **Alfred** 1898–1995; U.S. photojournalist, born in Germany.

El Cid see CID, EL.

El·ea·nor /élənər, –nawr/ **of Aq·ui·taine** /ákwitayn/ c. 1122–1204; queen of France (1137–52) and England (1154–89).

El·gar /élgaar, –gər/, (**Sir**) **Edward William** 1857–1934; English composer.

El Gre·co see GRECO, EL.

E·li·a /eélee₃/ see LAMB, CHARLES.

El·i·ot /éleeət/, **George** (pseudonym of **Mary Ann Evans**) 1819–80; English novelist.

El·i·ot, T(**homas**) **S**(**tearns**) 1888–1965; British poet and critic, born in U.S.

El·iz·a·beth /ilízəbəth/ name of two British monarchs: **1 Elizabeth I** 1533–1603; reigned 1558–1603; **2 Elizabeth II** 1926– ; reigned 1952– .

El·ling·ton /élingtən/, **Duke** (**Edward Kennedy**) 1899–1974; U.S. jazz pianist, bandleader, and composer.

El·lis /éləs/, (**Henry**) **Havelock** 1859–1939; English psychologist.

Em·er·son /émərsən/, **Ralph Waldo** 1803–82; U.S. essayist and poet.

Em·ped·o·cles /empédəkleez/ c. 493–c. 433 B.C.; Greek philosopher.

En·gels /éng-gəlz/, **Friedrich** 1820–95; German political philosopher in England.

En·ni·us /éneeəs/, **Quintus** 239–169 B.C.; Roman poet and playwright.

En·ver Pa·sha /énver paáshə, pəshaá/ 1881–1922; Turkish statesman and military leader.

E·pi·cu·rus /epikyŏŏrəs/ 341–270 B.C.; Greek philosopher.

E·ras·mus /irázməs/, **Desiderius** c. 1469–1536; Dutch theologian and humanist.

Er·ic /érik/ (called **"the Red"**) c. 940–c. 1010; Norse explorer.

Er·ic·son /ériksən/ (also **Er'ics·son**; **Er'iks·son**), **Leif** early 11th cent.; Norse explorer.

Ernst /ernst/, **Max** 1891–1976; German artist.

Eth·el·red II /éthəlred/ (called **"the Unready"**) c. 969–1016; king of England (978–1016).

Eu·clid /yŏŏklid/ 3rd cent. B.C.; Greek mathematician.

Eu·gé·nie /yŏŏjənee, yŏŏjáynee/ 1826–1920; empress of France (1853–71), born in Spain; wife of Napoleon III.

Eu·rip·i·des /yŏŏrípideez/ 480–c. 406 B.C.; Greek playwright.

Ev·ans /évənz/, (**Sir**) **Arthur John** 1851–1941; British archaeologist.

Ev·ans, (**Dame**) **Edith** 1888–1976; English actress.

Ev·ans, Mary Ann see ELIOT, GEORGE.

Fa·ber·gé /fabərzháy/, **Peter Carl** 1846–1920; Russian goldsmith and jeweler.

Fahd /faad/ 1922– ; king of Saudi Arabia (1982–).

Fair·field /fáirfeeld/, **Cicily Isabel** see WEST, REBECCA.

Fal·la /faáyə/, **Manuel de** 1876–1946; Spanish composer.

Far·a·day /fárədee, –day/, **Michael** 1791–1867; British chemist and physicist.

Fa·rouk /fərŏŏk/ 1920–65; king of Egypt (1936–52).

Far·ra·gut /fárəgət/, **David Glasgow** (born **James Glasgow Farragut**) 1801–70; U.S. naval commander.

Faulk·ner /fáwknər/, **William Cuthbert** 1897–1962; U.S. novelist.

Fau·ré /fawráy/, **Gabriel** 1845–1924; French composer.

Faust /fowst/ (also **Faus·tus**) died c. 1540; German astronomer and necromancer.

Fer·ber /fárbər/, **Edna** 1885–1968; U.S. author.

Fer·di·nand II /fárd'nand/ (called **"the Catholic"**) 1452–1516; W European king who founded the Spanish monarchy; husband of Isabella I.

Fer·mi /férmee/, **Enrico** 1901–54; U.S. nuclear physicist, born in Italy.

Fied·ler /feédlər/, **Arthur** 1894–1979; U.S. conductor.

Field·ing /feélding/, **Henry** 1707–54; English novelist.

Fields /feeldz/, **W. C.** (born **William Claude Dukenfield**) 1880–1946; U.S. vaudevillian and comedic actor.

Fill·more /fílmawr, –mōr/, **Millard** 1800–74; 13th president of the U.S. (1850–53).

Fitz·ger·ald /fitsjérəld/, **Ella** 1918–96; U.S. jazz singer.

Fitz·ger·ald, **F(rancis) Scott Key** 1896–1940; U.S. author.

Flau·bert /flōbér/, **Gustave** 1821–80; French author.

Flem·ing /fléming/, **(Sir) Alexander** 1881–1955; Scottish bacteriologist; discovered and developed penicillin.

Flem·ing, **Ian Lancaster** 1908–64; English novelist.

Fletch·er /fléchər/, **John** 1579–1625; English playwright.

Foch /fawsh/, **Ferdinand** 1851–1929; French general.

Fon·da /faándə/ family of U.S. actors, including: **1 Henry** 1905–82; father of: **2 Jane** 1937– .

Fon·teyn /faantáyn/, **(Dame) Margot** (born **Margaret Hookham**) 1919–91; English prima ballerina.

Ford /fawrd/, **Ford Madox** (born **Ford Hermann Hueffer**) 1873–1939; English novelist.

Ford, **Gerald Rudolph, Jr.** (born **Leslie Lynch King, Jr.**) 1913– ; 38th president of the U.S. (1974–77).

Ford, **Henry** 1863–1947; U.S. automobile manufacturer.

For·ster /fáwrstər/, **E(dward) M(organ)** 1879–1970; English novelist.

For·syth /fáwrsīth, fawrsíth/, **Frederick** 1938– ; English novelist.

Fos·ter /fáwstər, faástər/, **Stephen Collins** 1826–64; U.S. songwriter.

Fou·cault /fookó/, **Michel** 1929–84; French philosopher.

Fowles /fowlz/, **John** 1926– ; English novelist.

Fox /faaks/, **George** 1624–91; English founder of the Society of Friends (Quakers).

Fra·go·nard /fragənaár/, **Jean-Honoré** 1732–1806; French artist.

France /frans/, **Anatole** (pseudonym of **Jacques Anatole Thibault**) 1844–1924; French author.

Fran·cis /fránsis/ **of As·si·si** /əsísee, əseéezee/, **St.** c. 1181–1226; Italian monk; founder of Franciscan religious order.

Franck /fraangk/, **César** 1822–90; French composer, born in Belgium.

Fran·co /frángkō, fraáng–/, **Francisco** 1892–1975; Spanish general; dictator of Spain (1939–75).

Frank /frangk/, **Anne** 1929–45; Jewish diarist, born in Germany; wrote diary while in hiding from the Nazis.

Frank·furt·er /frángkfərtər/, **Felix** 1882–1965; U.S. Supreme Court justice (1939–62), born in Austria.

Frank·lin /frángklən/, **Aretha** 1943– ; U.S. soul and gospel singer.

Frank·lin, **Benjamin** 1706–90; U.S. statesman, author, and inventor.

Franz Jo·sef I /fraanz yōzəf/ 1830–1916; emperor of Austria (1848–1916).

Fra·zer /fráyzər/, **(Sir) James George** 1854–1941; Scottish anthropologist.

Fred·er·ick I /fréd(ə)rik/ (called **"Barbarossa"**) c. 1123–90; Holy Roman emperor (1152–90).

Fred·er·ick II (called **"the Great"**) 1712–86; king of Prussia (1740–86).

Fred·er·ick Wil·liam /wílyəm/ (called **"the Great Elector"**) 1620–88; elector of Brandenburg (1640–88).

Fré·mont /freémaant/, **John Charles** 1813–90; U.S. explorer and politician.

Freud /froyd/, **Lucian** 1922– ; British artist, born in Germany.

Freud, **Sigmund** 1856–1939; Austrian neurologist; founder of psychoanalysis.

Frie·dan /freedán/, **Betty** (born **Naomi Goldstein**) 1921– ; U.S. feminist and author.

Fried·man /freédmən/, **Milton** 1912– ; U.S. economist.

Frost /frawst/, **Robert Lee** 1874–1963; U.S. poet.

Frye /frī/, **(Herman) Northrop** 1912–91; Canadian literary critic.

Fu·ad /foō-aád/ name of two kings of Egypt: **1 Fuad I** 1868–1936; reigned 1922–36. **2 Fuad II** 1952– ; reigned 1952–53.

Fuen·tes /fwéntays/, **Carlos** 1928– ; Mexican author.

Ful·bright /foólbrīt/, **(James) William** 1905–95; U.S. senator.

Ful·ler /foólər/, **R(ichard) Buckminster** 1895–1983; U.S. engineer and architect.

Ful·ler, **(Sarah) Margaret** 1810–50; U.S. critic and social reformer.

Ful·ton /foólt'n/, **Robert** 1765–1815; U.S. engineer; developed first commercially successful steamboat.

Ga·ble /gáybəl/, (**William**) **Clark** 1901–60; U.S. actor.

Gad·da·fi /gədaáfee/ see QADHAFI, MUAMMAR.

Ga·ga·rin /gəgaárən/, **Yuri** 1934–68; Soviet cosmonaut; first human in space.

Gage /gayj/, **Thomas** 1721–87; British general.

Gains·bor·ough /gáynzbrō, –bərə/, **Thomas** 1727–88; English artist.

Gal·braith /gálbrayth/, **John Kenneth** 1908– ; U.S. economist, born in Canada.

Ga·len /gáylən/ c. 130–c. 201; Greek physician.

Gal·i·le·o /galəláyō, –leéō/ 1564–1642; Italian astronomer.

Gals·wor·thy /gáwlzwərthee/, **John** 1867–1933; English novelist and playwright.

Ga·ma /gaámə/, **Vasco da** c. 1469–1524; Portuguese navigator.

Gan·dhi /gaándee/ two Indian prime ministers: **1 Indira Priyadarshini Nehru** 1917–84; in office 1966–77; 1980–84; assassinated; mother of: **2 Rajiv** 1944–91; in office 1984–89; assassinated.

Gan·dhi, **Mahatma** (born **Mohandes Karamchand**) 1869–1948; Indian nationalist and spiritual leader.

Gar·bo /gaárbō/, **Greta** (born **Greta Louisa Gustafsson**) 1905–90; U.S. actress, born in Sweden.

Gar·cí·a Lor·ca /gaarseéə láwrkə/, **Federico** 1899–1936; Spanish poet and playwright.

Gar·cí·a Már·quez /gaarseéə maárkays/, **Gabriel** 1928– ; Colombian author.

Gard·ner /gaárdnər/, **Erle Stanley** 1899–1970; U.S. author.

Gar·field /gaárfeeld/, **James Abram** 1831–81; 20th president of the U.S. (1881); assassinated.

Gar·i·bal·di /garəbáwldee/, **Giuseppe** 1807–82; Italian nationalist.

Gar·land /gárlənd/, **Judy** (born **Frances Gumm**) 1922–69; U.S. singer and actress.

Gar·ri·son /gárəsən/, **William Lloyd** 1805–79; U.S. editor and abolitionist.

Gar·vey /gaárvee/, **Marcus Mosiah** 1887–1940; Jamaican black nationalist.

Gates /gayts/, **Bill** (**William Henry**) 1955– ; U.S. computer executive.

Gates, **Horatio** c. 1728–1806; American Revolutionary War general, born in England.

Gau·guin /gōgáN/, (**Eugène**) **Paul** 1848–1903; French artist.

Gaulle see DE GAULLE.

Gau·ta·ma /gówtəmə, gáw–/ see BUDDHA.

Geh·rig /gérig/, **Lou** (**Henry Louis**) (called **"the Iron Horse"**) 1903–41; U.S. baseball player.

Gei·sel /gízəl/, **Theodor Seuss** see SEUSS, DR.

Gen·ghis Khan /géng-gəs, jeng-gəs kaán/ c. 1162–1227; ruler of the Mongols; conquered most of Asia.

George III /jawrj/ 1738–1820; king of England (1760–1820); reigned during American Revolution.

George, St. died c. 337; patron saint of England.

Ge·ron·i·mo /jəraánəmō/ c. 1829–1909; Apache Indian leader.

Gersh·win /górshwən/ **1 Ira** 1896–1983; U.S. lyricist; brother of: **2 George** 1898–1937; U.S. composer.

Get·ty /gétee/, **J**(**ean**) **Paul** 1892–1976; U.S. industrialist.

Gib·bon /gíbən/, **Edward** 1737–94; English historian.

Gib·ran /jibraán/, **Kahlil** 1883–1931; Lebanese author and artist.

Gide /zheed/, **André** 1869–1951; French author.

Giel·gud /geélgōōd/, (**Sir**) (**Arthur**) **John** 1904– ; English actor and director.

Gil·bert /gílbərt/, (**Sir**) **W**(**illiam**) **S**(**chwenck**) 1836–1911; English playwright and librettist; collaborated with composer (**Sir**) Arthur Sullivan.

Gil·les·pie /gəléspee/, **Dizzy** (**John Birks**) 1917–93; U.S. jazz musician.

Ging·rich /gíngrich/, **Newt**(**on Leroy**) 1943– ; U.S. politician.

Gins·berg /gínzbərg/, **Allen** 1926–97; U.S. poet.

Gins·berg, **Ruth Bader** 1933– ; U.S. Supreme Court justice (1993–).

Gior·gio·ne /jawrjónay/ c. 1478–1511; Italian artist.

Giot·to /jaátō, jee-aátō/ c. 1267–1337; Florentine artist.

Gis·card d'Es·taing /zheeskaár destáN/, **Valéry** 1926– ; president of France (1974–81).

Gish /gish/, **Lillian** 1896–1993; U.S. actress.

Glad·stone /gládstōn, –stən/, **William Ewart** 1809–98; prime minister of Great Britain (1868–74; 1880–85; 1886; 1892–94).

Glea·son /gleésən/, **Jackie** 1916–87; U.S. entertainer.

Glen·dow·er /glendówər/ (also **Glyn·dwr'**) /glindōōr/, **Owen** c. 1355–c. 1417; legendary Welsh rebel.

Glenn /glen/, **John Herschel, Jr.** 1921– ; U.S. astronaut and politician; first American to orbit the earth (1962).

God·dard /gaádərd/, **Robert Hutchings** 1882–1945; U.S. rocket scientist.

Go·di·va /gədívə/, **Lady** died 1080; legendary English noblewoman.

Go·du·nov /gŏd'n-awf, gáwd–/, **Boris** 1550–1605; czar of Russia (1598–1605).

Goeb·bels /gŏbəlz, gŏr–/, (**Paul**) **Joseph** 1897–1945; German director of Nazi propaganda.

Goe·ring /gŏring, gŏr–/, **Hermann Wilhelm** 1893–1946; German Nazi leader; directed the air force.

Goe·the /gŏtə, gŏr–/, **Johann Wolfgang von** 1749–1832; German poet and statesman.

Go·gol /gŏgawl, gáwgəl/, **Nikolai Vasilievich** 1809–52; Russian novelist and playwright.

Gol·ding /gŏlding/, (**Sir**) **William** 1911–93; English author.

Gold·smith /gŏldsmith/, **Oliver** 1728–74; Irish author.

Go·li·ath /gəlíəth/ biblical giant killed by David.

Gom·pers /gaámpərz/, **Samuel** 1850–1924; U.S. labor leader, born in England.

Good·man /gŏŏdmən/, **Benny** (**Benjamin David**) (called **"the King of Swing"**) 1909–86; U.S. jazz clarinetist and bandleader.

Good·year /gŏŏdyeer/, **Charles** 1800–60; U.S. inventor; developed vulcanized rubber.

Gor·ba·chev /gáwrbəchawf, –chawv/, **Mikhail Sergeyevich** 1931– ; president of the Soviet Union (1988–91).

Gordimer /gáwrdimər/, **Nadine** 1923– ; South African novelist.

Gor·don /gáwrd'n/, **Charles George** 1833–85; British general and colonial administrator.

Gore /gawr/, **Albert, Jr.** 1948– ; U.S. vice president (1993–).

Gor·ky /gáwrkee/, **Maxim** (pseudonym of **Aleksei Maksimovich Peshkov**) 1868–1936; Russian author and revolutionary.

Gou·nod /gŏŏnó/, **Charles François** 1818–93; French composer.

Go·ya /góyə/, **Francisco** 1746–1828; Spanish artist.

Gra·ham /gráyəm, gram/, **Billy** (**William Franklin**) 1918– ; U.S. evangelical preacher.

Gra·ham, Katherine 1917– ; U.S. newspaper executive.

Gra·ham, Martha 1893–1991; U.S. dancer and choreographer.

Gra·hame /gráyəm/, **Kenneth** 1859–1932; Scottish author.

Grant /grant/, **Cary** (born **Archibald Alexander Leach**) 1904–86; U.S. actor, born in England.

Grant, Ulysses S(**impson**) (born **Hiram Ulysses Grant**) 1822–85; Union general in the American Civil War; 18th president of the U.S. (1869–77).

Grass /graas/, **Günter** 1927– ; German novelist and playwright.

Graves /grayvz/, **Robert** 1895–1985; English poet, novelist, and critic.

Gray /gray/, **Thomas** 1716–71; English poet.

Gre·co /grékō/, **El** (born **Domenikos Theotokopoulos**) 1541–1614; Spanish artist, born in Crete.

Gree·ley /greélee/, **Horace** 1811–72; U.S. journalist and politician.

Greene /green/, (**Henry**) **Graham** 1904–91; English novelist.

Greene, Nathanael 1742–86; American Revolutionary War general.

Green·span /geénspan/, **Alan** 1926– ; U.S. economist.

Greer /greer/, **Germaine** 1939– ; Australian feminist and author.

Greg·o·ry /grégəree/ name of sixteen popes, including: **1 Gregory I, St.** (called **"the Great"**) c. 540–604; pope (590–604); developed the Gregorian chant. **2 Gregory XIII** 1502–85; pope (1572–85); introduced the modern calendar.

Gren·ville /grénvil/, **George** 1712–70; prime minister of Great Britain (1763–65).

Grey /gray/, (**Lady**) **Jane** 1537–54; queen of England (1553); executed by Mary I.

Grey, Zane 1875–1939; U.S. author.

Grieg /greeg/, **Edvard** 1843–1907; Norwegian composer.

Grif·fith /grífith/, **D**(**avid Lewelyn**) **W**(**ark**) 1875–1948; U.S. film director.

Grimm /grim/ two German philologists and folklorists: **1 Jacob Ludwig Karl** 1785–1863; brother of: **2 Wilhelm Karl** 1786–1859.

Gro·my·ko /grəmeékō/, **Andrei** 1909–89; Russian diplomat.

Gro·pi·us /grópeeəs/, **Walter** 1883–1969; U.S. architect, born in Germany.

Gue·va·ra /g(w)əvaárə, gay–/, **Che** (**Ernesto**) 1928–67; Cuban revolutionary, born in Argentina.

Guin·ness /gínəs/, (**Sir**) **Alec** 1914– ; British actor.

Gus·tav·us A·dol·phus /gustaávəs ədáwlfəs/ 1594–1632; king of Sweden (1611–32).

Gut·en·berg /gŏŏt'n-bərg/, **Johannes** c. 1400–68; German inventor of printing with movable type.

Guth·rie /gúthree/, **Woody** (**Woodrow Wilson**) 1912–67; U.S. folk musician, singer, and songwriter.

Hai·le Se·las·sie /híle səlaásee, –lás–/ (born **Tafari Makonnen**) 1892–1975; emperor of Ethiopia (1930–74).

Hak·luyt /háklo͞ot, háklit/, **Richard** c. 1552–1616; English geographer.

Hale/hayl/, **Nathan** 1755–76; American Revolutionary hero; hanged as a spy by British.

Ha·ley /háylee/, **Alex Palmer** 1921–92; U.S. author.

Hal·ley /hálee, háylee/, **Edmund** 1656–1742; English astronomer.

Hals /haals/, **Frans** c. 1580–1666; Dutch artist.

Hal·sey /háwlzee/, **William Frederick** (called **"Bull"**) 1882–1959; U.S. admiral.

Ham·il·ton /hámiltən/, **Alexander** 1755–1804; first U.S. secretary of the treasury (1789–95).

Ham·mar·skjold /haámərshəld, hám–/, **Dag** 1905–61; Swedish statesman; secretary-general of the United Nations (1953–61).

Ham·mer·stein /hámərstīn/, **Oscar, II** 1895–1960; U.S. lyricist and librettist.

Ham·mett /hámit/, (**Samuel**) **Dashiell** 1894–1961; U.S. author.

Ham·mu·ra·bi /haməraábee, haam–/ fl. 18th cent. B.C.; king of Babylon (1792–1750 B.C.); instituted early code of laws.

Ham·sun /haámsən/, **Knut** (pseudonym of **Knut Pedersen**) 1859–1952; Norwegian novelist.

Han·cock /hánkaak/, **John** 1737–93; American politician; first signer of the U.S. Declaration of Independence.

Han·del /hándəl/, **George Frederick** 1685–1759; British composer, born in Germany.

Han·dy /hándee/, **W(illiam) C(hristopher)** 1873–1958; U.S. blues musician and composer.

Hanks /hangks/, **Tom** (**Thomas J.**) 1956– ; U.S. actor.

Han·ni·bal /hánibəl/ 247–182 B.C.; Carthaginian general.

Har·ding /haárding/, **Warren Gamaliel** 1865–1923; 29th president of the U.S. (1921–23).

Har·dy /haárdee/, **Thomas** 1840–1928; English author.

Harms·worth /haármzwərth/, **Alfred** (**Viscount Northcliffe**) 1865–1922; English publisher and politician.

Har·ris /háris/, **Joel Chandler** 1848–1908; U.S. author.

Har·ri·son/hárisən/, **George** 1943– ; British pop and rock guitarist, singer, and songwriter.

Har·ri·son, (**Sir**) **Rex** 1908–90; English actor.

Har·ri·son, family of U.S. politicians, including: **1 William Henry** 1773–1841; 9th president of the U.S. (1841); grandfather of: **2 Benjamin** 1833–1901; 23rd president of the U.S. (1889–93).

Hart /haart/, **Lorenz** 1895–1943; U.S. lyricist.

Harte /haart/, (**Francis**) **Bret** 1836–1902; U.S. author.

Har·vey /haárvee/, **William** 1578–1657; English physician and anatomist.

Hath·a·way /háthəway/, **Anne** c. 1557–1623; wife of William Shakespeare.

Haupt·mann /hówptmaan/, **Gerhart** 1862–1946; German playwright.

Ha·vel /haávəl/, **Václav** 1936– ; Czech author and politician.

Hawke /hawk/, **Bob** (**Robert James Lee**) 1929– ; prime minister of Australia (1983–91).

Hawk·ing /háwking/, **Stephen William** 1942– ; British scientist.

Haw·thorne /háwthawrn/, **Nathaniel** 1804–64; U.S. author.

Hay /hay/, **John Milton** 1838–1905; U.S. statesman.

Hay·dn /hīd'n/, **Franz Joseph** 1732–1809; Austrian composer.

Hayes/hayz/, **Helen** (born **Helen Hayes Brown**) 1900–93; U.S. actress.

Hayes, Rutherford B(irchard) 1822–93; 19th president of the U.S. (1877–81).

Hearst /hərst/, **William Randolph** 1863–1951; U.S. newspaper publisher.

Heath /heeth/, (**Sir**) **Edward** 1916– ; prime minister of Great Britain (1970–74).

He·gel /háygəl/, **Georg Wilhelm Friedrich** 1770–1831; German philosopher.

Hei·deg·ger /hídigər/, **Martin** 1889–1976; German philosopher.

Hei·fetz /hífəts/, **Jascha** 1901–87; U.S. violinist, born in Lithuania.

Hei·ne /hínə/, (**Christian**) **Heinrich** 1797–1856; German poet.

Heinz /hīnz/, **Henry John** 1844–1919; U.S. manufacturer of processed foods.

Hel·ler /hélər/, **Joseph** 1923– ; U.S. author.

Hell·man /hélmən/, **Lillian Florence** 1905–84; U.S. playwright.

Hem·ing·way /hémingway/, **Ernest Miller** 1899–1961; U.S. author.

Hen·drix /héndriks/, **Jimi** 1942–70; U.S. rock guitarist, singer, and songwriter.

Hen·ry /hénree/ (called **"the Navigator"**) 1394–1460; prince of Portugal; sponsor of geographic expeditions.

Hen·ry VIII 1491–1547; king of England (1509–47).

Hen·ry, O. (pseudonym of **William Sydney Porter**) 1862–1910; U.S. author.

Hen·ry, Patrick 1736–99; American patriot and orator.

Hen·son /hénsən/, **Jim** (**James Maury**) 1936–90; U.S. puppeteer; creator of the Muppets.

Hep·burn /hépbərn/, **Audrey** 1929–93; U.S. actress, born in Belgium.

Hep·burn, Katharine 1909– ; U.S. actress.

Her·a·cli·tus /herəklítəs/ c. 500 B.C.; Greek philosopher.

Her·od /hérəd/ several rulers of ancient Palestine, including: **1 Herod I** (called **"the Great"**) c. 74–4 B.C.; king of Judea (37–4 B.C.); father of: **2 Herod Antipas** 22 B.C.–A.D. c. 40; ruler of Galilee (4 B.C.–A.D. 40). **3 Herod Agrippa I** 10 B.C.–A.D. 44; king of Judea (41–44); grandson of Herod I.

He·rod·o·tus /hərádətəs/ (called **"the Father of History"**) fl. 5th cent. B.C.; Greek historian.

Her·rick /hérik/, **Robert** 1591–1674; English poet.

Her·zl /hértsəl/, **Theodor** 1860–1904; Austrian founder of the Zionist movement, born in Hungary.

He·si·od /héseeəd, hésee–/ fl. 8th cent. B.C.; Greek poet.

Hess /hes/, (**Walter Richard**) **Rudolf** 1894–1987; German Nazi official, born in Egypt.

Hes·se /hésə/, **Hermann** 1877–1962; Swiss author, born in Germany.

Hey·er·dahl /híərdaal/, **Thor** 1914– ; Norwegian explorer and ethnologist.

Hick·ok /híkaak/, **James Butler** (called **"Wild Bill Hickock"**) 1837–76; U.S. frontiersman.

Hil·la·ry /híləree/, (**Sir**) **Edmund Percival** 1919– ; New Zealand mountaineer; climbed Mt. Everest (1953).

Hil·ton /hílt'n/, **James** 1900–54; English novelist.

Himm·ler /hímlər/, **Heinrich** 1900–45; German head of the Nazi secret police.

Hin·de·mith /híndəmit/, **Paul** 1895–1963; German composer.

Hin·den·burg /híndinbərg/, **Paul von** 1847–1934; German field marshal; 2nd president of Germany (1925–32).

Hip·poc·ra·tes /hipákrəteez/ (called **"the Father of Medicine"**) c. 460–c. 377 B.C.; Greek physician.

Hi·ro·hi·to /heerōheétō/ (also known as **Sho'wa**) 1901–89; emperor of Japan (1926–89).

Hitch·cock /híchkaak/, (**Sir**) **Alfred Joseph** 1899–1980; British film director.

Hit·ler /hítlər/, **Adolf** (born **Adolf Schicklgruber**) (called **"Der Führer"**) 1889–1945; dictator of Nazi Germany (1934–45), born in Austria.

Ho Chi Minh /hó cheé mín/ (born **Nguyen That Thanh**) 1890–1969; Vietnamese revolutionary; president of North Vietnam (1954–1969).

Hobbes /haabz/, **Thomas** 1588–1679; English philosopher.

Ho·garth /hógaarth/, **William** 1697–1764; English artist and engraver.

Hol·bein /hólbīn, háwl–/ name of two German artists: **1 Hans** (called **"the Elder"**) c. 1465–1524; father of: **2 Hans** (called **"the Younger"**) c. 1497–1543; worked in England.

Hol·ins·hed /haálins-hed, –inshed/, **Raphael** died c. 1580; English chronicler.

Holmes /hōlmz, hōmz/ **1 Oliver Wendell** 1809–94; U.S. author and physician; father of: **2 Oliver Wendell** 1841–1935; U.S. Supreme Court justice (1902–32).

Holst /hōlst/, **Gustav** 1874–1934; English composer.

Ho·mer /hómər/ 8th cent. B.C.; Greek epic poet.

Ho·mer, Winslow 1836–1910; U.S. artist.

Ho·neck·er /hónəkər/, **Erich** 1912–94; head of state of East Germany (1976–89).

Hoo·ver /hoʻovər/, **Herbert Clark** 1874–1964; 31st president of the U.S. (1929–33).

Hoo·ver, J(ohn) Edgar 1895–1972; director of the Federal Bureau of Investigation (1924–72).

Hope /hōp/, **Bob** (born **Leslie Townes Hope**) 1903– ; U.S. comedian and actor, born in England.

Hop·kins /haápkinz/, **Gerard Manley** 1844–89; English poet.

Hop·per /haápər/, **Edward** 1882–1967; U.S. artist.

Hor·ace /háwrəs/ (**Quintus Horatius Flaccus**) 65–8 B.C.; Roman poet.

Hor·o·witz /háwrəwits, haár–/, **Vladimir** 1904–89; U.S. pianist, born in Russia.

Hou·di·ni /hoōdeénee/, **Harry** (born **Ehrich Weiss**) 1874–1926; U.S. magician and escape artist, born in Hungary.

Hous·man /hówsmən/, **A(lfred) E(dward)** 1859–1936; English poet.

Hous·ton /hyoʻostən/, **Samuel** 1793–1863; U.S. general and president of the Republic of Texas (1836–38).

Howe /how/, **Elias** 1819–67; U.S. inventor of the sewing machine.

Howe, Julia Ward 1819–1910; U.S. social reformer and author.

How·ells /hówəlz/, **William Dean** 1837–1920; U.S. author and editor.

Hox·ha /háwjə/, **Enver** 1908–85; Albanian Communist political leader.

Hud·son /húdsən/, **Henry** died 1611?; English explorer.

Hughes /hyoōz, yoōz/, **Howard Robard** 1905–76; U.S. aviator and industrialist.

Hughes, **(James) Langston** 1902–67; U.S. author.

Hughes, Ted 1930– ; English poet.

Hu·go /hyō/gō/, **Victor** 1802–85; French author.

Hume /hyōom, yōom/, **David** 1711–76; Scottish philosopher and historian.

Hum·per·dinck /húmpərdingk/, **Engelbert** 1854–1921; German composer.

Hus·sein I /hōosayn/ (also **Hu'sain**) 1935– ; king of Jordan (1953–).

Hus·sein, Saddam 1937– ; political leader of Iraq.

Hus·serl /húsərl/, **Edmund** 1859–1938; German philosopher.

Hutch·in·son /húchinsən/, **Anne** 1591–1643; American religious leader, born in England.

Hux·ley /húkslee/, **Aldous Leonard** 1894–1963; English novelist.

Ibn Sa·ud /íbən saa-ōod/, **Abdul-Aziz** c. 1880–1953; king of Saudi Arabia (1932–53).

Ib·sen /íbsən/, **Henrik** 1828–1906; Norwegian playwright.

Ig·na·tius /ignáyshəs/ **of Loy·o·la** /loyólə/, **St.** 1491–1556; Spanish founder of the Jesuit religious order.

Ikh·na·ton /iknaátən/ see *Amenhotep IV* (AMENHOTEP).

Inge /inj/, **William Motter** 1913–73; U.S. playwright.

In·gres /aNgr/, **Jean** 1780–1867; French artist.

Io·nes·co /yənéskō, eeə–/, **Eugène** 1912–94; French playwright, born in Romania.

Ir·ving /ə́rving/, **Washington** 1783–1859; U.S. author.

I·sa·bel·la I /izəbélə/ 1474–1504; queen of Castile and Aragon; sponsor of Christopher Columbus.

Ish·er·wood /íshərwŏod/, **Christopher William Bradshaw** 1904–86; U.S. novelist, born in England.

I·van IV /ívən/ (called **"Ivan the Terrible"**) 1530–84; first czar of Russia (1547–84).

Ives /īvz/, **Charles Edward** 1874–1954; U.S. composer.

Jack·son /jáksən/, **Andrew** (called **"Old Hickory"**) 1767–1845; U.S. general; 7th president of the U.S. (1828–37).

Jack·son, Jesse Louis 1941– ; U.S. clergyman and civil-rights activist.

Jack·son, Michael 1958– ; U.S. pop singer and songwriter.

Jack·son, Shirley 1919–65; U.S. author.

Jack·son, Thomas Jonathan (called **"Stonewall Jackson"**) 1824–63; Confederate general in the American Civil War.

Jag·ger /jágər/, **Mick (Michael Philip)** 1944– ; English rock singer.

James I /jaymz/, 1566–1625; king of England and Ireland (1603–25). □□ **Ja·co·be'an** *adj. & n.*

James, Henry 1843–1916; British novelist and critic, born in the U.S.

James, Jesse Woodson 1847–82; U.S. outlaw.

James, P(hyliss) D(orothy) 1920– ; British author.

James, William 1842–1910; U.S. philosopher and psychologist.

Jef·fer·son /jéfərsən/, **Thomas** 1743–1826; U.S. patriot and statesman; 3rd president of the U.S. (1801–09). □□ **Jef·fer·so'ni·an** /–só-neeən/ *adj.*

Je·rome /jəróm/, **St.** c. 342–420; early Christian scholar; published the Vulgate Bible.

Je·sus /jéezəs, –zəz/ (also known as **Je'sus Christ'** or **Je'sus of Naz'a·reth**) c. 4 B.C.–c. A.D. 30; source of the Christian religion.

Joan /jōn/ **of Arc, St.** (called **"the Maid of Orleans"**) c. 1412–31; French national heroine and Christian martyr.

John /jaan/ (called **"John Lackland"**) 1165–1216; king of England (1199–1216); signed the Magna Carta (1215).

John Paul II /jaan páwl/ (born **Karol Jozef Wojtyla**) 1920– ; pope (1978–), born in Poland.

Johns /jaanz/, **Jasper** 1930– ; U.S. artist.

John·son /jaánsən/, **Andrew** 1808–75; 17th president of the U.S. (1865–69).

John·son, Lyndon Baines (called **"L.B.J."**) 1908–73; 36th president of the U.S. (1963–69).

John·son, Samuel 1709–84; English lexicographer and author.

Jo·li·et /zhawlyáy/, **Louis** 1645–1700; French-Canadian explorer.

Jones /jōnz/, **Inigo** 1573–1652; English architect.

Jones, John Paul (born **John Paul**) 1747–92; American naval hero, born in Scotland.

Jong /jong/, **Erica** 1942– ; U.S. author.

Jon·son /jaánsən/, **Ben(jamin)** 1572–1637; English playwright and poet.

Jordan /jáwrd'n/, **Michael Jeffrey** 1963– ; U.S. basketball player.

Jo·se·phus /jōseéfəs/, **Flavius** c. 37–c. 100; Jewish historian and general.

Joyce /joys/, **James** 1882–1941; Irish author.

Juan Car·los /waan kaárlōs, hwaan/ 1938– ; king of Spain (1975–).

Ju·das Is·car·i·ot /jo͞odəs iskáireeət/ died c. 30; apostle who betrayed Jesus.

Jul·ius /jo͞olyəs/, **Caesar** see CAESAR, (GAIUS) JULIUS.

Jung /yo͞ong/, **Carl Gustav** 1875–1961; Swiss psychologist. ▢▢ **Jung'i·an** /–eeən/ *adj.*

Jus·tin·i·an /justíneeən/ 483–565; Byzantine emperor (527–565); codified Roman law.

Ju·ve·nal /jo͞ovən'l/ c. 60–c. 140; Roman satirist.

Kaf·ka /kaáfkə/, **Franz** 1883–1924; Czech author.

Ka·me·ha·me·ha I /kəmayəmáyhə/ c. 1758–1819; king of Hawaii (1810–19).

Kan·din·sky /kandínskee/, **Wassily** 1866–1944; Russian artist.

Kant /kaant, kant/, **Immanuel** 1724–1804; German philosopher.

Ka·wa·ba·ta /kaawəbaátə, kawaábətə/, **Yasunari** 1899–1972; Japanese author.

Keats /keets/, **John** 1795–1821; English poet.

Kel·ler /kélər/, **Helen Adams** 1880–1968; U.S. author, educator, and social reformer; deaf and blind from infancy.

Kel·ly /kélee/, **Grace** 1928–82; U.S. actress; princess of Monaco (1956–82).

Kem·pis /kémpis/, **Thomas à** (born **Thomas Hemerken**) c. 1379–1471; German monk and author.

Ken·ne·dy U.S. political family, including three brothers: **1 John Fitzgerald** (called **"J.F.K."**) 1917–63; 35th president of the U.S. (1961–63); assassinated; **2 Robert Francis** 1925–68; U.S. politician; assassinated; and **3 Ted** (**Edward Moore**) 1932– ; U.S. politician.

Ken·ne·dy /kénədee/, **Anthony Mcleod** 1936– ; U.S. Supreme Court justice (1988–).

Ken·yat·ta /kenyaátə/, **Jomo** c. 1891–1978; Kenyan political leader.

Kep·ler /képlər/, **Johannes** 1571–1630; German astronomer.

Kern /kərn/, **Jerome** 1885–1945; U.S. composer.

Ker·ou·ac /kéro͞o-ak/, **Jack** 1922–69; U.S. author.

Key /kee/, **Francis Scott** 1779–1843; U.S. lawyer; wrote lyrics to "The Star-Spangled Banner."

Keynes /kaynz/, **John Maynard** 1883–1946; English economist. ▢▢ **Keynes·i·an** /káynzeeən/ *adj. & n.*

Kho·mei·ni /k͟homáynee, kō–/, (**Ayatollah**) **Ruhollah** c. 1900–89; Islamic head of state of Iran (1979–89).

Khrush·chev /kro͞oshchef, –chawf/, **Nikita Sergeyevich** 1894–1971; Russian politician; premier of the Soviet Union (1958–64).

Kidd /kid/, **William** (called **"Captain Kidd"**) 1645–1701; Scottish pirate.

Kier·ke·gaard /ke͞erkəgaard, –gawr/, **Sören** 1813–55; Danish philosopher.

Kil·mer /kílmər/, (**Alfred**) **Joyce** 1886–1918; U.S. poet.

Kim Il Sung /kim il so͞ong/ 1912–94; premier (1948–72) and president (1972–94) of North Korea.

King /king/, **Martin Luther, Jr.** 1929–68; U.S. civil-rights leader; assassinated.

King, Stephen 1947– ; U.S. author.

Kip·ling /kípling/, (**Joseph**) **Rudyard** 1865–1936; English author, born in India.

Kis·sin·ger /kísinjər/, **Henry Alfred** 1923– ; U.S. statesman, born in Germany.

Kitch·e·ner /kíchənər/, (**Horatio**) **Herbert** (**1st Earl Kitchener of Khartoum**) 1850–1916; British soldier and statesman.

Klee /klay/, **Paul** 1879–1940; Swiss artist.

Knox /naaks/, **Henry** 1750–1806; first U.S. secretary of war (1785–94).

Knox, John 1505–72; Scottish religious leader.

Knut, /kano͞ot, –nyo͞ot/, see CANUTE.

Kohl /kōl/, **Helmut** 1930– ; German political leader.

Kos·ci·us·ko /kawshcho͞oshkō, kaasee-o͞oskō, kaaz–/, **Thaddeus** 1746–1817; Polish patriot; American Revolutionary War general in the Continental army.

Kos·suth /kaáso͞oth, kaaso͞oth/, **Lajos** 1802–94; Hungarian patriot and statesman.

Kroc /kraak/, **Ray**(**mond Albert**) 1902–1984; U.S. entrepreneur; founder of McDonald's restaurant chain.

Ku·blai Khan /ko͞oblə kaán, ko͞oblī/ c. 1215–94; founder of the Mongol dynasty in China.

K'ung Fu-tzu /ko͞ongfo͞odzə/ see CONFUCIUS.

La·fa·yette (also **La Fa·yette**) /laafee-ét, laf–/, **Marie Joseph** (**Marquis de**) 1757–1834; French statesman; American Revolutionary War general in the Continental army.

La·Fol·lette /ləfaálit/, **Robert Marion** 1855–1925; U.S. politician.

La Fon·taine /laa fawNtén/, **Jean de** 1621–95; French author.

Lamb /lam/, **Charles** (pseudonym **"Elia"**) 1775–1834; English critic and essayist.

Lang·land /lánglənd/, **William** c. 1330–c. 1400; English poet.

Lao-tse /lówdzo͞o/ (also **Lao-tsze, Lao-tsu**) c. 604–c. 531 B.C.; Chinese philosopher.

La Roche·fou·cauld /laa rawshfo͞okó/, **François** (**Duc de**) 1613–80; French author.

La·rousse /laaróos, lə–/, **Pierre** 1817–75; French lexicographer and encyclopedist.

La Salle /laa saál, lə sál/, **René Robert Cavalier** (**Sieur de**) 1643–87; French explorer.

Law·rence /láwrəns, laár–/, **D(avid) H(erbert)** 1885–1930; English author.

Law·rence, T(homas) E(dward) (called **"Lawrence of Arabia"**) 1888–1935; British soldier and author.

Lay·a·mon /líəmən, láy–/ late 12th cent.; English poet.

Lea·key /leékee/ **1 Louis Seymour Bazett** 1903–72; British archaeologist and anthropologist; husband of: **2 Mary Douglas** 1913–96; British archaeologist; their son: **3 Richard Erskine Frere** Kenyan paleontologist.

Lear /leer/, **Edward** 1812–88; English artist and writer of humorous verse.

Lee /lee/, **Henry** (called **"Light-horse Harry"**) 1756–1818; American Revolutionary War cavalry commander.

Lee, Robert E(dward) 1807–70; Confederate commander in the American Civil War.

Leib·niz /lípnits, líbnəts/, **Gottfried Wilhelm** 1646–1716; German philosopher and mathematician.

L'En·fant /laaɴfaáɴ/, **Pierre Charles** 1754–1825; American soldier and engineer, born in France; designed Washington, D.C.

Le·nin /lénin/ (born **Vladimir Ilich Ulyanov**) 1870–1924; Russian Communist leader.

Len·non /lénən/, **John Winston** 1940–80; English pop and rock musician, singer, and songwriter.

Le·o·nar·do da Vin·ci /leeənaárdō də vínchee/ 1452–1519; Italian artist, inventor, and engineer.

Ler·ner /lɔ́rnər/, **Alan Jay** 1918–86; U.S. lyricist and librettist.

Les·seps /léseps, leséps/, **Ferdinand** (**Vicomte de**) 1805–94; French diplomat; promoter of the Suez Canal.

Lew·is /lóois/, **C(ecil) Day** 1904–72; English poet and critic.

Lew·is, C(live) S(taples) 1898–1963; English author.

Lew·is, (Harry) Sinclair 1885–1951; U.S. author.

Lew·is, Meriwether 1774–1809; U.S. explorer (with William Clark) of the North American continent (1804–06).

Lin·coln /língkən/, **Abraham** 1809–65; 16th president of the U.S. (1861–65); assassinated.

Lind·bergh /líndbərg, lín–/, **Charles Augustus** 1902–74; U.S. aviator; made first solo transatlantic flight (1927).

Lind·say /líndzee, lín–/, (**Nicholas**) **Vachel** 1879–1931; U.S. poet.

Lin·nae·us /ləneéəs, –náy–/, **Carolus** 1707–78; Swedish botanist.

Lis·ter /lístər/, **Joseph** 1827–1912; English surgeon; developed antiseptic surgery.

Liszt /list/, **Franz** 1811–86; Hungarian composer.

Liv·ing·stone /lívingstən/, **David** 1813–73; Scottish missionary and explorer.

Liv·y /lívee/ (Latin name **Titus Livius**) 59 B.C.–A.D. 17; Roman historian.

Lloyd George /loyd jáwrj/, **David** 1863–1945; prime minister of Great Britain (1916–22).

Lloyd Web·ber /loyd wébər/, (**Sir**) **Andrew** 1948– ; English composer.

Locke /laak/, **John** 1632–1704; English philosopher.

Loewe /lō/, **Frederick** 1904–88; U.S. composer, born in Austria.

Lon·don /lúndən/, **Jack** (**John Griffith**) 1876–1916; U.S. author.

Long /lawng/, **Huey Pierce** (called **"the Kingfish"**) 1893–1935; U.S. politician; assassinated.

Long·fel·low /láwngfelō/, **Henry Wadsworth** 1807–82; U.S. poet.

Lor·rain, Claude see CLAUDE LORRAIN.

Lou·is /lóoee, lweé/ name of eighteen kings of France, including: **1 Louis XIV** (called **"the Sun King"**) 1638–1715; reigned 1643–1715. **2 Louis XVI** 1754–93; reigned 1774–92.

Lou·is /lóoəs/, **Joe** (born **Joseph Louis Barrow**) (called **"the Brown Bomber"**) 1914–81; U.S. boxer.

Lou·is Phi·lippe /lweé fileép, lóoee/ 1773–1850; king of France (1830–48).

Low·ell /lóəl/, **Amy** 1874–1925; U.S. poet.

Low·ell, James Russell 1819–91; U.S. poet and critic.

Low·ell, Robert 1917–77; U.S. poet.

Lu·cre·tius /lookreéshəs/ (**Titus Lucretius Carus**) c. 94–c. 55 B.C.; Roman poet and philosopher.

Lu·ther /lóothər/, **Martin** 1483–1546; German theologian; key figure of the Protestant Reformation.

Ly·cur·gus /līkɔ́rgəs/ fl. 9th cent. B.C.; Spartan lawgiver.

Lyl·y /lílee/, **John** c. 1554–1606; English author.

Ly·on /líən/, **Mary** 1797–1849; U.S. educator.

Mac·Ar·thur /məkaárthər/, **Douglas** 1880–1964; U.S. general.

Ma·cau·lay /məkáwlee/, **Thomas Babington** 1800–59; English author and historian.

Mac·beth /məkbéth, mak–/ c. 1005–57; king

of Scotland (1040–57); Shakespearean tragic hero.

Mac·ca·be·us /makəbéəs/, **Judas** died 160 B.C.; Jewish patriot.

Mac·Don·ald /məkdaánld/, (**James**) **Ramsay** 1866–1937; prime minister of Great Britain (1924; 1929–35).

Mach /maakh, maak/, **Ernst** 1836–1916; Austrian physicist.

Mach·i·a·vel·li /makeeəvélee/, **Niccolò di Bernardo** 1469–1527; Italian political theorist.

Mac·ken·zie /məkénzee/, **Alexander** 1822–92; prime minister of Canada (1873–78).

Mac·ken·zie, (**Sir**) **Alexander** 1764–1820; Scottish explorer of Canada.

Mac·Leish /makleésh/, **Archibald** 1892–1982; U.S. poet and playwright.

Mac·mil·lan /məkmílən/, (**Maurice**) **Harold** 1895–1987; prime minister of Great Britain (1957–63).

Mad·i·son /mádisən/, **James** 1751–1836; 4th president of the U.S. (1809–17).

Mae·ter·linck /máytərlingk, met–/, (**Count**) **Maurice** 1862–1947; Belgian poet and playwright.

Ma·gel·lan /məjélən/, **Ferdinand** c. 1480–1521; Portuguese navigator.

Ma·gritte /maagreét/, **René** 1898–1967; Belgian artist.

Mahfouz /maáfooz/, **Naguib** 1911– ; Egyptian author.

Mah·ler /maálər/, **Gustav** 1860–1911; Austrian composer.

Mail·er /máylər/, **Norman** 1923– ; U.S. author.

Mai·mon·i·des /mīmaánideez/, **Moses** (born **Moses ben Maimon**) 1135–1204; Jewish theologian and scholastic philosopher, born in Spain.

Ma·jor /máyjər/, **John** 1943– ; prime minister of Great Britain (1990–97).

Mal·a·mud /máləməd/, **Bernard** 1914–86; U.S. author.

Mal·colm X /málkəm éks/ (born **Malcolm Little**) 1925–65; U.S. civil-rights activist; assassinated.

Ma·li·now·ski /malináwfskee/, **Bronislaw** 1884–1942; U.S. anthropologist, born in Poland.

Mal·lar·mé /maalaarmáy/, **Stéphane** 1842–98; French poet.

Mal·o·ry /máləree/, (**Sir**) **Thomas** died 1471; English author.

Mal·raux /malró/, **André** 1901–76; French statesman and author.

Mal·thus /málthəs, máwl–/, **Thomas Robert** 1766–1834; English economist.

Man·de·la /mandélə/, **Nelson** 1918– ; president of South Africa (1994–).

Man·et /manáy, maa–/, **Édouard** 1832–83; French artist.

Mann /man/, **Horace** 1796–1859; U.S. educator.

Mann /maan/, **Thomas** 1875–1955; German author.

Man Ray see RAY, MAN.

Mans·field /mánsfeeld/, **Katherine** (born **Kathleen Beauchamp**) 1888–1923; British author, born in New Zealand.

Man·son /mánsən/, **Charles** 1934– ; U.S. cult leader and criminal.

Mao Ze·dong /mów dzədoóng/ (also **Mao Tse-tung**) 1893–1976; Chinese Communist leader.

Ma·rat /maaraá/, **Jean Paul** 1743–93; French revolutionary leader, born in Switzerland; assassinated.

Mar·ci·a·no /maarsee-ánō, –shee–, –aánō/, **Rocky** (born **Rocco Francis Marchegiano**) 1923–69; U.S. boxer.

Mar·co Po·lo see POLO, MARCO.

Mar·co·ni /maarkónee/, **Guglielmo** 1874–1937; Italian inventor; pioneered wireless telegraphy.

Mar·cos /maárkōs/, **Ferdinand** 1917–89; president of the Philippines (1965–86).

Mar·cus Au·re·li·us /maárkəs awreéleeəs/ 121–180; Roman emperor and Stoic philosopher.

Mar·cuse /maarkoózə/, **Herbert** 1898–1979; U.S. philosopher, born in Germany.

Mare, Walter de la see DE LA MARE, WALTER.

Mar·gre·the II /maargrétə/ 1940– ; queen of Denmark (1972–).

Ma·rie An·toi·nette /məreé antwənét/ 1755–93; queen of France (1774–92), wife of Louis XVI.

Ma·rie de Mé·di·cis /məreé də maydeeseés/ (Italian name **Ma·ri·a de' Med·i·ci** /máydəchee/) 1573–1642; queen of France (1610–17).

Mark An·to·ny see ANTONY, MARK.

Mark·ham /maárkəm/, (**Charles**) **Edwin** 1852–1940; U.S. poet.

Marl·bor·ough /márlbərō, máwlbrə/, **1st Duke of** see CHURCHILL, JOHN.

Mar·lowe /maárlō/, **Christopher** 1564–93; English playwright and poet.

Mar·quand /maarkwaánd/, **J**(**ohn**) **P**(**hillips**) 1893–1960; U.S. author.

Mar·quette /maarkét/, **Jacques** 1637–75; Jesuit missionary and explorer of North America, born in France.

Mar·quez, Gabriel García see GARCÍA MÁRQUEZ, GABRIEL.

Mar·shall /maárshəl/, George C(atlett) 1880–1959; U.S. general and statesman.

Mar·shall, John 1755–1835; Chief Justice of the U.S. (1801–35).

Mar·shall, Thurgood 1908–93; U.S. Supreme Court justice (1967–91).

Mar·tel, Charles see CHARLES MARTEL.

Mar·tial /maárshəl/ 1st cent. A.D.; Roman writer of epigrams, born in Spain.

Marx /maarks/, Karl Heinrich 1818–83; German political philosopher.

Mar·y /máiree/ (called "the Virgin Mary" or "Blessed Virgin Mary") 1st cent. B.C.–A.D. 1st cent.; mother of Jesus.

Mar·y I (also known as Mary Tu·dor) (called "Bloody Mary") 1516–58; queen of England (1553–58).

Mar·y, Queen of Scots (also known as Mary Stu·art) 1542–87; queen of Scotland (1542–67).

Ma·sa·ryk /maásaarik/, Tomáš 1850–1937; president of Czechoslovakia (1918–35).

Mase·field /máysfeeld/, John Edward 1878–1967; English poet, playwright, and novelist.

Mas·ters /mástərz/, Edgar Lee 1869–1950; U.S. poet.

Ma·tisse /maateés/, Henri 1869–1954; French artist.

Maugham /mawm/, (William) Somerset 1874–1965; English author.

Mau·pas·sant /mōpaasaáN/, (Henri) Guy de 1850–93; French author.

Mau·riac /mawr-yaák/, François 1885–1970; French author.

Max·i·mil·ian /maksimílyən/ 1832–67; emperor of Mexico (1864–67).

Maz·a·rin /maazaaráN/, Jules 1602–61; French cardinal and statesman, born in Italy.

Mboy·a /embóyə/, Tom (Thomas Joseph) 1930–69; Kenyan political leader; assassinated.

Mc·Car·thy /məkaárthee/, Joseph Raymond 1908–57; U.S. politician.

Mc·Car·thy, Mary 1912–89; U.S. author.

Mc·Cart·ney /məkaártnee/, (James) Paul 1942– ; English pop and rock musician, singer, and songwriter.

Mc·Clel·lan /məklélən/, George Brinton 1826–85; Union general in the American Civil War.

Mc·Cor·mick /məkáwrmik/, Cyrus Hall 1809–84; U.S. developer of the mechanical reaper.

Mc·Kin·ley /məkínlee/, William 1843–1901; 25th president of the U.S. (1897–1901); assassinated.

Mc·Lu·han /məkloՂoən/, (Herbert) Marshall 1911–80; Canadian communications theorist.

Mead /meed/, Margaret 1901–78; U.S. anthropologist.

Meade /meed/, George Gordon 1815–72; Union general in the American Civil War.

Med·i·ci /médichee, médeechee/ powerful Italian family, including: 1 Cosimo de' (called "the Elder") 1389–1464; Florentine ruler, banker, and art patron. 2 Lorenzo de' (called "the Magnificent") 1449–92; Florentine ruler and art patron. 3 Caterina de' see CATHERINE DE MÉDICIS. 4 Cosimo de' (called "the Great") 1519–74; duke of Florence (1537–74). 5 Maria de' see MARIE DE MÉDICIS.

Mei·ji Ten·no /máyjee ténnō/ (born Mutsuhito) 1852–1912; emperor of Japan (1867–1912).

Me·ir /me-eՂr/, Golda (born Goldie Mabovitch) 1898–1978; prime minister of Israel (1969–74), born in Russia.

Mel·ba /mélbə/, (Dame) Nellie (born Helen Porter Mitchell) 1861–1931; Australian operatic soprano.

Mel·lon /mélən/, Andrew William 1855–1937; U.S. financier and art patron; U.S. secretary of the treasury (1921–32).

Mel·ville /mélvil/, Herman 1819–91; U.S. author.

Me·nan·der /mənándər/ c. 342–292 B.C.; Greek playwright.

Men·ci·us /méncheeəs/ (Latinized name of Meng-tzu' or Meng·zi') c. 371–c. 289 B.C.; Chinese philosopher.

Menck·en /méngkən/, H(enry) L(ouis) 1880–1956; U.S. journalist and critic.

Men·del /méndəl/, Gregor Johann 1822–84; Austrian monk and botanist.

Men·dels·sohn /méndəlsən/, Felix 1809–47; German composer.

Me·nes /meՂneez/ king of Egypt (c. 3100 B.C.).

Meng-tzu /múng dzoՂo/ (also Meng·zi') see MENCIUS.

Me·not·ti /mənáwtee/, Gian Carlo 1911– ; U.S. composer, born in Italy.

Men·u·hin /ményoՂohin/, Yehudi 1916– ; U.S. violinist.

Mer·ca·tor /mərkáytər/, Gerardus 1512–94; Flemish cartographer.

Mer·e·dith /mérədith/, George 1828–1909; English novelist and poet.

Met·ter·nich /métərnik, –nikh/, (Prince) Klemens 1773–1859; Austrian statesman.

Mi·chel·an·ge·lo /mīkəlánjəlō, mikəl–/ (surname Buonarroti) 1475–1564; Italian artist and architect.

Mich·en·er /míchənər, míchnər/, **James A(lbert)** 1907–97; U.S. author.

Mies van der Rohe /mees vaan də róə/, **Ludwig** 1886–1969; U.S. architect and designer, born in Germany.

Mill /mil/, **J(ohn) S(tuart)** 1806–73; English philosopher and economist.

Mil·lay /məláy/, **Edna St. Vincent** 1892–1950; U.S. poet.

Mil·ler /mílər/, **Arthur** 1915– ; U.S. playwright.

Mil·ler, (Alton) Glenn 1904–44; U.S. jazz trombonist and bandleader.

Mil·ler, Henry 1891–1980; U.S. author.

Mil·let /meeláy/, **Jean François** 1814–75; French artist.

Milne /miln/, **A(lan) A(lexander)** 1882–1956; English author.

Mil·ton /mílt'n/, **John** 1608–74; English poet.

Min·u·it /mínyōoit/, **Peter** 1580–1638; Dutch colonial administrator in America.

Mi·ró /mee-ró/, **Joan** 1893–1983; Spanish artist.

Mitch·ell /míchəl/, **Margaret** 1900–49; U.S. author.

Mit·ford /mítfərd/ **1 Nancy** 1904–73; English author; sister of: **2 Jessica** 1917–96; U.S. author, born in England.

Mith·ri·da·tes VI /mithrədáyteez/ (called **"the Great"**) c. 132–63 B.C.; king of Pontus (120–63 B.C.).

Mit·ter·rand /meeteráaN/, **François** 1916–96; president of France (1981–95).

Mo·bu·tu Se·se Se·ko /məbōotōo sésay sékō/ 1930–97; president of (the former) Zaire (1965–97).

Mo·di·glia·ni /mōdeel-yaánee/, **Amedeo** 1884–1920; Italian artist.

Mo·ham·med /mōháamid/ see MUHAMMAD.

Mo·lière /mōlyér/ (pseudonym of **Jean-Baptiste Poquelin**) 1622–73; French playwright.

Mol·nár /mōlnaár/, **Ferenc** 1878–1952; Hungarian author.

Momm·sen /mómsən/, **Theodor** 1817–1903; German historian.

Mon·dale /móndayl/, **Walter Frederick** 1928– ; vice president of the U.S. (1977–81).

Mon·dri·an /máwndree-aan/, **Piet** 1872–1944; Dutch artist.

Mo·net /mawnáy/, **Claude** 1840–1926; French artist.

Mon·roe /mənró/, **James** 1758–1831; 5th president of the U.S. (1817–25).

Mon·roe, Marilyn 1926–62; U.S. actress.

Mon·taigne /mawNtén, –tényə/, **Michel de** 1533–92; French essayist.

Mont·calm /mōNkaálm/, **Louis Joseph** 1712–59; French general.

Mon·tes·quieu /maantəskyóo/ 1689–1755; French political philosopher.

Mon·tes·so·ri /maantəsáwree/, **Maria** 1870–1952; Italian educator.

Mon·te·ver·di /maantəvérdee/, **Claudio** 1567–1643; Italian composer.

Mon·te·zu·ma II /maantəzóomə/ 1466–1520; Aztec emperor (1502–20).

Moon /mōon/, **Sun Myung** 1920– ; Korean religious leader.

Moore /mawr, mōor/, **G(eorge) E(dward)** 1873–1958; English philosopher.

Moore, Henry 1898–1986; English sculptor.

Moore, Marianne 1887–1972; U.S. poet.

More /mawr/, **(Sir) Thomas** 1478–1535; English scholar and statesman.

Mor·gan /máwrgən/, **J(ohn) P(ierpont)** 1837–1913; U.S. financier and philanthropist.

Mor·i·son /máwrisən/, **Samuel Eliot** 1887–1976; U.S. historian.

Mo·ri·sot /mawrisó/, **Berthe** 1841–95; French artist.

Mor·ris /máwrəs, maár–/, **Gouverneur** 1752–1816; U.S. statesman.

Mor·ris /máwrəs, maár–/, **Robert** 1734–1806; U.S. statesman and financier, born in England.

Mor·ri·son /máwrisən, maár–/, **Jim** 1943–1971; U.S. singer and songwriter.

Mor·ri·son, Toni 1931– ; U.S. novelist.

Morse /mawrs/, **Samuel F(inley) B(reese)** 1791–1872; U.S. artist and inventor; devised telegraphic code.

Mo·ses /mōziz/ c. 14th cent. B.C.; Hebrew prophet and lawgiver.

Mo·ses /mōziz/, **Anna Mary** (called **"Grandma Moses"**) 1860–1961; U.S. artist.

Mo·ses ben Mai·mon see MAIMONIDES.

Mo·ther Te·re·sa see TERESA, MOTHER.

Mott /maat/, **Lucretia Coffin** 1793–1880; U.S. social reformer.

Mount·bat·ten /mowntbát'n/, **Louis (1st Earl Mountbatten of Burma)** 1900–79; British admiral and statesman.

Mous·sorg·sky /mōosáwrgskee/ (also **Mus·sorg'sky**), **Modest** 1839–81; Russian composer.

Mo·zart /mótsaart/, **Wolfgang Amadeus** 1756–91; Austrian composer.

Mu·ga·be /mōogaábee/, **Robert** 1924– ; prime minister (1980–87) and president (1987–) of Zimbabwe.

Mu·ham·mad A·li see ALI, MUHAMMAD.

Mu·ham·mad /mo͞oha'aməd, mō–/ (also **Mo·ham'med**; **Ma·hom'et**) c. 570–632; Arab prophet, founder of Islam.

Muir /myo͞or/, **John** 1838–1914; U.S. naturalist and explorer, born in Scotland.

Mun·ro /mənró/, **H(ector) H(ugh)** (pseudonym **"Saki"**) 1870–1916; Scottish author, born in Burma.

Mu·rat /myo͞oraá/, **Joachim** c. 1767–1815; French general and king of Naples (1808–15).

Mur·doch /mə́rdaak/, **Rupert** 1931– ; Australian media executive.

Mur·ray /mə́ree/, **(Sir) James Augustus Henry** 1837–1915; British philologist and lexicographer.

Mus·so·li·ni /mo͞osəle'enee, mo͞ósə–/, **Benito** (called **"Il Duce"**) 1883–1945; Fascist dictator of Italy (1922–43).

Mus·sorg·sky see MOUSSORGSKY.

My·ron /mírən/ fl. c. 480–440 B.C.; Greek sculptor.

Na·bo·kov /nábəkawf, nəbáwkəf/, **Vladimir** 1899–1977; U.S. novelist, born in Russia.

Na·der /náydər/, **Ralph** 1934– ; U.S. consumer advocate.

Na·po·le·on I /nəpóleeən/ (surname **Bonaparte**) 1769–1821; French general, born in Corsica; emperor of France (1804–15). □□ **Na·po·le·on'ic** /–leea'ánək/ adj.

Na·po·le·on III (**Louis Napoleon Bonaparte**) 1808–73; president (1848–52) and emperor (1852–70) of France.

Nash /nash/, **Ogden** 1902–71; U.S. writer of humorous verse.

Nas·ser /násər/, **Gamal Abdel** 1918–70; president of Egypt (1956–58).

Na·tion /náyshən/, **Carry Amelia Moore** 1846–1911; U.S. temperance activist.

Neb·u·chad·nez·zar /nebəkədnézər/ king of Babylon (605–562 B.C.).

Neh·ru /néro͞o, náyro͞o/, **Jawaharlal** 1889–1964; prime minister of India (1947–64).

Nel·son /nélsən/, **Horatio** 1758–1805; British admiral.

Ne·ro /ne'erō/ 37–68; Roman emperor (54–68).

Net·an·ya·hu /netaanyaáho͞o/, **Benjamin** 1949– ; prime minister of Israel (1996–).

Neu·mann /nóymaan/, **John von** 1903–57; U.S. mathematician, born in Hungary.

New·man /no͞ómən, nyo͞o–/, **John Henry** 1801–91; English theologian.

New·ton /no͞ot'n, nyo͞o–/, **(Sir) Isaac** 1642–1727; English mathematician and physicist.

Ngo Dinh Di·em /nó dín dee-ém/ 1901–63; president of South Vietnam (1956–63).

Nich·o·las II /níkələs, nikləs/ 1868–1918; last Russian czar (1894–1917); assassinated.

Nich·o·las, St. fl. 4th cent.; Christian bishop in Asia Minor.

Nick·laus /níkləs/, **Jack (William)** (called **"the Golden Bear"**) 1940– ; U.S. golfer.

Nie·buhr /ne'ebo͞or/, **Reinhold** 1892–1971; U.S. theologian.

Nie·tzsche /ne'echə, –chee/, **Friedrich Wilhelm** 1844–1900; German philosopher.

Night·in·gale /nít'n-gayl/, **Florence** 1820–1910; English nurse.

Ni·jin·sky /nəzhínskee, –jín–/, **Vaslav** 1890–1950; Russian ballet dancer and choreographer.

Nim·itz /nímits/, **Chester William** 1885–1966; U.S. admiral.

Nix·on /níksən/, **Richard Milhous** 1913–94; 37th president of the U.S. (1969–74); resigned.

Nkru·mah /enkro͞'omə/, **Kwame** 1909–72; Ghanaian political leader.

No·bel /nōbél/, **Alfred Bernhard** 1833–96; Swedish inventor; endowed Nobel Prizes.

North /nawrth/, **Frederick** (called **"Lord North"**) 1732–92; prime minister of Great Britain (1770–82).

Nos·tra·da·mus /naastrədáyməs, naws–, –daáməs/ 1503–66; French astrologer and prophet.

Noyes /noyz/, **Alfred** 1880–1958; English poet and critic.

Nu·re·yev /no͞oráyəf, no͞'oree-ef/, **Rudolf Hametovich** 1939–93; Russian ballet dancer.

O'Ca·sey /ōkáysee/, **Sean** 1880–1964; Irish playwright.

O'Con·nell /ōka'ánl/, **Daniel** 1775–1847; Irish nationalist leader.

O'Con·nor /ōka'ánər/, **(Mary) Flannery** 1925–1964; U.S. author.

O'Con·nor, Sandra Day 1930– ; U.S. Supreme Court justice (1981–); first woman appointed to Court.

Oc·ta·vi·an /oktávee-ən/ see AUGUSTUS.

O·dets /ōdéts/, **Clifford** 1906–63; U.S. playwright.

Of·fen·bach /áwfənbaakh, –baak/, **Jacques** 1819–80; French composer, born in Germany.

O·gle·thorpe /ógəlthawrp/, **James Edward** 1696–1785; English colonizer of Georgia.

O'Hig·gins /ōhíginz/, **Bernardo** (called **"the Liberator of Chile"**) c. 1778–1842; Chilean revolutionary; dictator of Chile (1817–23).

O'Keeffe /ōke'ef/, **Georgia** 1887–1986; U.S. artist.

O·liv·i·er /əlívee-ay, ō–/, **(Sir) Laurence Kerr** 1907–89; English actor.

Olm·sted /ómstid/, **Frederick Law** 1822–1903; U.S. landscape architect.

O·mar Khay·yám /ōmaar kī-aám, kī-ám/ died 1123; Persian poet and astronomer.

O·nas·sis /ōnásis/ **1 Aristotle Socrates** c. 1900–75; Greek shipping tycoon, born in Turkey; husband of: **2 Jacqueline Lee Bouvier Kennedy** 1929–94; wife of John F. Kennedy (1953–63) and Aristotle Onassis (1968–75).

O'Neill /ōneél/, **Eugene Gladstone** 1888–1953; U.S. playwright.

Op·pen·heim·er /aápənhīmər/, **J(ulius) Robert** 1904–67; U.S. nuclear physicist.

Or·well /áwrwel, –wəl/, **George** (pseudonym of **Eric Arthur Blair**) 1903–50; English author, born in India.

Os·man I /aázmən, aás–/ (also **Oth′man**) 1259–1326; Turkish ruler; founder of the Ottoman Empire.

Os·wald /aázwawld, –wəld/, **Lee Harvey** 1939–63; accused assassin of U.S. president John F. Kennedy.

O·tis /ótis/, **James** 1725–83; American Revolutionary War patriot.

Ov·id /aávid/ (born **Publius Ovidius Naso**) 43 B.C.–c. A.D. 17; Roman poet.

Ow·en /óən/, **David** 1938– ; British politician.

Ow·en, Wilfred 1893–1918; English poet.

Ow·ens /óənz/, **Jesse** (born **James Cleveland Owens**) 1913–80; U.S. Olympic athlete.

Pa·de·rew·ski /padəréfskee, –rév–/, **Ignace** 1860–1941; Polish pianist, composer, and statesman.

Pa·ga·ni·ni /pagəneénee/, **Nicolò** 1782–1840; Italian violinist and composer.

Pah·la·vi /paáləvee/, **Mohammed Reza** 1919–80; shah of Iran (1941–79); exiled.

Paine /payn/, **Thomas** 1737–1809; American patriot and political philosopher, born in England.

Pal·la·dio /pəlaádee-ō/, **Andrea** 1508–80; Italian architect.

Pal·mer /paámər, paálmər/, **Arnold** 1929– ; U.S. golfer.

Pank·hurst /pángkhərst/, **Emmeline Goulden** 1858–1928; English suffragist.

Pa·pan·dre·ou /paapaandráyōō/, **George** 1888–1968; premier of Greece (1963; 1964–65).

Par·ker /paárkər/, **Dorothy Rothschild** 1893–1967; U.S. author and critic.

Park·man /paárkmən/, **Francis** 1823–93; U.S. historian.

Par·men·i·des /paarménideez/ early 5th cent. B.C.; Greek philosopher.

Par·nell /paarnél, paárn'l/, **Charles Stewart** 1846–91; Irish nationalist.

Pas·cal /paskál/, **Blaise** 1623–62; French mathematician and philosopher.

Pas·ter·nak /pástərnak/, **Boris** 1890–1960; Russian poet and novelist.

Pas·teur /pastöór/, **Louis** 1822–95; French chemist and microbiologist.

Pat·rick /pátrik/, **St.** 5th cent.; patron saint of Ireland.

Pat·ton /pát'n/, **George S(mith)** 1885–1945; U.S. general.

Paul /pawl/, **St.** died c. 67; early Christian missionary.

Paul·ing /páwling/, **Linus Carl** 1901–94; U.S. chemist.

Pa·va·rot·ti /paavəraátee, pav–/, **Luciano** 1935– ; Italian operatic tenor.

Pav·lov /paávlawf, páv–, –lawv/, **Ivan** 1849–1936; Russian physiologist.

Pav·lo·va /pávləvə, pavlóvə/, **Anna** 1881–1931; Russian prima ballerina.

Peale /peel/, **Charles Willson** 1741–1827; U.S. artist.

Peale, Norman Vincent 1898–1994; U.S. religious leader.

Pea·ry /peéree/, **Robert Edwin** 1856–1920; U.S. Arctic explorer.

Pe·der·sen /páydərsən/, **Knut** see HAMSUN, KNUT.

Peel /peel/, **(Sir) Robert** 1788–1850; prime minister of Great Britain (1834–35; 1841–46).

Pei /pay/, **I(eoh) M(ing)** 1917– ; U.S. architect, born in China.

Penn /pen/, **William** 1644–1718; English Quaker and founder of Pennsylvania (1682).

Pep·in III /pépin/ (called **"the Short"**) c. 714–768; king of the Franks (751–768); father of Charlemagne.

Pepys /peeps/, **Samuel** 1633–1703; English diarist.

Pé·rez de Cué·llar /pérez de kwáyyaar/, **Javier** 1920– ; Peruvian diplomat; secretary-general of the United Nations (1982–92).

Per·i·cles /périkleez/ c. 495–429 B.C.; Athenian statesman and general.

Per·kins /pérkinz/, **Frances** 1882–1965; U.S. secretary of labor (1933–45); first woman cabinet member.

Pe·rón /pərón, pay–/ **1 Juan Domingo** 1895–1974; president of Argentina (1946–55; 1973–74); husband of: **2 (Maria) Evita Duarte Ibarguren** (called **"Evita"**) 1919–52; Argentine political figure.

Pe·rot /pəró/, **H(enry) Ross** 1930– ; U.S. business executive and politician.

Per·ry /péree/ **1 Oliver Hazard** 1785–1819; U.S. naval officer; brother of: **2 Matthew Calbraith** 1794–1858; U.S. commodore.

Per·shing /pə́rshing, –zhing/, **John J(oseph)** (called **"Black Jack"**) 1860–1948; U.S. commander of American forces during World War I.

Pesh·kov /pyáyshkəf/, **Aleksei Maksimovich** see GORKY, MAXIM.

Pé·tain /paytáN/, **Henri Philippe** 1856–1951; premier of Fascist Vichy France (1940–44).

Pe·ter I /peétər/ (called **"the Great"**) 1672–1725; emperor of Russia (1682–1725).

Pe·ter, St. (also known as **Si′mon Pe′ter**) died c. 67; apostle of Jesus.

Pe·ter·son /peétərsən/, **Roger Tory** 1908–1996; U.S. ornithologist, artist, and author.

Pe·trarch /peétraark, pé–/ 1304–74; Italian poet. □□ **Pe·trarch·an** /pətraárkən/ *adj.*

Phid·i·as /fídeeəs/ fl. 5th cent. B.C.; Athenian sculptor.

Phil·ip II /fíləp/ c. 382–336 B.C.; king of Macedonia; father of Alexander the Great.

Pi·af /pee-aáf/, **Edith** (born **Edith Giovanna Gassion**) 1915–63; French singer.

Pia·get /pyaazháy/, **Jean** 1897–1980; Swiss psychologist.

Pi·cas·so /pikaásō, –kás–/, **Pablo** 1881–1973; Spanish artist.

Pick·ett /píkət/, **George Edward** 1825–75; Confederate general in the American Civil War.

Pierce /peers/, **Franklin** 1804–69; 14th president of the U.S. (1853–57).

Pi·late /pílət/, **Pontius** 1st cent. A.D.; Roman procurator of Judea (26–c. 36).

Pin·dar /píndər, –daar/ 518–438 B.C.; Greek lyric poet.

Pink·er·ton /píngkərtən/, **Allan** 1819–84; U.S. detective, born in Scotland.

Pi·no·chet U·gar·te /peenōchét ōōgaártay/, **Augusto** 1915– ; president of Chile (1973–89).

Pin·ter /píntər/, **Harold** 1930– ; English playwright.

Pi·ran·del·lo /peerəndélō/, **Luigi** 1867–1936; Italian author.

Pi·sis·tra·tus /pisístrətəs/ died c. 527 B.C.; Athenian ruler.

Pis·sar·ro /pisaárō/, **Camille** 1830–1903; French artist.

Pitt /pit/ **1 William** (**1st Earl of Chatham**) (called **"the Elder Pitt"** and **"the Great Commoner"**) 1708–78; British political leader; father of: **2 William** (called **"the Younger Pitt"**) 1759–1806; prime minister of Great Britain (1783–1801; 1804–06).

Pi·zar·ro /pizaárō/, **Francisco** c. 1478–1541; Spanish conquistador; conqueror of Peru.

Planck /plaangk, plangk/, **Max** 1858–1947; German physicist.

Plan·tag·e·net /plantájinit/ British ruling dynasty (1154–1485).

Plath /plath/, **Sylvia** 1932–63; U.S. poet and novelist.

Pla·to /pláytō/ 429–347 B.C.; Greek philosopher.

Plau·tus /pláwtəs/, **Titus Maccius** c. 250–184 B.C.; Roman comic playwright.

Plin·y /plínee/ **1** (called **"the Elder"**) c. 23–79; Roman scholar; uncle of: **2** (called **"the Younger"**) c. 61–c. 112; Roman author.

Plu·tarch /plōōtaark/ c. 46–c. 120; Greek biographer.

Po·ca·hon·tas /pōkəhaántəs/ (English name **Rebecca Rolfe**) c. 1595–1617; Native American princess; daughter of Powhatan.

Poe /pō/, **Edgar Allan** 1809–49; U.S. short-story author and poet.

Pol Pot /paal paát, pōl/ c. 1925– ; prime minister of Cambodia (1976–79).

Polk /pōk/, **James Knox** 1795–1849; 11th president of the U.S. (1845–49).

Pol·lock /paálək/, (**Paul**) **Jackson** 1912–56; U.S. artist.

Po·lo /pólō/, **Marco** 1254–1324; Venetian traveler in E Asia.

Pom·pey /paámpee/ (called **"the Great"**) 106–48 B.C.; Roman general and politician.

Pom·pi·dou /pōNpeedōō/, **Georges** 1911–74; president of France (1969–74).

Ponce de Le·ón /paans də leéən, pónsə daylee-ón, paants, pōntsə/, **Juan** c. 1460–1521; Spanish explorer; discovered Florida (1513).

Pon·ti·ac /paántee-ak/ c. 1720–69; Ottawa Indian chief.

Pope /pōp/, **Alexander** 1688–1744; English poet.

Po·que·lin /pōkláN/, **Jean-Baptiste** see MOLIÈRE.

Porsche /páwrshə/, **Ferdinand** 1875–1952; Austrian car designer.

Por·ter /páwrtər, pór–/, **Cole Albert** 1891–1964; U.S. composer.

Por·ter, Katherine Anne Maria Veronica Callista Russell 1890–1980; U.S. author.

Por·ter, William Sydney see HENRY, O.

Pot·ter /paátər/, (**Helen**) **Beatrix** 1866–1943; English author.

Pound /pownd/, **Ezra** (**Loomis**) 1885–1972; U.S. poet and critic.

Pow·ell /pów'l/, **Colin** 1937– ; U.S. general.

Pow·ha·tan /powətán, pow-hát'n/ c. 1550–1618; Native American chief in early colonial Virginia.

Prax·it·e·les /praksít'l-eez/ fl. 370–330 B.C.; Athenian sculptor.

Pres·ley /prézlee, prés–/, **Elvis Aron** (called **"the King of Rock and Roll"**) 1935–77; U.S. pop and rock singer.

Pre·vin /prévin/, **André** (born **Andreas Priwin**) 1929– ; U.S. composer and conductor, born in Germany.

Price /prīs/, (**Mary**) **Leontyne** 1927– ; U.S. operatic soprano.

Priest·ley /preéstlee/, **J**(**ohn**) **B**(**oynton**) 1894–1984; English author.

Priest·ley, **Joseph** 1733–1804; English scientist and theologian.

Pro·ko·fiev /prəkáwfyev, –yef, –yəf/, **Sergei** 1891–1953; Russian composer.

Prou·dhon /proōodóN/, **Pierre Joseph** 1809–65; French author.

Proust /proōost/, **Marcel** 1871–1922; French author and critic.

Ptol·e·my /taálimee/ fl. 127–151; ancient astronomer and geographer in Alexandria.

Puc·ci·ni /poōcheénee/, **Giacomo** 1858–1924; Italian opera composer.

Pu·las·ki /pəláskee, pyoō–/, (**Count**) **Casimir** c. 1748–79; Polish patriot; American Revolutionary War general in Continental army.

Pu·litz·er /poōolitsər, pyoō–/, **Joseph** 1847–1911; U.S. newspaper publisher, born in Hungary.

Push·kin /poōoshkin/, **Alexander** 1799–1837; Russian author.

Py·thag·o·ras /pəthág(ə)rəs, pī–/ fl. late 6th cent. B.C.; Greek philosopher.

Qa·dha·fi /kədaáfee, –dáf–/ (also **Gad·da'fi**), **Muammar** (**Muhammad**) **al-** 1942– ; chief of state of Libya (1969–).

Rab·e·lais /rabəláy/, **François** c. 1494–1553; French satirical author.

Ra·bin /raabeén/, **Yitzhak** 1922–95; prime minister of Israel (1974–77; 1992–95); assassinated.

Rach·ma·ni·noff /raakmaáninawf/, **Sergei** 1873–1943; Russian composer.

Ra·leigh /ráwlee, raálee/ (also **Ra'legh**), (**Sir**) **Walter** c. 1552–1618; English courtier, explorer, and poet.

Ram·ses /rámseez/ (also **Ram'e·ses**) name of eleven pharaohs of Egypt, including: **1 Ramses I** reigned 1320–1318 B.C.; grandfather of: **2 Ramses II** reigned 1304–1237 B.C. **3 Ramses III** reigned 1198–1166 B.C.

Rand /rand/, **Ayn** 1905–82; U.S. author, born in Russia.

Raph·a·el /ráfeeəl, ráyfee–, raáfee–/ (surname **Sanzio**) 1483–1520; Italian artist.

Ra·spu·tin /raspyoŏt'n/, **Grigori** 1871–1916; Russian mystic; influential in the court of Czar Nicholas II.

Ra·vel /rəvél/, **Maurice** 1875–1937; French composer.

Ray /ray/, **Man** (born **Emmanuel Rudnitsky**) 1890–1976; U.S. artist and photographer.

Rea·gan /ráygən/, **Ronald Wilson** 1911– ; 40th president of the U.S. (1981–89).

Reed /reed/, **Walter C.** 1851–1902; U.S. army physician.

Rehn·quist /rénkwist/, **William H**(**ubbs**) 1924– ; Chief Justice of the U.S. (1986–).

Re·marque /rəmaárk/, **Erich Maria** 1898–1970; U.S. author, born in Germany.

Rem·brandt /rémbrant/ (surname **Harmensz van Rijn**) 1606–69; Dutch artist.

Re·nault /rənáwlt/, **Mary** (pseudonym of **Mary Challans**) 1905–83; British novelist.

Re·no /reénō/, **Janet** 1938– ; U.S. attorney general (1993–).

Re·noir /rənwaár/, **Pierre Auguste** 1841–1919; French artist.

Re·vere /rəveér/, **Paul** 1735–1818; American patriot and silversmith.

Reyn·olds /rén'ldz/, (**Sir**) **Joshua** 1723–92; English artist.

Rhee /ree/, **Syngman** 1875–1965; president of South Korea (1948–60).

Rhodes /rōdz/, **Cecil John** 1853–1902; British colonial administrator in S Africa.

Ri·chard /ríchərd/ name of three kings of England: **1 Richard I** (called **"the Heart"**) 1157–99; reigned 1189–99. **2 Richard II** 1367–1400; reigned 1377–99. **3 Richard III** 1452–85; reigned 1483–85.

Rich·ard·son /ríchərdsən/, **Samuel** 1689–1761; English author.

Rich·e·lieu /ríshəloō, –lyoō/, **Armand Jean du Plessis** (**Duc de**) 1585–1642; French cardinal and statesman.

Rick·o·ver /ríkōvər/, **Hyman George** 1900–86; U.S. admiral.

Ride /rīd/, **Sally Kristen** 1951– ; U.S. astronaut.

Rim·sky-Kor·sa·kov /rimskee káwrsəkawf/, **Nikolai** 1844–1908; Russian composer.

Ri·ve·ra /rivérə/, **Diego** 1886–1957; Mexican artist.

Rob·bins /raábinz/, **Jerome** 1918– ; U.S. ballet dancer and choreographer.

Robert I /róbərt/ (called **"Robert the Bruce"**) 1274–1329; king of Scotland (1306–29).

Robe·son /róbsən/, **Paul** 1898–1976; U.S. actor and singer.

Robes·pierre /róbzpeer, –pyer/, **Maximilien** 1758–94; French revolutionary leader.

Rob·in·son /raábinsən/, **Edwin Arlington** 1869–1935; U.S. poet.

Rob·in·son, Jackie (**John Roosevelt**) 1919–72; U.S. baseball player.

Rock·e·fel·ler /rókəfelər/ U.S. family prominent in industry, philanthropy, and politics, including: **1 John D**(**avison**) 1839–1937; oil magnate; father of: **2 John D**(**avison**), **Jr.** 1874–1960; philanthropist; father of: **3 Nelson** 1908–79; politician.

Rock·well /rókwel/, **Norman** 1894–1978; U.S. artist.

Rodg·ers /rójərz/, **Richard** 1902–79; U.S. composer.

Ro·din /rōdáN/, (**François**) **Auguste** 1840–1917; French sculptor.

Roent·gen see RÖNTGEN, WILHELM CONRAD.

Rog·ers /rójərz/, **Will**(**iam Penn Adair**) 1879–1935; U.S. humorist.

Röl·vaag /rólvaag/, **Ole Edvart** 1876–1931; U.S. author, born in Norway.

Rom·berg /rómbərg/, **Sigmund** 1887–1951; U.S. composer, born in Hungary.

Rom·mel /róməl/, **Erwin Johannes Eugen** (called **"the Desert Fox"**) 1891–1944; German general.

Rönt·gen/réntgən, rénchən/ (also **Roent′gen**), **Wilhelm Conrad** 1845–1923; German physicist; discovered X rays.

Roo·se·velt /rózəvelt, –vəlt, ró͞o–/ **1 Franklin Delano** 1882–1945; 32nd president of the U.S. (1933–45); husband of: **2** (**Anna**) **Eleanor** 1884–1962; U.S. diplomat and author.

Roo·se·velt, Theodore 1858–1919; 26th president of the U.S. (1901–08).

Ross /raws/, **Betsy** (**Elizabeth Griscom**) 1752–1836; reported maker of the first American flag (1776).

Ros·set·ti /rōzétee, –sét–/ **1 Dante Gabriel** 1828–82; English poet and artist; brother of: **2 Christina Georgina** 1830–94; English poet.

Ros·si·ni /rəseénee, raw–/, **Gioachino** 1792–1868; Italian composer.

Ros·tand/rawstaáN, rostánd/, **Edmond** 1868–1918; French playwright.

Roth /rawth/, **Philip** 1933– ; U.S. novelist.

Roth·schild/rawth-chīld, ráwths–/ European-based family prominent in banking and finance, including: **1 Mayer Amschel** 1743–1812; German financier. **2 Lionel Nathan, Baron de** 1809–79; British financier.

Rous·seau /rōo͞só/, **Jean-Jacques** 1712–78; French philosopher and author, born in Switzerland.

Ru·bens /ró͞obənz/, **Peter Paul** 1577–1640; Flemish artist.

Ru·bin·stein/ró͞obinstīn/, **Arthur** (also **Artur**) 1886–1982; U.S. concert pianist, born in Poland.

Rush·die /ró͞oshdee, rúsh–/, (**Ahmed**) **Salman** 1947– ; British novelist, born in India.

Rus·kin /rúskin/, **John** 1819–1900; English art and social critic.

Rus·sell /rúsəl/, **Bertrand** 1873–1970; British philosopher, mathematician, and social reformer.

Ruth /ró͞oth/, **Babe** (**George Herman**) 1895–1948; U.S. baseball player.

Ruth·er·ford /rúthərfərd, –əfərd/, (**Sir**) **Ernest** 1871–1937; British nuclear physicist, born in New Zealand.

Ryle /rīl/, **Gilbert** 1900–76; English philosopher.

Saa·ri·nen /saárənən/ two U.S. architects, born in Finland: **1** (**Gottlieb**) **Eliel** 1873–1950; father of: **2 Eero** 1910–61.

Sa·bin /sáybin/, **Albert Bruce** 1906–93; U.S. microbiologist, born in Russia; developed oral vaccine for polio.

Sac·a·ja·we·a /sakəjəweéə, –wáyə/ (also **Sa·ca·ga·we′a**) c. 1788–1812; Shoshone Indian guide for the Lewis and Clark expedition.

Sa·dat /sədaát, –dát/, **Anwar el-** 1918–81; president of Egypt (1970–81); assassinated.

Sade /saad/, **Donatien** (**Comte de**) (called **"Marquis de Sade"**) 1740–1814; French novelist and notorious sexual deviant.

Sa·gan /sáygən/, **Carl Edward** 1934–96; U.S. astronomer and author.

Saint-Gau·dens /saynt gáwdnz/, **Augustus** 1848–1907; U.S. sculptor, born in Ireland.

Saint-Saëns /saN saáNs/, (**Charles**) **Camille** 1835–1921; French composer.

Sa·kha·rov /saákhərawf, sák–/, **Andrei Dmitrievich** 1921–89; Russian nuclear physicist.

Sa·ki /saákee/ see MUNRO, H(ECTOR) H(UGH).

Sal·a·din /sálədeen, –ədin/ 1137–93; sultan of Egypt and Syria (1175–93).

Sa·la·zar /sáləzaar/, **António de Oliveira** 1899–1970; premier of Portugal (1932–68).

Sal·in·ger /sálinjər/, **J**(**erome**) **D**(**avid**) 1919– ; U.S. author.

Salk /saw(l)k/, **Jonas** 1914–95; U.S. physician and microbiologist; developed first polio vaccine (1955).

Sal·lust /sáləst/, (Latin name **Gaius Sallustius Crispus**) 86–34 B.C.; Roman historian and politician.

Sand /sand/, **George** (pseudonym of **Amandine-Aurore-Lucile Dupin Dudevant**) 1804–76; French novelist.

Sand·burg /sánbərg, sánd–/, **Carl** 1878–1967; U.S. poet and biographer.

Sang·er /sángər/, **Margaret Louise Higgins** 1883–1966; U.S. reformer; proponent of birth control.

San·ta An·na /sántə ánə/ (also **San'ta An'a**), **Antonio López de** c. 1795–1876; Mexican military and political leader.

San·ta·ya·na /santəyaánə/, **George** 1863–1952; U.S. philosopher and poet, born in Spain.

Sap·pho /sáfō/ fl. 7th cent.–6th cent. B.C.; Greek lyric poet.

Sar·gent /saárjənt/, **John Singer** 1856–1925; U.S. portrait artist.

Sa·roy·an /səróyən/, **William** 1908–81; U.S. author.

Sar·tre /saártrə, saart/, **Jean-Paul** 1905–80; French philosopher and author.

Saus·sure /sōsóōr/, **Ferdinand de** 1857–1913; Swiss linguist.

Sav·o·na·ro·la /savənəróla/, **Girolamo** 1452–98; Italian religious reformer.

Sca·li·a /skəleéə/, **Antonin** 1936–   ; U.S. Supreme Court justice (1986–   ).

Scar·lat·ti /skaarlaátee/ two Italian composers: **1 Alessandro** 1659–1725; father of: **2 (Giuseppe) Domenico** 1685–1757.

Schles·in·ger /shlésinjər/ two U.S. historians: **1 Arthur Meier** 1888–1965; father of: **2 Arthur Meier, Jr.** 1917–   .

Schil·ler /shílər/, **Johann Christoph Friedrich von** 1759–1805; German playwright and poet.

Schlie·mann /shleémaan/, **Heinrich** 1822–90; German archaeologist.

Schön·berg /shərnbərg/, **Arnold Franz Walter** 1874–1951; U.S. composer, born in Austria.

Scho·pen·hau·er /shópənhowər/, **Arthur** 1788–1860; German philosopher.

Schrö·ding·er /shráydingər, shród–/, **Erwin** 1887–1961; German theoretical physicist.

Schu·bert /shoóbərt/, **Franz** 1797–1828; Austrian composer.

Schulz /shoōlts/, **Charles M(onroe)** 1922–   ; U.S. cartoonist.

Schu·mann /shoómaan, –mən/, **Robert** 1810–56; German composer.

Schwarz·kopf /shwáwrtskawf/, **H. Norman** 1934–   ; U.S. general.

Schweit·zer /shwítsər/, **Albert** 1875–1965; French theologian, organist, and medical missionary in Africa.

Scip·i·o /sípee-ō, skíp–/ name of two Roman generals: **1 Publius Cornelius Scipio Africanus Major** 236–c. 184 B.C.; defeated Hannibal; adoptive grandfather of: **2 Publius**

Cornelius Scipio Aemilianus Africanus 185–129 B.C.; destroyed Carthage.

Scott /skot/, **Dred** c. 1795–1858; U.S. slave; subject of a controversial U.S. Supreme Court proslavery decision (1857).

Scott, (Sir) Walter 1771–1832; Scottish novelist and poet.

Scott, Winfield (called **"Old Fuss and Feathers"**) 1786–1866; U.S. general.

Sea·borg /seébawrg/, **Glenn Theodor** 1912–   ; U.S. chemist.

Se·go·vi·a /səgóveeə/, **Andrés** 1893–1987; Spanish classical guitarist.

Se·leu·cus I /səloókəs/ c. 358–280 B.C.; Macedonian general; founded Seleucid Empire of Syria and Asia Minor.

Sen·e·ca /sénikə/, **Lucius Annaeus** c. 4 B.C.–A.D. 65; Roman philosopher and author.

Sen·nach·er·ib /sənakərib/ died 681 B.C.; king of Assyria (704–681 B.C.).

Se·quoy·a /sikwóyə/ c. 1770–1843; Cherokee Indian scholar.

Se·ton /seét'n/, **St. Elizabeth Ann Bayley** (called **"Mother Seton"**) 1774–1821; U.S. religious leader and educator.

Seu·rat /səraá/, **Georges** 1859–91; French artist.

Seuss /soōs/, **Dr.** (pseudonym of **Theodor Seuss Geisel**) 1904–91; U.S. children's author and illustrator.

Sew·ard /soóərd/, **William Henry** 1801–72; U.S. politician; advocated U.S. purchase of Alaska.

Shake·speare /sháykspeer/, **William** 1564–1616; English poet and playwright. □□ **Shake·spear'e·an** adj. **Shake·spear'i·an** adj.

Sha·li·kash·vi·li /shaaleekaashveélee/, **John Malchase** 1936–   ; U.S. general, born in Poland; chairman of the Joint Chiefs of Staff (1993–   ).

Shan·kar /shaángkaar/, **Ravi** 1920–   ; Indian sitar player.

Shaw /shaw/, **George Bernard** 1856–1950; Irish playwright, novelist, and critic.

Shel·ley /shélee/ **1 Percy Bysshe** 1792–1822; English poet; husband of: **2 Mary Wollstonecraft** 1797–1851; English novelist.

Sher·i·dan /shérid'n/, **Phillip Henry** 1831–88; Union general in the American Civil War.

Sher·i·dan, Richard Brinsley 1751–1816; Irish playwright.

Sher·man /shərmən/, **Roger** 1721–93; American statesman and patriot.

Sher·man, William Tecumseh 1820–91; Union general in the American Civil War.

Shev·ard·na·dze /shevərdnaádzə/, **Eduard** 1928–   ; president of the Georgian Republic (1992–   ).

Sho·sta·ko·vich /shostəkóvich/, **Dmitri** 1906–75; Russian composer.

Sho·wa /shówə/ see HIROHITO.

Si·be·li·us /sibáyleeəs/, **Jean** 1865–1957; Finnish composer.

Sid·dhart·ha Gau·ta·ma /sidaártə, –thə; gówtəmə/ see BUDDHA.

Sie·mens /seémənz, zeé–/, (**Ernst**) **Werner von** 1816–92; German electrical engineer and inventor.

Si·kor·sky /sikáwrskee/, **Igor** 1889–1972; U.S. aircraft designer, born in Russia.

Sills /silz/, **Beverly** (born **Belle Silverman**) 1929– ; U.S. operatic soprano.

Si·mon Pe·ter see PETER, ST.

Si·mon /símən/, (**Marvin**) **Neil** 1927– ; U.S. playwright.

Simp·son /símpsən/, **O(renthal) J(ames)** 1947– ; U.S. football player and actor.

Si·na·tra /sinaátrə/, **Frank** (**Francis Albert**) 1915– ; U.S. singer and actor.

Sin·clair /sínklair, –kláir/, **Upton** 1878–1968; U.S. novelist.

Sing·er /síng-ər/, **Isaac Bashevis** 1904–91; U.S. author, born in Poland.

Sing·er, Isaac Merritt 1811–75; U.S. inventor.

Sit·ting Bull /síting bŏŏl/ c. 1831–90; Sioux Indian leader.

Skin·ner /skínər/, **B(urrhus) F(rederic)** 1904–90; U.S. psychologist.

Sme·ta·na /smét'nə/, **Bedřich** 1824–84; Czech composer.

Smith /smith/, **Adam** 1723–90; Scottish philosopher and economist.

Smith, John 1580–1631; English colonist of Virginia.

Smith, Joseph 1805–44; founder of the Mormon Church (1830).

Smol·lett /smólit/, **Tobias George** 1721–71; English novelist.

Smuts /smʏts, smuts/, **Jan Christiaan** 1870–1950; prime minister of South Africa (1919–24; 1939–48).

Soc·ra·tes /sókrəteez/ 469–399 B.C.; Greek philosopher. □□ **So·crat·ic** /səkrátik/ adj.

So·lon /sólən/ c. 638–559 B.C.; Athenian lawgiver.

Sol·zhe·ni·tsyn /sólzhəneétsin, sawl–/, **Alexander** 1918– ; Russian novelist.

Sond·heim /sóndhīm/, **Stephen Joshua** 1930– ; U.S. songwriter.

Son·tag /sóntag/, **Susan** 1933– ; U.S. author and critic.

Soph·o·cles /sófəkleez/ c. 496–406 B.C.; Greek tragedian.

Sou·sa /sóŏzə/, **John Philip** 1854–1932; U.S. bandmaster and composer.

Sou·ter /sóŏtər/, **David Hackett** 1939– ; U.S. Supreme Court justice (1990–).

Sou·they /súthee, sówthee/, **Robert** 1774–1843; English author.

So·yin·ka /shaw-yíngkə/, **Wole** 1934– ; Nigerian author.

Spar·ta·cus /spaártəkəs/ died 71 B.C.; Thracian gladiator; leader of a slave revolt against Rome.

Spen·ser /spénsər/, **Edmund** c. 1552–99; English poet.

Spiel·berg /speélbərg/, **Steven** 1947– ; U.S. film director, writer, and producer.

Spi·no·za /spinózə/, **Baruch** (**Benedict de**) 1632–77; Dutch philosopher.

Spock /spok/, **Benjamin** 1903– ; U.S. pediatrician and author.

Squan·to /skwaántō/ died 1622; Pawtuxet Indian who befriended Pilgrims at Plymouth Colony in Massachusetts.

Sta·lin /staálən, stál–/, **Joseph** (born **Iosif Vissarionovich Dzhugashvili**) 1879–1953; Soviet political leader.

Stan·dish /stándish/, **Myles** (or **Miles**) c. 1584–1656; English colonist in New England.

Stan·i·slav·sky /stanislaávskee/, **Konstantin** 1863–1938; Russian director and teacher of acting.

Stan·ley /stánlee/, (**Sir**) **Henry Morton** (born **John Rowlands**) 1841–1904; U.S. explorer and author, born in Wales.

Stan·ton /stánt'n/, **Elizabeth Cady** 1815–1902; U.S. social reformer.

Starr /staar/, **Ringo** (born **Richard Starkey**) 1940– ; British pop and rock drummer and singer.

Stein /stīn/, **Gertrude** 1874–1946; U.S. author.

Stein·beck /stínbek/, **John Ernst** 1902–68; U.S. author.

Stein·em /stínəm/, **Gloria** 1934– ; U.S. journalist, editor, and women's rights activist.

Sten·dhal /stendaál, staʌdaál/ (pseudonym of **Henri Beyle**) 1783–1842; French novelist.

Sterne /stərn/, **Laurence** 1713–68; British novelist.

Steu·ben /styóŏbən, stŏŏ–, shtóy–/, (**Baron**) **Friedrich von** 1730–94; Prussian military leader; American Revolutionary War general in the Continental army.

Ste·vens /steévənz/, **John Paul** 1920– ; U.S. Supreme Court justice (1975–).

Ste·vens, Wallace 1878–1955; U.S. poet.

Ste·ven·son /steévənsən/, **Adlai Ewing** 1900–65; U.S. politician and statesman.

Ste·ven·son, Robert Louis Balfour 1850–94; British novelist.

Stone /stōn/, **Lucy** 1818–93; U.S. suffragist.

Stop·pard /stópaard, –ərd/, **Tom** (born Thomas Straussler) 1937– ; English playwright, born in Czechoslovakia.

Stowe /stō/, **Harriet Beecher** 1811–96; U.S. author.

Stra·di·va·ri /stradəvaáree, –vár–/, **Antonio** c. 1644–1737; Italian violin-maker.

Strauss/strows, shtrows/, **Johann** (called **"the Waltz King"**) 1825–99; Austrian composer.

Strauss, Richard Georg 1864–1949; German composer.

Stra·vin·sky /strəvínskee/, **Igor** 1882–1971; U.S. composer, born in Russia.

Strind·berg /strín(d)bərg/, **(Johan) August** 1849–1912; Swedish author.

Stu·art /stóoərt/, **Gilbert Charles** 1755–1828; U.S. portrait artist.

Stu·art, Jeb (James Ewell Brown) 1833–64; Confederate general in the American Civil War.

Stuy·ve·sant /stívəsənt/, **Peter** 1592–1672; Dutch colonial administrator in America.

Sue·to·ni·us /sweetóneeəs/ 75–150; Roman historian.

Su·kar·no /sookaárnō/, **Achmed** 1901–70; president of Indonesia (1949–67).

Su·har·to /soohaártō/, **Raden** 1921– ; president of Indonesia (1968–).

Su·lei·man I /sóolaymaan, –li–/ (called **"the Magnificent"**) c. 1495–1566; sultan of the Ottoman Empire.

Sul·la /súlə/, **Lucius Cornelius** c. 138–78 B.C.; Roman general and political leader.

Sun Yat-sen /sóon yaátsén/ (also **Sun Yi-xian**) 1866–1925; Chinese political leader.

Suth·er·land /súthərlənd/, **Joan** 1926– ; Australian operatic soprano.

Swift /swift/, **Jonathan** 1667–1745; English clergyman and satirist, born in Ireland.

Swin·burne /swínbərn/, **Algernon Charles** 1837–1909; English poet and critic.

Synge /sing/, **(Edmund) John Millington** 1871–1909; Irish playwright.

Tac·i·tus /tásitəs/, **Cornelius** c. 55–c. 120; Roman historian.

Taft /taft/ **1 William Howard** 1857–1930; 27th president of the U.S. (1909–13); Chief Justice of the U.S. (1921–30); father of: **2 Robert A(lphonse)** 1889–1953; U.S. politician.

Ta·gore /təgáwr, –gór/, **(Sir) Rabindranath** 1861–1941; Indian poet.

Tal·ley·rand-Pé·ri·gord/táleerand perəgáwr/, **Charles Maurice de (Prince de Bénévent)** 1754–1838; French diplomat.

Tam·er·lane /támərlayn/ c. 1336–1405; Mongol ruler.

Tar·king·ton /taárkingtən/, **(Newton) Booth** 1869–1946; U.S. author.

Tay·lor /táylər/, **Elizabeth** 1932– ; U.S. actress, born in England.

Tay·lor, Zachary 1784–1850; 12th president of the U.S. (1849–50).

Tchai·kov·sky /chīkáwfskee, –káwv–/, **Peter Ilyich** 1840–93; Russian composer.

Te Ka·na·wa/tay kaánəwə/, **Kiri** 1944– ; New Zealand operatic soprano.

Te·cum·seh /təkúmsə/ c. 1768–1813; Shawnee Indian leader.

Teil·hard de Char·din /tay-yaár də shaardá-N/, **Pierre** 1881–1955; French Jesuit philosopher.

Tel·ler /télər/, **Edward** 1908– ; U.S. nuclear physicist, born in Hungary.

Tem·ple/témpəl/, **Shirley** see BLACK, SHIRLEY TEMPLE.

Teng Hsiao-p'ing/dúng shyówpíng/ see DENG XIAOPING.

Ten·ny·son /ténəsən/, **Alfred, Lord** 1809–92; English poet.

Te·re·sa /təreésə, –ráyzə/, **Mother** (born Agnes Gonxha Bojaxhiu) 1910–97; Roman Catholic missionary nun, born in Albania.

Tes·la /téslə/, **Nikola** 1856–1943; U.S. engineer and inventor.

Thack·er·ay/thákəree/, **William Makepeace** 1811–63; English author.

Tha·les/tháyleez/ fl. early 6th cent. B.C.; Greek philosopher.

Thant /t(h)aánt, t(h)ánt/, **U** 1909–74; Burmese diplomat; secretary-general of the United Nations (1962–71).

Thatch·er /tháchər/, **(Lady) Margaret Hilda Roberts** (called **"the Iron Lady"**) 1925– ; prime minister of Great Britain (1979–90).

Thi·bault /teebō/, **Jacques Anatole** see FRANCE, ANATOLE.

Thom·as à Kem·pis see KEMPIS, THOMAS À.

Thom·as /taáməs/, **Clarence** 1948– ; U.S. Supreme Court justice (1991–).

Thom·as, Dylan 1914–53; Welsh poet.

Tho·reau /thəró, tháwrō/, **Henry David** (born David Henry Thoreau) 1817–62; U.S. author.

Thu·cyd·i·des /thoōsídədeez, thyoō–/ c. 455–c. 400 B.C.; Greek historian.

Thur·ber /thárbər/, **James Grover** 1894–1961; U.S. cartoonist and author.

Ti·be·ri·us /tībeéreeəs/ 42 B.C.–A.D. 37; Roman emperor (A.D. 14–37).

Til·lich /tílik/, **Paul Johannes** 1886–1965; U.S. theologian, born in Germany.

Tin·to·ret·to /tintərétō/ 1518–94; Italian artist.

Ti·tian /tíshən/ c. 1488–1576; Italian artist.

Ti·to /téetō/, (born **Josip Broz**) 1892–1980; president of Yugoslavia (1953–80).

Tocque·ville /tókvil/, **Alexis de** 1805–59; French statesman and author.

Tof·fler /táwflǝr/, **Alvin** 1928– ; U.S. author.

To·jo /tōjō/, **Hideki** 1885–1948; war minister (1940–41) and prime minister (1941–44) of Japan; executed.

Tol·kien /taálkeen, tōl–/, **J(ohn) R(onald) R(euel)** 1892–1973; English author.

Tol·stoy /táwlstoy, tōl–, taál–/, (**Count**) **Leo** (or **Lev**) **Nikolaevich** 1828–1910; Russian author.

Tor·que·ma·da /tawrkǝmaádǝ/, **Tomás de** c. 1420–98; Spanish cleric; led Spanish Inquisition.

Tos·ca·ni·ni /toskǝneénee/, **Arturo** 1867–1975; Italian conductor.

Tou·louse-Lau·trec /tōōlōos lōtrék/, **Henri de** 1864–1901; French artist.

Toyn·bee /tóynbee/, **Arnold Joseph** 1889–1975; English historian.

Tra·cy /tráysee/, **Spencer** 1900–67; U.S. actor.

Trev·i·thick /trévǝthik/, **Richard** 1771–1833; British engineer.

Trol·lope /trólǝp/, **Anthony** 1815–82; English novelist.

Trot·sky /trótskee/, **Leon** (born **Lev Davidovich Bronstein**) 1879–1940; Russian revolutionary.

Tru·deau /trōōdó/, **Pierre Elliott** 1919– ; prime minister of Canada (1968–79; 1980–84).

Tru·man /troóomǝn/, **1 Harry S** 1884–1972; 33rd president of the U.S. (1945–53); father of: **2 Margaret** 1924– ; U.S. author.

Trump /trump/, **Donald** 1946– ; U.S. business executive.

Tub·man /túbmǝn/, **Harriet** 1820–1913; U.S. abolitionist.

Tuch·man /túkmǝn/, **Barbara** 1912–89; U.S. historian.

Tur·ge·nev /tōōrgáynyǝf, –gén–/, **Ivan** 1818–83; Russian novelist.

Tur·ner /tɔ́rnǝr/, **Joseph Mallord William** 1775–1851; English landscape artist.

Tur·ner, Nat 1800–31; U.S. slave insurrectionist.

Tur·ner, Ted (**Robert Edward**) 1938– ; U.S. media executive.

Tut·ankh·a·men /tōōtaangkaámǝn, –tang–/ 14th cent. B.C.; Egyptian king.

Tu·tu /tóōtōō/, **Desmond** (born **Mpilo**) 1931– ; South African archbishop and civil-rights leader.

Twain /twayn/, **Mark** (pseudonym of **Samuel Langhorne Clemens**) 1835–1910; U.S. author.

Tweed /tweed/, **Boss** (**William Marcy**) 1823–78; U.S. politician.

Ty·ler /tílǝr/, **John** 1790–1862; 10th president of the U.S. (1841–45).

Tyn·dale /tíndǝl, –dayl/, **William** c. 1494–1536; English translator of the Bible.

Up·dike /úpdīk/, **John Hoyer** 1932– ; U.S. novelist.

Va·lé·ry /valǝreé/, **Paul Ambroise** 1871–1945; French poet and philosopher.

Van Bu·ren /van byōōrǝn/, **Martin** (called "**Old Kinderhook**") 1782–1862; 8th president of the U.S. (1837–41).

Van·der·bilt /vándǝrbilt/, **Cornelius** 1794–1877; U.S. industrialist.

Van Dyck /van dík/, (**Sir**) **Anthony** 1599–1641; Flemish artist.

Van Eyck /van ík/, **Jan** died 1441; Flemish artist.

Van Gogh /van gó, gaákh/, **Vincent** 1853–90; Dutch artist.

Vaughan /vawn/, **Sarah** 1924–90; U.S. jazz singer.

Vaughan Wil·liams /vawn wílyǝmz/, **Ralph** 1872–1958; English composer.

Ve·láz·quez /vǝláskǝs, –kwez/, **Diego** 1599–1660; Spanish artist.

Ver·di /vérdee/, **Giuseppe** 1813–1901; Italian opera composer.

Ver·gil /vɔ́rjǝl/ see VIRGIL.

Ver·meer /vǝrmeér/, **Jan** 1632–75; Dutch artist.

Verne /vǝrn/, **Jules** 1828–1905; French author.

Ves·puc·ci /vespóōchee/, **Amerigo** 1451–1512; Italian explorer.

Vic·to·ri·a /viktáwreeǝ/ 1819–1901; queen of Great Britain (1837–1901).

Vi·dal /vidaál, –dáwl/, **Gore** (born **Eugene Luther Vidal**) 1925– ; U.S. author.

Vil·la /veé–ǝ/, **Pancho** (**Francisco**) 1877–1923; Mexican revolutionary.

Vil·lon /vee-yóN/, **François** 1431–c. 1463; French poet.

Vir·gil /vɔ́rjǝl/ (also **Ver′gil**) 70–19 B.C.; Roman poet.

Vir·gin Mar·y see MARY.

Vi·val·di /vivaáldee/, **Antonio** 1678–1741; Italian composer.

Vol·ta /vówltǝ/, (**Count**) **Alessandro** 1745–1827; Italian physicist.

Vol·taire /vōltáir, vawl–, –tér/, (pseudonym of **François-Marie Arouet**) 1694–1778; French author.

Von·ne·gut /vónigǝt/, **Kurt** 1922– ; U.S. author.

Wag·ner /vaágnǝr/, **Richard** 1813–83; German composer.

Wald·heim /vaáldhīm/, **Kurt** 1918–　; Austrian political leader and diplomat; secretary-general of the United Nations (1972–82).

Wa·le·sa /vəlénsə, vəwénsə/, **Lech** 1943–　; Polish labor and political leader.

Wal·lace /waáləs/, **Alfred Russel** 1823–1913; British naturalist.

Wal·lace, George Corley 1919–　; U.S. politician.

Wal·pole /wáwlpōl/, **Horace** (**4th Earl of Orford**) 1717–97; English author.

Wal·ton /wáwlt'n/, **Izaak** 1593–1683; English author.

Wan·kel /vaángkəl/, **Felix** 1902–88; German engineer.

War·hol /wáwrhawl, –hōl/, **Andy** (born **Andrew Warhola**) c. 1930–87; U.S. artist and filmmaker.

War·ren /wáwrən, waár–/, **Earl** 1891–1974; Chief Justice of the U.S. (1953–69).

Wash·ing·ton /waáshingtən, wáwsh–/, **Booker T**(**aliaferro**) 1856–1915; U.S. educator and reformer.

Wash·ing·ton, George 1732–99; American patriot and Revolutionary War general; 1st president of the U.S. (1789–97).

Wat·son /waátsən/, **James Dewey** 1928–　; U.S. biologist.

Watt /waat/, **James** 1736–1819; Scottish inventor.

Wat·teau /vaató, waa–/, **Jean Antoine** 1684–1721; French artist.

Waugh /waw/, **Evelyn** 1903–66; English novelist.

Wayne /wayn/, **Anthony** (called "**Mad Anthony**") 1745–96; American Revolutionary War general.

Wayne, John (born **Marion Michael Morrison**) 1907–79; U.S. actor.

We·ber /váybər/, **Max** 1864–1920; German sociologist.

We·ber /wébər/, **Max** 1881–1961; U.S. artist, born in Russia.

Web·ster /wébstər/, **Daniel** 1782–1852; U.S. politician and orator.

Web·ster, Noah 1758–1843; U.S. lexicographer.

Wedg·wood /wéjwŏŏd/, **Josiah** 1730–95; English potter.

Weill /vīl/, **Kurt** 1900–50; German composer.

Weiz·mann /vítsmən/, **Chaim** 1874–1952; president of Israel (1949–52).

Wel·ling·ton /wélingtən/, **1st Duke of** (**Arthur Wellesley**) (called "**the Iron Duke**") 1769–1852; British general and statesman; prime minister of Great Britain (1828–30).

Wells /welz/, **H**(**erbert**) **G**(**eorge**) 1866–1946; English author.

Wel·ty /wéltee/, **Eudora** 1909–　; U.S. author.

Wes·ley /wéslee, wéz–/, **John** 1703–91; English evangelical leader; founder of Methodism.

West /west/, **Benjamin** 1738–1820; U.S. artist.

West, Rebecca (pseudonym of **Cicily Isabel Fairfield**) 1892–1983; English author.

Whar·ton /(h)wáwrt'n/, **Edith Newbold Jones** 1862–1937; U.S. novelist.

Wheat·ley /(h)weétlee/, **Phillis** c. 1753–84; American poet, probably born in Senegal.

Wheat·stone /(h)weétstōn/, (**Sir**) **Charles** 1802–75; English physicist and inventor.

Whis·tler /(h)wíslər/, **James Abbott McNeill** 1834–1903; U.S. artist.

White·head /(h)wít-hed/, **Alfred North** 1861–1947; English mathematician and philosopher.

Whit·man /(h)wítmən/, **Walt**(**er**) 1819–92; U.S. poet.

Whit·ney /(h)wítnee/, **Eli** 1765–1825; U.S. inventor and manufacturer.

Whit·tier /(h)wíteeər/, **John Greenleaf** 1807–92; U.S. poet.

Wie·sel /veezél, wizél/, **Elie** 1928–　; U.S. author and educator, born in Romania.

Wilde /wīld/, **Oscar** 1854–1900; Irish poet and playwright.

Wil·der /wíldər/, **Thornton Niven** 1897–1975; U.S. author.

Wil·lard /wílərd/, **Emma Hart** 1787–1870; U.S. educational reformer.

Wil·liam /wílyəm/ name of four kings of England, including: **1 William I** (called "**the Conqueror**") c. 1027–87; reigned 1066–87. **2 William III** 1650–1702; reigned 1689–1702 with his wife, Mary II.

Wil·liams /wílyəmz/, **Roger** c. 1603–83; English clergyman; established Rhode Island colony (1636).

Wil·liams, Tennessee (born **Thomas Lanier Williams**) 1911–83; U.S. playwright.

Wil·liams, William Carlos 1883–1963; U.S. poet.

Wil·son /wilsən/, **Edmund** 1895–1972; U.S. critic and author.

Wil·son, (**Lord**) (**James**) **Harold** 1916–95; prime minister of Great Britain (1964–70; 1974–76).

Wil·son, (**Thomas**) **Woodrow** 1856–1924; 28th president of the U.S. (1913–21).

Win·frey /wínfree/, **Oprah** 1954–　; U.S. television personality and actress.

Witt·gen·stein /vítgənshtīn, –stīn/, **Ludwig** 1889–1951; British philosopher, born in Austria.

Wode·house /wo͝odhows/, (**Sir**) **P(elham) G(renville)** 1881–1975; English author.
Wolfe /wo͝olf/, **Thomas** 1900–38; U.S. author.
Wol·las·ton /wo͝oləstən/, **William Hyde** 1766–1828; English scientist.
Wol·sey /wo͝olzee/, **Thomas** c. 1474–1530; English cleric and statesman.
Won·der /wúndər/, **Stevie** (born **Stephen Judkins**) 1950– ; U.S. pop singer and songwriter.
Wood /wo͝od/, **Grant** 1892–1942; U.S. artist.
Woods /wo͝odz/, **Tiger** (**Eldrick**) 1975– ; U.S. golfer.
Woolf /wo͝olf/, (**Adeline**) **Virginia** 1882–1941; English author.
Words·worth /wɔ́rdzwərth/, **William** 1770–1850; English poet.
Wouk /wōk/, **Herman** 1915– ; U.S. author.
Wren /ren/, (**Sir**) **Christopher** 1632–1723; English architect.
Wright /rīt/, **Frank Lloyd** 1869–1959; U.S. architect.
Wright, Richard 1908–60; U.S. author.
Wright two U.S. aviation pioneers: **1 Wilbur** 1867–1912; brother of: **2 Orville** 1871–1948.
Wy·eth /wíəth/ family of U.S. artists, including: **1 N(ewell) C(onvers)** 1882–1945; father of: **2 Andrew Newell** 1917– ; father of: **3 Jamie** (**James Browning**) 1946– .

Xa·vi·er /záyvyər, igzáy–/, **St. Francis** (**Francisco Javier**) 1506–52; Spanish Jesuit missionary of the Far East.
Xen·o·phon /zénəfən, –fon/ c. 428–c. 354 B.C.; Greek author.
Xerx·es I /zɔ́rkseez/ c. 519–465 B.C.; king of Persia (486–465 B.C.).
Yeats /yayts/, **William Butler** 1865–1939; Irish poet and playwright.
Yelt·sin /yéltsin/, **Boris** 1931– ; president of the Russian federation (1991–).
Young /yung/, **Brigham** 1801–77; U.S. Mormon leader.
Za·pa·ta /zəpaátə/, **Emiliano** c. 1877–1919; Mexican revolutionary.
Zar·a·thus·tra /zaarəthoo͝ostrə/ see ZOROASTER.
Zep·pe·lin /zépəlin/, (**Count**) **Ferdinand von** 1838–1917; German airship developer.
Zhou En·lai /jố enlí/ see CHOU EN-LAI.
Zhu·kov /zhoo͝okawf, –kawv/, **Georgi Konstantinovich** 1896–1974; Soviet military leader in World War II.
Zieg·feld /zígfeld, zee̍g–/, **Flo(renz)** 1867–1932; U.S. theater producer.
Zo·la /zólə, zōlaá/, **Émile** 1840–1902; French author.
Zo·ro·as·ter /záwrō-astər, zór–/ (also **Zar·at·hus'tra**) c. 628–551 B.C.; Persian prophet; founder of Zoroastrianism.

Geographical Entries

Aa·chen /aákhən/ city in W Germany. Pop. 241,900.

Ab·er·deen /abərdeén/ port city in E Scotland, United Kingdom. Pop. 218,200.

Ab·i·djan /abijaán/ port city and commercial capital of Ivory Coast. Pop. 2,797,000.

Ab·i·lene /ábəleen/ city in central Texas. Pop. 106,654.

A·bu Dha·bi /aábōō daábee/ capital of the United Arab Emirates. Pop. 363,400.

A·bu·ja /aabóójaa/ capital of Nigeria, in the central part. Pop. 339,100.

A·ca·di·a /akáydeeə/ **Na·tion·al Park** scenic area on the coast of Maine; includes parts of Mount Desert Island, Schoodic Peninsula, and Isle au Haut.

A·ca·pul·co /akəpoólkō, aak–, –poól–/ port city in S Mexico. Pop. 515,400.

Ac·cra /aákraá/ port city and capital of Ghana. Pop. 1,781,100.

A·con·ca·gua /aakənkaágwə/ mountain in the Andes range, in W Argentina; highest in W hemisphere: 22,831 ft.

Ad·dis A·ba·ba /ádis ábəbə/ capital of Ethiopia, in the central part. Pop. 2,200,200.

Ad·e·laide /ád'layd/ capital of South Australia, Australia, in the SE part. Pop. 1,023,600.

A·den /aád'n, áyd'n/ port city and economic capital of Yemen. Pop. 318,000.

A·den, Gulf of arm of the Arabian Sea, S of Yemen.

Ad·i·ron·dack /adəraándak/ **Moun·tains** mountain range in NE New York; part of the Appalachian range.

A·dri·at·ic /aydree-átik/ **Sea** arm of the Mediterranean Sea, between Italy and the Balkan Peninsula.

Ae·ge·an /ijeéən, ee–/ **Sea** arm of the Mediterranean Sea, between Greece and Turkey.

Af·ghan·i·stan /afgánistan/ republic in central Asia. Pop. 22,664,000. Capital: Kabul.

Af·ri·ca /áfrikə/ continent between the Atlantic and Indian oceans, S of Europe. □□ **Af'ri·can** *n. & adj.*

A·gra /aágrə/ city in N central India; site of the Taj Mahal. Pop. 899,200.

A·guas·ca·lien·tes /aagwaaskaalyéntays/ state in central Mexico. Pop. 719,700. Capital: Aguascalientes.

Ah·mad·a·bad /aámədəbaad/ city in W India. Pop. 2,872,900.

Aix-en-Pro·vence /ayks aaɴ prōvaáɴs, eks/ city in SE France. Pop. 126,900.

Ak·ron /ákrən/ city in N Ohio. Pop. 223,019.

Al·a·bam·a /aləbámə/ state in SE U.S. Pop. 4,040,587. Capital: Montgomery. Abbr. **AL**; **Ala.** □□ **Al·a·bam'i·an, Al·a·bam'an** *n. & adj.*

A·las·ka /əláskə/ state in NW U.S. Pop. 550,043. Capital: Juneau. Abbr. **AK** □□ **A·las'kan** *n. & adj.*

A·las·ka, Gulf of arm of the N Pacific, on the S coast of Alaska.

Al·ba·ni·a /albáyneeə, awl–/ republic in S Europe, on the Balkan Peninsula. Pop. 3,249,000. Capital: Tiranë. □□ **Al·ba'ni·an** *n. & adj.*

Al·ba·ny /áwlbənee/ capital of New York, in the E part. Pop. 101,082.

Al·ber·ta /albúrtə/ province in W Canada. Pop. 2,662,000. Capital: Edmonton. □□ **Al·ber'tan** *n. & adj.*

Al·bu·quer·que /álbəkərkee/ city in central New Mexico. Pop. 384,736.

Al·ca·traz /álkətraz/ island in in San Francisco Bay; site of a former federal penitentiary.

A·lep·po /əlépō/ city in N Syria. Pop. 1,591,400.

A·leu·tian /əloóshən/ **Is·lands** (also called **the A·leu'tians**) island chain in Alaska, between the Bering Sea and the Pacific.

Al·ex·an·dri·a /aligzándreeə/ **1** port city in N Egypt. Pop. 3,382,000. **2** city in NE Virginia; Pop. 111,183.

Al·ge·ri·a /aljeéreeə/ republic in NW Africa. Pop. 29,183,000. Capital: Algiers. □□ **Al·ge'ri·an** *n. & adj.*

Al·giers /aljeérz/ port city and capital of Algeria. Pop. 1,507,200.

Al·lah·a·bad /áləhəbad, –baad/ city in N India. Pop. 806,400.

Al·le·ghe·ny /aləgáynee/ **Moun·tains** mountain range in E U.S., extending from Pennsylvania to Virginia; part of the Appalachian range.

Al·len·town /áləntown/ city in E Pennsylvania. Pop. 105,090.

al-Ma·nam·ah /al mənámə/ see MANAMA.

Al·ma·ty /aalmaateé/ (formerly **Alma-Ata** /aalmaá aataá/) capital of Kazakhstan, in the SE part. Pop. 1,164,000.

Alps /alps/ mountain range in S Europe,

extending from France through Switzerland and to the Balkan Peninsula.

Am·a·ril·lo /amərílō/ city in NW Texas. Pop. 157,615.

Am·a·zon /ámazaan, –zən/ **Riv·er** river in N South America, flowing 3,900 mi. from the Andes to the Atlantic; largest river in the world.

A·mer·i·ca /əmérikə, –már–/ **1** popular term for the United States of America. **2** (also called **the A·mer'i·cas**) the continents of North and South America, considered together. □□ **A·mer'i·can** n. & adj.

A·mer·i·can Sa·mo·a /səmóə/ (also **East'ern Sa·mo'a**) island group in the S Pacific, comprising the E islands of Samoa; a U.S. territory. Pop. 60,000. Capital: Pago Pago. See also WESTERN SAMOA. □□ **Sa·mo'an** n. & adj.

Am·i·ens /aámyaɴ, aamyáɴ/ city in N France. Pop. 136,200.

Am·man /aamaán/ capital of Jordan. Pop. 963,500.

Am·rit·sar /əmrítsər/ city in NW India. Pop. 709,500.

Am·ster·dam /ámstərdam/ port city and capital of the Netherlands. Pop. 724,100.

An·a·heim /ánəhīm/ city in SW California. Pop. 266,406.

An·chor·age /ángkərij/ port city in S Alaska. Pop. 226,338.

An·da·man /ándəmən, –man/ **Is·lands** island group in the Bay of Bengal, W of the Malay Peninsula.

An·des /ándeez/ mountain range in W South America, extending from Colombia to Cape Horn. □□ **An'de·an** n. & adj.

An·dor·ra /andáwrə/ republic in W Europe, on the border between France and Spain. Pop. 73,000. Capital: Andorra la Vella.

An·gel /áynjəl/ **Falls** waterfall in SE Venezuela; highest in the world: 3,212 ft.

An·go·la /ang-gólə, an–/ republic in SW Africa. Pop. 10,343,000. Capital: Luanda. □□ **An·go'lan** n. & adj.

An·guil·la /anggwílə/ island in the E West Indies; dependent territory of the United Kingdom. Pop. 8,700.

An·ka·ra /aángkərə, áng–/ capital of Turkey, in the central part. Pop. 2,720,000.

An·nap·o·lis /ənápələs/ capital of Maryland, in the central part; site of U.S. Naval Academy. Pop. 33,187.

Ann Ar·bor /an aárbər/ city in SE Michigan. Pop. 109,592.

An·ta·na·na·ri·vo /antənanəreévō/ capital of Madagascar, in the E central part. Pop. 1,052,800.

Ant·arc·ti·ca /antaárktikə, –aártikə/ **1** largely ice-covered continent surrounding the South Pole. **2** (**the Antarctic**) region of Antarctica and surrounding oceans. □□ **ant·arc'tic** adj.

An·ti·gua /anteégwə/ **and Bar·bu·da** /baarbo͞odə/ island state in the E West Indies. Pop. 66,000. Capital: St. John's.

An·til·les /antíleez/ island chain in the West Indies, comprising the Greater Antilles and the Lesser Antilles.

An·tip·o·des /antípədeez/ **1** collective term for Australia and New Zealand. **2** island group in the S Pacific, SE of New Zealand.

Ant·werp /ántwərp/ port city in N Belgium. Pop. 462,900.

Ap·en·nines /ápənīnz/ mountain range extending the length of the Italian peninsula.

A·pi·a /əpeéə/ port city and capital of Western Samoa. Pop. 32,900.

Ap·pa·la·chi·an /apəláychən, –lách–, –cheeən/ **Moun·tains** mountain range in E North America, extending from Quebec to Alabama.

Ap·po·mat·tox /apəmátəks/ **Court·house** hist. former town in central Virginia, at present-day Appomattox; site of Lee's surrender to Grant ending the American Civil War (1865).

A·ra·bi·an /əráybeeən/ **Pen·in·su·la** (also called **A·ra'bi·a**) peninsula in SW Asia, bounded by the Red Sea and the Persian Gulf, and comprising Kuwait, Oman, Qatar, Saudi Arabia, United Arab Emirates, and Yemen.

A·ra·bi·an Sea part of the Indian Ocean, between the Arabian Peninsula and India.

Ar·al /árəl/ **Sea** inland sea in W Asia.

Ar·a·rat /árərat/, **Mount** mountain in E Turkey; traditional landing site of Noah's Ark.

Arch·an·gel see ARKHANGELSK.

Arc·tic /aárktik, aártik/ region delimited by the Arctic Circle.

Arc·tic Cir·cle imaginary line at latitude 66° 32′ N, delimiting the Arctic region.

Arc·tic O·cean ocean N of North America, Asia, and Europe. Area 5,540,000 sq. mi.

Ar·gen·ti·na /aarjənteénə/ republic in SE South America. Pop. 34,673,000. Capital: Buenos Aires. □□ **Ar·gen·tine** /aárjənteen, –tīn/ n. & adj. **Ar·gen·tin·e·an** /aarjəntíneeən/ n. & adj.

Ar·i·zo·na /arəzónə/ state in SW U.S. Pop. 3,665,118. Capital: Phoenix. Abbr. **Ariz.; AZ** □□ **Ar·i·zo'nan, Ar·i·zo'ni·an** n. & adj.

Ar·kan·sas /aárkənsaw/ state in S central U.S. Pop. 2,350,725. Capital: Little Rock. Abbr. **AR; Ark.** □□ **Ar·kan·san** /aarkánsən/ n. & adj.

Ar·khan·gelsk /aarkangélsk/ (also **Arch·an' gel**) port city in NW Russia. Pop. 407,100.

Ar·ling·ton /aárlingtən/ **1** city in N Texas. Pop. 261,721. **2** city in NE Virginia. Pop. 170,936.

Ar·me·ni·a /aarme'eneeə/ republic in W Asia. Pop. 3,464,000. Capital: Yerevan. □□ **Ar·me'ni·an** *n. & adj.*

A·ru·ba /aaroóbaa/ self-governing Caribbean island, NW of Venezuela. Pop. 68,000.

Ash·ga·bat /áshkəbat/ (also **Ashkh'a·bad**) capital of Turkmenistan, in the S part. Pop. 518,000.

A·sia /áyzhə/ continent bounded by Europe, the Mediterranean and Red seas, and the Indian, Pacific, and Arctic oceans. □□ **A'sian** *n. & adj.*

A·sia Mi·nor *hist.* peninsula in W Asia, bounded by the Black and Mediterranean seas; roughly equivalent to present-day Turkey.

As·ma·ra /aasmaárə/ (also **As·me'ra**) capital of Eritrea, in the central part. Pop. 367,300.

A·sun·ción /aasoōnsee-ón/ capital of Paraguay, in the SW part. Pop. 502,400.

As·wan /áswaan, –waán/ city in SE Egypt. Pop. 220,000.

A·syut /aasyoót/ city in E central Egypt. Pop. 321,000.

A·ta·ca·ma /aatəkaámə, at–/ **Des·ert** arid region in N Chile.

Ath·a·bas·ka /athəbáskə/, **Lake** lake in W Canada.

Ath·ens /áthənz/ capital of Greece, in the E part. Pop. 748,100. □□ **A·the·ni·an** /əthee'neeən/ *n. & adj.*

At·lan·ta /ətlántə, at–/ capital of Georgia, in the NW central part. Pop. 394,017.

At·lan·tic /ətlántik, at–/ **In·tra·coast·al Wa·ter·way** system of sheltered waterways along the E seaboard of the U.S.

At·lan·tic O·cean ocean separating the Americas from Europe and Africa. Area 31,530,000 sq. mi.

At·las /átləs/ **Moun·tains** mountain range in NW Africa, extending from SW Morocco to NE Tunisia.

Auck·land /áwklənd/ port city in N New Zealand. Pop. 336,500.

Augs·burg /ówksboōrk, áwgzbərg/ city in S Germany. Pop. 264,800.

Au·gus·ta /əgústə/ capital of Maine, in the SW part. Pop. 21,325.

Au·ro·ra /əráwrə, –rórə/ **1** city in NE central Colorado. Pop. 222,103. **2** city in NE Illinois. Pop. 99,581.

Aus·tin /áwstən/ capital of Texas, in the E central part. Pop. 465,622.

Aus·tral·a·sia /awstrəláyzhə, aas–, –shə/ region including Australia, New Zealand, and neighboring islands in the S Pacific.

Aus·tral·ia /awstráylyə, aas–/ **1** continent SE of Asia, bounded by the Indian and Pacific oceans. **2** commonwealth of the states and territories of Australia and Tasmania. Pop. 18,261,000. Capital: Canberra. □□ **Aus·tral'i·an** *n. & adj.*

Aus·tri·a /áwstreeə, aás–/ republic in central Europe. Pop. 8,023,000. Capital: Vienna. □□ **Aus'tri·an** *n. & adj.*

Az·er·bai·jan /azərbīzhaán, –jaán/ republic in SW Asia; formerly part of the USSR. Pop. 7,677,000. Capital: Baku. □□ **Az·er·bai·ja'ni** *n. & adj.*

A·zores /áyzawrz/ island group in the Atlantic, W of Portugal; autonomous region of Portugal.

A·zov /ázawf, áyzawf/, **Sea of** N arm of the Black Sea.

Bad·lands /bádlanz, –landz/ barren region in SW South Dakota and NW Nebraska.

Baf·fin /báfin/ **Bay** inlet of the Arctic Ocean, between Baffin Island and Greenland.

Baf·fin Is·land island in NE Canada, W of Greenland.

Bagh·dad /bágdad, bagdád/ (also **Bag'dad**) capital of Iraq, in the E central part. Pop. 4,044,000.

Ba·ha·mas /bəhaáməz/ island nation in the N West Indies, SE of Florida. Pop. 259,000. Capital: Nassau. □□ **Ba·ha·mi·an** /bəháymeeən/ *n. & adj.*

Bah·rain /baaráyn, baakhráyn/ sheikdom consisting of islands in the Persian Gulf. Pop. 590,000. Capital: Manama.

Bai·kal /bīkaál, –káwl/, **Lake** lake in S Russia; deepest in the world: 5,700 ft.

Ba·ja Ca·li·for·nia /baáhaa kalifáwrnyə/ **1** peninsula in NW Mexico, bounded by the Pacific and the Gulf of California. **2** (formerly **Ba'ja Ca·li·for'nia Nor·te** /náwrtay/) state in NW Mexico; N part of Baja California peninsula. Pop. 1,886,000. Capital: Mexicali.

Ba·ja Ca·li·for·nia Sur /soōr/ state in NW Mexico; S part of Baja California peninsula. Pop. 317,800. Capital: La Paz.

Ba·kers·field /báykərzfeeld/ city in S California. Pop. 174,820.

Ba·ku /baakoó/ port city and capital of Azerbaijan. Pop. 1,080,500.

Bal·e·ar·ic /balee-árik/ **Is·lands** island group in the W Mediterranean Sea; province of Spain.

Ba·li /baálee, bálee/ island in Indonesia, E of Java.

Bal·kan /báwlkən/ **Pen·in·su·la** peninsula in S Europe, bounded by the Adriatic and Black seas, and comprising the Balkan States.

Bal·kan States (also called **the Bal'kans**)

countries of the Balkan Peninsula: Albania, Bulgaria, Greece, Romania, Croatia, Bosnia and Herzegovina, Yugoslavia (including Serbia), Macedonia, and European Turkey.

Bal·tic /báwltik/ **Sea** sea in N Europe, S of Scandinavian Peninsula.

Bal·ti·more /báwltəmawr/ port city in N central Maryland. Pop. 736,014.

Ba·ma·ko /báməkō/ capital of Mali, in the SW part. Pop. 745,800.

Ban·dung /baándōōng/ city in Indonesia, on Java. Pop. 2,026,900.

Ban·ga·lore /baánggəlawr/ city in SW India. Pop. 2,650,700.

Bang·kok /bángkaak/ port city and capital of Thailand. Pop. 5,572,700.

Ban·gla·desh /banggládésh, baang–/ republic in S Asia. Pop. 123,063,000. Capital: Dhaka. □□ **Ban·gla·desh′i** n. & adj.

Ban·gui /baang-geé/ capital of Central African Republic, in the SW part. Pop. 524,000.

Ban·jul /baánjōōl/ port city and capital of Gambia. Pop. 44,200.

Bar·ba·dos /baarbáydōs, –ōz/ island nation in the E West Indies. Pop. 257,000. Capital: Bridgetown. □□ **Bar·ba′di·an** n. & adj.

Bar·ba·ry /baárbəree/ Mediterranean coast of the former Barbary States, in N Africa.

Bar·ba·ry States hist. Morocco, Algiers, Tunis, and Tripoli; refuge for pirates between 1520 and 1830.

Bar·ce·lo·na /baarsəlónə/ port city in NE Spain. Pop. 1,630,900.

Ba·ri /baáree/ (also called **Ba′ri del·le Pu·glie** /delə poólyee/) port city in SE Italy. Pop. 339,000.

Ba·ro·da /bəródə/ city in W India. Pop. 1,021,100.

Bar·ran·qui·lla /baaraankeéyə, –keélyə/ port city in N Colombia. Pop. 1,064,300.

Ba·sel /baázəl/ city in W Switzerland. Pop. 176,200.

Bas·ra /baásrə, baáz–/ city in SE Iraq. Pop. 616,700.

Basse·terre /baastér/ port city and capital of St. Kitts and Nevis. Pop. 15,000.

Basse-Terre /baas tér/ port city and capital of Guadeloupe. Pop. 14,100.

Ba·su·to·land /bəsoótōōland, –tōland/ see LE-SOTHO.

Bat·oɴ Rouge /bat'n roózh/ capital of Louisiana, in the SE central part. Pop. 219,531.

Bat·tle /bát'l/ **Creek** city in S Michigan. Pop. 53,540.

Ba·ya·món /bīəmón/ city in N Puerto Rico. Pop. 202,100.

Beau·fort /bófərt/ **Sea** part of the Arctic Ocean, NE of Alaska.

Beau·mont /bómaant/ city in SE Texas. Pop. 114,323.

Bea·ver·ton /beévərtən/ city in NW Oregon. Pop. 53,310.

Beer·she·ba /beersheébə/ city in S Israel. Pop. 141,400.

Bei·jing /bayjíng, –zhíng/ (formerly **Peking**) capital of China, in the NE part. Pop. 5,769,600.

Bei·rut /bayrōót/ capital of Lebanon, in the W part. Pop. 1,100,000.

Bel·a·rus /belərōós/ republic in E Europe; formerly, as Byelorussia, part of the USSR. Pop. 10,416,000. Capital: Minsk.

Bel·fast /bélfast, belfást/ port city and capital of Northern Ireland, United Kingdom. Pop. 296,700.

Bel·gium /béljəm/ kingdom in W Europe. Pop. 10,170,000. Capital: Brussels. □□ **Bel′gian** n. & adj.

Bel·go·rod /bélgəraad, byél–/ city in W Russia. Pop. 317,900.

Bel·grade /bélgrayd, –graad/ capital of Serbia, in the N part; capital of former Yugoslavia. Pop. 1,168,500.

Be·lize /bəleéz/ country in N Central America. Pop. 219,000. Capital: Belmopan.

Belle·vue /bélvyōō/ city in W central Washington. Pop. 86,874.

Bel·mo·pan /belmōpán/ capital of Belize, in the central part. Pop. 3,900.

Be·lo Ho·ri·zon·te /báylō hawrizaántee/ city in SE Brazil. Pop. 1,529,600.

Be·na·res /bənaáris, –eez/ see VARANASI.

Ben·e·lux /bén′ləks/ collective term for Belgium, the Netherlands, and Luxembourg.

Ben·gal /ben-gáwl, beng; n–/, **Bay of** inlet of the Indian Ocean, between India and Burma.

Ben·gha·zi /ben-gaázee/ port city in N Libya. Pop. 446,300.

Be·nin /bəneén, –nín/ republic in W Africa. Pop. 5,710,000. Capital: Porto-Novo.

Ber·gen /bérgən/ port city in SW Norway. Pop. 221,700.

Ber·ing /beéring, bér–/ **Sea** extension of the N Pacific, between Russia and Alaska.

Ber·ing Strait body of water separating Asia (Russia) from North America (Alaska).

Berke·ley /búrklee/ city in W California. Pop. 102,724.

Ber·lin /bərlín/ capital of Germany, in the NE part. Pop. 3,475,400. □□ **Ber·lin′er** n.

Ber·mu·da /bərmyōódə/ (also called **the Ber·mu′das**) island group in the Atlantic, E of North Carolina; British colony. Pop. 62,000.

Capital: Hamilton. □□ **Ber·mu′dan, Ber·mu′ di·an** *n. & adj.*

Ber·mu·da Tri·an·gle area in the Atlantic bounded by Puerto Rico, Bermuda, and Florida, where many ships and planes are said to have disappeared mysteriously.

Bern /bərn, bern/ (also **Berne**) capital of Switzerland, in the W central part. Pop. 134,600. □□ **Ber·nese** /bərneèz, –neès/ *n. & adj.*

Be·thes·da /bəthézdə/ city in central Maryland. Pop. 62,936.

Bho·pal /bōpaàl/ city in central India. Pop. 1,063,700.

Bhu·tan /booˈtán, –taàn/ monarchy in the Himalayas, NE of India. Pop. 1,823,000. Capital: Thimphu.

Bia·ly·stok /bee-aàleestawk/ city in E Poland. Pop. 276,100.

Bie·le·feld /beèləfelt/ city in W central Germany. Pop. 324,700.

Big Sur /big sər/ Pacific coastal region of California, from Carmel to San Simeon.

Bil·ba·o /bilbów, –báyō/ port city in N Spain. Pop. 371,800.

Bil·lings /bílingz/ city in S central Montana. Pop. 81,151.

Bir·ming·ham 1 /búrmingham/ city in N central Alabama. Pop. 265,968. **2** /búrmingəm/ city in central England. Pop. 1,024,100.

Bis·cay /biskáy/, **Bay of** inlet of the Atlantic, between France and Spain.

Bish·kek /bishkék/ capital of Kyrgyzstan, in the N part. Pop. 597,000.

Bis·marck /bízmaark/ capital of North Dakota, in the S central part. Pop. 49,256.

Bis·sau /bisów/ port city and capital of Guinea-Bissau. Pop. 200,000.

Black /blak/ **Hills** mountains in NE Wyoming and W South Dakota.

Black·pool /blákpool/ city in NW England. Pop. 146,100.

Black /blak/ **Sea** sea enclosed by Turkey, the Balkan Peninsula, Ukraine, SW Russia, and Georgia.

Blanc /blaaN/, **Mont** /mawn/ mountain on the France-Italy-Switzerland border; highest in the Alps: 15,771 ft.

Bloem·fon·tein /bloóofaanten/ judicial capital of South Africa, in the central part. Pop. 126,900.

Bloo·ming·ton /bloóomingtən/ **1** city in SE central Minnesota. Pop. 86,335. **2** city in S central Indiana. Pop. 60,633.

Blue·grass /bloóogras/ **Re·gion** area of central Kentucky noted for thoroughbred horse breeding.

Blue Ridge /bloó rij/ **Moun·tains** mountain range in E U.S., extending from West Virginia to N Georgia; part of the Appalachian range.

Bo·go·tá /bōgətaà/ capital of Colombia, in the central part. Pop. 5,237,600.

Boi·se /bóysee, –zee/ capital of Idaho, in the SW part. Pop. 125,738.

Bo·liv·i·a /bəliveeə/ republic in W South America. Pop. 7,165,000. Capitals: La Paz; Sucre. □□ **Bo·liv′i·an** *n. & adj.*

Bo·lo·gna /bəlónyə/ city in N Italy. Pop. 395,000. □□ **Bo·lo·gnese** /bōləneèz/ *n. & adj.*

Bom·bay /baambáy/ port city in W India. Pop. 14,496,000.

Bonn /baan, bawn/ city in W Germany; seat of government. Pop. 296,900.

Bon·ne·ville /baanivil/ **Salt Flats** barren salt flatland in NW Utah.

Bor·deaux /bawrdó/ port city in SW France. Pop. 213,300.

Bor·ne·o /báwrnee-ō/ island in the Malay Archipelago.

Bos·ni·a /baàzneeə/ **and Her·ze·go·vi·na** /hərtsəgōveènə, –góvinə/ (also called **Bos′ni·a-Her·ze·go·vi′na**) republic in S Europe, on the Balkan Peninsula; formerly part of Yugoslavia. Pop. 2,656,000. Capital: Sarajevo.

Bos·po·rus /baàspərəs/ strait connecting the Sea of Marmara and the Black Sea.

Bos·ton /báwstən/ capital of Massachusetts, in the E part. Pop. 574,283. □□ **Bos·ton′i·an** /bawstóneeən/ *n. & adj.*

Both·ni·a /baàthneeə/, **Gulf of** arm of the Baltic Sea, between Finland and Sweden.

Bot·swa·na /baatswaànə/ republic in S Africa. Pop. 1,478,000. Capital: Gaborone.

Boul·der /bóldər/ city in N central Colorado. Pop. 83,312.

Bourne·mouth /báwrnməth/ city in S England. Pop. 151,300.

Bramp·ton /brámtən, brámp–/ city in SE Ontario, Canada. Pop. 234,400.

Bra·sil·ia /brəzílyə/ capital of Brazil, in the S central part. Pop. 411,300.

Bra·ti·sla·va /braatislaàvə/ capital of Slovakia, in the W part. Pop. 446,700.

Bra·zil /brəzíl/ republic in E South America. Pop. 162,661,000. Capital: Brasilia. □□ **Bra· zil′ian** *n. & adj.*

Braz·za·ville /brázəvil/ capital of the Republic of the Congo, in the SE part. Pop. 937,600.

Brem·en /brémən/ port city in NW Germany. Pop. 551,600.

Brem·er·ha·ven /brémərhaavən/ port city in NW Germany. Pop. 131,500.

Bre·scia /bráyshə/ city in N Italy. Pop. 191,900.

Brest /brest/ **1** port city in W France. Pop. 153,100. **2** city in SW Belarus. Pop. 284,000.

Brid·al·veil /bríd'lvayl/ waterfall in Yosemite National Park, California: 620 ft. high.

Bridge·port /bríjpawrt, –pōrt/ city in SW Connecticut. Pop. 141,686.

Bridge·town /bríjtown/ port city and capital of Barbados. Pop. 6,100.

Brigh·ton /brít'n/ city in SE England. Pop. 143,600.

Bris·bane /brízbən, –bayn/ port city and capital of Queensland, Australia. Pop. 786,400.

Bris·tol /brístəl/ port city in SW England. Pop. 399,200.

Brit·ain /brít'n/ see GREAT BRITAIN.

Brit·ish Co·lum·bi·a /brítish kəlúmbeeə/ province in W Canada. Pop. 3,535,000. Capital: Victoria. □□ **Brit'ish Co·lum'bi·an** *n. & adj.*

Brit·ish Em·pire *hist.* countries under the control or leadership of the British Crown.

Brit·ish Vir·gin /vɔ́rjin/ **Is·lands** island group in the E West Indies; British possession.

Br·no /búrnō/ city in E Czech Republic. Pop. 388,000.

Brock·ton /braˈaktən/ city in SE Massachusetts. Pop. 92,788.

Bronx /braangks/ (also **the Bronx**) one of the five boroughs of New York City. Pop. 1,203,789.

Brook·lyn /broˈoklən/ one of the five boroughs of New York City. Pop. 2,300,664.

Browns·ville /brównzvil/ city in S Texas. Pop. 98,962.

Bruges /bro͞ozh, bryzh/ (also called **Brug·ge** /brúgə/) city in NW Belgium. Pop. 116,800.

Bru·nei /bro͞oníˈ/ sultanate on the NW coast of Borneo. Pop. 300,000. Capital: Bandar Seri Begawan.

Brus·sels /brúsəlz/ capital of Belgium, in the central part; site of European parliament. Pop. 949,100.

Bry·ansk /bree-aˈansk/ city in W Russia. Pop. 460,900.

Bryce /brīs/ **Can·yon Na·tion·al Park** area in S Utah noted for its extensive natural rock formations.

Bu·cha·rest /boˈokərest/ capital of Romania, in the S part. Pop. 2,064,500.

Bu·da·pest /boˈodəpest/ capital of Hungary, in the N central part. Pop. 1,996,000.

Bue·nos Ai·res /bwaynəs éreez/ port city and capital of Argentina. Pop. 2,961,000.

Buf·fa·lo /búfəlō/ port city in W New York. Pop. 328,123.

Bu·jum·bu·ra /bo͞ojəmbo͞orə/ capital of Burundi, in the E part. Pop. 300,000.

Bul·gar·i·a /bəlgáreeə, bul–/ republic in SE Europe. Pop. 8,613,000. Capital: Sofia. □□ **Bul·gar'i·an** *n. & adj.*

Bur·bank /búrbangk/ city in SW California. Pop. 93,643.

Bur·gos /boˈorgōs/ city in N Spain. Pop. 166,300.

Bur·ki·na Fa·so /bo͞orkeˈenə faˈasō/ republic in W Africa. Pop. 10,623,000. Capital: Ouagadougou.

Bur·ma /búrmə/ (also called **My·an'mar**) republic in SE Asia. Pop. 45,976,000. Capital: Rangoon. □□ **Bur·mese** /bərmeˈez/ *n. & adj.*

Bur·sa /bo͞orsaˈa/ city in NW Turkey. Pop. 996,600.

Bu·run·di /bəroˈondee/ republic in central Africa. Pop. 5,943,000. Capital: Bujumbura.

Bye·lo·rus·sia /byelōrúshə/ see BELARUS.

Byz·an·tine /bízanteen, –tīn/ *hist.* term for the Eastern Roman Empire from the fall of the Western Empire (476) to the fall of Constantinople (1453).

By·zan·ti·um /bizánshee-əm, –tee-əm/ see ISTANBUL.

Cá·diz /kədíz/ port city in SW Spain. Pop. 155,400.

Caen /kaaN/ city in NW France. Pop. 115,600.

Ca·guas /kaˈawaas, –gwaas/ city in E central Puerto Rico. Pop. 139,800.

Cai·ro /kírō/ capital of Egypt, in the N part. Pop. 6,849,000.

Cal·cut·ta /kalkútə/ port city in E India. Pop. 4,399,800.

Cal·ga·ry /kálgəree/ city in S Alberta, Canada. Pop. 710,700.

Ca·li /kaˈalee/ city in SW Colombia. Pop. 1,718,900.

Cal·i·for·nia /kalifáwrnyə/ state in W U.S. Pop. 29,760,021. Capital: Sacramento. Abbr. **CA**; **Cal.**; **Calif.** □□ **Cal·i·for'ni·an** *n. & adj.*

Cal·i·for·nia, Gulf of arm of the Pacific, enclosed by Baja California.

Ca·ma·güey /kaaməgwáy/ city in central Cuba. Pop. 279,000.

Cam·bo·di·a /cambódeeə/ (also called **Kam·pu·che'a**) republic in SE Asia. Pop. 10,861,000. Capital: Phnom Penh. □□ **Cam·bo'di·an** *n. & adj.*

Cam·bridge /káymbrij/ **1** city in NE Massachusetts. Pop. 95,802. **2** city in SE England. Pop. 113,800.

Cam·den /kámdən/ city in SW New Jersey. Pop. 87,492.

Cam·e·roon /kaməroˈon/ republic in W Africa. Pop. 14,262,000. Capital: Yaoundé.

Camp Da·vid /dáyvid/ U.S. presidential retreat in Catoctin Mountains of Maryland, NW of Washington, D.C.

Cam·pe·che /kampáychay, –peéchee/ state in SE Mexico. Pop. 535,200. Capital: Campeche.

Cam·pi·nas /kampeénəs/ city in SE Brazil. Pop. 748,100.

Can·a·da /kánədə/ country in N North America. Pop. 28,821,900. Capital: Ottawa. □□ **Ca·na·di·an** /kənáydee-ən/ *n. & adj.*

Ca·nar·y /kənáiree/ **Is·lands** island group in the Atlantic, off the NW coast of Africa.

Can·ber·ra /kánbərə, –brə/ capital of Australia, in the SE part. Pop. 303,700.

Can·ter·bur·y /kántərberee, –bree/ city in SE England; seat of the archbishop who heads the Anglican Church. Pop. 132,400.

Can·ton /kánt'n/ city in NE Ohio. Pop. 84,161.

Cape Ca·nav·er·al /kənávrəl, –návər–/ cape on the E central coast of Florida; site of Kennedy Space Center.

Cape Cod /kaad/ peninsula in SE Massachusetts, bounded by Cape Cod Bay, the Atlantic, and Nantucket Sound.

Cape Hat·ter·as /hátərəs/ cape on the North Carolina coast.

Cape Horn /hawrn/ headland of a S Chilean island; the southernmost tip of South America.

Cape of Good Hope /goॅod hōp/ cape at the SW tip of South Africa.

Cape Town port city and legislative capital of South Africa, in the SW part. Pop. 854,600.

Cape Verde /vərd/ republic in NW Africa, comprising an island group W of Senegal. Pop. 449,000. Capital: Praia.

Ca·ra·cas /kərákəs, –raák–/ capital of Venezuela, in the N part. Pop. 1,822,500.

Car·diff /kaárdif/ port city and capital of Wales, United Kingdom. Pop. 300,000.

Car·ib·be·an /karəbeéən, kəríbeeən/ **Sea** arm of the Atlantic, enclosed by the West Indies, N South America, and Central America.

Carls·bad /kaárlzbad/ **Cav·erns** network of subterranean limestone caves in SE New Mexico.

Car·o·li·na /karəlínə/ **1** (also called **the Car·o·li·nas**) North and South Carolina. **2** /kaárə-leénə/ city in NE Puerto Rico. Pop. 187,100.

Car·o·line /kárəlīn, kér–, –lin/ **Is·lands** island group in the Pacific, E of the Philippines; U.S. trusteeship.

Car·pa·thi·an /kaarpáytheeən/ **Moun·tains** mountain range in central Europe.

Car·son /kaársən/ **Cit·y** capital of Nevada, in the W part. Pop. 40,443.

Car·ta·ge·na /kaartəjeénə, –háynə/ port city in N Colombia. Pop. 745,700.

Car·thage /kaárthij/ *hist.* ancient city-state near present-day Tunis, in N Africa. □□ **Car·tha·gin'i·an** *n. & adj.* □□

Cas·a·blan·ca /kasəblángkə, kaz–/ *n.* port city in NW Morocco. Pop. 2,943,000.

Cas·cade /kaskáyd/ **Range** mountain range in W U.S., extending from N California into Canada.

Cas·pi·an /káspeeən/ **Sea** inland salt lake between Europe and Asia, N of Iran.

Cas·tries /kastreé, kaástrees/ port city and capital of St. Lucia. Pop. 11,100.

Cat·a·li·na /kat'l-eénə/ **Is·land** see SANTA CATALINA ISLAND.

Ca·ta·nia /kətaányə, –táyn–/ port city in E Sicily, Italy. Pop. 327,200.

Cats·kill /kátskil/ **Moun·tains** mountain range in SE New York; part of the Appalachian range.

Cau·ca·sus /káwkəsəs/ **Moun·tains** mountain range dividing Russia from Georgia and Azerbaijan; traditional division between Europe and Asia.

Cay·enne /kī-én, kay–/ port city and capital of French Guiana. Pop. 41,700.

Cay·man /káymən/ **Is·lands** island group in the NW Caribbean; dependent territory of the United Kingdom. Pop. 35,000.

Ce·dar /seédər/ **Rap·ids** city in E Iowa. Pop. 108,751.

Cel·e·bes /sélebeez/ see SULAWESI.

Cen·tral Af·ri·can Re·pub·lic republic in central Africa. Pop. 3,274,000. Capital: Bangui.

Cen·tral A·mer·i·ca portion of continental North America between Mexico and South America.

Cen·tral Val·ley valley in W central California, between the San Joaquin and Sacramento rivers.

Cey·lon /silón, say–/ see SRI LANKA.

Chad /chad/ republic in N central Africa. Pop. 6,977,000. Capital: N'Djamena. **Chad'i·an**

Cham·paign /shampáyn/ city in E central Illinois. Pop. 63,502.

Cham·plain /shampláyn/, **Lake** lake in NE U.S., between New York and Vermont.

Chang /chang/ **Riv·er** (formerly **Yangtze River**) river in central China, flowing 3,400 mi. from Tibet to the East China Sea; longest river in China.

Chan·nel /chánəl/ **Is·lands** group of British islands in the English Channel, near the coast of France; includes Guernsey and Jersey.

Charles·ton /chaárlstən/ **1** capital of West Virginia, in the W central part. Pop. 57,287. **2** port city in SE South Carolina. Pop. 80,414.

Char·lotte /shaárlət/ city in S North Carolina. Pop. 395,934.

Char·lotte·town /shaárlət-town/ capital of Prince Edward Island, Canada, in the central part. Pop. 15,400.

Chat·ta·hoo·chee /chatəhoóchee/ **Riv·er** river in SE U.S., flowing 440 mi. from NE Georgia to the Gulf of Mexico.

Chat·ta·noo·ga /chatənoógə/ city in S Tennessee. Pop. 152,466.

Chel·ya·binsk /chelyaábinsk/ city in S Russia. Pop. 1,086,000.

Chem·nitz /khémnits/ (formerly **Karl-Marx-Stadt**) city in E central Germany. Pop. 274,200.

Ches·a·peake /chésəpeek/ city in SE Virginia. Pop. 151,976.

Ches·a·peake Bay inlet of the Atlantic, on the E coast of the U.S.

Che·tu·mal /chaytoōmaál/ capital of Quintana Roo, Mexico, in the S part. Pop. 111,400.

Chey·enne /shīán, –én/ capital of Wyoming, in the SE part. Pop. 50,008.

Chi·a·pas /chee-aápəs, chaápəs/ state in S Mexico. Pop. 3,210,500. Capital: Tuxtla.

Chi·ba /cheébə/ city in Japan, on Honshu. Pop. 856,900.

Chi·ca·go /shikaágō, –káwgō/ city in NE Illinois. Pop. 2,783,726. □□ **Chi·ca'go·an**

Chi·hua·hua /chəwaáwaa, –wə/ state in N central Mexico. Pop. 2,441,900. Capital: Chihuahua.

Chil·e /chílee, cheélay/ republic in W South America. Pop. 14,333,000. Capital: Santiago. □□ **Chil'e·an** n. & adj.

Chil·pan·cin·go /chilpənsínggō/ capital of Guerrero, Mexico, in the E central part. Pop. 136,200.

Chi·lung /jeéloōng/ (formerly **Keelung**) port city in N Taiwan. Pop. 352,900.

Chi·na /chínə/ (official name **People's Republic of China**; abbr. **PRC**) republic in E and central Asia. Pop. 1,210,005,000. Capital: Beijing.

Chi·nan /jénán/ see JINAN.

Chis·holm /chízəm/ **Trail** hist. cattle trail from San Antonio, Texas, to Abilene, Kansas, used after the Civil War.

Chi·și·nă·u /keesheenúoō/ see KISHINEV.

Chit·ta·gong /chítəgaang, –gawng/ port city in SE Bangladesh. Pop. 1,599,000.

Chong·qing /chúngchíng, –king/ (formerly **Chungking**) city in S central China. Pop. 2,980,000.

Chon·ju /júnjoó/ city in SW South Korea. Pop. 563,400.

Christ·church /krístchərch, kríst–/ city in E central New Zealand. Pop. 314,000.

Chuk·chi /chúkchee, choók–/ **Sea** arm of the Arctic Ocean, N of the Bering Strait.

Chu·la Vis·ta /choólə vístə/ city in SW California. Pop. 135,163.

Chung·king /chúngkíng, chən–/ see CHONGQING.

Cin·cin·nat·i /sinsinátee/ port city in SW Ohio. Pop. 364,040.

Cit·rus /sítrəs/ **Heights** city in central California. Pop. 107,439.

Ciu·dad Gua·ya·na /seeoōdaád gwaayaánaa, seeyoō–/ see SANTO TOMÉ DE GUAYANA.

Ciu·dad Juá·rez /waáres, hwaáres/ city in N Mexico. Pop. 544,500.

Ciu·dad Vic·to·ria /veektáwree-ə/ capital of Tamaulipas, Mexico, in the W central part. Pop. 195,000.

Clear·wa·ter /kleérwawtər, –waatər/ city in W Florida. Pop. 98,784.

Cleve·land /kleévlənd/ city in N Ohio. Pop. 505,616.

Co·a·hui·la /kōəweélə, kwaaweélə/ state in N Mexico. Pop. 1,972,300. Capital: Saltillo.

Co·blenz /kóblens/ (also **Ko'blenz**) city in W Germany. Pop. 109,600.

Co·li·ma /kəleémə/ state in W Mexico. Pop. 428,500. Capital: Colima.

Co·logne /kəlón/ (German name **Köln**) city in W Germany. Pop. 963,800.

Co·lom·bi·a /kəlúmbeeə/ republic in NW South America. Pop. 36,813,000. Capital: Bogotá. □□ **Co·lom'bi·an**

Co·lom·bo /kəlúmbō/ port city and capital of Sri Lanka. Pop. 615,000.

Col·o·ra·do /kaalərádō, –raádō/ state in W U.S. Pop. 3,294,394. Capital: Denver. Abbr. **Colo.**; **CO** □□ **Col·o·ra'dan**, **Col·o·ra'do·an** n. & adj.

Col·o·rad·o Riv·er river in W U.S., flowing 1,450 mi. from Colorado through the Grand Canyon and into the Gulf of California.

Col·o·rad·o Springs city in E central Colorado. Pop. 281,140.

Co·lum·bi·a /kəlúmbeeə/ **1** capital of South Carolina, in the central part. Pop. 98,052. **2** city in central Missouri. Pop. 69,101.

Co·lum·bi·a Riv·er river in W North America, flowing 1,200 mi. from W Canada through Washington and Oregon and into the Pacific.

Co·lum·bus /kəlúmbəs/ capital of Ohio, in the central part. Pop. 632,910.

Com·o·ros /kaámərōz, kəmáwrōz/ island republic in the Indian Ocean, between Africa and Madagascar. Pop. 569,000. Capital: Moroni. □□ **Com'o·ran**, **Co·mo'ri·an** n. & adj.

Co·na·kry /kaánəkree/ port city and capital of Guinea. Pop. 1,508,000.

Con·cep·ción /kənsepsee-ón/ city in S central Chile. Pop. 350,300.

Con·cord /ka'ángkərd, –kawrd/ **1** capital of New Hampshire, in the S part. Pop. 36,006. **2** city in W California. Pop. 111,348.

Con·go /ka'ánggō/ **1** (formerly **Zaire**) republic in central Africa. Pop. 41,151,000. Capital: Kinshasa. **2** (official name **Re·pub'lic of the Con'go**) republic in central Africa. Pop. 2,528,000. Capital: Brazzaville. □□ **Con·go·lese** /kaanggəleéz, –leés/ *n. & adj.*

Con·go Riv·er river in central Africa, flowing 3,000 mi. from SE Congo (formerly Zaire) to the Atlantic.

Con·nect·i·cut /kənétikət/ state in NE U.S. Pop. 3,287,116. Capital: Hartford. Abbr. **Conn.; CT; Ct.** □□ **Con·nect'i·cut·ter** *n.*

Con·nect·i·cut Riv·er river in New England, flowing 400 mi. from N New Hampshire to Long Island Sound.

Con·stan·tine /ka'ánstənteen, kawnstaanteén/ city in NE Algeria. Pop. 440,900.

Con·stan·ti·no·ple /kaanstantənópəl/ see Is-TANBUL.

Con·ti·nen·tal Di·vide (also called **Great Di·vide**) High ridge of the Rocky Mountains; watershed of the North American continent, separating the river systems flowing either W or E and S.

Cook /kŏŏk/ **Is·lands** island group in the S Pacific, belonging to New Zealand. Pop. 20,000.

Co·pen·ha·gen /kópənhaygən, –haagən/ port city and capital of Denmark. Pop. 1,353,300.

Cor·al /káwrəl/ **Sea** arm of the S Pacific, NE of Australia.

Cór·do·ba /káwrdəbə, –əvə/ **1** (also **Cor'do·va**) city in S Spain. Pop. 315,900. **2** city in central Argentina. Pop. 1,208,700.

Cor·fu /kawrfŏŏ/ island in Greece, SW of Albania.

Cork /kawrk/ port city in S Ireland. Pop. 127,000.

Cor·pus Chris·ti /káwrpəs krístee/ port city in S Texas. Pop. 257,453.

Cor·si·ca /káwrsikə/ island in the Mediterranean Sea, W of Italy; a department of France. Capital: Ajaccio □□ **Cor'si·can** *n. & adj.*

Cos·ta Bra·va /kóstə braávə/ region on the NE coast of Spain.

Cos·ta del Sol /del sól/ region on the S coast of Spain.

Cos·ta Me·sa /kóstə máysə, káwstə/ city in SW California. Pop. 96,357.

Cos·ta Ri·ca /kóstə reékə, káws–/ republic in S Central America. Pop. 3,463,000. Capital: San José. □□ **Cos'ta Ric'an** *n. & adj.*

Côte d'A·zur /kōt dəzŏŏr/ region on the SE coast of France.

Côte d'I·voire /kōt deevwaár/ see Ivory Coast.

Co·to·nou /kōt'n-ŏŏ/ port city and government center of Benin. Pop. 533,200.

Cov·en·try /ka'ávəntree, kúv–/ city in central England. Pop. 302,500.

Crac·ow /krákow, kraákŏŏf/ (also **Kra'ków**) city in S central Poland. Pop. 746,000.

Cra·ter /kráytər/ **Lake** lake in S Oregon formed by an ancient volcanic crater.

Crete /kreet/ (also called **Can'di·a**) Greek island in the Mediterranean Sea, SE of the mainland.

Cri·me·a /krīmeéə/ peninsula in S Ukraine, bounded by the Black Sea and the Sea of Azov. □□ **Cri·me'an** *adj.*

Cro·a·tia /krōáyshə/ republic in S Europe, on the Balkan Peninsula; formerly part of Yugoslavia. Pop. 5,004,000. Capital: Zagreb.

Cu·ba /kyŏŏbə, kŏŏbə/ island republic in the W West Indies. Pop. 10,951,000. Capital: Havana. □□ **Cu'ban** *n. & adj.*

Cuer·na·va·ca /kwernəvaákə/ capital of Morelos, Mexico, in the N part. Pop. 279,200.

Cu·lia·cán /kŏŏlyəkaán/ capital of Sinaloa, Mexico, in the central part. Pop. 415,000.

Cum·ber·land /kúmbərlənd/ **Gap** natural pass through the Appalachian Mountains in Kentucky and Virginia.

Cum·ber·land Road see National Road.

Cu·ra·çao /kŏŏrəsōw, –sów, kyŏŏrə–/ largest island of the Netherlands Antilles, NW of Venezuela. Capital: Willemstad.

Cy·prus /síprəs/ island republic in the E Mediterranean Sea. Pop. 745,000. Capital: Nicosia.

Czech·o·slo·va·ki·a /chekəsləvaákeeə/ former republic of central Europe (1918–93); divided into Czech Republic and Slovakia.

Czech /chek/ **Re·pub·lic** republic in central Europe; formerly the W part of Czechoslovakia. Pop. 10,321,000. Capital: Prague.

Cze·sto·cho·wa /chenstəkóvə/ city in S Poland. Pop. 259,800.

Da·kar /dəkaár, dákaar/ port city and capital of Senegal. Pop. 785,100.

Da·lian /daályén/ (formerly **Talien; Lüda**) port city in NE China. Pop. 2,400,300.

Dal·las /dáləs/ city in NE Texas. Pop. 1,006,877. □□ **Dal'las·ite** *n.*

Da·mas·cus /dəmáskəs/ capital of Syria, in the SW part. Pop. 1,550,000.

Da·nang /daanaáng, dənáng/ port city in central Vietnam. Pop. 382,700.

Dan·ube /dányŏŏb/ **Riv·er** river in central Europe, flowing 1,720 mi. from SW Germany to the Black Sea.

Dar·da·nelles /daard'nélz/ strait in Turkey,

connecting the Aegean Sea with the Sea of Marmara.

Dar es Sa·laam /daar es səlaám/ port city and capital of Tanzania. Pop. 1,360,900.

Dav·en·port /dávənpawrt/ city in E Iowa. Pop. 95,333.

Day·ton /dáyt'n/ city in SW Ohio. Pop. 182,044.

D.C. (also **DC**) District of Columbia. See also WASHINGTON, D.C.

Dead /ded/ **Sea** inland salt lake, between Israel and Jordan.

Dear·born /deérbawrn, –bərn/ city in SE Michigan. Pop. 89,286.

Death /deth/ **Val·ley** desert basin in E California; lowest point is 282 ft. below sea level.

De·ca·tur /dikáytər/ city in central Illinois. Pop. 83,885.

Del·a·ware /déləwair, –wer/ state in E U.S. Pop. 666,168. Capital: Dover. Abbr. **DE; Del.** □□ **Del·a·war′e·an** n. & adj.

Del·a·ware Bay inlet of the Atlantic, between Delaware and New Jersey.

Del·a·ware Riv·er river in E U.S., flowing 280 mi. from S New York to Delaware Bay.

Del·hi /délee/ city in N India. Pop. 7,206,700.

Del·mar·va /delmaárvə/ **Pen·in·su·la** peninsula in E U.S., bounded by the Atlantic and Chesapeake Bay, and comprising parts of Delaware, Maryland, and Virginia.

De·na·li /denaálee/ **Na·tion·al Park** U.S. national park in S central Alaska; contains North America's highest peak, Mount McKinley.

Den·mark /dénmaark/ kingdom in N Europe. Pop. 5,250,000. Capital: Copenhagen.

Den·ver /dénvər/ capital of Colorado, in the central part. Pop. 467,610.

Der·by /daárbee/ city in central England. Pop. 230,500.

Des Moines /di móin/ capital of Iowa, in the central part. Pop. 193,187.

De·troit /ditróyt/ city in SE Michigan. Pop. 1,027,974.

Dha·ka /daákə/ capital of Bangladesh, in the central part. Pop. 3,839,000.

Di·a·mond /dímənd, díə–/ **Head** extinct volcano on SE coast of Oahu, Hawaii.

Di·jon /dee-zháwN, –zhaán/ city in E France. Pop. 151,600.

Dis·trict of Co·lum·bi·a /kəlúmbeeə/ federal district in E U.S., on the Potomac River; coextensive with the national capital, Washington. Abbr. **DC; D.C.**

Dji·bou·ti /jibóotee/ **1** republic in E Africa. Pop. 428,000. Capital: Djibouti. **2** capital of Djibouti, in the E part. Pop. 290,000.

Dni·pro·pe·trovsk /neprōpətráwfsk, dənye-prō–/ city in E central Ukraine. Pop. 1,147,000.

Do·ha /dóhə/ port city and capital of Qatar. Pop. 313,600.

Dom·i·ni·ca /daaminee'ekə, dəmínikə/ island republic in the E West Indies. Pop. 83,000. Capital: Roseau.

Dom·i·ni·can /dəmínikən/ **Re·pub·lic** republic in the central West Indies, comprising the E part of Hispaniola. Pop. 8,089,000. Capital: Santo Domingo.

Do·netsk /dənétsk, –nyétsk/ city in E Ukraine. Pop. 1,088,000.

Don /daan/ **Riv·er** river in SW Russia, flowing 1,200 mi. from Tula to the Sea of Azov.

Dort·mund /dáwrtmōōnt, –mənd/ city in W Germany. Pop. 600,900.

Do·ver /dóvər/ **1** capital of Delaware, in the central part. Pop. 27,630. **2** port city in SE England. Pop. 32,800.

Dres·den /drézdən/ city in SE Germany. Pop. 474,400.

Du·bai /dōōbí/ port city in N United Arab Emirates. Pop. 585,200.

Dub·lin /dúblin/ capital of the Republic of Ireland, in the E part. Pop. 478,400. □□ **Dub′lin·er** n. & adj.

Du·buque /dəbyóōk/ city in E Iowa. Pop. 57,546.

Duis·burg /dōōsbōōrk, dyōōs–, –bərg/ port city in W Germany. Pop. 536,100.

Du·luth /dəlóōth/ city in NE Minnesota. Pop. 85,493.

Dun·dee /dəndeé/ port city in E Scotland, United Kingdom. Pop. 167,600.

Du·ran·go /dōōránggō, dyōōráng–/ state in N central Mexico. Pop. 1,349,400. Capital: Durango.

Dur·ban /dúrbən/ port city in SE South Africa. Pop. 715,700.

Dur·ham /dúrəm, dōōr–/ city in NE central North Carolina. Pop. 136,600.

Du·shan·be /dōōshaánbay, dyōō–, –sham–/ capital of Tadzhikistan, in the W part. Pop. 524,000.

Düs·sel·dorf /dōōsəldawrf, dyōōs–/ port city in W Germany. Pop. 572,600.

Dust Bowl agricultural region of about 50 million acres in central U.S.; site of great dust storms 1935–38.

East Chi·na Sea arm of the N Pacific, E of mainland China and N of Taiwan.

East Ger·ma·ny (also called **German Democratic Republic**) German state created in 1949, under Communist government; unified with West Germany in 1990.

East Los An·ge·les /laws ánjələs, –leez/ city in SW California. Pop. 126,379.

Ec·ua·dor /ékwədawr/ republic in NW South America. Pop. 11,466,000. Capital: Quito. □□ **Ec·ua·dor'an, Ec·ua·do'ri·an** /-reeən/ *n. & adj.*

Ed·in·burgh /éd'nbərə, –brə/ capital of Scotland, in the United Kingdom. Pop. 447,600.

Ed·mon·ton /édməntən/ capital of Alberta, Canada, in the central part. Pop. 616,700.

E·gypt /eéjipt/ republic in NE Africa. Pop. 63,575,000. Capital: Cairo.

Eir·e /érə, írə/ see IRELAND 2.

El·ba /élbə/ Italian island in the Mediterranean Sea, E of Corsica.

El·brus /elbro͞oz/, **Mount** mountain in the Caucasus range, on the border between Russia and Georgia; highest peak in Europe: 18,481 ft.

El Gi·za see GIZA.

E·liz·a·beth /ilízəbəth/ city in NE New Jersey. Pop. 110,002.

El·lis /éləs/ **Is·land** island in New York Harbor; former arrival point for European immigrants.

El Mon·te /el maántee/ city in SW California. Pop. 106,209.

El Ni·ño /neényō/ periodic occasional warm Pacific current that alters climate patterns.

El Pas·o /pásō/ city in W Texas. Pop. 515,342.

El Sal·va·dor /sálvədawr/ republic in NW Central America. Pop. 5,829,000. Capital: San Salvador. □□ **Sal·va·do'ran, Sal·va·do' ri·an** /-reeən/ *n. & adj.*

Eng·land /ínggglənd/ largest division of the United Kingdom. Pop. 44,876,000. Capital: London. ¶ See note at GREAT BRITAIN.

Eng·lish /íngglish/ **Chan·nel** strait between S England and N France, connecting the Atlantic and the North Sea.

En·sche·de /énskədə/ city in the E Netherlands. Pop. 147,900.

E·qua·to·ri·al Guin·ea /ekwətóree-əl gínee/ mainland and island republic in W Africa. Pop. 431,000. Capital: Malabo.

Er·furt /érfo͞ort/ city in central Germany. Pop. 213,500.

E·rie /eéree/ city in NW Pennsylvania. Pop. 108,718.

E·rie, Lake one of the Great Lakes, N of Ohio.

E·rie Ca·nal canal in New York between Albany and Buffalo, connecting the Hudson River with Lake Erie.

Er·i·tre·a /eritreéə, –tráyə/ republic in E Africa; formerly a province of Ethiopia. Pop. 3,428,000. Capital: Asmara.

Es·con·di·do /eskəndeédō/ city in SW California. Pop. 108,635.

Es·fa·han /ésfəhaan/ see ISFAHAN.

Es·sen /ésən/ city in W Germany. Pop. 618,000.

Es·to·ni·a /estóneeə/ republic in N Europe; formerly part of the USSR. Pop. 1,459,000. Capital: Tallinn.

E·thi·o·pi·a /eethee-óˈpeeə/ republic in E Africa. Pop. 57,172,000. Capital: Addis Ababa. □□ **E·thi·o'pi·an** *n. & adj.*

Et·na /étnə/, **Mount** active volcano on Sicily: 11,122 ft. high.

Eu·gene /yo͞ojeén/ city in W Oregon. Pop. 112,669.

Eu·phra·tes /yo͞ofráyteez/ **Riv·er** river in SW Asia, flowing 1,700 mi. from central Turkey to the Persian Gulf.

Eu·rope /yo͞orəp/ continent bounded by the Arctic and Atlantic oceans, Asia, the Caucasus Mountains, and the Black, Mediterranean, Baltic, and North seas.

Eu·ro·pe·an /yo͞orəpeéən/ **Un·ion** (formerly **Eu·ro·pe'an Com·mu'ni·ty**) official name of a confederation of independent European countries.

Ev·ans·ton /évənstən/ city in NE Illinois. Pop. 73,233.

Ev·ans·ville /évənzvil/ city in SW Indiana. Pop. 126,272.

Ev·er·est /évrəst, évərəst/, **Mount** mountain in the Himalayas, on the Tibet-Nepal border; highest in the world: 29,028 ft.

Ev·er·glades /évərglaydz/ large area of swampland in S Florida.

Faer·oe /fárō, férō/ **Is·lands** cluster of Danish islands in the N Atlantic, between Iceland and Great Britain.

Fair·banks /fáirbangks, fér–/ city in central Alaska. Pop. 30,843.

Fai·sa·la·bad /fīsaaləbaàd/ (formerly **Lyallpur**) city in E Pakistan. Pop. 1,104,200.

Falk·land /fáwklənd, fáwlk–/ **Is·lands** (Spanish name **Is·las Mal·vin·as** /eésləs maalveénəs/) island group in the Atlantic, E of Argentina; British possession.

Far East term for E Asia, including China, Japan, Korea, Mongolia, and adjacent areas.

Far·go /faàrgō/ city in E North Dakota. Pop. 74,111.

Fay·ette·ville /fáyətvəl, –vil/ city in S central North Carolina. Pop. 75,695.

Fed·er·al Dis·trict of Mex·i·co national government district in Mexico, in the central part.

Fer·ra·ra /fərəàrə/ city in NE Italy. Pop. 137,400.

Fez /fez, fes/ (also **Fès**) city in N central Morocco. Pop. 564,800.

Fi·ji /feéjee/ independent archipelago in the S Pacific, N of New Zealand. Pop. 782,000. Capital: Suva. □□ **Fi'ji·an** *n. & adj.*

Fin·ger /fínggər/ **Lakes** chain of long, thin lakes in central New York.

Fin·land /fínlənd/ republic in N Europe. Pop. 5,105,000. Capital: Helsinki.

Flan·ders /flándərz/ Atlantic coastal region of Europe in Belgium, France, and the Netherlands.

Flint /flint/ city in SE central Michigan. Pop. 140,761.

Flor·ence /fláwrəns, flaár–/ (Italian name **Fi·ren·ze** /feeréntsay, fərénzə/) city in central Italy. Pop. 392,900. □□ **Flor·en·tine** /fláwrənteen, -tīn/ n. & adj.

Flor·i·da /fláwrədə, flaár–/ peninsular state in SE U.S. Pop. 12,937,926. Capital: Tallahassee. Abbr. **FL; Fla.** □□ **Flo·rid·i·an** /flərídeeən/ n. & adj.

Flor·i·da Keys island chain in Florida, extending from the S tip of Florida into the Gulf of Mexico.

Flor·i·da, Straits of channel separating Florida from Cuba.

For·mo·sa /fawrmósə/ see TAIWAN.

Fort Col·lins /kaálinz/ city in N Colorado. Pop. 87,758.

Fort Lau·der·dale /láwdərdayl/ city in SE Florida. Pop. 149,377.

Fort Wayne /wayn/ city in NE Indiana. Pop. 173,072.

Fort Worth /wúrth/ city in N Texas. Pop. 447,619.

France /frans/ republic in W Europe. Pop. 58,041,000. Capital: Paris.

Frank·fort /frángkfərt/ capital of Kentucky, in the N central part. Pop. 25,968.

Frank·furt /frángkfərt/ **1** (also called **Frank′furt am Main** /aam mín/) city in W Germany. Pop. 652,400. **2** (also called **Frank′furt an der O·der** /aan dər ódər/) city in E Germany. Pop. 70,000.

Fred·er·ic·ton /frédriktən/ capital of New Brunswick, Canada, in the S part. Pop. 46,500.

Free·town /fréetown/ port city and capital of Sierra Leone. Pop. 469,800.

Fre·mont /fréemaant/ city in W California. Pop. 173,339.

French Gui·an·a /geeaánə/ overseas department of France, on the NE coast of South America. Pop. 151,180. Capital: Cayenne.

French Pol·y·ne·sia /paalənéezhə, –shə/ island group in the S Pacific; territory of France. Pop. 225,000. Capital: Papeete.

Fres·no /fréznō/ city in central California. Pop. 354,202.

Fu·ji /fóojee/, **Mount** dormant volcano in central Japan: 12,388 ft. high.

Fu·ku·o·ka /fookoō-ókə/ city in Japan, on Kyushu. Pop. 1,284,700.

Ful·ler·ton /fóolərtən/ city in SW California. Pop. 114,144.

Fu·na·fu·ti /foonəfóotee, fyoonəfyóotee/ capital of Tuvalu, in the central part. Pop. 3,800.

Fun·dy /fúndee/, **Bay of** inlet of the Atlantic, between New Brunswick and Nova Scotia.

Fu·shun /fóoshoōn/ city in NE China. Pop. 1,350,000.

Ga·bon /gabáwɴ/ republic in W Africa. Pop. 1,253,000. Capital: Libreville. □□ **Gab·o·nese** /gabəneéz, –neés/ n. & adj.

Ga·bo·ro·ne /gaabərónee/ capital of Botswana, in the SE part. Pop. 156,800.

Gaines·ville /gáynzvəl, –vıl/ city in N Florida. Pop. 84,770.

Ga·lá·pa·gos /gəlaápəgəs/ **Is·lands** archipelago in the Pacific, W of Ecuador; province of Ecuador.

Gal·i·lee /gálilee/, **Sea of** lake in NE Israel.

Gal·ves·ton /gálvəstən/ **Bay** inlet of the Gulf of Mexico, SE of Houston, Texas.

Gam·bi·a /gámbeeə, gaám–/ (also **the Gambia**) republic in W Africa. Pop. 1,205,000. Capital: Banjul.

Gan·ges /gánjeez/ **Riv·er** river in India, flowing 1,560 mi. from the Himalayas to the Bay of Bengal at Calcutta.

Gar·den Grove /gaárdən grōv/ city in SW California. Pop. 143,050.

Gar·land city in SW Texas. Pop. 180,650.

Gar·y /géree/ city in NW Indiana. Pop. 116,646.

Ga·tun /gətoōn/ **Lake** artificial lake forming part of the Panama Canal.

Gaul /gawl/ hist. province of the ancient Roman Empire, in W Europe.

Ga·za Strip /gaázə/ area of land along the Mediterranean Sea, between Egypt and Israel.

Gdansk /gədaánsk, –dánsk/ port city in N Poland. Pop. 463,100.

Gdy·nia /gədíneeə/ port city in N Poland. Pop. 251,500.

Ge·ne·va /jənéevə/ city in SW Switzerland. Pop. 172,700.

Ge·ne·va, Lake (also called **Lake Le′man**) lake between Switzerland and France.

Gen·o·a /jénəwə/ port city in N Italy. Pop. 659,800.

George·town /jáwrjtown/ port city and capital of Guyana. Pop. 248,500.

Geor·gia /jáwrjə/ **1** state in SE U.S. Pop. 6,478,216. Capital: Atlanta. Abbr. **GA; Ga. 2** republic in E Europe; formerly part of the USSR. Pop. 5,220,000. Capital: Tbilisi. □□ **Geor′gian** n. & adj.

Ger·ma·ny /júrmənee/ republic in W Europe. Pop. 83,536,000. Capital: Berlin.

Get·tys·burg /géteezbərg/ borough in S central Pennsylvania; site of a Civil War battle. Pop. 7,025.

Gha·na /gaánə/ republic in W Africa. Pop. 17,698,000. Capital: Accra. □□ **Gha'na·ian, Ghan'i·an** n. & adj.

Ghent /gent/ port city in NW central Belgium. Pop. 227,500.

Gi·bral·tar /jibráwltər/ British crown colony near the S tip of Spain. Pop. 29,000.

Gi·bral·tar, Strait of strait between Europe and Africa, at the Atlantic entrance to the Mediterranean Sea.

Gi·jón /heehón/ port city in N Spain, on the Bay of Biscay. Pop. 269,600.

Gi·za /geézə/ (also called **El Gi'za**) city in N Egypt. Pop. 2,144,000.

Glas·gow /gláskō, glázgō/ port city in SW Scotland, United Kingdom. Pop. 674,800. □□ **Glas·we·gian** /glasweéjən, -jeeən/ n. & adj.

Glen·dale /gléndayl/ **1** city in SW California. Pop. 180,038. **2** city in SW central Arizona. Pop. 148,134.

Glouces·ter /glaástər, gláws–/ port city in SW central England. Pop. 104,800.

Go·bi /góbee/ desert in E Asia, mostly in Mongolia.

Gö·te·borg /yótəbawr, –bawryə/ (also **Go·then·burg** /gaáthənberg/) port city in SW Sweden. Pop. 449,200.

Got·land /gaátlənd/ island province in SE Sweden, in the Baltic Sea.

Gra·na·da /grənaádə/ city in S Spain. Pop. 271,200.

Grand Banks extensive shoal and fishing grounds SE of Newfoundland.

Grand Can·yon extensive gorge of the Colorado River, in NW Arizona.

Grand Cou·lee Dam dam on the Columbia River, in NE central Washington; largest concrete dam in U.S.

Grand Rap·ids city in W Michigan. Pop. 189,126.

Grand Te·ton /teéton/ highest peak in the Teton range: 13,770 ft.

Graz /graats/ city in SE Austria. Pop. 237,800.

Great Ba·sin extensive desert region in W U.S.

Great Brit·ain /brít'n/ **1** island of NW Europe, comprising England, Scotland, and Wales. **2** popular term for the United Kingdom. ¶ *Great Britain* is the overall name given to the island that comprises *England, Scotland, Wales*; the *United Kingdom* includes the preceding and *Northern Ireland*; the *British Isles* include the *United Kingdom* together with the *Channel Islands* and all the other surrounding islands—the *Isles of Scilly*, the *Isle of Man*,

749   **Germany ~ Guadalajara**

and the *Orkney* and *Shetland* islands. The all-encompassing adjective is *British*, which is unlikely to offend anyone. *Welsh, Scottish,* and *English* should be used with care; it is safest to use *British* if unsure.

Great Di·vide see CONTINENTAL DIVIDE.

Great·er An·til·les /antíleez/ term for the larger islands of the West Indies: Cuba, Hispaniola, Jamaica, and Puerto Rico. See also LESSER ANTILLES.

Great·er Sun·da Is·lands island chain in the Malay Archipelago; includes Borneo, Java, and Sumatra.

Great Lakes series of five freshwater lakes between the U.S. and Canada: Superior, Michigan, Huron, Erie, and Ontario.

Great Plains dry, grassy region E of the Rocky Mountains, in Canada and the U.S.

Great Salt Lake inland salt sea in NW Utah.

Great Salt Lake Des·ert arid region in NW Utah.

Great Slave Lake lake in S central Northwest Territories, Canada.

Great Smo·ky Moun·tains mountain range in E U.S., between Tennessee and North Carolina; part of the Appalachian range.

Greece /grees/ republic in S Europe, on the Balkan Peninsula. Pop. 10,539,000. Capital: Athens.

Green Bay city in E Wisconsin. Pop. 96,466.

Green·land /greénlənd, –land/ island territory of Denmark, NE of Canada; largest island in the world. Pop. 58,000. □□ **Green'land·er** n. **Green·land'ic** adj.

Green·land Sea arm of the Arctic Ocean, NE of Greenland.

Green Moun·tains mountain range in E North America, extending from S Quebec through Vermont into W Massachusetts; part of the Appalachian range.

Greens·bo·ro /greénzbərə/ city in N central North Carolina. Pop. 183,521.

Gre·na·da /grənáydə/ island country in the E West Indies. Pop. 95,000. Capital: St. George's.

Gre·no·ble /grənóbəl/ city in SE France. Pop. 154,000.

Gro·ning·en /gróningən/ city in the N Netherlands. Pop. 170,700.

Groz·ny /gráwznee, graáz–/ city in S Russia. Pop. 364,000.

Gua·da·la·ja·ra /gwaad'ləhaárə/ capital of Jalisco, Mexico, in the N central part. Pop. 1,650,042.

Gua·dal·ca·nal /gwaad'lkənál/ island in the W Pacific; largest of the Solomon Islands; site of a World War II battle.

Gua·da·lu·pe /gwaad'lŏopay/ city in NE Mexico. Pop. 535,300.

Gua·de·loupe /gwaad'lŏop/ island in the E West Indies; dependency of France. Pop. 408,000. Capital: Basse-Terre.

Guam /gwaam/ island in the W Pacific; largest of the Mariana Islands; territory of the U.S. Pop. 157,000. □□ **Gua·ma′ni·an** /-máyneeən/ *n. & adj.*

Gua·na·jua·to /gwaanəwaátō, –nəhwaá–/ state in central Mexico. Pop. 3,982,600. Capital: Guanajuato.

Guan·tá·na·mo /gwaantaánəmō/ city in SE Cuba; site of a U.S. naval base. Pop. 207,800.

Gua·te·ma·la /gwaatəmaálə/ republic in N Central America. Pop. 11,278,000. Capital: Guatemala City. □□ **Gua·te·ma′lan** *n. & adj.*

Gua·te·ma·la Cit·y capital of Guatemala, in the S central part. Pop. 823,300.

Guay·a·quil /gwīəkeél/ port city in Ecuador. Pop. 1,508,400.

Guern·sey /gúrnzee/ island in the English Channel; British crown dependency. Pop. 63,000. Capital: St. Peter Port.

Guer·re·ro /ger-rérō/ state in S Mexico. Pop. 2,620,600. Capital: Chilpancingo.

Guin·ea /gínee/ republic in W Africa. Pop. 7,412,000. Capital: Conakry.

Guin·ea-Bis·sau /bisów/ republic in W Africa. Pop. 1,151,000. Capital: Bissau.

Guin·ea, Gulf of arm of the Atlantic, on the W coast of Africa.

Gui·yang /gwáyyaáng/ (formerly **Kuei-yang**) city in S China. Pop. 1,018,600.

Gulf Stream warm Atlantic current flowing from Gulf of Mexico along the E coast of North America toward Europe.

Guy·a·na /gī-aánə, -ánə/ republic in NE South America. Pop. 712,000. Capital: Georgetown.

Gyan·dzha /gyaánjə/ city in W Azerbaijan. Pop. 282,200.

Haar·lem /haárləm/ city in the W Netherlands. Pop. 149,000.

Hague /hayg/, **The** city in the SW Netherlands; seat of government. Pop. 444,200.

Hai·fa /hífə/ port city in NW Israel. Pop. 252,300.

Hai·phong /hífáwng/ port city in N Vietnam. Pop. 456,000.

Hai·ti /háytee/ republic in the central West Indies, comprising the W part of Hispaniola. Pop. 6,732,000. Capital: Port-au-Prince. □□ **Hai·tian** /háyshən/ *n. & adj.*

Hal·i·fax /hálifaks/ capital of Nova Scotia, Canada, in the E part. Pop. 320,500.

Hal·le /haálə/ city in E central Germany. Pop. 290,100.

Ham·a·dan /hamədáan, -dán/ city in W Iran. Pop. 349,700.

Ham·burg /haámbərg/ port city in N Germany. Pop. 1,705,900.

Hamp·ton /hámptən/ city in SE Virginia. Pop. 133,793.

Ha·noi /hanóy/ capital of Vietnam, in the N part. Pop. 2,154,900.

Han·o·ver /hánōvər/ city in N central Germany. Pop. 525,800.

Ha·ra·re /həraárray/ capital of Zimbabwe, in the N part. Pop. 1,184,200.

Har·bin /haarbín/ city in NE China. Pop. 2,830,000.

Har·ris·burg /hárəsbərg/ capital of Pennsylvania, in the SE central part. Pop. 52,376.

Hart·ford /haártfərd/ capital of Connecticut, in the N central part. Pop. 139,739.

Ha·van·a /həvánə/ port city and capital of Cuba. Pop. 2,241,000.

Ha·wai·i /həwaáee, –wíee, –wáwee/ **1** state in the U.S. comprising eight Pacific islands. Pop. 1,108,229. Capital: Honolulu. Abbr. **HI 2** largest island of the state of Hawaii. □□ **Ha·wai′ian** /-waáyən, -wíən/ *n. & adj.*

Hay·ward /háywərd/ city in W California. Pop. 111,498.

Heb·ri·des /hébrədeez/ island group in the Atlantic, off the W coast of Scotland.

Hei·del·berg /hʃd'lbərg/ city in SW Germany. Pop. 139,000.

Hel·e·na /hélənə/ capital of Montana, in the W central part. Pop. 24,569.

Hel·sin·ki /hélsingkee/ port city and capital of Finland. Pop. 525,000.

Hē·rá·klei·on /herákleeaan/ see IRÁKLION.

Her·mo·si·llo /ermōseéyō/ capital of Sonora, Mexico, in the central part. Pop. 406,417.

Hi·a·le·ah /hīəleéə/ city in SE Florida. Pop. 188,004.

Hi·dal·go /hidálgō/ state in E central Mexico. Pop. 1,888,400. Capital: Pachuca.

Him·a·la·yas /himəláyəz, himaályəz, –ləyəz/ mountain range in S Asia, along the border between India and Tibet.

Hin·du Kush /híndōo kŏósh/ mountain range in central Asia, extending W from the Himalayas.

Hi·ro·shi·ma /heerəsheémə, heeróshimə/ port city in Japan, on Honshu; target of first atomic bomb. Pop. 1,108,900.

His·pan·io·la /hispənyólə/ island in the central West Indies, comprising the republic of Haiti and the Dominican Republic.

Ho·bart /hóbaart/ capital of Tasmania, Australia, in the SE part. Pop. 129,000.

Ho Chi Minh /hō chee mín/ **Cit·y** (formerly **Saigon**) city in S Vietnam. Pop. 4,322,300.

Hok·kai·do /haakídō/ (formerly **Yezo**) island in N Japan.

Hol·land /haálənd/ see NETHERLANDS, THE.

Hol·ly·wood /haáleewŏŏd/ **1** city in SE Florida. Pop. 121,697. **2** section of Los Angeles, California; center of U.S. motion-picture industry.

Ho·ly /hólee/ **Land** see PALESTINE.

Ho·ly Ro·man Em·pire *hist.* empire of W central Europe from 800 to 1806.

Hon·du·ras /haandŏŏrəs, –dyŏŏ–/ republic in N Central America. Pop. 5,605,000. Capital: Tegucigalpa. �□□ **Hon·du′ran** *n. & adj.*

Hong Kong /haáng kaáng, háwng káwng/ city and commercial center of SE China; formerly (to 1997) a British crown colony. Pop. 6,305,000. Capital: Victoria.

Ho·ni·a·ra /hōnee-aárə/ capital of the Solomon Islands, on Guadalcanal. Pop. 43,600.

Hon·o·lu·lu /haanəlŏŏlŏŏ, hōn–/ capital of Hawaii, on the S coast of Oahu. Pop. 365,272.

Hon·shu /haánshŏŏ/ largest island in Japan, in the central part.

Hood /hŏŏd/, **Mount** inactive volcanic peak in NW Oregon, in the Cascade range.

Hoo·ver /hŏŏvər/ **Dam** dam on the Colorado River, along the Arizona-Nevada border.

Hous·ton /hyŏŏstən, yŏŏs–/ city in SE Texas. Pop. 1,630,553.

Huang /hwaang/ **Riv·er** (also called **Yel′low Riv′er**) river in China, flowing 2,800 mi. from Qinghai to the Yellow Sea.

Hud·son /hədsən/ **Bay** inland sea in NE Canada; an arm of the Atlantic.

Hud·son Riv·er river in E New York, flowing 300 mi. from the Adirondacks to New York Bay.

Hull /həl/ (official name **Kings′ton up·on′ Hull**) port city on the Humber River in England. Pop. 269,100.

Hun·ga·ry /húnggəree/ republic in central Europe. Pop. 10,003,000. Capital: Budapest.

Hun·ting·ton /húntingtən/ city in SE New York. Pop. 191,474.

Hun·ting·ton Beach city in SW California. Pop. 181,519.

Hunts·ville /húntsvəl, –vil/ city in N Alabama. Pop. 159,789.

Hu·ron /hyŏŏraan, yŏŏraan, –ən/, **Lake** one of the Great Lakes, W of Michigan.

Hy·der·a·bad /hídərəbaad/ **1** city in W India. Pop. 3,145,900. **2** city in S Pakistan. Pop. 751,500.

I·ba·dan /ibaád′n/ city in SW Nigeria. Pop. 1,365,000.

I·be·ri·an /ībeéreeən/ **Pen·in·su·la** (also called **I·be′ri·a**) peninsula in SW Europe, bounded by the Bay of Biscay, the Atlantic, and the Mediterranean Sea, and comprising Portugal and Spain.

Ice·land /íslənd/ island republic in the N Atlantic, between Scandinavia and Greenland. Pop. 270,000. Capital: Reykjavik.

I·da·ho /ídəhō/ state in NW U.S. Pop. 1,006,749. Capital: Boise. Abbr. **ID; Ida.** �□□ **I′da·ho·an** *n. & adj.*

I·guas·sú /eegwaasŏŏ/ **Falls** waterfall on the Argentina-Brazil border: 210 ft. high.

Il·li·nois /ilənóy, –nóyz/ state in central U.S. Pop. 11,430,602. Capital: Springfield. Abbr. **IL; Ill.** �□□ **Il·li·nois′an**, **Il·li·noi′an** /–nóyən/ *n. & adj.*

Im·pe·ri·al /impéereeəl/ **Val·ley** valley in S central California.

In·chon /ínchaan/ port city in NW South Korea. Pop. 2,307,600.

In·de·pend·ence /indipéndəns/ city in W Missouri. Pop. 112,301.

In·di·a /índeeə/ republic in S Asia. Pop. 952,108,000. Capital: New Delhi.

In·di·an·a /indee-ánə/ state in central U.S. Pop. 5,544,159. Capital: Indianapolis. Abbr. **IN; Ind.** �□□ **In·di·an′an** *n. & adj.*

In·di·an·ap·o·lis /indeeənápələs/ capital of Indiana, in the central part. Pop. 731,327.

In·di·an /índeeən/ **O·cean** ocean between Africa and Australia, S of Asia. Area 28,350,500 sq. mi.

In·do·chi·na /indōchínə/ peninsula in SE Asia, bounded by the Bay of Bengal and the S China Sea, and comprising Burma, W Malaysia, Thailand, Cambodia, Laos, and Vietnam.

In·do·ne·sia /indəneéezhə/ republic of the Malay Archipelago in SE Asia. Pop. 206,612,000. Capital: Jakarta. �□□ **In·do·ne′sian** *n. & adj.*

In·dus /índəs/ **Riv·er** river in Asia, flowing 1,900 mi. from Tibet through Pakistan and into the Arabian Sea.

Inglewood /inggəlwŏŏd/ city in SW California. Pop. 109,602.

Inns·bruck /ínzbrŏŏk/ city in W Austria. Pop. 118,100.

I·o·ni·an /ī-óneeən/ **Sea** arm of the Mediterranean Sea, between Greece and Italy.

I·o·wa /íəwə/ state in central U.S. Pop. 2,776,755. Capital: Des Moines. Abbr. **IA; Ia.** �□□ **I′o·wan** *n. & adj.*

I·o·wa Cit·y city in E Iowa. Pop. 59,738.

Ips·wich /ipswich/ city in E England. Pop. 114,800.

I·rá·kli·on /irákleeon/ (also Hē·rá′klei·on) port city and capital of Crete. Pop. 117,200.

I·ran /irán, iraŕn, īrán/ (formerly Persia) republic in SW Asia. Pop. 66,094,000. Capital: Teheran. □□ I·ra·ni·an /iráyneeən/ n. & adj.

I·raq /irák, iraŕk, īrák/ republic in SW Asia. Pop. 21,422,000. Capital: Baghdad. □□ I·ra·qi /irákee/ n. & adj.

Ir·bid /eŕbid/ city in N Jordan. Pop. 314,700.

Ire·land /írlənd/ 1 island in the N Atlantic, W of England. 2 (official name Re·pub′lic of Ire′land; also called Eir′e) republic in NW Europe; occupies most of the island of Ireland. Pop. 3,567,000. Capital: Dublin. See also NORTHERN IRELAND.

I·rish /írish/ Sea arm of the Atlantic, between England and Ireland.

Ir·kutsk /eerkoŕotsk/ city in S Russia. Pop. 654,000.

Ir·vine /úrvīn/ city in SW California. Pop. 110,330.

Ir·ving /úrving/ city in NE Texas. Pop. 155,037.

Is·fa·han /isfəhaŕn/ (also Esfahan or Ispahan) city in central Iran; former capital of Persia. Pop. 1,127,000.

Is·lam·a·bad /islaŕməbaad/ capital of Pakistan, in the NE part. Pop. 204,400.

Is·ra·el /ízreeəl, –rayel/ 1 republic in SW Asia; formed in 1948 as a Jewish state. Pop. 5,422,000 (excluding territory occupied after 1967). Capital: Jerusalem. 2 hist. ancient biblical country of the Hebrews. □□ Is·rae·li /izráylee/ n. & adj.

Is·tan·bul /istaanboŕol/ (formerly Constantinople; ancient name Byzantium) port city in NW Turkey. Pop. 7,615,500.

It·a·ly /ít′lee/ republic in S Europe. Pop. 57,460,000. Capital: Rome.

I·vo·ry /ívəree, –vree/ Coast (official name Côte d′I·voire′) republic in W Africa. Pop. 14,762,000. Capital: Abidjan. □□ I·vo·ri·an /iváwreeən/ n. & adj.

I·wo Ji·ma /eewə jeŕmə, eewō/ island S of Japan; site of World War II battle.

Iz·mir /izmeŕr/ (formerly Smyrna) port city in E Turkey. Pop. 1,985,300.

Jack·son /jáksən/ capital of Mississippi, in the central part. Pop. 196,637.

Ja·kar·ta /jəkaŕrtə/ capital of Indonesia, on NW coast of Java. Pop. 6,503,400.

Ja·la·pa /həlaŕpə/ capital of Veracruz, Mexico, in the central part. Pop. 111,800.

Ja·lis·co /həlískō/ state in W Mexico. Pop. 5,302,700. Capital: Guadalajara.

Ja·mai·ca /jəmáykə/ island republic in the W West Indies, S of Cuba. Pop. 2,595,000. Capital: Kingston.

Ja·pan /jəpán/ island nation E of mainland Asia. Pop. 125,450,000. Capital: Tokyo.

Ja·pan, Sea of arm of the Pacific, between Japan and mainland Asia.

Ja·va /jaŕavə, jávə/ main island of Indonesia, SE of Sumatra.

Jef·fer·son /jéfərsən/ City capital of Missouri, in the central part. Pop. 35,481.

Je·na /yáynə/ city in E central Germany. Pop. 102,200.

Jer·sey /júrzee/ island in the English Channel; British crown dependency. Pop. 88,000. Capital: St. Helier.

Jer·sey Cit·y city in NE New Jersey. Pop. 228,537.

Je·ru·sa·lem /jəroŕosələm, –sləm/ capital of Israel, in the E central part. Pop. 504,100.

Jid·da /jídə/ port city in W Saudi Arabia. Pop. 1,800,000.

Ji·nan /jeenaan/ (also Chi·nan) city in NE China. Pop. 1,100,000.

Jodh·pur /jaŕdpoōr/ city in NW India. Pop. 666,300.

Jo·han·nes·burg /jōhánəsbərg/ city in NE South Africa. Pop. 712,500.

Jo·li·et /jōlee-ét/ city in NE Illinois. Pop. 76,836.

Jor·dan /jáwrd′n/ kingdom in SW Asia, E of Israel. Pop. 4,212,000. Capital: Amman. □□ Jor·da·ni·an /jawrdáyneeən/ n. & adj.

Jor·dan Riv·er river in SW Asia, flowing 200 mi. from S Lebanon to the Dead Sea.

Juan de Fu·ca /waan də foŕokə, fyoŕo–/, Strait of channel separating Vancouver Island, Canada, from U.S.

Ju·neau /joŕonō/ capital of Alaska, in the SE part. Pop. 26,751.

Jung·frau /yoŕongfrow/ mountain in the Alps, in S Switzerland: 13,642 ft. high.

Ka·bul /kaaboŕol, kaŕabəl/ capital of Afghanistan, in the E part. Pop. 700,000.

Ka·go·shi·ma /kaagōsheŕemə, kaagósheemə/ port city in S Japan, on Kyushu. Pop. 546,300.

Ka·la·ha·ri /kaləhaŕaree, kaal–/ desert in SW Africa, mainly in Botswana.

Kal·a·ma·zoo /kaləməzoŕo/ city in SW Michigan. Pop. 80,277.

Ka·li·nin /kəleŕenin, –nyin/ (formerly Tver) city in W Russia. Pop. 455,000.

Ka·li·nin·grad /kəleŕeningrad, –nyingrad/ port city in W Russia. Pop. 419,000.

Kam·chat·ka /kamchaŕatkə/ peninsula in E Russia, bounded by the Sea of Okhotsk and the Bering Sea.

Kam·pa·la /kaampaŕalə/ capital of Uganda, in the SE part. Pop. 773,500.

Kam·pu·che·a /kampoŕocheeə/ see CAMBODIA.

Ka·no /kaánō/ city in N central Nigeria. Pop. 657,300.

Kan·pur /kaánpōōr/ city in N India. Pop. 1,874,400.

Kan·sas /kánzəs/ state in central U.S. Pop. 2,477,574. Capital: Topeka. Abbr. **KS; Kan.**; **Kans.** □□ **Kan′san** *n.* & *adj.*

Kan·sas Cit·y 1 city in W Missouri. Pop. 435,146. **2** city in E Kansas. Pop. 149,767.

Kao·hsiung /gówshee-ōóng/ port city in SW Taiwan. Pop. 1,426,518.

Ka·ra·chi /kəraáchee/ port city in S Pakistan. Pop. 5,208,100.

Karl-Marx-Stadt /kaarl maárks shtaat/ see CHEMNITZ.

Karls·ruh·e /kaárlzrōōə/ city in SW Germany. Pop. 277,000.

Kath·man·du /katmandōó/ (also **Kat·man·du′**) capital of Nepal, in the central part. Pop. 235,200.

Ka·to·wi·ce /kaatəveétsə/ city in S Poland. Pop. 355,100.

Kau·nas /kównəs/ city in S central Lithuania. Pop. 429,000.

Ka·wa·sa·ki /kaawəsaákee/ port city in Japan, on Honshu. Pop. 1,202,800.

Kay·se·ri /kīzəreé/ city in central Turkey. Pop. 454,000.

Ka·zakh·stan /kəzaakstaán/ republic in central Asia; formerly part of the USSR. Pop. 16,916,000. Capital: Almaty. □□ **Ka·zakh′** *n.*

Kee·lung /keélōōng/ see CHILUNG.

Ken·tuck·y /kəntúkee/ state in E central U.S. Pop. 3,685,296. Capital: Frankfort. Abbr. **KY; Ky.** □□ **Ken·tuck′i·an** *n.* & *adj.*

Ken·ya /kényə, keén-/ republic in E Africa. Pop. 28,177,000. Capital: Nairobi.

Khar·kiv /kaárkif/ (formerly **Khar′kov**) city in NE Ukraine. Pop. 1,555,000.

Khar·toum /kaartōóm/ capital of Sudan, in the E central part. Pop. 476,200.

Ki·ev /keé-ef, -ev/ capital of Ukraine, in the N central part. Pop. 2,630,000.

Ki·ga·li /kigaálee/ capital of Rwanda, in the central part. Pop. 232,700.

Ki·lau·e·a /kiləwáyə/ active volcano on the island of Hawaii.

Kil·i·man·ja·ro /kilimənjaárō/, **Mount** volcanic mountain in N Tanzania; highest peak in Africa: 19,340 ft.

Kings·ton /kíngstən/ port city and capital of Jamaica. Pop. 103,800.

Kings·ton up·on Hull see HULL.

Kings·town /kíngztown/ port city and capital of St. Vincent and the Grenadines. Pop. 15,500.

Kin·sha·sa /kinshaásə/ capital of the Congo

(formerly Zaire), in the W part. Pop. 4,655,300.

Ki·ri·ba·ti /keereebaátee, kíribas/ island republic in the W Pacific, along the equator, comprising thirty-three islands. Pop. 81,000. Capital: Tarawa.

Kir·kuk /keerkóók/ city in N Iraq. Pop. 570,000.

Ki·shi·nev /kíshinef/ (also called **Chi·și·nă′u**) capital of Moldova, in the central part. Pop. 662,000.

Ki·ta·kyu·shu /keetaakee-óóshōō/ port city in Japan, on Kyushu. Pop. 1,019,600.

Kitch·e·ner /kíchənər, kíchnər/ city in SE Ontario, Canada. Pop. 168,300.

Knox·ville /naáksvil/ city in E Tennessee. Pop. 165,121.

Ko·be /kóbay, -bee/ port city in Japan, on Honshu. Pop. 1,488,600.

Ko·blenz /kóblents/ see COBLENZ.

Ko·di·ak /kódee-ak/ **Is·land** island in Alaska, in the NW Gulf of Alaska.

Köln /köln/ see COLOGNE.

Kol·we·zi /kōlwáyzee/ city in S Congo (formerly Zaire). Pop. 417,800.

Kon·ya /kawnyaà/ city in SW central Turkey. Pop. 576,000.

Ko·re·a /kəreéə/ peninsula in E Asia, bounded by the Yellow Sea and the Sea of Japan; divided into two countries: **1 North Korea** Pop. 23,904,000. Capital: Pyongyang. **2 South Korea** Pop. 45,482,000. Capital: Seoul . □□ **Ko·re′an** *n.* & *adj.*

Kra·ka·to·a /krakətóə/ (also **Kra·ka·tau** /krákətow/) island volcano in Indonesia; noted for its violent eruption in 1883.

Kra·ków /krákow, kraákōōf/ see CRACOW.

Kras·no·yarsk /kraasnəyaársk/ city in central Russia. Pop. 869,400.

K2 (also called **God·win Aus·ten** /gaádwin áwstən/) mountain in N Kashmir; second highest in the world: 28,250 ft.

Kua·la Lum·pur /kwaálə ləmpōór/ capital of Malaysia, on the SW Malay Peninsula. Pop. 1,100,000.

Kuei·yang /gwáy-yáng/ (also **Kwei·yang**) see GUIYANG.

Kui·by·shev /kweébəshef, -shev/ see SAMARA.

Ku·ma·mo·to /kōōməmótō/ city in Japan, on Kyushu. Pop. 650,300.

Ku·ma·si /kōōmaásee/ city in S central Ghana. Pop. 385,200.

Ku·wait /kəwáyt/ **1** monarchy in W Asia, on the Persian Gulf. Pop. 1,950,000. **2** (also called **Ku·wait′ Cit′y**) port city and capital of Kuwait. Pop. 44,200. □□ **Ku·wai′ti** /-tee/ *n.* & *adj.*

Kwang·ju /gwaángjŏō/ city in SW South Korea. Pop. 1,257,500.

Kyo·to /kee-ŏtō/ city in Japan, on Honshu. Pop. 1,463,600.

Kyr·gyz·stan /kirgistaán, –stán/ republic in W central Asia; formerly part of the USSR. Pop. 4,530,000. Capital: Bishkek.

Kyu·shu /kyŏōshŏō/ island in SW Japan.

La·do·ga /laádəgə, lád–/, **Lake** lake N of St. Petersburg, Russia; largest lake in Europe.

La·hore /ləháwr, –hŏr/ city in E Pakistan. Pop. 2,952,700.

Lake Dis·trict noted scenic region in NW England.

Lake·wood /láykwŏōd/ city in central Colorado. Pop. 126,481.

La Ma·tan·za /laa mətaánsə/ city in E Argentina. Pop. 1,111,800.

Lan·sing /lánsing/ capital of Michigan, in the S part. Pop. 127,321.

La·os /laáōs/ country in SE Asia, between Thailand and Vietnam. Pop. 4,976,000. Capital: Vientiane. □□ **La·o·tian** /lay-ŏshən/ *n. & adj.*

La Paz /lə paáz, paás/ **1** administrative capital of Bolivia, in the W part. Pop. 785,000 **2** capital of Baja California Sur, Mexico, in the S part. Pop. 161,000.

La Pla·ta /plaátə/ port city in E Argentina. Pop. 643,000.

La·re·do /ləráydō/ city in S Texas. Pop. 122,899.

Las Cru·ces /laas krŏōsəs/ city in S New Mexico. Pop. 62,126.

Las Pal·mas /paálməs/ port city of the Canary Islands, off the coast of Morocco. Pop. 342,000.

Las Ve·gas /váygəs/ city in SE Nevada. Pop. 258,295.

Lat·a·ki·a /latəkeéə/ port city in W Syria. Pop. 306,500.

Lat·vi·a /látveeə/ republic in N Europe; formerly part of the USSR. Pop. 2,469,000. Capital: Riga. □□ **Lat′vi·an** *n. & adj.*

Lau·sanne /lōzaán, –zán/ city in W Switzerland. Pop. 116,800.

La·val /laavaál, ləvál/ city in S Quebec, Canada. Pop. 314,400.

Law·rence /láwrəns, laár–/ city in NE Massachusetts. Pop. 70,207.

Leb·a·non /lébənaan, –nən/ republic in SW Asia. Pop. 3,776,000. Capital: Beirut. □□ **Leb·a·nese** /–neéz/ *n. & adj.*

Leeds /leedz/ city in N England. Pop. 724,400.

Lee·ward /leéwərd, lŏōərd/ **Is·lands** island group in the E West Indies, extending from Dominica NW to the U.S. Virgin Islands.

Leg·horn /léghawrn/ (Italian name **Li·vor′ no**) port city in W Italy. Pop. 165,500.

Le Ha·vre /lə haáv, haávrə/ port city in N France. Pop. 197,200.

Leices·ter /léstər/ city in central England. Pop. 293,400.

Lei·den /lifd′n/ city in the SW Netherlands. Pop. 115,500.

Leip·zig /lífpsig, –sik/ city in E Germany. Pop. 481,100.

Le·man /leémən/, **Lake** see GENEVA, LAKE.

Le Mans /lə maaN/ city in NW France. Pop. 148,500.

Le·nin·grad /léningrad/ see SAINT PETERSBURG 1.

Le·ón /lay-áwn/ **1** city in NW Spain. Pop. 147,300. **2** city in central Mexico. Pop. 758,300.

Le·so·tho /ləsótō, –sŏōtō/ (formerly **Basutoland**) monarchy in S Africa. Pop. 1,971,000. Capital: Maseru.

Less·er An·til·les /antíleez/ term for the smaller islands of the West Indies, comprising the Leeward and Windward islands, SE of Puerto Rico. See also GREATER ANTILLES.

Le·vant /ləvánt/ term for the countries on the E coast of the Mediterranean Sea; includes Israel, Syria, and Lebanon.

Lev·it·town /lévit-town/ city in SE New York, on Long Island. Pop. 53,286.

Lex·ing·ton /léksingtən/ **1** city in NE central Kentucky. Pop. 225,366. **2** town in NE Massachusetts; site of the first battle of the American Revolution (1775). Pop. 29,000.

Li·be·ri·a /lībeéreeə/ republic in W Africa. Pop. 2,110,000. Capital: Monrovia. □□ **Li·ber′i·an** *n. & adj.*

Li·bre·ville /leébrəvil/ port city and capital of Gabon. Pop. 362,400.

Lib·y·a /libeeə/ republic in N Africa. Pop. 5,445,000. Capital: Tripoli. □□ **Lib′y·an** *n. & adj.*

Liech·ten·stein /líkhtənshtīn, líktənstīn/ principality in central Europe. Pop. 31,000. Capital: Vaduz. □□ **Liech′ten·stein·er** *n. & adj.*

Li·ège /lee-ézh/ city in E Belgium. Pop. 192,400.

Lille /leel/ city in N France. Pop. 178,300.

Li·long·we /lil’áwngway/ administrative capital of Malawi, in the central part. Pop. 395,500.

Li·ma /leémə/ capital of Peru, in the W part. Pop. 421,600.

Li·moges /leemŏzh/ city in central France. Pop. 136,400.

Lin·coln /língkən/ capital of Nebraska, in the E part. Pop. 191,972.

Linz /lins/ port city in NW Austria. Pop. 203,000.

Lis·bon /lízbən/ port city and capital of Portugal. Pop. 677,800.

Lith·u·a·ni·a /lithəwáyneeə/ republic in N Europe; formerly part of the USSR. Pop. 3,646,000. Capital: Vilnius.

Lit·tle Rock /lítəl raak/ capital of Arkansas, in the central part. Pop. 175,795.

Liv·er·pool /lívərpōol/ port city in W England. Pop. 474,000. □□ **Liv·er·pud·li·an** /livərpúdleeən/ n. & adj.

Li·vo·ni·a /livōneeə/ city in SE Michigan. Pop. 100,850.

Li·vor·no /leeváwrnaw/ see LEGHORN.

Lju·blja·na /lōoblee-aanə, lyōō-/ capital of Slovenia. Pop. 276,100.

Lla·no Es·ta·ca·do /laanō estəkaadō/ (also called **Staked Plain**) extensive plateau in Texas and New Mexico.

Loch Ness /laak nes/ lake in NW Scotland.

Lódz /lōoj/ city in central Poland. Pop. 828,500.

Lo·mas de Za·mo·ra /lómaas də zəmáwrə/ city in E Argentina. Pop. 572,800.

Lo·mé /lōmáy/ port city and capital of Togo. Pop. 366,500.

Lon·don /lúndən/ **1** capital of England and of the United Kingdom, in the S part of England. Pop. 6,967,500. **2** city in SE Ontario, Canada. Pop. 303,200.

Long /lawng/ **Beach** city in SW California. Pop. 429,433.

Long Is·land island in SE New York; includes portions of New York City.

Long Is·land Sound arm of the Atlantic, separating Connecticut from Long Island, New York.

Look·out /lōokowt/ **Moun·tain** ridge near Chattanooga in SE Tennessee; site of Civil War battle.

Los An·ge·les /laws ánjələs, –leez/ city in S California. Pop. 3,485,398. □□ **An·ge·le·no** /anjəleenō/, **Los An·ge·le·no, Los An·ge·le·an** /anjəleeən/ n.

Lou·ise /lōo-eez, lōō-/, **Lake** glacial lake in SW Alberta, Canada, in the Canadian Rocky Mountains.

Lou·i·si·an·a /lōo-eezee-ánə/ state in S U.S. Pop. 4,219,973. Capital: Baton Rouge. Abbr. **LA; La.** □□ **Lou·i·si·an'an, Lou·i·si·an'i·an** /–áneeən/ n. & adj.

Lou·is·ville /lōoeevil, –əvəl/ city in N central Kentucky. Pop. 269,063. □□ **Lou·is·vill·ian** /lōoivílyən/ n.

Lourdes /lōordz, lōord/ town in SW France; site of a Roman Catholic shrine noted for miraculous cures. Pop. 18,100.

Lou·ren·ço Mar·ques /lərénsō maarkés, maárkəs/ see MAPUTO.

Low Coun·tries term for low-lying countries along the North Sea; includes Belgium, Luxembourg, and the Netherlands.

Low·ell /lóəl/ city in NE Massachusetts. Pop. 103,439.

Lu·an·da /lōo-aándə/ port city and capital of Angola. Pop. 2,000,000.

Lub·bock /lúbək/ city in NW Texas. Pop. 186,206.

Lü·beck /lýbek/ port city in N Germany. Pop. 216,900.

Lu·blin /lōoblin/ city in E Poland. Pop. 352,500.

Lu·bum·ba·shi /lōobōombaáshee/ city in S Congo (formerly Zaire). Pop. 851,400.

Luck·now /lúknow/ city in N India. Pop. 1,619,100.

Lü·da /lōodaá/ see DALIAN.

Lu·gansk /lōogaánsk/ (formerly **Voroshilovgrad**) city in E Ukraine. Pop. 487,000.

Lu·sa·ka /lōosaákə/ capital of Zambia, in the SE part. Pop. 982,400.

Lux·em·bourg /lúksəmbərg/ **1** country and grand duchy in W Europe. Pop. 416,000. **2** capital of Luxembourg, in the S part. Pop. 76,400. **3** province in SE Belgium. □□ **Lux' em·bourg·er** n. **Lux' em·bourg·i·an** /–bərgeeən/ n. & adj.

Lviv /ləveéf/ (also **Lvov**) city in W Ukraine. Pop. 802,000.

Ly·all·pur /líəlpōor/ see FAISALABAD.

Lyd·i·a /lídeeə/ hist. ancient kingdom of W Asia Minor. □□ **Lyd'i·an** n. & adj.

Lynn /lin/ city in NE Massachusetts. Pop. 81,245.

Ly·ons /lee-áwɴ/ (also **Lyon**) in E France. Pop. 422,400.

Maas·tricht /maástrikht/ city in the SE Netherlands. Pop. 118,300.

Ma·cau /məków/ overseas territory of Portugal (to 1999), consisting of a peninsula and two islands off the S coast of China. Pop. 497,000. Capital: Macau City.

Mac·e·do·ni·a /masədóneeə/ **1** hist. ancient country on the Balkan Peninsula, N of Greece. **2** independent state of N Greece; formerly part of Yugoslavia. Pop. 2,104,000. Capital: Skopje. □□ **Mace·do'ni·an** /–neeən/ n. & adj.

Mac·ken·zie /məkénzee/ **Riv·er** river in NW Canada, flowing 1,120 mi. from Great Slave Lake to the Beaufort Sea.

Ma·con /máykən/ city in central Georgia. Pop. 106,612.

Mad·a·gas·car /madəgáskər/ (formerly **Malagasy Republic**) island country in the Indian

Ocean, E of Mozambique. Pop. 13,671,000.
Capital: Antananarivo. □□ **Ma·da·gas′can** *n.*
& adj.

Ma·dei·ra /mədeérə, –dérə/ **1** island group off
the NW coast of Africa; part of Portugal. **2**
the major island of this group.

Mad·i·son /mádisən/ capital of Wisconsin, in
the S part. Pop. 191,262.

Ma·dras /mədrás, –draás/ port city in SE India.
Pop. 3,841,400.

Ma·drid /mədríd/ capital of Spain, in the central part. Pop. 3,041,100. □□ **Mad·ri·le·ni·an**
/madrileéneeən/ *n. & adj.*

Mag·de·burg /mágdəbərg/ city in E central
Germany. Pop. 265,400.

Ma·hal·la al-Ku·bra /məhálə al koóbrə/ city
in N Egypt. Pop. 408,000.

Maine /mayn/ state in NE U.S. Pop.
1,227,928. Capital: Augusta. Abbr. **ME; Me.**
□□ **Main′er** *n.*

Mainz /mīnts/ port city in W Germany. Pop.
184,600.

Ma·ju·ro /məjoóró/ capital of the Marshall
Islands, in the SE part. Pop. 20,000.

Ma·la·bo /məlaábō/ capital of Equatorial
Guinea, on the island of Bioko. Pop. 58,000.

Má·la·ga /máləgə/ port city in S Spain. Pop.
531,400.

Mal·a·gas·y /máləgásee/ **Re·pub·lic** see
MADAGASCAR.

Ma·lang /məlaáng/ city in Indonesia, on Java.
Pop. 650,300.

Ma·la·wi /məlaáwee/ republic in SE Africa.
Pop. 9,453,000. Capitals: Lilongwe; Zomba.

Ma·la·wi, Lake see NYASA, LAKE.

Ma·lay·a /məláyə/ **1** see MALAY PENINSULA.
2 former federation of eleven states on the
Malay Peninsula; now part of Malaysia.

Ma·lay /máylay/ **Ar·chi·pel·a·go** (formerly
Malaysia) extensive group of islands between
Australia and mainland Asia; includes the
Philippines and Indonesia.

Ma·lay Pen·in·su·la (also called **Ma·lay′a**)
peninsula in SE Asia, bounded by the South
China Sea and the Strait of Malacca, and
comprising parts of Burma, Malaysia, and
Thailand.

Ma·lay·sia /məláyzhə/ **1** constitutional mon-
archy in SE Asia. Pop. 19,963,000 Capital:
Kuala Lumpur. **2** see MALAY ARCHIPELAGO.
□□ **Ma·lay′sian** *n. & adj.*

Mal·dives /máwldeevz/ republic com-
prising about 2,000 islands in the Indian
Ocean, SW of India. Pop. 271,000. Capital:
Male. □□ **Mal·div′i·an** /–díveeən/ *n. & adj.*

Ma·le /maálee/ capital of the Maldives, in the
central part. Pop. 63,000.

Ma·li /maálee/ republic in W Africa. Pop.
9,653,000. Capital: Bamako. □□ **Ma′li·an** *n.*
& adj.

Mal·mö /maálmə, –mər/ port city in S Sweden.
Pop. 245,700.

Mal·ta /máwltə/ island state in the Mediterranean Sea, S of Sicily. Pop. 376,000. Capital:
Valletta.

Mal·vi·nas, Is·las see FALKLAND ISLANDS.

Mam·moth /máməth/ **Cave** series of limestone caverns in central Kentucky; longest
cave system in the world: more than 300 mi.
of passages.

Man /man/, **Isle of** British island in the Irish
Sea, between Britain and Ireland. Pop.
74,000. Capital: Douglas. □□ **Manx** /mangks/
n. & adj.

Ma·na·gua /mənaágwə/ capital of Nicaragua,
in the W part. Pop. 682,000.

Ma·na·ma /mənámə/ (also called **al-Ma·nam′**
ah) capital of Bahrain. Pop. 140,400.

Ma·náos /maanóws/ (also **Ma·naus′**) port city
in W Brazil. Pop. 613,000.

Man·ches·ter /mánchestər/ **1** city in S New
Hampshire. Pop. 99,600. **2** city in NW England. Pop. 431,100.

Man·da·lay /mandəláy/ city in N Burma. Pop.
532,900.

Man·hat·tan /manhát′n/ one of the five boroughs of New York City. Pop. 1,487,536.

Ma·nil·a /mənílə/ port city and capital of the
Philippines. Pop. 1,894,700.

Man·i·to·ba /manitóbə/ province in central
Canada. Pop. 1,116,000. Capital: Winnipeg.
□□ **Man·i·to′ban** *n. & adj.*

Mann·heim /maánhīm/ city in SW Germany.
Pop. 316,200.

Ma·pu·to /maapoótō/ (formerly **Lourenço**
Marques) port city and capital of Mozambique. Pop. 931,600.

Mar·a·cai·bo /marəkíbō/ port city in NW Venezuela. Pop. 1,249,700.

Ma·ra·cay /maarəkí/ city in NE Venezuela.
Pop. 354,200.

Mar·i·an·a /maree-ánə, mer–/ **Trench** Pacific
depression SW of the Mariana Islands and
E of the Philippines; greatest known ocean
depth: 36,201 ft.

Mar·i·time /máritīm/ **Prov·in·ces** Canadian
provinces of New Brunswick, Nova Scotia,
and Prince Edward Island.

Ma·ri·u·pol /maaree-oópawl/ (formerly **Zhda-**
nov) city in S Ukraine. Pop. 510,000.

Mar·ma·ra /maármərə/, **Sea of** sea in W Turkey, between the Black and Mediterranean
seas.

Mar·ra·kesh /márəkesh/ city in W central
Morocco. Pop. 602,000.

Mar·seilles /maarsáy/ port city in SE France. Pop. 807,700.

Mar·shall /maárshəl/ **Is·lands** republic comprising a group of islands in the Pacific, NE of New Guinea. Pop. 58,000. Capital: Majuro.

Mar·tha's /maárthəz/ **Vine·yard** island in Massachusetts, S of Cape Cod.

Mar·ti·nique /maart'n-eék/ island in the E West Indies; department of France. Pop. 399,000. Capital: Fort-de-France.

Mar·y·land /mérələnd/ state in E central U.S. Pop. 4,781,468. Capital: Annapolis. Abbr. **MD; Md.** □□ **Mar′y·land·er** *n.*

Ma·se·ru /maázərōō/ capital of Lesotho, in the W part. Pop. 109,400.

Ma·son-Dix·on /máysən díksən/ **Line** boundary between Pennsylvania and Maryland; traditional division between the North and the South.

Mas·sa·chu·setts /masəchóōsits/ state in NE U.S. Pop. 6,016,425. Capital: Boston. Abbr. **MA; Mass.**

Mat·a·mo·ros /matəmáwrəs/ city in NE Mexico. Pop. 266,100.

Mat·ter·horn /mátərhawrn/ mountain in the Alps, on the border of Switzerland and Italy: 14,692 ft. high.

Mau·i /mówee/ island of central Hawaii.

Mau·na Lo·a /mownə lóə/ mountain on the island of Hawaii; includes Kilauea volcano.

Mau·ri·ta·ni·a /mawritáyneeə/ republic in W Africa. Pop. 2,336,000. Capital: Nouakchott.

Mau·ri·tius /mawrishəs/ island republic in the Indian Ocean, E of Madagascar. Pop. 1,140,000. Capital: Port Louis.

Ma·ya·güez /mīəgwáys/ port city in W Puerto Rico. Pop. 100,400.

Ma·za·tlán /maazətlaán/ port city in W Mexico. Pop. 262,700.

Mba·bane /m-bəbaán, em–/ capital of Swaziland, in the W central part. Pop. 47,000.

Mc·Al·len /məkálən/ city in S Texas. Pop. 84,000.

Mc·Kin·ley /məkínlee/, **Mount** mountain in central Alaska; highest in North America: 20,320 ft.

Mead /meed/, **Lake** largest artificial lake in U.S.; formed by Hoover Dam.

Mec·ca /mékə/ city in W Saudi Arabia; holy site in Islam. Pop. 550,000.

Me·dan /maydaán/ city in Indonesia, on Sumatra. Pop. 1,686,000.

Me·del·lín /medəyeén/ city in NW Colombia. Pop. 1,621,400.

Me·di·na /mədeénə/ city in W Saudi Arabia. Pop. 290,000.

Med·i·ter·ra·ne·an /meditəráyneeən/ **Sea** sea with coastlines along Europe, Asia, and Africa.

Mek·nès /meknés/ city in NE Morocco. Pop. 401,000.

Me·kong /máykáwng/ **Riv·er** river in SE Asia, flowing 2,600 mi. from S China to the South China Sea.

Mel·a·ne·sia /meləneétzhə, –shə/ island region in the Pacific, NE of Australia.

Mel·bourne /mélbərn, –bawrn/ port city and capital of Victoria, Australia. Pop. 3,218,100.

Mem·phis /mémfis/ city in SW Tennessee. Pop. 610,337.

Mé·ri·da /méridə/ capital of Yucatán, Mexico, in the NW part. Pop. 523,400.

Mer·sin /merseén/ port city in S Turkey. Pop. 523,000.

Me·sa /máysə/ city in central Arizona. Pop. 288,091.

Me·shed /məshéd/ city in NE Iran. Pop. 1,759,200.

Mes·o·po·ta·mi·a /mesəpətáymeeə/ region in SW Asia, between the Tigris and Euphrates rivers; part of present-day Iraq.

Mes·quite /məskeét/ city in NE Texas. Pop. 101,484.

Mes·si·na /məseénə/ port city in NE Sicily. Pop. 233,800.

Met·air·ie /métəree/ city in SE Louisiana. Pop. 149,428.

Metz /mets/ city in NE France. Pop. 123,900.

Mex·i·cal·i /meksikálee/ capital of Baja California, Mexico, in the NE part. Pop. 438,400.

Mex·i·co /méksikō/ country in S North America. Pop. 95,772,000. Capital: Mexico City. □□ **Mex′i·can** *n. & adj.*

Mex·i·co, Gulf of arm of the Atlantic, S of the U.S. and E of Mexico.

Mex·i·co Cit·y capital of Mexico, in the central part. Pop. 9,815,800.

Mi·am·i /mī-ámee/ city in SE Florida. Pop. 358,548.

Mi·am·i Beach city in SE Florida. Pop. 92,639.

Mich·i·gan /míshigən/ peninsular state in N central U.S. Pop. 9,295,297. Capital: Lansing. Abbr. **MI; Mich.** □□ **Mich·i·gan·der** /mishigándər/, **Mich′i·gan·ite** /–gənīt/ *n.*

Mich·i·gan, Lake one of the Great Lakes, between Wisconsin and the lower peninsula of Michigan.

Mi·cho·a·cán /meéchō-aakaán/ state in SW Mexico. Pop. 3,548,200. Capital: Morelia.

Mi·cro·ne·sia /mīkrəneétzhə, –shə/ **1** region of Pacific islands E of the Philippines and N of the equator. **2** (official name **Federated States of Micronesia**) federation of islands in the S Pacific. Pop. 125,000. Capital: Palikir.

Mid·dle East (also **Near East**) region of SW

Asia and N Africa, roughly from Afghanistan to Libya.

Mid·land /mídlənd/ city in W Texas. Pop. 89,443.

Mid·west /mídwést/ (also called **Mid'dle West**) region of N central U.S., from the Great Plains to the Allegheny Mountains.

Mi·lan /milán, –lȧan/ city in N Italy. Pop. 1,334,200. □□ **Mil·an·ese** /miləneéz/ n. & adj.

Mil·wau·kee /milwáwkee/ city in SE Wisconsin. Pop. 628,088.

Min·ne·ap·o·lis /minee-ápələs/ city in E Minnesota. Pop. 368,383.

Min·ne·so·ta /minəsótə/ state in N central U.S. Pop. 4,375,099. Capital: St. Paul. Abbr. **Minn.**; **MN** □□ **Min·ne·so'tan** n. & adj.

Minsk /minsk/ capital of Belarus. Pop. 1,700,600.

Mis·sis·sau·ga /misisáwgə/ city in Ontario, Canada. Pop. 463,400.

Mis·sis·sip·pi /misisípee/ state in S U.S. Pop. 2,573,216. Capital: Jackson. Abbr. **Miss.**; **MS** □□ **Mis·sis·sip'pi·an** n. & adj.

Mis·sis·sip·pi Riv·er river in central U.S., flowing 2,470 mi. from Minnesota to the Gulf of Mexico; largest river in U.S.

Mis·sour·i /mizŏóree, –ə/ state in central U.S. Pop. 5,117,073. Capital: Jefferson City. Abbr. **MO**; **Mo.** □□ **Mis·sour'i·an** n. & adj.

Mis·sour·i Riv·er river in central U.S., flowing 2,700 mi. from Montana to the Mississippi River near St. Louis, Missouri.

Mo·bile /mōbeél, móbeel/ port city in SW Alabama. Pop. 196,278.

Mo·bile /mōbeél/ **Bay** arm of the Gulf of Mexico, S of Alabama.

Mo·de·na /máwd'nə/ city in N Italy. Pop. 176,600.

Mo·des·to /mədéstō/ city in central California. Pop. 164,730.

Mo·ga·di·shu /mōgədíshoō, –deéshoō/ port city and capital of Somalia. Pop. 900,000.

Mo·ja·ve /məhȧavee, mō–/ **Des·ert** arid basin in SE California.

Mol·do·va /məldóvə/ (formerly **Mol·da'vi·an** /mawldáyvee-ən/ **Soviet Socialist Republic**) republic in SE Europe; formerly part of the USSR. Pop. 4,464,000. Capital: Kishinev.

Mo·lo·kai /maaləkí, mō–/ island in central Hawaii.

Mo·luc·cas /məlúkəz/ (also called **Spice Is'lands**) island group in the S Pacific, in the Malay Archipelago, between New Guinea and Sulawesi.

Mom·ba·sa /maambȧasə/ port city in SE Kenya. Pop. 600,000.

Mon·a·co /mȧanəkō/ principality on the Mediterranean Sea, near Nice, France. Pop. 32,300. Capital: Monaco. □□ **Mon'a·can**, **Mon·e·gasque'** n. & adj.

Mön·chen·glad·bach /mönkhən-glȧatbaakh/ city in W Germany. Pop. 266,100.

Mon·go·li·a /maan-góleeə, maang–/ republic in E central Asia. Pop. 2,497,000. Capital: Ulan Bator. □□ **Mon·go'li·an** n.

Mon·ro·vi·a /mənróveeə/ port city and capital of Liberia. Pop. 421,100.

Mon·tan·a /maantánə/ state in NW U.S. Pop. 799,065. Capital: Helena. Abbr. **Mont.**; **MT**. □□ **Mon·tan'an** n. & adj.

Mon·te·ne·gro /məntəneégrō, –negrō/ republic in SE Europe; formerly part of Yugoslavia. Pop. 635,000. Capital: Podgorica. □□ **Mon·te·ne'gran** n. & adj.

Mon·ter·rey /maantəráy/ capital of Nuevo León, Mexico, in the W part. Pop. 1,069,000.

Mon·te·vi·de·o /maantəvidáyō/ port city and capital of Uruguay. Pop. 1,378,700.

Mont·gom·er·y /məntgúməree, maant–, –gúmree/ capital of Alabama, in the E central part. Pop. 187,106.

Mont·pel·ier 1 (/maantpeélyər/) capital of Vermont, in the N central part. Pop. 8,247. 2 (/mawɴpelyáy/) city in S France. Pop. 210,900.

Mont·re·al /maantree-áwl/ city in S Quebec, Canada. Pop. 1,017,700.

Mont·ser·rat /montsərȧat/ island in the E West Indies; dependent territory of the United Kingdom. Pop. 13,000. Capital: Plymouth.

Mo·re·lia /məráylyə/ capital of Michoacán, Mexico, in the N part. Pop. 428,500.

Mo·re·los /məráyləs/ state in S central Mexico. Pop. 1,195,100. Capital: Cuernavaca.

Mo·re·no /məreénō/ **Val·ley** city in SW California. Pop. 118,779.

Mo·roc·co /məraákō/ kingdom in NW Africa. Pop. 29,779,000. Capital: Rabat. □□ **Mo·roc'can** n. & adj.

Mo·rón /mawrón/ city in E Argentina. Pop. 641,500.

Mo·ro·ni /mawrónee/ capital of Comoros, on Grande Comore Island. Pop. 30,000.

Mos·cow /mȧaskow, –kō/ capital of Russia, in the W part; former capital of the USSR. Pop. 8,717,000.

Mo·sul /mōsoól/ city in W Iraq. Pop. 664,200.

Mo·zam·bique /mōzambeék/ republic in SE Africa. Pop. 17,878,000. Capital: Maputo. □□ **Mo·zam·bi'can** n. & adj.

Mul·tan /moóltaan/ city in central Pakistan. Pop. 730,100.

Mu·nich /myoόnik, –nikh/ city in SW Germany. Pop. 1,244,700.

Mün·ster /mýnstər, mún–/ city in NW Germany. Pop. 264,900.

Mur·cia /múrshə, –sheeə/ city in SE Spain. Pop. 341,500.

Mur·mansk /mo͞ormánsk/ port city in NW Russia. Pop. 407,000.

Mus·cat /múskaat, –kət/ port city and capital of Oman. Pop. 52,000.

My·an·mar /myaánmaar/ see BURMA.

My·sore /mīsáwr/ city in S India. Pop. 480,700.

Myu·ko·la·yiv /myo͞okəlíif/ (formerly **Nikolayev**) city in Ukraine. Pop. 508,000.

Na·ga·sa·ki /naagəsaákee/ port city in Japan, on Kyushu. Pop. 438,700.

Na·go·ya /nəgóyə, naágəyaa/ city in Japan, on Honshu. Pop. 2,152,300.

Nag·pur /naágpo͞or/ city in central India. Pop. 1,624,800.

Nai·ro·bi /nīróbee/ capital of Kenya, in the S central part. Pop. 2,000,000.

Na·mib·i·a /nəmíbeeə/ republic in SW Africa. Pop. 1,677,000. Capital: Windhoek. □□ **Na·mib'i·an** n. & adj.

Nam·p'o /námpɔ́/ city in SW North Korea. Pop. 370,000.

Nam·pu·la /nampo͞ólə/ city in E Mozambique. Pop. 250,500.

Nan·chang /naánchaáng/ city in SE China. Pop. 1,350,000.

Nan·cy /naaNseé, nánsee/ city in NE France. Pop. 102,400.

Nan·jing /naánjíng/ (formerly **Nan·king**) port city in E China. Pop. 2,500,000.

Nantes /naaNt/ port city in W France. Pop. 252,000.

Nan·tuck·et /nantúkit/ island in Massachusetts, S of Cape Cod.

Na·ples /náypəlz/ (Italian name **Na'po·li**) port city in SW Italy. Pop. 1,061,600.

Nash·u·a /násho͞oə/ city in S New Hampshire. Pop. 79,662.

Nash·ville /náshvil, –vəl/ capital of Tennessee, in the N central part. Pop. 487,969.

Nas·sau /násaw/ capital of the Bahamas, on New Providence Island. Pop. 172,200.

Na·tion·al /náshənəl/ **Road** (also called **National Old Trail Road; Cumberland Road**) first federal road in U.S., extending from Cumberland, Maryland, W to St. Louis, Missouri.

Na·u·ru /naa–o͞óro͞o/ island republic in the Pacific, W of Kiribati. Pop. 10,000.

Na·ya·rit /nīəreét/ state in W Mexico. Pop. 824,600. Capital: Tepic.

N'Dja·me·na /enjəmáynə, –meénə/ capital of Chad, in the W part. Pop. 531,000.

Ndo·la /en-dólə/ city in N Zambia. Pop. 376,300.

Near East see MIDDLE EAST.

Ne·bras·ka /nəbráskə/ state in central U.S. Pop. 1,578,385. Capital: Lincoln. Abbr. **NE; Nebr.** □□ **Ne·bras'kan** n. & adj.

Neg·ev /négev/ **Des·ert** arid region in S Israel.

Ne·pal /nipáwl, –pál/ constitutional monarchy in S Asia. Pop. 22,094,000. Capital: Kathmandu. □□ **Ne·pa·lese** /nepəleéz, –leés/ n. & adj.

Neth·er·lands /nétʰərləndz/ (also called **Hol'land**) kingdom in W Europe. Capital: Amsterdam. Seat of government: The Hague. Pop. 15,568,000. □□ **Neth'er·land·er** n.

Neth·er·lands An·til·les /antíleez/ island group in the West Indies, comprised of islands off the NW coast of Venezuela and islands among the NW Leeward Islands; territory of the Netherlands. Pop. 209,000. Capital: Willemstad.

Ne·tza·hual·có·yotl /netsaawaalkóyōt'l/ city in central Mexico. Pop. 1,255,500.

Ne·vad·a /nəvádə, –vaádə/ state in W U.S. Pop. 1,201,833. Capital: Carson City. Abbr. **Nev.; NV** □□ **Ne·vad' an, Ne·vad'i·an** /–deeən/ n. & adj.

New·ark /no͞óərk, nyo͞ó–/ city in N New Jersey. Pop. 275,221.

New Bed·ford /no͞o bédfərd, nyo͞o/ city in SE Massachusetts. Pop. 99,922.

New Bruns·wick /brúnzwik/ province in SE Canada. Pop. 751,000. Capital: Fredericton.

New Cal·e·do·ni·a /kalidóneea, –dónyə/ island group in the S Pacific; territory of France. Pop. 188,000. Capital: Nouméa.

New·cas·tle /no͞ókasəl, no͞okás–, nyo͞ó–, nyo͞o–/ port city in SE Australia. Pop. 427,700.

New·cas·tle up·on Tyne /tīn/ port city in N England. Pop. 283,600.

New Del·hi /délee/ capital of India, in the N central part. Pop. 301,300.

New Eng·land /íngglənd/ region of the NE U.S.; includes Connecticut, Maine, Massachusetts, New Hampshire, Rhode Island, and Vermont.

New·found·land /no͞ofənlánd, no͞ofənlənd, nyo͞o–, nyo͞ó–, –fənd–/ **1** island off the Atlantic coast of Canada. **2** province in E Canada, comprising Labrador and the island of Newfoundland. Pop. 581,000. Capital: St. John's. □□ **New'found·land·er** n.

New Guin·ea /gínee/ island in the East Indies, N of Australia; comprises parts of Papua New Guinea and Indonesia.

New Hamp·shire /hámpshər/ state in NE U.S. Pop. 1,109,252. Capital: Concord. Abbr. **NH; N.H.; N. Hamp.** □□ **New Hamp'shir·ite, New Hamp'shire·man** /–mən/ n.

New Ha·ven /háyvən/ city in S Connecticut. Pop. 130,474.

New Jer·sey /júrzee/ state in E U.S. Pop. 7,730,188. Capital: Trenton. Abbr. **NJ; N.J.** □□ **New Jer'sey·ite, New Jer'sey·an** *n.*

New Mex·i·co /méksikō/ state in SW U.S. Pop. 1,515,069. Capital: Santa Fe. Abbr. **NM; N. Mex.** □□ **New Mex'i·can** *n. & adj.*

New Or·le·ans /áwrleeənz, áwrlənz, awrleê-nz/ port city in SE Louisiana. Pop. 496,938. □□ **New Or·lea'ni·an** /awrlíneeən/ *n.*

New·port News /nóōpawrt nóōz, –pərt, ny-óō–/ city in SE Virginia. Pop. 170,045.

New South Wales /waylz/ state in SE Australia. Pop. 5,426,200. Capital: Sydney.

New York /yáwrk/ **1** state in NE U.S. Pop. 17,990,455. Capital: Albany. Abbr. **NY; N.Y. 2** (also **New York Cit'y**) city in SE New York. Pop. 7,322,564. Abbr. **NYC.** □□ **New York'er** *n.*

New Zea·land /zéélənd/ island country in the S Pacific, SE of Australia. Pop. 3,548,000. Capital: Wellington. □□ **New Zea'land·er** *n.*

Ni·ag·a·ra /nī-ágrə, –ágərə/ **Falls** falls of the Niagara River, along the U.S.-Canada border.

Nia·mey /nee-aámay/ capital of Niger, in the SW part. Pop. 391,900.

Nic·a·ra·gua /nikəraágwə/ republic in central Central America. Pop. 4,272,000. Capital: Managua. □□ **Nic·a·ra'guan** *n. & adj.*

Nice /nees/ port city in SE France. Pop. 345,700.

Nic·o·si·a /nikəseéə/ capital of Cyprus, in the central part. Pop. 186,400.

Ni·ger /níjər, neezhér/ republic in NW Africa. Pop. 9,113,000. Capital: Niamey. □□ **Ni·ge·ri·en** /nījeèreeən/ *n. & adj.*

Ni·ge·ri·a /nījeèreeə/ republic in W Africa. Pop. 103,912,000. Capital: Abuja. □□ **Ni·ge'ri·an** *n. & adj.*

Ni·ger /níjər/ **Riv·er** river in W Africa, flowing 2,600 mi. from S Guinea to the Gulf of Guinea.

Ni·ko·la·yev /nikəlaáyəf/ see MYUKOLAYIV.

Nile /nīl/ **Riv·er** river in E Africa, flowing 3,470 mi. from Lake Victoria to the Mediterranean Sea; longest river in the world.

Nîmes /neem/ city in S France. Pop. 133,600.

Nome /nōm/ city in W Alaska. Pop. 3,500.

Nor·folk /náwrfək, –fawk/ city in SE Virginia. Pop. 261,229.

Nor·man /náwrmən/ city in central Oklahoma. Pop. 80,071.

North Af·ri·ca term for region of Africa N of the Sahara Desert.

North A·mer·i·ca continent in the W hemisphere, comprising Canada, the United States, Mexico, and Central America. □□ **North A·mer'i·can** *n. & adj.*

North·amp·ton /nawrthámtən, –hámptən/ city in central England. Pop. 187,200.

North Car·o·li·na /karəlínə/ state in SE U.S. Pop. 6,628,637. Capital: Raleigh. Abbr. **NC; N.C.; N. Car.** □□ **North Car·o·lin'i·an** /–líneeən/ *n.*

North Da·ko·ta /dəkótə/ state in N central U.S. Pop. 638,800. Capital: Bismarck. Abbr. **ND; N.D.; N. Dak.** □□ **North Da·ko'tan** /–kót'n/ *n.*

North·ern Ire·land /írlənd/ the NE part of the island of Ireland; part of the United Kingdom. Pop. 1,583,000. Capital: Belfast. ¶ See note at GREAT BRITAIN.

North·ern Mar·i·an·a /maree-ánə, mer–/ **Is·lands** island group in the Pacific, N of Guam; U.S. possession. Pop. 52,000.

North Ko·re·a see KOREA.

North Pole N end of the earth's axis, in the Arctic Ocean.

North Sea arm of the Atlantic, between Britain and N Europe.

North·west Ter·ri·to·ries territory of Canada, in the NW part. Pop. 63,000. Capital: Yellowknife.

Nor·way /náwrway/ kingdom of N Europe. Pop. 4,384,000. Capital: Oslo.

Nor·we·gian /nawrweêjən/ **Sea** arm of the Arctic Ocean, between Greenland and Norway.

Nor·wich /náwrij, –ich/ city in E England. Pop. 128,100.

Not·ting·ham /naátingəm/ city in central England. Pop. 282,400.

Nou,dot>ak·chott /nóō-aákshaat/ capital of Mauritania, in the SW part. Pop. 393,300.

No·va Sco·tia /nōvə skóshə/ province in E Canada. Pop. 923,000. Capital: Halifax. □□ **No'va Sco'tian** *n. & adj.*

Nov·go·rod /naávgəraad/ city in W Russia. Pop. 233,000.

No·vo·si·birsk /nōvōsibeérsk/ city in SW Russia. Pop. 1,369,000.

Nu·bi·an /nóōbeeən, nyóō–/ **Des·ert** arid region in NE Sudan.

Nue·vo La·re·do /nóō-áyvō ləráydō/ city in E Mexico, across the Rio Grande from Laredo, Texas. Pop. 218,400.

Nue·vo Le·ón /lay-ón/ state in NE Mexico. Pop. 3,098,700. Capital: Monterrey.

Nu·ku·a·lo·fa /nōōkōōaláwfə, –lófə/ port city and capital of Tonga. Pop. 34,000.

Nu·rem·berg /nóōrəmbərg/ (German name **Nürnberg** /nÝrnbərk/) city in S Germany. Pop. 495,800.

Nya·sa /nī-ásə/, **Lake** (also called **Lake Malawi**) freshwater lake in SE Africa, E of Malawi.

O·a·hu /ō-aáhōō/ Hawaiian island; includes Honolulu.

Oak·land /ṓklənd/ city in W California. Pop. 372,242.

Oa·xa·ca /waahaákə/ state in S Mexico. Pop. 3,019,600. Capital: Oaxaca.

O·ce·an·i·a /ōshee-áneeə/ collective term for Australia and the Pacific islands.

O·cean·side /ṓshənsīd/ city in SW California. Pop. 128,398.

O·den·se /ṓd'n-sə/ port city in S Denmark. Pop. 182,600.

O·der /ṓdər/ **Riv·er** river in central Europe, flowing 570 mi. from E Czech Republic to the Baltic Sea.

O·des·sa /ōdésə/ port city in S Ukraine. Pop. 1,046,000.

Og·bo·mo·sho /aagbəmṓshō/ city in SW Nigeria. Pop. 711,900.

O·hi·o /ōhī́ō/ state in E central U.S. Pop. 10,847,115. Capital: Columbus. Abbr. **O.**; **OH** □□ **O·hi′o·an** *n. & adj.*

O·hi·o Riv·er river in E central U.S., flowing 980 mi. from W Pennsylvania into the Mississippi River at Cairo, Illinois.

O·ka·ya·ma /ōkəyaámə/ city in Japan, on Honshu. Pop. 616,100.

O·kee·cho·bee /ōkəchṓbee/, **Lake** lake in S Florida, in the N part of the Everglades.

O·ke·fe·no·kee /ōkeefənṓkee/ **Swamp** extensive wooded swamp area in S Georgia.

O·khotsk /əkháwtsk, ōkaátsk/, **Sea of** arm of the N Pacific, enclosed by the Kamchatka Peninsula and the Kuril Islands.

O·ki·na·wa /ōkinaáwə/ Japanese island between the East China Sea and the Pacific; largest of the Ryukyu Islands.

O·kla·ho·ma /ōkləhṓmə/ state in S central U.S. Pop. 3,145,585. Capital: Oklahoma City. Abbr. **OK**; **Okla.** □□ **O·kla·ho′man** *n. & adj.*

O·kla·ho·ma Cit·y capital of Oklahoma, in the central part. Pop. 444,719.

Old Faith·ful /fáythfŏŏl/ regularly erupting geyser in Yellowstone National Park, Wyoming.

O·lym·pi·a /ōlímpeeə/ **1** capital of Washington, in the W part. Pop. 33,840. **2** *hist.* ancient Greek city; site of the ancient Olympic games.

O·lym·pus /ōlímpəs/ mountain in N Greece; home of the gods in Greek mythology.

O·ma·ha /ṓməhaa, –haw/ city in E Nebraska. Pop. 335,795.

O·man /ōmaán/ independent sultanate on the SE Arabian Peninsula. Pop. 2,187,000. Capital: Muscat.

O·man, Gulf of arm of the Arabian Sea, at the entrance to the Persian Gulf.

Om·dur·man /aamdərmán/ city in NE central Sudan. Pop. 526,300.

Omsk /awmsk, aamsk/ city in SW Russia. Pop. 1,163,000.

On·tar·i·o /aantéreeō, –tár–/ province in S Canada. Pop. 10,746,000. Capital: Toronto. □□ **On·tar′i·an** *n. & adj.*

On·tar·i·o, Lake easternmost and smallest of the Great Lakes, N of W New York.

O·por·to /ōpáwrtō/ (also **Pôr′to**) port city in NW Portugal. Pop. 310,600.

O·ran /ōraán/ port city in NW Algeria. Pop. 609,800.

Or·ange /áwrinj, ór–/ city in SW California. Pop. 110,658.

O·ran·je·stad /awraányəstaad, –jəstad/ city in W Aruba. Pop. 20,000.

Or·e·gon /áwrigən, aàr–, –gaan/ state in NW U.S. Pop. 2,842,321. Capital: Salem. Abbr. **OR**; **Ore.** □□ **Or·e·go·ni·an** /awrigōneeən, aar–/ *n. & adj.*

Or·e·gon Trail 19th-century pioneer route extending W 2,000 mi. from Independence, Missouri, to Oregon.

Ork·ney /áwrknee/ **Is·lands** island group in the N Atlantic, off the NE tip of Scotland.

Or·lan·do /awrlándō/ city in central Florida. Pop. 164,693.

Or·lé·ans /awrlayaáN/ city in central France. Pop. 108,000.

O·sa·ka /ōsaákə/ city in Japan, on Honshu. Pop. 2,602,400.

Osh·kosh /aáshkaash/ city in E Wisconsin. Pop. 55,006.

Os·lo /aázlō, aàs–/ capital of Norway, in the SE part. Pop. 487,900.

O·stra·va /áwstrəvə/ city in E Czech Republic. Pop. 325,800.

Ot·ta·wa /aátəwə, –waa, –waw/ capital of Canada, in the SE part of Ontario. Pop. 314,000.

Oua·ga·dou·gou /waagədŏŏgōō/ capital of Burkina Faso, in the central part. Pop. 690,000.

O·ver·land /ōvərland, –lənd/ **Park** city in NE Kansas. Pop. 111,790.

O·vi·e·do /ōvee-áydō/ city in N Spain. Pop. 201,700.

Ox·ford /aáksfərd/ city in S England. Pop. 132,000.

Ox·nard /aáksnaard/ city in SW California. Pop. 142,216.

O·zark /ṓzaark/ **Moun·tains** mountain range in S central U.S.

Pa·chu·ca /pəchŏŏkə/ capital of Hidalgo, Mexico, in the central part. Pop. 174,000.

Pa·cif·ic /pəsífik/ **O·cean** ocean separating Asia and Australia from the Americas. Area 70,000,000 sq. mi.

Pa·cif·ic Rim the Pacific coastal regions of Asia, Australia, North America, and South America.

Pa·dang /paádaang/ port city in Indonesia, on Sumatra. Pop. 477,300.

Pad·u·a /pájəwə/ city in NE Italy. Pop. 212,600.

Pa·go Pa·go /paanggō paánggō/ capital of American Samoa, on Tutuila Island. Pop. 3,500.

Paint·ed /páyntəd/ **Des·ert** arid region in N central Arizona featuring multicolored rock surfaces.

Pa·ki·stan /pákistan, paakistaán/ republic in central Asia. Pop. 129,276,000. Capital: Islamabad. □□ **Pa·ki·stan′i** *n. & adj.*

Pa·lat·i·nate /pəlát'nayt/ district in Germany, W of the Rhine.

Pa·lem·bang /paaləmbaáng/ port city in Indonesia, on Sumatra. Pop. 1,084,500.

Pa·ler·mo /pəlérmō/ port city in W Sicily. Pop. 694,700.

Pal·es·tine /páləstīn, –steen/ **1** *hist.* ancient country on the E coast of the Mediterranean Sea. **2** (also called **Ho′ly Land**) area controlled by British 1923–48; now divided among Egypt, Israel, and Jordan. □□ **Pal·es·tin′i·an** /–stíneeən/ *n. & adj.*

Pal·ma /paálmə/ (also **Pal′ma de Ma·llor·ca** /day maayáwrkə, maalyáwrkə/) port city on island of Majorca, Spain. Pop. 296,754.

Pal·o Al·to /palō áltō/ city in W California. Pop. 55,900.

Pam·plo·na /pamplṓnə/ city in N Spain. Pop. 182,500.

Pan·a·ma /pánəmaa, –maw/ **1** republic in S Central America. Pop. 2,655,000. **2** (also **Pan′a·ma Cit′y**) port city and capital of Panama. Pop. 411,500. □□ **Pa·na·ma·ni·an** /panəmáyneeən/ *n. & adj.*

Pan·a·ma Ca·nal canal through the Isthmus of Panama, connecting the Pacific and Atlantic oceans.

Pan·chi·ao /paánchee-ów/ city in N Taiwan. Pop. 539,100.

Pa·pe·e·te /paapayáytay, paapétee/ port city and capital of French Polynesia, on Tahiti. Pop. 23,600.

Pap·u·a New Guin·ea /paápōōə nōō gínee, nyōō/ republic in the W Pacific, comprising the E part of New Guinea and nearby islands. Pop. 4,395,000. Capital: Port Moresby.

Par·a·dise /párədīs/ city in N California. Pop. 124,682.

Par·a·guay /párəgwī, –gway/ republic in central South America. Pop. 5,504,000. Capital: Asunción. □□ **Par·a·guay′an** *n. & adj.*

Par·a·mar·i·bo /parəmáribō/ port city and capital of Suriname. Pop. 77,600.

Par·is /páris, paareé/ port city and capital of France. Pop. 2,175,200. □□ **Pa·ri·sian** /pəreézhən/ *n. & adj.*

Par·ma /paármə/ city in N Italy. Pop. 169,300.

Pas·a·de·na /pásədeenə/ city in S California. Pop. 131,591.

Pat·er·son /pátərsən/ city in N New Jersey. Pop. 140,891.

Pat·na /pútnə/ city in NE India. Pop. 917,200.

Pearl /pərl/ **Har·bor** inlet on the S coast of Oahu, Hawaii.

Pe·king /paykíng, pee–/ see BEIJING.

Penn·syl·va·nia /pensəlváynyə/ state in NE U.S. Pop. 11,881,643. Capital: Harrisburg. Abbr. **PA**; **Pa.**; **Penn.**; **Penna.** □□ **Penn·syl·va′nian** *n. & adj.*

Pen·sa·co·la /pensəkṓlə/ city in NW Florida. Pop. 58,165.

Pe·o·ri·a /pee-áwreeə, –ṓr–/ city in NW central Illinois. Pop. 113,504.

Perm /perm/ city in W Russia. Pop. 1,032,000.

Per·nam·bu·co /pərnambóōkō/ see RECIFE.

Per·sia /púrzha/ **1** *hist.* ancient empire in W Asia. **2** official name (until 1935) of Iran.

Per·sian Gulf arm of the Arabian Sea, between the Arabian Peninsula and Iran.

Perth /pərth/ port city and capital of Western Australia, Australia. Pop. 809,000.

Pe·ru /pəróō/ republic in W South America. Pop. 24,523,000. Capital: Lima. □□ **Pe·ru′vi·an** /–veeən/ *n. & adj.*

Pe·sha·war /pəshaáwər/ city in N Pakistan. Pop. 566,300.

Pet·ri·fied /pétrifīd/ **For·est** part of the Painted Desert in E Arizona; contains prehistoric fossilized tree trunks.

Phil·a·del·phi·a /filədélfeeə/ city in SE Pennsylvania. Pop. 1,585,577.

Phil·ip·pines /filipeenz, filipeénz/ republic consisting of about 7,100 islands in the Pacific, SE of China. Pop. 63,609,000. Capital: Manila.

Phnom Penh /pənaam pén/ port city and capital of Cambodia. Pop. 920,000.

Phoe·nix /feéniks/ capital of Arizona, in the central part. Pop. 983,403.

Pierre /peer/ capital of South Dakota, in the central part. Pop. 12,906.

Pikes /pīks/ **Peak** mountain in the Rocky Mountains, in E central Colorado.

Pi·rae·us /pīreéəs, piráy–/ port city in E Greece. Pop. 169,600.

Pi·sa /peézə/ city in W Italy. Pop. 101,500.

Pitts·burgh /pítsbərg/ city in W Pennsylvania. Pop. 369,879.

Piu·ra /pyóōraa/ city in N Peru. Pop. 278,000.

Pla·no /pláynō/ city in NE Texas. Pop. 128,713.

Plo·es·ti /plaw-yéshtee, –yésht/ (also **Plo·ies'ti**) city in SE central Romania. Pop. 254,300.

Plym·outh /plímǝth/ **1** port city in SW England. Pop. 255,800. **2** city in SE Massachusetts. Pop. 45,608.

Pod·go·ri·ca /páwdgawreetsaa/ capital of Montenegro, in the SE part. Pop. 54,500.

Point Bar·row /bárō/ the N tip of Alaska; the northernmost point of the U.S.

Pointe-Noire /pwaant nwaár, nǝwaár/ port city in the SW Republic of the Congo. Pop. 576,200.

Po·land /pólǝnd/ republic in central Europe. Pop. 38,643,000. Capital: Warsaw.

Pol·y·ne·sia /paalǝneéezhǝ, –shǝ/ islands in the central Pacific, from New Zealand N to the Hawaiian Islands; a subdivision of Oceania. □□ **Pol·y·ne'sian** *n.* & *adj.*

Po·mo·na /pǝmónǝ/ city in S California. Pop. 131,723.

Pom·pa·no /paámpǝnō/ **Beach** city in SE Florida. Pop. 72,411.

Pon·ce /páwnsay/ port city in S Puerto Rico. Pop. 190,500.

Pont·char·train /paánchǝrtrayn, paanchǝrtráyn/, **Lake** shallow inlet of the Gulf of Mexico, N of New Orleans, Louisiana.

Poo·na /póônǝ/ city in W India. Pop. 1,559,600.

Po·po·cat·e·petl /pōpǝkaatépit'l/ volcanic peak in SW Mexico: 17,887 ft. high.

Port-au-Prince /pawrt ō príns, práNs/ port city and capital of Haiti. Pop. 846,200.

Port E·liz·a·beth /ilízǝbǝth/ port city in S South Africa. Pop. 303,400.

Port·land /páwrtlǝnd/ **1** city in NW Oregon. Pop. 437,319. **2** city in SW Maine. Pop. 64,358.

Port Lou·is /lóóis, lōō-eé/ port city and capital of Mauritius. Pop. 144,800.

Port Mores·by /máwrzbee/ port city and capital of Papua New Guinea. Pop. 193,200.

Pôr·to /páwrtōō/ see OPORTO.

Pôr·to A·le·gre /ǝlégrǝ/ port city in S Brazil. Pop. 1,237,200.

Port-of-Spain /spayn/ port city and capital of Trinidad and Tobago. Pop. 52,500.

Por·to-No·vo /pawrtō nóvō/ port city and capital of Benin. Pop. 177,700.

Port Sa·id /saa-eéd/ port city in NE Egypt. Pop. 460,000.

Ports·mouth /páwrtsmǝth/ **1** port city in SE Virginia. Pop. 103,907. **2** port city in S England. Pop. 189,100.

Por·tu·gal /páwrchǝgǝl/ republic in SW Europe, on the Iberian Peninsula. Pop. 9,865,000. Capital: Lisbon.

Port-Vi·la /pawrt veéla/ (also **Vi'la**) port city and capital of Vanuatu.

Po·to·mac /pǝtómik/ **Riv·er** river in E U.S., flowing 290 mi. from West Virginia to Chesapeake Bay.

Pots·dam /paátsdam/ city in NE Germany. Pop. 138,300.

Poz·nan /póznan, –nanyǝ/ city in W central Poland. Pop. 582,300.

Prague /praag/ capital of the Czech Republic, in the W central part. Pop. 1,213,300.

Prai·a /príǝ/ capital of Cape Verde, on São Tiago Island. Pop. 61,600.

Prai·rie /práiree/ **Prov·in·ces** term for the Canadian provinces of Alberta, Manitoba, and Saskatchewan.

Pres·i·den·tial Range mountain range in N New Hampshire; part of the White Mountain range.

Pre·to·ri·a /pritáwreeǝ/ administrative capital of South Africa, in the N part. Pop. 525,600.

Prince Ed·ward /prins édwǝrd/ **Is·land** island province in E Canada, in the Gulf of St. Lawrence. Pop. 132,000. Capital: Charlottetown.

Prince Wil·liam /wílyǝm/ **Sound** arm of the Gulf of Alaska, off the S coast of Alaska.

Prov·i·dence /praávǝdǝns/ capital of Rhode Island, in the NE part. Pop. 160,728.

Pro·vo /próvō/ city in N central Utah. Pop. 86,835.

Pue·bla /pwéblaa/ state in E central Mexico. Pop. 4,126,100. Capital: Puebla.

Pueb·lo /pwéblō, pwéblō-éblō/ city in SE central Colorado. Pop. 98,640.

Puer·to Ri·co /páwrtǝ reékō, pwértō/ island in the E central West Indies; self-governing commonwealth of the U.S. Pop. 3,819,000. Capital: San Juan. □□ **Puer'to Ri'can** /–kǝn/ *n.* & *adj.*

Puer·to Ri·co Trench Atlantic depression N of Puerto Rico; deepest part of the Atlantic: 28,374 ft.

Pu·get /pyóójit/ **Sound** arm of the Pacific, in NW Washington.

Pu·san /póósaán/ port city in SE South Korea. Pop. 3,813,800.

Pyong·yang /pyáwng-yaáng/ capital of North Korea, in the W part. Pop. 2,355,000.

Pyr·e·nees /peérǝneez/ mountain range in SW Europe, between France and Spain.

Qa·tar /kaátǝr, gútǝr/ peninsular emirate on the Persian Gulf. Pop. 548,000. Capital: Doha. □□ **Qa·tar'i** *n.* & *adj.*

Qing·dao /chíngdów/ (also **Tsing'tao'**) port city in E China. Pop. 1,459,200.

Qom /kōm/ city in NW Iran; Islamic holy site. Pop. 681,300.

Que·bec /kwibék, kibék/ **1** principally French-speaking province in E Canada. Pop. 7,209,000. **2** (also **Que·bec' Cit'y**) capital of Quebec, in the S part. Pop. 645,600. □□ **Que·beck'er, Que·bec·ois** /kaybekwaa/ *n.*

Queens /kweenz/ one of the five boroughs of New York City. Pop. 1,951,598.

Queens·land /kweénzlənd, –land/ state in NE Australia. Pop. 2,395,100. Capital: Brisbane.

Que·ré·ta·ro /kəráytərō/ state in central Mexico. Pop. 1,051,200. Capital: Querétaro.

Que·zon /kaysón/ **Cit·y** city in the Philippines, on Luzon. Pop. 1,676,600.

Quil·mes /keélmays/ city in E Argentina. Pop. 509,400.

Quin·ta·na Ro·o /keentaánə rố-ō/ state in E Mexico. Pop. 493,300. Capital: Chetumal.

Qui·to /keétō/ capital of Ecuador, in the N central part. Pop. 1,444,400.

Ra·bat /rəbaát/ port city and capital of Morocco. Pop. 518,600.

Ra·cine /rəseén, ray–/ city in SE Wisconsin. Pop. 84,298.

Rai·nier /rəneér, ray–/, **Mount** inactive volcano in W central Washington.

Ra·leigh /ráwlee, raálee/ capital of North Carolina, in the central part. Pop. 207,951.

Ran·cho Cu·ca·mon·ga /ránchō kōōkəmaánggə/ city in SW California. Pop. 101,409.

Ran·goon /ranggốn/ (also **Yan'gon**) port city and capital of Burma. Pop. 3,851,000.

Rap·id /rápid/ **Cit·y** city in SW South Dakota. Pop. 54,523.

Ra·ven·na /rəvénə/ city in NE Italy. Pop. 133,600.

Ra·wal·pin·di /raawəlpíndee/ city in N Pakistan. Pop. 794,800.

Read·ing /réding/ **1** city in SE Pennsylvania. Pop. 78,380. **2** city in S England. Pop. 137,700.

Re·ci·fe /rəseéfə/ (formerly **Pernambuco**) port city in NE Brazil. Pop. 1,297,000.

Red /red/ **Riv·er 1** river in S central U.S., flowing 1,300 mi. from E New Mexico through Texas and into the Mississippi River in Louisiana. **2** (also called **Red Riv'er of the North**) river in N central U.S., flowing 530 mi. along the Minnesota–North Dakota border into Lake Winnipeg in Canada.

Red Sea arm of the Indian Ocean, between the Arabian Peninsula and Africa.

Re·gi·na /rijínə/ capital of Saskatchewan, Canada, in the S part. Pop. 179,200.

Reims /reɴs, reemz/ city in NE France. Pop. 185,200.

Rennes /ren/ city in NW France. Pop. 203,500.

Re·no /reénō/ city in W Nevada. Pop. 133,850.

Ré·u·nion /ree-yốnyən/ island in the Indian Ocean; overseas department of France. Pop. 679,000. Capital: Saint-Denis.

Rey·kja·vik /ráykyəvik/ port city and capital of Iceland. Pop. 104,300.

Rhine /rīn/ **Riv·er** river in W Europe, flowing 820 mi. from Switzerland to the North Sea.

Rhode /rōd/ **Is·land** (official name **Rhode Island and Providence Plantations**) state in NE U.S. Pop. 1,003,464. Capital: Providence. Abbr. **RI; R.I.** □□ **Rhode Is'land·er** *n.*

Rhodes /rōdz/ Greek island in the Aegean Sea, off the SW coast of Turkey.

Rho·de·sia /rōdeézhə, –shə/ former region of S Africa under British control; in 1965 became independent countries of Southern Rhodesia (now Zimbabwe) and Northern Rhodesia (now Zambia).

Rhone /rōn/ **Riv·er** river in W Europe, flowing 500 mi. from Switzerland to the Mediterranean Sea.

Rich·mond /ríchmənd/ capital of Virginia, in the E part. Pop. 203,056.

Ri·ga /reégə/ port city and capital of Latvia. Pop. 839,700.

Rim·i·ni /ríminee/ port city in N Italy. Pop. 130,000.

Ri·o de Ja·nei·ro /reéō day zhənérō/ port city in SE Brazil. Pop. 5,473,900.

Ri·o Gran·de /gránd, grándee/ river in North America, flowing 1,800 mi. from Colorado to the Gulf of Mexico; forms the border between Texas and Mexico.

Riv·er·side /rívərsīd/ city in SW California. Pop. 226,505.

Ri·yadh /reeaád, reeyaád/ capital of Saudi Arabia, in the E central part. Pop. 1,800,000.

Ro·a·noke /rố·ənōk/ city in W Virginia. Pop. 96,397.

Roch·es·ter /raáchestər, –əstər/ city in W New York. Pop. 231,636.

Rock·ford /raákfərd/ city in N Illinois. Pop. 173,645.

Rock·y Moun·tains (also called the **Rock'ies**) mountain range in W North America, extending from New Mexico to Alaska.

Ro·ma·ni·a /rōmáyneeə, rōō–/ (also **Ru·ma'ni·a**) republic in SE Europe. Pop. 21,657,000. Capital: Bucharest.

Rome /rōm/ capital of Italy, in the W central part. Pop. 2,687,900.

Ro·sa·ri·o /rōsaáreeō, –zaár–/ port city in E central Argentina. Pop. 875,700.

Ro·seau /rōzố/ port city and capital of Dominica. Pop. 15,900.

Ross /raws, raas/ **Sea** arm of the S Pacific, extending into Antarctica, S of New Zealand.

Ros·tock /raástaak, –tawk/ city in N Germany. Pop. 232,600.

Ro·stov /rəstáwf/ port city in SW Russia. Pop. 1,026,000.

Rot·ter·dam /rȧtərdam/ port city in the W Netherlands. Pop. 599,400.

Rou·en /roōo-aȧN/ city in NW France. Pop. 105,500.

Ru·ma·ni·a /roōomáyneeə/ var. of ROMANIA.

Rush·more /rúshmawr/, **Mount** peak in the Black Hills of South Dakota, with carving of the faces of four U.S. presidents: Washington, Jefferson, T. Roosevelt, and Lincoln.

Rus·sia /rúshə/ republic in E Europe and Asia; chief republic of the former USSR. Pop. 148,178,000. Capital: Moscow.

Rwan·da /roōo-aȧndə/ republic in central Africa. Pop. 6,853,000. Capital: Kigali. □□ **Rwan'dan** *n.* & *adj.*

Sac·ra·men·to /sakrəméntō/ capital of California, in the N central part. Pop. 369,365.

Sa·har·a /səhárə, -haȧrə/ **Des·ert** extensive arid region in N Africa.

Sa·hel /səháyl, -heȯel/ arid region extending S from Senegal to Chad, S of the Sahara Desert.

Sai·gon /sīgaȧn, sígaan/ see HO CHI MINH CITY.

Saint Cath·a·rines /káthərinz, káthrinz/ city in S Ontario, Canada. Pop. 129,300.

St. Chris·to·pher /krístəfər/ **and Nevis** /neȯe-vis/ see ST. KITTS AND NEVIS.

Saint Geor·ge's /jórjəz/ capital of Grenada, on Grenada Island. Pop. 4,600.

St. Hel·ens, /hélənz/, **Mount** active volcano in the Cascade Mountains of Washington.

St. John's /jaȧnz/ **1** capital of Antigua and Barbuda, on NW Antigua. Pop. 21,500. **2** capital of Newfoundland, Canada, in the NE part. Pop. 171,900.

St. Jo·seph /jósəf, -zəf/ city in NW Missouri. Pop. 71,852.

St. Kitts /kits/ **and Ne·vis** /neȯevis/ (formerly **St. Christopher and Nevis**) two-island state in the E West Indies. Pop. 41,000. Capital: Basseterre.

St. Law·rence /láwrəns, laȧr-/ **Riv·er** river in SE Canada, flowing 760 mi. from Lake Ontario to the Atlantic.

St. Law·rence Sea·way international waterway for oceangoing ships, connecting the Great Lakes to the Atlantic.

St. Lou·is /loȯois/ city in E Missouri. Pop. 396,685.

St. Lu·cia /loȯoshə/ island country in the E West Indies. Pop. 158,000. Capital: Castries.

St. Paul /pawl/ capital of Minnesota, in the E part. Pop. 272,235.

St. Pe·ters·burg /peȯetərzbərg/ **1** (formerly **Leningrad** 1924–91) port city in NW Russia. Pop. 4,838,000. **2** city in W central Florida. Pop. 238,629.

St. Vin·cent /vínsənt/ **and the Gren·a·dines** /grénədeenz/ island state in the SE West Indies. Pop. 118,000. Capital: Kingstown.

Sa·kai /saȧkī/ port city in Japan, on Honshu. Pop. 808,100.

Sa·kha·lin /sakəleȯen/ **Is·land** island in SE Russia, N of Japan.

Sal·a·man·ca /saaləmaȧngkə/ city in W Spain. Pop. 167,400.

Sa·lem /sáyləm/ capital of Oregon, in the NW part. Pop. 107,786.

Sa·ler·no /səlérnō/ port city in W Italy. Pop. 146,500.

Sa·li·nas /səleȯenəs/ city in W California. Pop. 108,777.

Sa·lon·i·ka /səlaȧnikə/ see THESSALONIKE.

Sal·ti·llo /saalteȯeō, -teȯeyō/ capital of Coahuila, Mexico, in the SW part. Pop. 420,900.

Salt Lake Cit·y capital of Utah, in the N central part. Pop. 159,936.

Sal·ton /sáwlt'n/ **Sea** shallow salt lake in S California; 240 ft. below sea level.

Sal·va·dor /sálvədawr, salvədáwr/ port city in E Brazil. Pop. 2,070,300.

Salz·burg /sáwlzbərg, saȧlz-, zaȧlts-/ city in central Austria. Pop. 144,000.

Sa·ma·ra /səmaȧrə/ (formerly **Kuibyshev** 1935–91) port city in E Russia. Pop. 1,239,000.

Sam·ar·kand /sámərkand/ city in E Uzbekistan. Pop. 368,000.

Sa·mo·a /səmóə/ (also **Sa·mo'a Is'lands**) see AMERICAN SAMOA; WESTERN SAMOA.

Sa·naa /sanaȧ/ political capital of Yemen, in the W part. Pop. 503,600.

San An·dre·as /san andráyəs/ **Fault** earthquake zone extending S to N along the California coast.

San An·to·ni·o /san antóneeō, əntó-/ city in S central Texas. Pop. 935,933.

San Ber·nar·di·no /san bərnədeȯenō, -nər-/ city in SE California. Pop. 164,164.

San Bue·na·ven·tu·ra /san bwenəventoȯorə, -ventyoȯo-/ (also **Ventura**) port city in SW California. Pop. 92,575.

San Di·e·go /san dee-áygō/ city in S California. Pop. 1,110,549.

San Fran·cis·co /san frənsískō, fran-/ port city in W California. Pop. 723,959. □□ **San Fran·cis'can** *n.*

San Fran·cis·co Bay inlet of the Pacific, in W central California.

San Joa·quin /san waakeȯen/ **Val·ley** rich agricultural area in the S part of California's Central Valley.

San Jo·sé /saan hōzáy/ capital of Costa Rica, in the central part. Pop. 299,500.

San Jo·se /san hōzáy, əzáy/ city in W California. Pop. 782,248.

San Juan /san waán, hwaán/ port city and capital of Puerto Rico. Pop. 438,100.

San Jus·to /saan hóóstō/ city in E Argentina. Pop. 946,700.

San Lu·is Po·to·sí /saan lōōees pōtəseé/ state in central Mexico. Pop. 2,003,200. Capital: San Luis Potosí.

San Ma·ri·no /san məreénō/ republic in S Europe, surrounded by Italy; oldest independent country in Europe. Pop. 25,000. □□ **San Mar·i·nese'** /marəneéz, –neés/ n. & adj.

San Ni·co·lás de los Gar·zas /saan neekōlaás de laws gaársaas/ city in NE Mexico. Pop. 436,600.

San Pe·dro Su·la /saan páydrō sóólaa/ city in NW Honduras. Pop. 368,500.

San Sal·va·dor /san sálvədawr/ capital of El Salvador, in the S central part. Pop. 422,600.

San·ta An·a /santə ánə/ city in SW California. Pop. 293,742.

San·ta Bar·ba·ra /baárbərə, –brə/ city in SW California. Pop. 85,571.

San·ta Cat·a·li·na /kat'leénə/ **Is·land** (also **Cat·a·li'na Island**) island in SW California.

San·ta Cla·ra /klárə, klérə/ city in W California. Pop. 93,613.

San·ta Cla·ri·ta /kləreétə/ city in S California. Pop. 110,642.

San·ta Cruz /saántaa króóz/ city in central Bolivia. Pop. 767,300.

San·ta Cruz de Te·ne·rife /day tenəreéf, –ríf, –reéfay/ port city on Tenerife Island, Spain. Pop. 203,900.

San·ta Fe /santə fáy/ capital of New Mexico, in the N central part. Pop. 55,859.

San·ta Mon·i·ca /maánikə/ city in SW California. Pop. 86,905.

San·ta Ro·sa /rózə/ city in W California. Pop. 113,313.

San·ti·a·go /saantee–aágō, sant–/ capital of Chile, in the central part. Pop. 5,076,800.

San·ti·a·go de Cu·ba /saantyaágō day kóóbaa, kyóó–/ port city in SE Cuba. Pop. 440,100.

San·to Do·min·go /sáantō dəmínggō/ port city and capital of the Dominican Republic. Pop. 1,600,000.

San·to To·mé de Gua·ya·na /tōmáy daygwaayaánə/ (also **Ciu·dad' Gua·ya'na** /seeōō–daad, seeyōō–/) city in NE Venezuela. Pop. 453,000.

São Pau·lo /sow pówlō/ city in SE Brazil. Pop. 9,393,800.

São To·mé /təmáy/ capital of São Tomé and Principe, on NE São Tomé Island. Pop. 35,000.

São To·mé and Prin·ci·pe /prínsəpə/ island republic in W Africa, in the Gulf of Guinea. Pop. 144,000. Capital: São Tomé.

Sap·po·ro /saapórō, –páwrō/ city in Japan, on Hokkaido. Pop. 1,757,000.

Sar·a·gos·sa /sarəgósə/ (also **Za·ra·go'za**) city in NE Spain. Pop. 606,600.

Sa·ra·je·vo /sarəyáyvō, saar–/ capital of Bosnia and Herzegovina, in the E central part. Pop. 526,000.

Sar·a·so·ta /sarəsótə/ city in W central Florida. Pop. 50,961.

Sar·din·i·a /saardíneeə/ Italian island in the Mediterranean Sea, W of Italy. Pop. 1,645,192. Capital: Cagliari.

Sas·katch·e·wan /səskáchəwən, sas–, –waan/ province in central Canada. Pop. 1,003,000. Capital: Regina.

Sas·ka·toon /saskətóón/ city in S central Saskatchewan, Canada. Pop. 186,100.

Sau·di A·ra·bi·a /sówdee əráybeeə, sáwdee/ kingdom in SW Asia, on the Arabian Peninsula. Pop. 19,409,000. Capital: Riyadh. □□ **Sau'di, Sau·di A·ra'bi·an** n. & adj.

Sa·van·nah /səvánə/ city in E Georgia. Pop. 137,560.

Sa·van·nah Riv·er river in S U.S., flowing 300 mi. from NW South Carolina to the Atlantic; forms the boundary between South Carolina and Georgia.

Say·da /sídə/ see SIDON.

Scan·di·na·vi·a /skandináyveeə/ **1** region of N Europe; includes Denmark, Norway, Sweden, and sometimes Finland, Iceland, and the Faeroe Islands. **2** (also called **Scan·di·na' vi·an Pen·in'su·la**) peninsula in N Europe, bounded by the Norwegian, North, and Baltic seas and the Gulf of Bothnia, and comprising Norway and Sweden. □□ **Scan·di·na'vi·an** n. & adj.

Scar·bor·ough /skaárbərō, –brə/ city in SE Ontario, Canada. Pop. 524,600.

Sche·nec·ta·dy /skənéktədee/ city in E New York. Pop. 65,566.

Schuyl·kill /skóólkil, skóókəl, skóólkəl/ **Riv·er** river in Pennsylvania, flowing 130 mi. from E central Pennsylvania into the Delaware River at Philadelphia.

Scil·ly /sílee/, **Isles of** island group in the Atlantic, off the SW coast of England.

Scot·land /skaátlənd/ division of the United Kingdom, N of England. Pop. 4,770,600. Capital: Edinburgh.

Scotts·dale /skaátsdayl/ city in SW central Arizona. Pop. 130,069.

Scran·ton /skránt'n/ city in NE Pennsylvania. Pop. 81,805.

Se·at·tle /seeát'l/ port city in W central Washington. Pop. 516,259.

Seine /sayn, sen/ **Riv·er** river in France, flowing 480 mi. from E France through Paris and into the English Channel.

Se·ma·rang /səmaáraang/ port city in Indonesia, on Java. Pop. 1,005,300.

Sen·dai /séndī/ city in Japan, on Honshu. Pop. 971,300.

Sen·e·gal /senəgáwl/ republic in W Africa. Pop. 9,093,000. Capital: Dakar. □□ **Sen·e·gal·ese** /–eéz/ n. & adj.

Seoul /sōl/ capital of South Korea, in the NW part. Pop. 10,229,300.

Ser·bi·a /súrbeeə/ republic in SE Europe; formerly part of Yugoslavia. Pop. 9,979,000. Capital: Belgrade. □□ **Serb** n. & adj.

Se·vas·to·pol /səvástəpōl, –pawl/ port city in S Ukraine. Pop. 365,000.

Se·ville /səvíl/ port city in SW Spain. Pop. 714,100.

Sey·chelles /sayshél, –shélz/ island republic in the Indian Ocean, NE of Madagascar. Pop. 78,000. Capital: Victoria.

Shang·hai /shanghí, shánghī/ port city in E China. Pop. 7,830,000.

Shef·field /shéfeeld/ city in N England. Pop. 530,100.

Shen·yang /shúnyaáng/ city in NE China. Pop. 4,540,000.

Shet·land /shétlənd/ **Is·lands** island group in the N Atlantic, off the NE coast of Scotland.

Shi·ko·ku /shikōkōō/ island in Japan, S of Honshu.

Shi·raz /shiraáz/ city in SW Iran. Pop. 965,100.

Shreve·port /shreévpawrt, –pōrt/ city in NW Louisiana. Pop. 198,525.

Shub·ra al-Khay·mah /shōōbraá al kīmaá, –maákh/ city in N Egypt. Pop. 834,000.

Si·am /sī-ám/ see THAILAND.

Si·an /sheéaán/ see XIAN.

Sic·i·ly /sísəlee/ Italian island in the Mediterranean Sea, off the SW tip of Italy. Pop. 4,910,000. Capital: Palermo.

Si·don /sīd'n/ (also **Say′da**) port city in SW Lebanon. Pop. 100,000.

Si·er·ra Le·one /see-érə lee-ón/ republic in W Africa. Pop. 4,793,000. Capital: Freetown. □□ **Si·er′ra Le·o′ne·an** /–neeən/ n. & adj.

Si·er·ra Ne·va·da /nəvádə, –vaádə/ **1** mountain range in E California. **2** mountain range in S Spain.

Sil·i·con Val·ley area in W California, from San Jose to Palo Alto.

Si·mi /simeé, seémee/ **Val·ley** city in SW California. Pop. 100,217.

Si·nai /sínī/ **Pen·in·su·la** peninsula in NE Egypt, bounded by the gulfs of Suez and Aqaba and the Red Sea.

Si·na·lo·a /seenəlóə/ state in NW Mexico. Pop. 2,204,100. Capital: Culiacán.

Sin·ga·pore /síngəpawr, sínggə–/ republic in SE Asia, at the S tip of the Malay Peninsula. Pop. 3,397,000. Capital: Singapore. □□ **Sin·ga·po′re·an** /–reeən/ n.

Sioux /sōō/ **Cit·y** city in W Iowa. Pop. 80,505.

Sioux Falls city in SE South Dakota. Pop. 100,814.

Skop·je /skáwpye, –yay/ capital of Macedonia, in the N part. Pop. 541,300.

Skye /skī/ island in the Hebrides, off the NW coast of Scotland.

Slo·va·ki·a /sləvaákeeə, slō–/ (also called **Slo′vak Re·pub′lic**) republic in central Europe; formerly part of Czechoslovakia. Pop. 5,374,000. Capital: Bratislava.

Slo·ve·ni·a /sləveéneeə, slō–/ republic in S Europe; formerly part of Yugoslavia. Pop. 1,951,000. Capital: Ljubljana. □□ **Slo·ve′ni·an** n. & adj.

Smo·lensk /sməlénsk/ city in W Russia. Pop. 355,000.

Smyr·na /smúrnə/ see IZMIR.

Snake /snayk/ **Riv·er** river in NW U.S., flowing 1,040 mi. from Yellowstone National Park, Wyoming, to the Columbia River in Washington.

So·ci·e·ty /səsíətee/ **Is·lands** island group in the S Pacific, forming part of French Polynesia.

So·fi·a /sōfeéə, sō–/ capital of Bulgaria, in the W part. Pop. 1,116,800.

Sol·o·mon /saáləmən/ **Is·lands** island country, in the Pacific, E of New Guinea. Pop. 413,000. Capital: Honiara.

So·ma·li·a /səmaályə, –eeə/ republic in E Africa. Pop. 9,639,000. Capital: Mogadishu. □□ **So·ma′li** n. **So·ma′li·an** adj.

So·no·ra /sənáwrə/ state in NW Mexico. Pop. 1,823,600. Capital: Hermosillo.

So·no·ran /sənáwrən/ **Des·ert** arid region in SW Arizona, SE California, and NW Mexico.

South Af·ri·ca republic in S Africa. Capitals: Bloemfontein; Cape Town; Pretoria. Pop. 41,743,000. □□ **South′ Af′ri·can** n. & adj.

South A·mer·i·ca continent in the W hemisphere, S of Panama. □□ **South′ A·mer′i·can** n. & adj.

South·amp·ton /sowthámtən, sowth-hámp–/ port city in S England. Pop. 211,700.

South Aus·tral·ia state in S central Australia. Pop. 1,285,000. Capital: Adelaide.

South Bend /bend/ city in N Indiana. Pop. 105,511.

South Car·o·li·na /karəlínə/ state in SE U.S. Pop. 3,486,703. Capital: Columbia. Abbr. **SC; S.C.; S. Car.** □□ **South Car·o·lin·i·an** /–líneeən/ *n. & adj.*

South Chi·na Sea arm of the W Pacific, enclosed by Borneo and the Philippines.

South Da·ko·ta /dəkótə/ state in N central U.S. Pop. 696,004. Capital: Pierre. Abbr. **SD; S.D.; S. Dak.** □□ **South' Da·ko'tan** *n. & adj.*

South Ko·re·a see KOREA.

South Pole S end of the earth's axis, on Antarctica.

So·vi·et /sóvee–ət/ **Un·ion** see UNION OF SOVIET SOCIALIST REPUBLICS.

So·we·to /səwétō, –wáytō/ group of townships in N South Africa. Pop. 596,600.

Spain /spayn/ monarchy in SW Europe, on the Iberian Peninsula. Pop. 39,181,000. Capital: Madrid.

Spice /spīs/ **Is·lands** see MOLUCCAS.

Spo·kane /spōkán/ city in E Washington. Pop. 177,196.

Spring·field /spríngfeeld/ **1** capital of Illinois, in the central part. Pop. 105,227. **2** city in SW Massachusetts. Pop. 156,983. **3** city in SW Missouri. Pop. 140,494.

Sri Lan·ka /sree laángkə, shree/ (formerly **Ceylon**) island republic in the Indian Ocean, off the S tip of India. Pop. 18,553,000. Capital: Colombo. □□ **Sri Lank'an** *n. & adj.*

Staked /staykt/ **Plain** see LLANO ESTACADO.

Sta·lin·grad /staálingrad/ see VOLGOGRAD.

Stam·ford /stámfərd/ city in SW Connecticut. Pop. 108,056.

Stat·en /stát'n/ **Is·land** island in New York Bay; one of the five boroughs of New York City. Pop. 378,977.

Stav·ro·pol /staavráwpəl, –ró–/ city in S Russia. Pop. 342,000.

Stock·holm /staákhōlm, –hōm/ port city and capital of Sweden. Pop. 711,100.

Stock·ton /staáktən/ city in central California. Pop. 210,943.

Stoke-on-Trent /stōk aan trént/ city in W central England. Pop. 254,200.

Stras·bourg /straasbóōrg, straásbərg/ city in NE France. Pop. 255,900.

Stutt·gart /shtóōtgaart/ city in SW Germany. Pop. 588,500.

Su·cre /sóōkray/ legislative capital of Bolivia, in the S part. Pop. 145,000.

Su·dan /sōōdán, –daán/ republic in NE Africa. Pop. 31,548,000. Capital: Khartoum.

Su·ez /sōō-éz, sóōez/ port city in NE Egypt. Pop. 388,000.

Su·ez Ca·nal canal in NE Egypt, connecting the Mediterranean and Red seas.

Su·la·we·si /sōōlaawáysee/ (formerly **Celebes**) island in central Indonesia, in the Malay Archipelago.

Su·ma·tra /sōōmaátrə/ island in W Indonesia.

Sum·ga·it /sōōmgaa-eét/ city in E Azerbaijan. Pop. 236,200.

Sun·chon /sóōncháwn/ city in S South Korea. Pop. 136,000.

Sun·da /sə́ndə, sóōndaa/ **Is·lands** island chain in the Malay Archipelago; includes Borneo, Java, Sumatra, and smaller islands.

Sun·ny·vale /sə́neevayl/ city in W California. Pop. 117,229.

Su·pe·ri·or /sōōpeéreeər/, **Lake** northernmost and largest of the Great Lakes, N of Michigan.

Su·ra·ba·ya /sōōrəbíə/ port city in Indonesia, on Java. Pop. 2,421,000.

Su·rat /sōōrət, sōōraát/ port city in W India. Pop. 1,498,800.

Su·ri·na·me /sōōrinaám, –nám/ republic in N South America. Pop. 436,000. Capital: Paramaribo. □□ **Su·ri·na·mese** /sōōrənəmeéz, –meés/ *n. & adj.*

Su·va /sóōvə/ port city and capital of Fiji. Pop. 69,700.

Su·won /sóōwə́n/ city in NW South Korea. Pop. 755,500.

Sverd·lovsk /sferdláwfsk/ (also called **Ye·ka' te·rin·burg**) city in W Russia. Pop. 1,280,000.

Swan·sea /swaánzee/ port city in S Wales, United Kingdom. Pop. 189,300.

Swa·zi·land /swaázeeland/ kingdom in S Africa. Pop. 999,000. Capital: Mbabane.

Swe·den /sweéd'n/ kingdom in N Europe. Pop. 8,901,000. Capital: Stockholm. □□ **Swede** /sweed/ *n.* **Swed'ish** *adj.*

Switz·er·land /swítsərlənd/ republic in central Europe. Pop. 6,779,000. Capital: Bern.

Syd·ney /sídnee/ port city and capital of New South Wales, Australia. Pop. 3,772,700.

Syr·a·cuse /seérəkyōōs, sér–, –kyōōz/ city in central New York. Pop. 163,860.

Syr·i·a /seéreeə/ republic in SW Asia. Pop. 15,609,000. Capital: Damascus. □□ **Syr'i·an** *n. & adj.*

Szcze·cin /shchétseen/ port city in NW Poland. Pop. 419,600.

Ta·bas·co /təbáskō/ state in SE Mexico. Capital: Villahermosa. Pop. 1,501,700.

Ta·briz /təbreéz/ city in NW Iran. Pop. 1,089,000.

Ta·co·ma /təkómə/ port city in W central Washington. Pop. 176,664.

Ta·dzhik·i·stan /taajhèkistán, –taán/ republic in central Asia; formerly part of the USSR. Pop. 5,916,000. Capital: Dushanbe. □□ **Ta· dzhik'** *n.*

Tae·gu /tágóo/ city in SE South Korea. Pop. 2,449,100.

Tae·jon /tájáwn/ city in central South Korea. Pop. 1,272,100.

Ta·gus /táygəs/ **Riv·er** river on the Iberian Peninsula, flowing 570 mi. from E central Spain through Portugal and into the Atlantic.

Ta·hi·ti /təheétee/ island in the S Pacific; one of the Society Islands. □□ **Ta·hi'tian** /–shən/ *n. & adj.*

Ta·hoe /taáhō/, **Lake** glacial lake in the Sierra Nevada range, on the California-Nevada border: 6,228 ft. above sea level.

Tai·chung /tíchóng/ city in W central Taiwan. Pop. 761,800.

Ta·if /taáif/ city in W Saudi Arabia. Pop. 300,000.

Tai·nan /tínaán/ city in SW Taiwan. Pop. 683,300.

Tai·pei /típáy, –báy/ capital of Taiwan, in the N part. Pop. 2,626,100.

Tai·wan /tīwaán/ (also called **For·mo'sa**) island nation in SE China. Pop. 21,466,000. Capital: Taipei. □□ **Tai·wan·ese** /tīwəneéz/ *n. & adj.*

Tai·yuan /tíyōō-aán/ city in N China. Pop. 1,533,900.

Ta·lien /daálee-én/ see DALIAN.

Tal·la·has·see /taləhásee/ capital of Florida, in the NW part. Pop. 124,773.

Tal·linn /taályin, tál–, –lin/ port city and capital of Estonia. Pop. 434,800.

Ta·mau·li·pas /taamowleépaas/ state in NE Mexico. Pop. 2,249,600. Capital: Ciudad Victoria.

Tam·pa /támpə/ city in W central Florida. Pop. 280,015.

Tam·pi·co /tampeékō/ port city in E Mexico. Pop. 272,700.

Tan·gan·yi·ka /tangənyeékə, tanggən–/, **Lake** freshwater lake in central Africa, between Tanzania and Congo (formerly Zaire).

Tan·gier /tanjeér/ (also **Tan·giers** /–jeérz/) port city in N Morocco. Pop. 307,000.

Tang·shan /taángshaán/ city in NE China. Pop. 1,500,000.

Tan·za·ni·a /tanzəneéə/ republic in E Africa, formed by the merger of Tanganyika and Zanzibar. Pop. 29,058,000. Capital: Dar es Salaam. □□ **Tan·za·ni'an** *n. & adj.*

Tash·kent /tashként/ capital of Uzbekistan, in the E part. Pop. 2,106,000.

Tas·ma·ni·a /tazmáyneeə/ island state in SE Australia, S of Victoria. Pop. 452,800. Capital: Hobart.

Tbi·li·si /təbəleésee/ capital of the republic of Georgia, in the SE part. Pop. 1,279,000.

Te·gu·ci·gal·pa /təgōōsigálpə, –gaál–/ capital of Honduras, in the S part. Pop. 608,100.

Teh·ran /tayrán, –raán, tayə–/ (also **Te·he·ran**) capital of Iran, in the NW central part. Pop. 6,042,600.

Tel A·viv-Jaf·fa /tel əveev jaáfə/ (also called **Tel A·viv'**) city in W central Israel. Pop. 321,700.

Tem·pe /témpee/ city in central Arizona. Pop. 141,865.

Ten·nes·see /tenəseé/ state in S central U.S. Pop. 4,877,185. Capital: Nashville. Abbr. **Tenn.**; **TN** □□ **Ten·nes·see'an** *n. & adj.*

Ten·nes·see Riv·er river in E central U.S., flowing 650 mi. from E Tennessee through Alabama and W Tennessee and Kentucky and into the Ohio River.

Te·pic /taypeék/ capital of Nayarit, Mexico, in the W part. Pop. 207,000.

Ter·re Haute /terə hót, hót/ city in W Indiana. Pop. 57,483.

Te·ton /teéton/ **Range** mountain range in W Wyoming, part of the Rocky Mountain range.

Tex·as /téksəs/ state in S U.S. Pop. 16,986,510. Capital: Austin. Abbr. **Tex.**; **TX** □□ **Tex'an** *n. & adj.*

Thai·land /tílənd, –land/ (formerly **Siam**) kingdom in SE Asia. Pop. 58,851,000. Capital: Bangkok.

Thai·land, Gulf of arm of the South China Sea, S and W of Thailand.

Thames /temz/ **Riv·er** river in S England, flowing 210 mi. from Gloucestershire through London and into the North Sea.

Thana /taánə/ city in W India. Pop. 803,400.

Thes·sa·lo·ni·ke /thesəlawneékee/ (also called **Salon'ika**) port city in NE Greece. Pop. 378,000.

Thim·phu /thimpóo/ official capital of Bhutan. Pop. 30,300.

Thou·sand Is·lands group of about 1,700 islands in the St. Lawrence River, between Ontario, Canada, and New York.

Thou·sand Oaks /ōks/ city in SW California. Pop. 104,352.

Tian·jin /tee-aánjín, tee-én–/ (formerly **Tientsin**) port city in NE China. Pop. 5,770,000.

Ti·bet /tibét/ autonomous region of W China. Capital: Lhasa.

Tien·tsin /tíntsín/ see TIANJIN.

Ti·er·ra del Fue·go /tee-érə del fwáygō/ island group at the S tip of South America; divided between Chile and Argentina.

Ti·gris /tígris/ **Riv·er** river in SW Asia, flowing 1,150 mi. from Turkey to the Euphrates River in Iraq.

Ti·jua·na /tihwaánə, teeəwaánə/ city in NW Mexico. Pop. 698,800.

Til·burg /tílbərg/ city in the S Netherlands. Pop. 164,100.

Ti·mi·soa·ra /teemishwaárǝ/ city in W Romania. Pop. 325,400.

Ti·ra·në /tiraánǝ/ capital of Albania, in the central part. Pop. 300,000.

Ti·ti·ca·ca /titeekaáka/, **Lake** lake on the Bolivia-Peru border: 12,508 ft. above sea level.

Tlax·ca·la /tlaaskaálǝ, tǝlaa–/ state in central Mexico. Pop. 761,300. Capital: Tlaxcala.

To·go /tógō/ country in W Africa. Pop. 4,571,000. Capital: Lomé.

To·ky·o /tókeeō/ capital of Japan, on Honshu. Pop. 7,966,200.

To·le·do /tǝleédō/ city in NW Ohio. Pop. 332,943.

To·lu·ca /tǝlóōkǝ/ capital of Mexico, Mexico, in the S part. Pop. 827,300.

Ton·ga /taánggǝ, táwng–/ island kingdom in the S Pacific, NE of New Zealand. Pop. 106,000. Capital: Nukualofa. □□ **Ton'gan** n. & adj.

To·pe·ka /tǝpeékǝ/ capital of Kansas, in the NE part. Pop. 119,883.

To·ri·no /tǝreénō/ see TURIN.

To·ron·to /tǝraántō/ capital of Ontario, Canada, in the SE part. Pop. 3,893,000.

Tor·rance /táwrǝns, taár–/ city in SW California. Pop. 133,107.

Tor·re·ón /tawray-ón/ city in N Mexico. Pop. 328,100.

Tou·lon /tōōláwN/ port city in SE France. Pop. 170,200.

Tou·louse /tōōlóōz/ city in S France. Pop. 365,900.

Tours /tōōr/ city in NW central France. Pop. 133,400.

Trans·vaal /tranzvaál/ province in NE South Africa.

Tran·syl·va·nia /transilváyneeǝ/ a region and former province of central Romania.

Tren·ton /trént'n/ capital of New Jersey, in the W central part. Pop. 88,675.

Tri·este /tree-ést/ port city in NE Italy. Pop. 226,700.

Trin·i·dad /trínidad/ **and To·ba·go** /tǝbáygō/ island republic in the SE West Indies. Pop. 1,272,000. Capital: Port-of-Spain.

Trip·o·li /trípǝlee/ **1** capital of Libya, in the NW part. Pop. 591,100. **2** port city in NW Lebanon. Pop. 240,000.

Trond·heim /traánhaym/ port city in central Norway. Pop. 143,700.

Troy /troy/ **1** hist. ancient city in NW Asia Minor (present-day Turkey). **2** city in E New York. Pop. 72,884. □□ **Tro·jan** /trójǝn/ adj.

Tru·ji·llo /trōōheéyō/ port city in NW Peru. Pop. 509,300.

Tsing·tao /tsíngtów/ see QINGDAO.

Tuc·son /tóōsaan/ city in S central Arizona. Pop. 405,390.

Tul·sa /túlsǝ/ city in NE Oklahoma. Pop. 367,302.

Tu·nis /tóōnis, tyōō–/ port city and capital of Tunisia. Pop. 674,100.

Tu·ni·sia /tōōneézhǝ, tyōō–, –nízhǝ/ republic in N Africa. Pop. 9,020,000. Capital: Tunis. □□ **Tu·ni'sian** n. & adj.

Tu·rin /tōōrin, tōōrín, tyōō–, tyōō–/ (Italian name **To·ri'no**) city in NW Italy. Pop. 945,600.

Tur·key /tǝrkee/ republic in W Asia and SE Europe. Pop. 62,484,000. Capital: Ankara.

Turk·me·ni·stan /tǝrkménistan/ republic in S Asia; formerly part of the USSR. Pop. 4,149,000. Capital: Ashgabat. □□ **Turk·men** n.

Turks /túrks/ **and Cai·cos** /kíkōs, káykōs/ **Is·lands** two island groups in the N Atlantic, SE of the Bahamas; dependent territory of the United Kingdom. Pop. 14,000. Capital: Grand Turk.

Tus·ca·loo·sa /tǝskǝlóōsǝ/ city in W Alabama. Pop. 77,759.

Tu·va·lu /tōōvaálōō, tyōō–, –vaár–/ island nation in the S Pacific, N of Fiji. Pop. 10,000. Capital: Funafuti.

Tux·tla /tóōstlaa/ (official name **Tux'tla Gu·ti·ér·rez** /gōōtyérays/) capital of Chiapas, Mexico, in the W central part. Pop. 289,600.

Tver /tver/ see KALININ.

U·fa /ōōfaá/ city in W Russia. Pop. 1,094,000.

U·gan·da /ōōgándǝ, yōō–/ republic in E Africa. Pop. 20,158,000. Capital: Kampala. □□ **U·gan'dan** n. & adj.

U·jung Pan·dang /óōjōōng paadaáng/ port city in Indonesia, on Sulawesi. Pop. 913,200.

U·kraine /yōōkráyn/ republic in E Europe; formerly part of the USSR. Pop. 50,864,000. Capital: Kiev.

U·lan Ba·tor /óōlaan baátawr/ (also **U·laan·baa'tar**) capital of Mongolia, in the N central part. Pop. 619,000.

Ulm /ōōlm/ city in S Germany. Pop. 115,100.

Ul·san /óōlsaán/ city in SE South Korea. Pop. 967,400.

Un·ion of So·vi·et So·cial·ist Re·pub·lics (also called **So'vi·et Un'ion**) former union of fifteen constituent republics under Soviet direction, in E Europe and Asia; dissolved in 1991. Abbr. USSR □□ **So'vi·et** n. & adj.

U·nit·ed Ar·ab E·mir·ates /árǝb émǝrǝts, –rayts/ independent federation of seven emirates on the Persian Gulf. Pop. 3,057,000. Capital: Abu Dhabi.

U·nit·ed King·dom monarchy in NW Europe; includes England, Northern Ireland, Scotland, and Wales. Pop. 58,490,000. Capital: London. Abbr. **UK; U.K.**

U·nit·ed States of A·mer·i·ca federal republic of 50 states: 49 states in North America and the island state of Hawaii in the N Pacific. Pop. 265,563,000. Capital: Washington, D.C. Abbr. **US; U.S.; USA; U.S.A.**

Upp·sa·la /ə́psəlaa, –saalə/ city in E Sweden. Pop. 183,500.

U·ral /yoŏrəl/ **Moun·tains** mountain range in W Russia; considered part of the boundary between Europe and Asia.

Ur·fa /ŏŏrfaa/ city in SE Turkey. Pop. 357,900.

U·ru·guay /ŏŏrəgwī, yŏŏ–, –gway/ republic in SE South America. Pop. 3,239,000. Capital: Montevideo. □□ **U·ru·guay'an** n. & adj.

Ü·rüm·qi /ŏŏrŏŏm-chee/ city in W China. Pop. 1,160,000.

USSR see UNION OF SOVIET SOCIALIST REPUBLICS.

U·tah /yoŏtaa, –taw/ state in W U.S. Pop. 1,722,850. Capital: Salt Lake City. Abbr. **UT; Ut.** □□ **U·tah·an** /yoŏtaáən, –táwən, yoŏtaan, –tawn/ n. & adj.

U·trecht /oŏtrekt, yoŏ–/ city in the central Netherlands. Pop. 235,400.

Uz·bek·i·stan /ŏŏzbékistaan, –stan/ republic in S central Asia; formerly part of the USSR. Pop. 23,418,000. Capital: Tashkent. □□ **Uz' bek** n.

Va·duz /faadoŏts/ capital of Liechtenstein, in the W part. Pop. 5,100.

Va·len·ci·a /vaalénseeə, –thyaa/ 1 port city in E Spain. Pop. 752,900. 2 city in N Venezuela. Pop. 903,100.

Va·lla·do·lid /valədəlíd, –leéd/ city in NW central Spain. Pop. 336,900.

Val·le·jo /vəláyō/ city in central California. Pop. 109,199.

Val·let·ta /vəlétə/ port city and capital of Malta. Pop. 9,100.

Val·pa·rai·so /valpərízō/ port city in central Chile. Pop. 282,200.

Van·cou·ver /vankoŏvər/ 1 island in SW Canada, off the SW coast of British Columbia. 2 port city in S British Columbia. Pop. 471,800.

Va·nu·a·tu /vaánəwaátŏŏ, vaányə–/ island republic in the Pacific, NE of Australia. Pop. 178,000. Capital: Port-Vila.

Va·ra·na·si /vəraánəsee/ (formerly **Benares**) city in NE India. Pop. 929,300.

Var·na /vaárnə/ port city in E Bulgaria. Pop. 301,400.

Vat·i·can /vátikən/ **Cit·y** independent seat of the Roman Catholic Church, within the city of Rome, Italy.

Ve·ne·zia /vənétseeə/ see VENICE.

Ven·e·zue·la /venəzəwáylə, –zwáylə/ republic in N South America. Pop. 21,983,000. Capital: Caracas. □□ **Ven·e·zue' lan** n. & adj.

Ven·ice /vénis/ (Italian name **Ve·ne·zia** /vənétseeə/) port city in NE Italy. Pop. 306,400. □□ **Ve·ne·tian** /neéshən/ n. & adj.

Ven·tu·ra /ventyoŏrə, –choŏr–/ See SAN BUENAVENTURA.

Ve·ra·cruz /verəkroŏs, –kroŏz/ 1 state in E central Mexico. Pop. 6,228,200. Capital: Jalapa. 2 port city in E Veracruz, Mexico. Pop. 438,800.

Ver·mont /vərmaánt/ state in NE U.S. Pop. 562,758. Capital: Montpelier. Abbr. **VT; Vt.** □□ **Ver·mont' er** n.

Ve·ro·na /vərónə/ city in N Italy. Pop. 256,800.

Ve·su·vi·us /vəsoŏveeəs/ active volcano near Naples, Italy.

Vic·to·ri·a /viktáwreeə/ 1 capital of British Columbia, Canada, on Vancouver Island. Pop. 71,200. 2 state in SE Australia. Pop. 3,832,400. Capital: Melbourne. 3 port city and capital of Seychelles. Pop. 25,000.

Vic·to·ri·a, Lake freshwater lake in E central Africa; main source of the Nile River.

Vic·to·ri·a Falls waterfall in S Africa, on the Zambezi River: 420 ft. high.

Vi·en·na /vee-énə/ capital of Austria, in the NE part. Pop. 1,533,200. □□ **Vi·en·nese** /veeəneéz/ n. & adj.

Vien·tiane /vyentyaán/ capital of Laos, in the NW part. Pop. 178,200.

Vi·et·nam /vee-étnaám, veeət–, –nám/ republic in SE Asia, on the S China Sea. Pop. 73,977,000. Capital: Hanoi.

Vi·go /veégō/ port city in NW Spain. Pop. 288,600.

Vi·la /veélə/ see PORT-VILA.

Vi·lla·her·mo·sa /veeyə-ermósə, veelyə–/ capital of Tabasco, Mexico, in the S central part. Pop. 261,200.

Vil·ni·us /vílneeəs/ capital of Lithuania, in the SE part. Pop. 590,100.

Vir·gin·ia /vərjínyə/ state in E U.S. Pop. 6,187,358. Capital: Richmond. Abbr. **VA; Va.** □□ **Vir·gin' ian** n. & adj.

Vir·gin·ia Beach city in SE Virginia. Pop. 393,069.

Vir·gin /vərjin/ **Is·lands of the U·nit·ed States** island group in the E West Indies; U.S. possession. Pop. 101,800. Capital: Charlotte Amalie.

Vi·sa·kha·pat·nam /visaakəpátnəm/ port city in E India. Pop. 752,000.

Vla·di·kav·kaz /vlaadəkaáfkaaz/ city in S Russia. Pop. 325,000.

Vla·di·vos·tok /vladivaástaak, –vəstaák/ port city in SE Russia. Pop. 632,000.

Vol·ga /vaálgə, váwl–, vól–/ **Riv·er** river in E

Europe, flowing 2,320 mi. from W Russia to the Caspian Sea; longest river in Europe.

Vol·go·grad /va'algəgrad, vól–/ (formerly **Stalingrad**) city in SW Russia. Pop. 1,003,000.

Vo·ro·shi·lov·grad /vərawshe'eləfgraad/ see LUGANSK.

Wa·bash /wáwbash/ **Riv·er** river in central U.S., flowing 475 mi. from W Ohio through Indiana and into the Ohio River; forms S Indiana-Illinois border.

Wa·co /wáykō/ city in central Texas. Pop. 103,590.

Wales /waylz/ division of the United Kingdom, W of England. Capital: Cardiff. Pop. 2,719,200. ¶ See note at GREAT BRITAIN.

War·ren /wáwrən, wa'ar–/ city in SE Michigan. Pop. 144,864.

War·saw /wáwrsaw/ capital of Poland, in the E central part. Pop. 1,640,700.

Wash·ing·ton /wa'ashingtən, wáwsh–/ state in NW U.S. Pop. 4,866,692. Capital: Olympia. Abbr. **WA**; **Wash.** □□ **Wash·ing·ton·i·an** /–tóneeən/ n. & adj.

Wash·ing·ton, D.C. capital of the U.S.; coextensive with the District of Columbia, between Virginia and Maryland. Pop. 606,900.

Wash·ing·ton, Mount mountain in the White Mountains in N New Hampshire; highest peak in NE U.S.: 6,288 ft.

Wa·ter·bur·y /wáwtərberee, wa'at–/ city in W Connecticut. Pop. 108,961.

Wed·dell /wədél, wéd'l/ **Sea** arm of the Atlantic, E of the Antarctic Peninsula.

Wel·ling·ton /wélingtən/ capital of New Zealand, on S North Island. Pop. 158,600.

West Bank disputed area in the Middle East, W of the Jordan River and the Dead Sea. Pop. 1,428,000.

West·ern Aus·tral·ia state in W Australia. Pop. 1,273,600. Capital: Perth.

West·ern Sa·mo·a /səmóə/ island country in the S Pacific, comprising the W islands of Samoa. Pop. 214,000. Capital: Apia. See also AMERICAN SAMOA. □□ **Sa·mo'an** n. & adj.

West Ger·man·y /júrmənee/ (also called **Federal Republic of Germany**) German state created in 1949, under parliamentary government; unified with East Germany in 1990.

West In·dies /índeez/ island group off the E coast of North and South America, between the Atlantic and the Caribbean Sea; includes the Greater Antilles, the Lesser Antilles, and the Bahamas.

West Palm /paam, paw(1)m/ **Beach** city in SE Florida. Pop. 67,643.

West Vir·gin·ia /vərjínyə/ state in E central

U.S. Pop. 1,793,477. Capital: Charleston. Abbr. **WV; W. Va.** □□ **West Vir·gin'ian** n. & adj.

Whee·ling /wee'ling, hwee–/ city in N West Virginia. Pop. 148,641.

White·horse /wít-hawrs, hwít–/ capital of Yukon Territory, Canada, in the S part. Pop. 17,900.

White /wīt/ **Moun·tains** mountain range in N New Hampshire; part of the Appalachian range. Highest peak: Mount Washington.

Whit·ney /wítnee, hwit–/, **Mount** mountain in the Sierra Nevada range, in central California; highest peak in conterminous U.S.: 14,495 ft.

Whit·ti·er /wíteeər, hwítee–/ city in SW California. Pop. 77,671.

Wich·i·ta /wíchətaw, –taa/ city in S central Kansas. Pop. 304,011.

Wies·ba·den /vee'sbaad'n/ city in W Germany. Pop. 266,100.

Wight /wīt/, **Isle of** island in S England, in the English Channel.

Wil·ming·ton /wílmingtən/ city in N Delaware. Pop. 71,529.

Wind·hoek /vínthōōk/ capital of Namibia, in the central part. Pop. 161,000.

Wind·sor /wínzər/ city in S Ontario, Canada. Pop. 191,400.

Wind·ward /wíndwərd/ **Is·lands** island group in the E West Indies, extending from Grenada N to Martinique.

Win·ni·peg /wínipeg/ capital of Manitoba, Canada, in the S part. Pop. 616,800.

Win·ston-Sa·lem /wínstən sáyləm/ city in N central North Carolina. Pop. 143,485.

Wis·con·sin /wiskaánsən/ state in N central U.S. Pop. 4,891,769. Capital: Madison. Abbr. **WI; Wis.** □□ **Wis·con'sin·ite** n.

Wol·ver·hamp·ton /wōōlvərhamptən, –vəramptən, –amtən/ city in W England. Pop. 245,100.

Worces·ter /wōōstər/ city in central Massachusetts. Pop. 169,759.

Wroc·law /vráwtslaaf/ city in SW Poland. Pop. 642,900.

Wu·han /wōoha'an/ city in E China. Pop. 3,750,000.

Wup·per·tal /vōōpərtaal/ city in W Germany. Pop. 383,800.

Wy·o·ming /wīóming/ state in W U.S. Pop. 453,588. Capital: Cheyenne. Abbr. **WY; Wyo.** □□ **Wy·o'ming·ite** n.

Xi·an /shee'a'an/ (also **Si·an**) city in central China. Pop. 2,760,000.

Ya·mous·sou·kro /yaamōōsōōókrō/ capital of Ivory Coast, in the S central part. Pop. 106,800.

Yan·gon /ya'angōōn/ see RANGOON.

Yang·tze /yangtse'e, –se'e/ **Riv·er** see CHANG.

Ya·oun·dé /yowndáy/ capital of Cameroon, in the S part. Pop. 800,000.

Ya·ren /yaárən/ district in SW Nauru; seat of government. Pop. 600.

Ye·ka·te·rin·burg /yikaátərinbŏŏrg/ see SVERDLOVSK.

Yel·low·knife /yélōnīf/ capital of Northwest Territories, Canada, in the S part. Pop. 15,200.

Yel·low /yélō/ **Riv·er** see HUANG RIVER.

Yel·low Sea arm of the N Pacific, between Korea and China.

Yel·low·stone /yéləstōn/ **Falls** waterfall of the Yellowstone River, in NW Wyoming.

Yem·en /yémən, yáymən/ republic on the SW Arabian Peninsula. Capitals: Aden; Sanaa. Pop. 13,483,000. □□ **Yem′en·ite, Yem′en·i** *n. & adj.*

Ye·re·van /yerəvaán/ capital of Armenia, in the W part. Pop. 1,226,000.

Ye·zo /ye'ezaw/ see HOKKAIDO.

Yo·ko·ha·ma /yōkəhaámə/ port city in Japan, on Honshu. Pop. 3,307,400.

Yo·ko·su·ka /yōkəsŏ'kə/ port city in Japan, on Honshu. Pop. 432,200.

Yon·kers /yaángkərz/ city in SE New York. Pop. 188,082.

York /yawrk/ **1** city in NE England. Pop. 104,000. **2** city in SE Ontario, Canada. Pop. 140,500.

York·town /yáwrktown/ village in E Virginia; site of British surrender to Washington (1781).

Yo·sem·i·te /yōsémitee/ **Na·tion·al Park** scenic mountain region in E California.

Youngs·town /yə́ngstown/ city in NE Ohio. Pop. 95,732.

Yu·ca·tán /yōōkətán, –taán/ state in SE Mexico. Pop. 1,362,900. Capital: Mérida.

Yu·go·sla·vi·a /yōōgōslaáveeə/ federation (1918–92) in SE Europe that included Serbia, Croatia, Bosnia and Herzegovina, Montenegro, Macedonia, and Slovenia.

Yu·kon /yōōkaan/ **Riv·er** river in NW North America, flowing 2,000 mi. from Yukon Territory, Canada, through Alaska and into the Bering Sea.

Yu·kon Ter·ri·to·ry territory in NW Canada, bordering Alaska. Pop. 32,000. Capital: Whitehorse.

Za·ca·te·cas /zaakətáykəs/ state in N central Mexico. Pop. 1,276,300. Capital: Zacatecas.

Za·greb /zaágreb/ capital of Croatia, in the N part. Pop. 867,700.

Za·ire /zaa-e'er/ see CONGO 1.

Zam·be·zi /zambe'ezee/ **Riv·er** river in S Africa, flowing 1,650 mi. from NW Zambia to the Indian Ocean.

Zam·bi·a /zámbeeə/ republic in S central Africa. Pop. 9,159,000. Capital: Lusaka. □□ **Zam′bi·an** *n. & adj.*

Zan·zi·bar /zánzibaar/ island in the Indian Ocean, off the E coast of Tanzania; part of Tanzania.

Za·ra·go·za /saaraagáwsaa/ see SARAGOSSA.

Zhdan·ov /zhdaánəf/ see MARIUPOL.

Zim·bab·we /zimbaábway/ republic in S central Africa. Pop. 11,271,000. Capital: Harare.

Zom·ba /zaámbə/ legislative capital of Malawi, in the S part. Pop. 62,700.

Zu·rich /zŏ'orik/ city in N Switzerland. Pop. 342,900.

Special Reference Sections

Standard Weights and Measures
with Metric Equivalents

Linear Measure

1 inch	= 25.4 millimeters
1 foot = 12 inches	= 0.3048 meter
1 yard = 3 feet	= 0.9144 meter
= 36 inches	
1 (statute) mile = 1,760 yards	= 1.609 kilometers
= 5,280 feet	

Square Measure

1 sq. inch	= 6.45 sq. centimeters
1 sq. foot = 144 sq. inches	= 9.29 sq. decimeters
1 sq. yard = 9 sq. feet	= 0.836 sq. meter
1 acre = 4,840 sq. yards	= 0.405 hectare
1 sq. mile = 640 acres	= 259 hectares

Cubic Measure

1 cu. inch	= 16.4 cu. centimeters
1 cu. foot = 1,728 cu. inches	= 0.0283 cu. meter
1 cu. yard = 27 cu. feet	= 0.765 cu. meter

Capacity Measure

DRY MEASURE

1 pint = 33.60 cu. inches	= 0.550 liter
1 quart = 2 pints	= 1.101 liters
1 peck = 8 quarts	= 8.81 liters
1 bushel = 4 pecks	= 35.3 liters

LIQUID MEASURE

1 fluid ounce	= 29.573 milliliters
1 gill = 4 fluid ounces	= 118.294 milliliters
1 pint = 16 fluid ounces	= 0.473 liter
	= 28.88 cu. inches
1 quart = 2 pints	= 0.946 liter
1 gallon = 4 quarts	= 3.785 liters

Avoirdupois Weight

1 grain	= 0.065 gram
1 dram	= 1.772 grams
1 ounce = 16 drams	= 28.35 grams
1 pound = 16 ounces	= 0.4536 kilograms
= 7,000 grains	(0.45359237 exactly)
1 stone (British) = 14 pounds	= 6.35 kilograms
1 ton	= 2,000 pounds
1 hundred weight (US)	= 100 pounds
20 hundred weight (US)	= 2,000 pounds

Conversion from Standard to Metric Measurements

Standard	Multiply By	To Get Metric
Length		
inches	2.54	centimeters
feet	30.48	centimeters
yards	0.91	meters
miles	1.61	kilometers
Area		
sq. inches	6.45	sq. centimeters
sq. feet	0.09	sq. meters
sq. yards	0.84	sq. meters
sq. miles	2.59	sq. kilometers
acres	0.4	hectares
Weight		
ounces	28.35	grams
pounds	0.45	kilograms
short tons	0.89	metric tons
Volume		
teaspoons	4.93	milliliters
tablespoons	14.79	milliliters
cu. inches	16.38	milliliters
fluid ounces	29.57	milliliters
cups	0.24	liters
pints	0.47	liters
quarts	0.95	liters
gallons	3.79	liters
cu. feet	0.03	cu. meters
cu. yards	0.76	cu. meters

778

Metric Weights and Measures
with Standard Equivalents

Linear Measure

1 millimeter (mm)	= 0.039 inch
1 centimeter (cm) = 10 millimeters	= 0.394 inch
1 decimeter (dm) = 10 centimeters	= 3.94 inches
1 meter (m) = 10 decimeters	= 1.094 yards
1 decameter = 10 meters	= 10.94 yards
1 hectometer = 100 meters	= 109.4 yards
1 kilometer (km) = 1,000 meters	= 0.6214 mile

Square Measure

1 sq. centimeter	= 0.155 sq. inch
1 sq. meter	= 10,000 sq. centimeters
	= 1.196 sq. yards
1 are = 100 sq. meters	= 119.6 sq. yards
1 hectare = 100 ares	= 2.471 acres
1 sq. kilometer	= 0.386 sq. mile
	= 100 hectares

Cubic Measure

1 cu. centimeter	= 0.061 cu. inch
1 cu. meter = 1,000,000 cu. centimeters	= 1.308 cu. yards

Capacity Measure

1 milliliter (ml)	= 0.034 fluid ounces
1 centiliter (cl) = 10 milliliters	= 0.34 fluid ounces
1 deciliter (dl) = 10 centiliter	= 3.38 fluid ounces
1 liter (l) = 10 deciliters	= 1.06 quarts
1 decaliter = 10 liters	= 2.20 gallons
1 hectoliter = 100 liters	= 2.75 bushels

Weight

1 milligram (mg)	= 0.015 grain
1 centigram = 10 milligrams	= 0.154 grain
1 decigram (dg) = 10 centigrams	= 1.543 grains
1 gram (g) = 10 decigrams	= 15.43 grains
1 decagram = 10 grams	= 5.64 drams
1 hectogram = 100 grams	= 3.527 ounces
1 kilogram (kg) = 1,000 grams	= 2.205 pounds
1 ton (metric ton) = 1,000 kilograms	= 0.984 (long) ton

Conversion from Metric to Standard Measurements

Metric	Multiply By	To Get Standard
Length		
millimeters	0.039	inches
centimeters	0.39	inches
meters	3.28	feet
meters	1.09	yards
kilometers	0.62	miles
Area		
sq. centimeters	0.16	sq. inches
sq. meters	1.19	sq. yards
sq. kilometers	0.39	sq. miles
hectares	2.5	acres
Weight		
grams	0.035	ounces
kilograms	2.2	pounds
metric tons	1.1	short tons
Volume		
milliliters	0.03	fluid ounces
milliliters	0.06	cu. inches
liters	2.11	pints
liters	1.06	quarts
liters	0.26	gallons
cu. meters	35.32	cu. feet
cu. meters	1.31	cu. yards

Signs and Symbols

General

&	and	×	by, as in *an 8′ × 12′ room*
&c.	et cetera (and so forth)	w/	with
©	copyright(ed)	w/o	without
®	registered; of a trademark or service mark	§	section (of a text)
†	death; died	″	ditto marks; repeat the word or sign located in the line above
℞	take (Latin *recipe*); used on prescriptions	☢	radioactive; radiation
#	1. number (before a figure) 2. pound(s) (after a figure) 3. space (in printing)		

Science and Mathematics

♂	male	=	equal to
♀	female	≠	not equal to
+	1. plus	>	greater than
	2. positive (number or charge)	<	less than
		≥	greater than or equal to
−	1. minus	≤	less than or equal to
	2. negative (number or charge)	≡	identical with
±	plus or minus	≈	approximately equal to
× *or* · *or* ∗	multiplied by	≅	congruent to (in geometry)
÷	divided by	:	is to; the ratio of
Σ	sum	!	factorial of
π	pi; the ratio of the circumference of a circle to its diameter (3.14159265+)	⊥	perpendicular to
		√	radical sign; root
		°	degree
		′	1. minute(s) of arc 2. foot, feet
∞	infinity	″	1. second(s) of arc 2. inch(es)
∴	therefore		
∥	parallel to	∅	empty set

Commerce and Finance

$	dollar(s)		@	at the rate of
¢	cent(s)		%	percent
£	pound(s) sterling (UK)		DM	Deutsche mark (Germany)
p	(new) pence (UK)		F	franc (France)
¥	yen (Japan)			

Signs of the Zodiac

Spring

♈	Aries, the Ram
♉	Taurus, the Bull
♊ *or* II	Gemini, the Twins

Summer

♋	Cancer, the Crab
♌	Leo, the Lion
♍	Virgo, the Virgin

Autumn

♎	Libra, the Balance
♏	Scorpio, the Scorpion
♐	Sagittarius, the Archer

Winter

♑	Capricorn, the Goat
♒	Aquarius, the Water Bearer
♓	Pisces, the Fishes

Diacritical Marks
(to distinguish sounds or values of letters)

´	acute (as in the French word *née*)
`	grave (as in the French word *père*)
~	tilde (as in the Spanish word *piñata*)
^	circumflex (as in the French word *fête*)
‾	macron (as used in pronunciation: *āge, īce*)
˘	breve (as used in pronunciation: *tăp, rĭp*)
¨	dieresis (as in the word *naïve*)
¸	cedilla (as in the word *façade*)

Temperature

Fahrenheit: Water boils at 212° and freezes at 32°.

Celsius or Centigrade: Water boils at 100° and freezes at 0°.

Kelvin: Water boils at 373.15 K and freezes at 273.15 K.

Celsius	Fahrenheit	Fahrenheit	Celsius
-17.8°	0°	0°	-17.8°
-10°	14°	10°	-12.2°
0°	32°	20°	-6.6°
10°	50°	32°	0.0°
20°	68°	40°	3.5°
30°	86°	50°	10.0°
40°	104°	60°	15.5°
50°	122°	70°	21.1°
60°	140°	80°	26.6°
70°	158°	90°	32.2°
80°	176°	100°	37.6°
90°	194°	212°	100.0°
100°	212°		

To convert Celsius into Fahrenheit: multiply by 9, divide by 5, and add 32.

To convert Fahrenheit into Celsius: subtract 32, multiply by 5, and divide by 9.

Heat Index

As humidity increases, the air at a given temperature feels warmer. The combination of heat and high humidity reduces the body's natural ability to cool itself. For example, when the actual temperature is 85 degrees Fahrenheit with a relative humidity of 80 percent, the air feels like dry air at 97 degrees.

						Temperature (°F)						
	70	75	80	85	90	95	100	105	110	115	120
Humidity (%)						*Equivalent Temperature (°F)*					
0	64	69	73	78	83	87	91	95	99	103	107
10	65	70	75	80	85	90	95	100	105	111	116
20	66	72	77	82	87	93	99	105	112	120	130
30	67	73	78	84	90	96	104	113	123	120	148
40	68	74	79	86	93	101	110	123	137	135	
50	69	75	81	88	96	107	120	135	150		
60	70	76	82	90	100	114	132	149			
70	70	77	85	93	106	124	144				
80	71	78	86	97	113	136					
90	71	79	88	102	122						
100	72	80	91	108							

Windchill Temperatures

The chart below illustrates the effect of wind speed on perceived air temperature. "Windchill," or the perceived feeling of coldness of the air, increases with higher wind speed.

Air temperature (°F)	*Wind speed in miles per hour*								
	0	5	10	15	20	25	30	35	40
	Equivalent windchill temperatures								
35	35	32	22	16	12	8	6	4	3
30	30	27	16	9	4	1	-2	-4	-5
25	25	22	10	2	-3	-7	-10	-12	-13
20	20	16	3	-5	-10	-15	-18	-20	-21
15	15	11	-3	-11	-17	-22	-25	-27	-29
10	10	6	-9	-18	-24	-29	-33	-35	-37
5	5	0	-15	-25	-31	-36	-41	-43	-45
0	0	-5	-22	-31	-39	-44	-49	-52	-53
-5	-5	-10	-27	-38	-46	-51	-56	-58	-60
-10	-10	-15	-34	-45	-53	-59	-64	-67	-69
-15	-15	-21	-40	-51	-60	-66	-71	-74	-76
-20	-20	-26	-46	-58	-67	-74	-79	-82	-84
-25	-25	-31	-52	-65	-74	-81	-86	-89	-92

Mathematical Notation

Mathematical Power	Name	Prefix (symbol)
10^{18} or 1,000,000,000,000,000,000	one quintillion	exa- (E)
10^{15} or 1,000,000,000,000,000	one quadrillion	peta- (P)
10^{12} or 1,000,000,000,000	one trillion	tera- (T)
10^{9} or 1,000,000,000	one billion	giga- (G)
10^{6} or 1,000,000	one million	mega- (M)
10^{3} or 1,000	one thousand	kilo- (K, k)
10^{2} or 100	one hundred	hecto- (H, h)
10^{1} or 10	ten	—
1	one	—
10^{-1} or 0.1	one tenth	deci- (d)
10^{-2} or 0.01	one hundredth	centi- (c)
10^{-3} or 0.001	one thousandth	milli- (m)
10^{-6} or 0.000 001	one millionth	micro- (μ)
10^{-9} or 0.000 000 001	one billionth	nano- (n)
10^{-12} or 0.000 000 000 001	one trillionth	pico- (p)
10^{-15} or 0.000 000 000 000 001	one quadrillionth	femto- (f)
10^{-18} or 0.000 000 000 000 000 001	one quintillionth	atto- (a)

Multiplication Tables

×	1	2	3	4	5	6	7	8	9	10	11	12
1	1	2	3	4	5	6	7	8	9	10	11	12
2	2	4	6	8	10	12	14	16	18	20	22	24
3	3	6	9	12	15	18	21	24	27	30	33	36
4	4	8	12	16	20	24	28	32	36	40	44	48
5	5	10	15	20	25	30	35	40	45	50	55	60
6	6	12	18	24	30	36	42	48	54	60	66	72
7	7	14	21	28	35	42	49	56	63	70	77	84
8	8	16	24	32	40	48	56	64	72	80	88	96
9	9	18	27	36	45	54	63	72	81	90	99	108
10	10	20	30	40	50	60	70	80	90	100	110	120
11	11	22	33	44	55	66	77	88	99	110	121	132
12	12	24	36	48	60	72	84	96	108	120	132	144

Multiplication Tables

×12				×13				×14			
1	12	13	156	1	13	13	169	1	14	13	182
2	24	14	168	2	26	14	182	2	28	14	196
3	36	15	180	3	39	15	195	3	42	15	210
4	48	16	192	4	52	16	208	4	56	16	224
5	60	17	204	5	65	17	221	5	70	17	238
6	72	18	216	6	78	18	238	6	84	18	252
7	84	19	228	7	91	19	247	7	98	19	266
8	96	25	300	8	104	25	325	8	112	25	350
9	108	35	420	9	117	35	455	9	126	35	490
10	120	45	540	10	130	45	585	10	140	45	630
11	132	55	660	11	143	55	715	11	154	55	770
12	144	65	780	12	156	65	845	12	168	65	910
		75	900			75	975			75	1050
		85	1020			85	1105			85	1190
		95	1140			95	1235			95	1330

×15		×16		×17		×18		×19	
1	15	1	16	1	17	1	18	1	19
2	30	2	32	2	34	2	36	2	38
3	45	3	48	3	51	3	54	3	57
4	60	4	64	4	68	4	72	4	76
5	75	5	80	5	85	5	90	5	95
6	90	6	96	6	102	6	108	6	114
7	105	7	112	7	119	7	126	7	133
8	120	8	128	8	136	8	144	8	152
9	135	9	144	9	153	9	162	9	171
10	150	10	160	10	170	10	180	10	190
11	165	11	176	11	187	11	198	11	209
12	180	12	192	12	204	12	216	12	228
13	195	13	208	13	221	13	234	13	247
14	210	14	224	14	238	14	252	14	266
15	225	15	240	15	255	15	270	15	285
16	240	16	256	16	272	16	288	16	304
17	255	17	272	17	289	17	306	17	323
18	270	18	288	18	306	18	324	18	342
19	285	19	304	19	323	19	342	19	361
25	375	25	400	25	425	25	450	25	475
35	525	35	560	35	595	35	630	35	665
45	675	45	720	45	765	45	810	45	855
55	825	55	880	55	935	55	990	55	1045
65	975	65	1040	65	1105	65	1170	65	1235
75	1125	75	1200	75	1275	75	1350	75	1425
85	1275	85	1360	85	1445	85	1530	85	1615
95	1425	95	1520	95	1615	95	1710	95	1805

786

Arabic and Roman Numerals

Arabic	Roman	Arabic	Roman
0		17	XVII
1	I	18	XVIII
2	II	19	XIX
3	III	20	XX
4	IV or IIII	30	XXX
5	V	40	XL
6	VI	50	L
7	VII	60	LX
8	VIII	70	LXX
9	IX or VIIII	80	LXXX
10	X	90	XC
11	XI	100	C
12	XII	400	CD
13	XIII	500	D
14	XIV	900	CM
15	XV	1,000	M
16	XVI	2,000	MM

Greek Alphabet

Letter name	Lowercase	Uppercase
alpha	α	A
beta	β	B
gamma	γ	Γ
delta	δ	Δ
epsilon	ε	E
zeta	ζ	Z
eta	η	H
theta	θ	Θ
iota	ι	I
kappa	κ	K
lambda	λ	Λ
mu	μ	M
nu	ν	N
xi	ξ	Ξ
omicron	o	O
pi	π	Π
rho	ρ	P
sigma	σ, ς	Σ
tau	τ	T
upsilon	υ	Y
phi	φ	Φ
chi	χ	X
psi	ψ	Ψ
omega	ω	Ω

Books of the Bible

787

Old Testament

Genesis (Gen.)
Exodus (Exod.)
Leviticus (Lev.)
Numbers (Num.)
Deuteronomy (Deut.)
Joshua (Josh.)
Judges (Judg.)
Ruth
First Book of Samuel
(1 Sam.)
Second Book of Samuel
(2 Sam.)
First Book of Kings
(1 Kgs.)
Second Book of Kings
(2 Kgs.)

First Book of
Chronicles (1 Chr.)
Second Book of Chronicles
(2 Chr.)
Ezra
Nehemiah (Neh.)
Esther
Job
Psalms (Ps.)
Proverbs (Prov.)
Ecclesiastes (Eccles.)
Song of Songs, Song of
Solomon, Canticles
(S. of S., Cant.)
Isaiah (Isa.)
Jeremiah (Jer.)

Lamentations (Lam.)
Ezekiel (Ezek.)
Daniel (Dan.)
Hosea (Hos.)
Joel
Amos
Obadiah (Obad.)
Jonah
Micah (Mic.)
Nahum (Nah.)
Habakkuk (Hab.)
Zephaniah (Zeph.)
Haggai (Hag.)
Zechariah (Zech.)
Malachi (Mal.)

Apocrypha

First Book of Esdras
(1 Esd.)
Second Book of Esdras
(2 Esd.)
Tobit
Judith
Rest of Esther
(Rest of Esth.)
Wisdom of Solomon
(Wisd.)

Ecclesiasticus, Wisdom of
Jesus the Son of Sirach
(Ecclus., Sir.)
Baruch
Song of the Three Children
(S. of III Ch.)
Susanna (Sus.)
Bel and the Dragon
(Bel & Dr.)

Prayer of Manasseh
(Pr. of Man.)
First Book of Maccabees
(1 Macc.)
Second Book of Maccabees
(2 Macc.)

New Testament

Gospel according to St.
Matthew (Matt.)
Gospel according to St.
Mark (Mark)
Gospel according to St.
Luke (Luke)
Gospel according to
St. John (John)
Acts of the Apostles (Acts)
Epistle to the Romans
(Rom.)
First Epistle to the
Corinthians (1 Cor.)
Second Epistle to the
Corinthians (2 Cor.)
Epistle to the Galatians
(Gal.)
Epistle to the Ephesians
(Eph.)

Epistle to the Philippians
(Phil.)
Epistle to the Colossians
(Col.)
First Epistle to the
Thessalonians
(1 Thess.)
Second Epistle to the
Thessalonians
(2 Thess.)
First Epistle to Timothy
(1 Tim.)
Second Epistle to Timothy
(2 Tim.)
Epistle to Titus (Tit.)
Epistle to Philemon
(Philem.)

Epistle to the Hebrews
(Heb.)
Epistle of James (Jas.)
First Epistle of Peter
(1 Pet.)
Second Epistle of Peter
(2 Pet.)
First Epistle of John
(1 John)
Second Epistle of John
(2 John)
Third Epistle of John
(3 John)
Epistle of Jude (Jude)
Revelation, Apocalypse
(Rev., Apoc.)

Chemical Elements

Element	Symbol	Atomic Number	Element	Symbol	Atomic Number
actinium	Ac	89	helium	He	2
aluminum	Al	13	holmium	Ho	67
americium	Am	95	hydrogen	H	1
antimony	Sb	51	indium	In	49
argon	Ar	18	iodine	I	53
arsenic	As	33	iridium	Ir	77
astatine	At	85	iron	Fe	26
barium	Ba	56	krypton	Kr	36
berkelium	Bk	97	lanthanum	La	57
beryllium	Be	4	lawrencium	Lr	103
bismuth	Bi	83	lead	Pb	82
bohrium	Bh	107	lithium	Li	3
boron	B	5	lutetium	Lu	71
bromine	Br	35	magnesium	Mg	12
cadmium	Cd	48	manganese	Mn	25
calcium	Ca	20	meitnerium	Mt	109
californium	Cf	98	mendelevium	Md	101
carbon	C	6	mercury	Hg	80
cerium	Ce	58	molybdenum	Mo	42
cesium	Cs	55	neodymium	Nd	60
chlorine	Cl	17	neon	Ne	10
chromium	Cr	24	neptunium	Np	93
cobalt	Co	27	nickel	Ni	28
copper	Cu	29	niobium	Nb	41
curium	Cm	96	nitrogen	N	7
dubnium	Db	105	nobelium	No	102
dysprosium	Dy	66	osmium	Os	76
einsteinium	Es	99	oxygen	O	8
erbium	Er	68	palladium	Pd	46
europium	Eu	63	phosphorus	P	15
fermium	Fm	100	platinum	Pt	78
fluorine	F	9	plutonium	Pu	94
francium	Fr	87	polonium	Po	84
gadolinium	Gd	64	potassium	K	19
gallium	Ga	31	praseodymium	Pr	59
germanium	Ge	32	promethium	Pm	61
gold	Au	79	protactinium	Pa	91
hafnium	Ha	105	radium	Ra	88
hassium	Hs	108	radon	Rn	86

Element	Symbol	Atomic Number	Element	Symbol	Atomic Number
rhenium	Re	75	tellurium	Te	52
rhodium	Rh	45	terbium	Tb	65
rubidium	Rb	37	thallium	Tl	81
ruthenium	Ru	44	thorium	Th	90
rutherfordium	Rf	104	thulium	Tm	69
samarium	Sm	62	tin	Sn	50
scandium	Sc	21	titanium	Ti	22
seaborgium	Sg	106	tungsten		
selenium	Se	34	(wolfram)	W	74
silicon	Si	14	uranium	U	92
silver	Ag	47	vanadium	V	23
sodium	Na	11	xenon	Xe	54
strontium	Sr	38	ytterbium	Yb	70
sulfur	S	16	yttrium	Y	39
tantalum	Ta	73	zinc	Zn	30
technetium	Tc	43	zirconium	Zr	40

States of the United States of America

State (traditional; postal abbreviations)	Capital	Area codes
Alabama (Ala.; AL)	Montgomery	205, 334
Alaska (Alas.; AK)	Juneau	907
Arizona (Ariz.; AZ)	Phoenix	520, 602
Arkansas (Ark.; AR)	Little Rock	501, 870
California (Calif.; CA)	Sacramento	209, 213, 310, 408, 415, 510, 562, 619, 626, 650, 707, 714, 760, 805, 818, 909, 916, 949
Colorado (Col.; CO)	Denver	303, 719, 970
Connecticut (Conn.; CT)	Hartford	203, 860
Delaware (Del.; DE)	Dover	302
District of Columbia (D.C., DC)		202
Florida (Fla.; FL)	Tallahassee	305, 352, 407, 561, 813, 904, 941, 954
Georgia (Ga.; GA)	Atlanta	404, 706, 770, 912
Hawaii (HI)	Honolulu	808
Idaho (Id.; ID)	Boise	208
Illinois (Ill.; IL)	Springfield	217, 309, 312, 618, 630, 708, 773, 815, 847
Indiana (Ind.; IN)	Indianapolis	219, 317, 765, 812
Iowa (Ia.; IA)	Des Moines	319, 515, 712
Kansas (Kan.; KS)	Topeka	316, 913
Kentucky (Ky.; KY)	Frankfort	502, 606
Louisiana (La.; LA)	Baton Rouge	318, 504
Maine (Me.; ME)	Augusta	207
Maryland (Md.; MD)	Annapolis	240, 301, 410, 443
Massachusetts (Mass.; MA)	Boston	413, 508, 617
Michigan (Mich.; MI)	Lansing	248, 313, 517, 616, 810, 906
Minnesota (Minn.; MI)	St. Paul	218, 320, 507, 612
Mississippi (Miss.; MS)	Jackson	601

State (traditional; postal abbreviations)	Capital	Area codes
Missouri (Mo.; MO)	Jefferson City	314, 417, 573, 816
Montana (Mont.; MT)	Helena	406
Nebraska (Nebr.; NE)	Lincoln	308, 402
Nevada (Nev.; NV)	Carson City	702
New Hampshire (N.H.; NH)	Concord	603
New Jersey (N.J.; NJ)	Trenton	201, 609, 732, 908, 973
New Mexico (N. Mex.; NM)	Santa Fe	505
New York (N.Y.; NY)	Albany	212, 315, 516, 518, 607, 716, 718 914, 917
North Carolina (N.C.; NC)	Raleigh	704, 910, 919
North Dakota (N. Dak.; ND)	Bismarck	701
Ohio (O.; OH)	Columbus	216, 330, 419, 440, 513, 614, 937
Oklahoma (Okla.; OK)	Oklahoma City	405, 918
Oregon (Ore.; OR)	Salem	503, 541
Pennsylvania (Pa.; PA)	Harrisburg	215, 412, 610, 717, 724, 814
Rhode Island (R.I.; RI)	Providence	401
South Carolina (S.C.; SC)	Columbia	803, 864
South Dakota (S. Dak.; SD)	Pierre	605
Tennessee (Tenn.; TN)	Nashville	423, 615, 901
Texas (Tex.; TX)	Austin	210, 214, 254, 281, 409, 512, 713, 806, 817, 830, 903, 915, 940, 956, 972
Utah (Ut.; UT)	Salt Lake City	801
Vermont (Vt.; VT)	Montpelier	802
Virginia (Va.; VA)	Richmond	540, 703, 757, 804
Washington (Wash.; WA)	Olympia	206, 253, 360, 425, 509
West Virginia (W. Va.; WV)	Charleston	304
Wisconsin (Wis.; WI)	Madison	414, 608, 715, 920
Wyoming (Wyo.; WY)	Cheyenne	307

Presidents of the United States of America

1.	George Washington 1732–99	Federalist 1789–97
2.	John Adams 1735–1826	Federalist 1797–1801
3.	Thomas Jefferson 1743–1826	Democratic–Republican 1801–09
4.	James Madison 1751–1836	Democratic–Republican 1809–17
5.	James Monroe 1758–1831	Democratic–Republican 1817–25
6.	John Quincy Adams 1767–1848	Democratic-Republican 1825–29
7.	Andrew Jackson 1767–1845	Democrat 1829–37
8.	Martin Van Buren 1782–1862	Democrat 1837–41
9.	William H. Harrison 1773–1841	Whig 1841
10.	John Tyler 1790–1862	Whig, then Democrat 1841–45
11.	James K. Polk 1795–1849	Democrat 1845–49
12.	Zachary Taylor 1784–1850	Whig 1849–50
13.	Millard Fillmore 1800–74	Whig 1850–53
14.	Franklin Pierce 1804–69	Democrat 1853–57
15.	James Buchanan 1791–1868	Democrat 1857–61
16.	Abraham Lincoln 1809–65	Republican 1861–65
17.	Andrew Johnson 1808–75	Democrat 1865–69
18.	Ulysses S. Grant 1822–85	Republican 1869–77
19.	Rutherford B. Hayes 1822–93	Republican 1877–81
20.	James A. Garfield 1831–81	Republican 1881
21.	Chester A. Arthur 1830–86	Republican 1881–85
22.	Grover Cleveland 1837–1908	Democrat 1885–89
23.	Benjamin Harrison 1833–1901	Republican 1889–93
24.	Grover Cleveland (see above)	Democrat 1893–97
25.	William McKinley 1843–1901	Republican 1897–1901
26.	Theodore Roosevelt 1858–1919	Republican 1901–09
27.	William H. Taft 1857–1930	Republican 1909–13
28.	Woodrow Wilson 1856–1924	Democrat 1913–21
29.	Warren G. Harding 1865–1923	Republican 1921–23
30.	Calvin Coolidge 1872–1933	Republican 1923–29
31.	Herbert Hoover 1874–1964	Republican 1929–33
32.	Franklin D. Roosevelt 1882–1945	Democrat 1933–45
33.	Harry S Truman 1884–1972	Democrat 1945–53
34.	Dwight D. Eisenhower 1890–1969	Republican 1953–61
35.	John F. Kennedy 1917–63	Democrat 1961–63
36.	Lyndon B. Johnson 1908–73	Democrat 1963–69
37.	Richard M. Nixon 1913–94	Republican 1969–74
38.	Gerald R. Ford 1913–	Republican 1974–77
39.	James Earl Carter 1924–	Democrat 1977–81
40.	Ronald W. Reagan 1911–	Republican 1981–89
41.	George H.W. Bush 1924–	Republican 1989–93
42.	William J. Clinton 1946–	Democrat 1993–

Countries of the World

Country	Capital	Continent/Area	Nationality
Afghanistan	Kabul	Asia	Afghan
Albania	Tirane	Europe	Albanian
Algeria	Algiers	Africa	Algerian
Andorra	Andorra la Vella	Europe	Andorran
Angola	Luanda	Africa	Angolan
Antigua and Barbuda	Saint John's	North America	Antiguan, Barbudan
Argentina	Buenos Aires	South America	Argentine
Armenia	Yerevan	Asia	Armenian
Australia	Canberra	Australia	Australian
Austria	Vienna	Europe	Austrian
Azerbaijan	Baku	Asia	Azerbaijani
Bahamas, The	Nassau	North America	Bahamian
Bahrain	Manama	Asia	Bahraini
Bangladesh	Dhaka	Asia	Bangaldeshi
Barbados	Bridgetown	North America	Barbadian
Belarus	Minsk	Europe	Belarusian
Belgium	Brussels	Europe	Belgian
Belize	Belmopan	North America	Belizean
Benin	Porto-Novo	Africa	Beninese
Bhutan	Thimphu	Asia	Bhutanese
Bolivia	La Paz; Sucre	South America	Bolivian
Bosnia and Herzegovina	Sarajevo	Europe	Bosnian, Herzegovinian
Botswana	Gaborone	Africa	Motswana, *sing.*, Batswana, *pl.*
Brazil	Brasilia	South America	Brazilian
Brunei	Bandar Seri Begawan	Asia	Bruneian
Bulgaria	Sofia	Europe	Bulgarian
Burkina	Ouagadougou	Africa	Burkinabe
Burma (Myanmar)	Rangoon	Asia	Burmese
Burundi	Bujumbura	Africa	Burundian, *n.*; Burundi, *adj.*
Cambodia	Phnom Penh	Asia	Cambodian
Cameroon	Yaoundé	Africa	Cameroonian
Canada	Ottawa	North American	Canadian
Cape Verde	Praia	Africa	Cape Verdean
Central African Republic	Bangui	Africa	Central African
Chad	N'Djamena	Africa	Chadian
Chile	Santiago	South America	Chilean

Country	Capital	Continent/Area	Nationality
China	Beijing	Asia	Chinese
Colombia	Bogotá	South America	Colombian
Comoros	Moroni	Africa	Comoran
Congo	Brazzaville	Africa	Congolese, n.; Congolese or Congo, adj.
Congo (Zaire)	Kinsasha	Africa	
Costa Rica	San José	North America	Costa Rican
Côte d'Ivoire (Ivory Coast)	Yamoussoukro	Africa	Ivorian
Croatia	Zagreb	Europe	Croat, n.; Croatian, adj.
Cuba	Havana	North America	Cuban
Cyprus	Nicosia	Europe	Cypriot
Czech Republic	Prague	Europe	Czech
Denmark	Copenhagen	Europe	Dane, n.; Danish, adj.
Djibouti	Djibouti	Africa	Djiboutian
Dominica	Roseau	North America	Dominican
Dominican Republic	Santo Domingo	North America	Dominican
Ecuador	Quito	South America	Ecuadorian
Egypt	Cairo	Africa	Egyptian
El Salvador	San Salvador	North America	Salvadoran
Equatorial Guinea	Malabo	Africa	Equatorial Guinean or Equatoguinean
Eritrea	Asmara	Africa	Eritrean
Estonia	Tallinn	Europe	Estonian
Ethiopia	Addis Ababa	Africa	Ethiopian
Fiji	Suva	Oceania	Fijian
Finland	Helsinki	Europe	Finn, n.; Finnish, adj.
France	Paris	Europe	French
Gabon	Libreville	Africa	Gabonese
Gambia, The	Banjul	Africa	Gambian
Georgia	T'bilisi	Asia	Georgian
Germany	Berlin	Europe	German
Ghana	Accra	Africa	Ghanaian
Greece	Athens	Europe	Greek
Grenada	Saint George's	North America	Grenadian
Guatemala	Guatemala	North America	Guatemalan
Guinea	Conakry	Africa	Guinean
Guinea-Bissau	Bissau	Africa	Guinea-Bissauan
Guyana	Georgetown	South America	Guyanese
Haiti	Port-au-Prince	North America	Haitian

Country	Capital	Continent/Area	Nationality
Holy See	Vatican City	Europe	
Honduras	Tegucigalpa	North America	Honduran
Hungary	Budapest	Europe	Hungarian
Iceland	Reykjavik	Europe	Icelander, n.; Icelandic, adj.
India	New Delhi	Asia	Indian
Indonesia	Jakarta	Asia	Indonesian
Iran	Tehran	Asia	Iranian
Iraq	Baghdad	Asia	Iraqi
Ireland	Dublin	Europe	Irish
Israel	Jerusalem	Asia	Israeli
Italy	Rome	Europe	Italian
Ivory Coast (see Côte d'Ivoire)			
Jamaica	Kingston	North America	Jamaican
Japan	Tokyo	Asia	Japanese
Jordan	Amman	Asia	Jordanian
Kazakhstan	Almaty	Asia	Kazakhstani
Kenya	Nairobi	Africa	Kenyan
Kiribati	Tarawa	Oceania	I-Kiribati
Korea, North	P'yongyang	Asia	North Korean
Korea, South	Seoul	Asia	South Korean
Kuwait	Kuwait	Asia	Kuwaiti
Kyrgyzstan	Bishkek	Asia	Kyrgyz
Laos	Vientiane	Asia	Lao or Laotian
Latvia	Riga	Europe	Latvian or Lett
Lebanon	Beirut	Asia	Lebanese
Lesotho	Maseru	Africa	Mosotho, sing.; Basotho, pl.; Basotho, adj.
Liberia	Monrovia	Africa	Liberian
Libya	Tripoli	Africa	Libyan
Liechtenstein	Vaduz	Europe	Liechtensteiner, n.; Liechtenstein, adj.
Lithuania	Vilnius	Europe	Lithuanian
Luxembourg	Luxembourg	Europe	Luxembourger, n.; Luxembourg, adj.
Macedonia, The Former Yugoslav Republic of	Skopje	Europe	Macedonian
Madagascar	Antananarivo	Africa	Malagasy
Malawi	Lilongwe	Africa	Malawian
Malaysia	Kuala Lumpur	Asia	Malaysian

Country	Capital	Continent/Area	Nationality
Maldives	Male	Asia	Maldivian
Mali	Bamako	Africa	Malian
Malta	Valletta	Europe	Maltese
Marshall Islands	Majuro	Oceania	Marshallese
Mauritania	Nouakchott	Africa	Mauritanian
Mauritius	Port Louis	Africa	Mauritian
Mexico	Mexico	North America	Mexican
Micronesia, Federated States of	Kolonia	Oceania	Micronesian
Moldova	Chisinau	Europe	Moldovan
Monaco	Monaco	Europe	Monacan or Monegasque
Mongolia	Ulaanbaatar	Asia	Mongolian
Morocco	Rabat	Africa	Moroccan
Mozambique	Maputo	Africa	Mozambican
Myanmar (see Burma)			
Namibia	Windhoek	Africa	Namibian
Nauru	Yaren District	Oceania	Nauruan
Nepal	Kathmandu	Asia	Nepalese
Netherlands	Amsterdam; The Hague	Europe	Dutchman or Dutchwoman, n.; Dutch, adj.
New Zealand	Wellington	Oceania	New Zealander, n.; New Zealand, adj.
Nicaragua	Managua	North America	Nicaraguan
Niger	Niamey	Africa	Nigerien
Nigeria	Abuja	Africa	Nigerian
Norway	Oslo	Europe	Norwegian
Oman	Muscat	Asia	Omani
Pakistan	Islamabad	Asia	Pakistani
Palau	Koror	Oceania	Palauan
Panama	Panama	North America	Panamanian
Papua New Guinea	Port Moresby	Oceania	Papua New Guinean
Paraguay	Asunción	South America	Paraguayan
Peru	Lima	South America	Peruvian
Philippines	Manila	Asia	Filipino, n.; Philippine, adj.
Poland	Warsaw	Europe	Pole, n.; Polish, adj.
Portugal	Lisbon	Europe	Portuguese
Qatar	Doha	Asia	Quatari
Romania	Bucharest	Europe	Romanian

Country	Capital	Continent/Area	Nationality
Russia	Moscow	Europe & Asia	Russian
Rwanda	Kigali	Africa	Rwandan
Saint Kitts and Nevis	Basseterre	North America	Kittsian; Nevisian
Saint Lucia	Castries	North America	St. Lucian
Saint Vincent and the Grenadines	Kingstown	North America	St. Vincentian or Vincentian
San Marino	San Marino	Europe	Sammarinese
Sao Tome and Principe	Sao Tome	Africa	Sao Tomean
Saudi Arabia	Riyadh	Asia	Saudi or Saudi Arabian
Senegal	Dakar	Africa	Senegalese
Seychelles	Victoria	Indian Ocean	Seychellois, n.; Seychelles, adj.
Sierra Leone	Freetown	Africa	Sierra Leonean
Singapore	Singapore	Asia	Singaporean, n.; Singapore, adj.
Slovakia	Bratislava	Europe	Slovak
Slovenia	Ljubljana	Europe	Slovene, n.; Slovenian, adj.
Solomon Islands	Honiara	Oceania	Solomon Islander
Somalia	Mogadishu	Africa	Somali
South Africa	Pretoria; Cape Town; Bloemfontein	Africa	South African
Spain	Madrid	Europe	Spanish
Sri Lanka	Colombo	Asia	Sri Lankan
Sudan	Khartoum	Africa	Sudanese
Suriname	Paramaribo	South America	Surinamer, n.; Surinamese, adj.
Swaziland	Mbabane	Africa	Swazi
Sweden	Stockholm	Europe	Swede, n.; Swedish, adj.
Switzerland	Bern	Europe	Swiss
Syria	Damascus	Asia	Syrian
Tajikistan	Dushanbe	Asia	Tajik
Tanzania	Dar es Salaam	Africa	Tanzanian
Thailand	Bangkok	Asia	Thai
Togo	Lome	Africa	Togolese
Tonga	Nuku'alofa	Oceania	Tongan
Trinidad and Tobago	Port-of-Spain	South America	Trinidadian; Tobagonian
Tunisia	Tunis	Africa	Tunisian

Country	Capital	Continent/Area	Nationality
Turkey	Ankara	Asia & Europe	Turk, *n.*; Turkish, *adj.*
Turkmenistan	Ashgabat	Asia	Turkmen
Tuvalu	Funafuti	Oceania	Tuvaluan
Uganda	Kampala	Africa	Ugandan
Ukraine	Kiev	Europe	Ukrainian
United Arab Emirates	Abu Dhabi	Africa	Emirian
United Kingdom	London	Europe	Briton, *n.*; British, collective pl. & *adj.*
United States	Washington, DC	North America	American
Uruguay	Montevideo	South America	Uruguayan
Uzbekistan	Tashkent	Asia	Uzbek
Vanuatu	Port-Vila	Oceania	Ni-Vanuatu
Venezuela	Caracas	South America	Venezuelan
Vietnam	Hanoi	Asia	Vietnamese
Western Samoa	Apia	Oceania	Western Samoan
Yemen	Sanaa	Asia	Yemeni
Yugoslavia (Serbia and Montenegro)	Belgrade	Europe	Yugoslav; Serb, *n.*; Serbian, *adj.*; Montenegran
Zambia	Lusaka	Africa	Zambian
Zimbabwe	Harare	Africa	Zimbabwean